X mas
1992
Janet Tresish
VC

Familiar
Quotations

Familiar Quotations

*A collection of passages, phrases,
and proverbs traced to their
sources in ancient and
modern literature*

SIXTEENTH EDITION

John Bartlett

JUSTIN KAPLAN, GENERAL EDITOR

Little, Brown and Company

BOSTON TORONTO LONDON

First Edition Published 1855
Sixteenth Edition Published 1992

LIBRARY OF CONGRESS CATALOGING-IN-PUBLICATION DATA

Bartlett, John, 1820–1905.
    Familiar quotations: a collection of passages, phrases, and proverbs traced to
their sources in ancient and modern literature / John Bartlett; edited by Justin
Kaplan.—16th ed., rev. and enl.
        p.   cm.
    Includes indexes.
    ISBN 0-316-08277-5
    1. Quotations, English.   I. Kaplan, Justin.   II. Little, Brown
and Company.   III. Title.
PN6081.B27   1992
808.88′2—dc20   91-21170

RRD-OH

Published simultaneously in Canada
by Little, Brown & Company (Canada) Limited

PRINTED IN THE UNITED STATES OF AMERICA

Contents

Preface to the
Sixteenth Edition

JOHN BARTLETT, born in 1820, lived to see his name become as generic for quotations as Noah Webster's for definitions. Starting at the age of sixteen, he worked himself up from apprentice bookbinder in Cambridge, Massachusetts, to bookstore clerk to bookstore owner. He read widely, kept notes on his reading, and in time made himself an information bank for the local academic and literary community. The commonplace books he kept over many years of answering questions about who said what, when, and where were the basis of the first edition of *Familiar Quotations*. He published it himself in 1855, a year that also saw the publication of his neighbor Henry Wadsworth Longfellow's *Hiawatha*, Walt Whitman's *Leaves of Grass*, and *Maud: A Monodrama* by Queen Victoria's poet laureate, Alfred Lord Tennyson.

The first *Bartlett,* issued in an edition of one thousand copies, was a relatively small volume of 258 pages of prose and verse quotations, chiefly from the Bible, Shakespeare, and British writers. A few American writers were also represented —Washington Irving, William Cullen Bryant, Longfellow, and (another Cambridge neighbor) James Russell Lowell. Bartlett contributed an editor's preface and an index of authors and key words. He sold his bookstore when the Civil War started, served for a while as volunteer paymaster in the United States Navy, and, in 1863, joined the Boston publishing house of Little, Brown and Company. Little, Brown took over the publication of *Familiar Quotations* (already in a fourth enlarged, enriched, and revised edition) and has kept it on the list ever since. By the end of his life (he died in 1905) Bartlett had brought out, in all, nine editions of his famous book but found time, nonetheless, to pursue many other interests. He was an acknowledged expert on fishing, chess, and whist and estimated he had also spent sixteen thousand hours compiling, with the help of his wife, Hannah, a *Complete Concordance to Shakespeare's Dramatic Works and Poems.*

"The object of this work," Bartlett wrote in the preface to the 1855 *Familiar Quotations,* "is to show, to some extent, the obligations our language owes to various authors for numerous phrases and familiar quotations which have become 'household words.'" Like him, his editorial successors do their best to be practical (in answering readers' needs) and authoritative (in supplying reliable, verified texts and precise citations). But we recognize—and hope that readers will also—that comprehensive as it is, a book of this sort reflects both personal judgment and changing usage and can never be "definitive."

John Bartlett arranged the quotations in his book chronologically, by author's birth date. His arrangement gave, and continues to give, *Familiar Quotations* a double nature. Like a dictionary or atlas, it is a reference book of first resort. But also, as I discovered for myself at an early age with my first copy, *Bartlett* is an enormously rich and attractive *reading* book, a unique sort of anthology that ranges in time from ancient Egypt to the present. One of the simplest, most spontaneous ways to map experience, chronology invites readers to travel over land masses and archaeological layers of remembered words. A quotation book is both intellectual history and cultural montage, a key to past and present taste, memory, and enthusiasms as they themselves change and, in changing, reach out for new material and put a different light on some of the old. Three hundred forty of the 2,550 authors in the present edition are newcomers to *Bartlett;* 245 of the "older" ones have been retired.

The editors who succeeded Bartlett broadened his original criterion, "familiar quotations which have become 'household words.'" It now extends to quotations chosen as well for their literary power, intellectual and historical significance, originality, and timeliness. Some quotations, of course, become "familiar" simply because they appear in a book of familiar quotations; this may be a partial instance of what sociologist Robert K. Merton calls a "self-fulfilling prophecy." Whatever their eventual staying power, some quotations may be on everyone's tongue for a few seasons. Andy Warhol's "In the future everyone will be world-famous for fifteen minutes" was probably the most popular quotation of the 1970s. Its counterpart for the 1980s was "The opera ain't over till the fat lady sings." On the other hand, a quotation such as "God is in the details" has proved its staying power over many decades but continues to resist efforts to track it to a rumored original source in Gustave Flaubert. Other quotations remain uncertain as far as demonstrable authenticity is concerned and fall into that guarded and elastic category called "attributed."[1]

Several quotation books (including the fifteenth edition of *Bartlett*) credit the Hartford editor and essayist Charles Dudley Warner with, "Everybody talks about the weather, but nobody does anything about it." I put my chips on Mark Twain as the author of that famous quip. But I've restored to its rightful author, the American humorist Bill Nye, "Wagner's music is better than it sounds," an observation previously credited to Mark Twain. This edition includes a number of quotations that could not be described as "familiar" but, one might argue, *deserve* to be "familiar" because they crystallize decisive events: for example, the passages from James D. Watson and Francis P. Crick's paper on the double helix structure of the DNA molecule, Alan Turing's inquiry into the nature of artificial intelligence, and the defining contexts of "psychoanalytic," "final solution," "genocide," "WASP," and "AIDS."

John Bartlett's readers on both sides of the Atlantic enjoyed a common language —a so-called lingua franca—enriched with direct or oblique references to Shakespeare and the Bible, the classics, and "standard authors." In the United States, for example, from 1836 on William Holmes McGuffey's *Eclectic Readers* spurred generations of schoolchildren to recite, often from memory, literary texts like Gray's "Elegy Written in a Country Churchyard," Bryant's "Thanatopsis," Longfellow's "Evangeline," and Dickens's "Death of Little Nell" (see Oscar Wilde's comment on this celebrated three-handkerchief episode). British soldiers in World War I carried

---

[1]*The Quote Sleuth: A Manual for the Tracer of Lost Quotations,* by Anthony W. Shipps (Urbana, Illinois, 1990), is a valuable resource on such matters.

The Oxford Book of English Verse with them into the trenches and quoted from it in their journals and letters home. "The Great War" was "a literary war," Paul Fussell writes, fought at a time when "the belief in the educative powers of classical and English literature was still extremely strong."[2] During World War II *The Pocket Book of Verse* was one of the six or seven paperbacks most popular with American troops; British troops had equivalent Penguin anthologies.

The distinctive common language of the Vietnam era, however, came from non-traditional sources—movies, street slogans ("Make love not war"), television ("Sorry about that," a catchline from the comedy series *Get Smart*), and especially rock lyrics. The "war and its music," Michael Herr wrote, "had run power off the same circuit for so long they didn't even have to fuse." As electronic and visual media continue to grow in their shaping influence, traditional book culture, the wellspring of a work such as *Bartlett's Familiar Quotations*, finds its age-old primacy seriously challenged. According to a much-publicized recent survey, nearly 60 percent of all adult Americans have never read a book, and the better part of the remaining 40 percent read no more than one book a year.[3] Within the university, once its undisputed seat of power, traditional book culture is often attacked for being anachronistic, repressive, unrepresentative, sexist, hegemonic, phallocentric, eurocentric, racist, or, in some other alleged respect, "incorrect."

Public speakers today are afraid of sounding "literary" or "elitist" and feel most comfortable when citing Casey Stengel or Yogi Berra (whose popularity as comic oracle now surpasses that of malaprop movie mogul Samuel Goldwyn). A newsletter distributed to professional speechwriters in 1989 advises them to junk "all cultural references, literary allusions, or great thoughts and quotations from the past." The newsletter goes on to give a list of writers whom the speaker "should never, never quote, no matter what the provocation or temptation. These include: Yeats, Pound, and Eliot, naturally, but also Dylan Thomas, Samuel Beckett, Sartre, Camus, Kafka, etc., etc. If you even *mention* these writers you lay yourselves open to ridicule. The businessman who will quote Mallarmé or Rimbaud is capable of anything."[4] Political leaders speak in headlines or captions, television "sound bites" that become briefer with each presidential campaign and leave no time for flowers of rhetoric.[5] (In contrast to this language of fragment, slogan, and "bitespeak" the last sentence alone of Abraham Lincoln's Gettysburg Address runs to seventy-four words.)

Nevertheless, like Molière's Would-Be Gentleman, who discovered that for forty years he had been "speaking prose without knowing it," we speak a language that draws on quotations. They are telegraphic, a form of shorthand. We use them to lend point and luster to what we say, and in converting other people's words to our own use often give them meanings quite different from what their authors may have intended. We cherish and like to repeat, simply for the reassurance they give, proverbs, nursery rhymes, song lyrics, and the like that have so much talismanic force they function on a nearly pre-intellectual level. We use quotations, like the Biblical Shibboleth, as passwords and secret handshakes, socially strategic signals that say, "I understand you. We speak the same language." Quotations have always been supremely effective rhetorical devices, instruments of one-upmanship, ways of support-

---

[2]*The Great War and Modern Memory* (New York, 1975), pp. 155–161. See also Fussell's *Wartime* (New York, 1989), pp. 236–251.

[3]See, for example, Alvin Kernan, *The Death of Literature* (New Haven, 1990).

[4]*Speechwriter's Newsletter: The Weekly Voice of the Silent Profession,* May 12, 1989.

[5]"They shrank from an average of roughly 45 seconds 10 years ago to 14.7 seconds in 1984 to about 9 seconds in 1988." *Newsweek,* November 21, 1988, p. 14.

ing any position under the sun with borrowed or stolen authority. But please remember that "The devil can cite Scripture for his purpose" and that quoting can be a shabby substitute for thinking. "I hate quotation," Emerson wrote in his journal. "Tell me what you know." The Fowlers' *Dictionary of Modern English Usage* offers further cautions about using other people's words.

What has changed in the century and a half since John Bartlett first brought out his book is not the practice of quoting but what we quote and the mood or need it corresponds to. John Donne's magnificent "Death be not proud" belongs in *Bartlett*. But so, too, does Woody Allen's "It's not that I'm afraid to die. I just don't want to be there when it happens." Lending what George Orwell called "an appearance of solidity to pure wind," euphemism, evasion, and doubletalk ("revenue enhancement," "collateral damage") form a tide that laps at our grasp of reality. To turn back this tide we need to be much more vernacular, skeptical, and ironic than earlier readers of *Bartlett* and consequently less tolerant of self-evident propositions, ceremonial boilerplate, gassy platitudes, and fortune cookie sentiments. Such exhibits of "the conventional wisdom" (see John Kenneth Galbraith) tend to bulk large in quotation books. Readers will find somewhat fewer of them in this edition.

In order to be descriptive, to reflect the way we talk and think, a book called *Familiar Quotations,* edited and published for the 1990s, has to look beyond as well as to traditional sources. This is not to say that these non-canonical sources necessarily pan out. Given the amount of time the general population spends watching television, one might expect television to be a heavy contributor to the common quotation vocabulary. However, with a few notable exceptions (*Star Trek, Monty Python,* and *Sesame Street* among them), I haven't found this to be the case. Viewers I queried (through the columns of the magazine *TV Entertainment Monthly*) turned out to have retained in their memories only a few pathetic tatters, first among them being the semi-apocryphal "Beam me up, Scotty." "Up your nose with a rubber hose" (from *Welcome Back, Kotter*) and "Thanks, I needed that" (from a Mennen commercial) were distant seconds.

By contrast with television, the movies (*Casablanca,* for one) continue to be a rich quotation source. "Nowadays, when literary people get together they are at least as likely to argue or reminisce about films as about novels. . . . For a long time now, the experience of the cinema has been woven into most people's lives, usually since childhood."[6] Although the "nowadays" here refers to 1969, the statement has even more force today. Movie tags like "Win one for the Gipper," "Go ahead, make my day," and "Evil Empire" were vital components of Ronald Reagan's presidential vocabulary. The movies themselves have become almost as "intertextual" as Dante's *Divine Comedy* or Eliot's *The Wasteland* and count on the audience's quickness to recognize verbal and visual allusions (the shower scene in Alfred Hitchcock's *Psycho* is now as archetypal in its way as Hamlet stalking Claudius at prayer).

This sixteenth edition includes over fifty new quotations (with screenwriter credits) that come directly from the movies and many more that are related, such as Woodrow Wilson's dramatic response to D. W. Griffith's *The Birth of a Nation* when it was screened at the White House. Rock and pop lyrics, politics, public affairs, business, and sports are among the other nonliterary quotation sources represented here, to list only a few authors, by Jimi Hendrix, Elvis Presley, Bruce Springsteen,

---

[6]John Gross, *The Rise and Fall of the Man of Letters* (New York, 1969). The twenty-three writers who contributed essays to David Rosenberg's collection *The Movie That Changed My Life* (New York, 1991) provide further testimony on these points.

Chuck Berry, the Doors, Jack Dempsey, Joe Louis, Prince Charles, Deng Xiaoping, and Mikhail Gorbachev.

As for literary sources, some of the 340 authors who now appear in *Bartlett* for the first time are Nelson Algren, Russell Baker, Walter Benjamin, Saint Bonaventure, Martin Buber, Anthony Burgess, Kate Chopin, Noam Chomsky, Annie Dillard, Frantz Fanon, M. F. K. Fisher, Nadine Gordimer, Günter Grass, Václav Havel, Stephen Hawking, Seamus Heaney, Hillel, Zora Neale Hurston, Shirley Jackson, Alice James, Milan Kundera, Ursula K. LeGuin, Primo Levi, Claude Lévi-Strauss, Rosa Luxemburg, Norman Mailer, Bernard Malamud, Toni Morrison, Robert Musil, Joe Orton, Harold Pinter, V. S. Pritchett, Philip Roth, Salman Rushdie, Susan Sontag, the Talmud, Paul Tillich, Alice Walker, Elie Wiesel, Ludwig Wittgenstein. Some authors who appeared in the fifteenth edition are now more fully represented in the sixteenth, among them George Orwell, Evelyn Waugh, Philip Larkin, Allen Ginsberg, Woody Allen, S. J. Perelman, Franz Kafka, and Sigmund Freud. The Melville, Whitman, and Mark Twain sections have been thoroughly revised. Shakespeare (with 1,960 quotations) and the Bible (with 1,591) are still the dominant presences they were for John Bartlett in 1855. The sixteenth edition of *Familiar Quotations* continues to reaffirm the culture we're told is so gravely at risk but at the same time casts a wider net than its predecessors.

Bartlett's Familiar Quotations welcomes suggestions and comments from its readers, and I am grateful for information I've received in this way. I owe special thanks to the following for generous help that they either volunteered or allowed me to solicit from them: Daniel Aaron, Frank Avruch, Jim Barnes, Bill Blackbeard, Sissela Bok, Jerome H. Buckley, Steven Cohen, George C. Cronemiller, Frank Deford, Byron Dobell, David Herbert Donald, Scott Donaldson, John H. Dorenkamp, Donald Fanger, Victor Ford, Robert H. Hirst, Joy Johannessen, Joseph P. Kahn, Ralph Keyes, Corby Kummer, Anthony F. Lazzara, Bill Littlefield, Edward L. Mark, Jeffrey McQuain, Cable Neuhaus, Robert W. Pitha, Richard Rhodes, Robert D. Richardson, Jr., William Safire, Lloyd Schwartz, Peter Schwed, Laurence Senelick, Anthony W. Shipps, David Sills, Mark Starr, Michael D. Stein, Brita Stendahl, Ross Terrill, John Updike, Helen Vendler, Aileen Ward, Elizabeth Erb Ward, Helen Whall.

Emily Morison Beck, editor of the fourteenth (1968) and fifteenth (1980) editions of *Bartlett,* graciously shared with me her knowledge and continuing enthusiasm. Stephen Haas and Hester Kaplan contributed indispensable research. As always, I thank Anne Bernays for her discriminating review of a manuscript. At Little, Brown, I thank William D. Phillips, who invited me to take on this irresistible project; Ellen Denison, who oversaw the early stages; Jean Crockett and Jackie Serafino, for their scrupulous checking and proofing; Kate Schwartz, who assisted in copyediting; and, first and last, Betsy Pitha, chief copy editor, for the pleasure of working with her and for seeing this book through with such personal dedication and professional skill.

JUSTIN KAPLAN

Cambridge, Massachusetts

Guide to the Use of *Familiar Quotations*

BASIC INFORMATION

AUTHORS APPEAR chronologically in the order of their birth dates; authors born in the same year are arranged alphabetically. The quotations for each author are generally in chronological order according to the date of publication (in some instances according to the date of composition). Poetry generally precedes prose for authors who wrote both.

Anonymous quotations are located as follows: early miscellaneous and Latin quotations are placed at about A.D. 670. General anonymous quotations come immediately after the last dated author and are arranged in roughly chronological order (no precise dates of origin being known). Specific groupings of anonymous quotations—African, Ballads, Cowboy Songs, and so on—follow the general Anonymous section in alphabetical order according to the heading.

A document without a specific author appears near the people with whom it is associated; for example, the Constitution of the United States (1787) appears among its creators, such as George Washington (born in 1732), John Adams (1735), James Madison (1751), and Alexander Hamilton (1755).

To find a particular author, consult the Index of Authors, page xv; to find a particular quotation, consult the Index, page 795.

QUOTATION SOURCES

Each quotation has a source line supplying title, date (most often that of publication) and any other helpful information. *Ibid.*, short for *ibidem*, "in the same place," covers everything in the preceding source line that would have to be repeated in the next. For example, in the source line *Ibid.* 13 following the source line *Light in August* [*1932*], *ch. 4*, the only change is the chapter number. Instead of *ibid.*, full source lines are provided in the left-hand columns of left-hand pages. In the quotations from the Bible and from Shakespeare, the page headings provide blanket sources for the quotations on the particular page.

FOOTNOTES

The footnotes supply information about a quotation, such as the original text of a translated quotation, the name of the translator, background comments for the quotation, other quotations related in phrase or content to the footnoted quotation, and cross-references to similar quotations that may not readily be found through the Index.

INDEX OF AUTHORS

The Index of Authors provides birth and death dates and the page number for the quotations by each author, as well as the page numbers for any additional quotations by that author in the footnotes. Bracketed parts of a name as listed in this index are those not used in the author's typical "signature"—for example, T[homas] S[tearns] Eliot. The Index of Authors also lists many pseudonyms, with cross-references from the less familiar name to the more familiar—for example, Karen Blixen is cross-referred to Isak Dinesen, the pseudonym under which she wrote. Authors who are quoted only in footnotes have their full names and birth and death dates given in the footnotes; authors in the main text are cited in footnotes only by surname and without dates (full names and sometimes dates are given when necessary to avoid confusion with another person of the same name).

To find a particular book of the Bible, see the Bible entry, where the books are listed alphabetically. The same is true for Shakespeare; to find any work, consult the Shakespeare entry. Anonymous quotations are listed under the heading "Anonymous," as well as by specific groupings, such as Ballads (Anonymous), Cowboy Songs (Anonymous), and so on.

INDEX

The *Bartlett* index is arranged by keywords, not topics. The keywords are spelled according to *Webster's Ninth New Collegiate Dictionary* and *Webster's Third New International Dictionary*. The spelling and capitalization in the entry line following are those of the quotation. Some older or variant spellings are indexed, as are "made" words, such as "hitherandthithering," "slithy," acronyms, and dialectal words. Compound expressions not found in *Webster's* are sometimes indexed: the hyphenated form "good-night," for example, is so indexed to allow grouping under this key expression rather than under "good" and "night." ("Human" and "being," however, are separately indexed.) Compound names, such as "Long Island," "South Vietnam," "United States," are indexed as one word. The elided *e* found in many quotations as '*d* is supplied in all the index entries. Quotations from other languages generally are indexed, usually at a keyword specific to the other language, but sometimes at a keyword that is also in English; see, for example, the entries at "Bourgeois."

Alphabetization is word-for-word, not letter-by-letter. Thus "New Zealand" precedes "Newborn." The order of plural and possessive keywords is from singular possessive to plural to plural possessive: for example, *Lover's, Lovers, Lovers'*.

The number at the end of each index entry shows the page on which the quotation starts and the number of the quotation on the page—224:4, for example. Entries for footnote quotations are cited by page and note number: 224:*n*2.

The index entry line is usually a short form of the indexed phrase, and the words in general appear in the same order, with the keyword abbreviated unless it starts the entry:

Hope, all we h. in Heaven, 451:6
Americans h. of world, 327:12
animated by faith and h., 314:18
is waking dream, 77:9
the thing with feathers, 511:20
to see Pilot, 460:13

Occasionally words not in the actual quotations are supplied in the index entries to make the entries clear.

Readers who cannot find a particular quotation under one keyword are advised to scan any keyword entry in its entirety, since there are many ways of indexing one phrase, or to try other keywords.

BETSY PITHA
Editor, Little, Brown and Company

Index of Authors

Familiar Quotations

The Song of the Harper[1,2]

c. 2650–2600 B.C.

1 There is no one who can return from there,
To describe their nature, to describe their
  dissolution,
That he may still our desires,
Until we reach the place where they have gone.
St. 5

2 Remember: it is not given to man to take his
  goods with him.
No one goes away and then comes back.
St. 10

Ptahhotpe

Twenty-fourth century B.C.

3   Teach him what has been said in the past; then he
will set a good example to the children of the magistrates, and judgment and all exactitude shall enter
into him. Speak to him, for there is none born wise.
*The Maxims of Ptahhotpe [c. 2350 B.C.],[3]
introduction*

4   Do not be arrogant because of your knowledge,
but confer with the ignorant man as with the
learned. . . . Good speech is more hidden than
malachite, yet it is found in the possession of women
slaves at the millstones.   *Ibid. maxim no. 1*

5   Truth is great and its effectiveness endures.[4]
Ibid. 5

6   Follow your desire as long as you live and do not
perform more than is ordered; do not lessen the time
of following desire, for the wasting of time is an
abomination to the spirit. . . . When riches are
gained, follow desire, for riches will not profit if one
is sluggish.   *Ibid. 11*

7   Beware an act of avarice; it is a bad and incurable
disease.   *Ibid. 19*

[1]Ancient Egyptian quotations from *The Song of the Harper*,
Ptahhotpe, *The Teaching for Merikare*, *The Man Who Was
Tired of Life*, and *Love Songs of the New Kingdom* are from
WILLIAM KELLY SIMPSON, ed., *The Literature of Ancient Egypt*
[1973]. Those from *The Book of the Dead*, Queen Hatshepsut,
Suti and Hor, *The Great Hymn to the Aten*, and Amenemope
are from MIRIAM LICHTHEIM, *Ancient Egyptian Literature*,
vol. II, *The New Kingdom* [1976].
[2]From the tomb of King Inyotef.
Translated by WILLIAM KELLY SIMPSON.
[3]Translated from the earliest manuscript of the *Maxims* (the
Prisse Papyrus in Paris) by R. O. FAULKNER.
[4]See *I Esdras 4:41*, 30:13, and Patmore, 503:10.

8   Do not repeat slander; you should not hear it, for
it is the result of hot temper.   *Ibid. 23*

9   One who is serious all day will never have a good
time, while one who is frivolous all day will never
establish a household.   *Ibid. 25*

10   Be cheerful while you are alive.   *Ibid. 34*

The Teaching for Merikare[5]

c. 2135–2040 B.C.

11   Be skillful in speech, that you may be strong;
[. . .][6] it is the strength of [. . .] the tongue, and
words are braver than all fighting . . . a wise man
is a school for the magnates, and those who are
aware of his knowledge do not attack him.
Par. 4

12   Copy your forefathers, for work is carried out
through knowledge; see, their words endure in writing. . . . Do not be evil, for patience is good; make
your lasting monument in the love of you.
Par. 5

13   Wretched is he who has bound the land to himself
[. . .]; a fool is he who is greedy when others
possess. Life on earth passes away, it is not long; he
is fortunate who has a good remembrance in it.
Par. 6

14   Do justice, that you may live long upon earth.
Calm the weeper, do not oppress the widow, do not
oust a man from his father's property, do not degrade magnates from their seats. Beware of punishing wrongfully; do not kill, for it will not profit you.
Par. 8

15   More acceptable is the character of the straightforward man than the ox of the wrongdoer. Serve
God, that He may do the like for you. . . . Provide
for men, the cattle of God, for He made heaven and
earth at their desire. He suppressed the greed of the
waters, He gave the breath of life to their noses, for
they are likenesses of Him which issued from His
flesh.   *Par. 22*

16   Instill the love of you into all the world, for a
good character is what is remembered.   *Par. 24*

[5]A treatise on kingship addressed by a king of Heracleopolis,
whose name is lost, to his son and successor Merikare.
Translated by R. O. FAULKNER.
[6]Three bracketed dots represent an unfilled gap in the original; unbracketed dots represent our own omission from the
text.

The Man Who Was Tired of Life[1]
c. 1990 B.C.

1 To whom can I speak today?
Brothers are evil
And the friends of today unlovable.

Song, st. 9

2 To whom can I speak today?
Gentleness has perished
And the violent man has come down on everyone.

Ibid. st. 11

3 To whom can I speak today?
The wrong which roams the earth,
There is no end to it.

Ibid. st. 24

4 Death is in my sight today
As when a man desires to see home
When he has spent many years in captivity.

Ibid. st. 30

The Book of the Dead[2]
c. 1700–1000 B.C.

5 Hail to you gods . . .
On that day of the great reckoning.
Behold me, I have come to you,
Without sin, without guilt, without evil,
Without a witness against me,
Without one whom I have wronged. . . .
Rescue me, protect me,
Do not accuse me before the great god!

I am one pure of mouth, pure of hands.

The Address to the Gods

Love Songs of the New Kingdom[3]
c. 1550–1080 B.C.

6 My love for you is mixed throughout my
body . . .

So hurry to see your lady,
like a stallion on the track,
or like a falcon swooping down to its papyrus
marsh.

Heaven sends down the love of her
as a flame falls in the hay.

Song no. 2

7 The voice of the wild goose,
caught by the bait, cries out.

Love of you holds me back,
and I can't loosen it at all. . . .

I did not set my traps today;
love of you has thus entrapped me.

Ibid. 10

8 Now must I depart from the brother . . .
and as I long for your love,
my heart stands still inside me. . . .

Sweet pomegranate wine in my mouth
is bitter as the gall of birds.

But your embraces
alone give life to my heart;
may Amun give me what I have found
for all eternity.

Ibid. 12

9 The voice of the turtledove speaks out. It says:
Day breaks, which way are you going?
Lay off, little bird,
must you so scold me?

I found my lover on his bed,
and my heart was sweet to excess.

Ibid. 14

Queen Hatshepsut[4]
d. 1468 B.C.

10 So as regards these two great obelisks,[5]
Wrought with electrum[6] by my majesty for my
father Amun,
In order that my name may endure in this temple,
For eternity and everlastingness,
They are each of one block of hard granite,
Without seam, without joining together!

Speech of the Queen

Suti and Hor[7]
Fifteenth–fourteenth centuries B.C.

11 Creator uncreated.
Sole one, unique one, who traverses eternity,
Remote one, with millions under his care;
Your splendor is like heaven's splendor.

First Hymn to the Sun God

[1]Translated by R. O. FAULKNER.
[2]Translated by MIRIAM LICHTHEIM.
"The coming forth by day" . . . the Egyptians called it.
— MIRIAM LICHTHEIM, *Ancient Egyptian Literature, vol. II,
The New Kingdom* [1976], *pt. III, introduction*
[3]Translated by WILLIAM KELLY SIMPSON.

[4]Translated by MIRIAM LICHTHEIM.
[5]Queen Hatshepsut erected four obelisks in the temple of
Amun at Karnak, two of which have disappeared entirely.
. . . The obelisks are of pink Assuan granite. — MIRIAM LICH-
THEIM, *Ancient Egyptian Literature, vol. II, The New Kingdom*
[1976], *pt. I, sec. 2*
[6]"Electrum," or "fine gold," designated the gold with a high
silver content which was especially prized. — *Ibid. note to
Speech of the Queen*
[7]Architects to Amenhotep III (reigned c. 1411–1375 B.C.).
Translated by MIRIAM LICHTHEIM.

1 Beneficent mother of gods and men . . .
Valiant shepherd who drives his flock,
Their refuge, made to sustain them. . . .
He makes the seasons with the months,
Heat as he wishes, cold as he wishes. . . .
Every land rejoices at his rising,
Every day gives praise to him.

Second Hymn to the Sun God

The Great Hymn to the Aten[1]
c. 1350 B.C.

2 Splendid you rise in heaven's lightland,
O living Aten, creator of life!

St. 1

3 When you set in western lightland,
Earth is in darkness as if in death.[2]

St. 2

4 Every lion comes from its den,
All the serpents bite;
Darkness hovers, earth is silent,
As their maker rests in lightland.

Earth brightens when you dawn in lightland,
When you shine as Aten of daytime;
As you dispel the dark,
As you cast your rays,
The Two Lands are in festivity.
Awake they stand on their feet,
You have roused them.

St. 2, 3

5 The entire land sets out to work,
All beasts browse on their herbs;
Trees, herbs are sprouting,
Birds fly from their nests . . .
Ships fare north, fare south as well,
Roads lie open when you rise;
The fish in the river dart before you,
Your rays are in the midst of the sea.

St. 3

6 How many are your deeds,
Though hidden from sight,
O Sole God beside whom there is none!
You made the earth as you wished, you alone.

St. 5

¹From the reign [1365–1349 B.C.] of Amenhotep IV Akhenaten.
Translated by MIRIAM LICHTHEIM.
Amenhotep IV . . . converted the supreme god [Aten, the sun disk] into the sole god by denying the reality of all the other gods. — LICHTHEIM, *ibid. pt. II*
²See *Psalm 104:20–24, 19:6.*
The resemblances [between the Great Hymn to the Aten and Psalm 104] are . . . likely to be the result of the generic similarity between Egyptian hymns and Biblical psalms. A specific literary interdependence is not probable. — LICHTHEIM, *ibid. note to The Great Hymn to the Aten*

I Ching[3]
[The Book of Changes]
c. Twelfth century B.C.[4]

7 The mountain rests on the earth: the image of splitting apart. Thus those above can insure their position only by giving generously to those below.

Bk. I, ch. 25, Po / Splitting Apart

8 Fire in the lake: the image of revolution.

Ibid. 49, Ko / Revolution (Molting)

9 Wind over lake: the image of inner truth.

Ibid. 61, Chung Fu / Inner Truth

Amenemope
c. Eleventh century B.C.

10 Beginning of the teaching for life,
The instructions for well-being . . .
Knowing how to answer one who speaks,
To reply to one who sends a message.[5]

The Instruction of Amenemope,[6] prologue

11 Give your ears, hear the sayings,
Give your heart to understand them;
It profits to put them in your heart.[7]

Ibid. ch. 1

12 Beware of robbing a wretch,
Of attacking a cripple.[8]

Ibid. 2

13 The truly silent, who keep apart,
He is like a tree grown in a meadow.
It greens, it doubles its yield,
It stands in front of its lord.
Its fruit is sweet, its shade delightful,
Its end comes in the garden.[9]

Ibid. 4

14 Do not move the markers on the border of the fields.[10]

Ibid. 6

15 Better is poverty in the hand of the god,
Than wealth in the storehouse;
Better is bread with a happy heart
Than wealth with vexation.[11]

Ibid.

³Translated from Chinese into German by RICHARD WILHELM, and into English by CARY F. BAYNES.
⁴Traditional date of the present collection of sixty-four hexagrams (some of which reach into legendary antiquity) credited to Wen Wang, whose son Wu Wang was the first ruler of the Chou dynasty [c. 1027–256 B.C.].
⁵See *Proverbs 22:20–21, 22:12.*
⁶Translated by MIRIAM LICHTHEIM.
⁷See *Proverbs 22:17–18, 22:11.*
⁸See *Proverbs 22:22, 22:13,* and *Ecclesiasticus 4:1, 31:6.*
⁹See *Psalm 1:1–3, 15:29,* and *Jeremiah 17:8, 28:29.*
¹⁰See *Proverbs 22:28, 22:14.*
¹¹See *Proverbs 15:16–17, 21:26.*

1 Do not set your heart on wealth . . .
Do not strain to seek increases,
What you have, let it suffice you.[1]
If riches come to you by theft,
They will not stay the night with you. . . .
They made themselves wings like geese,
And flew away to the sky.[2]
                    The Instruction of Amenemope, ch. 7

2 Look to these thirty chapters,
They inform, they educate.[3]
                                        Ibid. 30

3 The scribe who is skilled in his office,
He is found worthy to be a courtier.[4]
                                        Ibid.

The Holy Bible[5]
The Old Testament[6]

4   In the beginning God created the heaven and the earth.
    And the earth was without form, and void; and darkness was upon the face of the deep. And the Spirit of God moved upon the face of the waters.
    And God said, Let there be light:[7] and there was light.
    The First Book of Moses, Called Genesis,
    chapter 1, verses 1–3

5   And the evening and the morning were the first day.   *1:5*

6   And God saw that it was good.   *1:10*

7   And God said, Let us make man in our image, after our likeness.   *1:26*

8   Male and female created he them.   *1:27*

9   Be fruitful, and multiply, and replenish the earth, and subdue it: and have dominion over the fish of the sea, and over the fowl of the air, and over every living thing that moveth upon the earth.   *1:28*

10   And on the seventh day God ended his work which he had made.   *2:2*

11   And the Lord God formed man of the dust of the ground, and breathed into his nostrils the breath of life; and man became a living soul.   *2:7*

12   And the Lord God planted a garden eastward in Eden.   *2:8*

13   The tree of life also in the midst of the garden.
                                            2:9

14   But of the tree of the knowledge of good and evil, thou shalt not eat of it: for in the day that thou eatest thereof thou shalt surely die.   *2:17*

15   It is not good that the man should be alone; I will make him an help meet for him.   *2:18*

16   And the Lord God caused a deep sleep to fall upon Adam, and he slept: and he took one of his ribs, and closed up the flesh instead thereof.
    And the rib, which the Lord God had taken from man, made he a woman.   *2:21–22*

17   Bone of my bones, and flesh of my flesh.
                                            2:23

18   Therefore shall a man leave his father and his mother, and shall cleave unto his wife: and they shall be one flesh.
    And they were both naked, the man and his wife, and were not ashamed.   *2:24–25*

19   Now the serpent was more subtile than any beast of the field.   *3:1*

20   Your eyes shall be opened, and ye shall be as gods, knowing good and evil.   *3:5*

21   And they sewed fig leaves together, and made themselves aprons.[8]
    And they heard the voice of the Lord God walking in the garden in the cool of the day.   *3:7–8*

22   The woman whom thou gavest to be with me, she gave me of the tree, and I did eat.   *3:12*

23   What is this that thou hast done? And the woman said, The serpent beguiled me, and I did eat.
    And the Lord God said unto the serpent, Because thou hast done this, thou art cursed above all cattle, and above every beast of the field; upon thy belly shalt thou go, and dust shalt thou eat all the days of thy life.   *3:13–14*

24   And I will put enmity between thee and the woman, and between thy seed and her seed; it shall bruise thy head, and thou shalt bruise his heel.
                                            3:15

25   In sorrow thou shalt bring forth children.
                                            3:16

26   In the sweat of thy face shalt thou eat bread, till thou return unto the ground; for out of it wast thou taken: for dust thou art, and unto dust shalt thou return.
    And Adam called his wife's name Eve; because she was the mother of all living.   *3:19–20*

---

[1]See *Proverbs 23:4, 22:17.*
[2]See *Proverbs 23:5, 22:18.*
[3]See *Proverbs 22:20, 22:12.*
[4]See *Proverbs 22:29, 22:15.*
[5]The oldest part of the Bible, Song of the Sea (*Exodus 15:1–18; see 9:2–9:5*) dates from the tenth century B.C., the era of Solomon, but the material used by the author (called J, or the Yahwist) was much older. Next oldest is the Song of Deborah (*Judges 5:1–12, 11:1–11:2*).
    Bible quotations are from the Authorized (King James) Version [1611]. Numbers in Bible citations represent chapter and verse.
[6]The Hebrew Scriptures. The first five books (the Pentateuch, or the five books of Moses) are the Jewish Torah, embodying the Law revealed to Moses on Mount Sinai.
[7]Fiat lux.— *The Vulgate*

[8]The Geneva Bible [1560] was known sometimes as the Breeches Bible because in this passage "aprons" is rendered as "breeches."

1 So he drove out the man: and he placed at the east of the garden of Eden cherubims, and a flaming sword which turned every way, to keep the way of the tree of life. *3:24*

2 And Abel was a keeper of sheep, but Cain was a tiller of the ground. *4:2*

3 Am I my brother's keeper? *4:9*

4 The voice of thy brother's blood crieth unto me from the ground. *4:10*

5 A fugitive and a vagabond shalt thou be in the earth. *4:12*

6 My punishment is greater than I can bear. *4:13*

7 And the Lord set a mark upon Cain. *4:15*

8 And Cain went out from the presence of the Lord, and dwelt in the land of Nod. *4:16*

9 Jabal: he was the father of such as dwell in tents. *4:20*

10 Jubal: he was the father of all such as handle the harp and organ. *4:21*

11 Tubal-cain, an instructor of every artificer in brass and iron. *4:22*

12 And Enoch walked with God. *5:24*

13 And all the days of Methuselah were nine hundred sixty and nine years. *5:27*

14 And Noah begat Shem, Ham, and Japheth. *5:32*

15 There were giants in the earth in those days . . . mighty men which were of old, men of renown. *6:4*

16 Make thee an ark of gopher wood. *6:14*

17 And of every living thing of all flesh, two of every sort shalt thou bring into the ark. *6:19*

18 And the rain was upon the earth forty days and forty nights. *7:12*

19 But the dove found no rest for the sole of her foot. *8:9*

20 And, lo, in her mouth was an olive leaf pluckt off. *8:11*

21 For the imagination of man's heart is evil from his youth. *8:21*

22 While the earth remaineth, seedtime and harvest, and cold and heat, and summer and winter, and day and night shall not cease. *8:22*

23 Whoso sheddeth man's blood, by man shall his blood be shed: for in the image of God made he man. *9:6*

24 I do set my bow in the cloud, and it shall be for a token of a covenant between me and the earth. *9:13*

25 Even as Nimrod the mighty hunter before the Lord. *10:9*

26 Therefore is the name of it called Babel; because the Lord did there confound the language of all the earth. *11:9*

27 Let there be no strife, I pray thee, between me and thee . . . for we be brethren. *13:8*

28 Abram dwelled in the land of Canaan, and Lot dwelled in the cities of the plain, and pitched his tent toward Sodom. *13:12*

29 In a good old age. *15:15*

30 His [Ishmael's] hand will be against every man, and every man's hand against him. *16:12*

31 Thy name shall be Abraham; for a father of many nations have I made thee. *17:5*

32 My Lord, if now I have found favor in thy sight, pass not away, I pray thee, from thy servant. *18:3*

33 But his [Lot's] wife looked back from behind him, and she became a pillar of salt. *19:26*

34 My son, God will provide himself a lamb for a burnt offering. *22:8*

35 Behold behind him a ram caught in a thicket by his horns. *22:13*

36 Esau was a cunning hunter, a man of the field; and Jacob was a plain man, dwelling in tents. *25:27*

37 And he [Esau] sold his birthright unto Jacob.
Then Jacob gave Esau bread and pottage of lentils. *25:33–34*

38 The voice is Jacob's voice, but the hands are the hands of Esau. *27:22*

39 Thy brother came with subtilty, and hath taken away thy blessing. *27:35*

40 He [Jacob] dreamed, and behold a ladder set up on the earth, and the top of it reached to heaven: and behold the angels of God ascending and descending on it. *28:12*

41 Surely the Lord is in this place; and I knew it not. *28:16*

42 This is none other but the house of God, and this is the gate of heaven. *28:17*

43 Jacob served seven years for Rachel; and they seemed unto him but a few days, for the love he had to her. *29:20*

44 And Laban said, This heap [of stones] is a witness between me and thee this day. Therefore was the name of it called Galeed;
And Mizpah; for he said, The Lord watch between me and thee, when we are absent one from another. *31:48–49*

45 And Jacob was left alone; and there wrestled a man with him until the breaking of the day. *32:24*

1   I will not let thee go, except thou bless me.

Genesis 32:26

2   And Jacob called the name of the place Peniel: for I have seen God face to face, and my life is preserved.[1]

32:30

3   Behold, this dreamer cometh.   *37:19*

4   They stript Joseph out of his coat, his coat of many colors.   *37:23*

5   The Lord made all that he did to prosper in his hand.   *39:3*

6   And she [Potiphar's wife] caught him by his garment, saying, Lie with me: and he left his garment in her hand, and fled, and got him out.   *39:12*

7   The seven good kine are seven years; and the seven good ears are seven years: the dream is one.
And the seven thin and ill-favored kine that came up after them are seven years; and the seven empty ears blasted with the east wind shall be seven years of famine.   *41:26–27*

8   Then shall ye bring down my gray hairs with sorrow to the grave.   *42:38*

9   But Benjamin's mess was five times so much as any of theirs.   *43:34*

10   Wherefore have ye rewarded evil for good?

44:4

11   God forbid.   *44:7*[2]

12   The man in whose hand the cup is found, he shall be my servant.   *44:17*

13   And he fell upon his brother Benjamin's neck, and wept; and Benjamin wept upon his neck.

45:14

14   And ye shall eat the fat of the land.   *45:18*

15   And they came into the land of Goshen.

46:28

16   But I will lie with my fathers, and thou shalt carry me out of Egypt, and bury me in their buryingplace. And he said, I will do as thou hast said.   *47:30*

17   Unstable as water, thou shalt not excel.

49:4

18   I have waited for thy salvation, O Lord.

49:18

19   Unto the utmost bound of the everlasting hills.

49:26

20   Now there arose up a new king over Egypt, which knew not Joseph.
The Second Book of Moses, Called Exodus 1:8

21   She took for him an ark of bulrushes, and daubed it with slime and with pitch.   *2:3*

22   I have been a stranger in a strange land.[3]

2:22

23   Behold, the bush burned with fire, and the bush was not consumed.   *3:2*

24   Put off thy shoes from off thy feet, for the place whereon thou standest is holy ground.   *3:5*

25   And Moses hid his face; for he was afraid to look upon God.   *3:6*

26   A land flowing with milk and honey.[4]   *3:8*

27   And God said unto Moses, I AM THAT I AM.

3:14

28   I am slow of speech, and of a slow tongue.

4:10

29   Let my people go.   *5:1*

30   Ye shall no more give the people straw to make brick.   *5:7*

31   Thou shalt say unto Aaron, Take thy rod, and cast it before Pharaoh, and it shall become a serpent.

7:9

32   They [Pharaoh's wise men] cast down every man his rod, and they became serpents: but Aaron's rod swallowed up their rods.
And he hardened Pharaoh's heart.   *7:12–13*

33   This is the finger of God.   *8:19*

34   Darkness which may be felt.   *10:21*

35   Yet will I bring one plague more upon Pharaoh, and upon Egypt.   *11:1*

36   Your lamb shall be without blemish.   *12:5*

37   And they shall eat the flesh in that night, roast with fire, and unleavened bread; and with bitter herbs they shall eat it.[5]   *12:8*

38   And thus shall ye eat it; with your loins girded, your shoes on your feet, and your staff in your hand; and ye shall eat it in haste: it is the Lord's passover.
For I will pass through the land of Egypt this night, and will smite all the firstborn in the land of Egypt, both man and beast; and against all the gods of Egypt I will execute judgment: I am the Lord.

12:11–12

39   This day [Passover] shall be unto you for a memorial; and ye shall keep it a feast to the Lord throughout your generations.   *12:14*

40   Seven days shall ye eat unleavened bread.

12:15

41   There was a great cry in Egypt; for there was not a house where there was not one dead.   *12:30*

42   Remember this day, in which ye came out from Egypt, out of the house of bondage.   *13:3*

43   And the Lord went before them by day in a pillar of a cloud, to lead them the way; and by night in a pillar of fire, to give them light.   *13:21*

---

[1]See *I Corinthians 13:12, 43:16.*
[2]*Passim* in the Old Testament.
[3]See Sophocles, *67:5.*

[4]Also in *Exodus 33:3* and *Jeremiah 11:5.*
[5]The feast of the Passover.

1 And the children of Israel went into the midst of the sea upon the dry ground: and the waters were a wall unto them on their right hand, and on their left.
14:22

2 I will sing unto the Lord, for he hath triumphed gloriously: the horse and his rider hath he thrown into the sea.
The Lord is my strength and song, and he is become my salvation.
15:1-2

3 The Lord is a man of war.
15:3

4 Thy right hand, O Lord, is become glorious in power: thy right hand, O Lord, hath dashed in pieces the enemy.
15:6

5 Thou sentest forth thy wrath, which consumed them as stubble.
And with the blast of thy nostrils the waters were gathered together, the floods stood upright as an heap, and the depths were congealed in the heart of the sea.
15:7-8

6 Would to God we had died by the hand of the Lord in the land of Egypt, when we sat by the flesh-pots, and when we did eat bread to the full.
16:3

7 It is manna.
16:15

8 I am the Lord thy God.
20:2[1]

9 Thou shalt have no other gods before me.
Thou shalt not make unto thee any graven image.
20:3-4

10 For I the Lord thy God am a jealous God, visiting the iniquity of the fathers upon the children unto the third and fourth generation of them that hate me;[2]
And showing mercy unto thousands of them that love me, and keep my commandments.
Thou shalt not take the name of the Lord thy God in vain.
20:5-7

11 Remember the sabbath day, to keep it holy.
Six days shalt thou labor, and do all thy work:
But the seventh day . . . thou shalt not do any work.
20:8-10

12 Honor thy father and thy mother: that thy days may be long upon the land which the Lord thy God giveth thee.[3]
Thou shalt not kill.
Thou shalt not commit adultery.
Thou shalt not steal.
Thou shalt not bear false witness against thy neighbor.
Thou shalt not covet thy neighbor's house, thou shalt not covet thy neighbor's wife, nor his manser-vant, nor his maidservant, nor his ox, nor his ass, nor any thing that is thy neighbor's.
20:12-17

13 But let not God speak with us, lest we die.
20:19

14 He that smiteth a man, so that he die, shall be surely put to death.
21:12

15 Eye for eye, tooth for tooth,[4] hand for hand, foot for foot.
21:24

16 Behold, I send an Angel before thee, to keep thee in the way.
23:20

17 A stiffnecked people.
32:9

18 Who is on the Lord's side? let him come unto me.
32:26

19 Thou canst not see my face: for there shall no man see me, and live.
33:20

20 And he [Moses] was there with the Lord forty days and forty nights; he did neither eat bread, nor drink water. And he wrote upon the tables the words of the covenant, the ten commandments.
34:28

21 Whatsoever parteth the hoof, and is cloven-footed, and cheweth the cud, among the beasts, that shall ye eat.
The Third Book of Moses, Called Leviticus 11:3

22 And the swine . . . is unclean to you.
Of their flesh shall ye not eat.
11:7-8

23 Let him go for a scapegoat into the wilderness.
16:10

24 And when ye reap the harvest of your land, thou shalt not wholly reap the corners of thy field, neither shalt thou gather the gleanings of thy harvest.
And thou shalt not glean thy vineyard, neither shalt thou gather every grape of thy vineyard; thou shalt leave them for the poor and stranger.
19:9-10

25 Thou shalt not go up and down as a talebearer among thy people.
19:16

26 Thou shalt love thy neighbor as thyself.[5]
19:18

27 Ye shall hallow the fiftieth year, and proclaim liberty throughout all the land unto all the inhabitants thereof:[6] it shall be a jubilee unto you.
25:10

28 The Lord bless thee, and keep thee:
The Lord make his face shine upon thee, and be gracious unto thee:
The Lord lift up his countenance upon thee, and give thee peace.
The Fourth Book of Moses, Called Numbers 6:24-26

29 Sent to spy out the land.
13:16

---

[1]*Exodus 20:2-17* contains the Ten Commandments (the Decalogue), as handed down by God to Moses on Mount Sinai. Also in *Deuteronomy 5:6-21*.
[2]See Euripides, 69:17.
[3]See Aeschylus, 63:2.

[4]Also in *Matthew 5:38*.
[5]Also in *Matthew 19:19* and 22:39 (36:1), *Mark 12:31* and 33, *Romans 13:9*, *Galatians 5:14*, *James 2:8*.
[6]From "proclaim" through "thereof": inscription on the Liberty Bell, Philadelphia [1751].

1   And your children shall wander in the wilderness forty years.   *Numbers 14:33*

2   Moses lifted up his hand, and with his rod he smote the rock twice: and the water came out abundantly.   *20:11*

3   He whom thou blessest is blessed.   *22:6*

4   The Lord opened the mouth of the ass, and she said unto Balaam, What have I done unto thee?   *22:28*

5   Let me die the death of the righteous, and let my last end be like his!   *23:10*

6   God is not a man, that he should lie.[1]   *23:19*

7   What hath God wrought![2]   *23:23*

8   How goodly are thy tents, O Jacob, and thy tabernacles, O Israel!   *24:5*

9   Be sure your sin will find you out.   *32:23*

10   I call heaven and earth to witness.
     The Fifth Book of Moses, Called Deuteronomy
     4:26

11   Thou shalt love the Lord thy God with all thine heart, and with all thy soul, and with all thy might.[3]
     And these words, which I command thee this day, shall be in thine heart:
     And thou shalt teach them diligently unto thy children.   *6:5–7*

12   Ye shall not tempt the Lord your God.[4]
                                                  6:16

13   The Lord thy God hath chosen thee to be a special people unto himself.   *7:6*

14   Man doth not live by bread only,[5] but by every word that proceedeth out of the mouth of the Lord doth man live.   *8:3*

15   For the Lord thy God bringeth thee into a good land.   *8:7*

16   A land of wheat, and barley, and vines, and fig trees, and pomegranates; a land of oil olive, and honey;
     A land wherein thou shalt eat bread without scarceness, thou shalt not lack any thing in it; a land whose stones are iron, and out of whose hills thou mayest dig brass.   *8:8–9*

17   A dreamer of dreams.   *13:1*

18   The wife of thy bosom.   *13:6*

19   The poor shall never cease out of the land.[6]
                                                 15:11

20   Thou shalt not move a sickle unto thy neighbor's standing corn.   *23:25*

21   Thou shalt not muzzle the ox when he treadeth out the corn.   *25:4*

22   And thou shalt become an astonishment, a proverb, and a byword, among all nations.   *28:37*

23   In the morning thou shalt say, Would God it were even! and at even thou shalt say, Would God it were morning!   *28:67*

24   The secret things belong unto the Lord our God.   *29:29*

25   I have set before you life and death, blessing and cursing: therefore choose life, that both thou and thy seed may live.   *30:19*

26   He is the Rock, his work is perfect: for all his ways are judgment: a God of truth.   *32:4*

27   Jeshurun waxed fat, and kicked.   *32:15*

28   As thy days, so shall thy strength be.   *33:25*

29   The eternal God is thy refuge, and underneath are the everlasting arms.   *33:27*

30   No man knoweth of his [Moses'] sepulcher unto this day.   *34:6*

31   Be strong and of a good courage;[7] be not afraid, neither be thou dismayed: for the Lord thy God is with thee whithersoever thou goest.
     The Book of Joshua 1:9

32   And the priests that bare the ark of the covenant of the Lord stood firm on dry ground in the midst of Jordan, and all the Israelites passed over on dry ground, until all the people were passed clean over Jordan.   *3:17*

33   Mighty men of valor.   *6:2*

34   And it came to pass, when the people heard the sound of the trumpet, and the people shouted with a great shout, that the wall fell down flat, so that the people went up into the city [Jericho].   *6:20*

35   His fame was noised throughout all the country.
                                                 6:27

36   Hewers of wood and drawers of water.
                                                 9:21

37   Sun, stand thou still upon Gibeon; and thou, Moon, in the valley of Ajalon.   *10:12*

38   Old and stricken in years.[8]   *13:1*

39   I am going the way of all the earth.   *23:14*

40   They shall be as thorns in your sides.[9]
     The Book of Judges 2:3

41   Then Jael, Heber's wife, took a nail of the tent, and took an hammer in her hand, and went softly unto him [Sisera], and smote the nail into his tem-

---

[1]See Aeschylus, 63:7.
[2]Quoted by Samuel F. B. Morse in the first telegraph message he sent to his partner, Alfred Vail, from Washington to Baltimore [May 24, 1844].
[3]See *Matthew 22:37, 36:1.*
[4]Also in *Matthew 4:7.*
[5]Man shall not live by bread alone.—*Matthew 4:4*
[6]See *Matthew 26:11, 36:22.*

[7]Also in *Deuteronomy 31:6, 7, 23.*
[8]Also in *I Kings 1:1.*
[9]See *II Corinthians 12:7, 44:11.*

ples, and fastened it into the ground; for he was fast asleep, and weary: so he died.   4:21

1   I Deborah arose . . . I arose a mother in Israel.[1]
                                                    5:7

2   Awake, awake, Deborah: awake, awake, utter a song: arise, Barak, and lead thy captivity captive.
                                                    5:12

3   The stars in their courses fought against Sisera.
                                                    5:20

4   She [Jael] brought forth butter in a lordly dish.
                                                    5:25

5   At her feet he bowed, he fell, he lay down: at her feet he bowed, he fell: where he bowed, there he fell down dead.   5:27

6   The mother of Sisera looked out at a window, and cried through the lattice, Why is his chariot so long in coming? why tarry the wheels of his chariots?
                                                    5:28

7   Have they not divided the prey; to every man a damsel or two?   5:30

8   The sword of the Lord, and of Gideon.
                                                    7:18

9   Is not the gleaning of the grapes of Ephraim better than the vintage of Abiezer?   8:2

10 Say now Shibboleth: and he said Sibboleth: for he could not frame to pronounce it right.   12:6

11 There was a swarm of bees and honey in the carcass of the lion.   14:8

12 Out of the eater came forth meat, and out of the strong came forth sweetness.   14:14

13 If ye had not plowed with my heifer, ye had not found out my riddle.   14:18

14 He smote them hip and thigh.   15:8

15 With the jawbone of an ass . . . have I slain a thousand men.   15:16

16 The Philistines be upon thee, Samson.   16:9

17 The Philistines took him [Samson], and put out his eyes, and brought him down to Gaza, and bound him with fetters of brass; and he did grind in the prison house.   16:21

18 Strengthen me, I pray thee, only this once, O God, that I may be . . . avenged of the Philistines for my two eyes.   16:28

19 So the dead which he slew at his death were more than they which he slew in his life.   16:30

20 From Dan even to Beersheba.   20:1

21 All the people arose as one man.   20:8

22 In those days there was no king in Israel: every man did that which was right in his own eyes.
                                                    21:25

23 Whither thou goest, I will go; and where thou lodgest, I will lodge: thy people shall be my people, and thy God my God.   *The Book of Ruth 1:16*

24 Let me glean and gather after the reapers among the sheaves.   2:7

25 Go not empty unto thy mother in law.
                                                    3:17

26 In the flower of their age.
                                The First Book of Samuel 2:33

27 The Lord called Samuel: and he answered, Here am I.   3:4

28 Speak, Lord; for thy servant heareth.   3:9

29 Be strong, and quit yourselves like men.[2]
                                                    4:9

30 And she named the child Ichabod, saying, The glory is departed from Israel: because the ark of God was taken.   4:21

31 Is Saul also among the prophets?   10:11

32 God save the king.   10:24

33 A man after his own heart.   13:14

34 Every man's sword was against his fellow.
                                                    14:20

35 But Jonathan heard not when his father charged the people with the oath: wherefore he put forth the end of the rod that was in his hand, and dipped it in an honeycomb, and put his hand to his mouth; and his eyes were enlightened.   14:27

36 For the Lord seeth not as man seeth; for man looketh on the outward appearance, but the Lord looketh on the heart.   16:7

37 I know thy pride, and the naughtiness of thine heart.   17:28

38 Let no man's heart fail because of him [Goliath].
                                                    17:32

39 Go, and the Lord be with thee.   17:37

40 And he [David] . . . chose him five smooth stones out of the brook.   17:40

41 So David prevailed over the Philistine with a sling and with a stone.   17:50

42 Saul hath slain his thousands, and David his ten thousands.   18:7

43 And Jonathan . . . loved him [David] as he loved his own soul.   20:17

44 Wickedness proceedeth from the wicked.
                                                    24:13

45 I have played the fool.   26:21

46 Tell it not in Gath, publish it not in the streets of Askelon.   *The Second Book of Samuel 1:20*

47 Saul and Jonathan were lovely and pleasant in their lives, and in their death they were not divided:

---

[1]The Song of Deborah; see 6:*n*5.

[2]See *I Corinthians 16:13*, 43:29.

they were swifter than eagles, they were stronger than lions.   *II Samuel 1:23*

1   How are the mighty fallen in the midst of the battle!   *1:25*

2   Thy love to me was wonderful, passing the love of women.

How are the mighty fallen, and the weapons of war perished!   *1:26–27*

3   Abner . . . smote him under the fifth rib.
2:23

4   Know ye not that there is a prince and a great man [Abner] fallen this day in Israel?   *3:38*

5   And David and all the house of Israel played before the Lord on all manner of instruments made of fir wood, even on harps, and on psalteries, and on timbrels, and on cornets, and on cymbals.[1]
6:5

6   Uzzah put forth his hand to the ark of God, and took hold of it . . . and the anger of the Lord was kindled against Uzzah.   *6:6*

7   David danced before the Lord.   *6:14*

8   Tarry at Jericho until your beards be grown.[2]
10:5

9   Set ye Uriah in the forefront of the hottest battle.
11:15

10   The poor man had nothing, save one little ewe lamb.   *12:3*

11   Thou art the man.   *12:7*

12   Now he is dead, wherefore should I fast? Can I bring him back again? I shall go to him, but he shall not return to me.   *12:23*

13   For we must needs die, and are as water spilt on the ground, which cannot be gathered up again.
14:14

14   Would God I had died for thee, O Absalom, my son, my son!   *18:33*

15   The Lord is my rock, and my fortress, and my deliverer.   *22:2*

16   David the son of Jesse . . . the sweet psalmist of Israel.   *23:1*

17   Went in jeopardy of their lives.   *23:17*

18   A wise and an understanding heart.
The First Book of the Kings 3:12

19   Many, as the sand which is by the sea in multitude.   *4:20*

20   Judah and Israel dwelt safely, every man under his vine and under his fig tree.   *4:25*

21   He [Solomon] spake three thousand proverbs: and his songs were a thousand and five.   *4:32*

22   The wisdom of Solomon.   *4:34*

23   So that there was neither hammer nor axe nor any tool of iron heard in the house,[3] while it was in building.   *6:7*

24   A proverb and a byword among all people.
9:7

25   When the queen of Sheba heard of the fame of Solomon . . . she came to prove him with hard questions.   *10:1*

26   The half was not told me: thy wisdom and prosperity exceedeth the fame which I heard.   *10:7*

27   Once in three years came the navy of Tharshish, bringing gold, and silver, ivory, and apes, and peacocks.   *10:22*

28   King Solomon loved many strange women.
11:1

29   My father hath chastised you with whips, but I will chastise you with scorpions.   *12:11*

30   To your tents, O Israel.   *12:16*

31   He [Elijah] went and dwelt by the brook Cherith, that is before Jordan.   *17:5*

32   And the ravens brought him bread and flesh in the morning, and bread and flesh in the evening; and he drank of the brook.   *17:6*

33   An handful of meal in a barrel, and a little oil in a cruse.   *17:12*

34   And the barrel of meal wasted not, neither did the cruse of oil fail.   *17:16*

35   How long halt ye between two opinions?
18:21

36   Either he [Baal] is talking, or he is pursuing, or he is in a journey, or peradventure he sleepeth, and must be awaked.   *18:27*

37   There ariseth a little cloud out of the sea, like a man's hand.   *18:44*

38   And he girded up his loins, and ran before Ahab.
18:46

39   But the Lord was not in the wind: and after the wind an earthquake; but the Lord was not in the earthquake:

And after the earthquake a fire; but the Lord was not in the fire: and after the fire a still small voice.
19:11–12

40   Let not him that girdeth on his harness boast himself as he that putteth it off.   *20:11*

41   Hast thou found me, O mine enemy?   *21:20*

42   The dogs shall eat Jezebel by the wall of Jezreel.
21:23

[1]See *Psalm 150:3–6, 20:16.*
[2]Also in *I Chronicles 19:5.*

[3]Solomon's temple (the house of the Lord).

1 But there was none like unto Ahab, which did sell himself to work wickedness in the sight of the Lord, whom Jezebel his wife stirred up. *21:25*

2 I saw all Israel scattered upon the hills, as sheep that have not a shepherd. *22:17*

3 Feed him [Micajah] with bread of affliction, and with water of affliction, until I come in peace. *22:27*

4 There appeared a chariot of fire, and horses of fire, and parted them both asunder; and Elijah went up by a whirlwind into heaven. *The Second Book of the Kings 2:11*

5 The chariot of Israel, and the horsemen thereof. And he saw him no more. *2:12*

6 He [Elisha] took up also the mantle of Elijah. *2:13*

7 There is death in the pot. *4:40*

8 Is thy servant a dog, that he should do this great thing? *8:13*

9 What hast thou to do with peace? turn thee behind me. *9:18*

10 The driving is like the driving of Jehu the son of Nimshi; for he driveth furiously. *9:20*

11 Jezebel heard of it; and she painted her face, and tired her head, and looked out at a window. *9:30*

12 The angel of the Lord went out, and smote in the camp of the Assyrians an hundred fourscore and five thousand: and when they arose early in the morning, behold, they were all dead corpses.
So Sennacherib king of Assyria departed. *19:35–36*

13 Set thine house in order. *20:1*

14 I will wipe Jerusalem as a man wipeth a dish, wiping it, and turning it upside down. *21:13*

15 His mercy endureth for ever. *The First Book of the Chronicles 16:41*

16 The Lord searcheth all hearts, and understandeth all the imaginations of the thoughts. *28:9*

17 Thine, O Lord, is the greatness, and the power, and the glory, and the victory, and the majesty: for all that is in the heaven and in the earth is thine; thine is the kingdom, O Lord, and thou art exalted as head above all.[1] *29:11*

18 For all things come of thee, and of thine own have we given thee.[2] *29:14*

19 Our days on the earth are as a shadow. *29:15*

20 He [David] died in a good old age, full of days, riches, and honor. *29:28*

21 They which builded on the wall, and they that bare burdens, with those that laded, every one with one of his hands wrought in the work, and with the other hand held a weapon. *The Book of Nehemiah 4:17*

22 And he [Ezra] read therein before the street that was before the water gate from the morning until midday, before the men and the women, and those that could understand; and the ears of all the people were attentive unto the book of the law. *8:3*

23 Thou art a God ready to pardon, gracious and merciful, slow to anger, and of great kindness. *9:17*

24 Mordecai rent his clothes, and put on sackcloth with ashes. *The Book of Esther 4:1*

25 The man whom the king delighteth to honor. *6:6*

26 They hanged Haman on the gallows. *7:10*

27 One that feared God, and eschewed evil. *The Book of Job 1:1*

28 Satan came also. *1:6*

29 And the Lord said unto Satan, Whence comest thou? Then Satan answered the Lord, and said, From going to and fro in the earth, and from walking up and down in it. *1:7*

30 Doth Job fear God for nought? *1:9*

31 Naked came I out of my mother's womb, and naked shall I return thither:[3] the Lord gave, and the Lord hath taken away; blessed be the name of the Lord. *1:21*

32 Skin for skin, yea, all that a man hath will he give for his life. *2:4*

33 Curse God, and die. *2:9*

34 Let the day perish wherein I was born, and the night in which it was said, There is a man child conceived.[4] *3:3*

35 For now should I have lain still and been quiet, I should have slept: then had I been at rest,
With kings and counsellors of the earth, which built desolate places for themselves. *3:13–14*

36 There the wicked cease from troubling; and there the weary be at rest. *3:17*

37 Who ever perished, being innocent? or where were the righteous cut off? *4:7*

38 Fear came upon me, and trembling. *4:14*

39 Then a spirit passed before my face; the hair of my flesh stood up. *4:15*

40 Shall mortal man be more just than God? shall a man be more pure than his maker? *4:17*

[1]See *Matthew* 6:13, 33:12.
[2]See Marcus Aurelius, 111:5.

[3]See *Ecclesiastes* 5:15, 24:5.
[4]See Euripides, 68:5.

1   Wrath killeth the foolish man, and envy slayeth the silly one.   *Job 5:2*

2   Man is born unto trouble, as the sparks fly upward.   *5:7*

3   He taketh the wise in their own craftiness.   *5:13*

4   For thou shalt be in league with the stones of the field: and the beasts of the field shall be at peace with thee.   *5:23*

5   Thou shalt come to thy grave in a full age, like as a shock of corn cometh in in his season.   *5:26*

6   How forcible are right words!   *6:25*

7   My days are swifter than a weaver's shuttle, and are spent without hope.   *7:6*

8   He shall return no more to his house, neither shall his place know him any more.[1]   *7:10*

9   I would not live alway: let me alone: for my days are vanity.   *7:16*

10   But how should man be just with God?   *9:2*

11   The land of darkness and the shadow of death.   *10:21*

12   Canst thou by searching find out God?   *11:7*

13   And thine age shall be clearer than the noonday.   *11:17*

14   No doubt but ye are the people, and wisdom shall die with you.   *12:2*

15   The just upright man is laughed to scorn.   *12:4*

16   But ask now the beasts, and they shall teach thee; and the fowls of the air, and they shall tell thee:
Or speak to the earth, and it shall teach thee; and the fishes of the sea shall declare unto thee.   *12:7–8*

17   With the ancient is wisdom; and in length of days understanding.   *12:12*

18   He discovereth deep things out of darkness, and bringeth out to light the shadow of death.   *12:22*

19   Though he slay me, yet will I trust in him.   *13:15*

20   Man that is born of a woman is of few days, and full of trouble.
He cometh forth like a flower, and is cut down: he fleeth also as a shadow, and continueth not.   *14:1–2*

21   But man dieth, and wasteth away: yea, man giveth up the ghost, and where is he?   *14:10*

22   If a man die, shall he live again?   *14:14*

23   Should a wise man utter vain knowledge, and fill his belly with the east wind?   *15:2*

24   Miserable comforters are ye all.   *16:2*

25   My days are past.   *17:11*

26   I have said to corruption, Thou art my father: to the worm, Thou art my mother, and my sister.   *17:14*

27   The king of terrors.   *18:14*

28   I am escaped with the skin of my teeth.   *19:20*

29   Oh that my words were now written! oh that they were printed in a book!   *19:23*

30   I know that my redeemer liveth, and that he shall stand at the latter day upon the earth:[2]
And though, after my skin, worms destroy this body, yet in my flesh shall I see God.   *19:25–26*

31   Seeing the root of the matter is found in me.   *19:28*

32   Though wickedness be sweet in his mouth, though he hide it under his tongue.   *20:12*

33   Suffer me that I may speak; and after that I have spoken, mock on.   *21:3*

34   Shall any teach God knowledge?   *21:22*

35   They are of those that rebel against the light.   *24:13*

36   The womb shall forget him; the worm shall feed sweetly on him; he shall be no more remembered.   *24:20*

37   Yea, the stars are not pure in his sight.
How much less man, that is a worm? and the son of man, which is a worm?   *25:5–6*

38   But where shall wisdom be found? and where is the place of understanding?   *28:12*

39   The land of the living.   *28:13*

40   The price of wisdom is above rubies.[3]   *28:18*

41   Behold, the fear of the Lord, that is wisdom; and to depart from evil is understanding.   *28:28*

42   I caused the widow's heart to sing for joy.   *29:13*

43   I was eyes to the blind, and feet was I to the lame.   *29:15*

44   I know that thou wilt bring me to death, and to the house appointed for all living.   *30:23*

45   I am a brother to dragons, and a companion to owls.   *30:29*

46   My desire is, that the Almighty would answer me, and that mine adversary had written a book.   *31:35*

47   Great men are not always wise.   *32:9*

---

[1]When a few years are come, then I shall go the way whence I shall not return.—*Job 16:22*
The place thereof shall know it no more.—*Psalm 103:16*

[2]Also in *Book of Common Prayer, Burial of the Dead.*
[3][Wisdom] is more precious than rubies.—*Proverbs 3:15*
See Sophocles, 66:19.

1 For I am full of matter, the spirit within me constraineth me. *32:18*

2 One among a thousand. *33:23*

3 Far be it from God, that he should do wickedness. *34:10*

4 He multiplieth words without knowledge. *35:16*

5 Fair weather cometh out of the north. *37:22*

6 Then the Lord answered Job out of the whirlwind, and said,
Who is this that darkeneth counsel by words without knowledge?
Gird up now thy loins like a man. *38:1–3*

7 Where wast thou when I laid the foundations of the earth? declare, if thou hast understanding. *38:4*

8 The morning stars sang together, and all the sons of God shouted for joy. *38:7*

9 Hitherto shalt thou come, but no further: and here shall thy proud waves be stayed. *38:11*

10 Hast thou entered into the springs of the sea? or hast thou walked in the search of the depth? *38:16*

11 Hath the rain a father? or who hath begotten the drops of dew? *38:28*

12 Canst thou bind the sweet influences of Pleiades, or loose the bands of Orion? *38:31*

13 Canst thou guide Arcturus with his sons? *38:32*

14 Who can number the clouds in wisdom? or who can stay the bottles of heaven. *38:37*

15 Hast thou given the horse strength? hast thou clothed his neck with thunder? *39:19*

16 He paweth in the valley, and rejoiceth in his strength: he goeth on to meet the armed men. *39:21*

17 He swalloweth the ground with fierceness and rage; neither believeth he that it is the sound of the trumpet.
He saith among the trumpets, Ha, ha; and he smelleth the battle afar off, the thunder of the captains, and the shouting. *39:24–25*

18 Doth the eagle mount up at thy command, and make her nest on high?
She dwelleth and abideth on the rock, upon the crag of the rock, and the strong place.
From thence she seeketh the prey, and her eyes behold afar off.
Her young ones also suck up blood: and where the slain are, there is she. *39:27–30*

19 Behold, I am vile; what shall I answer thee? *40:4*

20 Behold now behemoth, which I made with thee; he eateth grass as an ox. *40:15*

21 Canst thou draw out leviathan with a hook? *41:1*

22 Who can open the doors of his face? his teeth are terrible round about.
His scales are his pride, shut up together as with a close seal. *41:14,15*

23 His heart is as firm as a stone; yea as hard as a piece of the nether millstone. *41:24*

24 He maketh the deep to boil like a pot. *41:31*

25 Upon earth there is not his like, who is made without fear. *41:33*

26 He is a king over all the children of pride. *41:34*

27 I have heard of thee by the hearing of the ear: but now mine eye seeth thee. *42:5*

28 So the Lord blessed the latter end of Job more than his beginning. *42:12*

29 Blessed is the man that walketh not in the counsel of the ungodly, nor standeth in the way of sinners, nor sitteth in the seat of the scornful.
But his delight is in the law of the Lord; and in his law doth he meditate day and night.
And he shall be like a tree planted by the rivers of water, that bringeth forth his fruit in his season; his leaf also shall not wither; and whatsoever he doeth shall prosper.
The ungodly are not so: but are like the chaff which the wind driveth away.
The Book of Psalms 1:1–4[1]

30 Why do the heathen rage, and the people imagine a vain thing? *2:1*

31 Blessed are all they that put their trust in him. *2:12*

32 Lord, lift thou up the light of thy countenance upon us. *4:6*

33 I will both lay me down in peace, and sleep.[2] *4:8*

34 Out of the mouth of babes and sucklings hast thou ordained strength, because of thine enemies; that thou mightest still the enemy and the avenger.
When I consider thy heavens, the work of thy fingers, the moon and the stars, which thou hast ordained;
What is man, that thou art mindful of him? and the son of man, that thou visitest him?
For thou hast made him a little lower than the angels. *8:2–5*

35 How excellent is thy name in all the earth. *8:9*

[1]See Amenemope, 5:13, and *Jeremiah* 17:5–8, 28:29.
[2]I will lay me down in peace, and take my rest.—*Book of Common Prayer*, Psalm 4:9

1   Flee as a bird to your mountain.

Psalms 11:1

2   How long wilt thou forget me, O Lord?

13:1

3   The fool hath said in his heart, There is no God.

14:1 and 53:1

4   Lord, who shall abide in thy tabernacle? who shall dwell in thy holy hill?

15:1

5   He that sweareth to his own hurt, and changeth not.

15:4

6   The lines are fallen unto me in pleasant places;[1] yea, I have a goodly heritage.

16:6

7   Keep me as the apple of the eye,[2] hide me under the shadow of thy wings.

17:8

8   He rode upon a cherub, and did fly: yea, he did fly upon the wings of the wind.

18:10

9   The heavens declare the glory of God; and the firmament showeth his handiwork.

Day unto day uttereth speech, and night unto night showeth knowledge.

19:1-2

10   Their line is gone out through all the earth, and their words to the end of the world. In them hath he set a tabernacle for the sun,

Which is as a bridegroom coming out of his chamber, and rejoiceth as a strong man to run a race.

His going forth is from the end of the heaven, and his circuit unto the ends of it: and there is nothing hid from the heat thereof.

19:4-6

11   The judgments of the Lord are true and righteous altogether.

More to be desired are they than gold, yea, than much fine gold: sweeter also than honey and the honeycomb.

19:9-10

12   Cleanse thou me from secret faults.

19:12

13   Let the words of my mouth, and the meditation of my heart, be acceptable in thy sight, O Lord, my strength, and my redeemer.

19:14

14   Thou hast given him his heart's desire.

21:2

15   My God, my God, why hast thou forsaken me?[3] why art thou so far from helping me, and from the words of my roaring?

22:1

16   They part my garments among them, and cast lots upon my vesture.

22:18

17   The Lord is my shepherd; I shall not want.

He maketh me to lie down in green pastures: he leadeth me beside the still waters.

He restoreth my soul: he leadeth me in the paths of righteousness for his name's sake.

Yea, though I walk through the valley of the shadow of death, I will fear no evil: for thou art with me; thy rod and thy staff they comfort me.

Thou preparest a table before me in the presence of mine enemies: thou anointest my head with oil; my cup runneth over.

Surely goodness and mercy shall follow me all the days of my life: and I will dwell in the house of the Lord for ever.

23

18   The earth is the Lord's, and the fullness thereof; the world, and they that dwell therein.[4]

For he hath founded it upon the seas, and established it upon the floods.

Who shall ascend into the hill of the Lord? or who shall stand in his holy place?

He that hath clean hands, and a pure heart; who hath not lifted up his soul unto vanity, nor sworn deceitfully.

24:1-4

19   Lift up your heads, O ye gates; and be ye lift up, ye everlasting doors; and the King of glory shall come in.

24:7

20   Who is this King of glory? The Lord of hosts, he is the King of glory.

24:10

21   The Lord is my light[5] and my salvation; whom shall I fear? the Lord is the strength of my life; of whom shall I be afraid?

27:1

22   Though an host should encamp against me, my heart shall not fear: though war should rise against me, in this will I be confident.

27:3

23   The Lord is my strength and my shield.

28:7

24   Worship the Lord in the beauty of holiness.

29:2

25   Weeping may endure for a night, but joy cometh in the morning.

30:5

26   I am forgotten as a dead man out of mind: I am like a broken vessel.

31:12

27   My times are in thy hand.

31:15

28   From the strife of tongues.

31:20

29   Sing unto him a new song; play skillfully with a loud noise.

33:3

30   O taste and see that the Lord is good.

34:8

31   Keep thy tongue from evil, and thy lips from speaking guile.

Depart from evil, and do good; seek peace, and pursue it.

34:13-14

32   Rescue my soul from their destructions, my darling from the lions.

35:17

33   How excellent is thy lovingkindness, O God!

36:7

34   The meek shall inherit the earth.[6]

37:11

---

[1] The lot is fallen unto me in a fair ground. — *Book of Common Prayer, Psalm 16:7*

[2] Also in *Deuteronomy 32:10* and *Proverbs 7:2.*

[3] This was the psalm Christ recited on the cross. See *Matthew 27:46, 37:12.*

[4] See *1 Corinthians 10:26, 43:9.*

[5] *Dominus illuminatio mea.* — *The Vulgate.* Motto of Oxford University.

[6] See *Matthew 5:5, 33:1.*

1 I have been young, and now am old; yet have I not seen the righteous forsaken, nor his seed begging bread.   *37:25*

2 I have seen the wicked in great power, and spreading himself[1] like a green bay tree.   *37:35*

3 Mark the perfect man, and behold the upright: for the end of that man is peace.[2]   *37:37*

4 For thine arrows stick fast in me, and thy hand presseth me sore.   *38:2*

5 I said, I will take heed to my ways, that I sin not with my tongue.   *39:1*

6 My heart was hot within me, while I was musing the fire burned.   *39:3*

7 Lord, make me to know mine end, and the measure of my days, what it is; that I may know how frail I am.   *39:4*

8 Every man at his best state is altogether vanity.
                                                       39:5

9 Surely every man walketh in a vain show: surely they are disquieted in vain: he heapeth up riches, and knoweth not who shall gather them.   *39:6*

10 For I am a stranger with thee, and a sojourner, as all my fathers were.
   O spare me, that I may recover strength, before I go hence, and be no more.   *39:12–13*

11 As the hart panteth after the water brooks, so panteth my soul after thee, O God.
   My soul thirsteth for God, for the living God.
                                                       42:1–2

12 Why art thou cast down, O my soul? and why art thou disquieted in me?   *42:5*[3]

13 Deep calleth unto deep.   *42:7*

14 My tongue is the pen of a ready writer.
                                                       45:1

15 The king's daughter is all glorious within.
                                                       45:13

16 God is our refuge and strength, a very present help in trouble.
   Therefore will we not fear, though the earth be removed, and though the mountains be carried into the midst of the sea.   *46:1–2*

17 There is a river, the streams whereof shall make glad the city of God, the holy place of the tabernacles of the most High.
   God is in the midst of her; she shall not be moved: God shall help her, and that right early.
                                                       46:4–5

18 Be still, and know that I am God.   *46:10*

19 Every beast of the forest is mine, and the cattle upon a thousand hills.   *50:10*

20 I was shapen in iniquity; and in sin did my mother conceive me.   *51*[4]*:5*

21 Purge me with hyssop, and I shall be clean: wash me, and I shall be whiter than snow.   *51:7*

22 Create in me a clean heart, O God; and renew a right spirit within me.   *51:10*

23 And take not thy holy spirit from me.   *51:11*

24 Open thou my lips; and my mouth shall show forth thy praise.   *51:15*

25 A broken and a contrite heart, O God, thou wilt not despise.   *51:17*

26 Oh that I had wings like a dove! for then would I fly away, and be at rest.[5]   *55:6*

27 We took sweet counsel together.   *55:14*

28 The words of his mouth were smoother than butter, but war was in his heart:[6] his words were softer than oil, yet were they drawn swords.   *55:21*

29 They are like the deaf adder that stoppeth her ear;
   Which will not hearken to the voice of charmers, charming never so wisely.   *58:4–5*

30 Thou hast showed thy people hard things: thou hast made us to drink the wine of astonishment.
                                                       60:3

31 Moab is my washpot; over Edom will I cast out my shoe: Philistia, triumph thou because of me.
                                                       60:8

32 Lead me to the rock that is higher than I.
                                                       61:2

33 He only is my rock and my salvation: he is my defense; I shall not be moved.   *62:6*

34 Thou renderest to every man according to his work.   *62:12*

35 My soul thirsteth for thee, my flesh longeth for thee in a dry and thirsty land, where no water is.
                                                       63:1

36 Thou crownest the year with thy goodness.
                                                       65:11

37 Make a joyful noise unto God, all ye lands.
                                                       66:1

38 We went through fire and through water.
                                                       66:12

39 God setteth the solitary in families.   *68:6*

40 Cast me not off in the time of old age; forsake me not when my strength faileth.   *71:9*

41 He shall come down like rain upon the mown grass: as showers that water the earth.   *72:6*

42 His enemies shall lick the dust.   *72:9*

---

[1]Flourishing.—*Book of Common Prayer, Psalm 37:36*
[2]For that shall bring a man peace at the last.—*Book of Common Prayer, Psalm 37:38*
[3]Also in *Psalms 42:11* and *43:5.*

[4]This psalm is known as the Miserere from its opening word in the Vulgate. The first line is: Have mercy upon me, O God.
[5]See Euripides, 68:19.
[6]The words of his mouth were softer than butter, having war in his heart.—*Book of Common Prayer, Psalm 50:22*

1   His name shall endure for ever.
Psalms 72:17

2   A stubborn and rebellious generation.   *78:8*

3   Man did eat angels' food.   *78:25*

4   But ye shall die like men, and fall like one of the princes.   *82:7*

5   How amiable are thy tabernacles, O Lord of hosts!   *84:1*

6   They go from strength to strength.   *84:7*

7   A day in thy courts is better than a thousand. I had rather be a doorkeeper in the house of my God, than to dwell in the tents of wickedness.   *84:10*

8   Mercy and truth are met together; righteousness and peace have kissed each other.   *85:10*

9   Lord, why castest thou off my soul? why hidest thou thy face from me?   *88:14*

10   Lord, thou hast been our dwelling place in all generations.
    Before the mountains were brought forth, or ever thou hadst formed the earth and the world, even from everlasting to everlasting, thou art God.
    Thou turnest man to destruction; and sayest, Return, ye children of men.
    For a thousand years in thy sight are but as yesterday when it is past, and as a watch in the night.
    Thou carriest them away as with a flood; they are as a sleep: in the morning they are like grass which groweth up.
    In the morning it flourisheth, and groweth up; in the evening it is cut down, and withereth.[1]
90:1–6

11   We spend our years as a tale that is told.[2]
90:9

12   The days of our years are threescore years and ten; and if by reason of strength they be fourscore years, yet is their strength labor and sorrow; for it is soon cut off, and we fly away.[3]   *90:10*

13   So teach us to number our days, that we may apply our hearts unto wisdom.   *90:12*

14   Establish thou the work of our hands upon us; yea, the work of our hands establish thou it.
90:17

15   He that dwelleth in the secret place of the most High shall abide under the shadow of the Almighty.
    I will say of the Lord, He is my refuge and my fortress: my God; in him will I trust.
    Surely he shall deliver thee from the snare of the fowler, and from the noisome pestilence.

[1]See *Isaiah 40:6* and *40:8, 27:17* and *27:18,* and *I Peter 1:24, 46:21.*
[2]We bring our years to an end, as it were a tale that is told.
—*Book of Common Prayer, Psalm 90:9*
[3]The days of our age are threescore and ten; and though men be so strong that they come to fourscore years, yet is their strength then but labor and sorrow; so soon passeth it away, and we are gone.—*Book of Common Prayer, Psalm 90:10*

He shall cover thee with his feathers, and under his wings shalt thou trust: his truth shall be thy shield and buckler.
    Thou shalt not be afraid for the terror by night; nor for the arrow that flieth by day.
    Nor for the pestilence that walketh in darkness; nor for the destruction that wasteth at noonday.
    A thousand shall fall at thy side, and ten thousand at thy right hand; but it shall not come nigh thee.
91:1–7

16   He shall give his angels charge over thee, to keep thee in all thy ways.
    They shall bear thee up in their hands, lest thou dash thy foot against a stone.[4]
    Thou shalt tread upon the lion and adder: the young lion and the dragon shalt thou trample under feet.   *91:11–13*

17   The righteous shall flourish like the palm tree: he shall grow like a cedar in Lebanon.   *92:12*

18   Mightier than the noise of many waters.[5]
93:4

19   O come, let us sing unto the Lord: let us make a joyful noise to the rock of our salvation.
    Let us come before his presence with thanksgiving, and make a joyful noise unto him with psalms.
    For the Lord is a great God, and a great King above all gods.
    In his hand are the deep places of the earth: the strength of the hills is his also.
    The sea is his, and he made it: and his hands formed the dry land.
    O come, let us worship and bow down: let us kneel before the Lord our maker.
    For he is our God; and we are the people of his pasture, and the sheep of his hand.[6]   *95:1–7*

20   O sing unto the Lord a new song.   *96:1*

21   The Lord reigneth; let the earth rejoice.
97:1

22   Make a joyful noise unto the Lord, all ye lands.
    Serve the Lord with gladness: come before his presence with singing.
    Know ye that the Lord he is God: it is he that hath made us, and not we ourselves; we are his people, and the sheep of his pasture.
    Enter into his gates with thanksgiving, and into his courts with praise: be thankful unto him, and bless his name.
    For the Lord is good; his mercy is everlasting; and his truth endureth to all generations.   *100*

23   My days are consumed like smoke.   *102:3*

24   I watch, and am as a sparrow alone upon the house top.   *102:7*

[4]See *Luke 4:10–11, 38:10.* Also in *Matthew 4:6.*
[5]See *Revelation 14:2, 47:30.*
[6]See *Ephesians 5:19, 44:26,* and *Book of Common Prayer, Morning Prayer (Venite), 48:20.*

1   As the heaven is high above the earth, so great is his mercy toward them that fear him.   *103:11*

2   As for man, his days are as grass: as a flower of the field, so he flourisheth.

For the wind passeth over it, and it is gone; and the place thereof shall know it no more.[1]   *103:15–16*

3   Who layeth the beams of his chambers in the waters: who maketh the clouds his chariot: who walketh upon the wings of the wind.   *104:3*

4   Wine that maketh glad the heart of man.   *104:15*

5   The cedars of Lebanon.   *104:16*

6   He appointed the moon for seasons: the sun knoweth his going down.

Thou makest darkness, and it is night: wherein all the beasts of the forest do creep forth.[2]

The young lions roar after their prey, and seek their meat from God.

The sun ariseth, they gather themselves together, and lay them down in their dens.

Man goeth forth unto his work and to his labor until the evening.

O Lord, how manifold are thy works! in wisdom hast thou made them all: the earth is full of thy riches.

So is this great and wide sea, wherein are things creeping innumerable, both small and great beasts.

There go the ships: there is that leviathan, whom thou hast made to play therein.

These wait all upon thee; that thou mayest give them their meat in due season.   *104:19–27*

7   The people asked, and he brought quails, and satisfied them with the bread of heaven.[3]   *105:40*

8   Such as sit in darkness and in the shadow of death.[4]   *107:10*

9   They that go down to the sea in ships, that do business in great waters.   *107:23*

10   They mount up to the heaven, they go down again to the depths.   *107:26*

11   They reel to and fro, and stagger like a drunken man, and are at their wit's end.   *107:27*

12   For I am poor and needy, and my heart is wounded within me.

I am gone like the shadow when it declineth: I am tossed up and down as the locust.   *109:22–23*

13   Thou hast the dew of thy youth.   *110:3*

14   The fear of the Lord is the beginning of wisdom.   *111:10*

15   From the rising of the sun unto the going down of the same the Lord's name is to be praised.   *113:3*

16   The mountains skipped like rams, and the little hills like lambs.   *114:4*

17   They have mouths, but they speak not: eyes have they, but they see not.

They have ears, but they hear not.[5]   *115:5–6*

18   I said in my haste, All men are liars.   *116:11*

19   Precious in the sight of the Lord is the death of his saints.   *116:15*

20   The stone which the builders refused is become the head stone of the corner.[6]   *118:22*

21   This is the day which the Lord hath made.   *118:24*

22   Blessed be he that cometh in the name of the Lord.[7]   *118:26*

23   Thy word is a lamp unto my feet, and a light unto my path.   *119:105*

24   I am for peace: but when I speak, they are for war.   *120:7*

25   I will lift up mine eyes unto the hills, from whence cometh my help.[8]

My help cometh from the Lord, which made heaven and earth.

He will not suffer thy foot to be moved: he that keepeth thee will not slumber.

Behold, he that keepeth Israel shall neither slumber nor sleep.

The Lord is thy keeper: the Lord is thy shade upon thy right hand.

The sun shall not smite thee by day, nor the moon by night.

The Lord shall preserve thee from all evil: he shall preserve thy soul.

The Lord shall preserve thy going out and thy coming in from this time forth, and even for evermore.   *121*

26   I was glad when they said unto me, Let us go into the house of the Lord.   *122:1*

27   Peace be within thy walls, and prosperity within thy palaces.   *122:7*

28   They that sow in tears shall reap in joy.

He that goeth forth and weepeth, bearing precious seed, shall doubtless come again with rejoicing, bringing his sheaves with him.   *126:5–6*

29   Except the Lord build the house, they labor in vain that build it: except the Lord keep the city, the watchman waketh but in vain.   *127:1*

30   He giveth his beloved sleep.   *127:2*

---

[1]See Homer, 54:8.
[2]See *The Great Hymn to the Aten*, 5:3.
[3]See *John* 6:35, 40:4.
[4]See *Matthew* 4:16, 32:36, and *Luke* 1:79, 38:1.

[5]Also in *Psalm* 135:16–17.
[6]Also in *Matthew* 21:42.
[7]Also in *Matthew* 21:9, 23:39, *Mark* 11:9, and *Luke* 13:35.
[8]I lift up my eyes to the hills. From whence does my help come?—*Revised Standard Version*

1   As arrows are in the hand of a mighty man; so are children of the youth.

Happy is the man that hath his quiver full of them.

Psalms 127:4–5

2   Out of the depths have I cried unto thee, O Lord.

130:1

3   My soul waiteth for the Lord more than they that watch for the morning.   *130:6*

4   I will not give sleep to mine eyes, or slumber to mine eyelids.[1]   *132:4*

5   Behold, how good and how pleasant it is for brethren to dwell together in unity!   *133:1*

6   By the rivers of Babylon, there we sat down, yea, we wept, when we remembered Zion.[2]

We hanged our harps upon the willows in the midst thereof.

For there they that carried us away captive required of us a song; and they that wasted us required of us mirth, saying, Sing us one of the songs of Zion.

How shall we sing the Lord's song in a strange land?

If I forget thee, O Jerusalem, let my right hand forget her cunning.

If I do not remember thee, let my tongue cleave to the roof of my mouth.   *137:1–6*

7   O Lord, thou hast searched me, and known me.

Thou knowest my downsitting and mine uprising; thou understandest my thought afar off.

139:1–2

8   Whither shall I go from thy Spirit? or whither shall I flee from thy presence?

If I ascend up into heaven, thou art there: if I make my bed in hell, behold, thou art there.

If I take the wings of the morning, and dwell in the uttermost parts of the sea;

Even there shall thy hand lead me, and thy right hand shall hold me.   *139:7–10*

9   The darkness and the light are both alike to thee.

139:12

10   I am fearfully and wonderfully made.

139:14

11   They have sharpened their tongues like a serpent.

140:3

12   Thou openest thine hand, and satisfiest the desire of every living thing.   *145:16*

13   The Lord is nigh unto all them that call upon him, to all that call upon him in truth.   *145:18*

14   Put not your trust in princes.   *146:3*

15   He telleth the number of the stars; he calleth them all by their names.   *147:4*

16   Praise him with the sound of the trumpet: praise him with the psaltery and harp.

Praise him with the timbrel and dance: praise him with stringed instruments and organs.

Praise him upon the loud cymbals: praise him upon the high sounding cymbals.[3]

Let every thing that hath breath praise the Lord.

150:3–6

17   To give subtilty to the simple, to the young man knowledge and discretion.   *The Proverbs 1:4*

18   My son, if sinners entice thee, consent thou not.

1:10

19   Wisdom crieth without; she uttereth her voice in the streets.   *1:20*

20   Length of days is in her right hand; and in her left hand riches and honor.   *3:16*

21   Her ways are ways of pleasantness, and all her paths are peace.   *3:17*

22   Be not afraid of sudden fear.   *3:25*

23   Wisdom is the principal thing; therefore get wisdom: and with all thy getting get understanding.

4:7

24   The path of the just is as the shining light, that shineth more and more unto the perfect day.

4:18

25   Keep thy heart with all diligence; for out of it are the issues of life.   *4:23*

26   The lips of a strange woman drop as a honeycomb, and her mouth is smoother than oil:

But her end is bitter as wormwood, sharp as a two-edged sword.   *5:3–4*

27   Go to the ant, thou sluggard; consider her ways, and be wise:

Which having no guide, overseer, or ruler,

Provideth her meat in the summer, and gathereth her food in the harvest.   *6:6–8*

28   Yet a little sleep, a little slumber, a little folding of the hands to sleep:[4]

So shall thy poverty come as one that traveleth, and thy want as an armed man.   *6:10–11*

29   Lust not after her beauty in thine heart; neither let her take thee with her eyelids.   *6:25*

30   Can a man take fire in his bosom, and his clothes not be burned?

Can one go upon hot coals, and his feet not be burned?   *6:27–28*

31   Jealousy is the rage of a man: therefore he will not spare in the day of vengeance.   *6:34*

32   He goeth after her straightway, as an ox goeth to the slaughter.   *7:22*

33   I love them that love me; and those that seek me early shall find me.   *8:17*

[1]Also in *Proverbs 6:4.*

[2]By the waters of Babylon we sat down and wept, when we remembered thee, O Sion.—*Book of Common Prayer, Psalm 137:1*

[3]See *II Samuel 6:5, 12:5.*

[4]Also in *Proverbs 24:33.*

1   Wisdom hath builded her house, she hath hewn out her seven pillars.   *9:1*

2   Reprove not a scorner, lest he hate thee: rebuke a wise man, and he will love thee.   *9:8*

3   Stolen waters are sweet, and bread eaten in secret is pleasant.   *9:17*

4   A wise son maketh a glad father: but a foolish son is the heaviness of his mother.   *10:1*

5   Blessings are upon the head of the just: but violence covereth the mouth of the wicked.
The memory of the just is blessed: but the name of the wicked shall rot.   *10:6−7*

6   Hatred stirreth up strifes: but love covereth all sins.   *10:12*

7   In the multitude of counsellors there is safety.[1]
He that is surety for a stranger shall smart for it.   *11:14−15*

8   As a jewel of gold in a swine's snout, so is a fair woman which is without discretion.   *11:22*

9   He that trusteth in his riches shall fall.   *11:28*

10 He that troubleth his own house shall inherit the wind.   *11:29*

11 A virtuous woman is a crown to her husband.   *12:4*

12 A righteous man regardeth the life of his beast: but the tender mercies of the wicked are cruel.   *12:10*

13 The way of a fool is right in his own eyes.   *12:15*

14 Hope deferred maketh the heart sick.   *13:12*

15 The way of transgressors is hard.   *13:15*

16 The desire accomplished is sweet to the soul.   *13:19*

17 He that spareth his rod hateth his son: but he that loveth him chasteneth him betimes.[2]   *13:24*

18 Fools make a mock at sin.   *14:9*

19 The heart knoweth his own bitterness; and a stranger doth not intermeddle with his joy.   *14:10*

20 Even in laughter the heart is sorrowful.   *14:13*

21 The prudent man looketh well to his going.   *14:15*

22 In all labor there is profit: but the talk of the lips tendeth only to penury.   *14:23*

23 Righteousness exalteth a nation.   *14:34*

24 A soft answer turneth away wrath.   *15:1*

25 A merry heart maketh a cheerful countenance: but by sorrow of the heart the spirit is broken.   *15:13*

26 He that is of a merry heart hath a continual feast.
Better is little with the fear of the Lord, than great treasure, and trouble therewith.
Better is a dinner of herbs where love is, than a stalled ox and hatred therewith.   *15:15−17*

27 A wrathful man stirreth up strife: but he that is slow to anger appeaseth strife.   *15:18*

28 A word spoken in due season, how good is it!   *15:23*

29 Before honor is humility.   *15:33 and 18:12*

30 A man's heart deviseth his way: but the Lord directeth his steps.   *16:9*

31 Pride goeth before destruction, and an haughty spirit before a fall.[3]   *16:18*

32 The hoary head is a crown of glory, if it be found in the way of righteousness.
He that is slow to anger is better than the mighty; and he that ruleth his spirit than he that taketh a city.
                                                                                                          16:31−32

33 Whoso mocketh the poor reproacheth his Maker.   *17:5*

34 He that repeateth a matter separateth very friends.   *17:9*

35 Whoso rewardeth evil for good, evil shall not depart from his house.   *17:13*

36 A merry heart doeth good like a medicine.   *17:22*

37 He that hath knowledge spareth his words: and a man of understanding is of an excellent spirit.
Even a fool, when he holdeth his peace, is counted wise.   *17:27−28*

38 A fool's mouth is his destruction.   *18:7*

39 A wounded spirit who can bear?   *18:14*

40 A brother offended is harder to be won than a strong city: and their contentions are like the bars of a castle.   *18:19*

41 Whoso findeth a wife findeth a good thing.   *18:22*

42 A man that hath friends must show himself friendly: and there is a friend that sticketh closer than a brother.   *18:24*

43 Wealth maketh many friends.   *19:4*

44 A foolish son is the calamity of his father: and the contentions of a wife are a continual dropping. *19:13*

45 He that hath pity upon the poor lendeth unto the Lord.   *19:17*

[1]Also in *Proverbs 24:6*.
[2]See Menander, 81:7, and Samuel Butler [1612−1680], 263:-21.

[3]See Sophocles, 65:18 and 66:22.

1   Wine is a mocker, strong drink is raging.

Proverbs 20:1

2   It is an honor for a man to cease from strife: but every fool will be meddling.   *20:3*

3   Even a child is known by his doings, whether his work be pure, and whether it be right.
The hearing ear, and the seeing eye, the Lord hath made even both of them.   *20:11–12*

4   It is naught, it is naught, saith the buyer: but when he is gone his way, then he boasteth.

20:14

5   Bread of deceit is sweet to a man; but afterwards his mouth shall be filled with gravel.   *20:17*

6   Meddle not with him that flattereth with his lips.

20:19

7   It is better to dwell in a corner of the housetop, than with a brawling woman in a wide house.

21:9 and 25:24

8   A good name is rather to be chosen than great riches.   *22:1*

9   Train up a child in the way he should go; and when he is old, he will not depart from it.   *22:6*

10   The borrower is servant to the lender.   *22:7*

11   Bow down thine ear, and hear the words of the wise, and apply thine heart unto my knowledge.
For it is a pleasant thing if thou keep them within thee; they shall withal be fitted in thy lips.[1]

22:17–18

12   Have I not written to thee excellent things in counsels and knowledge,
That I might make thee know the certainty of the words of truth; that thou mightest answer the words of truth to them that send unto thee?[2]

22:20–21

13   Rob not the poor, because he is poor: neither oppress the afflicted in the gate.[3]   *22:22*

14   Remove not the ancient landmark.[4]   *22:28*

15   Seest thou a man diligent in his business? He shall stand before kings.[5]   *22:29*

16   Put a knife to thy throat, if thou be a man given to appetite.   *23:2*

17   Labor not to be rich: cease from thine own wisdom.[6]   *23:4*

18   Riches certainly make themselves wings; they fly away as an eagle toward heaven.[6]   *23:5*

19   As he thinketh in his heart, so is he.   *23:7*

20   The drunkard and the glutton shall come to poverty: and drowsiness shall clothe a man with rags.

23:21

21   Despise not thy mother when she is old.

23:22

22   Look not thou upon the wine when it is red, when it giveth his color in the cup, when it moveth itself aright.
At the last it biteth like a serpent, and stingeth like an adder.   *23:31–32*

23   A wise man is strong; yea, a man of knowledge increaseth strength.   *24:5*

24   If thou faint in the day of adversity, thy strength is small.   *24:10*

25   A word fitly spoken is like apples of gold in pictures of silver.   *25:11*

26   If thine enemy be hungry, give him bread to eat; and if he be thirsty, give him water to drink:
For thou shalt heap coals of fire upon his head.[7]

25:21–22

27   As cold waters to a thirsty soul, so is good news from a far country.   *25:25*

28   For men to search their own glory is not glory.

25:27

29   Answer a fool according to his folly.   *26:5*

30   As a dog returneth to his vomit, so a fool returneth to his folly.
Seest thou a man wise in his own conceit? There is more hope of a fool than of him.
The slothful man saith, There is a lion in the way; a lion is in the streets.   *26:11–13*

31   Whoso diggeth a pit shall fall therein: and he that rolleth a stone, it will return upon him.   *26:27*

32   Boast not thyself of tomorrow; for thou knowest not what a day may bring forth.[8]   *27:1*

33   Let another man praise thee, and not thine own mouth.   *27:2*

[1]See Amenemope, 5:11.

[2]Here I have written out for you thirty sayings, / full of knowledge and wise advice, / to impart to you a knowledge of the truth, / that you may take back a true report to him who sent you.—*The New English Bible with the Apocrypha: Oxford Study Edition* [1976], *Proverbs 22:20–21*.
Thirty wise sayings [*Proverbs 22:17–24:22*]. This section is dependent on the Egyptian work by Amenemope, from which ten sayings have been derived and adapted to the Israelite setting. . . . The Masoretic Text reading . . . formerly rendered "excellent things" [22:20] has been corrected to "thirty sayings"—a very minor change in the Hebrew—on the basis of the Amenemope.—*Ibid.*, note to Proverbs 22:17–24:22.
See Amenemope, 5:10 and 6:2.

[3]See Amenemope, 5:12, and *Ecclesiasticus 4:1, 31:6*.

[4]Also in *Proverbs 23:10*.
See Amenemope, 5:14.

[5]See Amenemope, 6:3.

[6]See Amenemope, 6:1.

[7]Also in *Romans 12:20*.
See Marcus Aurelius, 111:20.

[8]See Sophocles, 67:3.

1 Open rebuke is better than secret love.
Faithful are the wounds of a friend; but the kisses of an enemy are deceitful.   *27:5–6*

2 To the hungry soul every bitter thing is sweet.
27:7

3 Better is a neighbor that is near than a brother far off.   *27:10*

4 Iron sharpeneth iron; so a man sharpeneth the countenance of his friend.   *27:17*

5 The wicked flee when no man pursueth: but the righteous are bold as a lion.   *28:1*

6 He that maketh haste to be rich shall not be innocent.   *28:20*

7 He that trusteth in his own heart is a fool.
28:26

8 He that giveth unto the poor shall not lack.
28:27

9 A fool uttereth all his mind.   *29:11*

10 Where there is no vision, the people perish.
29:18

11 A man's pride shall bring him low: but honor shall uphold the humble in spirit.   *29:23*

12 Give me neither poverty nor riches.   *30:8*

13 Accuse not a servant unto his master.   *30:10*

14 The horseleach hath two daughters, crying, Give, give.   *30:15*

15 There be three things which are too wonderful for me, yea, four which I know not:
The way of an eagle in the air; the way of a serpent upon a rock; the way of a ship in the midst of the sea; and the way of a man with a maid.   *30:18–19*

16 Give strong drink unto him that is ready to perish, and wine unto those that be of heavy hearts.
Let him drink, and forget his poverty, and remember his misery no more.   *31:6–7*

17 Who can find a virtuous woman? for her price is far above rubies.
The heart of her husband doth safely trust in her.
31:10–11

18 Her husband is known in the gates, when he sitteth among the elders of the land.   *31:23*

19 Strength and honor are her clothing.   *31:25*

20 In her tongue is the law of kindness.
She looketh well to the ways of her household, and eateth not the bread of idleness.
Her children arise up, and call her blessed.
31:26–28

21 Many daughters have done virtuously, but thou excellest them all.
Favor is deceitful, and beauty is vain: but a woman that feareth the Lord, she shall be praised.
Give her of the fruit of her hands; and let her own works praise her in the gates.   *31:29–31*

22 Vanity of vanities, saith the Preacher, vanity of vanities; all is vanity.
What profit hath a man of all his labor which he taketh under the sun?
One generation passeth away, and another generation cometh: but the earth abideth for ever.
The sun also ariseth.
Ecclesiastes; or, The Preacher 1:2–5

23 All the rivers run into the sea; yet the sea is not full.   *1:7*

24 The eye is not satisfied with seeing, nor the ear filled with hearing.   *1:8*

25 The thing that hath been, it is that which shall be; and that which is done is that which shall be done: and there is no new thing under the sun.   *1:9*

26 There is no remembrance of former things; neither shall there be any remembrance of things that are to come with those that shall come after.
1:11

27 I have seen all the works that are done under the sun; and, behold, all is vanity and vexation of spirit.
That which is crooked cannot be made straight: and that which is wanting cannot be numbered.
1:14–15

28 In much wisdom is much grief: and he that increaseth knowledge increaseth sorrow.   *1:18*

29 Wisdom excelleth folly, as far as light excelleth darkness.   *2:13*

30 One event happeneth to them all.   *2:14*

31 How dieth the wise man? as the fool.   *2:16*

32 To every thing there is a season, and a time to every purpose under the heaven.
A time to be born, and a time to die; a time to plant, and a time to pluck up that which is planted;
A time to kill, and a time to heal; a time to break down, and a time to build up;
A time to weep, and a time to laugh; a time to mourn, and a time to dance;
A time to cast away stones, and a time to gather stones together; a time to embrace, and a time to refrain from embracing;
A time to get, and a time to lose; a time to keep, and a time to cast away;
A time to rend, and a time to sew; a time to keep silence, and a time to speak;
A time to love, and a time to hate; a time of war, and a time of peace.   *3:1–8*

33 Wherefore I praised the dead which are already dead more than the living which are yet alive.
4:2

34 Better is a handful with quietness, than both the hands full with travail and vexation of spirit.
4:6

35 A threefold cord is not quickly broken.
4:12

1   Better is a poor and a wise child than an old and foolish king.   *Ecclesiastes 4:13*

2   God is in heaven, and thou upon earth: therefore let thy words be few.   *5:2*

3   Better is it that thou shouldest not vow, than that thou shouldest vow and not pay.   *5:5*

4   The sleep of a laboring man is sweet . . . but the abundance of the rich will not suffer him to sleep.   *5:12*

5   As he came forth of his mother's womb, naked shall he return to go as he came,[1] and shall take nothing of his labor, which he may carry away in his hand.   *5:15*

6   A good name is better than precious ointment; and the day of death than the day of one's birth.   *7:1*

7   It is better to go to the house of mourning, than to go to the house of feasting.   *7:2*

8   As the crackling of thorns under a pot, so is the laughter of the fool.   *7:6*

9   Better is the end of a thing than the beginning thereof.   *7:8*

10   In the day of prosperity be joyful, but in the day of adversity consider.   *7:14*

11   Be not righteous over much.   *7:16*

12   There is not a just man upon earth, that doeth good, and sinneth not.   *7:20*

13   And I find more bitter than death the woman, whose heart is snares and nets, and her hands as bands.   *7:26*

14   One man among a thousand have I found; but a woman among all those have I not found.   *7:28*

15   God hath made man upright; but they have sought out many inventions.   *7:29*

16   There is no discharge in that war.   *8:8*

17   A man hath no better thing under the sun, than to eat, and to drink, and to be merry.[2]   *8:15*

18   A living dog is better than a dead lion.
For the living know that they shall die: but the dead know not any thing, neither have they any more a reward; for the memory of them is forgotten.   *9:4–5*

19   Whatsoever thy hand findeth to do, do it with thy might; for there is no work, nor device, nor knowledge, nor wisdom, in the grave, whither thou goest.   *9:10*

20   I returned, and saw under the sun, that the race is not to the swift, nor the battle to the strong, neither yet bread to the wise, nor yet riches to men of understanding, nor yet favor to men of skill; but time and chance happeneth to them all.
For man also knoweth not his time: as the fishes that are taken in an evil net, and as the birds that are caught in the snare; so are the sons of men snared in an evil time, when it falleth suddenly upon them.   *9:11–12*

21   A feast is made for laughter, and wine maketh merry: but money answereth all things.   *10:19*

22   A bird of the air shall carry the voice, and that which hath wings shall tell the matter.   *10:20*

23   Cast thy bread upon the waters: for thou shalt find it after many days.   *11:1*

24   He that observeth the wind shall not sow; and he that regardeth the clouds shall not reap.   *11:4*

25   In the morning sow thy seed, and in the evening withhold not thine hand.   *11:6*

26   Rejoice, O young man, in thy youth.   *11:9*

27   Remember now thy Creator in the days of thy youth, while the evil days come not, nor the years draw nigh, when thou shalt say, I have no pleasure in them;
While the sun, or the light, or the moon, or the stars, be not darkened, nor the clouds return after the rain:
In the day when the keepers of the house shall tremble, and the strong men shall bow themselves, and the grinders cease because they are few, and those that look out of the windows be darkened,
And the doors shall be shut in the streets, when the sound of the grinding is low, and he shall rise up at the voice of the bird, and all the daughters of music shall be brought low.   *12:1–4*

28   The almond tree shall flourish, and the grasshopper shall be a burden, and desire shall fail; because man goeth to his long home, and the mourners go about the streets:
Or ever the silver cord be loosed, or the golden bowl be broken, or the pitcher be broken at the fountain, or the wheel broken at the cistern.
Then shall the dust return to the earth as it was: and the spirit shall return unto God who gave it.   *12:5–7*

29   The words of the wise are as goads, and as nails fastened by the masters of assemblies.   *12:11*

30   Of making many books there is no end; and much study is a weariness of the flesh.
Let us hear the conclusion of the whole matter: Fear God, and keep his commandments: for this is the whole duty of man.
For God shall bring every work into judgment, with every secret thing, whether it be good, or whether it be evil.   *12:12–14*

31   The song of songs, which is Solomon's.
    The Song of Solomon 1:1

---

[1]See *Job 1:21, 13:31.*
[2]See *Luke 12:19, 38:28.*

1   I am black, but comely, O ye daughters of Jerusalem, as the tents of Kedar, as the curtains of Solomon.   *1:5*

2   O thou fairest among women.   *1:8*

3   I am the rose of Sharon, and the lily of the valleys.   *2:1*

4   As the apple tree among the trees of the wood, so is my beloved among the sons.   *2:3*

5   His banner over me was love.
Stay me with flagons, comfort me with apples: for I am sick of love.   *2:4–5*

6   Rise up, my love, my fair one, and come away. For, lo, the winter is past, the rain is over and gone;
The flowers appear on the earth; the time of the singing of birds is come, and the voice of the turtle is heard in our land.   *2:10–12*

7   Take us the foxes, the little foxes, that spoil the vines: for our vines have tender grapes.   *2:15*

8   Until the day break, and the shadows flee away.   *2:17 and 4:6*

9   By night on my bed I sought him whom my soul loveth: I sought him, but I found him not.   *3:1*

10   Thy two breasts are like two young roes that are twins, which feed among the lilies.   *4:5*

11   Thou art all fair, my love; there is no spot in thee.   *4:7*

12   How much better is thy love than wine!   *4:10*

13   Awake, O north wind; and come, thou south; blow upon my garden, that the spices thereof may flow out. Let my beloved come into his garden, and eat his pleasant fruits.   *4:16*

14   My beloved put in his hand by the hole of the door, and my bowels were moved for him.   *5:4*

15   His mouth is most sweet: yea, he is altogether lovely. This is my beloved, and this is my friend, O daughters of Jerusalem.   *5:16*

16   Who is she that looketh forth as the morning, fair as the moon, clear as the sun, and terrible as an army with banners?   *6:10*

17   Return, return, O Shulamite.   *6:13*

18   Thy belly is like a heap of wheat set about with lilies.   *7:2*

19   Thy neck is as a tower of ivory.   *7:4*

20   Like the best wine . . . that goeth down sweetly, causing the lips of those that are asleep to speak.   *7:9*

21   I am my beloved's, and his desire is toward me.   *7:10*

22   Set me as a seal upon thine heart, as a seal upon thine arm: for love is strong as death; jealousy is cruel as the grave.   *8:6*

23   Many waters cannot quench love, neither can the floods drown it.   *8:7*

24   Make haste, my beloved, and be thou like to a roe or to a young hart upon the mountains of spices.   *8:14*

25   The ox knoweth his owner, and the ass his master's crib.   *The Book of the Prophet Isaiah 1:3*

26   The whole head is sick, and the whole heart faint.   *1:5*

27   As a lodge in a garden of cucumbers.   *1:8*

28   Bring no more vain oblations.   *1:13*

29   Learn to do well; seek judgment, relieve the oppressed, judge the fatherless, plead for the widow.
Come now, and let us reason together . . . though your sins be as scarlet, they shall be as white as snow.   *1:17–18*

30   They shall beat their swords into plowshares, and their spears into pruninghooks: nation shall not lift up sword against nation, neither shall they learn war any more.[1]   *2:4*

31   In that day a man shall cast his idols . . . to the moles and to the bats.   *2:20*

32   Cease ye from man, whose breath is in his nostrils.   *2:22*

33   The stay and the staff, the whole stay of bread, and the whole stay of water.   *3:1*

34   What mean ye that ye beat my people to pieces and grind the faces of the poor?   *3:15*

35   Walk with stretched forth necks and wanton eyes, walking and mincing as they go, and making a tinkling with their feet.   *3:16*

36   In that day seven women shall take hold of one man.   *4:1*

37   My wellbeloved hath a vineyard in a very fruitful hill.   *5:1*

38   And he looked for judgment, but behold oppression; for righteousness, but behold a cry.
Woe unto them that join house to house, that lay field to field, till there be no place, that they may be placed alone in the midst of the earth!   *5:7–8*

39   Woe unto them that rise up early in the morning, that they may follow strong drink.   *5:11*

40   Woe unto them that draw iniquity with cords of vanity, and sin as it were with a cart rope.   *5:18*

41   Woe unto them that call evil good, and good evil.   *5:20*

42   I saw also the Lord sitting upon a throne, high and lifted up, and his train filled the temple.

[1]Also in *Joel 3:10* and *Micah 4:3*.

Above it stood the seraphims: each one had six wings; with twain he covered his face, and with twain he covered his feet, and with twain he did fly.

Isaiah 6:1–2

1   Holy, holy, holy, is the Lord of hosts: the whole earth is full of his glory.   *6:3*

2   Woe is me! for I am undone; because I am a man of unclean lips, and I dwell in the midst of a people of unclean lips: for mine eyes have seen the King, the Lord of hosts.   *6:5*

3   I heard the voice of the Lord, saying, Whom shall I send, and who will go for us? Then said I, Here am I; send me.   *6:8*

4   Then said I, Lord, how long?   *6:11*

5   Behold, a virgin shall conceive, and bear a son, and shall call his name Immanuel.[1]   *7:14*

6   For a stone of stumbling and for a rock of offense.   *8:14*

7   The people that walked in darkness have seen a great light: they that dwell in the land of the shadow of death, upon them hath the light shined.   *9:2*

8   For unto us a child is born, unto us a son is given: and the government shall be upon his shoulder: and his name shall be called Wonderful, Counsellor, The mighty God, The everlasting Father, The Prince of Peace.
Of the increase of his government and peace there shall be no end.   *9:6–7*

9   The ancient and honorable, he is the head.   *9:15*

10   And there shall come forth a rod out of the stem of Jesse, and a Branch shall grow out of his roots:
And the Spirit of the Lord shall rest upon him, the spirit of wisdom and understanding, the spirit of counsel and might, the spirit of knowledge and of the fear of the Lord.   *11:1–2*

11   The wolf also shall dwell with the lamb, and the leopard shall lie down with the kid; and the calf and the young lion and the fatling together; and a little child shall lead them.
And the cow and the bear shall feed; their young ones shall lie down together: and the lion shall eat straw like the ox.
And the suckling child shall play on the hole of the asp, and the weaned child shall put his hand on the cockatrice' den.
They shall not hurt nor destroy in all my holy mountain: for the earth shall be full of the knowledge of the Lord, as the waters cover the sea.   *11:6–9*

12   For the Lord JEHOVAH is my strength and my song; he also is become my salvation.   *12:2*

[1]See *Matthew 1:23, 32:22.*

13   And I will punish the world for their evil, and the wicked for their iniquity; and I will cause the arrogancy of the proud to cease, and will lay low the haughtiness of the terrible.   *13:11*

14   How art thou fallen from heaven, O Lucifer, son of the morning!   *14:12*

15   Is this the man that made the earth to tremble, that did shake kingdoms.   *14:16*

16   The nations shall rush like the rushing of many waters.   *17:13*

17   And they shall fight every one against his brother.   *19:2*

18   The burden of the desert of the sea. As whirlwinds in the south pass through; so it cometh from the desert, from a terrible land.   *21:1*

19   Babylon is fallen, is fallen;[2] and all the graven images of her gods he hath broken unto the ground.   *21:9*

20   Watchman, what of the night?   *21:11*

21   Let us eat and drink; for tomorrow we shall die.   *22:13*

22   I will fasten him as a nail in a sure place.   *22:23*

23   Whose merchants are princes.   *23:8*

24   As with the maid, so with her mistress.   *24:2*

25   For thou hast been a strength to the poor, a strength to the needy in his distress.   *25:4*

26   A feast of fat things, a feast of wines on the lees.   *25:6*

27   He will swallow up death in victory;[3] and the Lord God will wipe away tears from off all faces.[4]   *25:8*

28   Open ye the gates, that the righteous nation which keepeth the truth may enter in.
Thou wilt keep him in perfect peace, whose mind is stayed on thee.   *26:2–3*

29   Awake and sing, ye that dwell in dust.   *26:19*

30   Hide thyself as it were for a little moment, until the indignation be overpast.   *26:20*

31   Leviathan that crooked serpent . . . the dragon that is in the sea.   *27:1*

32   For precept must be upon precept, precept upon precept; line upon line, line upon line; here a little, and there a little.   *28:10*

33   We have made a covenant with death, and with hell are we at agreement.   *28:15*

34   It shall be a vexation only to understand the report.   *28:19*

[2]See *Revelation 14:8, 47:31.*
[3]See *Hosea 13:14, 29:31,* and *I Corinthians 15:54, 43:28.*
[4]See *Revelation 21:4, 48:1.*

1 They are drunken, but not with wine; they stagger, but not with strong drink. *29:9*

2 Their strength is to sit still.
Now go, write it before them in a table, and note it in a book, that it may be for the time to come for ever and ever. *30:7−8*

3 The bread of adversity, and the water of affliction. *30:20*

4 This is the way, walk ye in it. *30:21*

5 Behold, a king shall reign in righteousness. *32:1*

6 And a man shall be as an hiding place from the wind, and a covert from the tempest; as rivers of water in a dry place, as the shadows of a great rock in a weary land. *32:2*

7 An habitation of dragons, and a court for owls. *34:13*

8 The desert shall rejoice, and blossom as the rose. *35:1*

9 Then the eyes of the blind shall be opened, and the ears of the deaf shall be unstopped.
Then shall the lame man leap as an hart, and the tongue of the dumb sing. *35:5−6*

10 Sorrow and sighing shall flee away. *35:10*

11 Thou trustest in the staff of this broken reed. *36:6*

12 Incline thine ear, O Lord, and hear. *37:17*

13 I shall go softly all my years in the bitterness of my soul. *38:15*

14 Comfort ye, comfort ye my people. *40:1*

15 Speak ye comfortably to Jerusalem, and cry unto her, that her warfare is accomplished, that her iniquity is pardoned: for she hath received of the Lord's hand double for all her sins.
The voice of him that crieth in the wilderness, Prepare ye the way of the Lord, make straight in the desert a highway for our God.[1] *40:2−3*

16 Every valley shall be exalted, and every mountain and hill shall be made low: and the crooked shall be made straight, and the rough places plain. *40:4*

17 The voice said, Cry. And he said, what shall I cry? All flesh is grass, and all the goodliness thereof is as the flower of the field.[2] *40:6*

18 The grass withereth, the flower fadeth;[2] but the word of our God shall stand for ever. *40:8*

19 Get thee up into the high mountain . . . say unto the cities of Judah, Behold your God! *40:9*

20 He shall feed his flock like a shepherd: he shall gather the lambs with his arm, and carry them in his bosom, and shall gently lead those that are with young. *40:11*

21 The nations are as a drop of a bucket, and are counted as the small dust of the balance. *40:15*

22 Have ye not known? have ye not heard? hath it not been told you from the beginning? *40:21*

23 They that wait upon the Lord shall renew their strength; they shall mount up with wings as eagles; they shall run, and not be weary, and they shall walk, and not faint. *40:31*

24 They helped every one his neighbor; and every one said to his brother, Be of good courage. *41:6*

25 A bruised reed shall he not break, and the smoking flax shall he not quench. *42:3*

26 Shall the clay say to him that fashioneth it, What makest thou? *45:9*

27 Behold, I have refined thee, but not with silver; I have chosen thee in the furnace of affliction. *48:10*

28 O that thou hadst hearkened to my commandments! then had thy peace been as a river, and thy righteousness as the waves of the sea. *48:18*

29 There is no peace, saith the Lord, unto the wicked. *48:22*

30 Therefore the redeemed of the Lord shall return, and come with singing unto Zion. *51:11*

31 Thou hast drunken the dregs of the cup of trembling. *51:17*

32 Therefore hear now this. *51:21*

33 How beautiful upon the mountains are the feet of him that bringeth good tidings, that publisheth peace. *52:7*

34 They shall see eye to eye. *52:8*

35 He is despised and rejected of men; a man of sorrows, and acquainted with grief. *53:3*

36 Surely he hath borne our griefs, and carried our sorrows. *53:4*

37 All we like sheep have gone astray.[3] *53:6*

38 He is brought as a lamb to the slaughter.[4] *53:7*

39 Ho, everyone that thirsteth, come ye to the waters. *55:1*

40 Behold, I have given him for a witness to the people, a leader and commander to the people. *55:4*

---

[1] See *Matthew 3:3*, 32:29. Also in *Mark 1:3*, *Luke 3:4*, and *John 1:23*.
[2] See *Psalm 90:5−6*, 18:10, and *I Peter 1:24*, 46:21.

[3] See *Book of Common Prayer, A General Confession*, 48:16.
[4] Also in *Acts 8:32*.

1   Let the wicked forsake his way, and the unrighteous man his thoughts.   *Isaiah 55:7*

2   For my thoughts are not your thoughts, neither are your ways my ways, saith the Lord.   *55:8*

3   Peace to him that is far off, and to him that is near.   *57:19*

4   Arise, shine; for thy light is come, and the glory of the Lord is risen upon thee.   *60:1*

5   A little one shall become a thousand, and a small one a strong nation.   *60:22*

6   Give unto them beauty for ashes, the oil of joy for mourning, the garment of praise for the spirit of heaviness.   *61:3*

7   I have trodden the winepress alone; and of the people there was none with me: for I will tread them in mine anger, and trample them in my fury; and their blood shall be sprinkled upon my garments, and I will stain all my raiment.   *63:3*

8   All our righteousnesses are as filthy rags; and we all do fade as a leaf.   *64:6*

9   We all are the work of thy hand.   *64:8*

10 I am holier than thou.   *65:5*

11 For, behold, I create new heavens and a new earth.[1]   *65:17*

12 And they shall build houses, and inhabit them; and they shall plant vineyards, and eat the fruit of them.
    They shall not build, and another inhabit; they shall not plant, and another eat.   *65:21-22*

13 As one whom his mother comforteth, so will I comfort you.   *66:13*

14 They were as fed horses in the morning: every one neighed after his neighbor's wife.
                  The Book of the Prophet Jeremiah 5:8

15 Hear now this, O foolish people, and without understanding; which have eyes, and see not; which have ears, and hear not.   *5:21*

16 But this people hath a revolting and a rebellious heart.   *5:23*

17 Saying, Peace, peace; when there is no peace.
                                           6:14 and 8:11

18 Stand ye in the ways, and see, and ask for the old paths, where is the good way, and walk therein.[2]
                                                    6:16

19 Amend your ways and your doings.
                                           7:3 and 26:13

20 The harvest is past, the summer is ended, and we are not saved.   *8:20*

21 Is there no balm in Gilead?   *8:22*

22 Oh that I had in the wilderness a lodging place of wayfaring men!   *9:2*

23 Thus saith the Lord, Let not the wise man glory in his wisdom, neither let the mighty man glory in his might, let not the rich man glory in his riches:
    But let him that glorieth glory in this, that he understandeth and knoweth me.   *9:23-24*

24 Can the Ethiopian change his skin, or the leopard his spots?   *13:23*

25 Our backslidings are many; we have sinned against thee.   *14:7*

26 Her sun is gone down while it was yet day.
                                                    15:9

27 A man of strife and a man of contention.
                                                    15:10

28 The sin of Judah is written with a pen of iron, and with the point of a diamond.   *17:1*

29 Cursed be the man that trusteth in man, and maketh flesh his arm, and whose heart departeth from the Lord.
    For he shall be like the heath in the desert, and shall not see when good cometh; but shall inhabit the parched places in the wilderness, in a salt land and not inhabited.
    Blessed is the man that trusteth in the Lord, and whose hope the Lord is.
    For he shall be as a tree planted by the waters, and that spreadeth out her roots by the river, and shall not see when heat cometh, but her leaf shall be green; and shall not be careful in the year of drought, neither shall cease from yielding fruit.[3]   *17:5-8*

30 The heart is deceitful above all things, and desperately wicked: who can know it?   *17:9*

31 As the partridge sitteth on eggs, and hatcheth them not; so he that getteth riches, and not by right, shall leave them in the midst of his days, and at his end shall be a fool.   *17:11*

32 Thou art my hope in the day of evil.   *17:17*

33 O earth, earth, earth, hear the word of the Lord.
                                                    22:29

34 A curse, and an astonishment, and a hissing, and a reproach.   *29:18*

35 The fathers have eaten a sour grape, and the children's teeth are set on edge.[4]   *31:29*

36 With my whole heart and with my whole soul.
                                                    32:41

37 And seekest thou great things for thyself? seek them not.   *45:5*

38 How doth the city sit solitary, that was full of people! how is she become as a widow!
                     The Lamentations of Jeremiah 1:1

---

[1]See *Revelation 21:1, 47:37.*
[2]Stare super vias antiquas.— *The Vulgate*

[3]See *Amenemope, 5:13,* and *Psalm 1:1-4, 15:29.*
[4]Also in *Ezekiel 18:2.*

1 She weepeth sore in the night, and her tears are on her cheeks: among all her lovers she hath none to comfort her. *1:2*

2 Is it nothing to you, all ye that pass by? behold, and see if there be any sorrow like unto my sorrow. *1:12*

3 Remembering mine affliction and my misery, the wormwood and the gall.[1] *3:19*

4 It is good for a man that he bear the yoke in his youth. *3:27*

5 As it were a wheel[2] in the middle of a wheel. *The Book of the Prophet Ezekiel 1:16*

6 As is the mother, so is her daughter. *16:44*

7 The king of Babylon stood at the parting of the way. *21:21*

8 The valley . . . was full of bones . . . and lo, they were very dry. *37:1–2*

9 Can these bones live? *37:3*

10 O ye dry bones, hear the word of the Lord. *37:4*

11 Every man's sword shall be against his brother. *38:21*

12 His legs of iron, his feet part of iron and part of clay. *The Book of Daniel 2:33*

13 Shadrach, Meshach, and Abednego, fell down bound into the midst of the burning fiery furnace. *3:23*

14 Nebuchadnezzar . . . was driven from men, and did eat grass as oxen. *4:33*

15 Belshazzar the king made a great feast to a thousand of his lords. *5:1*

16 And this is the writing that was written, MENE, MENE, TEKEL, UPHARSIN.
This is the interpretation of the thing: MENE; God hath numbered thy kingdom, and finished it.
TEKEL; Thou art weighed in the balances, and art found wanting.
PERES; Thy kingdom is divided, and given to the Medes and Persians. *5:25–28*

17 According to the law of the Medes and Persians, which altereth not. *6:12*

18 They brought Daniel, and cast him into the den of lions. *6:16*

19 So Daniel was taken up out of the den, and no manner of hurt was found upon him, because he believed in his God. *6:23*

20 The Ancient of days. *7:9 and 7:13*

21 Many shall run to and fro, and knowledge shall be increased. *12:4*

22 Ye are the sons of the living God. *Hosea 1:10*

23 Like people, like priest. *4:9*

24 After two days will he revive us: in the third day he will raise us up, and we shall live in his sight. *6:2*

25 He shall come unto us as the rain, as the latter and former rain unto the earth. *6:3*

26 For I desired mercy, and not sacrifice; and the knowledge of God more than burnt offerings. *6:6*

27 They have sown the wind, and they shall reap the whirlwind. *8:7*

28 Ye have plowed wickedness, ye have reaped iniquity. *10:13*

29 I drew them with . . . bands of love. *11:4*

30 I have multiplied visions, and used similitudes, by the ministry of the prophets. *12:10*

31 I will ransom them from the power of the grave; I will redeem them from death: O death, I will be thy plagues; O grave, I will be thy destruction.[3] *13:14*

32 Your old men shall dream dreams, your young men shall see visions. *Joel 2:28*

33 Multitudes in the valley of decision. *3:14*

34 They sold the righteous for silver, and the poor for a pair of shoes. *Amos 2:6*

35 Can two walk together, except they be agreed? *3:3*

36 Woe to them that are at ease in Zion. *6:1*

37 And Jonah was in the belly of the fish three days and three nights. *Jonah 1:17*

38 What doth the Lord require of thee, but to do justly, and to love mercy, and to walk humbly with thy God? *Micah 6:8*

39 The faces of them all gather blackness.[4] *Nahum 2:10*

40 Write the vision, and make it plain upon tables, that he may run that readeth it. *Habakkuk 2:2*

41 The stone shall cry out of the wall,[5] and the beam out of the timber shall answer it. *2:11*

42 The Lord is in his holy temple: let all the earth keep silence before him. *2:20*

43 Your fathers, where are they? And the prophets, do they live forever? *Zechariah 1:5*

44 I have spread you abroad as the four winds of the heaven. *2:6*

---

[1] I will feed them with wormwood, and make them drink the water of gall. — *Jeremiah 23:15* (also in *Jeremiah 9:15*)
[2] Also in *Ezekiel 10:10*.
[3] See *Isaiah 25:8, 26:27,* and *I Corinthians 15:54, 43:28.*
[4] The faces of them all are as the blackness of a kettle. — *Douay Bible* [1609], *Nahum 2:10.* The English version of the Roman Catholic Bible was first printed in Douay, France.
[5] See *Luke 19:40, 39:11.*

1   Not by might, nor by power, but by my spirit, saith the Lord of hosts.   *Zechariah 4:6*

2   For who hath despised the day of small things?   *4:10*

3   Behold, thy King cometh unto thee . . . lowly, and riding upon an ass.   *9:9*

4   Prisoners of hope.   *9:12*

5   So they weighed for my price thirty pieces of silver.[1]   *11:12*

6   What are these wounds in thine hands? . . . Those with which I was wounded in the house of my friends.   *13:6*

7   Have we not all one father? hath not one God created us?   *Malachi 2:10*

8   Behold, I will send my messenger, and he shall prepare the way before me.   *3:1*

9   Behold, the day cometh, that shall burn as an oven.   *4:1*

10   Unto you that fear my name shall the Sun of righteousness arise with healing in his wings.   *4:2*

11   Behold, I will send you Elijah the prophet before the coming of the great and dreadful day of the Lord.   *4:5*

The Apocrypha[2]

12   And when they are in their cups, they forget their love both to friends and brethren, and a little after draw out swords.   *I Esdras 3:22*

13   Great is Truth, and mighty above all things.[3]   *4:41*

14   What is past I know, but what is for to come I know not.   *II Esdras 4:46*

15   Now therefore keep thy sorrow to thyself, and bear with a good courage that which hath befallen thee.   *10:15*

16   I shall light a candle of understanding in thine heart, which shall not be put out.   *14:25*

[1]See *Matthew 26:15, 36:23.*

[2]The Apocrypha (The Hidden Books) is a term used to describe the books found in the Alexandrine Greek Scripture (the Septuagint) but absent from the Orthodox Hebrew Scripture (the Masoretic Text). In the light of recent archaeological discoveries it appears that this difference reflects a conscious exclusion of the debatable books by developing Orthodox Judaism. These books are regarded as canonical only by Roman Catholics.

[3]Magna est veritas et praevalet.—*The Vulgate, Book III* (uncanonical)

For great is truth, and shall prevail.—THOMAS BROOKS [1608–1680], *The Crown and Glory of Christianity* [1662]

See Ptahhotpe, 3:5, and Patmore, 503:10.

17   If thou hast abundance, give alms accordingly: if thou have but a little, be not afraid to give according to that little.   *Tobit 4:8*

18   Put on her garments of gladness.   *Judith 10:3*

19   The ear of jealousy heareth all things.   *The Wisdom of Solomon 1:10*

20   Our time is a very shadow that passeth away.   *2:5*

21   Let us crown ourselves with rosebuds, before they be withered.   *2:8*

22   For God created man to be immortal, and made him to be an image of his own eternity.
Nevertheless through envy of the devil came death into the world.   *2:23–24*

23   The souls of the righteous are in the hand of God, and there shall no torment touch them.
In the sight of the unwise they seemed to die: and their departure is taken for misery,
And their going from us to be utter destruction: but they are in peace.
For though they be punished in the sight of men, yet is their hope full of immortality.
And having been a little chastised, they shall be greatly rewarded: for God proved them, and found them worthy for himself.   *3:1–5*

24   They that put their trust in him shall understand the truth.   *3:9*

25   Even so we in like manner, as soon as we were born, began to draw to our end.   *5:13*

26   For the hope of the ungodly is like dust that is blown away with the wind . . . and passeth away as the remembrance of a guest that tarrieth but a day.   *5:14*

27   For the very true beginning of her [wisdom] is the desire of discipline; and the care of discipline is love.   *6:17*

28   And when I was born, I drew in the common air, and fell upon the earth, which is of like nature; and the first voice which I uttered was crying, as all others do.   *7:3*

29   All men have one entrance into life, and the like going out.   *7:6*

30   The light that cometh from her [wisdom] never goeth out.   *7:10*

31   Who can number the sand of the sea, and the drops of rain, and the days of eternity?
    The Wisdom of Jesus the Son of Sirach, or Ecclesiasticus, 1:2

32   To whom hath the root of wisdom been revealed?   *1:6*

33   For the Lord is full of compassion and mercy, long-suffering, and very pitiful, and forgiveth sins, and saveth in time of affliction.   *2:11*

1   The greater thou art, the more humble thyself.
3:18

2   Many are in high place, and of renown: but mysteries are revealed unto the meek.   *3:19*

3   Seek not out the things that are too hard for thee, neither search the things that are above thy strength.
3:21

4   Be not curious in unnecessary matters: for more things are showed unto thee than men understand.
3:23

5   Profess not the knowledge . . . that thou hast not.
A stubborn heart shall fare evil at the last.
3:25–26

6   Defraud not the poor of his living, and make not the needy eyes to wait long.[1]   *4:1*

7   Wisdom exalteth her children, and layeth hold of them that seek her.
He that loveth her loveth life.   *4:11–12*

8   Observe the opportunity.   *4:20*

9   Be not as a lion in thy house, nor frantic among thy servants.
Let not thine hand be stretched out to receive, and shut when thou shouldest repay.   *4:30–31*

10   Set not thy heart upon thy goods; and say not, I have enough for my life.   *5:1*

11   Winnow not with every wind, and go not into every way.   *5:9*

12   Let thy life be sincere.   *5:11*

13   Be not ignorant of any thing in a great matter or a small.   *5:15*

14   If thou wouldest get a friend, prove him first.
6:7

15   A faithful friend is a strong defense: and he that hath found such an one hath found a treasure.
6:14

16   A faithful friend is the medicine of life.
6:16

17   If thou seest a man of understanding, get thee betimes unto him, and let thy foot wear the steps of his door.   *6:36*

18   Whatsoever thou takest in hand, remember the end, and thou shalt never do amiss.   *7:36*

19   Rejoice not over thy greatest enemy being dead, but remember that we die all.   *8:7*

20   Miss not the discourse of the elders.   *8:9*

21   Forsake not an old friend; for the new is not comparable to him: a new friend is as new wine; when it is old, thou shalt drink it with pleasure.
9:10

22   Pride is hateful before God and man.   *10:7*

23   He that is today a king tomorrow shall die.
10:10

24   Pride was not made for men, nor furious anger for them that are born of a woman.   *10:18*

25   Be not overwise in doing thy business.
10:26

26   Many kings have sat down upon the ground; and one that was never thought of hath worn the crown.
11:5

27   In the day of prosperity there is a forgetfulness of affliction: and in the day of affliction there is no more remembrance of prosperity.   *11:25*

28   Judge none blessed before his death.[2]   *11:28*

29   A friend cannot be known in prosperity: and an enemy cannot be hidden in adversity.   *12:8*

30   He that toucheth pitch shall be defiled therewith.
13:1

31   How agree the kettle and the earthen pot together?   *13:2*

32   All flesh consorteth according to kind, and a man will cleave to his like.[3]   *13:16*

33   A rich man beginning to fall is held up of his friends: but a poor man being down is thrust also away by his friends.   *13:21*

34   The heart of a man changeth his countenance, whether it be for good or evil.   *13:25*

35   So is a word better than a gift.   *18:16*

36   Be not made a beggar by banqueting upon borrowing.   *18:33*

37   He that contemneth small things shall fall by little and little.   *19:1*

38   Whether it be to friend or foe, talk not of other men's lives.   *19:8*

39   A man's attire, and excessive laughter, and gait, show what he is.   *19:30*

40   A tale out of season [is as] music in mourning.
22:6

41   I will not be ashamed to defend a friend.
22:25

42   All wickedness is but little to the wickedness of a woman.   *25:19*

43   The discourse of fools is irksome.   *27:13*

44   Many have fallen by the edge of the sword: but not so many as have fallen by the tongue.
28:18

[2]See Solon, 55:20; Aeschylus, 63:14; and Sophocles, 66:2.
[3]See Homer, 54:2; John Heywood, 141:5; and Robert Burton, 235:12.

[1]See Amenemope, 5:12, and *Proverbs* 22:22, 22:13.

1   Better is the life of a poor man in a mean cottage, than delicate fare in another man's house.
Ecclesiasticus 29:22

2   There is no riches above a sound body.
30:16

3   Gladness of the heart is the life of a man, and the joyfulness of a man prolongeth his days.   *30:22*

4   Envy and wrath shorten the life, and carefulness bringeth age before the time.   *30:24*

5   Watching for riches consumeth the flesh, and the care thereof driveth away sleep.   *31:1*

6   Let thy speech be short, comprehending much in few words.   *32:8*

7   Consider that I labored not for myself only, but for all them that seek learning.   *33:17*

8   Leave not a stain in thine honor.   *33:22*

9   Let the counsel of thine own heart stand.
37:13

10   Honor a physician with the honor due unto him for the uses which ye may have of him: for the Lord hath created him.   *38:1*

11   When the dead is at rest, let his remembrance rest; and be comforted for him, when his spirit is departed from him.   *38:23*

12   How can he get wisdom . . . whose talk is of bullocks?   *38:25*

13   Let us now praise famous men, and our fathers that begat us.   *44:1*

14   All these were honored in their generations, and were the glory of their times.
There be of them, that have left a name behind them, that their praises might be reported.
And some there be, which have no memorial; who are perished, as though they had never been; and are become as though they had never been born; and their children after them.   *44:7–9*

15   Their bodies are buried in peace; but their name liveth for evermore.   *44:14*

16   His word burned like a lamp.   *48:1*

17   O all ye works of the Lord, bless ye the Lord: praise him and exalt him above all[1] for ever.
The Song of the Three Holy Children 35

18   Daniel had convicted them of false witness by their own mouth.   *The History of Susanna 61*

19   It is a foolish thing to make a long prologue, and to be short in the story itself.
The Second Book of the Maccabees 2:32

20   When he was at the last gasp.   *7:9*

21   Speech finely framed delighteth the ears.
15:39

[1]In the *Book of Common Prayer (The Benedicite)*: magnify him.

The New Testament[2]

22   Behold, a virgin shall be with child, and shall bring forth a son, and they shall call his name Emmanuel, which being interpreted is, God with us.[3]
The Gospel According to Saint Matthew 1:23

23   Now when Jesus was born in Bethlehem of Judaea in the days of Herod the king, behold, there came wise men from the east to Jerusalem,
Saying, Where is he that is born King of the Jews? for we have seen his star in the east, and are come to worship him.   *2:1–2*

24   They saw the young child with Mary his mother, and fell down, and worshipped him: and . . . they presented unto him gifts; gold, and frankincense, and myrrh.
And being warned of God in a dream that they should not return to Herod, they departed into their own country another way.   *2:11–12*

25   Out of Egypt have I called my son.   *2:15*

26   Rachel weeping for her children, and would not be comforted, because they are not.[4]   *2:18*

27   He shall be called a Nazarene.   *2:23*

28   Repent ye: for the kingdom of heaven is at hand.
3:2

29   The voice of one crying in the wilderness, Prepare ye the way of the Lord, make his paths straight.[5]
3:3

30   And his meat was locusts and wild honey.
3:4

31   O generation of vipers, who hath warned you to flee from the wrath to come?   *3:7*

32   Now also the axe is laid unto the root of the trees: therefore every tree which bringeth not forth good fruit is hewn down, and cast into the fire.
3:10

33   The Spirit of God descending like a dove.
3:16

34   This is my beloved Son, in whom I am well pleased.   *3:17*

35   And when he had fasted forty days and forty nights, he was afterward an hungred.   *4:2*

36   The people which sat in darkness saw great light.[6]   *4:16*

37   Follow me, and I will make you fishers of men.
4:19

[2]The earliest Christian writings [A.D. c. 50–c. 64] are the Letters (Epistles) of Paul the Apostle. The Gospels are later, between the years 70 and 100.
[3]See *Isaiah 7:14, 26:5.*
[4]Rachel weeping for her children refused to be comforted . . . because they were not.—*Jeremiah 31:15*
[5]See *Isaiah 40:3, 27:15.*
[6]See *Psalm 107:10, 19:8,* and *Luke 1:79, 38:1.*

1   Blessed are the poor in spirit: for theirs is the kingdom of heaven.

Blessed are they that mourn: for they shall be comforted.

Blessed are the meek: for they shall inherit the earth.[1]

Blessed are they which do hunger and thirst after righteousness: for they shall be filled.

Blessed are the merciful: for they shall obtain mercy.

Blessed are the pure in heart: for they shall see God.

Blessed are the peacemakers: for they shall be called the children of God.

Blessed are they which are persecuted for righteousness' sake: for theirs is the kingdom of heaven.

Blessed are ye, when men shall revile you, and persecute you, and shall say all manner of evil against you falsely, for my sake.   *5:3–11*[2]

2   Ye are the salt of the earth: but if the salt have lost his savor, wherewith shall it be salted?   *5:13*

3   Ye are the light of the world. A city that is set on an hill cannot be hid.

Neither do men light a candle, and put it under a bushel, but on a candlestick; and it giveth light unto all that are in the house.

Let your light so shine before men, that they may see your good works, and glorify your Father which is in heaven.

Think not that I am come to destroy the law, or the prophets: I am not come to destroy, but to fulfill.   *5:14–17*

4   Till heaven and earth pass, one jot or one tittle shall in no wise pass from the law, till all be fulfilled.   *5:18*

5   Whosoever looketh on a woman to lust after her hath committed adultery with her already in his heart.

And if thy right eye offend thee, pluck it out, and cast it from thee: for it is profitable for thee that one of thy members should perish, and not that thy whole body should be cast into hell.

And if thy right hand offend thee, cut it off.   *5:28–30*

6   Swear not at all; neither by heaven; for it is God's throne:

Nor by the earth; for it is his footstool.   *5:34–35*

7   Resist not evil: but whosoever shall smite thee on thy right cheek, turn to him the other also.   *5:39*

8   Love your enemies, bless them that curse you, do good to them that hate you, and pray for them which despitefully use you, and persecute you.   *5:44*

9   He maketh his sun to rise on the evil and on the good, and sendeth rain on the just and on the unjust.   *5:45*

10   Be ye therefore perfect, even as your Father which is in heaven is perfect.   *5:48*

11   When thou doest alms, let not thy left hand know what thy right hand doeth.   *6:3*

12   After this manner therefore pray ye: Our Father which art in heaven, Hallowed be thy name.

Thy kingdom come. Thy will be done in earth, as it is in heaven.

Give us this day our daily bread.

And forgive us our debts, as we forgive our debtors.[3]

And lead us not into temptation, but deliver us from evil: For thine is the kingdom, and the power, and the glory,[4] for ever. Amen.   *6:9–13*[5]

13   Lay not up for yourselves treasures upon earth, where moth and rust doth corrupt, and where thieves break through and steal:

But lay up for yourselves treasures in heaven.   *6:19–20*

14   For where your treasure is, there will your heart be also.   *6:21*

15   The light of the body is the eye.   *6:22*

16   If therefore the light that is in thee be darkness, how great is that darkness!   *6:23*

17   No man can serve two masters: for either he will hate the one, and love the other; or else he will hold to the one, and despise the other. Ye cannot serve God and mammon.   *6:24*

18   Is not the life more than meat, and the body than raiment?

Behold the fowls of the air: for they sow not, neither do they reap, nor gather into barns.   *6:25–26*

19   Which of you by taking thought can add one cubit unto his stature?   *6:27*

20   Consider the lilies of the field, how they grow; they toil not, neither do they spin.   *6:28*

21   Even Solomon in all his glory was not arrayed like one of these.   *6:29*

22   Seek ye first the kingdom of God, and his righteousness; and all these things shall be added unto you.   *6:33*

---

[1]See *Psalm 37:11*, 16:34.

[2]The Beatitudes are the opening of the Sermon on the Mount, which continues through *Matthew 7*.

[3]And forgive us our trespasses, As we forgive those who trespass against us.—*Book of Common Prayer, Morning Prayer*

[4]See *Chronicles 29:11*, 13:17.

[5]The Lord's Prayer.

1   Take therefore no thought for the morrow: for the morrow shall take thought for the things of itself. Sufficient unto the day is the evil thereof.

Matthew 6:34

2   Judge not, that ye be not judged.   7:1

3   With what measure ye mete, it shall be measured to you again.

And why beholdest thou the mote that is in thy brother's eye, but considerest not the beam that is in thine own eye?   7:2–3

4   Thou hypocrite, first cast out the beam out of thine own eye.   7:5

5   Neither cast ye your pearls before swine.

7:6

6   Ask, and it shall be given you; seek, and ye shall find; knock, and it shall be opened unto you.

7:7

7   Or what man is there of you, whom if his son ask bread, will he give him a stone?   7:9

8   Therefore all things whatsoever ye would that men should do to you, do ye even so to them: for this is the law and the prophets.[1]   7:12

9   Wide is the gate, and broad is the way, that leadeth to destruction, and many there be which go in thereat:

Because strait is the gate, and narrow is the way, which leadeth unto life, and few there be that find it.

7:13–14

10   Beware of false prophets, which come to you in sheep's clothing, but inwardly they are ravening wolves.   7:15

11   Ye shall know them by their fruits. Do men gather grapes of thorns, or figs of thistles?

7:16

12   By their fruits ye shall know them.   7:20

13   Not every one that saith unto me, Lord, Lord, shall enter into the kingdom of heaven; but he that doeth the will of my Father which is in heaven.

7:21

14   [The house] fell not: for it was founded upon a rock.   7:25

15   A foolish man, which built his house upon the sand.   7:26

16   But the children of the kingdom shall be cast out into outer darkness: there shall be weeping and gnashing of teeth.   8:12

17   The foxes have holes, and the birds of the air have nests; but the Son of man hath not where to lay his head.   8:20

18   Follow me; and let the dead bury their dead.

8:22

19   Why are ye fearful, O ye of little faith?

8:26

20   He saw a man, named Matthew, sitting at the receipt of custom.   9:9

21   They that be whole need not a physician, but they that are sick.   9:12

22   I am not come to call the righteous, but sinners to repentance.   9:13

23   Can the children of the bridechamber mourn, as long as the bridegroom is with them?   9:15

24   Neither do men put new wine into old bottles.

9:17

25   The maid is not dead, but sleepeth.   9:24

26   The harvest truly is plenteous, but the laborers are few.   9:37

27   Go rather to the lost sheep of the house of Israel.

10:6

28   Freely ye have received, freely give.   10:8

29   Whosoever shall not receive you, nor hear your words, when ye depart out of that house or city, shake off the dust of your feet.   10:14

30   Be ye therefore wise as serpents, and harmless as doves.[2]   10:16

31   Ye shall be hated of all men for my name's sake.

10:22

32   The disciple is not above his master, nor the servant above his lord.   10:24

33   Are not two sparrows sold for a farthing? and one of them shall not fall on the ground without your Father.

But the very hairs of your head are all numbered.

10:29–30

34   I came not to send peace, but a sword.

10:34

35   He that taketh not his cross, and followeth after me, is not worthy of me.

He that findeth his life shall lose it: and he that loseth his life for my sake shall find it.[3]

10:38–39

36   He that hath ears to hear, let him hear.

11:15

37   The Son of man came eating and drinking, and they say, Behold a man gluttonous, and a winebibber, a friend of publicans and sinners. But wisdom is justified of her children.   11:19

38   Come unto me, all ye that labor and are heavy laden, and I will give you rest.

Take my yoke upon you, and learn of me; for I am

---

[1]The Golden Rule. Common form: Do unto others as you would have others do unto you.

See Confucius, 61:30; Aristotle, 77:15; Hillel, 102:7; and Chesterfield, 304:21.

[2]Often quoted as: Wise as the serpent, and harmless as the dove.

[3]See *Matthew 16:25, 35:30.*

meek and lowly in heart: and ye shall find rest unto your souls.

For my yoke is easy, and my burden is light.

11:28–30

1   He that is not with me is against me.   *12:30*

2   The tree is known by his fruit.   *12:33*

3   Out of the abundance of the heart the mouth speaketh.   *12:34*

4   Behold, a greater than Solomon is here.

12:42

5   Some seeds fell by the way side.   *13:4*

6   Because they had no root, they withered away.

13:6

7   But other fell into good ground, and brought forth fruit, some an hundredfold, some sixtyfold, some thirtyfold.   *13:8*

8   The care of this world, and the deceitfulness of riches.   *13:22*

9   The kingdom of heaven is like to a grain of mustard seed.   *13:31*

10   Pearl of great price.   *13:46*

11   The kingdom of heaven is like unto a net, that was cast into the sea, and gathered of every kind.[1]

13:47

12   Is not this the carpenter's son?   *13:55*

13   A prophet is not without honor, save in his own country.   *13:57*

14   [Salome] the daughter of Herodias danced before them, and pleased Herod.   *14:6*

15   Give me here John Baptist's head in a charger.

14:8

16   We have here but five loaves, and two fishes.

14:17

17   And they did all eat, and were filled: and they took up of the fragments that remained twelve baskets full.   *14:20*

18   And in the fourth watch of the night Jesus went unto them, walking on the sea.   *14:25*

19   Be of good cheer; it is I; be not afraid.

14:27

20   O thou of little faith, wherefore didst thou doubt?

14:31

21   Of a truth thou art the Son of God.   *14:33*

22   Not that which goeth into the mouth defileth a man; but that which cometh out of the mouth, this defileth a man.   *15:11*

23   They be blind leaders of the blind. And if the blind lead the blind, both shall fall into the ditch.

15:14

24   The dogs eat of the crumbs which fall from their masters' table.   *15:27*

25   When it is evening, ye say, It will be fair weather: for the sky is red.   *16:2*

26   The signs of the times.   *16:3*

27   Thou art the Christ, the Son of the living God.

16:16

28   Thou art Peter, and upon this rock I will build my church; and the gates of hell shall not prevail against it.

And I will give unto thee the keys of the kingdom of heaven.   *16:18–19*

29   Get thee behind me, Satan.   *16:23*

30   Whosoever will save his life shall lose it: and whosoever will lose his life for my sake shall find it.[2]

For what is a man profited, if he shall gain the whole world, and lose his own soul?   *16:25–26*

31   Except ye be converted, and become as little children, ye shall not enter into the kingdom of heaven.

18:3

32   He rejoiceth more of that sheep, than of the ninety and nine which went not astray.   *18:13*

33   Where two or three are gathered together in my name, there am I in the midst of them.[3]   *18:20*

34   Until seventy times seven.   *18:22*

35   What therefore God hath joined together, let not man put asunder.[4]   *19:6*

36   If thou wilt be perfect, go and sell that thou hast, and give to the poor, and thou shalt have treasure in heaven.   *19:21*

37   It is easier for a camel to go through the eye of a needle, than for a rich man to enter into the kingdom of God.   *19:24*

38   Many that are first shall be last; and the last shall be first.   *19:30*

39   Borne the burden and heat of the day.

20:12

40   Is it not lawful for me to do what I will with mine own?   *20:15*

41   Overthrew the tables of the moneychangers.

21:12

42   My house shall be called the house of prayer; but ye have made it a den of thieves.   *21:13*

43   They made light of it.   *22:5*

44   Many are called, but few are chosen.   *22:14*

45   Render therefore unto Caesar the things which are Caesar's; and unto God the things that are God's.   *22:21*

[1]See *Lao-tzu, 58:3.*

[2]See *Matthew 10:39, 34:35.*

[3]See *Book of Common Prayer, A Prayer of Saint Chrysostom, 49:6.*

[4]See *Book of Common Prayer, Solemnization of Matrimony, 50:6.*

1   Thou shalt love the Lord thy God with all thy heart, and with all thy soul, and with all thy mind.[1]

This is the first and great commandment.

And the second is like unto it, Thou shalt love thy neighbor as thyself.[2]

On these two commandments hang all the law and the prophets.   *Matthew 22:37–40*

2   Whosoever shall exalt himself shall be abased; and he that shall humble himself shall be exalted.
                                        23:12

3   Woe unto you, scribes and Pharisees, hypocrites! for ye pay tithe of mint and anise and cumin.
                                        23:23

4   Blind guides, which strain at a gnat, and swallow a camel.   *23:24*

5   Whited sepulchers, which indeed appear beautiful outward, but are within full of dead men's bones.
                                        23:27

6   O Jerusalem, Jerusalem, thou that killest the prophets, and stonest them which are sent unto thee, how often would I have gathered thy children together, even as a hen gathereth her chickens under her wings, and ye would not!   *23:37*

7   Ye shall hear of wars and rumors of wars: see that ye be not troubled: for all these things must come to pass, but the end is not yet.

For nation shall rise against nation.   *24:6–7*

8   Abomination of desolation.   *24:15*

9   Wheresoever the carcase is, there will the eagles be gathered together.   *24:28*

10   And he shall send his angels with a great sound of a trumpet.   *24:31*

11   Heaven and earth shall pass away, but my words shall not pass away.   *24:35*

12   The one shall be taken, and the other left.
                                        24:40

13   Then shall the kingdom of heaven be likened unto ten virgins, which took their lamps, and went forth to meet the bridegroom.

And five of them were wise, and five were foolish.
                                        25:1–2

14   Well done, thou good and faithful servant . . . enter thou into the joy of thy lord.   *25:21*

15   Unto every one that hath shall be given, and he shall have abundance: but from him that hath not shall be taken away even that which he hath.
                                        25:29

16   Cast ye the unprofitable servant into outer darkness.   *25:30*

17   And before him shall be gathered all nations: and he shall separate them one from another, as a shepherd divideth his sheep from the goats.   *25:32*

18   For I was an hungred, and ye gave me meat: I was thirsty, and ye gave me drink: I was a stranger, and ye took me in:

Naked, and ye clothed me: I was sick, and ye visited me: I was in prison, and ye came unto me.
                                        25:35–36

19   Inasmuch as ye have done it unto one of the least of these my brethren, ye have done it unto me.
                                        25:40

20   There came unto him [Jesus] a woman having an alabaster box of very precious ointment, and poured it on his head, as he sat at meat.   *26:7*

21   To what purpose is this waste?   *26:8*

22   For ye have the poor always with you; but me ye have not always.[3]   *26:11*

23   What will ye give me, and I will deliver him unto you? And they covenanted with him for thirty pieces of silver.[4]   *26:15*

24   My time is at hand.   *26:18*

25   Verily I say unto you, that one of you shall betray me.   *26:21*

26   And they were exceeding sorrowful, and began every one of them to say unto him, Lord, is it I?
                                        26:22

27   It had been good for that man [Judas] if he had not been born.   *26:24*

28   Jesus took bread, and blessed it, and brake it, and gave it to the disciples, and said, Take, eat; this is my body.

And he took the cup, and gave thanks, and gave it to them, saying, Drink ye all of it;

For this is my blood of the new testament, which is shed for many for the remission of sins.

But I say unto you, I will not drink henceforth of this fruit of the vine, until that day when I drink it new with you in my Father's kingdom.[5]
                                        26:26–29

29   My soul is exceeding sorrowful, even unto death.
                                        26:38

30   O my Father, if it be possible, let this cup pass from me: nevertheless, not as I will, but as thou wilt.
                                        26:39

31   Could ye not watch with me one hour?

Watch and pray, that ye enter not into temptation: the spirit indeed is willing, but the flesh is weak.
                                        26:40–41

32   Behold, the hour is at hand, and the Son of man is betrayed into the hands of sinners.   *26:45*

33   He came to Jesus, and said, Hail, Master; and kissed him.   *26:49*

[1]See *Deuteronomy 6:5*, 10:11.
[2]See *Leviticus 19:18*, 9:26.
[3]See *Deuteronomy 15:11*, 10:19.
[4]See *Zechariah 11:12*, 30:5.
[5]See *I Corinthians 11:24*, 25, 43:11 and 43:12.

1 All they that take the sword shall perish with the sword. 26:52

2 Thy speech bewrayeth thee. 26:73

3 Then began he to curse and to swear, saying, I know not the man. And immediately the cock crew.
And Peter remembered the word of Jesus . . . Before the cock crow, thou shalt deny me thrice.[1] And he went out, and wept bitterly. 26:74–75

4 The potter's field, to bury strangers in. 27:7

5 Have thou nothing to do with that just man. 27:19

6 Let him be crucified. 27:22

7 [Pilate] took water, and washed his hands before the multitude, saying, I am innocent of the blood of this just person: see ye to it. 27:24

8 His blood be on us, and on our children. 27:25

9 A place called Golgotha, that is to say, a place of a skull. 27:33

10 This is Jesus the King of the Jews. 27:37

11 He saved others; himself he cannot save. 27:42

12 Eli, Eli, lama sabachthani? that is to say, My God, my God, why hast thou forsaken me?[2] 27:46

13 And, behold, the veil of the temple was rent in twain from the top to the bottom; and the earth did quake, and the rocks rent. 27:51

14 His countenance was like lightning, and his raiment white as snow. 28:3

15 Go ye therefore, and teach all nations, baptizing them in the name of the Father, and of the Son, and of the Holy Ghost. 28:19

16 Lo, I am with you alway, even unto the end of the world. 28:20

17 There cometh one mightier than I[3] after me, the latchet of whose shoes I am not worthy to stoop down and unloose.
The Gospel According to Saint Mark 1:7

18 Arise, and take up thy bed, and walk. 2:9

19 The sabbath was made for man, and not man for the sabbath. 2:27

20 If a house be divided against itself, that house cannot stand. 3:25

21 The earth bringeth forth fruit of herself; first the blade, then the ear, after that the full corn in the ear. 4:28

22 What manner of man is this? 4:41

23 They came . . . into the country of the Gadarenes. 5:1

24 My name is Legion: for we are many. 5:9

25 And the unclean spirits went out, and entered the swine: and the herd ran violently down a steep place into the sea . . . and were choked in the sea. 5:13

26 Clothed, and in his right mind. 5:15

27 My little daughter lieth at the point of death. 5:23

28 Knowing in himself that virtue had gone out of him. 5:30

29 I see men as trees, walking. 8:24

30 Lord, I believe; help thou mine unbelief. 9:24

31 Suffer the little children to come unto me, and forbid them not; for of such is the kingdom of God. 10:14

32 Which devour widows' houses, and for a pretense make long prayers. 12:40

33 And there came a certain poor widow, and she threw in two mites. 12:42

34 Watch ye therefore: for ye know not when the master of the house cometh, at even, or at midnight, or at the cockcrowing, or in the morning:
Lest coming suddenly he find you sleeping. 13:35–36

35 He is risen.[4] 16:6

36 Go ye into all the world, and preach the gospel to every creature. 16:15

37 Hail, thou that art highly favored, the Lord is with thee: blessed art thou among women.
The Gospel According to Saint Luke 1:28

38 For with God nothing shall be impossible. 1:37

39 Blessed is the fruit of thy womb. 1:42

40 My soul doth magnify the Lord. 1:46

41 For he hath regarded the low estate of his handmaiden: for, behold, from henceforth all generations shall call me blessed. 1:48

42 He hath scattered the proud in the imagination of their hearts.
He hath put down the mighty from their seats, and exalted them of low degree. 1:51–52

43 He hath filled the hungry with good things; and the rich he hath sent empty away. 1:53

44 Blessed be the Lord God of Israel; for he hath visited and redeemed his people. 1:68

45 As he spake by the mouth of his holy prophets, which have been since the world began:

[1]This night, before the cock crow, thou shalt deny me thrice.
—*Matthew 26:34*
[2]See *Psalm 22:1, 16:15.*
[3]John the Baptist.

[4]See *Luke 24:34, 39:28,* and *Book of Common Prayer, 48:14.*

That we should be saved from our enemies, and from the hand of all that hate us.

Luke 1:70–71

1   Through the tender mercy of our God; whereby the dayspring from on high hath visited us,

To give light to them that sit in darkness and in the shadow of death.[1]   *1:78–79*

2   And she brought forth her firstborn son, and wrapped him in swaddling clothes, and laid him in a manger; because there was no room for them in the inn.   *2:7*

3   There were in the same country shepherds abiding in the field, keeping watch over their flock by night.

And, lo, the angel of the Lord came upon them, and the glory of the Lord shone round about them: and they were sore afraid.

And the angel said unto them, Fear not: for, behold, I bring you good tidings of great joy, which shall be to all people.

For unto you is born this day in the city of David a Savior, which is Christ the Lord.   *2:8–11*

4   Glory to God in the highest, and on earth peace, good will toward men.[2]   *2:14*

5   Lord, now lettest thou thy servant depart in peace.   *2:29*

6   A light to lighten the Gentiles, and the glory of thy people Israel.   *2:32*

7   Wist ye not that I must be about my Father's business?   *2:49*

8   Jesus increased in wisdom and stature, and in favor with God and man.   *2:52*

9   [The devil] showed unto him all the kingdoms of the world in a moment of time.   *4:5*

10   For it is written, He shall give his angels charge over thee, to keep thee:

And in their hands they shall bear thee up, lest at any time thou dash thy foot against a stone.

4:10–11[3]

11   Physician, heal thyself.   *4:23*

12   Woe unto you, when all men shall speak well of you!   *6:26*

13   Her sins, which are many, are forgiven; for she loved much.   *7:47*

14   And he said to the woman, Thy faith hath saved thee; go in peace.   *7:50*

15   Nothing is secret, that shall not be made manifest.   *8:17*

16   No man, having put his hand to the plow, and looking back, is fit for the kingdom of God.

9:62

17   Nor scrip, nor shoes.   *10:4*

18   Peace be to this house.   *10:5*

19   The laborer is worthy of his hire.   *10:7*

20   I beheld Satan as lightning fall from heaven.

10:18

21   Many prophets and kings have desired to see those things which ye see, and have not seen them; and to hear those things which ye hear, and have not heard them.   *10:24*

22   A certain man went down from Jerusalem to Jericho, and fell among thieves.   *10:30*

23   A certain Samaritan . . . had compassion on him.   *10:33*

24   Go, and do thou likewise.   *10:37*

25   But Martha was cumbered about much serving.

10:40

26   But one thing is needful: and Mary hath chosen that good part, which shall not be taken away from her.   *10:42*

27   This is an evil generation: they seek a sign.

11:29

28   Soul, thou hast much goods laid up for many years; take thine ease, eat, drink, and be merry.[4]

12:19

29   Thou fool, this night thy soul shall be required of thee.   *12:20*

30   Let your loins be girded about, and your lights burning.   *12:35*

31   For unto whomsoever much is given, of him shall be much required: and to whom men have committed much, of him they will ask the more.   *12:48*

32   The poor, and the maimed, and the halt, and the blind.   *14:21*

33   Which of you, intending to build a tower, sitteth not down first, and counteth the cost, whether he have sufficient to finish it?   *14:28*

34   Rejoice with me; for I have found my sheep which was lost.   *15:6*

35   [The prodigal son] wasted his substance with riotous living.   *15:13*

36   Bring hither the fatted calf, and kill it.

15:23

37   For this my son was dead, and is alive again; he was lost, and is found.   *15:24*

38   Son, thou art ever with me, and all that I have is thine.   *15:31*

39   What shall I do? . . . I cannot dig; to beg I am ashamed.   *16:3*

40   The children of this world are in their generation wiser than the children of light.   *16:8*

---

[1]See *Psalm 107:10, 19:8,* and *Matthew 4:16, 32:36.*
[2]The Douay Bible has "peace to men of good will."
[3]See *Psalm 91:11–12, 18:16.* Also in *Matthew 4:6.*

[4]See *Ecclesiastes 8:15, 24:17.*

1   He that is faithful in that which is least is faithful also in much: and he that is unjust in the least is unjust also in much.   *16:10*

2   The beggar died, and was carried by the angels into Abraham's bosom.   *16:22*

3   Between us and you there is a great gulf fixed.   *16:26*

4   It were better for him that a millstone were hanged about his neck, and he cast into the sea.   *17:2*

5   The kingdom of God is within you.   *17:21*

6   Remember Lot's wife.   *17:32*

7   Two men went up into the temple to pray; the one a Pharisee, and the other a publican.   *18:10*

8   God, I thank thee, that I am not as other men are.   *18:11*

9   God be merciful to me a sinner.   *18:13*

10   Out of thine own mouth will I judge thee.   *19:22*

11   If these should hold their peace, the stones would immediately cry out.[1]   *19:40*

12   He is not a God of the dead, but of the living.   *20:38*

13   In your patience possess ye your souls.   *21:19*

14   The Son of man coming in a cloud with power and great glory.   *21:27*

15   This do in remembrance of me.[2]   *22:19*

16   Not my will, but thine, be done.   *22:42*

17   For if they do these things in a green tree, what shall be done in the dry?   *23:31*

18   The place, which is called Calvary.   *23:33*

19   Father, forgive them; for they know not what they do.   *23:34*

20   Lord, remember me when thou comest into thy kingdom.   *23:42*

21   To day shalt thou be with me in paradise.   *23:43*

22   Father, into thy hands I commend my spirit.   *23:46*

23   He gave up the ghost.   *Ibid.*

24   He was a good man, and a just.   *23:50*

25   Why seek ye the living among the dead?   *24:5*

26   Their words seemed to them as idle tales.   *24:11*

27   Did not our heart burn within us, while he talked with us?   *24:32*

[1]See *Habakkuk 2:11, 29:41.*
[2]See *I Corinthians 11:24, 43:11.*

28   The Lord is risen indeed.[3]   *24:34*

29   In the beginning was the Word, and the Word was with God, and the Word was God.
The Gospel According to Saint John 1:1

30   And the light shineth in darkness; and the darkness comprehended it not.   *1:5*

31   There was a man sent from God, whose name was John.   *1:6*

32   The true Light, which lighteth every man that cometh into the world.   *1:9*

33   The Word was made flesh, and dwelt among us . . . full of grace and truth.   *1:14*

34   No man hath seen God at any time.   *1:18*

35   Behold the Lamb of God, which taketh away the sin of the world.[4]   *1:29*

36   Can there any good thing come out of Nazareth?   *1:46*

37   Hereafter ye shall see heaven open, and the angels of God ascending and descending upon the Son of man.   *1:51*

38   Woman, what have I to do with thee? mine hour is not yet come.   *2:4*

39   The water that was made wine.   *2:9*

40   This beginning of miracles did Jesus in Cana of Galilee,[5] and manifested forth his glory; and his disciples believed on him.   *2:11*

41   When he had made a scourge of small cords, he drove them all out of the temple.   *2:15*

42   Make not my Father's house an house of merchandise.   *2:16*

43   Except a man be born again, he cannot see the kingdom of God.   *3:3*

44   The wind bloweth where it listeth, and thou hearest the sound thereof, but canst not tell whence it cometh, and whither it goeth: so is every one that is born of the Spirit.   *3:8*

45   How can these things be?   *3:9*

46   God so loved the world, that he gave his only begotten Son, that whosoever believeth in him should not perish, but have everlasting life.   *3:16*

47   There cometh a woman of Samaria to draw water: Jesus saith unto her, Give me to drink.   *4:7*

48   The hour cometh, and now is, when the true worshippers shall worship the Father in spirit and in truth.   *4:23*

49   He was a burning and a shining light.   *5:35*

[3]See *Mark 16:6, 37:35,* and *Book of Common Prayer, 48:14.*
[4]Spoken by John the Baptist.
See *The Missal, 48:9.*
[5]There was a marriage in Cana of Galilee.—*John 2:1*

1   Search the scriptures.   *John 5:39*

2   What are they among so many?   *6:9*

3   Gather up the fragments that remain, that nothing be lost.   *6:12*

4   I am the bread of life:[1] he that cometh to me shall never hunger; and he that believeth on me shall never thirst.   *6:35*

5   It is the spirit that quickeneth; the flesh profiteth nothing.   *6:63*

6   Judge not according to the appearance.   *7:24*

7   Never man spake like this man.   *7:46*

8   He that is without sin among you, let him first cast a stone at her.   *8:7*

9   Neither do I condemn thee: go, and sin no more.   *8:11*

10   I am the light of the world: he that followeth me shall not walk in darkness, but shall have the light of life.   *8:12*

11   The truth shall make you free.   *8:32*

12   Ye are of your father the devil . . . there is no truth in him. . . . he is a liar, and the father of it.   *8:44*

13   I must work the works of him that sent me, while it is day: the night cometh, when no man can work.   *9:4*

14   Whether he be a sinner or no, I know not: one thing I know, that, whereas I was blind, now I see.   *9:25*

15   I am the door.   *10:9*

16   I am come that they might have life, and that they might have it more abundantly.   *10:10*

17   I am the good shepherd: the good shepherd giveth his life for the sheep.   *10:11*

18   Other sheep I have, which are not of this fold.   *10:16*

19   I am the resurrection, and the life: he that believeth in me, though he were dead, yet shall he live:
And whosoever liveth and believeth in me shall never die.[2]   *11:25–26*

20   Jesus wept.   *11:35*

21   It is expedient for us, that one man should die for the people.   *11:50*

22   Then saith one of his disciples, Judas Iscariot, Simon's son, which should betray him,
Why was not this ointment sold for three hundred pence, and given to the poor?[3]   *12:4–5*

23   Yet a little while is the light with you. Walk while ye have the light, lest darkness come upon you.   *12:35*

24   That thou doest, do quickly.   *13:27*

25   A new commandment I give unto you, That ye love one another.   *13:34*

26   Let not your heart be troubled: ye believe in God, believe also in me.
In my Father's house are many mansions: if it were not so, I would have told you. I go to prepare a place for you.   *14:1–2*

27   I will come again, and receive you unto myself; that where I am, there ye may be also.   *14:3*

28   I am the way, the truth, and the life.   *14:6*

29   I will not leave you comfortless.   *14:18*

30   Peace I leave with you, my peace I give unto you: not as the world giveth, give I unto you. Let not your heart be troubled, neither let it be afraid.   *14:27*

31   Greater love hath no man than this, that a man lay down his life for his friends.   *15:13*

32   Ye have not chosen me, but I have chosen you.   *15:16*

33   Whither goest thou?[4]   *16:5*

34   Ask, and ye shall receive, that your joy may be full.   *16:24*

35   Be of good cheer; I have overcome the world.   *16:33*

36   Pilate saith unto him, What is truth?   *18:38*

37   Now Barabbas was a robber.   *18:40*

38   Behold the man![5]   *19:5*

39   Woman, behold thy son!   *19:26*

40   It is finished.   *19:30*

41   Touch me not.[6]   *20:17*

42   Then saith he to Thomas . . . be not faithless, but believing.   *20:27*

43   Blessed are they that have not seen, and yet have believed.   *20:29*

44   Suddenly there came a sound from heaven as of a rushing mighty wind.
The Acts of the Apostles 2:2

45   There appeared unto them cloven tongues like as of fire, and it sat upon each of them.
And they were all filled with the Holy Ghost, and began to speak with other tongues.   *2:3–4*

46   Silver and gold have I none; but such as I have give I thee.   *3:6*

47   And distribution was made unto every man according as he had need.   *4:35*

---

[1]See *Psalm 105:40, 19:7.*
[2]Also in *Book of Common Prayer, Burial of the Dead.*
[3]See *Matthew 26:7* and *26:8, 36:20* and *36:21.*

[4]*Quo vadis?* — *The Vulgate*
[5]*Ecce homo.* — *The Vulgate*
[6]*Noli me tangere.* — *The Vulgate*

1   If this counsel or this work be of men, it will come to nought:

But if it be of God, ye cannot overthrow it.

5:38–39

2   Thy money perish with thee.   *8:20*

3   In the gall of bitterness, and in the bond of iniquity.   *8:23*

4   Saul, yet breathing out threatenings and slaughter against the disciples of the Lord.   *9:1*

5   Saul, Saul, why persecutest thou me?   *9:4*

6   It is hard for thee to kick against the pricks.[1]   *9:5*

7   He is a chosen vessel unto me.   *9:15*

8   Immediately there fell from his eyes as it had been scales.   *9:18*

9   What God hath cleansed, that call not thou common.   *10:15*

10   God is no respecter of persons.[2]   *10:34*

11   The gods are come down to us in the likeness of men.   *14:11*

12   We also are men of like passions with you.   *14:15*

13   Come over into Macedonia, and help us.   *16:9*

14   Certain lewd fellows of the baser sort.   *17:5*

15   Ye men of Athens, I perceive that in all things ye are too superstitious.

For as I passed by, and beheld your devotions, I found an altar with this inscription, TO THE UNKNOWN GOD.   *17:22–23*

16   God that made the world, and all things therein, seeing that he is Lord of heaven and earth, dwelleth not in temples made with hands;

Neither is worshipped with men's hands, as though he needed any thing, seeing he giveth to all life, and breath, and all things;

And hath made of one blood all nations of men for to dwell on all the face of the earth.   *17:24–26*

17   For in him we live, and move, and have our being; as certain also of your own poets have said, For we are also his offspring.[3]   *17:28*

18   Your blood be upon your own heads.   *18:6*

19   And Gallio cared for none of those things.   *18:17*

20   Mighty in the Scriptures.   *18:24*

21   We have not so much as heard whether there be any Holy Ghost.   *19:2*

22   All with one voice about the space of two hours cried out, Great is Diana of the Ephesians.   *19:34*

23   It is more blessed to give than to receive.   *20:35*

24   I [Paul] am . . . a Jew of Tarsus, a city in Cilicia, a citizen of no mean city.   *21:39*

25   Brought up in this city at the feet of Gamaliel.   *22:3*

26   And the chief captain answered, With a great sum obtained I this freedom. And Paul said, But I was free born.   *22:28*

27   God shall smite thee, thou whited wall.   *23:3*

28   Revilest thou God's high priest?   *23:4*

29   I [Paul] am a Pharisee, the son of a Pharisee.   *23:6*

30   A conscience void of offense toward God, and toward men.   *24:16*

31   When I have a convenient season, I will call for thee.   *24:25*

32   I appeal unto Caesar.   *25:11*

33   Paul, thou art beside thyself; much learning doth make thee mad.   *26:24*

34   I am not mad . . . but speak forth the words of truth and soberness.   *26:25*

35   For this thing was not done in a corner.   *26:26*

36   Almost thou persuadest me to be a Christian.   *26:28*

37   Wherein thou judgest another, thou condemnest thyself.

*The Epistle of Paul the Apostle to the Romans
2:1*

38   These, having not the law, are a law unto themselves.   *2:14*

39   The things that are more excellent.   *2:18*

40   Where no law is, there is no transgression.   *4:15*

41   Who against hope believed in hope.   *4:18*

42   Where sin abounded, grace did much more abound.   *5:20*

43   Death hath no more dominion over him.   *6:9*

44   I speak after the manner of men.   *6:19*

45   The wages of sin is death; but the gift of God is eternal life.   *6:23*

46   The good that I would I do not: but the evil which I would not, that I do.[4]   *7:19*

---

[1] See Aeschylus, 63:18.
[2] For there is no respect of persons with God. — *Romans 2:11*
[3] See Aeschylus, 63:17; Cleanthes, 82:2; and Aratus, 82:12.

[4] See Euripides, 68:14, and Ovid, 101:25.

1   Who shall deliver me from the body of this death?
Romans 7:24

2   Heirs of God, and joint-heirs with Christ.
8:17

3   For we know that the whole creation groaneth and travaileth in pain together until now.   *8:22*

4   All things work together for good to them that love God.   *8:28*

5   For whom he did foreknow, he also did predestinate to be conformed to the image of his Son, that he might be the firstborn among many brethren.

Moreover whom he did predestinate, them he also called: and whom he called, them he also justified: and whom he justified, them he also glorified.
8:29 – 30

6   If God be for us, who can be against us?
8:31

7   Who shall lay any thing to the charge of God's elect? It is God that justifieth.   *8:33*

8   Who shall separate us from the love of Christ?
8:35

9   Neither death, nor life, nor angels, nor principalities, nor powers, nor things present, nor things to come,

Nor height, nor depth, nor any other creature, shall be able to separate us from the love of God, which is in Christ Jesus our Lord.   *8:38 – 39*

10   Hath not the potter power over the clay, of the same lump to make one vessel unto honor, and another unto dishonor?   *9:21*

11   For who hath known the mind of the Lord?
11:34

12   I beseech you therefore, brethren . . . that ye present your bodies a living sacrifice, holy, acceptable unto God, which is your reasonable service.[1]
12:1

13   Let love be without dissimulation.   *12:9*

14   Be kindly affectioned one to another with brotherly love.   *12:10*

15   Given to hospitality.   *12:13*

16   Be not wise in your own conceits.
Recompense to no man evil for evil.
12:16 – 17

17   If it be possible, as much as lieth in you, live peaceably with all men.   *12:18*

18   Vengeance is mine; I will repay, saith the Lord.
12:19

19   Be not overcome of evil, but overcome evil with good.   *12:21*

20   The powers that be are ordained of God.
13:1

21   Render therefore to all their dues: tribute to whom tribute is due; custom to whom custom; fear to whom fear; honor to whom honor.

Owe no man anything, but to love one another.
13:7 – 8

22   Love is the fulfilling of the law.   *13:10*

23   The night is far spent, the day is at hand: let us therefore cast off the works of darkness, and let us put on the armor of light.

Let us walk honestly, as in the day; not in rioting and drunkenness, not in chambering and wantonness, not in strife and envying.

But put ye on the Lord Jesus Christ, and make not provision for the flesh, to fulfil the lusts thereof.[2]
13:12 – 14

24   Doubtful disputations.   *14:1*

25   Let every man be fully persuaded in his own mind.   *14:5*

26   For none of us liveth to himself, and no man dieth to himself.

For whether we live, we live unto the Lord; and whether we die, we die unto the Lord: whether we live therefore, or die, we are the Lord's.   *14:7 – 8*

27   Let us therefore follow after the things which make for peace.   *14:19*

28   We then that are strong ought to bear the infirmities of the weak, and not to please ourselves.
15:1

29   God hath chosen the foolish things of the world to confound the wise; and God hath chosen the weak things of the world to confound the things which are mighty.
*The First Epistle of Paul the Apostle
to the Corinthians 1:27*

30   As it is written,[3] Eye hath not seen, nor ear heard.
2:9

31   I have planted, Apollos watered; but God gave the increase.   *3:6*

32   We are laborers together with God: ye are God's husbandry.   *3:9*

33   Every man's work shall be made manifest: for the day shall declare it, because it shall be revealed by fire; and the fire shall try every man's work of what sort it is.   *3:13*

34   For the temple of God is holy, which temple ye are.   *3:17*

35   We are made a spectacle unto the world, and to angels, and to men.   *4:9*

36   Absent in body, but present in spirit.   *5:3*

37   A little leaven leaveneth the whole lump.
5:6

---

[1]See *Book of Common Prayer*, 49:17.

[2]See Saint Augustine, 114:24, and note.

[3]Men have not heard, nor perceived by the ear, neither hath the eye seen. —*Isaiah 64:4*

1   For even Christ our Passover is sacrificed for us.
5:7

2   It is better to marry than to burn.   *7:9*

3   The fashion of this world passeth away.
7:31

4   Knowledge puffeth up, but charity edifieth.
8:1

5   I am made all things to all men.   *9:22*

6   Know ye not that they which run in a race run all, but one receiveth the prize?   *9:24*

7   Let him that thinketh he standeth take heed lest he fall.   *10:12*

8   All things are lawful for me, but all things are not expedient.   *10:23*

9   The earth is the Lord's, and the fullness thereof.[1]
10:26

10   If a woman have long hair, it is a glory to her.
11:15

11   Take, eat: this is my body, which is broken for you: this do in remembrance of me.[2]   *11:24*

12   This cup is the new testament in my blood: this do ye, as oft as ye drink it, in remembrance of me.[3]
11:25

13   Though I speak with the tongues of men and of angels, and have not charity,[4] I am become as sounding brass, or a tinkling cymbal.   *13:1*

14   Though I have all faith, so that I could remove mountains, and have not charity, I am nothing.
And though I bestow all my goods to feed the poor, and though I give my body to be burned, and have not charity, it profiteth me nothing.
Charity suffereth long, and is kind; charity envieth not; charity vaunteth not itself, is not puffed up.
13:2–4

15   Beareth all things, believeth all things, hopeth all things, endureth all things.
Charity never faileth.   *13:7–8*

16   We know in part, and we prophesy in part.
But when that which is perfect is come, then that which is in part shall be done away.
When I was a child, I spake as a child, I understood as a child, I thought as a child: but when I became a man, I put away childish things.[5]
For now we see through a glass, darkly; but then face to face:[6] now I know in part; but then shall I know even as also I am known.

And now abideth faith, hope, charity, these three; but the greatest of these is charity.   *13:9–13*

17   If the trumpet give an uncertain sound, who shall prepare himself to the battle?   *14:8*

18   Let all things be done decently and in order.
14:40

19   And last of all he was seen of me also, as of one born out of due time.
For I am the least of the apostles, that am not meet to be called an apostle, because I persecuted the church of God.
But by the grace of God I am what I am.
15:8–10

20   But now is Christ risen from the dead, and become the firstfruits of them that slept.
For since by man came death, by man came also the resurrection of the dead.
For as in Adam all die, even so in Christ shall all be made alive.   *15:20–22*

21   The last enemy that shall be destroyed is death.
15:26

22   Evil communications corrupt good manners.
15:33

23   Thou fool, that which thou sowest is not quickened, except it die.   *15:36*

24   One star differeth from another star in glory.
15:41

25   It is sown in corruption; it is raised in incorruption.   *15:42*

26   The first man is of the earth, earthy.   *15:47*

27   Behold, I show you a mystery; We shall not all sleep, but we shall all be changed,
In a moment, in the twinkling of an eye, at the last trump: for the trumpet shall sound, and the dead shall be raised incorruptible, and we shall be changed.
For this corruptible must put on incorruption, and this mortal must put on immortality.
15:51–53

28   Death is swallowed up in victory.[7]
O death, where is thy sting? O grave, where is thy victory?[8]   *15:54–55*

29   Watch ye, stand fast in the faith, quit you like men, be strong.[9]   *16:13*

30   If any man love not the Lord Jesus Christ, let him be Anathema Maranatha.   *16:22*

31   Not of the letter, but of the spirit: for the letter killeth, but the spirit giveth life.
The Second Epistle of Paul the Apostle to the Corinthians 3:6

[1]See *Psalm 24:1*, 16:18.
[2]See *Matthew 26:26, 36:28*, and *Luke 22:19*, 39:15.
[3]See *Matthew 26:27–29*, 36:28.
[4]In the Revised Standard Version *charity* throughout this chapter is translated as *love* — the love of mankind in the sense of the Greek *agapé* and the Latin *caritas*.
[5]See *Homer*, 52:31.
[6]See *Genesis 32:30*, 8:2.
[7]See *Isaiah 25:8, 26:27*, and *Hosea 13:14*, 29:31.
[8]See *Mitford*, 744:8.
[9]See *I Samuel 4:9*, 11:29.

1   Seeing then that we have such hope, we use great plainness of speech.   *II Corinthians 3:12*

2   The things which are seen are temporal; but the things which are not seen are eternal.   *4:18*

3   We walk by faith, not by sight.   *5:7*

4   Now is the accepted time.   *6:2*

5   By honor and dishonor, by evil report and good report.   *6:8*

6   As having nothing, and yet possessing all things.[1]   *6:10*

7   God loveth a cheerful giver.   *9:7*

8   Though I be rude in speech.   *11:6*

9   For ye suffer fools gladly, seeing ye yourselves are wise.   *11:19*

10   Forty stripes save one.   *11:24*

11   A thorn in the flesh.[2]   *12:7*

12   My strength is made perfect in weakness.   *12:9*

13   The grace of the Lord Jesus Christ, and the love of God, and the communion of the Holy Ghost, be with you all.[3]   *13:14*

14   The right hands of fellowship.
    The Epistle of Paul the Apostle to the Galatians 2:9

15   Weak and beggarly elements.   *4:9*

16   It is good to be zealously affected always in a good thing.   *4:18*

17   Ye are fallen from grace.   *5:4*

18   For the flesh lusteth against the Spirit, and the Spirit against the flesh: and these are contrary the one to the other: so that ye cannot do the things that ye would.   *5:17*

19   The fruit of the Spirit is love, joy, peace, long-suffering, gentleness, goodness, faith,
    Meekness, temperance.   *5:22–23*

20   Every man shall bear his own burden.   *6:5*

21   Be not deceived; God is not mocked: for whatsoever a man soweth, that shall he also reap.   *6:7*

22   Let us not be weary in well doing.   *6:9*

23   To be strengthened with might by his Spirit in the inner man.
    The Epistle of Paul the Apostle to the Ephesians 3:16

24   Carried about with every wind of doctrine.   *4:14*

25   We are members one of another.
    Be ye angry, and sin not: let not the sun go down upon your wrath.   *4:25–26*

26   Speaking to yourselves in psalms and hymns and spiritual songs, singing and making melody in your heart to the Lord.[4]   *5:19*

27   Put on the whole armor of God.   *6:11*

28   For we wrestle not against flesh and blood, but against principalities, against powers, against the rulers of the darkness of this world, against spiritual wickedness in high places.
    Wherefore take unto you the whole armor of God, that ye may be able to withstand in the evil day, and having done all, to stand.   *6:12–13*

29   To live is Christ, and to die is gain.
    The Epistle of Paul the Apostle to the Philippians 1:21

30   Work out your own salvation with fear and trembling.   *2:12*

31   For it is God which worketh in you both to will and to do of his good pleasure.   *2:13*

32   This one thing I do, forgetting those things which are behind, and reaching forth unto those things which are before,
    I press toward the mark.   *3:13–14*

33   Whose end is destruction, whose God is their belly, and whose glory is in their shame, who mind earthly things.   *3:19*

34   The peace of God, which passeth all understanding, shall keep your hearts and minds through Christ Jesus.[5]   *4:7*

35   Whatsoever things are true, whatsoever things are honest, whatsoever things are just, whatsoever things are pure, whatsoever things are lovely, whatsoever things are of good report; if there be any virtue, and if there be any praise, think on these things.   *4:8*

36   I have learned, in whatsoever state I am, therewith to be content.   *4:11*

37   By him were all things created, that are in heaven, and that are in earth, visible and invisible . . . all things were created by him, and for him:
    And he is before all things, and by him all things consist.
    The Epistle of Paul the Apostle to the Colossians 1:16–17

38   Touch not; taste not; handle not.   *2:21*

39   Set your affection on things above, not on things on the earth.   *3:2*

40   Where there is neither Greek nor Jew, circumcision nor uncircumcision, Barbarian, Scythian, bond nor free: but Christ is all, and in all.   *3:11*

41   Fathers, provoke not your children to anger, lest they be discouraged.   *3:21*

[1]See Terence, 86:5, and Wotton, 227:8.
[2]See *Judges 2:3, 10:40*.
[3]Also in *Book of Common Prayer, Morning Prayer* (end).
[4]See *Psalm 95:1–2, 18:19*, and *Book of Common Prayer, Morning Prayer (Venite)*, 48:20.
[5]Also in *Book of Common Prayer, Holy Communion* (Blessing).

1 Let your speech be alway with grace, seasoned with salt. *4:6*

2 Luke, the beloved physician. *4:14*

3 Labor of love.
The First Epistle of Paul the Apostle to the Thessalonians 1:3

4 Study to be quiet, and to do your own business. *4:11*

5 The day of the Lord so cometh as a thief in the night. *5:2*

6 Ye are all the children of light, and the children of the day: we are not of the night, nor of darkness. *5:5*

7 Putting on the breastplate of faith and love; and for an helmet, the hope of salvation. *5:8*

8 Pray without ceasing. *5:17*

9 Prove all things; hold fast that which is good. *5:21*

10 The law is good, if a man use it lawfully.
The First Epistle of Paul the Apostle to Timothy 1:8

11 Christ Jesus came into the world to save sinners; of whom I am chief. *1:15*

12 For if a man know not how to rule his own house, how shall he take care of the church of God?[1] *3:5*

13 Not greedy of filthy lucre. *3:8*

14 Speaking lies in hypocrisy; having their conscience seared with a hot iron. *4:2*

15 Every creature of God is good, and nothing to be refused, if it be received with thanksgiving. *4:4*

16 Refuse profane and old wives' fables. *4:7*

17 Let them learn first to show piety at home. *5:4*

18 But if any provide not for his own, and specially for those of his own house, he hath denied the faith, and is worse than an infidel. *5:8*

19 They learn to be idle, wandering about from house to house; and not only idle, but tattlers also and busybodies, speaking things which they ought not. *5:13*

20 Drink no longer water, but use a little wine for thy stomach's sake. *5:23*

21 We brought nothing into this world, and it is certain we can carry nothing out.[2] *6:7*

22 The love of money is the root of all evil.[3] *6:10*

23 Fight the good fight of faith, lay hold on eternal life. *6:12*

24 Rich in good works. *6:18*

25 O Timothy, keep that which is committed to thy trust, avoiding profane and vain babblings, and oppositions of science falsely so called. *6:20*

26 For God hath not given us the spirit of fear; but of power, and of love, and of a sound mind.
The Second Epistle of Paul the Apostle to Timothy 1:7

27 A workman that needeth not to be ashamed. *2:15*

28 Be instant in season, out of season. *4:2*

29 I have fought a good fight, I have finished my course, I have kept the faith. *4:7*

30 The Lord reward him according to his works. *4:14*

31 Unto the pure all things are pure.
The Epistle of Paul to Titus 1:15

32 Making mention of thee always in my prayers.
The Epistle of Paul to Philemon 1:4

33 Who maketh his angels spirits, and his ministers a flame of fire.
The Epistle of Paul the Apostle to the Hebrews 1:7

34 The word of God is quick, and powerful, and sharper than any two-edged sword, piercing even to the dividing asunder of soul and spirit, and of the joints and marrow, and is a discerner of the thoughts and intents of the heart. *4:12*

35 Strong meat belongeth to them that are of full age. *5:14*

36 They crucify to themselves the Son of God afresh, and put him to an open shame. *6:6*

37 Without shedding of blood is no remission. *9:22*

38 Faith is the substance of things hoped for, the evidence of things not seen. *11:1*

39 Wherefore seeing we also are compassed about with so great a cloud of witnesses . . . let us run with patience the race that is set before us,
Looking unto Jesus the author and finisher of our faith. *12:1–2*

40 Whom the Lord loveth he chasteneth. *12:6*

41 The spirits of just men made perfect. *12:23*

42 Let brotherly love continue.
Be not forgetful to entertain strangers: for thereby some have entertained angels unawares. *13:1–2*

43 The Lord is my helper, and I will not fear what man shall do unto me. *13:6*

[1]See Sophocles, 66:14.
[2]Also in *Book of Common Prayer, Burial of the Dead.*
[3]Radix malorum est cupiditas.—CHAUCER, *The Canterbury Tales* [c. 1387], *The Pardoner's Prologue, l. 6*
See Sophocles, 66:7, and Plato, 75:12.

1   Jesus Christ the same yesterday, and to day, and for ever.   *Hebrews 13:8*

2   For here have we no continuing city, but we seek one to come.   *13:14*

3   To do good and to communicate forget not: for with such sacrifices God is well pleased.   *13:16*

4   Let patience have her perfect work, that ye may be perfect and entire, wanting nothing.
If any of you lack wisdom, let him ask of God.
The General Epistle of James 1:4–5

5   Blessed is the man that endureth temptation: for when he is tried, he shall receive the crown of life.
1:12

6   Every good gift and every perfect gift is from above, and cometh down from the Father of lights, with whom is no variableness, neither shadow of turning.   *1:17*

7   Be swift to hear, slow to speak, slow to wrath:
For the wrath of man worketh not the righteousness of God.   *1:19–20*

8   Be ye doers of the word, and not hearers only.[1]
1:22

9   Unspotted from the world.   *1:27*

10   As the body without the spirit is dead, so faith without works is dead also.   *2:26*

11   How great a matter a little fire kindleth!
3:5

12   The tongue can no man tame; it is an unruly evil.
3:8

13   This wisdom descendeth not from above, but is earthly, sensual, devilish.   *3:15*

14   Resist the devil, and he will flee from you.
4:7

15   What is your life? It is even a vapor, that appeareth for a little time, and then vanisheth away.
4:14

16   Be patient therefore, brethren, unto the coming of the Lord. Behold, the husbandman waiteth for the precious fruit of the earth, and hath long patience for it, until he receive the early and latter rain.
5:7

17   Ye have heard of the patience of Job.   *5:11*

18   The effectual fervent prayer of a righteous man availeth much.   *5:16*

19   Hope to the end.
The First Epistle General of Peter 1:13

20   The Father, who without respect of persons judgeth according to every man's work.   *1:17*

21   All flesh is as grass, and all the glory of man as the flower of grass. The grass withereth, and the flower thereof falleth away:
But the word of the Lord endureth for ever.[2]
1:24–25

22   Abstain from fleshly lusts, which war against the soul.   *2:11*

23   Honor all men. Love the brotherhood. Fear God. Honor the king.   *2:17*

24   Ornament of a meek and quiet spirit.   *3:4*

25   Giving honor unto the wife, as unto the weaker vessel.   *3:7*

26   Charity shall cover the multitude of sins.
4:8

27   A crown of glory that fadeth not away.
5:4

28   Be sober, be vigilant; because your adversary the devil, as a roaring lion, walketh about, seeking whom he may devour.   *5:8*

29   And the day star arise in your hearts.
The Second Epistle General of Peter 1:19

30   The dog is turned to his own vomit again.
2:22

31   God is light, and in him is no darkness at all.
The First Epistle General of John 1:5

32   If we say that we have no sin, we deceive ourselves, and the truth is not in us.   *1:8*

33   If any man sin, we have an advocate with the Father, Jesus Christ the righteous:
And he is the propitiation for our sins:[3] and not for ours only, but also for the sins of the whole world.
2:1–2

34   He is antichrist, that denieth the Father and the Son.   *2:22*

35   Whoso hath this world's good, and seeth his brother have need, and shutteth up his bowels of compassion from him, how dwelleth the love of God in him?   *3:17*

36   He that loveth not, knoweth not God; for God is love.   *4:8*

37   There is no fear in love; but perfect love casteth out fear.   *4:18*

38   Raging waves of the sea, foaming out their own shame; wandering stars, to whom is reserved the blackness of darkness for ever.
The General Epistle of Jude 13

[1]See Homer, 51:32.

[2]See *Psalm 90:5–6*, 18:10, and *Isaiah 40:6* and 40:8, 27:17 and 27:18.

[3]Also in *Book of Common Prayer*, Holy Communion.

1 I John, who also am your brother, and companion in tribulation, and in the kingdom and patience of Jesus Christ, was in the isle that is called Patmos, for the word of God, and for the testimony of Jesus Christ.
The Revelation of Saint John the Divine 1:9

2 What thou seest, write in a book, and send it unto the seven churches which are in Asia. *1:11*

3 And being turned, I saw seven golden candlesticks. *1:12*

4 His feet like unto fine brass, as if they burned in a furnace; and his voice as the sound of many waters. *1:15*

5 When I saw him, I fell at his feet as dead. *1:17*

6 I am he that liveth, and was dead; and, behold, I am alive for evermore, Amen; and have the keys of hell and of death. *1:18*

7 I have somewhat against thee, because thou hast left thy first love. *2:4*

8 To him that overcometh will I give to eat of the tree of life. *2:7*

9 Be thou faithful unto death, and I will give thee a crown of life. *2:10*

10 He shall rule them with a rod of iron. *2:27*

11 I will give him the morning star. *2:28*

12 I will not blot out his name out of the book of life. *3:5*

13 I know thy works, that thou art neither cold nor hot: I would thou wert cold or hot.
So then because thou art lukewarm, and neither cold nor hot, I will spew thee out of my mouth. *3:15–16*

14 Behold, I stand at the door, and knock. *3:20*

15 The first beast was like a lion, and the second beast like a calf, and the third beast had a face as a man, and the fourth beast was like a flying eagle.
And the four beasts had each of them six wings about him; and they were full of eyes within: and they rest not day and night, saying, Holy, holy, holy, Lord God Almighty, which was, and is, and is to come. *4:7–8*

16 Thou hast created all things, and for thy pleasure they are and were created. *4:11*

17 A book . . . sealed with seven seals. *5:1*

18 He went forth conquering, and to conquer. *6:2*

19 Behold a pale horse: and his name that sat on him was Death, and Hell followed with him. *6:8*

20 Four angels standing on the four corners of the earth, holding the four winds of the earth. *7:1*

21 Hurt not the earth, neither the sea, nor the trees. *7:3*

22 All nations, and kindreds, and people, and tongues. *7:9*

23 These are they which came out of great tribulation, and have washed their robes, and made them white in the blood of the lamb. *7:14*

24 They shall hunger no more, neither thirst any more; neither shall the sun light on them, nor any heat. *7:16*

25 The name of the star is called Wormwood. *8:11*

26 The kingdoms of this world are become the kingdoms of our Lord and of his Christ. *11:15*

27 There was war in heaven: Michael and his angels fought against the dragon; and the dragon fought and his angels,
And prevailed not. *12:7–8*

28 The great dragon was cast out, that old serpent, called the Devil, and Satan, which deceiveth the whole world. *12:9*

29 No man might buy or sell, save he that had the mark, or the name of the beast. *13:17*

30 The voice of many waters.[1] *14:2*

31 Babylon is fallen, is fallen, that great city.[2] *14:8*

32 Blessed are the dead which die in the Lord . . . that they may rest from their labours.[3] *14:13*

33 And he gathered them together into a place called in the Hebrew tongue Armageddon. *16:16*

34 He is Lord of lords, and King of kings. *17:14*

35 He treadeth the winepress of the fierceness and wrath of Almighty God. *19:15*

36 Another book was opened, which is the book of life. *20:12*

37 I saw a new heaven and a new earth:[4] for the first heaven and the first earth were passed away; and there was no more sea.
And I John saw the holy city, new Jerusalem, coming down from God out of heaven, prepared as a bride adorned for her husband. *21:1–2*

[1]See *Psalm 93:4*, 18:18.
[2]See *Isaiah 21:9*, 26:19.
[3]Also in *Book of Common Prayer, Burial of the Dead.*
[4]See *Isaiah 65:17*, 28:11.

1 God shall wipe away all tears[1] from their eyes; and there shall be no more death, neither sorrow, nor crying, neither shall there be any more pain: for the former things are passed away. *Revelation 21:4*

2 There shall be no night there. *22:5*

3 He that is unjust, let him be unjust still: and he which is filthy, let him be filthy still: and he that is righteous, let him be righteous still: and he that is holy, let him be holy still.
And, behold, I come quickly. *22:11–12*

4 I am Alpha and Omega, the beginning and the end, the first and the last. *22:13*

The Missal

5 Dominus vobiscum [The Lord be with you].
Et cum spiritu tuo [And with your spirit].
Antiphon

6 Mea culpa, mea culpa, mea maxima culpa [Through my fault, through my fault, through my most grievous fault]. *Confession of Sins*

7 Kyrie, eleison [Lord, have mercy on us].
Kyrie

8 Gloria in excelsis Deo. Et in terra pax hominibus bonae voluntatis [Glory to God in the highest. And on earth peace to men of good will].[2] *Gloria*

9 Domine Deus, Agnus Dei, Filius Patris: qui tollis peccata mundi, miserere nobis [O Lord God, Lamb of God, Son of the Father: who takes away the sins of the world, have mercy on us].[3] *Ibid.*

10 Hoc est enim Corpus meum [For this is My Body].[4] *The Consecration*

11 Hic est enim Calix Sanguinis mei, novi et aeterni testamenti: mysterium fidei: qui pro vobis et pro multis effundetur in remissionem peccatorum [For this is the chalice of My Blood, of the new and eternal covenant; the mystery of faith; which shall be shed for you and for many unto the forgiveness of sins].[5] *Ibid.*

12 O felix culpa, quae talem ac tantum meruit habere Redemptorem [O happy fault, which has deserved to have such and so mighty a Redeemer].[6] *Exsultet on Holy Saturday*

---

[1]See *Isaiah 25:8, 26:27.*
[2]See *Luke 2:14, 38:4.*
[3]See *John 1:29, 39:35.*
[4]See *Matthew 26:26, 36:28,* and *I Corinthians 11:24, 43:11.*
[5]See *Matthew 26:27–29, 36:28,* and *I Corinthians 11:25, 43:-12.*
[6]This dates from the seventh century at the latest, and may be much older. It has been attributed to Saint Augustine and Saint Ambrose.

The Book of Common Prayer [1928][7]

13 Movable feasts. *Tables and Rules, p. xxxi*

14 He is risen. The Lord is risen indeed.[8] *Morning Prayer, Easter, p. 5*

15 The Scripture moveth us, in sundry places, to acknowledge and confess our manifold sins and wickedness. *Ibid. Minister's Opening Words, p. 5*

16 We have erred, and strayed from thy ways like lost sheep.[9] *Ibid. A General Confession, p. 6*

17 We have left undone those things which we ought to have done; And we have done those things which we ought not to have done. *Ibid.*

18 Have mercy upon us, miserable offenders. *Ibid.*

19 Who desireth not the death of a sinner, but rather that he may turn from his wickedness and live. *Ibid. The Declaration of Absolution, p. 7*

20 Let us come before his presence with thanksgiving; and show ourselves glad in him with psalms.[10] *Ibid. Venite, p. 9*

21 In his hand are all the corners of the earth; and the strength of the hills is his also.
The sea is his, and he made it; and his hands prepared the dry land. *Ibid.*

22 Glory be to the Father, and to the Son, and to the Holy Ghost;
As it was in the beginning, is now, and ever shall be, world without end. Amen. *Ibid. Gloria Patri, p. 9*

23 We praise thee, O God [Te deum laudamus]. *Ibid. Te Deum, p. 10*

24 The noble army of Martyrs. *Ibid.*

25 I believe in God the Father Almighty, Maker of heaven and earth:
And in Jesus Christ his only Son our Lord: Who was conceived by the Holy Ghost, Born of the Virgin Mary: Suffered under Pontius Pilate, Was crucified, dead, and buried: He descended into hell; The third day he rose again from the dead: He ascended into heaven, And sitteth on the right hand of God the

---

[7]THOMAS CRANMER [1489–1556] gathered the western Latin rites as used in England, notably the Sarum rite of Salisbury Cathedral, when he compiled [1549] the English Prayer Book, known as the first Prayer Book of Edward VI. A revised second Prayer Book of Edward VI [1552] was revised again [1559]; finally, the present English Book of Common Prayer was published [1662]. The American Book of Common Prayer [1789], which derives from the English Prayer Book, was revised in 1892 and again in 1928. It is this revision from which the quotations in *Bartlett* are taken.
See Newman, 426:22.
[8]See *Mark 16:6, 37:35,* and *Luke 24:34, 39:28.*
[9]See *Isaiah 53:6, 27:37.*
[10]See *Psalm 95:1–2, 18:19,* and *Ephesians 5:19, 44:26.*

Father Almighty: From thence he shall come to judge the quick and the dead.

I believe in the Holy Ghost: The holy Catholic Church; The Communion of Saints: The Forgiveness of sins: The Resurrection of the body: And the Life everlasting. *Ibid. Apostles' Creed, p. 15*

1 Begotten of his Father before all worlds, God of God, Light of Light, Very God of very God; Begotten, not made; Being of one substance with the Father; By whom all things were made: Who for us men and for our salvation came down from heaven, And was incarnate by the Holy Ghost of the Virgin Mary, And was made man. *Ibid. Nicene Creed, p. 16*

2 O God, who art the author of peace and lover of concord, in knowledge of whom standeth our eternal life, whose service is perfect freedom; Defend us thy humble servants in all assaults of our enemies. *Ibid. A Collect for Peace, p. 17*

3 O God, the Creator and Preserver of all mankind, we humbly beseech thee for all sorts and conditions of men; that thou wouldest be pleased to make thy ways known unto them, thy saving health unto all nations. *Ibid. A Prayer for All Conditions of Men, p. 18*

4 We commend to thy fatherly goodness all those who are any ways afflicted, or distressed, in mind, body, or estate. *Ibid. p. 19*

5 We, thine unworthy servants, do give thee most humble and hearty thanks for all thy goodness and loving-kindness to us, and to all men; We bless thee for our creation, preservation, and all the blessings of this life; but above all, for thine inestimable love in the redemption of the world by our Lord Jesus Christ; for the means of grace, and for the hope of glory. *Ibid. A General Thanksgiving, p. 19*

6 Almighty God, who . . . dost promise that when two or three are gathered together in thy Name[1] thou wilt grant their requests; Fulfill now, O Lord, the desires and petitions of thy servants, as may be most expedient for them. *Ibid. A Prayer of Saint Chrysostom, p. 20*

7 Lighten our darkness, we beseech thee, O Lord; and by thy great mercy defend us from all perils and dangers of this night. *Evening Prayer, A Collect for Aid against Perils, p. 31*

8 From all blindness of heart, from pride, vainglory, and hypocrisy; from envy, hatred, and malice, and all uncharitableness,
Good Lord, deliver us. *The Litany, p. 54*

9 From all the deceits of the world, the flesh, and the devil. *Ibid.*

10 From battle and murder, and from sudden death. *Ibid.*

11 Give to all nations unity, peace, and concord. *Ibid. p. 56*

12 The kindly fruits of the earth. *Ibid. p. 57*

13 Almighty God, unto whom all hearts are open, all desires known, and from whom no secrets are hid; Cleanse the thoughts of our hearts by the inspiration of thy Holy Spirit, that we may perfectly love thee, and worthily magnify thy holy Name. *Holy Communion, The Collect, p. 67*

14 Ye who do truly and earnestly repent you of your sins, and are in love and charity with your neighbors, and intend to lead a new life. *Ibid. To those who come to receive the Holy Communion, p. 75*

15 We acknowledge and bewail our manifold sins and wickedness, Which we, from time to time, most grievously have committed, By thought, word, and deed, Against thy Divine Majesty, Provoking most justly thy wrath and indignation against us. We do earnestly repent, And are heartily sorry for these our misdoings; The remembrance of them is grievous unto us; The burden of them is intolerable. *Ibid. General Confession, p. 75*

16 Therefore with Angels and Archangels, and with all the company of heaven, we laud and magnify thy glorious Name; evermore praising thee. *Ibid. Proper Preface, p. 77*

17 And here we offer and present unto thee, O Lord, our selves, our souls and bodies, to be a reasonable, holy, and living sacrifice unto thee.[2] *Ibid. The Invocation, p. 81*

18 The Peace of God, which passeth all understanding, keep your hearts and minds in the knowledge and love of God, and of his Son Jesus Christ our Lord. *Ibid. Blessing, p. 84*

19 Miserable sinners. *Ibid. The Exhortations, p. 86*

20 Read, mark, learn, and inwardly digest [the Scriptures]. *The Second Sunday in Advent. The Collect, p. 92*

21 Dost thou, therefore, in the name of this Child, renounce the devil and all his works, the vain pomp and glory of the world, with all covetous desires of the same, and the sinful desires of the flesh, so that thou wilt not follow, nor be led by them? *Holy Baptism. To the Godfathers and Godmothers, p. 276*

22 An outward and visible sign of an inward and spiritual grace. *Offices of Instruction, Questions on the Sacraments, p. 292*

[1] See *Matthew* 18:20, 35:33.

[2] See *Romans* 12:1, 42:12.

1   Is not by any to be entered into unadvisedly or lightly; but reverently, discreetly, advisedly, soberly, and in the fear of God.
Solemnization of Matrimony, p. 300

2   If any man can show just cause, why they may not lawfully be joined together, let him now speak, or else hereafter for ever hold his peace.   *Ibid.*

3   Wilt thou . . . forsaking all others, keep thee only unto [him; her], so long as ye both shall live?
Ibid. p. 301

4   To have and to hold from this day forward, for better for worse, for richer for poorer, in sickness and in health, to love and to cherish, till death us do part.   *Ibid.*

5   With this Ring I thee wed.   *Ibid. p. 302*

6   Those whom God hath joined together let no man put asunder.[1]   *Ibid. p. 303*

7   In the midst of life we are in death.[2]
Burial of the Dead, p. 332

8   Earth to earth, ashes to ashes, dust to dust; in sure and certain hope of the Resurrection unto eternal life.   *Ibid. p. 333*

9   The iron entered into his soul.
The Psalter, Psalm 105:18, p. 471

The Book of Common Prayer [English]

10   Give peace in our time, O Lord.
Morning Prayer, Versicles

11   Grant that the old Adam in this Child may be so buried, that the new man may be raised up in him.
Public Baptism of Infants, Blessing on the Child

12   To love, cherish, and to obey.
Solemnization of Matrimony

13   With all my worldly goods I thee endow.
Ibid.

The Upanishads
800–500 B.C.[3]

14   Thou art that.[4]
Chandogya Upanishad, 6.8.7, etc.

[1]See *Matthew* 19:6, 35:35.

[2]This is derived from a Latin antiphon, said to have been composed by Notker, a monk of Saint Gall, in 911, while watching some workmen building a bridge at Martinsbrücke, in peril of their lives. It forms the groundwork of Luther's antiphon *De Morte.*

[3]Ancient Indian literary chronology is conjectural. The dates given are approximate.

[4]Tat tvam asi (Sanskrit). The context: That which is that subtle essence is the self of this All; it is the true; it is the Self. "Thou art that, O Svetaketu."

15   Lead me from the unreal to the real!
Lead me from darkness to light!
Lead me from death to immortality![5]
Brihadaranyaka Upanishad, 1.3.28

16   Not thus, not thus.[6]   *Ibid. 2.3.6*

17   This Self is the honey of all beings, and all beings are the honey of this Self.   *Ibid. 2.5.14*

18   The gods love the obscure and hate the obvious.[7]
Ibid. 4.2.2

19   Da da da[8] (that is) Be subdued, Give, Be merciful.[5]
Ibid. 5.2.3

20   If the slayer thinks he slays,
If the slain thinks he is slain,
Both these do not understand:
He slays not, is not slain.[9]
Katha Upanishad, 2.19

21   Om.[10]   *Passim*

22   Shanti.[11]   *Passim*

Homer
c. 700 B.C.

23   Sing, goddess, the wrath of Peleus' son Achilles, a destroying wrath which brought upon the Achaeans myriad woes, and sent forth to Hades many valiant souls of heroes.   *The Iliad, bk. I, l. 1*

24   And the plan of Zeus was being accomplished.
Ibid. l. 5

25   A dream, too, is from Zeus.   *Ibid. l. 63*

26   He knew the things that were and the things that would be and the things that had been before.
Ibid. l. 70

27   If you are very valiant, it is a god, I think, who gave you this gift.   *Ibid. l. 178*

28   Speaking, he addressed her winged words.
Ibid. l. 201

29   Whoever obeys the gods, to him they particularly listen.   *Ibid. l. 218*

30   From his tongue flowed speech sweeter than honey.   *Ibid. l. 249*

[5]Translated by F. MAX MÜLLER.

[6]Neti neti. The only possible description of the world soul self. The context: Not thus, not thus; for there is nothing else higher than this "not thus."

[7]Translated by R. C. ZAEHNER.

[8]The voice of the thunder. The full Sanskrit is: Da da da iti. Damyata datta dayadhvamiti.
"Datta, dayadhvam, damyata" (Give, sympathize, control).
—T. S. ELIOT, *The Waste Land* [1922], *note to line 401*
See T. S. Eliot, 669:6.

[9]See Emerson, 430:10.

[10]Om is a sacred syllable used especially to begin and end a scriptural recitation.

[11]Shanti means "peace." T. S. Eliot, in his note to line 434 of *The Waste Land,* says, " 'The Peace which passeth understanding' is our equivalent to this word."

1 Rosy-fingered dawn appeared, the early-born.[1]
Ibid. l. 477 and elsewhere

2 The son of Kronos [Zeus] spoke, and nodded with his darkish brows, and immortal locks fell forward from the lord's deathless head, and he made great Olympus tremble. *Ibid. l. 528*

3 The Olympian is a difficult foe to oppose.
Ibid. l. 589

4 Uncontrollable laughter arose among the blessed gods.[2] *Ibid. l. 599*

5 A councilor ought not to sleep the whole night through, a man to whom the populace is entrusted, and who has many responsibilities.
Ibid. II, l. 24

6 Proud is the spirit of Zeus-fostered kings—their honor comes from Zeus, and Zeus, god of council, loves them. *Ibid. l. 196*

7 A multitude of rulers is not a good thing. Let there be one ruler, one king. *Ibid. l. 204*

8 He [Thersites] was the ugliest man who came to Ilium. *Ibid. l. 216*

9 I could not tell nor name the multitude, not even if I had ten tongues, ten mouths, not if I had a voice unwearying and a heart of bronze were in me.[3]
Ibid. l. 488

10 Yet with his powers of augury he [Chromis] did not save himself from dark death. *Ibid. l. 859*

11 The glorious gifts of the gods are not to be cast aside. *Ibid. III, l. 65*

12 Young men's minds are always changeable, but when an old man is concerned in a matter, he looks both before and after. *Ibid. l. 108*

13 Like cicadas, which sit upon a tree in the forest and pour out their piping voices, so the leaders of the Trojans were sitting on the tower. *Ibid. l. 151*

14 There is no reason to blame the Trojans and the well-greaved Achaeans that for such a woman they long suffer woes. *Ibid. l. 156*

15 Words like winter snowflakes. *Ibid. l. 222*

16 The sun, which sees all things and hears all things. *Ibid. l. 277*

17 Son of Atreus, what manner of speech has escaped the barrier of your teeth? *Ibid. IV, l. 350*

18 Far away in the mountains a shepherd hears their thundering. *Ibid. l. 455*

19 He lives not long who battles with the immortals, nor do his children prattle about his knees when he has come back from battle and the dread fray.[4]
Ibid. V, l. 407

20 Not at all similar are the race of the immortal gods and the race of men who walk upon the earth.[5]
Ibid. l. 441

21 Great-hearted Stentor with brazen voice, who could shout as loud as fifty other men.
Ibid. l. 785

22 He was a wealthy man, and kindly to his fellow men; for dwelling in a house by the side of the road, he used to entertain all comers.[6] *Ibid. VI, l. 14*

23 A generation of men is like a generation of leaves: the wind scatters some leaves upon the ground, while others the burgeoning wood brings forth— and the season of spring comes on. So of men one generation springs forth and another ceases.
Ibid. l. 146

24 Always to be bravest and to be preeminent above others. *Ibid. l. 208*

25 Victory shifts from man to man. *Ibid. l. 339*

26 May men say, "He is far greater than his father," when he returns from battle. *Ibid. l. 479*

27 Smiling through tears. *Ibid. l. 484*

28 Attach a golden chain from heaven, and all of you take hold of it, you gods and goddesses, yet would you not be able to drag Zeus the most high from heaven to earth. *Ibid. VIII, l. 19*

29 Hades is relentless and unyielding.
Ibid. IX, l. 158

30 Hateful to me as the gates of Hades is that man who hides one thing in his heart and speaks another.
Ibid. l. 312

31 Even when someone battles hard, there is an equal portion for one who lingers behind, and in the same honor are held both the coward and the brave man; the idle man and he who has done much meet death alike. *Ibid. l. 318*

32 To be both a speaker of words and a doer of deeds.[7] *Ibid. l. 443*

33 Prayers are the daughters of mighty Zeus, lame and wrinkled and slanting-eyed. *Ibid. l. 502*

34 A companion's words of persuasion are effective.
Ibid. XI, l. 793

35 It was built against the will of the immortal gods, and so it did not last for long. *Ibid. XII, l. 8*

36 The single best augury is to fight for one's country. *Ibid. l. 243*

37 There is a strength in the union even of very sorry men. *Ibid. XIII, l. 237*

38 There is a fullness of all things, even of sleep and of love. *Ibid. l. 636*

---

[1]See Milton, 259:16.
[2]Also in *The Odyssey*, bk. *VIII, l. 326.*
[3]See Virgil, 94:11.
[4]See Thomas Gray, 322:6.

[5]See Xenophanes, 60:6.
[6]He held his seat; a friend to human race. / Fast by the road, his ever-open door / Obliged the wealthy and relieved the poor.
—POPE, *translation of The Iliad* [1715]
[7]See *James* 1:22, 46:8.

1   You will certainly not be able to take the lead in all things yourself, for to one man a god has given deeds of war, and to another the dance, to another the lyre and song, and in another wide-sounding Zeus puts a good mind.   *Iliad, bk. XIII, l. 729*

2   It is not possible to fight beyond your strength, even if you strive.   *Ibid. l. 787*

3   She [Aphrodite] spoke and loosened from her bosom the embroidered girdle of many colors into which all her allurements were fashioned. In it was love and in it desire and in it blandishing persuasion which steals the mind even of the wise.
    Ibid. XIV, l. 214

4   There she met sleep, the brother of death.[1]
    Ibid. l. 231 and XVI, l. 672

5   Ocean, who is the source of all.
    Ibid. XIV, l. 246

6   The hearts of the noble may be turned [by entreaty].   *Ibid. XV, l. 203*

7   It is not unseemly for a man to die fighting in defense of his country.[2]   *Ibid. l. 496*

8   Of men who have a sense of honor, more come through alive than are slain, but from those who flee comes neither glory nor any help.   *Ibid. l. 563*

9   The outcome of the war is in our hands; the outcome of words is in the council.
    Ibid. XVI, l. 630

10   But he, mighty man, lay mightily in the whirl of dust, forgetful of his horsemanship.   *Ibid. l. 775*

11   Once harm has been done, even a fool understands it.   *Ibid. XVII, l. 32*

12   The most preferable of evils.[3]   *Ibid. l. 105*

13   Surely there is nothing more wretched than a man, of all the things which breathe and move upon the earth.   *Ibid. l. 446*

14   Sweeter it [wrath] is by far than the honeycomb dripping with sweetness, and spreads through the hearts of men.   *Ibid. XVIII, l. 109*

15   I too shall lie in the dust when I am dead, but now let me win noble renown.   *Ibid. l. 120*

16   Zeus does not bring all men's plans to fulfillment.
    Ibid. l. 328

17   The Erinyes, who exact punishment of men underground if one swears a false oath.
    Ibid. XIX, l. 259

18   Not even Achilles will bring all his words to fulfillment.   *Ibid. XX, l. 369*

19   Miserable mortals who, like leaves, at one moment flame with life, eating the produce of the land, and at another moment weakly perish.
    Ibid. XXI, l. 463

20   It is entirely seemly for a young man killed in battle to lie mangled by the bronze spear. In his death all things appear fair. But when dogs shame the gray head and gray chin and nakedness of an old man killed, it is the most piteous thing that happens among wretched mortals.   *Ibid. XXII, l. 71*

21   Then the father held out the golden scales, and in them he placed two fates of dread death.
    Ibid. l. 209

22   There are no compacts between lions and men, and wolves and lambs have no concord.
    Ibid. l. 262

23   By the ships there lies a dead man, unwept, unburied: Patroclus.   *Ibid. l. 386*

24   Remembering this, he wept bitterly, lying now on his side, now on his back, now on his face.
    Ibid. XXIV, l. 9

25   The fates have given mankind a patient soul.
    Ibid. l. 49

26   Thus have the gods spun the thread for wretched mortals: that they live in grief while they themselves are without cares; for two jars stand on the floor of Zeus of the gifts which he gives, one of evils and another of blessings.   *Ibid. l. 525*

27   Tell me, muse, of the man of many resources[4] who wandered far and wide after he sacked the holy citadel of Troy, and he saw the cities and learned the thoughts of many men, and on the sea he suffered in his heart many woes.   *The Odyssey, bk. I, l. 1*

28   By their own follies they perished, the fools.
    Ibid. l. 7

29   Look now how mortals are blaming the gods, for they say that evils come from us, but in fact they themselves have woes beyond their share because of their own follies.   *Ibid. l. 32*

30   Surely these things lie on the knees of the gods.[5]
    Ibid. l. 267

31   You ought not to practice childish ways, since you are no longer that age.[6]   *Ibid. l. 296*

32   For rarely are sons similar to their fathers: most are worse, and a few are better than their fathers.
    Ibid. II, l. 276

---

[1]Sleep, the brother of Death.—HESIOD, *The Theogony*, l. 756

Sleep, Death's twin brother.—TENNYSON, *In Memoriam* [1850], pt. LXVIII

[2]See Horace, 96:14.

[3]See Aristotle, 78:4.

Of two evils, the least should be chosen.—CICERO, *De Officiis*, III, 1

Of harmes two, the lesse is for to chese.—CHAUCER, *Troilus and Criseyde* [c. 1385], bk. II, l. 470

Of two evils the less is always to be chosen.—THOMAS à KEMPIS, *Imitation of Christ*, bk. III, ch. 12

[4]See Pope, 299:25.

[5]Also familiar as: In the lap of the gods.

[6]See I Corinthians 13:11, 43:16.

1   Gray-eyed Athena sent them a favorable breeze, a fresh west wind, singing over the wine-dark sea.
Ibid. 420

2   A young man is embarrassed to question an older one.
Ibid. III, l. 24

3   All men have need of the gods.   *Ibid. l. 48*

4   The minds of the everlasting gods are not changed suddenly.
Ibid. l. 147

5   A small rock holds back a great wave.
Ibid. l. 296

6   No mortal could vie with Zeus, for his mansions and his possessions are deathless.
Ibid. IV, l. 78

7   She [Helen] threw into the wine which they were drinking a drug which takes away grief and passion and brings forgetfulness of all ills.   *Ibid. l. 220*

8   The immortals will send you to the Elysian plain at the ends of the earth, where fair-haired Rhadamanthys is. There life is supremely easy for men. No snow is there, nor ever heavy winter storm, nor rain, and Ocean is ever sending gusts of the clear-blowing west wind to bring coolness to men.
Ibid. l. 563

9   Olympus, where they say there is an abode of the gods, ever unchanging: it is neither shaken by winds nor ever wet with rain, nor does snow come near it, but clear weather spreads cloudless about it, and a white radiance stretches above it.[1]
Ibid. VI, l. 42

10   May the gods grant you all things which your heart desires, and may they give you a husband and a home and gracious concord, for there is nothing greater and better than this—when a husband and wife keep a household in oneness of mind, a great woe to their enemies and joy to their friends, and win high renown.   *Ibid. l. 180*

11   All strangers and beggars are from Zeus, and a gift, though small, is precious.[2]   *Ibid. l. 207*

12   Their ships are swift as a bird or a thought.
Ibid. VII, l. 36

13   We are quick to flare up, we races of men on the earth.   *Ibid. l. 307*

14   So it is that the gods do not give all men gifts of grace—neither good looks nor intelligence nor eloquence.   *Ibid. VIII, l. 167*

15   Evil deeds do not prosper; the slow man catches up with the swift.   *Ibid. l. 329*

16   Even if you gods, and all the goddesses too, should be looking on, yet would I be glad to sleep with golden Aphrodite.   *Ibid. l. 341*

17   Among all men on the earth bards have a share of honor and reverence, because the muse has taught them songs and loves the race of bards.
Ibid. l. 479

18   Thus she spoke; and I longed to embrace my dead mother's ghost. Thrice I tried to clasp her image, and thrice it slipped through my hands, like a shadow, like a dream.[3]   *Ibid. XI, l. 204*

19   They strove to pile Ossa on Olympus, and on Ossa Pelion with its leafy forests, that they might scale the heavens.[4]   *Ibid. l. 315*

20   There is a time for many words, and there is also a time for sleep.   *Ibid. l. 379*

21   There is nothing more dread and more shameless than a woman who plans such deeds in her heart as the foul deed which she plotted when she contrived her husband's murder.   *Ibid. l. 427*

22   In the extravagance of her evil she has brought shame both on herself and on all women who will come after her, even on one who is virtuous.
Ibid. l. 432

23   Therefore don't you be gentle to your wife either. Don't tell her everything you know, but tell her one thing and keep another thing hidden.[5]
Ibid. l. 441

24   There is no more trusting in women.
Ibid. l. 456

25   I should rather labor as another's serf, in the home of a man without fortune, one whose livelihood was meager, than rule over all the departed dead.   *Ibid. l. 489*

26   Friends, we have not till now been unacquainted with misfortunes.   *Ibid. XII, l. 208*

27   It is tedious to tell again tales already plainly told.[6]   *Ibid. l. 452*

28   The wine urges me on, the bewitching wine, which sets even a wise man to singing and to laughing gently and rouses him up to dance and brings forth words which were better unspoken.
Ibid. XIV, l. 463

29   It is equally wrong to speed a guest who does not want to go, and to keep one back who is eager. You

---

[1]The majesty of the gods is revealed, and their peaceful abodes, which neither the winds shake nor clouds soak with showers, nor does the snow congealed with biting frost besmirch them with its white fall, but an ever cloudless sky vaults them over, and smiles with light bounteously spread abroad. —LUCRETIUS, *De Rerum Natura, bk. III, l. 18*

[2]See Theocritus, 82:17.

[3]See Virgil, 93:36.

[4]See Virgil, 92:25.
Then the omnipotent Father with his thunder made Olympus tremble, and from Ossa hurled Pelion. —OVID, *Metamorphoses, I, l. 154*
I would have you call to mind the strength of the ancient giants, that undertook to lay the high mountain Pelion on the top of Ossa, and set among those the shady Olympus. —RABELAIS, *Works, bk. IV* [1548], *ch. 38*

[5]See Thomas Fuller, 250:10.

[6]See Shakespeare, 170:5.

ought to make welcome the present guest, and send forth the one who wishes to go.[1]

Odyssey, bk. XV, l. 72

1   Even his griefs are a joy long after to one that remembers all that he wrought and endured.[2]

Ibid. l. 400

2   God always pairs off like with like.[3]

Ibid. XVII, l. 218

3   Bad herdsmen ruin their flocks.   *Ibid. l. 246*

4   Wide-sounding Zeus takes away half a man's worth on the day when slavery comes upon him.

Ibid. l. 322

5   Then dark death seized Argus, as soon as he had seen Odysseus in the twentieth year.

Ibid. l. 326

6   The gods, likening themselves to all kinds of strangers, go in various disguises from city to city, observing the wrongdoing and the righteousness of men.   *Ibid. l. 485*

7   Nothing feebler than a man does the earth raise up, of all the things which breathe and move on the earth, for he believes that he will never suffer evil in the future, as long as the gods give him success and he flourishes in his strength; but when the blessed gods bring sorrows too to pass, even these he bears, against his will, with steadfast spirit, for the thoughts of earthly men are like the day which the father of gods and men brings upon them.

Ibid. XVIII, l. 130

8   Men flourish only for a moment.[4]

Ibid. XIX, l. 328

9   Dreams surely are difficult, confusing, and not everything in them is brought to pass for mankind. For fleeting dreams have two gates: one is fashioned of horn and one of ivory. Those which pass through the one of sawn ivory are deceptive, bringing tidings which come to nought, but those which issue from the one of polished horn bring true results when a mortal sees them.[5]   *Ibid. l. 560*

10   Endure, my heart: you once endured something even more dreadful.   *Ibid. XX, l. 18*

11   Your heart is always harder than a stone.

Ibid. XXIII, l. 103

12   Therefore the fame of her excellence will never perish, and the immortals will fashion among earthly men a gracious song in honor of faithful Penelope.   *Ibid. XXIV, l. 196*

[1]See Pope, 299:26 and 302:22.
[2]See Virgil, 93:17.
[3]See *Ecclesiasticus 13:16, 31:32*; John Heywood, 141:5; and Robert Burton, 235:12.
   Like to like.—ARISTOTLE, *Rhetoric, bk. I, ch. 2, sec. 25*
[4]See *Psalm 103:15, 19:2.*
[5]See Virgil, 94:17.

Hesiod

c. 700 B.C.

13   With the muses of Helicon let us begin our singing.   *The Theogony, l. 1*

14   They once taught Hesiod beauteous song, when he was shepherding his sheep below holy Helicon.

Ibid. l. 22

15   We know how to speak many falsehoods which resemble real things, but we know, when we will, how to speak true things.   *Ibid. l. 27*

16   On his tongue they pour sweet dew, and from his mouth flow gentle words.[6]   *Ibid. l. 83*

17   Love, who is most beautiful among the immortal gods, the melter of limbs, overwhelms in their hearts the intelligence and wise counsel of all gods and all men.   *Ibid. l. 120*

18   From their eyelids as they glanced dripped love.

Ibid. l. 910

19   There was not after all a single kind of strife, but on the earth there are two kinds: one of them a man might praise when he recognized her, but the other is blameworthy.   *Works and Days, l. 11*

20   Potter bears a grudge against potter, and craftsman against craftsman, and beggar is envious of beggar, and bard of bard.   *Ibid. l. 25*

21   Fools, they do not even know how much more is the half than the whole.[7]   *Ibid. l. 40*

22   Often an entire city has suffered because of an evil man.   *Ibid. l. 240*

23   He harms himself who does harm to another, and the evil plan is most harmful to the planner.

Ibid. l. 265

24   Badness you can get easily, in quantity: the road is smooth, and it lies close by. But in front of excellence the immortal gods have put sweat, and long and steep is the way to it, and rough at first. But when you come to the top, then it is easy, even though it is hard.   *Ibid. l. 287*

25   A bad neighbor is a misfortune, as much as a good one is a great blessing.   *Ibid. l. 346*

26   Do not seek evil gains; evil gains are the equivalent of disaster.   *Ibid. l. 352*

27   If you should put even a little on a little, and should do this often, soon this too would become big.[8]   *Ibid. l. 361*

28   At the beginning of a cask and at the end take your fill; in the middle be sparing.   *Ibid. l. 368*

29   The dawn speeds a man on his journey, and speeds him too in his work.   *Ibid. l. 579*

[6]See Coleridge, 382:25.
[7]See Robert Browning, 466:4.
[8]See Chaucer, 132:8, and Cervantes, 150:28.

1 Observe due measure, for right timing is in all things the most important factor. *Ibid. l. 694*

2 Gossip is mischievous, light and easy to raise, but grievous to bear and hard to get rid of. No gossip ever dies away entirely, if many people voice it: it too is a kind of divinity. *Ibid. l. 761*

Archilochus
Early seventh century B.C.

3 I have saved myself—what care I for that shield? Away with it! I'll get another one no worse.
Fragment 6

4 Old women should not seek to be perfumed.
Fragment 27

5 The fox knows many things, but the hedgehog knows one great thing.[1] *Fragment 103*

Mimnermus
c. 650 – c. 590 B.C.

6 What life is there, what delight, without golden Aphrodite? *Fragment 1*

The Seven Sages[2]
c. 650 – c. 550 B.C.

7 Know thyself.
Inscription at the Delphic Oracle. From PLUTARCH, Morals

8 Hesiod might as well have kept his breath to cool his pottage.[3]
PERIANDER. From PLUTARCH, The Banquet of the Seven Wise Men, sec. 14

9 Every one of you hath his particular plague, and my wife is mine; and he is very happy who hath this only.
PITTACUS. From PLUTARCH, Morals, On the Tranquillity of the Mind

10 Nothing too much.[4]
From DIOGENES LAERTIUS, Lives of Eminent Philosophers, bk. I, sec. 63

11 Do not speak ill of the dead.[5] *Ibid. 70*

[1]The fox has many tricks, and the hedgehog has only one, but that is the best of all.—ERASMUS, *Adagia* [1500]

[2]Sayings throughout antiquity were variously attributed to the figures known as the Seven Sages. The list is commonly given as Thales, Solon, Periander, Cleobulus, Chilon, Bias, Pittacus. (See Solon, below.)

[3]Spare your breath to cool your porridge.—RABELAIS, *Works, bk. V* [1552], *ch. 28*

[4]See Terence, 85:12; Horace, 95:2 and 96:7; Lucan, 105:21; and Anonymous: Latin, 119:15.

[5]The Latin form: De mortuis nil nisi bonum [Of the dead, nothing but good].
See Propertius, 100:31.

12 Not even the gods fight against necessity.[6]
Ibid. 77

13 Know the right moment.[7] *Ibid. 79*

14 Rule will show the man.
BIAS. From ARISTOTLE, Nicomachean Ethics, bk. V, ch. 1

Solon
c. 638 – c. 559 B.C.

15 Many evil men are rich, and good men poor, but we shall not exchange with them our excellence for riches. *Fragment 4*

16 Poets tell many lies. *Fragment 21*

17 I grow old ever learning many things.[8]
Fragment 22

18 Speech is the image of actions.
From DIOGENES LAERTIUS, Lives of Eminent Philosophers, bk. I, sec. 58

19 Let us sacrifice to the Muses.
From PLUTARCH, The Banquet of the Seven Wise Men

20 Until he is dead, do not yet call a man happy, but only lucky.[9] *From HERODOTUS,[10] bk. I, ch. 32*

Stesichorus
c. 630 – c. 555 B.C.

21 This tale is not true: you [Helen] did not even board the well-benched ships, and you did not go to the citadel of Troy.[11] *Fragment 11*

Alcaeus
c. 625 – c. 575 B.C.

22 Wine, dear boy, and truth.[12] *Fragment 66*

23 Wine is a peep-hole on a man.[12]
Fragment 104

24 Let us run into a safe harbor.[13]
Fragment 120

[6]See Euripides, 69:5.
[7]Occasionem cognosce.
[8]See Plato, 75:20.
[9]See *Ecclesiasticus 11:28, 31:28*; Aeschylus, 63:14; and Sophocles, 66:2.
[10]Herodotus attributed these words to Solon.
[11]Stesichorus allegedly went blind after writing an account of Helen's perfidy to Menelaus in his *Helen*, but was cured after he composed a palinode, denying that Helen ever went to Troy and blaming Homer for the story.
[12]Earliest references to what became the proverb In vino veritas (In wine is truth), which was known to Plato (*Symposium, 217*) and to Pliny the Elder, *Natural History, XIV, 141*.
See Anonymous: Latin, 119:9.
[13]Part of what is probably the oldest poem using the image of the ship of state.
See Sophocles, 66:4.

Anacharsis
fl. c. 600 B.C.

1   [On learning that the sides of a ship were four fingers thick:] The passengers are just that distance from death.[1]

From DIOGENES LAERTIUS, *Lives of Eminent Philosophers, Anacharsis, 5*

2   [Anacharsis] laughed at him [Solon] for imagining the dishonesty and covetousness of his countrymen could be restrained by written laws, which were like spiders' webs, and would catch, it is true, the weak and poor, but easily be broken by the mighty and rich.[2]   *From* PLUTARCH, *Lives, Life of Solon*

3   In Greece wise men speak and fools decide.[3]

Ibid.

Sappho[4]
c. 612 B.C.

4   Deathless Aphrodite on your rich-wrought throne.[5]   *Fragment 1*

5   Equal to the gods seems to me that man who sits facing you and hears you nearby sweetly speaking and softly laughing. This sets my heart to fluttering in my breast, for when I look on you a moment, then can I speak no more, but my tongue falls silent, and at once a delicate flame courses beneath my skin, and with my eyes I see nothing, and my ears hum, and a cold sweat bathes me, and a trembling seizes me all over, and I am paler than grass, and I feel that I am near to death.[6]   *Fragment 2*

6   The stars about the lovely moon hide their shining forms when it lights up the earth at its fullest.

Fragment 4

7   I loved you once long ago, Athis . . . you seemed to me a small, ungainly child.

Fragments 40–41

8   The moon has set, and the Pleiades; it is midnight, and time passes, and I sleep alone.[7]

Fragment 94

9   Sweet mother, I cannot ply the loom, vanquished by desire for a youth through the work of soft Aphrodite.   *Fragment 114*

---

[1]"How thick do you judge the planks of our ship to be?" "Some two good inches and upward," returned the pilot. "It seems, then, we are within two fingers' breadth of damnation." —RABELAIS, *Works, bk. IV* [1548], *ch. 23*

[2]See Swift, 288:18.

[3]Literally: Anacharsis said [to Solon] that in Greece wise men spoke and fools decided.

[4]Some say there are nine Muses: but they're wrong. / Look at Sappho of Lesbos; she makes ten. —PLATO, *no. 36;* translated by PETER JAY in his edition of *The Greek Anthology* [1973]

[5]Or "with your intricate charms."

[6]See Catullus, 91:4.

[7]See Housman, 580:5.

10   As an apple reddens on the high bough; high atop the highest bough the apple pickers passed it by— no, not passed it by, but they could not reach it.   *Fragment 116*

11   Hesperus, you herd homeward whatever Dawn's light dispersed: you herd sheep—herd goats—herd children home to their mothers.[8]   *Fragment 120*

Lao-tzu[9]
c. 604 – c. 531 B.C.

12 The Tao [Way] that can be told of is not the
  eternal Tao;
The name that can be named is not the eternal
  name.
The Nameless is the origin of Heaven and Earth;
The Named is the mother of all things.
Therefore let there always be non-being, so we
  may see their subtlety,
And let there always be being, so we may see
  their outcome.
The two are the same,
But after they are produced, they have different
  names.
They both may be called deep and profound.
Deeper and more profound,
The door of all subtleties!

The Way of Lao-tzu, 1

13 When the people of the world all know beauty as
  beauty,
There arises the recognition of ugliness.
When they all know the good as good,
There arises the recognition of evil.

Ibid. 2

14 In the government of the sage,
  He keeps their hearts vacuous,
  Fills their bellies,
  Weakens their ambitions,
  And strengthens their bones,
He always causes his people to be without
    knowledge [cunning] or desire,
And the crafty to be afraid to act.

Ibid. 3

15 Heaven and Earth are not humane.
They regard all things as straw dogs.[10]

Ibid. 5

16 The spirit of the valley never dies.
It is called the subtle and profound female.
The gate of the subtle and profound female
Is the root of Heaven and Earth.
It is continuous, and seems to be always existing.
Use it and you will never wear it out.

Ibid. 6

---

[8]Translated by MARY BARNARD [1962]. See Meleager, 87:5, and Housman, 579:22.

[9]Translated by WING-TSIT CHAN.

[10]Straw dogs were used in sacrifices and then discarded.

1 The best [man] is like water.
  Water is good; it benefits all things and does not
    compete with them.
  It dwells in [lowly] places that all disdain.
  This is why it is so near to Tao.
                                        Ibid. 8

2 To produce things and to rear them,
  To produce, but not to take possession of them,
  To act, but not to rely on one's own ability,
  To lead them, but not to master them—
  This is called profound and secret virtue.
                                        Ibid. 10

3 He who loves the world as his body may be
    entrusted with the empire.
                                        Ibid. 13

4 We look at it [Tao] and do not see it;
  Its name is The Invisible.
  We listen to it and do not hear it;
  Its name is The Inaudible.
  We touch it and do not find it;
  Its name is The Subtle [formless].
                                        Ibid. 14

5 It is The Vague and Elusive.
  Meet it and you will not see its head.
  Follow it and you will not see its back.
                                        Ibid.

6 Manifest plainness,
  Embrace simplicity,
  Reduce selfishness,
  Have few desires.
                                        Ibid. 19

7 Abandon learning and there will be no sorrow.
                                        Ibid. 20

8 To yield is to be preserved whole.
  To be bent is to become straight.
  To be empty is to be full.
  To be worn out is to be renewed.
  To have little is to possess.
  To have plenty is to be perplexed.
                                        Ibid. 22

9 He who knows others is wise;
  He who knows himself is enlightened.
                                        Ibid. 33

10 [The sage] never strives himself for the great, and
    thereby the great is achieved.
                                        Ibid. 34

11 Tao invariably takes no action, and yet there is
    nothing left undone.
  Reversion is the action of Tao.
  Weakness is the function of Tao.
  All things in the world come from being.
  And being comes from non-being.
                                        Ibid. 40

12 When the highest type of men hear Tao,
  They diligently practice it.
  When the average type of men hear Tao,
  They half believe in it.
  When the lowest type of men hear Tao,
  They laugh heartily at it.
                                        Ibid. 41

13 The softest things in the world overcome the
    hardest things in the world.
  Non-being penetrates that in which there is no
    space.
  Through this I know the advantage of taking no
    action.
                                        Ibid. 43

14 There is no calamity greater than lavish desires.
  There is no greater guilt than discontentment.
  And there is no greater disaster than greed.
                                        Ibid. 46

15 One may know the world without going out of
    doors.
  One may see the Way of Heaven without looking
    through the windows.
  The further one goes, the less one knows.[1]
  Therefore the sage knows without going about,
  Understands without seeing,
  And accomplishes without any action.
                                        Ibid. 47

16 He who possesses virtue in abundance
  May be compared to an infant.
                                        Ibid. 55

17 He who knows does not speak.
  He who speaks does not know.
                                        Ibid. 56

18 The more laws and order are made prominent,
  The more thieves and robbers there will be.
                                        Ibid. 57

19 Tao is the storehouse of all things.
  It is the good man's treasure and the bad man's
    refuge.
                                        Ibid. 62

20 A journey of a thousand miles must begin with a
    single step.[2]
                                        Ibid. 64

21 People are difficult to govern because they have
    too much knowledge.
                                        Ibid. 65

22 I have three treasures. Guard and keep them:
  The first is deep love,
  The second is frugality,
  And the third is not to dare to be ahead of the
    world.
  Because of deep love, one is courageous.
  Because of frugality, one is generous.

[1]I.e., the more one studies, the further one is from the Tao.
[2]Traditional translation.

Because of not daring to be ahead of the world,
one becomes the leader of the world.
The Way of Lao-tzu, 67

1 When armies are mobilized and issues joined,
The man who is sorry over the fact will win.
Ibid. 69

2 To know that you do not know is the best.
To pretend to know when you do not know is a
disease.[1]
Ibid. 71

3 Heaven's net is indeed vast.
Though its meshes are wide, it misses nothing.[2]
Ibid. 73

4 To undertake executions for the master
executioner [Heaven] is like hewing wood for
the master carpenter.
Whoever undertakes to hew wood for the master
carpenter rarely escapes injuring his own
hands.
Ibid. 74

5 The Way of Heaven has no favorites.
It is always with the good man.
Ibid. 79

6 Let there be a small country with few
people. . . .
Though neighboring communities overlook one
another and the crowing of cocks and
barking of dogs can be heard,
Yet the people there may grow old and die
without ever visiting one another.
Ibid. 80

7 True words are not beautiful;[3]
Beautiful words are not true.
A good man does not argue;
He who argues is not a good man.
A wise man has no extensive knowledge;
He who has extensive knowledge is not a wise
man.
The sage does not accumulate for himself.
The more he uses for others, the more he has
himself.
The more he gives to others, the more he possesses
of his own.
The Way of Heaven is to benefit others and not to
injure.
The Way of the sage is to act but not to compete.
Ibid. 81

Epimenides
Sixth century B.C.

8   All Cretans are liars.   *Attributed*

---

[1]See Confucius, 60:24.
[2]See *Matthew 13:47, 35:11.*
[3]I.e., they are not "fine-sounding."

Pythagoras
c. 582–500 B.C.

9   Friends share all things.[4]
*From DIOGENES LAERTIUS, Lives of Eminent
Philosophers,[5] bk. VIII, sec. 10*

10   Don't eat your heart.   *Ibid. 17*

11   Reason is immortal, all else mortal.   *Ibid. 30*

Ibycus[6]
c. 580 B.C.

12   There is no medicine to be found for a life which
has fled.   *Fragment 23*

13   An argument needs no reason, nor a friendship.
Fragment 40

Aesop[7]
fl. c. 550 B.C.

14   The lamb . . . began to follow the wolf in
sheep's clothing.   *The Wolf in Sheep's Clothing*

15   Appearances often are deceiving.   *Ibid.*

16   Do not count your chickens before they are
hatched.[8]   *The Milkmaid and Her Pail*

17   I am sure the grapes are sour.[9]
The Fox and the Grapes

18   No act of kindness, no matter how small, is ever
wasted.   *The Lion and the Mouse*

19   Slow and steady wins the race.
The Hare and the Tortoise

20   Familiarity breeds contempt.[10]
The Fox and the Lion

21   The boy cried "Wolf, wolf!" and the villagers
came out to help him.
The Shepherd Boy and the Wolf

---

[4]See Plato, 74:11, and Sallust, 91:25.
[5]Translated by R. D. HICKS (Loeb Classical Library).
[6]Associated with Ibycus is the phrase: the cranes of Ibycus.
It derives from the legend that Ibycus was murdered at sea and
his murderers were discovered through cranes that followed
the ship. Hence, "the cranes of Ibycus" became a term for the
agency of the gods in revealing crime.
[7]Animal fables from before Aesop's time and after were
attributed to him. The first collection was made two hundred
years after his death. See also La Fontaine, 267.
[8]To swallow gudgeons ere they're catched / And count their
chickens ere they're hatched.—SAMUEL BUTLER, *Hudibras,
pt. II* [1664], *canto III, l. 923*
[9]The fox, when he cannot reach the grapes, says they are not
ripe.—GEORGE HERBERT, *Jacula Prudentum* [1651]
   "They are too green," he said, "and only good for fools."
—LA FONTAINE, *Fables, bk. III* [1668], *fable 11, The Fox and
the Grapes*
[10]Familiarity breeds contempt—and children.—TWAIN,
Notebooks [1935]

1   A crust eaten in peace is better than a banquet partaken in anxiety.[1]
The Town Mouse and the Country Mouse

2   Borrowed plumes.   *The Jay and the Peacock*

3   It is not only fine feathers that make fine birds. *Ibid.*

4   Self-conceit may lead to self-destruction.
The Frog and the Ox

5   People often grudge others what they cannot enjoy themselves.   *The Dog in the Manger*

6   It is thrifty to prepare today for the wants of tomorrow.   *The Ant*[2] *and the Grasshopper*

7   Be content with your lot; one cannot be first in everything.   *Juno and the Peacock*[3]

8   A huge gap appeared in the side of the mountain. At last a tiny mouse came forth.[4]
The Mountain in Labor

9   Any excuse will serve a tyrant.
The Wolf and the Lamb

10   Beware lest you lose the substance by grasping at the shadow.   *The Dog and the Shadow*

11   Who shall bell the cat?
The Rats and the Cat

12   I will have nought to do with a man who can blow hot and cold with the same breath.
The Man and the Satyr

13   Thinking to get at once all the gold the goose could give, he killed it and opened it only to find —nothing.   *The Goose with the Golden Eggs*

14   Put your shoulder to the wheel.
Hercules and the Wagoner

15   The gods help them that help themselves.[5]
Ibid.

16   We would often be sorry if our wishes were gratified.[6]   *The Old Man and Death*

17   Union gives strength.[7]   *The Bundle of Sticks*

18   While I see many hoof marks going in, I see none coming out. It is easier to get into the enemy's toils than out again.
The Lion, the Fox, and the Beasts

19   The haft of the arrow had been feathered with one of the eagle's own plumes. We often give our enemies the means of our own destruction.[8]
The Eagle and the Arrow

Theognis

fl. c. 545 B.C.

20   One finds many companions for food and drink, but in a serious business a man's companions are very few.   *Elegies, l. 115*

21   Even to a wicked man a divinity gives wealth, Cyrnus, but to few men comes the gift of excellence.
Ibid. l. 149

22   Surfeit begets insolence, when prosperity comes to a bad man.   *Ibid. l. 153*

23   Adopt the character of the twisting octopus, which takes on the appearance of the nearby rock. Now follow in this direction, now turn a different hue.   *Ibid. l. 215*

24   The best of all things for earthly men is not to be born and not to see the beams of the bright sun; but if born, then as quickly as possible to pass the gates of Hades, and to lie deep buried.[9]   *Ibid. l. 425*

25   No man takes with him to Hades all his exceeding wealth.   *Ibid. l. 725*

26   Bright youth passes swiftly as a thought.
Ibid. l. 985

---

[1]See *Proverbs* 15:17, 21:26.

[2]See *Proverbs* 6:6–8, 20:27.

[3]See O'Casey, 654:11.

[4]A mountain was in labor, sending forth dreadful groans, and there was in the region the highest expectation. After all, it brought forth a mouse.—PHAEDRUS, *Fables, IV*, 22:1

See Horace, 98:10.

[5]God loves to help him who strives to help himself.—AESCHYLUS, *Fragment 223*

Heaven helps not the men who will not act.—SOPHOCLES, *Fragment 288*

Try first thyself, and after call in God; / For to the worker God himself lends aid.—EURIPIDES, *Hippolytus, Fragment 435*

Help thyself, and God will help thee.—GEORGE HERBERT, *Jacula Prudentum* [1651]

God helps those who help themselves.—ALGERNON SIDNEY, *Discourses on Government* [1698], *sec. 23*, and FRANKLIN, *Poor Richard's Almanac* [1733–1758]

See Hippocrates, 71:17.

[6]Granting our wish one of Fate's saddest jokes is!—JAMES RUSSELL LOWELL, *Two Scenes from the Life of Blondel, sc. II, st. 2*

Beware, my lord! Beware lest stern Heaven hate you enough to hear your prayers!—FRANCE, *The Crime of Sylvestre Bonnard* [1881], *pt. II, ch. 4*

When the gods wish to punish us they answer our prayers.—WILDE, *An Ideal Husband* [1895], *act II*

[7]See John Dickinson, 336:10.

[8]So in the Libyan fable it is told / That once an eagle, stricken with a dart, / Said, when he saw the fashion of the shaft, / "With our own feathers, not by others' hands, / Are we now smitten."—AESCHYLUS, *Fragment 135*; translated [1868] by EDWARD HAYES PLUMPTRE

That eagle's fate and mine are one, / Which on the shaft that made him die / Espied a feather of his own, / Wherewith he wont to soar so high.—EDMUND WALLER, *To a Lady Singing a Song of His Composing*

[9]See Sophocles, 67:9; Francis Bacon, 160:15; Yeats, 598:3; and Auden, 720:5.

Anacreon
c. 570 – c. 480 B.C.

1   Bring water, bring wine, boy! Bring flowering garlands to me! Yes, bring them, so that I may try a bout with love.   *Fragment 27*

2   I both love and do not love, and am mad and am not mad.[1]   *Fragment 79*

3   War spares not the brave, but the cowardly.[2]
     *Fragment 101. From The Palatine Anthology,
     VII, 160*

Xenophanes
c. 570 – c. 475 B.C.

4   Homer and Hesiod attributed to the gods everything that is a shame and a reproach among men.
                         Fragment 11

5   If cattle and horses, or lions, had hands, or were able to draw with their feet and produce the works which men do, horses would draw the forms of gods like horses, and cattle like cattle, and they would make the gods' bodies the same shape as their own.[3]
                         Fragment 15

6   One god, greatest among gods and men, similar to mortals neither in shape nor even in thought.[4]
                         Fragment 23

7   It takes a wise man to recognize a wise man.
     *From DIOGENES LAERTIUS, Lives of Eminent
     Philosophers, Xenophanes, IX*

Simonides
c. 556 – 468 B.C.

8   It is hard to be truly excellent, four-square in hand and foot and mind, formed without blemish.
                         Fragment 4

9   The city is the teacher of the man.
                         Fragment 53

10   Fighting in the forefront of the Greeks, the Athenians crushed at Marathon the might of the gold-bearing Medes.   *Fragment 88*

11   Go tell the Spartans, thou who passest by,
     That here, obedient to their laws, we lie.[5]
                         Fragment 92

[1]See Catullus, 91:16.
[2]See Sophocles, 67:4.
[3]See Montesquieu, 304:9.
[4]See Homer, 51:20.
[5]Translated by W. L. BOWLES.
     Epitaph for the Lacedaemonian [Spartan] king Leonidas and his small force at Thermopylae, who all died fighting to hold the pass against the invading Persian army [480 B.C.].
     Ruskin said of this epitaph that it was the noblest group of words uttered by man.

12   If to die honorably is the greatest
     Part of virtue, for us fate's done her best.
     Because we fought to crown Greece with freedom
     We lie here enjoying timeless fame.
               For the Athenian Dead at Plataia[6]

13   We did not flinch but gave our lives to save
     Greece when her fate hung on a razor's edge.
               Cenotaph at the Isthmos[6]

14   Painting is silent poetry, and poetry painting that speaks.
     *From PLUTARCH, De Gloria Atheniensium, III,
     346*

Confucius
551 – 479 B.C.

15   Fine words and an insinuating appearance are seldom associated with true virtue.
               The Confucian Analects,[7] bk. 1:3

16   A youth, when at home, should be filial, and, abroad, respectful to his elders.   *Ibid. 1:6*

17   If a man withdraws his mind from the love of beauty, and applies it as sincerely to the love of the virtuous; if, in serving his parents, he can exert his utmost strength; if, in serving his prince, he can devote his life; if, in his intercourse with his friends, his words are sincere—although men say that he has not learned, I will certainly say that he has.
                         Ibid. 1:7

18   Hold faithfulness and sincerity as first principles.
                         Ibid. 1:8, ii

19   Have no friends not equal to yourself.
                         Ibid. 1:8, iii

20   When you have faults, do not fear to abandon them.   *Ibid. 1:8, iv*

21   He who exercises government by means of his virtue may be compared to the north polar star, which keeps its place and all the stars turn towards it.   *Ibid. 2:1*

22   [The superior man] acts before he speaks, and afterwards speaks according to his actions.
                         Ibid. 2:13

23   Learning without thought is labor lost; thought without learning is perilous.   *Ibid. 2:15*

24   When you know a thing, to hold that you know it; and when you do not know a thing, to allow that you do not know it—this is knowledge.[8]
                         Ibid. 2:17

[6]Translated by PETER JAY in his edition of *The Greek Anthology* [1973].
[7]Sayings attributed to Confucius and his followers; from *The Chinese Classics* [1861–1886], vol. I, *The Confucian Analects*, translated by JAMES LEGGE.
[8]See Lao-tzu, 58:2.

1 Things that are done, it is needless to speak about . . . things that are past, it is needless to blame. *Ibid. 3:21, ii*

2 I have not seen a person who loved virtue, or one who hated what was not virtuous. He who loved virtue would esteem nothing above it. *Ibid. 4:6, i*

3 If a man in the morning hear the right way, he may die in the evening without regret. *Ibid. 4:8*

4 The superior man . . . does not set his mind either for anything, or against anything; what is right he will follow. *Ibid. 4:10*

5 When we see men of worth, we should think of equaling them; when we see men of a contrary character, we should turn inwards and examine ourselves. *Ibid. 4:17*

6 The cautious seldom err. *Ibid. 4:23*

7 Virtue is not left to stand alone. He who practices it will have neighbors. *Ibid. 4:25*

8 Man is born for uprightness. If a man lose his uprightness, and yet live, his escape from death is the effect of mere good fortune. *Ibid. 6:16*

9 The man of virtue makes the difficulty to be overcome his first business, and success only a subsequent consideration. *Ibid. 6:20*

10 With coarse rice to eat, with water to drink, and my bended arm for a pillow—I have still joy in the midst of these things. Riches and honors acquired by unrighteousness are to me as a floating cloud.[1] *Ibid. 7:15*

11 I am not one who was born in the possession of knowledge; I am one who is fond of antiquity, and earnest in seeking it there. *Ibid. 7:19*

12 Is virtue a thing remote? I wish to be virtuous, and lo! virtue is at hand. *Ibid. 7:29*

13 The superior man is satisfied and composed; the mean man is always full of distress. *Ibid. 7:36*

14 The people may be made to follow a path of action, but they may not be made to understand it. *Ibid. 8:9*

15 While you are not able to serve men, how can you serve spirits [of the dead]? . . . While you do not know life, how can you know about death? *Ibid. 11:11*

16 To go beyond is as wrong as to fall short. *Ibid. 11:15, iii*

17 He with whom neither slander that gradually soaks into the mind, nor statements that startle like a wound in the flesh, are successful may be called intelligent indeed. *Ibid. 12:6*

18 In carrying on your government, why should you use killing [the unprincipled for the good of the unprincipled] at all? Let your evinced desires be for what is good, and the people will be good. The relation between superiors and inferiors is like that between the wind and the grass. The grass must bend when the wind blows across it. *Ibid. 12:19*

19 Good government obtains when those who are near are made happy, and those who are far off are attracted. *Ibid. 13:16, ii*

20 The firm, the enduring, the simple, and the modest are near to virtue. *Ibid. 13:27*

21 The scholar who cherishes the love of comfort is not fit to be deemed a scholar. *Ibid. 14:3*

22 The man who in the view of gain thinks of righteousness; who in the view of danger is prepared to give up his life; and who does not forget an old agreement however far back it extends—such a man may be reckoned a complete man. *Ibid. 14:13, ii*

23 He who speaks without modesty will find it difficult to make his words good. *Ibid. 14:21*

24 The superior man is modest in his speech, but exceeds in his actions. *Ibid. 14:29*

25 Recompense injury with justice, and recompense kindness with kindness. *Ibid. 14:36, iii*

26 The determined scholar and the man of virtue will not seek to live at the expense of injuring their virtue. They will even sacrifice their lives to preserve their virtue complete. *Ibid. 15:8*

27 If a man take no thought about what is distant, he will find sorrow near at hand. *Ibid. 15:11*

28 The superior man is distressed by his want of ability. *Ibid. 15:18*

29 What the superior man seeks is in himself. What the mean man seeks is in others. *Ibid. 15:20*

30 What you do not want done to yourself, do not do to others.[2] *15:23*

31 When a man's knowledge is sufficient to attain, and his virtue is not sufficient to enable him to hold, whatever he may have gained, he will lose again. *Ibid. 15:32, i*

32 The superior man cannot be known in little matters, but he may be entrusted with great concerns. The small man may not be entrusted with great concerns, but he may be known in little matters. *Ibid. 15:33*

33 Virtue is more to man than either water or fire. I have seen men die from treading on water and fire,

[1]See *Proverbs 15:16–17, 21:26.*

[2]See *Matthew 7:12, 34:8;* Aristotle, 77:15; Hillel, 102:7; and Chesterfield, 304:21.

but I have never seen a man die from treading the course of virtue.   *Confucian Analects, bk. 15:34*

1   By nature, men are nearly alike; by practice, they get to be wide apart.   *Ibid. 17:2*

2   To be able to practice five things everywhere under heaven constitutes perfect virtue. . . . [They are] gravity, generosity of soul, sincerity, earnestness, and kindness.   *Ibid. 17:6*

3   There are three things which the superior man guards against. In youth . . . lust. When he is strong . . . quarrelsomeness. When he is old . . . covetousness.   *Ibid. 17:8*

4   Without recognizing the ordinances of Heaven, it is impossible to be a superior man.   *Ibid. 20:3, i*

5   Without an acquaintance with the rules of propriety, it is impossible for the character to be established.   *Ibid. 20:3, ii*

6   Without knowing the force of words, it is impossible to know men.   *Ibid. 20:3, iii*

Heraclitus
c. 540 – c. 480 B.C.

7   All is flux, nothing stays still.
From DIOGENES LAERTIUS, Lives of Eminent Philosophers, bk. IX, sec. 8, and PLATO, Cratylus, 402A

8   Nothing endures but change.   *Ibid.*

9   It is wise to listen, not to me but to the Word, and to confess that all things are one.
On the Universe,[1] fragment 1

10   Nature is wont to hide herself.   *Ibid. 10*

11   Much learning does not teach understanding.   *Ibid. 16*

12   This world . . . ever was, and is, and shall be, ever-living Fire, in measures being kindled and in measures going out.   *Ibid. 20*

13   God is day and night, winter and summer, war and peace, surfeit and hunger.   *Ibid. 36*

14   You could not step twice into the same rivers;[2] for other waters are ever flowing on to you.
Ibid. 41

15   The opposite is beneficial; from things that differ comes the fairest attunement; all things are born through strife.   *Ibid. 46*

16   Couples are wholes and not wholes, what agrees disagrees, the concordant is discordant. From all things one and from one all things.   *Ibid. 59*

17   The road up and the road down is one and the same.   *Ibid. 69*

[1]Translated by W. H. S. JONES (Loeb Classical Library).
[2]Usually quoted as: river. See Kamo no Chomei, 122:16.

18   Man, like a light in the night, is kindled and put out.   *Ibid. 77*

19   For when is death not within ourselves? . . . Living and dead are the same, and so are awake and asleep, young and old.[3]   *Ibid. 78*

20   The people should fight for their law as for a wall.   *Ibid. 100*

21   It is better to hide ignorance, but it is hard to do this when we relax over wine.   *Ibid. 108*

22   A man's character is his fate.   *Ibid. 121*

Themistocles
c. 528 – c. 462 B.C.

23   Tuning the lyre and handling the harp are no accomplishments of mine, but rather taking in hand a city that was small and inglorious and making it glorious and great.
From PLUTARCH, Lives, Themistocles, sec. 2

24   The wooden wall is your ships.[4]   *Ibid. 10*

25   Strike, but hear me.[5]   *Ibid. 11*

26   [Of his son] The boy is the most powerful of all the Hellenes; for the Hellenes are commanded by the Athenians, the Athenians by myself, myself by the boy's mother, and the mother by her boy.
Ibid. 18

27   [Of two suitors for his daughter's hand] I choose the likely man in preference to the rich man; I want a man without money rather than money without a man.
From PLUTARCH, Lives, Themistocles, sec. 18

28   I have with me two gods, Persuasion and Compulsion.[6]   *Ibid. 21*

29   The speech of man is like embroidered tapestries, since like them this too has to be extended in order to display its patterns, but when it is rolled up it conceals and distorts them.   *Ibid. 29*

30   He who commands the sea has command of everything.[7]   *From CICERO, Ad Atticum, X, 8*

31   [Upon being asked whether he would rather be Achilles or Homer] Which would you rather be—

[3]See Euripides, 69:15.
[4]This was Themistocles' interpretation to the Athenians in 480 B.C. of the second oracle at Delphi: "Safe shall the wooden wall continue for thee and thy children." The account appears in full in HERODOTUS, Histories, bk. VII, sec. 141–143.
[5]Said in reply to Eurybiades, commander of the Spartan fleet, when he raised his staff as though to strike.
[6]Said to the Andrians, when demanding money from them, to which they replied that they already had two great gods, Penury and Powerlessness, who hindered them from giving him money.
[7]See Francis Bacon, 160:7; Edmund Waller, 249:27; Washington, 336:17; and Mahan, 541:3.

a victor in the Olympic games, or the announcer of the victor?

From PLUTARCH, *Apothegms, Themistocles*

Aeschylus
525–456 B.C.

1   I would far rather be ignorant than knowledgeable of evils.   *The Suppliants, l. 453*

2   "Reverence for parents" stands written among the three laws of most revered righteousness.[1]
Ibid. l. 707

3   Myriad laughter of the ocean waves.
Prometheus Bound, l. 89

4   For somehow this is tyranny's disease, to trust no friends.   *Ibid. l. 224*

5   Words are the physicians of a mind diseased.[2]
Ibid. l. 378

6   Time as he grows old teaches all things.
Ibid. l. 981

7   God's mouth knows not how to speak falsehood, but he brings to pass every word.[3]   *Ibid. l. 1030*

8   On me the tempest falls. It does not make me tremble. O holy Mother Earth, O air and sun, behold me. I am wronged.[4]   *Ibid. l. 1089*

9   I pray the gods some respite from the weary task of this long year's watch that lying on the Atreidae's roof on bended arm, doglike, I have kept, marking the conclave of all the night's stars, those potentates blazing in the heavens that bring winter and summer to mortal men, the constellations, when they wane, when they rise.   *Agamemnon, l. 1*

10   A great ox stands on my tongue.[5]   *Ibid. l. 36*

11   He who learns must suffer. And even in our sleep pain that cannot forget falls drop by drop upon the heart, and in our own despair, against our will, comes wisdom to us by the awful grace of God.
Ibid. l. 177

12   She [Helen] brought to Ilium her dowry, destruction.   *Ibid. l. 406*

13   It is in the character of very few men to honor without envy a friend who has prospered.
Ibid. l. 832

14   Only when man's life comes to its end in prosperity can one call that man happy.[6]   *Ibid. l. 928*

15   Alas, I am struck a deep mortal blow!
Ibid. l. 1343

16   Death is better, a milder fate than tyranny.[7]
Ibid. l. 1364

17   Zeus, first cause, prime mover; for what thing without Zeus is done among mortals?[8]
Ibid. l. 1485

18   Do not kick against the pricks.[9]
Ibid. l. 1624

19   I know how men in exile feed on dreams of hope.
Ibid. l. 1668

20   Good fortune is a god among men, and more than a god.   *The Libation Bearers, l. 59*

21   Destiny waits alike for the free man as well as for him enslaved by another's might.   *Ibid. l. 103*

22   For a deadly blow let him pay with a deadly blow: it is for him who has done a deed to suffer.[10]
Ibid. l. 312

23   What is pleasanter than the tie of host and guest?
Ibid. l. 702

24   His resolve is not to seem, but to be, the best.
The Seven Against Thebes, l. 592

Pheidippides
d. 490 B.C.

25   Rejoice, we are victorious.
From LUCAN, *Pro Lapsu in Salutado, 3*

Pindar
c. 518 – c. 438 B.C.

26   Water is best. But gold shines like fire blazing in the night, supreme of lordly wealth.
Olympian Odes, I, l. 1

27   The days that are still to come are the wisest witnesses.   *Ibid. l. 51*

28   If any man hopes to do a deed without God's knowledge, he errs.   *Ibid. l. 104*

29   Do not peer too far.[11]   *Ibid. l. 184*

30   I have many swift arrows in my quiver which speak to the wise, but for the crowd they need interpreters. The skilled poet is one who knows much through natural gift, but those who have learned their art chatter turbulently, vainly, against the divine bird of Zeus.   *Ibid. II, l. 150*

31   I will not steep my speech in lies; the test of any man lies in action.[12]   *Ibid. IV, l. 27*

---

[1]See *Exodus* 20:12, 9:12.
[2]See Milton, 261:11.
[3]See *Numbers* 23:19, 10:6.
[4]Translated by EDITH HAMILTON.
[5]A proverbial expression of uncertain origin for enforced silence.
[6]See *Ecclesiasticus* 11:28, 31:28; Solon, 55:20; and Sophocles, 66:2.
[7]See Patrick Henry, 339:10.
[8]See *Acts* 17:28, 41:17; Cleanthes, 82:2; and Aratus, 82:12.
[9]Also in PINDAR, *Pythian Odes, II, l. 174*, and EURIPIDES, *Bacchae, l. 795*. See *Acts* 9:5, 41:6.
[10]See *Exodus* 21:12, 9:14.
[11]Do not set your eyes on things far off.—*Pythian Odes, III, l. 39*
See Euripides, 68:9.
[12]Translated by RICHMOND LATTIMORE.

1   The issue is in God's hands.
Olympian Odes, XIII, l. 147

2   Zeus, accomplisher, to all grant grave restraint and attainment of sweet delight.   *Ibid. last line*

3   Seek not, my soul, the life of the immortals; but enjoy to the full the resources that are within thy reach.   *Pythian Odes, III, l. 109*

4   They say that this lot is bitterest: to recognize the good but by necessity to be barred from it.[1]
Ibid. IV, l. 510

5   Creatures of a day, what is a man? What is he not? Mankind is a dream of a shadow. But when a god-given brightness comes, a radiant light rests on men, and a gentle life.   *Ibid. VIII, l. 135*

6   When toilsome contests have been decided, good cheer is the best physician, and songs, the sage daughters of the Muses, soothe with their touch.
Nemean Odes, IV, l. 1

7   Words have a longer life than deeds.
Ibid. l. 10

8   Not every truth is the better for showing its face undisguised; and often silence is the wisest thing for a man to heed.   *Ibid. V, l. 30*

9   One race there is of men, one of gods, but from one mother we both draw our breath.
Ibid. VI, l. 1

10   If one but tell a thing well, it moves on with undying voice, and over the fruitful earth and across the sea goes the bright gleam of noble deeds ever unquenchable.   *Isthmian Odes, IV, l. 67*

11   It is not possible with mortal mind to search out the purposes of the gods.   *Fragment 61*

12   O bright and violet-crowned and famed in song, bulwark of Greece, famous Athens, divine city!
Fragment 76

13   Unsung, the noblest deed will die.[2]
Fragment 120

14   What is God? Everything.   *Fragment 140d*

15   Convention is the ruler of all.   *Fragment 169*

16   Hope, which most of all guides the changeful mind of mortals.   *Fragment 214*

Anaxagoras
c. 500–428 B.C.

17   The descent to Hades is the same from every place.
From DIOGENES LAERTIUS, Lives of Eminent Philosophers, Anaxagoras, 2

[1]See Boethius, 115:10; Dante, 125:18; Chaucer, 128:19; and Tennyson, 455:13.
[2]See Horace, 97:1, and Pope, 303:13.

The Pali Canon[3]
c. 500 – c. 250 B.C.[4]

18   All that is comes from the mind; it is based on the mind, it is fashioned by the mind.[5]
Suttapitaka. Dhammapada, ch. 1, verse 1

19   For hatred does not cease by hatred at any time: hatred ceases by love—this is the eternal law.[5]
Ibid. 1:5

20   Avoid what is evil; do what is good; purify the mind—this is the teaching of the Awakened One [Buddha].[5]   *Ibid. 14:183*

21   Better to live alone; with a fool there is no companionship. With few desires live alone and do no evil, like an elephant in the forest roaming at will.
Ibid. 23:330

22   I have preached the truth without making any distinction between exoteric and esoteric doctrine: for in respect of truths, Ananda, the Tathagata[6] has no such thing as the closed fist of a teacher, who keeps some things back.[7]
Ibid. Mahaparinibbana-sutta, 2:32

23   Be lamps [or islands] unto yourselves. Be a refuge unto yourselves. Do not turn to any external refuge. Hold fast to the teaching [dhamma] as a lamp.[5]
Ibid. 2:33

24   Few and far between are the Tathagatas,[6] the Arahat Buddhas, who appear in the world.[5]
Ibid. 5:10

25   Decay is inherent in all component things! Work out your salvation with diligence.[8]   *Ibid. 6:10*

26   This is the noble truth of sorrow. Birth is sorrow, age is sorrow, disease is sorrow, death is sorrow . . . in short, all the five components of individuality [khandas] are sorrow.
    And this is the noble truth of the arising of sorrow. It arises from craving, which leads to rebirth, which brings delight and passion . . .
    And this is the noble truth of the stopping of sorrow. It is the complete stopping of that craving . . . being emancipated from it . . .
    And this is the noble truth of the way which leads to the stopping of sorrow. It is the noble eightfold path.[9]   *Ibid. Samyutta-nikaya, 5:421*

27   The law that I have preached . . . and the discipline that I have established, will be your master after my disappearance.[5]   *Ibid. Digha Nikaya, II*

[3]The sacred scriptures of Theravada Buddhists.
[4]Ancient Indian literary chronology is conjectural.
[5]Translated by JAN NATTIER-BARBARO.
[6]Tathagata: Thus-come-one, an Indian term designating an enlightened being.
[7]Translated by T. W. RHYS DAVIDS.
[8]Translated by T. W. RHYS DAVIDS.
The last words of the Buddha.
[9]Translated by WILLIAM THEODORE DE BARY.

1   This noble eightfold path . . . right views, right aspirations, right speech, right conduct, right livelihood, right effort, right mindfulness, and right contemplation.[1]

Ibid. Dhammacakkappavattanasutta, verse 4

2 The wise and moral man
Shines like a fire on a hilltop,
Making money like the bee,
Who does not hurt the flower.[2]

Ibid. Singalavada-sutta, Digha-nikaya, 3:180

3   It would be absurd to say of the [enlightened] monk, with his heart set free, that he believes that the perfected being survives after death — or indeed that he does not survive, or that he does and yet does not, or that he neither does nor does not. Because the monk is free his state transcends all expression, predication, communication, and knowledge.[3]

Ibid. Digha-nikaya, 2:65

4   If, Ananda, women had not received permission to go out from the household life and enter the homeless state[4] . . . then would the pure religion, Ananda, have lasted long, the good law would have stood fast for a thousand years. But since, Ananda, women have now received that permission, the pure religion, Ananda, will not now last so long, the good law will now stand fast for only five hundred years.[1]

Vinayapitaka. Cullavagga, bk. X, ch. 1, verse 6

5   I go for refuge to the Buddha.
I go for refuge to the Doctrine.
I go for refuge to the Order [of monks].

Traditional (liturgical), passim

Pericles[5]

c. 495–429 B.C.

6   Wait for that wisest of all counselors, Time.

From PLUTARCH, *Lives, Pericles, sec. 18*

7   Trees, though they are cut and lopped, grow up again quickly,[6] but if men are destroyed, it is not easy to get them again.   *Ibid. 33*

Sophocles[7]

c. 495–406 B.C.

8 Silence gives the proper grace to women.

Ajax, l. 293

9 Nobly to live, or else nobly to die,
Befits proud birth.[8]

Ibid. l. 480

10   Of all human ills, greatest is fortune's wayward tyranny.   *Ibid. l. 486*

11 For kindness begets kindness evermore,
But he from whose mind fades the memory
Of benefits, noble is he no more.

Ibid. l. 522

12 Sleep that masters all.

Ibid. l. 675

13 I, whom proof hath taught of late
How so far only should we hate our foes
As though we soon might love them, and so far
Do a friend service as to one most like
Someday to prove our foe, since oftenest men
In friendship but a faithless haven find.[9]

Ibid. l. 678

14 Men of ill judgment oft ignore the good
That lies within their hands, till they have lost it.

Ibid. l. 964

15 It is not righteousness to outrage
A brave man dead, not even though you hate him.

Ibid. l. 1344

16 Ships are only hulls, high walls are nothing,
When no life moves in the empty passageways.

Oedipus Rex,[10] *l. 56*

17 How dreadful knowledge of the truth can be
When there's no help in truth!

Ibid. l. 316

18 The tyrant is a child of Pride
Who drinks from his great sickening cup
Recklessness and vanity,
Until from his high crest headlong
He plummets to the dust of hope.[11]

Ibid. l. 872

19 The greatest griefs are those we cause ourselves.

Ibid. l. 1230

20 Time eases all things.[12]

Ibid. l. 1515

[8]See Euripides, 69:10, and the Duc de Lévis, 367:8.
[9]They love as though they will someday hate and hate as though they will someday love. — ARISTOTLE quoting BIAS [6th century B.C.], *Rhetoric, II, 13*
See Publilius Syrus, 99:20.
[10]Translated by DUDLEY FITTS and ROBERT FITZGERALD.
[11]Pride will have a fall. — *English proverb* [c. 1509]
A variant is: Pride goeth before a fall.
Pride goeth before, and shame cometh behind. — *Treatise of a Gallant* [c. 1510]
Pride will have a fall;/For pride goeth before and shame cometh after. — JOHN HEYWOOD, *Proverbs* [1546], *pt. I, ch. 10*
See *Proverbs* 16:18, 21:31.
[12]See Terence, 85:18, and La Fontaine, 268:4.

[1]Translated by T. W. RHYS DAVIDS and H. OLDENBERG.
[2]Translated by WILLIAM THEODORE DE BARY.
A text addressed — exceptionally in the early Buddhist literature — to laity rather than monks.
[3]Translated by WILLIAM THEODORE DE BARY.
[4]Enter the Buddhist order.
[5]See Thucydides, *Funeral Oration of Pericles,* 72:2–72:9.
[6]The lopped tree in time may grow again. — SOUTHWELL, *Times Go by Turns* [c. 1595]
[7]Sophocles said he drew men as they ought to be, and Euripides as they were. — ARISTOTLE, *Poetics, ch. 25*

1   Look upon Oedipus
This is the king who solved the famous riddle [of
    the Sphinx].[1]

Oedipus Rex, l. 1524

2 Let every man in mankind's frailty
Consider his last day; and let none
Presume on his good fortune until he find
Life, at his death, a memory without pain.[2]

Ibid. l. 1529

3 For God hates utterly
The bray of bragging tongues.

Antigone[3] [c. 442 B.C.], l. 123

4   Our ship of state, which recent storms have
threatened to destroy, has come safely to harbor at
last.[4]   *Ibid. l. 163*

5   I have nothing but contempt for the kind of governor who is afraid, for whatever reason, to follow
the course that he knows is best for the State; and as
for the man who sets private friendship above the
public welfare—I have no use for him, either.

Ibid. l. 181

6   Nobody likes the man who brings bad news.[5]

Ibid. l. 277

7   Money: There's nothing in the world so demoralizing as money.[6]   *Ibid. l. 295*

8   How dreadful it is when the right judge judges
wrong!   *Ibid. l. 323*

9 Numberless are the world's wonders, but none
More wonderful than man.

Ibid. l. 333 (Ode I)

10   It is a good thing
To escape from death, but it is not great pleasure
To bring death to a friend.

Ibid. l. 437

11 But all your[7] strength is weakness itself against
The immortal unrecorded laws of God.

---

[1]The riddle of the Sphinx: What creature walks in the morning on four feet, at noon upon two, and at evening upon three?
Oedipus solved it: Man as a baby crawls on hands and knees,
then strides erect on his feet, and in old age walks with a staff.
The Sphinx, a monster with a woman's head and bust and a
lion's body with wings, waylaid passers on the road to Thebes
to propound the riddle, destroying anyone who failed to guess
the answer. Oedipus solved the riddle, the Sphinx destroyed
herself, and the grateful Thebans made him king.
    See Seferis, 706:7.
[2]See *Ecclesiasticus 11:28, 31:28*; Solon, 55:20; and Aeschylus,
63:14.
    There is a saying among men, put forth of old, that you
cannot rightly judge whether a mortal's lot is good or evil, until
he dies.—SOPHOCLES, *Trachiniae, l. 1*
[3]Translated by DUDLEY FITTS and ROBERT FITZGERALD.
[4]See Alcaeus, 55:24.
[5]Don't shoot the messenger.—*Saying*
See Shakespeare, 183:11 and 217:19.
[6]See *I Timothy 6:10*, 45:22, and Plato, 75:12.
[7]Creon.

They are not merely now: they were and shall be
Forever, beyond man utterly.

Ibid. l. 452

12 Grief teaches the steadiest minds to waver.

Ibid. l. 563

13 All that is and shall be,
And all the past, is his [Zeus's].

Ibid. l. 611 (Ode II)

14 Show me the man who keeps his house in hand,
He's fit for public authority.[8]

Ibid. l. 660

15 Anarchy, anarchy! Show me a greater evil!
This is why cities tumble and the great houses
    rain down,
This is what scatters armies!

Ibid. l. 672

16 Reason is God's crowning gift to man.

Ibid. l. 684

17 The ideal condition
Would be, I admit, that men should be right by
    instinct;
But since we are all likely to go astray,
The reasonable thing is to learn from those who
    can teach.

Ibid. l. 720

18 Love, unconquerable,[9]
Waster of rich men, keeper
Of warm lights and all-night vigil
In the soft face of a girl:
Sea-wanderer, forest-visitor!
Even the pure immortals cannot escape you,
And mortal man, in his one day's dusk,
Trembles before your glory.

Ibid. l. 781 (Ode III)

19 Wisdom outweighs any wealth.[10]

Ibid. l. 1050

20 There is no happiness where there is no wisdom;[11]
No wisdom but in submission to the gods.
Big words are always punished,
And proud men in old age learn to be wise.

Ibid. l. 1347, closing lines

21 Death is not the worst; rather, in vain
To wish for death, and not to compass it.

Electra, l. 1008

22   A prudent mind can see room for misgiving, lest
he who prospers should one day suffer reverse.[12]

Trachiniae, l. 296

---

[8]See *I Timothy 3:5*, 45:12.
[9]See Sophocles, 67:1; Virgil, 92:20; and Chaucer, 129:14.
[10]See *Job 28:18*, 14:40.
[11]See Epicurus, 81:20.
[12]See *Proverbs 16:18*, 21:31.

1   They are not wise, then, who stand forth to buffet against Love; for Love rules the gods as he will, and me.[1]
Ibid. l. 441

2   Knowledge must come through action; you can have no test which is not fanciful, save by trial.
Ibid. l. 592

3   Rash indeed is he who reckons on the morrow, or haply on days beyond it; for tomorrow is not, until today is past.[2]
Ibid. l. 943

4   War never slays a bad man in its course,
But the good always![3]
Philoctetes, l. 436

5   Stranger in a strange country.[4]
Oedipus at Colonus[5] *[406 B.C.], l. 184*

6   The good befriend themselves.
Ibid. l. 309

7   The immortal
Gods alone have neither age nor death!
All other things almighty Time disquiets.
Ibid. l. 607

8   Athens, nurse of men.
Ibid. l. 701

9   Not to be born surpasses thought and speech.
The second best is to have seen the light
And then to go back quickly whence we came.[6]
Ibid. l. 1224

10   One word
Frees us of all the weight and pain of life:
That word is love.
Ibid. l. 1616

11   It made our hair stand up in panic fear.
Ibid. l. 1625

12   A remedy too strong for the disease.
Tereus, fragment 514[7]

13   Truly, to tell lies is not honorable;
But when the truth entails tremendous ruin,
To speak dishonorably is pardonable.
Creusa, fragment 323

14   Sons are the anchors of a mother's life.
Phaedra, fragment 612

15   To him who is in fear everything rustles.
Acrisius, fragment 58

16   No falsehood lingers on into old age.
Ibid. 59

17   No man loves life like him that's growing old.[8]
Ibid. 64

18   A woman's vows I write upon the wave.
Unknown Dramas, fragment 694

Empedocles
c. 490 – c. 430 B.C.

19   At one time through love all things come together into one, at another time through strife's hatred they are borne each of them apart.
Fragment 17

20   The blood around men's heart is their thinking.
Fragment 105

Euripides[9]
c. 485–406 B.C.

21   Never say that marriage has more of joy than pain.
Alcestis[10] *[438 B.C.], l. 238*

22   A second wife
is hateful to the children of the first;
a viper is not more hateful.
Ibid. l. 309

23   A sweet thing, for whatever time,
to revisit in dreams the dear dead we have lost.
Ibid. l. 355

24   Oh, if I had Orpheus' voice and poetry
with which to move the Dark Maid and her Lord,
I'd call you back, dear love, from the world below.
I'd go down there for you. Charon or the grim
King's dog could not prevent me then
from carrying you up into the fields of light.
Ibid. l. 358

25   Light be the earth upon you, lightly rest.[11]
Ibid. l. 462

26   God, these old men!
How they pray for death! How heavy
they find this life in the slow drag of days!
And yet, when Death comes near them,
You will not find one who will rise and walk with
him, not one whose years are still a burden
to him.[12]
Ibid. l. 669

---

[8]See Euripides, 67:26.

[9]All Greece is his monument, though his grave / Lies in Macedon, refuge of his last days. / Hellas of Hellas, Athens his land, who gave / so much joy by his art, whom so many praise. —THUCYDIDES, *Euripides;* translated by PETER JAY in his edition of *The Greek Anthology* [1973]

Sophocles said he drew men as they ought to be, and Euripides as they were. —ARISTOTLE, *Poetics, ch. 25*

[10]Translated by DUDLEY FITTS and ROBERT FITZGERALD.

[11]See Anonymous: Latin, 119:31, and Beaumont and Fletcher, 238:16.

[12]See Sophocles, 67:17.

---

[1]See Sophocles, 66:18; Virgil, 92:20; and Chaucer, 129:14.

[2]See *Proverbs 27:1, 22:32.*

[3]Translated by SIR GEORGE YOUNG.
See Anacreon, 60:3.

[4]See *Exodus 2:22, 8:22.*

[5]Translated by ROBERT FITZGERALD.

[6]See Theognis, 59:24; Francis Bacon, 160:15; Yeats, 598:3; and Auden, 720:5.

[7]The fragments are from the Everyman edition of *The Dramas of Sophocles.*

1 You love the daylight: do you think your
father does not?

Alcestis, l. 691

2 Dishonor will not trouble me, once I am dead.

Ibid. l. 726

3 Today's today. Tomorrow, we may be
ourselves gone down the drain of Eternity.

Ibid. l. 788

4 O mortal man, think mortal thoughts!

Ibid. l. 799

5 My mother was accursed the night she bore me,
and I am faint with envy of all the dead.[1]

Ibid. l. 865

6 You were a stranger to sorrow: therefore Fate
has cursed you.

Ibid. l. 927

7 I have found power in the mysteries of thought,
exaltation in the chanting of the Muses;
I have been versed in the reasonings of men;
but Fate is stronger than anything I have known.

Ibid. l. 962

8 Time cancels young pain.

Ibid. l. 1085

9 Slight not what's near through aiming at
what's far.[2]

Rhesus [c. 435 B.C.], l. 482

10 There is no benefit in the gifts of a bad man.

Medea [431 B.C.], l. 618

11 When love is in excess it brings a man nor honor
nor any worthiness.

Ibid. l. 627

12 What greater grief than the loss of one's
native land.

Ibid. l. 650

13 I know indeed what evil I intend to do,
but stronger than all my afterthoughts is my fury,
fury that brings upon mortals the greatest evils.

Ibid. l. 1078

14 We know the good, we apprehend it clearly,
but we can't bring it to achievement.[3]

Hippolytus [428 B.C.],[4] l. 380

15 There is one thing alone
that stands the brunt of life throughout its course:
a quiet conscience.

Ibid. l. 426

16 In this world second thoughts, it seems, are best.[5]

Ibid. l. 435

17 Love distills desire upon the eyes,
love brings bewitching grace into the heart
of those he would destroy.
I pray that love may never come to me
with murderous intent,
in rhythms measureless and wild.
Not fire nor stars have stronger bolts
than those of Aphrodite sent
by the hand of Eros, Zeus's child.

Ibid. l. 525

18 My tongue swore, but my mind was still
unpledged.[6]

Ibid. l. 612

19 Would that I were under the cliffs, in the secret
hiding-places of the rocks,
that Zeus might change me to a winged bird.[7]

Ibid. l. 732

20 I would win my way to the coast,
apple-bearing Hesperian coast
of which the minstrels sing,
where the Lord of the Ocean
denies the voyager further sailing,
and fixes the solemn limit of Heaven
which giant Atlas upholds.
There the streams flow with ambrosia
by Zeus's bed of love,
and holy Earth, the giver of life,
yields to the gods rich blessedness.[8]

Ibid. l. 742

21   In a case of dissension, never dare to judge till
you've heard the other side.[9]

*Heraclidae[10] [c. 428 B.C.] (quoted by
ARISTOPHANES, The Wasps)*

22   Leave no stone unturned.   *Ibid.*

23   I care for riches, to make gifts
To friends, or lead a sick man back to health
With ease and plenty. Else small aid is wealth
For daily gladness; once a man be done
With hunger, rich and poor are all as one.

Electra [413 B.C.],[8] l. 427

24   A coward turns away, but a brave man's choice
is danger.

Iphigenia in Tauris [c. 412 B.C.], l. 114

25   The day is for honest men, the night for thieves.

Ibid. l. 1026

26   Mankind . . . possesses two supreme blessings.
First of these is the goddess Demeter, or Earth—
whichever name you choose to call her by. It was she
who gave to man his nourishment of grain. But after
her there came the son of Semele, who matched her
present by inventing liquid wine as his gift to man.
For filled with that good gift, suffering mankind
forgets its grief; from it comes sleep; with it oblivion

---

[1]See *Job 3:3, 13:34.*
[2]See Pindar, 63:29.
[3]See *Romans 7:19*, 41:46, and Ovid, 101:25.
[4]Translated by DAVID GRENE.
[5]Second thoughts, they say, are best. —DRYDEN, *The Spanish Friar* [1681], *act II, sc. ii*

Is it so true that second thoughts are best? —TENNYSON, *Sea Dreams* [1864]

[6]See Sallust, 91:23.
[7]See *Psalm 55:6, 17:26.*
[8]Translated by GILBERT MURRAY.
[9]See Protagoras, 70:16, and Saint Augustine, 114:27.
[10]Translated by MORRIS HICKEY MORGAN.

of the troubles of the day. There is no other medicine for misery.[1]   *The Bacchae [c. 407 b.c.], l. 274*

1   Talk sense to a fool and he calls you foolish.
Ibid. l. 480

2   Slow but sure moves the might of the gods.[2]
Ibid. l. 882

3 What is wisdom? What gift of the gods
is held in glory like this:
to hold your hand victorious
over the heads of those you hate?
Glory is precious forever.
Ibid. l. 877

4 Humility, a sense of reverence before the sons of
heaven—
of all the prizes that a mortal man might win,
these, I say, are wisest; these are best.
Ibid. l. 1150

5   Yet do I hold that mortal foolish who strives
against the stress of necessity.[3]
Mad Heracles, l. 281

6   The company of just and righteous men is better
than wealth and a rich estate.
Aegeus,[4] fragment 7

7   A bad beginning makes a bad ending.
Aeolus,[4] fragment 32

8   Time will explain it all. He is a talker, and needs
no questioning before he speaks.
Ibid. fragment 38

9   Waste not fresh tears over old griefs.
Alexander,[4] fragment 44

10   The nobly born must nobly meet his fate.[5]
Alcymene,[4] fragment 100

11   Man's best possession is a sympathetic wife.
Antigone,[4] fragment 164

12 When good men die their goodness does not
perish,
But lives though they are gone. As for the bad,
All that was theirs dies and is buried with them.[6]
Temenidae,[4] fragment 734

13 An old man weds a tyrant, not a wife.
*Phoenix (quoted by Aristophanes,
Thesmophoriazusae), fragment 413*

14   Every man is like the company he is wont to
keep.[7]   *Ibid. 809*

[1]Translated by William Arrowsmith.
[2]See George Herbert, 244:38, and von Logau, 247:15.
[3]See The Seven Sages, 55:12.
[4]Translated by Morris Hickey Morgan.
[5]If there be any good in nobility, I trow it to be only this, that it imposeth a necessity upon those which are noble, that they should not suffer their nobility to degenerate from the virtues of their ancestors.—Boethius, *De Consolatione Philosophiae, III, 6, 25*
See Sophocles, 65:9, and the Duc de Lévis, 367:8.
[6]See Shakespeare, 188:28.
[7]Translated by Morris Hickey Morgan.
Familiar form: A man is known by the company he keeps.

15 Who knows but life be that which men call death,
And death what men call life?[8]
Phrixus,[4] fragment 830

16 Whoso neglects learning in his youth,
Loses the past and is dead for the future.[9]
Ibid. 927

17   The gods
Visit the sins of the fathers upon the children.[10]
Ibid. 970

18   Those whom God wishes to destroy, he first
makes mad.[11]   *Fragment*

19   These men won eight victories over the Syracusans when the favor of the gods was equal for both
sides.   *Epitaph for the Athenians Slain in Sicily*

Herodotus
c. 485 – c. 425 b.c.

20   Men trust their ears less than their eyes.
The Histories of Herodotus, bk. I, ch. 8

21   A woman takes off her claim to respect along
with her garments.[12]   *Ibid.*

22   In peace, children inter their parents; war violates
the order of nature and causes parents to inter their
children.   *Ibid. 87*

23   [The Persians] are accustomed to deliberate
about the most important matters when they are
drunk.   *Ibid. 133*

24   It was a kind of Cadmean victory.[13]
Ibid. 166

25   For great wrongdoing there are great punishments from the gods.   *Ibid. II, 120*

[8]See Heraclitus, 62:19.
[9]See Thucydides, 71:19, and Santayana, 588:6.
[10]For the sins of your fathers you, though guiltless, must suffer.—Horace, *Odes, III, 6:1*
The sins of the father are to be laid upon the children.—Shakespeare, *The Merchant of Venice, act III, sc. v, l. 1*
See *Exodus* 20:5, 9:10.
[11]In Boswell's *Life of Johnson* [1791], vol. 2, pp. 442–443 (Everyman edition), this is quoted as a saying which everybody repeats but nobody knows where to find.
Whom Fortune wishes to destroy she first makes mad.—Publilius Syrus, *Maxim 911*
When falls on man the anger of the gods, / First from his mind they banish understanding.—Lycurgus [fl. 820 b.c.]
For those whom God to ruin has designed, / He fits for fate, and first destroys their mind.—Dryden, *The Hind and the Panther* [1687], *pt. III, l. 1093*
Whom the Gods would destroy they first make mad.—Longfellow, *The Masque of Pandora* [1875], *VI*
See Anonymous: Latin, 119:25.
[12]See Chaucer, 131:8.
[13]Polyneices and Eteocles, sons of Oedipus and descendants of Cadmus, fought for the possession of Thebes and killed each other. Hence, a Cadmean victory means one where victor and vanquished suffer alike.
See also Pyrrhus, 82:11 ("Pyrrhic victory").

1   If a man insisted always on being serious, and never allowed himself a bit of fun and relaxation, he would go mad or become unstable without knowing it.   *Histories, bk. II, ch. 173*

2   It is better to be envied than pitied.[1]
Ibid. III, 52

3   Envy is born in a man from the start.
Ibid. 80

4   Force has no place where there is need of skill.
Ibid. 127

5   From the foot, Hercules.[2]   *Ibid. IV, 82*

6   It is the gods' custom to bring low all things of surpassing greatness.[3]   *Ibid. VII, 10*

7   Haste in every business brings failures.   *Ibid.*

8   When life is so burdensome, death has become for man a sought-after refuge.   *Ibid. 46*

9   Circumstances rule men; men do not rule circumstances.   *Ibid. 49*

10   Great deeds are usually wrought at great risks.
Ibid. 50

11   Not snow, no, nor rain, nor heat, nor night keeps them from accomplishing their appointed courses with all speed.[4]   *Ibid. VIII, 98*

12   The king's might is greater than human, and his arm is very long.   *Ibid. 140*

13   This is the bitterest pain among men, to have much knowledge but no power.   *Ibid. IX, 16*

14   In soft regions are born soft men.   *Ibid. 122*

Protagoras
c. 485 – c. 410 B.C.

15   Man is the measure of all things.
Fragment 1

16   There are two sides to every question.[5]
From DIOGENES LAERTIUS, *Lives of Eminent Philosophers, Protagoras, bk. IX, sec. 51*

[1]Also in PINDAR, *Pythian Odes, I, 164.*
[2]*Ex pede, Herculem.* From AULUS GELLIUS [c. 123–165] (*Noctes Atticae, I, 1*), who tells how Pythagoras deduced the stature of Hercules from the length of his foot.
See Anonymous: Latin, 119:1.
[3]It is the lofty pine that by the storm / Is oftener tossed; / towers fall with heavier crash / Which higher soar.—HORACE, *Odes, II, 10:9*
The bigger they come, the harder they fall.—*Boxing expression attributed to* ROBERT FITZSIMMONS [1862–1917] *and to* JOHN L. SULLIVAN [1858–1918]; *probably much earlier than either*
[4]Neither snow, nor rain, nor heat, nor gloom of night stays these couriers from the swift completion of their appointed rounds.—*Inscription, New York City Post Office, adapted from* HERODOTUS
[5]See Euripides, 68:21, and Saint Augustine, 114:27.

Agis
Fifth century B.C.

17   The Lacedemonians are not wont to ask how many the enemy are, but where they are.
From PLUTARCH, *Apothegms, Agis*

Socrates[6]
469–399 B.C.

18   Often when looking at a mass of things for sale, he would say to himself, "How many things I have no need of!"
From DIOGENES LAERTIUS, *Lives of Eminent Philosophers, bk. II, sec. 25*

19   Having the fewest wants, I am nearest to the gods.   *Ibid. 27*

20   There is only one good, knowledge, and one evil, ignorance.   *Ibid. 31*

21   My divine sign indicates the future to me.
Ibid. 32

22   I know nothing except the fact of my ignorance.[7]
Ibid.

23   Bad men live that they may eat and drink, whereas good men eat and drink that they may live.[8]
From PLUTARCH, *How a Young Man Ought to Hear Poems, 4*

24   I am not an Athenian or a Greek, but a citizen of the world.   *From* PLUTARCH, *Of Banishment*

25   Crito, I owe a cock to Asclepius; will you remember to pay the debt?
From PLATO, *Phaedo (Socrates' last words)*

Democritus
c. 460 – c. 370 B.C.

26   Whatever a poet writes with enthusiasm and a divine inspiration is very fine.[9]   *Fragment 18*

27   In truth we know nothing, for truth lies in the depth.   *Fragment 117*

28   By convention there is color, by convention sweetness, by convention bitterness, but in reality there are atoms and space.   *Fragment 125*

29   Word is a shadow of deed.   *Fragment 145*

[6]Much of Plato, especially in the *Apology* and *Phaedo,* is thought to be direct quotation from Socrates. See Plato, 74:19.
[7]See Milton, 261:3.
[8]He used to say that other men lived to eat, but that he ate to live.—DIOGENES LAERTIUS, *Lives of Eminent Philosophers, Socrates, sec. 14*
We must eat to live and live to eat.—FIELDING, *The Miser, act III, sc. iii*
See Molière, 269:20, and Franklin, 309:6.
[9]Apparently the earliest reference to the madness or divine inspiration of poets.
See Robert Burton, 234:13; Wordsworth, 374:9; and Robert Lowell, 742:16.

Hippocrates

c. 460–377 B.C.

1   I swear by Apollo Physician, by Asclepius, by Health, by Panacea, and by all the gods and goddesses, making them my witnesses, that I will carry out, according to my ability and judgment, this oath and this indenture. . . . I will use treatment to help the sick according to my ability and judgment, but never with a view to injury and wrongdoing. Neither will I administer a poison to anybody when asked to do so, nor will I suggest such a course. Similarly, I will not give to a woman a pessary to cause abortion. I will keep pure and holy both my life and my art. . . . In whatsoever houses I enter, I will enter to help the sick, and I will abstain from all intentional wrongdoing and harm, especially from abusing the bodies of man or woman, bond or free. And whatsoever I shall see or hear in the course of my profession in my intercourse with men, if it be what should not be published abroad, I will never divulge, holding such things to be holy secrets. Now if I carry out this oath, and break it not, may I gain forever reputation among all men for my life and for my art.

The Physician's Oath[1]

2   As to diseases make a habit of two things—to help, or at least, to do no harm.[2]

Epidemics, bk. I, ch. 11

3   Healing is a matter of time, but it is sometimes also a matter of opportunity.   *Precepts,*[1] *ch. 1*

4   Time is that wherein there is opportunity, and opportunity is that wherein there is no great time.

Ibid.

5   Sometimes give your services for nothing, calling to mind a previous benefaction or present satisfaction. And if there be an opportunity of serving one who is a stranger in financial straits, give full assistance to all such. For where there is love of man, there is also love of the art. For some patients, though conscious that their condition is perilous, recover their health simply through their contentment with the goodness of the physician. And it is well to superintend the sick to make them well, to care for the healthy to keep them well, also to care for one's own self, so as to observe what is seemly.[3]

Ibid. 6

6   If for the sake of a crowded audience you do wish to hold a lecture, your ambition is no laudable one, and at least avoid all citations from the poets, for to quote them argues feeble industry.   *Ibid. 12*

7   Opposites are cures for opposites.

Breaths, bk. I

8   Medicine is the most distinguished of all the arts, but through the ignorance of those who practice it,

and of those who casually judge such practitioners, it is now of all the arts by far the least esteemed.

Law, bk. I

9   There are in fact two things, science and opinion; the former begets knowledge, the latter ignorance.

Ibid. IV

10   Things that are holy are revealed only to men who are holy.[4]   *Ibid. V*

11   Idleness and lack of occupation tend—nay are dragged—towards evil.   *Decorum, bk. I*

12   A wise man should consider that health is the greatest of human blessings, and learn how by his own thought to derive benefit from his illnesses.

Regimen in Health,[5] *bk. IX*

13   Life is short, the art long,[6] opportunity fleeting, experiment treacherous, judgment difficult.

Aphorisms,[5] *sec. I, 1*

14   For extreme diseases extreme strictness of treatment is most efficacious.[7]   *Ibid. 6*

15   Many admire, few know.

Regimen,[5] *bk. I, sec. 24*

16   Male and female have the power to fuse into one solid, both because both are nourished in both and because soul is the same thing in all living creatures, although the body of each is different.   *Ibid. 28*

17   Prayer indeed is good, but while calling on the gods a man should himself lend a hand.[8]

Ibid. IV, 87

Thucydides[9]

c. 460–400 B.C.

18   Thucydides, an Athenian, wrote the history of the war between the Peloponnesians and the Athenians; he began at the moment that it broke out, believing that it would be a great war, and more memorable than any that had preceded it.

The History of the Peloponnesian War [431–413 B.C.], bk. I, sec. 1

19   With reference to the narrative of events, far from permitting myself to derive it from the first source that came to hand, I did not even trust my own impressions, but it rests partly on what I saw myself, partly on what others saw for me, the accuracy of the report being always tried by the most severe and detailed tests possible. My conclusions have cost me some labor from the want of coincidence between accounts of the same occurrences by different eyewitnesses, arising sometimes from imperfect memory, sometimes from undue partiality for one side or

---

[1]Translated by W. H. S. JONES (Loeb Classical Library).
[2]Often cited in Latin: primum non nocere.
See Nightingale, 492:3.
[3]See Plato, 75:5.

[4]See Manilius, 103:16.
[5]Translated by W. H. S. JONES (Loeb Classical Library).
[6]Vita brevis est, ars longa.—SENECA, *De Brevitate Vitae, I, 1*
[7]See Shakespeare, 198:9.
[8]See Aesop, 59:15.
[9]Translated by RICHARD LIVINGSTONE.

the other. The absence of romance in my history will, I fear, detract somewhat from its interest; but I shall be content if it is judged useful by those inquirers who desire an exact knowledge of the past as an aid to the interpretation of the future,[1] which in the course of human things must resemble if it does not reflect it. My history has been composed to be an everlasting possession, not the showpiece of an hour.[2]   *Peloponnesian War, bk. I, sec. 22*

1   The great wish of some is to avenge themselves on some particular enemy, the great wish of others to save their own pocket. Slow in assembling, they devote a very small fraction of the time to the consideration of any public object, most of it to the prosecution of their own objects. Meanwhile each fancies that no harm will come of his neglect, that it is the business of somebody else to look after this or that for him; and so, by the same notion being entertained by all separately, the common cause imperceptibly decays.[3]   *Ibid. 141*

2   Our constitution is named a democracy, because it is in the hands not of the few but of the many. But our laws secure equal justice for all in their private disputes, and our public opinion welcomes and honors talent in every branch of achievement, not for any sectional reason but on grounds of excellence alone. And as we give free play to all in our public life, so we carry the same spirit into our daily relations with one another. . . . Open and friendly in our private intercourse, in our public acts we keep strictly within the control of law. We acknowledge the restraint of reverence; we are obedient to whomsoever is set in authority, and to the laws, more especially to those which offer protection to the oppressed and those unwritten ordinances whose transgression brings admitted shame.
      Ibid. II (Funeral Oration of Pericles), 37

3   We are lovers of beauty without extravagance, and lovers of wisdom without unmanliness. Wealth to us is not mere material for vainglory but an opportunity for achievement; and poverty we think it no disgrace to acknowledge but a real degradation to make no effort to overcome.   *Ibid. 40*

4   But the bravest are surely those who have the clearest vision of what is before them, glory and danger alike, and yet notwithstanding go out to meet it.   *Ibid.*

5   We secure our friends not by accepting favors but by doing them.[4]   *Ibid.*

[1]See Euripides, 69:16, and Santayana, 588:6.
[2]See Ranke, 418:22.
[3]Quoted by President John F. Kennedy in Frankfurt [June 25, 1963].
[4]Rather by conferring than by accepting favors, they [the Romans] established friendly relations.—SALLUST, *The War with Catiline* [c. 40 B.C.], 6

6   In a word I claim that our city as a whole is an education to Greece.   *Ibid. 41*

7   Fix your eyes on the greatness of Athens as you have it before you day by day, fall in love with her, and when you feel her great, remember that this greatness was won by men with courage, with knowledge of their duty, and with a sense of honor in action . . . So they gave their bodies to the commonwealth and received, each for his own memory, praise that will never die, and with it the grandest of all sepulchers, not that in which their mortal bones are laid, but a home in the minds of men, where their glory remains fresh to stir to speech or action as the occasion comes by. For the whole earth is the sepulcher of famous men; and their story is not graven only on stone over their native earth, but lives on far away, without visible symbol, woven into the stuff of other men's lives. For you now it remains to rival what they have done and, knowing the secret of happiness to be freedom and the secret of freedom a brave heart, not idly to stand aside from the enemy's onset.   *Ibid. 43*

8   Great is the glory of the woman who occasions the least talk among men, whether of praise or of blame.   *Ibid. 45*

9   For human nature is as surely made arrogant by consideration as it is awed by firmness.
      Ibid. III, 39

10   Men make the city, and not walls or ships without men in them.
      Ibid. VII, 77 (Address of Nicias to the Athenians at Syracuse)

11   This or the like was the cause of the death of a man [Nicias] who, of all the Greeks in my time, least deserved such a fate, for he had lived in the practice of every virtue.   *Ibid. VIII, 86*

12   This was the greatest event in the war, or, in my opinion, in Greek history; at once most glorious to the victors and most calamitous to the conquered. They were beaten at all points and altogether; their sufferings in every way were great. They were totally destroyed—their fleet, their army, everything—and few out of many returned home. So ended the Sicilian expedition.   *Ibid. 87*

Aristophanes
c. 450–385 B.C.

13 For then, in wrath, the Olympian Pericles
      Thundered and lightened, and confounded Hellas
      Enacting laws which ran like drinking songs.[5]
            Acharnians [425 B.C.], l. 530

14 When men drink, then they are rich and successful
      and win lawsuits and are happy and help
      their friends.

[5]Translated by B. B. ROGERS (Loeb Classical Library).

Quickly, bring me a beaker of wine, so that I may
 wet my mind and say something clever.
       Knights [424 B.C.], l. 92

1 You have all the characteristics of a popular
 politician: a horrible voice, bad breeding, and
 a vulgar manner.
         Ibid. l. 217

2 To make the worse appear the better reason.[1]
   Clouds [423 B.C.], l. 114 and elsewhere

3 Haven't you sometimes seen a cloud that looked
 like a centaur?
 Or a leopard perhaps? Or a wolf? Or a bull?[2]
         Ibid. l. 346

4 Old men are children for a second time.[3]
        Ibid. l. 1417

5 This is what extremely grieves us, that a man who
 never fought
 Should contrive our fees to pilfer, one who for his
 native land
 Never to this day had oar, or lance, or blister in
 his hand.
      Wasps[4] *[422 B.C.], l. 1117*

6 Let each man exercise the art he knows.
        Ibid. l. 1431

7 You cannot teach a crab to walk straight.
     Peace [421 B.C.], l. 1083

8 [On the nightingale] Lord Zeus, listen to the little
 bird's voice; he has filled the whole thicket
 with honeyed song.
      Birds [414 B.C.], l. 223

9 Bringing owls to Athens.[5]
        Ibid. l. 301

10 The wise learn many things from their enemies.
        Ibid. l. 375

11 Full of wiles, full of guile, at all times, in all ways,
 Are the children of Men.[4]
        Ibid. l. 451

12 Mankind, fleet of life, like tree leaves, weak
 creatures of clay, unsubstantial as shadows,
 wingless, ephemeral, wretched, mortal and
 dreamlike.
        Ibid. l. 685

13 Somewhere, what with all these clouds, and all
 this air,
 There must be a rare name, somewhere . . .
 How do you like "Cloud-Cuckoo-Land"?[6]
        Ibid. l. 817

14 Halcyon days.[7]
        Ibid. l. 1594

15 A woman's time of opportunity is short, and if
 she doesn't seize it, no one wants to marry
 her, and she sits watching for omens.
    Lysistrata [411 B.C.], l. 596

16 There is no animal more invincible than a
 woman, nor fire either, nor any wildcat so
 ruthless.
        Ibid. l. 1014

17 These impossible women! How they do get
 around us!
 The poet was right: can't live with them, or
 without them![8]
        Ibid. l. 1038

18 Under every stone lurks a politician.[9]
   Thesmophoriazusae [410 B.C.], l. 530

19 There's nothing worse in the world than
 shameless woman—save some other woman.
        Ibid. l. 531

20 Shall I crack any of those old jokes, master,
 At which the audience never fail to laugh?
      Frogs[4] *[405 B.C.], l. 1*

21 Brekekekex, ko-ax, ko-ax.[10]
     Ibid. l. 209 and elsewhere

22 A savage-creating stubborn-pulling fellow,
 Uncurbed, unfettered, uncontrolled of speech,
 Unperiphrastic, bombastiloquent.[11]
        Ibid. l. 837

23 High thoughts must have high language.[6]
        Ibid. l. 1058

24 Who knows whether living is dying, and breathing
 Is eating, and sleeping is a wool blanket?
        Ibid. l. 1477

25 Blest the man who possesses a
 Keen intelligent mind.
        Ibid. l. 1482

26 I am amazed that anyone who has made a fortune
 should send for his friends.
    Plutus [c. 388 B.C.], l. 340

27 We say that poverty is the sister of beggary.
        Ibid. l. 549

28 Even if you persuade me, you won't persuade me.
        Ibid. l. 600

---

[1]See Milton, 257:1.
[2]Translated by DUDLEY FITTS.
See Shakespeare, 197:18 and 218:3.
[3]See Shakespeare, 195:32.
[4]Translated by B. B. ROGERS (Loeb Classical Library).
[5]See Horace, 95:8.
[6]Translated by DUDLEY FITTS.

[7]The appellation of Halcyon days, which was applied to a
rare and bloodless week of repose. —GIBBON, *Decline and Fall
of the Roman Empire* [1776–1788], *ch.* 48
See Shakespeare, 163:7.
[8]Translated by DUDLEY FITTS.
See Ovid, 101:12, and Martial, 106:24.
[9]A play on the proverb: Under every stone lurks a scorpion.
[10]Adopted as a Yale College cheer.
[11]Refers to Aeschylus.

1 A man's homeland is wherever he prospers.
Plutus, l. 1151

Agathon
c. 448–400 B.C.

2   This only is denied to God: the power to undo the past.
From ARISTOTLE, *Nicomachean Ethics, bk. VI, ch. 2*

Agesilaus
444–400 B.C.

3   If all men were just, there would be no need of valor.   *From* PLUTARCH, *Lives, Agesilaus, sec. 23*

4   It is circumstance and proper timing that give an action its character and make it either good or bad.
Ibid. 36

Xenophon
c. 430 – c. 355 B.C.

5   Apollo said that everyone's true worship was that which he found in use in the place where he chanced to be.
Recollections of Socrates, bk. I, ch. 3, sec. 1

6   The sea! The sea![1]   *Anabasis, IV, 7, 24*

7   I knew my son was mortal.[2]
From DIOGENES LAERTIUS, *Lives of Eminent Philosophers, Xenophon, bk. II, sec. 55*

Zeuxis
fl. 400 B.C.

8   Criticism comes easier than craftsmanship.
From PLINY THE ELDER, *Natural History*

Plato[3]
c. 428–348 B.C.

9   We who of old left the booming surge of the Aegean lie here in the mid-plain of Ecbatana: farewell, renowned Eretria once our country; farewell, Athens nigh to Euboea; farewell, dear sea.[4]
The Greek Anthology [1906],[5] III, 10

10   Beloved Pan, and all ye other gods who haunt this place, give me beauty in the inward soul; and may

the outward and inward man be at one. May I reckon the wise to be the wealthy, and may I have such a quantity of gold as none but the temperate can carry.   *Dialogues, Phaedrus, sec. 279*

11   Friends have all things in common.[6]   *Ibid.*

12   And the true order of going, or being led by another, to the things of love, is to begin from the beauties of earth and mount upwards for the sake of that other beauty, using these steps only, and from one going on to two, and from two to all fair forms to fair practices, and from fair practices to fair notions, until from fair notions he arrives at the notion of absolute beauty, and at last knows what the essence of beauty is.   *Ibid. Symposium, 211*

13   Beholding beauty with the eye of the mind, he will be enabled to bring forth, not images of beauty, but realities (for he has hold not of an image but of a reality), and bringing forth and nourishing true virtue to become the friend of God and be immortal, if mortal man may.   *Ibid. 212*

14   Socrates is a doer of evil, who corrupts the youth; and who does not believe in the gods of the state, but has other new divinities of his own. Such is the charge.   *Ibid. Apology, 24*

15   The life which is unexamined is not worth living.
Ibid. 38

16   Either death is a state of nothingness and utter unconsciousness, or, as men say, there is a change and migration of the soul from this world to another. . . . Now if death be of such a nature, I say that to die is to gain; for eternity is then only a single night.   *Ibid. 40*

17   No evil can happen to a good man, either in life or after death.   *Ibid. 41*

18   The hour of departure has arrived, and we go our ways—I to die, and you to live. Which is better God only knows.   *Ibid. 42*

19   Man is a prisoner who has no right to open the door of his prison and run away. . . . A man should wait, and not take his own life until God summons him.   *Ibid. Phaedo,[7] 62*

20   Must not all things at the last be swallowed up in death?   *Ibid. 72*

21   Will you not allow that I have as much of the spirit of prophecy in me as the swans? For they, when they perceive that they must die, having sung all their life long, do then sing more lustily than ever, rejoicing in the thought that they are going to the god they serve.[8]   *Ibid. 85*

---

[1]Thalatta! Thalatta! / Hail to thee, O Sea, ageless and eternal!—HEINE, *Thalatta! Thalatta!, st. 1*

[2]When his son was killed in battle.

[3]Translated by BENJAMIN JOWETT unless otherwise noted.
Asclepius cured the body: to make men whole / Phoebus sent Plato, healer of the soul.—*On Plato's Grave,* anonymous inscription translated by WILLIAM J. PHILBIN in *The Greek Anthology* [1973], edited by PETER JAY

[4]On the Eretrian exiles settled in Persia by Darius.

[5]Edited by J. W. MACKAIL.

[6]Also in EURIPIDES, *Orestes, l. 735.*
See Pythagoras, 58:9, and Sallust, 91:25.

[7]See Socrates, 70:n6.

[8]The jalous swan, ayens his deth that singeth.—CHAUCER, *The Parliament of Fowls* [1380–1386], *l. 342*
I will play the swan and die in music.—SHAKESPEARE, *Othello, act V, sc. ii, l. 245*

1   The partisan, when he is engaged in a dispute, cares nothing about the rights of the question, but is anxious only to convince his hearers of his own assertions.   *Ibid. 91*

2   False words are not only evil in themselves, but they infect the soul with evil.   *Ibid.*

3   The soul takes nothing with her to the other world but her education and culture; and these, it is said, are of the greatest service or of the greatest injury to the dead man, at the very beginning of his journey thither.   *Ibid. 107*

4   He who is of a calm and happy nature will hardly feel the pressure of age, but to him who is of an opposite disposition youth and age are equally a burden.   *The Republic, bk. I, 329–D*

5   No physician, insofar as he is a physician, considers his own good in what he prescribes, but the good of his patient; for the true physician is also a ruler having the human body as a subject, and is not a mere moneymaker.[1]   *Ibid. 342–D*

6   When there is an income tax, the just man will pay more and the unjust less on the same amount of income.   *Ibid. 343–D*

7   Mankind censure injustice fearing that they may be the victims of it, and not because they shrink from committing it.   *Ibid. 344–C*

8   The beginning is the most important part of the work.[2]   *Ibid. 377–B*

9   The judge should not be young; he should have learned to know evil, not from his own soul, but from late and long observation of the nature of evil in others: knowledge should be his guide, not personal experience.   *Ibid. III, 409–B*

10   Everything that deceives may be said to enchant.   *Ibid. 413–C*

11   How, then, might we contrive . . . one noble lie to persuade if possible the rulers themselves, but failing that the rest of the city?[3]   *Ibid. 414–C*

12   Wealth is the parent of luxury and indolence, and poverty of meanness and viciousness, and both of discontent.[4]   *Ibid. IV, 422–A*

13   The direction in which education starts a man will determine his future life.   *Ibid. 425–B*

14   What is the prime of life? May it not be defined as a period of about twenty years in a woman's life, and thirty in a man's?   *Ibid. V, 460–E*

15   Until philosophers are kings, or the kings and princes of this world have the spirit and power of philosophy, and political greatness and wisdom meet in one, and those commoner natures who pursue either to the exclusion of the other are compelled to stand aside, cities will never have rest from their evils—no, nor the human race, as I believe—and then only will this our State have a possibility of life and behold the light of day.   *Ibid. 473–C*

16   Let there be one man who has a city obedient to his will, and he might bring into existence the ideal polity about which the world is so incredulous.   *Ibid. 502–B*

17   Behold! human beings living in an underground den . . . Like ourselves . . . they see only their own shadows, or the shadows of one another, which the fire throws on the opposite wall of the cave.   *Ibid. VII, 515–B*

18   Astronomy compels the soul to look upwards and leads us from this world to another.   *Ibid. 529*

19   I have hardly ever known a mathematician who was capable of reasoning.   *Ibid. 531–E*

20   Solon was under a delusion when he said that a man when he grows old may learn many things[5]—for he can no more learn much than he can run much; youth is the time for any extraordinary toil.   *Ibid. 536–D*

21   Bodily exercise, when compulsory, does no harm to the body; but knowledge which is acquired under compulsion obtains no hold on the mind.   *Ibid. 536–E*

22   Let early education be a sort of amusement; you will then be better able to find out the natural bent.   *Ibid. 537*

23   Oligarchy: A government resting on a valuation of property, in which the rich have power and the poor man is deprived of it.   *Ibid. VIII, 550–C*

24   Democracy, which is a charming form of government, full of variety and disorder, and dispensing a sort of equality to equals and unequals alike.   *Ibid. 558–C*

25   Democracy passes into despotism.[6]   *Ibid. 562–A*

26   The people have always some champion whom they set over them and nurse into greatness. . . . This and no other is the root from which a tyrant springs; when he first appears he is a protector.   *Ibid. 565–C*

27   In the early days of his power, he is full of smiles, and he salutes everyone whom he meets.   *Ibid. 566–D*

28   When the tyrant has disposed of foreign enemies by conquest or treaty, and there is nothing to fear

---

See Shakespeare, 170:20 and 181:2; and Anonymous, 777:6.

[1]See Hippocrates, 71:5.

[2]Proverbial. Also in *Laws, VI, 2.*
See Aristotle, 78:26; Horace, 97:8; and John Heywood, 141:-21.

[3]Translated by Paul Shorey (Loeb Classical Library).

[4]See *I Timothy 6:10*, 45:22, and Sophocles, 66:7.

[5]See Solon, 55:17.

[6]Translated by F. M. Cornford.

from them, then he is always stirring up some war or other, in order that the people may require a leader.
Republic, bk. VIII, 566 – E

1   There are three arts which are concerned with all things: one which uses, another which makes, a third which imitates them.   *Ibid. X, 601 – D*

2   No human thing is of serious importance.
Ibid. 604 – C

3   The soul of man is immortal and imperishable.
Ibid. 608 – D

4   If a person shows that such things as wood, stones, and the like, being many are also one, we admit that he shows the coexistence of the one and many, but he does not show that the many are one or the one many; he is uttering not a paradox but a truism.   *Dialogues, Parmenides, 129*

5   The absolute natures or kinds are known severally by the absolute idea of knowledge.
Ibid. 134

6   If a man, fixing his attention on these and the like difficulties, does away with ideas of things and will not admit that every individual thing has its own determinate idea which is always one and the same, he will have nothing on which his mind can rest; and so he will utterly destroy the power of reasoning.
Ibid. 135

7   You cannot conceive the many without the one.
Ibid. 166

8   Let us affirm what seems to be the truth, that, whether one is or is not, one and the others in relation to themselves and one another, all of them, in every way, are and are not, and appear to be and appear not to be.   *Ibid.*

9   Well, my art of midwifery is in most respects like theirs; but differs, in that I attend men and not women, and I look after their souls when they are in labor, and not after their bodies: and the triumph of my art is in thoroughly examining whether the thought which the mind of the young man brings forth is a false idol or a noble and true birth.
Ibid. Theaetetus, 150

10   He [the philosopher] does not hold aloof in order that he may gain a reputation; but the truth is, that the outer form of him only is in the city: his mind, disdaining the littlenesses and nothingnesses of human beings, is "flying all abroad" as Pindar says, measuring earth and heaven and the things which are under and on the earth and above the heaven, interrogating the whole nature of each and all in their entirety, but not condescending to anything which is within reach.   *Ibid. 173*

11   I would have you imagine, then, that there exists in the mind of man a block of wax, which is of different sizes in different men; harder, moister, and having more or less of purity in one than another, and in some of an intermediate quality. . . . Let us

say that this tablet is a gift of Memory, the mother of the Muses; and that when we wish to remember anything which we have seen, or heard, or thought in our own minds, we hold the wax to the perceptions and thoughts, and in that material receive the impression of them as from the seal of a ring; and that we remember and know what is imprinted as long as the image lasts; but when the image is effaced, or cannot be taken, then we forget and do not know.   *Ibid. 191*

12   Let us now suppose that in the mind of each man there is an aviary of all sorts of birds — some flocking together apart from the rest, others in small groups, others solitary, flying anywhere and everywhere. . . . We may suppose that the birds are kinds of knowledge, and that when we were children, this receptacle was empty; whenever a man has gotten and detained in the enclosure a kind of knowledge, he may be said to have learned or discovered the thing which is the subject of the knowledge: and this is to know.   *Ibid. 197*

13   The greatest penalty of evildoing — namely, to grow into the likeness of bad men.   *Laws, 728*

14   Of all the animals, the boy is the most unmanageable.   *Ibid. 808*

15   You are young, my son, and, as the years go by, time will change and even reverse many of your present opinions. Refrain therefore awhile from setting yourself up as a judge of the highest matters.
Ibid. 888

16   And this which you deem of no moment is the very highest of all: that is whether you have a right idea of the gods, whereby you may live your life well or ill.   *Ibid.*

17   Not one of them who took up in his youth with this opinion that there are no gods ever continued until old age faithful to his conviction.   *Ibid.*

Iphicrates
c. 419 – 348 b.c.

18   My family history begins with me, but yours ends with you.[1]
From PLUTARCH, Apothegms, Iphicrates

Phocion
c. 402 – 317 b.c.

19   Have I inadvertently said some evil thing?[2]
From PLUTARCH, Apothegms, Phocion, sec. 10

---

[1]Iphicrates, a shoemaker's son who became a famous general, said this to Harmodius of distinguished ancestry when he reviled him for his mean birth.
Curtius Rufus seems to be descended from himself. — TIBERIUS [42 B.C. – A.D. 37]. From TACITUS, *Annals, XI, 21*
I am my own ancestor [Moi, je suis mon ancêtre]. — ANDOCHE JUNOT [1771 – 1813]
[2]Said when an opinion he delivered pleased the people.

1 The good have no need of an advocate.

Ibid.

Diogenes the Cynic
c. 400 – c. 325 B.C.

2 [When asked by Alexander if he wanted anything:] Stand a little out of my sun.

From PLUTARCH, *Lives, Alexander, sec. 14*

3 Plato having defined man to be a two-legged animal without feathers,[1] Diogenes plucked a cock and brought it into the Academy, and said, "This is Plato's man."[2] On which account this addition was made to the definition: "With broad flat nails."

From DIOGENES LAERTIUS, *Lives of Eminent Philosophers, Diogenes, sec. 6*

4 [When asked what was the proper time for supper:] If you are a rich man, whenever you please; and if you are a poor man, whenever you can.[3]

Ibid.

5 I am looking for an honest man.[4] *Ibid.*

6 The sun too penetrates into privies, but is not polluted by them.[5] *Ibid.*

Antiphanes
c. 388 – c. 311 B.C.

7 We must have richness of soul.

Greek Comic Fragments, no. 570

Aristotle[6]
384–322 B.C.

8 Liars when they speak the truth are not believed.

From DIOGENES LAERTIUS, *Lives of Eminent Philosophers, bk. V, sec. 17*

9 Hope is a waking dream. *Ibid. 18*

10 What soon grows old? Gratitude. *Ibid.*

11 Beauty is the gift of God. *Ibid. 19*

12 Educated men are as much superior to uneducated men as the living are to the dead.[7] *Ibid.*

13 What is a friend? A single soul dwelling in two bodies.[8] *Ibid. 20*

14 I have gained this by philosophy: that I do without being commanded what others do only from fear of the law.[9] *Ibid. 21*

15 We should behave to our friends as we would wish our friends to behave to us.[10] *Ibid.*

16 Education is the best provision for old age.

Ibid.

17 If purpose, then, is inherent in art, so is it in Nature also. The best illustration is the case of a man being his own physician, for Nature is like that —agent and patient at once.

Physics,[11] *bk. II, ch. 8*

18 Time crumbles things; everything grows old under the power of Time and is forgotten through the lapse of Time. *Ibid. IV, 12*

19 The least initial deviation from the truth is multiplied later a thousandfold.

On the Heavens, bk. I, ch. 5

20 In all things of nature there is something of the marvelous. *Parts of Animals, bk. I, ch. 5*

21 All men by nature desire knowledge.

Metaphysics, bk. I, ch. 1

22 The final cause, then, produces motion through being loved.[12] *Ibid. 7*

23 The actuality of thought is life. *Ibid. XII, 7*

24 It is of itself that the divine thought thinks (since it is the most excellent of things), and its thinking is a thinking on thinking. *Ibid. 9*

25 Every science and every inquiry, and similarly every activity and pursuit, is thought to aim at some good. *Nicomachean Ethics, bk. I, ch. 1*

26 While both [Plato and truth] are dear, piety requires us to honor truth above our friends.[13]

Ibid. 6

---

[1]See Dryden, 274:5.

[2]Seeing that the human race falls into the same classification as the feathered creatures, we must divide the biped class into featherless and feathered.—PLATO, *The Statesman, 266–E*

[3]The rich when he is hungry, the poor when he has anything to eat.—RABELAIS, *Works, bk. IV* [1548], *ch. 64*

[4]Attributed also to AESOP.

[5]The spiritual virtue of a sacrament is like light: although it passes among the impure, it is not polluted.—SAINT AUGUSTINE, *Tract on Saint John, ch. 5:15*

The sun shineth upon the dunghill, and is not corrupted.—LYLY, *Euphues* [1579]

The sun, which passeth through pollutions and itself remains as pure as before.—FRANCIS BACON, *Advancement of Learning* [1605], *bk. II*

Truth is as impossible to be soiled by any outward touch as the sunbeam.—MILTON, *The Doctrine and Discipline of Divorce* [1643]

[6]Chiefly from *The Basic Works of Aristotle*, edited by RICHARD MCKEON.

[7]This used to be quoted "with great warmth" by Dr. Johnson, according to BOSWELL, *Life of Johnson* [1791].

[8]Andrágathos, my soul's half.—MELEAGER. From *The Greek Anthology* [1906], edited by J. W. MACKAIL, *XII, 52*

See Zeno, 81:22; Cicero, 88:9; Horace, 95:16; and Donne, 229:12.

[9]Also attributed to Xenocrates [396–314 B.C.] by Cicero.

[10]See *Matthew 7:12,* 34:8; Confucius, 61:30; Hillel, 102:7; and Chesterfield, 304:21.

[11]Translated by PHILIP H. WICKSTEED and FRANCIS CORNFORD (Loeb Classical Library).

[12]See Dante, 127:4.

[13]Amicus Plato, sed magis amica veritas [Plato is dear to me, but dearer still is truth]. Adapted from a medieval life of Aristotle.

1   One swallow does not make a summer.[1]
Nicomachean Ethics, bk. I, ch. 7

2   For the things we have to learn before we can do them, we learn by doing them.   *Ibid. II, 1*

3   It is possible to fail in many ways . . . while to succeed is possible only in one way (for which reason also one is easy and the other difficult—to miss the mark easy, to hit it difficult).   *Ibid. 6*

4   We must as second best . . . take the least of the evils.[2]   *Ibid. 9*

5   A man is the origin of his action.[3]
Ibid. III, 3

6   Without friends no one would choose to live, though he had all other goods.   *Ibid. VIII, 1*

7   To be conscious that we are perceiving or thinking is to be conscious of our own existence.[4]
Ibid. IX, 9

8   To enjoy the things we ought and to hate the things we ought has the greatest bearing on excellence of character.   *Ibid. X, 1*

9   If happiness is activity in accordance with excellence, it is reasonable that it should be in accordance with the highest excellence.   *Ibid. 7*

10   We make war that we may live in peace.
Ibid.

11   With regard to excellence, it is not enough to know, but we must try to have and use it.
Ibid. 9

12   Man is by nature a political animal.
Politics, bk. I, ch. 2

13   Nature does nothing uselessly.[5]   *Ibid.*

14   He who is unable to live in society, or who has no need because he is sufficient for himself, must be either a beast or a god.   *Ibid.*

15   The two qualities which chiefly inspire regard and affection [are] that a thing is your own and that it is your only one.   *Ibid. II, 4*

16   It is the nature of desire not to be satisfied, and most men live only for the gratification of it. The beginning of reform is not so much to equalize property as to train the noble sort of natures not to desire more, and to prevent the lower from getting more.
Ibid. 7

17   Even when laws have been written down, they ought not always to remain unaltered.   *Ibid. 8*

18   Again, men in general desire the good, and not merely what their fathers had.   *Ibid.*

19   They should rule who are able to rule best.
Ibid. 11

20   A state is not a mere society, having a common place, established for the prevention of mutual crime and for the sake of exchange. . . . Political society exists for the sake of noble actions, and not of mere companionship.   *Ibid. III, 9*

21   If liberty and equality, as is thought by some, are chiefly to be found in democracy, they will be best attained when all persons alike share in the government to the utmost.   *Ibid. IV, 4*

22   The best political community is formed by citizens of the middle class.   *Ibid. 11*

23   Democracy arises out of the notion that those who are equal in any respect are equal in all respects; because men are equally free, they claim to be absolutely equal.   *Ibid. V, 1*

24   Inferiors revolt in order that they may be equal, and equals that they may be superior. Such is the state of mind which creates revolutions.   *Ibid. 2*

25   In revolutions the occasions may be trifling but great interests are at stake.   *Ibid. 3*

26   Well begun is half done.[6]   *Ibid. 4*

27   The basis of a democratic state is liberty.
Ibid. VI, 2

28   Law is order, and good law is good order.
Ibid. VII, 4

29   Evils draw men together.[7]
Rhetoric, bk. I, ch. 6

30   It is this simplicity that makes the uneducated more effective than the educated when addressing popular audiences.   *Ibid. II, 22*

31   A tragedy is the imitation of an action that is serious and also, as having magnitude, complete in itself . . . with incidents arousing pity and fear, wherewith to accomplish its catharsis of such emotions.   *Poetics, ch. 6*

32   A whole is that which has beginning, middle, and end.   *Ibid. 7*

33   Poetry is something more philosophic and of graver import than history, since its statements are of the nature of universals, whereas those of history are singulars.   *Ibid. 9*

34   A likely impossibility is always preferable to an unconvincing possibility.   *Ibid. 24*

---

[1]One swallow maketh not summer.—JOHN HEYWOOD, *Proverbs* [1546], *pt. II, ch. 5*
One swallow makes a summer.—ROBERT LOWELL, *Fall, 1961*
[2]See Homer, 52:12.
[3]See Sallust, 92:1.
[4]See Descartes, 246:18.
[5]God and nature do nothing uselessly.—*On the Heavens, bk. I, ch. 4*

[6]Aristotle is quoting a proverb.
See Plato, 75:8; Horace, 97:8; and John Heywood, 141:21.
[7]Aristotle is quoting a proverb.

1   Misfortune shows those who are not really friends.[1]   *Eudemian Ethics, bk. VII, ch. 2*

Demosthenes
c. 384–322 B.C.

2   Every advantage in the past is judged in the light of the final issue.   *First Olynthiac, sec. 11*

3   Nothing is easier than self-deceit. For what each man wishes, that he also believes to be true.[2]
    Third Olynthiac, sec. 19

4   You cannot have a proud and chivalrous spirit if your conduct is mean and paltry; for whatever a man's actions are, such must be his spirit.
    Ibid. 33

5   I decline to buy repentance at the cost of ten thousand drachmas.[3]
    From AULUS GELLIUS, *Noctes Atticae, bk. I, ch. 8*

Antigonus
c. 382–301 B.C.

6   But how many ships do you reckon my presence to be worth?[4]
    From PLUTARCH, *Apothegms, Antigonus*

7   [When described by Hermodotus as "Son of the Sun":] My valet is not aware of this.[5]   *Ibid.*

Mencius[6]
372–289 B.C.

8   When one by force subdues men, they do not submit to him in heart. They submit, because their strength is not adequate to resist.
    Works, bk. II, 1:3.2

9   There is no attribute of the superior man greater than his helping men to practice virtue.
    Ibid. 1:8.5

10   The superior man will not manifest either narrow-mindedness or the want of self-respect.
    Ibid. 1:9.3

11   To give the throne to another man would be easy; to find a man who shall benefit the kingdom is difficult.   *Ibid. III, 1:4.10*

12   Never has a man who has bent himself been able to make others straight.   *Ibid. 2:1.5*

13   If you know that [a] thing is unrighteous, then use all dispatch in putting an end to it—why wait till next year?   *Ibid. 2:8.3*

14   The compass and square produce perfect circles and squares. By the sages, the human relations are perfectly exhibited.   *Ibid. IV, 1:2.1*

15   The root of the kingdom is in the state. The root of the state is in the family. The root of the family is in the person of its head.   *Ibid. 1:5*

16   The people turn to a benevolent rule as water flows downwards, and as wild beasts fly to the wilderness.   *Ibid. 1:9.2*

17   Benevolence is the tranquil habitation of man, and righteousness is his straight path.
    Ibid. 1:10.2

18   The path of duty lies in what is near, and man seeks for it in what is remote.   *Ibid. 1:11*

19   Sincerity is the way of Heaven.   *Ibid. 1:12.2*

20   There are three things which are unfilial, and to have no posterity is the greatest of them.
    Ibid. 1:26.1

21   Men must be decided on what they will not do, and then they are able to act with vigor in what they ought to do.   *Ibid. 2:8*

22   The great man does not think beforehand of his words that they may be sincere, nor of his actions that they may be resolute—he simply speaks and does what is right.   *Ibid. 2:11*

23   The great man is he who does not lose his child's-heart.[7]   *Ibid. 2:12*

24   Friendship with a man is friendship with his virtue, and does not admit of assumptions of superiority.   *Ibid. 2:13.1*

25   The tendency of man's nature to good is like the tendency of water to flow downwards.
    Ibid. VI, 1:2.2

26   From the feelings proper to it, [man's nature] is constituted for the practice of what is good.
    Ibid. 1:6.5–6

27   Benevolence, righteousness, propriety, and knowledge are not infused into us from without.
    Ibid. 1:6.7

28   Benevolence is man's mind, and righteousness is man's path.   *Ibid. 1:11.1*

29   The great end of learning is nothing else but to seek for the lost mind.   *Ibid. 1:11.4*

---

[1]In prosperity it is very easy to find a friend, but in adversity it is the most difficult of all things.—EPICTETUS, *Fragment 127*
  See Cicero, 88:8; Publilius Syrus, 100:18; Ovid, 102:3; and John Heywood, 142:5.

[2]See Julius Caesar, 88:17, and Dryden, 273:19.

[3]In reply to the courtesan Laïs.

[4]His pilot had told him that the enemy outnumbered him in ships.

[5]See Montaigne, 146:17, and Cornuel, 249:8.

[6]From *The Chinese Classics* [1861–1886], vol. II, *The Works of Mencius*, translated by JAMES LEGGE.

[7]"Except ye be converted, and become as little children, ye shall not enter into the kingdom of heaven" [*Matthew 18:3*]. But Christ speaks of the child's-heart as a thing to be regained; Mencius speaks of it as a thing not to be lost.—JAMES LEGGE

1   All men have in themselves that which is truly honorable. Only they do not think of it.
Works, bk. VI, 1:17.1

2   If a scholar have not faith [in his principles], how shall he take a firm hold of things?   *Ibid. 2:12*

3   When Heaven is about to confer a great office on any man, it first exercises his mind with suffering, and his sinews and bones with toil.   *Ibid. 2:15.2*

4   Kindly words do not enter so deeply into men as a reputation for kindness.   *Ibid. VII, 1:14.1*

5   Is it only the mouth and belly which are injured by hunger and thirst? Men's minds are also injured by them.   *Ibid. 1:27.1*

6   The people are the most important element in a nation; the spirits of the land and grain are next; the sovereign is the lightest.   *Ibid. 2:14.1*

Chuang-tzu[1]
369–286 B.C.

7   Great wisdom is generous; petty wisdom is contentious. Great speech is impassioned, small speech cantankerous.   *On Leveling All Things*

8   Take, for instance, a twig and a pillar, or the ugly person and the great beauty, and all the strange and monstrous transformations. These are all leveled together by Tao. Division is the same as creation; creation is the same as destruction.   *Ibid.*

9   I do not know whether I was then a man dreaming I was a butterfly, or whether I am now a butterfly dreaming I am a man.   *Ibid.*

10   All men know the utility of useful things; but they do not know the utility of futility.
This Human World

11   He who pursues fame at the risk of losing his self is not a scholar.   *The Great Supreme*

12   Those who seek to satisfy the mind of man by hampering it with ceremonies and music and affecting charity and devotion have lost their original nature.   *Joined Toes*

13   In the days of perfect nature, man lived together with birds and beasts, and there was no distinction of their kind . . . they were in a state of natural integrity. . . . When Sages appeared, crawling for charity and limping with duty, doubt and confusion entered men's minds. . . . Destruction of Tao and virtue in order to introduce charity and duty — this is the error of the Sages.   *Horses' Hoofs*

14   Banish wisdom, discard knowledge, and gangsters will stop!
Opening Trunks; or, A Protest Against Civilization

[1]From *The Wisdom of China and India* [1942], edited by LIN YUTANG.

15   For all men strive to grasp what they do not know, while none strive to grasp what they already know; and all strive to discredit what they do not excel in, while none strive to discredit what they do excel in. This is why there is chaos.   *Ibid.*

16   Cherish that which is within you, and shut off that which is without; for much knowledge is a curse.   *On Tolerance*

17   "The prince keeps [a] tortoise carefully enclosed in a chest in his ancestral temple. Now would this tortoise rather be dead and have its remains venerated, or would it rather be alive and wagging its tail in the mud?"
    "It would rather be alive . . . and wagging its tail in the mud."
    "Begone!" cried Chuang-tzu. "I too will wag my tail in the mud."   *Autumn Floods*

Sun-tzu[2]
c. Fourth century B.C.

18   A military operation involves deception. Even though you are competent, appear to be incompetent. Though effective, appear to be ineffective.
The Art of War. Strategic Assessments

19   Victorious warriors win first and then go to war, while defeated warriors go to war first and then seek to win.   *Ibid.*

20   The best victory is when the opponent surrenders of its own accord before there are any actual hostilities. . . . It is best to win without fighting.
Ibid. Planning a Siege

21   Be extremely subtle, even to the point of formlessness. Be extremely mysterious, even to the point of soundlessness. Thereby you can be the director of the opponent's fate.
Ibid. Emptiness and Fullness

Pytheas[3]
fl. 330 B.C.

22   They smell of the lamp.[4]
From PLUTARCH, *Lives, Demosthenes*

Alexander the Great
356–323 B.C.

23   [At Achilles' tomb:] O fortunate youth, to have found Homer as the herald of your glory![5]
From CICERO, *Pro Archia, 24*

24   If I were not Alexander, I would be Diogenes.
From PLUTARCH, *Lives, Alexander, 14*

[2]Translated by THOMAS CLEARY.
[3]See Virgil, 92:*n*11.
[4]Pytheas refers to the orations of Demosthenes, who worked in an underground cave lighted only by a lamp. See Cardozo, 609:11.
[5]See Chateaubriand, 369:16.

Apelles
fl. 325 B.C.

1 Not a day without a line.[1]
Proverbial from PLINY THE ELDER, *Natural History, XXXV, 36*

2 A cobbler should not judge above his last.[2]
Ibid. 85

Menander[3]
c. 342–292 B.C.

3 We live, not as we wish to, but as we can.
Lady of Andros, fragment 50

4 Riches cover a multitude of woes.
The Boeotian Girl, fragment 90

5 Whom the gods love dies young.[4]
The Double Deceiver, fragment 125

6 At times discretion should be thrown aside, and with the foolish we should play the fool.[5]
Those Offered for Sale, fragment 421

7 The man who has never been flogged has never been taught.[6]
The Girl Who Gets Flogged, fragment 422

8 The truth sometimes not sought for comes forth to the light.
Ibid. 433

9 This is living, not to live unto oneself alone.
The Brothers in Love, fragment 508

10 Deus ex machina [A god from the machine].
The Woman Possessed with a Divinity, fragment 227

11 I call a fig a fig, a spade a spade.[7]
Unidentified fragment 545

12 Even God lends a hand to honest boldness.[8]
Ibid. 572

13 Marriage, if one will face the truth, is an evil, but a necessary evil.[9]
Ibid. 651

14 It is not white hair that engenders wisdom.
Ibid. 639

15 Health and intellect are the two blessings of life.
Monostikoi (Single Lines)

16 The man who runs may fight again.[10]   *Ibid.*

17 Conscience is a God to all mortals.   *Ibid.*

Epicurus
341–270 B.C.

18 Death is nothing to us, since when we are, death has not come, and when death has come, we are not.
From DIOGENES LAERTIUS, *Lives of Eminent Philosophers, bk. X, sec. 125*

19 Pleasure is the beginning and the end of living happily.
Ibid. 128

20 It is impossible to live pleasurably without living wisely, well, and justly, and impossible to live wisely, well, and justly without living pleasurably.[11]
Ibid. 140

Theophrastus
d. 278 B.C.

21 Time is the most valuable thing a man can spend.[12]
From DIOGENES LAERTIUS, *Lives of Eminent Philosophers, bk. V, sec. 40*

Zeno
335–263 B.C.

22 [When asked, "What is a friend?"] Another I.[13]
From DIOGENES LAERTIUS, *Lives of Eminent Philosophers, bk. VII, sec. 23*

---

[1]Nulla dies sine linea.
See Trollope, 476:5.
[2]Ne supra crepidam sutor iudicaret.
The more common rendering is: Cobbler, stick to your last.
[3]Translated by F. C. ALLINSON (Loeb Classical Library).
[4]Also in PLAUTUS, *Bacchides*, IV, 7:18.
Those that God loves do not live long. — GEORGE HERBERT, *Jacula Prudentum* [2nd edition, 1651]
Heaven gives its favorites — early death. — BYRON, *Childe Harold*, canto IV [1818], st. 102
See Wordsworth, 376:20.
[5]See Horace, 97:3; Montaigne, 147:2; and Francis Bacon, 160:1.
[6]They spare the rod and spoil the child. — RALPH VENNING [c. 1621–1674], *Mysteries and Revelations* [1649]
Also in LUCIAN, *Hermotimus*, sec. 86.
See *Proverbs* 13:24, 21:17, and Samuel Butler [1612–1680], 263:21.
[7]Also attributed to Aristophanes by LUCIAN, *De Conscribend. Hist.*, 41.
The Macedonians are a rude and clownish people that call a spade a spade. — PLUTARCH, *Apothegms, Philip of Macedon*
I think it good plain English, without fraud, To call a spade a spade, a bawd a bawd. — JOHN TAYLOR [1580–1653], *A Kicksey Winsey*
[8]See Terence, 86:12, and Virgil, 94:25.

[9]Marriage is an evil that most men welcome. — *Monostikoi (Single Lines)*
Motto of *The Spectator* [December 29, 1711].
[10]He who flees will fight again. — TERTULLIAN, *De Fuga in Persecutione*, 10
That same man that runneth away / May again fight another day. — ERASMUS, *Apothegms* [1542], translated by NICHOLAS UDALL [1505–1556]
Celuy qui fuit de bonne heure / Peut combattre derechef / [Who flies in good time / Can fight anew]. — ANONYMOUS [1594]; *translated from* VARRO, *Saturae Menippeae*
For he who fights and runs away / May live to fight another day; / But he who is in battle slain / Can never rise and fight again. — GOLDSMITH, *The Art of Poetry on a New Plan* [1761]
A version similar to Goldsmith's appears in JAMES RAY, *History of the Rebellion* [1752].
[11]See Sophocles, 66:20.
[12]Nothing is so dear and precious as time. — RABELAIS, *Works*, bk. V [1564], *ch. 5*
See Franklin, 310:12.
[13]Alter ego.
See Aristotle, 77:13; Cicero, 88:9; Horace, 95:16; and Donne, 229:12.

1   The goal of life is living in agreement with nature.[1]

> From DIOGENES LAERTIUS, *Lives, bk. VII, sec. 87*

Cleanthes
c. 330–232 B.C.

2   For we are your offspring.[2]

> *Hymn to Zeus, l. 4*

3   Lead me, Zeus, and you, Fate, wherever you have assigned me. I shall follow without hesitation; but even if I am disobedient and do not wish to, I shall follow no less surely.

> From EPICTETUS, *Enchiridion, sec. 53*

Euclid
fl. 300 B.C.

4   Q.E.D. [Quod erat demonstrandum: Which was to be proved.]   *Elements, bk. I, proposition 5*[3]

5   [To Ptolemy I] There is no royal road to geometry.[4]

> From PROCLUS, *Commentary on Euclid, Prologue*

Bion
c. 325 – c. 255 B.C.

6   Old age is the harbor of all ills.

> From DIOGENES LAERTIUS, *Lives of Eminent Philosophers, bk. IV, sec. 47*

7   Wealth is the sinews of affairs.[5]   *Ibid. 48*

8   The road to Hades is easy to travel.[6]

> *Ibid. 49*

9   He has not acquired a fortune; the fortune has acquired him.   *Ibid. 50*

10   Though boys throw stones at frogs in sport, the frogs do not die in sport, but in earnest.[7]

> From PLUTARCH, *Water and Land Animals, 7*

Pyrrhus
c. 318–272 B.C.

11   Another such victory over the Romans, and we are undone.[8]

> From PLUTARCH, *Lives, Pyrrhus, sec. 21*

---

[1]See Marcus Aurelius, 111:5.
[2]Possibly the source of *Acts 17:28, 41:17.* See also Aeschylus, 63:17, and Aratus, 82:12.
[3]Proposition 5, too difficult for many students to pass beyond, became known as the asses' bridge [pons asinorum].
[4]Often quoted as: There is no royal road to learning.
[5]See Cicero, 88:13; Rabelais, 139:10; and Churchill, 622:3.
[6]A passage broad, / Smooth, easy, inoffensive, down to Hell. —MILTON, *Paradise Lost* [1667], *bk. II, l. 432*
[7]See L'Estrange, 266:12.
[8]Pyrrhus, king of Epirus, refers to the dearly bought victory at Asculum, 280 B.C. Hence the phrase: Pyrrhic victory. See also Herodotus, 69:24 ("Cadmean victory").

Aratus
c. 315–240 B.C.

12   From Zeus let us begin, whom we mortals never leave unnamed: full of Zeus are all streets and all gathering places of men, and full are the sea and harbors. Everywhere we all have need of Zeus. For we are also his offspring.[9]   *Phaenomena, sec. 1*

Theocritus[10]
c. 310–250 B.C.

13   Sweet is the whispering music of yonder pine that sings.

> *Idylls, I*

14   Our concern be peace of mind: some old crone let us seek,
To spit on us for luck and keep unlovely things afar.

> *Ibid. VII*

15   Cicala to cicala is dear, and ant to ant,
And kestrels dear to kestrels, but to me the Muse and song.

> *Ibid. IX*

16   The frog's life is most jolly, my lads; he has no care
Who shall fill up his cup; for he has drink enough to spare.

> *Ibid. X*

17   Verily great grace may go
With a little gift; and precious are all things that come from friends.[11]

> *Ibid. XXVIII*

Callimachus
c. 300–240 B.C.

18   Big book, big bore.[12]

> From *The Greek Anthology* [1973], PETER JAY, ed., introduction to Callimachus

19   You're walking by the tomb of Battiades,[13]
Who knew well how to write poetry, and enjoy
Laughter at the right moment, over the wine.

> *Ibid. no. 150, On Himself*[14]

20   Someone spoke of your death, Heraclitus.[15] It brought me
Tears, and I remembered how often together

---

[9]Possibly the source of *Acts 17:28, 41:17.* See also Aeschylus, 63:17, and Cleanthes, 82:2.
[10]Translated by R. C. TREVELYAN.
[11]See Homer, 53:11.
[12]In reference to the traditional epics.
[13]Callimachus.
[14]Translated by PETER JAY.
[15]Elegiac poet from Halicarnassus, author of a collection of poems, *Nightingales,* and a friend of Callimachus.

We ran the sun down with talk . . . somewhere
You've long been dust, my Halicarnassian friend.
But your *Nightingales* live on. Though the
    Death-world
Claws at everything, it will not touch them.[1]
                        Ibid. 152

Leonidas of Tarentum
c. 290 – c. 220 B.C.

1 Far from Italy, far from my native Tarentum
I lie; and this is the worst of it—worse than
    death.
An exile's life is no life. But the Muses loved me.
For my suffering they gave me a honeyed gift:
My name survives me. Thanks to the sweet Muses
Leonidas will echo throughout all time.[2]
    From The Greek Anthology [1973], PETER JAY,
    ed., no. 189

2 The season of ships is here,
  The west wind and the swallows;
Flowers in the fields appear,
  And the ocean of hills and hollows
Has calmed its waves and is clear.

Free that anchor and chain!
  Set your full canvas flying,
O men in the harbor lane:
  It is I, Priapus, crying.
Sail out on your trades again![3]

                        Ibid. 197

Archimedes
c. 287–212 B.C.

3 Eureka! [I have found it!][4]
    From VITRUVIUS POLLIO *[first century B.C.], De*
    Architectura, bk. IX, 215

4 Give me where to stand, and I will move the
earth.[5]
    From PAPPUS OF ALEXANDRIA, *Collectio,*
    bk. VIII, prop. 10, sec. 11

Quintus Fabius Maximus
c. 275–203 B.C.

5 To be turned from one's course by men's opinions, by blame, and by misrepresentation shows a
man unfit to hold an office.[6]
    From PLUTARCH, *Lives, Fabius Maximus, sec. 5*

---

[1]Translated by PETER JAY.
See Cory, 502:9.
[2]Translated by FLEUR ADCOCK.
[3]Translated by CLIVE SANSOM.
[4]On discovery of a method to test the purity of gold.
[5]Said with reference to the lever.
[6]See Horace, 96:15.

Lacydes
fl. c. 241 B.C.

6 [When asked late in life why he was studying
geometry] If I should not be learning now, when
should I be?
    From DIOGENES LAERTIUS, *Lives of Eminent*
    Philosophers, Lacydes, sec. 5

Titus Maccius Plautus
254–184 B.C.

7 What is yours is mine, and all mine is yours.[7]
           Trinummus, act II, sc. ii, l. 48

8 Not by age but by capacity is wisdom acquired.
                      Ibid. l. 88

9 You are seeking a knot in a bulrush.[8]
           Menaechmi, act II, sc. i, l. 22

10 In the one hand he is carrying a stone, while he
shows the bread in the other.[9]
           Aulularia, act II, sc. ii, l. 18

11 There are occasions when it is undoubtedly better
to incur loss than to make gain.
           Captivi, act II, sc. ii, l. 77

12 Patience is the best remedy for every trouble.
           Rudens, act II, sc. v, l. 71

13 Consider the little mouse, how sagacious an animal it is which never entrusts its life to one hole
only.[10]   *Truculentus, act IV, sc. iv, l. 15*

14 No guest is so welcome in a friend's house that he
will not become a nuisance after three days.[11]
           Miles Gloriosus, act III, sc. i

15 No man is wise enough by himself.   *Ibid. iii*

16 Nothing is there more friendly to a man than a
friend in need.[12]   *Epidicus, act III, sc. iii, l. 44*

---

[7]See Shakespeare, 205:7.
[8]A proverbial expression implying a desire to create doubts
and difficulties where there really are none. It occurs in TER-
ENCE, *Andria*, V, 4:38; also in ENNIUS, *Saturae*, 46.
[9]See *Matthew* 7:9, 34:7.
[10]I holde a mouses herte nat worth a leek / That hath but oon
hole for to sterte to, / And if that faille, thanne is al ydo.—
CHAUCER, *The Canterbury Tales* [c. 1387], *The Wife of Bath's
Prologue, l. 572*
  The mouse that hath but one hole is quickly taken.—
GEORGE HERBERT, *Jacula Prudentum* [1651]
  The mouse that always trusts to one poor hole / Can never
be a mouse of any soul.—POPE, *Paraphrase of the Prologue*
[1714], *l. 298*
[11]Fish and guests in three days are stale.—LYLY, *Euphues*
[1579]
  Fish and visitors stink in three days.—FRANKLIN, *Poor
Richard's Almanac* [1736], *January*
[12]A friend in need is a friend indeed.—HAZLITT, *English
Proverbs*

1   Things which you do not hope happen more frequently than things which you do hope.[1]
Mostellaria, act I, sc. iii, l. 40

2   To blow and swallow at the same moment is not easy.
Ibid. III, ii, l. 104

3   Practice yourself what you preach.[2]
Asinaria, act III, sc. iii, l. 644

Maharbal [Barca the Carthaginian]
fl. 210 B.C.

4   You know how to win a victory, Hannibal, but not how to use it.[3]
From LIVY, *History, XXII, 51*

Bhagavad Gita[4]
250 B.C.–A.D. 250[5]

5   For certain is death for the born
And certain is birth for the dead;
Therefore over the inevitable
Thou shouldst not grieve.[6]
Chapter 2, verse 27

6   This embodied [soul] is eternally unslayable
In the body of everyone, son of Bharata;
Therefore all beings
Thou shouldst not mourn.

Likewise having regard for thine own [caste] duty
Thou shouldst not tremble;
For another, better thing than a fight required of duty
Exists not for a warrior.
2:30

7   On action alone be thy interest,
Never on its fruits.
Let not the fruits of action be thy motive,
Nor be thy attachment to inaction.[7]
2:47

8   Better one's own duty, [though] imperfect,
Than another's duty well performed.[8]
3:35 and 18:47

9   In whatsoever way any come to Me,
In that same way I grant them favor.[8]
4:11

10   Who sees Me in all,
And sees all in Me,
For him I am not lost,
And he is not lost for Me.[8]
6:30

11   Whatsoever state [of being] meditating upon
He leaves the body at death,[9]
To just that he goes, son of Kunti,
Always being made to be in the condition of that.[8]
8:6

12   If the radiance of a thousand suns were to burst forth at once in the sky, that would be like the splendor of the Mighty One [Krishna].[10]   *11:12*

13   I am mighty, world-destroying Time.
11:32

Quintus Ennius
239–169 B.C.

14   No sooner said than done—so acts your man of worth.   *Annals, bk. 9 (quoted by* PRISCIANUS)

15   I never indulge in poetics
Unless I am down with rheumatics.
Fragment of a satire (quoted by PRISCIANUS)

16   By delaying he preserved the state.[11]
From CICERO, *De Senectute, IV*

17   Let no one pay me honor with tears, nor celebrate my funeral rites with weeping.   *Ibid. XX*

18   The ape, vilest of beasts, how like to us.[12]
From CICERO, *De Natura Deorum, bk. I, ch. 35*

19   No one regards what is before his feet; we all gaze at the stars.
Iphigenia. From CICERO, *De Divinatione, bk. II, ch. 13*

20   The idle mind knows not what it is it wants.
Ibid.

21   Whom they fear they hate.
Thyestes. From CICERO, *De Officiis, II, 7*

---

[1] The unexpected always happens.—*Common saying*
[2] Facias ipse quod faciamus suades.
See Saint Jerome, 113:17.
[3] Vincere scis, Hannibal, victoria uti nescis.
Maharbal was commander of cavalry under Hannibal, who had insisted on a day's rest for the army after the victory at Cannae [216 B.C.], thereby enabling the enemy to recoup.
See Polybius, 85:10.
[4] Sanskrit: The Lord's Song.
[5] Ancient Indian literary chronology is conjectural. The dates given are approximate.
[6] Translated by ANNIE BESANT.
[7] Translated by F. EDGERTON.
At the moment which is not of action or inaction / You can receive this: "on whatever sphere of being / The mind of a man may be intent / At the time of death"—that is the one action / (And the time of death is every moment) / Which shall fructify in the lives of others: / And do not think of the fruit of action, / Fare forward.—T. S. ELIOT, *Four Quartets* [1943], *The Dry Salvages, pt. III*

[8] Translated by F. EDGERTON.
[9] See Eliot's lines from *The Dry Salvages* quoted in the note to *Gita* 2:47, 84:7.
[10] Translated by SWAMI NIKHILANANDA.
See Oppenheimer, 714:*n*3.
[11] This refers to Quintus Fabius Maximus, "Cunctator." Hence the "Fabian policy" of waiting.
[12] Simia quam similis, turpissima bestia, nobis!

Marcus Porcius Cato [Cato the Elder][1]
234–149 B.C.

1   A farm is like a man—however great the income, if there is extravagance but little is left.
On Agriculture,[2] *bk. I, sec. 6*

2   Even though work stops, expenses run on.
Ibid. XXXIX, 2

3   It is a hard matter, my fellow citizens, to argue with the belly, since it has no ears.[3]
From PLUTARCH, *Lives, Cato, sec. 8*

4   Wise men profit more from fools than fools from wise men; for the wise men shun the mistakes of fools, but fools do not imitate the successes of the wise.
Ibid. 9

5   I would much rather have men ask why I have no statue, than why I have one.
Ibid. 19

6   Carthage must be destroyed.[4]
Ibid. 27

7   Grasp the subject, the words will follow.[5]
From CAIUS JULIUS VICTOR, *Ars Rhetorica, I [4th century A.D.]*

8   An orator is a good man who is skilled in speaking.
From SENECA THE ELDER *[c. 45 B.C.–A.D. 40], Controversiae, I, Preface, and elsewhere*

Caecilius Statius
220–168 B.C.

9   He plants trees to benefit another generation.[6]
Synephebi. Quoted by CICERO *in De Senectute, VII*

Polybius
c. 200 – c. 118 B.C.

10   Those who know how to win are much more numerous than those who know how to make proper use of their victories.[7]
History, bk. X, 36

---

[1]Also known as Cato the Censor.
[2]Translated by WILLIAM D. HOOPER, revised by HARRISON BOYD ASH (Loeb Classical Library).
[3]The belly has no ears nor is it to be filled with fair words. —RABELAIS, *Works, IV* [1548], 67
See La Fontaine, 268:8, and Adlai Stevenson, 706:12.
[4]*Delenda est Carthago.*
These words were added to every speech Cato made in the senate, preceded by *ceterum censeo* [in my opinion].
[5]*Rem tene; verba sequentur.*
[6]*Serit arbores quae alteri seculo prosint.*
John Quincy Adams used *Alteri seculo* for his seal [c. 1830].
He that plants trees loves others beside himself. —THOMAS FULLER [1654–1734], *Gnomologia* [1732]
A man does not plant a tree for himself; he plants it for posterity. —ALEXANDER SMITH, *Dreamthorp* [1863], ch. 11
See John Adams, 338:10.
[7]See Maharbal, 84:4.

11   There is no witness so dreadful, no accuser so terrible as the conscience that dwells in the heart of every man.
Ibid. XVIII, 43

Terence[8] [Publius Terentius Afer]
c. 190–159 B.C.

12   Moderation in all things.[9]
Andria (The Lady of Andros), l. 61

13   Hence these tears.[10]
Ibid. l. 126

14   Lovers' quarrels are the renewal of love.[11]
Ibid. l. 555

15   Charity begins at home.[12]
Ibid. l. 635

16   I am a man: nothing human is alien to me.[13]
Heauton Timoroumenos (The Self-Tormentor), l. 77

17   Draw from others the lesson that may profit yourself.[14]
Ibid. l. 221

18   Time removes distress.[15]
Ibid. l. 421

19   Nothing is so difficult but that it may be found out by seeking.[16]
Ibid. l. 675

20   Some people ask, "What if the sky were to fall?"[17]
Ibid. l. 719

---

[8]Translated by JOHN SARGEAUNT (Loeb Classical Library), with occasional adaptations.
[9]*Ne quid nimis.*
See The Seven Sages, 55:10; Horace, 95:2 and 96:7; Lucan, 105:21; and Anonymous: Latin, 119:15.
[10]*Hinc illae lacrimae.*
The phrase is proverbial for "That's the cause of it," and was often quoted, by Horace in *Epistles, I, xix, 41,* and by others.
Hence rage and tears [Inde irae et lacrimae]. —JUVENAL, *Satires, bk. I, l. 168*
[11]*Amantium irae amoris integratio est.*
This was quoted by Winston Churchill in a message to Franklin D. Roosevelt.
The anger of lovers renews the strength of love. —PUBLILIUS SYRUS, *Maxim 24*
The falling out of faithful friends renewing is of love.— RICHARD EDWARDS [c. 1523–1566], *The Paradise of Dainty Devices* [1576]
Let the falling out of friends be a renewing of affection. —LYLY, *Euphues* [1579]
The falling out of lovers is the renewing of love.—ROBERT BURTON, *Anatomy of Melancholy* [1621–1651], *pt. III, sec. 2*
[12]*Proximus sum egomet mihi.*
See I Timothy 5:4, 45:17, and Thomas Browne, 248:18.
[13]*Homo sum: humani nil a me alienum puto.* Quoted by CICERO in *De Officiis, I, 30.*
[14]*Periculum ex aliis facito tibi quod ex usu siet.* (A saying.)
[15]*Diem adimere aegritudinem hominibus.* (A saying: Time heals all wounds.)
See Sophocles, 65:20, and La Fontaine, 268:4.
[16]*Nil tam difficile est quin quaerendo investigari possiet.*
[17]*Quid si nunc caelum ruat?*
Some ambassadors from the Celtae, being asked by Alexander what in the world they dreaded most, answered, that they feared lest the sky should fall upon them. —FLAVIUS ARRIANUS [c. 100–170], *bk. I, 4*

1   Extreme law is often extreme injustice.[1]
Heauton Timoroumenos, l. 796

2   There is nothing so easy but that it becomes difficult when you do it reluctantly.   *Ibid. l. 805*

3   While there's life, there's hope.[2]   *Ibid. l. 981*

4   In fact, nothing is said that has not been said before.[3]   *Eunuchus, l. 41 (Prologue)*

5   I have everything, yet have nothing; and although I possess nothing, still of nothing am I in want.[4]
Ibid. l. 243

6   There are vicissitudes in all things.[5]
Ibid. l. 276

7   I don't care one straw.[6]   *Ibid. l. 411*

8   Take care and say this with presence of mind.[7]
Ibid. l. 769

9   He is wise who tries everything before arms.
Ibid. l. 789

10   I know the disposition of women: when you will, they won't; when you won't, they set their hearts upon you of their own inclination.   *Ibid. l. 812*

11   I took to my heels as fast as I could.
Ibid. l. 844

12   Fortune helps the brave.[8]   *Phormio, l. 203*

13   So many men, so many opinions; every one his own way.[9]   *Ibid. l. 454*

14   I bid him look into the lives of men as though into a mirror, and from others to take an example for himself.   *Adelphoe (The Brothers), l. 415*

[1]Ius summum saepe summa est malitia.
Extreme law, extreme injustice, is now become a stale proverb in discourse.—CICERO, *De Officiis, I, 33*
Extreme justice is often injustice.—RACINE, *La Thébaïde* [1664], *act IV, sc. iii*
Mais l'extrême justice est une extrême injure.—VOLTAIRE, *Oedipe* [1718], *act III, sc. iii*
See Anonymous: Latin, 119:32.
[2]Modo liceat vivere, est spes.
See Cicero, 87:23, and Goldsmith, 328:4.
[3]See *Ecclesiastes 1:9*, 23:25; Robert Burton, 234:6; and La Bruyère, 283:11.
[4]See *II Corinthians 6:10*, 44:6, and Wotton, 227:8.
[5]See Francis Bacon, 160:11, and Sterne, 320:5.
[6]Ego non flocci pendere.
Nor do they care a straw.—CERVANTES, *Don Quixote, pt. I* [1605], *bk. III, ch. 9*
[7]Fac animo haec praesenti dicas. Literally, "with a present mind"—equivalent to Caesar's "praesentia animi" (*De Bello Gallico, V, 43, 4*).
[8]Pliny the Younger says (*bk. VI, letter 16*) that Pliny the Elder said this during the eruption of Vesuvius: "Fortune favors the brave."
See Menander, 81:12, and Virgil, 94:25.
[9]Quot homines tot sententiae: suo quoque mos.
So many heads so many wits.—JOHN HEYWOOD, *Proverbs* [1546], *pt. I, ch. 2*
So many men so many minds.—GEORGE GASCOIGNE [c. 1525–1577], *The Glass of Government* [1575]

Huai-nan Tzu[10] [Liu An][11]
Second century B.C.

15   Before heaven and earth had taken form all was vague and amorphous. Therefore it was called the Great Beginning. The Great Beginning produced emptiness and emptiness produced the universe. . . . The combined essences of heaven and earth became the yin and yang, the concentrated essences of the yin and yang became the four seasons, and the scattered essences of the four seasons became the myriad creatures of the world.
Huai-nan Tzu, 3:1a

Tung Chung-shu[10]
c. 179 – c. 104 B.C.

16   He who is the ruler of men takes nonaction as his way and considers impartiality as his treasure. He sits upon the throne of non-action and rides upon the perfection of his officials.
Ch'un-ch'iu fan-lu

Lucius Accius
170–86 B.C.

17   Let them hate, so long as they fear.[12]
Fragment

Han Wu-ti[13]
157–87 B.C.

18   The sound of her silk skirt has stopped.
On the marble pavement dust grows.
Her empty room is cold and still.
Fallen leaves are piled against the doors.
   Longing for that lovely lady
How can I bring my aching heart to rest?
On the death of his mistress[14]

Marcus Terentius Varro
116–27 B.C.

19   The longest part of the journey is said to be the passing of the gate.
On Agriculture [De Re Rustica],[15] *bk. I, ii, 2*

[10]From *Sources of Chinese Tradition* [1960], edited by WILLIAM THEODORE DE BARY.
[11]*Huai-nan Tzu* is from the scholarly court of Liu An (d. 122 B.C.), prince of Huai-nan, known also as Huai-nan Tzu.
[12]Oderint dum metuant.
From a lost tragedy. Frequently cited by Cicero and others. Suetonius (*Gaius Caligula, 30*) says that the Emperor Caligula was fond of quoting it.
[13]Sixth emperor of the Han dynasty.
[14]From *Chinese Poems*, ARTHUR WALEY, translator.
[15]Translated by WILLIAM D. HOOPER, revised by HARRISON BOYD ASH (Loeb Classical Library).

1 When people come to inspect . . . farmsteads, it is not to see collections of pictures . . . but collections of fruit. *Ibid.* 10

2 Not all who own a harp are harpers. *Ibid. II, i, 3*

3 It was divine nature which gave us the country, and man's skill that built the cities.[1] *Ibid. III, i, 4*

Marcus Licinius Crassus

fl. 70 B.C.

4 Those who aim at great deeds must also suffer greatly. *From* PLUTARCH, *Lives, Crassus, ch.* 26

Meleager

First century B.C.

5 Farewell, Morning Star, herald of dawn, and quickly come as the Evening Star, bringing again in secret her whom thou takest away.[2]
The Greek Anthology [1906], J. W. MACKAIL, *ed., sec. 1, no. 21*

Marcus Tullius Cicero

106–43 B.C.

6 How long, Catiline, will you abuse our patience?[3] *In Catilinam, I, 1*

7 O tempora! O mores! [Oh the times! The customs!] *Ibid.*

8 He has departed, withdrawn, gone away, broken out.[4] *Ibid. II, 1*

9 I am a Roman citizen.[5] *In Verrem, V, 57*

10 Law stands mute in the midst of arms.[6] *Pro Milone, IV, 11*

11 Cui bono? [To whose advantage?][7] *Ibid. XII, 32*

12 These studies are a spur to the young, a delight to the old; an ornament in prosperity, a consoling refuge in adversity; they are pleasure for us at home, and no burden abroad; they stay up with us at night, they accompany us when we travel, they are with us in our country visits. *Pro Archia Poeta, VII, 16*

13 Leisure with dignity.[8]
Pro Publio Sestio, sec. 45

14 History is the witness that testifies to the passing of time; it illumines reality, vitalizes memory, provides guidance in daily life, and brings us tidings of antiquity. *Ibid. II, 36*

15 The first law for the historian is that he shall never dare utter an untruth. The second is that he shall suppress nothing that is true. Moreover, there shall be no suspicion of partiality in his writing, or of malice. *Ibid. 62*

16 The freedom of poetic license.[9] *Ibid. III, 153*

17 If a man aspires to the highest place, it is no dishonor to him to halt at the second, or even at the third. *Orator, 4*

18 For just as some women are said to be handsome though without adornment, so this subtle manner of speech, though lacking in artificial graces, delights us.[10] *Ibid. 78*

19 Nothing quite new is perfect. *Brutus, 71*

20 There were poets before Homer. *Ibid.*

21 The aim of forensic oratory is to teach, to delight, to move. *De Optimo Genere Oratorum, 16*

22 The dregs of Romulus.[11] *Ad Atticum, II, 1*

23 While there's life, there's hope.[12]
Ibid. IX, 10

24 What is more agreeable than one's home?[13]
Ad Familiares, IV, 8

25 I like myself, but I won't say I'm as handsome as the bull that kidnapped Europa.
De Natura Deorum, I, 78

26 It was ordained at the beginning of the world that certain signs should prefigure certain events.
De Divinatione, I, 118

27 There is nothing so ridiculous but some philosopher has said it.[14] *Ibid. II, 119*

28 I would rather be wrong with Plato than right with such men as these [the Pythagoreans].
Tusculanae Disputationes, I, 17

29 O philosophy, you leader of life.[15]
Ibid. V, 2

30 Socrates was the first to call philosophy down from the heavens and to place it in cities, and even to introduce it into homes and compel it to inquire about life and standards and goods and evils.
Ibid. V, 4

---

[1]Divina natura dedit agros, ars humana aedificavit urbes.
[2]See Sappho, 56:11, and Housman, 579:22.
[3]Quo usque, Catilina, abutere patientia nostra?
[4]Abiit, excessit, evasit, erupit.
  Depart — be off — excede — evade — erump! — OLIVER WENDELL HOLMES, *The Autocrat of the Breakfast-Table* [1858], *Aestivation, ch. II*
[5]Civis Romanus sum.
[6]Silent enim leges inter arma.
[7]In full: Cui bono fuerit? [To whose advantage was it?]
[8]Otium cum dignitate.

[9]Poetarum licentiae liberiora.
[10]See Milton, 258:24, and James Thomson, 308:7.
[11]In Romuli faece. That is, the lowest order of society.
[12]Dum anima est, spes est.
  See Terence, 86:3, and Goldsmith, 328:4.
[13]Quae est domestica sede iucundior?
[14]See Descartes, 246:17, and Goethe, 350:23.
[15]O vitae philosophia dux.
  See Heath, 360:8.

1   The highest good.[1]   *De Officiis, I, 2*

2   Let arms yield to the toga, the laurel crown to praise.[2]   *Ibid. I, 22*

3   Never less idle than when wholly idle, nor less alone than when wholly alone.   *Ibid. III, 1*

4   Rome, fortunately natal 'neath my consulship![3]
                                    De Consultatu Suo

5   The people's good is the highest law.[4]
                                    De Legibus, III, 3

6   He used to raise a storm in a teapot.[5]
                                                      Ibid. 16

7   Let the punishment match the offense.[6]
                                                      Ibid. 20

8   The shifts of Fortune test the reliability of friends.[7]   *De Amicitia, XVII*

9   A friend is, as it were, a second self.[8]
                                                      Ibid. XXI

10   Give me a young man in whom there is something of the old, and an old man with something of the young: guided so, a man may grow old in body, but never in mind.   *De Senectute, XI*

11   Old men are garrulous by nature.   *Ibid. XVI*

12   Old age: the crown of life, our play's last act.
                                                    Ibid. XXIII

13   Endless money forms the sinews of war.[9]
                                          Philippics, V, 2:5

[1]Summum bonum.
The nature of the good and the highest good.—HORACE, *Satires, II, 6, 76*
    See Lucretius, 90:12.
[2]Cedant arma togae, concedat laurea laudi.
He is quoting from his own poem *De suis temporibus*, bk. III.
[3]O fortunatam natam me consule Romam!
The verse is quoted disparagingly by Juvenal (*X, 122*), Quintilian (*XI, 1, 24*), and others.
[4]Salus populi suprema est lex.
[5]Excitabat enim fluctus in simpulo.
A tempest in a teapot.—*Proverb*
[6]Noxiae poena par esto.
See W. S. Gilbert, 531:3.
[7]See Aristotle, 79:1; Publilius Syrus, 100:18; Ovid, 102:3; and John Heywood, 142:5.
[8]See Aristotle, 77:13; Zeno, 81:22; Horace, 95:16; and Donne, 229:12.
[9]He who first called money the sinews of affairs seems to have spoken with special reference to the affairs of war.—PLUTARCH, *Lives, Cleomenes 27*
    Neither is money the sinews of war (as it is trivially said).—FRANCIS BACON, *Essays* [1625], *Of the True Greatness of Kingdoms*
    Money is the sinew of love as well as of war.—THOMAS FULLER [1654–1734], *Gnomonologia* [1732], *no. 3442*
    See Bion, 82:7; Rabelais, 139:10; and Winston Churchill, 622:3.

Pompey [Gnaeus Pompeius]
106–48 B.C.

14   More worship the rising than the setting sun.[10]
                    From PLUTARCH, Lives, Pompey, 14

15   A dead man cannot bite.   *Ibid. 77*

Julius Caesar
100–44 B.C.

16   All Gaul is divided into three parts.[11]
                                    De Bello Gallico, I, 1

17   Men willingly believe what they wish.[12]
                                                  Ibid. III, 18

18   I love treason but hate a traitor.[13]
                From *PLUTARCH, Lives, Romulus, sec. 17*

19   I wished my wife to be not so much as suspected.[14]   *Ibid. Caesar, sec. 10*

20   I had rather be the first man among these fellows than the second man in Rome.   *Ibid. 11*

21   The die is cast.[15]   *Ibid. 32*

22   Go on, my friend, and fear nothing; you carry Caesar and his fortune in your boat.   *Ibid. 38*

23   The Ides of March have come.[16]   *Ibid. 63*

24   [In answer to a question as to what sort of death was the best:] A sudden death.   *Ibid.*

25   I came, I saw, I conquered.[17]
    From *SUETONIUS, Lives of the Caesars, Julius, sec. 37*

26   You also, Brutus my son.[18]   *Ibid. 82*

[10]Addressed to Sulla.
See Garrick, 323:17.
[11]Gallia est omnis divisa in partes tres.
[12]Fere libenter homines id quod volunt credunt.
See Demosthenes, 79:3, and Dryden, 273:19.
[13]Princes in this case do hate the traitor, though they love the treason.—DANIEL, *Tragedy of Cleopatra* [1594], *act IV, sc. i*
    This principle is old, but true as fate, / Kings may love treason, but the traitor hate.—DEKKER, *The Honest Whore* [1604], *pt. I, act IV, sc. iv*
    Though I love the treason, I hate the traitor.—PEPYS, *Diary, March 7, 1667*
    See Dryden, 275:22.
[14]Caesar's wife must be above suspicion.—*Traditional saying*
[15]Iacta alea est. Proverb quoted by Caesar as he crossed the Rubicon.
    Also in SUETONIUS, *Lives of the Caesars, Julius.*
[16]See Shakespeare, 187:18.
[17]Veni, vidi, vici. Inscription displayed in Caesar's Pontic triumph.
    Also in PLUTARCH, *Apothegms, Caesar.*
[18]Et tu, Brute. Suetonius reports that Caesar said this in Greek.
    See Shakespeare, 188:16.

1 It is not these well-fed long-haired men that I fear, but the pale and the hungry-looking.[1]
From PLUTARCH, *Lives, Antony, sec. 11*

Lucretius[2] [Titus Lucretius Carus]
99–55 B.C.

2 Mother of Aeneas and his race, darling of men and gods, nurturing Venus.
De Rerum Natura (On the Nature of Things), bk. I, l. 1 (Invocation)

3 For thee the wonder-working earth puts forth sweet flowers. *Ibid. l. 7*

4 The lively power of his mind prevailed, and forth he marched far beyond the flaming walls of the heavens,[3] as he traversed the immeasurable universe in thought and imagination. *Ibid. l. 72*

5 Such evil deeds could religion prompt.[4]
Ibid. l. 101

6 Nothing can be created from nothing.[5]
Ibid. l. 155

7 The first beginnings of things cannot be distinguished by the eye. *Ibid. l. 268*

8 The ring on the finger becomes thin beneath by wearing, the fall of dripping water hollows the stone.[6] *Ibid. l. 312*

9 Nature works by means of bodies unseen.
Ibid. l. 328

10 Material objects are of two kinds, atoms and compounds of atoms. The atoms themselves cannot

be swamped by any force, for they are preserved indefinitely by their absolute solidity.[7]
Ibid. l. 518

11 On a dark theme I trace verses full of light, touching all the muses' charm.[8] *Ibid. l. 933*

12 Truths kindle light for truths. *Ibid. l. 1117*

13 Pleasant it is, when over a great sea the winds trouble the waters, to gaze from shore upon another's great tribulation: not because any man's troubles are a delectable joy, but because to perceive what ills you are free from yourself is pleasant.[9]
Ibid. II, l. 1

14 O miserable minds of men! O blind hearts! In what darkness of life, in what great dangers ye spend this little span of years![10] *Ibid. l. 14*

15 Life is one long struggle in the dark.
Ibid. l. 54

16 Thus the sum of things is ever being renewed, and mortals live dependent one upon another. Some nations increase, others diminish, and in a short space the generations of living creatures are changed and like runners pass on the torch of life.[11]
Ibid. l. 75

17 So far as it goes, a small thing may give analogy of great things, and show the tracks of knowledge.
Ibid. l. 123

18 All things must needs be borne on through the calm void, moving at equal rate with unequal weights.[8] *Ibid. l. 238*

19 Never trust her at any time when the calm sea shows her false alluring smile. *Ibid. l. 558*

20 What once sprung from the earth sinks back into the earth.[12] *Ibid. l. 999*

21 That fear of Acheron be sent packing which troubles the life of man from its deepest depths, suffuses all with the blackness of death, and leaves no delight clean and pure. *Ibid. III, l. 37*

22 So it is more useful to watch a man in times of peril, and in adversity to discern what kind of man he is; for then at last words of truth are drawn from

[1]The reference is to Brutus and Cassius.
See Shakespeare, 187:24.
[2]Translated by W. H. D. ROUSE (Loeb Classical Library), with adaptations.
[3]Flammantia moenia mundi.
[4]Tantum religio potuit suadere malorum.
The reference is to Agamemnon's sacrifice of his daughter Iphigenia.
Translated by CYRIL BAILEY.
[5]Nil posse creari de nilo.
See Shakespeare, 208:20.
[6]Anulus in digito subter tenuatur habendo, / Stilicidi casus lapidem cavat.
See also the concluding lines of *Book IV:*
Nonne vides etiam guttas in saxa cadentis / Umoris longo in spatio pertundere saxa? [Do you not see that even drops of water falling upon a stone in the long run beat a way through the stone?]
Drops of water hollow out a stone, a ring is worn thin by use.
—OVID, *Ex Ponto, IV,* 10:5
Also in PLUTARCH, *Of the Training of Children.*
The drop of rain maketh a hole in the stone, not by violence, but by oft falling.—LATIMER, *Seventh Sermon Before Edward VI* [1549]
The soft droppes of rain perce the hard marble.—LYLY, *Euphues* [1579]
And drizling drops that often doe redound, / The firmest flint doth in continuance wear.—SPENSER, *Amoretti* [1595], sonnet 18

[7]Translated by R. E. LATHAM.
[8]Translated by CYRIL BAILEY.
[9]It is a pleasure to stand upon the shore, and to see ships tost upon the sea: a pleasure to stand in the window of a castle, and to see a battle and the adventures thereof below: but no pleasure is comparable to the standing upon the vantage ground of truth . . . and to see the errors, and wanderings, and mists, and tempests, in the vale below.—FRANCIS BACON, *Essays* [1625], *Of Truth*
[10]Translated by CYRIL BAILEY.
Insensate care of mortals! Oh how false the argument which makes thee downward beat thy wings.—DANTE, *Divine Comedy* [c. 1310–1321], *Paradiso, canto XI,* 1
[11]Et quasi cursores vitae lampada tradunt.
[12]Translated by CYRIL BAILEY.
See *Book of Common Prayer,* 50:8.

the depths of his heart, and the mask is torn off, reality remains.   *De Rerum Natura, bk. III, l. 55*

1   For as children tremble and fear everything in the blind darkness, so we in the light sometimes fear what is no more to be feared than the things children in the dark hold in terror and imagine will come true.[1]   *Ibid. l. 87*

2   A tree cannot grow in the sky, nor clouds be in the deep sea, nor fish live in the fields, nor can blood be in sticks nor sap in rocks.   *Ibid. l. 784*

3   Therefore death is nothing to us, it matters not one jot, since the nature of the mind is understood to be mortal.[2]   *Ibid. l. 830*

4   When immortal Death has taken mortal life.[3]   *Ibid. l. 869*

5   Why dost thou not retire like a guest sated with the banquet of life, and with calm mind embrace, thou fool, a rest that knows no care?[4]   *Ibid. l. 938*

6   By protracting life, we do not deduct one jot from the duration of death.[5]   *Ibid. l. 1087*

7   What is food to one, is to others bitter poison.[6]   *Ibid. IV, l. 637*

8   From the heart of this fountain of delights wells up some bitter taste to choke them even amid the flowers.[4]   *Ibid. l. 1133*

9   But if one should guide his life by true principles, man's greatest riches is to live on a little with contented mind; for a little is never lacking.   *Ibid. V, l. 1117*

10   Men are eager to tread underfoot what they have once too much feared.   *Ibid. l. 1140*

11   Violence and injury enclose in their net all that do such things, and generally return upon him who began.[7]   *Ibid. l. 1152*

12   [Epicurus] set forth what is the highest good, towards which we all strive, and pointed out the past, whereby along a narrow track we may strain on towards it in a straight course.[8]   *Ibid. VI, l. 26*

[1]See Francis Bacon, 159:4.
[2]Nil igitur mors est ad nos neque pertinet hilum, / Quandoquidem natura animi mortalis habetur.
[3]Mortalem vitam mors cum immortalis ademit.
Translated by CYRIL BAILEY.
[4]Translated by CYRIL BAILEY.
[5]See Montaigne, 145:13.
[6]Ut quod ali cibus est aliis fuat acre venenum.
What's one man's poison, signor, / Is another's meat or drink.—BEAUMONT AND FLETCHER, *Love's Cure* [1647], act III, sc. ii
One man's meat is another's poison.—OSWALD DYKES [fl. c. 1709], *English Proverbs* [1709]
[7]See *Matthew* 26:52, 37:1.
[8]Translated by CYRIL BAILEY.
The highest good [summum bonum]. See Cicero, 88:1.

13   [The people] were given over in troops to disease[9] and death.   *Ibid. l. 1144*

Gaius Valerius Catullus[10]
87 – c. 54 B.C.

14   To whom am I to present my pretty new book, freshly smoothed off with dry pumice stone? To you, Cornelius: for you used to think that my trifles were worth something, long ago.   *Carmina, I, l. 1*

15   May it live and last for more than one century.   *Ibid. l. 10*

16   Mourn, ye Graces and Loves, and all you whom the Graces love. My lady's sparrow is dead, the sparrow, my lady's pet.[11]   *Ibid. III, l. 1*

17   Now he goes along the dark road, thither whence they say no one returns.   *Ibid. l. 11*

18   But these things are past and gone.[12]   *Ibid. IV, l. 25*

19   Let us live and love, my Lesbia, and value at a penny all the talk of crabbed old men. Suns may set and rise again: for us, when our brief light has set, there's the sleep of perpetual night.[13] Give me a thousand kisses.[14]   *Ibid. V, l. 1*

20   Poor Catullus, you should cease your folly.   *Ibid. VIII, l. 1*

21   But you, Catullus, be resolved and firm.   *Ibid. l. 19*

22   And let her not look to find my love, as before; my love, which by her fault has dropped like a flower on the meadow's edge, when it has been touched by the plow passing by.   *Ibid. XI, l. 21*

23   Over head and heels.[15]   *Ibid. XX, l. 9*

24   Ah, what is more blessed than to put cares away!   *Ibid. XXXI, l. 7*

25   Whatever it is, wherever he is, whatever he is doing, he smiles: it is a malady he has, neither an elegant one as I think, nor in good taste.   *Ibid. XXXIX, l. 6*

26   There is nothing more silly than a silly laugh.   *Ibid. l. 16*

[9]The devastating Athenian plague [430 B.C.] described by Thucydides.
[10]Translated by F. W. CORNFORD (Loeb Classical Library).
[11]Passer, deliciae meae puellae.
This is also the opening line of *Carmina, II.*
[12]Sed haec prius fuere.
[13]See Shakespeare, 165:31; Campion, 226:13; Jonson, 232:4; and Herrick, 241:19.
[14]Vivamus, mea Lesbia, atque amemus . . . / Soles occidere et redire possunt: / Nobis cum semel occidit brevis lux / Nox est perpetua una dormienda. / Da mi basia mille.
See Herrick, 241:8.
[15]Per caputque pedesque.

1   Oh this age! How tasteless and ill-bred it is!
Ibid. XLIII, l. 8

2   Now spring brings back balmy warmth.[1]
Ibid. XLVI, l. 1

3   Catullus, the worst of all poets, gives you [Marcus Tullius] his warmest thanks; he being as much the worst of all poets as you are the best of all patrons.
Ibid. XLIX, l. 4

4   He seems to me to be equal to a god, he, if it may be, seems to surpass the very gods, who sitting opposite you again gazes at you and hears you sweetly laughing.[2]
Ibid. LI, l. 1

5   What an eloquent manikin![3]
Ibid. LIII, l. 5

6   I would see a little Torquatus, stretching his baby hands from his mother's lap, smile a sweet smile at his father with lips half parted.
Ibid. LXI, l. 216

7   The evening is come; rise up, ye youths. Vesper from Olympus now at last is just raising his long-looked-for light.
Ibid. LXII, l. 1

8   What is given by the gods more desirable than the fortunate hour?[4]
Ibid. l. 30

9   Not unknown am I to the goddess [Venus] who mingles with her cares a sweet bitterness.
Ibid. LXVIII, l. 17

10   It is not fit that men should be compared with gods.
Ibid. l. 141

11   What a woman says to her ardent lover should be written in wind and running water.
Ibid. LXX

12   Leave off wishing to deserve any thanks from anyone, or thinking that anyone can ever become grateful.
Ibid. LXXIII, l. 1

13   If a man can take any pleasure in recalling the thought of kindnesses done.
Ibid. LXXVI, l. 1

14   It is difficult suddenly to lay aside a long-cherished love.
Ibid. l. 13

15   O ye gods, grant me this in return for my piety.
Ibid. l. 26

16   I hate and I love. Why I do so, perhaps you ask. I know not, but I feel it and I am in torment.[5]
Ibid. LXXXV, l. 1

17   Wandering through many countries and over many seas, I come, my brother, to these sorrowful obsequies, to present you with the last guerdon of death, and speak, though in vain, to your silent ashes.
Ibid. CI, l. 1

[1]Iam ver egelidos refert tepores.
[2]See Sappho, 56:5.
[3]Salaputtium disertum!
[4]Quid datur a divis felici optatius hora?
[5]Odi et amo. Quare id faciam, fortasse requiris. / Nescio, sed fieri sentio et excrucior.
   See Anacreon, 60:2.

18   And forever, O my brother, hail and farewell![6]
Ibid. l. 10

19   But you shall not escape my iambics.[7]
Fragment

Sallust[8] [Gaius Sallustius Crispus]
86–34 B.C.

20   All our power lies in both mind and body; we employ the mind to rule, the body rather to serve; the one we have in common with the Gods, the other with the brutes.
The War with Catiline [c. 40 B.C.], sec. 1

21   The renown which riches or beauty confer is fleeting and frail; mental excellence is a splendid and lasting possession.
Ibid.

22   Covetous of others' possessions, he [Catiline] was prodigal of his own.[9]
Ibid. 5

23   Ambition drove many men to become false; to have one thought locked in the breast, another ready on the tongue.[10]
Ibid. 10

24   In truth, prosperity tries the souls even of the wise.[11]
Ibid. 11

25   To like and dislike the same things, that is indeed true friendship.[12]
Ibid. 20

26   Thus in the highest position there is the least freedom of action.[13]
Ibid. 51

27   On behalf of their country, their children, their altars, and their hearths.[14]
Ibid. 59

28   The soul is the captain and ruler of the life of mortals.[15]
The War with Jugurtha [c. 41 B.C.], sec. 1

29   The splendid achievements of the intellect, like the soul, are everlasting.
Ibid. 2

30   A city for sale and soon to perish if it finds a buyer![16]
Ibid. 35

31   Punic faith.[17]
Ibid. 108

[6]Atque in perpetuum, frater, ave atque vale.
[7]At non effugies meos iambos.
[8]Translated by J. C. ROLFE (Loeb Classical Library).
[9]Alieni appetens, sui profusus.
[10]See Euripides, 68:18.
[11]Quippe secundae res sapientium animos fatigant.
[12]Idem velle atque idem nolle, ea demum firma amicitia est. See Pythagoras, 58:9, and Plato, 74:11.
[13]Ita in maxima fortuna minima licentia est.
[14]Pro patria, pro liberis, pro aris atque focis suis.
[15]Dux atque imperator vitae mortalium animus est.
   Be the proud captain still of thine own fate. — J. B. KENYON [1858–1924], *The Black Camel*
   See Sallust, 92:1; Francis Bacon, 160:4; Shakespeare, 187:22; Tennyson, 459:9; Henley, 557:10; and Nehru, 677:7.
[16]Jugurtha's remark as he looked back at Rome upon being ordered by the senate to leave Italy.
[17]Punica fide (treachery).

1   Experience has shown that to be true which Appius[1] says in his verses, that every man is the architect of his own fortune.[2]

Speech to Caesar on the State, sec. 1

Virgil [Publius Vergilius Maro]

70–19 B.C.

2   A god has brought us this peace.

Eclogues, I, l. 6

3   To compare great things with small.

Ibid. l. 23

4   Happy old man![3]   *Ibid. l. 46*

5   Ah Corydon, Corydon, what madness has caught you?   *Ibid. II, l. 69*

6   With Jove I begin.[4]   *Ibid. III, l. 60*

7   A sad thing is a wolf in the fold, rain on ripe corn, wind in the trees, the anger of Amaryllis.

Ibid. l. 80

8   A snake lurks in the grass.[5]   *Ibid. l. 93*

9   Let us raise a somewhat loftier strain![6]

Ibid. IV, l. 1

10   The great cycle of the ages is renewed. Now Justice returns, returns the Golden Age; a new generation now descends from on high.[7]   *Ibid. l. 5*

11   We have made you [Priapus] of marble for the time being.   *Ibid. VII, l. 35*

12   We are not all capable of everything.[8]

Ibid. VIII, l. 63

13   Draw Daphnis from the town, my songs, draw Daphnis home.   *Ibid. l. 68*

14   Hylax barks in the doorway.   *Ibid. l. 107*

15   Your descendants shall gather your fruits.[9]

Ibid. IX, l. 50

16   Time bears away all things, even our minds.

Ibid. l. 51

17   Let us go singing as far as we go: the road will be less tedious.   *Ibid. l. 64*

18   This last labor grant me, O Arethusa.

Ibid. X, l. 1

19   What if Amyntas is dark? Violets are dark, too, and hyacinths.   *Ibid. l. 38*

20   Love conquers all things; let us too surrender to Love.[10]   *Ibid. l. 69*

21   Utmost [farthest] Thule.[11]   *Georgics, I, l. 30*

22   Look with favor upon a bold beginning.[12]

Ibid. l. 40

23   O farmers, pray that your summers be wet and your winters clear.   *Ibid. l. 100*

24   Practice and thought might gradually forge many an art.   *Ibid. l. 133*

25   Thrice they tried to pile Ossa on Pelion, yes, and roll up leafy Olympus upon Ossa; thrice the Father of Heaven split the mountains apart with his thunderbolt.[13]   *Ibid. l. 281*

26   Frogs in the marsh mud drone their old lament.

Ibid. l. 378

27   Not every soil can bear all things.

Ibid. II, l. 109

28   Ah too fortunate farmers, if they knew their own good fortune!   *Ibid. l. 458*

29   May the countryside and the gliding valley streams content me. Lost to fame, let me love river and woodland.   *Ibid. l. 485*

30   Happy the man who could search out the causes of things.[14]   *Ibid. l. 490*

---

[1]Appius Claudius Caecus, consul in 307 B.C., the earliest Roman writer known to us.

[2]His own character is the arbiter of everyone's fortune. —PUBLILIUS SYRUS, *Maxim 283*

The brave man carves out his fortune, and every man is the son of his own works.—CERVANTES, *Don Quixote, pt. I* [1605], *bk. I, ch. 4*

See Aristotle, 78:5, and Sallust, 91:28.

[3]Fortunate senex!

[4]Ab Iove principium.

[5]Latet anguis in herba.

[6]Paulo maiora canamus!

[7]Magnus ab integro saeclorum nascitur ordo. / Iam redit et Virgo, redeunt Saturnia regna; / Iam nova progenies caelo demittitur alto.

Interpreted by the Middle Ages as a prophecy of the birth of Christ. Dante cites the lines in *Purgatorio, canto XXII, l. 70.*

A phrase altered from the first line (Novus ordo seclorum) appears on the reverse of the Great Seal of the United States of America (first used on the silver dollar certificates, series of 1935). Virgil supplied the Latin for other phrases of the Great Seal.

See Virgil, 92:22 and 94:29, and Shelley, 408:10.

[8]Non omnia possumus omnes.

[9]Carpent tua poma nepotes.

[10]Omnia vincit amor: et nos cedamus amori.

See Sophocles, 66:18 and 67:1, and Chaucer, 129:14.

[11]Ultima Thule.

The phrase, designating a far-off land, has been in use since the Greek mariner Pytheas discovered in the fourth century B.C. an island he named Thule six days north of England, thought to be Iceland.

See Seneca, 103:13, and Thomson, 308:8.

[12]Audacibus annue coeptis.

This phrase also (see note 7) was adapted for use on the reverse of the Great Seal of the United States of America: Annuit coeptis. See Virgil, 94:n14, for the Latin on the face of the Great Seal.

[13]See Homer, 53:19.

[14]Felix qui potuit rerum cognoscere causas.

The reference is apparently to the scientist-philosopher-poet Lucretius (see 89).

1 And no less happy he who knows the rural gods.[1]
Ibid. l. 493

2 This life the old Sabines knew long ago; Remus knew it, and his brother.
Ibid. l. 532

3 The best day . . . is the first to flee.[2]
Ibid. III, l. 66

4 Years grow cold to love.   *Ibid. l. 97*

5 Time is flying never to return.[3]   *Ibid. l. 284*

6 All aglow is the work.[4]   *Ibid. IV, l. 169*

7 A sudden madness came down upon the unwary lover [Orpheus]—forgivable, surely, if Death knew how to forgive.
Ibid. l. 488

8 Sweet Parthenope nourished me, flourishing in studies of ignoble ease.[5]   *Ibid. l. 563*

9 I who once played shepherds' songs and in my brash youth sang of you, O Tityrus, beneath the spreading beech.[6]   *Ibid. l. 565*

10 Arms and the man I sing.[7]   *Aeneid, bk. I, l. 1*

11 Can heavenly minds yield to such rage?
Ibid. l. 11

12 So vast was the struggle to found the Roman state.   *Ibid. l. 33*

13 Night, pitch-black, lies upon the deep.[8]
Ibid. l. 89

14 O thrice and four times blessed![9]   *Ibid. l. 94*

15 Fury provides arms.   *Ibid. l. 150*

16 You have suffered worse things; God will put an end to these also.   *Ibid. l. 199*

17 Perhaps someday it will be pleasant to remember even this.[10]   *Ibid. l. 203*

18 The organizer a woman.[11]   *Ibid. l. 364*

19 Her walk revealed her as a true goddess.
Ibid. l. 405

20 How happy those whose walls already rise!
Ibid. l. 437

21 Here are the tears of things; mortality touches the heart.[12]   *Ibid. l. 462*

22 I make no distinction between Trojan and Tyrian.   *Ibid. l. 574*

23 A mind aware of its own rectitude.[13]
Ibid. l. 604

24 As long as rivers shall run down to the sea, or shadows touch the mountain slopes, or stars graze in the vault of heaven, so long shall your honor, your name, your praises endure.   *Ibid. l. 607*

25 I have known sorrow and learned to aid the wretched.   *Ibid. l. 630*

26 Unspeakable, O Queen, is the sorrow you bid me renew.   *Ibid. II, l. 3*

27 Whatever it is, I fear Greeks even when they bring gifts.[14]   *Ibid. l. 49*

28 From a single crime know the nation.
Ibid. l. 65

29 I shudder to say it.[15]   *Ibid. l. 204*

30 O fatherland, O Ilium home of the gods, O Troy walls famed in battle!   *Ibid. l. 241*

31 Ucalegon's afire next door.[16]   *Ibid. l. 311*

32 We have been Trojans; Troy has been.
Ibid. l. 325

33 There is but one safety to the vanquished—to hope not safety.   *Ibid. l. 354*

34 Our foes will provide us with arms.
Ibid. l. 391

35 The gods thought otherwise.[17]   *Ibid. l. 428*

36 Thrice would I have thrown my arms about her neck, and thrice the ghost embraced fled from my grasp: like a fluttering breeze, like a fleeting dream.[18]
Ibid. l. 793

37 O accurst craving for gold!   *Ibid. III, l. 57*

38 Rumor flies.[19]   *Ibid. l. 121*

39 I feel again a spark of that ancient flame.[20]
Ibid. IV, l. 23

40 Deep in her breast lives the silent wound.
Ibid. l. 67

---

[1]Fortunatus et ille deos qui novit agrestis.
[2]Optima . . . dies . . . prima fugit.
[3]Fugit inreparabile tempus.
[4]Fervet opus.
[5]Me . . . dulcis alebat / Parthenope, studiis florentem ignobilis otii.
Parthenope: ancient name of Naples.
[6]Tityrus is also referred to in *Eclogues I, 1.*
[7]Arma virumque cano.
See Dryden, 276:5.
[8]See *Genesis 1:2, 6:4.*
[9]O terque quaterque beati!
[10]Forsan et haec olim meminisse iuvabit.
See Homer, 54:1.
[11]Dux femina facti.
[12]Sunt lacrimae rerum et mentem mortalia tangunt.

[13]The mind, conscious of rectitude, laughed to scorn the falsehood of report. —OVID, *Fasti, bk. IV, l. 311*
[14]Quidquid id est, timeo Danaos et dona ferentis.
[15]Horresco referens.
[16]Iam proximus ardet / Ucalegon.
Ucalegon was one of the ancient counselors who sat with Priam on the wall. His house was next to that of Anchises, father of Aeneas.
[17]Dis aliter visum.
[18]Virgil here translates HOMER, *Odyssey, bk. XI, l. 204.* See 53:18.
[19]Fama volat.
[20]Agnosco veteris vestigia flammae.
See Dante, 126:18.

1   A woman is always a fickle, unstable thing.[1]
Aeneid, bk. IV, l. 569

2   Arise from my bones, avenger of these wrongs!
Ibid. l. 625

3   Thus, thus, it is joy to pass to the world below.[2]
Ibid. l. 660

4   Naked in death upon an unknown shore.
Ibid. V, l. 871

5   Yield not to evils, but attack all the more boldly.
Ibid. VI, l. 95

6   It is easy to go down into Hell; night and day, the gates of dark Death stand wide; but to climb back again, to retrace one's steps to the upper air— there's the rub, the task.[3]
Ibid. l. 126

7   Faithful Achates.[4]   *Ibid. l. 158 and elsewhere*

8   Death's brother, Sleep.   *Ibid. l. 278*

9   The swamp of Styx, by which the gods take oath.
Ibid. l. 323

10   Unwillingly I left your land, O Queen.[5]
Ibid. l. 460

11   Had I a hundred tongues, a hundred mouths, a voice of iron and a chest of brass, I could not tell all the forms of crime, could not name all the types of punishment.[6]
Ibid. l. 625

12   That happy place, the green groves of the dwelling of the blest.   *Ibid. l. 638*

13   The spirit within nourishes, and the mind, diffused through all the members, sways the mass and mingles with the whole frame.   *Ibid. l. 726*

14   Each of us bears his own Hell.   *Ibid. l. 743*

15   Others, I take it, will work better with breathing bronze and draw living faces from marble; others will plead at law with greater eloquence, or measure the pathways of the sky, or forecast the rising stars. Be it your concern, Roman, to rule the nations under law (this is your proper skill) and establish the way of peace; to spare the conquered and put down the mighty from their seat.[7]
Ibid. l. 847

16   Give me handfuls of lilies to scatter.[8]
Ibid. l. 883

17   There are two gates of Sleep. One is of horn, easy of passage for the shades of truth; the other, of gleaming white ivory, permits false dreams to ascend to the upper air.[9]   *Ibid. l. 893*

18   Prayed to the Genius of the place.
Ibid. VII, l. 136

19   We descend from Jove; in ancestral Jove Troy's sons rejoice.   *Ibid. l. 219*

20   If I cannot bend Heaven, I shall move Hell.
Ibid. l. 312

21   An old story, but the glory of it is forever.
Ibid. IX, l. 79

22   To have died once is enough.   *Ibid. l. 140*

23   I cannot bear a mother's tears.   *Ibid. l. 289*

24   Good speed to your youthful valor, boy! So shall you scale the stars![10]   *Ibid. l. 641*

25   Fortune favors the brave.[11]   *Ibid. X, l. 284*

26   Dying dreams of his sweet Argos.[12]
Ibid. l. 782

27   Believe one who has proved it. Believe an expert.[13]   *Ibid. XI, l. 283*

28   His limbs were cold in death; his spirit fled with a groan, indignant, to the shades below.
Ibid. XII, l. 951

29   One composed of many.[14]
Minor Poems. Moretum, l. 104

30   Death twitches my ear. "Live," he says; "I am coming."   *Ibid. Copa, l. 38*

Horace [Quintus Horatius Flaccus]
65–8 B.C.

31   How comes it, Maecenas, that no man living is content with the lot that either his choice has given

---

[1]Varium et mutabile semper femina.
Woman often changes; foolish the man who trusts her. —FRANCIS I OF FRANCE, written by him with his ring on a window of the château of Chambord (BRANTÔME, *Oeuvres, VII, 395*)
La donna è mobile.—FRANCESCO MARIA PIAVE [1810– 1879], *libretto of Verdi's Rigoletto, Duke's song*
See Walter Scott, 378:14.
[2]Sic, sic, iuvat ire sub umbras.
[3]Facilis descensus Averni: / Noctes atque dies patet atri ianua Ditis; / Sed revocare gradum superasque evadere ad auras, / Hoc opus, hic labor est.
[4]Fidus Achates. Proverbial for a trusty friend; Achates was the faithful comrade of Aeneas.
[5]Aeneas to the ghost of Dido, who had killed herself when he left her.
[6]See Homer, 51:9.
[7]See Milton, 254:18.

[8]Quoted by DANTE in *The Divine Comedy, Purgatorio, canto XXX, l. 21.*
[9]See Homer, 54:9.
[10]Macte nova virtute, puer, sic itur ad astra.
See Dante, 126:20.
[11]Audentes fortuna iuvat.
See Menander, 81:12, and Terence, 86:12.
[12]Dulces moriens reminiscitur Argos.
[13]Experto credite.
Believe an expert; believe one who has had experience.— SAINT BERNARD, *Epistle 106*
Believe the experienced Robert. Believe Robert, who has tried it.—ROBERT BURTON, *Anatomy of Melancholy* [1621– 1651], *Introduction*
[14]E pluribus unus.
Adapted (E pluribus unum) for the motto on the face of the Great Seal of the United States, adopted June 20, 1782. For the Latin on the reverse of the Great Seal, see Virgil, 92:*n*7 and 92:*n*12.

him, or chance has thrown in his way, but each has praise for those who follow other paths?

Satires, bk. I [35 B.C.], satire i, l. 1

1   The story's about you.[1]   *Ibid. l. 69*

2   There is measure in all things.[2]   *Ibid. l. 106*

3   We rarely find anyone who can say he has lived a happy life, and who, content with his life, can retire from the world like a satisfied guest.

Ibid. l. 117

4   And all that tribe.[3]   *Ibid. ii, l. 2*

5   The limbs of a dismembered poet.[4]

Ibid. iv, l. 62

6   A man without a flaw.[5]   *Ibid. v, l. 32*

7   Life grants nothing to us mortals without hard work.   *Ibid. ix, l. 59*

8   As crazy as hauling timber into the woods.[6]

Ibid. x, l. 34

9   Simplicity and charm.[7]   *Ibid. l. 44*

10   This used to be among my prayers[8] — a piece of land not so very large, which would contain a garden, and near the house a spring of ever-flowing water, and beyond these a bit of wood.[9]

Ibid. II [30 B.C.], vi, l. 1

11   O nights and feasts of the gods![10]   *Ibid. l. 65*

12   In Rome you long for the country; in the country —oh inconstant!—you praise the distant city to the stars.   *Ibid. vii, l. 28*

13   Happy the man who far from schemes of business, like the early generations of mankind, works his ancestral acres with oxen of his own breeding, from all usury free.[11]

Epodes [c. 29 B.C.], II, st. 1

14   You ask me why a soft numbness diffuses all my inmost senses with deep oblivion, as though with thirsty throat I'd drained the cup that brings the sleep of Lethe.[12]   *Ibid. XIV, st. 1*

15   But if you name me among the lyric bards, I shall strike the stars with my exalted head.

Odes, bk. I [23 B.C.], ode i, last lines

16   The half of my own soul.[13]   *Ibid. iii, l. 8*

17   No ascent is too steep for mortals. Heaven itself we seek in our folly.   *Ibid. l. 37*

18   Pale Death with impartial tread beats at the poor man's cottage door and at the palaces of kings.[14]

Ibid. iv, l. 13

19   Life's brief span forbids us to enter on far-reaching hopes.[15]   *Ibid. l. 15*

20 What slender youth, bedewed with liquid odors, Courts thee on roses in some pleasant cave, Pyrrha? For whom bind'st thou In wreaths thy golden hair, Plain in thy neatness?[16]

Ibid. v, l. 1

21   Never despair.[17]   *Ibid. vii, l. 27*

22   Tomorrow once again we sail the Ocean Sea.[18]

Ibid. last line

23   Leave all else to the gods.[19]   *Ibid. ix, l. 9*

24   Cease to ask what the morrow will bring forth, and set down as gain each day that Fortune grants.[20]

Ibid. l. 13

25   Seize the day, put no trust in the morrow![21]

Ibid. xi, last line

26   Happy, thrice happy and more, are they whom an unbroken bond unites and whose love shall know no sundering quarrels so long as they shall live.

Ibid. xiii, l. 17

27   O fairer daughter of a fair mother![22]

Ibid. xvi, l. 1

28   The pure in life and free from sin.[23]

Ibid. xxii, l. 1

29   What restraint or limit should there be to grief for one so dear?   *Ibid. xxiv, l. 1*

30   Grant me, sound of body and of mind, to pass an old age lacking neither honor nor the lyre.[24]

Ibid. xxxi, last lines

---

[13]Animae dimidium meae.
The reference is to Virgil.
See Aristotle, 77:13; Zeno, 81:22; Cicero, 88:9; and Donne, 229:12.

[14]See Publilius Syrus, 98:29, and Shirley, 246:23.

[15]Vitae summa brevis spem nos vetat incohare longam.
See Dowson, 602:10.

[16]Simplex munditiis.
Translated by JOHN MILTON.

[17]Nil desperandum.

[18]Cras ingens iterabimus aequor.
Translated by S. E. MORISON.

[19]Permitte divis cetera.

[20]See *Matthew 6:34*, 34:1; Publilius Syrus, 100:6; and Marcus Aurelius, 110:15.

[21]Carpe diem, quam minimum credula postero.
See *The Wisdom of Solomon 2:8*, 30:21; Ronsard, 144:3; Spenser, 153:11; and Herrick, 241:9.

[22]O matre pulchra filia pulchrior.

[23]Integer vitae scelerisque purus.

[24]Not to be tuneless in old age!—DOBSON, *Henry Wadsworth Longfellow*

---

[1]De te fabula.

[2]Est modus in rebus.
See The Seven Sages, 55:10; Terence, 85:12; Horace, 96:7; Lucan, 105:21; and Anonymous: Latin, 119:15.

[3]Hoc genus omne.

[4]Disiecti membra poetae.
The reference is to Orpheus torn apart by the Maenads.

[5]Ad unguem factus homo.

[6]Carrying coals to Newcastle.—*Proverb*
See Aristophanes, 73:9.

[7]Molle atque facetum. This refers to Virgil's poetry.

[8]Hoc erat in votis.

[9]See Pope, 302:23.

[10]O noctes cenaeque deum!

[11]See Pope, 298:5.

[12]See Keats, 415:9.

1   A grudging and infrequent worshipper of the gods.[1]
Odes, bk. I, ode xxxiv, l. 1

2   Now is the time for drinking, now the time to beat the earth with unfettered foot.[2]
Ibid. xxxvii, l. 1

3   Persian luxury, boy, I hate.[3]
Ibid. xxxviii, l. 1

4   Cease your efforts to find where the last rose lingers.[4]
Ibid. l. 3

5   In adversity remember to keep an even mind.[5]
Ibid. II [23 B.C.], iii, l. 1

6   We are all driven into the same fold.[6]
Ibid. l. 25

7   Whoever cultivates the golden mean[7] avoids both the poverty of a hovel and the envy of a palace.
Ibid. x, l. 5

8   It is the mountaintop that the lightning strikes.[8]
Ibid. l. 11

9   Nor does Apollo always stretch the bow.[8]
Ibid. l. 19

10   Alas, Postumus, Postumus, the fleeting years slip by.[9]
Ibid. xiv, l. 1

11   No lot is altogether happy.[10]
Ibid. xvi, l. 27

12   I hate the common herd of men and keep them afar. Let there be sacred silence: I, the Muses' priest, sing for girls and boys songs not heard before.
Ibid. III [23 B.C.], i, l. 1

13   Dark Care sits enthroned behind the Knight.[11]
Ibid. l. 40

14   It is sweet and honorable to die for one's country.[12]
Ibid. ii, l. 13

15   The man who is tenacious of purpose in a rightful cause is not shaken from his firm resolve by the frenzy of his fellow citizens clamoring for what is wrong, or by the tyrant's threatening countenance.[13]
Ibid. iii, l. 1

16   Force without wisdom falls of its own weight.
Ibid. iv, l. 65

17   Our sires' age was worse than our grandsires'. We their sons are more worthless than they: so in our turn we shall give the world a progeny yet more corrupt.
Ibid. vi, l. 46

18   Skilled in the works of both languages.
Ibid. viii, l. 5

19   With you I should love to live, with you be ready to die.[14]
Ibid. ix, last line

20   Gloriously perjured,[15] a maiden famous to all time.[16]
Ibid. xi, l. 35

21   O fount Bandusian, more sparkling than glass.[17]
Ibid. xiii, l. 1

22   I would not have borne this in my hot youth when Plancus was consul.[18]
Ibid. xiv, l. 27

23   A pauper in the midst of wealth.[19]
Ibid. xvi, l. 28

24   He will through life be master of himself and a happy man who from day to day can have said, "I have lived: tomorrow the Father may fill the sky with black clouds or with cloudless sunshine."[20]
Ibid. xxix, l. 41

25   I have built a monument more lasting than bronze.[21]
Ibid. xxx, l. 1

26   I shall not wholly die.[22]
Ibid. l. 6

27   I am not what I was in the reign of the good Cinara. Forbear, cruel mother of sweet loves.[23]
Ibid. IV [13 B.C.], i, l. 3

28   The centuries roll back to the ancient age of gold.
Ibid. ii, l. 39

29   We are but dust and shadow.
Ibid. vii, l. 16

---

[1]Parcus deorum cultor et infrequens.

[2]Nunc est bibendum, nunc pede libero pulsanda tellus.
Ode on the death of Cleopatra.

[3]Persicos odi, puer, apparatus.

[4]Mitte sectari, rosa quo locorum / Sera moretur.

[5]Aequam memento rebus in arduis / Servare mentem.

[6]Omnes eodem cogimur.

[7]Auream quisquis mediocritatem / Diliget.
Keep the golden mean. — PUBLILIUS SYRUS, *Maxim 1072*
See The Seven Sages, 55:10; Terence, 85:12; Horace, 95:2; Lucan, 105:21; and Anonymous: Latin, 119:15.

[8]Neque semper arcum / Tendit Apollo.

[9]Eheu fugaces, Postume, Postume, / Labuntur anni.

[10]Nihil est ab omni / Parte beatum.

[11]Post equitem sedet atra cura.

[12]Dulce et decorum est pro patria mori.
See Homer, 52:7.

[13]See Fabius Maximus, 83:5, and Addison, 292:3.

[14]Tecum vivere amem, tecum obeam libens.

[15]Splendide mendax.
Chosen by Swift as Gulliver's motto.

[16]Hypermestra.

[17]O fons Bandusiae splendidior vitro.

[18]In my hot youth, when George the Third was king. — BYRON, *Don Juan* [1819–1824], canto 1, st. 212

[19]Magnus inter opes inops.

[20]Ille potens sui / Laetusque deget, cui licet in diem / Dixisse "Vixi: cras vel atra / Nube polum pater occupato / Vel sole puro."
Tomorrow let my sun his beams display / Or in clouds hide them; I have lived my day. — COWLEY, *Discourse XI, Of Myself* [1661], st. 11
See Dryden, 274:29, and Sydney Smith, 380:18.

[21]Exegi monumentum aere perennius.

[22]Non omnis moriar.

[23]Non sum qualis eram bonae / Sub regno Cinarae. Desine, dulcium / Mater saeva Cupidinum.
Mater saeva Cupidinum. — *Odes, bk. I, xix, l. 1*
See Dowson, 602:7.

1   Many brave men lived before Agamemnon; but all are overwhelmed in eternal night, unwept, unknown, because they lack a sacred poet.[1]

Ibid. ix, l. 25

2   It is not the rich man you should properly call happy, but him who knows how to use with wisdom the blessings of the gods, to endure hard poverty, and who fears dishonor worse than death, and is not afraid to die for cherished friends or fatherland.

Ibid. l. 45

3   It is sweet to let the mind unbend on occasion.[2]

Ibid. xii, l. 27

4   I am not bound over to swear allegiance to any master; where the storm drives me I turn in for shelter.   *Epistles, bk. I, epistle i, l. 14*

5   To flee vice is the beginning of virtue, and to have got rid of folly is the beginning of wisdom.

Ibid. l. 41

6   Make money, money by fair means if you can, if not, by any means money.[3]   *Ibid. l. 66*

7   The people are a many-headed beast.[4]

Ibid. l. 76

8   He who has begun has half done. Dare to be wise; begin![5]   *Ibid. ii, l. 40*

9   The covetous man is ever in want.

Ibid. l. 56

10   Anger is a short madness.   *Ibid. l. 62*

11   Think to yourself that every day is your last; the hour to which you do not look forward will come as a welcome surprise. As for me, when you want a good laugh, you will find me, in a fine state, fat and sleek, a true hog of Epicurus' herd.[6]

Ibid. iv, l. 13

12   You may drive out Nature with a pitchfork, yet she still will hurry back.   *Ibid. l. 24*

13   They change their clime, not their disposition, who run across the sea.[7]   *Ibid. xi, l. 27*

14   He is not poor who has enough of things to use. If it is well with your belly, chest and feet, the wealth of kings can give you nothing more.

Ibid. xii, l. 4

15   Harmony in discord.[8]   *Ibid. l. 19*

16   For joys fall not to the rich alone, nor has he lived ill, who from birth to death has passed unknown.

Ibid. xvii, l. 9

17   It is not everyone that can get to Corinth.[9]

Ibid. l. 36

18   Once a word has been allowed to escape, it cannot be recalled.[10]   *Ibid. xviii, l. 71*

19   It is your concern when your neighbor's wall is on fire.   *Ibid. l. 84*

20   No poems can please for long or live that are written by water-drinkers.   *Ibid. xix, l. 2*

21   O imitators, you slavish herd!   *Ibid. l. 19*

22   And seek for truth in the groves of Academe.[11]

Ibid. II [14 B.C.], ii, l. 45

23   Barefaced poverty drove me to writing verses.

Ibid. l. 51

[1]How many, famous while they lived, are utterly forgotten for want of writers! — BOETHIUS, *De Consolatione Philosophiae*, II, 7

Brave men were living before Agamemnon / And since, exceeding valorous and sage, / A good deal like him too, but quite the same none; / But then they shone not on the poet's page. — BYRON, *Don Juan* [1819–1824], canto I, st. 5

See Pindar, 64:13, and Pope, 303:13.

[2]See Menander, 81:6; Montaigne, 147:2; and Francis Bacon, 160:1.

[3]Get money; still get money, boy, no matter by what means. — JONSON, *Every Man in His Humour* [1598], act II, sc. iii

See Pope, 303:4.

[4]Belua multorum es capitum.

Plato describes the multitude as a "great strong beast." — *The Republic*, bk. VI, 493–B

The multitude of the gross people, being a beast of many heads. — ERASMUS, *Adagia, no. 122*

O weak trust of the many-headed multitude. — PHILIP SIDNEY, *The Arcadia* [1580], bk. II

The beast of many heads, the staggering multitude. — MARSTON AND WEBSTER, *The Malcontent* [1604], act III, sc. iii

If there be any among those common objects of hatred I do contemn and laugh at, it is that great enemy of reason, virtue, and religion, the multitude . . . one great beast and a monstrosity more prodigious than Hydra. — THOMAS BROWNE, *Religio Medici* [1643], pt. II, sec. 1

Sir, your people is a great beast. — *Attributed to* ALEXANDER HAMILTON

See Machiavelli, 137:3; Shakespeare, 183:9, 219:3, and 219:10; and Pope, 303:10.

[5]See Plato, 75:8; Aristotle, 78:26; and John Heywood, 141:21.

[6]See Chaucer, 129:24.

[7]See Kipling, 592:18.

[8]Concordia discors.

[9]A rendering of a Greek proverb, "It's not everyone that can make the voyage to Corinth," which referred to the expense of the life there.

There is but one road that leads to Corinth. — PATER, *Marius the Epicurean* [1885], *ch. 24*

[10]Semel emissum volat irrevocabile verbum.

The written word, unpublished, can be destroyed, but the spoken word can never be recalled. — *Ars Poetica* [c. 8 B.C.], *l. 389*

It is as easy to recall a stone thrown violently from the hand as a word which has left your tongue. — MENANDER, *Fragment 1092K*

Four things come not back: the spoken word; the sped arrow; time past; the neglected opportunity. — OMAR IBN AL-HALIF, *Aphorism*

A word once spoken revoked cannot be. — ALEXANDER BARCLAY [c. 1475–1552], *The Ship of Fools* [1509]

Thoughts unexpressed may sometimes fall back dead; / But God Himself can't kill them when they're said. — CARLETON, *The First Settler's Story, st. 21*

See Chaucer, 132:7.

[11]Atque inter silvas Academi quaerere verum.

See Milton, 261:1.

1   The years as they pass plunder us of one thing after another.   *Epistles, bk. II, epistle ii, l. 55*

2   I have to submit to much in order to pacify the touchy tribe of poets.[1]   *Ibid. l. 102*

3   "Painters and poets," you say, "have always had an equal license in bold invention." We know; we claim the liberty for ourselves and in turn we give it to others.   *Ibid. III (Ars Poetica) [c. 8 B.C.], l. 9*

4   It was a wine jar when the molding began: as the wheel runs round why does it turn out a water pitcher?   *Ibid. l. 21*

5   It is when I struggle to be brief that I become obscure.   *Ibid. l. 25*

6   Scholars dispute and the case is still before the courts.[2]   *Ibid. l. 78*

7   Foot-and-a-half-long words.[3]   *Ibid. l. 97*

8 If you wish me to weep, you yourself
Must first feel grief.[4]
         Ibid. l. 102

9   Taught or untaught, we all scribble poetry.   *Ibid. l. 117*

10   The mountains will be in labor, and a ridiculous mouse will be brought forth.[5]   *Ibid. l. 139*

11   From the egg.[6]   *Ibid. l. 147*

12   In the midst of things.[7]   *Ibid. l. 148*

13   A praiser of past time.[8]   *Ibid. l. 173*

14   Let a play have five acts, neither more nor less.   *Ibid. l. 189*

15   Turn the pages of your Greek models night and day.[9]   *Ibid. l. 268*

16   He wins every hand who mingles profit with pleasure, by delighting and instructing the reader at the same time.   *Ibid. l. 343*

17   Sometimes even good old Homer nods.[10]   *Ibid. l. 359*

18   As in painting, so in poetry.[11]   *Ibid. l. 361*

19   He has defiled his father's grave.   *Ibid. l. 471*

[1]Genus irritabile vatum.
[2]Grammatici certant et adhuc sub iudice lis est.
[3]Sesquipedalia verba.
[4]Si vis me flere, dolendum est / Primum ipsi tibi.
[5]Parturient montes, nascetur ridiculus mus.
See Aesop, 59:8.
[6]Ab ovo.
Helen, the cause of the Trojan War, sprang from an egg engendered by Leda and the Swan (Zeus).
[7]In medias res.
[8]Laudator temporis acti.
[9]See Hsieh Ho, 115:8, and Fujiwara no Teika, 123:3.
[10]Quandoque bonus dormitat Homerus.
Homer himself, in a long work, may sleep.—HERRICK, *Hesperides* [1648], *no. 95*
See Pope, 298:12.
[11]Ut pictura poesis.

Augustus Caesar
63 B.C.–A.D. 14

20   Quintilius Varus, give me back my legions![12]   *From SUETONIUS, Augustus, sec. 23*

21   More haste, less speed.[13]   *Ibid. 25*

22   Well done is quickly done.[14]   *Ibid.*

23   I found Rome a city of bricks and left it a city of marble.   *Ibid. 28*

24   After this time I surpassed all others in authority, but I had no more power than the others who were also my colleagues in office.   *Res Gestae, 34*

25   Young men, hear an old man to whom old men hearkened when he was young.   *From PLUTARCH, Apothegms, Caesar Augustus*

Livy [Titus Livius]
59 B.C.–A.D. 17

26   We can endure neither our evils nor their cures.[15]   *History, Prologue*

27   Better late than never.[16]   *Ibid. bk. IV, sec. 23*

28   Beyond the Alps lies Italy.[17]   *Ibid. XXI, 30*

Publilius Syrus[18]
First century B.C.

29   As men, we are all equal in the presence of death.[19]   *Maxim 1*

30   He doubly benefits the needy who gives quickly.[20]   *Maxim 6*

31   To do two things at once is to do neither.   *Maxim 7*

32   A god could hardly love and be wise.[21]   *Maxim 25*

[12]Quintili Vare, legiones redde!
[13]A Greek proverb, a familiar rendering of which is: Festina lente.
[14]A Latin proverb: Sat celeriter fieri quidquid fiat satis bene. See Publilius Syrus, 98:30, and Anonymous: Latin, 118:18.
[15]The two reasons for writing a history.
[16]Potius sero quam numquam.
It is better to learn late than never.—PUBLILIUS SYRUS, *Maxim 864*
[17]In conspectu Alpes habeant, quarum alterum latus Italiae sit.
Au-delà des Alpes est l'Italie.—NAPOLEON [1797]
[18]Commonly called Publius, but spelled Publilius by Pliny in his *Natural History, 35, sec. 199.* Translated mainly by DARIUS LYMAN. The numbers are those of the translator.
[19]See Horace, 95:18, and Shirley, 246:23.
[20]See Augustus Caesar, 98:22, and Anonymous: Latin, 118:-18.
[21]It is impossible to love and be wise.—FRANCIS BACON, *Essays* [1597–1625], *Of Love*

1 The loss which is unknown is no loss at all.[1]
Maxim 38

2 A good reputation is more valuable than money.
Maxim 108

3 It is well to moor your bark with two anchors.
Maxim 119

4 Many receive advice, few profit by it.
Maxim 149

5 While we stop to think, we often miss our opportunity.
Maxim 185

6 Whatever you can lose, you should reckon of no account.
Maxim 191

7 For a good cause, wrongdoing is virtuous.[2]
Maxim 244

8 You should hammer your iron when it is glowing hot.[3]
Maxim 262

9 What is left when honor is lost? *Maxim 265*

10 A fair exterior is a silent recommendation.
Maxim 267

11 Fortune is not satisfied with inflicting one calamity.
Maxim 274

12 When Fortune is on our side, popular favor bears her company.
Maxim 275

13 When Fortune flatters, she does it to betray.[4]
Maxim 277

14 Fortune is like glass — the brighter the glitter, the more easily broken.
Maxim 280

15 It is more easy to get a favor from Fortune than to keep it.
Maxim 282

16 There are some remedies worse than the disease.[5]
Maxim 301

17 A cock has great influence on his own dunghill.[6]
Maxim 357

18 Anyone can hold the helm when the sea is calm.[7]
Maxim 358

19 The bow too tensely strung is easily broken.
Maxim 388

20 Treat your friend as if he might become an enemy.[8]
Maxim 402

21 No pleasure endures unseasoned by variety.[9]
Maxim 406

22 The judge is condemned when the criminal is absolved.[10]
Maxim 407

23 Practice is the best of all instructors.[11]
Maxim 439

24 He who is bent on doing evil can never want occasion.
Maxim 459

25 Never find your delight in another's misfortune.
Maxim 467

26 It is a bad plan that admits of no modification.
Maxim 469

27 It is an unhappy lot which finds no enemies.
Maxim 499

28 The fear of death is more to be dreaded than death itself.[12]
Maxim 511

29 A rolling stone gathers no moss.[13]
Maxim 524

30 Never promise more than you can perform.
Maxim 528

31 No one should be judge in his own case.[14]
Maxim 545

32 Necessity knows no law except to prevail.[15]
Maxim 553

33 Nothing can be done at once hastily and prudently.[16]
Maxim 557

34 We desire nothing so much as what we ought not to have.
Maxim 559

35 It is only the ignorant who despise education.
Maxim 571

[8]Treat your friend as if he will one day be your enemy, and your enemy as if he will one day be your friend. — LABERIUS [105–43 B.C.], *Fragment*
See Sophocles, 65:13.

[9]See Samuel Johnson, 314:7, and Cowper, 334:28.

[10]Iudex damnatur ubi nocens absolvitur. — *Motto adopted for the Edinburgh Review*

[11]Practice makes perfect. — *Proverb*
The saying "Practice is everything" is Periander's. — DIOGENES LAERTIUS, *Lives of Eminent Philosophers, Periander, 6*

[12]See Shakespeare, 204:11.

[13]The rolling stone never gathereth mosse. — JOHN HEYWOOD, *Proverbs* [1546], *pt. I, ch. 2*
The stone that is rolling can gather no moss. — TUSSER, *A Hundred Good Points of Husbandry* [1557]

[14]It is not permitted to the most equitable of men to be a judge in his own cause. — PASCAL, *Pensées* [1670], *ch. 4, 1*

[15]Proverbial; attributed to Syrus.
Necessity gives the law and does not itself receive it. — *Maxim 399*
See Saint Augustine, 114:29, and Cromwell, 247:3.

[16]See Chaucer, 131:22, and John Heywood, 140:15.

[1]See Shakespeare, 207:7.

[2]Honesta turpitudo est pro causa bona.

[3]Strike while the iron is hot. — RABELAIS, *Gargantua and Pantagruel, bk. II* [1534], *ch. 31*
When the iron is hot, strike. — JOHN HEYWOOD, *Proverbs* [1546], *pt. I, ch. 2*
Nothing like striking while the iron is hot. — CERVANTES, *Don Quixote, pt. II* [1615], *bk. IV, ch. 71*

[4]See Shakespeare, 170:6.

[5]Marius said, "I see the cure is not worth the pain." — PLUTARCH, *Lives, Caius Marius*
The remedy is worse than the disease. — FRANCIS BACON, *Essays* [1597–1625], *Of Seditions*
I find the medicine worse than the malady. — BEAUMONT AND FLETCHER, *Love's Cure* [1647], *act III, sc. ii*

[6]Every cock is proud on his own dunghill. — JOHN HEYWOOD, *Proverbs* [1546], *pt. I, ch. 2*

[7]See Shakespeare, 200:6.

1 Do not turn back when you are just at the goal.[1]
Maxim 580

2 It is not every question that deserves an answer.
Maxim 581

3 No man is happy who does not think himself so.[2]
Maxim 584

4 Never thrust your own sickle into another's corn.[3]
Maxim 593

5 You cannot put the same shoe on every foot.
Maxim 596

6 Every day should be passed as if it were to be our last.[4]
Maxim 633

7 Money alone sets all the world in motion.
Maxim 656

8 You should go to a pear tree for pears, not to an elm.[5]
Maxim 674

9 It is a very hard undertaking to seek to please everybody.
Maxim 675

10 Look for a tough wedge for a tough log.
Maxim 723

11 Pardon one offense, and you encourage the commission of many.
Maxim 750

12 In every enterprise consider where you would come out.[6]
Maxim 777

13 It takes a long time to bring excellence to maturity.
Maxim 780

14 No one knows what he can do till he tries.
Maxim 786

15 It is vain to look for a defense against lightning.
Maxim 835

16 Everything is worth what its purchaser will pay for it.[7]
Maxim 847

17 Better be ignorant of a matter than half know it.[8]
Maxim 865

18 Prosperity makes friends, adversity tries them.[9]
Maxim 872

19 Let a fool hold his tongue and he will pass for a sage.
Maxim 914

20 You need not hang up the ivy branch over the wine that will sell.[10]
Maxim 968

21 It is a consolation to the wretched to have companions in misery.[11]
Maxim 995

22 Unless degree is preserved, the first place is safe for no one.[12]
Maxim 1042

23 Confession of our faults is the next thing to innocence.
Maxim 1060

24 I have often regretted my speech, never my silence.[13]
Maxim 1070

25 Speech is a mirror of the soul: as a man speaks, so is he.
Maxim 1073

Dionysius of Halicarnassus
c. 54 – c. 7 B.C.

26 The contact with manners then is education; and this Thucydides appears to assert when he says history is philosophy learned from examples.
Ars Rhetorica, XI, 2

Sextus Propertius
c. 54 B.C. – A.D. 2

27 Never change when love has found its home.
Elegies, I, i, 36

28 The seaman's story is of tempest, the plowman's of his team of bulls; the soldier tells his wounds, the shepherd his tale of sheep.
Ibid. II, i, 43

29 Let each man pass his days in that wherein his skill is greatest.
Ibid. 46

30 What though strength fails? Boldness is certain to win praise. In mighty enterprises, it is enough to have had the determination.[14]
Ibid. x, 5

31 Let no one be willing to speak ill of the absent.[15]
Ibid. xix, 32

---

[1]When men are arrived at the goal, they should not turn back. — PLUTARCH, *Of the Training of Children*

[2]No man can enjoy happiness without thinking that he enjoys it. — SAMUEL JOHNSON, *The Rambler* [1750–1752]

[3]Did thrust as now in others' corn his sickle. — DU BARTAS, *Divine Weeks and Works* [1578], *Second Week, pt. 2*

Not presuming to put my sickle in another man's corn. — NICHOLAS YONGE [d. 1619], *Musica Transalpina, Epistle Dedicatory* [1588]

See *Deuteronomy* 23:25, 10:20.

[4]See *Matthew* 6:34, 34:1; Horace, 95:24; and Marcus Aurelius, 110:15.

[5]You may as well expect pears from an elm. — CERVANTES, *Don Quixote, pt. II* [1615], *bk. IV, ch. 40*

[6]In every affair, consider what precedes and what follows and then undertake it. — EPICTETUS, *That Everything Is to Be Undertaken with Circumspection, ch. 15*

[7]See Samuel Butler [1612–1680], 263:19.

[8]See Pope, 298:13.

[9]See Aristotle, 79:1; Cicero, 88:8; Ovid, 102:3; and John Heywood, 142:5.

[10]Good wine needs no bush. — SHAKESPEARE, *As You Like It, Epilogue, l. 4*

Good wine needs neither bush nor preface / To make it welcome. — WALTER SCOTT, *Peveril of the Peak* [1822], *ch. 4*

Bush . . . *archaic:* a bunch or branch of ivy, formerly hung outside a tavern to indicate wine for sale. — *Webster's Third New International Dictionary* [1966]

I.e., good wine needs no advertising.

[11]See Ray, 272:7.

[12]See Shakespeare, 200:8.

[13]Simonides said that "he never repented that he held his tongue, but often that he had spoken." — PLUTARCH, *Rules for the Preservation of Health*

See Plutarch, 107:8.

[14]Quod si deficiant vires, audacia certe / Laus erit: in magnis et voluisse sat est.

[15]Absenti nemo non nocuisse velit.

See The Seven Sages, 55:11.

1   Let each man have the wit to go his own way.
Ibid. xxv, 38

2   Absence makes the heart grow fonder.[1]
Ibid. xxxiii, 43

3   There is something beyond the grave; death does not end all, and the pale ghost escapes from the vanquished pyre.[2]   *Ibid. IV, vii, 1*

Albius Tibullus
c. 54 – c. 19 B.C.

4   May I look on you when my last hour comes; may I hold you, as I sink, with my failing hand.[3]
Elegies, I, i, 59

5   Jupiter laughs at the perjuries of lovers.[4]
Ibid. III, vi, 49

6   Jove the Rain-giver.   *Ibid. vii, 26*

Ovid [Publius Ovidius Naso]
43 B.C.–A.D. c. 18

7   I have faith that yields to none, and ways without reproach, and unadorned simplicity, and blushing modesty.   *Amores, I, iii, 13*

8   The rest who does not know?[5]   *Ibid. v, 25*

9   Every lover is a warrior, and Cupid has his camps.[6]   *Ibid. ix, 1*

10   Run slowly, horses of the night.[7]
Ibid. xiii, 39

11   Stay far hence, far hence, you prudes![8]
Ibid. II, i, 3

12   So I can't live either without you or with you.[9]
Ibid. III, xi, 39

---

[1]Semper in absentes felicior aestus amantes.

[2]Our souls survive this death. — OVID, *Metamorphoses,* XV, *l.* 158

[3]Te spectem, suprema mihi cum venerit hora. / Te teneam moriens deficiente manu.

[4]Periuria ridet amantum Iupiter.
Also in OVID, *Ars Amatoria, I, 633*
And Jove but laughs at lovers' perjury. — DRYDEN, *Palamon and Arcite* [1680], *bk. II, l.* 758, and *Amphitryon* [1690], act I, sc. ii
See Shakespeare, 175:4.

[5]Cetera quis nescit?

[6]Love is a kind of warfare. — OVID, *Ars Amatoria, II, 233*
A batallas de amor campo de pluma [A field of feathers for the strife of love]. — LUIS DE GÓNGORA Y ARGOTE [1561–1627], *Soledad, I*

[7]At si, quem malis, Cephalum complexa teneres, / Clamares "lente currite noctis equi."
See Marlowe, 162:23.

[8]Procul hinc, procul este, severi!

[9]Sic ego nec sine te nec tecum vivere possum.
See Aristophanes, 73:17, and Martial, 106:24.

---

13   They come to see; they come that they themselves may be seen.[10]   *Ars Amatoria, I, 99*

14   It is convenient that there be gods, and, as it is convenient, let us believe there are.[11]   *Ibid. 637*

15   To be loved, be lovable.   *Ibid. II, 107*

16   Nothing is stronger than habit.   *Ibid. 345*

17   Perhaps too my name will be joined to theirs[12] [the names of famous poets].   *Ibid. III, 339*

18   Now there are fields of corn where Troy once was.   *Heroides, I, i, 2*

19   [Chaos] A rough, unordered mass of things.[13]
Metamorphoses, I, 7

20   Your lot is mortal: not mortal is what you desire.
Ibid. II, 56

21   You will be safest in the middle.[14]   *Ibid. 137*

22   I am Actaeon: recognize your master![15]
Ibid. III, 230

23   The cause is hidden, but the result is well known.[16]   *Ibid. IV, 287*

24   We can learn even from our enemies.[17]
Ibid. 428

25   I see and approve better things, but follow worse.[18]   *Ibid. VII, 20*

26   The gods have their own rules.[19]
Ibid. IX, 500

27   Time the devourer of all things.[20]
Ibid. XV, 234

28   And now I have finished a work that neither the wrath of love, nor fire, nor the sword, nor devouring age shall be able to destroy.   *Ibid. 871*

29   Resist beginnings; the prescription comes too late when the disease has gained strength by long delays.[21]   *Remedia Amoris, 91*

---

[10]Spectatum veniunt, veniunt spectentur ut ipsae.
And for to se, and eek for to be seye. — CHAUCER, *The Canterbury Tales* [c. 1387], *The Wife of Bath's Prologue, l.* 552
To see and to be seen. — JONSON, *Epithalamion, III, 4*

[11]See Tillotson, 273:7, and Voltaire, 306:25.

[12]Forsitan et nostrum nomen miscebitur istis.

[13]Rudis indigestaque moles.

[14]Medio tutissimus ibis.

[15]Actaeon ego sum, dominum cognoscite vestrum!

[16]Causa latet, vis est notissima.

[17]Fas est et ab hoste doceri. Imitated from ARISTOPHANES, *The Birds, l.* 370: People before this have learned from their enemies.

[18]Video meliora, proboque, deteriora sequor.
I know and love the good, yet, ah! the worst pursue. — PETRARCH, *Sonnet 225, Canzone 21, To Laura in Life* [c. 1327]
See Romans 7:19, 41:46, and Euripides, 68:14.

[19]Sunt superis sua iura.

[20]Tempus edax rerum.

[21]See Persius, 104:18.

1   Love yields to business. If you seek a way out of love, be busy; you'll be safe then.[1]

Remedia Amoris, 143

2   Poetry comes fine-spun from a mind at peace.

Tristia, I, i, 39

3   So long as you are secure you will count many friends; if your life becomes clouded you will be alone.[2]

Ibid. ix, 5

4   Whatever I tried to write was verse.

Ibid. IV, x, 26

5   It is annoying to be honest to no purpose.

Ex Ponto, II, iii, 14

6   Note too that a faithful study of the liberal arts humanizes character and permits it not to be cruel.

Ibid. ix, 47

Hillel

fl. 30 B.C.–A.D. 10

7   What is hateful to you do not do to your neighbor. That is the whole Torah. The rest is commentary.[3]

*From Talmud [compiled sixth century].
Shabbath*

8   God says: If you come to My House, I will come to yours.   *Ibid. Sukkah*[4]

9   If I am not for myself, who is for me? And when I am for myself, what am I? And if not now, when?

Ibid. The Wisdom of the Fathers[5]

10   The more flesh, the more worms. The more possessions, the more worry.   *Ibid.*

Phaedrus[6]

fl. A.D. c. 8

11   Submit to the present evil, lest a greater one befall you.   *Fables, bk. I, fable 2, l. 31*

12   He was the author, our hand finished it.

Ibid. 6, l. 20

13   It has been related that dogs drink at the river Nile running along, that they may not be seized by the crocodiles.[7]   *Ibid. 25, l. 3*

14   Come of it what may, as Sinon said.

Ibid. III, prologue, l. 27

15   Things are not always what they seem.[8]

Ibid. IV, 2, l. 5

16   To add insult to injury.   *Ibid. V, l. 3*

17   Once lost, Jupiter himself cannot bring back opportunity.[9]   *Ibid. VII, l. 4*

Lucius Annaeus Seneca[10]

c. 4 B.C.–A.D. 65

18   What fools these mortals be.[11]   *Epistles, 1, 3*

19   It is not the man who has too little, but the man who craves more, that is poor.   *Ibid. 2, 2*

20   Live among men as if God beheld you; speak to God as if men were listening.   *Ibid. 10, 5*

21   The best ideas are common property.

Ibid. 12, 11

22   Men do not care how nobly they live, but only how long, although it is within the reach of every man to live nobly, but within no man's power to live long.   *Ibid. 22, 17*

23   A great pilot can sail even when his canvas is rent.

Ibid. 30, 3

24   Man is a reasoning animal.   *Ibid. 41, 8*

25   It is quality rather than quantity that matters.[12]

Ibid. 45, 1

26   You can tell the character of every man when you see how he receives praise.   *Ibid. 52, 12*

27   Not lost, but gone before.[13]   *Ibid. 63, 16*

28   All art is but imitation of nature.   *Ibid. 65, 3*

29   It is a rough road that leads to the heights of greatness.   *Ibid. 84, 13*

30   The pilot . . . who has been able to say, "Neptune, you shall never sink this ship except on an even keel," has fulfilled the requirements of his art.[14]

Ibid. 85, 33

31   I was shipwrecked before I got aboard.

Ibid. 87, 1

32   It is better, of course, to know useless things than to know nothing.   *Ibid. 88, 45*

---

[1]Qui finem quaeris amoris / Cedit amor rebus; res age, tutus eris.

[2]See Aristotle, 79:1; Cicero, 88:8; Publilius Syrus, 100:18; and John Heywood, 142:5.

[3]See *Matthew 7:12*, 34:8; Confucius, 61:30; Aristotle, 77:15; and Chesterfield, 304:21.

[4]Translated by ISRAEL W. SLOTKIN.

[5]Translated by JACOB NEUSNER.

[6]Translated by HENRY THOMAS RILEY [1816–1878].

[7]Pliny the Elder in his *Natural History (bk. VIII, sec. 148)* and Aelian in his *Various Histories* relate the same fact as to the dogs drinking from the Nile. "To treat a thing as the dogs do the Nile" was a common proverb, signifying superficial treatment.

[8]Non semper ea sunt quae videntur.

[9]Opportunity knocks only once.—*Proverb*

[10]Translated by R. M. GUMMERE, J. W. BASORE, W. H. D. ROUSE, and F. J. MILLER (Loeb Classical Library).

[11]Tanta stultitia mortalium est.

See Shakespeare, 173:18.

[12]See Anonymous: Latin, 119:16.

[13]Non amittuntur, sed praemittuntur.

Not dead, but gone before.—SAMUEL ROGERS, *Human Life* [1819]

[14]The mariner of old said thus to Neptune in a great tempest, "O God! thou mayest save me if thou wilt, and if thou wilt, thou mayest destroy me; but whether or no, I will steer my rudder true."—MONTAIGNE, *Essays* [1580–1595], *bk. II, ch. 16*

1   Do not ask for what you will wish you had not got.   *Ibid. 95, 1*

2   We are mad, not only individually, but nationally. We check manslaughter and isolated murders; but what of war and the much vaunted crime of slaughtering whole peoples?   *Ibid. 95, 30*

3   A great step towards independence is a good-humored stomach, one that is willing to endure rough treatment.   *Ibid. 123, 3*

4   Fire is the test of gold; adversity, of strong men.[1]
Moral Essays. On Providence, 5, 9

5   Time discovers truth.[2]   *Ibid. On Anger, 2, 22*

6   Whom they have injured they also hate.[3]
Ibid. 33

7   There is no great genius without some touch of madness.[4]
Ibid. On Tranquillity of the Mind, 17, 10

8   A great fortune is a great slavery.
Ibid. To Polybius on Consolation, 6, 5

9   Wherever the Roman conquers, there he dwells.
Ibid. To Helvia on Consolation, 7, 7

10   You roll my log, and I will roll yours.
Apocolocyntosis, sec. 9

11   Do you seek Alcides' equal? None is, except himself.[5]   *Hercules Furens, 1, 1, 84*

12   Successful and fortunate crime is called virtue.[6]
Ibid. 255

13   An age will come after many years when the Ocean will loose the chains of things, and a huge

---

land lie revealed; when Tiphys[7] will disclose new worlds and Thule[8] no more be the ultimate.[9]
Medea, l. 374

14   A good mind possesses a kingdom.[10]
Thyestes, 380

Marcus Manilius
First century A.D.

15   [Human reason] freed men's minds from wondering at portents by wresting from Jupiter his bolts and power of thunder, and ascribing to the winds the noise and to the clouds the flame.[11]
Astronomica,[12] bk. I, l. 102

16   Who could know heaven save by heaven's gift and discover God save one who shares himself in the divine?[13]   *Ibid. II, l. 115*

Caligula [Gaius Caesar]
A.D. 12–41

17   Strike so that he may feel he is dying.[14]
From Suetonius, The Lives of the Caesars, sec. 30

18   Would that the Roman people had a single neck [to cut off their head].[15]   *Ibid.*

Pliny the Elder
[Gaius Plinius Secundus][16]
A.D. 23–79

19   In comparing various authors with one another, I have discovered that some of the gravest and latest

---

[1]See Beaumont and Fletcher, 238:19.

[2]Veritatem dies aperit. Omnia tempus revelat [Time reveals all].—Tertullian, *Apologeticus, 7*

Time reveals all things.—Erasmus, *Adagia*

[3]It is human nature to hate those whom you have injured. —Tacitus, *Agricola, 42, 15*

Chi fa ingiuria non perdona mai [He never pardons those he injures].—*Italian proverb*

The offender never pardons.—George Herbert, *Jacula Prudentum* [1651]

Forgiveness to the injured does belong; / But they ne'er pardon who have done the wrong.—Dryden, *The Conquest of Granada* [1670], *pt. II, act I, sc. ii*

[4]An ancient commonplace, which Seneca says he quotes from Aristotle, *Problemata, 30, 1:* "No excellent soul is exempt from a mixture of madness." It is also in Plato, *Phaedrus, 245-A.*

Good sense travels on the well-worn paths; genius, never. And that is why the crowd, not altogether without reason, is so ready to treat great men as lunatics.—Lombroso, *The Man of Genius,* preface

See Dryden, 274:3.

[5]And but herself admits no parallel.—Massinger, *Duke of Milan* [1623], *act IV, sc. iii*

None but himself can be his parallel.—Lewis Theobald [1688–1744], *The Double Falsehood*

[6]See Harington, 160:16.

[7]Jason's pilot.

[8]See Virgil, 92:21, and Thomson, 308:8.

[9]Venient annis / Saecula seris, quibus Oceanus / Vincula rerum laxet, et ingens / Pateat tellus, Tiphysque novos / Detegat orbes nec sit terris / Ultima Thule.

Translated by S. E. Morison.

As one much addicted to prophecies, and who had already voyaged beyond Thule (Iceland), Columbus was much impressed by the passage in Seneca's *Medea.*—S. E. Morison, *Admiral of the Ocean Sea* [1942], *vol. I, ch. 6*

Next to these lines from *Medea* in an early edition of Seneca's tragedies that belonged to Columbus's son Ferdinand, there is this annotation in the son's hand: Haec profetia impleta est per patrem meum . . . almirantem anno 1492 [The prophecy was fulfilled by my father the Admiral in the year 1492]. —*Ibid. 5*

[10]See Dyer, 148:2.

[11]Cur imbres ruerent, ventosque causa moveret pervidit, solvitque animis miracula rerum eripuitque Jovi fulmen viresque tonandi et sonitum ventis concessit, nubibus ignem.

See Shakespeare, 219:9, and Franklin, 309:*n*1.

[12]Translated by G. P. Gould (Loeb Classical Library).

[13]See Hippocrates, 71:10.

[14]Ita feri ut se mori sentiat.

Translated by J. C. Rolfe (Loeb Classical Library).

[15]Utinam populus Romanus cervicem haberet.

[16]With some alterations, translated by John Bostock [1773–1846] and Henry Thomas Riley [1816–1878].

See also Pliny the Younger, 109:24.

writers have transcribed, word for word, from former works, without making acknowledgment.
Natural History, bk. I, dedication, sec. 22

1   Everything is soothed by oil, and this is the reason why divers send out small quantities of it from their mouths, because it smooths every part which is rough.[1]   *Ibid. II, 234*

2   It is far from easy to determine whether she [Nature] has proved to man a kind parent or a merciless stepmother.[2]   *Ibid. VII, 1*

3   Man alone at the very moment of his birth, cast naked upon the naked earth, does she abandon to cries and lamentations.[3]   *Ibid. 2*

4   To laugh, if but for an instant only, has never been granted to man before the fortieth day from his birth, and then it is looked upon as a miracle of precocity.[4]   *Ibid.*

5   Man is the only one that knows nothing, that can learn nothing without being taught. He can neither speak nor walk nor eat, and in short he can do nothing at the prompting of nature only, but weep.
Ibid. VII, 4

6   With man, most of his misfortunes are occasioned by man.[5]   *Ibid. 5*

7   Indeed, what is there that does not appear marvelous when it comes to our knowledge for the first time?[6] How many things, too, are looked upon as quite impossible until they have been actually effected?   *Ibid. 6*

8   The human features and countenance, although composed of but some ten parts or little more, are so fashioned that among so many thousands of men there are no two in existence who cannot be distinguished from one another.[7]   *Ibid. 8*

9   There is always something new out of Africa.[8]
Ibid. VIII, 17

10   When a building is about to fall down, all the mice desert it.[9]   *Ibid. 103*

11   Bears when first born are shapeless masses of white flesh a little larger than mice, their claws alone being prominent. The mother then licks them gradually into proper shape.[10]   *Ibid. 126*

12   The best plan is to profit by the folly of others.
Ibid. XVIII, 31

13   With a grain of salt.[11]   *Ibid. XXIII, 8*

14   Why is it that we entertain the belief that for every purpose odd numbers are the most effectual?[12]
Ibid. XXVIII, 23

Persius [Aulus Persius Flaccus]
A.D. 34–62

15   The stomach is the teacher of the arts and the dispenser of invention.[13]   *Satires, prologue, l. 10*

16   Tell, priests, what is gold doing in a holy place?
Ibid. II, l. 69

17   Let them look upon virtue and pine because they have lost her.   *Ibid. III, l. 38*

18   Meet the disease at its first stage.[14]
Ibid. l. 64

---

[1]Why does pouring oil on the sea make it clear and calm? Is it for that the winds, slipping the smooth oil, have no force, nor cause any waves?—PLUTARCH, *Natural Questions, IX*

Bishop Adain [651] gave to a company about to take a journey by sea "some holy oil, saying, 'I know that when you go abroad you will meet with a storm and contrary wind; but do you remember to cast this oil I give you into the sea, and the wind shall cease immediately.'"—BEDE, *Ecclesiastical History, bk. III, ch. 14*

[2]To man the earth seems altogether / No more a mother, but a stepdame rather.—DU BARTAS, *Divine Weeks and Works* [1578], *First Week, Third Day*

[3]He is born naked, and falls a-whining at the first.—ROBERT BURTON, *Anatomy of Melancholy* [1621–1651], *pt. I, sec. 2, member 3, subsec. 10*

See *The Wisdom of Solomon* 7:3, 30:28.

[4]This term of forty days is mentioned by Aristotle in his *Natural History.*

[5]See Burns, 361:8, and Wordsworth, 372:18.

[6]See Tacitus, 109:20.

[7]It is the common wonder of all men, how among so many millions of faces there should be none alike.—THOMAS BROWNE, *Religio Medici* [1643], *pt. II, sec. 2*

Of a thousand shavers, two do not shave so much alike as not to be distinguished.—SAMUEL JOHNSON [1777]; from BOSWELL, *Life of Johnson* [1791], *vol. II, p. 120* (Everyman edition)

[8]Ex Africa semper aliquid novi.

Quoted as a Greek proverb.

[9]This is alluded to by Cicero in his letters to Atticus, and is mentioned by Aelian *(Animated Nature, bk. VI, ch. 41).* Compare the modern proverb: Rats desert a sinking ship.

[10]Not unlike the bear which bringeth forth / In the end of thirty days a shapeless birth; / But after licking, it in shape she draws, / And by degrees she fashions out the paws, / The head, and neck, and finally doth bring / To a perfect beast that first deformed thing.—DU BARTAS, *Divine Weeks and Works* [1578], *First Week, First Day*

I had not time to lick it into form, as a bear doth her young ones.—ROBERT BURTON, *Anatomy of Melancholy* [1621–1651], *Democritus to the Reader*

[11]Cum grano salis.

Pompey's antidote against poison was "to be taken fasting, a grain of salt being added."

[12]The god delights in an odd number.—VIRGIL, *Eclogues, VIII, 75*

[13]Magister artis ingeniique largitor venter.

Necessity, mother of invention.—WILLIAM WYCHERLEY [c. 1640–1716], *Love in a Wood* [1671], *act III, sc. iii*

Art imitates Nature, and necessity is the mother of invention.—RICHARD FRANCK [c. 1624–1708], *Northern Memoirs* [written 1658, published 1694]

Sheer necessity—the proper parent of an art so nearly allied to invention.—R. B. SHERIDAN, *The Critic* [1779], *act I, sc. ii*

See Anonymous: Latin, 119:12.

[14]Venienti occurrite morbo.

A stitch in time saves nine.—*Proverb*

Also in Publilius Syrus, *Maxim 866.*

See Ovid, 101:29.

Gaius Petronius [Petronius Arbiter[1]]

d. A.D. c. 66

1   He has joined the great majority.[2]

Satyricon, sec. 42

2   A man who is always ready to believe what is told him will never do well.   *Ibid. 43*

3   One good turn deserves another.   *Ibid. 45*

4   A man must have his faults.   *Ibid.*

5   Not worth his salt.   *Ibid. 57*

6   My heart was in my mouth.   *Ibid. 62*

7   Beauty and wisdom are rarely conjoined.

Ibid. 94

8   The studied spontaneity of Horace.[3]

Ibid. 118

9   Natural curls.[4]   *Ibid. 126*

Quintilian [Marcus Fabius Quintilianus]

A.D. c. 35–c. 100

10   We give to necessity the praise of virtue.[5]

De Institutione Oratoria, bk. I, 8, 14

11   A liar should have a good memory.[6]

Ibid. IV, 2, 91

12   Vain hopes are often like the dreams of those who wake.   *Ibid. VI, 2, 30*

13   For it is feeling and force of imagination that makes us eloquent.[7]   *Ibid. X, 7, 15*

14   Those who wish to appear wise among fools, among the wise seem foolish.[8]   *Ibid. 21*

[1]Pliny calls Petronius Titus in *Natural History, XXXVII, 8.* See Tacitus, 109:15.

[2]*Abiit ad plures.*

[3]*Horatii curiosa felicitas.*

[4]*Crines ingenio suo flexi.*

[5]*Seize the opportunity, I beg, and make a virtue of necessity* [fac de necessitate virtutem].—SAINT JEROME, *Letter 54*

In the additions of Hadrianus Julius to the *Adagia* of Erasmus he remarks under the head of *Necessitatem edere* that a very familiar proverb was current among his countrymen: Necessitatem in virtutem commutare [To make necessity a virtue].

Thus maketh vertue of necessitee.—CHAUCER, *Troilus and Criseyde* [c. 1385], bk. IV, l. 1586

Make a virtue of necessity.—ROBERT BURTON, *Anatomy of Melancholy* [1621–1651], pt. III, sec. 3, member 4, subsec. l

See Shakespeare, 171:1.

[6]He who has not a good memory should never take upon him the trade of lying.—MONTAIGNE, *Essays* [1580–1595], bk. I, ch. 9, *Of Liars*

Il faut bonne mémoire, après qu'on a menti [You must have a good memory after you have lied].—CORNEILLE, *Le Menteur* [1642], act IV, sc. v

Liars ought to have good memories.—ALGERNON SIDNEY, *Discourses on Government* [1698], ch. 2, sec. 15

[7]*Pectus est enim, quod disertos facit.*

[8]A fool with judges, amongst fools a judge.—COWPER, *Conversation* [1782], l. 298

See Pope, 303:30.

Flavius Josephus[9]

A.D. 37–95?

15   Everyone ought to worship God according to his own inclinations, and not to be constrained by force.

Life, ch. 23

16   While I am alive I shall never be in such slavery as to forgo my own kindred, or forget the laws of our forefathers.

The Wars of the Jews, bk. VI, ch. 8

Eleazar ben Jair[9]

d. A.D. 73

17   Let us spare nothing but our provisions. For they will be a testimonial when we are dead, that we were not subdued for want of necessaries; but that, according to our original resolution, we have preferred death before slavery.

Speech at Masada. From JOSEPHUS, *The Wars of the Jews, bk. VII, ch. 8*

Nero

A.D. 37–68

18   What an artist dies with me![10]

From SUETONIUS, *Nero, sec. 49*

Lucan

A.D. 39–65

19   If the victor had the gods on his side, the vanquished had Cato.[11]   *The Civil War, bk. I, 128*

20   There stands the shadow of a glorious name.[12]

Ibid. 135

21   Keep to moderation, keep the end in view, follow nature.[13]   *Ibid. II, 381*

22   Thinking nothing done while anything remained to be done.[14]   *Ibid. 657*

23   More was lost than mere life and existence.[15]

Ibid. VII, 639

24   We all praise fidelity; but the true friend pays the penalty when he supports those whom Fortune crushes.[16]   *Ibid. VIII, 485*

[9]Translated by WILLIAM WHISTON.

[10]*Qualis artifex pereo!*

[11]*Victrix causa deis placuit, sed victa Catoni.*

[12]*Stat magni nominis umbra.*

[13]*Servare modum, finemque tenere, / Naturamque sequi.*

See The Seven Sages, 55:10; Terence, 85:12; Horace, 95:2 and 96:7; and Anonymous: Latin, 119:15.

[14]The reference is to Caesar.

[15]*Plus est quam vita salusque / Quod perit.*

[16]"*Dat poenas laudata fides, dum sustinet*," inquit, / "*Quos fortuna premit*" / [A praised faith / Is her own scourge, when it sustains their states / Whom fortune hath depressed].—JONSON, *Anglia, 39, 247*

1   A name illustrious and revered by nations.[1]
Civil War, bk. IX, 203

2   Is the dwelling place of God anywhere but in the earth and sea, the air and sky, and virtue? Why seek we further for deities? Whatever you see, whatever you touch, that is Jupiter.   *Ibid. 578*

3   The very ruins have been destroyed.[2]
Ibid. 969

Longinus
First century A.D.

4   It frequently happens that where the second line is sublime, the third, in which he [Lucan] meant to rise still higher, is perfect bombast.
On the Sublime, sec. 3

5   Sublimity is the echo of a noble mind.
Ibid. 9

6   In the Odyssey one may liken Homer to the setting sun, of which the grandeur remains without the intensity.   *Ibid.*

Martial[3] [Marcus Valerius Martialis]
A.D. c. 40 – c. 104

7   My poems are naughty, but my life is pure.[4]
Epigrams, I, 4

8   Tomorrow's life is too late. Live today.
Ibid. 15

9   Some good, some so-so, and lots plain bad: that's how a book of poems is made, my friend.
Ibid. 16

10   I don't like you, Sabidius, I can't say why; But I can say this: I don't like you, Sabidius.[5]
Ibid. 32

11   Stop abusing my verses, or publish some of your own.   *Ibid. 91*

12   You complain, friend Swift, of the length of my epigrams, but you yourself write nothing. Yours are shorter.   *Ibid. 110*

13   Conceal a flaw, and the world will imagine the worst.   *Ibid. III, 42*

14   The bee is enclosed, and shines preserved in amber, so that it seems enshrined in its own nectar.[6]
Ibid. IV, 32

15   They praise those verses, yes, but read something else.   *Ibid. 49*

16   You ask what a nice girl will do? She won't give an inch, but she won't say no.   *Ibid. 71*

17   Our days pass by, and are scored against us.[7]
Ibid. V, 20

18   What's a wretched man? A man whom no man pleases.   *Ibid. 28*

19   A man who lives everywhere lives nowhere.
Ibid. 73

20   You puff the poets of other days,
The living you deplore.
Spare me the accolade: your praise
Is not worth dying for.
Ibid. VIII, 69

21   Virtue extends our days: he lives two lives who relives his past with pleasure.[8]   *Ibid. X, 23*

22   Neither fear your death's day nor long for it.
Ibid. 47

23   You'll get no laurel crown for outrunning a burro.   *Ibid. XII, 36*

24   You're obstinate, pliant, merry, morose, all at once. For me there's no living with you, or without you.[9]   *Ibid. 47*

25   The country in town.[10]   *Ibid. 57*

26   I know these are nothing.[11]   *Ibid. XIII, 2*

Titus Vespasianus
A.D. c. 41–81

27   Friends, I have lost a day.[12]
From SUETONIUS, Titus, sec. 8

---

[6]Whence we see spiders, flies, or ants entombed preserved forever in amber, a more than royal tomb.—FRANCIS BACON, *Historia Vitae et Mortis* [1623], *Sylva Sylvarum, cent. I, exper. 100*

I saw a fly within a bead / Of amber cleanly buried.—HERRICK, *On a Fly Buried in Amber*

[7]Nobis pereunt et imputantur.

[8]Thus would I double my life's fading space; / For he that runs it well, runs twice his race.—COWLEY, *Discourse XI, Of Myself, st. 11*

For he lives twice who can at once employ / The present well, and ev'n the past enjoy.—POPE, *Imitation of Martial*

[9]Difficilis facilis fucundus acerbus es idem: / Nec tecum possum vivere nec sine te.

See Aristophanes, 73:17, and Ovid, 101:12.

[10]Rus in urbe.

[11]Nos haec novimus esse nihil.

Said of his own poems. The phrase was used by John Gay as an epigraph for *The Beggar's Opera* [1728].

[12]Amici, diem perdidi.

And faith though praised, is punished, that supports / Such as good fate forsakes.—JOHN FLETCHER, *The False One* [1647], *act 1, sc. i, l. 303*

[1]Clarum et venerabile nomen / Gentibus.

Cato's tribute to the fallen Pompey.

[2]Etiam periere ruinae.

The reference is to Troy.

[3]Translated by DUDLEY FITTS.

[4]Lasciva est nobis pagina, vita proba.

[5]See Tom Brown, 286:25.

Plutarch

A.D. 46–120

1 As geographers, Sosius, crowd into the edges of their maps parts of the world which they do not know about, adding notes in the margin to the effect that beyond this lies nothing but sandy deserts full of wild beasts, and unapproachable bogs.[1]

Lives, Aemilius Paulus, sec. 5

2 A Roman divorced from his wife, being highly blamed by his friends, who demanded, "Was she not chaste? Was she not fair? Was she not fruitful?" holding out his shoe, asked them whether it was not new and well made. "Yet," added he, "none of you can tell where it pinches me."[2] *Ibid. 29*

3 Where the lion's skin will not reach, you must patch it out with the fox's.[3]

Ibid. Lysander, sec. 7

4 Perseverance is more prevailing than violence; and many things which cannot be overcome when they are together, yield themselves up when taken little by little. *Ibid. Sertorius, sec. 16*

5 Medicine, to produce health, has to examine disease; and music, to create harmony, must investigate discord. *Ibid. Demetrius, sec. 1*

6 The very spring and root of honesty and virtue lie in good education.

Morals. Of the Training of Children

7 It is indeed desirable to be well descended, but the glory belongs to our ancestors. *Ibid.*

8 It is wise to be silent when occasion requires, and better than to speak, though never so well.[4]

Ibid.

9 An old doting fool, with one foot already in the grave. *Ibid.*

10 He is a fool who leaves things close at hand to follow what is out of reach.[5] *Ibid. Of Garrulity*

11 All men whilst they are awake are in one common world; but each of them, when he is asleep, is in a world of his own.[6] *Ibid. Of Superstition*

12 Spintharus, speaking in commendation of Epaminondas, says he scarce ever met with any man who knew more and spoke less.

Ibid. Of Hearing, sec. 6

13 Antiphanes said merrily that in a certain city the cold was so intense that words were congealed as soon as spoken, but that after some time they thawed and became audible; so that the words spoken in winter were articulated next summer.[7]

Ibid. Of Man's Progress in Virtue

14 When the candles are out all women are fair.[8]

Ibid. Conjugal Precepts

15 Like watermen, who look astern while they row the boat ahead.[9]
Ibid. Whether 'Twas Rightfully Said, Live Concealed

16 The great-god Pan is dead.[10]
Ibid. Why the Oracles Cease to Give Answers

17 I am whatever was, or is, or will be; and my veil no mortal ever took up.[11]

Ibid. Of Isis and Osiris

18 For to err in opinion, though it be not the part of wise men, is at least human.[12]

Ibid. Against Colotes

19 Pythagoras, when he was asked what time was, answered that it was the soul of this world.

Ibid. Platonic Questions

---

[6]A saying attributed to Heraclitus.

[7]Rabelais gives a somewhat similar account, referring to Antiphanes, in *Works*, bk. IV [1548], chs. 55–56.

See Raspe (Baron Munchausen), 341:12.

[8]When all candles be out, all cats be gray. —JOHN HEYWOOD, *Proverbs* [1546], pt. I, ch. 5

See Herrick, 241:7.

[9]Like rowers, who advance backward. —MONTAIGNE, *Essays* [1580–1595], *Of Profit and Honor, bk. III, ch. 1*

Like the watermen that row one way and look another. —ROBERT BURTON, *Anatomy of Melancholy* [1621–1651], *Democritus to the Reader*

See Bunyan, 272:22.

[10]Plutarch says in *Of Isis and Osiris* that a ship well laden with passengers drove with the tide near the Isles of Paxi, when a loud voice was heard by most of the passengers calling one Thanus. The voice then said aloud to him, "When you are arrived at Palodes, take care to make it known that the great god Pan is dead."

Great Pan is dead. —ELIZABETH BARRETT BROWNING, *The Dead Pan, st. 26*

[11]I am the things that are, and those that are to be, and those that have been. No one ever lifted my skirts; the fruit which I bore was the sun. —PROCLUS [c. 411–485], *On Plato's Timaeus* (inscription in the temple of Neith at Sais, in Egypt)

[12]See Anonymous: Latin, 118:30; Shirley, 246:20; Pope, 299:4; and Burns, 362:5.

---

[1]So geographers, in Afric maps, / With savage pictures fill their gaps, / And o'er unhabitable downs / Place elephants for want of towns. —SWIFT, *On Poetry, A Rhapsody* [1733]

[2]The wearer knows where the shoe wrings. —GEORGE HERBERT, *Jacula Prudentum* [1651]

I can tell where my own shoe pinches. —CERVANTES, *Don Quixote, pt. I* [1605], *bk. IV, ch. 5*

[3]The prince must be a lion, but he must also know how to play the fox. —MACHIAVELLI, *The Prince* [1532]

[4]Closed lips hurt no one, speaking may. —CATO THE CENSOR, *On Agriculture, bk. I, distich 12*

See Publilius Syrus, 100:24.

[5]Better one bird in hand than ten in the wood. —JOHN HEYWOOD, *Proverbs* [1546], pt. I, ch. 2

One bird in the hand is worth two in the wood. —THOMAS LODGE, *Rosalynde* [1590]

A bird in hand is worth two in the bush. —CERVANTES, *Don Quixote, pt. I* [1605], bk. IV, ch. 4

A feather in hand is better than a bird in the air. —GEORGE HERBERT, *Jacula Prudentum* [1651]

Epictetus[1]
A.D. c. 55–135

1   When you close your doors, and make darkness within, remember never to say that you are alone, for you are not alone;[2] nay, God is within, and your genius is within. And what need have they of light to see what you are doing?

Discourses, bk. I, ch. 14

2   No thing great is created suddenly, any more than a bunch of grapes or a fig. If you tell me that you desire a fig, I answer you that there must be time. Let it first blossom, then bear fruit, then ripen.

Ibid. 15

3   Any one thing in the creation is sufficient to demonstrate a Providence to a humble and grateful mind.   *Ibid. 16*

4   Were I a nightingale, I would sing like a nightingale; were I a swan, like a swan. But as it is, I am a rational being, therefore I must sing hymns of praise to God.   *Ibid.*

5   Practice yourself, for heaven's sake, in little things; and thence proceed to greater.   *Ibid. 18*

6   Appearances to the mind are of four kinds. Things either are what they appear to be; or they neither are, nor appear to be; or they are, and do not appear to be; or they are not, and yet appear to be. Rightly to aim in all these cases is the wise man's task.   *Ibid. 27*

7   Only the educated are free.   *Ibid. II, 1*

8   Shall I show you the sinews of a philosopher? "What sinews are those?"—A will undisappointed; evils avoided; powers daily exercised; careful resolutions; unerring decisions.   *Ibid. 8*

9   What is the first business of one who practices philosophy? To get rid of self-conceit. For it is impossible for anyone to begin to learn that which he thinks he already knows.   *Ibid. 17*

10   Be not swept off your feet by the vividness of the impression, but say, "Impression, wait for me a little. Let me see what you are and what you represent. Let me try you."   *Ibid. 18*

11   First say to yourself what you would be; and then do what you have to do.   *Ibid. III, 23*

12   Remember that you ought to behave in life as you would at a banquet. As something is being passed around it comes to you; stretch out your hand, take a portion of it politely. It passes on; do not detain it. Or it has not come to you yet; do not project your desire to meet it, but wait until it comes in front of you. So act toward children, so toward a wife, so toward office, so toward wealth.

The Encheiridion, 15

13   Where do you suppose he got that high brow?

Ibid. 22

14   Everything has two handles—by one of which it ought to be carried and by the other not.[3]

Ibid. 43

Juvenal [Decimus Junius Juvenalis]
A.D. c. 55 – c. 130

15   It is hard not to write satire.[4]

Satires, I, l. 30

16   Honesty is praised and starves.[5]   *Ibid. l. 74*

17   If nature refuses, indignation will produce verses.[6]   *Ibid. l. 79*

18   All the doings of mankind, their wishes, fears, anger, pleasures, joys, and varied pursuits, form the motley subject of my book.   *Ibid. l. 85*

19   Censure pardons the raven, but is visited upon the dove.[7]   *Ibid. II, l. 63*

20   No one becomes depraved in a moment.[8]

Ibid. l. 83

21   Grammarian, rhetorician, geometrician, painter, trainer, soothsayer, rope-dancer, physician, magician—he knows everything. Tell the hungry little Greek to go to heaven; he'll go.[9]   *Ibid. III, l. 76*

22   Bitter poverty has no harder pang than that it makes men ridiculous.[10]   *Ibid. l. 152*

23   It is not easy for men to rise whose qualities are thwarted by poverty.   *Ibid. l. 164*

24   We all live in a state of ambitious poverty.

Ibid. l. 182

25   A rare bird on earth, comparable to a black swan.[11]   *Ibid. VI, l. 165*

[1]Translated by W. A. OLDFATHER (Loeb Classical Library).
[2]Though in a wilderness, a man is never alone.—THOMAS BROWNE, *Religio Medici* [1643], *p. 82* (Everyman edition)

[3]There is a right and wrong handle to everything.—RASPE, *Travels of Baron Munchausen* [1785], *ch. 30*
[4]Difficile est saturam non scribere.
Translated by G. G. RAMSAY (Loeb Classical Library).
[5]Probitas laudatur et alget.
A favorite quotation of Linnaeus.
[6]Si natura negat, facit indignatio versum.
[7]Dat veniam corvis, vexat censura columbas.
[8]Nemo repente fuit turpissimus.
Translated by GILBERT HIGHET.
See Beaumont and Fletcher, 238:15, and Racine, 281:12.
[9]See Dryden, 274:11.
[10]Nil habet infelix paupertas durius in se, quam quod ridiculos homines facit.
[11]Rara avis in terris nigroque simillima cycno.

1 I wish it, I command it. Let my will take the place of reason.[1] *Ibid. l. 223*

2 We are now suffering the evils of a long peace. Luxury, more deadly than war, broods over the city, and avenges a conquered world.[2] *Ibid. l. 292*

3 But who is to guard the guards themselves?[3] *Ibid. l. 347*

4 An inveterate and incurable itch for writing besets many, and grows old in their sick hearts. *Ibid. VII, l. 51*

5 Nobility is the one and only virtue.[4] *Ibid. VIII, l. 20*

6 Count it the greatest sin to prefer life to honor, and for the sake of living to lose what makes life worth having.[5] *Ibid. l. 83*

7 The people that once bestowed commands, consulships, legions, and all else, now concerns itself no more, and longs eagerly for just two things—bread and circuses![6] *Ibid. X, l. 79*

8 Put Hannibal in the scales.[7] *Ibid. l. 147*

9 You should pray for a sound mind in a sound body.[8] *Ibid. l. 356*

10 For revenge is always the delight of a mean spirit, of a weak and petty mind! You may immediately draw proof of this—that no one rejoices more in revenge than a woman. *Ibid. XIII, l. 189*

11 The greatest reverence is due the young.[9] *Ibid. XIV, 47*

Cornelius Tacitus
A.D. c. 56 – c. 120

12 The images of the most illustrious families . . . were carried before it [the bier of Julia]. Those of Brutus and Cassius were not displayed; but for that reason they shone with preeminent luster. *Annals, bk. III, 76*

13 He had talents equal to business, and aspired no higher. *Ibid. VI, 39*

14 What is today supported by precedents will hereafter become a precedent. *Ibid. XI, 24*

15 [Of Petronius:] Arbiter of taste.[10] *Ibid. XVI, 18*

16 It is the rare fortune of these days that one may think what one likes and say what one thinks. *Histories, bk. I, 1*

17 [Of Servius Galba:] He seemed more important than a private citizen while he was a private citizen, and in the opinion of all he was capable of rule—if he had not ruled. *Ibid. 49*

18 The desire for glory clings even to the best men longer than any other passion.[11] *Ibid. IV, 6*

19 The gods are on the side of the stronger.[12] *Ibid. 17*

20 Whatever is unknown is taken for marvelous;[13] but now the limits of Britain are laid bare. *Agricola, sec. 30*

21 Where they make a desert, they call it peace.[14] *Ibid.*

22 Think of your forefathers and posterity.[15] *Ibid. 32*

23 Fortune favored him . . . in the opportune moment of his death. *Ibid. 45*

Pliny the Younger
[Gaius Plinius Caecilius Secundus]
A.D. c. 61 – c. 112

24 Modestus said of Regulus that he was "the biggest rascal that walks upon two legs." *Letters,[16] bk. I, letter 5*

25 There is nothing to write about, you say. Well then, write and let me know just this—that there is nothing to write about; or tell me in the good old style if you are well. That's right. I am quite well.[17] *Ibid. 11*

[1]Hoc volo, sic iubeo, sit pro ratione voluntas.
[2]Nunc patimur longae pacis mala, saevior armis / Luxuria incubuit victumque ulciscitur orbem.
[3]Sed quis custodiet ipsos custodes?
What an absurd idea—a guardian to need a guardian!—PLATO, *The Republic, bk. III, 403–E*
[4]Nobilitas sola est atque unica virtus.
[5]Summum crede nefas animam praeferre pudori, / Et propter vitam vivendi perdere causas.
[6]Panem et circenses.
[7]Expende Hannibalem.
[8]Mens sana in corpore sano.
See Locke [1632–1704], 277:10.
[9]Maxima debetur puero reverentia.
See Locke, 277:12.

[10]Elegantiae arbiter.
See Petronius, 105.
[11]See Milton, 253:20.
[12]Deos fortioribus adesse.
See Bussy-Rabutin, 266:13; Boileau, 280:17; Frederick the Great, 318:20; and Gibbon, 340:6.
[13]Omne ignotum pro magnifico est.
See Pliny the Elder, 104:7.
[14]Calgacus, addressing the Britons at the battle of the Grampians, referring to the Romans.
See Byron, 401:9.
[15]Et maiores vestros et posteros cogitate.
[16]*Book VI, letter 16,* contains the description of the eruption of Vesuvius [79], as witnessed by Pliny the Elder.
[17]This comes to inform you that I am in a perfect state of health, hoping you are in the same. Ay, that's the old beginning.
—GEORGE COLMAN THE YOUNGER, *The Heir-at-Law* [1797], *act III, sc. ii*

1   An object in possession seldom retains the same charm that it had in pursuit.[1]
Letters, bk. II, letter 15

2   He [Pliny the Elder] used to say that "no book was so bad but some good might be got out of it."[2]
Ibid. III, 5

3   This expression of ours, "Father of a family."[3]
Ibid. V, 19

4   That indolent but agreeable condition of doing nothing.[4]
Ibid. VIII, 9

5   His only fault is that he has no fault.[5]
Ibid. IX, 26

Suetonius
[Gaius Suetonius Tranquillus]
A.D. c. 69 – c. 140

6   Hail, Emperor, we who are about to die salute you.[6]
Life of Claudius, 21

Hadrian [Publius Aelius Hadrianus]
A.D. 76–138

7   Little soul, wandering, gentle guest and companion of the body, into what places will you now go, pale, stiff, and naked, no longer sporting as you did![7]
Ad Animam Suam

Chang Heng[8]
A.D. 78–139

8   Heaven is like an egg, and the earth is like the yolk of the egg.
Saying

[1]It has been a thousand times observed, and I must observe it once more, that the hours we pass with happy prospects in view are more pleasing than those crowned with fruition. — GOLDSMITH, *The Vicar of Wakefield* [1766], ch. 10

[2]"There is no book so bad," said the bachelor, "but something good may be found in it." — CERVANTES, *Don Quixote*, pt. II [1615], ch. 3

[3]Paterfamilias.

[4]Dolce far niente [Sweet doing-nothing]. — *Italian proverb*

[5]The greatest of faults, I should say, is to be conscious of none. — CARLYLE, *On Heroes and Hero Worship* [1841], *The Hero as Prophet*

[6]Ave, Caesar, morituri te salutamus.
Also rendered "te salutant": those about to die salute you.

[7]Animula vagula blandula, / Hospes comesque corporis, / Quae nunc abibis in loca / Pallidula rigida nudula, / Nec ut soles dabis iocosi.
Amelette Ronsardelette, / mignonelette doucelette, / très chère hostesse de mon corps, / tu descens là bas foibelette, / pasle, maigrelette, seulette, / dans le froid Royaulme des mors. — RONSARD, *A son âme* [dictated on his deathbed, December 27, 1585]
See Pope, 299:8.

[8]From *Sources of Chinese Tradition* [1960], edited by WILLIAM THEODORE DE BARY.

Lucius Annaeus Florus
fl. 125

9   Each year new consuls and proconsuls are made; but not every year is a king or a poet born.[9]
De Qualitate Vitae, fragment 8

Ptolemy [Claudius Ptolemaeus]
c. 100–178

10   Everything that is hard to attain is easily assailed by the generality of men.
Tetrabiblos,[10] bk. I, sec. 1

11   The length of life takes the leading place among inquiries about events following birth.
Ibid. III, 10

12   As material fortune is associated with the properties of the body, so honor belongs to those of the soul.
Ibid. IV, 1

13   There are three classes of friendship and enmity, since men are so disposed to one another either by preference or by need or through pleasure and pain.
Ibid. 7

Marcus Aurelius Antoninus[11]
121–180

14   This Being of mine, whatever it really is, consists of a little flesh, a little breath, and the part which governs.
Meditations, II, 2

15   You will find rest from vain fancies if you perform every act in life as though it were your last.[12]
Ibid. 5

16   Remember that no man loses other life than that which he lives, nor lives other than that which he loses.
Ibid. 14

17   Each thing is of like form from everlasting and comes round again in its cycle.
Ibid.

18   The longest-lived and the shortest-lived man, when they come to die, lose one and the same thing.
Ibid.

19   As for life, it is a battle and a sojourning in a strange land; but the fame that comes after is oblivion.
Ibid. 17

20   Never esteem anything as of advantage to you that will make you break your word or lose your self-respect.
Ibid. III, 7

[9]From this derived the proverb: Poeta nascitur, non fit (The poet is born, not made).
See Jonson, 232:24.

[10]Translated by F. E. ROBBINS (Loeb Classical Library).

[11]Translated by MORRIS HICKEY MORGAN, with some adaptations.

[12]See *Matthew* 6:34, 34:1; Horace, 95:24; and Publilius Syrus, 100:6.

1   By a tranquil mind I mean nothing else than a mind well ordered.   *Ibid. IV, 3*

2   The universe is change; our life is what our thoughts make it.   *Ibid.*

3   How much time he gains who does not look to see what his neighbor says or does or thinks, but only at what he does himself, to make it just and holy.   *Ibid. 18*

4   Whatever is in any way beautiful hath its source of beauty in itself, and is complete in itself; praise forms no part of it. So it is none the worse nor the better for being praised.   *Ibid. 20*

5   All that is harmony for you, my Universe, is in harmony with me as well.[1] Nothing that comes at the right time for you is too early or too late for me. Everything is fruit to me that your seasons bring, Nature. All things come of you, have their being in you, and return to you.[2]   *Ibid. 23*

6   "Let your occupations be few," says the sage,[3] "if you would lead a tranquil life."   *Ibid. 24*

7   Love the little trade which you have learned, and be content with it.   *Ibid. 31*

8   All is ephemeral—fame and the famous as well.   *Ibid. 35*

9   Search men's governing principles, and consider the wise, what they shun and what they cleave to.   *Ibid. 38*

10   Time is a sort of river of passing events, and strong is its current; no sooner is a thing brought to sight than it is swept by and another takes its place, and this too will be swept away.[4]   *Ibid. 43*

11   All that happens is as usual and familiar as the rose in spring and the crop in summer.   *Ibid. 44*

12   Mark how fleeting and paltry is the estate of man—yesterday in embryo, tomorrow a mummy or ashes. So for the hairsbreadth of time assigned to thee, live rationally, and part with life cheerfully, as drops the ripe olive, extolling the season that bore it and the tree that matured it.   *Ibid. 48*

13   In the morning, when you are sluggish about getting up, let this thought be present: "I am rising to a man's work."   *Ibid. V, 1*

14   A man makes no noise over a good deed, but passes on to another as a vine to bear grapes again in season.[5]   *Ibid. 6*

15   Nothing happens to anybody which he is not fitted by nature to bear.   *Ibid. 18*

16   Live with the gods.   *Ibid. 27*

[1]See Zeno, 82:1.
[2]See *I Chronicles 29:14, 13:18.*
[3]Democritus, *Fragment 3;* also quoted by Seneca in *On Anger, III, 6,* and *On the Happy Life, 13.*
[4]See Watts, 294:16, and Anonymous, 783:18.
[5]See *Matthew 6:3, 33:11.*

17   The controlling intelligence understands its own nature, and what it does, and whereon it works.   *Ibid. VI, 5*

18   What is not good for the swarm is not good for the bee.   *Ibid. 54*

19   One universe made up of all that is; and one God in it all, and one principle of being, and one law, the reason, shared by all thinking creatures, and one truth.   *Ibid. VII, 9*

20   It is man's peculiar duty to love even those who wrong him.[6]   *Ibid. 22*

21   Very little is needed to make a happy life.   *Ibid. 67*

22   To change your mind and to follow him who sets you right is to be nonetheless the free agent that you were before.   *Ibid. VIII, 16*

23   Look to the essence of a thing, whether it be a point of doctrine, of practice, or of interpretation.   *Ibid. 22*

24   Be not careless in deeds, nor confused in words, nor rambling in thought.   *Ibid. 51*

25   Think not disdainfully of death, but look on it with favor; for even death is one of the things that Nature wills.   *Ibid. IX, 3*

26   A wrongdoer is often a man who has left something undone, not always one who has done something.[7]   *Ibid. 5*

27   Blot out vain pomp; check impulse; quench appetite; keep reason under its own control.   *Ibid. 7*

28   Whatever may befall you, it was preordained for you from everlasting.   *Ibid. X, 5*

Galen
129–199

29   The chief merit of language is clearness, and we know that nothing detracts so much from this as do unfamiliar terms.
   On the Natural Faculties,[8] bk. I, sec. 2

30   It was, of course, a grand and impressive thing to do, to mistrust the obvious, and to pin one's faith in things which could not be seen!   *Ibid. 13*

31   Praxiteles and Phidias . . . were unable to . . . reach and handle all portions of the material. It is not so, however, with nature. Every part of a bone she makes bone, every part of the flesh she makes flesh, and so with fat and all the rest; there is no part she has not touched, elaborated, and embellished.   *Ibid. II, 3*

32   That which *is* grows, while that which *is not* becomes.   *Ibid.*

[6]See *Proverbs 25:21, 22:26.*
[7]See *Book of Common Prayer, 48:17.*
[8]Translated by Arthur J. Brock (Loeb Classical Library).

Diogenes Laertius
fl. c. 200

1   Time is the image of eternity.   *Plato, 41*

2   There is a written and an unwritten law. The one by which we regulate our constitutions in our cities is the written law; that which arises from custom is the unwritten law.   *Ibid. 51*

Tertullian
[Quintus Septimius Tertullianus]
c. 160–240

3   O witness of the soul naturally Christian.
    Apologeticus, 17

4   See how these Christians love one another.[1]
    Ibid. 39

5   We multiply whenever we are mown down by you; the blood of Christians is seed.[2]   *Ibid. 50*

6   Man is one name belonging to every nation upon earth. In them all is one soul though many tongues. Every country has its own language, yet the subjects of which the untutored soul speaks are the same everywhere.   *Testimony of the Soul*

7   Mother Church.[3]   *Ad Martyras, 1*

8   Truth persuades by teaching, but does not teach by persuading.   *Adversus Valentinianos, 1*

9   Truth does not blush.[4]   *Ibid. 3*

10   It is to be believed because it is absurd.[5]
    De Carne Christi, 5

11   It is certain because it is impossible.[6]   *Ibid.*

12   Out of the frying pan into the fire.[7]   *Ibid. 6*

[1]Tertullian is sarcastically repeating what the enemies of Christianity are saying.
[2]Plures efficimur, quoties metimur a vobis; semen est sanguis christianorum.
    This is often rendered as: The blood of the martyrs is the seed of the Church.
    The Church of Christ has been founded by shedding its own blood, not that of others; by enduring outrage, not by inflicting it. Persecutions have made it grow; martyrdoms have crowned it.—SAINT JEROME, *letter 82*
    The blood of martyrs is the seed of Christians.—LAURENS BEYERLINCK [1578–1627], *Magnum Theatrum Vitae Humanorum* [1665]
    The seed of the Church, I mean the blood of primitive martyrs.—THOMAS FULLER, *Church History of Britain* [1655], *pt. IV, bk. I*
[3]Domina mater ecclesia.
    See Saint Cyprian, 112:18.
[4]Veritas non erubescit.
[5]Prorsus credibile est, quia ineptum est.
[6]Certum est, quia impossibile est.
    This is called Tertullian's rule of faith. It is sometimes rendered as: Credo quia impossibile [I believe because it is impossible]. Saint Augustine expresses the same idea in *Confessions*, VI, 5, 7.
[7]De calcaria in carbonarium.

13   One man's religion neither harms nor helps another man.   *Ad Scapulam, 2*

14   It is certainly no part of religion to compel religion.   *Ibid.*

15   I must dispel vanity with vanity.
    Adversus Marcionem, IV, 30

The Sayings of Jesus
Third century

16   Jesus saith, Wherever there are two, they are not without God, and wherever there is one alone, I say, I am with him.[8] Raise the stone, and there thou shalt find Me, cleave the wood and there am I.
    The Oxyrhynchus Papyri,[9] *Part I [1898], no. 1,* ΛΟΓΙΑ ΙΗΣΟΥ *[Logia Iesou], logion 5*

17   Jesus saith, Ye ask who are those that draw us to the kingdom, if the kingdom is in Heaven? . . . The fowls of the air, and all beasts that are under the earth or upon the earth, and the fishes of the sea, these are they which draw you, and the kingdom of Heaven is within you.[10]
    Ibid. IV [1904], no. 654, New Sayings of Jesus, second saying

Saint Cyprian
d. 258

18   He cannot have God for his father who has not the Church for his Mother.[11]
    De Unitate Ecclesiae [251], ch. 6

19   There is no salvation outside the Church.[12]
    Letter 73 [c. 256]

Plotinus
205–270

20   All things are filled full of signs, and it is a wise man who can learn about one thing from another.
    Enneads,[13] *bk. II, treatise iii, sec. 7*

21   One principle must make the universe a single complex living creature, one from all.   *Ibid. 8*

    Leap out of the frying pan into the fire.—JOHN HEYWOOD, *Proverbs* [1546], *pt. II, ch. 5*
[8]See *Matthew 18:20, 35:33.*
[9]Translated and edited by BERNARD P. GRENFELL and ARTHUR H. HUNT, who also discovered the papyri. The *Logia* were first published [1897] as ΛΟΓΙΑ ΙΗΣΟΥ: *Sayings of Our Lord.*
[10]See *Luke 17:21, 39:5.*
[11]Habere non potest deum patrem qui ecclesiam non habet matrem.
    See Tertullian, 112:7.
[12]Salus extra ecclesiam non est.
    Quoted by Saint Augustine in *De Baptismo*, hence sometimes attributed to him.
[13]Translated by A. H. ARMSTRONG (Loeb Classical Library).

Longus

Third century

1 There was never any yet that wholly could escape love, and never shall there be any, never so long as beauty shall be, never so long as eyes can see.

Daphnis and Chloe, proem, ch. 2

2 He is so poor that he could not keep a dog.

Ibid. 15

Constantine[1]

c. 288–337

3 In this sign shalt thou conquer.[2]

From EUSEBIUS, *Life of Constantine, I, 28*

Ammianus Marcellinus

c. 330–395

4 Rose among thorns.

History, bk. XVI, ch. 17

Julian [Flavius Claudius Julianus][3]

332–363

5 You have conquered, Galilean.[4]

From THEODORET, *Church History, III, 20*

Saint Ambrose

c. 340–397

6 When you are at Rome live in the Roman style; when you are elsewhere live as they live elsewhere.[5]

Advice to Saint Augustine. From JEREMY TAYLOR, *Ductor Dubitantium [1660], I, 1, 5*

Saint Jerome[6]

c. 342–420

7 The friendship that can cease has never been real.

Letter 3

8 It is easier to mend neglect than to quicken love.

Letter 7

9 Love knows nothing of order.

Ibid.

10 The fact is that my native land is a prey to barbarism, that in it men's only God is their belly,[7] that they live only for the present, and that the richer a man is the holier he is held to be.

Ibid.

11 An unstable pilot steers a leaking ship, and the blind is leading the blind straight to the pit.[8] The ruler is like the ruled.

Ibid.

12 No athlete is crowned but in the sweat of his brow.

Letter 14

13 If there is but little water in the stream, it is the fault, not of the channel, but of the source.

Letter 17

14 You are a Ciceronian, not a Christian.[9]

Letter 22

15 It is idle to play the lyre for an ass.[10]

Letter 27

16 The line, often adopted by strong men in controversy, of justifying the means by the end.[11]

Letter 48

17 Do not let your deeds belie your words, lest when you speak in church someone may say to himself, "Why do you not practice what you preach?"[12]

Ibid.

18 Avoid, as you would the plague, a clergyman who is also a man of business.[13]

Letter 52

19 A fat paunch never breeds fine thoughts.[14]

Ibid.

20 That clergyman soon becomes an object of contempt who being often asked out to dinner never refuses to go.

Ibid.

21 The best almoner is he who keeps back nothing for himself.

Ibid.

22 It is worse still to be ignorant of your ignorance.

Letter 53

23 Even brute beasts and wandering birds do not fall into the same traps or nets twice.[13]

Letter 54

---

[1]Flavius Valerius Aurelius Constantinus.

[2]In hoc signo vinces.

The alleged words of Constantine's vision before his battle with Maxentius at Saxa Rubra, near Rome [312].

[3]Known as Julian the Apostate.

[4]Vicisti, Galilaee.

The Latin translation of the alleged dying words of the emperor.

See Swinburne, 534:4.

[5]Si fueris Romae, Romano vivito more; / Si fueris alibi, vivito sicut ibi.

My mother, having joined me at Milan, found that the church there did not fast on Saturdays as at Rome, and was at a loss what to do. I consulted Saint Ambrose, of holy memory, who replied, "When I am at Rome, I fast on a Saturday; when I am at Milan, I do not. Follow the custom of the church where you are." — SAINT AUGUSTINE, *Epistle to Januarius (Epistle 2), sec. 18.* Also *Epistle to Casualanus (Epistle 36), sec. 32*

When in Rome, do as the Romans do. — *Proverb*

[6]Translated by W. H. FREMANTLE.

[7]See *Philippians 3:19, 44:33.*

[8]See *Matthew 15:14, 35:23.*

[9]This was addressed to Jerome in a dream by Christ the Judge, censuring him for loving the classics more than the Fathers.

[10]A Greek proverb frequently quoted by Jerome.

[11]See Prior, 287:17.

[12]Cur ergo haec ipse non facis?

See Plautus, 84:3.

[13]Translated by F. A. WRIGHT (Loeb Classical Library).

[14]This is a Greek proverb.

Fat paunches have lean pates, and dainty bits / Make rich the ribs, but bankrupt quite the wits. — SHAKESPEARE, *Love's Labour's Lost, act I, sc. i, l. 26*

1   Sometimes the character of the mistress is inferred from the dress of her maids.   *Letter 54*

2   The face is the mirror of the mind, and eyes without speaking confess the secrets of the heart.   *Ibid.*

3   The scars of others should teach us caution.   *Ibid.*

4   I have always revered not crude verbosity but holy simplicity.[1]   *Letter 57*

5   When the stomach is full, it is easy to talk of fasting.   *Letter 58*

6   The Roman world is falling, yet we hold our heads erect instead of bowing our necks.[2]   *Letter 60*

7   Every day we are changing, every day we are dying, and yet we fancy ourselves eternal.   *Ibid.*

8   Early impressions are hard to eradicate from the mind. When once wool has been dyed purple, who can restore it to its previous whiteness?   *Letter 107*

9   Christians are not born but made.[3]   *Ibid.*

10   The tired ox treads with a firmer step.[4]   *Letter 112*

11   For they wished to fill the winepress of eloquence not with the tendrils of mere words but with the rich grape juice of good sense.   *Letter 125*

12   Preferring to store her money in the stomachs of the needy rather than hide it in a purse.[5]   *Letter 127*

13   The privileges of a few do not make common law.[6]   *Exposition on Jona*

14   Never look a gift horse in the mouth.[7]   *On the Epistle to the Ephesians*

Saint John Chrysostom
c. 345–407

15   Hell is paved with priests' skulls.   *De Sacerdotio [c. 390]*

16   No one can harm the man who does himself no wrong.[8]   *Letter to Olympia*

Vegetius [Flavius Vegetius Renatus]
fl. c. 375

17   Let him who desires peace prepare for war.[9]   *De Rei Militari, III, prologue*

Saint Augustine
354–430

18   Will is to grace as the horse is to the rider.[10]   *De Libero Arbitrio [388–395]*

19   The weakness of little children's limbs is innocent, not their souls.   *Confessions [397–401], I, 7*

20   To Carthage I came, where all about me resounded a caldron of dissolute loves.[11]   *Ibid. III, 1*

21   I was in love with loving.   *Ibid.*

22   In the usual course of study I had come to a book of a certain Cicero.   *Ibid. 4*

23   Give me chastity and continence, but not just now.   *Ibid. VIII, 7*

24   Take up, read! Take up, read![12]   *Ibid. 12*

25   Too late I loved you, O Beauty ever ancient and ever new! Too late I loved you! And, behold, you were within me, and I out of myself, and there I searched for you.   *Ibid. X, 27*

26   Give what you command, and command what you will.   *Ibid. 29*

27   Hear the other side.[13]   *De Duabus Animabus, XIV, 2*

28   I would not have believed the gospel had not the authority of the Church moved me.   *Contra Epistulam Fundamenti [c. 410], ch. 5*

29   Necessity has no law.[14]   *Soliloquiorum. Animae ad Deum [c. 410], 2*

30   We make a ladder of our vices, if we trample those same vices underfoot.   *Sermones, 3*

31   Anger is a weed; hate is the tree.   *Ibid. 58*

32   The dove loves when it quarrels; the wolf hates when it flatters.   *Ibid. 64*

33   Rome has spoken; the case is closed.[15]   *Ibid. 131*

[9]Qui desiderat pacem, praeparet bellum.

[10]This is considered the most important definition of the relation of grace to free will in the Middle Ages.

[11]To Carthage then I came.—T. S. ELIOT, *The Waste Land* [1922], *III, l. 307 and note*

[12]Tolle lege, tolle lege.
   What the bell seemed to say to Augustine at the moment of his conversion. When he opened the Bible, his eyes fell on *Romans 13:12–14, 42:23.*

[13]Audi partem alteram.
   See Euripides, 68:21, and Protagoras, 70:16.

[14]See Publilius Syrus, 99:32, and Oliver Cromwell, 247:3.

[15]Roma locuta est; causa finita est.

[1]Venerationi mihi semper fuit non verbosa rusticas sed sancta simplicitas.
   See Huss, 132:11.

[2]Romanus orbis ruit.

[3]Fiunt, non nascuntur Christiani.

[4]An old Roman proverb quoted by Saint Jerome to Saint Augustine after the latter criticized the elder Jerome.

[5]Translated by F. A. WRIGHT (Loeb Classical Library).

[6]Privilegia paucorum non faciunt legem.

[7]Noli equi dentes inspicere donati.

[8]No one is injured save by himself.—ERASMUS, *Adagia*

1   He who created you without you will not justify you without you.   *Ibid. 169*

2   The most glorious city of God.
De Civitate Dei [415], I, preface

3   Two cities have been formed by two loves: the earthly by the love of self, even to the contempt of God; the heavenly by the love of God, even to the contempt of self.   *Ibid. XIV, 28*

Saint Vincent of Lérins
d. c. 450

4   [That faith is catholic] which has been believed always, everywhere, and by all.[1]
Commonitorium, ch. 2

5   Every word [of Tertullian] almost was a sentence; every sentence a victory.   *Ibid. 18*

Saint Remy [Remigius]
c. 438 – c. 533

6   Henceforward burn what thou hast worshipped, and worship what thou hast burned.[2]
Said to Clovis at his baptism [496]

Clovis
466 – 511

7   God of Clotilda,[3] if you grant me victory I shall become a Christian.[4]
Legendary vow before battle

Hsieh Ho[5]
fl. 500

8   By copying, the ancient models should be perpetuated.[6]
Notes Concerning the Classification of Old Paintings, Sixth Principle

Saint Benedict[7]
480 – 543

9   We are therefore about to establish a school of the Lord's service in which we hope to introduce nothing harsh or burdensome.
Rule of Saint Benedict, prologue

[1]Quod semper, quod ubique, quod ab omnibus creditum est. The definition of the traditional articles of faith.
[2]See Clovis, 115:7.
[3]Saint Clotilda, wife of Clovis.
[4]Clovis defeated the Alemanni in 496, and following his vow was baptized with three thousand followers by Saint Remy at Rheims.
See Saint Remy, 115:6.
[5]From *The Spirit of the Brush*, translated by SHIO SAKANISHI [Wisdom of the East Series, 1957].
[6]See Horace, 98:15, and Fujiwara no Teika, 123:3.
[7]Founder of Western monasticism.

Boethius
480 – 524

10   In every adversity of fortune, to have been happy is the most unhappy kind of misfortune.[8]
De Consolatione Philosophiae, bk. II, 4, 4

11   Who hath so entire happiness that he is not in some part offended with the condition of his estate?
Ibid. 41

12   Nothing is miserable but what is thought so, and contrariwise, every estate is happy if he that bears it be content.   *Ibid. 64*

13   From thee, great God, we spring, to thee we tend—
Path, motive, guide, original and end.[9]
Ibid. III, 9, 27

14   Who can give law to lovers? Love is a greater law to itself.   *Ibid. 12, 47*

Pope Gregory I
540 – 604

15   [They answered that they were called Angles.] It is well, for they have the faces of angels, and such should be the co-heirs of the angels in heaven.[10]
From BEDE, Ecclesiastical History of the English People, II, 1

Talmud
compiled c. sixth century A.D.

16   The day is short, the labor long, the workers are idle, and reward is great, and the Master is urgent.
Mishna. The Wisdom of the Fathers

17   Whoever destroys a single life is as guilty as though he had destroyed the entire world; and whoever rescues a single life earns as much merit as though he had rescued the entire world.
Mishna. Sanhedrin

Ali ibn-Abi-Talib[11]
c. 602 – 661

18   He who has a thousand friends has not a friend to spare,
And he who has one enemy will meet him everywhere.
A Hundred Sayings

[8]See Pindar, 64:4; Dante, 125:18; Chaucer, 128:19; and Tennyson, 455:13.
[9]Translated by SAMUEL JOHNSON, and used as motto to *The Rambler, no. 7* [1750].
[10]Traditionally quoted "Non Angli sed angeli" (Not Angles but angels), these were the words of Pope Gregory when he beheld two English slaves in a Roman slave market.
[11]Ali ibn-Abi-Talib, son-in-law of Muhammad and fourth caliph, who was called the Lion of God, was murdered in 661.

The Koran[1]

1   In the name of the most merciful God: Praise be to God, the Lord of all Being; the most merciful, the Master of the day of judgment. Thee do we worship, and of Thee do we beg assistance. Direct us in the right path, in the path of those to whom Thou hast been gracious; not of those against whom Thou art incensed, nor of those who go astray.

Chapter 1, verses 1–3

2   Do not veil the truth with falsehood, nor conceal the truth knowingly.   *2:42*

3   We believe in God, and in that which has been sent down on us and sent down on Abraham, Ishmael, Isaac and Jacob, and the Tribes, and that which was given to Moses and Jesus and the Prophets, of their Lord; we make no division between any of them, and to Him we surrender.[2]   *2:135–136*

4   A believing slave is better than an idolater, even though ye admire him.   *2:221*

5   God will not take you to task for vain words in your oaths, but He will take you to task for what your hearts have amassed.   *2:225*

6   I [Muhammad] have no power over benefit or hurt to myself except as God willeth . . . I am only a warner, and a bringer of good tidings to a people who believe.   *7:188*

7   God sufficeth me: there is no God but He. In Him I put my trust.   *9:129*

8   In the alternation of night and day, and what God has created in the heavens and the earth—surely there are signs for a god-fearing people.   *10:6*

9   Surely God wrongs not men, but themselves men wrong.   *10:44*

10   Not so much as the weight of an ant in earth or heaven escapes from the Lord, neither is aught smaller than that, or greater, but is clearly written in God's book.   *10:61*

11   God changes not what is in a people, until they change what is in themselves.   *13:11*

12   We [God] never sent a messenger save with the language of his folk, that he might make (the message)[3] clear for them.   *14:4*

13   Seest thou not how God hath coined a parable? A good word is like a good tree whose root is firmly fixed, and whose top is in the sky. And it produces its edible fruit every season, by the permission of its Lord. . . . And a corrupt word is like a corrupt tree which has been torn off the ground, and has no fixity. God makes those who believe stand firm in this life and the next by His firm Word.

14:24–27

14   Our [God's] word to a thing when We will it, is but to say, "Be," and it is.   *16:40*

15   Glory be to Him who carried His servant by night from the sacred temple of Mecca to the temple of Jerusalem that is more remote, whose precinct We have blessed, that We might show him of Our tokens.   *17:1*

16   Thy Lord hath decreed that ye worship none save Him, and (that ye show) kindness to parents. . . . Lower unto them the wing of submission through mercy, and say, "My Lord, have mercy on them both as they took care of me when I was little."

17:23–24

17   Walk not on the earth exultantly, for thou canst not cleave the earth, neither shalt thou reach to the mountains in height.   *17:37*

18   They will question thee concerning the soul. Say: "The soul is the concern of my Lord, and you have been given of knowledge but a little."   *17:85*

19   They say: "We will not believe thee till thou makest a spring to gush forth from the earth for us, or . . . bringest God and the angels as a surety." . . . And naught prevented men from believing when the guidance came to them, but that they said, "Has God sent forth a mortal as messenger?" Say: "Had there been in the earth angels walking at peace, We would have sent down upon them out of heaven an angel as messenger."   *17:90–95*

20   And do not say, regarding anything, "I am going to do that tomorrow," but only, "if God will."[4]

18:23–24

21   Wealth and children are the adornment of this present life: but good works, which are lasting, are better in the sight of thy Lord as to recompense, and better as to hope.   *18:46*

22   Man says: "How is it possible, when I am dead, that I shall then be brought forth alive?" Does he not remember that We have created him once, and that he was nothing then?   *19:66–67*

---

[1]Also spelled Qur'an; Quran. Muslims believe that the Koran is of divine origin, revealed by God to the prophet Muhammad [c. 570–632].

The word Koran, derived from the verb *karaa,* to read, signifies properly in Arabic "the reading," or rather, "that which ought to be read." . . . The Koran is divided into 114 larger portions of very unequal length, which we call chapters, but the Arabians *sowar,* in the singular *sura,* a word rarely used on any other occasion.—GEORGE SALE, *The Koran* [1734], *The Preliminary Discourse, sec. III*

Translations by GEORGE SALE [1734], E. H. PALMER [1900], J. M. RODWELL [1909], RICHARD BELL [1927], M. M. PICKTHALL [1953], and A. J. ARBERRY [1955], edited and adapted by SARI NUSEIBAH.

[2]"Surrender" is the literal translation of the word Islam.

[3]Throughout the Koran, parentheses indicate additions to the Arabic.

[4]In Arabic: Inshallah.

1   Do not the unbelievers see that the skies and the earth were both a solid mass, and that We clave them asunder, and that by means of water We give life to everything? Will they not then believe?

21:30

2   O men, if you are in doubt as to the Resurrection, surely We created you of dust, then of a sperm drop, then of a blood clot, then of a lump of flesh. . . . And thou beholdest the earth blackened; then, when We send down water upon it, it quivers, and swells, and puts forth herbs of every joyous kind.

22:5

3   We [God] charge not any soul save to its ability.

23:62

4   God is the light of the heavens and of the earth. His light is like a niche in which is a lamp—the lamp encased in glass—the glass, as it were, a glistening star. From a blessed tree it is lighted, the olive neither from the East nor of the West, whose oil would well nigh shine out, even though fire touched it not. It is light upon light. God guideth whom He will to His light, and God setteth forth parables to men.

24:35

5   As for the unbelievers, their works are as a mirage in a spacious plain which the man athirst supposes to be water, till, when he comes to it, he finds it is nothing; there indeed he finds God, and He pays him his account in full; and God is swift at the reckoning.

Or they are as shadows upon a sea obscure, covered by a billow above which is a billow, above which are clouds, shadows piled upon one another; when he puts forth his hand, wellnigh he cannot see it. And to whomsoever God assigns no light, no light has he.

24:39–40

6   Thou seest the mountains and thou deemest them affixed, (verily) they are as fleeting as the clouds.

27:88

7   Thou truly canst not guide whom thou lovest; but God guideth whom He will; and He best knoweth those who yield to guidance.

28:55

8   The present life is naught but a diversion and a sport; surely the Last Abode is Life, did they but know.

29:64

9   Whosoever surrenders his face to God and performs good deeds, he verily has grapsed the surest handle, and unto God is the sequel of all things.

31:22

10   If whatever trees are in the earth were pens, and He should after that swell the seas into seven seas of ink, the Words of God would not be exhausted.

31:27

11   We offered this trust[1] to the heavens and the earth and the mountains, but they were humbled by it, and

[1] The message conveyed in the Koran.

shrank from bearing it. Yet, man bore it. Truly he is ever in the darkness of injustice, and of ignorance.

33:72

12   He makes the night seep into the day, and makes the day seep into the night; He has subordinated the sun and the moon, making each of them journey towards a preordained time.   *35:13*

13   And on that day no soul shall be wronged at all, nor shall ye be rewarded for aught but that which ye have done.   *36:54*

14   They say: "We only have the life of this world. We die and we live, and nothing destroys us but time." Yet, not true knowledge have they of this; only belief.   *45:24*

15   O true believers, let not men laugh other men to scorn, who peradventure may be better than themselves. . . . Neither let the one of you speak ill of another in his absence.   *49:10–13*

16   The Arabs of the desert say, We believe. Answer, Ye do by no means believe; but say, We have embraced Islam: for the faith hath not yet entered into your hearts.   *49:14*

17   We [God] created Man, and We know what his soul whispereth within him; and We are nearer unto him than his jugular vein.   *50:16*

18   The heart of Muhammad did not falsely represent that which he saw. Will you therefore dispute with him concerning that which he saw?

53:11–12

19   O tribe of spirits and of men, if you are able to slip through the parameters of the skies and the earth, then do so. You shall not pass through them save with My [the Lord's] authority.   *55:33*

20   He is the first and the last, the manifest and the hidden: and He knoweth all things.   *57:3*

21   Let every soul look upon the morrow for the deed it has performed.   *59:18*

22   Is he, therefore, who goeth groveling upon his face, better directed than he who walketh upright in a straight way?   *67:22*

23   Man is a witness unto his deeds.   *75:14*

24   Recite: In the name of thy Lord who created, Created Man of a blood clot.
Recite: And thy Lord is the most Generous, who taught by the Pen,
Taught Man that he knew not.

96:1–5

25   Whoso has done an atom's weight of good shall see it; and whoso has done an atom's weight of evil shall see it.   *99:7–8*

26   Say: "He is God, One God, the Everlasting Refuge, who has not begotten, and has not been begotten, and equal to Him is not anyone."   *112*

Anonymous: Early Miscellaneous

1   Whatever kind of word thou speakest the like shalt thou hear.
The Greek Anthology,[1] bk. IX, 382

2   Envy slays itself by its own arrows.
Ibid. X, 111

3   Give a sop to Cerberus.
Greek and Roman saying

4   Give me today, and take tomorrow.
Quoted, and condemned, by Saint Chrysostom

5   Keep a green tree in your heart and perhaps the singing bird will come.   *Chinese proverb*

6   On the day of victory no one is tired.
Arab proverb

7   Death is afraid of him because he has the heart of a lion.   *Arab proverb*

8   I came to the place of my birth, and cried, "The friends of my youth, where are they?" And echo answered, "Where are they?"   *Arab saying*

9   If you have two loaves of bread, sell one and buy a hyacinth.   *Persian saying[2]*

10 If only, when one heard
That Old Age was coming
One could bolt the door,
Answer "Not at home"
And refuse to meet him!
Kokinshu (Collection of Ancient and Modern Poems) [905][3]

Anonymous: Latin

11 Ab urbe condita [Since the founding of the city (Rome)].   *Saying*

12 Absit omen [May it not be an omen].
Saying

13 Acta est fabula [The play is over].
Said at ancient dramatic performances and quoted by Augustus on his deathbed

14 Actus non facit reum, nisi mens sit rea [The act is not criminal unless the intent is criminal].
Legal maxim

15 Ad astra per aspera [To the stars through hardships].   *Proverb*

16 Adeste, fideles,
Laeti triumphantes;
Venite, venite in Bethlehem.

[O come, all ye faithful,
Joyful and triumphant,
O come ye, O come ye to Bethlehem.]
Hymn [18th century]

17 Anno aetatis suae . . . [In the year of his age].
Phrase

18 Bis dat qui cito dat [He gives twice who gives promptly].[4]   *Saying*

19 Cave ab homine unius libri [Beware the man of one book].[5]
Quoted by ISAAC D'ISRAELI in Curiosities of Literature [1791–1793]

20 Cave canem [Beware of the dog].   *Proverb*

21 Caveat emptor [Let the buyer beware].
Proverb

22 Cras amet qui nunquam amavit quique amavit cras amet [Tomorrow let him love who has never loved and tomorrow let him who has loved love].[6]
Pervigilium Veneris [c. 350], refrain

23 Cucullus non facit monachum [The cowl does not make a monk].[7]   *Medieval proverb*

24 Cuius regio eius religio [He who controls the area controls the religion].   *Proverb*

25 De gustibus non disputandum [There is no accounting for tastes].   *Proverb*

26 De minimis non curat lex [The law is not concerned with trifles].   *Legal maxim*

27 Deus vult [God wills it].
Motto of the Crusades [1095]

28 Dis manibus sacrum[8] [Sacred to the departed spirit(s)].   *Tombstone inscription*

29 Divide et impera [Divide and rule].
Ancient political maxim cited by MACHIAVELLI

30 Errare humanum est [To err is human].[9]
Saying

31 Et in Arcadia ego [I too am in Arcadia].[10]
Inscription on a tomb in a painting [c. 1623] by GUERCINO [1591–1666]

---

[1]Translated by W. R. PATON (Loeb Classical Library).
[2]Quoted also as a Chinese or Greek saying, and in various versions, including: If you have two pieces of silver, take one and buy a lily.

If thou of fortune be bereft, / And in thy store there be but left / Two loaves—sell one, and with the dole / Buy hyacinths to feed thy soul.— JAMES TERRY WHITE [1845–1920], *Not by Bread Alone* [1907]

[3]Translated by ARTHUR WALEY in *Anthology of Japanese Literature* [1955], edited by DONALD KEENE.

[4]See Augustus Caesar, 98:22, and Publilius Syrus, 98:30.
[5]See Sydney Smith, 380:14.
[6]See Parnell, 295:20.
[7]It takes more than a hood and sad eyes to make a monk.
—*Albanian proverb*
[8]Abbreviated DMS.
[9]See Plutarch, 107:18; Shirley, 246:20; Pope, 299:4; and Burns, 362:5.
[10]That is, Even in Arcadia there am I [Death].

Bartolommeo Schidoni [1560–1616] wrote: Et ego in Arcadia vixi [I too have lived in Arcadia]. Poussin, Reynolds, and others used this phrase in their paintings. Erwin Panofsky discusses the phrase in *Philosophy and History: Essays Presented to E. Cassirer* [1936].

1   Ex ungue leonem [From his claw one can tell a lion].[1]   *Saying*

2   Fiat justitia ruat coelum [Let justice be done though heaven should fall].[2]
Proverb, sometimes attributed to Lucius Calpurnius Piso Caesoninus *[d. 43 B.C.]*

3   Finis coronat opus [The end crowns the work].[3]
Saying

4   Flagrante delicto ["Red-handed"].   *Saying*

5   Fluctuat nec mergitur [It tosses but doesn't sink].
Saying

6 Gaudeamus igitur,
Iuvenes dum sumus.

[Let us live then and be glad
While young life is before us.]
Students' song [c. 1267]

7   Habeas corpus [You are to produce the person[4]].
Legal phrase

8   Hannibal ad portas! [Hannibal is at the gates!]
Saying

9   In vino veritas [In wine is truth].[5]
Proverb quoted by Plato, *Symposium 217*

10   Ipse dixit [He himself said it].
Phrase of "proof"

11   Ius est ars boni et aequi [Legal justice is the art of the good and the fair].   *Saying*

12   Mater artium necessitas [Necessity is the mother of invention].[6]   *Saying*

13   Mors ultima ratio [Death is the final accounting].
Saying

14   Nemo me impune lacessit [No one provokes me with impunity].
Motto of the Crown of Scotland

15   Nihil nimis [Nothing in excess].[7]   *Saying*

16   Non multa sed multum [Not many but much].[8]
Proverb

17   Orare est laborare, laborare est orare [To pray is to work, to work is to pray].
Ancient motto of the Benedictine order

18   Parvis e glandibus quercus [Tall oaks from little acorns grow].   *Saying*

19   Pereant qui nostra ante nos dixerunt [May they perish who have used our words before us].
Saying

20   Piscem natare doces [You're teaching a fish to swim].   *Saying*

21   Post coitum omne animal triste [Every creature is sad after coitus].   *Saying*

22   Post hoc, ergo propter hoc [After this, therefore because of this].
Definition of fallacy in logic

23   Primus inter pares [First among equals].
Saying

24   Pro bono publico [For the public good].
Saying

25   Quos [or Quem] deus vult perdere prius dementat [Those whom God wishes to destroy, he first makes mad].[9]   *Saying*

26   Requiescat in pace[10] [May he rest in peace; May she rest in peace].   *Saying*

27   Res iudicata pro veritate habetur [A matter which has been legally decided is considered true].
Legal maxim

28   Ruat coelum, fiat voluntas tua [Though heaven should fall, let thy will be done].   *Proverb*

29   Semper fidelis [Ever faithful].   *Saying*

30   Sic semper tyrannis[11] [Thus always to tyrants].
Saying

31   Sit tibi terra levis [May the earth rest lightly on you].[12]   *Tombstone inscription*

32   Summum ius summa iniuria [Extreme justice is extreme injustice].[13]
Legal maxim cited by Cicero *in De Officiis, I, 10, 33*

33   Tempora mutantur, nos et mutamur in illis [Times change, and we change with them too].[14]
From Owen's *Epigrammata [1615]*

34   Testis unus testis nullus [A single witness is no witness].   *Legal maxim*

35   Ubi bene ibi patria [Where one is happy, there's one's homeland].   *Saying*

[1]Literally: From the claw a lion.
See Herodotus, 70:5.
[2]Also familiar as: Fiat justitia et ruant coeli [Let justice be done though the heavens fall].
And as: Fiat justitia et pereat mundus [Let justice be done though the world perish].
See J. Q. Adams, 368:14.
[3]See John Heywood, 141:20; Shakespeare, 201:12 and 203:-17; Herrick, 241:2; and Quarles, 242:13.
[4]The person of the accused.
[5]See Alcaeus, 55:22.
[6]See Persius, 104:15, and Christie, 677:17.
[7]Also quoted as: Ne quid nimis.
See The Seven Sages, 55:10; Terence, 85:12; Horace, 95:2 and 96:7; and Lucan, 105:21.
[8]I.e., Not quantity but quality.
See Seneca, 102:25.

[9]See Euripides, 69:18.
[10]Abbreviated RIP.
[11]Motto of Virginia.
See John Wilkes Booth, 536:5.
[12]Abbreviated STTL.
See Euripides, 67:25, and Beaumont and Fletcher, 238:16.
[13]I.e., Extreme legal justice.
See Terence, 86:1.
[14]Translated by John Owen in *Epigrams* [1615]. Also quoted by Raphael Holinshed in *Chronicles of England* [1578].
See Spenser, 154:3.

1   Urbi et orbi [To the city[1] and to the world].
Apostolic blessing

2   Vade in pace [Go in peace].
End of confessional absolution

3   Vae victis! [Woe to the conquered!]
From LIVY, *History, bk. V, sec. 48, as said by
Brennus to the Romans*

4   Volenti non fit iniuria [To a person who consents
no injustice is done].   *Legal maxim*

Bede [Venerable Bede]
c. 672 – c. 735

5   No reptiles are found there [in Ireland], and no
snake can live there; for, though often carried thither
out of Britain, as soon as the ship comes near the
shore, and the scent of the air reaches them, they die.
*Ecclesiastical History of the English People,
bk. I, ch. 1*

6   The present life of man, O king, seems to me, in
comparison of that time which is unknown to us,
like to the swift flight of a sparrow through the room
wherein you sit at supper in winter, with your com-
manders and ministers, and a good fire in the midst,
whilst the storms of rain and snow prevail abroad;
the sparrow, I say, flying in at one door, and immediately out at another, whilst he is within, is safe
from the wintry storm; but after a short space of fair
weather, he immediately vanishes out of your sight,
into the dark winter from which he had emerged. So
this life of man appears for a short space, but of
what went before, or what is to follow, we are utterly ignorant.   *Ibid. II, 13*

Saint John of Damascus
c. 675 – c. 749

7   God is a sea of infinite substance.[2]
De Fide Orthodoxa, bk. I, ch. 9

Alcuin
c. 732–804

8   The voice of the people is the voice of God [Vox
populi vox Dei].[3]
Letter to Charlemagne [A.D. 800]

9 Here halt, I pray you, make a little stay,
O wayfarer, to read what I have writ,
And know by my fate what thy fate shall be.
What thou art now, wayfarer, world renowned,
I was: what I am now, so shall thou be.

[1]Rome.
[2]This is the most frequently quoted definition of God in the
Middle Ages. It is based on SAINT GREGORY OF NAZIANZUS
[c. 330–390], *Oration 38.*
[3]See Pope, 303:5.

The world's delight I followed with a heart
Unsatisfied: ashes am I, and dust.
His Own Epitaph[4]

10   Alcuin was my name: learning I loved.   *Ibid.*

Ono no Komachi
Ninth century

11 The flowers withered,
Their color faded away,
While meaninglessly
I spent my days in the world
And the long rains were falling.
Kokinshu [905][5]

12 This night of no moon
There is no way to meet him.
I rise in longing—
My breast pounds, a leaping flame,
My heart is consumed in fire.
Ibid.

Ching Hao
fl. 925

13   There are Six Essentials in painting. The first is
called *spirit;* the second, *rhythm;* the third, *thought;*
the fourth, *scenery;* the fifth, the *brush;* and the last
is the *ink.*   *Notes on Brushwork*[6]

14   Resemblance reproduces the formal aspect of objects, but neglects their spirit; truth shows the spirit
and substance in like perfection.   *Ibid.*

Murasaki Shikibu
c. 978–c. 1031

15   [The art of the novel] happens because the storyteller's own experience of men and things, whether
for good or ill—not only what he has passed
through himself, but even events which he has only
witnessed or been told of—has moved him to an
emotion so passionate that he can no longer keep it
shut up in his heart.
The Tale of Genji [c. 1000][7]

16   Anything whatsoever may become the subject of
a novel, provided only that it happens in this mun-
dane life and not in some fairyland beyond our
human ken.   *Ibid.*

[4]Translated by HELEN WADDELL.
[5]Translated by DONALD KEENE in his *Anthology of Japanese
Literature* [1955].
[6]From *The Spirit of the Brush,* translated by SHIO SAKANISHI
[Wisdom of the East Series, 1957].
[7]Translated by ARTHUR WALEY.
See Motoori, 333:10.

The Primary Chronicle[1]
1040–1118

1   The Chuds, the Slavs and the Krivchians then said to the peoples of Rus: "Our whole land is great and rich, but there is no order in it. Come to rule and reign over us."
Annal for the years 860–862: Invitation of the Varangians to Novgorod

2   Then we went to Greece, and the Greeks led us to the edifices where they worship their God, and we knew not whether we were in heaven or on earth. For on earth there is no such splendor or such beauty, and we are at a loss how to describe it. We only know that God dwells there among men, and their service is fairer than the ceremonies of other nations.
Annal for the year 987: Vladimir's Christianization of Russia

3   It is the Russians' joy to drink; we cannot do without it.
Ibid.

Saint Anselm
c. 1033–1109

4   God is that, the greater than which cannot be conceived.[2]
Proslogion, ch. 3

Abu Muhammad al-Kasim al-Hariri
1054–1122

5 We praise Thee, O God,
For whatever perspicuity of language Thou hast taught us
And whatever eloquence Thou hast inspired us with.
Makamat. Prayer

Peter Abelard
1079–1142

6 O what their joy and their glory must be,
Those endless sabbaths the blessed ones see![3]
Hymnus Paraclitensis

[1]The earliest of the Russian chronicles or annals, begun in 1040 and continued through 1118 by various annalists, gives the record of Russian history since 852. It was copied several times and incorporated into later chronicles as the beginning. These quotations are from the Laurentian version, copied in 1377, translated by SAMUEL CROSS.

[2]This is commonly referred to as the ontological argument for the existence of God, and derives from SAINT AUGUSTINE, *De Doctrina Christiana, bk. I, ch. 7*. It is also to be found in DESCARTES, *Third Meditation*.

[3]O quanta qualia sunt illa sabbata, / Quae semper celebrat superna curia.
Translated by JOHN MASON NEALE [1884].

7   Against the disease of writing one must take special precautions, since it is a dangerous and contagious disease.
Letter 8, Abelard to Héloïse[4]

Saint Bernard
1091–1153

8   You will find something more in woods than in books. Trees and stones will teach you that which you can never learn from masters.[5]
Epistle 106

9   I have liberated my soul.[6]
Ibid. 371

10   Hell is full of good intentions or desires.[7]
Attributed. From SAINT FRANCIS DE SALES, *Letter 74*

Héloïse
c. 1098 – c. 1164

11   Riches and power are but gifts of blind fate, whereas goodness is the result of one's own merits.
Letter 2, Héloïse to Abelard[8]

Song of Roland
Eleventh century

12   Friend Roland, sound your horn.[9]
La Chanson de Roland, l. 1070

13   Roland is valorous and Oliver is wise.[10]
Ibid. l. 1093

Gratian [Franciscus Gratianus]
Twelfth century

14   Paintings are the Bible of the laity.[11]
Decretum, pt. III

[4]See Héloïse, below.
[5]See Shakespeare, 190:7 and 191:5, and Wordsworth, 372:21.
[6]Liberavi animam meam.
[7]Hell is full of good meanings and wishings.—GEORGE HERBERT, *Jacula Prudentum* [1651], no. 170
Hell is paved with good intentions.—RAY, *English Proverbs* [1670]
Quoted by SAMUEL JOHNSON [1775]; from BOSWELL, *Life of Johnson* [1791], *vol. I, p. 555* (Everyman edition)
Hell is paved with good intentions, not with bad ones.—SHAW, *Maxims for Revolutionists*
[8]See Abelard, 121:7.
[9]Compagnon Roland sonnez de votre oliphant.
[10]Roland est preux et Oliver est sage.
A Roland for an Oliver—i.e., a blow for a blow, tit for tat, referring to the drawn combat between Roland and Oliver.
[11]Also attributed to GREGORY SERENO, bishop of Massilia (Marseilles), *Letter 9*.

Poem of the Cid[1]
Twelfth century

1   Were his lord but worthy, God, how fine a vassal.
l. 20

2   Thus parted the one from the others as the nail from the flesh.   *l. 375*

3   Who serves a good lord lives always in luxury.
l. 850

4   One would grow poor staying in one place always.   *l. 948*

Frederick I [Barbarossa]
c. 1122–1190

5   An emperor is subject to no one but God and Justice.
From JULIUS WILHELM ZINCGREF,
Apophthegmata, bk. 1 [1626]

Averroës
1126–1198

6   Knowledge is the conformity of the object and the intellect.[2]   *Destructio Destructionum*

Henry II
1133–1189

7   Who will free me from this turbulent priest?[3]
Attributed

Maimonides
[Moses ben Maimon]
1135–1204

8   Anticipate charity by preventing poverty; assist the reduced fellowman, either by a considerable gift, or a sum of money, or by teaching him a trade, or by putting him in the way of business, so that he may earn an honest livelihood, and not be forced to the dreadful alternative of holding out his hand for charity. This is the highest step and the summit of charity's golden ladder.   *Charity's Eight Degrees*

9   Astrology is a disease, not a science.
Laws of Repentance [1170–1180]

10   When I find the road narrow, and can see no other way of teaching a well-established truth except by pleasing one intelligent man and displeasing ten thousand fools—I prefer to address myself to the one man.[4]
*The Guide for the Perplexed [1190].
Introduction*

11   The spiritual perfection of man consists in his becoming an intelligent being—one who knows all that he is capable of learning.   *Ibid. ch. 3*

12   In the realm of Nature there is nothing purposeless, trivial, or unnecessary.   *Ibid. ch. 15*

13   Thou has endowed man with the wisdom to relieve the suffering of his brother, to recognize his disorders, to extract the healing substances, to discover their powers and to apply them to suit every ill.   *Attributed*

Walter Map [Mapes]
c. 1140 – c. 1210

14   I intend to die in a tavern; let the wine be placed near my dying mouth,[5] so that when the choirs of angels come, they may say, "God be merciful to this drinker!"   *De Nugis Curialium*

Alain de Lille [Alanus de Insulis]
d. 1202

15   Do not hold as gold all that shines as gold.[6]
Parabolae

Kamo no Chōmei
1153–1216

16   The flow of the river is ceaseless and its water is never the same.[7] The bubbles that float in the pools, now vanishing, now forming, are not of long duration: so in the world are man and his dwellings. . . . [People] die in the morning, they are born in the evening, like foam on the water.
Hojoki (An Account of My Hut) [1212][8]

---

[1]Translated by W. S. MERWIN.
[2]The classic definition of epistemology, still commented on today and used by the Neo-Thomists.
[3]Thomas à Becket.
[4]Translated from the Arabic by M. FRIEDLANDER.
[5]Meum est propositum in taberna mori;/Vinum sit appositum morientis ori.
[6]Non teneas aurum totum quod splendet ut aurum.
Hyt is not al gold that glareth.—CHAUCER, *The House of Fame* [1374–1385], *bk. I, l. 272*
But al thyng which that shineth as the gold / Nis nat gold, as that I have herd it told.—CHAUCER, *The Canterbury Tales* [c. 1387], *The Canon's Yeoman's Tale, l. 962*
All is not gold that outward showeth bright.—JOHN LYDGATE [c. 1370–c. 1451], *On the Mutability of Human Affairs*
Non omne quod fulget est aurum.—GABRIEL BIEL [c. 1420–1495], *Expositio Canonis Messe, lecture 77*, derived from WILLIAM OF AUVERGNE [d. 1249].
All that glisters is not gold— / Often have you heard that told.—SHAKESPEARE, *The Merchant of Venice, act II, sc. vii, l. 65*
[7]See Heraclitus, 62:14.
[8]Translated by DONALD KEENE in his *Anthology of Japanese Literature* [1955].

1   My body is like a drifting cloud—I ask for nothing, I want nothing.   *Ibid.*

Fujiwara no Teika
1162–1241

2   In the expression of the emotions originality merits the first consideration. . . . The words used, however, should be old ones.
Guide to the Composition of Poetry[1]

3   There are no teachers of Japanese poetry. But they who take the old poems as their teachers, steep their minds in the old style, and learn their words from the masters of former time—who of them will fail to write poetry?[2]   *Ibid.*

Walther von der Vogelweide
c. 1170 – c. 1230

4 Now the summer came to pass
And flowers through the grass
Joyously sprang,
While all the tribes of birds sang.[3]
Dream Song, st. 1

5 The sun no longer shows
His face; and treason sows
His secret seeds that no man can detect;
Fathers by their children are undone;
The brother would the brother cheat;
And the cowled monk is a deceit . . .
Might is right, and justice there is none.[4]
Millennium

Eike von Repkow
fl. c. 1220

6   He who comes first, eats first.[5]
Sachsenspiegel [1219–1233]

Saint Francis of Assisi[6]
c. 1181–1226

7 Praise to thee, my Lord, for all thy creatures,
Above all Brother Sun
Who brings us the day and lends us his light.
The Song of Brother Sun and of All His Creatures [1225]

8 Love is he, radiant with great splendor,
And speaks to us of Thee, O Most High.
Ibid.

9   Where there is charity and wisdom, there is neither fear nor ignorance. Where there is patience and humility, there is neither anger nor vexation. Where there is poverty and joy, there is neither greed nor avarice. Where there is peace and meditation, there is neither anxiety nor doubt.
The Counsels of the Holy Father Saint Francis. Admonition 27

10   Lord, make me an instrument of Your peace. Where there is hatred let me sow love; where there is injury, pardon; where there is doubt, faith; where there is despair, hope; where there is darkness, light; and where there is sadness, joy.
   O divine Master, grant that I may not so much seek to be consoled as to console; to be understood as to understand; to be loved as to love. For it is in giving that we receive; it is in pardoning that we are pardoned; and it is in dying that we are born to eternal life.   *Attributed*

11   I have sinned against my brother the ass.
Dying words

Magna Carta
1215

12   No freeman shall be taken, or imprisoned, or outlawed, or exiled, or in any way harmed, nor will we go upon him nor will we send upon him, except by the legal judgment of his peers or by the law of the land.   *Clause 39*

13   To none will we sell, to none deny or delay, right or justice.   *Clause 40*

Tommaso di Celano
c. 1185 – c. 1255

14 Day of wrath! O day of mourning!
See fulfilled the prophets' warning,
Heaven and earth in ashes burning![7]
Dies Irae

Saint Bonaventure
c. 1217–1274

15   An example from the monkey: The higher it climbs, the more you see of its behind.[8]
Conferences on the Gospel of John

---

[1]From *Sources of Japanese Tradition* [1960], edited by WILLIAM THEODORE DE BARY.
[2]See Horace, 98:15, and Hsieh Ho, 115:8.
[3]Dô der sumer komen was, / Und die blumen dur daz gras / Wünneclâchen sprungen, / Aedâ die vogele sungen.
[4]Translated by JETHRO BITHELL.
[5]Familiar as: First come first served.
[6]Translated by LEO SHERLEY-PRICE.

[7]Dies irae, dies illa / Solvet saeclum in favilla, / Teste David cum Sibylla.
   Translated by W. J. IRONS [1849]. This has been attributed also to SAINT GREGORY and SAINT BERNARD.
   See Roscommon, 278:25.
[8]Exemplum de simia, quae, quanto plus ascendit, tanto plus apparent posteriora eius.
   Translated by the REV. WALTER J. BURGHARDT, S.J.

Roger Bacon
c. 1220 – c. 1292

1   If in other sciences we should arrive at certainty without doubt and truth without error, it behooves us to place the foundations of knowledge in mathematics.[1]   *Opus Majus,*[2] *bk. I, ch. 4*

Alfonso X [Alfonso the Wise]
1221–1284

2   Had I been present at the creation, I would have given some useful hints for the better ordering of the universe.[3]   *Attributed*

Rutebeuf
d. 1285

3   What became of the friends I had
With whom I was always so close
    And loved so dearly?
    La Complainte Rutebeuf

4   Friendship is dead:
They were friends who go with the wind,
And the wind was blowing at my door.   *Ibid.*

Saint Thomas Aquinas
c. 1225–1274

5   Sing, my tongue, the Savior's glory,
Of His Flesh the mystery sing;
Of the Blood, all price exceeding,
Shed by our immortal King.[4]
    Pange, Lingua (hymn for Vespers on the Feast of Corpus Christi), st. 1

6   Down in adoration falling,
Lo! the sacred Host we hail;
Lo! o'er ancient forms departing,
Newer rites of grace prevail;
Faith for all defects supplying,
Where the feeble senses fail.
    Ibid. st. 5 (Tantum Ergo)

7   Thus Angels' Bread is made
The Bread of man today:

---

[1]See Galileo, 161:15.
[2]Translated by ROBERT BURKE.
[3]Carlyle says, in his *History of Frederick the Great, bk. II, ch. 7,* that this saying of Alfonso about Ptolemy's astronomy, "that it seemed a crank machine; that it was pity the Creator had not taken advice," is still remembered by mankind— this and no other of his many sayings.
[4]Pange, lingua, gloriosi / Corporis mysterium / Sanguinisque pretiosi, / Quem in mundi pretium / Fructus ventris generosi / Rex effudit gentium.
    Translated by EDWARD CASWALL.
    Now, my tongue, the mystery telling / Of the glorious Body sing.—*Hymnal of the Protestant Episcopal Church*
    Pange, lingua, gloriosi proelium certáminis [Sing, my tongue, the glorious battle].—SAINT VENANTIUS FORTUNATUS [c. 530–c. 610], bishop of Poitiers

---

The Living Bread from Heaven
With figures doth away:
O wondrous gift indeed!
The poor and lowly may
Upon their Lord and Master feed.[5]
    Sacris Solemniis Juncta Sint Gaudia (Matins hymn for Corpus Christi), st. 6 (Panis Angelicus)

8   O saving Victim, opening wide
The gate of heaven to man below,
Our foes press on from every side,
Thine aid supply, Thy strength bestow.[6]
    Verbum Supernum Prodiens (hymn for Lauds on Corpus Christi), st. 5 (O Salutaris Hostia)

9   Lord Jesu, blessed Pelican.
    Adoro Te Devote (hymn appointed for the Thanksgiving after Mass), st. 6 (Pie Pellicane Jesu Domine)

10   Three things are necessary for the salvation of man: to know what he ought to believe; to know what he ought to desire; and to know what he ought to do.   *Two Precepts of Charity [1273]*

11   Law: an ordinance of reason for the common good, made by him who has care of the community.   *Summa Theologica [1273]*

12   Concerning perfect blessedness which consists in a vision of God.[7]   *Ibid.*

13   Reason in man is rather like God in the world.
    Opuscule 11, De Regno

Meister Eckhart
c. 1260 – c. 1327

14   In silence man can most readily preserve his integrity.   *Directions for the Contemplative Life*

15   The more wise and powerful a master, the more directly is his work created, and the simpler it is.
    Of the Eternal Birth

16   One must not always think so much about what one should do, but rather what one should be. Our works do not ennoble us; but we must ennoble our works.   *Work and Being*

Dante Alighieri
1265–1321

17   In that part of the book of my memory before which is little that can be read, there is a rubric, saying, "Incipit Vita Nova [The new life begins]."
    La Vita Nuova [1293][8]

---

[5]Translated by J. D. CHAMBERS.
See *Psalm 78:25, 18:3.*
[6]Translated by EDWARD CASWALL.
[7]Probably the origin of the phrase: beatific vision.
[8]Translated by DANTE GABRIEL ROSSETTI.

1 Love hath so long possessed me for his own
And made his lordship so familiar.

Ibid.

2 Love with delight discourses in my mind
Upon my lady's admirable gifts . . .
Beyond the range of human intellect.

Il Convito.[1] *Trattato Terzo, l. 1*

3 In the middle of the journey of our life I came to myself within a dark wood where the straight way was lost.[2]

The Divine Comedy [c. 1310–1321]. Inferno,[3]
canto I, l. 1

4 And as he, who with laboring breath has escaped from the deep to the shore, turns to the perilous waters and gazes. *Ibid. l. 22*

5 Thou [Virgil] art my master and my author, thou art he from whom alone I took the style whose beauty has done me honor. *Ibid. l. 85*

6 All hope abandon, ye who enter here![4]

Ibid. III, l. 9

7 Here must all distrust be left behind; all cowardice must be ended. *Ibid. l. 14*

8 There sighs, lamentations and loud wailings resounded through the starless air, so that at first it made me weep; strange tongues, horrible language, words of pain, tones of anger, voices loud and hoarse, and with these the sound of hands, made a tumult which is whirling through that air forever dark, as sand eddies in a whirlwind. *Ibid. l. 22*

9 This miserable state is borne by the wretched souls of those who lived without disgrace and without praise. *Ibid. l. 34*

10 Let us not speak of them; but look, and pass on.[5]

Ibid. l. 51

11 These wretches, who never were alive.

Ibid. l. 64

12 Into the eternal darkness, into fire and into ice.[5]

Ibid. l. 87

13 Without hope we live in desire.

Ibid. IV, l. 42

14 I came into a place void of all light, which bellows like the sea in tempest, when it is combated by warring winds.[5] *Ibid. V, l. 28*

15 As in the cold season their wings bear the starlings along in a broad, dense flock, so does that blast the wicked spirits. Hither, thither, downward, upward, it drives them.[6] *Ibid. l. 40*

16 Love, which is quickly kindled in the gentle heart, seized this man for the fair form that was taken from me, and the manner still hurts me. Love, which absolves no beloved one from loving, seized me so strongly with his charm that, as thou seest, it does not leave me yet. *Ibid. l. 100*

17 What sweet thoughts, what longing led them to the woeful pass.[7] *Ibid. l. 113*

18 There is no greater sorrow
Than to be mindful of the happy time
In misery.[8]

Ibid. l. 121

19 Galeotto was the book and he that wrote it; that day we read in it no farther.[9] *Ibid. l. 137*

20 I fell as a dead body falls. *Ibid. Last line*

21 Pride, Envy, and Avarice are the three sparks that have set these hearts on fire. *Ibid. VI, l. 74*

22 But when thou shalt be in the sweet world, I pray thee bring me to men's memory. *Ibid. l. 88*

23 Ye that are of good understanding, note the doctrine that is hidden under the veil of the strange verses! *Ibid. IX, l. 61*

24 Already I had fixed my look on his; and he rose upright with breast and countenance, as if he entertained great scorn of Hell.[7] *Ibid. X, l. 34*

25 Necessity brings him [Dante] here, not pleasure.
Ibid. XII, l. 87

26 If thou follow thy star, thou canst not fail of a glorious haven. *Ibid. XV, l. 55*

27 So my conscience chide me not, I am ready for Fortune as she wills. *Ibid. l. 91*

28 He listens well who takes notes. *Ibid. l. 99*

29 A fair request should be followed by the deed in silence. *Ibid. XXIV, l. 77*

30 Consider your origin; you were not born to live like brutes, but to follow virtue and knowledge.
Ibid. XXVI, l. 118

31 If I thought my answer were to one who would ever return to the world, this flame should stay without another movement; but since none ever returned

---

[1]Translated by CHARLES LYELL.
The first line is also in *The Divine Comedy, Purgatorio, canto II, l. 112.*

[2]Nel mezzo del cammin di nostra vita / Mi ritrovai per una selva oscura, / Che la diritta via era smarrita.

[3]Translated by JOHN D. SINCLAIR unless otherwise noted.

[4]Lasciate ogni speranza, voi ch'entrate.
Traditional translation.

[5]Translated by JOHN AITKEN CARLYLE, *The Temple Classics* [1900].

[6]Di qua, di là, di giù, di su li mena.

[7]Translated by JOHN AITKEN CARLYLE, *The Temple Classics* [1900].

[8]Nessun maggior dolore / Che ricordarsi del tempo felice / Nella miseria.
Translated by LONGFELLOW.
See Pindar, 64:4; Boethius, 115:10; Chaucer, 128:19; and Tennyson, 455:13.

[9]Galeotto fu il libro e chi lo scrisse: / Quel giorno più non vi leggemmo avante.

alive from this depth, if what I hear is true, I answer thee without fear of infamy.

Divine Comedy. Inferno, canto XXVII, l. 60

1   And thence we came forth, to see again the stars.[1]
Ibid. XXXIV, l. 139

2   To run over better waters the little vessel of my genius now hoists her sails, as she leaves behind her a sea so cruel.[2]   *Ibid. Purgatorio,[3] canto I, l. 1*

3   He goes seeking liberty, which is so dear, as he knows who for it renounces life.   *Ibid. l. 71*

4   O conscience, upright and stainless, how bitter a sting to thee is a little fault!   *Ibid. III, l. 8*

5   For to lose time is most displeasing to him who knows most.   *Ibid. l. 78*

6   The Infinite Goodness has such wide arms that it takes whatever turns to it.   *Ibid. l. 121*

7   Unless, before then, the prayer assist me which rises from a heart that lives in grace: what avails the other, which is not heard in heaven?
Ibid. IV, l. 133

8   "Why is thy mind so entangled," said the Master [Virgil], "that thou slackenest thy pace? What is it to thee what they whisper there? Come after me and let the people talk. Stand like a firm tower that never shakes its top for blast of wind."
Ibid. V,[4] l. 10

9   Go right on and listen as thou goest.
Ibid. l. 45

10   [Beatrice] who shall be a light between truth and intellect.   *Ibid. VI, l. 45*

11   It was now the hour that turns back the longing of seafarers and melts their hearts, the day they have bidden dear friends farewell, and pierces the new traveler with love if he hears in the distance the bell that seems to mourn the dying day.[4]
Ibid. VIII, l. 1

12   Give us this day the daily manna,[5] without which, in this rough desert, he backward goes, who toils most to go on.   *Ibid. XI, l. 13*

13   Worldly renown is naught but a breath of wind, which now comes this way and now comes that, and changes name because it changes quarter.
Ibid. l. 100

14   O human race, born to fly upward, wherefore at a little wind dost thou so fall?   *Ibid. XII, l. 95*

15   To a greater force, and to a better nature, you, free, are subject, and that creates the mind in you, which the heavens have not in their charge. There-

fore if the present world go astray, the cause is in you, in you it is to be sought.   *Ibid. XVI, l. 79*

16   Everyone confusedly conceives of a good in which the mind may be at rest, and desires it; wherefore everyone strives to attain to it.
Ibid. XVII, l. 127

17   Love kindled by virtue always kindles another, provided that its flame appear outwardly.
Ibid. XXII, l. 10

18   Less than a drop of blood remains in me that does not tremble; I recognize the signals of the ancient flame.[6]   *Ibid. XXX, l. 46*

19   But so much the more malign and wild does the ground become with bad seed and untilled, as it has the more of good earthly vigor.   *Ibid. l. 118*

20   Pure and disposed to mount unto the stars.[7]
Ibid. XXXIII, l. 145

21   The glory of Him who moves everything penetrates through the universe, and is resplendent in one part more and in another less.
Ibid. Paradiso,[8] canto I, l. 1

22   A great flame follows a little spark.
Ibid. l. 34

23   And in His will is our peace.[9]   *Ibid. III, l. 85*

24   The greatest gift that God in His bounty made in creation, and the most conformable to His goodness, and that which He prizes the most, was the freedom of the will, with which the creatures with intelligence, they all and they alone, were and are endowed.   *Ibid. V, l. 19*

25   Thou shalt prove how salt is the taste of another's bread and how hard is the way up and down another man's stairs.   *Ibid. XVII, l. 58*

26   Overcoming me with the light of a smile, she [Beatrice] said to me: "Turn and listen, for not only in my eyes is Paradise."[10]   *Ibid. XVIII, l. 19*

27   Therefore the sight that is granted to your world penetrates within the Eternal Justice as the eye into the sea; for though from the shore it sees the bottom, in the open sea it does not, and yet the bottom is there but the depth conceals it.   *Ibid. XIX, l. 73*

28   The experience of this sweet life.[11]
Ibid. XX, l. 47

---

[1]E quindi uscimmo a riveder le stelle.
[2]See Pope, 302:3.
[3]Translated [1902] by Charles Eliot Norton unless otherwise noted.
[4]Translated by John D. Sinclair.
[5]See *Matthew* 6:11, 33:12.

[6]Men che dramma / Di sangue m'è rimaso, che no tremi; / Conosco i segni dell' antica fiamma.
See Virgil, 93:39.
[7]Puro e disposto a salire alle stelle.
See Virgil, 94:24.
[8]Translated by John D. Sinclair.
[9]E'n la sua volontade e nostra pace.
[10]See Chaucer, 128:25.
[11]L'esperienza di questa dolce vita.

1 Like the lark that soars in the air, first singing, then silent, content with the last sweetness that satiates it, such seemed to me that image, the imprint of the Eternal Pleasure.   *Ibid. l. 73*

2 The night that hides things from us.
Ibid. XXIII, l. 3

3 With the color that paints the morning and evening clouds that face the sun I saw then the whole heaven suffused.   *Ibid. XXVII, l. 28*

4 The Love that moves the sun and the other stars.[1]
Ibid. XXXIII, l. 145

Yoshida Kenko
1283–1350

5 One should write not unskillfully in the running hand, be able to sing in a pleasing voice and keep good time to music; and, lastly, a man should not refuse a little wine when it is pressed upon him.
Tsurezure-Gusa (Essays in Idleness) [c. 1340][2]

6 A certain recluse, I know not who, once said that no bonds attached him to this life, and the only thing he would regret leaving was the sky.   *Ibid.*

William of Occam [Ockham]
c. 1285 – c. 1349

7 Entities should not be multiplied unnecessarily.[3]
Quodlibeta Septem [c. 1320]

Philip VI [Philip of Valois]
1293–1350

8 He who loves me, let him follow me.[4]
Attributed

Petrarch[5] [Francesco Petrarca]
1304–1374

9 Who overrefines his argument brings himself to grief.   *To Laura in Life, canzone 11*

10 A good death does honor to a whole life.
To Laura in Death, canzone 16

11 To be able to say how much you love is to love but little.   *Ibid. 137*

---

[1]*L'amor che muove il sole e l'altre stelle.*
See Aristotle, 77:22.
[2]Translated by DONALD KEENE in his *Anthology of Japanese Literature* [1955].
[3]Translated [seventeenth century] by JOHN PONCE of Cork. The axiom became known as "Occam's Razor."
[4]*Qui m'aime me suive.*
[5]Chaucer translated *Sonnet 88 (In Vita), S'amor non è.* See 128:12.

12 Rarely do great beauty and great virtue dwell together.   *De Remedies, bk. II*

Edward III
1312–1377

13 Honi soit qui mal y pense. [Evil to him who evil thinks].   *Motto of the Order of the Garter [1349]*

14 Let the boy win his spurs.
Said of the Black Prince at the battle of Crécy [1345]

John Barbour
c. 1316–1395

15 Freedom all solace to man gives;
He lives at ease that freely lives.
The Bruce [c. 1375], l. 227

William of Wykeham
1324–1404

16 Manners maketh man.
Motto of his two foundations, Winchester College and New College, Oxford

William Langland
c. 1330 – c. 1400

17 In a summer season when soft was the sun.[6]
The Vision of Piers Plowman [1362–1390]

18 A fair field full of folk found I there.   *Ibid.*

19 Who will bell the cat?   *Ibid.*

John Wycliffe
c. 1330–1384

20 I believe that in the end the truth will conquer.
To the Duke of Lancaster [1381]. From J. R. GREEN, A Short History of the English People [1874], ch. 5

Juliana of Norwich
c. 1342–after 1416

21 It behoved that there should be sin; but all shall be well, and all shall be well, and all manner of thing shall be well.[7]
Revelations of Divine Love [1373–c. 1393], ch. 27, The Thirteenth Revelation

---

[6]See Chaucer, 128:10.
[7]Sin is Behovely . . . —T. S. ELIOT, *Four Quartets. Little Gidding* [1942], *III*
See T. S. Eliot, 672:7.

1   He said not "Thou shalt not be tempested, thou
shalt not be travailed, thou shalt not be dis-eased";
but he said, "Thou shalt not be overcome."
Revelations of Divine Love, ch. 68

Geoffrey Chaucer[1]
c. 1343–1400

2   Soun ys noght but eyr ybroken,
And every speche that ys spoken,
Lowd or pryvee, foul or fair,
In his substaunce ys but air.
The House of Fame [1374–1385], bk. II, l. 765

3   Venus clerk, Ovide,
That hath ysowen wonder wide
The grete god of Loves name.
Ibid. III, l. 1487

4   Hard is the herte that loveth nought
In May.
The Romaunt of the Rose [c. 1380],[2] l. 85

5   For nakid as a worm was she.
Ibid. l. 454

6   As round as appil was his face.
Ibid. l. 819

7   The lyf so short, the craft so long to lerne,
Th' assay so hard, so sharp the conquerynge.
The Parliament of Fowls [1380–1386], l. 1

8   For out of olde feldes, as men seyth,
Cometh al this newe corn fro yer to yere;[3]
And out of olde bokes, in good feyth,
Cometh al this newe science that men lere.
Ibid. l. 22

9   Nature, the vicaire of the almyghty lorde.
Ibid. l. 379

10   Now welcome, somer, with thy sonne softe,
That hast this wintres wedres overshake.
Ibid. l. 680

11   But the Troian gestes, as they felle,
In Omer, or in Dares, or in Dite,
Whoso that kan may rede hem as they write.
Troilus and Criseyde [c. 1385], bk. I, l. 145

12   If no love is, O God, what fele I so?
And if love is, what thing and which is he?
If love be good, from whennes cometh my woo?[4]
•   *Ibid. l. 400 (Canticus Troili)*

13   Unknowe, unkist, and lost, that is unsought.
Ibid. l. 809

14   O wynd, o wynd, the weder gynneth clere.
Ibid. II, l. 2

15   Til crowes feet be growen under youre yë.
Ibid. l. 403

16   Lord, this is an huge rayn!
This were a weder for to slepen inne!
Ibid. III, l. 656

17   For I have seyn, of a ful misty morwe
Folowen ful often a myrie someris day.
Ibid. l. 1060

18   Right as an aspes leef she gan to quake.
Ibid. l. 1200

19   For of fortunes sharpe adversitee
The worste kynde of infortune is this,
A man to han ben in prosperitee,
And it remembren, whan it passed is.[5]
Ibid. l. 1625

20   Oon ere it herde, at tothir out it wente.[6]
Ibid. IV, l. 434

21   But manly sette the world on six and sevene;[7]
And if thow deye a martyr, go to hevene!
Ibid. l. 622

22   For tyme ylost may nought recovered be.
Ibid. l. 1283

23   They take it wisly, faire, and softe.[8]
Ibid. V, l. 347

24   For he that naught n' assaieth, naught
n' acheveth.[9]
Ibid. l. 784

25   That Paradis stood formed in her yën.[10]
Ibid. l. 817

26   Trewe as stiel.
Ibid. l. 831

27   This sodeyn Diomede.
Ibid. l. 1024

28   Ye, fare wel al the snow of ferne yere![11]
Ibid. l. 1176

29   Ek gret effect men write in place lite;
Th' entente is al, and nat the lettres space.
Ibid. 1629

---

[1]From the text of F. N. Robinson, *The Works of Geoffrey Chaucer*, 2nd edition [1957].

[2]Chaucer, and probably others, translated the French *Roman de la Rose* by Guillaume de Lorris [begun 1237] and Jean de Meun [continued c. 1277].

[3]John Bartlett quoted this line at the head of his preface to the ninth edition of *Familiar Quotations* [1891].

[4]The *Canticus Troili (Song of Troilus)* is a fairly close rendering of Petrarch's *Sonnet 88 (In Vita), S'amor non è.*

[5]See Pindar, 64:4; Boethius, 115:10; Dante, 125:18; and Tennyson, 455:13.

[6]Commonly quoted: In one ear and out the other.

[7]All is uneven, / And everything is left at six and seven.— Shakespeare, *Richard II*, act II, sc. ii, l. 120
Things going on at sixes and sevens.—Goldsmith, *The Good-Natur'd Man* [1768], *act I*

[8]The proverb is: Fair and softly goes far.
See Shakespeare, 175:18.

[9]See John Heywood, 141:33, and W. S. Gilbert, 530:16.

[10]See Dante, 126:26.

[11]See Villon, 134:1.

1 Go, litel bok, go, litel myn tragedye.[1]
> *Ibid. l. 1786*

2 O yonge, fresshe folkes, he or she,
In which that love up groweth with youre age,
Repeyreth hom fro worldly vanyte.
> *Ibid. l. 1835*

3 O moral Gower, this book I directe
To the.
> *Ibid. l. 1856*

4   Whan that the month of May
Is comen, and that I here the foules synge,
And that the floures gynnen for to sprynge,
Farewel my bok, and my devocioun!
> *The Legend of Good Women* [c. 1386], l. 36

5 That, of al the floures in the mede,
Thanne love I most thise floures white and rede,
Swiche as men callen daysyes in our toun.
> *Ibid. l. 41*

6 Whan that Aprille with his shoures soote
The droghte of March hath perced to the roote.
> *The Canterbury Tales* [c. 1387]. Prologue, l. 1

7 And smale foweles maken melodye,
That slepen al the nyght with open yë,
(So priketh hem nature in hir corages);
Thanne longen folk to goon on pilgrimages.
> *Ibid. l. 9*

8 He was a verray, parfit gentil knyght.
> *Ibid. l. 72*

9 He was as fressh as is the month of May.
> *Ibid. l. 92*

10 He koude songes make and wel endyte.
> *Ibid. l. 95*

11 Curteis he was, lowely, and servysable,
And carf biforn his fader at the table.
> *Ibid. l. 99*

12 Ful weel she soong the service dyvyne,
Entuned in hir nose ful semely;
And Frenssh she spak ful faire and fetisly,

After the scole of Stratford atte Bowe
For Frenssh of Parys was to hir unknowe.
> *Ibid. l. 122*

13 She wolde wepe, if that she saugh a mous
Kaught in a trappe, if it were deed or bledde.
> *Ibid. l. 144*

14 And theron heng a brooch of gold ful sheene,
On which ther was first write a crowned *A,*
And after *Amor vincit omnia.*[2]
> *Ibid. l. 160*

15 His palfrey was as broun as is a berye.
> *Ibid. l. 207*

16 A Frere ther was, a wantowne and a merye.
> *Ibid. l. 208*

17 He knew the tavernes wel in every toun.
> *Ibid. l. 240*

18 Somwhat he lipsed, for his wantownesse,
To make his Englissh sweete upon his tonge.
> *Ibid. l. 264*

19 A Clerk ther was of Oxenford also.
> *Ibid. l. 285*

20 As leene was his hors as is a rake.
> *Ibid. l. 287*

21 For hym was levere have at his beddes heed
Twenty bookes, clad in blak or reed,
Of Aristotle and his philosophie,
Than robes riche, or fithele, or gay sautrie,
But al be that he was a philosophre,
Yet hadde he but litel gold in cofre.
> *Ibid. l. 293*

22 And gladly wolde he lerne, and gladly teche.[3]
> *Ibid. l. 308*

23 Nowher so bisy a man as he ther nas,
And yet he semed bisier than he was.
> *Ibid. l. 321*

24 For he was Epicurus owene sone.[4]
> *Ibid. l. 336*

25 It snewed in his hous of mete and drynke.
> *Ibid. l. 345*

26   He was a good felawe.[5]
> *Ibid. l. 395*

27 His studie was but litel on the Bible.
> *Ibid. l. 438*

28 For gold in phisik is a cordial,
Therefore he lovede gold in special.
> *Ibid. l. 443*

---

[1] Off with you down where you want to go. — HORACE, *Epistles, I, xx, 5*

Little book, you will go without me — I don't mind — to the city. — OVID, *Tristia, I, i, 1*

Vade salutatem pro me, liber [Go forth, my book, to bear my greetings]. — MARTIAL, *Epigrams, I, 70*

Go now, my little book, to every place / Where my first pilgrim has but shown his face. — BUNYAN, *The Pilgrim's Progress* [1678], *Apology*

Go, little Book! From this my solitude / I cast thee on the Waters — go thy ways. — SOUTHEY, *Lay of the Laureate* [1815], *L'Envoi*

These lines of Southey's and the next two were quoted by BYRON in *Don Juan* [1818], *canto I, stanza 222*, which ends: The four first rhymes are Southey's, every line: / For God's sake, reader! take them not for mine!

Go, little book, and wish to all / Flowers in the garden, meat in the hall. — R. L. STEVENSON, *Underwoods* [1887], *Envoy*

[2] See Sophocles, 66:18 and 67:1, and Virgil, 92:20.
[3] See Pope, 299:7.
[4] See Horace, 97:11.
[5] If he be not fellow with the best king, thou shalt find the best king of good fellows. — SHAKESPEARE, *King Henry V, act V, sc. ii, l. 259*

1 She was a worthy womman al hir lyve,
Housbondes at chirche dore she hadde fyve.
Canterbury Tales. Prologue, l. 459

2 This noble ensample to his sheep he yaf,
That first he wroghte, and afterward he taughte.
Ibid. l. 496

3 If gold ruste, what shal iren do?
Ibid. l. 500

4 But Cristes loore and his apostles twelve
He taughte, but first he folwed it hymselve.
Ibid. l. 527

5 And yet he hadde a thombe of gold.[1]
Ibid. l. 563

6 That hadde a fyr-reed cherubynnes face.
Ibid. l. 624

7 Wel loved he garleek, oynons, and eek lekes,
And for to drynken strong wyn, reed as blood.
Ibid. l. 634

8 And whan that he wel dronken hadde the wyn,
Than wolde he speke no word but Latyn.
Ibid. l. 637

9 Whoso shal telle a tale after a man,
He moot reherce as ny as evere he kan
Everich a word, if it be in his charge,
Al speke he never so rudeliche and large,
Or ellis he moot telle his tale untrewe,
Or feyne thyng, or fynde wordes new.
Ibid. l. 731

10 For May wol have no slogardie anyght.
The sesoun priketh every gentil herte,
And maketh hym out of his slep to sterte.[2]
Ibid. The Knight's Tale, l. 1042

11 Ech man for hymself.
Ibid. l. 1182

12 The bisy larke, messager of day.
Ibid. l. 1491

13 May, with alle thy floures and thy grene,
Welcome be thou, faire, fresshe May.
Ibid. l. 1510

14 That "feeld hath eyen, and the wode hath eres."[3]
Ibid. l. 1522

15 Now up, now doun, as boket in a welle.
Ibid. l. 1533

16 For pitee renneth soone in gentil herte.
Ibid. l. 1761

17   Cupido,
Upon his shuldres wynges hadde he two;
And blynd he was, as it is often seene;
A bowe he bar and arwes brighte and kene.
Ibid. l. 1963

18 The smylere with the knyf under the cloke.
Ibid. l. 1999

19 Up roos the sonne, and up roose Emelye.
Ibid. l. 2273

20 Myn be the travaille, and thyn be the glorie!
Ibid. l. 2406

21 And was al his chiere, as in his herte.
Ibid. l. 2683

22 What is this world? what asketh men to have?
Now with his love, now in his colde grave
Allone, withouten any compaignye.
Ibid. l. 2777

23 This world nys but a thurghfare ful of wo,
And we been pilgrymes, passing to and fro.
Deeth is an ende of every worldly soore.
Ibid. l. 2847

24 Jhesu Crist, and seiynte Benedight,
Blesse this hous from every wikked wight.
Ibid. The Miller's Tale, l. 3483

25 And broghte of myghty ale a large quart.
Ibid. l. 3497

26 "Tehee!" quod she, and clapte the wyndow to.
Ibid. l. 3740

27 Yet in our asshen olde is fyr yreke.[4]
Ibid. The Reeve's Prologue, l. 3882

28 The gretteste clerkes been noght the wisest men.
Ibid. The Reeve's Tale, l. 4054

29 Thurgh thikke and thurgh thenne.[5]
Ibid. l. 4066

30 So was hir joly whistle wel ywet.
Ibid. l. 4155

31 She is mirour of alle curteisye.[6]
Ibid. The Man of Law's Tale, l. 166

32 For in the sterres, clerer than is glas,
Is writen, God woot, whoso koude it rede,
The deeth of every man.
Ibid. l. 194

---

[1]In allusion to the proverb: An honest miller hath a golden thumb.

[2]See Malory, 133:11.

[3]The proverb also occurs in the Latin form: Campus habet lumen, et habet nemus auris acumen [The field has sight, and the wood a sharp ear].

Wode has erys, felde has sigt. — *King Edward and the Shepherd, MS* [c. 1300]

Fields have eyes and woods have ears. — JOHN HEYWOOD, *Proverbs* [1546], *pt. II, ch. 5*

Walls have ears. — CERVANTES, *Don Quixote, pt. II* [1615], *ch.* 48

Woods have tongues / As walls have ears. — TENNYSON, *Idylls of the King, Balin and Balan* [1885], *l.* 522

[4]See Thomas Gray, 322:20.

[5]Through thick and thin. — DU BARTAS, *Divine Weeks and Works* [1578], *Second Week, Fourth Day*

[6]Call him bounteous Buckingham, / The mirror of all courtesy. — SHAKESPEARE, *Henry VIII, act II, sc. i, l.* 52

1 Sathan, that evere us waiteth to bigile.
Ibid. l. 582

2 But, Lord Crist! whan that it remembreth me
Upon my yowthe, and on my jolitee,
It tikleth me aboute myn herte roote.
Unto this day it dooth myn herte boote
That I have had my world as in my tyme.
Ibid. The Wife of Bath's Prologue, l. 469

3 In his owene grece I made hym frye.[1]
Ibid. l. 487

4 By God! in erthe I was his purgatorie,
For which I hope his soule be in glorie.
Ibid. l. 489

5 What thyng we may nat lightly have,
Thereafter wol we crie al day and crave.
Ibid. l. 517

6 Greet prees at market maketh deere ware,
And to greet cheep is holde at litel prys.
Ibid. l. 522

7 But yet I hadde alwey a coltes tooth.
Gat-toothed I was, and that bicam me weel.
Ibid. l. 601

8 A womman cast hir shame away,
Whan she cast of hir smok.[2]
Ibid. l. 782

9 As thikke as motes in the sonne-beem.
Ibid. The Wife of Bath's Tale, l. 868

10 "My lige lady, generally," quod he,
"Wommen desiren have sovereynetee
As well over hir housbond as hir love."
Ibid. l. 1037

11 Looke who that is moost vertuous alway,
Pryvee and apert, and most entendeth ay
To do the gentil dedes that he kan;
Taak hym for the grettest gentil man.
Ibid. l. 1113

12 That he is gentil that dooth gentil dedis.[3]
Ibid. l. 1170

13 For thogh we slepe, or wake, or rome, or ryde,
Ay fleeth the tyme, it nyl no man abyde.[4]
Ibid. The Clerk's Tale, l. 118

14 Ye been oure lord, dooth with youre owene thyng
Right as yow list.
Ibid. l. 652

[1] Proverbial.
Fryeth in her own grease. — JOHN HEYWOOD, *Proverbs* [1546], *pt. I, ch. 11*
The best way were to entertain him with hope, till the wicked fire of lust have melted him in his own grease. — SHAKESPEARE, *The Merry Wives of Windsor, act II, sc. i, l. 69*
[2] See Herodotus, 69:21.
[3] See Goldsmith, 328:20.
[4] See John Heywood, 140:21.

15 Love is noght oold as whan that it is newe.
Ibid. l. 857

16 This flour of wyfly pacience.
Ibid. l. 919

17 O stormy peple! unsad and evere untrewe!
Ibid. l. 995

18 No wedded man so hardy be t'assaille
His wyves pacience, in trust to fynde
Grisildis, for in certein he shal faille!
Ibid. l. 1180

19 It is no childes pley
To take a wyf withouten avysement.
Ibid. The Merchant's Tale, l. 1530

20 For love is blynd.[5]
Ibid. l. 1598

21 My wit is thynne.
Ibid. l. 1682

22 Ther nys no werkman, whatsoevere he be,
That may bothe werke wel and hastily;[6]
This wol be doon at leyser parfitly.[7]
Ibid. l. 1832

23 Therfore bihoveth hire a ful long spoon
That shal ete with a feend.[8]
Ibid. The Squire's Tale, l. 602

24 Men loven of propre kynde newefangelnesse.
Ibid. l. 610

25 Fy on possessioun
But if a man be vertuous withal.
Ibid. l. 686

26 Pacience is an heigh vertu, certeyn.
Ibid. The Franklin's Tale, l. 773

27 Servant in love and lord in marriage.
Ibid. l. 793

28 It is agayns the proces of nature.
Ibid. l. 1345

29 Trouthe is the hyeste thyng that men may
kepe.
Ibid. l. 1479

30 For dronkenesse is verray sepulture
Of mannes wit and his discrecioun.
Ibid. The Pardoner's Tale, l. 558

[5] Proverbial.
See Shakespeare, 172:21, and 180:20.
[6] See Publilius Syrus, 99:33, and John Heywood, 140:15.
[7] Ease and speed in doing a thing do not give the work lasting solidity or exactness of beauty. — PLUTARCH, *Life of Pericles*
[8] Proverbial.
He must have a long spoon that must eat with the devil.
— SHAKESPEARE, *The Comedy of Errors, act IV, sc. iii, l. 64*

1 Mordre wol out, certeyn, it wol nat faille.[1]
  Canterbury Tales. The Prioress's Tale, l. 1766

2 This may wel be rym dogerel.
  Ibid. Chaucer's Tale of Sir Thopas, l. 2115

3 Ful wys is he that kan hymselven knowe![2]
  Ibid. The Monk's Tale, l. 3329

4 He was of knyghthod and of fredom flour.
  Ibid. l. 3832

5 For whan a man hath over-greet a wit,
  Ful oft hym happeth to mysusen it.
  Ibid. The Canon Yeoman's Prologue, l. 648

6 My sone, keep wel thy tonge, and keep thy
  freend.
  Ibid. The Manciple's Tale, l. 319

7 Thing that is seyd is seyd; and forth it gooth.[3]
  Ibid. l. 355

8 For the proverbe seith that "manye smale maken
  a greet."[4]
  Ibid. The Parson's Tale, l. 361

9 Reule wel thyself, that other folk canst rede.
  And trouthe thee shal delivere, it is no drede.
  Truth [c. 1390], l. 6

10 The wrastling for this world axeth a fal.
  Ibid. l. 16

John Huss [Jan Hus]
c. 1372–1415

11   O holy simplicity![5]   *Last words, at the stake*

Thomas à Kempis
1380–1471

12   Sic transit gloria mundi [So passes away the glory
of this world].[6]
  Imitation of Christ [c. 1420], bk. I, ch. 3

[1]Proverbial.
  Also in *The Nun's Priest's Tale, ll. 4242 and 4247.*
  How easily murder is discovered! —SHAKESPEARE, *Titus
Andronicus, act II, sc. iii, l. 287*
  Truth will come to light; murder cannot be hid long. —
SHAKESPEARE, *The Merchant of Venice, act II, sc. ii, l. 86*
  Murder, though it have no tongue, will speak / With most
miraculous organ. —SHAKESPEARE, *Hamlet, act II, sc. ii, l. 630*
  Murder will out. —CERVANTES, *Don Quixote, pt. I [1605],
bk. III, ch. 8*
  Carcasses bleed at the sight of the murderer. —ROBERT
BURTON, *Anatomy of Melancholy [1621–1651], pt. I, sec. I
member 2, subsec. 5*
  Other sins only speak; murder shrieks out. —JOHN WEB-
STER, *The Duchess of Malfi [1623], act IV, sc. ii*
  [2]See The Seven Sages, 55:7.
  [3]See Horace, 97:18.
  [4]The proverb goes back to Saint Augustine.
  Many small make a great. —JOHN HEYWOOD, *Proverbs
[1546], pt. I, ch. II*
  See Hesiod, 54:27, and Cervantes, 150:28.
  [5]O sancta simplicitas!
  See Saint Jerome, 114:4.
  [6]These words are used in the crowning of the pope.

13   Be not angry that you cannot make others as you
wish them to be, since you cannot make yourself as
you wish to be.   *Ibid. 16*

14   Man proposes, but God disposes.[7]   *Ibid. 19*

15   What canst thou see elsewhere which thou canst
not see here? Behold the heaven and the earth and all
the elements; for of these are all things created.
  Ibid. 20

16   No man ruleth safely but he that is willingly
ruled.   *Ibid.*

17   And when he is out of sight, quickly also is he out
of mind.[8]   *Ibid. 23*

18   O that we had spent but one day in this world
thoroughly well!   *Ibid.*

19   First keep the peace within yourself, then you can
also bring peace to others.   *Ibid. II, 3*

20   Love is swift, sincere, pious, pleasant, gentle,
strong, patient, faithful, prudent, long-suffering,
manly and never seeking her own; for wheresoever
a man seeketh his own, there he falleth from love.[9]
  Ibid. III, 5

Charles d'Orléans
1394–1465

21   I am dying of thirst by the side of the fountain.[10]
  Ballades, 2

22   The season has shed its mantle of wind and chill
and rain.[11]   *Rondeaux, 63*

23 All by myself, wrapped in my thoughts,
  And building castles in Spain and in France.[12]
  Ibid. 109

[7]Homo proponet et Deus disponit. —LANGLAND, *The Vi-
sion of Piers Plowman, l. 13,994 [1550 edition]*
  Man appoints, and God disappoints. —CERVANTES, *Don
Quixote, pt. II [1615], bk. IV, ch. 55*
  See Proverbs 16:9, 21:30.
  [8]Fer from eze, fer from herte, / Quoth Hendyng. —HEN-
DYNG [1272–1307], *Proverbs, MS*
  Out of sight, out of mind. —BARNABE GOOGE [1540–1594],
Eglogs [1563]
  And out of mind as soon as out of sight. —GREVILLE, *Sonnet 56*
  I do perceive that the old proverbs be not always true, for I
do find that the absence of my Nath. doth breed in me the more
continual remembrance of him. —LADY ANN BACON [1528–
1610], *letter to Lady Jane Cornwallis*
  [9]See I Corinthians 13:4 and 13:7, 43:14 and 43:15.
  [10]Je meurs de soif auprès de la fontaine.
  [11]Le temps a laissé son manteau / De vent, de froidure et de
pluie.
  [12]Translated by NORBERT GUTERMAN.
  Thou shalt make castels thanne in Spayne, / And dreme of
joye, all but in vayne. —JEAN DE MEUN [13th cent.], *The Romaunt of the Rose [c. 1277], fragment B, l. 2573, translated by
CHAUCER*

John Fortescue
c. 1395 – c. 1479

1   Much cry and no wool.[1]
      De Laudibus Legum Angliae [1471], ch. 10

2   Comparisons are odious.[2]   *Ibid. 19*

Sir Thomas Malory
d. 1471

3   The noble history of the Sangreal,[3] and of the most renowned Christian king . . . King Arthur.
    Le Morte d'Arthur [1485]. Preface by William Caxton [c. 1422–1491], the first English printer

4   Whoso pulleth out this sword of this stone and anvil, is rightwise king born of all England.
      Ibid. bk. I, ch. 5

5   And with that the king saw coming toward him the strangest beast that ever he saw or heard of; so the beast went to the well and drank, and the noise was in the beast's belly like unto the questing of thirty couple hounds; but all the while the beast drank there was no noise in the beast's belly: and therewith the beast departed with a great noise . . . Pellinore, that time king, followed the questing beast.   *Ibid. 19*

6   In the midst of the lake Arthur was ware of an arm clothed in white samite, that held a fair sword in that hand.   *Ibid. 25*

7   Always Sir Arthur lost so much blood that it was marvel he stood on his feet, but he was so full of knighthood that knightly he endured the pain.
      Ibid. IV, 9

8   What, nephew, said the king, is the wind in that door?   *Ibid. VII, 34*

9   The joy of love is too short, and the sorrow thereof, and what cometh thereof, dureth over long.
      Ibid. X, 56

10   It is his day.   *Ibid. 70*

11   The month of May was come, when every lusty heart beginneth to blossom, and to bring forth fruit; for like as herbs and trees bring forth fruit and flourish in May, in likewise every lusty heart that is in any manner a lover, springeth and flourisheth in lusty deeds. For it giveth unto all lovers courage, that lusty month of May.[4]   *Ibid. XVIII, 25*

12   All ye that be lovers call unto your remembrance the month of May, like as did Queen Guenever, for whom I make here a little mention, that while she lived she was a true lover, and therefore she had a good end.   *Ibid.*

13   Such a fellowship of good knights shall never be together in no company.   *Ibid. XX, 9*

14   I shall curse you with book and bell and candle.[5]
      Ibid. XXI, 1

15   Through this man [Launcelot] and me [Guenever] hath all this war been wrought, and the death of the most noblest knights of the world; for through our love that we have loved together is my most noble lord slain.   *Ibid. 9*

16   For as well as I have loved thee, mine heart will not serve me to see thee, for through thee and me is the flower of kings and knights destroyed.
      Ibid.

17   Thou were the meekest man and the gentlest that ever ate in hall among ladies. And thou were the sternest knight to thy mortal foe that ever put spear in the rest.   *Ibid. 13*

18   Yet some men say in many parts of England that King Arthur is not dead, but had by the will of our Lord Jesu into another place. And men say that he shall come again and he shall win the Holy Cross. Yet I will not say that it shall be so, but rather I will say, Here in this world he changed his life. And many men say that there is written upon his tomb this verse: *Hic iacet Arthurus, rex quondam, rexque futurus.*[6]   *Ibid. XXXI, 7*

Henry VI
1421–1471

19 Kingdoms are but cares,
State is devoid of stay;
Riches are ready snares,
And hasten to decay.
    From Sir John Harington, Nugae Antiquae [1769]

François Villon
1431 – c. 1465

20 Ah God! Had I but studied
In the days of my foolish youth.[7]
    Le Grand Testament, 26

---

[1] A great cry, but little wool.—Cervantes, *Don Quixote, pt. II [1615], bk. III, ch. 13*
    All cry and no wool.—Samuel Butler, *Hudibras, pt. I [1663], canto 1, l. 852*
[2] This was a well-known phrase in the fourteenth century, and has been repeated by many, including Lydgate, Shakespeare, and Swift.
    See Donne, 230:6.
[3] The Holy Grail.
[4] See Chaucer, 130:10.

[5] The reference is to the ceremony of excommunication, current since the eighth century, performed with bell, book, and candle.
[6] Here lies Arthur, the once and future king.
[7] Hé Dieu! si j'eusse étudié / Au temps de ma jeunesse folle.

1 But where are the snows of yesteryear?[1]
　Le Grand Testament. Ballade des Dames du
　Temps Jadis

2 In this faith I will to live and die.
　　　Ibid. Ballade de l'Homage à Notre Dame

3 There's no good speech save in Paris.[2]
　　　Ibid. Ballade des Femmes de Paris

4 But pray God that he absolve us all![3]
　　　　　　　　　　　　Codicile

5 I know all except myself.[4]
　　　　　Ballade des Menus Propres

Aldus Manutius
1449–1515

6　Talk of nothing but business, and dispatch that
business quickly.
　Placard on the door of the Aldine Press, Venice,
　established about 1490[5]

Christopher Columbus
1451–1506

7　Here the people could stand it no longer and
complained of the long voyage; but the Admiral
cheered them as best he could, holding out good
hope of the advantages they would have. He added
that it was useless to complain, he had come [to go]
to the Indies, and so had to continue it until he found
them, with the help of Our Lord.
　Journal of the First Voyage,[6] October 10, 1492

8　At two hours after midnight appeared the land, at
a distance of 2 leagues. They handed all sails and set
the *treo*, which is the mainsail without bonnets, and
lay-to waiting for daylight Friday, when they arrived
at an island of the Bahamas that was called in the
Indians' tongue Guanahaní [San Salvador].
　　　　　　　　　Ibid. October 12, 1492

9　The two Christians met on the way many people
who were going to their towns, women and men,
with a firebrand in the hand, [and] herbs to drink the
smoke thereof, as they are accustomed.[7]
　　　　　　　　　Ibid. November 6, 1492

10　And I say that Your Highnesses ought not to
consent that any foreigner does business or sets foot
here, except Christian Catholics, since this was the
end and the beginning of the enterprise, that it
should be for the enhancement and glory of the
Christian religion, nor should anyone who is not a
good Christian come to these parts.[8]
　　　　　　　　　Ibid. November 27, 1492

11　And they know neither sect nor idolatry, with the
exception that all believe that the source of all power
and goodness is in the sky, and they believe very
firmly that I, with these ships and people, came from
the sky, and in this belief they everywhere received
me, after they had overcome their fear.
　Letter to the Sovereigns on the First Voyage,
　February 15–March 4, 1493[9]

12　I have always read that the world, both land and
water, was spherical, as the authority and researches
of Ptolemy and all the others who have written on
this subject demonstrate and prove, as do the
eclipses of the moon and other experiments that are
made from east to west, and the elevation of the
North Star from north to south.
　Letter to the Sovereigns on the Third Voyage,
　October 18, 1498[10]

13　I should be judged as a captain who went from
Spain to the Indies to conquer a people numerous
and warlike, whose manners and religion are very
different from ours, who live in sierras and mountains, without fixed settlements, and where by divine
will I have placed under the sovereignty of the King
and Queen our Lords, an Other World, whereby
Spain, which was reckoned poor, is become the richest of countries.
　Letter to Doña Juana de Torres, October 1500[11]

14　I came to serve you at the age of 28 and now I
have not a hair on me that is not white, and my body
is infirm and exhausted. All that was left to me and
my brothers has been taken away and sold, even to
the cloak that I wore, without hearing or trial, to my
great dishonor.
　Lettera Rarissima to the Sovereigns, July 7, 1503
　(Fourth Voyage)[12]

Leonardo da Vinci
1452–1519

15　Man and the animals are merely a passage and
channel for food, a tomb for other animals, a haven

---

[1]Mais où sont les neiges d'antan?
Translated by DANTE GABRIEL ROSSETTI.
See Chaucer, 128:28.
[2]Il n'est bon bec que de Paris.
[3]Mais priez Dieu que tous nous veuille absoudre.
[4]Je connais tout, fors moi-même.
[5]Quoted by THOMAS FROGNALL DIBDIN in *Introduction to
the Knowledge of Rare and Valuable Editions of the Greek and
Latin Classics* [1802], *vol. I, p. 436.*
[6]BARTOLOMÉ DE LAS CASAS [1474–1566] made an abstract
of Columbus's *Journal of the First Voyage (El Libro de la
Primera Navegación),* which is the nearest thing to an original
journal that we have.
Translated by SAMUEL ELIOT MORISON.
[7]The first certain reference in history to smoking tobacco.

[8]Here may be found the first suggestion of the exclusive
colonial policy that Spain and other nations followed. —SAM-
UEL ELIOT MORISON, *Journals and Other Documents on the
Life and Voyages of Christopher Columbus* [1963]
[9]This letter, the first and rarest of all printed Americana,
describes the scenery and the natives of Hispaniola.
[10]Translated by MORISON and MILTON ANASTOS.
[11]Columbus is coming from the Indies as a prisoner to Cadiz.
[12]Translated by MILTON ANASTOS.

for the dead, giving life by the death of others, a coffer full of corruption.

The Notebooks [1508–1518],[1] *vol. I, ch. 1*

1   Intellectual passion drives out sensuality.

Ibid.

2   As a well-spent day brings happy sleep, so life well used brings happy death.   *Ibid.*

3   Life well spent is long.   *Ibid.*

4   Shun those studies in which the work that results dies with the worker.   *Ibid.*

5   Whoever in discussion adduces authority uses not intellect but rather memory.   *Ibid. 2*

6   Iron rusts from disuse; stagnant water loses its purity and in cold weather becomes frozen; even so does inaction sap the vigor of the mind.   *Ibid.*

7   Savage is he who saves himself.   *Ibid.*

8   It is easier to resist at the beginning than at the end.   *Ibid.*

9   Necessity is the mistress and guardian of nature.

Ibid.

10   Human subtlety . . . will never devise an invention more beautiful, more simple or more direct than does nature, because in her inventions nothing is lacking, and nothing is superfluous.   *Ibid. 3*

11   Mechanics is the paradise of the mathematical sciences because by means of it one comes to the fruits of mathematics.   *Ibid. 20*

12   O speculators about perpetual motion, how many vain chimeras have you created in the like quest? Go and take your place with the seekers after gold.   *Ibid. II, 25*

13   O neglectful Nature, wherefore art thou thus partial, becoming to some of thy children a tender and benignant mother, to others a most cruel and ruthless stepmother? I see thy children given into slavery to others without ever receiving any benefit, and in lieu of any reward for the services they have done for them they are repaid by the severest punishments.

Ibid. 45

14   The Medici created and destroyed me.

Ibid. 46

Amerigo Vespucci
1454–1512

15   Those new regions [America] which we found and explored with the fleet . . . we may rightly call a New World . . . a continent more densely peopled and abounding in animals than our Europe or

[1]Translated by EDWARD MACCURDY.

Asia or Africa; and, in addition, a climate milder than in any other region known to us.[2]

Letter called Mundus Novus [1503] to Lorenzo Pier Francesco de'Medici

Sebastian Brant
c. 1458–1521

16   The world wants to be deceived.

The Ship of Fools (Das Narrenschiff) [1494]

John Skelton
c. 1460–1529

17 I say, thou mad March hare.[3]

Replication Against Certain Young Scholars

18 He ruleth all the roost.[4]

Why Come Ye Not to Court, l. 198

19 The wolf from the door.[5]

Ibid. l. 1531

20   Old proverb says,
That bird is not honest
That filleth his own nest.[6]

Poems Against Garnesche

21 Maid, widow, or wife.

Philip Sparrow

22 Vengeance I ask and cry,
By way of exclamation,
On the whole nation
Of cats wild and tame:
God send them sorrow and shame!

Ibid.

23 Merry Margaret,
As midsummer flower,

[2]Translated by G. T. NORTHUP, *Vespucci Reprints and Studies* [1916], and S. E. MORISON, *The European Discovery of America: The Southern Voyages* [1974].

This, and a letter of Vespucci to his friend Pier Soderini [1504], led geography professor Martin Waldseemüller to credit Vespucci with discovering "a fourth part of the world" and to issue a map [1507] with a bold AMERICA on the continent now called South America. Vespucci had invented a voyage of 1497, a year before Columbus's Third Voyage to the mainland of South America.

[3]Mad as a March hare. — JOHN HEYWOOD, *Proverbs* [1546], *pt. II, ch. 5*

[4]Rule the rost. — JOHN HEYWOOD, *Proverbs* [1546], *pt. I, ch. 5*

Rules the roast. — JONSON, CHAPMAN, MARSTON, *Eastward Ho* [1605], *act II, sc. ii*

Her that ruled the rost. — THOMAS HEYWOOD, *History of Women* [ed. 1624]

[5]To keep the wolf from the door. — JOHN HEYWOOD, *Proverbs* [1546], *pt. II, ch. 7*

See Charlotte Perkins Gilman, 583:8.

[6]It is a foul bird that filleth his own nest. — JOHN HEYWOOD, *Proverbs* [1546], *pt. II, ch. 5*

Gentle as falcon
Or hawk of the tower.
To Mistress Margaret Hussey

Giovanni Pico della Mirandola
1463–1494

1   We have made thee neither of heaven nor of earth, neither mortal nor immortal, so that with freedom of choice and with honor, as though the maker and molder of thyself, thou mayest fashion thyself in whatever shape thou shalt prefer. Thou shalt have the power to degenerate into the lower forms of life, which are brutish. Thou shalt have the power, out of thy soul's judgment, to be reborn into the highest forms, which are divine.[1]
On the Dignity of Man [1496]

William Dunbar
c. 1465 – c. 1530

2 London, thou art the flower of Cities all.
London, refrain

3 Gem of all joy, jasper of jocundity.
Ibid. st. 3

4 I that in heill wes and gladnes
Am trublit now with gret seiknes
And feblit with infermite:
Timor Mortis conturbat me.[2]
Lament for the Makers (Makaris)[3] [c. 1508], refrain

5 Our plesance here is all vain glory,
This false world is but transitory.
Ibid. st. 2

Desiderius Erasmus
c. 1466–1536

6   In the country of the blind the one-eyed man is king.[4]
Adagia [1500]

7   It is folly alone that stays the fugue of Youth and beats off louring Old Age.
The Praise of Folly [1509]

8   They may attack me with an army of six hundred syllogisms; and if I do not recant, they will proclaim me a heretic.
Ibid.

Niccolò Machiavelli[5]
1469–1527

9   There is nothing more difficult to take in hand, more perilous to conduct, or more uncertain in its success, than to take the lead in the introduction of a new order of things.
The Prince [1532],[6] ch. 6

10   Since love and fear can hardly exist together, if we must choose between them, it is far safer to be feared than loved.
Ibid. 8

11   The chief foundations of all states, new as well as old or composite, are good laws and good arms; and as there cannot be good laws where the state is not well armed, it follows that where they are well armed they have good laws.
Ibid. 12

12   A prince should therefore have no other aim or thought, nor take up any other thing for his study, but war and its organization and discipline, for that is the only art that is necessary to one who commands.
Ibid. 14

13   Among other evils which being unarmed brings you, it causes you to be despised.
Ibid.

14   Many have imagined republics and principalities which have never been seen or known to exist in reality; for how we live is so far removed from how we ought to live, that he who abandons what is done for what ought to be done, will rather bring about his own ruin than his preservation.
Ibid. 15

15   A prince being thus obliged to know well how to act as a beast must imitate the fox and the lion, for the lion cannot protect himself from traps, and the fox cannot defend himself from wolves. One must therefore be a fox to recognize traps, and a lion to frighten wolves.
Ibid. 17

16   When neither their property nor their honor is touched, the majority of men live content.
Ibid. 19

17   There are three classes of intellects: one which comprehends by itself; another which appreciates what others comprehend; and a third which neither comprehends by itself nor by the showing of others; the first is the most excellent, the second is good, the third is useless.
Ibid. 22

18   There is no other way of guarding oneself against flattery than by letting men understand that they will not offend you by speaking the truth; but when everyone can tell you the truth, you lose their respect.
Ibid. 23

---

[1]Translated by ELIZABETH LIVERMORE FORBES.
[2]Fear of Death troubles me.
[3]Makers: poets.
[4]*In regione caecorum rex est luscus.*
  In the country of the blind the one-eyed man is king; I passed for a good teacher, because the rest in town were bad. — ROUSSEAU, *Confessions [1781–1788], pt. 1, bk. 5*

[5]Every Country hath its Machiavel. — THOMAS BROWNE, *Religio Medici [1643], pt. 1, sec. 20*
  Out of his surname they have coined an epithet for a knave, and out of his Christian name a synonym for the Devil. — MACAULAY, *On Machiavelli [1827]*
  See Samuel Butler [1612–1680], 263:30.
[6]Translated by W. K. MARRIOTT.

1   God is not willing to do everything, and thus take away our free will and that share of glory which belongs to us.   *Ibid. 26*

2   Whoever desires to found a state and give it laws, must start with assuming that all men are bad and ever ready to display their vicious nature, whenever they may find occasion for it.
Discourse upon the First Ten Books of Livy, bk. I, ch. 3

3   The people resemble a wild beast,[1] which, naturally fierce and accustomed to live in the woods, has been brought up, as it were, in a prison and in servitude, and having by accident got its liberty, not being accustomed to search for its food, and not knowing where to conceal itself, easily becomes the prey of the first who seeks to incarcerate it again.   *Ibid. 16*

4   He who establishes a tyranny and does not kill Brutus, and he who establishes a democratic regime and does not kill the sons of Brutus, will not last long.[2]   *Ibid. III, 3*

Charles VIII
1470–1498

5   This is our gracious will.[3]
Royal Order of March 12, 1497

Nicholas Copernicus
1473–1543

6   Finally we shall place the Sun himself at the center of the Universe. All this is suggested by the systematic procession of events and the harmony of the whole Universe, if only we face the facts, as they say, "with both eyes open."
De Revolutionibus Orbium Coelestium [1543][4]

Ludovico Ariosto
1474–1533

7   Nature made him, and then broke the mold.[5]
Orlando Furioso [1532], canto X, st. 84

Michelangelo [Buonarroti]
1475–1564

8   The more the marble wastes, the more the statue grows.   *Sonnet*

[1]See Horace, 97:7; Shakespeare, 183:9, 219:3, and 219:10; and Pope, 303:10.
[2]Translated by LESLIE J. WALKER, S.J.
[3]Tel est notre bon plaisir.
[4]Translated by JOHN F. DOBSON.
[5]Natura il fece, e poi ruppe la stampa.
See Byron, 401:21.

9   If it be true that any beautiful thing raises the pure and just desire of man from earth to God, the eternal fount of all, such I believe my love.
Sonnet

10   The power of one fair face makes my love sublime, for it has weaned my heart from low desires.
Sonnet

11   I live and love in God's peculiar light.   *Ibid.*

Sir Thomas More[6]
1478–1535

12   They wonder much to hear that gold, which in itself is so useless a thing, should be everywhere so much esteemed, that even men for whom it was made, and by whom it has its value, should yet be thought of less value than it is.
Utopia [1516]. Of Jewels and Wealth

13   They have no lawyers among them, for they consider them as a sort of people whose profession it is to disguise matters.
Ibid. Of Law and Magistrates

14   Plato by a goodly similitude declareth, why wise men refrain to meddle in the commonwealth. For when they see the people swarm into the streets, and daily wet to the skin with rain, and yet cannot persuade them to go out of the rain, they do keep themselves within their houses, seeing they cannot remedy the folly of the people.[7]
Ibid. Concerning the Best State of a Commonwealth

15   A little wanton money, which burned out the bottom of his purse.   *Works [c. 1530]*

16   This is a fair tale of a tub told of his election.[8]
Confutation of Tyndale's Answers [1532]

17   For men use, if they have an evil turn, to write it in marble: and whoso doth us a good turn we write it in dust.
Richard III and His Miserable End [1543]

18   See me safe up, and for my coming down let me shift for myself.
On ascending the scaffold. From WILLIAM ROPER, *Life of Sir Thomas More [1626]*

19   This hath not offended the king.
As he drew his beard aside upon placing his head on the block. From BACON, *Apothegms, no. 22*

[6]Canonized [1935] by Pope Pius XI.
See Whittinton, 138:1.
[7]In the modern phrase: Not sense enough to come in out of the rain.
[8]A tale of a tub is a cock-and-bull story. Jonson used it as the title of a comedy [1633], and Swift as the title of a satire [1696].

Robert Whittinton
c. 1480 – c. 1530

1   [Sir Thomas] More is a man of angel's wit and singular learning; I know not his fellow. For where is the man of that gentleness, lowliness and affability? And as time requireth, a man of marvelous mirth and pastimes; and sometimes of as sad a gravity; a man for all seasons.
Passage composed for schoolboys to put into Latin

Martin Luther
1483–1546

2   If it were an art to overcome heresy with fire, the executioners would be the most learned doctors on earth.
To the Christian Nobility of the German States [1520]

3   Here I stand; I can do no other. God help me. Amen.[1]
Speech at the Diet of Worms [April 18, 1521]

4   The mad mob does not ask how it could be better, only that it be different. And when it then becomes worse, it must change again. Thus they get bees for flies, and at last hornets for bees.
Whether Soldiers Can Also Be in a State of Grace [1526]

5 A mighty fortress is our God,
A bulwark never failing.
Our helper He amid the flood
Of mortal ills prevailing.[2]
Ein' Feste Burg [1529]

6   What can only be taught by the rod and with blows will not lead to much good; they will not remain pious any longer than the rod is behind them.
The Great Catechism. Second Command [1529]

7   Peace is more important than all justice; and peace was not made for the sake of justice, but justice for the sake of peace.
On Marriage [1530]

8   Justice is a temporary thing that must at last come to an end; but the conscience is eternal and will never die.
Ibid.

---

[1]Hier stehe ich, ich kann nicht anders. Gott helfe mir. Amen. Inscribed on his monument at Worms.
Also translated as: Here I stand, I cannot do otherwise. And: God helping me, I can do no other.
[2]Ein' feste burg is unser Gott, / ein gute wehr und waffen. / Er hilft uns frei aus aller not, / die uns itzt hat betroffen.
Translated by FREDERICK HENRY HEDGE.
Great God! there is no safety here below; / Thou art my fortress, thou that seem'st my foe. — QUARLES, *Divine Poems*
See *Psalm* 46:1, 17:16.

9   Superstition, idolatry, and hypocrisy have ample wages, but truth goes a-begging.
Table Talk [1569], 53

10   For where God built a church, there the Devil would also build a chapel[3] . . . Thus is the Devil ever God's ape.
Ibid. 67

11   The Mass is the greatest blasphemy of God, and the highest idolatry upon earth, an abomination the like of which has never been in Christendom since the time of the Apostles.
Ibid. 171

12   There is no more lovely, friendly and charming relationship, communion or company than a good marriage.
Ibid. 292

13   A theologian is born by living, nay dying and being damned, not by thinking, reading, or speculating.
Ibid. 352

14   Reason is the greatest enemy that faith has: it never comes to the aid of spiritual things, but — more frequently than not — struggles against the divine Word, treating with contempt all that emanates from God.
Ibid. 353

15   If I had heard that as many devils would set on me in Worms as there are tiles on the roofs, I should nonetheless have ridden there.
Works [1745], XVI, 14

16   It makes a difference whose ox is gored.
Works [1854], LXII

Hernán Cortés [Hernando Cortez]
1485–1547

17   [The Aztecs] said that by no means would they give themselves up, for as long as one of them was left he would die fighting, and that we would get nothing of theirs because they would burn everything or throw it into the water.
Third Dispatch [May 15, 1522]. To Charles V

Hugh Latimer
c. 1485–1555

18   Play the man, Master Ridley; we shall this day light such a candle, by God's grace, in England, as I trust shall never be put out.[4]
To Nicholas Ridley [1500–1555] as they were being burned alive at Oxford for heresy [October 16, 1555]. From J. R. GREEN, A Short History of the English People [1874], ch. 7

---

[3]Where God hath a temple, the Devil will have a chapel. — ROBERT BURTON, *Anatomy of Melancholy* [1621–1651], pt. III, sec. 4, member I, subsec. I
No sooner is a temple built to God but the Devil builds a chapel hard by. — GEORGE HERBERT, *Jacula Prudentum* [1651]
See Defoe, 285:14.
[4]See *II Esdras* 14:25, 30:16.

Pope Julius III
1487–1555

1   Do you not know, my son, with what little understanding the world is ruled?[1]
To a Portuguese monk who sympathized with the pope's burdens of office

Jacques Cartier
1491–1557

2   I am rather inclined to believe that this is the land God gave to Cain.[2]   *La Première Relation*

Saint Ignatius of Loyola
1491–1556

3 Teach us, good Lord, to serve Thee as Thou
      deservest:
To give and not to count the cost;
To fight and not to heed the wounds;
To toil and not to seek for rest;
To labor and not ask for any reward
Save that of knowing that we do Thy will.
Prayer for Generosity [1548]

Bernal Díaz del Castillo
c. 1492 – c. 1581

4   To me it appears that the names of those[3] ought to be written in letters of gold, who died so cruel a death, for the service of God and His Majesty, to give light to those who were in darkness, and to procure wealth which all men desire.[4]
The True History of the Conquest of New Spain (Historia Verdadera de la Conquista de la Nueve España) [1800], pt. II, ch. 10

Philippus Aureolus Paracelsus
c. 1493–1541

5   Every experiment is like a weapon which must be used in its particular way—a spear to thrust, a club to strike. Experimenting requires a man who knows when to thrust and when to strike, each according to need and fashion.[5]
Surgeon's Book (Chirurgische Bucher) [1605]

Francis [François] I
1494–1547

6   All is lost save honor.[6]
Letter to his mother after his defeat at Pavia [February 23, 1525]

François Rabelais
c. 1494–1553

7   Break the bone and suck out the substantific marrow.
Gargantua and Pantagruel,[7] bk. I [1532], prologue

8   To laugh is proper to man.[8]
Ibid. Rabelais to the Reader

9   Appetite comes with eating[9] . . . but the thirst goes away with drinking.   *Ibid. ch. 5*

10   War begun without good provision of money beforehand for going through with it is but as a breathing of strength and blast that will quickly pass away. Coin is the sinews of war.[10]   *Ibid. 46*

11   How shall I be able to rule over others, that have not full power and command of myself?[11]
Ibid. 52

12   Do what thou wilt.[12]   *Ibid. 57*

13   Wisdom entereth not into a malicious mind, and science without conscience is but the ruin of the soul.
Ibid. II [1534], 8

14   Subject to a kind of disease, which at that time they called lack of money.[13]   *Ibid. 16*

15   So much is a man worth as he esteems himself.
Ibid. 29

16   A good crier of green sauce.   *Ibid. 31*

17   This flea which I have in mine ear.
Ibid. III [1545], 31

[1]An nescis, mi fili, quantilla prudentia mundus regatur?
[2]J'estime mieux que autrement, que c'est la terre que Dieu donna à Cain.
Upon discovering the bleak shore of the Gulf of St. Lawrence, today's Labrador and Quebec [summer 1534].
[3]The five hundred and fifty soldiers who came to Mexico with Cortés [1519], all but five of whom were dead at the time Díaz was writing [1568].
[4]Translated by MAURICE KEATINGE.
[5]Translated by HENRY M. PACHTER.

[6]Tout est perdu fors l'honneur.
The actual words written were: De toutes choses ne m'est demeuré que l'honneur et la vie qui est sauvé. The letter is in DULAURE, *Histoire Civile, Physique et Morale de Paris* [1821–1825].
[7]Translated by SIR THOMAS URQUHART and PETER ANTHONY MOTTEUX [1653–1694].
[8]Pour ce que rire est le propre de l'homme.
[9]My appetite comes to me while eating.—MONTAIGNE, *Essays* [1580–1595], III, 9
[10]See Bion, 82:7; Cicero, 88:13; and Churchill, 622:3.
[11]He is most powerful who has power over himself.—SENECA, *Epistles*, 90, 34
[12]Fais ce que voudras.
[13]Or that eternal want of pence, / Which vexes public men.— TENNYSON, *Will Waterproof's Lyrical Monologue* [1842], st. 6
See Shakespeare, 183:24.

1   Oh thrice and four times happy those who plant cabbages![1]

> *Gargantua and Pantagruel, bk. IV [1548], ch. 18*

2   Which was performed to a T.[2]   *Ibid. 41*

3   He that has patience may compass anything.
                                                 Ibid. 48

4   We will take the good will for the deed.[3]
                                                 Ibid. 49

5   Speak the truth and shame the Devil.[4]

> *Ibid. V [1552], author's prologue*

6   Plain as a nose in a man's face.[5]   *Ibid.*

7   Like hearts of oak.[6]   *Ibid.*

8   Go hang yourselves [critics] . . . you shall never want rope enough.[7]   *Ibid.*

9   Looking as like . . . as one pea does like another.[8]   *Ibid. ch. 2*

10   It is meat, drink, and cloth to us.   *Ibid. 7*

11   I am going to seek a grand perhaps; draw the curtain, the farce is played.[9]

> *Alleged last words. From* MOTTEUX, *Life of Rabelais*

[1]See Montaigne, 145:11, and Voltaire, 306:12.

[2]We could manage this matter to a T.—STERNE, *Tristram Shandy, bk. II [1760], ch. 5*

You see they'd have fitted him to a T.—SAMUEL JOHNSON; from BOSWELL, *Life of Johnson* [1791]

You will find it shall echo my speech to a T.—THOMAS MOORE, *Address for the Opening of the New Theatre of St. Stephen*

[3]The will for deed I do accept.—DU BARTAS, *Divine Weeks and Works* [1578], *Second Week, Third Day, pt. 2*

You must take the will for the deed.—SWIFT, *Polite Conversation* [1738], *Dialogue 2*

[4]While you live, tell truth and shame the devil!—SHAKESPEARE, *Henry IV, pt. I, act III, sc. i, l. 62*

I'd tell the truth, and shame the devil.—SAMUEL JOHNSON; from BOSWELL, *Life of Johnson* [1791], *vol. I, p. 460* (Everyman edition)

Truth being truth, / Tell it and shame the devil.—ROBERT BROWNING, *The Ring and the Book* [1868–1869], *III, The Other Half-Rome*

[5]As clear and as manifest as the nose in a man's face.—ROBERT BURTON, *Anatomy of Melancholy* [1621–1651], *pt. III, sec. 3, member 4, subsec. I*

See Shakespeare, 168:2.

[6]See Garrick, 323:18.

[7]They were suffered to have rope enough till they had haltered themselves.—THOMAS FULLER, *The Historie of the Holy Warre* [1639], *bk. 5, ch. 7*

Give a man enough rope and he'll hang himself.—*Proverb*

[8]As like as one pease is to another.—JOHN LYLY, *Euphues* [1579]

They say we are / Almost as like as eggs. — SHAKESPEARE, *The Winter's Tale, act I, sc. ii, l. 130*

As one egg is like another.—CERVANTES, *Don Quixote, pt. II [1615], bk. III, ch. 14*

[9]Je m'en vais chercher un grand peut-être; tirez le rideau, la farce est jouée.

His religion, at best, is an anxious wish; like that of Rabelais, "a great Perhaps."—CARLYLE, *Essays, Burns* [1828]

The grand perhaps.—ROBERT BROWNING, *Bishop Blougram's Apology* [1855]

See Leoncavallo, 575:4.

John Heywood[10]
c. 1497 – c. 1580

12   All a green willow, willow, willow,
All a green willow is my garland.[11]

> *The Green Willow*

13   The loss of wealth is loss of dirt,
As sages in all times assert;
The happy man's without a shirt.[12]

> *Be Merry Friends*

14   Let the world slide,[13] let the world go;
A fig for care, and a fig for woe!
If I can't pay, why I can owe,
And death makes equal the high and low.

> *Ibid.*

15   Haste maketh waste.[14]

> *Proverbs [1546], pt. I, ch. 2*

16   Good to be merry and wise.   *Ibid.*

17   Look ere ye leap.[15]   *Ibid.*

18   While between two stools my tail go to the ground.[16]   *Ibid.*

19   The fat is in the fire.   *Ibid. 3*

20   When the sun shineth, make hay.   *Ibid.*

21   The tide tarrieth no man.[17]   *Ibid.*

22   And while I at length debate and beat the bush,
There shall step in other men and catch the birds.[18]

> *Ibid.*

[10]John Heywood's *Proverbs*, first printed in 1546, is the earliest collection of English colloquial sayings. The selection here given is from the edition of 1874 (a reprint of 1598), edited by JULIAN SHARMAN.

See also *Oxford Dictionary of English Proverbs* [3rd edition, 1970], compiled by WILLIAM G. SMITH and edited by F. P. WILSON, and *A Dictionary of the Proverbs in English in the 16th and 17th Centuries* [1950], compiled by MORRIS PALMER TILLEY.

[11]The earliest known of the "willow" songs (see Shakespeare, 208:4).

[12]This line is the theme of many poems.

[13]Let the world slide.—*Towneley Mysteries* [1420].

Let the world slide.—SHAKESPEARE, *The Taming of the Shrew, Induction, sc. i, l. 6*

[14]In wikked haste is no profit.—CHAUCER, *The Canterbury Tales* [c. 1387], *Melibee, 2240*

See Publilius Syrus, 99:33, and Chaucer, 131:22.

[15]Thou shouldst have looked before thou hadst leapt.—JONSON, CHAPMAN, MARSTON, *Eastward Ho* [1605], *act V, sc. i*

See Samuel Butler [1612–1680], 263:25.

[16]Between two stools one sits on the ground.—*Les Proverbes del Vilain, MS Bodleian* [c. 1303]

[17]Time nor tide tarrieth no man.—ROBERT GREENE, *Disputations* [1592]

Hoist up sail while gale doth last, / Tide and wind stay no man's pleasure.—SOUTHWELL, *St. Peter's Complaint* [1595]

Nae man can tether time or tide.—BURNS, *Tam o' Shanter* [1791]

See Chaucer, 131:13.

[18]It is this proverb which Henry V is reported to have uttered at the siege of Orléans: Shall I beat the bush and another take the bird?

1 Wedding is destiny,
And hanging likewise.[1]

Ibid.

2 Happy man, happy dole.[2] *Ibid.*

3 God never send'th mouth but he sendeth meat.[3]

Ibid. 4

4 A hard beginning maketh a good ending.

Ibid.

5 Like will to like.[4] *Ibid.*

6 More afraid than hurt. *Ibid.*

7 Nothing is impossible to a willing heart.

Ibid.

8 Let the world wag, and take mine ease in mine inn. *Ibid. 5*

9 Hold their noses to grindstone. *Ibid.*

10 Cut my coat after my cloth. *Ibid. 8*

11 The nearer to the church, the further from God.[5]

Ibid. 9

12 Now for good luck, cast an old shoe after me.

Ibid.

13 Better is to bow than break.[6] *Ibid.*

14 it hurteth not the tongue to give fair words.[7]

Ibid.

15 Two heads are better than one. *Ibid.*

16 A short horse is soon curried. *Ibid. 10*

17 To tell tales out of school. *Ibid.*

18 To hold with the hare and run with the hound.

Ibid.

19 Neither fish nor flesh, nor good red herring.

Ibid.

20 All is well that ends well.[8] *Ibid.*

21 Of a good beginning cometh a good end.[9]

Ibid.

22 When the steed is stolen, shut the stable door.[10]

Ibid.

23 She looketh as butter would not melt in her mouth. *Ibid.*

24 Ill weed groweth fast.[11] *Ibid.*

25 Beggars should be no choosers. *Ibid.*

26 Merry as a cricket. *Ibid. 11*

27 To rob Peter and pay Paul.[12] *Ibid.*

28 A man may well bring a horse to the water,
But he cannot make him drink without he will.[13]

Ibid.

29 Rome was not built in one day. *Ibid.*

30 Ye have many strings to your bow.[14] *Ibid.*

31 Children learn to creep ere they can learn to go.

Ibid.

32 Better is half a loaf than no bread. *Ibid.*

33 Nought venture nought have.[15] *Ibid.*

34 Children and fools cannot lie.[16] *Ibid.*

35 All is fish that cometh to net.[17] *Ibid.*

---

[1]Hanging and wiving go by destiny. — *The Schole-hous for Women* [1541]

Marriage and hanging go by destiny; matches are made in heaven. — ROBERT BURTON, *Anatomy of Melancholy* [1621–1651], *pt. III, sec. 2, member 5, subsec. 5*

See Lyly, 155:22.

[2]Happy man be his dole. — SHAKESPEARE, *The Merry Wives of Windsor, act III, sc. iv, l. 68,* and *The Winter's Tale, act I, sc. ii, l. 163*

[3]God sendeth and giveth both mouth and the meat. — TUSSER, *A Hundred Good Points of Husbandry* [1557]

God sends meat, and the Devil sends cooks. — JOHN TAYLOR [1580–1653], *Works* [1630], *vol. II, p. 85*

The holy prophet Zoroaster said, / The Lord who made thy teeth shall give thee bread. — *Persian couplet*

[4]See *Ecclesiasticus 13:16,* 31:32; Homer, 54:2; and Robert Burton, 235:12.

[5]Qui est près de l'église est souvent loin de Dieu [He who is near the Church is often far from God]. — *Les Proverbes Communs* [c. 1500]

See Spenser, 153:3.

[6]Rather to bow than break is profitable: / Humility is a thing commendable. — *The Moral Proverbs of Cristyne* [1390]

[7]Fair words never hurt the tongue. — JONSON, CHAPMAN, MARSTON, *Eastward Ho* [1605], *act IV, sc. i*

[8]Si finis bonus est, totum bonum erit [If the end is good, all will be good]. — *Gesta Romanorum* [1472], *tale 67*

See Anonymous: Latin, 119:3; Shakespeare, 190:12 and 203:-17; Herrick, 241:2; and Quarles, 242:13.

[9]Who that well his warke beginneth, / The rather a good end he winneth. — JOHN GOWER [c. 1325–1408], *Confessio Amantis* [c. 1386–1390]

See Plato, 75:8; Aristotle, 78:26; and Horace, 97:8.

[10]Quant le cheval est emblé dounke ferme fols l'estable [When the horse has been stolen, the fool shuts the stable]. — *Les Proverbes del Vilain,* MS Bodleian [c. 1303]

[11]Ewyl weed ys sone y-growe. — *MS Harleian* [c. 1490]

Great weeds do grow apace. — SHAKESPEARE, *Richard III, act II, sc. iv, l. 13*

An ill weed grows apace. — GEORGE CHAPMAN, *An Humorous Day's Mirth* [1599]

[12]Give not Saint Peter so much, to leave Saint Paul nothing. — GEORGE HERBERT, *Jacula Prudentum* [1640]

"To rob Peter and pay Paul" is said to have had its origin in the reign of Edward VI when the lands of St. Peter at Westminster were appropriated to raise money for the repair of St. Paul's in London.

The French form of the proverb is: Découvrir saint Pierre pour couvrir saint Paul.

[13]You may bring a horse to the river, but he will drink when and what he pleaseth. — GEORGE HERBERT, *Jacula Prudentum* [1651]

[14]Two strings to his bow. — HOOKER, *Laws of Ecclesiastical Polity, bk. V* [1597], *ch. 80*

[15]See Chaucer, 128:24, and W. S. Gilbert, 530:16.

[16]'Tis an old saw, children and fools speak true. — LYLY, *Endymion* [1591]

[17]All's fish they get that cometh to net. — TUSSER, *A Hundred Good Points of Husbandry* [1557], *February Abstract*

1   Who is worse shod than the shoemaker's wife?[1]
Proverbs, pt. I, ch. 11

2   One good turn asketh another.   *Ibid.*

3   A dog hath a day.   *Ibid.*

4   A hair of the dog that bit us.[2]   *Ibid.*

5   But in deed,
A friend is never known till a man have need.[3]
Ibid.

6   Burnt child fire dreadeth.[4]   *Ibid. II, 2*

7   There is no fool to the old fool.[5]   *Ibid.*

8   A woman hath nine lives like a cat.   *Ibid. 4*

9   A penny for your thought.   *Ibid.*

10   You cannot see the wood for the trees.
Ibid.

11   You stand in your own light.   *Ibid.*

12   Tit for tat.[6]   *Ibid.*

13   Three may keep counsel, if two be away.[7]
Ibid. 5

14   Small pitchers have wide ears.[8]   *Ibid.*

15   Many hands make light work.   *Ibid.*

16   Out of God's blessing into the warm sun.[9]
Ibid.

17   There is no fire without some smoke.[10]
Ibid.

18   A cat may look on a king.   *Ibid.*

19   Much water goeth by the mill
That the miller knoweth not of.[11]
Ibid.

20   He must needs go whom the devil doth drive.
Ibid. 7

21   Set the cart before the horse.   *Ibid.*

22   The more the merrier.   *Ibid.*

23   Be the day never so long,
Evermore at last they ring to even-song.[12]
Ibid.

24   The moon is made of a green cheese.[13]   *Ibid.*

25   I know on which side my bread is buttered.
Ibid.

26   The wrong sow by th' ear.   *Ibid. 9*

27   An ill wind that bloweth no man to good.[14]
Ibid.

28   For when I gave you an inch, you took an ell.[15]
Ibid.

29   Would ye both eat your cake and have your cake?[16]   *Ibid.*

30   Every man for himself and God for us all.[17]
Ibid.

31   Though he love not to buy the pig in the poke.[18]   *Ibid.*

32   This hitteth the nail on the head.   *Ibid. 11*

33   Enough is as good as a feast.   *Ibid.*

[1]Him that makes shoes go barefoot himself. — ROBERT BURTON, *Anatomy of Melancholy* [1621–1651], *Democritus to the Reader*

[2]Old receipt books advised that an inebriate should drink sparingly in the morning some of the same kind of liquor which he had drunk to excess the night before.

[3]See Aristotle, 79:1; Cicero, 88:8; Publilius Syrus, 100:18; and Ovid, 102:3.

[4]Brend child fur dredth, / Quoth Hendyng. — HENDYNG [1272–1307], *Proverbs, MS*

[5]There is no fool like an old fool. — LYLY, *Mother Bombie* [1590], *act IV, sc. ii*, and in frequent use thereafter.

[6]This is a corruption of *Tant pour tant.*

[7]Two may keep counsel when the third's away. — SHAKESPEARE, *Titus Andronicus, act IV, sc. ii, l. 145*
Three can hold their peace if two be away. — GEORGE HERBERT, *Jacula Prudentum* [1651]

[8]Pitchers have ears. — SHAKESPEARE, *The Taming of the Shrew, act IV, sc. iv, l. 52*, and *Richard III, act II, sc. iv, l. 37*
Little pitchers have wide ears. — GEORGE HERBERT, *Jacula Prudentum* [1640]

[9]Thou shalt come out of a warm sun into God's blessing. — LYLY, *Euphues* [1579]
Thou out of Heaven's benediction com'st / To the warm sun. — SHAKESPEARE, *King Lear, act II, sc. ii, l. 168*

[10]There can no great smoke arise, but there must be some fire. — LYLY, *Euphues* [1579]

[11]More water glideth by the mill / Than wots the miller of. — SHAKESPEARE, *Titus Andronicus, act II, sc. i, l. 85*
The miller sees not all the water that goes by his mill. — ROBERT BURTON, *Anatomy of Melancholy* [1621–1651], *pt. III, sec. 3, member 4, subsec. 1*

[12]Be the day short or never so long, / At length it ringeth to evensong. — *Quoted at the stake by George Tankerfield* [1555]. From JOHN FOXE [1516–1587], *Actes and Monuments (The Book of Martyrs)* [1563], *ch. 7*

[13]They would make me believe that the moon was made of green cheese. — JOHN FRITH [1503–1533], *A Pistle to the Christian Reader* [1529]

[14]Except wind stands as never it stood, / It is an ill wind turns none to good. — TUSSER, *A Description of the Properties of Winds*
Falstaff. What wind blew you hither, Pistol?
Pistol. Not the ill wind which blows no man to good. — SHAKESPEARE, *Henry IV, Part II, act V, sc. iii, l. 87*

[15]Give an inch, he'll take an ell. — JOHN WEBSTER, *Sir Thomas Wyatt*

[16]Wouldst thou both eat thy cake and have it? — GEORGE HERBERT, *The Size* [1633]

[17]Every man for himself, his own ends, the Devil for all. — ROBERT BURTON, *Anatomy of Melancholy* [1621–1651], *pt. III, sec. 1, member 3*

[18]For buying or selling of pig in a poke. — TUSSER, *A Hundred Good Points of Husbandry* [1557], *September Abstract*

Charles V
1500–1558

1 Iron hand in a velvet glove.
Attributed. From THOMAS CARLYLE, *Latter-Day
Pamphlets, 11*

2 I make war on the living, not on the dead.
*Said when advised to hang Luther's corpse on
the gallows [1546]*

3 I speak Spanish to God, Italian to women, French
to men, and German to my horse.[1] *Attributed*

Pope Gregory XIII
1502–1585

4 To the greater glory of God.[2]
*From The Canons and Decrees of the Council
of Trent [1542–1560]*

Sir Thomas Wyatt
c. 1503–1542

5 Forget not yet the tried intent
Of such a truth as I have meant;
My great travail so gladly spent,
Forget not yet!
Forget Not Yet

6 My lute, awake! perform the last
Labor that thou and I shall waste,
And end that I have now begun;
For when this song is sung and past,
My lute, be still, for I have done.
*The Lover Complaineth the Unkindness of His
Love*

7 They flee from me, that sometime did me seek
With naked foot, stalking in my chamber.
*The Lover Showeth How He Is Forsaken of
Such as He Sometime Enjoyed*

8 And graven with diamonds in letters plain
There is written her fair neck round about:
Noli me tangere, for Caesar's I am,
And wild for to hold, though I seem tame.
Whoso List to Hunt

John Bradford
c. 1510–1555

9 The familiar story, that, on seeing evildoers taken
to the place of execution, he was wont to exclaim:
"But for the grace of God there goes John Bradford," is a universal tradition, which has overcome
the lapse of time.[3]
*Biographical notice, Parker Society edition, The
Writings of John Bradford [1853]*

[1] Je parle espagnol à Dieu, italien aux femmes, français aux
hommes, et allemand à mon cheval.
[2] Ad maiorem Dei gloriam. Motto of the Society of Jesus.
[3] There but for the grace of God goes God. — *Anonymous
saying, attributed to* ORSON WELLES, *among others*

Ambroise Paré
1510–1590

10 I treated him, God cured him.[4]
His favorite saying

Sir Thomas Vaux
1510–1556

11 Companion none is like
Unto the mind alone;
For many have been harmed by speech,
Through thinking, few or none.
Of a Contented Mind [1557]

12 But age, with his stealing steps,
Hath claw'd me in his clutch.[5]
The Aged Lover Renounceth Love, st. 3

Richard Grafton
c. 1513–1572

13 Thirty days hath November,
April, June, and September,
February hath twenty-eight alone,
And all the rest have thirty-one.[6]
Chronicles of England [1562]

John Knox
c. 1513–1572

14 The First Blast of the Trumpet Against the Monstrous Regiment [Regimen] of Women.
Title of pamphlet [1558]

15 A man with God is always in the majority.[7]
*Inscription on Reformation Monument, Geneva,
Switzerland*

Mary Tudor [Mary I]
1516–1558

16 When I am dead and opened, you shall find
"Calais" lying in my heart.[8]
From HOLINSHED, *Chronicles [1577], III, 1160*

[4] Je le soignay, Dieu le guérit.
[5] Quoted by First Clown in SHAKESPEARE, *Hamlet,* act V,
sc. i, l. 77.
[6] Thirty days hath September, / April, June, and November; /
All the rest have thirty-one, / Excepting February alone, /
Which hath but twenty-eight, in fine, / Till leap year gives it
twenty-nine. — *Common in the New England states*
Compare the old Latin class mnemonic:
In March, July, October, May, / The Ides are on the fifteenth
day, / The Nones the seventh: all other months besides / Have
two days less for Nones and Ides.
[7] Un homme avec Dieu est toujours dans la majorité.
See Phillips, 462:17.
[8] See Robert Browning, 465:12.

Joachim du Bellay
1522–1560

1   Happy he who like Ulysses has made a glorious voyage.[1]
Les Regrets [1559], XXXI

Pierre de Ronsard
1524–1585

2 When you are old, at evening candlelit,
Beside the fire bending to your wool,
Read out my verse and murmur, "Ronsard writ
This praise for me when I was beautiful."[2]
Sonnets pour Hélène, I, 43

3 Live now, believe me, wait not till tomorrow;
Gather the roses of life today.[3]
Ibid.

4 Sweetheart, come see if the rose
Which at morning began to unclose
Its damask gown to the sun
Has not lost, now the day is done,
The folds of its damasked gown
And its colors so like your own.
Odes [1553]. À Cassandre[4]

5 Harvest, oh! harvest your hour
While life is abloom with youth!
For age with bitter ruth
Will fade your beauty's flower.[5]
Ibid. last lines

Thomas Tusser
c. 1524–1580

6 At Christmas play and make good cheer,
For Christmas comes but once a year.
A Hundred Good Points of Husbandry [1557].
The Farmer's Daily Diet

7 Such mistress, such Nan,
Such master, such man.[6]
Ibid. April's Abstract

[1]Heureux qui, comme Ulysse, a fait un beau voyage.
[2]Quand vous serez bien vieille, au soir à la chandelle, / Assise auprès du feu, devidant et filant, / Direz, chantant mes vers, en vous émerveillant: / "Ronsard me célébrait du temps que j'étais belle."
Translated by HUMBERT WOLFE.
See the adaptation by Yeats: When you are old and gray and full of sleep, 595:1.
[3]Vivez, si m'en croyez, n'attendez à demain: / Cueillez des aujourd'hui les roses de la vie.
See *The Wisdom of Solomon 2:8,* 30:21; Horace, 95:25; Spenser, 153:11; and Herrick, 241:9.
[4]Mignonne, allons voir si la rose / Qui, ce matin, avoit déclose / Sa robe de pourpre au soleil, / A point perdu, cette vesprée / Les plis de sa robe pourprée / Et son teint au vôtre pareil.
Translated by CURTIS HIDDEN PAGE.
[5]Cueillez, cueillez votre jeunesse: / Comme à cette fleur, la vieillesse / Fera ternir votre beauté.
[6]Tel maître, tel valet. — *Attributed to* PIERRE TERRÀIL, SEIGNEUR DE BAYARD [c. 1473–1524], *known as the* CHEVALIER BAYARD

8 Sweet April showers
Do spring May flowers.
Ibid. April's Husbandry

9 'Tis merry in hall
Where beards wag all.
Ibid. August's Abstract

Gabriel Meurier
1530–1601

10   He who excuses himself accuses himself.[7]
Trésor des Sentences

William Stevenson
c. 1530–1575

11 I cannot eat but little meat,
My stomach is not good;
But sure I think that I can drink
With him that wears a hood.
Gammer Gurton's Needle [1566], drinking song, act II

12 Back and side go bare, go bare,
Both foot and hand go cold;
But, belly, God send thee good ale enough,
Whether it be new or old.
Ibid. refrain

Henri Estienne
c. 1531–1598

13   Si jeunesse savait, si vieillesse pouvait [If youth but knew, if old age but could].
Les Prémices [1594]

14   God tempers the wind to the shorn lamb.[8]
Ibid.

Elizabeth I
1533–1603

15   I know I have the body of a weak and feeble woman, but I have the heart and stomach of a king, and of a king of England too; and think foul scorn that Parma or Spain, or any prince of Europe, should dare to invade the borders of my realm.
Speech to the troops at Tilbury on the approach of the Armada [1588]

16   I am your anointed Queen. I will never be by violence constrained to do anything. I thank God I am endued with such qualities that if I were turned out of the Realm in my petticoat I were able to live in any place in Christendom.
From CHAMBERLIN, Sayings of Queen Elizabeth

[7]Qui s'excuse, s'accuse.
See Shakespeare, 170:10, and 174:11.
[8]Dieu mesure le froid à la brebis tondue.
See Sterne, 321:2.

1 I will make you shorter by the head. *Ibid.*

2 The daughter of debate, that eke discord doth sow.[1] *Ibid.*

3 [To the Countess of Nottingham] God may forgive you, but I never can.
From HUME, *History of England Under the House of Tudor, vol. II, ch. 7*

4 Though God hath raised me high, yet this I count the glory of my crown: that I have reigned with your loves. *The Golden Speech [1601]*

5 Semper eadem [Ever the same]. *Motto*

6 'Twas God the word that spake it,
He took the Bread and brake it;
And what the word did make it,
That I believe, and take it.[2]
From S. CLARKE, *Marrow of Ecclesiastical History [ed. 1675], pt. II, Life of Queen Elizabeth*

7 Must! Is *must* a word to be addressed to princes? Little man, little man!
On her deathbed, to Robert Cecil, her principal secretary [March 24, 1603]

Michel Eyquem de Montaigne[3]
1533–1592

8 I want to be seen here in my simple, natural, ordinary fashion, without straining or artifice; for it is myself that I portray. . . . I am myself the matter of my book.[4]
Essays,[5] bk. I [1580], To the Reader

9 Truly man is a marvelously vain, diverse, and undulating object. It is hard to found any constant and uniform judgment on him.[6] *Ibid. ch. 1*

10 The thing I fear most is fear.[7] *Ibid. 18*

11 I want death to find me planting my cabbages.[8] *Ibid. 20*

12 He who would teach men to die would teach them to live.[9] *Ibid.*

13 Live as long as you please, you will strike nothing off the time you will have to spend dead.[10] *Ibid.*

14 Wherever your life ends, it is all there. The advantage of living is not measured by length, but by use; some men have lived long, and lived little; attend to it while you are in it. It lies in your will, not in the number of years, for you to have lived enough. *Ibid.*

15 I do not speak the minds of others except to speak my own mind better. *Ibid. 26*

16 Since I would rather make of him [the child] an able man than a learned man, I would also urge that care be taken to choose a guide [tutor] with a well-made rather than a well-filled head.[11] *Ibid.*

17 If you press me to say why I loved him, I can say no more than it was because he was he and I was I.[12] *Ibid. 28*

18 Nothing is so firmly believed as what is least known. *Ibid. 32*

19 A man of understanding has lost nothing, if he has himself.[13] *Ibid. 39*

20 We must reserve a back shop all our own,[14] entirely free, in which to establish our real liberty and our principal retreat and solitude. *Ibid.*

21 The greatest thing in the world is to know how to belong to oneself.[15] *Ibid.*

22 It is a thorny undertaking, and more so than it seems, to follow a movement so wandering as that of our mind, to penetrate the opaque depths of its innermost folds, to pick out and immobilize the innumerable flutterings that agitate it.[16]
Ibid. II [1580], 6

---

[1]Mary, Queen of Scots.

[2]Answer on being asked her opinion of Christ's presence in the Sacrament.

[3]Translated by DONALD M. FRAME unless otherwise noted.

[4]Je veux qu'on m'y voit en ma façon simple, naturelle, et ordinaire, sans étude et artifice; car c'est moi que je peins. . . . Je suis moi-même la matière de mon livre.

[5]Books I and II of the *Essays* were published in 1580; republished [1588] with the addition of book III and with many interpolations in books I and II; the whole republished posthumously [1595], incorporating material based on Montaigne's marginal annotations in the 1588 edition.
This book of Montaigne the world has endorsed by translating it into all tongues. — EMERSON, *Representative Men* [1850], *Montaigne*

[6]Certes, c'est un subject [sic] merveilleusement vain, divers, et ondoyant, que l'homme. Il est malaisé d'y fonder jugement constant et uniforme.

[7]C'est de quoi j'ai le plus de peur que la peur.
See *Proverbs* 3:25, 20:22; Francis Bacon, 158:18; Wellington, 371:9; Thoreau, 476:26; and F. D. Roosevelt, 648:18.

[8]Je veux que la mort me trouve plantant mes choux.
See Rabelais, 140:1, and Voltaire, 306:12.

[9]I have taught you, my dear flock, for above thirty years how to live, and I will show you in a very short time how to die.
— SIR EDWIN SANDYS [1561–1629], *Anglorum Speculum*
Teach him how to live, / And, oh still harder lesson! how to die. — PORTEUS, *Death, l. 316*
In teaching me the way to live / It taught me how to die.
— GEORGE POPE MORRIS, *My Mother's Bible, st. 4*

[10]See Lucretius, 90:6.

[11]Plutôt la tête bien faite que bien pleine.

[12]Parce que c'était lui; parce que c'était moi.
Translated by CHARLES COTTON, revised by HAZLITT and WIGHT.

[13]L'homme d'entendement n'a rien perdu, s'il a soi-même.

[14]Il se faut réserver une arrière boutique toute notre.

[15]La plus grande chose du monde, c'est de savoir être à soi.

[16]C'est une épineuse entreprise, et plus qu'il ne semble, de suivre une allure si vagabonde que celle de nôtre esprit; de pénétrer les profondeurs opaques de ses replis internes; de choisir et arrêter tant de menus de ses agitations.

1   My trade and my art is living.[1]

Essays, bk. II, ch. 6

2   The easy, gentle, and sloping path . . . is not the path of true virtue. It demands a rough and thorny road.

Ibid. 11

3   When I play with my cat, who knows if I am not a pastime to her more than she is to me?

Ibid. 12

4   The souls of emperors and cobblers are cast in the same mold. . . . The same reason that makes us bicker with a neighbor creates a war between princes.

Ibid.

5   Their [the Skeptics'] way of speaking is: "I settle nothing . . . I do not understand it . . . Nothing seems true that may not seem false." Their sacramental word is Επεχω, which is to say, I suspend my judgment.[2]

Ibid.

6   This notion [skepticism] is more clearly understood by asking "What do I know?"[3]

Ibid.

7   Man is certainly crazy. He could not make a mite, and he makes gods by the dozen.[4]

Ibid.

8   What of a truth that is bounded by these mountains and is falsehood to the world that lives beyond?[5]

Ibid.

9   Those who have compared our life to a dream were right. . . . We sleeping wake, and waking sleep.[6]

Ibid.

10   How many valiant men we have seen to survive their own reputation![7]

Ibid. 16

11   A man may be humble through vainglory.

Ibid. 17

12   I find that the best goodness I have has some tincture of vice.

Ibid. 20

13   Saying is one thing and doing is another.

Ibid. 31

14   There were never in the world two opinions alike, any more than two hairs or two grains. Their most universal quality is diversity.

Ibid. 37

15   I will follow the good side right to the fire, but not into it if I can help it.

Ibid. III [1595], 1

16   I speak the truth, not my fill of it, but as much as I dare speak; and I dare to do so a little more as I grow old.

Ibid.

17   Few men have been admired by their own households.[8]

Ibid.

18   Every man bears the whole stamp of the human condition.[9]

Ibid.

19   It [marriage] happens as with cages: the birds without despair to get in, and those within despair of getting out.[10]

Ibid. 5

20   Everyone recognizes me in my book, and my book in me.

Ibid.

21   It takes so much to be a king that he exists only as such. That extraneous glare that surrounds him hides him and conceals him from us; our sight breaks and is dissipated by it, being filled and arrested by this strong light.[11]

Ibid. 7

22   Our wisdom and deliberation for the most part follow the lead of chance.[12]

Ibid. 8

23   Not because Socrates said so,[13] but because it is in truth my own disposition—and perchance to some

---

[1]Mon métier et mon art, c'est vivre.

[2]Je suspends mon jugement.
Translated by E. J. Trechmann.
Greek word (*epecho*) inscribed on a bay in Montaigne's library.—Maurice Rat, *Oeuvres Complètes de Montaigne, La Pléiade Edition* [1962], *note*
This is one of a dozen maxims from Sextus Empiricus, third-century Greek philosopher, which together with Biblical and Latin quotations comprise the fifty-seven sentences painted on the roof bays of Montaigne's library. About two thirds of the sentences are in *Apologie de Raimond Sebond* (chapter 12 of book II of the *Essays*).
See also the next quotation (Montaigne, 146:6).

[3]Que sais-je?
Translated by E. J. Trechmann.
This phrase appeared on a medal Montaigne had struck, which showed also his coat of arms and the collar of the order of Saint Michael, and on the reverse side a pair of scales in perfect balance, the date [1576], his age (forty-two), and the Skeptics' motto Επεχω (see Montaigne, 146:5).

[4]L'homme est bien insensé. Il ne saurait forger un ciron, et forge des Dieux à douzaines.

[5]Quelle vérité que ces montagnes bornent, qui est mensonge qui se tient au delà?

[6]Ceux qui ont apparié notre vie à un songe ont eu de la raison. . . . Nous veillons dormants et veillants dormons.
Translated by E. J. Trechmann.
See Calderón de la Barca, 247:7.

[7]See Richard Bentley, 286:9.

[8]See Antigonus, 79:7, and Cornuel, 249:8.

[9]Chaque homme porte la forme, entière de l'humaîne condition.
Translated by Charles Cotton, revised by Hazlitt and Wight.

[10]Translated by Charles Cotton, revised by Hazlitt and Wight.
I myself have loved a lady and pursued her with a great deal of under-age protestation, whom some three or four gallants that have enjoyed would with all their hearts have been glad to have been rid of. 'Tis just like a summer bird-cage in a garden: the birds that are without despair to get in, and the birds that are within despair and are in a consumption for fear they shall never get out.— John Webster, *The White Devil* [1612], act I, sc. ii
Wedlock, indeed, hath oft comparèd been / To public feasts, where meet a public rout— / Where they that are without would fain go in, / And they that are within would fain go out. —Sir John Davies [1569–1626], *Contention Betwixt a Wife, etc.*
See Emerson, 432:28.

[11]See Shakespeare, 198:22, and Tennyson, 459:3.

[12]Although men flatter themselves with their great actions, they are not so often the result of great design as of chance. —La Rochefoucauld, *Maxim 57*

[13]See Socrates, 70:24.

excess—I look upon all men as my compatriots, and embrace a Pole as a Frenchman, making less account of the national than of the universal and common bond.[1]   *Ibid. 9*

1   There is no man so good that if he placed all his actions and thoughts under the scrutiny of the laws, he would not deserve hanging ten times in his life.[2]   *Ibid.*

2   A man must be a little mad if he does not want to be even more stupid.[3]   *Ibid.*

3   I have seen no more evident monstrosity and miracle in the world than myself.   *Ibid. 11*

4   I have here only made a nosegay of culled flowers, and have brought nothing of my own but the thread that ties them together.[4]   *Ibid. 12*

5   It is more of a job to interpret the interpretations than to interpret the things, and there are more books about books than about any other subject: we do nothing but write glosses about each other.   *Ibid. 13*

6   For truth itself does not have the privilege to be employed at any time and in every way; its use, noble as it is, has its circumscriptions and limits.   *Ibid.*

7   No matter that we may mount on stilts, we still must walk on our own legs. And on the highest throne in the world, we still sit only on our own bottom.[5]   *Ibid.*

8   Let us give Nature a chance; she knows her business better than we do.   *Ibid.*

William I [William the Silent]
1533–1584

9   My God, have mercy on my soul and on my poor people.[6]

Last words as he fell under an assassin's bullets

[1]Translated by CHARLES COTTON, revised by HAZLITT and WIGHT.

See Montesquieu, 304:12.

[2]See Shakespeare, 196:3.

[3]See Menander, 81:6; Horace, 97:3; and Bacon, 160:1.

[4]Translated by CHARLES COTTON, revised by HAZLITT and WIGHT.

John Bartlett used this passage as an epigraph for the fourth edition of *Familiar Quotations* [1864].

I am but a gatherer and disposer of other men's stuff, at my best value.—WOTTON, *The Elements of Architecture* [1624], *preface*

[5]Si, avons nous beau monter sur des échasses, car sur des échasses encore faut-il marcher de nos jambes. Et au plus élevé trône du monde, si ne sommes assis que sur notre cul.

Translated by WALTER KAISER.

See Bunyan, 272:14.

[6]Mon Dieu, ayez pitié de mon âme et de mon pauvre peuple.

William Butler[7]
1535–1618

10   It is unseasonable and unwholesome in all months that have not an *r* in their name to eat an oyster.   *Dyet's Dry Dinner [1599]*

Sir Humphrey Gilbert
c. 1539–1583

11   We are as near to heaven by sea as by land![8]
From HAKLUYT, *Voyages, vol. III [1600], p. 159*

Saint John of the Cross
[San Juan de la Cruz]
1542–1591

12   The Dark Night of the Soul.[9]
Title of treatise [c. 1583] based on his poem[10]
Songs of the Soul Which Rejoices at Having
Reached . . . Union with God by the Road of
Spiritual Negation [c. 1578]

Mary Stuart [Mary, Queen of Scots]
1542–1587

13   In my end is my beginning.   *Motto*

14 O Lord my God, I have trusted in thee;
O Jesu my dearest one, now set me free.
In prison's oppression, in sorrow's obsession,
I weary for thee.
With sighing and crying bowed down as dying,
I adore thee, I implore thee, set me free![11]
Prayer written in her Book of Devotion before her execution

[7]Styled by Thomas Fuller in his *Worthies of England* [1662], the "Aesculapius of our age."

See Walton, 245:27.

[8]The way to heaven out of all places is of like length and distance.—MORE, *Utopia* [1516]

Gilbert, on the last day of his life, was seen in his tiny pinnace *Squirrel* with a book in hand, probably More's *Utopia*, which inspired his last utterance. He was homeward bound from Newfoundland, which he had just taken possession of in the name of the queen [August 1583].

"Do not fear! Heaven is as near," / He said, "by water as by land!"—LONGFELLOW, *Sir Humphrey Gilbert* [1849], *st. 6*

[9]La noche oscura del alma.

See Fitzgerald, 694:18.

[10]The poem, often called *Noche oscura* from its first line (En una noche oscura; In a dark night), is one of three poems made up of *canciones del alma* (songs of the soul), on which the author wrote spiritual treatises. *The Dark Night of the Soul* is sometimes used as a group title for the poems.

[11]O Domine Deus! speravi in te; / O care mi Jesu! nunc libera me. / In dura catena, in misera poena, / Disidero te. / Languendo, gemendo, et genuflectendo, / Adoro, imploro, ut liberes me!

Translated by SWINBURNE.

Jan Zamoyski
1542–1605

1   The king reigns, but does not govern.[1]
Speech in the Polish Parliament [1605], referring to King Sigismund III

Sir Edward Dyer
1543–1607

2 My mind to me a kingdom is;
Such present joys therein I find
That it excels all other bliss
That earth affords or grows by kind:
Though much I want which most would have,
Yet still my mind forbids to crave.
Rawlinson Poetry MS 85,[2] p. 17

Guillaume de Salluste, Seigneur Du Bartas
1544–1590

3 For where's the state beneath the firmament
That doth excel the bees for government?[3]
Divine Weeks and Works [1578], First Week, Fifth Day, pt. 1

4 Or almost like a spider, who, confined
In her web's center, shakt with every wind,
Moves in an instant if the buzzing fly
Stir but a string of her lawn canapie.[4]
Ibid. Sixth Day

5 Living from hand to mouth.
Ibid. Second Week, First Day, pt. 4

6 In the jaws of death.[5]
Ibid.

---

[1]Adolphe Thiers adopted the epigram as the motto for his journal *Le National*, which he established with François-Auguste Mignet and Armand Carrel in 1830.

[2]This poem became popular as a song, altered thus:
My mind to me a kingdom is;/ Such perfect joy therein I find,/ As far exceeds all earthly bliss/ That God and Nature hath assigned./ Though much I want that most would have,/ Yet still my mind forbids to crave.—WILLIAM BYRD [1543–1623], *Psalms, Sonnets, and Songs of Sadness and Piety* [1588]
See Seneca, 103:14.

[3]See Shakespeare, 184:23.

[4]Much like a subtle spider which doth sit/ In middle of her web, which spreadeth wide;/ If aught do touch the utmost thread of it/ She feels it instantly on every side.—SIR JOHN DAVIES [1569–1626], *The Immortality of the Soul* [1599]
Our souls sit close and silently within,/ And their own webs from their own entrails spin;/ And when eyes meet far off, our sense is such/ That, spider-like, we feel the tenderest touch.—DRYDEN, *Marriage à la Mode* [1673], act II, sc. i
The spider's touch, how exquisitely fine!/ Feels at each thread, and lives along the line.—POPE, *An Essay on Man* [1733–1734], epistle I, l. 217

[5]Out of the jaws of death.—SHAKESPEARE, *Twelfth-Night*, act III, sc. iv, l. 396

7   Only that he may conform
To tyrant custom.
Ibid. Third Day, pt. 2

8 Who well lives, long lives; for this age of ours
Should not be numbered by years, days, and hours.
Ibid. Fourth Day, bk. 2

9   My lovely living boy,
My hope, my hap, my love, my life, my joy.[6]
Ibid.

10 Out of the book of Nature's learned breast.[7]
Ibid.

11 Flesh of thy flesh, nor yet bone of thy bone.
Ibid.

William Gilbert
1544–1603

12   Philosophy is for the few.[8]
De Magnete (On the Magnet) [1600]

13   In the discovery of secret things and in the investigation of hidden causes, stronger reasons are obtained from sure experiments and demonstrated arguments than from probable conjectures and the opinions of philosophical speculators of the common sort.[8]
Ibid.

Miguel de Cervantes
1547–1616

14   You are a king by your own fireside, as much as any monarch in his throne.
Don Quixote de la Mancha [1605–1615][9] author's preface, p. xix

15   I was so free with him as not to mince the matter.[10]
p. xx

16   They can expect nothing but their labor for their pains.[11]
p. xxiii

17   Time out of mind.[12]
Pt. I [1605], bk. I, ch. 1, p. 4

---

[6]My fair son!/ My life, my joy, my food, my all the world!—SHAKESPEARE, *King John*, act III, sc. iv, l. 103

[7]The book of Nature is that which the physician must read; and to do so he must walk over the leaves.—PARACELSUS. From *Encyclopaedia Britannica* (11th edition), vol. XX, p. 749

[8]Translated by P. F. MOTTELAY.

[9]Translated [1700–1703] by PETER ANTHONY MOTTEUX. Page numbers are those of the Modern Library Giant edition.

[10]You mince matters.—MOLIÈRE, *Tartuffe* [1667], act I, sc. i
See Shakespeare, 206:19.

[11]Nothing is to be gotten without pains (labor).—*Old Proverb*
See Shakespeare, 200:3.

[12]Time out o' mind.—SHAKESPEARE, *Romeo and Juliet*, act I, sc. iv, l. 70

1 Which I have earned with the sweat of my brows.[1] *I, 4, p. 22*

2 By a small sample we may judge of the whole piece. *p. 25*

3 Put you in this pickle.[2] *I, 5, p. 30*

4 Can we ever have too much of a good thing? *I, 6, p. 37*

5 The charging of his enemy was but the work of a moment.[3] *I, 8, p. 50*

6 I don't know that ever I saw one in my born days. *II, 2, p. 57*

7 Those two fatal words, Mine and Thine.[4] *II, 3, p. 63*

8 The eyes those silent tongues of Love. *p. 65*

9 And had a face like a benediction.[5] *II, 4, p. 69*

10 There's not the least thing can be said or done, but people will talk and find fault.[6] *p. 70*

11 Without a wink of sleep.[7] *p. 72*

12 Fortune leaves always some door open to come at a remedy. *III, 1, p. 94*

13 Thank you for nothing. *p. 94*

14 No limits but the sky.[8] *III, 3, p. 110*

15 To give the devil his due. *p. 111*

16 You're leaping over the hedge before you come to the stile. *III, 4, p. 117*

17 Paid him in his own coin. *p. 119*

18 The famous Don Quixote de la Mancha, otherwise called the Knight of the Sorrowful Countenance.[9] *III, 5, p. 126*

19 You are come off now with a whole skin. *p. 127*

20 Fear is sharp-sighted, and can see things underground, and much more in the skies. *III, 6, p. 131*

21 A finger in every pie.[10] *p. 133*

22 No better than she should be.[11] *Ibid.*

23 That's the nature of women . . . not to love when we love them, and to love when we love them not. *Ibid.*

24 You may go whistle for the rest. *p. 134*

25 Ill luck, you know, seldom comes alone.[12] *p. 135*

26 Why do you lead me a wild-goose chase? *p. 136*

27 Experience, the universal Mother of Sciences. *III, 7, p. 140*

28 Give me but that, and let the world rub, there I'll stick. *p. 148*

29 Sing away sorrow, cast away care. *III, 8, p. 153*

30 Of good natural parts, and of a liberal education. *p. 154*

31 Let every man mind his own business. *p. 157*

32 Those who'll play with cats must expect to be scratched. *p. 159*

33 Raise a hue and cry. *Ibid.*

34 'Tis the part of a wise man to keep himself today for tomorrow, and not venture all his eggs in one basket. *III, 9, p. 162*

35 The ease of my burdens, the staff of my life. *p. 163*

36 Within a stone's throw of it. *p. 170*

37 The very remembrance of my former misfortune proves a new one to me. *III, 10, p. 174*

38 Absence, that common cure of love. *p. 177*

39 From pro's and con's they fell to a warmer way of disputing. *p. 181*

40 Little said is soon amended.[13] *p. 184*

41 Thou hast seen nothing yet. *III, 11, p. 190*

42 Between jest and earnest. *Ibid.*

43 My love and hers have always been purely Platonic. *p. 192*

44 'Tis ill talking of halters in the house of a man that was hanged. *p. 195*

[1]See *Genesis* 3:19, 6:26.

[2]How cam'st thou in this pickle? — SHAKESPEARE, *The Tempest*, act V, sc. i, l. 281

[3]Don Quixote has mistaken windmills for giants, the "enemy," and attacks them. The expression "tilting at windmills" alludes to this incident.

[4]See Boileau, 280:17.

[5]The more familiar translation.

[6]Do you think you could keep people from talking? — MO-LIÈRE, *Tartuffe* [1667], act I, sc. viii

Take wife, or cowl; ride you, or walk: / Doubt not but tongues will have their talk. — LA FONTAINE, *The Miller, His Son, and the Donkey* [1694]

[7]See Shakespeare, 219:30, and Pope, 302:19.

[8]Modern saying: The sky's the limit.

[9]El Caballero de la Triste Figura.

Translated by TOBIAS SMOLLETT.

[10]No pie was baked at Castlewood but her little finger was in it. — THACKERAY, *The Virginians* [1857–1859], ch. 5

[11]An old proverb.

You are no better than you should be. — BEAUMONT AND FLETCHER, *The Coxcomb* [1647], act IV, sc. iii

[12]See Shakespeare, 198:20.

[13]Often rendered: Least said soonest mended.

1 My memory is so bad that many times I forget my own name!   *Don Quixote, bk. III, ch. 11, p. 195*

2 'Twill grieve me so to the heart that I shall cry my eyes out.   *p. 197*

3 Ready to split his sides with laughing.   *III, 13, p. 208*

4 My honor is dearer to me than my life.   *IV, 1, p. 226*

5 On the word of a gentleman, and a Christian.   *p. 236*

6 Think before thou speakest.   *IV, 3, p. 252*

7 Let us forget and forgive injuries.   *p. 254*

8 I must speak the truth, and nothing but the truth.   *p. 255*

9 More knave than fool.   *IV, 4, p. 261*

10 Here's the devil-and-all to pay.   *IV, 10, p. 319*

11 I begin to smell a rat.   *Ibid.*

12 The proof of the pudding is in the eating.   *p. 322*

13 Let none presume to tell me that the pen is preferable to the sword.   *p. 325*

14 There's no striving against the stream; and the weakest still goes to the wall.   *IV, 20, p. 404*

15 The bow cannot always stand bent, nor can human frailty subsist without some lawful recreation.   *IV, 21, p. 412*

16 It is not the hand but the understanding of a man that may be said to write.[1]
Pt. II [1615], bk. III, author's preface, p. 441

17 When the head aches, all the members partake of the pains.[2]   *III, 2, p. 455*

18 Youngsters read it [Don Quixote's story], grown men understand it, and old people applaud it.   *III, 3, p. 464*

19 History is in a manner a sacred thing, so far as it contains truth; for where truth is, the supreme Father of it may also be said to be, at least, inasmuch as concerns truth.   *p. 465*

20 Every man is as Heaven made him, and sometimes a great deal worse.   *III, 4, p. 468*

21 There's no sauce in the world like hunger.   *III, 5, p. 473*

22 He casts a sheep's eye at the wench.   *p. 474*

23 I ever loved to see everything upon the square.   *p. 475*

24 Neither will I make myself anybody's laughing-stock.   *Ibid.*

25 Journey over all the universe in a map, without the expense and fatigue of traveling, without suffering the inconveniences of heat, cold, hunger, and thirst.   *III, 6, p. 479*

26 Presume to put in her oar.   *p. 480*

27 The fair sex.[3]   *Ibid.*

28 A little in one's own pocket is better than much in another man's purse. 'Tis good to keep a nest egg. Every little makes a mickle.[4]   *III, 7, p. 486*

29 Remember the old saying, "Faint heart ne'er won fair lady."[5]   *III, 10, p. 501*

30 Forewarned forearmed.   *p. 502*

31 As well look for a needle in a bottle of hay.[6]   *Ibid.*

32 Are we to mark this day with a white or a black stone?

33 The very pink of courtesy.[7]   *III, 13, p. 521*

34 I'll turn over a new leaf.   *p. 524*

35 He's [Don Quixote's] a muddled fool, full of lucid intervals.   *III, 18, p. 556*

36 Marriage is a noose.   *III, 19, p. 564*

37 There are only two families in the world, the Haves and the Have-Nots.   *III, 20, p. 574*

38 He preaches well that lives well, quoth Sancho; that's all the divinity I understand.   *p. 575*

39 Love and War are the same thing, and stratagems and policy are as allowable in the one as in the other.   *III, 21, p. 580*

40 A private sin is not so prejudicial in this world as a public indecency.   *III, 22, p. 582*

41 There is no love lost, sir.   *Ibid.*

42 Come back sound, wind and limb.   *p. 587*

43 Patience, and shuffle the cards.[8]
III, 23, p. 592

---

[1]Cervantes's left hand was maimed for life by gunshot wounds in the battle of Lepanto.

[2]When the head is not sound, the rest cannot be well.—Du Bartas, *Divine Weeks and Works* [1578]

For let our finger ache, and it indues / Our other healthful members ev'n to that sense / Of pain.—Shakespeare, *Othello, act III, sc. iv, l. 145*

[3]That sex which is therefore called fair.—Steele, *The Spectator, no. 302* [February 15, 1712]

[4]See Hesiod, 54:27, and Chaucer, 132:8.

[5]See William S. Gilbert, 530:16.

[6]A needle in a haystack.

[7]*La mesma cortesía.*
See Shakespeare, 175:21.

[8]But patience, cousin, and shuffle the cards, till our hand is a stronger one.—Walter Scott, *Quentin Durward* [1823], ch. 8

Cut the fiercest quarrels short / With "Patience, gentlemen, and shuffle."—Winthrop Mackworth Praed [1802–1839], *Quince, st. 5*

Men disappoint me so, I disappoint myself so, yet courage, patience, shuffle the cards.—Margaret Fuller, *letter to the Reverend W. H. Channing*

1   Tell me thy company, and I'll tell thee what thou art.[1]   *p. 594*

2   Tomorrow will be a new day.   *III, 26, p. 618*

3   I can see with half an eye.   *III, 29, p. 632*

4   Great persons are able to do great kindnesses.   *III, 32, p. 662*

5   Honesty's the best policy.[2]   *III, 33, p. 666*

6   An honest man's word is as good as his bond.   *IV, 34, p. 674*

7   A blot in thy scutcheon to all futurity.   *IV, 35, p. 681*

8   They had best not stir the rice, though it sticks to the pot.   *IV, 37, p. 691*

9   Good wits jump;[3] a word to the wise is enough.   *p. 692*

10   Diligence is the mother of good fortune.   *IV, 38, p. 724*

11   What a man has, so much he's sure of.   *p. 725*

12   The pot calls the kettle black.   *p. 727*

13   Mum's the word.[4]   *IV, 44, p. 729*

14   I shall be as secret as the grave.   *IV, 62, p. 862*

15   Now blessings light on him that first invented this same sleep! It covers a man all over, thoughts and all, like a cloak;[5] 'tis meat for the hungry, drink for the thirsty, heat for the cold, and cold for the hot. 'Tis the current coin that purchases all the pleasures of the world cheap; and the balance that sets the king and the shepherd, the fool and the wise man even.   *IV, 68, p. 898*

16   The ass will carry his load, but not a double load; ride not a free horse to death.   *IV, 71, p. 917*

17   He . . . got the better of himself, and that's the best kind of victory one can wish for.   *IV, 72, p. 924*

18   Every man was not born with a silver spoon in his mouth.   *IV, 73, p. 926*

19   Ne'er look for birds of this year in the nests of the last.[6]   *IV, 74, p. 933*

20   There is a strange charm in the thoughts of a good legacy, or the hopes of an estate, which wondrously alleviates the sorrow that men would otherwise feel for the death of friends.   *p. 934*

21   For if he like a madman lived,
At least he like a wise one died.
        p. 935 (Don Quixote's epitaph)

22   Don't put too fine a point to your wit for fear it should get blunted.   *The Little Gypsy (La Gitanilla)*

23   My heart is wax molded as she pleases, but enduring as marble to retain.[7]   *Ibid.*

Giordano Bruno
1548–1600

24   Time takes all and gives all.[8]
        The Candle Bearer [1582],[9] dedication

25   It is Unity that doth enchant me. By her power I am free though thrall, happy in sorrow, rich in poverty, and quick even in death.
        On the Infinite Universe and Worlds [1584],[10] introductory epistle

26   Our bodily eye findeth never an end, but is vanquished by the immensity of space.
        Ibid. Fifth Dialogue

27   There is in the universe neither center nor circumference.   *Ibid.*

Charles IX
1550–1574

28   Horses and poets should be fed, not overfed.[11]
        Saying

William Camden
1551–1623

29 My friend, judge not me,
Thou seest I judge not thee.
Betwixt the stirrup and the ground
Mercy I asked, and mercy found.
        Remains Concerning Britain. Epitaph for a man killed by falling from his horse

---

[1]Show me your garden and I shall tell you what you are. —ALFRED AUSTIN [1835–1913], *The Garden That I Love* [1905]

[2]I hold the maxim no less applicable to public than to private affairs, that honesty is always the best policy. —WASHINGTON, *Farewell Address* [1796]

[3]Great wits jump. —STERNE, *Tristram Shandy, vol. III* [1761–1762], *ch.* 9

[4]"Cry 'mum.'" —SHAKESPEARE, *The Merry Wives of Windsor, act V, sc. ii, l.* 6

[5]"God's blessing," said Sancho Panza, "be upon the man who first invented this self-same thing called sleep; it covers a man all over like a cloak." —LAURENCE STERNE, *Tristram Shandy*

[6]For Time will teach thee soon the truth, / There are no birds in last year's nest! —LONGFELLOW, *It Is Not Always May, st.* 6

[7]See Byron, 402:3.

[8]See T. S. Eliot, 671:16.

[9]Translated by J. B. HALLE.

[10]Translated by DOROTHEA SINGER.

[11]Equi et poetae alendi, non saginandi.

Sir Edward Coke
1552–1634

1   Reason is the life of the law; nay, the common law itself is nothing else but reason. . . . The law, which is perfection of reason.[1]

First Institute [1628]

2   The gladsome light of jurisprudence.

Ibid. epilogue

3   For a man's house is his castle, *et domus sua cuique tutissimum refugium.*[2]

Third Institute [1644]

4   The house of everyone is to him as his castle and fortress, as well for his defense against injury and violence as for his repose.

Semayne's Case. 5 Report 91

5   They [corporations] cannot commit treason, nor be outlawed nor excommunicate, for they have no souls.   *Case of Sutton's Hospital. 10 Report 32*

6   Magna Carta is such a fellow that he will have no sovereign.

Debate in the Commons [May 17, 1628]

7 Six hours in sleep, in law's grave study six,
Four spend in prayer, the rest on Nature fix.[3]
Translation quoted by COKE. *From The Pandects (Digest of Justinian). De in Ius Vocando*

Sir Walter Ralegh
c. 1552–1618

8 Like to an hermit poor in place obscure,
I mean to spend my days of endless doubt,
To wail such woes as time cannot recure,
Where none but Love shall ever find me out.
The Phoenix Nest [1593]. Sonnet

9 As you came from the holy land
Of Walsinghame,
Met you not with my true Love
By the way as you came?
As You Came from the Holy Land [c. 1599], st. 1

10 But true love is a durable fire,
In the mind ever burning,
Never sick, never old, never dead,
From itself never turning.

Ibid. st. 11

11 If all the world and love were young,
And truth in every shepherd's tongue,
These pretty pleasures might me move
To live with thee, and be thy love.[4]
The Nymph's Reply to the Passionate Shepherd[5]
(printed in England's Helicon) [1600], st. 1

12 Fain would I climb, yet fear I to fall.
Written on a windowpane[6]

13 Our passions are most like to floods and streams,
The shallow murmur, but the deep are dumb.[7]
Sir Walter Ralegh to the Queen [c. 1599], st. 1

14 Silence in love bewrays more woe
Than words, though ne'er so witty;
A beggar that is dumb, you know,
Deserveth double pity.

Ibid. st. 5

15 Go, Soul, the body's quest,
Upon a thankless arrant:
Fear not to touch the best,
The truth shall be thy warrant:
Go, since I needs must die,
And give the world the lie.
The Lie (printed in FRANCIS DAVISON, *Poetical Rhapsody) [1608; manuscript copy traced to 1595], st. 1*

16 Give me my scallop shell of quiet,
My staff of faith to walk upon,
My scrip of joy, immortal diet,
My bottle of salvation,
My gown of glory, hope's true gage
And thus I'll take my pilgrimage.
Diaphantus [1604]. The Passionate Man's Pilgrimage

17 Methought I saw the grave where Laura lay.
Verses to Edmund Spenser

18 Shall I, like a hermit, dwell
On a rock or in a cell?

Poem

19   [History] hath triumphed over time, which besides it nothing but eternity hath triumphed over.
History of the World [1614], preface

20   Whosoever, in writing a modern history, shall follow truth too near the heels, it may haply strike out his teeth.   *Ibid.*

---

[4]See Donne, 229:10.
[5]An answer to MARLOWE, *The Passionate Shepherd to His Love* (see 162:2).
[6]Under this Queen Elizabeth wrote, "If thy heart fails thee, climb not at all."—THOMAS FULLER, *Worthies of England* [1662]
[7]Altissima quaeque flumina minimo sono labi [The deepest rivers flow with the least sound].—QUINTUS CURTIUS [first century A.D.], *VII, 4, 13*
Where the stream runneth smoothest, the water is deepest.—LYLY, *Euphues and his England* [1580]
Smooth runs the water where the brook is deep.—SHAKESPEARE, *Henry VI, Part II, act III, sc. i, l. 53*
Take heed of still waters, the quick pass away.—GEORGE HERBERT, *Jacula Prudentum* [1651]

---

[1]Let us consider the reason of the case. For nothing is law that is not reason.—SIR JOHN POWELL [1645–1713], *Coggs v. Bernard, 2 Ld. Raym. Rep., p. 911*
[2]One's home is the safest refuge to everyone.—*Pandects* [533], *lib. II, tit. IV, De in Ius Vocando*
I in mine own house am an emperor / And will defend what's mine.—MASSINGER, *The Roman Actor* [1629], *act I, sc. ii*
[3]Seven hours to law, to soothing slumber seven; / Ten to the world allot, and all to heaven.—SIR WILLIAM JONES [1746–1794]

1   O eloquent, just, and mighty Death! whom none could advise, thou hast persuaded; what none hath dared, thou hast done; and whom all the world hath flattered, thou only hast cast out of the world and despised. Thou hast drawn together all the far-stretched greatness, all the pride, cruelty, and ambition of man, and covered it all over with these two narrow words, *Hic jacet!*
Ibid. bk. V, pt. I, ch. 6, conclusion

2 Even such is time, that takes in trust
Our youth, our joys, our all we have,
And pays us but with age and dust;
Who in the dark and silent grave,
When we have wandered all our ways,
Shuts up the story of our days.
And from which earth, and grave, and dust,
The Lord shall raise me up, I trust.
A version of one of his earlier poems, found at his death in his Bible in the Gatehouse at Westminster

Edmund Spenser
1552–1599

3 To kirk the nearer, from God more far,
Has been an old-said saw.
And he that strives to touch the stars,
Oft stumbles at a straw.[1]
The Shepherd's Calendar [1579]. July, l. 97

4 Fierce wars and faithful loves shall moralize my song.[2]
The Faerie Queene [1590], introduction, st. 1

5 A gentle knight was pricking on the plain.
Ibid. bk. I, canto 1, st. 1

6 A bold bad man.
Ibid. st. 37

7   Her angel's face
As the great eye of heaven shined bright,
And made a sunshine in the shady place.
Ibid. 3, st. 4

8 Ay me, how many perils do enfold
The righteous man, to make him daily fall.[3]
Ibid. 8, st. 1

9 Sleep after toil, port after stormy seas,
Ease after war, death after life does greatly please.[4]
Ibid. 9, st. 40

10 All for love, and nothing for reward.
Ibid. II, 8, st. 2

11 Gather therefore the Rose, whilst yet is prime,
For soon comes age, that will her pride deflower:
Gather the Rose of love, whilst yet is time.[5]
Ibid. 12, st. 75

12 Her birth was of the womb of morning dew.[6]
Ibid. III, 6, st. 3

13   Roses red and violets blue,
And all the sweetest flowers, that in the forest grew.
Ibid. st. 6

14 All that in this delightful garden grows,
Should happy be, and have immortal bliss.
Ibid. st. 41

15 That Squire of Dames.
Ibid. 8, st. 44

16 And painful pleasure turns to pleasing pain.
Ibid. 10, st. 60

17 How over that same door was likewise writ,
Be bold, be bold, and everywhere *Be bold.*
Ibid. 11, st. 54

18 Another iron door, on which was writ,
Be not too bold.[7]
Ibid.

19 Dan Chaucer, well of English undefiled,
On Fame's eternal beadroll worthy to be filed.
Ibid. IV [1596], 2, st. 32

20 For all that nature by her mother wit
Could frame in earth.
Ibid. 10, st. 21

21 Ill can he rule the great, that cannot reach the small.
Ibid. V, 2, st. 43

22 Who will not mercy unto others show,
How can he mercy ever hope to have?[8]
Ibid. VI, 1, st. 42

23 The gentle mind by gentle deeds is known.
For a man by nothing is so well bewrayed,
As by his manners.
Ibid. 3, st. 1

24 That here on earth is no sure happiness.
Ibid. 11, st. 1

[1]See John Heywood, 141:11.

[2]And moralized his song.—POPE, *Epistle to Dr. Arbuthnot* [1735], *l. 340*

[3]Ay me! what perils do environ / The man that meddles with cold iron!—SAMUEL BUTLER, *Hudibras*, pt. I [1663], canto III, *l. 1*

[4]These lines are cut on Joseph Conrad's gravestone at Canterbury.

[5]See *The Wisdom of Solomon 2:8, 30:21*; Horace, 95:25; Ronsard, 144:3; and Herrick, 241:9.

[6]The dew of thy birth is of the womb of the morning.— *Book of Common Prayer, Psalter, Psalm 110:3*

[7]Jockey of Norfolk, be not too bold, / For Dickon thy master is bought and sold.—SHAKESPEARE, *Richard III*, act V, sc. iii, *l. 305*

Forbear, said I: be not too bold. / Your fleece is white but 'tis too cold.—CRASHAW, *Hymn of the Nativity* [1652], *l. 50*

Write on your doors the saying wise and old, / "Be bold! be bold!" and everywhere—"Be bold; / Be not too bold!"— LONGFELLOW, *Morituri Salutamus* [1875]

[8]See *Matthew 5:7, 33:1*.

1   The ever-whirling wheel
Of Change; the which all mortal things doth
sway.
> *The Faerie Queene, bk. VII, canto 6, st. 1*

2 Wars and alarums unto nations wide.
> *Ibid. st. 3*

3 But times do change and move continually.[1]
> *Ibid. st. 47*

4 For deeds do die, however nobly done,
And thoughts of men do as themselves decay,
But wise words taught in numbers for to run,
Recorded by the Muses, live for ay.
> *The Ruines of Time [1591], l. 400*

5 Full little knowest thou that hast not tried,
What hell it is, in suing long to bide:
To lose good days, that might be better spent;
To waste long nights in pensive discontent;
To speed today, to be put back tomorrow;
To feed on hope, to pine with fear and sorrow.
> *Mother Hubberd's Tale [1591], l. 895*

6 To fret thy soul with crosses and with cares;
To eat thy heart through comfortless despairs;
To fawn, to crouch, to wait, to ride, to run,
To spend, to give, to want, to be undone.
Unhappy wight, born to disastrous end,
That doth his life in so long tendance spend.
> *Ibid. l. 903*

7 What more felicity can fall to creature,
Than to enjoy delight with liberty.
> *Muiopotmos; or, The Fate of the Butterfly*
> *[1591], l. 209*

8 I hate the day, because it lendeth light
To see all things, and not my love to see.
> *Daphnaida [1591], l. 407*

9 Death slew not him, but he made death his ladder
to the skies.
> *An Epitaph upon Sir Philip Sidney [1591], l. 20*

10 Though last not least.[2]
> *Colin Clouts Come Home Again [1595], l. 144*

11 Tell her the joyous time will not be stayed
Unlesse she do him by the forelock take.[3]
> *Amoretti [1595]. Sonnet 70*

12 The woods shall to me answer, and my Echo ring.
> *Epithalamion [1595], l. 18*

13 Ah! when will this long weary day have end,
And lend me leave to come unto my love?
> *Ibid. l. 278*

14 For of the soul the body form doth take:
For soul is form, and doth the body make.
> *Hymn in Honor of Beauty [1596], l. 132*

---

[1]See Anonymous: Latin, 119:33.
[2]The last, not least in honor or applause. — POPE, *The Dunciad* [1728], bk. IV, l. 577
See Shakespeare, 188:21 and 208:24.
[3]Take Time by the forelock. — THALES [c. 640–c. 546 B.C.]

15 For all that fair is, is by nature good;[4]
That is a sign to know the gentle blood.
> *Ibid. l. 139*

16 Sweet Thames! run softly, till I end my Song.[5]
> *Prothalamion [1596], refrain*

17 I was promised on a time
To have reason for my rhyme;
From that time unto this season,
I received nor rhyme nor reason.
> *Lines on his promised pension. From* THOMAS
> FULLER, *Worthies of England [1662]*

John Florio
c. 1553–1625

18   England is the paradise of women, the purgatory
of men, and the hell of horses.
> *Second Frutes [1591]*

19   Praise the sea; on shore remain.   *Ibid.*

Henri IV [Henry of Navarre]
1553–1610

20   I want there to be no peasant in my realm so poor
that he will not have a chicken in his pot every
Sunday.   *Attributed*

21   Paris is well worth a Mass.[6]   *Attributed*[7]

22   Hang yourself, brave Crillon; we fought at
Arques and you were not there.[8]
> *Letter [1597]. From Lettres missives de Henri*
> *IV, Collection des Documents Inédits de*
> *l'Histoire de France, vol. IV [1847]*

23   The wisest fool in Christendom [James I of En-
gland].   *Attributed*[9]

George Keith, Fifth Earl Marischal
c. 1553–1623

24   Thai half said. Quhat say thai? Let thame say.[10]
> *Family motto, Mitchell Tower, Marischal*
> *College, Aberdeen, Scotland [founded 1593]*

---

[4]See Shakespeare, 204:16.
[5]Sweet Thames, run softly till I end my song, / Sweet Thames, run softly, for I speak not loud or long. — T. S. ELIOT, *The Waste Land* [1922], pt. III
[6]Paris vaut bien une messe.
[7]Attributed also to Henri's minister Sully.
[8]Pends-toi, brave Crillon, nous avons combattu à Arques et tu n'y étais pas.
Louis de Balbes de Berton de Crillon [c. 1541–1615], French soldier of legendary courage, fought as captain under Henri IV in the battle of Ivry and the siege of Paris.
[9]Attributed also to Henri's minister Sully.
[10]They say. What say they? Let them say. — *Motto over the fireplace in George Bernard Shaw's home*

Fulke Greville, Lord Brooke
1554–1628

1 Oh wearisome condition of humanity!
Born under one law, to another bound.
Mustapha [1609], V, 4

2   Fulke Greville, Servant to Queen Elizabeth,
Councillor to King James, and Friend to Sir Philip
Sidney.   *Epitaph, on his monument in Warwick*

Richard Hooker
c. 1554–1600

3   Of Law there can be no less acknowledged than
that her seat is the bosom of God, her voice the
harmony of the world. All things in heaven and
earth do her homage—the very least as feeling her
care, and the greatest as not exempted from her
power.
Laws of Ecclesiastical Polity [1593], bk. 1

4   That to live by one man's will became the cause
of all men's misery.   *Ibid.*

John Lyly
c. 1554–1606

5   Be valiant, but not too venturous. Let thy attire
be comely, but not costly.
*Euphues: The Anatomy of Wit [1579]. Arber's
reprint, p. 39*

6   The finest edge is made with the blunt whetstone.
Ibid. p. 47

7   Delays breed dangers.[1]   *Ibid. p. 65*

8   It seems to me (said she) that you are in some
brown study.   *Ibid. p. 80*

9   Many strokes overthrow the tallest oaks.[2]
Ibid. p. 81

10   Let me stand to the main chance.[3]
Ibid. p. 104

11   It is a world to see.   *Ibid. p. 116*

12   A clear conscience is a sure card.
Ibid. p. 207

13   Go to bed with the lamb, and rise with the lark.[4]
Euphues and His England [1580], p. 229

---

[1]*Periculum in mora.—Latin proverb*
All delays are dangerous in war.—DRYDEN, *Tyrannic Love*
[1669], *act I, sc. i*
See Shakespeare, 163:14.
[2]Many strokes, though with a little axe, / Hew down and fell
the hardest-timber'd oak.—SHAKESPEARE, *Henry VI, Part III,
act II, sc. i, l. 54*
See Franklin, 310:4.
[3]See Samuel Butler [1612–1680], 263:25.
[4]To rise with the lark and go to bed with the lamb.—NICHO-
LAS BRETON [c. 1553–c. 1625], *Court and Country* [1618]
Rise with the lark, and with the lark to bed.—JAMES HUR-
DIS [1763–1801], *The Village Curate*

14   A comely old man as busy as a bee.
Ibid. p. 252

15   Maidens, be they never so foolish, yet being fair
they are commonly fortunate.   *Ibid. p. 279*

16   Your eyes are so sharp that you cannot only look
through a millstone, but clean through the mind.
Ibid. p. 289

17   I am glad that my Adonis hath a sweet tooth in
his head.   *Ibid. p. 308*

18   A rose is sweeter in the bud than full-blown.[5]
Ibid. p. 314

19 Cupid and my Campaspe played
At cards for kisses: Cupid paid.
Alexander and Campaspe [1584], act III, sc. v

20 How at heaven's gates she claps her wings,
The morn not waking till she sings.[6]
Ibid. V, i

21 Night hath a thousand eyes.
Maides Metamorphosis, III, 1

22   Marriages are made in heaven and consummated
on earth.[7]   *Mother Bombie [1590], act IV, sc. i*

Sir Philip Sidney
1554–1586

23   High-erected thoughts seated in the heart of courtesy.   *The Arcadia [written 1580], bk. 1*

24   They are never alone that are accompanied with
noble thoughts.[8]   *Ibid.*

25   My dear, my better half.   *Ibid. III*

26 My true-love hath my heart, and I have his,
By just exchange one for the other given:
I hold his dear, and mine he cannot miss,
There never was a better bargain driven.
Ibid. Sonnet

27 Ring out your bells! Let mourning shows be
spread!
For Love is dead.
Ibid. Song

28 Leave me, O Love, which reachest but to dust,
And thou, my mind, aspire to higher things;
Grow rich in that which never taketh rust:
Whatever fades, but fading pleasure brings.
Ibid. Sonnet

---

[5]The rose is fairest when 'tis budding new.—WALTER
SCOTT, *The Lady of the Lake* [1810], *canto III, st. 1*
[6]See Shakespeare, 219:24.
[7]*Les mariages se font au ciel, et se consomment sur la terre.*
—French proverb
If marriages / Are made in heaven, they should be happier.
—THOMAS SOUTHERNE [1660–1746], *The Fatal Marriage*
[1694]
See John Heywood, 141:n1.
[8]He never is alone that is accompanied with noble thoughts.
—BEAUMONT AND FLETCHER, *Love's Cure* [1647], *act III, sc. iii*

1   Sweet food of sweetly uttered knowledge.
The Defense of Poesy [written c. 1580]

2   He cometh unto you with a tale which holdeth children from play, and old men from the chimney corner. *Ibid.*

3   I never heard the old song of Percy and Douglas that I found not my heart moved more than with a trumpet. *Ibid.*

4   "Fool!" said my muse to me, "look in thy heart, and write."
Astrophel and Stella [1591]

5   With how sad steps, O Moon, thou climb'st the skies!
How silently, and with how wan a face![1]
Ibid.

6   Have I caught my heav'nly jewel.[2]
Ibid. Second Song

7   Thy necessity[3] is yet greater than mine.
Said on the battlefield of Zutphen [September 22, 1586] on giving his water bottle to a dying soldier

François de Malherbe[4]
1555–1628

8   And a rose, she lived as roses do, the space of a morn.[5]   *Consolation à Monsieur du Périer [1599]*

9   And the fruits will outdo what the flowers have promised.[6]
Prière pour le roi Henri le Grand [1605]

10   What Malherbe writes will endure forever.
Sonnet à Louis XIII [1624]

Philip Nicolai
1556–1608

11   Wake, awake, for night is flying:
The watchmen on the heights are crying.[7]
Hymn [1597]

George Peele
1556 – 1596

12   Fair and fair, and twice so fair,
As fair as any may be.
The Arraignment of Paris [1584]

[1]Wordsworth begins a sonnet [1802] with these two lines.
[2]Quoted by SHAKESPEARE in *The Merry Wives of Windsor*, *act III, sc. iii, l. 45.*
[3]More often quoted as: Thy need.
[4]See Boileau, 280:5.
[5]Et rose, elle a vécu ce que vivent les roses, / L'espace d'un matin.
[6]Et les fruits passeront la promesse des fleurs.
[7]Wachet auf, ruft uns die stimme.
Translated by CATHERINE WINKWORTH.

13   My merry, merry, merry roundelay
Concludes with Cupid's curse:
They that do change old love for new,
Pray gods, they change for worse!
Ibid.

14   His golden locks time hath to silver turned;
O time too swift, O swiftness never ceasing!
His youth 'gainst time and age hath ever spurned,
But spurned in vain; youth waneth by increasing.
Polyhymnia [1590]. Farewell to Arms, st. 1

15   His helmet now shall make a hive for bees,
And lovers' sonnets turned to holy psalms,
A man-at-arms must now serve on his knees,
And feed on prayers, which are age his alms.
Ibid. 2

Thomas Kyd
1558–1594

16   What outcries call me from my naked bed?
The Spanish Tragedy [1594], act II, sc. v, l. 1

17   O eyes, no eyes, but fountains fraught with tears;
O life, no life, but lively form of death;
O world, no world, but mass of public wrongs,
Confused and filled with murder and misdeeds.
Ibid. III, ii, 1

18   Hieronymo, beware: go by, go by.
Ibid. III, xii, 31

19   Why then I'll fit you, say no more.
When I was young, I gave my mind
And plied myself to fruitless poetry:
Which though it profit the professor naught
Yet it is passing pleasing to the world.
Ibid. IV, ii, 70

Thomas Lodge
c. 1558–1625

20   Love in my bosom like a bee
Doth suck his sweet.
Rosalynde [1590]

21   Devils are not so black as they are painted.
A Margarite of America [1596]

Chidiock Tichborne[8]
c. 1558–1586

22   My prime of youth is but a frost of cares;
My feast of joy is but a dish of pain;
My crop of corn is but a field of tares;
And all my good is but vain hope of gain:
The day is past, and yet I saw no sun;
And now I live, and now my life is done.
Tichborne's Elegy [1586]

[8]He was executed for an attempt on Queen Elizabeth's life.

George Chapman
c. 1559–1634

1 Promise is most given when the least is said.
Hero and Leander [1598]

2 Love calls to war;
Sighs his alarms,
Lips his swords are,
The field his arms.
Ibid. Epithalamion Teratos, refrain

3 Young men think old men are fools; but old men know young men are fools.
All Fools [1605], act V, sc. i

4 Keep thy shop, and thy shop will keep thee. Light gains make heavy purses.[1]
Eastward Ho [1605],[2] act I, sc. i

5 Why, do nothing, be like a gentleman, be idle.
. . . Make ducks and drakes with shillings.
Ibid.

6 I will neither yield to the song of the siren nor the voice of the hyena, the tears of the crocodile[3] nor the howling of the wolf.
Ibid. V, i

7 For one heat, all know, doth drive out another,
One passion doth expel another still.[4]
Monsieur d'Olive [1606], act V, sc. i

8 To put a girdle round about the world.[5]
Bussy d'Ambois [1607], act I, sc. i

9 Speed his plow.[6]
Ibid.

10 So our lives
In acts exemplary, not only win
Ourselves good names, but doth to others give
Matter for virtuous deeds, by which we live.
Ibid.

11 Who to himself is law no law doth need,
Offends no law, and is a king indeed.
Ibid. II, i

12 Be free, all worthy spirits,
And stretch yourselves, for greatness and for height.
The Conspiracy of Charles, Duke of Byron [1608], act III, sc. i

13 Give me a spirit that on this life's rough sea
Loves t' have his sails filled with a lusty wind,
Even till his sail-yards tremble, his masts crack,

And his rapt ship run on her side so low
That she drinks water, and her keel plows air.
Ibid.

14 Danger, the spur of all great minds.
The Revenge of Bussy d'Ambois [1610], act V, sc. i

15 We have watered our horses in Helicon.
May-Day [1611], act III, sc. iii

Maximilien de Béthune, Duc de Sully[7]
1559–1641

16 Tilling and grazing are the two breasts that feed France.[8]
Economies Royales, III

17 The English take their pleasures sadly after the fashion of their country.[9]
Memoirs

Robert Greene
c. 1560–1592

18 Sweet are the thoughts that savor of content;
The quiet mind is richer than a crown.[10]
Farewell to Folly [1591], st. 1

19 A mind content both crown and kingdom is.[10]
Ibid. st. 2

20 For there is an upstart crow, beautified with our feathers, that with his tiger's heart wrapped in a player's hide,[11] supposes he is as well able to bumbast out a blank verse as the best of you; and being an absolute *Johannes fac totum*, is in his own conceit the only Shake-scene in a country.[12]
The Croatsworth of Wit [1592]

21 Hangs in the uncertain balance of proud time.
Friar Bacon and Friar Bungay [acted 1594], act III

22 Hell's broken loose.[13]
Ibid. IV

Francis Bacon[14]
1561–1626

23 I have taken all knowledge to be my province.
Letter to Lord Burleigh [1592]

24 The monuments of wit survive the monuments of power.
Essex's Device [1595]

---

[1]Quoted by Benjamin Franklin in *Poor Richard's Almanac* [1735], *June.*
[2]By Chapman, Jonson, and Marston.
[3]These crocodile tears.—ROBERT BURTON, *Anatomy of Melancholy* [1621–1651], *pt. III, sec. 2, member 2, subsec. 4*
She's false, false as the tears of crocodiles.—SUCKLING, *The Sad One, act IV, sc. v*
See Francis Bacon, 159:26.
[4]See Shakespeare, 174:16.
[5]See Shakespeare, 173:7.
[6]Usually quoted: Speed the plow.

[7]See Henri IV of France, 154:21.
[8]Labourage et pâturage sont les deux mamelles dont la France est alimentée.
[9]Les anglais s'amusent tristement selon l'usage de leur pays.
[10]See stanza 2 (Greene, 157:19) and Shakespeare, 164:19.
[11]See Shakespeare, 164:13.
[12]First known literary reference to Shakespeare.
[13]See Milton, 259:2.
[14]If parts allure thee, think how Bacon shined, / The wisest, brightest, meanest of mankind.—POPE, *Essay on Man [1733–1734], epistle IV, l. 281*
See Walton, 246:1.

1   Knowledge is power [*Nam et ipsa scientia potestas est*].[1]

     Meditationes Sacrae [1597]. De Haeresibus

2   For all knowledge and wonder (which is the seed of knowledge) is an impression of pleasure in itself.

     The Advancement of Learning [1605], bk. I, i, 3

3   Time, which is the author of authors.

     Ibid. iv, 12

4   If a man will begin with certainties, he shall end in doubts; but if he will be content to begin with doubts he shall end in certainties.   *Ibid. v, 8*

5   *Antiquitas saeculi juventus mundi.*[2] These times are the ancient times, when the world is ancient, and not those which we account ancient *ordine retrogrado,* by a computation backward from ourselves.[3]

     Ibid.

6   [Knowledge] is a rich storehouse for the glory of the Creator and the relief of man's estate.

     Ibid. 11

7   It [Poesy] was ever thought to have some participation of divineness, because it doth raise and erect the mind by submitting the shows of things to the desires of the mind.   *Ibid. II, iv, 2*

8   They are ill discoverers that think there is no land, when they can see nothing but sea.

     Ibid. vii, 5

9   But men must know that in this theater of man's life it is reserved only for God and angels to be lookers on.   *Ibid. xx, 8*

10   We are much beholden to Machiavel and others, that write what men do, and not what they ought to do.   *Ibid. xxi, 9*

11   All good moral philosophy is but the handmaid to religion.   *Ibid. xxii, 14*

12   There are and can be only two ways of searching into and discovering truth. The one flies from the senses and particulars to the most general axioms

. . . this way is now in fashion. The other derives axioms from the senses and particulars, rising by a gradual and unbroken ascent, so that it arrives at the most general axioms last of all. This is the true way, but as yet untried.   *Novum Organum [1620]*

13   There are four classes of Idols which beset men's minds. To these for distinction's sake I have assigned names—calling the first class, Idols of the Tribe; the second, Idols of the Cave; the third, Idols of the Market-Place; the fourth, Idols of the Theater.

     Ibid. Aphorism 39

14   The human understanding is like a false mirror, which, receiving rays irregularly, distorts and discolors the nature of things by mingling its own nature with it.   *Ibid. 41*

15   Nature, to be commanded, must be obeyed.

     Ibid. 129

16   I do plainly and ingenuously confess that I am guilty of corruption, and do renounce all defense. I beseech your Lordships to be merciful to a broken reed.[4]

     On being charged by Parliament with corruption in office [1621]

17   Lucid intervals and happy pauses.
     History of King Henry VII [1622], III

18   Nothing is terrible except fear itself.[5]
     De Augmentis Scientiarum, bk. II, Fortitudo [1623]

19   Riches are a good handmaid, but the worst mistress.   *Ibid. Antitheta*

20   Hope is a good breakfast, but it is a bad supper.
     Apothegms [1624], no. 36

21   Like strawberry wives, that laid two or three great strawberries at the mouth of their pot, and all the rest were little ones.   *Ibid. 54*

22   Sir Amice Pawlet, when he saw too much haste made in any matter, was wont to say, "Stay a while, that we may make an end the sooner."

     Ibid. 76

23   Alonso of Aragon was wont to say in commendation of age, that age appears to be best in four things —old wood best to burn, old wine to drink, old friends to trust, and old authors to read.[6]

     Ibid. 97

24   Cosmus, Duke of Florence, was wont to say of perfidious friends, that "We read that we ought to forgive our enemies; but we do not read that we ought to forgive our friends."   *Ibid. 206*

25   Cato said the best way to keep good acts in memory was to refresh them with new.   *Ibid. 247*

---

[1]Knowledge is more than equivalent to force.—SAMUEL JOHNSON, *Rasselas [1759], ch. 13*
     See *Proverbs 24:5, 22:23.*
     [2]The age of antiquity is the youth of the world.
     [3]As in the little, so in the great world, reason will tell you that old age or antiquity is to be accounted by the farther distance from the beginning and the nearer approach to the end—the times wherein we now live being in propriety of speech the most ancient since the world's creation.—GEORGE HAKEWILL [1578–1649], *An Apologie or Declaration of the Power and Providence of God in the Government of the World [1627]*
     For as old age is that period of life most remote from infancy, who does not see that old age in this universal man ought not to be sought in the times nearest his birth, but in those most remote from it?—PASCAL, *Preface to the Treatise on Vacuum*
     It is worthy of remark that a thought which is often quoted from Francis Bacon occurs in [Giordano] Bruno's *Cena di Cenere,* published in 1584: I mean the notion that the later times are more aged than the earlier.—WHEWELL, *Philosophy of the Inductive Sciences [1840], vol. II, p. 198*
     We are Ancients of the earth, / And in the morning of the times.—TENNYSON, *The Day Dream [1842], L'Envoi*

[4]See *Isaiah 36:6, 27:11.*
     [5]*Nil terribile nisi ipse timor.*
     See *Proverbs 3:25, 20:22;* Montaigne, 145:10; Wellington, 371:9; Thoreau, 476:26; and F. D. Roosevelt, 648:18.
     [6]See John Webster, 237:11; Selden, 238:22; and Goldsmith, 329:25.

1 My essays . . . come home to men's business and bosoms. *Essays [1625],*[1] *dedication*

2 What is truth? said jesting Pilate,[2] and would not stay for an answer. *Ibid. Of Truth*

3 No pleasure is comparable to the standing upon the vantage-ground of truth. *Ibid.*

4 Men fear death as children fear to go in the dark; and as that natural fear in children is increased with tales, so is the other.[3] *Ibid. Of Death*

5 Revenge is a kind of wild justice, which the more man's nature runs to, the more ought law to weed it out. *Ibid. Of Revenge*

6 It was a high speech of Seneca (after the manner of the Stoics), that "The good things which belong to prosperity are to be wished, but the good things that belong to adversity are to be admired." *Ibid. Of Adversity*

7 Prosperity is the blessing of the Old Testament; adversity is the blessing of the New. *Ibid.*

8 Prosperity is not without many fears and distastes; and adversity is not without comforts and hopes. *Ibid.*

9 Prosperity doth best discover vice, but adversity doth best discover virtue. *Ibid.*

10 Virtue is like precious odors—most fragrant when they are incensed or crushed.[4] *Ibid.*

11 He that hath wife and children hath given hostages to fortune; for they are impediments to great enterprises, either of virtue or mischief. *Ibid. Of Marriage and Single Life*

12 Wives are young men's mistresses, companions for middle age, and old men's nurses. *Ibid.*

13 A good name is like a precious ointment; it filleth all around about, and will not easily away; for the odors of ointments are more durable than those of flowers.[5] *Ibid. Of Praise*

14 In charity there is no excess. *Ibid. Of Goodness and Goodness of Nature*

15 If a man be gracious and courteous to strangers, it shows he is a citizen of the world, and that his heart is no island cut off from other lands, but a continent that joins to them.[6] *Ibid.*

16 The desire of power in excess caused the angels to fall; the desire of knowledge in excess caused man to fall.[7] *Ibid.*

17 Money is like muck, not good except it be spread. *Ibid. Of Seditions and Troubles*

18 I had rather believe all the fables in the legends and the Talmud and the Alcoran, than that this universal frame is without a mind. *Ibid. Of Atheism*

19 A little philosophy inclineth man's mind to atheism, but depth in philosophy bringeth men's minds about to religion.[8] *Ibid.*

20 Travel, in the younger sort, is a part of education; in the elder, a part of experience. He that traveleth into a country before he hath some entrance into the language, goeth to school, and not to travel. *Ibid. Of Travel*

21 Princes are like to heavenly bodies, which cause good or evil times, and which have much veneration but no rest.[9] *Ibid. Of Empire*

22 Fortune is like the market, where many times, if you can stay a little, the price will fall. *Ibid. Of Delays*

23 Nothing doth more hurt in a state than that cunning men pass for wise. *Ibid. Of Cunning*

24 Be so true to thyself, as thou be not false to others.[10] *Ibid. Of Wisdom for a Man's Self*

25 It is the nature of extreme self-lovers, as they will set an house on fire, and it were but to roast their eggs. *Ibid.*

26 It is the wisdom of the crocodiles, that shed tears when they would devour.[11] · *Ibid.*

27 He that will not apply new remedies must expect new evils; for time is the greatest innovator. *Ibid. Of Innovations*

28 Cure the disease and kill the patient. *Ibid. Of Friendship*

29 Riches are for spending. *Ibid. Of Expense*

30 There is a wisdom in this beyond the rules of physic. A man's own observation, what he finds good of and what he finds hurt of, is the best physic to preserve health. *Ibid. Of Regimen of Health*

---

[1]First edition, 1597; first complete edition, 1625.

[2]See *John 18:38,* 40:36.

[3]See Lucretius, 90:1.

[4]As aromatic plants bestow / No spicy fragrance while they grow; / But crushed or trodden to the ground, / Diffuse their balmy sweets around.—GOLDSMITH, *The Captivity* [1764], *act I*

The good are better made by ill, / As odors crushed are sweeter still.—SAMUEL ROGERS, *Jacqueline* [1814], *st. 3*

[5]See *Ecclesiastes 7:1,* 24:6.

[6]See *Romans 14:7,* 42:26; Donne, 231:8; and Quarles, 242:5.

[7]Pride still is aiming at the blest abodes; / Men would be angels, angels would be gods. / Aspiring to be gods if angels fell, / Aspiring to be angels men rebel.—POPE, *Essay on Man, epistle I* [1733], *l. 125*

[8]A little skill in antiquity inclines a man to Popery; but depth in that study brings him about again to our religion.—THOMAS FULLER, *The Holy State and the Profane State* [1642], *The True Church Antiquary*

[9]See Shelley, 408:9.

[10]See Shakespeare, 194:1.

[11]See George Chapman, 157:6.

1   Intermingle . . . jest with earnest.[1]
Essays. Of Discourse

2   Nature is often hidden; sometimes overcome; seldom extinguished.   *Ibid. Of Nature in Men*

3   If a man look sharply and attentively, he shall see Fortune; for though she is blind, she is not invisible.[2]
Ibid. Of Fortune

4   Chiefly the mold of a man's fortune is in his own hands.[3]   *Ibid.*

5   There is no excellent beauty that hath not some strangeness in the proportion.   *Ibid. Of Beauty*

6   God Almighty first planted a garden.[4]
Ibid. Of Gardens

7   He that commands the sea is at great liberty, and may take as much and as little of the war as he will.[5]
Ibid. Of the True Greatness of Kingdoms

8   Some books are to be tasted, others to be swallowed, and some few to be chewed and digested.
Ibid. Of Studies

9   Reading maketh a full man, conference a ready man, and writing an exact man.   *Ibid.*

10   Histories make men wise; poets, witty; the mathematics, subtile; natural philosophy, deep; moral, grave; logic and rhetoric, able to contend.
Ibid.

11   The greatest vicissitude of things amongst men is the vicissitude of sects and religions.[6]
Ibid. Of Vicissitude of Things

12   I bequeath my soul to God. . . . My body to be buried obscurely. For my name and memory, I leave it to men's charitable speeches, and to foreign nations, and the next age.   *From his will [1626]*

13   The world's a bubble, and the life of man
Less than a span.[7]
The World [1629]

[1]See Menander, 81:6; Horace, 97:3; and Montaigne, 147:2.
[2]Fortune is painted blind, with a muffler afore her eyes, to signify to you that Fortune is blind.—SHAKESPEARE, *King Henry V*, act III, sc. vi, l. 31
[3]See Sallust, 91:28 and 92:1; Shakespeare, 187:22; Tennyson, 459:9; Henley, 557:10; and Nehru, 677:7.
[4]Gardens were before gardeners, and but some hours after the earth.—THOMAS BROWNE, *The Garden of Cyrus* [1658], *ch. 1*
[5]He that is master of the sea, may, in some sort, be said to be Master of every country; at least such as are bordering on the sea. For he is at liberty to begin and end War, where, when, and on what terms he pleaseth, and extend his conquests even to the Antipodes.— JOSEPH GANDER [fl. c. 1703], *The Glory of Her Sacred Majesty Queen Anne in the Royal Navy* [1703]
  See Themistocles, 62:30; Edmund Waller, 249:27; Washington, 336:17; and Mahan, 541:3.
[6]See Terence, 86:6; and Sterne, 320:5.
[7]Whose life is a bubble, and in length a span.—WILLIAM BROWNE, *Britannia's Pastorals* [1613], *bk. I, song*
  See Sir John Davies, 227:15, and *The New England Primer*, 287:13.

14   Who then to frail mortality shall trust
But limns on water, or but writes in dust.
Ibid.

15   What then remains but that we still should cry
For being born, and, being born, to die?[8]
Ibid.

Sir John Harington
1561–1612

16   Treason doth never prosper: what's the reason?
For if it prosper, none dare call it treason.[9]
Epigrams. Of Treason

17   The readers and the hearers like my books,
But yet some writers cannot them digest;
But what care I? for when I make a feast
I would my guests should praise it, not the cooks.
Ibid. Of Writers Who Carp at Other Men's Books

Robert Southwell
c. 1561–1595

18   Times go by turns, and chances change by course,
From foul to fair, from better hap to worse.
Times Go by Turns [c. 1595], st. 1

19   As I in hoary winter night stood shivering in the snow,
Surprised was I with sudden heat which made my heart to glow;
And lifting up a fearful eye to view what fire was near
A pretty Babe all burning bright did in the air appear.
The Burning Babe [written c. 1595]

20   With this he vanished out of sight, and swiftly shrunk away,
And straight I called unto mind that it was Christmas Day.
Ibid.

Samuel Daniel
c. 1562–1619

21   Care-charmer Sleep, son of the sable Night,
Brother to Death, in silent darkness born.
Sonnets to Delia [1592]

22   Make me to say, when all my griefs are gone,
"Happy the heart that sighed for such a one!"
Ibid. Sonnet: I Must Not Grieve

[8]This line frequently occurs in almost exactly the same shape among the minor poems of the time: "Not to be born, or, being born, to die."—WILLIAM DRUMMOND [1585–1649], *Poems* [1656]
  See Theognis, 59:24; Sophocles, 67:9; Yeats, 598:3; and Auden, 720:5.
[9]See Seneca, 103:12.

1 Let others sing of knights and paladins
In aged accents and untimely words.
Ibid.

2 These are the arks, the trophies, I erect,
That fortify thy name against old age.
Ibid.

3 And for the few that only lend their ear,
That few is all the world.
Musophilus [1599], st. 97

4 This is the thing that I was born to do.
Ibid. st. 100

5 Unless above himself he can
Erect himself, how poor a thing is man!
To the Countess of Cumberland [c. 1600], st. 12

6 Love is a sickness full of woes,
All remedies refusing.
Hymen's Triumph [1615]

Lope de Vega
1562–1635

7 Harmony is pure love, for love is complete agreement.
Fuenteovejuna [c. 1613],[1] act I, l. 381

8 Except for God, the King's our only lord.
Ibid. l. 1701

Michael Drayton
1563–1631

9 Fair stood the wind for France.
The Ballad of Agincourt [1606], st. 1

10 O, when shall Englishmen
With such acts fill a pen,
Or England breed again
Such a King Harry?
Ibid. st. 15

11 Since there's no help, come let us kiss and part—
Nay, I have done: you get no more of me,
And I am glad, yea glad with all my heart,
That thus so cleanly I myself can free.
Shake hands forever, cancel all our vows,
And when we meet at any time again,
Be it not seen in either of our brows
That we one jot of former love retain.
Poems [1619]. Idea

12 The coast was clear.
Nymphidia [1627]

13 Had in him those brave translunary things
That the first poets had.
Said of MARLOWE. To Henry Reynolds, Of Poets and Poesy [1627]

[1] Translated by ANGEL FLORES and MURIEL KITTEL. From *Spanish Drama* [1962].

14 For that fine madness still he did retain
Which rightly should possess a poet's brain.
Ibid.

Galileo Galilei
1564–1642

15 Philosophy is written in this grand book—I mean the universe—which stands continually open to our gaze, but it cannot be understood unless one first learns to comprehend the language and interpret the characters in which it is written. It is written in the language of mathematics, and its characters are triangles, circles, and other geometrical figures, without which it is humanly impossible to understand a single word of it; without these, one is wandering about in a dark labyrinth.[2]
Il Saggiatore [1623][3]

16 But it does move![4]
Attributed. From ABBÉ IRAILH, Querelles littéraires [1761], vol. III, p. 49

17 Facts which at first seem improbable will, even on scant explanation, drop the cloak which has hidden them and stand forth in naked and simple beauty.
Dialogues Concerning Two New Sciences [1638],[5] Day 1

Christopher Marlowe
1564–1593

18 Our swords shall play the orators for us.
Tamburlaine the Great [c. 1587], pt. I, l. 328

19 Accurst be he that first invented war.
Ibid. l. 664

20 Is it not passing brave to be a king,
And ride in triumph through Persepolis?
Ibid. l. 758

21 Nature that framed us of four elements,
Warring within our breasts for regiment,
Doth teach us all to have aspiring minds:
Our souls, whose faculties can comprehend
The wondrous Architecture of the world:
And measure every wandering planet's course,
Still climbing after knowledge infinite,
And always moving as the restless Spheres,
Will us to wear ourselves and never rest,
Until we reach the ripest fruit of all,
That perfect bliss and sole felicity,
The sweet fruition of an earthly crown.
Ibid. l. 869

[2] See Roger Bacon, 124:1.
[3] The Assayer in *The Controversy on the Comets of 1618* [1960], translated by STILLMAN DRAKE and C. D. O'MALLEY.
[4] E pur si muove!
Alleged to have been whispered by him after recanting before the Inquisition his claim that the earth revolved around the sun.
[5] Translated by HENRY CREW and ALFONSO DE SALVIO.

1 Tamburlaine, the Scourge of God, must die.
Tamburlaine the Great, pt. I, l. 4641

2 Come live with me, and be my love;
And we will all the pleasures prove
That valleys, groves, hills, and fields,[1]
Woods or steepy mountain yields.[2]
The Passionate Shepherd to His Love [c. 1589]

3 By shallow rivers, to whose falls
Melodious birds sing madrigals.[3]
Ibid.

4 And I will make thee beds of roses
And a thousand fragrant posies.[3]
Ibid.

5 I count religion but a childish toy,
And hold there is no sin but ignorance.
The Jew of Malta [c. 1589], prologue

6 Infinite riches in a little room.[4]
Ibid. act I, sc. i

7 Excess of wealth is cause of covetousness.
Ibid. ii

8   Now will I show myself to have more of the
serpent than the dove;[5] that is, more knave than fool.
Ibid. II, iii

9 *Friar Barnadine:* Thou hast committed—
Barabas: Fornication—but that was in another
country;
And besides, the wench is dead.
Ibid. IV, i

10 My men, like satyrs grazing on the lawns,
Shall with their goat feet dance the antic hay.
Edward II [1593], act I, sc. i

11 Who ever loved that loved not at first sight?[6]
Hero and Leander [1598]

12 Like untuned golden strings all women are,
Which long time lie untouched, will harshly jar.
Vessels of brass oft handled brightly shine.
Ibid.

13 Live and die in Aristotle's works.
*The Tragical History of Doctor Faustus [1604],
act I, sc. i*

14 Unhappy spirits that fell with Lucifer,
Conspired against our God with Lucifer,
And are forever damned with Lucifer.
Ibid. iii

---

[1] Also given as: Hills and valleys, dales, and fields.
[2] See Ralegh, 152:11, and Donne, 229:10.
[3] To shallow rivers, to whose falls / Melodious birds sing madrigals; / There will we make our peds of roses, / And a thousand fragrant posies.—SHAKESPEARE, *The Merry Wives of Windsor*, act III, sc. i, l. 17
[4] Here lyeth muche rychnesse in lytell space.—JOHN HEYWOOD, *The Foure PP* [1521–1525]
[5] See *Matthew* 10:16, 34:30.
[6] Quoted in SHAKESPEARE, *As You Like It*, act III, sc. v, l. 82. None ever loved but at first sight they loved.—GEORGE CHAPMAN, *The Blind Beggar of Alexandria* [1598]

---

15 Why this is hell, nor am I out of it:
Think'st thou that I who saw the face of God,
And tasted the eternal joys of Heaven,
Am not tormented with ten thousand hells,
In being deprived of everlasting bliss?
Ibid.

16 Hell hath no limits, nor is circumscribed
In one self place; for where we are is hell,
And where hell is there must we ever be.
Ibid. II, i

17   When all the world dissolves,
And every creature shall be purified,
All places shall be hell that is not Heaven.
Ibid.

18 Have not I made blind Homer sing to me?
Ibid. ii

19 Was this the face that launched a thousand ships,
And burnt the topless towers of Ilium?[7]
Sweet Helen, make me immortal with a kiss.
Her lips suck forth my soul;[8] see, where it flies!
Ibid. V, i

20 Oh, thou art fairer than the evening air
Clad in the beauty of a thousand stars.
Ibid.

21   Pray for me! and what noise soever ye hear, come
not unto me, for nothing can rescue me.
Ibid. ii

22 Now hast thou but one bare hour to live,
And then thou must be damned perpetually!
Stand still, you ever-moving spheres of Heaven,
That time may cease, and midnight never come.
Ibid.

23 *O lente, lente currite noctis equi:*[9]
The stars move still, time runs, the clock will
strike,
The Devil will come, and Faustus must be
damned.
O, I'll leap up to my God! Who pulls me down?
See, see where Christ's blood streams in the
firmament!
One drop would save my soul—half a drop: ah,
my Christ!
Ibid.

24 O soul, be changed into little waterdrops,
And fall into the ocean—ne'er to be found.
My God! my God! look not so fierce on me!
Ibid.

25 I'll burn my books!
Ibid.

---

[7] Was this fair face the cause, quoth she, / Why the Grecians sacked Troy?—SHAKESPEARE, *All's Well That Ends Well*, act I, sc. iii, l. 75
[8] Once he drew / With one long kiss my whole soul through / My lips.—TENNYSON, *Fatima* [1833], st. 3
[9] Slowly, slowly run, O horses of the night.
See Ovid, 101:10.

1 Cut is the branch that might have grown full
    straight,
And burned is Apollo's laurel bough,
That sometime grew within this learned man.
Ibid. iii

Matthew Roydon
c. 1564 – c. 1622

2 You knew—who knew not Astrophil?
*The Phoenix Nest [1593]; An Elegy, or Friend's
Passion for His Astrophil (on the death of Sir
Philip Sidney)*

3 A sweet attractive kind of grace,
A full assurance given by looks,
Continual comfort in a face,
The lineaments of Gospel books;
I trow that countenance cannot lie.
Whose thoughts are legible in the eye.
Ibid.

4 Was never eye, did see that face,
Was never ear, did hear that tongue,
Was never mind, did mind his grace,
That ever thought the travel long,
But eyes, and ears, and ev'ry thought,
Were with his sweet perfections caught.
Ibid.

William Shakespeare[1]
1564–1616

5 Hung be the heavens with black, yield day to
    night!
*King Henry the Sixth, Part I [1589–1590], act I,
sc. i, l. 1*

6 Fight till the last gasp.
I, ii, 127

7 Expect Saint Martin's summer, halcyon days.[2]
I, ii, 131

8 Glory is like a circle in the water,
Which never ceaseth to enlarge itself,
Till by broad spreading it disperse to nought.
I, ii, 133

9   Unbidden guests
Are often welcomest when they are gone.
II, ii, 55

10 Between two hawks, which flies the higher pitch;
Between two dogs, which hath the deeper mouth;
Between two blades, which bears the better
    temper;
Between two horses, which doth bear him best;

[1]From the text of W. J. CRAIG, Oxford University Press
[1935]. For the dating and sequence of the plays and poems see
E. K. CHAMBERS, *William Shakespeare* (1930), and JAMES G.
MCMANAWAY, "Recent Studies in Shakespeare's Chronology," *Shakespeare Survey*, III (1950).
[2]See Aristophanes, 73:14.

Between two girls, which hath the merriest eye;
I have perhaps, some shallow spirit of judgment;
But in these nice sharp quillets of the law,
Good faith, I am no wiser than a daw.
II, iv, 12

11 I'll note you in my book of memory.
II, iv, 101

12 Just death, kind umpire of men's miseries.
II, v, 29

13 Chok'd with ambition of the meaner sort.
II, v, 123

14 Delays have dangerous ends.[3]
III, ii, 33

15 Of all base passions, fear is most accurs'd.
V, ii, 18

16 She's beautiful and therefore to be woo'd,
She is a woman, therefore to be won.[4]
V, iii, 78

17 For what is wedlock forced, but a hell,
An age of discord and continual strife?
Whereas the contrary bringeth bliss,
And is a pattern of celestial peace.
V, v, 62

18 'Tis not my speeches that you do mislike,
But 'tis my presence that doth trouble ye.
Rancor will out.
*King Henry the Sixth, Part II [1590–1591], act I,
sc. i, l. 141*

19 Could I come near your beauty with my nails
I'd set my ten commandments in your face.
I, iii, 144

20 Blessed are the peacemakers on earth.[5]
II, i, 34

21 Now, God be prais'd, that to believing souls
Gives light in darkness, comfort in despair!
II, i, 66

22 God defend the right!
II, iii, 55

23 Sometimes hath the brightest day a cloud;
And after summer evermore succeeds
Barren winter, with his wrathful nipping cold:
So cares and joys abound, as seasons fleet.
II, iv, 1

24 Now 'tis the spring, and weeds are
    shallow-rooted;
Suffer them now and they'll o'ergrow the garden.
III, i, 31

25   In thy face I see
The map of honor, truth, and loyalty.
III, i, 202

[3]See Lyly, 155:7.
[4]A similar passage is in *Titus Andronicus*, act II, sc. i, l. 82.
[5]See *Matthew* 5:9, 33:1.

1 What stronger breastplate than a heart untainted!
Thrice is he arm'd that hath his quarrel just,
And he but naked, though lock'd up in steel,
Whose conscience with injustice is corrupted.[1]
King Henry VI, Pt. II, III, ii, 232

2 He dies, and makes no sign.
III, iii, 29

3 Forbear to judge, for we are sinners all.[2]
Close up his eyes, and draw the curtain close;
And let us all to meditation.
III, iii, 31

4 The gaudy, blabbing, and remorseful day
Is crept into the bosom of the sea.
IV, i, 1

5 Small things make base men proud.
IV, i, 106

6 True nobility is exempt from fear.
IV, i, 129

7   I will make it felony to drink small beer.[3]
IV, ii, 75

8   The first thing we do, let's kill all the lawyers.
IV, ii, 86

9   Is not this a lamentable thing, that of the skin of
an innocent lamb should be made parchment? that
parchment, being scribbled o'er, should undo a
man?   *IV, ii, 88*

10   Adam was a gardener.   *IV, ii, 146*

11   Thou hast most traitorously corrupted the youth
of the realm in erecting a grammar-school; and
whereas, before, our forefathers had no other books
but the score and the tally, thou hast caused printing
to be used; and, contrary to the king, his crown, and
dignity, thou hast built a paper-mill.   *IV, vii, 35*

12 Beggars mounted run their horse to death.[4]
*King Henry the Sixth, Part III [1590–1591],
act I, sc. iv, l. 127*

13 O tiger's heart wrapp'd in a woman's hide![5]
I, iv, 137

14 To weep is to make less the depth of grief.
II, i, 85

15 The smallest worm will turn being trodden on.
II, ii, 17

16   Didst thou never hear
That things ill got had ever bad success?
II, ii, 45

17 Thou [Death] setter up and plucker down of
kings.[6]
II, iii, 37

18 And what makes robbers bold but too much
lenity?
II, vi, 22

19 My crown is in my heart, not on my head;
Not deck'd with diamonds and Indian stones,
Nor to be seen: my crown is call'd content;
A crown it is that seldom kings enjoy.[7]
III, i, 62

20   'Tis a happy thing
To be the father unto many sons.
III, ii, 104

21 Like one that stands upon a promontory,
And spies a far-off shore where he would tread,
Wishing his foot were equal with his eye.
III, ii, 135

22   Yield not thy neck
To fortune's yoke, but let thy dauntless mind
Still ride in triumph over all mischance.
III, iii, 16

23 For how can tyrants safely govern home,
Unless abroad they purchase great alliance?
III, iii, 69

24 Having nothing, nothing can he lose.
III, iii, 152

25 Hasty marriage seldom proveth well.
IV, i, 18

26 What fates impose, that men must needs abide;
It boots not to resist both wind and tide.
IV, iii, 57

27 Now join your hands, and with your hands your
hearts.
IV, vi, 39

28 For many men that stumble at the threshold
Are well foretold that danger lurks within.
IV, vii, 11

29 A little fire is quickly trodden out,
Which, being suffer'd, rivers cannot quench.
IV, viii, 7

30   When the lion fawns upon the lamb,
The lamb will never cease to follow him.
IV, viii, 49

31   What is pomp, rule, reign, but earth and
dust?
And, live we how we can, yet die we must.
V, ii, 27

---

[1]See Milton, 253:2 and 257:14.
[2]See *Matthew* 7:1, 34:2.
[3]Doth it not show vilely in me to desire small beer?—*King
Henry IV, Part II, act II, sc. ii, l. 7*
    That questionable superfluity—small beer.—Jerrold,
The Tragedy of the Till
    See *Othello*, 206:9.
[4]Set a beggar on horseback and he will ride a gallop.—
Robert Burton, *Anatomy of Melancholy* [1621–1651], *pt. II,
sec. 2, member 2*
    Set a beggar on horseback, and he'll outride the Devil.—
Henry George Bohn [1796–1884], *Foreign Proverbs, German*
[1855]
[5]See Robert Greene, 157:20.

[6]Proud setter up and puller down of kings. — *King Henry VI,
Part III, act III, sc. iii, l. 157*
[7]See Robert Greene, 157:18 and 157:19.

1 For every cloud engenders not a storm.
> *V, iii, 13*

2 What though the mast be now blown overboard,
The cable broke, the holding anchor lost,
And half our sailors swallow'd in the flood?
Yet lives our pilot still.
> *V, iv, 3*

3 So part we sadly in this troublous world,
To meet with joy in sweet Jerusalem.
> *V, v, 7*

4 Men ne'er spend their fury on a child.
> *V, v, 57*

5 He's sudden if a thing comes in his head.
> *V, v, 86*

6 Suspicion always haunts the guilty mind;
The thief doth fear each bush an officer.
> *V, vi, 11*

7 This word "love," which greybeards call divine.
> *V, vi, 81*

8 Bid me discourse, I will enchant thine ear.
> *Venus and Adonis [1592], l. 145*

9 Love is a spirit all compact of fire,
Not gross to sink, but light, and will aspire.
> *l. 149*

10 "Fondling," she saith, "since I have hemm'd thee
here
Within the circuit of this ivory pale,
I'll be a park, and thou shalt be my deer;
Feed where thou wilt, on mountain, or in dale:
Graze on my lips, and if those hills be dry,
Stray lower, where the pleasant fountains lie."
> *1. 229*

11 O! what a war of looks was then between them.
> *l. 355*

12 Like a red morn, that ever yet betoken'd
Wrack to the seaman, tempest to the field.
> *l. 453*

13 The owl, night's herald.
> *l. 531*

14 Love comforteth like sunshine after rain.
> *l. 799*

15 The text is old, the orator too green.
> *l. 806*

16 For he being dead, with him is beauty slain,
And, beauty dead, black chaos comes again.[1]
> *l. 1019*

17 The grass stoops not, she treads on it so light.
> *l. 1028*

18 Now is the winter of our discontent
Made glorious summer by this sun of York.
> *King Richard the Third [1592–1593], act I,
sc. i, l. 1*

[1]See *Othello*, 206:27.

19 Grim-visag'd war hath smooth'd his wrinkled
front.
> *I, i, 9*

20 He capers nimbly in a lady's chamber
To the lascivious pleasing of a lute.
> *I, i, 12*

21 This weak piping time of peace.
> *I, i, 24*

22 No beast so fierce but knows some touch of pity.
> *I, ii, 71*

23 Look, how my ring encompasseth thy finger,
Even so thy breast encloseth my poor heart;
Wear both of them, for both of them are thine.
> *I, ii, 204*

24 Was ever woman in this humor woo'd?
Was ever woman in this humor won?
> *I, ii, 229*

25   The world is grown so bad
That wrens make prey where eagles dare not
perch.[2]
> *I, iii, 70*

26 The day will come that thou shalt wish for me
To help thee curse this pois'nous bunch-back'd
toad.
> *I, iii, 245*

27 And thus I clothe my naked villany
With odd old ends stol'n forth of holy writ,
And seem a saint when most I play the devil.
> *I, iii, 336*

28 Talkers are no good doers.
> *I, iii, 351*

29 O, I have pass'd a miserable night,
So full of ugly sights, of ghastly dreams,
That, as I am a Christian faithful man,
I would not spend another such a night,
Though 'twere to buy a world of happy days.
> *I, iv, 2*

30 Lord, Lord! methought what pain it was to
drown:
What dreadful noise of water in mine ears!
What sights of ugly death within mine eyes!
Methought I saw a thousand fearful wracks;
A thousand men that fishes gnaw'd upon.
> *I, iv, 21*

31 The kingdom of perpetual night.[3]
> *I, iv, 47*

32 Sorrow breaks seasons and reposing hours,
Makes the night morning, and the noontide night.
> *I, iv, 76*

33 A parlous boy.
> *II, iv, 35*

[2]See Pope, 299:6.
[3]See Catullus, 90:19; Campion, 226:13; Jonson, 232:4; and
Herrick, 241:19.

1 So wise so young, they say, do never live long.[1]
King Richard III, III, i, 79

2 Off with his head![2]
III, iv, 75

3 Lives like a drunken sailor on a mast;
Ready with every nod to tumble down
Into the fatal bowels of the deep.
III, iv, 98

4 I am not in the giving vein today.
IV, ii, 115

5 The sons of Edward sleep in Abraham's bosom.[3]
IV, iii, 38

6 A grievous burden was thy birth to me;
Tetchy and wayward was thy infancy.
IV, iv, 168

7 An honest tale speeds best being plainly told.
IV, iv, 359

8 Harp not on that string.
IV, iv, 365

9 Relenting fool, and shallow changing woman!
IV, iv, 432

10 Is the chair empty? is the sword unsway'd?
Is the king dead? the empire unpossess'd?
IV, iv, 470

11 True hope is swift, and flies with swallow's wings;
Kings it makes gods, and meaner creatures kings.
V, ii, 23

12 The king's name is a tower of strength.
V, iii, 12

13 Give me another horse! bind up my wounds!
V, iii, 178

14 O coward conscience, how dost thou afflict me!
V, iii, 180

15 My conscience hath a thousand several tongues,
And every tongue brings in a several tale,
And every tale condemns me for a villain.
V, iii, 194

16 Conscience is but a word that cowards use,
Devis'd at first to keep the strong in awe.
V, iii, 310

17 A horse! a horse! my kingdom for a horse!
V, iv, 7

18   I have set my life upon a cast,
And I will stand the hazard of the die.
I think there be six Richmonds in the field.
V, iv, 9

19 The pleasing punishment that women bear.
*The Comedy of Errors [1592–1594], act I, sc. i,
l. 46*

20 For we may pity, though not pardon thee.
I, i, 97

21 Why, headstrong liberty is lash'd with woe.
There's nothing situate under heaven's eye
But hath his bound, in earth, in sea, in sky.
II, i, 15

22   Every why hath a wherefore.[4]   *II, ii, 45*

23   There's no time for a man to recover his hair that
grows bald by nature.   *II, ii, 74*

24   What he hath scanted men in hair, he hath given
them in wit.   *II, ii, 83*

25   Small cheer and great welcome makes a merry
feast.   *III, i, 26*

26 There is something in the wind.
III, i, 69

27 We'll pluck a crow together.
III, i, 83

28 For slander lives upon succession,
Forever housed where it gets possession.
III, i, 105

29 Be not thy tongue thy own shame's orator.
III, ii, 10

30 Ill deeds are doubled with an evil word.
III, ii, 20

31 A back-friend, a shoulder-clapper.
IV, ii, 37

32 The venom clamors of a jealous woman
Poison more deadly than a mad dog's tooth.
V, i, 69

33 Unquiet meals make ill digestions.
V, i, 74

34   One Pinch, a hungry lean-fac'd villain,
A mere anatomy, a mountebank,
A threadbare juggler, and a fortune-teller,
A needy, hollow-ey'd, sharp-looking wretch,
A living-dead man.
V, i, 238

35 Beauty itself doth of itself persuade
The eyes of men without an orator.
The Rape of Lucrece [1593–1594], l. 29

36 This silent war of lilies and of roses,
Which Tarquin view'd in her fair face's field.
l. 71

37 One for all, or all for one we gage.
l. 144

38 Who buys a minute's mirth to wail a week?
Or sells eternity to get a toy?
For one sweet grape who will the vine destroy?
l. 213

39 Extreme fear can neither fight nor fly.
l. 230

---

[1] A little too wise, they say, do ne'er live long. — MIDDLETON, *The Phoenix*, act I, sc. i
[2] See Cibber, 291:21, and Carroll, 517:23.
[3] See *Luke* 16:22, 39:2.

[4] For every why he had a wherefore. — SAMUEL BUTLER, *Hudibras*, pt. I [1663], canto 1, l. 132
See *King Henry V*, 185:25.

1 All orators are dumb when beauty pleadeth.
l. 268

2 Time's glory is to calm contending kings,
To unmask falsehood and bring truth to light.
l. 939

3 For greatest scandal waits on greatest state.
l. 1006

4 To see sad sights moves more than hear them told.
l. 1324

5 Cloud-kissing Ilion.
l. 1370

6 Lucrece swears he did her wrong.[1]
l. 1462

7 Sweet mercy is nobility's true badge.
*Titus Andronicus [1593–1594], act I, sc. i,
l. 119*

8 These words are razors to my wounded heart.
I, i, 314

9 He lives in fame that died in virtue's cause.
I, i, 390

10 These dreary dumps.[2]
I, i, 391

11 The eagle suffers little birds to sing,
And is not careful what they mean thereby.
IV, iv, 82

12 Tut! I have done a thousand dreadful things
As willingly as one would kill a fly.
V, i, 141

13   I'll not budge an inch.
*The Taming of the Shrew [1593–1594],
Induction, sc. i, l. 13*

14 And if the boy have not a woman's gift
To rain a shower of commanded tears,
An onion will do well for such a shift.
i, 124

15 No profit grows where is no pleasure ta'en;
In brief, sir, study what you most affect.
Act I, sc. i, l. 39

16   There's small choice in rotten apples.
I, i, 137

17 To seek their fortunes further than at home,
Where small experience grows.
I, ii, 51

18 I come to wive it wealthily in Padua.
I, ii, 75

19   Nothing comes amiss, so money comes withal.
I, ii, 82

20 And do as adversaries do in law,
Strive mightily, but eat and drink as friends.
I, ii, 281

21 I must dance barefoot on her wedding day,
And, for your love to her, lead apes in hell.
II, i, 33

22 Asses are made to bear, and so are you.
II, i, 200

23 Kiss me, Kate, we will be married o' Sunday.
II, i, 318

24 Old fashions please me best.
III, i, 81

25 Who woo'd in haste and means to wed at leisure.[3]
III, ii, 11

26 Such an injury would vex a very saint.
III, ii, 28

27   A little pot and soon hot.[4]   *IV, i, 6*

28 Sits as one new-risen from a dream.
IV, i, 189

29 This is a way to kill a wife with kindness.
IV, i, 211

30 Kindness in women, not their beauteous looks,
Shall win my love.
IV, ii, 41

31 Our purses shall be proud, our garments poor:
For 'tis the mind that makes the body rich;
And as the sun breaks through the darkest clouds,
So honor peereth in the meanest habit.
IV, iii, 173

32 Forward, I pray, since we have come so far,
And be it moon, or sun, or what you please.
An if you please to call it a rush-candle,
Henceforth I vow it shall be so for me.
IV, v, 12

33 He that is giddy thinks the world turns round.
V, ii, 20

34 A woman mov'd is like a fountain troubled,
Muddy, ill-seeming, thick, bereft of beauty.
V, ii, 143

35 Such duty as the subject owes the prince,
Even such a woman oweth to her husband.
V, ii, 156

36 Home-keeping youth have ever homely wits.
*The Two Gentlemen of Verona [1594], act I,
sc. i, l. 2*

37 I have no other but a woman's reason:
I think him so, because I think him so.
I, ii, 23

38 *Julia:* They do not love that do not show their love.

---

[1]Some villain hath done me wrong.—*King Lear, act I, sc. ii, l. 186*

[2]And doleful dumps the mind oppress.—*Romeo and Juliet, act IV, sc. v, l. 130*

[3]See Congreve, 290:34.

[4]He is a little chimney, and heated hot in a moment.—LONGFELLOW, *The Courtship of Miles Standish* [1858]

Lucetta: O! they love least that let men know their
　love.
　　　The Two Gentlemen of Verona, I, ii, 31

1 O! how this spring of love resembleth
The uncertain glory of an April day!
　　　I, iii, 84

2 O jest unseen, inscrutable, invisible,
As a nose on a man's face,[1] or a weathercock on a
　steeple!
　　　II, i, 145

3 He makes sweet music with th' enamell'd stones.
　　　II, vii, 28

4 That man that hath a tongue, I say, is no man,
If with his tongue he cannot win a woman.
　　　III, i, 104

5 Except I be by Silvia in the night,
There is no music in the nightingale.
　　　III, i, 178

6 Much is the force of heaven-bred poesy.
　　　III, ii, 72

7 Who is Silvia? what is she,
That all our swains commend her?
Holy, fair, and wise is she;
The heaven such grace did lend her,
That she might admired be.
　　　IV, ii, 40

8 Alas, how love can trifle with itself!
　　　IV, iv, 190

9 Black men are pearls in beauteous ladies' eyes.
　　　V, ii, 12

10 How use doth breed a habit in a man![2]
　　　V, iv, 1

11 Spite of cormorant devouring Time.
　　　*Love's Labour's Lost [1594–1595], act I, sc. i,
　　　l. 4*

12 Make us heirs of all eternity.
　　　I, i, 7

13 Why, all delights are vain; but that most vain
Which, with pain purchas'd doth inherit pain.
　　　I, i, 72

14 Light seeking light doth light of light beguile.
　　　I, i, 77

15 Study is like the heaven's glorious sun,
That will not be deep-search'd with saucy looks;
Small have continual plodders ever won,
Save base authority from others' books.
These earthly godfathers of heaven's lights
That give a name to every fixed star,
Have no more profit of their shining nights
Than those that walk and wot not what they are.
　　　I, i, 84

[1]See Rabelais, 140:6.
[2]*Custom is almost second nature.*—Plutarch, *Rules for
the Preservation of Health, 18*

16 At Christmas I no more desire a rose
Than wish a snow in May's newfangled mirth;
But like of each thing that in season grows.
　　　I, i, 105

17 And men sit down to that nourishment which is
called supper.
　　　I, i, 237

18 That unlettered small-knowing soul.
　　　I, i, 251

19 A child of our grandmother Eve, a female; or, for
thy more sweet understanding, a woman.
　　　I, i, 263

20 Affliction may one day smile again; and till then,
sit thee down, sorrow!　　　*I, i, 312*

21 Devise, wit; write, pen; for I am for whole
volumes in folio.　　　*I, ii, 194*

22 Beauty is bought by judgment of the eye,
Not utter'd by base sale of chapmen's tongues.
　　　II, i, 15

23 　　A merrier man,
Within the limit of becoming mirth,
I never spent an hour's talk withal.
　　　II, i, 66

24 Your wit's too hot, it speeds too fast, 'twill tire.
　　　II, i, 119

25 Warble, child; make passionate my sense of hearing.　　　*III, i, 1*

26 Remuneration! O! that's the Latin word for three
farthings.　　　*III, i, 143*

27 A very beadle to a humorous sigh.
　　　III, i, 185

28 This wimpled, whining, purblind, wayward boy,
This senior-junior, giant-dwarf, Dan Cupid;
Regent of love-rimes, lord of folded arms,
The anointed sovereign of sighs and groans,
Liege of all loiters and malcontents.
　　　III, i, 189

29 He hath not fed of the dainties that are bred of a
book; he hath not eat paper, as it were; he hath not
drunk ink.　　　*IV, ii, 25*

30 Many can brook the weather that love not the
　wind.
　　　IV, ii, 34

31 You two are book-men.　　　*IV, ii, 35*

32 These are begot in the ventricle of memory, nourished in the womb of pia mater, and delivered upon
the mellowing of occasion.　　　*IV, ii, 70*

33 By heaven, I do love, and it hath taught me to
rime, and to be melancholy.　　　*IV, iii, 13*

34 The heavenly rhetoric of thine eye.
　　　IV, iii, 60

35 For where is any author in the world
Teaches such beauty as a woman's eye?
Learning is but an adjunct to ourself.
　　　IV, iii, 312

1 But love, first learned in a lady's eyes,
Lives not alone immured in the brain.

IV, iii, 327

2 It adds a precious seeing to the eye.

IV, iii, 333

3　　　　As sweet and musical
As bright Apollo's lute,[1] strung with his hair;
And when Love speaks, the voice of all the gods
Makes heaven drowsy with the harmony.

IV, iii, 342

4 From women's eyes this doctrine I derive:
They sparkle still the right Promethean fire;
They are the books, the arts, the academes,
That show, contain, and nourish all the world.

IV, iii, 350

5　He draweth out the thread of his verbosity finer
than the staple of his argument.　*V, i, 18*

6　*Moth:* They have been at a great feast of languages, and stolen the scraps.
　　Costard: O! they have lived long on the almsbasket of words. I marvel thy master hath not eaten thee for a word; for thou art not so long by the head as *honorificabilitudinitatibus:* thou art easier swallowed than a flap-dragon.　*V, i, 39*

7　In the posteriors of this day, which the rude multitude call the afternoon.　*V, i, 96*

8 Taffeta phrases, silken terms precise,
Three-pil'd hyperboles, spruce affectation,
Figures pedantical.

V, ii, 407

9　Let me take you a button-hole lower.

V, ii, 705

10　The naked truth of it is, I have no shirt.

V, ii, 715

11 A jest's prosperity lies in the ear
Of him that hears it, never in the tongue
Of him that makes it.

V, ii, 869

12 When daisies pied and violets blue,
And lady-smocks all silver-white,
And cuckoo-buds of yellow hue
Do paint the meadows with delight,
The cuckoo then, on every tree,
Mocks married men; for thus sings he,
　　Cuckoo;
Cuckoo, cuckoo: O word of fear,
Unpleasing to a married ear!

V, ii, 902

13 When icicles hang by the wall,
And Dick the shepherd blows his nail,
And Tom bears logs into the hall,
And milk comes frozen home in pail,
When blood is nipp'd and ways be foul,
Then nightly sings the staring owl,

[1]See Milton, 253:3.

　　Tu-who;
Tu-whit, tu-who—a merry note,
While greasy Joan doth keel the pot.

V, ii, 920

14 When all aloud the wind doth blow,
And coughing drowns the parson's saw,
And birds sit brooding in the snow,
And Marian's nose looks red and raw,
When roasted crabs hiss in the bowl.

V, ii, 929

15　The words of Mercury are harsh after the songs of Apollo.　*V, ii, 938*

16 For new-made honor doth forget men's names.

King John [1594–1596], act I, sc. i, l. 187

17 Sweet, sweet, sweet poison for the age's tooth.

I, i, 213

18 Bearing their birthrights proudly on their backs,
To make a hazard of new fortunes here.

II, i, 70

19 For courage mounteth with occasion.

II, i, 82

20　　　The hare of whom the proverb goes,
Whose valor plucks dead lions by the beard.[2]

II, i, 137

21 A woman's will.

II, i, 194

22 Saint George, that swing'd the dragon, and e'er since
Sits on his horse back at mine hostess' door.

II, i, 288

23 He is the half part of a blessed man,
Left to be finished by such a she;
And she a fair divided excellence,
Whose fullness of perfection lies in him.

II, i, 437

24 'Zounds! I was never so bethump'd with words
Since I first call'd my brother's father dad.

II, i, 466

25 Mad world! mad kings! mad composition!

II, i, 561

26 That smooth-fac'd gentleman, tickling Commodity,
Commodity, the bias of the world.

II, i, 573

27 I will instruct my sorrows to be proud;
For grief is proud and makes his owner stoop.

III, i, 68

28 Thou wear a lion's hide! doff it for shame,
And hang a calf's-skin on those recreant limbs.

III, i, 128

29 The sun's o'ercast with blood: fair day, adieu!
Which is the side that I must go withal?
I am with both: each army hath a hand;

[2]So hares may pull dead lions by the beard.—KYD, *The Spanish Tragedy* [1594], *act I, sc. ii, l. 172*

And in their rage, I having hold of both,
They whirl asunder and dismember me.
King John, III, i, 326

1 Bell, book, and candle shall not drive me back.
III, iii, 12

2 Look, who comes here! a grave unto a soul.
III, iv, 17

3 Death, death: O, amiable lovely death!
III, iv, 25

4 Grief fills the room up of my absent child,
Lies in his bed, walks up and down with me,
Puts on his pretty looks, repeats his words,
Remembers me of all his gracious parts,
Stuffs out his vacant garments with his form.
III, iv, 93

5 Life is as tedious as a twice-told tale,[1]
Vexing the dull ear of a drowsy man.
III, iv, 108

6 When Fortune means to men most good,
She looks upon them with a threatening eye.[2]
III, iv, 119

7 A scepter snatch'd with an unruly hand
Must be as boisterously maintain'd as gain'd;
And he that stands upon a slippery place
Makes nice of no vile hold to stay him up.
III, iv, 135

8 As quiet as a lamb.
IV, i, 80

9 To gild refined gold, to paint the lily,
To throw a perfume on the violet,
To smooth the ice, or add another hue
Unto the rainbow, or with taper-light
To seek the beauteous eye of heaven to garnish,
Is wasteful and ridiculous excess.
IV, ii, 11

10 And oftentimes excusing of a fault
Doth make the fault the worse by the excuse.[3]
IV, ii, 30

11 We cannot hold mortality's strong hand.
IV, ii, 82

12 There is no sure foundation set on blood,
No certain life achiev'd by others' death.
IV, ii, 104

13 Make haste; the better foot before.[4]
IV, ii, 170

14 Another lean unwash'd artificer.
IV, ii, 201

[1]See Homer, 53:27.
[2]See Publilius Syrus, 99:13.
[3]See Meurier, 144:10, and *A Midsummer-Night's Dream*, 174:11.
[4]'Put forward your best foot!—ROBERT BROWNING, *Respectability* [1855], st. 3

15 How oft the sight of means to do ill deeds
Makes ill deeds done!
IV, ii, 219

16 Heaven take my soul, and England keep my
bones!
IV, iii, 10

17 I am amaz'd, methinks, and lose my way
Among the thorns and dangers of this world.
IV, iii, 140

18 Unthread the rude eye of rebellion,
And welcome home again discarded faith.
V, iv, 11

19 The day shall not be up so soon as I,
To try the fair adventure of tomorrow.
V, v, 21

20   'Tis strange that death should sing.
I am the cygnet to this pale faint swan,
Who chants a doleful hymn to his own death.[5]
V, vii, 20

21 Now my soul hath elbow-room.
V, vii, 28

22   I do not ask you much:
I beg cold comfort.[6]
V, vii, 41

23 This England never did, nor never shall,
Lie at the proud foot of a conqueror.
V, vii, 112

24 Come the three corners of the world in arms,
And we shall shock them. Nought shall make us
rue,
If England to itself do rest but true.
V, vii, 116

25 The purest treasure mortal times afford
Is spotless reputation.
*King Richard the Second [1595], act 1, sc. i,
l. 177*

26 Mine honor is my life; both grow in one;
Take honor from me, and my life is done.
I, i, 182

27 We were not born to sue, but to command.
I, i, 196

28 The daintiest last, to make the end most sweet.
I, iii, 68

29 Truth hath a quiet breast.
I, iii, 96

30 How long a time lies in one little word!
I, iii, 213

31 Things sweet to taste prove in digestion sour.
I, iii, 236

32 Must I not serve a long apprenticehood
To foreign passages, and in the end,

[5]See Plato, 74:21; *The Merchant of Venice*, 181:2; and Anonymous, 777:6.
[6]See *The Tempest*, 224:3, and Gibbons, 708:7.

Having my freedom, boast of nothing else
But that I was a journeyman to grief?

I, iii, 271

1 All places that the eye of heaven visits
Are to a wise man ports and happy havens.
Teach thy necessity to reason thus;
There is no virtue like necessity.[1]
Think not the king did banish thee,
But thou the king.

I, iii, 275

2 For gnarling sorrow hath less power to bite
The man that mocks at it and sets it light.

I, iii, 292

3 O! who can hold a fire in his hand
By thinking on the frosty Caucasus?
Or cloy the hungry edge of appetite
By bare imagination of a feast?
Or wallow naked in December snow
By thinking on fantastic summer's heat?
O, no! the apprehension of the good
Gives but the greater feeling to the worse.

I, iii, 294

4 Where'er I wander, boast of this I can,
Though banish'd, yet a true-born Englishman.[2]

I, iii, 308

5   The tongues of dying men
Enforce attention like deep harmony.

II, i, 5

6 The setting sun, and music at the close,
As the last taste of sweets, is sweetest last,
Writ in remembrance more than things long past.

II, i, 12

7 Report of fashions in proud Italy,
Whose manners still our tardy apish nation
Limps after in base imitation.

II, i, 21

8 For violent fires soon burn out themselves;
Small showers last long, but sudden storms are
   short.

II, i, 34

9 This royal throne of kings, this scepter'd isle,
This earth of majesty, this seat of Mars,
This other Eden, demi-paradise,
This fortress built by Nature for herself
Against infection and the hand of war,
This happy breed of men, this little world,
This precious stone set in the silver sea,
Which serves it in the office of a wall,
Or as a moat defensive to a house,
Against the envy of less happier lands,
This blessed plot, this earth, this realm, this
   England,

This nurse, this teeming womb of royal kings,
Fear'd by their breed and famous by their birth.

II, i, 40

10 England, bound in with the triumphant sea,
Whose rocky shore beats back the envious siege
Of watery Neptune.

II, i, 61

11 That England, that was wont to conquer others,
Hath made a shameful conquest of itself.

II, i, 65

12 The ripest fruit first falls.

II, i, 154

13 Each substance of a grief hath twenty shadows.

II, ii, 14

14 I count myself in nothing else so happy
As in a soul remembering my good friends.

II, iii, 46

15 Evermore thanks, the exchequer of the poor.

II, iii, 65

16 Grace me no grace, nor uncle me no uncle.

II, iii, 87

17 The caterpillars of the commonwealth,
Which I have sworn to weed and pluck away.

II, iii, 166

18 Things past redress are now with me past care.

II, iii, 171

19 I see thy glory like a shooting star
Fall to the base earth from the firmament.

II, iv, 19

20 Eating the bitter bread of banishment.[3]

III, i, 21

21 Not all the water in the rough rude sea
Can wash the balm from an anointed king.

III, ii, 54

22 O! call back yesterday, bid time return.[4]

III, ii, 69

23 The worst is death, and death will have his day.

III, ii, 103

24   Of comfort no man speak:
Let's talk of graves, of worms, and epitaphs;
Make dust our paper, and with rainy eyes
Write sorrow on the bosom of the earth;
Let's choose executors and talk of wills.

III, ii, 144

25 And nothing can we call our own but death,
And that small model of the barren earth
Which serves as paste and cover to our bones.
For God's sake, let us sit upon the ground
And tell sad stories of the death of kings:
How some have been depos'd, some slain in war,
Some haunted by the ghosts they have depos'd,
Some poison'd by their wives, some sleeping
   kill'd;

---

[1]See Quintilian, 105:10.
[2]A stern, a true-born Englishman. —SAMUEL JOHNSON; from
BOSWELL, *Life of Johnson* [1791]
The True-born Englishman [1701]. Title of satire by DEFOE.

[3]See *Isaiah 30:20, 27:3.*
[4]See Thomas Heywood, 233:19.

All murder'd: for within the hollow crown
That rounds the mortal temples of a king
Keeps Death his court.
                King Richard II, III, ii, 152

1 Comes at the last, and with a little pin
Bores through his castle wall, and farewell king!
                III, ii, 169

2   He is come to open
The purple testament of bleeding war.
                III, iii, 93

3   O! that I were as great
As is my grief, or lesser than my name,
Or that I could forget what I have been,
Or not remember what I must be now.
                III, iii, 136

4 I'll give my jewels for a set of beads,
My gorgeous palace for a hermitage,
My gay apparel for an almsman's gown.
                III, iii, 147

5 And my large kingdom for a little grave,
A little little grave, an obscure grave.
                III, iii, 153

6   And there at Venice gave
His body to that pleasant country's earth,
And his pure soul unto his captain Christ,
Under whose colors he had fought so long.
                IV, i, 97

7 Peace shall go sleep with Turks and infidels.
                IV, i, 139

8 So Judas did to Christ: but he, in twelve,
Found truth in all but one; I, in twelve thousand,
    none.
God save the king! Will no man say, amen?
                IV, i, 170

9 Now is this golden crown like a deep well
That owes two buckets filling one another;
The emptier ever dancing in the air,
The other down, unseen and full of water:
That bucket down and full of tears am I,
Drinking my griefs, whilst you mount up on high.
                IV, i, 184

10 You may my glories and my state depose,
But not my griefs; still am I king of those.
                IV, i, 192

11   Some of you with Pilate wash your hands,[1]
Showing an outward pity.
                IV, i, 239

12 A mockery king of snow.
                IV, i, 260

13 As in a theater, the eyes of men,
After a well-grac'd actor leaves the stage,
Are idly bent on him that enters next,
Thinking his prattle to be tedious.
                V, ii, 23

14   How sour sweet music is
When time is broke and no proportion kept!
So is it in the music of men's lives.
                V, v, 42

15 I wasted time, and now doth time waste me;
For now hath time made me his numbering clock:
My thoughts are minutes.
                V, v, 49

16 This music mads me: let it sound no more.
                V, v, 61

17 Mount, mount, my soul! thy seat is up on high,
Whilst my gross flesh sinks downward, here to
    die.
                V, v, 112

18 To live a barren sister all your life,
Chanting faint hymns to the cold fruitless moon.
                *A Midsummer-Night's Dream [1595–1596],
                act I, sc. i, l. 72*

19   For aught that I could ever read,
Could ever hear by tale or history,
The course of true love never did run smooth.
                I, i, 132

20 Swift as a shadow, short as any dream,
Brief as the lightning in the collied night,
That, in a spleen, unfolds both heaven and earth,
And ere a man hath power to say, "Behold!"
The jaws of darkness do devour it up:
So quick bright things come to confusion.
                I, i, 144

21 Love looks not with the eyes, but with the mind,
And therefore is wing'd Cupid painted blind.[2]
                I, i, 234

22   The most lamentable comedy, and most cruel
death of Pyramus and Thisby.   *I, ii, 11*

23   Masters, spread yourselves.   *I, ii, 16*

24   This is Ercles' vein, a tyrant's vein.   *I, ii, 43*

25   I'll speak in a monstrous little voice.
                I, ii, 55

26   I am slow of study.   *I, ii, 70*

27   That would hang us, every mother's son.
                I, ii, 81

28   I will aggravate my voice so that I will roar you
as gently as any sucking dove; I will roar you as
'twere any nightingale.   *I, ii, 85*

29   A proper man, as one shall see in a summer's day;
a most lovely, gentleman-like man.   *I, ii, 89*

30 Over hill, over dale,[3]
Thorough bush, thorough brier,

---

[1]See *Matthew* 27:24, 37:7.

[2]I have heard of reasons manifold / Why Love must needs be
blind, / But this the best of all I hold — / His eyes are in his
mind. — COLERIDGE, *Reason for Love's Blindness* [1828]
    See Chaucer, 131:20, and *The Merchant of Venice*, 180:20.
[3]See Gruber, 636:15.

Over park, over pale,
Thorough flood, thorough fire.

II, i, 2

1 I must go seek some dew drops here,
And hang a pearl in every cowslip's ear.

II, i, 14

2 I am that merry wanderer of the night.
I jest to Oberon, and make him smile
When I a fat and bean-fed horse beguile,
Neighing in likeness of a filly foal:
And sometimes lurk I in a gossip's bowl,
In very likeness of a roasted crab.

II, i, 43

3 Ill met by moonlight, proud Titania.

II, i, 60

4 These are the forgeries of jealousy.

II, i, 81

5 Since once I sat upon a promontory,
And heard a mermaid on a dolphin's back
Uttering such dulcet and harmonious breath,
That the rude sea grew civil at her song,
And certain stars shot madly from their spheres
To hear the sea-maid's music.

II, i, 149

6 And the imperial votaress passed on,
In maiden meditation, fancy-free.
Yet mark'd I where the bolt of Cupid fell:
It fell upon a little western flower,
Before milk-white, now purple with love's wound,
And maidens call it, Love-in-idleness.

II, i, 163

7 I'll put a girdle round about the earth
In forty minutes.[1]

II, i, 175

8 For you in my respect are all the world:
Then how can it be said I am alone,
When all the world is here to look on me?

II, i, 224

9 I know a bank whereon the wild thyme blows,
Where oxlips and the nodding violet grows
Quite over-canopied with luscious woodbine,
With sweet musk-roses, and with eglantine:
There sleeps Titania some time of the night,
Lull'd in these flowers with dances and delight;
And there the snake throws her enamell'd skin,
Weed wide enough to wrap a fairy in.

II, i, 249

10 Some to kill cankers in the musk-rose buds,
Some war with rere-mice for their leathern wings,
To make my small elves coats.

II, ii, 3

11 The clamorous owl, that nightly hoots, and
  wonders
At our quaint spirits.

II, ii, 6

[1]See George Chapman, 157:8.

12 You spotted snakes with double tongue,
Thorny hedge-hogs, be not seen;
Newts, and blind-worms, do no wrong;
Come not near our fairy queen.

II, ii, 9

13 Night and silence! who is here?
Weeds of Athens he doth wear.

II, ii, 70

14 As a surfeit of the sweetest things
The deepest loathing to the stomach brings.[2]

II, ii, 137

15 To bring in—God shield us!—a lion among ladies, is a most dreadful thing; for there is not a more
fearful wild-fowl than your lion living.

III, i, 32

16 A calendar, a calendar! look in the almanack; find
out moonshine.

III, i, 55

17 Bless thee, Bottom! bless thee! thou art translated.

III, i, 124

18 Lord, what fools these mortals be![3]

III, ii, 115

19   So we grew together,
Like to a double cherry, seeming parted,
But yet an union in partition;
Two lovely berries molded on one stem.

III, ii, 208

20 Though she be but little, she is fierce.

III, ii, 325

21 I have a reasonable good ear in music: let us have
the tongs and the bones.

IV, i, 32

22 Truly, a peck of provender: I could munch your
good dry oats. Methinks I have a great desire to a
bottle of hay: good hay, sweet hay, hath no fellow.

IV, i, 36

23 I have an exposition of sleep come upon me.

IV, i, 44

24 My Oberon! what visions have I seen!
Methought I was enamor'd of an ass.

IV, i, 82

25   I never heard
So musical a discord, such sweet thunder.

IV, i, 123

26 I have had a dream, past the wit of man to say
what dream it was.

IV, i, 211

27 The eye of man hath not heard, the ear of man
hath not seen,[4] man's hand is not able to taste, his
tongue to conceive, nor his heart to report, what my
dream was.

IV, i, 218

28 Eat no onions nor garlic, for we are to utter sweet
breath.

IV, ii, 44

[2]See *King Henry IV, Part I*, 178:11.
[3]See Seneca, 102:18.
[4]See *I Corinthians 2:9*, 42:30.

1 The lunatic, the lover, and the poet,
Are of imagination all compact:
One sees more devils than vast hell can hold,
That is, the madman; the lover, all as frantic,
Sees Helen's beauty in a brow of Egypt:
The poet's eye, in a fine frenzy rolling,
Doth glance from heaven to earth, from earth to
    heaven;
And, as imagination bodies forth
The forms of things unknown, the poet's pen
Turns them to shapes, and gives to airy nothing
A local habitation and a name.
Such tricks hath strong imagination,
That, if it would but apprehend some joy,
It comprehends some bringer of that joy;
Or in the night, imagining some fear,
How easy is a bush suppos'd a bear!
        A Midsummer-Night's Dream, V, i, 7

2 But all the story of the night told over,
And all their minds transfigur'd so together,
More witnesseth than fancy's images,
And grows to something of great constancy,
But, howsoever, strange and admirable.
                    V, i, 23

3 Very tragical mirth.
                    V, i, 57

4 The true beginning of our end.[1]
                    V, i, 111

5 The best in this kind are but shadows.
                    V, i, 215

6 A very gentle beast, and of a good conscience.
                    V, i, 232

7 All that I have to say, is, to tell you that the
lanthorn is the moon; I, the man in the moon; this
thorn-bush, my thorn-bush; and this dog, my dog.
                    V, i, 263

8 Well roared, Lion.   *V, i, 272*

9 This passion, and the death of a dear friend,
would go near to make a man look sad.
                    V, i, 295

10 With the help of a surgeon, he might yet recover,
and prove an ass.   *V, i, 318*

11 No epilogue, I pray you, for your play needs no
excuse. Never excuse.[2]   *V, i, 363*

12 The iron tongue of midnight hath told twelve;
Lovers, to bed; 'tis almost fairy time.
                    V, i, 372

13 If we shadows have offended,
Think but this, and all is mended,
That you have but slumber'd here
While these visions did appear.
                    V, ii, 54

14 A pair of star-cross'd lovers.
    Romeo and Juliet [1595–1596], prologue, l. 6

15 Saint-seducing gold.
                  Act I, sc. i, l. 220

16 One fire burns out another's burning,[3]
One pain is lessen'd by another's anguish.
                    I, ii, 47

17 I will make thee think thy swan a crow.
                    I, ii, 92

18 For I am proverb'd with a grandsire phrase.
                    I, iv, 37

19 We burn daylight.
                    I, iv, 43

20 O! then, I see, Queen Mab hath been with
    you! . . .
She is the fairies' midwife, and she comes
In shape no bigger than an agate-stone
On the forefinger of an alderman,
Drawn with a team of little atomies
Athwart men's noses as they lie asleep.
                    I, iv, 53

21 True, I talk of dreams,
Which are the children of an idle brain,
Begot of nothing but vain fantasy.
                    I, iv, 97

22 For you and I are past our dancing days.[4]
                    I, v, 35

23 It seems she hangs upon the cheek of night
Like a rich jewel in an Ethiop's ear;
Beauty too rich for use, for earth too dear!
                    I, v, 49

24 My only love sprung from my only hate!
Too early seen unknown, and known too late!
                    I, v, 142

25 Young Adam Cupid, he that shot so trim
When King Cophetua lov'd the beggarmaid.[5]
                    II, i, 13

26 He jests at scars, that never felt a wound.
But, soft! what light through yonder window
    breaks?
It is the east, and Juliet is the sun!
                    II, ii, 1

27 She speaks, yet she says nothing.
                    II, ii, 12

28 See! how she leans her cheek upon her hand:
O! that I were a glove upon that hand,
That I might touch that cheek.
                    II, ii, 23

---

[1] I see the beginning of my end.—MASSINGER, *The Virgin Martyr* [1622], *act III, sc. iii*
[2] See Meurier, 144:10, and *King John*, 170:10.
[3] See George Chapman, 157:7.
[4] My dancing days are done.—BEAUMONT AND FLETCHER, *The Scornful Lady* [1616], *act V, sc. iii*
[5] See Tennyson, 456:5, and Anonymous, 776:13.

1 O Romeo, Romeo! wherefore art thou Romeo?[1]
Deny thy father, and refuse thy name;
Or, if thou wilt not, be but sworn my love,
And I'll no longer be a Capulet.

II, ii, 33

2 What's in a name? that which we call a rose
By any other name would smell as sweet.

II, ii, 43

3 For stony limits cannot hold love out.

II, ii, 67

4   At lovers' perjuries,
They say, Jove laughs.[2]

II, ii, 92

5 In truth, fair Montague, I am too fond.

II, ii, 98

6   I'll prove more true
Than those that have more cunning to be strange.

II, ii, 100

7 *Romeo:* Lady, by yonder blessed moon I swear
That tips with silver all these fruit-tree tops—
Juliet: O! swear not by the moon, the inconstant
moon,
That monthly changes in her circled orb,
Lest that thy love prove likewise variable.

II, ii, 107

8   Do not swear at all;
Or, if thou wilt, swear by thy gracious self,
Which is the god of my idolatry.

II, ii, 112

9 It is too rash, too unadvis'd, too sudden;
Too like the lightning, which doth cease to be
Ere one can say it lightens.

II, ii, 118

10 This bud of love, by summer's ripening breath,
May prove a beauteous flower when next we
meet.

II, ii, 121

11 Love goes toward love, as schoolboys from their
books;
But love from love, toward school with heavy
looks.

II, ii, 156

12   O! for a falconer's voice,
To lure this tassel-gentle back again.

II, ii, 158

13 How silver-sweet sound lovers' tongues by night,
Like softest music to attending ears!

II, ii, 165

14   I would have thee gone;
And yet no further than a wanton's bird,
Who lets it hop a little from her hand,
Like a poor prisoner in his twisted gyves,
And with a silk thread plucks it back again,
So loving-jealous of his liberty.

II, ii, 176

15 Good night, good night! parting is such sweet
sorrow,
That I shall say good night till it be morrow.

II, ii, 184

16 Virtue itself turns vice, being misapplied;
And vice sometime's by action dignified.

II, iii, 21

17 Care keeps his watch in every old man's eye,
And where care lodges, sleep will never lie.

II, iii, 35

18 Wisely and slow; they stumble that run fast.[3]

II, iii, 94

19   One, two, and the third in your bosom.

II, iv, 24

20   O flesh, flesh, how art thou fishified!

II, iv, 41

21   The very pink of courtesy.[4]   *II, iv, 63*

22   A gentleman, nurse, that loves to hear himself
talk, and will speak more in a minute than he will
stand to in a month.   *II, iv, 156*

23 These violent delights have violent ends.

II, vi, 9

24 Therefore love moderately; long love doth so;
Too swift arrives as tardy as too slow.

II, vi, 14

25   Thy head is as full of quarrels as an egg is full of
meat.[5]   *III, i, 23*

26   A word and a blow.[6]   *III, i, 44*

27   No, 'tis not so deep as a well, nor so wide as a
church door; but 'tis enough, 'twill serve: ask for me
tomorrow, and you shall find me a grave man.

III, i, 101

28   A plague o' both your houses!
They have made worms' meat of me.

III, i, 112

29 O! I am Fortune's fool.

III, i, 142

30 Gallop apace, you fiery-footed steeds,
Towards Phoebus' lodging.

III, ii, 1

---

[1]*Huncamunca:* O Tom Thumb! Tom Thumb! wherefore art thou Tom Thumb?—FIELDING, *Tom Thumb* [1730], act II, sc. iii

[2]And Jove but laughs at lovers' perjury.—DRYDEN, *Palamon and Arcite* [1680], bk. II, l. 758, and *Amphitryon* [1690], act I, sc. ii

See Tibullus, 101:5.

[3]See Chaucer, 128:23.

[4]See Cervantes, 150:33.

[5]It's as full of good-nature as an egg's full of meat. —RICHARD BRINSLEY SHERIDAN, *A Trip to Scarborough* [1777], act III, sc. iv

[6]Word and a blow.—BUNYAN, *The Pilgrim's Progress* [1678], pt. I

1   When he shall die,
Take him and cut him out in little stars,
And he will make the face of heaven so fine
That all the world will be in love with night,
And pay no worship to the garish sun.
                              Romeo and Juliet, III, ii, 21

2   He was not born to shame:
Upon his brow shame is asham'd to sit.
                              III, ii, 91

3 Adversity's sweet milk, philosophy.
                              III, iii, 54

4   Hang up philosophy!
Unless philosophy can make a Juliet.
                              III, iii, 56

5 The lark, the herald of the morn.
                              III, v, 6

6 Night's candles are burnt out, and jocund day
Stands tiptoe on the misty mountaintops.
                              III, v, 9

7 Thank me no thankings, nor proud me no prouds.
                              III, v, 153

8 Is there no pity sitting in the clouds,
That sees into the bottom of my grief?
                              III, v, 198

9 Past hope, past cure, past help!
                              IV, i, 45

10   'Tis an ill cook that cannot lick his own fingers.
                              IV, ii, 6

11 *Apothecary:* My poverty, but not my will,
     consents.
Romeo: I pay thy poverty, and not thy will.
                              V, i, 75

12   The strength
Of twenty men.
                              V, i, 78

13 The time and my intents are savage-wild,
More fierce and more inexorable far
Than empty tigers or the roaring sea.
                              V, iii, 39

14 Tempt not a desperate man.
                              V, iii, 59

15 One writ with me in sour misfortune's book.
                              V, iii, 82

16 How oft when men are at the point of death
Have they been merry!
                              V, iii, 88

17   Beauty's ensign yet
Is crimson in thy lips and in thy cheeks,
And death's pale flag is not advanced there.
                              V, iii, 94

18   O! here
Will I set up my everlasting rest,
And shake the yoke of inauspicious stars

From this world-wearied flesh. Eyes, look your
     last!
Arms, take your last embrace!
                              V, iii, 109

19   O true apothecary!
Thy drugs are quick.
                              V, iii, 119

20 See what a scourge is laid upon your hate,
That heaven finds means to kill your joys with
     love.
                              V, iii, 292

21 For never was a story of more woe
Than this of Juliet and her Romeo.
                              V, iii, 309

22 So shaken as we are, so wan with care.
     *King Henry the Fourth, Part I [1596–1597], act
     I, sc. i, l. 1*

23   In those holy fields
Over whose acres walk'd those blessed feet
Which fourteen hundred years ago were nail'd
For our advantage on the bitter cross.
                              I, i, 24

24   Unless hours were cups of sack, and minutes capons, and clocks the tongues of bawds, and dials the
signs of leaping houses, and the blessed sun himself
a fair hot wench in flame-color'd taffeta, I see no
reason why thou shouldst be so superfluous to demand the time of the day.   *I, ii, 7*

25   Diana's foresters, gentlemen of the shade, minions of the moon.   *I, ii, 29*

26   A purse of gold most resolutely snatched on
Monday night and most dissolutely spent on Tuesday morning.   *I, ii, 38*

27   Thy quips and thy quiddities.   *I, ii, 51*

28   So far as my coin would stretch; and where it
would not, I have used my credit.   *I, ii, 61*

29   Old father antick the law.   *I, ii, 69*

30   I am as melancholy as a gib cat, or a lugged bear.
                              I, ii, 82

31   I would to God thou and I knew where a commodity of good names were to be bought.
                              I, ii, 92

32   O! thou hast damnable iteration, and art indeed
able to corrupt a saint.   *I, ii, 101*

33   Now am I, if a man should speak truly, little
better than one of the wicked.   *I, ii, 105*

34   'Tis my vocation, Hal; 'tis no sin for a man to
labor in his vocation.   *I, ii, 116*

35   There's neither honesty, manhood, nor good fellowship in thee.   *I, ii, 154*

36   Well then, once in my days I'll be a madcap.
                              I, ii, 158

37 I know you all, and will a while uphold
The unyok'd humor of your idleness:

Yet herein will I imitate the sun,
Who doth permit the base contagious clouds
To smother up his beauty from the world,
That when he please again to be himself,
Being wanted, he may be more wonder'd at,
By breaking through the foul and ugly mists
Of vapors that did seem to strangle him.
If all the year were playing holidays,
To sport would be as tedious as to work.

I, ii, 217

1 You tread upon my patience.

I, iii, 4

2 Came there a certain lord, neat, and trimly
　　dress'd,
Fresh as a bridegroom; and his chin new-reap'd,
Show'd like a stubble-land at harvest-home:
He was perfumed like a milliner,
And 'twixt his finger and his thumb he held
A pouncet-box, which ever and anon
He gave his nose and took 't away again.

I, iii, 33

3 And as the soldiers bore dead bodies by,
He call'd them untaught knaves, unmannerly,
To bring a slovenly unhandsome corpse
Betwixt the wind and his nobility.

I, iii, 42

4 So pester'd with a popinjay.

I, iii, 50

5 God save the mark!

I, iii, 56

6 To put down Richard, that sweet lovely rose,
And plant this thorn, this canker, Bolingbroke.

I, iii, 176

7 Or sink or swim.

I, iii, 194

8 O! the blood more stirs
To rouse a lion than to start a hare!

I, iii, 197

9 By heaven methinks it were an easy leap
To pluck bright honor from the pale-fac'd moon,
Or dive into the bottom of the deep,
Where fathom-line could never touch the ground,
And pluck up drowned honor by the locks.

I, iii, 201

10 Why, what a candy deal of courtesy
This fawning greyhound then did proffer me!

I, iii, 251

11 I know a trick worth two of that. *II, i, 40*

12 If the rascal have not given me medicines to make
me love him, I'll be hanged. *II, ii, 20*

13 I'll starve ere I'll rob a foot further.

II, ii, 24

14 It would be argument for a week, laughter for a
month, and a good jest forever. *II, ii, 104*

15 Falstaff sweats to death
And lards the lean earth as he walks along.

II, ii, 119

16 Out of this nettle, danger, we pluck this flower,
safety. *II, iii, 11*

17 I could brain him with his lady's fan.

II, iii, 26

18 Constant you are,
But yet a woman: and for secrecy,
No lady closer; for I well believe
Thou wilt not utter what thou dost not know;
And so far will I trust thee, gentle Kate.

II, iii, 113

19 A Corinthian, a lad of mettle, a good boy.

II, iv, 13

20 I am not yet of Percy's mind, the Hotspur of the
North; he that kills me some six or seven dozen of
Scots at a breakfast, washes his hands, and says to
his wife, "Fie upon this quiet life! I want work."

II, iv, 116

21 A plague of all cowards, I say. *II, iv, 129*

22 There live not three good men unhanged in England, and one of them is fat and grows old.

II, iv, 146

23 You care not who sees your back: call you that
backing of your friends? A plague upon such backing! *II, iv, 168*

24 I have peppered two of them. . . . I tell thee
what, Hal, if I tell thee a lie, spit in my face, call me
horse. *II, iv, 216*

25 Give you a reason on compulsion! if reasons were
as plenty as blackberries, I would give no man a
reason upon compulsion, I. *II, iv, 267*

26 Mark now, how a plain tale shall put you down.

II, iv, 285

27 What doth gravity out of his bed at midnight?

II, iv, 328

28 A plague of sighing and grief! it blows a man up
like a bladder. *II, iv, 370*

29 I must speak in passion, and I will do it in King
Cambyses' vein. *II, iv, 429*

30 That reverend vice, that gray iniquity, that father
ruffian, that vanity in years. *II, iv, 505*

31 If sack and sugar be a fault, God help the wicked!
If to be old and merry be a sin, then many an old
host that I know is damned: if to be fat be to be
hated, then Pharaoh's lean kine are to be loved.

II, iv, 524

32 Banish plump Jack, and banish all the world.

II, iv, 534

33 Play out the play. *II, iv, 539*

34 O, monstrous! but one half-penny-worth of
bread to this intolerable deal of sack!

II, iv, 597

1 Diseased nature oftentimes breaks forth
In strange eruptions.
King Henry IV, Pt. I, III, i, 27

2 I am not in the roll of common men.
III, i, 43

3 *Glendower:* I can call spirits from the vasty deep.
Hotspur: Why, so can I, or so can any man;
But will they come when you do call for them?
III, i, 53

4 I had rather be a kitten and cry mew,
Than one of these same meter ballad-mongers.
III, i, 128

5 Mincing poetry:
'Tis like the forc'd gait of a shuffling nag.
III, i, 133

6 But in the way of bargain, mark you me,
I'll cavil on the ninth part of a hair.
III, i, 138

7 A deal of skimble-skamble stuff.
III, i, 153

8 I understand thy kisses and thou mine,
And that's a feeling disputation.
III, i, 204

9 *Lady Percy:* . . . Lie still, ye thief, and hear the
lady sing in Welsh.
Hotspur: I had rather hear Lady, my brach, howl
in Irish. *III, i, 238*

10 A good mouth-filling oath.
III, i, 258

11 They surfeited with honey and began
To loathe the taste of sweetness, whereof a little
More than a little is by much too much.[1]
III, ii, 71

12 He was but as the cuckoo is in June,
Heard, not regarded.
III, ii, 75

13 My near'st and dearest enemy.[2]
III, ii, 123

14 The end of life cancels all bands.
III, ii, 157

15 An I have not forgotten what the inside of a
church is made of, I am a peppercorn, a brewer's
horse. *III, iii, 8*

16 Company, villanous company, hath been the
spoil of me. *III, iii, 10*

17 I have more flesh than another man, and therefore more frailty. *III, iii, 187*

18 The very life-blood of our enterprise.
IV, i, 28

19 Were it good
To set the exact wealth of all our states
All at one cast? to set so rich a main
On the nice hazard of one doubtful hour?
IV, i, 45

20 Baited like eagles having lately bath'd . . .
As full of spirit as the month of May,
And gorgeous as the sun at midsummer.
IV, i, 99

21 I saw young Harry, with his beaver on.
IV, i, 104

22 To turn and wind a fiery Pegasus
And witch the world with noble horsemanship.
IV, i, 109

23 Worse than the sun in March
This praise doth nourish agues.
IV, i, 111

24 Doomsday is near; die all, die merrily.
IV, i, 134

25 The cankers of a calm world and a long peace.
IV, ii, 32

26 Tut, tut, good enough to toss; food for powder,
food for powder; they'll fill a pit as well as better.
IV, ii, 72

27 To the latter end of a fray and the beginning of a
feast
Fits a dull fighter and a keen guest.
IV, ii, 86

28 Greatness knows itself.
IV, iii, 74

29 I could be well content
To entertain the lag-end of my life
With quiet hours.
V, i, 23

30 Rebellion lay in his way, and he found it.
V, i, 28

31 Never yet did insurrection want
Such water-colors to impaint his cause.
V, i, 79

32 I would it were bed-time, Hal, and all well.
V, i, 126

33 Honor pricks me on. Yea, but how if honor prick
me off when I come on? how then? Can honor set to
a leg? No. Or an arm? No. Or take away the grief of
a wound? No. Honor hath no skill in surgery then?
No. What is honor? a word. What is that word,
honor? Air. A trim reckoning! Who hath it? he that
died o' Wednesday. Doth he feel it? No. Doth he
hear it? No. It is insensible then? Yea, to the dead.
But will it not live with the living? No. Why? Detraction will not suffer it. Therefore I'll none of it: honor
is a mere scutcheon; and so ends my catechism.
V, i, 131

---

[1]See *A Midsummer-Night's Dream*, 173:14.
[2]See *Hamlet*, 193:14.

1 Suspicion all our lives shall be stuck full of eyes;
  For treason is but trusted like the fox.
  V, ii, 8

2 Let me tell the world.[1]
  V, ii, 65

3   The time of life is short;
  To spend that shortness basely were too long.
  V, ii, 81

4 Two stars keep not their motion in one sphere.
  V, iv, 65

5 But thought's the slave of life, and life time's fool;
  And time, that takes survey of all the world,
  Must have a stop. O! I could prophesy,
  But that the earthy and cold hand of death
  Lies on my tongue.
  V, iv, 81

6   This earth, that bears thee dead,
  Bears not alive so stout a gentleman.
  V, iv, 92

7 Thy ignominy sleep with thee in the grave,
  But not remember'd in thy epitaph!
  V, iv, 100

8 I could have better spar'd a better man.
  V, iv, 104

9   The better part of valor is discretion.[2]
  V, iv, 120

10   Full bravely hast thou flesh'd
  Thy maiden sword.
  V, iv, 132

11   Lord, Lord, how this world is given to lying!
  V, iv, 148

12   I'll purge, and leave sack, and live cleanly.
  V, iv, 168

13 Your mind is tossing on the ocean.
  The Merchant of Venice [1596–1597], *act I,
  sc. i, l. 8*

14 My ventures are not in one bottom trusted,
  Nor to one place.
  I, i, 42

15 Nature hath fram'd strange fellows in her time.
  I, i, 51

16 You have too much respect upon the world:
  They lose it that do buy it with much care.
  I, i, 74

[1]I'll tell the world.—*Measure for Measure, act II, sc. iv, l. 154*
  Ay, tell the world!—ROBERT BROWNING, *Paracelsus* [1835], *pt. II*

[2]It showed discretion the best part of valor.—BEAUMONT AND FLETCHER, *A King and No King* [1619], *act II, sc. iii*

17 I hold the world but as the world, Gratiano;
  A stage where every man must play a part,[3]
  And mine a sad one.
  I, i, 77

18 Why should a man, whose blood is warm within,
  Sit like his grandsire cut in alabaster?
  I, i, 83

19 There are a sort of men whose visages
  Do cream and mantle like a standing pond.
  I, i, 88

20   I am Sir Oracle,
  And when I ope my lips let no dog bark!
  I, i, 93

21   I do know of these,
  That therefore only are reputed wise
  For saying nothing.
  I, i, 95

22 Fish not, with this melancholy bait,
  For this fool-gudgeon, this opinion.
  I, i, 101

23   Gratiano speaks an infinite deal of nothing, more than any man in all Venice. His reasons are as two grains of wheat hid in two bushels of chaff: you shall seek all day ere you find them, and, when you have them, they are not worth the search.   *I, i, 114*

24 In my school-days, when I had lost one shaft,
  I shot his fellow of the selfsame flight
  The selfsame way with more advised watch,
  To find the other forth, and by adventuring both,
  I oft found both.
  I, i, 141

25   They are as sick that surfeit with too much as they that starve with nothing.   *I, ii, 5*

26   Superfluity comes sooner by white hairs, but competency lives longer.   *I, ii, 9*

27   If to do were as easy as to know what were good to do, chapels had been churches, and poor men's cottages princes' palaces.   *I, ii, 13*

28   The brain may devise laws for the blood, but a hot temper leaps o'er a cold decree.   *I, ii, 19*

29   He doth nothing but talk of his horse.   *I, ii, 43*

30   I fear he will prove the weeping philosopher when he grows old, being so full of unmannerly sadness in his youth.   *I, ii, 51*

31   God made him, and therefore let him pass for a man.   *I, ii, 59*

32   When he is best, he is a little worse than a man, and when he is worst, he is little better than a beast.
  I, ii, 93

33   I dote on his very absence.   *I, ii, 118*

[3]See *As You Like It*, 191:3.

1   Ships are but boards, sailors but men: there be land-rats and water-rats, land-thieves and water-thieves.   *The Merchant of Venice, I, iii, 22*

2   Yes, to smell pork; to eat of the habitation which your prophet the Nazarite[1] conjured the devil into. I will buy with you, sell with you, talk with you, walk with you, and so following; but I will not eat with you, drink with you, nor pray with you. What news on the Rialto?   *I, iii, 34*

3   How like a fawning publican he looks!
I hate him for he is a Christian.
    I, iii, 42

4   If I can catch him once upon the hip,
I will feed fat the ancient grudge I bear him.
    I, iii, 47

5   Cursed be my tribe,
If I forgive him!
    I, iii, 52

6   The devil can cite Scripture for his purpose.
    I, iii, 99

7   A goodly apple rotten at the heart.
O, what a goodly outside falsehood hath!
    I, iii, 102

8   For sufferance is the badge of all our tribe.
You call me misbeliever, cut-throat dog,
And spet upon my Jewish gaberdine.
    I, iii, 111

9   Shall I bend low, and in a bondman's key,
With bated breath, and whispering humbleness,
Say this.
    I, iii, 124

10   I'll seal to such a bond,
And say there is much kindness in the Jew.
    I, iii, 153

11   O father Abram! what these Christians are,
Whose own hard dealing teaches them suspect
The thoughts of others.
    I, iii, 161

12   I like not fair terms and a villain's mind.
    I, iii, 180

13   Mislike me not for my complexion,
The shadow'd livery of the burnish'd sun.
    II, i, 1

14   O heavens! this is my true-begotten father.
    II, ii, 36

15   An honest, exceeding poor man.   *II, ii, 54*

16   The very staff of my age, my very prop.
    II, ii, 71

17   It is a wise father that knows his own child.
    II, ii, 83

18   And the vile squealing of the wry-neck'd fife.
    II, v, 30

19   Who riseth from a feast
With that keen appetite that he sits down?
    II, vi, 8

20   But love is blind,[2] and lovers cannot see
The pretty follies that themselves commit.
    II, vi, 36

21   Must I hold a candle to my shames?
    II, vi, 41

22   Men that hazard all
Do it in hope of fair advantages:
A golden mind stoops not to shows of dross.
    II, vii, 18

23   Young in limbs, in judgment old.
    II, vii, 71

24   My daughter! O my ducats! O my daughter!
Fled with a Christian! O my Christian ducats!
Justice! the law! my ducats, and my daughter!
A sealed bag, two sealed bags of ducats,
Of double ducats, stol'n from me by my daughter!
    II, viii, 15

25   The fool multitude, that choose by show.
    II, ix, 26

26   I will not jump with common spirits
And rank me with the barbarous multitude.
    II, ix, 32

27   Let none presume
To wear an undeserved dignity.
O! that estates, degrees, and offices
Were not deriv'd corruptly, and that clear honor
Were purchas'd by the merit of the wearer.
    II, ix, 39

28   Some there be that shadows kiss;
Such have but a shadow's bliss.
    II, ix, 66

29   Let him look to his bond.   *III, i, 49*

30   I am a Jew. Hath not a Jew eyes? hath not a Jew hands, organs, dimensions, senses, affections, passions?   *III, i, 62*

31   If you prick us, do we not bleed? if you tickle us, do we not laugh? if you poison us, do we not die? and if you wrong us, shall we not revenge?
    III, i, 65

32   The villainy you teach me I will execute, and it shall go hard but I will better the instruction.
    III, i, 76

33   I would not have given it for a wilderness of monkeys.   *III, i, 130*

---

[1]That hee shall be called a Nazarite.—*The Geneva Bible* [1557–1560], *Matthew 2:23*
The Geneva version of the Bible is the one Shakespeare was familiar with.

[2]See Chaucer, 131:20, and *A Midsummer-Night's Dream*, 172:21.

1 There's something tells me, but it is not love,
   I would not lose you; and you know yourself,
   Hate counsels not in such a quality.

III, ii, 4

2   Makes a swanlike end,
   Fading in music.[1]

III, ii, 44

3 Tell me where is fancy bred,
   Or in the heart or in the head?
   How begot, how nourished?
       Reply, reply.

III, ii, 63

4 In law, what plea so tainted and corrupt
   But, being season'd with a gracious voice,
   Obscures the show of evil?

III, ii, 75

5 There is no vice so simple but assumes
   Some mark of virtue on his outward parts.

III, ii, 81

6 The seeming truth which cunning times put on
   To entrap the wisest.

III, ii, 100

7 How all the other passions fleet to air,
   As doubtful thoughts, and rash-embrac'd despair,
   And shuddering fear, and green-ey'd jealousy.

III, ii, 108

8 An unlesson'd girl, unschool'd, unpractic'd;
   Happy in this, she is not yet so old
   But she may learn.

III, ii, 160

9 Here are a few of the unpleasant'st words
   That ever blotted paper.

III, ii, 252

10 Thou call'dst me dog before thou hadst a cause,
   But, since I am a dog, beware my fangs.

III, iii, 6

11   Thus when I shun Scylla, your father, I fall into
   Charybdis, your mother.[2]   *III, v, 17*

12 Some men there are love not a gaping pig;
   Some, that are mad if they behold a cat.

IV, i, 47

13 A harmless necessary cat.

IV, i, 55

14 *Bassanio:* Do all men kill the things they do not
       love?

Shylock: Hates any man the thing he would not
   kill?

IV, i, 66

15 What! wouldst thou have a serpent sting thee
       twice?

IV, i, 69

16   The weakest kind of fruit
   Drops earliest to the ground.

IV, i, 115

17 To hold opinion with Pythagoras,
   That souls of animals infuse themselves
   Into the trunks of men.[3]

IV, i, 131

18   I never knew so young a body with so old a head.[4]

IV, i, 163

19 The quality of mercy is not strain'd,
   It droppeth as the gentle rain from heaven
   Upon the place beneath: it is twice bless'd;
   It blesseth him that gives and him that takes:
   'Tis mightiest in the mightiest; it becomes
   The throned monarch better than his crown;
   His scepter shows the force of temporal power,
   The attribute to awe and majesty,
   Wherein doth sit the dread and fear of kings;[5]
   But mercy is above this sceptered sway,
   It is enthroned in the hearts of kings,
   It is an attribute to God himself,
   And earthly power doth then show likest God's
   When mercy seasons justice.[6] Therefore, Jew,
   Though justice be thy plea, consider this,
   That in the course of justice none of us
   Should see salvation: we do pray for mercy,
   And that same prayer doth teach us all to render
   The deeds of mercy.

IV, i, 184

20 To do a great right, do a little wrong.

IV, i, 216

21 A Daniel come to judgment! yea, a Daniel!

IV, i, 223

22 How much more elder art thou than thy looks!

IV, i, 251

23 Is it so nominated in the bond?

IV, i, 260

24 'Tis not in the bond.

IV, i, 263

25 For herein Fortune shows herself more kind
   Than is her custom: it is still her use

---

[1]See Plato, 74:21; *King John*, 170:20; and Anonymous, 777:6.
[2]Scylla to port, and on our starboard beam Charybdis, dire
gorge of the salt sea tide.—HOMER, *Odyssey*, bk. XII, l. 232
   Scylla guards the right side; implacable Charybdis the left.
—VIRGIL, *Aeneid*, bk. III, l. 420
   Incidis in Scyllam cupiens vitare Charybdim [You fall into
Scylla in seeking to avoid Charybdis].—PHILIPPE GUALTIER [fl.
c. 1300], *Alexandreis* [c. 1300], bk. V, l. 301

[3]*Clown:* What is the opinion of Pythagoras concerning wild
fowl? / *Malvolio:* That the soul of our grandam might haply
inhabit a bird.—*Twelfth-Night*, act IV, sc. ii, l. 55
[4]He is young, but take it from me, a very staid head.—
THOMAS WENTWORTH, EARL OF STRAFFORD [1593–1641], *letter commending the Earl of Ormond to Charles I for appointment as councilor*
[5]See *Measure for Measure*, 204:1.
[6]See Milton, 260:13.

To let the wretched man outlive his wealth,
To view with hollow eye and wrinkled brow
An age of poverty.
The Merchant of Venice, IV, i, 268

1   I have a daughter;
Would any of the stock of Barabbas
Had been her husband rather than a Christian!
IV, i, 296

2 An upright judge, a learned judge!
IV, i, 324

3 Now, infidel, I have thee on the hip.
IV, i, 334

4 A Daniel, still say I; a second Daniel!
I thank thee, Jew, for teaching me that word.
IV, i, 341

5 You take my house when you do take the prop
That doth sustain my house; you take my life
When you do take the means whereby I live.
IV, i, 376

6 He is well paid that is well satisfied.
IV, i, 416

7 *Lorenzo:* The moon shines bright: in such a night
    as this . . .
Troilus methinks mounted the Troyan walls,
And sigh'd his soul toward the Grecian tents,
Where Cressid lay that night.
Jessica: In such a night
Did Thisbe fearfully o'ertrip the dew,
And saw the lion's shadow ere himself,
And ran dismay'd away.
Lorenzo: In such a night
Stood Dido with a willow in her hand
Upon the wild sea-banks, and waft her love
To come again to Carthage.
Jessica: In such a night
Medea gather'd the enchanted herbs
That did renew old Aeson.
V, i, 1

8 How sweet the moonlight sleeps upon this bank!
Here we will sit, and let the sounds of music
Creep in our ears: soft stillness and the night
Become the touches of sweet harmony.
Sit, Jessica: look, how the floor of heaven
Is thick inlaid with patines of bright gold:
There's not the smallest orb which thou behold'st
But in his motion like an angel sings,
Still quiring to the young-eyed cherubins.
Such harmony is in immortal souls;
But, whilst this muddy vesture of decay
Doth grossly close it in, we cannot hear it.
V, i, 54

9 I am never merry when I hear sweet music.
V, i, 69

10 The man that hath no music in himself,
Nor is not mov'd with concord of sweet sounds,
Is fit for treasons, stratagems, and spoils;
The motions of his spirit are dull as night,

And his affections dark as Erebus:
Let no such man be trusted.
V, i, 83

11 How far that little candle throws his beams!
So shines a good deed in a naughty world.[1]
V, i, 90

12 How many things by season season'd are
To their right praise and true perfection!
V, i, 107

13 This night methinks is but the daylight sick.
V, i, 124

14 A light wife doth make a heavy husband.
V, i, 130

15 These blessed candles of the night.
V, i, 220

16   I will make a Star Chamber matter of it.
*The Merry Wives of Windsor [1597; revised
1600–1601], act 1, sc. i, l. 2*

17   She has brown hair, and speaks small like a
woman.
I, i, 48

18   Seven hundred pounds and possibilities is goot
gifts.
I, i, 65

19   I had rather than forty shillings I had my Book of
Songs and Sonnets here.
I, i, 205

20   "Convey," the wise it call. "Steal!" foh! a fico for
the phrase!
I, iii, 30

21   I am almost out at heels.
I, iii, 32

22   Thou art the Mars of malcontents.
I, iii, 111

23   Here will be an old abusing of God's patience and
the king's English.
I, iv, 5

24   Dispense with trifles.
II, i, 47

25   Faith, thou hast some crotchets in thy head now.
II, i, 158

26 Why, then the world's mine oyster,
Which I with sword will open.
II, ii, 2

27   This is the short and the long of it.
II, ii, 62

28   Like a fair house built upon another man's
ground.
II, ii, 229

29   Better three hours too soon than a minute too
late.
II, ii, 332

30   I cannot tell what the dickens his name is.
III, ii, 20

31   He capers, he dances, he has eyes of youth, he
writes verses, he speaks holiday, he smells April and
May.
III, ii, 71

32 O, what a world of vile ill-favor'd faults
Looks handsome in three hundred pounds a year!
III, iv, 32

[1]See *Matthew* 5:15, 33:3, and William Bradford, 240:12.

1 A woman would run through fire and water for such a kind heart. *III, iv, 106*

2 I have a kind of alacrity in sinking. *III, v, 13*

3 As good luck would have it.[1] *III, v, 86*

4 A man of my kidney. *III, v, 119*

5 [He] curses all Eve's daughters, of what complexion soever. *IV, ii, 24*

6 Wives may be merry, and yet honest too. *IV, ii, 110*

7 This is the third time; I hope good luck lies in odd numbers. . . . There is divinity in odd numbers, either in nativity, chance or death. *V, i, 2*

8 Better a little chiding than a great deal of heartbreak. *V, iii, 10*

9   Rumor is a pipe
Blown by surmises, jealousies, conjectures,
And of so easy and so plain a stop
That the blunt monster with uncounted heads,
The still-discordant wavering multitude,[2]
Can play upon it.
King Henry the Fourth, Part II [1598],
Induction, l. 15

10 Even such a man, so faint, so spiritless,
So dull, so dead in look, so woe-begone,
Drew Priam's curtain in the dead of night,
And would have told him half his Troy was
    burn'd.
Act I, sc. i, l. 70

11 Yet the first bringer of unwelcome news
Hath but a losing office, and his tongue
Sounds ever after as a sullen bell,
Remember'd knolling a departing friend.[3]
I, i, 100

12 I am not only witty in myself, but the cause that wit is in other men.[4] *I, ii, 10*

13 A rascally yea-forsooth knave. *I, ii, 40*

14 You lie in your throat. *I, ii, 97*

15 Your lordship, though not clean past your youth, hath yet some smack of age in you, some relish of the saltness of time. *I, ii, 112*

16 It is the disease of not listening, the malady of not marking, that I am troubled withal. *I, ii, 139*

17 I am as poor as Job, my lord, but not so patient. *I, ii, 145*

18 We that are in the vaward of our youth. *I, ii, 201*

19 Have you not a moist eye, a dry hand, a yellow cheek, a white beard, a decreasing leg, an increasing belly? *I, ii, 206*

20 Every part about you blasted with antiquity. *I, ii, 210*

21 For my voice, I have lost it with hollaing and singing of anthems. *I, ii, 215*

22 It was always yet the trick of our English nation, if they have a good thing, to make it too common. *I, ii, 244*

23 I were better to be eaten to death with rust than to be scoured to nothing with perpetual motion. *I, ii, 249*

24 I can get no remedy against this consumption of the purse: borrowing only lingers and lingers it out, but the disease is incurable.[5] *I, ii, 267*

25   Who lin'd himself with hope,
Eating the air on promise of supply.
I, iii, 27

26 A habitation giddy and unsure
Hath he that buildeth on the vulgar heart.
I, iii, 89

27 Past and to come seem best; things present worst. *I, iii, 108*

28 A poor lone woman. *II, i, 37*

29 Away, you scullion! you rampallian! you fustilarian! I'll tickle your catastrophe. *II, i, 67*

30 He hath eaten me out of house and home. *II, i, 82*

31 Let the end try the man. *II, ii, 52*

32 Thus we play the fools with the time, and the spirits of the wise sit in the clouds and mock us. *II, ii, 155*

33   He was indeed the glass
Wherein the noble youth did dress themselves.
II, iii, 21

34 And let the welkin roar. *II, iv, 181*

35 Is it not strange that desire should so many years outlive performance? *II, iv, 283*

36   O sleep! O gentle sleep![6]
Nature's soft nurse, how have I frighted thee,
That thou no more wilt weigh my eyelids down
And steep my senses in forgetfulness?
III, i, 5

37 With all appliances and means to boot. *III, i, 29*

38 Uneasy lies the head that wears a crown. *III, i, 31*

---

[1]As ill luck would have it.—Cervantes, *Don Quixote, pt. I* [1605], *bk. I, ch. 2*
[2]See Horace, 97:7; Machiavelli, 137:3; *Coriolanus*, 219:3 and 219:10; and Pope, 303:10.
[3]See Sophocles, 66:6, and *Antony and Cleopatra*, 217:19.
[4]See Foote, 324:6.

[5]See Rabelais, 139:14.
[6]Sleep, most gentle sleep.—Ovid, *Metamorphoses, bk. II, l. 624*

1 O God! that one might read the book of fate.
King Henry IV, Pt. II, III, i, 45

2 There is a history in all men's lives.
III, i, 80

3   Death, as the Psalmist saith, is certain to all; all shall die.
III, ii, 41

4   We have heard the chimes at midnight.
III, ii, 231

5   A man can die but once; we owe God a death.
III, ii, 253

6 We see which way the stream of time doth run
And are enforc'd from our most quiet sphere
By the rough torrent of occasion.
IV, i, 70

7   We ready are to try our fortunes
To the last man.
IV, ii, 43

8   I may justly say with the hook-nosed fellow of Rome, "I came, saw, and overcame."[1]
IV, iii, 44

9 O polish'd perturbation! golden care!
That keep'st the ports of slumber open wide
To many a watchful night!
IV, v, 22

10   See, sons, what things you are!
How quickly nature falls into revolt
When gold becomes her object!
IV, v, 63

11 Thy wish was father, Harry, to that thought.[2]
IV, v, 91

12 Before thy hour be ripe.
IV, v, 95

13   Commit
The oldest sins the newest kind of ways.
IV, v, 124

14 His cares are now all ended.
V, ii, 3

15 This is the English, not the Turkish court;
Not Amurath an Amurath succeeds,
But Harry Harry.
V, ii, 47

16 I know thee not, old man: fall to thy prayers;
How ill white hairs become a fool and jester!
V, v, 52

17   Master Shallow, I owe you a thousand pound.
V, v, 78

18 O! for a Muse of fire, that would ascend
The brightest heaven of invention!
King Henry the Fifth [1598–1599], Chorus, l. 1

19   Or may we cram
Within this wooden O the very casques
That did affright the air at Agincourt?
l. 12

20 Consideration like an angel came,
And whipp'd the offending Adam out of him.[3]
Act I, sc. i, l. 28

21 Hear him debate of commonwealth affairs,
You would say it hath been all in all his study.
I, i, 41

22 Turn him to any cause of policy,
The Gordian knot of it he will unloose,
Familiar as his garter; that, when he speaks,
The air, a charter'd libertine, is still.
I, i, 45

23   Therefore doth heaven divide
The state of man in divers functions,
Setting endeavor in continual motion;
To which is fixed, as an aim or butt,
Obedience: for so work the honeybees,
Creatures that by a rule in nature teach
The act of order to a peopled kingdom.
I, ii, 183

24 The singing masons building roofs of gold.
I, ii, 198

25   Many things, having full reference
To one consent, may work contrariously;
As many arrows, loosed several ways,
Fly to one mark; as many ways meet in one town;
As many fresh streams meet in one salt sea;
As many lines close in the dial's center;
So may a thousand actions, once afoot,
End in one purpose, and be all well borne
Without defeat.
I, ii, 205

26   'Tis ever common
That men are merriest when they are from home.
I, ii, 271

27 Now all the youth of England are on fire,
And silken dalliance in the wardrobe lies.
II, Chorus, 1

28 O England! model to thy inward greatness,
Like little body with a mighty heart,
What mightst thou do, that honor would thee do,
Were all thy children kind and natural!
II, Chorus, 16

29 That's the humor of it.
II, i, 63

30   He's [Falstaff's] in Arthur's bosom, if ever man went to Arthur's bosom. A' made a finer end and went away an it had been any christom child; a' parted even just between twelve and one, even at the turning o' the tide: for after I saw him fumble with the sheets and play with flowers and smile upon his fingers' ends, I knew there was but one way; for his

---

[1]See *Julius Caesar*, 88:25.

[2]Men's thoughts are much according to their inclination, their discourse and speeches according to their learning and infused opinions.—FRANCIS BACON, *Essays* [1597–1625], *Of Custom and Education*

[3]See *Book of Common Prayer (English)*, 50:11.

nose was as sharp as a pen, and a' babbled of green fields. *II, iii, 11*

1   As cold as any stone. *II, iii, 26*

2 Trust none;
For oaths are straws, men's faiths are wafer-cakes,
And hold-fast is the only dog, my duck.
II, iii, 53

3 Once more unto the breach, dear friends, once
        more;
Or close the wall up with our English dead!
In peace there's nothing so becomes a man
As modest stillness and humility:
But when the blast of war blows in our ears,
Then imitate the action of the tiger;
Stiffen the sinews, summon up the blood,
Disguise fair nature with hard-favor'd rage;
Then lend the eye a terrible aspect.
III, i, 1

4 And sheath'd their swords for lack of argument.
III, i, 21

5 I see you stand like greyhounds in the slips,
Straining upon the start. The game's afoot:[1]
Follow your spirit; and, upon this charge
Cry "God for Harry! England and Saint George!"
III, i, 31

6   I would give all my fame for a pot of ale, and safety. *III, ii, 14*

7   Men of few words are the best men.
III, ii, 40

8   He will maintain his argument as well as any military man in the world. *III, ii, 89*

9   I know the disciplines of wars. *III, ii, 156*

10 I thought upon one pair of English legs
Did march three Frenchmen.
III, vi, 161

11 We are in God's hand. *III, vi, 181*

12   That island of England breeds very valiant creatures: their mastiffs are of unmatchable courage.
III, vii, 155

13   Give them great meals of beef and iron and steel, they will eat like wolves and fight like devils.
III, vii, 166

14 The hum of either army stilly sounds,
That the fix'd sentinels almost receive
The secret whispers of each other's watch:
Fire answers fire, and through their paly flames
Each battle sees the other's umber'd face:
Steed threatens steed, in high and boastful neighs
Piercing the night's dull ear; and from the tents
The armorers, accomplishing the knights,
With busy hammers closing rivets up,
Give dreadful note of preparation.
IV, Chorus, 5

15 A little touch of Harry in the night.
IV, Chorus, 47

16 There is some soul of goodness in things evil,
Would men observingly distill it out.
IV, i, 4

17   Every subject's duty is the king's; but every subject's soul is his own. *IV, i, 189*

18   What infinite heart's ease
Must kings neglect that private men enjoy!
And what have kings that privates have not too,
Save ceremony, save general ceremony?
And what art thou, thou idol[2] ceremony?
What kind of god art thou, that suffer'st more
Of mortal griefs than do thy worshippers?
What are thy rents? what are thy comings-in?
O ceremony! show me but thy worth.
IV, i, 256

19 'Tis not the balm, the scepter and the ball,
The sword, the mace, the crown imperial,
The intertissued robe of gold and pearl,
The farced title running 'fore the king,
The throne he sits on, nor the tide of pomp
That beats upon the high shore of this world,
No, not all these, thrice-gorgeous ceremony,
Not all these, laid in bed majestical,
Can sleep so soundly as the wretched slave,
Who with a body fill'd and vacant mind
Gets him to rest, cramm'd with distressful bread.
IV, i, 280

20 O God of battles! steel my soldiers' hearts;
Possess them not with fear; take from them now
The sense of reckoning, if the opposed numbers
Pluck their hearts from them.
IV, i, 309

21 But if it be a sin to covet honor,
I am the most offending soul alive.
IV, iii, 28

22 This day is call'd the feast of Crispian:
He that outlives this day, and comes safe home,
Will stand a tip-toe when this day is nam'd.
And rouse him at the name of Crispian.
IV, iii, 40

23 We few, we happy few, we band of brothers;
For he today that sheds his blood with me
Shall be my brother.
IV, iii, 60

24   The saying is true, "The empty vessel makes the greatest sound." *IV, iv, 72*

25   There is occasions and causes why and wherefore[3] in all things. *V, i, 3*

26   By this leek, I will most horribly revenge. I eat and eat, I swear. *V, i, 49*

27   All hell shall stir for this. *V, i, 72*

---

[1]See Conan Doyle, 577:26.

[2]Sometimes rendered: idle.
[3]See *The Comedy of Errors*, 166:22.

1   The naked, poor, and mangled Peace,
Dear nurse of arts, plenties, and joyful births.
King Henry V, V, ii, 34

2   Grow like savages—as soldiers will,
That nothing do but meditate on blood.
V, ii, 59

3   For these fellows of infinite tongue, that can rime themselves into ladies' favors, they do always reason themselves out again.   *V, ii, 162*

4   My comfort is, that old age, that ill layer-up of beauty, can do no more spoil upon my face.
V, ii, 246

5   O Kate! nice customs curtsy to great kings.
V, ii, 291

6   He hath indeed better bettered expectation than you must expect of me to tell you how.
Much Ado About Nothing [1598–1600], act I, sc. i, l. 15

7   How much better is it to weep at joy than to joy at weeping!   *I, i, 28*

8   A very valiant trencher-man.   *I, i, 52*

9   There's a skirmish of wit between them.
I, i, 64

10   He wears his faith but as the fashion of his hat.
I, i, 76

11   I see, lady, the gentleman is not in your books.
I, i, 79

12   What! my dear Lady Disdain, are you yet living?
I, i, 123

13   Shall I never see a bachelor of threescore again?
I, i, 209

14   In time the savage bull doth bear the yoke.
I, i, 271

15   Benedick the married man.   *I, i, 278*

16   I could not endure a husband with a beard on his face: I had rather lie in the woollen.   *II, i, 31*

17   As merry as the day is long.   *II, i, 52*

18   Would it not grieve a woman to be over-mastered with a piece of valiant dust? to make an account of her life to a clod of wayward marl?   *II, i, 64*

19   I have a good eye, uncle: I can see a church by daylight.   *II, i, 86*

20   Speak low, if you speak love.   *II, i, 104*

21   Friendship is constant in all other things
Save in the office and affairs of love:
Therefore all hearts in love use their own tongues;
Let every eye negotiate for itself
And trust no agent.
II, i, 184

22   She speaks poniards, and every word stabs: if her breath were as terrible as her terminations, there were no living near her; she would infect to the north star.   *II, i, 257*

23   Silence is the perfectest herald of joy: I were but little happy, if I could say how much.   *II, i, 319*

24   It keeps on the windy side of care.[1]
II, i, 328

25   There was a star danced, and under that was I born.   *II, i, 351*

26   I will tell you my drift.[2]   *II, i, 406*

27   He was wont to speak plain and to the purpose.
II, iii, 19

28   Sigh no more, ladies, sigh no more.
Men were deceivers ever;
One foot in sea, and one on shore,
To one thing constant never.
II, iii, 65

29   Sits the wind in that corner?   *II, iii, 108*

30   Bait the hook well: this fish will bite.
II, iii, 121

31   Shall quips and sentences and these paper bullets of the brain awe a man from the career of his humor? No; the world must be peopled. When I said I would die a bachelor, I did not think I should live till I were married.   *II, iii, 260*

32   From the crown of his head to the sole of his foot, he is all mirth.   *III, ii, 9*

33   He hath a heart as sound as a bell, and his tongue is the clapper; for what his heart thinks his tongue speaks.   *III, ii, 12*

34   Everyone can master a grief but he that has it.
III, ii, 28

35   Are you good men and true?   *III, iii, 1*

36   To be a well-favored man is the gift of fortune; but to write and read comes by nature.
III, iii, 14

37   If they make you not then the better answer, you may say they are not the men you took them for.
III, iii, 49

38   They that touch pitch will be defiled.[3]
III, iii, 61

39   The fashion wears out more apparel than the man.   *III, iii, 147*

40   A good old man, sir; he will be talking: as they say, When the age is in, the wit is out.
III, v, 36

41   O! what men dare do! what men may do! what men daily do, not knowing what they do!
IV, i, 19

---

[1] The windy side of the law. — *Twelfth-Night, act III, sc. iv, l. 183*

[2] We know your drift. — *Coriolanus, act III, sc. iii, l. 114*

[3] This pitch, as ancient writers do report, doth defile; so doth the company thou keepest. — *King Henry IV, Part I, act II, sc. iv, l. 460*

See *Ecclesiasticus 13:1, 31:30.*

1 O! what authority and show of truth
Can cunning sin cover itself withal.

IV, i, 35

2   For it so falls out
That what we have we prize not to the worth
Whiles we enjoy it, but being lack'd and lost,
Why, then we rack the value, then we find
The virtue that possession would not show us
Whiles it was ours.

IV, i, 219

3   Masters, it is proved already that you are little
better than false knaves, and it will go near to be
thought so shortly.   *IV, ii, 23*

4   Flat burglary as ever was committed.

IV, ii, 54

5   Thou wilt be condemned into everlasting redemption for this.   *IV, ii, 60*

6   O that he were here to write me down an ass!

IV, ii, 80

7 Patch griefs with proverbs.

V, i, 17

8 Charm ache with air and agony with words.

V, i, 26

9 For there was never yet philosopher
That could endure the toothache patiently.

V, i, 35

10 Some of us will smart for it.

V, i, 108

11   What though care killed a cat,[1] thou hast mettle
enough in thee to kill care.   *V, i, 135*

12   I was not born under a riming planet.

V, ii, 40

13   The trumpet of his own virtues.   *V, ii, 91*

14 Done to death by slanderous tongues.

V, iii, 3

15   A surgeon to old shoes.
Julius Caesar [1599], act I, sc. i, l. 26

16   As proper men as ever trod upon neat's leather.

I, i, 27

17 Have you not made a universal shout,
That Tiber trembled underneath her banks,
To hear the replication of your sounds
Made in her concave shores?

I, i, 48

18 Beware the ides of March.[2]

I, ii, 18

19 Set honor in one eye and death i' the other,
And I will look on both indifferently.

I, ii, 86

20 Well, honor is the subject of my story.
I cannot tell what you and other men
Think of this life; but, for my single self,
I had as lief not be as live to be
In awe of such a thing as I myself.

I, ii, 92

21 Stemming it with hearts of controversy.

I, ii, 109

22 Why, man, he doth bestride the narrow world
Like a Colossus; and we petty men
Walk under his huge legs, and peep about
To find ourselves dishonorable graves.
Men at some time are masters of their fates:[3]
The fault, dear Brutus, is not in our stars,
But in ourselves, that we are underlings.

I, ii, 134

23 Upon what meat doth this our Caesar feed,
That he is grown so great?

I, ii, 148

24 Let me have men about me that are fat;
Sleek-headed men and such as sleep o' nights.
Yond Cassius has a lean and hungry look;[4]
He thinks too much: such men are dangerous.

I, ii, 191

25   He reads much;
He is a great observer, and he looks
Quite through the deeds of men.

I, ii, 200

26 Seldom he smiles, and smiles in such a sort
As if he mock'd himself, and scorn'd his spirit
That could be mov'd to smile at anything.

I, ii, 204

27 But, for my own part, it was Greek to me.[5]

I, ii, 288

28   Yesterday the bird of night did sit,
Even at noonday, upon the marketplace,
Hooting and shrieking.

I, iii, 26

29 So every bondman in his own hand bears
The power to cancel his captivity.

I, iii, 101

30 O! he sits high in all the people's hearts:
And that which would appear offense in us,
His countenance, like richest alchemy,
Will change to virtue and to worthiness.

I, iii, 157

31 The abuse of greatness is when it disjoins
Remorse from power.

II, i, 18

32   'Tis a common proof,
That lowliness is young ambition's ladder,

---

[1] Let care kill a cat, / We'll laugh and grow fat.—*Shirburn
Ballads* [1585], 91
     Hang sorrow, care'll kill a cat. — JONSON, *Every Man in His
Humour* [1598], act I, sc. i
[2] See Julius Caesar, 88:23.

[3] See Sallust, 91:28 and 92:1; Bacon, 160:4; Tennyson, 459:9;
Henley, 557:10; and Nehru, 677:7.
[4] See Julius Caesar, 89:1.
[5] This geare is Greeke to me.—GEORGE GASCOIGNE
[c. 1525–1577], *Supposes, I* [1573]

Whereto the climber-upward turns his face;
But when he once attains the upmost round,
He then unto the ladder turns his back,
Looks in the clouds, scorning the base degrees
By which he did ascend.

Julius Caesar, II, i, 21

1 Therefore think him as a serpent's egg
Which, hatch'd, would, as his kind, grow
  mischievous,
And kill him in the shell.

II, i, 32

2 Between the acting of a dreadful thing
And the first motion, all the interim is
Like a phantasma, or a hideous dream:
The genius and the mortal instruments
Are then in council; and the state of man,
Like to a little kingdom, suffers then
The nature of an insurrection.

II, i, 63

3   O conspiracy!
Sham'st thou to show thy dangerous brow by
  night,
When evils are most free?

II, i, 77

4 Let's carve him as a dish fit for the gods,
Not hew him as a carcass fit for hounds.

II, i, 173

5 But when I tell him he hates flatterers,
He says he does, being then most flattered.

II, i, 207

6 Enjoy the honey-heavy dew of slumber.

II, i, 230

7   Dwell I but in the suburbs
Of your good pleasure?

II, i, 285

8 You are my true and honorable wife,
As dear to me as are the ruddy drops
That visit my sad heart.[1]

II, i, 288

9 Think you I am no stronger than my sex,
Being so father'd and so husbanded?

II, i, 296

10 When beggars die there are no comets seen;
The heavens themselves blaze forth the death of
  princes.

II, ii, 30

11 Cowards die many times before their deaths;
The valiant never taste of death but once.
Of all the wonders that I yet have heard,
It seems to me most strange that men should fear;
Seeing that death, a necessary end,
Will come when it will come.

II, ii, 32

12 Antony, that revels long o' nights.

II, ii, 116

13 How hard it is for women to keep counsel!

II, iv, 9

14 But I am constant as the northern star,
Of whose true-fix'd and resting quality
There is no fellow in the firmament.

III, i, 60

15 Speak, hands, for me!

III, i, 76

16 Et tu, Brute?[2]

III, i, 77

17 Some to the common pulpits, and cry out,
"Liberty, freedom, and enfranchisement!"

III, i, 79

18   How many ages hence
Shall this our lofty scene be acted o'er,
In states unborn and accents yet unknown!

III, i, 111

19 O mighty Caesar! dost thou lie so low?
Are all thy conquests, glories, triumphs, spoils,
Shrunk to this little measure?

III, i, 148

20 The choice and master spirits of this age.

III, i, 163

21 Though last, not least in love.[3]

III, i, 189

22 O! pardon me, thou bleeding piece of earth,
That I am meek and gentle with these butchers;
Thou art the ruins of the noblest man
That ever lived in the tide of times.

III, i, 254

23 Cry "Havoc!" and let slip the dogs of war.

III, i, 273

24   Romans, countrymen, and lovers! hear me for my
cause; and be silent, that you may hear.

III, ii, 13

25   Not that I loved Caesar less, but that I loved
Rome more.   *III, ii, 22*

26   As he was valiant, I honor him; but, as he was
ambitious, I slew him.   *III, ii, 27*

27   If any, speak; for him have I offended. I pause for
a reply.   *III, ii, 36*

28 Friends, Romans, countrymen, lend me your ears;
I come to bury Caesar, not to praise him.
The evil that men do lives after them,
The good is oft interred with their bones.[4]

III, ii, 79

29 For Brutus is an honorable man;
So are they all, all honorable men.

III, ii, 88

[1]Dear as the ruddy drops that warm my heart.—THOMAS
GRAY, *The Bard* [1757], *act I, sc. iii, l. 12*

[2]See Julius Caesar, 88:26.
[3]See Spenser, 154:10, and *King Lear*, 208:19.
[4]See Euripides, 69:12.

1 When that the poor have cried, Caesar hath wept;
  Ambition should be made of sterner stuff.
  III, ii, 97

2 O judgment! thou art fled to brutish beasts,
  And men have lost their reason.
  III, ii, 110

3 But yesterday the word of Caesar might
  Have stood against the world; now lies he there,
  And none so poor to do him reverence.
  III, ii, 124

4 If you have tears, prepare to shed them now.
  III, ii, 174

5 See what a rent the envious Casca made.
  III, ii, 180

6 This was the most unkindest cut of all.
  III, ii, 188

7   Great Caesar fell.
  O! what a fall was there, my countrymen;
  Then I, and you, and all of us fell down,
  Whilst bloody treason flourish'd over us.
  III, ii, 194

8 What private griefs they have, alas! I know not.
  III, ii, 217

9 I come not, friends, to steal away your hearts:
  I am no orator, as Brutus is;
  But, as you know me all, a plain blunt man.
  III, ii, 220

10 For I have neither wit, nor words, nor worth,
  Action, nor utterance, nor the power of speech,
  To stir men's blood: I only speak right on.
  III, ii, 225

11   Put a tongue
  In every wound of Caesar, that should move
  The stones of Rome to rise and mutiny.
  III, ii, 232

12 When love begins to sicken and decay,
  It useth an enforced ceremony.
  There are no tricks in plain and simple faith.
  IV, ii, 20

13 An itching palm.
  IV, iii, 10

14 I had rather be a dog, and bay the moon,
  Than such a Roman.
  IV, iii, 27

15 I'll use you for my mirth, yea, for my laughter,
  When you are waspish.
  IV, iii, 49

16 There is no terror, Cassius, in your threats;
  For I am arm'd so strong in honesty
  That they pass by me as the idle wind,
  Which I respect not.
  IV, iii, 66

17 A friend should bear his friend's infirmities,
  But Brutus makes mine greater than they are.
  IV, iii, 85

18   All his faults observ'd,
  Set in a notebook, learn'd, and conn'd by rote.
  IV, iii, 96

19 There is a tide in the affairs of men,
  Which, taken at the flood, leads on to fortune;
  Omitted, all the voyage of their life
  Is bound in shallows and in miseries.
  IV, iii, 217

20 We must take the current when it serves,
  Or lose our ventures.
  IV, iii, 222

21 The deep of night is crept upon our talk,
  And nature must obey necessity.
  IV, iii, 225

22 But for your words, they rob the Hybla bees,
  And leave them honeyless.
  V, i, 34

23 Forever, and forever, farewell, Cassius!
  If we do meet again, why, we shall smile;
  If not, why then, this parting was well made.
  V, i, 117

24   O! that a man might know
  The end of this day's business, ere it come.
  V, i, 123

25 O Julius Caesar! thou art mighty yet!
  Thy spirit walks abroad, and turns our swords
  In our own proper entrails.
  V, iii, 94

26 The last of all the Romans, fare thee well!
  V, iii, 99

27 This was the noblest Roman of them all.
  V, v, 68

28 His life was gentle, and the elements
  So mix'd in him that Nature might stand up
  And say to all the world, "This was a man!"[1]
  V, v, 73

29   What's the new news at the new court?
  As You Like It [1599–1600], act I, sc. i, 1. 103

30   Fleet the time carelessly, as they did in the golden
  world.
  I, i, 126

31   Always the dullness of the fool is the whetstone
  of the wits.
  I, ii, 59

32   The little foolery that wise men have makes a
  great show.
  I, ii, 97

33   Well said: that was laid on with a trowel.
  I, ii, 113

34   Your heart's desires be with you!   *I, ii, 214*

35 One out of suits with fortune.
  I, ii, 263

36 My pride fell with my fortunes.
  I, ii, 269

[1]See *Hamlet*, 193:16.

1 Hereafter, in a better world than this,
I shall desire more love and knowledge of you.
As You Like It, I, ii, 301

2 Heavenly Rosalind!

I, ii, 306

3 O, how full of briers is this working-day world!

I, iii, 12

4 Beauty provoketh thieves sooner than gold.

I, iii, 113

5 We'll have a swashing and a martial outside,
As many other mannish cowards have.

I, iii, 123

6 Hath not old custom made this life more sweet
Than that of painted pomp? Are not these woods
More free from peril than the envious court?

II, i, 2

7 Sweet are the uses of adversity,
Which, like the toad, ugly and venomous,
Wears yet a precious jewel in his head;
And this our life exempt from public haunt,
Finds tongues in trees, books in the running
   brooks,
Sermons in stones, and good in everything.[1]

II, i, 12

8   The big round tears
Cours'd one another down his innocent nose
In piteous chase.

II, i, 38

9 Sweep on, you fat and greasy citizens.

II, i, 55

10   And He that doth the ravens feed,
Yea, providently caters for the sparrow,
Be comfort to my age!

II, iii, 43

11 Though I look old, yet I am strong and lusty;
For in my youth I never did apply
Hot and rebellious liquors in my blood.

II, iii, 47

12 Therefore my age is as a lusty winter,
Frosty, but kindly.

II, iii, 52

13 Thou art not for the fashion of these times,
Where none will sweat but for promotion.

II, iii, 59

14 Ay, now am I in Arden; the more fool I: when I
was at home, I was in a better place: but travelers
must be content.   *II, iv, 16*

15 If you remember'st not the slightest folly
That ever love did make thee run into,
Thou hast not lov'd.

II, iv, 34

16 We that are true lovers run into strange capers.

II, iv, 53

17 I shall ne'er be ware of mine own wit, till I break
my shins against it.   *II, iv, 59*

18 Under the greenwood tree
Who loves to lie with me,
And turn his merry note
Unto the sweet bird's throat,
Come hither, come hither, come hither:
Here shall he see
No enemy
But winter and rough weather.

II, v, 1

19 I can suck melancholy out of a song as a weasel
sucks eggs.   *II, v, 12*

20 Who doth ambition shun,
And loves to live i' the sun,
Seeking the food he eats,
And pleas'd with what he gets.

II, v, 38

21   I met a fool i' the forest,
A motley fool.

II, vii, 12

22 And then he drew a dial from his poke,
And, looking on it with lack-luster eye,
Says very wisely, "It is ten o'clock;
Thus may we see," quoth he, "how the world
   wags."[2]

II, vii, 20

23 And so, from hour to hour we ripe and ripe,
And then from hour to hour we rot and rot,
And thereby hangs a tale.[3]

II, vii, 26

24 My lungs began to crow like chanticleer,
That fools should be so deep-contemplative,
And I did laugh sans intermission
An hour by his dial.

II, vii, 30

25 Motley's the only wear.

II, vii, 34

26   If ladies be but young and fair,
They have the gift to know it.

II, vii, 37

27   I must have liberty
Withal, as large a charter as the wind,
To blow on whom I please.

II, vii, 47

28 The "why" is plain as way to parish church.

II, vii, 52

29   But whate'er you are
That in this desert inaccessible,
Under the shade of melancholy boughs,
Lose and neglect the creeping hours of time;
If ever you have look'd on better days,
If ever been where bells have knoll'd to church,

---

[1] See Saint Bernard, 121:8; *As You Like It*, 191:5; and Wordsworth, 372:21.

[2] So wags the world.—WALTER SCOTT, *Ivanhoe* [1819],
ch. 37

[3] Also elsewhere in Shakespeare.

If ever sat at any good man's feast,
If ever from your eyelids wip'd a tear,
And know what 'tis to pity, and be pitied,
Let gentleness my strong enforcement be.

II, vii, 109

1 True is it that we have seen better days.

II, vii, 120

2 Oppress'd with two weak evils, age and hunger.

II, vii, 132

3   All the world's a stage,
And all the men and women merely players:[1]
They have their exits and their entrances;
And one man in his time plays many parts,
His acts being seven ages. At first the infant,
Mewling and puking in the nurse's arms.
And then the whining school-boy, with his satchel,
And shining morning face, creeping like snail
Unwillingly to school. And then the lover,
Sighing like furnace, with a woful ballad
Made to his mistress' eyebrow. Then a soldier,
Full of strange oaths, and bearded like the pard,
Jealous in honor, sudden and quick in quarrel,
Seeking the bubble reputation
Even in the cannon's mouth. And then the justice,
In fair round belly with good capon lin'd,
With eyes severe, and beard of formal cut,
Full of wise saws and modern instances;
And so he plays his part. The sixth age shifts
Into the lean and slipper'd pantaloon,
With spectacles on nose and pouch on side,
His youthful hose well sav'd, a world too wide
For his shrunk shank; and his big manly voice,
Turning again toward childish treble, pipes
And whistles in his sound. Last scene of all,
That ends this strange eventful history,
Is second childishness and mere oblivion,
Sans teeth, sans eyes, sans taste, sans everything.

II, vii, 139

4 Blow, blow, thou winter wind,
Thou art not so unkind
As man's ingratitude.

II, vii, 174

5 These trees shall be my books.[2]

III, ii, 5

6 The fair, the chaste, and unexpressive she.

III, ii, 10

7   It goes much against my stomach. Hast any philosophy in thee, shepherd?   *III, ii, 21*

8   He that wants money, means, and content, is without three good friends.   *III, ii, 25*

---

[1] See *The Merchant of Venice*, 179:17.
   The world's a theater, the earth a stage, / Which God and Nature do with actors fill.— THOMAS HEYWOOD, *Apology for Actors* [1612]
   The world's a stage on which all the parts are played.— MIDDLETON, *A Game of Chess* [1624], act V, sc. i

[2] See Saint Bernard, 121:8; *As You Like It*, 190:7; and Wordsworth, 372:21.

9   I am a true laborer: I earn that I eat, get that I wear, owe no man hate, envy no man's happiness, glad of other men's good, content with my harm.

III, ii, 78

10 From the east to western Ind,
No jewel is like Rosalind.

III, ii, 94

11   This is the very false gallop of verses.

III, ii, 120

12   Let us make an honorable retreat; though not with bag and baggage, yet with scrip and scrippage.

III, ii, 170

13   O, wonderful, wonderful, and most wonderful, wonderful! and yet again wonderful! and after that, out of all whooping.   *III, ii, 202*

14   Answer me in one word.   *III, ii, 238*

15   Do you not know I am a woman? when I think, I must speak.   *III, ii, 265*

16   I do desire we may be better strangers.

III, ii, 276

17   *Jacques:* What stature is she of?
    Orlando: Just as high as my heart.

III, ii, 286

18   Time travels in divers paces with divers persons. I'll tell you who Time ambles withal, who Time trots withal, who Time gallops withal, and who he stands still withal.   *III, ii, 328*

19   Every one fault seeming monstrous till his fellow fault came to match it.   *III, ii, 377*

20   Everything about you demonstrating a careless desolation.   *III, ii, 405*

21   Truly, I would the gods had made thee poetical.

III, iii, 16

22   The wounds invisible
That love's keen arrows make.

III, v, 30

23   Down on your knees,
And thank heaven, fasting, for a good man's love.

III, v, 57

24 Sell when you can, you are not for all markets.

III, v, 60

25 I am falser than vows made in wine.

III, v, 73

26   It is a melancholy of mine own, compounded of many simples, extracted from many objects, and indeed the sundry contemplation of my travels, which, by often rumination, wraps me in a most humorous sadness.   *IV, i, 16*

27   I had rather have a fool to make me merry than experience to make me sad.   *IV, i, 28*

28   Farewell, Monsieur Traveler: look you lisp, and wear strange suits, disable all the benefits of your own country, be out of love with your nativity, and almost chide God for making you that countenance

you are; or I will scarce think you have swam in a gondola.   *As You Like It, IV, i, 35*

1   I'll warrant him heart-whole.   *IV, i, 51*

2   Men have died from time to time, and worms have eaten them, but not for love.   *IV, i, 110*

3   Forever and a day.   *IV, i, 151*

4   Men are April when they woo, December when they wed: maids are May when they are maids, but the sky changes when they are wives.
    IV, i, 153

5   My affection hath an unknown bottom, like the bay of Portugal.   *IV, i, 219*

6   The horn, the horn, the lusty horn
Is not a thing to laugh to scorn.
    IV, ii, 17

7   Chewing the food of sweet and bitter fancy.
    IV, iii, 103

8   "So so," is good, very good, very excellent good: and yet it is not; it is but so so.   *V, i, 30*

9   The fool doth think he is wise, but the wise man knows himself to be a fool.   *V, i, 35*

10   No sooner met, but they looked; no sooner looked but they loved; no sooner loved but they sighed; no sooner sighed but they asked one another the reason; no sooner knew the reason but they sought the remedy.   *V, ii, 37*

11   But, O! how bitter a thing it is to look into happiness through another man's eyes!   *V, ii, 48*

12   It was a lover and his lass,
With a hey, and a ho, and a hey nonino,
That o'er the green corn-field did pass,
In the spring time, the only pretty ring time,
When birds do sing, hey ding a ding, ding;
Sweet lovers love the spring.
    V, iii, 18

13   Here comes a pair of very strange beasts, which in all tongues are called fools.   *V, iv, 36*

14   An ill-favored thing, sir, but mine own.[1]
    V, iv, 60

15   Rich honesty dwells like a miser, sir, in a poor house, as your pearl in your foul oyster.
    V, iv, 62

16   "The retort courteous." . . . "the quip modest." . . . "the reply churlish." . . . "the reproof valiant" . . . "the countercheck quarrelsome." . . . "the lie circumstantial," and "the lie direct."
    V, iv, 75

17   Your "if" is the only peacemaker; much virtue in "if."   *V, iv, 108*

18   He uses his folly like a stalking horse, and under the presentation of that he shoots his wit.
    V, iv, 112

---

[1]"A poor thing but mine own" is the popular version.

19   For this relief much thanks; 'tis bitter cold,
And I am sick at heart.
    Hamlet [1600–1601], act I, sc. i, l. 8

20   Not a mouse stirring.[2]
    I, i, 10

21   Thou art a scholar; speak to it, Horatio.
    I, i, 42

22   But in the gross and scope of my opinion,
This bodes some strange eruption to our state.
    I, i, 68

23   Whose sore task
Does not divide the Sunday from the week.
    I, i, 75

24   This sweaty haste
Doth make the night joint-laborer with the day.
    I, i, 77

25   In the most high and palmy state of Rome,
A little ere the mightiest Julius fell,
The graves stood tenantless and the sheeted dead
Did squeak and gibber in the Roman streets.
    I, i, 113

26   And then it started like a guilty thing
Upon a fearful summons.
    I, i, 148

27   The cock, that is the trumpet to the morn.
    I, i, 150

28   Whether in sea or fire, in earth or air,
The extravagant and erring spirit hies
To his confine.
    I, i, 153

29   It faded on the crowing of the cock.
Some say that ever 'gainst that season comes
Wherein our Savior's birth is celebrated,
The bird of dawning singeth all night long;
And then, they say, no spirit can walk abroad;
The nights are wholesome; then no planets strike,
No fairy takes, nor witch hath power to charm,
So hallow'd and so gracious is the time.
    I, i, 157

30   But, look, the morn in russet mantle clad,
Walks o'er the dew of yon high eastern hill.
    I, i, 166

31   The memory be green.[3]
    I, ii, 2

32   With one auspicious and one dropping eye,
With mirth in funeral and with dirge in marriage,
In equal scale weighing delight and dole.
    I, ii, 11

33   So much for him.
    I, ii, 25

34   A little more than kin, and less than kind.
    I, ii, 65

---

[2]See Clement Clarke Moore, 391:6.
[3]See Thomas Moore, 391:11.

1 Thou know'st 'tis common; all that live must die,
Passing through nature to eternity.

I, ii, 72

2 Seems, madam! Nay, it is; I know not "seems."
'Tis not alone my inky cloak, good mother,
Nor customary suits of solemn black.

I, ii, 76

3 But I have that within which passeth show;
These but the trappings and the suits of woe.

I, ii, 85

4   To persever
In obstinate condolement is a course
Of impious stubbornness; 'tis unmanly grief:
It shows a will most incorrect to heaven,
A heart unfortified, a mind impatient.

I, ii, 92

5 O! that this too too solid[1] flesh would melt,
Thaw and resolve itself into a dew;
Or that the Everlasting had not fix'd
His canon 'gainst self-slaughter! O God! O God!
How weary, stale, flat, and unprofitable
Seem to me all the uses of this world.

I, ii, 129

6   Things rank and gross in nature
Possess it merely. That it should come to this!

I, ii, 136

7 So excellent a king; that was, to this,
Hyperion to a satyr; so loving to my mother
That he might not beteem the winds of heaven
Visit her face too roughly.

I, ii, 139

8   Why, she would hang on him,
As if increase of appetite had grown
By what it fed on.

I, ii, 143

9 Frailty, thy name is woman!

I, ii, 146

10 Like Niobe, all tears.

I, ii, 149

11 A beast, that wants discourse of reason.

I, ii, 150

12 It is not nor it cannot come to good.

I, ii, 158

13 A truant disposition.

I, ii, 169

14 Thrift, thrift, Horatio! the funeral bak'd meats
Did coldly furnish forth the marriage tables.
Would I had met my dearest foe[2] in heaven
Ere I had ever seen that day.

I, ii, 180

15 In my mind's eye, Horatio.

I, ii, 185

16 He was a man, take him for all in all,[3]
I shall not look upon his like again.

I, ii, 187

17 Season your admiration for a while.

I, ii, 192

18 In the dead vast and middle of the night.

I, ii, 198

19 Armed at points exactly, cap-a-pe.

I, ii, 200

20   Distill'd
Almost to jelly with the act of fear.

I, ii, 204

21 A countenance more in sorrow than in anger.

I, ii, 231

22 *Hamlet:*   His beard was grizzled, no?
Horatio: It was, as I have seen it in his life,
A sable silver'd.

I, ii, 239

23 Give it an understanding, but no tongue.

I, ii, 249

24   All is not well;
I doubt some foul play.

I, ii, 254

25   Foul deeds will rise,
Though all the earth o'erwhelm them, to men's
    eyes.

I, ii, 256

26 The chariest maid is prodigal enough
If she unmask her beauty to the moon;
Virtue itself 'scapes not calumnious strokes;
The canker galls the infants of the spring
Too oft before their buttons be disclos'd,
And in the morn and liquid dew of youth
Contagious blastments are most imminent.

I, iii, 36

27 Do not, as some ungracious pastors do,
Show me the steep and thorny way to heaven,
Whiles, like a puff'd and reckless libertine,
Himself the primrose path of dalliance treads,
And recks not his own rede.[4]

I, iii, 47

28 Give thy thoughts no tongue.

I, iii, 59

29 Be thou familiar, but by no means vulgar;
Those friends thou hast, and their adoption tried,
Grapple them to thy soul with hoops of steel.

I, iii, 61

30   Beware
Of entrance to a quarrel, but, being in,
Bear 't that th' opposed may beware of thee.

[1]Alternative readings are "sallied" and "sullied."
[2]See *Henry IV, Part I*, 178:13.

[3]See *Julius Caesar*, 189:28.
[4]Wel oghte a preest ensample for to yive. / By his clennesse,
how that his sheep shold live.—CHAUCER, *The Canterbury
Tales* [c. 1387], *prologue, l. 504*
   And may ye better reck the rede, / Than ever did th' adviser.
—BURNS, *Epistle to a Young Friend* [1786]

Give every man thy ear, but few thy voice;
Take each man's censure, but reserve thy
    judgment.
Costly thy habit as thy purse can buy,
But not express'd in fancy; rich, not gaudy;[1]
For the apparel oft proclaims the man.

Hamlet, I, iii, 65

1 Neither a borrower, nor a lender be;
For loan oft loses both itself and friend,
And borrowing dulls the edge of husbandry.
This above all: to thine own self be true,
And it must follow, as the night the day,
Thou canst not then be false to any man.[2]

I, iii, 75

2   'Tis in my memory lock'd,
And you yourself shall keep the key of it.

I, iii, 85

3   You speak like a green girl,
Unsifted in such perilous circumstance.

I, iii, 101

4 Springes to catch woodcocks.

I, iii, 115

5 When the blood burns, how prodigal the soul
Lends the tongue vows.

I, iii, 116

6 Be somewhat scanter of your maiden presence.

I, iii, 121

7 The air bites shrewdly.

I, iv, 1

8 But to my mind,—though I am native here
And to the manner born—it is a custom
More honor'd in the breach than the observance.

I, iv, 14

9 Angels and ministers of grace defend us!

I, iv, 39

10 Be thy intents wicked or charitable,
Thou com'st in such a questionable shape
That I will speak to thee.

I, iv, 42

11   What may this mean,
That thou, dead corse, again in complete steel
Revisit'st thus the glimpses of the moon,
Making night hideous;[3] and we fools of nature
So horridly to shake our disposition
With thoughts beyond the reaches of our souls?

I, iv, 51

12 I do not set my life at a pin's fee.

I, iv, 65

13   The dreadful summit of the cliff
That beetles o'er his base into the sea.

I, iv, 70

---

[1]See Samuel Wesley, 286:24.
[2]See Francis Bacon, 159:24.
[3]And makes night hideous.—Pope, *The Dunciad*, bk. III
[1728], *l. 166*

14   My fate cries out,
And makes each petty artery in this body
As hardy as the Nemean lion's nerve.

I, iv, 81

15   Unhand me, gentlemen,
By heaven! I'll make a ghost of him that lets me.

I, iv, 84

16 Something is rotten in the state of Denmark.

I, iv, 90

17 I could a tale unfold whose lightest word
Would harrow up thy soul, freeze thy young
    blood,
Make thy two eyes, like stars, start from their
    spheres,
Thy knotted and combined locks to part,
And each particular hair to stand an end,
Like quills upon the fretful porpentine.

I, v, 15

18 Murder most foul, as in the best it is.

I, v, 27

19 And duller shouldst thou be than the fat weed
That rots itself in ease on Lethe wharf.

I, v, 32

20   O my prophetic soul!
My uncle!

I, v, 40

21 O Hamlet! what a falling-off was there.

I, v, 47

22 But virtue, as it never will be mov'd,
Though lewdness court it in a shape of heaven,
So lust, though to a radiant angel link'd,
Will sate itself in a celestial bed,
And prey on garbage.

I, v, 53

23 In the porches of mine ears.

I, v, 63

24 Cut off even in the blossoms of my sin,
Unhousel'd, disappointed, unanel'd,
No reckoning made, but sent to my account
With all my imperfections on my head.

I, v, 76

25   Leave her to heaven,
And to those thorns that in her bosom lodge,
To prick and sting her.

I, v, 86

26 The glowworm shows the matin to be near,
And 'gins to pale his uneffectual fire.

I, v, 89

27   While memory holds a seat
In this distracted globe. Remember thee!
Yea, from the table of my memory
I'll wipe away all trivial fond records.

I, v, 96

28 Within the book and volume of my brain.

I, v, 103

1 O villain, villain, smiling, damned villain!
My tables—meet it is I set it down,
That one may smile, and smile, and be a villain;
At least I'm sure it may be so in Denmark.
I, v, 106

2 There's ne'er a villain dwelling in all Denmark,
But he's an arrant knave.
I, v, 123

3 There are more things in heaven and earth,
Horatio,
Than are dreamt of in your philosophy.
I, v, 166

4 To put an antic disposition on.
I, v, 172

5 Rest, rest, perturbed spirit!
I, v, 182

6 The time is out of joint; O cursed spite,
That ever I was born to set it right!
I, v, 188

7 Your bait of falsehood takes this carp of truth;
And thus do we of wisdom and of reach,
With windlasses and with assays of bias,
By indirections find directions out.
II, i, 63

8 Ungarter'd, and down-gyved to his ankle.
II, i, 80

9 This is the very ecstasy of love.
II, i, 102

10 Brevity is the soul of wit.
II, ii, 90

11 More matter, with less art.
II, ii, 95

12 That he is mad, 'tis true; 'tis true 'tis pity;
And pity 'tis 'tis true.
II, ii, 97

13 Find out the cause of this effect,
Or rather say, the cause of this defect,
For this effect defective comes by cause.
II, ii, 101

14 Doubt thou the stars are fire;
Doubt that the sun doth move;
Doubt truth to be a liar;
But never doubt I love.
II, ii, 115

15 *Polonius:* Do you know me, my lord?
Hamlet: Excellent well; you are a fishmonger.
II, ii, 173

16 To be honest, as this world goes, is to be one man
picked out of ten thousand.   *II, ii, 179*

17 *Hamlet:* For if the sun breed maggots in a dead
dog, being a god[1] kissing carrion,—Have you a
daughter?

[1]In some editions: good.

Polonius: I have, my lord.
Hamlet: Let her not walk i' the sun.
II, ii, 183

18 Still harping on my daughter.   *II, ii, 190*

19 *Polonius:* What do you read, my lord?
Hamlet: Words, words, words.   *II, ii, 195*

20 They have a plentiful lack of wit.   *II, ii, 204*

21 Though this be madness, yet there is method in 't.
II, ii, 211

22 These tedious old fools!   *II, ii, 227*

23 The indifferent children of the earth.
II, ii, 235

24 Happy in that we are not over happy.
II, ii, 236

25 There is nothing either good or bad, but thinking
makes it so.   *II, ii, 259*

26 O God! I could be bounded in a nutshell, and
count myself a king of infinite space, were it not that
I have bad dreams.   *II, ii, 263*

27 Beggar that I am, I am even poor in thanks.
II, ii, 286

28 This goodly frame, the earth, seems to me a sterile promontory; this most excellent canopy, the air,
look you, this brave o'erhanging firmament, this
majestical roof fretted with golden fire, why, it appears no other thing to me but a foul and pestilent
congregation of vapors. What a piece of work is a
man! How noble in reason! how infinite in faculty!
in form, in moving, how express and admirable! in
action how like an angel! in apprehension how like
a god!   *II, ii, 317*

29 And yet, to me, what is this quintessence of dust?
man delights not me; no, nor woman neither.
II, ii, 328

30 There is something in this more than natural, if
philosophy could find it out.   *II, ii, 392*

31 I am but mad north-northwest: when the wind is
southerly I know a hawk from a handsaw.[2]
II, ii, 405

32 They say an old man is twice a child.[3]
II, ii, 413

33 One fair daughter and no more,
The which he loved passing well.
II, ii, 435

34 Come, give us a taste of your quality.
II, ii, 460

[2]The *hawk* was a basic tool of the plasterer and the *handsaw*
a basic tool of the carpenter. . . . The tools are quite easy to
distinguish. I know that *heronshaw* [a young heron] is the
classic answer but why go all round Robin Hood's barn for an
answer to a simple comparison of common tools?—*Morris
Dictionary of Word and Phrase Origins* [1977], quoting FRAN-
CIS W. SHERIDAN
[3]See Aristophanes, 73:4.

1   The play, I remember, pleased not the million;
'twas caviare to the general.   *Hamlet, II, ii, 465*

2   They are the abstracts and brief chronicles of the
time: after your death you were better have a bad
epitaph than their ill report while you live.
II, ii, 555

3   Use every man after his desert, and who should
'scape whipping?[1]   *II, ii, 561*

4 O! what a rogue and peasant slave am I.
II, ii, 584

5 What's Hecuba to him or he to Hecuba,
That he should weep for her?
II, ii, 593

6 Who calls me villain? breaks my pate across?
Plucks off my beard and blows it in my face?
II, ii, 607

7 But I am pigeon-liver'd, and lack gall
To make oppression bitter.
II, ii, 613

8   The play's the thing
Wherein I'll catch the conscience of the king.
II, ii, 641

9   With devotion's visage
And pious action we do sugar o'er
The devil himself.
III, i, 47

10 To be, or not to be: that is the question:
Whether 'tis nobler in the mind to suffer
The slings and arrows of outrageous fortune,
Or to take arms against a sea of troubles,
And by opposing end them? To die: to sleep;
No more; and, by a sleep to say we end
The heartache and the thousand natural shocks
That flesh is heir to, 'tis a consummation
Devoutly to be wish'd. To die, to sleep;
To sleep: perchance to dream: ay, there's the rub;
For in that sleep of death what dreams may come
When we have shuffled off this mortal coil,
Must give us pause. There's the respect
That makes calamity of so long life;
For who would bear the whips and scorns of
time,
The oppressor's wrong, the proud man's
contumely,
The pangs of dispriz'd love, the law's delay.
The insolence of office, and the spurns
That patient merit of the unworthy takes,
When he himself might his quietus make
With a bare bodkin? who would fardels bear,
To grunt and sweat under a weary life,
But that the dread of something after death,
The undiscover'd country from whose bourn
No traveler returns, puzzles the will,
And makes us rather bear those ills we have
Than fly to others that we know not of?

[1]See Montaigne, 147:1.

Thus conscience does make cowards of us all;
And thus the native hue of resolution
Is sicklied o'er with the pale cast of thought,
And enterprises of great pith and moment
With this regard their currents turn awry,
And lose the name of action.
III, i, 56

11   Nymph, in thy orisons
Be all my sins remember'd.
III, i, 89

12   To the noble mind
Rich gifts wax poor when givers prove unkind.
III, i, 100

13   Get thee to a nunnery.   *III, i, 124*

14   What should such fellows as I do crawling between heaven and earth? We are arrant knaves, all.
III, i, 128

15   Be thou as chaste as ice, as pure as snow, thou
shalt not escape calumny.   *III, i, 142*

16   I have heard of your paintings too, well enough;
God has given you one face, and you make yourselves another.   *III, i, 150*

17 O! what a noble mind is here o'erthrown:
The courtier's, soldier's, scholar's, eye, tongue,
sword.
III, i, 159

18 The glass of fashion and the mould of form,
The observ'd of all observers!
III, i, 162

19 Now see that noble and most sovereign reason,
Like sweet bells jangled, out of tune and harsh.
III, i, 166

20   O! woe is me,
To have seen what I have seen, see what I see!
III, i, 169

21   Speak the speech, I pray you, as I pronounced it
to you, trippingly on the tongue; but if you mouth it,
as many of your players do, I had as lief the town-
crier spoke my lines. Nor do not saw the air too
much with your hand, thus; but use all gently: for in
the very torrent, tempest, and—as I may say—
whirlwind of passion, you must acquire and beget a
temperance, that may give it smoothness. O! it offends me to the soul to hear a robustious periwig-
pated fellow tear a passion to tatters, to very rags, to
split the ears of the groundlings, who for the most
part are capable of nothing but inexplicable dumbshows and noise: I would have such a fellow
whipped for o'erdoing Termagant; it out-herods
Herod.   *III, ii, 1*

22   Suit the action to the word, the word to the action; with this special observance, that you o'erstep
not the modesty of nature.   *III, ii, 20*

23   To hold, as 'twere, the mirror up to nature; to
show virtue her own feature, scorn her own image,

and the very age and body of the time his form and pressure. *III, ii, 25*

1 I have thought some of nature's journeymen had made men and not made them well, they imitated humanity so abominably. *III, ii, 38*

2 No; let the candied tongue lick absurd pomp, And crook the pregnant hinges of the knee Where thrift may follow fawning. *III, ii, 65*

3 A man that fortune's buffets and rewards Hast ta'en with equal thanks. *III, ii, 72*

4 They are not a pipe for fortune's finger To sound what stop she please. Give me that man That is not passion's slave, and I will wear him In my heart's core, ay, in my heart of heart, As I do thee. Something too much of this. *III, ii, 75*

5 My imaginations are as foul As Vulcan's stithy. *III, ii, 88*

6 The chameleon's dish: I eat the air, promise-crammed; you cannot feed capons so. *III, ii, 98*

7 Nay, then, let the devil wear black, for I'll have a suit of sables. *III, ii, 138*

8 There's hope a great man's memory may outlive his life half a year. *III, ii, 141*

9 Marry, this is miching mallecho; it means mischief. *III, ii, 148*

10 *Ophelia:* 'Tis brief, my lord.
Hamlet: As woman's love. *III, ii, 165*

11 Where love is great, the littlest doubts are fear; When little fears grow great, great love grows there. *III, ii, 183*

12 Wormwood, wormwood.[1] *III, ii, 193*

13 The lady doth protest too much, methinks. *III, ii, 242*

14 Let the galled jade wince, our withers are unwrung. *III, ii, 256*

15 Why, let the stricken deer go weep, The hart ungalled play; For some must watch, while some must sleep: So runs the world away. *III, ii, 287*

16 You would pluck out the heart of my mystery. *III, ii, 389*

17 Do you think I am easier to be played on than a pipe? *III, ii, 393*

18 *Hamlet:* Do you see yonder cloud that's almost in shape of a camel?

Polonius: By the mass, and 'tis like a camel, indeed.
Hamlet: Methinks it is like a weasel.
Polonius: It is backed like a weasel.
Hamlet: Or like a whale?
Polonius: Very like a whale.[2] *III, ii, 400*

19 They fool me to the top of my bent. *III, ii, 408*

20 By and by is easily said. *III, ii, 411*

21 'Tis now the very witching time of night, When churchyards yawn and hell itself breathes out Contagion to this world. *III, ii, 413*

22 I will speak daggers to her, but use none. *III, ii, 421*

23 O! my offense is rank, it smells to heaven; It hath the primal eldest curse upon 't; A brother's murder! *III, iii, 36*

24 Now might I do it pat, now he is praying; And now I'll do 't: and so he goes to heaven; And so I am reveng'd. *III, iii, 73*

25 With all his crimes broad blown, as flush as May. *III, iii, 81*

26 My words fly up, my thoughts remain below: Words without thoughts never to heaven go. *III, iii, 97*

27 How now! a rat? Dead, for a ducat, dead! *III, iv, 23*

28 False as dicers' oaths. *III, iv, 45*

29 A rhapsody of words. *III, iv, 48*

30 See, what a grace was seated on this brow; Hyperion's curls, the front of Jove himself, An eye like Mars, to threaten and command, A station like the herald Mercury New-lighted on a heaven-kissing hill, A combination and a form indeed, Where every god did seem to set his seal, To give the world assurance of a man. *III, iv, 55*

31 At your age The heyday in the blood is tame, it's humble. *III, iv, 68*

32 O shame! where is thy blush? Rebellious hell, If thou canst mutine in a matron's bones, To flaming youth let virtue be as wax, And melt in her own fire: proclaim no shame When the compulsive ardor gives the charge,

---

[1]See *Lamentations of Jeremiah 3:19, 29:3.*

[2]See Aristophanes, 73:3, and *Antony and Cleopatra,* 218:3.

Since frost itself as actively doth burn,
And reason panders will.

Hamlet, III, iv, 82

1 A king of shreds and patches.[1]

III, iv, 102

2 Lay not that flattering unction to your soul.

III, iv, 145

3   Confess yourself to heaven;
Repent what's past; avoid what is to come.

III, iv, 149

4 For in the fatness of these pursy times
Virtue itself of vice must pardon beg.

III, iv, 153

5 Assume a virtue, if you have it not.

III, iv, 160

6   Refrain tonight;
And that shall lend a kind of easiness
To the next abstinence: the next more easy;
For use almost can change the stamp of nature.

III, iv, 165

7 I must be cruel only to be kind.

III, iv, 178

8 For 'tis the sport to have the enginer
Hoist with his own petar.

III, iv, 206

9   Diseases desperate grown
By desperate appliance are relieved,
Or not at all.[2]

IV, iii, 9

10   A man may fish with the worm that hath eat of
a king, and eat of the fish that hath fed of that worm.

IV, iii, 29

11 We go to gain a little patch of ground
That hath in it no profit but the name.

IV, iv, 18

12 How all occasions do inform against me,
And spur my dull revenge! What is a man,
If his chief good and market of his time
Be but to sleep and feed? a beast, no more.[3]
Sure he that made us with such large discourse,
Looking before and after, gave us not
That capability and godlike reason
To fust in us unus'd.

IV, iv, 32

13   Some craven scruple
Of thinking too precisely on the event.

IV, iv, 40

14   Rightly to be great
Is not to stir without great argument,

---

¹See W. S. Gilbert, 530:18.
²See Hippocrates, 71:14.
³The unmotivated herd that only sleep and feed. — JAMES
RUSSELL LOWELL, *Under the Old Elm, pt. VII, st. 3*

But greatly to find quarrel in a straw
When honor's at the stake.

IV, iv, 53

15 So full of artless jealousy is guilt,
It spills itself in fearing to be spilt.

IV, v, 19

16 How should I your true love know
From another one?
By his cockle hat and staff,
And his sandal shoon.[4]

IV, v, 23

17 He is dead and gone, lady,
He is dead and gone;
At his head a grass-green turf
At his heels a stone.

IV, v, 29

18   We know what we are, but know not what we
may be.   *IV, v, 43*

19   Come, my coach! Good night, ladies; good night,
sweet ladies; good night, good night.   *IV, v, 72*

20 When sorrows come, they come not single spies,
But in battalions.[5]

IV, v, 78

21   We have done but greenly,
In hugger-mugger to inter him.

IV, v, 84

22 There's such divinity doth hedge a king,
That treason can but peep to what it would.[6]

IV, v, 123

23   There's rosemary, that's for remembrance . . .
and there is pansies, that's for thoughts.

IV, v, 174

24   O! you must wear your rue with a difference.
There's a daisy; I would give you some violets, but
they withered all when my father died.

IV, v, 181

25 A very riband in the cap of youth.

IV, vii, 77

26   Nature her custom holds,
Let shame say what it will.

IV, vii, 188

27   There is no ancient gentlemen but gardeners,
ditchers, and grave-makers; they hold up Adam's
profession.   *V, i, 32*

28   Cudgel thy brains no more about it.

V, i, 61

---

⁴Ophelia is quoting a version of a poem by Walter Ralegh.
⁵One woe doth tread upon another's heel, / So fast they follow. — *Hamlet, act IV, sc. vii, l. 164*
   Thus woe succeeds a woe, as wave a wave. — HERRICK,
Sorrows Succeed [1648]
   Woes cluster; rare are solitary woes; / They love a train, they
tread each other's heel. — EDWARD YOUNG, *Night Thoughts*
[1742–1745], *Night III, l. 63*
   See Cervantes, 149:25.
⁶See Montaigne, 146:21, and Tennyson, 459:3.

1   Has this fellow no feeling of his business, that he sings at grave-making?   *V, i, 71*

2   Custom hath made it in him a property of easiness.   *V, i, 73*

3   A politician . . . one that would circumvent God.   *V, i, 84*

4   Why may not that be the skull of a lawyer? Where be his quiddities now, his quillets, his cases, his tenures, and his tricks?   *V, i, 104*

5   One that was a woman, sir; but, rest her soul, she's dead.   *V, i, 145*

6   How absolute the knave is! we must speak by the card, or equivocation will undo us.   *V, i, 147*

7   The age is grown so picked that the toe of the peasant comes so near the heel of the courtier, he galls his kibe.   *V, i, 150*

8   Alas! poor Yorick. I knew him, Horatio; a fellow of infinite jest, of most excellent fancy; he hath borne me on his back a thousand times; and now, how abhorred in my imagination it is! my gorge rises at it. Here hung those lips that I have kissed I know not how oft. Where be your gibes now? your gambols? your songs? your flashes of merriment, that were wont to set the table on a roar? Not one now, to mock your own grinning? quite chapfallen? Now get you to my lady's chamber, and tell her, let her paint an inch thick, to this favor she must come; make her laugh at that.   *V, i, 201*

9   To what base uses we may return, Horatio! Why may not imagination trace the noble dust of Alexander, till he find it stopping a bung-hole?   *V, i, 222*

10 Imperious Caesar, dead and turn'd to clay,
Might stop a hole to keep the wind away.
       V, i, 235

11   Lay her i' the earth;
And from her fair and unpolluted flesh
May violets spring!
       V, i, 260

12 A ministering angel shall my sister be.[1]
       V, i, 263

13 Sweets to the sweet: farewell!
       V, i, 265

14 I thought thy bride-bed to have deck'd, sweet maid,
And not have strew'd thy grave.
       V, i, 267

15 Though I am not splenetive and rash
Yet have I in me something dangerous.
       V, i, 283

16 I lov'd Ophelia: forty thousand brothers
Could not, with all their quantity of love,
Make up my sum.
       V, i, 291

17   Nay, an thou'lt mouth,
I'll rant as well as thou.
       V, i, 305

18 Let Hercules himself do what he may,
The cat will mew and dog will have his day.
       V, i, 313

19 There's a divinity that shapes our ends,
Rough-hew them how we will.
       V, ii, 10

20 I once did hold it, as our statists do,
A baseness to write fair.
       V, ii, 33

21 It did me yeoman's service.
       V, ii, 36

22   Not a whit, we defy augury; there's a special providence in the fall of a sparrow.[2] If it be now, 'tis not to come; if it be not to come, it will be now; if it be not now, yet it will come: the readiness is all.
       V, ii, 232

23 A hit, a very palpable hit.
       V, ii, 295

24   This fell sergeant, death,
Is strict in his arrest.
       V, ii, 350

25 Report me and my cause aright.
       V, ii, 353

26 I am more an antique Roman than a Dane.
       V, ii, 355

27 O God! Horatio, what a wounded name,
Things standing thus unknown, shall live behind me.
If thou didst ever hold me in thy heart,
Absent thee from felicity awhile,
And in this harsh world draw thy breath in pain,
To tell my story.
       V, ii, 358

28 The rest is silence.
       V, ii, 372

29 Now cracks a noble heart. Good night, sweet prince,
And flights of angels sing thee to thy rest!
       V, ii, 373

30   O proud death![3]
What feast is toward in thine eternal cell?
       V, ii, 378

31 Property was thus appall'd,
That the self was not the same;

[1] See Walter Scott, 378:14.

[2] See *Matthew* 10:29, 34:33, and Pope, 301:5.
[3] See Donne, 230:22.

Single nature's double name
Neither two nor one was call'd.
The Phoenix and the Turtle [1601], l. 37

1 Reason, in itself confounded,
Saw division grow together.
l. 41

2 The chance of war.
Troilus and Cressida [1601–1602], prologue,
l. 31

3   I have had my labor for my travail.[1]
Act I, sc. i, l. 73

4   Women are angels, wooing:
Things won are done; joy's soul lies in the doing.
I, ii, 310

5 Men prize the thing ungain'd more than it is.
I, ii, 313

6   The sea being smooth,
How many shallow bauble boats dare sail
Upon her patient breast.[2]
I, iii, 34

7 The heavens themselves, the planets, and this
center
Observe degree, priority, and place,
Insisture, course, proportion, season, form,
Office, and custom, in all line of order.
I, iii, 85

8   O! when degree is shaked,
Which is the ladder to all high designs,
The enterprise is sick.[3]
I, iii, 101

9 Take but degree away, untune that string,
And, hark! what discord follows; each thing meets
In mere oppugnancy: the bounded waters
Should lift their bosoms higher than the shores,
And make a sop of all this solid globe.
I, iii, 109

10 Then everything includes itself in power,
Power into will, will into appetite;
And appetite, a universal wolf,
So doubly seconded with will and power,
Must make perforce a universal prey,
And last eat up himself.
I, iii, 119

11 Like a strutting player, whose conceit
Lies in his hamstring, and doth think it rich
To hear the wooden dialogue and sound
'Twixt his stretch'd footing and the scaffoldage.
I, iii, 153

12 And in such indexes, although small pricks
To their subsequent volumes, there is seen

The baby figure of the giant mass
Of things to come.
I, iii, 343

13   Who wears his wit in his belly, and his guts in his
head.   *II, i, 78*

14   Modest doubt is call'd
The beacon of the wise, the tent that searches
To the bottom of the worst.
II, ii, 15

15   'Tis mad idolatry
To make the service greater than the god.
II, ii, 56

16   He that is proud eats up himself; pride is his own
glass, his own trumpet, his own chronicle.
II, iii, 165

17 I am giddy, expectation whirls me round.
The imaginary relish is so sweet
That it enchants my sense.
III, ii, 17

18   Words pay no debts.   *III, ii, 56*

19   To fear the worst oft cures the worse.
III, ii, 77

20   All lovers swear more performance than they are
able, and yet reserve an ability that they never perform; vowing more than the perfection of ten and
discharging less than the tenth part of one.
III, ii, 89

21   For to be wise, and love,
Exceeds man's might; that dwells with gods
above.
III, ii, 163

22 If I be false, or swerve a hair from truth,
When time is old and hath forgot itself,
When waterdrops have worn the stones of Troy,
And blind oblivion swallow'd cities up.
And mighty states characterless are grated
To dusty nothing, yet let memory,
From false to false, among false maids in love
Upbraid my falsehood! when they have said "as
false
As air, as water,[4] wind, or sandy earth,
As fox to lamb, as wolf to heifer's calf,
Pard to the hind, or stepdame to her son";
Yea, let them say, to stick the heart of falsehood,
"As false as Cressid."
III, ii, 191

23 Time hath, my lord, a wallet at his back,
Wherein he puts alms for oblivion.
III, iii, 145

24   Perseverance, dear my lord,
Keeps honor bright: to have done, is to hang

[1]See Cervantes, 148:16.
[2]See Publilius Syrus, 99:18.
[3]See Publilius Syrus, 100:22.

[4]See *Othello*, 208:12.

Quite out of fashion, like a rusty mail
In monumental mockery.

III, iii, 150

1 For honor travels in a strait so narrow
Where one but goes abreast.

III, iii, 154

2   Time is like a fashionable host,
That slightly shakes his parting guest by the hand,
And with his arms outstretch'd, as he would fly,
Grasps in the comer: welcome ever smiles,
And farewell goes out sighing.

III, iii, 168

3   Beauty, wit,
High birth, vigor of bone, desert in service,
Love, friendship, charity, are subjects all
To envious and calumniating time.
One touch of nature makes the whole world kin.

III, iii, 171

4 And give to dust that is a little gilt
More laud than gilt o'er-dusted.

III, iii, 178

5 My mind is troubled, like a fountain stirr'd;
And I myself see not the bottom of it.

III, iii, 314

6   You do as chapmen do,
Dispraise the thing that you desire to buy.

IV, i, 75

7 As many farewells as be stars in heaven.

IV, iv, 44

8 And sometimes we are devils to ourselves
When we will tempt the frailty of our powers,
Presuming on their changeful potency.

IV, iv, 95

9 The kiss you take is better than you give.

IV, v, 38

10   Fie, fie upon her!
There's language in her eye, her cheek, her lip,
Nay, her foot speaks; her wanton spirits look out
At every joint and motive of her body.

IV, v, 54

11 What's past and what's to come is strew'd with
    husks
And formless ruin of oblivion.

IV, v, 165

12   The end crowns all,[1]
And that old common arbitrator, Time,
Will one day end it.

IV, v, 223

13 Words, words, mere words, no matter from the
    heart.

V, iii, 109

14 Hector is dead; there is no more to say.

V, x, 22

15   O world! world! world! thus is the poor agent
despised.

V, x, 36

16 If music be the food of love,[2] play on;
Give me excess of it, that, surfeiting,
The appetite may sicken, and so die.
That strain again! it had a dying fall:
O! it came o'er my ear like the sweet sound
That breathes upon a bank of violets,
Stealing and giving odor!

    Twelfth-Night [1601–1602], act I, sc. i, l. 1

17 O spirit of love! how quick and fresh art thou,
That, notwithstanding thy capacity
Receiveth as the sea, nought enters there,
Of what validity and pitch soe'er,
But falls into abatement and low price,
Even in a minute: so full of shapes is fancy,
That it alone is high fantastical.

I, i, 9

18 When my tongue blabs, then let mine eyes not see.

I, ii, 61

19   I am sure care's an enemy to life.   *I, iii, 2*

20   Let them hang themselves in their own straps.

I, iii, 13

21   I am a great eater of beef, and I believe that does
harm to my wit.   *I, iii, 92*

22   Wherefore are these things hid?   *I, iii, 135*

23   Is it a world to hide virtues in?   *I, iii, 142*

24   God give them wisdom that have it; and those
that are fools, let them use their talents.

I, v, 14

25   One draught above heat makes him a fool, the
second mads him, and a third drowns him.

I, v, 139

26 'Tis beauty truly blent, whose red and white
Nature's own sweet and cunning hand laid on:
Lady, you are the cruel'st she alive,
If you will lead these graces to the grave
And leave the world no copy.

I, v, 259

27 Make me a willow cabin at your gate,
And call upon my soul within the house.

I, v, 289

28 Holla your name to the reverberate hills,
And make the babbling gossip of the air
Cry out, "Olivia!"

I, v, 293

29 Farewell, fair cruelty.

I, v, 309

30 O mistress mine! where are you roaming?

II, iii, 42

---

[1] See Anonymous: Latin, 119:3; John Heywood, 141:20; *All's Well That Ends Well*, 203:17; Herrick, 241:2; and Quarles, 242:13.

[2] Is not music the food of love? — RICHARD BRINSLEY SHERIDAN, *The Rivals* [1775], act II, sc. i
See *Antony and Cleopatra*, 217:18.

1 Journeys end in lovers meeting,
Every wise man's son doth know.

Twelfth-Night, II, iii, 46

2 What is love? 'tis not hereafter;
Present mirth hath present laughter.
What's to come is still unsure:
In delay there lies no plenty;
Then come kiss me, sweet and twenty,
Youth's a stuff will not endure.

II, iii, 50

3   He does it with a better grace, but I do it more
natural.   *II, iii, 91*

4   Is there no respect of place, persons, nor time, in
you?[1]   *II, iii, 100*

5   *Sir Toby:* Dost thou think, because thou art virtuous, there shall be no more cakes and ale?
    Clown: Yes, by Saint Anne; and ginger shall be
hot i' the mouth too.   *II, iii, 124*

6   The devil a puritan that he is, or anything constantly but a time-pleaser; an affectioned ass.

II, iii, 161

7   My purpose is, indeed, a horse of that color.[2]

II, iii, 184

8 These most brisk and giddy-paced times.

II, iv, 6

9   If ever thou shalt love,
In the sweet pangs of it remember me;
For such as I am all true lovers are:
Unstaid and skittish in all motions else
Save in the constant image of the creature
That is belov'd.

II, iv, 15

10   Let still the woman take
An elder than herself, so wears she to him,
So sways she level in her husband's heart:
For, boy, however we do praise ourselves,
Our fancies are more giddy and unfirm,
More longing, wavering, sooner lost and worn,
Than women's are.

II, iv, 29

11 Then, let thy love be younger than thyself,
Or thy affection cannot hold the bent;
For women are as roses, whose fair flower
Being once display'd, doth fall that very hour.

II, iv, 36

12 The spinsters and the knitters in the sun,
And the free maids that weave their thread with
        bones,
Do use to chant it: it is silly sooth,
And dallies with the innocence of love,
Like the old age.

II, iv, 44

13 Come away, come away, death,
And in sad cypress let me be laid;

---

[1] See *Acts 10:34, 41:10.*
[2] A play on "a horse of a different color."

Fly away, fly away, breath;
I am slain by a fair cruel maid.

II, iv, 51

14 *Duke:*   And what's her history?
Viola: A blank, my lord. She never told her love,
But let concealment, like a worm i' the bud,
Feed on her damask cheek: she pin'd in thought,
And with a green and yellow melancholy,
She sat like Patience on a monument,
Smiling at grief.

II, iv, 112

15 I am all the daughters of my father's house,
And all the brothers too.

II, iv, 122

16   Here comes the trout that must be caught with
tickling.   *II, v, 25*

17 I may command where I adore.

II, v, 116

18   Be not afraid of greatness: some are born great,
some achieve greatness, and some have greatness
thrust upon them.   *II, v, 159*

19   Remember who commended thy yellow stockings, and wished to see thee ever cross-gartered.

II, v, 168

20   Foolery, sir, does walk about the orb like the sun;
it shines everywhere.   *III, i, 44*

21 This fellow's wise enough to play the fool,
And to do that well craves a kind of wit.

III, i, 68

22 Music from the spheres.[3]

III, i, 122

23 How apt the poor are to be proud.

III, i, 141

24 Then westward-ho!

III, i, 148

25 O! what a deal of scorn looks beautiful
In the contempt and anger of his lip.

III, i, 159

26 Love sought is good, but giv'n unsought is better.

III, i, 170

27   You will hang like an icicle on a Dutchman's
beard.   *III, ii, 30*

28   Let there be gall enough in thy ink.

III, ii, 54

29   Laugh yourselves into stitches.   *III, ii, 75*

30   I think we do know the sweet Roman hand.

III, iv, 31

31   This is very midsummer madness.   *III, iv, 62*

32   More matter for a May morning.

III, iv, 158

---

[3] The music of the spheres.—*Pericles, act V, sc. i, l. 231*
A phrase that stems from the Pythagorean Theory (sixth
century B.C.) of the music or harmony of the spheres.
See Thomas Browne, 248:20.

1   He's a very devil.   *III, iv, 304*

2 Out of my lean and low ability
I'll lend you something.
III, iv, 380

3 I hate ingratitude more in a man
Than lying, vainness, babbling drunkenness,
Or any taint of vice whose strong corruption
Inhabits our frail blood.
III, iv, 390

4   As the old hermit of Prague, that never saw pen
and ink, very wittily said to a niece of King Gorboduc, "That, that is, is."   *IV, ii, 14*

5   I say there is no darkness but ignorance, in which
thou art more puzzled than the Egyptians in their
fog.   *IV, ii, 47*

6   Thus the whirligig of time brings in his revenges.
V, i, 388

7 When that I was and a little tiny boy,
With hey, ho, the wind and the rain;
A foolish thing was but a toy,
For the rain it raineth every day.[1]

V, i, 404

8   Love all, trust a few,
Do wrong to none: be able for thine enemy
Rather in power than use, and keep thy friend
Under thy own life's key: be check'd for silence,
But never tax'd for speech.
*All's Well That Ends Well [1602–1604], act I,
sc. i, l. 74*

9   It were all one
That I should love a bright particular star
And think to wed it, he is so above me.
I, i, 97

10 The hind that would be mated by the lion
Must die for love.
I, i, 103

11 My friends were poor, but honest.[2]
I, iii, 203

12 Oft expectation fails, and most oft there
Where most it promises.
II, i, 145

13   They say miracles are past.   *II, iii, 1*

14 A young man married is a man that's marr'd.
II, iii, 315

15   The web of our life is of a mingled yarn, good and
ill together.   *IV, iii, 83*

16 There's place and means for every man alive.
IV, iii, 379

17 All's well that ends well: still the fine's the crown;
Whate'er the course, the end is the renown.[3]
IV, iv, 35

18   I am a man whom Fortune hath cruelly scratched.
V, ii, 28

19   Praising what is lost
Makes the remembrance dear.
V, iii, 19

20 The inaudible and noiseless foot of time.
V, iii, 41

21   Love that comes too late,
Like a remorseful pardon slowly carried.
V, iii, 57

22   All impediments in fancy's course
Are motives of more fancy.
V, iii, 216

23   Good counselors lack no clients.
Measure for Measure [1604], act I, sc. ii, l. 115

24 And liberty plucks justice by the nose.
I, iii, 29

25 I hold you as a thing ensky'd and sainted.
I, iv, 34

26   A man whose blood
Is very snow-broth; one who never feels
The wanton stings and motions of the sense.
I, iv, 57

27   Our doubts are traitors,
And make us lose the good we oft might win,
By fearing to attempt.[4]
I, iv, 78

28 We must not make a scarecrow of the law,
Setting it up to fear the birds of prey,
And let it keep one shape, till custom make it
Their perch and not their terror.
II, i, 1

29 The jury, passing on the prisoner's life,
May in the sworn twelve have a thief or two
Guiltier than him they try.
II, i, 19

30 Some rise by sin, and some by virtue fall.
II, i, 38

31   Great with child, and longing . . . for stewed
prunes.   *II, i, 94*

32 This will last out a night in Russia,
When nights are longest there.
II, i, 144

33   His face is the worst thing about him.
II, i, 167

34 Condemn the fault, and not the actor of it?
II, ii, 37

---

[1]Parodied by the Fool in *King Lear*, 210:1.
[2]Though I be poor, I'm honest.—MIDDLETON, *The Witch*
[c. 1627], *III, 2*
See Anonymous, 782:17.

[3]See Anonymous: Latin, 119:3; John Heywood, 141:20;
Troilus and Cressida, 201:12; Herrick, 241:2; and Quarles,
242:13.
[4]See *Macbeth*, 213:9.

1 No ceremony that to great ones 'longs,
Not the king's crown, nor the deputed sword,
The marshal's truncheon, nor the judge's robe,
Become them with one half so good a grace
As mercy does.[1]

Measure for Measure, II, ii, 59

2 The law hath not been dead, though it hath slept.

II, ii, 90

3   O! it is excellent
To have a giant's strength, but it is tyrannous
To use it like a giant.

II, ii, 107

4   But man, proud man,
Drest in a little brief authority,
Most ignorant of what he's most assur'd,
His glassy essence, like an angry ape,
Plays such fantastic tricks before high heaven
As make the angels weep.

II, ii, 117

5 That in the captain's but a choleric word,
Which in the soldier is flat blasphemy.

II, ii, 130

6   It oft falls out,
To have what we would have, we speak not what
we mean.

II, iv, 118

7 The miserable have no other medicine
But only hope.

III, i, 2

8 Be absolute for death.

III, i, 5

9   A breath thou art,
Servile to all the skyey influences.

III, i, 8

10   Thou hast nor youth nor age;
But, as it were, an after-dinner's sleep,
Dreaming on both; for all thy blessed youth
Becomes as aged, and doth beg the alms
Of palsied eld; and when thou art old and rich,
Thou hast neither heat, affection, limb, nor
beauty,
To make thy riches pleasant.

III, i, 32

11 The sense of death is most in apprehension,[2]
And the poor beetle, that we tread upon,
In corporal sufferance finds a pang as great
As when a giant dies.

III, i, 76

12   If I must die,
I will encounter darkness as a bride,
And hug it in my arms.

III, i, 81

13 The cunning livery of hell.

III, i, 93

14 Ay, but to die, and go we know not where;
To lie in cold obstruction and to rot;
This sensible warm motion to become
A kneaded clod; and the delighted spirit
To bathe in fiery floods, or to reside
In thrilling region of thick-ribbed ice;
To be imprison'd in the viewless winds,
And blown with restless violence round about
The pendant world.

III, i, 116

15 The weariest and most loathed worldly life
That age, ache, penury, and imprisonment
Can lay on nature is a paradise
To what we fear of death.

III, i, 127

16   The hand that hath made you fair hath made you
good.[3]   *III, i, 182*

17   Virtue is bold, and goodness never fearful.

III, i, 214

18   There, at the moated grange, resides this dejected
Mariana.[4]   *III, i, 279*

19   This news is old enough, yet it is every day's
news.   *III, ii, 249*

20 He, who the sword of heaven will bear
Should be as holy as severe.

III, ii, 283

21 O, what may man within him hide,
Though angel on the outward side!

III, ii, 293

22 Take, O take those lips away,
That so sweetly were forsworn;
And those eyes, the break of day,
Lights that do mislead the morn:
But my kisses bring again, bring again,
Seals of love, but seal'd in vain, seal'd in vain.[5]

IV, i, 1

23   Music oft hath such a charm
To make bad good, and good provoke to harm.[6]

IV, i, 16

24   Every true man's apparel fits your thief.

IV, ii, 46

25   The old fantastical duke of dark corners.

IV, iii, 167

26   I am a kind of burr; I shall stick.

IV, iii, 193

---

[3]See Spenser, 154:15.
[4]"Mariana in the moated grange." —*Motto used by* TENNY-
SON *for the poem* Mariana [1830]
[5]This song occurs in act V, sc. ii, of FLETCHER's *Bloody
Brother* [c. 1616], with an additional stanza:
Hide, O hide those hills of snow, / Which thy frozen bosom
bears, / On whose tops the pinks that grow / Are of those that
April wears! / But first set my poor heart free, / Bound in those
icy chains by thee.
[6]See Congreve, 291:7.

---

[1]See *The Merchant of Venice*, 181:19.
[2]See Publilius Syrus, 99:28.

1 We would, and we would not.
IV, iv, 37

2 A forted residence 'gainst the tooth of time
And razure of oblivion.
V, i, 12

3   Truth is truth
To the end of reckoning.
V, i, 45

4 Neither maid, widow, nor wife.
V, i, 173

5 Haste still pays haste, and leisure answers leisure,
Like doth quit like, and Measure still for
Measure.
V, i, 411

6 They say best men are molded out of faults,
And, for the most, become much more the better
For being a little bad.
V, i, 440

7 What's mine is yours, and what is yours is mine.[1]
V, i, 539

8 Horribly stuff'd with epithets of war.
Othello [1604–1605], act I, sc. i, l. 14

9 A fellow almost damn'd in a fair wife.
I, i, 21

10 The bookish theoric.
I, i, 24

11 We cannot all be masters.
I, i, 43

12 And when he's old, cashier'd.
I, i, 48

13 In following him, I follow but myself.
I, i, 58

14 But I will wear my heart upon my sleeve
For daws to peck at.
I, i, 64

15   An old black ram
Is tupping your white ewe.
I, i, 88

16   You are one of those that will not serve God if the
devil bid you.   *I, i, 108*

17   Your daughter and the Moor are now making the
beast with two backs.   *I, i, 117*

18 Keep up your bright swords, for the dew will rust
them.
I, ii, 59

19 The wealthy curled darlings of our nation.
I, ii, 68

20   The bloody book of law
You shall yourself read in the bitter letter
After your own sense.
I, iii, 67

[1] See Plautus, 83:7.

21   Rude am I in my speech,
And little bless'd with the soft phrase of peace.
I, iii, 81

22   Little shall I grace my cause
In speaking for myself. Yet, by your gracious
patience,
I will a round unvarnish'd tale deliver
Of my whole course of love.
I, iii, 88

23   A maiden never bold;
Of spirit so still and quiet, that her motion
Blush'd at herself.
I, iii, 94

24 Still question'd me the story of my life
From year to year, the battles, sieges, fortunes
That I have pass'd.
I, iii, 129

25 Wherein I spake of most disastrous chances,
Of moving accidents by flood and field,
Of hair-breadth 'scapes i' the imminent deadly
breach.
I, iii, 134

26 Hills whose heads touch heaven.
I, iii, 141

27 And of the Cannibals that each other eat,
The Anthropophagi, and men whose heads
Do grow beneath their shoulders.
I, iii, 143

28   My story being done,
She gave me for my pains a world of sighs:
She swore, in faith, 'twas strange, 'twas passing
strange;
'Twas pitiful, 'twas wondrous pitiful:
She wish'd she had not heard it, yet she wish'd
That heaven had made her such a man; she
thank'd me,
And bade me, if I had a friend that lov'd her,
I should but teach him how to tell my story,
And that would woo her. Upon this hint I spake:
She lov'd me for the dangers I had pass'd,
And I lov'd her that she did pity them.
This only is the witchcraft I have us'd.
I, iii, 158

29 I do perceive here a divided duty.
I, iii, 181

30 To mourn a mischief that is past and gone
Is the next way to draw new mischief on.
I, iii, 204

31 The robb'd that smiles steals something from the
thief.
I, iii, 208

32   Our bodies are our gardens, to the which our
wills are gardeners.   *I, iii, 324*

33   Put money in thy purse.   *I, iii, 345*

1 The food that to him now is as luscious as locusts, shall be to him shortly as bitter as coloquintida.   *Othello, I, iii, 354*

2 Framed to make women false.
                                    I, iii, 404

3 The enchafed flood.
                                    II, i, 17

4 One that excels the quirks of blazoning pens.
                                    II, i, 63

5   You are pictures out of doors,
Bells in your parlors, wildcats in your kitchens,
Saints in your injuries, devils being offended,
Players in your housewifery, and housewives in
    your beds.
                                    II, i, 109

6 For I am nothing if not critical.
                                    II, i, 119

7 I am not merry, but I do beguile
The thing I am by seeming otherwise.
                                    II, i, 122

8 She that was ever fair and never proud,
Had tongue at will and yet was never loud.
                                    II, i, 148

9 *Iago:* To suckle fools and chronicle small beer.[1]
Desdemona: O most lame and impotent
            conclusion!
                                    II, i, 160

10   You may relish him more in the soldier than in
the scholar.   *II, i, 165*

11   If it were now to die,
'Twere now to be most happy.
                                    II, i, 192

12   Base men being in love have then a nobility in
their natures more than is native to them.
                                    II, i, 218

13 Egregiously an ass.
                                    II, i, 321

14   I have very poor and unhappy brains for drinking.   *II, iii, 34*

15 Potations pottle deep.
                                    II, iii, 57

16   Well, God's above all; and there be souls must be
saved, and there be souls must not be saved.
                                    II, iii, 106

17 Silence that dreadful bell! it frights the isle
From her propriety.
                                    II, iii, 177

18 But men are men; the best sometimes forget.
                                    II, iii, 243

19 Thy honesty and love doth mince this matter.[2]
                                    II, iii, 249

20   Reputation, reputation, reputation! O! I have lost
my reputation. I have lost the immortal part of myself, and what remains is bestial.   *II, iii, 264*

21   Reputation is an idle and most false imposition;
oft got without merit, and lost without deserving.
                                    II, iii, 270

22   O thou invisible spirit of wine! if thou hast no
name to be known by, let us call thee devil!
                                    II, iii, 285

23   O God! that men should put an enemy in their
mouths to steal away their brains; that we should,
with joy, pleasance, revel, and applause, transform
ourselves into beasts.   *II, iii, 293*

24   Good wine is a good familiar creature if it be well
used.   *II, iii, 315*

25 Play the villain.
                                    II, iii, 345

26 How poor are they that have not patience!
What wound did ever heal but by degrees?
                                    II, iii, 379

27 Excellent wretch! Perdition catch my soul
But I do love thee! and when I love thee not,
Chaos is come again.[3]
                                    III, iii, 90

28 Men should be what they seem.
                                    III, iii, 126

29   Speak to me as to thy thinkings,
As thou dost ruminate, and give thy worst of
        thoughts
The worst of words.
                                    III, iii, 131

30 Good name in man and woman, dear my lord,
Is the immediate jewel of their souls:
Who steals my purse steals trash; 'tis something,
        nothing;
'Twas mine, 'tis his, and has been slave to
        thousands;
But he that filches from me my good name
Robs me of that which not enriches him,
And makes me poor indeed.
                                    III, iii, 155

31   O! beware, my lord, of jealousy;
It is the green-ey'd monster which doth mock
The meat it feeds on; that cuckold lives in bliss
Who, certain of his fate, loves not his wronger;
But, O! what damned minutes tells he o'er
Who dotes, yet doubts; suspects, yet soundly
        loves!
                                    III, iii, 165

32 Poor and content is rich, and rich enough.
                                    III, iii, 172

33 Think'st thou I'd make a life of jealousy,
To follow still the changes of the moon

---

[1]See *King Henry VI, Part II*, 164:7.
[2]See Cervantes, 148:15.

[3]See *Venus and Adonis*, 165:16.

With fresh suspicions? No; to be once in doubt
Is once to be resolved.

III, iii, 177

1 I humbly do beseech you of your pardon
For too much loving you.

III, iii, 212

2   If I do prove her haggard,
Though that her jesses were my dear heart-strings,
I'd whistle her off and let her down the wind,
To prey at fortune.

III, iii, 260

3   I am declin'd
Into the vale of years.

III, iii, 265

4   O curse of marriage!
That we can call these delicate creatures ours,
And not their appetites. I had rather be a toad,
And live upon the vapor of a dungeon,
Than keep a corner in the thing I love
For others' uses.

III, iii, 268

5   Trifles light as air
Are to the jealous confirmations strong
As proofs of holy writ.

III, iii, 323

6   Not poppy, nor mandragora,[1]
Nor all the drowsy syrups of the world,
Shall ever medicine thee to that sweet sleep
Which thou ow'dst yesterday.

III, iii, 331

7 He that is robb'd, not wanting what is stol'n,
Let him not know 't and he's not robb'd at all.[2]

III, iii, 343

8   O! now, forever
Farewell the tranquil mind; farewell content!
Farewell the plumed troop and the big wars
That make ambition virtue! O, farewell!
Farewell the neighing steed, and the shrill trump,
The spirit-stirring drum, the ear-piercing fife,
The royal banner, and all quality,
Pride, pomp, and circumstance of glorious war!
And, O you mortal engines, whose rude throats
The immortal Jove's dread clamors counterfeit,
Farewell! Othello's occupation's gone!

III, iii, 348

9 Be sure of it; give me the ocular proof.

III, iii, 361

10   No hinge nor loop
To hang a doubt on.

III, iii, 366

11 On horror's head horrors accumulate.

III, iii, 371

[1] See *Antony and Cleopatra*, 217:4.
[2] See Publilius Syrus, 99:1.

12   Take note, take note, O world!
To be direct and honest is not safe.

III, iii, 378

13 But this denoted a foregone conclusion.

III, iii, 429

14   Swell, bosom, with thy fraught,
For 'tis of aspics' tongues!

III, iii, 450

15   Like to the Pontick sea,
Whose icy current and compulsive course
Ne'er feels retiring ebb, but keeps due on
To the Propontic and the Hellespont,
Even so my bloody thoughts, with violent pace,
Shall ne'er look back, ne'er ebb to humble love,
Till that a capable and wide revenge
Swallow them up.

III, iii, 454

16 Our new heraldry is hands not hearts.

III, iv, 48

17 But jealous souls will not be answer'd so;
They are not ever jealous for the cause,
But jealous for they are jealous; 'tis a monster
Begot upon itself, born on itself.

III, iv, 158

18   'Tis the strumpet's plague
To beguile many and be beguil'd by one.

IV, i, 97

19   They laugh that win.   *IV, i, 123*

20   My heart is turned to stone; I strike it, and it
hurts my hand. O! the world hath not a sweeter
creature; she might lie by an emperor's side and
command him tasks.   *IV, i, 190*

21   O, she will sing the savageness out of a bear.
IV, i, 198

22   But yet the pity of it, Iago! O! Iago, the pity of it,
Iago!   *IV, i, 205*

23   Is this the noble nature
Whom passion could not shake? whose solid
    virtue
The shot of accident nor dart of chance
Could neither graze nor pierce?

IV, i, 276

24 I understand a fury in your words,
But not the words.

IV, ii, 31

25 Steep'd me in poverty to the very lips.

IV, ii, 49

26   But, alas! to make me
A fixed figure for the time of scorn
To point his slow and moving finger at.

IV, ii, 52

27 Patience, thou young and rose-lipp'd cherubin.

IV, ii, 62

1 O thou weed!
Who art so lovely fair and smell'st so sweet
That the sense aches at thee, would thou hadst
    ne'er been born.

Othello, IV, ii, 66

2 O heaven! that such companions thou'dst unfold,
And put in every honest hand a whip
To lash the rascals naked through the world.

IV, ii, 141

3 Unkindness may do much;
And his unkindness may defeat my life,
But never taint my love.

IV, ii, 159

4 The poor soul sat sighing by a sycamore tree,
Sing all a green willow;[1]
Her hand on her bosom, her head on her knee,
Sing willow, willow, willow.

IV, iii, 41

5 It makes us, or it mars us.

V, i, 4

6 Every way makes my gain.

V, .i, 14

7 He hath a daily beauty in his life.

V, i, 19

8 This is the night
That either makes me or fordoes me quite.

V, i, 128

9 And smooth as monumental alabaster.

V, ii, 5

10 Put out the light, and then put out the light:
If I quench thee, thou flaming minister,
I can again thy former light restore,
Should I repent me; but once put out thy light,
Thou cunning'st pattern of excelling nature,
I know not where is that Promethean heat
That can thy light relume.

V, ii, 7

11 It is the very error of the moon;
She comes more near the earth than she was
    wont,
And makes men mad.

V, ii, 107

12 She was as false as water.[2]

V, ii, 132

13 Curse his better angel from his side,
And fall to reprobation.

V, ii, 206

14 Here is my journey's end, here is my butt,
And very sea-mark of my utmost sail.

V, ii, 266

15 An honorable murderer, if you will;
For nought I did in hate, but all in honor.

V, ii, 293

16 I have done the state some service, and they
    know 't;
No more of that. I pray you, in your letters,
When you shall these unlucky deeds relate,
Speak of me as I am; nothing extenuate,
Nor set down aught in malice: then, must you
    speak
Of one that lov'd not wisely but too well;
Of one not easily jealous, but, being wrought,
Perplex'd in the extreme; of one whose hand,
Like the base Indian, threw a pearl away
Richer than all his tribe; of one whose subdu'd
    eyes
Albeit unused to the melting mood,
Drop tears as fast as the Arabian trees
Their med'cinable gum.

V, ii, 338

17 In Aleppo once,
Where a malignant and a turban'd Turk
Beat a Venetian and traduc'd the state,
I took by the throat the circumcised dog,
And smote him thus.

V, ii, 354

18 My love's
More richer than my tongue.

King Lear [1605], act I, sc. 1, l. 79

19 Now, our joy,
Although our last, not least.[3]

I, i, 84

20 Nothing will come of nothing.[4]

I, i, 92

21 Mend your speech a little,
Lest you may mar your fortunes.

I, i, 96

22 *Lear:* So young, and so untender?
Cordelia: So young, my lord, and true.

I, i, 108

23 Come not between the dragon and his wrath.

I, i, 124

24 Kill thy physician, and the fee bestow
Upon the foul disease.

I, i, 166

25 I want that glib and oily art
To speak and purpose not.

I, i, 227

26 A still-soliciting eye.

I, i, 234

27 Time shall unfold what plighted cunning hides;
Who covers faults, at last shame them derides.

I, i, 282

28 The infirmity of his age. *I, i, 296*

29 Who in the lusty stealth of nature take
More composition and fierce quality

---

[1]See John Heywood, 140:12.
[2]See *Troilus and Cressida*, 200:22.

[3]See Spenser, 154:10, and *Julius Caesar*, 188:21.
[4]See Lucretius, 89:6.

Than doth, within a dull, stale, tired bed,
Go to the creating a whole tribe of fops.

I, ii, 11

1 Now, gods, stand up for bastards!

I, ii, 22

2 We have seen the best of our time: machinations, hollowness, treachery, and all ruinous disorders, follow us disquietly to our graves. *I, ii, 125*

3 This is the excellent foppery of the world, that, when we are sick in fortune,—often the surfeit of our own behavior,—we make guilty of our disasters the sun, the moon, and the stars; as if we were villains by necessity, fools by heavenly compulsion, knaves, thieves, and treachers by spherical predominance, drunkards, liars, and adulterers by an enforced obedience of planetary influence.

I, ii, 129

4 Edgar—
[*Enter Edgar*]
and pat he comes, like the catastrophe of the old comedy: my cue is villainous melancholy, with a sigh like Tom o' Bedlam. *I, ii, 149*

5 *Lear:* Dost thou know me, fellow?
Kent: No, sir, but you have that in your countenance which I would fain call master.
Lear: What's that?
Kent: Authority. *I, iv, 28*

6 That which ordinary men are fit for, I am qualified in, and the best of me is diligence. *I, iv, 36*

7 Truth's a dog must to kennel; he must be whipped out when Lady the brach may stand by the fire and stink. *I, iv, 125*

8 Have more than thou showest,
Speak less than thou knowest,
Lend less than thou owest.

I, iv, 132

9 Can you make no use of nothing, nuncle?

I, iv, 144

10 Ingratitude, thou marble-hearted fiend,
More hideous, when thou show'st thee in a child,
Than the sea-monster.

I, iv, 283

11 How sharper than a serpent's tooth it is
To have a thankless child!

I, iv, 312

12 Striving to better, oft we mar what's well.

I, iv, 371

13 The son and heir of a mongrel bitch.

II, ii, 23

14 I have seen better faces in my time
Than stands on any shoulder that I see
Before me at this instant.

II, ii, 99

15 A good man's fortune may grow out at heels.

II, ii, 164

16 Fortune, good night, smile once more; turn thy wheel!

II, ii, 180

17 *Hysterica passio!* down, thou climbing sorrow!
Thy element's below.

II, iv, 57

18 That sir which serves and seeks for gain,
And follows but for form,
Will pack when it begins to rain,
And leave thee in the storm.

II, iv, 79

19 Nature in you stands on the very verge
Of her confine.

II, iv, 149

20 Necessity's sharp pinch!

II, iv, 214

21 Our basest beggars
Are in the poorest thing superfluous:
Allow not nature more than nature needs,
Man's life is cheap as beast's.

II, iv, 267

22 Let not women's weapons, waterdrops,
Stain my man's cheeks!

II, iv, 280

23 I have full cause of weeping, but this heart
Shall break into a hundred thousand flaws
Or ere I'll weep. O fool! I shall go mad.

II, iv, 287

24 Blow, winds, and crack your cheeks! rage! blow!
You cataracts and hurricanoes, spout
Till you have drench'd our steeples, drown'd the cocks!
You sulphurous and thought-executing fires,
Vaunt-couriers to oak-cleaving thunderbolts,
Singe my white head! And thou, all-shaking thunder,
Strike flat the thick rotundity o' the world!
Crack nature's molds, all germens spill at once
That make ingrateful man!

III, ii, 1

25 I tax not you, you elements, with unkindness.

III, ii, 16

26 A poor, infirm, weak, and despis'd old man.

III, ii, 20

27 There was never yet fair woman but she made mouths in a glass. *III, ii, 35*

28 I will be the pattern of all patience.

III, ii, 37

29 I am a man
More sinn'd against than sinning.

III, ii, 59

30 The art of our necessities is strange,
That can make vile things precious.

III, ii, 70

1 He that has and a little tiny wit,
With hey, ho, the wind and the rain,
Must make content with his fortunes fit,
Though the rain it raineth every day.[1]
King Lear, III, ii, 76

2 O! that way madness lies; let me shun that.
III, iv, 21

3 Poor naked wretches, wheresoe'er you are,
That bide the pelting of this pitiless storm,
How shall your houseless heads and unfed sides,
Your loop'd and window'd raggedness, defend
 you
From seasons such as these? O! I have ta'en
Too little care of this. Take physic, pomp;
Expose thyself to feel what wretches feel,
That thou mayst shake the superflux to them,
And show the heavens more just.
III, iv, 28

4 Pillicock sat on Pillicock-hill:
Halloo, halloo, loo, loo!
III, iv, 75

5   Out-paramoured the Turk.   *III, iv, 91*

6   Is man no more than this? Consider him well.
Thou owest the worm no silk, the beast no hide, the
sheep no wool, the cat no perfume. Ha! here's three
on 's are sophisticated; thou art the thing itself;
unaccommodated man is no more but such a poor,
bare, forked animal as thou art. Off, off, you lend-
ings! Come; unbutton here.   *III, iv, 105*

7   'Tis a naughty night to swim in.   *III, iv, 113*

8   The green mantle of the standing pool.
III, iv, 137

9 But mice and rats and such small deer
Have been Tom's food for seven long year.
III, iv, 142

10 The prince of darkness is a gentleman.[2]
III, iv, 147

11 Poor Tom's a-cold.
III, iv, 151

12 Child Rowland to the dark tower came,[3]
His word was still, Fie, foh, and fum,
I smell the blood of a British man.
III, iv, 185

13   He's mad that trusts in the tameness of a wolf, a
horse's health, a boy's love, or a whore's oath.
III, vi, 20

[1]See *Twelfth-Night*, 203:7.
[2]The Devil is a gentleman.—SHELLEY, *Peter Bell the Third*
[1819], *pt. II, st. 2*
[3]Child Roland to the dark tower came.—WALTER SCOTT,
The Bridal of Triermain [1813]
 Dauntless the slug-horn to my lips I set, / And blew. "*Childe
Roland to the Dark Tower came.*"—ROBERT BROWNING,
Child Roland to the Dark Tower Came [1855], *st. 34*

14   The little dogs and all,
Tray, Blanch, and Sweetheart, see, they bark at
 me.
III, vi, 65

15   Is there any cause in nature that makes these hard
hearts?   *III, vi, 81*

16 I am tied to the stake, and I must stand the
 course.
III, vii, 54

17 Out, vile jelly!
III, vii, 83

18 The lowest and most dejected thing of fortune.
IV, i, 3

19   The worst is not,
So long as we can say, "This is the worst."
IV, i, 27

20 As flies to wanton boys, are we to the gods;
They kill us for their sport.
IV, i, 36

21 You are not worth the dust which the rude wind
Blows in your face.
IV, ii, 30

22 She that herself will sliver and disbranch
From her material sap, perforce must wither
And come to deadly use.
IV, ii, 34

23 Wisdom and goodness to the vile seem vile;
Filths savor but themselves.
IV, ii, 38

24 Tigers, not daughters.
IV, ii, 39

25   It is the stars,
The stars above us, govern our conditions.
IV, iii, 34

26 Our foster-nurse of nature is repose.
IV, iv, 12

27   How fearful
And dizzy 'tis to cast one's eyes so low!
The crows and choughs that wing the midway air
Show scarce so gross as beetles; halfway down
Hangs one that gathers samphire, dreadful trade!
Methinks he seems no bigger than his head.
The fishermen that walk upon the beach
Appear like mice, and yond tall anchoring bark
Diminish'd to her cock, her cock a buoy
Almost too small for sight. The murmuring surge,
That on the unnumber'd idle pebbles chafes,
Cannot be heard so high.
IV, vi, 12

28   Nature's above art in that respect.
IV, vi, 87

29 Ay, every inch a king.
IV, vi, 110

1 The wren goes to 't, and the small gilded fly
Does lecher in my sight.
Let copulation thrive.

IV, vi, 115

2   Give me an ounce of civet, good apothecary, to
sweeten my imagination.   *IV, vi, 133*

3   A man may see how this world goes with no eyes.
Look with thine ears: see how yond justice rails
upon yon simple thief. Hark, in thine ear: change
places; and, handy-dandy, which is the justice,
which is the thief?   *IV, vi, 154*

4 Through tatter'd clothes small vices do appear;
Robes and furr'd gowns hide all. Plate sin with
    gold,
And the strong lance of justice hurtless breaks;
Arm it in rags, a pigmy's straw does pierce it.

IV, vi, 169

5   Get thee glass eyes;
And, like a scurvy politician, seem
To see the things thou dost not.

IV, vi, 175

6 When we are born, we cry that we are come
To this great stage of fools.

IV, vi, 187

7 Then, kill, kill, kill, kill, kill, kill!

IV, vi, 192

8   Mine enemy's dog,
Though he had bit me, should have stood that
    night
Against my fire.

IV, vii, 36

9 Thou art a soul in bliss; but I am bound
Upon a wheel of fire, that mine own tears
Do scald like molten lead.

IV, vii, 46

10 I am a very foolish fond old man,
Fourscore and upward, not an hour more or less;
And, to deal plainly,
I fear I am not in my perfect mind.

IV, vii, 60

11 Pray you now, forget and forgive.[1]

IV, vii, 84

12   Men must endure
Their going hence, even as their coming hither:
Ripeness is all.

V, ii, 9

13   Come, let's away to prison;
We two alone will sing like birds i' the cage:
When thou dost ask me blessing, I'll kneel down,
And ask of thee forgiveness: so we'll live,
And pray, and sing, and tell old tales, and laugh
At gilded butterflies, and hear poor rogues
Talk of court news; and we'll talk with them too,
Who loses and who wins; who's in, who's out;

[1] All our great fray . . . is forgiven and forgotten between
us quite. — JOHN HEYWOOD, *Proverbs* [1546], *pt. II, ch. 3*

And take upon's the mystery of things,
As if we were God's spies: and we'll wear out,
In a wall'd prison, packs and sets of great ones
That ebb and flow by the moon.

V, iii, 8

14 Upon such sacrifices, my Cordelia,
The gods themselves throw incense.

V, iii, 20

15 The gods are just, and of our pleasant vices
Make instruments to plague us.

V, iii, 172

16 The wheel is come full circle.

V, iii, 176

17 Howl, howl, howl, howl! O! you are men of
    stones:
Had I your tongues and eyes, I'd use them so
That heaven's vaults should crack. She's gone
    forever.

V, iii, 259

18   Her voice was ever soft,
Gentle and low, an excellent thing in woman.

V, iii, 274

19 And my poor fool is hang'd! No, no, no life!
Why should a dog, a horse, a rat, have life,
And thou no breath at all? Thou'lt come no more,
Never, never, never, never, never![2]
Pray you, undo this button.

V, iii, 307

20 Vex not his ghost: O! let him pass; he hates him
That would upon the rack of this tough world
Stretch him out longer.

V, iii, 315

21 The weight of this sad time we must obey;
Speak what we feel, not what we ought to say.
The oldest hath borne most: we that are young,
Shall never see so much, nor live so long.

V, iii, 325

22 'Tis not enough to help the feeble up,
But to support him after.
Timon of Athens [1605–1608], act I, sc. i, l. 108

23 I call the gods to witness.[3]

I, i, 138

24 I wonder men dare trust themselves with men.

I, ii, 45

25 Here's that which is too weak to be a sinner,
Honest water, which ne'er left man i' the mire.[4]

I, ii, 60

26 Immortal gods, I crave no pelf;
I pray for no man but myself:
Grant I may never prove so fond,
To trust man on his oath or bond.

I, ii, 64

[2] See William Pitt, 313:6, and Churchill, 621:5.
[3] See *Deuteronomy* 4:26, 10:10.
[4] Inscribed on the drinking fountain in the market square of
Stratford-on-Avon.

1 Men shut their doors against a setting sun.
Timon of Athens, I, ii, 152

2   Every man has his fault, and honesty is his.
III, i, 30

3 Nothing emboldens sin so much as mercy.
III, v, 3

4 You fools of fortune, trencher-friends, time's flies.
III, vi, 107

5 We have seen better days.
IV, ii, 27

6 O! the fierce wretchedness that glory brings us.
IV, ii, 30

7 I am Misanthropos, and hate mankind.
IV, iii, 53

8 Life's uncertain voyage.
V, i, 207

9 *First Witch:* When shall we three meet again
In thunder, lightning, or in rain?
Second Witch: When the hurlyburly's done,
When the battle's lost and won.
Macbeth [1606], act I, sc. i, l. 1

10 Fair is foul, and foul is fair:
Hover through the fog and filthy air.
I, i, 12

11 Banners flout the sky.
I, ii, 50

12 A sailor's wife had chestnuts in her lap,
And munch'd, and munch'd, and munch'd: "Give
me," quoth I:
"Aroint thee, witch!" the rump-fed ronyon cries.
I, iii, 4

13 Sleep shall neither night nor day
Hang upon his pent-house lid.
I, iii, 19

14 Dwindle, peak, and pine.
I, iii, 23

15 The weird sisters, hand in hand,
Posters of the sea and land,
Thus do go about, about:
Thrice to thine, and thrice to mine,
And thrice again, to make up nine.
Peace! The charm's wound up.
I, iii, 32

16 So foul and fair a day I have not seen.
I, iii, 38

17 If you can look into the seeds of time,
And say which grain will grow and which will
not,
Speak.
I, iii, 58

18   And to be king
Stands not within the prospect of belief.
I, iii, 73

19 The earth hath bubbles, as the water has,
And these are of them.
I, iii, 79

20 Or have we eaten on the insane root
That takes the reason prisoner?
I, iii, 84

21 And oftentimes, to win us to our harm,
The instruments of darkness tell us truths,
Win us with honest trifles, to betray 's
In deepest consequence.
I, iii, 123

22 As happy prologues to the swelling act
Of the imperial theme.
I, iii, 128

23   I am Thane of Cawdor:
If good, why do I yield to that suggestion
Whose horrid image doth unfix my hair
And make my seated heart knock at my ribs,
Against the use of nature? Present fears
Are less than horrible imaginings.
I, iii, 134

24 If chance will have me king, why, chance may
crown me,
Without my stir.
I, iii, 143

25   Come what come may,
Time and the hour runs through the roughest day.
I, iii, 146

26   Nothing in his life
Became him like the leaving it; he died
As one that had been studied in his death
To throw away the dearest thing he ow'd,
As 'twere a careless trifle.
I, iv, 7

27   There's no art
To find the mind's construction in the face:
He was a gentleman on whom I built
An absolute trust.
I, iv, 11

28 Glamis thou art, and Cawdor; and shalt be
What thou art promis'd. Yet do I fear thy nature;
It is too full o' the milk of human kindness[1]
To catch the nearest way.
I, v, 16

29   The raven himself is hoarse
That croaks the fatal entrance of Duncan
Under my battlements. Come, you spirits
That tend on mortal thoughts! unsex me here,
And fill me from the crown to the toe top full
Of direst cruelty; make thick my blood,
Stop up the access and passage to remorse,
That no compunctious visitings of nature
Shake my fell purpose, nor keep peace between

[1]The thunder of your words has soured the milk of human
kindness in my heart.—RICHARD BRINSLEY SHERIDAN, *The
Rivals* [1775], act III, sc. iv

The effect and it! Come to my woman's breasts,
And take my milk for gall, you murdering
    ministers.

I, v, 38

1 Nor heaven peep through the blanket of the dark,
To cry, "Hold, hold!"

I, v, 54

2 Your face, my thane, is as a book where men
May read strange matters.

I, v, 63

3   Look like the innocent flower,
But be the serpent under 't.

I, v, 66

4 *Duncan:* This castle hath a pleasant seat; the air
Nimbly and sweetly recommends itself
Unto our gentle senses.
Banquo: This guest of summer,
The temple-haunting martlet, does approve
By his lov'd mansionry that the heaven's breath
Smells wooingly here: no jutty, frieze,
Buttress, nor coign of vantage, but this bird
Hath made his pendent bed and procreant cradle:
Where they most breed and haunt, I have observ'd
The air is delicate.

I, vi, 1

5 If it were done when 'tis done, then 'twere well
It were done quickly; if the assassination
Could trammel up the consequence, and catch
With his surcease success; that but this blow
Might be the be-all and the end-all here,
·But here, upon this bank and shoal of time,
We'd jump the life to come.

I, vii, 1

6 This even-handed justice.

I, vii, 10

7   Besides, this Duncan
Hath borne his faculties so meek, hath been
So clear in his great office, that his virtues
Will plead like angels trumpet-tongu'd[1] against
The deep damnation of his taking-off;
And pity, like a naked new-born babe,
Striding the blast, or heaven's cherubin, hors'd
Upon the sightless couriers of the air,
Shall blow the horrid deed in every eye,
That tears shall drown the wind. I have no spur
To prick the sides of my intent, but only
Vaulting ambition, which o'erleaps itself
And falls on the other.

I, vii, 16

8   I have bought
Golden opinions from all sorts of people.

I, vii, 32

9 Letting "I dare not" wait upon "I would,"
Like the poor cat i' the adage.[2]

I, vii, 44

10 I dare do all that may become a man;
Who dares do more is none.

I, vii, 46

11   Nor time nor place
Did then adhere.

I, vii, 51

12   I have given suck, and know
How tender 'tis to love the babe that milks me:
I would, while it was smiling in my face,
Have pluck'd my nipple from his boneless gums,
And dash'd the brains out, had I so sworn as you
Have done to this.

I, vii, 54

13 *Macbeth:* If we should fail—
Lady Macbeth: We fail!
But screw your courage to the sticking-place,
And we'll not fail.

I, vii, 59

14 Memory, the warder of the brain.

I, vii, 65

15 Away, and mock the time with fairest show:
False face must hide what the false heart doth
     know.

I, vii, 81

16 The moon is down.

II, i, 2

17   There's husbandry in heaven;
Their candles are all out.

II, i, 4

18   Merciful powers!
Restrain in me the cursed thoughts that nature
Gives way to in repose.

II, i, 7

19   Shut up
In measureless content.

II, i, 16

20 Is this a dagger which I see before me,
The handle toward my hand? Come, let me clutch
     thee:
I have thee not, and yet I see thee still.
Art thou not, fatal vision, sensible
To feeling as to sight? or art thou but
A dagger of the mind, a false creation,
Proceeding from the heat-oppressed brain?

II, i, 33

21   Now o'er the one half-world
Nature seems dead, and wicked dreams abuse
The curtain'd sleep; witchcraft celebrates
Pale Hecate's offerings.

II, i, 49

22   Thou sure and firm-set earth,
Hear not my steps, which way they walk, for fear
The very stones prate of my whereabout.[3]

II, i, 56

---

[1]See *Matthew* 24:31, 36:10.
[2]See *Measure for Measure*, 203:27.

[3]See *Habakkuk* 2:11, 29:41, and *Luke* 19:40, 39:11.

1   The bell invites me.
Hear it not, Duncan; for it is a knell
That summons thee to heaven or to hell.
Macbeth, II, i, 62

2 It was the owl that shriek'd, the fatal bellman,
Which gives the stern'st good-night.
II, ii, 4

3   The attempt and not the deed
Confounds us.
II, ii, 12

4   Had he not resembled
My father as he slept I had done 't.
II, ii, 14

5 I had most need of blessing, and "Amen"
Stuck in my throat.
II, ii, 33

6 Methought I heard a voice cry "Sleep no more!
Macbeth does murder sleep," the innocent sleep,
Sleep that knits up the ravell'd sleave of care,
The death of each day's life, sore labor's bath,
Balm of hurt minds, great nature's second course,
Chief nourisher in life's feast.
II, ii, 36

7 Glamis hath murder'd sleep, and therefore
Cawdor
Shall sleep no more, Macbeth shall sleep no more!
II, ii, 43

8   Infirm of purpose!
Give me the daggers. The sleeping and the dead
Are but as pictures; 'tis the eye of childhood
That fears a painted devil.
II, ii, 53

9 Will all great Neptune's ocean wash this blood
Clean from my hand? No, this my hand will
rather
The multitudinous seas incarnadine,
Making the green one red.
II, ii, 61

10   The primrose way to the everlasting bonfire.
II, iii, 22

11   It [drink] provokes the desire, but it takes away
the performance.   *II, iii, 34*

12 The labor we delight in physics pain.
II, iii, 56

13 Confusion now hath made his masterpiece!
Most sacrilegious murder hath broke ope
The Lord's anointed temple, and stole thence
The life o' the building!
II, iii, 72

14 Shake off this downy sleep, death's counterfeit.
II, iii, 83

15 Had I but died an hour before this chance
I had liv'd a blessed time; for, from this instant,
There's nothing serious in mortality,

All is but toys; renown and grace is dead,
The wine of life is drawn, and the mere lees
Is left this vault to brag of.
II, iii, 98

16 Who can be wise, amaz'd, temperate and furious,
Loyal and neutral, in a moment? No man.
II, iii, 115

17 To show an unfelt sorrow is an office
Which the false man does easy.
II, iii, 143

18 A falcon, towering in her pride of place,
Was by a mousing owl hawk'd at and kill'd.
II, iv, 12

19 I must become a borrower of the night
For a dark hour or twain.
III, i, 27

20   To be thus is nothing;
But to be safely thus.
III, i, 48

21 *Murderer:*   We are men, my liege.
Macbeth: Ay, in the catalogue ye go for men.
III, i, 91

22   I am one, my liege,
Whom the vile blows and buffets of the world
Have so incens'd that I am reckless what
I do to spite the world.
III, i, 108

23 So weary with disasters, tugg'd with fortune,
That I would set my life on any chance,
To mend it or be rid on 't.
III, i, 112

24   Things without all remedy
Should be without regard: what's done is done.
III, ii, 11

25 We have scotch'd the snake, not kill'd it.
III, ii, 13

26   Duncan is in his grave;
After life's fitful fever he sleeps well;
Treason has done his worst: nor steel, nor poison,
Malice domestic, foreign levy, nothing
Can touch him further.
III, ii, 22

27 Then be thou jocund. Ere the bat hath flown
His cloister'd flight, ere, to black Hecate's
summons
The shard-borne beetle with his drowsy hums
Hath rung night's yawning peal, there shall be
done
A deed of dreadful note.
III, ii, 40

28   Come, seeling night,
Scarf up the tender eye of pitiful day,
And with thy bloody and invisible hand
Cancel and tear to pieces that great bond

Which keeps me pale! Light thickens, and the
   crow
Makes wing to the rooky wood.

III, ii, 46

1 Now spurs the lated traveler apace
To gain the timely inn.

III, iii, 6

2 But now I am cabin'd, cribb'd, confin'd, bound in
To saucy doubts and fears.

III, iv, 24

3 Now good digestion wait on appetite,
And health on both!

III, iv, 38

4 Thou canst not say I did it: never shake
Thy gory locks at me.

III, iv, 50

5 The air-drawn dagger.

III, iv, 62

6 I drink to the general joy of the whole table.

III, iv, 89

7   What man dare, I dare:
Approach thou like the rugged Russian bear,
The arm'd rhinoceros, or the Hyrcan tiger;
Take any shape but that, and my firm nerves
Shall never tremble.

III, iv, 99

8   Hence, horrible shadow!
Unreal mockery, hence!

III, iv, 106

9 Stand not upon the order of your going,
But go at once.

III, iv, 119

10 It will have blood, they say; blood will have
   blood:
Stones have been known to move and trees to
   speak.

III, iv, 122

11 *Macbeth:*   What is the night?
Lady Macbeth: Almost at odds with morning,
   which is which.

III, iv, 126

12   I am in blood
Stepp'd in so far, that, should I wade no more,
Returning were as tedious as go o'er.

III, iv, 136

13 Double, double toil and trouble;
Fire burn and cauldron bubble.

IV, i, 10

14 Eye of newt, and toe of frog,
Wool of bat, and tongue of dog.

IV, i, 14

15 Finger of birth-strangled babe,
Ditch-deliver'd by a drab.

IV, i, 30

16 By the pricking of my thumbs,
Something wicked this way comes.
Open, locks,
Whoever knocks!

IV, i, 44

17 How now, you secret, black, and midnight hags!

IV, i, 48

18 A deed without a name.

IV, i, 49

19 Be bloody, bold, and resolute; laugh to scorn
The power of man, for none of woman born
Shall harm Macbeth.

IV, i, 79

20 But yet I'll make assurance double sure,
And take a bond of fate.

IV, i, 83

21 Macbeth shall never vanquish'd be until
Great Birnam wood to high Dunsinane hill
Shall come against him.[1]

IV, i, 92

22 Show his eyes, and grieve his heart;
Come like shadows, so depart.

IV, i, 110

23 What! will the line stretch out to the crack of
   doom?

IV, i, 117

24   When our actions do not,
Our fears do make us traitors.

IV, ii, 3

25 He wants the natural touch.

IV, ii, 9

26 Angels are bright still, though the brightest fell.

IV, iii, 22

27 Pour the sweet milk of concord into hell,
Uproar the universal peace, confound
All unity on earth.

IV, iii, 98

28 Give sorrow words; the grief that does not speak
Whispers the o'er-fraught heart and bids it break.

IV, iii, 209

29   All my pretty ones?
Did you say all? O hell-kite! All?
What! all my pretty chickens and their dam
At one fell swoop?

IV, iii, 216

30 *Malcolm:* Dispute it like a man.
Macbeth: I shall do so;
But I must also feel it as a man:
I cannot but remember such things were,
That were most precious to me.

IV, iii, 219

---

[1]Till Birnam wood remove to Dunsinane / I cannot taint
with fear.—*Macbeth, act V, sc. iii, l. 2*

1   Out, damned spot! out, I say!
                              Macbeth, V, i, 38

2   Fie, my lord, fie! a soldier, and afeard?
                              V, i, 40

3   Who would have thought the old man to have
had so much blood in him?   V, i, 42

4   The Thane of Fife had a wife: where is she now?
                              V, i, 46

5   All the perfumes of Arabia will not sweeten this
little hand.   V, i, 56

6 Those he commands move only in command,
  Nothing in love; now does he feel his title
  Hang loose about him, like a giant's robe
  Upon a dwarfish thief.
                              V, ii, 19

7 The devil damn thee black, thou cream-fac'd loon!
  Where gott'st thou that goose look?
                              V, iii, 11

8 Thou lily-liver'd boy.
                              V, iii, 15

9 I have liv'd long enough: my way of life
  Is fall'n into the sere, the yellow leaf;[1]
  And that which should accompany old age,
  As honor, love, obedience, troops of friends,
  I must not look to have; but, in their stead,
  Curses, not loud but deep, mouth-honor, breath,
  Which the poor heart would fain deny, and dare
      not.
                              V, iii, 22

10 *Macbeth:* Canst thou not minister to a mind
      diseas'd,
  Pluck from the memory a rooted sorrow,
  Raze out the written troubles of the brain,
  And with some sweet oblivious antidote
  Cleanse the stuff'd bosom of that perilous stuff
  Which weighs upon the heart?
  Doctor: Therein the patient
  Must minister to himself.
  Macbeth: Throw physic to the dogs; I'll none of it.
                              V, iii, 40

11 I would applaud thee to the very echo,
   That should applaud again.
                              V, iii, 53

12 Hang out our banners on the outward walls;
   The cry is still, "They come"; our castle's strength
   Will laugh a siege to scorn.
                              V, v, 1

13   My fell of hair
   Would at a dismal treatise rouse and stir
   As life were in 't. I have supp'd full with horrors.
                              V, v, 11

14 She should have died hereafter;
   There would have been a time for such a word.
   Tomorrow, and tomorrow, and tomorrow,

[1]See Byron, 404:7.

Creeps in this petty pace from day to day,
To the last syllable of recorded time;
And all our yesterdays have lighted fools
The way to dusty death. Out, out, brief candle!
Life's but a walking shadow, a poor player
That struts and frets his hour upon the stage,
And then is heard no more; it is a tale
Told by an idiot, full of sound and fury,
Signifying nothing.
                              V, v, 17

15 I 'gin to be aweary of the sun,
   And wish the estate o' the world were now
      undone.
                              V, v, 49

16   Blow, wind! come, wrack!
   At least we'll die with harness on our back.
                              V, v, 51

17 Why should I play the Roman fool, and die
   On mine own sword?
                              V, vii, 30

18 I bear a charmed life.
                              V, vii, 41

19   Macduff was from his mother's womb
   Untimely ripp'd.
                              V, vii, 44

20 And be these juggling fiends no more believ'd,
   That palter with us in a double sense;
   That keep the word of promise to our ear
   And break it to our hope.
                              V, vii, 48

21 Live to be the show and gaze o' the time.
                              V, vii, 53

22   Lay on, Macduff,
   And damn'd be him that first cries, "Hold,
      enough!"
                              V, vii, 62

23   You shall see in him
   The triple pillar of the world transform'd
   Into a strumpet's fool.
       Antony and Cleopatra [1606–1607], act I, sc. i,
       l. 12

24 There's beggary in the love that can be reckon'd.
                              I, i, 15

25 Let Rome in Tiber melt, and the wide arch
   Of the rang'd empire fall! Here is my space.
   Kingdoms are clay.
                              I, i, 33

26 In nature's infinite book of secrecy
   A little I can read.
                              I, ii, 11

27 I love long life better than figs.
                              I, ii, 34

28   On the sudden
   A Roman thought hath struck him.
                              I, ii, 90

1 Eternity was in our lips and eyes,
　Bliss in our brows bent.

I, iii, 35

2　　　Good now, play one scene
　Of excellent dissembling, and let it look
　Like perfect honor.

I, iii, 78

3 O! my oblivion is a very Antony,
　And I am all forgotten.

I, iii, 90

4 Give me to drink mandragora.[1] . . .
　That I might sleep out this great gap of time
　My Antony is away.

I, v, 4

5 O happy horse, to bear the weight of Antony!

I, v, 21

6 The demi-Atlas of this earth, the arm
　And burgonet of men.

I, v, 23

7 Where's my serpent of old Nile?

I, v, 25

8 A morsel for a monarch.

I, v, 31

9 My man of men.

I, v, 71

10　　　My salad days,
　When I was green in judgment.

I, v, 73

11　　　We, ignorant of ourselves,
　Beg often our own harms, which the wise powers
　Deny us for our good; so find we profit
　By losing of our prayers.

II, i, 5

12　　　Epicurean cooks
　Sharpen with cloyless sauce his appetite.

II, i, 24

13 No worse a husband than the best of men.

II, ii, 135

14 The barge she sat in, like a burnish'd throne,
　Burn'd on the water; the poop was beaten gold,
　Purple the sails, and so perfumed, that
　The winds were love-sick with them; the oars
　　　were silver,
　Which to the tune of flutes kept stroke, and made
　The water which they beat to follow faster,
　As amorous of their strokes. For her own person,
　It beggar'd all description.

II, ii, 199

15 Age cannot wither her, nor custom stale
　Her infinite variety; other women cloy
　The appetites they feed, but she makes hungry

[1] See *Othello*, 207:6.

Where most she satisfies; for vilest things
Become themselves in her, that the holy priests
Bless her when she is riggish.

II, ii, 243

16 I have not kept my square, but that to come
　Shall all be done by the rule.

II, iii, 6

17　　　I will to Egypt
　And though I make this marriage for my peace,
　I' the East my pleasure lies.

II, iii, 38

18　　　Music, moody food
　Of us that trade in love.[2]

II, v, 1

19 Though it be honest, it is never good
　To bring bad news.[3]

II, v, 85

20 He will to his Egyptian dish again.

II, vi, 133

21 Come, thou monarch of the vine,
　Plumpy Bacchus, with pink eyne!

II, vii, 120

22　　　Ambition,
　The soldier's virtue.

III, i, 22

23 Celerity is never more admir'd
　Than by the negligent.

III, vii, 24

24　　　We have kiss'd away
　Kingdoms and provinces.

III, viii, 17

25　　　He wears the rose
　Of youth upon him.

III, xi, 20

26　　　Men's judgments are
　A parcel of their fortunes, and things outward
　Do draw the inward quality after them,
　To suffer all alike.

III, xi, 31

27 I found you as a morsel, cold upon
　Dead Caesar's trencher.

III, xi, 116

28 Let's have one other gaudy night.

III, xi, 182

29 Now he'll outstare the lightning. To be furious
　Is to be frighted out of fear.

III, xi, 194

30 To business that we love we rise betime,
　And go to 't with delight.

IV, iv, 20

[2] See *Twelfth-Night*, 201:16.
[3] See Sophocles, 66:6, and *King Henry IV, Part II*, 183:11.

¹ O infinite virtue! com'st thou smiling from
The world's great snare uncaught?
Antony and Cleopatra, IV, viii, 17

² The shirt of Nessus is upon me.
IV, x, 56

³ Sometimes we see a cloud that's dragonish;
A vapor sometime like a bear or lion,
A tower'd citadel, a pendant rock,
A forked mountain, or blue promontory
With trees upon 't.¹
IV, xii, 2

⁴ Unarm, Eros; the long day's task is done,
And we must sleep.
IV, xii, 35

⁵   But I will be
A bridegroom in my death, and run into 't
As to a lover's bed.
IV, xii, 99

⁶   O sun!
Burn the great sphere thou mov'st in; darkling
stand
The varying shore² o' the world.
IV, xiii, 10

⁷ I am dying, Egypt, dying; only
I here importune death awhile, until
Of many thousand kisses the poor last
I lay upon thy lips.
IV, xiii, 18

⁸ O! wither'd is the garland of the war,
The soldier's pole is fall'n; young boys and girls
Are level now with men; the odds is gone,
And there is nothing left remarkable
Beneath the visiting moon.
IV, xiii, 64

⁹ Let's do it after the high Roman fashion,
And make death proud to take us.
IV, xiii, 87

¹⁰   And it is great
To do that thing that ends all other deeds,
Which shackles accidents, and bolts up change.
V, ii, 4

¹¹ His legs bestrid the ocean; his rear'd arm
Crested the world; his voice was propertied
As all the tuned spheres, and that to friends;
But when he meant to quail and shake the orb,
He was as rattling thunder. For his bounty,
There was no winter in 't, an autumn 'twas
That grew the more by reaping; his delights
Were dolphin-like, they show'd his back above
The element they liv'd in; in his livery
Walk'd crowns and crownets, realms and islands
were
As plates dropp'd from his pocket.
V, ii, 82

¹² The bright day is done,
And we are for the dark.
V, ii, 192

¹³   The quick comedians
Extemporally will stage us, and present
Our Alexandrian revels. Antony
Shall be brought drunken forth, and I shall see
Some squeaking Cleopatra boy my greatness
I' the posture of a whore.
V, ii, 215

¹⁴   A woman is a dish for the gods, if the devil dress
her not.   *V, ii, 274*

¹⁵   I wish you joy of the worm.
V, ii, 280

¹⁶   I have
Immortal longings in me.
V, ii, 282

¹⁷ Husband, I come.
V, ii, 289

¹⁸ If thou and nature can so gently part,
The stroke of death is as a lover's pinch,
Which hurts, and is desir'd.
V, ii, 296

¹⁹ Dost thou not see my baby at my breast,
That sucks the nurse asleep?
V, ii, 311

²⁰ Now boast thee, death, in thy possession lies
A lass unparallel'd.
V, ii, 317

²¹ *First Guard:* . . . Charmian, is this well done?
Charmian: It is well done, and fitting for a
princess
Descended of so many royal kings.³
V, ii, 327

²² As she would catch another Antony
In her strong toil of grace.
V, ii, 348

²³   The gods sent not
Corn for the rich men only.
Coriolanus [1607–1608], act I, sc. i, l. 213

²⁴   They threw their caps
As they would hang them on the horns o' the
moon,
Shouting their emulation.
I, i, 218

²⁵   All the yarn she spun in Ulysses' absence did but
fill Ithaca full of moths.   *I, iii, 93*

²⁶   Nature teaches beasts to know their friends.
II, i, 6

---

¹See Aristophanes, 73:3, and *Hamlet*, 197:18.
²In some editions: star.

³One of the soldiers seeing her, angrily said unto her: Is that
well done Charmian? Very well said she again, and meet for a
princess descended of so many noble kings.—PLUTARCH,
Lives; translated [1579] by THOMAS NORTH

1   A cup of hot wine with not a drop of allaying
Tiber in 't.[1]   *II, i, 52*

2 My gracious silence, hail!
                                                   II, i, 194

3   He himself stuck not to call us the many-headed
multitude.[2]   *II, iii, 18*

4   Bid them wash their faces,
And keep their teeth clean.
                                                   II, iii, 65

5 I thank you for your voices, thank you,
    Your most sweet voices.
                                                   II, iii, 179

6 The mutable, rank-scented many.
                                                   III, i, 65

7 Hear you this Triton of the minnows? mark you
His absolute "shall"?
                                                   III, i, 88

8 What is the city but the people?
                                                   III, i, 198

9 His nature is too noble for the world:
    He would not flatter Neptune for his trident,
    Or Jove for 's power to thunder.[3] His heart's his
        mouth:
    What his breast forges, that his tongue must vent.
                                                   III, i, 254

10   The beast
    With many heads butts me away.[4]
                                                   IV, i, 1

11   O! a kiss
    Long as my exile, sweet as my revenge![5]
                                                   V, iii, 44

12   Chaste as the icicle
    That's curdied by the frost from purest snow,
    And hangs on Dian's temple.
                                                   V, iii, 65

13   He wants nothing of a god but eternity and a
heaven to throne in.   *V, iv, 25*

14 They'll give him death by inches.
                                                   V, iv, 43

15 If you have writ your annals true, 'tis there,
    That, like an eagle in a dovecote, I
    Flutter'd your Volscians in Corioli:
    Alone I did it.
                                                   V, v, 114

16 Thou hast done a deed whereat valor will weep.
                                                   V, v, 135

17 He shall have a noble memory.
                                                   V, v, 155

18 See, where she comes apparell'd like the spring.
                    Pericles [1608–1609], act I, sc. i, l. 12

19 Few love to hear the sins they love to act.
                                                   I, i, 92

20 The sad companion, dull-ey'd melancholy.
                                                   I, ii, 2

21   *Third Fisherman:* . . . Master, I marvel how the
fishes live in the sea.
    First Fisherman: Why, as men do a-land; the great
ones eat up the little ones.[6]   *II, i, 29*

22   Lest the bargain should catch cold and starve.
            Cymbeline [1609–1610], act I, sc. iv, l. 186

23   Hath his bellyful of fighting.   *II, i, 24*

24 Hark! hark! the lark at heaven's gate sings,
    And Phoebus 'gins arise,[7]
    His steeds to water at those springs
    On chalic'd flowers that lies;
    And winking Mary-buds begin
    To ope their golden eyes:
    With everything that pretty is,
    My lady sweet, arise.
                                                   II, iii, 22

25 As chaste as unsunn'd snow.
                                                   II, v, 13

26 Some griefs are med'cinable.
                                                   III, ii, 33

27 O! for a horse with wings!
                                                   III, ii, 49

28 The game is up.
                                                   III, iii, 107

29   Slander,
    Whose edge is sharper than the sword, whose
        tongue
    Outvenoms all the worms of Nile, whose breath
    Rides on the posting winds and doth belie
    All corners of the world.
                                                   III, iv, 35

30 I have not slept one wink.[8]
                                                   III, iv, 103

31   Weariness
    Can snore upon the flint when resty sloth
    Finds the down pillow hard.
                                                   III, vi, 33

32   An angel! or, if not,
    An earthly paragon!
                                                   III, vi, 42

---

[1]See Lovelace, 267:17.
[2]See Horace, 97:7; Machiavelli, 137:3; *King Henry IV, Part II*, 183:9; *Coriolanus*, 219:10; and Pope, 303:10.
[3]See Manilius, 103:15, and Franklin, 309:*n*1.
[4]See Horace, 97:7; Machiavelli, 137:3; *King Henry IV, Part II*, 183:9; *Coriolanus*, 219:3; and Pope, 303:10.
[5]See Byron, 402:12.

[6]Men lived like fishes; the great ones devoured the small.
—ALGERNON SIDNEY, *Discourses on Government* [1698], *ch. 2, sec. 18*
[7]See Lyly, 155:20.
[8]See Cervantes, 149:11, and Pope, 302:19.

1   Society is no comfort
To one not sociable.

Cymbeline, IV, ii, 12

2   I wear not
My dagger in my mouth.

IV, ii, 78

3 Fear no more the heat o' the sun,
Nor the furious winter's rages;
Thou thy worldly task hast done,
Home art gone, and ta'en thy wages;
Golden lads and girls all must,
As chimney-sweepers, come to dust.

IV, ii, 258

4 Quiet consummation have;
And renowned be thy grave!

IV, ii, 280

5 Fortune brings in some boats that are not steer'd.

IV, iii, 46

6 Hang there like fruit, my soul,
Till the tree die!

V, v, 264

7 From fairest creatures we desire increase,
That thereby beauty's rose might never die.

Sonnets[1] [1609], 1, l. 1

8 When forty winters shall besiege thy brow,
And dig deep trenches in thy beauty's field.

Sonnet 2, l. 1

9 Thou art thy mother's glass, and she in thee
Calls back the lovely April of her prime.

Sonnet 3, l. 9

10 Music to hear, why hear'st thou music sadly?
Sweets with sweet war not, joy delights in joy.

Sonnet 8, l. 1

11   Everything that grows
Holds in perfection but a little moment.

Sonnet 15, l. 1

12 Shall I compare thee to a summer's day?
Thou art more lovely and more temperate:

[1]The sonnets were written definitely before 1598, according to the *Palladis Tamia* [1598] of Francis Mere [1565–1647], and according to Leslie Hotson in *Mr. W. H.* [1964] they bear strong evidence of all being written in 1588–1589. They were published [1609] by THOMAS THORPE, who wrote the dedication:

TO THE ONLIE BEGETTER OF
THESE INSUING SONNETS
MR. W. H., ALL HAPPINESSE
AND THAT ETERNITIE
PROMISED
BY
OUR EVER-LIVING POET
WISHETH
THE WELL-WISHING
ADVENTURER IN
SETTING
FORTH
T.T.

Rough winds do shake the darling buds of May,
And summer's lease hath all too short a date.

Sonnet 18, l. 1

13 But thy eternal summer shall not fade.

l. 9

14 The painful warrior famoused for fight,
After a thousand victories, once foil'd,
Is from the books of honor razed quite,
And all the rest forgot for which he toil'd.

Sonnet 25, l. 9

15 When in disgrace with fortune and men's eyes
I all alone beweep my outcast state,
And trouble deaf heaven with my bootless cries.

Sonnet 29, l. 1

16 Desiring this man's art, and that man's scope,
With what I most enjoy contented least;
Yet in these thoughts myself almost despising,
Haply I think on thee.

Sonnet 29, l. 7

17 For thy sweet love remember'd such wealth brings
That then I scorn to change my state with kings.

l. 13

18 When to the sessions of sweet silent thought
I summon up remembrance of things past,
I sigh the lack of many a thing I sought,
And with old woes new wail my dear times'
waste.

Sonnet 30, l. 1

19 But if the while I think on thee, dear friend,
All losses are restor'd and sorrows end.

l. 13

20 Full many a glorious morning have I seen.

Sonnet 33, l. 1

21 Roses have thorns, and silver fountains mud;
Clouds and eclipses stain both moon and sun,
And loathsome canker lives in sweetest bud.
All men make faults.

Sonnet 35, l. 2

22 Be thou the tenth Muse.

Sonnet 38, l. 9

23 For nimble thought can jump both sea and land.

Sonnet 44, l. 7

24 Against that time when thou shalt strangely pass,
And scarcely greet me with that sun, thine eye,
When love, converted from the thing it was,
Shall reasons find of settled gravity.

Sonnet 49, l. 5

25 Not marble, nor the gilded monuments
Of princes, shall outlive this powerful rime.

Sonnet 55, l. i.

26 Like as the waves make towards the pebbled
shore,
So do our minutes hasten to their end.

Sonnet 60, l. 1

1 Time doth transfix the flourish set on youth
And delves the parallels in beauty's brow.

l. 9

2 When I have seen by Time's fell hand defac'd
The rich-proud cost of outworn buried age.

Sonnet 64, l. 1

3 When I have seen the hungry ocean gain
Advantage on the kingdom of the shore,
And the firm soil win of the watery main,
Increasing store with loss, and loss with store.

l. 5

4 Tir'd with all these, for restful death I cry.

Sonnet 66, l. 1

5 And art made tongue-tied by authority.

l. 9

6 And simple truth miscall'd simplicity,
And captive good attending captain ill.

l. 11

7 No longer mourn for me when I am dead
Than you shall hear the surly sullen bell
Give warning to the world that I am fled
From this vile world, with vilest worms to dwell.

Sonnet 71, l. 1

8 That time of year thou mayst in me behold
When yellow leaves, or none, or few, do hang
Upon those boughs which shake against the cold,[1]
Bare ruin'd choirs, where late the sweet birds sang.

Sonnet 73, l. 1

9 Clean starved for a look.

Sonnet 75, l. 10

10 Who is it that says most? which can say more
Than this rich praise,—that you alone are you?

Sonnet 84, l. 1

11 Farewell! thou art too dear for my possessing,
And like enough thou know'st thy estimate.

Sonnet 87, l. 1

12 In sleep a king, but, waking, no such matter.

l. 14

13 Ah! do not, when my heart hath 'scap'd this
sorrow,
Come in the rearward of a conquer'd woe;
Give not a windy night a rainy morrow,
To linger out a purpos'd overthrow.

Sonnet 90, l. 5

14 They that have power to hurt and will do none,
That do not do the thing they most do show,
Who, moving others, are themselves as stone,
Unmoved, cold, and to temptation slow.

Sonnet 94, l. 1

15 They are the lords and owners of their faces,
Others but stewards of their excellence.

[1]See Byron, 404:7.

The summer's flower is to the summer sweet,
Though to itself it only live and die.

l. 7

16 Lilies that fester smell far worse than weeds.[2]

l. 14

17 The hardest knife ill-used doth lose his edge.

Sonnet 95, l. 14

18 How like a winter hath my absence been.

Sonnet 97, l. 1

19 From you have I been absent in the spring,
When proud-pied April, dress'd in all his trim,
Hath put a spirit of youth in everything.

Sonnet 98, l. 1

20 Sweets grown common lose their dear delight.

Sonnet 102, l. 12

21 To me, fair friend, you never can be old,
For as you were when first your eye I ey'd,
Such seems your beauty still.

Sonnet 104, l. 1

22 When in the chronicle of wasted time
I see descriptions of the fairest wights,
And beauty making beautiful old rime,
In praise of ladies dead and lovely knights,
Then, in the blazon of sweet beauty's best,
Of hand, of foot, of lip, of eye, of brow,
I see their antique pen would have express'd
Even such a beauty as you master now.

Sonnet 106, l. 1

23 Not mine own fears, nor the prophetic soul
Of the wide world dreaming on things to come,
Can yet the lease of my true love control,
Suppos'd as forfeit to a confin'd doom.
The mortal moon hath her eclipse endur'd,
And the sad augurs mock their own presage;
Incertainties now crown themselves assur'd,
And peace proclaims olives of endless age.

Sonnet 107, l. 1

24 O! never say that I was false of heart,
Though absence seem'd my flame to qualify.

Sonnet 109, l. 1

25 That is my home of love: if I have rang'd,
Like him that travels, I return again.

l. 5

26 Alas! 'tis true I have gone here and there,
And made myself a motley to the view,
Gor'd mine own thoughts, sold cheap what is
most dear,
Made old offenses of affections new.

Sonnet 110, l. 1

[2]As in the nature of things, those which most admirably
flourish, most swiftly fester or putrefy, as roses, lilies, violets,
while others last: so in the lives of men, those that are most
blooming, are soonest turned into the opposite.—PLINY THE
ELDER, *Natural History, bk. XVI, ch. 15*

1
      My nature is subdu'd
To what it works in, like the dyer's hand.
                                        Sonnet 111, l. 6

2 Let me not to the marriage of true minds
Admit impediments. Love is not love
Which alters when it alteration finds,
Or bends with the remover to remove:
O, no! it is an ever-fixèd mark,
That looks on tempests and is never shaken;
It is the star to every wandering bark,
Whose worth's unknown, although his height be
      taken.
Love's not Time's fool, though rosy lips and
      cheeks
Within his bending sickle's compass come;
Love alters not with his brief hours and weeks,
But bears it out even to the edge of doom.
If this be error, and upon me prov'd,
I never writ, nor no man ever lov'd.
                                        Sonnet 116

3 What potions have I drunk of Siren tears,
Distill'd from limbecks foul as hell within.
                                        Sonnet 119, l. 1

4 O benefit of ill!
                                        l. 9

5 And ruin'd love, when it is built anew,
Grows fairer than at first, more strong, far
      greater.
                                        l. 11

6 'Tis better to be vile than vile esteem'd,
When not to be receives reproach of being.
                                        Sonnet 121, l. 1

7 The expense of spirit in a waste of shame
Is lust in action; and till action, lust
Is perjur'd, murderous, bloody, full of blame,
Savage, extreme, rude, cruel, not to trust;
Enjoy'd no sooner but despised straight;
Past reason hunted; and no sooner had,
Past reason hated, as a swallow'd bait,
On purpose laid to make the taker mad:
Mad in pursuit, and in possession so;
Had, having, and in quest to have, extreme;
A bliss in proof,—and prov'd, a very woe;
Before, a joy propos'd; behind, a dream.
All this the world well knows; yet none knows
      well
To shun the heaven that leads men to this hell.
                                        Sonnet 129

8 My mistress' eyes are nothing like the sun;
Coral is far more red than her lips' red:
If snow be white, why then her breasts are dun;
If hairs be wires, black wires grow on her head.
                                        Sonnet 130, l. 1

9 When my love swears that she is made of truth,
I do believe her, though I know she lies.
                                        Sonnet 138, l. 1

10 Two loves I have of comfort and despair,
Which like two spirits do suggest me still.
                                        Sonnet 144, l. 1

11 Poor soul, the center of my sinful earth.
                                        Sonnet 146, l. 1

12 So shalt thou feed on Death, that feeds on men,
And Death once dead, there's no more dying then.
                                        l. 13

13 Past cure I am, now Reason is past care,
And frantic-mad with evermore unrest.
                                        Sonnet 147, l. 9

14 For I have sworn thee fair, and thought thee
      bright,
Who art as black as hell, as dark as night.
                                        l. 13

15   You pay a great deal too dear for what's given
freely.
      The Winter's Tale [1610–1611], act I, sc. i, l. 18

16 Two lads that thought there was no more behind
But such a day tomorrow as today,
And to be boy eternal.
                                        I, ii, 63

17 We were as twinn'd lambs that did frisk i' the
      sun,
And bleat the one at the other: what we chang'd
Was innocence for innocence.
                                        I, ii, 67

18 Paddling palms and pinching fingers.
                                        I, ii, 116

19 Affection! thy intention stabs the center:
Thou dost make possible things not so held,
Communicat'st with dreams.
                                        I, ii, 139

20 He makes a July's day short as December.
                                        I, ii, 169

21   A sad tale's best for winter.
I have one of sprites and goblins.
                                        II, i, 24

22 The silence often of pure innocence
Persuades when speaking fails.
                                        II, ii, 41

23 It is a heretic that makes the fire,
Not she which burns in 't.
                                        II, iii, 115

24 I am a feather for each wind that blows.
                                        II, iii, 153

25   What's gone and what's past help
Should be past grief.
                                        III, ii, 223

26   Exit, pursued by a bear.[1]   *III, iii, 57*

27   This is fairy gold, boy, and 'twill prove so.
                                        III, iii, 127

---

[1]Perhaps the most famous stage direction in English.

1 Then comes in the sweet o' the year.

IV, ii, 3

2 A snapper-up of unconsidered trifles.

IV, ii, 26

3 For the life to come, I sleep out the thought of it.

IV, ii, 30

4 Jog on, jog on, the footpath way,
   And merrily hent the stile-a:
   A merry heart goes all the day,
   Your sad tires in a mile-a.

IV, ii, 133

5 For you there's rosemary and rue; these keep
   Seeming and savor all the winter long.

IV, iii, 74

6   Here's flowers for you:
   Hot lavender, mints, savory, marjoram,
   The marigold, that goes to bed wi' the sun,
   And with him rises weeping: these are flowers
   Of middle summer, and I think they are given
   To men of middle age.

IV, iii, 103

7   Daffodils,
   That come before the swallow dares, and take
   The winds of March with beauty.

IV, iii, 118

8   What you do
   Still betters what is done.

IV, iii, 135

9   When you do dance, I wish you
   A wave o' the sea, that you might ever do
   Nothing but that.

IV, iii, 140

10 Lawn as white as driven snow.

IV, iii, 220

11   I love a ballad in print, a-life, for then we are sure
   they are true.   *IV, iii, 262*

12 The self-same sun that shines upon his court
   Hides not his visage from our cottage, but
   Looks on alike.

IV, iii, 457

13 I'll queen it no inch further,
   But milk my ewes and weep.

IV, iii, 462

14 Prosperity's the very bond of love,
   Whose fresh complexion and whose heart together
   Affliction alters.

IV, iii, 586

15   Let me have no lying; it becomes none but tradesmen.   *IV, iii, 747*

16   To purge melancholy.   *IV, iii, 792*

17 There's time enough for that.

V, iii, 128

18   He hath no drowning mark upon him; his complexion is perfect gallows.
   The Tempest [1611–1612], act I, sc. i, l. 33

19   Now would I give a thousand furlongs of sea for
   an acre of barren ground.   *I, i, 70*

20   I would fain die a dry death.   *I, i, 73*

21   What seest thou else
   In the dark backward and abysm of time?

I, ii, 49

22   By telling of it,
   Made such a sinner of his memory,
   To credit his own lie.

I, ii, 100

23 Your tale, sir, would cure deafness.

I, ii, 106

24   My library
   Was dukedom large enough.

I, ii, 109

25   The very rats
   Instinctively have quit it.

I, ii, 147

26 Knowing I lov'd my books, he furnish'd me,
   From mine own library with volumes that
   I prize above my dukedom.

I, ii, 166

27 From the still-vex'd Bermoothes.[1]

I, ii, 229

28 I [Ariel] will be correspondent to command,
   And do my spiriting gently.

I, ii, 297

29 You taught me language; and my profit on 't
   Is, I know how to curse: the red plague rid you,
   For learning me your language!

I, ii, 363

30 Come unto these yellow sands,
   And then take hands:
   Curtsied when you have, and kiss'd—
   The wild waves whist,—
   Foot it featly here and there.

I, ii, 375

31 This music crept by me upon the waters,
   Allaying both their fury, and my passion,
   With its sweet air.

I, ii, 389

32 Full fathom five thy father lies;
   Of his bones are coral made:
   Those are pearls that were his eyes:
   Nothing of him that doth fade,
   But doth suffer a sea-change
   Into something rich and strange.[2]

I, ii, 394

33 The fringed curtains of thine eye advance.

I, ii, 405

[1]See Richard Rich, 237:n2.
[2]The last three lines are inscribed on Shelley's gravestone.

1   Lest too light winning
Make the prize light.

The Tempest, I, ii, 448

2 There's nothing ill can dwell in such a temple:
If the ill spirit have so fair a house,
Good things will strive to dwell with 't.

I, ii, 454

3   He receives comfort like cold porridge.[1]

II, i, 10

4 I' the commonwealth I would by contraries
Execute all things; for no kind of traffic
Would I admit; no name of magistrate;
Letters should not be known; riches, poverty,
And use of service, none; contract, succession,
Bourn, bound of land, tilth, vineyard, none;
No use of metal, corn, or wine, or oil;
No occupation; all men idle, all;
And women too, but innocent and pure.[2]

II, i, 154

5 What's past is prologue.

II, i, 261

6 Open-ey'd Conspiracy
His time doth take.

II, i, 309

7   A very ancient and fish-like smell.   *II, ii, 27*

8   Misery acquaints a man with strange bedfellows.[3]   *II, ii, 42*

9   How cam'st thou to be the siege of this moon-
calf?   *II, ii, 115*

10   I shall laugh myself to death.   *II, ii, 167*

11 'Ban, 'Ban, Ca—Caliban,
Has a new master—Get a new man.

II, ii, 197

12   For several virtues
Have I lik'd several women.

III, i, 42

13 *Ferdinand:* . . . Here's my hand.
Miranda: And mine, with my heart in't.

III, i, 89

14   Thou deboshed fish thou.   *III, ii, 30*

15   Keep a good tongue in your head.   *III, ii, 41*

16 Flout 'em, and scout 'em; and scout 'em, and flout
'em;
Thought is free.[4]

III, ii, 133

---

[1]See *King John,* 170:22.

[2]It is a nation, would I answer Plato, that hath no kind of traffic, no knowledge of letters, no intelligence of numbers, no name of magistrate, nor of politic superiority; no use of service, of riches or poverty, no contracts, no successions, no partitions, no occupation but idle; no respect of kindred, but common, no apparel but natural, no manuring of lands, no use of wine, corn, or metal.—MONTAIGNE, *Essays, bk. I* [1580], *ch. 30, Of the Cannibals*

[3]See Charles Warner, 511:5.

[4]Thought is free.—*Twelfth-Night, act I, sc. iii, l. 73*

17   He that dies pays all debts.   *III, ii, 143*

18   The isle is full of noises,
Sounds and sweet airs, that give delight, and hurt
not.
Sometimes a thousand twangling instruments
Will hum about mine ears; and sometimes voices,
That, if I then had wak'd after long sleep,
Will make me sleep again.

III, ii, 146

19   A kind
Of excellent dumb discourse.

III, iii, 38

20   Do not give dalliance
Too much the rein.

IV, i, 51

21 Our revels now are ended. These our actors,
As I foretold you, were all spirits and
Are melted into air, into thin air:
And, like the baseless fabric of this vision,
The cloud-capp'd towers, the gorgeous palaces,
The solemn temples, the great globe itself,
Yea, all which it inherit, shall dissolve
And, like this insubstantial pageant faded,
Leave not a rack behind. We are such stuff
As dreams are made on, and our little life
Is rounded with a sleep.

IV, i, 148

22 With foreheads villainous low.

IV, i, 252

23   But this rough magic
I here abjure.

V, i, 50

24   I'll break my staff,
Bury it certain fathoms in the earth,
And, deeper than did ever plummet sound,
I'll drown my book.

V, i, 54

25 Where the bee sucks, there suck I
In a cowslip's bell I lie;
There I couch when owls do cry.
On the bat's back I do fly
After summer merrily:
Merrily, merrily shall I live now
Under the blossom that hangs on the bough.

V, i, 88

26   O brave new world,
That has such people in't!

V, i, 183

27 Let us not burden our remembrances
With a heaviness that's gone.

V, i, 199

28   This thing of darkness I
Acknowledge mine.

V, i, 274

29 And my ending is despair,
Unless I be reliev'd by prayer,

Which pierces so that it assaults
Mercy itself and frees all faults.

Epilogue, 1. 15

1   No man's pie is freed
From his ambitious finger.

    King Henry the Eighth [1613],[1] *act I, sc. i, l. 52*

2 The force of his own merit makes his way.

I, i, 64

3 Heat not a furnace for your foe so hot
That it do singe yourself.

I, i, 140

4 If I chance to talk a little wild, forgive me;
I had it from my father.

I, iv, 26

5 The mirror of all courtesy.

II, i, 53

6 Go with me, like good angels, to my end;
And, as the long divorce of steel falls on me,
Make of your prayers one sweet sacrifice,
And lift my soul to heaven.

II, i, 75

7 This bold bad man.

II, ii, 44

8   'Tis better to be lowly born,
And range with humble livers in content,
Than to be perk'd up in a glist'ring grief
And wear a golden sorrow.

II, iii, 19

9   I would not be a queen
For all the world.

II, iii, 45

10 Orpheus with his lute made trees,
And the mountain-tops that freeze,
Bow themselves, when he did sing.

III, i, 3

11 Heaven is above all yet; there sits a judge
That no king can corrupt.

III, i, 99

12   'Tis well said again;
And 'tis a kind of good deed to say well:
And yet words are no deeds.

III, ii, 153

13   And then to breakfast with
What appetite you have.

III, ii, 203

14 I have touch'd the highest point of all my
    greatness;
And from that full meridian of my glory,
I haste now to my setting: I shall fall
Like a bright exhalation in the evening,
And no man see me more.

III, ii, 224

[1]Written by Shakespeare and John Fletcher; see 236 and 238.

15 Press not a falling man too far.[2]

III, ii, 334

16 Farewell! a long farewell, to all my[3] greatness!
This is the state of man: today he puts forth
The tender leaves of hopes; tomorrow blossoms,
And bears his blushing honors thick upon him;
The third day comes a frost, a killing frost;
And, when he thinks, good easy man, full surely
His greatness is a-ripening, nips his root,
And then he falls, as I do. I have ventur'd,
Like little wanton boys that swim on bladders,
This many summers in a sea of glory,
But far beyond my depth: my high-blown pride
At length broke under me, and now has left me,
Weary and old with service, to the mercy
Of a rude stream, that must forever hide me.
Vain pomp and glory of this world,[4] I hate ye:
I feel my heart new open'd. O! how wretched
Is that poor man that hangs on princes' favors!
There is, betwixt that smile we would aspire to,
That sweet aspect of princes, and their ruin,
More pangs and fears than wars or women have;
And when he falls, he falls like Lucifer,
Never to hope again.

III, ii, 352

17 A peace above all earthly dignities,
A still and quiet conscience.

III, ii, 380

18 A load would sink a navy.

III, ii, 384

19 And sleep in dull cold marble.

III, ii, 434

20 Cromwell, I charge thee, fling away ambition:
By that sin fell the angels.

III, ii, 441

21 Love thyself last: cherish those hearts that hate
    thee;
Corruption wins not more than honesty.
Still in thy right hand carry gentle peace,
To silence envious tongues: be just, and fear not.
Let all the ends thou aim'st at be thy country's,
Thy God's, and truth's; then if thou fall'st, O
    Cromwell!
Thou fall'st a blessed martyr!

III, ii, 444

22 Had I but serv'd my God with half the zeal[5]
I serv'd my king, he would not in mine age
Have left me naked to mine enemies.

III, ii, 456

[2]'Tis a cruelty / To load a falling man. — *King Henry VIII,
act V, sc. iii, l. 76*

[3]Cardinal Wolsey.

[4]See *Book of Common Prayer,* 49:21.

[5]Had I served God as well in every part / As I did serve my
king and master still, / My scope had not this season been so
short, / Nor would have had the power to do me ill. — THOMAS
CHURCHYARD [c. 1520–1604], *Death of Morton* [1593]

1 An old man, broken with the storms of state,
Is come to lay his weary bones among ye;
Give him a little earth for charity.
King Henry VIII, IV, ii, 21

2 He gave his honors to the world again,
His blessed part to heaven, and slept in peace.
IV, ii, 29

3 So may he rest; his faults lie gently on him!
IV, ii, 31

4   He was a man
Of an unbounded stomach.
IV, ii, 33

5 Men's evil manners live in brass; their virtues
We write in water.
IV, ii, 45

6 He was a scholar, and a ripe and good one;
Exceeding wise, fair-spoken, and persuading;
Lofty and sour to them that lov'd him not;
But, to those men that sought him sweet as
summer.
IV, ii, 51

7 To dance attendance on their lordships' pleasures.
V, ii, 30

8 Nor shall this peace sleep with her; but as when
The bird of wonder dies, the maiden phoenix,
Her ashes new-create another heir
As great in admiration as herself.
V, v, 40

9 Wherever the bright sun of heaven shall shine,
His honor and the greatness of his name
Shall be, and make new nations.
V, v, 51

10   Some come to take their ease
And sleep an act or two.
Epilogue, l. 2

11 Good friend, for Jesus' sake forbear
To dig the dust enclosed here;
Blest be the man that spares these stones,
And curst be he that moves my bones.
Shakespeare's epitaph

John Davies of Hereford
c. 1565–1618

12 Beauty's but skin deep.[1]
*A Select Second Husband for Sir Thomas
Overburie's Wife* [1616], st. 13

[1]All the beauty of the world, 'tis but skin deep.—RALPH
VENNING [c. 1621–1674], *Orthodox Paradoxes* [3d edition,
1650], *The Triumph of Assurance*, p. 41
    Many a dangerous temptation comes to us in fine gay colors
that are but skin-deep.—MATTHEW HENRY, *Commentaries*,
Genesis 3

Thomas Campion
1567–1620

13 My sweetest Lesbia, let us live and love,
And though the sager sort our deeds reprove,
Let us not weigh them. Heaven's great lamps do
dive
Into their west, and straight again revive,
But soon as once set is our little light,
Then must we sleep one ever-during night.[2]
A Book of Airs [1601]. I

14 Then wilt thou speak of banqueting delights,
Of masks and revels which sweet youth did make.
Ibid. XX

15 Rose-cheeked Laura, come;
Sing thou smoothly with thy beauty's
Silent music, either other
Sweetly gracing.
Observations on the Art of English Poesie
[1602], ch. 8

16 The summer hath his joys,
And winter his delights;
Though love and all his pleasures are but toys,
They shorten tedious nights.
Third Book of Airs [1617]. XII

17 Never love unless you can
Bear with all the faults of man.
Ibid. XXVII

18 There is a garden in her face
Where roses and white lilies grow;
A heavenly paradise is that place
Wherein all pleasant fruits do flow.
There cherries grow which none may buy,
Till "cherry-ripe"[3] themselves do cry.
Fourth Book of Airs [1617]. VII, st. 1

19 Those cherries fairly do enclose
Of orient pearl a double row,
Which when her lovely laughter shows,
They look like rosebuds filled with snow.
Ibid. st. 2

Thomas Nashe
1567–1601

20 Spring, the sweet spring, is the year's pleasant
king;
Then blooms each thing, then maids dance in a
ring,
Cold doth not sting, the pretty birds do sing.
Cuckoo, jug-jug, pu-we, to-witta-woo!
Summer's Last Will and Testament [1600].
Spring, st. 1

[2]See Catullus, 90:19; Shakespeare, 165:31; Jonson, 232:4;
and Herrick, 241:19.
    [3]"Cherry-ripe" was a familiar street cry of the time. See
Herrick, 241:1.

1 From winter, plague and pestilence, good Lord,
    deliver us!
Ibid. Autumn, refrain

2 Brightness falls from the air;
  Queens have died young and fair;
  Dust hath closed Helen's eye.
  I am sick, I must die.
    Lord, have mercy on us!
Ibid. Adieu! Farewell Earth's Bliss!

Tommaso Campanella
1568–1639

3   Now that they are called masters, [they] are
ashamed again to become disciples.
The Defense of Galileo[1]

4   The new philosophy proceeds from the world,
the book of God.   *Ibid.*

Sir Henry Wotton
1568–1639

5 Love lodged in a woman's breast
  Is but a guest.
A Woman's Heart [1651]

6 How happy is he born and taught,
  That serveth not another's will;
  Whose armor is his honest thought,
  And simple truth his utmost skill!
The Character of a Happy Life [1614], st. 1

7 Who God doth late and early pray,
  More of his grace than gifts to send,
  And entertains the harmless day
  With a well-chosen book or friend.
Ibid. st. 5

8 Lord of himself, though not of lands;
  And having nothing, yet hath all.[2]
Ibid. st. 6

9 You meaner beauties of the night,
  That poorly satisfy our eyes
  More by your number than your light;
  You common people of the skies,
  What are you when the sun shall rise?
On His Mistress, the Queen of Bohemia,[3] *st. 1*

10 He first deceased; she for a little tried
  To live without him, liked it not, and died.
*Upon the Death of Sir Albert Morton's Wife
[1651]*

11   Hanging was the worst use a man could be put to.
*The Disparity Between Buckingham and Essex
[1651]*

[1]Translated by GRANT MCCOLLEY.
[2]See *II Corinthians* 6:10, 44:6, and Terence, 86:5.
[3]This was printed with music as early as 1624, in East's *Sixth
Set of Books,* and is found in many manuscripts.

12   An ambassador is an honest man sent to lie
abroad for the commonwealth.[4]
Reliquiae Wottonianae [1651]

13   The itch of disputing will prove the scab of
churches.[5]   *A Panegyric to King Charles [1651]*

Sir John Davies
1569–1626

14 I know my soul hath power to know all things,
  Yet is she blind and ignorant in all:
  I know I'm one of Nature's little kings,
  Yet to the least and vilest things am thrall.
Nosce Teipsum [1599], st. 44

15 I know my life's a pain, and but a span;[6]
  I know my sense is mocked in ev'ry thing:
  And to conclude, I know myself a man,
  Which is a proud, and yet a wretched thing.
Ibid. st. 45

Johannes Kepler
1571–1630

16   So long as the mother, Ignorance, lives, it is not
safe for Science, the offspring, to divulge the hidden
causes of things.[7]   *Somnium [1634]*[8]

Thomas Dekker
1572–1632

17 This age thinks better of a gilded fool
  Than of a threadbare saint in wisdom's school.
Old Fortunatus [1600], act I, sc. i

18 Honest labor bears a lovely face.
Patient Grissell [1603], act II, sc. i

19   The best of men
  That e'er wore earth about him, was a sufferer,
  A soft, meek, patient, humble, tranquil spirit,
  The first true gentleman that ever breathed.
*The Honest Whore, pt. I [1604] (in
collaboration with* THOMAS MIDDLETON),
act I, sc. ii

20 We are ne'er like angels till our passion dies.
Ibid. pt. II [1630], I, ii

[4]In a letter to Velserus [1612], Wotton says that this "merry
definition of an ambassador . . . I had chanced to set down
at my friend's, Mr. Christopher Fleckmore, in his Album."
[5]He directed that the stone over his grave be inscribed: Hic
jacet hujus sententiae primus auctor: DISPUTANDI PRURITUS
ECCLESIARUM SCABIES. Nomen alias quaere [Here lies the author of this phrase: "The itch for disputing is the sore of
churches." Seek his name elsewhere].—WALTON, *Life of Wotton* [1651]
[6]See Francis Bacon, 160:13, and *The New England Primer,*
287:13.
[7]A footnote of Kepler's in the text.
[8]Translated by PATRICIA KIRKWOOD.

1 Cast away care, he that loves sorrow
Lengthens not a day, nor can buy tomorrow;
Money is trash, and he that will spend it,
Let him drink merrily, fortune will send it.
    The Sun's Darling [1656] (in collaboration with
    JOHN FORD)

John Donne[1]
1572–1631

2 I wonder by my troth, what thou, and I
Did, till we lov'd? were we not wean'd till then?
But suck'd on country pleasures, childishly?
Or snorted we in the seven sleepers' den?
    The Good Morrow, st. 1[2]

3 And now good morrow to our waking souls,
Which watch not one another out of fear;
For love, all love of other sights controls,
And makes one little room, an everywhere.
Let sea-discoverers to new worlds have gone,
Let maps to other, worlds on worlds have shown,
Let us possess one world, each hath one, and is
    one.
    Ibid. st. 2

4 My face in thine eye, thine in mine appears,
And true plain hearts do in the faces rest,
Where can we find two better hemispheres
Without sharp North, without declining West?
    Ibid. st. 3

5 Go, and catch a falling star,
Get with child a mandrake root,
Tell me, where all past years are,
Or who cleft the Devil's foot.
Teach me to hear mermaids singing.[3]
    Song (Go and Catch a Falling Star), st. 1

6   And swear
      No where
Lives a woman true, and fair.
    Ibid. st. 2

7 Though she were true, when you met her,
And last, till you write your letter,
    Yet she
    Will be
False, ere I come, to two, or three.
    Ibid. st. 3

8 I have done one braver thing
Than all the Worthies did;

---

[1]See Walton, 245:11, and Carew, 246:3.
John Donne, Anne Donne, Un-done.—*Attributed; letter to his wife* [1602]

[2]The poems we quote from were published, for the first time unless otherwise noted, in Donne's posthumous *Poems* [1633; further editions 1635–1669]. The general composition dates are: Songs and Sonnets (through *Farewell to Love,* 230:2) about 1593–1601, with some considerably later; Elegies about 1593–1598; and Holy Sonnets about 1609–1611, 1615–1617.

[3]See T. S. Eliot, 667:19.

And yet a braver thence doth spring,
Which is, to keep that hid.
    The Undertaking, st. 1

9 But he who loveliness within
Hath found, all outward loathes,
For he who color loves, and skin,
Loves but their oldest clothes.
    Ibid. st. 4

10 And dare love that, and say so too,
And forget the He and She.
    Ibid. st. 5

11   Busy old fool, unruly Sun,
      Why dost thou thus,
Through windows, and through curtains call on
    us?
Must to thy motions lovers' seasons run?
    The Sun Rising, st. 1

12 Love, all alike, no season knows, nor clime,
Nor hours, days, months, which are the rags of
    time.
    Ibid.

13 She is all states, and all princes, I,
Nothing else is.
    Ibid. st. 3

14 For God sake hold your tongue, and let me love.
    The Canonization, st. 1

15 The Phoenix riddle hath more wit
By us, we two being one, are it.
So to one neutral thing both sexes fit,
We die and rise the same, and prove
Mysterious by this love.
    Ibid. st. 3

16 As well a well-wrought urn becomes
The greatest ashes, as half-acre tombs.
    Ibid. st. 4

17 I am two fools, I know,
For loving, and for saying so
In whining poetry.
    The Triple Fool, st. 1

18 Who are a little wise, the best fools be.
    Ibid. st. 2

19 Sweetest love, I do not go,
For weariness of thee,
Nor in hope the world can show
A fitter love for me;
    But since that I
Must die at last, 'tis best,
To use my self in jest
    Thus by feign'd deaths to die.
    Song (Sweetest Love, I Do Not Go), st. 1

20 Yesternight the sun went hence,
And yet is here today.
    Ibid. st. 2

21 But think that we
Are but turn'd aside to sleep.
    Ibid. st. 5

1 When I died last, and dear, I die
  As often as from thee I go.
                    The Legacy, st. 1

2 Oh do not die, for I shall hate
  All women so, when thou art gone.
                    A Fever, st. 1

3 Twice or thrice had I loved thee,
  Before I knew thy face or name.
                    Air and Angels, st. 1

4 'Tis true, 'tis day; what though it be?
  O wilt thou therefore rise from me?
  Why should we rise, because 'tis light?
  Did we lie down, because 'twas night?
  Love which in spite of darkness brought us hither
  Should in despite of light keep us together.
                    Break of Day, st. 1

5 All Kings, and all their favorites,
  All glory of honors, beauties, wits,
  The sun itself, which makes times, as they pass,
  Is elder by a year, now, than it was
  When thou and I first one another saw:
  All other things, to their destruction draw,
  Only our love hath no decay;
  This, no tomorrow hath, nor yesterday,
  Running, it never runs from us away,
  But truly keeps his first, last, everlasting day.
                    The Anniversary, st. 1

6 Send home my long strayed eyes to me,
  Which (Oh) too long have dwelt on thee.
                    The Message, st. 1

7 'Tis the year's midnight, and it is the day's.
  *A Nocturnal upon St. Lucy's Day, being the
  shortest day, st. 1*

8 The world's whole sap is sunk:
  The general balm th' hydroptic earth hath drunk,
  Whither, as to the bed's-feet, life is shrunk,
  Dead and interr'd; yet all these seem to laugh,
  Compared with me, who am their epitaph.
                    Ibid.

9 For I am every dead thing,
  In whom love wrought new alchemy.
  For his art did express
  A quintessence even from nothingness,
  From dull privations, and lean emptiness
  He ruin'd me, and I am re-begot
  Of absence, darkness, death; things which are not.
                    Ibid. st. 2

10 Come live with me, and be my love,
  And we will some new pleasures prove
  Of golden sands, and crystal brooks,
  With silken lines, and silver hooks.
                    The Bait,[1] st. 1

11 Dull sublunary lovers' love
  (Whose soul is sense) cannot admit
  Absence, because it doth remove
  Those things which elemented it.
                    A Valediction Forbidding Mourning, st. 4

12 Our two souls therefore which are one,[2]
  Though I must go, endure not yet
  A breach, but an expansion,
  Like gold to airy thinness beat.
                    Ibid. st. 6

13 If they be two, they are two so
  As stiff twin compasses are two,
  Thy soul the fixt foot, makes no show
  To move, but doth, if the other do.
                    Ibid. st. 7

14 Our eye-beams twisted, and did thread
  Our eyes, upon one double string;
  So to entergraft our hands, as yet
  Was all the means to make us one,
  And pictures in our eyes to get
  Was all our propagation.
                    The Extasy, l. 7

15 That subtle knot which makes us man:
  So must pure lovers' souls descend
  T' affections, and to faculties,
  Which sense may reach and apprehend,
  Else a great Prince in prison lies.
                    Ibid. l. 64

16 Love's mysteries in souls do grow,
  But yet the body is his book.
                    Ibid. l. 71

17 I long to talk with some old lover's ghost,
  Who died before the god of love was born.
                    Love's Deity, st. 1

18 To rage, to lust, to write to, to commend,
  All is the purlieu of the god of love.
                    Ibid. st. 3

19 Who ever comes to shroud me, do not harm
        Nor question much
  That subtle wreath of hair, which crowns my
        arm;
  The mystery, the sign you must not touch,
        For 'tis my outward soul,
  Viceroy to that, which then to heaven being gone,
        Will leave this to control,
  And keep these limbs, her provinces, from
        dissolution.
                    The Funeral, st. 1

20 A bracelet of bright hair about the bone.
                    The Relic, st. 1

21 Take heed of loving me.
                    The Prohibition, st. 1

[1]Included by Izaak Walton in *The Compleat Angler* [1653], *ch.9*, as "made by Dr. Donne, and made to shew the world that he could make soft verses, when he thought them fit and worth his labor."
See Ralegh, 152:11, and Marlowe, 162:2.

[2]See Aristotle, 77:13; Zeno, 81:22; Cicero, 88:9; and Horace, 95:16.

1 So, so, break off this last lamenting kiss,
  Which sucks two souls, and vapors both away.
                          The Expiration, st. 1

2   Ah cannot we
  As well as cocks and lions jocund be,
  After such pleasures?
                          Farewell to Love, st. 3

3 Love built on beauty, soon as beauty, dies.
                Elegies, no. 2, The Anagram, l. 27

4 Nature's lay idiot, I taught thee to love.
                Ibid. 7, Nature's Lay Idiot, l. 1

5   The Alphabet
  Of flowers.
                          Ibid. l. 9

6 She, and comparisons are odious.[1]
                Ibid. 8, The Comparison, l. 54

7 No spring, nor summer beauty hath such grace,
  As I have seen in one autumnal face.
                Ibid. 9, The Autumnal, l. 1

8 The heavens rejoice in motion, why should I
  Abjure my so much lov'd variety.
                Ibid. 17, Variety, l. 1

9 Who ever loves, if he do not propose
  The right true end of love, he's one that goes
  To sea for nothing but to make him sick.
                Ibid. 18, Love's Progress, l. 1

10 The Sestos and Abydos of her breasts
   Not of two lovers, but two loves the nests.
                          Ibid. l. 61

11 Those set our hairs, but these our flesh upright.
           Ibid. 19, To His Mistress Going to Bed, l. 24

12 O my America! my new-found land.
                          Ibid. l. 27

13 Full nakedness! All joys are due to thee,
   As souls unbodied, bodies unclothed must be,
   To taste whole joys.
                          Ibid. l. 33

14 Sir, more than kisses, letters mingle souls;
   For, thus friends absent speak.
           *Verse Letter to Sir Henry Wotton, written
           before April 1598, l. 1*

15 And new philosophy calls all in doubt,
   The element of fire is quite put out;
   The sun is lost, and the earth, and no man's wit
   Can well direct him where to look for it.
   And freely men confess that this world's spent,
   When in the planets, and the firmament
   They seek so many new; then see that this
   Is crumbled out again to his atomies.
   'Tis all in pieces, all coherence gone;

[1]See Fortescue, 133:2.

All just supply, and all relation:
Prince, subject, Father, Son, are things forgot.
           *An Anatomy of the World. The First
           Anniversary [first published 1611],[2] l. 205*

16   Her pure, and eloquent blood
   Spoke in her cheeks, and so distinctly wrought,
   That one might almost say, her body thought.
           *Of the Progress of the Soul. The Second
           Anniversary [first published 1612],[2] l. 244*

17 Nature's great masterpiece, an Elephant,
   The only harmless great thing; the giant
   Of beasts.
                The Progress of the Soul, st. 39

18 I am a little world made cunningly
   Of elements, and an angelic sprite.
                Holy Sonnets, no. 5, l. 1

19 At the round earth's imagin'd corners, blow
   Your trumpets, angels, and arise, arise
   From death, you numberless infinities
   Of souls.
                          Ibid. 7, l. 1

20 All whom war, dearth, age, agues, tyrannies,
   Despair, law, chance, hath slain.
                          Ibid. l. 6

21 If poisonous minerals, and if that tree,
   Whose fruit threw death on else immortal us,
   If lecherous goats, if serpents envious
   Cannot be damn'd; alas; why should I be?
                          Ibid. 9, l. 1

22 Death be not proud,[3] though some have called
         thee
   Mighty and dreadful, for thou art not so,
   For those whom thou think'st thou dost
         overthrow,
   Die not, poor death, nor yet canst thou kill me.
                          Ibid. 10, l. 1

23 Thou art slave to fate, chance, kings, and
         desperate men.
                          Ibid. l. 9

24 One short sleep past, we wake eternally,
   And death shall be no more;[4] death, thou shalt
         die.
                          Ibid. l. 13

25 What if this present were the world's last night?
                          Ibid. 13, l. 1

26 Batter my heart, three-person'd God; for you
   As yet but knock, breathe, shine, and seek to
         mend.
                          Ibid. 14, l. 1

[2]"Anniversary" of the death of Elizabeth Drury [c. 1595–
1610].
[3]See Shakespeare, 199:30.
[4]See *Revelation 21:4*, 48:1.

1 Show me, dear Christ, Thy spouse, so bright and
clear.

Ibid. 18,[1] *l. 1*

2 Since I am coming to that holy room,
Where, with thy choir of saints forevermore,
I shall be made thy music; as I come
I tune the instrument here at the door,
And what I must do then, think here before.

*Hymn to God My God, in My Sickness [written
c. 1623 or 1631], st. 1*

3 Whilst my physicians by their love are grown
Cosmographers, and I their map, who lie
Flat on this bed.

Ibid. st. 2

4 Wilt thou forgive that sin where I begun,
Which was my sin, though it were done before?
Wilt thou forgive that sin; through which I run,
And do run still: though still I do deplore?
When thou hast done, thou hast not done,
For, I have more.

*A Hymn to God the Father [first published
1633]*

5   I observe the physician with the same diligence as
he the disease.

*Devotions upon Emergent Occasions [1624],
no. 6*

6   I do nothing upon myself, and yet am mine own
executioner.[2]   *Ibid. 12*

7   The flea, though he kill none, he does all the harm
he can.   *Ibid.*

8   No man is an island, entire of itself; every man is
a piece of the continent,[3] a part of the main; if a clod
be washed away by the sea, Europe is the less, as well
as if a promontory were, as well as if a manor of thy
friends or of thine own were; any man's death diminishes me, because I am involved in mankind; and
therefore never send to know for whom the bell tolls;
it tolls for thee.   *Ibid. 17*

9   What gnashing is not a comfort, what gnawing of
the worm is not a tickling, what torment is not a
marriage bed to this damnation, to be secluded eternally, eternally, eternally from the sight of God?

*LXXX Sermons [1640], no. 76, preached to the
Earl of Carlisle, c. autumn 1622*

10   Now God comes to thee, not as in the dawning of
the day, not as in the bud of the spring, but as the
sun at noon to illustrate all shadows, as the sheaves
in harvest, to fill all penuries, all occasions invite his
mercies, and all times are his seasons.

Ibid. 3, preached on Christmas Day, 1625

11   I throw myself down in my chamber, and I call in
and invite God and his angels thither, and when they

are there, I neglect God and his angels, for the noise
of a fly, for the rattling of a coach, for the whining
of a door.

*Ibid. 80, preached at the funeral of Sir William
Cokayne, December 12, 1626*

12   And what is so intricate, so entangling as death?
Who ever got out of a winding sheet?

*Ibid. 54, preached to the King at Whitehall,
April 5, 1628*

13   Poor intricated soul! Riddling, perplexed, labyrinthical soul!

*Ibid. 48, preached upon the Day of St. Paul's
Conversion, January 25, 1629*

14   When my mouth shall be filled with dust, and the
worm shall feed, and feed sweetly upon me,[4] when
the ambitious man shall have no satisfaction if the
poorest alive tread upon him, nor the poorest receive
any contentment in being made equal to princes, for
they shall be equal but in dust.

*XXVI Sermons [1661], no. 26, Death's Duel,
last sermon, February 15, 1631*[5]

Ben Jonson[6]

c. 1573–1637

15 As sure as death.[7]

Every Man in His Humour [1598], act II, sc. i

16 As he brews, so shall he drink.

Ibid.

17 It must be done like lightning.

Ibid. IV, 5

18 Art hath an enemy called Ignorance.

*Every Man out of His Humour [1599], act I,
sc. i*

19 There shall be no love lost.

Ibid. II, i

20   True happiness
Consists not in the multitude of friends,
But in the worth and choice.

Cynthia's Revels [1600], act III, sc. ii

21 Queen and huntress, chaste and fair,
Now the sun is laid to sleep,
Seated in thy silver chair,
State in wonted manner keep:
Hesperus entreats thy light,
Goddess, excellently bright.

Ibid. V, iii

---

[4]See *Job* 24:20, 14:36.
[5]Called by His Majesty's household the Doctor's Own Funeral Sermon. —*Preface to the first edition [1632]*
[6]O rare Ben Jonson! —JOHN YOUNG, *Epitaph*
Which was done at the charge of Jack Young, who, walking
there when the grave was covering, gave the fellow 18 pence to
cut it. —AUBREY, *Brief Lives*
[7]Come del morire [Sure as death]. —GIOVANNI BOCCACCIO
[1313–1375], *Il Filostrato, canto IV, st. 140*

[1]First published in 1899.
[2]See Thomas Browne, 248:18.
[3]See *Romans 14:7, 42:26*; Francis Bacon, 159:15; and
Quarles, 242:5.

1 That old bald cheater, Time.
The Poetaster [1601], act I, sc. i

2   Of all wild beasts preserve me from a tyrant; and of all tame, a flatterer.   *Sejanus [1603], act I*

3 Calumnies are answered best with silence.
Volpone [1606], act II, sc. ii

4 Come my Celia, let us prove,
While we can, the sports of love;
Time will not be ours forever,
He at length our good will sever.
Spend not then his gifts in vain;
Suns that set may rise again,
But if once we lose this light,
'Tis with us perpetual night.[1]
Song, To Celia [1607]

5 Still to be neat, still to be drest,
As you were going to a feast.
Epicene; or, The Silent Woman [1609], act I, sc. i

6 Give me a look, give me a face,
That makes simplicity a grace;
Robes loosely flowing, hair as free,
Such sweet neglect more taketh me
Than all the adulteries of art:
They strike mine eyes, but not my heart.[2]
Ibid.

7 The dignity of truth is lost with much protesting.
Catiline's Conspiracy [1611], act III, sc. ii

8 Truth is the trial of itself
And needs no other touch,
And purer than the purest gold,
Refine it ne'er so much.
On Truth [1616], st. 1

9   Preserving the sweetness of proportion and expressing itself beyond expression.
The Masque of Hymen [1616]

10 Farewell, thou child of my right hand, and joy!
My sin was too much hope of thee, loved boy.
Epigrams [1616]. On My First Son [written c. 1603]

11 Rest in soft peace, and, asked, say here doth lie
Ben Jonson his best piece of poetry:
For whose sake, henceforth, all his vows be such,
As what he loves may never like too much.
Ibid.

12 Underneath this stone doth lie
As much beauty as could die;
Which in life did harbor give
To more virtue than doth live.
Ibid. Epitaph on Elizabeth, Lady H——

13 Follow a shadow, it still flies you;
Seem to fly it, it will pursue:

So court a mistress, she denies you;
Let her alone, she will court you.
The Forest [1616]. Follow a Shadow, st. 1

14 Whilst that for which all virtue now is sold,
And almost every vice—almighty gold.
Ibid. Epistle to Elizabeth, Countess of Rutland

15 Drink to me only with thine eyes,
And I will pledge with mine;
Or leave a kiss but in the cup
And I'll not look for wine.[3]
The thirst that from the soul doth rise
Doth ask a drink divine;
But might I of Jove's nectar sup,
I would not change for thine.
Ibid. To Celia, st. 1

16 I sent thee late a rosy wreath,
Not so much honoring thee
As giving it a hope that there
It could not wither'd be.
But thou thereon didst only breathe,
And sent'st it back to me;
Since when it grows and smells, I swear,
Not of itself, but thee.
Ibid. st. 2

17   Reader, look,
Not at his picture, but his book.
On the portrait of Shakespeare prefixed to the First Folio [1623]

18   Soul of the age!
The applause, delight, the wonder of our stage!
My Shakespeare, rise; I will not lodge thee by
Chaucer or Spenser, or bid Beaumont lie
A little further, to make thee a room;
Thou art a monument, without a tomb,
And art alive still, while thy book doth live,
And we have wits to read, and praise to give.
To the Memory of My Beloved, the Author, Mr. William Shakespeare [1623]

19 Marlowe's mighty line.
Ibid.

20 And though thou hadst small Latin and less Greek.
Ibid.

21 Call forth thundering Aeschylus.
Ibid.

22 He was not of an age but for all time.
Ibid.

23 Who casts to write a living line, must sweat.
Ibid.

24 For a good poet's made, as well as born.[4]
Ibid.

---

[1]See Catullus, 90:19; Shakespeare, 165:31; Campion, 226:13; and Herrick, 241:19.
[2]See Herrick, 241:5.
[3]Drink to me with your eyes alone. . . . And if you will, take the cup to your lips and fill it with kisses, and give it so to me.—PHILOSTRATUS [c. 181–250], *Letter 24*
[4]See Florus, 110:9.

1 Sweet Swan of Avon!

               Ibid.

2 Those that merely talk and never think,
  That live in the wild anarchy of drink.[1]
> *Underwoods [1640]. An Epistle, Answering to
> One That Asked to Be Sealed of the Tribe of
> Ben*

3 In small proportions we just beauties see,
  And in short measures life may perfect be.
> *Ibid. To the Immortal Memory of Sir Lucius
> Cary and Sir Henry Morison*

4   The players have often mentioned it as an honor
to Shakespeare that in his writing (whatsoever he
penned) he never blotted out a line. My answer hath
been, "Would he had blotted a thousand."
> *Timber; or, Discoveries Made upon Men and
> Matter [1640]*

5   I loved the man [Shakespeare] and do honor his
memory, on this side idolatry, as much as any.

               Ibid.

6   Greatness of name in the father oft-times overwhelms the son; they stand too near one another.
The shadow kills the growth: so much, that we see
the grandchild come more and oftener to be heir of
the first.   *Ibid.*

7   Though the most be players, some must be spectators.   *Ibid.*

8   Talking and eloquence are not the same: to
speak, and to speak well, are two things. A fool may
talk, but a wise man speaks.   *Ibid.*

Richard Barnfield
1574–1627

9 The waters were his winding sheet, the sea was
    made for his tomb;
  Yet for his fame the ocean sea, was not sufficient
    room.
> *Epitaph on Hawkins*[2] *[1595]*

10 As it fell upon a day
  In the merry month of May,
  Sitting in a pleasant shade
  Which a grove of myrtles made.
> *Poems: In Divers Humours [1598]. Ode*

11 King Pandion, he is dead,
  All thy friends are lapp'd in lead.

               Ibid.

12 Every one that flatters thee
  Is no friend in misery.
  Words are easy, like the wind;
  Faithful friends are hard to find.

Every man will be thy friend
Whilst thou hast wherewith to spend;
But if store of crowns be scant,
No man will supply thy want.

               Ibid.

13 If music and sweet poetry agree.
> *Ibid. To His Friend, Mr. R. L.*

Joseph Hall
1574–1656

14 So little in his purse, so much upon his back.
> *Portrait of a Poor Gallant*

15 'Mongst all these stirs of discontented strife,
  O, let me lead an academic life;
  To know much, and to think for nothing, know
  Nothing to have, yet think we have enow.
> *Discontent of Men with Their Condition*

16   Death borders upon our birth, and our cradle
stands in the grave.
> *Epistles [1608–1611]. Decade III, epistle 2*

Thomas Heywood
c. 1574 – c. 1641

17 Within the red-leaved table of my heart.
> *A Woman Killed with Kindness [1607], sc. vi*

18 I will walk on eggs.

               Ibid. xiii

19 O God! O God! that it were possible
  To undo things done; to call back yesterday![3]
  That Time could turn up his swift sandy glass,
  To untell the days, and to redeem these hours.

               Ibid.

20 Pack clouds away, and welcome day,
  With night we banish sorrow.
> *Pack Clouds Away [1630], st. 1*

21 I hold he loves me best that calls me Tom.
> *Hierarchie of the Blessed Angels [1635]*

22 Seven cities warr'd for Homer being dead,
  Who living had no roof to shroud his head.[4]

               Ibid.

John Marston
c. 1575 – c. 1634

23   Oblivioni sacrum [Sacred to oblivion].

               Epitaph

---

[1]They never taste who always drink; / They always talk who
never think. — PRIOR, *Upon a Passage in the Scaligerana*
  See Dryden, 274:10.
[2]Sir John Hawkins [1532–1595], second in command to
Drake on the expedition to the West Indies, died at sea off
Puerto Rico.

[3]See Shakespeare, 171:22.
[4]Seven cities strive for the learned root of Homer: / Smyrna,
Chios, Colophon, Ithaca, Pylos, Argos, Athens. — ANONY-
MOUS; *from The Greek Anthology [1906], ed.* J. W. MACKAIL,
bk. VI, epigram 298
  Seven wealthy towns contend for Homer dead, / Through
which the living Homer begged his bread. — THOMAS SEWARD
[1708–1790], *On Homer*

Cyril Tourneur
1575–1626

1 Does the silkworm expend her yellow labors
For thee? For thee does she undo herself?
Are lordships sold to maintain ladyships,
For the poor benefit of a bewildering minute?
The Revenger's Tragedy [1607], act III, sc. iv

Henry Peacham
c. 1576 – c. 1643

2   Affect not as some do that bookish ambition to be stored with books and have well-furnished libraries, yet keep their heads empty of knowledge; to desire to have many books, and never to use them, is like a child that will have a candle burning by him all the while he is sleeping.
The Compleat Gentleman [1622]

Robert Burton
1577–1640

3 All my joys to this are folly,
Naught so sweet as melancholy.[1]
The Anatomy of Melancholy [1621–1651]. The Author's Abstract

4   I would help others, out of a fellow-feeling.[2]
Ibid. Democritus to the Reader

5   They lard their lean books with the fat of others' works.   *Ibid.*

6   We can say nothing but what hath been said.[3] Our poets steal from Homer. . . . Our story-dressers do as much; he that comes last is commonly best.   *Ibid.*

7   A dwarf standing on the shoulders of a giant may see farther than a giant himself.[4]   *Ibid.*

8   It is most true, *stilus virum arguit*—our style betrays us.[5]   *Ibid.*

9   Old friends become bitter enemies on a sudden for toys and small offenses.[6]   *Ibid.*

10   Penny wise, pound foolish.   *Ibid.*

11   Women wear the breeches . . . in a word, the world turned upside downward.   *Ibid.*

12   Like Aesop's fox, when he had lost his tail, would have all his fellow foxes cut off theirs.   *Ibid.*

13   All poets are mad.[7]   *Ibid.*

14   Every man hath a good and a bad angel attending on him in particular, all his life long.
Ibid. pt. I, sec. 2, member 1, subsec. 2

15   That which Pythagoras said to his scholars of old, may be forever applied to melancholy men, *A fabis abstinete*, eat no beans.
Ibid. member 2, subsec. 1

16   Cookery is become an art, a noble science; cooks are gentlemen.   *Ibid. subsec. 2*

17   No rule is so general, which admits not some exception.[8]   *Ibid. subsec. 3*

18   Idleness is an appendix to nobility.
Ibid. subsec. 6

19   Why doth one man's yawning make another yawn?   *Ibid. member 3, subsec. 2*

20   They do not live but linger.   *Ibid. subsec. 10*

21   [Desire is] a perpetual rack, or horsemill, according to Austin [Saint Augustine], still going round as in a ring.   *Ibid. subsec. 11*

22   [The rich] are indeed rather possessed by their money than possessors.   *Ibid. subsec. 12*

23   Were it not that they are loath to lay out money on a rope, they would be hanged forthwith, and sometimes die to save charges.   *Ibid.*

24   A mere madness, to live like a wretch and die rich.   *Ibid.*

25   I may not here omit those two main plagues and common dotages of human kind, wine and women, which have infatuated and besotted myriads of people; they go commonly together.
Ibid. subsec. 13

26   All our geese are swans.[9]   *Ibid. subsec. 14*

27   They are proud in humility; proud in that they are not proud.   *Ibid.*

28   We can make mayors and officers every year, but not scholars.   *Ibid. subsec. 15*

29   *Hinc quam sic calamus saevior ense, patet.* The pen worse than the sword.
Ibid. member 4, subsec. 4

30   See one promontory (said Socrates of old), one mountain, one sea, one river, and see all.[10]
Ibid. subsec. 7

31   One was never married, and that's his hell; another is, and that's his plague.   *Ibid.*

---

[1]See Fletcher, 236:13; Milton, 251:22; and Hood, 422:22.
[2]A fellow-feeling makes one wondrous kind.—GARRICK, *Prologue on Quitting the Stage* [1776]
[3]See *Ecclesiastes 1:9*, 23:25; Terence, 86:4; and La Bruyère, 283:11.
[4]See Newton, 281:25.
[5]Latin proverb.
See Buffon, 311:7.
[6]See Pope, 299:9.

[7]See Democritus, 70:*n*9; Wordsworth, 374:9; and Robert Lowell, 742:16.
[8]The exception proves the rule.—*Proverb*
[9]Every man thinks his own geese swans.—DICKENS, *The Cricket on the Hearth* [1845], *Chirp the Second*
See Matthew Arnold, 500:2.
[10]A blade of grass is always a blade of grass, whether in one country or another.—SAMUEL JOHNSON, in Hester Piozzi, *Anecdotes of Samuel Johnson* [1786]

1 Aristotle said melancholy men of all others are most witty. *Ibid. sec. 3, member 1, subsec. 3*

2 Seneca thinks the gods are well pleased when they see great men contending with adversity. *Ibid. pt. II, sec. 2, member 1, subsec. 1*

3 Machiavel says virtue and riches seldom settle on one man. *Ibid. member 2*

4 As he said in Machiavel, *omnes eodem patre nati,* Adam's sons, conceived all and born in sin, etc. "We are by nature all as one, all alike, if you see us naked; let us wear theirs and they our clothes, and what is the difference?" *Ibid.*

5 Who cannot give good counsel? 'Tis cheap, it costs them nothing. *Ibid. member 3*

6 Many things happen between the cup and the lip.[1] *Ibid.*

7 All places are distant from heaven alike. *Ibid. member 4*

8 The commonwealth of Venice in their armory have this inscription: "Happy is that city which in time of peace thinks of war." *Ibid. member 6*

9 Every man, as the saying is, can tame a shrew but he that hath her. *Ibid.*

10 Tobacco, divine, rare, superexcellent tobacco, which goes far beyond all the panaceas, potable gold, and philosopher's stones, a sovereign remedy to all diseases . . . but as it is commonly abused by most men, which take it as tinkers do ale, 'tis a plague, a mischief, a violent purger of goods, lands, health, hellish, devilish and damned tobacco, the ruin and overthrow of body and soul. *Ibid. sec. 4, member 2, subsec. 2*

11 "Let me not live," said Aretine's Antonia, "if I had not rather hear thy discourse than see a play." *Ibid. pt. III, sec. 1, member 1, subsec. 1*

12 Birds of a feather will gather together.[2] *Ibid. subsec. 2*

13 No cord nor cable can so forcibly draw, or hold so fast, as love can do with a twined thread.[3] *Ibid. sec. 2, member 1, subsec. 2*

14 To enlarge or illustrate this power and effect of love is to set a candle in the sun.[4] *Ibid.*

15 [Quoting Seneca:] Cornelia kept her in talk till her children came from school, "and these," said she, "are my jewels." *Ibid. member 2, subsec. 3*

16 Diogenes struck the father when the son swore. *Ibid. subsec. 5*

17 For "ignorance is the mother of devotion," as all the world knows. *Ibid. sec. 4, member 1, subsec. 2*

18 The fear of some divine and supreme powers keeps men in obedience.[5] *Ibid.*

19 One religion is as true as another. *Ibid. member 2, subsec. 1*

20 Melancholy and despair, though often, do not always concur; there is much difference: melancholy fears without a cause, this upon great occasion; melancholy is caused by fear and grief, but this torment procures them and all extremity of bitterness. *Ibid. subsec. 3*

21 A good conscience is a continual feast. *Ibid.*

22 Our conscience, which is a great ledger book, wherein are written all our offenses . . . grinds our souls with the remembrance of some precedent sins, makes us reflect upon, accuse and condemn ourselves. *Ibid.*

23 What physic, what chirurgery, what wealth, favor, authority can relieve, bear out, assuage, or expel a troubled conscience? A quiet mind cureth all. *Ibid. subsec. 5*

24 Be not solitary, be not idle.[6] *Ibid. subsec. 6*

William Harvey
1578–1657

25 The heart of animals is the foundation of their life, the sovereign of everything within them, the sun of their microcosm. *De Motu Cordis et Sanguinis [1628],[7] dedication to King Charles*

26 All we know is still infinitely less than all that still remains unknown. *Ibid. dedication to Dr. Argent and Other Learned Physicians*

[1]A very ancient proverb, sometimes attributed to Homer.
There is many a slip 'twixt the cup and the lip.—PALLADAS [fl. 400], in *The Greek Anthology* [1906], ed. J. W. MACKAIL, *bk. X, epigram 32*
Though men determine, the gods do dispose; and ofttimes many things fall out between the cup and the lip.—ROBERT GREENE, *Perimedes the Blacksmith* [1588]
[2]Birds of a feather flock together.—WITHER, *Abuses* [1613], 72
See *Ecclesiasticus 13:16, 31:32;* Homer, *54:2;* and John Heywood, *141:5.*
[3]One hair of a woman can draw more than a hundred pair of oxen.—HOWELL, *Letters* [1645–1655], *bk. II, 4*
She knows her man, and when you rant and swear, / Can draw you to her with a single hair.—DRYDEN, *Persius* [1693], *satire V, l. 246*
See Pope, *299:12.*
[4]And hold their farthing candle to the sun.—EDWARD YOUNG, *Love of Fame* [1725–1728], *Satire VII, l. 99*
And hold their glimmering tapers to the sun.—CRABBE, *The Parish Register* [1807], *pt. I, Introduction*
See Algernon Sidney, *270:1.*
[5]The fear o' hell's a hangman's whip / To haud the wretch in order.—BURNS, *Epistle to a Young Friend*
[6]See Samuel Johnson, *317:15.*
[7]*An Anatomical Disquisition on the Motion of the Heart and Blood in Animals.*
Translated by ROBERT WILLIS.

1   I profess both to learn and to teach anatomy, not from books but from dissections; not from positions of philosophers but from the fabric of nature.
De Motu Cordis et Sanguinis, dedication

2   I appeal to your own eyes as my witness and judge.
De Generatione Animalium (On the Generation of Animals) [1651],[1] *introduction*

John Fletcher[2]
1579–1625

3   Drink today, and drown all sorrow;
You shall perhaps not do 't tomorrow.
Rollo, Duke of Normandy [1639] (in collaboration with JONSON and others), act II, sc. ii

4   And he that will to bed go sober
Falls with the leaf in October.[3]
Ibid.

5   Three merry boys, and three merry boys,
And three merry boys are we.[4]
As ever did sing in a hempen string
Under the gallows tree.
Ibid. III, ii

6   O woman, perfect woman! what distraction
Was meant to mankind when thou wast made a devil!
Monsieur Thomas [1639], act III, sc. i

7   That soul that can
Be honest is the only perfect man.
The Honest Man's Fortune [1647] (in collaboration with three other authors), epilogue

8   Weep no more, nor sigh, nor groan,
Sorrow calls no time that's gone;
Violets plucked, the sweetest rain
Makes not fresh nor grow again.
The Queen of Corinth [1647] (in collaboration with MASSINGER and a third author), act III, sc. ii

9   Of all the paths lead to a woman's love
Pity's the straightest.
The Knight of Malta [1647] (in collaboration with MASSINGER), act I, sc. i

10   Go to grass.
The Little French Lawyer [1647] (in collaboration with MASSINGER), act IV, sc. vii

[1]Translated by ROBERT WILLIS.
[2]See also Shakespeare, 225:*n*1, and Beaumont and Fletcher, 238.
[3]The following well-known catch, or glee, is formed on this song:
He who goes to bed, and goes to bed sober, / Falls as the leaves do, and dies in October; / But he who goes to bed, and goes to bed mellow, / Lives as he ought to do, and dies an honest fellow.
[4]Three merry men be we. — PEELE, *Old Wives' Tale* [1595]

11   There is no jesting with edge tools.
Ibid.

12   Let's meet, and either do or die.[5]
The Island Princess [1647], act II, sc. ii

13   Hence, all you vain delights,
As short as are the nights
Wherein you spend your folly!
There's naught in this life sweet
But only melancholy;
O sweetest melancholy!
The Nice Valor [1647]. Melancholy[6]

Thomas Middleton
1580–1627

14   Better the day, better the deed.[7]
Michaelmas Term [1607], act III, sc. i

15   Since the worst comes to the worst.[8]
Ibid. III, iv

16   What is got over the Devil's back (that's by knavery), is spent under the belly (that's by lechery).[9]
Ibid. IV, i

17   As true as I live.
The Family of Love [1608], act V, sc. iii

18   Have you summoned your wits from woolgathering?[10]
Ibid.

19   By my faith the fool has feathered his nest well.[11]
The Roaring Girl [1611], act I, sc. i

20   That disease of which all old men sicken — avarice.[12]
Ibid.

21   I that am of your blood was taken from you
For your better health; look no more upon 't,
But cast it to the ground regardlessly,
Let the common sewer take it from distinction.
The Changeling [written 1622], act V, sc. iii

[5]This expression is a kind of common property, being the motto, we believe, of a Scottish family. — WALTER SCOTT, review of Thomas Campbell's *Gertrude of Wyoming* [1809], where it appears (*pt. III, l. 37*): Tomorrow let us do or die!
See Burns, 363:20.
[6]This poem is frequently and with some likelihood attributed to WILLIAM STRODE [1602–1645].
See Robert Burton, 234:3; Milton, 251:22; and Hood, 422:-22.
[7]The better the day, the worse deed. — MATTHEW HENRY, *Commentaries, Genesis* 3
[8]If the worst comes to the worst. — *Discovery of the Knights of the Poste* [1597]
[9]What is got over the Devil's back is spent under the belly. — RABELAIS, *Works,* bk. V [1552], ch. 11
Isocrates was in the right to insinuate that what is got over the Devil's back is spent under his belly. — LESAGE, *Gil Blas* [1715–1735], bk. VIII, ch. 9
[10]My understanding has forsook me, and is gone a-woolgathering. — CERVANTES, *Don Quixote,* pt. II [1605–1615], bk. IV, ch. 38
[11]We will feather our nests ere time may us espy. — *A Merry Interlude Entitled Respublica* [1553], act III, sc. vi
[12]So for a good old-gentlemanly vice / I think I must take up with avarice. — BYRON, *Don Juan* [1818–1824], *canto I, st.* 216

1 As the case stands.
The Old Law [1656], act II, sc. i

2 On his last legs. *Ibid. V, i*

3 'Tis a stinger.
More Dissemblers Besides Women [1657],
act III, sc. ii

4 How many honest words have suffered corruption since Chaucer's days!
No Wit, No Help, Like a Woman's [1657],
act II, sc. i

5 By many a happy accident. *Ibid. IV, i*

6 Anything for a Quiet Life.
Title of play [1662]

7 This was a good week's labor.
Anything for a Quiet Life, act V, sc. ii

8 There's no hate lost between us.
The Witch [written c. 1627], act IV, sc. iii

9 Black spirits and white, red spirits and gray,
Mingle, mingle, mingle, you that mingle may.[1]
Ibid. V, ii

Richard Rich
fl. 1610

10 God will not let us fall . . .
For . . . our work is good,
We hope to plant a nation,
Where none before hath stood.
Newes from Virginia: The Flock Triumphant
[1610][2]

John Webster
c. 1580 – c. 1625

11 Is not old wine wholesomest, old pippins toothsomest, old wood burn brightest, old linen wash whitest? Old soldiers, sweethearts, are surest, and old lovers are soundest.[3]
Westward Hoe [1607], (in collaboration with
DEKKER), *act II, sc. ii*

12 I saw him now going the way of all flesh.
Ibid.

13 Call for the robin redbreast and the wren,
Since o'er shady groves they hover,
And with leaves and flowers do cover
The friendless bodies of unburied men.
The White Devil [1612], act V, sc. iv

14 But keep the wolf far thence, that's foe to men,
For with his nails he'll dig them up again.
Ibid.

15 Prosperity doth bewitch men, seeming clear;
But seas do laugh, show white, when rocks are
near.
Ibid. V, vi

16 I am Duchess of Malfi still.
Duchess of Malfi [1623], act IV, sc. ii

17 I know death hath ten thousand several doors
For men to take their exits.[4]
Ibid.

18 Heaven-gates are not so highly arch'd
As princes' palaces; they that enter there
Must go upon their knees.
Ibid.

19 *Ferdinand:* Cover her face; mine eyes dazzle; she
died young.
Bosola: I think not so; her infelicity
Seemed to have years too many.
Ibid.

20 Vain the ambition of kings
Who seek by trophies and dead things
To leave a living name behind,
And weave but nets to catch the wind.[5]
The Devil's Law Case [1623], song

Sir Thomas Overbury
1581–1613

21 Give me, next good, an understanding wife,
By nature wise, not learned much by art.
A Wife [1614]

22 He disdains all things above his reach, and preferreth all countries before his own.
An Affectate Traveller [1614]

James Ussher
1581–1656

23 According to our chronology, [the creation of the world] fell upon the entrance of the night preceding the twenty third day of October in the year of the Julian Calendar, 710 [4004 B.C.].
The Annals of the World [1658]

---

[1] These lines are introduced into *Macbeth*, act IV, sc. i. According to George Steevens, "the song was, in all probability, a traditional one."

[2] Narrative poem about Rich's voyage to Virginia [1609] with Captain Christopher Newport. Its account of a shipwreck on the Bermudas may have been a source for scenes in Shakespeare's *The Tempest*.

[3] See Francis Bacon, 158:23; Selden, 238:22; and Goldsmith, 329:25.

[4] The thousand doors that lead to death. — THOMAS BROWNE, *Religio Medici* [1643], *pt. 1, sec. 44*
Death hath so many doors to let out life. — FLETCHER AND MASSINGER, *The Custom of the Country* [1647], *act II, sc. ii*
Death hath a thousand doors to let out life. — MASSINGER, *A Very Woman* [1665], *act V, sc. iv*
See Swift, 288:13.

[5] Since in a net I seek to hold the wind. — WYATT, *Sonnet, Whoso List to Hunt*

Richard Corbet
1582–1635

1 Farewell, rewards and fairies,
  Good housewives now may say.
                    The Fairies Farewell, st. 1

2   Who of late for cleanliness,
  Finds sixpence in her shoe?
                                        Ibid.

3 Nor too much wealth nor wit come to thee,
  So much of either may undo thee.
                    To His Son, Vincent Corbet

Jacques du Laurens
1583–1650

4   I do not attack fools, but foolishness.
                                  Satires [1624]

Philip Massinger
1583–1640

5   Be wise;
  Soar not too high to fall; but stoop to rise.
                    Duke of Milan [1623], act I, sc. ii

6 He that would govern others, first should be
  The master of himself.
                    The Bondman [1624], act I, sc. iii

7   To be nobly born
  Is now a crime.
                    The Roman Actor [1629], act I, sc. i

8   Whose wealth
  Arithmetic cannot number.
                                    Ibid. iii

9 Grim death.[1]
                                    Ibid. IV, ii

10   A New Way to Pay Old Debts.
                          Title of play [1632]

Francis Beaumont[2]
c. 1584–1616

11   What things have we seen
  Done at the Mermaid! heard words that have
      been
  So nimble, and so full of subtle flame,
  As if that everyone from whence they came,
  Had meant to put his whole wit in a jest,
  And resolv'd to live a fool, the rest
  Of his dull life.
                    Letter to Ben Jonson [1640]

[1]See Milton, 257:18.
[2]See also Beaumont and Fletcher.

Beaumont and Fletcher[3]
[Francis Beaumont c. 1584–1616]
[John Fletcher 1579–1625][4]

12   It is always good
  When a man has two irons in the fire.
              The Faithful Friends [c. 1608], act I, sc. ii

13 As cold as cucumbers.
              Cupid's Revenge [1615], act I, sc. i

14 Kiss till the cow comes home.[5]
              The Scornful Lady [1616], act III, sc. i

15 There is a method in man's wickedness—
  It grows up by degrees.[6]
              A King and No King [1619], act V, sc. iv

16 Upon my buried body lie lightly, gentle earth.[7]
              The Maid's Tragedy [1619], act II, sc. ii

17 The devil take the hindmost!
              Philaster [1620], act V, sc. iii

18 Whistle, and she'll come to you.[8]
              Wit Without Money [1639], act IV, sc. iv

19 Calamity is man's true touchstone.[9]
  *Four Plays in One. The Triumph of Honour
  [1647], sc. i*

20 Though I say it that should not say it.
  *Wit at Several Weapons (probably in
  collaboration with WILLIAM ROWLEY [c. 1585–
  c. 1642]), act II, sc. ii*

John Selden
1584–1654

21   *Scrutamini scripturas* [Let us look at the scriptures]. These two words have undone the world.
              Table Talk [1689]. Bible, Scripture

22   Old friends are best. King James used to call for his old shoes; they were easiest for his feet.[10]
                              Ibid. Friends

23   Humility is a virtue all preach, none practice; and yet everybody is content to hear.
                              Ibid. Humility

24   Tis not the drinking that is to be blamed, but the excess.   *Ibid.*

25   Ignorance of the law excuses no man; not that all men know the law, but because 'tis an excuse every

[3]Of whose partnership John Aubrey said: "There was a wonderful consimility of fancy. They lived together not far from the playhouse, had one wench in the house between them, the same clothes and cloak, &c."
[4]Also on 236.
[5]Also familiar as: Till the cows come home.
[6]See Juvenal, 108:20, and Racine, 281:12.
[7]See Euripides, 67:25, and Anonymous: Latin, 119:31.
[8]See Burns, 362:18.
[9]See Seneca, 103:4.
[10]See Francis Bacon, 158:23; John Webster, 237:11; and Goldsmith, 329:25.

man will plead, and no man can tell how to refute
him. *Ibid. Law*

1 Wit and wisdom are born with a man.
Ibid. Learning

2 Few men make themselves masters of the things
they write or speak. *Ibid.*

3 Take a straw and throw it up into the air—you
shall see by that which way the wind is.
Ibid. Libels

4 Marriage is a desperate thing.
Ibid. Marriage

5 Pleasure is nothing else but the intermission of
pain. *Ibid. Pleasure*

6 Thou little thinkest what a little foolery governs
the whole world.[1] *Ibid. Pope*

7 They that govern most make the least noise.
Ibid. Power

8 Syllables govern the world. *Ibid.*

9 Wise men say nothing in dangerous times.
Ibid. Wisdom

10 Preachers say, Do as I say, not as I do.
Ibid. Preaching

11 A king is a thing men have made for their own
sakes, for quietness' sake. Just as in a family one
man is appointed to buy the meat.
Ibid. Of a King

Tirso de Molina [Gabriel Téllez]
c. 1584–1648

12 Through his honor I conquered him. For these
peasants carry their honor in their hands so that they
may constantly consult it; this same honor that once
felt so much at home in the city but now has taken
refuge in a more rural setting.
El Burlador de Sevilla (The Rogue of Seville)
[1630],[2] act III, sc. iii

John Ford
c. 1586–1639

13 Diamond cut diamond.
The Lover's Melancholy [1629], act I, sc. i

14 Remember
When we last gathered roses in the garden,
I found my wits; but truly you lost yours.
The Broken Heart [1629], act IV, sc. ii

15 'Tis Pity She's a Whore. *Title of play [1633]*

[1]Behold, my son, with how little wisdom the world is governed.—AXEL OXENSTIERN [1583–1654]
[2]Translated by ROBERT O'BRIEN.
This is the original Don Juan play.

Thomas Rainsborough
d. 1648

16 The poorest he that is in England hath a life to
live as the greatest he.
*In the army debates at Putney [October 29,
1647]*

Thomas Hobbes
1588–1679

17 Words are wise men's counters, they do but
reckon with them, but they are the money of fools.
Leviathan [1651], pt. I, ch. 4

18 The privilege of absurdity; to which no living
creature is subject but man only. *Ibid. 5*

19 Sudden glory is the passion which maketh those
grimaces called laughter. *Ibid. 6*

20 The secret thoughts of a man run over all things,
holy, profane, clean, obscene, grave, and light, without shame or blame. *Ibid. 8*

21 During the time men live without a common
power to keep them all in awe, they are in that
condition which is called *war;* and such a war, as is
of every man, against every man.[3] *Ibid. 13*

22 [In a state of nature] No arts; no letters; no society; and which is worst of all, continual fear and
danger of violent death; and the life of man, solitary,
poor, nasty, brutish, and short. *Ibid.*

23 The Papacy is not other than the Ghost of the
deceased Roman Empire, sitting crowned upon the
grave thereof. *Ibid. pt. IV, ch. 47*

24 The praise of ancient authors proceeds not from
the reverence of the dead, but from the competition
and mutual envy of the living.
Ibid. A Review and Conclusion

25 Such truth as opposeth no man's profit nor pleasure is to all men welcome. *Ibid.*

26 I am about to take my last voyage, a great leap in
the dark. *Last words*

John Winthrop
1588–1649

27 For we must consider that we shall be as a city
upon a hill.[4] The eyes of all people are upon us, so
that if we shall deal falsely with our God in this work
we have undertaken, and so cause Him to withdraw
His present help from us, we shall be made a story
and a byword through the world.
*A Model of Christian Charity [1630], a sermon
delivered on board the Arbella*

[3]See Swift, 289:19.
[4]See *Matthew 5:14, 33:3.*

George Wither
1588–1667

1 Shall I wasting in despair
Die because a woman's fair?
Or make pale my cheeks with care
'Cause another's rosy are?
Be she fairer than the day,
Or the flow'ry meads in May,
If she be not so to me,
What care I how fair she be?
Fair Virtue [1622]. Sonnet 4, st. 1

2 'Twas I that beat the bush,
The bird to others flew.
A Love Sonnet [1622], st. 11

3 Though I am young, I scorn to flit
On the wings of borrowed wit.
The Shepherd's Hunting [1622]. Eclogue 4

Honorat de Bueil, Marquis de Racan
1589–1670

4 Nothing in the world lasts
Save eternal change.[1]
Odes. The Coming of Spring

5   The good effect of Fortune may be short-lived.
To build on it is to build on sand.[2]
Poésies Diverses

William Bradford
1590–1657

6   They knew they were pilgrims.[3]
Of Plymouth Plantation [1620–1647], ch. 7

7   So they committed themselves to the will of God
and resolved to proceed.
Ibid. 9

8   Being thus arrived in a good harbor, and brought
safe to land, they fell upon their knees[4] and blessed
the God of Heaven who had brought them over the
vast and furious ocean, and delivered them from all
the perils and miseries thereof, again to set their feet
on the firm and stable earth, their proper element.
Ibid.

9   And for the season it was winter, and they that
know the winters of that country know them to be
sharp and violent, and subject to cruel and fierce
storms, dangerous to travel to known places, much
more to search an unknown coast. . . . For summer being done, all things stand upon them with a
weather-beaten face, and the whole country, full of

woods and thickets, represented a wild and savage
hue.
Ibid.

10   But it pleased God to visit us then with death
daily, and with so general a disease that the living
were scarce able to bury the dead.
Ibid. 12

11   Behold, now, another providence of God. A ship
comes into the harbor.
Ibid. 13

12   Thus out of small beginnings greater things have
been produced by His hand that made all things of
nothing,[5] and gives being to all things that are; and,
as one small candle may light a thousand, so the light
here kindled hath shone unto many, yea in some sort
to our whole nation.[6]
Ibid. 21

William Basse
d. c. 1653

13 Renowned Spenser, lie a thought more nigh
To learned Chaucer; and rare Beaumont, lie
A little nearer Spenser; to make room
For Shakespeare in your threefold fourfold tomb.
On Mr. Wm. Shakespeare [c. 1616]

William Browne
1591–c. 1645

14 Underneath this sable hearse
Lies the subject of all verse:
Sidney's sister, Pembroke's mother.
Death, ere thou hast slain another
Fair and learned and good as she,
Time shall throw a dart at thee.
Epitaph on the Countess of Pembroke [1621]

15 There is no season such delight can bring,
As summer, autumn, winter, and the spring.
Variety

Robert Herrick
1591–1674

16 I sing of brooks, of blossoms, birds, and bowers:
Of April, May, of June, and July flowers.
I sing of Maypoles, Hock-carts, wassails, wakes,
Of bridegrooms, brides, and of their bridal cakes.
Hesperides [1648]. Argument of His Book

17 What is a kiss? Why this, as some approve:
The sure, sweet cement, glue, and lime of love.
Ibid. A Kiss

18 Bid me to live, and I will live
Thy Protestant to be,
Or bid me love, and I will give
A loving heart to thee.
Ibid. To Anthea, Who May Command Him
Any Thing

---

[1]Rien au monde ne dure / Qu'un éternel changement.
[2]Le bien de la fortune est un bien périssable; quand on bâtit
sur elle, on bâtit sur le sable.
See *Matthew 7:26, 34:15.*
[3]It was owing to this passage, first printed in 1669, that the
Mayflower's company came eventually to be called the Pilgrim
Fathers.
[4]See Evarts, 481:4.
[5]See Dryden, 273:10.
[6]See *Matthew 5:15, 33:3,* and Shakespeare, 182:11.

1 Cherry ripe,[1] ripe, ripe, I cry,
  Full and fair ones; come and buy!
  If so be you ask me where
  They do grow, I answer, there,
  Where my Julia's lips do smile;
  There's the land, or cherry-isle.
  Ibid. Cherry Ripe

2 It is the end that crowns us, not the fight.[2]
  Ibid. The End

3 Some asked how pearls did grow, and where?
  Then spoke I to my girl
  To part her lips, and showed them there
  The quarelets of pearl.
  *Ibid. The Rock of Rubies, and the Quarrie of
  Pearls*

4 A sweet disorder in the dress
  Kindles in clothes a wantonness.
  Ibid. Delight in Disorder

5 A winning wave, deserving note,
  In the tempestuous petticoat,
  A careless shoestring, in whose tie
  I see a wild civility,
  Do more bewitch me than when art
  Is too precise in every part.[3]
  Ibid.

6 You say to me-wards your affection's strong;
  Pray love me little, so you love me long.
  Ibid. Love Me Little, Love Me Long

7 Night makes no difference 'twixt the Priest and
      Clerk;
  Joan as my Lady is as good i' the dark.[4]
  Ibid. No Difference i' th' Dark

8 Give me a kiss, and to that kiss a score;
  Then to that twenty, add a hundred more:
  A thousand to that hundred: so kiss on,[5]
  To make that thousand up a million.
  Treble that million, and when that is done,
  Let's kiss afresh, as when we first begun.
  Ibid. To Anthea: Ah, My Anthea!

9 Gather ye rosebuds while ye may,
  Old Time is still a-flying,
  And this same flower that smiles today
  Tomorrow will be dying.[6]
  Ibid. To the Virgins to Make Much of Time

10 Fair daffodils, we weep to see
   You haste away so soon.
   Ibid. To Daffodils

11 Her pretty feet, like snails, did creep
   A little out, and then,[7]

As if they played at bo-peep,
Did soon draw in again.
  *Ibid. To Mistress Susanna Southwell: Upon Her
  Feet*

12 Her eyes the glowworm lend thee,
   The shooting stars attend thee;
     And the elves also,
     Whose little eyes glow
   Like the sparks of fire, befriend thee.
   Ibid. The Night Piece to Julia

13 Thus times do shift, each thing his turn does hold;
   New things succeed, as former things grow old.
   Ibid. Ceremonies for Candlemas Eve

14 Made us nobly wild, not mad.
   Ibid. Ode for Ben Jonson

15 Outdid the meat, outdid the frolic wine.
   Ibid.

16 Attempt the end, and never stand to doubt;
   Nothing's so hard but search will find it out.
   Ibid. Seek and Find

17 Get up, sweet Slug-a-bed, and see
   The dew bespangling herb and tree.
   Ibid. Corinna's Going A-Maying

18   'Tis sin,
   Nay, profanation to keep in.
   Ibid.

19 So when or you or I are made
   A fable, song, or fleeting shade,
   All love, all liking, all delight
   Lies drowned with us in endless night.[8]
   Ibid.

20 Whenas in silks my Julia goes,
   Then, then (methinks) how sweetly flows
   That liquefaction of her clothes.

   Next, when I cast mine eyes and see
   That brave vibration each way free;
   Oh how that glittering taketh me!
   Ibid. Upon Julia's Clothes

21 Here a little child I stand
   Heaving up my either hand.
   Cold as paddocks though they be,
   Here I lift them up to Thee,
   For a benison to fall
   On our meat, and on us all.
   *His Noble Numbers [1648]. Another Grace for
   a Child*

Henry King
1592–1669

22   Thou art the book,
   The library whereon I look.
   The Exequy [1657]

---

[1]See Campion, 226:18.
[2]See Anonymous: Latin, 119:3; John Heywood, 141:20;
Shakespeare, 201:12 and 203:17; and Quarles, 242:13.
[3]See Jonson, 232:6.
[4]See Plutarch, 107:14.
[5]See Catullus, 90:19.
[6]See *Wisdom of Solomon 2:8*, 30:21; Horace, 95:25; Ronsard, 144:3; and Spenser, 153:11.
[7]See Suckling, 262:5.

[8]See Catullus, 90:19; Shakespeare, 165:31; Campion, 226:13;
and Jonson, 232:4.

1   Then we shall rise
And view ourselves with clearer eyes
In that calm region where no night
Can hide us from each other's sight.

The Exequy

2 Sleep on, my Love, in thy cold bed,
Never to be disquieted!
My last good-night! Thou wilt not wake,
Till I thy fate shall overtake;
Till age, or grief, or sickness, must
Marry my body to that dust
It so much loves, and fill the room
My heart keeps empty in thy tomb.
Stay for me there; I will not fail
To meet thee in that hollow vale.

Ibid.

3 But hark! my pulse like a soft drum
Beats my approach, tells thee I come.

Ibid.

4 We that did nothing study but the way
To love each other, with which thoughts the day
Rose with delight to us, and with them set,
Must learn the hateful art, how to forget.

The Surrender

Francis Quarles
1592–1644

5 No man is born unto himself alone;[1]
Who lives unto himself, he lives to none.

Esther [1621], sec. 1, Meditation 1

6 The way to bliss lies not on beds of down,
And he that had no cross deserves no crown.[2]

Ibid. sec. 9, Meditation 9

7 We spend our midday sweat, our midnight oil;
We tire the night in thought, the day in toil.

Emblems [1635], bk. II, no. 2

8 Be wisely worldly, be not worldly wise.

Ibid.

9 This house is to be let for life or years;
Her rent is sorrow, and her income tears.
Cupid, 't has long stood void; her bills make
known,
She must be dearly let, or let alone.

Ibid. 10, Epigram

10 The slender debt to Nature's quickly paid,[3]
Discharged, perchance, with greater ease than
made.

Ibid. 13

[1]See *Romans 14:7*, 42:26; Francis Bacon, 159:15; and Donne, 231:8.
[2]See *Matthew 10:38*, 34:35; Penn, 282:17; and Bennard, 616:2.
[3]To die is a debt we must all of us discharge.—EURIPIDES, *Alcestis, l. 418*

11 The road to resolution lies by doubt:
The next way home's the farthest way about.[4]

Ibid. IV, 2, Epigram

12 It is the lot of man but once to die.

Ibid. V, 7

13 My soul, sit thou a patient looker-on;
Judge not the play before the play is done:
Her plot hath many changes; every day
Speaks a new scene; the last act crowns the play.[5]

Epigram. Respice Finem

14 And what's a life?—a weary pilgrimage,
Whose glory in one day doth fill the stage
With childhood, manhood, and decrepit age.

What Is Life?

15 Let all thy joys be as the month of May,
And all thy days be as a marriage day:
Let sorrow, sickness, and a troubled mind
Be stranger to thee.

To a Bride

Thomas Ravenscroft
c. 1592 – c. 1635

16 Nose, nose, nose, nose!
And who gave thee this jolly red nose?
Nutmegs and ginger, cinnamon and cloves,
And they gave me this jolly red nose.

Deuteromelia [1609]. Song no. 7[6]

George Herbert
1593–1633

17 A verse may find him who a sermon flies.[7]

The Temple [1633]. The Church Porch, st. 1

18 Drink not the third glass, which thou canst not
tame
When once it is within thee.

Ibid. st. 5

19 Dare to be true: nothing can need a lie:
A fault, which needs it most, grows two thereby.[8]

Ibid. st. 13

20 By all means use sometimes to be alone.

Ibid. st. 25

[4]The longest way round is the shortest way home.—*Proverb*
[5]See Anonymous: Latin, 119:3; John Heywood, 141:20; Shakespeare, 201:12 and 203:17; and Herrick, 241:2.
[6]Quoted by Beaumont and Fletcher, *The Knight of the Burning Pestle* [1613], act I, sc. iii. Ravenscroft's *Deuteromelia* was a supplement to his *Pammelia*, which was the earliest collection of rounds, catches, and canons printed in England.
[7]That many people read a song / Who will not read a sermon.—WINTHROP MACKWORTH PRAED [1802–1839], *The Chant of the Brazenhead, st. 1*
[8]And he that does one fault at first, / And lies to hide it, makes it two.—WATTS, *Song 15*

1 By no means run in debt: take thine own measure.
  Who cannot live on twenty pound a year,
  Cannot on forty.
  Ibid. st. 30

2 Wit's an unruly engine, wildly striking
  Sometimes a friend, sometimes the engineer.
  Ibid. st. 41

3 Be useful where thou livest.
  Ibid. st. 55

4 Man is God's image; but a poor man is
  Christ's stamp to boot: both images regard.
  Ibid. st. 64

5 Was ever grief like mine?
  Ibid. The Church. The Sacrifice, refrain

6 For thirty pence he did my death devise,[1]
  Who at three hundred did the ointment prize.[2]
  Ibid. st. 3

7 Man stole the fruit, but I must climb the tree.
  Ibid. st. 49

8 I got me flowers to strew Thy way,
  I got me boughs off many a tree:
  But Thou wast up by break of day,
  And brought'st Thy sweets along with Thee.
  Ibid. Easter, st. 4

9 Who says that fictions only and false hair
  Become a verse? Is there in truth no beauty?[3]
  Ibid. Jordan, st. 1

10 Sweet day, so cool, so calm, so bright,
  The bridal of the earth and sky.
  Ibid. Virtue, st. 1

11 Sweet spring, full of sweet days and roses,
  A box where sweets compacted lie.
  Ibid. st. 3

12 Only a sweet and virtuous soul,
  Like season'd timber, never gives.
  Ibid. st. 4

13 Who goes to bed and does not pray,
  Maketh two nights to every day.
  Ibid. Charms and Knots, st. 4

14 Nothing wears clothes, but Man; nothing doth
  need
  But he to wear them.
  Ibid. Providence, st. 28

15 Most things move th' under-jaw, the crocodile
  not.[4]
  Most things sleep lying, th' elephant leans or
  stands.[5]
  Ibid. st. 35

[1]See *Zechariah 11:12, 30:5,* and *Matthew 26:15, 36:23.*
[2]See *John 12:4–5, 40:22.*
[3]See Keats, 416:7.
[4]The crocodile does not move the lower jaw, but is the only
animal that brings down its upper jaw to the under one. —
HERODOTUS, *Customs of the Egyptians*
[5]Leans the huge elephant. — JAMES THOMSON, *The Seasons,
Summer* [1727], *l. 725*

16 I struck the board, and cried, No more:
      I will abroad.
  What? shall I ever sigh and pine?
  My lines and life are free; free as the road,
  Loose as the wind, as large as store.
      Shall I be still in suit?
  Have I no harvest but a thorn
  To let me blood, and not restore
  What I have lost with cordial fruit?
      Sure there was wine
  Before my sighs did dry it; there was corn
  Before my tears did drown it;
  Is the year only lost to me?
  Have I no bays to crown it?
  Ibid. The Collar

17 Call in thy death's head there: tie up thy fears.
  Ibid.

18 But as I rav'd and grew more fierce and wild
      At every word,
  Methought I heard one calling, *Child!*
      And I replied, *My Lord.*
  Ibid.

19 He would adore my gifts instead of me,
      And rest in Nature, not the God of Nature:
  So both should losers be.
  Ibid. The Pulley, st. 3

20 Let him be rich and weary, that at least,
      If goodness lead him not, yet weariness
  May toss him to my breast.
  Ibid. st. 4

21   Grief melts away
        Like snow in May,
  As if there were no such cold thing.
  Ibid. The Flower, st. 1

22 Who would have thought my shrivel'd heart
  Could have recovered greenness?
  Ibid. st. 2

23 And now in age I bud again,
  After so many deaths I live and write;
  I once more smell the dew and rain,
  And relish versing: O my only light,
      It cannot be
      That I am he
  On whom thy tempests fell all night.
  Ibid. st. 6

24 The harbingers are come. See, see their mark;
  White is their color, and behold my head.
  Ibid. The Forerunners, st. 1

25 Teach me, my God and King,
  In all things thee to see
  And what I do in any thing,
  To do it as for thee.
  Ibid. The Elixir, st. 1

26 A servant with this clause
  Makes drudgery divine:

Who sweeps a room, as for thy laws,
Makes that and th' action fine.
The Temple. The Elixir, st. 5

1 Love bade me welcome: yet my soul drew back,
Guilty of dust and sin.
But quick-ey'd Love, observing me grow slack
From my first entrance in,
Drew nearer to me, sweetly questioning,
If I lack'd anything.
Ibid. Love, st. 1

2 You must sit down, says Love, and taste my meat:
So I did sit and eat.
Ibid. st. 3

3 Religion stands on tiptoe in our land,
Ready to pass to the American strand.
The Church Militant [1633], l. 235

4 Love, and a cough, cannot be hid.[1]
Jacula Prudentum [1651], no. 49

5 Ill ware is never cheap. Pleasing ware is half sold.
Ibid. 61

6 When a dog is drowning, everyone offers him drink.
Ibid. 77

7 Deceive not thy physician, confessor, nor lawyer.
Ibid. 105

8 Who would do ill ne'er wants occasion.
Ibid. 116

9 A snow year, a rich year.
Ibid. 125

10 Well may he smell fire, whose gown burns.
Ibid. 138

11 Love your neighbor, yet pull not down your hedge.[2]
Ibid. 141

12 Marry your son when you will; your daughter when you can.
Ibid. 149

13 The mill cannot grind with the water that's past.
Ibid. 153

14 Good words are worth much, and cost little.
Ibid. 155

15 Hell is full of good meanings and wishings.[3]
Ibid. 170

16 Where the drink goes in, there the wit goes out.
Ibid. 187

17 Whose house is of glass, must not throw stones at another.[4]
Ibid. 196

18 By suppers more have been killed than Galen ever cured.
Ibid. 272

19 The lion is not so fierce as they paint him.[5]
Ibid. 289

20 Go not for every grief to the physician, nor for every quarrel to the lawyer, nor for every thirst to the pot.
Ibid. 290

21 The best mirror is an old friend.
Ibid. 296

22 When you are an anvil, hold you still; when you are a hammer, strike your fill.[6]
Ibid. 338

23 He that lies with the dogs, riseth with fleas.
Ibid. 343

24 He that is not handsome at twenty, nor strong at thirty, nor rich at forty, nor wise at fifty, will never be handsome, strong, rich, or wise.
Ibid. 349

25 The buyer needs a hundred eyes, the seller not one.
Ibid. 390

26 My house, my house, though thou art small, thou art to me the Escurial.
Ibid. 413

27 Trust not one night's ice.
Ibid. 453

28 For want of a nail the shoe is lost, for want of a shoe the horse is lost, for want of a horse the rider is lost.[7]
Ibid. 499

29 Pension never enriched young man.
Ibid. 515

30 One enemy is too much.
Ibid. 523

31 Living well is the best revenge.
Ibid. 524

32 Thursday come, and the week is gone.
Ibid. 587

33 Time is the rider that breaks youth.
Ibid. 615

34 Show me a liar, and I'll show thee a thief.
Ibid. 652

35 One father is more than a hundred schoolmasters.
Ibid. 686

36 Reason lies between the spur and the bridle.
Ibid. 711

37 One sword keeps another in the sheath.
Ibid. 723

38 God's mill grinds slow, but sure.[8]
Ibid. 747

39 He that lends, gives.
Ibid. 787

40 Words are women, deeds are men.[9]
Ibid. 843

41 Poverty is no sin.
Ibid. 844

[1]See Anonymous: Spanish, 794:7.
[2]See Frost, 622:21.
[3]Sir, Hell is paved with good intentions. — SAMUEL JOHNSON [1775]; from BOSWELL, *Life of Johnson* [1791], *vol. I, p. 555* (Everyman edition)
[4]People in glass houses shouldn't throw stones. — *Proverb*
See Franklin, 309:21.

[5]The lion is not so fierce as painted. — THOMAS FULLER, *Expecting Preferment*
[6]Stand like an anvil when it is beaten upon. — SAINT IGNATIUS THEOPHORUS, bishop of Antioch [fl. c. 100]
When you are the anvil, bear— / When you are the hammer, strike. — MARKHAM, *Preparedness*
[7]See Franklin, 310:10.
[8]See Euripides, 69:2, and von Logau, 247:15.
[9]Fatti maschii parole femine [Manly deeds, womanly words]. — *Motto of Maryland*
See Samuel Johnson, 313:27.

1　None knows the weight of another's burthen.
Ibid. 880

2　One hour's sleep before midnight is worth three after.
Ibid. 882

3　He hath no leisure who useth it not.
Ibid. 897

4　Half the world knows not how the other half lives.
Ibid. 907

5　Life is half spent before we know what it is.
Ibid. 917

6　Every mile is two in winter.
Ibid. 949

7　The eye is bigger than the belly.
Ibid. 1018

8　His bark is worse than his bite.
Ibid. 1090

9　There is an hour wherein a man might be happy all his life, could he find it.
Ibid. 1143

10　Woe be to him that reads but one book.
Ibid. 1146

Izaak Walton
1593–1683

11　But God, who is able to prevail, wrestled with him, as the Angel did with Jacob, and marked him; marked him for his own.[1]　*Life of Donne [1640]*

12　I have laid aside business, and gone a-fishing.
The Compleat Angler [1653–1655]. Epistle to the Reader

13　Angling may be said to be so like the mathematics that it can never be fully learnt.　*Ibid.*

14　As no man is born an artist, so no man is born an angler.　*Ibid.*

15　I shall stay him no longer than to wish him a rainy evening to read this following discourse; and that if he be an honest angler, the east wind may never blow when he goes a-fishing.　*Ibid.*

16　I am, Sir, a brother of the Angle.
Ibid. pt. I, ch. 1

17　Doubt not but angling will prove to be so pleasant that it will prove to be, like virtue, a reward to itself.[2]

Sir Henry Wotton . . . was a most dear lover, and a frequent practicer of the art of angling; of which he would say, "it was an employment for his

---

[1]See *Genesis 32:24, 7:45,* and Gray, *322:22.*

[2]*Ipsa quidem virtus sibimet pulcherrima merces* [Virtue herself is her own fairest reward].—SILIUS ITALICUS [A.D. c. 25–99], *Punica, bk. XIII, l. 663*

Virtue was sufficient of herself for happiness.—DIOGENES LAERTIUS, *Lives of Eminent Philosophers, XLII, Plato*

That virtue is her own reward, is but a cold principle.—THOMAS BROWNE, *Religio Medici [1643], pt. I, sec. 47*

Virtue is its own reward.—PRIOR, *Imitations of Horace, bk. III, ode 2*

I think mankind by thee would be less bored / If only thou wert not thine own reward.—JOHN KENDRICK BANGS [1862–1922], *A Hint to Virtue*

---

idle time, which was then not idly spent . . . a rest to his mind, a cheerer of his spirits, a diverter of sadness, a calmer of unquiet thoughts, a moderator of passions, a procurer of contentedness; and that it begat habits of peace and patience in those that professed and practiced it."　*Ibid.*

18　You will find angling to be like the virtue of humility, which has a calmness of spirit and a world of other blessings attending upon it.[3]　*Ibid.*

19　I remember that a wise friend of mine did usually say, "That which is everybody's business is nobody's business."　*Ibid. 2*

20　Good company and good discourse are the very sinews of virtue.　*Ibid.*

21　An honest ale-house where we shall find a cleanly room, lavender in the windows, and twenty ballads stuck about the wall.　*Ibid.*

22　The Chavender or Chub.　*Ibid. 3*

23　An excellent angler, and now with God.
Ibid. 4

24　Old-fashioned poetry, but choicely good.
Ibid.

25　I love such mirth as does not make friends ashamed to look upon one another next morning.
Ibid. 5

26　No man can lose what he never had.　*Ibid.*

27　We may say of angling as Dr. Boteler[4] said of strawberries: "Doubtless God could have made a better berry, but doubtless God never did"; and so, if I might be judge, God never did make a more calm, quiet, innocent recreation than angling.　*Ibid.*

28　Thus use your frog. . . . Put your hook through his mouth, and out at his gills; . . . and then with a fine needle and silk sew the upper part of his leg, with only one stitch, to the arming-wire of your hook; or tie the frog's leg, above the upper joint, to the armed-wire; and in so doing use him as though you loved him.　*Ibid. 8*

29　This dish of meat is too good for any but anglers, or very honest men.　*Ibid.*

30　Look to your health; and if you have it, praise God, and value it next to a good conscience; for health is the second blessing that we mortals are capable of; a blessing that money cannot buy.
Ibid. 21

31　Let the blessing of Saint Peter's Master be . . . upon all that are lovers of virtue, and dare trust in his Providence, and be quiet and go a-angling.
Ibid.

---

[3]There is certainly something in angling . . . that tends to produce a gentleness of spirit, and a pure serenity of mind.—IRVING, *The Sketch-Book [1819–1820], The Angler*

[4]This praise of the strawberry first appeared in the second edition of *The Angler* [1655].

See William Butler, *147.*

1   The great secretary of Nature and all learning, Sir Francis Bacon.   *Life of Herbert [1670]*

James Howell
c. 1594–1666

2   All work and no play makes Jack a dull boy.   *Proverbs [1659]*

Thomas Carew
c. 1595 – c. 1639

3 Here lies a King that rul'd, as he thought fit
The universal monarchy of wit;
Here lies two flamens, and both those the best:
Apollo's first, at last the true God's priest.
An Elegy upon the Death of Dr. Donne [1633]

4 Ask me no more where Jove bestows,
When June is past, the fading rose;
For in your beauty's orient deep
These flowers, as in their causes, sleep.
Poems [1640]. To Celia, st. 1

5 Ask me no more whither doth haste
The nightingale when May is past;
For in your sweet dividing throat
She winters and keeps warm her note.
Ibid. st. 3

6 Ask me no more if east or west
The Phoenix builds her spicy nest;
For unto you at last she flies,
And in your fragrant bosom dies.
Ibid. st. 5

7 Give me more love or more disdain;
The torrid or the frozen zone:
Bring equal ease unto my pain;
The temperate affords me none.
Ibid. Mediocrity in Love Rejected, st. 1

8 Thou shalt confess the vain pursuit
Of human glory yields no fruit
        But an untimely grave.
Ibid. On the Duke of Buckingham

9 He that loves a rosy cheek,
Or a coral lip admires,
Or, from starlike eyes, doth seek
Fuel to maintain his fires;
As old Time makes these decay,
So his flames must waste away.
Ibid. Disdain Returned, st. 1

10 The firstling of the infant year.
Ibid. The Primrose

11 Then fly betimes, for only they
Conquer Love that run away.
Ibid. Conquest by Flight

12 The magic of a face.
Ibid. Epitaph on the Lady S——

René Descartes
1596–1650

13   Good sense is of all things in the world the most equally distributed, for everybody thinks he is so well supplied with it, that even those most difficult to please in all other matters never desire more of it than they already possess.
Le Discours de la Méthode [1637], I

14   It is not enough to have a good mind. The main thing is to use it well.   *Ibid.*

15   The greatest minds are capable of the greatest vices as well as of the greatest virtues.   *Ibid.*

16   The first precept was never to accept a thing as true until I knew it as such without a single doubt.
Ibid.

17   One cannot conceive anything so strange and so implausible that it has not already been said by one philosopher or another.[1]   *Ibid. II*

18   I think, therefore I am [Cogito, ergo sum; Je pense, donc je suis].[2]   *Ibid. IV*

James Shirley
1596–1666

19   How little room
Do we take up in death that, living, know
No bounds!
The Wedding [1626], act IV, sc. iv

20 I presume you're mortal, and may err.[3]
The Lady of Pleasure [1635]

21 Only the actions of the just
Smell sweet and blossom in their dust.
Ibid.

22 Death calls ye to the crowd of common men.
Cupid and Death [1653]

23 The glories of our blood and state
Are shadows, not substantial things;
There is no armor against fate;
Death lays his icy hand on kings.[4]
Contention of Ajax and Ulysses [1659], sc. iii

Oliver Cromwell
1599–1658

24   A few honest men are better than numbers.
Letter to Sir W. Spring [September 1643]

25   The State, in choosing men to serve it, takes no notice of their opinions. If they be willing faithfully to serve it, that satisfies.
Before the battle of Marston Moor [July 2, 1644]

[1]See Cicero, 87:27, and Goethe, 350:23.
[2]See Aristotle, 78:7.
[3]See Plutarch, 107:18; Anonymous: Latin, 118:30; Pope, 299:4; and Burns, 362:5.
[4]See Horace, 95:18, and Publilius Syrus, 98:29.

1   I beseech you, in the bowels of Christ, think it possible you may be mistaken.[1]
Letter to the General Assembly of the Church of Scotland [August 3, 1650]

2   You have sat too long here for any good you have been doing lately. . . . Depart, I say; and let us have done with you. In the name of God, go!
To the Rump Parliament [April 20, 1653]

3   Necessity hath no law.[2] Feigned necessities, imaginary necessities . . . are the greatest cozenage that men can put upon the Providence of God, and make pretenses to break known rules by.
To Parliament [September 12, 1654]

4   I would have been glad to have lived under my woodside, and to have kept a flock of sheep, rather than to have undertaken this government.
To Parliament [1658]

5   Mr. Lely, I desire you would use all your skill to paint my picture truly like me, and not flatter me at all; but remark all these roughnesses, pimples, warts, and everything as you see me, otherwise I will never pay a farthing for it.[3]
From HORACE WALPOLE, *Anecdotes of Painting in England [1762–1771]*

6   It is not my design to drink or to sleep, but my design is to make what haste I can to be gone.
Dying words

Pedro Calderón de la Barca
1600–1681

7   What is life? A madness. What is life? An illusion, a shadow, a story. And the greatest good is little enough: for all life is a dream, and dreams themselves are only dreams.[4]
Life Is a Dream, act II, l. 1195

8   But whether it be dream or truth, to do well is what matters. If it be truth, for truth's sake. If not, then to gain friends for the time when we awaken.
Ibid. III, 236

9   The treason past, the traitor is no longer needed.
Ibid. III, 1109

10   What surprises you, if a dream taught me this wisdom, and if I still fear I may wake up and find myself once more confined in prison? And even if this should not happen, merely to dream it is enough. For this I have come to know, that all human happiness finally ceases, like a dream.
Ibid. III, 1114

[1]See Hand, 615:4.
[2]See Publilius Syrus, 99:32, and Saint Augustine, 114:29.
[3]Warts and all.—*Saying*
[4]Que es la pequeño: / Que toda la vida es sueño, / y los sueños sueños son.
Translated by EDWARD AND ELIZABETH HUBERMAN.
See Montaigne, 146:9.

Martin Parker
c. 1600 – c. 1656

11 Ye gentlemen of England
That live at home at ease,
Ah! little do you think upon
The dangers of the seas.
Song

Jules Cardinal Mazarin
1602–1661

12   I must leave all that! Farewell, dear paintings that I have loved so much and which have cost me so much.[5]
Remark shortly before his death

Roger Williams
c. 1603–1683

13   There goes many a ship to sea, with many hundred souls in one ship, whose weal and woe is common, and is a true picture of a commonwealth or a human combination or society. It hath fallen out sometimes that both Papists and Protestants, Jews and Turks may be embarked in one ship; upon which supposal I affirm that all the liberty of conscience that ever I pleaded for turns upon these two hinges—that none of the papists, Protestants, Jews or Turks be forced to come to the ship's prayers or worship, nor compelled from their own particular prayers or worship, if they practice any.
Letter to the Town of Providence [January 1655]

Friedrich von Logau
1604–1655

14 Armed peace.
Poetic Aphorisms (Sinngedichten) [1654]

15 Though the mills of God grind slowly, yet they grind exceeding small.[6]
Ibid. Retribution

Sir Thomas Browne
1605–1682

16   I dare, without usurpation, assume the honorable style of a Christian.
Religio Medici [1643], pt. I, sec. 1

17   I could never divide myself from any man upon the difference of an opinion, or be angry with his judgment for not agreeing with me in that from which perhaps within a few days I should dissent myself.
Ibid. 6

[5]Il faut quitter tout cela! Adieu, chers tableaux que j'ai tant aimés et qui m'ont tant coûté.
[6]Translated by LONGFELLOW.
See Euripides, 69:2, and Herbert, 244:38.

1   Many . . . have too rashly charged the troops of error, and remain as trophies unto the enemies of truth.   *Religio Medici, pt. I, sec. 6*

2   A man may be in as just possession of truth as of a city, and yet be forced to surrender.   *Ibid.*

3   As for those wingy mysteries in divinity, and airy subtleties in religion, which have unhinged the brains of better heads, they never stretched the *pia mater* of mine.   *Ibid. 9*

4   I love to lose myself in a mystery, to pursue my Reason to an *O altitudo!*[1]   *Ibid.*

5   Rich with the spoils of Nature.   *Ibid. 13*

6   We carry with us the wonders we seek without us: There is all Africa and her prodigies in us.   *Ibid. 15*

7   All things are artificial, for nature is the art of God.[2]   *Ibid. 16*

8   Obstinacy in a bad cause is but constancy in a good.[3]   *Ibid. 25*

9   Persecution is a bad and indirect way to plant religion.   *Ibid.*

10   Thus is man that great and true *Amphibium,* whose nature is disposed to live . . . in divided and distinguished worlds; for though there be but one [world] to sense, there are two to reason; the one visible; the other invisible.   *Ibid. 34*

11   Not picked from the leaves of any author, but bred amongst the weeds and tares of mine own brain.   *Ibid. 36*

12   This reasonable moderator, and equal piece of justice, Death.   *Ibid. 38*

13   I am not so much afraid of death, as ashamed thereof. 'Tis the very disgrace and ignominy of our natures, that in a moment can so disfigure us, that our nearest friends, wife, and children, stand afraid and start at us.   *Ibid. 40*

14   How shall the dead arise, is no question of my faith; to believe only possibilities, is not faith, but mere philosophy.   *Ibid. 48*

15   The heart of man is the place the devil dwells in: I feel sometimes a hell within myself.   *Ibid. 51*

16   There is no road or ready way to virtue.   *Ibid. 55*

17   All places, all airs make unto me one country; I am in England, everywhere, and under any meridian.   *Ibid. II, 1*

18   But how shall we expect charity towards others, when we are uncharitable to ourselves? Charity begins at home,[4] is the voice of the world; yet is every man his greatest enemy, and, as it were, his own executioner.[5]   *Ibid. 4*

19   I could be content that we might procreate like trees, without conjunction, or that there were any way to perpetuate the World without this trivial and vulgar way of coition.   *Ibid. 9*

20   Sure there is music even in the beauty, and the silent note which Cupid strikes, far sweeter than the sound of an instrument. For there is a music wherever there is a harmony, order, or proportion; and thus far we may maintain the music of the spheres.[6]   *Ibid.*

21   For the world, I count it not an inn, but a hospital; and a place not to live, but to die in.   *Ibid. 11*

22   There is surely a piece of divinity in us, something that was before the elements, and owes no homage unto the sun.   *Ibid.*

23   When we desire to confine our words, we commonly say they are spoken under the rose.[7]   *Vulgar Errors [1645]*

24   An old and gray-headed error.   *Ibid.*

25   Times before you, when even living men were antiquities; when the living might exceed the dead, and to depart this world could not be properly said to go unto the greater number.   *Urn-Burial; or, Hydriotaphia [1658]. Dedication*

26   With rich flames, and hired tears, they solemnized their obsequies.   *Ibid. ch. 3*

27   Were the happiness of the next world as closely apprehended as the felicities of this, it were a martyrdom to live.   *Ibid. 4*

28   These dead bones have . . . quietly rested under the drums and tramplings of three conquests.   *Ibid. 5*

29   Time which antiquates antiquities, and hath an art to make dust of all things.   *Ibid.*

30   What song the Sirens sang, or what name Achilles assumed when he hid himself among women, though puzzling questions, are not beyond all conjecture.   *Ibid.*

31   The long habit of living indisposeth us for dying.   *Ibid.*

---

[1]See Aiken, 675:4.

[2]The course of Nature is the art of God.—EDWARD YOUNG, *Night Thoughts* [1742–1745], *Night IX, l.* 1267

[3]See Sterne, 320:12.

[4]See *I Timothy* 5:4, 45:17, and Terence, 85:15.

[5]See Donne, 231:6.

[6]See Shakespeare, 202:22.

[7]*Sub rosa.*

In strict confidence. The origin of the phrase is obscure but the story is that Cupid gave Harpocrates (the god of silence) a rose, to bribe him not to betray the amours of Venus. Hence the flower became the emblem of silence and was sculptured on the ceilings of banquet-rooms, to remind the quests that what was spoken *sub vino* was not to be repeated *sub divo.* In the sixteenth century it was placed over confessionals.—*Brewer's Dictionary of Phrase and Fable*, 14th ed. [1989]

1 The iniquity of oblivion blindly scattereth her poppy, and deals with the memory of men without distinction to merit of perpetuity. *Ibid.*

2 Oblivion is not to be hired: the greater part must be content to be as though they had not been, to be found in the register of God, not in the record of man. *Ibid.*

3 The night of time far surpasseth the day, and who knows when was the equinox? *Ibid.*

4 Man is a noble animal, splendid in ashes, and pompous in the grave. *Ibid.*

5 That unextinguishable laugh in heaven.
The Garden of Cyrus [1658], ch. 2

6 Life itself is but the shadow of death, and souls departed but the shadows of the living. All things fall under this name. The sun itself is but the dark simulacrum, and light but the shadow of God.
Ibid. 4

7 To keep our eyes open longer were but to act our Antipodes. The huntsmen are up in America, and they are already past their first sleep in Persia. But who can be drowsy at that hour which freed us from everlasting sleep? or have slumbering thoughts at that time, when sleep itself must end, and, as some conjecture, all shall awake again? *Ibid. 5*

Anne Bigot Cornuel
1605–1694

8 No man is a hero to his valet.[1]
Attributed

Pierre Corneille
1606–1684

9 To conquer without risk is to triumph without glory. *Le Cid [1636], act II, sc. ii*

10 Brave men are brave from the very first.
Ibid. II, iii

11 And the combat ceased for want of combatants.
Ibid. IV, iii

12 Do your duty, and leave the rest to heaven.
Horace [1639], act II, sc. viii

13 All evils are equal when they are extreme.
Ibid. III, iv

14 The worst of all states is the people's state.
Cinna [1640], act II, sc. i

15 Who is all-powerful should fear everything.
Ibid. IV, ii

16 By speaking of our misfortunes we often relieve them. *Polyeucte [1640], act I, sc. iii*

17 The manner of giving is worth more than the gift.
Le Menteur [1642], act I, sc. i

18 A liar is always lavish of oaths. *Ibid. III, v*

19 The fire which seems extinguished often slumbers beneath the ashes.
Rodogune [1644], act III, sc. iv

20 Guess if you can, choose if you dare.
Héraclius [1646], act IV, sc. iv

21 A service beyond all recompense
Weighs so heavy that it almost gives offense.
Suréna [1674], act III, sc. i

22 I owe my fame only to myself.
Poésies Diverses, 23

Sir William Davenant
1606–1668

23 The lark now leaves his wat'ry nest
And, climbing, shakes his dewy wings.
Song [1638], st. 1

24 I shall ask leave to desist, when I am interrupted by so great an experiment as dying.
His apology, in illness, for not having finished Gondibert

25 How much pleasure they lose (and even the pleasures of heroic poesy are not unprofitable) who take away the liberty of a poet, and fetter his feet in the shackles of a historian.
Prefatory letter to Thomas Hobbes. From S. T. COLERIDGE, Biographia Literaria [1817], ch. 22

Edmund Waller
1606–1687

26 Illustrious acts high raptures do infuse,
And every conqueror creates a muse.
Panegyric to My Lord Protector

27 Guarded with ships, and all our sea our own.[2]
To My Lord of Falkland

28 To man, that was in th' evening made,
Stars gave the first delight;
Admiring, in the gloomy shade,
Those little drops of light.
An Apology for Having Loved Before [1664]

29 That which her slender waist confin'd
Shall now my joyful temples bind;
No monarch but would give his crown
His arms might do what this has done.
On a Girdle [1664]

30 My joy, my grief, my hope, my love,
Did all within this circle move!
Ibid.

[1] Il n'y avoit point de héros pour les valets de chambre. See Antigonus, 79:7, and Montaigne, 146:17.

[2] See Themistocles, 62:30; Francis Bacon, 160:7; Washington, 336:17; and Mahan, 541:3.

1   Go, lovely rose!
Tell her that wastes her time and me
    That now she knows,
When I resemble her to thee,
How sweet and fair she seems to be.
Go, Lovely Rose [1664]

2   So all we know
Of what they do above
Is that they happy are, and that they love.
Upon the Death of My Lady Rich [1664]

3 Poets that lasting marble seek
Must carve in Latin or in Greek.
Of English Verse [1668]

4 And keeps the palace of the soul.
Of Tea

5 Poets lose half the praise they should have got,
Could it be known what they discreetly blot.
Upon Roscommon's Translation of HORACE, De Arte Poetica

6 The soul's dark cottage, batter'd and decay'd,
Lets in new light through chinks that Time has made;
Stronger by weakness, wiser, men become
As they draw near to their eternal home.
Leaving the old, both worlds at once they view,
That stand upon the threshold of the new.
On the Divine Poems [1686]

Paul Gerhardt
1607–1676

7 O sacred head, now wounded,
With grief and shame bowed down;
Now scornfully surrounded
With thorns, thy only crown.[1]
Passion Chorale [1656], based on twelfth-century Latin hymn, st. 1

Thomas Fuller
1608–1661

8   Drawing near her death, she sent most pious thoughts as harbingers to heaven; and her soul saw a glimpse of happiness through the chinks of her sickness-broken body.   *Life of Monica [1642]*

9   He was one of a lean body and visage, as if his eager soul, biting for anger at the clog of his body, desired to fret a passage through it.[2]
Life of the Duke of Alva [1642]

[1]O Haupt vol Blut und Wunden / Vol Schmerz und voller Hohn! / O Haupt zum Spott gebunden / Mit einer Dornen Krohn!
Translated by JAMES WADDELL ALEXANDER.
[2]See Dryden, 274:3.

10   He knows little who will tell his wife all he knows.[3]
The Holy State and the Profane State [1642]. The Good Husband

11   One that will not plead that cause wherein his tongue must be confuted by his conscience.
Ibid. The Good Advocate

12   Light, God's eldest daughter,[4] is a principal beauty in a building.   *Ibid. Of Building*

13   Learning hath gained most by those books by which the printers have lost.   *Ibid. Of Books*

14   Deceive not thyself by overexpecting happiness in the married estate. . . . Remember the nightingales which sing only some months in the spring, but commonly are silent when they have hatched their eggs.   *Ibid. Of Marriage*

15   They that marry ancient people, merely in expectation to bury them, hang themselves in hope that one will come and cut the halter.   *Ibid.*

16   Fame sometimes hath created something of nothing.   *Ibid. Fame*

17   Anger is one of the sinews of the soul; he that wants it hath a maimed mind.   *Ibid. Of Anger*

18   It is always darkest just before the day dawneth.
Pisgah Sight [1650], bk. II, ch. 2

John Milton[5]
1608–1674

19 This is the month, and this the happy morn,
Wherein the Son of Heav'n's eternal King,
Of wedded maid and virgin mother born,
Our great redemption from above did bring;
For so the holy sages once did sing,
That He our deadly forfeit should release,
And with His Father work us a perpetual peace.
On the Morning of Christ's Nativity [1629], st. 1, l. 1

20 It was the winter wild
While the Heav'n-born child
All meanly wrapt in the rude manger lies.
Ibid. Hymn, st. 1, l. 29

21 No war, or battle's sound
Was heard the world around.
The idle spear and shield were high up hung.
Ibid. st. 4, l. 53

22 Time will run back and fetch the Age of Gold.
Ibid. st. 14, l. 135

23 The Oracles are dumb.
Ibid. st. 19, l. 173

[3]See Homer, 53:23.
[4]See *Genesis* 1:3, 6:4, and Milton, 257:23.
[5]See Wordsworth, 374:19.

1 Peor and Baalim
Forsake their temples dim.
Ibid. st. 22, l. 197

2 What needs my Shakespeare for his honor'd
bones,
The labor of an age in piled stones,
Or that his hallow'd relics should be hid
Under a star-y-pointing pyramid?
Dear son of memory, great heir of fame,
What need'st thou such weak witness of thy
name?
On Shakespeare [1630]

3 How soon hath Time, the subtle thief of youth,
Stol'n on his wing my three-and-twentieth year.
*On His Having Arrived at the Age of
Twenty-three [1631]*

4 As ever in my great Taskmaster's eye.
Ibid.

5 Such sweet compulsion doth in music lie.
Arcades [1630–1634], l. 68

6 Hence, loathed Melancholy,
Of Cerberus and blackest Midnight born,
In Stygian cave forlorn,
'Mongst horrid shapes, and shrieks, and sights
unholy.
L'Allegro [1631], l. 1

7 So buxom, blithe, and debonair.
Ibid. l. 24

8 Haste thee, Nymph, and bring with thee
Jest, and youthful jollity,
Quips and cranks and wanton wiles,
Nods and becks and wreathed smiles.
Ibid. l. 25

9 Sport, that wrinkled Care derides,
And Laughter, holding both his sides.
Come, and trip it, as you go,
On the light fantastic toe.
Ibid. l. 31

10 The mountain nymph, sweet liberty.
Ibid. l. 36

11 Mirth, admit me of thy crew,
To live with her, and live with thee,
In unreproved pleasures free.
Ibid. l. 38

12 While the cock with lively din
Scatters the rear of darkness thin,
And to the stack, or the barn door,
Stoutly struts his dames before,
Oft list'ning how the hounds and horn
Cheerly rouse the slumb'ring morn.
Ibid. l. 49

13 And every shepherd tells his tale
Under the hawthorn in the dale.
Ibid. l. 67

14 Meadows trim, with daisies pied,
Shallow brooks, and rivers wide;
Towers and battlements it sees
Bosom'd high in tufted trees,
Where perhaps some beauty lies,
The cynosure of neighboring eyes.
Ibid. l. 75

15 And the jocund rebecks sound
To many a youth, and many a maid,
Dancing in the checkered shade.
And young and old come forth to play
On a sunshine holiday.
Ibid. l. 94

16 Then to the spicy nut-brown ale.
Ibid. l. 100

17 Tower'd cities please us then,
And the busy hum of men.
Ibid. l. 117

18   Ladies, whose bright eyes
Rain influence, and judge the prize.
Ibid. l. 121

19 And pomp, and feast, and revelry,
With mask, and antique pageantry,
Such sights as youthful poets dream
On summer eves by haunted stream.
Then to the well-trod stage anon,
If Jonson's learned sock be on,
Or sweetest Shakespeare, Fancy's child,
Warble his native wood-notes wild,
And ever, against eating cares,
Lap me in soft Lydian airs,
Married to immortal verse[1]
Such as the meeting soul may pierce,
In notes with many a winding bout
Of linked sweetness long drawn out.
Ibid. l. 127

20 Such strains as would have won the ear
Of Pluto, to have quite set free
His half-regain'd Eurydice.
These delights, if thou canst give,
Mirth, with thee, I mean to live.
Ibid. l. 148

21 Hence vain deluding Joys,
The brood of Folly without father bred!
Il Penseroso [1631], l. 1

22 Hail divinest Melancholy.[2]
Ibid. l. 12

23 Sober, steadfast, and demure.
Ibid. l. 32

24 And looks commercing with the skies,
Thy rapt soul sitting in thine eyes.
Ibid. l. 39

[1]Wisdom married to immortal verse. — WORDSWORTH, *The
Excursion* [1814], *bk. VII*
[2]See Robert Burton, 234:3; Fletcher, 236:13; and Hood, 422:-
22.

1 And add to these retired Leisure,
That in trim gardens takes his pleasure.

Il Penseroso, l. 49

2 Sweet bird, that shunn'st the noise of folly,
Most musical, most melancholy!

Ibid. l. 61

3   I walk unseen
On the dry smooth-shaven green,
To behold the wandering moon,
Riding near her highest noon,
Like one that had been led astray
Through the heav'n's wide pathless way,
And oft, as if her head she bow'd,
Stooping through a fleecy cloud.

Ibid. l. 65

4 Oft, on a plat of rising ground,
I hear the far-off curfew sound
Over some wide-watered shore,
Swinging low with sullen roar.

Ibid. l. 73

5 Where glowing embers through the room
Teach light to counterfeit a gloom,
Far from all resort of mirth,
Save the cricket on the hearth.

Ibid. l. 79

6 Sometime let gorgeous Tragedy
In sceptered pall come sweeping by,
Presenting Thebes, or Pelops' line,
Or the tale of Troy divine.

Ibid. l. 97

7 Or bid the soul of Orpheus sing
Such notes as, warbled to the string,
Drew iron tears down Pluto's cheek.

Ibid. l. 105

8 Or call up him that left half told
The story of Cambuscan bold.

Ibid. l. 109

9 Where more is meant than meets the ear.

Ibid. l. 120

10 And storied windows richly dight,
Casting a dim religious light.
There let the pealing organ blow,
To the full-voiced choir below,
In service high, and anthems clear
As may, with sweetness, through mine ear
Dissolve me into ecstasies,
And bring all Heaven before mine eyes.

Ibid. l. 159

11 Before the starry threshold of Jove's Court
My mansion is.

Comus [1634], l. 1

12 Above the smoke and stir of this dim spot
Which men call earth.

Ibid. l. 5

13 Yet some there be that by due steps aspire
To lay their just hands on that golden key
That opes the palace of Eternity.

Ibid. l. 12

14 An old, and haughty nation proud in arms.

Ibid. l. 33

15 What never yet was heard in tale or song,
From old or modern bard, in hall or bower.

Ibid. l. 44

16 Bacchus, that first from out the purple grape
Crush'd the sweet poison of misused wine.

Ibid. l. 46

17 These my sky-robes, spun out of Iris' woof.

Ibid. l. 83

18 The star that bids the shepherd fold.

Ibid. l. 93

19 And the gilded car of day,
His glowing axle doth allay
In the steep Atlantic stream.

Ibid. l. 95

20 Midnight shout and revelry,
Tipsy dance and jollity.

Ibid. l. 103

21 What hath night to do with sleep?

Ibid. l. 122

22 Ere the blabbing eastern scout,
The nice morn on th' Indian steep,
From her cabin'd loophole peep.

Ibid. l. 138

23 Come, knit hands, and beat the ground,
In a light fantastic round.

Ibid. l. 143

24   A thousand fantasies
Begin to throng into my memory,
Of calling shapes, and beck'ning shadows dire,
And airy tongues that syllable men's names
On sands and shores and desert wildernesses.

Ibid. l. 205

25 Was I deceiv'd or did a sable cloud
Turn forth her silver lining on the night?

Ibid. l. 221

26 Sweet Echo, sweetest nymph, that liv'st unseen
Within thy airy shell
By slow Meander's margent green,
And in the violet-embroider'd vale.

Ibid. l. 230

27 How sweetly did they float upon the wings
Of silence, through the empty-vaulted night,
At every fall smoothing the raven down
Of darkness till it smil'd!

Ibid. l. 249

28 Such sober certainty of waking bliss.

Ibid. l. 263

29 Virtue could see to do what Virtue would
By her own radiant light, though sun and moon

Were in the flat sea sunk. And Wisdom's self
Oft seeks to sweet retired solitude,
Where, with her best nurse Contemplation,
She plumes her feathers, and lets grow her wings.
Ibid. l. 373

1   The unsunn'd heaps
Of miser's treasure.
Ibid. l. 398

2 Tis Chastity, my brother, Chastity:
She that has that, is clad in complete steel.[1]
Ibid. l. 420

3 How charming is divine philosophy!
Not harsh and crabbed, as dull fools suppose,
But musical as is Apollo's lute,[2]
And a perpetual feast of nectar'd sweets
Where no crude surfeit reigns.
Ibid. l. 476

4 Fill'd the air with barbarous dissonance.
Ibid. l. 550

5   I was all ear,
And took in strains that might create a soul
Under the ribs of Death.
Ibid. l. 560

6   That power
Which erring men call Chance.
Ibid. l. 587

7 Thou canst not touch the freedom of my mind.
Ibid. l. 663

8 Praising the lean and sallow abstinence.
Ibid. l. 709

9 Beauty is Nature's coin, must not be hoarded,
But must be current, and the good thereof
Consists in mutual and partaken bliss.
Ibid. l. 739

10 Beauty is Nature's brag, and must be shown
In courts, at feasts, and high solemnities,
Where most may wonder at the workmanship;
It is for homely features to keep home—
They had their name thence; coarse complexions
And cheeks of sorry grain will serve to ply
The sampler, and to tease the huswife's wool.
What need a vermeil-tinctur'd lip for that,
Love-darting eyes, or tresses like the morn?
Ibid. l. 745

11 Sabrina fair,
Listen where thou art sitting
Under the glassy, cool, translucent wave,
In twisted braids of lilies knitting
The loose train of thy amber-dropping hair;
Listen for dear honor's sake,
Goddess of the silver lake,
    Listen and save.
Ibid. l. 859

12 But now my task is smoothly done:
I can fly, or I can run.
Ibid. l. 1012

13 Love Virtue, she alone is free,
She can teach ye how to climb
Higher than the sphery chime;
Or, if Virtue feeble were,
Heav'n itself would stoop to her.
Ibid. l. 1019

14 Yet once more, O ye laurels, and once more
Ye myrtles brown, with ivy never sere,
I come to pluck your berries harsh and crude,
And with forc'd fingers rude
Shatter your leaves before the mellowing year.
Lycidas [1637], l. 1

15   He knew
Himself to sing, and build the lofty rhyme.
Ibid. l. 10

16 Hence with denial vain, and coy excuse.
Ibid. l. 18

17 Under the opening eyelids of the morn,
We drove afield; and both together heard
What time the gray-fly winds her sultry horn,
Batt'ning our flocks with the fresh dews of night.
Ibid. l. 26

18 But O the heavy change, now thou art gone,
Now thou art gone and never must return!
Ibid. l. 37

19 As killing as the canker to the rose.
Ibid. l. 45

20 Alas! what boots it with incessant care
To tend the homely slighted shepherd's trade,
And strictly meditate the thankless Muse?
Were it not better done as others use,
To sport with Amaryllis in the shade,
Or with the tangles of Neaera's hair?
Fame is the spur that the clear spirit doth raise[3]
(That last infirmity of noble mind)[4]
To scorn delights, and live laborious days;
But the fair guerdon when we hope to find,
And think to burst out into sudden blaze,
Comes the blind Fury with th' abhorred shears,
And slits the thin-spun life.
Ibid. l. 64

21 Fame is no plant that grows on mortal soil.
Ibid. l. 78

22 It was that fatal and perfidious bark,
Built in th' eclipse, and rigg'd with curses dark,
That sunk so low that sacred head of thine.
Ibid. l. 100

---

[1]See Shakespeare, 164:1.
[2]See Shakespeare, 169:3.

[3]See Tacitus, 109:18.
[4]That thirst [for applause], if the last infirmity of noble minds, is also the first infirmity of weak ones; and on the whole, the strongest impulsive influence of average humanity.
—RUSKIN, *Sesame and Lilies* [1865], *Of Kings' Treasuries, sec. 3*

1 Last came, and last did go,
The Pilot of the Galilean lake;
Two massy keys he bore of metals twain,
(The golden opes, the iron shuts amain).
Lycidas, l. 108

2 Blind mouths! That scarce themselves know how
  to hold
A sheep-hook.
Ibid. l. 119

3 The hungry sheep look up, and are not fed,
But swoln with wind and the rank mist they
  draw,
Rot inwardly, and foul contagion spread:
Besides what the grim wolf with privy paw
Daily devours apace, and nothing said;
But that two-handed engine at the door
Stands ready to smite once, and smite no more.
Ibid. l. 123

4 Whether beyond the stormy Hebrides,[1]
Where thou perhaps under the whelming tide
Visit'st the bottom of the monstrous world.
Ibid. l. 156

5 Look homeward, Angel, now, and melt with
  ruth.[2]
Ibid. l. 163

6 For Lycidas your sorrow is not dead,
Sunk though he be beneath the watery floor;
So sinks the day-star in the ocean bed;
And yet anon repairs his drooping head,
And tricks his beams, and with new-spangled ore
Flames in the forehead of the morning sky.
So Lycidas sunk low, but mounted high,
Through the dear might of him that walk'd the
  waves.
Ibid. l. 166

7 He touch'd the tender stops of various quills,
With eager thought warbling his Doric lay.
Ibid. l. 188

8 At last he rose, and twitch'd his mantle blue:
Tomorrow to fresh woods and pastures new.
Ibid. l. 192

9 O nightingale, that on yon bloomy spray
Warbl'st at eve, when all the woods are still.
Sonnet, To the Nightingale [c. 1637]

10 Thy liquid notes that close the eye of day.
Ibid. l. 5

11 Where the bright seraphim in burning row
Their loud uplifted angel trumpets blow.
At a Solemn Music [c. 1637]

12   A poet soaring in the high region of his fancies,
with his garland and singing robes about him.
*The Reason of Church Government [1641],
bk. II, introduction*

13   By labor and intent study (which I take to be my
portion in this life), joined with the strong propensity of nature, I might perhaps leave something so
written to after-times, as they should not willingly
let it die.
Ibid.

14   Beholding the bright countenance of truth in the
quiet and still air of delightful studies.   *Ibid.*

15   He who would not be frustrate of his hope to
write well hereafter in laudable things ought himself
to be a true poem.
Apology for Smectymnuus [1642]

16   His words . . . like so many nimble and airy
servitors trip about him at command.   *Ibid.*

17   Truth . . . never comes into the world but like
a bastard, to the ignominy of him that brought her
forth.[3]
*The Doctrine and Discipline of Divorce [1643],
introduction*

18   Let not England forget her precedence of teaching
nations how to live.[4]   *Ibid.*

19   Litigious terms, fat contentions, and flowing fees.
Tractate of Education [1644]

20   Inflamed with the study of learning and the admiration of virtue; stirred up with high hopes of living
to be brave men and worthy patriots, dear to God,
and famous to all ages.   *Ibid.*

21   Ornate rhetoric taught out of the rule of Plato.
. . . To which poetry would be made subsequent,
or indeed rather precedent, as being less subtle and
fine, but more simple, sensuous, and passionate.
Ibid.

22   In those vernal seasons of the year, when the air
is calm and pleasant, it were an injury and sullenness
against Nature not to go out, and see her riches, and
partake in her rejoicing with heaven and earth.
Ibid.

23   As good almost kill a man as kill a good book:
who kills a man kills a reasonable creature, God's
image; but he who destroys a good book kills reason
itself.   *Areopagitica [1644]*

24   A good book is the precious lifeblood of a master
spirit, embalmed and treasured up on purpose to a
life beyond life.   *Ibid.*

25   I cannot praise a fugitive and cloistered virtue,
unexercised and unbreathed, that never sallies out
and sees her adversary, but slinks out of the race,
where that immortal garland is to be run for, not
without dust and heat.   *Ibid.*

26   Where there is much desire to learn, there of
necessity will be much arguing, much writing, many

---

[1]See James Thomson, 308:8.
[2]See Thomas Wolfe, 706:16.

[3]Still rule those minds on earth / At whom sage Milton's
wormwood words were hurled: / "Truth like a bastard comes
into the world / Never without ill-fame to him who gives her
birth"? —HARDY, *Lausanne* [1897]
[4]See Virgil, 94:15.

opinions; for opinion in good men is but knowledge in the making.   *Ibid.*

1   God is decreeing to begin some new and great period in His Church, even to the reforming of Reformation itself: what does He then but reveal Himself to His servants, and as His manner is, first to His Englishmen?   *Ibid.*

2   Methinks I see in my mind a noble and puissant nation rousing herself like a strong man after sleep, and shaking her invincible locks. Methinks I see her as an eagle mewing her mighty youth, and kindling her undazzled eyes at the full midday beam.
                                            Ibid.

3   Give me the liberty to know, to utter, and to argue freely according to conscience, above all liberties.   *Ibid.*

4   Though all the winds of doctrine[1] were let loose to play upon the earth, so Truth be in the field, we do injuriously, by licensing and prohibiting, to misdoubt her strength. Let her and Falsehood grapple; who ever knew Truth put to the worse, in a free and open encounter?[2]   *Ibid.*

5   Men of most renowned virtue have sometimes by transgressing most truly kept the law.
                             Tetrachordon [1644–1645]

6 That would have made Quintilian stare and gasp.
          *On the Detraction Which Followed upon My
          Writing Certain Treatises [1645]*

7   For such kind of borrowing as this, if it be not bettered by the borrower, among good authors is accounted Plagiarè.   *Eikonoklastes [1649], ch. 23*

8   None can love freedom heartily, but good men; the rest love not freedom, but license.
                    Tenure of Kings and Magistrates [1649]

9   No man who knows aught, can be so stupid to deny that all men naturally were born free.
                                            Ibid.

10   Peace hath her victories
No less renown'd than war.
                    To the Lord General Cromwell [1652]

11 When I consider how my light is spent,
Ere half my days, in this dark world and wide,
And that one talent which is death to hide
Lodg'd with me useless.
                            On His Blindness [1652]

12 Doth God exact day-labor, light denied?
                                            Ibid.

13   Who best
Bear his mild yoke, they serve him best: his state
Is kingly; thousands at his bidding speed,

And post o'er land and ocean without rest;
They also serve who only stand and wait.
                                            Ibid.

14 Avenge, O Lord, thy slaughter'd saints, whose
      bones
Lie scatter'd on the Alpine mountains cold;
Ev'n them who kept thy truth so pure of old
When all our fathers worshipp'd stocks and stones
Forget not.
          On the Late Massacre in Piedmont [1655]

15   Yet I argue not
Against Heav'n's hand or will, nor bate one jot
Of heart or hope; but still bear up, and steer
Right onward.
          *To Cyriack Skinner, upon His Blindness
          [c. 1655]*

16 Methought I saw my late espoused saint
Brought to me like Alcestis from the grave.
                    On His Deceased Wife [c. 1658]

17 But oh! as to embrace me she inclin'd,
I wak'd, she fled, and day brought back my night.
                                            Ibid.

18 Of Man's first disobedience, and the fruit
Of that forbidden tree whose mortal taste
Brought death into the world, and all our woe,
With loss of Eden.
                    Paradise Lost [1667], bk. I, l. 1

19 Things unattempted yet in prose or rhyme.
                                    Ibid. l. 16

20   What in me is dark
Illumine, what is low raise and support;
That to the height of this great argument
I may assert eternal Providence,
And justify the ways of God to men.[3]
                                    Ibid. l. 22

21 The infernal serpent; he it was, whose guile,
Stirr'd up with envy and revenge, deceiv'd
The mother of mankind.
                                    Ibid. l. 34

22   Him the Almighty Power
Hurl'd headlong flaming from th' ethereal sky[4]
With hideous ruin and combustion down
To bottomless perdition, there to dwell
In adamantine chains and penal fire,
Who durst defy th' Omnipotent to arms.
                                    Ibid. l. 44

23 No light, but rather darkness visible.
                                    Ibid. l. 63

24 Regions of sorrow, doleful shades, where peace
And rest can never dwell, hope never comes
That comes to all.
                                    Ibid. l. 65

---

[1]See *Ephesians 4:14*, 44:24.
[2]See Jefferson, 344:5, and Oliver Wendell Holmes, Jr., 542:-25.

[3]See *Samson Agonistes*, 261:12; Pope, 301:2; and Housman, 579:15.
[4]See *Luke 10:18*, 38:20.

1   What though the field be lost?
All is not lost; th' unconquerable will,
And study of revenge, immortal hate,
And courage never to submit or yield.
Paradise Lost, bk. I, l. 105

2   To be weak is miserable,
Doing or suffering.
Ibid. l. 157

3 And out of good still to find means of evil.
Ibid. l. 165

4 The seat of desolation, void of light.
Ibid. l. 181

5 A mind not to be chang'd by place or time.
The mind is its own place, and in itself
Can make a heav'n of hell, a hell of heav'n.
Ibid. l. 253

6 To reign is worth ambition though in hell:
Better to reign in hell than serve in heav'n.
Ibid. l. 262

7 His spear, to equal which the tallest pine
Hewn on Norwegian hills, to be the mast
Of some great ammiral, were but a wand,
He walk'd with, to support uneasy steps
Over the burning marle.
Ibid. l. 292

8 Thick as autumnal leaves that strow the brooks
In Vallombrosa.
Ibid. l. 302

9 Awake, arise, or be forever fallen!
Ibid. l. 330

10   Spirits, when they please,
Can either sex assume, or both.
Ibid. l. 423

11   When night
Darkens the streets, then wander forth the sons
Of Belial, flown with insolence and wine.
Ibid. l. 500

12 Th' imperial ensign, which, full high advanc'd,
Shone like a meteor, streaming to the wind.[1]
Ibid. l. 536

13 Sonorous metal blowing martial sounds:
At which the universal host up sent
A shout that tore hell's concave, and beyond
Frighted the reign of Chaos and old Night.
Ibid. l. 540

14   Anon they move
In perfect phalanx, to the Dorian mood
Of flutes and soft recorders.
Ibid. l. 549

15   His form had yet not lost
All her original brightness, nor appear'd

---

[1]Streamed like a meteor to the troubled air.—THOMAS
GRAY, *The Bard* [1757], *sec. I, st. 2, l. 6*

Less than archangel ruin'd, and th' excess
Of glory obscur'd.
Ibid. l. 591

16   The sun . . .
In dim eclipse, disastrous twilight sheds
On half the nations, and with fear of change
Perplexes monarchs.
Ibid. l. 594

17   Care
Sat on his faded cheek, but under brows
Of dauntless courage.
Ibid. l. 601

18 Thrice he assay'd, and thrice, in spite of scorn,
Tears, such as angels weep, burst forth.
Ibid. l. 619

19   Who overcomes
By force hath overcome but half his foe.
Ibid. l. 648

20 Mammon, the least erected spirit that fell
From heaven; for ev'n in heaven his looks and
    thoughts
Were always downward bent, admiring more
The riches of heaven's pavement, trodden gold,
Than aught divine or holy else enjoyed
In vision beatific.
Ibid. l. 679

21   Let none admire
That riches grow in hell; that soil may best
Deserve the precious bane.
Ibid. l. 690

22   From morn
To noon he fell, from noon to dewy eve,
A summer's day; and with the setting sun
Dropp'd from the zenith like a falling star.
Ibid. l. 742

23 High on a throne of royal state, which far
Outshone the wealth of Ormus and of Ind,
Or where the gorgeous East with richest hand
Showers on her kings barbaric pearl and gold,
Satan exalted sat, by merit rais'd
To that bad eminence; and from despair
Thus high uplifted beyond hope, aspires
Beyond thus high, insatiate to pursue
Vain war with heav'n.
Ibid. II, l. 1

24   Moloch, scepter'd king,
Stood up, the strongest and the fiercest spirit
That fought in heav'n; now fiercer by despair.
Ibid. l. 44

25   Rather than be less
Car'd not to be at all.
Ibid. l. 47

26 My sentence is for open war.
Ibid. l. 51

27 Which if not victory is yet revenge.
Ibid. l. 105

1 But all was false and hollow; through his tongue
Dropp'd manna, and could make the worse
    appear
The better reason.[1]

Ibid. l. 112

2   For who would lose,
Though full of pain, this intellectual being,
Those thoughts that wander through eternity,
To perish rather, swallow'd up and lost
In the wide womb of uncreated night,
Devoid of sense and motion?

Ibid. l. 146

3 His red right hand.[2]

Ibid. l. 174

4 Unrespited, unpitied, unrepriev'd.

Ibid. l. 185

5   The never-ending flight
Of future days.

Ibid. l. 221

6 Thus Belial with words cloth'd in reason's garb
Counsel'd ignoble ease, and peaceful sloth,
Not peace.

Ibid. l. 226

7   With grave
Aspect he rose, and in his rising seem'd
A pillar of state; deep on his front engraven
Deliberation sat and public care;
And princely counsel in his face yet shone,
Majestic though in ruin.

Ibid. l. 300

8   To sit in darkness here
Hatching vain empires.

Ibid. l. 377

9 The palpable obscure.

Ibid. l. 406

10   Long is the way
And hard, that out of hell leads up to light.

Ibid. l. 432

11 Their rising all at once was as the sound
Of thunder heard remote.

Ibid. l. 476

12 Others apart sat on a hill retir'd,
In thoughts more elevate, and reason'd high
Of Providence, foreknowledge, will, and fate,
Fix'd fate, free will, foreknowledge absolute,
And found no end, in wand'ring mazes lost.

Ibid. l. 557

13 Vain wisdom all, and false philosophy.

Ibid. l. 565

14   Arm th' obdur'd breast
With stubborn patience as with triple steel.[3]

Ibid. l. 568

15 Far off from these a slow and silent stream,
Lethe the river of oblivion rolls.

Ibid. l. 582

16 At certain revolutions all the damn'd
Are brought: and feel by turns the bitter change
Of fierce extremes, extremes by change more
    fierce.

Ibid. l. 597

17 Whence and what art thou, execrable shape?

Ibid. l. 681

18 Before mine eyes in opposition sits
Grim Death[4] my son and foe.

Ibid. l. 803

19 Hot, cold, moist, and dry, four champions fierce,[5]
Strive here for mast'ry.

Ibid. l. 898

20   To compare
Great things with small.

Ibid. l. 921

21 With ruin upon ruin, rout on rout,
Confusion worse confounded.

Ibid. l. 995

22 And fast by hanging in a golden chain,
This pendent world, in bigness as a star
Of smallest magnitude close by the moon.

Ibid. l. 1051

23 Hail, holy light! offspring of heav'n firstborn.[6]

Ibid. III, l. 1

24   Thus with the year
Seasons return; but not to me returns
Day, or the sweet approach of ev'n or morn,
Or sight of vernal bloom, or summer's rose,
Or flocks, or herds, or human face divine;[7]
But cloud instead, and ever-during dark
Surrounds me, from the cheerful ways of men
Cut off, and for the book of knowledge fair
Presented with a universal blank
Of Nature's works to me expung'd and raz'd,
And wisdom at one entrance quite shut out.

Ibid. l. 40

25 See golden days, fruitful of golden deeds,
With Joy and Love triumphing.

Ibid. l. 337

26 Dark with excessive bright.

Ibid. l. 380

---

[4]See Massinger, 238:9.
[5]Hot and cold, and moist and dry.—DU BARTAS, *Divine Weeks and Works* [1578], *Second Day*
  See Dryden, 275:7.
[6]God's first creature, which was light.—FRANCIS BACON, *The New Atlantis* [1626]
  Light, the prime work of God.—MILTON, *Samson Agonistes* [1671], *l. 70*
  See *Genesis* 1:3, 6:4, and Thomas Fuller, 250:12.
[7]See Blake, 356:13 and 358:13.

---

[1]See Aristophanes, 73:2.
[2]*Rubente dextera.*—HORACE, *Odes, I, ii, 2, To Caesar Augustus*
[3]See Shakespeare, 164:1.

1 Into a limbo large and broad, since called
The Paradise of Fools, to few unknown.
Paradise Lost, bk. III, l. 495

2 The hell within him.
Ibid. IV, l. 20

3   At whose sight all the stars
Hide their diminish'd heads.[1]
Ibid. l. 34

4   A grateful mind
By owing owes not, but still pays, at once
Indebted and discharg'd.
Ibid. l. 55

5 Me miserable! which way shall I fly
Infinite wrath, and infinite despair?
Which way I fly is hell; myself am hell;
And in the lowest deep a lower deep,
Still threat'ning to devour me, opens wide,
To which the hell I suffer seems a heaven.
Ibid. l. 73

6 So farewell hope, and with hope farewell fear,
Farewell remorse: all good to me is lost;
Evil, be thou my good.
Ibid. l. 108

7   And on the Tree of Life,
The middle tree and highest there that grew,
Sat like a cormorant.
Ibid. l. 194

8 A heaven on earth.
Ibid. l. 208

9 Flowers of all hue, and without thorn the rose.
Ibid. l. 256

10   Not that fair field
Of Enna, where Proserpin gathering flowers
Herself a fairer flower by gloomy Dis
Was gathered, which cost Ceres all that pain
To seek her through the world.
Ibid. l. 268

11 Two of far nobler shape erect and tall,
Godlike erect, with native honor clad
In naked majesty seem'd lords of all.
Ibid. l. 288

12 For contemplation he and valor form'd,
For softness she and sweet attractive grace;
He for God only, she for God in him.
Ibid. l. 297

13   Implied
Subjection, but requir'd with gentle sway,
And by her yielded, by him best receiv'd,
Yielded with coy submission, modest pride,
And sweet reluctant amorous delay.
Ibid. l. 307

14 Adam the goodliest man of men since born
His sons, the fairest of her daughters Eve.
Ibid. l. 323

15 So spake the Fiend, and with necessity,
The tyrant's plea,[2] excus'd his devilish deeds.
Ibid. l. 393

16 Imparadis'd in one another's arms.
Ibid. l. 506

17   Live while ye may,
Yet happy pair.
Ibid. l. 533

18 Now came still evening on, and twilight gray
Had in her sober livery all things clad.
Ibid. l. 598

19   The wakeful nightingale,
She all night long her amorous descant sung;
Silence was pleas'd: now glow'd the firmament
With living sapphires: Hesperus, that led
The starry host, rode brightest, till the moon,
Rising in clouded majesty, at length
Apparent queen unveil'd her peerless light,
And o'er the dark her silver mantle threw.
Ibid. l. 602

20 The timely dew of sleep.
Ibid. l. 614

21 With thee conversing I forget all time,
All seasons, and their change; all please alike.
Sweet is the breath of morn, her rising sweet,
With charm of earliest birds.
Ibid. l. 639

22   Sweet the coming on
Of grateful ev'ning mild, then silent night
With this her solemn bird, and this fair moon,
And these the gems of heaven, her starry train.
Ibid. l. 646

23 Millions of spiritual creatures walk the earth
Unseen, both when we wake, and when we sleep.
Ibid. l. 677

24   In naked beauty more adorn'd,
More lovely, than Pandora.[3]
Ibid. l. 713

25   Eas'd the putting off
These troublesome disguises which we wear.
Ibid. l. 739

26 Hail wedded love, mysterious law, true source
Of human offspring.
Ibid. l. 750

27 Squat like a toad, close at the ear of Eve.
Ibid. l. 800

28 Not to know me argues yourselves unknown.
Ibid. l. 830

[1]Ye little stars! hide your diminished rays.—POPE, *Moral Essays* [1731–1735], *Epistle III, l. 282*

[2]See William Pitt [1759–1806], 364:9.
[3]See Cicero, 87:18, and James Thomson, 308:7.

1   Abash'd the Devil stood,
And felt how awful goodness is, and saw
Virtue in her shape how lovely.
Ibid. l. 846

2 All hell broke loose.[1]
Ibid. l. 918

3 Like Teneriff or Atlas unremoved.
Ibid. l. 987

4   The starry cope
Of heaven.
Ibid. l. 992

5   His sleep
Was airy light from pure digestion bred.
Ibid. V, l. 3

6   My latest found,
Heaven's last, best gift, my ever new delight!
Ibid. l. 18

7 These are thy glorious works, Parent of good.
Ibid. l. 153

8 Him first, him last, him midst, and without end.
Ibid. l. 165

9 A wilderness of sweets.
Ibid. l. 294

10 So saying, with dispatchful looks in haste
She turns, on hospitable thoughts intent.
Ibid. l. 331

11   Freely we serve,
Because we freely love, as in our will
To love or not; in this we stand or fall.
Ibid. l. 538

12   What if earth
Be but the shadow of heaven, and things therein
Each to other like, more than on earth is thought?
Ibid. l. 574

13 Hear all ye Angels, progeny of light,
Thrones, Dominations, Princedoms, Virtues,
Powers.
Ibid. l. 600

14 All seem'd well pleas'd, all seem'd but were not
all.
Ibid. l. 617

15 Among the faithless, faithful only he.
Ibid. l. 897

16   Morn,
Wak'd by the circling hours, with rosy hand[2]
Unbarr'd the gates of light.
Ibid. VI, l. 2

17 Servant of God, well done,[3] well hast thou fought
The better fight, who single hast maintained
Against revolted multitudes the cause
Of truth, in word mightier than they in arms.
Ibid. l. 29

18 He onward came; far off his coming shone.
Ibid. l. 768

19 More safe I sing with mortal voice, unchang'd
To hoarse or mute, though fall'n on evil days,
On evil days though fall'n, and evil tongues;
In darkness, and with dangers compass'd round,
And solitude.
Ibid. VII, l. 24

20   Out of one man a race
Of men innumerable.
Ibid. l. 155

21   There Leviathan
Hugest of living creatures, on the deep
Stretch'd like a promontory sleeps or swims,
And seems a moving land, and at his gills
Draws in, and at his trunk spouts out a sea.
Ibid. l. 412

22 The planets in their stations list'ning stood,
While the bright pomp ascended jubilant.
Open, ye everlasting gates, they sung,
Open, ye heavens, your living doors;[4] let in
The great Creator from his work return'd
Magnificent, his six days' work, a world.
Ibid. l. 563

23 The angel ended, and in Adam's ear
So charming left his voice that he awhile
Thought him still speaking, still stood fix'd to
hear.
Ibid. VIII, l. 1

24   To know
That which before us lies in daily life
Is the prime wisdom.
Ibid. l. 192

25 Liquid lapse of murmuring streams.
Ibid. l. 263

26 And feel that I am happier than I know.
Ibid. l. 282

27 Her virtue and the conscience of her worth,
That would be woo'd, and not unsought be won.
Ibid. l. 502

28 The sum of earthly bliss.
Ibid. l. 522

29   So absolute she seems
And in herself complete, so well to know
Her own, that what she wills to do or say,
Seems wisest, virtuousest, discreetest, best.
Ibid. l. 547

30 Accuse not Nature, she hath done her part;
Do thou but thine.
Ibid. l. 561

31 My unpremeditated verse.
Ibid. IX, l. 24

32   Unless an age too late, or cold
Climate, or years damp my intended wing.

---

[1]See Robert Greene, 157:22.
[2]See Homer, 51:1.
[3]See *Matthew 25:21*, 36:14.

[4]See *Psalm 24:7*, 16:19.

1   Unless an age too late, or cold
Climate, or years damp my intended wing.
Paradise Lost, bk. IX, l. 44

2 The serpent subtlest beast of all the field.[1]
Ibid. l. 86

3 For solitude sometimes is best society,
And short retirement urges sweet return.
Ibid. l. 249

4 At shut of evening flowers.
Ibid. l. 278

5 As one who long in populous city pent.[2]
Ibid. l. 445

6 God so commanded, and left that command
Sole daughter of his voice;[3] the rest, we live
Law to ourselves, our reason is our law.
Ibid. l. 652

7   Her rash hand in evil hour
Forth reaching to the fruit, she pluck'd, she eat:
Earth felt the wound, and Nature from her seat,
Sighing through all her works, gave signs of woe
That all was lost.
Ibid. l. 780

8 So dear I love him, that with him all deaths
I could endure, without him live no life.
Ibid. l. 832

9   In her face excuse
Came prologue, and apology too prompt.
Ibid. l. 853

10 O fairest of creation! last and best
Of all God's works! creature in whom excell'd
Whatever can to sight or thought be form'd,
Holy, divine, good, amiable, or sweet!
How art thou lost, how on a sudden lost,
Defac'd, deflower'd, and now to Death devote?
Ibid. l. 896

11   I feel
The link of nature draw me: flesh of flesh,
Bone of my bone thou art,[4] and from thy state
Mine never shall be parted, bliss or woe.
Ibid. l. 913

12 Our state cannot be sever'd; we are one,
One flesh; to lose thee were to lose myself.
Ibid. l. 958

13   I shall temper so
Justice with mercy.[5]
Ibid. X, l. 77

14 Pandemonium, city and proud seat
Of Lucifer.
Ibid. l. 424

15 A dismal universal hiss, the sound
Of public scorn.
Ibid. l. 508

16 Death . . . on his pale horse.[6]
Ibid. l. 588

17 Demoniac frenzy, moping melancholy,
And moon-struck madness.
Ibid. XI, l. 485

18 Nor love thy life, nor hate; but what thou liv'st
Live well; how long or short permit to Heaven.
Ibid. l. 553

19 A bevy of fair women.
Ibid. l. 582

20   The evening star,
Love's harbinger.
Ibid. l. 588

21 The brazen throat of war.
Ibid. l. 713

22   For now I see
Peace to corrupt no less than war to waste.
Ibid. l. 783

23 An olive leaf he brings, pacific sign.
Ibid. l. 860

24 The world was all before them, where to choose
Their place of rest, and Providence their guide:
They hand in hand with wand'ring steps and slow
Through Eden took their solitary way.
Ibid. XII, l. 646

25   Most men admire
Virtue who follow not her lore.
Paradise Regained [1671], bk. I, l. 482

26 Skill'd to retire, and in retiring draw
Hearts after them tangled in amorous nets.
Ibid. II, l. 161

27   Beauty stands
In the admiration only of weak minds
Led captive.
Ibid. l. 220

28 Rocks whereon greatest men have oftest wreck'd.
Ibid. l. 228

29 Of whom to be disprais'd were no small praise.
Ibid. III, l. 56

30 Elephants endorsed with towers.
Ibid. l. 329

31 Dusk faces with white silken turbans wreath'd.
Ibid. IV, l. 76

32   The childhood shows the man,
As morning shows the day.[7]
Ibid. l. 220

33 Athens, the eye of Greece, mother of arts
And eloquence.
Ibid. l. 240

[1]See *Genesis 3:1, 6:19.*
[2]See Keats, 413:22.
[3]See Wordsworth, 376:2.
[4]See *Genesis 2:23, 6:17.*
[5]See Shakespeare, 181:19.

[6]See *Revelation 6:8, 47:19.*
[7]See Wordsworth, 374:7.

1　　　The olive grove of Academe,[1]
Plato's retirement, where the Attic bird
Trills her thick-warbled notes the summer long.
Ibid. l. 244

2　　　Socrates . . .
Whom well inspir'd the oracle pronounc'd
Wisest of men.
Ibid. l. 274

3 The first and wisest of them all professed
To know this only, that he nothing knew.[2]
Ibid. l. 293

4 Deep vers'd in books and shallow in himself.
Ibid. l. 327

5　　　Till morning fair
Came forth with pilgrim steps, in amice gray.
Ibid. l. 426

6 Eyeless in Gaza, at the mill with slaves.[3]
Samson Agonistes [1671], l. 41

7 O dark, dark, dark, amid the blaze of noon,
Irrecoverably dark, total eclipse
Without all hope of day!
Ibid. l. 80

8 The sun to me is dark
And silent as the moon,
When she deserts the night,
Hid in her vacant interlunar cave.
Ibid. l. 86

9 To live a life half dead, a living death.
Ibid. l. 100

10 Ran on embattled armies clad in iron,
And, weaponless himself,
Made arms ridiculous.
Ibid. l. 129

11　　　Apt words have power to suage
The tumors of a troubled mind.[4]
Ibid. l. 184

12 Just are the ways of God,
And justifiable to men;[5]
Unless there be who think not God at all.
Ibid. l. 293

13 A grain of manhood.
Ibid. l. 408

14 What boots it at one gate to make defense,
And at another to let in the foe?
Ibid. l. 560

15 My race of glory run, and race of shame,
And I shall shortly be with them at rest.
Ibid. l. 597

[1]See Horace, 97:22.
[2]See Socrates, 70:22.
[3]See *Judges 16:21*, 11:17.
[4]See Aeschylus, 63:5.
[5]See *Paradise Lost*, 255:20; Pope, 301:2; and Housman, 579:-15.

16 But who is this, what thing of sea or land?
Female of sex it seems,
That so bedeck'd, ornate, and gay,
Comes this way sailing
Like a stately ship
Of Tarsus, bound for th' isles
Of Javan or Gadire,
With all her bravery on, and tackle trim,
Sails fill'd, and streamers waving,
Courted by all the winds that hold them play;
An amber scent of odorous perfume
Her harbinger?
Ibid. l. 710

17 *Dalila:* In argument with men a woman ever
Goes by the worse, whatever be her cause.
Samson: For want of words, no doubt, or lack of
breath!
Ibid. l. 903

18 Fame, if not double-faced, is double-mouthed,
And with contrary blast proclaims most deeds;
On both his wings, one black, the other white,
Bears greatest names in his wild airy flight.
Ibid. l. 971

19 Yet beauty, though injurious, hath strange power,
After offense returning, to regain
Love once possess'd.
Ibid. l. 1003

20 Love-quarrels oft in pleasing concord end;
Not wedlock-treachery.
Ibid. l. 1008

21 Boast not of what thou would'st have done, but
do
What then thou would'st.
Ibid. l. 1104

22 He's gone; and who knows how he may report
Thy words by adding fuel to the flame?
Ibid. l. 1350

23 For evil news rides post, while good news baits.
Ibid. l. 1538

24 Suspense in news is torture.
Ibid. l. 1569

25 Nothing is here for tears, nothing to wail
Or knock the breast, no weakness, no contempt,
Dispraise, or blame, nothing but well and fair,
And what may quiet us in a death so noble.
Ibid. l. 1721

26 All is best, though we oft doubt,
What the unsearchable dispose
Of highest Wisdom brings about.
Ibid. l. 1745

27 Calm of mind, all passion spent.
Ibid. l. 1758

28　　　Such bickerings to recount, met often in these our
writers, what more worth is it than to chronicle the
wars of kites or crows flocking and fighting in the
air?　　　*The History of England [1670], bk. IV*

Edward Hyde, Earl of Clarendon
1609–1674

1   He [Hampden] had a head to contrive, a tongue to persuade, and a hand to execute any mischief.
History of the Rebellion [1702–1704], vol. III, bk. VII, sec. 84

Sir John Suckling
1609–1642

2 Why so pale and wan, fond lover?
Prithee, why so pale?
Will, when looking well can't move her,
Looking ill prevail?
Aglaura [1638]. Song, st. 1

3 Quit, quit, for shame, this will not move,
This cannot take her.
If of herself she will not love,
Nothing can make her.
The devil take her!
Ibid. st. 3

4 High characters (cries one), and he would see
Things that ne'er were, nor are, nor ne'er will be.[1]
The Goblins [1639], epilogue

5 Her feet beneath her petticoat
Like little mice, stole in and out,[2]
As if they feared the light;
But oh, she dances such a way!
No sun upon an Easter-day
Is half so fine a sight.
A Ballad upon a Wedding [1641], st. 8

6 Her lips were red, and one was thin,
Compared to that was next her chin,
Some bee had stung it newly.
Ibid. st. 11

7 I prithee send me back my heart,
Since I cannot have thine;
For if from yours you will not part,
Why then shouldst thou have mine?
Fragmenta Aurea [1646]. Song, st. 1

8 'Tis not the meat, but 'tis the appetite
Makes eating a delight.
Ibid. Of Thee, Kind Boy, st. 3

9 Out upon it, I have loved
Three whole days together;
And am like to love three more,
If it prove fair weather.
Ibid. A Poem with the Answer, st. 1

10 'Tis expectation makes a blessing dear,
Heaven were not heaven, if we knew what it were.
Ibid. Against Fruition, st. 4

[1]There's no such thing in Nature, and you'll draw / A faultless monster which the world ne'er saw. — JOHN SHEFFIELD, DUKE OF BUCKINGHAM AND NORMANBY, *Essay on Poetry*
[2]See Herrick, 241:11.

Anne Bradstreet
c. 1612–1672

11   Youth is the time of getting, middle age of improving, and old age of spending.
Meditations Divine and Moral [1664], 3

12   Authority without wisdom is like a heavy axe without an edge, fitter to bruise than polish.
Ibid. 12

13   If we had no winter, the spring would not be so pleasant: if we did not sometimes taste of adversity, prosperity would not be so welcome.   *Ibid. 14*

14   Sore laborers have hard hands and old sinners have brawny consciences.   *Ibid. 36*

15 If ever two were one, then surely we.
If ever man were loved by wife, then thee;
If ever wife was happy in a man,
Compare with me ye women if you can.
To My Dear and Loving Husband [1678]

Samuel Butler
1612–1680

16 When civil fury first grew high,
And men fell out they knew not why.
Hudibras, pt. I [1663], canto I, l. 1

17 And pulpit, drum ecclesiastic,[3]
Was beat with fist, instead of a stick.
Ibid. l. 11

18 Beside, 'tis known he could speak Greek
As naturally as pigs squeak:[4]
That Latin was no more difficile
Than to a blackbird 'tis to whistle.
Ibid. l. 51

19 He could distinguish and divide
A hair 'twixt south and southwest side,
On either which he would dispute,
Confute, change hands, and still confute.
Ibid. l. 67

20 He'd run in debt by disputation,
And pay with ratiocination.
Ibid. l. 77

21 For rhetoric, he could not ope
His mouth, but out there flew a trope.
Ibid. l. 81

22 For all a rhetorician's rules
Teach nothing but to name his tools.
Ibid. l. 89

[3]This is the first we hear of the "drum ecclesiastic" beating up for recruits in worldly warfare in our country. — IRVING, *Knickerbocker's History of New York* [1809], bk. V, ch. 7
[4]He Greek and Latin speaks with greater ease / Than hogs eat acorns, and tame pigeons peas. — LIONEL CRANFIELD, EARL OF MIDDLESEX [1575–1645], *Panegyric on Tom Coriate*

1 A Babylonish dialect
Which learned pedants much affect.
Ibid. l. 93

2 For he by geometric scale,
Could take the size of pots of ale.
Ibid. l. 121

3 And wisely tell what hour o' th' day
The clock doth strike, by algebra.
Ibid. l. 125

4 Where entity and quiddity,
The ghosts of defunct bodies, fly.
Ibid. l. 145

5 'Twas Presbyterian true blue.
Ibid. l. 191

6 Such as do build their faith upon
The holy text of pike and gun.
Ibid. l. 195

7 And prove their doctrine orthodox,
By apostolic blows and knocks.
Ibid. l. 199

8 Compound for sins they are inclin'd to,
By damning those they have no mind to.
Ibid. l. 215

9 The trenchant blade, Toledo trusty,
For want of fighting was grown rusty,
And ate into itself, for lack
Of somebody to hew and hack.
Ibid. l. 357

10 For rhyme the rudder is of verses,
With which like ships they steer their courses.
Ibid. l. 463

11 And force them, though it was in spite
Of Nature and their stars, to write.
Ibid. l. 647

12 Great actions are not always true sons
Of great and mighty resolutions.
Ibid. l. 885

13   I'll make the fur
Fly 'bout the ears of the old cur.
Ibid. canto III, l. 277

14 These reasons made his mouth to water.
Ibid. l. 379

15 I am not now in fortune's power:
He that is down can fall no lower.[1]
Ibid. l. 877

16 Cheer'd up himself with ends of verse,
And sayings of philosophers.
Ibid. l. 1011

17 Cleric before, and Lay behind;
A lawless linsey-woolsey brother,
Half of one order, half another.
Ibid. l. 1226

[1]See Bunyan, 272:28.

18 Some have been beaten till they know
What wood a cudgel's of by th' blow;
Some kick'd, until they can feel whether
A shoe be Spanish or neat's leather.
Ibid. pt. II [1664], canto I, l. 221

19 For what is worth in anything
But so much money as 'twill bring?[2]
Ibid. l. 465

20 She that with poetry is won
Is but a desk to write upon.
Ibid. l. 591

21 Love is a boy by poets styled;
Then spare the rod, and spoil the child.[3]
Ibid. l. 843

22 Oaths are but words, and words but wind.
Ibid. canto II, l. 107

23 For truth is precious and divine—
Too rich a pearl for carnal swine.
Ibid. l. 257

24 He that imposes an oath makes it,
Not he that for convenience takes it;
Then how can any man be said
To break an oath he never made?
Ibid. l. 377

25   As the ancients
Say wisely, have a care o' th' main chance,[4]
And look before you ere you leap;[5]
For as you sow, ye are like to reap.[6]
Ibid. l. 501

26 Doubtless the pleasure is as great
Of being cheated as to cheat.
Ibid. canto III, l. 1

27 He made an instrument to know
If the moon shine at full or no.
Ibid. l. 261

28 As men of inward light are wont
To turn their optics in upon 't.
Ibid. pt. III [1678], canto I, l. 481

29 What makes all doctrines plain and clear?
About two hundred pounds a year.
And that which was proved true before,
Prove false again? Two hundred more.
Ibid. l. 1277

30 Nick Machiavel had ne'er a trick,
Though he gave his name to our Old Nick.
Ibid. l. 1313

31 True as the dial to the sun,[7]
Although it be not shined upon.
Ibid. canto II, l. 175

[2]See Publilius Syrus, 100:16.
[3]See *Proverbs*, 13:24, 21:17, and Menander, 81:7.
[4]See Lyly, 155:10.
[5]See John Heywood, 140:17.
[6]See *Galatians* 6:7, 44:21.
[7]True as the needle to the pole, / Or as the dial to the sun.
—BARTON BOOTH [1681–1733], *Song*

1 He that complies against his will
Is of his own opinion still.
                    Hudibras, pt. III, canto III, l. 547

2 Neither have the hearts to stay,
Nor wit enough to run away.
                    Ibid. l. 569

3 And poets by their sufferings grow,[1]
As if there were no more to do,
To make a poet excellent,
But only want and discontent.
                    Fragments

James Graham, Marquess of Montrose
1612–1650

4 He either fears his fate too much,
Or his deserts are small,
That puts it not unto the touch
To win or lose it all.
                    My Dear and Only Love, st. 2

5 I'll make thee glorious by my pen,
And famous by my sword.[2]
                    Ibid. st. 5

Richard Crashaw
c. 1613–1649

6 The conscious water saw its God, and blushed.[3]
                    Epigrammata Sacra [1634]. Aquae in Vinum Versae

7 Two went to pray? Oh, rather say
One went to brag, the other to pray.
                    Steps to the Temple [1648]. Two Went Up into the Temple to Pray[4]

8 Whoe'er she be,
That not impossible she
That shall command my heart and me.
                    Ibid. Wishes to His Supposed Mistress, l. 1

9 Where'er she lie,
Locked up from mortal eye,
In shady leaves of destiny.
                    Ibid. l. 4

10 Life that dares send
A challenge to his end,
And when it comes, say, Welcome, friend!
                    Ibid. l. 85

[1]See Shelley, 407:11.
[2]I'll make thee famous by my pen, / And glorious by my sword.—WALTER SCOTT, *The Legend of Montrose* [1819], ch. 15
[3]Nympha pudica Deum vidit, et erubuit.—Quoted by SAMUEL JOHNSON [1778]; from BOSWELL, *Life of Johnson* [1791], vol. II, p. 218 (Everyman edition).
   The bashful stream hath seen its God and blushed.—AARON HILL
   The water hears thy faintest word, / And blushes into wine.—JOHN SAMUEL BEWLEY MONSELL [1811–1875], *Mysterious Is Thy Presence, Lord, st. 1*
[4]See *Luke 18:10, 39:7.*

11 Sidnaeian showers
Of sweet discourse, whose powers
Can crown old Winter's head with flowers.
                    Ibid. l. 88

12 I would be married, but I'd have no wife,
I would be married to a single life.
                    Ibid. On Marriage

13 All is Caesar's, and what odds
So long as Caesar's self is God's?
                    Ibid. Mark XII

14 All those fair and flagrant things.
                    The Flaming Heart upon the Book of Saint Teresa [1652], l. 34

15 Love's passives are his activ'st part.
The wounded is the wounding heart.
                    Ibid. l. 73

16 O thou undaunted daughter of desires!
                    Ibid. l. 93

17 By all the eagle in thee, all the dove.
                    Ibid. l. 95

18 Poor world (said I) what wilt thou do
To entertain this starry stranger?
Is this the best thou canst bestow?
A cold, and not too cleanly, manger?
Contend, ye powers of heav'n and earth,
To fit a bed for this huge birth.
                    Hymn of the Nativity [1652], st. 6

19 Proud world, said I, cease your contest,
And let the mighty babe alone.
The phoenix builds the phoenix' nest.
Love's architecture is his own.
The babe whose birth embraves this morn,
Made his own bed ere he was born.
                    Ibid. st. 7

20 Welcome, all wonders in one sight!
Eternity shut in a span.
                    Ibid. Full Chorus

21 The modest front of this small floor,
Believe me, reader, can say more
Than many a braver marble can—
"Here lies a truly honest man!"
                    Epitaph upon Mr. Ashton

François, Duc de La Rochefoucauld
1613–1680

22   Self-love is the greatest of all flatterers.
                    Reflections; or, Sentences and Moral Maxims [1678], maxim 2

23   We all have strength enough to endure the misfortunes of others.[5]
                    Ibid. 19

24   Philosophy triumphs easily over past evils and future evils; but present evils triumph over it.
                    Ibid. 22

[5]See Pope, 303:20.

1 We need greater virtues to sustain good fortune than bad. *Ibid. 25*

2 If we had no faults of our own, we would not take so much pleasure in noticing those of others. *Ibid. 31*

3 Jealousy feeds upon suspicion, and it turns into fury or it ends as soon as we pass from suspicion to certainty. *Ibid. 32*

4 Self-interest speaks all sorts of tongues, and plays all sorts of roles, even that of disinterestedness. *Ibid. 39*

5 We are never so happy nor so unhappy as we imagine. *Ibid. 49*

6 To succeed in the world, we do everything we can to appear successful. *Ibid. 56*

7 There is no disguise which can for long conceal love where it exists or simulate it where it does not. *Ibid. 70*

8 There are very few people who are not ashamed of having been in love when they no longer love each other. *Ibid. 71*

9 True love is like ghosts, which everybody talks about and few have seen. *Ibid. 76*

10 The love of justice in most men is simply the fear of suffering injustice. *Ibid. 78*

11 Silence is the best tactic for him who distrusts himself. *Ibid. 79*

12 It is more ignominious to mistrust our friends than to be deceived by them. *Ibid. 84*

13 Everyone complains of his memory, and no one complains of his judgment. *Ibid. 89*

14 Old people like to give good advice, as solace for no longer being able to provide bad examples. *Ibid. 93*

15 A man who is ungrateful is sometimes less to blame for it than his benefactor. *Ibid. 96*

16 The mind is always the dupe of the heart.[1] *Ibid. 102*

17 Nothing is given so profusely as advice. *Ibid. 110*

18 The true way to be deceived is to think oneself more clever than others. *Ibid. 127*

19 We would rather speak ill of ourselves than not talk about ourselves at all. *Ibid. 138*

20 Usually we praise only to be praised. *Ibid. 146*

21 Our repentance is not so much regret for the ill we have done as fear of the ill that may happen to us in consequence. *Ibid. 180*

[1]The Mind lives on the Heart / Like any Parasite.—EMILY DICKINSON, *The Mind Lives on the Heart* [c. 1876]

22 Who lives without folly is not so wise as he thinks. *Ibid. 209*

23 Most people judge men only by their success or their good fortune. *Ibid. 212*

24 Hypocrisy is the homage that vice pays to virtue. *Ibid. 218*

25 Too great haste in paying off an obligation is a kind of ingratitude. *Ibid. 226*

26 There is great skill in knowing how to conceal one's skill. *Ibid. 245*

27 The pleasure of love is in loving. We are happier in the passion we feel than in that we arouse. *Ibid. 259*

28 Absence diminishes mediocre passions and increases great ones, as the wind blows out candles and fans fire. *Ibid. 276*

29 We always like those who admire us; we do not always like those whom we admire. *Ibid. 294*

30 The gratitude of most men is merely a secret desire to receive greater benefits.[2] *Ibid. 298*

31 We frequently forgive those who bore us, but cannot forgive those whom we bore. *Ibid. 304*

32 Lovers never get tired of each other, because they are always talking about themselves. *Ibid. 312*

33 In jealousy there is more self-love than love. *Ibid. 324*

34 We confess to little faults only to persuade ourselves that we have no great ones. *Ibid. 327*

35 We pardon to the extent that we love. *Ibid. 330*

36 We rarely find that people have good sense unless they agree with us.[3] *Ibid. 347*

37 Jealousy is always born together with love, but it does not always die when love dies. *Ibid. 361*

38 Mediocre minds usually dismiss anything which reaches beyond their own understanding. *Ibid. 375*

39 The greatest fault of a penetrating wit is to go beyond the mark. *Ibid. 377*

40 We may give advice, but we do not inspire conduct. *Ibid. 378*

41 The veracity which increases with old age is not far from folly. *Ibid. 416*

42 Few people know how to be old. *Ibid. 423*

43 Nothing prevents our being natural so much as the desire to appear so. *Ibid. 431*

[2]A lively sense of future favors.—ROBERT WALPOLE, *definition of the gratitude of place-expectants;* from WILLIAM HAZLITT, *English Comic Writers* [1819], *Wit and Humor*

[3]"That was excellently observed," say I when I read a passage in another where his opinion agrees with mine. When we differ, then I pronounce him to be mistaken.—SWIFT, *Thoughts on Various Subjects*

1   In their first passion women love their lovers, in the others they love love.[1]   *Maxim 471*

2   Quarrels would not last long if the fault were only on one side.   *Ibid. 496*

3   In the misfortune of our best friends we often find something that is not displeasing.[2]   *Ibid. 583*

Jeremy Taylor
1613–1667

4   Too quick a sense of constant infelicity.
    Holy Dying [1650–1651]

5   Every schoolboy knows it.
    On the Real Presence, V

6   The union of hands and hearts.
    Sermons [1653], The Marriage Ring, pt. I

7   No man ever repented that he arose from the table sober, healthful, and with his wits about him.
    Ibid.

Thomas Ady
fl. 1655

8   Matthew, Mark, Luke, and John,
The bed be blest that I lie on.
Four angels to my bed,
Four angels round my head,[3]
One to watch, and one to pray,
And two to bear my soul away.
    A Candle in the Dark [1655]

Richard Baxter
1615–1691

9   I preached as never sure to preach again,
And as a dying man to dying men.
    Poetical Fragments [1681]. Love Breathing Thanks and Praise

10   In necessary things, unity; in doubtful things, liberty; in all things, charity.[4]   *Motto*

Sir John Denham
1615–1669

11   Oh, could I flow like thee,[5] and make thy stream
My great example, as it is my theme!

Though deep yet clear, though gentle yet not dull;
Strong without rage, without o'erflowing full.
    Cooper's Hill [1642], l. 189

Sir Roger L'Estrange
1616–1704

12   Though this may be play to you, 'tis death to us.[6]
    Fables [1692]. Fable 398, Boys and Frogs

Roger de Bussy-Rabutin
1618–1693

13   God is usually on the side of the big squadrons and against the small ones.[7]
    Letter to the Comte de Limoges [October 18, 1677]

Abraham Cowley
1618–1667

14   What shall I do to be forever known,
And make the age to come my own?
    The Motto

15   This only grant me, that my means may lie
Too low for envy, for contempt too high.
    A Vote [1636]

16   Well then; I now do plainly see
This busy world and I shall ne'er agree;
The very honey of all earthly joy
Does of all meats the soonest cloy,
And they (methinks) deserve my pity,
Who for it can endure the stings,
The crowd, and buzz and murmurings,
Of this great hive, the city.
    The Wish [1647]

17   Ah yet, ere I descend to the grave
May I a small house and large garden have;
And a few friends, and many books, both true,
Both wise, and both delightful too!
    Ibid.

18   A mistress moderately fair.
    Ibid.

19   The world's a scene of changes, and to be
Constant, in Nature were inconstancy.
    Inconstancy [1647]

20   The thirsty earth soaks up the rain,
And drinks, and gapes for drink again.
The plants suck in the earth, and are
With constant drinking fresh and fair.
    Anacreon [1656], II, Drinking

---

[1]See Byron, 402:21.

[2]*Maxim 583* is one of the "maximes supprimées" discarded before the 1678 edition.
In all distresses of our friends / We first consult our private ends; / While Nature, kindly bent to ease us, / Points out some circumstance to please us. — SWIFT, *A Paraphrase of Rochefoucauld's Maxim*

[3]Usual version: Bless the bed that I lie on. / Four corners to my bed, / Four angels round my head.

[4]In necessariis, unitas; in dubiis libertas; in omniis caritas.

[5]The river Thames.

[6]See Bion, 82:10.

[7]"It is said that God is always for the big battalions. — VOLTAIRE, *letter to M. le Riche* [February 6, 1770]
Providence is always on the side of the last reserve. — *Attributed to* NAPOLEON
See Tacitus, 109:19; Boileau, 280:17; Frederick the Great, 318:20; and Gibbon, 340:6.

1 Fill all the glasses there, for why
  Should every creature drink but I,
  Why, man of morals, tell me why?
  Ibid.

2 A mighty pain to love it is,
  And 'tis a pain that pain to miss;
  But of all pains, the greatest pain
  It is to love, but love in vain.
  Ibid. VII, Gold

3 His time is forever, everywhere his place.
  Friendship in Absence

4 Nothing is there to come, and nothing past,
  But an eternal now does always last.
  Davideis [1656], bk. I, l. 361

5 Life is an incurable disease.
  To Dr. Scarborough [1656]

6 Ye fields of Cambridge, our dear Cambridge, say,
  Have ye not seen us walking every day?
  Was there a tree about which did not know
  The love betwixt us two?
  On the Death of Mr. William Harvey [1657][1]

7 God the first garden made, and the first city.
  The Garden [1664], essay 5

8 Hence ye profane! I hate ye all,
  Both the great vulgar and the small.[2]
  Horace, bk. III, ode 1

9 Charm'd with the foolish whistlings of a name.
  Virgil, Georgics, bk. II, l. 72

10 Words that weep and tears that speak.[3]
  The Prophet

11 Poet and Saint! to thee alone are given
  The two most sacred names of earth and Heaven.
  On the Death of Mr. Crashaw[4] *[1668]*

12 His faith, perhaps, in some nice tenets might
  Be wrong; his life, I'm sure, was in the right.
  Ibid.

Richard Lovelace
1618–1658

13 Oh, could you view the melody
    Of every grace
    And music of her face,[5]
  You'd drop a tear;
    Seeing more harmony
    In her bright eye
  Than now you hear.
  Lucasta [1649]. Orpheus to Beasts

14 Tell me not, sweet, I am unkind,
    That from the nunnery

Of thy chaste breast and quiet mind,
    To war and arms I fly.
  Ibid. To Lucasta: Going to the Wars, st. 1

15 I could not love thee, dear, so much,
    Lov'd I not honor more.
  Ibid. st. 3

16 When I lie tangled in her hair,
    And fettered to her eye,
  The gods that wanton in the air
  Know no such liberty.
  Ibid. To Althea: From Prison, st. 1

17 When flowing cups run swiftly round
  With no allaying Thames.[6]
  Ibid. st. 2

18 Stone walls do not a prison make,[7]
    Nor iron bars a cage;
  Minds innocent and quiet take
    That for an hermitage;
  If I have freedom in my love,
    And in my soul am free,
  Angels alone that soar above
    Enjoy such liberty.
  Ibid. st. 4

19 If to be absent were to be
    Away from thee;
  Or that when I am gone,
    You and I were alone;
  Then, my Lucasta, might I crave
  Pity from blust'ring wind, or swallowing wave.
  Ibid. To Lucasta: Going Beyond the Seas, st. 1

Ninon de L'Enclos
1620–1705

20 Old age is woman's hell.[8]   *Attributed*

Jean de La Fontaine
1621–1695

21 We believe no evil till the evil's done.
  Fables, bk. I [1668], fable 8

22 We heed no instincts but our own.   *Ibid.*

23 The opinion of the strongest is always the best.
  Ibid. 10

24 Better to suffer than to die: that is mankind's
  motto.   *Ibid. 16*

25 By the work one knows the workman.
  Ibid. 21

26 I bend but do not break.   *Ibid. 22*

27 It is a double pleasure to deceive the deceiver.
  Ibid. II [1668], fable 15

---

[1] See Harvey, 235.
[2] Odi profanum vulgus.
[3] See Thomas Gray, 323:5.
[4] See Crashaw, 264.
[5] The mind, the music breathing from her face. —BYRON,
The Bride of Abydos [1813], canto I, st. 6

[6] See Shakespeare, 219:1.
[7] Stone walls a prisoner make, but not a slave. —WORDS-
WORTH, *Humanity*
[8] La vieillesse est l'enfer des femmes.

1   It is impossible to please all the world and one's father.   *Fables, bk. III [1668], fable 1*

2   In everything one must consider the end.[1]   *Ibid. 5*

3   Beware, as long as you live, of judging people by appearances.   *Ibid. VI [1668], fable 5*

4   On the wings of Time grief flies away.[2]   *Ibid. 21*

5   The sign brings customers.   *Ibid. VII [1678–1679], fable 15*

6   People who make no noise are dangerous.   *Ibid. VIII [1678–1679], fable 23*

7   He knows the universe, and himself he does not know.   *Ibid. 26*

8   A hungry stomach cannot hear.[3]   *Ibid. IX [1678–1679], fable 17*

Andrew Marvell
1621–1678

9 The inglorious arts of peace.
Upon Cromwell's Return from Ireland [1650]

10 He[4] nothing common did or mean
Upon that memorable scene,
But with his keener eye
The axe's edge did try.
Ibid.

11 But bowed his comely head
Down as upon a bed.
Ibid.

12 So much one man can do,
That does both act and know.
Ibid.

13 Had we but world enough, and time,
This coyness, lady, were no crime.
To His Coy Mistress [1650–1652]

14   I would
Love you ten years before the Flood,
And you should, if you please, refuse
Till the conversion of the Jews.
My vegetable love should grow
Vaster than empires, and more slow.
Ibid.

15 But at my back I always hear
Time's winged chariot hurrying near;
And yonder all before us lie
Deserts of vast eternity.
Ibid.

16   Then worms shall try
That long preserved virginity,

And your quaint honor turn to dust,
And into ashes all my lust.
The grave's a fine and private place,
But none, I think, do there embrace.
Ibid.

17 Thus, though we cannot make our sun
Stand still, yet we will make him run.
Ibid.

18 Annihilating all that's made
To a green thought in a green shade.[5]
The Garden [1650–1652]

19 Casting the body's vest aside,
My soul into the boughs does glide.
Ibid.

20 The world in all doth but two nations bear—
The good, the bad; and these mixed everywhere.
The Loyal Scot [1650–1652]

21 My love is of a birth as rare
As 'tis for object strange and high;
It was begotten by despair
Upon impossibility.
The Definition of Love [1650–1652], st. 1

22 As lines, so loves oblique, may well
Themselves in every angle greet;
But ours, so truly parallel,
Though infinite, can never meet.
Ibid. st. 7

23 Where the remote Bermudas ride,
In th' ocean's bosom unespied.
Bermudas [1657]

24 Here hangs in shades the orange bright,
Like golden lamps in a green night.
Ibid.

25 And all the way, to guide their chime,
With falling oars they kept the time.[6]
Ibid.

Molière [Jean Baptiste Poquelin]
1622–1673

26   To pull the chestnuts out of the fire with the cat's paw.[7]   *L'Étourdi [1655], act III, sc. vi*

27   We die only once, and for such a long time!   *Le Dépit Amoureux [1656], act V, sc. iii*

28   I always make the first verse well, but I have trouble making the others.   *Les Précieuses Ridicules [1659], act I, sc. xi*

29   The world, dear Agnes, is a strange affair.   *L'École des Femmes [1662], act II, sc. vi*

30   There is no rampart that will hold out against malice.   *Tartuffe [1664], act I, sc. i*

---

[1]See *Ecclesiasticus 7:36, 31:18.*
[2]See Sophocles, 65:20, and Terence, 85:18.
[3]*Ventre affamé n'a point d'oreilles.*
See Cato the Elder, 85:3, and Adlai Stevenson, 706:12.
[4]King Charles I.

[5]The same phrase is in VIRGIL, *Eclogues, IX,* 20.
[6]See Thomas Moore, 391:8.
[7]*Tirer les marrons du feu avec la patte du chat. —Proverb in many languages*

1 Those whose conduct gives room for talk are always the first to attack their neighbors.   *Ibid.*

2 You are an ass in three letters, my son.[1]
                                                    Ibid.

3 She is laughing up her sleeve at you.
                                                    Ibid. vi

4 A woman always has her revenge ready.
                                                    Ibid. II, ii

5 Cover that bosom that I must not see: souls are wounded by such things.[2]   *Ibid. III, ii*

6 Although I am a pious man, I am not the less a man.   *Ibid. III, iii*

7 To create a public scandal is what's wicked; to sin in private is not a sin.   *Ibid. IV, v*

8 I saw him, I say, saw him with my own eyes.
                                                    Ibid. V, iii

9 We have changed all that.[3]
        Le Médecin Malgré Lui [1666], act II, sc. vi

10 On some preference esteem is based; to esteem everything is to esteem nothing.
        Le Misanthrope [1666], act I, sc. i

11 He's a wonderful talker, who has the art of telling you nothing in a great harangue.   *Ibid. II, v*

12 He makes his cook his merit, and the world visits his dinners and not him.   *Ibid.*

13 You see him laboring to produce *bons mots*.
                                                    Ibid.

14 The more we love our friends, the less we flatter them; it is by excusing nothing that pure love shows itself.   *Ibid.*

15 Doubts are more cruel than the worst of truths.
                                                    Ibid. III, vii

16 Anyone may be an honorable man, and yet write verse badly.   *Ibid. IV, i*

17 If everyone were clothed with integrity, if every heart were just, frank, kindly, the other virtues would be well-nigh useless, since their chief purpose is to make us bear with patience the injustice of our fellows.   *Ibid. V, i*

18 It is a wonderful seasoning of all enjoyments to think of those we love.   *Ibid. iv*

19 I prefer an accommodating vice to an obstinate virtue.   *Amphitryon [1666], act I, sc. iv*

20 One must eat to live, and not live to eat.[4]
                                                    Ibid. III, i

21 The true Amphitryon is the Amphitryon who gives dinners.[5]   *Ibid. v*

22 My Lord Jupiter knows how to sugarcoat the pill.   *Ibid. x*

23 You've asked for it, Georges Dandin, you've asked for it.[6]
        Georges Dandin [1668], act I, sc. ix

24 Good Heavens! For more than forty years I have been speaking prose without knowing it.
        Le Bourgeois Gentilhomme [1670], act II, sc. iv

25 All that is not prose is verse; and all that is not verse is prose.   *Ibid.*

26 My fair one, let us swear an eternal friendship.[7]
                                                    Ibid. IV, i

27 I will maintain it before the whole world.
                                                    Ibid. IV, v

28 What the devil was he doing in that galley?[8]
        Les Fourberies de Scapin [1671], act II, sc. xi

29 Grammar, which knows how to control even kings.[9]   *Les Femmes Savantes [1672], act II, sc. vi*

30 It is seasoned throughout with Attic salt.
                                                    Ibid. III, ii

31 A learned fool is more foolish than an ignorant one.   *Ibid. IV, iii*

32 Ah, there are no longer any children!
        Le Malade Imaginaire [1673], act II, sc. xi

33 Nearly all men die of their remedies, and not of their illnesses.   *Ibid. III, iii*

Algernon Sidney
1622–1683

34 This hand, unfriendly to tyrants,
   Seeks with the sword placid repose under liberty.[10]
        Life and Memoirs of Algernon Sidney

[1]Vous êtes un sot en trois lettres, mon fils.
[2]Couvrez ce sein que je ne saurais voir: / Par de pareils objets les âmes sont blessées.
[3]Nous avons changé tout cela.
[4]See Socrates, 70:23, and Franklin, 309:6.
[5]Le véritable Amphitryon est l'Amphitryon où l'on dine. See Dryden, 275:29.
[6]Vous l'avez voulu, Georges Dandin, vous l'avez voulu.
[7]Madam, I have been looking for a person who disliked gravy all my life; let us swear eternal friendship.—SYDNEY SMITH, *Lady Holland's Memoir*, [1855], *vol. I, ch. 9*
[8]Que diable allait-il faire dans cette galère?
    Que diable aller faire aussi dans la galère d'un Turc? d'un Turc! [What the deuce did he want on board a Turk's galley? A Turk!]—CYRANO DE BERGERAC [1619–1655], *Le Pédant Joué* [1654], *act II, sc. iv*
    The saying of Molière came into his head: "But what the devil was he doing in that galley?" and he laughed at himself.—TOLSTOI, *War and Peace* [1865–1872], *bk. IV, ch. 6*
[9]SIGISMUND [1368–1437], Holy Roman emperor, at the Council of Constance [1414] said to a prelate who had objected to His Majesty's grammar: Ego sum rex Romanus, et supra grammaticam [I am the Roman king, and am above grammar].
[10]Manus haec, inimica tyrannis, / Ense petit placidam sub libertate quietem.
    The second line is the motto of the Commonwealth of Massachusetts: By the sword we seek peace, but peace only under liberty.

1   It is not necessary to light a candle to the sun.[1]
     Discourses on Government [1698], ch. 2, sec. 23

Henry Vaughan
1622–1695

2   Dear Night! this world's defeat;
     The stop to busy fools; care's check and curb;
     The day of spirits; my soul's calm retreat
         Which none disturb!
     Christ's progress, and His prayer-time;
     The hours to which high Heaven doth chime.
         Silex Scintillans, pt. I [1650]. The Night, l. 25

3   There is in God, some say,
     A deep but dazzling darkness.
         Ibid. l. 49

4   Happy those early days, when I
     Shin'd in my angel-infancy!
     Before I understood this place
     Appointed for my second race.
         Ibid. The Retreat, l. 1

5   But felt through all this fleshly dress
     Bright shoots of everlastingness.
         Ibid. l. 19

6   Some men a forward motion love,
     But I by backward steps would move.
         Ibid. l. 29

7   I saw Eternity the other night
     Like a great ring of pure and endless light.
         All calm, as it was bright;
     And round beneath it, Time in hours, days, years,
         Driv'n by the spheres
     Like a vast shadow mov'd; in which the world
     And all her train were hurl'd.
         Ibid. The World

8   My soul, there is a country
     Far beyond the stars
     Where stands a winged sentry
     All skillful in the wars:
     There, above noise and danger,
     Sweet Peace is crown'd with smiles,
     And One born in a manger
     Commands the beauteous files.
         Ibid. Peace, st. 1

9   They are all gone into the world of light!
     And I alone sit lingering here;
     Their very memory is fair and bright,
     And my sad thoughts doth clear.
         *Silex Scintillans, pt. II [1655]. They Are All
         Gone, st. 1*

10   I see them walking in an air of glory
     Whose light doth trample on my days,
     My days, which are at best but dull and hoary,
     Mere glimmering and decays.
         Ibid. st. 3

[1]See Robert Burton, 235:14.

11   Dear, beauteous death, the jewel of the just!
     Shining nowhere but in the dark;
     What mysteries do lie beyond thy dust,
     Could man outlook that mark!
         Ibid. st. 5

12   I cannot reach it, and my striving eye
     Dazzles at it, as at eternity.
         Ibid. Childhood

Blaise Pascal
1623–1662

13   Things are always at their best in their beginning.
         Lettres Provinciales [1656–1657], no. 4

14   I have made this letter longer than usual, because
     I lack the time to make it short.[2]   *Ibid. 16*

15   True eloquence takes no heed of eloquence, true
     morality takes no heed of morality.
         Pensées [1670], no. 4

16   Do you wish people to think well of you? Don't
     speak well of yourself.   *Ibid. 44*

17   Physical science will not console me for the igno-
     rance of morality in the time of affliction.
         Ibid. 67

18   What is man in nature? Nothing in relation to the
     infinite, everything in relation to nothing, a mean
     between nothing and everything.[3]   *Ibid. 72*

19   I lay it down as a fact that if all men knew what
     others say of them, there would not be four friends
     in the world.   *Ibid. 101*

20   The state of man: inconstancy, boredom, anxi-
     ety.[4]   *Ibid. 127*

21   I have discovered that all human evil comes from
     this, man's being unable to sit still in a room.
         Ibid. 139

22   Cleopatra's nose, had it been shorter, the whole
     face of the world would have been changed.
         Ibid. 162

23   The eternal silence of these infinite spaces terrifies
     me.[5]   *Ibid. 206*

24   We shall die alone.[6]   *Ibid. 211*

25   The heart has its reasons which reason knows
     nothing of.[7]   *Ibid. 277*

[2]Je n'ai fait celle-ci plus longue parceque je n'ai pas eu le
loisir de la faire plus courte.
     Not that the story need be long, but it will take a long while
to make it short. —THOREAU, *Letter to Mr. B* [November 16,
1857]
     See Woodrow Wilson, 572:15.
[3]Qu'est-ce que l'homme dans la nature? Un néant à l'égard
de l'infini, un tout à l'égard du néant, un milieu entre rien et
tout.
[4]Condition de l'homme: inconstance, ennui, inquiétude.
See Bossuet, 272:1.
[5]Le silence éternel de ces espaces infinis m'effraie.
[6]On mourra seul.
[7]Le coeur a ses raisons que la raison ne connaît point.

1   We know the truth, not only by the reason, but by the heart.   *Ibid. 282*

2   Justice without strength is helpless, strength without justice is tyrannical. . . . Unable to make what is just strong, we have made what is strong just.   *Ibid. 298*

3   Man is but a reed, the weakest in nature, but he is a thinking reed.[1]   *Ibid. 347*

4   Man is neither angel nor beast; and the misfortune is that he who would act the angel acts the beast.[2]   *Ibid. 358*

5   Evil is easy, and has infinite forms.   *Ibid. 408*

6   To ridicule philosophy is really to philosophize.[3]   *Ibid. 430*

7   What a chimera then is man! What a novelty! What a monster, what a chaos, what a contradiction, what a prodigy! Judge of all things, feeble earthworm, depository of truth, a sink of uncertainty and error, the glory and the shame of the universe.[4]   *Ibid. 434*

8   Self is hateful.[5]   *Ibid. 455*

9   Men blaspheme what they do not know.   *Ibid. 556*

10   Men never do evil so completely and cheerfully as when they do it from religious conviction.   *Ibid. 894*

11   "The God of Abraham, the God of Isaac, the God of Jacob," not of philosophers and scholars.   *Writing found in Pascal's effects after his death*

George Fox[6]
1624–1691

12   The Lord showed me, so that I did see clearly, that he did not dwell in these temples which men had commanded and set up, but in people's hearts . . . his people were his temple, and he dwelt in them.[7]   *Journal [1694]*

13   When the Lord sent me forth into the world, He forbade me to put off my hat to any, high or low.   *Ibid.*

14   [It was] Justice Bennet of Derby, who was the first that called us Quakers, because we bid them tremble at the word of the Lord. This was in the year 1650.   *Ibid.*

[1]L'homme n'est qu'un roseau, le plus faible de la nature, mais c'est un roseau pensant.
[2]L'homme n'est ni ange ni bête; et le malheur veut que qui veut faire l'ange fait la bête.
[3]Se moquer de la philosophie, c'est vraiment philosopher.
[4]See Pope, 301:13.
[5]Le moi est haïssable.
[6]Founder of the Society of Friends (Quakers).
[7]See I Corinthians 3:17, 42:34.

15   He [Oliver Cromwell] said: "I see there is a people risen and come up that I cannot win either with gifts, honors, offices or places; but all other sects and people I can."   *Ibid.*

Thomas Sydenham
1624–1689

16   Fever itself is Nature's instrument.   *Quoted in Bulletin of the New York Academy of Medicine, vol. IV [1928], p. 922*

17   Gout, unlike any other disease, kills more rich men than poor, more wise men than simple.   *Ibid. 993*

18   A man is as old as his arteries.   *Ibid.*

John Aubrey
1626–1697

19   I have heard him [William Harvey] say, that after his book of the circulation of the blood came out, that he fell mightily in his practice, and that 'twas believed by the vulgar that he was crack-brained; and all the physicians were against his opinion.   *Brief Lives [1690]. William Harvey*

20   He [Thomas Hobbes] had read much, if one considers his long life; but his contemplation was more than his reading. He was wont to say that if he had read as much as other men, he should have known no more than other men.   *Ibid. Thomas Hobbes*

21   He [John Milton] was so fair that they called him *the Lady of Christ's College.*   *Ibid. John Milton*

22   Mr. William Shakespeare was born at Stratford upon Avon in the County of Warwick. His father was a butcher, and I have been told heretofore by some of the neighbors, that when he was a boy he exercised his father's trade, but when he killed a calf he would do it in a high style and make a speech.   *Ibid. William Shakespeare*

Marie de Rabutin-Chantal, Marquise de Sévigné
1626–1696

23   True friendship is never serene.   *Lettres. À Madame de Grignan [September 10, 1671]*

24   Racine will go out of style like coffee.   *Attributed*

Jacques Bénigne Bossuet
1627–1704

25   The greatest weakness of all weaknesses is to fear too much to appear weak.   *Politique Tirée de l'Écriture Sainte*

1   The inexorable boredom that is at the core of life.[1]   *From M. A. COUTURIER, Se Garder Libre*

Robert Boyle
1627–1691

2   I am not ambitious to appear a man of letters: I could be content the world should think I had scarce looked upon any other book than that of nature.
The Philosophical Works of Robert Boyle [1738], vol. I, preliminary discourse

John Ray
1627–1705

3   In a calm sea every man is a pilot.
English Proverbs [1670]

4   If wishes were horses, beggars might ride.
Ibid.

5   Money begets money.   *Ibid.*

6   Blood is thicker than water.[2]   *Ibid.*

7   Misery loves company.[3]   *Ibid.*

8   To go like a cat upon a hot bakestone.[4]
Ibid.

John Bunyan
1628–1688

9   Some said, "John, print it"; others said, "Not so."
   Some said, "It might do good"; others said, "No."
The Pilgrim's Progress [1678]. Apology for His Book

10   As I walked through the wilderness of this world.
Ibid. pt. I

11   I saw a man clothed with rags . . . a book in his hand, and a great burden upon his back.   *Ibid.*

12   The name of the one was Obstinate and the name of the other Pliable.   *Ibid.*

13   The name of the slough was Despond.   *Ibid.*

14   Every fat [vat] must stand upon his bottom.[5]
Ibid.

15   The gentleman's name was Mr. Worldly-Wise-Man.   *Ibid.*

16   A very stately palace before him, the name of which was Beautiful.   *Ibid.*

17   The valley of Humiliation.   *Ibid.*

18   A foul Fiend coming over the field to meet him; his name is Apollyon.   *Ibid.*

19   I will talk of things heavenly, or things earthly; things moral, or things evangelical; things sacred, or things profane; things past, or things to come; things foreign, or things at home; things more essential, or things circumstantial.   *Ibid.*

20   It beareth the name of Vanity Fair, because the town where 'tis kept is lighter than vanity.
Ibid.

21   Hanging is too good for him, said Mr. Cruelty.
Ibid.

22   My great-grandfather was but a water-man, looking one way, and rowing another.[6]   *Ibid.*

23   A castle called Doubting Castle, the owner whereof was Giant Despair.   *Ibid.*

24   They came to the Delectable Mountains.
Ibid.

25   A great horror and darkness fell upon Christian.
Ibid.

26   So I awoke, and behold it was a dream.
Ibid.

27   A man that could look no way but downwards with a muckrake in his hand.[7]   *Ibid. pt. II*

28   He that is down, needs fear no fall,
   He that is low, no pride.[8]
Ibid. Shepherd Boy's Song

29   Who would true valor see,
   Let him come hither;
   One here will constant be,
   Come wind, come weather.[9]
   There's no discouragement
   Shall make him once relent
   His first avow'd intent
      To be a pilgrim.

Ibid.

30   My sword I give to him that shall succeed me in my pilgrimage, and my courage and skill to him that can get it. My marks and scars I carry with me, to be a witness for me, that I have fought His battles who now will be my rewarder.   *Ibid.*

31   So he passed over, and all the trumpets sounded for him on the other side.   *Ibid.*

32   The captain of all these men of death that came against him to take him away, was the Consumption, for it was that that brought him down to the grave.
The Life and Death of Mr. Badman [1680]

---

[1]See Pascal, 270:20.
[2]See W. S. Gilbert, 530:16.
[3]See Publilius Syrus, 100:21.
[4]*Cat on a Hot Tin Roof*—TENNESSEE WILLIAMS, *title of play* [1955]
[5]Every tub must stand upon its bottom.—CHARLES MACKLIN, *The Man of the World* [1781], act I, sc. ii
   See Montaigne, 147:7.
[6]See Plutarch, 107:15.
[7]See Theodore Roosevelt, 576:4.
[8]See Samuel Butler [1612–1680], 263:15.
[9]He who would valiant be / 'Gainst all disaster, / Let him in constancy / Follow the Master.—*Alternate version, as a hymn* [1906]

Sir William Temple
1628–1699

1   Books, like proverbs, receive their chief value from the stamp and esteem of ages through which they have passed.
> *Miscellanea, pt. II [1690]. Ancient and Modern Learning*

2   When all is done, human life is, at the greatest and the best, but like a froward child, that must be played with and humored a little to keep it quiet till it falls asleep, and then the care is over.
> *Ibid. Of Poetry*

George Villiers, Duke of Buckingham
1628–1687

3   Ay, now the plot thickens very much upon us.
> *The Rehearsal [written 1663, performed 1671], act III, sc. ii*

Charles II
1630–1685

4   This is very true: for my words are my own, and my actions are my ministers'.
> *Reply to John Wilmot, Earl of Rochester* [1]

5   Let not poor Nelly starve.
> *On his deathbed. From GILBERT BURNET, The History of My Own Times [1724–1734], vol. I, bk. 2, ch. 17*

6   He had been, he said, an unconscionable time dying; he hoped that they would excuse it.
> *From MACAULAY, History of England [1849], vol. I, ch. 4*

John Tillotson
1630–1694

7   If God were not a necessary Being of Himself, He might almost seem to be made for the use and benefit of men.[2]
> *Sermon*

8   They who are in highest places, and have the most power, have the least liberty, because they are most observed.
> *Reflections*

Richard Cumberland
1631–1718

9   It is better to wear out than to rust out.
> *From BISHOP GEORGE HORNE [1730–1792], Sermon on the Duty of Contending for the Truth*

[1]See Rochester, 283:21.
[2]See Ovid, 101:14, and Voltaire, 306:25.

John Dryden
1631–1700

10 By viewing Nature, Nature's handmaid Art,
Makes mighty things from small beginnings grow.[3]
> *Annus Mirabilis [1667], st. 155*

11 He [Shakespeare] was the man who of all modern, and perhaps ancient poets, had the largest and most comprehensive soul.
> *Essay of Dramatic Poesy [1668]*

12 He was naturally learned; he needed not the spectacles of books to read Nature; he looked inwards, and found her there.
> *Ibid.*

13 Pains of love be sweeter far
Than all other pleasures are.
> *Tyrannic Love [1669], act IV, sc. i*

14 I am as free as Nature first made man,
Ere the base laws of servitude began,
When wild in woods the noble savage ran.
> *The Conquest of Granada [1669–1670], pt. I, act I, sc. i*

15 Death in itself is nothing; but we fear
To be we know not what, we know not where.
> *Aureng-Zebe [1676], act IV, sc. i*

16 When I consider life, 'tis all a cheat;
Yet, fool'd with hope, men favor the deceit;
Trust on, and think tomorrow will repay.
Tomorrow's falser than the former day.
> *Ibid.*

17 The wretched have no friends.
> *All for Love [1678], act III, sc. i*

18 Your Cleopatra; Dolabella's Cleopatra; every man's Cleopatra.
> *Ibid. IV, i*

19 With how much ease believe we what we wish![4]
Whatever is, is in its causes just.
> *Oedipus [1679] (with NATHANIEL LEE), act III, sc. i*

20   His hair just grizzled,
As in a green old age.[5]
> *Ibid.*

21 Of no distemper, of no blast he died,
But fell like autumn fruit that mellow'd long—
Even wondered at, because he dropp'd no sooner.
Fate seem'd to wind him up for fourscore years,
Yet freshly ran he on ten winters more;
Till like a clock worn out with eating time,
The wheels of weary life at last stood still.
> *Ibid. IV, i*

[3]See William Bradford, 240:12.
[4]See Demosthenes, 79:3, and Julius Caesar, 88:17.
[5]*A green old age, unconscious of decays.*—POPE, *Translation of the Iliad [1715], bk. XXIII, l. 929*

1 In pious times, ere priestcraft did begin,
Before polygamy was made a sin.
Absalom and Achitophel, pt. I [1680], l. 1

2 Whate'er he did was done with so much ease,
In him alone, 'twas natural to please.
Ibid. l. 27

3 Of these the false Achitophel was first,
A name to all succeeding ages curs'd.
For close designs and crooked counsels fit,
Sagacious, bold, and turbulent of wit,
Restless, unfix'd in principles and place,
In power unpleas'd, impatient of disgrace;
A fiery soul, which working out its way,
Fretted the pygmy-body to decay:[1]
And o'er-inform'd the tenement of clay.
A daring pilot in extremity;
Pleased with the danger, when the waves went
    high
He sought the storms; but for a calm unfit,
Would steer too nigh the sands to boast his wit.
Great wits are sure to madness near allied,
And thin partitions do their bounds divide.[2]
Ibid. l. 150

4 Bankrupt of life, yet prodigal of ease.
Ibid. l. 168

5 And all to leave what with his toil he won
To that unfeather'd two-legg'd thing,[3] a son.
Ibid. l. 169

6 In friendship false, implacable in hate,
Resolved to ruin or to rule the state.
Ibid. l. 173

7 His courage foes, his friends his truth proclaim.
Ibid. l. 357

8 All empire is no more than power in trust.
Ibid. l. 411

9 Better one suffer, than a nation grieve.
Ibid. l. 416

10 Who think too little, and who talk too much.[4]
Ibid. l. 534

11 A man so various that he seem'd to be
Not one, but all mankind's epitome:
Stiff in opinions, always in the wrong;
Was everything by starts, and nothing long:
But, in the course of one revolving moon,
Was chemist, fiddler, statesman, and buffoon.[5]
Ibid. l. 545

12 So over violent, or over civil,
That every man with him was God or Devil.
Ibid. l. 557

13 His tribe were God Almighty's gentlemen.
Ibid. l. 645

14 Nor is the people's judgment always true:
The most may err as grossly as the few.
Ibid. l. 781

15 Of ancient race by birth, but nobler yet
In his own worth.
Ibid. l. 900

16 Beware the fury of a patient man.
Ibid. l. 1005

17 Made still a blund'ring kind of melody;
Spurr'd boldly on, and dash'd through thick and
    thin,
Through sense and nonsense, never out nor in.
Free from all meaning, whether good or bad,
And in one word, heroically mad.
Ibid. pt. II [1682],[6] *l.* 413

18 For every inch that is not fool is rogue.
Ibid. l. 463

19   There is a pleasure sure
In being mad which none but madmen know.[7]
The Spanish Friar [1681], act II, sc. i

20 And, dying, bless the hand that gave the blow.[8]
Ibid.

21   He's a sure card.   *Ibid. iii*

22   They say everything in the world is good for
something.   *Ibid. III, ii*

23   Dead men tell no tales.[9]   *Ibid. IV, ii*

24 Or break the eternal Sabbath of his rest.
Ibid. V, ii

25 All human things are subject to decay,
And, when fate summons, monarchs must obey.
Mac Flecknoe [1682], l. 1

26 The rest to some faint meaning make pretense,
But Shadwell[10] never deviates into sense.
Some beams of wit on other souls may fall,
Strike through and make a lucid interval;
But Shadwell's genuine night admits no ray,
His rising fogs prevail upon the day.
Ibid. l. 19

27 And torture one poor word ten thousand ways.
Ibid. l. 208

28   Wit will shine
Through the harsh cadence of a rugged line.
To the Memory of Mr. Oldham [1684], l. 15

29 Happy the man, and happy he alone,
He who can call today his own;

---

[1]See Thomas Fuller, 250:9.

[2]Remembrance and reflection how allied! / What thin partitions sense from thought divide! —POPE, *An Essay on Man* [1733–1734], *epistle I, l.* 225

    See Seneca, 103:7.

[3]See Diogenes the Cynic, 77:3.

[4]See Jonson, 233:*n*1.

[5]See Juvenal, 108:21.

[6]In collaboration with NAHUM TATE. See 284.

[7]There is a pleasure in poetic pains / Which only poets know. —COWPER, *The Task* [1785], II, *The Timepiece, l.* 285

[8]Adore the hand that gives the blow. —POMFRET, *Verses to His Friend*

[9]Cited in the play text as a proverb.

[10]See Shadwell, 282.

He who, secure within, can say,
Tomorrow, do thy worst, for I have liv'd today.[1]
Imitation of Horace, bk. III, ode 29 [1685], l. 65

1 Not heaven itself upon the past has power;
But what has been, has been, and I have had my
hour.
Ibid. l. 71

2 I can enjoy her [Fortune] while she's kind;
But when she dances in the wind,
And shakes the wings and will not stay,
I puff the prostitute away.
Ibid. l. 81

3 And virtue, though in rags, will keep me warm.
Ibid. l. 87

4 Since heaven's eternal year is thine.
*To the Pious Memory of Mrs. Anne Killegrew
[1686], l. 15*

5 O gracious God! how far have we
Profaned thy heavenly gift of poesy!
Ibid. l. 56

6 Her wit was more than man, her innocence a
child.[2]
Ibid. l. 70

7 Then cold, and hot, and moist, and dry,[3]
In order to their stations leap,
And Music's power obey.
From harmony, from heavenly harmony,
This universal frame began:
From harmony to harmony
Through all the compass of the notes it ran,
The diapason closing full in Man.
A Song for Saint Cecilia's Day [1687], st. 1

8 What passion cannot Music raise and quell?
Ibid. st. 2

9 The trumpet's loud clangor
Excites us to arms.
Ibid. st. 3

10 The soft complaining flute,
In dying notes, discovers
The woes of hopeless lovers.
Ibid. st. 4

11 The trumpet shall be heard on high
The dead shall live, the living die,
And Music shall untune the sky!
Ibid. Grand Chorus

12 She fear'd no danger, for she knew no sin.
The Hind and the Panther [1687], pt. I, l. 4

13 For truth has such a face and such a mien
As to be lov'd needs only to be seen.[4]
Ibid. l. 33

14 Of all the tyrannies on human kind
The worst is that which persecutes the mind.
Ibid. l. 239

15 Reason to rule, mercy to forgive:
The first is law, the last prerogative.
Ibid. l. 261

16 And kind as kings upon their coronation day.
Ibid. l. 271

17 All have not the gift of martyrdom.
Ibid. II, l. 59

18 War seldom enters but where wealth allures.
Ibid. l. 706

19 Much malice mingled with a little wit.
Ibid. III, l. 1

20 Jealousy, the jaundice of the soul.
Ibid. l. 73

21 For present joys are more to flesh and blood
Than a dull prospect of a distant good.
Ibid. l. 364

22 T' abhor the makers, and their laws approve,
Is to hate traitors and the treason love.[5]
Ibid. l. 706

23 Secret guilt by silence is betrayed.
Ibid. l. 763

24 Possess your soul with patience.[6]
Ibid. l. 839

25 Three poets, in three distant ages born,
Greece, Italy, and England did adorn.
The first in loftiness of thought surpass'd;
The next, in majesty; in both the last.
The force of Nature could no further go.
To make a third, she joined the former two.
Under Mr. Milton's Picture [1688]

26 This is the porcelain clay of humankind.[7]
Don Sebastian [1690], act I, sc. i

27 A knockdown argument: 'tis but a word and a
blow. *Amphitryon [1690], act I, sc. i*

28 Whistling to keep myself from being afraid.[8]
Ibid. III, iii, i

29 I am the true Amphitryon.[9] *Ibid. V, i*

30 Fairest Isle, all isles excelling,
Seat of pleasures, and of loves;
Venus here will choose her dwelling,
And forsake her Cyprian groves.
King Arthur [1691], act II, sc. v, Song of Venus

---

[1] See Horace, 96:24, and Sydney Smith, 380:18.
[2] See Pope, 300:28.
[3] See Milton, 257:19.
[4] See Pope, 301:14.

[5] See Julius Caesar, 88:18.
[6] See Luke 21:19, 39:13.
[7] The precious porcelain of human clay. — BYRON, *Don Juan*
[1818–1824], canto IV, st. 11
[8] Whistling aloud to bear his courage up. — ROBERT BLAIR
[1699–1746], *The Grave* [1743], l. 58
[9] See Molière, 269:21.

1 Theirs was the giant race, before the flood.[1]
> *Epistle to Congreve [1693], l. 5*

2 Genius must be born, and never can be taught.
> *Ibid. l. 60*

3 Be kind to my remains; and oh defend,
Against your judgment, your departed friend!
> *Ibid. l. 72*

4 Look round the habitable world: how few
Know their own good, or knowing it, pursue.
> *Juvenal, Satire X [1693]*

5 Arms, and the man I sing,[2] who, forced by fate,
And haughty Juno's unrelenting hate.
> *Virgil, Aeneid [1697], bk. I, l. 1*

6 None but the brave deserves the fair.
> *Alexander's Feast [1697], l. 15*

7   With ravish'd ears
The monarch hears;
Assumes the god,
Affects to nod,
And seems to shake the spheres.
> *Ibid. l. 37*

8 Sound the trumpets; beat the drums . . .
Now give the hautboys breath; he comes, he
comes.[3]
> *Ibid. l. 50*

9 Bacchus, ever fair and ever young.
> *Ibid. l. 54*

10   Rich the treasure,
Sweet the pleasure—
Sweet is pleasure after pain.
> *Ibid. l. 58*

11   The king grew vain;
Fought all his battles o'er again;
And thrice he routed all his foes, and thrice he
slew the slain.
> *Ibid. l. 66*

12 Fallen, fallen, fallen, fallen,
Fallen from his high estate,
And welt'ring in his blood;
Deserted, at his utmost need,
By those his former bounty fed,
On the bare earth expos'd he lies,
With not a friend to close his eyes.
> *Ibid. l. 77*

13 Sigh'd and look'd, and sigh'd again.
> *Ibid. l. 120*

14 And, like another Helen, fir'd another Troy.
> *Ibid. l. 154*

15 Could swell the soul to rage, or kindle soft desire.
> *Ibid. l. 160*

16 He rais'd a mortal to the skies,
She drew an angel down.
> *Ibid. l. 169*

17 Words, once my stock, are wanting to
commend
So great a poet and so good a friend.
> *To My Friend Mr. Motteux [1698], l. 54*

18 Lord of yourself, uncumber'd with a wife.
> *Epistle to John Driden of Chesterton [1700],
l. 18*

19 Better to hunt in fields, for health unbought,
Than fee the doctor for a nauseous draught.
The wise, for cure, on exercise depend;
God never made his work for man to mend.
> *Ibid. l. 92*

20 A very merry, dancing, drinking,
Laughing, quaffing, and unthinking time.
> *The Secular Masque [1700], l. 39*

21 The sword within the scabbard keep,
And let mankind agree.
> *Ibid. l. 69*

22 All, all of a piece throughout:
Thy chase had a beast in view;
Thy wars brought nothing about;
Thy lovers were all untrue.
'Tis well an old age is out,
And time to begin a new.
> *Ibid. l. 96*

23 Ill habits gather by unseen degrees—
As brooks make rivers, rivers run to seas.
> *Ovid, Metamorphoses [1700], bk. XV, The
Worship of Aesculapius, l. 155*

24   [Of Chaucer's *Canterbury Tales:*] Here is God's
plenty.
> *Fables Ancient and Modern [1700], preface*

25 For Art may err, but Nature cannot miss.
> *Ibid. The Cock and the Fox, l. 452*

26 Old as I am, for ladies' love unfit,
The power of beauty I remember yet.
> *Ibid. Cymon and Iphigenia, l. 1*

27 He trudg'd along unknowing what he sought,
And whistled as he went, for want of thought.
> *Ibid. l. 84*

28 She hugg'd the offender, and forgave the offense:
Sex to the last.[4]
> *Ibid. l. 367*

29 Of seeming arms to make a short essay,
Then hasten to be drunk—the business of the
day.
> *Ibid. l. 407*

---

[1] See *Genesis* 6:4, 7:15.
[2] See Virgil, 93:10.
[3] See Morell, 308:23.

[4] And love the offender, yet detest the offense. —POPE, *Eloisa to Abelard* [1717], l. 192

1 He was exhal'd; his great Creator drew
His spirit, as the sun the morning dew.[1]
> *On the Death of a Very Young Gentleman*
> *[1700]*

2 Here lies my wife: here let her lie!
Now she's at rest, and so am I.
> *Epitaph intended for his wife*

William Stoughton
1631–1701

3 God hath sifted a nation that he might send choice grain into this wilderness.[2]
> *Election sermon at Boston [April 29, 1669]*

Anton van Leeuwenhoek
1632–1723

4 We cannot in any better manner glorify the Lord and Creator of the universe than that in all things, how small soever they appear to our naked eyes, but which have yet received the gift of life and power of increase, we contemplate the display of his omnificence and perfections with the utmost admiration.
> *The Select Works of Anthony van Leeuwenhoek*
> *[1798]*[3]

John Locke
1632–1704

5 New opinions are always suspected, and usually opposed, without any other reason but because they are not already common.
> *Essay Concerning Human Understanding [1690],*
> *dedicatory epistle*

6 No man's knowledge here can go beyond his experience.   *Ibid. bk. II, ch. 1, sec. 19*

7 It is one thing to show a man that he is in an error, and another to put him in possession of truth.
> *Ibid. IV, 7, 11*

8 All men are liable to error; and most men are, in many points, by passion or interest, under temptation to it.   *Ibid. 20, 17*

9 Wherever Law ends, Tyranny begins.[4]
> *Second Treatise of Government [1690], sec. 202*

10 A sound mind in a sound body,[5] is a short but full description of a happy state in this world.
> *Some Thoughts Concerning Education [1693],*
> *sec. 1*

11 Good and evil, reward and punishment, are the only motives to a rational creature: these are the spur and reins whereby all mankind are set on work, and guided.[6]   *Ibid. 54*

12 He that will have his son have a respect for him and his orders, must himself have a great reverence for his son.[7]   *Ibid. 65*

13 Virtue is harder to be got than a knowledge of the world; and, if lost in a young man, is seldom recovered.   *Ibid. 70*

14 The only fence against the world is a thorough knowledge of it.   *Ibid. 88*

Benedict [Baruch] Spinoza[8]
1632–1677

15 Peace is not an absence of war, it is a virtue, a state of mind, a disposition for benevolence, confidence, justice.
> *Theological-Political Treatise [1670]*

16 Nature abhors a vacuum.
> *Ethics [1677],*[9] *pt. I, proposition 15: note*

17 God and all the attributes of God are eternal.
> *Ibid. 19*

18 Nothing exists from whose nature some effect does not follow.   *Ibid. 36*

19 He who would distinguish the true from the false must have an adequate idea of what is true and false.
> *Ibid. II, 42: proof*

20 Will and Intellect are one and the same thing.
> *Ibid. 49: corollary*

21 He that can carp in the most eloquent or acute manner at the weakness of the human mind is held by his fellows as almost divine.
> *Ibid. III: preface*

22 Surely human affairs would be far happier if the power in men to be silent were the same as that to speak. But experience more than sufficiently teaches

---

[6]By education, then, I mean goodness in the form in which it is first acquired by a child . . . the rightly disciplined state of pleasures and pains whereby a man from his first beginnings on will abhor what he should abhor and relish what he should relish.—PLATO, *Laws, bk. II*

In educating the young we use pleasure and pain as rudders to steer their course.—ARISTOTLE, *Nichomachean Ethics, bk. X*

[7]See Juvenal, 109:11.

[8]Ein Gottbetrunkener Mensch [A God-intoxicated man]. —NOVALIS (FRIEDRICH VON HARDENBERG)

The Lord blot out his name under heaven. The Lord set him apart for destruction from all the tribes of Israel, with all the curses of the firmament which are written in the Book of the Law. . . . There shall no man speak to him, no man write to him, no man show him any kindness, no man stay under the same roof with him, no man come nigh him.—*Amsterdam synagogue's curse on Spinoza [1656]*

[9]Everyman edition, translated by ANDREW BOYLE.

---

[1]Early, bright, transient, chaste as morning dew, / She sparkled, was exhaled, and went to heaven.—EDWARD YOUNG, *Night Thoughts [1742–1745], Night V, l. 600*

[2]God had sifted three kingdoms to find the wheat for this planting.—LONGFELLOW, *The Courtship of Miles Standish [1858], IV*

[3]Translated by SAMUEL HOOLE.

[4]See William Pitt, 313:2.

[5]See Juvenal, 109:9.

that men govern nothing with more difficulty than their tongues.   *Ethics, pt. III, proposition 2: note*

1   Pride is therefore pleasure arising from a man's thinking too highly of himself.   *Ibid. 26: note*

2   It may easily come to pass that a vain man may become proud and imagine himself pleasing to all when he is in reality a universal nuisance.
        Ibid. 30: note

3   Self-complacency is pleasure accompanied by the idea of oneself as cause.   *Ibid. 51: note*

4   It therefore comes to pass that everyone is fond of relating his own exploits and displaying the strength both of his body and his mind, and that men are on this account a nuisance one to the other.
        Ibid. 54: note

5   I refer those actions which work out the good of the agent to courage, and those which work out the good of others to nobility. Therefore temperance, sobriety, and presence of mind in danger, etc., are species of courage; but modesty, clemency, etc., are species of nobility.   *Ibid. 59: note*

6   Fear cannot be without hope nor hope without fear.   *Ibid. definition 13: explanation*

7   So long as a man imagines that he cannot do this or that, so long is he determined not to do it: and consequently, so long it is impossible to him that he should do it.   *Ibid. 28: explanation*

8   Those who are believed to be most abject and humble are usually most ambitious and envious.
        Ibid. proposition 29: explanation

9   One and the same thing can at the same time be good, bad, and indifferent, e.g., music is good to the melancholy, bad to those who mourn, and neither good nor bad to the deaf.   *Ibid. IV: preface*

10   Man is a social animal.[1]
        Ibid. proposition 35: note

11   Men will find that they can prepare with mutual aid far more easily what they need, and avoid far more easily the perils which beset them on all sides, by united forces.   *Ibid.*

12   Avarice, ambition, lust, etc., are nothing but species of madness.[2]   *Ibid. 44: note*

13   He whose honor depends on the opinion of the mob must day by day strive with the greatest anxiety, act and scheme in order to retain his reputation. For the mob is varied and inconstant, and therefore if a reputation is not carefully preserved it dies quickly.   *Ibid. 58: note*

14   In refusing benefits caution must be used lest we seem to despise or to refuse them for fear of having to repay them in kind.   *Ibid. 70: note*

[1]See Blackstone, 325:19.
[2]To me, avarice seems not so much a vice, as a deplorable piece of madness. — THOMAS BROWNE, *Religio Medici* [1643]

15   To give aid to every poor man is far beyond the reach and power of every man. . . . Care of the poor is incumbent on society as a whole.
        Ibid. appendix, 17

16   None are more taken in by flattery than the proud, who wish to be the first and are not.
        Ibid. 21

17   Those are most desirous of honor and glory who cry out the loudest of its abuse and the vanity of the world.   *Ibid. V, proposition 10: note*

18   We feel and know that we are eternal.
        Ibid. 23: note

19   All excellent things are as difficult as they are rare.   *Ibid. 42: note*

20   The things which . . . are esteemed as the greatest good of all . . . can be reduced to these three headings: to wit, Riches, Fame, and Pleasure. With these three the mind is so engrossed that it cannot scarcely think of any other good.
    Tractatus de Intellectus Emendatione [1677], I, 3

Sir Christopher Wren[3]
1632–1723

21   Si monumentum requiris circumspice [If you would see the man's monument, look around].
    Inscription in St. Paul's Cathedral, London. Written by Wren's son

Wentworth Dillon, Earl of Roscommon
c. 1633–1685

22 Choose an author as you choose a friend.
        Essay on Translated Verse [1684], l. 96

23 Immodest words admit of no defense,
For want of decency is want of sense.
        Ibid. l. 113

24 The multitude is always in the wrong.
        Ibid. l. 183

25 My God, my Father, and my Friend,
Do not forsake me in my end.
        Translation of Dies Irae[4]

Samuel Pepys
1633–1703

26   I pray God to keep me from being proud.
        Diary, March 22, 1660

27   This morning came home my fine camlet cloak, with gold buttons, and a silk suit, which cost me much money, and I pray God to make me able to pay for it.   *Ibid. July 1, 1660*

[3]See E. C. Bentley, 627:18.
[4]See Tommaso di Celano, 123:14.

1 And so to bed. *Ibid. July 22, 1660, passim*

2 I am unwilling to mix my fortune with him that is going down the wind.
Ibid. September 6, 1660

3 I went out to Charing Cross, to see Major-General Harrison hanged, drawn, and quartered; which was done there, he looking as cheerful as any man could do in that condition.
Ibid. October 13, 1660

4 A good honest and painful sermon.
Ibid. March 17, 1661

5 One, by his own confession to me, that can put on two several faces, and look his enemies in the face with as much love as his friends. But, good God! what an age is this, and what a world is this! that a man cannot live without playing the knave and dissimulation. *Ibid. September 1, 1661*

6 Though he be a fool, yet he keeps much company, and will tell all he sees or hears, and so a man may understand what the common talk of the town is. *Ibid. September 2, 1661*

7 My wife, poor wretch.
Ibid. September 18, 1661, passim

8 Thanks be to God, since my leaving drinking of wine, I do find myself much better, and do mind my business better, and do spend less money, and less time lost in idle company.
Ibid. January 26, 1662

9 As happy a man as any in the world, for the whole world seems to smile upon me.
Ibid. October 31, 1662

10 To the Trinity House, where a very good dinner among the old soakers. *Ibid. February 15, 1665*

11 But Lord! how everybody's looks, and discourse in the street, is of death, and nothing else; and few people going up and down, that the town is like a place distressed and forsaken.[1]
Ibid. August 30, 1665

12 Strange to see how a good dinner and feasting reconciles everybody. *Ibid. November 9, 1665*

13 Saw a wedding in the church . . . and strange to see what delight we married people have to see these poor fools decoyed into our condition.
Ibid. December 25, 1665

14 Musick and women I cannot but give way to, whatever my business is. *Ibid. March 9, 1666*

15 Home, and, being washing-day, dined upon cold meat. *Ibid. April 4, 1666*

16 Musick is the thing of the world that I love most.
Ibid. July 30, 1666

[1]The time of the Great Plague.

17 Did satisfy myself mighty fair in the truth of the saying that the world do not grow old at all, but is in as good condition in all respects as ever it was.
Ibid. February 3, 1667

18 This day I am, by the blessing of God, 34 years old, in very good health and mind's content, and in condition of estate much beyond whatever my friends could expect of a child of theirs, this day 34 years. The Lord's name be praised! and may I be ever thankful for it. *Ibid. February 23, 1667*

19 But it is pretty to see what money will do.
Ibid. March 21, 1667

20 To church; and with my mourning, very handsome, and new periwig, make a great show.
Ibid. March 31, 1667

21 But to think of the clatter they make with his coach, and his own fine clothes, and yet how meanly they live within doors, and nastily, and borrowing everything of neighbors. *Ibid. April 1, 1667*

22 Whose red nose makes me ashamed to be seen with him. *Ibid. May 3, 1667*

23 Gives me some kind of content to remember how painful it is sometimes to keep money, as well as to get it. *Ibid. October 11, 1667*

24 I find my wife hath something in her gizzard, that only waits an opportunity of being provoked to bring up; but I will not, for my content-sake, give it.
Ibid. June 17, 1668

25 In appearance, at least, he being on all occasions glad to be at friendship with me, though we hate one another, and know it on both sides.
Ibid. September 22, 1668

26 I do hate to be unquiet at home.
Ibid. January 21, 1669

27 And so I betake myself to that course, which is almost as much as to see myself go into my grave; for which, and all the discomforts that will accompany my being blind, the good God prepare me!
Ibid. May 31, 1669 (final entry)

George Savile, Marquess of Halifax
1633–1695

28 Children and fools want everything, because they want wit to distinguish; there is no stronger evidence of a crazy understanding than the making too large a catalogue of things necessary.
Advice to a Daughter [1688]

29 Popularity is a crime from the moment it is sought; it is only a virtue where men have it whether they will or no.
Political, Moral, and Miscellaneous Reflections [1750]

30 Misspending a man's time is a kind of self-homicide. *Ibid.*

1   Men are not hanged for stealing horses, but that horses may not be stolen.   *Reflections*

Robert South
1634–1716

2   Speech was given to the ordinary sort of men whereby to communicate their mind; but to wise men, whereby to conceal it.[1]   *Sermon [1676]*

Robert Hooke
1635–1703

3   The truth is, the science of Nature has been already too long made only a work of the brain and the fancy: It is now high time that it should return to the plainness and soundness of observations on material and obvious things.   *Micrographia [1665]*

Nicolas Boileau-Despréaux
1636–1711

4   Happy who in his verse can gently steer
From grave to light, from pleasant to severe.[2]
   The Art of Poetry [1674], canto I, l. 75

5   At last comes Malherbe[3] and, the first to do so in France, brings to his verse a smooth cadence.   *Ibid. l. 131*

6   Whate'er is well conceived is clearly said,
And the words to say it flow with ease.   *Ibid. l. 153*

7   Every age has its pleasures, its style of wit, and its own ways.   *Ibid. III, l. 374*

8   The wisest man is he who does not fancy that he is so at all.   *Satire 1, l. 46*

9   A Cat's a cat, and Rolet is a knave.   *Ibid. l. 52*

10   He [Molière] pleases all the world, but cannot please himself.   *Ibid. l. 94*

11   In spite of every sage whom Greece can show,
Unerring wisdom never dwelt below;
Folly in all of every age we see,
The only difference lies in the degree.   *Satire 4, l. 37*

12   Greatest fools are oft most satisfied.   *Ibid. l. 128*

13   If your descent is from heroic sires,
Show in your life a remnant of their fires.   *Satire 5, l. 43*

14   Of all the creatures that creep, swim, or fly,
Peopling the earth, the waters, and the sky,
From Rome to Iceland, Paris to Japan,
I really think the greatest fool is man.   *Satire 8, l. 1*

15   But satire, ever moral, ever new,
Delights the reader and instructs him, too.
She, if good sense refine her sterling page,
Oft shakes some rooted folly of the age.   *Satire 8, l. 257*

16   Honor is like an island, rugged and without a beach; once we have left it, we can never return.   *Satire 10, l. 167*

17   Now two punctilious envoys, Thine and Mine,
Embroil the earth about a fancied line;
And, dwelling much on right and much on wrong,
Prove how the right is chiefly with the strong.[4]   *Satire 11, l. 141*

18   Nothing but truth is lovely, nothing fair.   *Epistle 9*

19   The terrible burden of having nothing to do.   *Epistle 11*

Thomas Ken
1637–1711

20   Awake, my soul, and with the sun
Thy daily stage of duty run.   *Morning Hymn [1695]*

21   Praise God, from whom all blessings flow!
Praise Him, all creatures here below!
Praise Him above, ye heavenly host!
Praise Father, Son, and Holy Ghost!   *Doxology [1709]*

Thomas Traherne
c. 1637–1674

22   You never enjoy the world aright, till the sea itself floweth in your veins, till you are clothed with the heavens, and crowned with the stars: and perceive yourself to be the sole heir of the whole world.   *Centuries of Meditations [1908], Century I, sec. 29*

23   The corn was orient and immortal wheat, which never should be reaped, nor was ever sown. I thought it had stood from everlasting to everlasting.[5]   *Ibid. III, 3*

---

[1]Speech was made to open man to man, and not to hide him; to promote commerce, and not betray it.—DAVID LLOYD [1635–1692], *The Statesmen and Favorites of England Since the Reformation* [1665, edited by WHITWORTH], *vol. I, p. 503*
Men talk only to conceal the mind.—EDWARD YOUNG, *Love of Fame* [1725–1728], satire II, l. 208
The true use of speech is not so much to express our wants as to conceal them.—GOLDSMITH, *The Bee, no. 3* [October 20, 1759]
See Voltaire, 306:21.
[2]Translated by DRYDEN.
See Pope, 302:2.
[3]Enfin Malherbe vint.
[4]See Tacitus, 109:19; Bussy-Rabutin, 266:13; Frederick the Great, 318:20; and Gibbon, 340:6.
[5]See *Psalm 90:2*, 18:10.

1 How like an angel came I down!
> *Wonder [1910], st. 1*

2 I within did flow
With seas of life like wine.
> *Ibid. st. 3*

Louis XIV
1638–1715

3 I am the state.[1]
> *Attributed remark before the parliament in 1651*

4 Has God forgotten all I have done for him?[2]
> *Attributed remark upon hearing the news of the French defeat at Malplaquet [1709]*

5 I almost had to wait.[3]
> *Attributed remark when a coach he had ordered arrived just in time*

Jean Racine
1639–1699

6 I loved him too much not to hate him at all!
> *Andromaque [1667], act II*

7 You are Emperor, my lord, and yet you weep?
> *Bérénice [1670], act IV, sc. v*

8 My only hope lies in my despair.
> *Bajazet [1672], act I, sc. iv*

9 You have named him, not I.[4]
> *Phèdre [1677], act I, sc. iii*

10 It is no longer a passion hidden in my heart: it is Venus herself fastened to her prey.[5] *Ibid.*

11 Innocence has nothing to dread. *Ibid. III, vi*

12 Crime like virtue has its degrees; and timid innocence was never known to blossom suddenly into extreme license.[6] *Ibid. IV, ii*

13 To repair the irreparable ravages of time.
> *Athalie [1691], act II, sc. v*

Sir Charles Sedley
c. 1639–1701

14 Phyllis is my only joy,
Faithless as the winds or seas;
Sometimes coming, sometimes coy,
Yet she never fails to please.
> *Song [1702], st. 1*

---

¹L'état c'est moi.
See Napoleon, 370:11.
²Dieu a donc oublié tout ce que j'ai fait pour lui?
³J'ai failli attendre.
⁴C'est toi qui l'a nommé.
⁵Ce n'est plus une ardeur dans mes veines cachée: / C'est Vénus toute entière à sa proie attachée.
⁶See Juvenal, 108:20, and Beaumont and Fletcher, 238:15.

Aphra Behn
1640–1689

15 A brave world, sir, full of religion, knavery, and change: we shall shortly see better days.
> *The Roundheads [1677]*

16 Variety is the soul of pleasure.
> *The Rover, Part II [1680], act I*

17 Come away; poverty's catching. *Ibid.*

18 Money speaks sense in a language all nations understand. *Ibid. III, sc. i*

19 Beauty unadorned. *Ibid. IV, ii*

20 Faith, sir, we are here today, and gone tomorrow.
> *The Lucky Chance [1686–1687], act IV*

21 Oh, what a dear ravishing thing is the beginning of an Amour!
> *The Emperor of the Moon [1687], act I, sc. i*

Ihara Saikaku
1642–1693

22 Take care! Kingdoms are destroyed by bandits, houses by rats, and widows by suitors.
> *The Japanese Family Storehouse; or, The Millionaires' Gospel,[7] bk. I, ch. 5*

23 When you send a clerk on business to a distant province, a man of rigid morals is not your best choice. *Ibid. II, 5*

24 For each of the four hundred and four bodily ailments celebrated physicians have produced infallible remedies, but the malady which brings the greatest distress to mankind—to even the wisest and cleverest of us—is the plague of poverty.
> *Ibid. III, 1*

Sir Isaac Newton
1642–1727

25 If I have seen further (than you and Descartes) it is by standing upon the shoulders of Giants.[8]
> *Letter to Robert Hooke, February 5, 1675 / 1676*

26 I frame no hypotheses; for whatever is not deduced from the phenomena is to be called an hypothesis; and hypotheses, whether metaphysical or physical, whether of occult qualities or mechanical, have no place in experimental philosophy.
> *Ibid.*

27 Errors are not in the art but in the artificers.
> *Philosophiae Naturalis Principia Mathematica [1687],[9] preface*

---

⁷Edited and translated by G. W. SARGENT.
⁸See Robert Burton, 234:7.
For the history (and pseudo-history) of this celebrated aphorism see ROBERT K. MERTON, *On the Shoulders of Giants* [1965].
⁹*Mathematical Principles of Natural Philosophy* [1729], translated by ANDREW MOTTE.

1   Every body continues in its state of rest, or of uniform motion in a right line, unless it is compelled to change that state by forces impressed upon it.
Principia Mathematica. Laws of Motion, I

2   The change of motion is proportional to the motive force impressed; and is made in the direction of the right line in which that force is impressed.[1]
Ibid. II

3   To every action there is always opposed an equal reaction: or, the mutual actions of two bodies upon each other are always equal, and directed to contrary parts.
Ibid. III

4   God in the beginning formed matter in solid, massy, hard, impenetrable, movable particles, of such sizes and figures, and with such other properties, and in such proportion to space, as most conduced to the end for which he formed them.
Optics [1704]

5   I do not know what I may appear to the world; but to myself I seem to have been only like a boy playing on the seashore, and diverting myself in now and then finding a smoother pebble or a prettier shell than ordinary, whilst the great ocean of truth lay all undiscovered before me.
From BREWSTER, *Memoirs of Newton [1855], vol. II, ch. 27*

6   O Diamond! Diamond! thou little knowest the mischief done!
Said to a pet dog who knocked over a candle and set fire to his papers

Thomas Shadwell[2]
c. 1642–1692

7   And wit's the noblest frailty of the mind.
A True Widow [1679], act II, sc. i

8   The haste of a fool is the slowest thing in the world.
Ibid. III, i

9   I am, out of the ladies' company, like a fish out of the water.
Ibid.

10   Every man loves what he is good at.
Ibid. V, i

Matsuo Bashō
1644–1694

11   The months and days are the travelers of eternity. The years that come and go are also voyagers. . . . I too for years past have been stirred by the sight of a solitary cloud drifting with the wind to ceaseless thoughts of roaming.
The Narrow Road of Oku (Oku no Hosomichi)[3]

12   Such stillness—
The cries of the cicadas
Sink into the rocks.
Ibid.

13   The white chrysanthemum
Even when lifted to the eye
Remains immaculate.[4]
Conversations with Bashō. From the collection Kyoraisho Hyokai

14   Clear cascades!
Into the waves scatter
Blue pine needles.
Ibid.

15   An old pond—
A frog leaping in—
The sound of water.[5]
Poem

16   A rough sea!
Stretched out over Sado
The Milky Way.[5]
Poem

William Penn
1644–1718

17   No Cross, No Crown.[6]
Title of pamphlet [1669]

18   Any government is free to the people under it where the laws rule and the people are a party to the laws.   *Frame of Government [1682]*

19   Truth often suffers more by the heat of its defenders than from the arguments of its opposers.
Some Fruits of Solitude [1693]

20   It is a reproach to religion and government to suffer so much poverty and excess.   *Ibid. 52*

21   They that love beyond the world cannot be separated by it. Death is but crossing the world, as friends do the seas; they live in one another still.
Ibid.

22   Men are generally more careful of the breed of their horses and dogs than of their children.
Ibid. 85

23   It were endless to dispute upon everything that is disputable.   *Ibid. 184*

---

[1]In modern terms, acceleration is directly proportional to applied force.
[2]See Dryden, 274:26.
[3]From *Anthology of Japanese Literature* [1955], edited by DONALD KEENE.
[4]From *Sources of Japanese Tradition* [1960], edited by WILLIAM THEODORE DE BARY.
[5]Translated by DANA B. YOUNG.
[6]See *Matthew 10:38, 34:35*; Quarles, 242:6; and Bennard, 616:2.

1 Have a care therefore where there is more sail than ballast. *Ibid.* 260

2 Passion is a sort of fever in the mind, which ever leaves us weaker than it found us. *Ibid.* 279

3 The public must and will be served. *Ibid.*

Edward Taylor
c. 1644–1729

4 Who spread its canopy? Or curtains spun?
Who in this bowling alley bowled the sun?
Poetical Works [1939]. God's Determinations Touching His Elect, preface

5 For in Christ's coach saints sweetly sing
As they to glory ride therein.
Ibid. The Joy of Church Fellowship Rightly Attended

6 Make me, O Lord, thy spinning-wheel complete.
Ibid. Housewifery

7 It's food too fine for angels; yet come, take
And eat thy fill! It's Heaven's sugar cake.[1]
Ibid. Sacramental Meditations, 8

8 This bread of life dropped in thy mouth doth cry:
Eat, eat me, soul, and thou shalt never die.
Ibid.

9 Is Christ thy advocate to plead thy cause?[2]
Art thou his client? Such shall never slide.
He never lost his case.
Ibid. 38

10 My case is bad. Lord, be my advocate.
My sin is red: I'm under God's arrest.
Ibid.

Jean de La Bruyère
1645–1696

11 We come too late to say anything which has not been said already.[3]
Les Caractères [1688]. Des Ouvrages de l'Esprit

12 Liberality consists less in giving a great deal than in gifts well timed. *Ibid. Du Coeur*

13 Time, which strengthens friendship, weakens love. *Ibid.*

14 We must laugh before we are happy, for fear we die before we laugh at all.[4] *Ibid.*

15 To laugh at men of sense is the privilege of fools.
Ibid. De la Société

16 There are but three events in a man's life: birth, life and death. He is not conscious of being born, he dies in pain, and he forgets to live.
Ibid. De l'Homme

17 Most men make use of the first part of their life to render the last part miserable. *Ibid.*

18 Women run to extremes; they are either better or worse than men. *Ibid. Des Femmes*

Baron Gottfried Wilhelm von Leibniz
1646–1716

19 I often say a great doctor kills more people than a great general.[5]
Quoted in Bulletin of the New York Academy of Medicine, vol. V [1929], p. 152

Henry Aldrich
1647–1710

20 If all be true that I do think,
There are five reasons we should drink:
Good wine—a friend—or being dry—
Or lest we should be by and by—
Or any other reason why.
Five Reasons for Drinking

John Wilmot, Earl of Rochester
1647–1680

21 Here lies our sovereign lord the King,
Whose promise none relies on;
He never said a foolish thing,
Nor ever did a wise one.
Written on the bedchamber door of Charles II[6]

22 For pointed satire I would Buckhurst choose,
The best good man with the worst-natured muse.[7]
An Allusion to Horace, bk. I, satire X

23 A merry monarch, scandalous and poor.
A Satire on King Charles II

24 There's not a thing on earth that I can name,
So foolish, and so false, as common fame.
Did E'er This Saucy World

25 Reason, which fifty times for one does err,
Reason, an ignis fatuus of the mind.
A Satire Against Mankind [1675], l. 11

26 Books bear him up a while, and make him try
To swim with bladders of philosophy.
Ibid. l. 20

27 Then Old Age and Experience, hand in hand,
Lead him to death, and make him understand,

---

[1]Based on *John 6:51.*
[2]See *1 John 2:1–2*, 46:33.
[3]See *Ecclesiastes 1:9*, 23:25; Terence, 86:4, and Robert Burton, 234:6.
[4]See Beaumarchais, 336:5, and Byron, 403:2.

[5]See Prior, 287:22.
[6]See Charles II, 273.
[7]Thou best-humored man with the worst-humored muse!
—Goldsmith, *Retaliation [1774], Postscript*

After a search so painful and so long,
That all his life he has been in the wrong.
                    A Satire Against Mankind, l. 25

1 Dead, we become the lumber of the world.
                    Seneca's Troas, act 2, chorus

John Sheffield,
Duke of Buckingham and Normanby
1648–1721

2 Of all those arts in which the wise excel,
Nature's chief masterpiece is writing well.
                    Essay on Poetry [1682]

3 Read Homer once, and you can read no more;
For all books else appear so mean, so poor,
Verse will seem prose; but still persist to read,
And Homer will be all the books you need.
                    Ibid.

4 And when I feigned an angry look,
Alas! I loved you best.
                    The Reconcilement [1701]

William III[1]
1650–1702

5 There is one certain means by which I can be sure
never to see my country's ruin: I will die in the last
ditch.
                    From HUME, *History of England [1754–1757],
                    ch. 65*

6 Every bullet has its billet.
                    From JOHN WESLEY, *Journal [June 6, 1765]*

Juana Inés de la Cruz
1651–1695

7 Foolish men who accuse
a woman mindlessly—
you cannot even see
you cause what you abuse.
                    Hombres Necios (Foolish Men),[2] st. 1

8 Has anyone ever seen
a stranger moral fervor?
You who dirty the mirror
cry that it isn't clean.
                    Ibid. st. 6

9 I became a nun, because although I recognized it
as having many ramifications . . . foreign to my
temperament, still, given my completely negative
feelings about marriage, it was the least dispropor-
tionate and most fitting thing I could do.
                    Reply to Sor Filotea de la Cruz[3] [1691]

---

[1]Prince of Orange; joint sovereign of England with his wife,
Mary II.
[2]Translated by WILLIS and ALICKI BARNSTONE.
[3]Name used by Manuel Fernández de la Cruz, bishop of
Puebla, in signing an angry letter attacking Sor Juana's scholarly work as inappropriate.
Translated by RACHEL PHILLIPS.

10 Since I first gained the use of reason my inclination towards learning has been so violent and strong
that neither the scoldings of other people . . .
nor my own reflections . . . have been able to stop
me from following this natural impulse that God
gave me. He alone must know why; and He knows
too that I have begged Him to take away the light of
my understanding, leaving only enough for me to
keep His law, for anything else is excessive in a
woman, according to some people, and others say it
is even harmful.
                    Ibid.

François de Salignac
de la Mothe Fénelon
1651–1715

11 Do not men die fast enough without being destroyed by each other? Can any man be insensible of
the brevity of life? and can he who knows it, think
life too long!   *Télémaque [1699], bk. VII*

12 To be always ready for war, said Mentor, is the
surest way to avoid it.   *Ibid. X*

13 Some of the most dreadful mischiefs that afflict
mankind proceed from wine; it is the cause of disease, quarrels, sedition, idleness, aversion to labor,
and every species of domestic disorder.   *Ibid.*

14 Mankind, by the perverse depravity of their nature, esteem that which they have most desired as of
no value the moment it is possessed, and torment
themselves with fruitless wishes for that which is
beyond their reach.   *Ibid. XVIII*

Thomas Otway
1652–1685

15 What mighty ills have not been done by woman!
Who was 't betrayed the Capitol?—A woman!
Who lost Mark Antony the world?—A woman!
Who was the cause of a long ten years' war,
And laid at last old Troy in ashes?—Woman!
Destructive, damnable, deceitful woman!
                    The Orphan [1680], act III, sc. i

16 Let us embrace, and from this very moment vow
an eternal misery together.   *Ibid. IV, ii*

17 O woman! lovely woman! Nature made thee
To temper man: we had been brutes without you;
Angels are painted fair, to look like you.
                    Venice Preserved [1682], act I, sc. i

Nahum Tate
1652–1715

18 When I am laid in earth.
                    Dido and Aeneas [c. 1690][4]

---

[4]Libretto for the opera by Henry Purcell.

1 While shepherds watch'd their flocks by night,
All seated on the ground,
The angel of the Lord came down,
And glory shone around.[1]
Christmas Hymn [1700], st. 1

2 Glad tidings of great joy I bring
To you and all mankind.[2]
Ibid.

Nahum Tate
1652–1715

and Nicholas Brady
1659–1726

3 Through all the changing scenes of life,
In trouble and in joy.
*New Version of the Psalms of David [1696],
Psalm 34*

4 As pants the hart for cooling streams
When heated in the chase.
Ibid. Psalm 42

5 Jesus Christ is risen today,
Alleluia!
*Easter Hymn [1698], translated from the Latin
[fourteenth century]*

Nathaniel Lee[3]
c. 1653–1692

6 Then he will talk—good gods! how he will
talk!
*The Rival Queens; or, The Death of Alexander
the Great [1677], act I, sc. iii*

7 When Greeks joined Greeks, then was the tug of
war.
Ibid. IV, ii

8 'Tis beauty calls, and glory shows the way.
Ibid.

9 Man, false man, smiling, destructive man!
Theodosius [1680], act III, sc. ii

Ransetsu
1653–1708

10 Against the blue stands
A pine tree etched
By tonight's moon.[4]
Harvest Moon

Andrew Fletcher of Saltoun
1655–1716

11 If a man were permitted to make all the ballads,
he need not care who should make the laws of a
nation.
*Conversation Concerning a Right Regulation of
Governments for the Common Good of
Mankind [1704]*

John Dennis
1657–1734

12 A man who could make so vile a pun would not
scruple to pick a pocket.
*The Gentleman's Magazine, vol. LI [1781],
p. 324*

13 They will not let my play run, and yet they steal
my thunder![5]
Remark

Daniel Defoe
1660–1731

14 Wherever God erects a house of prayer,
The Devil always builds a chapel there;[6]
And 'twill be found, upon examination,
The latter has the largest congregation.
The True-Born Englishman [1701], pt. I, l. 1

15 From this amphibious ill-born mob began
That vain, ill-natur'd thing, an Englishman.
Ibid. l. 132

16 Great families of yesterday we show,
And lords whose parents were the Lord knows
who.
Ibid. l. 374

17 In their religion they are so uneven,
That each man goes his own byway to heaven.
Ibid. II, l. 104

18 And of all plagues with which mankind are
curs'd,
Ecclesiastic tyranny's the worst.
Ibid. l. 299

19 When kings the sword of justice first lay down,
They are no kings, though they possess the crown.

---

[1]See *Luke 2:8–9, 38:3.*
[2]See *Luke 2:10, 38:3.*
[3]Lee collaborated with Dryden on *Oedipus* (see 273:19).
[4]Translated by Prescott B. Wintersteen, Jr.

[5]For his play *Appius and Virginia* [1709], Dennis had invented a new species of thunder. "The tragedy however was coldly received, notwithstanding such assistance, and was acted but a short time. Some nights after, Mr. Dennis, being in the pit at the representation of *Macbeth*, heard his own thunder made use of; upon which he rose in a violent passion, and exclaimed, with an oath, that it was his thunder. 'See,' said he, 'how the rascals use me! They will not let my play run, and yet they steal my thunder!'"—*Biographia Britannica, vol. V, p. 103*
[6]See Luther, 138:10.

Titles are shadows, crowns are empty things,
The good of subjects is the end of kings.
        The True-Born Englishman, pt. II, l. 313

1 All men would be tyrants if they could.[1]
        The Kentish Petition [1712–1713]

2 The best of men cannot suspend their fate:
The good die early, and the bad die late.
        Character of the Late Dr. S. Annesley [1715]

3   He bid me [Robinson Crusoe] observe it, and I
should always find that the calamities of life were
shared among the upper and lower part of mankind;
but that the middle station had the fewest disasters.
        Robinson Crusoe[2] *[1719]*

4   One day, about noon, going towards my boat, I
was exceedingly surprised with the print of a man's
naked foot on the shore, which was very plain to be
seen in the sand.   *Ibid.*

5   My man Friday.   *Ibid.*

Sir Samuel Garth
1661–1719

6 A barren superfluity of words.
        The Dispensary [1699], canto II, l. 95

7 Hard was their lodging, homely was their food;
For all their luxury was doing good.[3]
        Claremont, l. 148

Kikaku
1661–1707

8 A harvest moon!
And on the mats—
Shadows of pine boughs.[4]

        Harvest Moon

Richard Bentley
1662–1742

9   No man was ever written out of reputation but
by himself.[5]
        From J. H. Monk, Life of Bentley [1831]

10   It is a pretty poem, Mr. Pope, but you must not
call it Homer.[6]   *From Johnson, Life of Pope*

[1]See Abigail Adams, 347:1.
[2]See Rousseau, 319:16.
[3]And learn the luxury of doing good.—Goldsmith, *The
Traveller* [1764], *l. 22*
[4]Translated by Prescott B. Wintersteen, Jr.
[5]See Montaigne, 146:10.
[6]The reference is to Pope's translation of *The Iliad.*
See Pope, 299:23.

Matthew Henry
1662–1714

11   He rolls it under his tongue as a sweet morsel.
        Commentaries [1708–1710], Psalm 36

12   Our creature comforts.   *Ibid. Psalm 37*

13   They that die by famine die by inches.
                    Ibid. Psalm 59

14   To fish in troubled waters.   *Ibid. Psalm 60*

15   Here is bread, which strengthens man's heart,
and therefore called the staff of life.[7]
                    Ibid. Psalm 104

16   Hearkeners, we say, seldom hear good of themselves.   *Ibid. Ecclesiastes 7*

17   It was a common saying among the Puritans,
"Brown bread and the Gospel is good fare."
                    Ibid. Isaiah 30

18   None so blind as those that will not see.[8]
                    Ibid. Jeremiah 20

19   Judas had given them the slip.   *Ibid. Luke 22*

20   After a storm comes a calm.   *Ibid. Acts 9*

21   Men of polite learning and a liberal education.
                        Ibid. 10

22   It is good news, worthy of all acceptation! and yet
not too good to be true.   *Ibid. Timothy 1*

23   All this and heaven too.   *Life of Philip Henry*

Samuel Wesley
1662–1735

24 Style is the dress of thought;[9] a modest dress,
Neat, but not gaudy,[10] will true critics please.
        An Epistle to a Friend Concerning Poetry [1700]

Thomas [Tom] Brown
1663–1704

25 I do not love thee, Doctor Fell.
The reason why I cannot tell;
But this alone I know full well,
I do not love thee, Doctor Fell.[11]
        *Written while a student at Christ Church,
        Oxford*

[7]Bread is the staff of life.—Swift, *A Tale of a Tub* [1704]
Corn, which is the staff of life.—Edward Winslow [1595–
1655], *Good News from New England* [1624]
    See *Isaiah 3:1, 25:33.*
[8]See *Jeremiah 5:21, 28:15.*
[9]See Chesterfield, 305:10.
[10]See Shakespeare, 193:30.
[11]Je ne vous aime pas, Hylas; / Je n'en saurois dire la cause, /
Je sais seulement une chose; / C'est que je ne vous aime pas.
—Roger de Bussy-Rabutin
    See Martial, 106:10.

1 To treat a poor wretch with a bottle of Burgundy, and fill his snuffbox, is like giving a pair of laced ruffles to a man that has never a shirt on his back.[1]
Laconics [1707]

Mary de la Rivière Manley
1663–1724

2 No time like the present.
The Lost Lover [1696], act IV, sc. i

Cotton Mather
1663–1728

3 I write the wonders of the Christian religion, flying from the depravations of Europe, to the American strand: and, assisted by the Holy Author of that religion, I do, with all conscience of truth, required therein by Him, who is the Truth itself, report the wonderful displays of His infinite power, wisdom, goodness, and faithfulness, wherewith his Divine Providence hath irradiated an Indian wilderness.
Magnalia Christi Americana [1702], introduction

William Walsh
1663–1708

4 Of all the plagues a lover bears, Sure rivals are the worst.
Song, st. 1

5 I can endure my own despair, But not another's hope.
Ibid. st. 2

The New England Primer[2]

6 In Adam's fall
We sinned all.

7 My book and heart
Must never part.

8 Young Obadias,
David, Josias—
All were pious.

9 Peter denied
His Lord, and cried.

10 Young Timothy
Learnt sin to fly.

11 Xerxes did die,
And so must I.

12 Zaccheus he
Did climb the tree
Our Lord to see.

13 Our days begin with trouble here,
Our life is but a span,[3]
And cruel death is always near,
So frail a thing is man.

14 Now I lay me down to sleep,[4]
I pray the Lord my soul to keep;
If I should die before I wake,
I pray the Lord my soul to take.

Matthew Prior
1664–1721

15 All jargon of the schools.[5]
I Am That I Am, An Ode [1688]

16 Our hopes, like towering falcons, aim
At objects in an airy height;
The little pleasure of the game
Is from afar to view the flight.
To the Honorable Charles Montague [1692]

17 The end must justify the means.[6]
Hans Carvel [1700]

18 Lays the rough paths of peevish Nature even,
And opens in each heart a little heaven.
Charity [1703]

19 Be to her virtues very kind;
Be to her faults a little blind;
Let all her ways be unconfin'd;
And clap your padlock—on her mind!
An English Padlock [1707]

20 And thought the nation ne'er would thrive
Till all the whores were burnt alive.
Paulo Purganti and His Wife [1708]

21 He rang'd his tropes, and preach'd up patience;
Back'd his opinion with quotations.
Ibid.

22 Cured yesterday of my disease,
I died last night of my physician.[7]
The Remedy Worse than the Disease [1714]

23 And often took leave, but was loth to depart.
The Thief and the Cordelier [1718]

---

[1]See Goldsmith, 330:15.

[2]As early as 1691, Benjamin Harris of Boston advertised the forthcoming second impression of the *New England Primer*. The oldest known copy extant is dated 1737.

[3]See Francis Bacon, 160:13, and Sir John Davies, 227:15.

[4]The first record of this prayer is found in the *Enchiridion Leonis* [1160]. The early editions of the *Primer* give the first line of the prayer as: Now I lay me down to take my sleep. The familiar version of the line appeared in the edition of 1784. In the edition of 1814 the second line reads: I pray thee, Lord, my soul to keep.

[5]Noisy jargon of the schools.—POMFRET, *Reason*
The sounding jargon of the schools.—COWPER, *Truth* [1782], *l.* 367

[6]See Saint Jerome, 113:16.

[7]See Leibniz, 283:19.

1 His noble negligences teach
What others' toils despair to reach.
Alma [1718], canto II, l. 7

2 Till their own dreams at length deceive 'em,
And oft repeating, they believe 'em.
Ibid. III, l. 13

3 To John I ow'd great obligation;
But John, unhappily, thought fit
To publish it to all the nation:
Sure John and I are more than quit.
Epigram [1718]

4 Venus, take my votive glass;
Since I am not what I was,
What from this day I shall be,
Venus, let me never see.
*The Lady Who Offers Her Looking-Glass to
Venus [1718]*

5 Nobles and heralds, by your leave,
Here lies what once was Matthew Prior;
The son of Adam and of Eve:
Can Bourbon or Nassau go higher?
Epitaph [1721]

Sir John Vanbrugh[1]
1664–1726

6   Once a woman has given you her heart you can
never get rid of the rest of her.
The Relapse [1697], act III, sc. i

7   No man worth having is true to his wife, or can
be true to his wife, or ever was, or ever will be so.
Ibid. ii

8   *Belinda:* Ay, but you know we must return good
for evil.
   Lady Brute: That may be a mistake in the translation.   *The Provok'd Wife [1698], act I, sc. i*

9   He laughs best who laughs last.[2]
The Country House [1706], act II, sc. v

10   Much of a muchness.
*The Provok'd Husband [1728] (completed by
Colley Cibber) act I, sc. i*

Susannah Centlivre
c. 1667–1723

11   The real Simon Pure.
A Bold Stroke for a Wife [1718], act V, sc. i

---

[1]Under this stone, Reader, survey/Dead Sir John Vanbrugh's house of clay./Lie heavy on him, Earth! for he/Laid
many heavy loads on thee!—Abel Evans [1679–1737]. Vanbrugh was the architect of Blenheim Palace.
[2]Better the last smile than the first laughter.—Ray, *Proverbs*
[1670]

John Pomfret
1667–1702

12 We live and learn, but not the wiser grow.[3]
Reason, l. 112

Jonathan Swift
1667–1745

13   Books, like men their authors, have no more than
one way of coming into the world, but there are ten
thousand to go out of it, and return no more.[4]
A Tale of a Tub [1704], dedication

14   Books, the children of the brain.   *Ibid. sec. 1*

15   As boys do sparrows, with flinging salt upon their
tails.   *Ibid. 7*

16   Satire is a sort of glass, wherein beholders do
generally discover everybody's face but their own.
The Battle of the Books [1704]

17   Instead of dirt and poison we have rather chosen
to fill our hives with honey and wax; thus furnishing
mankind with the two noblest of things, which are
sweetness and light.[5]   *Ibid.*

18   Laws are like cobwebs, which may catch small
flies, but let wasps and hornets break through.[6]
*A Critical Essay upon the Faculties of the Mind
[1707]*

19   There is nothing in this world constant, but inconstancy.   *Ibid.*

20   'Tis very warm weather when one's in bed.
Journal to Stella [November 8, 1710]

21   With my own fair hands.
Ibid. [January 4, 1711]

22   We are so fond of one another, because our ailments are the same.   *Ibid. [February 1, 1711]*

23   I love good creditable acquaintance; I love to be
the worst of the company.   *Ibid. [May 17, 1711]*

24   We were to do more business after dinner; but
after dinner is after dinner—an old saying and a
true, "much drinking, little thinking."
Ibid. [February 26, 1712]

25   We have just religion enough to make us hate, but
not enough to make us love one another.
*Thoughts on Various Subjects; from
Miscellanies [1711]*

---

[3]It is good to live and learn.—Cervantes, *Don Quixote*,
pt. II [1615], *ch.* 32
   Live and learn,/Not first learn and then live.—Robert
Browning, *Parleyings with Certain People, With Christopher
Smart* [1887], IX
[4]See John Webster, 237:17.
[5]See Matthew Arnold, 500:14.
[6]See Anacharsis, 56:2.

1 Censure is the tax a man pays to the public for being eminent. *Ibid.*

2 Every man desires to live long, but no man would be old. *Ibid.*

3 A nice man is a man of nasty ideas. *Ibid.*

4 Vision is the art of seeing things invisible. *Ibid. [1726]*

5 'Tis an old maxim in the schools,
That flattery's[1] the food of fools;
Yet now and then your men of wit
Will condescend to take a bit.
Cadenus and Vanessa [1713][2]

6 Proper words in proper places, make the true definition of a style.
Letter to a Young Clergyman [January 9, 1720]

7 If Heaven had looked upon riches to be a valuable thing, it would not have given them to such a scoundrel.
Letter to Miss Vanhomrigh [August 12, 1720]

8 He [the Emperor] is taller by almost the breadth of my nail, than any of his court, which alone is enough to strike an awe into the beholders.
Gulliver's Travels [1726]. Voyage to Lilliput, ch. 2

9 *All true believers shall break their eggs at the convenient end:* and which is the convenient end, seems, in my humble opinion, to be left to every man's conscience. *Ibid. ch. 4*

10 I cannot but conclude the bulk of your natives to be the most pernicious race of little odious vermin that nature ever suffered to crawl upon the surface of the earth. *Ibid. Voyage to Brobdingnag, ch. 6*

11 And he gave it for his opinion, that whoever could make two ears of corn or two blades of grass to grow upon a spot of ground where only one grew before, would deserve better of mankind, and do more essential service to his country, than the whole race of politicians put together.[3] *Ibid. 7*

12 He had been eight years upon a project for extracting sunbeams out of cucumbers, which were to be put in vials hermetically sealed, and let out to warm the air in raw inclement summers.
Ibid. Voyage to Laputa, ch. 5

[1]"Vanity's" in some texts.
[2]When the poem of "Cadenus and Vanessa" was the general topic of conversation, someone said, "Surely that Vanessa must be an extraordinary woman that could inspire the Dean to write so finely upon her." Mrs. Johnson smiled, and answered that "she thought that point not quite so clear; for it was well known the Dean could write finely upon a broomstick."—SAMUEL JOHNSON, *Lives of the Poets* [1779–1781], *Life of Swift*
[3]He who makes two blades of grass grow in place of one renders a service to the state.—VOLTAIRE, *Letter to M. Moreau* [1765]

13 I said the thing which was not. (For they have no word in their language to express lying or falsehood.)[4] *Ibid. Voyage to the Houyhnhnms, ch. 3*

14 I told him . . . that we ate when we were not hungry, and drank without the provocation of thirst.
Ibid. 6

15 A set of phrases learnt by rote;
A passion for a scarlet coat;
When at a play to laugh, or cry,
Yet cannot tell the reason why:
Never to hold her tongue a minute;
While all she prates has nothing in it.
The Furniture of a Woman's Mind [1727]

16 For conversation well endu'd;
She calls it witty to be rude;
And, placing raillery in railing,
Will tell aloud your greatest failing.
Ibid.

17 Not die here in a rage, like a poisoned rat in a hole. *Letter to Bolingbroke [March 21, 1729]*

18 Yet malice never was his aim;
He lash'd the vice but spar'd the name.
No individual could resent,
Where thousands equally were meant.
His satire points at no defect
But what all mortals may correct;
For he abhorr'd that senseless tribe
Who call it humor when they gibe.
Verses on the Death of Dr. Swift [1731], l. 459

19 Hobbes clearly proves that every creature
Lives in a state of war by nature.[5]
On Poetry. A Rhapsody [1733]

20 So, naturalists observe, a flea
Hath smaller fleas that on him prey;
And these have smaller still to bite 'em;
And so proceed *ad infinitum.*
Thus every poet, in his kind,
Is bit by him that comes behind.
Ibid.

21 Conversation is but carving!
Give no more to every guest
Than he's able to digest.
Give him always of the prime,
And but little at a time.
Carve to all but just enough,
Let them neither starve nor stuff,
And that you may have your due,
Let your neighbor carve for you.
Conversation

22 Under an oak, in stormy weather,
I joined this rogue and whore together;

[4]Gulliver has been trying to describe his voyage in a ship to his Houyhnhnm "Master," who doesn't believe him, and accuses him of being mistaken or of saying "the thing which was not."
[5]See Hobbes, 239:21.

And none but he who rules the thunder
Can put this rogue and whore asunder.
> *Marriage certificate. From The Oxford Book of Literary Anecdotes, JAMES SUTHERLAND, ed. [1975], no. 77*

1   The sight of you is good for sore eyes.[1]
> *Polite Conversation [1738], dialogue 1*

2   'Tis as cheap sitting as standing.   *Ibid.*

3   I hate nobody: I am in charity with all the world.[2]
> *Ibid.*

4   You were half seas over.   *Ibid.*

5   I won't quarrel with my bread and butter.
> *Ibid.*

6   She's no chicken; she's on the wrong side of thirty, if she be a day.   *Ibid.*

7   She wears her clothes, as if they were thrown on her with a pitchfork.   *Ibid.*

8   He was a bold man that first eat an oyster.
> *Ibid. 2*

9   That's as well said, as if I had said it myself.
> *Ibid.*

10   Fingers were made before forks, and hands before knives.   *Ibid.*

11   She has more goodness in her little finger, than he has in his whole body.   *Ibid.*

12   Lord, I wonder what fool it was that first invented kissing!   *Ibid.*

13   The best doctors in the world are Doctor Diet, Doctor Quiet, and Doctor Merryman.   *Ibid.*

14   May you live all the days of your life.   *Ibid.*

15   I always love to begin a journey on Sundays, because I shall have the prayers of the church to preserve all that travel by land, or by water.
> *Ibid.*

16   I thought you and he had been hand-and-glove.
> *Ibid.*

17   She watches him, as a cat would watch a mouse.
> *Ibid. 3*

18   She pays him in his own coin.   *Ibid.*

19   There was all the world and his wife.   *Ibid.*

20 Hail, fellow, well met,
All dirty and wet:
Find out if you can,
Who's master, who's man.
> *My Lady's Lamentation [1765], l. 171*

21   I shall be like that tree, I shall die at the top.
> *From SIR WALTER SCOTT, Life of Swift [1814]*

22   Good God! What a genius I had when I wrote that book [*A Tale of a Tub*].   *Ibid.*

23   Ubi saeva indignatio ulterius cor lacerare nequit [Where savage indignation can lacerate his heart no more].[3]
> *Epitaph. Inscribed on Swift's grave, Saint Patrick's, Dublin*

Alain René Lesage
1668–1747

24   It may be said that his wit shines at the expense of his memory.
> *Gil Blas [1715–1735], bk. III, ch. 11*

25   A flatterer can risk everything with great personages.   *Ibid. IV, 7*

26   Pride and conceit were the original sin of man.
> *Ibid. VII, 3*

27   I wish you all sorts of prosperity with a little more taste.   *Ibid. 4*

28   The pleasure of talking is the inextinguishable passion of a woman, coeval with the act of breathing.   *Ibid. 7*

29   Facts are stubborn things.   *Ibid. X, 1*

Giovanni Battista [Giambattista] Vico
1668–1744

30   The nature of things is nothing other than that they come into being at certain times and in certain ways. Wherever the same circumstances are present, the same phenomena arise and no others.
> *Scienza Nuova [1725][4]*

31   In that dark night which shrouds from our eyes the most remote antiquity, a light appears which cannot lead us astray; I speak of this incontestable truth: the social world is certainly the work of man.
> *Ibid.*

32   Governments must be conformable to the nature of the governed; governments are even a result of that nature.[5]   *Ibid.*

William Congreve
1670–1729

33   Eternity was in that moment.
> *The Old Bachelor [1693], act IV, sc. vii*

34   Married in haste, we may repent at leisure.[6]
> *Ibid. V, viii*

35   It is the business of a comic poet to paint the vices and follies of human kind.
> *The Double Dealer [1694], epistle dedicatory*

36   Retired to their tea and scandal, according to their ancient custom.[7]   *Ibid. act I, sc. i*

---

[3]See Yeats, 598:9.
[4]Translated by JULES MICHELET.
[5]See John Adams, 338:1, and Jefferson, 343:2.
[6]See Shakespeare, 167:25.
[7]See Fielding, 311:21.

[1]What a sight for sore eyes that would be!—HAZLITT, *Of Persons One Would Have Seen*
[2]See *Book of Common Prayer, Holy Communion*, 49:14.

1 Though marriage makes man and wife one flesh,
it leaves 'em still two fools. *Ibid. II, iii*

2 No mask like open truth to cover lies,
As to go naked is the best disguise.
Ibid. V, iv

3 Thou liar of the first magnitude.
Love for Love [1695], act II, sc. ii

4 I warrant you, if he danced till doomsday, he
thought I was to pay the piper.[1] *Ibid. v*

5 O fie, miss, you must not kiss and tell.
Ibid. x

6 Women are like tricks by sleight of hand,
Which, to admire, we should not understand.
Ibid. IV, xx

7 Music has charms to soothe a savage breast,[2]
To soften rocks, or bend a knotted oak.
The Mourning Bride [1697], act I, sc. i

8 By magic numbers and persuasive sound.
Ibid.

9 Heaven has no rage like love to hatred turned,
Nor hell a fury like a woman scorned.
Ibid. III, viii

10 Here she comes i' faith full sail, with her fan
spread and streamers out, and a shoal of fools for
tenders.—Ha, no, I cry her mercy!
The Way of the World [1700], act II, sc. iv

11 I nauseate walking; 'tis a country diversion, I
loathe the country. *Ibid. IV, iv*

12 Let us be very strange and well-bred: Let us be as
strange as if we had been married a great while; and
as well-bred as if we were not married at all.
Ibid.

13 If I continue to endure you a little longer, I may
by degrees dwindle into a wife. *Ibid.*

14 Thou art a retailer of phrases, and dost deal in
remnants of remnants. *Ibid. ix*

15 O, she is the antidote to desire. *Ibid. xiv*

16 Careless she is with artful care,
Affecting to seem unaffected.
Amoret

17 Defer not till tomorrow to be wise,
Tomorrow's sun to thee may never rise.[3]
Letter to Cobham

Colley Cibber
1671–1757

18 As good be out of the world as out of the fashion.
Love's Last Shift [1696], act II

19 Possession is eleven points in the law.
Woman's Wit [1697], act I

20 Words are but empty thanks. *Ibid. V*

21 Off with his head[4]—so much for Buckingham.
Richard III (altered) [1700], act IV, sc. iii

22 Perish the thought! *Ibid. V, v*

23 This business will never hold water.
She Wou'd and She Wou'd Not [1703], act IV

24 Old houses mended,
Cost little less than new before they're ended.
The Double Gallant [1707], prologue

25 Oh, how many torments lie in the small circle of
a wedding ring! *Ibid. act I, sc. ii*

26 Stolen sweets are best.
The Rival Fools [1709], act I

Anthony Ashley Cooper, Earl of Shaftesbury
1671–1713

27 How comes it to pass, then, that we appear such
cowards in reasoning, and are so afraid to stand the
test of ridicule?
A Letter Concerning Enthusiasm [1708], sec. 2

28 Truth, 'tis supposed, may bear all lights; and one
of those principal lights or natural mediums by
which things are to be viewed in order to a thorough
recognition is ridicule itself.
*Essay on the Freedom of Wit and Humor
[1709], pt. I, sec. 1*

Joseph Addison
1672–1719

29 For wheresoe'er I turn my ravish'd eyes,
Gay gilded scenes and shining prospects rise,
Poetic fields encompass me around,
And still I seem to tread on classic ground.
A Letter from Italy [1703]

30 And, pleas'd the Almighty's orders to perform,
Rides in the whirlwind and directs the storm.[5]
The Campaign [1704], l. 91

31 Reading is to the mind what exercise is to the
body. *Tatler [1709–1711], no. 147*

32 The spacious firmament on high,
With all the blue ethereal sky,
And spangled heavens, a shining frame,
Their great Original proclaim.[6]
*Ode [in The Spectator, no. 465, August 23,
1712]*

---

[1]Pay the piper: phrase for settling the score. He who pays the piper calls the tune.—*Proverb*
[2]See Shakespeare, 204:23.
[3]See Euripides, 68:3, and Edward Young, 296:10.
[4]See Shakespeare, 166:2, and Carroll, 517:23.
[5]This line is repeated by Pope in his *Dunciad*, bk. III [1728], l. 264. See 303:29.
[6]See Psalm 19:1, 16:9.

1 Soon as the evening shades prevail,
The moon takes up the wondrous tale,
And nightly to the listening earth
Repeats the story of her birth;
While all the stars that round her burn,
And all the planets in their turn,
Confirm the tidings as they roll,
And spread the truth from pole to pole.

Ode

2 Forever singing as they shine,
"The Hand that made us is divine."

Ibid.

3 Should the whole frame of Nature round him
break,
In ruin and confusion hurled,
He, unconcerned, would hear the mighty crack,
And stand secure amidst a falling world.

Horace, Odes, bk. III, ode iii[1]

4 'Tis not in mortals to command success,
But we'll do more, Sempronius; we'll deserve it.

Cato[2] *[1713], act I, sc. ii*

5 Blesses his stars and thinks it luxury.

Ibid. iv

6 'Tis pride, rank pride, and haughtiness of soul;
I think the Romans call it stoicism.

Ibid.

7 Were you with these, my prince, you'd soon
forget
The pale, unripened beauties of the north.

Ibid.

8 Beauty soon grows familiar to the lover,
Fades in his eye, and palls upon the sense.

Ibid.

9 My voice is still for war.
Gods! can a Roman senate long debate
Which of the two to choose, slavery or death?

Ibid. II, i

10 The woman that deliberates is lost.

Ibid. IV, i

11 Curse on his virtues! they've undone his
country.

Ibid. iv

12 What pity is it
That we can die but once to serve our country![3]

Ibid.

¹See Horace, 96:15.
²The *Massachusetts Spy* used the following lines from *Cato* as its motto from November 22, 1771, to April 6, 1775: Do thou Great Liberty inspire our Souls— / And make our Lives in thy Possession happy— / Or, our Deaths glorious in thy just Defense.
³See Nathan Hale, 354:16.

13 When vice prevails, and impious men bear sway,
The post of honor is a private station.[4]

Ibid.

14 It must be so—Plato, thou reasonest well!
Else whence this pleasing hope, this fond desire,
This longing after immortality?
Or whence this secret dread, and inward horror,
Of falling into naught? Why shrinks the soul
Back on herself, and startles at destruction?
'Tis the divinity that stirs within us;
'Tis heaven itself, that points out an hereafter,
And intimates eternity to man.
Eternity! thou pleasing, dreadful thought!

Ibid. V, i

15 Sweet are the slumbers of the virtuous man.

Ibid. iv

16 From hence, let fierce contending nations know
What dire effects from civil discord flow.

Ibid.

17 Round-heads and Wooden-shoes are standing
jokes.

The Drummer [1716], prologue, l. 8

18 Thus I live in the world rather as a spectator of
mankind than as one of the species.

The Spectator, no. 1 [March 1, 1711]

19 If I can any way contribute to the diversion or
improvement of the country in which I live, I shall
leave it, when I am summoned out of it, with the
secret satisfaction of thinking that I have not lived in
vain.[5]

Ibid.

20 I shall endeavor to enliven morality with wit, and
to temper wit with morality.

Ibid. 10 [March 12, 1711]

21 True happiness is of a retired nature, and an
enemy to pomp and noise; it arises, in the first place,
from the enjoyment of one's self; and, in the next,
from the friendship and conversation of a few select
companions.

Ibid. 15 [March 17, 1711]

22 There is not a more unhappy being than a superannuated idol.

Ibid. 73 [May 24, 1711]

23 A man that has a taste of music, painting, or
architecture, is like one that has another sense, when
compared with such as have no relish of those arts.

Ibid. 93 [June 16, 1711]

24 There is no defense against reproach but obscurity.

Ibid. 101 [June 26, 1711]

25 Much might be said on both sides.

Ibid. 122 [July 20, 1711]

26 Authors have established it as a kind of rule, that
a man ought to be dull sometimes; as the most severe

⁴Give me, kind Heaven, a private station, / A mind serene for contemplation! / Title and profit I resign; / The post of honor shall be mine.—GAY, *Fables, pt. II [1738], The Vulture, the Sparrow, and Other Birds*
⁵See Anonymous, 780:5.

reader makes allowances for many rests and nodding places in a voluminous writer.
Ibid. 124 [July 23, 1711]

1 Books are the legacies that a great genius leaves to mankind, which are delivered down from generation to generation, as presents to the posterity of those who are yet unborn.
Ibid. 166 [September 10, 1711]

2 Good nature is more agreeable in conversation than wit, and gives a certain air to the countenance which is more amiable than beauty.
Ibid. 169 [September 13, 1711]

3 Were I to prescribe a rule for drinking, it should be formed upon a saying quoted by Sir William Temple: the first glass for myself, the second for my friends, the third for good humor, and the fourth for mine enemies. *Ibid. 195 [October 13, 1711]*

4 A true critic ought to dwell rather upon excellencies than imperfections, to discover the concealed beauties of a writer, and communicate to the world such things as are worth their observation.
Ibid. 291 [February 2, 1712]

5 These widows, sir, are the most perverse creatures in the world. *Ibid. 335 [March 25, 1712]*

6 Mirth is like a flash of lightning, that breaks through a gloom of clouds, and glitters for a moment; cheerfulness keeps up a kind of daylight in the mind, and fills it with a steady and perpetual serenity. *Ibid. 381 [May 17, 1712]*

7 [Sir Roger] made several reflections on the greatness of the British Nation; as, that one Englishman could beat three Frenchmen; that we could never be in danger of Popery so long as we took care of our fleet; that the Thames was the noblest river in Europe . . . with many other honest prejudices which naturally cleave to the heart of a true Englishman. *Ibid. 383 [May 20, 1712]*

8 Our disputants put me in mind of the skuttle fish, that when he is unable to extricate himself, blackens all the water about him, till he becomes invisible.
Ibid. 476 [September 5, 1712]

9 The fraternity of the henpecked.
Ibid. 482 [September 12, 1712]

10 A man should always consider how much he has more than he wants; and secondly, how much more unhappy he might be than he really is.
Ibid. 574 [July 30, 1714]

11 We are always doing, says he, something for Posterity, but I would fain see Posterity do something for us. *Ibid. 583 [August 20, 1714]*

12 See in what peace a Christian can die.
Dying words [1719]. From EDWARD YOUNG, Conjectures on Original Composition [1759]

Edmond Hoyle[1]
1672–1769

13 When in doubt, win the trick.
Twenty-four Rules for Learners, rule 12

Sir Richard Steele
1672–1729

14 I am come to a tavern alone to eat a steak, after which I shall return to the office.
Letters to His Wife [October 28, 1707]

15 I was going home two hours ago, but was met by Mr. Griffith, who has kept me ever since. . . . I will come within a pint of wine.
Ibid. [Eleven at night, January 5, 1708]

16 A little in drink, but at all times yr faithful husband. *Ibid. [September 27, 1708]*

17 The finest woman in nature should not detain me an hour from you; but you must sometimes suffer the rivalship of the wisest men.
Ibid. [September 17, 1712]

18 Though her mien carries much more invitation than command, to behold her is an immediate check to loose behavior; and to love her is a liberal education.[2] *Tatler [1709–1711], no. 49*

19 When you fall into a man's conversation, the first thing you should consider is, whether he has a greater inclination to hear you, or that you should hear him.
The Spectator, no. 49 [April 26, 1711]

20 Of all the affections which attend human life, the love of glory is the most ardent.
Ibid. 139 [August 9, 1711]

21 Age in a virtuous person, of either sex, carries in it an authority which makes it preferable to all the pleasures of youth.
Ibid. 153 [August 25, 1711]

22 Among all the diseases of the mind there is not one more epidemical or more pernicious than the love of flattery. *Ibid. 238 [December 3, 1711]*

23 Will Honeycomb calls these over-offended ladies the outrageously virtuous.
Ibid. 266 [January 4, 1712]

24 A favor well bestowed is almost as great an honor to him who confers it as to him who receives it.
Ibid. 497 [September 30, 1712]

[1]Hoyle published a *Short Treatise on Whist* [1742], which in subsequent editions added rules for playing piquet, backgammon, chess, and other games. His *Laws* [1760] ruled whist playing until 1864; hence the saying, "according to Hoyle."
[2]Lady Elizabeth Hastings [1682–1739].

François Goyot de Pitavals
1673–1743

1   Causes Célèbres.
     *Title of book recounting famous trials and
     judgments*

Nicholas Rowe
1674–1718

2 As if Misfortune made the throne her seat,
  And none could be unhappy but the great.[1]
     The Fair Penitent [1703], prologue

3 At length the morn and cold indifference came.
     Ibid. act I, sc. i

4 Is this that haughty gallant, gay Lothario?
     Ibid. V, i

Isaac Watts
1674–1748

5 Were I so tall to reach the pole,
  Or grasp the ocean with my span,
  I must be measured by my soul;
  The mind's the standard of the man.
     Horae Lyricae [1706], bk. II, False Greatness

6 Let dogs delight to bark and bite,
  For God hath made them so;
     *Divine Songs [1715], 16, Against Quarreling and
     Fighting*

7 But, children, you should never let
  Such angry passions rise;
  Your little hands were never made
  To tear each other's eyes.
     Ibid.

8 Birds in their little nests agree;
  And 'tis a shameful sight,
  When children of one family
  Fall out, and chide, and fight.
     Ibid. 17, Love Between Brothers and Sisters

9 How doth the little busy bee
  Improve each shining hour,[2]
  And gather honey all the day
  From every opening flower!
     Ibid. 20, Against Idleness and Mischief

10 For Satan finds some mischief still
   For idle hands to do.
     Ibid.

11 Let me be dress'd fine as I will,
   Flies, worms, and flowers, exceed me still.
     Ibid. 22, Against Pride in Clothes

12 Hush! my dear, lie still and slumber,
   Holy angels guard thy bed!

Heavenly blessings without number
Gently falling on thy head.
     Ibid. 35, A Cradle Hymn

13 'Tis the voice of the sluggard; I heard him
      complain,
   "You have wak'd me too soon, I must slumber
      again."[3]
     Ibid. The Sluggard

14 O God, our help in ages past,
   Our hope for years to come,
   Our shelter from the stormy blast,
   And our eternal home.
     Psalm 90 [1719], st. 1

15 A thousand ages in Thy sight
   Are like an evening gone;
   Short as the watch that ends the night
   Before the rising sun.
     Ibid. st. 4

16 Time, like an ever-rolling stream,
   Bears all its sons away;
   They fly forgotten, as a dream
   Dies at the opening day.[4]
     Ibid. st. 5

17 Joy to the world! the Lord is come;
   Let earth receive her King.
   Let ev'ry heart prepare Him room,
   And heav'n and nature sing.
     Psalm 98 [1719], st. 1

18 When I can read my title clear
   To mansions in the skies,
   I'll bid farewell to every fear,
   And wipe my weeping eyes.
     Hymns and Spiritual Songs, bk. II, hymn 65

19 There is a land of pure delight,
   Where saints immortal reign;
   Infinite day excludes the night,
   And pleasures banish pain.
     Ibid. 66

William Somerville[5]
1675–1742

20 Let all the learned say what they can,
   'Tis ready money makes the man.
     Ready Money [1727]

21 There is something in a face,
   An air, and a peculiar grace,
   Which boldest painters cannot trace.
     The Lucky Hit [1727]

---

[1]None think the great unhappy, but the great.—EDWARD
YOUNG, *Love of Fame* [1725–1728], satire I, l. 238
[2]See Carroll, 517:5.
[3]See Carroll, 518:8.
[4]See Marcus Aurelius, 111:10, and Anonymous, 783:18.
[5]Of whom Samuel Johnson, in *Lives of the Poets*, made the
famous remark, "He writes very well for a gentleman."
See Johnson, 317:24.

1 The chase, the sport of kings;
Image of war, without its guilt.
The Chase [1735], I, 13

John Philips
1676–1709

2 Happy the man who, void of cares and strife,
In silken or in leathern purse retains
A Splendid Shilling.
The Splendid Shilling [1701], l. 1

Sir Robert Walpole
1676–1745

3 The balance of power.
Speech in the House of Commons [February 13, 1741]

4 All those men have their price.
From WILLIAM COXE, *Memoirs of Walpole [1798], vol. IV, p. 369*

5 Anything but history, for history must be false.
Walpoliana, no. 141

Henry St. John, Viscount Bolingbroke
1678–1751

6 Truth lies within a little and certain compass, but error is immense.   *Reflections upon Exile [1716]*

7 Nations, like men, have their infancy.
On the Study and Use of History [1752], letter 4

8 They [Thucydides and Xenophon] maintained the dignity of history.   *Ibid. 5*

9 It is the modest, not the presumptuous, inquirer who makes a real and safe progress in the discovery of divine truths. One follows Nature and Nature's God; that is, he follows God in his works and in his word.[1]   *Letter to Alexander Pope*

George Farquhar
1678–1707

10 Reason still keeps its throne, but it nods a little, that's all.
The Recruiting Officer [1706], act III, sc. ii

11 I have fed purely upon ale; I have eat my ale, and I always sleep upon ale.
The Beaux' Stratagem [1707], act I, sc. i

12 My Lady Bountiful.   *Ibid.*

13 I believe they talked of me, for they laughed consumedly.   *Ibid. III, i*

[1]See Pope, 302:1, and Jefferson, 343:2.

14 'Twas for the good of my country that I should be abroad.[2]—Anything for the good of one's country—I'm a Roman for that.   *Ibid. III, ii*

15 How a little love and good company improves a woman!   *Ibid. IV, i*

16 Spare all I have, and take my life.
Ibid. V, ii

Thomas Parnell
1679–1718

17 My days have been so wondrous free,
The little birds that fly
With careless ease from tree to tree,
Were but as bless'd as I.
Song [1714],[3] st. 1

18 Still an angel appear to each lover beside,
But still be a woman to you.
When Thy Beauty Appears [1722], st. 3

19 We call it only pretty Fanny's way.
An Elegy to an Old Beauty [1722], st. 4

20 Let those love now who never loved before;
Let those who always loved, now love the more.
Translation of the Pervigilium Veneris[4]

Destouches [Philippe Néricault]
1680–1754

21 Those not present are always wrong.[5]
L'Obstacle Imprévu [1717], act I, sc. vi

22 Criticism is easy, art is difficult.
Le Glorieux [1732], act II, sc. v

Edward Young
1683–1765

23 The love of praise, howe'er conceal'd by art,
Reigns more or less, and glows in ev'ry heart.
Love of Fame [1725–1728], satire I, l. 51

24 Some for renown, on scraps of learning dote,
And think they grow immortal as they quote.
Ibid. l. 89

25   Be wise with speed;
A fool at forty is a fool indeed.
Ibid. II, l. 282

[2]Leaving his country for his country's sake.—CHARLES FITZGEFFREY [c. 1575–1638], *The Life and Death of Sir Francis Drake [1596], st. 213*
True patriots all; for, be it understood, / We left our country for our country's good.—*Prologue for opening of playhouse at New South Wales [January 16, 1796]*; attributed to the famous pickpocket known as GEORGE BARRINGTON [1755–c. 1840]
[3]Set to music by Francis Hopkinson; one of the earliest American songs.
[4]See Anonymous: Latin, 118:22.
[5]Les absents ont toujours tort.

1 Forever most divinely in the wrong.
Love of Fame, satire VI, l. 105

2 For her own breakfast she'll project a scheme,
Nor take her tea without a stratagem.
Ibid. l. 187

3 One to destroy, is murder by the law;
And gibbets keep the lifted hand in awe;
To murder thousands takes a specious name,
War's glorious art, and gives immortal fame.
Ibid. VII, l. 55

4 The man that makes a character makes foes.
To Mr. Pope, epistle I, l. 28

5 In records that defy the tooth of time.
The Statesman's Creed

6 Tired nature's sweet restorer, balmy sleep!
Night Thoughts [1742–1745]. Night I, l. 1

7 Night, sable goddess! from her ebon throne,
In rayless majesty, now stretches forth
Her leaden scepter o'er a slumbering world.
Ibid. l. 18

8 Creation sleeps! 'Tis as the general pulse
Of life stood still, and Nature made a pause;
An awful pause! prophetic of her end.
Ibid. l. 23

9 The bell strikes one. We take no note of time
But from its loss.
Ibid. l. 55

10 Be wise today; 'tis madness to defer.[1]
Ibid. l. 390

11 Procrastination is the thief of time.
Ibid. l. 393

12 At thirty, a man suspects himself a fool;
Knows it at forty, and reforms his plan;
At fifty chides his infamous delay,
Pushes his prudent purpose to resolve;
In all the magnanimity of thought
Resolves, and re-resolves; then dies the same.
Ibid. l. 417

13 All men think all men mortal but themselves.
Ibid. l. 424

14 Man wants but little, nor that little long.[2]
Ibid. Night IV, l. 118

15 A God all mercy is a God unjust.
Ibid. l. 233

16 By night an atheist half believes a God.[3]
Ibid. Night V, l. 177

17   Like our shadows,
Our wishes lengthen as our sun declines.
Ibid. l. 661

18 Death loves a shining mark, a signal blow.
Ibid. l. 1011

19 Too low they build, who build beneath the stars.
Ibid. Night VIII, l. 215

20   Final Ruin fiercely drives
Her plowshare o'er creation.[4]
Ibid. Night IX, l. 167

21 An undevout astronomer is mad.
Ibid. l. 771

Sir William Pulteney, Earl of Bath
1684–1764

22 Since twelve honest men have decided the cause,
And were judges of facts, though not judges of
laws.
The Honest Jury [1731], III

George Berkeley
1685–1753

23   And what are these fluxions? The velocities of
evanescent increments. And what are these same
evanescent increments? They are neither finite quantities, nor quantities infinitely small, nor yet nothing.
May we not call them ghosts of departed quantities?
The Analyst [1734], sec. 35

24   [Tar water] is of a nature so mild and benign and
proportioned to the human constitution, as to warm
without heating, to cheer but not inebriate.[5]
Siris [1744], par. 217

25   Truth is the cry of all, but the game of the few.
Ibid. par. 368

26   He who says there is no such thing as an honest
man, you may be sure is himself a knave.
Maxims Concerning Patriotism

27 Westward the course of empire takes its way;[6]
The four first acts already past,
A fifth shall close the drama with the day:
Time's noblest offspring is the last.
*On the Prospect of Planting Arts and Learning
in America [1752], st. 6*

Jane Brereton
1685–1740

28 The picture placed the busts between,
Adds to the thought much strength,
Wisdom, and Wit are little seen,
But Folly's at full length.
*On Beau Nash's Picture at Full Length Between
the Busts of Sir Isaac Newton and Mr. Pope[7]*

---

[1]See Euripides, 68:3, and Congreve, 291:17.
[2]See Goldsmith, 328:22.
[3]See W. T. Cummings, 711:5.
[4]See Burns, 361:20.
[5]See Cowper, 335:3.
[6]Westward the star of empire takes its way. — JOHN QUINCY ADAMS, *Oration at Plymouth* [1802]
[7]In ALEXANDER DYCE [1798–1869], *Specimens of British Poetesses*. This epigram is often ascribed to CHESTERFIELD.

John Gay[1]
1685–1732

1 'Twas when the seas were roaring
  With hollow blasts of wind,
  A damsel lay deploring,
  All on a rock reclin'd.
  The What D'ye Call It [1715], act II, sc. viii

2 Now Cynthia, named fair regent of the night.
  Trivia [1716], bk. III

3 All in the Downs the fleet was moor'd.
  *Sweet William's Farewell to Black-eyed Susan
  [1720]*

4 Adieu! she cries; and waved her lily hand.
  Ibid.

5 My lodging is on the cold ground,
  And hard, very hard, is my fare,
  But that which grieves me more
  Is the coldness of my dear.
  My Lodging Is on the Cold Ground [1720], st. 1

6 Whence is thy learning? Hath thy toil
  O'er books consumed the midnight oil?
  *Fables, pt. I [1727]. The Shepherd and the
  Philosopher*

7 Where yet was ever found a mother
  Who'd give her booby for another?
  Ibid. The Mother, the Nurse, and the Fairy

8 When we risk no contradiction,
  It prompts the tongue to deal in fiction.
  Ibid. The Elephant and the Bookseller

9 In every age and clime we see
  Two of a trade can never agree.
  Ibid. The Rat-catcher and Cats

10 Those who in quarrels interpose
  Must often wipe a bloody nose.
  Ibid. The Mastiffs

11 I hate the man who builds his name
  On ruins of another's fame.
  Ibid. The Poet and the Rose

12 And when a lady's in the case,
  You know all other things give place.
  Ibid. The Hare and Many Friends

13 From wine what sudden friendship springs!
  Ibid. II [1738]. The Squire and His Cur

14 O Polly, you might have toy'd and kiss'd,
  By keeping men off, you keep them on.
  The Beggar's Opera [1728],[2] act I, sc. viii, air 9

15 If with me you'd fondly stray.
  Over the hills and far away.[3]
  Ibid. xiii, air 16

---

16 Fill ev'ry glass, for wine inspires us,
  And fires us
  With courage, love and joy.
  Women and wine should life employ.
  Is there ought else on earth desirous?
  Ibid. II, i, air 19

17 If the heart of a man is depress'd with cares,
  The mist is dispelled when a woman appears.
  Ibid. iii, air 21

18 Youth's the season made for joys,
  Love is then our duty.
  Ibid. iv, air 22

19 Man may escape from rope and gun;
  Nay, some have outliv'd the doctor's pill;
  Who takes a woman must be undone,
  That basilisk is sure to kill.
  The fly that sips treacle is lost in the sweets,
  So he that tastes woman, woman, woman,
  He that tastes woman, ruin meets.
  Ibid. viii, air 26

20 How happy could I be with either,
  Were t'other dear charmer away!
  Ibid. xiii, air 35

21 The charge is prepar'd; the lawyers are met;
  The Judges all ranged (a terrible show!)
  Ibid. III, xi, air 57

22 Life is a jest; and all things show it.
  I thought so once; but now I know it.
  My Own Epitaph

Aaron Hill
1685–1750

23 Tender-handed stroke a nettle,
  And it stings you for your pains;
  Grasp it like a man of mettle,
  And it soft as silk remains.[4]
  Verses Written on a Window in Scotland

Samuel Madden
1686–1765

24   In an orchard there should be enough to eat,
  enough to lay up, enough to be stolen, and enough
  to rot upon the ground.
  *Quoted by SAMUEL JOHNSON [1783]. From
  BOSWELL, Life of Johnson [1791], vol. II, p. 457
  (Everyman edition)*

Allan Ramsay
1686–1758

25 Farewell to Lochaber, farewell to my Jean.
  Lochaber No More [1724], st. 1

---

[1]See Pope's *Epitaph on Gay*, 300:28.
[2]See Brecht, 698:n1.
[3]'O'er the hills and far away.—THOMAS D'URFEY [1653–
1723], *Pills to Purge Melancholy* [1719]
See Tennyson, 456:2, and Anonymous, 790:4.

[4]The world's a nettle; disturb it, it stings: / Grasp it firmly, it
stings not.—OWEN MEREDITH [E. R. BULWER-LYTTON], *Lucile*
[1860], *pt. I, canto 3, st. 2*

Henry Carey

c. 1687–1743

1 Namby Pamby's little rhymes,
Little jingle, little chimes.

Namby Pamby[1]

2 Of all the girls that are so smart,
There's none like pretty Sally.
She is the darling of my heart,
And she lives in our alley.

Sally in Our Alley [1729], st. 1

3 God save our gracious king!
Long live our noble king!
God save the king!

God Save the King [c. 1740]

Pierre Carlet de Chamblain de Marivaux

1688–1763

4   In this world, you must be a bit too kind in order to be kind enough.

Le Jeu de l'Amour et du Hasard [1730], act I, sc. ii

Alexander Pope[2]

1688–1744

5 Happy the man whose wish and care
A few paternal acres bound,
Content to breathe his native air
In his own ground.[3]

Ode on Solitude [c. 1700], st. 1

6 Thus let me live, unseen, unknown,
Thus unlamented let me die,
Steal from the world, and not a stone
Tell where I lie.

Ibid. st. 5

7 Where'er you walk, cool gales shall fan the glade,
Trees, where you sit, shall crowd into a shade:
Where'er you tread, the blushing flow'rs shall rise,
And all things flourish where you turn your eyes.

Pastorals [written 1704]. Summer, l. 73

8 Nor Fame I slight, nor for her favors call;
She comes unlook'd for, if she comes at all.

The Temple of Fame [1711], l. 513

9 'Tis with our judgments as our watches, none
Go just alike, yet each believes his own.

An Essay on Criticism [1711], pt. I, l. 9

10 Let such teach others who themselves excel,
And censure freely who have written well.

Ibid. l. 15

11 Some are bewilder'd in the maze of schools,
And some made coxcombs nature meant but fools.

Ibid. l. 26

12 Those oft are stratagems which errors seem,
Nor is it Homer nods, but we that dream.[4]

Ibid. l. 179

13 A little learning is a dangerous thing;[5]
Drink deep, or taste not the Pierian spring:
There shallow draughts intoxicate the brain,
And drinking largely sobers us again.

Ibid. II, l. 15

14 True wit is nature to advantage dress'd,
What oft was thought, but ne'er so well express'd.

Ibid. l. 97

15 Words are like leaves; and where they most abound,
Much fruit of sense beneath is rarely found.

Ibid. l. 109

16 Such labored nothings, in so strange a style,
Amaze th' unlearn'd, and make the learned smile.

Ibid. l. 126

17 Be not the first by whom the new are tried,
Nor yet the last to lay the old aside.

Ibid. l. 135

18   As some to church repair,
Not for the doctrine, but the music there.
These equal syllables alone require,
Though oft the ear the open vowels tire;
While expletives their feeble aid do join,
And ten low words oft creep in one dull line.

Ibid. l. 142

19 Then, at the last and only couplet fraught
With some unmeaning thing they call a thought,
A needless Alexandrine ends the song,
That, like a wounded snake, drags its slow length along.

Ibid. l. 154

20 True ease in writing comes from art, not chance,
As those move easiest who have learn'd to dance.
'Tis not enough no harshness gives offense;
The sound must seem an echo to the sense.

Ibid. l. 162

21 At ev'ry trifle scorn to take offense.

Ibid. l. 186

---

[1]Ambrose Phillips . . . who had the honor of bringing into fashion a species of composition which has been called, after his name, Namby Pamby.—MACAULAY, *Review of Aikin's Life of Addison* [1843]

[2]A thousand years may elapse before there shall appear another man with a power of versification equal to that of Pope. —SAMUEL JOHNSON [1781]; *from* BOSWELL, *Life of Johnson* [1791]

[3]See Horace, 95:13.

[4]See Horace, 98:17.

[5]See Publilius Syrus, 100:17.

1 Some judge of authors' names, not works, and then
   Nor praise nor blame the writings, but the men.
                                                    Ibid. l. 212

2 What woeful stuff this madrigal would be,
   In some starv'd hackney sonneteer, or me!
   But let a lord once own the happy lines,
   How the wit brightens! how the style refines!
                                                    Ibid. l. 218

3 Some praise at morning what they blame at night,
   But always think the last opinion right.
                                                    Ibid. l. 230

4 To err is human, to forgive divine.[1]
                                                    Ibid. l. 325

5 All seems infected that th' infected spy,
   As all looks yellow to the jaundic'd eye.
                                                    Ibid. l. 358

6 For fools rush in where angels fear to tread.[2]
                                                    Ibid. III, l. 65

7 But where's the man who counsel can bestow,
   Still pleas'd to teach, and yet not proud to know?[3]
                                                    Ibid. l. 71

8 Vital spark of heav'nly flame!
   Quit, oh quit, this mortal frame:
   Trembling, hoping, ling'ring, flying,
   Oh the pain, the bliss of dying![4]
              The Dying Christian to His Soul [1712], st. 1

9 What dire offense from amorous causes springs,
   What mighty contests rise from trivial things![5]
              The Rape of the Lock [1712], canto I, l. 1

10 On her white breast a sparkling cross she wore,
   Which Jews might kiss, and infidels adore.
                                                    Ibid. II, l. 7

11 If to her share some female errors fall,
   Look on her face, and you'll forget 'em all.
                                                    Ibid. l. 17

12 Fair tresses man's imperial race ensnare,
   And beauty draws us with a single hair.[6]
                                                    Ibid. l. 27

13 Here thou, great Anna![7] whom three realms obey,
   Dost sometimes counsel take—and sometimes tea.
                                                    Ibid. III, l. 7

14 At every word a reputation dies.
                                                    Ibid. l. 16

15 The hungry judges soon the sentence sign,
   And wretches hang that jurymen may dine.
                                                    Ibid. l. 21

16 Let spades be trumps! she said, and trumps they were.
                                                    Ibid. l. 46

17 But when to mischief mortals bend their will,
   How soon they find fit instruments of ill!
                                                    Ibid. l. 125

18 The meeting points the sacred hair dissever
   From the fair head, forever, and forever!
   Then flash'd the living lightning from her eyes,
   And screams of horror rend th' affrighted skies.
                                                    Ibid. l. 153

19 To wake the soul by tender strokes of art,
   To raise the genius, and to mend the heart;
   To make mankind, in conscious virtue bold,
   Live o'er each scene, and be what they behold:
   For this the Tragic Muse first trod the stage.
         Prologue to Mr. Addison's Cato [1713], l. 1

20 Ignobly vain, and impotently great.
                                                    Ibid. l. 29

21 Here hills and vales, the woodland and the plain,
   Here earth and water seem to strive again,
   Not chaos-like together crush'd and bruis'd,
   But, as the world, harmoniously confus'd:
   Where order in variety we see,
   And where, though all things differ, all agree.
                           Windsor Forest [1713], l. 11

22   Party-spirit, which at best is but the madness of many for the gain of a few.[8]
              Letter to E. Blount [August 27, 1714]

23 The wrath of Peleus' son, the direful spring
   Of all the Grecian woes, O goddess sing![9]
              Translation of the Iliad [1715],[10] bk I, l. 1

24 She moves a goddess, and she looks a queen.
                                                    Ibid. III, 208

25 Tell me, Muse, of the man of many wiles.[11]
              Translation of the Odyssey [1725–1756], bk. I, l. 1

26 True friendship's laws are by this rule express'd,
   Welcome the coming, speed the parting guest.[12]
                                                    Ibid. XV, l. 83

27 Dear, damn'd, distracting town, farewell!
   Thy fools no more I'll tease:
   This year in peace, ye critics, dwell,
   Ye harlots, sleep at ease!
              A Farewell to London [1715], st. 1

[1]See Plutarch, 107:18; Anonymous: Latin, 118:30; Shirley, 246:20; and Burns, 362:5.
[2]See Shakespeare, 165:25.
[3]See Chaucer, 129:22.
[4]See Hadrian, 110:7.
[5]See Robert Burton, 234:9.
[6]See Robert Burton, 235:13.
[7]Queen Anne [1665–1714].

[8]See Pope, 303:23.
[9]Another version is:
Achilles' wrath, to Greece the direful spring / Of woes unnumbered, heavenly goddess, sing!
[10]See Richard Bentley, 286:10.
[11]See Homer, 52:27.
[12]See Homer, 53:29, and Pope, 302:22.

1 Luxurious lobster-nights, farewell,
For sober, studious days!
A Farewell to London, st. 12

2 Oh name forever sad! forever dear!
Still breath'd in sighs, still usher'd with a tear.
Eloisa to Abelard [1717], l. 31

3 Now warm in love, now with'ring in my bloom,
Lost in a convent's solitary gloom!
Ibid. l. 37

4 Speed the soft intercourse from soul to soul,
And waft a sigh from Indus to the Pole.
Ibid. l. 57

5 How happy is the blameless vestal's lot!
The world forgetting, by the world forgot.
Ibid. l. 207

6 He best can paint them who shall feel them most.
Ibid. l. 366

7 What beck'ning ghost, along the moonlight shade
Invites my steps, and points to yonder glade?
*Elegy to the Memory of an Unfortunate Lady
[1717], l. 1*

8 Is it, in Heav'n, a crime to love too well?
To bear too tender, or too firm a heart,
To act a lover's or a Roman's part?
Is there no bright reversion in the sky,
For those who greatly think, or bravely die?
Ibid. l. 6

9 How lov'd, how honor'd once, avails thee not,
To whom related, or by whom begot;
A heap of dust alone remains of thee;
'Tis all thou art, and all the proud shall be!
Ibid. l. 71

10 And yet the fate of all extremes is such,
Men may be read, as well as books, too much.
To observations which ourselves we make,
We grow more partial for th' observer's sake.
*Moral Essays [1731–1735]. Epistle I, To Lord
Cobham [1734], l. 9*

11 Not always actions show the man: we find
Who does a kindness is not therefore kind.
Ibid. l. 109

12 'Tis education forms the common mind:
Just as the twig is bent, the tree's inclin'd.
Ibid. l. 149

13 Most women have no characters at all.
Ibid. II, To Mrs. M. Blount [1735], l. 2

14 Chaste to her husband, frank to all beside,
A teeming mistress, but a barren bride.
Ibid. l. 71

15 Wise wretch! with pleasures too refin'd to please;
With too much spirit to be e'er at ease;
With too much quickness ever to be taught;
With too much thinking to have common
    thought.

You purchase pain with all that joy can give,
And die of nothing but a rage to live.
Ibid. l. 95

16 In men, we various ruling passions find;
In women, two almost divide the kind;
Those, only fix'd, they first or last obey,
The love of pleasure, and the love of sway.
Ibid. l. 207

17 Men, some to business, some to pleasure take;
But ev'ry woman is at heart a rake.
Ibid. l. 215

18 She who ne'er answers till a husband cools,
Or, if she rules him, never shows she rules;
Charms by accepting, by submitting, sways,
Yet has her humor most, when she obeys.
Ibid. l. 261

19 And mistress of herself, though china fall.
Ibid. l. 268

20 Woman's at best a contradiction still.
Ibid. l. 270

21 Who shall decide when doctors disagree?[1]
Ibid. III, To Lord Bathurst [1732], l. 1

22 But thousands die, without or this or that,
Die, and endow a college, or a cat.
Ibid. l. 95

23 The ruling passion, be it what it will,
The ruling passion conquers reason still.
Ibid. l. 153

24 Statesman, yet friend to truth! of soul sincere,
In action faithful, and in honor clear;
Who broke no promise, served no private end,
Who gain'd no title, and who lost no friend.
Ibid. V, To Mr. Addison [written 1720], l. 67

25   "Blessed is the man who expects nothing, for he
shall never be disappointed" was the ninth beatitude.[2]   *Letter to Fortescue [September 23, 1725]*

26 You beat your pate, and fancy wit will come:
Knock as you please, there's nobody at home.[3]
Epigram: An Empty House [1727]

27 Ye Gods! annihilate but space and time,
And make two lovers happy.
*Martinus Scriblerus on the Art of Sinking in
Poetry [1728], ch. 11*

28 In wit a man, simplicity a child.[4]
Epitaph on Gay [1732][5]

[1]When doctors differ who decides amid the milliard-headed
throng?—RICHARD FRANCIS BURTON, *The Kasîdah of Haji
Abdû El-Yazdi*, VIII, 29
[2]Blessed are those that nought expect, / For they shall not be
disappointed.— JOHN WOLCOT [PETER PINDAR], *Ode to Pitt*
[3]See Cowper, 334:12.
[4]See Dryden, 275:6.
[5]See Gay, 297.

1 Awake, my St. John![1] leave all meaner things
To low ambition, and the pride of kings.
Let us, since life can little more supply
Than just to look about us, and to die,
Expatiate free o'er all this scene of man;
A mighty maze! but not without a plan.
An Essay on Man [1733–1734]. Epistle I, l. 1

2 Eye Nature's walks, shoot folly as it flies,
And catch the manners living as they rise:
Laugh where we must, be candid where we can;
But vindicate the ways of God to man.[2]
Ibid. l. 13

3 Say first, of God above or man below,
What can we reason but from what we know?
Ibid. l. 17

4 Pleased to the last, he crops the flowery food,
And licks the hand just rais'd to shed his blood.
Ibid. l. 83

5 Who sees with equal eye, as God of all,
A hero perish or a sparrow fall,[3]
Atoms or systems into ruin hurl'd,
And now a bubble burst, and now a world.
Ibid. l. 87

6 Hope springs eternal in the human breast:
Man never is, but always to be blest.
Ibid. l. 95

7 Lo, the poor Indian! whose untutor'd mind
Sees God in clouds, or hears him in the wind;
His soul proud Science never taught to stray
Far as the solar walk or milky way;
Yet simple nature to his hope has giv'n,
Behind the cloud-topp'd hill, an humbler heav'n.
Ibid. l. 99

8 But thinks, admitted to that equal sky,
His faithful dog shall bear him company.
Ibid. l. 111

9 Seas roll to waft me, suns to light me rise;
My footstool earth, my canopy the skies.[4]
Ibid. l. 139

10 Die of a rose in aromatic pain?
Ibid. l. 200

11 All are but parts of one stupendous whole,
Whose body Nature is, and God the soul.
Ibid. l. 267

12 All nature is but art, unknown to thee;
All chance, direction which thou canst not see;
All discord, harmony not understood;
All partial evil, universal good;
And, spite of pride, in erring reason's spite,
One truth is clear, Whatever is, is right.
Ibid. l. 289

13 Know then thyself, presume not God to scan;
The proper study of mankind is man.[5]
Placed on this isthmus of a middle state,
A being darkly wise and rudely great:
With too much knowledge for the skeptic side,
With too much weakness for the stoic's pride,
He hangs between; in doubt to act or rest;
In doubt to deem himself a god, or beast;
In doubt his mind or body to prefer;
Born but to die, and reas'ning but to err;
Alike in ignorance, his reason such,
Whether he thinks too little or too much;
Chaos of thought and passion, all confus'd;
Still by himself abus'd, or disabus'd;
Created half to rise, and half to fall;
Great lord of all things, yet a prey to all;
Sole judge of truth, in endless error hurl'd;
The glory, jest, and riddle of the world![6]
Ibid. II, l. 1

14 Vice is a monster of so frightful mien,
As to be hated needs but to be seen;[7]
Yet seen too oft, familiar with her face,
We first endure, then pity, then embrace.
Ibid. l. 217

15 Behold the child, by Nature's kindly law,
Pleas'd with a rattle, tickled with a straw:
Some livelier plaything gives his youth delight,
A little louder, but as empty quite:
Scarfs, garters, gold, amuse his riper stage,
And beads and prayer books are the toys of age!
Pleas'd with this bauble still, as that before;
Till tir'd he sleeps, and life's poor play is o'er.
Ibid. l. 275

16 O happiness! our being's end and aim!
Good, pleasure, ease, content! whate'er thy name:
That something still which prompts the eternal
  sigh,
For which we bear to live, or dare to die.
Ibid. IV, l. 1

17 Worth makes the man, and want of it the fellow;
The rest is all but leather or prunella.
Ibid. l. 203

18 A wit's a feather, and a chief a rod;
An honest man's the noblest work of God.[8]
Ibid. l. 247

[5]Trees and fields tell me nothing: men are my teachers.—
PLATO, *Phaedrus*
  La vraie science et la vraie étude de l'homme, c'est l'homme
[The true science and the true study of man is man].—PIERRE
CHARRON [1541–1603], *Traité de la Sagesse* [1601], *bk. I,
preface*
  Das eigentliche Studium der Menschheit ist der Mensch
[The proper study of mankind is man].—GOETHE, *Elective
Affinities* [1808], *bk. II, ch. 7*
  See The Seven Sages, 55:7.
[6]See Pascal, 271:7.
[7]See Dryden, 275:13.
[8]See Burns, 361:10.

[1]Bolingbroke.
[2]See Milton, 255:20 and 261:12, and Housman, 579:15.
[3]See *Matthew 10:29*, 34:33, and Shakespeare, 199:22.
[4]See *Matthew 5:35*, 33:6; Wells, 601:15; and Day, 622:14.

1 Slave to no sect, who takes no private road,
  But looks through Nature up to Nature's God.[1]
  > *An Essay on Man. Epistle IV, l. 331*

2 Form'd by thy converse, happily to steer
  From grave to gay, from lively to severe.[2]
  > *Ibid. l. 379*

3 Say, shall my little bark attendant sail,
  Pursue the triumph and partake the gale?[3]
  > *Ibid. l. 385*

4 Thou wert my guide, philosopher, and friend.[4]
  > *Ibid. l. 390*

5 That true self-love and social are the same.[5]
  > *Ibid. l. 396*

6 Shut, shut the door, good John! fatigu'd, I said;
  Tie up the knocker! say I'm sick, I'm dead.
  The Dog-star rages!
  > *Epistle to Dr. Arbuthnot [1734]. Prologue to*
  > *Imitations of Horace, l. 1*

7 No creature smarts so little as a fool.
  > *Ibid. l. 84*

8 As yet a child, nor yet a fool to fame,
  I lisp'd in numbers, for the numbers came.
  > *Ibid. l. 127*

9 This long disease, my life.
  > *Ibid. l. 132*

10 Means not, but blunders round about a meaning;
   And he whose fustian's so sublimely bad,
   It is not poetry, but prose run mad.
   > *Ibid. l. 186*

11   Were there one whose fires
   True Genius kindles, and fair Fame inspires,
   Bless'd with each talent, and each art to please,
   And born to write, converse, and live with ease;
   Should such a man, too fond to rule alone,
   Bear, like the Turk, no brother near the throne;[6]
   View him with scornful, yet with jealous eyes,
   And hate for arts that caus'd himself to rise;
   Damn with faint praise, assent with civil leer,
   And, without sneering, teach the rest to sneer;[7]
   Willing to wound, and yet afraid to strike,
   Just hint a fault, and hesitate dislike;
   Alike reserv'd to blame or to commend,
   A tim'rous foe, and a suspicious friend;
   Dreading e'en fools, by flatterers besieged,

[1]See Bolingbroke, 295:9, and Jefferson, 343:2.
[2]See Boileau, 280:4.
[3]See Dante, 126:2.
[4]Is this my guide, philosopher, and friend?—*Imitations of Horace* [1733–1738], *Epistle I, bk. I, l. 177*
[5]See John Quincy Adams, 369:3.
[6]Nor is thy fame on lesser ruins built; / Nor needs thy juster title the foul guilt / Of Eastern kings, who, to secure their reign, / Must have their brothers, sons, and kindred slain.— DENHAM, *On Mr. John Fletcher's Works* [1668]
[7]When needs he must, yet faintly then he praises; / Somewhat the deed, much more the means he raises; / So marreth what he makes, and praising most, dispraises.—PHINEAS FLETCHER [1582–1650], *The Purple Island* [1633], *canto 7*

And so obliging that he ne'er oblig'd;
Like Cato, give his little Senate laws,[8]
And sit attentive to his own applause.
> *Ibid. l. 193*

12 Who but must laugh, if such a man there be?
   Who would not weep, if Atticus were he!
   > *Ibid. l. 213*

13 Curs'd be the verse, how well soe'er it flow,
   That tends to make one worthy man my foe.
   > *Ibid. l. 283*

14 Let Sporus tremble—"What? that thing of silk,
   Sporus, that mere white curd of ass's milk?
   Satire or sense, alas! can Sporus feel?
   Who breaks a butterfly upon a wheel?"
   > *Ibid. l. 305*

15 Yet let me flap this bug with gilded wings,
   This painted child of dirt, that stinks and stings;
   Whose buzz the witty and the fair annoys,
   Yet wit ne'er tastes, and beauty ne'er enjoys.
   > *Ibid. l. 309*

16 And he himself one vile antithesis.
   > *Ibid. l. 325*

17 Wit that can creep, and pride that licks the dust.
   > *Ibid. l. 333*

18 Unlearn'd, he knew no schoolman's subtle art,
   No language, but the language of the heart.
   > *Ibid. l. 398*

19 I cannot sleep a wink.[9]
   > *Imitations of Horace [1733–1738], satire I,*
   > *bk. II, l. 12*

20 Satire's my weapon, but I'm too discreet
   To run amuck, and tilt at all I meet.
   > *Ibid. l. 69*

21 There St. John mingles with my friendly bowl
   The feast of reason and the flow of soul.
   > *Ibid. l. 127*

22 For I, who hold sage Homer's rule the best,
   Welcome the coming, speed the going guest.[10]
   > *Ibid. II, II, l. 159*

23 I've often wish'd that I had clear,
   For life, six hundred pounds a year;
   A handsome house to lodge a friend,
   A river at my garden's end,
   A terrace walk, and half a rood
   Of land set out to plant a wood.[11]
   > *Ibid. VI, II, l. 1*

24 Give me again my hollow tree,
   A crust of bread, and liberty.
   > *Ibid. l. 220*

25 A patriot is a fool in ev'ry age.
   > *Ibid. Epilogue to the Satires, Dialogue I, l. 41*

[8]While Cato gives his little senate laws.—*Prologue to Mr. Addison's Cato* [1713], *l. 23*
[9]See Cervantes, 149:11, and Shakespeare, 219:30.
[10]See Homer, 53:29, and Pope, 299:26.
[11]See Horace, 95:10.

1 Never gallop Pegasus to death.
Ibid. Epistle I, bk. I, l. 14

2 Not to go back is somewhat to advance,
And men must walk, at least, before they dance.
Ibid. l. 53

3 He's arm'd without that's innocent within.
Ibid. l. 94

4 Get place and wealth, if possible with grace;
If not, by any means get wealth and place.[1]
Ibid. l. 103

5 The people's voice is odd,
It is, and it is not, the voice of God.[2]
Ibid. II, l. 89

6 In quibbles angel and archangel join,
And God the Father turns a school-divine.
Ibid. l. 101 (on Paradise Lost)

7 The mob of gentlemen who wrote with ease.
Ibid. l. 108

8 One simile that solitary shines
In the dry desert of a thousand lines.
Ibid. l. 111

9 Ev'n copious Dryden wanted, or forgot,
The last and greatest art—the art to blot.
Ibid. l. 280

10 There still remains, to mortify a wit,
The many-headed monster of the pit.[3]
Ibid. l. 304

11 We poets are (upon a poet's word)
Of all mankind the creatures most absurd:
The season when to come, and when to go,
To sing, or cease to sing, we never know.[4]
Ibid. l. 358

12 Call, if you will, bad rhyming a disease,
It gives men happiness, or leaves them ease.
Ibid. II, II, l. 182

13 Vain was the chief's, the sage's pride!
They had no poet, and they died.[5]
Ibid. Odes, bk. IV, ode 9, st. 4

14 Father of all! in every age,
In every clime ador'd,
By saint, by savage, and by sage,
Jehovah, Jove, or Lord!
The Universal Prayer [1738], st. 1

15 And binding Nature fast in fate,
Left free the human will.
Ibid. st. 3

16 I am his Highness'[6] dog at Kew;
Pray tell me, sir, whose dog are you?
On the collar of a dog

17 Nature and Nature's laws lay hid in night:
God said, Let Newton be! and all was light.
Epitaph intended for Sir Isaac Newton

18 Who dare to love their country, and be poor.
On his grotto at Twickenham [1740]

19 This is the Jew
That Shakespeare drew.
Of Macklin's performance in 1741 of Shylock in
The Merchant of Venice (attributed to Pope)

20 I never knew any man in my life who could not bear another's misfortunes perfectly like a Christian.[7]
Thoughts on Various Subjects; published in
Swift's Miscellanies [1727]

21 A man should never be ashamed to own he has been in the wrong, which is but saying, in other words, that he is wiser today than he was yesterday.
Ibid.

22 It is with narrow-souled people as with narrow-necked bottles; the less they have in them the more noise they make in pouring out. *Ibid.*

23 Party is the madness of many, for the gain of a few.[8] *Ibid.*

24 Whether thou choose Cervantes' serious air,
Or laugh and shake in Rabelais' easy chair.
The Dunciad [1728–1743], bk. I, l. 21

25 Poetic Justice, with her lifted scale,
Where, in nice balance, truth with gold she weighs,
And solid pudding against empty praise.
Ibid. l. 52

26 Next o'er his books his eyes began to roll,
In pleasing memory of all he stole.
Ibid. l. 127

27 A brain of feathers, and a heart of lead.
Ibid. II, l. 44

28 Peel'd, patch'd, and piebald, linsey-woolsey brothers,
Grave mummers! sleeveless some, and shirtless others.
That once was Britain.
Ibid. III, l. 115

29 And proud his mistress' orders to perform,
Rides in the whirlwind and directs the storm.[9]
Ibid. l. 263

30 A wit with dunces, and a dunce with wits.[10]
Ibid. IV, l. 90

31 The Right Divine of Kings to govern wrong.
Ibid. l. 188

32 Stuff the head
With all such reading as was never read:

[1]See Horace, 97:6.
[2]See Alcuin, 120:8.
[3]See Horace, 97:7; Machiavelli, 137:3; and Shakespeare, 183:9, 219:3, and 219:10.
[4]See Frost, 622:18.
[5]See Pindar, 64:13, and Horace, 97:1.
[6]Frederick, Prince of Wales.

[7]See La Rochefoucauld, 264:23.
[8]See Pope, 299:22.
[9]See Addison, 291:30.
[10]See Quintilian, 105:14.

For thee explain a thing till all men doubt it,
And write about it, Goddess, and about it.
The Dunciad, bk. IV, l. 249

1 To happy convents, bosom'd deep in vines,
Where slumber abbots, purple as their wines.
Ibid. l. 301

2 Religion blushing veils her sacred fires,
And unawares Morality expires.
Nor public flame, nor private, dares to shine;
Nor human spark is left, nor glimpse divine!
Lo! thy dread empire Chaos! is restor'd:
Light dies before thy uncreating word;
Thy hand, great Anarch! lets the curtain fall,
And universal darkness buries all.
Ibid. l. 649

Lady Mary Wortley Montagu
1689–1762

3 And we meet, with champagne and a chicken, at
last.
The Lover [1748]

4 Be plain in dress, and sober in your diet;
In short, my deary, kiss me, and be quiet.
A Summary of Lord Lyttelton's Advice

5 Satire should, like a polished razor keen,
Wound with a touch that's scarcely felt or seen.
*To the Imitator of the First Satire of Horace,
bk. II*

6 But the fruit that can fall without shaking
Indeed is too mellow for me.
Letters and Works [1837]. The Answer

Charles de Secondat,
Baron de Montesquieu[1]
1689–1755

7 How can anyone be Persian?
Lettres Persanes [1721], no. 30

8 A man should be mourned at his birth, not at his
death.
Ibid. 40

9 If triangles had a god, he would have three
sides.[2]
Ibid. 59

10 Liberty is the right of doing whatever the laws
permit.
De l'Esprit des Lois [1748], XI, 3

11 Useless laws weaken the necessary laws.
Ibid. XXIX, 16

12 If I knew of something that could serve my nation
but would ruin another, I would not propose it to

my prince, for I am first a man and only then a
Frenchman . . . because I am necessarily a man,
and only accidentally am I French.[3]
*Pensées et Fragments Inédits de Montesquieu
[1899], I*

13 You have to study a great deal to know a little.
Ibid.

John Byrom
1692–1763

14 God bless the King, I mean the Faith's Defender;
God bless—no harm in blessing—the Pretender;
But who Pretender is, or who is King,
God bless us all—that's quite another thing.
*Miscellaneous Poems [1773]. To an Officer in
the Army, Extempore; Intended to Allay the
Violence of Party Spirit*

15 Some say, that Signor Bononcini,
Compared to Handel's a mere ninny;
Others aver, to him, that Handel
Is scarcely fit to hold a candle.[4]
Strange! that such high dispute should be
'Twixt Tweedledum and Tweedledee.
*Ibid. On the Feuds Between Handel and
Bononcini*

16 As clear as a whistle.
Epistle to Lloyd

Philip Dormer Stanhope,
Earl of Chesterfield
1694–1773

17 Measures not men.[5]
Letters to His Son [1774]. March 6, 1742

18 Whatever is worth doing at all, is worth doing
well.
Ibid. March 10, 1746

19 The knowledge of the world is only to be acquired in the world, and not in a closet.
Ibid. October 4, 1746

20 An injury is much sooner forgotten than an insult.
Ibid. October 9, 1746

21 Do as you would be done by, is the surest method
that I know of pleasing.[6]   *Ibid. October 16, 1747*

22 Take the tone of the company that you are in.
Ibid.

[1]See Carlyle, 413:16.
[2]See Xenophanes, 60:5.
[3]See Montaigne, 146:23.
[4]See Lamb, 388:3.
[5]See Goldsmith, 329:6; Burke, 330:24; and John Adams,
337:18.
[6]See *Matthew* 7:12, 34:8; Confucius, 61:30; Aristotle, 77:15;
and Hillel, 102:7.

1   I knew once a very covetous, sordid fellow,[1] who used frequently to say, "Take care of the pence, for the pounds will take care of themselves."
Ibid. November 6, 1747

2   Advice is seldom welcome; and those who want it the most always like it the least.
Ibid. January 29, 1748

3   Speak of the moderns without contempt, and of the ancients without idolatry.
Ibid. February 22, 1748

4   Wear your learning, like your watch, in a private pocket: and do not pull it out and strike it, merely to show that you have one.   *Ibid.*

5   Manners must adorn knowledge, and smooth its way through the world. Like a great rough diamond, it may do very well in a closet by way of curiosity, and also for its intrinsic value.
Ibid. July 1, 1748

6   Women, then, are only children of a larger growth.   *Ibid. September 5, 1748*

7   Women who are either indisputably beautiful, or indisputably ugly, are best flattered upon the score of their understandings; but those who are in a state of mediocrity are best flattered upon their beauty, or at least their graces; for every woman who is not absolutely ugly thinks herself handsome.   *Ibid.*

8   Without some dissimulation no business can be carried on at all.   *Ibid. May 22, 1749*

9   Idleness is only the refuge of weak minds.
Ibid. July 20, 1749

10   Style is the dress of thoughts.[2]
Ibid. November 24, 1749

11   Dispatch is the soul of business.
Ibid. February 5, 1750

12   Knowledge may give weight, but accomplishments give luster, and many more people see than weigh.   *Ibid. May 8, 1750*

13   Let blockheads read what blockheads wrote.
Ibid. November 1, 1750

14   Every woman is infallibly to be gained by every sort of flattery, and every man by one sort or other.
Ibid. March 16, 1752

15   The chapter of knowledge is a very short, but the chapter of accidents is a very long one.[3]
To Solomon Dayrolles, February 16, 1753

16   I assisted at the birth of that most significant word "flirtation," which dropped from the most beautiful mouth in the world.
The World [December 5, 1754], no. 101

17 Unlike my subject will I frame my song,
It shall be witty, and it shan't be long.
Epigram on ("Long") Sir Thomas Robinson

18 The dews of the evening most carefully shun—
Those tears of the sky for the loss of the sun.
Advice to a Lady in Autumn

19   Give Dayrolles a chair.   *Last words*

Francis Hutcheson
1694–1746

20   That action is best which procures the greatest happiness for the greatest numbers.[4]
Inquiry Concerning Moral Good and Evil [1720], sec. 3

François Quesnay
1694–1774

21   Laissez faire, laissez passer.[5]   *Attributed*

Voltaire
[François Marie Arouet]
1694–1778

22   Virtue debases itself in justifying itself.
Oedipe [1718], act I, sc. iv

23   O what fine times, this age of iron!
Le Mondain [1736]

24   Paradise is where I am.   *Ibid.*

25   The superfluous, a very necessary thing.[6]
      Ibid.

26   The secret of being a bore is to tell everything.
Sept Discours en Vers sur l'Homme [1738]

27   Love truth, but pardon error.   *Ibid.*

28   He who is merely just is severe.
Letter to Frederick the Great [1740]

---

[1] William Lowndes [1652–1724], Secretary of the Treasury in the reigns of William III, Queen Anne, and George I. See Carroll, 518:1.
[2] See Samuel Wesley, 286:24.
[3] The Chapter of Accidents is the longest chapter in the book. — *Attributed to* JOHN WILKES *by* SOUTHEY, *The Doctor* [1834–1847], *ch. 118*

[4] The greatest happiness of the greatest number is the foundation of morals and legislation. — JEREMY BENTHAM [1748–1832], *Works, vol. X, p. 142*
[5] Let it be, let it pass.
The phrase is not readily translatable, and also appears as: Laissez faire, laissez aller. It has also been attributed to PIERRE LE PESANT BOISGUILLEBERT [1646–1714] and JEAN CLAUDE GOURNAY [1712–1759]. It was widely used by the Physiocrats in urging freedom from government interference, and was adopted by Adam Smith [1723–1790].
[6] See Oliver Wendell Holmes, Jr., 543:7.

1 The first who was king was a fortunate soldier:
Who serves his country well has no need of
ancestors.[1]

Mérope [1743], act I, sc. iii

2 It is better to risk saving a guilty person than to
condemn an innocent one.[2] *Zadig [1747], ch. 6*

3 They squeeze the orange and throw away the
skin.

*Letter to Madame Denis [September 2, 1751]
referring to his quarrel with Frederick the Great*

4 This agglomeration which was called and which
still calls itself the Holy Roman Empire is neither
holy, nor Roman, nor an Empire.

Essai sur les Moeurs [1756]

5 In this best of all possible worlds . . . everything is for the best.[3] *Candide [1759],[4] ch. 1*

6 If this is the best of all possible worlds, what are
the others like? *Ibid. 6*

7 [Optimism] is a mania for saying things are well
when one is in hell. *Ibid. 19*

8 You know that these two nations [France and
England] have been at war over a few acres of snow
near Canada, and that they are spending on this fine
struggle more than Canada itself is worth.

Ibid. 23

9 In this country [England] it is useful from time to
time to kill one admiral in order to encourage the
others.[5] *Ibid.*

10 This is the happiest of all men, for he is superior
to everything he possesses. *Ibid. 25*

11 Work keeps us from three great evils, boredom,
vice, and poverty.[6] *Ibid. 30*

12 We must cultivate our garden.[7] *Ibid.*

13 There are truths which are not for all men, nor
for all times.

Letter to Cardinal de Bernis [April 23, 1761]

14 One feels like crawling on all fours after reading
your work.

Letter to Rousseau [August 31, 1761]

15 Whatever you do, crush the infamous thing [su-
perstition], and love those who love you.[8]

Letter to d'Alembert [November 28, 1762]

16 Common sense is not so common.

Dictionnaire Philosophique [1764]. Self-Love

17 In general, the art of government consists in taking as much money as possible from one class of
citizens to give to the other. *Ibid. Money*

18 We have a natural right to make use of our pens
as of our tongue, at our peril, risk and hazard.

Ibid. Liberty of the Press

19 The best is the enemy of the good.[9]

Ibid. Dramatic Art

20 Very learned women are to be found, in the same
manner as female warriors; but they are seldom or
never inventors. *Ibid. Women*

21 Men use thought only to justify their wrongdoings, and speech only to conceal their thoughts.[10]

Dialogue 14. Le Chapon et la Poularde [1766]

22 I have never made but one prayer to God, a very
short one: "O Lord, make my enemies ridiculous."
And God granted it.

Letter to M. Damilaville [May 16, 1767]

23 History is no more than the portrayal of crimes
and misfortunes.[11] *L'Ingénu [1767], ch. 10*

24 Thought depends absolutely on the stomach, but
in spite of that, those who have the best stomachs
are not the best thinkers.

Letter to d'Alembert [August 20, 1770]

25 If God did not exist, it would be necessary to
invent him.[12]

*Épître à l'Auteur du Livre des Trois Imposteurs
[November 10, 1770]*

26 Change everything, except your loves.

Sur l'Usage de la Vie

27 I am very fond of truth, but not at all of martyrdom. *Letter to d'Alembert [February 1776]*

28 The embarrassment of riches.[13]

Le Droit du Seigneur, act II, sc. vi

29 He who thinks himself wise, O heavens! is a great
fool. *Ibid. IV, i*

30 Who has not the spirit of his age,
Of his age has all the unhappiness.[14]

Letter to Madame du Châtelet

---

[1]What can they see in the longest kingly line in Europe, save
that it runs back to a successful soldier?—WALTER SCOTT,
Woodstock [1826], *ch. 37*

[2]See Blackstone, 325:23.

[3]Dans ce meilleur des mondes possibles . . . tout est au
mieux.
Often quoted: All is for the best in the best of all possible
worlds.

[4]Translated by ROBERT M. ADAMS.

[5]Pour encourager les autres.
The reference is to Admiral John Byng, who was executed
in 1757 for failing to relieve Minorca.

[6]Le travail éloigne de nous trois grands maux, l'ennui, le
vice, et le besoin.

[7]Il faut cultiver notre jardin.
See Rabelais, 140:1, and Montaigne, 145:11.

[8]Quoi que vous fassiez, écrasez l'infâme, et aimez qui vous
aime.

[9]Le mieux est l'ennemi du bien.

[10]See South, 280:2.

[11]L'histoire n'est que le tableau des crimes et des malheurs.
See Gibbon, 340:3.

[12]See Ovid, 101:14, and Tillotson, 273:7.

[13]L'embarras des richesses.—ABBÉ D'ALLAINVAL [1700–
1753], *title of play* [1726]

[14]Qui n'a pas l'esprit de son âge, / De son âge a tout le malheur.

1   I advise you to go on living solely to enrage those
who are paying your annuities. It is the only pleasure
I have left.   *Letter to Madame du Deffand*

2   Liberty of thought is the life of the soul.
Essay on Epic Poetry (written in English)

3 Whoever you are, behold your master,
He is, or was, or has to be.[1]
On a statuette of Cupid in the Cirey Gardens

4   I disapprove of what you say, but I will defend to
the death your right to say it.   *Attributed*[2]

5   I die adoring God, loving my friends, not hating
my enemies, and detesting superstition.
Written February 28, 1778

Matthew Green
1696–1737

6 They politics like ours profess,
The greater prey upon the less.
The Grotto, l. 69

7 Fling but a stone, the giant dies.
Laugh and be well.
The Spleen [1737], l. 92

8 By happy alchemy of mind
They turn to pleasure all they find.
Ibid. l. 610

William Oldys
1696–1761

9 Busy, curious, thirsty fly,
Drink with me, and drink as I.
*On a Fly Drinking out of a Cup of Ale,
st. 1*

Marie de Vichy-Chamrond,
Marquise du Deffand
1697–1780

10   [Of Voltaire:] He has invented history.
From FOURNIER, L'Esprit dans l'Histoire [1857]

[1]Qui que tu sois, voici ton maître; / Il l'est — le fut — ou le
doit être.
[2]This sentence is not Voltaire's, but was first used in quoting
a letter from Voltaire to Helvétius in *The Friends of Voltaire*
[1906] by S. G. Tallentyre (E. Beatrice Hall). She claims it was
a paraphrase of Voltaire's words in the *Essay on Tolerance:*
Think for yourselves and let others enjoy the privilege to do so
too.
    Norbert Guterman, in *A Book of French Quotations* [1963],
suggests that the probable source for the quotation is from a
line in a letter to M. le Riche [February 6, 1770]: "Monsieur
l'abbé, I detest what you write, but I would give my life to make
it possible for you to continue to write."

11   The first step is the hardest.[3]
Letter to d'Alembert [July 7, 1763]

Charles Macklin
c. 1697–1797

12   The law is a sort of hocus-pocus science.[4]
Love à la Mode [1759], act II, sc. i

William Warburton
1698–1779

13   Orthodoxy is my doxy; heterodoxy is another
man's doxy.[5]
*From JOSEPH PRIESTLEY [1733–1804], Memoirs,
vol. I, p. 572*

John Dyer
1699–1757

14 A little rule, a little sway,
A sunbeam in a winter's day,
Is all the proud and mighty have
Between the cradle and the grave.
Grongar Hill [1726], l. 89

James Thomson
1700–1748

15 See, Winter comes to rule the varied year,[6]
Sullen and sad.
The Seasons. Winter [1726], l. 1

16   Welcome, kindred glooms!
Congenial horrors, hail!
Ibid. l. 5

17 Cruel as death, and hungry as the grave.
Ibid. l. 393

18   There studious let me sit,
And hold high converse with the mighty dead.
Ibid. l. 431

[3]This remark refers to the legend that Saint Denis, carrying
his head in his hands, walked from Montmartre to St. Denis,
a few miles north of Paris. Voltaire wrote to Madame du Deffand [January 1764] that one of her bons mots was quoted in
the notes of *La Pucelle, canto 1:* Il n'y a que le premier pas qui
coûte.
[4]Hocus was an old cunning attorney. — DR. JOHN ARBUTH-
NOT [1667–1735], *Law Is a Bottomless Pit; or, History of John
Bull* [1712], *ch. 5*
    The words of consecration, "Hoc est corpus," were traves-
tied into a nickname for jugglery, as "Hocus-pocus." — JOHN
RICHARD GREEN [1837–1883], *A Short History of the English
People* [1874], *ch. 7*
[5]Priestley relates that in a debate on the Test Laws, Lord
Sandwich said, "I have heard frequent use of the words 'orthodoxy' and 'heterodoxy' but I confess myself at a loss to
know precisely what they mean." Bishop Warburton whispered his definition to him.
    See Carlyle, 412:19.
[6]See Cowper, 335:5.

1 Ships dim-discover'd dropping from the clouds.
The Seasons. Summer [1727], l. 946

2 Sigh'd and look'd unutterable things.
Ibid. l. 1188

3 Come, gentle Spring! ethereal mildness, come.
Ibid. Spring [1728], l. 1

4 Delightful task! to rear the tender thought,
To teach the young idea how to shoot.
Ibid. l. 1152

5 An elegant sufficiency, content,
Retirement, rural quiet, friendship, books.
Ibid. l. 1161

6 Crown'd with the sickle, and the wheaten sheaf,
While Autumn, nodding o'er the yellow plain,
Comes jovial on.
Ibid. Autumn [1730], l. 1

7   For loveliness
Needs not the foreign aid of ornament,
But is when unadorned adorned the most.[1]
Ibid. l. 204

8 Or where the Northern ocean, in vast whirls,
Boils round the naked melancholy isles
Of farthest Thulè,[2] and th' Atlantic surge
Pours in among the stormy Hebrides.[3]
Ibid. l. 862

9 Come then, expressive silence, muse His praise.
A Hymn [1730], l. 118

10 O Sophonisba! Sophonisba, O![4]
Sophonisba [1730], act III, sc. ii

11 Forever, Fortune, wilt thou prove
An unrelenting foe to love,
And, when we meet a mutual heart,
Come in between and bid us part?
Song. Forever, Fortune

12 When Britain first, at Heaven's command,
Arose from out the azure main,
This was the charter of the land,
And guardian angels sung this strain:
Rule, Britannia, rule the waves;
Britons never will be slaves.
Alfred [1740], act II, sc. v

13 A pleasing land of drowsyhead it was.
The Castle of Indolence [1748], canto I, st. 6

14 A bard here dwelt, more fat than bard beseems,
Who, void of envy, guile, and lust of gain,
On virtue still, and nature's pleasing themes,
Poured forth his unpremeditated strain.
Ibid. st. 68

15 A little round, fat, oily man of God.
Ibid. st. 69

---

[1]See Cicero, 87:18, and Milton, 258:24.
[2]See Virgil, 92:21, and Seneca, 103:13.
[3]See Milton, 254:4.
[4]This line was parodied by Fielding in his *Tom Thumb* [1730]: O Huncamunca, Huncamunca, O.

Philip Doddridge
1702–1751

16 Awake my soul! stretch every nerve,
And press with vigor on;
A heavenly race demands thy zeal,
And an immortal crown.
Hymns [1755]. Zeal and Vigor in the Christian Race, st. 1

Jonathan Edwards
1703–1758

17   Resolved, never to do anything which I should be afraid to do if it were the last hour of my life.
Seventy Resolutions

18   Intend to live in continual mortification, and never to expect or desire any worldly ease or pleasure.
Diary [1723]

19   A little, wretched, despicable creature; a worm, a mere nothing, and less than nothing; a vile insect that has risen up in contempt against the majesty of Heaven and earth.
The Justice of God in the Damnation of Sinners [1734]

20   The God that holds you over the pit of hell, much as one holds a spider, or some loathsome insect over the fire, abhors you, and is dreadfully provoked: his wrath towards you burns like fire; he looks upon you as worthy of nothing else, but to be cast into the fire.
Sinners in the Hands of an Angry God [1741][5]

21   I assert that nothing ever comes to pass without a cause.
Freedom of Will [1754], sec. 3

22   This dictate of common sense.
Ibid.

Thomas Morell
1703–1784

23 See, the conquering hero comes!
Sound the trumpet, beat the drums![6]
Joshua [1748], pt. III

John Wesley
1703–1791

24   I look upon the world as my parish.
Journal [1909–1916]. June 11, 1739

25   That execrable sum of all villainies, commonly called the Slave Trade.
Ibid. February 12, 1772

26   Though I am always in haste, I am never in a hurry.
Letters [1831]. December 10, 1777

---

[5]See Robert Lowell, 742:12 and note.
[6]Handel used this in his oratorios *Judas Maccabaeus* [April 1, 1747] and *Joshua* [March 9, 1748], the libretti of which were written by Morell.
See Dryden, 276:8.

1 Let it be observed, that slovenliness is no part of religion; that neither this nor any text of Scripture, condemns neatness of apparel. Certainly this is a duty, not a sin. "Cleanliness is, indeed, next to godliness."
Sermon 93, On Dress

2 Do all the good you can,
By all the means you can,
In all the ways you can,
In all the places you can,
At all the times you can,
To all the people you can,
As long as ever you can.

John Wesley's Rule

Nathaniel Cotton
1705–1788

3 Yet still we hug the dear deceit.
Content. Vision IV

4 Hold the fleet angel fast until he bless thee.
Tomorrow

Benjamin Franklin[1]
1706–1790

5 The body of Benjamin Franklin, Printer (like the cover of an old book, its contents torn out and stripped of its lettering and gilding), lies here, food for worms; but the work shall not be lost, for it will (as he believed) appear once more in a new and more elegant edition, revised and corrected by the Author.
Epitaph on Himself [composed in 1728]

6 Eat to live, and not live to eat.[2]
Poor Richard's Almanac [1733]. May

7 After three days men grow weary, of a wench, a guest, and weather rainy.
Ibid. June

8 There is no little enemy.
Ibid. September

9 Without justice, courage is weak.
Ibid. [1734]. January

10 Blame-all and Praise-all are two blockheads.
Ibid. February

11 Where there's marriage without love, there will be love without marriage.
Ibid. May

12 Avarice and happiness never saw each other, how then should they become acquainted.
Ibid. November

13 A little house well filled, a little field well tilled, and a little wife well willed, are great riches.
Ibid. [1735]. February

14 Necessity never made a good bargain.
Ibid. April

15 Three may keep a secret, if two of them are dead.
Ibid. July

16 Opportunity is the great bawd.
Ibid. September

17 Early to bed and early to rise, makes a man healthy, wealthy, and wise.   *Ibid. October*

18 Here comes the orator! with his flood of words, and his drop of reason.   *Ibid.*

19 Some are weatherwise, some are otherwise.
Ibid. December

20 God helps them that help themselves.[3]
Ibid. [1736]. June

21 Don't throw stones at your neighbors', if your own windows are glass.[4]   *Ibid. August*

22 There are three faithful friends—an old wife, an old dog, and ready money.
Ibid. [1738]. January

23 If you would not be forgotten,
As soon as you are dead and rotten,
Either write things worthy reading,
Or do things worth the writing.
Ibid. May

24 Keep your eyes wide open before marriage, half shut afterwards.   *Ibid. June*

25 None but the well-bred man knows how to confess a fault, or acknowledge himself in an error.
Ibid. November

26 An empty bag cannot stand upright.
Ibid. [1740]. January

27 He that riseth late, must trot all day, and shall scarce overtake his business at night.
Ibid. [1742]. August

28 Experience keeps a dear school, but fools will learn in no other.[5]   *Ibid. [1743]. December*

29 The used key is always bright.
Ibid. [1744]. July

30 When the well's dry, we know the worth of water.   *Ibid. [1746]. January*

---

[1]*Eripuit coelo fulmen mox sceptra tyrannis* [He snatched the thunderbolt from heaven, then the scepter from tyrants].—*Attributed to* Turgot
This line was inscribed on Houdon's bust of Franklin in 1778.
See Manilius, 103:15, and Shakespeare, 219:9.
Antiquity would have rasied altars to this mighty genius, who, to the advantage of mankind, compassing in his mind the heavens and the earth, was able to restrain alike thunderbolts and tyrants.—Mirabeau, *Address upon the Death of Franklin*
I succeed him; no one could replace him.—Jefferson (to Charles Gravier, Comte de Vergennes, who had remarked, "You replace Mr. Franklin" as envoy to France)
See Byron, 404:4.
[2]See Socrates, 70:23, and Molière, 269:20.

[3]See Aesop, 59:15.
[4]See Herbert, 244:17.
[5]See Burke, 332:26.
[6]Do not let your chances like sunbeams pass you by,/For you never miss the water till the well runs dry.—Rowland Howard [fl. 1876], *You Never Miss the Water* [1876]

1   Dost thou love life? Then do not squander time; for that's the stuff life is made of.
Poor Richard's Almanac [1746]. June

2   Lost time is never found again.
Ibid. [1748]. January

3   He that's secure is not safe.   *Ibid. August*

4   Little strokes,
Fell great oaks.[1]
Ibid. [1750]. August

5   The cat in gloves catches no mice.
Ibid. [1754]. February

6   Work as if you were to live a hundred years,
Pray as if you were to die tomorrow.
Ibid. [1757]. May

7   A word to the wise is enough, and many words won't fill a bushel.
Ibid. [1758]. Preface: Courteous Reader

8   He that lives upon hope will die fasting.
Ibid.

9   Three removes is as bad as a fire.   *Ibid.*

10   A little neglect may breed great mischief . . . for want of a nail the shoe was lost; for want of a shoe the horse was lost; and for want of a horse the rider was lost.[2]   *Ibid.*

11   Eighth and lastly. They are so grateful!!
Reasons for Preferring an Elderly Mistress [1745]

12   Remember that time is money.[3]
Advice to a Young Tradesman [1748]

13   They that can give up essential liberty to obtain a little temporary safety deserve neither liberty nor safety.   *Historical Review of Pennsylvania* [1759]

14   Idleness and pride tax with a heavier hand than kings and parliaments. If we can get rid of the former, we may easily bear the latter.
Letter on the Stamp Act [July 11, 1765]

15   The grand leap of the whale up the Fall of Niagara is esteemed, by all who have seen it, as one of the finest spectacles in nature.
To the editor of a London newspaper [1765], *intended to chaff the English for their ignorance of America*

16   Here Skugg lies snug
As a bug in a rug.
Letter to Miss Georgiana Shipley [September 1772]

[1]See Lyly, 155:9.
[2]See Herbert, 244:28.
[3]We reckon hours and minutes to be dollars and cents.—
SAM SLICK [T. C. HALIBURTON], *The Clockmaker*
See Theophrastus, 81:21.

17   You and I were long friends: you are now my enemy, and I am

Yours,
B. Franklin
Letter to William Strahan [July 5, 1775]

18   We must all hang together, or assuredly we shall all hang separately.
At the signing of the Declaration of Independence [July 4, 1776]

19   Poor man, said I, you pay too much for your whistle.   *The Whistle* [1779]

20   Here you would know and enjoy what posterity will say of Washington. For a thousand leagues have nearly the same effect with a thousand years.
Letter to Washington [March 5, 1780]

21   George Washington, Commander of the American armies, who, like Joshua of old, commanded the sun and the moon to stand still, and they obeyed him.   *A toast at a dinner in Versailles*[4]

22   No nation was ever ruined by trade.
Thoughts on Commercial Subjects

23   There never was a good war or a bad peace.[5]
Letter to Josiah Quincy [September 11, 1783]

24   I wish the bald eagle had not been chosen as the representative of our country; he is a bird of bad moral character . . . like those among men who live by sharping and robbing, he is generally poor, and often very lousy . . .
The turkey . . . is a much more respectable bird, and withal a true original native of America.
Letter to Sarah Bache [January 26, 1784]

25   He [the sun] gives light as soon as he rises.
An Economical Project [1784][6]

26   A republic, if you can keep it.[7]
Response [September 18, 1787]

27   Our new Constitution is now established, and has an appearance that promises permanency; but in this world nothing can be said to be certain, except death and taxes.
Letter to Jean-Baptiste Leroy [November 13, 1789]

[4]The British minister had proposed a toast to George III, in which he likened him to the sun, and the French minister had toasted Louis XVI, comparing him with the moon.
[5]I cease not to advocate peace; even though unjust it is better than the most just war.—CICERO, *Epistolae ad Atticum, bk. VII, epistle 14*
It hath been said that an unjust peace is to be preferred before a just war.—SAMUEL BUTLER [1612–1680], *Butler's Remains* [1759], *Speeches in the Rump Parliament*
[6]Letter to the *Journal de Paris* advocating Daylight Saving Time.
[7]In Philadelphia, a Mrs. Powel "asked Dr. Franklin, Well Doctor what have we got a republic or a monarchy? A republic, replied the Doctor, if you can keep it." Recorded by James McHenry, one of Washington's aides, in his diary; published in the *American Historical Review, XI* [1906], *618.*

1   The next thing most like living one's life over again seems to be a recollection of that life, and to make that recollection as durable as possible by putting it down in writing.
Autobiography [1731–1759],[1] *ch. 1*

2   Eat not to dullness; drink not to elevation.
Ibid. 6

3   I shall never ask, never refuse, nor ever resign an office.
Ibid. 8

4   Human felicity is produced not so much by great pieces of good fortune that seldom happen, as by little advantages that occur every day.   *Ibid. 9*

5   When men are employed, they are best contented; for on the days they worked they were good-natured and cheerful, and, with the consciousness of having done a good day's work, they spent the evening jollily; but on our idle days they were mutinous and quarrelsome.   *Ibid. 10*

George Louis Leclerc de Buffon
1707–1788

6   [Of the horse:] The noblest conquest man has ever made.
L'Histoire des Mammifères. Le Cheval

7   The style is the man himself.[2]
Discourse (on his admission to the French Academy [1753])

8   Genius is nothing but a greater aptitude for patience.   *Attributed*[3]

Henry Fielding
1707–1754

9 All Nature wears one universal grin.
Tom Thumb [1730], act I, sc. i

10 Today it is our pleasure to be drunk;
And this our queen shall be as drunk as we.
Ibid. ii

---

[1]The *Autobiography*, begun in 1771, was first published (unauthorized, mangled, and in French) in 1791, and in complete form in 1868.
[2]Le style c'est l'homme même.
See Robert Burton, 234:8.
[3]Le génie n'est qu'une plus grande aptitude à la patience.
Hérault de Séchelles, in *Voyage à Montbard*, first attributed this to Buffon. It is quoted by Matthew Arnold in "A French Coleridge" [*Essays in Criticism*, 1865]. There is also a popular proverb: Genius is patience. Charles Thomson, Baron Sydenham [1799–1841], defined genius as a consummate sense of proportion.
Genius is an intuitive talent for labor. — JOHANNES WALAEUS [JAN VAN WALE] [1604–1699]
Patience is a necessary ingredient of genius. — DISRAELI, *The Young Duke* [1831]
Genius is capacity for taking trouble. — LESLIE STEPHEN [1832–1904]
See Carlyle, 413:15; Samuel Butler [1835–1902], 525:5; and Jane Ellice Hopkins, 532:2.

11 When I'm not thanked at all, I'm thanked enough;
I've done my duty, and I've done no more.
Ibid. iii

12 Oh, the roast beef of England,
And old England's roast beef![4]
The Grub Street Opera [1731], act III, sc. iii

13 I am as sober as a judge.
Don Quixote in England [1734], act III, sc. xiv

14 This story will never go down.
Tumble-Down Dick

15 The dusky night rides down the sky,
And ushers in the morn;
The hounds all join in glorious cry,
The huntsman winds his horn,
And a-hunting we will go.[5]
A-Hunting We Will Go [1734], st. 1

16   To whom nothing is given, of him can nothing be required.[6]   *Joseph Andrews [1742], bk. II, ch. 8*

17   I describe not men, but manners; not an individual, but a species.   *Ibid. III, 1*

18   They are the affectation of affectation.
Ibid. 3

19   Public schools are the nurseries of all vice and immorality.   *Ibid. 5*

20   Some folks rail against other folks, because other folks have what some folks would be glad of.
Ibid. IV, 6

21   Love and scandal are the best sweeteners of tea.[7]
Love in Several Masques [1743]

22   Every physician almost hath his favorite disease.
Tom Jones [1749],[8] *bk. II, ch. 9*

23   Thwackum was for doing justice, and leaving mercy to heaven.   *Ibid. III, 10*

24   Can any man have a higher notion of the rule of right and the eternal fitness of things?
Ibid. IV, 4

25   Distinction without a difference.
Ibid. VI, 13

26   O! more than Gothic ignorance.   *Ibid. VII, 3*

27   An amiable weakness.[9]   *Ibid. X, 8*

28   His designs were strictly honorable, as the phrase is; that is, to rob a lady of her fortune by way of marriage.   *Ibid. XI, 4*

---

[4]The Roast Beef of Old England. — RICHARD LEVERIDGE [c. 1670–1758], *title of poem*
[5]It's of three jovial huntsmen, and a-hunting they did go; / And they hunted, and they holloed, and they blew their horns also; / Look ye there! — *The Three Jovial Huntsmen* (old English ballad), st. 1
[6]See *Luke 12:48*, 38:31.
[7]See Congreve, 290:36.
[8]See Gibbon, 340:9.
[9]Amiable weaknesses of human nature. — GIBBON, *Decline and Fall of the Roman Empire* [1776–1788], *ch. 14*
It was an amiable weakness. — R. B. SHERIDAN, *The School for Scandal* [1777]

1　Hairbreadth missings of happiness look like the insults of Fortune.　*Tom Jones, bk. XIII, ch. 2*

2　The republic of letters.　*Ibid. XIV, 1*

3　It hath been often said, that it is not death, but dying which is terrible.　*Amelia [1751], bk. III, ch. 4*

4　These are called the pious frauds of friendship.　*Ibid. VI, 6*

5　When widows exclaim loudly against second marriages, I would always lay a wager that the man, if not the wedding day, is absolutely fixed on.　*Ibid. 8*

6　There is not in the universe a more ridiculous, nor a more contemptible animal, than a proud clergyman.　*Ibid. VI, 10*

7　One of my illustrious predecessors.[1]　*Covent Garden Journal [January 11, 1752]*

Linnaeus [Carl von Linné]
1707–1778

8　To live by medicine is to live horribly.　*Diaeta Naturalis, introduction*

9　Nature does not proceed by leaps.[2]　*Philosophia Botanica [1750], sec. 77*

10　A professor can never better distinguish himself in his work than by encouraging a clever pupil, for the true discoverers are among them, as comets amongst the stars.　*From biography of Linnaeus by Benjamin Daydon Jones, ch. 9*

11　Live innocently; God is here.　*Ibid. 15 (inscribed over the door of Linnaeus's bedchamber)*

12　If a tree dies, plant another in its place.　*Ibid.*

Charles Wesley
1707–1788

13　"Christ, the Lord, is risen today,"
Sons of men and angels say,
Raise your joys and triumphs high,
Sing, ye heavens, and earth reply.
　Hymns and Sacred Poems [1739]. Christ, the Lord, Is Risen Today

14　Jesus, lover of my soul,
Let me to Thy bosom fly,
While the waters nearer roll,

While the tempest still is high;
Hide me, O my Savior, hide,
Till the storm of life is past;
Safe into the haven glide,
O receive my soul at last.
　Ibid. [1740]. Jesus, Lover of My Soul

15　Gentle Jesus, meek and mild,
Look upon a little child;
Pity my simplicity,
Suffer me to come to thee.
　Ibid. [1742]. Gentle Jesus, Meek and Mild

16　Soldiers of Christ, arise,
And put your armor on.
　Ibid. [1749]. Soldiers of Christ, Arise

17　Hark! the herald angels sing
Glory to the newborn King;
Peace on earth, and mercy mild,
God and sinners reconciled!
Joyful all ye nations rise,
Join the triumph of the skies;
With th' angelic host proclaim
Christ is born in Bethlehem.[3]
　Ibid. [1753]. Christmas Hymn: Hark! the Herald Angels Sing

William Pitt, Earl of Chatham
1708–1778

18　The atrocious crime of being a young man, which the honorable gentleman [Walpole] has with such spirit and decency charged upon me, I shall neither attempt to palliate nor deny; but content myself with wishing that I may be one of those whose follies may cease with their youth, and not of that number who are ignorant in spite of experience.
　Speech in the House of Commons [March 6, 1741][4]

19　The poorest man may in his cottage bid defiance to all the forces of the Crown. It may be frail— its roof may shake—the wind may blow through it —the storm may enter—the rain may enter—but the King of England cannot enter—all his force dares not cross the threshold of the ruined tenement!
　Ibid. [1763]

20　I rejoice that America has resisted. Three millions of people, so dead to all the feelings of liberty, as voluntarily to submit to be slaves, would have been fit instruments to make slaves of the rest.
　Ibid. [January 14, 1766]

---

[1]Illustrious predecessor.—BURKE, *The Present Discontents* [1770]

I tread in the footsteps of illustrious men. . . . In receiving from the people the sacred trust twice confided to my illustrious predecessor [Andrew Jackson].—MARTIN VAN BUREN [1782–1862], *Inaugural Address* [March 4, 1837]

[2]Natura non facit saltus.

[3]GEORGE WHITEFIELD [1714–1770] altered lines 1 and 2, 7 and 8, from Wesley's original:
Hark, how all the welkin rings, / "Glory to the King of kings." . . . / Universal nature say, / "Christ the Lord is born today."

[4]This is the composition of Johnson, founded on some note or statement of the actual speech. Johnson said, "That speech I wrote in a garret, in Exeter Street."—BOSWELL, *Life of Johnson* [1791]

1　Confidence is a plant of slow growth in an aged bosom; youth is the season of credulity.
　　Speech in the House of Commons [January 14, 1766]

2　Unlimited power is apt to corrupt the minds of those who possess it;[1] and this I know, my lords, that where laws end, tyranny begins.[2]
　　Case of Wilkes. Speech [January 9, 1770]

3　There is something behind the throne greater than the King himself.
　　Speech in the House of Lords [March 2, 1770]

4　I love the Americans because they love liberty, and I love them for the noble efforts they made in the last war.　　*Ibid.*

5　Reparation for our rights at home, and security against the like future violations.[3]
　　Letter to the Earl of Shelburne [September 29, 1770]

6　If I were an American, as I am an Englishman, while a foreign troop was landed in my country, I never would lay down my arms—never—never—never![4] You cannot conquer America.
　　Speech [November 18, 1777]

7　I invoke the genius of the Constitution.
　　Ibid.

Samuel Johnson
1709–1784

8　Of all the griefs that harass the distrest,
　Sure the most bitter is a scornful jest.
　　London [1738] (an imitation of the Third Satire of Juvenal), l. 166

9　This mournful truth is ev'rywhere confessed—
　Slow rises worth, by poverty depress'd.[5]
　　Ibid. l. 176

10　When learning's triumph o'er her barb'rous foes
　First rear'd the stage, immortal Shakespeare rose;
　Each change of many-color'd life he drew,
　Exhausted worlds, and then imagin'd new:
　Existence saw him spurn her bounded reign,
　And panting Time toil'd after him in vain.
　　Prologue at the Opening of Drury Lane Theatre [1747]

11　Cold approbation gave the ling'ring bays,
　For those who durst not censure, scarce could praise.
　　Ibid.

12　Declamation roar'd, while Passion slept.
　　Ibid.

13　The wild vicissitudes of taste.
　　Ibid.

14　For we that live to please must please to live.
　　Ibid.

15　Studious to please, yet not ashamed to fail.
　　Prologue to the Tragedy of Irene [1749]

16　Let observation with extensive view
　Survey mankind, from China to Peru.[6]
　　Vanity of Human Wishes [1749], l. 1

17　Deign on the passing world to turn thine eyes,
　And pause a while from learning to be wise.
　There mark what ills the scholar's life assail—
　Toil, envy, want, the patron, and the jail.
　　Ibid. l. 157

18　A frame of adamant, a soul of fire,
　No dangers fright him, and no labors tire.
　　Ibid. l. 191

19　He left the name at which the world grew pale,
　To point a moral, or adorn a tale.
　　Ibid. l. 221

20　"Enlarge my life with multitude of days!"
　In health, in sickness, thus the suppliant prays:
　Hides from himself his state, and shuns to know
　That life protracted is protracted woe.
　　Ibid. l. 255

21　Superfluous lags the vet'ran on the stage.
　　Ibid. l. 308

22　Must helpless man, in ignorance sedate,
　Roll darkling down the torrent of his fate?
　　Ibid. l. 345

23　Secure, whate'er he gives, he gives the best.
　　Ibid. l. 356

24　With these celestial Wisdom calms the mind,
　And makes the happiness she does not find.
　　Ibid. l. 367

25　Curiosity is one of the permanent and certain characteristics of a vigorous mind.
　　The Rambler[7]*[March 12, 1751]*

26　No place affords a more striking conviction of the vanity of human hopes than a public library.
　　Ibid. [March 23, 1751]

27　I am not yet so lost in lexicography as to forget that words are the daughters of earth, and that things are the sons of heaven.[8]
　　Dictionary [1755], preface

---

[1]See Shelley, 406:8, and Acton, 521:5.
[2]See Locke, 277:9.
[3]Indemnity for the past and security for the future.— JOHN RUSSELL, *Life and Times of Charles James Fox* [1859–1860], *vol. III, p. 345, letter to the Honorable T. Maitland*
[4]See Shakespeare, 211:19, and Churchill, 621:5.
[5]Three years later Johnson wrote, "Mere unassisted merit advances slowly, if—what is not very common—it advances at all."

[6]De Quincey quotes with approval, but without naming him, the criticism of a writer who contends that this couplet amounts in effect to this: "Let observation with extensive observation observe mankind extensively."—*Rhetoric* [1828]
[7]For the *Rambler* motto, see Johnson's translation of BOETHIUS, *De Consolatione Philosophiae, III, 9, 27,* 115:13.
[8]See Herbert, 244:40.

1   CLUB—An assembly of good fellows, meeting under certain conditions.   *Dictionary*

2   ESSAY—A loose sally of the mind; an irregular indigested piece; not a regular and orderly composition.   *Ibid.*

3   EXCISE—A hateful tax levied upon commodities, and adjudged not by the common judges of property, but wretches hired by those to whom excise is paid.   *Ibid.*

4   GRUBSTREET—The name of a street near Moorsfield, London, much inhabited by writers of small histories, dictionaries, and temporary poems.   *Ibid.*

5   LEXICOGRAPHER—A writer of dictionaries, a harmless drudge.   *Ibid.*

6   OATS—A grain which in England is generally given to horses, but in Scotland supports the people.[1]   *Ibid.*

7   The joy of life is variety;[2] the tenderest love requires to be rekindled by intervals of absence.   *The Idler [1758–1760], no. 39*

8   He is no wise man who will quit a certainty for an uncertainty.   *Ibid. 57*

9   Ye who listen with credulity to the whispers of fancy, and pursue with eagerness the phantoms of hope; who expect that age will perform the promises of youth, and that the deficiencies of the present day will be supplied by the morrow; attend to the history of Rasselas, Prince of Abyssinia.   *Rasselas [1759], ch. 1*

10   To a poet nothing can be useless.   *Ibid. 10*

11   Human life is everywhere a state in which much is to be endured and little to be enjoyed.   *Ibid. 11*

12   Marriage has many pains, but celibacy has no pleasures.   *Ibid. 26*

13   Example is always more efficacious than precept.   *Ibid. 30*

14   The endearing elegance of female friendship.   *Ibid. 46*

15   How small, of all that human hearts endure,
That part which laws or kings can cause or cure!
Still to ourselves in every place consign'd,
Our own felicity we make or find.
    Lines added to OLIVER GOLDSMITH, *The Traveller [1763–1764]*

16   That man is little to be envied whose patriotism would not gain force upon the plain of Marathon, or

whose piety would not grow warmer among the ruins of Iona.
    Journey to the Western Islands [1775]. Inch Kenneth

17   Whoever wishes to attain an English style, familiar but not coarse, and elegant but not ostentatious, must give his days and nights to the volumes of Addison.
    Lives of the Poets [1779–1781]. Addison

18   To be of no church is dangerous. Religion, of which the rewards are distant, and which is animated only by faith and hope, will glide by degrees out of the mind unless it be invigorated and reimpressed by external ordinances, by stated calls to worship, and the salutary influence of example.
    Ibid. Milton

19   The father of English criticism.
    Ibid. Dryden

20   He delighted to tread upon the brink of meaning.
    Ibid.

21   The *Churchyard* abounds with images which find a mirror in every mind, and with sentiments to which every bosom returns an echo.   *Ibid. Gray*[3]

22   I am disappointed by that stroke of death [Garrick's], which has eclipsed the gaiety of nations, and impoverished the public stock of harmless pleasure.
    Ibid. Edmund Smith

23   New things are made familiar, and familiar things are made new.   *Ibid. Pope*

24   Tomorrow I purpose to regulate my room.
    Prayers and Meditations [1785]. 1764

25   Preserve me from unseasonable and immoderate sleep.   *Ibid. 1767*

26   Every man naturally persuades himself that he can keep his resolutions, nor is he convinced of his imbecility but by length of time and frequency of experiment.   *Ibid. 1770*

27   This world, where much is to be done and little to be known.
    Ibid. Against Inquisitive and Perplexing Thoughts

28   [Sunday] should be different from another day. People may walk, but not throw stones at birds. There may be relaxation, but there should be no levity.
    From BOSWELL, *Journal of a Tour to the Hebrides [1785]. August 20, 1773*

29   I have, all my life long, been lying till noon; yet I tell all young men, and tell them with great sincerity, that nobody who does not rise early will ever do any good.   *Ibid. September 14, 1773*

30   Wickedness is always easier than virtue; for it takes the short cut to everything.
    Ibid. September 17, 1773

---

[1]It was pleasant to me to find, that "oats," the "food of horses," were so much used as the food of the people in Dr. Johnson's own town.—BOSWELL, *Life of Johnson* [1791], *vol. I, p. 628* (Everyman edition)

I own that by my definition of *oats* I meant to vex them [the Scots].—JOHNSON, *ibid. II, 434*

[2]See Publilius Syrus, 99:21, and Cowper, 334:28.

[3]See Gray, 322:1.

1   Gratitude is a fruit of great cultivation; you do not find it among gross people.
Ibid. September 20, 1773

2 Here closed in death th' attentive eyes
That saw the manners in the face.
Epitaph on Hogarth [1786]

3 When the hoary Sage replied,
"Come, my lad, and drink some beer."
From MRS. PIOZZI, *Anecdotes of Samuel Johnson [1786]*

4 If the man who turnips cries,
Cry not when his father dies,
'Tis a proof that he had rather
Have a turnip than his father.[1]
Ibid.

5   He was a very good hater.
Ibid.

6   The law is the last result of human wisdom acting upon human experience for the benefit of the public.
Ibid.

7   The use of traveling is to regulate imagination by reality, and instead of thinking how things may be, to see them as they are.
Ibid.

8   Dictionaries are like watches; the worst is better than none, and the best cannot be expected to go quite true.
Ibid.

9   Books that you may carry to the fire, and hold readily in your hand, are the most useful after all.
From SIR JOHN HAWKINS, *Life of Johnson [1787]. Apothegms*

10 As with my hat[2] upon my head
I walk'd along the Strand,
I there did meet another man
With his hat in his hand.[3]
Anecdotes of Johnson by GEORGE STEEVENS

11   Abstinence is as easy to me as temperance would be difficult.
Anecdotes of Johnson by HANNAH MORE

12   *Boswell:* That, sir, was great fortitude of mind.
Johnson: No, sir; stark insensibility.
From JAMES BOSWELL, *Life of Johnson[4] [1791], November 5, 1728*

13   [Of Pembroke College:] Sir, we are a nest of singing birds.
Ibid. 1730

14   I'll come no more behind your scenes, David [Garrick]; for the silk stockings and white bosoms of your actresses excite my amorous propensities.
Ibid. 1749

15   A man may write at any time, if he will set himself doggedly to it.
Ibid. March 1750

[1]Burlesque of Lope de Vega's lines: "Se acquien los leones vence," etc.
[2]Elsewhere found: I put my hat.
[3]A parody on Thomas Percy's ballad *The Hermit of Warkworth*.
[4]Edited by G. B. HILL and revised by L. F. POWELL [1934].

16   Wretched un-idea'd girls.
Ibid. 1753

17   Is not a patron, my lord, one who looks with unconcern on a man struggling for life in the water, and when he has reached ground encumbers him with help? The notice which you have been pleased to take of my labors, had it been early, had been kind; but it has been delayed till I am indifferent, and cannot enjoy it; till I am solitary, and cannot impart it; till I am known, and do not want it.
Ibid. February 7, 1754 (Letter to Lord Chesterfield)

18   [Of Lord Chesterfield:] This man, I thought, had been a Lord among wits; but, I find, he is only a wit among Lords!
Ibid. 1754

19   Sir, he [Bolingbroke] was a scoundrel, and a coward: a scoundrel, for charging a blunderbuss against religion and morality; a coward, because he had not resolution to fire it off himself, but left half a crown to a beggarly Scotchman, to draw the trigger after his death.
Ibid. March 6, 1754

20   Ignorance, madame, pure ignorance.[5]
Ibid. 1755

21   If a man does not make new acquaintances as he advances through life, he will soon find himself left alone. A man, sir, should keep his friendship in a constant repair.[6]
Ibid. 1755

22   Towering in the confidence of twenty-one.
Ibid. January 9, 1758

23   Being in a ship is being in a jail, with the chance of being drowned.
Ibid. March 1759

24   Sir, I think all Christians, whether Papists or Protestants, agree in the essential articles, and that their differences are trivial, and rather political than religious.[7]
Ibid. 1763

25   The noblest prospect which a Scotchman ever sees is the high road that leads him to England!
Ibid. July 6, 1763

26   A man ought to read just as inclination leads him; for what he reads as a task will do him little good.
Ibid. July 14, 1763

27   If he does really think that there is no distinction between virtue and vice, why, sir, when he leaves our houses let us count our spoons.
Ibid.

[5]When asked by a lady why he defined "pastern" as the "knee" of a horse in his Dictionary.
[6]Keep your friendships in repair.—EMERSON, *Uncollected Lectures: Table-Talk* [1864]
[7]I do not find that the age or country makes the least difference; no, nor the language the actor spoke, nor the religion which they professed—whether Arab in the desert, or Frenchman in the Academy. I see that sensible men and conscientious men all over the world were of one religion of well-doing and daring.—EMERSON, *Lectures and Biographical Sketches* [1883], *The Preacher*
See Johnson, 316:10.

1   Sir, your levelers wish to level *down* as far as themselves; but they cannot bear leveling *up* to themselves.

From BOSWELL, *Life of Johnson, July 21, 1763*

2   Sherry[1] is dull, naturally dull; but it must have taken him a great deal of pains to become what we now see him. Such an excess of stupidity, sir, is not in Nature.   *Ibid. July 28, 1763*

3   Sir, a woman preaching is like a dog's walking on his hinder legs. It is not done well; but you are surprised to find it done at all.

Ibid. July 31, 1763

4   This was a good dinner enough, to be sure, but it was not a dinner to *ask* a man to.   *Ibid.*

5   [Of Sir John Hawkins:] A very unclubable man.

Ibid. 1764

6   It matters not how a man dies, but how he lives.

Ibid. October 26, 1769

7   That fellow seems to me to possess but one idea, and that is a wrong one.   *Ibid. 1770*

8   A gentleman who had been very unhappy in marriage, married immediately after his wife died: Johnson said, it was the triumph of hope over experience.   *Ibid.*

9   A decent provision for the poor is the true test of civilization.   *Ibid.*

10   All denominations of Christians have really little difference in point of doctrine, though they may differ widely in external forms.[2]   *Ibid. 1772*

11   Nobody can write the life of a man, but those who have eat and drunk and lived in social intercourse with him.   *Ibid. March 31, 1772*

12   I am a great friend to public amusements; for they keep people from vice.   *Ibid.*

13   There is more knowledge of the heart in one letter of Richardson's than in all *Tom Jones*.

Ibid. April 6, 1772

14   Why, sir, if you were to read Richardson for the story, your impatience would be so much fretted that you would hang yourself. But you must read him for the sentiment, and consider the story as only giving occasion to the sentiment.   *Ibid.*

15   A cow is a very good animal in the field; but we turn her out of a garden.   *Ibid. April 15, 1772*

16   Much may be made of a Scotchman if he be *caught* young.[3]   *Ibid. Spring 1772*

17   It is a foolish thing well done.[4]

Ibid. April 3, 1773

18   No, sir, do *you* read books *through?*[5]

Ibid. April 19, 1773

19   An old tutor of a college said to one of his pupils: Read over your compositions, and wherever you meet with a passage which you think is particularly fine, strike it out.[6]   *Ibid. April 30, 1773*

20   You are the most unscottified of your countrymen.   *Ibid. May 1, 1773*

21   The woman's a whore, and there's an end on 't.[7]

Ibid. May 7, 1773

22   Attack is the reaction; I never think I have hit hard unless it rebounds.   *Ibid. April 2, 1775*

23   Most vices may be committed very genteelly: a man may debauch his friend's wife genteelly: he may cheat at cards genteelly.   *Ibid. April 6, 1775*

24   A man will turn over half a library to make one book.   *Ibid.*

25   Patriotism is the last refuge of a scoundrel.

Ibid. April 7, 1775

26   Knowledge is of two kinds. We know a subject ourselves, or we know where we can find information upon it.   *Ibid. April 18, 1775*

27   In lapidary inscriptions a man is not upon oath.

Ibid. 1775

28   There is nothing which has yet been contrived by man by which so much happiness is produced as by a good tavern or inn.[8]   *Ibid. March 21, 1776*

29   No man but a blockhead ever wrote except for money.   *Ibid. April 5, 1776*

30   Life is a progress from want to want, not from enjoyment to enjoyment.   *Ibid. May 1776*

31   Sir, you have but two topics, yourself and me. I am sick of both.   *Ibid.*

32   Olivarii Goldsmith, Poetae, Physici, Historici, qui nullum fere scribendi genus non tetigit, Nullum quod tetigit non ornavit [To Oliver Goldsmith, Poet, Naturalist, Historian, who left scarcely any style of writing untouched, and touched nothing that he did not adorn].   *Ibid. June 22, 1776*

33   Life admits not of delays; when pleasure can be had, it is fit to catch it. Every hour takes away part

[1]Thomas Sheridan [1719–1788], actor, lecturer, and author.
[2]See Johnson, 315:24.
[3]Of Lord Mansfield, educated in England.
[4]Of Goldsmith's apology in the *London Chronicle* for beating Evans the bookseller.

[5]Upon being asked by Elphinstone if he had read a new book through.
[6]See Sydney Smith, 380:20.
[7]Of Lady Diana Beauclerk, divorced.
[8]Following this remark, Johnson quoted (not quite correctly):

Whoe'er has traveled life's dull round, / Whate'er his various tour has been, / May sigh to think how oft he found / His warmest welcome at an inn. — WILLIAM SHENSTONE [1714–1763]; *written on a window of an inn at Henley*

Robert Leighton [1611–1684], archbishop of Glasgow, often said that if he were to choose a place to die in, it should be an inn. — *Works, vol. I, p. 76* of the things that please us, and perhaps part of our disposition to be pleased.

Ibid. September 1, 1777

1 Depend upon it, sir, when a man knows he is to be hanged in a fortnight, it concentrates his mind wonderfully. *Ibid. September 19, 1777*

2 When a man is tired of London, he is tired of life; for there is in London all that life can afford.

Ibid. September 20, 1777

3 It is a man's own fault, it is from want of use, if his mind grows torpid in old age.

Ibid. April 9, 1778

4 Johnson had said that he could repeat a complete chapter of *The Natural History of Iceland,* from the Danish of Horrebow, the whole of which was exactly thus: "Ch. LXXII. *Concerning snakes.* There are no snakes to be met with throughout the whole island."[1]

Ibid. April 13, 1778

5 Every state of society is as luxurious as it can be. Men always take the best they can get.

Ibid. April 14, 1778

6 A country governed by a despot is an inverted cone. *Ibid.*

7 I am willing to love all mankind, except an American. *Ibid. April 15, 1778*

8 As the Spanish proverb says, "He, who would bring home the wealth of the Indies, must carry the wealth of the Indies with him." So it is in traveling, a man must carry knowledge with him if he would bring home knowledge. *Ibid. April 17, 1778*

9 It is better to live rich, than to die rich.

Ibid.

10 Were it not for imagination, sir, a man would be as happy in the arms of a chambermaid as of a duchess. *Ibid. May 9, 1778*

11 I would rather be attacked than unnoticed. For the worst thing you can do to an author is to be silent as to his works. *Ibid. March 26, 1779*

12 I remember a passage in Goldsmith's *Vicar of Wakefield,* which he was afterwards fool enough to expunge: "I do not love a man who is zealous for nothing." *Ibid.*

13 Claret is the liquor for boys; port for men; but he who aspires to be a hero must drink brandy.

Ibid. April 7, 1779

14 Worth seeing? yes; but not worth going to see.

Ibid. October 12, 1779

15 If you are idle, be not solitary; if you are solitary, be not idle.[2] *Ibid. October 27, 1779*

16 A Frenchman must be always talking, whether he knows anything of the matter or not; an Englishman is content to say nothing, when he has nothing to say. *Ibid. 1780*

17 Greek, sir, is like lace; every man gets as much of it as he can. *Ibid.*

18 [Of Oliver Goldsmith:] No man was more foolish when he had not a pen in his hand, or more wise when he had. *Ibid.*

19 The applause of a single human being is of great consequence. *Ibid.*

20 Come to me, my dear Bozzy, and let us be as happy as we can. *Ibid. March 14, 1781*

21 There are people whom one should like very well to drop, but would not wish to be dropped by.

Ibid. March 1781

22 We are not here to sell a parcel of boilers and vats, but the potentiality of growing rich beyond the dreams of avarice.[3] *Ibid. April 4, 1781*

23 Classical quotation is the *parole* of literary men all over the world. *Ibid. May 8, 1781*

24 My friend was of opinion that when a man of rank appeared in that character [as an author], he deserved to have his merit handsomely allowed.[4]

Ibid. May 1781

25 A jest breaks no bones. *Ibid. June 4, 1781*

26 Officious, innocent, sincere,
Of every friendless name the friend.
   Ibid. January 20, 1782 (on the death of Robert Levett)

27 To let friendship die away by negligence and silence, is certainly not wise. It is voluntarily to throw away one of the greatest comforts of this weary pilgrimage. *Ibid. March 20, 1782*

28 Whatever you have, spend less.

Ibid. December 7, 1782

29 I never have sought the world; the world was not to seek me. *Ibid. March 23, 1783*

30 Clear your mind of cant. *Ibid. May 15, 1783*

31 Who drives fat oxen should himself be fat.[5]

Ibid. June 1784

32 I have found you an argument; I am not obliged to find you an understanding. *Ibid.*

33 Blown about by every wind of criticism.[6]

Ibid.

34 Don't attitudenize. *Ibid.*

[1]Chapter XLII is still shorter: "There are no owls of any kind in the whole island."

[2]The great direction which Burton has left to men disordered like you, is this: Be not solitary, be not idle. — JOHNSON, *ibid.*
See Robert Burton, 235:24.

[3]See Edward Moore, 319:1.

[4]Usually quoted as: When a nobleman writes a book, he ought to be encouraged.
See Somerville, 294.

[5]Parody on: Who rules o'er freemen should himself be free.
—HENRY BROOKE [c. 1703–1783], *Gustavus Vasa* [1739]

[6]See *Ephesians* 4:14, 44:24.

1   I look upon every day to be lost, in which I do not make a new acquaintance.
    From BOSWELL, *Life of Johnson, November 1784*

2   God bless you, my dear!
    Ibid. December 13, 1784 (last words)

Julien Offray de La Mettrie
1709–1751

3   Man is a machine and . . . in the whole universe there is but a single substance variously modified.   *L'Homme Machine [1748],*[1] *conclusion*

George, Lord Lyttelton
1709–1773

4 Women, like princes, find few real friends.
    Advice to a Lady

5 What is your sex's earliest, latest care,
    Your heart's supreme ambition? To be fair.
    Ibid.

6 The lover in the husband may be lost.
    Ibid.

7 Where none admire, 'tis useless to excel;
    Where none are beaux, 'tis vain to be a belle.
    Soliloquy on a Beauty in the Country

Theodore Tronchin
1709–1781

8   In medicine, sins of commission are mortal, sins of omission venial.
    Quoted in Bulletin of New York Academy of Medicine, V [1929], 151

Oliver Edwards
1711–1791

9   I have tried too in my time to be a philosopher; but I don't know how, cheerfulness was always breaking in.
    From JAMES BOSWELL, *Life of Johnson [1791]. April 17, 1778*

David Hume
1711–1776

10   Generally speaking, the errors in religion are dangerous; those in philosophy only ridiculous.
    A Treatise of Human Nature [1739], bk. I, pt. iv, sec. vii

11   Avarice, the spur of industry.
    Essays [1741–1742]. Of Civil Liberty

[1]Translated by M. W. CALKINS.

12   Beauty in things exists in the mind which contemplates them.[2]   *Ibid. Of Tragedy*

13   Custom, then, is the great guide of human life.
    An Enquiry Concerning Human Understanding [1748], pt. 1

14   No testimony is sufficient to establish a miracle, unless the testimony be of such a kind that its falsehood would be more miraculous than the fact which it endeavors to establish.   *Ibid. Of Miracles*

15   Opposing one species of superstition to another, set them a-quarreling; while we ourselves, during their fury and contention, happily make our escape into the calm, though obscure, regions of philosophy.   *The Natural History of Religion [1757]*

16   Never literary attempt was more unfortunate than my Treatise of Human Nature. It fell dead-born from the press.   *My Own Life [1777], ch. 1*

Frederick the Great
1712–1786

17   By push of bayonets, no firing till you see the whites of their eyes.[3]   *At Prague [May 6, 1757]*

18   Rascals, would you live forever?[4]
    When the Guards hesitated at Kolin [June 18, 1757]

19   The prince is the first servant of his state.
    Memoirs of the House of Brandenburg [1758]

20   God is always with the strongest battalions.[5]
    Letter to the Duchess Luise Dorothea von Gotha [May 8, 1760]

21   I am tired of ruling over slaves.
    Last words [April 1, 1786]

George Grenville
1712–1770

22   A wise government knows how to enforce with temper or to conciliate with dignity.
    Speech against expulsion of John Wilkes, in Parliament [1769]

Edward Moore
1712–1757

23   This is adding insult to injury.
    The Foundling [1748], act V, sc. ii

[2]See Hungerford, 568:4.
[3]See William Prescott, 327:10.
[4]Ihr Racker, wollt ihr ewig leben?
Come on, you sons of bitches! Do you want to live forever?
—World War I American battle cry attributed to Marine Sergeant DANIEL DALY [1874–1937] at the battle of Belleau Wood, June 1918.
[5]See Tacitus, 109:19; Bussy-Rabutin, 266:13; Boileau, 280:-17; and Gibbon, 340:6.

1   I am rich beyond the dreams of avarice.[1]
The Gamester [1753], act II, sc. ii

Jean Jacques Rousseau[2]
1712–1778

2   The first man who, having fenced in a piece of land, said, "This is mine," and found people naïve enough to believe him, that man was the true founder of civil society.
Discourse upon the Origin and Foundation of the Inequality Among Mankind [1754]

3   Never exceed your rights, and they will soon become unlimited.   *Ibid.*

4   Money is the seed of money, and the first guinea is sometimes more difficult to acquire than the second million.   *Ibid.*

5   Man is born free, and everywhere he is in chains.[3]
The Social Contract [1762], I, ch. 1

6   The strongest is never strong enough to be always the master, unless he transforms his strength into right, and obedience into duty.   *Ibid. 3*

7   The right of conquest has no foundation other than the right of the strongest.   *Ibid. 4*

8   In the strict sense of the term, a true democracy has never existed, and never will exist.
Ibid. III, 4

9   The body politic, like the human body, begins to die from its birth, and bears in itself the causes of its destruction.   *Ibid. 11*

10   Good laws lead to the making of better ones; bad ones bring about worse.   *Ibid. 15*

11   Everything is good when it leaves the hands of the Creator; everything degenerates in the hands of man.   *Emile; or, On Education [1762], I*

12   I shall always maintain that whoso says in his heart, "There is no God," while he takes the name of God upon his lips, is either a liar or a madman.
Ibid.

13   People who know little are usually great talkers, while men who know much say little.   *Ibid.*

14   What wisdom can you find that is greater than kindness?   *Ibid. II*

15   Nature never deceives us; it is always we who deceive ourselves.   *Ibid. III*

16   There exists one book, which, to my taste, furnishes the happiest treatise of natural education. What then is this marvelous book? Is it Aristotle? Is it Pliny, is it Buffon? No—it is *Robinson Crusoe.*
Ibid.

17   Self-love makes more libertines than love.
Ibid. IV

18   Provided a man is not mad, he can be cured of every folly but vanity.   *Ibid.*

19   A man says what he knows, a woman says what will please.   *Ibid. V*

20   Where is the man who owes nothing to the land in which he lives? Whatever that land may be, he owes to it the most precious thing possessed by man, the morality of his actions and the love of virtue.
Ibid.

21   I have entered on an enterprise which is without precedent, and will have no imitator. I propose to show my fellows a man as nature made him, and this man shall be myself.
Confessions [1781–1788], I

22   Remorse sleeps during a prosperous period but wakes up in adversity.   *Ibid. II*

23   It is too difficult to think nobly when one only thinks to get a living.   *Ibid. II*

24   Hatred, as well as love, renders its votaries credulous.   *Ibid. V*

25   At length I recollected the thoughtless saying of a great princess, who, on being informed that the country people had no bread, replied, "Let them eat cake."[4]   *Ibid. VI*

26   The thirst after happiness is never extinguished in the heart of man.   *Ibid. IX*

27   He[5] thinks like a philosopher, but governs like a king.   *Ibid. XII*

Josiah Tucker
1712–1799

28   What is true of a shopkeeper is true of a shopkeeping nation.[6]
Tract Against Going to War for the Sake of Trade [1763]

Denis Diderot
1713–1784

29   My thoughts are my trollops.
Rameau's Nephew[7]

30   If your little savage were left to himself and to his native blindness, he would in time join the infant's reasoning to the grown man's passion—he would strangle his father and sleep with his mother.
Ibid.

---

[4]Qu'ils mangent de la brioche.
This remark is usually attributed to Marie Antoinette, after her arrival in France in 1770, but the sixth book of the *Confessions* was written two or three years before that date.
[5]Frederick the Great.
[6]See Adam Smith, 326:7.
[7]Translated by JACQUES BARZUN and RALPH H. BOWEN.

[1]See Samuel Johnson, 317:22.
[2]See Voltaire, 306:14.
[3]L'homme est né libre, et partout il est dans les fers.

1   I can be expected to look for truth but not to
find it.   *Pensées Philosophiques [1746], no. 29*

2   L'esprit de l'escalier [staircase wit].[1]
Paradoxe sur le Comédien

3   From fanaticism to barbarism is only one step.
Essai sur le Mérite de la Vertu

Laurence Sterne
1713–1768

4   Only the brave know how to forgive. . . . A
coward never forgave; it is not in his nature.
Sermons, vol. I [1760], no. 12

5   This sad vicissitude of things.[2]   *Ibid. 15*

6   I wish either my father or my mother, or indeed
both of them, as they were in duty both equally
bound to it, had minded what they were about when
they begot me.
Tristram Shandy, bk. I [1760], ch. 1

7   "Pray, my dear," quoth my mother, "have you
not forgot to wind up the clock?"—"Good G—!"
cried my father, making an exclamation, but taking
care to moderate his voice at the same time—"Did
ever woman, since the creation of the world, interrupt a man with such a silly question?"   *Ibid.*

8   So long as a man rides his hobbyhorse peaceably
and quietly along the king's highway, and neither
compels you or me to get up behind him—pray, sir,
what have either you or I to do with it?
Ibid. 7

9   For every ten jokes, thou hast got an hundred
enemies.   *Ibid. 12*

10   He was within a few hours of giving his enemies
the slip forever.   *Ibid.*

11   Whistled up to London, upon a Tom Fool's errand.   *Ibid. 16*

12   'Tis known by the name of perseverance in a
good cause—and of obstinacy in a bad one.[3]
Ibid. 17

13   Persuasion hung upon his lips.   *Ibid. 19*

14   Digressions, incontestably, are the sunshine—
they are the life, the soul of reading; take them out
of this book for instance—you might as well take
the book along with them.   *Ibid. 22*

15   The history of a soldier's wound beguiles the pain
of it.   *Ibid. 25*

16   But desire of knowledge, like the thirst of riches,
increases ever with the acquisition of it.
Ibid. II [1760], ch. 3

17   Writing, when properly managed (as you may be
sure I think mine is), is but a different name for
conversation.   *Ibid. 11*

18   Go, poor devil, get thee gone! Why should I hurt
thee? This world surely is wide enough to hold both
thee and me.   *Ibid. 12 (Uncle Toby to the fly)*

19   That's another story,[4] replied my father.
Ibid. 17

20   Trust that man in nothing who has not a conscience in everything.   *Ibid.*

21   Good—bad—indifferent.
Ibid. III [1761–1762], ch. 2

22   "Our armies swore terribly in Flanders," cried
my uncle Toby—"but nothing to this."
Ibid. 11

23   Of all the cants which are canted in this canting
world, though the cant of hypocrites may be the
worst, the cant of criticism is the most tormenting!
Ibid. 12

24   'Twould be as much as my life was worth.
Ibid. 20

25   One of the two horns of my dilemma.
Ibid. IV [1761–1762], ch. 26

26   The feather put into his cap of having been
abroad.   *Ibid. 31*

27   Now or never was the time.   *Ibid.*

28   There is a Northwest Passage to the intellectual
world.   *Ibid. V [1761–1762], ch. 42*

29   The Accusing Spirit, which flew up to heaven's
chancery with the oath, blushed as he gave it in; and
the Recording Angel, as he wrote it down, dropped
a tear upon the word and blotted it out forever.[5]
Ibid. VI [1761–1762], ch. 8

30   A man should know something of his own country, too, before he goes abroad.
Ibid. VII [1765], ch. 2

31   Ho! 'tis the time of salads.   *Ibid. 17*

32   L—d! said my mother, what is all this story
about?—A Cock and a Bull, said Yorick.
Ibid. IX [1767], ch. 33

33   They order, said I, this matter better in France.
A Sentimental Journey [1768], l. 1

34   I pity the man who can travel from Dan to Beersheba and cry, 'Tis all barren!
Ibid. In the Street, Calais

35   *Tant pis* and *tant mieux,* being two of the great
hinges in French conversation, a stranger would do
well to set himself right in the use of them before he
gets to Paris.   *Ibid. Montreuil*

---

[1]The witty retort thought of only after the conversation is
finished and one is on one's way downstairs.

[2]Revolves the sad vicissitude of things.—RICHARD GIFFORD
[1725–1807], *Contemplation*
    See Terence, 86:6, and Francis Bacon, 160:11.

[3]See Thomas Browne, 248:8.

[4]But that is another story.—KIPLING, *Plain Tales from the
Hills* [1888], *Three and—An Extra*

[5]But sad as angels for the good man's sin, / Weep to record,
and blush to give it in.—THOMAS CAMPBELL, *Pleasures of
Hope* [1799], *pt. II, l. 357*

1   Hail, ye small, sweet courtesies of life! for smooth do ye make the road of it.

Ibid. The Pulse, Paris

2   God tempers the wind, said Maria, to the shorn lamb.[1]

Ibid. Maria

Étienne Bonnot de Condillac
[L'Abbé de Condillac]
1715–1780

3   We cannot recollect the ignorance in which we were born.

Traité des Sensations [1754], dedication

4   The statue is therefore nothing but the sum of all it has acquired. May not this be the same with man?

Ibid. conclusion

Claude Adrien Helvétius
1715–1771

5   Truth is a torch that gleams through the fog without dispelling it.   *De l'Esprit [1758],[2] preface*

6   What makes men happy is liking what they have to do. This is a principle on which society is not founded.   *Ibid.*

7   We don't call a man mad who believes that he eats God, but we do the one who says he is Jesus Christ.   *Ibid.*

Luc de Clapiers,
Marquis de Vauvenargues
1715–1747

8   Great thoughts come from the heart.

Réflexions et Maximes [c. 1747], no. 127

9   Lazy people are always looking for something to do.   *Ibid. 458*

10   The things we know best are those we have not learned.   *Ibid. 479*

William Whitehead
1715–1785

11 Yes, I'm in love, I feel it now
And Caelia has undone me;
And yet I swear I can't tell how
The pleasing plague stole on me.

The Je ne sçay quoi song

12   An old tale which every schoolboy knows.

The Roman Father, prologue

[1]See Estienne, 144:14.
[2]Voltaire, when he read *De l'Esprit*, wrote the author: "Your book is dictated by the soundest reason. You had better get out of France as quickly as you can." The book was condemned by the *parlement* and burned.

Thomas Gray
1716–1771

13 Ye distant spires, ye antique towers,
That crown the wat'ry glade.

On a Distant Prospect of Eton College [1742], st. 1

14 Still as they run they look behind,
They hear a voice in every wind,
And snatch a fearful joy.

Ibid. st. 4

15 Alas, regardless of their doom,
The little victims play!
No sense have they of ills to come,
Nor care beyond today.

Ibid. st. 6

16 Grim-visag'd comfortless Despair.

Ibid. st. 7

17 To each his suff'rings: all are men,
Condemn'd alike to groan,
The tender for another's pain,
Th' unfeeling for his own.
Yet ah! why should they know their fate,
Since sorrow never comes too late,
And happiness too swiftly flies?
Thought would destroy their paradise.
No more; where ignorance is bliss,
'Tis folly to be wise.[3]

Ibid. st. 10

18 Daughter of Jove, relentless power,
Thou tamer of the human breast,
Whose iron scourge and tort'ring hour
The bad affright, afflict the best!

Hymn to Adversity [1742], st. 1

19 What sorrow was, thou bad'st her know,
And from her own she learn'd to melt at others' woe.

Ibid. st. 2

20 What female heart can gold despise?
What cat's averse to fish?

On the Death of a Favorite Cat [1747], st. 4

21 A fav'rite has no friend!

Ibid. st. 6

22 As sickly plants betray a niggard earth,
Whose barren bosom starves her gen'rous birth.

The Alliance of Education and Government [c. 1748], l. 1

23 The social smile, the sympathetic tear.

Ibid. l. 37

24 When love could teach a monarch to be wise,
And gospel-light first dawn'd from Bullen's eyes.[4]

Ibid. l. 108

[3]See *Ecclesiastes 1:18*, 23:28.
[4]The monarch is Henry VIII; Anne Boleyn's name is here spelled (as it is in Shakespeare's *Henry VIII*) as it is pronounced.

1 The curfew tolls the knell of parting day,
The lowing herd wind slowly o'er the lea,
The plowman homeward plods his weary way,
And leaves the world to darkness and to me.
  Elegy Written in a Country Churchyard [1750],[1]
  st. 1

2 Now fades the glimmering landscape on the sight,
And all the air a solemn stillness holds,
Save where the beetle wheels his droning flight,
And drowsy tinklings lull the distant folds.
  Ibid. st. 2

3 Save that from yonder ivy-mantled tow'r
The moping owl does to the moon complain.
  Ibid. st. 3

4 Each in his narrow cell forever laid,
The rude forefathers of the hamlet sleep.
  Ibid. st. 4

5 The breezy call of incense-breathing Morn.
  Ibid. st. 5

6 For them no more the blazing hearth shall burn,
Or busy housewife ply her evening care.[2]
  Ibid. st. 6

7 Let not ambition mock their useful toil,
Their homely joys, and destiny obscure;
Nor grandeur hear with a disdainful smile,
The short and simple annals of the poor.
  Ibid. st. 8

8 The boast of heraldry, the pomp of pow'r,
And all that beauty, all that wealth e'er gave,
Awaits alike the inevitable hour:
The paths of glory lead but to the grave.
  Ibid. st. 9

9 Where through the long-drawn aisle and fretted
    vault
The pealing anthem swells the note of praise.
  Ibid. st. 10

10 Can storied urn, or animated bust
Back to its mansion call the fleeting breath?
Can honor's voice provoke the silent dust,
Or flatt'ry soothe the dull cold ear of death?
  Ibid. st. 11

11 Hands, that the rod of empire might have sway'd,
Or wak'd to ecstasy the living lyre.
  Ibid. st. 12

12 But knowledge to their eyes her ample page
Rich with the spoils of time did ne'er unroll;
Chill penury repress'd their noble rage,
And froze the genial current of the soul.
  Ibid. st. 13

13 Full many a gem of purest ray serene,
The dark unfathom'd caves of ocean bear:
Full many a flower is born to blush unseen,
And waste its sweetness on the desert air.
  Ibid. st. 14

14 Some village Hampden, that with dauntless breast
The little tyrant of his fields withstood;
Some mute inglorious Milton here may rest,
Some Cromwell guiltless of his country's blood.[3]
  Ibid. st. 15

15 To scatter plenty o'er a smiling land,
And read their hist'ry in a nation's eyes.
  Ibid. st. 16

16 Forbade to wade through slaughter to a throne,
And shut the gates of mercy on mankind.
  Ibid. st. 17

17 Far from the madding crowd's ignoble strife,
Their sober wishes never learn'd to stray;
Along the cool sequester'd vale of life
They kept the noiseless tenor of their way.
  Ibid. st. 19

18 Implores the passing tribute of a sigh.
  Ibid. st. 20

19 For who to dumb forgetfulness a prey,
This pleasing anxious being e'er resign'd,
Left the warm precincts of the cheerful day,
Nor cast one longing ling'ring look behind?
  Ibid. st. 22

20 E'en from the tomb the voice of nature cries,
E'en in our ashes live their wonted fires.[4]
  Ibid. st. 23

21 Mindful of th' unhonor'd dead.
  Ibid. st. 24

22 Here rests his head upon the lap of Earth
A youth to fortune and to fame unknown.
Fair Science frown'd not on his humble birth.
And Melancholy mark'd him for her own.[5]
  Ibid. The Epitaph, st. 1

23 Large was his bounty, and his soul sincere,
Heav'n did a recompense as largely send:
He gave to mis'ry all he had, a tear,
He gain'd from Heav'n ('twas all he wish'd) a
    friend.
  Ibid. st. 2

24 No farther seek his merits to disclose,
Or draw his frailties from their dread abode,
(There they alike in trembling hope repose,)
The bosom of his Father and his God.
  Ibid. st. 3

25 The meanest floweret of the vale,
The simplest note that swells the gale,
The common sun, the air, the skies,
To him are opening paradise.
  *Ode on the Pleasure Arising from Vicissitude
  [1754], l. 49*

---

[1]See Samuel Johnson, 314:21.
[2]See Homer, 51:19.
[3]See Mencken, 642:16.
[4]See Chaucer, 130:27.
[5]See Walton, 245:11.

1 O'er her warm cheek and rising bosom move
The bloom of young Desire and purple light of
Love.
The Progress of Poesy [1754], I. 3, l. 16

2 Far from the sun and summer-gale,
In thy green lap was Nature's Darling[1] laid.
Ibid. III. 1, l. 1

3 Or ope the sacred source of sympathetic tears.
Ibid. l. 12

4 He[2] pass'd the flaming bounds of place and time:
The living throne, the sapphire-blaze,
Where angels tremble, while they gaze,
He saw; but blasted with excess of light,
Closed his eyes in endless night.
Ibid. 2, l. 4

5 Thoughts that breathe, and words that burn.[3]
Ibid. 3, l. 4

6 Ruin seize thee, ruthless King!
Confusion on thy banners wait,
Though fann'd by Conquest's crimson wing
They mock the air with idle state.
The Bard [1757], I. 1, l. 1

7 Weave the warp, and weave the woof,
The winding sheet of Edward's race.
Give ample room and verge enough,
The characters of hell to trace.
Ibid. II. 1, l. 1

8 Fair laughs the morn, and soft the zephyr blows,
While proudly riding o'er the azure realm
In gallant trim the gilded vessel goes;
Youth on the prow, and Pleasure at the helm;
Regardless of the sweeping whirlwind's sway,
That, hush'd in grim repose, expects his evening
prey.
Ibid. 2, l. 9

9 Visions of glory, spare my aching sight,
Ye unborn ages, crowd not on my soul!
Ibid. III. 1, l. 11

10 And truth severe, by fairy fiction drest.
Ibid. 3, l. 3

11 Now my weary lips I close;
Leave me, leave me to repose!
The Descent of Odin [1761], l. 71

12 Iron sleet of arrowy shower
Hurtle: in the darken'd air.
The Fatal Sisters [1761], l. 3

13 Too poor for a bribe, and too proud to
importune,
He had not the method of making a fortune.
On His Own Character [1761]

[1]Shakespeare.
[2]Milton.
[3]See Cowley, 267:10.

14 I shall be but a shrimp of an author.
Letter to Horace Walpole [February 25, 1768]

15 Sweet is the breath of vernal shower,
The bee's collected treasures sweet,
Sweet music's melting fall, but sweeter yet
The still small voice[4] of gratitude.
Ode for Music [1769], l. 61

Jean Le Rond d'Alembert
1717–1783

16   Nothing is more indisputable than the existence
of our senses.
*The Encyclopedia (L'Encyclopédie), vol. I
[1751], preliminary discourse[5]*

David Garrick
1717–1779

17 Let others hail the rising sun:
I bow to that whose course is run.[6]
On the Death of Mr. Pelham

18 Heart of oak[7] are our ships,
Heart of oak are our men:
    We always are ready;
    Steady, boys, steady;
We'll fight, and we'll conquer again and again.
Heart of Oak [c. 1770]

19 Here lies Nolly Goldsmith, for shortness called
Noll,
Who wrote like an angel, but talked like poor
Poll.
Impromptu epitaph on Oliver Goldsmith

Horace Walpole
1717–1797

20   Our supreme governors, the mob.
Letters. To Horace Mann [September 7, 1743]

21   Every drop of ink in my pen ran cold.
Ibid. To George Montagu [July 20, 1752]

22   It is charming to totter into vogue.
Ibid. To G. A. Selwyn [December 2, 1765]

23   The next Augustan age will dawn on the other
side of the Atlantic. There will, perhaps, be a Thu-
cydides at Boston, a Xenophon at New York, and,
in time, a Virgil at Mexico, and a Newton at Peru.
At last, some curious traveler from Lima will visit
England and give a description of the ruins of St.
Paul's, like the editions of Balbec and Palmyra.[8]
Ibid. To Mann [November 24, 1774]

[4]See *I Kings* 19:12, 12:39.
[5]Translated by R. N. SCHWAB.
[6]See Pompey, 88:14.
[7]See Rabelais, 140:7.
[8]See Macaulay, 425:7.

1   This world is a comedy to those that think, a tragedy to those that feel.
    Letters. To the Countess of Upper Ossory [August 16, 1776]

2   Prognostics do not always prove prophecies— at least the wisest prophets make sure of the event first.
    Ibid. To Thomas Walpole [February 19, 1785]

3   All his [Sir Joshua Reynolds's] own geese are swans, as the swans of others are geese.
    Ibid. [December 1, 1786]

Samuel Foote
1720–1777

4   Born in a cellar . . . and living in a garret.[1]
    The Author [1757], act II

5   Matt Minikin won't set fire to the Thames though he lives near the Bridge.
    Trip to Calais [1776]

6   He is not only dull himself, but the cause of dullness in others.[2]
    From JAMES BOSWELL, Life of Johnson [1791], 1783

7   So she went into the garden to cut a cabbage leaf to make an apple pie; and at the same time a great she-bear, coming up the street, pops its head into the shop. "What! no soap?" So he died, and she very imprudently married the barber; and there were present the Picninnies, and the Joblillies, and the Garyalies, and the grand Panjandrum himself, with the little round button at top, and they all fell to playing the game of catch as catch can, till the gunpowder ran out at the heels of their boots.
    Nonsense written to test the boasted memory of Charles Macklin, The Quarterly Review [1854]. Credited to Foote by MARIA EDGEWORTH, Harry and Lucy Concluded [1825], vol. II

Dennis O'Kelly
1720–1787

8   It will be Eclipse first, the rest nowhere.
    Declaration at Epsom [May 3, 1769], when the great racehorse Eclipse was to run his first race. Annals of Sporting, vol. II, p. 271

John Woolman
1720–1772

9   Though I felt uneasy at the thought of writing an instrument of slavery . . . through weakness I gave way and wrote it; but . . . said before my master and the Friend that I believed slavekeeping to be a practice inconsistent with the Christian religion.

[1]Born in the garret, in the kitchen bred.—BYRON, *A Sketch* [1816]
[2]See Shakespeare, 183:12.

This, in some degree, abated my uneasiness; yet . . . I should have been clearer if I had desired to be excused from it, as a thing against my conscience.
    Journal [1774]

William Collins
1721–1759

10   How sleep the brave, who sink to rest,
By all their country's wishes bless'd!
    Ode Written in the Beginning of the Year 1746, st. 1

11   By fairy hands their knell is rung,
By forms unseen their dirge is sung;
There Honor comes, a pilgrim gray,
To bless the turf that wraps their clay,
And Freedom shall awhile repair,
To dwell a weeping hermit there!
    Ibid. st. 2

12   In numbers warmly pure and sweetly strong.
    Ode to Simplicity [1747], st. 1

13   If aught of oaten stop or pastoral song
May hope, O pensive Eve, to soothe thine ear.
    Ode to Evening [1747], l. 1

14   Now air is hush'd, save where the weak-ey'd bat,
With short shrill shriek flits by on leathern wing,
Or where the beetle winds
His small but sullen horn.
    Ibid. l. 9

15   'Twas sad by fits, by starts 'twas wild.
    The Passions [1747], l. 28

16   With eyes uprais'd, as one inspir'd,
Pale Melancholy sate retir'd,
And from her wild sequester'd seat,
In notes by distance made more sweet,
Pour'd through the mellow horn her pensive soul.
    Ibid. l. 57

17   In hollow murmurs died away.
    Ibid. l. 68

18   O Music, sphere-descended maid,
Friend of Pleasure, Wisdom's aid!
    Ibid. l. 95

Jeanne Antoinette Poisson, Marquise de Pompadour
1721–1764

19   Après nous le déluge [After us the deluge].[3]
    Reputed reply to Louis XV [November 5, 1757] after the defeat of the French and Austrian armies by Frederick the Great in the battle of Rossbach

[3]The attribution to Madame de Pompadour is made by Després (*Mémoires de Madame de Hausset*); also by Sainte-Beuve and La Tour. Larousse (*Fleurs Historiques*) attributes the saying to the king. It was original with neither, for it is an old French proverb.

Tobias Smollett
1721–1771

1 He was formed for the ruin of our sex.
*The Adventures of Roderick Random [1748],
ch. 22*

2 That great Cham of literature, Samuel Johnson.
Letter to John Wilkes [March 16, 1759]

3 8 June. At London. I am pent up in frowsy lodgings, where there is not room enough to swing a cat.
*The Expedition of Humphry Clinker [1771],
vol. II*

Samuel Adams
1722–1803

4 Let us contemplate our forefathers, and posterity, and resolve to maintain the rights bequeathed to us from the former, for the sake of the latter. The necessity of the times, more than ever, calls for our utmost circumspection, deliberation, fortitude and perseverance. Let us remember that "if we suffer tamely a lawless attack upon our liberty, we encourage it, and involve others in our doom." It is a very serious consideration . . . that millions yet unborn may be the miserable sharers of the event.
Speech [1771]

5 What a glorious morning for America![1]
*Upon hearing the gunfire at Lexington,
Massachusetts [April 19, 1775]*

6 Driven from every other corner of the earth, freedom of thought and the right of private judgment in matters of conscience direct their course to this happy country as their last asylum.[2]
Speech, Philadelphia [August 1, 1776]

John Home
1722–1808

7 I'll woo her as the lion woos his brides.
Douglas [1756], act I, sc. i

8 My name is Norval; on the Grampian hills
My father feeds his flocks; a frugal swain,
Whose constant cares were to increase his store,
And keep his only son, myself, at home.
Ibid. III, i

9 Like Douglas conquer, or like Douglas, die.
Ibid. V, i

Christopher Smart
1722–1771

10 Tell them I Am, Jehovah said
To Moses; while earth heard in dread,
And smitten to the heart,

At once above, beneath, around,
All nature, without voice or sound,
Replied, O Lord, Thou art.
A Song to David [1763], st. 40

11 For adoration all the ranks
Of angels yield eternal thanks,
And David in the midst.
Ibid. st. 51

12 Where ask is have, where seek is find,
Where knock is open wide.[3]
Ibid. st. 77

13 And now the matchless deed's achiev'd,
Determin'd, dar'd, and done.
Ibid. st. 86

14 For I bless God in the libraries of the learned and
for all the booksellers in the world.
Jubilate Agno, frag. B1, l. 79

15 Let James rejoice with the Skuttle-Fish who foils
his foe by the effusion of his ink.
Ibid. l. 125

16 For the Mouse (mus) prevails in the Latin.
For Edi-mus, bibi-mus, vivi-mus, oremus.
Ibid. frag. B2, l. 636

17 For I will consider my Cat Jeoffrey,
For he is the servant of the Living God, duly and
daily serving him.
Ibid. l. 695

18 For he counteracts the Devil, who is Death, by
brisking about the life.
Ibid. l. 720

Sir William Blackstone[4]
1723–1780

19 Man was formed for society.[5]
Commentaries [1765–1769], introduction

20 The royal navy of England hath ever been its greatest defense and ornament; it is its ancient and natural strength; the floating bulwark of our island.
Ibid. bk. I, ch. 13

21 Time whereof the memory of man runneth not to the contrary.[6]   *Ibid. 18*

22 That the king can do no wrong is a necessary and fundamental principle of the English constitution.
Ibid. III, 17

23 It is better that ten guilty persons escape than one innocent suffer.[7]   *Ibid. IV, 27*

---

[3]See *Matthew 7:7, 34:6.*
[4]He it was that first gave the law the air of a science. He found it a skeleton, and clothed it with life, color, and complexion; he embraced the cold statue, and by his touch it grew into youth, health, and beauty.—BARRY YELVERTON, LORD AVONMORE [1736–1805], *On Blackstone*
[5]See Spinoza, 278:10.
[6]The favorite phrase of their law is "a custom whereof the memory of man runneth not back to the contrary."—EMERSON, *English Traits* [1856]
[7]See Voltaire, 306:2.

[1]The phrase was adopted by the town of Lexington as a legend for the town seal.
[2]See Thomas Paine, 340:21.

Adam Smith
1723–1790

1 It is not from the benevolence of the butcher, the brewer, or the baker that we expect our dinner, but from their regard to their own interest. We address ourselves, not to their humanity but to their self-love.
An Inquiry into the Nature and Causes of the Wealth of Nations [1776], vol. I, bk. I, ch. 2

2 A monopoly granted either to an individual or to a trading company has the same effect as a secret in trade or manufactures. *Ibid. ch. 7*

3 People of the same trade seldom meet together, even for merriment and diversion, but the conversation ends in a conspiracy against the public, or in some contrivance to raise prices. *Ibid. 10, pt. 2*

4 With the greater part of rich people, the chief enjoyment of riches consists in the parade of riches, which in their eyes is never so complete as when they appear to possess those decisive marks of opulence which nobody can possess but themselves.
Ibid. 11, pt. 2

5 It is the highest impertinence and presumption, therefore, in kings and ministers to pretend to watch over the economy of private people, and to restrain their expense. . . . They are themselves always, and without any exception, the greatest spendthrifts in the society. *Ibid. bk. II, ch. 3*

6 Every individual necessarily labors to render the annual revenue of the society as great as he can. He generally indeed neither intends to promote the public interest, nor knows how much he is promoting it. . . . He intends only his own gain, and he is in this, as in many other cases, led by an invisible hand to promote an end which was no part of his intention. . . . By pursuing his own interest he frequently promotes that of the society more effectually than when he really intends to promote it. I have never known much good done by those who affected to trade for the public good. *Ibid. bk. IV, ch. 2*

7 To found a great empire for the sole purpose of raising up a people of customers, may at first sight appear a project fit only for a nation of shopkeepers. It is, however, a project altogether unfit for a nation of shopkeepers; but extremely fit for a nation whose government is influenced by shopkeepers.[1]
Ibid. vol. II, bk. IV, ch. 7, pt. 3

[1]Let Pitt then boast of his victory to his nation of shopkeepers.—Bertrand Barère [1755–1841], *Speech* [June 11, 1794]
But it may be said as a rule, that every Englishman in the Duke of Wellington's army paid his way. The remembrance of such a fact surely becomes a nation of shopkeepers.—Thackeray, *Vanity Fair* [1847–1848], *vol. I, ch. 28*
See Josiah Tucker, 319:28.

8 Consumption is the sole end and purpose of all production; and the interest of the producer ought to be attended to only so far as it may be necessary for promoting that of the consumer.
Ibid. ch. 8

9 All systems either of preference or of restraint, therefore, being thus completely taken away, the obvious and simple system of natural liberty establishes itself of its own accord. Every man, as long as he does not violate the laws of justice, is left perfectly free to pursue his own interest his own way, and to bring both his industry and capital into competition with those of any other man or order of men. *Ibid. ch. 9*

Immanuel Kant
1724–1804

10 Two things fill the mind with ever-increasing wonder and awe, the more often and the more intensely the mind of thought is drawn to them: the starry heavens above me and the moral law within me. *Critique of Practical Reason [1788]*

11 Morality is not properly the doctrine of how we may make ourselves happy, but how we may make ourselves worthy of happiness. *Ibid.*

12 There is . . . only a single categorical imperative and it is this: Act only on that maxim through which you can at the same time will that it should become a universal law.
The Metaphysic of Morals [1797],[2] ch. 11

Robert, Lord Clive
1725–1774

13 By God, Mr. Chairman, at this moment I stand astonished at my own moderation!
Reply During Parliamentary Inquiry [1773]

Logan[3]
1725–1780

14 I appeal to any white man to say if he ever entered Logan's cabin hungry and he gave him not meat; if ever he came cold and naked and he clothed him not?
Message to Lord Dunmore, governor of Virginia [November 11, 1774]. From Thomas Jefferson, Notes on Virginia [1784–1785]

[2]Translated by A. D. Lindsay.
[3]Tah-gah-jute. Leader of the Mingo Indians.

George Mason
1725–1792

1   That all men are by nature equally free and independent, and have certain inherent rights, of which, when they enter into a state of society, they cannot by any compact deprive or divest their posterity; namely, the enjoyment of life and liberty, with the means of acquiring and possessing property, and pursuing and obtaining happiness and safety.
Virginia Bill of Rights[1] *[June 12, 1776], article 1*

2   Government is, or ought to be instituted for the common benefit, protection, and security of the people, nation, or community; of all the various modes and forms of government, that is best which is capable of producing the greatest degree of happiness and safety, and is most effectually secured against the danger of maladministration.[2]   *Ibid. 3*

3   The freedom of the press is one of the greatest bulwarks of liberty, and can never be restrained but by despotic governments.   *Ibid. 12*

John Newton[3]
1725–1807

4 Amazing grace! How sweet the sound
That saved a wretch like me!
I once was lost, but now am found,
Was blind, but now I see.
Olney Hymns [1779].[4] *Amazing Grace*

5 Glorious things of thee are spoken,
Zion, city of our God.
Ibid. Glorious Things

James Otis[5]
1725–1783

6   An act against the Constitution is void; an act against natural equity is void.
Argument Against the Writs of Assistance [1761]

7   Taxation without representation is tyranny.[6]
Attributed [1763]

[1]See Patrick Henry, 339:11. Henry drafted Article 16, on religious freedom.

[2]See Jefferson, 344:11.

[3]Newton wrote his own epitaph: John Newton, clerk, once an infidel and libertine, a servant of slaves in Africa, was by the rich mercy of our Lord and Savior Jesus Christ preserved, restored, pardoned, and appointed to preach the Faith he had long labored to destroy.

[4]See Cowper, 333:20.

[5][Otis arguing] was a flame of fire . . . the seeds of patriots and heroes were then and there sown. — JOHN ADAMS, *Works* [1850–1856], *vol. II, p. 522*

[6]This maxim was the guide and watchword of all the friends of liberty. Otis actually said: No parts of His Majesty's dominions can be taxed without their consent. — *Rights of the Colonies* [1764], *p. 64*

8   Ubi libertas ibi patria [Where liberty is, there is my country].   *His motto*

James Hutton
1726–1797

9   The result, therefore, of this physical inquiry [into the age of the earth] is, that we find no vestige of a beginning—no prospect of an end.
The Theory of the Earth [1795]

William Prescott
1726–1795

10   Don't one of you fire until you see the whites of their eyes.[7]   *At Bunker Hill [June 17, 1775]*

Jane Elliot
1727–1805

11 I've heard them lilting, at the ewe milking,
Lasses a' lilting, before dawn of day;
But now they are moaning, on ilka green loaning;
The flowers of the forest are a' wede away.
The Flowers of the Forest[8]

Anne Robert Jacques Turgot, Baron de l'Aulne
1727–1781

12   They [the Americans] are the hope of this world. They may become its model.
Letter to Dr. Richard Price [March 22, 1778]

John Wilkes
1727–1797

13   *Earl of Sandwich:* 'Pon my honor, Wilkes, I don't know whether you'll die on the gallows or of the pox.
Wilkes: That must depend, my Lord, upon whether I first embrace your Lordship's principles, or your Lordship's mistresses.
From SIR CHARLES PETRIE, *The Four Georges [1935]*

[7]Also attributed to ISRAEL PUTNAM [1718–1790].
Silent till you see the whites of their eyes. — PRINCE CHARLES OF PRUSSIA [fl. c. 1745], *at Jagerndorf* [May 23, 1745]
See Frederick the Great, 318:17.

[8]Walter Scott in *Minstrelsy of the Scottish Border* says that *The Flowers of the Forest* was written to an ancient tune and that the last line, the refrain, is indisputably ancient. The air was also used for verses by Alison Cockburn [1713–1794].

Oliver Goldsmith
c. 1728–1774

1   One writer excels at a plan or a title page, another works away the body of the book, and a third is a dab at an index.   *The Bee [1759], no. 1*

2   Good people all, with one accord,
Lament for Madame Blaize,
Who never wanted a good word—
From those who spoke her praise.
    Ibid. 4. Elegy on Mrs. Mary Blaize [1759], st. 1

3   As writers become more numerous, it is natural for readers to become more indolent.
    Ibid. 5. Upon Unfortunate Merit

4   To the last moment of his breath
On hope the wretch relies;
And e'en the pang preceding death
Bids expectation rise.[1]
    The Captivity, An Oratorio [1764], act II

5   Hope, like the gleaming taper's light,
Adorns and cheers our way;
And still, as darker grows the night,
Emits a brighter ray.
    Ibid.

6   Remote, unfriended, melancholy, slow,
Or by the lazy Scheldt, or wandering Po.
    The Traveller [1764], l. 1

7   Where'er I roam, whatever realms to see,
My heart untravel'd fondly turns to thee;
Still to my brother turns with ceaseless pain,
And drags at each remove a lengthening chain.
    Ibid. l. 7

8   Such is the patriot's boast, where'er we roam,
His first, best country ever is, at home.
    Ibid. l. 73

9   Where wealth and freedom reign contentment
    fails,
And honor sinks where commerce long prevails.
    Ibid. l. 91

10   Man seems the only growth that dwindles here.[2]
    Ibid. l. 126

11   They please, are pleas'd, they give to get esteem,
Till, seeming blest, they grow to what they seem.[3]
    Ibid. l. 265

12   To men of other minds my fancy flies,
Embosom'd in the deep where Holland lies.
Methinks her patient sons before me stand,
Where the broad ocean leans against the land.
    Ibid. l. 281

13   Pride in their port, defiance in their eye,
I see the lords of humankind[4] pass by.
    Ibid. l. 327

14   The land of scholars, and the nurse of arms.[5]
    Ibid. l. 356

15   For just experience tells; in every soil,
That those that think must govern those that toil.
    Ibid. l. 371

16   Laws grind the poor,[6] and rich men rule the law.
    Ibid. l. 386

17   A book may be very amusing with numerous errors, or it may be very dull without a single absurdity.   *The Vicar of Wakefield [1766], preface*

18   I . . . chose my wife, as she did her wedding gown, not for a fine glossy surface, but such qualities as would wear well.   *Ibid. ch. 1*

19   We sometimes had those little rubs which Providence sends to enhance the value of its favors.
    Ibid.

20   Handsome is that handsome does.[7]   *Ibid.*

21   I find you want me to furnish you with argument and intellects too.   *Ibid. 7*

22   Man wants but little here below,
Nor wants that little long.[8]
    Ibid. 8 [The Hermit (Edwin and Angelina), st. 8]

23   She was all of a muck of sweat.   *Ibid. 9*

24   They would talk of nothing but high life, and high-lived company, with other fashionable topics, such as pictures, taste, Shakespeare, and the musical glasses.   *Ibid.*

25   The naked every day he clad
When he put on his clothes.
    Ibid. 17. An Elegy on the Death of a Mad Dog, st. 3

26   And in that town a dog was found,
As many dogs there be,
Both mongrel, puppy, whelp, and hound,
And curs of low degree.
    Ibid. st. 4

27   The dog, to gain some private ends,
Went mad, and bit the man.
    Ibid. st. 5

28   The man recover'd of the bite,
The dog it was that died.
    Ibid. st. 8

29   When lovely woman stoops to folly,
And finds too late that men betray,
What charm can soothe her melancholy?
What art can wash her guilt away?[9]
    Ibid. 24. Song, st. 1

30   The only art her guilt to cover,
To hide her shame from every eye,

[1]See Terence, 86:3, and Cicero, 87:23.
[2]Italy.
[3]The character of the French.
[4]The British.
[5]England.
[6]See *Isaiah 3:15, 25:34.*
[7]See Chaucer, 131:12.
[8]See Edward Young, 296:14.
[9]See T. S. Eliot, 669:2.

To give repentance to her lover,
And wring his bosom, is—to die.
Ibid. st. 2

1   This same philosophy is a good horse in the stable, but an arrant jade on a journey.[1]
The Good-Natur'd Man [1768], act I

2   He calls his extravagance, generosity; and his trusting everybody, universal benevolence.
Ibid.

3   All his faults are such that one loves him still the better for them.   *Ibid.*

4   Friendship is a disinterested commerce between equals; love, an abject intercourse between tyrants and slaves.   *Ibid.*

5   Silence gives consent.   *Ibid. II*

6   Measures, not men, have always been my mark.[2]
Ibid.

7 Sweet Auburn! loveliest village of the plain.
The Deserted Village [1770], l. 1

8 Ill fares the land, to hastening ills a prey,
Where wealth accumulates, and men decay;
Princes and lords may flourish, or may fade;[3]
A breath can make them, as a breath has made;
But a bold peasantry, their country's pride,
When once destroy'd, can never be supplied.
Ibid. l. 51

9 His best companions, innocence and health;
And his best riches, ignorance of wealth.
Ibid. l. 61

10 How happy he who crowns in shades like these,
A youth of labor with an age of ease.
Ibid. l. 99

11 The watchdog's voice that bay'd the whispering wind,
And the loud laugh that spoke the vacant mind.[4]
Ibid. l. 121

12 A man he was to all the country dear,
And passing rich with forty pounds a year.
Ibid. l. 141

13 Careless their merits or their faults to scan,
His pity gave ere charity began.
Thus to relieve the wretched was his pride,
And e'en his failings leaned to Virtue's side.
Ibid. l. 161

14 And, as a bird each fond endearment tries
To tempt its new-fledg'd offspring to the skies,

[1]See La Rochefoucauld, 264:24.
[2]See Chesterfield, 304:17; Burke, 330:24; and John Adams, 337:18.
[3]See Burns, 361:10.
[4]Frequent and loud laughter is the characteristic of folly and ill manners: it is the manner in which the mob express their silly joy at silly things, and they call it being merry. In my mind there is nothing so illiberal and so ill-bred as audible laughter.—
CHESTERFIELD, *Letters* [MARCH 9, 1748]
See *Ecclesiastes* 7:6, 24:8.

He tried each art, reprov'd each dull delay,
Allur'd to brighter worlds, and led the way.
Ibid. l. 167

15 Truth from his lips prevail'd with double sway,
And fools, who came to scoff, remain'd to pray.
Ibid. l. 179

16 Even children follow'd with endearing wile,
And pluck'd his gown, to share the good man's smile.
Ibid. l. 183

17 A man severe he was, and stern to view;
I knew him well, and every truant knew:
Well had the boding tremblers learned to trace
The day's disasters in his morning face;
Full well they laugh'd with counterfeited glee,
At all his jokes, for many a joke had he;
Full well the busy whisper, circling round,
Convey'd the dismal tidings when he frown'd;
Yet he was kind; or if severe in aught,
The love he bore to learning was in fault;
The village all declar'd how much he knew;
'Twas certain he could write, and cipher too.
Ibid. l. 197

18 In arguing too, the parson own'd his skill,
For e'en though vanquish'd, he could argue still;
While words of learned length, and thundering sound
Amaz'd the gazing rustics rang'd around;
And still they gaz'd, and still the wonder grew,
That one small head could carry all he knew.
Ibid. l. 211

19 The whitewash'd wall, the nicely sanded floor,
The varnish'd clock that click'd behind the door;
The chest contriv'd a double debt to pay,
A bed by night, a chest of drawers by day.
Ibid. l. 227

20 To me more dear, congenial to my heart,
One native charm, than all the gloss of art.
Ibid. l. 253

21 And, ev'n while fashion's brightest arts decoy,
The heart distrusting asks, if this be joy.
Ibid. l. 263

22 Her modest looks the cottage might adorn,
Sweet as the primrose peeps beneath the thorn.
Ibid. l. 329

23 Thou source of all my bliss, and all my woe,
That found'st me poor at first, and keep'st me so.
Ibid. l. 413

24   In my time, the follies of the town crept slowly among us, but now they travel faster than a stagecoach.   *She Stoops to Conquer [1773], act I*

25   I love everything that's old: old friends, old times, old manners, old books, old wines.[5]   *Ibid.*

26   The very pink of perfection.   *Ibid.*

[5]See Francis Bacon, 158:23; John Webster, 237:11; and Selden, 238:22.

1 Let schoolmasters puzzle their brain,
With grammar, and nonsense, and learning;
Good liquor, I stoutly maintain,
Gives genius a better discerning.
She Stoops to Conquer, I

2   I'll be with you in the squeezing of a lemon.
Ibid.

3   A modest woman, dressed out in all her finery, is
the most tremendous object of the whole creation.
Ibid. II

4   This is Liberty Hall, gentlemen.   *Ibid.*

5   The first blow is half the battle.   *Ibid.*

6   We are the boys
That fear no noise
Where the thundering cannons roar.
Ibid.

7   They liked the book the better the more it made
them cry.   *Ibid.*

8   Ask me no questions, and I'll tell you no fibs.[1]
Ibid. III

9 Our Garrick's a salad; for in him we see
Oil, vinegar, sugar, and saltness agree!
Retaliation [1774], l. 11

10 Here lies our good Edmund,[2] whose genius was
such,
We scarcely can praise it, or blame it too much;
Who, born for the universe, narrow'd his mind,
And to party gave up what was meant for
mankind . . .
Who, too deep for his hearers, still went on
refining,
And thought of convincing, while they thought of
dining;
Though equal to all things, for all things unfit;
Too nice for a statesman, too proud for a wit.
Ibid. l. 29

11 His conduct still right, with his argument wrong.
Ibid. l. 46

12 On the stage he was natural, simple, affecting;
'Twas only that when he was off he was acting.
Ibid. l. 101

13 He cast off his friends as a huntsman his pack,
For he knew when he pleas'd he could whistle
them back.
Ibid. l. 107

14 When they talk'd of their Raphaels, Correggios,
and stuff,
He shifted his trumpet and only took snuff.[3]
Ibid. l. 145

---

[1]Them that asks no questions isn't told a lie. — KIPLING, *A
Smuggler's Song, st. 6*
[2]Edmund Burke.
[3]Sir Joshua Reynolds, who was exceedingly deaf.

15 Such dainties to them, their health it might hurt;
It's like sending them ruffles, when wanting a
shirt.[4]
The Haunch of Venison [1776], l. 33

16   There is no arguing with Johnson: for if his pistol
misses fire, he knocks you down with the butt end
of it.
From JAMES BOSWELL, *Life of Johnson [1791].
October 26, 1769*

17   [To Dr. Johnson:] If you were to make little fishes
talk, they would talk like whales.
Ibid. April 27, 1773

18   You may all go to pot.
*Verses in reply to an invitation to dine at Dr.
Baker's*

John Stark
1728–1822

19   My men, yonder are the Hessians. They were
bought for seven pounds and ten pence a man. Are
you worth more? Prove it. Tonight, the American
flag floats from yonder hill or Molly Stark sleeps a
widow!
*Before the battle of Bennington [August 16,
1777]*

Edmund Burke[5]
1729–1797

20   Custom reconciles us to everything.
On the Sublime and Beautiful [1756], sec. 18

21   There is, however, a limit at which forbearance
ceases to be a virtue.
*Observations on a Late Publication on the
Present State of the Nation [1769]*

22   The wisdom of our ancestors.[6]   *Ibid.*

23   When bad men combine, the good must associate; else they will fall one by one, an unpitied sacrifice in a contemptible struggle.
*Thoughts on the Cause of the Present
Discontents [April 23, 1770]*

24   Of this stamp is the cant of, Not men, but measures;[7] a sort of charm by which many people get
loose from every honorable engagement.   *Ibid.*

---

[4]See Tom Brown, 287:1.
[5]You could not stand five minutes with that man [Burke]
beneath a shed while it rained, but you must be convinced you
had been standing with the greatest man you had ever seen.
—SAMUEL JOHNSON, *Johnsonian Miscellanies [1897], edited
by G. B. HILL, vol. I, p. 290*
[6]*De Sapienta Veterum [The Wisdom of the Ancients].* —
FRANCIS BACON [1609], *title of work*
The phrase is also in Burke, *Discussion on the Traitorous
Correspondence Bill [1793].*
[7]See Chesterfield, 304:17; Goldsmith, 329:6; and John
Adams, 337:18.

1   So to be patriots as not to forget we are gentlemen.   *Ibid.*

2   Public life is a situation of power and energy; he trespasses against his duty who sleeps upon his watch, as well as he that goes over to the enemy.   *Ibid.*

3   Reflect how you are to govern a people who think they ought to be free, and think they are not. Your scheme yields no revenue; it yields nothing but discontent, disorder, disobedience; and such is the state of America, that after wading up to your eyes in blood, you could only end just where you begun; that is, to tax where no revenue is to be found, to —my voice fails me; my inclination indeed carries me no farther—all is confusion beyond it.
    First Speech on the Conciliation with America.
    American Taxation [April 19, 1774]

4   Your representative owes you, not his industry only, but his judgment; and he betrays instead of serving you if he sacrifices it to your opinion.
    Speech to the Electors of Bristol [November 3, 1774]

5   I have in general no very exalted opinion of the virtue of paper government.
    Second Speech on Conciliation with America.
    The Thirteen Resolutions [March 22, 1775]

6   The concessions of the weak are the concessions of fear.   *Ibid.*

7   Young man, there is America—which at this day serves for little more than to amuse you with stories of savage men and uncouth manners; yet shall, before you taste of death, show itself equal to the whole of that commerce which now attracts the envy of the world.   *Ibid.*

8   When we speak of the commerce with our colonies, fiction lags after truth; invention is unfruitful, and imagination cold and barren.   *Ibid.*

9   A people who are still, as it were, but in the gristle, and not yet hardened into the bone of manhood.   *Ibid.*

10   Through a wise and salutary neglect [of the colonies], a generous nature has been suffered to take her own way to perfection; when I reflect upon these effects, when I see how profitable they have been to us, I feel all the pride of power sink and all presumption in the wisdom of human contrivances melt and die away within me. My rigor relents. I pardon something to the spirit of liberty.   *Ibid.*

11   The use of force alone is but *temporary*. It may subdue for a moment; but it does not remove the necessity of subduing again: and a nation is not governed, which is perpetually to be conquered.
        Ibid.

12   Nothing less will content me, than *whole America*.   *Ibid.*

13   Abstract liberty, like other mere abstractions, is not to be found.   *Ibid.*

14   The religion most prevalent in our northern colonies is a refinement on the principle of resistance: it is the dissidence of dissent, and the protestantism of the Protestant religion.   *Ibid.*

15   In no country perhaps in the world is law so general a study [as in America]. . . . This study renders men acute, inquisitive, dexterous, prompt in attack, ready in defense, full of resources. . . . They augur misgovernment at a distance, and snuff the approach of tyranny in every tainted breeze.
        Ibid.

16   I do not know the method of drawing up an indictment against an whole people.   *Ibid.*

17   It is not, what a lawyer tells me I *may* do; but what humanity, reason, and justice, tell me I ought to do.   *Ibid.*

18   The march of the human mind is slow.
        Ibid.

19   Freedom and not servitude is the cure of anarchy; as religion, and not atheism, is the true remedy for superstition.   *Ibid.*

20   All government—indeed, every human benefit and enjoyment, every virtue and every prudent act —is founded on compromise and barter.   *Ibid.*

21   Slavery they can have anywhere. It is a weed that grows in every soil.   *Ibid.*

22   Deny them [the colonies] this participation of freedom, and you break that sole bond, which originally made, and must still preserve the unity of the empire.   *Ibid.*

23   It is the love of the [British] people; it is their attachment to their government, from the sense of the deep stake they have in such a glorious institution, which gives you both your army and your navy, and infuses into both that liberal obedience, without which your army would be a base rabble, and your navy nothing but rotten timber.   *Ibid.*

24   Magnanimity in politics is not seldom the truest wisdom; and a great empire and little minds go ill together.   *Ibid.*

25   By adverting to the dignity of this high calling our ancestors have turned a savage wilderness into a glorious empire: and have made the most extensive, and the only honorable conquests, not by destroying, but by promoting the wealth, the number, the happiness of the human race.   *Ibid.*

26   Corrupt influence, which is itself the perennial spring of all prodigality, and of all disorder; which loads us, more than millions of debt; which takes away vigor from our arms, wisdom from our councils, and every shadow of authority and credit from the most venerable parts of our constitution.
    Speech on the Economical Reform [1780]

1   He was not merely a chip of the old block, but the old block itself.
On Pitt's first speech [February 26, 1781]

2   A rapacious and licentious soldiery.
Speech on Fox's East India Bill [1783]

3   The people never give up their liberties but under some delusion.
Speech at County Meeting of Buckinghamshire [1784]

4   There never was a bad man that had ability for good service.
Impeachment of Warren Hastings [February 15, 1788]

5   Religious persecution may shield itself under the guise of a mistaken and over-zealous piety.
Ibid. [February 17, 1788]

6   An event has happened, upon which it is difficult to speak, and impossible to be silent.
Ibid. [May 5, 1789]

7   Resolved to die in the last dike of prevarication.
Ibid. [May 7, 1789]

8   There is but one law for all, namely, that law which governs all law, the law of our Creator, the law of humanity, justice, equity — the law of nature, and of nations.   *Ibid. [May 28, 1794]*

9   They made and recorded a sort of institute and digest of anarchy, called the Rights of Man.
On the Army Estimates [1790]

10   People will not look forward to posterity who never look backward to their ancestors.
Reflections on the Revolution in France [1790]

11   Government is a contrivance of human wisdom to provide for human wants. Men have a right that these wants should be provided for by this wisdom.
Ibid.

12   The age of chivalry has gone. That of sophisters, economists, and calculators has succeeded, and the glory of Europe is extinguished forever.   *Ibid.*

13   The unbought grace of life, the cheap defense of nations, the nurse of manly sentiment and heroic enterprise is gone!   *Ibid.*

14   That chastity of honor, which felt a stain like a wound.   *Ibid.*

15   Vice itself lost half its evil, by losing all its grossness.   *Ibid.*

16   Kings will be tyrants from policy, when subjects are rebels from principle.   *Ibid.*

17   Learning will be cast into the mire, and trodden down under the hoofs of a swinish multitude.
Ibid.

18   Because half a dozen grasshoppers under a fern make the field ring with their importunate chink, whilst thousands of great cattle, reposed beneath the shadow of the British oak, chew the cud and are silent, pray do not imagine that those who make the noise are the only inhabitants of the field; that, of course, they are many in number; or that, after all, they are other than the little shriveled, meager, hopping, though loud and troublesome *insects* of the hour.   *Ibid.*

19   Superstition is the religion of feeble minds.
Ibid.

20   He that wrestles with us strengthens our nerves, and sharpens our skill. Our antagonist is our helper.
Ibid.

21   To execute laws is a royal office; to execute orders is not to be a king. However, a political executive magistracy, though merely such, is a great trust.
Ibid.

22   You can never plan the future by the past.[1]
Letter to a member of the National Assembly [1791]

23   Old religious factions are volcanoes burnt out.
Speech on the Petition of the Unitarians [1792]

24   The cold neutrality of an impartial judge.
Preface to Brissot's Address [1794]

25   All men that are ruined, are ruined on the side of their natural propensities.
Letters on a Regicide Peace [1796], no. 1

26   Example is the school of mankind, and they will learn at no other.[2]   *Ibid.*

27   Mere parsimony is not economy. . . . Expense, and great expense, may be an essential part of true economy.   *Letter to a Noble Lord [1796]*

28   Economy is a distributive virtue, and consists not in saving but selection. Parsimony requires no providence, no sagacity, no powers of combination, no comparison, no judgment.   *Ibid.*

29   And having looked to Government for bread, on the very first scarcity they will turn and bite the hand that fed them.
Thoughts and Details on Scarcity [1800]

30   The only thing necessary for the triumph of evil is for good men to do nothing.   *Attributed[3]*

Gotthold Ephraim Lessing
1729–1781

31   He who doesn't lose his wits over certain things has no wits to lose.
Emilia Galotti [1772], act IV, sc. vii

32   No person must have to.
Nathan der Weise [1779], act I, sc. iii

[1]See Patrick Henry, 339:8.
[2]See Franklin, 309:28.
[3]Vigorous searches by many people have failed to locate this quotation anywhere in Burke's writings. In her preface to the fifteenth edition of *Bartlett* [1980, p. ix] Emily Morison Beck suggests that it may be "a twentieth-century paraphrase" of Burke, 330:23.

1   People are not always what they seem.
                                        Ibid. vi

2   The true beggar is the true king.
                                    Ibid. II, end

3   Not all are free who scorn their chains.
                                        Ibid. IV, iv

4   One can drink too much, but one never drinks enough.   *Lieder*

John Parker
1729–1775

5   Stand your ground. Don't fire unless fired upon, but if they mean to have a war let it begin here!
    To his Minute Men at Lexington, Massachusetts [April 19, 1775]

Speckled Snake[1]
c. 1729–1829

6   When the white man had warmed himself before the Indians' fire and filled himself with their hominy, he became very large. With a step he bestrode the mountains, and his feet covered the plains and the valleys. His hand grasped the eastern and the western sea, and his head rested on the moon.
    Statement when President Andrew Jackson recommended that the Cherokees, Chickasaws, Choctaws, Creeks, and Seminoles move west beyond the Mississippi [1829]

7   Brothers, I have listened to a great many talks from our great father.[2] But they always began and ended in this: "Get a little further; you are too near me."   *Ibid.*

Thomas Osbert Mordaunt
1730–1809

8   One crowded hour of glorious life
    Is worth an age without a name.
    Verses Written During the War [1756–1763]. From the Bee [October 12, 1791]

Motoori Norinaga[3]
1730–1801

9   Sages are superior to other people only in their cleverness. The fact is that they were all impostors. Among them the least blameworthy was Confucius.
                                    Arrowroot

10 *The Tale of Genji*[4] is simply a tale of human life which leaves aside and does not profess to take up at all the question of good and bad, and which dwells only upon the goodness of those who are aware of the sorrow of human existence.   *Tama no Ogushi*

Josiah Wedgwood
1730–1795

11 Am I not a man and a brother?
                            On a medallion[5] *[1787]*

Charles Churchill
1731–1764

12 Genius is of no country.
                            The Rosciad [1761], l. 207

13 Learn'd without sense, and venerably dull.
                                    Ibid. l. 591

14 Those who would make us feel—must feel themselves.
                                    Ibid. l. 962

15 Apt alliteration's artful aid.
                    The Prophecy of Famine [1763], l. 86

16   Fame
    Is nothing but an empty name.
                    The Ghost [1763], bk. I, l. 229

17 Just to the windward of the law.
                                    Ibid. III, l. 56

18 Though by whim, envy, or resentment led,
    They damn those authors whom they never read.
                    The Candidate [1764], l. 57

19   Be England what she will,
    With all her faults she is my country still.[6]
                            The Farewell, l. 27

William Cowper
1731–1800

20 Oh! for a closer walk with God.
        Olney Hymns [1779],[7] *no. 1, Walking with God*

21 What peaceful hours I once enjoy'd!
    How sweet their memory still!
    But they have left an aching void
    The world can never fill.
                                        Ibid.

22 God moves in a mysterious way
    His wonders to perform;
    He plants his footsteps in the sea
    And rides upon the storm.
            Ibid. 35, Light Shining out of Darkness

---

[1]A Creek.
[2]President Jackson.
[3]From *Sources of Japanese Tradition* [1960], edited by WILLIAM THEODORE DE BARY.
[4]See Murasaki Shikibu, 120:15.

[5]Representing a black man in chains, with one knee on the ground and both hands lifted up to heaven. This was adopted as a seal by the Anti-Slavery Society of London.
[6]England, with all thy faults I love thee still, / My country! —COWPER, *The Task* [1785], *bk. II, The Timepiece, l. 206*
    See John Quincy Adams, 368:14; Decatur, 390:22; and Schurz, 510:18.
[7]See John Newton, 327:4.

1 Behind a frowning providence
He hides a smiling face.
    Olney Hymns, no. 35, Light Shining out of Darkness

2 Thus happiness depends, as Nature shows,
Less on exterior things than most suppose.
    Table Talk [1782], l. 246

3 Freedom has a thousand charms to show,
That slaves, howe'er contented, never know.
    Ibid. l. 260

4 Manner is all in all, whate'er is writ,
The substitute for genius, sense, and wit.
    Ibid. l. 542

5 Low ambition and the thirst of praise.
    Ibid. l. 591

6 [Pope] Made poetry a mere mechanic art.
    Ibid. l. 656

7 Lights of the world, and stars of human race.
    The Progress of Error [1782], l. 97

8 How much a dunce that has been sent to roam
Excels a dunce that has been kept at home!
    Ibid. l. 415

9 A fool must now and then be right, by chance.
    Conversation [1782], l. 96

10 He would not, with a peremptory tone,
Assert the nose upon his face his own.
    Ibid. l. 121

11 I cannot talk with civet in the room,
A fine puss-gentleman that's all perfume.
    Ibid. l. 283

12 His wit invites you by his looks to come,
But when you knock it never is at home.[1]
    Ibid. l. 303

13 Our wasted oil unprofitably burns,
Like hidden lamps in old sepulchral urns.
    Ibid. l. 357

14 A business with an income at its heels
Furnishes always oil for its own wheels.
    Retirement [1782], l. 615

15 Absence of occupation is not rest,
A mind quite vacant is a mind distress'd.
    Ibid. l. 623

16 Built God a church, and laugh'd His word to
scorn.[2]
    Ibid. l. 688

17   Philologists, who chase
A panting syllable through time and space,
Start it at home, and hunt it in the dark
To Gaul, to Greece, and into Noah's ark.
    Ibid. l. 691

18 I praise the Frenchman,[3] his remark was shrewd—
How sweet, how passing sweet, is solitude!
But grant me still a friend in my retreat
Whom I may whisper—solitude is sweet.
    Ibid. l. 739

19 I am monarch of all I survey,
My right there is none to dispute.
    Verses Supposed to Be Written by Alexander Selkirk [1782], st. 1

20 O Solitude! where are the charms
That sages have seen in thy face?
    Ibid.

21   The British warrior queen,
Bleeding from the Roman rods.
    Boadicea [1782]

22   Though on pleasure she was bent,
She had a frugal mind.
    History of John Gilpin [1785], st. 8

23 A hat not much the worse for wear.
    Ibid. st. 46

24 Now let us sing—Long live the king,
And Gilpin, long live he;
And, when he next doth ride abroad,
May I be there to see!
    Ibid. st. 63

25 God made the country, and man made the town.
    The Task [1785], bk. I, The Sofa, l. 749

26 Oh for a lodge in some vast wilderness,[4]
Some boundless contiguity of shade,
Where rumor of oppression and deceit,
Of unsuccessful or successful war,
Might never reach me more.
    Ibid. II, The Timepiece, l. 1

27 Slaves cannot breathe in England; if their lungs
Receive our air, that moment they are free!
They touch our country, and their shackles fall.
    Ibid. l. 40

28 Variety's the very spice of life.[5]
    Ibid. l. 606

29   His head,
Not yet by time completely silver'd o'er,
Bespoke him past the bounds of freakish youth,
But strong for service still, and unimpair'd.
    Ibid. l. 702

30 Guilty splendor.
    Ibid. III, The Garden, l. 70

31 Great contest follows, and much learned dust
Involves the combatants.
    Ibid. l. 161

---

[1]See Pope, 300:26.
[2]Voltaire, who built a church at Ferney [1760–1761], with the inscription *Deo erexit Voltaire.*

[3]La Bruyère.
[4]See *Jeremiah* 9:2, 28:22, and Byron, 400:28.
[5]See Publilius Syrus, 99:21, and Samuel Johnson, 314:7.

1 From reveries so airy, from the toil
  Of dropping buckets into empty wells,
  And growing old in drawing nothing up.[1]
                              Ibid. l. 188

2 Who loves a garden loves a greenhouse too.
                              Ibid. l. 566

3 Now stir the fire, and close the shutters fast,
  Let fall the curtains, wheel the sofa round,
  And, while the bubbling and loud-hissing urn
  Throws up a steamy column, and the cups,
  That cheer but not inebriate,[2] wait on each,
  So let us welcome peaceful evening in.
                Ibid. IV, The Winter Evening, l. 36

4 'Tis pleasant, through the loopholes of retreat,
  To peep at such a world; to see the stir
  Of the great Babel, and not feel the crowd.
                              Ibid. l. 88

5 O Winter, ruler of the inverted year![3]
                              Ibid. l. 120

6 With spots quadrangular of diamond form,
  Ensanguin'd hearts, clubs typical of strife,
  And spades, the emblems of untimely graves.
                              Ibid. l. 217

7 It seems the part of wisdom.
                              Ibid. l. 336

8 All learned, and all drunk!
                              Ibid. l. 478

9 Gloriously drunk, obey th' important call.
                              Ibid. l. 510

10 But war's a game, which, were their subjects wise,
   Kings would not play at.
            Ibid. V, The Winter Morning Walk, l. 187

11 There is in souls a sympathy with sounds;
   And as the mind is pitch'd the ear is pleas'd
   With melting airs or martial, brisk, or grave:
   Some chord in unison with what we hear
   Is touch'd within us, and the heart replies.
          Ibid. VI, Winter Walk at Noon, l. 1

12   Here the heart
   May give a useful lesson to the head,
   And Learning wiser grow without his books.
                              Ibid. l. 85

13 Knowledge is proud that he has learn'd so much;
   Wisdom is humble that he knows no more.
                              Ibid. l. 96

14 Nature is but a name for an effect,
   Whose cause is God.
                              Ibid. l. 223

15 An honest man, close-button'd to the chin,
   Broadcloth without, and a warm heart within.
                Epistle to Joseph Hill [1785], l. 62

16 Shine by the side of every path we tread
   With such a luster, he that runs may read.[4]
                      Tirocinium [1785], l. 79

17 Toll for the brave—
   The brave! that are no more;
   All sunk beneath the wave,
   Fast by their native shore!
        On the Loss of the Royal George[5] [1791], st. 1

18 And still to love, though prest with ill,
   In wintry age to feel no chill,
   With me is to be lovely still,
     My Mary!
                      To Mary [1791], st. 12

19 Beware of desp'rate steps! The darkest day
   (Live till tomorrow) will have pass'd away.
                The Needless Alarm [1794]. Moral

20 I shall not ask Jean Jacques Rousseau
   If birds confabulate or no.
              Pairing Time Anticipated [c. 1794]

21 Misses! the tale that I relate
   This lesson seems to carry—
   Choose not alone a proper mate,
   But proper time to marry.
                              Ibid. Moral

22   Misery still delights to trace
   Its semblance in another's case.
                  The Castaway [1799], l. 59

Erasmus Darwin
1731–1802

23 Soon shall thy arm, unconquer'd steam! afar
   Drag the slow barge, or drive the rapid car;
   Or on wide-waving wings expanded bear
   The flying-chariot through the fields of air.
            The Botanic Garden, pt. I [1789], l. 289

24   Would it be too bold to imagine, that in the great length of time, since the earth began to exist, perhaps millions of ages before the commencement of the history of mankind, would it be too bold to imagine, that all warm-blooded animals have arisen from one living filament which the Great First Cause endued with animality . . . and thus possessing the faculty of continuing to improve by its own inherent activity, and of delivering down those improvements by generation to its posterity, world without end![6]
                              Zoonomia [1794]

---

[1]See Sydney Smith, 380:7.
[2]See Berkeley, 296:24.
[3]See James Thomson, 307:15.
[4]See *Habakkuk* 2:2, 29:40.
[5]The *Royal George* was an English man-of-war of 108 guns, which suddenly heeled over, under the strain caused by the shifting of her guns, while being refitted at Spithead, August 29, 1782. The commander, Admiral Kempenfeldt, and eight hundred of the sailors, marines, and visitors on board were drowned.
[6]Here the grandfather of Charles Darwin announces his own early theory of organic evolution.

Charles Lee
1731–1782

1   Beware that your Northern laurels do not change to Southern willows.[1]
To General Horatio Gates after the surrender of Burgoyne at Saratoga [October 17, 1777]

Beilby Porteus
1731–1808

2   One murder made a villain,
Millions, a hero.
Death [1759], l. 154

3   War its thousands slays, Peace, its ten thousands.[2]
Ibid. l. 178

Pierre de Beaumarchais
1732–1799

4   Judging by the virtues expected of a servant, does your Excellency know many masters who would be worthy valets?
Le Barbier de Séville [1775], act I, sc. ii

5   I quickly laugh at everything, for fear of having to cry.[3]
Ibid.

6   If you assure me that your intentions are honorable.
Ibid. IV, vi

7   If you are mediocre and you grovel, you shall succeed.
Le Mariage de Figaro [1784], act III, sc. iii

8   You went to some trouble to be born, and that's all.[4]
Ibid. V, iii

9   If censorship reigns there cannot be sincere flattery, and only small men are afraid of small writings.
Ibid.

John Dickinson
1732–1808

10 Then join hand in hand, brave Americans all!
By uniting we stand, by dividing we fall.[5]
The Liberty Song [1768]

Richard Henry Lee
1732–1794

11 That these united colonies are, and of right ought to be, free and independent states; that they are

absolved from all allegiance to the British crown; and that all political connection between them and the State of Great Britain is, and ought to be, totally dissolved.
Resolution moved at the Continental Congress [June 7, 1776; adopted July 2][6]

George Washington[7]
1732–1799

12 Discipline is the soul of an army. It makes small numbers formidable; procures success to the weak, and esteem to all.
Letter of Instructions to the Captains of the Virginia Regiments [July 29, 1759]

13 Let us therefore animate and encourage each other, and show the whole world that a Freeman, contending for liberty on his own ground, is superior to any slavish mercenary on earth.
General Orders, Headquarters, New York [July 2, 1776]

14 The time is now near at hand which must probably determine whether Americans are to be freemen or slaves; whether they are to have any property they can call their own; whether their houses and farms are to be pillaged and destroyed, and themselves consigned to a state of wretchedness from which no human efforts will deliver them. The fate of unborn millions will now depend, under God, on the courage and conduct of this army. Our cruel and unrelenting enemy leaves us only the choice of brave resistance, or the most abject submission. We have, therefore, to resolve to conquer or die.
Address to the Continental Army before the battle of Long Island [August 27, 1776]

15 There is nothing that gives a man consequence, and renders him fit for command, like a support that renders him independent of everybody but the State he serves.
Letter to the president of Congress, Heights of Harlem [September 24, 1776]

16 To place any dependence upon militia, is, assuredly, resting upon a broken staff.
Ibid.

17 Without a decisive naval force we can do nothing definitive. And with it, everything honorable and glorious.[8]
To Lafayette [November 15, 1781]

18 If men are to be precluded from offering their sentiments on a matter which may involve the most serious and alarming consequences that can invite the consideration of mankind, reason is of no use to

[1]Gates was later defeated by Cornwallis at Camden, South Carolina [August 16, 1780], and was relieved of his command.
[2]See *I Samuel* 18:7, 11:42.
[3]*Je me presse de rire de tout, de peur d'être obligé d'en pleurer.*
See La Bruyère, 283:14, and Byron, 403:2.
[4]*Vous vous êtes donné la peine de naître, et rien de plus.*
[5]United we stand, divided we fall.—*A watchword of the American Revolution*
See Aesop, 59:17.

[6]See John Adams, 338:4.
[7]The Father of your Country.—HENRY KNOX [1750–1806], *Letter to Washington [March 19, 1787]*
I can't tell a lie. I did cut it [the cherry tree] with my hatchet.
—*Attributed to Washington as a child;* MASON LOCKE WEEMS [1759–1825], *The Life of George Washington [1800]*
See Franklin, 310:21, and Henry (Light-Horse Harry) Lee, 355:16.
[8]See Themistocles, 62:30; Francis Bacon, 160:7; Edmund Waller, 249:27; and Mahan, 541:3.

us; the freedom of speech may be taken away, and dumb and silent we may be led, like sheep to the slaughter.

> *Address to officers of the Army [March 15, 1783]*

1   The preservation of the sacred fire of liberty, and the destiny of the republican model of government, are justly considered as deeply, perhaps as finally staked, on the experiment entrusted to the hands of the American people.

> *First Inaugural Address [April 30, 1789]*

2   Happily the Government of the United States, which gives to bigotry no sanction, to persecution no assistance, requires only that they who live under its protection should demean themselves as good citizens in giving it on all occasions their effectual support.

> *Letter to the Jewish congregation of Newport, Rhode Island [1790]*

3   To be prepared for war is one of the most effectual means of preserving peace.

> *First Annual Address [to both houses of Congress, January 8, 1790]*

4   The basis of our political systems is the right of the people to make and to alter their constitutions of government.

> *Farewell Address [September 17, 1796]*

5   Let me now . . . warn you in the most solemn manner against the baneful effects of the spirit of party.   *Ibid.*

6   Observe good faith and justice toward all nations. Cultivate peace and harmony with all. . . . The Nation which indulges toward another an habitual hatred or an habitual fondness is in some degree a slave. It is a slave to its animosity or to its affection, either of which is sufficient to lead it astray from its duty and its interest.   *Ibid.*

7   'Tis our true policy to steer clear of permanent alliances, with any portion of the foreign world.
              Ibid.

8   There can be no greater error than to expect or calculate upon real favors from nation to nation.
              Ibid.

9   It is well, I die hard, but I am not afraid to go.
> *Last words [December 14, 1799]*

John Adams[1]
1735–1826

10   Now to what higher object, to what greater character, can any mortal aspire than to be possessed of all this knowledge, well digested and ready at command, to assist the feeble and friendless, to discountenance the haughty and lawless, to procure

redress of wrongs, the advancement of right, to assert and maintain liberty and virtue, to discourage and abolish tyranny and vice?

> *Letter to Jonathan Sewall [October 1759]*

11   A pen is certainly an excellent instrument to fix a man's attention and to inflame his ambition.

> *Diary [November 14, 1760]*

12   I always consider the settlement of America with reverence and wonder, as the opening of a grand scene and design in providence, for the illumination of the ignorant and the emancipation of the slavish part of mankind all over the earth.

> *Notes for "A Dissertation on the Canon and Feudal Law" [1765]*

13   Liberty cannot be preserved without a general knowledge among the people, who have a right . . . and a desire to know; but besides this, they have a right, an indisputable, unalienable, indefeasible, divine right to that most dreaded and envied kind of knowledge, I mean of the characters and conduct of their rulers.

> *A Dissertation on the Canon and Feudal Law [1765]*

14   Let every sluice of knowledge be opened and set a-flowing.   *Ibid.*

15   Facts are stubborn things; and whatever may be our wishes, our inclinations, or the dictates of our passions, they cannot alter the state of facts and evidence.

> *Argument in Defense of the [British] Soldiers in the Boston Massacre Trials [December 1770]*

16   There is danger from all men. The only maxim of a free government ought to be to trust no man living with power to endanger the public liberty.

> *Notes for an Oration at Braintree, Massachusetts [Spring 1772]*

17   This is the most magnificent movement of all! There is a dignity, a majesty, a sublimity, in this last effort of the patriots that I greatly admire. The people should never rise without doing something to be remembered—something notable and striking. This destruction of the tea is so bold, so daring, so firm, intrepid and inflexible, and it must have so important consequences, and so lasting, that I can't but consider it as an epocha in history!

> *Diary [on the Boston Tea Party, December 17, 1773]*

18   A government of laws, and not of men.[2]

> *"Novanglus"* [3] *papers, Boston Gazette [1774], no. 7. Incorporated [1780] in the Massachusetts Constitution* [4]

---

[1]He is as disinterested as the being who made him: he is profound in his view; and accurate in his judgment, except where knowledge of the world is necessary to form a judgment. — JEFFERSON [January 30, 1787]

[2]Adams credits this formulation to James Harrington [1611–1677], with whose work *The Commonwealth of Oceana* [1656] he was familiar. Adams's use of the phrase gave it wide circulation in America.

See Chesterfield, 304:17; Goldsmith, 329:6; and Burke, 330:-24.

[3]Pseudonym of John Adams.

[4]Article 30 of the Declaration of Rights.

1   Metaphysicians and politicians may dispute forever, but they will never find any other moral principle or foundation of rule or obedience, than the consent of governors and governed.[1]
"Novanglus" papers, no. 7

2   I agree with you that in politics the middle way is none at all.
Letter to Horatio Gates [March 23, 1776]

3   You bid me burn your letters. But I must forget you first.
Letter to Abigail Adams [April 28, 1776]

4   Yesterday, the greatest question was decided which ever was debated in America, and a greater perhaps never was nor will be decided among men. A resolution was passed without one dissenting colony, "that these United Colonies are, and of right ought to be, free and independent States."[2]
Ibid. [July 3, 1776]

5   The second day of July, 1776,[3] will be the most memorable epoch in the history of America. I am apt to believe that it will be celebrated by succeeding generations as the great anniversary festival. It ought to be commemorated as the day of deliverance, by solemn acts of devotion to God Almighty. It ought to be solemnized with pomp and parade, with shows, games, sports, guns, bells, bonfires, and illuminations, from one end of this continent to the other, from this time forward forevermore.
Second Letter to Abigail Adams [July 3, 1776]

6   The happiness of society[4] is the end of government.   *Thoughts on Government [1776]*

7   The judicial power ought to be distinct from both the legislative and executive, and independent upon both, that so it may be a check upon both, as both should be checks upon that.   *Ibid.*

8   Virtue is not always amiable.
Diary [February 9, 1779]

9   By my physical constitution I am but an ordinary man. . . . Yet some great events, some cutting expressions, some mean hypocrisies, have at times thrown this assemblage of sloth, sleep, and littleness into rage like a lion.   *Ibid. [April 26, 1779]*

10   I must study politics and war that my sons may have liberty to study mathematics and philosophy. My sons ought to study mathematics and philosophy, geography, natural history, naval architecture, navigation, commerce, and agriculture, in order to give their children a right to study painting, poetry, music, architecture, statuary, tapestry, and porcelain.[5]   *Letter to Abigail Adams [May 12, 1780]*

11   You will never be alone with a poet in your pocket.
Letter to John Quincy Adams [May 14, 1781]

12   My country has in its wisdom contrived for me the most insignificant office [the vice-presidency] that ever the invention of man contrived or his imagination conceived; and as I can do neither good nor evil, I must be borne away by others and meet the common fate.[6]
Letter to Abigail Adams [December 19, 1793]

13   I pray Heaven to bestow the best of blessings on this house and all that shall hereafter inhabit it. May none but honest and wise men ever rule under this roof.[7]   *Ibid. [November 2, 1800]*

14   I had heard my father say that he never knew a piece of land [to] run away or break.
Autobiography [1802–1807]

15   You and I ought not to die before we have explained ourselves to each other.
Letter to Thomas Jefferson [July 15, 1813]

16   The fundamental article of my political creed is that despotism, or unlimited sovereignty, or absolute power, is the same in a majority of a popular assembly, an aristocratical council, an oligarchical junto, and a single emperor.
Ibid. [November 13, 1815]

17   Thomas — Jefferson — still surv —[8]
Last words [July 4, 1826]

Isaac Bickerstaffe
c. 1735 – c. 1812

18   There was a jolly miller once
Lived on the River Dee;
He worked and sang from morn till night
No lark more blithe than he.
Love in a Village [1762], act I, sc. ii

19   And this the burthen of his song
Forever used to be,
"I care for nobody, not I,
If no one cares for me."[9]

Ibid.

---

[1]See Vico, 290:32, and Jefferson, 343:2.
[2]See Richard Henry Lee, 336:11.
[3]On July 2, 1776, the resolution for independence, drafted by Richard Henry Lee of Virginia, was adopted by a committee including John Adams. On July 4 the Declaration of Independence was agreed to, engrossed, signed by John Hancock, and sent to the legislatures of the States.
[4]See Gibbon, 340:2, and Jefferson, 343:2.
[5]See Caecilius Statius, 85:9.
[6]See Jefferson, 344:2.
[7]Written the day after Adams moved into the new White House. President Franklin D. Roosevelt had it inscribed on the mantelpiece of the State Dining Room.
[8]Jefferson at Monticello died the same day — the fiftieth anniversary of the adoption of the Declaration of Independence.
[9]Naebody cares for me, / I care for naebody. — BURNS, *I Hae a Wife o' My Ain*, st. 4

Michel Guillaume Jean de Crèvecoeur [J. Hector St. John]
1735–1813

1 What then is the American, this new man? He is either an European, or the descendant of an European, hence that strange mixture of blood, which you will find in no other country. . . . Here individuals of all nations are melted into a new race of men, whose labors and posterity will one day cause great changes in the world.[1]
Letters from an American Farmer [1782], III

Charles Joseph, Prince de Ligne
1735–1814

2 The Congress doesn't run—it waltzes.[2]
Comment to Comte Auguste de La Garde–Chambonas [1814]

Paul Revere
1735–1818

3 To the memory of the glorious Ninety-two: members of the Honorable House of Representatives of the Massachusetts Bay who, undaunted by the insolent menaces of villains in power, from a strict regard to conscience and the liberties of their constituents on the 30th of June 1768 voted NOT TO RESCIND.
Inscription on Revere's silver "Liberty" bowl [1768]

4 If the British went out by water, to show two lanterns in the North Church steeple; and if by land, one as a signal, for we were apprehensive it would be difficult to cross the Charles River or get over Boston Neck.[3]
Signal code arranged with Colonel Conant of the Charlestown Committee of Safety [April 16, 1775]. Letter to Dr. Jeremy Belknap

Patrick Henry
1736–1799

5 Caesar had his Brutus; Charles the First his Cromwell; and George the Third ["Treason!" cried the Speaker]—*may profit by their example. If this be treason, make the most of it.*
Speech on the Stamp Act, House of Burgesses, Williamsburg, Virginia [May 29, 1765]

6 I am not a Virginian, but an American.
Speech in the First Continental Congress, Philadelphia [October 14, 1774]

7 It is natural for man to indulge in the illusions of hope. We are apt to shut our eyes against a painful truth, and listen to the song of that siren till she transforms us into beasts. Is this the part of wise men, engaged in a great and arduous struggle for liberty? Are we disposed to be the number of those who, having eyes, see not, and having ears, hear not,[4] the things which so nearly concern their temporal salvation? For my part, whatever anguish of spirit it may cost, I am willing to know the whole truth; to know the worst, and to provide for it.
Speech in Virginia Convention, Richmond [March 23, 1775]

8 I have but one lamp by which my feet are guided, and that is the lamp of experience. I know no way of judging of the future but by the past.[5] *Ibid.*

9 We are not weak if we make a proper use of those means which the God of Nature has placed in our power. . . . The battle, sir, is not to the strong alone;[6] it is to the vigilant, the active, the brave.
Ibid.

10 It is vain, sir, to extenuate the matter. The gentlemen may cry, Peace, peace! but there is no peace.[7] The war has actually begun! The next gale that sweeps from the north will bring to our ears the clash of resounding arms! Our brethren are already in the field! Why stand we here idle? What is it that the gentlemen wish? What would they have? Is life so dear or peace so sweet as to be purchased at the price of chains and slavery? Forbid it, Almighty God. I know not what course others may take, but as for me, give me liberty or give me death![8] *Ibid.*

11 That religion, or the duty which we owe to our Creator, and the manner of discharging it, can be directed only by reason and conviction, not by force or violence; and therefore all men are equally entitled to the free exercise of religion, according to the dictates of conscience; and that it is the mutual duty of all to practice Christian forbearance, love, and charity towards each other.
Virginia Bill of Rights [June 12, 1776],[9] article 16

Edward Gibbon
1737–1794

12 The various modes of worship, which prevailed in the Roman world, were all considered by the people, as equally true; by the philosopher, as

---

[1]See Zangwill, 590:6.
[2]Le Congrès ne marche pas, il danse [said of the Congress of Vienna].
[3]See Longfellow, 442:13.
[4]See *Jeremiah 5:21, 28:15.*
[5]See Burke, 332:22.
[6]See *Ecclesiastes 9:11, 24:20.*
[7]See *Jeremiah 6:14, 28:17.*
[8]See Aeschylus, 63:16.
[9]See George Mason, 327:n1. Mason drafted Articles 1, 3, and 12.

equally false; and by the magistrate, as equally useful.

*The History of the Decline and Fall of the
Roman Empire [1776–1788], ch. 2*

1   The principles of a free constitution are irrevoca-
bly lost, when the legislative power is nominated by
the executive.   *Ibid. 3*

2   Their united reigns [the Antonines'] are possibly
the only period of history in which the happiness of
a great people was the sole object of government.[1]
                                                 Ibid.

3   History . . . is indeed little more than the register of the crimes, follies, and misfortunes of mankind.[2]   *Ibid.*

4   Corruption, the most infallible symptom of constitutional liberty.   *Ibid. 21*

5   Our sympathy is cold to the relation of distant
misery.   *Ibid. 49*

6   The winds and waves are always on the side of
the ablest navigators.[3]   *Ibid. 68*

7   Vicissitudes of fortune, which spares neither man
nor the proudest of his works, which buries empires
and cities in a common grave.   *Ibid. 71*

8   All that is human must retrograde if it do not
advance.   *Ibid.*

9   The successors of Charles the Fifth may disdain
their brethren of England; but the romance of *Tom
Jones,* that exquisite picture of human manners, will
outlive the palace of the Escurial and the imperial
eagle of the house of Austria.

Memoirs (Autobiography) [1796]

10   Decent easy men, who supinely enjoyed the gifts
of the founder.   *Ibid.*

11   It was here [at the age of seventeen] that I suspended my religious inquiries.   *Ibid.*

12   I saw and loved.[4]   *Ibid.*

13   I sighed as a lover, I obeyed as a son.   *Ibid.*

14   [Of London:] Crowds without company, and dis-
sipation without pleasure.   *Ibid.*

15   The captain of the Hampshire grenadiers[5] . . .
has not been useless to the historian of the Roman
Empire.   *Ibid.*

16   It was at Rome, on the fifteenth of October 1764,
as I sat musing amidst the ruins of the Capitol, while
the barefoot friars were singing vespers in the Tem-

---

[1]Ah, might we read in America's signs / The Age restored of
the Antonines. — MELVILLE, *Timoleon* [1891], *The Age of the
Antonines,* st. 3
    See John Adams, 338:6, and Jefferson, 343:2.
[2]See Voltaire, 306:23.
[3]See Tacitus, 109:19; Bussy-Rabutin, 266:13; Boileau, 280:-
17; and Frederick the Great, 318:20.
[4]See Marlowe, 162:11.
[5]Gibbon was a captain in the Hampshire militia from June
12, 1759, to December 23, 1762.

ple of Jupiter, that the idea of writing the decline and
fall of the city first started to my mind.   *Ibid.*

Thomas Paine
1737–1809

17 From the east to the west blow the trumpet to
    arms!
Through the land let the sound of it flee;
Let the far and the near all unite, with a cheer,
In defense of our Liberty Tree.

The Liberty Tree [July 1775], st. 4

18   Society in every state is a blessing, but Government, even in its best state, is but a necessary evil; in
its worst state, an intolerable one.

Common Sense [1776]

19   Suspicion is the companion of mean souls, and
the bane of all good society.   *Ibid.*

20   When we are planning for posterity, we ought to
remember that virtue is not hereditary.   *Ibid.*

21   O! ye that love mankind! Ye that dare oppose not
only the tyranny but the tyrant, stand forth! Every
spot of the Old World is overrun with oppression.
Freedom hath been hunted round the globe. Asia
and Africa have long expelled her. Europe regards
her like a stranger and England hath given her warning to depart. O! receive the fugitive and prepare in
time an asylum for mankind.[6]   *Ibid.*

22   These are the times that try men's souls. The
summer soldier and the sunshine patriot will, in this
crisis, shrink from the service of their country; but he
that stands it *now,* deserves the love and thanks of
man and woman. Tyranny, like hell, is not easily
conquered; yet we have this consolation with us, that
the harder the conflict, the more glorious the triumph. What we obtain too cheap, we esteem too
lightly; it is dearness only that gives everything its
value. Heaven knows how to put a proper price upon
its goods; and it would be strange indeed, if so celestial an article as *Freedom* should not be highly rated.

The American Crisis, no. 1 [December 23, 1776]

23   Panics, in some cases, have their uses; they produce as much good as hurt. Their duration is always
short; the mind soon grows through them and acquires a firmer habit than before. But their peculiar
advantage is, that they are the touchstones of sincerity and hypocrisy, and bring things and men to light,
which might otherwise have lain forever undiscovered.   *Ibid.*

24   Not a place upon earth might be so happy as
America. Her situation is remote from all the wrangling world, and she has nothing to do but to trade
with them.   *Ibid.*

25   A bad cause will ever be supported by bad means
and bad men.   *Ibid. 2 [January 13, 1777]*

---

[6]See Samuel Adams, 325:6.

1 Those who expect to reap the blessings of freedom must, like men, undergo the fatigue of supporting it. *Ibid.* 4 [September 12, 1777]

2 It is not a field of a few acres of ground, but a cause, that we are defending, and whether we defeat the enemy in one battle, or by degrees, the consequences will be the same. *Ibid.*

3 We fight not to enslave, but to set a country free, and to make room upon the earth for honest men to live in. *Ibid.*

4 It is the object only of war that makes it honorable. And if there was ever a *just* war since the world began, it is this in which America is now engaged. *Ibid.* 5 [March 21, 1778]

5 War involves in its progress such a train of unforeseen and unsupposed circumstances . . . that no human wisdom can calculate the end. It has but one thing certain, and that is to increase taxes. *Prospects on the Rubicon* [1787]

6 [Burke] is not affected by the reality of distress touching his heart, but by the showy resemblance of it striking his imagination. He pities the plumage, but forgets the dying bird. *The Rights of Man, pt. I* [1791]

7 My country is the world and my religion is to do good. *Ibid.* II [1792], *ch.* 5

8 A thing moderately good is not so good as it ought to be. Moderation in temper is always a virtue; but moderation in principle is always a vice.[1] *Ibid.*

9 I believe in one God and no more, and I hope for happiness beyond this life. I believe in the equality of man; and I believe that religious duties consist in doing justice, loving mercy, and endeavoring to make our fellow creatures happy. *The Age of Reason* [1793], *pt. I*

10 It is with a pious fraud as with a bad action; it begets a calamitous necessity of going on. *Ibid.*

11 When authors and critics talk of the sublime, they see not how nearly it borders on the ridiculous.[2] *Ibid.* II, *note*

Rudolf Erich Raspe
1737–1794

12 His tunes were frozen up in the horn, and came out now by thawing.[3] *Travels of Baron Munchausen* [1785], *ch.* 6

13 If any of the company entertain a doubt of my veracity, I shall only say to such, I pity their want of faith. *Ibid.*

14 A traveler has a right to relate and embellish his adventures as he pleases, and it is very impolite to refuse that deference and applause they deserve. *Ibid.* 21

Ethan Allen
1738–1789

15 [Captain Delaplace[4]] gazed at Allen in bewildered astonishment. "By whose authority do you act?" exclaimed he. "In the name of the great Jehovah, and the Continental Congress!" replied Allen. *From* WASHINGTON IRVING, *Life of Washington* [1855–1859], *vol. I, ch.* 38

Jacques Delille
1738–1813

16 Fate chooses our relatives, we choose our friends.[5] *Malheur et Pitié* [1803], *canto I*

John Wolcot [Peter Pindar]
1738–1819

17 What rage for fame attends both great and small! Better be damned than mentioned not at all! *To the Royal Academicians* [1782–1785]

Daniel Bliss
1740–1806

18 God wills us free, man wills us slaves,
I will as God wills, God's will be done. *Epitaph on gravestone of John Jack, "A Native of Africa, who died March 1773, aged about 60 years. Tho' born in a land of slavery he was born free."*

James Boswell[6]
1740–1795

19 That favorite subject, Myself. *Letter to Temple* [July 26, 1763]

20 He who praises everybody, praises nobody. *Life of Johnson* [1791], *footnote* [March 30, 1778]

21 We cannot tell the precise moment when friendship is formed. As in filling a vessel drop by drop, there is at last a drop which makes it run over; so in

[1]Extremism in the defense of liberty is no vice. And . . . moderation in the pursuit of justice is no virtue.—BARRY GOLDWATER [1909–], *Acceptance speech, Republican presidential nomination* [July 16, 1964]

[2]See Napoleon, 370:9.

[3]See Plutarch, 107:13.

[4]Commandant at Fort Ticonderoga, New York [May 10, 1775].

[5]Le sort fait les parents, le choix fait les amis.

[6]See also excerpts from BOSWELL, *Life of Johnson* [1791], 315:12–318:2.

a series of kindnesses there is at last one which
makes the heart run over.
Life of Johnson [September 1777]

1   I think no innocent species of wit or pleasantry
should be suppressed; and that a good pun may be
admitted among the smaller excellencies of lively
conversation.   *Ibid. [June 1784]*

Louis Sébastien Mercier
1740–1814

2   Extremes Meet.[1]
Tableaux de Paris [1782], vol. IV, ch. 348, title

Augustus Montague Toplady
1740–1778

3 Rock of Ages, cleft for me,
Let me hide myself in thee.
Rock of Ages [1775],[2] st. 1

Sébastien Roch Nicolas Chamfort
1741–1794

4   The most wasted day of all is that on which we
have not laughed.   *Maxims and Thoughts, 1*

5   Chance is a nickname for Providence.
Ibid. 62

6   Be my brother, or I will kill you.[3]
From CARLYLE, *French Revolution [1837],
vol. II, pt. 1, ch. 12*

Johann Kaspar Lavater
1741–1801

7   Say not you know another entirely, till you have
divided an inheritance with him.
Aphorisms on Man [c. 1788], no. 157

8   Trust not him with your secrets, who, when left
alone in your room, turns over your papers.
Ibid. 449

9   The public seldom forgive twice.   *Ibid. 606*

Hester Lynch Thrale Piozzi
[Mrs. Thrale]
1741–1821

10   Johnson's conversation was by much too strong
for a person accustomed to obsequiousness and flattery; it was *mustard in a young child's mouth!*
From JAMES BOSWELL, *Life of Johnson [1791].*
May 1781

[1] "Extremes meet," as the whiting said with its tail in its
mouth.—HOOD, *The Doves and the Crows*
[2] Music by THOMAS HASTINGS [1784–1872].
[3] Sois mon frère ou je te tue.
A paraphrase of the revolutionary watchword: Fraternity or
death.

Gebhard Leberecht von Blücher
1742–1819

11   Ever forward, but slowly.
*While leading the Russians at Leipzig [October
19, 1813]*

12   May the pens of the diplomats not ruin again
what the people have attained with such exertions.
After the battle of Waterloo [1813]

Georg Christoph Lichtenberg
1742–1799

13   A knife without a blade, for which the handle is
missing.
*Göttingen Pocket Calendar [1798], describing an
impossible existence*

14   Nothing contributes more to peace of soul than
having no opinion at all.   *Aphorisms*

15   To do just the opposite is also a form of imitation.   *Ibid.*

16   A donkey appears to me like a horse translated
into Dutch.   *Ibid.*

17   I am always grieved when a man of real talent
dies. The world needs such men more than Heaven
does.   *Ibid.*

18   Soothsayers make a better living in the world
than truthsayers.   *Ibid.*

19   It may not be natural for man to walk on two
legs, but it was a noble invention.   *Ibid.*

20   The thing that astonished him was that cats
should have two holes cut in their coat exactly at the
place where their eyes are.   *Ibid.*

Anna Letitia Barbauld
1743–1825

21 Say not "Good night"; but in some brighter clime
Bid me "Good morning."

Ode to Life, st. 3

William Henry, Duke of Gloucester
1743–1805

22   Another damned, thick, square book! Always
scribble, scribble, scribble! Eh! Mr. Gibbon?
Upon receiving from EDWARD GIBBON *volume II
of the Decline and Fall of the Roman Empire
[1781]. From Best's Literary Memorials*

Thomas Jefferson
1743–1826

23   A lively and lasting sense of filial duty is more
effectually impressed on the mind of a son or daugh-

ter by reading *King Lear,* than by all the dry volumes of ethics, and divinity, that ever were written.

Letter to Robert Skipwith [August 3, 1771]

1   The God who gave us life, gave us liberty at the same time.

Summary View of the Rights of British America [1774]

2   When, in the course of human events, it becomes necessary for one people to dissolve the political bands which have connected them with another, and to assume among the powers of the earth the separate and equal station to which the laws of nature and of nature's God[1] entitle them, a decent respect to the opinions of mankind requires that they should declare the causes which impel them to the separation. We hold these truths to be self-evident; that all men are created equal; that they are endowed by their creator with certain unalienable[2] rights; that among these are life, liberty, and the pursuit of happiness;[3] that to secure these rights, governments are instituted among men, deriving their just powers from the consent of the governed;[4] that whenever any form of government becomes destructive of these ends, it is the right of the people to alter or to abolish it, and to institute new government, laying its foundation on such principles, and organizing its powers in such form, as to them shall seem most likely to effect their safety and happiness.

Declaration of Independence [July 4, 1776]

3   We must therefore . . . hold them [the British] as we hold the rest of mankind, enemies in war, in peace friends.   *Ibid.*

4   And for the support of this declaration, with a firm reliance on the protection of divine providence, we mutually pledge to each other our lives, our fortunes, and our sacred honor.   *Ibid.*

5   Ignorance is preferable to error; and he is less remote from the truth who believes nothing, than he who believes what is wrong.

Notes on the State of Virginia [1781–1785]. Query 6

6   The Newtonian principle of gravitation is now more firmly established, on the basis of reason, than it would be were the government to step in, and to make it an article of necessary faith. Reason and experiment have been indulged, and error has fled before them.   *Ibid. 17*

7   Subject opinion to coercion: whom will you make your inquisitors? Fallible men; men governed by bad passions, by private as well as public reasons.

Ibid. 17

8   Is uniformity [of opinion] attainable? Millions of innocent men, women, and children, since the introduction of Christianity, have been burnt, tortured, fined, imprisoned; yet we have not advanced one inch towards uniformity. What has been the effect of coercion? To make one half the world fools, and the other half hypocrites.   *Ibid.*

9   Indeed, I tremble for my country when I reflect that God is just.   *Ibid. 18*

10   Those who labor in the earth are the chosen people of God, if ever he had a chosen people, whose breasts He has made His peculiar deposit for substantial and genuine virtue.   *Ibid. 19*

11   He who permits himself to tell a lie once, finds it much easier to do it a second and third time, till at length it becomes habitual; he tells lies without attending to it, and truths without the world's believing him. This falsehood of the tongue leads to that of the heart, and in time depraves all its good dispositions.   *Letter to Peter Carr [August 19, 1785]*

12   The basis of our government being the opinion of the people, the very first object should be to keep that right; and were it left to me to decide whether we should have a government without newspapers, or newspapers without a government, I should not hesitate a moment to prefer the latter.

Letter to Colonel Edward Carrington [January 16, 1787]

13   Experience declares that man is the only animal which devours his own kind; for I can apply no milder term to the governments of Europe, and to the general prey of the rich on the poor.   *Ibid.*

14   I hold it, that a little rebellion, now and then, is a good thing, and as necessary in the political world as storms in the physical.

Letter to James Madison [January 30, 1787]

15   What country before ever existed a century and a half without a rebellion? . . . The tree of liberty must be refreshed from time to time with the blood of patriots and tyrants.[5] It is its natural manure.

Letter to William Stevens Smith [November 13, 1787]

16   The republican is the only form of government which is not eternally at open or secret war with the rights of mankind.

Letter to William Hunter [March 11, 1790]

17   We are not to expect to be translated from despotism to liberty in a featherbed.

Letter to Lafayette [April 2, 1790]

18   Let what will be said or done, preserve your *sang-froid* immovably, and to every obstacle, oppose patience, perseverance, and soothing language.

Letter to William Short [March 18, 1792]

19   Delay is preferable to error.

Letter to George Washington [May 16, 1792]

---

[1]See Bolingbroke, 295:9, and Pope, 302:1.

[2]Frequently quoted as "inalienable."
All men are born free and equal, and have certain natural, essential and unalienable rights. — *Constitution of Massachusetts* [1780]

[3]See John Adams, 338:6, and Gibbon, 340:2.

[4]See Vico, 290:32, and John Adams, 338:1.

[5]See Barère, 354:11.

1   We confide in our strength, without boasting of it; we respect that of others, without fearing it.
Letter to William Carmichael and William Short [June 30, 1793]

2   The second office of the government is honorable and easy, the first is but a splendid misery.[1]
Letter to Elbridge Gerry [May 13, 1797]

3   Offices are as acceptable here as elsewhere, and whenever a man has cast a longing eye on them, a rottenness begins in his conduct.
Letter to Tench Coxe [May 21, 1799]

4   I have sworn upon the altar of God, eternal hostility against every form of tyranny over the mind of man.
Letter to Dr. Benjamin Rush [September 23, 1800]

5   We are all Republicans — we are all Federalists. If there be any among us who would wish to dissolve this Union or to change its republican form, let them stand undisturbed as monuments of the safety with which error of opinion may be tolerated where reason is left free to combat it.[2]
First Inaugural Address [March 4, 1801]

6   But would the honest patriot, in the full tide of successful experiment, abandon a government which has so far kept us free and firm, on the theoretic and visionary fear that this government, the world's best hope, may by possibility want energy to preserve itself?   *Ibid.*

7   Sometimes it is said that man cannot be trusted with the government of himself. Can he, then, be trusted with the government of others? Or have we found angels in the forms of kings to govern him? Let history answer this question.   *Ibid.*

8   Still one thing more, fellow citizens — a wise and frugal government, which shall restrain men from injuring one another, which shall leave them otherwise free to regulate their own pursuits of industry and improvement, and shall not take from the mouth of labor the bread it has earned. This is the sum of good government, and this is necessary to close the circle of our felicities.   *Ibid.*

9   Equal and exact justice to all men, of whatever state or persuasion, religious or political; peace, commerce, and honest friendship with all nations, entangling alliances with none. . . . Freedom of religion; freedom of the press, and freedom of person under the protection of the *habeas corpus,* and trial by juries impartially selected. These principles form the bright constellation which has gone before us, and guided our steps through an age of revolution and reformation. The wisdom of our sages and the blood of our heroes have been devoted to their attainment. They should be the creed of our political faith, the text of civil instruction, the touchstone by which

to try the services of those we trust; and should we wander from them in moments of error or alarm, let us hasten to retrace our steps and to regain the road which alone leads to peace, liberty, and safety.
Ibid.

10   Whensoever hostile aggressions . . . require a resort to war, we must meet our duty and convince the world that we are just friends and brave enemies.
Letter to Andrew Jackson [December 3, 1806]

11   The care of human life and happiness, and not their destruction, is the first and only legitimate object of good government.[3]
To the Republican Citizens of Washington County, Maryland [March 31, 1809]

12   Politics, like religion, hold up the torches of martyrdom to the reformers of error.
Letter to James Ogilvie [August 4, 1811]

13   But though an old man, I am but a young gardener.
Letter to Charles Willson Peale [August 20, 1811]

14   The earth belongs to the living, not to the dead.
Letter to John W. Eppes [June 24, 1813]

15   I agree with you that there is a natural aristocracy among men. The grounds of this are virtue and talents.   *Letter to John Adams [October 28, 1813]*

16   Merchants have no country. The mere spot they stand on does not constitute so strong an attachment as that from which they draw their gains.
Letter to Horatio G. Spafford [March 17, 1814]

17   I cannot live without books.
Letter to John Adams [June 10, 1815]

18   If a nation expects to be ignorant and free, in a state of civilization, it expects what never was and never will be.
Letter to Colonel Charles Yancey [January 6, 1816]

19   Enlighten the people generally, and tyranny and oppressions of body and mind will vanish like evil spirits at the dawn of day.
Letter to Du Pont de Nemours [April 24, 1816]

20   I have the consolation to reflect that during the period of my administration not a drop of the blood of a single fellow citizen was shed by the sword of war or of the law.
Letter to papal nuncio Count Dugnani [February 14, 1818]

21   But this momentous question [the Missouri Compromise], like a firebell in the night awakened and filled me with terror. I considered it the knell of the Union.   *Letter to John Holmes [April 22, 1820]*

22   I know no safe depository of the ultimate powers of the society but the people themselves; and if we think them not enlightened enough to exercise their

[1]See John Adams, 338:12.
[2]See Milton, 255:4, and Oliver Wendell Holmes, Jr., 542:25.

[3]See George Mason, 327:2.

control with a wholesome discretion, the remedy is not to take it from them, but to inform their discretion.
> *Letter to William Charles Jarvis [September 28, 1820]*

1   We are not afraid to follow truth wherever it may lead, nor to tolerate any error so long as reason is left free to combat it.
> *Letter to William Roscoe [December 27, 1820]*

2   That one hundred and fifty lawyers should do business together ought not to be expected.
> *Autobiography [January 6, 1821], on the United States Congress*

3   And even should the cloud of barbarism and despotism again obscure the science and liberties of Europe, this country remains to preserve and restore light and liberty to them. In short, the flames kindled on the fourth of July, 1776, have spread over too much of the globe to be extinguished by the feeble engines of despotism; on the contrary, they will consume these engines and all who work them.
> *Letter to John Adams [September 12, 1821]*

4   Men by their constitutions are naturally divided into two parties: (1) Those who fear and distrust the people, and wish to draw all powers from them into the hands of the higher classes. (2) Those who identify themselves with the people, have confidence in them, cherish and consider them as the most honest and safe, although not the most wise depository of the public interests. In every country these two parties exist; and in every one where they are free to think, speak, and write, they will declare themselves.
> *Letter to Henry Lee [August 10, 1824]*

5   Never buy what you do not want, because it is cheap; it will be dear to you.
> *A Decalogue of Canons for Observation in Practical Life [February 21, 1825]*

6   When angry, count ten before you speak; if very angry, an hundred.   *Ibid.*

7   The good old Dominion, the blessed mother of us all.   *Thoughts on Lotteries [1826]*

8   This is the Fourth?
> *Last words [July 4, 1826][1]*

Antoine Laurent Lavoisier
1743–1794

9   It is impossible to dissociate language from science or science from language, because every natural science always involves three things: the sequence of phenomena on which the science is based; the abstract concepts which call these phenomena to mind; and the words in which the concepts are expressed. To call forth a concept a word is needed; to portray a phenomenon, a concept is needed. All three mirror one and the same reality.[2]
> *Traité Elémentaire de Chimie [1789]*

10   If, by the term *elements*, we mean to express the simple and indivisible molecules that compose bodies, it is probable that we know nothing about them; but if, on the contrary, we express by the term *elements* or *principles of bodies* the idea of the last point reached by analysis, all substances that we have not yet been able to decompose by any means are elements to us.[3]   *Ibid.*

William Paley
1743–1805

11   Who can refute a sneer?
> *Moral Philosophy [1785], vol. II, bk. V, ch. 9*

The Letters of Junius[4]
1769–1771

12   One precedent creates another. They soon accumulate and constitute law. What yesterday was fact, today is doctrine.
> *Dedication to the English Nation*

13   The liberty of the press is the palladium of all the civil, political, and religious rights of an Englishman.
> *Ibid.*

14   I believe there is yet a spirit of resistance in this country, which will not submit to be oppressed; but I am sure there is a fund of good sense in this country, which cannot be deceived.
> *No. 16, to the Printer of the Public Advertiser (H. S. Woodfall) [July 19, 1769]*

15   We owe it to our ancestors to preserve entire those rights, which they have delivered to our care: we owe it to our posterity, not to suffer their dearest inheritance to be destroyed.
> *No. 20, to the Printer of the Public Advertiser [August 8, 1769]*

16   When the constitution is openly invaded, when the first original right of the people, from which all laws derive their authority, is directly attacked, inferior grievances naturally lose their force, and are suffered to pass by without punishment or observation.
> *No. 30, to the Printer of the Public Advertiser [October 17, 1769]*

---

[2]Translated by J. Lipetz, D. E. Gershenson, and D. A. Greenberg.
[3]Translated by D. McKie.
[4]Pseudonym of the author of a series of letters [1769–1771] in the London *Public Advertiser* (published in book form, 1772). They have been attributed to, among others, Sir Philip Francis, Lord Shelburne, Lord George Sackville, and Lord Temple.

[1]John Adams died the same day. See his last words, 338:17.

1   There is a moment of difficulty and danger at which flattery and falsehood can no longer deceive, and simplicity itself can no longer be misled.

> *No. 35,*[1] *to the Printer of the Public Advertiser [December 19, 1769]*

2   They [the Americans] equally detest the pageantry of a king, and the supercilious hypocrisy of a bishop.   *Ibid.*

3   The least considerable man among us has an interest equal to the proudest nobleman, in the laws and constitution of his country, and is equally called upon to make a generous contribution in support of them—whether it be the heart to conceive, the understanding to direct, or the hand to execute.

> *No. 37, to the Printer of the Public Advertiser [March 19, 1770]*

4   We lament the mistakes of a good man, and do not begin to detest him until he affects to renounce his principles.

> *No. 41, to Lord Mansfield [November 14, 1770]*

5   The injustice done to an individual is sometimes of service to the public. Facts are apt to alarm us more than the most dangerous principles.   *Ibid.*

6   If individuals have no virtues, their vices may be of use to us.

> *No. 59, to the Printer of the Public Advertiser [October 5, 1771]*

Constitution of the United States
1787

7   We the people of the United States, in order to form a more perfect Union, establish justice, insure domestic tranquillity, provide for the common defense, promote the general welfare, and secure the blessings of liberty to ourselves and our posterity do ordain and establish this Constitution for the United States of America.   *Preamble*

8   The President, Vice-President, and all civil officers of the United States, shall be removed from office on impeachment for, and conviction of, treason, bribery, or other high crimes and misdemeanors.   *Article II, sec. 4*

9   Treason against the United States, shall consist only in levying war against them, or in adhering to their enemies, giving them aid and comfort. No person shall be convicted of treason unless on the testimony of two witnesses to the same overt act, or on confession in open court.   *Article III, sec. 3*

10   This Constitution, and the laws of the United States, which shall be made in pursuance thereof;

and all treaties made, or which shall be made, under the authority of the United States, shall be the Supreme Law of the land; and the judges in every State shall be bound thereby, any thing in the Constitution or laws of any State to the contrary notwithstanding.

> *Article VI, sec. 2*

11   Congress shall make no law respecting an establishment of religion, or prohibiting the free exercise thereof; or abridging the freedom of speech, or of the press; or the right of the people peaceably to assemble, and to petition the government for a redress of grievances.   *First Amendment [1791]*[2]

12   A well-regulated militia, being necessary to the security of a free State, the right of the people to keep and bear arms, shall not be infringed.

> *Second Amendment [1791]*

13   The right of the people to be secure . . . against unreasonable searches and seizures, shall not be violated, and no warrants shall issue, but upon probable cause.   *Fourth Amendment [1791]*

14   Nor shall any person be subject for the same offense to be twice put in jeopardy of life or limb; nor shall be compelled in any criminal case to be a witness against himself, nor be deprived of life, liberty, or property, without due process of law.

> *Fifth Amendment [1791]*

15   In all criminal prosecutions, the accused shall enjoy the right to a speedy and public trial, by an impartial jury of the State and district wherein the crime shall have been committed.

> *Sixth Amendment [1791]*

16   The right of trial by jury shall be preserved.

> *Seventh Amendment [1791]*

17   Excessive bail shall not be required, nor excessive fines imposed, nor cruel and unusual punishment inflicted.   *Eighth Amendment [1791]*

18   All persons born or naturalized in the United States, and subject to the jurisdiction thereof, are citizens of the United States and of the State wherein they reside. No State shall . . . abridge the privileges or immunities of citizens of the United States; nor shall any State deprive any person of life, liberty, or property, without due process of law; nor deny to any person within its jurisdiction the equal protection of the laws.

> *Fourteenth Amendment [1868], sec. 1*

19   The right of citizens of the United States to vote shall not be denied or abridged . . . on account of race, color, or previous condition of servitude.

> *Fifteenth Amendment [1870], sec. 1*

20   The right of citizens of the United States to vote shall not be denied or abridged . . . on account of sex.   *Nineteenth Amendment [1920], sec. 1*

---

[1]This letter is of great significance in the history of freedom of the press. The publisher was prosecuted for seditious libel, and the jury brought in a verdict of "guilty of printing and publishing only." After a second trial, Woodfall was freed on payment of costs.

[2]The first ten amendments are known as the Bill of Rights.

Abigail Adams[1]
1744–1818

1   In the new code of laws which I suppose it will be necessary for you to make I desire you would remember the ladies, and be more generous and favorable to them than your ancestors. Do not put such unlimited power into the hands of the husbands. Remember all men would be tyrants if they could.[2] If particular care and attention is not paid to the ladies we are determined to foment a rebellion, and will not hold ourselves bound by any laws in which we have no voice, or representation.
   Letter to John Adams [March 31, 1776]

2   Whilst you are proclaiming peace and good will to men, emancipating all nations, you insist upon retaining an absolute power over wives. But you must remember that arbitrary power is like most other things which are very hard, very liable to be broken—and notwithstanding all your wise laws and maxims we have it in our power not only to free ourselves but to subdue our masters, and without violence throw both your natural and legal authority at our feet.   *Ibid. [May 7, 1776]*

3   Deliver me from your cold phlegmatic preachers, politicians, friends, lovers and husbands.
   Ibid. [August 5, 1776]

4   If we mean to have heroes, statesmen and philosophers, we should have learned women. . . . If much depends as is allowed upon the early education of youth and the first principles which are instilled take the deepest root, great benefit must arise from literary accomplishments in women.
   Ibid. [August 14, 1776]

5   It is really mortifying, sir, when a woman possessed of a common share of understanding considers the difference of education between the male and female sex, even in those families where education is attended to. . . . Nay why should your sex wish for such a disparity in those whom they one day intend for companions and associates. Pardon me, sir, if I cannot help sometimes suspecting that this neglect arises in some measure from an ungenerous jealousy of rivals near the throne.[3]
   Letter to John Thaxter [February 15, 1778]

6   I regret the trifling narrow contracted education of the females of my own country.
   Letter to John Adams [June 30, 1778]

7   If we do not lay out ourselves in the service of mankind whom should we serve?
   Letter to John Thaxter [September 29, 1778]

[1]Had she lived to the age of the Patriarchs . . . every day of her life would have been filled with clouds of goodness and love.— JOHN QUINCY ADAMS, *Memoirs, vol. IV, 157–158, 202*
[2]See Defoe, 286:1.
[3]See Sand, 436:18.

8   These are times in which a genius would wish to live. It is not in the still calm of life, or in the repose of a pacific station, that great characters are formed. . . . Great necessities call out great virtues.
   Letter to John Quincy Adams [January 19, 1780]

9   A little of what you call frippery is very necessary towards looking like the rest of the world.
   Letter to John Adams [May 1, 1780]

10   Learning is not attained by chance, it must be sought for with ardor and attended to with diligence.
   Letter to John Quincy Adams [May 8, 1780]

11   Patriotism in the female sex is the most disinterested of all virtues. Excluded from honors and from offices, we cannot attach ourselves to the State or Government from having held a place of eminence. Even in the freest countries our property is subject to the control and disposal of our partners, to whom the laws have given a sovereign authority. Deprived of a voice in legislation, obliged to submit to those laws which are imposed upon us, is it not sufficient to make us indifferent to the public welfare? Yet all history and every age exhibit instances of patriotic virtue in the female sex; which considering our situation equals the most heroic of yours.
   Letter to John Adams [June 17, 1782]

Rowland Hill
1744–1833

12   He did not see any reason why the devil should have all the good tunes.
   Sermons. From E. W. BROOME, The Reverend Rowland Hill, p. 93

Jean Baptiste Lamarck
1744–1829

13   FIRST LAW. In every animal . . . a more frequent and continuous use of any organ gradually strengthens, develops and enlarges that organ . . . while the permanent disuse of any organ imperceptibly weakens and deteriorates it, and progressively diminishes its functional capacity, until it finally disappears.
   SECOND LAW. All the acquisitions or losses wrought by nature in individuals . . . are preserved by reproduction to the new individuals which arise.
   Philosophie Zoologique [1809],[4] pt. II, ch. 7

14   Habits form a second nature.[5]   *Ibid.*

[4]Translated by HUGH ELLIOT.
[5]Habit is a second nature and it destroys the first.—PASCAL, *Pensées [1670], no. 376*

Josiah Quincy
1744–1775

1   Blandishments will not fascinate us, nor will threats of a "halter" intimidate. For, under God, we are determined that wheresoever, whensoever, or howsoever we shall be called to make our exit, we will die free men.
Observations on the Boston Port Bill [1774]

Charles Dibdin
1745–1814

2 Did you ever hear of Captain Wattle?
He was all for love, and a little for the bottle.
Captain Wattle and Miss Roe

3 Here, a sheer hulk, lies poor Tom Bowling,
The darling of our crew;
No more he'll hear the tempest howling,
For death has broach'd him to.
Tom Bowling

Hannah More
1745–1833

4 Since trifles make the sum of human things,
And half our misery from our foibles springs.
Sensibility

5 Small habits well pursued betimes
May reach the dignity of crimes.
Florio and His Friend

William Scott, Lord Stowell
1745–1836

6   A dinner lubricates business.
From BOSWELL, Life of Johnson [1791]

7   The elegant simplicity of the three per cents.
From CAMPBELL, Lives of the Lord Chancellors [1857], vol. X, ch. 212

Francisco José de Goya y Lucientes
1746–1828

8   The sleep of reason produces monsters [El sueño de la razón produce monstruos].
Los Caprichos [1799]. Plate 43[1]

[1]Translated by HILDA HARRIS.
In plate 43 the artist rests, his head in his arms, on a desk inscribed with the Spanish line. Behind him hover monstrous owls, bats, and a great cat. Goya's text for the plate:
Imagination abandoned by Reason produces impossible monsters: united with her, she is the mother of the arts and the source of their wonders.

John Paul Jones
1747–1792

9   I wish to have no connection with any ship that does not sail *fast;* for I intend to go *in harm's way.*
Letter [November 16, 1778]

10   I have not yet begun to fight.
Attributed. Aboard the Bonhomme Richard [September 23, 1779]

François Alexandre Frédéric, Duc de La Rochefoucauld–Liancourt
1747–1827

11   *Louis XVI:* Is it a revolt?
La Rochefoucauld–Liancourt: No, Sire, it is a revolution.
Upon learning at Versailles of the fall of the Bastille [1789]

John O'Keeffe
1747–1833

12 Amo, amas,
I love a lass,
As a cedar tall and slender;
Sweet cowslip's grace
Is her nominative case,
And she's of the feminine gender!
The Agreeable Surprise [1783], act II, sc. ii, Song

13   You should always except the present company.
The London Hermit; or, Rambles in Dorsetshire [1793]

14   Fat, fair and forty[2] were all the toasts of the young men.
The Irish Mimic; or, Blunders at Brighton [1795]

Emmanuel Joseph Sieyès
1748–1836

15   I survived [J'ai vécu].
Upon being asked what he had done during the French Revolutionary Reign of Terror

Charles James Fox
1749–1806

16   [On the fall of the Bastille:] How much the greatest event it is that ever happened in the world! and how much the best!
Letter to Richard Fitzpatrick [July 30, 1789]. From LORD JOHN RUSSELL, Life and Times of C. J. Fox [1859–1866], vol. II, p. 361

[2]I am resolved to grow fat, and look young till forty!— DRYDEN, *Secret Love; or, The Maiden Queen [1667], act III, sc. i*

Johann Wolfgang von Goethe
1749–1832

1 There is strong shadow where there is much light.
Götz von Berlichingen [1773], act I

2 One lives but once in the world.
Clavigo [1774], act I, sc. i.

3 If you inquire what the people are like here,
I must answer, "The same as everywhere!"
The Sorrows of Young Werther [1] *[1774–1787].*
May 17

4 Getting along with women,
Knocking around with men,
Having more credit than money,
Thus one goes through the world.
Claudine von Villa Bella [1776]

5 Noble be man,
Helpful and good!
For that alone
Sets him apart
From every other creature
On earth.
The Divine [1783]

6 I sing as the bird sings
That lives in the boughs.[2]
Wilhelm Meister's Apprenticeship [1786–1830],
bk. II, ch. 11

7 Who ne'er his bread in sorrow ate,
Who ne'er the mournful midnight hours
Weeping upon his bed has sate,
He knows you not, ye Heavenly Powers.[3]
Ibid. 13

8 Knowst thou the land where the lemon trees
bloom,[4]
Where the gold orange glows in the deep thicket's
gloom,
Where a wind ever soft from the blue heaven
blows,
And the groves are of laurel and myrtle and rose?
Ibid. III, 1

9 If I love you, what business is it of yours?
Ibid. IV, 9

10 One ought, every day at least, to hear a little
song, read a good poem, see a fine picture, and, if it
were possible, to speak a few reasonable words.
Ibid. V, 1

11 To know of someone here and there whom we
accord with, who is living on with us, even in silence
—this makes our earthly ball a peopled garden.
Ibid. VII, 5

12 Art is long, life short; judgment difficult, opportunity transient.
Ibid. 9

13 Seeking with the soul the land of the Greeks.
Iphigenia in Tauris [1787], act I, sc. i

14 A useless life is an early death.
Ibid. ii

15 One says a lot in vain, refusing;
The other mainly hears the "No."
Ibid. iii

16 Pleasure and love are the pinions of great deeds.
Ibid. II, i

17 Life teaches us to be less harsh with ourselves and
with others.   *Ibid. IV, iv*

18 In art the best is good enough.[5]
Italian Journey. March 3, 1787

19 A noble person attracts noble people, and knows
how to hold on to them.
Torquato Tasso [1790], act I, sc. i

20 A talent is formed in stillness, a character in the
world's torrent.   *Ibid. ii*

21 We can't form our children on our own concepts;
we must take them and love them as God gives them
to us.   *Hermann and Dorothea [1797]*

22 The spirits that I summoned up
I now can't rid myself of.
The Sorcerer's Apprentice [1797]

23 Three things are to be looked to in a building:
that it stand on the right spot; that it be securely
founded; that it be successfully executed.
Elective Affinities [6] *[1808], bk. I, ch. 9*

24 The sum which two married people owe to one
another defies calculation. It is an infinite debt,
which can only be discharged through all eternity.
Ibid.

25 One is never satisfied with a portrait of a person
that one knows.   *Ibid. II, 2*

26 Time does not relinquish its rights, either over
human beings or over monuments.   *Ibid.*

27 The fate of the architect is the strangest of all.
How often he expends his whole soul, his whole
heart and passion, to produce buildings into which
he himself may never enter.   *Ibid. 3*

28 Let us live in as small a circle as we will, we are
either debtors or creditors before we have had time
to look round.   *Ibid. 4*

29 No one would talk much in society, if he knew
how often he misunderstands others.   *Ibid.*

---

[1] See Thackeray, 463:21.
[2] Ich singe, wie der Vogel singt / Der in den Zweigen wohnet.
See Tennyson, 457:9.
[3] Wer nie sein Brod mit Tränen ass, / Wer nie die kummervol-
len Nächte / Auf seinem Bette weinend sass, / Der kennt euch
nicht, ihr himmlischen Mächte.
Translated by LONGFELLOW as motto for book I of *Hyperion*
[1839].
[4] Kennst du das Land, wo die Zitronen blühn?

[5] In der Kunst ist das Beste gut genug.
[6] Translated by JAMES ANTHONY FROUDE.

1   A teacher who can arouse a feeling for one single good action, for one single good poem, accomplishes more than he who fills our memory with rows on rows of natural objects, classified with name and form.   *Elective Affinities, bk. II, ch. 7*

2   One never goes so far as when one doesn't know where one is going.
  Letter to Karl Friedrich Zelter [December 3, 1812]

3 Who wants to understand the poem
Must go to the land of poetry;
Who wishes to understand the poet
Must go to the poet's land.
  Divan of East and West [1819], motto

4   For I have been a man, and that means to have been a fighter.   *Ibid. Book of Paradise*

5   One must *be* something to be able to *do* something.
  Conversation with Johann Peter Eckermann [October 20, 1828]

6   If I work incessantly to the last, nature owes me another form of existence when the present one collapses.   *Letter to Eckermann [February 4, 1829]*

7   I call architecture frozen music.[1]
  Ibid. [March 23, 1829]

8   The artist may be well advised to keep his work to himself till it is completed, because no one can readily help him or advise him with it . . . but the scientist is wiser not to withhold a single finding or a single conjecture from publicity.
  Essay on Experimentation

9 Age does not make us childish, as they say.
It only finds us true children still.
  Faust [1808–1832]. The First Part. Prelude on the Stage

10 Man errs as long as he strives.[2]
  Ibid. Prologue in Heaven

11 And here, poor fool! with all my lore
I stand! no wiser than before.[3]
  Ibid. Night, Faust in His Study

12 Am I a god? I see so clearly!
  Ibid.

13 Two souls alas! dwell in my breast.
  Ibid. Outside the Gate of the Town

14 I am the Spirit that always denies![4]
  Ibid. Faust's Study

15 Dear friend, all theory is gray,
And green the golden tree of life.
  Ibid. Mephistopheles and the Student

16 Just trust yourself, then you will know how to live.
  Ibid.

17 A true German can't stand the French,
Yet willingly he drinks their wines.
  Ibid. Auerbach's Cellar

18 He who maintains he's right—if his the gift of tongues—
Will have the last word certainly.[5]
  Ibid. Faust and Gretchen. A Street

19 My peace is gone,
My heart is heavy.[6]
  Ibid. Gretchen's Room

20 Fair I was also, and that was my ruin.[7]
  Ibid. A Prison

21 Law is mighty, mightier necessity.
  Ibid. The Second Part, act I, A Spacious Hall

22 Once a man's thirty, he's already old,
He is indeed as good as dead.
It's best to kill him right away.
  Ibid. II, The Gothic Chamber

23 What wise or stupid thing can man conceive
That was not thought of in ages long ago?[8]
  Ibid.

24 I love those who yearn for the impossible.
  Ibid. Classical Walpurgis Night

25 The deed is everything, the glory nothing.
  Ibid. IV, A High Mountain Range

26 Of freedom and of life he only is deserving
Who every day must conquer them anew.[9]
  Ibid. V, Court of the Palace

27 Who strives always to the utmost,
For him there is salvation.[10]
  Ibid. Mountain Gorges

28 The Eternal Feminine draws us on.[11]
  Ibid. Heaven, last line

29 Do you wish to roam farther and farther?
See! The Good lies so near.
Only learn to seize good fortune,
For good fortune's always here.
  Remembrance

30 In limitations he first shows himself the master,
And the law can only bring us freedom.
  What We Bring [1802]

---

[1]Ich die Baukunst eine erstarrte Musik nenne.
  Since it [architecture] is music in space, as it were a frozen music. —FRIEDRICH VON SCHELLING [1775–1854], *Philosophie der Kunst, p. 576*
[2]Es irrt der Mensch, so lang er strebt.
[3]Da stehe ich nun, ich armer Thor! / Und bin so klug als wie zuvor.
  Translated by BAYARD TAYLOR.
[4]Ich bin der Geist der stets verneint.

[5]Translated by GEORGE MADISON PRIEST.
[6]Meine Ruh' ist hin, / Mein Herz ist schwer.
[7]Schön war ich auch, und das war mein Verderben.
[8]See Cicero, 87:27, and Descartes, 246:17.
[9]Nur der verdient sich Freiheit wie das Leben der täglich sie erobern muss.
[10]Wer immer strebend sich bemüht, / Den können wir erlösen.
[11]Das Ewig-Weibliche zieht uns hinan.

1 Create, artist! Do not talk!
Saying

2 O'er all the hilltops
Is quiet now,
In all the treetops
Hearest thou
Hardly a breath;
The birds are asleep in the trees:
Wait; soon like these
Thou too shalt rest.[1]
Wanderer's Nightsong

3 Individuality of expression is the beginning and end of all art.
Proverbs in Prose

4 Nothing is more damaging to a new truth than an old error.
Ibid.

5 Doubt grows with knowledge.
Ibid.

6 The greatest happiness for the thinking man is to have fathomed the fathomable, and to quietly revere the unfathomable.
Ibid.

7 First and last, what is demanded of genius is love of truth.
Ibid.

8 A man's manners are a mirror in which he shows his portrait.
Ibid.

9 All intelligent thoughts have already been thought; what is necessary is only to try to think them again.[2]
Ibid.

10 Nothing is more terrible than ignorance in action.[2]
Ibid.

11 Of all peoples the Greeks have dreamt the dream of life best.[3]
Ibid.

12 Everything that emancipates the spirit without giving us control over ourselves is harmful.
Ibid.

13 America, you have it better than our continent, the old one.[4]
Almanac for the Muses [1831]

14 Without haste, but without rest.
Motto

15 More light![5]
Last words

Pierre Simon de Laplace
1749–1827

16 Given for one instant an intelligence which could comprehend all the forces by which nature is animated and the respective positions of the beings which compose it, if moreover this intelligence were vast enough to submit these data to analysis, it would embrace in the same formula both the movements of the largest bodies in the universe and those of the lightest atom; to it nothing would be uncertain, and the future as the past would be present to its eyes.
Oeuvres, vol. VII, Théorie Analytique des Probabilités [1812–1820], introduction

17 The theory of probabilities is at bottom nothing but common sense reduced to calculus.
Ibid.

18 Sire, I have no need of that hypothesis.[6]
From ERIC TEMPLE BELL, Men of Mathematics [1937]

Honoré Gabriel Riqueti, Comte de Mirabeau
1749–1791

19 Go and tell those who have sent you that we are here by the will of the nation and that we shall not leave save at the point of bayonets.
Speech in the States-General [June 23, 1789]

John Philpot Curran
1750–1817

20 The condition upon which God hath given liberty to man is eternal vigilance;[7] which condition if he break, servitude is at once the consequence of his crime and the punishment of his guilt.
Speech upon the Right of Election of the Lord Mayor of Dublin [July 10, 1790]

James Madison
1751–1836

21 By a faction, understand a number of citizens, whether amounting to a majority or minority of the whole, who are united and actuated by some common impulse of passion, or of interest, adverse to the rights of other citizens, or to the permanent and aggregate interests of the community.
The Federalist [1787], no. 10

22 A zeal for different opinions concerning religion, concerning government, and many other points, as well of speculation as of practice; an attachment of different leaders ambitiously contending for preeminence and power; or to persons of other descriptions whose fortunes have been interesting to the

---

[1]Translated by LONGFELLOW.
[2]Translated by NORBERT GUTERMAN.
[3]Translated by BAILEY SAUNDERS.
[4]Amerika, du hast es besser—als unser Kontinent, das alte.
[5]Someday perhaps the inner light will shine forth from us, and then we shall need no other light.—*Elective Affinities, pt. II, ch. 3*

[6]Reply to Napoleon Bonaparte's remark upon receiving a copy of Laplace's *Mécanique Céleste:* You have written this huge book on the system of the world without once mentioning the author of the universe.
[7]Attributed also to JEFFERSON.
Commonly quoted: Eternal vigilance is the price of liberty.
There is one safeguard known generally to the wise, which is an advantage and security to all, but especially to democracies as against despots. What is it? Distrust.—DEMOSTHENES, *Philippic 2, sec. 24*

human passions, have, in turn, divided mankind into parties, inflamed them with mutual animosity, and rendered them much more disposed to vex and oppress each other than to cooperate for their common good. . . . But the most common and durable source of factions has been the various and unequal distribution of property.   *The Federalist, no. 10*

1   To secure the public good, and private rights, against the danger of . . . faction, and at the same time to preserve the spirit and form of popular government, is then the great object to which our inquiries are directed.   *Ibid.*

2   I believe there are more instances of the abridgment of the freedom of the people by gradual and silent encroachments of those in power than by violent and sudden usurpations.
Speech in the Virginia Convention [June 16, 1788]

Richard Brinsley Sheridan
1751–1816

3   *Mrs. Malaprop:* Illiterate him, I say, quite from your memory.   *The Rivals [1775], act I, sc. ii*

4   'Tis safest in matrimony to begin with a little aversion.   *Ibid.*

5   A progeny of learning.   *Ibid.*

6   Never say more than is necessary.   *Ibid. II, i*

7   I know you are laughing in your sleeve.
Ibid.

8   He is the very pineapple of politeness!
Ibid. III, iii

9   If I reprehend anything in this world, it is the use of my oracular tongue, and a nice derangement of epitaphs!   *Ibid.*

10   As headstrong as an allegory on the banks of the Nile.   *Ibid.*

11   Too civil by half.   *Ibid. iv*

12   Our ancestors are very good kind of folks; but they are the last people I should choose to have a visiting acquaintance with.   *Ibid. IV, i*

13   No caparisons, miss, if you please. Caparisons don't become a young woman.   *Ibid. ii*

14   You are not like Cerberus, three gentlemen at once, are you?   *Ibid.*

15   The quarrel is a very pretty quarrel as it stands; we should only spoil it by trying to explain it.
Ibid. iii

16   My valor is certainly going!—it is sneaking off! I feel it oozing out, as it were, at the palm of my hands!   *Ibid. V, iii*

17   I own the soft impeachment.   *Ibid.*

18   Through all the drama—whether damned or not—
Love gilds the scene, and women guide the plot.
Ibid. Epilogue

19   An apothecary should never be out of spirits.
St. Patrick's Day [1775], act I, sc. i

20   Death's a debt; his mandamus binds all alike—
no bail, no demurrer.   *Ibid. II, iv*

21   I ne'er could any luster see
In eyes that would not look on me.
The Duenna [1775], act I, sc. ii

22   I loved him for himself alone.   *Ibid. iii*

23   I was struck all on a heap.   *Ibid. II, ii*

24   A bumper of good liquor
Will end a contest quicker
Than justice, judge, or vicar.
Ibid. iii

25   Conscience has no more to do with gallantry than it has with politics.   *Ibid. iv*

26   Tale-bearers are as bad as the tale-makers.
The School for Scandal [1777], act I, sc. i

27   You shall see them on a beautiful quarto page, where a neat rivulet of text shall meander through a meadow of margin.   *Ibid.*

28   You had no taste when you married me.
Ibid. ii

29   Here's to the maiden of bashful fifteen;
Here's to the widow of fifty;
Here's to the flaunting, extravagant quean,
And here's to the housewife that's thrifty.
Let the toast pass—
Drink to the lass;
I'll warrant she'll prove an excuse for the glass.
Ibid. III, iii

30   An unforgiving eye, and a damned disinheriting countenance.   *Ibid. IV, i*

31   Be just before you're generous.   *Ibid.*

32   There is not a passion so strongly rooted in the human heart as envy.
The Critic [1779], act I, sc. i

33   The newspapers! Sir, they are the most villainous — licentious — abominable — infernal—Not that I ever read them—no—I make it a rule never to look into a newspaper.   *Ibid.*

34   Egad, I think the interpreter is the hardest to be understood of the two!   *Ibid. ii*

35   A practitioner in panegyric, or, to speak more plainly, a professor of the art of puffing.   *Ibid.*

36   The number of those who undergo the fatigue of judging for themselves is very small indeed.
Ibid.

37   Certainly nothing is unnatural that is not physically impossible.   *Ibid. II, i*

1 I wish, sir, you would practice this without me. I can't stay dying here all night. *Ibid. III, i*

2 You write with ease to show your breeding,
But easy writing's curst hard reading.
Clio's Protest [1819]

3 An oyster may be crossed in love.[1] *Ibid.*

4 The right honorable gentleman is indebted to his memory for his jests, and to his imagination for his facts.
Sheridaniana. Speech in Reply to Mr. Dundas

Johann Heinrich Voss
1751–1826

5 Who does not love wine, women, and song
Remains a fool his whole life long.[2]
Attributed

Thomas Chatterton[3]
1752–1770

6 Mie love ys dedde,
Gon to hys death-bedde,
Al under the wyllowe-tree.
Mynstrelles Songe[4]

Philip Freneau
1752–1832

7 Then rushed to meet the insulting foe;
They took the spear—but left the shield.[5]
To the Memory of the Brave Americans Who Fell at Eutaw Springs, S.C., September 8, 1781 [1786], st. 5

8 O come the time, and haste the day,
When man shall man no longer crush,
When Reason shall enforce her sway,
Nor these fair regions raise our blush,
Where still the African complains,
And mourns his yet unbroken chains.
On the Emigration to America and Peopling the Western Country [1786]

9 An age employed in edging steel
Can no poetic raptures feel . . .

[1]From the interpolated tragedy, *The Spanish Armada.*
[2]Wer nicht liebt Wein, Weib und Gesang,/ Der bleibt ein Narr sein Leben lang.
The couplet has also been attributed to Luther, apparently on no better authority than an eighteenth-century jingle in which "Luther" is needed to rhyme with "Futter."
[3]See Wordsworth, 374:9.
[4]This is from the poems of "Thomas Rowley," an imaginary fifteenth-century Bristol poet invented by Chatterton. Editions of the poems appeared in 1778 and 1782, and were exposed [1777–1778] by Thomas Tyrwhitt.
[5]When Prussia hurried to the field, / And snatched the spear, but left the shield.—WALTER SCOTT, *Marmion* [1808], canto III, introduction

No shaded stream, no quiet grove
Can this fantastic century move.
Poems [1795]. To an Author, st. 6

Friedrich Maximilian von Klinger
1752–1831

10 Sturm und Drang [Storm and Stress].
Title of play [1776]

Leonard MacNally
1752–1820

11 On Richmond Hill there lives a lass
More bright than Mayday morn;
Whose charms all other maids' surpass—
A rose without a thorn.
The Lass of Richmond Hill,[6] st. 1

Joseph de Maistre
1753–1821

12 Every nation has the government it deserves.
Letter to X [1811]

13 The sword of justice has no scabbard.
Les Soirées de Saint-Petersbourg [1821]. Premier Entretien

Antoine de Rivarol
1753–1801

14 What is not clear is not French.
Discours sur l'Universalité de la Langue Française [1784]

Joel Barlow
1754–1812

15 My morning incense, and my evening meal—
The sweets of Hasty Pudding.
The Hasty Pudding [1792], canto I

George Crabbe
1754–1832

16 Habit with him was all the test of truth,
"It must be right: I've done it from my youth."
The Borough [1810]. Letter 3, The Vicar

17 In idle wishes fools supinely stay;
Be there a will, and wisdom finds a way.
The Birth of Flattery [1807]

18 Cut and came again.
Tales [1812]. VII, The Widow's Tale

19 The ring, so worn as you behold,
So thin, so pale, is yet of gold.
His Mother's Wedding Ring

[6]Also attributed to JAMES UPTON [1670–1749] and W. HUDSON.

William Drennan
1754–1820

1 Nor one feeling of vengeance presume to defile
The cause, or the men, of the Emerald Isle.[1]
Erin [1795], st. 3

Jeanne Manon Roland
1754–1793

2   O liberty! O liberty! What crimes are committed
in thy name!
*Last words, before her death on the guillotine.
From LAMARTINE, Histoire des Girondins [1847]*

Charles Maurice de Talleyrand-Périgord
1754–1838

3 Black as the devil,
Hot as hell,
Pure as an angel,
Sweet as love.[2]

Recipe for coffee

4   [Of the Bourbons:] They have learned nothing,
and forgotten nothing.[3]
*From CHEVALIER DE PANAT, letter to Mallet du
Pan [January 1796]*

5   [Of the battle of Borodino, 1812:] It is the beginning of the end.[4]
*From EDOUARD FOURNIER, L'Esprit dans
l'Histoire [1857]*

6   The United States has thirty-two religions but
only one dish. *Attributed*

7   Women sometimes forgive a man who forces the
opportunity, but never a man who misses one.
Attributed

8   [To a young diplomat:] Don't be eager![5]
*From CHARLES AUGUSTIN SAINT-BEUVE, Portraits
de Femmes [1858]. Madame de Staël*

9   War is much too serious a matter to be entrusted
to the military.[6]
*Attributed. Quoted by Briand to Lloyd George
during World War I. Also attributed to
Clemenceau*

---

[1]The first known use of this appellation for Ireland.
[2]Noir comme le diable, / Chaud comme l'enfer, / Pur comme
un ange, / Doux comme l'amour.
This appears as an inscription on many old coffeepots.
[3]Ils n'ont rien appris, ni rien oublié.
[4]Voilà le commencement de la fin.
See Churchill, 621:12.
[5]Pas de zèle!
[6]La guerre! C'est une chose trop grave pour la confier à des
militaires. Sometimes quoted as: War is much too serious to
leave to the generals.

Benjamin Waterhouse
1754–1846

10 Tobacco is a filthy weed,
That from the devil does proceed;
It drains your purse, it burns your clothes,
And makes a chimney of your nose.
*From OLIVER WENDELL HOLMES [1809–1894],
who was vaccinated by Dr. Waterhouse*

Bertrand Barère de Vieuzac
1755–1841

11   The tree of liberty only grows when watered by
the blood of tyrants.[7]
*Speech in the National Convention [January 16,
1793]*

12   It is only the dead who do not return.
Speech [1794]

Anthelme Brillat-Savarin
1755–1826

13   Animals feed themselves, men eat; but only wise
men know the art of eating.
*La Physiologie du Goût (The Physiology of
Taste) [1825].[8] Aphorisms*

14   Tell me what you eat, and I shall tell you what
you are. *Ibid.*

15   The discovery of a new dish does more for human
happiness than the discovery of a star. *Ibid.*

Nathan Hale
1755–1776

16   I only regret that I have but one life to lose for my
country.[9]
*Last words, before being hanged by the British
as a spy [September 22, 1776]*

Alexander Hamilton
1755–1804

17   A national debt, if it is not excessive, will be to us
a national blessing.[10]
Letter to Robert Morris [April 30, 1781]

18   I believe the British government forms the best
model the world ever produced. . . . This govern-

---

[7]See Jefferson, 343:15.
[8]Translated by M. F. K. FISHER.
[9]See Addison, 292:12.
[10]At the time we were funding our national debt, we heard
much about "a public debt being a public blessing."—JEFFER-
SON, *Letter to John W. Epps* [November 6, 1813]
See Daniel Webster, 394:12.

ment has for its object public strength and individual security.

Debates of the Federal Convention [May 14–September 17, 1787].[1]*June 18, 1787*

1 All communities divide themselves into the few and the many. The first are the rich and wellborn, the other the mass of the people. . . . The people are turbulent and changing; they seldom judge or determine right. Give therefore to the first class a distinct, permanent share in the government. They will check the unsteadiness of the second, and as they cannot receive any advantage by a change, they therefore will ever maintain good government.

Ibid.

2 We are now forming a republican government. Real liberty is neither found in despotism or the extremes of democracy, but in moderate governments.

Ibid. June 26, 1787

3 Let Americans disdain to be the instruments of European greatness. Let the thirteen States, bound together in a strict and indissoluble Union, concur in erecting one great American system, superior to the control of all transatlantic force or influence, and able to dictate the terms of the connection between the old and the new world!

The Federalist [1787–1788], no. 11

4 Government implies the power of making laws. It is essential to the idea of a law, that it be attended with a sanction; or, in other words, a penalty or punishment for disobedience.

Ibid. 15

5 Why has government been instituted at all? Because the passions of men will not conform to the dictates of reason and justice, without constraint.

Ibid.

6 Every power vested in a government is in its nature sovereign, and includes by force of the term a right to employ all the means requisite . . . to the attainment of the ends of such power.

Opinion on the Constitutionality of the Bank [February 23, 1791]

7 If the end be clearly comprehended within any of the specified powers, and if the measure have an obvious relation to that end, and is not forbidden by any particular provision of the Constitution, it may safely be deemed to come within the compass of the national authority.

Ibid.

Louis XVIII
1755–1824

8 Punctuality is the politeness of kings.[2]

A favorite saying

John Marshall
1755–1835

9 It is emphatically the province and duty of the judicial department to say what the law is. . . . If two laws conflict with each other, the courts must decide on the operation of each. . . . This is of the very essence of judicial duty.

Marbury v. Madison, 1 Cranch, 1317 [1803]

10 We must never forget that it is a *constitution* we are expounding.

McCulloch v. Maryland, 4 Wheaton 316, 407 [1819]

11 This provision is made in a constitution, intended to endure for ages to come, and consequently, to be adapted to the various *crises* of human affairs.

Ibid. 415

12 Let the end be legitimate, let it be within the scope of the constitution, and all means which are appropriate, which are plainly adapted to that end, which are not prohibited, but consistent with the letter and spirit of the constitution, are constitutional.

Ibid. 421

13 The power to tax involves the power to destroy.[3]

Ibid. 431

14 The people made the Constitution, and the people can unmake it. It is the creature of their own will, and lives only by their will.

Cohens v. Virginia, 6 Wheaton (19 U.S.) 264, 389 [1821]

Martin Joseph Routh
1755–1854

15 You will find it a very good practice always to verify your references, sir.

From J. W. Burgon, Memoir of Dr. Routh, Quarterly Review [July 1878]

Henry [Light-Horse Harry] Lee
1756–1818

16 To the memory of the Man, first in war, first in peace, and first in the hearts of his countrymen.

Eulogy on the death of Washington [December 1799][4]

William Blake
1757–1827

17 How sweet I roam'd from field to field,
And tasted all the summer's pride,

[1] At which the Constitution was written.
[2] L'exactitude est la politesse des rois.

[3] See Oliver Wendell Holmes, Jr., 543:8.
[4] Based on resolutions presented to the House of Representatives a week earlier. In the resolutions, the statement ends with "fellow-citizens."

Till I the prince of love beheld,
Who in the sunny beams did glide!
        *Poetical Sketches [1783]. Song (How Sweet I
        Roamed), st. 1*

1 He loves to sit and hear me sing,
Then, laughing, sports and plays with me;
Then stretches out my golden wing,
And mocks my loss of liberty.
                            Ibid. st. 4

2 Like a fiend in a cloud,
With howling woe,
After night I do crowd,
And with night will go.
                    Ibid. Mad Song, st. 3

3 The languid strings do scarcely move!
The sound is forced, the notes are few!
                    Ibid. To the Muses, st. 4

4 Piping down the valleys wild,
Piping songs of pleasant glee,
On a cloud I saw a child,
And he laughing said to me:

"Pipe a song about a Lamb."
So I piped with merry cheer;
"Piper, pipe that song again."
So I piped; he wept to hear.
        *Songs of Innocence [1789–1790]. Introduction,
        st. 1, 2*

5 And I made a rural pen,
And I stain'd the water clear,
And I wrote my happy songs
Every child may joy to hear.
                            Ibid. st. 5

6 Little Lamb, who made thee?
Dost thou know who made thee?
Gave thee life and bid thee feed
By the stream and o'er the mead;
Gave thee clothing of delight,
Softest clothing, woolly, bright.
                    Ibid. The Lamb, st. 1

7 Little Lamb, I'll tell thee,
Little Lamb, I'll tell thee:
He is called by thy name,
For he calls himself a Lamb.
He is meek and he is mild;
He became a little child.
I a child, and thou a lamb,
We are called by his name.
Little Lamb, God bless thee!
Little Lamb, God bless thee!
                            Ibid. st. 2

8 My mother bore me in the southern wild,
And I am black, but O! my soul is white;
White as an angel is the English child,
But I am black as if bereav'd of light.
                Ibid. The Little Black Boy, st. 1

9 And we are put on earth a little space,
That we may learn to bear the beams of love,

And these black bodies and this sunburnt face
Is but a cloud, and like a shady grove.
                            Ibid. st. 4

10 I'll shade him from the heat till he can bear
To lean in joy upon our Father's knee;
And then I'll stand and stroke his silver hair,
And be like him and he will then love me.
                            Ibid. st. 7

11 When my mother died I was very young,
And my father sold me while yet my tongue
Could scarcely cry 'weep! 'weep! 'weep! 'weep!
So your chimneys I sweep, and in soot I sleep.
                Ibid. The Chimney Sweeper, st. 1

12 To Mercy, Pity, Peace, and Love
All pray in their distress;
And to these virtues of delight
Return their thankfulness.
                Ibid. The Divine Image, st. 1

13 For Mercy has a human heart,
Pity, a human face,
And Love, the human form divine,[1]
And Peace, the human dress.[2]
                            Ibid. st. 3

14 And all must love the human form,
In heathen, turk, or jew;
Where Mercy, Love, & Pity dwell
There God is dwelling too.
                            Ibid. st. 5

15 The moon like a flower
In heaven's high bower,
With silent delight,
Sits and smiles on the night.
                    Ibid. Night, st. 1

16 And there the lion's ruddy eyes
Shall flow with tears of gold,
And pitying the tender cries,
And walking round the fold,
Saying: "Wrath by his meekness,
And by his health, sickness,
Is driven away
From our immortal day."
                            Ibid. st. 5

17 When the voices of children are heard on the
        green
And laughing is heard on the hill,
My heart is at rest within my breast
And everything else is still.
                    Ibid. Nurse's Song, st. 1

18 Can I see another's woe,
And not be in sorrow too?
Can I see another's grief,
And not seek for kind relief?
                Ibid. On Another's Sorrow, st. 1

[1]See Milton, 257:24, and *A Divine Image*, 358:13.
[2]See *A Divine Image*, 358:13.

1 Does the Eagle know what is in the pit?
Or wilt thou go ask the Mole?
Can Wisdom be put in a silver rod?
Or Love in a golden bowl?
    The Book of Thel [1789–1792]. Thel's Motto

2   The reason Milton wrote in fetters when he
wrote of Angels and God, and at liberty when of
Devils and Hell, is because he was a true poet and of
the Devil's party without knowing it.
    *The Marriage of Heaven and Hell [1790–1793].
Note to The Voice of the Devil*

3 The road of excess leads to the palace of wisdom.
    Ibid. Proverbs of Hell, l. 3.

4 Eternity is in love with the production of time.
    Ibid. l. 10

5 No bird soars too high, if he soars with his own
    wings.
    Ibid. l. 15

6 The pride of the peacock is the glory of God.
The lust of the goat is the bounty of God.
The wrath of the lion is the wisdom of God.
The nakedness of woman is the work of God.
    Ibid. l. 22

7 The cistern contains: the fountain overflows.
    Ibid. l. 35

8 Think in the morning. Act in the noon. Eat in the
    evening. Sleep in the night.
    Ibid. l. 41

9 The tygers of wrath are wiser than the horses of
    instruction.
    Ibid. l. 44

10 You never know what is enough unless you know
    what is more than enough.
    Ibid. l. 46

11 Improvement makes straight roads; but the
    crooked roads without improvement are
    roads of genius.
    Ibid. l. 66

12 Sooner murder an infant in its cradle than nurse
    unacted desires.
    Ibid. l. 67

13 Truth can never be told so as to be understood,
    and not be believ'd.
    Ibid. l. 69

14 Enough! or too much.
    Ibid. l. 70

15 One Law for the Lion & Ox is Oppression.
    Ibid. A Memorable Fancy

16 For every thing that lives is Holy.
    Ibid. A Song of Liberty

17 Never seek to tell thy love
Love that never told can be;
For the gentle wind does move
Silently, invisibly.

I told my love, I told my love,
I told her all my heart;
Trembling, cold, in ghastly fears—
Ah, she doth depart.

Soon as she was gone from me
A traveler came by
Silently, invisibly—
Oh, was no deny.
    *Poems [written c. 1791–1792] from Blake's
Notebook. Never Seek to Tell*

18 I ask'd a thief to steal me a peach:
He turned up his eyes.
I ask'd a lithe lady to lie her down:
Holy and meek, she cries.

As soon as I went
An angel came.
He wink'd at the thief
And smil'd at the dame—

And without one word said
Had a peach from the tree,
And still as a maid
Enjoy'd the lady.
    Ibid. I Asked a Thief

19 Love to faults is always blind,
Always is to joy inclin'd,
Lawless, wing'd, and unconfin'd,
And breaks all chains from every mind.
    Ibid. Love to Faults

20 Abstinence sows sand all over
The ruddy limbs and flaming hair,
But Desire gratified
Plants fruits of life and beauty there.
    Ibid. Abstinence Sows Sand

21 If you trap the moment before it's ripe,
The tears of repentance you'll certainly wipe;
But if once you let the ripe moment go
You can never wipe off the tears of woe.
    Ibid. If You Trap the Moment

22 He who binds to himself a joy
Does the winged life destroy;
But he who kisses the joy as it flies
Lives in eternity's sunrise.
    *Ibid. Several Questions Answered, no. 1, He
Who Binds*

23 The look of love alarms
Because 'tis fill'd with fire;
But the look of soft deceit
Shall win the lover's hire.
    Ibid. 2, The Look of Love

24 What is it men in women do require?
The lineaments of Gratified Desire.
What is it women do in men require?
The lineaments of Gratified Desire.
    Ibid. 4, What Is It

25 Hear the voice of the Bard!
Who Present, Past, and Future sees,

Whose ears have heard
The Holy Word
That walk'd among the ancient trees.
Songs of Experience [1794]. Introduction, st. 1

1 Turn away no more.
Why wilt thou turn away?
The starry floor,
The wat'ry shore
Is giv'n thee till the break of day.
Ibid. st. 4

2 Love seeketh not itself to please,
Nor for itself hath any care,
But for another gives its ease,
And builds a Heaven in Hell's despair.
Ibid. The Clod and the Pebble, st. 1

3 Love seeketh only self to please,
To bind another to its delight,
Joys in another's loss of ease,
And builds a Hell in Heaven's despite.
Ibid. st. 3

4 O Rose, thou art sick.
The invisible worm
That flies in the night,
In the howling storm,

Has found out thy bed
Of crimson joy,
And his dark secret love
Does thy life destroy.
Ibid. The Sick Rose

5 Little Fly,
Thy summer's play
My thoughtless hand
Has brushed away.

Am not I
A fly like thee?
Or art not thou
A man like me?

For I dance
And drink and sing,
Till some blind hand
Shall brush my wing.
Ibid. The Fly, st. 1–3

6 Tyger! Tyger! burning bright
In the forests of the night,
What immortal hand or eye
Could frame thy fearful symmetry?

In what distant deeps or skies
Burnt the fire of thine eyes?
On what wings dare he aspire?
What the hand dare seize the fire?
Ibid. The Tyger, st. 1, 2

7 What the hammer? what the chain?
In what furnace was thy brain?
What the anvil? what dread grasp
Dare its deadly terrors clasp?

When the stars threw down their spears
And water'd heaven with their tears,
Did he smile his work to see?
Did he who made the Lamb make thee?
Ibid. st. 4, 5

8 In every cry of every man,
In every infant's cry of fear,
In every voice, in every ban,
The mind-forg'd manacles I hear.
Ibid. London, st. 2

9 But most through midnight streets I hear
How the youthful harlot's curse
Blasts the newborn infant's tear
And blights with plagues the marriage hearse.
Ibid. st. 4

10 Pity would be no more,
If we did not make somebody poor;
And Mercy no more could be,
If all were as happy as we.
Ibid. The Human Abstract, st. 1

11 My mother groan'd! my father wept.
Into the dangerous world I leapt:
Helpless, naked, piping loud,
Like a fiend hid in a cloud.
Ibid. Infant Sorrow, st. 1

12 I was angry with my friend;
I told my wrath, my wrath did end.
I was angry with my foe;
I told it not, my wrath did grow.
Ibid. A Poison Tree, st. 1

13 Cruelty has a human heart,
And Jealousy a human face;
Terror, the human form divine,[1]
And Secrecy, the human dress.
A Divine Image,[2] st. 1

14 Degrade first the arts if you'd mankind degrade,
Hire idiots to paint with cold light and hot shade.
*Annotations [c. 1798–1809] to Sir Joshua
Reynolds's Discourses,[3] title page*

15   To generalize is to be an idiot. To particularize is
the alone distinction of merit—general knowledges
are those knowledges that idiots possess.
Ibid. pp. xcvii–xcviii

16 My specter around me night and day
Like a wild beast guards my way.
My emanation far within
Weeps incessantly for my sin.
*Poems [written c. 1804] from Blake's Notebook.
My Specter, st. 1*

[1]See Milton, 257:24, and *The Divine Image*, 356:13.
[2]This poem was written and etched by Blake [1790–1791] as
a "Song of Experience" linked with *The Divine Image* in *Songs
of Innocence* (see 356:12 and 356:13), but in the published
Songs of Experience it was replaced by *The Human Abstract*
(358:10).
[3]Volume I of Reynolds's *Works*, edited by EDMOND MALONE
[second edition, 1798].

1 And throughout all eternity
　　I forgive you, you forgive me.
　　　　　　　　　　　　　　Ibid. st. 14

2 Mock on, mock on,[1] Voltaire, Rousseau.
　　Mock on, mock on—'tis all in vain!
　　You throw the sand against the wind,
　　And the wind blows it back again.
　　　　　　　　　　　　　Ibid. Mock On, st. 1

3 There is a smile of love,
　　And there is a smile of deceit,
　　And there is a smile of smiles
　　In which these two smiles meet.
　　　　Poems from the Pickering Manuscript [c. 1805].
　　　　The Smile, st. 1

4 For a tear is an intellectual thing,
　　And a sigh is the sword of an Angel King,
　　And the bitter groan of the martyr's woe
　　Is an arrow from the Almighty's bow.
　　　　　　　　　　　Ibid. The Gray Monk, st. 8

5 To see a world in a grain of sand
　　And a heaven in a wild flower,
　　Hold infinity in the palm of your hand
　　And eternity in an hour.
　　　　　　　Ibid. Auguries of Innocence, l. 1

6 A robin redbreast in a cage
　　Puts all Heaven in a rage.
　　　　　　　　　　　　　　　Ibid. l. 5

7 A dog starv'd at his master's gate
　　Predicts the ruin of the state.
　　　　　　　　　　　　　　　Ibid. l. 9

8 He who shall hurt the little wren
　　Shall never be belov'd by men.
　　　　　　　　　　　　　　　Ibid. l. 29

9 A truth that's told with bad intent
　　Beats all the lies you can invent.
　　　　　　　　　　　　　　　Ibid. l. 53

10 Man was made for joy and woe,
　　And when this we rightly know
　　Through the world we safely go.
　　　　　　　　　　　　　　　Ibid. l. 56

11 He who shall teach the child to doubt
　　The rotting grave shall ne'er get out.
　　　　　　　　　　　　　　　Ibid. l. 87

12 The Questioner, who sits so sly,
　　Shall never know how to Reply.
　　　　　　　　　　　　　　　Ibid. l. 93

13 The strongest poison ever known
　　Came from Caesar's laurel crown.
　　　　　　　　　　　　　　　Ibid. l. 97

14 He who doubts from what he sees
　　Will ne'er believe, do what you please.
　　If the sun and moon should doubt
　　They'd immediately go out.
　　　　　　　　　　　　　　　Ibid. l. 107

[1]See *Job 21:3, 14:33.*

15 The harlot's cry from street to street
　　Shall weave old England's winding sheet.
　　　　　　　　　　　　　　　Ibid. l. 115

16 God Appears and God is Light
　　To those poor Souls who dwell in Night,
　　But does a Human Form Display
　　To those who Dwell in Realms of day.
　　　　　　　　　　　　　　　Ibid l. 129

17 And did those feet in ancient time
　　Walk upon England's mountains green?
　　And was the holy Lamb of God
　　On England's pleasant pastures seen?

　　And did the Countenance Divine
　　Shine forth upon our clouded hills?
　　And was Jerusalem builded here
　　Among these dark Satanic mills?

　　Bring me my bow of burning gold,
　　Bring me my arrows of desire,
　　Bring me my spear—O clouds, unfold!
　　Bring me my chariot of fire!

　　I will not cease from mental fight,
　　Nor shall my sword sleep in my hand,
　　Till we have built Jerusalem
　　In England's green and pleasant land.
　　　　　　　Milton [c. 1809], prefatory poem

18 Great things are done when men and mountains
　　　　meet;
　　This is not done by jostling in the street.
　　　　Poems [written c. 1807–1809] from Blake's
　　　　Notebook. Great Things Are Done

19 If you have form'd a circle to go into,
　　Go into it yourself and see how you would do.
　　　　　　　　　　　　　　　Ibid. To God

20 The Angel that presided o'er my birth
　　Said, "Little creature, formed of joy and mirth,
　　Go love without the help of any thing on earth."
　　　　　　　　　Ibid. The Angel That Presided

21 Grown old in love from seven till seven times
　　　　seven,
　　I oft have wish'd for Hell for ease from Heaven.
　　　　　　　　　　　Ibid. Grown Old in Love

22 　　Poetry fettered fetters the human race. Nations
　　are destroyed, or flourish, in proportion as their
　　poetry, painting, and music are destroyed or flour-
　　ish!
　　　　　Jerusalem [c. 1818–1820]. To the Public, plate 1

23 He who would do good to another must do it in
　　　　minute particulars;
　　General good is the plea of the scoundrel,
　　　　hypocrite, and flatterer:
　　For art and science cannot exist but in minutely
　　　　organized particulars.
　　　　　　　　　　Ibid. ch. 3, plate 55, l. 60

24 England! awake! awake! awake!
　　Jerusalem thy sister calls!

Why wilt thou sleep the sleep of death
And close her from thy ancient walls?
> *Jerusalem, ch. 4, prefatory poem, plate 77, st. 1*

1 The vision of Christ that thou dost see
Is my vision's greatest enemy.
> *The Everlasting Gospel [written c. 1818], sec. 4, l. 1*

2 Both read the Bible day and night,
But thou read'st black where I read white.
> *Ibid. l. 13*

3 This life's dim windows of the soul
Distorts the heavens from pole to pole
And leads you to believe a lie
When you see with, not through, the eye.[1]
> *Ibid. 5, l. 101*

4 I am sure this Jesus will not do
Either for Englishman or Jew.
> *Ibid. 8*

James Gillray
c. 1757–1815

5   The Old Lady of Threadneedle Street.[2]
> *Title of cartoon [1797]*

John Philip Kemble
1757–1823

6 Perhaps it was right to dissemble your love,
But—why did you kick me down stairs?
> *The Panel, act I, sc. i*

Fisher Ames
1758–1808

7   A monarchy is a merchantman which sails well, but will sometimes strike on a rock, and go to the bottom; a republic is a raft which will never sink, but then your feet are always in the water.
> *Speech in the House of Representatives [1795]*

John Heath
1758–1810

8   Love of wisdom [philosophy] the guide of life.[3]
> *Greek phrase for Phi Beta Kappa, society founded at the College of William and Mary [December 5, 1776]*

[1]We are led to believe a lie / When we see not through the eye. — *Auguries of Innocence, l. 125*
[2]The Bank of England.
[3]*Philosophia biou kybernetes.* The name Phi Beta Kappa is from the Greek initial letters in the phrase. See Cicero, 87:29.

James Monroe
1758–1831

9   National honor is national property of the highest value.
> *First Inaugural Address [March 4, 1817]*

10   The American continents . . . are henceforth not to be considered as subjects for future colonization by any European powers.
> *Annual Message to Congress [December 2, 1823]. The Monroe Doctrine*

11   In the wars of the European powers in matters relating to themselves we have never taken any part, nor does it comport with our policy so to do.
> *Ibid.*

12   We owe it, therefore, to candor, and to the amicable relations existing between the United States and those powers to declare that we should consider any attempt on their part to extend their system to any portion of this hemisphere as dangerous to our peace and safety. With the existing colonies or dependencies of any European power we . . . shall not interfere. But with the governments . . . whose independence we have . . . acknowledged, we could not view any interposition for the purpose of oppressing them, or controlling, in any other manner, their destiny, by any European power, in any other light than as a manifestation of an unfriendly disposition toward the United States.   *Ibid.*

Horatio Nelson
1758–1805

13   Westminster Abbey, or victory!
> *At the battle of Cape St. Vincent [February 14, 1797]. From ROBERT SOUTHEY, Life of Nelson [1813], ch. 4*

14   I have only one eye, I have a right to be blind sometimes. . . . I really do not see the signal.
> *At the battle of Copenhagen [1801]. Ibid. 9*

15   Something must be left to chance; nothing is sure in a sea fight beyond all others.
> *Memorandum to the fleet, off Cadiz [October 9, 1805]*

16   But, in case signals can neither be seen or perfectly understood, no captain can do very wrong if he places his ship alongside that of the enemy.
> *Ibid.*

17   England expects every man will do his duty.[4]
> *At the battle of Trafalgar [October 21, 1805]. From ROBERT SOUTHEY, Life of Nelson [1813], ch. 9*

[4]This famous sentence is thus first reported: Say to the fleet, England confides that every man will do his duty. Captain Pasco, Nelson's flag lieutenant, suggested substituting "expects" for "confides," which was adopted. Captain Blackwood, who commanded the *Euryalus*, says that the correction suggested was from "Nelson expects" to "England expects."

1   Thank God, I have done my duty.   *Ibid.*

2   Kiss me, Hardy.   *Ibid.*

Red Jacket [Sagoyewatha][1]
c. 1758–1830

3   We first knew you a feeble plant which wanted a little earth whereon to grow. We gave it to you; and afterward, when we could have trod you under our feet, we watered and protected you; and now you have grown to be a mighty tree, whose top reaches the clouds, and whose branches overspread the whole land, whilst we, who were the tall pine of the forest, have become a feeble plant and need your protection.   *Statement [c. 1792]*

Robert Burns
1759–1796

4   Wee, sleekit, cow'rin, tim'rous beastie,
O, what a panic's in thy breastie!
Thou need na start awa sae hasty,
    Wi' bickering brattle!
            To a Mouse [1785], st. 1

5   I'm truly sorry man's dominion
Has broken Nature's social union.
            Ibid. st. 2

6   The best laid schemes o' mice and men
Gang aft a-gley.
            Ibid. st. 7

7   Nature's law,
That man was made to mourn.
        Man Was Made to Mourn [1786], st. 4

8   Man's inhumanity to man.[2]
Makes countless thousands mourn!
            Ibid. st. 7

9   He wales a portion with judicious care;
And "Let us worship God" he says, with solemn
    air.
        The Cotter's Saturday Night [1786], st. 12

10 From scenes like these, old Scotia's grandeur
    springs,
That makes her loved at home, revered abroad:
Princes and lords are but the breath of kings,[3]
"An honest man's the noblest work of God."[4]
            Ibid. st. 19

11 Gie me ae spark o' Nature's fire,
That's a' the learning I desire.
        First Epistle to J. Lapraik [1786], st. 13

12 The social, friendly, honest man,
Whate'er he be,

'Tis he fulfills great Nature's plan,
And none but he!
        Second Epistle to J. Lapraik [1786], st. 15

13 On ev'ry hand it will allow'd be,
He's just—nae better than he should be.
        A Dedication to Gavin Hamilton [1786]

14 It's hardly in a body's pow'r,
To keep, at times, frae being sour.
            Epistle to Davie [1786], st. 2

15 Misled by fancy's meteor ray,
By passion driven;
But yet the light that led astray
Was light from heaven.
            The Vision [1786], II, st. 18

16 His locked, lettered, braw brass collar
Showed him the gentleman an' scholar.
            The Twa Dogs [1786], st. 3

17 An' there began a lang digression
About the lords o' the creation.
            Ibid. st. 6

18 Oh wad some power the giftie gie us
To see oursels as ithers see us!
It wad frae monie a blunder free us,
    An' foolish notion.
            To a Louse [1786], st. 8

19 Wee, modest, crimson-tipped flow'r,
Thou's met me in an evil hour;
For I maun crush amang the stoure
Thy slender stem:
To spare thee now is past my pow'r,
Thou bonie gem.
        To a Mountain Daisy [1786], st. 1

20 Stern Ruin's plowshare drives elate,
Full on thy bloom.[5]
            Ibid. st. 9

21 Perhaps it may turn out a sang,
Perhaps turn out a sermon.
        Epistle to a Young Friend [1786], st. 1

22 I waive the quantum o' the sin,
The hazard of concealing:
But, och! it hardens a' within,
And petrifies the feeling!
            Ibid. st. 6

23 An atheist-laugh's a poor exchange
For Deity offended.
            Ibid. st. 9

24 There's nought but care on ev'ry han',
In every hour that passes, O:
What signifies the life o' man,
An' 't were nae for the lasses, O.
        Green Grow the Rashes, O [1787], st. 1

25 Auld Nature swears, the lovely dears
Her noblest work she classes, O:

---

[1]Seneca chief.
[2]See Pliny the Elder, 104:6, and Wordsworth, 372:18.
[3]See Goldsmith, 329:8.
[4]See Pope, 301:18.

[5]See Edward Young, 296:20.

Her prentice han' she tried on man,
An' then she made the lasses, O.
Green Grow the Rashes, O, st. 5

1 Green grow the rashes, O;
Green grow the rashes, O;
The sweetest hours that e'er I spend
Are spent among the lasses, O.
Ibid. chorus

2 I wasna fou, but just had plenty.
Death and Dr. Hornbook [1787], st. 3

3 John Barleycorn got up again,
And sore surprised them all.
John Barleycorn [1787], st. 3

4 The heart benevolent and kind
The most resembles God.
A Winter Night [1787]

5 Then gently scan your brother man,
Still gentler sister woman;
Tho' they may gang a kennin wrang,
To step aside is human.[1]
Address to the Unco Guid [1787], st. 7

6 O, my Luve is like a red, red rose,
That's newly sprung in June.
O, my Luve is like the melodie,
That's sweetly played in tune.
Johnson's Musical Museum [1787–1796]. A Red, Red Rose, st. 1

7 Contented wi' little and cantie wi' mair.
Ibid. Contented wi' Little, st. 1

8 Ye banks and braes o' bonny Doon,
How can ye bloom sae fresh and fair?
How can ye chant, ye little birds,
And I sae weary fu' o' care!
Thou'll break my heart, thou warbling bird,
That wantons thro' the flowering thorn!
Thou minds me o' departed joys,
Departed never to return.
Ibid. The Banks o' Doon, st. 1

9 Chords that vibrate sweetest pleasure
Thrill the deepest notes of woe.
Ibid. Sensibility How Charming, st. 4

10 Ae fond kiss, and then we sever;
Ae farewell and then forever![2]
Ibid. Ae Fond Kiss, st. 1

11 But to see her was to love her,
Love but her, and love forever.
Had we never lov'd sae kindly,
Had we never lov'd sae blindly,
Never met—or never parted—
We had ne'er been brokenhearted.
Ibid. st. 2

12 It was a' for our rightfu' King
We left fair Scotland's strand.
Ibid. It Was A' for Our Rightfu' King, st. 1

13 Now a' is done that men can do,
And a' is done in vain.
Ibid. st. 2

14 He turn'd him right and round about
Upon the Irish shore;
And gae his bridle reins a shake,
With adieu forevermore,
      My dear—
And adieu forevermore!
Ibid. st. 3

15 John Anderson my jo, John,
When we were first acquent,
Your locks were like the raven,
Your bonie brow was brent;
But now your brow is beld, John,
Your locks are like the snaw,
But blessings on your frosty pow,
John Anderson my jo!
Ibid. John Anderson My Jo, st. 1

16 Farewell to the Highlands, farewell to the North,
The birthplace of valor, the country of worth!
Wherever I wander, wherever I rove,
The hills of the Highlands for ever I love.
Ibid. My Heart's in the Highlands, st. 1

17 My heart's in the Highlands, my heart is not here,
My heart's in the Highlands a-chasing the deer;
A-chasing the wild deer, and following the roe,
My heart's in the Highlands wherever I go.
Ibid. chorus

18 O whistle, and I'll come to you,[3] my lad:
Tho' father and mither and a' should gae mad.
Whistle, and I'll Come to You, My Lad

19 Should auld acquaintance be forgot,
And never brought to min'?
Should auld acquaintance be forgot,
And days o' auld lang syne?
Auld Lang Syne [1788], st. 1

20 For auld lang syne, my dear,
For auld lang syne,
We'll tak a cup o' kindness yet
For auld lang syne!
Ibid. chorus

21 Flow gently, sweet Afton, among thy green braes,
Flow gently, I'll sing thee a song in thy praise.
My Mary's asleep by thy murmuring stream,
Flow gently, sweet Afton, disturb not her dream.
Afton Water [1789], st. 1

22 This day Time winds th' exhausted chain,
To run the twelvemonth's length again.
New Year's Day [1791], st. 1

23 The voice of Nature loudly cries,
And many a message from the skies,
That something in us never dies.
Ibid. st. 3

[1]See Plutarch, 107:18; Anonymous: Latin, 118:30; Shirley, 246:20; and Pope, 299:4.
[2]See Byron, 401:20.

[3]See Beaumont and Fletcher, 238:18.

1 When Nature her great masterpiece design'd,
   And fram'd her last, best work, the human mind,
   Her eye intent on all the mazy plan,
   She form'd of various stuff the various Man.
                    To Robert Graham [1791], st. 1

2 Whare sits our sulky, sullen dame,
   Gathering her brows like gathering storm,
   Nursing her wrath to keep it warm.
                    Tam o' Shanter [1791], l. 10

3 Ah, gentle dames! it gars me greet
   To think how monie counsels sweet,
   How monie lengthened, sage advices,
   The husband frae the wife despises.
                    Ibid. l. 33

4 His ancient, trusty, drouthy crony;
   Tam lo'ed him like a vera brither—
   They had been fou for weeks thegither.
                    Ibid. l. 43

5 Kings may be blest, but Tam was glorious,
   O'er a' the ills o' life victorious.
                    Ibid. l. 57

6 But pleasures are like poppies spread—
   You seize the flow'r, its bloom is shed;
   Or like the snow falls in the river—
   A moment white—then melts forever.
                    Ibid. l. 59

7 Inspiring bold John Barleycorn!
   What dangers thou canst make us scorn!
   Wi' tippenny, we fear nae evil;
   Wi' usquebae, we'll face the devil!
                    Ibid. l. 105

8 As Tammie glow'red, amazed, and curious,
   The mirth and fun grew fast and furious.
                    Ibid. l. 143

9 Her cutty sark, o' Paisley harn,
   That while a lassie she had worn,
   In longitude tho' sorely scanty,
   It was her best, and she was vauntie.
                    Ibid. l. 171

10 "Weel done, Cutty Sark!"[1]
                    Ibid. l. 189

11 Ah, Tam! Ah! Tam! Thou'll get thy fairin!
   In hell they'll roast you like a herrin!
                    Ibid. l. 201

12 She is a winsome wee thing,
   She is a handsome wee thing,
   She is a lo'esome wee thing,
      This sweet wee wife o' mine.
                    My Wife's a Winsome Wee Thing [1792],
                    chorus

13 The golden hours on angel wings
   Flew o'er me and my dearie;

For dear to me as light and life
   Was my sweet Highland Mary.
                    Highland Mary [1792], st. 2

14 But, oh! fell death's untimely frost,
   That nipt my flower sae early.
                    Ibid. st. 3

15 If there's a hole in a' your coats,
   I rede you tent it;
   A child's amang you takin' notes,
   And faith he'll prent it.
                    On the Late Captain Grose's Peregrinations
                    Thro' Scotland [1793], st. 1

16 Some hae meat and canna eat,
   And some wad eat that want it;
   But we hae meat, and we can eat,
   And sae the Lord be thankit.
                    The Selkirk Grace [1793] (attributed)

17 O Mary, at thy window be!
   It is the wish'd, the trysted hour.
                    Mary Morison [1793], st. 1

18 The lovely Mary Morison!
                    Ibid.

19 Scots wha hae wi' Wallace bled,
   Scots wham Bruce has aften led,
   Welcome to your gory bed
      Or to victorie.

   Now's the day, and now's the hour;
   See the front o' battle lour!
   See approach proud Edward's power—
      Chains and slaverie!
                    Scots Wha Hae [1794], st. 1, 2

20 Lay the proud usurpers low!
   Tyrants fall in every foe!
   Liberty's in every blow!
      Let us do or die![2]
                    Ibid. st. 6

21 The rank is but the guinea's stamp,
   The man's the gowd for a' that.
                    For A' That and A' That [1795], st. 1

22 A prince can mak a belted knight,
   A marquis, duke, and a' that;
   But an honest man's aboon his might,
   Guid faith, he mauna fa' that.
                    Ibid. st. 4

23 For a' that and a' that,
   It's coming yet, for a' that,
   That man to man the world o'er
   Shall brothers be for a' that.
                    Ibid. st. 5

24 For a' that, and a' that,
   An' twice as muckle 's a' that,
   I've lost but ane, I've twa behin',
   I've wife eneugh for a' that.
                    Posthumous Pieces [1799]. The Jolly Beggars,
                    chorus

---

[1]The famous tea clipper *Cutty Sark*, designed by Hercules Linton and built in 1869, had the story of Tam o' Shanter carved upon her bow and counter. Nannie, with flying locks and scanty shift, was the figurehead.

[2]See Fletcher, 236:12.

1 God knows, I'm no the thing I should be,
Nor am I even the thing I could be.
> *Posthumous Pieces. To the Reverend John
> M'Math, st. 8*

2 If there's another world, he lives in bliss;
If there is none, he made the best of this.
> *Ibid. Epitaph on William Muir*

3 In durance vile here must I wake and weep,
And all my frowsy couch in sorrow steep.
> *Ibid. Epistle from Esopus to Maria*

4 It's guid to be merry and wise,
It's guid to be honest and true,
It's guid to support Caledonia's cause
And bide by the buff and the blue.
> *Ibid. Here's a Health to Them That's Awa',
> st. 1*

Georges Jacques Danton
1759–1794

5 Everything belongs to the fatherland when the fatherland is in danger.
> *Speech to the Legislative Assembly [August 28,
> 1792]*

6 Audacity, more audacity, always audacity.[1]
> *Ibid. [September 2, 1792]*

7 Show my head to the people, it is worth seeing.
> *Last words, addressed to the executioner*

Joseph Fouché
1759–1820

8 Death is an eternal sleep.
> *Inscription placed by his orders on cemetery
> gates [1794]*

William Pitt
1759–1806

9 Necessity is the plea for every infringement of human freedom. It is the argument of tyrants; it is the creed of slaves.[2]
> *Speech in the House of Commons [November
> 18, 1783]*

Johann Christoph Friedrich von Schiller
1759–1805

10 I feel an army in my fist.
> *The Robbers [1781], act II, end*

11 The joke loses everything when the joker laughs himself.
> *The Conspiracy of Fiesco [1783], act I, sc. vii*

[1] *Il nous faut de l'audace, encore de l'audace, toujours de l'audace.*
[2] See Milton, 258:15.

12 Did you think the lion was sleeping because he didn't roar?
> *Ibid. xviii*

13 Joy, thou spark from Heav'n immortal,
Daughter of Elysium!
Drunk with fire, toward Heaven advancing
Goddess, to thy shrine we come.
Thy sweet magic brings together
What stern Custom spreads afar;
All men become brothers
Where thy happy wing-beats are.[3]
> *Ode to Joy [1785], st. 1*

14 There are three lessons I would write,
Three words as with a burning pen,
In tracings of eternal light
Upon the hearts of men.
> *Hope, Faith, and Love [c. 1786], st. 1*

15 World history is the world's court.[4]
> *Resignation [1786]*

16 What one refuses in a minute
No eternity will return.
> *Ibid.*

17 O who knows what slumbers in the background of the times?
> *Don Carlos [1787], act I, sc. i*

18 O the idea was childish, but divinely beautiful.
> *Ibid. ii*

19 Great souls suffer in silence.
> *Ibid. iv*

20 The richest monarch in the Christian world;
The sun in my own dominions never sets.[5]
> *Ibid. vi*

21 If you want to know yourself,
Just look how others do it;
If you want to understand others,
Look into your own heart.
> *Tabulae Votivae [1797]*

22 Posterity weaves no garlands for imitators.
> *Wallenstein's Camp [1798], prologue*

23 He who has done his best for his own time has lived for all times.
> *Ibid.*

[3] Alle Menschen werden Brüder, / Wo dein sanfter Flügel weilt.
Translated by THEODORE SPENCER (adapted).
Music by LUDWIG VAN BEETHOVEN.
[4] Die Weltgeschichte ist das Weltgericht.
[5] Why should the brave Spanish soldier brag the sun never sets in the Spanish dominions, but ever shineth on one part or other we have conquered for our king? — JOHN SMITH [1580–1631], *Advertisements for the Unexperienced, etc.* [1631]
It may be said of them [the Hollanders] as of the Spaniards, that the sun never sets on their dominions. — THOMAS GAGE [d. 1656], *New Survey of the West Indies* [1648], *Epistle Dedicatory*
The sun never sets on the immense empire of Charles V. — WALTER SCOTT, *Life of Napoleon* [1827]
His Majesty's dominions, on which the sun never sets. — JOHN WILSON [CHRISTOPHER NORTH, 1785–1854], *Noctes Ambrosianae, no. 20* [April 1829]

1   Life is earnest, art is gay.   *Ibid.*

2   Whatever is not forbidden is permitted.
                                    Ibid. sc. vi

3   Man is made of ordinary things, and habit is his
nurse.
            The Death of Wallenstein [1798], act I, sc. iv

4 Many a crown shines spotless now
That yet was deeply sullied in the winning.[1]
                                    Ibid. II, ii

5 There's no such thing as chance;
And what to us seems merest accident
Springs from the deepest source of destiny.[1]
                                    Ibid. iii

6   Time is man's angel.   *Ibid. V, xi*

7   What is the short meaning of the long speech?
                        The Piccolomini [1799], act I, sc. ii

8   War nourishes war.[2]   *Ibid.*

9   In thy breast are the stars of thy fate.
                                    Ibid. II, vi

10   You say it as you understand it.   *Ibid.*

11   When the wine goes in, strange things come out.
                                    Ibid. xii

12 O tender yearning, sweet hoping!
The golden time of first love!
The eye sees the open heaven,
The heart is intoxicated with bliss;
O that the beautiful time of young love
Could remain green forever.
                        The Song of the Bell [1799]

13 Appearance should never attain reality,
And if nature conquers, then must art retire.
            *To Goethe, when he put Voltaire's Mahomet on
            the stage [1800]*

14 Life is only error,
And death is knowledge.
                            Cassandra [1802]

15 I am better than my reputation.
                        Mary Stuart [1801], act III, sc. iv

16 For this should the singer accompany the king:
Both dwell on the heights of mankind.
                    The Maid of Orleans [1801], act I, sc. ii

17 Against stupidity the very gods
Themselves contend in vain.[3]
                                    Ibid. III, vi

18 Pain is short, and joy is eternal.
                                Ibid. last lines

19 On the mountains there is freedom!
The world is perfect everywhere,
Save where man comes with his torment.
                    The Bride of Messina [1803], act IV, sc. vii

---

[1]Translated by COLERIDGE.
[2]Der Krieg ernährt den Krieg.
[3]Against boredom even the gods themselves struggle in vain.
—NIETZSCHE, *The Antichrist [1888], 48*

20 The mountain cannot frighten one who was born
on it.
                        Wilhelm Tell [1804], act III, sc. i

21 Who reflects too much will accomplish little.
                                    Ibid.

22 You saw his weakness, and he will never forgive
you.
                                    Ibid.

23 This feat of Tell, the archer, will be told
While yonder mountains stand upon their base.
By heaven! The apple's cleft right through the
core.
                                    Ibid. iii

Mary Wollstonecraft
[Mary Wollstonecraft Godwin]
1759–1797

24   Nothing, I am sure, calls forth the faculties so
much as the being obliged to struggle with the
world.
            *Thoughts on the Education of Daughters [1787].
            Matrimony*

25   No man chooses evil because it is evil; he only
mistakes it for happiness, the good he seeks.
                A Vindication of the Rights of Men [1790]

26   Virtue can only flourish amongst equals.
                                    Ibid.

27   Till women are more rationally educated, the
progress in human virtue and improvement in
knowledge must receive continual checks.
                *A Vindication of the Rights of Women [1792],
                ch. 3*

28   If women be educated for dependence; that is, to
act according to the will of another fallible being,
and submit, right or wrong, to power, where are we
to stop?   *Ibid.*

29   How can a rational being be ennobled by anything that is not obtained by its own exertions?
                                    Ibid.

30   Women are systematically degraded by receiving
the trivial attentions which men think it manly to
pay to the sex, when, in fact, men are insultingly
supporting their own superiority.   *Ibid. 4*

31   It would be an endless task to trace the variety of
meannesses, cares, and sorrows into which women
are plunged by the prevailing opinion that they were
created rather to feel than reason, and that all the
power they obtain must be obtained by their charms
and weakness.   *Ibid.*

32   It is justice, not charity, that is wanting in the
world.   *Ibid.*

33   Women ought to have representatives, instead of
being arbitrarily governed without any direct share
allowed them in the deliberations of government.
                                    Ibid. 9

1   Till society is very differently constituted, parents, I fear, will still insist on being obeyed because they will be obeyed, and constantly endeavor to settle that power on a divine right which will not bear the investigation of reason.

> *A Vindication of the Rights of Women, ch. 11*

2   Every political good carried to the extreme must be productive of evil.

> *The French Revolution [1794], bk. V, ch. 4*

3   Executions, far from being useful examples to the survivors, have, I am persuaded, a quite contrary effect, by hardening the heart they ought to terrify. Besides, the fear of an ignominious death, I believe, never deterred anyone from the commission of a crime, because in committing it the mind is roused to activity about present circumstances.

> *Letters Written During a Short Residence
> in Sweden, Norway, and Denmark [1796].
> Letter 19*

4   The same energy of character which renders a man a daring villain would have rendered him useful to society, had that society been well organized.

> *Ibid.*

5   We reason deeply, when we forcibly feel.

> *Ibid.*

6   It is the preservation of the species, not of individuals, which appears to be the design of Deity throughout the whole of nature.   *Ibid. 22*

François Noël Babeuf [Gracchus]
1760–1797

7   Let the revolting distinction of rich and poor disappear once and for all, the distinction of great and small, of masters and valets, of governors and governed. Let there be no other difference between human beings than those of age and sex. Since all have the same needs and the same faculties, let there be one education for all, one food for all.

> *Manifesto of the Equals [c. 1795]*

8   We aim at something more sublime and more equitable—the common good, or the community of goods. . . . We demand, we would have, the communal enjoyment of the fruits of the earth, fruits which are for everyone.   *Ibid.*

Joseph Rouget de Lisle
1760–1836

9 Allons, enfants de la patrie,
Le jour de gloire est arrivé! . . .
Aux armes, citoyens!
Formez vos bataillons!
Marchons! Marchons! Qu'un sang impur
Abreuve nos sillons!

> *The Marseillaise [1792][1]*

[1]Forward, sons of France, the day of glory has come!
. . . To arms, citizens! Line up in battalions! Let us march on!

Antoine Boulay de la Meurthe
1761–1840

10   It is worse than a crime, it is a blunder [C'est pire qu'un crime, c'est une faute].[2]

> *On the execution of the Duc d'Enghien [1804]*

August Friedrich Ferdinand von Kotzebue
1761–1819

11 There is another and a better world.

> *The Stranger [1798], act I, sc. i*

William Lisle Bowles
1762–1850

12 The cause of Freedom is the cause of God!

> *The Right Honorable Edmund Burke [1791],
> l. 78*

George Colman the Younger
1762–1836

13   Tell 'em Queen Anne's dead.[3]

> *The Heir-at-Law [1797], act I, sc. i*

14   Not to be sneezed at.   *Ibid. II, i*

15 When taken,
To be well shaken.

> *Broad Grins [1802]. The Newcastle Apothecary*

16   John Bull;[4] or, The Englishman's Fireside.

> *Title of play [1803]*

17   His heart runs away with his head.

> *Who Wants a Guinea? [1805], act I, sc. i*

18   O Miss Bailey!
Unfortunate Miss Bailey!

> *Love Laughs at Locksmiths [1806], act II, song*

19 Says he, "I am a handsome man, but I'm a gay deceiver."

> *Ibid.*

Dorothea Jordan
1762–1816

20 "Oh where, and Oh! where is your Highland laddie gone?"

And let the impure blood [of our enemies] drench our fields.
  Composed in the garrison at Strasbourg and originally called *Chant de guerre de l'armée du Rhin*, the *Marseillaise* took its name from the patriots of Marseilles, who first made it known in Paris.

[2]Attributed also to TALLEYRAND and FOUCHÉ. Sainte-Beuve attributed it to BOULAY DE LA MEURTHE.

[3]The phrase became proverbial for telling what everybody knows.

[4]The origin of the supposed type of the British character.

"He's gone to fight the French, for King George
  upon the throne,
And it's Oh! in my heart, how I wish him safe at
  home!"

The Blue Bells of Scotland

Johann Paul Friedrich Richter
[Jean Paul]
1763–1825

1 Weltschmerz.[1]

Selina; or, Above Immortality [1827], 2

Samuel Rogers
1763–1855

2 Think nothing done while aught remains to do.

Human Life [1819], l. 49

3 Never less alone than when alone.

Ibid. l. 756

4 By many a temple half as old as Time.

Italy. A Farewell

5 Go! you may call it madness, folly;
  You shall not chase my gloom away!
  There's such a charm in melancholy
  I would not if I could be gay.

To —— [1814], st. 1

6   It doesn't much signify whom one marries, for
one is sure to find next morning that it was someone
else.   *Table Talk*

Robert Hall
1764–1831

7   Call things by their right names. . . . Glass of
brandy and water! That is the current but not the
appropriate name: ask for a glass of liquid fire and
distilled damnation.

From OLINTHUS GREGORY, *Brief Memoir of the
Life of Hall*

Gaston Pierre Marc, Duc de Lévis
1764–1830

8 Noblesse oblige [Rank has its obligations].[2]

Maxims and Reflections [1808]

Thomas Morton
1764–1838

9 Push on—keep moving.

A Cure for the Heartache [1797], act II, sc. i

[1]Literally, world pain.
[2]See Sophocles, 65:9, and Euripides, 69:10.

10 Approbation from Sir Hubert Stanley is praise
indeed.   *Ibid. V, ii*

11 What will Mrs. Grundy say? What will Mrs.
Grundy think?[3]

Speed the Plow [1798], act I, sc. i

Ann Radcliffe
1764–1823

12 Fate sits on these dark battlements and frowns,
  And as the portal opens to receive me,
  A voice in hollow murmurs through the courts
  Tells of a nameless deed.

The Mysteries of Udolpho [1794], motto

Robert Goodloe Harper
1765–1825

13   Millions for defense, but not one cent for tribute.[4]

*Toast at banquet for John Marshall [June 18,
1798]*

Sir James Mackintosh
1765–1832

14   Diffused knowledge immortalizes itself.

Vindiciae Gallicae [1791]

15   The Commons, faithful to their system, remained
in a wise and masterly inactivity.   *Ibid.*

16   The frivolous work of polished idleness.

*Dissertation on Ethical Philosophy [1830].
Remarks on Thomas Brown*

17   Disciplined inaction.

*History of the Revolution in England in 1688
[1834], ch. 7*

James Smithson
1765–1829

18   To found at Washington, under the name of the
Smithsonian Institution, an establishment for the increase and diffusion of knowledge among men.[5]

*Bequest [1829] with which the Smithsonian
Institution was established [1846]*

[3]See Herbert Spencer, 493:4.
[4]In 1797 a secret agent from Talleyrand told Charles Cotes-
worth Pinckney, minister to the French republic, that the
American commissioners in Paris to protest French attacks on
U.S. shipping would be received only if they paid a $50,000
bribe and made a large loan to the French government. Pinckney's reply was: "Not a sixpence, sir." Later, Harper's remark
was attributed to him.
[5]Quoted by John Quincy Adams in the *Committee Report
on the Smithson Bequest* [March 5, 1840].
See John Quincy Adams, 369:4.

Isaac D'Israeli
1766–1848

1   Whatever is felicitously expressed risks being worse expressed: it is a wretched taste to be gratified with mediocrity when the excellent lies before us.
Curiosities of Literature [1834]. On Quotation

Thomas Robert Malthus
1766–1834

2   Population, when unchecked, increases in a geometrical ratio. Subsistence increases only in an arithmetical ratio. A slight acquaintance with numbers will show the immensity of the first power in comparison of the second.
An Essay on the Principle of Population [1798]

Ernst Friedrich Herbert von Münster
1766–1839

3   Absolutism tempered by assassination.
Description of the Russian Constitution

Carolina Oliphant, Baroness Nairne
1766–1845

4 Better lo'ed ye canna be,
 Will ye no come back again?
  Life and Songs [1869]. Bonnie Charlie's Now Awa' [1]

5 Charlie is my darling, the young Chevalier.
  Ibid. Charlie Is My Darling [1]

6 We'll up an' gie them a blaw, a blaw,
 Wi' a hundred pipers an' a', an' a'.
  Ibid. The Hundred Pipers

7 Gude nicht, and joy be wi' you a'.
  Ibid. Gude Nicht

8 A penniless lass wi' a lang pedigree.
  Ibid. The Laird o' Cockpen

9 I'm wearin' awa'
 To the land o' the leal.
  Ibid. The Land o' the Leal

Germaine de Staël
[Anna Louise Germaine Necker, Baronne de Staël-Holstein]
1766–1817

10   Love is the whole history of a woman's life, it is but an episode in a man's. [2]
De l'Influence des Passions [1796]

[1] Also attributed to James Hogg.
[2] L'amour est l'histoire de la vie des femmes, c'est un épisode dans celle des hommes.

11   A man must know how to defy opinion; a woman how to submit to it.   *Delphine [1802]*

12   To understand everything makes one tolerant. [3]
Corinne [1807], bk. XVIII, ch. 5

13   I would gladly give half of the wit with which I am credited for half of the beauty you possess.
Letter to Juliette Récamier

John Quincy Adams
1767–1848

14   I can never join with my voice in the toast which I see in the papers attributed to one of our gallant naval heroes. I cannot ask of heaven success, even for my country, in a cause where she should be in the wrong. [4] *Fiat justitia, pereat coelum.* [5] My toast would be, may our country be always successful, but whether successful or otherwise, always right.
Letter to John Adams [August 1, 1816]

15   America, with the same voice which spoke herself into existence as a nation, proclaimed to mankind the inextinguishable rights of human nature, and the only lawful foundations of government.
Address [July 4, 1821]

16   America . . . well knows that by once enlisting under other banners than her own, were they even the banners of foreign independence, she would involve herself beyond the power of extraction, in all the wars of interest and intrigue, of individual avarice, envy, and ambition, which assume the colors and usurp the standard of freedom. The fundamental maxims of her policy would insensibly change from liberty to force. . . . She might become dictatress of the world. She would be no longer the ruler of her own spirit.   *Ibid.*

17   Individual liberty is individual power, and as the power of a community is a mass compounded of individual powers, the nation which enjoys the most freedom must necessarily be in proportion to its numbers the most powerful nation.
Letter to James Lloyd [October 1, 1822]

18 Who but shall learn that freedom is the prize
 Man still is bound to rescue or maintain;
 That nature's God commands the slave to rise,
 And on the oppressor's head to break the chain.
 Roll, years of promise, rapidly roll round,
 Till not a slave shall on this earth be found.
  Poem

[3] Tout comprendre rend très indulgent.
Attributed to Germaine de Staël are similar phrases: Comprendre c'est pardonner [To understand is to forgive]. Tout comprendre c'est tout pardonner [To know everything is to forgive everything].
[4] See Charles Churchill, 333:19; Decatur, 390:22; and Schurz, 510:18.
[5] See Anonymous: Latin, 119:2.

1 This house will bear witness to his piety; this town, his birthplace, to his munificence; history to his patriotism; posterity to the depth and compass of his mind.
From his epitaph for John Adams [1829][1]

2 In charity to all mankind, bearing no malice or ill will to any human being, and even compassionating those who hold in bondage their fellow men, not knowing what they do.[2]
Letter to A. Bronson [July 30, 1838]

3 The great problem of legislation is, so to organize the civil government of a community . . . that in the operation of human institutions upon social action, self-love and social may be made the same.[3]
Society and Civilization; in the American Review [July 1845]

4 To furnish the means of acquiring knowledge is . . . the greatest benefit that can be conferred upon mankind. It prolongs life itself and enlarges the sphere of existence.[4]
Report on the establishment of the Smithsonian Institution [c. 1846]

5 This is the last of earth! I am content.
Last words [February 21, 1848]

Black Hawk[5]
1767–1838

6 I saw my evil day at hand. The sun rose dim on us in the morning, and at night it sank in a dark cloud, and looked like a ball of fire. That was the last sun that shone on Black Hawk. His heart is dead. . . . He is now a prisoner to the white man.
Speech upon surrender, Prairie du Chien, Wisconsin [August 27, 1832]

7 [Black Hawk] has done nothing for which an Indian ought to be ashamed. He has fought for his countrymen, the squaws and papooses, against white men, who came year after year, to cheat them and take away their lands. You know the cause of our making war.[6] It is known to all white men. They ought to be ashamed of it. *Ibid.*

Andrew Jackson
1767–1845

8 The individual who refuses to defend his rights when called by his Government, deserves to be a slave, and must be punished as an enemy of his country and friend to her foe.
Proclamation to the people of Louisiana from Mobile [September 21, 1814]

9 The brave man inattentive to his duty, is worth little more to his country, than the coward who deserts her in the hour of danger.
To troops who had abandoned their lines during the battle of New Orleans [January 8, 1815]

10 Our Federal Union! it must be preserved!
Toast at Jefferson Birthday Celebration [1830]

11 Every man is equally entitled to protection by law; but when the laws undertake to add . . . artificial distinctions, to grant titles, gratuities, and exclusive privileges, to make the rich richer and the potent more powerful, the humble members of society—the farmers, mechanics, and laborers—who have neither the time nor the means of securing like favors to themselves, have a right to complain of the injustice of their government.
Veto of the Bank Bill [July 10, 1832]

12 There are no necessary evils in government. Its evils exist only in its abuses. If it would confine itself to equal protection, and, as Heaven does its rains, shower its favors alike on the high and the low, the rich and the poor, it would be an unqualified blessing. *Ibid.*

13 One man with courage makes a majority.
Attributed

François René de Chateaubriand
1768–1848

14 [On his conversion to Christianity:] I wept and I believed.[7] *Le Génie du Christianisme [1802]*

15 The original writer is not one who imitates nobody, but one whom nobody can imitate.[8]
Ibid.

16 Achilles exists only through Homer. Take away the art of writing from this world, and you will probably take away its glory.[9]
Les Natchez [1826], preface

Tecumseh[10]
1768–1813

17 These lands are ours. No one has a right to remove us, because we were the first owners. The Great Spirit above has appointed this place for us, on which to light our fires, and here we will remain.

---

[1]Inscribed on one of the portals of the United First Parish Church Unitarian (Church of the Presidents), Quincy, Massachusetts.
[2]See Lincoln, 450:11.
[3]See Pope, 302:5.
[4]See Smithson, 367:18.
[5]Ma-ke-tai-me-she-kia-kiak.
Chief of the Sauk and Fox Indians.
[6]The Black Hawk War [1832].
[7]J'ai pleuré et j'ai cru.
[8]L'écrivain original n'est pas celui qui n'imite personne, mais celui que personne ne peut imiter.
[9]See Alexander the Great, 80:23.
[10]Chief of the Shawnees.

As to boundaries, the Great Spirit knows no boundaries, nor will his red children acknowledge any.[1]

To Joseph Barron, messenger of President James Madison [1810]

1   My father! The Great Spirit is my father! The earth is my mother—and on her bosom I will recline.

Council at Vincennes, Indiana Territory [August 14, 1810]. Answer to request to sit at "his father's" (Governor William Henry Harrison's) side

2   I am a Shawnee. My forefathers were warriors. Their son is a warrior. From them I take only my existence. From my tribe I take nothing. I am the maker of my own fortune. And oh, that I might make the fortunes of my red people, and of my country, as great as the conceptions of my mind, when I think of the Great Spirit that rules this universe.   *Ibid. Speech to Harrison*

3   Once they were a happy race. Now they are made miserable by the white people, who are never contented but are always encroaching.   *Ibid.*

4   Sell a country! Why not sell the air, the clouds and the great sea, as well as the earth? Did not the Great Spirit make them all for the use of his children?   *Ibid.*

5   Our lives are in the hands of the Great Spirit. He gave to our ancestors the lands which we possess. We are determined to defend them, and if it is His will, our bones shall whiten on them, but we will never give them up.[2]

Speech to Major General Henry Procter, British commander, Fort Malden [September 1813]

Napoleon I [Napoleon Bonaparte]
1769–1821

6   Soldiers, from the summit of yonder pyramids forty centuries look down upon you.

In Egypt [July 21, 1798]

7   Go, sir, gallop, and don't forget that the world was made in six days. You can ask me for anything you like, except time.

To an aide [1803]. From R. M. JOHNSTON, The Corsican

8   A form of government that is not the result of a long sequence of shared experiences, efforts, and endeavors can never take root.

[1803]. From J. CHRISTOPHER HEROLD, The Mind of Napoleon [1955]

9   From the sublime to the ridiculous is but a step.[3]

To the Abbé du Pradt, on the return from Russia [1812], referring to the retreat from Moscow

10   You write to me that it's impossible; the word is not French.

Letter to General Lemarois [July 9, 1813]

11   What is the throne?—a bit of wood gilded and covered with velvet. I am the state[4]—I alone am here the representative of the people. Even if I had done wrong you should not have reproached me in public —people wash their dirty linen at home.[5] France has more need of me than I of France.

To the Senate [1814]

12   France is invaded; I am leaving to take command of my troops, and, with God's help and their valor, I hope soon to drive the enemy beyond the frontier.

At Paris [January 23, 1814]

13   The bullet that will kill me is not yet cast.

At Montereau [February 17, 1814]

14   The Allied Powers having proclaimed that the Emperor Napoleon is the sole obstacle to the reestablishment of peace in Europe, he, faithful to his oath, declares that he is ready to descend from the throne, to quit France, and even to relinquish life, for the good of his country.

Act of Abdication [April 4, 1814]

15   Unite for the public safety, if you would remain an independent nation.

Proclamation to the French People [June 22, 1815]

16   Wherever wood can swim, there I am sure to find this flag of England.   *At Rochefort [July 1815]*

17   Whatever shall we do in that remote spot? Well, we will write our memoirs. Work is the scythe of time.

On board H.M.S. Bellerophon [August 1815]

18   [Of his relations with the Empress Josephine:] I generally had to give in.

On St. Helena [May 19, 1816]

19   My maxim was, *la carrière est ouverte aux talents*, without distinction of birth or fortune.

Ibid. [March 3, 1817]

20   Our hour is marked, and no one can claim a moment of life beyond what fate has predestined.

To Dr. Arnott [April 1821]

21   Two o'clock in the morning courage: I mean unprepared courage.[6]

[December 4, 5, 1815]. From LAS CASES, Mémorial de Ste-Hélène [1823]

---

[1]He remembered the belligerent ants, who claimed their boundaries, and the pacific geese, who did not. . . . All those puffins, razorbills, guillemots and kittiwakes had lived together peacefully, preserving their own kinds of civilization without war—because they claimed no boundaries.—T. H. WHITE [1906–1964], *The Once and Future King* [1939], *bk. IV, ch. 14*

[2]Tecumseh was killed in the battle of the Thames River [October 5, 1813].

[3]Du sublime au ridicule il n'y a qu'un pas.
The saying has been attributed also to TALLEYRAND.
See Paine, 341:11.

[4]See Louis XIV, 281:3.

[5]Il faut laver son linge sale en famille [One should wash one's dirty linen at home].—*Saying current since about 1720*

[6]Le courage de l'improviste.

1   Madame Montholon having inquired what troops he considered the best, "Those which are victorious, Madame," replied the Emperor.

From BOURRIENNE, *Memoirs [1829]*

2   A silk stocking filled with mud.

Description of Talleyrand[1]

3   An army marches on its stomach.[2]

Attributed

4   Every French soldier carries a marshal's baton in his knapsack.[3]   *Attributed*

5   Perfidious Albion.[4]   *Attributed*

6   Chief of the Army.[5]   *Last words*

Arthur Wellesley, Duke of Wellington
1769–1852

7   Nothing except a battle lost can be half so melancholy as a battle won.

Dispatch from the field of Waterloo [June 1815]

8   I used to say of him [Napoleon] that his presence on the field made the difference of forty thousand men.

[November 2, 1831]. From PHILIP HENRY, EARL OF STANHOPE, *Notes of Conversations with the Duke of Wellington [1888]*

9   The only thing I am afraid of is fear.[6]

Ibid. [November 3, 1831]

10   Ours [our army] is composed of the scum of the earth—the mere scum of the earth.

Ibid. [November 4, 1831]

11   My rule always was to do the business of the day in the day.   *Ibid. [November 2, 1835]*

12   They wanted this iron fist to command them.

Ibid. [November 8, 1840]; of troops sent by Wellington to the Canadian frontier in the war with America

13   There is no mistake; there has been no mistake; and there shall be no mistake.

Wellingtoniana [1832], p. 78

14   I don't care a twopenny damn what becomes of the ashes of Napoleon Bonaparte.   *Attributed*

15   The battle of Waterloo was won on the playing fields of Eton.

From SIR WILLIAM FRASER, *Words on Wellington [1889]*

---

[1]Attributed by SAINTE-BEUVE.

[2]No man can be a patriot on an empty stomach.—BRANN, *The Iconoclast, Old Glory* [July 4, 1893]

[3]Tout soldat français porte dans sa giberne le bâton de maréchal de France.

[4]L'Angleterre, ah! la perfide Angleterre.—BOSSUET, *Sermon sur la Circoncision*

[5]Tête d'armée.

[6]See *Proverbs* 3:25, 20:22; Montaigne, 145:10; Francis Bacon, 158:18; Thoreau, 476:26; and F. D. Roosevelt, 648:18.

16   Publish and be damned.

Attributed; when the courtesan Harriette Wilson threatened to publish her memoirs and his letters

Ludwig van Beethoven
1770–1827

17   I want to seize fate by the throat.

Letter to Dr. Franz Wegeler [November 16, 1801]

18   Art! Who comprehends her? With whom can one consult concerning this great goddess?

Letter to Bettina von Arnim [August 11, 1810]

19   The world is a king, and, like a king, desires flattery in return for favor; but true art is selfish and perverse—it will not submit to the mold of flattery.

Conversations [March 1820]

Pierre Jacques Étienne, Count Cambronne
1770–1842

20   The Guards die, but never surrender.[7]

Attributed. Reply to surrender demand at Waterloo [1815]

George Canning
1770–1827

21   I give thee sixpence! I will see thee damned first.

The Anti-Jacobin, no. 11 [1797]. The Friend of Humanity and the Knife-Grinder, st. 9

22   I think of those companions true
Who studied with me at the U-
niversity of Göttingen.

Ibid. no. 30 [1798]. The Rovers, song, st. 1

23   A steady patriot of the world alone,
The friend of every country but his own.

Ibid. no 36 [1798]. New Morality, l. 113

24   And finds, with keen, discriminating sight,
Black's not so black—nor white so *very* white.

Ibid. l. 199

25   Give me th'avowed, th'erect, the manly foe,
Bold I can meet—perhaps may turn his blow;

---

[7]La Garde meurt, mais ne se rend pas.

Probably the invention of a French journalist; Cambronne denied ever having said it. "Merde!," a more likely reply also attributed to him, has been euphemized as "Le mot de Cambronne."

The finest word, perhaps, that a Frenchman ever uttered. . . . To speak that word, and then to die, what could be more grand! for to accept death is to die, and it is not the fault of this man, if, in the storm of grape, he survived.—HUGO, *Les Misérables* [1862], *Cosette, bk. I. Waterloo, ch. 15, translated by* CHARLES E. WILBOUR

But of all plagues, good Heav'n, thy wrath can
  send,
Save, save, oh! save me from the Candid Friend![1]
  The Anti-Jacobin, no. 36. New Morality, l. 207

1 When our perils are past, shall our gratitude
  sleep?
No—here's to the pilot that weathered the storm.
  *Song for the Inauguration of the Pitt Club [May
  25, 1802]*

2 In matters of commerce the fault of the Dutch
Is offering too little and asking too much.
  *Dispatch to Sir Charles Bagot, British minister
  at The Hague [January 31, 1826]*

3   I called the New World into existence to redress
the balance of the Old.
  The King's Message [December 12, 1826]

Georg Wilhelm Friedrich Hegel
1770–1831

4   What is reasonable is real; that which is real is
reasonable.   *Philosophy of Right [1821]*

5   The owl of Minerva spreads its wings only with
the falling of dusk.[2]   *Ibid.*

6   What experience and history teach is this—that
people and governments never have learned anything from history, or acted on principles deduced
from it.
  Philosophy of History [1832],[3] introduction

7   Amid the pressure of great events, a general principle gives no help.   *Ibid.*

8   To him who looks upon the world rationally, the
world in its turn presents a rational aspect. The
relation is mutual.   *Ibid.*

9   The history of the world is none other than the
progress of the consciousness of freedom.   *Ibid.*

10   We may affirm absolutely that nothing great in
the world has been accomplished without passion.
    Ibid.

11   It is easier to discover a deficiency in individuals,
in states, and in Providence, than to see their real
import and value.   *Ibid.*

12   Serious occupation is labor that has reference to
some want.   *Ibid. pt. I, sec. 2, ch. 1*

13   It is a matter of perfect indifference where a thing
originated; the only question is: "Is it true in and for
itself?"   *Ibid. III, 3, 2*

---

[1]Defend me from my friends; I can defend myself from my
enemies.—*Attributed to* CLAUDE LOUIS HECTOR, DUC DE VIL-
LARS [1653–1734], *when taking leave of Louis XIV*
[2]Translated by T. M. KNOX.
[3]Translated by J. SIBREE.
  Quoted by G. B. Shaw in *The Revolutionist's Handbook.*

James Hogg
1770–1835

14 We'll o'er the water, we'll o'er the sea,
We'll o'er the water to Charlie;
Come weal, come woe, we'll gather and go,
And live and die wi' Charlie.
  O'er the Water to Charlie

Joseph Hopkinson
1770–1842

15 Hail, Columbia! happy land!
Hail, ye heroes! heaven-born band!
Who fought and bled in Freedom's cause.
  Hail, Columbia [1798],[4] st. 1

William Wordsworth
1770–1850

16 And homeless near a thousand homes I stood,
And near a thousand tables pined and wanted
  food.
  Guilt and Sorrow [written 1791–1794],[5] st. 41

17 ——A simple child,[6]
That lightly draws its breath,
And feels its life in every limb,
What should it know of death?
  We Are Seven [1798], st. 1

18 Have I not reason to lament
What man has made of man?[7]
  Lines Written in Early Spring [1798], st. 6

19 Nor less I deem that there are Powers
Which of themselves our minds impress;
That we can feed this mind of ours
In a wise passiveness.
  Expostulation and Reply [1798], st. 6

20 Come forth into the light of things,
Let Nature be your teacher.
  The Tables Turned [1798], st. 4

21 One impulse from a vernal wood
May teach you more of man,
Of moral evil and of good,
Than all the sages can.[8]

  Ibid. st. 6

---

[4]The music, generally attributed to PHILIP PHILE, was Washington's inaugural march. Hopkinson supplied verses at a
singer's request, and the song won instant acclaim.
[5]Published 1842.
[6]In the first edition the line is: A simple child, dear brother
Jim. It was reduced to the current text in the 1815 edition of
Wordsworth's poems.
[7]See Pliny the Elder, 104:6, and Burns, 361:8.
[8]See Saint Bernard, 121:8, and Shakespeare, 190:7 and 191:5.

1
   That best portion of a good man's life,
His little, nameless, unremembered acts
Of kindness and of love.
> *Lines Composed a Few Miles Above Tintern*
> *Abbey [1798], l. 33*

2
   Blessed mood,
In which the burthen of the mystery,
In which the heavy and the weary weight
Of all this unintelligible world,
Is lightened.
> *Ibid. l. 37*

3
While with an eye made quiet by the power
Of harmony, and the deep power of joy,
We see into the life of things.
> *Ibid. l. 47*

4
   The sounding cataract
Haunted me like a passion: the tall rock,
The mountain, and the deep and gloomy wood,
Their colors and their forms, were then to me
An appetite; a feeling and a love,
That had no need of a remoter charm,
By thought supplied, nor any interest
Unborrowed from the eye.
> *Ibid. l. 76*

5
   I have learned
To look on nature, not as in the hour
Of thoughtless youth; but hearing oftentimes
The still, sad music of humanity,
Nor harsh nor grating, though of ample power
To chasten and subdue. And I have felt
A presence that disturbs me with the joy
Of elevated thoughts; a sense sublime
Of something far more deeply interfused,
Whose dwelling is the light of setting suns,
And the round ocean and the living air,
And the blue sky, and in the mind of man:
A motion and a spirit, that impels
All thinking things, all objects of all thought,
And rolls through all things.
> *Ibid. l. 88*

6 Knowing that Nature never did betray
The heart that loved her.
> *Ibid. l. 122*

7 Fair seedtime had my soul, and I grew up
Fostered alike by beauty and by fear.
> *The Prelude [written 1799–1805],*[1] *bk. I, l. 301*

8 Dust as we are, the immortal spirit grows
Like harmony in music; there is a dark
Inscrutable workmanship that reconciles
Discordant elements, makes them cling together
In one society.
> *Ibid. l. 340*

9
   The grim shape
Towered up between me and the stars, and still,
For so it seemed, with purpose of its own

[1] Published 1850.

And measured motion like a living thing,
Strode after me.
> *Ibid. l. 381*

10
   Where the statue stood
Of Newton with his prism and silent face,
The marble index of a mind forever
Voyaging through strange seas of thought, alone.
> *Ibid. III, l. 60*

11 But Europe at that time was thrilled with joy,
France standing on the top of golden hours,
And human nature seeming born again.
> *Ibid. VI, l. 339*

12 Bliss was it in that dawn to be alive,
But to be young was very heaven!
> *Ibid. XI, l. 108*

13
   There is
One great society alone on earth:
The noble Living and the noble Dead.
> *Ibid. l. 393*

14 Prophets of Nature, we to them will speak
A lasting inspiration, sanctified
By reason, blest by faith: what we have loved,
Others will love, and we will teach them how;
Instruct them how the mind of man becomes
A thousand times more beautiful than the earth
On which he dwells.
> *Ibid. XIV, l. 444*

15
   Poetry is the breath and finer spirit of all knowledge; it is the impassioned expression which is in the countenance of all Science.
> *Lyrical Ballads [2nd ed., 1800]. Preface*

16
   In spite of difference of soil and climate, of language and manners, of laws and customs—in spite of things silently gone out of mind, and things violently destroyed, the Poet binds together by passion and knowledge the vast empire of human society, as it is spread over the whole earth, and over all time.
> *Ibid.*

17
   I have said that poetry is the spontaneous overflow of powerful feelings: it takes its origin from emotion recollected in tranquillity.   *Ibid.*

18 What fond and wayward thoughts will slide
Into a lover's head!
"O mercy!" to myself I cried,
"If Lucy should be dead!"
> *Strange Fits of Passion Have I Known [1800],*
> *st. 7*

19 She dwelt among the untrodden ways
Beside the springs of Dove,
A maid whom there were none to praise
And very few to love:[2]

[2] He lived amidst th' untrodden ways / To Rydal Lake that lead; / A bard whom there were none to praise, / And very few to read. / Unread his works—his "Milk White Doe" / With dust is dark and dim; / It's still in Longmans' shop, and oh! / The difference to him!—*Parody by* HARTLEY COLERIDGE

A violet by a mossy stone
Half hidden from the eye!
—Fair as a star, when only one
Is shining in the sky.

She lived unknown, and few could know
When Lucy ceased to be;
But she is in her grave, and, oh,
The difference to me!
She Dwelt Among the Untrodden Ways [1800]

1 A slumber did my spirit seal;
I had no human fears:
She seemed a thing that could not feel
The touch of earthly years.

No motion has she now, no force;
She neither hears nor sees;
Rolled round in earth's diurnal course,
With rocks, and stones, and trees.
A Slumber Did My Spirit Seal [1800]

2   A fingering slave,
One that would peep and botanize
Upon his mother's grave?
A Poet's Epitaph [1800], st. 5

3 A reasoning, self-sufficing thing,
An intellectual All-in-all!
Ibid. st. 8

4 The harvest of a quiet eye.
Ibid. st. 13

5 Something between a hindrance and a help.
Michael [1800], l. 189

6 I traveled among unknown men,
In lands beyond the sea;
Nor, England! did I know till then
What love I bore to thee.
I Traveled Among Unknown Men [1807], st. 1

7 My heart leaps up when I behold
A rainbow in the sky:
So was it when my life began;
So is it now I am a man;
So be it when I shall grow old,
Or let me die!
The child is father of the man;[1]
And I could wish my days to be
Bound each to each by natural piety.
My Heart Leaps Up [1807][2]

8 Sweet childish days, that were as long
As twenty days are now.
*To a Butterfly (I've Watched You Now a Full
Half-Hour) [1807], st. 2*

9 I thought of Chatterton, the marvelous boy,
The sleepless soul that perished in his pride;
Of him[3] who walked in glory and in joy
Following his plow, along the mountainside:

[1]See Milton, 260:32.
[2]The last three lines are the epigraph for *Intimations of Immortality*, 375:3.
[3]Robert Burns.

By our own spirits are we deified:
We Poets in our youth begin in gladness;
But thereof come in the end despondency and
madness.[4]
Resolution and Independence [1807], st. 7

10 Choice word and measured phrase, above the
reach
Of ordinary men.
Ibid. st. 14

11 And mighty poets in their misery dead.
Ibid. st. 17

12 Earth has not anything to show more fair:
Dull would he be of soul who could pass by
A sight so touching in its majesty.
*Composed upon Westminster Bridge,
September 3, 1802 [1807], l. 1*

13 Ne'er saw I, never felt, a calm so deep!
The river glideth at his own sweet will!
Dear God! the very houses seem asleep;
And all that mighty heart is lying still!
Ibid. l. 11

14 Plain living and high thinking are no more:
The homely beauty of the good old cause
Is gone; our peace, our fearful innocence,
And pure religion breathing household laws.
Written in London, September 1802 [1807]

15 It is a beauteous evening, calm and free,
The holy time is quiet as a nun
Breathless with adoration.
It Is a Beauteous Evening [1807], l. 1

16 Thou liest in Abraham's bosom all the year;
And worship'st at the Temple's inner shrine,
God being with thee when we know it not.
Ibid. l. 12

17 Once did she hold the gorgeous east in fee:
And was the safeguard of the west.
*On the Extinction of the Venetian Republic
[1807], l. 1*

18   Thou hast great allies;
Thy friends are exultations, agonies,
And love, and man's unconquerable mind.
To Toussaint L'Ouverture [1807], l. 12

19 Milton! thou shouldst be living at this hour:
England hath need of thee: she is a fen
Of stagnant waters.
London, 1802 [1807], l. 1

20 Thy soul was like a star, and dwelt apart;
Thou hadst a voice whose sound was like the sea:
Pure as the naked heavens, majestic, free,
So didst thou travel on life's common way,
In cheerful godliness.
Ibid. l. 9

[4]See Democritus, 70:*n*9; Robert Burton, 234:13; and Robert
Lowell, 742:16.

1 We must be free or die, who speak the tongue
   That Shakespeare spake; the faith and morals
      hold
   Which Milton held.
   > *It Is Not to Be Thought Of [1807], l. 11*

2 The music in my heart I bore
   Long after it was heard no more.
   > *The Solitary Reaper [1807], st. 4*

3 There was a time when meadow, grove, and
      stream,
   The earth, and every common sight,
      To me did seem
      Appareled in celestial light,
   The glory and the freshness of a dream.
   It is not now as it hath been of yore—
      Turn wheresoe'er I may,
         By night or day,
   The things which I have seen I now can see no
      more.
   > *Ode. Intimations of Immortality from
   > Recollections of Early Childhood [1807], st. 1*

4 The Rainbow comes and goes,
   And lovely is the Rose.
   > *Ibid. st. 2*

5   The sunshine is a glorious birth;
      But yet I know, where'er I go,
   That there hath passed away a glory from the
      earth.
   > *Ibid.*

6 Whither is fled the visionary gleam?
   Where is it now, the glory and the dream?
   > *Ibid. st. 4*

7 Our birth is but a sleep and a forgetting:
   The soul that rises with us, our life's star,
      Hath had elsewhere its setting,
         And cometh from afar:
      Not in entire forgetfulness,
      And not in utter nakedness,
   But trailing clouds of glory do we come
      From God, who is our home:
   Heaven lies about us in our infancy!
   Shades of the prison-house begin to close
      Upon the growing boy.
   > *Ibid. st. 5*

8 The youth, who daily farther from the east
      Must travel, still is Nature's priest,
      And by the vision splendid
      Is on his way attended;
   At length the man perceives it die away,
   And fade into the light of common day.
   > *Ibid.*

9 As if his whole vocation
   Were endless imitation.
   > *Ibid. st. 7*

10 O joy! that in our embers
   Is something that doth live,

That nature yet remembers
What was so fugitive!
> *Ibid. st. 9*

11 High instincts before which our mortal nature
   Did tremble like a guilty thing surprised.
   > *Ibid.*

12   Truths that wake,
   To perish never.
   > *Ibid.*

13   Though inland far we be,
   Our souls have sight of that immortal sea
      Which brought us hither.
   > *Ibid.*

14 Though nothing can bring back the hour
   Of splendor in the grass, of glory in the flower.
   > *Ibid. st. 10*

15 The clouds that gather round the setting sun
   Do take a sober coloring from an eye
   That hath kept watch o'er man's mortality;
   Another race hath been, and other palms are won.
   Thanks to the human heart by which we live,
   Thanks to its tenderness, its joys, and fears,
   To me the meanest flower that blows can give
   Thoughts that do often lie too deep for tears.
   > *Ibid. st. 11*

16 She was a phantom of delight
   When first she gleamed upon my sight;
   A lovely apparition, sent
   To be a moment's ornament.
   > *She Was a Phantom of Delight [1807], st. 1*

17 And now I see with eye serene
   The very pulse of the machine.
   > *Ibid. st. 3*

18 A perfect woman, nobly planned,
   To warn, to comfort, and command.
   And yet a Spirit still, and bright
   With something of angelic light.
   > *Ibid.*

19 I wandered lonely as a cloud
   That floats on high o'er vales and hills,
   When all at once I saw a crowd,
   A host, of golden daffodils.[1]
   > *I Wandered Lonely as a Cloud [1807], st. 1*

20 Continuous as the stars that shine
   And twinkle on the milky way.
   > *Ibid. st. 2*

21 Ten thousand saw I at a glance,
   Tossing their heads in sprightly dance.
   > *Ibid.*

22 A poet could not but be gay,
   In such a jocund company.
   > *Ibid. st. 3*

[1]See Larkin, 751:2.

1   That inward eye
Which is the bliss of solitude.
            I Wandered Lonely as a Cloud, st. 4

2 Stern daughter of the voice of God![1]
  O Duty!
                   Ode to Duty [1807], st. 1

3   A light to guide, a rod
To check the erring, and reprove.
                       Ibid.

4 Me this unchartered freedom tires;
  I feel the weight of chance desires;
  My hopes no more must change their name,
  I long for a repose that ever is the same.
                  Ibid. st. 5

5 Thou dost preserve the stars from wrong;
  And the most ancient heavens, through Thee, are
    fresh and strong.
                  Ibid. st. 7

6 The light that never was, on sea or land,
  The consecration, and the poet's dream.
    Elegiac Stanzas. Suggested by a Picture of Peele
    Castle in a Storm [1807], st. 4

7   A deep distress hath humanized my Soul.
                  Ibid. st. 9

8 Who is the happy Warrior? Who is he
  That every man in arms should wish to be?
    Character of the Happy Warrior [1807], l. 1

9 Who, doomed to go in company with pain,
  And fear, and bloodshed, miserable train!
  Turns his necessity to glorious gain.
                  Ibid. l. 12

10 Nuns fret not at their convent's narrow room.
            Nuns Fret Not [1807], l. 1

11 The world is too much with us; late and soon,
  Getting and spending, we lay waste our powers:
  Little we see in Nature that is ours;
  We have given our hearts away, a sordid boon!
    The World Is Too Much with Us [1807], l. 1

12   Great God! I'd rather be
  A pagan suckled in a creed outworn;
  So might I, standing on this pleasant lea,
  Have glimpses that would make me less forlorn;
  Have sight of Proteus rising from the sea;
  Or hear old Triton blow his wreathèd horn.
                  Ibid. l. 9

13 Where lies the land to which yon ship must go?
  Fresh as a lark mounting at break of day,
  Festively she puts forth in trim array.
        Where Lies the Land [1807], l. 1

14 Dreams, books, are each a world; and books, we
    know,
  Are a substantial world, both pure and good:

[1]See Milton, 260:6.

Round these, with tendrils strong as flesh and
    blood,
Our pastime and our happiness will grow.
           Personal Talk [1807], sonnet 3

15 A power is passing from the earth.
    Lines on the Expected Dissolution of Mr. Fox
    [1807], st. 5

16 Two voices are there: one is of the sea,[2]
  One of the mountains; each a mighty voice.
    Thought of a Briton on the Subjugation of
    Switzerland [1807], l. 1

17 The silence that is in the starry sky,
  The sleep that is among the lonely hills.
    Song at the Feast of Brougham Castle [1807],
    l. 163

18   Every great and original writer, in proportion as
he is great or original, must himself create the taste
by which he is to be relished.
      Letter to Lady Beaumont [May 21, 1807]

19   Strongest minds
Are often those of whom the noisy world
Hears least.
          The Excursion [1814],[3] bk. I, l. 91

20   The good die first,[4]
And they whose hearts are dry as summer dust
Burn to the socket.
                  Ibid. l. 500

21   I have seen
A curious child, who dwelt upon a tract
Of inland ground, applying to his ear
The convolutions of a smooth-lipped shell,
To which, in silence hushed, his very soul
Listened intensely; and his countenance soon
Brightened with joy, for from within were heard
Murmurings, whereby the monitor expressed
Mysterious union with its native sea.
Even such a shell the universe itself
Is to the ear of Faith; and there are times,
I doubt not, when to you it doth impart
Authentic tidings of invisible things;
Of ebb and flow, and ever-during power;
And central peace, subsisting at the heart
Of endless agitation.
                Ibid. IV, l. 1132

22   One in whom persuasion and belief
Had ripened into faith, and faith become
A passionate intuition.
                Ibid. l. 1293

[2]Two voices are there: one is of the deep; . . . / And one is
of an old half-witted sheep / Which bleats articulate monotony, / And indicates that two and one are three. . . . / And,
Wordsworth, both art thine.—JAMES KENNETH STEPHEN
[1859–1892], *Sonnet, Wordsworth* [1891]
   [3]This will never do.—FRANCIS JEFFREY [1773–1850], *opening sentence, review of* WORDSWORTH, *Excursion, Edinburgh
Review* [1814]
   [4]See Menander, 81:5.

1 Spires whose "silent finger points to heaven."[1]
                                        Ibid. VI, l. 19

2 A man he seems of cheerful yesterdays
    And confident tomorrows.
                                        Ibid. VII, l. 557

3 Surprised by joy—impatient as the wind.
                                        Surprised by Joy [1815], l. 1

4   The gods approve
    The depth, and not the tumult, of the soul.
                                        Laodamia [1815], st. 13

5 An ampler ether, a diviner air.
                                        Ibid. st. 18

6 Enough, if something from our hands have power
    To live, and act, and serve the future hour.
                                        *The River Duddon [1820], sonnet 34,
                                        Afterthought, l. 10*

7 We feel that we are greater than we know.
                                        Ibid. l. 14

8   The feather, whence the pen
    Was shaped that traced the lives of these good
            men,
    Dropped from an angel's wing.[2]
                                        *Ecclesiastical Sonnets [1822], pt. III, sonnet 5,
                                        Walton's Book of Lives, l. 2*

9 The unimaginable touch of Time.
                                        Ibid. 34. Mutability

10 Give all thou canst; high Heaven rejects the lore
    Of nicely calculated less or more.
                                        *Ibid. 43. Inside of King's College Chapel,
                                        Cambridge, l. 6*

11 But hushed be every thought that springs
    From out the bitterness of things.
                                        *Elegiac Stanzas. Addressed to Sir G. H. B.
                                        [1827], st. 7*

12 Type of the wise who soar, but never roam,
    True to the kindred points of heaven and home!
                                        To a Skylark [1827]

13 Scorn not the sonnet; Critic, you have frowned,
    Mindless of its just honors; with this key
    Shakespeare unlocked his heart.
                                        Scorn Not the Sonnet [1827], l. 1

14 Small service is true service while it lasts:
    Of humblest friends, bright creature! scorn not
            one:
    The daisy, by the shadow that it casts,
    Protects the lingering dewdrop from the sun.
                                        To a Child. Written in Her Album [1835]

[1] An instinctive taste teaches men to build their churches in
flat countries with spire steeples, which, as they cannot be
referred to any other object, point as with silent finger to the
sky and stars.—COLERIDGE, *The Friend* [1809], *no. 14*
    [2] The pen wherewith thou dost so heavenly sing / Made of a
quill from an angel's wing.—HENRY CONSTABLE [1562–1613],
Sonnet

Thomas John Dibdin
1771–1841

15 Oh, it's a snug little island!
    A right little, tight little island.
                                        The Snug Little Island

James Montgomery
1771–1854

16 Give me the hand that is honest and hearty,
    Free as the breeze and unshackled by party.
                                        Give Me Thy Hand, st. 2

17 Here in the body pent,
    Absent from Him I roam,
    Yet nightly pitch my moving tent
    A day's march nearer home.
                                        At Home in Heaven

18 Prayer is the soul's sincere desire,
    Uttered or unexpressed;
    The motion of a hidden fire
    That trembles in the breast.
                                        What Is Prayer? st. 1

Sir Walter Scott
1771–1832

19 The way was long, the wind was cold,
    The Minstrel was infirm and old;
    His withered cheek, and tresses gray,
    Seem'd to have known a better day.
                                        *The Lay of the Last Minstrel [1805],
                                        introduction*

20 The unpremeditated lay.
                                        Ibid.

21 Such is the custom of Branksome Hall.
                                        Ibid. canto I, st. 7

22 Steady of heart, and stout of hand.
                                        Ibid. st. 21

23 If thou would'st view fair Melrose aright,
    Go visit it by the pale moonlight.
                                        Ibid. II, st. 1

24 I cannot tell how the truth may be;
    I say the tale as 'twas said to me.
                                        Ibid. II, st. 22

25 In peace, Love tunes the shepherd's reed;
    In war, he mounts the warrior's steed;
    In halls, in gay attire is seen;
    In hamlets, dances on the green.
    Love rules the court, the camp, the grove,
    And men below, and saints above;
    For love is heaven, and heaven is love.
                                        Ibid. III, st. 2

26   For ne'er
    Was flattery lost on poet's ear:

A simple race! they waste their toil
For the vain tribute of a smile.
> *The Lay of the Last Minstrel, canto IV,*
> *conclusion*

1 Breathes there the man, with soul so dead,
Who never to himself hath said,
This is my own, my native land!
Whose heart hath ne'er within him burn'd[1]
As home his footsteps he hath turn'd
From wandering on a foreign strand!
If such there breathe, go, mark him well;
For him no Minstrel raptures swell;
High though his titles, proud his name,
Boundless his wealth as wish can claim;
Despite those titles, power, and pelf,
The wretch, concentered all in self,
Living, shall forfeit fair renown,
And, doubly dying, shall go down
To the vile dust, from whence he sprung,
Unwept, unhonor'd, and unsung.
> *Ibid.* VI, *st.* 1

2 O Caledonia! stern and wild,
Meet nurse for a poetic child!
Land of brown heath and shaggy wood;
Land of the mountain and the flood!
> *Ibid. st.* 2

3 November's sky is chill and drear,
November's leaf is red and sear.
> *Marmion [1808], canto I, introduction, st.* 1

4 Stood for his country's glory fast,
And nail'd her colors to the mast!
> *Ibid. st.* 10

5 But search the land of living men,
Where wilt thou find their like again?
> *Ibid. st.* 11

6 And come he slow, or come he fast,
It is but Death who comes at last.
> *Ibid.* II, *st.* 30

7 Oh, young Lochinvar is come out of the West,
Through all the wide Border his steed was the
best.
> *Ibid.* V, *st.* 12 *[Lochinvar, st.* 1]

8 So faithful in love, and so dauntless in war,
There never was knight like the young Lochinvar.
> *Ibid.*

9 For a laggard in love, and a dastard in war,
Was to wed the fair Ellen of brave Lochinvar.
> *Ibid. [Lochinvar, st.* 2]

10 With a smile on her lips, and a tear in her eye.
> *Ibid. [Lochinvar, st.* 5]

11 Heap on more wood!—the wind is chill;
But let it whistle as it will,
We'll keep our Christmas merry still.
> *Ibid.* VI, *introduction, st.* 1

[1]See *Luke* 24:32, 39:27.

12 And dar'st thou, then,
To beard the lion in his den,
The Douglas in his hall?
> *Ibid. st.* 14

13 Oh, what a tangled web we weave,
When first we practice to deceive!
> *Ibid. st.* 17

14 O Woman! in our hours of ease,
Uncertain, coy, and hard to please,
And variable as the shade[2]
By the light quivering aspen made;
When pain and anguish wring the brow,
A ministering angel thou![3]
> *Ibid. st.* 30

15 "Charge, Chester, charge! On, Stanley, on!"
Were the last words of Marmion.
> *Ibid. st.* 32

16 To all, to each, a fair goodnight,
And pleasing dreams, and slumbers light!
> *Ibid. L'Envoy*

17 The stag at eve had drunk his fill,
Where danced the moon on Monan's rill,
And deep his midnight lair had made
In lone Glenartney's hazel shade.
> *The Lady of the Lake [1810], canto I, st.* 1

18 In listening mood she seemed to stand,
The guardian Naiad of the strand.
> *Ibid. st.* 17

19 The will to do, the soul to dare.
> *Ibid. st.* 21

20 Soldier, rest! thy warfare o'er,
Sleep the sleep that knows not breaking,
Dream of battled fields no more,
Days of danger, nights of waking.
> *Ibid. st.* 31

21 Hail to the Chief who in triumph advances![4]
> *Ibid.* II, *st.* 19

22 Like the dew on the mountain,
Like the foam on the river,
Like the bubble on the fountain,
Thou art gone, and forever!
> *Ibid.* III, *st.* 16 *[Coronach, st.* 3]

23 And, Saxon—I am Roderick Dhu!
> *Ibid.* V, *st.* 9

24 Come one, come all! this rock shall fly
From its firm base as soon as I.
> *Ibid. st.* 10

25 Respect was mingled with surprise,
And the stern joy which warriors feel
In foemen worthy of their steel.
> *Ibid.*

[2]See Virgil, 94:1.
[3]See Shakespeare, 199:12.
[4]The verses beginning with this line were set to music by
JAMES SANDERSON [1769–c. 1841]. The march has become traditionally attached to the President of the United States.

1 Where, where was Roderick then!
One blast upon his bugle horn
Were worth a thousand men!
Ibid. VI, st. 18

2 Still are the thoughts to memory dear.
Rokeby [1813], canto I, st. 33

3 A mother's pride, a father's joy.
Ibid. III, st. 15

4 Oh, Brignal banks are wild and fair,
And Greta woods are green,
And you may gather garlands there
Would grace a summer queen.
Ibid. st. 16

5 O! many a shaft at random sent
Finds mark the archer little meant!
And many a word, at random spoken,
May soothe or wound a heart that's broken!
The Lord of the Isles [1815], canto V, st. 18

6 Randolph, thy wreath has lost a rose.[1]
Ibid. VI, st. 18

7 A lawyer without history or literature is a mechanic, a mere working mason; if he possesses some knowledge of these, he may venture to call himself an architect. *Guy Mannering [1815], ch. 37*

8 It's no fish ye're buying, it's men's lives.
The Antiquary [1816], ch. 11

9 Come as the winds come, when
Forests are rended,
Come as the waves come, when
Navies are stranded.
Pibroch of Donald Dhu [1816], st. 4

10 Time will rust the sharpest sword,
Time will consume the strongest cord;
That which molders hemp and steel,
Mortal arm and nerve must feel.
Harold the Dauntless [1817], canto I, st. 4

11 Sea of upturned faces.
Rob Roy [1817], ch. 20

12 There's a gude time coming. *Ibid. 32*

13 My foot is on my native heath, and my name is MacGregor. *Ibid. 34*

14 Jock, when ye hae naething else to do, ye may be ay sticking in a tree; it will be growing, Jock, when ye're sleeping.
The Heart of Midlothian [1818], ch. 8

15 Vacant heart, and hand, and eye,
Easy live and quiet die.
The Bride of Lammermoor [1819], ch. 3. Lucy Ashton's Song

16 There is a southern proverb — fine words butter no parsnips.
The Legend of Montrose [1819], ch. 3

17 The happy combination of fortuitous circumstances.
The Monastery [1820]. Answer of the Author of Waverley to the Letter of Captain Clutterbuck

18 As old as the hills. *Ibid. ch. 9*

19 And better had they ne'er been born,
Who read to doubt, or read to scorn.
Ibid. 12

20 Spur not an unbroken horse; put not your plowshare too deep into new land. *Ibid. 25*

21 Oh, poverty parts good company.
The Abbot [1820], ch. 7

22 Tell that to the marines — the sailors won't believe it.[2] *Redgauntlet [1824], vol. II, ch. 7*

23 Rouse the lion from his lair.
The Talisman [1825], heading, ch. 6

24 Recollect that the Almighty, who gave the dog to be companion of our pleasures and our toils, hath invested him with a nature noble and incapable of deceit. *Ibid. 24*

25 A miss is as good as a mile.
Journal [December 3, 1825]

26 If you keep a thing seven years, you are sure to find a use for it. *Woodstock [1826], ch. 28*

27 Come fill up my cup, come fill up my can,
Come saddle your horses, and call up your men;
Come open the West Port, and let me gang free,
And it's room for the bonnets of Bonny Dundee!
The Doom of Devorgoil [1830]. Bonny Dundee, chorus

Sydney Smith
1771–1845

28 In the four quarters of the globe, who reads an American book, or goes to an American play, or looks at an American picture or statue? . . . Under which of the old tyrannical governments of Europe is every sixth man a slave, whom his fellow-creatures may buy, and sell, and torture?
In Edinburgh Review [January–May 1820]

29 If you choose to represent the various parts in life by holes upon a table, of different shapes — some circular, some triangular, some square, some oblong — and the persons acting these parts by bits of wood of similar shapes, we shall generally find that the triangular person has got into the square hole, the oblong into the triangular, and a square person has squeezed himself into the round hole.[3]
Sketches of Moral Philosophy [1850]

---

[1]Robert Bruce's censure of Randolph for permitting a body of English cavalry to pass his flank on the day before the battle of Bannockburn [June 24, 1314].

[2]"Right," quoth Ben, "that will do for the marines." —
BYRON, *The Island [1823], canto II, last line*
"That will do for the marines, but the sailors won't believe it" is an old saying.

[3]Generally accepted as the origin of the phrase: A square peg in a round hole.

1   That knuckle-end of England—that land of Calvin, oatcakes, and sulphur.
    Lady Holland's Memoir [1855], vol. I, ch. 2

2   Preaching has become a byword for long and dull conversation of any kind; and whoever wishes to imply, in any piece of writing, the absence of everything agreeable and inviting, calls it a sermon.
    Ibid. 3

3   Avoid shame, but do not seek glory—nothing so expensive as glory.   *Ibid. 4*

4   Take short views, hope for the best, and trust in God.[1]   *Ibid. 6*

5   Looked as if she had walked straight out of the ark.   *Ibid. 7*

6   Not body enough to cover his mind decently with; his intellect is improperly exposed.
    Ibid. 9

7   He has spent all his life in letting down empty buckets into empty wells; and he is frittering away his age in trying to draw them up again.[2]   *Ibid.*

8   Ah, you flavor everything; you are the vanilla of society.   *Ibid.*

9   As the French say, there are three sexes—men, women, and clergymen.   *Ibid.*

10   My living in Yorkshire was so far out of the way, that it was actually twelve miles from a lemon.
    Ibid.

11   Daniel Webster struck me much like a steam engine in trousers.   *Ibid.*

12   Live always in the best company when you read.
    Ibid. 10

13   Never give way to melancholy; resist it steadily, for the habit will encroach.   *Ibid.*

14   He was a one-book man. Some men have only one book in them; others, a library.[3]   *Ibid. 11*

15   Marriage resembles a pair of shears, so joined that they can not be separated; often moving in opposite directions, yet always punishing anyone who comes between them.[4]   *Ibid.*

16   Macaulay is like a book in breeches. . . . He has occasional flashes of silence, that make his conversation perfectly delightful.   *Ibid.*

17   Let onion atoms lurk within the bowl
And, scarce suspected, animate the whole.
    Ibid. Recipe for Salad

[1]See Auden, 720:21.
[2]See Cowper, 335:1.
[3]See Anonymous: Latin, 118:19.
[4]We are the two halves of a pair of scissors, when apart, Pecksniff, but together we are something.—DICKENS, *Martin Chuzzlewit* [1843–1844], *ch. 11*

18   Serenely full, the epicure would say,
Fate cannot harm me, I have dined today.[5]
    Ibid.

19   What you don't know would make a great book.
    Ibid.

20   In composing, as a general rule, run your pen through every other word you have written; you have no idea what vigor it will give your style.[6]
    Ibid.

21   Thank God for tea! What would the world do without tea?—how did it exist? I am glad I was not born before tea.   *Ibid.*

22   That sign of old age, extolling the past at the expense of the present.   *Ibid.*

23   We know nothing of tomorrow; our business is to be good and happy today.   *Ibid. 12*

Samuel Taylor Coleridge
1772–1834

24 O the one life within us and abroad,
Which meets all motion and becomes its soul,
A light in sound, a sound-like power in light,
Rhythm in all thought, and joyance everywhere—
Methinks, it should have been impossible
Not to love all things in a world so filled.
    The Eolian Harp [1795], l. 26

25   And what if all of animated nature
Be but organic harps diversely fram'd,
That tremble into thought, as o'er them sweeps
Plastic and vast, one intellectual breeze,
At once the Soul of each, and God of All?
    Ibid. l. 44

26 It is an ancient Mariner,
And he stoppeth one of three.
"By thy long gray beard and glittering eye,
Now wherefore stopp'st thou me?"
    The Rime of the Ancient Mariner [1798], pt. I, st. 1

27 The guests are met, the feast is set:
May'st hear the merry din.
    Ibid. st. 2

28 He holds him with his glittering eye—
The Wedding Guest stood still,
And listens like a three years' child:
The Mariner hath his will.
    Ibid. st. 4

29 The ship was cheered, the harbor cleared,
Merrily did we drop
Below the kirk, below the hill,
Below the lighthouse top.
    Ibid. st. 6

[5]See Horace, 96:24, and Dryden, 274:29.
[6]See Samuel Johnson, 316:19.

1 The Wedding Guest here beat his breast,
For he heard the loud bassoon.

Ibid. st. 8

2 The bride hath paced into the hall,
Red as a rose is she.

Ibid. st. 9

3 And now there came both mist and snow,
And it grew wondrous cold:
And ice, mast-high, came floating by,
As green as emerald.

Ibid. st. 13

4 The ice was here, the ice was there,
The ice was all around:
It cracked and growled, and roared and howled,
Like noises in a swound!

Ibid. st. 15

5 "God save thee, ancient Mariner!
From the fiends, that plague thee thus!—
Why look'st thou so?"—"With my crossbow
I shot the Albatross."

Ibid. st. 20

6 The fair breeze blew, the white foam flew,
The furrow followed free;
We were the first that ever burst
Into that silent sea.

Ibid. II, st. 5

7 As idle as a painted ship
Upon a painted ocean.

Ibid. st. 8

8 Water, water, everywhere,
Nor any drop to drink.

Ibid. st. 9

9 The very deep did rot: O Christ!
That ever this should be!
Yea, slimy things did crawl with legs
Upon the slimy sea.

Ibid. st. 10

10 About, about, in reel and rout
The death fires danced at night.

Ibid. st. 11

11 I bit my arm, I sucked the blood,
And cried, A sail! a sail!

Ibid. III, st. 4

12 Her lips were red, her looks were free,
Her locks were yellow as gold:
Her skin was white as leprosy,
The nightmare Life-in-Death was she,
Who thicks man's blood with cold.

Ibid. st. 11

13 "The game is done! I've won, I've won!"
Quoth she, and whistles thrice.

Ibid. st. 12

14 The sun's rim dips, the stars rush out:
At one stride comes the dark;

With far-heard whisper o'er the sea
Off shot the specter bark.

Ibid. st. 13

15 We listened and looked sideways up!
Fear at my heart, as at a cup,
My lifeblood seemed to sip.

Ibid. st. 14

16 The hornèd Moon, with one bright star
Within the nether tip.

Ibid.

17 Each turned his face with a ghastly pang,
And cursed me with his eye.

Ibid. st. 15

18 I fear thee, ancient Mariner!
I fear thy skinny hand!
And thou art long, and lank, and brown,
As is the ribbed sea-sand.[1]

Ibid. IV, st. 1

19 Alone, alone, all, all alone;
Alone on a wide, wide sea.

Ibid. st. 3

20 The moving moon went up the sky,
And nowhere did abide;
Softly she was going up,
And a star or two beside.

Ibid. st. 10

21 Her beams bemocked the sultry main,
Like April hoarfrost spread;
But where the ship's huge shadow lay,
The charmed water burnt alway
A still and awful red.

Ibid. st. 11

22 O happy living things! no tongue
Their beauty might declare:
A spring of love gushed from my heart,
And I blessed them unaware.

Ibid. st. 14

23 Oh sleep! it is a gentle thing,
Beloved from pole to pole.

Ibid. V, st. 1

24 A noise like of a hidden brook
In the leafy month of June,
That to the sleeping woods all night
Singeth a quiet tune.

Ibid. st. 18

25   The man hath penance done,
And penance more will do.

Ibid. st. 26

26 Like one that on a lonesome road
Doth walk in fear and dread,
And having once turned round walks on,
And turns no more his head;

[1] A note by Coleridge in *Sibylline Leaves* [1817] says: "For [these] lines I am indebted to Mr. Wordsworth."

Because he knows a frightful fiend
Doth close behind him tread.
The Ancient Mariner, pt. VI, st. 10

1 Is this the hill? is this the kirk?
Is this mine own countree?
Ibid. st. 14

2 No voice; but oh! the silence sank
Like music on my heart.
Ibid. st. 22

3 And the owlet whoops to the wolf below,
That eats the she-wolf's young.
Ibid. VII, st. 5

4 "Ha! ha!" quoth he, "full plain I see,
The Devil knows how to row."
Ibid. st. 12

5 I pass, like night, from land to land;
I have strange power of speech;
That moment that his face I see,
I know the man that must hear me:
To him my tale I teach.
Ibid. st. 17

6 O Wedding Guest! This soul hath been
Alone on a wide wide sea:
So lonely 'twas, that God himself
Scarce seemèd there to be.
Ibid. st. 19

7 He prayeth well who loveth well
Both man and bird and beast.
Ibid. st. 22

8 He prayeth best who loveth best
All things both great and small;
For the dear God who loveth us,
He made and loveth all.
Ibid. st. 23

9 A sadder and a wiser man
He rose the morrow morn.
Ibid. st. 25

10 'Tis a month before the month of May,
And the Spring comes slowly up this way.
Christabel [1797–1800], pt. I, l. 21

11 The one red leaf, the last of its clan,
That dances as often as dance it can.
Ibid. l. 49

12 Her gentle limbs did she undress,
And lay down in her loveliness.
Ibid. l. 237

13 A sight to dream of, not to tell!
Ibid. l. 252

14 That saints will aid if men will call:
For the blue sky bends over all!
Ibid. l. 330

15 Alas! they had been friends in youth;
But whispering tongues can poison truth;
And constancy lives in realms above;
And life is thorny; and youth is vain;

And to be wroth with one we love
Doth work like madness in the brain.
Ibid. II, l. 408

16 The frost performs its secret ministry,
Unhelped by any wind.
Frost at Midnight [1798], l. 1

17 Therefore all seasons shall be sweet to thee,
Whether the summer clothe the general earth
With greenness, or the redbreast sit and sing
Betwixt the tufts of snow on the bare branch
Of mossy apple-tree, while the nigh thatch
Smokes in the sun-thaw; whether the eave-drops
    fall
Heard only in the trances of the blast,
Or if the secret ministry of frost
Shall hang them up in silent icicles,
Quietly shining to the quiet moon.
Ibid. l. 65

18 Forth from his dark and lonely hiding place
(Portentous sight!) the owlet Atheism,
Sailing on obscene wings athwart the noon,
Drops his blue-fringèd lids, and holds them close,
And hooting at the glorious sun in Heaven,
Cries out, "Where is it?"
Fears in Solitude [1798], l. 81

19 In Xanadu did Kubla Khan
A stately pleasure dome decree:
Where Alph, the sacred river, ran
Through caverns measureless to man
Down to a sunless sea.
So twice five miles of fertile ground
With walls and towers were girdled round.
Kubla Khan [1798]

20 A savage place! as holy and enchanted
As e'er beneath a waning moon was haunted
By woman wailing for her demon-lover!
Ibid.

21 Five miles meandering with a mazy motion.
Ibid.

22 Ancestral voices prophesying war!
Ibid.

23 It was a miracle of rare device,
A sunny pleasure dome with caves of ice!
Ibid.

24 A damsel with a dulcimer
In a vision once I saw:
It was an Abyssinian maid,
And on her dulcimer she played,
Singing of Mount Abora.
Ibid.

25 Could I revive within me
Her symphony and song,
To such a deep delight 'twould win me,
That with music loud and long,

I would build that dome in air,
That sunny dome! those caves of ice!
And all who heard should see them there,
And all should cry, Beware! Beware!
His flashing eyes, his floating hair!
Weave a circle round him thrice,
And close your eyes with holy dread,
For he on honeydew hath fed,[1]
And drunk the milk of Paradise.

Ibid.

1 Strongly it bears us along in swelling and limitless
  billows,
Nothing before and nothing behind but the sky
  and the ocean.
   The Homeric Hexameter (translated from
   SCHILLER) [1799?]

2 In the hexameter rises the fountain's silvery
  column;
In the pentameter aye falling in melody back.
   The Ovidian Elegiac Metre (translated from
   SCHILLER) [1799]

3 All thoughts, all passions, all delights,
Whatever stirs this mortal frame,
All are but ministers of Love,
And feed his sacred flame.
                              Love [1799], st. 1

4 Earth, with her thousand voices, praises God.
   Hymn Before Sunrise, in the Vale of Chamouni
   [1802], last line

5 What is an epigram? A dwarfish whole,
Its body brevity, and wit its soul.[2]
                              An Epigram [1802]

6 I see, not feel, how beautiful they are!
                    Dejection: An Ode [1802], st. 2

7   It were a vain endeavor,
      Though I should gaze forever
On that green light that lingers in the west:
I may not hope from outward forms to win
The passion and the life, whose fountains are
      within.
                              Ibid. st. 3

8 O lady! we receive but what we give
And in our life alone does Nature live.
                              Ibid. st. 4

9 A light, a glory, a fair luminous cloud
Enveloping the earth.
                              Ibid.

10 Joy is the sweet voice, joy the luminous cloud—
We in ourselves rejoice!
And thence flows all that charms or ear or sight,
All melodies the echoes of that voice,
All colors a suffusion from that light.
                              Ibid. st. 5

11 Trochee trips from long to short;
From long to long in solemn sort
Slow Spondee stalks.
                              Metrical Feet [1806]

12 With Donne, whose muse on dromedary trots,
Wreathe iron pokers into true-love knots.
                    On Donne's Poetry [c. 1818]

13 Flowers are lovely; love is flower-like;
Friendship is a sheltering tree.
                    Youth and Age [1823–1832], st. 2

14 All Nature seems at work. Slugs leave their lair—
The bees are stirring—birds are on the wing—
And Winter slumbering in the open air,
Wears on his smiling face a dream of Spring!
And I the while, the sole unbusy thing,
Nor honey make, nor pair, nor build, nor sing.
          Work Without Hope [February 21, 1825], l. 1

15 Work without Hope draws nectar in a sieve,
And Hope without an object cannot live.
                              Ibid. l. 13

16 I counted two and seventy stenches,
All well defined, and several stinks.
                              Cologne [1828]

17   In looking at objects of Nature while I am thinking, as at yonder moon dim-glimmering through the
dewy window-pane, I seem rather to be seeking, as
it were *asking* for, a symbolical language for something within me that already and forever exists, than
observing anything new.
                    Anima Poetae [1805], ch. 4

18   Poetry is not the proper antithesis to prose, but to
science. Poetry is opposed to science, and prose to
metre. The proper and immediate object of science
is the acquirement, or communication, of truth; the
proper and immediate object of poetry is the communication of immediate pleasure.
                    Definitions of Poetry [1811]

19   Reviewers are usually people who would have
been poets, historians, biographers, etc., if they
could; they have tried their talents at one or at the
other, and have failed; therefore they turn critics.
   Lectures on Shakespeare and Milton [1811–
   1812]

20   The last speech [Iago's soliloquy], the motive-
hunting of a motiveless malignity—how awful!
                    Notes on Shakespeare [c. 1812]

21   The most general definition of beauty . . .
Multeity in Unity.
          On the Principles of Genial Criticism [1814]

22   The Good consists in the congruity of a thing
with the laws of the reason and the nature of the
will, and in its fitness to determine the latter to
actualize the former: and it is always discursive. The
Beautiful arises from the perceived harmony of an
object, whether sight or sound, with the inborn and

---

[1]See Hesiod, 54:16.
[2]See Shakespeare, 195:10.

constitutive rules of the judgment and imagination: and it is always intuitive.   *Genial Criticism*

1   The imagination . . . that reconciling and mediatory power, which incorporating the reason in images of the sense and organizing (as it were) the flux of the senses by the permanence and self-circling energies of the reason, gives birth to a system of symbols, harmonious in themselves, and consubstantial with the truths of which they are the conductors.   *The Statesman's Manual [1816]*

2   Not the poem which we have *read*, but that to which we *return*, with the greatest pleasure, possesses the genuine power, and claims the name of *essential poetry*.
Biographia Literaria [1817], ch. 1

3   Every reform, however necessary, will by weak minds be carried to an excess, that itself will need reforming.   *Ibid.*

4   Until you understand a writer's ignorance, presume yourself ignorant of his understanding.
Ibid. 12

5   During the act of knowledge itself, the objective and subjective are so instantly united, that we cannot determine to which of the two the priority belongs.   *Ibid.*

6   The primary imagination I hold to be the living power and prime agent of all human perception, and as a repetition in the finite mind of the eternal act of creation in the infinite I Am.   *Ibid. 13*

7   The secondary [imagination] . . . dissolves, diffuses, dissipates, in order to re-create; or where this process is rendered impossible, yet still at all events it struggles to idealize and to unify. It is essentially vital, even as all objects (*as* objects) are essentially fixed and dead.   *Ibid.*

8   The fancy is indeed no other than a mode of memory emancipated from the order of time and space.   *Ibid.*

9   The two cardinal points of poetry, the power of exciting the sympathy of the reader by a faithful adherence to the truth of nature, and the power of giving the interest of novelty by the modifying colors of imagination.   *Ibid. 14*

10   That willing suspension of disbelief for the moment, which constitutes poetic faith.   *Ibid.*

11   A poem is that species of composition, which is opposed to works of science, by proposing for its immediate object pleasure, not truth; and from all other species (having this object in common with it) it is discriminated by proposing to itself such delight from the whole, as is compatible with a distinct gratification from each component part.[1]   *Ibid.*

12   A poem of any length neither can be, or ought to be, all poetry.   *Ibid.*

13   The poet, described in *ideal* perfection, brings the whole soul of man into activity, with the subordination of its faculties to each other, according to their relative worth and dignity. He diffuses a tone and spirit of unity, that blends, and (as it were) *fuses*, each into each, by that synthetic and magical power . . . imagination.   *Ibid.*

14   [Imagination] reveals itself in the balance or reconciliation of opposite or discordant qualities: of sameness, with difference; of the general, with the concrete; the idea, with the image; the individual, with the representative; the sense of novelty and freshness, with old and familiar objects; a more than usual state of emotion, with more than usual order; judgment ever awake and steady self-possession, with enthusiasm and feeling profound or vehement; and while it blends and harmonizes the natural and the artificial, still subordinates art to nature; the manner to the matter; and our admiration of the poet to our sympathy with the poetry.   *Ibid.*

15   No man was ever yet a great poet, without being at the same time a profound philosopher.
Ibid. 15

16   While [Shakespeare] darts himself forth and passes into all the forms of human character and passion, the one Proteus of the fire and the flood, [Milton] attracts all forms and things to himself, into the unity of his own *Ideal*. All things and modes of action shape themselves anew in the being of Milton; while Shakespeare becomes all things, yet for ever remaining himself.   *Ibid.*

17   Our myriad-minded Shakespeare.[2]   *Ibid.*

18   The best part of human language, properly so called, is derived from reflection on the acts of the mind itself.[3]   *Ibid. 17*

19   Now Art, used collectively for painting, sculpture, architecture and music, is the mediatress between, and reconciler of, nature and man. It is, therefore, the power of humanizing nature, of infusing the thoughts and passions of man into everything which is the object of his contemplation.
On Poesy or Art [1818]

20   The artist must imitate that which is within the thing, that which is active through form and figure, and discourses to us by symbols.   *Ibid.*

21   The heart should have fed upon the truth, as insects on a leaf, till it be tinged with the color, and show its food in every . . . minutest fiber.
Ibid.

22   Schiller has the material sublime.
Table Talk [December 29, 1822]

[1]See the similar idea expressed some years earlier in *Definitions of Poetry,* 383:18.

[2]A phrase which I have borrowed from a Greek monk, who applies it to a patriarch of Constantinople.—COLERIDGE's *footnote*

[3]The poem of the act of the mind.—WALLACE STEVENS, *Of Modern Poetry*

1   I wish our clever young poets would remember my homely definitions of prose and poetry; that is, prose = words in their best order; poetry = the best words in their best order.   *Ibid. [July 12, 1827]*

2   The man's desire is for the woman; but the woman's desire is rarely other than for the desire of the man.   *Ibid. [July 23, 1827]*

3   That passage is what I call the sublime dashed to pieces by cutting too close with the fiery four-in-hand round the corner of nonsense.   *Ibid.*

4   The happiness of life is made up of minute fractions—the little soon forgotten charities of a kiss or smile, a kind look, a heartfelt compliment, and the countless infinitesimals of pleasurable and genial feeling.   *The Friend. The Improvisatore [1828]*

5   Beneath this sod
A poet lies, or that which once seemed he—
Oh, lift a thought in prayer for S.T.C.!
That he, who many a year, with toil of breath,
Found death in life, may here find life in death.
   Epitaph written for himself [1833]

Novalis
[Baron Friedrich von Hardenberg]
1772–1801

6   We are near awakening when we dream that we dream.   *Pollen [1798]*

Josiah Quincy, Jr.
1772–1864

7   If this bill [for the admission of Orleans Territory as a State] passes, I am compelled to declare it as my deliberate opinion that the bonds of this Union are virtually dissolved; that the States which compose it are free from their moral obligations; and that, as it will be the right of all, so it will be the duty of some, to prepare definitely for a separation—amicably if they can; violently if they must.[1]
   Speech in the House of Representatives [January 14, 1811]

William Barnes Rhodes
1772–1826

8 *Bombastes:* So have I heard on Afric's burning shore
A hungry lion give a grievous roar;
The grievous roar echoed along the shore.
Artaxaminous: So have I heard on Afric's burning shore

---

[1]The gentleman [Quincy] cannot have forgotten his own sentiment, uttered even on the floor of this House, "Peaceably if we can, forcibly if we must."—HENRY CLAY, *Speech [January 8, 1813]*

Another lion give a grievous roar;
And the first lion thought the last a bore.
   Bombastes Furioso [1810], act I, sc. iv

David Ricardo
1772–1823

9   Labor, like all other things which are purchased and sold, and which may be increased or diminished in quantity, has its natural and its market price. The natural price of labor is that price which is necessary to enable the laborers, one with another, to subsist and perpetuate their race, without either increase or diminution.
   On the Principles of Political Economy and Taxation [1817], ch. 5

10   There is no way of keeping profits up but by keeping wages down.
   On Protection to Agriculture [1820], sec. 6

Friedrich von Schlegel
1772–1829

11   The historian is a prophet in reverse.
   Athenaeum [1798–1800]

William Henry Harrison[2]
1773–1841

12   We admit of no government by divine right . . . the only legitimate right to govern is an express grant of power from the governed.
   Inaugural Address [March 4, 1841]

13   A decent and manly examination of the acts of government should be not only tolerated, but encouraged.   *Ibid.*

John Randolph
1773–1833

14   The surest way to prevent war is not to fear it.
   Speech in the House of Representatives [March 5, 1806]

15   Never were abilities so much below mediocrity so well rewarded; no, not when Caligula's horse was made Consul.[3]   *Speech [February 1, 1828]*

---

[2]Tippecanoe and Tyler, Too.—A. C. ROSS [fl. c. 1840], *Presidential campaign song [1840]*
   The iron-armed soldier, the true-hearted soldier,/ The gallant old soldier of Tippecanoe.—GEORGE POPE MORRIS, *campaign song for Harrison [1840], sung to the tune of* The Old Oaken Bucket
[3]Referring to President John Quincy Adams's appointment of Richard Rush as Secretary of the Treasury. According to Suetonius, Emperor Gaius Caligula (see 103) was said to have intended awarding his horse Incitatus a consulship.

1   [Of Edward Livingston:] He is a man of splendid abilities, but utterly corrupt. He shines and stinks like rotten mackerel by moonlight.
From W. CABELL BRUCE, John Randolph of Roanoke [1923], vol. II, p. 197

2   [Of Martin Van Buren:] He rowed to his object with muffled oars.   *Ibid. p. 203*

Robert Southey
1774–1843

3 It was a summer evening;
Old Kaspar's work was done,
And he before his cottage door
Was sitting in the sun;
And by him sported on the green
His little grandchild Wilhelmine.
The Battle of Blenheim [1798], st. 1

4 He came to ask what he had found,
That was so large, and smooth, and round.
Ibid. st. 2

5 " 'Tis some poor fellow's skull," said he,
"Who fell in the great victory."
Ibid. st. 3

6 But what they fought each other for,
I could not well make out.
Ibid. st. 6

7 "And everybody praised the duke,
Who this great fight did win."
"But what good came of it at last?"
Quoth little Peterkin.
"Why, that I cannot tell," said he;
"But 'twas a famous victory."
Ibid. st. 11

8 "You are old, Father William," the young man cried,
"The few locks which are left you are gray;
You are hale, Father William—a hearty old man:
Now tell me the reason, I pray."
The Old Man's Comforts and How He Gained Them [1799],[1] st. 1

9 "In the days of my youth, I remembered my God,
And he hath not forgotten my age."
Ibid. st. 6

10 And then they knew the perilous rock,
And blessed the Abbot of Aberbrothok.
The Inchcape Rock [1802],[2] st. 4

11 Till the vessel strikes with a shivering shock—
"O Christ! It is the Inchcape Rock."
Ibid. st. 15

---

[1]Of several parodies of this poem, the one by Lewis Carroll is probably better known than the original. See 517:9–517:11.
[2]A rock in the North Sea, off the Firth of Tay, Scotland, dangerous to navigators because it is covered with every tide. There is a tradition that a warning bell was fixed on the rock by the Abbot of Aberbrothok, which was stolen by a sea pirate, who perished on the rock a year later.

12 Curses are like young chickens, they always come home to roost.
The Curse of Kehama [1810], motto

13 They sin who tell us love can die;
With life all other passions fly,
All others are but vanity.
Ibid. canto X, st. 10

14 Thou hast been called, O sleep! the friend of woe;
But 'tis the happy that have called thee so.
Ibid. XV, st. 12

15 My days among the dead are past;
Around me I behold,
Where'er these casual eyes are cast,
The mighty minds of old.
My Days Among the Dead Are Past [1818], st. 1

16 Yet leaving here a name, I trust,
That will not perish in the dust.
Ibid. st. 4

17   Agreed to differ.   *Life of Wesley [1820]*

18   The Satanic school.
Vision of Judgment [1821], original preface

19   The arts babblative and scribblative.
Colloquies on the Progress and Prospects of Society [1829], no. 1, pt. 2

20   The march of intellect.   *Ibid. 14*

21 From his brimstone bed, at break of day,
A-walking the Devil is gone,
To look at his little snug farm of the world,
And see how his stock went on.
The Devil's Walk [1830], st. 1

22 His coat was red, and his breeches were blue,
And there was a hole where his tail came through.
Ibid. st. 3

Jane Austen[3]
1775–1817

23   It is a truth universally acknowledged, that a single man in possession of a good fortune, must be in want of a wife.   *Pride and Prejudice [1813], ch. 1*

24   She [Mrs. Bennet] was a woman of mean understanding, little information, and uncertain temper.
Ibid.

25   A lady's imagination is very rapid; it jumps from admiration to love, from love to matrimony in a moment.   *Ibid. 6*

26   Mr. Collins had only to change from Jane to Elizabeth—and it was soon done—done while Mrs. Bennet was stirring the fire.   *Ibid. 15*

---

[3][Miss Austen] had a talent for describing the involvements and feelings and characters of ordinary life which is to me the most wonderful I ever met with. The Big Bow-Wow strain I can do myself like any now going; but the exquisite touch, which renders ordinary commonplace things and characters interesting, from the truth of the description and the sentiment, is denied to me.—WALTER SCOTT, *Journal* [March 14, 1826]

1   You have delighted us long enough.
Ibid. 18

2   Mrs. Bennet was restored to her usual querulous serenity.   *Ibid. 42*

3   You ought certainly to forgive them, as a Christian, but never to admit them in your sight, or allow their names to be mentioned in your hearing.
Ibid. 57

4   For what do we live, but to make sport for our neighbors, and laugh at them in our turn?
Ibid.

5   I have been a selfish being all my life, in practice, though not in principle.   *Ibid. 58*

6   One half of the world cannot understand the pleasures of the other.   *Emma [1815], ch. 9*

7   It was a delightful visit—perfect, in being much too short.   *Ibid. 13*

8   Nobody who has not been in the interior of a family can say what the difficulties of any individual of that family may be.   *Ibid. 18*

9   Business, you know, may bring money, but friendship hardly ever does.   *Ibid. 34*

10   "Only a novel" . . . in short, only some work in which the greatest powers of the mind are displayed, in which the most thorough knowledge of human nature, the happiest delineation of its varieties, the liveliest effusions of wit and humor are conveyed to the world in the best chosen language.
Northanger Abbey [1818], ch. 5

11   She had been forced into prudence in her youth, she learned romance as she grew older—the natural sequence of an unnatural beginning.
Persuasion [1818], ch. 4

12   I do not want people to be very agreeable, as it saves me the trouble of liking them a great deal.
Letters. To her sister Cassandra [December 24, 1798]

13   The little bit (two inches wide) of ivory on which I work with so fine a brush as produces little effect after much labor.
Ibid. To J. Edward Austen [December 16, 1816]

Charles Lamb
1775–1834

14 I have had playmates, I have had companions,
In my days of childhood, in my joyful school
   days—
All, all are gone, the old familiar faces.
Old Familiar Faces [1798]

15   For God's sake (I never was more serious) don't make me ridiculous any more by terming me gentle-

hearted in print[1] . . . substitute drunken dog, ragged head, seld-shaven, odd-eyed, stuttering, or any other epithet which truly and properly belongs to the gentleman in question.
Letter to Coleridge [August 1800]

16   Separate from the pleasure of your company, I don't much care if I never see a mountain in my life.
Letter to Wordsworth [1801]

17   The man must have a rare recipe for melancholy, who can be dull in Fleet Street.
Letter to Thomas Manning [February 15, 1802]

18   Gone before
To that unknown and silent shore.
Hester [1803], st. 7

19   A good-natured woman, though, which is as much as you can expect from a friend's wife, whom you got acquainted with a bachelor.
Letter to Hazlitt [1805]

20   This very night I am going to leave off tobacco! Surely there must be some other world in which this unconquerable purpose shall be realized.
Letter to Thomas Manning [1815]

21   Anything awful makes me laugh. I misbehaved once at a funeral.   *Letter to Southey [1815]*

22   [Of Coleridge:] An archangel a little damaged.
Letter to Wordsworth [1816]

23   The red-letter days, now become, to all intents and purposes, dead-letter days.
Essays of Elia [1823]. Oxford in the Vacation

24   The human species, according to the best theory I can form of it, is composed of two distinct races, the men who borrow, and the men who lend.
Ibid. The Two Races of Men

25   Your borrowers of books—those mutilators of collections, spoilers of the symmetry of shelves, and creators of odd volumes.   *Ibid.*

26   A clear fire, a clean hearth, and the rigor of the game.   *Ibid. Mrs. Battle's Opinions on Whist*

27   I have no ear.   *Ibid. A Chapter on Ears*

28   Sentimentally I am disposed to harmony; but organically I am incapable of a tune.   *Ibid.*

29   Credulity is the man's weakness, but the child's strength.   *Ibid. Witches, and Other Night Fears*

30   Not many sounds in life, and I include all urban and all rural sounds, exceed in interest a knock at the door.   *Ibid. Valentine's Day*

31   It is good to love the unknown.   *Ibid.*

32   Presents, I often say, endear absents.
Ibid. A Dissertation upon Roast Pig

[1]For thee, my gentlehearted Charles, to whom / No sound is dissonant which tells of life.—COLERIDGE, *This Lime Tree Bower My Prison* [1797]

1   I came home forever!
   Letter to Bernard Barton [1825], on leaving his
   "33 years' desk" at the East India House

2 Who first invented work, and bound the free
   And holiday-rejoicing spirit down?
                                        Work

3 Some cry up Haydn, some Mozart,
   Just as the whim bites. For my part,
   I do not care a farthing candle
   For either of them, nor for Handel.[1]
                Letter to Mrs. William Hazlitt [1830]

4 For thy sake, Tobacco, I
   Would do anything but die.
                       A Farewell to Tobacco

5   A poor relation—is the most irrelevant thing in
   nature.
              Last Essays of Elia [1833]. Poor Relations

6   I love to lose myself in other men's minds.
        Ibid. Detached Thoughts on Books and Reading

7   Books think for me.   *Ibid.*

8   Things in books' clothing.   *Ibid.*

9   How sickness enlarges the dimensions of a man's
   self to himself.   *Ibid. The Convalescent*

10   Your absence of mind we have borne, till your
   presence of body came to be called in question by it.
                           Ibid. Amicus Redivivus

11   A pun is a pistol let off at the ear; not a feather
   to tickle the intellect.
        Ibid. Popular Fallacies: IX, That the Worst Puns
        Are the Best

12   A presentation copy . . . is a copy of a book
   which does not sell, sent you by the author, with his
   foolish autograph at the beginning of it; for which,
   if a stranger, he only demands your friendship; if a
   brother author, he expects from you a book of
   yours, which does not sell, in return.
        Ibid. XI, That We Must Not Look a Gift Horse
        in the Mouth

13   The good things of life are not to be had singly,
   but come to us with a mixture.
        Ibid. XIII, That You Must Love Me and Love
        My Dog

14   The greatest pleasure I know is to do a good
   action by stealth, and to have it found out by accident.   *Table Talk. In the Athenaeum [1834]*

Walter Savage Landor
1775–1864

15 Ah what avails the sceptered race,
   Ah what the form divine!
                           Rose Aylmer [1806]

16 Rose Aylmer, whom these wakeful eyes
   May weep, but never see,
   A night of memories and of sighs
   I consecrate to thee.
                                        Ibid.

17   Of all failures, to fail in a witticism is the worst,
   and the mishap is the more calamitous in a drawn-
   out and detailed one.
        Imaginary Conversations [1824–1829].
        Chesterfield and Chatham

18   'Tis verse that gives
   Immortal youth to mortal maids.
                                        Verse

19 When we play the fool, how wide
   The theatre expands! beside,
   How long the audience sits before us!
   How many prompters! what a chorus!
                           Plays [1846], st. 2

20 There is delight in singing, though none hear
   Beside the singer.
                    To Robert Browning [1846]

21 I strove with none, for none was worth my strife;
   Nature I loved; and next to Nature, Art.
   I warm'd both hands before the fire of life;
   It sinks, and I am ready to depart.
                    I Strove with None [1853]

Thomas Campbell
1777–1844

22 'Tis distance lends enchantment to the view,
   And robes the mountain in its azure hue.[2]
                Pleasures of Hope [1799], pt. I, l. 7

23 Hope, for a season, bade the world farewell,
   And Freedom shriek'd—as Kosciusko fell!
                                   Ibid. l. 381

24 And muse on Nature with a poet's eye.
                                Ibid. II, l. 98

25 On the green banks of Shannon, when Sheelah
        was nigh,
   No blithe Irish lad was so happy as I;
   No harp like my own could so cheerily play,
   And wherever I went was my poor dog Tray.[3]
                       The Harper [1799], st. 1

26 Ye mariners of England,
   That guard our native seas;
   Whose flag has braved, a thousand years,
   The battle and the breeze!
                Ye Mariners of England [1800], st. 1

---

[1]See John Byrom, 304:15.

[2]The mountains too, at a distance, appear airy masses and
smooth, but seen near at hand they are rough.—DIOGENES
LAERTIUS, *Pyrrho, sec. 9*

[3]My Old Dog Tray.—STEPHEN C. FOSTER, *title of song*

1 Britannia needs no bulwarks,
No towers along the steep;
Her march is o'er the mountain waves,
Her home is on the deep.

Ibid. st. 3

2 The meteor flag of England
Shall yet terrific burn,
Till danger's troubled night depart,
And the star of peace return.

Ibid. st. 4

3 'Tis the sunset of life gives me mystical lore,
And coming events cast their shadows before.[1]

Lochiel's Warning [1802]

4 The combat deepens. On, ye brave,
Who rush to glory or the grave!
Wave, Munich! all thy banners wave,
And charge with all thy chivalry!

Hohenlinden [1802], st. 7

5 There was silence deep as death,
And the boldest held his breath,
For a time.

Battle of the Baltic [1805], st. 2

6 Ye are brothers! ye are men!
And we conquer but to save.

Ibid. st. 5

7 Oh, how hard it is to find
The one just suited to our mind!

Song, st. 1

8 Oh leave this barren spot to me!
Spare, woodman, spare the beechen tree![2]

The Beech Tree's Petition, st. 1

9 A stoic of the woods — a man without a tear.

Gertrude of Wyoming [1809], pt. I, st. 23

10 Oh! once the harp of Innisfail
Was strung full high to notes of gladness;
But yet it often told a tale
Of more prevailing sadness.

O'Connor's Child [1810], st. 1

Henry Clay
1777–1852

11   How often are we forced to charge fortune with
partiality towards the unjust!

Letter [December 4, 1801]

12   If you wish to avoid foreign collision, you had
better abandon the ocean.

Speech in the House of Representatives [January 22, 1812]

13   Government is a trust, and the officers of the
government are trustees; and both the trust and the
trustees are created for the benefit of the people.

Speech at Ashland, Kentucky [March 1829]

14   The arts of power and its minions are the same in
all countries and in all ages. It marks its victim;
denounces it; and excites the public odium and the
public hatred, to conceal its own abuses and encroachments.

Speech in the Senate [March 14, 1834]

15   I have heard something said about allegiance to
the South. I know no South, no North, no East, no
West, to which I owe any allegiance. . . . The
Union, sir, is my country.

Speech in the Senate [1848]

16   The Constitution of the United States was made
not merely for the generation that then existed, but
for posterity — unlimited, undefined, endless, perpetual posterity.

Speech in the Senate [January 29, 1850]

17   I would rather be right than be President.[3]

Speech in the Senate [1850]

Lorenzo Dow
1777–1834

18   You will be damned if you do.—And you will be
damned if you don't [definition of Calvinism].

Reflections on the Love of God

Carl Friedrich Gauss
1777–1855

19   Mathematics is the queen of the sciences.

*From SARTORIUS VON WALTERSHAUSEN, Gauss
zum Gedächtniss [1856]*

Valentine Blacker
1778–1823

20   Put your trust in God, my boys, and keep your
powder dry!

*From EDWARD HAYES, Ballads of Ireland [1856].
Oliver's Advice, An Orange Ballad*

Henry Peter Brougham,
Baron Brougham and Vaux
1778–1868

21   What is valuable is not new, and what is new is
not valuable.

*From The Edinburgh Review [c. 1802], The
Work of Thomas Young*

---

[1]Often do the spirits / Of great events stride on before the
events, / And in today already walks tomorrow.—SCHILLER,
Wallenstein [1799–1800], *pt. II, act V, sc. i*
Translated by COLERIDGE.
[2]See George Pope Morris, 428:10.

[3]Said when told that his defense of the Compromise of 1850
would endanger his chances for the presidency.

1   The schoolmaster is abroad,[1] and I trust to him, armed with his primer, against the soldier in full military array.

    Speech, Opening of Parliament [January 29, 1828]

2   In my mind, he was guilty of no error—he was chargeable with no exaggeration—he was betrayed by his fancy into no metaphor, who once said that all we see about us, Kings, Lords, and Commons, the whole machinery of the State, all the apparatus of the system, and its varied workings, end in simply bringing twelve good men into a box.

    Present State of the Law [February 7, 1828]

3   Pursuit of Knowledge Under Difficulties.

    Title of book [1830]

4   Education makes a people easy to lead, but difficult to drive; easy to govern but impossible to enslave.   *Attributed*

5   The great unwashed.   *Attributed*

William Hazlitt
1778–1830

6   One has no notion of him [William Cobbett] as making use of a fine pen, but a great mutton-fist; his style stuns readers. . . . He is too much for any single newspaper antagonist; "lays waste" a city orator or Member of Parliament, and bears hard upon the government itself. He is a kind of *fourth estate* in the politics of the country.[2]

    Table Talk [1821–1822]. Character of Cobbett

7   It is better to be able neither to read nor write than to be able to do nothing else.

    Ibid. On the Ignorance of the Learned

8   What I mean by living to one's self is living in the world, as in it, not of it. . . . It is to be a silent spectator of the mighty scene of things; . . . to take a thoughtful, anxious interest in what is passing in the world, but not to feel the slightest inclination to make or meddle with it.

    Ibid. On Living to One's Self

9   Even in the common affairs of life, in love, friendship, and marriage, how little security have we when we trust our happiness in the hands of others!

    Ibid.

10   There is not a more mean, stupid, dastardly, pitiful, selfish, spiteful, envious, ungrateful animal than the Public. It is the greatest of cowards, for it is afraid of itself.   *Ibid.*

11   When a man is dead, they put money in his coffin, erect monuments to his memory, and celebrate the anniversary of his birthday in set speeches. Would they take any notice of him if he were living? No!

    Ibid.

12   One of the pleasantest things in the world is going a journey; but I like to go by myself.

    Ibid. On Going a Journey

13   When I am in the country I wish to vegetate like the country.   *Ibid.*

14   The soul of a journey is liberty, perfect liberty, to think, feel, do just as one pleases.   *Ibid.*

15   Give me the clear blue sky over my head, and the green turf beneath my feet, a winding road before me, and a three hours' march to dinner—and then to thinking! It is hard if I cannot start some game on these lone heaths.   *Ibid.*

16   No young man ever thinks he shall die.

    Ibid. On the Fear of Death

17   *Horus non numero nisi serenas*[3] is the motto of a sundial near Venice. There is a softness and a harmony in the words and in the thought unparalleled.

    Ibid. Of a Sundial in Venice

18   The love of liberty is the love of others; the love of power is the love of ourselves.

    Political Essays. The Times Newspaper

19   We never do anything well till we cease to think about the manner of doing it.

    Sketches and Essay. On Prejudice

20   Men of genius do not excel in any profession because they labor in it, but they labor in it because they excel.   *Characteristics, no. 416 [c. 1821]*

21   We are not hypocrites in our sleep.

    On Dreams

Stephen Decatur
1779–1820

22   Our country! In her intercourse with foreign nations may she always be in the right; but our country, right or wrong.[4]

    Toast given at Norfolk [April 1816]. From Alexander Slidell Mackenzie, *Life of Stephen Decatur [1848]*[5]

---

[1]At the first meeting of the London Mechanics' Institution [1825], John Reynolds, head of a school in Clerkenwell, acted as secretary of the meeting. Lord Brougham, who spoke at this meeting, said in the course of his remarks, "Look out, gentlemen, the schoolmaster is abroad." The phrase attracted little attention at that time, but when used in a speech three years later, it at once became popular.

[2]See Carlyle, 411:18; Macaulay, 424:17; and Thackeray, 463:16.

[3]I count only the hours that are serene.—*Proverb*
Also quoted as: I count only the sunny hours.

[4]I hope to find my country in the right: however, I will stand by her, right or wrong.—John Jordan Crittenden [1787–1863], *On the Mexican War*
    See Charles Churchill, 333:19; John Quincy Adams, 368:14; and Schurz, 510:18.

[5]*Niles' Weekly Register* [Baltimore; April 20, 1816] gives a slightly different reading: *Our Country*—In her intercourse with foreign nations may she always be in the *right*, and always *successful, right* or *wrong*.

Thomas, Lord Denman
1779–1854

1 Trial by jury, instead of being a security to persons who are accused, will be a delusion, a mockery, and a snare.
O'Connell v. The Queen [September 4, 1844]

Francis Scott Key
1779–1843

2 Oh, say, can you see by the dawn's early light,
What so proudly we hailed at the twilight's last
gleaming?
Whose broad stripes and bright stars, through the
perilous fight,
O'er the ramparts we watched were so gallantly
streaming?
And the rockets' red glare, the bombs bursting in
air,
Gave proof through the night that our flag was
still there.
Oh, say, does that star-spangled banner yet wave
O'er the land of the free and the home of the
brave?
*The Star-Spangled Banner [September 14, 1814],
st. 1*

3 Blessed with victory and peace, may the
Heaven-rescued land
Praise the Power that hath made and preserved us
a nation.
Then conquer we must, when our cause it is just,
And this be our motto, "In God is our trust."
Ibid. st. 4

William Lamb, Viscount Melbourne
1779–1848

4 I wish I was as cocksure of anything as Tom
Macaulay is of everything.
*From Melbourne's Papers [1889]. Preface by
EARL COWPER*

5 Things have come to a pretty pass when religion
is allowed to invade the sphere of private life.
*From G. W. E. RUSSELL, Collections and
Recollections [1898]*

Clement Clarke Moore
1779–1863

6 'Twas the night before Christmas, when all
through the house
Not a creature was stirring—not even a mouse;[1]
The stockings were hung by the chimney with
care,
In hopes that St. Nicholas soon would be there.
A Visit from St. Nicholas [December 1823]

[1]See Shakespeare, 192:20.

7 "Happy Christmas to all, and to all a goodnight!"
Ibid.

Thomas Moore
1779–1852

8 Faintly as tolls the evening chime,
Our voices keep tune and our oars keep time.[2]
*Poems Relating to America. A Canadian Boat
Song, st. 1*

9 Go where glory waits thee!
But while fame elates thee,
Oh, still remember me!
*Irish Melodies [1807–1834]. Go Where Glory
Waits Thee, st. 1*

10 Oh, breathe not his name! let it sleep in the shade,
Where cold and unhonor'd his relics are laid.
Ibid. Oh, Breathe Not His Name, st. 1

11 And the tear that we shed, though in secret it
rolls,
Shall long keep his memory green in our souls.[3]
Ibid. st. 2

12 The harp that once through Tara's halls
The soul of music shed,
Now hangs as mute on Tara's walls
As if that soul were fled.
*Ibid. The Harp That Once Through Tara's
Halls, st. 1*

13 Believe me, if all those endearing young charms
Which I gaze on so fondly today,
Were to change by tomorrow and fleet in my
arms,
Like fairy gifts fading away,
Thou would'st still be ador'd as this moment thou
art,
Let thy loveliness fade as it will,
And around the dear ruin each wish of my heart
Would entwine itself verdantly still.
*Ibid. Believe Me, If All Those Endearing Young
Charms, st. 1*

14 But there's nothing half so sweet in life
As love's young dream.
Ibid. Love's Young Dream, st. 1

15 Eyes of unholy blue.
Ibid. By That Lake Whose Gloomy Shore, st. 2

16 'Tis the last rose of summer,
Left blooming alone;
All her lovely companions
Are faded and gone.
Ibid. The Last Rose of Summer, st. 1

17 The Minstrel Boy to the war is gone,
In the ranks of death you'll find him.
His father's sword he has girded on,
And his wild harp slung behind him.
Ibid. The Minstrel Boy, st. 1

[2]See Marvell, 268:25.
[3]See Shakespeare, 192:31.

1   And the best of all ways
To lengthen our days
Is to steal a few hours from the night, my dear.
Irish Melodies. The Young May Moon, st. 1

2 You may break, you may shatter the vase, if you
will,
But the scent of the roses will hang round it still.[1]
Ibid. Farewell! But Whenever, st. 3

3 No eye to watch, and no tongue to wound us,
All earth forgot, and all heaven around us.
Ibid. Come O'er the Sea, st. 2

4 The light that lies
In woman's eyes,
Has been my heart's undoing.
Ibid. The Time I've Lost in Wooing, st. 1

5   My only books
Were woman's looks,
And folly's all they've taught me.
Ibid.

6 A Persian's heaven is easily made:
'Tis but black eyes and lemonade.
*Intercepted Letters; or, The Two Penny Post
Bag [1813], VI*

7 Oft in the stilly night,
Ere Slumber's chain has bound me,
Fond Memory brings the light
Of other days around me;
The smiles, the tears,
Of boyhood's years,
The words of love then spoken;
The eyes that shone
Now dimmed and gone,
The cheerful hearts now broken.
*National Airs [1815]. Oft in the Stilly Night,
st. 1*

8   I feel like one,
Who treads alone
Some banquet hall deserted,
Whose lights are fled,
Whose garlands dead,
And all but he departed.
Ibid. st. 2

9 What though youth gave love and roses,
Age still leaves us friends and wine.
Ibid. Spring and Autumn, st. 1

10 Oh, call it by some better name,
For friendship sounds too cold.
*Ballads and Songs. Oh, Call It by Some Better
Name, st. 1*

[1]The jar will long keep the fragrance of what it was once
steeped in when new.—HORACE, *Epistles, I, ii, 69*
That flavor, absorbed when new, remains.—QUINTILIAN
But, somehow or other, though you fill it with water, the jar
retains the odor which it acquired when first used.—SAINT
JEROME
The image was frequently used in the classical period; un-
glazed ware is more absorbent than glazed.

11 There's a bower of roses by Bendemeer's stream,
And the nightingale sings round it all the day
long.
Lalla Rookh [1817], pt. II

12 Some flow'rets of Eden ye still inherit,
But the trail of the serpent is over them all.
Ibid.

13 Oh! ever thus, from childhood's hour,
I've seen my fondest hope decay;
I never loved a tree or flower,
But 'twas the first to fade away.
I never nurs'd a dear gazelle
To glad me with its soft black eye,
But when it came to know me well,
And love me, it was sure to die.
Ibid. V

14 Like Dead Sea fruits, that tempt the eye,
But turn to ashes on the lips.[2]
Ibid.

15   Paradise itself were dim
And joyless, if not shared with him!
Ibid. VI

Joseph Story
1779–1845

16   [The law] is a jealous mistress, and requires a
long and constant courtship. It is not to be won by
trifling favors, but by lavish homage.
*The Value and Importance of Legal Studies
[August 5, 1829]*

William Ellery Channing
1780–1842

17   We do, then, with all earnestness, though without
reproaching our brethren, protest against the irrational and unscriptural doctrine of the Trinity. "To
us," as to the Apostle and the primitive Christians,
"there is one God, even the Father." With Jesus, we
worship the Father, as the only living and true God.
We are astonished, that any man can read the New
Testament, and avoid the conviction, that the Father
alone is God.
Unitarian Christianity [Baltimore, 1819]

18   I see the marks of God in the heavens and the
earth, but how much more in a liberal intellect, in
magnanimity, in unconquerable rectitude, in a philanthropy which forgives every wrong, and which
never despairs of the cause of Christ and human
virtue! I do and I must reverence human nature.
. . . I thank God that my own lot is bound up with
that of the human race.
*Likeness to God [Providence, Rhode Island,
1828]*

[2]See Byron, 399:23.

1   There are seasons, in human affairs, of inward and outward revolution, when new depths seem to be broken up in the soul, when new wants are unfolded in multitudes, and a new and undefined good is thirsted for. These are periods when . . . *to dare* is the highest wisdom.
        Complete Works [1879]. The Union [1829]

2   I call that mind free which jealously guards its intellectual rights and powers, which calls no man master, which does not content itself with a passive or hereditary faith, which opens itself to light whencesoever it may come, which receives new truth as an angel from Heaven.   *Spiritual Freedom*

Karl von Clausewitz
1780–1831

3   War is not merely a political act, but also a political instrument, a continuation of political relations, a carrying out of the same by other means.[1]
        Vom Kriege (On War) [1833]

Charles Caleb Colton
1780–1832

4   When you have nothing to say, say nothing.
        Lacon [1820–1822], vol. I, no. 183

5   Imitation is the sincerest of flattery.
        Ibid. 217

6   That debt which cancels all others.
        Ibid. II, 66

Philip Hone
1780–1851

7   By and by we shall have balloons and pass over to Europe between sun and sun. Oh, for the good old days of heavy post-coaches and speed at the rate of six miles an hour!   *Diary [November 28, 1844]*

Charles Miner
1780–1865

8   When I see a merchant overpolite to his customers, begging them to taste a little brandy and throwing half his goods on the counter—thinks I, that man has an ax to grind.
        Essays from the Desk of Poor Robert the Scribe [1815]. Who'll Turn Grindstones[2]

[1]Der Krieg ist nichts anderes als die Fortsetzung der Politik mit anderen Mitteln.
    See Mao Tse-tung, 686:14.
[2]First published in *Luzerne Federalist* [September 7, 1810]. Because of the similarity of the title to *Poor Richard*, the phrase "an ax to grind" has often been attributed to FRANKLIN.

Frances Trollope
1780–1863

9   Let no one who wishes to receive agreeable impressions of American manners, commence their travels in a Mississippi steamboat.
        Domestic Manners of the Americans [1832]

Ebenezer Elliott
1781–1849

10   Not kings and lords, but nations!
     Not thrones and crowns, but men!
        Corn Law Rhymes [1828]. When Wilt Thou Save the People? st. 1

11   God save the people!
        Ibid.

12   What is a communist? One who hath yearnings
     For equal division of unequal earnings.
        Poetical Works [1846]. Epigram

James Lawrence
1781–1813

13   Tell the men to fire faster and not to give up the ship; fight her till she sinks.[3]
        On board the U.S. frigate Chesapeake [June 1, 1813]

John Caldwell Calhoun
1782–1850

14   The very essence of a free government consists in considering offices as public trusts, bestowed for the good of the country, and not for the benefit of an individual or a party.
        Speech [February 13, 1835]

15   A power has risen up in the government greater than the people themselves, consisting of many and various and powerful interests, combined into one mass, and held together by the cohesive power of the vast surplus in the banks.[4]
        Speech [May 27, 1836]

16   The surrender of life is nothing to sinking down into acknowledgment of inferiority.
        Speech in the Senate [February 19, 1847]

Thomas H. Palmer
1782–1861

17   'Tis a lesson you should heed,
     Try, try again.

[3]Usually quoted as "Don't give up the ship"; Captain Lawrence's final order as he was carried below, fatally wounded, before the capture of his ship by the British frigate *Shannon*.
[4]From this speech comes the phrase: Cohesive power of public plunder.

If at first you don't succeed,
Try, try again.

Teacher's Manual [1840][1]

Ann Taylor
1782–1866
Jane Taylor
1783–1824

1 Who ran to help me when I fell,
And would some pretty story tell,
Or kiss the place to make it well?
  My mother.
Original Poems for Infant Minds [1804]. My Mother [by ANN TAYLOR*], st. 6*

2 Twinkle, twinkle, little star,
How I wonder what you are,
Up above the world so high,
Like a diamond in the sky![2]
Rhymes for the Nursery [1806]. The Star, st. 1

3 I like little pussy, her coat is so warm;
And if I don't hurt her she'll do me no harm.
Ibid. I Like Little Pussy [by JANE TAYLOR*], st. 1*

4 Oh, that it were my chief delight
To do the things I ought!
Then let me try with all my might
To mind what I am taught.
Hymns for Infant Minds [1810]. For a Very Little Child

Daniel Webster[3]
1782–1852

5 It is, sir, as I have said, a small college, and yet there are those who love it.
Dartmouth College Case [1818]

6 Whatever makes men good Christians, makes them good citizens.
Speech at Plymouth, Massachusetts [December 22, 1820]

7 Labor in this country is independent and proud. It has not to ask the patronage of capital, but capital solicits the aid of labor. *Speech [April 2, 1824]*

8 We wish that this column, rising towards heaven among the pointed spires of so many temples dedicated to God, may contribute also to produce in all minds a pious feeling of dependence and gratitude. We wish, finally, that the last object to the sight of him who leaves his native shore, and the first to gladden his who revisits it, may be something which

shall remind him of the liberty and the glory of his country.
Address on Laying the Cornerstone of the Bunker Hill Monument [June 17, 1825]

9 Sink or swim, live or die, survive or perish, I give my hand and my heart to this vote.[4]
Discourse in Commemoration of Adams and Jefferson, Faneuil Hall, Boston [August 2, 1826]

10 It is my living sentiment, and by the blessing of God it shall be my dying sentiment—Independence now and Independence forever.[5]   *Ibid.*

11 Washington is in the clear upper sky.   *Ibid.*

12 The gentleman has not seen how to reply to this, otherwise than by supposing me to have advanced the doctrine that a national debt is a national blessing.[6]
Second Speech on Foote's Resolution [January 26, 1830]

13 I shall enter on no encomium upon Massachusetts; she needs none. There she is.[7] Behold her, and judge for yourselves. There is her history; the world knows it by heart. The past, at least, is secure. There is Boston and Concord and Lexington and Bunker Hill; and there they will remain forever.   *Ibid.*

14 The people's government, made for the people, made by the people, and answerable to the people.[8]
Ibid.

15 When my eyes shall be turned to behold for the last time the sun in heaven, may I not see him shining on the broken and dishonored fragments of a once glorious Union; on States dissevered, discordant, belligerent; on a land rent with civil feuds, or drenched, it may be, in fraternal blood.   *Ibid.*

16 Liberty and Union, now and forever, one and inseparable.   *Ibid.*

17 There is no refuge from confession but suicide; and suicide is confession.
Argument on the murder of Captain White [April 6, 1830]

18 He smote the rock of the national resources, and abundant streams of revenue gushed forth.[9] He touched the dead corpse of the Public Credit, and it sprung upon its feet.
Speech on Hamilton [March 10, 1831]

19 On this question of principle, while actual suffering was yet afar off, they [the Colonies] raised their

---

[1]Later popularized by EDWARD HICKSON [1803–1870] in his *Moral Songs [1857]* and often attributed to him or cited as a proverb.

[2]See Carroll, 517:20.

[3]See Sydney Smith, 380:11.

[4]Live or die, sink or swim.—GEORGE PEELE, *Edward I* [c. 1584]

[5]On the day of his [John Adams's] death, hearing the noise of bells and cannon, he asked the occasion. On being reminded that it was "Independent Day," he replied, "Independence forever."—DANIEL WEBSTER, *Works* [1903], *vol. I, p. 150*

[6]See Hamilton, 354:17.

[7]Generally misquoted as "Massachusetts, there she stands."

[8]Our sovereign, the people.—CHARLES JAMES FOX, toast [1798], *for which his name was erased from the Privy Council*

[9]See *Numbers 20:11, 10:2.*

flag against a power, to which, for purposes of foreign conquest and subjugation, Rome in the height of her glory is not to be compared—a power which has dotted over the surface of the whole globe with her possessions and military posts, whose morning drumbeat, following the sun, and keeping company with the hours, circles the earth with one continuous and unbroken strain of the martial airs of England.

Speech [May 7, 1834]

1   God grants liberty only to those who love it, and are always ready to guard and defend it.

Speech [June 3, 1834]

2   One country, one constitution, one destiny.

Speech [March 15, 1837]

3   When tillage begins, other arts follow. The farmers therefore are the founders of human civilization.

On Agriculture [January 13, 1840]

4   America has furnished to the world the character of Washington. And if our American institutions had done nothing else, that alone would have entitled them to the respect of mankind.

On the Completion of the Bunker Hill Monument [June 17, 1843]

5   Justice, sir, is the great interest of man on earth.

On Mr. Justice Story [September 12, 1845]

6   Inconsistencies of opinion, arising from changes of circumstances, are often justifiable.

Speech [July 25 and 27, 1846]

7   Liberty exists in proportion to wholesome restraint.

Speech at the Charleston Bar Dinner [May 10, 1847]

8   The law: It has honored us; may we honor it.

Ibid.

9   I was born an American; I will live an American; I shall die an American.   *Speech [July 17, 1850]*

10   Faneuil Hall, the cradle of American liberty.

Letter [April 1851]

11   Men hang out their signs indicative of their respective trades: shoemakers hang out a gigantic shoe; jewelers, a monster watch; and the dentist hangs out a gold tooth; but up in the mountains of New Hampshire, God Almighty has hung out a sign to show that there He makes men.

On the Old Man of the Mountain[1]; attributed

12   I still live.   *Last words [October 24, 1852]*

Simón Bolívar
1783–1830

13   A state too extensive in itself, or by virtue of its dependencies, ultimately falls into decay; its free government is transformed into a tyranny; it disregards the principles which it should preserve, and finally degenerates into despotism. The distinguishing characteristic of small republics is stability: the character of large republics is mutability.

Letter from Jamaica [Summer, 1815]

14   Those who have served the cause of the revolution have plowed the sea.   *Attributed*

15   The three greatest dolts in the world: Jesus Christ, Don Quixote, and I.   *Attributed*

Reginald Heber
1783–1826

16 Brightest and best of the sons of the morning,
Dawn on our darkness, and lend us thine aid.

Hymns. Epiphany [1811], st. 1

17 The Son of God goes forth to war,
A kingly crown to gain;
His blood-red banner streams afar;
Who follows in His train?

Ibid. The Son of God Goes Forth to War [1812], st. 1

18 From Greenland's icy mountains,
From India's coral strand,
Where Afric's sunny fountains
Roll down their golden sand.

Ibid. Missionary Hymn [1819], st. 1

19 Though every prospect pleases,
And only man is vile.[2]

Ibid. st. 2

20 The heathen in his blindness
Bows down to wood and stone.

Ibid.

21 Holy, Holy, Holy! Lord God Almighty!
Early in the morning our song shall rise to Thee:
Holy, Holy, Holy! Merciful and Mighty!
God in Three Persons, Blessed Trinity.

Ibid. Holy, Holy, Holy! [1827]

Washington Irving
1783–1859

22   How convenient it would be to many of our great men and great families of doubtful origin, could they have the privilege of the heroes of yore, who, whenever their origin was involved in obscurity, modestly announced themselves descended from a god.

Knickerbocker's History of New York [1809], bk. II, ch. 3

23   His wife "ruled the roast," and in governing the governor, governed the province, which might thus be said to be under petticoat government.

Ibid. IV, 4

---

[1]Natural rock formation in the shape of a human profile, in the Presidential Range of the White Mountains. It gave Hawthorne the theme of his story *The Great Stone Face.*

[2]Stanza 2 was dropped from the Episcopal *Hymnal* in 1940.

1   They claim to be the first inventors of those recondite beverages, cocktail, stonefence, and sherry cobbler.
    Knickerbocker's History, bk. IV, ch. 241

2   There is in every true woman's heart a spark of heavenly fire, which lies dormant in the broad daylight of prosperity; but which kindles up, and beams and blazes in the dark hour of adversity.
    The Sketch-Book [1819–1820]. The Wife

3   Those men are most apt to be obsequious and conciliating abroad, who are under the discipline of shrews at home.   *Ibid. Rip Van Winkle*[1]

4   A sharp tongue is the only edged tool that grows keener with constant use.   *Ibid.*

5   That happy age when a man can be idle with impunity.   *Ibid.*

6   A woman's whole life is a history of the affections.   *Ibid. The Broken Heart*

7   His [the author's] renown . . . has been purchased, not by deeds of violence and blood, but by the diligent dispensation of pleasure.
    Ibid. Westminster Abbey [The Poets' Corner]

8   Whenever a man's friends begin to compliment him about looking young, he may be sure that they think he is growing old.
    Bracebridge Hall [1822]. Bachelors

9   I am always at a loss to know how much to believe of my own stories.
    Tales of a Traveler [1824]. To the Reader

10   The almighty dollar, that great object of universal devotion throughout our land.
    Wolfert's Roost [1855]. The Creole Village

Stendhal [Henri Beyle]
1783–1842

11   Almost all our misfortunes in life come from the wrong notions we have about the things that happen to us. To know men thoroughly, to judge events sanely, is, therefore, a great step towards happiness.
    Journal [December 10, 1801]

12   I call "crystallization" that action of the mind that discovers fresh perfections in its beloved at every turn of events.   *De l'Amour [1822], ch. 1*

13   A wise woman never yields by appointment. It should always be an unforeseen happiness.
    Ibid. 60

14   Prudery is a kind of avarice, the worst of all.
    Ibid. Fragments

15   In matters of sentiment, the public has very crude ideas; and the most shocking fault of women is that they make the public the supreme judge of their lives.   *Ibid.*

16   A novel is a mirror that strolls along a highway. Now it reflects the blue of the skies, now the mud puddles underfoot.
    Le Rouge et le Noir (The Red and the Black)[2]
    [1830]

17   There is no such thing as "natural law": this expression is nothing but old nonsense. Prior to laws, what is natural is only the strength of the lion, or the need of the creature suffering from hunger or cold, in short, need.   *Ibid.*

18   I see but one rule: to be clear. If I am not clear, all my world crumbles to nothing.
    Reply to Balzac [October 30, 1840]

19   Wit lasts no more than two centuries.   *Ibid.*

20   It is the nobility of their style which will make our writers of 1840 unreadable forty years from now.
    Manuscript note [1840]

21   Love has always been the most important business in my life, I should say the only one.
    La Vie d'Henri Brulard [1890]

Allan Cunningham
1784–1842

22   A wet sheet and a flowing sea,
    A wind that follows fast,
    And fills the white and rustling sail,
    And bends the gallant mast.
    The Songs of Scotland [1825]. A Wet Sheet and a Flowing Sea, st. 1

Leigh Hunt
1784–1859

23   This Adonis in loveliness was a corpulent man of fifty.[3]   *The Examiner [March 22, 1812]*

24   Where the light woods go seaward from the town.
    The Story of Rimini [1816], canto I, l. 18

25   Green little vaulter in the sunny grass.
    To the Grasshopper and the Cricket [1817]

26   There lived a knight, when knighthood was in flow'r,
    Who charmed alike the tilt-yard and the bower.
    The Gentle Armour [1832], canto I

---

[1]The theme of Irving's story derives from DIOGENES LAERTIUS, *Epimenides* [c. 200]. Epimenides was sent by his father into the field to look for a sheep; he turned out of the road at midday and lay down in a certain cave and fell asleep, and slept there fifty-seven years; and after that, when awake, he went on looking for the sheep, thinking that he had been taking a short nap.

[2]Translated by NORBERT GUTERMAN.
[3]For this reference to the Prince Regent, Hunt was imprisoned. But he was allowed to redecorate the walls of his prison with a trellis of roses, had his family with him, and visitors were freely admitted; Byron, indeed, gave a dinner party in his honor at the jail.

1 Abou Ben Adhem (may his tribe increase!)
Awoke one night from a deep dream of peace.
Abou Ben Adhem [1838]

2 An angel writing in a book of gold.
Ibid.

3 Write me as one that loves his fellow men.
Ibid.

4 And showed the names whom love of God had
bless'd,
And lo! Ben Adhem's name led all the rest.
Ibid.

5 Jenny kissed me when we met,
Jumping from the chair she sat in;
Time, you thief, who love to get
Sweets into your list, put that in:
Say I'm weary, say I'm sad,
Say that health and wealth have missed me,
Say I'm growing old, but add,
Jenny kissed me.[1]
Rondeau [1838]

6 A Venus grown fat!
Blue-Stocking Revels

7 "No love," quoth he, "but vanity, sets love a task
like that."
The Glove and the Lions, st. 4

8   A pleasure so exquisite as almost to amount to
pain.   *Letter to Alexander Ireland [June 2, 1848]*

Henry John Temple, Viscount Palmerston
1784–1865

9   We have no eternal allies and we have no perpetual enemies. Our interests are eternal and perpetual,
and these interests it is our duty to follow.
*Speech in the House of Commons on foreign
policy [March 1, 1848]*

Zachary Taylor
1784–1850

10   Hurrah for Old Kentuck! That's the way to do it.
Give 'em hell, damn 'em.
*Shouted to the 2nd Kentucky Regiment on
seeing them rally in battle [Buena Vista,
Mexico, February 23, 1847]*

11   A little more grape, Captain Bragg.
Attributed [ibid.]

12   Tell him to go to hell.
*Reply to Santa Anna's demand for surrender
[ibid.]*

---

[1] Jenny was Jane Welsh Carlyle, who kissed Hunt when he
brought Carlyle good news.

Thomas De Quincey
1785–1859

13   The burden of the incommunicable.
*Confessions of an English Opium Eater [1822–
1856], pt. I*

14   So, then, Oxford Street, stonyhearted stepmother, thou that listenest to the sighs of orphans,
and drinkest the tears of children, at length I was
dismissed from thee.   *Ibid.*

15   Thou only givest these gifts to man, and thou
hast the keys of Paradise, O just, subtle, and mighty
opium!   *Ibid. II*

16   Everlasting farewells! and again, and yet again
reverberated—everlasting farewells!   *Ibid. III*

17   Dyspepsy is the ruin of most things: empires,
expeditions, and everything else.
Letter to Hessey [1823]

18   If once a man indulges himself in murder, very
soon he comes to think little of robbing; and from
robbing he comes next to drinking and Sabbath-
breaking, and from that to incivility and procrastination.
*Murder Considered as One of the Fine Arts
[1827]*

Lady Caroline Lamb
1785–1828

19   [Of Byron:] Mad, bad, and dangerous to know.
Journal [March 1812]

Thomas Love Peacock
1785–1866

20 Not drunk is he who from the floor
Can rise alone and still drink more;
But drunk is he who prostrate lies,
Without the power to drink or rise.
*The Misfortunes of Elphin [1829], ch. 3,
heading (translated from the Welsh)*

21 The mountain sheep are sweeter,
But the valley sheep are fatter;
We therefore deemed it meeter
To carry off the latter.
Ibid. 11

22   Ancient sculpture is the true school of modesty.
But where the Greeks had modesty, we have cant;
where they had poetry, we have cant; where they
had patriotism, we have cant; where they had anything that exalts, delights, or adorns humanity, we
have nothing but cant, cant, cant.
Crotchet Castle [1831], ch. 7

23   A book that furnishes no quotations is, *me judice,*
no book—it is a plaything.   *Ibid. 9*

Oliver Hazard Perry
1785–1819

1   We have met the enemy, and they are ours.[1]
*Dispatch from U.S. brig Niagara to General
William Henry Harrison, announcing his victory
at the battle of Lake Erie [September 10, 1813]*

Samuel Woodworth
1785–1842

2 How dear to this heart are the scenes of my
    childhood,
When fond recollection presents them to view!
The Old Oaken Bucket

3 The old oaken bucket, the iron-bound bucket,
The moss-covered bucket which hung in the well.
Ibid.

David Crockett
1786–1836

4 I leave this rule for others when I'm dead,
Be always sure you're right—then go ahead.[2]
Narrative of the Life of Colonel Crockett [1834]

5   My love was so hot as mighty nigh to burst my
boilers.   *Ibid.*

6   If I could rest anywhere it would be in Arkansaw
where the men are of the real half-horse, half-
alligator breed such as grows nowhere else on the
face of the earth.   *Ibid.*

7   Don't shoot, Colonel, I'll come down: I know I'm
a gone coon.[3]
Story told by Crockett of a treed raccoon

William Learned Marcy
1786–1857

8   They see nothing wrong in the rule that to the
victor belong the spoils of the enemy.
Speech in the Senate [January 1832]

Winfield Scott
1786–1866

9   The enemy say that Americans are good at a long
shot, but cannot stand the cold iron. I call upon you
instantly to give a lie to the slander. Charge!
*Address to the 11th Infantry Regiment
[Chippewa, Canada, June 5, 1814]*

---

[1]We have met the enemy and he is us.—WALT KELLY [1913–
1973], 1970 *Pogo* cartoon, used in 1971 Earth Day poster
[2]Crockett's motto in the War of 1812.
[3]A humorous Revolutionary War expression referring to a
story about a backwoods spy dressed in raccoon skins who said
to the British soldiers who discovered him, "I'm a gone coon."
—STUART BERG FLEXNER, *I Hear America Talking* (1976)

10   Say to the seceded States, "Wayward sisters, depart in peace."
Letter to W. H. Seward [March 3, 1861]

Seattle[4]
c. 1786–1866

11   When the last red man has vanished from this
earth, and his memory is only a story among the
whites, these shores will still swarm with the invisible dead of my people. And when your children's
children think they are alone in the fields, the forests,
the shops, the highways, or the quiet of the woods,
they will not be alone. There is no place in this
country where a man can be alone. At night when
the streets of your town and cities are quiet, and you
think they are empty, they will throng with the returning spirits that once thronged them, and that
still love these places. The white man will never be
alone.
*Speech to governor of Washington Territory
[c. 1855]*

François Guizot
1787–1874

12   Enrich yourselves![5]   *Speech [March 1, 1843]*

Emma Willard
1787–1870

13 Rocked in the cradle of the deep.
The Cradle of the Deep [1831]

George Noel Gordon, Lord Byron
1788–1824

14 "Friendship is Love without his wings!"
L'Amitié Est l'Amour sans Ailes[6] [written 1806]

15 I only know we loved in vain;
I only feel—farewell! farewell!
Farewell! If Ever Fondest Prayer [1808], st. 2

16   Near this spot are deposited the remains of one
who possessed beauty without vanity, strength without insolence, courage without ferocity, and all the
virtues of Man, without his vices. This praise, which
would be unmeaning flattery if inscribed over
human ashes, is but a just tribute to the memory of
Boatswain, a dog.
*Inscription on the monument of a
Newfoundland dog [1808]*

17 The poor dog, in life the firmest friend,
The first to welcome, foremost to defend.
Ibid.

---

[4]Chief of the Dwamish and allied tribes of Puget Sound. The
city of Seattle was named for him.
[5]Enrichissez-vous!
[6]A French proverb.

1   I'll publish right or wrong:
Fools are my theme, let satire be my song.
English Bards and Scotch Reviewers [1809], l. 5

2 'Tis pleasant, sure, to see one's name in print;
A book's a book, although there's nothing in 't.
Ibid. l. 51

3 A man must serve his time to every trade
Save censure—critics all are ready-made.
Ibid. l. 63

4 With just enough of learning to misquote.
Ibid. l. 66

5   As soon
Seek roses in December, ice in June;
Hope constancy in wind, or corn in chaff;
Believe a woman or an epitaph,
Or any other thing that's false, before
You trust in critics.
Ibid. l. 75

6 Better to err with Pope, than shine with Pye.
Ibid. l. 102

7 Maid of Athens, ere we part,
Give, oh give me back my heart!
Maid of Athens [1810], st. 1

8 Vex'd with mirth the drowsy ear of night.
Childe Harold's Pilgrimage, canto I [1812], st. 2

9 Had sigh'd to many, though he loved but one.
Ibid. st. 5

10 Maidens, like moths, are ever caught by glare,
And Mammon wins his way where seraphs might
despair.
Ibid. st. 9

11 Might shake the saintship of an anchorite.[1]
Ibid. st. 11

12 War, war is still the cry, "War even to the
knife!"[2]
Ibid. st. 86

13 Gone—glimmering through the dream of things
that were.
Ibid. canto II [1812], st. 2

14 A schoolboy's tale, the wonder of an hour!
Ibid.

15 Who would be free themselves must strike the
blow.
Ibid. st. 76

16 Where'er we tread 'tis haunted, holy ground.
Ibid. st. 88

17 What is the worst of woes that wait on age?
What stamps the wrinkle deeper on the brow?

To view each loved one blotted from life's page,
And be alone on earth, as I am now.
Ibid. st. 98

18 Once more upon the waters, yet once more!
And the waves bound beneath me as a steed
That knows his rider!
Ibid. canto III [1816], st. 2

19   Years steal
Fire from the mind as vigor from the limb;
And life's enchanted cup but sparkles near the
brim.
Ibid. st. 8

20 And Harold stands upon this place of skulls.
Ibid. st. 18

21 There was a sound of revelry by night,
And Belgium's capital had gather'd then
Her beauty and her chivalry, and bright
The lamps shone o'er fair women and brave men.
A thousand hearts beat happily; and when
Music arose with its voluptuous swell,
Soft eyes look'd love to eyes which spake again,
And all went merry as a marriage bell.
But hush! hark! a deep sound strikes like a rising
knell!
Ibid. st. 21

22 Did ye not hear it?—No! 'twas but the wind,
Or the car rattling o'er the stony street.
On with the dance! let joy be unconfined;
No sleep till morn, when Youth and Pleasure meet
To chase the glowing hours with flying feet.
Ibid. st. 22

23 Like to the apples on the Dead Sea's shore,
All ashes to the taste.[3]
Ibid. st. 34

24   Thou fatal Waterloo.
Millions of tongues record thee, and anew
Their children's lips shall echo them, and say—
"Here, where the sword united nations drew,
Our countrymen were warring on that day!"
And this is much, and all which will not pass
away.[4]
Ibid. st. 35

25 He who ascends to mountaintops, shall find
The loftiest peaks most wrapt in clouds and snow;
He who surpasses or subdues mankind
Must look down on the hate of those below.
Ibid. st. 45

26 All tenantless, save to the crannying wind.
Ibid. st. 47

27 History's purchased page to call them great.
Ibid. st. 48

---

[1]*Such lips would tempt a saint; such hands as those / Would make an anchorite lascivious.*— JOHN FORD, *'Tis Pity She's a Whore* [1633], *act I, sc. iii, l. 196*

[2]*War even to the knife!*— JOSÉ DE PALAFOX Y MELZI [1775–1847]
    Palafox, governor of Saragossa, had been summoned by the besieging French to surrender the city [1808].

[3]See Thomas Moore, 392:14.

[4]This was the passage Sir Winston Churchill quoted to President Franklin D. Roosevelt when both agreed to substitute the term United Nations for Associated Powers in the pact that the two leaders wished all the free nations to sign. [In a conference at the White House, January 1942.]

1 The castled crag of Drachenfels
Frowns o'er the wide and winding Rhine.
Childe Harold's Pilgrimage, canto III, st. 55

2 To fly from, need not be to hate, mankind.
Ibid. st. 69

3 By the blue rushing of the arrowy Rhone.
Ibid. st. 71

4 I live not in myself, but I become
Portion of that around me: and to me
High mountains are a feeling, but the hum
Of human cities torture.
Ibid. st. 72

5 Sapping a solemn creed with solemn sneer.
Ibid. st. 107

6 Fame is the thirst of youth.
Ibid. st. 112

7 I have not loved the world, nor the world me;
I have not flatter'd its rank breath, nor bow'd
To its idolatries a patient knee.
Ibid. st. 113

8   I stood
Among them, but not of them; in a shroud
Of thoughts which were not their thoughts.
Ibid.

9 I stood in Venice on the Bridge of Sighs,
A palace and a prison on each hand.
Ibid. canto IV [1818], st. 1

10 Where Venice sate in state, throned on her
hundred isles.
Ibid.

11 She looks a sea Cybele, fresh from ocean,
Rising with her tiara of proud towers
At airy distance, with majestic motion,
A ruler of the waters and their powers.
Ibid. st. 2

12 The beings of the mind are not of clay;
Essentially immortal, they create
And multiply in us a brighter ray
And more beloved existence.
Ibid. st. 5

13 'Tis solitude should teach us how to die;
It hath no flatterers; vanity can give
No hollow aid; alone—man with his God must
strive.
Ibid. st. 33

14 The Ariosto of the North.[1]
Ibid. st. 40

15 Italia! O Italia! thou who hast
The fatal gift of beauty.[2]
Ibid. st. 42

16 Let these describe the undescribable.
Ibid. st. 53

17 The starry Galileo, with his woes.
Ibid. st. 54

18 The poetry of speech.
Ibid. st. 58

19 Then farewell, Horace; whom I hated so,
Not for thy faults, but mine.
Ibid. st. 77

20 O Rome! my country! city of the soul!
Ibid. st. 78

21 The Niobe of nations! there she stands,
Childless and crownless, in her voiceless woe.
Ibid. st. 79

22 Yet, Freedom! yet thy banner, torn, but flying,
Streams like the thunderstorm *against* the wind.
Ibid. st. 98

23 Alas! our young affections run to waste,
Or water but the desert.
Ibid. st. 120

24 Of its own beauty is the mind diseased.
Ibid. st. 122

25 Time, the avenger! unto thee I lift
My hands, and eyes, and heart, and crave of thee
a gift.
Ibid. st. 130

26 Butcher'd to make a Roman holiday!
Ibid. st. 141

27 "While stands the Coliseum, Rome shall stand;
When falls the Coliseum, Rome shall fall;
And when Rome falls—the world."[3]
Ibid. st. 145

28 Oh! that the desert were my dwelling place.[4]
Ibid. st. 177

29 There is a pleasure in the pathless woods,
There is a rapture on the lonely shore,
There is society, where none intrudes,
By the deep sea, and music in its roar:
I love not man the less, but Nature more.
Ibid. st. 178

30 Roll on, thou deep and dark blue ocean—roll!
Ten thousand fleets sweep over thee in vain;
Man marks the earth with ruin—his control
Stops with the shore.
Ibid. st. 179

31 He sinks into thy depths with bubbling groan,
Without a grave, unknell'd, uncoffin'd, and
unknown.
Ibid.

[1]Walter Scott.
[2]Based on the famous sonnet of VINCENZO DA FILICAJA [1642–1707]: Italia, Italia! O tu cui feo la sorte.
[3]The saying of the ancient pilgrims, quoted from Bede by Gibbon in *Decline and Fall of the Roman Empire* [1776–1788], ch. 71.
[4]See *Jeremiah* 9:2, 28:22, and Cowper, 334:26.

1 Time writes no wrinkle on thine azure brow—
Such as creation's dawn beheld, thou rollest now.
Ibid. st. 182

2 Thou glorious mirror, where the Almighty's form
Glasses itself in tempests.
Ibid. st. 183

3 Dark-heaving—boundless, endless, and sublime—
The image of Eternity.
Ibid.

4 And I have loved thee, Ocean! and my joy
Of youthful sports was on thy breast to be
Borne, like thy bubbles, onward: from a boy
I wanton'd with thy breakers.
Ibid. st. 184

5 And trusted to thy billows far and near,
And laid my hand upon thy mane—as I do here.
Ibid.

6 I awoke one morning and found myself famous.
*Entry in Memoranda after publication of first
two cantos of Childe Harold's Pilgrimage. From
Thomas Moore, Life of Byron [1830], ch. 14*

7 Clime of the unforgotten brave!
The Giaour [1813], l. 103

8 I die—but first I have possess'd,
And come what may, I have been bless'd.
Ibid. l. 1114

9 Mark! where his carnage and his conquests cease!
He makes a solitude, and calls it—peace![1]
The Bride of Abydos [1813], canto II, st. 20

10 The fatal facility of the octosyllabic verse.
The Corsair [1814]. Dedication

11 Such hath it been—shall be—beneath the sun
The many still must labor for the one.
Ibid. canto I, st. 8

12 The Cincinnatus of the West,
Whom envy dared not hate,
Bequeathed the name of Washington
To make man blush there was but one![2]
Ode to Napoleon Bonaparte [1814], II

13 Lord of himself—that heritage of woe.
Lara [1814], canto I, st. 2

14 She walks in beauty, like the night
Of cloudless climes and starry skies;
And all that's best of dark and bright
Meet in her aspect and her eyes:
Thus mellow'd to that tender light
Which heaven to gaudy day denies.
*Hebrew Melodies [1815]. She Walks in Beauty,
st. 1*

15 The Assyrian came down like the wolf on the
fold,
And his cohorts were gleaming in purple and
gold;

And the sheen of their spears was like stars on the
sea,
When the blue wave rolls nightly on deep Galilee.
Ibid. The Destruction of Sennacherib,[3] st. 1

16 And the might of the Gentile, unsmote by the
sword,
Hath melted like snow in the glance of the Lord!
Ibid. st. 6

17 There's not a joy the world can give like that it
takes away,
When the glow of early thought declines in
feeling's dull decay.
Stanzas for Music [1815], st. 1

18 The glory and the nothing of a name.
Churchill's Grave, l. 43

19 For years fleet away with the wings of the dove.
The First Kiss of Love, st. 7

20 Fare thee well! and if forever,
Still forever, fare thee well.[4]
Fare Thee Well [1816], st. 1

21 Sighing that Nature form'd but one such man,
And broke the die, in molding Sheridan.[5]
Monody on the Death of Sheridan [1816], l. 117

22 Eternal Spirit of the chainless Mind!
Brightest in dungeons, Liberty! thou art.
*The Prisoner of Chillon [1816]. Sonnet on
Chillon, l. 1*

23 A light broke in upon my brain—
It was the carol of a bird;
It ceased, and then it came again,
The sweetest song ear ever heard.
Ibid. st. 10

24 There be none of Beauty's daughters
With a magic like thee;
And like music on the waters
Is thy sweet voice to me.
Stanzas for music [1816], st. 1

25 I had a dream which was not all a dream.
Darkness [1816]

26 Though the day of my destiny's over,
And the star of my fate hath declined.
Stanzas to Augusta [1816], st. 1

27 My boat is on the shore,
And my bark is on the sea;
But, before I go, Tom Moore,
Here's a double health to thee!

Here's a sigh to those who love me,
And a smile to those who hate;
And, whatever sky's above me,
Here's a heart for every fate.
To Thomas Moore [1817], st. 1, 2

[1]See *Tacitus, 109:21.*
[2]See *The Age of Bronze, 404:4.*
[3]See *II Kings, 19:35, 13:12.*
[4]See *Burns, 362:10.*
[5]See *Ariosto, 137:7.*

1 So we'll go no more a-roving
　So late into the night,
　Though the heart be still as loving,
　And the moon be still as bright.

　For the sword outwears its sheath,
　And the soul wears out the breast,
　And the heart must pause to breathe,
　And love itself have rest.

　Though the night was made for loving,
　And the day returns too soon,
　Yet we'll go no more a-roving
　By the light of the moon.
　　　　So We'll Go No More A-Roving [1817]

2 Sorrow is knowledge: they who know the most
　Must mourn the deepest o'er the fatal truth,
　The Tree of Knowledge is not that of Life.
　　　　Manfred [1817], act I, sc. i

3 His heart was one of those which most enamor
　　　us,
　Wax to receive, and marble to retain.[1]
　　　　Beppo [1818], st. 34

4 I love the language, that soft bastard Latin,
　Which melts like kisses from a female mouth.
　　　　Ibid. st. 44

5 I wish he[2] would explain his explanation.
　　　　Don Juan. Dedication [written 1818], st. 2

6 But—Oh! ye lords of ladies intellectual,
　Inform us truly, have they not henpeck'd you all?
　　　　Ibid. canto I, st. 22

7 Her stature tall—I hate a dumpy woman.
　　　　Ibid. st. 61

8 What men call gallantry, and gods adultery,
　Is much more common where the climate's sultry.
　　　　Ibid. st. 63

9 Christians have burnt each other, quite persuaded
　That all the Apostles would have done as they
　　　did.
　　　　Ibid. st. 83

10 A little still she strove, and much repented,
　And whispering "I will ne'er consent"—
　　　consented.
　　　　Ibid. st. 117

11 'Tis sweet to hear the watchdog's honest bark
　Bay deep-mouth'd welcome as we draw near
　　　home;
　'Tis sweet to know there is an eye will mark
　Our coming, and look brighter when we come.
　　　　Ibid. st. 123

12 Sweet is revenge—especially to women.[3]
　　　　Ibid. st. 124

13 Pleasure's a sin, and sometimes sin's a pleasure.
　　　　Ibid. st. 133

14 Man's love is of man's life a thing apart,
　'Tis woman's whole existence.
　　　　Ibid. st. 194

15 What is the end of fame? 'tis but to fill
　A certain portion of uncertain paper:
　Some liken it to climbing up a hill,
　Whose summit, like all hills, is lost in vapor.
　　　　Ibid. st. 218

16 There's nought, no doubt, so much the spirit
　　　calms
　As rum and true religion.
　　　　Ibid. canto II [1819], st. 34

17 A solitary shriek, the bubbling cry
　Of some strong swimmer in his agony.
　　　　Ibid. st. 53

18 Let us have wine and women, mirth and laughter,
　Sermons and soda water the day after.
　　　　Ibid. st. 178

19 Man, being reasonable, must get drunk;
　The best of life is but intoxication.
　　　　Ibid. st. 179

20　　　For man, to man so oft unjust,
　Is always so to women; one sole bond
　Awaits them, treachery is all their trust;
　Taught to conceal, their bursting hearts despond
　Over their idol, till some wealthier lust
　Buys them in marriage—and what rests beyond?
　A thankless husband, next a faithless lover,
　Then dressing, nursing, praying, and all's over.
　　　　Ibid. st. 200

21 In her first passion woman loves her lover,
　In all the others, all she loves is love.[4]
　　　　Ibid. canto III [1821], st. 3

22 Think you, if Laura had been Petrarch's wife,
　He would have written sonnets all his life?
　　　　Ibid. st. 8

23 Even good men like to make the public stare.
　　　　Ibid. st. 81

24 The isles of Greece, the isles of Greece![5]
　Where burning Sappho loved and sung.
　　　　Ibid. st. 86 [song, st. 1]

25 Eternal summer gilds them yet,
　But all, except their sun, is set.
　　　　Ibid.

26 The mountains look on Marathon,
　And Marathon looks on the sea;
　And musing there an hour alone,
　I dreamed that Greece might still be free.
　　　　Ibid. [st. 3]

27 Earth! render back from out thy breast
　A remnant of our Spartan dead!

[1]See Cervantes, 151:23.
[2]Coleridge.
[3]See Shakespeare, 219:11.

[4]See La Rochefoucauld, 266:1.
[5]From isles of Greece / The princes orgulous, their high blood chaf'd, / Have to the port of Athens sent their ships.
—SHAKESPEARE, *Troilus and Cressida*, prologue

Of the three hundred grant but three,
To make a new Thermopylae.

Ibid. [st. 7]

1 What, silent still? and silent all?
Ah! no;—the voices of the dead
Sound like a distant torrent's fall.

Ibid. [st. 8]

2 And if I laugh at any mortal thing,
'Tis that I may not weep.[1]

Ibid. canto IV [1821], st. 4

3 These two hated with a hate
Found only on the stage.

Ibid. st. 93

4 I've stood upon Achilles' tomb,
And heard Troy doubted; time will doubt of
Rome.

Ibid. st. 101

5 There's not a sea the passenger e'er pukes in,
Turns up more dangerous breakers than the
Euxine.

Ibid. canto V [1821], st. 5

6 And put himself upon his good behavior.

Ibid. st. 47

7 The women pardon'd all except her face.

Ibid. st. 113

8 A lady of "a certain age," which means
Certainly aged.

Ibid. canto VI, st. 69

9 Not so Leonidas and Washington,
Whose every battlefield is holy ground,
Which breathes of nations saved, not worlds
undone.

Ibid. canto VIII [1823], st. 5

10 "Gentlemen farmers"—a race worn out quite.

Ibid. canto IX [1823], st. 32

11 When Bishop Berkeley said "there was no
matter,"
And proved it—'twas no matter what he said.

Ibid. canto XI [1823], st. 1

12 And, after all, what is a lie? 'Tis but
The truth in masquerade.

Ibid. st. 37

13 'Tis strange the mind, that very fiery particle,
Should let itself be snuff'd out by an article.

Ibid. st. 60 (of John Keats)[2]

14 Ready money is Aladdin's lamp.

Ibid. canto XII [1823], st. 12

15 Cervantes smil'd Spain's chivalry away.

Ibid. canto XIII [1823], st. 11

16 The English winter—ending in July,
To recommence in August.

Ibid. st. 42

17 Society is now one polish'd horde,
Formed of two mighty tribes, the *Bores* and
Bored.

Ibid. st. 95

18 All human history attests
That happiness for man—the hungry sinner!—
Since Eve ate apples, much depends on dinner.

Ibid. st. 99

19 Of all the horrid, hideous notes of woe,
Sadder than owl songs or the midnight blast,
Is that portentous phrase, "I told you so."

Ibid. canto XIV [1823], st. 50

20 'Tis strange—but true; for truth is always
strange;
Stranger than fiction.[3]

Ibid. st. 101

21 The Devil hath not, in all his quiver's choice,
An arrow for the heart like a sweet voice.

Ibid. canto XV [1824], st. 13

22 The antique Persians taught three useful things—
To draw the bow, to ride, and speak the truth.

Ibid. canto XVI [1824], st. 1

23 Oh, talk not to me of a name great in story;
The days of our youth are the days of our glory;
And the myrtle and ivy of sweet two-and-twenty
Are worth all your laurels, though ever so plenty.
*Stanzas Written on the Road Between Florence
and Pisa [1821], st. 1*

24 All farewells should be sudden.

Sardanapalus [1821], act V

25 The best of prophets of the future is the past.

Journal [January 28, 1821]

26 The world is a bundle of hay,
Mankind are the asses that pull,
Each tugs in a different way—
And the greatest of all is John Bull!

Letter to Thomas Moore [June 22, 1821]

27 Because
He is all-powerful, must all-good, too, follow?
I judge but by the fruits—and they are bitter—
Which I must feed on for a fault not mine.

Cain [1821], act I, sc. i

28 Who killed John Keats?
"I," says the Quarterly,
So savage and Tartarly;
" 'Twas one of my feats."[4]

John Keats [c. 1821]

---

[3]Le vrai peut quelquefois n'être pas vraisemblable [Truth
may sometimes be improbable].—BOILEAU, *L'Art Poétique,
III, l. 48*

Truth is stranger than fiction, but not so popular.—*Anonymous*

[4]See *Don Juan,* 403:13; Shelley, 408:14; and Anonymous,
789:1.

[1]See La Bruyère, 283:14, and Beaumarchais, 336:5.
[2]See Byron, 403:28, and Shelley, 408:14.

1   He seems
To have seen better days, as who has not
Who has seen yesterday?
Werner [1822], act I, sc. i

2 The "good old times"—all times when old are
good—
Are gone.
The Age of Bronze [1823], st. 1

3 Whose[1] game was empires and whose stakes were
thrones,
Whose table earth—whose dice were human
bones.
Ibid. st. 3

4 While Franklin's quiet memory climbs to heaven,
Calming the lightning which he thence had riven,
Or drawing from the no less kindled earth
Freedom and peace to that which boasts his
birth;[2]
While Washington's a watchword, such as ne'er
Shall sink while there's an echo left to air.[3]
Ibid. st. 5

5 Sublime tobacco! which from east to west
Cheers the tar's labor or the Turkman's rest.[4]
The Island [1823], canto II, st. 19

6   What's drinking?
A mere pause from thinking!
The Deformed Transformed [1824], act III, sc. i

7 My days are in the yellow leaf;[5]
The flowers and fruits of love are gone;
The worm, the canker, and the grief
Are mine alone!
On My Thirty-sixth Year [1824], st. 2

8 Seek out—less often sought than found—
A soldier's grave, for thee the best;
Then look around, and choose thy ground,
And take thy rest.
Ibid. st. 10

9   Now Barabbas was a publisher.
Alleged alteration in the Bible, John 18:40[6]

Sarah Josepha Hale
1788–1879

10 Mary had a little lamb,
Its fleece was white as snow,

[1]Napoleon.
[2]See Franklin, 309:*n*1.
[3]See *Ode to Napoleon*, 401:12.
[4]"Let Aristotle and all your philosophers say what they like,
there is nothing to be compared with tobacco.—Molière,
Dom Juan; ou Le Festin de Pierre [1665], act I, sc. i
Translated by Curtis Hidden Page.
[5]See Shakespeare, 216:9 and 221:8.
[6]The publisher John Murray sent Byron a Bible in acknowledgment of a favor, and the poet returned it with the word
"robber" changed to "publisher."

And everywhere that Mary went,
The lamb was sure to go.
*Mary's Lamb,[7] st. 1. From The Juvenile
Miscellany [September 1830]*

Arthur Schopenhauer
1788–1860

11   To marry is to halve your rights and double your
duties.
The World as Will and Idea [1819], vol. II

12   Hatred comes from the heart; contempt from the
head; and neither feeling is quite within our control.
*Studies in Pessimism [1851].[8] Psychological
Observations*

13   Every man takes the limits of his own field of
vision for the limits of the world.   *Ibid.*

14   Every parting gives a foretaste of death;[9] every
coming together again a foretaste of the resurrection.
Ibid.

15   Dissimulation is innate in woman, and almost as
much a quality of the stupid as of the clever.
Ibid. On Women

16   The two foes of human happiness are pain and
boredom.
Essays. Personality; or, What a Man Is

17   A man who has no mental needs, because his
intellect is of the narrow and normal amount, is, in
the strict sense of the word, what is called a philistine.[10]   *Ibid.*

18   Intellect is invisible to the man who has none.
Ibid. Our Relation to Others, sec. 23

19   There is no more mistaken path to happiness
than worldliness, revelry, high life.
Ibid. Our Relation to Ourselves, sec. 24

20   Do not shorten the morning by getting up late;
look upon it as the quintessence of life, as to a
certain extent sacred.
Counsels and Maxims, ch. 2

James Fenimore Cooper
1789–1851

21   Few men exhibit greater diversity, or, if we may
so express it, greater antithesis of character than the
native warrior of North America. In war, he is dar-

[7]According to *The Story of Mary's Little Lamb* [1928], published by Mr. and Mrs. Henry Ford, the first three stanzas of
the poem are by John Roulstone [1805–1822]; Sarah Josepha
Hale's "genius completed the poem in its present form" (six
stanzas); "Mary" was Mary Elizabeth Sawyer [1806–1889] of
Sterling, Massachusetts; and the events of the poem are true.
[8]Translated by T. Bailey Saunders.
[9]See Haraucourt, 570:4.
[10]See Matthew Arnold, 499:12.

ing, boastful, cunning, ruthless, self-denying, and self-devoted; in peace, just, generous, hospitable, revengeful, superstitious, modest, and commonly chaste.   *The Last of the Mohicans [1826]*

1   'Tis grand! 'tis solemn! 'tis an education of itself to look upon!   *The Deerslayer [1841], ch. 2*

2   Those families, you know, are our upper crust —not upper ten thousand.[1]
           The Ways of the Hour [1850], ch. 6

Astolphe Louis Léonard, Marquis de Custine
1790–1857

3   This empire [Russia], vast as it is, is only a prison to which the emperor holds the key.[2]
           La Russie en 1839.[3] Peterhof, July 23, 1839

4   Whoever has really seen Russia will find himself content to live anywhere else. It is always good to know that a society exists where no happiness is possible because, by a law of nature, man cannot be happy unless he is free.   *Ibid. Conclusion*

Fitz-Greene Halleck
1790–1867

5   Green be the turf above thee,
Friend of my better days!
None knew thee but to love thee,
Nor named thee but to praise.
           On the Death of Joseph Rodman Drake [1820], st. 1

6   One of the few, the immortal names
That were not born to die.
           Ibid. Marco Bozzaris [1855], st. 7

Alphonse de Lamartine
1790–1869

7   O time, arrest your flight! and you, propitious hours, arrest your course! Let us savor the fleeting delights of our most beautiful days![4]
           The Lake [1820], st. 6

8   I say to this night: "Pass more slowly"; and the dawn will come to dispel the night.[5]   *Ibid. st. 8*

9   Limited in his nature, infinite in his desires, man is a fallen god who remembers the heavens.
           Méditations Poétiques [1820]. Sermon 2

10   What is our life but a succession of preludes to that unknown song whose first solemn note is sounded by death?[6]   *Ibid. 2nd series. Sermon 15*

11   The more I see of the representatives of the people, the more I admire my dogs.
           From A. G. G. D'ORSAY, Letter to John Forster [1850]

Samuel Gilman
1791–1858

12 Fair Harvard! Thy sons to thy Jubilee throng.
           Ode, Bicentennial, Harvard University [September 8, 1836], st. 1

13 First flower of their wilderness, star of their night,
Calm rising through change and through storm.
           Ibid.

John Howard Payne
1791–1852

14 'Mid pleasures and palaces though we may roam,
Be it ever so humble, there's no place like home.[7]
           Home, Sweet Home. From the opera Clari, the Maid of Milan [1823]

Charles Wolfe
1791–1823

15 Not a drum was heard, not a funeral note,
As his corse to the rampart we hurried.
           The Burial of Sir John Moore at Corunna [1817], st. 1

16 But he lay like a warrior taking his rest,
With his martial cloak around him.
           Ibid. st. 3

17 We carved not a line, and we raised not a stone—
But we left him alone with his glory.
           Ibid. st. 8

Victor Cousin
1792–1867

18   We need religion for religion's sake, morality for morality's sake, art for art's sake.
           Cours de Philosophie [1818]

John Keble
1792–1866

19 The voice that breathed o'er Eden
That earliest wedding day.
           Poems [1869]. Holy Matrimony, st. 1

---

[1]See Sam Slick, 419:9.
[2]See Stalin, 638:10.
[3]Translated by PHYLLIS PENN KOHLER.
[4]O temps, suspends ton vol! et vous, heures propices, / Suspendez votre cours! / Laissez-nous savourer les rapides délices / Des plus beaux de nos jours!
[5]Je dis à cette nuit: "Sois plus lente"; et l'aurore / Va dissiper la nuit.

[6]This passage was used by Franz Liszt as a heading for his tone poem *Les Préludes.*
[7]Home is home, be it never so homely.—*English proverb* [c. 1300]

Frederick Marryat
1792–1848

1 All zeal, Mr. Easy.
Midshipman Easy [1836], ch. 9

2 I haven't the gift of the gab, my sons—because I'm bred to the sea.
The Old Navy, st. 1

3 It's just six of one and half a dozen of the other.
The Pirate, ch. 4

4 Every man paddle his own canoe.
Settlers in Canada [1844], ch. 8

Joseph Mohr
1792–1848

5 Silent night! Holy night![1]
All is calm, all is bright.
Holy Night [1818]

Lord John Russell
1792–1878

6 If peace cannot be maintained with honor, it is no longer peace.[2]
Speech at Greenock [September 19, 1853]

7 Among the defects of the bill, which were numerous, one provision was conspicuous by its presence and another by its absence.
Speech to the electors of the City of London [April 1859]

Percy Bysshe Shelley
1792–1822

8 Power, like a desolating pestilence,
Pollutes whate'er it touches;[3] and obedience,
Bane of all genius, virtue, freedom, truth,
Makes slaves of men, and, of the human frame,
A mechanized automaton.
Queen Mab [1813], III

9 The awful shadow of some unseen Power
Floats though unseen among us—visiting
This various world with as inconstant wing
As summer winds that creep from flower to flower.
Hymn to Intellectual Beauty [1816], st. 1

10 Spirit of Beauty, that dost consecrate
With thine own hues all thou dost shine upon
Of human thought or form.
Ibid. st. 2

11 Some say that gleams of a remoter world
Visit the soul in sleep—that death is slumber,

[1]Stille Nacht! Heilige Nacht!
Music by FRANZ GRÜBER [1787–1863].
[2]See Disraeli, 435:14, and Neville Chamberlain, 606:10.
[3]See William Pitt, 313:2, and Acton, 521:5.

And that its shapes the busy thoughts outnumber
Of those who wake and live.
Mont Blanc [1816], st. 3

12 Man's yesterday may ne'er be like his morrow;
Nought may endure but Mutability.
Mutability [1816], I, st. 4

13 I met a traveler from an antique land
Who said: Two vast and trunkless legs of stone
Stand in the desert. Near them, on the sand,
Half sunk, a shattered visage lies, whose frown,
And wrinkled lip, and sneer of cold command,
Tell that its sculptor well those passions read.
Which yet survive, stamped on these lifeless things,
The hand that mocked them and the heart that fed:
And on the pedestal these words appear:
"My name is Ozymandias, king of kings:
Look on my works, ye Mighty, and despair!"
Nothing beside remains. Round the decay
Of that colossal wreck, boundless and bare,
The lone and level sands stretch far away.
Ozymandias [1817]

14 With hue like that when some great painter dips
His pencil in the gloom of earthquake and eclipse.
The Revolt of Islam [1817], canto V, st. 23

15 I could lie down like a tired child,
And weep away the life of care
Which I have borne and yet must bear,
Till death like sleep might steal on me.
Stanzas Written in Dejection near Naples [1818], st. 4

16 Ere Babylon was dust,
The Magus Zoroaster, my dead child,
Met his own image walking in the garden,
That apparition, sole of men, he saw.
Prometheus Unbound [1818–1819], act I, l. 191

17 The good want power, but to weep barren tears.
The powerful goodness want: worse need for them.
The wise want love; and those who love want wisdom;
And all best things are thus confused with ill.
Ibid. l. 625

18 Peace is in the grave.
The grave hides all things beautiful and good:
I am a God and cannot find it there.
Ibid. l. 638

19 From the dust of creeds outworn.
Ibid. l. 697

20 Forms more real than living man,
Nurslings of immortality!
Ibid. l. 748

21 To know nor faith, nor love nor law; to be
Omnipotent but friendless is to reign.
Ibid. act II, sc. iv, l. 47

1
        All love is sweet,
Given or returned. Common as light is love,
And its familiar voice wearies not ever. . . .
They who inspire it most are fortunate,
As I am now; but those who feel it most
Are happier still.
                                  Ibid. v, 39

2 Death is the veil which those who live call life:
They sleep, and it is lifted.[1]
                                  Ibid. III, iii, 113

3 Nor yet exempt, though ruling them like slaves,
From chance, and death, and mutability,
The clogs of that which else might overscar
The loftiest star of unascended heaven,
Pinnacled dim in the intense inane.
                                  Ibid. iv, 200

4 Familiar acts are beautiful through love.
                                  Ibid. IV, l. 403

5 Man, who wert once a despot and a slave;
A dupe and a deceiver; a decay;
A traveler from the cradle to the grave
Through the dim light of this immortal day.
                                  Ibid. l. 549

6 To suffer woes which Hope thinks infinite;
To forgive wrongs darker than death or night;
To defy Power, which seems omnipotent;
To love, and bear; to hope till Hope creates
From its own wreck the thing it contemplates;
Neither to change, nor falter, nor repent;
This, like thy glory, Titan, is to be
Good, great and joyous, beautiful and free;
This is alone Life, Joy, Empire, and Victory.
                                  Ibid. l. 570

7
        I love all waste
And solitary places; where we taste
The pleasure of believing what we see
Is boundless, as we wish our souls to be.
                                  Julian and Maddalo [1819], l. 14

8 Thou Paradise of exiles, Italy!
                                  Ibid. l. 57

9
        It is our will
That thus enchains us to permitted ill—
We might be otherwise—we might be all
We dream of happy, high majestical.
Where is the love, beauty and truth we seek,
But in our mind?
                                  Ibid. l. 170

10 *Me*—who am as a nerve o'er which do creep
The else unfelt oppressions of this earth.
                                  Ibid. l. 449

11
        Most wretched men
Are cradled into poetry by wrong;
They learn in suffering what they teach in song.[2]
                                  Ibid. l. 543

12 Chameleons feed on light and air:
Poets' food is love and fame.
                                  An Exhortation [1819], st. 1

13 O wild West Wind, thou breath of Autumn's
        being,
Thou, from whose unseen presence the leaves
        dead
Are driven, like ghosts from an enchanter fleeing,
Yellow, and black, and pale, and hectic red,
Pestilence-stricken multitudes.
                                  Ode to the West Wind [1819], l. 1

14 Wild Spirit, which art moving everywhere;
Destroyer and preserver; hear, oh, hear!
                                  Ibid. l. 13

15
        Thou dirge
Of the dying year, to which this closing night
Will be the dome of a vast sepulcher.
                                  Ibid. l. 23

16 Oh, lift me as a wave, a leaf, a cloud!
I fall upon the thorns of life! I bleed!
                                  Ibid. l. 44

17 Make me thy lyre, even as the forest is:
What if my leaves are falling like its own!
The tumult of thy mighty harmonies
Will take from both a deep, autumnal tone,
Sweet though in sadness. Be thou, Spirit fierce,
My spirit! Be thou me, impetuous one!
                                  Ibid. l. 57

18 The trumpet of a prophecy! O Wind,
If winter comes, can spring be far behind?
                                  Ibid. l. 68

19 Men of England, wherefore plow
For the lords who lay ye low?
                                  Song to the Men of England [1819], st. 1

20 Nothing in the world is single,
All things by a law divine
In one spirit meet and mingle.
                                  Love's Philosophy [1819], st. 1

21 I arise from dreams of thee
In the first sweet sleep of night,
When the winds are breathing low,
And the stars are shining bright.
                                  The Indian Serenade [1819], st. 1

22 Hell is a city much like London—
A populous and smoky city.
                                  Peter Bell the Third [1819], pt. III, st. 1

23
        Teas,
Where small talk dies in agonies.
                                  Ibid. st. 12

24 An old, mad, blind, despised and dying king.[3]
                                  England in 1819 [written 1819], l. 1

25 I met Murder on the way—
He had a mask like Castlereagh.
                                  The Mask of Anarchy [written 1819], st. 2

---

[1]Lift not the painted veil which those who live / Call Life.
—SHELLEY, *Sonnet* [1818]
[2]See Samuel Butler [1612–1680], 264:3.

[3]George III.

1   One by one, and two by two,
He tossed them human hearts to chew.
                              The Mask of Anarchy, st. 3

2 Rise like Lions after slumber
In unvanquishable number—
Shake your chains to earth like dew
Which in sleep had fallen on you—
Ye are many—they are few.
                              Ibid. st. 38, 91

3 A lovely lady, garmented in light
From her own beauty.
                              The Witch of Atlas [1820], st. 5

4 Hail to thee, blithe spirit!
Bird thou never wert,
That from Heaven, or near it,
Pourest thy full heart
In profuse strains of unpremeditated art.
                              To a Skylark [1821], st. 1

5 And singing still dost soar, and soaring ever
    singest.
                              Ibid. st. 2

6 Thou art unseen—but yet I hear thy shrill
    delight.
                              Ibid. st. 4

7 We look before and after,
And pine for what is not;
Our sincerest laughter
With some pain is fraught;
Our sweetest songs are those that tell of saddest
    thought.
                              Ibid. st. 18

8 Teach me half the gladness
That thy brain must know,
Such harmonious madness,
From my lips would flow,
The world should listen then, as I am listening
now.
                              Ibid. st. 21

9 Kings are like stars—they rise and set, they have
The worship of the world, but no repose.[1]
                              Hellas [1821], l. 195

10 The world's great age begins anew,
The golden years return,[2]
The earth doth like a snake renew
Her winter weeds outworn.
                              Ibid. l. 1060

11 The world is weary of the past,
Oh, might it die or rest at last!
                              Ibid. final chorus

12 What! alive, and so bold, O earth?
                              *Written on Hearing the News of the Death of
                              Napoleon [1821], st. 1*

[1]See Francis Bacon, 159:21.
[2]See Virgil, 92:10.

13 I never was attached to that great sect,
Whose doctrine is, that each one should select
Out of the crowd a mistress or a friend,
And all the rest, though fair and wise, commend
To cold oblivion, though 'tis in the code
Of modern morals, and the beaten road
Which those poor slaves with weary footsteps
    tread
Who travel to their home among the dead
By the broad highway of the world, and so
With one chained friend, perhaps a jealous foe,
The dreariest and the longest journey go.
True love in this differs from gold and clay,
That to divide is not to take away.
                              Epipsychidion [1821], l. 149

14 I weep for Adonais[3]—he is dead!
Oh, weep for Adonais! though our tears
Thaw not the frost which binds so dear a head!
                              Adonais [1821], st. 1

15   Till the Future dares
Forget the Past, his fate and fame shall be
An echo and a light unto eternity!
                              Ibid.

16 To that high capital, where kingly Death
Keeps his pale court in beauty and decay,
He came.
                              Ibid. st. 7

17 Lost Angel of a ruined Paradise!
                              Ibid. st. 10

18 Ah woe is me! Winter is come and gone,
But grief returns with the revolving year.
                              Ibid. st. 18

19   The intense atom glows
A moment, then is quenched in a most cold
    repose.
                              Ibid. st. 20

20 Alas! that all we loved of him should be,
But for our grief, as if it had not been,
And grief itself be mortal!
                              Ibid. st. 21

21 As long as skies are blue, and fields are green,
Evening must usher night, night urge the morrow,
Month follow month with woe, and year wake
    year to sorrow.
                              Ibid.

22 The Pilgrim of Eternity,[4] whose fame
Over his living head like heaven is bent,
An early but enduring monument,

[3]John Keats.
    Morning star, you shone among the living; and now in death
you shine, evening star, on the dead.—PLATO, *Aster (Star)*,
epigraph (in Greek) for Shelley's *Adonais*
    See Byron, 403:13 and 403:28.
[4]Byron.

Came, veiling all the lightnings of his song
In sorrow.

Ibid. st. 30

1 A pardlike spirit, beautiful and swift.

Ibid. st. 32

2 In mockery of monumental stone.

Ibid. st. 35

3 He hath awakened from the dream of life.

Ibid. st. 39

4 He has outsoared the shadow of our night;
Envy and calumny and hate and pain,
And that unrest which men miscall delight
Can touch him not and torture not again;
From the contagion of the world's slow stain
He is secure, and now can never mourn
A heart grown cold, a head grown gray in vain.

Ibid. st. 40

5 He lives, he wakes—'tis Death is dead, not he.

Ibid. st. 41

6 He is made one with Nature: there is heard
His voice in all her music, from the moan
Of thunder to the song of night's sweet bird.

Ibid. st. 42

7 He is a portion of the loveliness
Which once he made more lovely.

Ibid. st. 43

8 The One remains, the many change and pass;
Heaven's light forever shines, earth's shadows fly;
Life, like a dome of many-colored glass,
Stains the white radiance of eternity,
Until Death tramples it to fragments—Die,
If thou wouldst be with that which thou dost
seek!

Ibid. st. 52

9 The soul of Adonais, like a star,
Beacons from the abode where the Eternal are.

Ibid. st. 55

10 Music, when soft voices die,
Vibrates in the memory;
Odors, when sweet violets sicken,
Live within the sense they quicken.

Rose leaves, when the rose is dead,
Are heaped for the beloved's bed;
And so thy thoughts, when thou art gone,
Love itself shall slumber on.

To ——— : Music, When Soft Voices Die [1821]

11 One word is too often profaned
For me to profane it,
One feeling too falsely disdained
For thee to disdain it.

*To ——— : One Word Is Too Often Profaned
[1821], st. 1*

12 The desire of the moth for the star,
Of the night for the morrow,
The devotion to something afar
From the sphere of our sorrow.

Ibid. st. 2

13 Swiftly walk o'er the western wave, Spirit of
Night!

To Night [1821], st. 1

14 I ask of thee, beloved Night—
Swift be thine approaching flight,
Come soon, soon!

Ibid. st. 5

15 Rarely, rarely, comest thou,
Spirit of Delight!

Song: Rarely, Rarely, Comest Thou [1821], st. 1

16 Let me set my mournful ditty
To a merry measure;
Thou wilt never come for pity,
Thou wilt come for pleasure.

Ibid. st. 4

17 I love tranquil solitude
And such society
As is quiet, wise, and good.

Ibid. st. 7

18 There is no sport in hate when all the rage
Is on one side.

Lines to a Reviewer [1821]

19 When the lamp is shattered
The light in the dust lies dead—
When the cloud is scattered
The rainbow's glory is shed.

When the Lamp Is Shattered [1822], st. 1

20 Best and brightest,[1] come away!

To Jane: The Invitation [1822], l. 1

21 Away, away, from men and towns,
To the wild wood and the downs.

Ibid. l. 21

22 I am gone into the fields
To take what this sweet hour yields—
Reflection, you may come tomorrow,
Sit by the fireside with Sorrow.—
You with the unpaid bill, Despair—
You, tiresome verse-reciter, Care—
I will pay you in the grave.

Ibid. l. 31

23 A tone
Of some world far from ours,
Where music and moonlight and feeling
Are one.

*To Jane: The Keen Stars Were Twinkling
[1822], st. 4*

24 The great secret of morals is love; or a going out
of our own nature, and an identification of ourselves

[1]See Heber, 395:16.

with the beautiful which exists in thought, action, or person not our own. . . . The great instrument of moral good is the imagination; and poetry administers to the effect by acting upon the cause.

A Defense of Poetry [1821]

1   Poetry is the record of the best and happiest moments of the happiest and best minds.   *Ibid.*

2   Poets are the hierophants of an unapprehended inspiration; the mirrors of the gigantic shadows which futurity casts upon the present.   *Ibid.*

3   Poets are the unacknowledged legislators of the world.   *Ibid.*

Thaddeus Stevens
1792–1868

4   Though the President is Commander-in-Chief, Congress is his commander; and, God willing, he shall obey. He and his minions shall learn that this is not a Government of kings and satraps, but a Government of the people, and that Congress is the people.

Speech in House of Representatives [January 3, 1867]

John Clare
1793–1864

5 I am! yet what I am who cares, or knows? My friends forsake me like a memory lost.

I Am

6 Untroubling and untroubled where I lie— The grass below—above the vaulted sky.

Ibid.

7 The wind and clouds, now here, now there, Hold no such strange dominion As woman's cold, perverted will, And soon estranged opinion.

When Lovers Part

8 Till kicked and torn and beaten out he lies And leaves his hold and cackles, groans, and dies.

Badger

9   If life had a second edition, how I would correct the proofs.

Letter to a friend. From J. W. AND ANNE TIBBLE, John Clare: A Life [1932]

Felicia Dorothea Hemans
1793–1835

10 The stately homes of England! How beautiful they stand,

Amidst their tall ancestral trees, O'er all the pleasant land!¹

The Homes of England, st. 1

11 The breaking waves dashed high On a stern and rock-bound coast, And the woods, against a stormy sky, Their giant branches tossed.

The Landing of the Pilgrim Fathers, st. 1

12 A band of exiles moored their bark On a wild New England shore.

Ibid. st. 2

13 The boy² stood on the burning deck, Whence all but he had fled.

Casabianca, st. 1

14 The flames rolled on; he would not go Without his father's word.

Ibid. st. 3

15 In the busy haunts of men.

Tale of the Secret Tribunal, pt. I

16 He Never Smiled Again.

Title and refrain of poem

Henry Francis Lyte
1793–1847

17 Abide with me: fast falls the eventide; The darkness deepens; Lord, with me abide: When other helpers fail, and comforts flee, Help of the helpless, O abide with me.

Eventide [1847], st. 1

Lucretia Mott
1793–1880

18   Let woman then go on—not asking favors, but claiming as a right the removal of all hindrances to her elevation in the scale of being—let her receive encouragement for the proper cultivation of all her powers, so that she may enter profitably into the active business of life . . . Then in the marriage union, the independence of the husband and wife will be equal, their dependence mutual, and their obligations reciprocal.

Discourse on Woman [delivered December 17, 1849], last paragraph

---

¹The stately homes of England, / How beautiful they stood / Before their recent owners / Relinquished them for good.— E. V. KNOX [1881–1971], *The Stately Homes*
   I became one of the stately homos of England.—QUENTIN CRISP [1908–], *The Naked Civil Servant*
   See Woolf, 650:17.
²Giacomo Casabianca, whose father, Louis, at the battle of the Nile [1798], commanded the flagship *Orient*. It took fire and blew up, the commander was mortally wounded, and when most of the crew fled, Giacomo remained aboard, in an effort to help his gallant father.

William Cullen Bryant
1794–1878

1 To him who in the love of Nature holds
  Communion with her visible forms, she speaks
  A various language.
    Thanatopsis [1817–1821], l. 1

2 Go forth, under the open sky, and list
  To Nature's teachings.
    Ibid. l. 14

3   The hills,
  Rock-ribbed, and ancient as the sun.
    Ibid. l. 37

4 So live, that when thy summons comes to join
  The innumerable caravan which moves
  To that mysterious realm, where each shall take
  His chamber in the silent halls of death,
  Thou go not, like the quarry-slave at night,
  Scourged to his dungeon, but, sustained and
      soothed
  By an unfaltering trust, approach thy grave,
  Like one that wraps the drapery of his couch
  About him, and lies down to pleasant dreams.
    Ibid. l. 73

5 He who, from zone to zone,
  Guides through the boundless sky thy certain
      flight,
  In the long way that I must tread alone,
  Will lead my steps aright.
    To a Waterfowl [1818], st. 8

6 The groves were God's first temples.
    A Forest Hymn [1824]

7 Loveliest of lovely things are they,
  On earth, that soonest pass away.
  The rose that lives its little hour
  Is prized beyond the sculptured flower.
    *A Scene on the Banks of the Hudson [1828],
    st. 3*

8 The melancholy days are come, the saddest of the
      year,
  Of wailing winds, and naked woods, and
      meadows brown and sere.
    The Death of the Flowers [1832], st. 1

9 These are the gardens of the desert, these
  The unshorn fields, boundless and beautiful,
  For which the speech of England has no name—
  The prairies.
    The Prairies [1833]

10 Truth, crushed to earth, shall rise again.
    The Battlefield [1839], st. 9

Cornelius Vanderbilt
1794–1877

11   You have undertaken to cheat me. I won't sue
  you, for the law is too slow. I'll ruin you.
    Letter to former business associates [1853]

William Whewell
1794–1866

12   And so no force however great can stretch a cord
  however fine into an horizontal line which is accurately straight.
    *Elementary Treatise on Mechanics [1819]. The
    Equilibrium of Forces on a Point*

13   Man is the interpreter of nature, science the right
  interpretation.
    *Philosophy of the Inductive Sciences [1840],
    aphorism 17*

14   It is a test of true theories not only to account for
  but to predict phenomena.   *Ibid. 39*

Narcisse Achille, Comte de Salvandy
1795–1856

15   We are dancing on a volcano.
    *At a fête given by the Duc d'Orléans for the
    King of Naples [1830]*

Thomas Carlyle
1795–1881

16   Aesop's Fly, sitting on the axle of the chariot, has
  been much laughed at for exclaiming: What a dust I
  do raise!   *On Boswell's Life of Johnson [1832]*

17   Whoso belongs only to his own age, and reverences only its gilt Popinjays or soot-smeared Mum-
  bojumbos, must needs die with it.   *Ibid.*

18   The stupendous Fourth Estate, whose wide
  world-embracing influences what eye can take in?[1]
    Ibid.

19   All work is as seed sown; it grows and spreads,
  and sows itself anew.   *Ibid.*

20   The courage we desire and prize is not the courage to die decently, but to live manfully.   *Ibid.*

21   No man who has once heartily and wholly
  laughed can be altogether irreclaimably bad.
    Sartor Resartus [1833–1834], bk. I, ch. 4

22   He who first shortened the labor of copyists by
  device of movable types was disbanding hired armies, and cashiering most kings and senates, and
  creating a whole new democratic world: he had invented the art of printing.   *Ibid. 5*

23   Man is a tool-using animal. . . . Without tools
  he is nothing, with tools he is all.   *Ibid.*

24   Be not the slave of Words.   *Ibid. 8*

[1]Burke said there were Three Estates in Parliament; but, in
the Reporters' Gallery yonder, there sat a Fourth Estate more
important far than they all.—*On Heroes and Hero Worship*
[1841], *The Hero as Man of Letters*
  See Hazlitt, 390:6; Macaulay, 424:17; and Thackeray,
463:16.

1 What you see, yet can not see over, is as good as infinite.   *Sartor Resartus, bk. II, ch. 1*

2 Sarcasm I now see to be, in general, the language of the Devil; for which reason I have long since as good as renounced it.   *Ibid. 4*

3 The Everlasting No.   *Ibid. 7 (chapter title)*

4 With stupidity and sound digestion man may front much.   *Ibid.*

5 Great men are the inspired (speaking and acting) texts of that divine Book of Revelations, whereof a chapter is completed from epoch to epoch, and by some named History.   *Ibid. 8*

6 The Everlasting Yea.   *Ibid. 9 (chapter title)*

7 Man's unhappiness, as I construe, comes of his greatness; it is because there is an Infinite in him, which with all his cunning he cannot quite bury under the Finite.   *Ibid.*

8 Close thy Byron; open thy Goethe.   *Ibid.*

9 Love not Pleasure; love God.   *Ibid.*

10 As the Swiss inscription says: *Sprechen ist silbern, Schweigen ist golden*—"Speech is silvern, Silence is golden"; or, as I might rather express it, speech is of time, silence is of eternity.[1]   *Ibid. III, 3*

11 It is now almost my sole rule of life to clear myself of cants and formulas, as of poisonous Nessus shirts.   *Letter to His Wife [1835]*

12 France was long a despotism tempered by epigrams.   *History of the French Revolution [1837], pt. I, bk. I, ch. 1*

13 No lie you can speak or act but it will come, after longer or shorter circulation, like a bill drawn on Nature's Reality, and be presented there for payment—with the answer, No effects.   *Ibid. III, 1*

14 To a shower of gold most things are penetrable.   *Ibid. 7*

15 A whiff of grapeshot.   *Ibid. V, 3*

16 O poor mortals, how ye make this earth bitter for each other.   *Ibid. 5*

17 Battles, in these ages, are transacted by mechanism; with the slightest possible development of human individuality or spontaneity; men now even die, and kill one another, in an artificial manner.   *Ibid. VII, 4*

18 History a distillation of rumor.   *Ibid. 5*

19 The difference between Orthodoxy or My-doxy and Heterodoxy or Thy-doxy.[2]   *Ibid. pt. II, bk. IV, ch. 2*

20 The sea-green Incorruptible [Robespierre].   *Ibid. VI, 7*

21 Aristocracy of the Moneybag.   *Ibid. VII, 7*

22 Democracy is, by the nature of it, a self-canceling business; and gives in the long run a net result of zero.   *Chartism [1839], ch. 6, Laissez-Faire*

23 A well-written Life is almost as rare as a well-spent one.[3]   *Critical and Miscellaneous Essays [1839–1857]. Richter*

24 The great law of culture is: Let each become all that he was created capable of being.   *Ibid.*

25 The three great elements of modern civilization, gunpowder, printing, and the Protestant religion.   *Ibid. The State of German Literature*

26 In every man's writings, the character of the writer must lie recorded.   *Ibid. Goethe*

27 There is no heroic poem in the world but is at bottom a biography, the life of a man; also, it may be said, there is no life of a man, faithfully recorded, but is a heroic poem of its sort, rhymed or unrhymed.   *Ibid. Sir Walter Scott*

28 No man lives without jostling and being jostled; in all ways he has to elbow himself through the world, giving and receiving offense.   *Ibid.*

29 The uttered part of a man's life, let us always repeat, bears to the unuttered, unconscious part a small unknown proportion. He himself never knows it, much less do others.   *Ibid.*

30 Nothing that was worthy in the past departs; no truth or goodness realized by man ever dies, or can die.   *Ibid.*

31 No sadder proof can be given by a man of his own littleness than disbelief in great men.   *On Heroes and Hero Worship [1841]. The Hero as Divinity*

32 The history of the world is but the biography of great men.[4]   *Ibid.*

33 A vein of poetry exists in the hearts of all men.   *Ibid. The Hero as Poet*

34 The Age of Miracles is forever here!   *Ibid. The Hero as Priest*

35 All that mankind has done, thought, gained or been: it is lying as in magic preservation in the pages of books.   *Ibid. The Hero as Man of Letters*

---

[1]Silence is deep as Eternity; speech is shallow as Time.—*Critical and Miscellaneous Essays, Sir Walter Scott*

[Carlyle] loves silence somewhat platonically.—GIUSEPPI MAZZINI [1805–1872]; *from* JANE WELSH CARLYLE, *Letter to Mrs. Stirling* [October 1843]

[2]See William Warburton, 307:13.
[3]See Strachey, 643:17.
[4]History is the essence of innumerable biographies.—*On History* [1830]
See Emerson, 431:17.

1   The true university of these days is a collection of books.   *Ibid.*

2   The suffering man ought really to consume his own smoke; there is no good in emitting smoke till you have made it into fire.[1]   *Ibid.*

3   Adversity is sometimes hard upon a man; but for one man who can stand prosperity, there are a hundred that will stand adversity.   *Ibid.*

4   "A fair day's wages for a fair day's work": it is as just a demand as governed men ever made of governing. It is the everlasting right of man.
                          Past and Present [1843], bk. I, ch. 3

5   Fire is the best of servants; but what a master![2]
                                            Ibid. II, 9

6   All work, even cotton spinning, is noble; work is alone noble. . . . A life of ease is not for any man, nor for any god.   *Ibid. III, 4*

7   Every noble crown is, and on earth will forever be, a crown of thorns.   *Ibid. 8*

8   He who takes not counsel of the Unseen and Silent, from him will never come real visibility and speech.   *Ibid. 12*

9   Captains of Industry.
                          Ibid. IV, 4 (chapter title)

10   There is endless merit in a man's knowing when to have done.   *Francia [1845]*

11   He that works and *does* some Poem, not he that merely *says* one, is worthy of the name of Poet.
                          Introduction to Cromwell's Letters and Speeches [1845]

12   Respectable Professors of the Dismal Science.[3]
                          Latter Day Pamphlets, no. 1 [1850]

13   A Parliament speaking through reporters to Buncombe and the twenty-seven millions, mostly fools.
                                            Ibid. 6

14   A healthy hatred of scoundrels.   *Ibid. 12*

15   "Genius" (which means transcendent capacity of taking trouble, first of all).[4]
                          Life of Frederick the Great [1858–1865], bk. IV, ch. 3

16   Happy the people whose annals are blank in history books![5]   *Ibid. XVI, 1*

---

[1]Would that he consumed his own smoke. — MELVILLE, *Moby-Dick [1851], ch. 96*
Consume your own smoke. — ROBERT BROWNING, *Pacchiarotto [1876], 25*
[2]Mammon is like fire: the usefulest of all servants, if the frightfulest of all masters! — CARLYLE, *ibid. IV, 7*
[3]Referring to political economy and social science, Carlyle also in his *Occasional Discourse on the Negro Question [1849]* speaks of: What we might call, by way of eminence, the Dismal Science.
[4]See Buffon, 311:8; Samuel Butler [1835–1902], 525:5; and Jane Ellice Hopkins, 532:2.
[5]Carlyle identifies this as "Montesquieu's aphorism." See George Eliot, 483:22.

17 So here hath been dawning
    Another blue day:
    Think, wilt thou let it
    Slip useless away?
                                            Today

18   Lord Bacon could as easily have created the planets as he could have written Hamlet.
                          Remark in discussion

Joseph Rodman Drake
1795–1820

19 When Freedom from her mountain height,
    Unfurled her standard to the air,
    She tore the azure robe of night,
    And set the stars of glory there.
                          The American Flag [1819], st. 1

John Woodcock Graves
1795–1886

20 D' ye ken John Peel with his coat so gay?
    D' ye ken John Peel at the break of day?
    D' ye ken John Peel when he's far far away
    With his hounds and his horn in the morning?

    'Twas the sound of his horn brought me from my bed,
    And the cry of his hounds, has me ofttimes led;
    For Peel's view-hollo would waken the dead,
    Or the fox from his lair in the morning.
                          John Peel [1832]

John Keats
1795–1821

21 How many bards gild the lapses of time!
                          Poems [1817]. Sonnet. How Many Bards Gild the Lapses of Time

22 To one who has been long in city pent,[6]
    'Tis very sweet to look into the fair
    And open face of heaven.
                          Ibid. Sonnet. To One Who Has Been Long in City Pent

23 He mourns that day so soon has glided by:
    E'en like the passage of an angel's tear
    That falls through the clear ether silently.
                                            Ibid.

24 Much have I travel'd in the realms of gold,
    And many goodly states and kingdoms seen;
    Round many western islands have I been
    Which bards in fealty to Apollo hold.
    Oft of one wide expanse had I been told
    That deep-brow'd Homer ruled as his demesne;
    Yet did I never breathe its pure serene

---

[6]See Milton, 260:5.

Till I heard Chapman speak out loud and bold:
Then felt I like some watcher of the skies
When a new planet swims into his ken;
Or like stout Cortez when with eagle eyes
He star'd at the Pacific—and all his men
Look'd at each other with a wild surmise—
Silent, upon a peak in Darien.

> *Poems [1817]. Sonnet. On First Looking into Chapman's Homer*

1 And other spirits there are standing apart
Upon the forehead of the age to come;
These, these will give the world another heart,
And other pulses. Hear ye not the hum
Of mighty workings —— ?
Listen awhile, ye nations, and be dumb.

> *Ibid. Sonnet. Addressed to the Same (Benjamin Robert Haydon)*

2 The poetry of earth is never dead.

> *Ibid. Sonnet. On the Grasshopper and the Cricket*

3 O for ten years, that I may overwhelm
Myself in poesy; so I may do the deed
That my own soul has to itself decreed.

> *Ibid. Sleep and Poetry, l. 96*

4 And can I ever bid these joys farewell?
Yes, I must pass them for a nobler life,
Where I may find the agonies, the strife
Of human hearts.

> *Ibid. l. 122*

5　　　　A drainless shower
Of light is poesy; 'tis the supreme of power;
'Tis might half slumb'ring on its own right arm.

> *Ibid. l. 235*

6 But strength alone though of the Muses born
Is like a fallen angel: trees uptorn,
Darkness, and worms, and shrouds, and sepulchers
Delight it; for it feeds upon the burrs
And thorns of life; forgetting the great end
Of poesy, that it should be a friend
To soothe the cares, and lift the thoughts of man.

> *Ibid. l. 241*

7　　There is not a fiercer hell than the failure in a great object.

> *Endymion [1818], preface*

8　　The imagination of a boy is healthy, and the mature imagination of a man is healthy; but there is a space of life between, in which the soul is in a ferment, the character undecided, the way of life uncertain, the ambition thicksighted: thence proceeds mawkishness, and the thousand bitters which those men I speak of must necessarily taste in going over the following pages.

> *Ibid.*

9 A thing of beauty is a joy forever:
Its loveliness increases; it will never
Pass into nothingness; but still will keep
A bower quiet for us, and a sleep

Full of sweet dreams, and health, and quiet breathing.

> *Ibid. bk. I, l. 1*

10　　　　The grandeur of the dooms
We have imagined for the mighty dead.

> *Ibid. l. 20*

11 Wherein lies happiness? In that which becks
Our ready minds to fellowship divine,
A fellowship with essence; till we shine,
Full alchemiz'd, and free of space. Behold
The clear religion of heaven!

> *Ibid. l. 777*

12　　　　The crown of these
Is made of love and friendship, and sits high
Upon the forehead of humanity.

> *Ibid. l. 800*

13 A hope beyond the shadow of a dream.

> *Ibid. l. 857*

14　　　　'Tis the pest
Of love, that fairest joys give most unrest.

> *Ibid. II, l. 365*

15 A virgin purest lipp'd, yet in the lore
Of love deep learned to the red heart's core.

> *Poems [1820]. Lamia, pt. I, l. 189*

16 Let the mad poets say whate'er they please
Of the sweets of Fairies, Peris, Goddesses,
Haunters of cavern, lake, and waterfall,
As a real woman, lineal indeed
From Pyrrha's pebbles or old Adam's seed.

> *Ibid. l. 328*

17 Love in a hut, with water and a crust,
Is—Love, forgive us!—cinders, ashes, dust.

> *Ibid. II, l. 1*

18 Do not all charms fly
At the mere touch of cold philosophy?

> *Ibid. l. 229*

19 Philosophy will clip an angel's wings.

> *Ibid. l. 234*

20 For them the Ceylon diver held his breath,
And went all naked to the hungry shark;
For them his ears gush'd blood; for them in death
The seal on the cold ice with piteous bark
Lay full of darts; for them alone did seethe
A thousand men in troubles wide and dark:
Half-ignorant, they turn'd an easy wheel,
That set sharp racks at work, to pinch and peel.

> *Ibid. Isabella; or, The Pot of Basil, st. 15*

21 St. Agnes' Eve—Ah, bitter chill it was!
The owl, for all his feathers, was a-cold.
The hare limp'd trembling through the frozen grass,
And silent was the flock in woolly fold.

> *Ibid. The Eve of St. Agnes, st. 1*

22 The silver, snarling trumpets 'gan to chide.

> *Ibid. st. 4*

1 The music, yearning like a God in pain.

Ibid. st. 7

2 Asleep in lap of legends old.

Ibid. st. 15

3 Sudden a thought came like a full-blown rose,
  Flushing his brow, and in his pained heart
  Made purple riot.

Ibid. st. 16

4 Full on this casement shone the wintry moon,
  And threw warm gules on Madeline's fair breast.

Ibid. st. 25

5 Unclasps her warmed jewels one by one;
  Loosens her fragrant bodice; by degrees
  Her rich attire creeps rustling to her knees.

Ibid. st. 26

6 And still she slept an azure-lidded sleep,
  In blanched linen, smooth, and lavender'd,
  While he from forth the closet brought a heap
  Of candied apple, quince, and plum, and gourd;
  With jellies soother than the creamy curd,
  And lucent syrops, tinct with cinnamon;
  Manna and dates, in argosy transferr'd
  From Fez; and spiced dainties, every one,
  From silken Samarcand to cedar'd Lebanon.

Ibid. st. 30

7 Beyond a mortal man impassion'd far
  At these voluptuous accents, he arose,
  Ethereal, flush'd, and like a throbbing star
  Seen mid the sapphire heaven's deep repose;
  Into her dream he melted, as the rose,
  Blendeth its odour with the violet,—
  Solution sweet: meantime the frost-wind blows
  Like Love's alarum pattering the sharp sleet
  Against the window-panes; St. Agnes' moon hath
  set.

Ibid. st. 36

8 And they are gone: aye, ages long ago
  These lovers fled away into the storm.

Ibid. st. 42

9 My heart aches, and a drowsy numbness pains
  My sense, as though of hemlock I had drunk,
  Or emptied some dull opiate to the drains
  One minute past, and Lethe-wards had sunk.[1]

Ibid. Ode to a Nightingale, st. 1

10 That thou, light-winged Dryad of the trees,
   In some melodious plot
  Of beechen green, and shadows numberless,
  Singest of summer in full-throated ease.

Ibid.

11 O, for a draught of vintage! that hath been
  Cool'd a long age in the deep-delved earth,
  Tasting of Flora and the country green,
  Dance, and Provençal song, and sunburnt mirth!
  O, for a beaker full of the warm South,
  Full of the true, the blushful Hippocrene,

[1]See Horace, 95:14.

With beaded bubbles winking at the brim,
  And purple-stained mouth.

Ibid. st. 2

12 Fade far away, dissolve, and quite forget
  What thou among the leaves hast never known,
  The weariness, the fever, and the fret
  Here, where men sit and hear each other groan;
  Where palsy shakes a few, sad, last gray hairs,
  Where youth grows pale, and specter-thin, and
    dies;
  Where but to think is to be full of sorrow
    And leaden-eyed despairs.

Ibid. st. 3

13 Already with thee! tender is the night.

Ibid. st. 4

14 I cannot see what flowers are at my feet,
  Nor what soft incense hangs upon the boughs,
  But, in embalmed darkness, guess each sweet.

Ibid. st. 5

15 The murmurous haunt of flies on summer eves.

Ibid.

16 Darkling I listen; and, for many a time
  I have been half in love with easeful Death,
  Call'd him soft names in many a mused rhyme,
  To take into the air my quiet breath;
  Now more than ever seems it rich to die,
  To cease upon the midnight with no pain,
  While thou art pouring forth thy soul abroad
    In such an ecstasy!
  Still wouldst thou sing, and I have ears in vain—
  To thy high requiem become a sod.

Ibid. st. 6

17 Thou wast not born for death, immortal Bird!
  No hungry generations tread thee down;
  The voice I hear this passing night was heard
  In ancient days by emperor and clown:
  Perhaps the self-same song that found a path
  Through the sad heart of Ruth, when, sick for
    home,
  She stood in tears amid the alien corn;
  The same that oft-times hath
  Charm'd magic casements, opening on the foam
  Of perilous seas, in faery lands forlorn.

Ibid. st. 7

18 Forlorn! the very word is like a bell
  To toll me back from thee to my sole self!

Ibid. st. 8

19 Was it a vision, or a waking dream?
  Fled is that music:—Do I wake or sleep?

Ibid.

20 Thou still unravish'd bride of quietness,
   Thou foster-child of silence and slow time,
   Sylvan historian, who canst thus express
   A flowery tale more sweetly than our rhyme:
   What leaf-fring'd legend haunts about thy shape?

Ibid. Ode on a Grecian Urn, st. 1

1 What men or gods are these? What maidens loth?
  What mad pursuit? What struggle to escape?
  What pipes and timbrels? What wild ecstasy?
  Poems [1820]. Ode on a Grecian Urn, st. 1

2 Heard melodies are sweet, but those unheard
  Are sweeter.
  Ibid. st. 2

3 Forever wilt thou love, and she be fair!
  Ibid.

4 Forever piping songs forever new.
  Ibid. st. 3

5 Who are these coming to the sacrifice?
  To what green altar, O mysterious priest,
  Lead'st thou that heifer lowing at the skies,
  And all her silken flanks with garlands drest?
  Ibid. st. 4

6 O Attic shape! Fair attitude!
  Ibid. st. 5

7 When old age shall this generation waste,
  Thou shalt remain, in midst of other woe
  Than ours, a friend to man, to whom thou say'st,
  "Beauty is truth, truth beauty,"[1]—that is all
  Ye know on earth, and all ye need to know.
  Ibid.

8   To make delicious moan
  Upon the midnight hours.
  Ibid. Ode to Psyche, st. 3

9 A bright torch, and a casement ope at night,
  To let the warm Love in!
  Ibid. st. 5

10 Ever let the fancy roam,
  Pleasure never is at home.
  Ibid. Fancy, l. 1

11 Bards of Passion and of Mirth,
  Ye have left your souls on earth!
  Have ye souls in heaven too,
  Double-lived in regions new?
  Ibid. Ode written on the blank page before
  BEAUMONT AND FLETCHER, *The Fair Maid of the Inn*

12 Souls of Poets dead and gone,
  What Elysium have ye known,
  Happy field or mossy cavern,
  Choicer than the Mermaid Tavern?

  [1]If asked who said "Beauty is truth, truth beauty!" a great many readers would answer "Keats." But Keats said nothing of the sort. It is what he said the Grecian Urn said, his description and criticism of a certain kind of work of art, the kind from which the evils and problems of this life, the "heart high sorrowful and cloyed," are deliberately excluded. The Urn, for example, depicts, among other beautiful sights, the citadel of a hill town; it does not depict warfare, the evil which makes the citadel necessary.—AUDEN, *The Dyer's Hand* [1962], *Robert Frost*
  See Herbert, 243:9.

Have ye tippled drink more fine
  Than mine host's Canary wine?
  Ibid. Lines on the Mermaid Tavern

13 Season of mists and mellow fruitfulness,
  Close bosom-friend of the maturing sun.
  Ibid. To Autumn, st. 1

14 Who hath not seen thee oft amid thy store?
  Sometimes whoever seeks abroad may find
  Thee sitting careless on a granary floor,
  Thy hair soft-lifted by the winnowing wind;
  Or on a half-reap'd furrow sound asleep,
  Drows'd with the fume of poppies while thy hook
  Spares the next swath and all its twined flowers.
  Ibid. st. 2

15 Where are the songs of Spring? Ay, where are
      they?
  Think not of them, thou hast thy music too,—
  While barred clouds bloom the soft-dying day,
  And touch the stubble-plains with rosy hue;
  Then in a wailful choir the small gnats mourn
  Among the river sallows, borne aloft
  Or sinking as the light wind lives or dies;
  And full-grown lambs loud bleat from hilly bourn;
  Hedge-crickets sing; and now with treble soft
  The red-breast whistles from a garden-croft;
  And gathering swallows twitter in the skies.
  Ibid. st. 3

16 No, no, go not to Lethe, neither twist
  Wolf's-bane, tight-rooted, for its poisonous wine.
  Ibid. Ode on Melancholy, st. 1

17 Then glut thy sorrow on a morning rose.
  Ibid. st. 2

18 She dwells with Beauty—Beauty that must die;
  And Joy, whose hand is ever at his lips
  Bidding adieu; and aching Pleasure nigh,
  Turning to poison while the bee-mouth sips:
  Ay, in the very temple of Delight
  Veil'd Melancholy has her sovran shrine,
  Though seen of none save him whose strenuous
      tongue
  Can burst Joy's grape against his palate fine;
  His soul shall taste the sadness of her might,
  And be among her cloudy trophies hung.
  Ibid. st. 3

19 Deep in the shady sadness of a vale
  Far sunken from the healthy breath of morn,
  Far from the fiery noon, and eve's one star,
  Sat gray-hair'd Saturn, quiet as a stone.
  Ibid. Hyperion: A Fragment, bk. I, l. 1

20 How beautiful, if sorrow had not made
  Sorrow more beautiful than Beauty's self.
  Ibid. l. 35

21 For to bear all naked truths,
  And to envisage circumstance, all calm,
  That is the top of sovereignty.
  Ibid. II, l. 203

1 Knowledge enormous makes a God of me.
  Names, deeds, gray legends, dire events, rebellions,
  Majesties, sovran voices, agonies,
  Creations and destroyings, all at once
  Pour into the wide hollows of my brain,
  And deify me, as if some blithe wine
  Or bright elixir peerless I had drunk,
  And so become immortal.
      Ibid. III, l. 113

2 My spirit is too weak—mortality
  Weighs heavily on me like unwilling sleep,
  And each imagin'd pinnacle and steep
  Of godlike hardship, tells me I must die
  Like a sick Eagle looking at the sky.[1]
      Life, Letters and Literary Remains of John Keats, edited by RICHARD MONCKTON MILNES *[1848]. On Seeing the Elgin Marbles*

3 This living hand, now warm and capable
  Of earnest grasping, would, if it were cold
  And in the icy silence of the tomb,
  So haunt thy days and chill thy dreaming nights
  That thou would wish thine own heart dry of blood
  So in my veins red life might stream again,
  And thou be conscience-calm'd—see here it is—
  I hold it towards you.
      Ibid. Fragment: This Living Hand

4 O, what can ail thee, knight-at-arms,
  Alone and palely loitering?
  The sedge has withered from the lake,
  And no birds sing!
      Ibid. La Belle Dame Sans Merci,[2] st. 1

5 I met a lady in the meads
  Full beautiful, a faery's child;
  Her hair was long, her foot was light,
  And her eyes were wild.
      Ibid. st. 4

6 She looked at me as she did love,
  And made sweet moan.
      Ibid. st. 5

7 I saw pale kings and princes too,
  Pale warriors, death-pale were they all;
  They cried—"La Belle Dame sans Merci
  Hath thee in thrall!"
      Ibid. st. 10

8 It keeps eternal whisperings around
  Desolate shores, and with its mighty swell
  Gluts twice ten thousand caverns.
      Ibid. On the Sea[3]

9 When I have fears that I may cease to be
  Before my pen has glean'd my teeming brain.
      Ibid. Sonnet. When I Have Fears

10 When I behold, upon the night's starr'd face,
   Huge cloudy symbols of a high romance.
      Ibid.

11   Then on the shore
   Of the wide world I stand alone, and think
   Till love and fame to nothingness do sink.
      Ibid.

12 Bright star, would I were steadfast as thou art—
   Not in lone splendor hung aloft the night
   And watching, with eternal lids apart,
   Like nature's patient, sleepless Eremite,
   The moving waters at their priestlike task
   Of pure ablution round earth's human shores.
      Ibid. Sonnet. Bright Star[4]

13 None can usurp this height . . .
   But those to whom the miseries of the world
   Are misery, and will not let them rest.
      The Fall of Hyperion: A Dream, canto I, l. 147

14   I am certain of nothing but of the holiness of the Heart's affections and the truth of Imagination— What the imagination seizes as Beauty must be truth —whether it existed before or not.
      Letter to Benjamin Bailey [November 22, 1817]

15   The Imagination may be compared to Adam's dream—he awoke and found it truth.   *Ibid.*

16   O for a Life of Sensations rather than of Thoughts!   *Ibid.*

17   I scarcely remember counting upon any Happiness—I look not for it if it be not in the present hour —nothing startles me beyond the Moment. The setting sun will always set me to rights—or if a Sparrow come before my Window I take part in its existence and pick about the Gravel.   *Ibid.*

18   At once it struck me, what quality went to form a Man of Achievement especially in Literature & which Shakespeare possessed so enormously—I mean *Negative Capability,* that is, when man is capable of being in uncertainties, Mysteries, doubts, without any irritable reaching after fact & reason.
      Letter to George and Thomas Keats [December 22, 1817]

19   We hate poetry that has a palpable design upon us—and if we do not agree, seems to put its hand in its breeches pocket. Poetry should be great & unobtrusive, a thing which enters into one's soul, and does not startle it or amaze it with itself, but with its subject.
      Letter to John Hamilton Reynolds [February 3, 1818]

---

[1]Printed in the *Examiner* [February 23, 1817].
[2]Title of a French poem by ALAIN CHARTIER [c. 1385–c. 1433].
  First printed by Leigh Hunt in the *Indicator* [May 10, 1820].
[3]From want of regular rests, I have been rather *narvus,* and the passage in *Lear*—"Do you not hear the sea?"—has haunted me intensely.—KEATS, *Letter to John Hamilton Reynolds* [April 17, 1817]

  Edgar: . . . Hark! do you hear the sea?—SHAKESPEARE, *King Lear, act IV, sc. vi, l. 4*
[4]Written on a blank page in Shakespeare's *Poems.*

1   Poetry should surprise by a fine excess and not by Singularity—it should strike the Reader as a wording of his own highest thoughts, and appear almost a Remembrance.
Letter to John Taylor [February 27, 1818]

2   If poetry comes not as naturally as the Leaves to a tree it had better not come at all.   *Ibid.*

3   Scenery is fine—but human nature is finer.
Letter to Benjamin Bailey [March 13, 1818]

4   Axioms in philosophy are not axioms until they are proved upon our pulses: We read fine—things but never feel them to the full until we have gone the same steps as the Author.
Letter to John Hamilton Reynolds [May 3, 1818]

5   I compare human life to a large Mansion of Many Apartments, two of which I can only describe, the doors of the rest being as yet shut upon me.
Ibid.

6   I begin to get a little acquainted with my own strength and weakness.—Praise or blame has but a momentary effect on the man whose love of beauty in the abstract makes him a severe critic on his own Works.
Letter to James Hessey [October 8, 1818]

7   The Genius of Poetry must work out its own salvation in a man: It cannot be matured by law & precept, but by sensation & watchfulness in itself—That which is creative must create itself—In Endymion, I leaped headlong into the Sea, and thereby have become better acquainted with the Soundings, the quicksands, & the rocks, than if I had stayed upon the green shore, and piped a silly pipe, and took tea & comfortable advice.—I was never afraid of failure; for I would sooner fail than not be among the greatest.   *Ibid.*

8   I think I shall be among the English Poets after my death.
Letter to George and Georgiana Keats [October 14, 1818]

9   As to the poetical character itself . . . it is not itself—it has no self—it is every thing and nothing. . . . It has as much delight in conceiving an Iago as an Imogen.
Letter to Richard Woodhouse [October 27, 1818]

10   A Poet is the most unpoetical of anything in existence; because he has no Identity—he is continually infor[ming]—and filling some other Body.
Ibid.

11   A Man's life of any worth is a continual allegory—and very few eyes can see the Mystery of his life—a life like the scriptures, figurative. . . . Lord Byron cuts a figure, but he is not figurative—Shakespeare led a life of Allegory: his works are the comments on it.
Letter to George and Georgiana Keats [February 14–May 3, 1819]

12   I myself am pursuing the same instinctive course as the veriest human animal you can think of—I am however young writing at random—straining at particles of light in the midst of a great darkness—without knowing the bearing of any one assertion of any one opinion. Yet may I not in this be free from sin?   *Ibid. [March 19, 1819]*

13   Though a quarrel in the streets is a thing to be hated, the energies displayed in it are fine; the commonest Man shows a grace in his quarrel.
Ibid.

14   Nothing ever becomes real till it is experienced—Even a proverb is no Proverb to you till your Life has illustrated it.   *Ibid.*

15   Call the world if you Please "The vale of Soul-making."   *Ibid. [April 21, 1819]*

16   Do you not see how necessary a World of Pains and troubles is to School an Intelligence and make it a soul? A Place where the heart must feel and suffer in a thousand diverse ways!   *Ibid.*

17   I have two luxuries to brood over in my walks, your Loveliness and the hour of my death. O that I could have possession of them both in the same minute.   *To Fanny Brawne [July 25, 1819]*

18   "If I should die," said I to myself, "I have left no immortal work behind me—nothing to make my friends proud of my memory—but I have lov'd the principle of beauty in all things, and if I had had time I would have made myself remember'd."
Ibid. [c. February 1820]

19   You might curb your magnanimity and be more of an artist, and "load every rift"[1] of your subject with ore.   *Letter to Shelley [August 16, 1820]*

20   I can scarcely bid you good bye even in a letter. I always made an awkward bow. God bless you!
Letter to Charles Armitage Brown; Keats's last letter [November 30, 1820]

21   Here lies one whose name was writ in water.[2]
Epitaph for himself [1821]

Leopold von Ranke

1795–1886

22   You have reckoned that history ought to judge the past and to instruct the contemporary world as-

[1]Keats is quoting Spenser, *The Faerie Queene, bk. II, canto 7, st. 28.*

[2]Among the many things he has requested of me tonight, this is the principal—that on his gravestone shall be this inscription.—*Letter from* Joseph Severn [1793–1879], *in* Richard Monckton Milnes, *Life, Letters, and Literary Remains of John Keats* [1848]

to the future. The present attempt does not yield to that high office. It will merely tell how it really was.[1]

Geschichten der Romanischen und Germanischen Volker (History of the Romanic and Germanic Peoples) von 1492 bis 1535 [1824], preface

Alfred Bunn
1796–1860

1 I dreamt that I dwelt in marble halls,
With vassals and serfs at my side.
The Bohemian Girl [1843], act II, song

David Hartley Coleridge
1796–1849

2 The soul of man is larger than the sky,
Deeper than ocean, or the abysmal dark
Of the unfathomed center.
To Shakespeare

3 But what is Freedom? Rightly understood,
A universal license to be good.
Liberty [1833]

Horace Mann
1796–1859

4 Lost, yesterday, somewhere between sunrise and sunset, two golden hours, each set with sixty diamond minutes. No reward is offered, for they are gone forever. *Aphorism*

5 Be ashamed to die until you have won some victory for humanity.
Commencement Address, Antioch College [1859]

James Robinson Planché
1796–1880

6 It would have made a cat laugh.
The Queen of the Frogs [1879], act I, sc. iv

William Hickling Prescott
1796–1859

7 What, then, must have been the emotions of the Spaniards, when, after working their toilsome way into the upper air, the cloudy tabernacle parted before their eyes, and they beheld these fair scenes in all their pristine magnificence and beauty![2] It was like the spectacle which greeted the eyes of Moses from the summit of Pisgah, and, in the warm glow of

their feelings, they cried out, "It is the promised land!"
The Conquest of Mexico [1843], bk. III, ch. 8

8 Drawing his sword he [Pizarro] traced a line with it on the sand from East to West. Then, turning towards the South, "Friends and comrades!" he said, "on that side are toil, hunger, nakedness, the drenching storm, desertion, and death; on this side ease and pleasure. There lies Peru with its riches; here, Panama and its poverty. Choose, each man, what best becomes a brave Castilian. For my part, I go to the South." So saying, he stepped across the line. *The Conquest of Peru [1847], II, 4*

Sam Slick
[Thomas Chandler Haliburton]
1796–1865

9 I want you to see Peel, Stanley, Graham, Shiel, Russell, Macaulay, Old Joe, and so on. These men are all upper crust here.[3]
Sam Slick in England [1843–1844],[4] ch. 24

10 Circumstances alter cases.
The Old Judge [1849], ch. 15

Thomas Haynes Bayly
1797–1839

11 Tell me the tales that to me were so dear,
Long, long ago, long, long ago.
Long, Long Ago

Heinrich Heine
1797–1856

12 On wings of song, my dearest,
I will carry you off.
Auf Flügeln des Gesanges[5]

13 I will not mourn, although my heart is torn,
Oh, love forever lost! I will not mourn.
Ich grolle nicht[6]

14 I cannot tell why this imagined
Despair has fallen upon me;
The ghost of an ancient legend
That will not let me be.
Lorelei[7]

---

[1] Wie es eigentlich gewesen ist.
See Thucydides, 71:19.

[2] From this summit [Popocatépetl, 17,887 feet] could be seen the great city of Mexico, and the whole of the lake, and all the towns which were built in it. —Díaz del Castillo, *Historia Verdadera de la Conquista de la Nueva España*, pt. IV, ch. 53

[3] See James Fenimore Cooper, 405:2.

[4] The "Sam Slick" papers first appeared in a weekly paper in Nova Scotia [1836].

[5] Auf Flügeln des Gesanges, / Herzliebchen, trag ich dich fort.
Translated by Louis Untermeyer.

[6] Ich grolle nicht, und wenn das Herz auch bricht, / Ewig verlornes Lieb! Ich grolle nicht.
Translated by Louis Untermeyer.

[7] Ich weiss nicht, was soll es bedeuten, / Dass ich so traurig bin; / Ein Märchen aus alten Zeiten, / Das kommt mir nicht aus dem Sinn.
Translated by Louis Untermeyer.

1 Child, you are like a flower,
So sweet and pure and fair.
I look at you, and sadness
Touches me with a prayer.
Du bist wie eine Blume[1]

2 A knight of the holy spirit. *Harzreise*

3 Wherever they burn books they will also, in the end, burn human beings.
Almansor: A Tragedy [1823]

4 Every woman is the gift of a world to me.
Ideas: The Book Le Grand [1826]

5 Don't send a poet to London.
English Fragments [1828], ch. 2, London

6 Christianity is an idea, and as such is indestructible and immortal, like every idea.
History of Religion and Philosophy in Germany [1834], vol. I

7 Mark this well, you proud men of action: You are nothing but the unwitting agents of the men of thought who often, in quiet self-effacement, mark out most exactly all your doings in advance.
Ibid. III

8 People in those old times had convictions; we moderns only have opinions. And it needs more than a mere opinion to erect a Gothic cathedral.
The French Stage [1837], ch. 9

9 Wild, dark times are rumbling toward us, and the prophet who wishes to write a new apocalypse will have to invent entirely new beasts, and beasts so terrible that the ancient animal symbols of Saint John will seem like cooing doves and cupids in comparison.[2]
Lutetia; or, Paris [1842]. From the Augsberg Gazette, 12, VII

10 The future smells of Russian leather, of blood, of godlessness and of much whipping. I advise our grandchildren to come into the world with very thick skin on their backs. *Ibid.*

11 Ordinarily he is insane, but he has lucid moments when he is only stupid.
Of Savoye, appointed ambassador to Frankfurt by Lamartine [1848]

12 So we keep asking, over and over,
Until a handful of earth
Stops our mouths—
But is that an answer?
Lazarus, I [1854]

13 Of course he [God] will forgive me; that's his business [Bien sûr, il me pardonnera; c'est son métier].
Last words [1856]

14 No author is a man of genius to his publisher.
Attributed

[1]*Du bist wie eine Blume, / So hold und schön und rein; / Ich schau dich an, und Wehmut / Schleicht mir ins Herz hinein.*
Translated by Louis Untermeyer.
[2]See Yeats, 596:20.

Samuel Lover
1797–1868

15 Reproof on her lip, but a smile in her eye.
Rory O'More [1836], st. 1

16 "For there's luck in odd numbers," says Rory O'More.[3]
Ibid. st. 3

Sir Charles Lyell[4]
1797–1875

17 Although we are mere sojourners on the surface of the planet, chained to a mere point in space, enduring but for a moment of time, the human mind is not only enabled to number worlds beyond the unassisted ken of mortal eye, but to trace the events of indefinite ages before the creation of our race, and is not even withheld from penetrating into the dark secrets of the ocean, or the interior of the solid globe; free, like the spirit which the poet described as animating the universe.
Principles of Geology, vol. I [1830], ch. 13

18 It may be said that, so far from having a materialistic tendency, the supposed introduction into the earth at successive geological periods of life—sensation, instinct, the intelligence of the higher mammalia bordering on reason, and lastly, the improvable reason of Man himself—presents us with a picture of the ever-increasing dominion of mind over matter.
The Geological Evidences of the Antiquity of Man [1863]

Mary Wollstonecraft Shelley
1797–1851

19 Nothing contributes so much to tranquilize the mind as a steady purpose—a point on which the soul may fix its intellectual eye.
Frankenstein [1818], Letter I

20 I beheld the wretch—the miserable monster whom I had created. *Ibid. ch. 5*

Sojourner Truth
[Isabella Van Wagener]
c. 1797–1883

21 Frederick, is God dead?
Question to speaker Frederick Douglass [c. 1850]

22 That man . . . says that women need to be helped into carriages, and lifted over ditches, and to have the best place everywhere. Nobody ever helps me into carriages, or over mud puddles, or gives me

[3]See Pliny the Elder, 104:14, and Shakespeare, 183:7.
[4]See Gosse, 557:5.

any best place, and aren't I a woman? . . . I have plowed, and planted, and gathered into barns, and no man could head me—and aren't I a woman? I could work as much and eat as much as a man (when I could get it), and bear the lash as well—and aren't I a woman? I have borne thirteen children and seen them most all sold off into slavery, and when I cried out with a mother's grief, none but Jesus heard—and aren't I a woman?

Speech at Woman's Rights Convention, Akron, Ohio [1851]

1   That . . . man . . . says women can't have as much rights as man, cause Christ wasn't a woman. Where did your Christ come from? . . . From God and a woman. Man had nothing to do with him.
Ibid.

2   The rich rob the poor and the poor rob one another.
Saying

Alfred de Vigny
1797–1863

3   I love the sound of the horn, at night, in the depth of the woods.[1]
Le Cor [1826]

4   God! how sad is the sound of the horn deep in the woods![2]
Ibid.

5   I [Nature] am called a mother, but I am a grave.
La Maison du Berger [1864]

6   Love that which will never be seen twice.
Ibid.

7   Silence alone is great; all else is weakness.
La Mort du Loup [1864]

Auguste Comte
1798–1857

8   Love our principle, order our foundation, progress our goal.
Système de Politique Positive [1851–1854]

9   Nothing at bottom is real except humanity.[3]
Ibid.

10   The dead govern the living.
Catéchisme Positiviste [1852]

Eugène Delacroix
1798–1863

11   O young artist, you search for a subject—everything is a subject. Your subject is yourself, your impressions, your emotions in the presence of nature.
Oeuvres Littéraires

12   The first virtue of a painting is to be a feast for the eyes.
Journal [1893–1895]

[1]J'aime le son du cor, le soir, au fond des bois.
[2]Dieu! que le son du cor est triste au fond des bois!
[3]Il n'y a, au fond, de réel que l'humanité.

13   Painting is only a bridge linking the painter's mind with that of the viewer.
Ibid.

August Heinrich Hoffmann
[Hoffmann von Fallersleben]
1798–1874

14   Deutschland, Deutschland über Alles.[4]
Title of poem [September 1, 1841]

Jules Michelet
1798–1874

15   England is an empire, Germany is a nation, a race, France is a person.
Histoire de France [1833–1867]

16   What is the first part of politics? Education. The second? Education. And the third? Education.
Le Peuple [1846]

David Macbeth Moir
1798–1851

17   From the lone sheiling of the misty island
Mountains divide us, and the waste of seas—
Yet still the blood is strong, the heart is Highland,
And we in dreams behold the Hebrides.[5]
The Lone Sheiling [Canadian Boat Song, 1829]

Dionysios Solomos
1798–1857

18   We knew thee of old,
O divinely restored,
By the light of thine eyes
And the light of thy sword.

From the graves of our slain
Shall thy valor prevail
As we greet thee again—
Hail, Liberty! Hail!
Hymn to Liberty [1823],[6] *st.* 1, 2

19   On the blackened spine of Psara,
Glory, pacing alone,
Broods on her shining heroes;
She crowns her hair with a band
Born from the spare, few grasses
That are left in the ruined land.
The Destruction of Psara [1825][7]

[4]Germany before everything.
[5]This poem, entitled *Canadian Boat Song*, appeared [September 1829] anonymously in the *Noctes Ambrosianae* series in *Blackwood's Edinburgh Magazine*. It has been attributed to (among others) John Wilson ("Christopher North"), John Galt, John Lockhart, Scott, and to David Macbeth Moir, who is now generally accepted as the author.
[6]Translated by RUDYARD KIPLING.
Out of a total of 158 stanzas in the hymn, the first four have been adopted as the Greek national anthem.
[7]Translated by CEDRIC WHITMAN.

1   Enclose in your soul Greece (or something equal) and you shall feel every kind of grandeur.
Note to "Free Besieged" [c. 1833][1]

Amos Bronson Alcott
1799–1888

2   The true teacher defends his pupils against his own personal influence. He inspires self-trust. He guides their eyes from himself to the spirit that quickens him. He will have no disciple.
Orphic Sayings. From The Dial [July 1840]. The Teacher

3   Who loves a garden still his Eden keeps,
Perennial pleasures plants, and wholesome
harvests reaps.
Tablets [1868]

4   One must be a wise reader to quote wisely and well.   *Table Talk [1877]. Quotation*

5   To be ignorant of one's ignorance is the malady of the ignorant.   *Ibid. Discourse*

6   I press thee to my heart as Duty's faithful child.
Sonnet to Louisa May Alcott [1882]

Honoré de Balzac
1799–1850

7   It is easier to be a lover than a husband for the simple reason that it is more difficult to be witty every day than to say pretty things from time to time.   *Physiologie du Mariage [1829]*

8   I am a galley slave to pen and ink.
Lettres [1832]

9   Fame is the sun of the dead.
La Recherche de l'Absolu [1834]

10   Our heart is a treasury; if you spend all its wealth at once you are ruined. We find it as difficult to forgive a person for displaying his feeling in all its nakedness as we do to forgive a man for being penniless.   *Le Père Goriot [1835]*[2]

11   Man is no angel. He is sometimes more of a hypocrite and sometimes less, and then fools say that he has or has not principles.   *Ibid.*

12   "Temptations can be got rid of." "How?" "By yielding to them."   *Ibid.*

13   I believe in the incomprehensibility of God.
Letter to Éveline Hanska [1837]

14   Those sweetly smiling angels with pensive looks, innocent faces, and cash-boxes for hearts.
La Cousine Bette [1846], ch. 15

Simon Cameron
1799–1889

15   An honest politician is one who when he's bought stays bought.   *Attributed*

Rufus Choate
1799–1859

16   The courage of New England was the "courage of conscience." It did not rise to that insane and awful passion, the love of war for itself.
Address at Ipswich, Massachusetts, Centennial [1834]

17   We join ourselves to no party that does not carry the flag and keep step to the music of the Union.
Letter to the Whig Convention, Worcester, Massachusetts [October 1, 1855]

Thomas Hood
1799–1845

18   They went and told the sexton, and
The sexton tolled the bell.
Faithless Sally Brown [1826], st. 17

19   I remember, I remember
The house where I was born,
The little window where the sun
Came peeping in at morn.
I Remember, I Remember [1827], st. 1

20   Now 'tis little joy
To know I'm farther off from heaven
Than when I was a boy.
Ibid. st. 4

21   And there is even a happiness
That makes the heart afraid.
Ode to Melancholy [1827]

22   There's not a string attuned to mirth
But has its chord in melancholy.[3]
Ibid.

23   But evil is wrought by want of thought,
As well as want of heart.
The Lady's Dream [1827], st. 16

24   I saw old Autumn in the misty morn
Stand shadowless like silence, listening
To silence.
Ode: Autumn [1827], st. 1

25   Straight down the Crooked Lane,
And all round the Square.
A Plain Direction, st. 1

26   Never go to France
Unless you know the lingo,
If you do, like me,
You will repent, by jingo.
French and English [1839], st. 1

---

[1]Translated by GEORGE SAVIDIS.
[2]Translated by MARION AYTON CRAWFORD.

[3]See Robert Burton, 234:3; Fletcher, 236:13; and Milton, 251:22.

1 No warmth, no cheerfulness, no healthful ease,
  No comfortable feel in any member—
  No shade, no shine, no butterflies, no bees,
  No fruits, no flowers, no leaves, no birds,
  November!

          No!

2 Seem'd washing his hands with invisible soap
  In imperceptible water.

    Miss Kilmansegg and Her Precious Leg [1841–
    1843]. Her Christening, st. 10

3 O bed! O bed! delicious bed!
  That heaven upon earth to the weary head.

         Ibid. Her Dream, st. 8

4 With fingers weary and worn,
  With eyelids heavy and red,
  A woman sat in unwomanly rags
  Plying her needle and thread—
    Stitch! stitch! stitch!
  In poverty, hunger, and dirt.

      The Song of the Shirt [1843], st. 1

5 She sang the Song of the Shirt.

         Ibid.

6 Work! work! work!

        Ibid. st. 2

7 O men, with sisters dear!
  O men, with mothers and wives!
  It is not linen you're wearing out,
  But human creatures' lives!

        Ibid. st. 4

8 O God! that bread should be so dear,
  And flesh and blood so cheap!

        Ibid. st. 5

9 One more unfortunate,
  Weary of breath,
  Rashly importunate,
  Gone to her death!

  Take her up tenderly,
  Lift her with care;
  Fashioned so slenderly,
  Young, and so fair!

    The Bridge of Sighs [1844], st. 1, 2

10 Alas for the rarity
    Of Christian charity
      Under the sun!

        Ibid. st. 9

Mary Howitt

1799–1888

11 "Will you walk into my parlor?" said the Spider
    to the Fly;
  " 'Tis the prettiest little parlor that ever you did
    spy."

    The Spider and the Fly [1844]

Thomas Noel

1799–1861

12 Rattle his bones over the stones!
  He's only a pauper, whom nobody owns!

      The Pauper's Drive, st. 1

Alexander Pushkin

1799–1837

13   Reason's icy intimations,
  and records of a heart in pain.

    Eugene Onegin [1823],[1] *dedication*

14 Unforced, as conversation passed,
  he had the talent of saluting
  felicitously every theme,
  of listening like a judge supreme
  while serious topics were disputing,
  or, with an epigram-surprise,
  of kindling smiles in ladies' eyes.

    Ibid. ch. 1, st. 5

15 Always contented with his life,
  and with his dinner, and his wife.

      Ibid. st. 12

16 Why fight what's known to be decisive?
  Custom is despot of mankind.

      Ibid. st. 25

17 The illness with which he'd been smitten
  should have been analyzed when caught,
  something like *spleen*, that scourge of Britain,
  or Russia's *chondria,* for short.

      Ibid. st. 38

18 Habit is Heaven's own redress:
  it takes the place of happiness.

      Ibid. 2, st. 31

19 Love passed, the muse appeared, the weather
  of mind got clarity newfound;
  now free, I once more weave together
  emotion, thought, and magic sound.

      Ibid. st. 59

20 *Pimen [writing by lamplight]:* One more, the final
    record, and my annals
  Are ended, and fulfilled the duty laid
  By God on me, a sinner. Not in vain
  Hath God appointed me for many years
  A witness, teaching me the art of letters;
  A day will come when some laborious monk
  Will bring to light my zealous, nameless toil,
  Kindle, as I, his lamp, and from the parchment
  Shaking the dust of ages, will transcribe
  My chronicles.

    Boris Godunov [written 1825][2]

[1]Translated by CHARLES JOHNSTON.
[2]Translated by ALFRED HAYES.

1 Like to some magistrate grown gray in office
Calmly he contemplates alike the just
And unjust, with indifference he notes
Evil and good, and knows not wrath nor pity.
Boris Godunov

2   *Mosalsky:* Good folk! Maria Godunov and her son Feodor have poisoned themselves. We have seen their dead bodies. [*The people are silent with horror.*] Why are you silent? Cry, Long live Czar Dimitri Ivanovich! [*The people are speechless.*]   *Ibid.*

3 And thus he[1] mused: "From here, indeed
Shall we strike terror in the Swede;
And here a city, by our labor
Founded, shall gall our haughty neighbor;
'Here cut'—so Nature gives command—
'Your window through on Europe: stand
Firm-footed by the sea, unchanging!' "
The Bronze Horseman [written 1833][2]

John Brown
1800–1859

4   Had I so interfered in behalf of the rich, the powerful, the intelligent, the so-called great, or in behalf of any of their friends . . . every man in this court would have deemed it an act worthy of reward rather than punishment.
Last speech to the court [November 2, 1859]

5   I am yet too young to understand that God is any respecter of persons.[3] I believe that to have interfered as I have done . . . in behalf of His despised poor, was not wrong, but right. Now, if it is deemed necessary that I should forfeit my life for the furtherance of the ends of justice, and mingle my blood further with the blood of my children, and with the blood of millions in this slave country whose rights are disregarded by wicked, cruel, and unjust enactments, I submit: so let it be done!   *Ibid.*

6   This *is* a beautiful country.
Remark as he rode to the gallows, seated on his coffin [December 2, 1859]

Julia Crawford
1800–1885

7 Kathleen Mavourneen! the gray dawn is breaking,
The horn of the hunter is heard on the hill.
Kathleen Mavourneen [1835], st. 1

8 Oh! hast thou forgotten this day we must part?
It may be for years, and it may be forever;
Then why art thou silent, thou voice of my heart?
Ibid.

---

[1]Peter I (the Great) [1672–1725].
[2]Translated by OLIVER ELTON.
[3]See *Acts 10:34*, 41:10, and *I Peter 1:17*, 46:20.

Thomas Babington, Lord Macaulay
1800–1859

9   That is the best government which desires to make the people happy, and knows how to make them happy.
Essay on Mitford's History of Greece [1824]

10   Free trade, one of the greatest blessings which a government can confer on a people, is in almost every country unpopular.   *Ibid.*

11   Nobles by the right of an earlier creation, and priests by the imposition of a mightier hand.
On Milton [1825]

12   The dust and silence of the upper shelf.
Ibid.

13   As civilization advances, poetry almost necessarily declines.   *Ibid.*

14   Perhaps no person can be a poet, or can even enjoy poetry, without a certain unsoundness of mind.   *Ibid.*

15   There is only one cure for the evils which newly acquired freedom produces, and that cure is freedom.   *Ibid.*

16   Nothing is so useless as a general maxim.
On Machiavelli [1827]

17   The gallery in which the reporters sit has become a fourth estate of the realm.[4]
On Hallam's Constitutional History [1828]

18   The English Bible—a book which if everything else in our language should perish, would alone suffice to show the whole extent of its beauty and power.   *On John Dryden [1828]*

19   His imagination resembled the wings of an ostrich. It enabled him to run, though not to soar.
Ibid.

20   Men are never so likely to settle a question rightly as when they discuss it freely.
Southey's Colloquies on Society [1830]

21   A single breaker may recede; but the tide is evidently coming in.   *Ibid.*

22   That wonderful book, while it obtains admiration from the most fastidious critics, is loved by those who are too simple to admire it.
On Southey's edition of Bunyan's Pilgrim's Progress [1830]

23   We know no spectacle so ridiculous as the British public in one of its periodical fits of morality.
On Moore's Life of Lord Byron [1831]

24   From the poetry of Lord Byron they drew a system of ethics compounded of misanthropy and voluptuousness—a system in which the two great

---

[4]See Hazlitt, 390:6; Carlyle, 411:18; and Thackeray, 463:16.

commandments were to hate your neighbor and to love your neighbor's wife. *Ibid.*

1 Reform, that you may preserve.
Debate on the First Reform Bill [March 2, 1831]

2 Ye diners-out from whom we guard our spoons.[1]
Political Georgics

3 The conformation of his mind was such that whatever was little seemed to him great, and whatever was great seemed to him little.
On Horace Walpole [1833]

4 Such night in England ne'er had been, nor ne'er again shall be.
The Armada [1833], l. 34

5 An acre in Middlesex is better than a principality in Utopia. *On Lord Bacon [1837]*

6 Every schoolboy knows who imprisoned Montezuma, and who strangled Atahualpa.
On Lord Clive [1840]

7 She [the Roman Catholic Church] may still exist in undiminished vigor when some traveler from New Zealand shall, in the midst of a vast solitude, take his stand on a broken arch of London Bridge to sketch the ruins of St. Paul's.[2]
On Leopold von Ranke's History of the Popes [1840]

8 She [the Catholic Church] thoroughly understands what no other Church has ever understood, how to deal with enthusiasts. *Ibid.*

9 The Chief Justice was rich, quiet, and infamous.
On Warren Hastings [1841]

10 I shall not be satisfied unless I produce something which shall for a few days supersede the last fashionable novel on the tables of young ladies.
Letter to Macvey Napier [November 5, 1841]

11 In order that he might rob a neighbor whom he had promised to defend, black men fought on the coast of Coromandel and red men scalped each other by the great lakes of North America.
On Frederick the Great [1842]

12 We hardly know an instance of the strength and weakness of human nature so striking and so grotesque as the character of this haughty, vigilant, resolute, sagacious blue-stocking, half Mithridates and half Trissotin, bearing up against a world in arms,

[1]The louder he talked of his honor, the faster we counted our spoons.—EMERSON, *The Conduct of Life [1860], Worship*

[2]Who knows but that hereafter some traveler like myself will sit down upon the banks of the Seine, the Thames, or the Zuyder Zee, where now, in the tumult of enjoyment, the heart and the eyes are too slow to take in the multitude of sensations? Who knows but he will sit down solitary amid silent ruins, and weep a people inurned and their greatness changed into an empty name?—CONSTANTIN DE VOLNEY [1757–1820], *Ruins, ch. 11*

See Horace Walpole, 323:23.

with an ounce of poison in one pocket and a quire of bad verses in the other. *Ibid.*

13 Lars Porsena of Clusium
By the Nine Gods he swore
That the great house of Tarquin
Should suffer wrong no more.
By the Nine Gods he swore it,
And named a trysting day,
And bade his messengers ride forth
East and west and south and north,
To summon his array.
Lays of Ancient Rome [1842]. Horatius, st. 1

14 To every man upon this earth
Death cometh soon or late;
And how can man die better
Than facing fearful odds
For the ashes of his fathers,
And the temples of his gods?
Ibid. st. 27

15 He [Richard Steele] was a rake among scholars, and a scholar among rakes.
Review of Lucy Aikin's Life and Writings of Addison [1843]

16 A man who has never looked on Niagara has but a faint idea of a cataract; and he who has not read Barère's *Memoirs* may be said not to know what it is to lie. *On Mémoires de Bertrand Barère [1844]*

17 Those who compare the age in which their lot has fallen with a golden age which exists only in imagination, may talk of degeneracy and decay; but no man who is correctly informed as to the past will be disposed to take a morose or desponding view of the present.
History of England [1849–1861], vol. I, ch. 1

18 I shall cheerfully bear the reproach of having descended below the dignity of history if I can succeed in placing before the English of the nineteenth century a true picture of the life of their ancestors.
Ibid.

19 The Puritan hated bear-baiting, not because it gave pain to the bear, but because it gave pleasure to the spectators. *Ibid. 2*

20 There were gentlemen and there were seamen in the navy of Charles II. But the seamen were not gentlemen, and the gentlemen were not seamen.
Ibid. 3

21 He [Richard Rumbold, c. 1622–1685] never would believe that Providence had sent a few men into the world ready booted and spurred to ride, and millions ready saddled and bridled to be ridden.
Ibid. 5

22 The ambassador [of Russia] and the grandees who accompanied him were so gorgeous that all London crowded to stare at them, and so filthy that nobody dared to touch them. They came to the court balls dropping pearls and vermin. *Ibid. V, 23*

1   Your Constitution is all sail and no anchor.
Letter to H. S. Randall, author of a Life of Thomas Jefferson [May 23, 1857]

2   Soon fades the spell, soon comes the night;
Say will it not be then the same,
Whether we played the black or white,
Whether we lost or won the game?
Sermon in a Churchyard, st. 8

Helmuth von Moltke
1800–1891

3   First ponder, then dare.[1]   *Attributed*

4   The fate of every nation rests in its own power.
To the German Reichstag [March 1, 1880]

5   A war, even the most victorious, is a national misfortune.   *Letter [1880]*

Richard Bethell, Lord Westbury
1800–1873

6   Take a note of that; his Lordship says he will turn it over in what he is pleased to call his mind.
Attributed[2]

Jane Welsh Carlyle
1801–1866

7   A positive engagement to marry a certain person at a certain time, at all haps and hazards, I have always considered the most ridiculous thing on earth.   *To Thomas Carlyle [January 1825]*

8   In spite of the honestest efforts to annihilate my *I-ity*, or merge it in what the world doubtless considers my better half, I still find myself a self-subsisting and alas! self-seeking *me*.
To John Sterling [June 4, 1835]

9   Oh Lord! If you but knew what a brimstone of a creature I am behind all this beautiful amiability!
To Eliza Stodart [February 29, 1836]

10   Instead of boiling up individuals into the species, I would draw a chalk circle round every individuality, and preach to it to keep within that, and preserve and cultivate its identity.
To John Sterling [August 5, 1845]

11   I can see that the Lady has a genius for ruling, whilst I have a genius for *not being ruled*.
To Thomas Carlyle [September 28, 1845]

12   The surest way to get a thing in this life is to be prepared for doing without it, to the exclusion even of hope.   *Journal, August 1849*

[1]Erst wägen, dann wagen.
[2]Reportedly an audible aside from the barristers' table in reference to a presiding judge. According to T. A. Nash, *Life of Lord Westbury* [1888], *vol. I, p. 158,* Westbury disclaimed invention of the mot.

13   Not a hundredth part of the thoughts in my head have ever been or ever will be spoken or written —as long as I keep my senses, at least.
Ibid. July 16, 1858

14   The triumphal procession air which, in our manners and customs, is given to marriage at the outset —that singing of *Te Deum* before the battle has begun.   *To Miss Barnes [August 24, 1859]*

Thomas Cole
1801–1848

15   Over all, rocks, wood, and water, brooded the spirit of repose, and the silent energy of nature stirred the soul to its inmost depths.
Essay on American Scenery [1835]

David Glasgow Farragut
1801–1870

16   Damn the torpedoes—full speed ahead!
At the battle of Mobile Bay [August 5, 1864]

John Henry Cardinal Newman
1801–1890

17   Time hath a taming hand.
Persecution [1832], st. 3

18   Lead, kindly Light, amid the encircling gloom;
Lead thou me on!
The night is dark, and I am far from home;
Lead thou me on!
Keep thou my feet: I do not ask to see
The distant scene; one step enough for me.
The Pillar of Cloud [1833]. Lead Kindly Light, st. 1

19   Growth is the only evidence of life.
Apologia pro Vita Sua [1864]

20   It is thy very energy of thought
Which keeps thee from thy God.
Dream of Gerontius [1866], pt. III

21   Living Nature, not dull Art
Shall plan my ways and rule my heart.
Nature and Art [1868], st. 12

22   O Lord, support us all the day long, until the shadows lengthen and the evening comes, and the busy world is hushed, and the fever of life is over, and our work is done. Then in thy mercy grant us a safe lodging, and a holy rest, and peace at the last.
Sermon [1834]. Included in the Book of Common Prayer

23   There is a knowledge which is desirable, though nothing come of it, as being of itself a treasure, and a sufficient remuneration of years of labor.
The Idea of a University [1873]. Discourse V, pt. 6

1　It is almost a definition of a gentleman to say that he is one who never inflicts pain.　*Ibid. VIII*

2　The world is content with setting right the surface of things.　*Ibid.*

3　Ex umbris et imaginibus in veritatem [From shadows and symbols into the truth]!
　　　　His own epitaph at Edgbaston

Brigham Young
1801–1877

4　This is the place!
　　On first seeing the valley of the Great Salt Lake [July 24, 1847]

Lydia Maria Child
1802–1880

5　We first crush people to the earth, and then claim the right of trampling on them forever, because they are prostrate.
　　An Appeal on Behalf of That Class of Americans Called Africans [1833]

6　They [the slaves] have stabbed themselves for freedom—jumped into the waves for freedom—starved for freedom—fought like very tigers for freedom! But they have been hung, and burned, and shot—and their tyrants have been their historians!
　　　　Ibid.

7　Over the river and through the wood,
To grandfather's house we go;
　The horse knows the way
　To carry the sleigh,
Through the white and drifted snow.
　　Flowers for Children [1844–1846]. Thanksgiving Day, st. 1

8　Woman stock is rising in the market. I shall not live to see women vote, but I'll come and rap at the ballot box.
　　Letter to Sarah Shaw [August 3, 1856]

9　The United States is . . . a warning rather than an example to the world.
　　To the twenty-fifth-anniversary meeting of the Massachusetts Anti-Slavery Society [1857]

10　Yours for the unshackled exercise of every faculty by every human being.
　　Message to woman suffrage supporters [c. 1875]

David Christy
1802 – c. 1868

11　Cotton Is King; or, The Economical Relations of Slavery.　*Title of book [1855]*[1]

[1] Take away *time is money*, and what is left of England? take away *cotton is king*, and what is left of America?—HUGO, *Les Misérables* [1862], *Marius, bk. IV, ch. 4*

Alexandre Dumas the Elder
1802–1870

12　All for one, one for all, that is our motto.
　　The Three Musketeers [1844], ch. 9

13　Nothing succeeds like success.[2]
　　　　Ange Pitou [1854], vol. I

14　Let us look for the woman.[3]
　　The Mohicans of Paris [1854–1855], vol. III, ch. 10, 11

Victor Hugo
1802–1885

15　These two halves of God, the Pope and the emperor.　*Hernani [1830], act IV, sc. ii*

16　God became a man, granted. The devil became a woman.[4]　*Ruy Blas [1838], act II, sc. v*

17　Popularity? It is glory's small change.
　　　　Ibid. III, v

18　An invasion of armies can be resisted, but not an idea whose time has come.[5]
　　Histoire d'un Crime [written 1852], conclusion

19　Waterloo! Waterloo! Waterloo! Dismal plain![6]
　　Les Châtiments [1853]. L'Expiation

20　The eye was in the tomb and stared at Cain.
　　　　La Conscience [1859]

21　You have created a new thrill.[7]
　　Letter to Baudelaire [October 6, 1859]

22　The supreme happiness of life is the conviction that we are loved.
　　Les Misérables [1862].[8] Fantine, bk. V, ch. 4

23　Great grief is a divine and terrible radiance which transfigures the wretched.　*Ibid. 13*

24　Napoleon . . . mighty somnambulist of a vanished dream.　*Ibid. Cosette, bk. I, ch. 13*

25　Waterloo is a battle of the first rank won by a captain of the second.　*Ibid. 16*

26　Would you realize what Revolution is, call it Progress; and would you realize what Progress is, call it Tomorrow.　*Ibid. 17*

27　Great blunders are often made, like large ropes, of a multitude of fibers.　*Ibid. V, 10*

28　Upon the first goblet he read this inscription, *monkey wine;* upon the second, *lion wine;* upon the

[2] Rien ne réussit comme le succès.—*French proverb*
[3] The phrase "Cherchez la femme" is attributed to FOUCHÉ.
[4] Dieu s'est fait homme; soit. Le diable s'est fait femme.
[5] On résiste à l'invasion des armées; on ne résiste pas à l'invasion des idées. (Literally, one can resist the invasion of armies, but not the invasion of ideas.)
[6] Waterloo! Waterloo! Waterloo! Morne plaine!
[7] Vous créez un frisson nouveau.
[8] Translated by CHARLES E. WILBOUR.

third, *sheep wine;* upon the fourth, *swine wine.* These four inscriptions expressed the four descending degrees of drunkenness: the first, that which enlivens; the second, that which irritates; the third, that which stupefies; finally the last, that which brutalizes.   *Les Misérables. Cosette, bk. VI, ch. 9*

1   A man is not idle because he is absorbed in thought. There is a visible labor and there is an invisible labor.   *Ibid. VII, 8*

2   No one ever keeps a secret so well as a child.   *Ibid. VIII, 8*

3   Social prosperity means man happy, the citizen free, the nation great.   *Ibid. Saint Denis, bk. I, ch. 4*

4   Thought is the labor of the intellect, reverie is its pleasure.   *Ibid. II, 1*

5   Where the telescope ends, the microscope begins. Which of the two has the grander view?   *Ibid. III, 3*

6 To rise at six, to dine at ten,
To sup at six, to sleep at ten,
Makes a man live for ten times ten.
     Inscription over the door of Hugo's study

7   I represent a party which does not yet exist: the party of revolution, civilization.
This party will make the twentieth century.
There will issue from it first the United States of Europe, then the United States of the World.
     On the wall of the room in which Hugo died, Place des Vosges, Paris

Letitia Elizabeth Landon
1802–1838

8 Few, save the poor, feel for the poor.
     The Poor

9 Were it not better to forget
Than but remember and regret?
     Despondency

George Pope Morris
1802–1864

10 Woodman, spare that tree!
Touch not a single bough![1]
In youth it sheltered me,
And I'll protect it now.
     Woodman, Spare That Tree [1830], st. 1

11 The union of hearts—the union of hands—
And the flag of our Union forever!
     The Flag of Our Union [1851]

[1]See Campbell, 389:8.

William Allen
1803–1879

12   Fifty-four forty, or fight![2]
     Speech in the Senate [1844]

Thomas Lovell Beddoes
1803–1849

13 The anchor heaves, the ship swings free,
The sails swell full. To sea, to sea!
     Death's Jest-Book [1850]. Song from the Ship, st. 2

14 If there were dreams to sell,
What would you buy?
Some cost a passing-bell;
Some a light sigh.

     Dream Pedlary

George Borrow
1803–1881

15   There's night and day, brother, both sweet things; sun, moon, and stars, brother, all sweet things; there's likewise a wind on the heath. Life is very sweet, brother; who would wish to die?
     Lavengro [1851], ch. 25

16   I learned . . . to fear God, and to take my own part.   *Ibid. 86*

17   Youth will be served, every dog has his day, and mine has been a fine one.   *Ibid. 92*

18   Youth is the only season for enjoyment, and the first twenty-five years of one's life are worth all the rest of the longest life of man, even though those five-and-twenty be spent in penury and contempt, and the rest in the possession of wealth, honors, respectability.   *The Romany Rye [1857], ch. 30*

Edward Bulwer-Lytton, Baron Lytton
1803–1873

19   In other countries poverty is a misfortune—with us it is a crime.   *England and the English [1833]*

20 Rank is a great beautifier.
     The Lady of Lyons [1838], act II, sc. i

21 Love, like Death,
Levels all ranks, and lays the shepherd's crook
Beside the scepter.
     Ibid. III, ii

22 Beneath the rule of men entirely great,
The pen is mightier than the sword.
     Richelieu [1839], act II, sc. ii

[2]Slogan of expansionist Democrats in the 1844 presidential campaign, in which the Oregon boundary definition was a pressing issue. The new Democratic President, James K. Polk, compromised [1846] with Great Britain on the 49th parallel.

1 In the lexicon of youth, which fate reserves
For a bright manhood, there is no such word
As—*fail*.

Ibid.

2 It was a dark and stormy night.[1]

Paul Clifford [1840], opening words

3 [Tennyson:] Out-babying Wordsworth and
outglittering Keats.

The New Timon [1846], pt. 1

4   In science, address the few, in literature the many.
In science, the few must dictate opinion to the many;
in literature, the many, sooner or later, force their
judgment on the few.

Caxtonia. Readers and Writers

William Driver

1803–1886

5   I name thee Old Glory.

*As the flag was hoisted to the masthead of his
brig*[2]

Ralph Waldo Emerson

1803–1882

6 Good-bye, proud world! I'm going home;
Thou art not my friend and I'm not thine.

Poems [1847]. Good-bye, st. 1

7 Nor knowest thou what argument
Thy life to thy neighbor's creed has lent.
All are needed by each one;
Nothing is fair or good alone.

Ibid. Each and All, st. 1

8 I wiped away the weeds and foam,
I fetched my sea-born treasures home;
But the poor, unsightly, noisome things
Had left their beauty on the shore,
With the sun and the sand and the wild uproar.

Ibid. st. 3

9 I like a church; I like a cowl;
I love a prophet of the soul;
And on my heart monastic aisles
Fall like sweet strains or pensive smiles;
Yet not for all his faith can see
Would I that cowlèd churchman be.

Ibid. The Problem, st. 1

10 The hand that rounded Peter's dome,
And groined the aisles of Christian Rome,
Wrought in a sad sincerity;
Himself from God he could not free;

---

[1]See Schulz, 751:10.
[2]On August 10, 1831, a large American flag was presented to
Driver, captain of the *Charles Doggett,* by a band of women in
recognition of his bringing the British mutineers of the ship
Bounty from Tahiti back to their former home, Pitcairn Island.

He builded better than he knew—
The conscious stone to beauty grew.

Ibid. st. 2

11 Line in nature is not found;
Unit and universe are round;
In vain produced, all rays return;
Evil will bless, and ice will burn.

Ibid. Uriel, st. 2

12 Announced by all the trumpets of the sky,
Arrives the snow.

Ibid. The Snowstorm

13   Enclosed
In a tumultuous privacy of storm.

Ibid.

14 In May, when sea winds pierced our solitudes,
I found the fresh Rhodora in the woods.

Ibid. The Rhodora

15 Rhodora! if the sages ask thee why
This charm is wasted on the earth and sky,
Tell them, dear, that if eyes were made for seeing,
Then Beauty is its own excuse for being.

Ibid.

16 Things are of the snake.

Ibid. Ode Inscribed to W. H. Channing

17 Things are in the saddle,
And ride mankind.

Ibid.

18 There are two laws discrete,
Not reconciled—
Law for man, and law for thing.

Ibid.

19 Give all to love;
Obey thy heart;
Friends, kindred, days,
Estate, good fame,
Plans, credit and the Muse,
Nothing refuse.

Ibid. Give All to Love, st. 1

20 Heartily know,
When half-gods go,
The gods arrive.

Ibid. st. 6

21 Love not the flower they pluck, and know it not,
And all their botany is Latin names.

Ibid. Blight

22 By the rude bridge that arched the flood,
Their flag to April's breeze unfurled,
Here once the embattled farmers stood,
And fired the shot heard round the world.

*Ibid. Hymn Sung at the Completion of the
Battle Monument, Concord, Massachusetts
[July 4, 1837], st. 1*

23 "Pass in, pass in," the angels say,
"In to the upper doors,
Nor count compartments of the floors,

But mount to paradise
By the stairway of surprise."

Poems. Merlin I

1 God said, I am tired of kings,
I suffer them no more;
Up to my ear the morning brings
The outrage of the poor.
*May-Day and Other Pieces [1867]. Boston
Hymn, st. 2*

2 Today unbind the captive,
So only are ye unbound;
Lift up a people from the dust,
Trump of their rescue, sound!

Ibid. st. 17

3 I think no virtue goes with size.

Ibid. The Titmouse

4 So nigh is grandeur to our dust,
So near is God to man,
When Duty whispers low, *Thou must,*
The youth replies, *I can.*

Ibid. Voluntaries, III

5 Wilt thou seal up the avenues of ill?
Pay every debt, as if God wrote the bill.

Ibid. "Suum Cuique"

6 Daughters of Time, the hypocritic Days,
Muffled and dumb like barefoot dervishes,
And marching single in an endless file,
Bring diadems and fagots in their hands.

Ibid. Days

7   I, too late,
Under her solemn fillet saw the scorn.

Ibid.

8 It is time to be old,
To take in sail.

Ibid. Terminus

9 Obey the voice at eve obeyed at prime.

Ibid.

10 If the red slayer think he slays,
Or if the slain think he is slain,
They know not well the subtle ways
I keep, and pass, and turn again.[1]

Ibid. Brahma

11 They reckon ill who leave me out;
When me they fly, I am the wings;
I am the doubter and the doubt,
And I the hymn the Brahmin sings.

Ibid.

12 I am the owner of the sphere,
Of the seven stars and the solar year,
Of Caesar's hand, and Plato's brain,
Of Lord Christ's heart, and Shakespeare's strain.

Ibid. History

13   To different minds, the same world is a hell, and
a heaven.   *Journal. December 20, 1822*

[1]See *The Upanishads*, 50:20.

14   Four snakes gliding up and down a hollow for no
purpose that I could see—not to eat, not for love,
but only gliding.   *Ibid. April 11, 1834*

15   I wish to write such rhymes as shall not suggest
a restraint, but contrariwise the wildest freedom.

Ibid. June 27, 1839

16   You shall have joy, or you shall have power, said
God; you shall not have both.

Ibid. October 1842

17   The sky is the daily bread of the eyes.

Ibid. May 25, 1843

18   Poetry must be as new as foam, and as old as the
rock.   *Ibid. March 1845*

19   *Immortality.* I notice that as soon as writers
broach this question they begin to quote. I hate quotation. Tell me what you know.

Ibid. May 1849

20   Blessed are those who have no talent!

Ibid. February 1850

21   The word *liberty* in the mouth of Mr. Webster
sounds like the word *love* in the mouth of a courtesan.   *Ibid. February 12 (?), 1851*

22   I trust a good deal to common fame, as we all
must. If a man has good corn, or wood, or boards,
or pigs, to sell, or can make better chairs or knives,
crucibles or church organs, than anybody else, you
will find a broad hard-beaten road to his house,
though it be in the woods.[2]   *Ibid. February 1855*

23   The blazing evidence of immortality is our dissatisfaction with any other solution.

Ibid. July 1855

24   The foregoing generations beheld God and nature face to face; we, through their eyes. Why should
not we also enjoy an original relation to the universe?   *Nature [1836, 1849]. Introduction*

25   Undoubtedly we have no questions to ask which
are unanswerable. We must trust the perfection of
the creation so far, as to believe that whatever curiosity the order of things has awakened in our minds,
the order of things can satisfy.   *Ibid.*

26   Crossing a bare common, in snow puddles, at
twilight, under a clouded sky, without having in my
thoughts any occurrence of special good fortune, I
have enjoyed a perfect exhilaration. I am glad to the
brink of fear.   *Ibid. sec. 1*

27   Standing on the bare ground . . . all mean ego-
tism vanishes. I become a transparent eyeball; I am
nothing; I see all; the currents of the Universal Being
circulate through me; I am part or particle of God.

Ibid.

[2]If a man can write a better book, preach a better sermon,
or make a better mousetrap than his neighbor, though he builds
his house in the woods the world will make a beaten path to his
door.—*Attributed to* EMERSON *(in a lecture) by* SARAH S. B.
YULE *and* MARY S. KEENE, *Borrowings* [1889]

1 Give me health and a day, and I will make the pomp of emperors ridiculous. *Ibid.* 3

2 Every natural fact is a symbol of some spiritual fact. *Ibid.* 4

3 A man is a god in ruins. *Ibid.*

4 All that Adam had, all that Caesar could, you have and can do. . . . Build, therefore, your own world. *Ibid.*

5 The scholar is the delegated intellect. In the right state he is *Man Thinking.*
The American Scholar [1837], introduction

6 Meek young men grow up in libraries, believing it their duty to accept the views which Cicero, which Locke, which Bacon have given, forgetful that Cicero, Locke and Bacon were only young men in libraries when they wrote these books.
Ibid. sec. 2

7 There is then creative reading as well as creative writing. *Ibid.*

8 Character is higher than intellect. *Ibid.* 3

9 In self-trust all the virtues are comprehended.
Ibid.

10 Wherever Macdonald[1] sits, there is the head of the table. *Ibid.*

11 This time, like all times, is a very good one, if we but know what to do with it. *Ibid.*

12 I embrace the common, I explore and sit at the feet of the familiar, the low. Give me insight into to-day, and you may have the antique and future worlds. What would we really know the meaning of? The meal in the firkin; the milk in the pan; the ballad in the street; the news of the boat. *Ibid.*

13 If the single man plant himself indomitably on his instincts, and there abide, the huge world will come round to him.[2] *Ibid.*

14 If utterance is denied, the thought lies like a burden on the man. Always the seer is a sayer.
Divinity School Address [1838]

15 Men grind and grind in the mill of a truism, and nothing comes out but what was put in. But the moment they desert the tradition for a spontaneous thought, then poetry, wit, hope, virtue, learning, anecdote, all flock to their aid.
Literary Ethics [1838]

16 I have no expectation that any man will read history aright who thinks that what was done in a remote age, by men whose names have resounded far, has any deeper sense than what he is doing today. *Essays: First Series [1841]. History*

17 We are always coming up with the emphatic facts of history in our private experience and verifying them here. All history becomes subjective; in other words, there is properly no history; only biography.[3]
Ibid.

18 It is the fault of our rhetoric that we cannot strongly state one fact without seeming to belie some other. *Ibid.*

19 To believe your own thought, to believe that what is true for you in your private heart is true for all men—that is genius. *Ibid. Self-Reliance*

20 Society everywhere is in conspiracy against the manhood of every one of its members. . . . The virtue in most request is conformity. Self-reliance is its aversion. It loves not realities and creators, but names and customs. *Ibid.*

21 Whoso would be a man must be a nonconformist. *Ibid.*

22 It is easy in the world to live after the world's opinion; it is easy in solitude to live after our own; but the great man is he who in the midst of the crowd keeps with perfect sweetness the independence of solitude. *Ibid.*

23 A foolish consistency is the hobgoblin of little minds, adored by little statesmen and philosophers and divines. With consistency a great soul has simply nothing to do. *Ibid.*

24 To be great is to be misunderstood. *Ibid.*

25 An institution is the lengthened shadow of one man. *Ibid.*

26 I like the silent church before the service begins, better than any preaching. *Ibid.*

27 Discontent is the want of self-reliance: it is infirmity of will. *Ibid.*

28 For every Stoic was a Stoic; but in Christendom where is the Christian? *Ibid.*

29 Nothing can bring you peace but yourself.
Ibid.

30 Every sweet hath its sour; every evil its good.
Ibid. Compensation

31 For everything you have missed, you have gained something else; and for everything you gain, you lose something. *Ibid.*

32 Everything in Nature contains all the powers of Nature. Everything is made of one hidden stuff.
Ibid.

33 All mankind love a lover. *Ibid. Love*

34 Thou art to me a delicious torment.
Ibid. Friendship

35 Almost all people descend to meet. *Ibid.*

36 Happy is the house that shelters a friend.
Ibid.

37 A friend is a person with whom I may be sincere. Before him, I may think aloud. *Ibid.*

---

[1]Often quoted as "Macgregor."

[2]All things come round to him who will but wait. —LONGFELLOW, *Tales of a Wayside Inn, The Student's Tale* [1863]

[3]See Carlyle, 412:32.

1   A friend may well be reckoned the masterpiece of Nature.   *Essays: First Series. Friendship*

2   Two may talk and one may hear, but three cannot take part in a conversation of the most sincere and searching sort.   *Ibid.*

3   The only reward of virtue is virtue; the only way to have a friend is to be one.   *Ibid.*

4   I do then with my friends as I do with my books. I would have them where I can find them, but I seldom use them.   *Ibid.*

5   In skating over thin ice our safety is in our speed.   *Ibid. Prudence*

6   Heroism feels and never reasons and therefore is always right.   *Ibid. Heroism*

7   Beware when the great God lets loose a thinker on this planet.   *Ibid. Circles*

8   One man's justice is another's injustice; one man's beauty another's ugliness; one man's wisdom another's folly.   *Ibid.*

9   Nature abhors the old, and old age seems the only disease;[1] all others run into this one.   *Ibid.*

10   Nothing great was ever achieved without enthusiasm.   *Ibid.*

11   Nothing astonishes men so much as common sense and plain dealing.   *Ibid. Art*

12   A man may love a paradox without either losing his wit or his honesty.
    Walter Savage Landor. From The Dial [1841], XII

13   Literature is the effort of man to indemnify himself for the wrongs of his condition.   *Ibid.*

14   There is always a certain meanness in the argument of conservatism, joined with a certain superiority in its fact.   *The Conservative [1842]*

15   For it is not meters, but a metermaking argument that makes a poem—a thought so passionate and alive that like the spirit of a plant or an animal it has an architecture of its own, and adorns nature with a new thing.
    Essays: Second Series [1844]. The Poet

16   Language is the archives of history. . . . Language is fossil poetry.   *Ibid.*

17   Nature and books belong to the eyes that see them.   *Ibid. Experience*

18   The less government we have, the better—the fewer laws, and the less confided power.
    Ibid. Politics

19   Money, which represents the prose of life, and which is hardly spoken of in parlors without an apology, is, in its effects and laws, as beautiful as roses.   *Ibid. Nominalist and Realist*

20   Every man is wanted, and no man is wanted much.   *Ibid.*

21   The reward of a thing well done, is to have done it.   *Ibid.*

22   As to what are called the masses, and common men—there are no common men. All men are at last of a size.
    Representative Men [1850]. The Uses of Great Men

23   He is great who is what he is from Nature, and who never reminds us of others.   *Ibid.*

24   Every hero becomes a bore at last.   *Ibid.*

25   Great geniuses have the shortest biographies.
    Ibid. Plato; or, The Philosopher

26   Things added to things, as statistics, civil history, are inventories. Things used as language are inexhaustibly attractive.   *Ibid.*

27   Keep cool: it will be all one a hundred years hence.[2]   *Ibid. Montaigne; or, The Skeptic*

28   Is not marriage an open question, when it is alleged, from the beginning of the world, that such as are in the institution wish to get out, and such as are out wish to get in?[3]   *Ibid.*

29   Self-reliance, the height and perfection of man, is reliance on God.   *The Fugitive Slave Law [1854]*

30   Great men, great nations, have not been boasters and buffoons, but perceivers of the terror of life, and have manned themselves to face it.
    The Conduct of Life [1860]. Fate

31   Men are what their mothers made them.
    Ibid.

32   Coal is a portable climate.   *Ibid. Wealth*

33   The world is his, who has money to go over it.
    Ibid.

34   Art is a jealous mistress.   *Ibid.*

35   Solitude, the safeguard of mediocrity, is to genius the stern friend.   *Ibid. Culture*

36   There is always a best way of doing everything, if it be to boil an egg. Manners are the happy ways of doing things.   *Ibid. Behavior*

37   Fine manners need the support of fine manners in others.   *Ibid.*

38   Shallow men believe in luck.   *Ibid. Worship*

39   I wish that life should not be cheap, but sacred. I wish the days to be as centuries, loaded, fragrant.
    Ibid. Considerations by the Way

40   Our chief want in life is somebody who shall make us do what we can.   *Ibid.*

41   Make yourself necessary to somebody.   *Ibid.*

---

[1]Old age is an incurable disease.—SENECA, *Epistulae ad Lucilium, no. 108*

[2]What matters what anybody thinks? "It will be all the same a hundred years hence." That is the most sensible proverb ever invented.—GEORGE DU MAURIER, *Peter Ibbetson* [1891]
[3]See Montaigne, 146:19.

1   Beauty without grace is the hook without the bait.   *Ibid. Beauty*

2   Never read any book that is not a year old.   *Ibid. In Praise of Books*

3   There are always two parties, the party of the Past and the party of the Future; the Establishment and the Movement.
   Historic Notes of Life and Letters in New England [1867]

4   The key to the period appeared to be that the mind had become aware of itself. . . . The young men were born with knives in their brain, a tendency to introversion, self-dissection, anatomizing of motives.   *Ibid.*

5   Hitch your wagon to a star.
   Society and Solitude [1870]. Civilization

6   The true test of civilization is, not the census, nor the size of cities, nor the crops—no, but the kind of man the country turns out.   *Ibid.*

7   Every genuine work of art has as much reason for being as the earth and the sun.   *Ibid. Art*

8   A masterpiece of art has in the mind a fixed place in the chain of being, as much as a plant or a crystal.   *Ibid.*

9   We boil at different degrees.   *Ibid. Eloquence*

10   The best university that can be recommended to a man of ideas is the gauntlet of the mobs.   *Ibid.*

11   The ornament of a house is the friends who frequent it.   *Ibid. Domestic Life*

12   Can anybody remember when the times were not hard and money not scarce?   *Ibid. Works and Days*

13   'Tis the good reader that makes the good book; . . . in every book he finds passages which seem confidences or asides hidden from all else and unmistakably meant for his ear.   *Ibid. Success*

14   We do not count a man's years until he has nothing else to count.   *Ibid. Old Age*

15   A mollusk is a cheap edition [of man] with a suppression of the costlier illustrations, designed for dingy circulation, for shelving in an oyster-bank or among the seaweed.
   Power and Laws of Thought [c. 1870]

16   Life is not so short but that there is always time enough for courtesy.
   Letters and Social Aims [1876]. Social Aims

17   I have heard with admiring submission the experience of the lady who declared that the sense of being perfectly well-dressed gives a feeling of inward tranquillity which religion is powerless to bestow.   *Ibid.*

18   Great men are they who see that spiritual is stronger than any material force, that thoughts rule the world.
   Ibid. Progress and Culture, Phi Beta Kappa Address [July 18, 1876]

19   Next to the originator of a good sentence is the first quoter of it.[1]
   Ibid. Quotation and Originality

20   When Shakespeare is charged with debts to his authors, Landor replies, "Yet he was more original than his originals. He breathed upon dead bodies and brought them into life."   *Ibid.*

21   By necessity, by proclivity, and by delight, we all quote.   *Ibid.*

22   Wit makes its own welcome, and levels all distinctions.   *Ibid. The Comic*

23   The perception of the comic is a tie of sympathy with other men.   *Ibid.*

24   What is a weed? A plant whose virtues have not yet been discovered.
   Fortune of the Republic [1878]

25   To live without duties is obscene.
   Lectures and Biographical Sketches [1883]. Aristocracy

26   Speak the affirmative; emphasize your choice by utter ignoring of all that you reject.
   Ibid. The Preacher

27   Genius has no taste for weaving sand.
   Ibid. The Scholar

28   This world we live in is but thickened light.   *Ibid.*

29   All the thoughts of a turtle are turtles, and of a rabbit, rabbits.
   The Natural History of Intellect [1893]

30   When you strike at a king, you must kill him.
   Recollected by OLIVER WENDELL HOLMES, JR. From MAX LERNER, The Mind and Faith of Justice Holmes [1943]

Robert Stephen Hawker
1803–1875

31 And shall Trelawny die?
Here's twenty thousand Cornish men
Will know the reason why.
   The Song of the Western Men [1825],[2] st. 1

---

[1]There is not less wit nor less invention in applying rightly a thought one finds in a book, than in being the first author of that thought.—PIERRE BAYLE [1647–1706], *Dictionnaire Historique et Critique* [1697–1702]

[2]"And shall Trelawny die?" has been a popular phrase throughout Cornwall since the imprisonment in the Tower of London [1688] of Sir Jonathan Trelawny [1650–1721] with six other prelates for refusing to recognize the Declaration of Indulgence issued by James II.

Richard Henry Hengist Horne
1803–1884

1   'Tis always morning somewhere in the world.
Orion [1843], bk. III, canto 2

Douglas Jerrold
1803–1857

2   Dogmatism is puppyism come to its full growth.
Wit and Opinions of Douglas Jerrold [1859]

3   That fellow would vulgarize the day of judgment.
Ibid. A Comic Author

4   Some people are so fond of ill luck that they run halfway to meet it.
Ibid. Meeting Troubles Halfway

5   Talk to him of Jacob's ladder, and he would ask the number of the steps.
Ibid. A Matter-of-fact Man

Robert Smith Surtees
1803–1864

6   Jorrocks' Jaunts and Jollities.
Title of novel [1838]

7   Full o' beans and benevolence.
Handley Cross [1843], ch. 27

8   Three things I never lends—my 'oss, my wife, and my name.   *Hillingdon Hall [1845], ch. 33*

9   More people are flattered into virtue than bullied out of vice.
The Analysis of the Hunting Field [1846], ch. 1

10   Better be killed than frightened to death.
Mr. Facey Romford's Hounds [1864], ch. 32

Fëdor Tiutchev
1803–1873

11   A thought, once uttered, is a lie.
Silentium [1830]

12   Like first love, the heart of Russia will not forget you.   *Tribute to Pushkin [January 29, 1837]*

13   Homeland of patience, land of the Russian people.   *These Poor Villages [1855]*

Benjamin Disraeli, Earl of Beaconsfield
1804–1881

14   The microcosm of a public school.
Vivian Grey [1826], bk. I, ch. 2

15   I hate definitions.   *Ibid. II, 6*

16   Variety is the mother of Enjoyment.
Ibid. V, 4

17   There is moderation even in excess.
Ibid. VI, 1

18   I repeat . . . that all power is a trust; that we are accountable for its exercise; that, from the people, and for the people, all springs, and all must exist.   *Ibid. 7*

19   Man is not the creature of circumstances. Circumstances are the creatures of men.   *Ibid.*

20   A *dark* horse, which had never been thought of, and which the careless St. James had never even observed in the list, rushed past the grandstand in sweeping triumph.
The Young Duke [1831], bk. II, ch. 5

21   Yes, I am a Jew, and when the ancestors of the right honorable gentleman were brutal savages in an unknown island, mine were priests in the temple of Solomon.[1]   *Reply to a taunt by Daniel O'Connell*

22   What we anticipate seldom occurs; what we least expected generally happens.
Henrietta Temple [1837], bk. II, ch. 4

23   Though I sit down now, the time will come when you will hear me.
Maiden speech in the House of Commons [1837]

24   A government of statesmen or of clerks? Of Humbug or Humdrum?
Coningsby [1844], bk. II, ch. 4

25   I rather like bad wine . . . one gets so bored with good wine.
Sybil; or, The Two Nations [1845], bk. I, ch. 1

26   Two nations, between whom there is no intercourse and no sympathy; who are as ignorant of each other's habits, thoughts, and feelings as if they were dwellers in different zones, or inhabitants of different planets; who are formed by a different breeding, are fed by a different food, are ordered by different manners, and are not governed by the same laws . . . *the rich and the poor.*   *Ibid. II, 5*

27   Property has its duties as well as its rights.[2]
Ibid. 11

28   Little things affect little minds.   *Ibid. III, 2*

29   The right honorable gentleman [Sir Robert Peel] caught the Whigs bathing and walked away with their clothes.
Speech in the House of Commons [February 28, 1845]

30   Duty cannot exist without faith.
Tancred [1847], bk. II, ch. 1

---

[1]The gentleman will please remember that when his half-civilized ancestors were hunting the wild boar in the forests of Silesia, mine were the princes of the earth.— JUDAH P. BENJAMIN [1811–1884], *reply to a senator; from* BEN PERLEY POORE, *Reminiscences of Sixty Years in the National Metropolis* [1886]

[2]Property has its duties as well as its rights.— CAPTAIN THOMAS DRUMMOND [1797–1840; inventor of the Drummond light], *Letter to the Landlords of Tipperary* [May 22, 1838]

1   He was fresh and full of faith that "something would turn up." *Ibid. III, 6*

2   A precedent embalms a principle.
Speech on the expenditures of the country [February 22, 1848]

3   How much easier it is to be critical than to be correct. *Speech [January 24, 1860]*

4   Is man an ape or an angel? I, my lord, I am on the side of the angels. I repudiate with indignation and abhorrence those newfangled theories.
Speech at Oxford Diocesan Conference [November 25, 1864]

5   Individualities may form communities, but it is institutions alone that can create a nation.
Speech at Manchester [1866]

6   I have climbed to the top of the greasy pole.
To friends, on being made prime minister [1868]

7   When a man fell into his anecdotage, it was a sign for him to retire.   *Lothair [1870], ch. 28*

8   Every woman should marry—and no man.
Ibid. 30

9   You know who the critics are? The men who have failed in literature and art.   *Ibid. 35*

10   "My idea of an agreeable person," said Hugo Bohun, "is a person who agrees with me."
Ibid. 41

11   Increased means and increased leisure are the two civilizers of man.
Speech to the Conservatives of Manchester [April 3, 1872]

12   The secret of success is constancy to purpose.
Speech [June 24, 1872]

13   The health of the people is really the foundation upon which all their happiness and all their powers as a state depend.   *Speech [July 24, 1877]*

14   Lord Salisbury and myself have brought you back peace—but a peace I hope with honor.[1]
Speech in the House of Commons [July 16, 1878]

15   A series of congratulatory regrets.
Speech at Knightsbridge [July 27, 1878]

16   A sophistical rhetorician [Gladstone], inebriated with the exuberance of his own verbosity, and gifted with an egotistical imagination that can at all times command an interminable and inconsistent series of arguments to malign an opponent and to glorify himself.   *Ibid.*

17   The harebrained chatter of irresponsible frivolity.
Speech at the Guildhall, London [November 9, 1878]

[1]See John Russell, 406:6, and Neville Chamberlain, 606:10.

18   The Athanasian Creed is the most splendid ecclesiastical lyric ever poured forth by the genius of man.   *Endymion [1880], ch. 52*

19   "As for that," said Waldershare, "sensible men are all of the same religion." "And pray, what is that?" inquired the prince. "Sensible men never tell."   *Ibid. 81*

20   No, it is better not. She would only ask me to take a message to Albert.
On his deathbed, declining a visit from Queen Victoria

Gavarni [Sulpice Guillaume Chevalier]
1804–1866

21   Les Enfants Terribles [The Terrible Children].
Title of series of prints [1865]

Nathaniel Hawthorne
1804–1864

22   By the sympathy of your human hearts for sin ye shall scent out all the places—whether in church, bedchamber, street, field, or forest—where crime has been committed, and shall exult to behold the whole earth one stain of guilt, one mighty blood spot.   *Young Goodman Brown [1835]*

23   As the moral gloom of the world overpowers all systematic gaiety, even so was their home of wild mirth made desolate amid the sad forest.
The Maypole of Merrymount [1836]

24   If a man, sitting all alone, cannot dream strange things, and make them look like truth, he need never try to write romances.
The Scarlet Letter [1850]. The Custom-House

25   On the breast of her gown, in fine red cloth, surrounded with an elaborate embroidery and fantastic flourishes of gold thread, appeared the letter A.   *Ibid. ch. 2*

26   My heart was a habitation large enough for many guests, but lonely and chill, and without a household fire. I longed to kindle one! It seemed not so wild a dream.   *Ibid. 4*

27   There is a fatality, a feeling so irresistible and inevitable that it has the force of doom, which almost invariably compels human beings to linger around and haunt, ghostlike, the spot where some great and marked event has given the color to their lifetime; and still the more irresistibly, the darker the tinge that saddens it.   *Ibid. 5*

28   Let the black flower blossom as it may!
Ibid. 14

29   Let men tremble to win the hand of woman, unless they win along with it the utmost passion of her heart.   *Ibid. 15*

1 "Never, never!" whispered she. "What we did had a consecration of its own."
The Scarlet Letter, ch. 17

2 The scarlet letter was her passport into regions where other women dared not tread. Shame, Despair, Solitude! These had been her teachers—stern and wild ones—and they had made her strong, but taught her much amiss. *Ibid. 18*

3 At some brighter period, when the world should have grown ripe for it, in Heaven's own time, a new truth would be revealed, in order to establish the whole relation between man and woman on a surer ground of mutual happiness. *Ibid. 24*

4 The book, if you would see anything in it, requires to be read in the clear, brown, twilight atmosphere in which it was written; if opened in the sunshine, it is apt to look exceedingly like a volume of blank pages.
Twice-Told Tales [1851], preface

5 Not to be deficient in this particular, the author has provided himself with a moral—the truth, namely, that the wrongdoing of one generation lives into the successive ones.
The House of the Seven Gables [1851], preface

6 God will give him blood to drink! *Ibid. ch. 1*

7 Life is made up of marble and mud. *Ibid. 2*

8 What other dungeon is so dark as one's own heart! What jailer so inexorable as one's self! *Ibid. 11*

9 Of all the events which constitute a person's biography, there is scarcely one . . . to which the world so easily reconciles itself as to his death. *Ibid. 21*

10 The greatest obstacle to being heroic is the doubt whether one may not be going to prove one's self a fool; the truest heroism is, to resist the doubt; and the profoundest wisdom, to know when it ought to be resisted, and when to be obeyed.
The Blithedale Romance [1852], ch. 2

11 In youth men are apt to write more wisely than they really know or feel; and the remainder of life may be not idly spent in realizing and convincing themselves of the wisdom which they uttered long ago. *The Snow Image [1852], preface*

12 No author, without a trial, can conceive of the difficulty of writing a romance about a country where there is no shadow, no antiquity, no mystery, no picturesque and gloomy wrong, nor anything but a commonplace prosperity, in broad and simple daylight, as is happily the case with my dear native land.
The Marble Faun [1860], preface

13 Mountains are earth's undecaying monuments.
Sketches from Memory [1868]. The Notch of the White Mountains

Charles Augustin Sainte-Beuve
1804–1869

14 Vigny, more secret,
As if in his tower of ivory, retired before noon.[1]
Pensées d'Août, à M. Villemain [1837], st. 3

15 Silence is the sovereign contempt.[2]
Mes Poisons

George Sand
[Amandine Aurore Lucile Dupin, Baronne Dudevant]
1804–1876

16 Love, bumping his head blindly against all the obstacles of civilization. *Indiana [1832], preface*

17 No human creature can give orders to love.
Jacques [1834]

18 Deliberately, women are given a deplorable education. . . . While man frees himself from constraining civil and religious bonds, he is only too glad to have woman hold tightly to the Christian principle of suffering and keeping her silence.[3]
Letters to Marcie [1837]

19 We cannot tear out a single page of our life, but we can throw the whole book in the fire.
Mauprat [1837]

20 Charity degrades those who receive it and hardens those who dispense it. *Consuelo [1842]*

21 They [the peasants] were born kings of the earth far more truly than those who possess it only from having bought it. *The Haunted Pool [1851]*

22 Life in common among people who love each other is the ideal of happiness.
Histoire de Ma Vie [1856]

23 In our wholly factitious society, to have no cash at all means frightful want or absolute powerlessness. *Ibid.*

24 Revolutions . . . have put one half of France in mourning for the other. *Ibid.*

25 There is only one happiness in life, to love and be loved.
Letter to Lina Calamatta [March 31, 1862]

26 Faith is an excitement and an enthusiasm: it is a condition of intellectual magnificence to which we must cling as to a treasure, and not squander . . .

---

[1]Vigny, plus secret, / Comme en sa tour d'ivoire, avant midi, rentrait.

The poet, retired in his Tower of Ivory, isolated, according to his desire, from the world of man, resembles, whether he so wishes or not, another solitary figure, the watcher enclosed for months at a time in a lighthouse at the head of a cliff.— JULES DE GAULTIER [b. 1858], *La Guerre et les Destinées de l'Art*

[2]Le silence seul est le souverain mépris.

[3]See Abigail Adams, 347:5.

in the small coin of empty words, or in exact and priggish argument.
Letter to Des Planches [May 25, 1866]

1   The whole secret of the study of nature lies in learning how to use one's eyes.
Nouvelles Lettres d'un Voyageur [1869]

2   Art for art's sake is an empty phrase. Art for the sake of the true, art for the sake of the good and the beautiful, that is the faith I am searching for.
Letter to Alexandre Saint-Jean [1872]

3   I would rather believe that God did not exist than believe that He was indifferent.
Impressions et Souvenirs [1896]

Sarah Flower Adams
1805–1848

4 E'en though it be a cross
That raiseth me;
Still all my song would be,
Nearer, My God, to Thee,
Nearer, My God, to Thee,
Nearer to Thee.
Nearer, My God, to Thee, st. 1

Hans Christian Andersen
1805–1875

5   They could see she was a real princess and no question about it, now that she had felt one pea all the way through twenty mattresses and twenty more feather beds. Nobody but a princess could be so delicate.
Fairy Tales [1835].[1] The Princess and the Pea

6   Many, many steeples would have to be stacked one on top of another to reach from the bottom to the surface of the sea. It is down there that the sea folk live.
Ibid. The Little Mermaid

7   We [sea folk] can live to be three hundred years old, but when we perish we turn into mere foam on the sea.
Ibid.

8   The Emperor's New Clothes.
Ibid. Title of story

9   "But he hasn't got anything on," a little child said.
Ibid. The Emperor's New Clothes

10   The little live nightingale . . . had come to sing of comfort and hope. As he sang, the phantoms grew pale, and still more pale, and the blood flowed quicker and quicker through the Emperor's feeble body. Even Death listened, and said, "Go on, little nightingale, go on!"
Ibid. The Nightingale

11   His own image . . . was no longer the reflection of a clumsy, dirty, gray bird, ugly and offensive. He himself was a swan! Being born in a duck yard does

[1]Translated by JEAN HERSHOLT.

not matter, if only you are hatched from a swan's egg.
Ibid. The Ugly Duckling

William Lloyd Garrison
1805–1879

12   Our country is the world—our countrymen are all mankind.
Motto of The Liberator [1831]

13   Let Southern oppressors tremble—let their secret abettors tremble—let their Northern apologists tremble—let all the enemies of the persecuted blacks tremble.
The Liberator, no. 1 [January 1, 1831]

14   I will be as harsh as truth and as uncompromising as justice. On this subject I do not wish to think, or speak, or write, with moderation. No! No! Tell a man whose house is on fire to give a moderate alarm; tell him to moderately rescue his wife from the hands of the ravisher; tell the mother to gradually extricate her babe from the fire into which it has fallen; but urge me not to use moderation.
Ibid.

15   I am in earnest—I will not equivocate—I will not excuse—I will not retreat a single inch; and I will be heard!
Ibid.

16   The compact which exists between the North and the South is a covenant with death and an agreement with hell.[2]
Resolution adopted by the Anti-Slavery Society [January 27, 1843]

17   With reasonable men, I will reason; with humane men I will plead; but to tyrants I will give no quarter, nor waste arguments where they will certainly be lost.
W. P. and F. J. T. GARRISON, *William Lloyd Garrison [1885–1889], vol. I, p. 188*

18   Wherever there is a human being, I see God-given rights inherent in that being, whatever may be the sex or complexion.
Ibid. III, p. 390

19   You cannot possibly have a broader basis for any government than that which includes all the people, with all their rights in their hands, and with an equal power to maintain their rights.
Ibid. IV, p. 224

Sidney Sherman
1805–1873

20   Remember the Alamo![3]
Battle cry, San Jacinto [April 21, 1836]; attributed

[2]See *Isaiah 28:15, 26:33.*
[3]On March 6, 1836, five days after Texas declared her independence from Mexico, President Antonio López de Santa Anna attacked the Alamo, the fortified mission at San Antonio; captured it after every Texan had been killed or wounded; and put the wounded to death. He was defeated and captured at San Jacinto [April 21, 1836] by the Texas army under Commander in Chief Samuel Houston. Sidney Sherman was a colonel in the army.

Alexis de Tocqueville
1805–1859

1   I know of no country, indeed, where the love of money has taken stronger hold on the affections of men and where a profounder contempt is expressed for the theory of the permanent equality of property.
Democracy in America,[1] *pt. I [1835], ch. 3*

2   Within these limits the power vested in the American courts of justice of pronouncing a statute to be unconstitutional forms one of the most powerful barriers that have ever been devised against the tyranny of political assemblies.   *Ibid. 6*

3   I have never been more struck by the good sense and the practical judgment of the Americans than in the manner in which they elude the numberless difficulties resulting from their Federal Constitution.
Ibid. 8

4   In order to enjoy the inestimable benefits that the liberty of the press ensures, it is necessary to submit to the inevitable evils that it creates.   *Ibid. 9*

5   They [the Americans] have all a lively faith in the perfectibility of man, they judge that the diffusion of knowledge must necessarily be advantageous, and the consequences of ignorance fatal; they all consider society as a body in a state of improvement, humanity as a changing scene, in which nothing is, or ought to be, permanent; and they admit that what appears to them today to be good, may be superseded by something better tomorrow.   *Ibid. 18*

6   America is a land of wonders, in which everything is in constant motion and every change seems an improvement. The idea of novelty is there indissolubly connected with the idea of amelioration.
Ibid.

7   There are at the present time two great nations in the world. . . . I allude to the Russians and the Americans. . . . Their starting-point is different and their courses are not the same; yet each of them seems marked out by the will of Heaven to sway the destinies of half the globe.   *Ibid.*

8   Democratic nations care but little for what has been, but they are haunted by visions of what will be; in this direction their unbounded imagination grows and dilates beyond all measure. . . . Democracy, which shuts the past against the poet, opens the future before him.
Ibid. pt. II [1840], bk. I, ch. 17

9   Thus not only does democracy make every man forget his ancestors, but it hides his descendants and separates his contemporaries from him; it throws him back forever upon himself alone and threatens in the end to confine him entirely within the solitude of his own heart.   *Ibid. II, 2*

[1]The Henry Reeve text, as revised by Francis Bowen, corrected and edited by Phillips Bradley [1945].

10   If I were asked . . . to what the singular prosperity and growing strength of that people [the Americans] ought mainly to be attributed, I should reply: To the superiority of their women.
Ibid. III, 12

11   The love of wealth is therefore to be traced, as either a principal or accessory motive, at the bottom of all that the Americans do; this gives to all their passions a sort of family likeness.   *Ibid. 17*

12   Never was any such event [the French Revolution], stemming from factors so far back in the past, so inevitable yet so completely unforeseen.
The Old Regime and the French Revolution [1856],[2] *pt. I, ch. 1*

13   When a people which has put up with an oppressive rule over a long period without protest suddenly finds the government relaxing its pressure, it takes up arms against it.   *Ibid. III*

Elizabeth Barrett Browning
1806–1861

14 Thou large-brained woman and large-hearted man.
To George Sand, A Desire [1844]

15 Knowledge by suffering entereth,
And life is perfected by death.
A Vision of Poets [1844], last lines

16 Do ye hear the children weeping, O my brothers,
Ere the sorrow comes with years?
The Cry of the Children [1844], st. 1

17 I tell you hopeless grief is passionless.
Grief [1844], l. 1

18 Therefore to this dog will I,
Tenderly not scornfully,
Render praise and favor.
To Flush, My Dog [1844], st. 14

19 "Yes," I answered you last night;
"No," this morning, sir, I say:
Colors seen by candlelight
Will not look the same by day.
The Lady's "Yes" [1844], st. 1

20 By thunders of white silence overthrown.
Hiram Power's Greek Slave [1850], last line

21 "Guess now who holds thee?"—"Death," I said.
But there
The silver answer rang—"Not Death, but Love."
Sonnets from the Portuguese [1850], no. 1

22 Because God's gifts put man's best dreams to shame.
Ibid. 26

23 How do I love thee? Let me count the ways.
I love thee to the depth and breadth and height

[2]Translated by STUART GILBERT.

My soul can reach, when feeling out of sight
For the ends of Being and ideal Grace.

Ibid. 43

1   I love thee with the breath,
Smiles, tears, of all my life!—and, if God choose,
I shall but love thee better after death.

Ibid.

2   Life, struck sharp on death,
Makes awful lightning.

Aurora Leigh[1] *[1857], bk. I, l. 210*

3 I should not dare to call my soul my own.

Ibid. II, l. 786

4 God answers sharp and sudden on some prayers,
And thrusts the thing we have prayed for in our
        face,
A gauntlet with a gift in 't.

Ibid. l. 952

5 A little sunburnt by the glare of life.

Ibid. IV, l. 1140

6 Since when was genius found respectable?

Ibid. VI, l. 275

7   Earth's crammed with heaven,
And every common bush afire with God.

Ibid. VII, l. 820

8 What was he doing, the great god Pan,
        Down in the reeds by the river?
Spreading ruin and scattering ban,
Splashing and paddling with hoofs of a goat,
And breaking the golden lilies afloat
        With the dragonfly on the river.

A Musical Instrument [1860]

Friedrich Halm
[Eligius Franz Josef von
Münch-Bellinghausen]
1806–1871

9 Two souls with but a single thought,
Two hearts that beat as one.[2]

Der Sohn der Wildness [1842], act II

Matthew Fontaine Maury
1806–1873

10   There is a river in the ocean: in the severest
droughts it never fails, and in the mightiest floods it
never overflows; its banks and its bottom are of cold
water, while its current is of warm; the Gulf of
Mexico is its fountain, and its mouth is the Arctic
Seas. It is the Gulf Stream. There is in the world no
other such majestic flow of waters.

The Physical Geography of the Sea and Its
Meteorology [1855], ch. 2

[1]See Edward FitzGerald, 446:11.
[2]Zwei Sellen und en Gedanke, / Zwei Herzen und ein Schlag!
Translated by MARIA LOVELL.

John Stuart Mill
1806–1873

11   The sole end for which mankind are warranted,
individually or collectively, in interfering with the
liberty of action of any of their number is self-
protection.   *On Liberty [1859], introduction*

12   If all mankind minus one were of one opinion,
and only one person were of the contrary opinion,
mankind would be no more justified in silencing that
one person than he, if he had the power, would be
justified in silencing mankind.   *Ibid. ch. 2*

13   There is no such thing as absolute certainty, but
there is assurance sufficient for the purposes of
human life.   *Ibid.*

14   He who knows only his own side of the case,
knows little of that.   *Ibid.*

15   The fatal tendency of mankind to leave off thinking about a thing when it is no longer doubtful is the
cause of half their errors.   *Ibid.*

16   We can never be sure that the opinion we are
endeavoring to stifle is a false opinion; and if we
were sure, stifling it would be an evil still.

Ibid.

17   The liberty of the individual must be thus far
limited; he must not make himself a nuisance to
other people.   *Ibid. 3*

18   All good things which exist are the fruits of originality.   *Ibid.*

19   Whatever crushes individuality is despotism, by
whatever name it may be called.   *Ibid.*

20   Everyone who receives the protection of society
owes a return for the benefit.   *Ibid. 4*

21   The individual is not accountable to society for
his actions, insofar as these concern the interests of
no person but himself.   *Ibid. 5*

22   The worth of a state, in the long run, is the worth
of the individuals composing it.   *Ibid.*

23   Liberty consists in doing what one desires.

Ibid.

24   Unearned increment.

Dissertations and Discussions [1859]

25   Instead of the function of governing, for which it
is radically unfit, the proper office of a representative
assembly is to watch and control the government.

Ibid.

26   The creed which accepts as the foundation of
morals Utility, or the Greatest Happiness Principle,
holds that actions are right in proportion as they
tend to promote happiness, wrong as they tend to
produce the reverse of happiness.

Utilitarianism [1863], ch. 2

27   It is better to be a human being dissatisfied than
a pig satisfied; better to be Socrates dissatisfied than
a fool satisfied.   *Ibid.*

1 The social state is at once so natural, so necessary, and so habitual to man, that . . . he never conceives himself otherwise than as a member of a body.   *Utilitarianism, ch. 3*

2 It is only a man here and there who has any tolerable knowledge of the character even of the women of his own family.
The Subjection of Women [1869], ch. 1

3 The generality of the male sex cannot yet tolerate the idea of living with an equal.   *Ibid. 2*

4 Marriage is the only actual bondage known to our law. There remain no legal slaves, except the mistress of every house.   *Ibid. 4*

5 The moral regeneration of mankind will only really commence, when the most fundamental of the social relations [marriage] is placed under the rule of equal justice, and when human beings learn to cultivate their strongest sympathy with an equal in rights and in cultivation.   *Ibid.*

6 Ask yourself whether you are happy, and you cease to be so.   *Autobiography [1873], ch. 5*

Johann Bernhard, Graf von Rechberg
1806–1899

7 Guarantees which are not worth the paper they are written on.
In a dispatch concerning the recognition of Italy [1861]

Charles Francis Adams
1807–1886

8 It would be superfluous in me to point out to your Lordship that this is war.
Dispatch to Earl Russell [September 5, 1863]

Jean Louis Rodolphe Agassiz
1807–1873

9 The eye of the trilobite tells us that the sun shone on the old beach where he lived; for there is nothing in nature without a purpose, and when so complicated an organ was made to receive the light, there must have been light to enter it.
Geological Sketches [1870], ch. 2

10 The world has arisen in some way or another. How it originated is the great question, and Darwin's theory, like all other attempts to explain the origin of life, is thus far merely conjectural. I believe he has not even made the best conjecture possible in the present state of our knowledge.
Evolution and Permanence of Type [1874]

Giuseppe Garibaldi
1807–1882

11 I offer neither pay, nor quarters, nor provisions; I offer hunger, thirst, forced marches, battles and death. Let him who loves his country in his heart, and not with his lips only, follow me.
From G. M. Trevelyan, Garibaldi's Defense of the Roman Republic [1907–1911]

Robert Edward Lee
1807–1870

12 It is well that war is so terrible, or we should grow too fond of it.
On seeing a Federal charge repulsed at Fredericksburg [December 1862]

13 Strike the tent.
Last words [October 12, 1870]

Henry Wadsworth Longfellow
1807–1882

14 I heard the trailing garments of the Night
Sweep through her marble halls.
Hymn to Night [1839], st. 1

15 Tell me not, in mournful numbers,
Life is but an empty dream!
For the soul is dead that slumbers,
And things are not what they seem.

Life is real! Life is earnest!
And the grave is not its goal;
Dust thou art, to dust returnest,
Was not spoken of the soul.
A Psalm of Life [1839], st. 1, 2

16 Art is long, and Time is fleeting,
And our hearts, though stout and brave,
Still, like muffled drums, are beating
Funeral marches to the grave.
Ibid. st. 4

17 Lives of great men all remind us
We can make our lives sublime.
And, departing, leave behind us
Footprints on the sands of time.
Ibid. st. 7

18 Let us, then, be up and doing,
With a heart for any fate;
Still achieving, still pursuing,
Learn to labor and to wait.
Ibid. st. 9

19 Skoal! to the Northland! skoal!
Thus the tale ended.
The Skeleton in Armor [1841], st. 20

20 It was the schooner Hesperus,
That sailed the wintry sea;

And the skipper had taken his little daughter,
To bear him company.
The Wreck of the Hesperus [1842], st. 1

1 But the father answered never a word,
A frozen corpse was he.
Ibid. st. 12

2 Christ save us all from a death like this,
On the reef of Norman's Woe!
Ibid. st. 22

3 Under the spreading chestnut tree
The village smithy stands;
The smith a mighty man is he
With large and sinewy hands.
And the muscles of his brawny arms
Are strong as iron bands.
The Village Blacksmith [1842], st. 1

4 His brow is wet with honest sweat,
He earns whate'er he can,
And looks the whole world in the face,
For he owes not any man.
Ibid. st. 2

5 Something attempted, something done,
Has earned a night's repose.
Ibid. st. 7

6 Into each life some rain must fall,
Some days must be dark and dreary.
The Rainy Day [1842], st. 3

7 Standing with reluctant feet,
Where the brook and river meet,
Womanhood and childhood fleet!
Maidenhood [1842], st. 3

8 A banner with the strange device,
Excelsior!
Excelsior [1842], st. 1

9 Stars of the summer night!
Far in yon azure deeps.
The Spanish Student [1843], act I, sc. iii
(serenade)

10 The day is done, and the darkness
Falls from the wings of Night,
As a feather is wafted downward
From an eagle in his flight.
The Day Is Done [1845], st. 1

11 The bards sublime,
Whose distant footsteps echo
Through the corridors of Time.
Ibid. st. 5

12 And the night shall be filled with music,
And the cares, that infest the day,
Shall fold their tents, like the Arabs,
And as silently steal away.
Ibid. st. 11

13 I shot an arrow into the air,
It fell to earth, I knew not where.
The Arrow and the Song [1845], st. 1

14 And the song, from beginning to end,
I found again in the heart of a friend.
Ibid. st. 3

15 This is the forest primeval. The murmuring pines
and the hemlocks . . .
Stand like Druids of old.
Evangeline [1847], l. 1

16 Build me straight, O worthy Master!
Staunch and strong, a goodly vessel.
The Building of the Ship [1849], l. 1

17 And see! she stirs!
She starts—she moves—she seems to feel
The thrill of life along her keel.
Ibid. l. 349

18 Sail on, O Ship of State!
Sail on, O Union, strong and great!
Humanity with all its fears,
With all the hopes of future years,
Is hanging breathless on thy fate!
Ibid. l. 378

19 Our hearts, our hopes, our prayers, our tears,
Our faith triumphant o'er our fears,
Are all with thee—are all with thee!
Ibid. l. 397

20 Nothing useless is, or low.
The Builders [1849], st. 2

21 God sent his Singers upon earth
With songs of sadness and of mirth.
The Singers [1849], st. 1

22 But the great Master said, "I see
No best in kind, but in degree;
I gave a various gift to each,
To charm, to strengthen, and to teach."
Ibid. st. 6

23 All your strength is in your union.
All your danger is in discord;
Therefore be at peace henceforward,
And as brothers live together.
The Song of Hiawatha [1855], pt. I

24 By the shores of Gitche Gumee,
By the shining Big-Sea-Water,
Stood the wigwam of Nokomis,
Daughter of the Moon, Nokomis.
Ibid. III

25 From the waterfall he named her,
Minnehaha, Laughing Water.
Ibid. IV

26 As unto the bow the cord is,
So unto the man is woman,
Though she bends him, she obeys him,
Though she draws him, yet she follows,
Useless each without the other!
Ibid. X

1　If we could read the secret history of our enemies, we should find in each man's life sorrow and suffering enough to disarm all hostility.

Driftwood [1857]

2 If I am not worth the wooing, I surely am not worth the winning.

The Courtship of Miles Standish [1858], pt. III

3 "Why don't you speak for yourself, John?"

Ibid.

4 The long mysterious Exodus of death.

The Jewish Cemetery at Newport [1858], st. 1

5　　A boy's will is the wind's will,
And the thoughts of youth are long, long thoughts.

My Lost Youth [1858], refrain

6 I remember the black wharves and the slips,
And the sea-tides tossing free;
And Spanish sailors with bearded lips,
And the beauty and majesty of the ships,
And the magic of the sea.

Ibid. st. 3

7 A Lady with a Lamp[1] shall stand
In the great history of the land,
A noble type of good,
Heroic womanhood.

Santa Filomena [1858], st. 10

8 Between the dark and the daylight,
When the night is beginning to lower,
Comes a pause in the day's occupations,
That is known as the Children's Hour.

The Children's Hour [1860], st. 1

9 I hear in the chamber above me
The patter of little feet.

Ibid. st. 2

10 Grave Alice, and laughing Allegra,
And Edith with golden hair.

Ibid. st. 3

11　　A solid man of Boston.
A comfortable man with dividends,
And the first salmon and the first green peas.

The New England Tragedies [1868]. John Endicott, act IV, sc. i

12 Listen, my children, and you shall hear,
Of the midnight ride of Paul Revere,
On the eighteenth of April, in Seventy-five;
Hardly a man is now alive
Who remembers that famous day and year.

Tales of a Wayside Inn [1863–1874], pt. I, The Landlord's Tale: Paul Revere's Ride, st. 1

13 One if by land, and two if by sea;[2]
And I on the opposite shore will be,
Ready to ride and spread the alarm
Through every Middlesex village and farm.

Ibid. st. 2

14 The fate of a nation was riding that night.

Ibid. st. 8

15 He seemed the incarnate "Well, I told you so!"

Ibid. The Poet's Tale: The Birds of Killingworth, st. 9

16 Ships that pass in the night, and speak each other in passing,
Only a signal shown and a distant voice in the darkness;
So on the ocean of life we pass and speak one another,[3]
Only a look and a voice; then darkness again and a silence.

Ibid. III, The Theologian's Tale: Elizabeth, IV

17　　Time has laid his hand
Upon my heart, gently, not smiting it,
But as a harper lays his open palm
Upon his harp to deaden its vibrations.

The Golden Legend [1872], pt. IV, The Cloisters

18 Let him not boast who puts his armor on
As he who puts it off, the battle done.

Morituri Salutamus [1875], st. 9

19 The love of learning, the sequestered nooks,
And all the sweet serenity of books.

Ibid. st. 21

20 For age is opportunity no less
Than youth itself.

Ibid. st. 24

21 Not in the clamor of the crowded street,
Not in the shouts and plaudits of the throng,
But in ourselves, are triumph and defeat.

The Poets

22 Three silences there are: the first of speech,
The second of desire, the third of thought.

The Three Silences of Molinos

23 In the long, sleepless watches of the night.

The Cross of Snow [1879]

24 The holiest of all holidays are those
Kept by ourselves in silence and apart;
The secret anniversaries of the heart.

Holidays

25 There was a little girl
Who had a little curl
Right in the middle of her forehead;
And when she was good
She was very, very good,
But when she was bad she was horrid.

There Was a Little Girl

---

[1]Florence Nightingale [1820–1910].
[2]See Revere, 339:4.

[3]Two lives that once part are as ships that divide.—Bulwer-Lytton, *A Lament*
　　As vessels starting from ports thousands of miles apart pass close to each other in the naked breadths of the ocean, nay, sometimes even touch in the dark.—Oliver Wendell Holmes, *Professor at the Breakfast-Table [1860]*

John Greenleaf Whittier
1807–1892

1 No fetters in the Bay State—no slave upon our
land!
Massachusetts to Virginia [1843], st. 24

2 The Night is mother of the Day,
The Winter of the Spring,
And ever upon old Decay
The greenest mosses cling.
A Dream of Summer [1847], st. 4

3 So fallen! so lost! the light withdrawn
Which once he wore!
The glory from his gray hairs gone
Forevermore!
Ichabod [1850],[1] st. 1

4   From those great eyes
The soul has fled:
When faith is lost, when honor dies,
The man is dead!
Ibid. st. 8

5 Blessings on thee, little man,
Barefoot boy, with cheek of tan!
The Barefoot Boy [1856], st. 1

6 Health that mocks the doctor's rules,
Knowledge never learned of schools.
Ibid. st. 2

7 The age is dull and mean. Men creep,
Not walk.
*Lines Inscribed to Friends under Arrest for
Treason Against the Slave Power [1856], st. 1*

8 For of all sad words of tongue or pen,
The saddest are these: "It might have been!"[2]
Maud Muller [1856], st. 53

9 Up from the meadows rich with corn,
Clear in the cool September morn.
Barbara Frietchie [1864], st. 1

10 The clustered spires of Frederick stand
Green-walled by the hills of Maryland.
Ibid. st. 2

11 "Shoot, if you must, this old gray head,
But spare your country's flag," she said.
Ibid. st. 18

12 "Who touches a hair of yon gray head
Dies like a dog! March on!" he said.
Ibid. st. 21

13 The sun that brief December day
Rose cheerless over hills of gray,

---

[1]This poem was the outcome of the surprise and grief and
forecast of evil consequences which I felt on reading the seventh
of March speech of Daniel Webster in support of the "compromise," and the Fugitive Slave Law. No partisan or personal
enmity dictated it.—WHITTIER'S *Note*
  See *1 Samuel* 4:21, 11:30.
[2]See Guiterman, 611:17.

And, darkly circled, gave at noon
A sadder light than waning moon.
Snowbound [1866], l. 1

14 Shut in from all the world without,
We sat the clean-winged hearth about.
Ibid. l. 155

15 Angel of the backward look.
Ibid. l. 714

16 God is and all is well.
My Birthday [1871], st. 2

17 Dear Lord and Father of mankind,
Forgive our foolish ways!
Reclothe us in our rightful mind,
In purer lives Thy service find,
In deeper reverence, praise.
The Brewing of Soma [1872]

Salmon Portland Chase
1808–1873

18   The Constitution, in all its provisions, looks to an
indestructible Union composed of indestructible
States.
*Decision in Texas v. White, 7 Wallace 725
[1868]*

Alphonse Karr
1808–1890

19   The more things change, the more they remain
the same.[3] *Les Guêpes [Janvier 1849]*

Maurice de MacMahon
1808–1893

20 Here I am, and here I stay.[4]
At Sevastopol [September 1855]

Gérard de Nerval [Gérard Labrunie]
1808–1855

21   Despair and suicide are the result of certain fatal
situations for those who have no faith in immortality, its joys and sorrows. *Le Rêve et la Vie, II*

22   The jailer is another kind of captive—is the jailer
envious of his prisoner's dreams?
Fragments de Faust

23 I am the somber one, the unconsoled widower,
The Prince of Aquitaine whose tower was
destroyed.[5]

---

[3]Plus ça change, plus c'est la même chose.
[4]J'y suis, j'y reste.
[5]Je suis le ténébreux, le veuf, l'inconsolé, / Le Prince d'Aquitaine à la tour abolie.
  T. S. Eliot quotes the second line in *The Waste Land* [1922],
line 429.

My only star is dead, and my star-studded lute
Wears the black sun of Melancholy.
Les Chimères [1854]. El Desdichado

Caroline Sheridan Norton
1808–1877

1 A soldier of the Legion lay dying in Algiers.
Bingen on the Rhine, st. 1

George Washington Patten
c. 1808–1882

2 If we must perish in the fight,
Oh! let us die like men.
Oh! Let Us Die Like Men, st. 4

Samuel Francis Smith
1808–1895

3 My country, 'tis of thee,
Sweet land of liberty,
Of thee I sing:
Land where my fathers died,
Land of the pilgrims' pride,
From every mountainside
Let freedom ring.
America [1831], st. 1

4 Long may our land be bright
With freedom's holy light;
Protect us by thy might,
Great God, our King!
Ibid. st. 4

Charles Robert Darwin
1809–1882

5   I have called this principle, by which each slight variation, if useful, is preserved, by the term Natural Selection.   *On the Origin of Species [1859], ch. 3*

6   The expression often used by Mr. Herbert Spencer, of the Survival of the Fittest, is more accurate, and is sometimes equally convenient.[1]   *Ibid.*

7   We will now discuss in a little more detail the Struggle for Existence.[2]   *Ibid.*

8   It is interesting to contemplate an entangled bank, clothed with many plants of many kinds, with birds singing on the bushes, with various insects flitting about, and with worms crawling through the damp earth, and to reflect that these elaborately constructed forms, so different from each other, and dependent on each other in so complex a manner, have all been produced by laws acting around us.
Ibid.

[1]See Spencer, 493:9.
[2]The perpetual struggle for room and food. — MALTHUS, *On Population* [1798], *ch. 3*

9   Each organic being is striving to increase in a geometrical ratio . . . each at some period of its life, during some season of the year, during each generation or at intervals, has to struggle for life and to suffer great destruction. . . . The vigorous, the healthy, and the happy survive and multiply.
Ibid.

10   From the war of nature, from famine and death, the most exalted object which we are capable of conceiving, namely, the production of the higher animals, directly follows. There is grandeur in this view of life, with its several powers, having been originally breathed by the Creator into a few forms or into one, and that . . . from so simple a beginning endless forms most beautiful and most wonderful have been and are being evolved.   *Ibid. 15*

11   When the views advanced by me in this volume . . . are generally admitted, we can dimly foresee that there will be a considerable revolution in natural history.   *Ibid.*

12   The Simiadae then branched off into two great stems, the New World and Old World monkeys; and from the latter at a remote period, Man, the wonder and the glory of the universe, proceeded.[3]
The Descent of Man [1871], ch. 6

13   A hairy quadruped, furnished with a tail and pointed ears, probably arboreal in its habits.
Ibid. 21

14   For my own part I would as soon be descended from that heroic little monkey, who braved his dreaded enemy in order to save the life of his keeper; or from that old baboon, who, descending from the mountains, carried away in triumph his young comrade from a crowd of astonished dogs — as from a savage who delights to torture his enemies, offers up bloody sacrifices, practices infanticide without remorse, treats his wives like slaves, knows no decency, and is haunted by the grossest superstitions.
Ibid.

15   Man with all his noble qualities . . . with his godlike intellect which has penetrated into the movements and constitution of the solar system . . . still bears in his bodily frame the indelible stamp of his lowly origin.   *Ibid.*

16   The plow is one of the most ancient and most valuable of man's inventions; but long before he existed the land was in fact regularly plowed, and still continues to be thus plowed by earthworms. It may be doubted whether there are many other animals which have played so important a part in the history of the world, as have these lowly organized creatures.
The Formation of Vegetable Mold Through the Action of Worms [1881], ch. 7

[3]I confess freely to you, I could never look long upon a monkey, without very mortifying reflections. — CONGREVE, *Letter to Dennis* [1695]

1   As for a future life, every man must judge for himself between conflicting vague probabilities.
        From Life and Letters of Charles Darwin [1887],
        edited by FRANCIS DARWIN

2   I love fools' experiments. I am always making them.   *Ibid.*

Edward FitzGerald
1809–1883

3 Wake! For the Sun who scatter'd into flight
The Stars before him from the Field of night,
Drives Night along with them from Heav'n and strikes
The Sultan's Turret with a Shaft of Light.
        The Rubáiyát of Omar Khayyám,[1] *st. 1*

4 Awake! for Morning in the Bowl of Night
Has flung the Stone that puts the Stars to flight:
And Lo! the Hunter of the East has caught
The Sultan's Turret in a Noose of Light.
                        Ibid. [first edition]

5 Now the New Year reviving old Desires,
The thoughtful Soul to Solitude retires.
                        Ibid. st. 4

6 Come, fill the Cup, and in the fire of Spring
The Winter garment of Repentance fling:
The Bird of Time has but a little way
To fly—and Lo! the Bird is on the Wing.
                Ibid. st. 7 [first edition]

7 The Leaves of Life keep falling one by one.
                        Ibid. st. 8

8 Each Morn a thousand Roses brings, you say:
Yes, but where leaves the Rose of Yesterday?
                        Ibid. st. 9

9 A Book of Verses underneath the Bough,
A Jug of Wine, a Loaf of Bread—and Thou
Beside me singing in the Wilderness—
Oh, Wilderness were Paradise enow!
                        Ibid. st. 12

10 Ah, take the Cash, and let the Credit go,
Nor heed the rumble of a distant Drum!
                        Ibid. st. 13

11 Think, in this batter'd Caravanserai
Whose Portals are alternate Night and Day,
How Sultan after Sultan with his Pomp
Abode his destin'd Hour, and went his way.
                        Ibid. st. 17

12 They say the Lion and the Lizard keep
The Courts where Jamshyd gloried and drank deep:
And Bahram, that great Hunter—the Wild Ass
Stamps o'er his Head, but cannot break his sleep.
                        Ibid. st. 18

13 I sometimes think that never blows so red
The Rose as where some buried Caesar bled;
That every Hyacinth the Garden wears
Dropt in her Lap from some once lovely Head.
                        Ibid. st. 19

14 Ah, my Belovèd, fill the Cup that clears
Today of past Regrets and future Fears:
Tomorrow!—Why, Tomorrow I may be
Myself with Yesterday's Sev'n thousand Years.
                        Ibid. st. 21

15 For some we loved, the loveliest and the best
That from his Vintage rolling Time hath prest.
                        Ibid. st. 22

16 Ah, make the most of what we yet may spend,
Before we too into the Dust descend;
Dust into Dust, and under Dust, to lie,
Sans Wine, sans Song, sans Singer, and—sans End!
                        Ibid. st. 24

17 Myself when young did eagerly frequent
Doctor and Saint, and heard great argument
About it and about: but evermore
Came out by the same door wherein I went.
                        Ibid. st. 27

18 And this was all the Harvest that I reap'd—
"I came like Water, and like Wind I go."
                        Ibid. st. 28

19 There was the Door to which I found no Key;
There was the Veil through which I might not see.
Some little talk awhile of Me and Thee
There was—and then no more of Thee and Me.
                        Ibid. st. 32

20   "While you live,
Drink!—for, once dead, you never shall return."
                        Ibid. st. 35

21 For I remember stopping by the way
To watch a Potter thumping his wet Clay:
And with its all-obliterated Tongue
It murmured—"Gently, Brother, gently, pray!"
                        Ibid. st. 37

22 And fear not lest Existence closing your
Account, and mine, should know the like no more;
The Eternal Saki from that Bowl has pour'd
Millions of Bubbles like us, and will pour.
                        Ibid. st. 46

23 'Tis all a Checkerboard of Nights and Days
Where Destiny with Men for Pieces plays:
Hither and thither moves, and mates, and slays,
And one by one back in the Closet lays.
                Ibid. st. 49 [first edition]

24   Striking from the Calendar
Unborn Tomorrow and dead Yesterday.
                        Ibid. st. 57

25 The Moving Finger writes; and, having writ,
Moves on: nor all your Piety nor Wit

[1]Translated from the Persian of OMAR KHAYYÁM [died c. 1123] in four editions, 1859, 1868, 1872, and 1879. The fourth edition is used here, unless otherwise stated.

Shall lure it back to cancel half a Line,
Nor all your Tears wash out a Word of it.
The Rubáiyát of Omar Khayyám, st. 71

1   That inverted Bowl we call The Sky,
Whereunder crawling coop'd we live and die.
Ibid. st. 52 [first edition]

2 Ah, Moon of my Delight who know'st no wane.
Ibid. st. 74 [first edition]

3 And He that with his hand the Vessel made
Will surely not in after Wrath destroy.
Ibid. st. 85

4 After a momentary silence spake
Some Vessel of a more ungainly Make;
"They sneer at me for leaning all awry:
What! did the Hand then of the Potter shake?"
Ibid. st. 86

5 Who *is* the Potter, pray, and who the Pot?
Ibid. st. 87

6 Indeed the Idols I have loved so long
Have done my credit in this World much wrong:
Have drown'd my Glory in a shallow Cup,
And sold my Reputation for a Song.
Ibid. st. 93

7 I wonder often what the Vintners buy
One half so precious as the stuff they sell.
Ibid. st. 95

8 Ah Love! could you and I with Him conspire
To grasp this Sorry Scheme of Things entire,
Would not we shatter it to bits—and then
Remold it nearer to the Heart's Desire!
Ibid. st. 99

9 And when like her, O Saki, you shall pass
Among the Guests Star-scatter'd on the Grass,
And in your joyous errand reach the spot
Where I made One—turn down an empty Glass!
Ibid. st. 101

10 The King in a carriage may ride,
And the Beggar may crawl at his side;
But in the general race,
They are traveling all the same pace.
Chronomoros

11   Mrs. Browning's death was rather a relief to me,
I must say; no more Aurora Leighs, thank God!
Letter [July 15, 1861][1]

William Ewart Gladstone
1809–1898

12   Decision by majorities is as much an expedient as
lighting by gas.
Speech in the House of Commons [1858]

13   You cannot fight against the future. Time is on
our side.   *Speech on the Reform Bill [1866]*

14   Out of the range of practical politics.
Speech at Dalkeith [November 26, 1879]

15   The resources of civilization are not yet exhausted.   *Speech at Leeds [October 7, 1881]*

16   All the world over, I will back the masses against
the classes.   *Speech at Liverpool [June 28, 1886]*

17   I have always regarded that Constitution as the
most remarkable work known to me in modern
times to have been produced by the human intellect,
at a single stroke (so to speak), in its application to
political affairs.
*Letter to the committee in charge of the
celebration of the centennial of the American
Constitution [July 20, 1887]*

18   Justice delayed is justice denied.   *Attributed*

Nikolai Gogol
1809–1852

19   It is no use to blame the looking glass if your face
is awry.   *The Inspector-General [1836], epigraph*

20   Of course, Alexander the Great was a hero, but
why smash the chairs?   *Ibid.*

21   The more destruction there is everywhere, the
more it shows the activity of town authorities.
Ibid. act I, sc. i

22   I tell everyone very plainly that I take bribes, but
what kind of bribes? Why, greyhound puppies.
That's a totally different matter.   *Ibid.*

23   The sergeant's widow told you a lie when she
said I flogged her. I never flogged her. She flogged
herself.   *Ibid. IV, xv*

24   What are you laughing at? You are laughing at
yourselves!   *Ibid. V, viii*

25   And for a long time yet, led by some wondrous
power, I am fated to journey hand in hand with my
strange heroes and to survey the surging immensity
of life, to survey it through the laughter that all can
see and through the tears unseen and unknown by
anyone.   *Dead Souls [1842], vol. I, ch. 7*

26   Rus! Rus! I see you, from my lovely enchanted
remoteness I see you: a country of dinginess, and
bleakness and dispersal; no arrogant wonders of nature crowned by the arrogant wonders of art appear
within you to delight or terrify the eyes. . . . So
what is the incomprehensible secret force driving me
towards you? Why do I constantly hear the echo of
your mournful song as it is carried from sea to sea
through your entire expanse? . . . And since you
are without end yourself, is it not within you that a
boundless thought will be born?[2]   *Ibid. II, 11*

27   Oh troika, winged troika, tell me who invented
you? Surely, nowhere but among a nimble nation
could you have been born: in a country which has

---

[1]See Elizabeth Barrett Browning, 439:2.

[2]Translated by VLADIMIR NABOKOV.

taken itself in earnest and has evenly spread far and wide over half of the globe, so that once you start counting the milestones you may count on till a speckled haze dances before your eyes. . . .

Rus, are you not similar in your headlong motion to one of those nimble troikas that none can overtake? The flying road turns into smoke under you, bridges thunder and pass, all falls back and is left behind! . . . And what does this awesome motion mean? What is the passing strange force contained in these passing strange steeds? Steeds, steeds, what steeds! Has the whirlwind a home in your manes? . . . Rus, whither are you speeding so? Answer me. No answer. The middle bell trills out in a dream its liquid soliloquy; the roaring air is torn to pieces and becomes wind; all things on earth fly by and other nations and states gaze askance as they step aside and give her the right of way.[1]

> *Ibid. II, concluding paragraphs*

1   In the course of the reading he [Pushkin] became more and more melancholy and finally became completely gloomy. When the reading was over he uttered in a voice full of sorrow: "Goodness, how sad is our Russia!"

> *Four Letters Concerning Dead Souls [1843]*

2   I shall laugh my bitter laugh.

> *Epitaph on Gogol's tombstone*

Oliver Wendell Holmes
1809–1894

3 Ay, tear her tattered ensign down!
Long has it waved on high,
And many an eye has danced to see
That banner in the sky;
Beneath it rung the battle shout,
And burst the cannon's roar—
The meteor of the ocean air
Shall sweep the clouds no more.

> *Old Ironsides [1830],[2] st. 1*

4 And silence, like a poultice, comes
To heal the blows of sound.

> *The Music Grinders, st. 10*

5 There is no time like the old time, when you and
   I were young.

> *No Time Like the Old Time, st. 1*

6   A thought is often original, though you have uttered it a hundred times.

> *The Autocrat of the Breakfast-Table [1858], ch. 1*

7   Insanity is often the logic of an accurate mind overtasked.

> *Ibid. 2*

8   Man has his will—but woman has her way!

> *Ibid.*

---

[1]Translated by Vladimir Nabokov.
[2]This poem roused such popular feeling that it is generally credited with saving the frigate *Constitution* from being dismantled as unfit for service.

9   Put not your trust in money, but put your money in trust.

> *Ibid.*

10   I find the great thing in this world is not so much where we stand, as in what direction we are moving: To reach the port of heaven, we must sail sometimes with the wind and sometimes against it—but we must sail, and not drift, nor lie at anchor.

> *Ibid. 4*

11 Build thee more stately mansions, O my soul,
As the swift seasons roll!
Leave thy low-vaulted past!

> *Ibid. [The Chambered Nautilus, st. 5]*

12   Sin has many tools, but a lie is the handle which fits them all.

> *Ibid. ch. 6*

13   Boston State-House is the hub of the solar system. You couldn't pry that out of a Boston man, if you had the tire of all creation straightened out for a crowbar.

> *Ibid.*

14   The axis of the earth sticks out visibly through the center of each and every town or city.

> *Ibid.*

15   The world's great men have not commonly been great scholars, nor its great scholars great men.

> *Ibid.*

16 Have you heard of the wonderful one-hoss shay,
That was built in such a logical way
It ran a hundred years to a day?

> *Ibid. 11 [The Deacon's Masterpiece, st. 1]*

17 End of the wonderful one-hoss shay.
Logic is logic. That's all I say.

> *Ibid. [st. 12]*

18   He comes of the Brahmin caste of New England. This is the harmless, inoffensive, untitled aristocracy.

> *The Brahmin Caste of New England [1860]*

19   Science is a first-rate piece of furniture for a man's upper chamber, if he has common sense on the ground floor.

> *The Poet at the Breakfast-Table [1872], ch. 5*

20 And if I should live to be
The last leaf upon the tree
In the spring,
Let them smile, as I do now,
At the old forsaken bough
Where I cling.

> *The Last Leaf [1831], st. 8*

Abraham Lincoln
1809–1865

21   If the good people, in their wisdom, shall see fit to keep me in the background, I have been too familiar with disappointments to be very much chagrined.

> *Address at New Salem, Illinois [March 9, 1832]*

22   Politicians [are] a set of men who have interests aside from the interests of the people, and who, to say the most of them, are, taken as a mass, at least

one long step removed from honest men. I say this with the greater freedom because, being a politician myself, none can regard it as personal.

Speech in the Illinois Legislature [January 11, 1837]

1   If destruction be our lot we must ourselves be its author and finisher. As a nation of freemen we must live through all time, or die by suicide.

Address at the Young Men's Lyceum, Springfield, Illinois [January 27, 1838]

2   There is no grievance that is a fit object of redress by mob law.   *Ibid.*

3   Any people anywhere, being inclined and having the power, have the *right* to rise up, and shake off the existing government, and form a new one that suits them better.

Speech in the House of Representatives [January 12, 1848]

4   No man is good enough to govern another man without that other's consent.

Speech at Peoria, Illinois [October 16, 1854]

5   I hate [slavery] because it deprives the republican example of its just influence in the world—enables the enemies of free institutions, with plausibility, to taunt us as hypocrites—causes the real friends of freedom to doubt our sincerity.   *Ibid.*

6   The ballot is stronger than the bullet.

Speech at Bloomington, Illinois [May 19, 1856]

7   "A house divided against itself cannot stand."[1] I believe this government cannot endure permanently half slave and half free. I do not expect the Union to be dissolved—I do not expect the house to fall— but I do expect it will cease to be divided. It will become all one thing, or all the other.

Speech at the Republican State Convention, Springfield, Illinois [June 16, 1858]

8   Nobody has ever expected me to be President. In my poor, lean, lank face nobody has ever seen that any cabbages were sprouting out.[2]

Second campaign speech against Douglas, Springfield, Illinois [July 17, 1858]

9   As I would not be a *slave,* so I would not be a *master.* This expresses my idea of democracy. Whatever differs from this, to the extent of the difference, is no democracy.

Fragment [August 1, 1858?]. From ROY P. BASLER, The Collected Works of Abraham Lincoln [1953], vol. II, p. 532

10   When . . . you have succeeded in dehumanizing the Negro; when you have put him down and made it forever impossible for him to be but as the

beasts of the field; when you have extinguished his soul and placed him where the ray of hope is blown out in darkness like that which broods over the spirits of the damned, are you quite sure that the demon you have roused will not turn and rend you?

Speech at Edwardsville, Illinois [September 11, 1858]

11   That is the issue that will continue in this country when these poor tongues of Judge Douglas and myself shall be silent. It is the eternal struggle between these two principles—right and wrong—throughout the world. They are the two principles that have stood face to face from the beginning of time; and will ever continue to struggle. The one is the common right of humanity, and the other the divine right of kings. It is the same principle in whatever shape it develops itself.

Reply, seventh and last joint debate, Alton, Illinois [October 15, 1858]

12   This is a world of compensations; and he who would be no slave must consent to have no slave. Those who deny freedom to others deserve it not for themselves, and, under a just God, cannot long retain it.

Letter to H. L. Pierce and others [April 6, 1859]

13   Public opinion in this country is everything.

Speech at Columbus, Ohio [September 16, 1859]

14   It is said an Eastern monarch once charged his wise men to invent him a sentence, to be ever in view, and which should be true and appropriate in all times and situations. They presented him the words: "And this, too, shall pass away." How much it expresses! How chastening in the hour of pride! How consoling in the depths of affliction!

Address to the Wisconsin State Agricultural Society, Milwaukee [September 30, 1859]

15   Let us have faith that right makes might, and in that faith let us to the end dare to do our duty as we understand it.

Address at Cooper Union, New York [February 27, 1860]

16   No one, not in my situation, can appreciate my feeling of sadness at this parting. To this place, and the kindness of these people, I owe everything. Here I have lived a quarter of a century, and have passed from a young to an old man. Here my children have been born, and one is buried. I now leave, not knowing when or whether ever I may return, with a task before me greater than that which rested upon Washington. Without the assistance of that Divine Being who ever attended him, I cannot succeed. With that assistance I cannot fail. Trusting in Him who can go with me, and remain with you, and be everywhere for good, let us confidently hope that all will yet be well.

Farewell Address, Springfield, Illinois [February 11, 1861]

---

[1]See *Mark* 3:25, 37:20.

[2]They have seen in his [Douglas's] round, jolly, fruitful face, post offices, land offices, marshalships and cabinet appointments, chargeships and foreign missions, bursting and sprouting out in wonderful exuberance, ready to be laid hold of by their greedy hands.—LINCOLN, *ibid.*

1   If we do not make common cause to save the good old ship of the Union on this voyage, nobody will have a chance to pilot her on another voyage.
Address at Cleveland, Ohio [February 15, 1861]

2   It is safe to assert that no government proper ever had a provision in its organic law for its own termination.   *First Inaugural Address [March 4, 1861]*

3   If by the mere force of numbers a majority should deprive a minority of any clearly written constitutional right, it might, in a moral point of view, justify revolution—certainly would if such a right were a vital one.   *Ibid.*

4   This country, with its institutions, belongs to the people who inhabit it. Whenever they shall grow weary of the existing government, they can exercise their constitutional right of amending it, or their revolutionary right to dismember or overthrow it.
Ibid.

5   Why should there not be a patient confidence in the ultimate justice of the people? Is there any better or equal hope in the world?   *Ibid.*

6   While the people retain their virtue and vigilance, no administration, by any extreme of wickedness or folly, can very seriously injure the government in the short space of four years.   *Ibid.*

7   I think the necessity of being *ready* increases. Look to it.
Letter (this is the whole message) to Governor Andrew G. Curtin of Pennsylvania [April 8, 1861]

8   This is essentially a people's contest. . . . It is a struggle for maintaining in the world that form and substance of government whose leading object is to elevate the condition of men—to lift artificial weights from all shoulders—to clear the paths of laudable pursuit for all—to afford all an unfettered start, and a fair chance, in the race of life.
Message to Congress in Special Session [July 4, 1861]

9   Labor is prior to, and independent of, capital. Capital is only the fruit of labor, and could never have existed if labor had not first existed. Labor is the superior of capital, and deserves much the higher consideration. Capital has its rights, which are as worthy of protection as any other rights.
First Annual Message to Congress [December 3, 1861]

10   It is called the Army of the Potomac but it is only McClellan's bodyguard. . . . If McClellan is not using the army, I should like to borrow it for a while.
Washington, D.C. [April 9, 1862]

11   My paramount object in this struggle is to save the Union, and is not either to save or to destroy slavery. If I could save the Union without freeing any slave, I would do it; and if I could save it by freeing all the slaves, I would do it; and if I could do it by freeing some and leaving others alone, I would also do that.
Letter to Horace Greeley [August 22, 1862]

12   I shall try to correct errors when shown to be errors; and I shall adopt new views so fast as they shall appear to be true views. . . . I intend no modification of my oft-expressed personal wish that all men, everywhere, could be free.   *Ibid.*

13   On the first day of January in the year of our Lord, one thousand eight hundred and sixty-three, all persons held as slaves within any state, or designated part of a state, the people whereof shall then be in rebellion against the United States shall be then, thenceforward, and forever free.
Preliminary Emancipation Proclamation [September 22, 1862][1]

14   [I feel] somewhat like the boy in Kentucky who stubbed his toe while running to see his sweetheart. The boy said he was too big to cry, and far too badly hurt to laugh.
Reply as to how he felt about the New York elections. From Frank Leslie's Illustrated Weekly [November 22, 1862]

15   If there ever could be a proper time for mere catch arguments, that time surely is not now. In times like the present, men should utter nothing for which they would not willingly be responsible through time and in eternity.
Second Annual Message to Congress [December 1, 1862]

16   Fellow citizens, we cannot escape history. We of this Congress and this administration will be remembered in spite of ourselves. No personal significance or insignificance can spare one or another of us. The fiery trial through which we pass will light us down in honor or dishonor to the last generation. We say we are for the Union. The world will not forget that we say this. We know how to save the Union. The world knows we do know how to save it. We, even we here, hold the power and bear the responsibility. In giving freedom to the slave, we assure freedom to the free—honorable alike in what we give and what we preserve. We shall nobly save or meanly lose the last, best hope of earth. Other means may succeed; this could not fail. The way is plain, peaceful, generous, just—a way which if followed the world will forever applaud and God must forever bless.   *Ibid.*

17   Beware of rashness, but with energy and sleepless vigilance go forward and give us victories.
Letter to Major General Joseph Hooker [January 26, 1863]

18   The Father of Waters again goes unvexed to the sea.
Letter to James C. Conkling [August 26, 1863]

[1]The Emancipation Proclamation was issued one hundred days later [January 1, 1863].

1   I have endured a great deal of ridicule without much malice; and have received a great deal of kindness, not quite free from ridicule. I am used to it.
  Letter to James H. Hackett [November 2, 1863]

2   Fourscore and seven years ago our fathers brought forth on this continent, a new nation, conceived in Liberty, and dedicated to the proposition that all men are created equal.

  Now we are engaged in a great civil war, testing whether that nation or any nation so conceived and so dedicated can long endure. We are met on a great battlefield of that war. We have come to dedicate a portion of that field, as a final resting place for those who here gave their lives that that nation might live. It is altogether fitting and proper that we should do this.

  But, in a larger sense, we cannot dedicate — we cannot consecrate — we cannot hallow — this ground. The brave men, living and dead, who struggled here, have consecrated it far above our poor power to add or detract. The world will little note nor long remember what we say here, but it can never forget what they did here. It is for us, the living, rather to be dedicated here to the unfinished work which they who fought here have thus far so nobly advanced. It is rather for us to be here dedicated to the great task remaining before us — that from these honored dead we take increased devotion to that cause for which they gave the last full measure of devotion; that we here highly resolve that these dead shall not have died in vain; that this nation, under God, shall have a new birth of freedom; and that government of the people, by the people, for the people, shall not perish from the earth.
  Address at Gettysburg [November 19, 1863]

3   The President last night had a dream. He was in a party of plain people and as it became known who he was they began to comment on his appearance. One of them said, "He is a common-looking man." The President replied, "Common-looking people are the best in the world: that is the reason the Lord makes so many of them."
  From Letters of John Hay and Extracts from His Diary, edited by C. L. HAY [December 23, 1863]

4   I claim not to have controlled events, but confess plainly that events have controlled me.
  Letter to A. G. Hodges [April 4, 1864]

5   I do not allow myself to suppose that either the convention or the League have concluded to decide that I am either the greatest or best man in America, but rather they have concluded that it is not best to swap horses while crossing the river, and have further concluded that I am not so poor a horse that they might not make a botch of it in trying to swap.
  Reply to the National Union League [June 9, 1864]

6   Truth is generally the best vindication against slander.
  Letter to Secretary Stanton, refusing to dismiss Postmaster-General Montgomery Blair [July 18, 1864]

7   It has long been a grave question whether any government, not too strong for the liberties of its people, can be strong enough to maintain its existence in great emergencies.
  Response to a serenade [November 10, 1864]

8   I desire so to conduct the affairs of this administration that if at the end, when I come to lay down the reins of power, I have lost every other friend on earth, I shall at least have one friend left, and that friend shall be down inside me.
  Reply to the Missouri Committee of Seventy [1864]

9   Dear Madam, I have been shown in the files of the War Department a statement of the Adjutant-General of Massachusetts that you are the mother of five[1] sons who have died gloriously on the field of battle. I feel how weak and fruitless must be any words of mine which should attempt to beguile you from the grief of a loss so overwhelming. But I cannot refrain from tendering to you the consolation that may be found in the thanks of the Republic they died to save. I pray that our heavenly Father may assuage the anguish of your bereavement, and leave you only the cherished memory of the loved and lost, and the solemn pride that must be yours to have laid so costly a sacrifice upon the altar of freedom.
  Letter to Mrs. Bixby [November 21, 1864]

10   It may seem strange that any men should dare to ask a just God's assistance in wringing their bread from the sweat of other men's faces,[2] but let us judge not, that we be not judged.[3]
  Second Inaugural Address [March 4, 1865]

11   Fondly do we hope, fervently do we pray, that this mighty scourge of war may speedily pass away. Yet, if God wills that it continue until all the wealth piled by the bondsman's two hundred and fifty years of unrequited toil shall be sunk, and until every drop of blood drawn with the lash shall be paid by another drawn with the sword, as was said three thousand years ago, so still it must be said, "The judgments of the Lord are true and righteous altogether."[4]

  With malice toward none, with charity for all, with firmness in the right as God gives us to see the right,[5] let us strive on to finish the work we are in, to bind up the nation's wounds, to care for him who shall have borne the battle and for his widow and his

[1]Later, the records were revised; the correct number was two.
[2]See *Genesis* 3:19, 6:26.
[3]See *Matthew* 7:1, 34:2.
[4]See *Psalms* 19:9, 16:11.
[5]See John Quincy Adams, 369:2.

orphan, to do all which may achieve and cherish a just and lasting peace among ourselves and with all nations.   *Ibid.*

1   I have always thought that all men should be free; but if any should be slaves, it should be first those who desire it for themselves, and secondly those who desire it for others. Whenever I hear anyone arguing for slavery, I feel a strong impulse to see it tried on him personally.
    Address to an Indiana Regiment [March 17, 1865]

2   Important principles may and must be inflexible.
    Last public address, Washington, D.C. [April 11, 1865]

3   If you once forfeit the confidence of your fellow citizens, you can never regain their respect and esteem. It is true that you may fool all the people some of the time; you can even fool some of the people all the time; but you can't fool all of the people all the time.
    To a caller at the White House. From ALEXANDER K. McCLURE, *Lincoln's Yarns and Stories [1904]*

4   If I were to try to read, much less answer, all the attacks made on me, this shop might as well be closed for any other business. I do the very best I know how—the very best I can; and I mean to keep doing so until the end. If the end brings me out all right, what is said against me won't amount to anything. If the end brings me out wrong, ten angels swearing I was right would make no difference.
    Conversation at the White House. From FRANCIS B. CARPENTER, *Six Months at the White House with Abraham Lincoln [1866]*

Benjamin Peirce
1809–1880

5   Mathematics is the science which draws necessary conclusions.
    Linear Associative Algebra [1870], first sentence

Edgar Allan Poe[1]
1809–1849

6 O, human love! thou spirit given,
On Earth, of all we hope in Heaven!
    Tamerlane [1827], l. 177

7 All that we see or seem
Is but a dream within a dream.
    A Dream Within a Dream [1827, revised 1849], l. 10

8 The happiest day—the happiest hour
My sear'd and blighted heart hath known,

The highest hope of pride and power,
I feel hath flown.
    The Happiest Day [1827], st. 1

9 From childhood's hour I have not been
As others were—I have not seen
As others saw.
    Alone [written 1829, published 1875], l. 1

10 Hast thou not torn the Naiad from her flood,
The Elfin from the green grass, and from me
The summer dream beneath the tamarind tree?
    Sonnet. To Science [1829], l. 12

11   It is with literature as with law or empire—an established name is an estate in tenure, or a throne in possession.
    Poems [1831]. Preface, Letter to Mr. B——

12 Helen, thy beauty is to me
Like those Nicean barks of yore,
That gently, o'er a perfumed sea,
The weary, wayworn wanderer bore
To his own native shore.

On desperate seas long wont to roam,
Thy hyacinth hair, thy classic face,
Thy Naiad airs have brought me home
To the glory that was Greece,
And the grandeur that was Rome.
    To Helen [1831], st. 1, 2

13 If I could dwell
Where Israfel[2]
Hath dwelt, and he where I,
He might not sing so wildly well
A mortal melody,
While a bolder note than this might swell
From my lyre within the sky.
    Israfel [1831], st. 8

14 Lo! Death has reared himself a throne
In a strange city, lying alone
Far down within the dim West,
Where the good and the bad and the worst and
    the best
Have gone to their eternal rest.
    The City in the Sea [1831], st. 1

15 The viol, the violet, and the vine.
    Ibid. st. 2

16 While from a proud tower in the town
Death looks gigantically down.
    Ibid. st. 3

17 And when, amid no earthly moans,
Down, down that town shall settle hence,
Hell, rising from a thousand thrones,
Shall do it reverence.
    Ibid. st. 5

[1]See James Russell Lowell, 485:8.

[2]Poe's epigraph for the poem: And the angel Israfel, whose heartstrings are a lute, and who has the sweetest voice of all God's creatures.—*Koran*

1 A dirge for the most lovely dead
  That ever died so young!

Lenore [1831], st. 1

2 Thou wast that all to me, love,
  For which my soul did pine—
  A green isle in the sea, love,
  A fountain and a shrine,
  All wreathed with fairy fruits and flowers,
  And all the flowers were mine.

To One in Paradise [1834], st. 1

3 And all my days are trances,
  And all my nightly dreams
  Are where thy gray eye glances,
  And where thy footstep gleams—
  In what ethereal dances,
  By what eternal streams.

Ibid. st. 4

4   During the whole of a dull, dark, and soundless
  day in the autumn of the year, when the clouds hung
  oppressively low in the heavens, I had been passing
  alone, on horseback, through a singularly dreary
  tract of country, and at length found myself, as the
  shades of the evening drew on, within view of the
  melancholy House of Usher.

The Fall of the House of Usher [1839]

5 In the greenest of our valleys
  By good angels tenanted,
  Once a fair and stately palace—
  Radiant palace—reared its head.

The Haunted Palace [1839], st. 1

6   They who dream by day are cognizant of many
  things which escape those who dream only by night.

Eleonora [1841]

7 And much of Madness, and more of Sin,
  And Horror the soul of the plot.

The Conqueror Worm [1843], st. 3

8 While the angels, all pallid and wan,
  Uprising, unveiling, affirm
  That the play is the tragedy, "Man,"
  And its hero the Conqueror Worm.

Ibid. st. 5

9   There is something in the unselfish and self-sacrificing love of a brute, which goes directly to the heart
  of him who has had frequent occasion to test the
  paltry friendship and gossamer fidelity of mere Man.

The Black Cat [1843]

10   The boundaries which divide Life from Death are
  at best shadowy and vague. Who shall say where the
  one ends, and where the other begins?

The Premature Burial [1844]

11 From a wild weird clime that lieth, sublime,
  Out of Space—out of Time.

Dreamland [1845], st. 1

12   With me poetry has been not a purpose, but a
  passion; and the passions should be held in reverence: they must not—they cannot at will be excited,
  with an eye to the paltry compensations, or the more
  paltry commendations, of mankind.

The Raven and Other Poems [1845], preface

13 Once upon a midnight dreary, while I pondered,
    weak and weary,
  Over many a quaint and curious volume of
    forgotten lore—
  While I nodded, nearly napping, suddenly there
    came a tapping,
  As of someone gently rapping, rapping at my
    chamber door.

The Raven [1845], st. 1

14 Ah, distinctly I remember it was in the bleak
    December;
  And each separate dying ember wrought its ghost
    upon the floor.

Ibid. st. 2

15   Sorrow for the lost Lenore—
  For the rare and radiant maiden whom the angels
    name Lenore—
  Nameless *here* for evermore.

Ibid.

16 The silken, sad, uncertain rustling of each purple
    curtain.

Ibid. st. 3

17 Deep into that darkness peering, long I stood
    there wondering, fearing,
  Doubting, dreaming dreams no mortal ever dared
    to dream before.

Ibid. st. 5

18 "Ghastly grim and ancient Raven wandering from
    the Nightly shore—
  Tell me what thy lordly name is on the Night's
    Plutonian shore!"
  Quoth the Raven, "Nevermore."

Ibid. st. 8

19 "Prophet!" said I, "thing of evil!—prophet still, if
    bird or devil!"

Ibid. st. 15

20 "Take thy beak from out my heart, and take thy
    form from off my door!"
  Quoth the Raven, "Nevermore."

Ibid. st. 17

21 And the Raven, never flitting, still is sitting, *still* is
    sitting
  On the pallid bust of Pallas just above my
    chamber door.

Ibid. st. 18

22 And my soul from out that shadow that lies
    floating on the floor
  Shall be lifted—nevermore!

Ibid.

23   The Imp of the Perverse.[1]

Title of story [1845]

---

[1]Perverseness is one of the primitive impulses of the human
heart.—*The Black Cat* [1843]

1 The skies they were ashen and sober;
   The leaves they were crispèd and sere—
   The leaves they were withering and sere:
   It was night in the lonesome October
   Of my most immemorial year.
                              Ulalume [1847], st. 1

2 It was down by the dank tarn of Auber,
   In the ghoul-haunted woodland of Weir.
                              Ibid.

3 Here once, through an alley Titanic,
   Of cypress, I roamed with my Soul—
   Of cypress, with Psyche, my Soul.
                              Ibid. st. 2

4 Thus I pacified Psyche and kissed her,
   And tempted her out of her gloom.
                              Ibid. st. 8

5 "Over the Mountains
   Of the Moon,
   Down the Valley of the Shadow,
   Ride, boldly ride,"
   The shade replied—
   "If you seek for Eldorado!"
                              Eldorado [1849], st. 4

6 And the fever called "Living"
   Is conquered at last.
                              For Annie [1849], st. 1

7 And this maiden she lived with no other thought
   Than to love and be loved by me.
                              Annabel Lee [1849], st. 1

8 *I* was a child and *she* was a child,
   In this kingdom by the sea,
   But we loved with a love that was more than
        love—
   I and my Annabel Lee—
   With a love that the wingèd seraphs of Heaven
   Coveted her and me.
                              Ibid. st. 2

9 And neither the angels in Heaven above
   Nor the demons down under the sea,
   Can ever dissever my soul from the soul
   Of the beautiful Annabel Lee.
                              Ibid. st. 5

10 In her sepulcher there by the sea—
   In her tomb by the sounding sea.
                              Ibid. st. 6

11 Keeping time, time, time,
   In a sort of Runic rhyme,
   To the tintinnabulation that so musically wells
   From the bells, bells, bells, bells,
   Bells, bells, bells.
                              The Bells [1849], st. 1

12   I hold that a long poem does not exist. I maintain
   that the phrase "a long poem" is simply a flat contradiction in terms.   *The Poetic Principle [1850]*

13   There neither exists nor can exist any work more
   thoroughly dignified—more supremely noble than

this very poem—this poem *per se*—this poem
which is a poem and nothing more—this poem written solely for the poem's sake.   *Ibid.*

14   I would define, in brief, the poetry of words as the
rhythmical creation of Beauty. Its sole arbiter is
taste. With the intellect or with the conscience, it has
only collateral relations. Unless incidentally, it has
no concern whatever either with duty or with truth.[1]
                                                Ibid.

Pierre Joseph Proudhon
1809–1865

15   Property is theft [La propriété c'est le vol]!
              Qu'est-ce que la Propriété? [1840], ch. 1

Alfred, Lord Tennyson
1809–1892

16 Weeded and worn the ancient thatch
   Upon the lonely moated grange.
                              Mariana[2] [1830], st. 1

17 She said, "I am aweary, aweary,
   I would that I were dead!"
                              Ibid. refrain

18 A still small voice[3] spake unto me,
   "Thou art so full of misery,
   Were it not better not to be?"
                              The Two Voices [1832], st. 1

19 Though thou wert scattered to the wind,
   Yet is there plenty of the kind.
                              Ibid. st. 11

20 I know that age to age succeeds,
   Blowing a noise of tongues and deeds,
   A dust of systems and of creeds.
                              Ibid. st. 69

21 Like glimpses of forgotten dreams.
                              Ibid. st. 127

22 No life that breathes with human breath
   Has ever truly longed for death.
                              Ibid. st. 132

23   In after-dinner talk,
   Across the walnuts and the wine.
                              The Miller's Daughter [1832], st. 4

24 Self-reverence, self-knowledge, self-control,
   These three alone lead life to sovereign power.
                              Oenone [1832], l. 142

25 The daughter of a hundred Earls,
   You are not one to be desired.
                              Lady Clara Vere de Vere [1832], st. 1

[1]Poe first published this passage in his review of Longfellow's *Ballads and Other Poems, Graham's Magazine* [April
1842].
[2]See Shakespeare, 204:18.
[3]See *I Kings 19:12, 12:39.*

1 The lion on your old stone gates
Is not more cold to you than I.
Lady Clara Vere de Vere, st. 3

2 The gardener Adam and his wife
Smile at the claims of long descent.
Ibid. st. 7

3 'Tis only noble to be good.
Kind hearts are more than coronets,
And simple faith than Norman blood.
Ibid.

4 You must wake and call me early, call me early,
mother dear;
Tomorrow 'ill be the happiest time of all the glad
New Year;
Of all the glad New Year, mother, the maddest,
merriest day;
For I'm to be Queen o' the May, mother, I'm to
be Queen o' the May.
The May Queen [1832], st. 1

5 In the afternoon they came unto a land
In which it seemed always afternoon.
The Lotos-Eaters [1832], st. 1

6 Music that gentlier on the spirit lies,
Than tir'd eyelids upon tir'd eyes.
Ibid. Choric Song, st. 1

7 There is no joy but calm!
Ibid. st. 2

8   Ah, why
Should life all labor be?
Ibid. st. 4

9 Let us alone. Time driveth onward fast,
And in a little while our lips are dumb.
Let us alone. What is it that will last?
All things are taken from us, and become
Portions and parcels of the dreadful Past.
Ibid.

10 Give us long rest or death, dark death or dreamful
ease.
Ibid.

11 Surely, surely, slumber is more sweet than toil, the
shore
Than labor in the deep mid-ocean, wind and wave
and oar;
Oh rest ye, brother mariners, we will not wander
more.
Ibid. last lines

12 Dan Chaucer, the first warbler, whose sweet
breath
Preluded those melodious bursts that fill
The spacious times of great Elizabeth
With sounds that echo still.
A Dream of Fair Women [1832]

13 A daughter of the gods, divinely tall,
And most divinely fair.
Ibid. st. 22

14 Many-tower'd Camelot.
The Lady of Shalott [1832], pt. I, st. 1

15 "Tirra lirra," by the river
Sang Sir Lancelot.
Ibid. III, st. 4

16 She left the web, she left the loom,
She made three paces thro' the room,
She saw the water lily bloom,
She saw the helmet and the plume,
She look'd down to Camelot.
Out flew the web and floated wide;
The mirror cracked from side to side.
"The curse has come upon me," cried
The Lady of Shalott.
Ibid. st. 5

17 But Lancelot mused a little space;
He said, "She has a lovely face;
God in his mercy lend her grace,
The Lady of Shalott."
Ibid. IV, st. 6

18   The great brand
Made lightnings in the splendor of the moon,
And flashing round and round, and whirled in an
arch,
Shot like a streamer of the northern morn,
Seen where the moving isles of winter shock
By night, with noises of the northern sea,
So flashed and fell the brand Excalibur.
Morte d'Arthur [1842], l. 136

19   Lo! the level lake
And the long glories of the winter moon.
Ibid. l. 191

20   Half light, half shade,
She stood, a sight to make an old man young.
The Gardener's Daughter [1842], l. 139

21 The long mechanic pacings to and fro,
The set gray life, and apathetic end.
Love and Duty [1842], l. 17

22 Meet is it changes should control
Our being, lest we rest in ease.
Love Thou Thy Land [1842], st. 11

23   Ah! when shall all men's good
Be each man's rule, and universal peace
Lie like a shaft of light across the land,
And like a lane of beams athwart the sea,
Through all the circle of the golden year?
The Golden Year [1842], l. 47

24 It little profits that an idle king,
By this still hearth, among these barren crags,
Match'd with an aged wife, I mete and dole
Unequal laws unto a savage race.
Ulysses [1842], l. 1

25   I will drink
Life to the lees.
Ibid. l. 6

1 Much have I seen and known; cities of men
  And manners, climates, councils, governments,
  Myself not least, but honor'd of them all;
  And drunk delight of battle with my peers,
  Far on the ringing plains of windy Troy.
  I am a part of all that I have met;
  Yet all experience is an arch wherethrough
  Gleams that untravel'd world.

  > *Ibid. l. 13*

2 How dull it is to pause, to make an end,
  To rust unburnished, not to shine in use,
  As though to breathe were life!

  > *Ibid. l. 22*

3 And this gray spirit yearning in desire
  To follow knowledge like a sinking star,
  Beyond the utmost bound of human thought.

  > *Ibid. l. 30*

4 This is my son, mine own Telemachus.

  > *Ibid. l. 33*

5 Death closes all: but something ere the end,
  Some work of noble note, may yet be done,
  Not unbecoming men that strove with gods.

  > *Ibid. l. 51*

6   The deep
  Moans round with many voices. Come, my
      friends,
  'Tis not too late to seek a newer world.
  Push off, and sitting well in order smite
  The sounding furrows, for my purpose holds
  To sail beyond the sunset, and the baths
  Of all the western stars, until I die.
  It may be that the gulfs will wash us down;
  It may be we shall touch the Happy Isles,
  And see the great Achilles, whom we knew.

  > *Ibid. l. 55*

7 To strive, to seek, to find, and not to yield.

  > *Ibid. l. 70*

8 Comrades, leave me here a little, while as yet 'tis
      early morn:
  Leave me here, and when you want me, sound
      upon the bugle horn.

  > *Locksley Hall [1842], l. 1*

9 In the spring a young man's fancy lightly turns to
      thoughts of love.

  > *Ibid. l. 20*

10 He will hold thee, when his passion shall have
      spent its novel force,
  Something better than his dog, a little dearer than
      his horse.

  > *Ibid. l. 49*

11 The many-winter'd crow that leads the clanging
      rookery home.

  > *Ibid. l. 68*

12 Such a one do I remember, whom to look at was
      to love.

  > *Ibid. l. 72*

13   This is the truth the poet sings,
  That a sorrow's crown of sorrow is remembering
      happier things.[1]

  > *Ibid. l. 75*

14 Like a dog, he hunts in dreams.

  > *Ibid. l. 79*

15 With a little hoard of maxims preaching down a
      daughter's heart.

  > *Ibid. l. 94*

16 But the jingling of the guinea helps the hurt that
      Honor feels.

  > *Ibid. l. 105*

17 For I dipp'd into the future, far as human eye
      could see,
  Saw the Vision of the world, and all the wonder
      that would be;
  Saw the heavens fill with commerce, argosies of
      magic sails,
  Pilots of the purple twilight, dropping down with
      costly bales;
  Heard the heavens fill with shouting, and there
      rain'd a ghastly dew
  From the nations' airy navies grappling in the
      central blue.

  > *Ibid. l. 119*

18 Till the war drum throbbed no longer and the
      battle flags were furled
  In the Parliament of man, the Federation of the
      world.

  > *Ibid. l. 127*

19 And the kindly earth shall slumber, lapp'd in
      universal law.

  > *Ibid. l. 130*

20 Yet I doubt not through the ages one increasing
      purpose runs,
  And the thoughts of men are widened with the
      process of the suns.

  > *Ibid. l. 137*

21 Knowledge comes, but wisdom lingers.

  > *Ibid. l. 141*

22 Woman is the lesser man, and all thy passions,
      match'd with mine,
  Are as moonlight unto sunlight, and as water unto
      wine.

  > *Ibid. l. 151*

23 I will take some savage woman, she shall rear my
      dusky race.

  > *Ibid. l. 168*

24 I the heir of all the ages, in the foremost files of
      time.

  > *Ibid. l. 178*

25 Let the great world spin forever down the ringing
      grooves of change.

  > *Ibid. l. 182*

[1]See Pindar, 64:4; Boethius, 115:10; Dante, 125:18; and
Chaucer, 128:19.

1 Better fifty years of Europe than a cycle of
Cathay.
Locksley Hall, l. 184

2 And o'er the hills and far away[1]
Beyond their utmost purple rim,
Beyond the night, across the day,
Through all the world she followed him.
The Day Dream [1842]. The Departure, st. 4

3 My strength is as the strength of ten,
Because my heart is pure.
Sir Galahad [1842], st. 1

4 Or that eternal lack of pence,
Which vexes public men.
*Will Waterproof's Lyrical Monologue [1842],
st. 6*

5 Cophetua sware a royal oath;
"This beggar maid shall be my queen!"[2]
The Beggar Maid [1842], st. 2

6 A little grain of conscience made him sour.
The Vision of Sin [1842], sec. 5

7 Break, break, break,
On thy cold gray stones, O Sea!
And I would that my tongue could utter
The thoughts that arise in me.

O, well for the fisherman's boy,
That he shouts with his sister at play!
O, well for the sailor lad,
That he sings in his boat on the bay!

And the stately ships go on
To their haven under the hill;
But O, for the touch of a vanish'd hand,
And the sound of a voice that is still!
Break, Break, Break [1842], st. 1–3

8 But the tender grace of a day that is dead
Will never come back to me.
Ibid. st. 4

9 And quoted odes, and jewels five-words-long
That on the stretched forefinger of all Time
Sparkle forever.
The Princess [1847], pt. II, l. 355

10 Sweet and low, sweet and low,
Wind of the western sea,
Low, low, breathe and blow,
Wind of the western sea!
Over the rolling waters go,
Come from the dying moon, and blow,
Blow him again to me;
While my little one, while my pretty one, sleeps.
Ibid. III [song, Sweet and Low, st. 1]

11 The splendor falls on castle walls
And snowy summits old in story:
The long light shakes across the lakes,
And the wild cataract leaps in glory.

Blow, bugle, blow, set the wild echoes flying,
Blow, bugle; answer, echoes, dying, dying, dying.
Ibid. IV [song, The Splendor Falls, st. 1]

12 The horns of Elfland faintly blowing.
Ibid. [st. 2]

13 Tears, idle tears, I know not what they mean,
Tears from the depth of some divine despair
Rise in the heart, and gather to the eyes,
In looking on the happy autumn fields,
And thinking of the days that are no more.
Ibid. [song, Tears, Idle Tears, st. 1]

14 Dear as remember'd kisses after death,
And sweet as those by hopeless fancy feign'd
On lips that are for others; deep as love,
Deep as first love, and wild with all regret;
O Death in Life, the days that are no more.
Ibid. [st. 4]

15 O Swallow, Swallow, flying, flying South,
Fly to her, and fall upon her gilded eaves,
And tell her, tell her, what I tell to thee.
Ibid. [song, O Swallow, st. 1]

16 Man is the hunter; woman is his game.
Ibid. V, l. 147

17 Man for the field and woman for the hearth:
Man for the sword and for the needle she:
Man with the head and woman with the heart:
Man to command and woman to obey;
All else confusion.
Ibid. l. 437

18 Home they brought her warrior dead.
She nor swoon'd nor utter'd cry:
All her maidens, watching, said,
"She must weep or she will die."
*Ibid. VI [song, Home They Brought Her
Warrior, st. 1]*

19 Ask me no more: thy fate and mine are seal'd:
I strove against the stream and all in vain:
Let the great river take me to the main:
No more, dear love, for at a touch I yield;
Ask me no more.
Ibid. VII [song, Ask Me No More, st. 3]

20 Now sleeps the crimson petal, now the white;
Nor waves the cypress in the palace walk;
Nor winks the gold fin in the porphyry font:
The firefly wakens: waken thou with me.
*Ibid. [song, Now Sleeps the Crimson Petal,
st. 1]*

21 Now lies the Earth all Danaë to the stars,
And all thy heart lies open unto me.
Ibid. [st. 3]

22 Sweet is every sound,
Sweeter thy voice, but every sound is sweet;
Myriads of rivulets hurrying through the lawn,
The moan of doves in immemorial elms,
And murmuring of innumerable bees.
Ibid. l. 203

[1]See Gay, 297:15, and Anonymous, 790:4.
[2]See Shakespeare, 174:25, and Anonymous, 776:13.

1 Some sense of duty, something of a faith,
Some reverence for the laws ourselves have made,
Some patient force to change them when we will,
Some civic manhood firm against the crowd.

Ibid. Conclusion, l. 54

2 Believing where we cannot prove.

In Memoriam[1] *[1850]. Prologue, st. 1*

3 Our little systems have their day.

Ibid. st. 5

4 Let knowledge grow from more to more,
But more of reverence in us dwell;
That mind and soul, according well,
May make one music as before.

Ibid. st. 7

5 I held it truth, with him who sings[2]
To one clear harp in divers tones,
That men may rise on stepping-stones
Of their dead selves to higher things.

Ibid. 1, st. 1

6 I sometimes hold it half a sin
To put in words the grief I feel;
For words, like Nature, half reveal
And half conceal the Soul within.

Ibid. 5, st. 1

7 But, for the unquiet heart and brain
A use in measured language lies;
The sad mechanic exercise,
Like dull narcotics numbing pain.

Ibid. st. 2

8 And from his ashes may be made
The violet of his native land.

Ibid. 18, st. 1

9 I do but sing because I must,
And pipe but as the linnets sing.[3]

Ibid. 21, st. 6

10 And Thought leap'd out to wed with Thought
Ere Thought could wed itself with Speech.

Ibid. 23, st. 4

11 'Tis better to have loved and lost
Than never to have loved at all.[4]

Ibid. 27, st. 4

12 How fares it with the happy dead?

Ibid. 44, st. 1

13 Be near me when my light is low.

Ibid. 50, st. 1

[1] In memory of Arthur Henry Hallam [1811–1833].
[2] Goethe.
[3] See Goethe, 349:6.
[4] Say what you will, 'tis better to be left than never to have been loved. — CONGREVE, *The Way of the World* [1700], *act II, sc. vi*

Better to love amiss than nothing to have loved. — CRABBE, *Tales* [1812], *XIV, The Struggles of Conscience*

'Tis better to have fought and lost / Than never to have fought at all. — CLOUGH, *Peschiera*

14 And Time, a maniac scattering dust,
And Life, a Fury slinging flame.

Ibid. st. 2

15 Do we indeed desire the dead
Should still be near us at our side?

Ibid. 51, st. 1

16 Hold thou the good; define it well;
For fear divine Philosophy
Should push beyond her mark, and be
Procuress to the Lords of Hell.

Ibid. 53, st. 4

17 Oh yet we trust that somehow good
Will be the final goal of ill.

Ibid. 54, st. 1

18 But what am I?
An infant crying in the night:
An infant crying for the light:
And with no language but a cry.

Ibid. st. 5

19 So careful of the type she seems,
So careless of the single life.

Ibid. 55, st. 2

20 The great world's altar-stairs,
That slope through darkness up to God.

Ibid. st. 4

21 Nature, red in tooth and claw.

Ibid. 56, st. 4

22 O Sorrow, wilt Thou live with me
No casual mistress, but a wife.

Ibid. 59, st. 1

23 So many worlds, so much to do,
So little done, such things to be.

Ibid. 73, st. 1

24 God's finger touch'd him, and he slept.

Ibid. 85, st. 5

25 Fresh from brawling courts
And dusty purlieus of the law.

Ibid. 89, st. 3

26 There lives more faith in honest doubt,
Believe me, than in half the creeds.

Ibid. 96, st. 3

27 He seems so near, and yet so far.

Ibid. 97, st. 6

28 Ring out, wild bells, to the wild sky!

Ibid. 106, st. 1

29 Ring out the old, ring in the new,
Ring, happy bells, across the snow:
The year is going, let him go;
Ring out the false, ring in the true.

Ibid. st. 2

30 Ring out old shapes of foul disease,
Ring out the narrowing lust of gold;
Ring out the thousand wars of old,
Ring in the thousand years of peace.

Ibid. st. 7

1 Love is and was my lord and king.
> *In Memoriam, 126, st. 1*

2   Wearing all that weight
Of learning lightly like a flower.
> *Ibid. Epilogue, st. 10*

3 One God, one law, one element,
And one far-off divine event,
To which the whole creation moves.
> *Ibid. st. 36*

4 He clasps the crag with crooked hands;
Close to the sun in lonely lands,
Ring'd with the azure world he stands.

The wrinkled sea beneath him crawls;
He watches from his mountain walls,
And like a thunderbolt he falls.
> *The Eagle [1851]*

5 Bury the Great Duke
With an empire's lamentation.
> *Ode on the Death of the Duke of Wellington*
> *[1852], st. 1*

6 The last great Englishman is low.
> *Ibid. st. 3*

7 O iron nerve to true occasion true,
O fall'n at length, that tower of strength
Which stood four-square to all the winds that
    blew.
> *Ibid. st. 4*

8 Speak no more of his renown.
Lay your earthly fancies down,
And in the vast cathedral leave him.
God accept him, Christ receive him.
> *Ibid. st. 9*

9 Half a league, half a league,
Half a league onward,
All in the valley of death
Rode the six hundred.
> *The Charge of the Light Brigade [1854],*[1] *st. 1*

10 "Forward, the Light Brigade!"
Was there a man dismay'd?
> *Ibid. st. 2*

11 Someone had blundered.
> *Ibid.*

12 Theirs not to make reply,
Theirs not to reason why,
Theirs but to do and die.
> *Ibid.*

13 Cannon to right of them,
Cannon to left of them,
Cannon in front of them
Volley'd and thunder'd.
> *Ibid. st. 3*

14 Into the jaws of death,
Into the mouth of hell
Rode the six hundred.
> *Ibid.*

15 I come from haunts of coot and hern,
I make a sudden sally
And sparkle out among the fern,
To bicker down a valley.
> *The Brook [1855], song, st. 1*

16 For men may come and men may go,
But I go on forever.
> *Ibid. st. 6*

17 Faultily faultless, icily regular, splendidly null,
Dead perfection, no more.
> *Maud [1855], pt. I, sec. ii*

18 And ah for a man to arise in me,
That the man I am may cease to be!
> *Ibid. st. 6*

19 Gorgonized me from head to foot,
With a stony British stare.
> *Ibid. xiii, st. 2*

20 Come into the garden, Maud,
For the black bat, night, has flown,
Come into the garden, Maud,
I am here at the gate alone.
> *Ibid. xxii, st. 1*

21 For a breeze of morning moves,
And the planet of Love is on high,
Beginning to faint in the light that she loves
On a bed of daffodil sky.
> *Ibid. st. 2*

22 All night have the roses heard
The flute, violin, bassoon;
All night has the casement jessamine stirr'd
To the dancers dancing in tune;
Till a silence fell with the waking bird,
And a hush with the setting moon.
> *Ibid. st. 3*

23 There has fallen a splendid tear
From the passion-flower at the gate.
> *Ibid. st. 10*

24 She is coming, my own, my sweet;
Were it ever so airy a tread,
My heart would hear her and beat,
Were it earth in an earthy bed;
My dust would hear her and beat,
Had I lain for a century dead;
Would start and tremble under her feet,
And blossom in purple and red.
> *Ibid. st. 11*

25 Ah Christ, that it were possible
For one short hour to see
The souls we loved, that they might tell us
What and where they be.
> *Ibid. II, iv, st. 3*

[1]See Bosquet, 460:19.

1 The woods decay, the woods decay and fall,
The vapors weep their burthen to the ground,
Man comes and tills the field and lies beneath,
And after many a summer dies the swan.
Tithonus [1860], l. 1

2 Here at the quiet limit of the world.
Ibid. l. 7

3 Wearing the white flower of a blameless life,
Before a thousand peering littlenesses,
In that fierce light which beats upon a throne,[1]
And blackens every blot.
Idylls of the King [1859–1885], dedication, l. 24

4 Man's word is God in man.
Ibid. The Coming of Arthur, l. 132

5 Large, divine, and comfortable words.[2]
Ibid. l. 267

6 Clothed in white samite, mystic, wonderful.
Ibid. l. 284

7 Live pure, speak true, right wrong, follow the
King—
Else, wherefore born?
Ibid. Gareth and Lynette, l. 117

8 Our hoard is little, but our hearts are great.
Ibid. The Marriage of Geraint, l. 352

9 For man is man and master of his fate.[3]
Ibid. l. 355

10 It is the little rift within the lute,
That by and by will make the music mute,
And ever widening slowly silence all.
Ibid. Merlin and Vivien, l. 388

11 Blind and naked Ignorance
Delivers brawling judgments, unashamed,
On all things all day long.
Ibid. l. 662

12 Elaine the fair, Elaine the lovable,
Elaine, the lily maid of Astolat.
Ibid. Lancelot and Elaine, l. 1

13 But, friend, to me
He is all fault who hath no fault at all.
For who loves me must have a touch of earth.
Ibid. l. 131

14 In me there dwells
No greatness, save it be some far-off touch
Of greatness to know well I am not great.
Ibid. l. 447

15 The shackles of an old love straitened him,
His honor rooted in dishonor stood,
And faith unfaithful kept him falsely true.
Ibid. l. 870

16 He makes no friend who never made a foe.
Ibid. l. 1082

17 The greater man the greater courtesy.
Ibid. The Last Tournament, l. 628

18 The vow that binds too strictly snaps itself.
Ibid. l. 652

19 For manners are not idle, but the fruit
Of loyal nature and of noble mind.
Ibid. Guinevere, l. 333

20 No more subtle master under Heaven
Than is the maiden passion for a maid,
Not only to keep down the base in man,
But teach high thought, and amiable words
And courtliness, and the desire of fame,
And love of truth, and all that makes a man.
Ibid. l. 475

21 The days will grow to weeks, the weeks to
months,
The months will add themselves and make the
years,
The years will roll into the centuries,
And mine will ever be a name of scorn.
Ibid. l. 619

22 I found Him in the shining of the stars,
I mark'd Him in the flowering of His fields,
But in His ways with men I find Him not.
Ibid. The Passing of Arthur, l. 9

23 For why is all around us here
As if some lesser god had made the world,
But had not force to shape it as he would?
Ibid. l. 13

24 So all day long the noise of battle roll'd
Among the mountains by the winter sea.
Ibid. l. 170

25 Authority forgets a dying king.
Ibid. l. 289

26 And slowly answer'd Arthur from the barge:
The old order changeth, yielding place to new;
And God fulfills himself in many ways,
Lest one good custom should corrupt the world.
Ibid. l. 407

27 More things are wrought by prayer
Than this world dreams of. Wherefore, let thy
voice
Rise like a fountain for me night and day.
Ibid. l. 415

28 From the great deep to the great deep he goes.
Ibid. l. 445

29 Cast all your cares on God; that anchor holds.
Enoch Arden [1864], l. 222

30 Insipid as the queen upon a card.
Aylmer's Field [1864], l. 28

31 The worst is yet to come.
Sea Dreams [1864], l. 301

[1]See Montaigne, 146:21, and Shakespeare, 198:22.
[2]Hear what comfortable words our Saviour Christ saith unto all who truly turn to him.—*Book of Common Prayer, Holy Communion*
[3]See Sallust, 91:28 and 92:1; Francis Bacon, 160:4; Shakespeare, 187:22; Henley, 557:10; and Nehru, 677:7.

1   He said likewise
That a lie which is half a truth is ever the blackest
of lies,
That a lie which is all a lie may be met and
fought with outright,
But a lie which is part a truth is a harder matter
to fight.

The Grandmother [1864], st. 8

2 Doẓn't thou 'ear my 'erse's legs, as they canters
awaäy?
Proputty, proputty, proputty—that's what I 'ears
'em saäy.

Northern Farmer: New Style [1869], st. 1

3 Doänt thou marry for munny, but goä wheer
munny is!

Ibid. st. 5

4 Speak to Him thou for He hears, and Spirit with
Spirit can meet—
Closer is He than breathing, and nearer than
hands and feet.

The Higher Pantheism [1869], st. 6

5 Flower in the crannied wall,
I pluck you out of the crannies,
I hold you here, root and all, in my hand,
Little flower—but *if* I could understand
What you are, root and all, and all in all,
I should know what God and man is.

Flower in the Crannied Wall [1869]

6 At Flores in the Azores Sir Richard Grenville lay,
And a pinnace, like a flutter'd bird, came flying
from far away;
"Spanish ships of war at sea! we have sighted
fifty-three!"

The Revenge [1878], st. 1

7 All the charm of all the Muses often flowering in
a lonely word.

To Virgil [1882], st. 3

8 Cleave ever to the sunnier side of doubt.

The Ancient Sage [1885], l. 68

9 That man's the best Cosmopolite
Who loves his native country best.

Hands All Round [1885], l. 3

10 I am Merlin
Who follow the Gleam.

Merlin and the Gleam [1889], st. 1

11 Sunset and evening star,
And one clear call for me!
And may there be no moaning of the bar,
When I put out to sea,

But such a tide as moving seems asleep,
Too full for sound and foam,
When that which drew from out the boundless
deep
Turns again home.

Crossing the Bar [1889], st. 1, 2

12 Twilight and evening bell,
And after that the dark.

Ibid. st. 3

13 I hope to see my Pilot face to face
When I have crossed the bar.

Ibid. st. 4

Robert Charles Winthrop
1809–1894

14   Our Country—whether bounded by the St.
John's and the Sabine, or however otherwise
bounded[1] or described, and be the measurements
more or less—still our Country, to be cherished in all
our hearts, to be defended by all our hands.

Toast at Faneuil Hall [Fourth of July, 1845]

15   A star for every State, and a State for every star.

Address on Boston Common [1862]

Henry Alford
1810–1871

16 Come, ye thankful people, come,
Raise the song of harvest-home;
All is safely gathered in,
Ere the winter storms begin.

Come, Ye Thankful People, Come [1844]

17 Ten thousand times ten thousand
In sparkling raiment bright,
The armies of the ransomed saints
Throng up the steeps of light:
'Tis finished! all is finished,
Their fight with death and sin:
Fling open wide the golden gates,
And let the victors in.

Hymn [1867], st. 1

Phineas Taylor Barnum
1810–1891

18   There's a sucker born every minute.

Attributed

Pierre Jean François Joseph Bosquet
1810–1861

19   It is magnificent, but it is not war.[2]

*On the charge of the Light Brigade at Balaklava
[October 25, 1854]*

---

[1]The United States—bounded on the north by the Aurora
Borealis, on the south by the precession of the equinoxes, on
the east by the primeval chaos, and on the west by the Day of
Judgment.—JOHN FISKE [1842–1901], *Bounding the United
States*

[2]C'est magnifique, mais ce n'est pas la guerre.
See Tennyson, 458:9.

Sir Francis Hastings Doyle
1810–1888

1 Last night, among his fellow roughs,
He jested, quaffed, and swore;
A drunken private of the Buffs,
Who never looked before.
Today, beneath the foeman's frown,
He stands in Elgin's place,
Ambassador from Britain's crown,
And type of all her race.
The Private of the Buffs, st. 1

Margaret Fuller
1810–1850

2   I myself am more divine than any I see.
Letter to Emerson [March 1, 1838]

3   It does not follow because many books are written by persons born in America that there exists an American literature. Books which imitate or represent the thoughts and life of Europe do not constitute an American literature. Before such can exist, an original idea must animate this nation and fresh currents of life must call into life fresh thoughts along its shores.
Papers on Literature and Art [1846]

4   I now know all the people worth knowing in America, and I find no intellect comparable to my own.
Memoirs of Margaret Fuller Ossoli [1852], vol. I, pt. 4

5   For precocity some great price is always demanded sooner or later in life.
Diary. From THOMAS WENTWORTH HIGGINSON, Life of Margaret Fuller Ossoli [1884], ch. 18

6   Genius will live and thrive without training, but it does not the less reward the watering pot and pruning knife.   *Ibid.*

7   I accept the universe.[1]   *Attributed*

Elizabeth Cleghorn Gaskell
1810–1865

8   A man is *so* in the way in the house.
Cranford [1851–1853], ch. 1

9   A little credulity helps one on through life very smoothly.   *Ibid. ch. 11*

10   I'll not listen to reason. . . . Reason always means what someone else has got to say.
Ibid. ch. 14

[1]By God! she'd better.—*Carlyle's reported comment*

James Sloan Gibbons
1810–1892

11 We are coming, Father Abraham, three hundred thousand more.
Three Hundred Thousand More [1862],[2] st. 1

William Miller
1810–1872

12 Wee Willie Winkie rins through the town,
Upstairs and downstairs, in his nichtgown,
Tirlin' at the window, cryin' at the lock,
"Are the weans in their bed? for it's now ten o'clock."
Willie Winkie

Alfred de Musset
1810–1857

13 I have come too late into a world too old.[3]
Rolla [1833]

14   Do Not Trifle with Love.[4]
Title of a comedy [1834]

15 The most despairing songs are the loveliest of all,
I know immortal ones composed only of tears.
Poésies Nouvelles. La Nuit de Mai [1835]

16   How glorious it is, but how painful it is also, to be exceptional in this world!
La Merle Blanc [1842]

Theodore Parker
1810–1860

17   Truth never yet fell dead in the streets; it has such affinity with the soul of man, the seed however broadcast will catch somewhere and produce its hundredfold.
A Discourse of Matters Pertaining to Religion [1842]

18   A democracy—that is a government of all the people, by all the people, for all the people;[5] of course, a government of the principles of eternal justice, the unchanging law of God; for shortness' sake I will call it the idea of Freedom.
The American Idea [May 29, 1850][6]

[2]Song to help raise volunteers for the Union Army.
[3]Je suis venu trop tard dans un monde trop vieux.
[4]On Ne Badine Pas avec l'Amour.
[5]Parker used the same phrase in a speech delivered in Boston [May 31, 1854] and in a sermon in the Music Hall, Boston [July 4, 1858]. William H. Herndon visited Boston and on his return to Springfield, Illinois, took with him some of Parker's sermons and addresses. In his *Abraham Lincoln, vol. II, p. 65*, Herndon says that Lincoln marked with pencil the portion of the Music Hall address, "Democracy is direct self-government, over all the people, by all the people, for all the people."
[6]Speech at the New England Anti-Slavery Convention, Boston.

Robert Schumann
1810–1856

1   Hats off, gentlemen—a genius!
      On first hearing Frédéric Chopin's music [1831]

Edmund Hamilton Sears
1810–1876

2 It came upon the midnight clear,
  That glorious song of old,
  From angels bending near the earth
  To touch their harps of gold:
  "Peace on the earth, good will to men
  From heav'n's all-gracious King."
  The world in solemn stillness lay
  To hear the angels sing.
      The Angel's Song [1850], st. 1

Martin Farquhar Tupper
1810–1889

3 Error is a hardy plant: it flourisheth in every soil.
  Proverbial Philosophy [1838–1842]. Of Truth in Things False

4 Well-timed silence hath more eloquence than
  speech.
      Ibid. Of Discretion

5 A good book is the best of friends, the same
  today and forever.
      Ibid. Of Reading

6 Nature's own Nobleman, friendly and frank,
  Is a man with his heart in his hand!
      Nature's Nobleman [1844], st. 1

John Bright
1811–1889

7   Force is not a remedy.
      Speech at Birmingham [November 16, 1880]

8   My opinion is that the Northern States will man-
     age somehow to muddle through.
      *Said during the American Civil War. From
      JUSTIN MCCARTHY, Reminiscences [1899]*

9   He [Benjamin Disraeli] is a self-made man and
     worships his creator.   *Attributed*

Fanny Fern
[Sara Payson Willis Parton]
1811–1872

10   The way to a man's heart is through his stomach.
      Fern Leaves [1853]

Théophile Gautier
1811–1872

11 Everything passes—Robust art
   Alone is eternal.
   The bust
   Survives the city.[1]
      L'Art [1832]

Horace Greeley
1811–1872

12   The best business you can go into you will find on
      your father's farm or in his workshop. If you have
      no family or friends to aid you, and no prospect
      opened to you there, turn your face to the great
      West,[2] and there build up a home and fortune.
      *From JAMES PARTON, Life of Horace Greeley
      [1855]. To Aspiring Young Men*

13   The illusion that times that were are better than
      those that are, has probably pervaded all ages.
      The American Conflict [1864–1866]

14   I never said all Democrats were saloon keepers.
      What I said was that all saloon keepers were Demo-
      crats.   *Attributed*

Wendell Phillips
1811–1884

15   Revolutions are not made; they come. A revolu-
      tion is as natural a growth as an oak. It comes out
      of the past. Its foundations are laid far back.
      Speech [January 8, 1852]

16   The best use of laws is to teach men to trample
      bad laws under their feet.
      Speech [April 12, 1852]

17   One on God's side is a majority.[3]
      Speech [November 1, 1859]

18   Every man meets his Waterloo at last.   *Ibid.*

19   Whether in chains or in laurels, Liberty knows
      nothing but victories.   *Ibid.*

20   Truth is one forever absolute, but opinion is truth
      filtered through the moods, the blood, the disposi-
      tion of the spectator.   *Idols [October 4, 1859]*

21   Revolutions never go backward.[4]
      Speech [February 17, 1861]

---

[1]Tout passe—L'art robuste / Seul a l'éternité; / Le buste / Survit à la cité.
[2]See Soule, 475:4.
[3]See John Knox, 143:15.
[4]I know, and all the world knows, that revolutions never go backward.—WILLIAM HENRY SEWARD [1801–1872], *Speech at Rochester, New York, on the Irrepressible Conflict* [October 1858]

Harriet Beecher Stowe
1811–1896

1 Eliza made her desperate retreat across the river just in the dusk of twilight. The gray mist of evening, rising slowly from the river, enveloped her as she disappeared up the bank, and the swollen current and floundering masses of ice presented a hopeless barrier between her and her pursuer.
Uncle Tom's Cabin [1852], ch. 8

2 I [Topsy] 'spect I growed. Don't think nobody never made me.   *Ibid. 20*

3 My soul an't yours, Mas'r! You haven't bought it,—ye can't buy it! It's been bought and paid for, by one that is able to keep it.   *Ibid. 33*

Charles Sumner
1811–1874

4 Where Slavery is, there Liberty cannot be; and where Liberty is, there Slavery cannot be.
Slavery and the Rebellion; speech at Cooper Institute [November 5, 1864]

5 There is the National flag. He must be cold, indeed, who can look upon its folds rippling in the breeze without pride of country. If in a foreign land, the flag is companionship, and country itself, with all its endearments.
Are We a Nation? [November 19, 1867]

William Makepeace Thackeray
1811–1863

6 This I set down as a positive truth. A woman with fair opportunities, and without a positive hump, may marry whom she likes.[1]
Vanity Fair [1847–1848], vol. I, ch. 4

7 Them's my sentiments.   *Ibid. 21*

8 Everybody in Vanity Fair must have remarked how well those live who are comfortably and thoroughly in debt; how they deny themselves nothing; how jolly and easy they are in their minds.
Ibid. 22

9 How to Live Well on Nothing a Year.
Ibid. 36 (title)

10 I think I could be a good woman if I had five thousand a year.   *Ibid. II, 1*

11 Ah! *Vanitas vanitatum!* Which of us is happy in this world? Which of us has his desire? or, having it,

[1]I should like to see any kind of a man, distinguishable from a gorilla, that some good and even pretty woman could not shape a husband out of.—OLIVER WENDELL HOLMES, *The Professor at the Breakfast-Table* [1860]
The whole world is strewn with snares, traps, gins and pitfalls for the capture of men by women.—SHAW, *Man and Superman* [1903], *Epistle Dedicatory*

is satisfied?—Come, children, let us shut up the box and the puppets, for our play is played out.
Ibid. 27

12 He who meanly admires mean things is a Snob.
The Book of Snobs [1848], ch. 2

13 Rake's Progress.[2]
Pendennis [1848–1850], ch. 19 (title)

14 Yes, I am a fatal man, Madame Fribsbi. To inspire hopeless passion is my destiny.   *Ibid. 23*

15 Remember, it's as easy to marry a rich woman as a poor woman.   *Ibid. 28*

16 Of the Corporation of the Goosequill—of the Press . . . of the fourth estate.[3] . . . There she is —the great engine—she never sleeps. She has her ambassadors in every quarter of the world—her couriers upon every road. Her officers march along with armies, and her envoys walk into statesmen's cabinets. They are ubiquitous.   *Ibid. 30*

17 'Tis not the dying for a faith that's so hard, Master Harry—every man of every nation has done that —'tis the living up to it that's difficult.
Henry Esmond [1852], bk. I, ch. 6

18 'Tis strange what a man may do, and a woman yet think him an angel.   *Ibid. 7*

19 The wicked are wicked, no doubt, and they go astray and they fall, and they come by their deserts; but who can tell the mischief which the very virtuous do?   *The Newcomes [1853–1855], ch. 20*

20 This Bouillabaisse a noble dish is—
A sort of soup, or broth, or brew.
Ballads [1855]. The Ballad of Bouillabaisse, st. 2

21 Charlotte, having seen his body
Borne before her on a shutter,
Like a well-conducted person,
Went on cutting bread and butter.
Ibid. Sorrows of Werther[4]

22 A pedigree reaching as far back as the Deluge.
The Rose and the Ring [1855], ch. 2

23 The book of female logic is blotted all over with tears, and Justice in their courts is forever in a passion.   *The Virginians [1857–1859], ch. 4*

24 Women like not only to conquer, but to be conquered.   *Ibid.*

25 Next to the very young, I suppose the very old are the most selfish.   *Ibid. 61*

26 To endure is greater than to dare; to tire out hostile fortune; to be daunted by no difficulty; to keep heart when all have lost it; to go through in-

[2]The Rake's Progress.—WILLIAM HOGARTH [1697–1764], *title of series of paintings and engravings* [1735]
[3]See Hazlitt, 390:6; Carlyle, 411:18; and Macaulay, 424:17.
[4]See Goethe, 349:3.

trigue spotless; to forgo even ambition when the end is gained—who can say this is not greatness?

Ibid. 92

1   Bravery never goes out of fashion.

The Four Georges [1860]. George II

2   It is to the middle class we must look for the safety of England.

Ibid. George III

3   George, be a King!

Ibid. Princess Augusta to her son George III

Robert Browning
1812–1889

4 The year's at the spring
And day's at the morn;
Morning's at seven;
The hillside's dew-pearled;
The lark's on the wing;
The snail's on the thorn:
God's in his heaven—
All's right with the world.

Pippa Passes [1841], pt. I

5 Speak to me—not of me!

Ibid.

6 Some unsuspected isle in far-off seas.

Ibid. II

7 In the morning of the world,
When earth was nigher heaven than now.

Ibid. III

8 All service ranks the same with God:
With God, whose puppets, best and worst,
Are we; there is no last nor first.

Ibid. IV

9 You know, we French stormed Ratisbon.

Incident of the French Camp [1842], st. 1

10 "You're wounded!" "Nay," the soldier's pride
Touched to the quick, he said:
"I'm killed, Sire!" And his chief beside,
Smiling the boy fell dead.

Ibid. st. 5

11 That's my last Duchess painted on the wall,
Looking as if she were alive.

My Last Duchess [1842], l. 1

12   She had
A heart—how shall I say?—too soon made glad.

Ibid. l. 21

13   I gave commands;
Then all smiles stopped together.

Ibid. l. 45

14 Marching along, fifty-score strong,
Great-hearted gentlemen, singing this song.

Cavalier Tunes [1842]. Marching Along, st. 1

15 Boot, saddle, to horse, and away!

Ibid. Boot and Saddle, refrain

16   Just my vengeance complete,
The man sprang to his feet,
Stood erect, caught at God's skirts, and prayed!
—So, *I* was afraid!

Instans Tyrannus [1845], st. 7

17 Hamelin Town's in Brunswick,
By famous Hanover city.

The Pied Piper of Hamelin [1845], st. 1

18 Rats!
They fought the dogs and killed the cats,
And bit the babies in the cradles,
And ate the cheeses out of the vats,
And licked the soup from the cooks' own ladles.

Ibid. st. 2

19 And out of the houses the rats came tumbling.
Great rats, small rats, lean rats, brawny rats,
Brown rats, black rats, gray rats, tawny rats,
Grave old plodders, gay young friskers,
Fathers, mothers, uncles, cousins,
Cocking tails and pricking whiskers,
Families by tens and dozens,
Brothers, sisters, husbands, wives—
Followed the Piper for their lives.

Ibid. st. 7

20 When the liquor's out, why clink the cannikin?

The Flight of the Duchess [1845], st. 16

21 It's a long lane that knows no turnings.

Ibid. st. 17

22 Just for a handful of silver he left us,
Just for a riband to stick in his coat.

The Lost Leader [1] [1845], st. 1

23 We that had loved him so, followed him, honored him,
Lived in his mild and magnificent eye,
Learned his great language, caught his clear accents,
Made him our pattern to live and to die!

Ibid.

24 Shakespeare was of us, Milton was for us,
Burns, Shelley, were with us—they watch from their graves!

Ibid.

25 One more devils'-triumph and sorrow for angels,
One more wrong to man, one more insult to God!

Ibid. st. 2

26   Let him never come back to us!
There would be doubt, hesitation and pain,
Forced praise on our part—the glimmer of twilight,
Never glad confident morning again!

Ibid.

27 It was roses, roses all the way.

The Patriot [1845], st. 1

---

[1]Often assumed to refer to Wordsworth.

1 I sprang to the stirrup, and Joris, and he;
  I galloped, Dirck galloped, we galloped all three.
  > *How They Brought the Good News from Ghent
  > to Aix [1845], st. 1*

2 Round the cape of a sudden came the sea,
  And the sun looked over the mountain's rim:
  And straight was a path of gold for him,
  And the need of a world of men for me.
  > *Parting at Morning [1845]*

3 Oh, to be in England now that April's there,
  And whoever wakes in England sees, some
      morning, unaware,
  That the lowest boughs and the brushwood sheaf
  Round the elm tree bole are in tiny leaf,
  While the chaffinch sings on the orchard bough
  In England—now!
  > *Home Thoughts, from Abroad [1845], l. 1*

4 That's the wise thrush; he sings each song twice
      over,
  Lest you should think he never could recapture
  The first fine careless rapture!
  > *Ibid. l. 14*

5 Nobly, nobly Cape Saint Vincent to the northwest
      died away;
  Sunset ran, one glorious blood-red, reeking into
      Cadiz Bay.
  > *Home Thoughts, from the Sea [1845], l. 1*

6 The Savior at his sermon on the mount,
  Saint Praxed in a glory, and one Pan
  Ready to twitch the Nymph's last garment off.
  > *The Bishop Orders His Tomb at Saint Praxed's
  > Church [1845], l. 59*

7 And then how I shall lie through centuries,
  And hear the blessed mutter of the mass,
  And see God made and eaten all day long,
  And feel the steady candle flame, and taste
  Good strong thick stupefying incense smoke!
  > *Ibid. l. 80*

8 Let's contend no more, Love,
  Strive nor weep:
  All be as before, Love,
  —Only sleep!
  > *A Woman's Last Word [1855], st. 1*

9 Where the quiet-colored end of evening smiles.
  > *Love Among the Ruins [1855], st. 1*

10 Oh heart! oh blood that freezes, blood that burns!
      Earth's returns
  For whole centuries of folly, noise and sin!
      Shut them in,
  With their triumphs and their glories and the rest!
      Love is best!
  > *Ibid. st. 7*

11 Your ghost will walk, you lover of trees,
      (If our loves remain)
  In an English lane.
  > *De Gustibus [1855], st. 1*

12 Open my heart, and you will see
  Graved inside of it, "Italy."[1]
  > *Ibid. st. 2*

13   Only I discern
  Infinite passion, and the pain
  Of finite hearts that yearn.
  > *Two in the Campagna [1855], st. 12*

14 Escape me?
  Never—
  Beloved!
  While I am I, and you are you.
  > *Life in a Love [1855]*

15 To dry one's eyes and laugh at a fall,
  And baffled, get up and begin again.
  > *Ibid.*

16 Ah, did you once see Shelley plain,
  And did he stop and speak to you,
  And did you speak to him again?
  How strange it seems, and new![2]
  > *Memorabilia [1855], st. 1*

17 What's become of Waring
  Since he gave us all the slip?
  > *Waring [1855], pt. I, st. 1*

18 In Vishnu-land what Avatar?
  > *Ibid. st. 6*

19 Who knows but the world may end tonight?
  > *The Last Ride Together [1855], st. 2*

20 Sing, riding's a joy! For me I ride.
  > *Ibid. st. 7*

21 The instant made eternity—
  And heaven just prove that I and she
  Ride, ride together, forever ride?
  > *Ibid. st. 10*

22 He said, "What's time? Leave Now for dogs and
      apes!
  Man has Forever."
  > *A Grammarian's Funeral [1855], l. 81*

23 He ventured neck or nothing—heaven's success
  Found, or earth's failure.
  > *Ibid. l. 109*

24 That low man seeks a little thing to do,
  Sees it and does it;
  This high man, with a great thing to pursue,
  Dies ere he knows it.
  That low man goes on adding one to one,
  His hundred's soon hit;
  This high man, aiming at a million,
  Misses an unit.
  That, has the world here—should he need the
      next,
  Let the world mind him!

[1]See Mary Tudor, 143:16.
[2]And did you once find Browning plain? / And did he really
seem quite clear? / And did you read the book again? / How
strange it seems, and queer.—Charles William Stubbs
[1845–1912], *Parody*

This, throws himself on God, and unperplexed
Seeking shall find Him.
A Grammarian's Funeral. l. 113

1 A common grayness silvers everything.
Andrea del Sarto [1855], l. 35

2　　　Days decrease,
And autumn grows, autumn in everything.
Ibid. l. 44

3 So free we seem, so fettered fast we are.
Ibid. l. 51

4 Less is more.[1]
Ibid. l. 78

5 Ah, but a man's reach should exceed his grasp,
Or what's a heaven for?
Ibid. l. 97

6 I am grown peaceful as old age tonight.
Ibid. l. 244

7　　　Truth that peeps
Over the glasses' edge when dinner's done.
Bishop Blougram's Apology [1855], l. 17

8 The common problem, yours, mine, everyone's,
Is—not to fancy what were fair in life
Provided it could be—but, finding first
What may be, then find how to make it fair
Up to our means.
Ibid. l. 87

9 Just when we are safest, there's a sunset touch,
A fancy from a flower bell, someone's death,
A chorus ending from Euripides.
Ibid. l. 183

10 Our interest's on the dangerous edge of things.
The honest thief, the tender murderer,
The superstitious atheist, demirep
That loves and saves her soul in new French
books.
Ibid. l. 396

11　　　You call for faith:
I show you doubt, to prove that faith exists.
The more of doubt, the stronger faith, I say,
If faith o'ercomes doubt.
Ibid. l. 601

12 No, when the fight begins within himself,
A man's worth something.
Ibid. l. 693

13 While you sat and played toccatas, stately at the
clavichord.
A Toccata of Galuppi's [1855], st. 6

14 What of soul was left, I wonder, when the kissing
had to stop?
Ibid. st. 14

---

[1] A popular aphorism with the architect Ludwig Mies van der
Rohe.
　　Not so honest would be more honest.—G. E. Lessing,
Emilia Galotti [1772], *act I, sc. iv*
　　See Hesiod, 54:21.

15 Dear dead women, with such hair, too—what's
become of all the gold
Used to hang and brush their bosoms? I feel chilly
and grown old.
Ibid. st. 15

16 Stake your counter as boldly every whit,
Venture as warily, use the same skill,
Do your best, whether winning or losing it,
If you choose to play!
The Statue and the Bust [1855], l. 238

17 How good is man's life, the mere living! how fit
to employ
All the heart and the soul and the senses forever
in joy!
Saul [1855], st. 9

18 Death was past, life not come: so he waited.
Ibid. st. 10

19　　　God is seen God
In the star, in the stone, in the flesh, in the soul
and the clod.
Ibid. st. 17

20 Do I find love so full in my nature, God's ultimate
gift,
That I doubt his own love can compete with it?
Here, the parts shift?
Ibid.

21 'Tis not what man does which exalts him, but
what man would do!
Ibid. st. 18

22 Thou shalt love and be loved by, forever: a Hand
like this hand
Shall throw open the gates of new life to thee! See
the Christ stand!
Ibid.

23 Why stay we on the earth except to grow?
Cleon [1855], l. 114

24　　　We're made so that we love
First when we see them painted, things we have
passed
Perhaps a hundred times nor cared to see;
And so they are better, painted—better to us,
Which is the same thing. Art was given for that.
Fra Lippo Lippi [1855], l. 300

25 Rafael made a century of sonnets.
One Word More [1855], 2

26 Does he paint? he fain would write a poem—
Does he write? he fain would paint a picture.
Ibid. 8

27 Where my heart lies, let my brain lie also.
Ibid. 14

28 Oh, their Rafael of the dear Madonnas,
Oh, their Dante of the dread Inferno,
Wrote one song—and in my brain I sing it,
Drew one angel—borne, see, on my bosom!
Ibid. 19

1 That out of three sounds he frame, not a fourth
    sound, but a star.
Abt Vogler [1864], st. 7

2 On the earth the broken arcs; in the heaven, a
    perfect round.
Ibid. st. 9

3 The high that proved too high, the heroic for
    earth too hard,
    The passion that left the ground to lose itself in
    the sky,
    Are music sent up to God by the lover and the
    bard.
Ibid. st. 10

4 Each sufferer says his say, his scheme of the weal
    and woe.
Ibid. st. 11

5 The C Major of this life.
Ibid. st. 12

6 Grow old along with me!
    The best is yet to be,
    The last of life, for which the first was made.
    Our times are in his hand.
Rabbi Ben Ezra [1864], st. 1

7 Irks care the crop-full bird? Frets doubt the
    maw-crammed beast?
Ibid. st. 4

8 Then welcome each rebuff
    That turns earth's smoothness rough,
    Each sting that bids nor sit nor stand, but go!
    Be our joys three parts pain!
    Strive, and hold cheap the strain;
    Learn, nor account the pang; dare, never grudge
    the throe!
Ibid. st. 6

9 What I aspired to be,
    And was not, comforts me.
Ibid. st. 7

10 Therefore I summon age
    To grant youth's heritage.
Ibid. st. 13

11 Look not thou down but up!
Ibid. st. 30

12 Such ever was love's way: to rise, it stoops.
A Death in the Desert [1864], l. 134

13 To test man, the proofs shift.
Ibid. l. 295

14 Progress, man's distinctive mark alone,
    Not God's, and not the beasts': God is, they are;
    Man partly is, and wholly hopes to be.
Ibid. l. 586

15 Setebos, Setebos, and Setebos!
    'Thinketh, He dwelleth i' the cold o' the moon.
Caliban upon Setebos [1864], l. 24

16 The best way to escape His ire
    Is, not to seem too happy.
Ibid. l. 256

17 How sad and bad and mad it was—
    But then, how it was sweet!
Confessions [1864], st. 9

18 Fear death?—to feel the fog in my throat,
    The mist in my face.
Prospice [1864], l. 1

19 No! let me taste the whole of it, fare like my
    peers,
    The heroes of old,
    Bear the brunt, in a minute pay glad life's arrears
    Of pain, darkness, and cold.
Ibid. l. 17

20 Hold me but safe again within the bond
    Of one immortal look.
Eurydice to Orpheus [1864], l. 5

21 This could but have happened once—
    And we missed it, lost it forever.
Youth and Art [1864], st. 17

22 We find great things are made of little things,
    And little things go lessening till at last
    Comes God behind them.
Mr. Sludge, "The Medium" [1864], l. 1112

23 'Tis because stiffish cock-tail, taken in time,
    Is better for a bruise than arnica.
Ibid. l. 1478

24 O Lyric Love, half angel and half bird,
    And all a wonder and a wild desire.
The Ring and the Book [1868–1869], bk. I,
l. 1391

25 That's all we may expect of man, this side
    The grave: his good is—knowing he is bad.
Ibid. VI, Giuseppe Caponsacchi, l. 142

26 'Twas a thief said the last kind word to Christ:
    Christ took the kindness and forgave the theft.
Ibid. l. 869

27 All poetry is difficult to read,
    —The sense of it is, anyhow.
Ibid. VII, Pompilia, l. 1154

28 No work begun shall ever pause for death!
Ibid. l. 1787

29 Let him wait God's instant men call years.
Ibid. l. 1841

30   Through such souls alone
    God stooping shows sufficient of His light
    For us i' the dark to rise by. And I rise.
Ibid. l. 1843

31 Faultless to a fault.
Ibid. IX, Juris Doctor Johannes-Baptista
Bottinius, l. 1175

1   The curious crime, the fine
Felicity and flower of wickedness.
The Ring and the Book, bk. X, The Pope, l. 589

2   What I call God,
And fools call Nature.
Ibid. l. 1072

3 Why comes temptation, but for man to meet
And master and make crouch beneath his foot,
And so be pedestaled in triumph?
Ibid. l. 1184

4 White shall not neutralize the black, nor good
Compensate bad in man, absolve him so:
Life's business being just the terrible choice.
Ibid. l. 1235

5 You never know what life means till you die:
Even throughout life, 'tis death that makes life
live,
Gives it whatever the significance.
Ibid. XI, Guido, l. 2373

6 Save the squadron, honor France, love thy wife
the Belle Aurore!
Hervé Riel [1871], st. 11

7 A man in armor is his armor's slave.
Herakles [1871]

8 So absolutely good is truth, truth never hurts
The teller.
Fifine at the Fair [1872], st. 32

9   That far land we dream about,
Where every man is his own architect.
Red Cotton Nightcap Country [1873], II

10   A secret's safe
'Twixt you, me, and the gatepost!
The Inn Album [1875], II

11 Ignorance is not innocence but sin.
Ibid. V

12 Have you found your life distasteful?
My life did and does smack sweet.
Was your youth of pleasure wasteful?
Mine I saved and hold complete.
Do your joys with age diminish?
When mine fail me, I'll complain.
Must in death your daylight finish?
My sun sets to rise again.
At the "Mermaid" [1876], st. 10

13 Out of the wreck I rise.
Ixion [1883], l. 121

14 Never the time and the place
And the loved one all together!
Never the Time and the Place [1883]

15 But little do or can the best of us:
That little is achieved through Liberty.
Why I Am a Liberal [1885], l. 9

16 A minute's success pays the failure of years.
Apollo and the Fates [1886], st. 42

17 One who never turned his back but marched
breast forward,
Never doubted clouds would break,
Never dreamed though right were worsted, wrong
would triumph,
Held we fall to rise, are baffled to fight better,
Sleep to wake.
Asolando [1889]. Epilogue, st. 3

Samuel Dickinson Burchard
1812–1891

18   We are Republicans, and don't propose to leave
our party and identify ourselves with the party
whose antecedents have been Rum, Romanism, and
Rebellion.
*Speaking for a deputation of clergymen calling
upon James G. Blaine, the Republican
presidential candidate, in New York [October
29, 1884]*

Charles Dickens
1812–1870

19   A smattering of everything, and a knowledge of
nothing.
Sketches by Boz [1836–1837]. Tales, ch. 3

20   He had used the word [humbug] in its Pickwickian sense.   *Pickwick Papers [1836–1837], ch. 1*

21   "An observer of human nature, sir," said Mr.
Pickwick.   *Ibid. 2*

22   "It wasn't the wine," murmured Mr. Snodgrass,
in a broken voice. "It was the salmon."   *Ibid. 8*

23   I wants to make your flesh creep.   *Ibid.*

24   Tongue; well that's a wery good thing when it
an't a woman's.   *Ibid. 19*

25   Be wery careful o' widders all your life.
Ibid. 20

26   I took a good deal o' pains with his eddication,
sir; let him run in the streets when he was very
young, and shift for hisself. It's the only way to make
a boy sharp, sir.   *Ibid.*

27   The wictim o' connubiality, as Blue Beard's domestic chaplain said, with a tear of pity, ven he
buried him.   *Ibid.*

28   Dumb as a drum with a hole in it, sir.
Ibid. 25

29   Eccentricities of genius.   *Ibid. 30*

30   Keep yourself *to* yourself.   *Ibid. 32*

31   Poetry's unnat'ral; no man ever talked poetry
'cept a beadle on Boxin' Day.   *Ibid. 33*

32   She'll wish there was more, and that's the great
art o' letter-writin'.   *Ibid.*

33   Never mind the character, and stick to the al-
leybi.   *Ibid.*

1   She knows wot's wot, she does.   *Ibid. 37*

2   *They* don't mind it; it's a regular holiday to them —all porter and skittles.[1]   *Ibid. 41*

3   Anythin' for a quiet life, as the man said wen he took the sitivation at the lighthouse.   *Ibid. 43*

4   Right as a trivet.   *Ibid. 50*

5   Oliver Twist has asked for more!
          Oliver Twist [1837–1838], ch. 2

6   "The artful Dodger."   *Ibid. 8*

7   "Hard," replied the Dodger. "As nails," added Charley Bates.   *Ibid. 9*

8   There is a passion for hunting something deeply implanted in the human breast.   *Ibid. 10*

9   I'll eat my head.   *Ibid.*

10   I only know two sorts of boys. Mealy boys, and beef-faced boys.   *Ibid.*

11   There's light enough for wot I've got to do.   *Ibid. 47*

12   "If the law supposes that," said Mr. Bumble . . . "the law is a ass, a idiot."   *Ibid. 51*

13   He had but one eye, and the popular prejudice runs in favor of two.
          Nicholas Nickleby [1838–1839], ch. 4

14   Subdue your appetites, my dears, and you've conquered human natur.   *Ibid. 5*

15   There are only two styles of portrait painting; the serious and the smirk.   *Ibid. 10*

16   Oh! they're too beautiful to live, much too beautiful!   *Ibid. 14*

17   I pity his ignorance and despise him.   *Ibid. 15*

18   The infant phenomenon.   *Ibid. 23*

19   The unities, sir . . . are a completeness—a kind of universal dove-tailedness with regard to place and time.   *Ibid. 24*

20   The two countesses had no outlines at all, and the dowager's was a demd outline.   *Ibid. 34*

21   A demd, damp, moist, unpleasant body!   *Ibid.*

22   Bring in the bottled lightning, a clean tumbler, and a corkscrew.   *Ibid. 49*

23   All is gas and gaiters.   *Ibid.*

24   My life is one demd horrid grind.   *Ibid. 64*

25   He has gone to the demnition bowwows.   *Ibid.*

[1]Life is with such all beer and skittles; / They are not difficult to please / About their victuals.—CHARLES STUART CALVERLEY [1831–1884], *Contentment*
    Life ain't all beer and skittles, and more's the pity.— GEORGE DU MAURIER, *Trilby* [1894], *pt. I*
    See Thomas Hughes, 501:19.

26   What is the odds so long as the fire of soul is kindled at the taper of conwiviality, and the wing of friendship never moults a feather!
          The Old Curiosity Shop [1841], ch. 2

27   She's the ornament of her sex.   *Ibid. 5*

28   In love of home, the love of country has its rise.   *Ibid. 38*

29   That vague kind of penitence which holidays awaken next morning.   *Ibid. 40*

30   "Did you ever taste beer?" "I had a sip of it once," said the small servant. "Here's a state of things!" cried Mr. Swiveller. . . . "She *never* tasted it—it can't be tasted in a sip!"   *Ibid. 57*

31   It was a maxim with Foxey—our revered father, gentlemen—"Always suspect everybody."   *Ibid. 66*

32   Rather a tough customer in argyment.
          Barnaby Rudge [1841], ch. 1

33   "There are strings," said Mr. Tappertit, " . . . in the human heart that had better not be wibrated."   *Ibid. 22*

34   Oh gracious, why wasn't I born old and ugly?   *Ibid. 70*

35   Any man may be in good spirits and good temper when he's well dressed. There ain't much credit in that.   *Martin Chuzzlewit [1843–1844], ch. 5*

36   With affection beaming in one eye, and calculation shining out of the other.   *Ibid. 8*

37   "Do not repine, my friends," said Mr. Pecksniff, tenderly. "Do not weep for me. It is chronic."   *Ibid. 9*

38   Keep up appearances whatever you do.   *Ibid. 11*

39   "Do other men for they would do you." That's the true business precept.   *Ibid.*

40   Buy an annuity cheap, and make your life interesting to yourself and everybody else that watches the speculation.   *Ibid. 18*

41   Leave the bottle on the chimleypiece, and don't ask me to take none, but let me put my lips to it when I am so dispoged.   *Ibid. 19*

42   Rich folks may ride on camels, but it a'n't so easy for 'em to see out of a needle's eye [Sairey Gamp].   *Ibid. 25*

43   "She's the sort of woman now," said Mould . . . "one would almost feel disposed to bury for nothing: and do it neatly, too!"   *Ibid.*

44   He'd make a lovely corpse.   *Ibid.*

45   Gamp is my name, and Gamp my nater.   *Ibid. 26*

46   Our fellow-countryman is a model of a man, quite fresh from Natur's mold!   *Ibid. 34*

47   Oh Sairey, Sairey, little do we know wot lays afore us!   *Ibid. 40*

1   I don't believe there's no sich a person!
Martin Chuzzlewit, ch. 49

2   The words she spoke of Mrs. Harris, lambs could not forgive . . . nor worms forget.   *Ibid.*

3   Oh, but he was a tightfisted hand at the grindstone. Scrooge! a squeezing, wrenching, grasping, scraping, clutching, covetous old sinner! Hard and sharp as flint, from which no steel had ever struck out generous fire; secret, and self-contained, and solitary as an oyster.
A Christmas Carol [1843], stave 1

4   "Bah," said Scrooge. "Humbug!"   *Ibid.*

5   I wear the chain I forged in life [Marley's Ghost].   *Ibid.*

6   "I am the Ghost of Christmas Past." "Long past?" inquired Scrooge. . . . "No. Your past."
Ibid. 2

7   In came a fiddler . . . and tuned like fifty stomachaches. In came Mrs. Fezziwig, one vast substantial smile.   *Ibid.*

8   I am the Ghost of Christmas Present.
Ibid. 3

9   As good as gold [Tiny Tim].   *Ibid.*

10   "God bless us every one!" said Tiny Tim, the last of all.   *Ibid.*

11   "I am in the presence of the Ghost of Christmas Yet to Come?" said Scrooge.   *Ibid. 4*

12   I will honor Christmas in my heart, and try to keep it all the year.   *Ibid.*

13   It *was* a turkey! He could never have stood upon his legs, that bird! He would have snapped 'em off short in a minute, like sticks of sealing wax.
Ibid. 5

14 Oh let us love our occupations,
Bless the squire and his relations,
Live upon our daily rations,
And always know our proper stations.
The Chimes [1844], second quarter

15   He's tough, ma'am, tough, is J.B. Tough and devilish sly!   *Dombey and Son [1848], ch. 7*

16   "Wal'r, my boy," replied the Captain, "in the Proverbs of Solomon you will find the following words, 'May we never want a friend in need, nor a bottle to give him!' When found, make a note of."
Ibid. 15

17   Cows are my passion.   *Ibid. 21*

18   The bearings of this observation lays in the application on it.   *Ibid. 23*

19   You'll find us rough, sir, but you'll find us ready.
David Copperfield [1849–1850], ch. 3

20   I am a lone lorn creetur . . . and everythink goes contrary with me.   *Ibid.*

21   Barkis is willin'.   *Ibid. 5*

22   Experientia does it[1]—as Papa used to say.
Ibid. 11

23   "In case anything turned up," which was his [Mr. Micawber's] favorite expression.   *Ibid.*

24   I never will desert Mr. Micawber.   *Ibid. 12*

25   Annual income twenty pounds, annual expenditure nineteen nineteen six, result happiness. Annual income twenty pounds, annual expenditure twenty pounds ought and six, result misery.   *Ibid.*

26   It's a mad world. Mad as Bedlam.   *Ibid. 14*

27   Never . . . be mean in anything; never be false; never be cruel.   *Ibid. 15*

28   I'm a very umble person.[2]   *Ibid. 16*

29   The mistake was made of putting some of the trouble out of King Charles's head into my head.[3]
Ibid. 17

30   It was as true . . . as turnips is. It was as true . . . as taxes is. And nothing's truer than them.
Ibid. 21

31   What a world of gammon and spinnage it is, though, ain't it!   *Ibid. 22*

32   Nobody's enemy but his own.   *Ibid. 25*

33   Accidents will occur in the best-regulated families.   *Ibid. 28*

34   Ride on! Rough-shod if need be, smooth-shod if that will do, but ride on! Ride on over all obstacles, and win the race!   *Ibid.*

35   A long pull, and a strong pull, and a pull all together.   *Ibid. 30*

36   He's a-going out with the tide.   *Ibid.*

37   I ate umble pie with an appetite.   *Ibid. 39*

38   Let sleeping dogs lie—who wants to rouse 'em?
Ibid.

39   Skewered through and through with office pens, and bound hand and foot with red tape.
Ibid. 43

40   It's only my child-wife.   *Ibid. 44*

41   There can be no disparity in marriage like unsuitability of mind and purpose.   *Ibid. 45*

42   A man must take the fat with the lean.
Ibid. 51

43   Trifles make the sum of life.   *Ibid. 53*

44   The seamen said it blew great guns.
Ibid. 55

[1]Experientia docet [Experience teaches].—Tacitus, *History, bk. V, ch. 6*
[2]Not only humble but umble, which I look upon to be the comparative, or, indeed, superlative degree.—Anthony Trollope, *Doctor Thorne* [1858], *ch. 4*
[3]"King Charles's head" has passed into common use in the English language as a phrase meaning some whimsical obsession.—G. B. Stern [1890–1973], *Monogram* [1936]

1   He is an honorable, obstinate, truthful, high-spirited, intensely prejudiced, perfectly reasonable man.
Bleak House [1852–1858], ch. 2

2   This is a London particular. . . . A fog, miss.
Ibid. 3

3   Not to put too fine a point upon it.   *Ibid. 11*

4   [Old Mr. Turveydrop] was not like anything in the world but a model of Deportment.   *Ibid. 14*

5   Now, what I want is Facts. Teach these boys and girls nothing but Facts. Facts alone are wanted in life. Plant nothing else, and root out everything else.
Hard Times [1854], bk. I, ch. 1

6   There is a wisdom of the head, and . . . a wisdom of the heart.   *Ibid. III, 1*

7   I am the only child of parents who weighed, measured, and priced everything; for whom what could not be weighed, measured, and priced had no existence.   *Little Dorrit [1857–1858], bk. I, ch. 2*

8   Whatever was required to be done, the Circumlocution Office was beforehand with all the public departments in the art of perceiving—HOW NOT TO DO IT.   *Ibid. 10*

9   Papa, potatoes, poultry, prunes, and prism, are all very good words for the lips: especially prunes and prism.   *Ibid. II, 5*

10   Once a gentleman, and always a gentleman.
Ibid. 28

11   It was the best of times, it was the worst of times.
A Tale of Two Cities [1859], bk. I, ch. 1

12   A wonderful fact to reflect upon, that every human creature is constituted to be that profound secret and mystery to every other.   *Ibid. 3*

13   It is a far, far better thing that I do, than I have ever done; it is a far, far better rest that I go to, than I have ever known.   *Ibid. III, 15*

14   In the little world in which children have their existence, whosoever brings them up, there is nothing so finely perceived and so finely felt, as injustice.
Great Expectations [1860–1861], ch. 8

15   Ever been the best of friends!   *Ibid. 18*

16   My guiding star always is, Get hold of portable property.   *Ibid. 24*

17   Take nothing on its looks; take everything on evidence. There's no better rule.   *Ibid. 40*

18   Money and goods are certainly the best of references.
Our Mutual Friend [1864–1865], bk. I, ch. 4

19   People now call him the Golden Dustman [Mr. Boffin].   *Ibid. 11*

20   I want to be something so much worthier than the doll in the doll's house.[1]   *Ibid. 55*

21   I don't care whether I am a Minx or a Sphinx [Lavvy].   *Ibid. II, 8*

22   That's the state to live and die in! . . . R-r-rich!
Ibid. III, 5

23   We must scrunch or be scrunched.   *Ibid.*

Ivan Goncharov
1812–1891

24   "And he was as intelligent as other people, his soul was pure and clear as crystal; he was noble and affectionate—and yet he did nothing!"
"But why? What was the reason?"
"The reason . . . what reason was there? Oblomovism!"   *Oblomov [1859], pt. IV, ch. 12*

Alexander Ivanovich Herzen
1812–1870

25   Communism is a Russian autocracy turned upside down.
The Development of Revolutionary Ideas in Russia [1851]

26   Russia's future will be a great danger for Europe and a great misfortune for Russia if there is no emancipation of the individual. One more century of present despotism will destroy all the good qualities of the Russian people.   *Ibid.*

Edward Lear
1812–1888

27   There was an Old Man with a beard,
Who said: "It is just as I feared!
Two owls and a hen,
Four larks and a wren
Have all built their nests in my beard."
Book of Nonsense [1846]. Limerick

28   How pleasant to know Mr. Lear![2]
Who has written such volumes of stuff!
Some think him ill-tempered and queer,
But a few think him pleasant enough.
Nonsense Songs [1871]. Preface, st. 1

29   He has ears, and two eyes, and ten fingers,
Leastways if you reckon two thumbs;
Long ago he was one of the singers,
But now he is one of the dumbs.
Ibid. st. 3

30   His body is perfectly spherical,
He weareth a runcible hat.
Ibid. st. 5

31   The Owl and the Pussycat went to sea
In a beautiful pea-green boat,
They took some honey, and plenty of money,
Wrapped up in a five-pound note.

[1]See Ibsen, 507:18.

[2]See T. S. Eliot, 670:6.

The Owl looked up to the stars above,
And sang to a small guitar,
"O lovely Pussy! O Pussy, my love,
What a beautiful Pussy you are."
The Owl and the Pussycat [1871], st. 1

1 Pussy said to the Owl, "You elegant fowl!
How charmingly sweet you sing!
O let us be married! too long we have tarried:
But what shall we do for a ring?"
They sailed away, for a year and a day,
To the land where the Bong-tree grows
And there in a wood a Piggy-wig stood
With a ring at the end of his nose.
Ibid. st. 2

2 "Dear Pig, are you willing to sell for one shilling
Your ring?" Said the Piggy, "I will."
Ibid. st. 3

3 They dined on mince, and slices of quince,
Which they ate with a runcible spoon;
And hand in hand, on the edge of the sand,
They danced by the light of the moon.
Ibid.

4 Far and few, far and few,
Are the lands where the Jumblies live;
Their heads are green, and their hands are blue,
And they went to sea in a sieve.
The Jumblies [1871], st. 1

5 Calico Pie,
The little Birds fly
Down to the calico tree,
Their wings were blue,
And they sang "Tilly-loo!"
Till away they flew—
And they never came back to me!
Calico Pie [1871], st. 1

6 Calico Jam,
The little Fish swam,
Over the syllabub sea.
Ibid. st. 2

7 Who, or why, or which, or what,
Is the Akond of Swat?
The Akond of Swat[1] [1877], l. 1

8 On the top of the Crumpetty Tree
The Quangle Wangle sat,
But his face you could not see,
On account of his Beaver Hat.
The Quangle Wangle's Hat [1877], st. 1

9 On the coast of Coromandel
Where the early pumpkins blow,
In the middle of the woods
Lived the Yonghy-Bonghy-Bò.
Two old chairs, and half a candle,

[1]Pray tell me, good reader, if tell me you can,/What's the Ahkoond of Swat to you folks or to me?—EUGENE FIELD, *The Ahkoond of Swat* [1884]

One old jug without a handle—
These were all his worldly goods.
The Courtship of the Yonghy-Bongy-Bò [1877], st. 1

10 There he heard a Lady talking,
To some milk-white Hens of Dorking—
'Tis the Lady Jingly Jones!
Ibid. st. 2

11 "I would be your wife most gladly!"
(Here she twirled her fingers madly),
"But in England I've a mate!"
Ibid. st. 5

12 When awful darkness and silence reign
Over the great Gromboolian plain,
Through the long, long wintry nights.
The Dong with the Luminous Nose [1877], st. 1

13 When storm-clouds brood on the towering heights
Of the hills of the Chankly Bore.
Ibid.

14 The Pobble who has no toes
Had once as many as we;
When they said, "Some day you may lose them
all"—
He replied, "Fish fiddle de-dee!"
The Pobble Who Has No Toes [1877], st. 1

15 It's a fact the whole world knows,
That Pobbles are happier without their toes.
Ibid. 6

16 Ploffskin, Pluffskin, Pelican jee!
We think no Birds so happy as we!
Plumpskin, Ploshkin, Pelican jill!
We think so then, and we thought so still.
The Pelican Chorus [1877], chorus

Samuel Smiles
1812–1904

17   The spirit of self-help is the root of all genuine growth in the individual; and, exhibited in the lives of many, it constitutes the true source of national vigor and strength.   *Self-Help [1859]*

William Edmondstoune Aytoun
1813–1865

18 Nowhere beats the heart so kindly
As beneath the tartan plaid!
Charles Edward at Versailles [1849], l. 219

19 The deep, unutterable woe
Which none save exiles feel.
The Island of the Scots [1849], st. 12

Henry Ward Beecher
1813–1887

20   Where is human nature so weak as in the book-store!
Star Papers [1855]. Subtleties of Book Buyers

1 A thoughtful mind, when it sees a nation's flag, sees not the flag only, but the nation itself; and whatever may be its symbols, its insignia, he reads chiefly in the flag the government, the principles, the truths, the history which belongs to the nation that sets it forth. *The National Flag [1861]*

2 Now comes the mystery.
Last words [March 8, 1887]

Claude Bernard
1813–1878

3 Observation is a passive science, experimentation an active science.
Introduction à l'Étude de la Médecine Expérimentale [1865][1]

4 The science of life . . . is a superb and dazzlingly lighted hall which may be reached only by passing through a long and ghastly kitchen.
Ibid.

5 Our ideas are only intellectual instruments which we use to break into phenomena; we must change them when they have served their purpose, as we change a blunt lancet that we have used long enough. *Ibid.*

6 A contemporary poet has characterized this sense of the personality of art and of the impersonality of science in these words—"Art is myself; science is ourselves." *Ibid.*

7 The stability of the *internal medium* is a primary condition for the freedom and independence of certain living bodies in relation to the environment surrounding them.
Leçons sur les Phénomènes de la Vie Communs aux Animaux et aux Végétaux [1878–1879][2]

8 All the vital mechanisms, varied as they are, have only one object, that of preserving constant the conditions of life in the internal environment.
Ibid.

9 The mental never influences the physical. It is always the physical that modifies the mental, and when we think that the mind is diseased, it is always an illusion. *Pensées [1937]*

Georg Büchner
1813–1837

10 The Revolution is like Saturn—it eats its own children. *Danton's Death [1835]*

[1]*An Introduction to the Study of Experimental Medicine*, translated by HENRY COPLEY GREENE.
[2]*Lessons on Reactions Common to Animals and Plants*, translated by J. M. D. OLMSTEAD.

John William Burgon
1813–1888

11 A rose-red city half as old as time.
Petra [1845]

Sören Kierkegaard
1813–1855

12 Philosophy is perfectly right in saying that life must be understood backward. But then one forgets the other clause—that it must be lived forward.
Journals and Papers [1843],[3] vol. I

13 The absurd . . . the fact that with God all things are possible. The absurd is not one of the factors which can be discriminated within the proper compass of the understanding: it is not identical with the improbable, the unexpected, the unforeseen.
Fear and Trembling [1843]. Problemata: Preliminary Expectoration

14 All essential knowledge relates to existence, or only such knowledge as has an essential relationship to existence is essential knowledge.
Concluding Unscientific Postscript [1846]

John Louis O'Sullivan
1813–1895

15 Our manifest destiny is to overspread the continent allotted by Providence for the free development of our yearly multiplying millions.
United States Magazine and Democratic Review [July–August 1845]

Richard Wagner
1813–1883

16 O thou, my gracious evening star.
Tannhäuser [1845]

17 To be German means to carry on a matter for its own sake.
Deutsche Kunst und Deutsche Politik [1867]

18 Ride of the Valkyries.
Die Walküre [1876]

Henry Stevenson Washburn
1813–1903

19 We shall meet, but we shall miss him,
There will be one vacant chair.
The Vacant Chair, st. 1

[3]Translated by HOWARD V. HONG and EDNA H. HONG.

Thomas Osborne Davis
1814–1845

1 Come in the evening, or come in the morning,
Come when you're looked for, or come without
warning.

The Welcome, st. 1

Frederick William Faber
1814–1863

2 Faith of our fathers! holy faith!
We will be true to thee till death.

A Pledge of Faithfulness [1849]

3 Hark! Hark! my soul, angelic songs are swelling
O'er earth's green fields, and ocean's wave-beat
shore;
How sweet the truth those blessed strains are
telling
Of that new life when sin shall be no more!

Pilgrims of the Night [1854][1]

Mikhail Lermontov
1814–1841

4 *A Hero of Our Time*, gentlemen, is indeed a portrait, but not of a single individual; it is a portrait
composed of all the vices of our generation in the
fullness of their development.

*A Hero of Our Time [1840]. Author's
Introduction*

5 A solitary sail that rises
White in the blue mist on the foam—
What is it in far lands it prizes?
What does it leave behind at home?

A Sail [1841],[2] *st. 1*

6 Beneath, the azure current floweth,
Above, the golden sunlight glows.
Rebellious, the storms it wooeth,
As if the storms could give repose.

Ibid. st. 3

Charles Mackay
1814–1889

7 There's a good time coming, boys!
A good time coming.

The Good Time Coming, st. 1

John Lothrop Motley
1814–1877

8 As long as he [William of Orange] lived, he was
the guiding-star of a whole brave nation, and when
he died the little children cried in the streets.

*The Rise of the Dutch Republic [1856], pt. VI,
ch. 7*

9 Give us the luxuries of life, and we will dispense
with its necessaries.

Quoted in OLIVER WENDELL HOLMES, *The
Autocrat of the Breakfast-Table [1858], ch. 6*

Edwin McMasters Stanton
1814–1869

10 Now he [Lincoln] belongs to the ages.

On the death of Lincoln [April 15, 1865]

Otto von Bismarck
1815–1898

11 The great questions of the time are not decided
by speeches and majority decisions—that was the
error of 1848 and 1849—but by iron and blood.[3]

*Speech to the Prussian Diet [September 30,
1862]*

12 Only a completely ready state can permit the
luxury of a liberal government.   *Speech [1866]*

13 Let us put Germany in the saddle, so to speak
—it already knows how to ride.

*Speech to the North German Reichstag [March
11, 1867]*

14 Politics is the art of the possible.[4]

Remark [August 11, 1867]

15 A conquering army on the border will not be
halted by the power of eloquence.

*Speech to the North German Reichstag
[September 24, 1867]*

16 The luxury of one's own opinion.

Speech to the Prussian Diet [December 17, 1873]

17 The right people in the right jobs.

Speech to the North German Reichstag [1875]

18 We Germans fear God, but nothing else in the
world.

Speech to the Reichstag [February 6, 1888]

Richard Henry Dana
1815–1882

19 Six days shalt thou labor and do all thou art able,
And on the seventh—holystone the decks and
scrape the cable.

Two Years Before the Mast [1840], ch. 3

20 If California ever becomes a prosperous country,
this bay [San Francisco] will be the center of its
prosperity.   *Ibid. 26*

David Davis
1815–1886

21 The Constitution of the United States is a law for
rulers and people, equally in war and in peace, and

---

[1] Music by HENRY T. SMART [1813–1879].
[2] Translated by C. M. BOWRA.

[3] Eisen und Blut.
[4] Die Politik ist die Lehre von Möglichen.

covers with the shield of its protection all classes of men, at all times, and under all circumstances. No doctrine, involving more pernicious consequences, was ever invented by the wit of man than that any of its provisions can be suspended during any of the great exigencies of government.

Ex Parte Milligan, 4 Wallace 2, 120–121 [1866]

Daniel Decatur Emmett
1815–1904

1 I wish I was in de land ob cotton,
Old times dar am not forgotten.
  Look away, look away,
  Look away, Dixie[1] Land.

Dixie's Land [1859], st. 1

2 In Dixie's land, we'll took our stand,
To lib an' die in Dixie!

Ibid. chorus

Johnson Jones Hooper
1815–1862

3 It is good to be shifty in a new country.

Some Adventures of Captain Simon Suggs [1845]

John Babsone Lane Soule
1815–1891

4 Go west, young man.[2]

Article in the Terre Haute (Indiana) Express [1851]

Elizabeth Cady Stanton
1815–1902

5 We hold these truths to be self-evident, that all men and women are created equal.

First Woman's Rights Convention, Seneca Falls, New York [July 19–20, 1848]. Declaration of Sentiments

6 Resolved, That it is the duty of the women of this country to secure to themselves their sacred right to the elective franchise.

Ibid. Resolution IX

7 The prejudice against color, of which we hear so much, is no stronger than that against sex. It is produced by the same cause, and manifested very much in the same way. The Negro's skin and the woman's sex are both prima facie evidence that they were intended to be in subjection to the white Saxon man.

Speech before the New York Legislature [February 18, 1860]

8 Woman's degradation is in man's idea of his sexual rights. Our religion, laws, customs, are all founded on the belief that woman was made for man. Come what will, my whole soul rejoices in the truth that I have uttered.[3]

Letter to Susan B. Anthony [June 14, 1860]

9 Our "pathway" is straight to the ballot box, with no variableness nor shadow of turning. . . . We demand in the Reconstruction suffrage for all the citizens of the Republic. I would not talk of Negroes or women, but of citizens.

Letter to Thomas Wentworth Higginson [January 13, 1868]

10 Women have crucified the Mary Wollstonecrafts, the Fanny Wrights, and the George Sands of all ages. Men mock us with the fact and say we are ever cruel to each other. . . . If this present woman [Victoria Woodhull] must be crucified, let men drive the spikes.   *Letter to Lucretia Mott [April 1, 1872]*

Anthony Trollope
1815–1882

11 The tenth Muse who now governs the periodical press.   *The Warden [1855], ch. 14*

12 One of her instructors in fashion had given her to understand that curls were not the thing. "They'll always pass muster," Miss Dunstable had replied, "when they are done up with bank notes."

Doctor Thorne [1858], ch. 16

13 There is no road to wealth so easy and respectable as that of matrimony.   *Ibid. 18*

14 I cannot hold with those who wish to put down the insignificant chatter of the world.

Framley Parsonage [1861]

15 She understood how much louder a cock can crow in its own farmyard than elsewhere.

The Last Chronicle of Barset [1867], vol. I, ch. 17

16 Always remember . . . that when you go into an attorney's office door, you will have to pay for it, first or last.   *Ibid. 20*

---

[1]*Dixie* comes from the ten-dollar notes issued by the Citizens' Bank in bilingual Louisiana before the Civil War and bearing the French word *dix,* ten, on the reverse side. Soon New Orleans, then Louisiana and the entire South were called "The land of Dixie," and later *Dixieland* and *Dixie.* The word became immensely popular with the song "Dixie" (whose actual title is "Dixie's Land").—STUART BERG FLEXNER, *I Hear America Talking* [1976]

[2]Horace Greeley used the expression in an editorial in the *New York Tribune.* As the saying "Go west, young man, and grow up with the country" gained popularity, Greeley printed Soule's article, to show the source of his inspiration. See Greeley, 462:12.

[3]Referring to resolutions she had introduced at the tenth National Woman's Rights Convention [May 10, 1860], declaring that under certain circumstances divorce was justifiable.

1   It's dogged as does it. It ain't thinking about it.
    The Last Chronicle of Barset, vol. I, ch. 61

2   She knew how to allure by denying, and to make the gift rich by delaying it.
    Phineas Finn [1869], ch. 57

3   There are worse things than a lie . . . I have found . . . that it may be well to choose one sin in order that another may be shunned.
    Doctor Wortle's School [1879], ch. 6

4   He must have known me had he seen me as he was wont to see me, for he was in the habit of flogging me constantly. Perhaps he did not recognize me by my face.   *An Autobiography [1883], ch. 1*

5   Three hours a day will produce as much as a man ought to write.[1]
    Ibid. 15

6   It had at this time become my custom . . . to write with my watch before me, and to require from myself 250 words every quarter of an hour. I have found that the 250 words have been forthcoming as regularly as my watch went.   *Ibid.*

7   Of all the needs a book has, the chief need is that it be readable.   *Ibid. 19*

Philip James Bailey
1816–1902

8   Let each man think himself an act of God,
    His mind a thought, his life a breath of God.
    Festus [1839]. Proem

9   America, thou half-brother of the world;
    With something good and bad of every land.
    Ibid. The Surface

Charlotte Brontë
1816–1855

10   We wove a web in childhood,
     A web of sunny air.
     Retrospection [1846], st. 1

11   The human heart has hidden treasures,
     In secret kept, in silence sealed.
     Evening Solace [1846], st. 1

12   Conventionality is not morality. Self-righteousness is not religion. To attack the first is not to assail the last.   *Jane Eyre [1847], preface*

13   Reader, I married him.   *Ibid. ch. 38*

14   An abundant shower of curates has fallen upon the north of England.   *Shirley [1849], ch. 1*

15   Unromantic as Monday morning.   *Ibid.*

16   I am neither a man nor a woman but an author.
     Letter to William Smith Williams [August 16, 1849]

[1]See Apelles, 81:1.

Ellen Sturgis Hooper
1816–1841

17   I slept and dreamed that life was beauty.
     I woke—and found that life was duty.
     Beauty and Duty

Eugène Pottier
1816–1887

18   Arise, ye prisoners of starvation,
     Arise, ye wretched of the earth,[2]
     For justice thunders condemnation—
     A better world's in birth.
     The Internationale [1871][3]

Henry David Thoreau
1817–1862

19   I am a parcel of vain strivings tied
     By a chance bond together.
     Sic Vita [1841], st. 1

20   We are as much as we see. Faith is sight and knowledge. The hands only serve the eyes.
     Journal [1906]. April 10, 1841

21   The Indian . . . stands free and unconstrained in Nature, is her inhabitant and not her guest, and wears her easily and gracefully. But the civilized man has the habits of the house. His house is a prison.
     Ibid. April 26, 1841

22   It is a great art to saunter.[4]   *Ibid.*

23   A slight sound at evening lifts me up by the ears, and makes life seem inexpressibly serene and grand. It may be in Uranus, or it may be in the shutter.
     Ibid. July 10–12, 1841

24   For many years I was self-appointed inspector of snowstorms and rainstorms, and did my duty faithfully, though I never received one cent for it.
     Ibid. February 22 [1845–1847][5]

25   Some circumstantial evidence is very strong, as when you find a trout in the milk.
     Ibid. November 11, 1850

26   Nothing is so much to be feared as fear.[6]
     Ibid. September 7, 1851

27   The bluebird carries the sky on his back.
     Ibid. April 3, 1852

28   The perception of beauty is a moral test.
     Ibid. June 21, 1852

[2]See Fanon, 754:21.
[3]Music by PIERRE DEGEYTER [1848–1932].
[4]*Sauntering* . . . derived "from idle people who roved about the country, in the Middle Ages, and asked charity, under pretense of going *à la Sainte Terre*," to the Holy Land, till the children exclaimed, "There goes a Sainte-Terrer."—*Walking* [1862]
[5]No year in Thoreau's dateline.
[6]See *Proverbs 3:25, 20:22*; Montaigne, 145:10; Francis Bacon, 158:18; Wellington, 371:9; and F. D. Roosevelt, 648:18.

1 The youth gets together his materials to build a bridge to the moon, or, perchance, a palace or temple on the earth, and, at length, the middle-aged man concludes to build a woodshed with them.
Ibid. July 14, 1852

2 Fire is the most tolerable third party.
Ibid. January 2, 1853

3 Nature is full of genius, full of the divinity; so that not a snowflake escapes its fashioning hand.
Ibid. January 5, 1856

4 The same law that shapes the earth-star shapes the snow-star. As surely as the petals of a flower are fixed, each of these countless snow-stars comes whirling to earth.
Ibid.

5 That man is the richest whose pleasures are the cheapest.
Ibid. March 11, 1856

6 The savage in man is never quite eradicated.
Ibid. September 26, 1859

7 Talk of mysteries! Think of our life in nature—daily to be shown matter, to come in contact with it—rocks, trees, wind on our cheeks! the *solid* earth! the *actual* world! the *common sense! Contact! Contact! Who* are we? *where* are we?
The Maine Woods, Ktaadn [1848]

8 I think that we should be men first, and subjects afterward. It is not desirable to cultivate a respect for the law, so much as for the right.
Civil Disobedience [1849]

9 How does it become a man to behave toward this American government today? I answer that he cannot without disgrace be associated with it.
Ibid.

10 A wise man will not leave the right to the mercy of chance, nor wish it to prevail through the power of the majority. There is but little virtue in the action of masses of men.
Ibid.

11 I came into this world, not chiefly to make this a good place to live in, but to live in it, be it good or bad.
Ibid.

12 Any man more right than his neighbors constitutes a majority of one.
Ibid.

13 Under a government which imprisons any unjustly, the true place for a just man is also a prison . . . the only house in a slave State in which a free man can abide with honor.
Ibid.

14 I saw that the State was half-witted, that it was timid as a lone woman with her silver spoons, and that it did not know its friends from its foes, and I lost all my remaining respect for it, and pitied it.
Ibid.

15 The vessel, though her masts be firm,
Beneath her copper bears a worm.
A Week on the Concord and Merrimack Rivers [1849]. Monday [Though All the Fates Should Prove Unkind, st. 2]

16 Methinks my own soul must be a bright invisible green.
Ibid. Wednesday

17 It takes two to speak the truth—one to speak, and another to hear.
Ibid.

18 Even the death of friends will inspire us as much as their lives. . . . Their memories will be encrusted over with sublime and pleasing thoughts, as monuments of other men are overgrown with moss; for our friends have no place in the graveyard.
Ibid.

19 Go where we will on the *surface* of things, men have been there before us.
Ibid. Thursday

20 The frontiers are not east or west, north or south, but wherever a man *fronts* a fact.
Ibid.

21 A true account of the actual is the rarest poetry, for common sense always takes a hasty and superficial view.
Ibid.

22 My life has been the poem I would have writ,
But I could not both live and utter it.
Ibid. My Life Has Been the Poem I Would Have Writ

23 As if our birth had at first sundered things, and we had been thrust up through into nature like a wedge, and not till the wound heals and the scar disappears, do we begin to discover where we are, and that nature is one and continuous everywhere.
Ibid. Friday

24 What are the earth and all its interests beside the deep surmise which pierces and scatters them?
Ibid.

25 It is so rare to meet with a man outdoors who cherishes a worthy thought in his mind, which is independent of the labor of his hands.
Ibid.

26 The eye may see for the hand, but not for the mind.
Ibid.

27 The fate of the country . . . does not depend on what kind of paper you drop into the ballot box once a year, but on what kind of man you drop from your chamber into the street every morning.
Slavery in Massachusetts [1854]

28 I should not talk so much about myself if there were anybody else whom I knew as well.
Walden [1854], 1, Economy

29 I have traveled a good deal in Concord.
Ibid.

30 Public opinion is a weak tyrant compared with our own private opinion. What a man thinks of himself, that it is which determines, or rather, indicates, his fate.
Ibid.

31 As if you could kill time without injuring eternity.
Ibid.

32 The mass of men lead lives of quiet desperation. What is called resignation is confirmed desperation.
Ibid.

1 It is a characteristic of wisdom not to do desperate things. *Walden, 1, Economy*

2 It is never too late to give up our prejudices. *Ibid.*

3 Age is no better, hardly so well, qualified for an instructor as youth, for it has not profited so much as it has lost. *Ibid.*

4 Most of the luxuries, and many of the so-called comforts, of life are not only not indispensable, but positive hindrances to the elevation of mankind. *Ibid.*

5 To be a philosopher is not merely to have subtle thoughts, nor even to found a school, but so to love wisdom as to live accordingly to its dictates, a life of simplicity, independence, magnanimity, and trust. *Ibid.*

6 Beware of all enterprises that require new clothes. *Ibid.*

7 In the long run men hit only what they aim at. *Ibid.*

8 The swiftest traveler is he that goes afoot. *Ibid.*

9 It is not necessary that a man should earn his living by the sweat of his brow unless he sweats easier than I do. *Ibid.*

10 When a man dies he kicks the dust. *Ibid.*

11 As for doing good, that is one of the professions which are full. *Ibid.*

12 There is no odor so bad as that which arises from goodness tainted. *Ibid.*

13 There are a thousand hacking at the branches of evil to one who is striking at the root. *Ibid.*

14 Philanthropy is almost the only virtue which is sufficiently appreciated by mankind. *Ibid.*

15 A man is rich in proportion to the number of things which he can afford to let alone.
Ibid. 2, Where I Lived, and What I Lived For

16 I know of no more encouraging fact than the unquestionable ability of man to elevate his life by a conscious endeavor. *Ibid.*

17 I went to the woods because I wished to live deliberately, to front only the essential facts of life, and see if I could not learn what it had to teach, and not, when I came to die, discover that I had not lived. *Ibid.*

18 Our life is frittered away by detail. . . . Simplify, simplify. *Ibid.*

19 We do not ride on the railroad; it rides upon us. *Ibid.*

20 Be it life or death, we crave only reality. *Ibid.*

21 Time is but the stream I go a-fishing in. *Ibid.*

22 Books must be read as deliberately and reservedly as they were written. *Ibid. 3, Reading*

23 How many a man has dated a new era in his life from the reading of a book. *Ibid.*

24 I love a broad margin to my life. *Ibid. 4, Sounds*

25 Our horizon is never quite at our elbows. *Ibid. 5, Solitude*

26 I never found the companion that was so companionable as solitude. We are for the most part more lonely when we go abroad among men than when we stay in our chambers. A man thinking or working is always alone, let him be where he will. *Ibid.*

27 I had three chairs in my house: one for solitude, two for friendship, three for society. *Ibid. 6, Visitors*

28 I was determined to know beans. *Ibid. 7, The Beanfield*

29 Through want of enterprise and faith men are where they are, buying and selling, and spending their lives like serfs. *Ibid. 10, Baker Farm*

30 They [wood stumps] warmed me twice—once while I was splitting them, and again when they were on the fire.[1] *Ibid. 13, Housewarming*

31 Heaven is under our feet as well as over our heads. *Ibid. 16, The Pond in Winter*

32 While men believe in the infinite, some ponds will be thought to be bottomless. *Ibid.*

33 Through our own recovered innocence we discern the innocence of our neighbors. *Ibid. 17, Spring*

34 It is not worth while to go round the world to count the cats in Zanzibar. *Ibid. 18, Conclusion*

35 As if there were safety in stupidity alone. *Ibid.*

36 If one advances confidently in the direction of his dreams, and endeavors to live the life which he has imagined, he will meet with a success unexpected in common hours. *Ibid.*

37 If a man does not keep pace with his companions, perhaps it is because he hears a different drummer. Let him step to the music which he hears, however measured or far away. *Ibid.*

38 It is life near the bone where it is sweetest. *Ibid.*

39 Rather than love, than money, than fame, give me truth. *Ibid.*

40 Only that day dawns to which we are awake. There is more day to dawn. The sun is but a morning star. *Ibid.*

[1]Who splits his own wood warms himself twice.—*Saying*

1 I hear many condemn these men because they were so few. When were the good and the brave ever in a majority?
A Plea for Captain John Brown [1859]

2 I speak for the slave when I say that I prefer the philanthropy of Captain Brown to that philanthropy which neither shoots me nor liberates me.
Ibid.

3 So we defend ourselves and our henroosts, and maintain slavery.
Ibid.

4 He is not Old Brown any longer; he is an angel of light.
Ibid.

5 Eastward I go only by force; but westward I go free.
Walking [1862]

6 In wildness is the preservation of the world.[1]
Ibid.

7 I believe in the forest, and in the meadow, and in the night in which the corn grows.
Ibid.

8 Life consists with wildness. The most alive is the wildest. Not yet subdued to man, its presence refreshes him.
Ibid.

9 Men will lie on their backs, talking about the fall of man, and never make an effort to get up.
Life Without Principle [1863]

10 A man may stand there [Cape Cod] and put all America behind him.
Cape Cod [1865], ch. 10

11 One world at a time.
Said a few days before his death

Alexei Konstantinovich Tolstoi
1817–1875

12 His pen is breathing revenge.
Vaska Shibanov [1855–1865]

13 No one can encompass the unencompassable.
Collected Works of Kosma Prutkov [1884][2]

14 If thou hast a fountain, shut it up: let even a fountain have a rest.
Ibid.

15 Many men are like unto sausages: whatever you stuff them with, that they will bear in them.
Ibid.

Alexander II
1818–1881

16 Better to abolish serfdom from above than to wait till it begins to abolish itself from below.
Speech in Moscow [March 30, 1856]

Cecil Frances Alexander
1818–1895

17 All things bright and beautiful,
All creatures great and small,
All things wise and wonderful,
The Lord God made them all.
All Things Bright and Beautiful [1848], st. 1

18 There is a green hill far away,
Without a city wall,
Where the dear Lord was crucified,
Who died to save us all.
There Is a Green Hill [1848], st. 1

19 Once in royal David's city
Stood a lowly cattle shed,
Where a mother laid her baby
In a manger for his bed:
Mary was that mother mild,
Jesus Christ her little child.
Once in Royal David's City [1848],[3] st. 1

Josh Billings [Henry Wheeler Shaw]
1818–1885

20 A sekret ceases tew be a sekret if it iz once confided—it iz like a dollar bill, once broken, it iz never a dollar agin.
Josh Billings: His Sayings [1865]. Affurisms

21 Love iz like the meazles; we kant have it bad but onst, and the later in life we have it the tuffer it goes with us.
Ibid.

22 Nature never makes any blunders; when she makes a fool she means it.
Ibid.

23 I don't care how much a man talks, if he only says it in a few words.
Ibid.

24 As scarce as truth is, the supply has always been in excess of the demand.
Ibid.

25 Poverty iz the stepmother ov genius.
Ibid.

26 The wheel that squeaks the loudest
Is the one that gets the grease.
The Kicker

27 It is better to know nothing than to know what ain't so.[4]
Proverb [1874]

28 If it want for faith, thare would be no living in this world. We couldn't even eat hash with enny safety, if it want for faith.
Essays [1876]. Faith

Emily Brontë
1818–1848

29 Sleep not, dream not; this bright day
Will not, cannot last for aye;

---

[1]Motto of the Wilderness Society.
See Muir, 537:14.
[2]Translated by B. G. GURNEY.

[3]Music by HENRY J. GAUNTLETT [1805–1876].
[4]Better know nothing than half-know many things.—
NIETZSCHE, *Thus Spake Zarathustra* [1883–1891], pt. IV, 64

Bliss like thine is bought by years
Dark with torment and with tears.
Sleep Not [1846], st. 1

1 Cold in the earth—and fifteen wild Decembers
From those brown hills have melted into spring.
Remembrance [1846], st. 3

2 Once drinking deep of that divinest anguish,
How could I seek the empty world again?
Ibid. st. 8

3 Yes, as my swift days near their goal,
'Tis all that I implore:
In life and death a chainless soul,
With courage to endure.
The Old Stoic [1846], st. 3

4 No coward soul is mine,
No trembler in the world's storm-troubled sphere:
I see Heaven's glories shine,
And faith shines equal, arming me from fear.
Last Lines [1846], st. 1

5 There is not room for Death.
Ibid. st. 7

6 I *am* Heathcliff.
Wuthering Heights [1847], ch. 9

7 I lingered round them, under that benign sky:
watched the moths fluttering among the heath and
harebells; listened to the soft wind breathing
through the grass; and wondered how anyone could
ever imagine unquiet slumbers for the sleepers in
that quiet earth.   *Ibid. last words*

Jacob Burckhardt
1818–1897

8 The picture I have formed of the *terribles simplificateurs* [terrible simplifiers] who are going to descend upon poor old Europe is not an agreeable one.
Letter to Friedrich von Preen [July 24, 1889][1]

Eliza Cook
1818–1889

9 I love it, I love it; and who shall dare
To chide me for loving that old armchair?
The Old Armchair

10 Better build schoolrooms for "the boy"
Than cells and gibbets for "the man."
A Song for the Ragged Schools, st. 12

Frederick Douglass
c. 1818–1895

11 Every tone [of the songs of the slaves] was a
testimony against slavery, and a prayer to God for
deliverance from chains.
*Narrative of the Life of Frederick Douglass
[1845], ch. 2*

[1]Translated by ALEXANDER DRU.

12 You have seen how a man was made a slave; you
shall see how a slave was made a man.
Ibid. ch. 10

13 What, to the American slave, is your Fourth of
July? I answer: A day that reveals to him, more than
all other days in the year, the gross injustice and
cruelty to which he is the constant victim. To him
your celebration is a sham.
Speech at Rochester, New York [July 4, 1852]

14 You profess to believe that "of one blood God
made all nations of men to dwell on the face of all
the earth"—and hath commanded all men, everywhere, to love one another—yet you notoriously
hate (and glory in your hatred!) all men whose skins
are not colored like your own!   *Ibid.*

15 The ground which a colored man occupies in this
country is, every inch of it, sternly disputed.
*Speech at the American and Foreign
Anti-Slavery Society annual meeting, New York
City [May 1853]*

16 The whole history of the progress of human liberty shows that all concessions yet made to her august claims have been born of earnest struggle.
. . . If there is no struggle, there is no progress.
Those who profess to favor freedom, and yet deprecate agitation, are men who want crops without plowing up the ground, they want rain without
thunder and lightning. They want the ocean without the awful roar of its many waters.
*Speech at Canandaigua, New York [August 3,
1857]*

17 The destiny of the colored American . . . is the
destiny of America.[2]
*Speech at the Emancipation League, Boston
[February 12, 1862]*

18 The relation subsisting between the white and
colored people of this country is the great, paramount, imperative, and all-commanding question
for this age and nation to solve.[2]
*Speech at the Church of the Puritans, New
York City [May 1863]*

19 Despite of it all, the Negro remains . . . cool,
strong, imperturbable, and cheerful.
*Speech on the twenty-first anniversary of
Emancipation in the District of Columbia,
Washington, D.C. [April 1883]*

20 In all the relations of life and death, we are met
by the color line.
*Speech at the Convention of Colored Men,
Louisville, Kentucky [September 24, 1883]*

21 No man can put a chain about the ankle of his
fellow man without at last finding the other end
fastened about his own neck.
*Speech at Civil Rights Mass Meeting,
Washington, D.C. [October 22, 1883]*

[2]See Du Bois, 604:19.

1   The life of the nation is secure only while the nation is honest, truthful, and virtuous.
> *Speech on the twenty-third anniversary of Emancipation in the District of Columbia, Washington, D.C. [April 1885]*

2   Where justice is denied, where poverty is enforced, where ignorance prevails, and where any one class is made to feel that society is in an organized conspiracy to oppress, rob, and degrade them, neither persons nor property will be safe.
> *Speech on the twenty-fourth anniversary of Emancipation in the District of Columbia, Washington, D.C. [April 1886]*

George Duffield
1818–1888

3 Stand up!—stand up for Jesus!
> *Hymn*

William Maxwell Evarts
1818–1901

4   The pious ones of Plymouth, who, reaching the Rock, first fell upon their own knees and then upon the aborigines.[1]
> *From* HENRY WATTERSON *in the Louisville Courier-Journal [July 4, 1913]*

Karl Marx
1818–1883

5   Religion . . . is the opium of the people.
> *Critique of the Hegelian Philosophy of Right [1844], introduction*

6   Hegel remarks somewhere that all great world-historic facts and personages appear, so to speak, twice. He forgot to add: the first time as tragedy, the second time as farce.
> *The Eighteenth Brumaire of Louis Napoleon [1852],[2] pt. 1*

7   What was new in what I did was: (1) to demonstrate that the *existence of classes* is tied only to *definite historical phases of development of production;* (2) that the class struggle necessarily leads to the *dictatorship of the proletariat;* (3) that this dictatorship is only a transition to the *dissolution of all classes* and leads to the formation of a *classless society.*
> *Letter to Joseph Weydemeyer [March 5, 1852][2]*

8   Nothing can have value without being an object of utility. If it be useless, the labor contained in it is useless, cannot be reckoned as labor, and cannot therefore create value.
> *Capital[3] [1867–1883], pt. II, ch. 3*

9   The intellectual desolation, artificially produced by converting immature human beings into mere machines.
> *Ibid. 10*

10   When commercial capital occupies a position of unquestioned ascendancy, it everywhere constitutes a system of plunder.
> *Ibid. 21*

11   From each according to his abilities, to each according to his needs.[4]
> *Critique of the Gotha Program [1875]*

12   The philosophers have only interpreted the world in various ways. The point, however, is to change it.[5]
> *Theses on Feuerbach [1888], xi*

13   All I know is that I am not a Marxist.[6]
> *Quoted in* FRIEDRICH ENGELS, *Letter to Conrad Schmidt [August 3, 1890]*

Karl Marx
1818–1883
and
Friedrich Engels
1820–1895

14   A specter is haunting Europe[7]—the specter of Communism. All the powers of old Europe have entered into a holy alliance to exorcise this specter: Pope and Czar, Meternich and Guizot, French Radicals and German police spies.
> *The Communist Manifesto [1848],[8] opening lines*

15   The history of all hitherto existing society is the history of class struggles. Freeman and slave, patrician and plebeian, lord and serf, guild master and journeyman, in a word, oppressor and oppressed, stood in constant opposition to each other, carried on an uninterrupted, now hidden, now open fight, a

---

[1]This pun has also been attributed to Oliver Wendell Holmes, Bill Nye, and George Frisbie Hoar.
See William Bradford, 240:8.
[2]Translated by SAUL K. PADOVER.

[3]Abridged edition prepared by JULIAN BORCHARDT, translated by STEPHEN L. TRASK.
[4]This phrase is in quotation marks, and it is believed that Marx is quoting or paraphrasing either Louis Blanc [1811–1882] or Morelly [fl. 1773]:
Let each produce according to his aptitudes and his force; let each consume according to his need.—LOUIS BLANC, *Organisation du Travail* [1840]
Nothing in society will belong to anyone, either as a personal possession or as capital goods, except the things for which the person has immediate use, for either his needs, his pleasures, or his daily work. Every citizen will make his particular contribution to the activities of the community according to his capacity, his talent and his age; it is on this basis that his duties will be determined, in conformity with the distributive laws.—MORELLY, *Le Code de la Nature* [1755]
See *Acts 4:35, 40:47.*
[5]Inscribed on his tomb at Highgate Cemetery, London.
[6]Translated by DONNA TORR.
[7]See Havel, 768:7.
[8]Translated by SAMUEL MOORE.

fight that each time ended, either in a revolutionary reconstitution of society at large, or in the common ruin of the contending classes.

The Communist Manifesto, sec. 1

1   The executive of the modern state is but a committee for managing the common affairs of the whole bourgeoisie.[1] The bourgeoisie has, historically, played a most revolutionary role.   *Ibid.*

2   The bourgeoisie, by the rapid improvement of all instruments of production, by the immensely facilitated means of communication, draws all, even the most barbarian, nations into civilization.   *Ibid.*

3   Of all the classes that stand face to face with the bourgeoisie today, the proletariat alone is a really revolutionary class. The other classes decay and finally disappear in the race of modern industry; the proletariat is its special and essential product.[2]
Ibid.

4   In this sense, the theory of the Communists may be summed up in the single sentence: Abolition of private property.   *Ibid. 2*

5   In proportion as the antagonism between classes within the nation vanishes, the hostility of one nation to another will come to an end.   *Ibid.*

6   The ruling ideas of each age have ever been the ideas of its ruling class.   *Ibid.*

7   The communists disdain to conceal their views and aims. They openly declare that their ends can be obtained only by forcible overthrow of all existing social conditions. Let the ruling classes tremble at a communist revolution. The proletarians have nothing to lose but their chains. They have a world to win. Working men of all countries, unite![3]
Ibid. 4

John Mason Neale
1818–1866

8 Good King Wenceslas looked out
On the feast of Stephen,
When the snow lay round about,
Deep and crisp and even.
Good King Wenceslas, st. 1

9 Brief life is here our portion.
Hymn from the Latin of SAINT BERNARD OF
CLUNY *[c. 1145], pt. II, Hic Breve Vivitur
[translated 1851], st. 1*

[1]By bourgeoisie is meant the class of modern capitalists, owners of the means of social production and employers of wage labor.—ENGELS, *notes to The Communist Manifesto* [1888 edition]

[2]By proletariat [is meant] the class of modern wage laborers who, having no means of production of their own, are reduced to selling their labor power in order to live.—ENGELS, *notes to The Communist Manifesto* [1888 edition]

[3]More familiar as: Workers of the world, unite!

10 Jerusalem the golden, with milk and honey blest,
Beneath thy contemplation sink heart and voice oppressed.
Ibid. III, Urbs Syon Aurea [translated 1858], st. 1

11 O come, O come, Emmanuel,
And ransom captive Israel.
*Hymn from the Latin, Veni, Veni, Emmanuel
[twelfth century], st. 1 [translated 1861]*

Francis Edward Smedley
1818–1864

12   You are looking as fresh as paint.
Frank Fairlegh [1850], ch. 41

13   All's fair in love and war.[4]   *Ibid. 50*

Ivan Sergeyevich Turgenev
1818–1883

14   A nihilist is a man who does not bow to any authorities, who does not take any principle on trust, no matter with what respect that principle is surrounded.   *Fathers and Sons [1862],[5] ch. 5*

15   That vague, crepuscular time, the time of regrets that resemble hopes, of hopes that resemble regrets, when youth has passed, but old age has not yet arrived.   *Ibid. 7*

16   I share no man's opinions; I have my own.
Ibid. 13

17   The courage not to believe in anything.
Ibid. 14

18   A picture shows me at a glance what it takes dozens of pages of a book to expound.[6]
Ibid. 16

19   Whatever a man prays for, he prays for a miracle. Every prayer reduces itself to this: "Great God, grant that twice two be not four."   *Prayer*

20   In days of doubt, in days of sad brooding on my country's fate, thou alone art my rod and my staff —mighty, true, free Russian speech! But for thee, how not to fall into despair, seeing all that happens at home? Yet who can think that such a tongue is not given to a great people?   *Senilia [1882]*

Arthur Hugh Clough
1819–1861

21 Grace is given of God, but knowledge is bought in the market.
The Bothie of Tober-na-Vuolich [1848], pt. IV

[4]All policy's allowed in war and love.—CENTLIVRE, *Love at a Venture* [1706], *act I*

[5]Translated by HARRY STEVENS.

[6]See Anonymous, 782:21.

1 A world where nothing is had for nothing.
Ibid. VIII

2 And almost everyone when age,
Disease, or sorrows strike him,
Inclines to think there is a God,
Or something very like Him.
Dipsychus [1862], pt. I, sc. v

3 Say not the struggle nought availeth,
The labour and the wounds are vain,
The enemy faints not, nor faileth,
And as things have been, things remain.

If hopes were dupes, fears may be liars;
It may be, in yon smoke concealed,
Your comrades chase e'en now the fliers,
And, but for you, possess the field.

For while the tired waves, vainly breaking,
Seem here no painful inch to gain,
Far back through creeks and inlets making
Came, silent, flooding in, the main,

And not by eastern windows only,
When daylight comes, comes in the light,
In front the sun climbs slow, how slowly,
But westward, look, the land is bright.
Say Not the Struggle Nought Availeth [1862]

4 No graven images may be
Worshipped, except the currency.
The Latest Decalogue [1862], l. 3

5 Thou shalt not covet, but tradition
Approves all forms of competition.
Ibid. l. 19

George Eliot [Marian Evans Cross]
1819–1880

6 'Tis God gives skill,
But not without men's hands: He could not make
Antonio Stradivari's violins
Without Antonio.
Stradivarius

7 O may I join the choir invisible
Of those immortal dead who live again
In minds made better by their presence.
O May I Join the Choir Invisible

8 These fellow mortals, every one, must be accepted as they are. *Adam Bede [1859], ch. 17*

9 There's no real making amends in this world, any more nor you can mend a wrong subtraction by doing your addition right. *Ibid. 18*

10 It's but little good you'll do a-watering the last year's crops. *Ibid.*

11 It was a pity he couldna be hatched o'er again, an' hatched different. *Ibid.*

12 A patronizing disposition always has its meaner side. *Ibid. 27*

13 It's them that take advantage that get advantage i' this world. *Ibid. 32*

14 He was like a cock who thought the sun had risen to hear him crow. *Ibid. 33*

15 Deep, unspeakable suffering may well be called a baptism, a regeneration, the initiation into a new state. *Ibid. 42*

16 We hand folks over to God's mercy, and show none ourselves. *Ibid.*

17 I'm not denyin' the women are foolish; God Almighty made 'em to match the men. *Ibid. 53*

18 The law's made to take care o' raskills.
The Mill on the Floss [1860], bk. III, ch. 4

19 There is no hopelessness so sad as that of early youth, when the soul is made up of wants, and has no long memories, no superadded life in the life of others. *Ibid. 5*

20 Not let them want bread, but only require them to eat it with bitter herbs.[1] *Ibid. IV, 1*

21 I've never any pity for conceited people, because I think they carry their comfort about with them.[2]
Ibid. V, 4

22 The happiest women, like the happiest nations, have no history.[3] *Ibid. VI, 3*

23 Nothing is so good as it seems beforehand.
Silas Marner [1861], ch. 18

24 In our springtime every day has its hidden growths in the mind, as it has in the earth when the little folded blades are getting ready to pierce the ground. *Felix Holt, the Radical [1866], ch. 18*

25 One way of getting an idea of our fellow-countrymen's miseries is to go and look at their pleasures.
Ibid. 28

26 Prophecy is the most gratuitous form of error.
Middlemarch [1871–1872], ch. 10

27 If we had a keen vision of all that is ordinary in human life, it would be like hearing the grass grow or the squirrel's heart beat, and we should die of that roar which is the other side of silence. *Ibid. 22*

28 If youth is the season of hope, it is often so only in the sense that our elders are hopeful about us.
Ibid. 55

29 There is no creature whose inward being is so strong that it is not greatly determined by what lies outside it. *Ibid. Finale*

30 Hostesses who entertain much must make up their parties as ministers make up their cabinets, on grounds other than personal liking.
Daniel Deronda [1876], bk. I, ch. 5

[1]See *Exodus* 12:8, 8:37.
[2]There is not enough of love and goodness in the world to throw any of it away on conceited people.—NIETZSCHE, *Human, All Too Human* [1878], 129
[3]See Carlyle, 413:16.

1   A difference of taste in jokes is a great strain on the affections.   *Daniel Deronda, bk. II, ch. 15*

2   Men's men: gentle or simple, they're much of a muchness.   *Ibid. IV, 31*

3   Blessed is the man who, having nothing to say, abstains from giving in words evidence of the fact.
Impressions of Theophrastus Such [1879]

4   Biographies generally are a disease of English literature.
Letter to Mrs. Thomas Adolphus Trollope [December 19, 1879]

Thomas Dunn English
1819–1902

5 Oh! don't you remember sweet Alice, Ben Bolt?
Sweet Alice, whose hair was so brown.
Ben Bolt [1843]

Julia Ward Howe
1819–1910

6 Mine eyes have seen the glory of the coming of
the Lord;
He is trampling out the vintage where the grapes
of wrath are stored;[1]
He hath loosed the fateful lightning of His terrible,
swift sword;
His truth is marching on.
Battle Hymn of the Republic [1862], st. 1

7 In the beauty of the lilies Christ was born across
the sea,
With a glory in His bosom that transfigures you
and me;
As He died to make men holy, let us die to make
men free.
Ibid. st. 5

Charles Kingsley[2]
1819–1875

8   Give me the political economist, the sanitary reformer, the engineer; and take your saints and virgins, relics and miracles. The spinning-jenny and the railroad, Cunard's liners and the electric telegraph, are to me . . . signs that we are, on some points at least, in harmony with the universe.
Yeast [1848], ch. 5

9 Oh Mary, go and call the cattle home . . .
Across the sands of Dee.
The Sands of Dee [1849], st. 1

10 The cruel crawling foam.[3]
Ibid. st. 4

---

[1]See *Isaiah 63:3, 28:7,* and *Revelation 19:15, 47:35.*
[2]See Anonymous, 780:n7.
[3]See Ruskin, 487:13.

---

11 For men must work, and women must weep,
And there's little to earn and many to keep,
Though the harbor bar be moaning.
The Three Fishers [1851], st. 1

12 And the sooner it's over, the sooner to sleep;
And good-bye to the bar and its moaning.
Ibid. st. 3

13 Be good, sweet maid, and let who will be clever;
Do noble things, not dream them, all day long;
And so make Life, and Death, and that For Ever
One grand sweet song.
A Farewell [1856], st. 3

14 Clear and cool, clear and cool,
By laughing shallow, and dreaming pool.
Water Babies [1863]. Song I, st. 1

15 When all the world is young, lad,
And all the trees are green;
And every goose a swan, lad,
And every lass a queen;
Then hey for boot and horse, lad,
And round the world away:
Young blood must have its course, lad,
And every dog his day.
Ibid. Song II, st. 1

16 God grant you find one face there
You loved when all was young!
Ibid.

17   Science frees us in many ways . . . from the bodily terror which the savage feels. But she replaces that, in the minds of many, by a moral terror which is far more overwhelming.
Sermon, The Meteor Shower [November 26, 1866]

18   Some say that the age of chivalry is past, that the spirit of romance is dead. The age of chivalry is never past, so long as there is a wrong left unredressed on earth, or a man or woman left to say, I will redress that wrong, or spend my life in the attempt.
From Charles Kingsley: His Letters and Memories of His Life [1879], vol. II, ch. 28

James Russell Lowell
1819–1891

19 Blessed are the horny hands of toil!
A Glance Behind the Curtain [1843]

20 They are slaves who fear to speak
For the fallen and the weak.
Stanzas on Freedom [1843], st. 4

21 They are slaves who dare not be
In the right with two or three.
Ibid.

22 The nurse of full-grown souls is solitude.
Columbus [1844]

1 Once to every man and nation comes the moment
　　to decide,
　In the strife of Truth with Falsehood, for the
　　good or evil side.
The Present Crisis [1844], st. 5

2 Truth forever on the scaffold, Wrong forever on
　　the throne—
　Yet that scaffold sways the future, and, behind the
　　dim unknown,
　Standeth God within the shadow, keeping watch
　　above his own.
Ibid. st. 8

3 Not only around our infancy
　Doth heaven with all its splendors lie;
　Daily, with souls that cringe and plot,
　We Sinais climb and know it not.
*The Vision of Sir Launfal [1848], prelude to
pt. I, st. 2*

4 For a cap and bells our lives we pay,
　Bubbles we buy with a whole soul's tasking:
　'Tis heaven alone that is given away,
　'Tis only God may be had for the asking.
Ibid. st. 4

5 And what is so rare as a day in June?
　Then, if ever, come perfect days.
Ibid. st. 5

6 In creating, the only hard thing's to begin;
　A grass-blade's no easier to make than an oak.
A Fable for Critics [1848]

7 And I honor the man who is willing to sink
　Half his present repute for the freedom to think,
　And, when he has thought, be his cause strong or
　　weak,
　Will risk t' other half for the freedom to speak.
Ibid.

8 There comes Poe, with his raven, like Barnaby
　　Rudge,
　Three fifths of him genius and two fifths sheer
　　fudge.[1]
Ibid.

9 Nature fits all her children with something to do,
　He who would write and can't write, can surely
　　review.
Ibid.

10 Ez fer war, I call it murder—
　There you hev it plain an' flat;
　I don't want to go no furder
　Than my Testament fer that.
The Biglow Papers. Series I [1848], no. 1, st. 5

11 　　You've gut to git up airly
　Ef you want to take in God.
Ibid.

12 A marciful Providunce fashioned us holler
　O' purpose thet we might our principles swaller.
Ibid. 4, st. 2

13 I du believe with all my soul
　In the gret Press's freedom,
　To pint the people to the goal
　An' in the traces lead 'em.
Ibid. 6, st. 7

14 I *don't* believe in princerple,
　But oh I *du* in interest.
Ibid. st. 9

15 God makes sech nights, all white an' still,
　Fur'z you can look or listen,
　Moonshine an' snow on field an' hill,
　All silence an' all glisten.
Ibid. Series II [1866]. The Courtin', st. 1

16 His heart kep' goin' pity-pat,
　But hern went pity-Zekle.
Ibid. st. 15

17 My gran'ther's rule was safer 'n 'tis to crow:
　Don't never prophesy—onless ye know.
Ibid. No. 2

18 It's 'most enough to make a deacon swear.
Ibid.

19 Ef you want peace, the thing you've gut tu du
　Is jes' to show you're up to fightin', tu.
Ibid.

20 Bad work follers ye ez long's ye live.
Ibid.

21 No, never say nothin' without you're compelled
　　tu,
　An' then don't say nothin' thet you can be held
　　tu.
Ibid. 5

22 They came three thousand miles, and died,
　To keep the Past upon its throne;
　Unheard, beyond the ocean tide,
　Their English mother made her moan.
*Graves of Two English Soldiers on Concord
Battleground [1849], st. 3*

23 　　There is nothing so desperately monotonous as
　the sea, and I no longer wonder at the cruelty of
　pirates.　　*Fireside Travels [1864]. At Sea*

24 　　It is by presence of mind in untried emergencies
　that the native metal of a man is tested.
Abraham Lincoln [1864]

25 When I was a beggarly boy,
　And lived in a cellar damp,
　I had not a friend nor a toy,
　But I had Aladdin's lamp.
Aladdin [1868], st. 1

26 Though old the thought and oft expressed,
　'Tis his at last who says it best.
For an Autograph [1868]

27 For me Fate gave, whate'er she else denied,
　A nature sloping to the southern side.
*Epistle to George William Curtis [1874].
Postscript*

[1]See Poe, 451.

1   The soil out of which such men as he are made is good to be born on, good to live on, good to die for and to be buried in.

> *Garfield [September 24, 1881]*

2   There is no good in arguing with the inevitable. The only argument available with an east wind is to put on your overcoat.

> *Democracy [October 6, 1884]*

3   These pearls of thought in Persian gulfs were bred,
Each softly lucent as a rounded moon;
The diver Omar plucked them from their bed,
Fitzgerald strung them on an English thread.

> *In a Copy of Omar Khayyám [1888], st. 1*

4   Things always seem fairer when we look back at them, and it is out of that inaccessible tower of the past that Longing leans and beckons.

> *Literary Essays, vol. I [1864–1890]. A Few Bits of Roman Mosaic*

5   Mishaps are like knives, that either serve us or cut us, as we grasp them by the blade or the handle.

> *Ibid. Cambridge Thirty Years Ago*

6   What a sense of security in an old book which Time has criticized for us!

> *Ibid. A Library of Old Authors*

7   There is no better ballast for keeping the mind steady on its keel, and saving it from all risk of crankiness, than business.

> *Ibid. II [1870–1890]. New England Two Centuries Ago*

8   Puritanism, believing itself quick with the seed of religious liberty, laid, without knowing it, the egg of democracy.

> *Ibid.*

9   It was in making education not only common to all, but in some sense compulsory on all, that the destiny of the free republics of America was practically settled.

> *Ibid.*

10   Every man feels instinctively that all the beautiful sentiments in the world weigh less than a single lovely action.

> *Ibid.*

11   An umbrella is of no avail against a Scotch mist.

> *Ibid. III [1870–1890]. On a Certain Condescension in Foreigners*

12   A wise skepticism is the first attribute of a good critic.

> *Ibid. Shakespeare Once More*

Herman Melville

1819–1891

13   Genius all over the world stands hand in hand, and one shock of recognition runs the whole circle round.

> *Hawthorne and His Mosses [1850]*

14   Are there no Moravians in the Moon, that not a missionary has yet visited this poor pagan planet of ours, to civilize civilization and christianize Christendom?

> *White Jacket [1850], ch. 64*

15   The grand truth about Nathaniel Hawthorne. He says NO! in thunder; but the Devil himself cannot make him say *yes.*

> *Letter to Nathaniel Hawthorne [April 16, 1851]*

16   Call me Ishmael.

> *Moby-Dick [1851], ch. 1*

17   Let the most absent-minded of men be plunged in his deepest reveries—stand that man upon his legs, set his feet a-going, and he will infallibly lead you to water, if water there be in all that region. . . . Meditation and water are wedded forever.

> *Ibid.*

18   There floated into my inmost soul, endless processions of the whale, and, mid most of them all, one grand hooded phantom, like a snow hill in the air.

> *Ibid.*

19   Better sleep with a sober cannibal than a drunken Christian.

> *Ibid. 3*

20   Woe to him who seeks to pour oil upon the waters when God has brewed them into a gale! Woe to him who seeks to please rather than to appall!

> *Ibid. 9*

21   A whale-ship was my Yale College and my Harvard.

> *Ibid. 24*

22   Thou great democratic God! . . . who didst pick up Andrew Jackson from the pebbles; who didst hurl him upon a war-horse; who didst thunder him higher than a throne!

> *Ibid. 26*

23   And this is what ye have shipped for, men! to chase that white whale on both sides of land, and over all sides of earth, till he spouts black blood and rolls fin out.

> *Ibid. 36*

24   All visible objects, man, are but as pasteboard masks . . . strike, strike through the mask!

> *Ibid.*

25   All that most maddens and torments; all that stirs up the lees of things; all truth with malice in it; all that cracks the sinews and cakes the brain; all the subtle demonisms of life and thought; all evil, to crazy Ahab, were visibly personified, and made practically assailable in Moby Dick. He piled upon the whale's white hump the sum of all the general rage and hate felt by his whole race from Adam down; and then, as if his chest had been a mortar, he burst his hot heart's shell upon it.

> *Ibid. 41*

26   Though in many of its aspects this visible world seems formed in love, the invisible spheres were formed in fright.

> *Ibid. 42*

27   For as this appalling ocean surrounds the verdant land, so in the soul of man there lies one insular Tahiti, full of peace and joy, but encompassed by all the horrors of the half known life.

> *Ibid. 58*

28   By heaven, man, we are turned round and round in this world, like yonder windlass, and Fate is the handspike.

> *Ibid. 132*

1 All collapsed, and the great shroud of the sea rolled on as it rolled five thousand years ago.
Ibid. 135

2 What we take to be our strongest tower of delight, only stands at the caprice of the minutest event —the falling of a leaf, the hearing of a voice, or the receipt of one little bit of paper scratched over with a few small characters by a sharpened feather.
Pierre [1852], bk. IV

3 One trembles to think of that mysterious thing in the soul, which seems to acknowledge no human jurisdiction, but in spite of the individual's own innocent self, will still dream horrid dreams, and mutter unmentionable thoughts.
Ibid.

4 A smile is the chosen vehicle for all ambiguities.
Ibid.

5 I would prefer not to.
Bartleby the Scrivener [1856]

6 The poor old Past,
The Future's slave.
Battle-Pieces [1866]. The Conflict of Convictions, st. 6

7 All wars are boyish, and are fought by boys.
Ibid. The March into Virginia

8 What troops
Of generous boys in happiness thus bred—
Saturnians through life's Tempe led,
Went from the North and came from the South,
With golden mottoes in the mouth,
To lie down midway on a bloody bed.
Ibid. On the Slain Collegians, st. 2

9 God bless Captain Vere!
Billy Budd, Sailor [1924], ch. 25

10 But me they'll lash in hammock, drop me deep.
Fathoms down, fathoms down, how I'll dream
fast asleep.
I feel it stealing now. Sentry, are you there?
Just ease these darbies[1] at the wrist,
And roll me over fair!
I am sleepy, and the oozy weeds about me twist.
Ibid.

John Ruskin
1819–1900

11 He is the greatest artist who has embodied, in the sum of his works, the greatest number of the greatest ideas. *Modern Painters, vol. I [1843], pt. I, ch. 2*

12 To know anything well involves a profound sensation of ignorance. *Ibid. 3*

13 The foam is not cruel.[2] . . . The state of mind which attributes to it these characters of a living creature is one in which the reason is unhinged by grief. All violent feelings . . . produce in us a falseness in

[1]Manacles.
[2]See Kingsley, 484:10.

all our impressions of external things, which I would generally characterize as the "Pathetic Fallacy."
Ibid. III [1856], pt. IV, ch. 12

14 The essence of lying is in deception, not in words.
Ibid. V, pt. IX, ch. 7

15 Remember that the most beautiful things in the world are the most useless; peacocks and lilies for instance.
The Stones of Venice [1851–1853], vol. I, ch. 2

16 All great art is the work of the whole living creature, body and soul, and chiefly of the soul.
Ibid. 4

17 Blue color is everlastingly appointed by the Deity to be a source of delight.
Lectures on Architecture and Painting [1853], I

18 There is no wealth but life.
Unto This Last [1862], sec. 77

19 Let us reform our schools, and we shall find little reform needed in our prisons. *Ibid. essay 2*

20 Value is the life-giving power of anything; cost, the quantity of labor required to produce it; price, the quantity of labor which its possessor will take in exchange for it. *Munera Pulveris [1862], ch. 1*

21 There is no law of history any more than of a kaleidoscope.
Letter to James Anthony Froude [February 1864]

22 Life being very short, and the quiet hours of it few, we ought to waste none of them in reading valueless books.
Sesame and Lilies [1865], preface

23 All books are divisible into two classes: the books of the hour, and the books of all time.
Ibid. Of Kings' Treasuries, sec. 8

24 Borrowers are nearly always ill-spenders, and it is with lent money that all evil is mainly done and all unjust war protracted.
The Crown of Wild Olive [1866], lecture 1

25 Give a little love to a child, and you get a great deal back. *Ibid.*

26 Taste . . . is the *only* morality. . . . Tell me what you like, and I'll tell you what you are.
Ibid. 2

27 Life without industry is guilt, industry without art is brutality.
Lectures on Art [1870]. III, The Relation of Art to Morals

28 Every increased possession loads us with a new weariness. *The Eagle's Nest [1872], ch. 5*

29 Architecture . . . the adaptation of form to resist force. *Val d'Arno [1874], ch. 6*

30 The first duty of government is to see that people have food, fuel, and clothes. The second, that they have means of moral and intellectual education.
Fors Clavigera [1876], letter 67

1   Great nations write their autobiographies in three manuscripts—the book of their deeds, the book of their words, and the book of their art.
St. Mark's Rest [1877], preface

Max Schneckenburger
1819–1849

2 Dear Fatherland, no danger thine:
Firm stands thy watch along the Rhine.[1]
The Watch on the Rhine (Die Wacht am Rhein) [1840], chorus

Victoria
1819–1901

3   I will be good.
On first seeing a chart of the line of succession to the throne [March 11, 1830]

4   *Great* events make me quiet and calm; it is only trifles that irritate my nerves.
Letter to King Leopold of Belgium [April 4, 1848]

5   We are not interested in the possibilities of defeat.
To A. J. Balfour [December 1899]

6   We are not amused.
Upon seeing an imitation of herself by the Honorable Alexander Grantham Yorke, groom-in-waiting to the Queen. From Notebooks of a Spinster Lady [January 2, 1900]

7   He [William Gladstone] speaks to me as if I was a public meeting.
From George W. E. Russell, Collections and Recollections [1898], ch. 14

William Ross Wallace
1819–1881

8 The hand that rocks the cradle
Is the hand that rules the world.
The Hand That Rules the World, st. 1

Walt Whitman
1819–1892

9   The United States themselves are essentially the greatest poem.
Preface to the first edition of Leaves of Grass [1855][2]

---

[1]Lieb Vaterland, magst ruhig sein,/ Fest steht und treu die Wacht am Rhein.

[2]The first edition of *Leaves of Grass,* published anonymously by its author in July 1855, contained a long preface and twelve untitled poems. Over the next four decades Whitman revised and enlarged his book. The texts and sequence of the verse quotations here are those of the so-called Deathbed Edition [Philadelphia, 1891–92].

10   All beauty comes from beautiful blood and a beautiful brain.
Ibid.

11   This is what you shall do: Love the earth and sun and the animals, despise riches, give alms to every one that asks, stand up for the stupid and crazy, devote your income and labor to others, hate tyrants, argue not concerning God.
Ibid.

12   The proof of a poet is that his country absorbs him as affectionately as he has absorbed it.
Ibid.

13 One's-Self I sing, a simple separate person,
Yet utter the word Democratic, the word
En-Masse.
One's-Self I Sing

14   O to be self-balanced for contingencies,
To confront night, storms, hunger, ridicule,
accidents, rebuffs, as the trees and animals
do.
Me Imperturbe

15 I hear America singing, the varied carols I hear.
I Hear America Singing

16 I celebrate myself, and sing myself,
And what I assume you shall assume,
For every atom belonging to me as good belongs
to you.

I loafe and invite my soul,
I lean and loafe at my ease observing a spear of
summer grass.
Song of Myself, 1

17 Stop this day and night with me and you shall
possess the origin of all poems.
Ibid. 2

18 Swiftly arose and spread around me the peace and
knowledge that pass all the argument of the
earth,
And I know that the hand of God is the promise
of my own,
And I know that the spirit of God is the brother
of my own,
And that all the men ever born are also my
brothers, and the women my sisters and
lovers,
And that a kelson of the creation is love.
Ibid. 5

19 A child said *What is the grass?* fetching it to me
with full hands;
How could I answer the child? I do not know
what it is any more than he.

I guess it must be the flag of my disposition, out of
hopeful green stuff woven.
Ibid. 6

20 And now it seems to me the beautiful uncut hair
of graves.
Ibid.

1 Has any one supposed it lucky to be born?
  I hasten to inform him or her it is just as lucky to
    die, and I know it.
                                                    Ibid. 7

2 And the look of the bay mare shames silliness out
  of me.
                                                    Ibid. 13

3 This is the grass that grows wherever the land is
    and the water is,
  This is the common air that bathes the globe.
                                                    Ibid. 17

4 Have you heard that it was good to gain the day?
  I also say it is good to fall, battles are lost in the
    same spirit in which they are won.
                                                    Ibid. 18

5 I find no sweeter fat than sticks to my own bones.
                                                    Ibid. 20

6 My foothold is tenon'd and mortis'd in granite,
  I laugh at what you call dissolution,
  And I know the amplitude of time.
                                                    Ibid.

7 I am the poet of the Body and I am the poet of
    the Soul.
                                                    Ibid. 21

8 I am he that walks with the tender and growing
    night,
  I call to the earth and sea half-held by the night.

  Press close bare-bosom'd night—press close
    magnetic nourishing night!
  Night of south winds—night of the large few
    stars!
  Still nodding night—mad naked summer night.
                                                    Ibid. 21

9 Walt Whitman, a kosmos, of Manhattan the son,
  Turbulent, fleshy, sensual, eating, drinking and
    breeding,
  No sentimentalist, no stander above men and
    women or apart from them,
  No more modest than immodest.

  Unscrew the locks from the doors!
  Unscrew the doors themselves from their jambs!
                                                    Ibid. 24

10 The scent of these arm-pits aroma finer than
    prayer,
  This head more than churches, bibles, and all the
    creeds.
                                                    Ibid.

11 I dote on myself, there is that lot of me and all so
    luscious.
                                                    Ibid.

12 Steep'd amid honey'd morphine, my windpipe
    throttled in fakes of death.
                                                    Ibid. 26

13 I merely stir, press, feel with my fingers, and am
    happy,

To touch my person to someone else's is about as
    much as I can stand.
                                                    Ibid. 27

14 Logic and sermons never convince,
  The damp of the night drives deeper into my soul.
                                                    Ibid. 30

15 I believe a leaf of grass is no less than the
    journey-work of the stars.
                                                    Ibid. 31

16 I think I could turn and live with animals, they
    are so placid and self-contain'd,
  I stand and look at them long and long.

  They do not sweat and whine about their
    condition,
  They do not lie awake in the dark and weep for
    their sins,
  They do not make me sick discussing their duty to
    God,
  Not one is dissatisfied, not one is demented with
    the mania of owning things,
  Not one kneels to another, nor to his kind that
    lived thousands of years ago,
  Not one is respectable or unhappy over the whole
    earth.
                                                    Ibid. 32

17 I am afoot with my vision.
                                                    Ibid. 33

18 I am the man, I suffer'd, I was there.
                                                    Ibid.

19 Agonies are one of my changes of garments.
                                                    Ibid.

20 I have said that the soul is not more than the
    body,
  And I have said that the body is not more than
    the soul,
  And nothing, not God, is greater to one than
    one's self is,
  And whoever walks a furlong without sympathy
    walks to his own funeral drest in his shroud.
                                                    Ibid. 48

21 Do I contradict myself?
  Very well then I contradict myself,
  (I am large, I contain multitudes.)
                                                    Ibid. 51

22 I sound my barbaric yawp over the roofs of the
    world.
                                                    Ibid. 52

23 I bequeath myself to the dirt to grow from the
    grass I love,
  If you want me again look for me under your
    boot-soles.
                                                    Ibid.

24 If anything is sacred the human body is sacred.
                                                    I Sing the Body Electric, 8

1 Through you I drain the pent-up rivers of myself,
In you I wrap a thousand onward years.
A Woman Waits for Me

2 As Adam early in the morning,
Walking forth from the bower refresh'd with
sleep,
Behold me where I pass, hear my voice, approach,
Touch me, touch the palm of your hand to my
body as I pass,
Be not afraid of my body.
As Adam Early in the Morning

3 Afoot and light-hearted I take to the open road,
Healthy, free, the world before me,
The long brown path before me leading wherever
I choose.

Henceforth I ask not good-fortune, I myself am
good-fortune.
Song of the Open Road, 1

4 The glories strung like beads on my smallest
sights and hearings, on the walk in the street
and the passage over the river.
Crossing Brooklyn Ferry, 2

5 A great city is that which has the greatest men
and women,
If it be a few ragged huts it is still the greatest city
in the whole world.
Song of the Broad-Axe, 4

6 Come Muse migrate from Greece and Ionia,
Cross out please those immensely overpaid
accounts,
That matter of Troy and Achilles' wrath, and
Aeneas', Odysseus' wanderings,
Placard "Removed" and "To Let" on the rocks of
your snowy Parnassus.
Song of the Exposition, 2

7 We must march my darlings, we must bear the
brunt of danger,
We the youthful sinewy races, all the rest on us
depend,
Pioneers! O pioneers!
Pioneers! O Pioneers!

8 Out of the cradle endlessly rocking,
Out of the mocking-bird's throat, the musical
shuttle,
Out of the Ninth-month midnight.
Out of the Cradle Endlessly Rocking

9 When I heard the learn'd astronomer,
When the proofs, the figures, were ranged in
columns before me,
When I was shown the charts and diagrams, to
add, divide, and measure them,
When I sitting heard the astronomer where he
lectured with much applause in the
lecture-room,
How soon unaccountable I became tired and sick,
Till rising and gliding out I wander'd off by
myself,

In the mystical moist night-air, and from time to
time,
Look'd up in perfect silence at the stars.
When I Heard the Learn'd Astronomer

10 Words! book-words! what are you?
Song of the Banner at Daybreak

11 Young man I think I know you—I think this face
is the face of the Christ himself,
Dead and divine and brother of all, and here
again he lies.
*A Sight in Camp in the Daybreak Gray and
Grim*

12 Many a soldier's loving arms about this neck have
cross'd and rested,
Many a soldier's kiss dwells on these bearded lips.
The Wound-Dresser

13 Give me the splendid silent sun with all his beams
full-dazzling.
Give Me the Splendid Silent Sun, 1

14 Word over all, beautiful as the sky,
Beautiful that war and all its deeds of carnage
must in time be utterly lost,
That the hands of the sisters Death and Night
incessantly softly wash again, and ever again,
this soil'd world;
For my enemy is dead, a man divine as myself is
dead.
Reconciliation

15 When lilacs last in the dooryard bloom'd,
And the great star early droop'd in the western
sky in the night,
I mourn'd, and yet shall mourn with
ever-returning spring.
When Lilacs Last in the Dooryard Bloom'd, 1

16 Nor for you, for one alone,
Blossoms and branches green to coffins all I bring,
For fresh as the morning, thus would I chant a
song for you O sane and sacred death.
Ibid. 7

17 Come lovely and soothing death,
Undulate round the world, serenely arriving,
arriving,
In the day, in the night, to all, to each,
Sooner or later delicate death.
Ibid. 14

18 Dark mother always gliding near with soft feet,
Have none chanted for thee a chant of fullest
welcome?
Ibid.

19 O Captain! my Captain! our fearful trip is done,
The ship has weather'd every rack, the prize we
sought is won,
The port is near, the bells I hear, the people all
exulting.
O Captain! My Captain!, st. 1

1 Exult O shores, and ring O bells!
   But I with mournful tread,
   Walk the deck my Captain lies,
   Fallen cold and dead.
                                    Ibid. st. 3

2 There was a child went forth every day,
   And the first object he look'd upon, that object he
      became.
                        There Was a Child Went Forth

3 The horizon's edge, the flying sea-crow, the
      fragrance of salt marsh and shore mud,
   These became part of that child who went forth
      every day, and who now goes, and will
      always go forth every day.
                                    Ibid.

4 To me every hour of the light and dark is a
      miracle,
   Every cubic inch of space is a miracle.
                                    Miracles

5 A batter'd, wreck'd old man,
   Thrown on this savage shore, far from home,
   Pent by the sea and dark rebellious brows, twelve
      dreary months,
   Sore, stiff with many toils, sicken'd and nigh to
      death,
   I take my way along the island's edge,
   Venting a heavy heart.
                                    Prayer of Columbus

6 I dream in my dream all the dreams of the other
      dreamers,
   And I become the other dreamers.
                                    The Sleepers, 1

7 I am she who adorn'd herself and folded her hair
      expectantly,
   My truant lover has come, and it is dark.
                                    Ibid.

8 A noiseless patient spider,
   I mark'd where on a little promontory it stood
      isolated,
   Mark'd how to explore the vacant vast
      surrounding,
   It launch'd forth filament, filament, filament out
      of itself,
   Ever unreeling them, ever tirelessly speeding them.
                        A Noiseless Patient Spider

9 Camerado, this is no book,
   Who touches this touches a man.
                                    So Long!

10 I depart from materials,
    I am as one disembodied, triumphant, dead.
                                    Ibid.

11 He [President Abraham Lincoln] has a face like a
    hoosier Michael Angelo, so awful ugly it becomes
    beautiful, with its strange mouth, its deep-cut, criss-
    cross lines, and its doughnut complexion.
                                    Letter [March 19, 1863]

12 Never was there, perhaps, more hollowness of
    heart than at present, and here in the United States.
    Genuine belief seems to have left us.
                                    Democratic Vistas [1871]

13 It [Democracy] is a great word, whose history, I
    suppose, remains unwritten, because that history
    has yet to be enacted.   *Ibid.*

14 *The Real War Will Never Get in the Books.* And
    so good-bye to the war.
                        *Specimen Days [1882]. The Real War Will
                        Never Get in the Books*

15 Such was the war. It was not a quadrille in a
    ball-room. Its interior history will not only never be
    written—its practicality, minutiae of deeds and pas-
    sions, will never even be suggested.   *Ibid.*

16 To have great poets, there must be great audi-
    ences, too.   *Collect [1882]. Notes Left Over*

17 So here I sit in the early candle-light of old age
    —I and my book—casting backward glances over
    our travel'd road.
                        *November Boughs [1888]. A Backward Glance
                        O'er Travel'd Roads*

18 The strongest and sweetest songs yet remain to be
    sung.   *Ibid.*

Susan Brownell Anthony
1820–1906

19 The men and women of the North are slavehold-
    ers, those of the South slaveowners. The guilt rests
    on the North equally with the South.
                Speech on No Union with Slaveholders [1857]

20 Cautious, careful people, always casting about to
    preserve their reputation and social standing, never
    can bring about a reform. Those who are really in
    earnest must be willing to be anything or nothing in
    the world's estimation.
                On the campaign for divorce law reform [1860]

21 Make [your employers] understand that you are
    in their service as workers, not as women.
                        *The Revolution (woman suffrage newspaper),
                        October 8, 1868*

22 Join the union, girls, and together say *Equal Pay
    for Equal Work.*   *Ibid. March 18, 1869*

23 Woman must not depend upon the protection of
    man, but must be taught to protect herself.
                        Speech in San Francisco [July 1871]

24 I shall work for the Republican party and call on
    all women to join me, precisely . . . for what that
    party has done and promises to do for women, noth-
    ing more, nothing less.
                Letter to Elizabeth Cady Stanton [autumn 1872]

25 Here, in the first paragraph of the Declaration [of
    Independence], is the assertion of the natural right of

all to the ballot; for how can "the consent of the governed" be given, if the right to vote be denied?
Is It a Crime for a Citizen of the United States to Vote? Speech [1873] before her trial for voting

1   Marriage, to women as to men, must be a luxury, not a necessity; an incident of life, not all of it. And the only possible way to accomplish this great change is to accord to women equal power in the making, shaping and controlling of the circumstances of life.
Speech on Social Purity [spring 1875]

Dion Boucicault
1820–1890

2   Yes, quit the house and never darken the threshold of its doors again.   *Flying Scud [1866], act I*

Florence Nightingale
1820–1910

3   It may seem a strange principle to enunciate as the very first requirement in a Hospital that it should do the sick no harm.[1]
Notes on Hospitals [1859], Preface

Theodore O'Hara
1820–1867

4 On Fame's eternal camping ground
Their silent tents are spread,
And Glory guards, with solemn round,
The bivouac of the dead.
The Bivouac of the Dead[2] [1847], st. 1

5 Sons of the dark and bloody ground.[3]
Ibid. st. 9

George Frederick Root
1820–1895

6 Tramp! Tramp! Tramp! the boys are marching,
Cheer up, comrades, they will come,
And beneath the starry flag
We shall breathe the air again
Of the free land in our own beloved home.
Tramp! Tramp! Tramp! [1862]

7 Yes, we'll rally round the flag, boys, we'll rally once again,
Shouting the battle cry of Freedom.
The Battle Cry of Freedom [1863]

[1]See Hippocrates, 71:2.
[2]Written to commemorate Americans slain in the battle of Buena Vista [February 22–23, 1847].
[3]Kentucky, from its history as a hunting and burial territory for warring Indian tribes.

Sir William Howard Russell
1820–1907

8   The Russians dashed on towards that thin red-line streak tipped with a line of steel.[4]
To The Times of London from the Crimea, describing the British infantry at Balaklava [October 25, 1854]

William Tecumseh Sherman
1820–1891

9   You cannot qualify war in harsher terms than I will. War is cruelty, and you cannot refine it.
Letter to James M. Calhoun, mayor of Atlanta, and others [September 12, 1864]

10   Hold the fort! I am coming![5]
Attributed signal from Kennesaw Mountain to General John Murray Corse at Allatoona Pass [October 5, 1864]

11   The legitimate object of war is a more perfect peace.   *Speech at St. Louis [July 20, 1865]*

12   War is at best barbarism. . . . Its glory is all moonshine. It is only those who have neither fired a shot nor heard the shrieks and groans of the wounded who cry aloud for blood, more vengeance, more desolation. War is hell.
Attributed to a graduation address at Michigan Military Academy [June 19, 1879]

13   I will not accept if nominated and will not serve if elected.[6]
Message to Republican National Convention [June 5, 1884]

Herbert Spencer
1820–1903

14   Progress, therefore, is not an accident, but a necessity. . . . It is a part of nature.
Social Statics [1851], pt. I, ch. 2

15   Education has for its object the formation of character.   *Ibid. II, 17*

16   The poverty of the incapable, the distresses that come upon the imprudent, the starvation of the idle, and those shoulderings aside of the weak by the

[4]Soon the men of the column began to see that though the scarlet line was slender, it was very rigid and exact. — A. W. KINGLAKE [1809–1891], *Invasion of the Crimea, vol. III, p. 455*
It's "Thin red line of 'eroes" when the drums begin to roll. — KIPLING, *Tommy, st. 3*
See Kipling, 591:17.
[5]He actually said: "Hold out. Relief is coming." General Corse replied: "I am short a cheekbone and an ear, but am able to whip all hell yet."
Hold the fort, for I am coming! — PHILIP PAUL BLISS [1838–1876], *Hold the Fort, refrain*
[6]The familiar version is: If nominated I will not run; if elected I will not serve.

strong, which leave so many "in shallows and in miseries,"[1] are the decrees of a large, farseeing benevolence. *Ibid. III, 25*

1 Opinion is ultimately determined by the feelings, and not by the intellect. *Ibid. IV, 30*

2 No one can be perfectly free till all are free; no one can be perfectly moral till all are moral; no one can be perfectly happy till all are happy. *Ibid.*

3 Every cause produces more than one effect. *Essays on Education [1861]. On Progress: Its Law and Cause*

4 The tyranny of Mrs. Grundy[2] is worse than any other tyranny we suffer under. *Ibid. On Manners and Fashion*

5 Old forms of government finally grow so oppressive that they must be thrown off even at the risk of reigns of terror. *Ibid.*

6 The fact disclosed by a survey of the past that majorities have been wrong must not blind us to the complementary fact that majorities have usually not been entirely wrong. *First Principles [1861]*

7 Volumes might be written upon the impiety of the pious. *Ibid.*

8 We have unmistakable proof that throughout all past time, there has been a ceaseless devouring of the weak by the strong. *Ibid.*

9 This survival of the fittest which I have here sought to express in mechanical terms, is that which Mr. Darwin has called "natural selection, or the preservation of favored races in the struggle for life."[3]
Principles of Biology [1864–1867], pt. III, ch. 12

10 The Republican form of government is the highest form of government: but because of this it requires the highest type of human nature—a type nowhere at present existing. *Essays [1891]. The Americans*

11 The ultimate result of shielding men from the effects of folly is to fill the world with fools. *Ibid. State Tamperings with Money Banks*

12 Time: That which man is always trying to kill, but which ends in killing him. *Definitions*

Harriet Tubman
c. 1820–1913

13 When I found I had crossed that line,[4] I looked at my hands to see if I was the same person. There was such a glory over everything.
To her biographer Sarah H. Bradford [c. 1868]

[1] See Shakespeare, 189:19.
[2] See Thomas Morton, 367:11.
[3] See Darwin, 444:6.
[4] On her first escape from slavery [1845].

14 I started with this idea in my head, "There's two things I've got a right to . . . death or liberty." *Ibid.*

15 'Twant me, 'twas the Lord. I always told him, "I trust to you. I don't know where to go or what to do, but I expect you to lead me," and he always did. *Ibid.*

John Tyndall
1820–1893

16 Heat Considered as a Mode of Motion. *Title of treatise [1863]*

17 Life is a wave, which in no two consecutive moments of its existence is composed of the same particles.[5] *Fragments of Science, vol. II, Vitality*

18 The brightest flashes in the world of thought are incomplete until they have been proved to have their counterparts in the world of fact. *Ibid. Scientific Materialism*

19 Charles Darwin, the Abraham of scientific men —a searcher as obedient to the command of truth as was the patriarch to the command of God. *Ibid. Science and Man*

20 Superstition may be defined as constructive religion which has grown incongruous with intelligence. *Ibid.*

21 Religious feeling is as much a verity as any other part of human consciousness; and against it, on the subjective side, the waves of science beat in vain. *Ibid. Professor Virchow and Evolution*

Henri-Frédéric Amiel
1821–1881

22 To know how to grow old is the masterwork of wisdom, and one of the most difficult chapters in the great art of living. *Journal Intime [1883]*

23 An error is the more dangerous the more truth it contains. *Ibid.*

24 Charm: the quality in others that makes us more satisfied with ourselves. *Ibid.*

Sir Henry Williams Baker
1821–1877

25 The King of love my shepherd is,
Whose goodness faileth never;
I nothing lack if I am his,
And he is mine forever.
Hymn [1868][6]

[5] See Heraclitus, 62:7.
[6] Music by JOHN BACCHUS DYKES [1823–1876].

Charles Baudelaire
1821–1867

1 Hypocrite lecteur—mon semblable—mon frère[1]
[Hypocrite reader—my double—my brother]!
Les Fleurs du Mal [1861]. Au Lecteur

2 The poet is like the prince of the clouds
Who haunts the tempest and laughs at the archer;
Exiled on the ground in the midst of jeers,
His giant wings prevent him from walking.[2]
Ibid. L'Albatros, st. 4

3 Perfumes, colors and sounds echo one another.[3]
Ibid. Correspondances

4 Mother of memories, mistress of mistresses.[4]
Ibid. Le Balcon, st. 1

5 There, there is nothing else but grace and
measure,
Richness, quietness and pleasure.[5]
Ibid. L'Invitation au Voyage, refrain

6 I have more memories than if I were a thousand
years old.[6]
Ibid. Spleen, l. 1

7 I am the wound and the knife!
I am the blow and the cheek!
I am the limbs and the wheel—
The victim and the executioner![7]
Ibid. L'Héautontimoroumenos

8 Here is the charming evening, the criminal's
friend;
It comes like an accomplice, with stealthy tread.[8]
Ibid. Le Crépuscule du Soir

9 What is that sad, dark island?—It is Cythera,
They tell us, a country famous in song,
Banal Eldorado of all the old bachelors.
Look! after all, it is a poor land![9]
Ibid. Un Voyage à Cythère

10 O Death, old captain, it is time! raise the anchor!
Ibid. Le Voyage, VIII

---

[1]You! hypocrite lecteur!—mon semblable—mon frère!—
T. S. ELIOT, *The Waste Land* [1922], l. 76
[2]Le Poète est semblable au prince des nuées / Qui hante la tempête et se rit de l'archer; / Exilé sur le sol au milieu des huées, / Ses ailes de géant l'empêchent de marcher.
[3]Les parfums, les couleurs, les sons se répondent.
[4]Mère des souvenirs, maîtresse des maîtresses.
[5]Là, tout n'est qu'ordre et beauté, / Luxe, calme et volupté.
Translated by RICHARD WILBUR.
[6]J'ai plus de souvenirs que si j'avais mille ans.
[7]Je suis la plaie et le couteau! / Je suis le soufflet et la joue! / Je suis les membres et la roue, / Et la victime et le bourreau!
[8]Voici le soir charmant, ami du criminel; / Il vient comme un complice, à pas de loup.
[9]Quelle est cette île triste et noire?—C'est Cythère, / Nous dit-on, un pays fameux dans les chansons, / Eldorado banal de tous les vieux garçons. / Regardez! après tout c'est une pauvre terre.

11 What do I care that you are good?
Be beautiful! and be sad![10]
*Nouvelles Fleurs du Mal [1866–1868]. Madrigal
Triste, st. 1*

12 There can be no progress (real, that is, moral)
except in the individual and by the individual himself. *Mon Coeur Mis à Nu [1887], XV*

13 There are in every man, at every hour, two simultaneous postulations, one towards God, the other
towards Satan. *Ibid. XIX*

14 There exist only three beings worthy of respect:
the priest, the soldier, the poet. To know, to kill, to
create.[11] *Ibid. XXII*

15 To be a great man and a saint for oneself, that is
the one important thing. *Ibid. LII*

16 Theory of the true civilization. It is not to be
found in gas or steam or table turning. It consists in
the diminution of the traces of original sin.
Ibid. LIX

17 You must shock the bourgeois.[12] *Attributed*

Sir Richard Francis Burton
1821–1890

18 Why meet we on the bridge of Time to 'change
one greeting and to part?
The Kasîdah of Haji Abdû El-Yazdi, pt. I, st. 11

19 Indeed he knows not how to know who knows
not also how to un-know.
Ibid. VI, 18

20 Do what thy manhood bids thee do, from none
but self expect applause;
He noblest lives and noblest dies who makes and
keeps his self-made laws.
Ibid. VIII, 37

Crowfoot[13]
1821–1890

21 What is life? It is the flash of a firefly in the night.
It is the breath of a buffalo in the wintertime. It is the
little shadow which runs across the grass and loses
itself in the sunset. *Last words [1890]*

Fëdor Mikhailovich Dostoevski
1821–1881

22 Petersburg, the most theoretical and intentional
town on the whole terrestrial globe.
Notes from the Underground [1864],[14] ch. 2

---

[10]Que m'importe que tu sois sage? / Sois belle! et sois triste!
[11]Il n'existe que trois êtres respectables: le prêtre, le guerrier, le poète. Savoir, tuer, et creer.
[12]Il faut épater le bourgeois.
[13]Blackfoot warrior and orator.
[14]Translated by CONSTANCE GARNETT.

1   Man is sometimes extraordinarily, passionately, in love with suffering. *Ibid. 9*

2   Man grows used to everything, the scoundrel!
Crime and Punishment [1866],[1] *book I, ch. 2*

3   If you were to destroy in mankind the belief in immortality, not only love but every living force maintaining the life of the world would at once be dried up.
The Brothers Karamazov [1879–1880],[1] *bk. II, ch. 6*

4   I want to tell you now about the insects to whom God gave "sensual lust." . . . I am that insect, brother, and it is said of me especially. All we Karamazovs are such insects, and, angel as you are, that insect lives in you too, and will stir a tempest in your blood. Tempests, because sensual lust is a tempest—worse than a tempest! Beauty is a terrible and awful thing! It is terrible because it has not been fathomed, for God sets us nothing but riddles. Here the boundaries meet and all contradictions exist side by side. *Ibid. III, 3*

5   What to the mind is shameful is beauty and nothing else to the heart. Is there beauty in Sodom? Believe me, that for the immense mass of mankind beauty is found in Sodom. Did you know that secret? The awful thing is that beauty is mysterious as well as terrible. God and devil are fighting there, and the battlefield is the heart of man. *Ibid.*

6   I want to travel in Europe . . . I know that I am only going to a graveyard, but it's a most precious graveyard. *Ibid. V, 3*

7   If the devil doesn't exist, but man has created him, he has created him in his own image and likeness. *Ibid. V, 4*

8   Is there in the whole world a being who would have the right to forgive and could forgive? I don't want harmony. From love of humanity I don't want it. . . . I would rather remain with my unavenged suffering and unsatisfied indignation, *even if I were wrong.* Besides, too high a price is asked for harmony; it's beyond our means to pay so much to enter on it. And so I hasten to give back my entrance ticket. . . . It's not God that I don't accept, Alyosha, only I most respectfully return Him the ticket. *Ibid.*

9   Imagine that you are creating a fabric of human destiny with the object of making men happy in the end, giving them peace and rest at last, but that it was essential and inevitable to torture to death only one tiny creature . . . and to found that edifice on its unavenged tears, would you consent to be the architect on those conditions? Tell me, and tell the truth.[2] *Ibid.*

[1]Translated by CONSTANCE GARNETT.
[2]"Do you remember the passage where he [Rousseau] asks the reader what he would do if he could make a fortune by

10   So long as man remains free he strives for nothing so incessantly and so painfully as to find someone to worship. *Ibid. 5*

11   We have corrected Thy work and have founded it upon *miracle, mystery* and *authority.* And men rejoiced that they were again led like sheep, and that the terrible gift that brought them such suffering, was, at last, lifted from their hearts. *Ibid.*

12   Men reject their prophets and slay them, but they love their martyrs and honor those whom they have slain. *Ibid. VI, 3*

13   The jealous are the readiest of all to forgive, and all women know it. *Ibid. VIII, 3*

14   Who doesn't desire his father's death?
Ibid. XII, 5

15   They have their Hamlets, but we still have our Karamazovs! *Ibid. 9*

16   But profound as psychology is, it's a knife that cuts both ways. *Ibid. 10*

17   For a moment the lie becomes truth.
Ibid. Epilogue, ch. 2

18   We have all come out of Gogol's *Overcoat.*[3]
Attributed

Mary Baker Eddy

1821–1910

19   Our Father-Mother God, all-harmonious.
Science and Health with Key to the Scriptures [1875], p. 16

20   Jesus of Nazareth was the most scientific man that ever trod the globe. He plunged beneath the material surface of things, and found the spiritual cause. *Ibid. p. 313*

21   Spirit is the real and eternal; matter is the unreal and temporal. *Ibid. p. 468*

22   Disease is an experience of so-called mortal mind. It is fear made manifest on the body.
Ibid. p. 493

killing an old mandarin in China by simply exerting his will, without stirring from Paris?" "Yes." "Well?" "Bah! I'm at my thirty-third mandarin." "Don't play the fool. Look here, if it were proved to you that the thing was possible and you only needed to nod your head, would you do it?" "Is your mandarin well stricken in years? But, bless you, young or old, paralytic or healthy, upon my word—The devil take it! Well, no."
—BALZAC, *Le Père Goriot* [1835]
[3]This statement, traditionally attributed to Dostoevski and quoted by most writers on Dostoevski and on Russian realism, appears in Eugène Melchior, vicomte de Vogüé [1848–1910], *Le Roman Russe* [1886], ch. 3: The more I read the Russians, the more I understand the observation one of them made to me: "We have all come out of Gogol's *Overcoat.*"

Gustave Flaubert
1821–1880

1   One must not always think that feeling is everything. Art is nothing without form.
Letter to Madame Louise Colet [August 12, 1846]

2   What a horrible invention, the bourgeois, don't you think?[1]   *Ibid. [September 22, 1846]*

3   One becomes a critic when one cannot be an artist, just as a man becomes a stool pigeon when he cannot be a soldier.   *Ibid. [October 22, 1846]*

4   There was an air of indifference about them [the male guests], a calm produced by the gratification of every passion . . . that special brutality which comes from the habit of breaking down half-hearted resistances that keep one fit and tickle one's vanity —the handling of blooded horses, the pursuit of loose women.
Madame Bovary [1857],[2] pt. I, ch. 8

5   It never occurred to her that if the drainpipes of a house are clogged, the rain may collect in pools on the roof; and she suspected no danger until suddenly she discovered a crack in the wall.   *Ibid. II, 5*

6   Human speech is like a cracked kettle on which we tap crude rhythms for bears to dance to, while we long to make music that will melt the stars.[3]
Ibid. 12

7   She [Madame Bovary] had that indefinable beauty that comes from happiness, enthusiasm, success—a beauty that is nothing more or less than a harmony of temperament and circumstances.
Ibid.

8   We shouldn't maltreat our idols: the gilt comes off on our hands.[4]   *Ibid. III, 6*

9   There isn't a bourgeois alive who in the ferment of his youth, if only for a day or for a minute, hasn't thought himself capable of boundless passions and noble exploits. The sorriest little woman-chaser has dreamed of Oriental queens; in a corner of every notary's heart lie the moldy remains of a poet.
Ibid.

10   Of all the icy blasts that blow on love, a request for money is the most chilling and havoc-wreaking.
Ibid. 8

11   Anyone's death always releases something like an aura of stupefaction, so difficult is it to grasp this irruption of nothingness and to believe that it has actually taken place.   *Ibid. 9*

12   Axiom: hatred of the bourgeois is the beginning of wisdom.
Letter to George Sand [May 10, 1867]

13   I call a bourgeois anyone whose thinking is vulgar.   *Quoted by Maupassant*

14   What is beautiful is moral, that is all there is to it.   *Letter to Maupassant [October 26, 1880]*

15   I am Madame Bovary.[5]
From RENÉ DESCHARNES, *Flaubert [1909]*

Nathan Bedford Forrest
1821–1877

16   Get there first with the most men.[6]
Reported by General Basil Duke and General Richard Taylor

Hermann Ludwig Ferdinand von Helmholtz
1821–1894

17   Nature as a whole possesses a store of force which cannot in any way be either increased or diminished . . . therefore, the quantity of force in Nature is just as eternal and unalterable as the quantity of matter. . . . I have named [this] general law "The Principle of the Conservation of Force."[7]
Über die Erhaltung der Kraft [1847]

18   Whoever, in the pursuit of science, seeks after immediate practical utility, may generally rest assured that he will seek in vain. All that science can achieve is a perfect knowledge and a perfect understanding of the action of natural and moral forces.
Academic discourse, Heidelberg [1862]

Nikolai Nekrasov
1821–1877

19   You do not have to be a poet, but you are obliged to be a citizen.   *Poet and Citizen*

20   Wretched and abundant,
Oppressed and powerful,
Weak and mighty,
Mother Russia!
Who Is Happy in Russia? [1873–1876]

William Henry Vanderbilt
1821–1885

21   The public be damned.
Reply to a newspaper reporter [October 2, 1882]

---

[1]Quelle atroce invention que celle du bourgeois, n'est-ce pas?
[2]Translated by FRANCIS STEEGMULLER.
[3]La parole humaine est comme un chaudron fêlé où nous battons des melodies à faire danser les ours, quand on voudrait attendrir les étoiles.
[4]Il ne faut pas toucher aux idoles: la dorure en reste aux mains.

[5]Madame Bovary, c'est moi!
[6]Erroneous version usually rendered: Git thar fustest with the mostest.
[7]Translated by E. ATKINSON.
Helmholtz's "force" is equivalent to the modern physicist's "energy."

Rudolf Virchow
1821–1902

1 I formulate the doctrine of pathological genera-tion . . . in simple terms: *omnis cellula a cellula.*[1]
Cellular Pathology [1858].[2] *Disease, Life and Man*

George John Whyte-Melville
1821–1878

2 In the choice of a horse and a wife, a man must please himself, ignoring the opinion and advice of friends.   *Riding Recollections [1878]*

Matthew Arnold
1822–1888

3   Be his[3]
My special thanks, whose even-balanced soul,
From first youth tested up to extreme old age,
Business could not make dull, nor passion wild:
Who saw life steadily and saw it whole.
                    To a Friend [1849], l. 8

4 Others abide our question. Thou art free.
We ask and ask: Thou smilest and art still,
Out-topping knowledge.
                    Shakespeare [1849], l. 1

5 Strong is the soul, and wise, and beautiful:
The seeds of godlike power are in us still:
Gods are we, bards, saints, heroes, if we will.
          Written in Emerson's Essays [1849], l. 11

6 Come, dear children, let us away;
Down and away below!
Now my brothers call from the bay,
Now the great winds shoreward blow,
Now the salt tides seaward flow;
Now the wild white horses play,
Champ and chafe and toss in the spray.
          The Forsaken Merman [1849], st. 1

7 Sand-strewn caverns, cool and deep,
Where the winds are all asleep.
                    Ibid. st. 4

8 Where great whales come sailing by,
Sail and sail, with unshut eye,
Round the world forever and aye.
                    Ibid.

9 Singing, "Here came a mortal,
But faithless was she.
And alone dwell forever
The kings of the sea."
                    Ibid. st. 8

[1]All cells come from [pre-existing] cells.
[2]Essays translated by LELLAND J. RATHER.
[3]Sophocles.

10 Fate gave, what Chance shall not control,
His sad lucidity of soul.
                    Resignation [1849], l. 197

11 The world in which we live and move
Outlasts aversion, outlasts love:
Outlasts each effort, interest, hope,
Remorse, grief, joy.
                    Ibid. l. 215

12 Yet they, believe me, who await
No gifts from Chance, have conquered Fate.
                    Ibid. l. 247

13 We cannot kindle when we will
The fire that in the heart resides,
The spirit bloweth and is still,
In mystery our soul abides.
                    Morality [1852], st. 1

14 Calm Soul of all things! make it mine
To feel, amid the city's jar,
That there abides a peace of thine,
Man did not make, and can not mar.
          Lines Written in Kensington Gardens [1852], st. 10

15 Goethe in Weimar sleeps, and Greece,
Long since, saw Byron's struggle cease.
          Memorial Verses, April 1850 [1852], st. 1

16 Physician of the Iron Age,
Goethe has done his pilgrimage.
He took the suffering human race,
He read each wound, each weakness clear;
And struck his finger on the place,
And said: Thou ailest here, and here!
                    Ibid. st. 3

17   This iron time
Of doubt, disputes, distractions, fears.
                    Ibid. st. 4

18 Hither and thither spins
The windborne, mirroring soul;
A thousand glimpses wins,
And never sees a whole.
          Empedocles on Etna [1852], act I, sc. ii, l. 82

19 Be neither saint- nor sophist-led, but be a man!
                    Ibid. l. 136

20 Thou hast no *right* to bliss.
                    Ibid. l. 160

21 We do not what we ought;
What we ought not, we do;
And lean upon the thought
That chance will bring us through.
                    Ibid. l. 237

22 Nature, with equal mind,
Sees all her sons at play;
Sees man control the wind,
The wind sweep man away.
                    Ibid. l. 257

23 So, loath to suffer mute,
We, peopling the void air,

Make Gods to whom to impute
The ills we ought to bear.
                    Empedocles on Etna, I, ii, l. 277

1 Is it so small a thing
To have enjoyed the sun,
To have lived light in the spring,
To have loved, to have thought, to have done;
To have advanced true friends, and beat down
        baffling foes?
                    Ibid. II, l. 397

2 The day in its hotness,
The strife with the palm;
The night in her silence,
The stars in their calm.
                    Ibid. l. 465

3 Yes, in the sea of life enisled,
With echoing straits between us thrown,
Dotting the shoreless watery wild,
We mortal millions live *alone*.
        To Marguerite. Continued [1852], l. 1

4 But often in the world's most crowded streets,
But often, in the din of strife,
There rises an unspeakable desire
After the knowledge of our buried life.
                    The Buried Life [1852], l. 45

5 And long we try in vain to speak and act
Our hidden self, and what we say and do
Is eloquent, is well—but 'tis not true!
                    Ibid. l. 64

6 What shelter to grow ripe is ours?
What leisure to grow wise?
        *Stanzas in Memory of the Author of
        "Obermann" [1852], st. 18*

7 Ah! two desires toss about
The poet's feverish blood;
One drives him to the world without,
And one to solitude.
                    Ibid. st. 24

8   What actions are the most excellent? Those, certainly, which most powerfully appeal to the great primary human affections: to those elementary feelings which subsist permanently in the race, and which are independent of time. These feelings are permanent and the same; that which interests them is permanent and the same also.
                    Preface to Poems [1853]

9 Go, for they call you, Shepherd, from the hill.
                    The Scholar Gypsy [1853], st. 1

10 Thou waitest for the spark from heaven: and we,
Light half-believers of our casual creeds,
Who never deeply felt, nor clearly willed . . .
Who hesitate and falter life away,
And lose tomorrow the ground won today—
Ah! do not we, wanderer! await it too?
                    Ibid. st. 18

11   And amongst us one,
Who most has suffered, takes dejectedly
His seat upon the intellectual throne.
                    Ibid. st. 19

12 Oh, born in days when wits were fresh and clear,
And life ran gaily as the sparkling Thames;
Before this strange disease of modern life,
With its sick hurry, its divided aims,
Its heads o'ertaxed, its palsied hearts, was rife.
                    Ibid. st. 21

13 Still nursing the unconquerable hope,
Still clutching the inviolable shade.
                    Ibid. st. 22

14 Strew on her roses, roses,
And never a spray of yew!
In quiet she reposes;
Ah, would that I did too!
                    Requiescat [1853], st. 1

15 Her cabined, ample spirit
It fluttered and failed for breath.
Tonight it doth inherit
The vasty hall of death.
                    Ibid. st. 4

16 Eternal passion!
Eternal pain!
                    Philomela [1853], st. 3

17 Truth sits upon the lips of dying men.
                    Sohrab and Rustum, l. 656

18   Sanity—that is the great virtue of the ancient literature; the want of that is the great defect of the modern, in spite of its variety and power.
                    Preface to Poems [1854]

19 For rigorous teachers seized my youth,
And purged its faith, and trimmed its fire,
Showed me the high, white star of Truth,
There bade me gaze, and there aspire.
        *Stanzas from the Grande Chartreuse [1855],
        st. 12*

20 Wandering between two worlds, one dead,
The other powerless to be born.
                    Ibid. st. 15

21 And we forget because we must
And not because we will.
                    Absence [1857], st. 3

22   The translator of Homer should above all be penetrated by a sense of four qualities of his author: that he is eminently rapid; that he is eminently plain and direct, both in the evolution of his thought and in the expression of it, that is, both in his syntax and in his words; that he is eminently plain and direct in the substance of his thought, that is, in his matter and ideas; and, finally, that he is eminently noble.
                    On Translating Homer [1861]

23   Of these two literatures [French and German], as of the intellect of Europe in general, the main effort, for now many years, has been a *critical* effort; the

endeavor, in all branches of knowledge—theology, philosophy, history, art, science—to see the object as in itself it really is.   *Ibid.*

1 The grand style arises in poetry, when a noble nature, poetically gifted, treats with simplicity or with severity a serious subject.   *Ibid.*

2 Nations are not truly great solely because the individuals composing them are numerous, free, and active; but they are great when these numbers, this freedom, and this activity are employed in the service of an ideal higher than that of an ordinary man, taken by himself.   *Democracy [1861]*

3 It is a very great thing to be able to think as you like; but, after all, an important question remains: *what* you think.   *Ibid.*

4 For the creation of a masterwork of literature two powers must concur, the power of the man and the power of the moment, and the man is not enough without the moment.
The Function of Criticism at the Present Time [1864]

5 The critical power . . . tends, at last, to make an intellectual situation of which the creative power can profitably avail itself . . . to make the best ideas prevail.   *Ibid.*

6 There is the world of ideas and there is the world of practice; the French are often for suppressing the one and the English the other; but neither is to be suppressed.   *Ibid.*

7 Burke is so great because, almost alone in England, he brings thought to bear upon politics, he saturates politics with thought.   *Ibid.*

8 The notion of the free play of the mind upon all subjects being a pleasure in itself, being an object of desire, being an essential provider of elements without which a nation's spirit, whatever compensations it may have for them, must, in the long run, die of inanition, hardly enters into an Englishman's thoughts.   *Ibid.*

9 I am bound by my own definition of criticism: *a disinterested endeavor to learn and propagate the best that is known and thought in the world.*
Ibid.

10 Whispering from her towers [Oxford] the last enchantments of the Middle Age. . . . Home of lost causes, and forsaken beliefs, and unpopular names, and impossible loyalties!
Essays in Criticism, first series [1865], preface

11 Poetry is simply the most beautiful, impressive and wisely effective mode of saying things, and hence its importance.   *Ibid. Heinrich Heine*

12 *Philistine* must have originally meant, in the mind of those who invented the nickname, a strong, dog-ged, unenlightened opponent of the chosen people, of the children of the light.[1]   *Ibid.*

13 On the breast of that huge Mississippi of falsehood called *History*, a foam-bell more or less is no consequence.[2]
Ibid. Literary Influence of Academies [1864]

14 The great apostle of the Philistines, Lord Macaulay.   *Ibid. Joubert*

15 Are ye too changed, ye hills?
See, 'tis no foot of unfamiliar men
Tonight from Oxford up your pathway strays!
Here came I often, often, in old days—
Thyrsis[3] and I; we still had Thyrsis then.
Thyrsis [1866], st. 1

16 That sweet city[4] with her dreaming spires.
Ibid. st. 2

17 The bloom is gone, and with the bloom go I.
Ibid. st. 6

18 Yes, thou art gone! and round me too the night
In ever-nearing circle weaves her shade.
Ibid. st. 14

19 The sea is calm tonight.
The tide is full, the moon lies fair
Upon the straits; on the French coast, the light
Gleams, and is gone; the cliffs of England stand,
Glimmering and vast, out in the tranquil bay.
Dover Beach [1867], st. 1

20 Listen! you hear the grating roar
Of pebbles which the waves draw back, and fling,
At their return, up the high strand,
Begin, and cease, and then again begin,
With tremulous cadence slow, and bring
The eternal note of sadness in.
Ibid.

21 Sophocles long ago
Heard it on the Aegean.
Ibid. st. 2

22 The sea of faith
Was once, too, at the full, and round earth's shore
Lay like the folds of a bright girdle furled.
But now I only hear
Its melancholy, long, withdrawing roar,
Retreating, to the breath
Of the night-wind, down the vast edges drear
And naked shingles of the world.

[1]See Schopenhauer, 404:17.
[2]This passage appeared only in the first appearance of the essay in *Cornhill Magazine* [August 1864].
 History is nothing more than the belief in the senses, the belief in falsehood.—NIETZSCHE, *The Twilight of the Idols* [1888], *"Reason" in Philosophy, 1*
 History is more or less bunk.—HENRY FORD [1863–1947], interview with Charles N. Wheeler, *Chicago Tribune* [May 25, 1916]
[3]Arthur Hugh Clough [1819–1861].
[4]Oxford.

Ah, love, let us be true
To one another! for the world, which seems
To lie before us like a land of dreams,
So various, so beautiful, so new,
Hath really neither joy, nor love, nor light,
Nor certitude, nor peace, nor help for pain;
And we are here as on a darkling plain
Swept with confused alarms of struggle and flight,
Where ignorant armies clash by night.

Dover Beach, st. 3, 4

1 Creep into thy narrow bed,
Creep, and let no more be said!

The Last Word [1867], st. 1

2 Let the long contention cease!
Geese are swans, and swans are geese.[1]

Ibid. st. 2

3 Charge once more, then, and be dumb!
Let the victors, when they come,
When the forts of folly fall,
Find thy body by the wall.

Ibid. st. 4

4 Cruel, but composed and bland,
Dumb, inscrutable and grand,
So Tiberius might have sat,
Had Tiberius been a cat.

Poor Matthias [1867]

5 Style . . . is a peculiar recasting and heightening, under a certain condition of spiritual excitement, of what a man has to say, in such a manner as to add dignity and distinction to it.

On the Study of Celtic Literature [1867], sec. 6

6 The Celts certainly have it [style] in a wonderful measure. *Ibid.*

7 The power of the Latin classic is in *character*, that of the Greek is in *beauty*. Now character is capable of being taught, learnt, and assimilated: beauty hardly.

Schools and Universities on the Continent [1868]

8 The whole scope of the essay is to recommend culture as the great help out of our present difficulties; culture being a pursuit of our total perfection by means of getting to know, on all the matters which most concern us, the best which has been thought and said in the world.

Culture and Anarchy [1869], preface

9 Our society distributes itself into Barbarians, Philistines, and Populace; and America is just ourselves, with the Barbarians quite left out, and the Populace nearly. *Ibid.*

10 I am a Liberal, yet I am a Liberal tempered by experience, reflection, and renouncement, and I am, above all, a believer in culture.

Ibid. Introduction

[1]See Robert Burton, 234:26.

11 Culture is then properly described not as having its origin in curiosity, but as having its origin in the love of perfection; it is *a study of perfection.*

Ibid. Sweetness and Light

12 Greatness is a spiritual condition worthy to excite love, interest, and admiration. *Ibid.*

13 Not a having and a resting, but a growing and a becoming is the character of perfection as culture conceives it. *Ibid.*

14 He who works for sweetness and light[2] united, works to make reason and the will of God prevail.

Ibid.

15 The men of culture are the true apostles of equality. *Ibid.*

16 Everything in our political life tends to hide from us that there is anything wiser than our ordinary selves. *Ibid. Barbarians, Philistines, Populace*

17 The governing idea of Hellenism is spontaneity of consciousness, that of Hebraism, strictness of conscience. *Ibid. Hebraism and Hellenism*

18 Below the surface stream, shallow and light,
Of what we say and feel—below the stream,
As light, of what we think we feel, there flows
With noiseless current, strong, obscure and deep,
The central stream of what we feel indeed.

St. Paul and Protestantism [1870]

19 Conduct is three-fourths of our life and its largest concern. *Literature and Dogma [1873], ch. 1*

20 The freethinking of one age is the common sense of the next. *God and the Bible [1875]*

21 Choose equality.

Mixed Essays [1879]. Equality

22 We have the religion of inequality. *Ibid.*

23 Inequality . . . has the natural and necessary effect, under the present circumstances, of materializing our upper class, vulgarizing our middle class, and brutalizing our lower class. *Ibid.*

24 For poetry the idea is everything; the rest is a world of illusion, of divine illusion. Poetry attaches its emotion to the idea; the idea *is* the fact. The strongest part of our religion today is its unconscious poetry.

Introduction to T. H. WARD, English Poets [1880]

25 *Eutrapelia.* "A happy and gracious flexibility," Pericles calls this quality of the Athenians . . . lucidity of thought, clearness and propriety of language, freedom from prejudice and freedom from stiffness, openness of mind, amiability of manners.

Irish Essays [1882]. A Speech at Eton

[2]See Swift, 288:17.

1 English civilization—the humanizing, the bringing into one harmonious and truly humane life, of the whole body of English society—that is what interests me.
Ibid. Ecce, Convertimur ad Gentes

2 That which in England we call the middle class is in America virtually the nation.
A Word About America [1882]

3 The American Philistine was a livelier sort of Philistine than ours.
A Word More About America [1885]

4 What really dissatisfies in American civilization is the want of the *interesting,* a want due chiefly to the want of those two great elements of the interesting, which are elevation and beauty.
Civilization in the United States [1888]

5 The best poetry will be found to have a power of forming, sustaining, and delighting us, as nothing else can.
Essays in Criticism, second series [1888]. The Study of Poetry

6 Coleridge, poet and philosopher wrecked in a mist of opium.   *Ibid. Byron*

7 [A] beautiful and ineffectual angel [Shelley], beating in the void his luminous wings in vain.
Ibid.

Rudolf Julius Emanuel Clausius
1822–1888

8 Heat cannot of itself pass from a colder to a hotter body.
The Second Law of Thermodynamics [1850][1]

Ulysses Simpson Grant
1822–1885

9 No terms except an unconditional and immediate surrender can be accepted. I propose to move immediately upon your works.
To General S. B. Buckner, Fort Donelson [February 16, 1862]

10 I propose to fight it out on this line, if it takes all summer.
Dispatch to Washington, before Spottsylvania Court House [May 11, 1864]

11 Wherever the enemy goes let our troops go also.
Dispatch to General Henry W. Halleck from City Point, Virginia [August 1, 1864]

[1]Translated by WALTER D. BROWN.
Heat will of its own accord flow only from a hot object to a cold object.—JOSIAH WILLARD GIBBS [1839–1903], *Scientific Papers [1906], The Second Law of Thermodynamics*

12 The war is over—the rebels are our countrymen again.
Upon stopping his men from cheering after Lee's surrender at Appomattox Court House [April 9, 1865]

13 Let us have peace.
Accepting nomination for the presidency [May 29, 1868]

14 Let no guilty man escape, if it can be avoided. No personal considerations should stand in the way of performing a public duty.
Indorsement of a letter relating to the Whiskey Ring [July 29, 1875]

15 Leave the matter of religion to the family altar, the church, and the private school, supported entirely by private contributions. Keep the church and the State forever separate.
Speech at Des Moines, Iowa [1875]

16 Labor disgraces no man; unfortunately you occasionally find men disgrace labor.
Speech at Midland International Arbitration Union, Birmingham, England [1877]

Edward Everett Hale
1822–1909

17 Behind all these men you have to do with, behind officers, and government, and people even, there is the country herself, your country, and . . . you belong to her as you belong to your own mother. Stand by her, boy, as you would stand by your mother.
The Man Without a Country [1863]

18 He loved his country as no other man has loved her, but no man deserved less at her hands.
Ibid. Epitaph of Philip Nolan

Thomas Hughes
1822–1896

19 Life isn't all beer and skittles;[2] but beer and skittles, or something better of the same sort, must form a good part of every Englishman's education.
Tom Brown's Schooldays [1857], pt. I, ch. 2

20 He never wants anything but what's right and fair; only when you come to settle what's right and fair, it's everything that he wants and nothing that you want.   *Ibid. II, 2*

William Porcher Miles
1822–1899

21 "Vote early and vote often," the advice openly displayed on the election banners in one of our northern cities.
Speech in the House of Representatives [March 31, 1858]

[2]See Dickens, 469:2.

Frederick Law Olmsted
1822–1903
and
Calvert Vaux
1824–1895

1   The Park [Central Park, New York City] throughout is a single work of art, and as such subject to the primary law of every work of art, namely, that it shall be framed upon a single, noble motive, to which the design of all its parts, in some more or less subtle way, shall be confluent and helpful.

Report submitted with "Greensward" [1] *Plan, awarded first prize by the Board of Commissioners of the Central Park [April 28, 1858]*

2   It is one great purpose of the Park to supply to the hundreds of thousands of tired workers, who have no opportunity to spend their summers in the country, a specimen of God's handiwork that shall be to them, inexpensively, what a month or two in the White Mountains or the Adirondacks is, at great cost, to those in easier circumstances.   *Ibid.*

Louis Pasteur
1822–1895

3   No, a thousand times no; there does not exist a category of science to which one can give the name applied science. There are science and the applications of science, bound together as the fruit to the tree which bears it.[2]

Pourquoi la France n'a pas trouvé des hommes supérieurs au moment du péril. From Revue Scientifique [1871]

4   In the fields of observation chance favors only the prepared mind.[3]

Inaugural lecture, University of Lille [December 7, 1854]

Red Cloud[4]
1822–1909

5   We were told that they [federal troops] wished merely to pass through our country . . . to seek for gold in the Far West . . . Yet before the ashes of the council fire are cold, the Great Father is building his forts among us. You have heard the sound of the white soldier's axe upon the Little Piney. His presence here is . . . an insult to the spirits of our ancestors. Are we then to give up their sacred graves to be plowed for corn? Dakotas, I am for war.

Speech at council at Fort Laramie, Wyoming [1866]

Heinrich Schliemann
1822–1890

6   I have gazed on the face of Agamemnon.
Telegram to the king of Greece, upon excavating the fifth and last grave at Mycenae [August 1876]

Théodore de Banville
1823–1891

7 We'll to the woods no more,
The laurels all are cut.[5]
Nous n'Irons Plus aux Bois

Julia A. Fletcher Carney
1823–1908

8 Little drops of water
Little grains of sand,
Make the mighty ocean
And the pleasant land.

Little Things [1845], st. 1

William Johnson Cory
1823–1892

9 They told me, Heraclitus, they told me you were dead;
They brought me bitter news to hear and bitter tears to shed.
I wept as I remembered how often you and I
Had tired the sun with talking and sent him down the sky.
And now that thou art lying, my dear old Carian guest,
A handful of gray ashes, long, long ago at rest,
Still are thy pleasant voices, thy *Nightingales,* awake,
For Death, he taketh all away, but them he cannot take.

Heraclitus. Translated from Callimachus[6]

Thomas Wentworth Higginson
1823–1911

10   When a thought takes one's breath away, a lesson on grammar seems an impertinence.

Preface to EMILY DICKINSON's Poems, first series [1890]

William Walsham How
1823–1897

11 For all the saints, who from their labors rest.
Hymn [1864], st. 1

---

[1] Pseudonym of Olmsted and Vaux in submitting their plan.
[2] Translated by I. BERNARD COHEN.
[3] Dans les champs de l'observation le hasard ne favorise que les esprits préparés.
[4] Mahpiua Luta, Oglala Sioux chief.

[5] Nous n'irons plus aux bois,/Les lauriers sont coupés. Translated by A. E. HOUSMAN. From an old nursery rhyme.
[6] See Callimachus, 82:20.

Leopold Kronecker

1823–1891

1 God made integers, all else is the work of man.
*Jahresberichte der Deutschen Mathematiker
Vereinigung, bk. 2*

George Martin Lane

1823–1897

2 The waiter roars it through the hall:
"We don't give bread with one fish ball!"
Lay of the Lone Fish Ball [1855], st. 10

Francis Parkman

1823–1893

3 The growth of New England was a result of the
aggregate efforts of a busy multitude, each in his
narrow circle toiling for himself, to gather competence or wealth. The expansion of New France was
the achievement of a gigantic ambition striving to
grasp a continent. It was a vain attempt.
*Pioneers of France in the New World [1865],
introduction*

4 A boundless vision grows upon us; an untamed
continent; vast wastes of forest verdure; mountains
silent in primeval sleep; river, lake, and glimmering
pool; wilderness oceans mingling with the sky. Such
was the domain which France conquered for civilization. Plumed helmets gleamed in the shade of its
forests, priestly vestments in its dens and fastnesses
of ancient barbarism. Men steeped in antique learning, pale with the close breath of the cloister, here
spent the noon and evening of their lives, ruled savage hordes with a mild, parental sway, and stood
serene before the direst shapes of death. Men of
courtly nurture, heirs to the polish of a far-reaching
ancestry, here, with their dauntless hardihood, put
to shame the boldest sons of toil.   *Ibid.*

5 Faithfulness to the truth of history involves far
more than a research, however patient and scrupulous, into special facts. Such facts may be detailed
with the most minute exactness, and yet the narrative, taken as a whole, may be unmeaning or untrue.
The narrator must seek to imbue himself with the
life and spirit of the time. He must study events in
their bearings near and remote; in the character,
habits, and manners of those who took part in them.
He must himself be, as it were, a sharer or a spectator of the action he describes.   *Ibid.*

6 For the student there is, in its season, no better
place than the saddle, and no better companion than
the rifle or the oar.   *Autobiography [1868]*

7 The most momentous and far-reaching question
ever brought to issue on this continent was: Shall
France remain here or shall she not?
Montcalm and Wolfe [1884], introduction

8 The [French] Revolution began at the top—in
the world of fashion, birth, and intellect—and
propagated itself downwards.   *Ibid.*

Coventry Patmore

1823–1896

9 A Woman is a foreign land,
Of which, though there he settle young,
A man will ne'er quite understand
The customs, politics, and tongue.
*The Angel in the House [1854–1856], bk. I,
canto 9. Prelude 2, Woman*

10 For want of me the world's course will not fail;
When all its work is done, the lie shall rot;
The truth is great, and shall prevail,[1]
When none cares whether it prevail or not.
The Unknown Eros [1877]. Magna Est Veritas

William Brighty Rands
[Matthew Browne]

1823–1882

11 Never do today what you can
Put off till tomorrow.[2]
Lilliput Levee

12 Great wide, beautiful, wonderful world,
With the wonderful water round you curled,
And the wonderful grass upon your breast,
World, you are beautifully dressed.
The Child's World, st. 1

Ernest Renan

1823–1892

13 The whole of history is incomprehensible without him [Jesus].
La Vie de Jésus [1863], introduction

14 O Lord, if there is a Lord, save my soul, if I have
a soul.   *Prière d'un Sceptique*

15 Religion is not a popular error; it is a great instinctive truth, sensed by the people, expressed by
the people.   *Les Apôtres [1866]*

16 Immortality is to labor at an eternal task.
L'Avenir de la Science [1890], preface

17 Nothing great is achieved without chimeras.
Ibid. ch. 19

John Sherman

1823–1900

18 I have come home to look after my fences.
Speech to his neighbors, Mansfield, Ohio

[1]See Ptahhotpe, 3:5, and *I Esdras* 4:41, 30:13.
[2]No idleness, no laziness, no procrastination; never put off
till tomorrow what you can do today.—CHESTERFIELD, *Letters* [December 26, 1749]

William Marcy Tweed
1823–1878

1   As long as I count the votes, what are you going to do about it?

Statement by the "Boss" of Tammany Hall on the ballot in New York City [November 1871]

William Allingham
1824–1889

2 Up the airy mountain,
Down the rushy glen,
We daren't go a-hunting
For fear of little men.

The Fairies, st. 1

3 Four ducks on a pond,
A grass bank beyond,
A blue sky of spring,
White clouds on the wing;
What a little thing
To remember for years—
To remember with tears!

Four Ducks on a Pond

Barnard Elliott Bee
1824–1861

4   There is Jackson, standing like a stone wall!

Of General T. J. Jackson at the battle of Bull Run [July 21, 1861]

Phoebe Cary
1824–1871

5 And though hard be the task,
"Keep a stiff upper lip."

Keep a Stiff Upper Lip

6 One sweetly solemn thought
Comes to me o'er and o'er;
I am nearer home today
Than I ever have been before.

Nearer Home, st. 1

Wilkie Collins
1824–1889

7   "I haven't much time to be fond of anything," says Sergeant Cuff. "But when I *have* a moment's fondness to bestow, most times . . . the roses get it."   *The Moonstone [1868]. First Period, ch. 12*

Alexandre Dumas the Younger
1824–1895

8   Business? It's quite simple. It's other people's money.[1]

La Question d'Argent [1857], act II, sc. vii

[1]Les affaires, c'est bien simple, c'est l'argent des autres.

Thomas Jonathan [Stonewall] Jackson
1824–1863

9   My duty is to obey orders.

A favorite aphorism

10   Let us cross over the river, and rest under the trees.   *Last words [May 10, 1863]*

William Thomson, Lord Kelvin
1824–1907

11   When you can measure what you are speaking about, and express it in numbers, you know something about it; but when you cannot measure it, when you cannot express it in numbers, your knowledge is of a meager and unsatisfactory kind: it may be the beginning of knowledge, but you have scarcely, in your thoughts, advanced to the stage of *science.*

Popular Lectures and Addresses [1891–1894]

Gustav Robert Kirchhoff
1824–1887

12   The highest object at which the natural sciences are constrained to aim, but which they will never reach, is the determination of the forces which are present in nature, and of the state of matter at any given moment—in one word, the reduction of all the phenomena of nature to mechanics.[2]

Über das Ziel der Naturwissenschaften [1865]

George Macdonald
1824–1905

13 Said the Wind to the Moon, "I will blow you out!"

The Wind and the Moon, st. 1

14 Here lie I, Martin Elginbrodde:
Hae mercy o' my soul, Lord God;
As I wad do, were I Lord God,
And ye were Martin Elginbrodde.

David Elginbrod [1863], bk. I, ch. 13

15   There is no feeling in a human heart which exists in that heart alone—which is not, in some form or degree, in every heart.

Unspoken Sermons, second series [1885]

16   You will be dead so long as you refuse to die.

What's Mine's Mine [1886], ch. 31

17   The world and my being, its life and mine, were one. The microcosm and macrocosm were at length atoned, at length in harmony. I lived in everything; everything entered and lived in me.

Lilith [1895], ch. 45

[2]Translated by J. B. STALLO.

Thomas Henry Huxley
1825–1895

1 I cannot but think that he who finds a certain proportion of pain and evil inseparably woven up in the life of the very worms, will bear his own share with more courage and submission.
On the Educational Value of the Natural History Sciences [1854]

2 To a person uninstructed in natural history, his country or seaside stroll is a walk through a gallery filled with wonderful works of art, nine-tenths of which have their faces turned to the wall.   *Ibid.*

3 Extinguished theologians lie about the cradle of every science as the strangled snakes beside that of Hercules.
Darwiniana. The Origin of Species [1860]

4 The method of scientific investigation is nothing but the expression of the necessary mode of working of the human mind.
Our Knowledge of the Causes of the Phenomena of Organic Nature [1863]

5 The improver of natural knowledge absolutely refuses to acknowledge authority, as such. For him, skepticism is the highest of duties, blind faith the one unpardonable sin.
On the Advisableness of Improving Natural Knowledge [1866]

6 The chess board is the world, the pieces are the phenomena of the universe, the rules of the game are what we call the laws of Nature. The player on the other side is hidden from us. We know that his play is always fair, just, and patient. But also we know, to our cost, that he never overlooks a mistake, or makes the smallest allowance for ignorance.
A Liberal Education [1868]

7 For every man the world is as fresh as it was at the first day, and as full of untold novelties for him who has the eyes to see them.   *Ibid.*

8 M. Comte's philosophy in practice might be compendiously described as Catholicism *minus* Christianity.   *On the Physical Basis of Life [1868]*

9 The great tragedy of Science—the slaying of a beautiful hypothesis by an ugly fact.
Biogenesis and Abiogenesis [1870]

10 If some great Power would agree to make me always think what is true and do what is right, on condition of being turned into a sort of clock and wound up every morning before I got out of bed, I should instantly close with the offer.
On Descartes' Discourse on Method [1870]. Method and Results

11 There is the greatest practical benefit in making a few failures early in life.
On Medical Education [1870]

12 That mysterious independent variable of political calculation, Public Opinion.
Universities, Actual and Ideal [1874]

13 Veracity is the heart of morality.   *Ibid.*

14 Logical consequences are the scarecrows of fools and the beacons of wise men.
Animal Automatism [1874]

15 Size is not grandeur, and territory does not make a nation.   *On University Education [1876]*

16 The great end of life is not knowledge but action.
Technical Education [1877]

17 If a little knowledge is dangerous, where is the man who has so much as to be out of danger?
On Elemental Instruction in Physiology [1877]

18 Irrationally held truths may be more harmful than reasoned errors.
The Coming of Age of The Origin of Species [1880]

19 It is the customary fate of new truths to begin as heresies and to end as superstitions.   *Ibid.*

20 I asserted—and I repeat—that a man has no reason to be ashamed of having an ape for his grandfather. If there were an ancestor whom I should feel shame in recalling it would rather be a man—a man of restless and versatile intellect—who, not content with an equivocal success in his own sphere of activity, plunges into scientific questions with which he has no real acquaintance, only to obscure them by an aimless rhetoric, and distract the attention of his hearers from the real point at issue by eloquent digressions and skilled appeals to religious prejudice.
Reply to Wilberforce's question.[1] From Leonard Huxley, *Life and Letters of Thomas Henry Huxley [1900], vol. 1*

George Edward Pickett
1825–1875

21 Up, men, and to your posts! Don't forget today that you are from Old Virginia.
Command at the beginning of his division's charge at Gettysburg [July 3, 1863]

Adelaide Anne Procter
1825–1864

22 Seated one day at the organ,
I was weary and ill at ease,
And my fingers wandered idly
Over the noisy keys.

A Lost Chord, st. 1[2]

---

[1]If anyone were to be willing to trace his descent through an ape as his *grandfather,* would he be willing to trace his descent similarly on the side of his *grandmother?*—Bishop Samuel Wilberforce [1805–1873], *at the British Association for the Advancement of Science* [1860]

[2]Music by Sir Arthur Sullivan [1842–1900].

1 But I struck one chord of music
Like the sound of a great Amen.
A Lost Chord, st. 2

Bayard Taylor
1825–1878

2 From the desert I come to thee
On a stallion shod with fire,
And the winds are left behind
In the speed of my desire.
Bedouin Song,[1] st. 1

3 Till the sun grows cold,
And the stars are old,
And the leaves of the Judgment Book unfold.
Ibid. refrain

William Whiting
1825–1878

4 Eternal Father, strong to save,
Whose arm doth bind the restless wave,
Who bidd'st the mighty ocean deep
Its own appointed limits keep,
O, hear us when we cry to Thee
For those in peril on the sea!
*The Hymn of the U.S. Navy [1860].[2] Eternal
Father, Strong to Save, st. 1*

Walter Bagehot
1826–1877

5   Writers, like teeth, are divided into incisors and
molars. Sydney Smith[3] was a "molar."
*Estimates of Some Englishmen and Scotchmen
[1858]. The First Edinburgh Reviewers*

6   The best reason why Monarchy is a strong government is, that it is an intelligible government. The
mass of mankind understand it, and they hardly
anywhere in the world understand any other.
The English Constitution [1867], ch. 3

7   [The British monarchy:]. Its mystery is its life. We
must not let in daylight upon magic. We must not
bring the Queen into the combat of politics, or she
will cease to be reverenced by all combatants.
Ibid. 4

8   One of the greatest pains to human nature is the
pain of a new idea.
Physics and Politics [1869], ch. 5

9   The most melancholy of human reflections, perhaps, is that on the whole it is a question whether the
benevolence of mankind does most good or harm.
Ibid.

10   A constitutional statesman is in general a man of
common opinions and uncommon abilities.
Biographical Studies [1907]. Sir Robert Peel

11   You may talk of the tyranny of Nero and Tiberius; but the real tyranny is the tyranny of your
next-door neighbor. . . . Public opinion is a per-
meating influence, and it exacts obedience to itself;
it requires us to think other men's thoughts, to speak
other men's words, to follow other men's habits.
Ibid.

Dinah Maria Mulock Craik
1826–1887

12 Douglas, Douglas, tender and true!
Douglas, Tender and True,[4] refrain

13 Oh, my son's my son till he gets him a wife,
But my daughter's my daughter all her life.
Young and Old

John Ellerton
1826–1893

14 Now the laborer's task is o'er;
Now the battle day is past;
Now upon the farther shore
Lands the voyager at last.
Hymn [1870],[2] st. 1

15 Father, in thy gracious keeping
Leave we now thy servant sleeping.
Ibid. refrain

16 The day thou gavest, Lord, is ended,
The darkness falls at thy behest;
To thee our morning hymns ascended,
Thy praise shall sanctify our rest.
Hymn [1870],[5] st. 1

Stephen Collins Foster
1826–1864

17 O, Susanna! O, don't you cry for me,
I've come from Alabama, with my banjo on my
knee.
O, Susanna[6] [1848], chorus

18 Gwine to run all night!
Gwine to run all day!
I'll bet my money on de bobtail nag—
Somebody bet on de bay.
Camptown Races [1850], chorus

19 Way down upon the Swanee River,
Far, far away,

[4]O Douglas, O Douglas! / Tendir and trewe.—Sir Richard
Holland [fl. 1450], *The Buke of the Howlat* [c. 1450], st. 31
[5]Music by C. C. Scholefield [1839–1904].
[6]Sung for the first time by Nelson Kneass in Andrews' Eagle
Ice Cream Saloon, Pittsburgh, Pennsylvania [September 11,
1847]. It shortly became a worldwide hit.

[1]Music by Ciro Pinsuti [1829–1888].
[2]Music by John Bacchus Dykes [1823–1876].
[3]See Sydney Smith, 379.

There's where my heart is turning ever;
There's where the old folks stay.
The Old Folks at Home [1851], st. 1

1 All the world is sad and dreary
Ev'rywhere I roam,
Oh! darkies, how my heart grows weary,
Far from the old folks at home.
Ibid. chorus

2 Weep no more, my lady,
Oh! weep no more today!
We will sing one song for the old Kentucky home,
For the old Kentucky home far away.
My Old Kentucky Home [1853], chorus

3 I dream of Jeanie with the light brown hair,
Floating, like a vapor, on the soft summer air.
Jeanie with the Light Brown Hair [1854], st. 1

4 I'm coming, I'm coming, for my head is bending
low;
I hear those gentle voices calling, "Old Black
Joe."
Old Black Joe [1860], st. 3

5 Beautiful dreamer, wake unto me,
Starlight and dewdrop are waiting for thee.
Beautiful Dreamer [1864], st. 1

G. W. Hunt
c. 1829–1904

6 We don't want to fight, but, by jingo, if we do,
We've got the ships, we've got the men, we've got
the money, too.
Song [1878][1]

George Brinton McClellan
1826–1885

7 All quiet along the Potomac.
*Frequent report from his Union headquarters
[1861]*

Edward Stuyvesant Bragg
1827–1912

8   They love him most for the enemies he has made.
*Speech seconding the presidential nomination of
Grover Cleveland [July 9, 1884]*

Charles Eliot Norton
1827–1908

9   A knowledge of Greek thought and life, and of
the arts in which the Greeks expressed their thought

and sentiment, is essential to high culture. A man
may know everything else, but without this knowledge he remains ignorant of the best intellectual and
moral achievements of his own race.
Letter to F. A. Tupper [1885]

10   The voice of protest, of warning, of appeal is
never more needed than when the clamor of fife and
drum, echoed by the press and too often by the
pulpit, is bidding all men fall in and keep step and
obey in silence the tyrannous word of command.
Then, more than ever, it is the duty of the good
citizen not to be silent.   *True Patriotism [1898]*

Lew [Lewis] Wallace
1827–1905

11   A man is never so on trial as in the moment of
excessive good fortune.
*Ben Hur: A Tale of the Christ [1880], bk. V,
ch. 7*

12   Would you hurt a man keenest, strike at his self-
love.   *Ibid. VI, 2*

Anna Bartlett Warner
1827–1915

13 Jesus loves me—this I know,
For the Bible tells me so.
The Love of Jesus [1858]

Septimus Winner [Alice Hawthorne]
1827–1902

14 Listen to the mockingbird, listen to the
mockingbird,
Still singing where the weeping willows wave.
Listen to the Mockingbird [1855]

Henrik Ibsen
1828–1906

15   All or nothing.   *Brand [1866]*[2]

16   Look into any man's heart you please, and you
will always find, in every one, at least one black spot
which he has to keep concealed.
Pillars of Society [1877],[3] *act III*

17   The spirit of truth and the spirit of freedom—
they are the pillars of society.   *Ibid. IV*

18   There can be no freedom or beauty about a home
life that depends on borrowing and debt.
A Doll's House [1879],[4] *act I*

19   Our house has never been anything but a playroom. I have been your doll wife, just as at home I

---

[1]Sung by Gilbert Hastings Macdermott (Farrell) [1845–
1901], "the Great Macdermott." The song gave the terms
"jingo" and "jingoism" to the political vocabulary, though the
phrase "by jingo" had been used earlier by Goldsmith and
Thomas Hood.

[2]Translated by C. H. HERFORD.
[3]Translated by WILLIAM ARCHER.
[4]Translated by WILLIAM ARCHER.
See Dickens, 471:20.

was Daddy's doll child. And the children in turn have been my dolls. I thought it was fun when you came and played with me, just as they thought it was fun when I went and played with them. That's been our marriage, Torvald.   *A Doll's House, act III*

1   If I'm ever to reach any understanding of myself and the things around me, I must learn to stand alone. That's why I can't stay here with you any longer.   *Ibid.*

2   I have another duty equally sacred . . . My duty to myself.   *Ibid.*

3   *Helmer:* First and foremost, you are a wife and mother.
     Nora: That I don't believe any more. I believe that first and foremost I am an individual, just as much as you are.   *Ibid.*

4   To crave for happiness in this world is simply to be possessed by a spirit of revolt. What right have we to happiness?   *Ghosts [1881],*[1] *act I*

5   I am half inclined to think we are all ghosts, Mr. Manders. It is not only what we have inherited from our fathers that exists again in us, but all sorts of old dead ideas and all kinds of old dead beliefs and things of that kind. They are not actually alive in us; but there they are dormant, all the same, and we can never be rid of them. Whenever I take up a newspaper and read it, I fancy I see ghosts creeping between the lines. There must be ghosts all over the world. They must be as countless as grains of the sands, it seems to me. And we are so miserably afraid of the light, all of us.   *Ibid. II*

6   Mother, give me the sun.   *Ibid. III*

7   I hold that man is in the right who is most closely in league with the future.
     Letter to Georg Brandes [January 3, 1882]

8   A community is like a ship; everyone ought to be prepared to take the helm.
     An Enemy of the People [1882],[1] *act I*

9   The minority is always right.   *Ibid. IV*

10   You should never wear your best trousers when you go out to fight for freedom and truth.
     Ibid. V

11   The strongest man in the world is he who stands most alone.   *Ibid.*

12   Always do that, wild ducks do. Go plunging right to the bottom . . . as deep as they can get . . . hold on with their beaks to the weeds and stuff— and all the other mess you find down there. Then they never come up again.
     The Wild Duck [1884],[2] *act II*

13   Take the life-lie away from the average man and straightaway you take away his happiness.
     Ibid. V

14   Our common lust for life.
     Hedda Gabler [1890],[2] *act II*

15   Oh courage . . . oh yes! If only one had that . . . Then life might be livable, in spite of everything.   *Ibid.*

16   Back he'll come . . . With vine leaves in his hair. Flushed and confident.   *Ibid.*

17   Everything I touch seems destined to turn into something mean and farcical.   *Ibid. IV*

18   The younger generation will come knocking at my door.   *The Master Builder [1892],*[3] *act I*

George Meredith
1828–1909

19   I expect that Woman will be the last thing civilized by Man.
     The Ordeal of Richard Feverel [1859], ch. 1

20   Who rises from prayer a better man, his prayer is answered.   *Ibid. 12*

21   The sun is coming down to earth, and the fields and the waters shout to him golden shouts.
     Ibid. 19

22   Kissing don't last; cookery do!   *Ibid. 28*

23   Speech is the small change of Silence.
     Ibid. 34

24 See ye not, courtesy
   Is the true alchemy,
   Turning to gold all it touches and tries?
     The Song of Courtesy [1859], IV

25 Not till the fire is dying in the grate,
   Look we for any kinship with the stars.
   Oh, wisdom never comes when it is gold,
   And the great price we pay for it full worth;
   We have it only when we are half earth.
     Modern Love [1862], 4

26 And if I drink oblivion of a day,
   So shorten I the stature of my soul.
     Ibid. 12

27 What are we first? First, animals; and next
   Intelligences at a leap; on whom
   Pale lies the distant shadow of the tomb.
     Ibid. 30

28   In tragic life, God wot,
   No villain need be! Passions spin the plot:
   We are betrayed by what is false within.
     Ibid. 43

29 More brain, O Lord, more brain! Or we shall mar
   Utterly this fair garden we might win.
     Ibid. 48

30 Ah, what a dusty answer gets the soul
   When hot for certainties in this our life!
     Ibid. 50

[1]Translated by WILLIAM ARCHER.
[2]Translated by A. G. CHATER.

[3]Translated by EDMUND GOSSE and WILLIAM ARCHER.

1 Into the breast that gives the rose
Shall I with shuddering fall!
The Spirit of Earth in Autumn [1862] st. 1

2   [Comedy] it is who proposes the correcting of
pretentiousness, of inflation, of dullness, and of the
vestiges of rawness and grossness yet to be found
among us. She is the ultimate civilizer, the polisher.
The Egoist [1879]. Prelude

3 Cynicism is intellectual dandyism.
Ibid. ch. 7

4   In . . . the book of Egoism, it is written, possession without obligation to the object possessed approaches felicity.   *Ibid. 14*

5 For singing till his heaven fills,
'Tis love of earth that he instills,
And ever winging up and up,
Our valley is his golden cup,
And he the wine which over flows
To lift us with him as he goes.
The Lark Ascending [1881], l. 65

6 The song seraphically free
Of taint of personality.
Ibid. l. 95

7 On a starred night Prince Lucifer uprose.
Tired of his dark dominion swung the fiend.
Lucifer in Starlight [1883]

8 Around the ancient track marched, rank on rank,
The army of unalterable law.[1]
Ibid.

9 Enter these enchanted woods,
You who dare.
The Woods of Westermain [1883], st. 1

10 She whom I love is hard to catch and conquer,
Hard, but O the glory of the winning were she
won!
Love in the Valley [1883], st. 2

11   A witty woman is a treasure; a witty beauty is a
power.   *Diana of the Crossways [1885], ch. 1*

12   What a woman thinks of women is the test of her
nature.   *Ibid.*

13   The well of true wit is truth itself.   *Ibid.*

14   Ireland gives England her soldiers, her generals
too.   *Ibid. 2*

15   How divine is utterance! . . . As we to the
brutes, poets are to us.   *Ibid. 16*

16 With patient inattention hear him prate.
Bellerophon [1887], st. 4

17 Full lasting is the song, though he,
The singer, passes.
The Thrush in February [1888], st. 17

18 Behold the life at ease; it drifts,
The sharpened life commands its course.
Hard Weather [1888], l. 71

[1]See T. S. Eliot, 668:1.

Dante Gabriel Rossetti
1828–1882

19 The blessed damozel leaned out
From the gold bar of Heaven;
Her eyes were deeper than the depth
Of waters stilled at even;
She had three lilies in her hand,
And the stars in her hair were seven.
The Blessed Damozel [1850], st. 1

20 And the souls mounting up to God
Went by her like thin flames.
Ibid. st. 7

21 One thing then learned remains to me—
The woodspurge has a cup of three.
The Woodspurge [1870], st. 4

22 Tell me now in what hidden way is
Lady Flora the lovely Roman?
Where's Hipparchia, and where is Thaïs,
Neither of them the fairer woman.
Where is Echo, beheld of no man
Only heard on river and mere—
She whose beauty was more than human? . . .
But where are the snows of yesteryear?
*The Ballad of Dead Ladies (After François
Villon) [1870], st. 1*

23 A sonnet is a moment's monument—
Memorial from the soul's eternity
To one dead deathless hour.
*Sonnets from the House of Life [1870–1881].[2]
Proem*

24 Beauty like hers is genius.
Ibid. 18, Genius in Beauty

25 And though thy soul sail leagues and leagues
beyond—
Still, leagues beyond those leagues, there is more
sea.
Ibid. 73, The Choice—III

26   My name is Might-have-been;
I am also called No-more, Too-late, Farewell.
Ibid. 97, A Superscription

27 When vain desire at last, and vain regret
Go hand in hand to death, and all is vain,
What shall assuage the unforgotten pain
And teach the unforgetful to forget?
Ibid. 101, The One Hope

28   The Stealthy School of Criticism.[3]
Letter to the Athenaeum [1871]

29 I have been here before,
But when or how I cannot tell;
I know the grass beyond the door,
The sweet keen smell,
The sighing sound, the lights around the shore.
Sudden Light [1881], st. 1

[2]See Buchanan, 541:15.
[3]Reply to Buchanan's attack.

Leo Nikolaevich Tolstoi
1828–1910

1 The hero of my tale, whom I love with all the power of my soul, whom I have tried to portray in all his beauty, who has been, is, and will be beautiful, is Truth.   *Sevastopol in May 1855 [1855]*

2 The old man . . . used to say that a nap "after dinner was silver—before dinner, golden."[1]
    War and Peace [1865–1869], bk. I, ch. 15

3 "What's this? am I falling? my legs are giving way under me," he thought, and fell on his back. He opened his eyes, hoping to see how the struggle of the French soldiers with the artilleryman was ending, and eager to know whether the red-haired artilleryman was killed or not, whether the cannons had been taken or saved. But he saw nothing of all that. Above him there was nothing but the sky—the lofty sky, not clear, but still immeasurably lofty, with gray clouds creeping quietly over it.
    Ibid.[2] *III, 16*

4 Three days afterwards the little princess was buried, and Prince Andrey went to the steps of the tomb to take his last farewell of her. Even in the coffin the face was the same, though the eyes were closed. "Ah, what have you done to me?" it still seemed to say.
    Ibid. IV, 9

5 In historical events great men—so called—are but the labels that serve to give a name to an event, and like labels, they have the least possible connection with the event itself. Every action of theirs, that seems to them an act of their own free will, is in an historical sense not free at all, but in bondage to the whole course of previous history, and predestined from all eternity.   *Ibid. IX, 1*

6 The strongest of all warriors are these two— Time and Patience.   *Ibid. X, 16*

7 He [Platon Karataev] did not understand, and could not grasp the significance of words taken apart from the sentence. Every word and every action of his was the expression of a force uncomprehended by him, which was his life.   *Ibid. XII, 13*

8 For us, with the rule of right and wrong given us by Christ, there is nothing for which we have no standard. And there is no greatness where there is not simplicity, goodness, and truth.
    Ibid. XIV, 18

9 Pure and complete sorrow is as impossible as pure and complete joy.   *Ibid. XV, 1*

10 The subject of history is the life of peoples and of humanity. To catch and pin down in words—that is, to describe directly the life, not only of humanity, but even of a single people, appears to be impossible.
    Ibid. epilogue, pt. II, ch. 1

11 Happy families are all alike; every unhappy family is unhappy in its own way.
    Anna Karenina [1875–1877], pt. I, ch. 1

12 Ivan Ilych's life had been most simple and most ordinary and therefore most terrible.
    The Death of Ivan Ilych [1886][3]

13 Ivan Ilych saw that he was dying, and he was in continuous despair.

In the depth of his heart he knew he was dying, but not only was he not accustomed to the thought, he simply did not and could not grasp it.

The syllogism he had learned from Kiezewetter's Logic: "Caius is a man, men are mortal, therefore Caius is mortal," had always seemed to him correct as applied to Caius, but certainly not as applied to himself. That Caius—man in the abstract—was mortal, was perfectly correct, but he was not Caius, not an abstract man, but a creature quite, quite separate from all others.   *Ibid.*

14 Six feet of land was all that he needed.
    How Much Land Does a Man Need? [1886]

15 The more is given the less the people will work for themselves, and the less they work the more their poverty will increase.[4]
    Help for the Starving, pt. III [January 1892]

16 Art is a human activity having for its purpose the transmission to others of the highest and best feelings to which men have risen.
    What Is Art? [1898], ch. 8

Geronimo
1829–1909

17 It [Arizona] is my land, my home, my father's land, to which I now ask to be allowed to return. I want to spend my last days there, and be buried among those mountains. If this could be I might die in peace, feeling that my people, placed in their native homes, would increase in numbers, rather than diminish as at present, and that our name would not become extinct.
    To President Grant from the reservation at Fort Sill, Oklahoma, after surrender [1877]

Carl Schurz
1829–1906

18 Our country, right or wrong.[5] When right, to be kept right; when wrong, to be put right.
    Address, Anti-Imperialistic Conference, Chicago [October 17, 1899]

---

[1]Translated by LOUISE AND AYLMER MAUDE.
[2]Translated by CONSTANCE GARNETT.

[3]Translated by AYLMER MAUDE.
[4]If you stop supporting that crowd, it will support itself. —SENECA, *Epistles, 20, 7*
[5]See Charles Churchill, 333:19; John Quincy Adams, 368:14; and Decatur, 390:22.

Ivan Mikhailovich Sechenov
1829–1905

1   All psychical acts without exception, if they are not complicated by elements of emotion . . . develop by way of reflex. Hence, all conscious movements resulting from these acts and usually described as voluntary, are reflex movements in the strict sense of the term.
Reflexes of the Brain [1863],[1] *ch. 2*

Charles Dudley Warner
1829–1900

2   To own a bit of ground, to scratch it with a hoe, to plant seeds, and watch the renewal of life—this is the commonest delight of the race, the most satisfactory thing a man can do.
My Summer in a Garden [1870]. Preliminary

3   No man but feels more of a man in the world if he have a bit of ground that he can call his own. However small it is on the surface, it is four thousand miles deep; and that is a very handsome property.
Ibid.

4   What a man needs in gardening is a cast-iron back, with a hinge in it.   *Ibid. Third Week*

5   Politics makes strange bedfellows.[2]
Ibid. Fifteenth Week

6   What small potatoes we all are, compared with what we might be!   *Ibid.*

7   The thing generally raised on city land is taxes.
Ibid. Sixteenth Week

Thomas Edward Brown
1830–1897

8 A Garden is a lovesome thing, God wot!
My Garden

9 Not God! in Gardens! when the eve is cool?
Nay, but I have a sign:
'Tis very sure God walks in mine.
Ibid.

Porfirio Díaz
1830–1915

10   Poor Mexico, so far from God and so close to the United States.   *Attributed*

Emily Dickinson[3]
1830–1886

11 Surgeons must be very careful
When they take the knife!

[1]Translated by S. BELSKY.
[2]See Shakespeare, 224:8.
[3]*The Complete Poems of Emily Dickinson* [1960], edited by THOMAS H. JOHNSON. Dates are of composition, not publication.

Underneath their fine incisions
Stirs the Culprit—*Life!*
No. 108 [c. 1859]

12 For each ecstatic instant
We must an anguish pay
In keen and quivering ratio
To the ecstasy.
No. 125 [c. 1859], st. 1

13 To fight aloud, is very brave—
But *gallanter*, I know
Who charge within the bosom
The Cavalry of Woe—
No. 126 [c. 1859], st. 1

14 These are the days when Birds come back—
A very few—a Bird or two—
To take a backward look.

These are the days when skies resume
The old—old sophistries of June—
A blue and gold mistake.
No. 130 [c. 1859], st. 1, 2

15 The thought beneath so slight a film—
Is more distinctly seen—
As laces just reveal the surge—
Or Mists—the Apennine—
No. 210 [c. 1860]

16 I taste a liquor never brewed,
From Tankards scooped in Pearl—
No. 214 [c. 1860], st. 1

17 Inebriate of Air—am I—
And Debauchee of Dew—
Reeling—through endless summer days—
From inns of Molten Blue—
Ibid. st. 2

18 Till Seraphs swing their snowy Hats—
And Saints—to windows run—
To see the little Tippler
Leaning against the—Sun—
Ibid. st. 4

19 Blazing in Gold and quenching in Purple
Leaping like Leopards to the Sky . . .
And the Juggler of Day is gone.
No. 228 [c. 1861]

20 "Hope" is the thing with feathers—[4]
That perches in the soul—
And sings the tune without the words—
And never stops—at all—
No. 254 [c. 1861], st. 1

21 There's a certain Slant of light,
Winter Afternoons—
That oppresses, like the Heft
Of Cathedral Tunes—
No. 258 [c. 1861], st. 1

22 I'm Nobody! Who are you?
Are you—Nobody—too?

[4]See Woody Allen, 767:12.

Then there's a pair of us!
Don't tell! they'd advertise—you know!

How dreary—to be—Somebody!
How public—like a Frog—
To tell one's name—the livelong June—
To an admiring Bog!

> No. 288 [c. 1861]

1 I tasted—careless—then—
I did not know the Wine
Came once a World—Did you?
Oh, had you told me so—
This Thirst would blister—easier—now—

> No. 296 [c. 1861], st. 3

2 The Soul selects her own Society—
Then—shuts the Door—
To her divine Majority—
Present no more—

> No. 303 [c. 1862], st. 1

3 I'll tell you how the Sun rose—
A Ribbon at a time—

> No. 318 [1862]

4 Some keep the Sabbath going to Church—
I keep it, staying at Home—
With a bobolink for a Chorister—
And an Orchard, for a Dome—

> No. 324 [1862], st. 1

5 So instead of getting to Heaven, at last—
I'm going, all along.

> Ibid. st. 3

6 After great pain, a formal feeling comes.

> No. 341 [c. 1862], st. 1

7 Of Course—I prayed—
And did God Care?
He cared as much as on the Air
A Bird—had stamped her foot—
And cried "Give Me"—

> No. 376 [c. 1862]

8 No Rack can torture me—
My Soul—at Liberty—
Behind this mortal Bone
There knits a bolder One—

> No. 384 [c. 1862], st. 1

9 Except Thyself may be
Thine Enemy—
Captivity is Consciousness—
So's Liberty.

> Ibid. st. 4

10 Good Morning—Midnight—
I'm coming Home—
Day—got tired of Me—
How could I—of Him?

> No. 425 [c. 1862], st. 1

11 Much Madness is divinest Sense—
To a discerning Eye—
Much Sense—the starkest Madness—
'Tis the Majority

In this, as All, prevail—
Assent—and you are sane—
Demur—you're straightway dangerous—
And handled with a Chain.

> No. 435 [c. 1862]

12 This is my letter to the World
That never wrote to Me—
The simple News that Nature told—
With tender Majesty.

> No. 441 [c. 1862], st. 1

13 I died for Beauty—but was scarce
Adjusted in the Tomb
When One who died for Truth, was lain
In an adjoining Room—

> No. 449 [c. 1862], st. 1

14 And so, as Kinsmen, met a Night—
We talked between the Rooms—
Until the Moss had reached our lips—
And covered up—our names—

> Ibid. st. 3

15 It was not Death, for I stood up,
And all the Dead, lie down—

> No. 510 [c. 1862], st. 1

16 I reckon—when I count at all—
First—Poets—Then the Sun—
Then Summer—Then the Heaven of God—
And then—the List is done—

But, looking back—the First so seems
To Comprehend the Whole—
The Others look a needless Show—
So I write—Poets—All—

> No. 569 [c. 1862], st. 1, 2

17 I like to see it lap the Miles—
And lick the Valleys up—

> No. 585 [c. 1862], st. 1

18 And neigh like Boanerges—
Then punctual as a Star
Stop—docile and omnipotent
At its own stable door—

> Ibid. st. 4

19 I asked no other thing—
No other—was denied—
I offered Being—for it—
The Mighty Merchant sneered—

Brazil? He twirled a Button—
Without a glance my way—
"But—Madam—is there nothing else—
That We can show—Today?"

> No. 621 [c. 1862]

20 The Brain—is wider than the Sky—
For—put them side by side—
The one the other will contain
With ease—and You—beside.

> No. 632 [1862], st. 1

21 I cannot live with You—
It would be Life—

And Life is over there—
Behind the Shelf.

No. 640 [c.1862], st. 1

1 And that White Sustenance—
Despair—

Ibid. st. 12

2 Pain—has an Element of Blank—
It cannot recollect
When it begun—or if there were
A time when it was not—

No. 650 [c.1862], st. 1

3 Because I could not stop for Death,
He kindly stopped for me—
The Carriage held but just Ourselves
And Immortality.

No. 712 [c.1863], st. 1

4 Alter! When the Hills do—
Falter! When the Sun
Question if His Glory
Be the Perfect One—

Surfeit! When the Daffodil
Doth of the Dew—
Even as Herself—Sir—
I will—of You—

No. 729 [c.1863]

5 God gave a Loaf to every Bird—
But just a Crumb—to Me—

No. 791 [c.1863], st. 1

6 This quiet Dust was Gentlemen and Ladies
And Lads and Girls—[1]
Was laughter and ability and Sighing,
And Frocks and Curls.

No. 813 [c.1864], st. 1

7 Adventure most unto itself
The Soul condemned to be—
Attended by a single Hound
Its own identity.

No. 822 [c.1864], st. 4

8 Dying! To be afraid of thee
One must to thine Artillery
Have left exposed a Friend—
Than thine old Arrow is a Shot
Delivered straighter to the Heart
The leaving Love behind.

No. 831 [c.1864], st. 1

9 Love—is anterior to Life—
Posterior—to Death—
Initial of Creation, and
The Exponent of Earth.

No. 917 [c.1864]

10 If I can stop one Heart from breaking
I shall not live in vain
If I can ease one Life the Aching
Or cool one Pain

[1]See Shakespeare, 220:3.

Or help one fainting Robin
Unto his Nest again
I shall not live in Vain.

No. 919 [c.1864]

11 A narrow Fellow in the Grass
Occasionally rides—

No. 986 [c.1865], st. 1

12 But never met this Fellow
Attended or alone
Without a tighter breathing
And Zero at the Bone—

Ibid. last stanza

13 The Dying, is a trifle, past
But living, this include
The dying multifold—without
The Respite to be dead.

No. 1013 [c.1865]

14 'Twas my one Glory—
Let it be
Remembered
I was owned of Thee—

No. 1028 [c.1865]

15 I never saw a Moor—
I never saw the Sea—
Yet know I how the Heather looks
And what a Billow be.

I never spoke with God
Nor visited in Heaven—
Yet certain am I of the spot
As if the Checks were given—

No. 1052 [c.1865]

16 Experiment to me
Is every one I meet
If it contain a Kernel?
The Figure of a Nut

Presents upon a Tree
Equally plausibly,
But Meat within, is requisite
To Squirrels, and to Me.

No. 1073 [c.1865]

17 The Bustle in a House
The Morning after Death
Is solemnest of industries
Enacted upon Earth—

The Sweeping up the Heart,
And putting Love away
We shall not want to use again
Until Eternity.

No. 1078 [c.1866]

18 We never know how high we are
Till we are called to rise
And then, if we are true to plan
Our statures touch the skies.

No. 1176 [c.1870], st. 1

1 A word is dead
When it is said,
Some say.
I say it just
Begins to live
That day.

No. 1212 [c. 1872]

2 There is no Frigate like a Book
To take us Lands away
Nor any Coursers like a Page
Of prancing Poetry—
This Traverse may the poorest take
Without oppress of Toll—
How frugal is the Chariot
That bears the Human Soul!

No. 1263 [c. 1873]

3 I thought that nature was enough
Till Human nature came
But that the other did absorb
As Parallax a Flame—

No. 1286 [c. 1873], st. 1

4 Until the Desert knows
That Water grows
His Sands suffice
But let him once suspect
That Caspian Fact
Sahara dies.

No. 1291 [c. 1873], st. 1

5 Not with a Club, the Heart is broken
Nor with a Stone—
A Whip so small you could not see it
I've known
To lash the Magic Creature
Till it fell.

No. 1304 [c. 1874], st. 1

6 A little Madness in the Spring
Is wholesome even for the King.

No. 1333 [c. 1875]

7 Love's stricken "why"
Is all that love can speak—
Built of but just a syllable
The hugest hearts that break.

No. 1368 [c. 1876]

8 Bees are Black, with Gilt Surcingles—
Buccaneers of Buzz.

No. 1405 [c. 1877], st. 1

9 The Pedigree of Honey
Does not concern the Bee—
A Clover, any time, to him,
Is Aristocracy.

No. 1627 [c. 1884], version II

10 A Drunkard cannot meet a Cork
Without a Revery—
And so encountering a Fly
This January Day

Jamaicas of Remembrance stir
That send me reeling in.

No. 1628 [c. 1884]

11 Eden is that old-fashioned House
We dwell in every day
Without suspecting our abode
Until we drive away.

No. 1657 [n.d.], st. 1

12 I took one Draught of Life—
I'll tell you what I paid—
Precisely an existence—
The market price, they said.

They weighed me, Dust by Dust—
They balanced Film with Film,
Then handed me my Being's worth—
A single Dram of Heaven!

No. 1725 [n.d.]

13 My life closed twice before its close—
It yet remains to see
If Immortality unveil
A third event to me

So huge, so hopeless to conceive
As these that twice befell.
Parting is all we know of heaven,
And all we need of hell.

No. 1732 [n.d.]

14 That it will never come again
Is what makes life so sweet.

No. 1741 [n.d.], st. 1

15 The only secret people keep
Is Immortality.

No. 1748 [n.d.]

16 To make a prairie it takes a clover and one bee,
One clover, and a bee,
And revery.
The revery alone will do,
If bees are few.

No. 1755 [n.d.]

17 Elysium is as far as to
The very nearest Room
If in that Room a Friend await
Felicity or Doom—

What Fortitude the Soul contains,
That it can so endure
The accent of a coming Foot—
The opening of a Door—

No. 1760 [n.d.]

18 That Love is all there is,
Is all we know of Love;
It is enough, the freight should be
Proportioned to the groove.

No. 1765 [n.d.]

19   If I read a book and it makes my whole body so
cold no fire can ever warm me, I know that is poetry.
If I feel physically as if the top of my head were taken

off, I know that is poetry. These are the only ways
I know it. Is there any other way?
From MARTHA GILBERT DICKINSON BIANCHI,
Life and Letters of Emily Dickinson [1924]

1   Little Cousins, Called back.
Last letter [May 1886]

Helen Hunt Jackson
1830–1885

2 O suns and skies and clouds of June,
   And flowers of June together,
   Ye cannot rival for one hour
   October's bright blue weather.
October's Bright Blue Weather, st. 1

Mother Jones [Mary Harris Jones]
1830–1930

3   Pray for the dead and fight like hell for the living!
Autobiography [1925]

Alexander Muir
1830–1906

4   And joined in love together,
   The Thistle, Shamrock, Rose entwine
   The Maple Leaf forever!
The Maple Leaf Forever [1867]

Christina Georgina Rossetti
1830–1894

5 My heart is like a singing bird.
A Birthday [1861], st. 1

6   The birthday of my life
   Is come, my love is come to me.
Ibid. st. 2

7 When I am dead, my dearest,
   Sing no sad songs for me;
   Plant thou no roses at my head,
   Nor shady cypress tree.
   Be the green grass above me
   With showers and dewdrops wet;
   And if thou wilt, remember
   And if thou wilt, forget.
Song [1862], st. 1

8 Remember me when I am gone away,
   Gone far away into the silent land.
Remember [1862], l. 1

9 Better by far you should forget and smile
   Than that you should remember and be sad.
Ibid. l. 13

10 In the bleak midwinter
   Frosty wind made moan,
   Earth stood hard as iron,
   Water like a stone;
   Snow had fallen, snow on snow,
   Snow on snow,
   In the bleak midwinter,
   Long ago.
A Christmas Carol

11 Oh roses for the flush of youth,
   And laurel for the perfect prime;
   But pluck an ivy branch for me
   Grown old before my time.
Song [1862]

12 Who has seen the wind?
   Neither you nor I:
   But when the trees bow down their heads,
   The wind is passing by.
Who Has Seen the Wind? [1872], st. 2

13 Sleeping at last, the trouble and turmoil over,
   Sleeping at last, the struggle and horror past,
   Cold and white, out of sight of friend and of
        lover,
   Sleeping at last.
Sleeping at Last [1893], st. 1

Robert Arthur Talbot Gascoyne-Cecil, Marquess of Salisbury
1830–1903

14   If you believe the doctors, nothing is wholesome;
   if you believe the theologians, nothing is innocent; if
   you believe the soldiers, nothing is safe.
Letter to Lord Lytton, Viceroy of India [June
15, 1877]

Alexander Smith
1830–1867

15   It is not of so much consequence what you say, as
   how you say it. Memorable sentences are memorable on account of some single irradiating word.
Dreamthorp [1863]. On the Writing of Essays

16   Death is the ugly fact which Nature has to hide,
   and she hides it well.
Ibid. Of Death and the Fear of Dying

George Graham Vest
1830–1904

17   The one absolutely unselfish friend that man can
   have in this selfish world, the one that never deserts
   him, the one that never proves ungrateful or treacherous, is his dog. . . . When all other friends desert, he remains.
Speech in the Senate [1884]

Ignatius Donnelly
1831–1901

1   The Democratic Party is like a mule—without pride of ancestry or hope of posterity.

Attributed

James Abram Garfield
1831–1881

2   Fellow citizens! God reigns, and the Government at Washington still lives!

Attributed speech on the assassination of Lincoln [April 15, 1865]

3   I am not willing that this discussion should close without mention of the value of a true teacher. Give me a log hut, with only a simple bench, Mark Hopkins[1] on one end and I on the other, and you may have all the buildings, apparatus and libraries without him.

Address to Williams College Alumni, New York [December 28, 1871]

Edward Robert Bulwer-Lytton, Earl of Lytton [Owen Meredith]
1831–1891

4 We may live without poetry, music and art;
We may live without conscience, and live without heart;
We may live without friends; we may live without books;
But civilized man cannot live without cooks.

Lucile [1860], pt. I, canto 2, st. 19

5 Genius does what it must, and talent does what it can.

Last Words of a Sensitive Second-Rate Poet

James Clerk Maxwell
1831–1879

6   All the mathematical sciences are founded on relations between physical laws and laws of numbers, so that the aim of exact science is to reduce the problems of nature to the determination of quantities by operations with numbers.

On Faraday's Lines of Force [1856]

7   When at last this little instrument appeared, consisting, as it does, of parts every one of which is familiar to us, and capable of being put together by

an amateur, the disappointment arising from its humble appearance was only partially relieved on finding that it was really able to talk.

The Telephone [1878]

Philip Henry Sheridan
1831–1888

8   The only good Indians I ever saw were dead.[2]

Attributed remark at Fort Cobb, Indian Territory [January 1869]

Sitting Bull[3]
c. 1831–1890

9   What treaty that the white man ever made with us have they kept? Not one. When I was a boy the Sioux owned the world; the sun rose and set on their land; they sent ten thousand men to battle. Where are the warriors today? Who slew them? Where are our lands? Who owns them? . . . What law have I broken? Is it wrong for me to love my own? Is it wicked for me because my skin is red? Because I am a Sioux; because I was born where my father lived; because I would die for my people and my country?

Statement

Louisa May Alcott
1832–1888

10   Christmas won't be Christmas without any presents.   *Little Women [1868], ch. 1*

11   If Mr. Clemens cannot think of something better to tell our pure-minded lads and lasses, he had best stop writing for them.

On Adventures of Huckleberry Finn [1885]

12   Resolved to take Fate by the throat and shake a living out of her.

From Ednah D. Cheney, Louisa May Alcott, Her Life, Letters, and Journals [1889], ch. 5

Elizabeth Akers Allen
1832–1911

13 Backward, turn backward, O Time, in your flight,
Make me a child again just for tonight!

Rock Me to Sleep [1860], st. 1

---

[1]Mark Hopkins [1802–1887], president of Williams College [1836–1872] and president of the American Board of Commissioners for Foreign Missions [1857–1881].

For Education is Making Men;/So is it now, so was it when/Mark Hopkins sat on one end of a log/And James Garfield sat on the other.—Guiterman, *Education*

[2]Edward Sylvester Ellis [1840–1916] reported that after Custer's fight with Black Kettle's band of Cheyenne Indians, the Comanche Chief Toch-a-way (Turtle Dove) was presented to General Sheridan. The Indian said: "Me Toch-a-way, me good Indian." The reply, as reported by Ellis but vehemently denied by Sheridan, is given in the text; the phrase is more often heard in the version: The only good Indian is a dead Indian.

[3]Tatanka Yotanka, Sioux warrior.

Lewis Carroll
[Charles Lutwidge Dodgson]
1832–1898

1 All in the golden afternoon
Full leisurely we glide,
For both our oars with little skill
By little arms are plied
While little hands make vain pretense
Our wanderings to guide.
> *Alice's Adventures in Wonderland* [1865],
> introduction, st. 1

2 "What is the use of a book," thought Alice, "without pictures or conversations?"
> *Ibid. ch. 1*

3 Do cats eat bats? . . . Do bats eat cats?
> *Ibid.*

4 Curiouser and curiouser!
> *Ibid. 2*

5 How doth the little crocodile
Improve his shining tail,
And pour the waters of the Nile
On every golden scale![1]

How cheerfully he seems to grin,
How neatly spreads his claws,
And welcomes little fishes in
With gently smiling jaws!
> *Ibid.*

6 "I'll be judge, I'll be jury," said cunning old Fury;
"I'll try the whole cause, and condemn you to
death."
> *Ibid. 3*

7 Oh my fur and whiskers!
> *Ibid. 4*

8 "I can't explain *myself*, I'm afraid, sir," said Alice, "because I'm not myself, you see."
"I don't see," said the Caterpillar.
> *Ibid. 5*

9 "You are old, Father William," the young man
said,
"And your hair has become very white;
And yet you incessantly stand on your head—
Do you think, at your age, it is right?"[2]
> *Ibid. [You Are Old, Father William, st. 1]*

10 "In my youth," said his father, "I took to the law,
And argued each case with my wife;
And the muscular strength which it gave to my
jaw,
Has lasted the rest of my life."
> *Ibid. [st. 6]*

11 "I have answered three questions, and that is
enough,"
Said his father. "Don't give yourself airs!
Do you think I can listen all day to such stuff?
Be off, or I'll kick you downstairs!"
> *Ibid. [st. 8]*

12 Those serpents! There's no pleasing them!
> *Ibid.*

13 "If everybody minded their own business," said the Duchess in a hoarse growl, "the world would go round a deal faster than it does."
> *Ibid. 6*

14 "Talking of axes," said the Duchess, "chop off her head!"
> *Ibid.*

15 Speak roughly to your little boy,
And beat him when he sneezes:
He only does it to annoy,
Because he knows it teases.
> *Ibid.*

16 "If it had grown up," she said to herself, "it would have made a dreadfully ugly child; but it makes rather a handsome pig, I think."
> *Ibid.*

17 "All right," said the [Cheshire] Cat; and this time it vanished quite slowly, beginning with the end of the tail, and ending with the grin, which remained some time after the rest of it had gone.
> *Ibid.*

18 "Then you should say what you mean," the March Hare went on.
"I do," Alice hastily replied; "at least—at least I mean what I say—that's the same thing, you know."
"Not the same thing a bit!" said the Hatter. "Why, you might just as well say that 'I see what I eat' is the same thing as 'I eat what I see'!"
> *Ibid. 7*

19 "It was the *best* butter," the March Hare meekly replied.
> *Ibid.*

20 Twinkle, twinkle, little bat!
How I wonder what you're at!
Up above the world you fly,
Like a teatray in the sky.[3]
> *Ibid.*

21 "Take some more tea," the March Hare said to Alice, very earnestly.
"I've had nothing yet," Alice replied in an offended tone: "so I can't take more."
"You mean you can't take *less*," said the Hatter: "it's very easy to take *more* than nothing."
> *Ibid.*

22 They drew all manner of things—everything that begins with an M . . . such as mousetraps, and the moon, and memory, and muchness—you know you say things are "much of a muchness."
> *Ibid.*

23 The Queen turned crimson with fury, and after glaring at her for a moment like a wild beast, began screaming, "Off with her head![4] Off with—"
> *Ibid. 8*

24 "Tut, tut, child," said the Duchess. "Everything's got a moral if only you can find it."
> *Ibid. 9*

---

[1]See Watts, 294:9.
[2]See Southey, 386:8.

[3]See Ann and Jane Taylor, 394:2.
[4]See Shakespeare, 166:2, and Cibber, 291:21.

1   Take care of the sense and the sounds will take care of themselves.[1]
Alice's Adventures in Wonderland, ch. 9

2   "We called him Tortoise because he taught us," said the Mock Turtle angrily. "Really you are very dull!"   *Ibid.*

3   "Reeling and Writhing, of course, to begin with," the Mock Turtle replied, "and the different branches of Arithmetic—Ambition, Distraction, Uglification, and Derision."   *Ibid.*

4   Advance twice, set to partners . . . change lobsters, and retire in same order.   *Ibid.* 10

5   "Will you walk a little faster?" said a whiting to a snail,
"There's a porpoise close behind us, and he's treading on my tail."
Ibid. [The Lobster-Quadrille, st. 1]

6   Will you, won't you, will you, won't you, will you join the dance?
Ibid.

7   The further off from England the nearer is to France—
Then turn not pale, beloved snail, but come and join the dance.
Ibid. [st. 3]

8   'Tis the voice of the Lobster: I heard him declare
"You have baked me too brown, I must sugar my hair."[2]
Ibid. ['Tis the Voice of the Lobster]

9   Soup of the evening, beautiful soup!
Ibid. [Turtle Soup]

10   Begin at the beginning . . . and go on till you come to the end: then stop.   *Ibid.* 12

11   Sentence first—verdict afterwards.   *Ibid.*

12   You're nothing but a pack of cards!   *Ibid.*

13   Child of the pure, unclouded brow
And dreaming eyes of wonder!
Though time be fleet and I and thou
Are half a life asunder,
Thy loving smile will surely hail
The love-gift of a fairy tale.
*Through the Looking-Glass [1872],
introduction, st. 1*

14   "The horror of that moment," the King went on, "I shall never, *never* forget!"
"You will, though," the Queen said, "if you don't make a memorandum of it."   *Ibid. ch. 1*

15   'Twas brillig, and the slithy toves
Did gyre and gimble in the wabe;
All mimsy were the borogoves,
And the mome raths outgrabe.

Beware the Jabberwock, my son!
The jaws that bite, the claws that catch!

Beware the Jubjub bird, and shun
The frumious Bandersnatch!
Ibid. [Jabberwocky, st. 1, 2]

16   And, as in uffish thought he stood,
The Jabberwock, with eyes of flame,
Came whiffling through the tulgey wood,
And burbled as it came!

One, two! One, two! And through and through
The vorpal blade went snicker-snack!
He left it dead, and with its head
He went galumphing back.

"And hast thou slain the Jabberwock?
Come to my arms, my beamish boy!
O frabjous day! Callooh! Callay!"
He chortled in his joy.
Ibid. [st. 4–6]

17   Curtsy while you're thinking what to say. It saves time.   *Ibid.* 2

18   "Now! Now!" cried the Queen. "Faster! Faster!"
Ibid.

19   "A slow sort of country!" said the Queen. "Now, *here*, you see, it takes all the running you can do, to keep in the same place. If you want to get somewhere else, you must run at least twice as fast as that!"
Ibid.

20   Speak in French when you can't think of the English for a thing—turn out your toes when you walk —and remember who you are!   *Ibid.*

21   "If you think we're waxworks," he said, "you ought to pay, you know. Waxworks weren't made to be looked at for nothing. Nohow!"   *Ibid.* 4

22   "Contrariwise," continued Tweedledee, "if it was so, it might be; and if it were so, it would be; but as it isn't, it ain't. That's logic."   *Ibid.*

23   The sun was shining on the sea,
Shining with all his might:
He did his very best to make
The billows smooth and bright—
And this was odd, because it was
The middle of the night.
Ibid. [The Walrus and the Carpenter, st. 1]

24   The Walrus and the Carpenter
Were walking close at hand:
They wept like anything to see
Such quantities of sand:
"If this were only cleared away,"
They said, "it would be grand!"

"If seven maids with seven mops
Swept it for half a year,
Do you suppose," the Walrus said,
"That they could get it clear?"
"I doubt it," said the Carpenter,
And shed a bitter tear.
Ibid. [st. 4, 5]

[1]See Chesterfield, 305:1.
[2]See Watts, 294:13.

1 "O Oysters, come and walk with us!"
The Walrus did beseech.
"A pleasant walk, a pleasant talk,
Along the briny beach."
Ibid. [st. 6]

2 And thick and fast they came at last,
And more, and more, and more—
All hopping through the frothy waves,
And scrambling to the shore.
Ibid. [st. 9]

3 "The time has come," the Walrus said,
"To talk of many things:
Of shoes—and ships—and sealing wax—
Of cabbages—and kings—
And why the sea is boiling hot—
And whether pigs have wings."
Ibid. [st. 11]

4 "But wait a bit," the Oysters cried,
"Before we have our chat;
For some of us are out of breath,
And all of us are fat!"
Ibid. [st. 12]

5 The Carpenter said nothing but
"The butter's spread too thick!"
Ibid. [st. 16]

6 "I weep for you," the Walrus said:
"I deeply sympathize."
With sobs and tears he sorted out
Those of the largest size,
Holding his pocket-handkerchief
Before his streaming eyes.
Ibid. [st. 17]

7 But answer came there none[1]—
And this was scarcely odd, because
They'd eaten every one.
Ibid. [st. 18]

8 Twopence a week, and jam every other day.
Ibid. 5

9 "The rule is, jam tomorrow, and jam yesterday
—but never jam today."
"It must come sometimes to 'jam today,'" Alice objected.
"No, it can't," said the Queen. "It's jam every other day: today isn't any other day, you know."
Ibid.

10 "It's a poor sort of memory that only works backwards," the Queen remarked. *Ibid.*

11 Consider anything, only don't cry! *Ibid.*

12 "There's no use trying," she said: "one *can't* believe impossible things."
"I daresay you haven't had much practice," said the Queen. "When I was your age, I always did it for half-an-hour a day. Why, sometimes I've believed as many as six impossible things before breakfast."
Ibid.

13 They gave it me—for an unbirthday present.
Ibid. 6

14 "But 'glory' doesn't mean 'a nice knockdown argument,'" Alice objected.
"When *I* use a word," Humpty Dumpty said, in rather a scornful tone, "it means just what I choose it to mean—neither more nor less."
"The question is," said Alice, "whether you *can* make words mean so many different things."
"The question is," said Humpty Dumpty, "which is to be master—that's all." *Ibid.*

15 It's as large as life and twice as natural.
Ibid. 7

16 His answer trickled through my head,
Like water through a sieve.
Ibid. 8

17 What's the French for fiddle-de-dee? *Ibid. 9*

18 It isn't etiquette to cut anyone you've been introduced to. Remove the joint! *Ibid.*

19 He would answer to "Hi!" or to any loud cry
Such as "Fry me!" or "Fritter my wig!"
To "What-you-may-call-um!" or
"What-was-his-name!"
But especially "Thing-um-a-jig!"
The Hunting of the Snark [1876]. Fit I, st. 9

20 "What's the good of Mercator's North Poles and
Equators,
Tropics, Zones and Meridian Lines?"
So the Bellman would cry: and the crew would
reply,
"They are merely conventional signs!"
Ibid. Fit II, st. 3

21 It frequently breakfasts at five-o'clock tea,
And dines on the following day.
Ibid. st. 17

22 There was silence supreme! Not a shriek, not a
scream,
Scarcely even a howl or a groan,
As the man they called "Ho!" told his story of
woe
In an antediluvian tone.
Ibid. Fit III, st. 3

23 It is this, it is this that oppresses my soul.
Ibid. st. 11

24 They sought it with thimbles, they sought it with
care;
They pursued it with forks and hope;
They threatened its life with a railway share;
They charmed it with smiles and soap.
Ibid. Fit V, st. 1

25 For the Snark *was* a Boojum, you see.
Ibid. Fit VIII, st. 9

[1]But answer came there none. —WALTER SCOTT, *The Bridal of Triermain* [1813], canto III, st. 10

1 He thought he saw an Elephant,
  That practiced on a fife:
  He looked again, and found it was
  A letter from his wife.
  "At length I realize," he said,
  "The bitterness of Life!"
                    Sylvie and Bruno [1889], ch. 5

2 He thought he saw a Buffalo
  Upon the chimneypiece:
  He looked again, and found it was
  His sister's husband's niece.
                                      Ibid. 6

3 He thought he saw an Albatross
  That fluttered round the lamp:
  He looked again, and found it was
  A penny postage stamp.
  "You'd best be getting home," he said,
  "The nights are very damp."
                                     Ibid. 12

William Croswell Doane
1832–1913

4 Ancient of Days, who sittest throned in glory,
  To thee all knees are bent, all voices pray.
                              Hymn [1886], st. 1

Henry Clay Work
1832–1884

5 Father, dear father, come home with me now,
  The clock in the belfry strikes one;
  You said you were coming right home from the
        shop
  As soon as your day's work was done.
                      Come Home, Father [1864], st. 1

6 "Hurrah! hurrah! we bring the Jubilee!
  Hurrah! Hurrah! the flag that makes you free!"
  So we sang the chorus from Atlanta to the sea,
  While we were marching through Georgia.
           Marching Through Georgia [1865], chorus

Wilhelm Max Wundt
1832–1920

7   We take issue . . . with every treatment of psychology that is based on simple self-observation or
on philosophical presuppositions.[1]
    *Grundzüge der Physiologischen Psychologie
    (Principles of Physiological Psychology) [1874]*

Isaac Hill Bromley
1833–1898

8 Conductor, when you receive a fare,
  Punch in the presence of the passenjare! . . .

[1]Translated by EDWARD TITCHENER.

Punch, brothers! Punch with care!
Punch in the presence of the passenjare!
                       Punch, Brother, Punch [1875][2]

Adam Lindsay Gordon
1833–1870

9 A little season of love and laughter,
  Of light and life, and pleasure and pain,
  And a horror of outer darkness after,
  And dust returneth to dust again.[3]
                                 The Swimmer

John Marshall Harlan
1833–1911

10   Our Constitution is color-blind, and neither
knows nor tolerates classes among citizens. In respect of civil rights, all citizens are equal before the
law. The humblest is the peer of the most powerful.
      *Dissenting opinion, Plessy v. Ferguson 163 U.S.
      537, 559 [1896]*

Robert Green Ingersoll
1833–1899

11   Like an armed warrior, like a plumed knight,
James G. Blaine marched down the halls of the
American Congress and threw his shining lance full
and fair against the brazen foreheads of the defamers
of his country and the maligners of his honor.
      *Speech nominating Blaine for President,
      National Republican Convention [June 15,
      1876]*

12   I am the inferior of any man whose rights I trample under foot. Men are not superior by reason of
the accidents of race or color. They are superior who
have the best heart—the best brain.   *Liberty*

13   Every cradle asks us, "Whence?" and every coffin, "Whither?" The poor barbarian, weeping above
his dead, can answer these questions as intelligently
as the robed priest of the most authentic creed.
                          Address at a child's grave

14   We, too, have our religion, and it is this: Help for
the living, hope for the dead.   *Ibid.*

15   An honest God is the noblest work of man.
                                    The Gods [1876]

16 Justice is the only worship.
   Love is the only priest.
   Ignorance is the only slavery.
   Happiness is the only good.

[2]Based on a New York streetcar sign. Erroneously attributed
to Mark Twain, who wrote about the verse in *A Literary
Nightmare* [1876].
[3]A little time for laughter, / A little time to sing, / A little time
to kiss and cling, / And no more kissing after.—PHILIP BOURKE
MARSTON [1850–1887], *After, st. 1*
See George du Maurier, 522:10.

The time to be happy is now,
The place to be happy is here,
The way to be happy is to make others so.
Creed

Petroleum V. Nasby
[David Ross Locke]
1833–1888

1 The contract 'twixt Hannah, God and me,
Was not for one or twenty years, but for eternity.
Hannah Jane [1871], st. 29

Alfred Nobel
1833–1896

2   My factories may make an end of war sooner than your congresses. The day when two army corps can annihilate each other in one second, all civilized nations, it is to be hoped, will recoil from war and discharge their troops.
From Bertha von Suttner, Memoiren [Stuttgart, 1909]

Alfred von Schlieffen
1833–1913

3   When you march into France, let the last man on the right brush the channel with his sleeve.
Of his envelopment plan for the German invasion of France in World War I

John Emerich Edward Dalberg-Acton,
Lord Acton
1834–1902

4   There is no error so monstrous that it fails to find defenders among the ablest men. Imagine a congress of eminent celebrities such as More, Bacon, Grotius, Pascal, Cromwell, Bossuet, Montesquieu, Jefferson, Napoleon, Pitt, etc. The result would be an Encyclopedia of Error.
Letter to Mary Gladstone [April 24, 1881]

5   Power tends to corrupt and absolute power corrupts absolutely.[1]
Letter to Bishop Mandell Creighton [April 5, 1887]

6   Advice to Persons About to Write History— Don't.[2]
Ibid. postscript

7   Liberty is not a means to a higher political end. It is itself the highest political end.
The History of Freedom and Other Essays [1907], ch. 1

[1]See William Pitt, 313:2, and Shelley, 406:8.
[2]See *Punch*, 554:14.

8   Writers the most learned, the most accurate in details, and the soundest in tendency, frequently fall into a habit which can neither be cured nor pardoned—the habit of making history into the proof of their theories.
Ibid. 8

George Arnold
1834–1865

9 Life for the living, and rest for the dead!
The Jolly Old Pedagogue, st. 2

Sabine Baring-Gould
1834–1924

10 Onward, Christian soldiers,
Marching as to war,
With the Cross of Jesus
Going on before!
Onward, Christian Soldiers [1864],[3] st. 1

11 Now the day is over,
Night is drawing nigh;
Shadows of the evening
Steal across the sky.
Now the Day Is Over [1865], st. 1

12 Through the night of doubt and sorrow
Onward goes the pilgrim band,
Singing songs of expectation,
Marching to the promised land.
Through the Night of Doubt and Sorrow [1867], st. 1[4]

Charles Farrar Browne [Artemus Ward]
1834–1867

13   I now bid you a welcome adoo.
Artemus Ward: His Book [1862]. The Shakers

14   My pollertics, like my religion, bein of a exceedin accommodatin character.
Ibid. The Crisis

15   I girdid up my Lions & fled the Seen.
Ibid. A Visit to Brigham Young

16   Did you ever hav the measels, and if so how many?
Ibid. The Census

17   The female woman is one of the greatest institooshuns of which this land can boste.
Ibid. Woman's Rights

18   I'm not a politician and my other habits air good.
Ibid. Fourth of July Oration

19   The prevailin weakness of most public men is to SLOP OVER! Washington never slopt over.
Ibid.

[3]Music by SIR ARTHUR SULLIVAN [1842–1900].
[4]Translated from the Danish of B. S. INGEMANN [1825].

1   The sun has a right to "set" where it wants to, and so, I may add, has a hen.
     Artemus Ward: His Travels [1865]. A Mormon Romance, ch. 4

2   I can't sing. As a singist I am not a success. I am saddest when I sing. So are those who hear me. They are sadder even than I am.
     Artemus Ward's Lecture [1866].

3   He [Brigham Young] is dreadfully married. He's the most married man I ever saw in my life.
     Ibid.

4   Why is this thus? What is the reason of this thusness?
     Ibid.

5   The Puritans nobly fled from a land of despotism to a land of freedim, where they could not only enjoy their own religion, but could prevent everybody else from enjoyin *his*.[1]
     London Punch Letters, no. 5 [1866]

6   Let us all be happy and live within our means, even if we have to borrow the money to do it with.
     Natural History

Edgar Degas
1834–1917

7   A picture is something which requires as much knavery, trickery, and deceit as the perpetration of a crime. Paint falsely, and then add the accent of nature.   *Attributed*

George Louis Palmella Busson du Maurier
1834–1896

8   The wretcheder one is, the more one smokes; and the more one smokes, the wretcheder one gets—a vicious circle!   *Peter Ibbetson [1891]*

9   Songs without words are best.   *Ibid.*

10   A little work, a little play,
     To keep us going—and so, good day!

     A little warmth, a little light,
     Of love's bestowing—and so, good night![2]

     A little fun, to match the sorrow
     Of each day's growing—and so, good morrow!

     A little trust that when we die
     We reap our sowing! and so—good-bye!
     Trilby [1894], pt. VIII

---

[1]The Puritan's idea of Hell is a place where everybody has to mind his own business.—*Attributed to* WENDELL PHILLIPS
[2]La vie est vaine:/Un peu d'amour,/Un peu de haine . . . /Et puis—bonjour!/La vie est brève,/Un peu d'espoir,/Un peu de rêve/Et puis—bonsoir!—LEON MONTENAEKEN [b. 1859], *Peu de Chose*
See Gordon, 520:9.

Charles William Eliot
1834–1926

11   In the modern world the intelligence of public opinion is the one indispensable condition of social progress.
     Inaugural address as president of Harvard [1869]

12   Enter to grow in wisdom.
     Depart to serve better thy country and thy kind.
     Inscriptions on the 1890 Gate to Harvard Yard

13   To the Fifty-fourth Regiment of Massachusetts Infantry:
     The white officers, taking life and honor in their hands, cast in their lot with men of a despised race unproved in war, and risked death as inciters of servile insurrection if taken prisoners, besides encountering all the common perils of camp march and battle.
     The black rank and file volunteered when disaster clouded the Union cause, served without pay for eighteen months till given that of white troops, faced threatened enslavement if captured, were brave in action, patient under heavy and dangerous labors, and cheerful amid hardships and privations.
     Together they gave to the nation and the world undying proof that Americans of African descent possess the pride, courage, and devotion of the patriot soldier. One hundred and eighty thousand such Americans enlisted under the Union flag in 1863–1865.
     Inscription on the Robert Gould Shaw Monument by Augustus Saint-Gaudens, Boston Common [1897][3]

Marshall Field
1834–1906

14   Give the lady what she wants!
     Instruction to manager of his Chicago department store

Ernst Heinrich Haeckel
1834–1919

15   Ontogenesis, or the development of the individual, is a short and quick recapitulation of phylogenesis,[4] or the development of the tribe to which it belongs, determined by the laws of inheritance and adaptation.   *The History of Creation [1868][5]*

16   The general theory of evolution . . . assumes that in nature there is a great, unital, continuous and everlasting process of development, and that all natural phenomena without exception, from the mo-

---

[3]See Dunbar, 615:1, and Robert Lowell, 743:10.
[4]Frequently quoted: Ontogeny recapitulates phylogeny. See Freud, 569:6.
[5]Translated by E. R. LANKESTER.

tion of the celestial bodies and the fall of the rolling stone up to the growth of the plant and the consciousness of man, are subject to the same great law of causation—that they are ultimately to be reduced to atomic mechanics.
Freie Wissenschaft und Freie Lehre [1878][1]

Walter Kittredge
1834–1905

1 We're tenting tonight on the old campground,
Give us a song to cheer
Our weary hearts, a song of home
And friends we love so dear.
Tenting on the Old Campground [1864], st. 1

William Morris
1834–1896

2 Well, if this is poetry, it is very easy to write.
Remark [1854]. From J. W. MACKAIL, Life of William Morris [1899]

3 I was half mad with beauty on that day.
The Defense of Guenevere [1858], l. 109

4 Had she come all the way for this,
To part at last without a kiss?
Yea, had she borne the dirt and rain
That her own eyes might see him slain
Beside the haystack in the floods?
The Haystack in the Floods [1858], l. 1

5 I know a little garden close,
Set thick with lily and red rose,
Where I would wander if I might
From dewy morn to dewy night.
The Life and Death of Jason [1867]. A Garden by the Sea, st. 1

6 The idle singer of an empty day.
The Earthly Paradise [1868–1870]. An Apology, st. 1

7 Dreamer of dreams, born out of my due time,
Why should I strive to set the crooked straight?
Ibid. st. 4

8 Love is enough, though the world be awaning.
Love Is Enough [1872]

9 If you want a golden rule that will fit everybody, this is it: Have nothing in your houses that you do not know to be useful, or believe to be beautiful.
The Beauty of Life [1880]

10 What I mean by Socialism is a condition of society in which there should be neither rich nor poor, neither master nor master's man, neither idle nor overworked, neither brain-sick brain workers nor heart-sick hand workers, in a word, in which all men would be living in equality of condition, and would

[1]Translated by J. B. STALLO.

manage their affairs unwastefully, and with the full consciousness that harm to one would mean harm to all—the realization at last of the meaning of the word *commonwealth*.
Written for "Justice" [1884]

11 The reward of labor is life.
News from Nowhere [1891], ch. 15

Frank Richard Stockton
1834–1902

12 Which came out of the opened door—the lady or the tiger? *The Lady or the Tiger? [1884]*

13 The board money is in the ginger jar and our conscience is clear.
The Casting Away of Mrs. Lecks and Mrs. Aleshine [1886]

James Thomson
1834–1882

14 Statues and pictures and verse may be grand,
But they are not the Life for which they stand.
Art [1865], st. 3, l. 19

15 Give a man a horse he can ride,
Give a man a boat he can sail.
Sunday Up the River [1869], st. 15

16 The City is of Night; perchance of Death,
But certainly of Night.
The City of Dreadful Night [1874], st. 1

17 I find no hint throughout the Universe
Of good or ill, of blessing or of curse;
I find alone Necessity Supreme.
Ibid. st. 14

James McNeill Whistler
1834–1903

18 Two and two the mathematician continues to make four, in spite of the whine of the amateur for three, or the cry of the critic for five.
Whistler v. Ruskin [1878]

19 The rare few, who, early in life, have rid themselves of the friendship of the many.
The Gentle Art of Making Enemies [1890]

20 To say of a picture, as is often said in its praise, that it shows great and earnest labor, is to say that it is incomplete and unfit for view. *Ibid.*

21 The masterpiece should appear as the flower to the painter—perfect in its bud as in its bloom—with no reason to explain its presence—no mission to fulfill—a joy to the artist, a delusion to the philanthropist—a puzzle to the botanist—an accident of sentiment and alliteration to the literary man.
Ibid.

1   Art should be independent of all claptrap— should stand alone, and appeal to the artistic sense of eye or ear, without confounding this with emotions entirely foreign to it, as devotion, pity, love, patriotism, and the like. All these have no kind of concern with it.
The Gentle Art of Making Enemies

2   One cannot continually disappoint a Continent.[1]
Ibid.

3   I am not arguing with you—I am telling you.
Ibid.

4   *Attorney-General Sir John Holker:* The labor of two days, then, is that for which you ask two hundred guineas?
Whistler: No;—I ask it for the knowledge of a lifetime.   *Ibid. Messieurs Les Enemis*[2]

5   *Wilde:* I wish I'd said that.
Whistler: You will, Oscar, you will.
From L. C. INGLEBY, Oscar Wilde [1907]

6   Had silicon been a gas I would have been a major general.
On failing chemistry at West Point. From JOSEPH PENNELL, The Life of James McNeill Whistler [1908]

Thomas Brigham Bishop
1835–1905

7   John Brown's body lies a-moldering in the grave, His soul is marching on.
John Brown's Body, st. 1

8   Shoo, fly! don't bodder me! I belong to Company G,
I feel like a morning star.
Shoo, Fly. Refrain

Phillips Brooks
1835–1893

9   O little town of Bethlehem!
How still we see thee lie;
Above thy deep and dreamless sleep
The silent stars go by;
Yet in thy dark streets shineth
The everlasting Light;
The hopes and fears of all the years
Are met in thee tonight.
O Little Town of Bethlehem [1867], st. 1

[1]Referring to a contemplated visit to the United States.
[2]Exchange in the 1878 trial of Whistler's libel suit against John Ruskin, who had written [*Fors Clavigera, Letter 79,* July 2, 1877] of the artist's *Nocturne in Black and Gold:* "I have seen, and heard, much of Cockney impudence before now; but never expected to hear a coxcomb ask two hundred guineas for flinging a pot of paint in the public's face."

10   Life comes before literature, as the material always comes before the work. The hills are full of marble before the world blooms with statues.
Literature and Life

Samuel Butler
1835–1902

11   The man who lets himself be bored is even more contemptible than the bore.
The Fair Haven [1873]. Memoir, ch. 3

12   A hen is only an egg's way of making another egg.
Life and Habit [1877], ch. 8

13   Stowed away in a Montreal lumber room
The Discobolus standeth and turneth his face to the wall;
Dusty, cobweb-covered, maimed and set at naught,
Beauty crieth in an attic and no man regardeth.
O God! O Montreal!
A Psalm of Montreal [1884], st. 1

14   The Discobolus is put here because he is vulgar— He has neither vest nor pants with which to cover his limbs.
Ibid. st. 5

15   It was very good of God to let Carlyle and Mrs. Carlyle marry one another and so make only two people miserable instead of four.
Letter to Miss E. M. A. Savage [November 21, 1884]

16   It is far safer to know too little than too much. People will condemn the one, though they will resent being called upon to exert themselves to follow the other.   *The Way of All Flesh [1903], ch. 5*

17   Taking numbers into account, I should think more mental suffering had been undergone in the streets leading from St. George's, Hanover Square, than in the condemned cells of Newgate.
Ibid. 13

18   Every man's work, whether it be literature or music or pictures or architecture or anything else, is always a portrait of himself.   *Ibid. 14*

19   One great reason why clergymen's households are generally unhappy is because the clergyman is so much at home or close about the house.
Ibid. 24

20   The advantage of doing one's praising for oneself is that one can lay it on so thick and exactly in the right places.   *Ibid. 34*

21   The best liar is he who makes the smallest amount of lying go the longest way.   *Ibid. 39*

22   A man's friendships are, like his will, invalidated by marriage—but they are also no less invalidated by the marriage of his friends.   *Ibid. 75*

1 Life is the art of drawing sufficient conclusions from insufficient premises.
Notebooks [1912]. Life

2 All progress is based upon a universal innate desire on the part of every organism to live beyond its income. *Ibid.*

3 Though analogy is often misleading, it is the least misleading thing we have.
Ibid. Music, Pictures, and Books

4 The phrase "unconscious humor" is the one contribution I have made to the current literature of the day. *Ibid. Homo Unius Libri*

5 Genius . . . has been defined as a supreme capacity for taking trouble.[1] . . . It might be more fitly described as a supreme capacity for getting its possessors into pains of all kinds and keeping them therein so long as the genius remains.
Ibid. Genius

6 An apology for the Devil: It must be remembered that we have only heard one side of the case. God has written all the books.
Ibid. Higgledy-Piggledy: An Apology for the Devil

7 God is Love—I dare say. But what a mischievous devil Love is! *Ibid. God Is Love*

8 [*The Ancient Mariner*] would not have taken so well if it had been called *The Old Sailor*.
Ibid. Titles and Subjects

9 The public buys its opinions as it buys its meat, or takes in its milk, on the principle that it is cheaper to do this than to keep a cow. So it is, but the milk is more likely to be watered.
Ibid. Sequel to "Alps and Sanctuaries"

10 I do not mind lying, but I hate inaccuracy.
Ibid. Truth and Convenience: Falsehood

Andrew Carnegie
1835–1919

11 While the law [of competition] may be sometimes hard for the individual, it is best for the race, because it insures the survival of the fittest in every department. We accept and welcome, therefore, as conditions to which we must accommodate ourselves, great inequality of environment, the concentration of business, industrial and commercial, in the hands of a few, and the law of competition between these, as being not only beneficial, but essential for the future progress of the race.
Wealth. From the North American Review [June 1889]

12 Upon the sacredness of property civilization itself depends—the right of the laborer to his hundred dollars in the savings bank, and equally the legal right of the millionaire to his millions. *Ibid.*

13 Surplus wealth is a sacred trust which its possessor is bound to administer in his lifetime for the good of the community. *Ibid.*

14 Those who would administer wisely must, indeed, be wise, for one of the serious obstacles to the improvement of our race is indiscriminate charity.
Ibid.

15 The man who dies . . . rich dies disgraced.
Ibid.

16 Three generations from shirtsleeves to shirtsleeves.[2] *Triumphant Democracy [1886]*

Fukuzawa Yukichi[3]
1835–1901

17 The final purpose of all my work was to create in Japan a civilized nation as well equipped in both the arts of war and peace as those of the Western world.
Autobiography [1898]

Mark Twain[4]
[Samuel Langhorne Clemens]
1835–1910

18 The serene confidence which a Christian feels in four aces.
Letter to The Golden Era (San Francisco) [May 22, 1864]

19 I *have* had a "call" to literature, of a low order —*i.e.* humorous. It is nothing to be proud of, but it is my strongest suit . . . seriously scribbling to excite the *laughter* of God's creatures.
Letter to Orion and Mary Clemens [October 19, 1865]

20 I don't see no p'ints about that frog that's any better'n any other frog.
The Notorious Jumping Frog of Calaveras County [1865][5]

21 I'll resk forty dollars that he can outjump any frog in Calaveras county. *Ibid.*

22 They spell it Vinci and pronounce it Vinchy; foreigners always spell better than they pronounce.
The Innocents Abroad [1869], ch. 19

23 There's millions in it!
The Gilded Age (stage version) [1874]

---

[1]See Buffon, 311:8; Carlyle, 413:15; and Jane Ellice Hopkins, 532:2.

[2]There's nobbut three generations atween clog and clog. —*Lancashire proverb, which Carnegie liked to quote*

[3]From *Sources of Japanese Tradition* [1960], edited by Wɪʟʟɪᴀᴍ Tʜᴇᴏᴅᴏʀᴇ ᴅᴇ Bᴀʀʏ.

[4]A pseudonym apparently derived from the Mississippi steamboating term signifying two fathoms (12 feet) of depth.

[5]Frequently cited as "The Celebrated Jumping Frog of Calaveras County."

1   Barring that natural expression of villainy which we all have, the man looked honest enough.
Sketches [1875]. A Mysterious Visit

2   Tom appeared on the sidewalk with a bucket of whitewash and a long-handled brush. He surveyed the fence, and all gladness left him and a deep melancholy settled down upon his spirit. Thirty yards of board fence nine feet high. Life to him seemed hollow, and existence but a burden.
The Adventures of Tom Sawyer [1876], ch. 2

3   Work consists of whatever a body is *obliged* to do. . . . Play consists of whatever a body is not obliged to do.   *Ibid.*

4   She makes me wash, they comb me all to thunder; she won't let me sleep in the woodshed. . . . The widder eats by a bell; she goes to bed by a bell; she gits up by a bell—everything's so awful reg'lar a body can't stand it.   *Ibid. ch. 35*

5   There is a sumptuous variety about the New England weather that compels the stranger's admiration—and regret. The weather is always doing something there; always attending strictly to business; always getting up new designs and trying them on the people to see how they will go. . . . Yes, one of the brightest gems in the New England weather is the dazzling uncertainty of it.
Speech, The Weather [1876]

6   I am a great & sublime fool. But then I am God's fool, & all His works must be contemplated with respect.
Letter to William Dean Howells [December 28(?), 1877]

7   I'm the man they call Sudden Death and General Desolation! Sired by a hurricane, dam'd by an earthquake. . . . When I'm playful I use the meridians of longitude and parallels of latitude for a seine, and drag the Atlantic Ocean for whales! I scratch my head with the lightning and purr myself to sleep with the thunder!   *Life on the Mississippi [1883], ch. 3*

8   The Child of Calamity.   *Ibid.*

9   I can picture that old time to myself now, just as it was then: the white town drowsing in the sunshine of a summer's morning . . . the great Mississippi, the majestic, the magnificent Mississippi, rolling its mile-wide tide along, shining in the sun.
Ibid. 4

10   I was gratified to be able to answer promptly, and I did. I said I didn't know.   *Ibid. 6*

11   Your true pilot cares nothing about anything on earth but the river, and his pride in his occupation surpasses the pride of kings.   *Ibid. 7*

12   By the Shadow of Death, but he's a lightning pilot!   *Ibid.*

13   I'll learn him or kill him.   *Ibid. 8*

14   When I find a well-drawn character in fiction or biography, I generally take a warm personal interest in him, for the reason that I have known him before—met him on the river.   *Ibid. 18*

15   The first time I ever saw St. Louis, I could have bought it for six million dollars, and it was the mistake of my life that I did not do it.   *Ibid. 22*

16   Give an Irishman lager for a month, and he's a dead man. An Irishman is lined with copper, and the beer corrodes it. But whiskey polishes the copper and is the saving of him.   *Ibid. 23*

17   All the modern inconveniences.   *Ibid. 43*

18   Persons attempting to find a motive in this narrative will be prosecuted; persons attempting to find a moral in it will be banished; persons attempting to find a plot in it will be shot.
Adventures of Huckleberry Finn [1885]. Notice

19   You don't know about me, without you have read a book by the name of "The Adventures of Tom Sawyer," but that ain't no matter. That book was made by Mr. Mark Twain, and he told the truth, mainly. There was things which he stretched, but mainly he told the truth. That is nothing. I never seen anybody but lied, one time or another.
Ibid. ch. 1

20   It was kind of solemn, drifting down the big still river, laying on our backs looking up at the stars, and we didn't ever feel like talking loud, and it warn't often that we laughed, only a little kind of a low chuckle. We had mighty good weather, as a general thing, and nothing ever happened to us at all, that night, nor the next, nor the next.
Ibid. 12

21   "Pilgrim's Progress," about a man that left his family it didn't say why. I read considerable in it now and then. The statements was interesting, but tough.   *Ibid. 17*

22   We said there warn't no home like a raft, after all. Other places do seem so cramped up and smothery, but a raft don't. You feel mighty free and easy and comfortable on a raft.   *Ibid. 18*

23   It was a monstrous big river down there.
Ibid. 19

24   All kings is mostly rapscallions.   *Ibid. 23*

25   Hain't we got all the fools in town on our side? and ain't that a big enough majority in any town?
Ibid. 26

26   You can't pray a lie.   *Ibid. 31*

27   I studied a minute, sort of holding my breath, and then says to myself: "All right, then, I'll *go* to hell."
Ibid.

1 He [George Washington Cable] has taught me to abhor and detest the Sabbath-day and hunt up new and troublesome ways to dishonor it.
Letter to William Dean Howells [February 27, 1885]

2 The difference between the *almost*-right word & the *right* word is really a large matter—it's the difference between the lightning bug and the lightning.
Letter to George Bainton [October 15, 1888]

3 We saw a faraway town sleeping in a valley by a winding river; and beyond it, on a hill, a vast gray fortress, with towers and turrets, the first I had ever seen, out of a picture.
   "Bridgeport?" said I, pointing.
   "Camelot," said he.
A Connecticut Yankee in King Arthur's Court [1889]. A Word of Explanation

4 Whenever the literary German dives into a sentence, that is the last you are going to see of him till he emerges on the other side of his Atlantic with his verb in his mouth.   *Ibid. ch. 22*

5 There ain't no way to find out why a snorer can't hear himself snore.
Tom Sawyer Abroad [1894], ch. 10

6 Tell the truth or trump—but get the trick.
Pudd'nhead Wilson [1894]. Pudd'nhead Wilson's Calendar, ch. 1

7 Adam was but human—this explains it all. He did not want the apple for the apple's sake, he wanted it only because it was forbidden.
   Ibid. 2

8 Training is everything. The peach was once a bitter almond; cauliflower is nothing but cabbage with a college education.   *Ibid. 5*

9 One of the most striking differences between a cat and a lie is that a cat has only nine lives.
   Ibid. 7

10 The holy passion of Friendship is of so sweet and steady and loyal and enduring a nature that it will last through a whole lifetime, if not asked to lend money.   *Ibid. 8*

11 Why is it that we rejoice at a birth and grieve at a funeral? It is because we are not the person involved.   *Ibid. 9*

12 When angry, count four; when very angry, swear.
   Ibid. 10

13 As to the Adjective: when in doubt, strike it out.
   Ibid. 11

14 Nothing so needs reforming as other people's habits.   *Ibid. 15*

15 Put all your eggs in the one basket and—WATCH THAT BASKET.   *Ibid. 15*

16 If you pick up a starving dog and make him prosperous, he will not bite you. This is the principal difference between a dog and a man.   *Ibid. 16*

17 Few things are harder to put up with than the annoyance of a good example.   *Ibid. 19*

18 It were not best that we should all think alike; it is difference of opinion that makes horse-races.
   Ibid. 19

19 [Citing a familiar "American joke":] In Boston they ask, How much does he know? in New York, How much is he worth? in Philadelphia, Who were his parents?
   What Paul Bourget Thinks of Us [1895]

20 He saw nearly all things as through a glass eye, darkly.
Fenimore Cooper's Literary Offenses [1895]

21 Be good and you will be lonesome.
Following the Equator [1897]. Pudd'nhead Wilson's New Calendar, frontispiece caption

22 When in doubt tell the truth.   *Ibid. ch. 2*

23 Noise proves nothing. Often a hen who has merely laid an egg cackles as if she had laid an asteroid.   *Ibid. 5*

24 Truth is the most valuable thing we have. Let us economize it.   *Ibid. 7*

25 It could probably be shown by facts and figures that there is no distinctly native American criminal class except Congress.   *Ibid. 8*

26 Everything human is pathetic. The secret source of Humor itself is not joy but sorrow. There is no humor in heaven.   *Ibid. 10*

27 We should be careful to get out of an experience only the wisdom that is in it—and stop there; lest we be like the cat that sits down on a hot stove-lid. She will never sit down on a hot stove-lid again— and that is well; but also she will never sit down on a cold one any more.   *Ibid. 11*

28 Pity is for the living, envy is for the dead.
   Ibid. 19

29 It is by the goodness of God that in our country we have those three unspeakably precious things: freedom of speech, freedom of conscience, and the prudence never to practice either of them.
   Ibid. 20

30 "*Classic.*" A book which people praise and don't read.   *Ibid. 25*

31 Man is the only animal that blushes. Or needs to.
   Ibid. 27

32 Each person is born to one possession which outvalues all his others—his last breath.   *Ibid. 42*

33 It takes your enemy and your friend, working together, to hurt you to the heart; the one to slander you and the other to get the news to you.
   ibid. 45

34 In statesmanship get the formalities right, never mind about the moralities.   *Ibid. 65*

1   Everyone is a moon, and has a dark side which he never shows to anybody.
Following the Equator, ch. 66

2   The report of my death was an exaggeration.
Note to London correspondent of the New York Journal [June 1, 1897]

3   Always do right. This will gratify some people, and astonish the rest.
Card sent to the Young People's Society, Greenpoint Presbyterian Church, Brooklyn [February 16, 1901]

4   I believe that our Heavenly Father invented man because he was disappointed in the monkey.
Autobiographical Dictation [November 24, 1906]

5   Laws are sand, customs are rock. Laws can be evaded and punishment escaped, but an openly transgressed custom brings sure punishment.
The Gorky Incident [1906]

6   Thunder is good, thunder is impressive; but it is the lightning that does the work.
Letter to an Unidentified Person [August 28, 1908]

7   Power, money, persuasion, supplication, persecution—these can lift at a colossal humbug—push it a little—weaken it a little, century by century, but only laughter can blow it to rags and atoms at a blast. Against the assault of laughter nothing can stand.   *The Mysterious Stranger [1922], ch. 10*

8   O kind missionary, O compassionate missionary, leave China! come home and convert these Christians!
Europe and Elsewhere [1923]. The United States of Lyncherdom

9   You tell me whar a man gits his corn pone, en I'll tell you what his 'pinions is.
Ibid. Corn-Pone Opinions

10   Biographies are but the clothes and buttons of the man—the biography of the man himself cannot be written.   *Autobiography [1924], vol. I*

11   [Man] has imagined a heaven, and has left entirely out of it the supremest of all his delights . . . sexual intercourse! . . . His heaven is like himself: strange, interesting, astonishing, grotesque. I give you my word, it has not a single feature in it that he *actually values.*
Letters from the Earth [1962], II

12   [The Bible] has noble poetry in it; and some clever fables; and some blood-drenched history; and a wealth of obscenity; and upwards of a thousand lies.   *Ibid. III*

13   When I was younger I could remember anything, whether it happened or not; but I am getting old, and soon I shall remember only the latter.
From ALBERT BIGELOW PAINE, Mark Twain, A Biography [1912]

14   Clothes make the man. Naked people have little or no influence in society.   *Attributed*

15   Everybody talks about the weather, but nobody does anything about it.[1]   *Attributed*

Thomas Bailey Aldrich
1836–1907

16 In street and alley, what strange tongues are loud,
Accents of menace alien to our air,
Voices that once the Tower of Babel knew!
O Liberty, white Goddess! Is it well
To leave the gates unguarded?
The Unguarded Gates [1892]

17   Though I am not genuine Boston, I am Boston-plated.
From FERRIS GREENSLET, The Life of Thomas Bailey Aldrich [1908]

Isabella Mary Beeton
1836–1865

18   A place for everything and everything in its place.[2]
The Book of Household Management [1861]

19   Clear as you go.   *Ibid.*

Edward Ernest Bowen
1836–1901

20 Forty years on, when afar and asunder
Parted are those who are singing today.
Forty Years On [1872][3]

Joseph Chamberlain
1836–1914

21   The day of small nations has long passed away. The day of Empires has come.
Speech, Birmingham [May 12, 1904]

Sir William Schwenck Gilbert
1836–1911

22 Oh, I am a cook and a captain bold
And the mate of the *Nancy* brig,

---

[1]A famously moot quotation frequently attributed instead to Charles Dudley Warner (see 511). A variant version—"We all grumble about the weather but nothing is *done* about it"—appears in Robert Underwood Johnson's recollections of Mark Twain (*Remembered Yesterdays* [1923]).

[2]In a well-conducted man-of-war . . . everything is in its place, and there is a place for everything.—MARRYAT, *Masterman Ready* [1842]

[3]Harrow school song.

And a bo'sun tight, and a midshipmite,
And the crew of the captain's gig.
  The "Bab" Ballads [1866–1871]. The Yarn of
  the "Nancy Bell," st. 3

1 As innocent as a new-laid egg.
           Engaged [1877], act I

2 I'm called Little Buttercup—dear little Buttercup,
Though I could never tell why.
        H.M.S. Pinafore [1878], act I

3 I am the Captain of the *Pinafore;*
And a right good captain too!
               Ibid.

4 And I'm never, never sick at sea!
 What, never?
 No, never!
 What, *never?*
 Hardly ever!
He's hardly ever sick at sea!
Then give three cheers, and one cheer more
For the hardy Captain of the *Pinafore!*
               Ibid.

5 And so do his sisters, and his cousins, and his
  aunts!
His sisters and his cousins,
Whom he reckons up by dozens,
And his aunts!
               Ibid.

6 When I was a lad I served a term
As office boy to an Attorney's firm.
I cleaned the windows and I swept the floor
And I polished up the handle of the big front
  door.
I polished up that handle so carefullee
That now I am the Ruler of the Queen's Navee!
               Ibid.

7 Stick close to your desks and *never go to sea,*
And you all may be Rulers of the Queen's Navee!
               Ibid.

8 Things are seldom what they seem,
Skim milk masquerades as cream.
             Ibid. II

9 He is an Englishman!
For he himself has said it,
And it's greatly to his credit,
That he is an Englishman!
               Ibid.

10 For he might have been a Roosian,
A French or Turk or Proosian,
Or perhaps Itali-an.
But in spite of all temptations
To belong to other nations,
He remains an Englishman.
               Ibid.

11 It is, it is a glorious thing
To be a Pirate King.
      Pirates of Penzance [1879], act I

12 I am the very model of a modern Major-General.
I've information vegetable, animal, and mineral,
I know the Kings of England, and I quote the
  fights historical,
From Marathon to Waterloo, in order categorical.
               Ibid.

13 When the foeman bares his steel,
  Tarantara, tarantara!
We uncomfortable feel,
  Tarantara.
              Ibid. II

14 When constabulary duty's to be done,
The policeman's lot is not a happy one.
               Ibid.

15 Come, friends, who plow the sea,
  Truce to navigation,
  Take another station;
Let's vary piracee
With a little burglaree.[1]
               Ibid.

16 Twenty love-sick maidens we,
Love-sick all against our will.
        Patience [1881], act I

17 You must lie upon the daisies and discourse in
  novel phrases of your complicated state of
  mind,
The meaning doesn't matter if it's only idle
  chatter of a transcendental kind.
And everyone will say,
As you walk your mystic way,
"If this young man expresses himself in terms too
  deep for *me,*
Why, what a very singularly deep young man this
  deep young man must be!"
               Ibid.

18 Though the Philistines may jostle, you will rank
  as an apostle in the high aesthetic band,
If you walk down Piccadilly with a poppy or a
  lily in your medieval hand.
And everyone will say,
As you walk your flowery way,
"If he's content with a vegetable love, which
  would certainly not suit *me,*
Why, what a most particularly pure young man
  this pure young man must be!"
               Ibid.

19 Prithee, pretty maiden, will you marry me?
(Hey, but I'm hopeful, willow, willow, waly!)
               Ibid.

20 While this magnetic,
Peripatetic
Lover he lived to learn,
By no endeavor,

[1]The roistering chorus "Hail, hail, the gang's all here" is
sung to Sir Arthur Sullivan's music for these lines.

Can magnet ever
Attract a silver churn!

Patience, act II

1 Francesca da Rimini, miminy, piminy,
Je-ne-sais-quoi young man!

Ibid.

2 A greenery-yallery, Grosvenor Gallery,
Foot-in-the-grave young man!

Ibid.

3 I see no objection to stoutness, in moderation.

Iolanthe [1882], act I

4 None shall part us from each other,
One in life and death are we:
All in all to one another—
I to thee and thou to me!
Thou the tree and I the flower—
Thou the idol; I the throng—
Thou the day and I the hour—
Thou the singer; I the song!

Ibid.

5 Bow, bow, ye lower middle classes!
Bow, bow, ye tradesmen, bow, ye masses.

Ibid.

6 The Law is the true embodiment
Of everything that's excellent.
It has no kind of fault or flaw,
And I, my Lords, embody the Law.

Ibid.

7 Pretty young wards in Chancery.

Ibid.

8 For I'm not so old, and not so plain,
And I'm quite prepared to marry again.

Ibid.

9 Hearts just as pure and fair
May beat in Belgrave Square
As in the lowly air
Of Seven Dials.

Ibid.

10 When I went to the Bar as a very young man
(Said I to myself, said I).

Ibid.

11 I often think it's comical
How nature always does contrive
That every boy and every gal,
That's born into the world alive,
Is either a little Liberal,
Or else a little Conservative!

Ibid. II

12 Here's a pretty kettle of fish!

Ibid.

13 The House of Peers, throughout the war,
Did nothing in particular,
And did it very well.

Ibid.

14 When you're lying awake with a dismal headache,
and repose is taboo'd by anxiety,
I conceive you may use any language you choose
to indulge in, without impropriety.

Ibid.

15 For you dream you are crossing the Channel, and
tossing about in a steamer from Harwich—
Which is something between a large bathing
machine and a very small second-class
carriage.

Ibid.

16 Faint heart never won fair lady![1]
Nothing venture, nothing win[2]—
Blood is thick, but water's thin[3]—
In for a penny, in for a pound[4]—
It's Love that makes the world go round![5]

Ibid.

17 I love my fellow creatures—I do all the good I
can—
Yet everybody says I'm such a disagreeable man!
And I can't think why!

Princess Ida [1884], act I

18 A wandering minstrel I—
A thing of shreds and patches,[6]
Of ballads, songs and snatches,
And dreamy lullaby!

The Mikado [1885], act I

19 I can't help it. I was born sneering.

Ibid.

20 As some day it may happen that a victim must be
found,
I've got a little list—I've got a little list.
Of society offenders who might well be
underground,
And who never would be missed—who never
would be missed.

Ibid.

21 Then the idiot who praises, with enthusiastic
tone,
All centuries but this, and every country but his
own.

Ibid.

22 Three little maids from school are we,
Pert as a schoolgirl well can be,
Filled to the brim with girlish glee.

Ibid.

[1]See Cervantes, 150:29.
[2]See Chaucer, 128:24, and John Heywood, 141:33.
[3]See Ray, 272:6.
[4]Well, then o'er shoes, o'er boots. And in for a penny, in for
a Pound.—EDWARD RAVENSCROFT [fl. 1671–1697], *The Canterbury Guests; Or, A Bargain Broken* [1695], act V, sc. 1
[5]See Anonymous: French, 786:18.
[6]See Shakespeare, 198:1.

1 Ah, pray make no mistake,
We are not shy;
We're very wide awake,
The moon and I!

Ibid. II

2 Here's a pretty state of things!
Here's a pretty how-de-do!

Ibid.

3 My object all sublime
I shall achieve in time—
To let the punishment fit the crime.[1]

Ibid.

4 A source of innocent merriment!

Ibid.

5   On a cloth untrue
    With a twisted cue
And elliptical billiard balls.

Ibid.

6 I seized him by his little pig-tail,
And on his knees fell he,
As he squirmed and struggled,
And gurgled and guggled,
I drew my snickersnee!

Ibid.

7   Merely corroborative detail, intended to give
artistic verisimilitude to an otherwise bald and unconvincing narrative.   *Ibid.*

8 The flowers that bloom in the spring, tra la,
Have nothing to do with the case.

Ibid.

9 On a tree by a river a little tomtit
Sang "Willow, titwillow, titwillow!"
And I said to him, "Dicky-bird, why do you sit
Singing 'Willow, titwillow, titwillow!'
"Is it weakness of intellect, birdie?" I cried,
"Or a rather tough worm in your little inside?"
With a shake of his poor little head he replied,
"Oh, willow, titwillow, titwillow!"

Ibid.

10   There's a fascination frantic
     In a ruin that's romantic;
Do you think you are sufficiently decayed?

Ibid.

11   He uses language that would make your hair
curl.   *Ruddigore [1887], act I*

12 When the footpads quail at the night-bird's wail,
     and black dogs bay at the moon,
Then is the specters' holiday—then is the ghosts'
     high noon!

Ibid. II

13 I have a song to sing, O!
Sing me your song, O!

The Yeomen of the Guard [1888], act I

[1]See Cicero, 88:7.

14 It's a song of a merryman, moping mum,
Whose soul was sad, and whose glance was glum,
Who sipped no sup, and who craved no crumb,
As he sighed for the love of a lady.

Ibid.

15 He led his regiment from behind—
He found it less exciting.

The Gondoliers [1889], act I

16   That celebrated,
     Cultivated,
     Underrated
     Nobleman,
The Duke of Plaza Toro!

Ibid.

17 No soldier in that gallant band
Hid half as well as he did.
He lay concealed throughout the war,
And so preserved his gore, O!

Ibid.

18 Of *that* there is no manner of doubt—
No probable, possible shadow of doubt—
No possible doubt whatever.

Ibid.

19 Life's a pudding full of plums;
Care's a canker that benumbs,
Wherefore waste our elocution
On impossible solution?
Life's a pleasant institution,
Let us take it as it comes!

Ibid.

20 The gratifying feeling that our duty has been
     done.

Ibid. II

21 Take a pair of sparkling eyes.

Ibid.

22 When everyone is somebodee,
Then no one's anybody!

Ibid.

23 The world has joked incessantly for over fifty
     centuries.
And every joke that's possible has long ago been
     made.
*His Excellency: The Played-Out Humorist
[1894]*

Bret Harte
[Francis Brett Harte]
1836–1902

24   Tell the boys I've got the Luck with me now.
The Luck of Roaring Camp [1868]

25   Beneath this tree lies the body of JOHN OAKHURST,
who struck a streak of bad luck on the 23rd of

November, 1850, and handed in his checks on the 7th of December, 1850.

The Outcasts of Poker Flat [1869]

1 Which I wish to remark,
And my language is plain,
That for ways that are dark
And for tricks that are vain,
The heathen Chinee is peculiar,
Which the same I would rise to explain.

Plain Language from Truthful James [1870]

Jane Ellice Hopkins
1836–1904

2 Genius is an infinite capacity for taking pains.[1]

Work Amongst Working Men [1870]

Cesare Lombroso
1836–1909

3 Klopstock was questioned regarding the meaning of a passage in his poem. He replied, "God and I both knew what it meant once; now God alone knows."[2]   *The Man of Genius [1891], pt. I, ch. 2*

4 The appearance of a single great genius is more than equivalent to the birth of a hundred mediocrities.   *Ibid. II, 2*

5 "Lawsuit mania" . . . a continual craving to go to law against others, while considering themselves the injured party.   *Ibid. III, 3*

John Burroughs
1837–1921

6 Serene, I fold my hands and wait,
Nor care for wind, nor tide, nor sea;
I rave no more 'gainst time or fate,
For lo! my own shall come to me.

Waiting [1876] st. 1

7 I was born with a chronic anxiety about the weather.   *Is It Going to Rain? [1877]*

8 One goes to Nature only for hints and half-truths. Her facts are crude until you have absorbed them or translated them. . . . It is not so much what we see as what the thing seen suggests.

Signs and Seasons [1886]. A Sharp Lookout

9 It is always easier to believe than to deny. Our minds are naturally affirmative.

The Light of Day [1900]. The Modern Skeptic

10 Nature teaches more than she preaches. There are no sermons in stones. It is easier to get a spark out of a stone than a moral.

Time and Change [1912]. The Gospel of Nature

---

[1]See Buffon, 311:8; Carlyle, 413:15; and Samuel Butler [1835–1902], 525:5.
[2]Also attributed to Browning, apropos of his *Sordello*.

11 I see on an immense scale, and as clearly as in a demonstration in a laboratory, that good comes out of evil; that the impartiality of the Nature Providence is best; that we are made strong by what we overcome; that man is man because he is as free to do evil as to do good; that life is as free to develop hostile forms as to develop friendly; that power waits upon him who earns it; that disease, wars, the unloosened, devastating elemental forces have each and all played their part in developing and hardening man and giving him the heroic fiber.

Accepting the Universe [1922]

Grover Cleveland
1837–1908

12 Your every voter, as surely as your chief magistrate, exercises a public trust.[3]

Inaugural Address [March 4, 1885]

George Dewey[4]
1837–1917

13 You may fire when you are ready, Gridley.

To the captain of Admiral Dewey's flagship at the battle of Manila Bay [May 1, 1898]

William Dean Howells
1837–1920

14 Lord, for the erring thought
Not into evil wrought:
Lord, for the wicked will
Betrayed and baffled still:
For the heart from itself kept,
Our thanksgiving accept.

A Thanksgiving

15 He who sleeps in continual noise is wakened by silence.

Pordenone, IV

16 The wrecks of slavery are fast growing a fungus crop of sentiment.

Their Wedding Journey [1872]

17 We invite our novelists . . . to concern themselves with the more smiling aspects of life, which are the more American.

Editor's Study: Dostoievski's Latest Novel, in Harper's Monthly [September 1886]

18 The mortality of all inanimate things is terrible to me, but that of books most of all.

Letter to Charles Eliot Norton [April 6, 1903]

19 Clemens was sole, incomparable, the Lincoln of our literature.   *My Mark Twain [1910]*

---

[3]"Public office is a public trust" was used by the Cleveland administration as its motto.
[4]See Ironquill, 544:6.

1   Some people can stay longer in an hour than others can in a week.   *Attributed*

John Pierpont Morgan
1837–1913

2   A man always has two reasons for what he does —a good one, and the real one.
From OWEN WISTER, *Roosevelt: The Story of a Friendship* [1930]

3   Any man who has to ask about the annual up-keep of a yacht can't afford one.   *Attributed*

4   Never be on the bear side but on the bull side when the United States is in question.[1]
Attributed

Horace Porter
1837–1921

5   A mugwump is a person educated beyond his intellect.
A slogan of the Cleveland-Blaine campaign [1884]

Innes Randolph
1837–1887

6 Oh, I'm a good old rebel, that's what I am.
A Good Old Rebel [c. 1870], st. 1

7 I won't be reconstructed, and I don't give a damn.
Ibid. st. 4

Algernon Charles Swinburne
1837–1909

8 When the hounds of spring are on winter's traces,
The mother of months in meadow or plain
Fills the shadows and windy places
With lisp of leaves and ripple of rain;
And the brown bright nightingale amorous
Is half assuaged for Itylus,
For the Thracian ships and the foreign faces,
The tongueless vigil, and all the pain.
Atalanta in Calydon [1865], chorus, st. 1

9 For winter's rains and ruins are over,
And all the season of snows and sins;
The days dividing lover and lover,
The light that loses, the night that wins;
And time remembered is grief forgotten,
And frosts are slain and flowers begotten,
And in green underwood and cover
Blossom by blossom the spring begins.
Ibid. st. 4

[1]Also attributed to Junius S. Morgan [1813–1890].

10 Before the beginning of years
There came to the making of man
Time, with a gift of tears;
Grief, with a glass that ran;
Pleasure, with pain for leaven;
Summer, with flowers that fell;
Remembrance fallen from heaven,
And madness risen from hell;
Strength without hands to smite;
Love that endures for a breath;
Night, the shadow of light,
And life, the shadow of death.
Ibid. chorus, st. 1

11 For words divide and rend;
But silence is most noble till the end.
Ibid.

12   Change in a trice
The lilies and languors of virtue
For the raptures and roses of vice.
Dolores [1866], st. 9

13 O splendid and sterile Dolores,
Our Lady of Pain.
Ibid.

14 The delight that consumes the desire,
The desire that outruns the delight.
Ibid. st. 14

15 For the crown of our life as it closes
Is darkness, the fruit there of dust.
Ibid. st. 20

16 What ailed us, O gods, to desert you
For creeds that refuse and restrain?
Come down and redeem us from virtue,
Our Lady of Pain.
Ibid. st. 35

17 Lo, this is she that was the world's delight.
Laus Veneris [1866], st. 3

18 Ah, yet would God this flesh of mine might be
Where air might wash and long leaves cover me;
Where tides of grass break into foam of flowers,
Or where the wind's feet shine along the sea.
Ibid. st. 14

19 O sad kissed mouth, how sorrowful it is!
Ibid. st. 79

20 To have known love, how bitter a thing it is.
Ibid. st. 103

21 There will no man do for your sake, I think,
What I would have done for the least word said.
I had wrung life dry for your lips to drink,
Broken it up for your daily bread.
The Triumph of Time [1866], st. 12

22 At the door of life, by the gate of breath,
There are worse things waiting for men than death.
Ibid. st. 20

1 I will go back to the great sweet mother,
Mother and lover of men, the sea.
The Triumph of Time, st. 33

2 I shall never be friends again with roses;
I shall loathe sweet tunes.
Ibid. st. 45

3 I have lived long enough, having seen one thing,
that love hath an end.
Hymn to Proserpine [1866]

4 Thou hast conquered, O pale Galilean;[1] the world
has grown gray from thy breath;
We have drunken of things Lethean, and fed on
the fullness of death.
Laurel is green for a season, and love is sweet for
a day;
But love grows bitter with treason, and laurel
outlives not May.
Sleep, shall we sleep after all? for the world is not
sweet in the end;
For the old faiths loosen and fall, the new years
ruin and rend.
Ibid.

5 I shall die as my fathers died, and sleep as they
sleep; even so.
For the glass of the years is brittle wherein we
gaze for a span.
Ibid.

6 For there is no God found stronger than death;
and death is a sleep.
Ibid.

7 If love were what the rose is,
And I were like the leaf,
Our lives would grow together
In sad or singing weather.
A Match [1866], st. 1

8 If you were April's lady,
And I were lord in May.
Ibid. st. 5

9 If you were queen of pleasure,
And I were king of pain,
We'd hunt down love together,
Pluck out his flying feather,
And teach his feet a measure,
And find his mouth a rein.
Ibid. st. 6

10 Forget that I remember,
And dream that I forget.
Rococo [1866], st. 2

11 For life is sweet, but after life is death.
This is the end of every man's desire.
A Ballad of Burdens [1866]. L'Envoy

12 Here, where the world is quiet;
Here, where all trouble seems

[1] See Julian, 113:5.

Dead winds' and spent waves' riot
In doubtful dreams of dreams.
The Garden of Proserpine [1866], st. 1

13 I am tired of tears and laughter,
And men that laugh and weep;
Of what may come hereafter
For men that sow and reap:
I am weary of days and hours,
Blown buds of barren flowers,
Desires and dreams and powers
And everything but sleep.
Ibid. st. 2

14 We are not sure of sorrow,
And joy was never sure.
Ibid. st. 10

15 From too much love of living,
From hope and fear set free,
We thank with brief thanksgiving
Whatever gods may be
That no life lives forever;
That dead men rise up never;
That even the weariest river
Winds somewhere safe to sea.
Ibid. st. 11

16 Ah that such sweet things should be fleet,
Such fleet things sweet!
Félise [1866], st. 22

17 I remember the way we parted,
The day and the way we met;
You hoped we were both broken-hearted
And knew we should both forget.
An Interlude [1866], st. 11

18 And the best and the worst of this is
That neither is most to blame,
If you have forgotten my kisses
And I have forgotten your name.
Ibid. st. 14

19 I am that which began;
Out of me the years roll;
Out of me God and man;
I am equal and whole;
God changes, and man, and the form of them
bodily; I am the soul.
Hertha [1871], st. 1

20 A creed is a rod,
And a crown is of night;
But this thing is God,
To be man with thy might,
To grow straight in the strength of thy spirit, and
to live out thy life as the light.
Ibid. st. 15

21 In the gray beginning of years, in the twilight of
things that began,
The word of the earth in the ears of the world,
was it God? was it man?
Hymn of Man [1871]

1 Glory to Man in the highest! for Man is the
master of things.
Ibid.

2 A blatant Bassarid of Boston, a rampant Maenad
of Massachusetts.[1]   *Under the Microscope [1872]*

3 Poor splendid wings so frayed and soiled and
torn!
A Ballad of François Villon [1878], st. 3

4 Villon, our sad bad glad mad brother's name.
Ibid. refrain

5 In a coign of the cliff between lowland and
highland,
At the sea-down's edge between windward and
lee,
Walled round with rocks as an inland island,
The ghost of a garden fronts the sea.
A Forsaken Garden [1878], st. 1

6 Sleep; and if life was bitter to thee, pardon,
If sweet, give thanks; thou hast no more to live;
And to give thanks is good, and to forgive.
*Ave Atque Vale: In Memory of Charles
Baudelaire [1878], st. 17*

7 Body and spirit are twins: God only knows which
is which.
*The Higher Pantheism in a Nutshell [1880],
st. 7*

8 God, whom we see not, is: and God, who is not,
we see:
Fiddle, we know, is diddle: and diddle, we take it,
is dee.
Ibid. st. 12

9 Mr. Whitman's Eve is a drunken apple-woman,
indecently sprawling in the slush and gutter amid the
rotten refuse of her overturned fruit-stall. . . .
Mr. Whitman's Venus is a Hottentot wench under
the influence of cantharides and adulterated rum.
Studies in Prose and Poetry [1894]. Whitmania

Henry Brooks Adams
1838–1918

10 Accident counts for much in companionship as in
marriage.
The Education of Henry Adams [1907], ch. 4

11 Women have, commonly, a very positive moral
sense; that which they will, is right; that which they
reject, is wrong; and their will, in most cases, ends by
settling the moral.
Ibid. 6

12 All experience is an arch, to build upon.
Ibid.

13 Only on the edge of the grave can man conclude
anything.
Ibid.

[1]Harriet Beecher Stowe, whose accusations against Byron in
"The True Story of Lady Byron's Life" [*Atlantic Monthly,*
September 1869] and in *Lady Byron Vindicated* [1870] aroused
strong protests in England.

14 Although the Senate is much given to admiring in
its members a superiority less obvious or quite invisible to outsiders, one Senator seldom proclaims his
own inferiority to another, and still more seldom
likes to be told of it.
Ibid. 7

15 Friends are born, not made.
Ibid.

16 A friend in power is a friend lost.
Ibid.

17 The effect of power and publicity on all men is
the aggravation of self, a sort of tumor that ends by
killing the victim's sympathies.
Ibid. 10

18 Young men have a passion for regarding their
elders as senile.
Ibid. 11

19 Knowledge of human nature is the beginning and
end of political education.
Ibid. 12

20 Intimates are predestined.
Ibid. 13

21 Chaos often breeds life, when order breeds habit.
Ibid.

22 At best, the renewal of broken relations is a nervous matter.
Ibid. 16

23 Sumner's[2] mind had reached the calm of water
which receives and reflects images without absorbing
them; it contained nothing but itself.
Ibid.

24 The difference is slight, to the influence of an
author, whether he is read by five hundred readers,
or by five hundred thousand; if he can select the five
hundred, he reaches the five hundred thousand.
Ibid. 17

25 The progress of Evolution from President Washington to President Grant was alone evidence
enough to upset Darwin.
Ibid.

26 A teacher affects eternity; he can never tell where
his influence stops.
Ibid. 20

27 One friend in a lifetime is much; two are many;
three are hardly possible. Friendship needs a certain
parallelism of life, a community of thought, a rivalry
of aim.
Ibid.

28 What one knows is, in youth, of little moment;
they know enough who know how to learn.
Ibid. 21

29 He had often noticed that six months' oblivion
amounts to newspaper death, and that resurrection
is rare. Nothing is easier, if a man wants it, than rest,
profound as the grave.
Ibid. 22

30 Morality is a private and costly luxury.
Ibid.

31 Practical politics consists in ignoring facts.
Ibid. 24

32 Nothing in education is so astonishing as the
amount of ignorance it accumulates in the form of
inert facts.
Ibid. 25

33 Power when wielded by abnormal energy is the
most serious of facts.
Ibid. 28

[2]Charles Sumner [1811–1874].

1   Modern politics is, at bottom, a struggle not of men but of forces.
Education of Henry Adams, ch. 28

2   We combat obstacles in order to get repose, and, when got, the repose is insupportable.   *Ibid. 29*

3   No one means all he says, and yet very few say all they mean, for words are slippery and thought is viscous.   *Ibid. 31*

4   Even in America, the Indian summer of life should be a little sunny and a little sad, like the season, and infinite in wealth and depth of tone—but never hustled.   *Ibid. 35*

John Wilkes Booth
1838–1865

5   Sic semper tyrannis![1] The South is avenged!
After shooting President Lincoln [April 14, 1865]

James Bryce
1838–1922

6   Europeans often ask, and Americans do not always explain, how it happens that this great office [the presidency], the greatest in the world, unless we except the Papacy, to which any man can rise by his own merits, is not more frequently filled by great and striking men.
The American Commonwealth [1888], vol. I, ch. 8

7   The government of cities is the one conspicuous failure of the United States.   *Ibid. 51*

8   To most people nothing is more troublesome than the effort of thinking.
Studies in History and Jurisprudence [1901]. Obedience

9   The greatest liberty that man has taken with Nature.[2]   *South America [1912]*

George Cooper
1838–1927

10   Sweet Genevieve,
The days may come, the days may go,
But still the hands of memory weave
The blissful dreams of long ago.
Sweet Genevieve [c. 1877][3]

John Milton Hay
1838–1905

11   I'll hold her nozzle agin the bank
Till the last galoot's ashore.
Pike County Ballads [1871]. Jim Bludso, st. 5

---

[1]See Anonymous: Latin, 119:30.
[2]The Panama Canal.
[3]Music by HENRY TUCKER.

---

12   And Christ ain't a-going to be too hard
On a man that died for men.
Ibid. st. 7

13   And I think that saving a little child,
And fotching him to his own,
Is a derned sight better business
Than loafing around The Throne.
Ibid. Little Breeches, last stanza

14   True luck consists not in holding the best of the cards at the table:
Luckiest he who knows just when to rise and go home.
Distichs, no. 15

15   It [the Spanish-American War] has been a splendid little war, begun with the highest motives, carried on with magnificent intelligence and spirit, favored by that fortune which loves the brave.
Letter to Theodore Roosevelt [July 27, 1898]

16   The open door.
To the Cabinet regarding completion of the trade policy he had negotiated with China [January 2, 1900]

George Washington Johnson
1838–1917

17   Let us sing of the days that are gone, Maggie,
When you and I were young.
When You and I Were Young, Maggie [1866],[4] refrain

William Edward Hartpole Lecky
1838–1903

18   The Augustinian doctrine of the damnation of unbaptized infants and the Calvinistic doctrine of reprobation . . . surpass in atrocity any tenets that have ever been admitted into any pagan creed.
History of European Morals [1869], vol. I, ch. 1

19   It had been boldly predicted by some of the early Christians that the conversion of the world would lead to the establishment of perpetual peace. In looking back, with our present experience, we are driven to the melancholy conclusion that, instead of diminishing the number of wars, ecclesiastical influence has actually and very seriously increased it.
Ibid. II, 4

George Leybourne
d. 1884

20   He flies through the air with the greatest of ease,
This daring young man on the flying trapeze;
His figure is handsome, all girls he can please,
And my love he purloined her away!
The Man on the Flying Trapeze [1860][5]

---

[4]Music by JAMES AUSTIN BUTTERFIELD.
[5]Music by ALFRED LEE.

Lydia Kamekeha Liliuokalani
1838–1917

1 Farewell to thee, farewell to thee . . .
Until we meet again.
Aloha Oe (Farewell to Thee) [1878]

Ernst Mach
1838–1916

2 Physics is experience, arranged in economical order.
The Economical Nature of Physical Inquiry [1882]

3 Intelligible as it is . . . that the efforts of thinkers have always been bent upon the "reduction of all physical processes to the motions of atoms," it must yet be affirmed that this is a chimerical ideal. This ideal has often played an effective part in popular lectures, but in the workshop of the serious inquirer it has discharged scarcely the least function.
On the Principle of the Conservation of Energy [1894]

John, Viscount Morley of Blackburn
1838–1923

4 Where it is a duty to worship the sun it is pretty sure to be a crime to examine the laws of heat.
Voltaire [1872]

5 Evolution is not a force but a process; not a cause but a law.
On Compromise [1874]

6 It is not enough to do good; one must do it the right way.
Rousseau [1876]

7 You have not converted a man because you have silenced him.
Ibid.

8 The great business of life is to be, to do, to do without, and to depart.
Address on Aphorisms [1887]

9 Simplicity of character is no hindrance to subtlety of intellect.
Life of Gladstone [1903]

10 No man can climb out beyond the limitations of his own character.
Critical Miscellanies [1908]. Robespierre

11 There are some books which cannot be adequately reviewed for twenty or thirty years after they come out.
Recollections [1917], vol. I, bk. 2, ch. 8

12 In my creed, waste of public money is like the sin against the Holy Ghost.
Ibid. II, 5, 3

13 Success depends on three things: who says it, what he says, how he says it; and of these three things, what he says is the least important.
Ibid. 4

John Muir
1838–1914

14 In God's wildness lies the hope of the world— the great fresh unblighted, unredeemed wilderness.[1]
Alaska Fragment [1890]

15 The clearest way into the Universe is through a forest wilderness.   *John of the Mountains [1938]*

16 The mountains are fountains of men as well as of rivers, of glaciers, of fertile soil. The great poets, philosophers, prophets, able men whose thought and deeds have moved the world, have come down from the mountains—mountain-dwellers who have grown strong there with the forest trees in Nature's workshops.
Ibid.

17 Most people are *on* the world, not in it—have no conscious sympathy or relationship to anything about them—undiffused, separate, and rigidly alone like marbles of polished stone, touching but separate.
Ibid.

18 How hard to realize that every camp of men or beast has this glorious starry firmament for a roof! In such places standing alone on the mountaintop it is easy to realize that whatever special nests we make —leaves and moss like the marmots and birds, or tents or piled stone—we all dwell in a house of one room—the world with the firmament for its roof —and are sailing the celestial spaces without leaving any track.
Ibid.

Philippe Auguste Villiers de L'Isle-Adam
1838–1889

19 Living? We'll leave that to the servants.[2]
Axel [1890]

20 I have thought too much to stoop to action![3]
Ibid.

Paul Cézanne
1839–1906

21 Treat nature in terms of the cylinder, the sphere, the cone, all in perspective.
From EMILE BERNARD, *Paul Cézanne [1925]*

22 Right now a moment of time is fleeting by! Capture its reality in paint! To do that we must put all else out of our minds. We must become that moment, make ourselves a sensitive recording plate . . . give the image of what we actually see, forgetting everything that has been seen before our time.
From JOACHIM GASQUET, *Paul Cézanne [1926]*[4]

---

[1] See Thoreau, 479:6.
[2] Vivre? Les serviteurs feront cela pour nous.
[3] J'ai trop pensé pour daigner agir!
[4] Translated by NORBERT GUTERMAN.

1   The day is coming when a single carrot, freshly observed [in a painting], will set off a revolution.
From JOACHIM GASQUET, *Paul Cézanne*

Francis Pharcellus Church
1839–1906

2   Yes, Virginia, there is a Santa Claus. . . . Thank God! he lives, and he lives forever. A thousand years from now, Virginia, nay ten times ten thousand years from now, he will continue to make glad the heart of childhood.[1]
Editorial in the New York Sun *[September 21, 1897]*

Henry George
1839–1897

3   So long as all the increased wealth which modern progress brings goes but to build up great fortunes, to increase luxury and make sharper the contrast between the House of Have and the House of Want, progress is not real and cannot be permanent.
Progress and Poverty [1879]. Introductory: The Problem

Walter Pater
1839–1894

4   Every intellectual product must be judged from the point of view of the age and the people in which it was produced.
Studies in the History of the Renaissance [1873]. Mirandola

5   Hers is the head upon which all "the ends of the world are come," and the eyelids are a little weary. It is a beauty wrought out from within upon the flesh, the deposit, little cell by cell, of strange thoughts and fantastic reveries and exquisite passions. Set it for a moment beside one of those white Greek goddesses or beautiful women of antiquity, and how would they be troubled by this beauty, into which the soul with all its maladies has passed?
Ibid. Leonardo da Vinci [Mona Lisa]

6   She is older than the rocks among which she sits; like the vampire, she has been dead many times, and learned the secrets of the grave; and has been a diver in deep seas, and keeps their fallen day about her; and trafficked for strange webs with Eastern merchants: and as Leda, was the mother of Helen of Troy, and, as Saint Anne, the mother of Mary; and all this has been to her but as the sound of lyres and flutes, and lives only in the delicacy with which it has molded the changing lineaments, and tinged the eyelids and the hands.
Ibid.

---

[1]Responding to a letter from eight-year-old Virginia O'Hanlon: "Please tell me the truth; is there a Santa Claus?"

7   All art constantly aspires towards the condition of music.
Ibid. The School of Giorgione

8   Not the fruit of experience, but experience itself, is the end.
Ibid. Conclusion

9   To burn always with this hard, gemlike flame, to maintain this ecstasy, is success in life.
Ibid.

10   Art comes to you proposing frankly to give nothing but the highest quality to your moments as they pass.
Ibid.

11   To know when one's self is interested, is the first condition of interesting other people.
Marius the Epicurean [1885], ch. 6

12   It is the addition of strangeness to beauty that constitutes the romantic character in art.
Appreciation [1889]. Postscript

Charles Sanders Peirce[2]
1839–1914

13   Do not block the way of inquiry.
Collected Papers [1931–1958], vol. I, par. 135

14   The idea does not belong to the soul; it is the soul that belongs to the idea.
Ibid. 216

15   Every man is fully satisfied that there is such a thing as truth, or he would not ask any question.
Ibid. V, 211

16   Let us not pretend to doubt in philosophy what we do not doubt in our hearts.
Ibid. 265

17   All the evolution we know of proceeds from the vague to the definite.
Ibid. VI, 191

18   Our whole past experience is continually in our consciousness, though most of it sunk to a great depth of dimness. I think of consciousness as a bottomless lake, whose waters seem transparent, yet into which we can clearly see but a little way.
Ibid. VII, 547

19   Unless man have a natural bent in accordance with nature's, he has no chance of understanding nature at all.
A Neglected Argument for the Reality of God [Hibbert Journal VII:90]

James Ryder Randall
1839–1908

20   Avenge the patriotic gore
That flecked the streets of Baltimore,
And be the battle queen of yore,
Maryland! My Maryland!
Maryland! My Maryland! [1861], st. 1

---

[2]See William James, 546:n2.

Thomas Brackett Reed
1839–1902

1 They [two fellow congressmen] never open their mouths without subtracting from the sum of human knowledge.

From SAMUEL W. McCALL, *The Life of Thomas Brackett Reed* [1914], ch. 21

John Davison Rockefeller
1839–1937

2 God gave me my money. I believe the power to make money is a gift from God. . . . I believe it is my duty to make money and still more money and to use the money I make for the good of my fellow man according to the dictates of my conscience.[1]

In an interview [1905]

Wilfrid Scawen Blunt
1840–1922

3 Ay, this is the famed rock, which Hercules
And Goth and Moor bequeathed us. At this
     door
England stands sentry.

Gibraltar

Timothy J. Campbell
1840–1904

4 What's the Constitution between friends?[2]

Attributed [c. 1885]

Henry Austin Dobson
1840–1921

5 Time goes, you say? Ah no!
Alas, Time stays, *we* go.

The Paradox of Time [1875], st. 1

6 The ladies of St. James's!
They're painted to the eyes;
Their white it stays forever,
Their red it never dies:
But Phyllida, my Phyllida!
Her color comes and goes;
It trembles to a lily—
It wavers to a rose.

The Ladies of St. James's [1883], st. 4

[1]He's kind iv a society f'r the privintion of croolty to money. If he finds a man misusing his money he takes it away fr'm him an' adopts it.—FINLEY PETER DUNNE, *Mr. Dooley Says* [1910]

[2]Reported comment to President Cleveland, who refused to support a bill on the grounds that it was unconstitutional.

Thomas Hardy
1840–1928

7 These purblind Doomsters had as readily strown
Blisses about my pilgrimage as pain.

Hap [1866]

8 When I set out for Lyonnesse,
    A hundred miles away,
    The rime was on the spray,
And starlight lit my lonesomeness.

When I Set Out for Lyonnesse [1870], st. 1

9 Good, but not religious-good.

Under the Greenwood Tree [1872], ch. 2

10 Like the British Constitution, she owes her success in practice to her inconsistencies in principle.

The Hand of Ethelberta [1876]

11 A lover without indiscretion is no lover at all.

Ibid.

12 In fact, precisely at this transitional point of its nightly roll into darkness the great and particular glory of the Egdon waste began, and nobody could be said to understand the heath who had not been there at such a time. It could best be felt when it could not clearly be seen.

The Return of the Native [1878], ch. 1

13 The place became full of a watchful intentness now; for when other things sank brooding to sleep the heath appeared slowly to awake and listen.

Ibid.

14 The great inviolate place had an ancient permanence which the sea cannot claim. Who can say of a particular sea that it is old? Distilled by the sun, kneaded by the moon, it is renewed in a year, in a day, or in an hour. The sea changed, the fields changed, the rivers, the villages, and the people changed, yet Egdon remained.

Ibid.

15 The hard, half-apathetic expression of one who deems anything possible at the hands of Time and Chance, except, perhaps, fair play.

The Mayor of Casterbridge [1886], ch. 1

16 And all her shining keys will be took from her, and her cupboards opened, and little things 'a didn't wish seen, anybody will see; and her wishes and ways will be as nothing!

Ibid. 18

17 Who is such a reprobate as I [Michael Henchard]! And yet it seems that even I be in Somebody's hand!

Ibid. 41

18 That Elizabeth-Jane Farfrae be not told of my death, or be made to grieve on account of me. And that I be not buried in consecrated ground. And that no sexton be asked to toll the bell. And that nobody is wished to see my dead body. And that no murners walk behind me at my funeral. And that no flours be

planted on my grave. And that no man remember me.

> *The Mayor of Casterbridge, ch. 45 [Henchard's will]*

1   That cold accretion called the world, which, so terrible in the mass, is so unformidable, even pitiable, in its units.

> *Tess of the D'Urbervilles [1891], ch. 13*

2   The chronic melancholy which is taking hold of the civilized races with the decline of belief in a beneficent power.   *Ibid. 18*

3   "Justice" was done, and the President of the Immortals (in Aeschylean phrase) had ended his sport with Tess.   *Ibid. 59*

4   But nobody did come, because nobody does.

> *Jude the Obscure [1895], pt. I, ch. 4*

5   The fundamental error of their matrimonial union; that of having based a permanent contract on a temporary feeling.   *Ibid. 11*

6   But sometimes a woman's love of being loved gets the better of her conscience.   *Ibid. IV, 5*

7   Done because we are too menny.   *Ibid. VI, 2*

8   Do not do an immoral thing for moral reasons.

> *Ibid. 3*

9 I leant upon a coppice gate
When Frost was specter-gray,
And Winter's dregs made desolate
The weakening eye of day.

> *The Darkling Thrush [1900], st. 1*

10 An aged thrush, frail, gaunt, and small,
In blast-beruffled plume.

> *Ibid. st. 3*

11 So little cause for carolings
Of such ecstatic sound
Was written on terrestrial things
Afar or nigh around,
That I could think there trembled through
His happy good-night air
Some blessed hope, whereof he knew
And I was unaware.

> *Ibid. st. 4*

12 Yes; quaint and curious war is!
You shoot a fellow down
You'd treat if met where any bar is,
Or help to half-a-crown.

> *The Man He Killed [1902], st. 5*

13 What of the Immanent Will and its designs?
It works unconsciously as heretofore,
External artistries in circumstance.

> *The Dynasts [1904–1908], pt. I, forescene*

14 A local cult called Christianity.

> *Ibid. Spirit of the Years, sc. vi*

15 Ere systemed suns were globed and lit
The slaughters of the race were writ.

> *Ibid. II, v, semichorus*

16   My argument is that War makes rattling good history; but Peace is poor reading.

> *Ibid. Spirit Sinister*

17 We two kept house, the Past and I,
The Past and I;
Through all my tasks it hovered nigh,
Leaving me never alone.

> *The Ghost of the Past, st. 1*

18 And as the smart ship grew
In stature, grace, and hue,
In shadowy silent distance grew the Iceberg too.

> *The Convergence of the Twain (Lines on the Loss of the Titanic) [1912], st. 8*

19 Woman much missed, how you call to me, call to me,
Saying that now you are not as you were
When you had changed from the one who was all to me,
But as at first, when our day was fair.

> *The Voice [1912], st 1*

20 What of the faith and fire within us
Men who march away
Ere the barn cocks say
Night is growing gray,
Leaving all that here can win us.

> *Men Who March Away [1914], st. 1*

21 That night your great guns, unawares,
Shook all our coffins as we lay,
And broke the chancel window-squares,
We thought it was the Judgment Day.

> *Channel Firing [1914], st. 1*

22 Only a man harrowing clods
In a slow silent walk
With an old horse that stumbles and nods
Half asleep as they stalk.

Only thin smoke without flame
From the heaps of couch grass:
Yet this will go onward the same
Though dynasties pass.

Yonder a maid and her wight
Come whispering by;
War's annals will cloud into night
Ere their story die.

> *In Time of "The Breaking of Nations" [1915]*

23 Ah, no; the years, the years;
Down their chiseled names the raindrop plows.

> *During Wind and Rain, st. 4*

24 This is the weather the shepherd shuns,
And so do I.

> *Weathers [1922], st. 2*

25 And meadow rivulets overflow,
And drops on gate bars hang in a row,
And rooks in families homeward go,
And so do I.

> *Ibid.*

Fanny Dixwell Holmes
1840–1929

1   Washington is full of famous men and the women they married when they were young.
>   From *CATHERINE DRINKER BOWEN, Yankee from Olympus [1944]*

Chief Joseph[1]
c. 1840–1904

2   Our chiefs are killed. . . . The old men are all dead. . . . The little children are freezing to death. My people, some of them have run away to the hills and have no blankets, no food. No one knows where they are, perhaps freezing to death. I want to have time to look for my children and see how many of them I can find. Maybe I can find them among the dead. Hear me, my chiefs. My heart is sick and sad. From where the sun now stands I will fight no more forever.
>   *To the Nez Percé tribe after surrender to General Nelson A. Miles [battle of Bear Paw Mountains, Montana, September 30–October 5, 1877]*

Alfred Thayer Mahan
1840–1914

3   The world has never seen a more impressive demonstration of the influence of sea power upon its history. Those far distant, storm-beaten ships, upon which the Grand Army never looked, stood between it and the dominion of the world.[2]
>   *The Influence of Sea Power upon the French Revolution and Empire, 1793–1812 [1892], vol. II, p. 118*

4   Whether they will or no, Americans must begin to look outward.
>   *The Interest of America in Sea Power [1897]*

William Graham Sumner
1840–1910

5   The Forgotten Man[3] . . . delving away in patient industry, supporting his family, paying his taxes, casting his vote, supporting the church and the school . . . but he is the only one for whom there is no provision in the great scramble and the big divide. Such is the Forgotten Man. He works, he votes, generally he prays—but his chief business in life is to pay. . . . Who and where is the Forgotten Man in this case, who will have to pay for it all?
>   *Speech, The Forgotten Man [1883]*

John Addington Symonds
1840–1893

6   These things shall be—a loftier race
Than e'er the world hath known shall rise
With flame of freedom in their souls,
And light of knowledge in their eyes.
>   *The Days That Are to Be*

7   They shall be gentle, brave and strong
To spill no drop of blood, but dare
All that may plant man's lordship firm
On earth and fire and sea and air.
>   *Ibid.*

John Wilson
d. 1889

8   Oh for a book and a shady nook, either in door or out.
>   *Poem for a catalogue of secondhand books*

Elizabeth Wordsworth
1840–1932

9   If all the good people were clever,
And all clever people were good,
The world would be nicer than ever
We thought that it possibly could.
>   *Good and Clever [1890]*

Émile Zola
1840–1902

10   I am little concerned with beauty or perfection. I don't care for the great centuries. All I care about is life, struggle, intensity. I am at ease in my generation.
>   *My Hates [1866]*

11   A work of art is a corner of creation seen through a temperament.
>   *Ibid.*

12   My own art is a negation of society, an affirmation of the individual, outside all rules and demands of society.
>   *Ibid.*

13   Truth is on the march and nothing can stop it.
>   *Article in Le Figaro [November 25, 1897]*

14   J'accuse.
>   *Title of letter to the president of the French Republic, L'Aurore [January 13, 1898]*

Robert Buchanan
1841–1901

15   The Fleshly School of Poetry.
>   *Title of article [1871][4]*

---

[1]Hinmaton-Yalaktit: Thunder Rolling in the Mountains.
[2]See Themistocles, 62:30; Francis Bacon, 160:7; Edmund Waller, 249:27; and Washington, 336:17.
[3]See F. D. Roosevelt, 648:14.

[4]Attack on the Pre-Raphaelites occasioned by some sonnets in Rossetti's *The House of Life.*
See D. G. Rossetti, 509:23 and 509:28.

Georges Clemenceau
1841–1929

1 The good Lord had only ten.
In reference to Woodrow Wilson's Fourteen Points

2 America is the only nation in history which miraculously has gone directly from barbarism to degeneration without the usual interval of civilization. *Attributed*

3 It is easier to make war than peace.[1]
Speech [1919]

Oliver Wendell Holmes, Jr.
1841–1935

4 The life of the law has not been logic: it has been experience. *The Common Law [1881], Lecture 1*

5 The law embodies the story of a nation's development through many centuries, and it cannot be dealt with as if it contained only the axioms and corollaries of a book of mathematics. *Ibid.*

6 I think that, as life is action and passion, it is required of a man that he should share the passion and action of his time at peril of being judged not to have lived. *Memorial Day Address [1884]*

7 Through our great good fortune, in our youth our hearts were touched with fire. *Ibid.*

8 I say to you in all sadness of conviction, that to think great thoughts you must be heroes as well as idealists. *The Profession of the Law [1886]*

9 Certainty generally is illusion, and repose is not the destiny of man. *The Path of the Law [1897]*

10 The remoter and more general aspects of the law are those which give it universal interest. It is through them that you not only become a great master in your calling, but connect your subject with the universe and catch an echo of the infinite, a glimpse of its unfathomable process, a hint of the universal law. *Ibid.*

11 The rule of joy and the law of duty seem to me all one. *Speech at Bar Association Dinner, Boston [1900]*

12 Life is an end in itself, and the only question as to whether it is worth living is whether you have enough of it.[2] *Ibid.*

13 A great man represents a great ganglion in the nerves of society, or, to vary the figure, a strategic point in the campaign of history, and part of his greatness consists in his being *there*.
John Marshall [1901]

14 Taxes are what we pay for civilized society.
Compañia de Tabacos v. Collector, 275 U.S. 87, 100 [1904]

15 Great cases like hard cases make bad law.
Northern Securities Co. v. United States, 193 U.S. 197, 400 [1904]

16 The Fourteenth Amendment does not enact Mr. Herbert Spencer's *Social Statics*.
Lochner v. New York, 198 U.S. 45, 75 [1905]

17 General propositions do not decide concrete cases. The decision will depend on a judgment or intuition more subtle than any articulate major premise. *Ibid. 78*

18 Life is painting a picture, not doing a sum.
The Class of '61. From Speeches [1913]

19 The only prize much cared for by the powerful is power. The prize of the general is not a bigger tent, but command. *Law and the Court [1913]*

20 The attacks upon the Court are merely an expression of the unrest that seems to wonder vaguely whether law and order pay. When the ignorant are taught to doubt, they do not know what they safely may believe. *Ibid.*

21 I recognize without hesitation that judges do and must legislate, but they can do so only interstitially; they are confined from molar to molecular motions.
Southern Pacific Co. v. Jensen, 244 U.S. 205, 221 [1917]

22 The common law is not a brooding omnipresence in the sky but the articulate voice of some sovereign or quasi sovereign that can be identified.
Ibid. 222

23 Certitude is not the test of certainty.
Natural Law [1918]

24 The most stringent protection of free speech would not protect a man in falsely shouting fire in a theater and causing a panic. . . . The question in every case is whether the words used are used in such circumstances and are of such a nature as to create a clear and present danger that they will bring about the substantive evils that Congress has a right to prevent.
Schenck v. United States, 249 U.S. 47 [1919]

25 When men have realized that time has upset many fighting faiths, they may come to believe even more than they believe the very foundations of their own conduct that the ultimate good desired is better reached by free trade in ideas — that the best test of truth is the power of the thought to get itself accepted in the competition of the market, and that truth is the only ground upon which their wishes safely can be carried out.[3] That at any rate is the

---

[1] Il est plus facile de faire la guerre que la paix.
[2] See William James, 546:8, and Santayana, 588:4.

[3] See Milton, 255:4, and Jefferson, 344:5.

theory of our Constitution. It is an experiment, as all life is an experiment.
Abrams v. United States, 250 U.S. 616, 630 [1919]

1 I dare say that I have worked off my fundamental formula on you that the chief end of man is to frame general propositions and that no general proposition is worth a damn.
Letter to Sir Frederick Pollock [1920]

2 If my fellow citizens want to go to Hell I will help them. It is my job.
Letter to Harold J. Laski [1920]

3 Have faith and pursue the unknown end.
Letter to John C. H. Wu [1924]

4 Upon this point a page of history is worth a volume of logic.
New York Trust Co. v. Eisner, 256 U.S. 345, 349 [1921]

5 It is said that this manifesto is more than a theory, that it was an incitement. Every idea is an incitement.
Gitlow v. New York, 268 U.S. 652, 673 [1925]

6 Three generations of imbeciles are enough.
Buck v. Bell, 274 U.S. 200, 207 [1927]

7 But if we are to yield to fashionable conventions, it seems to me that theaters are as much devoted to public use as anything well can be. We have not that respect for art that is one of the glories of France. But to many the superfluous is the necessary,[1] and it seems to me that Government does not go beyond its sphere in attempting to make life livable for them.
Tyson & Bro. v. Banton, 273 U.S. 418, 447 [1927]

8 The power to tax is not the power to destroy while this Court sits.[2]
Panhandle Oil Co. v. Knox, 277 U.S. 223 [1928]

9 For my part I think it a less evil that some criminals should escape than that the government should play an ignoble part. . . . If the existing code does not permit district attorneys to have a hand in such dirty business [wiretapping], it does not permit the judge to allow such iniquities to succeed.
Olmstead v. United States, 277 U.S. 438, 470 [1928]

10 If there is any principle of the Constitution that more imperatively calls for attachment than any other it is the principle of free thought—not free thought for those who agree with us but freedom for the thought that we hate.
United States v. Schwimmer, 279 U.S. 644, 653 [1928]

11 The riders in a race do not stop short when they reach the goal. There is a little finishing canter

[1]See Voltaire, 305:25.
[2]See John Marshall, 355:13.

before coming to a standstill. There is time to hear the kind voice of friends and to say to one's self: "The work is done." But just as one says that, the answer comes: "The race is over, but the work never is done while the power to work remains." The canter that brings you to a standstill need not be only coming to rest. It cannot be, while you still live. For to live is to function. That is all there is in living.
Radio address on his ninetieth birthday [March 8, 1931]

12 Young man, the secret of my success is that at an early age I discovered I was not God.
Reply to a reporter's question on his ninetieth birthday [March 8, 1931]

13 Oh, to be seventy again![3]
At ninety, upon seeing a beautiful young woman. Attributed

14 A second-class intellect. But a first-class temperament!
On President Franklin Delano Roosevelt [March 8, 1933]

William Henry Hudson
1841–1922

15 I . . . thanked the Author of my being for the gift of that wild forest, those green mansions where I had found so great a happiness!
Green Mansions [1904], ch. 5

16 In this wild solitary girl [Rima] I had at length discovered the mysterious warbler that so often followed me in the wood.
Ibid.

Joaquin [Cincinnatus Hiner or Heine] Miller
c. 1841–1913

17 Behind him lay the gray Azores,
Behind the Gates of Hercules;
Before him not the ghost of shores,
Before him only shoreless seas.
Columbus, st. 1

18 He gained a world; he gave that world
Its grandest lesson: "On! sail on!"[4]
Ibid. st. 5

Pierre Auguste Renoir
1841–1919

19 I have a predilection for painting that lends joyousness to a wall.
From AMBROISE VOLLARD, Renoir [1919]

[3]If only one were eighty!—COUNT FRIEDRICH VON WRANGEL [1784–1877]; *attributed*
[4]Actually, it was MARTÍN ALONSO PINZÓN [c. 1440–1493] who said, "Adelante, adelante, I can't hold with turning back without sighting land."

1 In a few generations you can breed a racehorse. The recipe for making a man like Delacroix is less well known.

From JEAN RENOIR, *Renoir My Father [1958]*

Clement William Scott
1841–1904

2 Oh, promise me that some day you and I
Will take our love together to some sky
Where we can be alone and faith renew,
And find the hollows where those flowers grew.

Oh, Promise Me [1888][1]

Edward Rowland Sill
1841–1887

3 At the punch bowl's brink
Let the thirsty think
What they say in Japan:
"First the man takes a drink,
Then the drink takes a drink,
Then the drink takes the man!"

An Adage from the Orient

4   But Lord,
Be merciful to me, a fool!

The Fool's Prayer

Sir Henry Morton Stanley
1841–1904

5   Doctor Livingstone, I presume?
On meeting David Livingstone in Ujiji, Central Africa [November 10, 1871]

Ironquill [Eugene Fitch Ware]
1841–1911

6 O Dewey[2] was the morning
Upon the first of May,
And Dewey was the Admiral
Down in Manila Bay;
And Dewey were the Regent's eyes,
"Them" orbs of royal blue!
And Dewey feel discouraged?
I Dew not think we Dew.

In the Topeka (Kansas) Daily Capital [May 3, 1898]

7 No evil deed live oN.

The Palindrome

George Frederick Baer
1842–1914

8   The rights and interests of the laboring man will be protected and cared for — not by the labor agita-tors, but by the Christian men to whom God in His infinite wisdom has given the control of the property interests of the country.   *Letter [July 17, 1902]*

Ambrose Bierce
1842 – c. 1914

9 Mark how my fame rings out from zone to zone:
A thousand critics shouting: "He's unknown!"

Couplet

10   Peyton Farquhar was dead; his body, with a broken neck, swung gently from side to side beneath the timbers of the Owl Creek bridge.

In the Midst of Life [1891].[3] *An Occurrence at Owl Creek Bridge*

11 To men a man is but a mind. Who cares
What face he carries or what form he wears?
But woman's body is the woman. O
Stay thou, my sweetheart, and do never go.

The Devil's Dictionary [1906][4]

12   *Achievement, n.* the death of endeavor and the birth of disgust.   *Ibid.*

13   *Advice, n.* the smallest current coin.   *Ibid.*

14   *Bore, n.* a person who talks when you wish him to listen.   *Ibid.*

15   *Cynic, n.* a blackguard whose faulty vision sees things as they are, not as they ought to be.

Ibid.

16   *Edible, adj.* good to eat, and wholesome to digest, as a worm to a toad, a toad to a snake, a snake to a pig, a pig to a man, and a man to a worm.[5]

Ibid.

17   *Habit, n.* a shackle for the free.   *Ibid.*

18   *Labor, n.* one of the processes by which A acquires property for B.   *Ibid.*

19   *Lawsuit, n.* a machine which you go into as a pig and come out as a sausage.   *Ibid.*

20   *Marriage, n.* a community consisting of a master, a mistress, and two slaves, making in all, two.

Ibid.

21   *Prejudice, n.* a vagrant opinion without visible means of support.   *Ibid.*

22   *Saint, n.* a dead sinner revised and edited.

Ibid.

23   Woman would be more charming if one could fall into her arms without falling into her hands.

Epigrams

24   You are not permitted to kill a woman who has wronged you, but nothing forbids you to reflect that she is growing older every minute. You are avenged 1440 times a day.   *Ibid.*

---

[1]Set to music by REGINALD DE KOVEN [1859–1920] and interpolated in his opera *Robin Hood* [1890].
[2]See George Dewey, 532:13.

[3]First published as *Tales of Soldiers and Civilians*, retitled in 1892.
[4]First published as *The Cynic's Word Book*, retitled in 1911.
[5]See Wallace Stevens, 639:2.

1   Self-denial is indulgence of a propensity to forego.   *Ibid.*

2   The covers of this book are too far apart.
Capsule book review. Attributed

Charles Edward Carryl
1842–1920

3 A capital ship for an ocean trip
Was the *Walloping Window Blind*—
No gale that blew dismayed her crew
Or troubled the captain's mind.
The man at the wheel was taught to feel
Contempt for the wildest blow.
And it often appeared, when the weather had
cleared,
That he'd been in his bunk below.
*Davy and the Goblin: A Nautical Ballad [1886],
st. 1*

Sir James Dewar
1842–1923

4   Minds are like parachutes. They only function when they are open.   *Attributed*

William James
1842–1910

5   I have often thought that the best way to define a man's character would be to seek out the particular mental or moral attitude in which, when it came upon him, he felt himself most deeply and intensely active and alive. At such moments there is a voice inside which speaks and says: "This is the real me!"
*The Letters of William James [1920]. To his
wife, Alice Gibbons James, 1878*

6   Most people live, whether physically, intellectually or morally, in a very restricted circle of their potential being. They *make use* of a very small portion of their possible consciousness, and of their soul's resources in general, much like a man who, out of his whole bodily organism, should get into a habit of using and moving only his little finger. Great emergencies and crises show us how much greater our vital resources are than we had supposed.
Ibid. To W. Lutoslawski, May 6, 1906

7   The moral flabbiness born of the exclusive worship of the bitch-goddess SUCCESS. That—with the squalid cash interpretation put on the word success —is our national disease.
Ibid. To H. G. Wells, September 11, 1906

8   The concrete man has but one interest—to be right. That to him is the art of all arts, and all means are fair which help him to it.
The Sentiment of Rationality [1882]

9   All our scientific and philosophic ideals are altars to unknown gods.
The Dilemma of Determinism [1884]

10   Habit is . . . the enormous flywheel of society, its most precious conservative agent. It alone is what keeps us all within the bounds of ordinance.
The Principles of Psychology [1890], ch. 4

11   There is no more miserable human being than one in whom nothing is habitual but indecision.
Ibid.

12   Keep the faculty of effort alive in you by a little gratuitous exercise every day. That is, be systematically ascetic or heroic in little unnecessary points, do every day or two something for no other reason than that you would rather not do it, so that when the hour of dire need draws nigh, it may find you not unnerved and untrained to stand the test.   *Ibid.*

13   The hell to be endured hereafter, of which theology tells, is no worse than the hell we make for ourselves in this world by habitually fashioning our characters in the wrong way.   *Ibid.*

14   We are spinning our own fates, good or evil, and never to be undone. Every smallest stroke of virtue or of vice leaves its never so little scar . . . Nothing we ever do is, in strict scientific literalness, wiped out.   *Ibid.*

15   Consciousness . . . does not appear to itself chopped up in bits. . . . A "river" or a "stream" are the metaphors by which it is most naturally described. In talking of it hereafter, let us call it the stream of thought, of consciousness, or of subjective life.   *Ibid. 9*

16   As we take, in fact, a general view of the wonderful stream of our consciousness, what strikes us first is this different pace of its parts. Like a bird's life, it seems to be made of an alternation of flights and perchings.   *Ibid.*

17   As the brain changes are continuous, so do all these consciousnesses melt into each other like dissolving views. Properly they are but one protracted consciousness, one unbroken stream.   *Ibid.*

18   The last peculiarity of consciousness to which attention is to be drawn in this first rough description of its stream is that . . . it is always interested more in one part of its object [thought] than in another, and welcomes and rejects, or chooses, all the while it thinks.   *Ibid.*

19   An act has no ethical quality whatever unless it be chosen out of several all equally possible.   *Ibid.*

20   In its widest possible sense, however, a man's Self is the sum total of all that he *can* call his, not only his body and his psychic powers, but his clothes and his house, his wife and children, his ancestors and friends, his reputation and works, his lands and horses, and yacht and bank account. All these things give him the same emotions. If they wax and prosper,

he feels triumphant; if they dwindle and die away, he feels cast down.

The Principles of Psychology, ch. 10

1   Let anyone try, I will not say to arrest, but to notice or attend to, the *present* moment of time. One of the most baffling experiences occurs. Where is it, this present? It has melted in our grasp, fled ere we could touch it, gone in the instant of becoming.

Ibid. 15

2   Genius . . . means little more than the faculty of perceiving in an unhabitual way.   *Ibid. 19*

3   The art of being wise is the art of knowing what to overlook.   *Ibid. 22*

4   The more rational statement is that we feel sorry because we cry, angry because we strike, afraid because we tremble, and not that we cry, strike, or tremble because we are sorry, angry, or fearful, as the case may be. Without the bodily states following on the perception, the latter would be purely cognitive in form, pale, colorless, destitute of emotional warmth.   *Ibid. 25*

5   A purely disembodied human emotion is a nonentity.   *Ibid.*

6   In the deepest heart of all of us there is a corner in which the ultimate mystery of things works sadly.

The Will to Believe [1897]. Is Life Worth Living?

7   It is only by risking our persons from one hour to another that we live at all. And often enough our faith beforehand in an uncertified result is the only thing that makes the result come true.   *Ibid.*

8   This life is worth living, we can say, since it is what we make it, from the moral point of view.[1]

Ibid.

9   Be not afraid of life. Believe that life *is* worth living, and your belief will help create the fact.

Ibid.

10   All the higher, more penetrating ideals are revolutionary. They present themselves far less in the guise of effects of past experience than in that of probable causes of future experience.

Ibid. The Moral Philosopher and the Moral Life

11   There is but one unconditional commandment, which is that we should seek incessantly, with fear and trembling, so to vote and to act as to bring about the very largest total universe of good which we can see.   *Ibid.*

12   An unlearned carpenter of my acquaintance once said in my hearing: "There is very little difference between one man and another; but what little there is, is very important." This distinction seems to me to go to the root of the matter.

Ibid. The Importance of Individuals

[1]See Oliver Wendell Holmes, Jr., 542:12, and Santayana, 588:4.

13   Religion . . . shall mean for us the feelings, acts, and experiences of individual men in their solitude.

The Varieties of Religious Experience [1902]. Lecture 2

14   Religion . . . is a man's total reaction upon life.   *Ibid.*

15   We can act *as if* there were a God; feel *as if* we were free; consider Nature *as if* she were full of special designs; lay plans *as if* we were to be immortal; and we find then that these words do make a genuine difference in our moral life.   *Ibid. 3*

16   The God whom science recognizes must be a God of universal laws exclusively, a God who does a wholesale, not a retail business. He cannot accommodate his processes to the convenience of individuals.   *Ibid. 20*

17   The philosophy which is so important in each of us is not a technical matter; it is our more or less dumb sense of what life honestly and deeply means. It is only partly got from books; it is our individual way of just seeing and feeling the total push and pressure of the cosmos.

Pragmatism [1907].[2] Lecture 1

18   No particular results then, so far, but only an attitude of orientation, is what the pragmatic method means. The attitude of looking away from first things, principles, "categories," supposed necessities; and of looking toward last things, fruits, consequences, facts.   *Ibid. 2*

19   I myself believe that the evidence for God lies primarily in inner personal experiences.   *Ibid. 3*

20   Our minds thus grow in spots; and like grease spots, the spots spread. But we let them spread as little as possible: we keep unaltered as much of our old knowledge, as many of our old prejudices and beliefs, as we can. We patch and tinker more than we renew. The novelty soaks in; it stains the ancient mass; but it is also tinged by what absorbs it.

Ibid. 5

21   Truth *happens* to an idea. It *becomes* true, is *made* true by events. Its verity *is* in fact an event, a process: the process namely of its verifying itself, its veri-*fication*. Its validity is the process of its valid-*ation*.   *Ibid. 6*

22   Pluralism lets things really exist in the each-form or distributively. Monism thinks that the all-form or collective-unit form is the only form that is rational.

A Pluralistic Universe [1909]. Lecture 8

23   So long as antimilitarists propose no substitute for war's disciplinary function, no *moral equivalent*

[2]The term [pragmatism] . . . was first introduced into philosophy by Mr. Charles Peirce in 1878 [in] an article entitled "How to Make Our Ideas Clear" in the *Popular Science Monthly* for January of that year. — *Pragmatism* [1907], *Lecture 1*

See Charles Sanders Peirce, 538.

of war, analogous, as one might say, to the mechanical equivalent of heat, so long they fail to realize the full inwardness of the situation.

Memories and Studies [1911]. The Moral Equivalent of War

1   The "through-and-through" universe seems to suffocate me with its infallible impeccable all-pervasiveness. . . . It seems too buttoned-up and white-chokered and clean-shaven a thing to speak in the name of the vast slow-breathing unconscious Kosmos with its dread abysses and its unknown tides.

Essays in Radical Empiricism [1912], ch. 12, Absolutism and Empiricism

2   The union of the mathematician with the poet, fervor with measure, passion with correctness, this surely is the ideal.

Collected Essays and Reviews [1920], ch. 11, Clifford's "Lectures and Essays" [1879]

3   I wished, by treating Psychology *like* a natural science, to help her to become one.

Ibid. A Plea for Psychology as a Natural Science [1892]

John Alexander Joyce
1842–1915

4 I shall love you in December
With the love I gave in May![1]

Question and Answer, st. 8

Prince Pëtr Alekseevich Kropotkin
1842–1921

5   Sociability is as much a law of nature as mutual struggle . . . mutual aid is as much a law of animal life as mutual struggle.   *Mutual Aid [1902]*

Sidney Lanier
1842–1881

6 Ye marshes, how candid and simple and
    nothing-withholding and free
Ye publish yourselves to the sky and offer
    yourselves to the sea!

The Marshes of Glynn [1877], l. 65

7 As the marsh hen secretly builds on the watery
    sod,
Behold I will build me a nest on the greatness of
    God:
I will fly in the greatness of God as the marsh hen
    flies

In the freedom that fills all the space 'twixt the
    marsh and the skies:
By so many roots as the marsh grass sends in the
    sod
I will heartily lay me a-hold on the greatness of
    God:
Oh, like to the greatness of God is the greatness
    within
The range of the marshes, the liberal marshes of
    Glynn.

Ibid. l. 71

8 Out of the hills of Habersham,
Down the valleys of Hall.

Song of the Chattahoochee [1877], st. 1

9 Into the woods my Master went,
Clean forspent, forspent.
Into the woods my Master came,
Forspent with love and shame.

A Ballad of Trees and the Master [1877], st. 1

Stéphane Mallarmé
1842–1898

10   The flesh is sad, alas, and I have read all the books.[2]   *Poésies. Brise Marine*

11   Such as into himself at last Eternity has changed him.[3]   *Ibid. Le Tombeau d'Edgar Poe*

12   A Throw of the Dice Will Never Abolish Chance.[4]   *Ibid. Title of poem*

13   To *name* an object is to take away three-fourths of the pleasure given by a poem. This pleasure consists in guessing little by little: to *suggest* it, that is the ideal.[5]

Réponse à une Enquête sur l'Évolution Littéraire [1891]

14   You don't make a poem with ideas, but with words.[6]

From PAUL VALÉRY, Degas, Danse, Dessin

Alfred Marshall
1842–1924

15   We might as reasonably dispute whether it is the upper or the under blade of a pair of scissors that cuts a piece of paper, as whether value is governed by utility or cost of production.

Principles of Economics [1890]

---

[1]Will you love me in December as you do in May?—JAMES J. WALKER [1881–1946]; *set to music by* ERNEST R. BALL [1905]

[2]La chair est triste, hélas! et j'ai lu tous les livres.
[3]Tel qu'en Lui-Même enfin l'éternité le change.
[4]Un coup de dés n'abolira jamais le hasard.
[5]*Nommer* un objet, c'est supprimer les trois-quarts de la jouissance du poème qui est fait peu à peu: le *suggérer*.
[6]Ce n'est point avec des idées que l'on fait des vers, c'est avec des mots.

T. A. Palmer
fl. 1868–1882

1   Dead, dead, dead! and he never knew me, never called me mother!   *East Lynne [1874], act III*[1]

George Washington Plunkitt
1842–1924

2   I seen my opportunities and I took 'em.
Definition of "honest graft." From WILLIAM L. RIORDON, *Plunkitt of Tammany Hall [1905]*

3   The politician who steals is worse than a thief. He is a fool. With all the grand opportunities around for the man with a political pull, there's no excuse for stealin' a cent.   *Ibid.*

Hugh Antoine D'Arcy
1843–1925

4   "Say, boys! if you give me just another whiskey I'll be glad,
And I'll draw right here a picture of the face that drove me mad.
Give me that piece of chalk with which you mark the baseball score,
You shall see the lovely Madeleine upon the bar-room floor."
The Face upon the Floor [1887][2]

Henry James
1843–1916

5   The face of nature and civilization in this our country is to a certain point a very sufficient literary field. But it will yield its secrets only to a really *grasping* imagination. . . . To write well and worthily of American things one need even more than elsewhere to be a *master*.
Letter to Charles Eliot Norton [January 16, 1871]

6   It's a complex fate, being an American, and one of the responsibilities it entails is fighting against a superstitious valuation of Europe.
Letter [1872] quoted in PERCY LUBBOCK, *Letters of Henry James [1920], vol. I, Biographical note*

7   It takes a great deal of history to produce a little literature.   *Hawthorne [1879], ch. 1*

8   Whatever question there may be of his [Thoreau's] talent, there can be none, I think, of his genius. It was a slim and crooked one, but it was eminently personal. He was unperfect, unfinished, inartistic; he was worse than provincial—he was parochial.   *Ibid. 4*

9   Cats and monkeys, monkeys and cats—all human life is there.
The Madonna of the Future [1879]

10   The real offense, as she ultimately perceived, was her having a mind of her own at all. Her mind was to be his—attached to his own like a small garden plot to a deer park.
The Portrait of a Lady [1881]

11   The only reason for the existence of a novel is that it does attempt to represent life.
The Art of Fiction [1888]

12   The only obligation to which in advance we may hold a novel, without incurring the accusation of being arbitrary, is that it be interesting.   *Ibid.*

13   If I should certainly say to a novice, "Write from experience and experience only," I should feel that this was rather a tantalizing monition if I were not careful immediately to add, "Try to be one of the people on whom nothing is lost."   *Ibid.*

14   We must grant the artist his subject, his idea, his *donnée*: our criticism is applied only to what he makes of it. . . . If we pretend to respect the artist at all, we must allow him his freedom of choice, in the face, in particular cases, of innumerable presumptions that the choice will not fructify. Art derives a considerable part of its beneficial exercise from flying in the face of presumptions.   *Ibid.*

15   There are few things more exciting to me . . . than a psychological reason.   *Ibid.*

16   The practice of "reviewing" . . . in general has nothing in common with the art of criticism.
Criticism [1893]

17   The critical sense is so far from frequent that it is absolutely rare, and the possession of the cluster of qualities that minister to it is one of the highest distinctions. . . . In this light one sees the critic as the real helper of the artist, a torchbearing outrider, the interpreter, the brother. . . . Just in proportion as he is sentient and restless, just in proportion as he reacts and reciprocates and penetrates, is the critic a valuable instrument.   *Ibid.*

18   We work in the dark—we do what we can—we give what we have. Our doubt is our passion, and our passion is our task. The rest is the madness of art.   *The Middle Years [1893]*

19   The time-honored bread sauce of the happy ending.   *Theatricals: Second Series [1895]*

20   Vereker's secret . . . the general intention of his books: the string the pearls were strung on, the buried treasure, the figure in the carpet.
The Figure in the Carpet [1896]

21   I caught him, yes, I held him—it may be imagined with what passion; but at the end of a minute I began to feel what it truly was that I held. We were

---

[1]Adapted from the novel *East Lynne [1861]* by ELLEN (Mrs. Henry) WOOD.
[2]Often called "The Face on the Barroom Floor."

alone with the quiet day, and his little heart, dispossessed, had stopped.

The Turn of the Screw [1898], ending

1 Live all you can; it's a mistake not to. It doesn't so much matter what you do in particular, so long as you have your life. If you haven't had that what *have* you had? . . . What one loses one loses; make no mistake about that. . . . The right time is *any* time that one is still so lucky as to have. . . . Live!

The Ambassadors [1903], bk. V, ch. 2

2 There is, I think, no more nutritive or suggestive truth . . . than that of the perfect dependence of the "moral" sense of a work of art on the amount of felt life concerned in producing it. The question comes back thus, obviously, to the kind and the degree of the artist's prime sensibility, which is the soil out of which his subject springs.

Prefaces [1907–1909]. *The Portrait of a Lady*

3 Life being all inclusion and confusion, and art being all discrimination and selection, the latter, in search of the hard latent *value* with which it alone is concerned, sniffs round the mass as instinctively and unerringly as a dog suspicious of some buried bone.

Ibid. The Spoils of Poynton

4 The fatal futility of Fact. *Ibid.*

5 The effort really to see and really to represent is no idle business in face of the *constant* force that makes for muddlement. The great thing is indeed that the muddled state too is one of the very sharpest of the realities, that it also has color and form and character, has often in fact a broad and rich comicality. *Ibid. What Maisie Knew*

6 To criticize is to appreciate, to appropriate, to take intellectual possession, to establish in fine a relation with the criticized thing and to make it one's own. *Ibid.*

7 The historian, essentially, wants more documents than he can really use; the dramatist only wants more liberties than he can really take.

Ibid. The Aspern Papers

8 The ever importunate murmur, "Dramatize it, dramatize it!" *Ibid. The Altar of the Dead*

9 In art economy is always beauty. *Ibid.*

10 The terrible *fluidity* of self-revelation.

Ibid. The Ambassadors

11 I'm glad you like adverbs—I adore them; they are the only qualifications I really much respect.

Letter to Miss M. Betham Edwards [January 5, 1912]

12 We must know, as much as possible, in our beautiful art . . . what we are talking about—and the only way to know is to have lived and loved and cursed and floundered and enjoyed and suffered. I think I don't regret a single "excess" of my responsive youth—I only regret, in my chilled age, certain occasions and possibilities I didn't embrace.

Letter to Hugh Walpole [August 21, 1913]

13 I still, in presence of life . . . have reactions—as many as possible. . . . It's, I suppose, because I am that queer monster, the artist, an obstinate finality, an inexhaustible sensibility. Hence the reactions—appearances, memories, many things, go on playing upon it with consequences that I note and "enjoy" (grim word!) noting. It all takes doing—and I *do*. I believe I shall do yet again—it is still an act of life.

Letter to Henry Adams [March 21, 1914]

14 It is art that *makes* life, makes interest, makes importance, for our consideration and application of these things, and I know of no substitute whatever for the force and beauty of its process.

Letter to H. G. Wells [July 10, 1915]

15 So it has come at last—the Distinguished Thing.

Of his final illness [December 2, 1915]

16 The full, the monstrous demonstration that Tennyson was not Tennysonian.

The Middle Years (autobiography) [1917], ch. 6

17 Summer afternoon—summer afternoon; to me those have always been the two most beautiful words in the English language.

Quoted by EDITH WHARTON, *A Backward Glance* [1934], *ch. 10*

William McKinley
1843–1901

18 There was nothing left for us to do but to take them all, and to educate the Filipinos, and uplift and civilize and Christianize them, and by God's grace do the very best we could for them, as our fellow-men for whom Christ also died.

On his decision to claim the Philippine Islands for the United States [1899]

Robert Bridges
1844–1930

19 Whither, O splendid ship, thy white sails crowding,
Leaning across the bosom of the urgent West,
That fearest nor sea rising, nor sky clouding,
Whither away, fair rover, and what thy quest?

Shorter Poems, bk. II [1879], no. 2 (A Passer-By), st. 1

20 When men were all asleep, the snow came flying,
In large white flakes falling on the city brown,
Stealthily and perpetually settling and loosely lying,
Hushing the latest traffic of the drowsy town.

Ibid. III [1880], no. 2 (London Snow)

1 I love all beauteous things,
  I seek and adore them;
  God hath no better praise,
  And man in his hasty days
  Is honored for them.
                    Shorter Poems, bk. IV [1890], no. 1, st. 1

2 Man, in the unsearchable darkness, knoweth one
    thing
  That as he is, so was he made.
                    The Testament of Beauty [1929]

Robert Jones Burdette
1844–1914

3   There are two days in the week about which and
upon which I never worry. Two carefree days, kept
sacredly free from fear and apprehension. One of
these days is Yesterday. . . . And the other day I
do not worry about is Tomorrow.
                    The Golden Day

Anatole France
[Jacques Anatole François Thibault]
1844–1924

4   I do not know any reading more easy, more fascinating, more delightful than a catalogue.
    The Crime of Sylvestre Bonnard [1881].[1] *The
    Log, December 24, 1849*

5   To know is nothing at all; to imagine is everything.   *Ibid. pt. II, ch. 2*

6   He flattered himself on being a man without any
prejudices; and this pretension itself is a very great
prejudice.   *Ibid. 4*

7   Those who have given themselves the most concern about the happiness of peoples have made their
neighbors very miserable.   *Ibid.*

8   Man is so made that he can only find relaxation
from one kind of labor by taking up another.
                    Ibid.

9   People who have no weaknesses are terrible;
there is no way of taking advantage of them.
                    Ibid.

10   The whole art of teaching is only the art of awakening the natural curiosity of young minds for the
purpose of satisfying it afterwards.   *Ibid.*

11   The good critic is one who tells of his mind's
adventures among masterpieces.
                    La Vie Littéraire [1888], preface

12   We reproach people for talking about themselves;
but it is the subject they treat best.
                    Ibid. Journal des Goncourt

13   The law, in its majestic equality, forbids the rich
as well as the poor to sleep under bridges, to beg in
the streets, and to steal bread.
                    The Red Lily [1894], ch. 7

14   A tale without love is like beef without mustard:
insipid.   *The Revolt of the Angels [1914], ch. 8*

Gerard Manley Hopkins
1844–1889

15 And I have asked to be
  Where no storms come,
  Where the green swell is in the havens dumb,
  And out of the swing of the sea.
                    Poems [1918].[2] *No. 20, Heaven-Haven, st. 2*

16 Elected Silence, sing to me
  And beat upon my whorlèd ear,
  Pipe me to pastures still and be
  The music that I care to hear.
                    No. 24, The Habit of Perfection, st. 1

17   Thou mastering me
        God! giver of breath and bread;
      World's strand, sway of the sea;
        Lord of living and dead;
  Thou hast bound bones and veins in me, fastened
      me flesh,
  And after it almost unmade, what with dread,
      Thy doing: and dost thou touch me afresh?
  Over again I feel thy finger and find thee.
                    No. 28, The Wreck of the Deutschland, st. 1

18 The world is charged with the grandeur of God.
                    No. 31, God's Grandeur, l. 1

19 Look at the stars! look, look up at the skies!
  O look at all the fire-folk sitting in the air!
                    No. 32, The Starlight Night, l. 1

20 I caught this morning morning's minion, king-
      dom of daylight's dauphin, dapple-dawn-drawn
      Falcon, in his riding
    Of the rolling level underneath him steady air,
      and striding
  High there, how he rung upon the rein of a
      wimpling wing
  In his ecstasy!
                    No. 36, The Windhover, l. 1

21 The achieve of, the mastery of the thing!
                    Ibid. l. 8

22 Brute beauty and valor and act, oh, air, pride,
      plume, here
  Buckle!
                    Ibid. l. 9

23 Glory be to God for dappled things.
                    No. 37, Pied Beauty, l. 1

[1] Translated by LAFCADIO HEARN.

[2] First published in 1918, edited by ROBERT BRIDGES. Poem
numbers are from the third edition [1948], edited by W. H.
GARDNER.

1 All things counter, original, spare, strange;
    Whatever is fickle, freckled (who knows how?)
    With swift, slow; sweet, sour; adazzle, dim;
He fathers-forth whose beauty is past change:
    Praise him.
                      Ibid. l. 7

2 Summer ends now; now, barbarous in beauty, the
    stooks arise
    Around; up above, what wind-walks! what
    lovely behavior
Of silk-sack clouds! Has wilder, willful-wavier
Meal-drift molded ever and melted across skies?
         No. 38, Hurrahing in Harvest, st. 1

3 Felix Randal the farrier, O he is dead then? My
    duty all ended,
Who have watched his mold of man, big-boned
    and hardy-handsome,
Pining, pining.
            No. 53, Felix Randal, st. 1

4 When thou at the random grim forge, powerful
    amidst peers,
Didst fettle for the great gray drayhorse his bright
    and battering sandal!
                 Ibid. st. 4

5 Margaret, are you grieving
Over Goldengrove unleaving?
    No. 55, Spring and Fall: To A Young Child, l. 1

6 Nor mouth had, no nor mind, expressed
What heart heard of, ghost guessed:
It is the blight man was born for,
It is Margaret you mourn for.
                Ibid. l. 12

7 As kingfishers catch fire, dragonflies draw flame.
                 No. 57, l. 1

8 How to keep—is there any any, is there none
    such, nowhere known some, bow or brooch
    or braid or brace, lace, latch or catch or key
    to keep
Back beauty, keep it, beauty, beauty, beauty . . .
    from vanishing away?
    No. 59, The Leaden Echo and the Golden Echo,
    l. 1

9 I say that we are wound
With mercy round and round
As if with air.
    No. 60, The Blessed Virgin Compared to the
    Air We Breathe, l. 34

10 World-mothering air, air wild,
Wound with thee, in thee isled,
Fold home, fast fold thy child.
               Ibid. l. 124

11 Not, I'll not, carrion comfort, Despair, not feast
    on thee;
Not untwist—slack they may be—these last
    strands of man
In me or, most weary, cry *I can no more.* I can;

Can something, hope, wish day come, not choose
    not to be.
         No. 64, Carrion Comfort, l. 1

12   That night, that year
Of now done darkness I wretch lay wrestling with
    (my God!) my God.
                Ibid. l. 13

13 No worst, there is none. Pitched past pitch of
    grief,
More pangs will, schooled at forepangs, wilder
    wring.
          No. 65, No Worst, l. 1

14 O the mind, mind has mountains; cliffs of fall
Frightful, sheer, no-man-fathomed.
                Ibid. l. 9

15 I wake and feel the fell of dark, not day.
What hours, O what black hours we have spent
This night.
         No. 69, I Wake and Feel, l. 1

16 I am gall, I am heartburn.
                Ibid. l. 9

17 I am all at once what Christ is, since he was what
    I am, and
This Jack, joke, poor potsherd, patch,
    matchwood, immortal diamond,
      Is immortal diamond.
    No. 72, That Nature Is a Heraclitean Fire and
    of the Comfort of the Resurrection, l. 22

18   No doubt my poetry errs on the side of oddness.
I hope in time to have a more balanced and Miltonic
style. But as air, melody, is what strikes me most of
all in music, and design in painting, so design, pattern, or what I am in the habit of calling *inscape* is
what I above all aim at in poetry. Now it is the virtue
of design, pattern, or inscape to be distinctive, and it
is the vice of distinctiveness to become queer. This
vice I cannot have escaped.
    Letter to Robert Bridges [February 15, 1879]

Andrew Lang
1844–1912

19 You can cover a great deal of country in books.
           To the Gentle Reader, st. 5

20 The surge and thunder of the Odyssey.
             Sonnet, The Odyssey

James Hilary Mulligan
1844–1916

21 The moonlight is the softest, in Kentucky,
Summer days come oftest, in Kentucky,
    Friendship is the strongest,
    Love's fires glow the longest,
    Yet a wrong is always wrongest,
      In Kentucky.
              In Kentucky, st. 1

Friedrich Wilhelm Nietzsche
1844–1900

1   Our destiny exercises its influence over us even when, as yet, we have not learned its nature: it is our future that lays down the law of our today.
Human, All Too Human [1878],[1] 7

2   One must have a good memory to be able to keep the promises one makes.   *Ibid.* 59

3   One will rarely err if extreme actions be ascribed to vanity, ordinary actions to habit, and mean actions to fear.   *Ibid.* 74

4   Every tradition grows ever more venerable—the more remote is its origin, the more confused that origin is. The reverence due to it increases from generation to generation. The tradition finally becomes holy and inspires awe.   *Ibid.* 96

5   When Zarathustra was alone . . . he said to his heart: "Could it be possible! This old saint in the forest hath not yet heard of it, that *God is dead!*"[2]
Thus Spake Zarathustra [1883–1891],[3]
prologue, ch. 2

6   Man is a rope stretched between the animal and the Superman—a rope over an abyss.   *Ibid.* 3

7   I want to teach men the sense of their existence, which is the Superman, the lightning out of the dark cloud man.   *Ibid.* 7

8   This is the hardest of all: to close the open hand out of love, and keep modest as a giver.
Ibid. pt. II, ch. 23

9   Distrust all in whom the impulse to punish is powerful.   *Ibid.* 29

10   We ought to learn from the kine one thing: ruminating.   *Ibid. IV, 68*

11   If ye would go up high, then use your own legs! Do not get yourselves *carried* aloft; do not seat yourselves on other people's backs and heads!
Ibid. 73

12   It is certainly not the least charm of a theory that it is refutable.
Beyond Good and Evil [1885–1886],[4] I, 18

13   No one is such a liar as the indignant man.
Ibid. II, 26

14   It is not the strength but the duration of great sentiments that makes great men.   *Ibid. IV, 72*

15   In revenge and in love woman is more barbarous than man.   *Ibid.* 139

16   Whoever fights monsters should see to it that in the process he does not become a monster. And

when you look long into an abyss, the abyss also looks into you.   *Ibid.* 146

17   The thought of suicide is a great consolation:[5] by means of it one gets successfully through many a bad night.   *Ibid.* 157

18   Blessed are the forgetful: for they get the better even of their blunders.   *Ibid.* 217

19   Is not life a hundred times too short for us to bore ourselves?   *Ibid.* 227

20   One does not know—cannot know—the best that is in one.   *Ibid.* 240

21   Mozart, the last chord of a centuries-old great European taste.   *Ibid.* 245

22   The melancholia of everything completed!
Ibid. IX, 277

23   The masters have been done away with; the morality of the common man has triumphed.
Genealogy of Morals [1887], essay 1,
aphorism 9

24   At the core of all these aristocratic races the beast of prey is not to be mistaken, the magnificent *blond beast*, avidly rampant for spoil and victory.
Ibid. 11

25   The broad effects which can be obtained by punishment in man and beast are the increase of fear, the sharpening of the sense of cunning, the mastery of the desires; so it is that punishment tames man, but does not make him "better."   *Ibid. 2, 15*

26   The sick are the greatest danger for the healthy; it is not from the strongest that harm comes to the strong, but from the weakest.   *Ibid. 3, 14*

27   A strong and well-constituted man digests his experiences (deeds and misdeeds all included) just as he digests his meats, even when he has some tough morsels to swallow.   *Ibid.* 16

28   Two great European narcotics, alcohol and Christianity.
The Twilight of the Idols [1888]. Things the
Germans Lack, 2

29   What is it: is man only a blunder of God, or God only a blunder of man?   *Ibid.*

30   If a man have a strong faith he can indulge in the luxury of skepticism.   *Ibid.* 12

31   Liberal institutions straightway cease from being liberal the moment they are soundly established: once this is attained no more grievous and more thorough enemies of freedom exist than liberal institutions.   *Ibid.* 38

32   It is my ambition to say in ten sentences what everyone else says in a whole book—what everyone else does *not* say in a whole book.   *Ibid.* 51

---

[1]Translated by ALEXANDER HARVEY.
[2]God is dead. God remains dead. And we have killed him.
—*The Gay Science (Die Fröhliche Wissenschaft) [1882]*, *ch.* 125
[3]Translated by THOMAS COMMON.
[4]Translated by HELEN ZIMMERN.

[5]We are in the power of no calamity while death is in our own.—THOMAS BROWNE, *Religio Medici [1643]*

1   Love is the state in which man sees things most widely different from what they are. The force of illusion reaches its zenith here, as likewise the sweetening and transfiguring power. When a man is in love he endures more than at other times; he submits to everything.

The Antichrist [1888],[1] aphorism 23

2   God created woman. And boredom did indeed cease from that moment—but many other things ceased as well! Woman was God's *second* mistake.

Ibid. 48

3   Life always gets harder toward the summit— the cold increases, responsibility increases.

Ibid. 57

4   I call Christianity the one great curse, the one enormous and innermost perversion, the one great instinct of revenge, for which no means are too venomous, too underhand, too underground and too petty—I call it the one immortal blemish of mankind.

Ibid. 62

5   My doctrine is: Live that thou mayest desire to live again—that is thy duty—for in any case thou wilt live again!   *Eternal Recurrence,[1] 27*

6   Even a thought, even a possibility, can shatter us and transform us.   *Ibid. 30*

7   Nothing on earth consumes a man more quickly than the passion of resentment.

Ecce Homo [1888][1]

8   I believe only in French culture, and regard everything else in Europe which calls itself "culture" as a misunderstanding. I do not even take the German kind into consideration.   *Ibid.*

9   Wherever Germany extends her sway, she ruins culture.   *Ibid.*

10   As an artist, a man has no home in Europe save in Paris.   *Ibid.*

11   Simply by being compelled to keep constantly on his guard, a man may grow so weak as to be unable any longer to defend himself.   *Ibid.*

12   My time has not yet come either; some are born posthumously.   *Ibid.*

13   No one can draw more out of things, books included, than he already knows. A man has no ears for that to which experience has given him no access.   *Ibid.*

14   The Germans are like women, you can scarcely ever fathom their depths—they haven't any.[2]

Ibid.

15   All prejudices may be traced back to the intestines. A sedentary life is the real sin against the Holy Ghost.[3]   *Ibid.*

16   One must separate from anything that forces one to repeat No again and again.   *Ibid.*

17   The Will to Power.[4]   *Title of book [1888]*

John Boyle O'Reilly
1844–1890

18   They who see the Flying Dutchman never, never reach the shore.

The Flying Dutchman

19   The red rose whispers of passion
And the white rose breathes of love;
O, the red rose is a falcon,
And the white rose is a dove.

A White Rose, st. 1

20   The organized charity, scrimped and iced,
In the name of a cautious, statistical Christ.

In Bohemia, st. 5

Arthur William Edgar O'Shaughnessy
1844–1881

21   We are the music-makers,
And we are the dreamers of dreams,
Wandering by lone sea breakers,
And sitting by desolate streams;
World-losers and world-forsakers,
On whom the pale moon gleams:
Yet we are the movers and shakers
Of the world forever, it seems.

Ode, st. 1

William Archibald Spooner[5]
1844–1930

22   Kinquering Congs their titles take.

Announcing the hymn in college chapel

23   You have deliberately tasted two worms and you can leave Oxford by the next town drain.

Dismissing a student. Attributed

Paul Verlaine
1844–1896

24   The long sobs
Of the violins

---

[1]Translated by ANTHONY M. LUDOVICI.
[2]Man thinks woman profound—why? Because he can never fathom her depths. Woman is not even shallow.—*The Twilight of the Idols, Maxims and Missiles, 27*
[3]Translated by CLIFTON P. FADIMAN.
[4]Der Wille zur Macht.
[5]Canon Spooner, for many years warden of New College, Oxford, was famous for unintentional transposition of (usually initial) word sounds, giving rise to the term "spoonerism."

Of autumn
Pierce my heart
With monotonous languor.[1]
　　　　Poèmes Saturniens [1866]. Chanson d'Automne

[1] There is weeping in my heart
Like the rain falling on the city.[2]
　　　　Romances sans Paroles [1874], III

[2] Here are fruits, flowers, leaves and branches,
And here is my heart which beats only for you.[3]
　　　　Ibid. Green

[3] What have you done, you there
Weeping without cease,
Tell me, yes you, what have you done
With all your youth?[4]
　　　　Sagesse [1881], III, st. 6

[4] Music above all, and for this
Choose the irregular.[5]
　　　　Jadis et Naguère [1884]. L'Art Poetique

[5] Take eloquence and wring its neck![6]
　　　　　　　　　Ibid.

[6] And all else is literature.[7]
　　　　　　　　　Ibid.

John B. Bogart[8]
1845–1921

[7]　When a dog bites a man, that is not news, because it happens so often. But if a man bites a dog, that is news.
　　From Frank M. O'Brien, *The Story of The (New York) Sun [1918]*

William McKendree [Will] Carleton
1845–1912

[8] Worm or beetle—drought or tempest—on a
　　farmer's land may fall,
Each is loaded full o' ruin, but a mortgage beats
　　'em all.
　　　　　　　The Tramp's Story

[9] Over the hill to the poorhouse I'm trudgin' my
　　weary way.
　　　　Over the Hill to the Poorhouse, st. 1

[1]Les sanglots longs / Des violons / De l'automne / Blessent mon coeur / D'une langueur / Monotone.
[2]Il pleure dans mon coeur / Comme il pleut sur la ville. See Rimbaud, 566:2.
[3]Voici des fruits, des fleurs, des feuilles et des branches, / Et puis voici mon coeur qui ne bat que pour vous.
[4]Qu'as-tu fait, O toi que voilà / Pleurant sans cesse, / Dis, qu'as-tu fait, toi que voilà / De ta jeunesse?
[5]De la musique avant toute chose, / Et pour cela préfère l'Impair.
[6]Prends l'éloquence et tords-lui son cou!
[7]Et tout le reste est littérature.
[8]City editor [1873–1890] of *The Sun,* New York.

William Kingdon Clifford
1845–1879

[10]　Remember, then, that it [science] is the guide of action; that the truth which it arrives at is not that which we can ideally contemplate without error, but that which we may act upon without fear; and you cannot fail to see that scientific thought is not an accompaniment or condition of human progress, but human progress itself.
　　Aims and Instruments of Scientific Thought [1872]

Daniel Webster Hoyt
1845–1936

[11] Why should good words ne'er be said
Of a friend till he is dead?
　　　　A Sermon in Rhyme [1878], st. 1

George Kennan
1845–1924

[12]　Heroism, the Caucasian mountaineers say, is endurance for one moment more.
　　Letter to Henry Munroe Rogers [July 25, 1921]

John Banister Tabb
1845–1909

[13] Out of the dusk a shadow,
　　Then a spark;
Out of the clouds a silence,
　　Then a lark;
Out of the heart a rapture,
　　Then a pain;
Out of the dead, cold ashes,
　　Life again.

　　　　　　　　Evolution

Punch

[14]　Advice to persons about to marry.—"Don't."[9]
　　　　　　　Vol. VIII, p. 1 [1845]

[15]　You pays your money and you takes your choice.
　　　　　　　X, 16 [1846]

[16]　What is Matter?—Never mind.
　　What is Mind?—No matter.
　　　　　　　XXIX, 19 [1855]

[17]　It ain't the 'unting as 'urts 'un, it's the 'ammer,
'ammer, 'ammer along the 'ard 'igh road.
　　　　　　　XXX, 218 [1856]

[18] There was an old owl lived in an oak,
The more he heard, the less he spoke;

[9]See Acton, 521:6.

The less he spoke, the more he heard,
O, if men were all like that wise bird!
LXVIII, 155 [1875]

1   It's worse than wicked, my dear, it's vulgar.
Almanac [1876]

2   Don't look at me, sir, with—ah—in that tone of
voice.   *XCVII, 38 [1884]*

3   I'm afraid you've got a bad egg, Mr. Jones.
Oh no, my Lord, I assure you! Parts of it are excellent!   *CIX, 222 [1895]*

Charles Dupee Blake
1846–1903

4 Rock-a-bye-baby on the tree top,
When the wind blows the cradle will rock,
When the bough breaks the cradle will fall,
And down will come baby, cradle and all.
Attributed

Léon Bloy
1846–1917

5   Suffering is an auxiliary of creation.
Pages de Léon Bloy [1951]

6   When you ask God to send you trials, you may be
sure your prayer will be granted.
Ibid. Pensées Détachées

Daniel Hudson Burnham
1846–1912

7   Make no little plans; they have no magic to stir
men's blood.   *Attributed[1]*

Charles Prestwich Scott
1846–1932

8   The primary office of a newspaper is the gathering of news . . . comment is free, but facts are sacred.   *In the Manchester Guardian [May 6, 1926]*

Edward Noyes Westcott
1846–1898

9   They say a reasonable amount o' fleas is good fer
a dog—keeps him from broodin' over *bein'* a dog.
David Harum [1898], ch. 32

10   The' ain't nothin' truer in the Bible 'n that sayin'
thet them that has gits.   *Ibid. 35*

[1]This quotation is now doubted. See HENRY M. SAYLOR,
" 'Make No Little Plans': Daniel Burnham Thought It but Did
He Say It?," *Journal of the American Institute of Architects*, 27
[1957]: 3.

Alexander Graham Bell
1847–1922

11   Mr. Watson, come here, I want you.[2]
To his assistant [March 10, 1876]

Thomas Alva Edison
1847–1931

12   There is no substitute for hard work.
Life [1932], ch. 24

13   Genius is one percent inspiration and ninety-nine
percent perspiration.   *Ibid.*

Henry Demarest Lloyd
1847–1903

14   Monopoly is Business at the end of its journey.
Wealth Against Commonwealth [1894]

15   Corporations have no souls, but they can love
each other.   *Ibid.*

John Locke
1847–1889

16 O Ireland, isn't it grand you look—
Like a bride in her rich adornin'?
And with all the pent-up love of my heart
I bid you the top o' the mornin'!
*The Exile's Return (Th' an'am an Dhia: My
Soul to God), st. 1*

Alice Meynell
1847–1922

17 She walks—the lady of my delight—
A shepherdess of sheep.

The Shepherdess, st. 1

Julia A. Moore
1847–1920

18 Leave off the agony, leave off style,
Unless you've got money by you all the while.
Leave Off the Agony in Style

Milton Nobles
1847–1924

19 The villain still pursued her.
The Phoenix [1875], act I, sc. iii

[2]The first intelligible words transmitted by telephone.

George Robert Sims
1847–1922

1 It was Christmas Day in the workhouse.
Christmas Day in the Workhouse, st. 1

Arthur James Balfour
1848–1930

2   His Majesty's Government view with favor the establishment in Palestine of a national home for the Jewish people, and will use their best endeavors to facilitate the achievement of this object, it being clearly understood that nothing shall be done which may prejudice the civil and religious rights of existing non-Jewish communities in Palestine, or the rights and political status enjoyed by Jews in any other country.
The Balfour Declaration. Letter to Lionel Walter, Lord Rothschild [November 2, 1917]

Sir Francis Darwin
1848–1925

3   But in science the credit goes to the man who convinces the world, not to the man to whom the idea first occurs.
First Galton Lecture before the Eugenics Society [1914]

Ludwig Max Goldberger
1848–1913

4   America, the land of unlimited possibilities.
Land of Unlimited Possibilities: Observations on Economic Life in the United States of America [1903]

Joel Chandler Harris
1848–1908

5   Hit look lak sparrer-grass, hit feel lak sparrer-grass, hit tas'e lak sparrer-grass, en I bless ef 'taint sparrer-grass.
Nights with Uncle Remus [1883], ch. 27

6   Tar-baby ain't sayin' nuthin', en Brer Fox, he lay low.   *Uncle Remus and His Friends [1892]*

7   Ez soshubble ez a baskit er kittens.   *Ibid.*

8   Bred en bawn in a brier-patch, Brer Fox.
Ibid.

9   You do de pullin', Sis Cow, en I'll do de gruntin'.
Ibid.

10   W'en ole man Rabbit say "scoot," dey scooted, en w'en old Miss Rabbit say "scat," dey scatted.
Ibid.

11   Lazy fokes' stummucks don't git tired.
Uncle Remus: Plantation Proverbs

12   Jaybird don't rob his own nes'.   *Ibid.*

13   Licker talks mighty loud w'en it gits loose fum de jug.   *Ibid.*

14   Hongry rooster don't cackle w'en he fine a wum.
Ibid.

15   Youk'n hide de fier, but w'at you gwine do wid de smoke?   *Ibid.*

16   Watch out w'en youer gittin' all you want. Fattenin' hogs ain't in luck.   *Ibid.*

17 Hop light, ladies,
Oh, Miss Loo!
Oh, swing dat yaller gal!
Do, boys, do!

Plantation Play Song

Joris Karl Huysmans
1848–1907

18   The loveliest tune imaginable becomes vulgar and insupportable as soon as the public begins to hum it and the hurdy-gurdies make it their own.
À Rebours (Against the Grain) [1884],[1] ch. 9

19   Art is the only clean thing on earth, except holiness.   *Crowds of Lourdes [1906]*

Alice James
1848–1892

20   When will women begin to have the first glimmer that above all other loyalties is the loyalty to Truth, *i.e.,* to yourself, that husband, children, friends and country are as nothing to that?
Diary [November 19, 1889]

Richard Jefferies
1848–1887

21   It is eternity now. I am in the midst of it. It is about me in the sunshine; I am in it, as the butterfly in the light-laden air. Nothing has to come; it is now. Now is eternity; now is the immortal life.
The Story of My Heart [1883]

Vilfredo Pareto
1848–1923

22   Give me a fruitful error any time, full of seeds, bursting with its own corrections. You can keep your sterile truth for yourself.
Comment on Kepler

[1]Translated by JOHN HOWARD.

Eben Eugene Rexford

1848–1916

1 Darling, I am growing old,
  Silver threads among the gold
  Shine upon my brow today;
  Life is fading fast away.
        Silver Threads Among the Gold [1873],[1] *st. 1*

Frederic Edward Weatherly

1848–1929

2 Always the same, Darby, my own,
  Always the same to your old wife Joan.
        Darby and Joan,[2] *refrain*

Bernhard von Bülow

1849–1929

3   A place in the sun.
        *A Promise for Germany. Speech before the
        Reichstag [December 6, 1897]*

Lord Randolph Spencer Churchill

1849–1895

4   The old gang [members of the Conservative government].
        *Speech in the House of Commons [March 7,
        1878]*

Sir Edmund Gosse

1849–1928

5   My father's theory[3] . . . was defined by a hasty press as being this—that God hid the fossils in the rocks in order to tempt geologists into infidelity.
        Father and Son [1907], ch. 5

William Ernest Henley

1849–1903

6 Bland as a Jesuit, sober as a hymn.
        In Hospital [1888]. No. 16, House Surgeon

7 Valiant in velvet, light in ragged luck,
  Most vain, most generous, sternly critical,
  Buffoon and poet, lover and sensualist:
  A deal of Ariel, just a streak of Puck,
  Much Antony, of Hamlet most of all,
  And something of the Shorter-Catechist.
        Ibid. 25, Apparition (Robert Louis Stevenson)

[1] Music by HART PEASE DANKS [1834–1903].
[2] Old Darby with Joan by his side, / You've often regarded with wonder; / He's dropsical, she is sore-eyed, / Yet they're ever uneasy asunder.—*Gentleman's Magazine* [March 1735]
[3] British naturalist Philip Henry Gosse [1810–1888], who opposed the uniformitarian geological theory of Charles Lyell [1797–1875].
See Lyell, 420:17.

8 As dust that drives, as straws that blow,
  Into the night go one and all.
        Ballade of Dead Actors [1888]

9 Out of the night that covers me,
  Black as the Pit from pole to pole,
  I thank whatever gods may be
  For my unconquerable soul.

  In the fell clutch of circumstance,
  I have not winced nor cried aloud;
  Under the bludgeonings of chance
  My head is bloody, but unbowed.
        *Echoes [1888]. No. 4, In Memoriam R. T.
        Hamilton Bruce ("Invictus"), st. 1, 2*

10 I am the master of my fate;
   I am the captain of my soul.[4]
        Ibid. st. 4

11 Night with her train of stars
   And her great gift of sleep.
        Ibid. 35, In Memoriam Margaritae Sororis, st. 2

12 Or ever the knightly years were gone
   With the old world to the grave,
   I was a King in Babylon
   And you were a Christian Slave.
        Ibid. 37, To W. A., st. 1

Sarah Orne Jewett

1849–1909

13   Captain Littlepage had overset his mind with too much reading.
        The Country of the Pointed Firs [1896], ch. 5

14   Wrecked on the lee shore of age.   *Ibid. 7*

15   We were standing where there was a fine view of the harbor and its long stretches of shore all covered by the great army of the pointed firs, darkly cloaked and standing as if they waited to embark. As we looked far seaward among the outer islands, the trees seemed to march seaward still, going steadily over the heights and down to the water's edge.
        Ibid.

16   Tact is after all a kind of mind-reading.
        Ibid. 10

17   In the life of each of us, I said to myself, there is a place remote and islanded, and given to endless regret or secret happiness.   *Ibid. 15*

18   'Tain't worthwhile to wear a day all out before it comes.   *Ibid. 16*

19   So we die before our own eyes; so we see some chapters of our lives come to their natural end.
        Ibid. 21

20   The thing that teases the mind over and over for years, and at last gets itself put down rightly on

[4] See Sallust, 91:28 and 92:1; Bacon, 160:4; Shakespeare, 187:-22; Tennyson, 459:9; and Nehru, 677:7.

paper—whether little or great, it belongs to Literature.

> *Letter to Willa Cather. Quoted in preface to The Country of the Pointed Firs and Other Stories [1925]*

Emma Lazarus
1849–1887

1   Give me your tired, your poor,
Your huddled masses yearning to breathe free,
The wretched refuse of your teeming shore,
Send these, the homeless, tempest-tost to me:
I lift my lamp beside the golden door.[1]

> *The New Colossus: Inscription for the Statue of Liberty, New York Harbor [1883]*

Sir William Osler
1849–1919

2   The greater the ignorance the greater the dogmatism.
> *Montreal Medical Journal [1902]*

3   The natural man has only two primal passions, to get and to beget.
> *Science and Immortality [1904], ch. 2*

4   The desire to take medicine is perhaps the greatest feature which distinguishes man from animals.
> *Ibid. 14*

5   Things cannot always go your way. Learn to accept in silence the minor aggravations, cultivate the gift of taciturnity and consume your own smoke with an extra draught of hard work, so that those about you may not be annoyed with the dust and soot of your complaints.
> *From HARVEY CUSHING, The Life of Sir William Osler [1925], vol. I, ch. 22*

6   Take the sum of human achievement in action, in science, in art, in literature—subtract the work of the men above forty, and while we should miss great treasures, even priceless treasures, we would practically be where we are today. . . . The effective, moving, vitalizing work of the world is done between the ages of twenty-five and forty.[2]
> *Ibid. 24 [The Fixed Period]*

7   My second fixed idea is the uselessness of men above sixty years of age, and the incalculable benefit it would be in commercial, political, and in professional life, if as a matter of course, men stopped work at this age.[3]
> *Ibid.*

[1] Set to music by IRVING BERLIN for *Miss Liberty*.
[2] Address at Johns Hopkins University, Baltimore [February 22, 1905].
[3] This valedictory address caused much discussion and misquotation. It was headlined in the press: OSLER RECOMMENDS CHLOROFORM AT SIXTY, and occasioned many columns of letters, caustic cartoons, and the like, until to "Oslerize" became a byword.

8   Nothing in life is more wonderful than faith—the one great moving force which we can neither weigh in the balance nor test in the crucible.
> *Ibid. II, 30*

Ivan Petrovich Pavlov
1849–1936

9   The naturalist must consider only one thing: what is the relation of this or that external reaction of the animal to the phenomena of the external world?
> *Scientific Study of So-Called Psychical Processes in the Higher Animals [1906]*

10   Mankind will possess incalculable advantages and extraordinary control over human behavior when the scientific investigator will be able to subject his fellow men to the same external analysis he would employ for any natural object, and when the human mind will contemplate itself not from within but from without.
> *Ibid.*

James Whitcomb Riley
1849–1916

11 O'er folded blooms
On swirls of musk,
The beetle booms adown the glooms
And bumps along the dusk.
> *The Beetle, st. 7*

12 The ripest peach is highest on the tree.
> *The Ripest Peach, st. 1*

13 There! little girl; don't cry!
> *A Life Lesson, st. 3*

14 That old sweetheart of mine.
> *An Old Sweetheart of Mine, st. 12*

15 An' all us other children, when the supper things
      is done,
We set around the kitchen fire an' has the mostest
      fun
A-list'nin' to the witch-tales 'at Annie tells about,
An' the Gobble-uns 'at gits you
Ef you
   Don't
      Watch
         Out!
> *Little Orphant Annie [1883], st. 1*

16 'Long about knee-deep in June,
'Bout the time strawberries melts
On the vine.
> *Knee-Deep in June [1883], st. 1*

17 Oh! the old swimmin' hole! When I last saw the
      place,
The scenes was all changed, like the change in my
      face.
> *The Old Swimmin' Hole [1883], st. 5*

1 O, it sets my heart a-clickin' like the tickin' of a
  clock,
When the frost is on the punkin and the fodder's
  in the shock.
> *When the Frost Is on the Punkin [1883], st. 3*

August Strindberg
1849–1912

2 I loathe people who keep dogs. They are cowards
who haven't got the guts to bite people themselves.
> *A Madman's Diary [1895], pt. 3*

Edward Bellamy
1850–1898

3 We hold the period of youth sacred to education,
and the period of maturity, when the physical forces
begin to flag, equally sacred to ease and agreeable
relaxation.
> *Looking Backward, 2000–1887 [1888], ch. 6*

4 The nation guarantees the nurture, education,
and comfortable maintenance of every citizen from
the cradle to the grave. *Ibid. 9*

5 Love of money . . . was the general impulse to
effort in your day. *Ibid.*

6 Badly off as the men . . . were in your day, they
were more fortunate than their mothers and wives.
> *Ibid. 11*

7 An American credit card . . . is just as good in
Europe as American gold used to be. *Ibid. 13*

8 Equal wealth and equal opportunities of culture
. . . have simply made us all members of one class.
> *Ibid. 14*

9 Your system was liable to periodical convulsions
. . . business crises at intervals of five to ten years,
which wrecked the industries of the nation.
> *Ibid. 22*

10 On no other stage are the scenes shifted with a
swiftness so like magic as on the great stage of history when once the hour strikes.
> *Ibid. Author's postscript*

11 *Looking Backward* was written in the belief that
the Golden Age lies before us and not behind us.
> *Ibid.*

Augustine Birrell
1850–1933

12 Libraries are not made; they grow.
> *Obiter Dicta. Book Buying*

13 That great dust heap called "history."
> *Ibid. Carlyle*

Hermann Ebbinghaus
1850–1909

14 From the most ancient subject we shall produce
the newest science.[1]
> *Inscription on the title page of Über das*
> *Gedachtnis (Memory) [1885]*

15 Psychology has a long past, but only a short history.
> *Abriss der Psychologie (Summary of*
> *Psychology) [1908], opening sentence*

Eugene Field
1850–1895

16 He could whip his weight in wildcats.
> *Modjesky as Cameel, st. 10*

17 The best of all physicians
  Is apple pie and cheese!
> *Apple Pie and Cheese, st. 5*

18 It always was the biggest fish I caught that got
  away.
> *Our Biggest Fish, st. 2*

19 When I demanded of my friend what viands he
    preferred,
  He quoth: "A large cold bottle, and a small hot
    bird!"
> *The Bottle and the Bird, st. 1*

20 Wynken, Blynken, and Nod one night
  Sailed off in a wooden shoe—
  Sailed on a river of crystal light
  Into a sea of dew.
> *Wynken, Blynken, and Nod, st. 1*

21 The little toy dog is covered with dust,
  But sturdy and staunch he stands;
  And the little toy soldier is red with rust,
  And his musket molds in his hands;
  Time was when the little toy dog was new,
  And the soldier was passing fair;
  And that was the time when our Little Boy Blue
  Kissed them and put them there.
> *Little Boy Blue, st. 1*

22 The gingham dog went "Bow-wow-wow!"
  And the calico cat replied "Mee-ow!"
  The air was littered, an hour or so,
  With bits of gingham and calico.
> *The Duel, st. 2*

23 'Most all the time, the whole year round, there
    ain't no flies on me,
  But jest 'fore Christmas I'm as good as I kin be!
> *Jest 'Fore Christmas, st. 1*

[1]De subjecto vetustissimo novissimam promovemus scien-
tiam.

Fred Gilbert
1850–1903

1   The Man Who Broke the Bank at Monte Carlo.
Title of song [1892]

Samuel Gompers
1850–1924

2   To protect the workers in their inalienable rights to a higher and better life; to protect them, not only as equals before the law, but also in their health, their homes, their firesides, their liberties as men, as workers, and as citizens; to overcome and conquer prejudices and antagonism; to secure to them the right to life, and the opportunity to maintain that life; the right to be full sharers in the abundance which is the result of their brain and brawn, and the civilization of which they are the founders and the mainstay. . . . The attainment of these is the glorious mission of the trade unions.   *Speech [1898]*

Mary Ellen [Mary Elizabeth] Lease
1850–1933

3   Raise less corn and more hell!
Attributed. Advice to Kansas farmers [1890]

Henry Cabot Lodge
1850–1924

4   Let us have done with British-Americans and Irish-Americans and German-Americans, and so on, and all be Americans. . . . If a man is going to be an American at all let him be so without any qualifying adjectives; and if he is going to be something else, let him drop the word American from his personal description.
The Day We Celebrate (Forefathers' Day). Address, New England Society of Brooklyn [December 21, 1888]

5   It is the flag just as much of the man who was naturalized yesterday as of the man whose people have been here many generations.
Address [1915]

Guy de Maupassant
1850–1893

6   A man who looks a part has the soul of that part.[1]
Mont-Oriol [1887]

7   Conversation . . . is the art of never appearing a bore, of knowing how to say everything interestingly, to entertain with no matter what, to be charming with nothing at all.
Sur l'Eau (On the Water) [1888]

8   History, that excitable and lying old lady.[2]
Ibid.

Bill [Edgar Wilson] Nye
1850–1896

9   Wagner's music is better than it sounds.
From Mark Twain's Autobiography [1924]

Laura Elizabeth Richards
1850–1943

10   Once there was an elephant
Who tried to use the telephant—
No! No! I mean an elephone
Who tried to use the telephone.
Eletelephony, l. 1

Robert Louis Stevenson
1850–1894

11   Mankind was never so happily inspired as when it made a cathedral.
An Inland Voyage [1878]. Noyon Cathedral

12   Every man is his own doctor of divinity, in the last resort.   *Ibid.*

13   For my part, I travel not to go anywhere, but to go. I travel for travel's sake. The great affair is to move.   *Travels with a Donkey [1878]*

14   Marriage is like life in this—that it is a field of battle, and not a bed of roses.
Virginibus Puerisque [1881], I, ch. 1

15   Man is a creature who lives not upon bread alone but principally by catchwords.   *Ibid. 2*

16   The cruelest lies are often told in silence.
Ibid. 4, Truth of Intercourse

17   Old and young, we are all on our last cruise.
Ibid. Crabbed Age and Youth

18   It is better to be a fool than to be dead.
Ibid.

19   Books are good enough in their own way, but they are a mighty bloodless substitute for life.
Ibid. An Apology for Idlers

20   Perpetual devotion to what a man calls his business, is only to be sustained by perpetual neglect of many other things.   *Ibid.*

21   There is no duty we so much underrate as the duty of being happy.   *Ibid.*

22   To travel hopefully is a better thing than to arrive.   *Ibid. El Dorado*

[1]Quand on a le physique d'un emploi, on en a l'âme.

[2]L'histoire, cette vieille dame exaltée et menteuse.

1 Fifteen men on the Dead Man's Chest—[1]
Yo-ho-ho, and a bottle of rum!
Drink and the devil had done for the rest—
Yo-ho-ho, and a bottle of rum!

Treasure Island [1883], ch. 1

2 Doctors is all swabs. *Ibid. 3*

3 "What is the Black Spot, Captain?" . . .
"That's a summons, mate." *Ibid.*

4 Pieces of eight, pieces of eight, pieces of eight!
Ibid. 10

5 Many's the long night I've dreamed of cheese
—toasted, mostly. *Ibid. 15*

6 Them that die'll be the lucky ones. *Ibid. 20*

7 In winter I get up at night
And dress by yellow candlelight.
In summer, quite the other way,
I have to go to bed by day.

A Child's Garden of Verses [1885]. Bed in Summer, st. 1

8 A child should always say what's true
And speak when he is spoken to,
And behave mannerly at table;
At least as far as he is able.

Ibid. Whole Duty of Children

9 Whenever the moon and stars are set,
Whenever the wind is high,
All night long in the dark and wet,
A man goes riding by.
Late in the night when the fires are out,
Why does he gallop and gallop about?

Ibid. Windy Nights, st. 1

10 I have a little shadow that goes in and out with
me,
And what can be the use of him is more than I
can see.
He is very, very like me from the heels up to the
head;
And I see him jump before me, when I jump into
my bed.

Ibid. My Shadow, st. 1

11 The friendly cow all red and white,
I love with all my heart:
She gives me cream with all her might,
To eat with apple tart.

Ibid. The Cow, st. 1

---

[1] Treasure Island came out of Kingsley's *At Last,* where I got the Dead Man's Chest—and that was the seed.—R. L. STE-VENSON, *Letter to Sidney Colvin*

We were crawling slowly along, looking out for Virgin Gorda; the first of those numberless isles which Columbus, so goes the tale, discovered on St. Ursula's day, and named them after the saint and her eleven thousand mythical virgins. Unfortunately, English buccaneers have since given to most of them less poetic names. The Dutchman's Cap, Broken Jerusalem, The Dead Man's Chest, Rum Island, and so forth, mark a time and race more prosaic.—CHARLES KINGSLEY, *At Last* [1870], *ch. 1*

12 The world is so full of a number of things,
I'm sure we should all be as happy as kings.

Ibid. Happy Thought

13 Dr. Jekyll and Mr. Hyde.

Title of novel [1886]

14 Am I no a bonny fighter?
Kidnapped [1886], ch. 10 (Alan Breck)

15 Let first the onion flourish there,
Rose among roots, the maiden-fair,
Wine-scented and poetic soul
Of the capacious salad bowl.

Underwoods [1887]. Bk. I, In English. To a Gardener

16 Under the wide and starry sky,
Dig the grave and let me lie.
Glad did I live and gladly die,
And I laid me down with a will.

This be the verse you grave for me:
Here he lies where he longed to be;
Home is the sailor, home from sea,
And the hunter home from the hill.

Ibid. Requiem

17 My body which my dungeon is,
And yet my parks and palaces.

Ibid. My Body Which My Dungeon Is

18 There's just ae thing I cannae bear,
An' that's my conscience.

Ibid. II, In Scots. My Conscience

19 I have thus played the sedulous ape to Hazlitt, to Lamb, to Wordsworth, to Sir Thomas Browne, to Defoe, to Hawthorne, to Montaigne, to Baudelaire and to Obermann.

Memories and Portraits [1887]. A College Magazine

20 A Penny Plain and Twopence Colored.

Ibid. Essay About Skelt's Juvenile Drama

21 Wealth I ask not, hope nor love,
Nor a friend to know me;
All I ask, the heaven above
And the road below me.

Songs of Travel. The Vagabond, st. 4

22 The untented Kosmos my abode,
I pass, a willful stranger;
My mistress still the open road
And the bright eyes of danger.

Ibid. Youth and Love

23 I will make you brooches and toys for your delight
Of birdsong at morning and starshine at night.

Ibid. Romance, st. 1

24 Bright is the ring of words
When the right man rings them.

Ibid. no. 14

25 Trusty, dusky, vivid, true,
With eyes of gold and bramble dew,

Steel-true and blade-straight
The great artificer
Made my mate.
> *Songs of Travel. 25, To My Wife, st. 1*

1 Be it granted me to behold you again in dying,
Hills of home!
> *Ibid. 45, To S. R. Crockett*

2 Not every man is so great a coward as he thinks
he is—nor yet so good a Christian.
> *The Master of Ballantrae [1889]. Mr.
Mackellar's Journey*

3 Nothing like a little judicious levity.
> *The Wrong Box [1889], ch. 7*

4 Do you know what the Governor of South Carolina said to the Governor of North Carolina? It's a
long time between drinks, observed that powerful
thinker.[1]
> *Ibid. 8*

5 So long as we love we serve; so long as we are
loved by others, I would almost say that we are
indispensable; and no man is useless while he has a
friend.
> *Across the Plains [1892]. Lay Morals*

6 If your morals make you dreary, depend upon it,
they are wrong. I do not say give them up, for they
may be all you have, but conceal them like a vice lest
they should spoil the lives of better and simpler people.
> *Ibid.*

7 Here lies one who meant well, tried a little, failed
much:—surely that may be his epitaph of which he
need not be ashamed.
> *Ibid.*

8 Ice and iron cannot be welded.
> *Weir of Hermiston [1896]*

9 Give us grace and strength to forbear and to
persevere. . . . Give us courage and gaiety and the
quiet mind, spare to us our friends, soften to us our
enemies.
> *Prayer[2]*

10 Youth is wholly experimental.
> *Letter to a Young Gentleman*

Rose Hartwick Thorpe
1850–1939

11 She breathed the husky whisper—
"Curfew must not ring tonight."
> *Curfew Must Not Ring Tonight [1882], st. 2*

12 Out she swung—far out; the city seemed a speck
of light below,

---

[1] Of the several traditions relating to the origin of this remark, the most reasonable one traces it to John Motley Morehead [1796–1866], who was Governor of North Carolina
1841–1845. He was visited by James H. Hammond [1807–
1864], who was Governor of South Carolina 1842–1844. They
engaged in discussion and argument, and when the latter
waxed hot, Governor Morehead was reported by a servant to
have exclaimed: "It's a long time between drinks."—JOHN
MOTLEY MOREHEAD, *letter* [November 21, 1934]

[2] On the bronze memorial to Stevenson in St. Giles Cathedral, Edinburgh, Scotland.

There 'twixt heaven and earth suspended as the
bell swung to and fro.
> *Ibid. st. 7*

Ella Wheeler Wilcox
1850–1919

13 One ship drives east and another drives west
With the selfsame winds that blow.
'Tis the set of sails and not the gales
Which tells us the way to go.
> *Winds of Fate*

14 No! the two kinds of people on earth that I mean
Are the people who lift and the people who lean.
> *To Lift or to Lean*

15 Laugh, and the world laughs with you;
Weep, and you weep alone.
> *Solitude,[3] st. 1*

16 So many gods, so many creeds,
So many paths that wind and wind,
When just the art of being kind
Is all this sad world needs.
> *The World's Need*

Kate O'Flaherty Chopin
1851–1904

17 Mrs. Pontellier was beginning to realize her position in the universe as a human being, and to recognize her relations as an individual to the world
within and about her.
> *The Awakening [1899], pt. VI*

18 For the first time in her life she stood naked in the
open air, at the mercy of the sun, the breeze that beat
upon her, and the waves that invited her.
> *Ibid. XXXIX*

Ferdinand Foch
1851–1929

19 My center is giving way, my right is pushed back,
situation excellent, I am attacking.[4]
> *At the second battle of the Marne [1918]. From
B. H. LIDDELL HART, Reputations Ten Years
After [1928]*

Henry Arthur Jones
1851–1929
and
Henry Herman
1832–1894

20 Oh God! put back Thy universe and give me
yesterday.
> *The Silver King [1882], act II, sc. 4*

---

[3] Music by LOUIS MOREAU GOTTSCHALK [1829–1869].
[4] Mon centre cède, ma droite recule, situation excellente,
j'attaque.

Edward Smith Ufford
1851–1929

1 Throw out the lifeline, throw out the lifeline,
Someone is sinking today.
Throw Out the Lifeline [1884], refrain

Francis William Bourdillon
1852–1921

2 The night has a thousand eyes,
And the day but one;
Yet the light of the bright world dies
With the dying sun.
The mind has a thousand eyes,
And the heart but one;
Yet the light of a whole life dies
When love is done.
*Among the Flowers [1878]. The Night Has a
Thousand Eyes*

Paul Bourget
1852–1935

3 Ideas are to literature what light is to painting.[1]
La Physiologie de l'Amour Moderne [1890]

Robert Bontine Cunninghame-Graham
1852–1936

4 God forbid that I should go to any heaven in
which there are no horses.
Letter to Theodore Roosevelt [1917]

Flying Hawk[2]
1852–1931

5 The tepee is much better to live in: always clean,
warm in winter, cool in summer; easy to move
. . . Indians and animals know better how to live
than white man; nobody can be in good health if he
does not have all the time fresh air, sunshine, and
good water.   *Statement in old age*

Edwin Markham
1852–1940

6 Bowed by the weight of centuries he leans
Upon his hoe and gazes on the ground,
The emptiness of ages in his face,
And on his back the burden of the world.
The Man with the Hoe [1899],[3] st. 1

---

[1]La pensée est à la littérature ce que la lumière est à la
peinture.
[2]Oglala Sioux chief.
[3]Inspired by Jean-François Millet's painting.

---

7 O masters, lords and rulers in all lands,
Is this the handiwork you give to God?
Ibid. st. 3

8 A man to match the mountains[4] and the sea.
Lincoln, The Man of the People [1901], st. 1

9 The color of the ground was in him, the red
earth,
The smack and tang of elemental things.
Ibid. st. 2

10   He went down
As when a lordly cedar, green with boughs,
Goes down with a great shout upon the hills,
And leaves a lonesome place against the sky.
Ibid. st. 4

George Moore
1852–1933

11 All reformers are bachelors—all extreme reformers have been bachelors.
The Bending of the Bough [1900], act I

12 After all there is but one race—humanity.
Ibid. III

13 A man travels the world over in search of what he
needs and returns home to find it.
The Brook Kerith [1916], ch. 11

Henry Van Dyke
1852–1933

14 The lintel low enough to keep out pomp and
pride:
The threshold high enough to turn deceit
aside.
For the Friends at Hurstmont. The Door

15 Self is the only prison that can ever bind the
soul.
The Prison and the Angel

16 The first day of spring is one thing, and the first
spring day is another. The difference between them
is sometimes as great as a month.
Fisherman's Luck [1899], ch. 5

James Davis [Owen Hall]
1853–1907

17 O tell me, pretty maiden, are there any more at
home like you?   *Florodora [1900], act II*

---

[4]A man to match his mountains, not to creep / Dwarfed and
abased below them.—WHITTIER, *Among the Hills [1869],
prelude*
Bring me men to match my mountains.—Foss, *The Coming
American*

Edgar Watson Howe
1853–1937

1   What people say behind your back is your standing in the community.

Country Town Sayings [1911]

2   There is nothing so well known as that we should not expect something for nothing—but we all do and call it Hope.   *Ibid.*

José Martí
1853–1895

3   Love is . . . born with the pleasure of looking at each other, it is fed with the necessity of seeing each other, it is concluded with the impossibility of separation!   *Amor [1881]*

4   A knowledge of different literatures is the best way to free one's self from the tyranny of any of them.   *On Oscar Wilde [1882]*

5   Man needs to suffer. When he does not have real griefs he creates them. Griefs purify and prepare him.   *Adúltera (Adulterous Thoughts) [1883]*

6   Terrible times in which priests no longer merit the praise of poets and in which poets have not yet begun to be priests.

On "El Poema de Niágara" of Pérez Bonalde [1883]

7   Men are products, expressions, reflections; they live to the extent that they coincide with their epoch, or to the extent that they differ markedly from it.

Henry Ward Beecher [1887]

8   A grain of poetry suffices to season a century.

Dedication of the Statue of Liberty [1887]

9   Others go to bed with their mistresses; I with my ideas.   *Letter [1890]*

10   Man needs to go outside himself in order to find repose and reveal himself.

Vivir en Sí (To Live in Oneself) [1891]

11   Mankind is composed of two sorts of men—those who love and create, and those who hate and destroy.   *Letter to a Cuban farmer [1893]*

12   Men have no special right because they belong to one race or another: the word man defines all rights.

Mi Raza (My Race) [1893]

13 I wish to leave the world
By its natural door;
In my tomb of green leaves
They are to carry me to die.
Do not put me in the dark
To die like a traitor;
I am good, and like a good thing
I will die with my face to the sun.

A Morir (To Die) [1894]

14   Only those who hate the Negro see hatred in the Negro.   *Manifesto of Montecristi [1895]*

15   The spirit of a government must be that of the country. The form of a government must come from the makeup of the country. Government is nothing but the balance of the natural elements of a country.

Our America [1891]

16   I have lived in the monster [the United States] and I know its insides; and my sling is the sling of David.

Letter to Manuel Mercado [1895]

Cecil John Rhodes
1853–1902

17   I desire to encourage and foster an appreciation of the advantages which will result from the union of the English-speaking peoples throughout the world, and to encourage in the students from the United States of America an attachment to the country from which they have sprung without I hope withdrawing them or their sympathies from the land of their adoption or birth.

His will, establishing the Rhodes Scholarships

18   So little done—so much to do.   *Last words*

James A. Bland
1854–1911

19 Carry me back to old Virginny,
There's where the cotton and the corn and taters grow;
There's where the birds warble sweet in the springtime,
There's where this old darky's heart am longed to go.

Carry Me Back to Old Virginny [1875], st. 1

Sir James George Frazer
1854–1941

20   Dwellers by the sea cannot fail to be impressed by the sight of its ceaseless ebb and flow, and are apt, on the principles of that rude philosophy of sympathy and resemblance . . . to trace a subtle relation, a secret harmony, between its tides and the life of man. . . . The belief that most deaths happen at ebb tide is said to be held along the east coast of England from Northumberland to Kent.

The Golden Bough [1922],[1] ch. 3

21   The heaviest calamity in English history, the breach with America, might never have occurred if George the Third had not been an honest dullard.

Ibid.

22   By religion, then, I understand a propitiation or conciliation of powers superior to man which are believed to direct and control the course of nature and of human life.   *Ibid. 4*

[1] Abridged one-volume edition. The original appeared in twelve volumes [1890–1915].

1 It is a common rule with primitive people not to waken a sleeper, because his soul is away and might not have time to get back.   *Ibid. 18*

2 The awe and dread with which the untutored savage contemplates his mother-in-law are amongst the most familiar facts of anthropology.   *Ibid.*

3 The world cannot live at the level of its great men.   *Ibid. 37*

Thomas Riley Marshall
1854–1925

4 What this country needs is a really good five-cent cigar.[1]   *Remark while presiding over the Senate*

Jules Henri Poincaré
1854–1912

5 To doubt everything or to believe everything are two equally convenient solutions; both dispense with the necessity of reflection.
Quoted by BERTRAND RUSSELL in preface to Science and Method [1913] (La Science et l'Hypothèse, 1903)[2]

6 Science is built up with facts, as a house is with stones. But a collection of facts is no more a science than a heap of stones is a house.   *Ibid.*

7 Sociology is the science with the greatest number of methods and the least results.   *Ibid. ch. 1*

Arthur Rimbaud
1854–1891

8 I went out under the sky, Muse! and I was your vassal.[3]
Ma Bohème. Fantaisie

9 My tavern was the Big Bear.
My stars in the sky rustled softly.[4]
Ibid.

10 My sad heart foams at the stern.[5]
Le Coeur Volé

11 Lighter than a cork I danced on the waves.[6]
Le Bateau Ivre [1871]

12 Sweeter than apples to children
The green water spurted through my wooden hull.[7]
Ibid.

[1]What this country needs is a good five-cent nickel.—FRANKLIN P. ADAMS
[2]Translated by G. B. HALSTED.
[3]J'allais sous le ciel, Muse! et j'étais ton féal.
[4]Mon auberge était à la Grande Ourse. / Mes étoiles au ciel avaient un doux frou-frou.
[5]Mon triste coeur bave à la poupe.
[6]Plus léger qu'un bouchon j'ai dansé sur les flots.
[7]Plus douce qu'aux enfants la chair des pommes sures, / L'eau verte pénétra ma coque de sapin.

13 I have bathed in the Poem
Of the Sea . . .
Devouring the green azures.[8]
Ibid.

14 I have seen the sunset, stained with mystic horrors,
Illumine the rolling waves with long purple forms,
Like actors in ancient plays.[9]
Ibid.

15 I long for Europe of the ancient parapets.[10]
Ibid.

16 I have seen starry archipelagoes! and islands
Whose raving skies are opened to the voyager:
Is it in these bottomless nights that you sleep, in exile,
A million golden birds, O future Vigor?[11]
Ibid.

17 Black A, white E, red I, green U, blue O: vowels,
Someday I shall recount your latent births.[12]
Voyelles [1871]

18 It is found again.
What? Eternity.
It is the sea
Gone with the sun.[13]
L'Éternité [1872]

19 O seasons, O châteaux,
What soul is without flaws?[14]
Bonheur, refrain

20 One evening, I sat Beauty in my lap.—And I found her bitter.—And I cursed her.
Une Saison en Enfer [1873]

21 I found I could extinguish all human hope from my soul.   *Ibid.*

22 Baptism enslaved me.   *Ibid. Nuit de l'Enfer*

23 I am the master of fantasy.   *Ibid.*

24 Old poetics played a large part in my alchemy of the word.   *Ibid. Délires*

25 I! I who fashioned myself a sorcerer or an angel, who dispensed with all morality, I have come back to the earth.   *Ibid. Adieu*

26 One must be absolutely modern.   *Ibid.*

[8]Je me suis baigné dans le Poème / De la Mer . . . / Dévorant les azurs verts.
[9]J'ai vu le soleil bas, taché d'horreurs mystiques, / Illuminant de longs figements violets, / Pareils à des acteurs des drames très antiques.
[10]Je regrette l'Europe aux anciens parapets!
[11]J'ai vu des archipels sidéraux! et des îles / Dont les cieux délirants sont ouverts au voyageur: / Est-ce en ces nuits sans fonds que tu dors et t'exiles, / Million d'oiseaux d'or, ô future Vigueur?
[12]A noir, E blanc, I rouge, U vert, O bleu: voyelles, / Je dirai quelque jour vos naissances latantes!
[13]Elle est retrouvée, / Quoi?—L'Éternité. / C'est la mer allée / Avec le soleil.
[14]O saisons, O châteaux / Quelle âme est sans défauts?

1   I have embraced the summer dawn.
Illuminations [1874]. Aube

2   It rains softly on the town.[1]
From a lost poem

3   I say one must be a *seer,* make oneself a *seer.* The poet makes himself a *seer* by an immense, long, deliberate *derangement* of all the senses.[2]
Letter to Paul Demeny [May 15, 1871]

Willard Duncan Vandiver
1854–1932

4   I come from a state that raises corn and cotton and cockleburs and Democrats, and frothy eloquence neither convinces nor satisfies me. I am from Missouri. You have got to show me.
Speech at a naval banquet in Philadelphia [1899]

Oscar Fingal O'Flahertie Wills Wilde
1854–1900

5 Tread lightly, she is near
Under the snow,
Speak gently, she can hear
The daisies grow.
Requiescat, st. 1

6 And down the long and silent street,
The dawn, with silver-sandaled feet,
Crept like a frightened girl.
The Harlot's House, st. 6

7   A poet can survive everything but a misprint.
The Children of the Poets

8   Meredith is a prose Browning, and so is Browning. He used poetry as a medium for writing in prose.   *The Critic as Artist [1891], pt. I*

9   As long as war is regarded as wicked, it will always have its fascination. When it is looked upon as vulgar, it will cease to be popular.   *Ibid. II*

10   There is no such thing as a moral or an immoral book. Books are well written, or badly written. That is all.
The Picture of Dorian Gray [1891], preface

11   All art is quite useless.   *Ibid.*

12   There is only one thing in the world worse than being talked about, and that is not being talked about.   *Ibid. ch. 1*

13   A man cannot be too careful in the choice of his enemies.   *Ibid.*

14   The only way to get rid of a temptation is to yield to it.   *Ibid. 2*

15   He knew the precise psychological moment[3] when to say nothing.   *Ibid.*

16   The only difference between a caprice and a life-long passion is that the caprice lasts a little longer.   *Ibid.*

17   Children begin by loving their parents; as they grow older they judge them; sometimes they forgive them.   *Ibid. 5*

18   Over the piano was printed a notice: Please do not shoot the pianist. He is doing his best.
Personal Impressions of America (Leadville) [1883]

19   Nowadays we are all of us so hard up that the only pleasant things to pay are compliments. They're the only things we can pay.
Lady Windermere's Fan [1892], act I

20   I can resist everything except temptation.
Ibid.

21   We are all in the gutter, but some of us are looking at the stars.   *Ibid. III*

22   In this world there are only two tragedies. One is not getting what one wants, and the other is getting it.[4]   *Ibid.*

23   What is a cynic? A man who knows the price of everything, and the value of nothing.   *Ibid.*

24   Experience is the name everyone gives to their mistakes.   *Ibid.*

25   I have never admitted that I am more than twenty-nine, or thirty at the most. Twenty-nine when there are pink shades, thirty when there are not.[5]   *Ibid. IV*

26   *Mrs. Allonby:* They say, Lady Hunstanton, that when good Americans die they go to Paris.[6]
Lady Hunstanton: Indeed? And when bad Americans die, where do they go to?
Lord Illingworth: Oh, they go to America.
A Woman of No Importance [1893], act I

---

[1]Il pleut doucement sur la ville.
Verlaine used this as an epigraph for his *Ariettes Oubliées,* III.
See Verlaine, 554:1.

[2]Je dis qu'il faut être *voyant,* se faire *voyant.* Le poète se fait *voyant* par un long, immense et raisonné *dérèglement* de tous les sens.

[3]In all considerations the psychological momentum or factor must be allowed to play a prominent part, for without its cooperation there is little to be hoped from the work of the artillery.—*Neue Preussische Kreuzzeitung* [December 16, 1870], *commenting upon the siege of Paris*
An error in translation gave us "psychological moment" (i.e., the critical moment). The Parisians ridiculed the phrase as an example of German pedantry, but it speedily became universal.

[4]See Shaw, 571:6.

[5]When you come to write my epitaph, Charles, let it be in these delicious words, "She had a long twenty-nine."—BARRIE, *Rosalind*

[6]Good Americans, when they die, go to Paris.—THOMAS GOLD APPLETON [1812–1884]; *from* OLIVER WENDELL HOLMES, *The Autocrat of the Breakfast-Table* [1858]

1　The youth of America is their oldest tradition. It has been going on now for three hundred years.
Ibid.

2　*Lord Illingworth:* The Book of Life begins with a man and a woman in a garden.
Mrs. Allonby: It ends with Revelations.
Ibid.

3　I suppose society is wonderfully delightful. To be in it is merely a bore. But to be out of it simply a tragedy.
Ibid. III

4　Really, if the lower orders don't set us a good example, what on earth is the use of them?
The Importance of Being Earnest [1895], act I

5　Her hair has turned quite gold from grief.
Ibid.

6　I have invented an invaluable permanent invalid called Bunbury, in order that I may be able to go down into the country whenever I choose.
Ibid.

7　Of course the music is a great difficulty. You see, if one plays good music, people don't listen, and if one plays bad music people don't talk.
Ibid.

8　To lose one parent, Mr. Worthing, may be regarded as a misfortune; to lose both looks like carelessness.
Ibid.

9　Relations are simply a tedious pack of people, who haven't got the remotest knowledge of how to live, nor the smallest instinct about when to die.
Ibid.

10　I never travel without my diary. One should always have something sensational to read in the train.
Ibid. II

11　Thirty-five is a very attractive age. London society is full of women of the very highest birth who have, of their own free choice, remained thirty-five for years.
Ibid. III

12　The fact is, that civilization requires slaves. The Greeks were quite right there. Unless there are slaves to do the ugly, horrible, uninteresting work, culture and contemplation become almost impossible. Human slavery is wrong, insecure, and demoralizing. On mechanical slavery, on the slavery of the machine, the future of the world depends.
The Soul of Man Under Socialism [1895]

13　Charity creates a multitude of sins.
Ibid.

14　Anybody can make history. Only a great man can write it.
Aphorisms

15　I never saw a man who looked
With such a wistful eye
Upon that little tent of blue
Which prisoners call the sky.
The Ballad of Reading Gaol [1898], pt. I, st. 3

16　When a voice behind me whispered low,
"That fellow's got to swing."
Ibid. st. 4

17　Yet each man kills the thing he loves,
By each let this be heard,
Some do it with a bitter look,
Some with a flattering word.
The coward does it with a kiss,
The brave man with a sword!
Ibid. st. 7

18　It is sweet to dance to violins
When Love and Life are fair:
To dance to flutes, to dance to lutes
Is delicate and rare:
But it is not sweet with nimble feet
To dance upon the air!
Ibid. II, st. 9

19　Something was dead in each of us,
And what was dead was Hope.
Ibid. III, st. 31

20　And the wild regrets, and the bloody sweats,
None knew so well as I:
For he who lives more lives than one
More deaths than one must die.
Ibid. st. 37

21　I know not whether laws be right,
Or whether laws be wrong;
All that we know who lie in gaol
Is that the wall is strong;
And that each day is like a year,
A year whose days are long.
Ibid. V, st. 1

22　The vilest deeds like poison weeds
Bloom well in prison air:
It is only what is good in man
That wastes and withers there:
Pale Anguish keeps the heavy gate
And the Warder is Despair.
Ibid. st. 5

23　How else but through a broken heart
May Lord Christ enter in?
Ibid. st. 14

24　Where there is sorrow there is holy ground.
De Profundis [1905]

25　One must have a heart of stone to read the death of Little Nell without laughing.
From RICHARD ELLMANN, Oscar Wilde [1988]

26　My wallpaper and I are fighting a duel to the death. One or the other of us has to go.　*Ibid.*

William Cowper Brann[1]
1855–1898

27　Boston runs to brains as well as to beans and brown bread. But she is cursed with an army of

---

[1]Known as "The Iconoclast" from the name of his paper, first published in Austin, Texas, and later in Waco.

cranks whom nothing short of a straitjacket or a swamp elm club will ever control.

From The Iconoclast. Beans and Blood

Henry Cuyler Bunner
1855–1896

1 Off with your hat as the flag goes by!

Airs from Arcady [1888]. The Old Flag, st. 1

Eugene Victor Debs
1855–1926

2   While there is a lower class I am in it, while there is a criminal element I am of it; while there is a soul in prison, I am not free.   *On labor and freedom*

3   The savings of many in the hands of one.

On wealth

Margaret Wolfe Hungerford
1855–1897

4   Beauty is in the eye of the beholder.[1]

Molly Bawn [1878]

Sir Arthur Wing Pinero
1855–1934

5   From forty till fifty a man is at heart either a stoic or a satyr.

The Second Mrs. Tanqueray [1893], act I

Olive Schreiner [Ralph Iron]
1855–1920

6   The barb in the arrow of childhood suffering is this: its intense loneliness, its intense ignorance.

The Story of an African Farm [1884], ch. 1

7   There never was a man who said one word for woman but he said two for man and three for the whole human race.   *Ibid. 4*

William Sharp [Fiona Macleod]
1855–1905

8 My heart is a lonely hunter that hunts on a lonely hill.

The Lonely Hunter, st. 6

Lyman Frank Baum
1856–1919

9   The wicked Witch of the East.

The Wonderful Wizard of Oz[2] [1900], ch. 2

[1]See Hume, 318:12.
[2]See Harburg, 699:16, and Langley, 730.

10   The road to the City of Emeralds is paved with yellow brick.   *Ibid.*

11   I'm really a very good man; but I'm a very bad Wizard.   *Ibid. 15*

Francis Bellamy
1856–1931

12   I pledge allegiance to the flag of the United States of America and to the republic for which it stands, one nation under God, indivisible, with liberty and justice for all.

The Pledge of Allegiance to the Flag [1892][3]

Theobald von Bethmann-Hollweg
1856–1921

13   Just for a word—"neutrality," a word which in wartime has so often been disregarded, just for a scrap of paper—Great Britain is going to make war.

To Sir Edward Goschen [August 4, 1914]

Louis Dembitz Brandeis
1856–1941

14   Those who won our independence believed that the final end of the State was to make men free to develop their faculties; and that in its government the deliberative forces should prevail over the arbitrary. They valued liberty both as an end and as a means. They believed liberty to be the secret of happiness and courage to be the secret of liberty.

Whitney v. California, 274 U.S. 357, 375 [1927]

15   Fear of serious injury cannot alone justify suppression of free speech and assembly. Men feared witches and burned women. It is the function of speech to free men from the bondage of irrational fears.   *Ibid. 376*

16   They [the makers of the Constitution] conferred, as against the Government, the right to be let alone—the most comprehensive of rights and the right most valued by civilized men.

Olmstead v. United States, 277 U.S. 438, 478 [1928]

17   If we would guide by the light of reason, we must let our minds be bold.

New State Ice Co. v. Liebmann, 285 U.S. 262, 311 [1932]

18   The Court bows to the lessons of experience and the force of better reasoning, recognizing that the

[3]In 1888 JAMES B. UPHAM [1845–1905] wrote a draft that Bellamy, chairman of a national celebration of the 400th anniversary of America's discovery, helped put in final form:
I pledge allegiance to my flag and to the republic for which it stands: one nation indivisible, with liberty and justice for all.
More than thirty years later, "my flag" was changed to "the flag of the United States of America"; in 1954 an act of Congress added "under God."

process of trial and error, so fruitful in the physical sciences, is appropriate also in the judicial function.
Burnet v. Coronado Oil and Gas Co., 285 U.S. 393, 406 [1932]

1 There is in most Americans some spark of idealism, which can be fanned into a flame. It takes sometimes a divining rod to find what it is; but when found, and that means often, when disclosed to the owners, the results are often most extraordinary.
The Words of Justice Brandeis [1953]

Sigmund Freud[1]
1856–1939

2 The new psychoanalytic method [is] . . . somewhat subtle but irreplaceable, so fruitful has it proved to be in explaining obscure unconscious mental processes.[2]
Heredity and the Aetiology of the Neuroses [1896]

3 The interpretation of dreams is the royal road to a knowledge of the unconscious activities of the mind.
The Interpretation of Dreams [1900], ch. 7

4 When a member of my family complains to me of having bitten his tongue, pinched a finger, or the like, he does not get the sympathy he hopes for but instead the question: "Why did you do that?"
The Psychopathology of Everyday Life [1901], ch. 8

5 Our hysterical patients suffer from reminiscences.
Five Lectures on Psychoanalysis [1910]. I

6 The psychic development of the individual is a short repetition of the course of development of the race.[3]
Leonardo da Vinci [1910]

7 At bottom God is nothing other than an exalted father.
Totem and Taboo [1913]. Pt. 4

8 We believe that civilization has been created under the pressure of the exigencies of life at the cost of satisfaction of the instincts.
Introductory Lectures on Psychoanalysis [1916–1917]. Lecture 1

9 If a man has been his mother's undisputed darling he retains throughout life the triumphant feeling, the confidence in success, which not seldom brings actual success with it.
A Childhood Memory of Goethe's [1917]

10 A culture which leaves unsatisfied and drives to rebelliousness so large a number of its members neither has a prospect of continued existence nor deserves it.
The Future of an Illusion [1927]

[1] Translated under the general editorship of JAMES STRACHEY, except for 569:2 and 569:17.
See Whitehead, 584:21, and Auden, 720:12.
[2] Translated by M. MEYER.
Apparently Freud's first published use of the root term "psychoanalytic."
[3] See Haeckel, 522:15.

11 Before the problem of the creative writer, analysis must lay down its arms.
Dostoevsky and Parricide [1928]

12 Men have gained control over the forces of nature to such an extent that with their help they could have no difficulty in exterminating one another to the last man. They know this, and hence comes a large part of their current unrest, their unhappiness and their mood of anxiety.
Civilization and Its Discontents [1930], pt. VIII

13 The ego's relation to the id might be compared with that of a rider to his horse. The horse supplies the locomotive energy, while the rider has the privilege of deciding on the goal and of guiding the powerful animal's movement. But only too often there arises between the ego and the id the not precisely ideal situation of the rider being obliged to guide the horse along the path by which it itself wants to go.
New Introductory Lectures on Psycho-analysis [1933]. Lecture 31

14 The poor ego . . . serves three severe masters and does what it can to bring their claims and demands into harmony with one another. No wonder that the ego so often fails in its task. Its three tyrannical masters are the external world, the super-ego and the id.
Ibid.

15 Where id was, there ego shall be.
Ibid.

16 Religion is an illusion and it derives its strength from its readiness to fit in with our instinctual wishful impulses.
Ibid. Lecture 35

17 It almost looks as if analysis were the third of those "impossible" professions in which one can be quite sure of unsatisfying results. The other two, much older-established, are the bringing-up of children and the government of nations.[4]
Analysis Terminable and Interminable [1937]

18 Judaism had been a religion of the father; Christianity became a religion of the son. The old God the Father fell back behind Christ; Christ, the Son, took his place, just as every son had hoped to do in primeval times.
Moses and Monotheism [1938], pt. III, sec. 1

19 The great question . . . which I have not been able to answer, despite my thirty years of research into the feminine soul, is "What does a woman want?"[5]
From Ernest Jones, Life and Work of Sigmund Freud, vol. II [1955], ch. 16

20 The poets and philosophers before me discovered the unconscious; what I discovered was the scientific method by which the unconscious can be studied.
On his seventieth birthday [1926]. From Lionel Trilling, The Liberal Imagination [1957]

[4] Translated by JOAN RIVIERE.
[5] Was will das Weib?

1   Yes, America is gigantic, but a giant mistake.
From Ernest Jones, Free Associations [1962]

2   To love and to work.[1]
From Erik H. Erikson, Childhood and Society [1963]

3   Sometimes a cigar is just a cigar.   *Attributed*

Edmond Haraucourt
1856–1941

4 To leave is to die a little;
To die to what we love.
We leave behind a bit of ourselves
Wherever we have been.[2]
Choix de Poésies [1891]. Rondel de l'Adieu

Elbert Hubbard
1856–1915

5   It is not book learning young men need, nor instruction about this and that, but a stiffening of the vertebrae which will cause them to be loyal to a trust, to act promptly, concentrate their energies, do a thing—"carry a message to Garcia."[3]
A Message to Garcia [March 1899]

Robert Edwin Peary
1856–1920

6   The Eskimo, Ootah, had his own explanation. Said he: "The devil is asleep or having trouble with his wife, or we should never have come back so easily."   *The North Pole [1910]*

Henri Philippe Pétain
1856–1951

7   They shall not pass.[4]
Attributed. Verdun [February 26, 1916]

[1]Lieben und arbeiten.
Describing "what he thought a normal person should be able to do well" [Erikson].

[2]Partir, c'est mourir un peu; / C'est mourir à ce qu'on aime. / On laisse un peu de soi-même / En toute heure et dans tout lieu.
Translated by NORBERT GUTERMAN. The first line is a French proverb.
See Schopenhauer, 404:14.

[3]After the declaration of the Spanish-American War, Andrew Summers Rowan, then lieutenant, United States Bureau of Military Intelligence, was sent to communicate with General Calixto Garcia. He landed in an open boat near Turquino Peak [April 24, 1898], executed the mission, and brought back information regarding the insurgent army.

[4]Ils ne passeront pas.
The first official record of the expression appears in General Nivelle's Order of the Day [June 23, 1916] to his troops at the height of battle: Vous ne les laisserez pas passer [You will not let them pass]!—ALAN HORNE, *New York Times Magazine* [February 20, 1966]
The inscription on the Verdun medal is: On ne passe pas.
See Ibarruri, 692:20.

George Bernard Shaw
1856–1950

8   My method is to take the utmost trouble to find the right thing to say, and then to say it with the utmost levity.   *Answers to Nine Questions*

9   It's well to be off with the Old Woman before you're on with the New.[5]
The Philanderer [1893], act II

10   The fickleness of the women I love is only equaled by the infernal constancy of the women who love me.   *Ibid.*

11   The test of a man or woman's breeding is how they behave in a quarrel.   *Ibid. IV*

12   People are always blaming their circumstances for what they are. I don't believe in circumstances. The people who get on in this world are the people who get up and look for the circumstances they want, and, if they can't find them, make them.
Mrs. Warren's Profession [1893], act II

13   There are no secrets better kept than the secrets that everybody guesses.   *Ibid. III*

14   A great devotee of the Gospel of Getting On.
Ibid. IV

15   We have no more right to consume happiness without producing it than to consume wealth without producing it.   *Candida [1898], act I*

16   I'm only a beer teetotaler, not a champagne teetotaler. I don't like beer.   *Ibid. III*

17   We don't bother much about dress and manners in England, because as a nation we don't dress well and we've no manners.
You Never Can Tell [1898], act I

18   The great advantage of a hotel is that it's a refuge from home life.   *Ibid. II*

19   There is only one religion, though there are a hundred versions of it.
Plays Pleasant and Unpleasant [1898], vol. II, preface

20   You're not a man, you're a machine.
Arms and the Man [1898], act III

21   The worst sin towards our fellow creatures is not to hate them, but to be indifferent to them: that's the essence of inhumanity.
The Devil's Disciple [1901], act II

22   This is the true joy in life, the being used for a purpose recognized by yourself as a mighty one; the being thoroughly worn out before you are thrown on the scrap heap; the being a force of nature instead of a feverish selfish little clod of ailments and grievances complaining that the world will not devote itself to making you happy.
Man and Superman [1903], epistle dedicatory

[5]See Anonymous, 779:20.

1 A lifetime of happiness! No man alive could bear it: it would be hell on earth. *Ibid. act I*

2 The more things a man is ashamed of, the more respectable he is. *Ibid.*

3 Marry Ann; and at the end of a week you'll find no more inspiration in her than in a plate of muffins. *Ibid. II*

4 Hell is full of musical amateurs: music is the brandy of the damned. *Ibid. III*

5 An Englishman thinks he is moral when he is only uncomfortable. *Ibid.*

6 There are two tragedies in life. One is to lose your heart's desire. The other is to gain it.[1] *Ibid. IV*

7 The golden rule is that there are no golden rules. *Ibid. Maxims for Revolutionists*

8 He who can, does. He who cannot, teaches. *Ibid.*

9 Marriage is popular because it combines the maximum of temptation with the maximum of opportunity. *Ibid.*

10 If you strike a child, take care that you strike it in anger, even at the risk of maiming it for life. A blow in cold blood neither can nor should be forgiven. *Ibid.*

11 Virtue consists, not in abstaining from vice, but in not desiring it. *Ibid.*

12 The greatest of our evils and the worst of our crimes is poverty. *Major Barbara [1905], preface*

13 I am a Millionaire. That is my religion. *Ibid. act II*

14 With the single exception of Homer, there is no eminent writer, not even Sir Walter Scott, whom I can despise so entirely as I despise Shakespeare when I measure my mind against his. . . . It would positively be a relief to me to dig him up and throw stones at him. *Dramatic Opinions and Essays [1907]. Blaming the Bard*

15 When two people are under the influence of the most violent, most insane, most delusive, and most transient of passions, they are required to swear that they will remain in that excited, abnormal, and exhausting condition continuously until death do them part. *Getting Married [1908], preface*

16 I like a bit of a mongrel myself, whether it's a man or a dog; they're the best for every day. *Misalliance [1910], episode I*

17 If parents would only realize how they bore their children! *Ibid.*

18 It is impossible for an Englishman to open his mouth, without making some other Englishman hate or despise him; English is not accessible even to Englishmen. *Pygmalion [1913],[2] preface*

19 Women upset everything. When you let them into your life, you find that the woman is driving at one thing and you're driving at another. *Ibid. act II*

20 *Pickering:* Have you no morals, man?
Doolittle: Can't afford them, Governor. *Ibid.*

21 I'm one of the undeserving poor. *Ibid.*

22 Gin was mother's milk to her. *Ibid. III*

23 All great truths begin as blasphemies. *Annajanska [1919]*

24 You see things; and you say, "Why?" But I dream things that never were; and I say, "Why not?" *Back to Methuselah [1921], pt. I, act I*

25 The nauseous sham goodfellowship our democratic public men get up for shop use. *Ibid. pt. II*

26 Everything happens to everybody sooner or later if there is time enough. *Ibid. pt. V*

27 Assassination is the extreme form of censorship. *The Rejected Statement, pt. I*

28 One man that has a mind and knows it can always beat ten men who haven't and don't. *The Apple Cart [1929], act I*

29 An American has no sense of privacy. He does not know what it means. There is no such thing in the country. *Speech at New York [April 11, 1933]*

Louis Henri Sullivan
1856–1924

30 Form ever follows function. *The Tall Office Building Artistically Considered. From Lippincott's Magazine [March 1896]*

Brandon Thomas
1856–1914

31 I am Charley's aunt from Brazil, where the nuts come from. *Charley's Aunt [1892], act I*

Booker Taliaferro Washington
1856–1915

32 In all things that are purely social we [black and white] can be as separate as the fingers, yet one as the hand in all things essential to mutual progress. *Speech at the Cotton States and International Exposition, Atlanta [September 18, 1895]*

33 No race can prosper till it learns that there is as much dignity in tilling a field as in writing a poem. *Up from Slavery [1901]*

[1]See Wilde, 566:22.

[2]See Lerner, 745:5–745:12.

1   You can't hold a man down without staying down with him.   *Attributed*

Woodrow Wilson
1856–1924

2   The United States must be neutral in fact as well as in name. . . . We must be impartial in thought as well as in action.
Message to the Senate [August 19, 1914]

3   You deal in the raw material of opinion, and, if my convictions have any validity, opinion ultimately governs the world.
Address to the Associated Press [April 20, 1915]

4   There is such a thing as a man being too proud to fight.
Address to Foreign-Born Citizens [May 10, 1915]

5   [The Civil War] created in this country what had never existed before—a national consciousness. It was not the salvation of the Union; it was the rebirth of the Union.   *Memorial Day Address [1915]*

6   We have stood apart, studiously neutral.
Message to Congress [December 7, 1915]

7   America cannot be an ostrich with its head in the sand.   *Speech at Des Moines [February 1, 1916]*

8   It must be a peace without victory. . . . Only a peace between equals can last.
Address to the Senate [January 22, 1917]

9   A little group of willful men, representing no opinion but their own, have rendered the great Government of the United States helpless and contemptible.
Statement made in reference to certain members of the Senate [March 4, 1917][1]

10   Armed neutrality is ineffectual enough at best.
Address to Congress, asking for a declaration of war [April 2, 1917]

11   The world must be made safe for democracy.
Ibid.

12   The day has come when America is privileged to spend her blood and her might for the principles that gave her birth and happiness and the peace which she has treasured.   *Ibid.*

13   1. Open covenants of peace, openly arrived at.
2. Absolute freedom of navigation upon the seas. . . .
5. A free, open-minded, and absolutely impartial adjustment of all colonial claims.
Address to Congress (The Fourteen Points) [January 8, 1918][2]

14   14. A general association of nations must be formed . . . for the purpose of affording mutual guarantees of political independence and territorial integrity to great and small states alike.   *Ibid.*

15   If I am to speak for ten minutes, I need a week for preparation; if fifteen minutes, three days; if half an hour, two days; if an hour, I am ready now.[3]
From JOSEPHUS DANIELS, The Wilson Era: Years of War and After [1946]

16   It is like writing history with lightning. And my only regret is that it is all so terribly true.
Attributed. On seeing D. W. GRIFFITH's movie The Birth of a Nation, at the White House [February 18, 1915]

Edward Francis Albee
1857–1930

17   Never give a sucker an even break.[4]
Remark

Joseph Conrad
1857–1924

18   A work that aspires, however humbly, to the condition of art should carry its justification in every line.   *The Nigger of the Narcissus [1898], preface*

19   But the artist appeals to that part of our being which is not dependent on wisdom; to that in us which is a gift and not an acquisition—and, therefore, more permanently enduring. He speaks to our capacity for delight and wonder, to the sense of mystery surrounding our lives: to our sense of pity, and beauty, and pain.   *Ibid.*

20   The ship, a fragment detached from the earth, went on lonely and swift like a small planet.
Ibid. ch. 2

21   Goodbye, brothers! You were a good crowd. As good a crowd as ever fisted with wild cries the beating canvas of a heavy foresail; or tossing aloft, invisible in the night, gave back yell for yell to a westerly gale.   *Ibid. 5*

22   I am a great foe to favoritism in public life, in private life, and even in the delicate relationship of an author to his works.
Lord Jim [1900], author's note

23   There is a weird power in a spoken word. . . . And a word carries far—very far—deals destruction through time as the bullets go flying through space.   *Ibid. ch. 15*

24   That faculty of beholding at a hint the face of his desire and the shape of his dream, without which the earth would know no lover and no adventurer.
Ibid. 16

---

[1]Eleven senators had conducted a filibuster against a bill authorizing the arming of American merchant vessels.
[2]See Clemenceau, 542:1.
[3]See Pascal, 270:14.
[4]According to the *Morris Dictionary of Word and Phrase Origins* [1977], this is often attributed to W. C. Fields, who uttered it in *Poppy* [1923]. He made the quote famous.

1   Only a moment; a moment of strength, of romance, of glamour—of youth! . . . A flick of sunshine upon a strange shore, the time to remember, the time for a sigh, and—goodbye!—Night—Goodbye . . . !   *Youth [1902]*

2   She strode like a grenadier, was strong and upright like an obelisk, had a beautiful face, a candid brow, pure eyes, and not a thought of her own in her head.   *Tales of Unrest [1902]. The Return*

3   Running . . . all over the sea trying to get behind the weather.   *Typhoon [1902], ch. 2*

4   We live, as we dream—alone.
       Heart of Darkness [1902],[1] I

5   I don't like work—no man does—but I like what is in work—the chance to find yourself. Your own reality—for yourself, not for others—what no other man can ever know.   *Ibid.*

6   No fear can stand up to hunger, no patience can wear it out, disgust simply does not exist where hunger is; and as to superstition, beliefs, and what you may call principles, they are less than chaff in a breeze.   *Ibid. II*

7   Exterminate all the brutes![2]   *Ibid.*

8   The horror! The horror!   *Ibid. III*

9   Mistah Kurtz—he dead.[3]   *Ibid.*

10   The air of the New World seems favorable to the art of declamation.   *Nostromo [1904], ch. 6*

11   The terrorist and the policeman both come from the same basket. Revolution, legality—countermoves in the same game; forms of idleness at bottom identical.   *The Secret Agent [1907], ch. 4*

12   A man's real life is that accorded to him in the thoughts of other men by reason of respect or natural love.   *Under Western Eyes [1911], pt. I, ch. 1*

13   Let a fool be made serviceable according to his folly.   *Ibid. ch. 3*

14   The belief in a supernatural source of evil is not necessary; men alone are quite capable of every wickedness.   *Ibid. II, 4*

---

[1]"Heart of Darkness" is experience . . . but it is experience pushed a little (and only very little) beyond the actual facts of the case for the perfectly legitimate, I believe, purpose of bringing it home to the minds and bosoms of the readers. . . . That somber theme had to be given a sinister resonance, a tonality of its own, a continued vibration that, I hoped, would hang in the air and dwell on the ear after the last note had been struck.—*Youth: A Narrative, and Two Other Stories, author's preface*

[2]For two hundred years, the Judges of England sat on the Bench, condemning to the penalty of death every man, woman, and child who stole property to the value of five shillings; and, during all that time, not one Judge ever remonstrated against the law. We English are a nation of brutes, and ought to be exterminated to the last man.—JOHN BRIGHT [1880]; in HENRY ADAMS, *The Education of Henry Adams* [1907], ch. 12

[3]Used by T. S. Eliot as an epigraph for *The Hollow Men* [1925].

15   All ambitions are lawful except those which climb upward on the miseries or credulities of mankind.   *A Personal Record [1912], preface*

16   Only in men's imagination does every truth find an effective and undeniable existence. Imagination, not invention, is the supreme master of art as of life.   *Ibid. ch. 1*

17   Historian of fine consciences.
       Notes on Life and Letters [1921]. Henry James, An Appreciation

Émile Coué
1857–1926

18   Every day, in every way, I'm getting better and better.[4]
       Formula of his faith cures, inscribed in his sanitarium, Nancy, France

Clarence Seward Darrow
1857–1938

19   I do not consider it an insult, but rather a compliment to be called an agnostic. I do not pretend to know where many ignorant men are sure—that is all that agnosticism means.
       Scopes trial, Dayton, Tennessee [July 13, 1925]

20   I don't believe in God because I don't believe in Mother Goose.   *Speech at Toronto [1930]*

21   There is no such thing as justice—in or out of court.   *Interview at Chicago [April 1936]*

John Davidson
1857–1909

22 In anguish we uplift
    A new unhallowed song:
    The race is to the swift;
    The battle to the strong.

                    War Song, st. 1

23 And blood in torrents pour
    In vain—always in vain,
    For war breeds war again.

                    Ibid. st. 7

Benjamin Franklin King, Jr.
1857–1894

24 Nowhere to go but out,
    Nowhere to come but back.

                    The Pessimist, st. 4

---

[4]Tous les jours, à tous les points de vue, je vais de mieux en mieux.

Edgar Smith
1857–1938

1 You may tempt the upper classes
With your villainous demitasses,
But Heaven will protect the working girl.
Heaven Will Protect the Working Girl

Frank Lebby Stanton
1857–1927

2 Jest a-wearyin' fer you—
All the time a-feelin' blue.
Wearyin' for You,[1] *st. 1*

3 Sweetes' li'l' feller—
Everybody knows;
Dunno what ter call 'im,
But he's mighty lak' a rose!
Mighty Lak' a Rose,[2] *st. 1*

Thorstein Veblen
1857–1929

4 Conspicuous consumption of valuable goods is a means of reputability to the gentleman of leisure.
The Theory of the Leisure Class [1899], ch. 4

5 With the exception of the instinct of self-preservation, the propensity for emulation is probably the strongest and most alert and persistent of the economic motives proper.
Ibid. 5

6 The dog . . . commends himself to our favor by affording play to our propensity for mastery, and as he is also an item of expense, and commonly serves no industrial purpose, he holds a well-assured place in men's regard as a thing of good repute.
Ibid. 6

7 The office of the leisure class in social evolution is to retard the movement and to conserve what is obsolescent.
Ibid. 7

8 Priestly vestments show, in accentuated form, all the features that have been shown to be evidence of a servile status and a vicarious life.
Ibid.

9 The walking-stick serves the purpose of an advertisement that the bearer's hands are employed otherwise than in useful effort, and it therefore has utility as an evidence of leisure. But it is also a weapon and it meets a felt need of barbarian man on that ground.
Ibid. 10

10 In point of substantial merit the law school belongs in the modern university no more than a school of fencing or dancing.
The Higher Learning in America [1918]

[1]Music by CARRIE JACOBS BOND.
[2]Music by ETHELBERT NEVIN [1862–1901].

Franz Boas
1858–1942

11 The behavior of an individual is therefore determined not by his racial affiliation, but by the character of his ancestry and his cultural environment.[3]
Race and Democratic Society [1945] ch. 4

12 No one has ever proved that a human being, through his descent from a certain group of people, must of necessity have certain mental characteristics.
Ibid. 7

Sam Walter Foss
1858–1911

13 The woods were made for the hunters of dreams,
The brooks for the fishers of song;
To the hunters who hunt for the gunless game
The streams and the woods belong.
The Bloodless Sportsman, st. 3

14 Let me live in my house by the side of the road
And be a friend to man.
The House by the Side of the Road, st. 5

Henry Watson Fowler
1858–1933
and
Francis George Fowler
1870–1918

15 Prefer geniality to grammar.
The King's English [1906], ch. 2

16 HACKNEYED PHRASES. . . . The purpose with which these phrases are introduced is for the most part that of giving a fillip to a passage that might be humdrum without them . . . but their true use when they come into the writer's mind is as danger signals; he should take warning that when they suggest themselves it is because what he is writing is bad stuff, or it would not need such help; let him see to the substance of his cake instead of decorating with sugarplums.
A Dictionary of Modern English Usage [1926][4]

17 QUOTATION. . . . A writer expresses himself in words that have been used before because they give his meaning better than he can give it himself, or because they are beautiful or witty, or because he expects them to touch a chord of association in his reader, or because he wishes to show that he is learned and well read. Quotations due to the last motive are invariably ill-advised; the discerning

[3]See Benedict, 662:12.
[4]To the memory of my brother Francis George Fowler . . . who shared with me the planning of this book, but did not live to share the writing.—H. W. FOWLER, *preface to the first edition*

reader detects it and is contemptuous; the undiscerning is perhaps impressed, but even then is at the same time repelled, pretentious quotations being the surest road to tedium.   *Ibid.*

1   THAT, *relative pronoun* . . .   The two kinds of relative clause, to one of which *that* and to the other of which *which* is appropriate, are the defining and the nondefining;[1] and if writers would agree to regard *that* as the defining relative pronoun, and *which* as the nondefining, there would be much gain both in lucidity and in ease. Some there are who follow this principle now, but it would be idle to pretend that it is the practice either of the most or of the best writers.
                                                      Ibid.

Remy de Gourmont
1858–1915

2   Aesthetic emotion puts man in a state favorable to the reception of erotic emotion. Art is the accomplice of love. Take love away and there is no longer art.   *Décadence*[2]

3   Man is a successful animal, that's all.
                          Promenades Philosophiques

Ruggiero Leoncavallo
1858–1919

4   The comedy is finished.[3]
                I Pagliacci (The Clowns) [1892], last words

John Trotwood Moore
1858–1929

5   Only the gamefish swims upstream.
                                         The Unafraid

Adolph Simon Ochs
1858–1935

6   All the news that's fit to print.
                        Motto of the New York Times

Ohiyesa [Charles Alexander Eastman][4]
1858–1939

7   [The Indian] sees no need for setting apart one day in seven as a holy day, since to him all days are God's.   *The Soul of the Indian [1911]*

[1]In American English, restrictive and nonrestrictive.
[2]Translated by W. A. BRADLEY.
[3]La commedia è finita.
See Rabelais, 140:11.
[4]Santee Dakota.

Max Planck
1858–1947

8   We have no right to assume that any physical laws exist, or if they have existed up to now, that they will continue to exist in a similar manner in the future.
                The Universe in the Light of Modern Physics [1931]

9   Anybody who has been seriously engaged in scientific work of any kind realizes that over the entrance to the gates of the temple of science are written the words: *Ye must have faith.* It is a quality which the scientist cannot dispense with.
                Where Is Science Going? [1932]

10   An important scientific innovation rarely makes its way by gradually winning over and converting its opponents: it rarely happens that Saul becomes Paul. What does happen is that its opponents gradually die out and that the growing generation is familiarized with the idea from the beginning.
                The Philosophy of Physics [1936]

Theodore Roosevelt
1858–1919

11   I wish to preach, not the doctrine of ignoble ease, but the doctrine of the strenuous life.
                Speech before the Hamilton Club, Chicago [April 10, 1899]

12   Far better it is to dare mighty things, to win glorious triumphs, even though checkered by failure, than to take rank with those poor spirits who neither enjoy much nor suffer much, because they live in the gray twilight that knows not victory nor defeat.
                                                      Ibid.

13   I am as strong as a bull moose and you can use me to the limit.
                Letter to Marcus Alonzo Hanna [June 27, 1900][5]

14   No man is justified in doing evil on the ground of expediency.
                The Strenuous Life: Essays and Addresses [1900]. The Strenuous Life

15   In life, as in a football game, the principle to follow is: Hit the line hard.
                            Ibid. The American Boy

16   There is a homely adage which runs, "Speak softly and carry a big stick; you will go far." If the American nation will speak softly and yet build and

[5]Now look, that damned cowboy is President of the United States. — MARCUS ALONZO HANNA [1837–1904], *on Roosevelt's accession [September 1901].*

keep at a pitch of the highest training a thoroughly efficient navy, the Monroe Doctrine will go far.
Speech at Minnesota State Fair [September 2, 1901]

1   The first requisite of a good citizen in this Republic of ours is that he shall be able and willing to pull his weight.
Speech at New York [November 11, 1902]

2   A man who is good enough to shed his blood for his country is good enough to be given a square deal afterwards. More than that no man is entitled to, and less than that no man shall have.
Speech at Springfield, Illinois [July 4, 1903]

3   No man is above the law and no man is below it; nor do we ask any man's permission when we require him to obey it. Obedience to the law is demanded as a right; not asked as a favor.
Third Annual Message [December 7, 1903]

4   The men with the muckrakes are often indispensable to the well-being of society, but only if they know when to stop raking the muck, and to look upward to the celestial crown above them. . . . If they gradually grow to feel that the whole world is nothing but muck their power of usefulness is gone.[1]
Address on the laying of the cornerstone of the House Office Building, Washington [April 14, 1906]

5   Malefactors of great wealth.
Speech at Provincetown, Massachusetts [August 20, 1907]

6   Nature-faker.
Everybody's Magazine [September 1907]

7   To waste, to destroy, our natural resources, to skin and exhaust the land instead of using it so as to increase its usefulness, will result in undermining in the days of our children the very prosperity which we ought by right to hand down to them amplified and developed.
Message to Congress [December 3, 1907]

8   Every man holds his property subject to the general right of the community to regulate its use to whatever degree the public welfare may require it.
Speech at Osawatomie [August 31, 1910]

9   I took the Isthmus, started the Canal, and then left Congress—not to debate the Canal, but to debate me. . . . While the debate goes on the Canal does too.
Speech at University of California, Berkeley [March 23, 1911]

10   We stand at Armageddon and we battle for the Lord.
Speech at Progressive Party Convention, Chicago [June 17, 1912]

11   The lunatic fringe in all reform movements.
Autobiography [1913]

12   There is no room in this country for hyphenated Americanism. . . . The one absolutely certain way of bringing this nation to ruin, of preventing all possibility of its continuing to be a nation at all, would be to permit it to become a tangle of squabbling nationalities.
Speech before the Knights of Columbus, New York [October 12, 1915]

13   One of our defects as a nation is a tendency to use what have been called "weasel words." When a weasel sucks eggs the meat is sucked out of the egg. If you use a "weasel word" after another there is nothing left of the other.
Speech at St. Louis [May 31, 1916]

14   Put out the light.
Last words [January 6, 1919]

Langdon Smith
1858–1908

15 When you were a tadpole and I was a fish,
In the Paleozoic time.
Evolution [1895], st. 1

Graham Wallas
1858–1932

16   The Great Society.   *Title of book [1914]*

17   The little girl had the making of a poet in her who, being told to be sure of her meaning before she spoke, said, "How can I know what I think till I see what I say?"   *The Art of Thought [1926], ch. 4*

Sir William Watson
1858–1935

18 April, April,
Laugh thy girlish laughter;
Then, the moment after,
Weep thy girlish tears.

Song

Katharine Lee Bates
1859–1929

19 O beautiful for spacious skies,
For amber waves of grain,
For purple mountain majesties
Above the fruited plain!
America! America!
God shed his grace on thee
And crown thy good with brotherhood
From sea to shining sea!
America the Beautiful [1893],[2] st. 1

---

[1]See Bunyan, 272:27.

[2]Music by SAMUEL A. WARD [1848–1903].

Henri Bergson
1859–1941

1   Laughter has no greater foe than emotion. . . .
To produce the whole of its effect, then, the comic
demands something like a momentary anesthesia of
the heart.[1]   *Laughter [1900], ch. 1, i*

2   The major task of the twentieth century will be to
explore the unconscious, to investigate the subsoil of
the mind.   *Le Rêve (The Dream) [1901]*

3   The present contains nothing more than the past,
and what is found in the effect was already in the
cause.
>   *L'Evolution Créatrice (Creative Evolution)
>   [1907], ch. 1*

4   Intelligence . . . is the faculty of making artificial objects, especially tools to make tools.
                                              Ibid. 2

5   L'élan vital [the vital spirit].   *Ibid.*

Harold Edwin Boulton
1859–1935

6 Speed, bonnie boat, like a bird on the wing;
Onward, the sailors cry:
Carry the lad that's born to be king
Over the sea to Skye.
                            Skye Boat Song, st. 1

Carrie Chapman Catt
1859–1947

7   No written law has ever been more binding than
unwritten custom supported by popular opinion.
>   *Speech, Why We Ask for the Submission of an
>   Amendment, at Senate hearing on woman's
>   suffrage [February 13, 1900]*

8   When a just cause reaches its flood tide . . .
whatever stands in the way must fall before its overwhelming power.
>   *Speech at Stockholm, Is Woman Suffrage
>   Progressing? [1911]*

John Dewey
1859–1952

9   We naturally associate democracy . . . with
freedom of action, but freedom of action without
freed capacity of thought behind it is only chaos.
>   *Democracy in Education, in The Elementary
>   School Teacher [December 1903]*

10   Every great advance in science has issued from a
new audacity of imagination.
                    The Quest for Certainty [1929], ch. 11

[1]Translated by CLOUDESLEY BRERETON and FRED ROTH-
WELL.

11   Education is not preparation for life; education is
life itself.   *Attributed*

Sir Arthur Conan Doyle
1859–1930

12   London, that great cesspool into which all the
loungers of the Empire are irresistibly drained.
                           A Study in Scarlet [1887]

13   When you have eliminated the impossible, whatever remains, *however improbable,* must be the
truth.   *The Sign of Four [1890], ch. 6*

14   The unofficial force—the Baker Street irregulars.
                                           Ibid. 8

15   To Sherlock Holmes she [Irene Adler] is always
the woman.
>   *The Adventures of Sherlock Holmes [1891]. A
>   Scandal in Bohemia*

16   Singularity is almost invariably a clue. The more
featureless and commonplace a crime is, the more
difficult is it to bring it home.
                    Ibid. The Boscombe Valley Mystery

17   My name is Sherlock Holmes. It is my business to
know what other people don't know.
                    Ibid. The Adventure of the Blue Carbuncle

18   The Speckled Band.   *Ibid. Title of story*

19   The lowest and vilest alleys of London do not
present a more dreadful record of sin than does the
smiling and beautiful countryside.
                    Ibid. The Adventure of the Copper Beeches

20   " . . . the curious incident of the dog in the
nighttime."
"The dog did nothing in the nighttime."
"That was the curious incident," remarked Sherlock Holmes.
>   *The Memoirs of Sherlock Holmes [1894]. Silver
>   Blaze*

21   Like all Holmes's reasoning the thing seemed
simplicity itself when it was once explained.
                    Ibid. The Stock-Broker's Clerk

22   You know my methods, Watson.
                    Ibid. The Crooked Man

23   "Excellent!" I [Watson] cried.
"Elementary," said he [Holmes].   *Ibid.*

24   [Professor Moriarty] is the Napoleon of crime,
Watson. He is the organizer of half that is evil and
of nearly all that is undetected in this great city.
                    Ibid. The Final Problem

25   They were the footprints of a gigantic hound!
                    The Hound of the Baskervilles [1902], ch. 2

26   Come, Watson, come! The game is afoot.[2]
>   *The Return of Sherlock Holmes [1904]. The
>   Adventure of the Abbey Grange*

[2]See Shakespeare, 185:5.

1 The fair sex is your department.
The Return of Sherlock Holmes. The Second Stain

2 We are dealing with an exceptionally astute and dangerous man . . . one of the most unscrupulous rascals that Australia has ever evolved—and for a young country it has turned out some very finished types.
His Last Bow [1917]. The Disappearance of Lady Frances Carfax

3 The giant rat of Sumatra, a story for which the world is not yet prepared.
The Case Book of Sherlock Holmes [1927]. The Adventure of the Sussex Vampire

Havelock Ellis
1859–1939

4 To be a leader of men one must turn one's back on men.
Introduction to HUYSMANS, *À Rebours (Against the Grain) [1884]*

5 The text of the Bible is but a feeble symbol of the Revelation held in the text of Men and Women.
Impressions and Comments

6 The omnipresent process of sex, as it is woven into the whole texture of our man's or woman's body, is the pattern of all the process of our life.
The New Spirit

7 Every artist writes his own autobiography.
Ibid.

8 All civilization has from time to time become a thin crust over a volcano of revolution.
Little Essays of Love and Virtue [1922], ch. 7

9 The greatest task before civilization at present is to make machines what they ought to be, the slaves, instead of the masters of men.
Ibid.

10 Dancing is the loftiest, the most moving, the most beautiful of the arts, because it is no mere translation or abstraction from life; it is life itself.
The Dance of Life [1923], ch. 2

11 The place where optimism most flourishes is the lunatic asylum.
Ibid. 3

12 A man must not swallow more beliefs than he can digest.
Ibid. 5

13 The Promised Land always lies on the other side of a wilderness.
Ibid.

14 The sun and the moon and the stars would have disappeared long ago . . . had they happened to be within the reach of predatory human hands.
Ibid. 7

15 Had there been a lunatic asylum in the suburbs of Jerusalem, Jesus Christ would infallibly have been shut up in it at the outset of his public career. That interview with Satan on a pinnacle of the Temple would alone have damned him, and everything that happened after could but have confirmed the diagnosis.
Impressions and Comments, series 3

Kenneth Grahame
1859–1932

16 There is *nothing*—absolutely nothing—half so much worth doing as simply messing about in boats . . . or with boats. . . . In or out of 'em, it doesn't matter.
The Wind in the Willows [1908], ch. 1

17 The clever men at Oxford
Know all that there is to be knowed.
But they none of them know one half as much
As intelligent Mr. Toad!
Ibid. 10

Alfred Edward Housman[1]
1859–1936

18 Loveliest of trees, the cherry now
Is hung with bloom along the bough.
A Shropshire Lad [1896], no. 2, st. 1

19 Now, of my threescore years and ten,
Twenty will not come again,
And take from seventy springs a score,
It only leaves me fifty more.

And since to look at things in bloom
Fifty springs are little room,
About the woodlands I will go
To see the cherry hung with snow.
Ibid. st. 2, 3

20 Clay lies still, but blood's a rover;
Breath's a ware that will not keep.
Up, lad: when the journey's over
There'll be time enough to sleep.
Ibid. 4 (Reveille), st. 6

21 Lovers lying two and two
Ask not whom they sleep beside,
And the bridegroom all night through
Never turns him to the bride.
Ibid. 12, st. 4

22 When I was one-and-twenty
I heard a wise man say,
"Give crowns and pounds and guineas
But not your heart away."
Ibid. 13, st. 1

23 When I was one-and-twenty
I heard him say again,
"The heart out of the bosom
Was never given in vain;
'Tis paid with sighs aplenty
And sold for endless rue."

[1] I am not a pessimist but a pejorist (as George Eliot said she was not an optimist but a meliorist); and that philosophy is founded on my observation of the world, not on anything so trivial and irrelevant as personal history.—*Autobiographical note written for a French translation of his poems*

And I am two-and-twenty,
And Oh, 'tis true, 'tis true.
Ibid. st. 2

1 His folly has not fellow
Beneath the blue of day
That gives to man or woman
His heart and soul away.
Ibid. 14, st. 3

2 Oh, when I was in love with you,
Then I was clean and brave,
And miles around the wonder grew
How well I did behave.

And now the fancy passes by,
And nothing will remain,
And miles around they'll say that I
Am quite myself again.
Ibid. 18, st. 1, 2

3 And silence sounds no worse than cheers
After earth has stopped the ears.
Ibid. 19 (To an Athlete Dying Young), st. 4

4 The bells they sound on Bredon,
And still the steeples hum.
"Come all to church, good people" —
Oh, noisy bells, be dumb;
I hear you, I will come.
Ibid. 21, st. 7

5 The lads that will die in their glory and never be
old.
Ibid. 23, st. 4

6 And fire and ice within me fight
Beneath the suffocating night.
Ibid. 30, st. 4

7 There, like the wind through woods in riot,
Through him the gale of life blew high;
The tree of man was never quiet:
Then 'twas the Roman, now 'tis I.
Ibid. 31, st. 4

8 Oh tarnish late on Wenlock Edge,
Gold that I never see.
Ibid. 39, st. 3

9 Into my heart an air that kills
From yon far country blows:
What are those blue remembered hills,
What spires, what farms are those?

That is the land of lost content,
I see it shining plain,
The happy highways where I went
And cannot come again.
Ibid. 40, st. 1, 2

10 Earth and high heaven are fixed of old and
founded strong.
Ibid. 48, st. 1

11 Far in a western brookland
That bred me long ago

The poplars stand and tremble
By pools I used to know.
Ibid. 52, st. 1

12 With rue my heart is laden
For golden friends I had,
For many a rose-lipped maiden
And many a lightfoot lad.
Ibid. 54, st. 1

13 By brooks too broad for leaping
The lightfoot boys are laid.
Ibid. st. 2

14 In all the endless road you tread
There's nothing but the night.
Ibid. 60

15 Oh many a peer of England brews
Livelier liquor than the Muse,
And malt does more than Milton can
To justify God's ways to man.[1]
Ale, man, ale's the stuff to drink
For fellows whom it hurts to think.
Ibid. 62, st. 2

16 Mithridates, he died old.[2]
Ibid. st. 4

17 Pass me the can, lad; there's an end of May.
Last Poems [1922], 9, st. 1

18 The troubles of our proud and angry dust
Are from eternity, and shall not fail.
Bear them we can, and if we can we must.
Shoulder the sky, my lad, and drink your ale.
Ibid. st. 7

19 The laws of God, the laws of man,
He may keep that will and can;
Not I: let God and man decree
Laws for themselves and not for me.
Ibid. 12

20 And how am I to face the odds
Of man's bedevilment and God's?
I, a stranger and afraid
In a world I never made.
Ibid.

21 Strapped, noosed, nighing his hour,
He stood and counted them and cursed his luck;
And then the clock collected in the tower
Its strength, and struck.
Ibid. 15 (Eight O'Clock), st. 2

22 Happy bridegroom, Hesper brings
All desired and timely things.
All whom morning sends to roam,
Hesper loves to lead them home.
Home return who him behold,
Child to mother, sheep to fold,

[1]See Milton, 255:20 and 261:12, and Pope, 301:2.
[2]Housman's passage is based on the belief of the ancients
that Mithridates the Great [c. 135–63 B.C.] had so saturated his
body with poisons that none could injure him. When captured
by the Romans he tried in vain to poison himself, then ordered
a Gallic mercenary to kill him.

Bird to nest from wandering wide:[1]
Happy bridegroom, seek your bride.
                  Last Poems, 24 (Epithalamium), st. 3

1 These, in the day when heaven was falling,
  The hour when earth's foundations fled,
  Followed their mercenary calling
  And took their wages and are dead.
            *Ibid. 37 (Epitaph on an Army of Mercenaries),[2]
            st. 1*

2 What God abandoned, these defended.
                                    Ibid. st. 2

3 They say my verse is sad: no wonder;
  Its narrow measure spans
  Tears of eternity, and sorrow,
  Not mine, but man's.
                      More Poems [1936], foreword

4 Hope lies to mortals
  And most believe her,
  But man's deceiver
  Was never mine.
                          Ibid. 6, st. 1

5 The rainy Pleiads wester,
  Orion plunges prone,
  And midnight strikes and hastens,
  And I lie down alone.[3]
                          Ibid. 11, st. 1

6 Life, to be sure, is nothing much to lose,
  But young men think it is, and we were young.
                          Ibid. 36

7 We now to peace and darkness
  And earth and thee restore
  Thy creature that thou madest
  And wilt cast forth no more.
                  Ibid. 47 (For My Funeral), st. 3

8 Good night; ensured release,
  Imperishable peace,
  Have these for yours.[4]
  While sky and sea and land
  And earth's foundations stand
  And heaven endures.
                  Ibid. 48 (Alta Quies), st. 1

9 Oh they're taking him to prison for the color of
  his hair.
                  Additional Poems [1937], 18, st. 1

10   Experience has taught me, when I am shaving of
  a morning, to keep watch over my thoughts, because, if a line of poetry strays into my memory, my
  skin bristles so that the razor ceases to act. . . .
  The seat of this sensation is the pit of the stomach.
                  The Name and Nature of Poetry [1933]

[1]See Sappho, 56:11, and Meleager, 87:5.
[2]The British regulars who made the retreat from Mons, beginning August 24, 1914.
[3]See Sappho, 56:8.
[4]These three lines are on the tablet over Housman's grave in
the parish church at Ludlow, Shropshire.

Jerome Klapka Jerome
1859–1927

11   Let your boat of life be light, packed with only
  what you need—a homely home and simple pleasures, one or two friends, worth the name, someone
  to love and someone to love you, a cat, a dog, and
  a pipe or two, enough to eat and enough to wear,
  and a little more than enough to drink; for thirst is
  a dangerous thing.
                  Three Men in a Boat [1889], ch. 3

12   I like work: it fascinates me. I can sit and look at
  it for hours. I love to keep it by me; the idea of
  getting rid of it nearly breaks my heart.
                          Ibid. 15

13   "Nothing, so it seems to me," said the stranger,
  "is more beautiful than the love that has weathered
  the storms of life. . . . The love of the young for
  the young, that is the beginning of life. But the love
  of the old for the old, that is the beginning of—
  of things longer."
          The Passing of the Third Floor Back [1908]

William James Lampton
1859–1917

14 Same old slippers,
  Same old rice,
  Same old glimpse of
  Paradise.
                  June Weddings, st. 10

15 Where the corn is full of kernels
  And the colonels full of corn.
                              Kentucky

Charles E. Stanton
1859–1933

16 Lafayette, we are here.[5]
          *Address at the tomb of Lafayette, Picpus
          Cemetery, Paris [July 4, 1917]*

James Kenneth Stephen
1859–1892

17 When the Rudyards cease from Kipling
  And the Haggards ride no more.
                          Lapsus Calami. To R. K.

18 Of sentences that stir my bile,
  Of phrases I detest,
  There's one beyond all others vile:
  "He did it for the best."
                  Ibid. The Malefactor's Plea, st. 1

[5]The remark has also been attributed to General JOHN JO-
SEPH PERSHING [1860–1948]; in *My Experiences in the World
War* [1931], Pershing denied having said "anything so splen-
did."

Francis Thompson
1859–1907

1 The fairest things have fleetest end,
  Their scent survives their close:
  But the rose's scent is bitterness
  To him that loved the rose.
  Daisy [1893], st. 10

2 Nothing begins, and nothing ends,
  That is not paid with moan;
  For we are born in other's pain,
  And perish in our own.
  Ibid. st. 15

3 Look for me in the nurseries of Heaven.[1]
  To My Godchild

4 I fled Him, down the nights and down the days;
  I fled Him, down the arches of the years;
  I fled Him, down the labyrinthine ways
  Of my own mind; and in the mist of tears
  I hid from Him, and under running laughter.
  The Hound of Heaven [1893], l. 1

5 But with unhurrying chase,
  And unperturbèd pace,
  Deliberate speed, majestic instancy,
  They beat—and a Voice beat
  More instant than the Feet—
  "All things betray thee, who betrayest Me."
  Ibid. l. 10

6 Across the margent of the world I fled,
  And troubled the gold gateways of the stars.
  Ibid. l. 25

7 I said to dawn, Be sudden; to eve, Be soon.
  Ibid. l. 30

8 My days have crackled and gone up in smoke.
  Ibid. l. 122

9 All which I took from thee I did but take,
  Not for thy harms,
  But just that thou might'st seek it in My arms.
  Ibid. l. 171

10 O world invisible, we view thee,
   O world intangible, we touch thee,
   O world unknowable, we know thee.
   *The Kingdom of God ("In No Strange Land")
   [1913], st. 1*

11 The angels keep their ancient places;
   Turn but a stone, and start a wing!
   'Tis ye, 'tis your estrangèd faces,
   That miss the many-splendored thing.
   Ibid. st. 4

12   Upon thy so sore loss
   Shall shine the traffic of Jacob's ladder
   Pitched betwixt Heaven and Charing Cross.
   Ibid. st. 5

[1]Inscribed on Thompson's tombstone in Kensal Green.

13 And lo, Christ walking on the water
   Not of Gennesareth, but Thames!
   Ibid. st. 6

14 Short arm needs man to reach to Heaven
   So ready is Heaven to stoop to him.
   Grace of the Way, st. 6

Sidney Webb, Lord Passfield
1859–1947

15   The inevitability of gradualness.
   Address to British Labor Party [1923]

Jane Addams
1860–1935

16   Private beneficence is totally inadequate to deal with the vast numbers of the city's disinherited.
   Twenty Years at Hull House [1910]

17   The common stock of intellectual enjoyment should not be difficult of access because of the economic position of him who would approach it.
   Ibid.

Sir James Matthew Barrie
1860–1937

18   Them that has china plates themsels is the maist careful no to break the china plates of others.
   The Little Minister [1891], ch. 26

19   We never understand how little we need in this world until we know the loss of it.
   Margaret Ogilvy [1896], ch. 8

20   Shall we make a new rule of life from tonight: always to try to be a little kinder than is necessary?
   The Little White Bird [1902], ch. 4

21   His lordship may compel us to be equal upstairs, but there will never be equality in the servants' hall.
   The Admirable Crichton [1903], act I

22   Do you believe in fairies? . . . If you believe, clap your hands!   *Peter Pan [1904], act IV*

23   It's a sort of bloom on a woman. If you have it [charm], you don't need to have anything else, and if you don't have it, it doesn't much matter what else you have. Some women, the few, have charm for all; and most have charm for one. But some have charm for none.
   What Every Woman Knows [1908], act I

24   The tragedy of a man who has found himself out.
   Ibid. IV

25   One's religion is whatever he is most interested in, and yours is Success.
   The Twelve-Pound Look [1910]

26   Peter and Wendy.   *Title of novel [1911]*

John Collins Bossidy
1860–1928

1 And this is good old Boston,
  The home of the bean and the cod,
  Where the Lowells talk to the Cabots
  And the Cabots talk only to God.[1]
      Toast, Holy Cross Alumni Dinner [1910]

William Jennings Bryan
1860–1925

2   The humblest citizen of all the land, when clad in
the armor of a righteous cause, is stronger than all
the hosts of Error.
      *Speech at the National Democratic Convention,
      Chicago [1896]*

3   Destroy our farms and the grass will grow in the
streets of every city in the country.   *Ibid.*

4   You shall not press down upon the brow of labor
this crown of thorns. You shall not crucify mankind
upon a cross of gold.[2]   *Ibid.*

Haddon Chambers
1860–1921

5   The long arm of coincidence.
      Captain Swift [1888], act II

Anton Pavlovich Chekhov
1860–1904

6   I feel more confident and more satisfied when I
reflect that I have two professions and not one. Medicine is my lawful wife and literature is my mistress.
When I get tired of one I spend the night with the
other. Though it's disorderly it's not so dull, and
besides, neither really loses anything through my
infidelity.
      Letter to A. S. Suvorin [September 11, 1888][3]

7   I would like to be a free artist and nothing else,
and I regret God has not given me the strength to be
one.
      Letter to Alexei Pleshcheev [October 4, 1888][3]

8   My holy of holies is the human body, health,
intelligence, talent, inspiration, love, and the most
absolute freedom imaginable, freedom from violence and lies, no matter what form the latter two

take. Such is the program I would adhere to if I were
a major artist.   *Ibid.*

9   An artist must pass judgment only on what he
understands; his range is limited as that of any other
specialist—that's what I keep repeating and insist-
ing upon. Anyone who says that the artist's field is
all answers and no questions has never done any
writing or had any dealings with imagery. An artist
observes, selects, guesses and synthesizes.
      Letter to A. S. Suvorin [October 27, 1888][3]

10   One must not put a loaded rifle on the stage if no
one is thinking of firing it.[4]
      *Letter to A. S. Lazarev-Gruzinsky [November 1,
      1889]*

11   I try to catch every sentence, every word you and
I say, and quickly lock all these sentences and words
away in my literary storehouse because they might
come in handy.   *The Seagull [1896],*[5] *act II*

12   People should be beautiful in every way—in their
faces, in the way they dress, in their thoughts and in
their innermost selves.
      Uncle Vanya [1897],[5] *act I*

13   We shall find peace. We shall hear the angels, we
shall see the sky sparkling with diamonds.
      Ibid. IV

14   To Moscow, to Moscow, to Moscow!
      Three Sisters [1901], act II

15   All Russia is our orchard.
      The Cherry Orchard [1904],[5] *act II*

Baron Corvo [Frederick William Rolfe]
1860–1913

16   He took one long slow breath: crossed right hand
over left upon his breast: became like a piece of a
pageant; and responded "I will."
      Hadrian the Seventh [1904], ch. 3

17   Pray for the repose of his soul. He was so tired.
      Ibid. closing lines

Harry Micajah Daugherty
1860–1941

18   In a smoke-filled room in some hotel.[6]
      Attributed

[1]Patterned on the toast given at the twenty-fifth anniversary
dinner of the Harvard Class of 1880, by a Westerner:
  Here's to old Massachusetts, / The home of the sacred cod, /
Where the Adamses vote for Douglas, / And the Cabots walk
with God.
  [2]I shall not help crucify mankind upon a cross of gold. I shall
not aid in pressing down upon the bleeding brow of labor this
crown of thorns.—BRYAN, *speech in the House of Representatives* [December 22, 1894]
  [3]Translated by SIMON KARLINSKY.

[4]A fuller version: If you say in the first chapter that there is
a rifle hanging on a wall, in the second or third chapter it
absolutely must go off. If it's not going to be fired, it shouldn't
be hanging there.—S. SHCHUKIN, *Memoirs* [1911]
  [5]Translated by RONALD HINGLY.
  [6]According to the *New York Times* [February 21, 1920],
Daugherty, presidential campaign manager for Senator Warren G. Harding, predicted that the convention would be dead-
locked and would be decided by a group of men who "will sit
down about two o'clock in the morning around a table in a
smoke-filled room." Daugherty maintained that he had not
said "smoke-filled." The room was in the suite occupied by
George Harvey, rooms 804–805 in the Blackstone Hotel.

Hamlin Garland
1860–1940

1 A Son of the Middle Border.
Title of autobiographical narrative [1917]

Charlotte Perkins Gilman
1860–1935

2 There are things in that wallpaper that nobody knows about but me, or ever will.

Behind that outside pattern the dim shapes get clearer every day.

It is always the same shape, only very numerous.

And it is like a woman stooping down and creeping about behind that pattern.
The Yellow Wallpaper [1892]

3 The labor of women in the house, certainly, enables men to produce more wealth than they otherwise could; and in this way women are economic factors in society. But so are horses.
Women and Economics [1898], ch. 1

4 There is no female mind. The brain is not an organ of sex. As well speak of a female liver.
Ibid. 8

5 Cried all, "Before such things can come,
You idiotic child,
You must alter human nature!"
And they all sat back and smiled.
In This Our World [1893]. Similar Cases

6 "I do not want to be a fly!
I want to be a worm!"
Ibid. A Conservative, st. 6

7 I ran against a Prejudice
That quite cut off the view.
Ibid. An Obstacle, st. 1

8 There's a whining at the threshold—
There's a scratching at the floor—
To work! To work! In Heaven's name!
The wolf is at the door![1]
Ibid. The Wolf at the Door, st. 6

9 The people people have for friends
Your common sense appall,
But the people people marry
Are the queerest folk of all.
Queer People

William Ralph Inge
1860–1954

10 A man may build himself a throne of bayonets, but he cannot sit on it.
From Wit and Wisdom of Dean Inge, edited by MARCHANT, *no. 108*

[1]See Skelton, 135:19.

James Ball Naylor
1860–1945

11 King David and King Solomon
Led merry, merry lives,
With many, many lady friends
And many, many wives;
But when old age crept over them—
With many, many qualms,
King Solomon wrote the Proverbs
And King David wrote the Psalms.
Ancient Authors

Sir D'Arcy Wentworth Thompson
1860–1948

12 Numerical precision is the very soul of science.
On Growth and Form [1917], ch. 1

13 The harmony of the world is made manifest in Form and Number, and the heart and soul and all the poetry of Natural Philosophy are embodied in the concept of mathematical beauty.
Ibid. Epilogue

Owen Wister
1860–1938

14 When you call me that, *smile!*
The Virginian [1902], ch. 2

William Bliss Carman
1861–1929

15 No fidget and no reformer, just
A calm observer of ought and must.
The Joys of the Road, st. 22

16 The scarlet of the maples can shake me like
a cry
Of bugles going by.
A Vagabond Song, st. 2

17 There is something in October sets the gypsy
blood astir.
Ibid. st. 3

Louise Imogen Guiney
1861–1920

18 He has done with roofs and men,
Open, Time, and let him pass.
Ballad of Kenelm

19 A short life in the saddle, Lord!
Not long life by the fire.
The Knight Errant, st. 2

John Luther Long
1861–1927

1   To die with honor when one can no longer live with honor.[1]   *Madame Butterfly [1897]*

Albert Bigelow Paine
1861–1937

2   The Great White Way.[2]
     Title of novel [1901]

Sir Walter Raleigh
1861–1922

3 I wish I loved the human race;
  I wish I loved its silly face;
  I wish I liked the way it walks;
  I wish I liked the way it talks;
  And when I'm introduced to one
  I wish I thought, *What jolly fun!*
     Wishes of an Elderly Man; wished at a garden party [June 1914]

Rabindranath Tagore
1861–1941

4   When one knows thee, then alien there is none, then no door is shut. Oh, grant me my prayer that I may never lose the touch of the one in the play of the many.   *Gitanjali [1913]*

5 At my dying hour, and over my long life,
  A clock strikes somewhere at the city's edge.
     Poem [1941]

Frederick Jackson Turner
1861–1932

6   The frontier is the outer edge of the wave—the meeting-point between savagery and civilization . . . the line of most rapid and effective Americanization. The wilderness masters the colonist.
     The Significance of the Frontier in American History [1894]

Alfred North Whitehead
1861–1947

7   The study of mathematics is apt to commence in disappointment. . . . We are told that by its aid the stars are weighed and the billions of molecules in a drop of water are counted. Yet, like the ghost of Hamlet's father, this great science eludes the efforts of our mental weapons to grasp it.
     An Introduction to Mathematics [1911], ch. 1

8   Civilization advances by extending the number of important operations which we can perform without thinking about them.   *Ibid. 5*

9   The science of pure mathematics, in its modern developments, may claim to be the most original creation of the human spirit.
     Science and the Modern World [1925], ch. 2

10   The greatest invention of the nineteenth century was the invention of the method of invention.
     Ibid. 6

11   The religious vision, and its history of persistent expansion, is our one ground for optimism. Apart from it, human life is a flash of occasional enjoyments lighting up a mass of pain and misery, a bagatelle of transient experience.   *Ibid. 12*

12   Rationalism is an adventure in the clarification of thought.
     Process and Reality [1929], pt. I, ch. 1, sec. 3

13   The safest general characterization of the European philosophical tradition is that it consists of a series of footnotes to Plato.   *Ibid. II, 1, 1*

14   The human body is an instrument for the production of art in the life of the human soul.
     Adventures of Ideas [1933], ch. 18

15   A general definition of civilization: a civilized society is exhibiting the five qualities of truth, beauty, adventure, art, peace.   *Ibid. 19*

16   The deliberate aim at Peace very easily passes into its bastard substitute, Anesthesia.   *Ibid. 20*

17   There are no whole truths; all truths are half-truths. It is trying to treat them as whole truths that plays the devil.
     Dialogues of Alfred North Whitehead [1953],[3] prologue

18   The vitality of thought is in adventure. *Ideas won't keep.* Something must be done about them. When the idea is new, its custodians have fervor, live for it, and, if need be, die for it.
     Ibid. ch. 12, April 28, 1938

19   A culture is in its finest flower before it begins to analyze itself.   *Ibid. 22, August 17, 1941*

20   What is morality in any given time or place? It is what the majority then and there happen to like, and immorality is what they dislike.
     Ibid. August 30, 1941

21   The ideas of Freud[4] were popularized by people who only imperfectly understood them, who were incapable of the great effort required to grasp them in their relationship to larger truths, and who there-

---

[1]Inscription on Samurai blade.
    One should die proudly when it is no longer possible to live proudly.—NIETZSCHE, *The Twilight of the Idols* [1888], *Skirmishes in a War with the Age, 36*
[2]Later a name for Broadway.

[3]As recorded by LUCIEN PRICE.
[4]See Freud, 569.

fore assigned to them a prominence out of all proportion to their true importance.
Ibid. 28, June 3, 1943

1   A philosopher of imposing stature doesn't think in a vacuum. Even his most abstract ideas are, to some extent, conditioned by what is or is not known in the time when he lives.
Ibid. 29, June 10, 1943

2   Intellect is to emotion as our clothes are to our bodies; we could not very well have civilized life without clothes, but we would be in a poor way if we had only clothes without bodies.   *Ibid.*

3   No period of history has ever been great or ever can be that does not act on some sort of high, idealistic motives, and idealism in our time has been shoved aside, and we are paying the penalty for it.
Ibid. 32, January 13, 1944

4   The English never abolish anything. They put it in cold storage.   *Ibid. 36, January 19, 1945*

Arthur Christopher Benson
1862–1925

5 Land of hope and glory, mother of the free,
How shall we extol thee, who are born of thee?
Wider still and wider shall thy bounds be set;
God, who made thee mighty, make thee mightier yet.
Land of Hope and Glory [1902],[1] *chorus*

Albert Jeremiah Beveridge
1862–1927

6   This party comes from the grass roots. It has grown from the soil of the people's hard necessities.
Address at the Bull Moose Convention, Chicago [August 5, 1912]

James W. Blake
1862–1935

7 East Side, West Side, all around the town,
The tots sang "Ring-a-rosie," "London Bridge is falling down";
Boys and girls together, me and Mamie O'Rorke,
Tripped the light fantastic on the sidewalks of New York.
The Sidewalks of New York [1894][2]

Carrie Jacobs Bond
1862–1946

8 Well, this is the end of a perfect day,
Near the end of a journey, too.
A Perfect Day, st. 2

[1]First *Pomp and Circumstance* march by Sir Edward Elgar.
[2]Music by Charles B. Lawlor.

9 For memory has painted this perfect day
With colors that never fade,
And we find at the end of a perfect day
The soul of a friend we've made.
Ibid.

Nicholas Murray Butler
1862–1947

10   An expert is one who knows more and more about less and less.
Commencement address, Columbia University

John Jay Chapman
1862–1933

11   The New Testament, and to a very large extent the Old, *is* the soul of man. You cannot criticize it. It criticizes you.   *Letter [March 26, 1898]*

12   The present in New York is so powerful that the past is lost.   *Ibid. [1909]*

13   Everybody in America is soft, and hates conflict. The cure for this, both in politics and social life, is the same—hardihood. Give them raw truth.
Practical Agitation [1898]

14   You get the satisfaction of being heard, and that is the whole possible scope of human ambition.
Learning and Other Essays [1910]. The Unity of Human Nature

Edward, Viscount Grey of Fallodon
1862–1933

15   The lamps are going out all over Europe; we shall not see them lit again in our lifetime.
Comment [August 3, 1914], on the eve of World War I

O. Henry [William Sydney Porter]
1862–1910

16   Perhaps there is no happiness in life so perfect as the martyr's.
The Trimmed Lamp [1907]. The Country of Elusion

17   It was beautiful and simple as all truly great swindles are.
The Gentle Grafter [1908]. The Octopus Marooned

18   Busy as a one-armed man with the nettle-rash pasting on wallpaper.   *Ibid. The Ethics of Pig*

19   Bagdad-on-the-Subway.[3]
Roads of Destiny [1909]. The Discounters of Money

[3]Also in *A Madison Square Arabian Night, A Night in New Arabia,* and *What You Want.*

1   History is bright and fiction dull with homely men who have charmed women.
Roads of Destiny. Next to Reading Matter

2   She plucked from my lapel the invisible strand of lint (the universal act of woman to proclaim ownership).
Strictly Business [1910]. A Ramble in Aphasia

3   East is East, and West is San Francisco, according to Californians. Californians are a race of people; they are not merely inhabitants of a State.
Ibid. A Municipal Report

4   It couldn't have happened anywhere but in little old New York.[1]
Whirligigs [1910]. A Little Local Color

5   A straw vote only shows which way the hot air blows.   *Rolling Stones [1913]. A Ruler of Men*

6   Take it from me—he's got the goods.
The Unprofitable Servant

7   Turn up the lights—I don't want to go home in the dark.[2]   *Last words [June 5, 1910]*

Charles Evans Hughes
1862–1948

8   We are under a Constitution, but the Constitution is what the judges say it is, and the judiciary is the safeguard of our liberty and of our property under the Constitution.
Speech at Elmira, New York [May 3, 1907]

9   How amazing it is that, in the midst of controversies on every conceivable subject, one should expect unanimity of opinion upon difficult legal questions! . . . The history of scholarship is a record of disagreements. And when we deal with questions relating to principles of law and their applications, we do not suddenly rise into a stratosphere of icy certainty.
Speech to the American Law Institute [May 7, 1936]

Maurice Maeterlinck
1862–1949

10   It is always a mistake not to close one's eyes, whether to forgive or to look better into oneself.
Pelléas et Mélisande [1892]

11   There are no dead.
The Blue Bird [1909], act IV, sc. ii

Sir Henry Newbolt
1862–1938

12 To set the cause above renown,
To love the game beyond the prize,

To honor, while you strike him down,
The foe that comes with fearless eyes;
To count the life of battle good
And dear the land that gave you birth,
And dearer yet the brotherhood
That binds the brave of all the earth.
The Island Race. Clifton Chapel, st. 2

13 *Qui procul hinc*, the legend's writ,
The frontier grave is far away—
Qui ante diem periit:
Sed miles, sed pro patria.[3]
Ibid. st. 4

14 Now the sunset breezes shiver,
And she's fading down the river,
But in England's song forever
She's the Fighting Téméraire.
The Fighting Téméraire, st. 6

15 Play up! play up! and play the game!
Vitaï Lampada

16 Keep the Nelson touch.
Minora Sidera

Robert Cameron Rogers
1862–1912

17 The hours I spent with thee, dear heart,
Are as a string of pearls to me;
I count them over, every one apart,
My rosary, my rosary.
The Rosary [1894], st. 1[4]

Edith Wharton
1862–1937

18 There are two ways of spreading light: to be
The candle or the mirror that reflects it.
Vesalius in Zante

19   Mrs. Ballinger is one of the ladies who pursue Culture in bands, as though it were dangerous to meet it alone.   *Xingu [1916]*

20   An unalterable and unquestioned law of the musical world required that the German text of French operas sung by Swedish artists should be translated into Italian for the clearer understanding of English-speaking audiences.
The Age of Innocence [1920], ch. 1

21   In the rotation of crops there was a recognized season for wild oats; but they were not sown more than once.   *Ibid. 31*

22   It was the old New York way of taking life "without effusion of blood": the way of people who dreaded scandal more than disease, who placed decency above courage, and who considered that noth-

---

[1]Also in *A Midsummer Knight's Dream, Past One at Rooney's,* and *The Rubber Plant's Story.*
[2]I'm Afraid to Go Home in the Dark.—HARRY H. WILLIAMS [1879–1922], *title of song [1907]*

[3]Who died far away, before his time: but as a soldier, for his country.
[4]Music by ETHELBERT NEVIN [1862–1901].

ing was more ill-bred than "scenes," except the behavior of those who gave rise to them. *Ibid. 33*

1 The worst of doing one's duty was that it apparently unfitted one for doing anything else. *Ibid. 34*

2 There's no such thing as old age; there is only sorrow. *A Backward Glance [1934]. A First Word*

3 In spite of illness, in spite even of the archenemy sorrow, one *can* remain alive long past the usual date of disintegration if one is unafraid of change, insatiable in intellectual curiosity, interested in big things, and happy in small ways. *Ibid.*

4 I was never allowed to read the popular American children's books of my day because, as my mother said, the children spoke bad English *without the author's knowing it.* *Ibid. ch. 3*

Black Elk [Hehaka Sapa]
1863–1950

5 Everything an Indian does is in a circle, and that is because the power of the world always works in circles, and everything tries to be round. In the old days when we were a strong and happy people, all our power came to us from the sacred hoop of the nation, and so long as the hoop was unbroken the people flourished.
Black Elk Speaks, Being the Life Story of a Holy Man of the Oglala Sioux, as told through JOHN G. NEIHARDT [1961]

Constantine Peter Cavafy
1863–1933

6 But Argos can do without the sons of Atreus.
Ancient houses are not eternal.
When the Watchman Saw the Light[1] [1900]

7 We won't be deceived
by titles such as Indispensable and Unique and Great.
Someone else indispensable and unique and great
can always be found at a moment's notice. *Ibid.*

8 Pleasure will have much to teach him.
He will not be afraid of the destructive act;
one half of the house must be pulled down.
This way he will grow virtuously into knowledge.
Strengthening the Spirit [1903]

9 What are we all waiting for
gathered together like this on the public square?
The Barbarians are coming today.
Waiting for the Barbarians [1904],[2] l. 1

[1]Translated by EDMUND KEELEY and GEORGE SAVIDIS.
[2]Translated by W. H. AUDEN and MARGUERITE YOURCENAR.

10 You'll not find another place, you'll not find another sea.
This city is going to follow you.
The City [1910],[3] l. 9

11 Setting out on the voyage to Ithaca
you must pray that the way be long,
full of adventures and experiences.
Ithaca [1911],[4] l. 11

12 Body, remember not only how much you were loved,
not only the beds you lay on,
but also those desires glowing openly
in eyes that looked at you,
trembling for you in voices.
Body, Remember [1918][5]

13 I created you while I was happy, while I was sad,
with so many incidents, so many details.

And, for me, the whole of you has been
transformed into feeling.
In the Same Space [1929][4]

William Randolph Hearst
1863–1951

14 You furnish the pictures and I'll furnish the war.
Attributed instructions to artist FREDERIC REMINGTON in Havana, Cuba [March 1898][6]

James Harvey Robinson
1863–1936

15 Political campaigns are designedly made into emotional orgies which endeavor to distract attention from the real issues involved, and they actually paralyze what slight powers of cerebration man can normally muster.
The Human Comedy [1937], ch. 9

16 With supreme irony, the war to "make the world safe for democracy" ended by leaving democracy more unsafe in the world than at any time since the collapse of the revolutions of 1848. *Ibid.*

George Santayana
1863–1952

17 O World, thou choosest not the better part!
It is not wisdom to be only wise,
And on the inward vision close the eyes,
But it is wisdom to believe the heart.
O World, Thou Choosest Not [1894]

[3]Translated by ROBERT LIDDELL.
[4]Translated by JOHN MAVROGORDATO.
[5]Translated by EDMUND KEELEY and PHILLIP SHERRARD.
[6]Hearst always denied sending such a telegram, and there is no proof that he ever did, even though it accurately reflects his views at the time.— JOYCE MILTON, *The Yellow Kids: Foreign Correspondents in the Heyday of Yellow Journalism* [1989]

1   Beauty as we feel it is something indescribable: what it is or what it means can never be said.
The Sense of Beauty [1896], pt. IV, Expression

2   Even the most inspired verse, which boasts not without a relative justification to be immortal, becomes in the course of ages a scarcely legible hieroglyphic; the language it was written in dies, a learned education and an imaginative effort are requisite to catch even a vestige of its original force. Nothing is so irrevocable as mind.
The Life of Reason [1905–1906], vol. I, Reason in Common Sense

3   Happiness is the only sanction of life; where happiness fails, existence remains a mad and lamentable experiment.   *Ibid.*

4   That life is worth living is the most necessary of assumptions, and, were it not assumed, the most impossible of conclusions.[1]   *Ibid.*

5   Fanaticism consists in redoubling your efforts when you have forgotten your aim.   *Ibid.*

6   Those who cannot remember the past are condemned to repeat it.[2]   *Ibid.*

7   When Socrates and his two great disciples composed a system of rational ethics they were hardly proposing practical legislation for mankind . . . They were merely writing an eloquent epitaph for their country.   *Ibid. V, Reason in Science*

8   Let a man once overcome his selfish terror at his own finitude, and his finitude is, in one sense, overcome.
The Ethics of Spinoza [1910], introduction

9   Perhaps the only true dignity of man is his capacity to despise himself.   *Ibid.*

10   Miracles are propitious accidents, the natural causes of which are too complicated to be readily understood.   *Ibid.*

11   The Bible is literature, not dogma.   *Ibid.*

12   American life is a powerful solvent. It seems to neutralize every intellectual element, however tough and alien it may be, and to fuse it in the native good will, complacency, thoughtlessness, and optimism.
Character and Opinion in the United States [1920]

13   All his life he [the American] jumps into the train after it has started and jumps out before it has stopped; and he never once gets left behind, or breaks a leg.   *Ibid.*

14   There is no cure for birth and death save to enjoy the interval.
Soliloquies in England and Later Soliloquies [1922]. War Shrines

15   I like to walk about amidst the beautiful things that adorn the world; but private wealth I should decline, or any sort of personal possessions, because they would take away my liberty.
Ibid. The Irony of Liberalism

16   My atheism, like that of Spinoza, is true piety towards the universe and denies only gods fashioned by men in their own image, to be servants of their human interests.   *Ibid. On My Friendly Critics*

17   Scepticism is the chastity of the intellect, and it is shameful to surrender it too soon or to the first comer.
Scepticism and Animal Faith [1923], ch. 9

18   The young man who has not wept is a savage, and the old man who will not laugh is a fool.
Dialogues in Limbo [1926], ch. 3

19   Religion in its humility restores man to his only dignity, the courage to live by grace.   *Ibid. 4*

20   There is nothing impossible in the existence of the supernatural: its existence seems to me decidedly probable.   *The Genteel Tradition at Bay [1931]*

21   There is no God and Mary is His Mother.
From ROBERT LOWELL, *Life Studies. For George Santayana [1953]*

Konstantin Sergeevich Alekseev Stanislavski
1863–1938

22   Our type of creativeness is the conception and birth of a new being—the person in the part. It is a natural act similar to the birth of a human being.
An Actor Prepares [1936],[3] ch. 16

23   In the creative process there is the father, the author of the play; the mother, the actor pregnant with the part; and the child, the role to be born.
Ibid.

Ernest Lawrence Thayer
1863–1940

24 There was ease in Casey's manner as he stepped
  into his place,
There was pride in Casey's bearing, and a smile
  on Casey's face,
And when, responding to the cheers, he lightly
  doffed his hat,
No stranger in the crowd could doubt 'twas Casey
  at the bat.
Casey at the Bat [1888], st. 6

25 Oh! somewhere in this favored land the sun is
  shining bright;
The band is playing somewhere, and somewhere
  hearts are light;

---

[1]See Oliver Wendell Holmes, Jr., 542:12, and William James, 546:8.
[2]See Euripides, 69:16, and Thucydides, 71:19.
[3]Translated by ELIZABETH REYNOLDS HAPGOOD.

And somewhere men are laughing and somewhere
children shout,
But there is no joy in Mudville—mighty Casey
has struck out.

Ibid. st. 13

Sir Roger Casement
1864–1916

1 Where all your rights become only an accumulated wrong; where men must beg with bated breath for leave to subsist in their own land, to think their own thoughts, to sing their own songs, to garner the fruits of their own labors . . . then surely it is braver, a saner and truer thing, to be a rebel in act and deed against such circumstances as these than tamely to accept it as the natural lot of men.

Statement from prison [June 29, 1916]

Joseph Hayden
fl. 1896

2 There'll be a hot time in the old town tonight.
A Hot Time in the Old Town [1896][1]

Richard Hovey
1864–1900

3 For it's always fair weather
When good fellows get together
With a stein on the table and a good song ringing
clear.

A Stein Song [1898], st. 1

4 O, Eleazer Wheelock was a very pious man;
He went into the wilderness to teach the
Indian. . . .
Eleazer was the faculty, and the whole curriculum
Was five hundred gallons of New England rum.

Eleazer Wheelock, st. 1

Andrew Barton [Banjo] Paterson
1864–1941

5 Once a jolly swagman camped by a billabong,
Under the shade of a coolibah tree,
And he sang as he sat and waited for his
billy-boil,
"Who'll come a-waltzing Matilda with me?"[2]

Waltzing Matilda

[1]Hayden's text for a march, *A Hot Time in the Old Town Tonight* [1886], by THEODORE AUGUST METZ [1848–1936], later a favorite of Theodore Roosevelt's Rough Riders in Cuba, and still later Roosevelt's campaign song.

[2]Swagman: tramp. Billabong: waterhole. Coolibah: eucalyptus. Billy: container used for brewing tea. Matilda: a bundle containing personal belongings.
Music by MARIE COWAN.

Jules Renard
1864–1910

6 To succeed you must add water to your wine, until there is no more wine. *Journal*

7 There are moments when everything goes well; don't be frightened, it won't last. *Ibid.*

8 I am not sincere even when I am saying that I am not sincere. *Ibid.*

9 We don't understand life any better at forty than at twenty, but we know it and admit it. *Ibid.*

Miguel de Unamuno
1864–1936

10 Consciousness is a disease.
The Tragic Sense of Life [1913], ch. 1

11 True science teaches, above all, to doubt and be ignorant. *Ibid. 5*

12 To believe in God is to yearn for His existence and, furthermore, it is to act as if He did exist.
Ibid. 8

13 Martyrs create faith, faith does not create martyrs. *Ibid. 9*

14 To fall into a habit is to begin to cease to be.
Ibid.

15 My work . . . is to shatter the faith of men here, there, and everywhere, faith in affirmation, faith in negation, and faith in abstention from faith, and this for the sake of faith in faith itself.[3]
Ibid. Conclusion

16 Warmth, warmth, more warmth! for we are dying of cold and not of darkness. It is not the night that kills, but the frost. *Ibid.*

17 The devil is an angel too. *Two Mothers*

18 And killing time is perhaps the essence of comedy, just as the essence of tragedy is killing eternity.
San Manuel Bueno, prologue

19 I would say that teleology is theology, and that God is not a "because," but rather an "in order to."
Ibid.

20 Let us go on committing suicide by working among our people, and let them dream life just as the lake dreams the sky. *Ibid.*

21 Use harms and even destroys beauty. The noblest function of an object is to be contemplated.
Mist [1914]

22 Every peasant has a lawyer inside of him, just as every lawyer, no matter how urbane he may be, carries a peasant within himself.
Civilization Is Civilism

[3]Translated by J. E. CRAWFORD FLITCH.

1   These terrible sociologists, who are the astrologers and alchemists of our twentieth century.
Fanatical Skepticism

2   Faith which does not doubt is dead faith.
The Agony of Christianity

3   We never know, believe me, when we have succeeded best.
Essays and Soliloquies

Max Weber
1864–1920

4   Charisma knows only inner determination and inner restraint. . . . The charismatic leader gains and maintains authority solely by proving his strength in life.[1]
Wirtschaft und Gesellschaft (Economy and Society) [1922], pt. III, ch. 9

Israel Zangwill
1864–1926

5   Scratch the Christian and you find the pagan—spoiled.   *Children of the Ghetto [1892]*

6   America is God's crucible, the great melting pot where all the races of Europe are melting and reforming![2]
The Melting Pot [1908], act I

Mrs. Patrick Campbell
[Beatrice Stella Tanner Campbell]
1865–1940

7   My dear, I don't care what they do, so long as they don't do it in the street and frighten the horses.
Attributed

Edith Cavell
1865–1915

8   I realize that patriotism is not enough. I must have no hatred or bitterness towards anyone.
Last words [October 12, 1915], before her execution by the Germans

Herbert Albert Laurens Fisher
1865–1940

9   All political decisions are taken under great pressure, and if a treaty serves its turn for ten or twenty years, the wisdom of its framers is sufficiently confirmed.   *Political Prophecies [1918]*

10   It is easier for eight or nine elderly men to feel their way towards unanimity if they are not compelled to conduct their converging maneuvers under the microscopes and telescopes of the press, but are permitted to shuffle about a little in slippers.
An International Experiment[3] [1921]

11   Purity of race does not exist. Europe is a continent of energetic mongrels.
A History of Europe [1934], ch. 1

12   Politics is the art of human happiness.
Ibid. 31

George V
1865–1936

13   How is the Empire?
Attributed last words [January 21, 1936][4]

Frederic William Goudy
1865–1947

14   I am the voice of today, the herald of tomorrow. . . . I am the leaden army that conquers the world—I am TYPE.   *The Type Speaks*

Laurence Hope
[Adela Florence Cory Nicolson]
1865–1904

15   To have—to hold—and—in time—let go!
India's Love Lyrics. The Teak Forest, st. 10

16   Pale hands I loved beside the Shalimar.
Ibid. Kashmiri Song, st. 1

Rudyard Kipling
1865–1936

17   I have eaten your bread and salt.
I have drunk your water and wine.
The deaths ye died I have watched beside
And the lives ye led were mine.
Departmental Ditties [1886]. Prelude, st. 1

18   Little Tin Gods on Wheels.
Ibid. Public Waste, st. 4

19   The toad beneath the harrow knows
Exactly where each tooth point goes;
The butterfly upon the road
Preaches contentment to that toad.
Ibid. Pagett, M.P., prelude

20   And a woman is only a woman, but a good cigar is a smoke.
Ibid. The Betrothed, st. 25

---

[1]Translated by H. H. GERTH and C. WRIGHT MILLS.
[2]The point about the melting pot . . . is that it did not happen.—NATHAN GLAZER [1925–] and DANIEL PATRICK MOYNIHAN [1927–], *Beyond the Melting Pot* [1963]
See Crèvecoeur, 339:1.

[3]The League of Nations.
[4]As reported by Buckingham Palace. As reported in the diary of LORD DAWSON, the king's physician, however, George's last words were "God damn you."

1   It takes a great deal of Christianity to wipe out uncivilized Eastern instincts, such as falling in love at first sight.

Plain Tales from the Hills [1888]. Lispeth

2   Never praise a sister to a sister, in the hope of your compliments reaching the proper ears.

Ibid. False Dawn

3   Many religious people are deeply suspicious. They seem—for purely religious purposes, of course—to know more about iniquity than the unregenerate.   *Ibid. Watches of the Night*

4   The silliest woman can manage a clever man; but it needs a very clever woman to manage a fool!

Ibid. Three and—an Extra

5   Lalun is a member of the most ancient profession in the world.

In Black and White [1888]. On the City Wall

6   Steady the Buffs.   *Soldiers Three [1888]*

7 Down to Gehenna or up to the Throne,
He travels the fastest who travels alone.[1]

Ibid. The Winners (L' Envoi: What Is the Moral?), st. 1

8   More men are killed by overwork than the importance of the world justifies.

The Phantom 'Rickshaw [1888]

9 Oh, East is East, and West is West, and never the
    twain shall meet,
Till Earth and Sky stand presently at God's great
    Judgment Seat;
But there is neither East nor West, border, nor
    breed, nor birth,
When two strong men stand face to face, though
    they come from the ends of the earth!

The Ballad of East and West [1889]

10   Bite on the bullet, old man, and don't let them think you're afraid.

The Light That Failed [1890–1891]

11 If I were damned of body and soul,
I know whose prayers would make me whole,
Mother o' mine, O mother o' mine.

Mother o' Mine [1891]

12 And the end of the fight is a tombstone white
    with the name of the late deceased,
And the epitaph drear: "A Fool lies here who
    tried to hustle the East."

The Naulahka [1892], ch. 5

13 When Earth's last picture is painted, and the tubes
    are twisted and dried,
When the oldest colors have faded, and the
    youngest critic has died,
We shall rest, and, faith, we shall need it—lie
    down for an eon or two,

Till the Master of All Good Workmen shall put
    us to work anew.

When Earth's Last Picture Is Painted [1892]

14 They rise to their feet as He passes by, gentlemen
    unafraid.

*Ballads and Barrack Room Ballads [1892, 1893].
Dedication, st. 5*

15 "What are the bugles blowin' for?" said
    Files-on-Parade.
"To turn you out, to turn you out," the
    Color-Sergeant said.

Ibid. Danny Deever,[2] st. 1

16 They've taken of his buttons off an' cut his stripes
    away,
An' they're hangin' Danny Deever in the mornin'.

Ibid.

17 We aren't no thin red 'eroes.[3]

Ibid. Tommy, st. 4

18 For it's Tommy this, an' Tommy that, an'
    "Chuck 'im out, the brute!"
But it's "Savior of 'is country" when the guns
    begin to shoot.

Ibid. st. 5

19 So 'ere's to you, Fuzzy-Wuzzy, at your 'ome in the
    Soudan;
You're a pore benighted 'eathen but a first-class
    fightin' man.

Ibid. Fuzzy-Wuzzy, st. 1

20 Though I've belted you an' flayed you,
By the livin' Gawd that made you,
You're a better man than I am, Gunga Din!

Ibid. Gunga Din, st. 5

21 'Ave you 'eard o' the Widow at Windsor
With a hairy gold crown on 'er 'ead?

Ibid. The Widow at Windsor, st. 1

22 By the old Moulmein Pagoda, lookin' eastward to
    the sea,
There's a Burma girl a-settin', and I know she
    thinks o' me;
For the wind is in the palm trees, and the temple
    bells they say:
"Come you back, you British soldier; come you
    back to Mandalay!"

Ibid. Mandalay,[4] st. 1

23 On the road to Mandalay,
Where the flyin' fishes play,
An' the dawn comes up like thunder outer China
    'crost the Bay!

Ibid.

24 Ship me somewheres east of Suez, where the best
    is like the worst,
Where there aren't no Ten Commandments, an' a
    man can raise a thirst.

Ibid. st. 6

---

[1]He may well win the race that runs by himself.—BENJAMIN FRANKLIN, *Poor Richard's Almanac* [1757]

[2]Music by WALTER DAMROSCH [1862–1950].
[3]See W. H. Russell, 492:8.
[4]Music by OLEY SPEAKS [1874–1948].

1 The Devil whispered behind the leaves, "It's pretty, but is it Art?"
Ballads and Barrack Room Ballads. The Conundrum of the Workshops, st. 1

2 To the legion of the lost ones, to the cohort of the damned.
Ibid. Gentlemen Rankers, st. 1

3 We're poor little lambs who've lost our way,
　Baa! Baa! Baa!
We're little black sheep who've gone astray,
　Baa—aa—aa!
Gentlemen rankers out on the spree,
Damned from here to Eternity,
God ha' mercy on such as we,
　Baa! Yah! Baa!
Ibid. refrain

4 We have done with Hope and Honor, we are lost to Love and Truth,
We are dropping down the ladder rung by rung;
And the measure of our torment is the measure of our youth.
God help us, for we knew the worst too young!
Ibid. st. 4

5 And what should they know of England who only England know?
Ibid. The English Flag, st. 1

6 The sin ye do by two and two ye must pay for one by one.
Ibid. Tomlinson, l. 60

7 There's a legion that never was 'listed,
That carries no colors or crest.
Ibid. The Lost Legion, st. 1

8 There are nine and sixty ways of constructing tribal lays,
And every single one of them is right.
Ibid. In the Neolithic Age, st. 5

9 There be triple ways to take, of the eagle or the snake,
Or the way of a man with a maid;[1]
But the sweetest way to me is a ship's upon the sea
In the heel of the Northeast Trade.
Ibid. The Long Trail, st. 5

10 　He wrapped himself in quotations—as a beggar would enfold himself in the purple of emperors.
Many Inventions [1893]. The Finest Story in the World

11 When 'Omer smote 'is bloomin' lyre,
He'd 'eard men sing by land an' sea;
An' what he thought 'e might require,
'E went an' took—the same as me!
When 'Omer Smote 'Is Bloomin' Lyre [1894], st. 1

12 Back to the Army again, sergeant,
Back to the Army again.
Out o' the cold an' the rain.
Back to the Army Again [1894], refrain

13 　We be of one blood, ye and I.
The Jungle Book [1894]. Kaa's Hunting

14 Brother, thy tail hangs down behind.
Ibid. Road Song of the Bandar-Log, refrain

15 Now this is the Law of the Jungle—as old and as true as the sky;
And the Wolf that shall keep it may prosper, but the Wolf that shall break it must die.
The Second Jungle Book [1895]. The Law of the Jungle, st. 1

16 When Pack meets with Pack in the Jungle, and neither will go from the trail,
Lie down till the leaders have spoken—it may be fair words shall prevail.
Ibid. st. 6

17 Now these are the Laws of the Jungle, and many and mighty are they;
But the head and the hoof of the Law and the haunch and the hump is—Obey!
Ibid. st. 19

18 They change their skies above them,
But not their hearts that roam.[2]
The Nativeborn [1895], st. 2

19 The Liner she's a lady, an' she never looks nor 'eeds—
The Man-o'-War's 'er 'usband, an' 'e gives 'er all she needs,
But, oh, the little cargo boats that sail the wet seas roun',
They're just the same as you an' me a-plyin' up and down!
The Liner She's a Lady [1895], st. 1

20 I've taken my fun where I've found it.
The Ladies [1895], st. 1

21 For the Colonel's Lady an' Judy O'Grady
Are sisters under their skins!
Ibid. st. 8

22 'E's a sort of a bloomin' cosmopolouse—soldier an' sailor too.
Soldier an' Sailor Too [1896], st. 2

23 A fool there was and he made his prayer
(Even as you and I!)
To a rag and a bone and a hank of hair
(We called her the woman who did not care)
But the fool he called her his lady fair—
(Even as you and I!)
The Vampire [1897], st. 1

24 Daughter am I in my mother's house;
But mistress in my own.
Our Lady of the Snows [1898], st. 1

25 God of our fathers, known of old,
Lord of our far-flung battle line,
Beneath whose awful Hand we hold

---

[1]See *Proverbs* 30:19, 23:15.

[2]See *Horace*, 97:13.

Dominion over palm and pine—
Lord God of Hosts, be with us yet,
Lest we forget—lest we forget!
Recessional [1899], st. 1

1 The tumult and the shouting dies;
The captains and the kings depart.
Ibid. st. 2

2 Lo, all our pomp of yesterday
Is one with Nineveh and Tyre!
Ibid. st. 3

3 Lesser breeds without the Law.
Ibid. st. 4

4 For frantic boast and foolish word—
Thy mercy on Thy People, Lord!
Ibid. st. 5

5 Take up the White Man's burden,[1]
Send forth the best ye breed—
Go, bind your sons to exile
To serve your captives' need.
The White Man's Burden [1899], st. 1

6 Little Friend of All the World.
Kim [1901], ch. 1

7 The flanneled fools at the wicket or the muddied
oafs at the goals.
The Islanders [1902], l. 31

8 I keep six honest serving men
(They taught me all I knew);
Their names are What and Why and When
And How and Where and Who.
The Just-So Stories [1902]. The Elephant's Child

9 The great gray-green, greasy Limpopo River, all
set about with fever-trees.   *Ibid.*

10 Rolling down to Rio.
Ibid. The Beginning of the Armadilloes, st. 2

11 The Cat. He walked by himself, and all places
were alike to him.
Ibid. The Cat That Walked By Himself

12 He went back through the wet wild woods, waving his wild tail, and walking by his wild lone. But
he never told anybody.   *Ibid.*

13 Who hath desired the sea?—the sight of salt
water unbounded.
The Sea and the Hills [1903], st. 1

14 Something hidden. Go and find it. Go and look
behind the Ranges—
Something lost behind the Ranges. Lost and
waiting for you. Go![2]
The Explorer [1903], st. 2

15 Boots—boots—boots—boots—movin' up and
down again!
There's no discharge in the war![3]
Boots [1903], st. 1

16 'Tisn't beauty, so to speak, nor good talk necessarily. It's just It. Some women'll stay in a man's
memory if they once walked down a street.
Traffics and Discoveries [1904]. Mrs. Bathurst

17 Of all the trees that grow so fair,
Old England to adorn,
Greater are none beneath the Sun,
Than oak, and ash, and thorn.[4]
Puck of Pook's Hill [1906]. A Tree Song, st. 1

18 Brothers and Sisters, I bid you beware
Of giving your heart to a dog to tear.
The Power of the Dog [1909]

19 If you can meet with Triumph and Disaster
And treat those two impostors just the same.
Rewards and Fairies [1910]. If, st. 2

20 If you can talk with crowds and keep your
virtue,
Or walk with Kings—nor lose the common
touch.
Ibid. st. 4

21 Yours is the Earth and everything that's in it,
And—which is more—you'll be a Man, my son!
Ibid.

22 The female of the species is more deadly than the
male.
The Female of the Species [1911], st. 1

23 Oh, Adam was a gardener, and God who made
him sees
That half a proper gardener's work is done upon
his knees.
The Glory of the Garden, st. 8

24 For all we have and are,
For all our children's fate,
Stand up and take the war.
The Hun is at the gate!
For All We Have and Are [1914], st. 1

25 What stands if Freedom fall?
Who dies if England live?
Ibid. st. 4

26 Hot and bothered.
*Independence. Rectorial Address at St. Andrews
[October 10, 1923]*

27 When your Daemon is in charge, do not try to
think consciously. Drift, wait, and obey.
*Something of Myself for My Friends Known
and Unknown [1937], ch. 8*

---

[1]Pile on the brown man's burden / To satisfy your greed.
—*London Truth; reprinted in Middlebury (Vermont) Register*
[March 17, 1899]

[2]*Because it is there.*—GEORGE LEIGH MALLORY [1886–
1924], *when asked why he wanted to climb Mount Everest*

[3]See *Ecclesiastes 8:8, 24:16.*

[4]See Anonymous: Ballads, 785:8.

Baroness Emmuska Orczy
1865–1947

1 We seek him here, we seek him there,
Those Frenchies seek him everywhere.
Is he in heaven?—Is he in hell?
That demmed, elusive Pimpernel?
The Scarlet Pimpernel [1905], ch. 12

Logan Pearsall Smith
1865–1946

2   There are two things to aim at in life: first, to get
what you want; and, after that, to enjoy it. Only the
wisest of mankind achieve the second.
Afterthoughts [1931]

3   How awful to reflect that what people say of us
is true!   *Ibid.*

4   Solvency is entirely a matter of temperament and
not of income.   *Ibid.*

5   There are few sorrows, however poignant, in
which a good income is of no avail.   *Ibid.*

6   The indefatigable pursuit of an unattainable perfection, even though it consist in nothing more than
in the pounding of an old piano, is what alone gives
a meaning to our life on this unavailing star.
Ibid.

7   What I like in a good author is not what he says,
but what he whispers.   *Ibid.*

8   People say that life is the thing, but I prefer reading.   *Ibid.*

9   There is more felicity on the far side of baldness
than young men can possibly imagine.   *Ibid.*

10   Thank heavens, the sun has gone in, and I don't
have to go out and enjoy it.   *Ibid.*

Arthur Symons
1865–1945

11 And I would have, now love is over,
An end to all, an end:
I cannot, having been your lover,
Stoop to become your friend!
After Love [1892], st. 3

12 My soul is like this cloudy, flaming opal ring.
Opals [1896]

13   He knew that the whole mystery of beauty can
never be comprehended by the crowd, and that
while clearness is a virtue of style, perfect explicitness is not a necessary virtue.
*The Symbolist Movement in Literature [1899].
Gérard de Nerval*

14   Without charm there can be no fine literature, as
there can be no perfect flower without fragrance.
Ibid. Stéphane Mallarmé

15   The mystic too full of God to speak intelligibly to
the world.   *Ibid. Arthur Rimbaud*

William Butler Yeats[1]
1865–1939

16 The woods of Arcady are dead,
And over is their antique joy;
Of old the world on dreaming fed;
Gray Truth is now her painted toy.
*Crossways [1889]. The Song of the Happy
Shepherd, st. 1*

17 Down by the salley gardens my love and I did
meet;
She passed the salley gardens with little
snow-white feet.
She bid me take love easy, as the leaves grow on
the tree;
But I, being young and foolish, with her would
not agree.
Ibid. Down by the Salley Gardens

18 She bid me take life easy, as the grass grows on
the weirs;
But I was young and foolish, and now am full of
tears.
Ibid.

19 The years like great black oxen tread the world,
And God the herdsman goads them on behind,
And I am broken by their passing feet.
The Countess Cathleen [1892] last lines

20 Red Rose, proud Rose, sad Rose of all my days!
Come near me, while I sing the ancient ways.
*The Rose [1893]. To the Rose Upon the Rood
of Time, st. 1*

21 I will arise and go now, and go to Innisfree,
And a small cabin build there, of clay and wattles
made:
Nine bean-rows will I have there, a hive for the
honeybee,
And live alone in the bee-loud glade.
Ibid. The Lake Isle of Innisfree,[2] st. 1

22 A pity beyond all telling
Is hid in the heart of love.
Ibid. The Pity of Love

23 The brawling of a sparrow in the eaves,
The brilliant moon and all the milky sky,
And all that famous harmony of leaves,
Had blotted out man's image and his cry.
Ibid. The Sorrow of Love, st. 1

[1]See Auden, 720:9.
[2]I had still the ambition, formed in Sligo in my teens, of living
in imitation of Thoreau on Innisfree, a little island in Lough
Gill, and when walking through Fleet Street very homesick I
heard a little tinkle of water and saw a fountain in a shop
window which balanced a little ball upon its jet, and began to
remember lake water. From the sudden remembrance came my
poem Innisfree.— *The Trembling of the Veil* [1926]

1 When you are old and gray and full of sleep,
And nodding by the fire, take down this book.[1]
> *Ibid. When You Are Old, st. 1*

2 How many loved your moments of glad grace,
And loved your beauty with love false or true,
But one man loved the pilgrim soul in you,
And loved the sorrows of your changing face.
> *Ibid. st. 2*

3   The Land of Faery,
Where nobody gets old and godly and grave,
Where nobody gets old and crafty and wise,
Where nobody gets old and bitter of tongue.
> *The Land of Heart's Desire [1894], l. 48*

4   Land of Heart's Desire,
Where beauty has no ebb, decay no flood,
But joy is wisdom, time an endless song.
> *Ibid. l. 373*

5 All things uncomely and broken, all things worn
        out and old,
The cry of a child by the roadway, the creak of a
        lumbering cart,
The heavy steps of the plowman, splashing the
        wintry mold,
Are wronging your image that blossoms a rose in
        the deeps of my heart.
> *The Wind Among the Reeds [1899]. The Lover
> Tells of the Rose in His Heart, st. 1*

6 And God stands winding His lonely horn,
And time and the world are ever in flight.
> *Ibid. Into the Twilight*

7 And pluck till time and times are done
The silver apples of the moon,
The golden apples of the sun.
> *Ibid. The Song of Wandering Aengus, st. 3*

8 Had I the heavens' embroidered cloths,
Enwrought with gold and silver light.
> *Ibid. He Wishes for the Cloths of Heaven*

9 But I, being poor, have only my dreams;
I have spread my dreams under your feet;
Tread softly because you tread on my dreams.
> *Ibid.*

10 When I play on my fiddle in Dooney,
Folk dance like a wave of the sea.
> *Ibid. The Fiddler of Dooney, st. 1*

11 O heart! O heart! if she'd but turn her head,
You'd know the folly of being comforted.
> *In the Seven Woods [1904]. The Folly of Being
> Comforted*

12 Never give all the heart, for love
Will hardly seem worth thinking of
To passionate women if it seem
Certain, and they never dream
That it fades out from kiss to kiss;

For everything that's lovely is
But a brief, dreamy kind delight.
> *Ibid. Never Give All the Heart*

13 I said, "A line will take us hours maybe;
Yet if it does not seem a moment's thought,
Our stitching and unstitching has been naught.
Better go down upon your marrow-bones
And scrub a kitchen pavement, or break stones."
> *Ibid. Adam's Curse, st. 1*

14 For to articulate sweet sounds together
Is to work harder than all these, and yet
Be thought an idler by the noisy set
Of bankers, schoolmasters, and clergymen
The martyrs call the world.
> *Ibid.*

15   It's certain there is no fine thing
Since Adam's fall but needs much laboring.
> *Ibid. st. 3*

16 I heard the old, old men say,
"All that's beautiful drifts away
Like the waters."
> *Ibid. The Old Men Admiring Themselves in the
> Water*

17 The friends that have it I do wrong
When ever I remake a song
Should know what issue is at stake,
It is myself that I remake.
> *The Collected Works in Verse and Prose of
> William Butler Yeats [1908], II, preliminary
> poem*

18 Why, what could she have done, being what she
        is?
Was there another Troy for her to burn?
> *The Green Helmet and Other Poems [1910]. No
> Second Troy*

19 The fascination of what's difficult
Has dried the sap out of my veins, and rent
Spontaneous joy and natural content
Out of my heart.
> *Ibid. The Fascination of What's Difficult*

20 Wine comes in at the mouth
And love comes in at the eye;
That's all we shall know for truth
Before we grow old and die.
> *Ibid. A Drinking Song*

21 Though leaves are many, the root is one;
Through all the lying days of my youth
I swayed my leaves and flowers in the sun;
Now I may wither into the truth.
> *Ibid. The Coming of Wisdom with Time*

22 In dreams begins responsibility.
> *Responsibilities [1914], epigraph (from an old
> play)*

23 Pardon, old fathers.
> *Ibid. preliminary poem*

[1] See Ronsard, 144:2.

1 Was it for this the wild geese spread
The gray wing upon every tide;
For this that all that blood was shed,
For this Edward Fitzgerald died,
And Robert Emmet and Wolfe Tone,
All that delirium of the brave?
Romantic Ireland's dead and gone,
It's with O'Leary in the grave.
> *Responsibilities. September 1913, st. 3*

2 Be secret and exult,
Because of all things known
That is most difficult.
> *Ibid. To a Friend Whose Work Has Come to Nothing*

3 The uncontrollable mystery on the bestial floor.
> *Ibid. The Magi, last line*

4 I made my song a coat
Covered with embroideries
Out of old mythologies
From heel to throat;
But the fools caught it,
Wore it in the world's eyes
As though they'd wrought it.
Song, let them take it,
For there's more enterprise
In walking naked.
> *Ibid. A Coat*

5 Upon the brimming water among the stones
Are nine-and-fifty swans.
> *The Wild Swans at Coole [1919]. The Wild Swans at Coole, st. 1*

6 Unwearied still, lover by lover,
They paddle in the cold
Companionable streams or climb the air;
Their hearts have not grown old.
> *Ibid. st. 4*

7 Some burn damp faggots, others may consume
The entire combustible world in one small room.
> *Ibid. In Memory of Major Robert Gregory, st. 11*

8 What made us dream that he could comb gray hair?
> *Ibid.*

9   A thought
Of that late death took all my heart for speech.
> *Ibid. st. 12*

10 I know that I shall meet my fate
Somewhere among the clouds above;
Those that I fight I do not hate,
Those that I guard I do not love;
My country is Kiltartan Cross,
My countrymen Kiltartan's poor.
> *Ibid. An Irish Airman Foresees His Death, l. 1*

11 Nor law, nor duty bade me fight,
Nor public men, nor cheering crowds,
A lonely impulse of delight
Drove to this tumult in the clouds.
> *Ibid. l. 9*

12 And I may dine at journey's end
With Landor and with Donne.
> *Ibid. To a Young Beauty, st. 3*

13 All the wild witches, those most noble ladies,
For all their broomsticks and their tears,
Their angry tears, are gone.
> *Ibid. Lines Written in Dejection l. 4*

14 I knew a phoenix in my youth, so let them have their day.
> *Ibid. His Phoenix, refrain*

15 Hands, do what you're bid:
Bring the balloon of the mind
That bellies and drags in the wind
Into its narrow shed.
> *Ibid. The Balloon of the Mind*

16 We have lit upon the gentle, sensitive mind
And lost the old nonchalance of the hand;
Whether we have chosen chisel, pen or brush,
We are but critics, or but half create.
> *Ibid. Ego Dominus Tuus, l. 12*

17 All changed, changed utterly:
A terrible beauty is born.
> *Michael Robartes and the Dancer [1921]. Easter 1916, st. 1*

18 Too long a sacrifice
Can make a stone of the heart.
O when may it suffice?
> *Ibid. st. 4*

19 Turning and turning in the widening gyre
The falcon cannot hear the falconer;
Things fall apart; the center cannot hold;
Mere anarchy is loosed upon the world,
The blood-dimmed tide is loosed, and everywhere
The ceremony of innocence is drowned;
The best lack all conviction, while the worst
Are full of passionate intensity.
> *Ibid. The Second Coming, st. 1*

20   Now I know
That twenty centuries of stony sleep
Were vexed to nightmare by a rocking cradle,
And what rough beast, its hour come round at last,
Slouches towards Bethlehem to be born?[1]
> *Ibid. st. 2*

21 Imagining in excited reverie
That the future years had come,
Dancing to a frenzied drum,
Out of the murderous innocence of the sea.
> *Ibid. A Prayer for My Daughter, st. 2*

22   For such,
Being made beautiful overmuch,
Consider beauty a sufficient end,

[1]See Heine, 420:9.

Lose natural kindness and maybe
The heart-revealing intimacy
That chooses right, and never find a friend.

Ibid. st. 3

1 It's certain that fine women eat
A crazy salad with their meat.

Ibid. st. 4

2 In courtesy I'd have her chiefly learned;
Hearts are not had as a gift but hearts are earned.

Ibid. st. 5

3 And many a poor man that has roved,
Loved and thought himself beloved,
From a glad kindness cannot take his eyes.

Ibid.

4 If there's no hatred in a mind
Assault and battery of the wind
Can never tear the linnet from the leaf.

Ibid. st. 7

5 An intellectual hatred is the worst,
So let her think opinions are accursed.
Have I not seen the loveliest woman born
Out of the mouth of Plenty's horn,
Because of her opinionated mind
Barter that horn and every good
By quiet natures understood
For an old bellows full of angry wind?

Ibid. st. 8

6   All hatred driven hence,
The soul recovers radical innocence
And learns at last that it is self-delighting,
Self-appeasing, self-affrighting,
And that its own sweet will is Heaven's will.

Ibid. st. 9

7 That is no country for old men. The young
In one another's arms, birds in the trees
—Those dying generations—at their song,
The salmon-falls, the mackerel-crowded seas,
Fish, flesh, or fowl, commend all summer long
Whatever is begotten, born, and dies.
Caught in that sensual music all neglect
Monuments of unaging intellect.

The Tower [1928]. Sailing to Byzantium, st. 1

8 An aged man is but a paltry thing,
A tattered coat upon a stick, unless
Soul clap its hands and sing, and louder sing
For every tatter in its mortal dress.

Ibid. st. 2

9 Consume my heart away; sick with desire
And fastened to a dying animal
It knows not what it is; and gather me
Into the artifice of eternity.

Ibid. st. 3

10 Once out of nature I shall never take
My bodily form from any natural thing,
But such a form as Grecian goldsmiths make
Of hammered gold and gold enameling
To keep a drowsy Emperor awake;

Or set upon a golden bough to sing
To lords and ladies of Byzantium
Of what is past, or passing, or to come.[1]

Ibid. st. 4

11 What shall I do with this absurdity—
O heart, O troubled heart—this caricature,
Decrepit age that has been tied to me
As to a dog's tail?

Ibid. The Tower, I

12 Does the imagination dwell the most
Upon a woman won or a woman lost?

Ibid. II, st. 13

13 The night can sweat with terror as before
We pieced our thoughts into philosophy,
And planned to bring the world under a rule,
Who are but weasels fighting in a hole.

Ibid. Nineteen Hundred and Nineteen, I, st. 4

14 But is there any comfort to be found?
Man is in love and loves what vanishes,
What more is there to say?

Ibid. st. 6

15 O but we dreamed to mend
Whatever mischief seemed
To afflict mankind, but now
That winds of winter blow
Learn that we were crack-pated when we
    dreamed.

Ibid. III, st. 3

16 Come let us mock at the great
That had such burdens on the mind
And toiled so hard and late
To leave some monument behind,
Nor thought of the leveling wind.

Ibid. V, st. 1

17 Much did I rage when young,
Being by the world oppressed,
But now with flattering tongue
It speeds the parting guest.

Ibid. Youth and Age

18 Odor of blood when Christ was slain
Made all Platonic tolerance vain
And vain all Doric discipline.

Ibid. Two Songs from a Play, II, st. 1

19 Everything that man esteems
Endures a moment or a day.
Love's pleasure drives his love away,
The painter's brush consumes his dreams.

Ibid. st. 2

20 Whatever flames upon the night
Man's own resinous heart has fed.

Ibid.

21 Locke sank into a swoon;
The Garden died;

[1] I have read somewhere that in the Emperor's palace at
Byzantium was a tree made of gold and silver, and artificial
birds that sang.—YEATS's *note*

God took the spinning-jenny
Out of his side.

The Tower. Fragments, I

1 A shudder in the loins engenders there
The broken wall, the burning roof and tower
And Agamemnon dead.

Ibid. Leda and the Swan, st. 3

2 Labor is blossoming or dancing where
The body is not bruised to pleasure soul,
Nor beauty born out of its own despair,
Nor blear-eyed wisdom out of midnight oil.
O chestnut tree, great-rooted blossomer,
Are you the leaf, the blossom or the bole?
O body swayed to music, O brightening glance,
How can we know the dancer from the dance?

Ibid. Among School Children, st. 8

3 Never to have lived is best, ancient writers say;
Never to have drawn the breath of life, never to
have looked into the eye of day;
The second best's a gay goodnight and quickly
turn away.[1]

From "Oedipus at Colonus," st. 3

4   That toil of growing up;
The ignominy of boyhood; the distress
Of boyhood changing into man;
The unfinished man and his pain.

*The Winding Stair and Other Poems [1933]. A
Dialogue of Self and Soul, II, st. 1*

5 I am content to live it all again
And yet again, if it be life to pitch
Into the frog-spawn of a blind man's ditch.

Ibid. st. 3

6 When such as I cast out remorse
So great a sweetness flows into the breast
We must laugh and we must sing,
We are blest by everything,
Everything we look upon is blest.

Ibid. st. 4

7   But what is Whiggery?
A leveling, rancorous, rational sort of mind
That never looked out of the eye of a saint
Or out of drunkard's eye.

Ibid. The Seven Sages

8   Only God, my dear,
Could love you for yourself alone
And not your yellow hair.

Ibid. For Anne Gregory, st. 3

9 Swift has sailed into his rest;
Savage indignation there
Cannot lacerate his breast,
Imitate him if you dare,
World-besotted traveler; he
Served human liberty.

Ibid. Swift's Epitaph[2]

[1]See Theognis, 59:24; Sophocles, 67:9; Francis Bacon, 160:-
15; and Auden, 720:5.
[2]See Swift, 290:23.

10 The intellect of man is forced to choose
Perfection of the life, or of the work,
And if it take the second must refuse
A heavenly mansion, raging in the dark.

Ibid. The Choice, st. 1

11 The unpurged images of day recede;
The Emperor's drunken soldiery are abed;
Night resonance recedes, night-walkers' song
After great cathedral gong.

Ibid. Byzantium, st. 1

12 At midnight on the Emperor's pavement flit
Flames that no faggot feeds, nor steel has lit.

Ibid. st. 4

13 An agony of flame that cannot singe a sleeve.

Ibid.

14 That dolphin-torn, that gong-tormented sea.

Ibid. st. 5

15 No man has ever lived that had enough
Of children's gratitude or woman's love.

Ibid. Vacillation, III, st. 1

16 Things said or done long years ago,
Or things I did not do or say
But thought that I might say or do,
Weigh me down, and not a day
But something is recalled,
My conscience or my vanity appalled.

Ibid. V, st. 2

17 Homer is my example and his unchristened heart.

Ibid. VIII

18 Somewhere beyond the curtain
Of distorting days
Lives that lonely thing
That shone before these eyes
Targeted, trod like Spring.

Ibid. Quarrel in Old Age, st. 2

19 I had wild Jack for a lover.

*Ibid. Words for Music Perhaps, V, Crazy Jane
on God, st. 4*

20 "Fair and foul are near of kin,
And fair needs foul," I cried.
"My friends are gone, but that's a truth
Nor grave nor bed denied."

*Ibid. VI, Crazy Jane Talks with the Bishop,
st. 2*

21 But Love has pitched his mansion in
The place of excrement
For nothing can be sole or whole
That has not been rent.

Ibid. st. 3

22 What were all the world's alarms
To mighty Paris when he found
Sleep upon a golden bed
That first dawn in Helen's arms?

Ibid. XVI, Lullaby, st. 1

23 Speech after long silence; it is right,
All other lovers being estranged or dead . . .

That we descant and yet again descant
Upon the supreme theme of Art and Song:
Bodily decrepitude is wisdom; young
We loved each other and were ignorant.
Ibid. XVII, After Long Silence

1 I carry the sun in a golden cup,
The moon in a silver bag.[1]
Ibid. XIX, Those Dancing Days Are Gone

2 I gave what other women gave
That stepped out of their clothes,
But when this soul, its body off,
Naked to naked goes,
He it has found shall find therein
What none other knows.
*Ibid. A Woman Young and Old, IX, A Last
Confession, st. 3*

3 He that sings a lasting song
Thinks in a marrowbone.
*A Full Moon in March [1935]. A Prayer for Old
Age, st. 1*

4 I pray—for fashion's word is out
And prayer comes round again—
That I may seem, though I die old,
A foolish, passionate man.
Ibid. st. 3

5   Whence had they come,
The hand and lash that beat down frigid Rome?
What sacred drama through her body heaved
When world-transforming Charlemagne was
    conceived?
*Ibid. Supernatural Songs, VIII, Whence Had
They Come?*

6 All perform their tragic play,
There struts Hamlet, there is Lear.
Last Poems [1936–1939]. Lapis Lazuli, st. 2

7   Heaven blazing into the head:
Tragedy wrought to its uttermost.
Though Hamlet rambles and Lear rages,
And all the drop-scenes drop at once
Upon a hundred thousand stages,
It cannot grow by an inch or an ounce.
Ibid.

8 Their eyes mid many wrinkles, their eyes,
Their ancient, glittering eyes, are gay.
Ibid. st. 5

9 If soul may look and body touch,
Which is the more blest?
Ibid. The Lady's Second Song, st. 3

10 My temptation is quiet.
Here at life's end
Neither loose imagination,
Nor the mill of the mind

Consuming its rag and bone,
Can make the truth known.
Ibid. An Acre of Grass, st. 2

11 Grant me an old man's frenzy,
Myself must I remake
Till I am Timon and Lear
Or that William Blake
Who beat upon the wall
Till Truth obeyed his call.
Ibid. st. 3

12 An old man's eagle mind.
Ibid. st. 4

13 Hurrah for revolution and more cannon-shot!
A beggar upon horseback lashes a beggar on foot.
Hurrah for revolution and cannon come again!
The beggars have changed places, but the lash
    goes on.
Ibid. The Great Day

14 You think it horrible that lust and rage
Should dance attention upon my old age;
They were not such a plague when I was young;
What else have I to spur me into song?
Ibid. The Spur

15 John Synge, I and Augusta Gregory, thought
All that we did, all that we said or sang
Must come from contact with the soil, from that
Contact everything Antaeus-like grew strong.
Ibid. The Municipal Gallery Revisited, st. 6

16 Think where man's glory most begins and ends,
And say my glory was I had such friends.
Ibid. st. 7

17 Down the mountain walls
From where Pan's cavern is
Intolerable music falls.
Foul goat-head, brutal arm appear,
Belly, shoulder, bum,
Flash fishlike; nymphs and satyrs
Copulate in the foam.
Ibid. News for the Delphic Oracle, st. 3

18 Like a long-legged fly upon the stream
His mind moves upon silence.
Ibid. Long-Legged Fly, refrain

19 What shall I do for pretty girls
Now my old bawd is dead?
*Ibid. John Kinsella's Lament for Mrs. Mary
Moore, refrain*

20 Fifteen apparitions have I seen;
The worst a coat upon a coat-hanger.
Ibid. The Apparitions, refrain

21 Players and painted stage took all my love,
And not those things that they were emblems of.
Ibid. The Circus Animals' Desertion, II, st. 3

22   Now that my ladder's gone,
I must lie down where all the ladders start,
In the foul rag-and-bone shop of the heart.
Ibid. III

[1]"The sun in a golden cup" . . . though not "the moon in a silver bag," is a quotation from the last of Mr. Ezra Pound's *Cantos.*—YEATS's note in *The Winding Stair and Other Poems*

1 Irish poets, learn your trade,
Sing whatever is well made.
Last Poems. Under Ben Bulben, V

2 Under bare Ben Bulben's head
In Drumcliff churchyard Yeats is laid.
Ibid. VI

3 On limestone quarried near the spot
By his command these words are cut:
Cast a cold eye
On life, on death.
Horseman, pass by![1]
Ibid.

4 I am still of opinion that only two topics can be of the least interest to a serious and studious mood —sex and the dead.   *The Letters of W. B. Yeats*

5 If a poet interprets a poem of his own he limits its suggestibility.   *Ibid.*

6 We poets would die of loneliness but for women, and we choose our men friends that we may have somebody to talk about women with.
Ibid. Letter to Olivia Shakespeare [1936]

7 In life courtesy and self-possession, and in the arts style, are the sensible impressions of the free mind, for both arise out of a deliberate shaping of all things and from never being swept away, whatever the emotion, into confusion or dullness.
Essays and Introductions [1961]. Poetry and the Tradition

George W. Young
fl. 1900

8 The lips that touch liquor must never touch mine!
The Lips That Touch Liquor, st. 5

George Ade
1866–1944

9 In uplifting, get underneath.
Fables in Slang [1899]. The Good Fairy

10 Stay with the procession or you will never catch up.
Forty Modern Fables [1901]. The Old-Time Pedagogue

11 Draw your salary before spending it.
Ibid. The People's Choice

12 Last night at twelve I felt immense,
But now I feel like thirty cents.
The Sultan of Sulu [1902]. Remorse

13 But, R - e - m - o - r - s - e!
The water-wagon is the place for me; . . .
It is no time for mirth and laughter,
The cold, gray dawn of the morning after!
Ibid.

[1]The last three lines are inscribed on Yeats's gravestone.

Tristan Bernard
1866–1947

14 To live happily with other people one should ask of them only what they can give.
L'Enfant Prodigue du Vesinet [1921]

15 Men are always sincere. They change sincerities, that's all.[2]
Ce Que l'On Dit aux Femmes [1922], act III

Gelett Burgess
1866–1951

16 I never saw a purple cow,
I never hope to see one;
But I can tell you, anyhow,
I'd rather see than be one.
The Purple Cow [1895]

17 Ah, yes, I wrote the "Purple Cow"—
I'm sorry, now, I wrote it!
But I can tell you, anyhow,
I'll kill you if you quote it.
Cinq Ans Après [1914]

Harry Dacre
d. 1922

18 Daisy, Daisy, give me your answer, do!
I'm half crazy, all for the love of you!
It won't be a stylish marriage,
I can't afford a carriage,
But you'll look sweet upon the seat
Of a bicycle built for two!
Daisy Bell [1892]

Thomas Lansing Masson
1866–1934

19 A Safe and Sane Fourth.   *Slogan*

Beatrix Potter
1866–1943

20 Once upon a time there were four little Rabbits, and their names were—Flopsy, Mopsy, Cottontail, and Peter.   *The Tale of Peter Rabbit [1902]*

21 But don't go into Mr. McGregor's garden.
Ibid.

22 No more twist!
The Tailor of Gloucester [1903]

23 The water was all slippy-sloppy in the larder and the back passage. But Mr. Jeremy liked getting his feet wet; nobody ever scolded him, and he never caught a cold.
The Tale of Mr. Jeremy Fisher [1906]

[2]Les hommes sont toujours sincères. Ils changent de sincérité, voilà tout.

Henry J. Sayers
d. 1932

1 Ta-ra-ra-boom-de-ay!
   *Title of minstrel show number [1891], made
   famous by Lottie Collins [1892]*

Lincoln Steffens
1866–1936

2 The Shame of the Cities.
   Title of book [1904]

3 "So you've been over into Russia?" said Bernard
Baruch, and I answered very literally, "I have been
over into the future, and it works."[1]
   Autobiography [1931], ch. 18

Sun Yat-sen[2]
1866–1925

4 The Chinese people have only family and clan
solidarity; they do not have national spirit . . .
they are just a heap of loose sand. . . . Other men
are the carving knife and serving dish; we are the fish
and the meat.
   China as a Heap of Loose Sand [1924]

Bert Leston Taylor
1866–1921

5 A bore is a man who, when you ask him how he
is, tells you.   *The So-Called Human Race [1922]*

Herbert George Wells
1866–1946

6 The Time Machine.   *Title of book [1895]*

7 The Social Contract is nothing more or less than
a vast conspiracy of human beings to lie to and
humbug themselves and one another for the general
Good. Lies are the mortar that bind the savage individual man into the social masonry.
   Love and Mr. Lewisham [1899], ch. 23

8 The past is but the beginning of a beginning, and
all that is and has been is but the twilight of the
dawn.   *The Discovery of the Future [1901]*

9 Nothing could have been more obvious to the
people of the early twentieth century than the rapid-
ity with which war was becoming impossible. And
as certainly they did not see it. They did not see it
until the atomic bombs burst in their fumbling
hands.   *The World Set Free [1914]*

10 The catastrophe of the atomic bombs which
shook men out of cities and businesses and economic
relations, shook them also out of their old-estab-
lished habits of thought, and out of the lightly held
beliefs and prejudices that came down to them from
the past.   *Ibid.*

11 The War That Will End War.
   Title of book [1914]

12 [A novel by Henry James] is like a church lit but
without a congregation to distract you, with every
light and line focused on the high altar. And on the
altar, very reverently placed, intensely there, is a
dead kitten, an egg-shell, a bit of string.
   Boon [1915], ch. 4, sect. 3

13 The professional military mind is by necessity an
inferior and unimaginative mind; no man of high
intellectual quality would willingly imprison his
gifts in such a calling.
   The Outline of History [1920], ch. 40

14 Human history becomes more and more a race
between education and catastrophe.   *Ibid. 41*

15 Life begins perpetually. Gathered together at last
under the leadership of man . . . unified, disciplined, armed with the secret powers of the atom
and with knowledge as yet beyond dreaming, Life,
forever dying to be born afresh, forever young and
eager, will presently stand upon this earth as upon a
footstool, and stretch out its realm amidst the stars.[3]
   Ibid.

16 The Shape of Things to Come.   *Title of book [1933]*

17 Queen Victoria was like a great paper-weight
that for half a century sat upon men's minds, and
when she was removed their ideas began to blow all
over the place haphazardly.
   *From NORMAN and JEAN MACKENZIE, H. G.
   Wells [1973]*

Stanley Baldwin
1867–1947

18 When you think about the defense of England
you no longer think of the chalk cliffs of Dover. You
think of the Rhine. That is where our frontier lies
today.
   *Speech in the House of Commons [July 30,
   1934]*

Julien Benda
1867–1956

19 Le Trahison des Clercs [The Treason of the Intel-
lectuals].   *Title of book [1927]*

---

[1]On Steffens's return from revolutionary Russia in 1919. Its
more familiar form is: I have seen the future, and it works
—*letter to* MARIE HOWE *[April 3, 1919]*.
[2]From *Sources of Chinese Tradition* [1960], edited by WIL-
LIAM THEODORE DE BARY.
[3]See *Matthew* 5:34–35, 33:6; Pope, 301:9; and Day,
622:14.

Enoch Arnold Bennett
1867–1931

1   The Old Wives' Tale.[1]   *Title of novel [1908]*

2   Being a husband is a whole-time job.
The Title [1918], act I

3   Pessimism, when you get used to it, is just as agreeable as optimism.
Things That Have Interested Me [1918]

4   The price of justice is eternal publicity.
Ibid. Second Series [1923]

Vicente Blasco-Ibáñez
1867–1928

5   It was the roar of the real, the only beast [the crowd in the arena].
Sangre y Arena (Blood and Sand) [1908]

6   Los Cuatro Jinetes del Apocalipsis [The Four Horsemen of the Apocalypse].[2]
Title of book [1916]

Ernest Dowson
1867–1900

7 Last night, ah, yesternight, betwixt her lips and mine
There fell thy shadow, Cynara! thy breath was shed
Upon my soul between the kisses and the wine;
And I was desolate and sick of an old passion,
Yea, I was desolate and bowed my head:
I have been faithful to thee, Cynara! in my fashion.[3]
Non Sum Qualis Eram Bonae Sub Regno Cynarae [1896],[4] st. 1

8 I have forgot much, Cynara! gone with the wind,
Flung roses, roses riotously with the throng.
Ibid. st. 3

9 I cried for madder music and for stronger wine,
But when the feast is finished and the lamps expire,
Then falls thy shadow, Cynara! the night is thine.
Ibid. st. 4

---

[1]A fool he is to believe the tales of an old wife. — ALEXANDER BARCLAY [c.1475–1552], *The Ship of Fools* [1509]
Old wives' foolish tales of Robin Hood. — NICHOLAS UDALL [1505–1556]
See *I Timothy 4:7, 45:16.*
[2]Phrase derived from the four allegorical horses in the Bible (*Revelation 6:1–8*).
See Rice, 643:15.
[3]See Cole Porter, 682:7.
[4]See Horace, 96:27.

10 They are not long, the weeping and the laughter,
Love and desire and hate:
I think they have no portion in us after
We pass the gate.

They are not long, the days of wine and roses;
Out of a misty dream
Our path emerges for a while, then closes
Within a dream.
Vitae Summa Brevis Spem Nos Vetat Incohare Longam[5] [1896]

Finley Peter Dunne [Mr. Dooley]
1867–1936

11   Life'd not be worth livin' if we didn't keep our inimies.
Mr. Dooley in Peace and in War [1898]. On New Year's Resolutions

12   Th' dead ar-re always pop'lar. I knowed a society wanst to vote a monyment to a man an' refuse to help his fam'ly, all in wan night.
Ibid. On Charity

13   "I think," said Mr. Dooley, "that if th' Christyan Scientists had some science an' th' doctors more Christianity, it wudden't make anny diff'rence which ye called in — if ye had a good nurse."
Mr. Dooley's Opinions [1900]. Christian Science

14   No matther whether th' constitution follows th' flag or not, th' supreme coort follows th' iliction returns.   *Ibid. The Supreme Court's Decisions*

15   I think a lie with a purpose is wan iv th' worst kind an' th' mos' profitable.   *Ibid. On Lying*

16   Th' dimmycratic party ain't on speakin' terms with itsilf.
Ibid. Mr. Dooley Discusses Party Politics

17   Th' raypublican party broke ye, but now that ye're down we'll not turn a cold shoulder to ye. Come in an' we'll keep ye — broke.   *Ibid.*

18   Hogan's r-right whin he says: "Justice is blind." Blind she is, an' deef an' dumb an' has a wooden leg.
Ibid. Cross-Examinations

19   No wan cares to hear what Hogan calls "Th' short an' simple scandals iv th' poor."   *Ibid.*

20   'Twas founded be th' Puritans to give thanks f'r bein' presarved fr'm th' Indyans, an' . . . we keep it to give thanks we are presarved fr'm th' Puritans.
Ibid. Thanksgiving

21   Vice . . . is a creature of such heejous mien . . . that th' more ye see it th' betther ye like it.
Ibid. The Crusade Against Vice

---

[5]See Horace, 95:19.

1   "D' ye think th' colledges has much to do with th' progress iv th' wurruld?" asked Mr. Hennessy.

"D' ye think," said Mr. Dooley, "'tis th' mill that makes th' wather run?"

Ibid. Colleges and Degrees

2   If ye live enough befure thirty ye won't care to live at all afther fifty.   *Ibid. Casual Observations*

3   Among men, Hinnissy, wet eye manes dhry heart.   *Ibid.*

4   A fanatic is a man that does what he thinks th' Lord wud do if He knew th' facts iv th' case.   *Ibid.*

5   'Tis as hard f'r a rich man to enther th' kingdom iv Hiven as it is f'r a poor man to get out iv Purgatory.   *Ibid.*

6   Thrust ivrybody, but cut th' ca-ards.   *Ibid.*

7   A man that'd expict to thrain lobsters to fly in a year is called a loonytic; but a man that thinks men can be tu-rrned into angels be an iliction is called a rayformer an' remains at large.   *Ibid.*

8   Miracles are laughed at be a nation that r-reads thirty millyon newspapers a day an' supports Wall sthreet.   *Ibid.*

9   If a man is wise, he gets rich, an' if he gets rich, he gets foolish, or his wife does. That's what keeps the money movin' around.

Observations by Mr. Dooley [1902]. Newport

10   But th' best thing about a little judicyous swearin' is that it keeps th' temper. 'Twas intinded as a compromise between runnin' away an' fightin'. Befure it was invinted they was on'y th' two ways out iv an argymint.   *Ibid. Swearing*

11   I don't think we injye other people's sufferin', Hinnissy. It isn't acshally injyement. But we feel betther f'r it.   *Ibid. Enjoyment*

12   Th' newspaper does ivrything f'r us. It runs th' polis foorce an' th' banks, commands th' milishy, conthrols th' ligislachure, baptizes th' young, marries th' foolish, comforts th' afflicted, afflicts th' comfortable, buries th' dead an' roasts thim aftherward.   *Ibid. Newspaper Publicity*

13   "Ye know a lot about [raising children]," said Mr. Hennessy.

"I do," said Mr. Dooley. "Not bein' an author, I'm a gr-reat critic."

Dissertations by Mr. Dooley [1906]. The Bringing Up of Children

14   Th' prisidincy is th' highest office in th' gift iv th' people. Th' vice-prisidincy is th' next highest an' th' lowest. It isn't a crime exactly. Ye can't be sint to jail f'r it, but it's a kind iv a disgrace. It's like writin' anonymous letters.   *Ibid. The Vice-President*

15   This home iv opporchunity where ivry man is th' equal iv ivry other man befure th' law if he isn't careful.   *Ibid. The Food We Eat*

16   "Ye ra-aly do think dhrink is a nicissry evil?" said Mr. Hennessy.

"Well," said Mr. Dooley, "if it's an evil to a man, it's not nicissry, an' if it's nicissry it's an evil."   *Ibid. The Bar*

17   "He made [money]," said Mr. Dooley, "because he honestly loved it with an innocint affiction. He was thrue to it. Th' reason ye have no money is because ye don't love it f'r itsilf alone. Money won't iver surrinder to such a flirt."

Mr. Dooley on Making a Will and Other Evil Necessities [1919]. On Making a Will

John Galsworthy
1867–1933

18   Nobody tells me anything.

Repeatedly spoken by James Forsyte in The Man of Property [1906] and In Chancery [1920]

19   Justice is a machine that, when someone has once given it the starting push, rolls on of itself.

Justice [1910], act II

20   Public opinion's always in advance of the law.

Windows [1922], act I

21   The value of a sentiment is the amount of sacrifice you are prepared to make for it.   *Ibid. II*

22   A man of action forced into a state of thought is unhappy until he can get out of it.

Maid in Waiting [1931], ch. 3

23   The beginnings and endings of all human undertakings are untidy, the building of a house, the writing of a novel, the demolition of a bridge, and, eminently, the finish of a voyage.

Over the River [1933], ch. 1

24   How to save the old that's worth saving, whether in landscape, houses, manners, institutions, or human types, is one of our greatest problems, and the one that we bother least about.   *Ibid. 39*

Edith Hamilton
1867–1963

25   They [the Greeks] were the first Westerners; the spirit of the West, the modern spirit, is a Greek discovery and the place of the Greeks is in the modern world.   *The Greek Way [1930], ch. 1*

26   To rejoice in life, to find the world beautiful and delightful to live in, was a mark of the Greek spirit which distinguished it from all that had gone before. It is a vital distinction.   *Ibid.*

Kaethe Kollwitz
1867–1945

1   I am gradually approaching the period in my life when work comes first. . . . No longer diverted by other emotions, I work the way a cow grazes.
Diary[1] *[April 1910]*

Charles Edward Montague
1867–1928

2   I was born below par to th' extent of two whiskies.   *Fiery Particles [1923]*

Luigi Pirandello
1867–1936

3   Right You Are If You Think You Are [Cosi è se vi pare].
Title of play [1917; English version, 1922]

4   Six Characters in Search of an Author [Sei personaggi in cerca d'autore].
Title of play [1921; English version, 1922]

5   Life is a very sad piece of buffoonery, because we have . . . the need to fool ourselves continuously by the spontaneous creation of a reality (one for each and never the same for everyone) which, from time to time, reveals itself to be vain and illusory.
Autobiographical Sketch in Le Lettere, Rome [October 15, 1924][2]

6   As You Desire Me [Come tu mi vuoi].
Title of play [1930; English version, 1931]

Henry Lewis Stimson
1867–1950

7   Gentlemen do not read each other's mail.[3]
On Active Service in Peace and War [1948]

Joseph Weber
1867–1942
and
Lew Fields
1867–1941

8 Who was that lady I saw you with last night? She ain't no lady; she's my wife.
Vaudeville routine [1887]

Harry Leon Wilson
1867–1939

9   I can be pushed just so far.
Ruggles of Red Gap [1915]

---

[1]Translated by RICHARD and CLARA WINSTON.
[2]Translated by WILLIAM MURRAY.
[3]Explaining his 1929 decision, as Secretary of State, to close down the department's codebreaking agency (the American "black chamber").

Wilbur Wright
1867–1912
and
Orville Wright
1871–1948

10   Success. Four flights Thursday morning. All against twenty-one-mile wind. Started from level with engine power alone. Average speed through air thirty-one miles. Longest fifty-nine seconds. Inform press. Home Christmas.
Telegram to the Reverend Milton Wright, from Kitty Hawk, N.C. [December 17, 1903]

Émile Auguste Chartier [Alain]
1868–1951

11   To think is to say *no.*
Le Citoyen contre les Pouvoirs

12   We prove what we want to prove, and the real difficulty is to know what we want to prove.
Système des Beaux-Arts [1920]

13   Nothing is more dangerous than an idea, when it's the only one we have.   *Libres-propos*

Paul Claudel
1868–1955

14   You explain nothing, O poet, but thanks to you all things become explicable.
La Ville [1897], act I

15 The words I use
Are everyday words and yet are not the same!
You will find no rhymes in my verse, no magic.
There are your very own phrases.
La Muse Qui Est la Grace [1910]

16   When man tries to imagine Paradise on earth, the immediate result is a very respectable Hell.
Conversations dans le Loir-et-Cher [1929]

Norman Douglas
1868–1952

17   You can tell the ideals of a nation by its advertisements.   *South Wind [1917], ch. 7*

18   Many a man who thinks to found a home discovers that he has merely opened a tavern for his friends.   *Ibid. 24*

William Edward Burghardt Du Bois
1868–1963

19   The problem of the twentieth century is the problem of the color line.[4]
To the Nations of the World; address to Pan-African conference, London [1900]

---

[4]See Frederick Douglass, 480:17 and 480:18.

1   Herein lies the tragedy of the age: not that men are poor—all men know something of poverty; not that men are wicked—who is good? Not that men are ignorant—what is truth? Nay, but that men know so little of men.

The Souls of Black Folk [1903]

2   It is a peculiar sensation, this double-consciousness, this sense of always looking at one's self through the eyes of others. . . . One feels his twoness—an American, a Negro; two souls, two thoughts, two unreconciled strivings; two warring ideals in one dark body, whose dogged strength alone keeps it from being torn asunder.   *Ibid.*

3   The cost of liberty is less than the price of repression.

John Brown [1909]. The Legacy of John Brown

4   Liberty trains for liberty. Responsibility is the first step in responsibility.   *Ibid.*

5   The dark world is going to submit to its present treatment just as long as it must and not one moment longer.

Darkwater [1920]. The Souls of White Folk

6   The return from your work must be the satisfaction which that work brings you and the world's need of that work. With this, life is heaven, or as near heaven as you can get. Without this—with work which you despise, which bores you, and which the world does not need—this life is hell.

To His Newborn Great-Grandson; address on his ninetieth birthday [1958]

7   Believe in life! Always human beings will live and progress to greater, broader, and fuller life.

Last message to the world [written 1957]. Read at his funeral [1963]

John Nance Garner
1868–1967

8   The vice-presidency isn't worth a pitcher of warm piss.   *Attributed*

Maxim Gorki[1]
[Aleksei Maksimovich Peshkov]
1868–1936

9   Former People [Creatures That Once Were Men].

Title of story [1897]

10   Let the storm rage ever stronger![2]

Song of a Stormy Petrel [1901]

11   Lies—there you have the religion of slaves and taskmasters.[3]   *The Lower Depths [1903]*

12   How marvelous is Man! How proud the word rings—Man!   *Ibid.*

13   In time I came to understand that out of the misery and murk of their lives the Russian people had learned to make sorrow a diversion, to play with it like a child's toy; seldom are they diffident about showing their happiness. And so, through their tedious weekdays, they made a carnival of grief; a fire is entertainment; and on a vacant face a bruise becomes an adornment.

Autobiography [1913]. Childhood

14   The proletarian state must bring up thousands of excellent "mechanics of culture," "engineers of the soul."[4]   *Speech at the Writers' Congress [1934]*

15   The basic hero of our books should be labor; that is, man organized by the processes of labor.

Ibid.

Frank McKinney "Kin" Hubbard
[Abe Martin]
1868–1930

16   It's no disgrace t' be poor, but it might as well be.

Abe Martin's Sayings and Sketches [1915]

17   When a fellow says it hain't the money but the principle o' the thing, it's th' money.

Hoss Sense and Nonsense [1926]

18   Nobuddy ever fergits where he buried a hatchet.

Abe Martin's Broadcast [1930]

19   If capital an' labor ever do git t'gether it's good night fer th' rest of us.   *Saying*

20   Now and then an innocent man is sent to the legislature.   *Ibid.*

Edward Verrall Lucas
1868–1938

21   The French never allow a distinguished son of France to lack a statue.

Wanderings and Diversions [1926]. Zigzags in France

22   Americans are people who prefer the Continent to their own country, but refuse to learn its languages.   *Ibid. The Continental Dictionary*

23   People in hotels strike no roots. The French phrase for chronic hotel guests even says so: they are called dwellers *sur la branche*.

Ibid. To Be Let or Sold

Edmond Rostand
1868–1918

24   A great nose indicates a great man—
Genial, courteous, intellectual,
Virile, courageous.

Cyrano de Bergerac [1897],[5] *act I*

---

[1]Gorki, "the bitter one," was the writer's pseudonym for his first sketch in a Tiflis newspaper [1892].

[2]This became a rallying cry of the revolutionaries.

[3]The censor forbade this line to be spoken on the stage.

[4]Attributed to Stalin in conversation with Gorki [October 26, 1934].

[5]Translated by BRIAN HOOKER.

1 I fall back dazzled at beholding myself all rosy
  red,
    At having, I myself, caused the sun to rise.
        Chantecler [1910], act II, sc. iii

Robert Falcon Scott
1868–1912

2   Had we lived, I should have had a tale to tell of
the hardihood, endurance, and courage of my companions which would have stirred the heart of every
Englishman. These rough notes and our dead bodies
must tell the tale.[1]
    *Diary of the Terra Nova Expedition to the
    Antarctic.[2] Message to the Public*

3   Every day we have been ready to start for our
depot *eleven miles* away, but outside the door of the
tent it remains a scene of whirling drift. I do not think
we can hope for any better things now. We shall stick
it out to the end, but we are getting weaker, of course,
and the end cannot be far.
    It seems a pity, but I do not think I can write more.

R. SCOTT

For God's sake look after our people.
    Ibid. Thursday, March 29, 1912 (last entry)

Luther Standing Bear[3]
1868–1939

4   Only to the white man was nature a "wilderness"
and only to him was the land "infested" with "wild"
animals and "savage" people. To us it was tame.
Earth was bountiful and we were surrounded with
the blessings of the Great Mystery. Not until the
hairy man from the east came and with brutal frenzy
heaped injustices upon us and the families that we
loved was it "wild" for us. When the very animals of
the forest began fleeing from his approach, then it
was that for us the "Wild West" began.
    Land of the Spotted Eagle [1933]

André Suarès
1868–1948

5   Heresy is the lifeblood of religions. It is faith that
begets heretics. There are no heresies in a dead religion.   *Péguy*

William Allen White
1868–1944

6   Tinhorn politicians.
        Emporia Gazette [October 25, 1901]

---

[1]Inscribed on the memorial to Captain Scott and his companions, Waterloo Place, London.
    [2]Found by searching party [November 1912]. First published
[1913] as *Scott's Last Expedition: Journals.*
    [3]Chief of the Oglala Tribe of the Sioux Nation.

7   All dressed up, with nowhere to go.
    *Of the Progressive party in 1916, after Theodore
    Roosevelt retired from presidential competition*

8   The talent of a meat-packer, the morals of a
moneychanger and the manners of an undertaker.
    *Obituary of Frank A. Munsey [December 23,
    1925]*

Laurence Binyon
1869–1943

9 They shall grow not old, as we that are left grow
  old:
  Age shall not weary them, nor the years condemn.
  At the going down of the sun and in the morning
  We will remember them.
                            For the Fallen, st. 4

Neville Chamberlain
1869–1940

10   For the second time in our history, a British Prime
Minister has returned from Germany bringing peace
with honor.[4] I believe it is peace for our time.[5]
. . . Go home and get a nice quiet sleep.
    *Address from 10 Downing Street, London
    [September 30, 1938], after returning from the
    Munich Conference*

11   Hitler has missed the bus.
    *Speech in the House of Commons [April 4,
    1940]*

Mohandas Karamchand [Mahatma] Gandhi[6]
1869–1948

12   Nonviolence is the first article of my faith. It is
also the last article of my creed.
    *Defense against charge of sedition [March 23,
    1922]*

13   The term *Satyagraha* was coined by me . . .
in order to distinguish it from the movement then
going on . . . under the name of Passive Resistance.
    Its root meaning is "holding on to truth," hence
"force of righteousness." I have also called it love
force or soul force. In the application of *Satyagraha,*
I discovered in the earliest stages that pursuit of truth
did not permit violence being inflicted on one's opponent, but that he must be weaned from error by patience and sympathy. For what appears truth to the
one may appear to be error to the other. And patience

---

[4]See John Russell, 406:6, and Disraeli, 435:14.
    [5]See *Book of Common Prayer (English),* 50:10.
    [6]Mahatma: Great Soul.

means self-suffering. So the doctrine came to mean vindication of truth, not by the infliction of suffering on the opponent, but on one's self.[1] *Ibid.*

1   Nonviolence and truth *(Satya)* are inseparable and presuppose one another. There is no god higher than truth.
True Patriotism: Some Sayings of Mahatma Gandhi [1939][2]

André Gide
1869–1951

2   Families, I hate you! Shut-in homes, closed doors, jealous possessions of happiness.[3]
Les Nourritures Terrestres (Fruits of the Earth) [1897], bk. IV

3   What another would have done as well as you, do not do it. What another would have said as well as you, do not say it; written as well, do not write it. Be faithful to that which exists nowhere but in yourself —and thus make yourself indispensable.
Ibid. Envoi

4   The most decisive actions of our life . . . are most often unconsidered actions.
Les Faux Monnayeurs (The Counterfeiters) [1926]

5   It is with noble sentiments that bad literature gets written.[4] *Letter to François Mauriac [1928]*

Strickland Gillilan
1869–1954

6 Bilin' down 's repoort, wuz Finnigin!
An' he writed this here: "Musther Flannigan—
Off agin, on agin,
Gone agin.—FINNIGIN."
Finnigin to Flannigan, st. 6

7 Adam
Had 'em.
Lines on the Antiquity of Microbes[5]

Stephen Butler Leacock
1869–1944

8   He flung himself from the room, flung himself upon his horse and rode madly off in all directions.
Nonsense Novels [1911]. Gertrude the Governess

1See Martin Luther King, 761:4.
2Edited by S. HOBHOUSE.
3Familles, je vous hais! foyers clos; portes refermées; possessions jalouses du bonheur.
4C'est avec de beaux sentiments qu'on fait de la mauvaise littérature.
5Said to be the shortest poem in the language.

9   The parent who could see his boy as he really is, would shake his head and say: "Willie is no good; I'll sell him."
Essays and Literary Studies [1916]. The Lot of the Schoolmaster

Edgar Lee Masters
1869–1950

10 All, all, are sleeping on the hill.
Spoon River Anthology [1915]. The Hill, refrain

11 Seeds in a dry pod, tick, tick, tick,
Tick, tick, tick, what little iambics,
While Homer and Whitman roared in the pines!
Ibid. Petit, the Poet

12 Degenerate sons and daughters,
Life is too strong for you—
It takes life to love life.
Ibid. Lucinda Matlock

13 Out of me unworthy and unknown
The vibrations of deathless music.
Ibid. Anne Rutledge

14 I am Anne Rutledge who sleep beneath these weeds,
Beloved in life of Abraham Lincoln.
Ibid.

Henri Matisse
1869–1954

15   I want to reach that state of condensation of sensations which constitutes a picture.
Notes d'un Peintre [1908]

16   What interests me most is neither still life nor landscape, but the human figure. It is through it that I best succeed in expressing the almost religious feeling I have towards life. *Ibid.*

William Vaughn Moody
1869–1910

17   Gigantic, willful, young,
Chicago sitteth at the northwest gates.
An Ode in Time of Hesitation [1901], st. 3

18   O ye who lead,
Take heed!
Blindness we may forgive, but baseness we will smite.
Ibid. st. 9

Edwin Arlington Robinson
1869–1935

19 I would have rid the earth of him
Once, in my pride.

I never knew the worth of him
Until he died.

An Old Story, st. 3

1 Life is the game that must be played.
Ballade by the Fire. Envoy

2 There is ruin and decay
In the House on the Hill:
They are all gone away,
There is nothing more to say.
The House on the Hill [1897], last stanza

3 Miniver Cheevy, child of scorn,
Grew lean while he assailed the seasons;
He wept that he was ever born,
And he had reasons.
Miniver Cheevy [1910], st. 1

4 Miniver Cheevy, born too late,
Scratched his head and kept on thinking;
Miniver coughed and called it fate,
And kept on drinking.

Ibid. st. 8

5 I shall have more to say when I am dead.
John Brown, last line

6 Here where the wind is always north-northeast
And children learn to walk on frozen toes.
New England, st. 1

7 He glittered when he walked.
Richard Cory, st. 2

8 So on we worked, and waited for the light,
And went without the meat, and cursed the bread;
And Richard Cory, one calm summer night,
Went home and put a bullet through his head.
Ibid. st. 4

William Strunk, Jr.
1869–1946

9   Omit needless words.
     Vigorous writing is concise. A sentence should
contain no unnecessary words, a paragraph no unnecessary sentences, for the same reason that a drawing should have no unnecessary lines and a machine
no unnecessary parts. This requires not that the
writer make all his sentences short, or that he avoid
all detail and treat his subjects only in outline, but
that every word tell.
The Elements of Style [1918], ch. 2, sec. 13

Booth Tarkington
1869–1946

10   There are two things that will be believed of any
man whatsoever, and one of them is that he has
taken to drink.   *Penrod [1914], ch. 10*

11   They were upon their great theme: "When I get
to be a man!" Being human, though boys, they con-

sidered their present estate too commonplace to be
dwelt upon. So, when the old men gather, they say:
"When I was a boy!" It really is the land of nowadays that we never discover.   *Ibid. 26*

Frank Lloyd Wright
1869–1959

12   No house should ever be *on* any hill or on anything. It should be *of* the hill, belonging to it, so hill
and house could live together each the happier for the
other.   *An Autobiography [1932]*

13   The physician can bury his mistakes, but the architect can only advise his client to plant vines.
New York Times Magazine [October 4, 1953]

Bernard Mannes Baruch
1870–1965

14   Behind the black portent of the new atomic age
lies a hope which, seized upon with faith, can work
out salvation. . . . Let us not deceive ourselves: we
must elect world peace or world destruction.
*Address to the United Nations Atomic Energy
Commission [June 14, 1946]*

15   We are in the midst of a cold war[1] which is getting warmer.
Speech before the Senate Committee [1948]

Hilaire Belloc
1870–1953

16 Child! do not throw this book about;
Refrain from the unholy pleasure
Of cutting all the pictures out!
Preserve it as your chiefest treasure.
A Bad Child's Book of Beasts [1896], dedication

17 When people call this beast to mind,
They marvel more and more
At such a little tail behind,
So large a trunk before.

Ibid. The Elephant

18 Whatever happens we have got
The Maxim Gun, and they have not.
The Modern Traveller [1898], VI

19 A smell of burning fills the startled air—
The Electrician is no longer there!
Newdigate Poem

20 How slow the shadow creeps: but when 'tis past
How fast the shadows fall. How fast! How fast!
For a Sundial

21 Of courtesy, it is much less
Than courage of heart or holiness,

[1]The phrase was first used by Baruch in 1947.

Yet in my walks it seems to me
That the Grace of God is in courtesy.

Courtesy

1 Do you remember an inn,
Miranda?

Tarantella

2 The chief defect of Henry King
Was chewing little bits of string.

Cautionary Tales [1907]. Henry King

3 Matilda told such dreadful lies,
It made one gasp and stretch one's eyes;
Her aunt, who, from her earliest youth,
Had kept a strict regard for truth,
Attempted to believe Matilda:
The effort very nearly killed her.

Ibid. Matilda

4 For every time she shouted "Fire!"
They only answered "Little liar!"
And therefore when her aunt returned,
Matilda, and the house, were burned.

Ibid.

5 Here richly, with ridiculous display,
The Politician's corpse was laid away.
While all of his acquaintance sneered and slanged
I wept: for I had longed to see him hanged.

Epitaph on the Politician Himself

6 I'm tired of Love: I'm still more tired of Rhyme.
But Money gives me pleasure all the time.

Fatigue

7 The Devil, having nothing else to do,
Went off to tempt My Lady Poltagrue.
My Lady, tempted by a private whim,
To his extreme annoyance, tempted him.

On Lady Poltagrue, a Public Peril

8 Of this bad world the loveliest and the best
Has smiled and said "Good Night," and gone to
  rest.

On a Dead Hostess

9 When I am dead, I hope it may be said:
"His sins were scarlet,[1] but his books were read."

On His Books

Benjamin Nathan Cardozo
1870–1938

10 What has once been settled by a precedent will
not be unsettled overnight, for certainty and uniformity are gains not lightly to be sacrificed.

The Paradoxes of Legal Science [1928]

11 As I search the archives of my memory, I seem to
discern six types or methods [of judicial writing]
which divide themselves from one another with
measurable distinctness. There is the type magiste-
rial or imperative; the type laconic or sententious;

the type conversational or homely; the type refined
or artificial, smelling of the lamp,[2] verging at times
upon preciosity or euphuism; the type demonstrative
or persuasive; and finally the type tonsorial or agglutinative, so called from the shears and the pastepot
which are its implements and emblem.

Law and Literature [1931]

12 [The Constitution] was framed upon the theory
that the peoples of the several states must sink or
swim together, and that in the long run prosperity
and salvation are in union and not division.

Baldwin v. Seelig, 294 U.S. 511, 523 [1935]

13 Freedom of expression is the matrix, the indispensable condition, of nearly every other form of
freedom.

Palko v. Connecticut, 302 U.S. 319, 327 [1937]

Lord Alfred Bruce Douglas
1870–1945

14 I am the Love that dare not speak its name.

Two Loves [1894]

Arthur J. Lamb
1870–1928

15 Her beauty was sold for an old man's gold,
She's a bird in a gilded cage.

A Bird in a Gilded Cage [1900]

Sir Harry Lauder
1870–1950

16 Oh, it's nice to get up in the mornin',
But it's nicer to lie in bed.

Song

17 Just a wee doch-an'-dorris
Before we gang awa' . . .
If y' can say
It's a braw brecht moonlecht necht,
Yer a' recht, that's a'.

Song

18 Roamin' in the gloamin'.

Song

19 I Love a Lassie.

Title of song

Vladimir Ilyich Lenin
[Vladimir Ilyich Ulyanov]
1870–1924

20 "The revolution's decisive victory over tsarism"
means the establishment of the *revolutionary-democratic dictatorship of the proletariat and the peasantry.*

Two Tactics of Social-Democracy [1905], ch. 6

[1]See *Isaiah 1:18, 25:29.*

[2]See Pytheas, 80:22.

1 We shall now proceed to construct the socialist order.
> *Speech at the Congress of Soviets [October 26, 1917]*[1]

2 Every cook has to learn how to govern the state.
> *Will the Bolsheviks Retain Government Power? [1917]*

3 The war is relentless: it puts the alternative in a ruthless relief: either to perish, or to catch up with the advanced countries and outdistance them, too, in economic matters.
> *The Impending Catastrophe and How to Fight It [1917]*

4 The suppression of the bourgeois state by the proletarian state is impossible without a violent revolution.　*The State and Revolution [1918], ch. 1*

5 So long as the state exists there is no freedom. When there is freedom, there will be no state.
> *Ibid. 5*

6 Communism is Soviet government plus the electrification of the whole country.
> *New External and Internal Position and the Problems of the Party [1920]*

7 It is true that liberty is precious—so precious that it must be rationed.
> *Attributed. Quoted by* SIDNEY AND BEATRICE WEBB, *Soviet Communism: A New Civilization? [1936], p. 1036*

Rosa Luxemburg
1870–1919

8 I hope to die at my post: in the streets or in prison.　*Letter from prison [c. 1917]*

9 Freedom is always freedom for the one who thinks differently.
> *The Russian Revolution [1922]*

Albert Jay Nock
1870–1945

10 As sheer casual reading matter, I still find the English dictionary the most interesting book in our language.
> *Memoirs of a Superfluous Man [1943], ch. 1, pt. 4*

11 All Souls College, Oxford, planned better than it knew when it limited the number of its undergraduates to four; four is exactly the right number for any college which is really intent on getting results.
> *Ibid. 3, 3*

12 Money does not pay for anything, never has, never will. It is an economic axiom as old as the hills that goods and services can be paid for only with goods and services.　*Ibid. 13, 3*

[1]Translated by MAX EASTMAN.

Roscoe Pound
1870–1964

13 The law must be stable, but it must not stand still.
> *Introduction to the Philosophy of Law [1922]*

Saki [Hector Hugh Munro]
1870–1916

14 The cook was a good cook, as cooks go; and as cooks go she went.
> *Reginald [1904]. Reginald on Besetting Sins*

15 Women and elephants never forget an injury.
> *Ibid.*

16 I might have been a goldfish in a glass bowl for all the privacy I got.
> *Ibid. The Innocence of Reginald*

17 The Western custom of one wife and hardly any mistresses.
> *Reginald in Russia [1910]. A Young Turkish Catastrophe*

18 Poverty keeps together more homes than it breaks up.　*The Chronicles of Clovis [1911]. Esmé*

19 Sredni Vashtar went forth,
His thoughts were red thoughts and his teeth were white.
His enemies called for peace, but he brought them death.
Sredni Vashtar the Beautiful.
> *Ibid. Sredni Vashtar*

20 The sacrifices of friendship were beautiful in her eyes as long as she was not asked to make them.
> *Beasts and Super-Beasts [1914]. Fur*

21 A little inaccuracy sometimes saves tons of explanation.
> *The Square Egg [1924]. Clovis on the Alleged Romance of Business*

T. Laurence Seibert
fl. 1900

22 Casey Jones! Orders in his hand.
Casey Jones! Mounted to the cabin,
Took his farewell journey to that promised land.
> *Casey Jones [1909]. Adapted from verses by* WALLACE SAUNDERS,[2] *set to music by* EDDIE NEWTON

[2]Of the many versions of this traditional ballad, the most familiar is printed in CARL SANDBURG, *The American Songbag* [1927]. It begins: Come all you rounders, for I want you to hear / The story of a brave engineer. / Casey Jones was the rounder's name, / On a big eight-wheeler of a mighty fame.

To the memory of the locomotive engineer whose name as "Casey Jones" became a part of folklore and the American language. "For I'm going to run till she leaves the rail—or make it on time with the southbound mail."—*Inscription on monument to* JOHN LUTHER JONES [1864–1900], *in Calvary Cemetery, Jackson, Tennessee*

Stephen Crane
1871–1900

1 They were going to look at war, the red animal —war, the blood-swollen god.
The Red Badge of Courage [1895], ch. 3

2 At times he regarded the wounded soldiers in an envious way. He conceived persons with torn bodies to be peculiarly happy. He wished that he, too, had a wound, a red badge of courage.   *Ibid. 9*

3 The red sun was pasted in the sky like a wafer.
Ibid.

4 He had fought like a pagan who defends his religion.   *Ibid. 17*

5 He had been to touch the great death, and found that, after all, it was but the great death. He was a man.   *Ibid. 24*

6 None of them knew the color of the sky.
The Open Boat [1897], first line

7 In the desert
I saw a creature, naked, bestial,
Who, squatting upon the ground,
Held his heart in his hands,
And ate of it.
I said, "Is it good, friend?"
"It is bitter—bitter," he answered;
"But I like it
"Because it is bitter,
"And because it is my heart."
The Black Riders [1895], III

8 Do not weep, maiden, for war is kind.
Because your lover threw wild hands toward the sky
And the affrighted steed ran on alone,
Do not weep.
War is kind.
War Is Kind [1899]. War Is Kind, st. 1

9 A man said to the universe:
"Sir, I exist!"
"However," replied the universe,
"The fact has not created in me
A sense of obligation."
Ibid. Fragment

William Henry Davies
1871–1940

10 What is this life if, full of care,
We have no time to stand and stare?
Leisure

Theodore Dreiser
1871–1945

11 Our civilization is still in a middle stage, scarcely beast, in that it is no longer wholly guided by instinct; scarcely human, in that it is not yet wholly guided by reason.   *Sister Carrie [1900]*

12 In your rocking chair by your window shall you dream such happiness as you may never feel.
Ibid. 50

13 I acknowledge the Furies, I believe in them, I have heard the disastrous beating of their wings.
To Grant Richards [1911]

14 An American Tragedy.   *Title of novel [1925]*

15 Oh, the moonlight's fair tonight along the Wabash,
From the fields there comes the breath of new-mown hay;
Through the sycamores the candle lights are gleaming
On the banks of the Wabash, far away.
On the Banks of the Wabash, chorus[1]

Arthur Guiterman
1871–1943

16 Amoebas at the start
Were not complex;
They tore themselves apart
And started Sex.
Sex, st. 1

17 Of all cold words of tongue or pen
The worst are these: "I knew him when—"[2]
Prophets in Their Own Country

Ralph Hodgson
1871–1962

18 'Twould ring the bells of Heaven
The wildest peal for years,
If Parson lost his senses
And people came to theirs,
And he and they together
Knelt down with angry prayers
For tamed and shabby tigers
And dancing dogs and bears,
And wretched, blind pit ponies,
And little hunted hares.
The Bells of Heaven

19 Time, you old gypsy man,
Will you not stay,
Put up your caravan
Just for one day?
Time, You Old Gypsy Man, st. 1

20 Oh, had our simple Eve
Seen through the make-believe!
Had she but known the
Pretender he was!
Eve, st. 5

---

[1]Written by Dreiser but credited to his songwriter brother, PAUL DRESSER (1857–1906).
[2]See Whittier, 443:8.

1 How they all pitied
Poor motherless Eve!

Eve, st. 7

2 I saw in vision
The worm in the wheat,
And in the shops nothing
For people to eat;
Nothing for sale in
Stupidity Street.

Stupidity Street, st. 2

James Weldon Johnson
1871–1938

3 We have come over a way that with tears has
been watered,
We have come, treading our path through the
blood of the slaughtered.

Lift Every Voice and Sing [1900], st. 2

4 The colored people of this country know and
understand the white people better than the white
people know and understand them.

*The Autobiography of an Ex-Colored Man
[1912], ch. 2*

5 Every race and every nation should be judged by
the best it has been able to produce, not by the
worst.

Ibid. 10

6 O black and unknown bards of long ago,
How came your lips to touch the sacred fire?
How, in your darkness, did you come to know
The power and beauty of the minstrels' lyre?

O Black and Unknown Bards [1917], st. 1

7 And God stepped out on space,
And He looked around and said,
"I'm lonely—
I'll make me a world."

God's Trombones [1927]. The Creation, st. 1

8 With His head in His hands,
God thought and thought,
Till He thought: I'll make me a man!

Ibid. st. 10

9 Find Sister Caroline . . .
And she's tired—
She's weary—
Go down, Death, and bring her to me.

Ibid. Go Down, Death, st. 5

10 It is from the blues that all that may be called
American music derives its most distinctive characteristic.   *Black Manhattan [1930], ch. 11*

Herbert George Ponting
1871–1935

11 On the outside grows the furside, on the inside
grows the skinside;

So the furside is the outside, and the skinside is
the inside.[1]

The Sleeping Bag[2]

Marcel Proust
1871–1922

12 For a long time I used to go to bed early.[3]
Remembrance of Things Past [1913–1927].[4]
Swann's Way, opening line

13 Once I had recognized the taste of the crumb of
madeleine soaked in her decoction of lime flowers
which my aunt used to give me . . . immediately
the old gray house upon the street, where her room
was, rose up like the scenery of a theater.   *Ibid.*

14 In his younger days a man dreams of possessing
the heart of the woman whom he loves; later, the
feeling that he possesses the heart of a woman may
be enough to make him fall in love with her.

Ibid.

15 What artists call posterity is the posterity of the
work of art.   *Ibid. Within a Budding Grove, pt. I*

16 Not only does one not retain all at once the truly
rare works, but even within such works it is the least
precious parts that one perceives first. Less deceptive
than life, these great masterpieces do not give us
their best at the beginning.   *Ibid.*

17 The time which we have at our disposal every day
is elastic; the passions that we feel expand it, those
that we inspire contract it; and habit fills up what
remains.   *Ibid.*

18 All the great things we know have come to us
from neurotics. It is they and only they who have
founded religions and created great works of art.

*Ibid. The Guermantes Way. My Grandmother's
Illness*

19 Like everybody who is not in love, he imagined
that one chose the person whom one loved after
endless deliberations and on the strength of various
qualities and advantages.

Ibid. Cities of the Plain, pt. I

20 They buried him, but all through the night of
mourning, in the lighted windows, his books arranged three by three kept watch like angels with
outspread wings and seemed, for him who was no
more, the symbol of his resurrection.

Ibid. The Captive, pt. I

[1]He, to get the cold side outside, / Put the warm side fur side
inside. / That's why he put the fur side inside, / Why he put the
skin side outside, / Why he turned them inside outside.—
Anonymous, The Modern Hiawatha
[2]For the *South Polar Times,* Midwinter Day [June 22, 1911],
prepared by the men of Captain Robert Falcon Scott's last
Antarctic expedition. Ponting was the photographer for the
Scott expedition.
[3]*Longtemps je me suis couché de bonne heure.*
[4]*À la Recherche du Temps Perdu,* translated by C. K. Scott
Montcrieff, except the last volume, *The Past Recaptured,*
translated by Frederick A. Blossom.

1   The bonds that unite another person to ourself exist only in our mind. Memory as it grows fainter relaxes them, and notwithstanding the illusion by which we would fain be cheated and with which, out of love, friendship, politeness, deference, duty, we cheat other people, we exist alone. Man is the creature that cannot emerge from himself, that knows his fellows only in himself; when he asserts the contrary, he is lying.   *Ibid. The Sweet Cheat Gone*

2   There is not a woman in the world the possession of whom is as precious as that of the truths which she reveals to us by causing us to suffer.   *Ibid.*

3   We are healed of a suffering only by experiencing it to the full.   *Ibid.*

4   Happiness is beneficial for the body but it is grief that develops the powers of the mind.
      Ibid. The Past Recaptured

5   Only through art can we get outside of ourselves and know another's view of the universe which is not the same as ours and see landscapes which would otherwise have remained unknown to us like the landscapes of the moon. Thanks to art, instead of seeing a single world, our own, we see it multiply until we have before us as many worlds as there are original artists.
      The Maxims of Marcel Proust [1948][1]

Ernest Rutherford
1871–1937

6   We cannot control atomic energy to an extent which would be of any value commercially, and I believe we are not likely ever to be able to do so.
      Speech to the British Association for the Advancement of Science [1933]

John Millington Synge
1871–1909

7   What is the price of a thousand horses against a son where there is one son only?
      Riders to the Sea [1904]

8   When I was writing *The Shadow of the Glen* . . . I got more aid than any learning could have given me from a chink in the floor of the old Wicklow house where I was staying, that let me hear what was being said by the servant girls in the kitchen.
      The Playboy of the Western World [1907], preface

9   May I meet him with one tooth and it aching, and one eye to be seeing seven and seventy divils in the twists of the road, and one old timber leg on him to limp into the scalding grave. There he is now cross-ing the strands, and that the Lord God would send a high wave to wash him from the world.[2]
      Ibid. act II

10   Oh my grief, I've lost him surely. I've lost the only Playboy of the Western World.
      Ibid. III, curtain line

11   A man who is not afraid of the sea will soon be drowned, he said, for he will be going out on a day he shouldn't. But we do be afraid of the sea, and we do only be drownded now and again.
      The Aran Islands [1907]

12   There is no language like the Irish for soothing and quieting.   *Ibid.*

13   A translation is no translation, he said, unless it will give you the music of a poem along with the words of it.   *Ibid.*

Paul Valéry
1871–1945

14   The folly of mistaking a paradox for a discovery, a metaphor for a proof, a torrent of verbiage for a spring of capital truths, and oneself for an oracle, is inborn in us.
      Introduction to the Method of Leonardo da Vinci [1895][3]

15   Collect all the facts that can be collected about the life of Racine and you will never learn from them the art of his verse. All criticism is dominated by the outworn theory that the man is the cause of the work as in the eyes of the law the criminal is the cause of the crime. Far rather are they both the effects.   *Ibid.*

16   The sea, the ever renewing sea![4]
      Charmes [1922]. Le Cimetière Marin

17   The wind is rising . . . we must attempt to live.[5]
      Ibid.

18   Poetry is simply literature reduced to the essence of its active principle. It is purged of idols of every kind, of realistic illusions, of any conceivable equivocation between the language of "truth" and the language of "creation."   *Littérature [1930]*

19   An intelligent woman is a woman with whom one can be as stupid as one wants.
      Mauvaises Pensées et Autres [1941]

---

[1]Edited and translated by JUSTIN O'BRIEN.

[2]May the grass grow at your door and the fox build his nest on your hearthstone. May the light fade from your eyes, so you never see what you love. May your own blood rise against you, and the sweetest drink you take be the bitterest cup of sorrow. May you die without benefit of clergy; may there be none to shed a tear at your grave, and may the hearthstone of hell be your best bed forever.— *Traditional Wexford curse*

[3]Translated by THOMAS MCGREEVY.

[4]La mer, la mer toujours recommencée!

[5]Le vent se lève . . . il faut tenter de vivre.

1   That which has always been accepted by everyone, everywhere, is almost certain to be false.
Tel Quel [1943]

2   God created man, and finding him not sufficiently alone, gave him a female companion so that he might feel his solitude more acutely.   *Ibid.*

3   A poem is never finished, only abandoned.
From W. H. AUDEN, A Certain World [1970]

Sir Norman Angell
1872–1967

4   The Great Illusion.
Title of book [1910] on the futility of war

Sir Max Beerbohm
1872–1956

5   Most women are not so young as they are painted.   *A Defense of Cosmetics*

6   To give an accurate and exhaustive account of that period would need a far less brilliant pen than mine.   *Eighteen Eighty [1895]*

7   Zuleika, on a desert island, would have spent most of her time in looking for a man's footprint.
Zuleika Dobson [1911], ch. 2

8   She was one of the people who say: "I don't know anything about music really, but I know what I like."   *Ibid. 9*

9   Of all the objects of hatred, a woman once loved is the most hateful.   *Ibid. 13*

10   The Socratic manner is not a game at which two can play. Please answer my question, to the best of your ability.   *Ibid. 15*

11   I have known no man of genius who had not to pay, in some affliction or defect either physical or spiritual, for what the gods had given him.
No. 2. The Pines

12   To say that a man is vain means merely that he is pleased with the effect he produces on other people. A conceited man is satisfied with the effect he produces on himself.   *Quia Imperfectum*

13   Strange, when you come to think of it, that of all the countless folk who have lived before our time on this planet not one is known in history or in legend as having died of laughter.   *Laughter*

Léon Blum
1872–1950

14   Life does not give itself to one who tries to keep all its advantages at once. I have often thought morality may perhaps consist solely in the courage of making a choice.   *On Marriage*

Patrick Reginald Chalmers
1872–1942

15   What's lost upon the roundabouts we pulls up on the swings!
Roundabouts and Swings, st. 2

Calvin Coolidge
1872–1933

16   There is no right to strike against the public safety by anybody, anywhere, any time.
Telegram to Samuel Gompers, president of the American Federation of Labor, on the Boston police strike [September 14, 1919]

17   The chief business of the American people is business.
Speech to the American Society of Newspaper Editors [January 17, 1925]

18   I do not choose to run for President in 1928.[1]
Statement to reporters [August 2, 1927]

19   He said he was against it.
On being asked what a clergyman preaching on sin had said

20   They hired the money, didn't they?
Attributed. Comment on European war debts [1925]

21   When a great many people are unable to find work, unemployment results.   *Attributed*

Edward Gordon Craig
1872–1966

22   That is what the title of artist means: one who perceives more than his fellows, and who records more than he has seen.
On the Art of the Theatre [1911]

Sergei Pavlovich Diaghilev
1872–1929

23   Astound me! I'll wait for you to astound me.
To Jean Cocteau [1912]. From FRANCIS STEEGMULLER, Cocteau [1970]

Paul Laurence Dunbar
1872–1906

24   It is not a carol of joy or glee,
But a prayer that he sends from his heart's deep core . . .
I know why the caged bird sings!
Sympathy [1899], st. 3

[1]See Will Rogers, 638:4.

1 Since thou[1] and those who died with thee for right
Have died, the Present teaches, but in vain!
Robert Gould Shaw, st. 2

2 It's easy 'nough to titter w'en de stew is smokin'
hot,
But hit's mighty ha'd to giggle w'en dey's nuffin'
in de pot.
Philosophy

Learned Hand
1872–1961

3   This much I think I do know—that a society so riven that the spirit of moderation is gone, no court *can* save; that a society where that spirit flourishes, no court *need* save; that in a society which evades its responsibility by thrusting upon the courts the nurture of that spirit, that spirit in the end will perish.
The Contribution of an Independent Judiciary to Civilization [1942]

4   "I beseech ye in the bowels of Christ, think that ye may be mistaken."[2] I should like to have that written over the portals of every church, every school, and every courthouse, and, may I say, of every legislative body in the United States. I should like to have every court begin, "I beseech ye in the bowels of Christ, think that we may be mistaken."
Morals in Public Life [1951]

5   I had rather take my chance that some traitors will escape detection than spread abroad a spirit of general suspicion and distrust, which accepts rumor and gossip in place of undismayed and unintimidated inquiry.
Speech to the Board of Regents, University of the State of New York [October 24, 1952]

6   That community is already in the process of dissolution where each man begins to eye his neighbor as a possible enemy, where nonconformity with the accepted creed, political as well as religious, is a mark of disaffection; where denunciation, without specification or backing, takes the place of evidence; where orthodoxy chokes freedom of dissent; where faith in the eventual supremacy of reason has become so timid that we dare not enter our convictions in the open lists, to win or lose. *Ibid.*

John McCrae
1872–1918

7 In Flanders fields the poppies blow
Between the crosses, row on row.
In Flanders Fields [1915], st. 1

8 To you from failing hands we throw
The torch; be yours to hold it high.
Ibid. st. 3

Bertrand Russell, Earl Russell
1872–1970

9   Mathematics may be defined as the subject in which we never know what we are talking about, nor whether what we are saying is true.
Recent Work on the Principles of Mathematics [1901]. In International Monthly, vol. 4, p. 84

10   Mathematics, rightly viewed, possesses not only truth, but supreme beauty—a beauty cold and austere, like that of sculpture, without appeal to any part of our weaker nature, without the gorgeous trappings of painting or music, yet sublimely pure, and capable of a stern perfection such as only the greatest art can show.
The Study of Mathematics [1902]

11   Mathematics takes us still further from what is human, into the region of absolute necessity, to which not only the actual world, but every possible world, must conform. *Ibid.*

12   It is undesirable to believe a proposition when there is no ground whatever for supposing it to be true. *Skeptical Essays [1928], ch. 1*

13   The psychology of adultery has been falsified by conventional morals, which assume, in monogamous countries, that attraction to one person cannot coexist with a serious affection for another. Everybody knows that this is untrue.
Marriage and Morals [1929], ch. 16

14   Fear is the main source of superstition, and one of the main sources of cruelty. To conquer fear is the beginning of wisdom.
An Outline of Intellectual Rubbish [1950]

15   Three passions, simple but overwhelmingly strong, have governed my life: the longing for love, the search for knowledge, and unbearable pity for the suffering of mankind.
Autobiography [1967], prologue

Ellery Sedgwick
1872–1960

16   Autobiographies ought to begin with Chapter Two. *The Happy Profession [1946], ch. 1*

17   In America, getting on in the world means getting out of the world we have known before. *Ibid.*

Carl Lotus Becker
1873–1945

18   Economic distress will teach men, if anything can, that realities are less dangerous than fancies, that fact-finding is more effective than fault-finding.
Progress and Power [1935]

---

[1]Colonel Robert Gould Shaw, white commander of the 54th Massachusetts regiment (first enlisted black regiment in the Civil War), died with many others of the regiment at Fort Wagner [July 18, 1863].
See Charles W. Eliot, 522:13, and Robert Lowell, 743:10.
[2]See Cromwell, 247:1.

1   The significance of man is that he is that part of the universe that asks the question, What is the significance of Man? He alone can stand apart imaginatively and, regarding himself and the universe in their eternal aspects, pronounce a judgment: The significance of man is that he is insignificant and is aware of it.   *Progress and Power*

George Bennard
1873–1958

2 I will cling to the old rugged cross,
And exchange it some day for a crown.[1]
            The Old Rugged Cross [1913], refrain

Willa Sibert Cather
1873–1947

3   No one can build his security upon the nobleness of another person.
            Alexander's Bridge [1912], ch. 8

4   There are only two or three human stories, and they go on repeating themselves as fiercely as if they had never happened before.
            O Pioneers! [1913], pt. II, ch. 4

5   The history of every country begins in the heart of a man or a woman.   *Ibid.*

6   I like trees because they seem more resigned to the way they have to live than other things do.
            Ibid. 8

7   I tell you there is such a thing as creative hate!
            The Song of the Lark [1915], pt. I

8   If there was a road I could not make it out in the faint starlight. There was nothing but land: not a country at all, but the material out of which countries are made.   *My Ántonia [1918], bk I, ch. 1*

9   That is happiness; to be dissolved into something complete and great.[2]   *Ibid. 2*

10   Winter lies too long in country towns; hangs on until it is stale and shabby, old and sullen.
            Ibid. II, 7

11   In New Mexico he always awoke a young man; not until he rose and began to shave did he realize that he was growing older. His first consciousness was a sense of the light dry wind blowing in through the windows, with the fragrance of hot sun and sagebrush and sweet clover; a wind that made one's body feel light and one's heart cry "To-day, to-day," like a child's.
            Death Comes for the Archbishop [1927], bk. IX, ch. 3

[1]See *Matthew 10*:38, 34:35; Quarles, 242:6; and Penn, 282:-17.
[2]Inscribed on Willa Cather's gravestone in Jaffrey, New Hampshire.

12   Only solitary men know the full joys of friendship. Others have their family; but to a solitary and an exile his friends are everything.
            Shadows on the Rock [1931], bk. III, ch. 5

Arthur Chapman
1873–1935

13 Out where the handclasp's a little stronger,
Out where the smile dwells a little longer,
  That's where the West begins.
            Out Where the West Begins, st. 1

Colette [Sidonie Gabrielle Colette]
1873–1954

14   Those pleasures so lightly called physical.
            Mélanges

15   Whether you are dealing with an animal or a child, to convince is to weaken.
            Le Pur et l'Impur [1932]

16   It was towards the end of June that incompatibility became established between them like a new season of the year.   *The Cat [1933], ch. 7*

17   One of the best things about love is just recognizing a man's step when he climbs the stairs.
            Occupation [1941][3]

18   The three great stumbling blocks in a girl's education . . . *homard a l'Américaine*, a boiled egg, and asparagus.   *Gigi [1942]*

19   The day after that wedding night I found that a distance of a thousand miles, abyss and discovery and irremediable metamorphosis, separated me from the day before.   *Noces [1945]*

Walter de la Mare
1873–1956

20 Slowly, silently, now the moon
Walks the night in her silver shoon.
                    Silver

21 Here lies a most beautiful lady,
Light of step and heart was she;
I think she was the most beautiful lady
That ever was in the West Country.
                    An Epitaph

22 "Is there anybody there?" said the Traveler,
Knocking on the moonlit door;
And his horse in the silence champed the grasses
Of the forest's ferny floor.
                    The Listeners

23 "Tell them that I came, and no one answered,
That I kept my word," he said.
                    Ibid.

[3]Translated by DAVID LE VAY.

1 Look thy last on all things lovely,
  Every hour—let no night
  Seal thy sense in deathly slumber
  Till to delight
  Thou hast paid thy utmost blessing.
  Fare Well [1918], st. 3

2 Nought but vast sorrow was there—
  The sweet cheat gone.
  The Ghost

3 Who said "Peacock Pie"?
  The old king to the sparrow:
  Who said "Crops are ripe"?
  Rust to the harrow.
  The Song of the Mad Prince

4 Poor Jim Jay
  Got stuck fast
  In Yesterday.
  Jim Jay

5 It's a very odd thing—
  As odd as can be—
  That whatever Miss T. eats
  Turns into Miss T.
  Miss T.

6 Bang! Now the animal
  Is dead and dumb and done.
  Nevermore to peep again, creep again, leap
    again,
  Eat or sleep or drink again, oh, what fun!
  Hi!

Mark Fenderson
1873–1944

7 What's the use? Yesterday an egg, tomorrow a feather duster.
  Caption for cartoon: The Dejected Rooster

Ford Madox [Hueffer] Ford
1873–1939

8 A fervent young admirer exclaimed: "By Jove, the Good Soldier is the finest novel in the English language!" whereupon my friend John Rodker, who has always had a properly tempered admiration for my work, remarked in his clear, slow drawl: "Ah, yes. It is, but you have left out a word. It is the finest French novel in the English language!"
  The Good Soldier [1915]. Dedicatory letter

9 This is the saddest story I have ever heard.
  Ibid. first line

10 Only two classes of books are of universal appeal: the very best and the very worst.
  Joseph Conrad [1924]

11 No more Hope, no more Glory, no more parades for you and me. . . . Na poo, finny![1]
  No More Parades [1925]

Lena Guilbert Ford
d. 1918

12 Keep the home fires burning,[2]
  While your hearts are yearning;
  Though your lads are far away
  They dream of home.
  There's a silver lining
  Through the dark cloud shining;
  Turn the dark cloud inside out,
  Till the boys come home.
  Keep the Home Fires Burning [1915]

Ellen Glasgow
1873–1945

13 No idea is so antiquated that it was not once modern. No idea is so modern that it will not someday be antiquated.
  Address to the Modern Language Association [1936]

14 Preserve, within a wild sanctuary, an inaccessible valley of reveries.   *A Certain Measure [1943]*

William Christopher Handy
1873–1958

15 I hate to see the evenin' sun go down.
  The St. Louis Blues [1914]

Otto Harbach
1873–1963

16 When a lovely flame dies,
  Smoke gets in your eyes.
  Roberta [1933].[3] Smoke Gets In Your Eyes

George Edward Moore
1873–1958

17 It appears to me that in Ethics, as in all other philosophical studies, the difficulties and disagreements, of which history is full, are mainly due to a very simple cause: namely to the attempt to answer questions, without first discovering precisely *what* question it is which you desire to answer.
  Principia Ethica [1903], preface

---

[1] World War I slang version of Il n'y a plus, fini.
[2] First line attributed to IVOR NOVELLO [1893–1951], who composed the music.
[3] Music by JEROME KERN.

Charles Péguy
1873–1914

1   Surrender is essentially an operation by means of which we set about explaining instead of acting.
Les Cahiers de la Quinzaine [1905]

2   Homer is new and fresh this morning, and nothing, perhaps, is as old and tired as today's newspaper.[1]
Note sur M. Bergson et la Philosophie Bergsonienne [1914]

3   Freedom is a system based on courage.
From HALÉVY, Life of Charles Péguy

Sime Silverman
1873–1933

4   Wall St. Lays an Egg.
Headline announcing stock market crash, Variety [October 30, 1929]

Alfred Emanuel Smith[2]
1873–1944

5   The kiss of death.
Alluding to Hearst's support of Ogden Mills, Smith's unsuccessful opponent for governor of New York State [1926]

6   Let's look at the record.
Campaign speeches [1928]

7   The Governor of New York State does not have to be an acrobat.
Speech in behalf of Franklin D. Roosevelt [1928]

8   Nobody shoots at Santa Claus.
Campaign speeches [1936]

9   No matter how thin you slice it, it's still baloney.
Ibid.

Henry Major Tomlinson
1873–1958

10   The sea is at its best at London, near midnight, when you are within the arms of a capacious chair, before a glowing fire, selecting phases of the voyages you will never make.
The Sea and the Jungle [1912]

11   As to the sea itself, love it you cannot. Why should you? I will never believe again the sea was ever loved by anyone whose life was married to it. It is the creation of Omnipotence, which is not of humankind and understandable, and so the springs of its behavior are hidden.
Ibid.

[1] Homère est nouveau ce matin, et rien n'est peut-être aussi vieux que le journal d'aujourd'hui.

[2] He is the Happy Warrior of the political battlefield.— FRANKLIN D. ROOSEVELT, *nominating speech, Democratic National Convention* [June 26, 1924]. See Wordsworth, 376:8.

Maurice Baring
1874–1945

12   All theories of what a good play is, or how a good play should be written, are futile. A good play is a play which when acted upon the boards makes an audience interested and pleased. A play that fails in this is a bad play.
Have You Anything to Declare?

Charles Austin Beard
1874–1948
and
Mary Ritter Beard
1876–1958

13   At no time, at no place, in solemn convention assembled, through no chosen agents, had the American people officially proclaimed the United States to be a democracy. The Constitution did not contain the word or any word lending countenance to it, except possibly the mention of "We, the people," in the preamble . . . When the Constitution was framed no respectable person called himself or herself a democrat.
America in Midpassage [1939], ch. 17

Arthur Henry Reginald Buller
1874–1944

14   There was a young lady named Bright,
Whose speed was far faster than light;
    She set out one day
    In a relative way,
And returned home the previous night.
Limerick. In Punch [December 19, 1923]

Gilbert Keith Chesterton
1874–1936

15   The Christian ideal has not been tried and found wanting. It has been found difficult; and left untried.
What's Wrong with the World [1910], pt. I, ch. 5

16   Nothing sublimely artistic has ever arisen out of mere art, any more than anything essentially reasonable has ever arisen out of pure reason. There must always be a rich moral soil for any great aesthetic growth.
A Defense of Nonsense [1911]

17   For the great Gaels of Ireland
Are the men that God made mad,
For all their wars are merry,
And all their songs are sad.
The Ballad of the White Horse [1911], bk. II

18   The whole difference between construction and creation is exactly this: that a thing constructed can

only be loved after it is constructed; but a thing created is loved before it exists.

Preface to DICKENS, *Pickwick Papers*

1   A good joke is the one ultimate and sacred thing which cannot be criticized. Our relations with a good joke are direct and even divine relations.

Ibid.

2 Strong gongs groaning as the guns boom far
(Don John of Austria is going to the war);
Stiff flags straining in the night blasts cold
In the gloom black-purple, in the glint old gold;
Torchlight crimson on the copper kettledrums,
Then the tuckets, then the trumpets, then the
    cannon, and he comes.

Lepanto [1915]

3 Cervantes on his galley sets the sword back in the
    sheath
(Don John of Austria rides homeward with a
    wreath).
And he sees across a weary land a straggling road
    in Spain,
Up which a lean and foolish knight forever rides
    in vain.

Ibid.

4 To an open house in the evening
Home shall men come,
To an older place than Eden
And a taller town than Rome.

The House of Christmas

5 Burn from my brain and from my breast
Sloth, and the cowardice that clings,
And stiffness and the soul's arrest:
And feed my brain with better things.

A Ballade of a Book Reviewer

6 St. George he was for England,
And before he killed the dragon
He drank a pint of English ale
Out of an English flagon.

The Englishman

7 Step softly, under snow or rain,
To find the place where men can pray;
The way is all so very plain
That we may lose the way.

The Wise Men

8 And Noah he often said to his wife when he sat
    down to dine,
"I don't care where the water goes if it doesn't get
    into the wine."

Wine and Water

9 Fools! For I also had my hour;
One far fierce hour and sweet:
There was a shout about my ears,
And palms before my feet.

The Donkey

Sir Winston Spencer Churchill[1]
1874–1965

10   I pass with relief from the tossing sea of Cause and Theory to the firm ground of Result and Fact.

The Malakand Field Force [1898]

11   It is better to be making the news than taking it; to be an actor rather than a critic.   *Ibid.*

12   Nothing in life is so exhilarating as to be shot at without result.   *Ibid.*

13   There are men in the world who derive as stern an exaltation from the proximity of disaster and ruin, as others from success.   *Ibid.*

14   Terminological inexactitude.

Speech in the House of Commons [February 22, 1906]

15   The maxim of the British people is "Business as usual."

Speech at the Guildhall [November 9, 1914]

16   Politics are almost as exciting as war, and quite as dangerous. In war you can only be killed once, but in politics many times.   *Remark [1920]*

17   By being so long in the lowest form [at Harrow] I gained an immense advantage over the cleverer boys. . . . I got into my bones the essential structure of the ordinary British sentence — which is a noble thing. . . . Naturally I am biased in favor of boys learning English; I would make them all learn English: and then I would let the clever ones learn Latin as an honor, and Greek as a treat.

Roving Commission: My Early Life [1930]

18   It is a good thing for an uneducated man to read books of quotations. Bartlett's *Familiar Quotations* is an admirable work, and I studied it intently. The quotations when engraved upon the memory give you good thoughts. They also make you anxious to read the authors and look for more.   *Ibid.*

19   You will make all kinds of mistakes; but as long as you are generous and true, and also fierce, you cannot hurt the world or even seriously distress her. She was made to be wooed and won by youth.

Ibid.

20   Decided only to be undecided, resolved to be irresolute, adamant for drift, solid for fluidity, all-powerful to be impotent.[2]

While England Slept [1936]

21   Dictators ride to and fro upon tigers which they dare not dismount. And the tigers are getting hungry.[3]   *Ibid.*

22   I have watched this famous island descending incontinently, fecklessly, the stairway which leads to a dark gulf.   *Ibid.*

[1]See Roosevelt and Churchill, 650.
[2]Of Stanley Baldwin's policies.
[3]He who rides a tiger is afraid to dismount. — WILLIAM SCARBOROUGH [fl. c. 1875], *Chinese Proverbs [1875], no. 2082*

1   The German dictator, instead of snatching the victuals from the table, has been content to have them served to him course by course.
      Speech on the Munich agreement, House of Commons [October 5, 1938]

2   That long [Canadian] frontier from the Atlantic to the Pacific Oceans, guarded only by neighborly respect and honorable obligations, is an example to every country and a pattern for the future of the world.
      Speech in honor of R. B. Bennett, Canada Club, London [April 20, 1939]

3   I cannot forecast to you the action of Russia. It is a riddle wrapped in a mystery inside an enigma.
      Radio broadcast [October 1, 1939]

4   For each and for all, as for the Royal Navy, the watchword should be, "Carry on, and dread nought."
      Speech on traffic at sea, House of Commons [December 6, 1939]

5   I have nothing to offer but blood, toil, tears and sweat.[1]
      First Statement as Prime Minister, House of Commons [May 13, 1940]

6   Victory at all costs, victory in spite of all terror, victory however long and hard the road may be; for without victory there is no survival.   *Ibid.*

7   We shall not flag or fail. We shall go on to the end. We shall fight in France, we shall fight on the seas and oceans, we shall fight with growing confidence and growing strength in the air, we shall defend our island, whatever the cost may be, we shall fight on the beaches, we shall fight on the landing grounds, we shall fight in the fields and in the streets, we shall fight in the hills; we shall never surrender.
      Speech on Dunkirk, House of Commons [June 4, 1940]

8   Let us . . . brace ourselves to our duties, and so bear ourselves that if the British Empire and its Commonwealth last for a thousand years, men will still say: "This was their finest hour."
      Speech in the House of Commons [June 18, 1940]

9   We shall defend every village, every town and every city. The vast mass of London itself, fought

[1]Mollify it with thy tears, or sweat, or blood.—DONNE, *An Anatomy of the World* [1611], *I, 430–431*
     Year after year they voted cent per cent, / Blood, sweat, and tear-wrung millions—why? for rent!—BYRON, *The Age of Bronze* [1823], *XIV*
     Their sweat, their tears, their blood bedewed the endless plain.— *The Unknown War* [1931], referring to the armies of the czar before the Russian Revolution
     Churchill alluded to his promise of blood, toil, tears, and sweat in subsequent speeches on October 8, 1940, May 7 and December 2, 1941, and January 27 and November 10, 1942.

street by street, could easily devour an entire hostile army; and we would rather see London laid in ruins and ashes than that it should be tamely and abjectly enslaved.   *Radio broadcast [July 14, 1940]*

10   Never in the field of human conflict was so much owed by so many to so few.
      Tribute to the Royal Air Force, House of Commons [August 20, 1940]

11   The British Empire and the United States will have to be somewhat mixed up together in some of their affairs for mutual and general advantage. For my own part, looking out upon the future, I do not view the process with any misgivings.   *Ibid.*

12   Death and sorrow will be the companions of our journey; hardship our garment; constancy and valor our only shield. We must be united, we must be undaunted, we must be inflexible.
      Report on the war, House of Commons [October 8, 1940]

13   We are waiting for the long-promised invasion. So are the fishes.
      Radio broadcast to the French people [October 21, 1940]

14   I do not at all resent criticism, even when, for the sake of emphasis, it for a time parts company with reality.
      Speech in the House of Commons [January 22, 1941]

15   Here is the answer which I will give to President Roosevelt. . . . Give us the tools, and we will finish the job.   *Radio broadcast [February 9, 1941]*

16   This is one of those cases in which the imagination is baffled by the facts.
      Remark in the House of Commons following the parachute descent in Scotland of Rudolf Hess [May 13, 1941]

17   The British nation is unique in this respect. They are the only people who like to be told how bad things are, who like to be told the worst.
      Report on the war, House of Commons [June 10, 1941]

18   A vile race of quislings[2]—to use the new word which will carry the scorn of mankind down the centuries.
      Speech at St. James's Palace, London [June 12, 1941]

19   The destiny of mankind is not decided by material computation. When great causes are on the move in the world . . . we learn that we are spirits, not animals, and that something is going on in space

[2]Vidkun Quisling, head of the Nasjonal Samling party in Norway, who cooperated and collaborated with the Nazis when Germany invaded Norway [April 9, 1940]. Quisling was executed [October 23, 1945].

and time, and beyond space and time, which, whether we like it or not, spells duty.
> *Radio broadcast to America on receiving the honorary degree of Doctor of Laws from the University of Rochester, New York [June 16, 1941]*

1   Hitler is a monster of wickedness, insatiable in his lust for blood and plunder. Not content with having all Europe under his heel, or else terrorized into various forms of abject submission, he must now carry his work of butchery and desolation among the vast multitudes of Russia and of Asia. . . . So now this bloodthirsty guttersnipe must launch his mechanized armies upon new fields of slaughter, pillage and devastation.
> *Radio broadcast on the German invasion of Russia [June 22, 1941]*

2   We will have no truce or parley with you [Hitler], or the grisly gang who work your wicked will. You do your worst—and we will do our best.
> *Speech to the London County Council [July 14, 1941]*

3   The V sign is the symbol of the unconquerable will of the occupied territories, and a portent of the fate awaiting the Nazi tyranny.
> *Message to the people of Europe on launching the V for Victory propaganda campaign [July 20, 1941]*

4   Nothing is more dangerous in wartime than to live in the temperamental atmosphere of a Gallup Poll,[1] always feeling one's pulse and taking one's temperature.
> *Report on the war, House of Commons [September 30, 1941]*

5   Never give in, never give in, never, never, never—in nothing, great or small, large or petty—never give in except to convictions of honor and good sense.[2]
> *Address at Harrow School [October 29, 1941]*

6   Do not let us speak of darker days; let us speak rather of sterner days. These are not dark days: these are great days—the greatest days our country has ever lived; and we must all thank God that we have been allowed, each of us according to our stations, to play a part in making these days memorable in the history of our race.
> *Ibid.*

7   In the past we have had a light which flickered, in the present we have a light which flames, and in the future there will be a light which shines over all the land and sea.
> *Speech on war with Japan, House of Commons [December 8, 1941]*

8   What kind of people do they [the Japanese] think we are?
> *Speech to the U.S. Congress [December 26, 1941]*

9   We have not journeyed all this way across the centuries, across the oceans, across the mountains, across the prairies, because we are made of sugar candy.
> *Speech to the Canadian Senate and House of Commons, Ottawa [December 30, 1941]*

10   When I warned [the French] that Britain would fight on alone whatever they did, their generals told their prime minister and his divided cabinet, "In three weeks England will have her neck wrung like a chicken." Some chicken; some neck.
> *Ibid.*

11   The late M. Venizelos[3] observed that in all her wars England—he should have said Britain, of course—always wins one battle—the last.
> *Speech at the Lord Mayor's Day Luncheon, London [November 10, 1942]*

12   Now this is not the end. It is not even the beginning of the end.[4] But it is, perhaps, the end of the beginning.
> *Ibid.*

13   I have not become the King's First Minister in order to preside over the liquidation of the British Empire.
> *Ibid.*

14   The soft underbelly of the Axis.
> *Report on the war, House of Commons [November 11, 1942]*

15   There was a man who sold a hyena skin while the beast still lived and who was killed in hunting it.
> *Speech on Allied war gains, House of Commons [August 2, 1944]*

16   "Not in vain" may be the pride of those who have survived and the epitaph of those who fell.[5]
> *Speech in the House of Commons [September 28, 1944]*

17   The United States is a land of free speech. Nowhere is speech freer—not even here where we sedulously cultivate it even in its most repulsive form.
> *Ibid.*

18   He [President Franklin D. Roosevelt] died in harness, and we may well say in battle harness, like his soldiers, sailors, and airmen, who side by side with

---

[1]Dr. George H. Gallup founded the British Institute of Public Opinion in 1936.

[2]See Shakespeare, 211:19, and William Pitt, 313:6.

[3]Eleutherios Venizelos [1864–1936], Greek statesman.

[4]See Talleyrand, 354:5.

[5]The eight thousand paratroopers of the First British Airborne Division who landed in Arnhem, Holland, behind the German lines and held the area for nine days and nights, with a loss of six thousand [September 1944]. MAJOR GENERAL R. E. URQUHART, the division commander, radioed to Field Marshal Bernard Montgomery: All will be ordered to break out rather than surrender.

ours are carrying on their task to the end all over the world. What an enviable death was his.
Speech in the House of Commons [April 17, 1945]

1   I think "No comment" is a splendid expression. I am using it again and again. I got it from Sumner Welles.
To reporters at the Washington airport, after conferring with President Truman at the White House [February 12, 1946]

2   From Stettin in the Baltic to Trieste in the Adriatic an iron curtain[1] has descended across the Continent.
Address at Westminster College, Fulton, Missouri [March 5, 1946]

3   This address to which I have given the title, "The Sinews of Peace."[2]
Ibid.

4   In War: Resolution. In Defeat: Defiance. In Victory: Magnanimity. In Peace: Good Will.
The Second World War: Moral of the Work, vol. I, The Gathering Storm [1948]

5   No one can guarantee success in war, but only deserve it.   *Ibid. II, Their Finest Hour [1949]*

6   When you have to kill a man it costs nothing to be polite.   *Ibid. III, The Grand Alliance [1950]*

7   Everyone has his day and some days last longer than others.
Speech in the House of Commons [January 1952]

8   To jaw-jaw is always better than to war-war.
At a White House luncheon [June 26, 1954]

9   A fanatic is one who can't change his mind and won't change the subject.   *Saying*

10   The inherent vice of capitalism is the unequal sharing of blessings; the inherent virtue of socialism is the equal sharing of miseries.   *Ibid.*

11   Short words are best and the old words when short are best of all.   *Ibid.*

[1]Between them [Germany] and me there is now a bloody iron curtain which has descended forever!—QUEEN ELISABETH OF BELGIUM [1876–1965], *in* 1914. Though German-born, she stood staunchly by her adopted country in World War I.
France . . . a nation of forty millions with a deep-rooted grievance and an iron curtain at its frontier.—GEORGE WASHINGTON CRILE [1864–1943], *A Mechanistic View of War and Peace* [1915]
With a rumble and a roar, an iron curtain is descending on Russian history.—VASILI ROZANOV [1856–1919], *Apocalypse of Our Time* [1918]
We were behind the "iron curtain" at last.—ETHEL ANNAKIN SNOWDEN [1881–1951], *Through Bolshevik Russia* [1920]
The Nazi minister of enlightenment and propaganda, Dr. JOSEPH GOEBBELS, used the phrase "iron curtain" in reference to the USSR in *Das Reich* [February 23, 1945].
CHURCHILL used it in a top-secret telegram to President Truman [May 12, 1945].
[2]See Bion, 82:7; Cicero, 88:13; and Rabelais, 139:10.

12   It is hard, if not impossible, to snub a beautiful woman—they remain beautiful and the rebuke recoils.   *Ibid.*

13   This is the sort of English up with which I will not put.   *Attributed*

Clarence Day
1874–1935

14   What fairy story, what tale from the Arabian Nights of the jinns, is a hundredth part as wonderful as this true fairy story of simians! It is so much more heartening, too, than the tales we invent. A universe capable of giving birth to many such accidents is —blind or not—a good world to live in, a promising universe. . . . We once thought we lived on God's footstool; it may be a throne.[3]
This Simian World [1920]. XIX

15   Aside from a few odd words in Hebrew, I took it completely for granted that God had never spoken anything but the most dignified English.
Life with Father [1935]. Father Interferes with the Twenty-third Psalm

16   "If you don't go to other men's funerals," he told Father stiffly, "they won't go to yours."
Ibid. Father Plans to Get Out

Robert Frost
1874–1963

17   They would not find me changed from him they knew—
Only more sure of all I thought was true.
Into My Own [1913], st. 4

18   Ah, when to the heart of man
Was it ever less than a treason
To go with the drift of things,
To yield with a grace to reason,
And bow and accept the end
Of a love or a season?[4]
Reluctance [1913], st. 4

19   I'm going out to clean the pasture spring;
I'll only stop to rake the leaves away
(And wait to watch the water clear, I may):
I shan't be gone long.—You come too.
The Pasture [1914], st. 1

20   Something there is that doesn't love a wall.
Mending Wall [1914]

21   My apple trees will never get across
And eat the cones under his pines, I tell him.
He only says, "Good fences make good neighbors."[5]
Ibid.

[3]See *Matthew 5:34–35, 33:6*; Pope, 301:9; and Wells, 601:15.
[4]See Pope, 303:11.
[5]See Herbert, 244:11.

1 Before I built a wall I'd ask to know
What I was walling in or walling out.
Ibid.

2 And nothing to look backward to with pride,
And nothing to look forward to with hope.
The Death of the Hired Man [1914]

3 Home is the place where, when you have to go
there,
They have to take you in.
Ibid.

4   The nearest friends can go
With anyone to death, comes so far short
They might as well not try to go at all.
Home Burial [1914]

5 Most of the change we think we see in life
Is due to truths being in and out of favor.
The Black Cottage [1914]

6 Pressed into service means pressed out of shape.
The Self-Seeker [1914]

7 I shall be telling this with a sigh
Somewhere ages and ages hence:
Two roads diverged in a wood, and I—
I took the one less traveled by,
And that has made all the difference.
The Road Not Taken [1916], st. 4

8 I'd like to get away from earth awhile
And then come back to it and begin over.
May no fate willfully misunderstand me
And half grant what I wish and snatch me away
Not to return. Earth's the right place for love:
I don't know where it's likely to go better.
Birches [1916]

9 One could do worse than be a swinger of birches.
Ibid.

10 I shall set forth for somewhere,
I shall make the reckless choice
Some say when they are in voice
And tossing so as to scare
The white clouds over them on,
I shall have less to say,
But I shall be gone.
The Sound of the Trees [1916]

11   Do you know,
Considering the market, there are more
Poems produced than any other thing?
No wonder poets sometimes have to *seem*
So much more businesslike than businessmen.
Their wares are so much harder to get rid of.
New Hampshire [1923]

12 The snake stood up for evil in the Garden.
The Ax-Helve [1923]

13 Why make so much of fragmentary blue
In here and there a bird, or butterfly,
Or flower, or wearing-stone, or open eye,
When heaven presents in sheets the solid hue?
Fragmentary Blue [1923], st. 1

14 Some say the world will end in fire,
Some say in ice.
From what I've tasted of desire
I hold with those who favor fire.
But if it had to perish twice,
I think I know enough of hate
To say that for destruction ice
Is also great
And would suffice.
Fire and Ice [1923]

15 The way a crow
Shook down on me
The dust of snow
From a hemlock tree

Has given my heart
A change of mood
And saved some part
Of a day I had rued.
Dust of Snow [1923]

16 Whose woods these are I think I know.
His house is in the village though;
He will not see me stopping here
To watch his woods fill up with snow.
Stopping by Woods on a Snowy Evening [1923], st. 1

17 My little horse must think it queer
To stop without a farmhouse near.
Ibid. st. 2

18 The woods are lovely, dark and deep.
But I have promises to keep,
And miles to go before I sleep,
And miles to go before I sleep.
Ibid. st. 4

19 Love at the lips was touch
As sweet as I could bear;
And once that seemed too much;
I lived on air.
To Earthward [1923], st. 1

20 Now no joy but lacks salt
That is not dashed with pain
And weariness and fault;
I crave the stain

Of tears, the aftermark
Of almost too much love,
The sweet of bitter bark
And burning clove.
Ibid. st. 5, 6

21 Keep cold, young orchard. Goodbye and keep
cold.
Dread fifty above more than fifty below.
Goodbye and Keep Cold [1923]

22 It looked as if a night of dark intent
Was coming, and not only a night, an age.
Someone had better be prepared for rage.
There would be more than ocean-water broken
Before God's last *Put out the Light* was spoken.
Once by the Pacific [1928]

1 Tree at my window, window tree,
  My sash is lowered when night comes on;
  But let there never be curtain drawn
  Between you and me.
  Tree at My Window [1928], st. 1

2 That day she put our heads together,
  Fate had her imagination about her,
  Your head so much concerned with outer,
  Mine with inner, weather.
  Ibid. st. 4

3 I have been one acquainted with the night.
  Acquainted with the Night [1928]

4 If, as they say, some dust thrown in my eyes
  Will keep my talk from getting overwise,
  I'm not the one for putting off the proof.
  Let it be overwhelming.
  Dust in the Eyes [1928]

5 Don't join too many gangs. Join few if any.
  Join the United States and join the family—
  But not much in between unless a college.
  Build Soil [1932]

6 The sun was warm but the wind was chill.
  You know how it is with an April day
  When the sun is out and the wind is still,
  You're one month on in the middle of May.
  But if you so much as dare to speak,
  A cloud comes over the sunlit arch,
  A wind comes off a frozen peak,
  And you're two months back in the middle of
     March.
  Two Tramps in Mud Time [1936], st. 3

7 But yield who will to their separation,
  My object in living is to unite
  My avocation and my vocation
  As my two eyes make one in sight.
  Only where love and need are one,
  And the work is play for mortal stakes,
  Is the deed ever really done
  For Heaven and the future's sakes.
  Ibid. st. 9

8 No memory of having starred
  Atones for later disregard,
  Or keeps the end from being hard.

  Better to go down dignified
  With boughten friendship by your side
  Than none at all. Provide, provide!
  Provide, Provide [1936], st. 6, 7

9 The old dog barks backward without getting up.
  I can remember when he was a pup.
  The Span of Life [1936]

10 The land was ours before we were the land's.
   She was our land more than a hundred years
   Before we were her people.
   The Gift Outright [1941][1]

[1]Read first before the Phi Beta Kappa Society at William and

11 She is as in a field a silken tent
   At midday when a sunny summer breeze
   Has dried the dew and all its ropes relent,
   So that in guys it gently sways at ease.
   The Silken Tent [1942]

12 But strictly held by none, is loosely bound
   By countless silken ties of love and thought
   To everything on earth the compass round,
   And only by one's going slightly taut
   In the capriciousness of summer air
   Is of the slightest bondage made aware.
   Ibid.

13 Happiness Makes Up in Height for What It Lacks
   in Length.   *Title of poem [1942]*

14 Far in the pillared dark
   Thrush music went—
   Almost like a call to come in
   To the dark and lament.

   But no, I was out for stars:
   I would not come in.
   I meant not even if asked,
   And I hadn't been.
   Come In [1942], st. 4, 5

15 And were an epitaph to be my story
   I'd have a short one ready for my own.
   I would have written of me on my stone:
   I had a lover's quarrel with the world.
   The Lesson for Today [1942]

16 We dance round in a ring and suppose,
   But the Secret sits in the middle and knows.
   The Secret Sits [1942]

17 First there's the children's house of make believe,
   Some shattered dishes underneath a pine,
   The playthings in the playhouse of the children.
   Weep for what little things could make them glad.
   Directive [1947]

18 Here are your waters and your watering place.
   Drink and be whole again beyond confusion.
   Ibid.

19 Have I not walked without an upward look
   Of caution under stars that very well
   Might not have missed me when they shot and
      fell?
   It was a risk I had to take—and took.
   Bravado [1947]

20 Any eye is an evil eye
   That looks in on to a mood apart.
   A Mood Apart [1947]

21 All those who try to go it sole alone,
   Too proud to be beholden for relief,
   Are absolutely sure to come to grief.
   Haec Fabula Docet [1947]

Mary College [December 5, 1941], later at the inauguration of
President John F. Kennedy [January 20, 1961].

1 It asks a little of us here.
It asks of us a certain height,
So when at times the mob is swayed
To carry praise or blame too far,
We may take something like a star
To stay our minds on and be staid.
Take Something Like a Star [1949]

2 Forgive, O Lord, my little jokes on Thee
And I'll forgive Thy great big one on me.
From In the Clearing [1962]

3 I am assured at any rate
Man's practically inexterminate.
Someday I must go into that.
There's always been an Ararat
Where someone someone else begat
To start the world all over at.
A-Wishing Well [1962]

4 It takes all sorts of in and outdoor schooling
To get adapted to my kind of fooling.
It Takes All Sorts [1962]

5 Unless I'm wrong
I but obey
The urge of a song:
I'm—bound—away![1]

And I may return
If dissatisfied
With what I learn
From having died.
Away! [1962], st. 5, 6

6 A poem . . . begins as a lump in the throat, a sense of wrong, a homesickness, a lovesickness. . . . It finds the thought and the thought finds the words.
Letter to Louis Untermeyer [January 1, 1916]

7 It is absurd to think that the only way to tell if a poem is lasting is to wait and see if it lasts. The right reader of a good poem can tell the moment it strikes him that he has taken an immortal wound—that he will never get over it.
The Poetry of Amy Lowell. From the Christian Science Monitor [May 16, 1925]

8 The figure a poem makes. It begins in delight and ends in wisdom . . . in a clarification of life—not necessarily a great clarification, such as sects and cults are founded on, but in a momentary stay against confusion.
Collected Poems [1939]. Preface

9 No tears in the writer, no tears in the reader.
Ibid.

10 Like a piece of ice on a hot stove the poem must ride on its own melting. . . . Read it a hundred times; it will forever keep its freshness as a metal keeps its fragrance. It can never lose its sense of a meaning that once unfolded by surprise as it went.
Ibid.

[1]See Anonymous: Shanties, 793:12.

11 How many times it thundered before Franklin took the hint! How many apples fell on Newton's head before he took the hint! Nature is always hinting at us. It hints over and over again. And suddenly we take the hint.
Comment

12 It is only a moment here and a moment there that the greatest writer has.
Ibid.

13 Poetry is a way of taking life by the throat.
Ibid.

14 Talking is a hydrant in the yard and writing is a faucet upstairs in the house. Opening the first takes all the pressure off the second.
Ibid.

15 The greatest thing in family life is to take a hint when a hint is intended—and not to take a hint when a hint isn't intended.
Ibid.

16 Always fall in with what you're asked to accept. Take what is given, and make it over your way. My aim in life has always been to hold my own with whatever's going. Not against: with.
Ibid.

17 I've given offense by saying I'd as soon write free verse as play tennis with the net down.
Interview [1959]

18 Education is . . . hanging around until you've caught on.
[January 30, 1963]

Harry Graham
1874–1936

19 Billy, in one of his nice new sashes,
Fell in the fire and was burnt to ashes;
Now, although the room grows chilly,
I haven't the heart to poke poor Billy.
Ruthless Rhymes [1901]. Tender-Heartedness

Herbert Clark Hoover
1874–1964

20 The American system of rugged individualism.[2]
Campaign speech, New York [October 22, 1928]

21 The grass will grow in the streets of a hundred cities.
Speech [October 31, 1932]

22 A good many things go around in the dark besides Santa Claus.
Address to the John Marshall Republican Club, St. Louis, Missouri [December 16, 1935]

[2]While I can make no claim for having introduced the term "rugged individualism," I should be proud to have invented it. It has been used by American leaders for over a half-century in eulogy of those God-fearing men and women of honesty whose stamina and character and fearless assertion of rights led them to make their own way in life.—HOOVER, *The Challenge to Liberty* [1934], *ch. 5*

1   Older men declare war. But it is youth that must fight and die. And it is youth who must inherit the tribulation, the sorrow, and the triumphs that are the aftermath of war.[1]
   Speech at the Republican National Convention, Chicago [June 27, 1944]

Harold L. Ickes
1874–1952

2   I am against government by crony.
   On resigning as secretary of the interior [February 1946]

Karl Kraus[2]
1874–1936

3   I and my public understand each other very well: it does not hear what I say, and I don't say what it wants to hear.   *Aphorism*

4   When the end of the world comes, I want to be living in retirement.   *Ibid.*

5   Heinrich Heine so loosened the corsets of the German language that today every little salesman can fondle her breasts.   *Ibid.*

6   An aphorism never coincides with the truth: it is either a half-truth or one-and-a-half truths.
   Ibid.

7   Psychoanalysis is that mental illness for which it regards itself as therapy.   *Ibid.*

8   A woman is, occasionally, quite a serviceable substitute for masturbation. It takes an abundance of imagination, to be sure.   *Ibid.*

Amy Lowell
1874–1925

9   A pattern called a war.
Christ! What are patterns for?

   Patterns

10 Sappho would speak, I think, quite openly,
And Mrs. Browning guard a careful silence,
But Emily would set doors ajar and slam them
And love you for your speed of observation.
   The Sisters

11 Heart-leaves of lilac all over New England,
Roots of lilac under all the soil of New
   England,
Lilac in me because I am New England.
   Lilacs

[1]See Rice, 643:14.
[2]Translated by HARRY ZOHN.

William Somerset Maugham
1874–1965

12   Like all weak men he laid an exaggerated stress on not changing one's mind.
   Of Human Bondage [1915], ch. 39

13   People ask you for criticism, but they only want praise.   *Ibid. 50*

14   There is nothing so degrading as the constant anxiety about one's means of livelihood. . . . Money is like a sixth sense without which you cannot make a complete use of the other five.
   Ibid. 51

15   I forget who it was that recommended men for their soul's good to do each day two things they disliked . . . it is a precept that I have followed scrupulously; for every day I have got up and I have gone to bed.
   The Moon and Sixpence [1919], ch. 2

16   Conscience is the guardian in the individual of the rules which the community has evolved for its own preservation.   *Ibid. 14*

17   Do you know that conversation is one of the greatest pleasures in life? But it wants leisure.
   The Trembling of a Leaf [1921], ch. 3

18   The tragedy of love is indifference.   *Ibid. 4*

19   I [Death] was astonished to see him in Baghdad, for I had an appointment with him tonight in Samarra.   *Sheppy [1933], act III*

20   She [Sadie Thompson] gathered herself together. No one could describe the scorn of her expression or the contemptuous hatred she put into her answer.
   "You men! You filthy dirty pigs! You're all the same, all of you. Pigs! Pigs!"
   Altogether [1934]. Rain

21   I would sooner read a timetable or a catalogue than nothing at all. They are much more entertaining than half the novels that are written.
   The Summing Up [1938]

22   If a nation values anything more than freedom, it will lose its freedom; and the irony of it is that if it is comfort or money that it values more, it will lose that too.   *Strictly Personal [1941], ch. 31*

Alice Duer Miller
1874–1942

23 The white cliffs of Dover, I saw rising steeply
Out of the sea that once made her [England]
   secure.
   The White Cliffs [1940], I

24 But in a world where England is finished and
   dead,
I do not wish to live.
   Ibid. LII

Robert William Service
1874–1958

1 This is the Law of the Yukon, that only the
strong shall thrive;
That surely the weak shall perish, and only the fit
survive.
Dissolute, damned and despairful, crippled and
palsied and slain,
This is the Will of the Yukon—Lo, how she
makes it plain!
The Law of the Yukon

2 Back of the bar, in a solo game, sat Dangerous
Dan McGrew,
And watching his luck was his light-o'-love, the
lady that's known as Lou.
The Shooting of Dan McGrew [1907], st. 1

3 The Northern Lights have seen queer sights,
But the queerest they ever did see
Was that night on the marge of Lake Lebarge
I cremated Sam McGee.
The Cremation of Sam McGee [1907], st. 1

Gertrude Stein
1874–1946

4 Rose is a rose is a rose is a rose.
Sacred Emily [written 1913]

5 You are all a lost generation.[1]
*Used by Ernest Hemingway as an epigraph for
The Sun Also Rises [1926]*

6 Pigeons on the grass alas.
Four Saints in Three Acts [written 1927]

7 Before the Flowers of Friendship Faded Friendship Faded.   *Title [written 1930]*

8 I murmured to Picasso that I liked his portrait of
Gertrude Stein. Yes, he said, everybody says that she
does not look like it but that does not make any
difference, she will.
The Autobiography of Alice B. Toklas [1933]

9 Remarks are not literature [said to Hemingway].
Ibid.

10 [Ezra Pound] was a village explainer, excellent if
you were a village, but if you were not, not.
Ibid.

11 America is my country and Paris is my home
town.   *An American and France [1936]*

12 In the United States there is more space where
nobody is than where anybody is.
This is what makes America what it is.
The Geographical History of America [1936]

13 [Of Oakland, California]: There is no there there.
Everybody's Autobiography [1937], ch. 4

[1]Hemingway stated that the remark was originally made by
a garage owner in the Midi to Gertrude Stein in reference to his
young mechanics, who were "une génération perdue."

14 What is the answer? [*I was silent.*] In that case,
what is the question?
Last words. From ALICE B. TOKLAS, *What Is
Remembered [1963]*

Harry Williams
1874–1924

15 It's a long way to Tipperary, it's a long way to
go;
It's a long way to Tipperary, to the sweetest girl I
know!
Goodbye, Piccadilly, farewell, Leicester Square,
It's a long, long way to Tipperary, but my heart's
right there!
Tipperary [1908][2]

16 In the Shade of the Old Apple Tree.
Title of song[2]

Edmund Clerihew[3] Bentley
1875–1956

17 The Art of Biography
Is different from Geography.
Geography is about Maps,
But Biography is about Chaps.
Biography for Beginners. Introduction

18 Sir Christopher Wren
Said "I am going to dine with some men.
If anybody calls
Say I am designing St. Paul's."
Ibid. Sir Christopher Wren[4]

19 John Stuart Mill
By a mighty effort of will
Overcame his natural bonhomie
And wrote *Principles of Political Economy.*
Ibid. John Stuart Mill

20 George the Third
Ought never to have occurred.
One can only wonder
At so grotesque a blunder.[5]
Ibid. George III

Mary McLeod Bethune
1875–1955

21 What does the Negro want? His answer is very
simple. He wants only what all other Americans

[2]Set to music by JACK JUDGE [1878–1938].
[3]A humorous quatrain in the form Bentley popularized is
known as a clerihew.
[4]See Wren, 278.
[5]George the First was always reckoned / Vile, but viler
George the Second; / And what mortal ever heard / Any good of
George the Third? / When from earth the Fourth descended /
God be praised, the Georges ended!—LANDOR, *epigram after
hearing Thackeray's lectures, The Four Georges [1855]*

want. He wants opportunity to make real what the Declaration of Independence and the Constitution and the Bill of Rights say, what the Four Freedoms establish. While he knows these ideals are open to no man completely, he wants only his equal chance to obtain them.[1]

> *"Certain Unalienable Rights." From What the Negro Wants [1944], edited by* RAYFORD W. LOGAN

1   If we accept and acquiesce in the face of discrimination, we accept the responsibility ourselves and allow those responsible to salve their conscience by believing that they have our acceptance and concurrence. We should, therefore, protest openly everything . . . that smacks of discrimination or slander.   *Ibid.*

John Buchan, Lord Tweedsmuir
1875–1940

2   We can only pay our debt to the past by putting the future in debt to ourselves.

> *Address to the people of Canada, on the coronation of George VI [May 12, 1937]*

3   Public life is regarded as the crown of a career, and to young men it is the worthiest ambition. Politics is still the greatest and the most honorable adventure.   *Pilgrim's Way [1940]*

Edgar Rice Burroughs
1875–1950

4   As the body rolled to the ground Tarzan of the Apes placed his foot upon the neck of his lifelong enemy, and raising his eyes to the full moon threw back his fierce young head and voiced the wild and terrible cry of his people.

> *Tarzan of the Apes [1914], ch. 7*

5   I am Tarzan of the Apes. I want you. I am yours. You are mine.[2]   *Ibid. ch. 18*

Hasegawa Nyozekan[3]
1875–1969

6   The war was started as the result of a mistaken intuitive "calculation" which transcended mathematics. We believed with a blind fervor that we could triumph over scientific weapons and tactics by means of our mystic will. . . . The characteristic reliance on intuition by Japanese had blocked the objective cognition of the modern world.

> *The Lost Japan [1952]*

[1]See Jordan, 768:10.
[2]Me Tarzan, you Jane—spoken by Johnny Weissmuller in the movie *Tarzan the Ape Man* [1932].
[3]From *Sources of Japanese Tradition* [1960], edited by WILLIAM THEODORE DE BARY.

Carl Gustav Jung
1875–1961

7   Without this playing with fantasy no creative work has ever yet come to birth. The debt we owe to the play of imagination is incalculable.

> *Psychological Types [1923], ch. 1, p. 82*

8   The great problems of life—sexuality, of course, among others—are always related to the primordial images of the collective unconscious. These images are really balancing or compensating factors which correspond with the problems life presents in actuality. This is not to be marveled at, since these images are deposits representing the accumulated experience of thousands of years of struggle for adaptation and existence.   *Ibid. 5, p. 271*

9   The meeting of two personalities is like the contact of two chemical substances: if there is any reaction, both are transformed.

> *Modern Man in Search of a Soul [1933], p. 57*

10   The great decisions of human life have as a rule far more to do with the instincts and other mysterious unconscious factors than with conscious will and well-meaning reasonableness. The shoe that fits one person pinches another; there is no recipe for living that suits all cases. Each of us carries his own life-form—an indeterminable form which cannot be superseded by any other.   *Ibid. p. 69*

11   Aging people should know that their lives are not mounting and unfolding but that an inexorable inner process forces the contraction of life. For a young person it is almost a sin—and certainly a danger—to be too much occupied with himself; but for the aging person it is a duty and a necessity to give serious attention to himself.   *Ibid. p. 125*

12   All ages before ours believed in gods in some form or other. Only an unparalleled impoverishment in symbolism could enable us to rediscover the gods as psychic factors, which is to say, as archetypes of the unconscious. No doubt this discovery is hardly credible as yet.

> *The Integration of the Personality [1939], p. 72*

13   If there is anything that we wish to change in the child, we should first examine it and see whether it is not something that could better be changed in ourselves.   *Ibid. p. 285*

14   The conscious mind allows itself to be trained like a parrot, but the unconscious does not—which is why St. Augustine thanked God for not making him responsible for his dreams.

> *Psychology and Alchemy [1953], p. 51*

15   The unconscious is not just evil by nature, it is also the source of the highest good: not only dark but also light, not only bestial, semihuman, and de-

monic but superhuman, spiritual, and, in the classical sense of the word, "divine."
The Practice of Psychotherapy [1953], p. 364

1 The little world of childhood with its familiar surroundings is a model of the greater world. The more intensively the family has stamped its character upon the child, the more it will tend to feel and see its earlier miniature world again in the bigger world of adult life.
From Psychological Reflections: A Jung Anthology [1953],[1] p. 83: Collected Works, vol. 4, The Theory of Psychoanalysis [1913]

2 This whole creation is essentially subjective, and the dream is the theater where the dreamer is at once scene, actor, prompter, stage manager, author, audience, and critic.
Ibid. p. 58: vol. 8, General Aspects of Dream Psychology [1928]

3 The dream is the small hidden door in the deepest and most intimate sanctum of the soul, which opens into that primeval cosmic night that was soul long before there was a conscious ego and will be soul far beyond what a conscious ego could ever reach.
Ibid. p. 46: vol. 10, The Meaning of Psychology for Modern Man [1934]

4 Emotion is the chief source of all becoming-conscious. There can be no transforming of darkness into light and of apathy into movement without emotion.
Ibid. p. 32: vol. 9, Psychological Aspects of the Modern Archetype [1938]

5 No one can flatter himself that he is immune to the spirit of his own epoch, or even that he possesses a full understanding of it. Irrespective of our conscious convictions, each one of us, without exception, being a particle of the general mass, is somewhere attached to, colored by, or even undermined by the spirit which goes through the mass. Freedom stretches only as far as the limits of our consciousness.
Ibid. p. 143: vol. 15, Paracelsus the Physician [1942]

6 Where love rules, there is no will to power; and where power predominates, there love is lacking. The one is the shadow of the other.
Ibid. p. 87: vol. 7, The Psychology of the Unconscious [1943]

Thomas Mann
1875–1955

7 We are most likely to get angry and excited in our opposition to some idea when we ourselves are not quite certain of our own position, and are inwardly tempted to take the other side.
Buddenbrooks [1903], pt. VIII, ch. 2

8 Beauty can pierce one like a pain.
Ibid. XI, 2

9 Space, like time, engenders forgetfulness; but it does so by setting us bodily free from our surroundings and giving us back our primitive, unattached state. . . . Time, we say, is Lethe; but change of air is a similar draught, and, if it works less thoroughly, does so more quickly.
The Magic Mountain [1924],[2] *ch. 1*

10 A man lives not only his personal life, as an individual, but also, consciously or unconsciously, the life of his epoch and his contemporaries.
Ibid. 2

11 The only religious way to think of death is as part and parcel of life; to regard it, with the understanding and the emotions, as the inviolable condition of life.
Ibid. 5

12 Time has no divisions to mark its passage, there is never a thunderstorm or blare of trumpets to announce the beginning of a new month or year. Even when a new century begins it is only we mortals who ring bells and fire off pistols.
Ibid.

13 Order and simplification are the first steps toward the mastery of a subject—the actual enemy is the unknown.
Ibid.

14 Opinions cannot survive if one has no chance to fight for them.
Ibid. 6

15 All interest in disease and death is only another expression of interest in life.
Ibid.

16 The invention of printing and the Reformation are and remain the two outstanding services of central Europe to the cause of humanity.
Ibid.

17 Speech is civilization itself. The word, even the most contradictory word, preserves contact—it is silence which isolates.
Ibid.

18 A man's dying is more the survivors' affair than his own.
Ibid.

19 What we call mourning for our dead is perhaps not so much grief at not being able to call them back as it is grief at not being able to want to do so.
Ibid. 7

20 Time cools, time clarifies; no mood can be maintained quite unaltered through the course of hours.
Ibid.

21 Death in Venice.
Stories of Three Decades [1936], *title of story*

22 Disorder and Early Sorrow.
Ibid.

23 In the Word is involved the unity of humanity, the wholeness of the human problem, which permits nobody to separate the intellectual and artistic from

---

[1]Edited by JOLANDE JACOBI.

[2]Translated by H. T. LOWE-PORTER.

the political and social, and to isolate himself within the ivory tower of the "cultural" proper.

Letter to the dean of the Philosophical Faculty, Bonn University [January 1937][1]

1   Hold fast the time! Guard it, watch over it, every hour, every minute! Unregarded it slips away, like a lizard, smooth, slippery, faithless, a pixy wife. Hold every moment sacred. Give each clarity and meaning, each the weight of thine awareness, each its true and due fulfillment.   *The Beloved Returns [1939]*

Hughes Mearns
1875–1965

2   As I was going up the stair
I met a man who wasn't there.
He wasn't there again today.
I wish, I wish he'd stay away.

The Psychoed

Rainer Maria Rilke
1875–1926

3   He was a poet and hated the approximate.
The Journal of My Other Self[2]

4   Love consists in this, that two solitudes protect and touch and greet each other.
Letters to a Young Poet[3]

5   The future enters into us, in order to transform itself in us, long before it happens.   *Ibid.*

6   Beauty's nothing
but beginning of Terror we're still just able to
    bear,
and why we adore it so is because it serenely
disdains to destroy us. Each single angel is
    terrible.
Duino Elegies,[4] *1*

7   We're never single-minded, unperplexed, like migratory birds.   *Ibid. 4*

8   The most visible joy can only reveal itself to us when we've transformed it, within.   *Ibid. 7*

9   Death is the side of life which is turned away from us.   *Letter to W. von Hulewicz*

10   A good marriage is that in which each appoints the other guardian of his solitude.   *Letters*[5]

11   Once the realization is accepted that even between the *closest* human beings infinite distances continue to exist, a wonderful living side by side can

grow up, if they succeed in loving the distance between them which makes it possible for each to see the other whole against the sky.   *Ibid.*

12   In the difficult are the friendly forces, the hands that work on us.   *Ibid.*

13   Works of art are indeed always products of having been in danger, of having gone to the very end in an experience, to where man can go no further.
Ibid.

Naomi Royde-Smith
c. 1875–1964

14   I know two things about the horse
And one of them is rather coarse.
The Horse [1928]

Rafael Sabatini
1875–1950

15   He was born with a gift of laughter and a sense that the world was mad. And that was all his patrimony.   *Scaramouche [1921], ch. 1*

Albert Schweitzer
1875–1965

16   Late on the third day, at the very moment when, at sunset, we were making our way through a herd of hippopotamuses, there flashed upon my mind, unforeseen and unsought, the phrase, "Reverence for Life."   *Out of My Life and Thought [1949]*

17   Affirmation of life is the spiritual act by which man ceases to live unreflectively and begins to devote himself to his life with reverence in order to raise it to its true value. To affirm life is to deepen, to make more inward, and to exalt the will to live.
Ibid.

18   Truth has no special time of its own. Its hour is now—always.   *Ibid.*

19   You don't live in a world all alone. Your brothers are here too.

On Receiving the Nobel Prize [1952]

Sherwood Anderson
1876–1941

20   All of the men and women the writer had ever known had become grotesques.
Winesburg, Ohio [1919]. The Book of the Grotesque

21   Everyone in the world is Christ and they are all crucified.   *Ibid. The Philosopher*

22   I am a lover and have not found my thing to love.
Ibid. Tandy

[1]Mann, who had left Germany [1933], wrote from Zurich after being informed that his name had been struck off the list of Honorary Doctors.
[2]Translated by JOHN LINTON.
[3]Translated by M. D. HERTER NORTON.
[4]Translated by J. B. LEISHMAN and STEPHEN SPENDER.
[5]Translated by JANE BARNARD GREENE and M. D. HERTER NORTON.

Sarah Norcliffe Cleghorn
1876–1959

1 The golf links lie so near the mill
That almost every day
The laboring children can look out
And watch the men at play.
The Golf Links Lie So Near the Mill [1915]

Irvin Shrewsbury Cobb
1876–1944

2 It smells like gangrene starting in a mildewed silo, it tastes like the wrath to come, and when you absorb a deep swig of it you have all the sensations of having swallowed a lighted kerosene lamp. A sudden, violent jolt of it has been known to stop the victim's watch, snap his suspenders and crack his glass eye right across.
Definition of "corn licker" given to the Distillers' Code Authority, NRA

Max Jacob
1876–1944

3 The poet's expression of joy conceals his despair at not having found the reality of joy.
La Défense de Tartufe [1919]

4 When you get to the point where you cheat for the sake of beauty, you're an artist.[1]
Art Poétique [1922]

5 What is called a sincere work is one that is endowed with enough strength to give reality to an illusion.
Ibid.

Charles Franklin Kettering
1876–1958

6 We should all be concerned about the future because we will have to spend the rest of our lives there.
Seed for Thought [1949]

Maxim Maximovich Litvinov
1876–1951

7 Peace is indivisible.[2]
Speech to the League of Nations, Geneva, condemning Italian aggression in Ethiopia [July 1, 1936]

[1] C'est au moment où l'on triche pour le beau que l'on est artiste.
[2] In an earlier speech at the League [September 5, 1935] during the Italian preparations for the invasion, Litvinov used a similar phrase: "The thesis of the indivisibility of peace. . . . It has now become clear to the whole world that each war is the creation of a preceding war and the generator of new present or future wars."

Wilson Mizner
1876–1933

8 Life's a tough proposition, and the first hundred years are the hardest.
Saying

9 Be nice to people on your way up because you'll meet them on your way down.
Ibid.

10 When you steal from one author, it's plagiarism; if you steal from many, it's research.
Ibid.

11 You sparkle with larceny.
Ibid.

12 You're a mouse studying to be a rat.
Ibid.

13 To my embarrassment, I was born in bed with a lady.
Ibid.

Pope Pius XII [Eugenio Pacelli]
1876–1958

14 Private property is a natural fruit of labor, a product of intense activity of man, acquired through his energetic determination to ensure and develop with his own strength his own existence and that of his family, and to create for himself and his own an existence of just freedom, not only economic, but also political, cultural and religious.
Radio broadcast [September 1, 1944]

George Macaulay Trevelyan
1876–1962

15 A man and what he loves and builds have but a day and then disappear; nature cares not—and renews the annual round untired. It is the old law, sad but not bitter. Only when man destroys the life and beauty of nature, there is the outrage.
Grey of Fallodon [1937], bk. I, ch. 3

16 Disinterested intellectual curiosity is the lifeblood of real civilization.
English Social History [1942], Introduction

17 Education . . . has produced a vast population able to read but unable to distinguish what is worth reading.
Ibid. ch. 18

Anthony Henderson Euwer
1877–1955

18 As a beauty I'm not a great star.
There are others more handsome, by far,
But my face—I don't mind it
For I am behind it;
It's the people in front get the jar.
Limeratomy

Rose Fyleman
1877–1957

1 There are fairies at the bottom of our garden!
The Fairies, st. 1

Sir James Hopwood Jeans
1877–1946

2 Taking a very gloomy view of the future of the human race, let us suppose that it can only expect to survive for two thousand million years longer, a period about equal to the past age of the earth. Then, regarded as a being destined to live for three-score years and ten, humanity, although it has been born in a house seventy years old, is itself only three days old.
The Wilder Aspects of Cosmogony [1928]

3 From the intrinsic evidence of his creation, the Great Architect of the Universe now begins to appear as a pure mathematician.
The Mysterious Universe [1930]

4 Physics tries to discover the pattern of events which controls the phenomena we observe. But we can never know what this pattern means or how it originates; and even if some superior intelligence were to tell us, we should find the explanation unintelligible.
Physics and Philosophy [1942]

McLandburgh Wilson
fl. 1915

5 'Twixt the optimist and pessimist
The difference is droll:
The optimist sees the doughnut
But the pessimist sees the hole.
Optimist and Pessimist

John Munro Woolsey
1877–1945

6 I am quite aware that owing to some of its scenes [James Joyce's] *Ulysses* is a rather strong draught to ask some sensitive, though normal, persons to take. But my considered opinion, after long reflection, is that whilst in many places the effect of *Ulysses* on the reader is somewhat emetic, nowhere does it tend to be an aphrodisiac.

Ulysses may, therefore, be admitted into the United States.
U.S. v. One Book Called "Ulysses," 5 Federal Supplement 182, 184 [1933], III

Emiliano Zapata
c. 1877–1919

7 Men of the South! It is better to die on your feet than to live on your knees![1]   *Attributed*

[1]Mejor morir a pie que vivir en rodillas.
Later a Republican watchword in the Spanish Civil War

Martin Buber
1878–1965

8 How would man exist if God did not need him, and how would you exist? You need God in order to be, and God needs you—for that is the meaning of your life.   *I and Thou[2] [1923]*

George Michael Cohan
1878–1942

9 Always Leave Them Laughing When You Say Goodbye.   *Mother Goose [1903], title of song*

10 Give my regards to Broadway,
Remember me to Herald Square,
Tell all the gang at Forty-second Street
That I will soon be there.
Little Johnny Jones [1904]. Give My Regards to Broadway

11 I'm a Yankee Doodle dandy,
A Yankee Doodle do or die;
A real live nephew of my Uncle Sam's
Born on the Fourth of July.
Ibid. Yankee Doodle Dandy

12 The Yanks are coming,
The drums rum-tumming everywhere.
Over There [1917]

13 And we won't come back till it's over over there.
Ibid.

14 What's all the shootin' for?
The Tavern [1920]

Adelaide Crapsey
1878–1914

15 These be
Three silent things:
The falling snow . . . the hour
Before the dawn . . . the mouth of one
Just dead.

Cinquain: Triad

Harry Emerson Fosdick
1878–1969

16 The Sea of Galilee and the Dead Sea are made of the same water. It flows down, clear and cool, from the heights of Hermon and the roots of the cedars of Lebanon. The Sea of Galilee makes beauty of it, for the Sea of Galilee has an outlet. It gets to give. It gathers in its riches that it may pour them out again to fertilize the Jordan plain. But the Dead Sea with

[1936–1939], especially identified with a speech at Madrid [July 18, 1936] by LA PASIONARIA [DOLORES IBARRURI], 692. See F. D. Roosevelt, 649:18.
[2]Translated by WALTER KAUFFMANN.

the same water makes horror. For the Dead Sea has no outlet. It gets to keep.

The Meaning of Service [1920]

Donald Robert Perry Marquis
1878–1937

1 I love you as New Englanders love pie!

Sonnets to a Red-Haired Lady [1922], XII

2 dedicated to babs
with babs knows what
and babs knows why

archy[1] and mehitabel [1927][2]

3 oh i should worry and fret
death and i will coquette
there s a dance in the old dame yet
toujours gai toujours gai

Ibid. the song of mehitabel

4 procrastination is the
art of keeping
up with yesterday

Ibid. certain maxims of archy

5 an optimist is a guy
that has never had
much experience

Ibid.

6   what in hell
have i done to deserve
all these kittens

Ibid. mehitabel and her kittens

7 dance mehitabel dance
caper and shake a leg
what little blood is left
will fizz like wine in a keg

Ibid. mehitabel dances with boreas

8 i have noticed
that when
chickens quit
quarrelling over their
food they often
find that there is
enough for all of them
i wonder if
it might not
be the same way
with the
human race

archy's life of mehitabel [1933]. random thoughts by archy

9   it is a cheering thought to think
that god is on the side of the best digestion[3]

archy does his part [1935]. the big bad wolf

[1]Archy, a cockroach, is unable to use the shift key on the typewriter for capitals and punctuation.
[2]Published later with other works by archy as *the lives and times of archy and mehitabel* [1943].
[3]Give me a good digestion, Lord, / And also something to digest.—ANONYMOUS, *A Pilgrim's Grace*, st. 1

10   there is always
a comforting thought
in time of trouble when
it is not our trouble

Ibid. comforting thoughts

11 it wont be long now it wont be long
man is making deserts of the earth
it wont be long now
before man will have it used up
so that nothing but ants
and centipedes and scorpions
can find a living on it

Ibid. what the ants are saying

12 what man calls civilization
always results in deserts

Ibid.

13 it wont be long now it wont be long
till earth is barren as the moon
and sapless as a mumbled bone

Ibid.

John Masefield
1878–1967

14 I must down to the seas again, to the lonely sea and the sky,
And all I ask is a tall ship and a star to steer her by,
And the wheel's kick and the wind's song and the white sail's shaking,
And a gray mist on the sea's face and a gray dawn breaking.

Sea Fever [1902], st. 1

15 I must down to the seas again, for the call of the running tide
Is a wild call and a clear call that may not be denied.

Ibid. st. 2

16 I must down to the seas again, to the vagrant gypsy life,
To the gull's way and the whale's way where the wind's like a whetted knife;
And all I ask is a merry yarn from a laughing fellow rover,
And quiet sleep and a sweet dream when the long trick's over.

Ibid. st. 3

17 It's a warm wind, the west wind, full of birds' cries.

The West Wind [1902], st. 1

18 Quinquireme of Nineveh from distant Ophir,
Rowing home to haven in sunny Palestine,
With a cargo of ivory,
And apes and peacocks,[4]
Sandalwood, cedarwood, and sweet white wine.

Cargoes, st. 1

[4]See *1 Kings* 10:22, 12:27.

1 Dirty British coaster with a salt-caked smokestack,
Butting through the Channel in the mad March
    days,
With a cargo of Tyne coal,
Road rail, pig lead,
Firewood, ironware, and cheap tin trays.
                                    Cargoes, st. 3

Paul Reynaud
1878–1966

2   We shall win because we are the stronger.[1]
                        Radio Speech [September 10, 1939]

Carl Sandburg
1878–1967

3 I am the people—the mob—the crowd—the
    mass.
Do you know that all the great work of the world
    is done through me?
                        I Am the People, the Mob [1916]

4 Hog butcher for the world,
Tool maker, stacker of wheat,
Player with railroads and the nation's freight
    handler;
Stormy, husky, brawling,
City of the big shoulders.
                                    Chicago [1916]

5 The fog comes
on little cat feet.
It sits looking
over the harbor and city
on silent haunches
and then moves on.
                                        Fog [1916]

6 Pile the bodies high at Austerlitz and Waterloo.
Shovel them under and let me work—
I am the grass; I cover all.
                                    Grass [1918]

7 I tell you the past is a bucket of ashes.
                                    Prairie [1918]

8 When Abraham Lincoln was shoveled into the
    tombs, he forgot the copperheads and the
    assassin . . . in the dust, in the cool tombs.
                                Cool Tombs [1918]

9 Lay me on an anvil, O God.
Beat me and hammer me into a crowbar.
Let me pry loose old walls.
Let me lift and loosen old foundations.
                            Prayers of Steel [1920]

10 Drum on your drums, batter on your banjos, sob
    on the long cool winding saxophones.
Go to it, O jazzmen.
                            Jazz Fantasia [1920]

11 The republic is a dream.
Nothing happens unless first a dream.
                    Washington Monument by Night [1922]

12 Sometime they'll give a war and nobody will
    come.[2]
                                The People, Yes [1936]

13   The people will live on.
The learning and blundering people will live on.
They will be tricked and sold and again sold
And go back to the nourishing earth for
    rootholds.
                                            Ibid.

14 The people know the salt of the sea
and the strength of the winds
lashing the corners of the earth.
The people take the earth
as a tomb of rest and a cradle of hope.
Who else speaks for the Family of Man?
                                            Ibid.

15 This old anvil laughs at many broken hammers.
There are men who can't be bought.
                    The People Will Live On [1936]

Upton Beall Sinclair
1878–1968

16   I aimed at the public's heart, and by accident I hit
it in the stomach.
                    On his novel The Jungle [1906]

Louis Edwin Thayer
1878–1956

17 I fancy when I go to rest someone will bring to
    light
Some kindly word or goodly act long buried out
    of sight;
But, if it's all the same to you, just give to me,
    instead,
The bouquets while I'm living and the knocking
    when I'm dead.
                    Of Post-Mortem Praises, st. 1

John Broadus Watson
1878–1958

18   Give me a dozen healthy infants, well-formed,
and my own specified world to bring them up in and
I'll guarantee to take any one at random and train
him to become any type of specialist I might select
—doctor, lawyer, artist, merchant chief and, yes,
even beggarman and thief, regardless of his talents,

---

[1]Nous vaincrons parce que nous sommes les plus forts.
The phrase became a war slogan.

[2]Suppose They Gave a War, and No One Came?—CHAR-
LOTTE KEYES [1914–], *article in McCall's* [October 1966]

penchants, tendencies, abilities, vocations, and race of his ancestors.   *Behaviorism [1925], ch. 5*

1   The universe will change if you bring up your children, not in the freedom of the libertine, but in behavioristic freedom.   *Ibid. 12*

Hans Zinsser
1878–1940

2   The scientist takes off from the manifold observations of predecessors, and shows his intelligence, if any, by his ability to discriminate between the important and the negligible, by selecting here and there the significant steppingstones that will lead across the difficulties to new understanding. The one who places the last stone and steps across to the terra firma of accomplished discovery gets all the credit.   *As I Remember Him [1940], ch. 20*

Nancy Witcher Langhorne Astor
1879–1964

3   I married beneath me. All women do.
    Attributed

Ethel Barrymore
1879–1959

4   That's all there is, there isn't any more.
    Signature curtain line added by her to the play Sunday *[1904] by* THOMAS RACEWARD

Sir William Henry Beveridge
1879–1963

5   There is no inherent mechanism in our present system which can with certainty prevent competitive sectional bargaining for wages from setting up a vicious spiral of rising prices under full employment.
    Full Employment in a Free Society [1945]

Louis Brownlow
1879–1963

6   They [the President's aides] should be possessed of high competence, great physical vigor, and a passion for anonymity.[1]
    Administrative Management in the Government of the United States: Report of the President's Committee on Administrative Management [January 1937]

[1]Tell the President that the way to solve his problem is to find that one man who would turn out to be . . . possessed of high competence, great physical vigor, and a passion for anonymity. —TOM JONES (private secretary to Prime Minister Stanley Baldwin) to Brownlow [1936]

James Branch Cabell
1879–1958

7   I am willing to taste any drink once.
    Jurgen [1919], ch. 16

8   The optimist proclaims that we live in the best of all possible worlds; and the pessimist fears this is true.   *The Silver Stallion [1926], ch. 26*

Ch'en Tu-hsiu[2]
1879–1942

9   The pulse of modern life is economic and the fundamental principle of economic production is individual independence.
    The New Youth [December 1916]

10   Man's happiness in life is the result of man's own effort and is neither the gift of God nor a spontaneous natural product.   *Ibid. [February 1918]*

Albert Einstein
1879–1955

11    $E = mc^2$.
    Statement of the mass-energy equivalence relationship[3]

12   The most beautiful thing we can experience is the mysterious. It is the source of all true art and science.
    What I Believe [1930]

13   Concern for man himself and his fate must always form the chief interest of all technical endeavors, concern for the great unsolved problems of the organization of labor and the distribution of goods —in order that the creations of our mind shall be a blessing and not a curse to mankind. Never forget this in the midst of your diagrams and equations.
    Address, California Institute of Technology [1931]

14   The whole of science is nothing more than a refinement of everyday thinking.
    Physics and Reality [1936]

15   Physical concepts are free creations of the human mind, and are not, however it may seem, uniquely determined by the external world.
    Evolution of Physics [1938]

16   Some recent work by E. Fermi and L. Szilard, which has been communicated to me in manuscript, leads me to expect that the element uranium may be turned into a new and important source of energy in the immediate future. Certain aspects of the

[2]From *Sources of Chinese Tradition* [1960], edited by WILLIAM THEODORE DE BARY. Ch'en was the founder [1921] of the Chinese Communist Party.
[3]Energy equals mass times the speed of light squared.
    The original statement is: If a body gives off the energy L in the form of radiation, its mass diminishes by L / c^2. —EINSTEIN, *Ist die Tragheit eines Korpers von Seinem Energieghalt Abhangig?* [1905]

situation which has arisen seem to call for watchfulness and, if necessary, quick action on the part of the Administration.

Letter to President Franklin D. Roosevelt [August 2, 1939] (the letter that resulted in the assignment of government funds for developing the atom bomb)

1   This new phenomena [atomic energy] would also lead to the construction of bombs. . . . A single bomb of this type, carried by boat and exploded in a port, might very well destroy the whole port, together with some of the surrounding territory. However, such bombs might very well prove to be too heavy for transportation by air.   *Ibid.*

2   As long as there are sovereign nations possessing great power, war is inevitable.
Einstein on the Atomic Bomb. From the Atlantic Monthly [November 1945]

3   I do not believe that civilization will be wiped out in a war fought with the atomic bomb. Perhaps two thirds of the people of the earth might be killed, but enough men capable of thinking, and enough books, would be left to start again, and civilization could be restored.   *Ibid.*

4   Since I do not foresee that atomic energy is to be a great boon for a long time, I have to say that for the present it is a menace. Perhaps it is well that it should be. It may intimidate the human race into bringing order into its international affairs, which, without the pressure of fear, it would not do.
Ibid.

5   I shall never believe that God plays dice with the world.
From PHILIPP FRANK, Einstein, His Life and Times [1947]

6   The Lord God is subtle, but malicious he is not.[1]
Inscription in Fine Hall, Princeton University

7   Every intellectual who is called before one of the committees ought to refuse to testify, i.e., he must be prepared . . . for the sacrifice of his personal welfare in the interest of the cultural welfare of his country. . . . This kind of inquisition violates the spirit of the Constitution.
If enough people are ready to take this grave step they will be successful. If not, then the intellectuals of this country deserve nothing better than the slavery which is intended for them.
Letter to William Frauenglass [May 16, 1953][2]

8   The unleashed power of the atom has changed everything save our modes of thinking, and we thus drift toward unparalleled catastrophes.
From RALPH E. LAPP, The Einstein Letter That Started It All. In the New York Times Magazine [August 2, 1964]

[1]Raffiniert ist der Herr Gott, aber Boshaft ist er nicht.
[2]Einstein's letter was published in the *New York Times* [June 12, 1953]. Frauenglass had been subpoenaed to testify before the Senate Internal Security Subcommittee.

9   Something deeply hidden had to be behind things.   *Ibid. [autobiographical handwritten note]*

Edward Morgan Forster
1879–1970

10   Only connect! That was the whole of her sermon. Only connect the prose and the passion, and both will be exalted, and human love will be seen at its height. Live in fragments no longer. Only connect, and the beast and the monk, robbed of the isolation that is life to either, will die.
Howards End [1910], ch. 22

11   The echo began in some indescribable way to undermine her hold on life. Coming at a moment when she chanced to be fatigued, it had managed to murmur, "Pathos, piety, courage—they exist, but are identical, and so is filth. Everything exists, nothing has value." If one had spoken vileness in that place, or quoted lofty poetry, the [echo's] comment would have been the same—"Ou-boum."
A Passage to India [1924]

12   If I had to choose between betraying my country and betraying my friend, I hope I should have the guts to betray my country.
Two Cheers for Democracy [1951]. What I Believe

13   Two cheers for Democracy: one because it admits variety and two because it permits criticism. Two cheers are quite enough: there is no occasion to give three.   *Ibid.*

[Stella Maria] Miles Franklin
1879–1954

14   Weariness! Weariness! This was life—my life —my career, my brilliant career! I was fifteen— fifteen! A few fleeting hours and I would be as old as those around me.
My Brilliant Career [1901], ch. 5

Edmund L. Gruber
1879–1941

15 Over hill, over dale,[3] we have hit the dusty trail
And those caissons go rolling along.
The Caisson Song[4] [1908]

16 Oh, it's hi-hi-yee! for the field artilleree,
Shout out your numbers loud and strong,

[3]See Shakespeare, 172:30.
[4]The 1st Battalion of the 5th Field Artillery relieved the 2nd Battalion in the Philippines [April 1908]. Gruber, then a lieutenant in the 5th, was asked to write a song that would symbolize the spirit of the reunited regiment. There are many variant wordings.

And where'er we go, you will always know
That those caissons are rolling along.
                                        Ibid.

Joe Hill [Joseph Hillstrom]
1879–1915

1 Work and pray, live on hay,
You'll get pie in the sky when you die.
                        The Preacher and the Slave

2   Don't waste any time mourning—organize!
     *Letter to William D. Haywood [November 18,
     1915, the day before Hill's execution]*

John Haynes Holmes
1879–1964

3   If Christians were Christians, there would be no
anti-Semitism. Jesus was a Jew. There is nothing
that the ordinary Christian so dislikes to remember
as this awkward historical fact.
          The Sensible Man's View of Religion [1933]

4   The universe is not hostile, nor yet is it friendly.
It is simply indifferent.   *Ibid.*

Vachel Lindsay
1879–1931

5 Booth died blind and still by faith he trod,
Eyes still dazzled by the ways of God.
     *General William Booth Enters into Heaven
     [1913], II*

6 Sleep softly . . . eagle forgotten . . . under the
stone.   *The Eagle That Is Forgotten[1] [1913], st. 5*

7 Factory windows are always broken.
Somebody's always throwing bricks,
Somebody's always heaving cinders,
Playing ugly Yahoo tricks.
                        Factory Windows, st. 1

8 Fat black bucks in a wine-barrel room,
Barrel-house kings; with feet unstable,
Sagged and reeled and pounded on the table,
Pounded on the table,
Beat an empty barrel with the handle of a broom.
                        The Congo [1914], pt. I

9 Then I saw the Congo, creeping through the
black,
Cutting through the forest with a golden track.
                                        Ibid.

10 Be careful what you do,
Or Mumbo-Jumbo, God of the Congo,
And all of the other
Gods of the Congo,
Mumbo-Jumbo will hoo-doo you.
                                        Ibid.

11 A bronzed, lank man! His suit of ancient black,
A famous high top-hat and plain worn shawl
Make him the quaint great figure that men love,
The prairie-lawyer, master of us all.
     *Abraham Lincoln Walks at Midnight [1914],
     st. 3*

12 Spring came on forever,
Spring came on forever,
Said the Chinese nightingale.
               The Chinese Nightingale [1917], end

13 Planting the trees that would march and train
On, in his name to the great Pacific,
Like Birnam Wood to Dunsinane,[2]
Johnny Appleseed[3] swept on.
                    In Praise of Johnny Appleseed

Dixon Lanier Merritt
1879–1972

14 A wonderful bird is the pelican,
His bill will hold more than his belican.
He can take in his beak
Food enough for a week,
But I'm damned if I see how the helican.
                             The Pelican [1910]

Jack Norworth
1879–1959

15 Take me out to the ball game,
Take me out with the crowd.
Buy me some peanuts and cracker-jack—
I don't care if I never get back.
               Take Me Out to the Ball Game [1908][4]

16 For it's one, two, three strikes you're out
At the old ball game.
                                        Ibid.

Will Rogers
1879–1935

17   All I know is just what I read in the papers.
                                    Prefatory remark

18   I tell you folks, all politics is applesauce.
                    The Illiterate Digest [1924], p. 30

---

[1] John Peter Altgeld [1847–1902; governor of Illinois, 1893–1897], widely criticized for pardoning, in June 1893, the anarchists who had been serving life terms since the Haymarket riot in Chicago on May 4, 1886. In pardoning them, Altgeld declared that "the judge conducted the trial with malicious ferocity."

[2] See Shakespeare, 215:21.
[3] John Chapman [1774–1847].
    Remember Johnny Appleseed, / All ye who love the apple; / He served his kind by word and deed, / In God's grand greenwood chapel.—WILLIAM HENRY VENABLE [1836–1920], *Johnny Appleseed, st. 25*
[4] Music by ALBERT VON TILZER [1878–1956].

1   Everything is funny as long as it is happening to somebody else.   *The Illiterate Digest, p. 131*

2   More men have been elected between sundown and sunup than ever were elected between sunup and sundown.   *Ibid. p. 152*

3   A comedian can only last till he either takes himself serious or his audience takes him serious.   *Syndicated newspaper article*

4   I not only "don't choose to run"[1] [for President] but I don't even want to leave a loophole in case I am drafted, so I won't "choose." I will say "won't run" no matter how bad the country will need a comedian by that time.   *Ibid.*

5   Politics has got so expensive that it takes lots of money to even get beat with.   *Ibid.*

6   My forefathers didn't come over on the *Mayflower*, but they met the boat.[2]   *Remark*

7   I joked about every prominent man in my lifetime, but I never met one I didn't like.   *Epitaph*

Joseph Stalin
[Iosif Vissarionovich Dzhugashvili]
1879–1953

8   Print is the sharpest and the strongest weapon of our party.   *Speech [April 19, 1923]*

9   The most remarkable thing about socialist competition is that it creates a basic change in people's view of labor, since it changes the labor from a shameful and heavy burden into a matter of honor, matter of fame, matter of valor and heroism.   *Speech [June 27, 1930]*

10   The Hitlerite blackguards . . . have turned Europe into a prison of nations,[3] and this they call the new order in Europe.   *Address to the Moscow Soviet [November 6, 1942]*

11   The Pope! How many divisions has *he* got?   *From* WINSTON CHURCHILL, *The Gathering Storm [1948]*

12   You cannot make a revolution with silk gloves.   *Attributed*

13   A single death is a tragedy, a million deaths is a statistic.   *Attributed*

Wallace Stevens
1879–1955

14   Twenty men crossing a bridge,
Into a village,

Are twenty men crossing twenty bridges,
Into twenty villages,
Or one man
Crossing a single bridge into a village.
    Metaphors of a Magnifico [1923]

15   The book of moonlight is not written yet.
    The Comedian as the Letter C [1923], III, 1

16   And as he came he saw that it was spring,
A time abhorrent to the nihilist
Or searcher for the fecund minimum.
    Ibid. III, 4

17   The natives of the rain are rainy men.
    Ibid. IV, 1

18   The plum survives its poems.
    Ibid. V, 1

19   Yet the quotidian saps philosophers.
    Ibid. V, 4

20   Green crammers of the green fruits of the world.
    Ibid. VI, 2

21   Poetry is the supreme fiction, madame.
    A High-toned Old Christian Woman [1923]

22   Let be be finale of seem.
The only emperor is the emperor of ice-cream.
    The Emperor of Ice-Cream [1923]

23   Only, here and there, an old sailor,
Drunk and asleep in his boots,
Catches tigers
In red weather.
    Disillusionment of Ten O'clock [1923]

24   Complacencies of the peignoir, and late
Coffee and oranges in a sunny chair.
    Sunday Morning [1923], st. 1

25   She says, "But in contentment I still feel
The need of some imperishable bliss."
Death is the mother of beauty; hence from her,
Alone, shall come fulfillment to our dreams
And our desires.
    Ibid. st. 5

26   We live in an old chaos of the sun,
Or old dependency of day and night,
Or island solitude, unsponsored, free,
Of that wide water, inescapable.
Deer walk upon our mountains, and the quail
Whistle about us their spontaneous cries;
Sweet berries ripen in the wilderness;
And, in the isolation of the sky,
At evening, casual flocks of pigeons make
Ambiguous undulations as they sink,
Downward to darkness, on extended wings.
    Ibid. st. 8

27   Chieftain Iffucan of Azcan in caftan
Of tan with henna hackles, halt!
    Bantams in Pine Woods [1923], st. 1

28   Damned universal cock, as if the sun
Was blackamoor to bear your blazing tail.
    Ibid. st. 2

---

[1]See Coolidge, 614:18.
[2]Rogers was part Cherokee.
[3] . . . The saying that Russia is a prison of nations.— V. I. LENIN, *On the Question of National Policy* (and elsewhere)
    See Custine, 405:3.

1 I placed a jar in Tennessee,
  And round it was, upon a hill.
  It made the slovenly wilderness
  Surround that hill.
                    Anecdote of the Jar [1923], st. 1

2   Frogs Eat Butterflies. Snakes Eat Frogs. Hogs Eat
  Snakes. Men Eat Hogs.[1]   *Title of poem [1923]*

3 Just as my fingers on these keys
  Make music, so the self-same sounds
  On my spirit make a music, too.
                    Peter Quince at the Clavier [1923], I

4 Beauty is momentary in the mind—
  The fitful tracing of a portal;
  But in the flesh it is immortal.

  The body dies; the body's beauty lives.
                                        Ibid. IV

5 Susanna's music touched the bawdy strings
  Of those white elders; but, escaping,
  Left only Death's ironic scraping.
  Now, in its immortality, it plays
  On the clear viol of her memory,
  And makes a constant sacrament of praise.
                                        Ibid.

6 I do not know which to prefer,
  The beauty of inflections
  Or the beauty of innuendoes,
  The blackbird whistling
  Or just after.
                    *Thirteen Ways of Looking at a Blackbird
                    [1923], st. 5*

7 She sang beyond the genius of the sea.
  The water never formed to mind or voice,
  Like a body wholly body, fluttering
  Its empty sleeves; and yet its mimic motion
  Made constant cry, caused constantly a cry,
  That was not ours although we understood,
  Inhuman, of the veritable ocean.
                    The Idea of Order at Key West [1936], st. 1

8 Poetry is the subject of the poem.
                    The Man with the Blue Guitar [1937], XXII

9 I am a native in this world
  And think in it as a native thinks.
                                        Ibid. XXVIII

10   Light
  Is the lion that comes down to drink.
                    The Glass of Water [1942], st. 2

11 A. A violent order is disorder; and
   B. A great disorder is an order. These
   Two things are one.
                    Connoisseur of Chaos [1942], st. 1

12 One's grand flights, one's Sunday baths,
   One's tootings at the weddings of the soul
   Occur as they occur.
                    *The Sense of the Sleight-of-Hand Man [1942],
                    st. 1*

¹See Bierce, 544:16.

13 And, capable, created in his mind,
   Eventual victor, out of the martyrs' bones
   The ultimate elegance: the imagined land.
                    Mrs. Alfred Uruguay [1942], st. 4

14 The prologues are over. It is a question, now,
   Of final belief. So, say that final belief
   Must be in a fiction. It is time to choose.
                    Asides on the Oboe [1942], st. 1

15   To get at the thing
   Without gestures is to get at it as
   Idea.
                    So-and-So Reclining on Her Couch [1947], st. 6

16 It was the last nostalgia: that he
   Should understand.
                    Esthétique du Mal [1947], X

17 The greatest poverty is not to live
   In a physical world, to feel that one's desire
   Is too difficult to tell from despair.
                                        Ibid. XV

18 Thus the theory of description matters most.
   It is the theory of the word for those

   For whom the word is the making of the world,
   The buzzing world and lisping firmament.

   It is a world of words to the end of it,
   In which nothing solid is its solid self.
                    Description Without Place [1947], VII

19   Torn by dreams,

   By the terrible incantations of defeats
   And by the fear that defeats and dreams are one.

   The whole race is a poet that writes down
   The eccentric propositions of its fate.
                    Men Made Out of Words [1947]

20 The inconceivable idea of the sun.

   You must become an ignorant man again
   And see the sun again with an ignorant eye
   And see it clearly in the idea of it.
                    *Notes Toward a Supreme Fiction [1947]. It
                    Must Be Abstract, I*

21 The death of one god is the death of all.
                                        Ibid.

22 It is the celestial ennui of apartments
   That sends us back to the first idea.
                                        Ibid. II

23 And still the grossest iridescence of ocean
   Howls hoo and rises and howls hoo and falls.
                                        Ibid. III

24 We are the mimics. Clouds are pedagogues.
                                        Ibid. IV

25 The President ordains the bee to be
   Immortal.
                    Ibid. It Must Change, II

26 Booming and booming of the new-come bee.
                                        Ibid.

1   He chose to include the things
That in each other are included, the whole,
The complicate, the amassing harmony.
    *Notes Toward a Supreme Fiction. It Must Give
    Pleasure, VI*

2 These external regions, what do we fill them with
Except reflections, the escapades of death,
Cinderella fulfilling herself beneath the roof.
    Ibid. VIII

3   Perhaps
The man-hero is not the exceptional monster,
But he that of repetition is most master.
    Ibid. IX

4 They will get it straight one day at the Sorbonne.
    Ibid. X

5 And one trembles to be so understood and, at
    last,
To understand, as if to know became
The fatality of seeing things too well.
    The Novel [1950], st. 16

6 We keep coming back and coming back
To the real: to the hotel instead of the hymns
That fall upon it out of the wind.
    An Ordinary Evening in New Haven [1950], IX

7 Total grandeur of a total edifice,
Chosen by an inquisitor of structures
For himself. He stops upon this threshold
As if the design of all his words takes form
And frame from thinking and is realized.
    To an Old Philosopher in Rome [1950], st. 16

8 Light the first light of evening, as in a room
In which we rest and, for small reason, think
The world imagined is the ultimate good.
    *Final Soliloquy of the Interior Paramour [1950],
    st. 1*

9 We say God and the imagination are one . . .
How high that highest candle lights the dark.
    Ibid. st. 5[1]

10 There it was, word for word,
The poem that took the place of a mountain.
    *The Poem That Took the Place of a Mountain
    [1952], st. 1*

11 Is it Ulysses that approaches from the east,
The interminable adventurer?
    The World as Meditation [1952], st. 1

12 That scrawny cry—It was
A chorister whose *c* preceded the choir.
It was part of the colossal sun.
    *Not Ideas About the Thing but the Thing Itself
    [1954], st. 5*

13 The palm at the end of the mind,
Beyond the last thought, rises . . .

A gold-feathered bird
Sings in the palm.
    Of Mere Being [1957], st. 1, 2

[1]Ellipses are in the original text.

14   The essential gaudiness of poetry.
    Stevens's note to The Emperor of Ice-Cream

15   The essential thing in form is to be free in whatever form is used. A free form does not assure freedom. As a form, it is just one more form. So that it
comes to this, I suppose, that I believe in freedom
regardless of form.   *A Note on Poetry [1937]*

16   What makes the poet the potent figure that he is,
or was, or ought to be, is that he creates the world
to which we turn incessantly and without knowing
it and that he gives to life the supreme fictions without which we are unable to conceive of it.
    *The Noble Rider and the Sound of Words
    [1942]*

17   The subject matter of poetry is not that "collection of solid, static objects extended in space" but
the life that is lived in the scene that it composes; and
so reality is not that external scene but the life that
is lived in it. Reality is things as they are.
    The Necessary Angel [1951]

18   His [the poet's] function is to make his imagination theirs [the people's] and he fulfills himself only
as he sees his imagination become the light in the
minds of others. His role, in short, is to help people
to live their lives.   *Ibid.*

19   The humble are they that move about the world
with the lure of the real in their hearts.
    Ibid. About One of Marianne Moore's Poems

20   Poetry is poetry, and one's objective as a poet is
to achieve poetry precisely as one's objective in
music is to achieve music.
    *On selecting Domination of Black as his best
    poem*

21   A poem is a meteor.
    Opus Posthumous [1957]. Adagia

22   Sentimentality is a failure of feeling.   *Ibid.*

23   A poem should be part of one's sense of life.
    Ibid.

24   A poet looks at the world as a man looks at a
woman.   *Ibid.*

25   All history is modern history.   *Ibid.*

26   All poetry is experimental poetry.   *Ibid.*

27   Poetry is a purging of the world's poverty and
change and evil and death. It is a present perfecting,
a satisfaction in the irremediable poverty of life.
    Ibid.

28   In the world of words, the imagination is one of
the forces of nature.   *Ibid.*

29   God is in me or else is not at all (does not exist).
    Ibid.

30   The world is a force, not a presence.   *Ibid.*

31   Poetry is a search for the inexplicable.   *Ibid.*

Simeon Strunsky
1879–1948

1 Famous remarks are very seldom quoted correctly. *No Mean City [1944], ch. 38*

Leon Trotsky
[Lev Davidovich Bronstein]
1879–1940

2 The literary "fellow travelers" of the Revolution. *Literature and Revolution [1923], ch. 2*

3 The dictatorship of the Communist Party is maintained by recourse to every form of violence. *Terrorism and Communism [1924], p. 71*

4 It was the supreme expression of the mediocrity of the apparatus that Stalin himself rose to his position. *My Life [1930], ch. 40*

5 The vengeance of history is more terrible than the vengeance of the most powerful General Secretary. *Stalin [1946], ch. 12*

Guillaume Apollinaire
[Wilhelm Apollinaris de Kostrowitsky]
1880–1918

6 Shepherdess, O Eiffel Tower, your flock of bridges is bleating this morning.[1] *Alcools [1913].[2] Zone*

7 Come night, strike hour.
Days go, I endure.[3]
Ibid. Le Pont Mirabeau (Mirabeau Bridge), refrain

8 I hibernated in my past.[4]
Ibid. La Chanson du Mal-Aimé (Song of the Poorly Loved), st. 10

9 O Milky Way, sister in whiteness
To Canaan's rivers and the bright
Bodies of lovers drowned,
Can we follow toilsomely
Your path to other nebulae?[5]
Ibid. st. 13 (also st. 27)

10 Pass on, let us pass, all is passing,
And I will look back many times:

[1] Bergère ô tour Eiffel le troupeau des ponts bêle ce matin.
[2] Translated by WILLIAM MEREDITH.
[3] Vienne la nuit sonne l'heure / Les jours s'en vont je demeure.
[4] J'ai hiverné dans mon passé.
Translated by ROGER SHATTUCK.
[5] Voie lactée ô soeur lumineuse / Des blancs ruisseaux de Chanaan / Et des corps blancs des amoureuses / Nageurs morts suivrons-nous d'ahan / Ton cours vers d'autres nébuleuses.

The sound of hunting horns, when it dies
On the wind, is like our memories.[6]
Ibid. Cors de Chasse (Hunting Horns), st. 2, 3

George Asaf [George H. Powell]
1880–1951

11 What's the use of worrying?
It never was worthwhile,
So, pack up your troubles in your old kit-bag,
And smile, smile, smile.
Pack Up Your Troubles in Your Old Kit-Bag [1915][7]

Alexander Blok
1880–1921

12 With your whole body, with your whole heart, with your whole conscience, listen to the Revolution. . . . This is the music everyone who has ears should hear.
The Intelligentsia and the Revolution [1918]

William Claude Fields
1880–1946

13 It ain't a fit night out for man or beast. *The Fatal Glass of Beer*

14 Anyone who hates children and dogs can't be all bad.[8] *Attributed*

15 On the whole, I'd rather be in Philadelphia. *His own epitaph*

George Joseph Herriman
1880–1944

16 I ain't a Kat . . . and I ain't Krazy . . . it's what's behind me that I am . . . it's the idea behind me, Ignatz, and that's wot I am. *Krazy Kat (comic strip) [1913 and after]*

17 In my Kosmis there will be no feeva of discord . . . all my immotions will function in hominy and kind feelings. *Ibid.*

Helen Keller
1880–1968

18 The mystery of language was revealed to me. I knew then that "w-a-t-e-r" meant the wonderful

[6] Passons passons puisque tout passe / Je me retournerai souvent / / Les souvenirs sont cors de chasse / Dont meurt le bruit parmi le vent.
See Anonymous: French, 786:16.
[7] Music by FELIX POWELL.
[8] Anyone who hates babies and dogs can't be all bad.— LEO C. ROSTEN [1908–], *in tribute to Fields at a banquet [1939]*
The quip has become more familiar in the form attributed to Fields.

cool something that was flowing over my hand. That living word awakened my soul, gave it light, joy, set it free!   *The Story of My Life [1902], ch. 4*

Douglas MacArthur
1880–1964

1   I shall return.
On arriving in Australia from the Philippines [March 30, 1942]

2   I have returned. By the grace of Almighty God, our forces stand again on Philippine soil.
On landing on Leyte [October 17, 1944]

3   I see that the old flagpole still stands. Have your troops hoist the colors to its peak, and let no enemy ever haul them down.
To Colonel George M. Jones and 503rd Regimental Combat Team, who recaptured Corregidor [March 2, 1945]

4   In war there is no substitute for victory.
Address to a Joint Meeting of Congress [April 19, 1951]

5   I still remember the refrain of one of the most popular barracks ballads of that day, which proclaimed most proudly that old soldiers never die; they just fade away. I now close my military career and just fade away.[1]   *Ibid.*

George Catlett Marshall
1880–1959

6   If man does find the solution for world peace it will be the most revolutionary reversal of his record we have ever known.
Biennial Report of the Chief of Staff, United States Army [September 1, 1945]

7   Our policy is directed not against any country or doctrine but against hunger, poverty, desperation and chaos. Its purpose should be the revival of a working economy in the world so as to permit the emergence of political and social conditions in which free institutions can exist.
Address at Harvard University [June 5, 1947], announcing the European Recovery Plan (Marshall Plan)

8   It is not enough to fight. It is the spirit which we bring to the fight that decides the issue. It is morale that wins the victory.
Military Review [October 1948]

Henry Louis Mencken
1880–1956

9   The virulence of the national appetite for bogus revelation.   *A Book of Prefaces [1917], ch. 1*

[1]See Anonymous, 782:15.

10   Time is a great legalizer, even in the field of morals.   *Ibid. 4*

11   The public . . . demands certainties. . . . But there *are* no certainties.
Prejudices, First Series [1919], ch. 3

12   All successful newspapers are ceaselessly querulous and bellicose. They never defend anyone or anything if they can help it; if the job is forced upon them, they tackle it by denouncing someone or something else.   *Ibid. 13*

13   The great artists of the world are never Puritans, and seldom even ordinarily respectable.
Ibid. 16

14   Philadelphia is the most pecksniffian of American cities, and thus probably leads the world.
The American Language [1919]

15   If, after I depart this vale, you ever remember me and have thought to please my ghost, forgive some sinner and wink your eye at some homely girl.
Epitaph. From Smart Set [December 1921]

16   There are no mute, inglorious Miltons,[2] save in the hallucinations of poets. The one sound test of a Milton is that he functions as a Milton.
Prejudices, Third Series [1922], ch. 3

17   Nine times out of ten, in the arts as in life, there is actually no truth to be discovered; there is only error to be exposed.   *Ibid.*

18   Injustice is relatively easy to bear; what stings is justice.   *Ibid.*

19   The older I grow the more I distrust the familiar doctrine that age brings wisdom.   *Ibid.*

20   Faith may be defined briefly as an illogical belief in the occurrence of the improbable.   *Ibid. 14*

21   To be happy one must be (*a*) well fed, unhounded by sordid cares, at ease in Zion,[3] (*b*) full of a comfortable feeling of superiority to the masses of one's fellow men, and (*c*) delicately and unceasingly amused according to one's taste. It is my contention that, if this definition be accepted, there is no country in the world wherein a man constituted as I am—a man of my peculiar weakness, vanities, appetites, and aversions—can be so happy as he can be in the United States.   *On Being An American [1922]*

22   The difference between a moral man and a man of honor is that the latter regrets a discreditable act, even when it has worked and he has not been caught.
Prejudices, Fourth Series [1924], ch. 11

23   Out where the grass grows high, and the horned cattle dream away the lazy afternoons, and men still fear the powers and principalities of the air—out

[2]See Gray, 322:14.
[3]See *Amos 6:1,* 29:36.

there between the corn-rows he held his old puissance to the end.

> *In Memoriam: W[illiam] J[ennings] B[ryan]*
> *[1925]*

1   No one in this world, so far as I know . . . has ever lost money by underestimating the intelligence of the great masses of the plain people.[1]

> *Notes on journalism, Chicago Tribune*
> *[September 19, 1926]*

2   Of all escape mechanisms, death is the most efficient.   *A Book of Burlesques [1928]*

3   When A annoys or injures B on the pretense of saving or improving X, A is a scoundrel.

> *Newspaper Days: 1899–1906 [1941]*

4   Conscience is the inner voice which warns us somebody may be looking.

> *A Mencken Chrestomathy [1949]. Sententiae*

5   Puritanism—The haunting fear that someone, somewhere, may be happy.   *Ibid.*

6   There are some people who read too much: the bibliobibuli. I know some who are constantly drunk on books, as other men are drunk on whiskey or religion. They wander through this most diverting and stimulating of worlds in a haze, seeing nothing and hearing nothing.

> *Minority Report: H. L. Mencken's Notebooks*
> *[1956]*

7   The booboisie.   *Passim*

Robert von Edler Musil
1880–1942

8   One spent tremendous amounts on the army; but just enough to assure one of remaining the second weakest among the great powers.

> *The Man Without Qualities [1930],[2] bk. 1, ch. 8*

9   The number of portraits one saw of [Emperor Franz Joseph] was almost as great as the number of inhabitants of his realms. . . . Believing in his existence was rather like seeing certain stars although they ceased to exist thousands of years ago.

> *Ibid. 20*

Alfred Noyes
1880–1958

10 Go down to Kew in lilac time (it isn't far from London!)
And you shall wander hand in hand with love in summer's wonderland.

> *Barrel Organ, st. 5*

11 The wind was a torrent of darkness among the gusty trees,

The moon was a ghostly galleon tossed upon cloudy seas,
The road was a ribbon of moonlight over the purple moor,
And the highwayman came riding—
    Riding—riding—
The highwayman came riding, up to the old inn-door.

> *The Highwayman*

12 I'll come to thee by moonlight, though hell should bar the way.

> *Ibid.*

Grantland Rice
1880–1954

13 When the One Great Scorer comes to write against your name—
He marks—not that you won or lost—but how you played the game.

> *Alumnus Football*

14 All wars are planned by old men
In council rooms apart.[3]

> *Two Sides of War, st. 1*

15 Outlined against a blue-gray October sky, the Four Horsemen[4] rode again. In dramatic lore they were known as Famine, Pestilence, Destruction, and Death. These are only aliases. Their real names are Stuhldreher, Miller, Crowley, and Layden.[5]

> *Story on Notre Dame football victory over*
> *Army, New York Tribune [October 19, 1924]*

Richard Rowland
1880–1947

16 The lunatics have taken charge of the asylum.

> *Comment on the formation of United Artists*
> *film corporation [1920]*

[Giles] Lytton Strachey
1880–1932

17 The art of biography seems to have fallen on evil times in England. . . . With us, the most delicate and humane of all the branches of the art of writing has been relegated to the journeymen of letters; we do not reflect that it is perhaps as difficult to write a good life as to live one.[6]

> *Eminent Victorians [1918]. Preface*

18 If this is dying, then I don't think much of it.

> *Last words. From* MICHAEL HOLROYD, *Lytton*
> *Strachey [1968], vol. II*

---

[1]Often misquoted as "No one ever went broke underestimating the intelligence of the American people."
[2]Translated by EITHNE WILKINS and ERNST KAISER.
[3]See Hoover, 626:1.
[4]See Blasco-Ibáñez, 602:6.
[5]Thereafter known as the Four Horsemen of Notre Dame.
[6]See Carlyle, 412:23.

Richard Henry Tawney
1880–1962

1   Industrialized communities neglect the very objects for which it is worth while to acquire riches in their feverish preoccupation with the means by which riches can be acquired.
The Acquisitive Society [1920]

Thomas Russell Ybarra
1880–1971

2 A Christian is a man who feels
Repentance on a Sunday
For what he did on Saturday
And is going to do on Monday.
The Christian

Franklin Pierce Adams [F.P.A.]
1881–1960

3   Christmas is over and Business is Business.
For the Other 364 Days

4 Up, to the office . . . and so to bed.
A Ballade of Mr. Samuel Pepys. Refrain

5 Ruthlessly pricking our gonfalon bubble,
Making a Giant hit into a double,
Words that are weighty with nothing but trouble:
"Tinker to Evers to Chance."
Baseball's Sad Lexicon

6 The best you get is an even break.
Ballade of Schopenhauer's Philosophy

7 Of making many books there is no end—
So Sancho Panza said, and so say I.
Thou wert my guide, philosopher and friend
When only one is shining in the sky.
Lines on and from Bartlett's Familiar Quotations

8 Go, lovely Rose that lives its little hour!
Go, little booke! and let who will be clever!
Roll on! From yonder ivy-mantled tower
The moon and I could keep this up forever.
Ibid.

Daisy Ashford
[Margaret Mary Norman]
1881–1972

9   Bernard always had a few prayers in the hall and some whiskey afterwards as he was rarther pious.
The Young Visiters [1919], ch. 3

10   Here on a golden chair was seated the prince of Wales in a lovely ermine cloak and a small but costly crown.
Ibid. 6

11   Taking the bull by both horns he kissed her violently on her dainty face. My bride to be he murmured several times.
Ibid. 9

Joseph Campbell
1881–1944

12 As a white candle
In a holy place,
So is the beauty
Of an aged face.
The Old Woman, st. 1

Padraic Colum
1881–1972

13   A little house—a house of my own—
Out of the wind's and the rain's way.
An Old Woman of the Roads, st. 6

Sir Alexander Fleming
1881–1955

14   It is the lone worker who makes the first advance in a subject: the details may be worked out by a team, but the prime idea is due to the enterprise, thought and perception of an individual.
Address at Edinburgh University [1951]

Edgar Albert Guest
1881–1959

15 Somebody said that it couldn't be done,
But he with a chuckle replied
That maybe it couldn't, but he would be one
Who wouldn't say so till he'd tried.
It Couldn't Be Done

16 It takes a heap o' livin' in a house t' make it home,
A heap o' sun an' shadder, an' ye sometimes have t' roam
Afore ye really 'preciate the things ye lef' behind,
An' hunger fer 'em somehow, with 'em allus on yer mind.
Home

Pope John XXIII
[Angelo Giuseppe Roncalli]
1881–1963

17   The social progress, order, security and peace of each country are necessarily connected with the social progress, order, security and peace of all other countries.
Pacem in Terris. Encyclical letter [April 11, 1963]

1 The representative of the highest spiritual authority of the earth is glad, indeed boasts, of being the son of a humble but robust and honest laborer.
Remark to the mayor of Fleury-sur-Loire. From Wit and Wisdom of Good Pope John, collected by HENRI FESQUET *[1963]*[1]

2 Learn how to be a policeman, because that cannot be improvised. As regards being pope, you will see later. Anybody can be pope; the proof of this is that I have become one.
Ibid. Letter to a young boy

Pablo Picasso
1881–1973

3 God is really only another artist. He invented the giraffe, the elephant, and the cat. He has no real style. He just keeps on trying other things.
From FRANÇOISE GILOT *and* CARLTON LAKE, *Life with Picasso [1964], ch. 1*

4 Painting isn't an aesthetic operation; it's a form of magic designed as a mediator between this strange hostile world and us, a way of seizing the power by giving form to our terrors as well as our desires.
Ibid. VI

5 I am only a public entertainer who has understood his time.
Remark

Pierre Teilhard de Chardin[2]
1881–1955

6 We have only to believe. And the more threatening and irreducible reality appears, the more firmly and desperately must we believe. Then, little by little, we shall see the universal horror unbend, and then smile upon us, and then take us in its more than human arms.
The Divine Milieu [1957], pt. III, ch. 3, sec. B

7 If there were no internal propensity to unite, even at a prodigiously rudimentary level—indeed in the molecule itself—it would be physically impossible for love to appear higher up.
The Phenomenon of Man [1959], bk. IV, ch. 2, sec. 2

8 From an evolutionary point of view, man has stopped moving, if he ever did move.
Ibid. Postscript

William Temple
1881–1944

9 There is no structural organization of society which can bring about the coming of the Kingdom of God on earth, since all systems can be perverted by the selfishness of man.
The Malvern Manifesto [1941]

Ludwig Edler von Mises
1881–1973

10 Unemployment as a mass phenomenon is the outcome of allegedly "pro-labor" policies of the governments and of labor union pressure and compulsion.
Bureaucracy [1944]

11 The market economy as such does not respect political frontiers. Its field is the world.
Human Action [1949]

12 Everybody thinks of economics whether he is aware of it or not. In joining a political party and in casting his ballot, the citizen implicitly takes a stand upon essential economic theories.
Ibid.

13 Statistical figures referring to economic events are historical data. They tell us what happened in a nonrepeatable historical case.
Ibid.

Sir Pelham Grenville Wodehouse
1881–1975

14 So always look for the silver lining
And try to find the sunny side of life.
Sally [1920].[3] *Look for the Silver Lining*

15 "Sir Jasper Finch-Farrowmere?" said Wilfred.
"ffinch-ffarrowmere," corrected the visitor, his sensitive ear detecting the capital letters.
Meet Mr. Mulliner [1927]. A Slice of Life

16 Into the face of the young man who sat on the terrace of the Hotel Magnifique at Cannes there had crept a look of furtive shame, the shifty, hangdog look which announces that an Englishman is about to talk French.
The Luck of the Bodkins [1936]. The Luck of the Bodkins

17 I could see that if not actually disgruntled, he was far from being gruntled.
The Code of the Woosters [1938]. The Code of the Woosters

18 "I hate you, I hate you!" cried Madeline, a thing I didn't know anyone ever said except in the second act of a musical comedy.
Stiff Upper Lip, Jeeves [1963]

Max Born
1882–1970

19 The human race has today the means for annihilating itself—either in a fit of complete lunacy, i.e., in a big war, by a brief fit of destruction, or by careless handling of atomic technology, through a

---

[1]Translated by SALVATOR ATTANASIO.
[2]Translated by BERNARD WALL.

[3]Music by JEROME KERN.
BUDDY DE SYLVA may have contributed lyrics.

slow process of poisoning and of deterioration in its genetic structure.

Bulletin of the Atomic Scientists [June 1957]

Georges Braque
1882–1963

1   Art upsets, science reassures.

Pensées sur l'Art

2   Truth exists, only falsehood has to be invented.

Ibid.

Percy Williams Bridgman
1882–1961

3   The concept of length is . . . fixed when the operations by which length is measured are fixed . . . The concept is synonymous with the corresponding set of operations.

The Logic of Modern Physics [1927]

Edward Arthur Burroughs, Bishop of Ripon
1882–1934

4   The sum of human happiness would not necessarily be reduced if for ten years every physical and chemical laboratory were closed and the patient and resourceful energy displayed in them transferred to the lost art of getting on together and finding the formula for making both ends meet in the scale of human life.

Sermon to the British Association for the Advancement of Science, Leeds [September 4, 1927]

Father Divine [George Baker]
c. 1882–1965

5   Peace, it's wonderful.

Motto of the Peace Mission Movement

Sir Arthur Stanley Eddington
1882–1944

6   It is one thing for the human mind to extract from the phenomena of nature the laws which it has itself put into them; it may be a far harder thing to extract laws over which it has no control. It is even possible that laws which have not their origin in the mind may be irrational, and we can never succeed in formulating them.

Space, Time, and Gravitation [1920], ch. 12

7   If an army of monkeys were strumming on typewriters they *might* write all the books in the British Museum.

The Nature of the Physical World [1928], ch. 4

8   The road to a knowledge of the stars leads through the atom; and important knowledge of the atom has been reached through the stars.

Stars and Atoms [1928], lecture 1

Felix Frankfurter
1882–1965

9   The [Fifteenth] Amendment nullifies sophisticated as well as simple-minded modes of discrimination.   *Lane v. Wilson, 307 U.S. 268, 275 [1939]*

10   The history of liberty has largely been the history of the observance of procedural safeguards.

McNabb v. United States, 318 U.S. 332, 347 [1943]

11   One who belongs to the most vilified and persecuted minority in history is not likely to be insensible to the freedoms guaranteed by our Constitution. . . . But as judges we are neither Jew nor Gentile, neither Catholic nor agnostic.

Flag Salute Cases, 319 U.S. 624, 646 [1943]

12   After all, this is the Nation's ultimate judicial tribunal, not a super-legal-aid bureau.

Uveges v. Pennsylvania, 335 U.S. 437, 449 [1948]

13   In a democratic society like ours, relief must come through an aroused popular conscience that sears the conscience of the people's representatives.

Baker v. Carr, 369 U.S. 186, 270 [1962]

14   I know of no title that I deem more honorable than that of Professor of the Harvard Law School.

Of Law and Life and Other Things [1965]

Jean Giraudoux
1882–1944

15   There are truths which can kill a nation.

Electra

16   Faithful women are all alike, they think only of their fidelity, never of their husbands.

Amphitryon 38 [1929]

Samuel Goldwyn[1]
1882–1974

17   Include me out.   *Attributed*

18   In two words: im-possible.   *Attributed*

19   I read part of it all the way through.

Attributed

20   Anybody who goes to see a psychiatrist ought to have his head examined.   *Attributed*

[1]Goldwynisms—as his colorful misuses of English were popularly referred to—abounded. With so many gag writers working for him, hardly a lunch in Hollywood went by without somebody's concocting a malapropism and passing it off as something Sam Goldwyn had just said to him.—A. SCOTT BERG, *Goldwyn: A Biography [1989], p. 396*

1   We've passed a lot of water since then.
Attributed

2   Anything that man says you've got to take with a dose of salts.
Attributed

3   A verbal agreement isn't worth the paper it's written on.
Attributed

William Frederick Halsey, Jr.
1882–1959

4   Attack—Repeat—Attack.
Dispatch [October 26, 1942] to the South Pacific Force before the battle of Santa Cruz Islands

5   Hit hard, hit fast, hit often.
Formula for waging war

6   Our ships have been salvaged and are retiring at high speed toward the Japanese fleet.
Radio message [October 1944] after Japanese claims that most of the U.S. Third Fleet had either been sunk or had retired

James Joyce
1882–1941

7   He was outcast from life's feast.
Dubliners [1916]. A Painful Case

8   Snow was general all over Ireland. It was falling on every part of the dark central plain, on the treeless hills, falling softly upon the Bog of Allen and, farther westward, softly falling into the dark mutinous Shannon waves. It was falling, too, upon every part of the lonely churchyard on the hill where Michael Furey lay buried. It lay thickly drifted on the crooked crosses and headstones, on the spears of the little gate, on the barren thorns. His soul swooned slowly as he heard the snow falling faintly through the universe and faintly falling, like the descent of their last end, upon all the living and the dead.
Ibid. The Dead

9   Ireland is the old sow that eats her farrow.
A Portrait of the Artist as a Young Man [1916], ch. 5

10   The artist, like the God of the creation, remains within or behind or beyond or above his handiwork, invisible, refined out of existence, indifferent, paring his fingernails.
Ibid.

11   Welcome, O life! I go to encounter for the millionth time the reality of experience and to forge in the smithy of my soul the uncreated conscience of my race.
April 27. Old father, old artificer, stand me now and ever in good stead.
Ibid. Concluding words of Stephen Dedalus

12   The snotgreen sea. The scrotumtightening sea.
Ulysses [1922]

13   Agenbite of inwit.[1] Conscience.
Ibid.

14   History, Stephen said, is a nightmare from which I am trying to awake.
Ibid.

15   My patience are exhausted [Martha Clifford].
Ibid.

16   A man of genius makes no mistakes. His errors are volitional and are the portals of discovery.
Ibid.

17   I thought well as well him as another and then I asked him with my eyes to ask again yes and then he asked me would I yes to say yes my mountain flower and first I put my arms around him yes and drew him down to me so he could feel my breasts all perfume yes and his heart was going like mad and yes I said yes I will Yes.
Ibid. last words

18   riverrun, past Eve and Adam's, from swerve of shore to bend of bay, brings us by a commodius vicus of recirculation back to Howth Castle and Environs.
Finnegans Wake [1939], pt. I (opening)

19   O
          tell me all about
      Anna Livia! I want to hear all
about Anna Livia. Well, you know Anna Livia? Yes, of course, we all know Anna Livia. Tell me all. Tell me now.
Ibid.

20   Can't hear with bawk of bats, all thim liffeying waters of. Ho, talk save us! My foos won't moos. I feel as old as yonder elm. A tale told of Shaun or Shem? All Livia's daughtersons. Dark hawks hear us. Night! Night! My ho head halls. I feel as heavy as yonder stone. Tell me of John or Shaun? Who were Shem and Shaun the living sons or daughters of? Night now! Tell me, tell me, tell me, elm! Night night! Telmetale of stem or stone. Beside the rivering waters of, hitherandthithering waters of. Night!
Ibid.

21   Three quarks[2] for Muster Mark!   *Ibid. II*

22   I am passing out. O bitter ending! I'll slip away before they're up. They'll never see. Nor know. Nor miss me. And it's old and old it's sad and old it's sad and weary I go back to you, my cold father, my cold mad father, my cold mad feary father, till the near sight of the mere size of him, the moyles and moyles of it, moananoaning, makes me seasilt saltsick and I rush, my only, into your arms, I see them rising! Save me from those therrble prongs!   *Ibid. IV*

[1] *Ayenbite of Inwyt* [remorse of conscience]—Title of treatise on the seven deadly sins by DAN MICHEL OF NORTHGATE [fourteenth century]
[2] The origin of physicist Murray Gell-Mann's name [1964] for the basic building block of matter.

Fiorello Henry La Guardia
1882–1947

1   Ticker tape ain't spaghetti.
*Speech to the United Nations Relief and
Rehabilitation Administration [March 29, 1946]*

2   When I make a mistake it's a beaut!
On an indefensible appointment

Winifred Mary Letts
1882–c. 1936

3 I saw the spires of Oxford
As I was passing by,
The gray spires of Oxford
Against a pearl-gray sky.
My heart was with the Oxford men
Who went abroad to die.
The Spires of Oxford, st. 1

Jacques Maritain
1882–1973

4   In the modern social order, the *person* is sacrificed to the *individual*. The individual is given universal suffrage, equality of rights, freedom of opinion;
while the person, isolated, naked, with no social
armor to sustain and protect him, is left to the mercy
of all the devouring forces which threaten the life of
the soul, exposed to relentless actions and reactions
of conflicting interests and appetites. . . . It is a
homicidal civilization.   *Three Reformers [1925]*

Alan Alexander Milne[1]
1882–1956

5 James James
Morrison Morrison
Weatherby George Dupree
Took great care of his Mother
Though he was only three.
James James
Said to his Mother,
"Mother," he said, said he,
"You must never go down to the end of the town
if you don't go down with me."
*When We Were Very Young [1924].
Disobedience*

6 I do like a little bit of butter to my bread!
Ibid. The King's Breakfast

7   I am a Bear of Very Little Brain, and long words
Bother me.   *Winnie-the-Pooh [1926], ch. 4*

8   Time for a little something.   *Ibid. 6*

[1]See Dorothy Parker, 687:12.

Sam [Taliaferro] Rayburn
1882–1961

9   I like to make running water walk.
On Conversation. From Valton J. Young, *The
Speaker's Agent [1956]*

10   The one thing besides people that I claim to know
is land.   *Ibid.*

11   A jackass can kick a barn down, but it takes a
carpenter to build one.   *Remark [c. 1953]*

12   To get along, go along.   *Attributed*

Franklin Delano Roosevelt[2]
1882–1945

13   There is nothing I love as much as a good fight.
*Interview in the New York Times [January 22,
1911]*

14   These unhappy times call for the building of
plans . . . that build from the bottom up and not
from the top down, that put their faith once more in
the forgotten man[3] at the bottom of the economic
pyramid.   *Radio address [April 7, 1932]*

15   The country needs and, unless I mistake its temper, the country demands bold, persistent experimentation. It is common sense to take a method and
try it. If it fails, admit it frankly and try another. But
above all, try something.
*Address at Oglethorpe University, Atlanta,
Georgia [May 22, 1932]*

16   I pledge you, I pledge myself, to a new deal for the
American people.[4]
*Speech accepting the Democratic nomination for
the presidency, Chicago [July 2, 1932]*

17   There is no indispensable man.[5]
*Campaign speech, New York [November 3,
1932]*

18   The only thing we have to fear is fear itself.[6]
First Inaugural Address [March 4, 1933]

19   In the field of world policy I would dedicate this
nation to the policy of the good neighbor.[7]
Ibid.

20   If I were asked to state the great objective which
Church and State are both demanding for the sake of

[2]See Oliver Wendell Holmes, Jr., 543:14, and Lippmann,
677:1.
[3]All honor to the one that in this hour / Cries to the world as
from a lighted tower— / Cries for the Man Forgotten.—
Markham, *The Forgotten Man*
     See William Graham Sumner, 541:5.
[4]It seemed to me that what the nine hundred and ninety-four
dupes needed was a new deal.—Mark Twain, *A Connecticut
Yankee in King Arthur's Court* [1889], *ch. 13*
[5]Il n'y a point d'homme nécessaire.—*French proverb*
[6]See *Proverbs* 3:25, 20:22; Montaigne, 145:10; Francis
Bacon, 158:18; Wellington, 371:9; and Thoreau, 476:26.
[7]I am as desirous of being a good neighbor as I am of being
a bad subject.—Thoreau, *Civil Disobedience* [1849]

every man and woman and child in this country, I would say that that great objective is "a more abundant life."

Address to the Federal Council of Churches of Christ [December 6, 1933]

1   We are moving forward to greater freedom, to greater security for the average man than he has ever known before in the history of America.

Fireside Chat [September 30, 1934]

2   Out of this modern civilization economic royalists carved new dynasties. . . . The royalists of the economic order have conceded that political freedom was the business of the Government, but they have maintained that economic slavery was nobody's business.

Speech accepting renomination [June 27, 1936]

3   This generation of Americans has a rendezvous with destiny.   *Ibid.*

4   I have seen war. . . . I hate war.

Address at Chautauqua, New York [August 14, 1936]

5   I have not sought, I do not seek, I repudiate the support of any advocate of Communism or of any other alien "ism" which would by fair means or foul change our American democracy.

Address at Syracuse [September 29, 1936]

6   I should like to have it said of my first Administration that in it the forces of selfishness and of lust for power met their match. I should like to have it said of my second Administration that in it these forces met their master.

Speech at Madison Square Garden [October 31, 1936]

7   I see one-third of a nation ill-housed, ill-clad, ill-nourished.

Second Inaugural Address [January 20, 1937]

8   The test of our progress is not whether we add more to the abundance of those who have much; it is whether we provide enough for those who have too little.   *Ibid.*

9   The epidemic of world lawlessness is spreading. When an epidemic of physical disease starts to spread, the community approves and joins in a quarantine of the patients in order to protect the health of the community against the spread of the disease.

Speech at Chicago [October 5, 1937][1]

10   War is a contagion.   *Ibid.*

11   The only sure bulwark of continuing liberty is a government strong enough to protect the interests of the people, and a people strong enough and well enough informed to maintain its sovereign control over its government.

Fireside Chat [April 14, 1938]

12   A program whose basic thesis is not that the system of free private enterprise for profit has failed in this generation, but that it has not yet been tried.

Message on Concentration of Economic Power [April 29, 1938]

13   The Soviet Union, as everybody who has the courage to face the fact knows, is run by a dictatorship as absolute as any other dictatorship in the world.

Address to the American Youth Congress [February 10, 1940]

14   On this tenth day of June 1940 the hand that held the dagger has struck it into the back of its neighbor.[2]

Address at the University of Virginia, Charlottesville [June 10, 1940]

15   I have said this before, but I shall say it again and again and again: Your boys are not going to be sent into any foreign wars.

Campaign speech in Boston [October 30, 1940]

16   We must be the great arsenal of democracy.

Fireside Chat [December 29, 1940]

17   We look forward to a world founded upon four essential human freedoms. The first is freedom of speech and expression—everywhere in the world. The second is freedom of every person to worship God in his own way—everywhere in the world. The third is freedom from want . . . everywhere in the world. The fourth is freedom from fear . . . anywhere in the world.[3]

Message to Congress [January 6, 1941]

18   We, too, born to freedom, and believing in freedom, are willing to fight to maintain freedom. We, and all others who believe as deeply as we do, would rather die on our feet than live on our knees.[4]

On receiving the degree of Doctor of Civil Law from Oxford University [June 19, 1941]

19   Yesterday, December 7, 1941—a date which will live in infamy—the United States of America was suddenly and deliberately attacked by naval and air forces of the Empire of Japan.

War Message to Congress [December 8, 1941]

20   Never before have we had so little time in which to do so much.

Fireside Chat [February 23, 1942]

21   Books cannot be killed by fire. People die, but books never die. No man and no force can abolish memory. . . . In this war, we know, books are weapons.

Message to the American Booksellers Association [April 23, 1942]

[2]Italian Foreign Minister Count Galeazzo Ciano had just notified the French ambassador that Italy considered herself at war with France beginning June 11.

[3]See Roosevelt and Churchill, 650:8.

[4]See Zapata, 632:7.

[1]The "Quarantine the Aggressors" speech.

1   It is not a tax bill but a tax relief bill providing relief not for the needy but for the greedy.
Tax bill veto message [February 22, 1944]

2   I think I have a right to resent, to object to libelous statements about my dog.[1]
Speech at the Teamsters' Dinner, Washington [September 23, 1944]

3   All of our people all over the country—except the pure-blooded Indians—are immigrants or descendants of immigrants, including even those who came over here on the *Mayflower*.
Campaign speech in Boston [November 4, 1944]

4   The American people are quite competent to judge a political party that works both sides of a street.   *Ibid.*

5   We have learned that we cannot live alone, at peace; that our own well-being is dependent on the well-being of other nations, far away. We have learned that we must live as men, and not as ostriches, nor as dogs in the manger. We have learned to be citizens of the world, members of the human community.
Fourth Inaugural Address [January 20, 1945]

6   More than an end to war, we want an end to the beginnings of all wars.
Address written for Jefferson Day broadcast [April 13, 1945][2]

Franklin Delano Roosevelt and Winston Churchill

7   First, their countries seek no aggrandizement, territorial or other.
Second, they desire to see no territorial changes that do not accord with the freely expressed wishes of the peoples concerned.
Atlantic Charter, drawn up aboard the U.S.S. Augusta in Argentia Harbor, Newfoundland [issued August 14, 1941]

8   Sixth, after the final destruction of the Nazi tyranny, they hope to see established a peace which will afford to all nations the means of dwelling in safety within their own boundaries, and which will afford assurance that all the men in all the lands may live out their lives in freedom from fear and want.[3]
Ibid.

9   Eighth, they believe that all of the nations of the world, for realistic as well as spiritual reasons, must come to the abandonment of the use of force. Since no future peace can be maintained if land, sea or air armaments continue to be employed by nations

which threaten, or may threaten, aggression outside of their frontiers, they believe, pending the establishment of a wider and permanent system of general security, that the disarmament of such nations is essential.   *Ibid.*

James Stephens
1882–1950

10 I hear a sudden cry of pain!
There is a rabbit in a snare.
The Snare

11 Forgive us all our trespasses,
Little creatures, everywhere!
Little Things, st. 5

12 And, in cloud, and clod, to Sing
Of Everything and Anything!
The Pit of Bliss

13   Women are wiser than men because they know less and understand more.
The Crock of Gold [1912], ch. 2

14   They fell out over pigs, let them fall in over pigs.
In the Land of Youth [1924]

Virginia Woolf
1882–1941

15   On or about December, 1910, human character changed. I am not saying that one went out, as one might into a garden, and there saw that a rose had flowered, or that a hen had laid an egg. The change was not sudden and definite like that.
Mr. Bennett and Mrs. Brown [1924]

16   In people's eyes, in the swing, tramp, and trudge; in the bellow and uproar; the carriages, motor cars, omnibuses, vans, sandwich men shuffling and swinging; brass bands; barrel organs; in the triumph and the jingle and the strange high singing of some aeroplane overhead was what she loved; life; London; this moment in June.   *Mrs. Dalloway [1925]*

17   Those comfortably padded lunatic asylums which are known, euphemistically, as the stately homes of England.[4]
The Common Reader [1925]. Lady Dorothy Nevill

18   Trivial personalities decomposing in the eternity of print.   *Ibid. The Modern Essay*

19   There is no room for the impurities of literature in an essay.   *Ibid.*

20   That complete statement which is literature.
Ibid. How It Strikes a Contemporary

21   The word-coining genius, as if thought plunged into a sea of words and came up dripping.
Ibid. An Elizabethan Play

---

[1]It had been charged that the President's Scottie, Fala, allegedly stranded in the Aleutian Islands, had been brought home by a destroyer at a cost of millions.
[2]President Roosevelt died on April 12, at Warm Springs, Georgia.
[3]See F. D. Roosevelt, 649:17.

[4]See Hemans, 410:10 and note.

1 A biography is considered complete if it merely accounts for six or seven selves, whereas a person may well have as many thousand.
Orlando [1928], ch. 6

2 The beauty of the world has two edges, one of laughter, one of anguish, cutting the heart asunder.
A Room of One's Own [1929]

3 Women have served all these centuries as looking-glasses possessing the magic and delicious power of reflecting the figure of man at twice its natural size.
Ibid.

4 Death is the enemy. . . . Against you I will fling myself, unvanquished and unyielding, O Death.
The Waves [1931]

5 Surely it was time someone invented a new plot, or that the author came out from the bushes.
Between the Acts [1941]

Eubie [James Herbert] Blake
1883–1983

6 If I'd known I was going to live this long, I'd have taken better care of myself.
Attributed [1983]

Coco [Gabrielle] Chanel
1883–1971

7 How many cares one loses when one decides not to be something but to be someone.
Remark

8 There are people who have money and people who are rich.
Remark

9 As long as you know that most men are like children you know everything.
Remark

10 Fashion is architecture: it is a matter of proportions.
Remark

11 I wanted to give a woman comfortable clothes that would flow with her body. A woman is closest to being naked when she is well dressed.
Remark

Kahlil Gibran
1883–1931

12 Let there be spaces in your togetherness.
The Prophet [1923]. On Marriage

13 Work is love made visible. And if you cannot work with love but only with distaste, it is better that you should leave your work and sit at the gate of the temple and take alms of those who work with joy.
Ibid. On Work

14 You pray in your distress and in your need; would that you might pray also in the fullness of your joy and in your days of abundance.
Ibid. On Prayer

15 I have learned silence from the talkative, toleration from the intolerant, and kindness from the unkind; yet strange, I am ungrateful to those teachers.
Sand and Foam [1926]

Willie Howard
1883–1949

16 Comes de revolution, we'll eat strawberries and cream!
Ballyhoo of 1932 (vaudeville) [1932]

Franz Kafka
1883–1924

17 As Gregor Samsa awoke one morning from uneasy dreams he found himself transformed in his bed into a gigantic insect.[1]
The Metamorphosis [1915],[2] opening line

18 No one else could ever be admitted here, since this gate was made only for you. I am now going to shut it.
Parables. Before the Law[2]

19 The Messiah will come only when he is no longer necessary; he will come only on the day after his arrival; he will come, not on the last day, but on the very last.
Ibid. The Coming of the Messiah

20 "This village belongs to the Castle, and whoever lives here or passes the night here does so in a manner of speaking in the Castle itself. Nobody may do that without the Count's permission."
The Castle [1926][2]

21 The true way goes over a rope which is not stretched at any great height but just above the ground. It seems more designed to make people stumble than to be walked upon.
The Great Wall of China. Reflections

22 You do not need to leave your room. Remain sitting at your table and listen. Do not even listen, simply wait. Do not even wait, be quite still and solitary. The world will freely offer itself to you to be unmasked, it has no choice, it will roll in ecstasy at your feet.
Ibid.

23 I think we ought to read only the kind of books that wound and stab us. . . . We need the books that affect us like a disaster, that grieve us deeply, like the death of someone we loved more than ourselves, like being banished into forests far from everyone, like a suicide. A book must be the axe for the frozen sea inside us.
Letter to Oskar Pollak [January 27, 1904]

[1]When I read the line I thought to myself I didn't know anyone was allowed to write things like that. If I had known, I would have started writing a long time ago. So I immediately started writing short stories.—GARCÍA MÁRQUEZ
[2]Translated by WILLA and EDWIN MUIR.

1   Only our concept of time makes it possible for us to speak of the Day of Judgment by that name; in reality it is a summary court in perpetual session.
Letters. Quoted in MAX BROD, *Franz Kafka*

Nikos Kazantzakis
1883–1957

2   How simple and frugal a thing is happiness: a glass of wine, a roast chestnut, a wretched little brazier, the sound of the sea. . . . All that is required to feel that here and now is happiness is a simple, frugal heart.
Zorba the Greek [1946],[1] *ch. 7*

3   "Life is trouble," Zorba continued. "Death, no. To live—do you know what that means? To undo your belt and look for trouble!"   *Ibid. 8*

4   The highest point a man can attain is not Knowledge, or Virtue, or Goodness, or Victory, but something even greater, more heroic and more despairing: Sacred Awe!   *Ibid. 24*

5   The doors of heaven are adjacent and identical: both green, both beautiful. Take care, Adam!
The Last Temptation of Christ [1960],[2] *ch. 18*

John Maynard Keynes
1883–1946

6   He [Clemenceau] had one illusion—France; and one disillusion—mankind, including Frenchmen.
Economic Consequences of the Peace [1919], ch. 3

7   He [Woodrow Wilson] could write Notes from Sinai or Olympus; he could remain unapproachable in the White House or even in the Council of Ten and be safe. But if he once stepped down to the intimate equality of the Four, the game was evidently up.   *Ibid.*

8   *Long run* is a misleading guide to current affairs. *In the long run* we are all dead.
A Tract on Monetary Reform [1923], ch. 3

9   Marxian Socialism must always remain a portent to the historians of opinion—how a doctrine so illogical and so dull can have exercised so powerful and enduring an influence over the minds of men, and, through them, the events of history.
The End of Laissez-Faire [1925], ch. 3

10   The engine which drives Enterprise is not Thrift, but Profit.   *A Treatise on Money [1930]*

11   Lenin is said to have declared that the best way to destroy the capitalist system was to debauch the currency. By a continuing process of inflation, governments can confiscate, secretly and unobserved, an important part of the wealth of their citizens. . . . Lenin was certainly right.
Essay in Persuasion [1931], pt. II

12   The love of money as a possession—as distinguished from the love of money as a means to the enjoyments and realities of life—will be recognized for what it is, a somewhat disgusting morbidity, one of those semi-criminal, semi-pathological propensities which one hands over with a shudder to the specialists in mental disease.   *Ibid. V*

13   Words ought to be a little wild for they are the assault of thoughts on the unthinking.
In the New Statesman and Nation [July 15, 1933]

14   His [Newton's] peculiar gift was the power of holding continuously in his mind a purely mental problem until he had seen through it.
Essays in Biography [1933]

15   Of the maxims of orthodox finance, none, surely, is more antisocial than the fetish of liquidity. . . . It forgets that there is no such thing as liquidity of investment for the community as a whole.
The General Theory of Employment, Interest and Money [1936], ch. 12

16   There are no intrinsic reasons for the scarcity of capital.   *Ibid. 24*

17   Practical men, who believe themselves to be quite exempt from any intellectual influences, are usually the slaves of some defunct economist. Madmen in authority, who hear voices in the air, are distilling their frenzy from some academic scribbler of a few years back.   *Ibid.*

Alfred Hart Miles
1883–1956

18   Anchors aweigh, my boys,
Anchors aweigh!
Farewell to college joys,
We sail at break of day.

Anchors Aweigh [1907][3]

Benito Mussolini
1883–1945

19   The Italian proletariat needs a blood bath for its force to be renewed.
Editorial, Popolo d'Italia [1920]

20   War alone brings up to its highest tension all human energy and puts the stamp of nobility upon the peoples who have the courage to face it.
Written for The Italian Encyclopedia. From GEORGE SELDES, *Sawdust Caesar [1935]*

21   We have buried the putrid corpse of liberty.
Speech. From MAURICE PARMELEE, *Bolshevism, Fascism and the Liberal-Democratic State [1934]*

---

[1]Translated by CARL WILDMAN.
[2]Translated by P. A. BIEN.
[3]Music by CHARLES A. ZIMMERMAN.

José Ortega y Gasset
1883–1955

1 Rancor is an outpouring of a feeling of inferiority. *Meditations on Quixote [1911]*

2 I am myself and what is around me, and if I do not save it, it shall not save me. *Ibid.*

3 The Mediterraneans, who do not think clearly, do see clearly. *Ibid.*

4 Culture is not life in its entirety, but just the moment of security, strength, and clarity. *Ibid.*

5 Nations are formed and are kept alive by the fact that they have a program for tomorrow. *Invertebrate Spain [1922], ch. 2*

6 A society without an aristocracy, without an elite minority, is not a society. *Ibid. 4*

7 Conversation is the socializing instrument par excellence, and in its style one can see reflected the capacities of a race. *Ibid. 7*

8 The choice of a point of view is the initial act of a culture. *The Modern Theme [1923], ch. 7*

9 To define is to exclude and negate. *Ibid. appendix*

10 Order is not pressure which is imposed on society from without, but an equilibrium which is set up from within. *Mirabeau and Politics [1927]*

11 Europe is really a swarm: many bees on a single course. *The Revolt of the Masses [1930], prologue*

12 America, far from being the future, was in truth a remote past because it was primitivism. *Ibid.*

13 Minorities are individuals or groups of individuals especially qualified. The masses are the collection of people not specially qualified. *Ibid. ch. 1*

14 Our life is at all times and before anything else the consciousness of what we can do. *Ibid. 4*

15 A revolution only lasts fifteen years, a period which coincides with the effectiveness of a generation. *Ibid. 10*

16 War is not an instinct but an invention. *Ibid. epilogue*

17 It is not the material of life which makes up Dostoevski's "realism," but rather the shape of life. *Notes on the Novel [1948]*

18 The person portrayed and the portrait are two entirely different things. *The Dehumanization of Art [1948]*

19 The masses feel that it is easy to flee from reality, when it is the most difficult thing in the world. *Ibid.*

20 The metaphor is probably the most fertile power possessed by man. *Ibid.*

21 I am a Spaniard, that is to say, a man without imagination. *Esthetic Essays [1956]*

22 Primitive man is by definition tactile man. *Ibid.*

Joseph Alois Schumpeter
1883–1950

23 Entrepreneurial profit . . . is the expression of the value of what the entrepreneur contributes to production in exactly the same sense that wages are the value expression of what the worker "produces." It is not a profit of exploitation any more than are wages. *The Theory of Economic Development [1934], ch. 4*

24 Marxism is essentially a product of the bourgeois mind. *Capitalism, Socialism and Democracy [1942], ch. 1*

25 Capitalism inevitably and by virtue of the very logic of its civilization creates, educates and subsidizes a vested interest in social unrest. *Ibid. 13*

26 As a matter of practical necessity, socialist democracy may eventually turn out to be more of a sham than capitalist democracy ever was. *Ibid. 23*

Joseph Warren Stilwell
1883–1946

27 I claim we got a hell of a beating. We got run out of Burma and it is humiliating as all hell. I think we ought to find out what caused it, go back and retake it. *Statement [New Delhi, May 24, 1942] on the American retreat from Burma*

William Carlos Williams
1883–1963

28 No wreaths please—
especially no hothouse flowers.
Some common memento is better,
something he prized and is known by:
his old clothes—a few books perhaps. *Tract [1917]*

29 Hell take curtains! Go with some show
of inconvenience; sit openly—
to the weather as to grief.
Or do you think you can shut grief in? *Ibid.*

30 Who shall say I am not
the happy genius of my household? *Danse Russe [1917]*

1 so much depends
upon

a red wheel
barrow

glazed with rain
water

beside the white
chickens
                    Spring and All [1923], no. XXI

2 Mothlike in mists, scintillant in the minute

brilliance of cloudless days, with broad bellying
    sails
they glide to the wind tossing green water
from their sharp prows while over them the crew
    crawls.
                    The Yachts [1935], st. 2, 3

3 It's the anarchy of poverty
delights me.
                    The Poor [1938], st. 1

4   THESE
are the desolate, dark weeks
when nature in its barrenness
equals the stupidity of man.

The year plunges into night
and the heart plunges
lower than night.
                    These [1938], st. 1, 2

Will Cuppy
1884–1949

5   The Dodo never had a chance. He seems to have
been invented for the sole purpose of becoming extinct and that was all he was good for.
        How to Become Extinct [1941]. The Dodo

Texas [Mary Louise Cecilia] Guinan
1884–1933

6   Hello, sucker!   *Greeting to nightclub patrons*

Bert Kalmar
1884–1947
Harry Ruby
1895–1974
and
S. J. Perelman
1904–1979

7   I'd horsewhip you if I had a horse.
    *Horse Feathers (screenplay) [1932], spoken by
    Groucho Marx*

Alice Lee Roosevelt Longworth
1884–1980

8   Harding was not a bad man. He was just a slob.
                    Crowded Hours [1933]

9   I do wish [Calvin Coolidge] did not look as if he
had been weaned on a pickle.
    *Ibid. Attributing the remark to a fellow-patient
    of her doctor's*

10   If you can't say anything good about someone, sit
right here by me.
        Embroidered on a pillow in her sitting room

Sean O'Casey
1884–1964

11   The whole worl's in a state o' chassis.
    Juno and the Paycock[1] [1924], act I and passim

12   One minute with him is all I ask; one minute
alone with him, while you're runnin' for th' priest
an' th' doctor.
            The Plough and the Stars [1926], act II

13   A few hundhred scrawls o' chaps with a couple o'
guns and Rosary beads, again' a hundhred thousand
thrained men with horse, fut an' artillery . . .
an' he wants us to fight fair!   *Ibid. IV*

Anna Eleanor Roosevelt[2]
1884–1962

14   No one can make you feel inferior without your
consent.   *This Is My Story [1937]*

15   You gain strength, courage and confidence by
every experience in which you really stop to look
fear in the face. You are able to say to yourself, "I
lived through this horror. I can take the next thing
that comes along." . . . You must do the thing you
think you cannot do.
                You Learn by Living [1960]

Damon Runyon
1884–1946

16   Always try to rub up against money, for if you
rub up against money long enough, some of it may
rub off on you.
        Guys and Dolls [1931]. A Very Honorable Guy

17   I long ago come to the conclusion that all life is
6 to 5 against.
            Money from Home [1935]. A Nice Price

[1]See Aesop, 59:7.
[2]She would rather light candles than curse the darkness and
her glow has warmed the world.—ADLAI E. STEVENSON [No-
vember 7, 1962]
    It is better to light one candle than curse the darkness.—
Motto of the Christopher Society

1 A freeloader is a confirmed guest. He is the man who is always willing to come to dinner.
Short Takes [1946]. Freeloading Ethics

Sara Teasdale
1884–1933

2 When I am dead and over me bright April
Shakes out her rain-drenched hair,
Though you should lean above me
    broken-hearted,
I shall not care.
I Shall Not Care, st. 1

Norman Mattoon Thomas
1884–1968

3 I'd rather see America save her soul than her face.
Speech before antiwar protest, Washington, D.C. [November 27, 1965]

Harry S. Truman
1884–1972

4 When they told me yesterday what had happened, I felt like the moon, the stars and all the planets had fallen on me.
To reporters the day after his accession to the presidency [April 13, 1945]

5 When Kansas and Colorado have a quarrel over the water in the Arkansas River they don't call out the National Guard in each state and go to war over it. They bring a suit in the Supreme Court of the United States and abide by the decision. There isn't a reason in the world why we cannot do that internationally. *Speech in Kansas City [April 1945]*

6 Sixteen hours ago an American airplane dropped one bomb on Hiroshima. . . . The force from which the sun draws its power has been loosed against those who brought war to the Far East.
First announcement of the atomic bomb [August 6, 1945]

7 The release of atomic energy constitutes a new force too revolutionary to consider in the framework of old ideas.
Message to Congress on atomic energy [October 3, 1945]

8 Means of destruction hitherto unknown, against which there can be no adequate military defense, and in the employment of which no single nation can in fact have a monopoly.
Declaration on Atomic Energy by President Truman and Prime Ministers Clement Attlee (Britain) and W. L. Mackenzie King (Canada) [November 15, 1945]

9 Effective, reciprocal, and enforceable safeguards acceptable to all nations. *Ibid.*

10 If you can't stand the heat, get out of the kitchen.
Saying

11 Once a decision was made, I did not worry about it afterward.
Memoirs [1955], vol. II, Years of Trial and Hope, ch. 1

12 Most of the problems a President has to face have their roots in the past. *Ibid.*

13 The Marshall Plan will go down in history as one of America's greatest contributions to the peace of the world. *Ibid. 8*

14 To me, party platforms are contracts with the people. *Ibid. 13*

15 A President needs political understanding to *run* the government, but he may be *elected* without it. *Ibid. 14*

16 The convention system has its faults, of course, but I do not know of a better method for choosing a presidential nominee. *Ibid.*

17 The Bill of Rights, contained in the first ten amendments to the Constitution, is every American's guarantee of freedom. *Ibid. 19*

18 If there is one basic element in our Constitution, it is civilian control of the military. *Ibid.*

19 There is a right kind and wrong kind of victory, just as there are wars for the right thing and wars that are wrong from every standpoint. . . . The kind of victory MacArthur had in mind—victory by the bombing of Chinese cities, victory by expanding the conflict to all of China—would have been the wrong kind of victory. *Ibid.*

20 The buck stops here.
Sign on Truman's desk when President. From ALFRED STEINBERG. The Man from Missouri [1962]

21 The only thing new in the world is the history you don't know.
From MERLE MILLER, Plain Speaking: An Oral Biography of Harry S. Truman [1974], ch. 23

22 Secrecy and a free, democratic government don't mix. *Ibid. 35*

Charter of the United Nations

23 We, the peoples of the United Nations
Determined to save succeeding generations from the scourge of war, which twice in our lifetime has brought untold sorrow to mankind, and
To reaffirm faith in fundamental human rights, in the dignity and worth of the human person, in the equal right of men and women and of nations large and small, and . . . for these ends
To practice tolerance and live together in peace with one another as good neighbors, and
To unite our strength to maintain international peace and security . . .

Have resolved to combine our efforts to accomplish these aims.
Charter of the United Nations [June 1945], preamble[1]

Sophie Tucker[2]
c. 1884–1966

1   From birth to age eighteen, a girl needs good parents. From eighteen to thirty-five, she needs good looks. From thirty-five to fifty-five, she needs a good personality. From fifty-five on, she needs good cash.
Said at sixty-nine

2   I have been poor and I have been rich. Rich is better.   *Attributed*

Niels Bohr
1885–1962

3   In our description of nature the purpose is not to disclose the real essence of the phenomena but only to track down, so far as it is possible, relations between the manifold aspects of our experience.
Atomic Theory and the Description of Nature [1934]

Arthur Wallace Calhoun
1885–1978

4   Gentlemen of the old régime in the South would say, "A woman's name should appear in print but twice—when she marries and when she dies."
Social History of the American Family [1918], citing MYRTA LOCKETT AVARY, *Dixie After the War [1906]*

Zechariah Chafee, Jr.
1885–1957

5   The press is a sort of wild animal in our midst —restless, gigantic, always seeking new ways to use its strength. . . . The sovereign press for the most part acknowledges accountability to no one except its owners and publishers.
The Press Under Pressure [Nieman Reports, April 1948]

Isak Dinesen [Karen Blixen]
1885–1962

6   What is man, when you come to think upon him, but a minutely set, ingenious machine for turning

with infinite artfulness, the red wine of Shiraz into urine?   *Seven Gothic Tales [1934]. The Dreamers*

7   That old saying which the peasants call the bachelors' prayer: "I pray thee, good Lord, that I may not be married. But if I am to be married, that I may not be a cuckold. But if I am to be a cuckold, that I may not know. But if I am to know, that I may not mind."   *Ibid. The Poet*

8   I had seen a herd of elephant traveling through dense native forest . . . pacing along as if they had an appointment at the end of the world.
Out of Africa [1937], pt. I, ch. 1

9   If I know a song of Africa—I thought—of the giraffe, and the African new moon lying on her back, of the plows in the fields, and the sweaty faces of the coffee-pickers, does Africa know a song of me? Would the air over the plain quiver with a color that I had had on, or the children invent a game in which my name was, or the full moon throw a shadow over the gravel of the drive that was like me, or would the eagles of Ngong look out for me?   *Ibid. 4*

10   I have before seen other countries, in the same manner, give themselves to you when you are about to leave them.   *Ibid. V, 1*

11   Man and woman are two locked caskets, of which each contains the key to the other.
Winter Tales [1942]. A Consolatory Tale

Will Durant
1885–1981

12   Once more, in the great systole and diastole of history, an age of freedom ended and an age of discipline began.
Caesar and Christ [1944], ch. 10

13   A great civilization is not conquered from without until it has destroyed itself within. The essential causes of Rome's decline lay in her people, her morals, her class struggle, her failing trade, her bureaucratic despotism, her stifling taxes, her consuming wars.   *Ibid. Epilogue*

William Norman Ewer
1885–1976

14 How odd
Of God
To choose
The Jews.

How Odd[3]

---

[1]The preamble is based on a draft by JAN CHRISTIAN SMUTS [1870–1950].

[2]Known as "The Last of the Red-Hot Mamas" from the title of a song by JACK YELLEN, which she introduced in 1928.

[3]But not so odd / As those who choose / A Jewish God, / But spurn the Jews.—CECIL BROWNE

Not odd / Of God. / Goyim / Annoy 'im.—LEO C. ROSTEN [1908–]

Karen Horney

1885–1952

1   Fortunately [psycho]analysis is not the only way to resolve inner conflicts. Life itself still remains a very effective therapist.

Our Inner Conflicts [1945], conclusion

Ishikawa Takuboku

1885–1912

2 Like a kite
Cut from the string,
Lightly the soul of my youth
Has taken flight.

Song of My Youth[1]

Frank Hyneman Knight

1885–1974

3   Market competition is the only form of organization which can afford a large measure of freedom to the individual.

Freedom and Reform [1947], ch. 13

4   Large scale collective bargaining . . . is merely a seductive name for bilateral monopoly . . . and means either adjudication of conflicts in terms of power, or deadlock and stoppage, usually injuring outside people more than the immediate parties to the dispute.

Ibid.

Ring Lardner

1885–1933

5   "Are you lost, daddy?" I asked tenderly.
"Shut up," he explained.

The Young Immigrunts [1920]

6   A good many young writers make the mistake of enclosing a stamped, self-addressed envelope, big enough for the manuscript to come back in. This is too much of a temptation to the editor.

How to Write Short Stories [1924]

David Herbert Lawrence

1885–1930

7   You love me so much, you want to put me in your pocket. And I should die there smothered.

Sons and Lovers [1913], ch. 15

8 Not I, not I, but the wind that blows through me!
A fine wind is blowing the new direction of Time.

Song of a Man Who Has Come Through [1920]

9 If only I am keen and hard like the sheer tip of a wedge
Driven by invisible blows,

The rock will split, we shall come at the wonder,
we shall find the Hesperides.

Ibid.

10   He was a little model, was Benjamin. Doctor Franklin. Snuff-colored little man! Immortal soul and all!

Studies in Classic American Literature [1922], ch. 2

11 I never saw a wild thing
Sorry for itself.

Self-Pity [1923]

12 A snake came to my water trough
On a hot, hot day, and I in pajamas for the heat,
To drink there.

Snake [1923]

13 For he seemed to me again like a king,
Like a king in exile, uncrowned in the underworld,
Now due to be crowned again.

Ibid.

14   Necessary, forever necessary, to burn out false shames and smelt the heaviest ore of the body into purity.   *Lady Chatterley's Lover [1928]*

15   This is John Thomas marryin' Lady Jane.

Ibid.

16 How beastly the bourgeois is
especially the male of the species.

How Beastly the Bourgeois Is [1929]

17 Now in November nearer comes the sun
down the abandoned heaven.

November by the Sea [1929]

18   Beauty is a mystery. You can neither eat it nor make flannel out of it.

Sex Versus Loveliness [1930]

19   Sex and beauty are inseparable, like life and consciousness. And the intelligence which goes with sex and beauty, and arises out of sex and beauty, is intuition.

Ibid.

20   How the horse dominated the mind of the early races, especially of the Mediterranean! You were a lord if you had a horse. Far back, far back in our dark soul the horse prances. . . . The horse, the horse! The symbol of surging potency and power of movement, of action, in man.

Apocalypse [1931]

21   For man, as for flower and beast and bird, the supreme triumph is to be most vividly, most perfectly alive.

Ibid.

22   Whales in mid-ocean, suspended in the waves of the sea
great heaven of whales in the waters, old hierarchies.
And enormous mother whales lie dreaming
suckling their whale-tender young

---

[1] From *Modern Japanese Literature* [1960], edited by DONALD KEENE.

and dreaming with strange whale eyes wide open
in the waters of the beginning and the end.
Whales Weep Not! [1932]

1 Reach me a gentian, give me a torch!
Let me guide myself with the blue, forked torch of
a flower
down the darker and darker stairs, where blue is
darkened on blueness
even where Persephone goes, just now, from the
frosted September
to the sightless realm where darkness is awake
upon the dark.
Bavarian Gentians [1932]

2 Build then the ship of death, for you must take
the longest journey, to oblivion.
The Ship of Death [1932], V

Sam M. Lewis
1885–1959
and
Joe Young
1889–1939

3   How You Gonna Keep 'Em Down on the Farm
After They've Seen Paree?
Title and refrain of song [1919][1]

Sinclair Lewis
1885–1951

4   His name was George F. Babbitt [and] . . .
he was nimble in the calling of selling houses for
more than people could afford to pay.
Babbitt [1922], ch. 1

5   A sensational event was changing from the
brown suit to the gray the contents of his pockets.
He was earnest about these objects. They were of
eternal importance, like baseball or the Republican
Party.   *Ibid.*

6   I've never done a single thing I've wanted to in my
whole life! I don't know 's I've accomplished anything except just get along.   *Ibid. 34*

7   Every compulsion is put upon writers to become
safe, polite, obedient, and sterile. In protest, I de-
clined election to the National Institute of Arts and
Letters some years ago, and now I must decline the
Pulitzer Prize.[2]
*Letter declining the Pulitzer Prize for his novel
Arrowsmith [1926]*

8   What is love? . . . It is the morning and the
evening star.   *Elmer Gantry [1927], ch. 20*

9   Our American professors like their literature
clear and cold and pure and very dead.
*The American Fear of Literature. Address in
Stockholm on receiving the Nobel Prize for
Literature [December 12, 1930]*

10   It Can't Happen Here.   *Title of book [1935]*

François Mauriac
1885–1970

11   There is no accident in our choice of reading. All
our sources are related.
Mémoires Intérieures [1959]

André Maurois
1885–1967

12   The minds of different generations are as impenetrable one by the other as are the monads of Leibniz.
Ariel [1924],[3] *ch. 12*

13   Modesty and unselfishness—these are virtues
which men praise—and pass by.   *Ibid. 24*

Chester William Nimitz
1885–1966

14   Uncommon valor was a common virtue.
*Of the Marines at Iwo Jima [February–May
1945]*

George Smith Patton
1885–1945

15   Wars may be fought with weapons, but they are
won by men. It is the spirit of the men who follow
and of the man who leads that gains the victory.
In the Cavalry Journal [September 1933]

16   Battle is the most magnificent competition in
which a human being can indulge. It brings out all
that is best; it removes all that is base.
Message to his troops [1943]

17   A pint of sweat will save a gallon of blood.[4]
*War As I Knew It [1947], Appendix D, letter
[April 3, 1944]*

Ezra Pound
1885–1972

18 Your mind and you are our Sargasso Sea.
Portrait d'une Femme [1916]

19 Haie! Haie!
These were the swift to harry;

---

[1]Music by WALTER DONALDSON [1893–1947].
[2]Lewis became a member of the Institute in 1935.

[3]Translated by ELLA D'ARCY.
[4]A drop of sweat on the drill ground will save many drops
of blood on the battlefield.—AUGUST WILLICH [1810–1878],
The Army: Standing Army or National Army? [1866]

These the keen-scented;
These were the souls of blood.
Slow on the leash,
      pallid the leash-men!
The Return [1916]

1 The apparition of these faces in the crowd;
Petals on a wet, black bough.
In a Station of the Metro [1916]

2 Winter is icumen in,
Lhude sing Goddamm,
Raineth drop and staineth slop,
And how the wind doth ramm!
Sing: Goddamm.[1]
Ancient Music

3 The leaves fall early this autumn, in wind.
The paired butterflies are already yellow with
    August
Over the grass in the West garden;
They hurt me. I grow older.
The River Merchant's Wife: A Letter (After Rihaku)

4 For three years, out of key with his time,
He strove to resuscitate the dead art
Of poetry; to maintain "the sublime"
In the old sense. Wrong from the start—
No, hardly, but seeing he had been born
In a half savage country, out of date.
Hugh Selwyn Mauberley. E.P. Ode pour l'élection de son sepulchre [1920], I

5 His true Penelope was Flaubert,
He fished by obstinate isles.
Ibid.

6 The age demanded an image
Of its accelerated grimace,
Something for the modern stage,
Not, at any rate, an Attic grace.
Ibid. II

7 Better mendacities
Than the classics in paraphrase!
Ibid.

8 Some quick to arm,
some for adventure,
some from fear of weakness,
some from fear of censure,
some for love of slaughter, in imagination,
learning later . . .
some in fear, learning love of slaughter;
Died some, pro patria,
    non "dulce" non "et decor" . . .
walked eye-deep in hell
believing in old men's lies, the unbelieving
came home, home to a lie.
Ibid. IV[2]

9 hysterias, trench confessions,
laughter out of dead bellies.
Ibid.

10 There died a myriad,
And of the best, among them,
For an old bitch gone in the teeth,
For a botched civilization.

Charm, smiling at the good mouth,
Quick eyes gone under earth's lid,

For two gross of broken statues,
For a few thousand battered books.
Ibid. V

11   As for literature
It gives no man a sinecure.
And no one knows, at sight, a masterpiece.
"And give up verse, my boy,
There's nothing in it."
Ibid. IX. Mr. Nixon

12 Hang it all, Robert Browning,
there can be but the one "Sordello."
Cantos [1925–1959], II

13 And the betrayers of language
      ......n and the press gang
And those who had lied for hire;
The perverts, the perverters of language, the
    perverts, who have set money-lust
Before the pleasures of the senses;
howling, as of a hen-yard in a printing-house,
    the clatter of presses,
the blowing of dry dust and stray paper,
foetor, sweat, the stench of stale oranges.
Ibid. XIV

14 With *Usura*
With usura hath no man a house of good stone
each block cut smooth and well fitting.
Ibid. XLV

15 No picture is made to endure nor to live with
but it is made to sell and sell quickly
with usura, sin against nature,
is thy bread ever more of stale rags
is thy bread dry as paper.
Ibid.

16 Usura slayeth the child in the womb
It stayeth the young man's courting
It hath brought palsey to bed, lyeth
between the young bride and her bridegroom
CONTRA NATURAM
Ibid.

17 What thou lovest well remains, the rest is dross
What thou lov'st well shall not be reft from thee
What thou lov'st well is thy true heritage
Whose world, or mine or theirs or is it of none?
First came the seen, then thus the palpable
    Elysium, though it were in the halls of
    hell.
What thou lovest well is thy true heritage.
Ibid. LXXXI

[1]See Anonymous, 775:10.
[2]Ellipses are in the original text.

1 The ant's a centaur in his dragon world.
Pull down thy vanity, it is not man
Made courage, or made order, or made grace,
  Pull down thy vanity, I say pull down.
Learn of the green world what can be thy place
In scaled invention or true artistry,
Pull down thy vanity,
        Paquin pull down!
The green casque has outdone your elegance.
                                Cantos, LXXXI

2   The history of an art is the history of masterwork, not of failures, or mediocrity.
                        The Spirit of Romance [1910]

3   Poetry must be as well written as prose.
                Letter to Harriet Monroe [January 1915]

4   Objectivity and again objectivity, and expression:
no hindside-before-ness, no straddled adjectives (as
"addled mosses dank"), no Tennysonianness of
speech; nothing—nothing that you couldn't, in
some circumstance, in the stress of some emotion,
actually say.   *Ibid.*

5   Literature is language charged with meaning.
                            ABC of Reading [1934], ch. 2

6   Literature is news that *stays* news.   *Ibid.*

7   Genius . . . is the capacity to see ten things
where the ordinary man sees one, and where the
man of talent sees two or three, *plus* the ability to
register that multiple perception in the material of his
art.   *Jefferson and / or Mussolini [1935]*

8   America, my country, is almost a continent and
hardly yet a nation.   *Patria Mia*

Harold Tucker Webster
1885–1952

9   Caspar Milquetoast: The Timid Soul.
                        Character in series of cartoons

10   The Thrill that Comes Once in a Lifetime.
                        Title of series of cartoons

Humbert Wolfe
1885–1940

11 Like a small gray
coffee pot
sits the squirrel.
                        The Gray Squirrel [1924], st. 1

12 Listen! the wind is rising,
and the air is wild with leaves,
We have had our summer evenings,
now for October eves!
                    Autumn (Resignation) [1926], st. 2

13 You cannot hope
to bribe or twist,
thank God! the
British journalist.

But, seeing what
the man will do
unbribed, there's
no occasion to.
        *The Uncelestial City [1930], bk. I, ii, 2. Over
        the Fire*

Elinor Hoyt Wylie
1885–1928

14 We shall walk in velvet shoes:
Wherever we go
Silence will fall like dews
On white silence below.
                        Velvet Shoes [1921], st. 4

15 Avoid the reeking herd,
Shun the polluted flock,
Live like that stoic bird
The eagle of the rock.
                    The Eagle and the Mole [1921], st. 1

16 If you would keep your soul
From spotted sight or sound,
Live like the velvet mole;
Go burrow underground.

And there hold intercourse
With roots of trees and stones,
With rivers at their source,
And disembodied bones.
                                    Ibid. st. 5, 6

17 I love the look, austere, immaculate,
Of landscapes drawn in pearly monotones.
                        Wild Peaches [1921], st. 4

18 I was, being human, born alone;
I am, being woman, hard beset;
I live by squeezing from a stone
The little nourishment I get.
                    Let No Charitable Hope [1923], st. 2

19 If any have a stone to throw
It is not I, ever or now.
                                    The Pebble

20 The worst and best are both inclined
To snap like vixens at the truth;
But, O, beware the middle mind
That purrs and never shows a tooth!
                            Nonsense Rhyme, st. 2

21   Honeyed words like bees,
Gilded and sticky, with a little sting.
                                Pretty Words

Zoë Akins
1886–1958

22   The Greeks Had a Word for It.
                            Title of play [1930]

Karl Barth
1886–1968

1   Conscience is the perfect interpreter of life.
The Word of God and the Word of Man [1957]

2   We have before us the fiendishness of business competition and the world war, passion and wrongdoing, antagonism between classes and moral depravity within them, economic tyranny above and the slave spirit below.   *Ibid.*

William Rose Benét
1886–1950

3 And now there is merely silence, silence, silence,
  saying
All we did not know.

Sagacity

David Ben-Gurion
1886–1973

4   In Israel, in order to be a realist you must believe in miracles.   *Interview [October 5, 1956]*

Hugo La Fayette Black
1886–1971

5   No higher duty, or more solemn responsibility, rests upon this Court than that of translating into living law and maintaining this constitutional shield deliberately planned and inscribed for the benefit of every human being subject to our Constitution— of whatever race, creed or persuasion.
Chambers v. Florida, 309 U.S. 227 [1938]

6   The First Amendment has erected a wall between church and state. That wall must be kept high and impregnable. We could not approve the slightest breach.
Everson v. Board of Education, 330 U.S. 1 [1947]

7   It is my belief that there *are* "absolutes" in our Bill of Rights, and that they were put there on purpose by men who knew what words meant and meant their prohibitions to be "absolutes."
Interview Before the American Jewish Congress [April 14, 1962]

8   An unconditional right to say what one pleases about public affairs is what I consider to be the minimum guarantee of the First Amendment.
New York Times Company v. Sullivan, 376 U.S. 254 [1964]

9   In revealing the workings of government that led to the Vietnam War, the newspapers nobly did precisely that which the Founders hoped and trusted they would do.
Concurring opinion on the publication of the Pentagon Papers [1971]

Randolph Silliman Bourne
1886–1918

10   War is the health of the state. It automatically sets in motion throughout society those irresistible forces for uniformity, for passionate cooperation with the Government in coercing into obedience the minority groups and individuals which lack the larger herd sense.   *The State [1918]*

Frances Cornford
1886–1960

11 Magnificently unprepared
For the long littleness of life.
Rupert Brooke[1] [1915]

12 O why do you walk through the fields in gloves,
Missing so much and so much?
O fat white woman whom nobody loves,
Why do you walk through the fields in gloves
When the grass is as soft as the breast of doves
And shivering-sweet to the touch?
To a Fat Lady Seen from the Train [1915]

Alain-Fournier [Henri Alban Fournier]
1886–1914

13   Le Grand Meaulnes [The Wanderer].
Title of novel [1913]

Al Jolson
1886–1950

14   You ain't heard nothin' yet, folks.
Ad lib remark in the first talking motion picture, The Jazz Singer [July 1927]

Gus Kahn
1886–1941
and
Raymond B. Egan
1890–1952

15 There's nothing surer,
The rich get rich and the poor get poorer,
In the meantime, in between time,
Ain't we got fun.

Ain't We Got Fun [1921]

Joyce Kilmer
1886–1918

16 I think that I shall never see
A poem lovely as a tree.

Trees[2] [1913]

[1]See Brooke, 662.
[2]See Broun, 666:23, and Nash, 709:10.

1 Poems are made by fools like me,
But only God can make a tree.

Trees

Aldo Leopold
1886–1948

2   We abuse land because we regard it as a commodity belonging to us. When we see land as a community to which we belong, we may begin to use it with love and respect.

A Sand County Almanac [1949], foreword

3   Conservation is a state of harmony between men and land.   *Ibid. Part III, The Land Ethic*

Siegfried Sassoon
1886–1967

4 Soldiers are citizens of death's gray land.

Dreamers [1918]

5 Soldiers are dreamers; when the guns begin
They think of firelit homes, clean beds, and wives.

Ibid.

6 And when the war is done and youth stone dead
I'd toddle safely home and die—in bed.

Base Details [1918]

7 Who will remember, passing through this gate,
The unheroic dead who fed the guns?
Who shall absolve the foulness of their fate—
Those doomed, conscripted, unvictorious ones?

On Passing the New Menin Gate [1918]

Tanizaki Junichiro
1886–1965

8   The Chinese love jade. That strange lump of stone with its faintly muddy light, like the crystallized air of the centuries, melting dimly, dully back, deeper and deeper—are not we Orientals the only ones who know its charm? We cannot say ourselves what it is that we find in this stone. It quite lacks the brightness of a ruby or an emerald or the glitter of a diamond. But this much we can say: when we see that shadowy surface, we think how Chinese it is, we seem to find in cloudiness the accumulated sediment of the long Chinese past, we think how appropriate it is that the Chinese should admire that surface and that shadow.   *In Praise of Shadows [1934]*[1]

Paul Johannes Tillich
1886–1965

9   The name of this infinite and inexhaustible depth and ground of all being is *God*.

The Shaking of the Foundations [1948], ch. 7

[1]From Edward Seidensticker's adaptation, *Atlantic Monthly* Supplement: *Perspective of Japan* [January 1955].

10   Grace strikes us when we are in great pain and restlessness. . . . Sometimes at that moment a wave of light breaks into our darkness, and it is as though a voice were saying: "You are accepted."

Ibid. 19

11   The basic anxiety, the anxiety of a finite being about the threat of non-being, cannot be eliminated. It belongs to existence itself.

The Courage to Be [1952], ch. 2

Ruth Fulton Benedict
1887–1948

12   From the moment of his birth the customs into which [an individual] is born shape his experience and behavior. By the time he can talk, he is the little creature of his culture.[2]

Patterns of Culture [1934], ch. 1

13   Our children are not individuals whose rights and tastes are casually respected from infancy, as they are in some primitive societies. . . . They are fundamentally extensions of our own egos and give a special opportunity for the display of authority.

Ibid. 7

14   In world history, those who have helped to build the same culture are not necessarily of one race, and those of the same race have not all participated in one culture. In scientific language, culture is not a function of race.   *Race: Science and Politics [1940], ch. 2*

15   Racism is the dogma that one ethnic group is condemned by nature to congenital inferiority and another group is destined to congenital superiority.

Ibid. 7

16   The tough-minded . . . respect difference. Their goal is a world made safe for differences, where the United States may be American to the hilt without threatening the peace of the world, and France may be France, and Japan may be Japan on the same conditions.

The Chrysanthemum and the Sword [1946], ch. 1

Rupert Brooke[3]
1887–1915

17 Breathless, we flung us on the windy hill,
Laughed in the sun, and kissed the lovely grass.

The Hill [1910]

18 And then you suddenly cried, and turned away.

Ibid.

19   Oh! yet
Stands the church clock at ten to three?
And is there honey still for tea?

The Old Vicarage, Grantchester [1912]

[2]See Boas, 574:11.
[3]See Cornford, 661:11.

1 Fish say, they have their stream and pond;
But is there anything beyond?

Heaven [1913]

2 Then, the cool kindliness of sheets, that soon
Smooth away trouble; and the rough male kiss
Of blankets; grainy wood; live hair that is
Shining and free; blue-massing clouds; the keen
Unpassioned beauty of a great machine;
The benison of hot water; furs to touch;
The good smell of old clothes.

The Great Lover [1914]

3 If I should die, think only this of me:
That there's some corner of a foreign field
That is forever England.

The Soldier [1914]

4 Now, God be thanked, Who has matched us with
His hour,
And caught our youth, and wakened us from
sleeping.

Peace

5 Blow out, you bugles, over the rich dead!
There's none of these so lonely and poor of old,
But, dying, has made us rarer gifts than gold.

The Dead [1914], I

Marc Chagall
1887–1985

6 Do not leave my hand without light.

Interview [1977]

Marcus Garvey
1887–1940

7 We are not engaged in domestic politics, in
church building or in social uplift work, but we are
engaged in nation building.

*Speech, The Principles of the Universal Negro
Improvement Association, at New York
[November 25, 1922]*

Isaac Goldberg
1887–1938

8 Diplomacy is to do and say
The nastiest thing in the nicest way.

The Reflex

Martin Luis Guzmán
1887–1976

9 Here lay the dilemma: either Villa would submit
to the idea of the revolution without understanding
it, in which case he and the true revolution would
succeed; or Villa would follow his instincts blindly,
and the revolution and he would both fail.[1]

*El Aguila y la Serpiente (The Eagle and the
Serpent) [1928], pt. II, bk. I, ch. 1*

Robinson Jeffers
1887–1962

10 Lend me the stone strength of the past and I will
lend you
The wings of the future, for I have them.

To the Rock That Will be a Cornerstone [1924]

11 The deep dark-shining
Pacific leans on the land,
Feeling his cold strength
To the outmost margins.

Night [1925]

12 The world's God is treacherous and full of
unreason.

Birth-Dues [1928]

13 I'd sooner, except the penalties, kill a man than a
hawk.

Hurt Hawks [1928]

14 I have grown to believe
A stone is a better pillow than many visions.

Clouds of Evening [1930]

15 The strong lean upon death as on a rock.

Gale in April [1930]

16 Give Your Heart to the Hawks.

Title of poem [1933]

17 I hate my verses, every line, every word.

Love the Wild Swan

18 Does it matter whether you hate your . . . self?[2]
At least
Love your eyes that can see, your mind that can
Hear the music, the thunder of the wings. Love the
wild swan.

Ibid.

19 Well: the day is a poem but too much
Like one of Jeffers's, crusted with blood and
barbaric omens,
Painful to excess, inhuman as a hawk's cry.

The Day Is a Poem (September 19, 1939) [1941]

20 As for me, I would rather
Be a worm in a wild apple than a son of man.

Original Sin [1948]

Le Corbusier
[Charles Édouard Jeanneret]
1887–1965

21 A house is a machine for living in.[3]

Vers une Architecture [1923]

[1] Translated by RACHEL PHILLIPS.
[2] Ellipses are in the original text.
[3] Une maison est une machine-à-habiter.

Emilio Mola
1887–1937

1   Fifth column.[1]
Phrase, Spanish Civil War [1936–1939]

Sir Bernard Montgomery,
Viscount Montgomery of Alamein
1887–1976

2   To us is given the honor of striking a blow for freedom which will live in history, and in the better days that lie ahead men will speak with pride of our doings.
Message to his troops, on the eve of the Allied invasion of Europe [June 5, 1944]

Marianne Moore
1887–1972

3 Dürer would have seen a reason for living in a town like this.
The Steeple-Jack [1935], st. 1

4   The sweet air coming into your house on a fine day, from water etched
with waves as formal as the scales on a fish.
Ibid.

5 Of the crow-blue mussel shells, one keeps adjusting the ash heaps;
opening and shutting itself like

an
injured fan.
The Fish [1935], st. 1, 2

6 I, too, dislike it.
Reading it, however, with a perfect contempt
for it, one discovers in
it, after all, a place for the genuine.
Poetry [1935; revised 1967]

7 Nor till the poets among us can be
"literalists of
the imagination"—above
insolence and triviality and can present

for inspection, "imaginary gardens with real
toads in them," shall we have
it.
Ibid. st. 4, 5 (excluded in 1967 revision)[2]

8 I wonder what Adam and Eve
think of it by this time.
Marriage [1935]

9   Ecstasy affords
the occasion and expediency determines the form.
The Past Is the Present [1935]

10 My father used to say,
"Superior people never make long visits,
have to be shown Longfellow's grave
or the glass flowers at Harvard."
Silence [1935]

11 "The deepest feeling always shows itself in
silence;
not in silence, but restraint."
Nor was he insincere in saying, "Make my house
your inn."[3]
Inns are not residences.
Ibid.

12   There is a great amount of poetry in unconscious
fastidiousness.   *Critics and Connoisseurs [1935]*

13   What is our innocence,
what is our guilt? All are
naked, none is safe.
What Are Years? [1941]

14 The power of the visible
is the invisible.
He "Digesteth Harde Yron" [1941], st. 8

15 I am troubled, I'm dissatisfied, I'm Irish.
Spenser's Ireland [1941], last line

16 Another armored animal—scale
lapping scale with spruce cone regularity until
they
form the uninterrupted central
tail row!
The Pangolin [1941], st. 1

17   Bedizened or stark
naked, man, the self, the being we call human,
writing
master to this world.
Ibid. st. 8

18   Among animals, *one* has a sense of humor.
Humor saves a few steps, it saves years.   *Ibid.*

19   The prey of fear, he, always
curtailed, extinguished, thwarted by the dusk,
work partly done,
says to the alternating blaze,
"Again the sun!
anew each day; and new and new and new,
that comes into and steadies my soul."
Ibid. st. 9

20   What sap
went through that little thread
to make the cherry red!
Nevertheless [1944], st. 11

---

[1]Mola, one of Franco's generals, boasted that he had four columns of troops to lead against Madrid and a fifth column of sympathizers inside Madrid.

[2]Omissions are not accidents.—MARIANNE MOORE, *Complete Poems* [1967], *author's note*

[3]Author's note: Edmund Burke, in *Burke's Life,* by Prior: "Throw yourself into a coach," said he. "Come down and make my house your inn."

1 They say there is a sweeter air
    where it was made, than we have here.
                    A Carriage from Sweden [1944]

2   THE MIND IS AN ENCHANTING THING
is an enchanted thing,
    like the glaze on a
katydid-wing
    subdivided by sun
      till the nettings are legion.
    The Mind Is an Enchanting Thing [1944], st. 1

3 I inwardly did nothing.
O Iscariot-like crime!
              In Distrust of Merits [1941], st. 8

4 We don't like flowers that do
    not wilt; they must die, and nine
    she-camel hairs aid memory.
           The Sycamore [1956], st. 2

5   O to be a dragon,
a symbol of the power of Heaven — of silkworm
size or immense; at times invisible.
    Felicitous phenomenon!
            O To Be a Dragon [1959]

6 To wear the arctic fox
you have to kill it.
      The Arctic Ox (Or Goat) [1959], st. 1

7 Camels are snobbish
and sheep, unintelligent;
    water buffaloes, neurasthenic —
even murderous.
Reindeer seem over-serious.
                  Ibid. st. 9

8   Why an inordinate interest in animals and athletes? They are subjects for art and exemplars of it, are they not? minding their own business. Pangolins, hornbills, pitchers, catchers, do not pry or prey — or prolong the conversation; do not make us self-conscious; look their best when caring least.
    A Marianne Moore Reader [1961], foreword

Samuel Eliot Morison
1887–1976

9   A tough but nervous, tenacious but restless race [the Yankees]; materially ambitious, yet prone to introspection, and subject to waves of religious emotion. . . . A race whose typical member is eternally torn between a passion for righteousness and a desire to get on in the world.
    Maritime History of Massachusetts [1921], ch. 2

10   He [Columbus] enjoyed long stretches of pure delight such as only a seaman may know, and moments of high, proud exultation that only a discoverer can experience.
    Admiral of the Ocean Sea [1942], ch. 49

11   A few hints as to literary craftsmanship may be useful to budding historians. First and foremost, *get writing!*
    History as a Literary Art. Old South Leaflets, ser. II, No. 1 [1946]

12   America was discovered accidentally by a great seaman who was looking for something else; when discovered it was not wanted; and most of the exploration for the next fifty years was done in the hope of getting through or around it. America was named after a man who discovered no part of the New World. History is like that, very chancy.
    The Oxford History of the American People [1965], ch. 2

13   If the American Revolution had produced nothing but the Declaration of Independence, it would have been worth while.   *Ibid. 14*

Georgia O'Keeffe
1887–1986

14   Where I was born and where and how I have lived is unimportant. It is what I have done with where I have been that should be of interest.
    Georgia O'Keeffe [1976]

15   I find that I have painted my life — things happening in my life — without knowing.   *Ibid.*

16   I had to create an equivalent for what I felt about what I was looking at — not copy it.   *Ibid.*

John Reed
1887–1920

17   Ten Days That Shook the World.
    Title of his eyewitness account of the Bolshevik Revolution [1919]

Edith Sitwell
1887–1964

18 Lily O'Grady,
    Silly and shady,
    Longing to be
    A lazy lady.
           Façade [1923].[1] *Popular Song*

19 Still falls the Rain —
    Dark as the world of man, black as our loss —
    Blind as the nineteen hundred and forty nails
Upon the Cross.
           Still Falls the Rain [1940]

20   Rhythm is one of the principal translators between dream and reality. Rhythm might be described as, to the world of sound, what light is to the world of sight. It shapes and gives new meaning.
    The Canticle of the Rose [1949]. Some Notes on My Own Poetry

[1]Music by WILLIAM WALTON.

Alexander Woollcott
1887–1943

1   The two oldest professions in the world—ruined by amateurs.
The Knock at the Stage Door. The Actor and the Streetwalker

2   All the things I really like to do are either immoral, illegal, or fattening.   *Remark*

3   Germany was the cause of Hitler just as much as Chicago is responsible for the Chicago *Tribune*.
Last words before the microphone [January 23, 1943], on the People's Platform program

Maxwell Anderson
1888–1959

4   Oh, it's a long, long while
From May to December,
But the days grow short,
When you reach September.
Knickerbocker Holiday [1938].[1] *September Song*

5   Oh, the days dwindle down
To a precious few . . .
And these few precious days
I'll spend with you.

Ibid.

Maxwell Anderson
1888–1959
and
Laurence Stallings
1894–1968

6   What Price Glory?   *Title of play [1924]*

Bruce Bairnsfather
1888–1959

7   Well, if you knows of a better 'ole, go to it.
Fragments from France [1915]. Caption for cartoon

Irving Berlin
1888–1989

8 You've got to get up, you've got to get up,
You've got to get up this morning!
Oh! How I Hate to Get Up in the Morning [1918]

9   A Pretty Girl Is Like a Melody.
Ziegfeld Follies [1919], title of song

10 Dancing cheek to cheek.
Top Hat [1935]. Cheek to Cheek

[1]Music by KURT WEILL.

11 God bless America,
Land that I love.

God Bless America [1938]

12 From the mountains to the prairies,
To the oceans white with foam,
God bless America,
My home sweet home!

Ibid.

13 I'm dreaming of a white Christmas.
Holiday Inn [1942]. White Christmas

14 This is the army, Mr. Jones,
No private baths or telephones.
This Is the Army [1942], title song

15   There's No Business Like Show Business.
Annie Get Your Gun [1946], title of song

16   Anything You Can Do, I Can Do Better.
Ibid.

Georges Bernanos
1888–1948

17   Hell, Madame, is to love no longer.
Le Journal d'un Curé de Campagne (The Diary of a Country Priest) [1936]

18   Democracies cannot dispense with hypocrisy any more than dictatorships can with cynicism.
Nous Autres Français (We French)

19   The most dangerous of our calculations are those we call illusions.   *Dialogue des Carmelites [1949]*

Henry Beston
1888–1968

20   The world today is sick to its thin blood for lack of elemental things, for fire before the hands, for water welling from the earth, for air, for the dear earth itself underfoot.
The Outermost House [1928], ch. 1

21   The three great elemental sounds in nature are the sound of rain, the sound of wind in a primeval wood, and the sound of outer ocean on a beach.
Ibid. 3

22   For a moment of night we have a glimpse of ourselves and of our world islanded in its stream of stars—pilgrims of mortality, voyaging between horizons across the eternal seas of space and time.
Ibid.

Heywood Broun
1888–1939

23   "Trees" maddens me, because it contains the most insincere line ever written by mortal man. Surely the Kilmer tongue must have been not far

from the Kilmer cheek when he wrote, "Poems are made by fools like me."[1]

> *It Seems to Me [1935]. "Trees," "If," and "Invictus"*

1   Life is a copycat and can be bullied into following the master artist who bids it come to heel.

> *Ibid. Nature the Copycat*

Dale Carnegie
1888–1955

2   How to Win Friends and Influence People.
> *Title of book [1938]*

Joyce Cary [Arthur Joyce Lunel]
1888–1957

3   She had a mannish manner of mind and face, able to feel hot and think cold.
> *Herself Surprised [1941], ch. 7*

4   Sara could commit adultery at one end and weep for her sins at the other, and enjoy both operations at once.   *The Horse's Mouth [1944], ch. 8*

Raymond Chandler
1888–1959

5   The Big Sleep.   *Title of novel [1939]*

6   A blonde to make a bishop kick a hole in a stained glass window.
> *Farewell, My Lovely [1940], ch. 13*

7   Down these mean streets a man must go who is not himself mean.
> *The Simple Art of Murder [1950]*

John Foster Dulles
1888–1959

8   You have to take chances for peace, just as you must take chances in war. . . . The ability to get to the verge without getting into the war is the necessary art. If you try to run away from it, if you are scared to go to the brink,[2] you are lost.

> *From* JAMES SHEPLEY, *How Dulles Averted War, in Life [January 16, 1956]*

Thomas Stearns Eliot
1888–1965

9 Let us go then, you and I,
When the evening is spread out against the sky
Like a patient etherized upon a table.
> *The Love Song of J. Alfred Prufrock [1917]*

[1]See Kilmer, 661:16.
[2]From the phrase "to the brink" developed "brinkmanship."

10 In the room the women come and go
Talking of Michelangelo.
> *Ibid.*

11 There will be time to murder and create.
> *Ibid.*

12 And indeed there will be time
To wonder, "Do I dare?" and, "Do I dare?"
> *Ibid.*

13 I have measured out my life with coffee spoons.
> *Ibid.*

14 I should have been a pair of ragged claws
Scuttling across the floors of silent seas.
> *Ibid.*

15 Should I, after tea and cakes and ices,
Have the strength to force the moment to its crisis?
> *Ibid.*

16 I have seen the moment of my greatness flicker,
And I have seen the eternal Footman hold my coat, and snicker,
And in short, I was afraid.
> *Ibid.*

17 No! I am not Prince Hamlet, nor was meant to be;
Am an attendant lord, one that will do
To swell a progress, start a scene or two,
Advise the prince; no doubt, an easy tool,
Deferential, glad to be of use,
Politic, cautious, and meticulous;
Full of high sentence, but a bit obtuse;
At times, indeed, almost ridiculous—
Almost, at times, the Fool.
> *Ibid.*

18 I grow old . . . I grow old . . .
I shall wear the bottoms of my trousers rolled.
> *Ibid.*

19 Shall I part my hair behind? Do I dare to eat a peach?
I shall wear white flannel trousers, and walk upon the beach.
I have heard the mermaids singing,[3] each to each.

I do not think that they will sing to me.
> *Ibid.*

20 Till human voices wake us, and we drown.
> *Ibid.*

21 And I must borrow every changing shape
To find expression.
> *Portrait of a Lady [1917], III*

22 I am aware of the damp souls of housemaids
Sprouting despondently at area gates.
> *Morning at the Window [1917]*

23 The readers of the *Boston Evening Transcript*
Sway in the wind like a field of ripe corn.
> *The Boston Evening Transcript [1917]*

[3]See Donne, 228:5.

1 Upon the glazen shelves kept watch
  Matthew and Waldo, guardians of the faith,
  The army of unalterable law.[1]
                              Cousin Nancy [1917]

2 His laughter tinkled among the teacups.
                              Mr. Apollinax [1917]

3 Stand on the highest pavement of the stair—
  Lean on a garden urn—
  Weave, weave the sunlight in your hair.
                La Figlia Che Piange [1917], st. 1

4 Simple and faithless as a smile and shake of the
      hand.
                              Ibid. st. 2

5 Sometimes these cogitations still amaze
  The troubled midnight and the noon's repose.
                              Ibid. st. 3

6 Here I am, an old man in a dry month,
  Being read to by a boy, waiting for rain.
                              Gerontion [1920]

7 After such knowledge, what forgiveness? Think
      now
  History has many cunning passages, contrived
      corridors
  And issues, deceives with whispering ambitions,
  Guides us by vanities.
                              Ibid.

8 Neither fear nor courage saves us. Unnatural vices
  Are fathered by our heroism. Virtues
  Are forced upon us by our impudent crimes.
  These tears are shaken from the wrath-bearing
      tree.
                              Ibid.

9 I shall not want Honor in Heaven
  For I shall meet Sir Philip Sidney
  And have talk with Coriolanus
  And other heroes of that kidney.
                A Cooking Egg [1920], st. 3

10 Over buttered scones and crumpets
   Weeping, weeping multitudes
   Droop in a hundred A.B.C.'s.
                              Ibid. st. 8

11 The hippopotamus's day
   Is passed in sleep; at night he hunts;
   God works in a mysterious way—
   The Church can sleep and feed at once.
                The Hippopotamus [1920], st. 6

12 Webster was much possessed by death
   And saw the skull beneath the skin.
                Whispers of Immortality [1920], st. 1

13 He knew the anguish of the marrow
   The ague of the skeleton;
   No contact possible to flesh
   Allayed the fever of the bone.
                         Ibid. st. 4 [of Donne]

14 Uncorseted, her friendly bust
   Gives promise of pneumatic bliss.
                              Ibid. st. 5

15 Reorganized upon the floor
   She yawns and draws a stocking up.
        Sweeney Among the Nightingales [1920], st. 4

16 The nightingales are singing near
   The Convent of the Sacred Heart,

   And sang within the bloody wood
   When Agamemnon cried aloud,
   And let their liquid siftings fall
   To stain the stiff dishonored shroud.
                         Ibid. st. 9, 10

17 April is the cruellest month, breeding
   Lilacs out of the dead land, mixing
   Memory and desire, stirring
   Dull roots with spring rain.
        *The Waste Land [1922]. I, The Burial of the
        Dead*

18   You know only
   A heap of broken images, where the sun beats,
   And the dead tree gives no shelter, the cricket no
       relief,
   And the dry stone no sound of water. Only
   There is shadow under this red rock,
   (Come in under the shadow of this red rock),
   And I will show you something different from
       either
   Your shadow at morning striding behind you
   Or your shadow at evening rising to meet you;
   I will show you fear in a handful of dust.
                              Ibid.

19 I had not thought death had undone so many.[2]
   Sighs, short and infrequent, were exhaled.[3]
                              Ibid.

20 I think we are in rats' alley
   Where the dead men lost their bones.
                Ibid. II, A Game of Chess

21 O O O O that Shakespeherian Rag—
   It's so elegant
   So intelligent.
                              Ibid.

22 Hurry up please its time.
                              Ibid.

23 But at my back from time to time I hear[4]
   The sound of horns and motors, which shall bring
   Sweeney to Mrs. Porter in the spring.
   O the moon shone bright on Mrs. Porter
   And on her daughter
   They wash their feet in soda water.
                Ibid. III, The Fire Sermon

[1]See Meredith, 509:8.

[2]DANTE, *Inferno, canto III, ll. 55–57.*
[3]DANTE, *Inferno, canto IV, ll. 25–27.*
[4]See Marvell, 268:15.

1   At the violet hour, when the eyes and back
Turn upward from the desk, when the human
    engine waits
Like a taxi throbbing waiting,
I Tiresias, though blind, throbbing between two
    lives.
                                    Ibid.

2 When lovely woman stoops to folly[1] and
Paces about her room again, alone,
She smooths her hair with automatic hand,
And puts a record on the gramophone.
                                    Ibid.

3 Phlebas the Phoenician, a fortnight dead,
Forgot the cry of gulls, and the deep sea swell
And the profit and loss.
              Ibid. IV, Death by Water

4 Here is no water but only rock.
           Ibid. V, What the Thunder Said

5 Who is the third who walks always beside you?
                                    Ibid.

6 *Dayadhvam:* I have heard the key
Turn in the door once and turn once only
We think of the key, each in his prison
Thinking of the key, each confirms a prison.[2]
                                    Ibid.

7 These fragments I have shored against my ruins.
                                  Ibid.

8 We are the hollow men
We are the stuffed men
Leaning together
Headpiece filled with straw. Alas!
               The Hollow Men [1925], I

9 Shape without form, shade without color,
Paralyzed force, gesture without motion;

      Those who have crossed
With direct eyes, to death's other Kingdom
Remember us—if at all—not as lost
Violent souls, but only
As the hollow men
The stuffed men.
                                    Ibid.

10 Between the idea
  And the reality
Between the motion
  And the act
Falls the Shadow.
                                Ibid. V

11 This is the way the world ends
Not with a bang but a whimper.
                                Ibid.

12 A cold coming we had of it,
Just the worst time of the year.
          Journey of the Magi [1927]

13 Because I do not hope to turn again[3]
Because I do not hope
Because I do not hope to turn.
               Ash-Wednesday [1930], I

14 Because these wings are no longer wings to fly
But merely vans to beat the air
The air which is now thoroughly small and dry
Smaller and dryer than the will
Teach us to care and not to care
Teach us to sit still.
                                Ibid.

15 Terminate torment
Of love unsatisfied
The greater torment
Of love satisfied.
                                Ibid. II

16 Blown hair is sweet, brown hair over the mouth
    blown,
Lilac and brown hair;
Distraction, music of the flute, stops and steps of
    the mind over the third stair,
Fading, fading; strength beyond hope and despair
Climbing the third stair.
                                Ibid. III

17   Redeem
The time. Redeem
The unread vision in the higher dream
While jeweled unicorns draw by the gilded hearse.
                              Ibid. IV

18 Against the Word the unstilled world still whirled
About the center of the silent Word.
                              Ibid. V

19 Wavering between the profit and the loss
In this brief transit where the dreams cross
The dreamcrossed twilight between birth and
    dying.
                                Ibid. VI

20 The white sails still fly seaward, seaward flying
Unbroken wings.

And the lost heart stiffens and rejoices
In the lost lilac and the lost sea voices
And the weak spirit quickens to rebel
For the bent goldenrod and the lost sea smell.
                                Ibid.

21 Even among these rocks,
Our peace in His will.
                                Ibid.

22 What seas what shores what gray rocks and what
    islands
What water lapping the bow
And scent of pine and the woodthrush singing
    through the fog

---

[1]See Goldsmith, 328:29.
[2]See *The Upanishads*, 50:19.
[3]GUIDO CAVALCANTI, *Perch' Io Non Spero.*

What images return
O my daughter.

Marina [1930]

1   I'll convert *you!*
Into a stew.
A nice little, white little, missionary stew!

Sweeney Agonistes

2 Birth, and copulation, and death.
That's all the facts when you come to brass tacks.

Ibid.

3 Two live as one
One live as two
Two live as three
Under the bam
Under the boo
Under the bamboo tree.

Ibid.

4 Stone, bronze, stone, steel, stone, oakleaves,
    horses' heels
Over the paving.

Coriolan I. Triumphal March

5 O hidden under the dove's wing, hidden in the
    turtle's breast,
Under the palmtree at noon, under the running
    water
At the still point of the turning world. O hidden.

Ibid.

6 How unpleasant to meet Mr. Eliot![1]
With his features of clerical cut,
And his brow so grim
And his mouth so prim.

Five-Finger Exercises, V

7 Yet we have gone on living,
Living and partly living.

Murder in the Cathedral [1935], pt. I

8 They know and do not know, what it is to act or
    suffer.
They know and do not know, that acting is
    suffering.

Ibid.

9 Saint and Martyr rule from the tomb.

Ibid.

10 The last temptation is the greatest treason:
To do the right deed for the wrong reason.

Ibid.

11 Human kind cannot bear very much reality.[2]

Ibid. II

12 Time present and time past
Are both perhaps present in time future,
And time future contained in time past.

Four Quartets. Burnt Norton [1935], I

13 Footfalls echo in the memory
Down the passage which we did not take

Towards the door we never opened
Into the rose garden.

Ibid.

14 Garlic and sapphires in the mud
Clot the bedded axle-tree.
The trilling wire in the blood
Sings below inveterate scars
And reconciles forgotten wars.

Ibid. II

15 At the still point of the turning world.
    Neither flesh nor fleshless.

Ibid.

16   Except for the point, the still point,
There would be no dance, and there is only the
    dance.

Ibid.

17 Only through time time is conquered.

Ibid.

18 Sudden in a shaft of sunlight
Even while the dust moves
There rises the hidden laughter
Of children in the foliage
Quick now, here, now, always—
Ridiculous the waste sad time
Stretching before and after.

Ibid. V

19 Macavity, Macavity, there's no one like Macavity,
He's broken every human law, he breaks the law
    of gravity.
His powers of levitation would make a fakir stare,
And when you reach the scene of the crime—
Macavity's not there!

Old Possum's Book of Practical Cats [1939].
Macavity: The Mystery Cat

20 In my beginning is my end.

Four Quartets. East Coker [1940], I

21   Keeping time,
Keeping the rhythm in their dancing
As in their living in the living seasons
The time of the seasons and the constellations
The time of milking and the time of harvest
The time of the coupling of man and woman
And that of beasts. Feet rising and falling.
Eating and drinking. Dung and death.

Ibid.

22 What is the late November doing
With the disturbance of the spring.

Ibid. II

23 A periphrastic study in a worn-out poetical
    fashion,
Leaving one still with the intolerable wrestle
With words and meanings. The poetry does not
    matter.

Ibid.

[1]See Lear, 471:28.
[2]Also in *Four Quartets. Burnt Norton*, pt. I.

1 The only wisdom we can hope to acquire
Is the wisdom of humility: humility is endless.
Ibid.

2 The houses are all gone under the sea.
Ibid.

3 The dancers are all gone under the hill.
Ibid.

4 O dark dark dark.[1] They all go into the dark,
The vacant interstellar spaces, the vacant into the
vacant.
Ibid. III

5 And we all go with them, into the silent funeral,
Nobody's funeral, for there is no one to bury.
I said to my soul, be still,[2] and let the dark come
upon you
Which shall be the darkness of God.
Ibid.

6 To arrive where you are, to get from where you
are not,
You must go by a way wherein there is no
ecstasy.
In order to arrive at what you do not know
You must go by the way which is the way of
ignorance.
Ibid.

7 The whole earth is our hospital
Endowed by the ruined millionaire.
Ibid. IV

8 We call this Friday good.
Ibid.

9   And so each venture
Is a new beginning, a raid on the inarticulate
With shabby equipment always deteriorating
In the general mess of imprecision of feeling,
Undisciplined squads of emotion.
Ibid. V

10 Home is where one starts from. As we grow older
The world becomes stranger, the pattern more
complicated
Of dead and living. Not the intense moment
Isolated, with no before and after,
But a lifetime burning in every moment
And not the lifetime of one man only
But of old stones that cannot be deciphered.
Ibid.

11 Love is most nearly itself
When here and now cease to matter.
Old men ought to be explorers[3]
Here and there does not matter
We must be still and still moving
Into another intensity
For a further union, a deeper communion
Through the dark cold and the empty desolation,

The wave cry, the wind cry, the vast waters
Of the petrel and the porpoise. In my end is my
beginning.[4]
Ibid.

12 I do not know much about gods; but I think that
the river
Is a strong brown god—sullen, untamed and
intractable.
Ibid. The Dry Salvages [1941], I

13 The sea is the land's edge also, the granite
Into which it reaches, the beaches where it tosses
Its hints of earlier and other creation:
The starfish, the hermit crab, the whale's
backbone;
The pools where it offers to our curiosity
The more delicate algae and the sea anemone.
It tosses up our losses, the torn seine,
The shattered lobsterpot, the broken oar
And the gear of foreign dead men. The sea has
many voices.
Ibid.

14 There is no end of it, the voiceless wailing,
No end to the withering of withered flowers.
Ibid. II

15 The backward look behind the assurance
Of recorded history, the backward halflook
Over the shoulder, towards the primitive terror.
Ibid.

16 Time the destroyer is time the preserver.[5]
Ibid.

17   Not fare well,
But fare forward, voyagers.
Ibid. III

18   Music heard so deeply
That it is not heard at all, but you are the music
While the music lasts.
Ibid. V

19   Only undefeated
Because we have gone on trying;
We, content at the last
If our temporal reversion nourish
(Not too far from the yew tree)
The life of significant soil.
Ibid.

20 What the dead had no speech for, when living,
They can tell you, being dead: the communication
Of the dead is tongued with fire beyond the
language of the living.
Ibid. Little Gidding [1942], I

21 Ash on an old man's sleeve
Is all the ash the burnt roses leave.
Dust in the air suspended
Marks the place where a story ended.
Dust inbreathed was a house—

[1]See Milton, 261:7.
[2]See *Psalm 46:10*, 17:18.
[3]See Roethke, 725:11.

[4]See Mary, Queen of Scots, 147:13.
[5]See Bruno, 151:24.

The wall, the wainscot and the mouse
The death of hope and despair,
   This is the death of air.
                              Four Quartets. Little Gidding, II

1 Water and fire shall rot
The marred foundations we forgot,
Of sanctuary and choir.
   This is the death of water and fire.
                                                        Ibid.

2 In the uncertain hour before the morning
Near the ending of interminable night
At the recurrent end of the unending
After the dark dove with the flickering tongue
Had passed below the horizon of his homing.
                                                        Ibid.

3 Since our concern was speech, and speech
      impelled us
To purify the dialect of the tribe.[1]
                                                        Ibid.

4 Who then devised the torment? Love.
Love is the unfamiliar Name
Behind the hands that wove
The intolerable shirt of flame
Which human power cannot remove.
   We only live, only suspire
   Consumed by either fire or fire.
                                                   Ibid. IV

5   A people without history
Is not redeemed from time, for history is a pattern
Of timeless moments. So, while the light fails
On a winter's afternoon, in a secluded chapel
History is now and England.
                                                   Ibid. V

6 We shall not cease from exploration
And the end of all our exploring
Will be to arrive where we started
And know the place for the first time.
                                                        Ibid.

7 A condition of complete simplicity
(Costing not less than everything)
And all shall be well and
All manner of thing shall be well[2]
When the tongues of flame are infolded
Into the crowned knot of fire
And the fire and the rose are one.
                                                        Ibid.

8   It [tradition] cannot be inherited, and if you want
it you must obtain it by great labor.
            Tradition and the Individual Talent [1919]

9   The progress of an artist is a continual self-sacrifice, a continual extinction of personality.   *Ibid.*

[1]Donner un sens plus pur aux mots de la tribu.—MAL-
LARMÉ, *Le Tombeau d'Edgar Poe*
[2]See Juliana of Norwich, 127:21.

10   Poetry is not a turning loose of emotion, but an
escape from emotion; it is not the expression of
personality, but an escape from personality. But, of
course, only those who have personality and emotions know what it means to want to escape from
these things.   *Ibid.*

11   The only way of expressing emotion in the form
of art is by finding an "objective correlative"; in
other words, a set of objects, a situation, a chain of
events which shall be the formula of that *particular*
emotion.   *Hamlet and His Problems [1919]*

12   Immature poets imitate; mature poets steal.
                                       Philip Massinger [1920]

13   Every vital development in language is a development of feeling as well.   *Ibid.*

14   In the seventeenth century a dissociation of sensibility set in, from which we have never recovered;
and this dissociation, as is natural, was aggravated
by the influence of the two most powerful poets of
the century, Milton and Dryden.
                           The Metaphysical Poets [1921]

15   Poets in our civilization, as it exists at present,
must be *difficult*. . . . The poet must become more
and more comprehensive, more allusive, more indirect, in order to force, to dislocate if necessary, language into its meaning.   *Ibid.*

16   The great poet, in writing himself, writes his
time.
             Shakespeare and the Stoicism of Seneca [1927]

17   We know too much, and are convinced of too
little. Our literature is a substitute for religion, and
so is our religion.
                    A Dialogue on Dramatic Poetry [1928]

18   The general point of view may be described as
classicist in literature, royalist in politics, and Anglo-
Catholic in religion.
                      For Lancelot Andrewes [1928], preface

19   We fight for lost causes because we know that our
defeat and dismay may be the preface to our successors' victory, though that victory itself will be temporary; we fight rather to keep something alive than
in the expectation that anything will triumph.
                           Ibid. Francis Herbert Bradley

20   Genuine poetry can communicate before it is understood.   *Dante [1929]*

21   More can be learned about how to write poetry
from Dante than from any English poet. . . . The
language of each great English poet is his own language; the language of Dante is the perfection of a
common language.   *Ibid.*

22   Sometimes, however, to be a "ruined man" is
itself a vocation.
             *The Use of Poetry and the Use of Criticism
             [1933]. Wordsworth and Coleridge*

1   As things are, and as fundamentally they must always be, poetry is not a career, but a mug's game. No honest poet can ever feel quite sure of the permanent value of what he has written: he may have wasted his time and messed up his life for nothing.
Ibid. Conclusion

2   Most editors are failed writers — but so are most writers.
From ROBERT GIROUX, *The Education of An Editor [1982]*

Jules Furthman
1888–1960
and
William Faulkner
1897–1962

3   Maybe just whistle. You know how to whistle, don't you, Steve? You just put your lips together and blow.
To Have and Have Not (screenplay) [1944], spoken by Lauren Bacall

Joseph Patrick Kennedy
1888–1969

4   Don't get mad, get even.   *Attributed*

Ronald Arbuthnott Knox
1888–1957

5   There once was a man who said, "God
Must think it exceedingly odd
If he finds that this tree
Continues to be
When there's no one about in the Quad."
Limerick on idealism[1]

William L. Laurence
1888–1977

6   A great ball of fire about a mile in diameter, changing colors as it kept shooting upward, from deep purple to orange, expanding, growing bigger, rising as it was expanding, an elemental force freed from its bonds after being chained for billions of years.
On the first atom bomb explosion.[2] *In the New York Times [September 26, 1945]*

7   At first it was a giant column that soon took the shape of a supramundane mushroom.   *Ibid.*

T. E. Lawrence[3]
1888–1935

8   I loved you, so I drew these tides of men into my hands and wrote my will across the sky in stars.
To earn you Freedom, the seven-pillared worthy house, that your eyes might be shining for me
When we came.
Seven Pillars of Wisdom[4] *[1926], dedication*

9   There could be no honor in a sure success, but much might be wrested from a sure defeat.
Revolt in the Desert [1927], ch. 19

Katherine Mansfield
1888–1923

10   If there was one thing that he hated more than another it was the way she had of waking him in the morning. She did it on purpose, of course. It was her way of establishing her grievance for the day.
Bliss [1920]. Mr. Reginald Peacock's Day

11   I want, by understanding myself, to understand others. I want to be all that I am capable of becoming. . . . This all sounds very strenuous and serious. But now that I have wrestled with it, it's no longer so. I feel happy — deep down. *All is well.*
Journal [1922], last entry

Eugene O'Neill
1888–1953

12   Dat ole davil, sea.
Anna Christie [1922], act I

13   Gimme a whiskey — ginger ale on the side. And don't be stingy, baby.[5]   *Ibid.*

14   We's all poor nuts and things happen, and we yust get mixed in wrong, that's all.   *Ibid. IV*

15   For de little stealin' dey gits you in jail soon or late. For de big stealin' dey makes you emperor and puts you in de Hall o' Fame when you croaks. If dey's one thing I learns in ten years on de Pullman cars listenin' to de white quality talk, it's dat same fact.   *The Emperor Jones [1920], sc. i*

16   *Yank:* Sure! Lock me up! Put me in a cage! Dat's de on'y answer yuh know. G'wan, lock me up!
Policeman: What you been doin'?
Yank: Enough to gimme life for! I was born, see?

---

[1]Dear Sir, Your astonishment's odd: / I am always about in the Quad; / And that's why the tree / Will continue to be, / Since observed by Yours Faithfully, God. — *Anonymous rejoinder*
[2]At Alamogordo, New Mexico [July 16, 1945]. See also Oppenheimer, 714:12.
[3]Lawrence changed his name to T. E. Shaw in 1927.
[4]See *Proverbs 9:1,* 21:1.
[5]Made famous in the movie version (1930) as silent film star Greta Garbo's first speech in a talkie.

Sure, dat's de charge. Write it in de blotter. I was born, get me!   *The Hairy Ape [1922], sc. vii*

1 Desire Under the Elms.   *Title of play [1924]*

2 God is a Mother.   *Strange Interlude [1928], pt. I, act V*

3 Strange interlude! Yes, our lives are merely strange dark interludes in the electrical display of God the Father!   *Ibid. II, IX*

4 Mourning Becomes Electra.   *Title of dramatic trilogy [1931]*

5 The sea hates a coward.   *Mourning Becomes Electra [1931]. The Hunted, act IV*

6 The damned don't cry.   *Ibid. The Haunted, act III*

7 The dead! Why can't the dead die!   *Ibid. IV*

8 A Long Day's Journey into Night.   *Title of play [1956]*

9 Born in a goddam hotel room and dying in a hotel room!   *Last words. From LOUIS SHAEFFER, O'Neill: Son and Artist [1973]*

John Crowe Ransom
1888–1974

10 Two evils, monstrous either one apart,
Possessed me, and were long and loath at going:
A cry of Absence, Absence, in the heart,
And in the wood the furious winter blowing.
    Winter Remembered

11 The lazy geese, like a snow cloud
Dripping their snow on the green grass,
Tricking and stopping, sleepy and proud,
Who cried in goose, Alas.
    Bells for John Whiteside's Daughter

12 Here lies a lady of beauty and high degree.
Of chills and fever she died, of fever and chills,
The delight of her husband, her aunts, an infant
    of three,
And of medicos marveling sweetly on her ills.
    Here Lies a Lady

13 God have mercy on the sinner
Who must write with no dinner,
No gravy and no grub,
No pewter and no pub,
No belly and no bowels,
Only consonants and vowels.
    Survey of Literature

14 Captain Carpenter rose up in his prime
Put on his pistols and went riding out.
    Captain Carpenter, st. 1

Knute Kenneth Rockne
1888–1931

15 Show me a good and gracious loser and I'll show you a failure.[1]
    Remark to Wisconsin basketball coach Walter Meanwell [1920s]

16 Win this one for the Gipper.   *Attributed*[2]

Alan Seeger
1888–1916

17 I have a rendezvous with Death
At some disputed barricade,
When spring comes back with rustling shade
And apple blossoms fill the air.
    I Have a Rendezvous with Death [1916]

18 And I to my pledged word am true,
I shall not fail that rendezvous.
    Ibid.

Bartolomeo Vanzetti
1888–1927

19 If it had not been for this thing, I might have lived out my life talking at street corners to scorning men. I might have died unmarked, unknown, a failure. Now we are not a failure. This is our career and our triumph. Never in our full life could we hope to do such work for tolerance, for justice, for man's understanding of man, as now we do by accident.
    Letter to his son [April 1927]

20 Our words—our lives—our pains: nothing! The taking of our lives—lives of a good shoemaker and a poor fish peddler—all! That last moment belongs to us—that agony is our triumph.   *Ibid.*

21 I found myself compelled to fight back from my eyes the tears, and quanch my heart trobling to my throat to not weep before him. But Sacco's name will live in the hearts of the people when your name, your laws, institutions and your false god are but a dim rememoring of a cursed past in which man was wolf to the man.   *Last speech to the court*[3]

Henry Agard Wallace
1888–1965

22 The century on which we are entering can be and must be the century of the common man.
    Address, The Price of Free World Victory [May 8, 1942]

[1]More familiar version: Show me a good loser and I'll show you a loser.
[2]See Buckner, 719:7.
[3]Vanzetti and Nicola Sacco, Italian anarchists, were executed August 23, 1927, by the Commonwealth of Massachusetts on charges, never conclusively proved, of murder and robbery.

Conrad Aiken
1889–1973

1 Music I heard with you was more than music,
And bread I broke with you was more than
  bread.
Now that I am without you, all is desolate;
All that was once so beautiful is dead.
Bread and Music [1914]

2 All lovely things will have an ending,
All lovely things will fade and die,
And youth, that's now so bravely spending,
Will beg a penny by and by.
All Lovely Things

3 The hiss was now becoming a roar—the whole
world was a vast moving screen of snow—but
even now it said peace, it said remoteness, it said
cold, it said sleep.
Silent Snow, Secret Snow [1932]

4 O Altitudo in the bloodstream swims.[1]
And in the Human Heart [1940]. Sonnet 6

5 Ice is the silent language of the peak;
and fire the silent language of the star.
Ibid. 10

Anna Akhmatova[2]
1889–1966

6 Who will grieve for this woman? Does she not
  seem
too insignificant for our concern?
Yet in my heart I never will deny her,
Who suffered death because she chose to turn.
Lot's Wife [composed 1922–1924]

7 No foreign sky protected me,
no stranger's wing shielded my face.
I stand as witness to the common lot,
survivor of that time, that place.
*Requiem [composed mainly 1935–1940].
Epigraph [composed 1961]*

8 In the terrible years of the Yezhov terror I spent
seventeen months waiting in line outside the prison
in Leningrad. One day somebody in the crowd identified me . . . and asked me in a whisper . . .
"Can you describe this?" And I said: "I can."
Ibid. Instead of a Preface [composed 1957]

9 That was a time when only the dead
could smile.
Ibid. Prologue [composed 1935–1940]

10 I should be proud to have my memory graced,
but only if the monument be placed . . .

[1]See Thomas Browne, 248:4.
[2]Translated by STANLEY KUNITZ with MAX HAYWARD.

here, where I endured three hundred hours
in line before the implacable iron bars.
Ibid. Epilogue [composed 1940], II

Robert Charles Benchley
1889–1945

11 Why don't you slip out of those wet clothes and
into a dry Martini?
Attributed[3]

12 Tell us your phobias and we will tell you what
you are afraid of.
Phobias

13 In America there are two classes of travel—
first-class, and with children.
Kiddie-Kar Travel

14 A great many people have come up to me and
asked me how I manage to get so much work done
and still keep looking so dissipated. My answer is
"Don't you wish you knew?"
How to Get Things Done

15 It took me fifteen years to discover that I had no
talent for writing, but I couldn't give it up because
by that time I was too famous.
Remark

Charlie [Sir Charles Spencer] Chaplin
1889–1977

16 [The tramp character:] A tramp, a gentleman, a
poet, a dreamer, a lonely fellow, always hopeful of
romance and adventure.
My Autobiography [1964], ch. 10

17 All I need to make a comedy is a park, a policeman, and a pretty girl.
Ibid.

18 I am known in parts of the world by people who
have never heard of Jesus Christ.[4]
*From Lita Grey Chaplin, My Life with Chaplin
[1966]*

Jean Cocteau
1889–1963

19 Mirrors should reflect a little before throwing
back images.
Des Beaux-Arts

20 The worst tragedy for a poet is to be admired
through being misunderstood.
Le Rappel à l'Ordre [1926]

21 The Blood of a Poet.
Title of film [1933]

22 The matters I relate
Are true lies.[5]
*The Journals of Jean Cocteau [1956]. Quoted
by WALLACE FOWLIE in the introduction*

[3]Spoken by him in the movie *The Major and the Minor*
[1942].
[4]See Lennon, 770:6.
[5]Les choses que je conte / Sont des mensonges vrais.

Christopher Dawson
1889–1970

1   As soon as men decide that all means are permitted to fight an evil, then their good becomes indistinguishable from the evil that they set out to destroy.
The Judgment of the Nations [1942]

Philip Guedalla
1889–1944

2   The work of Henry James has always seemed divisible by a simple dynastic arrangement into three reigns: James I, James II, and the Old Pretender.
Supers and Supermen [1920]

Adolf Hitler
1889–1945

3   My adversaries . . . applied the one means that wins the easiest victory over reason: terror and force.
Mein Kampf (My Battle) [1933], vol. I, ch. 2

4   A majority can never replace the man. . . . Just as a hundred fools do not make one wise man, an heroic decision is not likely to come from a hundred cowards.
Ibid. 3

5   Strength lies not in defense but in attack.
Ibid.

6   All propaganda has to be popular and has to adapt its spiritual level to the perception of the least intelligent of those towards whom it intends to direct itself.
Ibid. 6

7   The great masses of the people . . . will more easily fall victims to a big lie than to a small one.
Ibid. 10

8   Never tolerate the establishment of two continental powers in Europe.
Ibid. II, 14

9   After all, who remembers the Armenians?
Attributed remark, prior to the invasion of Poland [1939]

10   After fifteen years of work I have achieved, as a common German soldier and merely with my fanatical will power, the unity of the German nation, and have freed it from the death sentence of Versailles.[1]
Proclamation to the troops on taking over the leadership of the German armed forces [December 21, 1941]

11   This war no longer bears the characteristics of former inter-European conflicts. It is one of those

[1]The Allied and Associated Governments affirm and Germany accepts the responsibility of Germany and her Allies for causing all the loss and damage to which the Allied and Associated Governments and their nationals have been subjected as a consequence of the war imposed upon them by the aggression of Germany and her Allies.—*Article 231 (the "war guilt clause"), Treaty of Versailles [June 28, 1919]*

elemental conflicts which usher in a new millennium and which shake the world once in a thousand years.
Speech to the Reichstag [April 26, 1942]

12   Is Paris burning?[2]
Asked at the Oberkommando der Wehrmacht, Rastenburg, Germany [August 25, 1944]

George S. Kaufman
1889–1961

13   Satire is what closes Saturday night.   *Saying*

George S. Kaufman
1889–1961
and
Moss Hart
1904–1961

14   You Can't Take It with You.
Title of play [1936]

15   The Man Who Came to Dinner.
Title of play [1939]

16   George Washington Slept Here.
Title of play [1940]

Stoddard King
1889–1933

17 There's a long, long trail a-winding
Into the land of my dreams,
Where the nightingales are singing
And a white moon beams.
The Long, Long Trail[3] [1913]

Walter Lippmann
1889–1974

18   Whether we wish it or not we are involved in the world's problems, and all the winds of heaven blow through our land.
A Preface to Politics [1913], ch. 4

19   What each man does is based not on direct and certain knowledge, but on pictures made by himself or given to him. . . . The way in which the world is imagined determines at any particular moment what men will do.
Public Opinion [1922], ch. 1, The World Outside and the Pictures in Our Heads

20   In the great blooming, buzzing confusion of the outer world we pick out what our culture has already defined for us, and we tend to perceive that

[2]Brennt Paris?
[3]Music by Zo ELLIOTT.

which we have picked out in the form stereotyped for us by our culture. *Ibid. ch. 6, Stereotypes*

1 Franklin D. Roosevelt is no crusader. He is no tribune of the people. He is no enemy of entrenched privilege. He is a pleasant man who, without any important qualifications for the office, would very much like to be President.
Today and Tomorrow [January 8, 1932]

2 In government offices which are sensitive to the vehemence and passion of mass sentiment public men have no sure tenure. They are in effect perpetual office seekers, always on trial for their political lives, always required to court their restless constituents.
Essays in the Public Philosophy [1935]

3 The final test of a leader is that he leaves behind him in other men the conviction and the will to carry on. . . . The genius of a good leader is to leave behind him a situation which common sense, without the grace of genius, can deal with successfully.
Roosevelt Has Gone [April 14, 1945]

4 We have neglected our own affairs. Our education is inadequate, our cities are badly built, our social arrangements are unsatisfactory. We can't wait another generation. Unless we can surmount this crisis, and work and get going onto the path of a settlement in Asia, and a settlement in Europe, all of these plans of the Great Society here at home, all the plans for the rebuilding of backward countries in other continents will all be put on the shelf, because war interrupts everything like that.
Conversations with Walter Lippmann [1965]. Lippmann and Eric Sevareid [February 22, 1965]

5 A free press is not a privilege but an organic necessity in a great society. . . . A great society is simply a big and complicated urban society.
Address at the International Press Institute Assembly, London [May 27, 1965]

6 Responsible journalism is journalism responsible in the last analysis to the editor's own conviction of what, whether interesting or only important, is in the public interest. *Ibid.*

Jawaharlal Nehru
1889–1964

7 I want nothing to do with any religion concerned with keeping the masses satisfied to live in hunger, filth, and ignorance. I want nothing to do with any order, religious or otherwise, which does not teach people that they are capable of becoming happier and more civilized, on this earth, capable of becoming true *man*, master of his fate and captain of his soul.[1]
From EDGAR SNOW, Journey to the Beginning [1958]

[1]See Sallust, 91:28 and 92:1; Francis Bacon, 160:4; Shakespeare, 187:22; Tennyson, 459:9; and Henley, 557:10.

Arnold Toynbee
1889–1975

8 Civilizations, I believe, come to birth and proceed to grow by successfully responding to successive challenges. They break down and go to pieces if and when a challenge confronts them which they fail to meet. *Civilization on Trial [1948], ch. 4*

9 America is a large, friendly dog in a very small room. Every time it wags its tail it knocks over a chair. *Attributed*

Ludwig Wittgenstein
1889–1951

10 The world is all that is the case.
Tractatus Logico-Philosophicus [1922].[2] 1

11 What we cannot speak about we must pass over in silence.[3] *Ibid. 7*

Vannevar Bush
1890–1974

12 It was through the Second World War that most of us suddenly appreciated for the first time the power of man's concentrated efforts to understand and control the forces of nature. We were appalled by what we saw. *Science Is Not Enough [1967]*

Karel Čapek
1890–1938

13 Rossum's Universal Robots.[4] *R.U.R. [1920]*

Agatha Christie
1890–1976

14 "This affair must all be unraveled from within." He [Hercule Poirot] tapped his forehead. "These little gray cells. It is 'up to them'—as you say over here."
The Mysterious Affair at Styles [1920], ch. 10

15 Every murderer is probably somebody's old friend. *Ibid. 11*

16 It is completely unimportant. That is why it is so interesting.
The Murder of Roger Ackroyd [1926]

17 I don't think necessity is the mother of invention[5] —invention, in my opinion, arises directly from idle-

[2]Die Welt ist alles, was der Fall ist.
Translated by D. F. PEARS and B. F. McGUINNESS.
[3]Wovon man nicht sprechen kann, darüber muss man schweigen.
[4]The term "robot" came into English through Čapek's play.
[5]See Anonymous: Latin, 119:12.

ness, possibly also from laziness. To save oneself trouble.

> *An Autobiography [1977]. Pt. III, Growing Up*

1   If you love, you will suffer, and if you do not love, you do not know the meaning of a Christian life.

> *Ibid.*

Marcus Cook Connelly
1890–1980

2   Gangway for de Lawd God Jehovah!
> *The Green Pastures*[1] *[1930]*

3   *God:* I'll jest r'ar back an' pass a miracle.
> *Ibid.*

4   *Gabriel:* How about cleanin' up de whole mess of 'em and sta'tin' all over ag'in wid some new kind of animal?
> *God:* An' admit I'm licked?   *Ibid.*

5   Even bein' Gawd ain't a bed of roses.   *Ibid.*

Elmer Davis
1890–1958

6   The first and great commandment is, Don't let them scare you.
> *But We Were Born Free [1954], ch. 1*

7   This will remain the land of the free only so long as it is the home of the brave.   *Ibid.*

Charles André Joseph Marie de Gaulle
1890–1970

8   The sword is the axis of the world, and grandeur is indivisible.   *Le Fil de l'Épée [1934]*

9   France has lost a battle. But France has not lost the war.
> *Broadcast from London to the French people after the fall of France [June 18, 1940]*

10   Since those whose duty it was to hold the sword of France have let it fall, I have picked up its broken point.   *Radio address [July 13, 1940]*

11   If I live, I will fight, wherever I must, as long as I must, until the enemy is defeated and the national stain washed clean.
> *Les Mémoires de Guerre, vol. I [1954]*

12   France cannot be France without greatness.
> *Ibid.*

13   I always thought I was Jeanne d'Arc and Bonaparte. How little one knows oneself.
> *Reply to speaker who compared him to Robespierre. From Figaro Littéraire [1958]*

14   When I want to know what France thinks, I question myself.
> *From JEAN-RAYMOND TOURNOUX, Sons of France [1966]*

15   Only peril can bring the French together. One can't impose unity out of the blue on a country that has 265 different kinds of cheese.   *Attributed*

Dwight David Eisenhower
1890–1969

16   People of Western Europe: A landing was made this morning on the coast of France by troops of the Allied Expeditionary Force. This landing is part of the concerted United Nations plan for the liberation of Europe, made in conjunction with our great Russian allies. . . . I call upon all who love freedom to stand with us now. Together we shall achieve victory.   *Broadcast on D-Day [June 6, 1944]*

17   This conjunction of an immense military establishment and a large arms industry is new in the American experience. We must guard against the acquisition of unwarranted influence, whether sought or unsought, by the military-industrial complex. The potential for the disastrous rise of misplaced power exists and will persist.
> *Farewell Radio and Television Address to the American People [January 17, 1961]*

18   Biggest damfool mistake I ever made.
> *Recalling his appointment [1953] of Earl Warren as Chief Justice of the United States*

Gene Fowler
1890–1960

19   Writing is easy. All you do is stare at a blank sheet of paper until drops of blood form on your forehead.   *Attributed*[2]

Sir Alan Patrick Herbert
1890–1971

20   Holy Deadlock.
> *Title of novel [1934] satirizing the paradoxes of British divorce law*

21   The Common Law of England has been laboriously built upon a mythical figure—the figure of "The Reasonable Man."
> *Uncommon Law [1935], p. 1*

22   The critical period in matrimony is breakfast-time.   *Ibid. p. 98*

23   An Act of God was defined as something which no reasonable man could have expected.
> *Ibid. p. 316*

---

[1]Suggested by Roark Bradford's stories, *Ol' Man Adam an' His Chillun* [1928].

[2]Also attributed (in a variant form) to sports columnist RED [Walter Wellesley] SMITH [1905–1982].

Samuel Hoffenstein
1890–1947

1 Babies haven't any hair;
Old men's heads are just as bare;
Between the cradle and the grave
Lies a haircut and a shave.
Songs of Faith in the Year After Next, VIII

Gerald White Johnson
1890–1980

2   Heroes are created by popular demand, sometimes out of the scantiest materials, or none at all.
American Heroes and Hero-Worship [1943], ch. 1

3   In revolutionary times the rich are always the people who are most afraid.
American Freedom and the Press [1958]

Hanns Johst
1890–1978

4   When I hear the word "culture" . . . I reach for my pistol.[1]
Schlageter [1933]

Robert Ley
1890–1945

5   Strength through joy.[2]
Instruction for the German Labor Front [December 2, 1933]

Howard Phillips Lovecraft
1890–1937

6   The most merciful thing in the world, I think, is the inability of the human mind to correlate all its contents.   *The Call of Cthulhu [1928], ch. 1*

William Maguire
1890–1953

7   Praise the Lord and pass the ammunition.[3]
Attributed

Claude McKay
1890–1948

8 Upon the clothes behind the tenement,
That hang like ghosts suspended from the lines,

Linking each flat, but to each indifferent,
Incongruous and strange the moonlight shines.
A Song of the Moon

9 Although she feeds me bread of bitterness,
And sinks into my throat her tiger's tooth,
Stealing my breath of life, I must confess
I love this cultured hell that tests my youth!
Her vigor flows like tides into my blood,
Giving me strength erect against her hate.
Her bigness sweeps my being like a flood.
America

10 If we must die, let it not be like hogs
Hunted and penned in an inglorious spot.
If We Must Die

Christopher Morley
1890–1957

11   There is only one success—to be able to spend your life in your own way.
Where the Blue Begins [1922]

12   Life is a foreign language; all men mispronounce it.   *Thunder on the Left [1925], ch. 14*

13 There was so much handwriting on the wall
That even the wall fell down.
Around the Clock [1943]

14 Chattering voltage like a broken wire
The wild cicada cried, Six weeks to frost!
End of August

15   Why do they put the Gideon Bibles only in the bedrooms, where it's usually too late, and not in the barroom downstairs?
Contribution to a Contribution

Boris Pasternak
1890–1960

16   Art is unthinkable without risk and spiritual self-sacrifice.
On Modesty and Bravery [1936]. Speech at Writers' Conference[4]

17 I am alone; all drowns in the Pharisees' hypocrisy.
To live your life is not as simple as to cross a field.[5]
Hamlet [1946][6]

18 You are eternity's hostage
A captive of time.
Night [1957][6]

19 But what are pity, conscience, or fear
To the brazen pair, compared
With the living sorcery
Of their hot embraces?
Bacchanalia [1957],[6] *st. 4*

---

[1]Wenn ich Kultur höre . . . entsichere ich meinen Browning.
Often attributed to GOERING.
[2]Kraft durch Freude.
[3]Basis of the popular World War II song [1942] of that title by FRANK LOESSER [1910–1969].

[4]Translated by E. LEVIN.
[5]See Anonymous: Russian, 793:3.
[6]Translated by MAX HAYWARD.

1   During the last years of Mayakovski's life,[1] when all poetry had ceased to exist . . . literature had stopped.   *I Remember [1958]*[2]

2 It snowed and snowed, the whole world over,
Snow swept the world from end to end.
A candle burned on the table;
A candle burned.
    Doctor Zhivago [1958].[3] *The Poems of Yurii Zhivago (ch. 17),*[4] *Winter Night, st. 1*

3 A corner draft fluttered the flame
And the white fever of temptation
Upswept its angel wings that cast
A cruciform shadow.
                                Ibid. st. 7

4   Man is born to live, not to prepare for life. Life itself, the phenomenon of life, the gift of life, is so breathtakingly serious!   *Ibid. ch. 9*

5   And when the war broke out, its real horrors, its real dangers, its menace of real death were a blessing compared with the inhuman reign of the lie, and they brought relief because they broke the spell of the dead letter.   *Ibid. epilogue*

6   Departure beyond the borders of my country is for me equivalent to death.
                    Letter to Khrushchev [1958][5]

7 I am caught like a beast at bay.
Somewhere are people, freedom, light,
But all I hear is the baying of the pack,
There is no way out for me.
                    The Nobel Prize [1959][6]

"Red" Rowley
fl. 1915

8 Mademoiselle from Armenteers,
Hasn't been kissed in forty years,
    Hinky dinky, parley-voo.
            Mademoiselle from Armentières[7]

9 Mademoiselle from St. Nazaire,
She never heard of underwear.
                                Ibid.

George Seldes
1890–

10   Sawdust Caesar.[8]   *Title of book [1932]*

[1]Vladimir Mayakovski [1893–1930].
[2]Translated by MANYA HARARI.
[3]Translated by MAX HAYWARD and MANYA HARARI.
[4]The Poems of Yurii Zhivago translated by BERNARD GUILBERT GUERNEY.
[5]Translated by E. LEVIN.
[6]Translated by MAX HAYWARD.
[7]Soldiers' song of World War I, with innumerable versions. The tune and verse structure were based on a British Army song composed by ALFRED JAMES WALDEN ["HARRY WINCOTT," 1867–1947].
[8]Mussolini.

Casey [Charles Dillon] Stengel[9]
c. 1890–1975

11   I had many years that I was not so successful as a ballplayer, as it is a game of skill.
    Testimony before U.S. Senate Subcommittee on Antitrust and Monopoly [July 9, 1958]

12   There comes a time in every man's life and I've had many of them.   *Remark*

13   Most people my age are dead.   *Remark*

Joseph Nye Welch
1890–1960

14   Until this moment, Senator, I think I never really gauged your cruelty or your recklessness. . . . Have you no sense of decency, sir, at long last? Have you left no sense of decency?
    Response to Senator Joseph R. McCarthy during Senate hearings on alleged subversive activities in the U.S. Army [June 9, 1954]

Charles Erwin Wilson
1890–1961

15   For years I thought what was good for our country was good for General Motors, and vice versa. The difference did not exist.
    To the Senate Committee on Armed Services [1952]

Waldemar Young
1890–1938

16   We have ways of making men talk.
    Lives of a Bengal Lancer (screenplay) [1935]

Ely Culbertson
1891–1955

17   The bizarre world of cards . . . a world of pure power politics where rewards and punishments were meted out immediately. A deck of cards was built like the purest of hierarchies, with every card a master to those below it and a lackey to those above it. And there were "masses"—long suits—which always asserted themselves in the end, triumphing over the kings and aces.
                    Total Peace [1943], ch. 1

Karl Kelchner Darrow
1891–1982

18   One of the things which distinguishes ours from all earlier generations is this, that we have seen our atoms.   *The Renaissance of Physics [1936]*

[9]See Thurber, 690:15.

Al Dubin
1891–1945

1 Tip-Toe Thru' the Tulips with Me.
Title of song [1939][1]

Haile Selassie
1891–1975

2 Outside the kingdom of the Lord there is no nation which is greater than any other. God and history will remember your judgment.
Speech, the League of Nations [1936][2]

Hu Shih[3]
1891–1962

3 Only when we realize that there is no eternal, unchanging truth or absolute truth can we arouse in ourselves a sense of intellectual responsibility.
La Jeunesse Nouvelle [April 1919]

Jomo Kenyatta [Kamau Wa Ngengi]
1891–1978

4 The African is conditioned, by the cultural and social institutions of centuries, to a freedom of which Europe has little conception, and it is not in his nature to accept serfdom forever. He realizes that he must fight unceasingly for his own complete emancipation; for without this he is doomed to remain the prey of rival imperialisms.
Facing Mount Kenya: The Tribal Life of the Gikuyu (Kikuyu) [1938], Conclusion

5 We must try to trust one another. Stay and cooperate.[4]
Statement, as first president of the Republic of Kenya, to the white settlers [1964]

David Low
1891–1963

6 I have never met anybody who wasn't against war. Even Hitler and Mussolini were, according to themselves.
From the New York Times [February 10, 1946]

Osip Mandelstam
1891–1938

7 We live, deaf to the land beneath us,
Ten steps away no one hears our speeches,

But where there's so much as half a conversation
The Kremlin's mountaineer will get his mention.
Stalin [1934], st. 1, 2

8 One by one forging his laws, to be flung
Like horseshoes at the head, the eye, or the groin.

And every killing is a treat
For the broad-chested Ossete.
Ibid. st. 7, 8

Irene Rutherford McLeod
1891–1964

9 I'm a lean dog, a keen dog, a wild dog, and lone.
Songs to Save a Soul [1919]. Lone Dog

Henry Miller
1891–1980

10 Every man with a bellyful of the classics is an enemy to the human race.
Tropic of Cancer [1934]

11 It's good to be just plain happy; it's a little better to know that you're happy; but to understand that you're happy and to know why and how . . . and still be happy, be happy in the being and the knowing, well that is beyond happiness, that is bliss.
The Colossus of Maroussi [1941], pt. I

Elliot Paul
1891–1958

12 The last time I see Paris will be on the day I die. The city was inexhaustible, and so is its memory.
The Last Time I Saw Paris [1942],[5] pt. II, 23

Michael Polanyi
1891–1976

13 An art which has fallen into disuse for the period of a generation is altogether lost. . . . It is pathetic to watch the endless efforts — equipped with microscopy and chemistry, with mathematics and electronics — to reproduce a single violin of the kind the half-literate Stradivarius turned out as a matter of routine more than two hundred years ago.
Personal Knowledge [1958]

Cole Albert Porter
1891–1964

14 You do something to me,
Something that simply mystifies me.
Fifty Million Frenchmen [1929]. You Do Something to Me

---

[1]Music by JOE BURKE.
[2]He sought sanctions against Italy, which had invaded Ethiopia.
[3]From *Sources of Chinese Tradition* [1960], edited by WILLIAM THEODORE DE BARY.
[4]Harambee [Swahili for "Let's pull together"].—*National motto of Kenya*

[5]See Hammerstein, 692:7.

1 Night and day you are the one,
Only you beneath the moon and under the sun.
Gay Divorce [1932]. Night and Day

2 I get no kick from champagne.
Mere alcohol doesn't thrill me at all,
So tell me why should it be true
That I get a kick out of you.
Anything Goes [1934]. I Get a Kick Out of You

3 You're the Nile,
You're the Tower of Pisa,
You're the smile
On the Mona Lisa. . . .
But if, Baby, I'm the bottom you're the top!
Ibid. You're the Top!

4 It was great fun,
But it was just one of those things.
Jubilee [1935]. Just One of Those Things

5 It's delightful, it's delicious, it's de-lovely.
Red, Hot and Blue [1936]. It's De-Lovely

6   My Heart Belongs to Daddy.
Leave It to Me [1938], title of song

7 But I'm always true to you, darlin', in my fashion,[1]
Yes, I'm always true to you, darlin', in my way.
Kiss Me, Kate [1948]. Always True to You in My Fashion

Nicola Sacco[2]
1891–1927

8   Help the weak ones that cry for help, help the prosecuted and the victim . . . they are the comrades that fight and fall . . . for the conquest of the joy of freedom for all the poor workers. In this struggle for life you will find more love and you will be loved.   *Letter to his son Dante*

Earl Warren
1891–1974

9   To separate [black children] from others of similar age and qualifications solely because of their race generates a feeling of inferiority as to their status in the community that may affect their hearts and minds in a way unlikely ever to be undone. . . . We conclude that in the field of public education the doctrine of "separate but equal"[3] has no place. Separate educational facilities are inherently unequal.
Brown v. Board of Education of Topeka, 347 U.S. 483 [1954][4]

[1]See Dowson, 602:7.
[2]See Vanzetti, 674n3.
[3]All railway companies carrying passengers in their coaches in the state shall provide equal but separate accommodations for the white and colored races.—*Louisiana Acts of 1890, no. III, p. 152;* quoted by Mr. Justice HENRY B. BROWN in *Plessy v. Ferguson, 163 U.S. 537 [1896]*
[4]In a later implementation of the same case (*349 U.S. 294*

10   When an individual is taken into custody or otherwise deprived of his freedom by the authorities and is subjected to questioning . . . he must be warned prior to any questioning that he has the right to remain silent, that anything he says can be used against him in a court of law, that he has the right to the presence of an attorney, and that if he cannot afford an attorney one will be appointed for him prior to any questioning if he so desires.
Miranda v. Arizona, 384 U.S. 436 [1965]

George Aiken
1892–1984

11   The United States could well declare unilaterally that this stage of the Vietnam war is over—that we have "won" in the sense that our Armed Forces are in control of most of the field and no potential enemy is in a position to establish its authority over South Vietnam.
Speech in the U.S. Senate [October 19, 1966]

Walter Benjamin
1892–1940

12   Of all the ways of acquiring books, writing them oneself is regarded as the most praiseworthy method. . . . Writers are really people who write books not because they are poor, but because they are dissatisfied with the books which they could buy but do not like.   *Unpacking My Library [1931]*[5]

Stella Benson
1892–1933

13 Call no man foe, but never love a stranger.
To the Unborn, st. 3

Pearl S. Buck
1892–1973

14   Our society must make it right and possible for old people not to fear the young or be deserted by them, for the test of a civilization is the way that it cares for its helpless members.
My Several Worlds [1954]

Walter C. Hagen
1892–1969

15   You're only here for a short visit. Don't hurry. Don't worry. And be sure to smell the flowers along the way.   *The Walter Hagen Story [1956]*

[1955]), the Supreme Court asked that desegregation proceed "with all deliberate speed."
[5]Translated by HARRY ZOHN.

John Burdon Sanderson Haldane
1892–1964

1   Now, my suspicion is that the universe is not only queerer than we suppose, but queerer than we *can* suppose. . . . I suspect that there are more things in heaven and earth than are dreamed of, in any philosophy.[1] That is the reason why I have no philosophy myself, and must be my excuse for dreaming.

Possible Worlds [1927]

Robert Houghwout Jackson
1892–1954

2   If there is any fixed star in our constitutional constellation, it is that no official, high or petty, can prescribe what shall be orthodox in politics, nationalism, religion, or other matters of opinion or force citizens to confess by word or act their faith therein.

West Virginia State Board of Education v. Barnett, 319 U.S. 642 [1943]

3   The first trial in history for crimes against the peace of the world imposes a grave responsibility. The wrongs which we seek to condemn and punish have been so calculated, so malignant and so devastating that civilization cannot tolerate their being ignored because it cannot survive their being repeated.

Opening address before the International Military Tribunal, Nuremberg [1945]

4   There is danger that, if the Court does not temper its doctrinaire logic with a little practical wisdom, it will convert the constitutional Bill of Rights into a suicide pact.

Terminiello v. Chicago, 337 U.S. 1, 37 [1949]

5   The day that this country ceases to be free for irreligion, it will cease to be free for religion.

Dissenting opinion, Zorach v. Clausor, 343 U.S. 306, 325 [1952]

Robert Staughton Lynd
1892–1970
and
Helen Merrell Lynd
1896–1982

6   It is characteristic of mankind to make as little adjustment as possible in customary ways in the face of new conditions; the process of social change is epitomized in the fact that the first Packard car body delivered to the manufacturer had a whipstock on the dashboard.

Middletown [1929], pt. VI, ch. 29

[1]See Shakespeare, 195:3.

Archibald MacLeish
1892–1982

7 There with vast wings across the canceled skies,
There in the sudden blackness the black pall
Of nothing, nothing, nothing—nothing at all.

The End of the World [1926]

8 A poem should not mean
But be.

Ars Poetica [1926]

9 And here face downward in the sun
To feel how swift how secretly
The shadow of the night comes on.

You, Andrew Marvell [1930]

10 We were the first that found that famous country:
We marched by a king's name: we crossed the
    sierras:
Unknown hardships we suffered: hunger.

Conquistador [1932]. Bernál Díaz' Preface

11 She lies on her left side her flank golden:
Her hair is burned black with the strong sun.
The scent of her hair is of rain in the dust on her
    shoulders:
She has brown breasts and the mouth of no other
    country.

*Frescoes for Mr. Rockefeller's City [1933].
Landscape as a Nude, st. 1*

12 America was promises . . .
It was Man who had been promised.

America Was Promises [1939]

13   Races didn't bother the Americans. They were something a lot better than any race. They were a People. They were the first self-constituted, self-created People in the history of the world.

The American Cause [1940]

14 old age
level light
evening in the afternoon
love without the bitterness and so
good-night

Definitions of Old Age [1976]

Edna St. Vincent Millay
1892–1950

15 All I could see from where I stood
Was three long mountains and a wood.

Renascence [1912], l. 1

16 The world stands out on either side
No wider than the heart is wide;
Above the world is stretched the sky,—
No higher than the soul is high.
The heart can push the sea and land
Farther away on either hand;
The soul can split the sky in two,
And let the face of God shine through.
But East and West will pinch the heart

That can not keep them pushed apart;
And he whose soul is flat—the sky
Will cave in on him by and by.

Renascence, last lines

1 O world, I cannot hold thee close enough!

God's World [1917], st. 1

2 My candle burns at both ends;
It will not last the night;
But, ah, my foes, and, oh, my friends—
It gives a lovely light.[1]

A Few Figs from Thistles [1920]. First Fig

3 We were very tired, we were very merry—
We had gone back and forth all night on the
ferry.

Ibid. Recuerdo

4 I had a little sorrow,
Born of a little sin.

Ibid. The Penitent, st. 1

5 Whether or not we find what we are seeking
Is idle, biologically speaking.

Ibid. I Shall Forget You Presently, l. 13

6 Death devours all lovely things;
Lesbia with her sparrow
Shares the darkness—presently
Every bed is narrow.

Passer Mortuus Est [1921], st. 1

7 I know I am but summer to your heart,
And not the full four seasons of the year.

I Know I Am But Summer [1923], l. 1

8 I only know that summer sang in me
A little while, that in me sings no more.

What Lips My Lips Have Kissed [1923], l. 13

9   Euclid alone
Has looked on Beauty bare. Fortunate they
Who, though once only and then but far away,
Have heard her massive sandal set on stone.

*Euclid Alone Has Looked on Beauty Bare
[1923], l. 11*

10 If ever I said, in grief or pride,
I tired of honest things, I lied.

The Goose Girl [1923], l. 5

11 How strange a thing is death, bringing to his
knees, bringing to his antlers
The buck in the snow . . .
Life, looking out attentive from the eyes of the
doe.

The Buck in the Snow [1928]

12 I am not resigned to the shutting away of loving
hearts in the hard ground.
So it is, and so it will be, for so it has been, time
out of mind:

[1]I burned my candle at both ends,/ And now have neither
foes nor friends.—HOFFENSTEIN, *Songs of Fairly Utter Despair, 8*

Into the darkness they go, the wise and the lovely.
Crowned
With lilies and with laurel they go; but I am not
resigned.

Dirge Without Music [1928], st. 1

13 Love is not all: it is not meat nor drink
Nor slumber nor a roof against the rain;
Nor yet a floating spar to men that sink.

Love Is Not All [1931], l. 1

Reinhold Niebuhr
1892–1971

14   God, give us grace to accept with serenity the
things that cannot be changed, courage to change
the things which should be changed, and the wisdom
to distinguish the one from the other.

The Serenity Prayer [1934]

15   Goodness, armed with power, is corrupted; and
pure love without power is destroyed.

Beyond Tragedy [1938]

16   The prophet himself stands under the judgment
which he preaches. If he does not know that, he is a
false prophet.   *Ibid.*

17 Humor is a prelude to faith and
Laughter is the beginning of prayer.

Discerning the Signs of the Times [1949]

18   Nothing worth doing is completed in our lifetime; therefore, we must be saved by hope. Nothing
true or beautiful or good makes complete sense in
any immediate context of history; therefore, we
must be saved by faith. Nothing we do, however
virtuous, can be accomplished alone; therefore, we
are saved by love.

The Irony of American History [1952]

Martin Niemoeller
1892–1984

19   In Germany they came first for the Communists,
and I didn't speak up because I wasn't a Communist.
Then they came for the Jews, and I didn't speak up
because I wasn't a Jew. Then they came for the trade
unionists, and I didn't speak up because I wasn't a
trade unionist. Then they came for the Catholics,
and I didn't speak up because I was a Protestant.
Then they came for me, and by that time no one was
left to speak up.   *Attributed*

Harold Wallace Ross
1892–1951

20   *The New Yorker* will not be edited for the old
lady from Dubuque.[2]

Upon founding The New Yorker [1925]

[2]Later this became "the little old lady from Dubuque."

1   Is Moby Dick the whale or the man?

From JAMES THURBER, *The Years with Ross*
[1958]

2   I understand the hero [of Ernest Hemingway's *A Farewell to Arms*] keeps getting in bed with women, and the war wasn't fought that way.   *Ibid.*

John Ronald Reuel Tolkien
1892–1973

3   In a hole in the ground there lived a hobbit. Not a nasty, dirty, wet hole, filled with the ends of worms and an oozy smell, nor yet a dry, bare, sandy hole with nothing in it to sit down on or to eat: it was a hobbit-hole, and that means comfort.

The Hobbit; or There and Back Again [1937],
ch. 1

4 One Ring to rule them all, One Ring to find them,
One Ring to bring them all and in the darkness bind them.

The Fellowship of the Ring [1965], bk. I, ch. 2

Mae West
1892–1980

5   Goodness had nothing to do with it.[1]

Night After Night (screenplay) [1932]

6   Why don't you come up sometime and see me?[2]
. . . Come on up, I'll tell your fortune.

She Done Him Wrong (screenplay) [1933]

7   Beulah, peel me a grape.

I'm No Angel [1933]

8   When I'm good, I'm very good, but when I'm bad I'm better.   *Ibid.*

9   Between two evils, I always pick the one I never tried before.   *Klondike Annie (screenplay) [1936]*

Wendell Lewis Willkie
1892–1944

10   Freedom is an indivisible word. If we want to enjoy it, and fight for it, we must be prepared to extend it to everyone, whether they are rich or poor, whether they agree with us or not, no matter what their race or the color of their skin.

One World, ch. 13

11   The Constitution does not provide for first and second class citizens.

An American Program [1944], ch. 2

[1]In reply to "Goodness, what a lovely diamond!"
Also the title of her autobiography [1959].
[2]Frequently misquoted as "Come up and see me sometime."

Jack Yellen
1892–1991

12 Happy days are here again,
The skies above are clear again:
Let us sing a song of cheer again,
Happy days are here again!

Happy Days Are Here Again [1929][3]

Omar Bradley
1893–1981

13   The world has achieved brilliance without conscience. Ours is a world of nuclear giants and ethical infants.   *Address on Armistice Day [1948]*

14   In war there is no second prize for the runner-up.

In the Military Review [February 1950]

15   Red China is not the powerful nation seeking to dominate the world. Frankly, in the opinion of the Joint Chiefs of Staff, this strategy would involve us in the wrong war, at the wrong place, at the wrong time, and with the wrong enemy.

Testimony to the Committee on Armed Services and Committee on Foreign Affairs, U.S. Senate [May 15, 1951]

Lew Brown
1893–1958
and
Buddy [George Gard] De Sylva
1895–1950

16 And love can come to everyone,
The best things in life are free.

Good News [1927].[4] The Best Things in Life Are Free

17 Keep your sunny side up.

Sunny Side Up [1929],[4] title song

James Bryant Conant
1893–1978

18   He who enters a university walks on hallowed ground.   *Notes on the Harvard Tercentenary [1936]*

19   There is only one proved method of assisting the advancement of pure science—that of picking men of genius, backing them heavily, and leaving them to direct themselves.

Letter to the New York Times [August 13, 1945]

[3]With music by MILTON AGER [1893–1979], this song was played at the 1932 Democratic presidential convention and became a campaign song for Franklin D. Roosevelt.
[4]Music by RAY HENDERSON.

Jimmy [James Francis] Durante
1893–1980

1 Goodnight, Mrs. Calabash, wherever you are.
Radio series sign-off [1942]

2 Dese are de conditions dat prevail. *Saying*

3 Stop da music! *Saying*

Hermann Goering
1893–1946

4 Shoot first and inquire afterwards, and if you make mistakes, I will protect you.
Instruction for the Prussian police [1933]

5 Submit to me as soon as possible a draft showing . . . measures already taken for the execution of the intended final solution of the Jewish question.
Directive (drafted by Adolf Eichmann)[1] to Reinhard Heydrich [July 31, 1941]

Harold Joseph Laski
1893–1950

6 We live under a system by which the many are exploited by the few, and war is the ultimate sanction of that exploitation. *Plan or Perish [1945]*

7 It would be madness to let the purposes or the methods of private enterprise set the habits of the age of atomic energy. *Ibid.*

Anita Loos
1893–1981

8 Gentlemen always seem to remember blondes.
Gentlemen Prefer Blondes [1925], ch. 1

9 She always believed in the old adage, "Leave them while you're looking good." *Ibid.*

10 Kissing your hand may make you feel very, very good, but a diamond and sapphire bracelet lasts forever. *Ibid. 4*

Mao Tse-tung
1893–1976

11 A revolution is not the same as inviting people to dinner, or writing an essay, or painting a picture . . . A revolution is an insurrection, an act of violence by which one class overthrows another.
Selected Works of Mao Tse-tung [1965], vol. I, p. 28

12 Every Communist must grasp the truth: "Political power grows out of the barrel of a gun."
Ibid. II, 224

13 Weapons are an important factor in war, but not the decisive one; it is man and not materials that counts. *Lecture [1938]*

14 War cannot for a single minute be separated from politics.[2] *Ibid.*

15 The people are like water and the army is like fish.
Aspects of China's Anti-Japanese Struggle [1948]

16 The policy of letting a hundred flowers blossom and a hundred schools of thought contend is designed to promote the flourishing of the arts and the progress of science; it is designed to enable a socialist culture to thrive in our land.
Speech at Peking [February 27, 1957]

John Phillips Marquand
1893–1960

17 It is worthwhile for anyone to have behind him a few generations of honest, hard-working ancestry.
The Late George Apley [1937], ch. 3

18 Marriage . . . is a damnably serious business, particularly around Boston. *Ibid. 11*

Vladimir Mayakovski
1893–1930

19 If you wish,
I shall grow irreproachably tender:
Not a man, but a cloud in trousers!
Cloud in Trousers [1915][3]

20 Citizen!
Consider my traveling expenses:
Poetry—
    all of it—
        is a journey to the unknown.
Conversation with a Tax Collector about Poetry [1926][4]

21 Then there's amortization,
        the deadliest of all,
Amortization
        of the heart and soul.
Ibid.

22 But I subdued myself,
        setting my heel
On the throat
        of my own song.
At the Top of My Voice[3]

---

[1]See Eichmann, 718:*n*2.

[2]See Clausewitz, 393:3.
[3]Translated by GEORGE REAVEY.
[4]Translated by MAX HAYWARD.

Wilfred Owen
1893–1918

1 Above all, this book is not concerned with Poetry,
The subject of it is War, and the pity of War.
The Poetry is in the pity.
All a poet can do is warn.[1]
Poems [1920], preface

2 What passing bells for these who die as cattle?
Only the monstrous anger of the guns.
Only the stuttering rifles' rapid rattle
Can patter out their hasty orisons.
The Anthem for Doomed Youth, st. 1

3 And each slow dusk a drawing-down of blinds.
Ibid.

4 Red lips are not so red
As the stained stones kissed by the English dead.
Greater Love

5 Courage was mine, and I had mystery,
Wisdom was mine, and I had mastery:
To miss the march of this retreating world
Into vain citadels that are not walled.
Strange Meeting

Dorothy Parker
1893–1967

6 Four be the things I am wiser to know:
Idleness, sorrow, a friend, and a foe.
Enough Rope [1927]. Inventory, st. 1

7 Four be the things I'd been better without:
Love, curiosity, freckles, and doubt.
Ibid. st. 2

8 Scratch a lover, and find a foe.
Ibid. Ballade of a Great Weariness, st. 1

9 Men seldom make passes
At girls who wear glasses.
Ibid. News Item

10 Guns aren't lawful;
Nooses give;
Gas smells awful;
You might as well live.
Ibid. Résumé

11 Why is it no one ever sent me yet
One perfect limousine, do you suppose?
Ah no, it's always just my luck to get
One perfect rose.
Ibid. One Perfect Rose, st. 3

12 Tonstant Weader Fwowed up.
Review of A. A. MILNE, The House at Pooh Corner [1928][2]

[1]The last three lines serve as the motto for Benjamin Britten's *War Requiem (Op. 66)*, which uses the Latin text of the Mass for the Dead and some of the poems of Wilfred Owen.
[2]See Milne, 648.

13 Runs the gamut of emotions from A to B.
Attributed theater review, comment on a player

14 One more drink and I'll be under the host.
Attributed

15 Excuse my dust.
Epitaph, suggested by herself

Frederick Salomon Perls
1893–1970

16 I do my thing, and you do your thing . . .
You are you and I am I,
And if by chance we find each other, it's beautiful;
If not, it can't be helped.
Gestalt Therapy Verbatim [1969]

Robert Leroy Ripley
1893–1949

17 Believe It or Not.
Title of syndicated newspaper feature

Dorothy Leigh Sayers
1893–1957

18 The worst sin—perhaps the only sin—passion can commit, is to be joyless.
Gaudy Night [1936], ch. 23

Albert Szent-Györgyi von Nagyrapolt
1893–1986

19 The real scientist . . . is ready to bear privation and, if need be, starvation rather than let anyone dictate to him which direction his work must take.
Science Needs Freedom. From World Digest [1943]

20 Discovery consists of seeing what everybody has seen and thinking what nobody has thought.
From I. J. GOOD (ed.), The Scientist Speculates [1962]

Fred Allen
1894–1956

21 I have just returned from Boston. It is the only sane thing to do if you find yourself up there.
Letter to Groucho Marx [June 12, 1953]

22 California's a wonderful place to live—if you happen to be an orange.
From ROBERT TAYLOR, Fred Allen [1989]

Isaac Babel
1894–1941

1 A phrase is born into the world both good and bad at the same time. The secret lies in a slight, an almost invisible twist. The lever should rest in your hand, getting warm, and you can only turn it once, not twice.   *Guy de Maupassant [1924]*[1]

2 No steel can pierce the human heart so chillingly as a period at the right moment.[2]   *Ibid.*

3 Speaking of silence, we can't help talking about me, the past master of this genre.
    Speech at First Writers' Congress [1934]

4 The right to write badly was the privilege we widely used.   *Ibid.*

Louis Ferdinand Céline
[Louis Ferdinand Destouches]
1894–1961

5 Those who talk about the future are scoundrels. It is the present that matters. To evoke one's posterity is to make a speech to maggots.
    Voyage au Bout de la Nuit (Journey to the End of the Night) [1932]

Edward Estlin Cummings
1894–1962

6 All in green went my love riding
on a great horse of gold
into the silver dawn.
    All in green went my love riding [1923]

7 four lean hounds crouched low and smiling
my heart fell dead before.
    Ibid.

8 in Just-
spring when the world is mud-
luscious the little
lame balloonman
whistles far and wee
    Chansons Innocentes [1923], 1

9 when the world is puddle-wonderful
    Ibid.

10 Buffalo Bill's
defunct
        who used to
        ride a watersmooth-silver
                                stallion
and break onetwothreefourfive pigeons-
justlikethat
        Jesus
he was a handsome man
        and what i want to know is

[1]Translated by WALTER MORISON.
[2]Translated by MAX HAYWARD.

how do you like your blueeyed boy
Mister Death
    Portraits [1923], 8

11 the Cambridge ladies who live in furnished souls
are unbeautiful and have comfortable minds.
    Sonnets—Realities [1923], I

12 take it from me kiddo
believe me
my country, 'tis of

you, land of the Cluett
Shirt Boston Garter and Spearmint
Girl With The Wrigley Eyes (of you
land of the Arrow Ide
and Earl &
Wilson
Collars) of you i
sing: land of Abraham Lincoln and Lydia E.
        Pinkham,
land above all of Just Add Hot Water And
        Serve—
from every B.V.D.

let freedom ring

amen.
    Poem, Or Beauty Hurts Mr. Vinal [1926]

13   And there're a
hun-dred-mil-lion-oth-ers, like
all of you successfully if
delicately gelded (or spaded)
gentlemen (and ladies)
    Ibid.

14 a tiny violetflavored nuisance
    Ibid.

15 next to of course god america i
love you land of the pilgrims' and so forth
    next to of course god america i [1926]

16 i sing of Olaf glad and big
whose warmest heart recoiled at war
    i sing of Olaf glad and big [1931]

17 "I will not kiss your f.ing flag"
    Ibid.

18 "there is some s. I will not eat"
    Ibid.

19 unless statistics lie he was
more brave than me:more blond than you.
    Ibid.

20 somewhere i have never traveled, gladly beyond
any experience, your eyes have their silence.
    somewhere I have never traveled [1931]

21 nobody, not even the rain, has such small hands
    Ibid.

22 anyone lived in a pretty how town
(with up so floating many bells down)
spring summer autumn winter
he sang his didn't he danced his did.
    anyone lived in a pretty how town [1940]

1 my father moved through dooms of love
through sames of am through haves of give,
singing each morning out of each night
my father moved through depths of height
my father moved through dooms of love [1940]

2 and nothing quite so least as truth
—i say though hate were why men breathe—
because my father lived his soul
love is the whole and more than all
Ibid.

3 a politician is an arse upon
which everyone has sat except a man
One Times One [1944], 10

4 mr u will not be missed
who as an anthologist
sold the many on the few
not excluding mr u
Ibid. 11

5 pity this busy monster, manunkind,
not. Progress is a comfortable disease.
Ibid. 14

6   A world of made
is not a world of born
Ibid.

7   We doctors know
a hopeless case if—listen: there's a hell
of a good universe next door; let's go
Ibid.

8 —when skies are hanged and oceans drowned,
the single secret will still be man
Ibid. 20

9   For he has the territory of harmonicas, the acres
of flutes, the meadows of clarinets, the domain of
violins. And God says: Why did they put you in
prison? What did you do to the people? "I made
them dance and they put me in prison."
The Enormous Room [1922]. Surplice

10   Take me up into your mind once or twice before
I die (you know why: just because the eyes of you
and me will be full of dirt some day). Quickly take
me up into the bright child of your mind.
Ibid. Jean Le Nègre

Arthur Freed
1894–1973

11 Singin' in the rain, just singin' in the rain.
What a glorious feeling, I'm happy again.
Singin' in the Rain [1929][1]

Dashiell Hammett
1894–1961

12   That's the part of it I [Sam Spade] always liked.
He [Flitcraft] adjusted himself to beams falling, and

[1]Music by NACIO HERB BROWN.

then no more of them fell, and he adjusted himself
to their not falling.
The Maltese Falcon [1930], ch. 7

13   The Thin Man.   *Title of novel [1934]*

Ben Hecht
1894–1964
and
Charles MacArthur
1895–1956

14   Go on, Heathcliff, run away. Bring me back the
world!
*Wuthering Heights (screenplay) [1939], spoken
by Merle Oberon*

Herman Hupfeld
1894–1951

15 You must remember this, a kiss is still a kiss,
A sigh is just a sigh;
The fundamental things apply,
As time goes by.
*Everybody's Welcome [1931]. As Time Goes
By*[2]

16 It's still the same old story,
A fight for love and glory,
A case of do or die!
The world will always welcome lovers,
As time goes by.
Ibid.

Aldous Leonard Huxley
1894–1963

17   A bad book is as much of a labor to write as a
good one; it comes as sincerely from the author's
soul.   *Point Counter Point [1928], ch. 13*

18 A poor degenerate from the ape,
Whose hands are four, whose tail's a limb,
I contemplate my flaccid shape
And know I may not rival him
Save with my mind.
First Philosopher's Song

Nikita Sergeyevich Khrushchev
1894–1971

19   Cult of personality.
*Special Report to Twentieth Party Congress
[February 1956]*

20   About the capitalist states, it doesn't depend on
you whether or not we exist. If you don't like us,
don't accept our invitations, and don't invite us to

[2]Also in the film *Casablanca* [1943].

come and see you. Whether you like it or not, history is on our side. We will bury you.[1]

> *Reported statement at reception for Wladyslaw Gomulka at the Polish Embassy, Moscow [November 18, 1956]*

John Boynton Priestley
1894–1984

1   This country is geology by day and astronomy by night.   *Midnight on the Desert [1937]*

Elzie Crisler Segar
1894–1938

2   I yam what I yam, an' that's all I yam!
> *Thimble Theatre (comic strip) [c. 1932], Popeye speaking*

3   I will gladly pay you Tuesday for a hamburger today.
> *Ibid. [c. 1933], J. Wellington Wimpy speaking*

Genevieve Taggard
1894–1948

4 Try tropic for your balm,
Try storm,
And after storm, calm.
Try snow of heaven, heavy, soft, and slow,
Brilliant and warm.
Nothing will help, and nothing do much harm.
> *Of the Properties of Nature for Healing an Illness, st. 1*

James Thurber
1894–1961

5   Well, if I called the wrong number, why did you answer the phone?
> *Caption for cartoon in The New Yorker*

6   I love the idea of there being two sexes, don't you?   *Ibid.*

7   He knows all about art, but he doesn't know what he likes.   *Ibid.*

8   It's a naive domestic Burgundy without any breeding, but I think you'll be amused by its presumption.   *Ibid.*

9   The War Between Men and Women.
> *Series of cartoons*

10   Is Sex Necessary?
> *Title of book [1929] written with E. B. WHITE*

---

[1]Neither the original nor the translation of the last two sentences appeared in either *Pravda* or the *New York Times*, which carried the rest of the text. Another possible translation of the last sentence is: We shall be present at your funeral; i.e., we shall outlive you; but the above is the familiar version.

11   Let Your Mind Alone.   *Title of book [1937]*

12   Early to rise and early to bed makes a male healthy and wealthy and dead.
> *Fables for Our Time [1940]. The Shrike and the Chipmunks*

13   You might as well fall flat on your face as lean over too far backward.
> *Ibid. The Bear Who Let It Alone*

14   Don't count your boobies until they are hatched.
> *Ibid. The Unicorn in the Garden*

15   You Could Look It Up.[2]
> *Title of story [1941]*

16   Red Barber announces the Dodger games and he uses those expressions—picked them up down South. . . . "Tearing up the pea patch" means going on a rampage; "sitting in the catbird seat" means sitting pretty, like a batter with three balls and no strikes on him.
> *The Thurber Carnival [1945]. The Catbird Seat*

17   It is better to know some of the questions than all of the answers.   *Saying*

Jean Toomer
1894–1967

18 O can't you see it, O can't you see it,
Her skin is like dusk on the eastern horizon
. . . When the sun goes down.
> *Cane [1923]. Karintha*

19 Wind is in the cane. Come along.
Cane leaves swaying, rusty with talk,
Scratching choruses above the guinea's squawk,
Wind is in the cane. Come along.
> *Ibid. Carma*

20 A feast of moon and men and barking hounds,
An orgy for some genius of the South
With blood-hot eyes and cane-lipped scented mouth,
Surprised in making folk songs from soul sounds.
> *Ibid. Georgia Dusk, st. 2*

21 Beyond plants are animals,
Beyond animals is man,
Beyond man is the universe.

The Big Light,
Let the Big Light in!
> *The Blue Meridian*

22 What use bombs and antibombs,
Sovereign powers, brutal lives, ugly deaths?
Are men born to go down like this?
> *Ibid.*

---

[2]Subsequently popularized by and associated with CASEY STENGEL, 680, who used it as a conversation clincher.

1 Men,
Men and women—
Liberate!

The Blue Meridian

Mark Van Doren
1894–1972

2 Wit is the only wall
Between us and the dark.

Wit, st. 1

Norbert Wiener
1894–1964

3 We have decided to call the entire field of control and communication theory, whether in the machine or in the animal, by the name of Cybernetics, which we form from the Greek [for] steersman.

Cybernetics [1948]

4 The independent scientist who is worth the slightest consideration as a scientist has a consecration which comes entirely from within himself: a vocation which demands the possibility of supreme self-sacrifice.

The Human Use of Human Beings [1950]

5 The future offers very little hope for those who expect that our new mechanical slaves will offer us a world in which we may rest from thinking. Help us they may, but at the cost of supreme demands upon our honesty and our intelligence. The world of the future will be an ever more demanding struggle against the limitations of our intelligence, not a comfortable hammock in which we can lie down to be waited upon by our robot slaves.

God and Golem, Inc. [1964]

Edward, Duke of Windsor [Edward VIII]
1894–1972

6 I have found it impossible to carry the heavy burden of responsibility and to discharge my duties as King as I would wish to do without the help and support of the woman I love.[1]

Farewell broadcast after abdication [December 11, 1936]

Bud [William] Abbott
1895–1974
and
Lou Costello [Louis Francis Cristillo]
1906–1959

7 Who's on first, What's on second, I Don't Know's on third—

The Naughty Nineties [1945]

[1]Apparently written for Edward by Winston Churchill. See SARAH BRADFORD, *George VI* [1989], p. 202.

Jack [William Harrison] Dempsey
1895–1983

8 Honey, I just forgot to duck.
To his wife, after losing the heavyweight title to Gene Tunney [September 23, 1926]

Paul Éluard [Eugène Grindel]
1895–1952

9 I was born to know you
To give you your name
Freedom.[2]

Poésie et Vérité [1942]. Liberté

10 Farewell sadness
Good morning sadness.[3]

Ibid. La Vie Immédiate

Richard Buckminster Fuller
1895–1983

11 Don't fight forces; use them.   *Shelter [1932]*

12 God is a verb.
No More Secondhand God [1963]

13 For at least two million years men have been reproducing and multiplying on a little automated Spaceship Earth.   *Prospect for Humanity [1964]*

14 Synergy means behavior of whole systems unpredicted by the behavior of their parts.
What I Have Learned [1966]. How Little I Know

15 Thinking is a momentary dismissal of irrelevancies.   *Utopia or Oblivion [1969]*

16 Change the environment; do not try to change man.[4]   *Design Science [1969]*

17 Either man is obsolete or war is.
I Seem to Be a Verb [1970]

18 I am the only guinea pig I have.
Address to Engineering Society at Tel Aviv [June 16, 1972]

19 Dare to be naive.
Synergetics [1975]. Moral of the Work

20 Unity is plural and, at minimum, is two.
Ibid. sec. 224.12

21 Nature is trying very hard to make us succeed, but nature does not depend on us. We are not the only experiment.
Interview in the Minneapolis Tribune [April 30, 1978]

22 Universe to each must be
All that is, including me.

[2]Je suis né pour te connaître / Pour te nommer / Liberté.
[3]Adieu tristesse / Bonjour tristesse.
[4]See Bronowski, 722:15.

Environment in turn must be
All that is, excepting me.
*Synergetics 2 [1979], sec. 100.12, Universal
Requirements*

Robert Ranke Graves
1895–1985

1 As you are woman, so be lovely:
As you are lovely, so be various,
Merciful as constant, constant as various,
So be mine, as I yours for ever.
Pygmalion to Galatea

2   Goodbye to All That.
Title of autobiography [1929]

3   A well-chosen anthology is a complete dispensary
of medicine for the more common mental disorders,
and may be used as much for prevention as cure.
On English Poetry, 29

4   The reason why the hairs stand on end, the eyes
water, the throat is constricted, the skin crawls and
a shiver runs down the spine when one writes or
reads a true poem is that a true poem is necessarily
an invocation of the White Goddess, or Muse, the
Mother of All Living, the ancient power of fright
and lust—the female spider or the queen bee whose
embrace is death.[1]
The White Goddess [1948], ch. 1

Oscar Hammerstein II
1895–1960

5   Ol' Man River[2]
He just keeps rollin' along.
Show Boat [1927].[3] Ol' Man River

6 Can't help lovin' that man of mine.
Ibid. Can't Help Lovin' That Man

7 The last time I saw Paris, her heart was warm
and gay.
I heard the laughter of her heart in every street
café.
The Last Time I Saw Paris [1940][4]

8 Oh, what a beautiful mornin'
Oh, what a beautiful day.
I got a beautiful feelin'
Everything's going my way.
*Oklahoma! [1943].[5] Oh, What a Beautiful
Mornin'*

---

[1]See Dickinson, 514:19, and Housman, 580:10.
[2]The Mississippi.
[3]Based on the novel *Show Boat* [1926], by EDNA FERBER.
Music by JEROME KERN.
[4]Music by JEROME KERN.
See Paul, 681:12.
[5]Music by RICHARD RODGERS.

9 The corn is as high as an elephant's eye,
An' it looks like it's climbin' clear up to the sky.
Ibid.

10 Ev'rythin's up to date in Kansas City.
They've gone about as fur as they c'n go!
Ibid. Kansas City

11   June Is Bustin' Out All Over.
Carousel [1945],[5] title of song

12 Some enchanted evening . . .
You may see a stranger
Across a crowded room.
South Pacific [1949].[6] Some Enchanted Evening

13 Younger than springtime are you.
Ibid. Younger Than Springtime

14   I'm Gonna Wash That Man Right Outa My
Hair.
Ibid. Title of song

15   There Is Nothing Like a Dame.
Ibid. Title of song

Lorenz Milton Hart
1895–1943

16 We'll have Manhattan,
The Bronx and Staten
Island too.
Manhattan [1925][5]

17   That's why the lady is a tramp.
Babes in Arms [1937].[5] The Lady Is a Tramp

18   Bewitched, Bothered and Bewildered.
Pal Joey [1940],[5] title of song

Lesley Poles Hartley
1895–1972

19   The past is a foreign country; they do things
differently there.
The Go-Between [1953], prologue

Dolores Ibarruri [La Pasionaria][7]
1895–1989

20   No pasarán [They shall not pass]![8]
*Republican watchword in the Spanish Civil War
[1936–1939]*

Basil Henry Liddell Hart
1895–1970

21   Keep strong, if possible. In any case, keep cool.
Have unlimited patience. Never corner an opponent,
and always assist him to save his face. Put yourself

---

[6]Based on *Tales of the South Pacific* [1947], by JAMES A.
MICHENER. Music by RICHARD RODGERS.
[7]See Zapata, 632:7 and note.
[8]End of radio speech [July 18, 1936] calling on the women of
Spain to help defend the Republic.
See Pétain, 570:7.

in his shoes—so as to see things through his eyes. Avoid self-righteousness like the devil—nothing so self-blinding.

Deterrent or Defense [1960]. Advice to Statesmen

Groucho [Julius Henry] Marx
1895–1977

1 I never forget a face, but in your case I'll make an exception. *Saying*

2 Please accept my resignation. I don't care to belong to any club that will accept me as a member.
The Groucho Letters [1967]

John McNulty
1895–1956

3 They were talking about a certain hangout and Johnny said, "Nobody goes there anymore. It's too crowded."[1]
Some Nights When Nothing Happens Are the Best Nights in This Place [1943]

Lewis Mumford
1895–1990

4 The clock, not the steam-engine, is the key-machine of the modern industrial age.
Technics and Civilization [1934]

5 Layer upon layer, past times preserve themselves in the city until life itself is finally threatened with suffocation; then, in sheer defense, modern man invents the museum. *The Culture of Cities [1938]*

Edward E. Paramore, Jr.
1895–1956

6 Oh, the North Countree is a hard countree
That mothers a bloody brood;
And its icy arms hold hidden charms
For the greedy, the sinful and lewd.
And strong men rust, from the gold and the lust
That sears the Northland soul.
The Ballad of Yukon Jake [1921]

7 Oh, tough as a steak was Yukon Jake—
Hard-boiled as a picnic egg.
Ibid.

Andy Razaf
1895–1973

8 Ain't misbehavin',
I'm savin' my love for you.
Ain't Misbehavin' [1929][2]

9 Just 'cause you're black folks think you lack,
They laugh at you and scorn you too,
What did I do to be so black and blue?
Black and Blue [1929][2]

Morrie Ryskind
1895–1985

10 One morning I shot an elephant in my pajamas. How he got into my pajamas I'll never know.
Animal Crackers (screenplay) [1930], spoken by Groucho Marx

11 The calla lilies are in bloom again, mother. Such a strange flower, suitable for every occasion.
Stage Door (screenplay) [1937],[3] spoken by Katharine Hepburn

Edmund Wilson
1895–1972

12 I have had a good many more uplifting thoughts, creative and expansive visions—while soaking in comfortable baths or drying myself after bracing showers—in well-equipped American bathrooms than I have ever had in any cathedral.
A Piece of My Mind [1956], ch. 4

13 The cruellest thing that has happened to Lincoln since he was shot by Booth has been to fall into the hands of Carl Sandburg.[4]
Patriotic Gore [1962], ch. 3

14 I attribute such success as I have had to the use of the periodic sentence.
An Interview with Edmund Wilson [1962]

15 We tended to imagine Canada as a kind of vast hunting preserve convenient to the United States.
O Canada [1965]

Joseph Randolph Ackerley
1896–1967

16 What strained and anxious lives dogs must lead, so emotionally involved in the world of men, whose affections they strive endlessly to secure, whose authority they are expected unquestioningly to obey, and whose minds they can never do more than imperfectly reach and comprehend.
My Dog Tulip [1965]. Appendix

Edmund Blunden
1896–1974

17 I am for the woods against the world,
But are the woods for me?
The Kiss

---

[1]Often attributed to YOGI BERRA, 754.
[2]Music by THOMAS [FATS] WALLER and HARRY BROOKS.

[3]Written with ANTHONY VEILLER [1903–1965].
[4]Referring to Sandburg's six-volume biography, *Abraham Lincoln* [1926–1939].

1 Then is not Death at watch
Within those secret waters?
What wants he but to catch
Earth's heedless sons and daughters?
The Midnight Skaters

André Breton
1896–1966

2   Subjectivity and objectivity commit a series of assaults on each other during a human life out of which the first one suffers the worse beating.[1]
Nadja [1928], preface

3   It is at the movies that the only absolutely modern mystery is celebrated.
From J. H. MATHEWS, Surrealism and Film

Everett McKinley Dirksen
1896–1969

4   A billion here, a billion there, and pretty soon you're talking about real money.   *Attributed*

John Roderigo Dos Passos
1896–1970

5   Make sure he ain't a dinge, boys.
Make sure he ain't a guinea or a kike,
how can you tell a guy's a hunredpercent when all you've got's a gunnysack full of bones, bronze buttons stamped with the screaming eagle and a pair of roll puttees?
1919 [1932]. The Body of an American

6   America our nation has been beaten by strangers who have bought the laws and fenced off the meadows and cut down the woods for pulp and turned our pleasant cities into slums and sweated the wealth out of our people and when they want to they hire the executioner to throw the switch.
The Big Money [1936]. They have clubbed us off the streets

Francis Scott Fitzgerald
1896–1940

7   The victor belongs to the spoils.
The Beautiful and Damned [1922]

8   Everyone suspects himself of at least one of the cardinal virtues, and this is mine: I am one of the few honest people that I have ever known.
The Great Gatsby [1925], ch. 3

9   Jay Gatsby of West Egg, Long Island, sprang from his Platonic conception of himself. He was a son of God—a phrase which, if it means anything, means just that—and he must be about His Father's

business, the service of a vast, vulgar, and meretricious beauty.   *Ibid. 6*

10   Her voice is full of money.   *Ibid. 7*

11   They were careless people, Tom and Daisy—they smashed up things and creatures and then retreated back into their money or their vast carelessness, or whatever it was that kept them together, and let other people clean up the mess they had made.
Ibid. 9

12   Gatsby believed in the green light, the orgiastic future that year by year recedes before us.
Ibid.

13   So we beat on, boats against the current, borne back ceaselessly into the past.   *Ibid. last line*

14   Let me tell you about the very rich.[2] They are different from you and me. They possess and enjoy early, and it does something to them, makes them soft where we are hard, and cynical where we are trustful.   *The Rich Boy [1926]*

15   I remember riding in a taxi one afternoon between very tall buildings under a mauve and rosy sky; I began to bawl because I had everything I wanted and knew I would never be so happy again.
My Lost City [1932]

16   The hangover became a part of the day as well allowed-for as the Spanish siesta.   *Ibid.*

17   The test of a first-rate intelligence is the ability to hold two opposed ideas in the mind at the same time, and still retain the ability to function.
The Crack-up [1936]

18   In a real dark night of the soul it is always three o'clock in the morning.[3]   *Ibid.*

19   It was about then [1920] that I wrote a line which certain people will not let me forget: "She was a faded but still lovely woman of twenty-seven."
Early Success [1937]

20 Egyptian Proverb: The worst things:
To be in bed and sleep not,
To want for one who comes not,
To try to please and please not.
Notebooks [1978]

21   Show me a hero and I will write you a tragedy.
Ibid.

22   There are no second acts in American lives.
Ibid.

23   Draw your chair up close to the edge of the precipice and I'll tell you a story.   *Ibid.*

24   It is in the thirties that we want friends. In the forties we know they won't save us any more than love did.   *Ibid.*

[1] Translated by CESAR ALBINI.

[2] See Hemingway, 702:3 and note.
[3] See Saint John of the Cross, 147:12.

1 All good writing is swimming under water and holding your breath. *Undated letter*

Ira Gershwin[1]
1896–1983

2 Oh, lady be good
To me.
Lady Be Good [1924]. Oh, Lady Be Good

3 'S wonderful! 'S marvelous—
You should care for me!
Funny Face [1927]. 'S Wonderful

4 I got rhythm,
I got music,
I got my man—
Who could ask for anything more?
Girl Crazy [1930]. I Got Rhythm

5 Wintergreen for President.
Of Thee I Sing [1931],[2] title of song

6 Love Is Sweeping the Country.
Ibid. title of song

7 Of thee I sing, baby,
You have got that certain thing, baby,
Shining star and inspiration
Worthy of a mighty nation,
Of thee I sing!
Ibid. title song

8 Summertime
And the livin' is easy.
Porgy and Bess [1935].[3] Summertime

9 A Woman Is a Sometime Thing.
Ibid. title of song

10 I got plenty of nothin',
And nothin's plenty for me.
Ibid. I Got Plenty of Nothin'

11 It ain't necessarily so—
The things that you're liable
To read in the Bible—
It ain't necessarily so.
Ibid. It Ain't Necessarily So

12 Let's Call the Whole Thing Off!
Shall We Dance [1937], title of song

13 The memory of all that—
No, no! They can't take that away from me.
Ibid. They Can't Take That Away from Me

14 Nice work if you can get it,
And you can get it if you try.
A Damsel in Distress [1937]. Nice Work

[1]Music for all the lyrics is by GEORGE GERSHWIN.
[2]First musical to receive the Pulitzer Prize.
[3]Porgy and Bess.—*Title of play* [1927] *by* DuBOSE HEYWARD [1885–1940] *and* DOROTHY HEYWARD [1890–1961], *and of opera* [1935] *by* GEORGE GERSHWIN

Joe Jacobs
1896–1940

15 We wuz robbed!
After the heavyweight title fight between Max Schmeling and Jack Sharkey [June 21, 1932]

16 I should of stood in bed.
After leaving a sickbed to attend the World Series in Detroit [October 1935] and betting on the loser

Liam O'Flaherty
1896–1984

17 He [the informer] was a poor weak human being like themselves, a human soul, weak and helpless in suffering, shivering in the toils of the eternal struggle of the human soul with pain.
The Informer [1925]

Jean Piaget
1896–1980

18 If only we could know what was going on in a baby's mind while observing him in action we could certainly understand everything there is to psychology.
La Première Année de l'Enfant [1927]

Robert Emmet Sherwood
1896–1955

19 The trouble with me is, I belong to a vanishing race. I'm one of the intellectuals.
The Petrified Forest [1934]

20 Poor, dear God. Playing Idiot's Delight. The game that never means anything, and never ends.
Idiot's Delight [1936]

Lewis Lichtenstein Strauss
1896–1974

21 Our children will enjoy in their homes electrical energy too cheap to meter.
Speech on atomic energy [September 16, 1954]

Joseph Auslander
1897–1965

22 So there are no more words and all is ended;
The timbrel is stilled, the clarion laid away;
And Love with streaming hair goes unattended
Back to the loneliness of yesterday.
So There Are No More Words [1924]

Louise Bogan
1897–1970

1 I burned my life, that I might find
A passion wholly of the mind,
Thought divorced from eye and bone,
Ecstasy come to breath alone.

The Alchemist, st. 1

2 Women have no wilderness in them,
They are provident instead,
Content in the tight hot cell of their hearts
To eat dusty bread.

Women, st. 1

3 Up from the bronze, I saw
Water without a flaw
Rush to its rest in air,
Reach to its rest, and fall.

Roman Fountain, st. 1

4 —O remember
In your narrowing dark hours
That more things move
Than blood in the heart.

Night, st. 4

Bernard De Voto
1897–1955

5 The West begins where the average annual rainfall drops below twenty inches. When you reach the line which marks that drop—for convenience, the one hundredth meridian—you have reached the West.

The Plundered Province. In Harper's Magazine [August 1934]

6 Art is the terms of an armistice signed with fate.
Mark Twain at Work [1942]

7 The achieved West had given the United States something that no people had ever had before, an internal, domestic empire.

The Year of Decision [1943]

8 You can no more keep a martini in the refrigerator than you can keep a kiss there. The proper union of gin and vermouth is a great and sudden glory; it is one of the happiest marriages on earth and one of the shortest-lived. *The Hour [1951]*

9 The dawn of knowledge is usually the false dawn.
The Course of Empire [1952], ch. 2

William Faulkner
1897–1962

10 The Long Hot Summer.
Title of movie [1928]

11 Time is dead as long as it is being clicked off by little wheels; only when the clock stops does time come to life.
The Sound and the Fury [1929]. June Second 1910

12 I've seed de first en de last. . . . I seed de beginnin, en now I sees de endin.
Ibid. April Eighth 1928

13 Because no battle is ever won he said. They are not even fought. The field only reveals to man his own folly and despair, and victory is an illusion of philosophers and fools. *Ibid.*

14 They [the Negroes] will endure. They are better than we are. Stronger than we are. Their vices are vices aped from white men or that white men and bondage have taught them: improvidence and intemperance and evasion—not laziness: evasion: of what white men had set them to, not for their aggrandizement or even comfort but his own.
The Bear [1932], pt. IV

15 Poor man. Poor mankind.
Light in August [1932], ch. 4

16 Too much happens. . . . Man performs, engenders, so much more than he can or should have to bear. That's how he finds that he can bear anything. . . . That's what's so terrible. *Ibid. 13*

17 Gettysburg.[1] . . . You cant understand it. You would have to be born there.
Absalom, Absalom! [1936], ch. 9

18 Why do you hate the South?
I dont hate it. . . . I dont hate it. . . . I *dont hate it* he thought, panting in the cold air, the iron New England dark; *I dont. I dont! I dont hate it! I dont hate it!* *Ibid.*

19 JEFFERSON, YOKNAPATAWPHA CO., Mississippi. Area, 2400 Square Miles. Population, Whites, 6298; Negroes, 9313. WILLIAM FAULKNER, Sole Owner & Proprietor.
Ibid. Inscription on endpaper map drawn by author

20 He [the writer] must teach himself that the basest of all things is to be afraid; and, teaching himself that, forget it forever, leaving no room in his workshop for anything but the old verities and truths of the heart, the old universal truths lacking which any story is ephemeral and doomed—love and honor and pity and pride and compassion and sacrifice.
Speech upon receiving the Nobel Prize [December 10, 1950]

21 I decline to accept the end of man. *Ibid.*

22 I believe that man will not merely endure: he will prevail. *Ibid.*

23 He is immortal, not because he alone among creatures has an inexhaustible voice, but because he

[1]Representing, in context, the South.

has a soul, a spirit capable of compassion and sacrifice and endurance.   *Ibid.*

1   It is his [the poet's, the writer's] privilege to help man endure by lifting his heart, by reminding him of the courage and honor and hope and pride and compassion and pity and sacrifice which have been the glory of his past. The poet's voice need not merely be the record of man, it can be one of the props, the pillars to help him endure and prevail.   *Ibid.*

2   The writer's only responsibility is to his art. He will be completely ruthless if he is a good one. . . . If a writer has to rob his mother, he will not hesitate; the "Ode on a Grecian Urn" is worth any number of old ladies.
From Writers at Work: The Paris Review Interviews [1959]

3   Really the writer doesn't want success. . . . He knows he has a short span of life, that the day will come when he must pass through the wall of oblivion, and he wants to leave a scratch on that wall—Kilroy was here[1]—that somebody a hundred, or a thousand years later will see.
From Faulkner in the University [1959], Session 8

Paul Joseph Goebbels
1897–1945

4   We can do without butter, but, despite all our love of peace, not without arms. One cannot shoot with butter but with guns.[2]
Address in Berlin [January 17, 1936]

Herman Jacob Mankiewicz
1897–1953
and
Orson Welles
1915–1985

5   Mr. Kane was a man who got everything he wanted, and then lost it. Maybe Rosebud was something he couldn't get or something he lost. Anyway, it wouldn't have explained anything. I don't think any word can explain a man's life. No, I guess Rosebud is just a piece in a jigsaw puzzle, a missing piece.
Citizen Kane (screenplay) [1941]

David McCord
1897–

6 By and by
   God caught his eye.

Epitaphs: The Waiter

---

7 Still for us where Cottons mather
In the spring the Willas cather
   As of yore.
      And What's More: On Stopping at a New Hampshire Inn [1941]

8 The decent docent doesn't doze;
He teaches standing on his toes.
His student dassn't doze and does,
And that's what teaching is and was.
      What Cheer [1945]

9   Life is the garment we continually alter, but which never seems to fit.
      Whereas to Mr. Franklin [1956]

Horace McCoy
1897–1955

10   "Why did you kill her?" the policeman in the rear seat asked. . . . "They shoot horses, don't they?" I said.   *They Shoot Horses, Don't They? [1935]*

Thornton Niven Wilder
1897–1975

11   Even memory is not necessary for love. There is a land of the living and a land of the dead and the bridge is love, the only survival, the only meaning.
      The Bridge of San Luis Rey [1927], last lines

12 George Brush is my name
America's my nation
Luddington's my dwelling place
And Heaven's my destination.
      Heaven's My Destination [1934], title page poem[3]

13   Most everybody in the world climbs into their graves married.   *Our Town [1938], act II*

14   The dead don't stay interested in us living people for very long. Gradually, gradually, they let go hold of the earth . . . and the ambitions they had . . . and the pleasures they had . . . and the things they suffered . . . and the people they loved. They get weaned away from earth—that's the way I put it—weaned away.[4]   *Ibid. III*

15   Oh, earth, you're too wonderful for anybody to realize you. . . . Do any human beings ever realize life while they live it?—every, every minute?
      Ibid.

16   My advice to you is not to inquire why or whither, but just enjoy your ice cream while it's on your plate—that's my philosophy.
      The Skin of Our Teeth [1942], act I

17   Ninety-nine percent of the people in the world are fools and the rest of us are in great danger of contagion.   *The Matchmaker [1954], act I*

---

[1]See Anonymous, 783:10.
[2]Probably the origin of the slogan: Guns or butter.

[3]Labeled by Wilder: Doggerel verse which children of the Middle West were accustomed to write in their schoolbooks.
[4]Ellipses are in the original text.

1   The best part of married life is the fights. The rest
is merely so-so.   *The Matchmaker, II*

Walter Winchell
1897–1972

2   Good evening, Mr. and Mrs. America and all the
ships at sea! This is Walter Winchell in New York.
Let's go to press.
*Signature opening line for his weekly radio
broadcasts*

Stephen Vincent Benét
1898–1943

3   And I died in my boots like a pioneer
With the whole wide sky above me.
*A Ballad of William Sycamore, 1790–1880
[1923], st. 16*

4   Go play with the towns you have built of blocks,
The towns where you would have bound me!
I sleep in my earth like a tired fox,
And my buffalo have found me.
Ibid. st. 19

5   Oh, Georgia booze is mighty fine booze,
The best yuh ever poured yuh,
But it eats the soles right offen yore shoes,
For Hell's broke loose in Georgia.
The Mountain Whippoorwill [1923], st. 48

6   I have fallen in love with American names,
The sharp names that never get fat,
The snakeskin titles of mining claims,
The plumed war bonnet of Medicine Hat,
Tucson and Deadwood and Lost Mule Flat.
American Names [1927], st. 1

7   Bury my heart at Wounded Knee.
Ibid. st. 7

8   American Muse, whose strong and diverse heart
So many men have tried to understand
But only made it smaller with their art,
Because you are as various as your land.
John Brown's Body [1928]. Invocation, st. 1

9   Stonewall Jackson, wrapped in his beard and his
silence.
Ibid. bk. IV

10   Sherman's buzzin' along to de sea,
Like Moses ridin' on a bumblebee.
Ibid. VIII

11   If two New Hampshiremen aren't a match for the
devil, we might as well give the country back to the
Indians.   *The Devil and Daniel Webster [1936]*

12   Even the damned may salute the eloquence of
Mr. Webster.   *Ibid.*

13   When Daniel Boone goes by at night
The phantom deer arise
And all lost, wild America
Is burning in their eyes.
Daniel Boone [1942]

Bertolt Brecht
1898–1956

14   Oh, the shark has pretty teeth, dear—
And he shows them pearly white—
Just a jackknife has Macheath, dear—
And he keeps it out of sight.
*The Threepenny Opera (Die Dreigroschenoper)
[1928].*[1] *The Ballad of Mack the Knife (Moritat)*

15   Grub first: then ethics.   *Ibid. act II, sc. i*

16   Oh! Moon of Alabama
We now must say good-bye
We've lost our good old mama
And must have whiskey
Oh, you know why!
*Rise and Fall of the City of Mahagonny
(Aufstieg und Fall der Stadt Mahagonny)
[1931].*[2] *Alabama Song*

17   Alas, we
Who wished to lay the foundations of kindness,
Could not ourselves be kind.
But you, when at last it comes to pass
That man can help his fellow man,
Do not judge us
Too harshly.
*To Those Born Later (An Die Nachgeborenen)
[1938]*[3]

18   What they could do with round here is a good
war. What else can you expect with peace running
wild all over the place? You know what the trouble
with peace is? No organization.
Mother Courage and Her Children [1941], act I

19   One can describe the world of today to the people
of today only if one describes it as capable of alteration.
*Can Today's World Become Restored Through
Theater? [1955]*

William Orville Douglas
1898–1980

20   The Fifth Amendment is an old friend and a good
friend. It is one of the great landmarks in man's
struggle to be free of tyranny, to be decent and civilized.   *An Almanac of Liberty [1954]*

---

[1]Music by KURT WEILL. Translated by MARC BLITZSTEIN.
Based on the libretto of *The Beggar's Opera* by JOHN GAY. See
Gay, 297:14–297:21.
[2]Music by KURT WEILL.
[3]Translated by H. R. HAYS.

1   A Wilderness Bill of Rights.
Title of book [1965]

Federico García Lorca
1898–1936

2 In the parched path
I have seen the good lizard
(one drop of crocodile)
meditating.
The Old Lizard (El Lagarto Viejo) [1921][1]

3 Green, how much I want you green.
Green wind. Green branches.
The ship upon the sea
and the horse in the mountain.
Somnambule Ballad (Romance Sonámbulo)
[1928][2]

4 But I am no more I,
nor is my house now my house.
Ibid.

5 I touched her sleeping breasts,
and they opened to me suddenly
like spikes of hyacinth.
The Faithless Wife (La Casada Infiel) [1928][2]

6 Without silver light on their foliage
the trees had grown larger
and a horizon of dogs
barked very far from the river.
Ibid.

7 Black are the horses.
The horseshoes are black.
On the dark capes glisten
stains of ink and of wax.
Their skulls are leaden,
which is why they don't weep.
With their patent leather souls
they come down the street.
Ballad of the Spanish Civil Guard (Romance de
la Guardia Civil Española) [1928][3]

8 At five in the afternoon.
Ah, that fatal five in the afternoon!
It was five by all the clocks!
It was five in the shade of the afternoon!
Lament for Ignacio Sanchez Mejias (Llanto por
Ignacio Sanchez Mejias) [1935],[2] *I*

9 I will not see it!

Tell the moon to come
for I do not want to see the blood
of Ignacio on the sand.
Ibid. II

10 The New York dawn has
four columns of mud

[1]Translated by LYSANDER KEMP.
[2]Translated by STEPHEN SPENDER and J. L. GILL.
[3]Translated by A. L. LLOYD.

and a hurricane of black doves
that paddle in putrescent waters.
The Poet in New York (Poeta en Nueva York)
[1940]. The Dawn (La Aurora),[2] *st. 1*

11 The light is buried under chains and noises
in impudent challenge of rootless science.
Through the suburbs sleepless people stagger,
as though just delivered from a shipwreck of
blood.
Ibid. st. 5

George Gershwin[4]
1898–1937

12   Rhapsody in Blue.
Title of composition [1924]

13   True music . . . must repeat the thought and
inspirations of the people and the time. My people
are Americans. My time is today.
From EDWARD JABLONSKI and LAWRENCE D.
STEWART, The Gershwin Years [1926]

Horace Gregory
1898–1982

14 My boyhood saw
Greek islands floating over Harvard Square.[5]
Chorus for Survival [1935], 12

Edgar Y. Harburg
1898–1981

15 Once I built a railroad, now it's done.
Brother, can you spare a dime?
Americana [third edition, 1932].[6] *Brother, Can*
You Spare a Dime?

16 Somewhere over the rainbow
Bluebirds fly.
Birds fly over the rainbow—
Why then, oh why can't I?
The Wizard of Oz [1939].[7] *Over the Rainbow*

17 We gotta be free—
The eagle and me.
Bloomer Girl [1944].[8] *The Eagle and Me*

18 How are things in Glocca Morra this fine day?
Finian's Rainbow [1947].[9] *How Are Things in*
Glocca Morra?

[4]See Ira Gershwin, 695.
[5]The speaker in the poem is Emerson.
[6]Music by JAY GORNEY.
[7]Music by HAROLD ARLEN.
See Baum, 568:9.
[8]Music by HAROLD ARLEN.
The emancipation of woman from intemperance, injustice,
prejudice, and bigotry.—AMELIA JENKS BLOOMER [1818–
1894], *masthead of her paper The Lily*
[9]Music by BURTON LANE.

Clive Staples Lewis
1898–1963

1   The safest road to Hell is the gradual one—the gentle slope, soft underfoot, without sudden turnings, without milestones, without signposts.
The Screwtape Letters [1941], 12

2   The Future . . . something which everyone reaches at the rate of sixty minutes an hour, whatever he does, whoever he is.   *Ibid. 25*

3   The long, dull, monotonous years of middle-aged prosperity or middle-aged adversity are excellent campaigning weather [for the Devil].   *Ibid. 28*

Golda Meir
1898–1978

4   We only want that which is given naturally to all peoples of the world, to be masters of our own fate, only of our fate, not of others, and in cooperation and friendship with others.
Address to Anglo-American Committee of Inquiry [March 25, 1946]

Gunnar Myrdal
1898–1987

5   The American Negro problem is a problem in the heart of the American. It is there that the interracial tension has its focus. It is there that the decisive struggle goes on.   *An American Dilemma [1944]*

6   The treatment of the Negro is America's greatest and most conspicuous scandal.   *Ibid.*

Amelia Earhart Putnam
1898–1937

7 Courage is the price that life exacts for granting
      peace.
The soul that knows it not, knows no release
From little things;
Knows not the livid loneliness of fear,
Nor mountain heights where bitter joy can hear
The sound of wings.
Courage

Erich Maria Remarque
1898–1970

8   Monotonously the lorries sway, monotonously come the calls, monotonously falls the rain. It falls on our heads and on the heads of the dead up the line, on the body of the little recruit with the wound that is so much too big for his hip; it falls on Kemmerich's grave; it falls in our hearts.
All Quiet on the Western Front (Im Westen Nichts Neues) [1929]

Ben Shahn
1898–1969

9   Ever since I could remember I'd wished I'd been lucky enough to be alive at that great time—when something big was going on, like the Crucifixion. And suddenly I realized I was. Here I was living through another crucifixion. Here was something to paint!
On painting a gouache: Bartolomeo Vanzetti and Nicola Sacco [1932]

Jorge Luis Borges
1899–1986

10 Patio, heaven's watercourse.
The patio is the slope
down which the sky flows into the house.
Serenely
eternity waits at the crossway of the stars.
Fervor of Buenos Aires (Fervor de Buenos Aires) [1923]. Un Patio[1]

11   A man gradually identifies himself with the form of his fate; a man is, in the long run, his own circumstances.   *El Aleph [1949]. La Escritura de Dios*

12   It would be exaggerating to say that our relationship is hostile; I live, I let myself live, so that Borges can weave his literature and that literature justifies me. . . . I don't know which of us is writing this page.[2]
Personal Anthology (Antologia Personal) [1961]. Borges and Myself (Borges y Yo)

13   I have known what the Greeks did not: uncertainty.   *Ficciones [1962]. The Babylon Lottery*[3]

14   Writing is nothing more than a guided dream.
Doctor Brodie's Report [1972]. Preface[4]

Noël Coward
1899–1973

15 Mad dogs and Englishmen go out in the midday
      sun.
Mad Dogs and Englishmen

16 I'll see you again,
Whenever spring breaks through again.
Bittersweet [1929], act I, sc. ii

17   Strange how potent cheap music is.
Private Lives [1930], act I

18   Don't Let's Be Beastly to the Germans.
Title of song

19   Learn the lines and don't bump into the furniture.
Attributed. Advice on acting

---

[1]Translated by ROBERT FITZGERALD.
[2]Translated by RACHEL PHILLIPS.
[3]Translated by ANTHONY KERRIGAN.
[4]Translated by NORMAN THOMAS DI GIOVANNI.

Hart Crane
1899–1932

1 And yet this great wink of eternity,
Of rimless floods, unfettered leewardings.
Voyages [1926], II, st. 1

2 It was a kind and northern face
That mingled in such exile guise
The everlasting eyes of Pierrot
And, of Gargantua, the laughter.
Praise for an Urn: In Memoriam Ernest Nelson [1926]

3 Down Wall, from girder into street noon leaks,
A rip-tooth of the sky's acetylene.
The Bridge [1930]. To Brooklyn Bridge

4 And biased by full sails, meridians reel
Thy purpose—still one shore beyond desire!
The sea's green crying towers a-sway, Beyond.
Ibid. Ave Maria

5 Damp tonnage and alluvial march of days . . .
Tortured with history, its one will—flow!
Ibid. The River (Mississippi)

6 The swift red flesh, a winter king—
Who squired the glacier woman down the sky?
She ran the neighing canyons all the spring;
She spouted arms; she rose with maize—to die.
Ibid. The Dance

7 And why do I often meet your visage here,
Your eyes like agate lanterns—on and on
Below the toothpaste and the dandruff ads?
And did their riding eyes right through your side,
And did their eyes like unwashed platters ride?
And Death, aloft—gigantically down[1]
Probing through you toward me, O evermore!
Ibid. The Tunnel

Duke [Edward Kennedy] Ellington
1899–1974

8 It Don't Mean a Thing If It Ain't Got That Swing. *Title of song [1932]*

Friedrich August von Hayek
1899–1992

9 The system of private property is the most important guaranty of freedom, not only for those who own property, but scarcely less for those who do not. *The Road to Serfdom [1944], ch. 8*

10 I am certain that nothing has done so much to destroy the juridical safeguards of individual freedom as the striving after this mirage of social justice.
Economic Freedom and Representative Government [1973]

[1]See Poe, 451:16.

Ernest Hemingway
1899–1961

11 You and me, we've made a separate peace.
In Our Time [1924], ch. 6

12 It makes one feel rather good deciding not to be a bitch. . . . It's sort of what we have instead of God. *The Sun Also Rises [1926], ch. 19*

13 "Oh, Jake," Brett said, "we could have had such a damned good time together." . . .
"Yes," I said. "Isn't it pretty to think so?"
Ibid. last lines

14 I had seen nothing sacred, and the things that were glorious had no glory and the sacrifices were like the stockyards at Chicago if nothing was done with the meat except to bury it . . . Abstract words such as glory, honor, courage, or hallow were obscene. *A Farewell to Arms [1929], ch. 27*

15 The world breaks everyone and afterward many are strong at the broken places. But those that will not break it kills. It kills the very good and the very gentle and the very brave impartially. If you are none of these you can be sure that it will kill you too but there will be no special hurry. *Ibid. 34*

16 You never had time to learn. They threw you in and told you the rules and the first time they caught you off base they killed you. *Ibid. 41*

17 It was like saying good-bye to a statue. After a while I went out and left the hospital and walked back to the hotel in the rain. *Ibid.*

18 Grace under pressure.[2]
Definition of "guts." From DOROTHY PARKER, The Artist's Reward, in The New Yorker [November 30, 1929]

19 I know only that what is moral is what you feel good after and what is immoral is what you feel bad after. *Death in the Afternoon [1932], ch. 1*

20 I was trying to write then and I found the greatest difficulty, aside from knowing truly what you really felt, rather than what you were supposed to feel, had been taught to feel, was to put down what really happened in action; what the actual things were which produced the emotion that you experienced . . . the real thing, the sequence of motion and fact which made the emotion and which would be as valid in a year or in ten years or, with luck and if you stated it purely enough, always. *Ibid.*

21 If he wrote it he could get rid of it. He had gotten rid of many things by writing them.
Winner Take Nothing [1933]. Fathers and Sons

[2]After skiing with the Hemingways in 1926, Gerald Murphy was "absolutely elated" when Hemingway praised his courage in venturing down the slopes for the first time as "grace under pressure." See HONORIA MURPHY DONNELLY with RICHARD N. BILLINGS, *Sara & Gerald* [1982].

1 All good books are alike in that they are truer than if they had really happened and after you are finished reading one you will feel that all that happened to you and afterwards it all belongs to you: the good and the bad, the ecstasy, the remorse and sorrow, the people and the places and how the weather was. If you can get so that you can give that to people, then you are a writer.

Old Newsman Writes. From Esquire [December 1934]

2 All modern American literature comes from one book by Mark Twain called *Huckleberry Finn.*

Green Hills of Africa [1935], ch. 1

3 The rich were dull and they drank too much. . . . He remembered poor Julian[1] and his romantic awe of them and how he had started a story once that began, "The very rich are different from you and me." And how someone had said to Julian, Yes, they have more money.[2]

The Fifth Column and The First Forty-Nine Stories [1938]. The Snows of Kilimanjaro

4 Kilimanjaro is a snow-covered mountain 19,710 feet high, and is said to be the highest mountain in Africa. Its western summit is called the Masai "Ngàje Ngài," the House of God. Close to the western summit there is the dried and frozen carcass of a leopard. No one has explained what the leopard was seeking at that altitude. *Ibid. epigraph*

5 But did thee feel the earth move?

For Whom the Bell Tolls [1940], ch. 13

6 If we win here we will win everywhere. The world is a fine place and worth the fighting for and I hate very much to leave it. *Ibid. 43*

7 Cowardice, as distinguished from panic, is almost always simply a lack of ability to suspend the functioning of the imagination.

Men at War [1942], introduction

8 Time is the least thing we have of.

From The New Yorker profile by LILLIAN ROSS [May 13, 1950][3]

9 I must be worthy of the great DiMaggio who does all things perfectly even with the pain of the bone spur in his heel.

The Old Man and the Sea [1952]

10 A man can be destroyed but not defeated. *Ibid.*

[1]In original publication, "poor Scott Fitzgerald" [*Esquire,* August 1936].
[2]In 1936 Maxwell Perkins, the legendary editor of Fitzgerald and Hemingway at Charles Scribner's Sons, lunched with Hemingway and the critic Mary Colum. When Hemingway announced, "I am getting to know the rich," Mary Colum replied, "The only difference between the rich and other people is that the rich have more money."—MATTHEW J. BRUCCOLI [1931–], *Scott and Ernest* [1978]
See Fitzgerald, 694:14.
[3]Reprinted in book form: *Portrait of Hemingway* [1961].

11 The most essential gift for a good writer is a built-in, shock-proof, shit detector. This is the writer's radar and all great writers have had it.

Interview in Paris Review [Spring 1958]

12 You write until you come to a place where you still have your juice and know what will happen next and you stop and try to live through until the next day when you hit it again. *Ibid.*

13 If you are lucky enough to have lived in Paris as a young man, then wherever you go for the rest of your life, it stays with you, for Paris is a moveable feast.[4] *A Moveable Feast [1964], epigraph*

Robert Maynard Hutchins
1899–1977

14 The death of democracy is not likely to be an assassination from ambush. It will be a slow extinction from apathy, indifference, and undernourishment. *Great Books [1954]*

Nadezhda Mandelstam
1899–1980

15 I decided it is better to scream. This pitiful sound, which sometimes, goodness knows how, reaches into the remotest prison cell, is a concentrated expression of the last vestige of human dignity. It is a man's way of leaving a trace, of telling people how he lived and died. By his screams he asserts his right to live, sends a message to the outside world demanding help and calling for resistance. If nothing else is left, one must scream. Silence is the real crime against humanity.

Hope Against Hope [1970],[5] ch. 11

Charles W. Morton
1899–1967

16 It was around two decades ago, in the city room of the Boston *Evening Transcript,* that I first became aware of the elongated-yellow-fruit school of writing. The phrase turned up in a story . . . about some fugitive monkeys and the efforts of police to recapture them by using bananas as bait.

The Elongated Yellow Fruit [1954]

Vladimir Nabokov
1899–1977

17 The cradle rocks above an abyss, and common sense tells us that our existence is but a brief crack of light between two eternities of darkness.

Speak, Memory [1947], ch. 1

[4]See *Book of Common Prayer,* 48:13.
[5]Translated by MAX HAYWARD.

1   Lolita, light of my life, fire of my loins. My sin, my soul.   *Lolita [1955], pt. I, ch. 1*

2   Between the age limits of nine and fourteen there occur maidens who, to certain bewitched travelers, twice or many times older than they, reveal their nature, which is not human, but nymphic (that is, demoniac); and these chosen creatures I propose to designate as "nymphets."   *Ibid. 5*

3   I am thinking of aurochs and angels, the secret of durable pigments, prophetic sonnets, the refuge of art. And this is the only immortality you and I may share, my Lolita.   *Ibid. last paragraph*

4   In pornographic novels, action has to be limited to the copulation of clichés. Style, structure, imagery should never distract the reader from his tepid lust.
                    On a Book Entitled Lolita [1956]

5   For me a work of fiction exists only insofar as it affords me what I shall bluntly call aesthetic bliss.
                                                        Ibid.

6   Like so many aging college people, Pnin had long since ceased to notice the existence of students on the campus.   *Pnin [1957], ch. 3, sec. 6*

Elwyn Brooks White
1899–1985

7   All poets who, when reading from their own works, experience a choked feeling, are major. For that matter, all poets who read from their own works are major, whether they choke or not.
        How to Tell a Major Poet from a Minor Poet

8   "It's broccoli, dear."
    "I say it's spinach, and I say the hell with it."
        Caption for cartoon by Carl Rose in The New Yorker [December 8, 1928]

9   Commuter — one who spends his life
In riding to and from his wife;
A man who shaves and takes a train
And then rides back to shave again.
                                    Commuter [1929]

10   I have occasionally had the exquisite thrill of putting my finger on a little capsule of truth, and heard it give the faint squeak of mortality under my pressure.
        Letter to Stanley Hart White [January 1929]

11   I don't know which is more discouraging, literature or chickens.
        Letter to James Thurber [November 18, 1938]

12   When Mrs. Frederick C. Little's second son was born, everybody noticed that he was not much bigger than a mouse. The truth of the matter was, the baby looked very much like a mouse in every way. He was only two inches high; and he had a mouse's sharp nose, a mouse's tail, a mouse's whiskers, and the pleasant, shy manner of a mouse. Before he was many days old he was not only looking like a mouse but acting like one, too — wearing a gray hat and carrying a small cane.   *Stuart Little [1945], ch. 1*

13   "My name is Margalo," said the bird, softly, in a musical voice. "I come from fields once tall with wheat, from pastures deep in fern and thistle; I come from vales of meadowsweet, and I love to whistle."
                                                    Ibid. 8

14   Democracy is the recurrent suspicion that more than half of the people are right more than half of the time.   *The Wild Flag [1946]*

15   I am a member of a party of one, and I live in an age of fear. Nothing lately has unsettled my party and raised my fears so much as your editorial, on Thanksgiving Day, suggesting that employees should be required to state their beliefs in order to hold their jobs. The idea is inconsistent with our constitutional theory and has been stubbornly opposed by watchful men since the early days of the Republic.
        Letter to the New York Herald Tribune [November 29, 1947]

16   It was the best place to be, thought Wilbur, this warm delicious cellar, with the garrulous geese, the changing seasons, the heat of the sun, the passage of swallows, the nearness of rats, the sameness of sheep, the love of spiders, the smell of manure, and the glory of everything.
                        Charlotte's Web [1952], ch. 22

17   None of the new spiders ever quite took her place in his heart. She was in a class by herself. It is not often that someone comes along who is a true friend and a good writer. Charlotte was both.   *Ibid.*

18   An unhatched egg is to me the greatest challenge in life.   *Letter to Reginald Allen [March 5, 1973]*

19   The essayist . . . can pull on any sort of shirt, be any sort of person, according to his mood or his subject matter — philosopher, scold, jester, raconteur, confidant, pundit, devil's advocate, enthusiast.
                Essays of E. B. White [1977], foreword

Louis [Satchmo] Armstrong
1900–1971

20   Man, if you gotta ask you'll never know.[1]
                    Reply when asked what jazz is

Denis William Brogan
1900–1974

21   A people that has licked a more formidable enemy than Germany or Japan, primitive North

---

[1]Lady, if you got to ask you ain't got it. — THOMAS [FATS] WALLER [1904–1943], *when asked to explain rhythm*

America . . . a country whose national motto has been "root, hog, or die."
The American Character [1944]

1   Any well-established village in New England or the northern Middle West could afford a town drunkard, a town atheist, and a few Democrats.
Ibid.

Herbert Butterfield
1900–1979

2   It [the scientific revolution] outshines everything since the rise of Christianity and reduces the Renaissance and Reformation to the rank of mere episodes, mere internal displacements, within the system of medieval Christendom. . . . It looms so large as the real origin of the modern world and of the modern mentality that our customary periodization of European history has become an anachronism and an encumbrance.
The Origins of Modern Science [1949]

Lenore Coffee
1900–1984

3   What a dump!
Beyond the Forest (screenplay) [1949], spoken by Bette Davis

Theodosius Dobzhansky
1900–1975

4   Nature's stern discipline enjoins mutual help at least as often as warfare. The fittest may also be the gentlest.   *Mankind Evolving [1962]*

Elizabeth, Queen Mother of England
1900–

5   The children will not leave unless I do. I shall not leave unless their father does, and the King will not leave the country in any circumstances whatever.
Reported reply as to whether the princesses would leave England after the bombing of Buckingham Palace [1940]

Hans Frank
1900–1946

6   Our Constitution is the will of the Fuehrer.
In Volkischer Beobachter [May 20, 1936]

7   A thousand years will pass and the guilt of Germany will not be erased.
Before he was hanged at Nuremberg [October 16, 1946]

Erich Fromm
1900–1980

8   Freedom, although it has brought [modern man] independence and rationality, has made him isolated and, thereby, anxious and powerless.
Escape from Freedom [1941]. Foreword

9   Man's nature, his passions and anxieties, are a cultural product; as a matter of fact, man himself is the most important creation and achievement of the continuous human effort, the record of what we call history.   *Ibid. ch. 1*

Abel Green
1900–1973

10   Sticks Nix Hick Pix.
Headline about rural audiences' rejection of movies with rural themes, Variety [July 17, 1935]

James Hilton
1900–1954

11   The austere serenity of Shangri-La. Its forsaken courts and pale pavilions shimmered in repose from which all the fret of existence had ebbed away, leaving a hush as if moments hardly dared to pass.
Lost Horizon [1933], ch. 5

12   Anno domini—that's the most fatal complaint of all in the end.   *Goodbye, Mr. Chips [1934], ch. 1*

Ayatolla Ruholla Khomeini
1900–1989

13   The author of the Satanic Verses book [Salman Rushdie[1]], which is against Islam, the Prophet, and the Koran, and all those involved in its publication who were aware of its content, are sentenced to death. I ask all Moslems to execute them wherever they find them.   *Statement [February 14, 1989]*

Raphael Lemkin
1900–1959

14   By genocide[2] we mean the destruction of a nation or of an ethnic group.
Axis Rule in Occupied Europe [1944]

Margaret Mitchell
1900–1949

15   The usual masculine disillusionment in discovering that a woman has a brain.
Gone With the Wind [1936], pt. IV, ch. 36

---

[1]See Rushdie, 774:7.
[2]Lemkin coined the word (by combining a Greek and a Latin root) and introduced it in this passage.

1   Death and taxes[1] and childbirth! There's never any convenient time for any of them.   *Ibid. 38*

2   My dear, I don't give a damn [Rhett Butler to Scarlett O'Hara].[2]   *Ibid. V, 63*

3   I'll think of some way to get him back. After all, tomorrow is another day.   *Ibid. last line*

Wayne Lyman Morse
1900–1974

4   The liberal, emphasizing the civil and property rights of the individual, insists that the individual must remain so supreme as to make the state his servant.
Definition contributed to Nine Definitions of Liberalism. In the New Republic [July 22, 1946]

Stephen Potter
1900–1969

5   Gamesmanship: The Art of Winning Games Without Actually Cheating.   *Title of book [1947]*

6   One-Upmanship.   *Title of book [1952]*

V[ictor] S[awdon] Pritchett
1900–

7   The detective novel is the art-for-art's sake of our yawning Philistinism, the classic example of a specialized form of art removed from contact with the life it pretends to build on.
Books in General [1953]. The Roots of Detection

8   I come from a set of storytellers and moralists. . . . The storytellers were forever changing the tale and the moralists tampering with it in order to put it in an edifying light.   *A Cab at the Door [1967], ch. 1*

Ernie Pyle
1900–1945

9   I write from the worm's-eye point of view.
Here Is Your War [1943]

Leo Robin
1900–1984

10   Diamonds Are a Girl's Best Friend.
Gentlemen Prefer Blondes [1949],[3] title of song

[1]See Franklin, 310:27.
[2]Frankly, my dear, I don't give a damn.—SIDNEY HOWARD [1891–1939], *screenplay for Gone With the Wind* [1939]
[3]See Loos, 686:8.
Music by JULE STYNE.

Antoine de Saint-Exupéry
1900–1944

11   Although human life is priceless, we always act as if something had an even greater price than life. . . . But what is that something?
Night Flight [1931], ch. 14

12   Grown-ups never understand anything for themselves, and it is tiresome for children to be always and forever explaining things to them.
The Little Prince [1943],[4] ch. 1

13   It is only with the heart that one can see rightly; what is essential is invisible to the eye.   *Ibid. 21*

George Seferis [Giorgios Sefiriades]
1900–1971

14 Three years
we waited intently for the herald
closely watching
the pines the shore and the stars.
    Mythistorema [1935],[5] I

15 We were searching to rediscover the first seed
so that the ancient drama could begin again.
    Ibid.

16 We have no rivers, we have no wells, we have no
    springs,
only a few cisterns—and these empty—that echo,
    and we worship them.
A stagnant hollow sound, the same as our
    loneliness
the same as our love, the same as our bodies.
    Ibid. X

17 They were lovely, your eyes, but you didn't know
    where to look.
    Ibid. XVI

18 They're a burden for us
the friends who no longer know how to die.
    Ibid. XIX

19 Wherever I travel Greece wounds me.
    In the Manner of G.S. [1936]

20   Each of us earns his death, his own death,
      which belongs to no one else
and this game is life.
    The Last Day [1939]

21 Here where one meets the path of rain, wind, and
    ruin
does there exist the movement of the face, shape
    of the tenderness
of those who've shrunk so strangely in our lives,
those who remained the shadow of waves and
    thoughts with the sea's boundlessness
or perhaps no, nothing is left but the weight

[4]Translated by KATHERINE WOODS.
[5]Translated by EDMUND KEELEY and PHILIP SHERRARD.

the nostalgia for the weight of a living existence . . .
the poet a void.
> *The King of Asine [1940]*

1 It's painful and difficult, the living are not enough
for me.
> *Stratis Thalassinos Among the Agapanthi [1942]*

2 Sometimes it crosses my mind that the things I
write here are nothing
other than images that prisoners or sailors tattoo
on their skin.
> *Logbook II [1944], epigraph*

3 Great suffering descended on Greece.
So many bodies thrown
into the jaws of the sea, the jaws of the earth . . .
all for a linen undulation, a bit of cloud,
a butterfly's flicker, a swan's down,
an empty tunic—all for a Helen.
> *Helen [1953]*

4 He grew old between the fires of Troy
and the quarries of Sicily.
> *Euripides the Athenian [1953]*

5 They are children of many men, our words.
> *On Stage [1966],*[1] 6

6 As pines
keep the shape of the wind
even when the wind has fled and is no longer
there,
so words
guard the shape of man
even when man has fled and is no longer there.
> *Ibid.*

7 When, on the road to Thebes, Oedipus met the
Sphinx, who asked him her riddle, his answer was:
Man.[2] This simple word destroyed the monster. We
have many monsters to destroy. Let us think of Oedipus' answer.
> *Speech upon receiving the Nobel Prize [1963]*

Ignazio Silone [Secondo Tranquilli]
1900–1978

8 Liberty is the possibility of doubting, the possibility of making a mistake, the possibility of searching
and experimenting, the possibility of saying "No" to
any authority—literary, artistic, philosophic, religious, social, and even political.
> *Essay in The God That Failed [1950]*[3]

Adlai Ewing Stevenson
1900–1965

9 The problem of cat versus bird is as old as time.
If we attempt to resolve it by legislation who knows

but what we may be called upon to take sides as well
in the age old problems of dog versus cat, bird versus
bird, and even bird versus worm. . . . The State of
Illinois and its local governing bodies already have
enough to do without trying to control feline delinquency.
> *As governor of Illinois, vetoing a
> bird-protection bill [April 23, 1949]*

10 Let's talk sense to the American people.
> *Speech accepting the Democratic presidential
> nomination [July 26, 1952]*

11 When an American says that he loves his country,
he . . . means that he loves an inner air, an inner
light in which freedom lives and in which a man can
draw the breath of self-respect.
> *Speech at New York City [August 27, 1952]*

12 A hungry man is not a free man.[4]
> *Speech at Kasson, Minnesota [September 6,
> 1952]*

13 The time to stop a revolution is at the beginning,
not the end.
> *Speech at San Francisco [September 9, 1952]*

14 Your public servants serve you right.
> *Speech at Los Angeles [September 11, 1952]*

15 Unreason and anti-intellectualism abominate
thought. . . . But shouting is not a substitute for
thinking and reason is not the subversion but the
salvation of freedom.
> *Godkin Lectures, Harvard University [March
> 1954]*

Thomas Wolfe
1900–1938

16 A stone, a leaf, an unfound door.
> *Look Homeward, Angel*[5] *[1929], foreword*

17 Which of us has known his brother? Which of us
has looked into his father's heart? Which of us has
not remained forever prison-pent? Which of us is not
forever a stranger and alone?   *Ibid.*

18 O lost, and by the wind grieved, ghost, come
back again.   *Ibid.*

19 If a man has a talent and cannot use it, he has
failed. If he has a talent and uses only half of it, he
has partly failed. If he has a talent and learns somehow to use the whole of it, he has gloriously succeeded, and won a satisfaction and a triumph few
men ever know.
> *The Web and the Rock [1939], ch. 30*

20 I believe that we are lost here in America, but I
believe we shall be found.
> *You Can't Go Home Again [1940], ch. 48*

---

[1] Translated by WALTER KAISER.
[2] See *The Riddle of the Sphinx*, 66:n1.
[3] Edited by RICHARD CROSSMAN.

[4] See Cato, 85:3, and La Fontaine, 268:8.
[5] See Milton, 254:5.

Roy Campbell
1901–1957

1 You praise the firm restraint with which they
     write—
I'm with you there, of course.
They use the snaffle and the curb all right;
But where's the bloody horse?
                    On Some South African Novelists

Margaret Craven
1901–1980

2   The Indian knows his village and feels for his village as no white man for his country, his town, or even
for his own bit of land. His village is not the strip of
land four miles long and three miles wide that is his
as long as the sun rises and the moon sets. The myths
are the village, and the winds and rains. The river is
the village, and . . . the talking bird, the owl, who
calls the name of the man who is going to die.
           I Heard the Owl Call My Name [1973], pt. I

Werner Karl Heisenberg
1901–1976

3   Every tool carries with it the spirit by which it has
been created.   *Physics and Philosophy [1958]*

4   Since the measuring device has been constructed
by the observer . . . we have to remember that
what we observe is not nature in itself but nature
exposed to our method of questioning.   *Ibid.*

Zora Neale Hurston
c. 1901–1960

5   I am not tragically colored. There is no great
sorrow dammed up in my soul, nor lurking behind
my eyes. . . . I do not weep at the world—I am
too busy sharpening my oyster knife.
             How It Feels to Be Colored Me [1928]

6   Women forget all those things they don't want to
remember, and remember everything they don't
want to forget. The dream is the truth. Then they act
and do things accordingly.
           Their Eyes Were Watching God [1937], ch. 1

7   De nigger woman is de mule uh de world so fur
as Ah can see. Ah been prayin' fuh it tuh be different
wid you.   *Ibid. 2*

James Michael Kieran, Jr.
1901–1952

8   The brains trust.
     *In conversation with Franklin D. Roosevelt
     [August 1932], referring to the professors and
     other such advisers who served Roosevelt in his
     first campaign. The phrase later became "brain
     trust."*

André Malraux
1901–1976

9   The great mystery is not that we should have
been thrown down here at random between the profusion of matter and that of the stars; it is that from
our very prison we should draw, from our own
selves, images powerful enough to deny our nothingness.   *Man's Fate (La Condition Humaine) [1933]*

10   One cannot create an art that speaks to men
when one has nothing to say.
               Man's Hope (L'Espoir) [1938]

11   All art is a revolt against man's fate.
     The Voices of Silence (Les Voix du Silence) [1951]

12   The human mind invents its Puss-in-Boots and its
coaches that change into pumpkins at midnight because neither the believer nor the atheist is completely satisfied with appearances.
                  Anti-Memoirs [1967], preface

13   The genius of Christianity is to have proclaimed
that the path to the deepest mystery is the path of
love.   *Ibid. Anti-Memoirs, sec. 6*

14   The extermination camps, in endeavoring to turn
man into a beast, intimated that it is not life alone
which makes him man.
          Ibid. La Condition Humaine, sec. 2

15   The attempt to force human beings to despise
themselves . . . is what I call hell.   *Ibid.*

Margaret Mead
1901–1978

16   As the traveler who has once been from home is
wiser than he who has never left his own doorstep,
so a knowledge of one other culture should sharpen
our ability to scrutinize more steadily, to appreciate
more lovingly, our own.
          Coming of Age in Samoa [1928], introduction

17   If we are to achieve a richer culture, rich in contrasting values, we must recognize the whole gamut
of human potentialities, and so weave a less arbitrary social fabric, one in which each diverse human
gift will find a fitting place.
          *Sex and Temperament in Three Primitive
          Societies [1935], conclusion*

18   We know of no culture that has said, articulately,
that there is no difference between men and women
except in the way they contribute to the creation of
the next generation.   *Male and Female [1948]*

19   The mind is not sex-typed.
               Blackberry Winter [1972], ch. 5

20   Because of their age-long training in human relations—for that is what feminine intuition really is
—women have a special contribution to make to
any group enterprise, and I feel it is up to them to
contribute the kinds of awareness that relatively few
men . . . have incorporated through their education.   *Ibid. 14*

Linus Carl Pauling
1901–

1 Science is the search for truth—it is not a game in which one tries to beat his opponent, to do harm to others. We need to have the spirit of science in international affairs, to make the conduct of international affairs the effort to find the right solution, the just solution of international problems, not the effort by each nation to get the better of other nations, to do harm to them when it is possible.

No More War! [1958]

Arna Bontemps
1902–1973

2 Yet what I sowed and what the orchard yields
My brother's sons are gathering stalk and root,
Small wonder then my children glean in fields
They have not sown, and feed on bitter fruit.

A Black Man Talks of Reaping [1963], st. 3

3 Yet would we die as some have done:
Beating a way for the rising sun.

The Daybreakers [1963]

Thomas Edmund Dewey
1902–1971

4 That's why it's time for a change.[1]

Campaign speech at San Francisco [September 21, 1944]

Erik Homburger Erikson
1902–

5 This sense of identity provides the ability to experience one's self as something that has continuity and sameness, and to act accordingly.

Childhood and Society [1950]

6 The identity crisis . . . occurs in that period of the life cycle when each youth must forge for himself some central perspective and direction, some working unity, out of the effective remnants of his childhood and the hopes of his anticipated adulthood.

Young Man Luther [1958], ch. 1

Stella Gibbons
1902–1989

7 The farm was crouched on a bleak hillside, whence its fields, fanged with flints, dropped steeply to the village of Howling a mile away.

Cold Comfort Farm[2] [1932], ch. 3

8 Something nasty in the woodshed. *Ibid. 8*

---

[1]The phrase was used extensively in the campaigns of 1944, 1948, and 1952.
[2]See Shakespeare, 170:22.

Wolcott Gibbs
1902–1958

9 Backward ran sentences until reeled the mind.

More in Sorrow [1958]. Time . . . Fortune . . . Life . . . Luce

10 Where it will all end, knows God! *Ibid.*

Langston Hughes
1902–1967

11 It is the duty of the younger Negro artist . . . to change through the force of his art that old whispering "I want to be white," hidden in the aspirations of his people, to "Why should I want to be white? I am a Negro—and beautiful!"[3]

The Negro Artist and the Racial Mountain. In The Nation [June 23, 1926]

12 I've known rivers:
I've known rivers ancient as the world and older than the flow of human blood in human veins.
My soul has grown deep like the rivers.

The Negro Speaks of Rivers [1926]

13 I am a Negro:
Black as the night is black,
Black like the depths of my Africa.

Negro [1926]

14 Rest at pale evening . . .
A tall slim tree . . .
Night coming tenderly
Black like me.

Dream Variations [1926]

15 I got the Weary Blues
And I can't be satisfied.

The Weary Blues [1926]

16 Listen, Christ,
You did alright in your day, I reckon—
But that day's gone now.
They ghosted you up a swell story, too,
Called it Bible—
But it's dead now.

Goodbye Christ [1932]

17 Wear it
Like a banner
For the proud—
Not like a shroud.

Color [1943]

18 Good morning, daddy!
Ain't you heard
The boogie-woogie rumble
Of a dream deferred?

Dream Boogie [1951]

19 What happens to a dream deferred?
Does it dry up

---

[3]See Anonymous, 784:1.

like a raisin in the sun?
Or fester like a sore—
And then run?
Does it stink like rotten meat?
Or crust and sugar over—
like a syrupy sweet?

Maybe it just sags
like a heavy load.

Or does it explode?

Harlem [1951]

1 As I learn from you,
I guess you learn from me—
although you're older—and white—
and somewhat more free.

Theme for English B [1951]

2 Negro blood is sure powerful—because just *one* drop of black blood makes a colored man. *One* drop —you are a Negro! . . . Black is powerful.[1]

Simple Takes a Wife [1953]

Carlo Levi
1902–1975

3 Christ Stopped at Eboli.[2]

Title of book [1945]

Charles Augustus Lindbergh[3]
1902–1974

4 We (that's my ship and I) took off rather suddenly. We had a report somewhere around 4 o'clock in the afternoon before that the weather would be fine, so we thought we would try it.

Lindbergh's Own Story. In the New York Times [May 23, 1927]

5 I saw a fleet of fishing boats. . . . I flew down almost touching the craft and yelled at them, asking if I was on the right road to Ireland.

They just stared. Maybe they didn't hear me. Maybe I didn't hear them. Or maybe they thought I was just a crazy fool. An hour later I saw land.

Ibid.

Ogden Nash
1902–1971

6 Candy
Is dandy

But liquor
Is quicker.

Hard Lines [1931]. Reflections on Ice-Breaking

7 The turtle lives 'twixt plated decks
Which practically conceal its sex.
I think it clever of the turtle
In such a fix to be so fertile.

Ibid. The Turtle

8 The Bronx?
No, thonx!

Ibid. Geographical Reflection

9 A bit of talcum
Is always walcum.

Free Wheeling [1931]. The Baby

10 I think that I shall never see
A billboard lovely as a tree.
Indeed, unless the billboards fall
I'll never see a tree at all.[4]

Happy Days [1933]. Song of the Open Road.

11 There is something about a Martini,
Ere the dining and dancing begin,
And to tell you the truth,
It is not the vermouth—
I think that perhaps it's the gin.

The Primrose Path [1935]. A Drink with Something in It

12 There was a young belle of old Natchez
Whose garments were always in patchez.
When comment arose
On the state of her clothes,
She drawled, When Ah itchez, Ah scratchez!

I'm a Stranger Here Myself [1938]. Requiem

13 The trouble with a kitten is
THAT
Eventually it becomes a
CAT.

The Face Is Familiar [1941]. The Kitten

14 I believe a little incompatibility is the spice of life,
particularly if he has income and she is
pattable.

Versus [1949]. I Do, I Will, I Have

15 He tells you when you've got on too much
lipstick,
And helps you with your girdle when your hips
stick.

Ibid. The Perfect Husband

16 A door is what a dog is perpetually on the wrong side of.

The Private Dining Room [1953]. A Dog's Best Friend Is His Illiteracy

17 How confusing the beams from memory's lamp
are;
One day a bachelor, the next a grampa.

---

[1]See Carmichael and Hamilton, 771:2.
[2]Cristo Si è Fermato a Eboli.
[3]In the spring of '27, something bright and alien flashed across the sky. A young Minnesotan [Lindbergh] who seemed to have had nothing to do with his generation did a heroic thing, and for a moment people set down their glasses in country clubs and speakeasies and thought of their old best dreams.
—F. Scott Fitzgerald

[4]See Kilmer, 661:16.

What is the secret of the trick?
How did I get so old so quick?
>   *You Can't Get There from Here [1957]. Preface*
>   *to the Past*

1 Here lies my past. Good-bye I have kissed it;
Thank you, kids. I wouldn't have missed it.
>   *Ibid.*

2   Maybe I couldn't be dafter,
But I keep wondering if this time we couldn't
settle our differences before a war instead of
after.
>   *Everyone but Thee and Me [1962]. Is There an*
>   *Oculist in the House?*

3 I myself am more and more inclined to agree with
Omar and Satchel Paige as I grow older:
Don't try to rewrite what the moving finger has
writ, and don't ever look over your shoulder.
>   *There's Always Another Windmill [1968]. If a*
>   *Boder Meet a Boder, Need a Boder Cry? Yes*

4 Linguistics becomes an ever eerier area, like I feel
like I'm in Oz,
Just trying to tell it like it was.[1]
>   *The Old Dog Barks Backwards [1972]. What*
>   *Do You Want, A Meaningful Dialogue or a*
>   *Satisfactory Talk?*

Sir Karl Raimund Popper
1902–

5   Our belief in any particular natural law cannot
have a safer basis than our unsuccessful critical attempts to refute it.
>   *Conjectures and Refutations [1963]*

Stevie [Margaret Florence] Smith
1902–1971

6 I was much too far out all my life
And not waving but drowning.
>   *Not Waving but Drowning [1957]*

7 Why does my Muse only speak when she is
unhappy?
She does not, I only listen when I am unhappy.
>   *My Muse [1962]*

8 Yet a time may come when a poet or any person
Having a long life behind him, pleasure and
sorrow . . .
May fancy life comes to him with love and says:
We are friends enough now for me to give you
death;
Then he may commit suicide, then
He may go.
>   *Exeat [1966]*

[1]Tell it like it is. — *Youth slogan* [1960s]

John Ernst Steinbeck
1902–1968

9   Man, unlike any other thing organic or inorganic
in the universe, grows beyond his work, walks up
the stairs of his concepts, emerges ahead of his accomplishments.
>   *The Grapes of Wrath [1939], ch. 14*

10   Okie use' ta mean you was from Oklahoma.
Now it means you're scum. Don't mean nothing
itself, it's the way they say it.   *Ibid. 18*

Meredith Willson
1902–1984

11 Ya got trouble, folks,
Right here in River City.
Trouble with a capital "T"
And that rhymes with "P"
And that stands for Pool!
>   *The Music Man [1957]. Ya Got Trouble*

12   River City's gonna have her Boys Band! As sure
as the Lord made little green apples, and that band's
gonna be in uniform!   *Ibid.*

Tallulah Brockman Bankhead
1903–1968

13   There is less in this than meets the eye.
>   *Remark to Alexander Woollcott at Aglavaine*
>   *and Selysette by MAURICE MAETERLINCK*
>   *[January 3, 1922]*

Erskine Caldwell
1903–1987

14   Tobacco Road.   *Title of novel [1932]*[2]

Count Galeazzo Ciano
1903–1944

15   As always, victory finds a hundred fathers but
defeat is an orphan.[3]
>   *The Ciano Diaries 1939–1943 [1946].*
>   *[September 9, 1942]*

Cyril Vernon Connolly
1903–1974

16   Obesity is a mental state, a disease brought on by
boredom and disappointment.
>   *The Unquiet Grave [1945], pt. I*

[2]The play [1933], adapted by JACK KIRKLAND [1903–1969],
had one of the longest runs in American stage history.
[3]There's an old saying that victory has a hundred fathers and
defeat is an orphan. — JOHN F. KENNEDY, *after the debacle at*
the Bay of Pigs, Cuba [April 21, 1961]

1   Imprisoned in every fat man a thin one is wildly signaling to be let out.[1]   *Ibid. II*

Countee Cullen
1903–1946

2 One three centuries removed
From the scenes his fathers loved,
Spicy grove, cinnamon tree,
What is Africa to me?

Heritage [1925]

3 Jesus of the twice-turned cheek,
Lamb of God, although I speak
With my mouth thus, in my heart
Do I play a double part.
Even at Thy glowing altar
Must my heart grow sick and falter
Wishing He I served were black.

Ibid.

4 Not yet has my heart or head
In the least way realized
They and I are civilized.

Ibid.

William Thomas Cummings
1903–1944

5   There are no atheists in the foxholes.[2]
Field sermon, Bataan [1942]. From CARLOS P. ROMULO, *I Saw the Fall of the Philippines [1942]*

Malcolm Muggeridge
1903–1990

6   As Man alone, Jesus could not have saved us; as God alone, he would not; Incarnate, he could and did.   *Jesus [1975], pt. I*

Anaïs Nin
1903–1977

7   It's all right for a woman to be, above all, human. I am a woman first of all.
The Diary of Anaïs Nin, vol. I [1966], June 1933

8   Dreams are necessary to life.
Ibid. II [1967], June 1936 (letter to her mother)

9   Each friend represents a world in us, a world possibly not born until they arrive, and it is only by this meeting that a new world is born.
Ibid. March 1937

10   There are very few human beings who receive the truth, complete and staggering, by instant illumina-tion. Most of them acquire it fragment by fragment, on a small scale, by successive developments, cellu-larly, like a laborious mosaic.
Ibid. III [1969], Fall 1943

George Orwell [Eric Blair]
1903–1950

11   As for [Stanley] Baldwin, one could not even dig-nify him with the name of stuffed shirt. He was simply a hole in the air.
The Lion and The Unicorn [1940]

12   All animals are equal, but some animals are more equal than others.   *Animal Farm [1945], ch. 10*

13   The great enemy of clear language is insincerity.
Politics and the English Language [1946]

14   Political language . . . is designed to make lies sound truthful and murder respectable, and to give an appearance of solidity to pure wind.   *Ibid.*

15   It was a bright cold day in April and the clocks were striking thirteen.   *1984 [1948], opening line*

16   Big Brother is watching you.
Ibid. pt. I, ch. 1

17   War is peace. Freedom is slavery. Ignorance is strength.   *Ibid.*

18   Power is not a means; it is an end. One does not establish a dictatorship in order to safeguard a revo-lution; one makes the revolution in order to establish the dictatorship. The object of persecution is perse-cution. The object of torture is torture. The object of power is power.   *Ibid. III, 3*

19   If you want a picture of the future, imagine a boot stamping on a human face—forever.
Ibid.

Casey Robinson
1903–1979

20   Where's the rest of me?
Kings Row (screenplay) [1942], spoken by Ronald Reagan[3]

21   Oh, Jerry, don't ask for the moon. We have the stars.
Now Voyager (screenplay) [1942], spoken by Bette Davis

Benjamin Spock
1903–

22   The more people have studied different methods of bringing up children the more they have come to the conclusion that what good mothers and fathers

---

[1]Outside every fat man there was an even fatter man trying to close in.—KINGSLEY AMIS [1922–], *One Fat Englishman* [1963]

[2]See Edward Young, 296:16.

[3]Also the title of Reagan's autobiography [1965].

instinctively feel like doing for their babies is the best after all.

The Common Sense Book of Baby and Child Care [1946], ch. 1

Evelyn Waugh
1903–1966

1   I expect you'll be becoming a schoolmaster, sir. That's what most of the gentlemen does, sir, that gets sent down for indecent behavior.

Decline and Fall [1928], Prelude

2   Anyone who has been to an English public school will always feel comparatively at home in prison. It is the people brought up in the gay intimacy of the slums . . . who find prison so soul destroying.

Ibid. pt. III, ch. 4

3   "*What war?*" said the Prime Minister sharply. "No one has said anything to me about a war. I really think I should have been told. I'll be damned," he said defiantly, "if they shall have a war without consulting me. What's a cabinet for, if there's not more mutual confidence than that? What do they want a war for, anyway?"   *Vile Bodies [1930], ch. 8*

4   We will not have any Dickens today . . . but tomorrow, and the day after that, and the day after that. Let us read *Little Dorrit* again.

A Handful of Dust [1934], ch. 6

5   Feather-footed through the plashy fen passes the questing vole.   *Scoop [1938], bk. I, ch. 2, sec. 1*

6   He had aroused three irreconcilable feuds in Capri; he had practiced black art in Cefalu; he had been cured of drug taking in California and of an Oedipus complex in Vienna.

Brideshead Revisited [1945], bk. I, ch. 2

7   I caught a thin bat's squeak of sexuality, inaudible to any but me.   *Ibid. 3*

8   Her eyes greenish and remote, with a rich glint of lunacy. . . . "What did your Loved One pass on from?" she asked.   *The Loved One [1948], ch. 3*

9   Randolph Churchill went into hospital . . . to have a lung removed. It was announced that the trouble was not "malignant." . . . It was a typical triumph of modern science to find the only part of Randolph that was not malignant and remove it.

Diaries [March 1964]

Nathanael West
1903–1940

10   Are you in trouble?—Do-you-need-advice?— Write-to-Miss-Lonelyhearts-and-she-will-help-you.

Miss Lonelyhearts [1933]

11   The Miss Lonelyhearts are the priests of twentieth-century America.   *Ibid.*

12   The Day of the Locust.   *Title of novel [1939]*

Peter Arno
1904–1968

13   I consider your conduct unethical and lousy.

Caption for cartoon

14   Well, back to the old drawing board.

Caption for cartoon showing designer walking away from crashed plane

Joseph Campbell
1904–1987

15   Myth is the secret opening through which the inexhaustible energies of the cosmos pour into human cultural manifestation. Religions, philosophies, arts, the social forms of primitive and historic man, prime discoveries in science and technology, the very dreams that blister sleep, boil up from the basic, magic ring of myth.

The Hero with a Thousand Faces [1949]. Prologue

16   Follow your bliss.

The Power of Myth [1988]

Deng Xiaoping
1904–

17   Yellow cat, black cat, as long as it catches mice, it is a good cat.[1]   *Speech [1962]*

Richard Eberhart
1904–

18   I stood there in the whirling summer,
My hand capped a withered heart,
And thought of China and of Greece,
Of Alexander in his tent;
Of Montaigne in his tower,
Of Saint Theresa in her wild lament.

Collected Poems, 1930–1960 [1960]. The Groundhog

19   It is what man does not know of God
Composes the visible poem of the world.

Ibid. On a Squirrel Crossing the Road in Autumn in New England

Bergen Evans
1904–1978

20   Freedom of speech and freedom of action are meaningless without freedom to think. And there is no freedom of thought without doubt.

The Natural History of Nonsense [1946], ch. 19

[1]Translated by ROSS TERRILL.
Deng identified this as "a saying from Sichuan Province."

Clifton Fadiman
1904–

1 When you reread a classic you do not see more in the book than you did before; you see more in *you* than there was before.

Any Number Can Play [1957]

Cary Grant
[Archibald Alexander Leach]
1904–1986

2 Everybody wants to be Cary Grant. Even *I* want to be Cary Grant. *Attributed*

3 Old Cary Grant fine. How you?
Attributed answer to telegraphed query, How old Cary Grant?

Graham Greene
1904–1991

4 This Gun for Hire. *Title of novel [1936]*

5 There is always one moment in childhood when the door opens and lets the future in.
The Power and the Glory [1940], ch. 1

6 In human relations kindness and lies are worth a thousand truths.
The Heart of the Matter [1948], pt. I, ch. 2, sec. iv

7 No human being can really understand another, and no one can arrange another's happiness.
Ibid. III, 1, i

8 The Third Man. *Title of novel [1950]*

9 If we had not been taught how to interpret the story of the Passion, would we have been able to say from their actions alone whether it was the jealous Judas or the cowardly Peter who loved Christ?
The End of the Affair [1951], ch. 3

10 Have you seen a room from which faith has gone? . . . Like a marriage from which love has gone. . . . And patience, patience everywhere like a fog.
The Potting Shed [1957], act III

11 Our Man in Havana. *Title of novel [1958]*

12 Catholics and Communists have committed great crimes, but at least they have not stood aside, like an established society, and been indifferent. I would rather have blood on my hands than water like Pilate . . . if you have abandoned one faith, do not abandon all faith. There is always an alternative to the faith we lose. Or is it the same faith under another mask?
The Comedians [1966], pt. III, ch. 4, sec. 4

13 Our worst enemies here are not the ignorant and the simple, however cruel; our worst enemies are the intelligent and corrupt.
The Human Factor [1978], pt. III, ch. 3

Moss Hart[1]
1904–1961

14 Boredom is the keynote of poverty . . . for where there is no money there is no change of any kind, not of scene or of routine.
Act One [1959], pt. I

15 The only credential the city [New York] asked was the boldness to dream. For those who did, it unlocked its gates and its treasures, not caring who they were or where they came from. *Ibid. II*

Roman Hruska
1904–

16 Even if he is mediocre, there are a lot of mediocre judges and people and lawyers. They are entitled to a little representation, aren't they, and a little chance? We can't all have Brandeises, Cardozos and Frankfurters and stuff like that there.
Defending President Richard M. Nixon's proposed appointment of G. Harrold Carswell to the Supreme Court [1970]

Christopher William Bradshaw Isherwood
1904–1986

17 I am a camera with its shutter open, quite passive, recording, not thinking. Recording the man shaving at the window opposite and the woman in the kimono washing her hair. Some day, all this will have to be developed, carefully printed, fixed.
Goodbye to Berlin [1939], A Berlin Diary

George Frost Kennan
1904–

18 The main element of any United States policy toward the Soviet Union must be that of a long-term, patient but firm and vigilant containment of Russian expansive tendencies.
The Sources of Soviet Conduct, in Foreign Affairs [July 1947]

19 If we are to regard ourselves as a grown-up nation—and anything else will henceforth be mortally dangerous—then we must, as the Biblical phrase goes, put away childish things; and among these childish things the first to go, in my opinion, should be self-idealization and the search for absolutes in world affairs: for absolute security, absolute amity, absolute harmony.
Russia and the West under Lenin and Stalin [1961], ch. 25

20 There is no political or ideological difference between the Soviet Union and the United States—

[1]See also Kaufman and Hart, 676.

nothing which either side would like, or would hope, to achieve at the expense of the other—that would be worth the risks and sacrifices of a military encounter. *The Cloud of Danger [1977], ch. 11*

1 A war regarded as inevitable or even probable, and therefore much prepared for, has a very good chance of eventually being fought. *Ibid. 13*

Abbott Joseph Liebling
1904–1963

2 Freedom of the press is guaranteed only to those who own one.
Do You Belong in Journalism? in The New Yorker [May 14, 1960]

Pablo Neruda
[Neftalí Ricardo Reyes y Basualto]
1904–1973

3 Treacherous
generals:
look at my dead house,
look at broken Spain.
Residencia en la Tierra (Residence on Earth), series III [1947]. Explico Algunas Cosas (I Explain a Few Things)[1]

4 But from each hollow of Spain
Spain comes forth.
Ibid.

5 But from each crime are born bullets
that will one day seek out in you
where the heart lies.
Ibid.

6 What a great language I have, it's a fine language we inherited from the fierce Conquistadors . . . They carried everything off and left us everything . . . They left us the words.
Confieso Que He Vivido: Memorias (Memoirs) [1974],[2] *ch. 2*

7 Poetry is an act of peace. Peace goes into the making of a poet as flour goes into the making of bread. *Ibid. 6*

8 I continue to work with the materials I have, the materials I am made of. With feelings, beings, books, events, and battles, I am omnivorous. I would like to swallow the whole earth. I would like to drink the whole sea. *Ibid. 11*

9 Poetry is a deep inner calling in man; from it came liturgy, the psalms, and also the content of religions. *Ibid.*

[1]Translated by DONALD D. WALSH.
[2]Translated by HARDIE ST. MARTIN.

J. Robert Oppenheimer
1904–1967

10 It did not take atomic weapons to make man want peace, a peace that would last. But the atomic bomb was the turn of the screw. It has made the prospect of future war unendurable.
The Atomic Bomb and College Education [1946]

11 In some sort of crude sense which no vulgarity, no humor, no overstatement can quite extinguish, the physicists have known sin; and this is a knowledge which they cannot lose.
Physics in the Contemporary World, lecture at Massachusetts Institute of Technology [November 25, 1947]

12 We knew the world would not be the same. A few people laughed, a few people cried. Most people were silent. I remembered the line from the Hindu scripture, the *Bhagavad Gita*. . . . "I am become Death, the destroyer of worlds." I suppose we all thought that, one way or another.
Recalling the explosion of the first atomic bomb near Alamogordo, New Mexico [July 16, 1945].[3] *From LEN GIOVANITTI and FRED FREED, The Decision to Drop the Bomb [1965]*

Sidney Joseph Perelman
1904–1979

13 I have Bright's Disease and he has mine.
Caption for cartoon, in Judge [November 16, 1926]

14 Philomène was a dainty thing, built somewhat on the order of Lois De Fee, the lady bouncer. She had the rippling muscles of a panther, the stolidity of a water buffalo, and the lazy insolence of a shoe salesman. *Crazy Like a Fox [1944]. Kitchen Bouquet*

15 Outside of a spring lamb trotting into a slaughterhouse, there is nothing in the animal kingdom as innocent and foredoomed as the new purchaser of a country place. The moment he scratches his signature on the deed, it is open season and no limit to the bag. *Acres and Pains [1947], ch. 2*

16 The mere mention of Hollywood induces a condition in me like breakbone fever. It was a hideous and untenable place when I dwelt there, populated with few exceptions by Yahoos, and now that it has become the chief citadel of television, it's unspeakable. *Interview in Paris Review [1964]*

17 There are nineteen words in Yiddish that convey gradations of disparagement from a mild, fluttery helplessness to a state of downright, irreconcilable

[3]Oppenheimer also recalled another line from the *Bhavagad Gita*, "If the radiance of a thousand suns. . . . " See 84:12.
Now we are all sons of bitches.—KENNETH TOMPKINS BAINBRIDGE [1904–]. Oppenheimer later remarked that this was "the best thing anyone said after the test."

brutishness. All of them can be usefully employed to pinpoint the kind of individuals I write about.
Ibid.

1 Button-cute, rapier-keen, wafer-thin and pauper-poor. *Self-description*

Dr. Seuss [Theodor Seuss Geisel]
1904–1991

2 I meant what I said
And I said what I meant . . . [1]
An elephant's faithful
One hundred per cent!
Horton Hatches the Egg [1940]

3 You will see something new.
Two things. And I call them
Thing One and Thing Two.
The Cat in the Hat [1957]

Isaac Bashevis Singer
1904–1991

4 When literature becomes overly erudite, it means that interest in the art has gone and curiosity about the artist is what's most important. It becomes a kind of idolatry.
Isaac Bashevis Singer Talks . . . About Everything, interview with Richard Burgin in the New York Times Magazine [November 26, 1978]

5 It seems that the analysis of character is the highest human entertainment. And literature does it, unlike gossip, without mentioning real names.
Ibid.

6 There is a quiet humor in Yiddish and a gratitude for every day of life, every crumb of success, each encounter of love. . . . In a figurative way, Yiddish is the wise and humble language of us all, the idiom of a frightened and hopeful humanity.
Nobel lecture, Stockholm [December 8, 1978]

7 Children don't read to find their identity. They don't read to free themselves of guilt, to quench the thirst for rebellion, or to get rid of alienation. They have no use for psychology. They detest sociology. . . . They still believe in good, the family, angels, devils, witches, goblins, logic, clarity, punctuation and other such obsolete stuff.
Address at Nobel Prize banquet, Stockholm [December 10, 1978]

8 Buildings will collapse, power plants will stop generating electricity. Generals will drop atomic bombs on their own populations. Mad revolutionaries will run in the streets, crying fantastic slogans. I have often thought it would begin in New York.

[1] Ellipses are in the original text.

This metropolis has all the symptoms of a mind gone berserk. *Collected Stories [1986]. The Cafeteria*[2]

Burrhus Frederic Skinner
1904–1990

9 The one fact that I would cry from every housetop is this: the Good Life is waiting for us —here and now! . . . At this very moment we have the necessary techniques, both material and psychological, to create a full and satisfying life for everyone. *Walden Two [1948], ch. 23*

10 The real problem is not whether machines think but whether men do.
Contingencies of Reinforcement [1969], ch. 9

11 We are all controlled by the world in which we live, and part of that world has been and will be constructed by men. The question is this: are we to be controlled by accidents, by tyrants, or by ourselves in effective cultural design?
Cumulative Record [third edition, 1972], ch. 1

12 Physics does not change the nature of the world it studies, and no science of behavior can change the essential nature of man, even though both sciences yield technologies with a vast power to manipulate their subject matters. *Ibid. 5*

Betty Smith
1904–1972

13 There's a tree that grows in Brooklyn. Some people call it the Tree of Heaven. No matter where its seed falls, it makes a tree which struggles to reach the sky. *A Tree Grows in Brooklyn [1943]*

Jane Ace
1905–1974

14 Time wounds all heels.[3]
From GOODMAN ACE, The Fine Art of Hypochondria; or, How Are You? [1966]

Leo Durocher
1905–1991

15 Nice Guys Finish Last. *Title of book [1975]*

James William Fulbright
1905–

16 A policy that can be accurately, though perhaps not prudently, defined as one of "peaceful coexistence:" *Speech in the Senate [March 27, 1964]*

[2] Translated by ISAAC BASHEVIS SINGER and DOROTHEA STRAUS.
[3] Also attributed to FRANK CASE, proprietor of the Algonquin Hotel.
See Terence, 85:*n*16.

1   We must dare to think "unthinkable" thoughts. We must learn to explore all the options and possibilities that confront us in a complex and rapidly changing world. We must learn to welcome and not to fear the voices of dissent. We must dare to think about "unthinkable things" because when things become unthinkable, thinking stops and action becomes mindless.

Speech in the Senate [March 27, 1964]

Greta Garbo [Greta Gustafson]
1905–1990

2   I want to be alone.[1]   *Attributed*

Dag Hammarskjöld
1905–1961

3   What gives life its value you can find—and lose. But never possess. This holds good above all for "the Truth about Life."   *Markings*

4 The longest journey
Is the journey inwards
Of him who has chosen his destiny.

Ibid.

Lillian Hellman
1905–1984

5   There are people who eat the earth and eat all the people on it like in the Bible with the locusts. And other people who stand around and watch them eat it.   *The Little Foxes [1939], act III*

6   For every man who lives without freedom, the rest of us must face the guilt.

Watch on the Rhine [1941], act II

7   Lonely people talking to each other can make each other lonelier.

The Autumn Garden [1951], act I

8   I am most willing to answer all questions about myself . . . But . . . I am not willing, now or in the future, to bring bad trouble to people who, in my past association with them, were completely innocent of any talk or any action that was disloyal or subversive.

Letter to the House Committee on Un-American Activities [May 19, 1952]

9   I cannot and will not cut my conscience to fit this year's fashions.   *Ibid.*

10   A man should be jailed for telling lies to the young.   *Candide [1956],[2] act II, sc. iii*

11   We will not think noble because we are not noble. We will not live in beautiful harmony because there is no such thing in this world, nor should there be. We promise only to do our best and live out our lives. Dear God, that's all we can promise in truth.

Ibid.

Arthur Koestler
1905–1983

12   One may not regard the world as a sort of metaphysical brothel for emotions.

Darkness at Noon [1941].[3] The Second Hearing

13   The definition of the individual was: a multitude of one million divided by one million.

Ibid. The Grammatical Fiction

14   The Yogi and the Commissar.

Title of book [1945]

Stanley Kunitz
1905–

15   On the royal road to Thebes
I had my luck, I met a lovely monster,
And the story's this: I made the monster me.

The Approach to Thebes [1958]

16 I recognize the gods' capricious hand
And write this poem for money, rage, and love.

The Thief [1958]

17 The thing that eats the heart is mostly heart.

The Thing That Eats the Heart [1958], last line

18 Slime, in the grains of the State,
like smut in the corn,
from the top infected.
Hatred made law.

Around Pastor Bonhoeffer [1971]. Next to Last Things

19 That pack of scoundrels
tumbling through the gate
emerges
as the Order of the State.

The System [1971]

20 I've a long way to go
Who never learned to pray.

The Game [1971], st. 4

21 *Liebchen,*
with whom should I quarrel
except in the hiss of love,
that harsh, irregular flame?

The Quarrel [1979]

22 In every house of marriage
there's room for an interpreter.

Route Six [1979]

---

[1]Garbo maintains that her most famous remark has always been misquoted. . . . "I only said, 'I want to be *let* alone!' " —JOHN BAINBRIDGE, *in Life* [January 24, 1955]
[2]A comic operetta based upon Voltaire's satire. See Voltaire, 306:5–306:12, and Wilbur, 750:3.

[3]Translated by DAPHNE HARDY.

Phyllis McGinley
1905–1977

1 Meek-eyed parents hasten down the ramps
To greet their offspring, terrible from camps.
Ode to the End of Summer

2 Prince, I warn you, under the rose,
Time is the thief you cannot banish.
These are my daughters, I suppose.
But where in the world did the children vanish?
Ballade of Lost Objects [1954]

3 Always on Monday morning the press reports
God as revealed to His vicars in various guises—
Benevolent, stormy, patient, or out of sorts.
God knows which God is the God God
   recognizes.
The Day After Sunday [1954]

4 A mother's hardest to forgive.
Life is the fruit she longs to hand you,
Ripe on a plate. And while you live,
Relentlessly she understands you.
The Adversary

John O'Hara
1905–1970

5 Hot lead can be almost as effective coming from a linotype as from a firearm.
The Portable F. Scott Fitzgerald [1945],
introduction

6 An artist is his own fault.   *Ibid.*

Anthony Powell
1905–

7 All women are stimulated by the news that any wife has left any husband.
The Acceptance World [1955], ch. 4

8 In the break-up of a marriage the world inclines to take the side of the partner with the most vitality, rather than the one apparently least to blame.
Ibid. 5

Ayn Rand
1905–1982

9 Civilization is the progress toward a society of privacy. The savage's whole existence is public, ruled by the laws of his tribe. Civilization is the process of setting man free from men.
The Fountainhead [1943]

10 Great men can't be ruled.   *Ibid.*

11 Kill reverence and you've killed the hero in man.
Ibid.

Jean Paul Sartre
1905–1980

12 Everything is gratuitous, this garden, this city and myself. When you suddenly realize it, it makes you feel sick and everything begins to drift . . . that's nausea.   *La Nausée (Nausea) [1938]*

13 Man is not the sum of what he has but the totality of what he does not yet have, of what he might have.
Situations [1939], I

14 We do not do what we want and yet we are responsible for what we are—that is the fact.
Ibid. II

15 Man can will nothing unless he has first understood that he must count on no one but himself; that he is alone, abandoned on earth in the midst of his infinite responsibilities, without help, with no other aim than the one he sets himself, with no other destiny than the one he forges for himself on this earth.
L'Être et le Néant (Being and Nothingness)
[1943]

16 Hell is—other people![1]
Huis-Clos (No Exit) [1944], sc. v

17 I was escaping from Nature and at last becoming myself, that Other whom I was aspiring to be in the eyes of others.   *Les Mots (The Words) [1964][2]*

18 All the same, they [books] do serve some purpose. Culture doesn't save anything or anyone, it doesn't justify. But it's a product of man: he projects himself into it, he recognizes himself in it; that critical mirror alone offers him his image.   *Ibid.*

19 Never have I thought that I was the happy possessor of a "talent"; my sole concern has been to save myself by work and faith.   *Ibid.*

20 If I relegate impossible Salvation to the prop-room, what remains? A whole man, composed of all men and as good as all of them and no better than any.   *Ibid.*

Sir Charles Percy Snow
1905–1980

21 Literary intellectuals at one pole—at the other scientists. . . . Between the two a gulf of mutual incomprehension.
The Two Cultures and the Scientific Revolution
[1959]

22 No one is fit to be trusted with power. . . . No one. . . . Any man who has lived at all knows the follies and wickedness he's capable of. If he does not know it, he is not fit to govern others. And if he does know it, he knows also that neither he nor any

---

[1]L'enfer, c'est les Autres.
[2]Translated by BERNARD FRECHTMAN.

man ought to be allowed to decide a single human
fate.   *The Light and the Dark [1961]*

1   Corridors of Power.   *Title of novel [1965]*

Lionel Trilling
1905–1976

2   The poet is in command of his fantasy, while it is
exactly the mark of the neurotic that he is possessed
by his fantasy.
         *The Liberal Imagination [1950]. Freud and
         Literature*

3   There is no connection between the political
ideas of our educated class and the deep places of the
imagination.
              Ibid. The Function of the Little Magazine

4   Occasions are rare when the best literature becomes, as it were, the folk literature, and generally
speaking literature has always been carried on
within small limits and under great difficulties.
                                              Ibid.

5   We are all ill [i.e., neurotic]: but even a universal
sickness implies an idea of health.
                            Ibid. Art and Neurosis

6   The poet . . . may be used as the barometer,
but let us not forget that he is also part of the
weather.   *Ibid. The Sense of the Past*

Harold Adamson
1906–1980

7   Comin' In on a Wing and a Prayer.
                        Title of song [1943][1]

Hannah Arendt
1906–1975

8   Aristotle explicitly assures us that man, insofar as
he is a natural being and belongs to the species of
mankind, possesses immortality; through the recurrent cycle of life, nature assures the same kind of
being-forever to things that are born and die as to
things that are and do not change.
                   Between Past and Future [1961], ch. 2

9   It was as though in those last minutes he [Eich-
mann][2] was summing up the lessons that this long
course in human wickedness had taught us—the lesson of the fearsome, word-and-thought-defying *banality of evil.*
             *Eichmann in Jerusalem: A Report on the
             Banality of Evil [1963], ch. 15*

10   No punishment has ever possessed enough power
of deterrence to prevent the commission of crimes.
On the contrary, whatever the punishment, once a

[1]Music by JIMMY MCHUGH.
[2]To sum it all up, I must say I regret nothing.—ADOLF
EICHMANN [1906–1962], *while awaiting trial in Israel*

specific crime has appeared for the first time, its
reappearance is more likely than its initial emergence could have been.   *Ibid. epilogue*

11   The hypocrite's crime is that he bears false witness against himself. What makes it so plausible to
assume that hypocrisy is the vice of vices is that
integrity can indeed exist under the cover of all other
vices except this one. Only crime and the criminal,
it is true, confront us with the perplexity of radical
evil; but only the hypocrite is really rotten to the
core.   *On Revolution [1963], ch. 2*

Richard Armour
1906–1989

12   Shake and shake
The catsup bottle.
None will come,
And then a lot'll.

                          Going to Extremes [1949]

Samuel Beckett
1906–1989

13   That's how it is on this bitch of an earth.
                        Waiting for Godot [1952], act I

14   Nothing happens, nobody comes, nobody goes,
it's awful!   *Ibid.*

15   He can't think without his hat.   *Ibid.*

16   Some are born mad. Some remain so.
                                            Ibid. II

17   *Estragon:* I can't go on like this.
Vladimir: That's what you think.   *Ibid.*

18   Do you believe in the life to come? Mine was
always that.   *Endgame [1957]*

19   Nothing is funnier than unhappiness.
                                Endgame [1958]

20   Krapp's Last Tape.   *Title of play [1959]*

21   I could not have gone through the awful
wretched mess of life without having left a stain
upon the silence.
           From DEIRDRE BAIR, *Samuel Beckett [1978]*

John Betjeman
1906–1984

22   He rose, and he put down The Yellow Book.
He staggered—and, terrible-eyed,
He brushed past the palms on the staircase
And was helped to a hansom outside.
           *The Arrest of Oscar Wilde at the Cadogan
           Hotel [1937], st. 9*

23   Gracious Lord, oh bomb the Germans.
Spare their women for Thy Sake,
And if that is not too easy
We will pardon Thy Mistake.

But, gracious Lord, whate'er shall be,
Don't let anyone bomb me.
In Westminster Abbey [1940]

1 The sort of girl I like to see
Smiles down from her great height at me.
The Olympic Girl [1954]

2 Oh! would I were her racket pressed
With hard excitement to her breast.
Ibid.

3 Summoned by Bells.   *Title of book [1960]*

William Joseph Brennan, Jr.
1906–

4 Debate on public issues should be uninhibited, robust, and wide open, and that . . . may well include vehement, caustic, and sometimes unpleasantly sharp attacks on government and public officials.   *New York Times Co. v. Sullivan [1964]*

5 If the right of privacy means anything, it is the right of the individual, married or single, to be free from unwarranted governmental intrusion into matters so fundamentally affecting a person as the decision whether to bear or beget a child.
Eisenstadt v. Baird [1972]

6 Our nation has had a long and unfortunate history of sex discrimination . . . rationalized by an attitude of "romantic paternalism" which, in practical effect, put women not on a pedestal, but in a cage.   *Frontiero v. Richardson [1973]*

Robert Buckner
1906–

7 Some day, when things are tough, maybe you can ask the boys to go in there and win just one for the Gipper![1]
Knute Rockne—All-American (screenplay) [1940], spoken by Ronald Reagan as George Gipp

Curtis Emerson LeMay
1906–1990

8 My solution to the problem [of North Vietnam] would be to tell them frankly that they've got to draw in their horns and stop their aggression, or we're going to bomb them back into the Stone Age.
Mission with LeMay [1965]

Anne Morrow Lindbergh
1906–

9 The wave of the future is coming and there is no fighting it.   *The Wave of the Future [1940]*

[1]See Rockne, 674:16.

10 I . . . understand why the saints were rarely married women. I am convinced it has nothing inherently to do, as I once supposed, with chastity or children. It has to do primarily with distractions. . . . Woman's normal occupations in general run counter to creative life, or contemplative life or saintly life.   *Gift from the Sea [1955], ch. 2*

11 By and large, mothers and housewives are the only workers who do not have regular time off. They are the great vacationless class.   *Ibid. 3*

Satchel [Leroy] Paige
c. 1906–1982

12 Avoid fried meats which angry up the blood. If your stomach disputes you, lie down and pacify it with cool thoughts. Keep the juices flowing by jangling around gently as you move. Go very light on the vices, such as carrying on in society. The social ramble ain't restful. Avoid running at all times. Don't look back. Something might be gaining on you.   *How to Stay Young [1953]*

Roberto Rossellini
1906–1977

13 I am not a pessimist; to perceive evil where it exists is, in my opinion, a form of optimism.
Interview in Cahiers du Cinéma [1954]

Laurens Van der Post
1906–

14 Life is its own journey, presupposes its own change and movement, and one tries to arrest them at one's eternal peril.
Venture to the Interior [1951], pt. III, ch. 12

15 Africa has always walked in my mind proudly upright, an African giant among the other continents, toes well dug into the final ocean of one hemisphere, rising to its full height in the graying skies of the other; head and shoulders broad, square and enduring, making light of the bagful of blue Mediterranean slung over its back as it marches patiently through time.   *Flamingo Feather [1955], ch. 3*

16 Human beings are perhaps never more frightening than when they are convinced beyond doubt that they are right.
The Lost World of the Kalahari [1958], ch. 3

Elmer Wheeler
1906–1968

17 Don't sell the steak; sell the sizzle. It is the sizzle that sells the steak and not the cow, although the cow is, of course, mighty important.
Principle Number 1 of salesmanship [c. 1936]

Henny Youngman

1906–

1 Take my wife . . . please!   *Comedy line*

Wystan Hugh Auden

1907–1973

2 Let us honor if we can
The vertical man
Though we value none
But the horizontal one.

Epigraph for Poems [1930]

3 Sir, no man's enemy, forgiving all
But will his negative inversion, be prodigal.

Sir, No Man's Enemy [1930]

4 Harrow the house of the dead; look shining at
New styles of architecture, a change of heart.

Ibid.

5 The greater the love, the more false to its object,
Not to be born is the best for man;[1]
After the kiss comes the impulse to throttle,
Break the embraces, dance while you can.

O Who Can Ever Gaze His Fill [1937]

6 The stars are dead. The animals will not look.
We are left alone with our day, and the time is
    short, and History to the defeated
May say Alas but cannot help or pardon.

Spain [1937]

7 About suffering they were never wrong,
The Old Masters.

Musée des Beaux Arts [1940]

8 O plunge your hands in water,
Plunge them in up to the wrist;
Stare, stare in the basin
And wonder what you've missed.

The glacier knocks in the cupboard,
The desert sighs in the bed,
And the crack in the tea cup opens
A lane to the land of the dead.

As I Walked Out One Evening [1940], st. 10, 11

9 Earth, receive an honored guest;
William Yeats is laid to rest.
Let the Irish vessel lie
Emptied of its poetry.

In Memory of W. B. Yeats [1940],[2] III, st. 1

10 In the nightmare of the dark
All the dogs of Europe bark.

Ibid. st. 2

11 Intellectual disgrace
Stares from every human face,

And the seas of pity lie
Locked and frozen in each eye.

Ibid. st. 3

12 To us he is no more a person
Now but a whole climate of opinion.

In Memory of Sigmund Freud[3] [1940], st. 17

13 One rational voice is dumb: over a grave
The household of Impulse mourns one dearly
    loved.
    Sad is Eros, builder of cities,
    And weeping anarchic Aphrodite.

Ibid. st. 28

14 Law, says the judge as he looks down his nose,
Speaking clearly and most severely,
Law is as I've told you before,
Law is as you know I suppose,
Law is but let me explain it once more,
Law is The Law.

Law Like Love [1940], st. 4

15 Like love we don't know where or why
Like love we can't compel or fly
Like love we often weep
Like love we seldom keep.

Ibid. last stanza

16 Lay your sleeping head, my love,
Human on my faithless arm.

Lullaby [1940], st. 1

17 Every farthing of the cost,
All the dreaded cards foretell,
Shall be paid, but from this night
Not a whisper, not a thought,
Not a kiss nor look be lost.

Ibid. st. 3

18 At Dirty Dick's and Sloppy Joe's
We drank our liquor straight,
Some went upstairs with Margery,
And some, alas, with Kate.
    *The Sea and the Mirror [1944]. Master and
    Boatswain*

19 And children swarmed to him like settlers. He
    became a land.

Edward Lear [1945]

20 Thou shalt not sit
With statisticians nor commit
A social science.

Under Which Lyre [1946], st. 27

21 If thou must choose
Between the chances, choose the odd;
Read the *New Yorker;* trust in God;
And take short views.[4]

Ibid. last stanza

---

[1]See Theognis, 59:24; Sophocles, 67:9; Francis Bacon, 160:-15; and Yeats, 598:3.
[2]See Yeats, 594.

[3]See Freud, 569.
[4]See Sydney Smith, 380:4.

1 Sob, heavy world,
  Sob as you spin,
  Mantled in mist, remote from the happy.
  The Age of Anxiety [1947]

2 She looked over his shoulder
  For vines and olive trees,
  Marble, well-governed cities
  And ships upon untamed seas;
  But there on the shining metal
  His hands had put instead
  An artificial wilderness
  And a sky like lead.
  The Shield of Achilles [1955], st. 1

3 The mass and majesty of this world, all
  That carries weight and always weighs the same,
  Lay in the hands of others; they were small
  And could not hope for help, and no help came;
  What their foes liked to do was done, their shame
  Was all the worst could wish: they lost their pride
  And died as men before their bodies died.
  Ibid. st. 6

4 Our researchers into Public Opinion are content
  That he held the proper opinions for the time of
      year;
  When there was peace, he was for peace; when
      there was war, he went.
  *The Unknown Citizen (To JS/07/M/378 This
  Marble Monument Is Erected by the State)*

5 Was he free? Was he happy? The question is
      absurd:
  Had anything been wrong, we should certainly
      have heard.
  Ibid.

6 A culture is no better than its woods.
  Bucolics. Woods

7 Some books are undeservedly forgotten; none are
  undeservedly remembered.
  The Dyer's Hand[1] [1962]. Pt. I, Reading

8 It takes little talent to see clearly what lies under
  one's nose, a good deal of it to know in which
  direction to point that organ.   *Ibid. Writing*

9 Speaking for myself, the questions which interest
  me most when reading a poem are two. The first is
  technical: "Here is a verbal contraption. How does
  it work?" The second is, in the broadest sense,
  moral: "What kind of a guy inhabits this poem?
  What is his notion of the good life or the good place?
  His notion of the Evil One? What does he conceal
  from the reader? What does he conceal even from
  himself?"
  Ibid. II, Making, Knowing and Judging

10 Whatever its actual content and overt interest,
   every poem is rooted in imaginative awe. Poetry can
   do a hundred and one things, delight, sadden, disturb, amuse, instruct—it may express every possible

[1]See Shakespeare, 222:1.

shade of emotion, and describe every conceivable
kind of event, but there is only one thing that all
poetry must do; it must praise all it can for being and
for happening.   *Ibid.*

Jacques Barzun
1907–

11 Whoever wants to know the heart and mind of
America had better learn baseball, the rules and
realities of the game—and do it by watching first
some high school or small-town teams.
God's Country and Mine [1954], ch. 8

Lesley Blanch
1907–

12 She was an Amazon. Her whole life was spent
riding at breakneck speed along the wilder shores of
love. For her, each new affair was an encampment
set up along the way; sometimes a palace, sometimes
a tent, but always the supreme refuge.
*The Wilder Shores of Love [1954]. The
Honorable Jane Digby el Mezrah*

Rachel Louise Carson
1907–1964

13 The sea lies all about us. The commerce of all
lands must cross it. The very winds that move over
the lands have been cradled on its broad expanse and
seek ever to return to it. The continents themselves
dissolve and pass to the sea, in grain after grain of
eroded land. So the rains that rose from it return
again in rivers. In its mysterious past it encompasses
all the dim origins of life and receives in the end,
after, it may be, many transmutations, the dead
husks of that same life. For all at last returns to the
sea—to Oceanus, the ocean river, like the ever-
flowing stream of time, the beginning and the end.
The Sea Around Us [1951], ch. 14, ending

14 As crude a weapon as the cave man's club, the
chemical barrage has been hurled against the fabric
of life.   *Silent Spring [1962]*

Richard Crossman
1907–1974

15 Six intellectuals describe the journey into Communism and the return. They saw it first from a long
way off . . . as a vision of the Kingdom of God on
earth.   *The God that Failed [1950]. Introduction*

Daphne du Maurier
1907–1989

16 Last night I dreamt I went to Manderley again.
Rebecca [1938], first line

Christopher Fry
1907–

1 I travel light; as light,
That is, as a man can travel who will
Still carry his body around because
Of its sentimental value.

The Lady's Not for Burning [1950], act I

2 Religion
Has made an honest woman of the supernatural.

Ibid. II

3 Try thinking of love or something.
Amor vincit insomnia.[1]

A Sleep of Prisoners [1951]

Louis MacNeice
1907–1963

4 It's no go my honey love, it's no go my poppet;
Work your hands from day to day, the winds will
blow the profit.
The glass is falling hour by hour, the glass will
fall forever,
But if you break the bloody glass you won't hold
up the weather.

Bagpipe Music, last stanza

John Wayne
1907–1979

5   Talk low, talk slow, and don't say too much.

Advice on acting

Simone de Beauvoir
1908–1986

6   I wish that every human life might be pure transparent freedom.   *The Blood of Others [1946]*

7   This has always been a man's world, and none of the reasons hitherto brought forward in explanation of this fact has seemed adequate.

The Second Sex [1949–1950], pt. II, ch. 4

8   It is not in giving life but in risking life that man is raised above the animal; that is why superiority has been accorded in humanity not to the sex that brings forth but to that which kills.   *Ibid.*

9   One is not born a woman, one becomes one.[2]

Ibid. IV, 12

10   When we abolish the slavery of half of humanity, together with the whole system of hypocrisy that it implies, then the "division" of humanity will reveal its genuine significance and the human couple will find its true form.   *Ibid. VII. Conclusion*

11   It is for man to establish the reign of liberty in the midst of the world of the given. To gain the supreme victory, it is necessary, for one thing, that by and through their natural differentiation men and women unequivocally affirm their brotherhood.

Ibid.

12   The moment a woman gets power, she loses the solidarity she had with other women. She will want to be equal in a man's world and will become ambitious for her own sake.   *Interview [1984]*

Harry Andrew Blackmun
1908–

13   The right of privacy . . . is broad enough to encompass a woman's decision whether or not to terminate her pregnancy.

Roe v. Wade, 410 U.S. 153 [1973]

Jacob Bronowski
1908–1974

14   Man is a singular creature. He has a set of gifts which make him unique among the animals: so that, unlike them, he is not a figure in the landscape— he is a shaper of the landscape. In body and in mind he is the explorer of nature, the ubiquitous animal, who did not find but has made his home in every continent.   *The Ascent of Man [1973], ch. 1*

15   Nature—that is, biological evolution—has not fitted man to any specific environment. . . . Among the multitude of animals which scamper, fly, burrow, and swim around us, man is the only one who is not locked into his environment. His imagination, his reason, his emotional subtlety and toughness, make it possible for him not to accept the environment but to change it.[3] And that series of inventions by which man from age to age has remade his environment is a different kind of evolution— not biological, but cultural evolution. I call that brilliant sequence of cultural peaks *The Ascent of Man.*

Ibid.

Johnny Burke
1908–1964

16 Ev'ry time it rains it rains pennies from Heaven.
Don't you know each cloud contains pennies from
Heaven?

Pennies from Heaven [1936][4]

Henri Cartier-Bresson
1908–

17   The Decisive Moment.

Title of book of photographs [1952]

---

[1]See Virgil, 92:*n*10.
[2]*On ne naît pas femme, on le devient.*

[3]See R. B. Fuller, 691:16.
[4]Music by ARTHUR JOHNSTON.

Mary Frances Kennedy Fisher
1908–

1   When I write of hunger, I am really writing about love and the hunger for it, and warmth and the love of it and the hunger for it . . . and then the warmth and richness and fine reality of hunger satisfied . . . and it is all one.[1]
The Gastronomical Me [1943]. Foreword

Ian [Lancaster] Fleming
1908–1964

2   I would like a medium Vodka dry Martini— with a slice of lemon peel. Shaken and not stirred, please.
Dr. No [1958], ch. 14

John Kenneth Galbraith
1908–

3   One can relish the varied idiocy of human action during a panic to the full, for, while it is a time of great tragedy, nothing is being lost but money.
The Great Crash, 1929 [1955], ch. 1

4   Wealth is not without its advantages and the case to the contrary, although it has often been made, has never proved widely persuasive.
The Affluent Society [1958], ch. 1

5   Originality is something that is easily exaggerated, especially by authors contemplating their own work.
Ibid.

6   The hallmark of the conventional wisdom is acceptability. It has the approval of those to whom it is addressed.
Ibid. 2

7   It is a far, far better thing to have a firm anchor in nonsense than to put out on the troubled seas of thought.
Ibid. 11

8   Just as there must be balance in what a community produces, so there must also be balance in what the community consumes.
Ibid. 18

9   The leisure class has been replaced by another and much larger class to which work has none of the older connotation of pain, fatigue, or other mental or physical discomfort. We have failed to observe the emergence of this New Class, as it may be simply called.
Ibid. 24

10   The superior confidence which people repose in the tall man is well merited. Being tall, he is more visible than other men and being more visible, he is much more closely watched. In consequence, his behavior is far better than that of smaller men.
The Scotch [1964]

11   We are becoming the servants in thought, as in action, of the machine we have created to serve us.
The New Industrial State [1967], ch. 1

[1]Ellipses are in the original text.

12   The individual serves the industrial system not by supplying it with savings and the resulting capital; he serves it by consuming its products.   *Ibid. 4*

13   Much of the world's work, it has been said, is done by men who do not feel quite well. [Karl] Marx is a case in point.
The Age of Uncertainty [1977], ch. 3

Lyndon Baines Johnson
1908–1973

14   Come now, let us reason together.[2]   *Saying*

15   All I have I would have given gladly not to be standing here today.
First address to Congress as President [November 27, 1963]

16   We have talked long enough in this country about equal rights. We have talked for a hundred years or more. It is time now to write the next chapter— and to write in the books of law.   *Ibid.*

17   We still seek no wider war.
Radio / television speech [August 4, 1964] on the Gulf of Tonkin resolution

18   This nation, this generation, in this hour has man's first chance to build a Great Society, a place where the meaning of man's life matches the marvels of man's labor.
Address, accepting the presidential nomination [August 1964]

19   We are not about to send American boys 9 or 10,000 miles away from home to do what Asian boys ought to be doing for themselves.
Remark at Akron University, Akron, Ohio [October 21, 1964]

Otto Kerner, Jr.
1908–1976

20   Our nation is moving toward two societies, one black, one white—separate and unequal.
Report of the National Advisory Commission on Civil Disorders [1968], p. 1

Claude Lévi-Strauss
1908–

21   The world began without the human race and it will end without it. . . . Man has never—save only when he reproduces himself—done other than cheerfully dismantle million upon million of structures and reduce their elements to a state in which they can no longer be reintegrated.
Tristes Tropiques [1955].[3] Conclusion

[2]See *Isaiah* 1:18, 25:29.
[3]Translated by JOHN RUSSELL.

1   I therefore claim to show, not how men think in myths, but how myths operate in men's minds without their being aware of the fact.
The Raw and the Cooked [1964].[1] *Overture*

Abraham Harold Maslow
1908–1970

2   A musician must make music, an artist must paint, a poet must write, if he is to be ultimately at peace with himself. What a man can be, he must be.
Motivation and Personality [1954]

Joseph Raymond McCarthy
1908–1957

3   I have here in my hand a list of two hundred and five [people] that were known to the Secretary of State as being members of the Communist Party and who nevertheless are still working and shaping the policy of the State Department.
Speech, Wheeling, West Virginia [February 9, 1950]

Edward Roscoe Murrow
1908–1965

4   This—is London.
Opening phrase for broadcasts from·London during World War II [1939–1945]

5   I pray you to believe what I have said about Buchenwald. I have reported what I saw and heard, but only part of it. For most of it I have no words.
Broadcast report from London on Buchenwald concentration camp [April 15, 1945]

6   We must not confuse dissent with disloyalty.
See It Now (broadcast). Report on Senator Joseph R. McCarthy [March 7, 1954]

7   We will not be driven by fear into an age of unreason if we . . . remember that we are not descended from fearful men, not from men who feared to write, to speak, to associate and to defend causes which were, for the moment unpopular.
Ibid.

8   Unless we get off our fat surpluses and recognize that television in the main is being used to distract, delude, amuse and insulate us, then television and those who finance it, those who look at it and those who work at it, may see a totally different picture too late.
Speech at the Radio and Television News Directors Convention, Chicago [October 15, 1958]

[1]Translated by JOHN and DOREEN WEIGHTMAN.

Frank S. Nugent
1908–1965
and
Laurence Stallings
1894–1968

9   Never apologize and never explain—it's a sign of weakness.
She Wore a Yellow Ribbon (screenplay) [1949], spoken by John Wayne

Theodore Roethke
1908–1963

10 My secrets cry aloud.
I have no need for tongue.
My heart keeps open house,
My doors are widely flung.
Open House [1941], st. 1

11 This urge, wrestle, resurrection of dry sticks,
Cut stems struggling to put down feet,
What saint strained so much,
Rose on such lopped limbs to a new life?
Cuttings (later) [1948]

12 Nothing would sleep in that cellar.
Root Cellar [1948]

13 Nothing would give up life:
Even the dirt kept breathing a small breath.
Ibid.

14 Tugging all day at perverse life:
The indignity of it!
Weed Puller [1948]

15 The whiskey on your breath
Could make a small boy dizzy;
But I hung on like death:
Such waltzing was not easy.
My Papa's Waltz [1948], st. 1

16 I study the lives on a leaf: the little
Sleepers, numb nudgers in cold dimensions,
Beetles in caves, newts, stone-deaf fishes,
Lice tethered to long limp subterranean weeds,
Squirmers in bogs,
And bacterial creepers.
The Minimal [1948]

17 At Woodlawn I heard the dead cry;
I was lulled by the slamming of iron,
A slow drip over stones,
Toads brooding in wells.
All the leaves stuck out their tongues;
I shook the softening chalk of my bones,
Saying,
Snail, snail, glister me forward,
Bird, soft-sigh me home.
Worm, be with me.
This is my hard time.
The Lost Son [1948], 1. The Flight

1 Fear was my father, Father Fear.
His look drained the stones.
Ibid. 3. The Gibber

2 A lively understandable spirit
Once entertained you.
It will come again.
Be still.
Wait.
Ibid. 5. "It was beginning winter"

3 And the new plants, still awkward in their soil,
The lovely diminutives.
I could watch! I could watch!
I saw the separateness of all things!
A Field of Light [1948], III

4 I remember the neckcurls, limp and damp as
tendrils,
And her quick look, a sidelong pickerel smile.
Elegy for Jane [1953]

5 I take this cadence from a man named Yeats;
I take it, and I give it back again.
Four for Sir John Davies [1953], I. The Dance

6 I wake to sleep, and take my waking slow.
I feel my fate in what I cannot fear.
I learn by going where I have to go.
The Waking [1953]

7 I knew a woman, lovely in her bones,
When small birds sighed, she would sigh back at
them;
Ah, when she moved, she moved more ways than
one:
The shapes a bright container can contain!
I Knew a Woman [1958]

8 Each one's himself yet each one's everyone.
The Sententious Man [1958], st. 6

9 When I was a lark, I sang;
When I was a worm, I devoured.
What Can I Tell My Bones? [1958]

10 I long for the imperishable quiet at the heart of
form.
The Longing [1964]

11 Old men should be explorers?[1]
I'll be an Indian.
Ogalala?
Iroquois.
Ibid.

12 What I love is near at hand,
Always, in earth and air.
The Far Field [1964], III

13 All finite things reveal infinitude.
Ibid. IV

14 Light listened when she sang.
Light Listened [1964], st. 4

[1]See T. S. Eliot, 671:11.

15 In a dark time, the eye begins to see.
In a Dark Time [1964], st. 1

16 The soul has many motions, body one.
The Motion [1964], I

17 Love begets love. This torment is my joy.
Ibid. II

18 What's the worst portion in this mortal life?
A pensive mistress, and a yelping wife.
The Marrow [1964], I

19 Brooding on God, I may become a man.
Pain wanders through my bones like a lost fire;
What burns me now? Desire, desire, desire.
Ibid. II

20 Lord, hear me out, and hear me out this day:
From me to Thee's a long and terrible way.
Ibid. III

21 Now I adore my life
With the Bird, the abiding Leaf,
With the Fish, the questing Snail,
And the Eye altering all;
And I dance with William Blake
For love, for Love's sake.
Once More, the Round [1964]

William Saroyan
1908–1981

22 The Time of Your Life. *Title of play [1939]*

23 If you give to a thief he cannot steal from you,
and he is then no longer a thief.
The Human Comedy [1943], ch. 4

Victor Frederick Weisskopf
1908–

24 In man's brain the impressions from outside are
not merely registered; they produce concepts and
ideas. They are the imprint of the external world
upon the human brain. Therefore, it is not surprising
that, after a long period of searching and erring,
some of the concepts and ideas in human thinking
should have come gradually closer to the fundamental
laws of this world, that some of our thinking
should reveal the true structure of atoms and the
true movements of the stars. Nature, in the form of
man, begins to recognize itself.
Knowledge and Wonder [1962]

Richard Wright
1908–1960

25 Goddammit, look! We live here and they live
there. We black and they white. They got things and
we ain't. They do things and we can't. It's just like
living in jail. *Native Son [1940], bk. I*

1 Who knows when some slight shock, disturbing the delicate balance between social order and thirsty aspiration, shall send the skyscrapers in our cities toppling? *Native Son, bk. I*

2 If we had been allowed to participate in the vital processes of America's national growth, what would have been the textures of our lives, the pattern of our traditions, the routine of our customs, the state of our arts, the code of our laws, the function of our government! . . . We black folk say that America would have been stronger and greater.
Twelve Million Black Voices [1941]

James Agee
1909–1955

3 If I could do it, I'd do no writing at all here. It would be photographs; the rest would be fragments of cloth, bits of cotton, lumps of earth, records of speech, pieces of wood and iron, phials of odors, plates of food and of excrement. . . . A piece of the body torn out by the root might be more to the point.
Let Us Now Praise Famous Men [1941]. Preamble

4 All over Alabama the lamps are out. Every leaf drenches the touch; the spider's net is heavy. The roads lie there with nothing to use them. The fields lie there, with nothing at work in them, neither man nor beast. *Ibid. On the Porch: 1*

5 Nature, Mr. Allnut, is what we are put into this world to rise above.
The African Queen (screenplay) [1951], spoken by Katharine Hepburn

Nelson Algren
1909–1981

6 [Algren] shunts aside all rules, regulations, and dicta, except for three laws that he says a nice little old Negro lady once taught him: Never play cards with any man named "Doc." Never eat at any place called "Mom's." And never, ever, no matter what else you do in your life, *never* sleep with anyone whose troubles are worse than your own.
From H. E. F. DONOHUE, Conversations with Nelson Algren [1964]

Paul Brooks
1909–

7 In America today you can murder land for private profit. You can leave the corpse for all to see, and nobody calls the cops.
The Pursuit of Wilderness [1971], ch. 1

Dazai Osamu [Tsushima Shuji]
1909–1948

8 My unhappiness was the unhappiness of a person who could not say no. *No Longer Human*

Julius J. Epstein
1909–
Philip G. Epstein
1909–1952
and
Howard Koch
1916–

9 Of all the gin joints in all the towns in all the world, she walks into mine!
Casablanca (screenplay) [1943], spoken by Humphrey Bogart

10 Play it, Sam.[1]
Ibid. spoken by Ingrid Bergman

11 Here's looking at you, kid.
Ibid. spoken by Humphrey Bogart

12 Round up the usual suspects.
Ibid. spoken by Claude Rains

Edwin Herbert Land
1909–1991

13 The bottom line is in heaven.
Reply [1977] rejecting view that only the bottom line of the balance sheet shows the worth of a product

Stanislaw Jerzy Lec
1909–1966

14 One has to multiply thoughts to the point where there aren't enough policemen to control them.
Unkempt Thoughts [1962][2]

15 Proverbs contradict each other. That is the wisdom of a nation. *Ibid.*

16 No snowflake in an avalanche ever feels responsible. *More Unkempt Thoughts [1968][2]*

17 Get out of the way of Justice. She is blind.
Ibid.

18 Prolong human life only when you can shorten its miseries. *Ibid.*

19 Most of the sighs we hear have been edited.
Ibid.

[1]Play it!—*Ibid.* spoken by Humphrey Bogart.
See Woody Allen, 767:10.
[2]Translated by JACEK GALAZKA.

Malcolm Lowry
1909–1957

1 Malcolm Lowry
Late of the Bowery
His prose was flowery
And often glowery
He lived, nightly, and drank, daily,
And died playing the ukelele.

Epitaph

2   How alike are the groans of love, to those of the dying.   *Under the Volcano [1947], ch. 12*

3   Somebody threw a dead dog after him down the ravine.   *Ibid. last line*

4 Success is like some horrible disaster
Worse than your house burning.
After publication of Under the Volcano [1962]

Joseph Leo Mankiewicz
1909–

5   Fasten your seatbelts. It's going to be a bumpy night.
All About Eve (screenplay) [1950], spoken by Bette Davis

Elting Elmore Morison
1909–

6   The computer is no better than its program.
Men, Machines and Modern Times [1966]

Cyril Northcote Parkinson
1909–

7   Work expands so as to fill the time available for its completion.   *Parkinson's Law [1957], ch. 1*

David Riesman
1909–

8   While all people want and need to be liked by some of the people some of the time, it is only the modern other-directed types who make this their chief source of direction and chief area of sensitivity.
The Lonely Crowd [1950], ch. 1

9   The idea that men are created free and equal is both true and misleading: men are created different; they lose their social freedom and their individual autonomy in seeking to become like each other.
Ibid. 18

Stephen Spender
1909–

10 I think continually of those who were truly
   great . . .

The names of those who in their lives fought for
   life,
Who wore at their hearts the fire's center.
Born of the sun they traveled a short while
   towards the sun,
And left the vivid air signed with their honor.
I Think Continually of Those

11   He's still half with us
Conniving slyly, yet he knows he's gone
Into that cellar where they'll never find him,
Happy to be alone, his last work done,
Word freed from world, into a different wood.
Collected Poems [1986]. Auden's Funeral, sec. 1

Simone Weil
1909–1943

12   Attachment is the great fabricator of illusions; reality can be attained only by someone who is detached.
Gravity and Grace (La Pesanteur et la Grace) [1947]

13   Purity is the ability to contemplate defilement.
Ibid.

14   Man alone can enslave man.
Oppression and Liberty [1958]. Reflections Concerning the Causes of Liberty and Social Oppression

15   What a country calls its vital economic interests are not the things which enable its citizens to live, but the things which enable it to make war. Gasoline is much more likely than wheat to be a cause of international conflict.
The Need for Roots (L'Enracinement) [1949]

Eudora Welty
1909–

16   I haven't a literary life at all, not much of a confession, maybe. But I do feel that the people and things I love are of a true and human world, and there is no clutter about them. . . . I would not understand a literary life.
Selected Stories of Eudora Welty [1943], introduction

17   The storm had rolled away to faintness like a wagon crossing a bridge.
A Curtain of Green [1941]. A Piece of News

18   The excursion is the same when you go looking for your sorrow as when you go looking for your joy.   *The Wide Net [1943]. The Wide Net*

19   All they could see was sky, water, birds, light, and confluence. It was the whole morning world.
The Optimist's Daughter [1978]

20   Writing fiction has developed in me an abiding respect for the unknown in a human lifetime and a sense of where to look for the threads, how to fol-

low, how to connect, find in the thick of the tangle what clear line persists. The strands are all there: to the memory nothing is ever really lost.
One Writer's Beginnings [1984]. Finding a Voice

1   I am a writer who came of a sheltered life. A sheltered life can be a daring life as well. For all serious daring starts from within.   *Ibid.*

Jean Anouilh
1910–1987

2   Orpheus—they've gone on now, the good as well as the bad. . . . They've done their little song and dance in your life. . . . They are that way in you now, forever.   *Eurydice [1942]*

3   This horror and all these useless gestures, this grotesque adventure is ours. We must live it. Death is absurd also.   *Romeo and Jeannette [1946]*

4   And under this carnival disguise the heart of an old youngster who is still waiting to give his all. But how to be recognized under this mask? This is what they call a fine career.
The Waltz of the Toreadors [1952]. English version

Peter De Vries
1910–

5   We know the human brain is a device to keep the ears from grating on one another.
Comfort Me with Apples [1956], ch. 1

Tony [Two-Ton] Galento
1910–1979

6   I'll moider de bum.
Before his unsuccessful fight with Joe Louis for the heavyweight championship [June 28, 1939]

Jean Genet
1910–1986

7   To achieve harmony in bad taste is the height of elegance.
The Thief's Journal (Le Journal du Voleur) [1949]

8   I was already refusing to have taste. I forbade myself to have it. I knew that the cultivation of it would have not refined me but softened me.
Ibid.

9   I call saintliness not a state but the moral procedure leading to it.
Quoted by JEAN PAUL SARTRE in Saint Genet [1952]

Thomas Anthony Harris
1910–

10   I'm OK—You're OK.   *Title of book [1969]*

Frank Loesser
1910–1969

11   See what the boys in the back room will have And tell them I'm having the same.
Destry Rides Again [1939]. See What the Boys in the Back Room Will Have[1]

12   I'd love to get you On a slow boat to China. All to myself alone.
On a Slow Boat to China [1948]

Robert King Merton
1910–

13   The self-fulfilling prophecy is, in the beginning, a *false* definition of the situation evoking a new behavior which makes the originally false conception come *true*. The specious validity of the self-fulfilling prophecy perpetuates a reign of error. For the prophet will cite the actual course of events as proof that he was right from the very begining.
The Self-Fulfilling Prophecy [1948]

Wright Morris
1910–

14   In the dry places . . . towns, like weeds, spring up when it rains, dry up when it stops. But in a dry climate the husk of the plant remains. The stranger might find, as if preserved in amber, something of the green life that was once lived there, and the ghosts of men who have gone on to a better place. The withered towns are empty, but not uninhabited.
The Works of Love [1952], ch. 1

Robert Pirosh
1910–1989
and
George Seaton
1911–1970

15   Either he's dead, or my watch has stopped.
A Day at the Races (screenplay) [1937], spoken by Groucho Marx (feeling for a pulse)

David Morris Potter
1910–1971

16   Democracy is clearly most appropriate for countries which enjoy an economic surplus and least ap-

[1] Music by FREDERICK HOLLANDER.

propriate for countries where there is an economic insufficiency.

People of Plenty: Economic Abundance and the American Character [1954]

Elizabeth Bishop
1911–1979

1 This iceberg cuts its facets from within.
Like jewelry from a grave
it saves itself perpetually and adorns
Only itself.

The Imaginary Iceberg [1946], st. 3

2 Icebergs behoove the soul
(both being self-made from elements least visible)
to see them so: fleshed, fair, erected, indivisible.

Ibid.

3 Until everything
was rainbow, rainbow, rainbow!
And I let the fish go.

The Fish [1946]

4 Cold dark deep and absolutely clear,
element bearable to no mortal,
to fish and to seals . . .

At the Fishhouses [1955]

5 It is like what we imagine knowledge to be:
dark, salt, clear, moving, utterly free,
drawn from the cold hard mouth
of the world, derived from the rocky breasts
forever, flowing and drawn, and since
our knowledge is historical, flowing, and flown.

Ibid.

6 From Brooklyn, over the Brooklyn Bridge, on this
fine morning, please come flying.

Invitation to Miss Marianne Moore [1955], st. 1

7 Should we have stayed at home,
wherever that may be?

Questions of Travel [1965]

8 *Time to plant tears*, says the almanac.
The grandmother sings to the marvelous stove
and the child draws another inscrutable house.

Sestina [1965]

9 The staring sailor
that shakes his watch
that tells the time
of the poet, the man
that lies in the house of Bedlam.

Visits to St. Elizabeths [1965], st. 11

10 I knew that nothing stranger
had ever happened.

In the Waiting Room [1976]

11 How had I come to be here
like them, and overhear
a cry of pain that could have
got loud and worse but hadn't?

Ibid.

12 Home-made, home-made! But aren't we all?

Crusoe in England [1976]

13 I'd have
nightmares of other islands
stretching away from mine, infinities
of islands, islands spawning islands
like frogs' eggs turning into polliwogs
of islands, knowing that I had to live
on each and every one, eventually,
for ages, registering their flora,
their fauna, their geography.

Ibid.

14 —And Friday, my dear Friday, died of measles
seventeen years ago come March.

Ibid.

15 The art of losing isn't hard to master;
so many things seem filled with the intent
to be lost that their loss is no disaster.

Lose something every day. Accept the fluster
of lost door keys, the hour badly spent.
The art of losing isn't hard to master.

Geography III [1976]. One Art

16 Life and the memory of it cramped,
dim, on a piece of Bristol board.

Poem [1976]

Max Frisch
1911–1991

17 Technology . . . the knack of so arranging the world that we don't have to experience it.

Homo Faber [1957]

William Golding
1911–

18 Ralph wept for the end of innocence, the darkness of man's heart, and the fall through the air of the true, wise friend called Piggy.

The Lord of the Flies [1954], ch. 12

Hubert Horatio Humphrey
1911–1978

19 The politics of joy.

Presidential campaign slogan [1968]

20 Compassion is not weakness, and concern for the unfortunate is not socialism.　*Remark*

Clark Kerr
1911–

21 The university has become the multiversity and the nature of the presidency has followed this change. . . . The president of the multiversity is leader, educator, wielder of power, pump; he is also

officeholder, caretaker, inheritor, consensus seeker, persuader, bottleneck. But he is mostly a mediator.
The Uses of the University. The Godkin Lectures at Harvard University [1963]

Noel Langley

1911–

1 Toto, I've a feeling we're not in Kansas anymore.
The Wizard of Oz (screenplay) [1939],[1] spoken by Judy Garland

2 I'll get you, my pretty, and your little dog, too.
Ibid. spoken by Margaret Hamilton

Marshall Herbert McLuhan

1911–1980

3 The medium is the message.
Understanding Media [1964], title of first chapter

4 There is a basic principle that distinguishes a hot medium like radio from a cool one like the telephone, or a hot medium like the movie from a cool one like TV. . . . Hot media are . . . low in participation, and cool media are high in participation or completion by the audience.   *Ibid. ch. 2*

5 The new electronic interdependence recreates the world in the image of a global village.
The Medium is the Massage [1967]

David Ogilvy

1911–

6 The best headline I ever wrote contained *eighteen* words: At Sixty Miles an Hour the Loudest Noise in the New Rolls-Royce comes from the electric clock.
Confessions of an Advertising Man [1963], ch. 6

Kenneth Patchen

1911–1972

7 Let us have madness openly, O men
Of my generation. Let us follow
The footsteps of this slaughtered age.
Let Us Have Madness Openly [1936]

8 I'd like to die like this . . .
with the dark fingers of the water
closing and unclosing over these sleepy lights
and a sad bell somewhere murmuring good night.
Crossing on Staten Island Ferry [1939]

9 Do I not deal with angels
When her lips I touch.
For Miriam [1942]

[1]Written with FLORENCE RYERSON and EDGAR ALLAN WOLFE.
See Baum, 568.

10 Great mother of big apples it is a pretty World!
I Feel Drunk All the Time [1945]

11 I don't know how the rest of you feel,
But I feel drunk all the time.
Ibid.

12 I am the magical mouse
I don't eat cheese
I eat sunsets
And the tops of trees.
The Magical Mouse [1952], st. 1

13 Oh lonesome's a bad place
To get crowded into.
Lonesome Boy Blues [1952]

Ronald Reagan

1911–

14 Government is like a big baby—an alimentary canal with a big appetite at one end and no responsibility at the other.
Remark while campaigning for governor of California [1965]

15 We're the party that wants to see an America in which people can still get rich.
Remark at Republican congressional dinner, Washington, D.C. [May 4, 1982]

16 It's difficult to believe that people are starving in this country because food isn't available.
Press conference [June 11, 1986]

Ernst Friedrich Schumacher

1911–1977

17 Small Is Beautiful: Economics As If People Mattered.   *Title of book [1973]*

Tennessee Williams

1911–1983

18 Knowledge—Zzzzzp! Money—Zzzzzp!—Power! That's the cycle democracy is built on!
The Glass Menagerie [1945], sc. vii

19 Whoever you are—I have always depended on the kindness of strangers.
A Streetcar Named Desire [1947], sc. xi

20 Time rushes toward us with its hospital tray of infinitely varied narcotics, even while it is preparing us for its inevitably fatal operation.
The Rose Tattoo [1950]. Foreword, The Timeless World of a Play

21 It is a terrible thing for an old woman to outlive her dogs.   *Camino Real [1953]. Prologue*

22 *Make voyages!—Attempt them!*—there's nothing else . . .   *Ibid. Block 8*

1 Nothing's more determined than a cat on a tin roof—is there? Is there, baby?
Cat on a Hot Tin Roof[1] *[1955], act III, last line*

Jorge Amado
1912–

2 Color of cinnamon
Clove's sweet smell,
I've come a long way
To see Gabrielle.
Gabriela, Clove and Cinnamon (Gabriela, Cravo e Canela) [1958], epigraph

John Cheever
1912–1982

3 Fear tastes like a rusty knife and do not let her into your house. Courage tastes of blood. Stand up straight. Admire the world. Relish the love of a gentle woman. Trust in the Lord.
The Wapshot Chronicle [1957], ch. 36, end

4 The sea that morning was iridescent and dark. My wife and my sister were swimming—Diana and Helen—and I saw their uncovered heads, black and gold in the dark water. I saw them come out and I saw that they were naked, unshy, beautiful, and full of grace, and I watched the naked women walk out of the sea.   *Stories [1978]. Goodbye, My Brother*

5 Then it is dark; it is a night where kings in golden suits ride elephants over the mountains.
Ibid. The Country Husband

6 It was at the highest point in the arc of a bridge that I became aware suddenly of the depth and bitterness of my feelings about modern life, and of the profoundness of my yearning for a more vivid, simple, and peaceable world.
Ibid. The Angel of the Bridge

Lawrence George Durrell
1912–1990

7 So the riders of the darkness pass
On their circuit: the luminous island
Of the self trembles and waits,
Waits for us all, my friends,
Where the sea's big brush recolors
The dying lives, and the unborn smiles.
Fangbrand [1946], last stanza

8 I felt once more the strange equivocal power of the city—its flat alluvial landscape and exhausted airs . . . Alexandria; which is neither Greek, Syrian nor Egyptian, but a hybrid: a joint.
Justine [1957], pt. I

[1]See Ray, 272:8.

9 We are the children of our landscape; it dictates behavior and even thought in the measure to which we are responsive to it.   *Ibid.*

Milton Friedman
1912–

10 Positive economics is in principle independent of any particular ethical position or normative judgments . . . In short, positive economics is or can be an "objective" science.
Essays in Positive Economics [1953], pt. I, 1

11 Freedom in economic arrangements is itself a component of freedom broadly understood, so economic freedom is an end in itself. . . . Economic freedom is also an indispensable means toward the achievement of political freedom.
Capitalism and Freedom [1962], ch. 1

12 There's no such thing as a free lunch.
Attributed

Woody [Woodrow Wilson] Guthrie
1912–1967

13 This land is your land, this land is my land,
From California to the New York island,
From the redwood forest to the Gulf Stream
  waters,
This land was made for you and me.
This Land Is Your Land [1956]

Eugène Ionesco
1912–

14 Take a perfect circle, caress it and you'll have a vicious circle.
The Bald Soprano (La Cantatrice Chauve) [1950]

15 There are more dead people than living. And their numbers are increasing. The living are getting rarer.   *Rhinoceros [1960],*[2] *act I*

16 We haven't the time to take our time.
Exit the King (Le Roi Se Meurt) [1963]

Pope John Paul I [Albino Luciani]
1912–1978

17 He is Father. Even more, God is Mother, who does not want to harm us.
At Sunday Angelus blessing, St. Peter's Square [September 17, 1978]

18 I am only a poor man, accustomed to small things and silence.   *Illustrissimi [1978], epilogue*

[2]Translated by DEREK PROUSE.

Mary McCarthy
1912–1989

1   The Man in the Brooks Brothers Shirt.
The Company She Keeps [1942], title of story

2   Every word she [Lillian Hellman] writes is a lie, including "and" and "the."
Television interview [1980]

David Rousset
1912–

3   Concentration Camp Universe [L'Univers Concentrationnaire].
Title of book [1946][1]

Studs [Louis] Terkel
1912–

4   Perhaps it is this specter that most haunts working men and women: the planned obsolescence of people that is of a piece with the planned obsolescence of the things they make. Or sell.
Working [1972], introduction

Alan Mathison Turing
1912–1954

5   I propose to consider the question, "Can machines think?"
Computing Machinery and Intelligence [October 1950]

Patrick White
1912–1990

6   There's many benefits from a good read, just as some must sing a lungful of psalm, or take the bottle down from the shelf.
The Tree of Man [1955], ch. 1

7   Inspiration descends only in flashes, to clothe circumstances; it is not stored up in a barrel, like salt herrings, to be doled out.   *Voss [1957], ch. 2*

George Barker
1913–1991

8 She will not glance up at the bomber or
      condescend
To drop her gin and scuttle to a cellar,
But lean on the mahogany table like a mountain
Whom only faith can move, and so I send
O all my faith and all my love to tell her
That she will move from mourning into morning.
Eros in Dogma [1944]. To My Mother

[1]Translated as *The Other Kingdom* by RAMON GUTHRIE.

Menachem Begin
1913–1992

9   A great day in the annals of two ancient nations, Egypt and Israel, whose sons met in battle five times, fighting and falling. . . . It is thanks to our fallen heroes that we could have reached this day.
On signing the Egyptian-Israeli peace treaty, Washington, D.C. [March 26, 1979][2]

10   No more wars, no more bloodshed. Peace unto you. Shalom, salaam, forever.   *Ibid.*

Sammy Cahn
1913–

11 Love and marriage, love and marriage,
    Go together like a horse and carriage.
Our Town (television musical) [1955].[3] *Love and Marriage*

Albert Camus
1913–1960

12   Mother died today, or maybe it was yesterday.
The Stranger (L'Étranger) [1942], I

13   For the first time, the first, I laid my heart open to the benign indifference of the universe. To feel it so like myself, indeed, so brotherly, made me realize that I'd been happy, and that I was happy still.
Ibid. IV

14   The absurd is the essential concept and the first truth.
The Myth of Sisyphus (Le Mythe de Sisyphe) [1942]

15   The struggle to reach the top is itself enough to fulfill the heart of man. One must believe that Sisyphus is happy.   *Ibid.*

16   It is not rebellion itself which is noble but the demands it makes upon us.
The Plague (La Peste) [1947]

17   Can one be a saint if God does not exist? That is the only concrete problem I know of today.
Ibid.

18   In the depth of winter, I finally learned that within me there lay an invincible summer.
Summer (L'Été) [1954]. Return to Tipasa

19   I shall tell you a great secret, my friend. Do not wait for the last judgment. It takes place every day.
The Fall (La Chute) [1956]

20   A single sentence will suffice for modern man: he fornicated and read the papers.   *Ibid.*

[2]See Sadat, 745:22.
[3]Music by JIMMY VAN HEUSEN.

1   Freedom of the press is perhaps the freedom that has suffered the most from the gradual degradation of the idea of liberty.
Resistance, Rebellion, and Death [1960][1]

2   A free press can of course be good or bad, but, most certainly, without freedom it will never be anything but bad. . . . Freedom is nothing else but a chance to be better, whereas enslavement is a certainty of the worse.   *Ibid.*

Robertson Davies
1913–

3   Vaudeville audiences . . . could give the loudest sighs I have ever heard. Prisoners in the Bastille couldn't have touched them.
World of Wonders [1976]. A Bottle in the Smoke, pt. VIII

4   The magician Merlin had a strange laugh, and it was heard when nobody else was laughing. . . . He laughed because he knew what was coming next.
Ibid.

5   She was worse than a blabber; she was a hinter. It gave her pleasure to rouse curiosity and speculation about dangerous things.
What's Bred in the Bone [1985]. What would not Out of the Flesh?

6   About 60 years ago, I said to my father, "Old Mr. Senex is showing his age; he sometimes talks quite stupidly." My father replied, "That isn't age. He's always been stupid. He is just losing his ability to conceal it."
You're Not Getting Older, You're Getting Nosier, in the New York Times Book Review [May 12, 1991]

Gerald Rudolph Ford
1913–

7   I'm a Ford, not a Lincoln.
Comment after his nomination for the vice-presidency [October 12, 1973]

8   Our long national nightmare is over.
On being sworn in as President [August 9, 1974]

9   There is no Soviet domination of Eastern Europe.
Television debate with Jimmy Carter [October 6, 1976]

Donald Francis Mason
1913–

10   Sighted sub, sank same.
Radio message to U.S. Navy Base [January 28, 1942]

[1]Translated by JUSTIN O'BRIEN.

Richard Milhous Nixon
1913–

11   The kids, like all kids, loved the dog [Checkers], and I just want to say this, right now, that regardless of what they say about it, we are going to keep it.
Radio and TV speech responding to allegations of a political slush fund [September 23, 1952]

12   You won't have Nixon to kick around anymore, because, gentlemen, this is my last press conference.
To the press [November 7, 1962]

13   Bring us together again.
Speech in New York City [October 31, 1968]

14   The great silent majority.
Speech [November 3, 1969]

15   The Chinese are a great and vital people who should not remain isolated from the international community. . . . It is certainly in our interest, and in the interest of peace and stability in Asia and the world, that we take what steps we can toward improved practical relations with Peking.
First Foreign Policy Report to Congress [February 1970]

16   If when the chips are down, the world's most powerful nation . . . acts like a pitiful, helpless giant, the forces of totalitarianism and anarchy will threaten free nations and free institutions throughout the world.
Televised speech [April 30, 1970] announcing major United States offensive into Cambodia

17   I want you all to stonewall it.
Presidential transcript [March 22, 1973]

18   People have got to know whether or not their President is a crook. Well, I'm not a crook.
Press conference [November 11, 1973]

19   Always give your best, never get discouraged, never be petty; always remember, others may hate you. Those who hate you don't win unless you hate them. And then you destroy yourself.
Address to members of the administration on leaving office [August 9, 1974]

20   When the President does it, that means that it is not illegal.
Interview with David Frost [May 19, 1977]

Tillie Olsen
1913–

21   She would not exchange her solitude for anything. Never again to be forced to move to the rhythms of others.
Tell Me a Riddle [1961], title story, sec. 1

22   Only help her to know—help make it so there is cause for her to know—that she is more than this dress on the ironing board, helpless before the iron.
Ibid. I Stand Here Ironing

1   Women are traditionally trained to place others' needs first . . . their satisfaction to be in making it possible for others to use their abilities.
> *Silences [1978], pt. I*

Rosa Parks
1913–

2   I had felt for a long time, that if I was ever told to get up so a white person could sit, that I would refuse to do so.
> *Recalling her refusal to give up her seat on a Montgomery, Alabama, bus [December 1, 1955]*

Muriel Rukeyser
1913–1980

3 Fly down, Death: Call me:
I have become a lost name.
> *Madboy's Song, refrain*

4 What would happen if one woman told the truth about her life?
The world would split open
> *Käthe Kollwitz, sec. III*

Delmore Schwartz
1913–1966

5 Time is the school in which we learn,
Time is the fire in which we burn.
> *For Rhoda [1938]*

6 That inescapable animal walks with me.
Has followed me since the black womb held,
Moves where I move, distorting my gesture,
A caricature, a swollen shadow,
A stupid clown of the spirit's motive,
Perplexes and affronts with his own darkness,
The secret life of belly and bone.
> *The Heavy Bear Who Goes with Me, st. 3*

Karl Shapiro
1913–

7 Haul up the flag, you mourners,
Not half-mast but all the way;
The funeral is done and disbanded;
The devil's had the final say.
> *Elegy for Two Banjos, st. 1, 14*

Lewis Thomas
1913–

8   What is [the earth] *most* like? . . . It is *most* like a single cell.
> *The Lives of a Cell [1974]. The Lives of a Cell*

9   There is really no such creature as a single individual; he has no more life of his own than a cast-off cell marooned from the surface of your skin.
> *Ibid. Antaeus in Manhattan*

10   Viewed from the distance of the moon, the astonishing thing about the earth . . . is that it is alive. . . . Aloft, floating free beneath the moist, gleaming membrane of bright blue sky, is the rising earth, the only exuberant thing in this part of the cosmos. . . . It has the organized, self-contained look of a live creature, full of information, marvelously skilled in handling the sun.
> *Ibid. The World's Biggest Membrane*

11   We are a spectacular, splendid manifestation of life. We have language . . . We have affection. We have genes for usefulness, and usefulness is about as close to a "common goal" of nature as I can guess at. And finally, and perhaps best of all, we have music.
> *The Medusa and the Snail [1979]. The Youngest and Brightest Thing Around*

12   We are, perhaps, uniquely among the earth's creatures, the worrying animal. We worry away our lives, fearing the future, discontent with the present, unable to take in the idea of dying, unable to sit still.
> *Ibid.*

Philip Yordan
1913–

13   Lie to me. Tell me all these years you've waited. Tell me.
> *Johnny Guitar (screenplay) [1954], spoken by Sterling Hayden*

John Berryman
1914–1972

14 Mountainous, woman not breaks and will bend:
sways God nearby: anguish comes to an end.
Blossomed Sarah, and I
blossom. Is that thing alive? I hear a famisht howl.
> *Homage to Mistress Bradstreet [1953], st. 21*

15 Huffy Henry hid   the day,
Unappeasable Henry sulked.
> *77 Dream Songs [1964], poem no. 1*

16 I don't see how Henry, pried
open for all the world to see, survived.
> *Ibid.*

17 Life, friends, is boring. We must not say so.
> *Ibid. 14*

18   Two daiquiris
withdrew into a corner of the gorgeous room
and one told the other a lie.
> *Ibid. 16*

1 But never did Henry, as he thought he did,
   end anyone and hacks her body up
   and hide the pieces, where they may be found.
   He knows: he went over everyone, & nobody's
      missing.
   Often he reckons, in the dawn, them up.
   Nobody is ever missing.
                   Ibid. 29

2 He stared at ruin. Ruin stared straight back.
   He thought they were old friends.
                   Ibid. 45

3   Something can (has) been said for sobriety
   but very little.
                   Ibid. 57

4 But I do guess mos peoples gonna *lose.*
                   Ibid. 60

5 The world is gradually becoming a place
   where I do not care to be any more.
   His Toy, His Dream, His Rest [1968], poem
   no. 149

6 It is a true error to marry with poets
   or to be by them.
                 Ibid. 187

7   Decent fall the cloths
   over a high income.
                 Ibid. 196

8 I saw in my dream
   the great lost cities, Machu Picchu, Cambridge
      Mass., Angkor.
                 Ibid. 197

9 What was it missing, then, at the man's heart
   so that he does not wound?
        Ibid. 219 (So Long? Stevens)

10 Perhaps God resembles one of the last etchings of
      Goya
   & not Velasquez, never Rembrandt no.
     Ibid. 238 (Henry's Programme for God)

11 I always wanted to be old, I wanted to say
   "O I haven't read that for fifteen years."
                Ibid. 264

12 I haven't lost a battle yet but I am tense
   for the first losing.
                 Ibid. 315

13 Offering dragons quarter is no good,
   they regrow all their parts & come on again,
   they have to be killed.
                Ibid. 316

14 When will indifference come.
                Ibid. 384

Daniel Joseph Boorstin
1914–

15   A pseudo-event . . . comes about because someone has planned, planted, or incited it. Typically, it
is not a train wreck or an earthquake, but an interview.   *The Image [1962], ch. 1*

16   The celebrity is a person who is known for his
well-knownness.   *Ibid.*

William Seward Burroughs
1914–

17   The title means exactly what the words say:
NAKED Lunch—a frozen moment when everyone
sees what is on the end of every fork.
      Naked Lunch [1959]. Introduction

Ralph Ellison
1914–

18   I am an invisible man. . . . I am a man of substance, of flesh and bone, fiber and liquids—and I
might even be said to possess a mind. I am invisible,
understand, simply because people refuse to see me.
      The Invisible Man [1952], prologue

John Hersey
1914–

19   There was no sound of planes. The morning was
still; the place was cool and pleasant.
   Then a tremendous flash of light cut across the
sky. Mr. Tanimoto has a distinct recollection that it
traveled from east to west, from the city toward the
hills. It seemed a sheet of sun. Both he and Mr. Mat-
suo reacted in terror. . . . Under what seemed to be
a local dust cloud, the day grew darker and darker.
          Hiroshima [1946], ch. 1

20   There, in the tin factory, in the first moment of
the atomic age, a human being was crushed by
books.   *Ibid.*

Randall Jarrell
1914–1965

21 From my mother's sleep I fell into the State,
   And I hunched in its belly till my wet fur
      froze.
   Six miles from earth, loosed from its dream of
      life,
   I woke to black flak and the nightmare
      fighters.
   When I died they washed me out of the turret
      with a hose.
   The Death of the Ball Turret Gunner [1944]

22 The saris go by me from the embassies.
   Cloth from the moon. Cloth from another planet.
   They look back at the leopard like a leopard.
   The Woman at the Washington Zoo [1960]

1   You know what I was,
You see what I am: change me, change me!
                The Woman at the Washington Zoo

2   But I identify myself, as always,
With something that there's something wrong
        with,
With something human.
                The One Who Was Different [1965]

Robert Lindner
1914–1956

3   Rebel Without a Cause.
        *Title of book [1944] and movie [1955] starring
        James Dean*

4   The Fifty-Minute Hour.
                        Title of book [1954]

Joe Louis [Joseph Louis Borrow]
1914–1981

5   He can run, but he can't hide.
        *Remark before his heavyweight title fight with
        Billy Conn [June 19, 1941]*

Bernard Malamud
1914–1986

6   Levin wanted friendship and got friendliness; he
wanted steak and they offered spam.
                        A New Life [1961]

7   There comes a time in a man's life when to get
where he has to go—if there are no doors or windows—he walks through a wall.
        Rembrandt's Hat [1972]. Man in the Drawer

8   There is no life that can be recaptured wholly; as
it was. Which is to say that all biography is ultimately fiction. What does that tell you about the
nature of life, and does one really want to know?
                        Dubin's Lives [1979], ch. 1

9   One's fantasy goes for a walk and returns with a
bride.   *Long Work, Short Life [1985]*

Norman Panama
1914–
and
Melvin Frank
1913–

10   The pellet with the poison's in the flagon with the
dragon, the vessel with the pestle has the brew that
is true.
        *The Court Jester (screenplay) [1956], spoken by
        Danny Kaye*

Ross Parker
1914–
and
Hughie Charles
1907–

11   There'll Always Be an England.
                        Title of song [1939]

Octavio Paz
1914–

12   Would it not be true to say that North Americans
prefer to use reality rather than to know it?
        *The Labyrinth of Solitude (El Labrinto de la
        Soledad) [1950],[1] ch. 1*

13   Solitude lies at the lowest depth of the human
condition. Man is the only being who feels himself to
be alone and the only one who is searching for the
Other.   *Ibid. Appendix*

14   Touched by poetry, language is more fully language and at the same time is no longer language: it
is a poem.   *Claude Lévi-Strauss [1967],[1] ch. 3*

15   We are condemned
to kill time:
Thus we die
bit by bit
                Cuento de los Jardines [1968]

16   The supreme value is not the future but the present. The future is a deceitful time that always says
to us, "Not yet," and thus denies us. The future is
not the time of love: what man truly wants he wants
now. Whoever builds a house for future happiness
builds a prison for the present.
                Postscript (Posdata) [1970]

17   And the world is changed
if two people shaken by dizziness and enlaced
are fallen among the grass.
        *Configurations [1971]. Sun Stone (Piedra de
        Sol),[2] l. 432*

18   My steps along this street
Resound
            in another street
In which
            I hear my steps
Passing along this street
In which

Only the mist is real.

                        Ibid. Here (Aquí)[3]

19   The absolutes the eternities
Their outlying districts
            Are not my theme

[1]Translated by RACHEL PHILLIPS.
[2]Translated by MURIEL RUKEYSER.
[3]Translated by CHARLES TOMLINSON.

I am hungry for life and for death also
I know what I know and I write it.
Ibid. Vrindaban,[1] *l. 152*

1   Western civilization should be feminized.
Seven Voices [1972], interview

2   There can be a "boom" in petroleum or wheat,
but there can't be a boom in the novel and less still
in poetry.   *Ibid.*

Henry Reed
1914–

3 To-day we have naming of parts. Yesterday,
We had daily cleaning. And to-morrow morning,
We shall have what to do after firing. But to-day,
To-day we have naming of parts.
Lessons of the War [1946]. I. Naming of Parts

4 The early bees are assaulting and fumbling the
    flowers:
They call it easing the Spring.
Ibid.

5 And the various holds and rolls and throws and
    breakfalls
Somehow or other I always seemed to put
In the wrong place. And as for war, my wars
Were global from the start.
Ibid. III. Unarmed Combat

Budd Schulberg
1914–

6   I could've been a contender. I could've had class
and been somebody. Real class. Instead of a bum,
let's face it, which is what I am.
*On the Waterfront (screenplay) [1954], spoken
by Marlon Brando*

Jerry Siegel
1914–
and
Joe Shuster
1914–

7   Faster than a speeding bullet, more powerful than
a locomotive, able to leap tall buildings at a single
bound—look, up there in the sky, it's a bird, it's a
plane, it's Superman!
Superman (comic strip) [June 1938]

Dylan Thomas
1914–1953

8 The force that through the green fuse drives the
    flower
Drives my green age; that blasts the roots of trees

¹Translated by LYSANDER KEMP.

Is my destroyer.
And I am dumb to tell the crooked rose
My youth is bent by the same wintry fever.
*The Force That Through the Green Fuse Drives
the Flower [1934]*

9 Light breaks where no sun shines;
Where no sea runs, the waters of the heart
Push in their tides.
Light Breaks Where No Sun Shines [1934]

10 The hand that signed the paper felled a city;
Five sovereign fingers taxed the breath,
Doubled the globe of dead and halved a country;
These five kings did a king to death.
The Hand That Signed the Paper [1936]

11 And death shall have no dominion.[2]
Refrain and title of poem [1943]

12 After the first death there is no other.
*A Refusal to Mourn the Death, by Fire, of a
Child in London [1946]*

13 Forgotten mornings when he walked with his
    mother
Through the parables
    Of sunlight
And the legend of the green chapels.
Poem in October [1946]

14 Now as I was young and easy under the apple
    boughs
About the lilting house and happy as the grass
    was green.
Fern Hill, st. 1 [1946]

15 And honored among wagons I was prince of the
    apple towns.
Ibid.

16 In the sun that is young once only,
    Time let me play and be
Golden in the mercy of his means.
Ibid.

17   And the sabbath rang slowly
In the pebbles of the holy streams.
Ibid. st. 2

18 And honored among foxes and pheasants by the
    gay house
Under the new-made clouds and happy as the
    heart was long,
    In the sun born over and over,
        I ran my heedless ways.
Ibid. st. 5

19   Time held me green and dying
Though I sang in my chains like the sea.
Ibid. st. 6

20 Do not go gentle into that good night,
Old age should burn and rave at close of day;
Rage, rage against the dying of the light.
*Do Not Go Gentle into That Good Night
[1952]*

²See Romans 6:9, 41:43.

1   One Christmas was so much like another, in those years around the seatown corner now and out of all sound except the distant speaking of the voices I sometimes hear a moment before sleep, that I can never remember whether it snowed for six days and six nights when I was twelve or whether it snowed for twelve days and twelve nights when I was six.
Quite Early One Morning [1954]. A Child's Christmas in Wales

2   It is spring, moonless night in the small town, starless and bible-black.
Under Milk Wood [1954]

E[dward] Digby Baltzell
1915–

3   There is a crisis in American leadership in the middle of the twentieth century that is partly due, I think, to the declining authority of an establishment which is now based on an increasingly castelike White-Anglo Saxon-Protestant (WASP) upper class.
The Protestant Establishment [1964], ch. 1

Roland Barthes
1915–1980

4   I think that cars today are almost the exact equivalent of the great Gothic cathedrals: I mean the supreme creation of an era, conceived with passion by unknown artists, and consumed in image if not in usage by a whole population which appropriates them as a purely magical object.
Mythologies [1972].[1] *The New Citroën*

Saul Bellow
1915–

5   There was a disturbance in my heart, a voice that spoke there and said, *I want, I want, I want!* It happened every afternoon, and when I tried to suppress it it got even stronger. . . . It never said a thing except *I want, I want, I want!*
Henderson the Rain King [1959]

6   I am simply a human being, more or less.
Herzog [1964]

7   As though to be Jewish weren't trouble enough, the poor woman was German, too.
Mr. Sammler's Planet [1970], pt. I

8   New York makes one think of the collapse of civilization, about Sodom and Gomorrah, the end of the world. The end wouldn't come as a surprise here. Many people already bank on it.   *Ibid. VI*

[1]Translated by ANNETTE LAVERS.

9   The body, she says, is subject to the forces of gravity. But the soul is ruled by levity, pure.
Him with His Foot in His Mouth [1984], title story

Jerome Seymour Bruner
1915–

10   The shrewd guess, the fertile hypothesis, the courageous leap to a tentative conclusion—these are the most valuable coin of the thinker at work.
The Process of Education [1960]

11   Any subject can be taught effectively in some intellectually honest form to any child at any stage of development.   *Ibid.*

Alfred Kazin
1915–

12   A classic is a book that survives the circumstances that made it possible yet alone keeps those circumstances alive.
Review in The New Republic [August 29, 1988]

Sir Peter Brian Medawar
1915–1987

13   The scientist values research by the size of its contribution to that huge, logically articulated structure of ideas which is already, though not yet half built, the most glorious accomplishment of mankind.   *The Art of the Soluble [1967]*

14   Among scientists are collectors, classifiers, and compulsive tidiers-up; many are detectives by temperament and many are explorers; some are artists and others artisans. There are poet-scientists and philosopher-scientists and even a few mystics.
Ibid.

Arthur Miller
1915–

15   I don't say he's a great man. Willy Loman never made a lot of money. His name was never in the paper. He's not the finest character that ever lived. But he's a human being, and a terrible thing is happening to him. So attention must be paid. He's not to be allowed to fall into his grave like an old dog. Attention, attention must be finally paid to such a person.   *Death of a Salesman [1949], act I*

16   Never fight fair with a stranger, boy. You'll never get out of the jungle that way.   *Ibid.*

17   I have not moved from there to here without I think to please you, and still an everlasting funeral marches round your heart.
The Crucible [1953], act II

1 I am inclined to notice the ruin in things, perhaps because I was born in Italy.
A View from the Bridge [1955], act I

Paul A. Samuelson
1915–

2 Wall Street indexes predicted nine out of the last five recessions.
Column in Newsweek [September 19, 1966]

3 Man does not live by GNP alone.
Economics [1973], ch. 40

Jean Stafford
1915–1979

4 To her own heart, which was shaped exactly like a valentine, there came a winglike palpitation, a delicate exigency, and all the fragrance of all the flowery springtime love affairs that ever were seemed waiting for them in the whiskey bottle.
Children Are Bored on Sundays [1953], title story

Orson Welles
1915–1985

5 In Italy for thirty years under the Borgias they had warfare, terror, murder, bloodshed, but they produced Michelangelo, Leonardo da Vinci, and the Renaissance. In Switzerland they had brotherly love, they had five hundred years of democracy and peace. And what did that produce? The cuckoo-clock.
Speech written into The Third Man (screenplay by Graham Greene and Carol Reed) [1949]

John Malcolm Brinnin
1916–

6 I seek a father who most need a son.
Oedipus: His Cradle Song [1963]

7 In their big peppermint hotels.
News from the Islands [1963]

8 Another hill town:
another dry Cinzano in the sun.
Hotel Paradiso è Commerciale [1963]

9 We have all done this before; we're
bored and terrified.
Flight 539 [1963]

10 All of a sudden came the pelicans:
crazy old men in baseball caps, who flew
like jackknives and collapsed like fans.
Skin Diving in the Virgins [1970]

Walter Cronkite
1916–

11 And that's the way it is.
Sign-off sentence, CBS Evening News

Gavin Ewart
1916–

12 Miss Twye was soaping her breasts in her bath
When she heard behind her a meaning laugh
And to her amazement she discovered
A wicked man in the bathroom cupboard.
Miss Twye

Elizabeth Hardwick
1916–

13 Collaborating in the very private way of love or the highest kind of friendship . . . is the way for gifted, energetic wives of writers to a sort of composition of their own, this peculiar illusion of collaboration.
Seduction and Betrayal: Women in Literature [1974]. Amateurs

14 This is the unspoken contract of a wife and her works. In the long run wives are to be paid in a peculiar coin—consideration for their feelings. And it usually turns out this is an enormous, unthinkable inflation few men will remit, or if they will, only with a sense of being overcharged.
Ibid.

Shirley Jackson
1916–1965

15 "It isn't fair, it isn't right," Mrs. Hutchinson screamed, and then they were upon her.
The Lottery [1948], last line

Florynce R. Kennedy
1916–

16 Niggerization is the result of oppression—and it doesn't just apply to black people. Old people, poor people, and students can also get niggerized.
From GLORIA STEINEM, The Verbal Karate of Florynce R. Kennedy, Esq. [1973]

17 If men could get pregnant, abortion would be a sacrament.
Ibid.

Charles Wright Mills
1916–1962

18 By the power elite, we refer to those political, economic, and military circles which as an intricate set of overlapping cliques share decisions having at least national consequences. In so far as national

events are decided, the power elite are those who decide them.

> *The Power Elite [1956], ch. 1, The Higher Circles*

1   The sociological imagination enables us to grasp history and biography and the relations between the two within society.

> *The Sociological Imagination [1959], ch. 1*

Walker Percy
1916–1990

2   The fact is I am quite happy in a movie, even a bad movie. Other people, so I have read, treasure memorable moments in their lives.

> *The Moviegoer [1961]*

Gwendolyn Brooks
1917–

3   Maud went to college.
Sadie stayed at home.
Sadie scraped life
With a fine-tooth comb.

> *A Street in Bronzeville [1945]. Sadie and Maud, st. 1*

4   Abortions will not let you forget.
You remember the children you got that you did not get.

> *Ibid. The Mother, st. 1*

5   What shall I give my children? who are poor,
Who are adjudged the leastwise of the land.

> *Annie Allen [1949]. The Womanhood. The Children of the Poor, sonnet 2*

6   Exhaust the little moment. Soon it dies.
And be it gash or gold it will not come
Again in this identical disguise.

> *Ibid. Exhaust the Little Moment*

7   And remembering . . .
Remembering, with twinklings and twinges,
As they lean over the beans in their rented back
    room that is full of beads and receipts and
    dolls and cloths, tobacco crumbs, vases and
    fringes.

> *The Bean Eaters [1960]. The Bean Eaters, st. 3*

8   We real cool. We
Left school. We
Lurk late. We
Strike straight. We
Sing sin. We
Thin gin. We
Jazz June. We
Die soon.

> *Ibid. We Real Cool*

9   What else is there to say but everything?

> *In the Mecca [1968], st. 16*

10   He opened us—
who was a key,
who was a man.

> *Ibid. After Mecca. Malcolm X*

11   The time
cracks into furious flower. Lifts its face
all unashamed. And sways in wicked grace.

> *Ibid. The Second Sermon on the Warpland, st. 4*

12   Big Bessie's feet hurt like nobody's business,
but she stands—bigly—under the unruly
    scrutiny, stands in the wild weed.
In the wild weed
she is a citizen.

> *Ibid.*

13   Beware the easy griefs
that fool and fuel nothing.

> *Beckonings [1975]. Boys. Black, st. 7*

Anthony Burgess
[John Anthony Burgess Wilson]
1917–

14   What's it going to be then, eh?

> *A Clockwork Orange [1962], passim*

15   That shut her up real horrorshow and lovely.

> *Ibid.*

16   You have no idea how pleasant it is not to have any future. It's like having a totally efficient contraceptive.

> *Honey for the Bears [1964], pt. II, ch. 6*

Joe Darion
1917–

17   To dream the impossible dream,
To reach the unreachable star!

> *The Impossible Dream [1965][1]*

John Fitzgerald Kennedy
1917–1963

18   It was involuntary. They sank my boat.

> *Remark when asked how he became a hero. Quoted in ARTHUR M. SCHLESINGER, JR., A Thousand Days [1965], ch. 4*

19   A man does what he must—in spite of personal consequences, in spite of obstacles and dangers and pressures—and that is the basis of all human morality.

> *Profiles in Courage [1956], ch. 11*

20   The New Frontier of which I speak is not a set of promises—it is a set of challenges. It sums up not what I intend to offer the American people, but what I intend to ask of them.

> *Speech accepting the Democratic presidential nomination [July 15, 1960]*

[1]Music by MITCH LEIGH.

1   I am not the Catholic candidate for President. I am the Democratic Party's candidate for President, who happens also to be a Catholic.
Speech to Greater Houston Ministerial Association [September 12, 1960]

2   For of those to whom much is given, much is required. And when at some future date the high court of history sits in judgment on each of us, recording whether in our brief span of service we fulfilled our responsibilities to the state, our success or failure, in whatever office we hold, will be measured by the answers to four questions: First, were we truly men of courage . . . Second, were we truly men of judgment . . . Third, were we truly men of integrity . . . Finally, were we truly men of dedication?
Speech to the Massachusetts State Legislature [January 9, 1961]

3   Let the word go forth from this time and place, to friend and foe alike, that the torch has been passed to a new generation of Americans, born in this century, tempered by war, disciplined by a hard and bitter peace, proud of our ancient heritage, and unwilling to witness or permit the slow undoing of those human rights to which this nation has always been committed, and to which we are committed today at home and around the world.

Let every nation know, whether it wishes us well or ill, that we shall pay any price, bear any burden, meet any hardship, support any friend, oppose any foe to assure the survival and the success of liberty.
Inaugural address [January 20, 1961]

4   If a free society cannot help the many who are poor, it cannot save the few who are rich.   *Ibid.*

5   Let us never negotiate out of fear, but let us never fear to negotiate.   *Ibid.*

6   All this will not be finished in the first one hundred days. Nor will it be finished in the first one thousand days, nor in the life of this Administration, nor even perhaps in our lifetime on this planet. But let us begin.   *Ibid.*

7   And so, my fellow Americans, ask not what your country can do for you; ask what you can do for your country.[1]   *Ibid.*

---

[1]For, stripped of the temporary associations which gave rise to it, it is now the moment when by common consent we pause to become conscious of our national life and to rejoice in it, to recall what our country has done for each of us, and to ask ourselves what we can do for our country in return.—OLIVER WENDELL HOLMES, JR., *Address Before John Sedgwick Post No. 4, Grand Army of the Republic* [May 30, 1884]

As has often been said, the youth who loves his Alma Mater will always ask, not "What can she do for me?" but "What can I do for her?"—LE BARON RUSSELL BRIGGS [1855–1934], *Routine and Ideals* [1904], *College Life*

In the great fulfillment we must have a citizenship less concerned about what the government can do for it and more anxious about what it can do for the nation.—WARREN GAMALIEL HARDING [1865–1923], *Republican National Convention, Chicago* [June 7, 1916]

8   It is our task in our time and in our generation to hand down undiminished to those who come after us, as was handed down to us by those who went before, the natural wealth and beauty which is ours.
Address at the dedication ceremonies of the National Wildlife Federation Building [March 3, 1961]

9   I believe this nation should commit itself to achieving the goal, before this decade is out, of landing a man on the moon and returning him safely to earth.
Address to joint session of Congress [May 25, 1961]

10   Mankind must put an end to war or war will put an end to mankind.
Address to the United Nations [September 25, 1961]

11   Those who make peaceful revolution impossible will make violent revolution inevitable.
Address to Latin American diplomats, the White House [March 12, 1962]

12   There is always inequity in life. Some men are killed in a war and some men are wounded, and some men never leave the country . . . Life is unfair.   *Press conference [March 21, 1962]*

13   The wave of the future is not the conquest of the world by a single dogmatic creed but the liberation of the diverse energies of free nations and free men.
Address at the University of California, Berkeley [March 23, 1962]

14   I think this is the most extraordinary collection of talent, of human knowledge, that has ever been gathered together at the White House, with the possible exception of when Thomas Jefferson dined alone.
Address at a White House dinner and reception honoring Nobel Prize winners [April 1962]

15   My father always told me that all businessmen were sons of bitches, but I never believed it till now.
Comment on price increases proposed by U.S. Steel [April 1962]

16   We don't see the end of the tunnel, but I must say I don't think it is darker than it was a year ago, and in some ways lighter.[2]
Press conference [December 12, 1962]

17   Liberty without learning is always in peril and learning without liberty is always in vain.
Remarks on the ninetieth anniversary of Vanderbilt University [March 18, 1963]

This thought had lain in Kennedy's mind for a long time. As far back as 1945 he had noted down in a looseleaf notebook a quotation from Rousseau: "As soon as any man says of the affairs of the state, What does it matter to me? the state may be given up as lost."—ARTHUR M. SCHLESINGER, JR., *A Thousand Days* [1965], *prologue, footnote*

[2]If we see a light at the end of the tunnel, / It's the light of an oncoming train.—ROBERT LOWELL, *Since 1939* [1977]

1   If we cannot end now our differences, at least we can help make the world safe for diversity.
   Address at American University, Washington, D.C. [June 10, 1963]

2   Every American ought to have the right to be treated as he would wish to be treated, as one would wish his children to be treated. This is not the case.
   Television address on civil rights, after the registration of two Negroes at the University of Alabama [June 11, 1963]

3   No one has been barred on account of his race from fighting or dying for America—there are no "white" or "colored" signs on the foxholes or grave-yards of battle.
   Message to Congress on proposed civil rights bill [June 19, 1963]

4   All free men, wherever they may live, are citizens of Berlin. And therefore, as a free man, I take pride in the words "Ich bin ein Berliner."[1]
   Address at City Hall, West Berlin [June 26, 1963]

5   Yesterday, a shaft of light cut into the darkness. . . . For the first time, an agreement has been reached on bringing the forces of nuclear destruction under international control.
   Television address in Washington [July 26, 1963][2]

6   When power leads man toward arrogance, poetry reminds him of his limitations. When power narrows the areas of man's concern, poetry reminds him of the richness and diversity of his existence. When power corrupts, poetry cleanses, for art establishes the basic human truths which must serve as the touchstone of our judgment.
   Address at Amherst College [October 26, 1963]

7   Leadership and learning are indispensable to each other.
   Remarks prepared for delivery at the Trade Mart in Dallas [November 22, 1963]

8   Washington is a city of southern efficiency and northern charm.
   Remark. Quoted in ARTHUR M. SCHLESINGER, JR., *A Thousand Days [1965], ch. 25*

Walter Lord

1917–

9   A Night to Remember.   *Title of book [1955]*

[1]What [Kennedy's speech writers] did not know, but could easily have found out, was that such citizens never refer to themselves as "Berliners." They reserve that term for a favorite confection, often munched at breakfast. So while they understood and appreciated the sentiments behind the President's impassioned declaration, the residents tittered among themselves when he exclaimed, literally, "I am a jelly-filled dough-nut."—*New York Times [April 30, 1988]*

[2]In Moscow on July 25, Averell Harriman, Lord Hailsham, and Andrei Gromyko initialed the nuclear test ban treaty.

Robert Traill Spence Lowell

1917–1977

10 Christ walks on the black water. In Black Mud
   Darts the kingfisher. On Corpus Christi, heart,
   Over the drum-beat of St. Stephen's choir
   I hear him, *Stupor Mundi,* and the mud
   Flies from his hunching wings and beak—my heart,
   The blue kingfisher dives on you in fire.
   Colloquy in Black Rock [1946], st. 5

11 I will catch Christ with a greased worm.
   The Drunken Fisherman [1946], st. 5

12 I saw the spiders marching through air,
   Swimming from tree to tree that mildewed day
   In latter August when the hay
   Came creaking to the barn.[3]
   Mr. Edwards and the Spider [1946], st. 1

13 This is the Black Widow, death.
   Ibid. st. 5

14 I saw the sky descending, black and white,
   Not blue, on Boston.
   Where the Rainbow Ends [1946], st. 1

15 Now Paris, our black classic, breaking up
   like killer kings on an Etruscan cup.
   Beyond the Alps [1959]

16 You said:
   "We poets in our youth begin in sadness;
   thereof in the end come despondency and madness."[4]
   To Delmore Schwartz (Cambridge 1946) [1959]

17 Who asks for me, the Shelley of my age,
   must lay his heart out for my bed and board.
   Words for Hart Crane [1959]

18 I doodle handlebar
   moustaches on the last Russian Czar.
   Grandparents [1959]

19 We are old-timers,
   each of us holds a locked razor.
   Waking in the Blue [1959]

20 I keep no rank nor station.
   Cured, I am frizzled, stale and small.
   Home After Three Months Away [1959]

21 Only teaching on Tuesdays, bookworming
   in pajamas fresh from the washer each morning,
   I hog a whole house on Boston's
   "hardly passionate Marlborough Street."[5]
   Memories of West Street and Lepke [1959]

22 These are the tranquillized *Fifties,*
   and I am forty. Ought I to regret my seedtime?

[3]Jonathan Edwards [1703–1758], the Calvinist theologian, wrote at the age of twelve a series of scientific observations on the spider. See Edwards, 308:20.
[4]See Democritus, 70:n9; Robert Burton, 234:13; and Wordsworth, 374:9.
[5]The quotation is from Henry James.

I was a fire-breathing Catholic C.O.,
and made my manic statement,
telling off the state and president, and then
sat waiting sentence in the bull pen
beside a Negro boy with curlicues
of marijuana in his hair.

Ibid.

1 Flabby, bald, lobotomized,
he drifted in a sheepish calm,
where no agonizing reappraisal
jarred his concentration on the electric chair—
hanging like an oasis in his air
of lost connections.

Ibid.

2 Tamed by *Miltown,* we lie on Mother's bed.
Man and Wife [1959]

3   Oh my *Petite,*
clearest of all God's creatures, still all air and
nerve.

Ibid.

4 your old-fashioned tirade—
loving, rapid, merciless—
breaks like the Atlantic Ocean on my head.

Ibid.

5 Gored by the climacteric of his want,
he stalls above me like an elephant.
"To Speak of Woe That Is in Marriage" [1959]

6 My mind's not right.

A car radio bleats,
"Love, O careless Love. . . . " I hear
my ill-spirit sob in each blood cell,
as if my hand were at its throat. . . .
I myself am hell;
nobody's here.[1]

Skunk Hour [1959], st. 5, 6

7 Father, forgive me
my injuries,
as I forgive
those I
have injured!

You never climbed
Mount Sion, yet left
dinosaur
death-steps on the crust,
where I must walk.

Middle Age [1964], st. 3, 4

8 We are like a lot of wild
spiders crying together,
but without tears.

Fall 1961 [1964], st. 4

9 I am tired. Everyone's tired of my turmoil.
Eye and Tooth [1964], st. 9

10 Two months after marching through Boston,
half the regiment was dead;

[1]Ellipses are in the original text.

at the dedication,
William James could almost hear the bronze
Negroes[2] breathe.

Their monument sticks like a fishbone
in the city's throat.
Its Colonel is as lean
as a compass-needle.

He has an angry wrenlike vigilance,
a greyhound's gentle tautness;
he seems to wince at pleasure,
and suffocate for privacy.
For the Union Dead [1964], st. 7–9

11 on Boylston Street, a commercial photograph
shows Hiroshima boiling.

Ibid. st. 14

12 When I crouch to my television set,
the drained faces of Negro school-children rise
like balloons.

Ibid. st. 15

13 The Aquarium is gone. Everywhere,
giant finned cars nose forward like fish;
a savage servility
slides by on grease.

Ibid. st. 17

14 We beg delinquents for our life.
Central Park. In the New York Review
[October 1965]

15 O to break loose, like the chinook
salmon jumping and falling back,
nosing up to the impossible
stone and bone-crushing waterfall.
Waking Early Sunday Morning [1967], st. 1

16 Pity the planet, all joy gone
from this sweet volcanic cone;
peace to our children when they fall
in small war on the heels of small
war.

Ibid. last stanza

17 Rome, if built at all, must be built in a day.
Marcus Cato 234–149 B.C. [1973]

18 No one like one's mother and father ever lived.
Returning [1973]

19 After loving you so much, can I forget
you for eternity, and have no other choice?
Obit [1973]

20 The line must terminate.
Yet my heart rises, I know I've gladdened a
lifetime
knotting, undoing a fishnet of tarred rope;

[2]On the Saint-Gaudens monument to Colonel Robert Gould
Shaw and the 54th Massachusetts Regiment.
    There on foot go the dark outcasts, so true to nature
that one can almost hear them breathing as they march.—
WILLIAM JAMES, *Oration at Dedication of the Monument*
[May 31, 1897]
    See Charles W. Eliot, 522:13, and Dunbar, 615:1.

the net will hang on the wall when the fish are
    eaten,
nailed like illegible bronze on the futureless future.
              Fishnet [1973]

1 If I could go through it all again,
    the slender iron rungs of growing up,
    I would be as young as any,
    a child lost
    in unreality and loud music.
              Realities [1977]

2 It has taken me the time since you died
    to discover you are as human as I am . . .
    if I am.
              To Mother [1977]

3 I—
    really I can do little,
    as little now as then,
    about the infernal fires—
    I cannot blow out a match.
              Grass Fires [1977]

4 We are poor passing facts,
    warned by that to give
    each figure in the photograph
    his living name.
              Epilogue [1977]

Carson Smith McCullers
1917–1967

5   The Heart Is a Lonely Hunter.[1]
              Title of novel [1940]

6   This was the summer when for a long time she
had not been a member. She belonged to no club and
was a member of nothing in the world. Frankie had
become an unjoined person who hung around in the
doorways, and she was afraid.
        The Member of the Wedding [1946], ch. 1

7   If you walk along the main street on an August
afternoon there is nothing whatsoever to do.
        The Ballad of the Sad Cafe [1951]

Jessica Mitford
1917–

8   O grave, where is thy victory?[2] Where, indeed.
Many a badly stung survivor, faced with the aftermath of some relative's funeral, has ruefully concluded that the victory has been won hands down by
a funeral establishment.
        The American Way of Death [1963], ch. 1

[1]See Sharp, 568:8.
[2]See *I Corinthians* 15:54–55, 43:28.

Arthur Meier Schlesinger, Jr.
1917–

9   Above all he [John F. Kennedy] gave the world
for an imperishable moment the vision of a leader
who greatly understood the terror and the hope, the
diversity and the possibility, of life on this planet and
who made people look beyond nation and race to
the future of humanity.
          A Thousand Days [1965], ch. 37

10   The answer to the runaway Presidency is not the
messenger-boy Presidency. The American democracy must discover a middle ground between making
the President a czar and making him a puppet.
       The Imperial Presidency [1973], Preface

11   Suppose . . . that Lenin had died of typhus in
Siberia in 1895 and Hitler had been killed on the
western front in 1916. What would the twentieth
century have looked like now?
      The Cycles of American History [1986]

William Hollingsworth Whyte, Jr.
1917–

12   This book is about the organization man. If the
term is vague, it is because I can think of no other
way to describe the people I am talking about.
. . . They are the ones of our middle class who have
left home, spiritually as well as physically, to take
the vows of organization life, and it is they who are
the mind and soul of our great self-perpetuating
institutions.
      The Organization Man [1956], pt. I, ch. 1

Spiro Theodore Agnew
1918–

13   To some extent, if you've seen one city slum
you've seen them all.
      *Election campaign speech at Detroit [October
18, 1968]*

Leonard Bernstein
1918–1990

14   The key to the mystery of a great artist: that for
reasons unknown to him or to anyone else, he will
give away his energies and his life just to make sure
that one note follows another inevitably. . . .
The composer, by doing this, leaves us at the finish
with the feeling that something is right in the world,
that something checks throughout, something that
follows its own laws consistently, something we can
trust, that will never let us down.
    *The Joy of Music [1959]. Beethoven's Fifth
Symphony*

Otis Ray Bowen
1918–

1 When a person has sex, they're not just having it with that partner, they're having it with everybody that partner has had it with for the past ten years.
Statement on AIDS[1] *[1987]*

Harlan Cleveland
1918–

2 The Revolution of Rising Expectations.[2]
Title of speech at Colgate University [1949]

Corita Kent
1918–1986

3 There are so many hungry people that God cannot appear to them except in the form of bread.
Enriched Bread (silkscreen) [1965]

Ann Landers [Esther P. Lederer]
1918–

4 Women complain about sex more often than men. Their gripes fall into two major categories: (1) Not enough. (2) Too much.
Truth Is Stranger . . . [1968], ch. 2

Alan Jay Lerner
1918–1986

5 Oh, wouldn't it be loverly?
My Fair Lady [1956],[3] *act I, Wouldn't It Be Loverly?*

6 They're always throwing goodness at you
But with a little bit of luck
A man can duck.
Ibid. With a Little Bit of Luck

7 The rain in Spain stays mainly in the plain.
Ibid. The Rain in Spain

8 In Hertford, Hereford and Hampshire, hurricanes hardly happen. *Ibid.*

9 I could have danced all night!
Ibid. I Could Have Danced All Night!

10 Get me to the church on time!
Ibid. II, Get Me to the Church on Time

11 Why can't a woman be more like a man?
Ibid. A Hymn to Him

12 I've grown accustomed . . . to her face.[4]
Ibid. I've Grown Accustomed to Her Face

13 Don't let it be forgot
That once there was a spot
For one brief shining moment that was known
As Camelot.
Camelot [1960],[3] *end*

14 On a Clear Day You Can See Forever.
Title of musical [1965][5]

Nelson Rolihlahla Mandela
1918–

15 I have fought against white domination, and I have fought against black domination. I have cherished the ideal of a democratic and free society in which all persons will live together in harmony and with equal opportunities. It is an ideal which I hope to live for and achieve. But, if needs be, it is an ideal for which I am prepared to die.
Statement in the dock [April 20, 1964][6]

16 Only free men can negotiate; prisoners cannot enter into contracts.
Statement from prison [February 10, 1985]

Edwin O'Connor
1918–1968

17 "God be good to the man," she said. "He was mean as a panther, but good luck to him."
The Last Hurrah [1956], ch. 8

18 I'm not just an elected official of the city; I'm a tribal chieftain as well. *Ibid.*

Anwar al-Sadat
1918–1981

19 Land is immortal, for it harbors the mysteries of creation. *In Search of Identity [1978], ch. 1*

20 A man's village is his peace of mind. *Ibid. 2*

21 Peace is much more precious than a piece of land.
Speech in Cairo [March 8, 1978]

22 Let there be no more war or bloodshed between Arabs and Israelis. Let there be no more suffering or

[1][AIDS:] A disease, at least moderately predictive of a defect in cell-mediated immunity, occurring in a person with no known cause for diminished resistance to that disease. — *Morbidity and Mortality Weekly Report* [September 24, 1982]

[2]Remembering Edmund Burke's famous commentary on the turbulence of his time, I called [a speech at Colgate University] "Reflections on the Revolution of Rising Expectations." The phrase has since been attributed to nearly every literate American of our time, but I think this was the first time that phrase saw the light of day. — HARLAN CLEVELAND, *The Evolution of Rising Responsibility*, address before the U.N. [December 13, 1964]

[3]Music by FREDERICK LOEWE.
Musical based on GEORGE BERNARD SHAW's *Pygmalion*. See Shaw, 571:18–571:22.

[4]Ellipses are in the original text.
[5]Music by BURTON LANE.
[6]Also quoted by him on his release from prison [February 11, 1990].

denial of rights. Let there be no more despair or loss of faith.
> *On signing the Egyptian–Israeli peace treaty, Washington, D.C. [March 26, 1979]*[1]

Alexander Isayevich Solzhenitsyn
1918–

1   A great writer is, so to speak, a second government in his country. And for that reason no regime has ever loved great writers, only minor ones.
> *The First Circle [1964]*[2]

2   There was peace in their hearts. They were filled with the fearlessness of those who have lost *everything*, the fearlessness which is not easy to come by but which endures.
> *Ibid.*

3   The sole substitute for an experience which we have not ourselves lived through is art and literature.
> *Nobel Lecture [1972]*

4   Literature transmits incontrovertible condensed experience . . . from generation to generation. In this way literature becomes the living memory of a nation.
> *Ibid.*

5   Violence does not and cannot exist by itself; it is invariably intertwined with *the lie*.
> *Ibid.*

6   The Kolyma was the greatest and most famous island, the pole of ferocity of that amazing country of Gulag, which, though scattered in an archipelago geographically, was, in the psychological sense, fused into a continent—an almost invisible, almost imperceptible country inhabited by the Zek people.
> *The Gulag Archipelago 1918–1956 [1974, in translation]*,[2] *I, preface*

7   The Western world has lost its civil courage, both as a whole and separately, in each country, each government, each political party, and of course in the United Nations.
> *The Exhausted West. Commencement Address at Harvard University [June 8, 1978]*

8   I have spent all my life under a Communist regime, and I will tell you that a society without any objective legal scale is a terrible one indeed. But a society with no other scale but the legal one is not quite worthy of man either.
> *Ibid.*

Muriel Spark
1918–

9   The one certain way for a woman to hold a man is to leave him for religion.
> *The Comforters [1957], ch. 1*

[1]See Begin, 732:9.
[2]Translated by Thomas P. Whitney.

10   I am putting old heads on your young shoulders . . . and all my pupils are the *crème de la crème*.
> *The Prime of Miss Jean Brodie [1962], ch. 1*

11   Give me a girl at an impressionable age, and she is mine for life.
> *Ibid.*

12   One's prime is elusive. You little girls, when you grow up, must be on the alert to recognize your prime at whatever time of your life it may occur.
> *Ibid.*

13   It is one of the secrets of Nature in its mood of mockery that fine weather lays a heavier weight on the mind and hearts of the depressed and the inwardly tormented than does a really bad day with dark rain sniveling continuously and sympathetically from a dirty sky.
> *Territorial Rights [1979], ch. 3*

Daniel Bell
1919–

14   Capitalism, it is said, is a system wherein man exploits man. And communism—is vice versa.
> *The End of Ideology [1960]*

Robert L. Heilbroner
1919–

15   [The great economists] can be called the worldly philosophers, for they sought to embrace in a scheme of philosophy the most worldly of all of man's activities—his drive for wealth.
> *The Worldly Philosophers [1953]. Introduction*

16   Less than seventy-five years after it officially began, the contest between capitalism and socialism is over: capitalism has won.
> *Reflections: The Triumph of Capitalism, in The New Yorker [January 23, 1989]*

Pauline Kael
1919–

17   The words "Kiss Kiss Bang Bang," which I saw on an Italian movie poster, are perhaps the briefest statement imaginable of the basic appeal of movies.
> *Kiss Kiss Bang Bang [1968]. A Note on the Title*

Doris Lessing
1919–

18   A woman without a man cannot meet a man, any man, of any age, without thinking, even if it's for a half-second, Perhaps this is *the* man.
> *The Golden Notebook [1962]. Free Women, 5*

19   None of you [men] ask for anything—except everything, but just for so long as you need it.
> *Ibid.*

Primo Levi
1919–1987

1   The dark echoed with outlandish orders in that curt, barbaric barking of Germans in command which seems to give vent to a millennial anger.
Survival in Auschwitz [1960],[1] *ch. 2*

2   I am not even alive enough to know how to kill myself.   *Ibid. 15*

3   Today I think that if for no other reason than an Auschwitz existed, no one in our age should speak of Providence.   *Ibid. 17*

Wladziu Valentino [Lee] Liberace
1919–1987

4   I cried all the way to the bank.
Liberace: An Autobiography [1973], ch. 2

Laurence Johnston Peter
1919–1990

5   In a hierarchy, every employee tends to rise to his level of incompetence.
The Peter Principle [1969]

6   If you don't know where you're going, you will probably end up somewhere else.   *Ibid.*

7   *Lateral Arabesque*—a pseudo-promotion consisting of a new title and a new work place.   *Ibid.*

Jerome David Salinger
1919–

8   I keep picturing all these little kids playing some game in this big field of rye. . . . If they're running and they don't look where they're going I have to come out from somewhere and *catch* them. That's all I'd do all day. I'd just be the catcher in the rye and all. I know it's crazy.[2]
The Catcher in the Rye [1951], ch. 22

9   There isn't anyone *anywhere* that isn't Seymour's Fat Lady. Don't you know that? Don't you know that goddam secret yet? And don't you know—*listen* to me, now—*don't you know who that Fat Lady really is?* . . . Ah, buddy. Ah, buddy. It's Christ Himself. Christ Himself, buddy.[3]
Franny and Zooey [1961]

Pete [Peter] Seeger
1919–

10   Where have all the flowers gone?
The girls have picked them every one.
Oh, when will they ever learn?
Where Have All the Flowers Gone? [1961]

[1]Translated by STUART WOOLF.
[2]See Anonymous, 778:6.
[3]Ellipses are in the original text.

11   We're waist deep in the Big Muddy
And the big fool says to push on.
Waist Deep in the Big Muddy [1967]

May Swenson
1919–1989

12   Body my house
my horse my hound
what will I do
when you are fallen

Question [1954], st. 1

13   Where can I go
without my mount
all eager and quick
How will I know
in thicket ahead
is danger or treasure
when Body my good
bright dog is dead

Ibid. st. 3

14   The summer that I was ten—
Can it be there was only one
summer that I was ten?
The Centaur [1958]

15   Youth is given. One must put it away
like a doll in a closet,
take it out and play with it only
on holidays.
How to Be Old [1963]

16   It's done
on a diamond,
and for fun.
It's about
home, and it's
about run.

Analysis of Baseball [1963]

17   My face
a negative in the slate
window,
I sit
in a lit
corridor that races
through a dark
one.

Riding the "A" [1963]

George Corley Wallace
1919–

18   I draw the line in the dust and toss the gauntlet before the feet of tyranny. And I say, Segregation now! Segregation tomorrow! Segregation forever!
Inaugural address as governor of Alabama
[January 14, 1963]

Alex Comfort
1920–

1   The Joy of Sex.   *Title of book [1972]*

Phyllis Dorothy James
1920–

2   That's all one asks of a sermon. No possible relevance to anything but itself.
The Skull Beneath the Skin [1982], bk. V, ch. 1

Pope John Paul II [Karol Wojtyla]
1920–

3   The greatness of work is inside man.
Easter Vigil and Other Poems [1979]. The Quarry, I, Material

4   We must ask ourselves whether there will continue to accumulate over the heads of this new generation of children the threat of common extermination. . . . Are the children to receive the arms race from us as a necessary inheritance?
Speech at the United Nations [October 2, 1979]

5   You are our dearly beloved brothers, and in a certain way, it could be said that you are our elder brothers.
On visit to the Synagogue of Rome [April 13, 1986]

Timothy Leary
1920–

6   Turn On, Tune In, Drop Out.
Title of lecture [1967]

Howard Nemerov
1920–1991

7   Flaubert wanted to write a novel
About nothing.
Style [1967]

8   There is in space a small black hole
Through which, say our astronomers,
The whole damn thing, the universe,
Must one day fall. That will be all.
Cosmic Comics [1975]

9   When Moses in Horeb struck the rock,
And water came forth out of the rock,
Some of the people were annoyed with Moses
And said he should have used a fancier stick.
On Certain Wits [1977]

10   The world is full of mostly invisible things,
And there is no way but putting the mind's eye,
Or its nose, in a book, to find them out,
Things like the square root of Everest
Or how many times Byron goes into Texas,

Or whether the law of the excluded middle
Applies west of the Rockies.
To David, about His Education [1977]

Mario Puzo
1920–

11   I'll make him an offer he can't refuse.
The Godfather [1969]

Stewart Lee Udall
1920–

12   The most common trait of all primitive peoples is a reverence for the lifegiving earth, and the native American shared this elemental ethic: the land was alive to his loving touch, and he, its son, was brother to all creatures.   *The Quiet Crisis [1963], ch. 1*

13   A land ethic for tomorrow should be as honest as Thoreau's *Walden,* and as comprehensive as the sensitive science of ecology. It should stress the oneness of our resources and the live-and-help-live logic of the great chain of life. If, in our haste to "progress," the economics of ecology are disregarded by citizens and policy makers alike, the result will be an ugly America.   *Ibid. 14*

Sloan Wilson
1920–

14   The Man in the Gray Flannel Suit.
Title of novel [1955]

Rodney Dangerfield
1921–

15   I can't get no respect.   *Comedy signature line*

Alexander Dubček
1921–

16   Socialism with a human face.
Slogan of the Prague Spring [1968]

Betty Naomi Friedan
1921–

17   When she stopped conforming to the conventional picture of femininity she finally began to enjoy being a woman.
The Feminine Mystique [1963], ch. 14

18   The problem that has no name — which is simply the fact that American women are kept from growing to their full human capacities — is taking a far greater toll on the physical and mental health of our country than any known disease.   *Ibid.*

1   Who knows what women can be when they are finally free to become themselves? Who knows what women's intelligence will contribute when it can be nourished without denying love? . . . The time is at hand when the voices of the feminine mystique can no longer drown out the inner voice that is driving women on to become complete.

Ibid. end

2   This uneasy sense of battles won, only to be fought over again, of battles that should have been won, according to all the rules, and yet are not, of battles that suddenly one does not really want to win, and the weariness of battle altogether—how many women feel it?   *The Second Stage [1981]*

Bill [William Henry] Mauldin
1921–

3   I feel like a fugitive from th' law of averages.
Up Front [1945]. Caption for cartoon

4   Look at an infantryman's eyes and you can tell how much war he has seen.   *Ibid.*

5   Beautiful view. Is there one for the enlisted men?
Ibid.

Julius Kambarage Nyerere
1921–

6   The survival of our wildlife is a matter of grave concern to all of us in Africa. These wild creatures amid the wild places they inhabit are not only important as a source of wonder and inspiration but are an integral part of our natural resources and of our future livelihood and well-being.
The Arusha Declaration, Tanganyika [September 1961]

Gene [Eugene Wesley] Roddenberry
1921–1991

7   Space—the final frontier . . . These are the voyages of the starship *Enterprise*. Its five-year mission: to explore strange new worlds, to seek out new life and new civilizations, to boldly go where no man has gone before.
Star Trek (television series) [1966–1969][1]

Andrei Dmitrievich Sakharov
1921–1989

8   A thermonuclear war cannot be considered a continuation of politics by other means. It would be a means to universal suicide.
Progress, Coexistence, and Intellectual Freedom [1968]

[1]See also Anonymous, 784:10.

9   Intellectual freedom is the only guarantee of a scientific-democratic approach to politics, economic development, and culture.   *Ibid.*

10   Profound thoughts arise only in debate, with a possibility of counterargument, only when there is a possibility of expressing not only correct ideas but also dubious ideas.   *Ibid.*

Peter Ustinov
1921–

11   The young need old men. They need men who are not ashamed of age, not pathetic imitations of themselves. . . . Parents are the bones on which children sharpen their teeth.
Dear Me [1977], ch. 18

Richard Purdy Wilbur
1921–

12 But up in his room by artificial light
My father paints the summer.
My Father Paints the Summer [1947]

13 The beautiful changes as a forest is changed
By a chameleon's tuning his skin to it.
The Beautiful Changes [1947], st. 2

14 I dreamt the past was never past redeeming:
But whether this was false or honest dreaming
I beg death's pardon now. And mourn the dead.
The Pardon [1950], last stanza

15   The eyes open to a cry of pulleys,
And spirited from sleep, the astounded soul
Hangs for a moment bodiless and simple
as false dawn.
            Outside the open window
The morning air is all awash with angels.
Love Calls Us to the Things of This World [1956]

16   The soul shrinks
From all that it is about to remember,
From the punctual rape of every blessèd day,
And cries,
   "Oh, let there be nothing on earth but laundry,
Nothing but rosy hands in the rising steam
And clear dances done in the sight of heaven."
Ibid.

17 Mind in its purest play is like some bat
That beats about in caverns all alone,
Contriving by a kind of senseless wit
Not to conclude against a wall of stone.

It has no need to falter or explore;
Darkly it knows what obstacles are there,
And so may weave and flitter, dip and soar
In perfect courses through the blackest air.

And has this simile a like perfection?
The mind is like a bat. Precisely. Save

That in the very happiest intellection
A graceful error may correct the cave.
Mind [1956]

1 The werewolf's painful change. Turning his head
away
On the sweaty bolster, he tries to remember
The mood of manhood,

But lies at last, as always,
Letting it happen, the fierce fur soft to his face,
Hearing with sharper ears.
Beasts [1956], st. 3, 4

2 Ask us, prophet, how we shall call
Our natures forth when that live tongue is all
Dispelled, that glass obscured or broken

In which we have said the rose of our love and
the clean
Horse of our courage, in which beheld
The singing locust of the soul unshelled,
And all we mean or wish to mean.
Advice to a Prophet [1961], st. 7, 8

3 All bitter things conduce to sweet,
   As this example shows;
Without the little spirochete
We'd have no chocolate to eat,
Nor would tobacco's fragrance greet
   The European nose.
*Pangloss's Song: A Comic Opera Lyric
[1961]*[1]

4 What can I do but move
From folly to defeat,
And call that sorrow sweet
That teaches us to see
The final face of love
In what we cannot be?
*Someone Talking to Himself [1961], last
stanza*

5 All that we do
Is touched with ocean, yet we remain
On the shore of what we know.
For Dudley [1969]

6   What you hope for
Is that at some point of the pointless journey,
Indoors or out, and when you least expect it,
Right in the middle of your stride, like that,
So neatly that you never feel a thing,
The kind assassin Sleep will draw a bead
And blow your brains out.
Walking to Sleep [1969]

Whitney Moore Young, Jr.
1921–1971

7   Black is beautiful when it is a slum kid studying
to enter college, when it is a man learning new skills
for a new job, or a slum mother battling to give her

kids a chance for a better life. But white is beautiful,
too, when it helps change society to make our system
work for black people also. White is ugly when it
oppresses blacks — and so is black ugly when black
people exploit other blacks. No race has a monopoly
on vice or virtue, and the worth of an individual is
not related to the color of his skin.
*Beyond Racism: Building an Open Society
[1969], ch. 4*

Jack Kerouac
1922–1969

8   We're a *beat* generation.[2]
*Remark [November 1948]. From JOHN CLELLON
HOLMES, Nothing More to Declare [1967]*

9   But then they danced down the street like dingledodies, and I shambled after as I've been doing all
my life after people who interest me, because the
only people for me are the mad ones, the ones who
are mad to live, mad to talk, mad to be saved, desirous of everything at the same time, the ones who
never yawn or say a commonplace thing, but burn,
burn, burn like fabulous yellow roman candles ex-
ploding like spiders across the stars and in the middle you see the blue centerlight pop and everybody
goes "Awww!"   *On the Road [1957]*

Philip Larkin
1922–1985

10 Why should I let the toad *work*
Squat on my life?
Can't I use my wit as a pitchfork
And drive the brute off?
Toads [1955]

11 Marrying left your maiden name disused.
Maiden Name [1955]

12 Give me your arm, old toad;
Help me down Cemetery Road.
Toads Revisited [1964]

13 Sexual intercourse began
In nineteen sixty-three
(Which was rather late for me) —
Between the end of the *Chatterley* ban
And the Beatles' first LP.
Annus Mirabilis [1974]

14 One of those old-type *natural* fouled-up guys.
Posterity [1974]

15 They fuck you up, your mum and dad.
They may not mean to, but they do.

[1] See Hellman, 716:10.

[2] A man is beat whenever he goes for broke and wagers the
sum of his resources on a single number; and the young generation has done that continually from early youth. — JOHN CLEL-
LON HOLMES [1906–1988], "*This Is the Beat Generation,*"
New York Times Magazine [November 16, 1952].

They fill you with the faults they had
And add some extra, just for you.
This Be The Verse [1974]

1 Perhaps being old is having lighted rooms
Inside your head, and people in them, acting.
People you know, yet can't quite name.
The Old Fools [1974]

2   Deprivation is for me what daffodils were for
Wordsworth.[1]   *Remark, in interview [1979]*

John Gillespie Magee, Jr.
1922–1941

3 Oh! I have slipped the surly bonds of Earth
And danced the skies on laughter-silvered wings;
Sunward I've climbed, and joined the tumbling
    mirth
Of sun-split clouds,—and done a hundred things
You have not dreamed of—wheeled and soared
    and swung
High in the sunlit silence. Hov'ring there,
I've chased the shouting wind along, and flung
My eager craft through footless halls of air . . .

Up, up the long, delirious, burning blue
I've topped the wind-swept heights with easy
    grace
Where never lark nor ever eagle flew—
And, while with silent lifting mind I've trod
The high untrespassed sanctity of space,
Put out my hand, and touched the face of God.
High Flight [1941][2]

Bob Merrill
1922–

4 People, people who need people
Are the luckiest people in the world.
People [1963][3]

John A. Powers
1922–1980

5   All systems go. Everything is A-OK.
*Statement as public information officer for U.S.
space program [1959–1964]*

Alain Robbe-Grillet
1922–

6   The true writer has nothing to say. What counts
is the way he says it.[4]   *For a New Novel [1963]*

[1]See Wordsworth, 375:19–376:1.
[2]Ellipses are in the original text.
[3]Music by JULE STYNE.
[4]Le véritable écrivain n'a rien à dire, il a seulement une
manière de le dire.

Alice Schaerr Rossi
1922–

7   The single most impressive fact about the attempt by American women to obtain the right to
vote is how long it took.
*The Feminist Papers [1973]. Along the Suffrage
Trail*

Charles Monroe Schulz
1922–

8   Happiness Is a Warm Puppy.
Title of book [1962]

9   You're a Good Man, Charlie Brown.
*Title of play [1967] based on Peanuts (comic
strip)*

10   *It was a dark and stormy night.*[5] *Suddenly a
scream pierced the air. . . .*   Good writing takes
enormous concentration.   *Peanuts [1988]*

Joseph Stefano
1922–

11   A boy's best friend is his mother.
*Psycho (screenplay) [1960], spoken by Anthony
Perkins*

Kurt Vonnegut, Jr.
1922–

12   So it goes.
Slaughterhouse-Five [1969], ch. 1 and passim

13   You know—we've had to imagine the war here,
and we have imagined that it was being fought by
aging men like ourselves. We had forgotten that
wars were fought by babies. When I saw those
freshly shaved faces, it was a shock. "My God, my
God—" I said to myself, "it's the Children's Crusade."   *Ibid. ch. 5*

14   High school is closer to the core of the American
experience than anything else I can think of.
*From his introduction to Our Time Is Now:
Notes from the High School Underground,
edited by JOHN BIRMINGHAM [1970]*

Italo Calvino
1923–1985

15   I have tried to remove weight, sometimes from
people, sometimes from heavenly bodies, sometimes
from cities; above all I have tried to remove weight
from the structure of stories and from language.
Six Memos for the Next Millennium [1988]

[5]See Bulwer-Lytton, 429:2.

Paddy Chayevsky
1923–1981

1   I'm mad as hell, and I'm not going to take it any more.   *Network, screenplay [1976]*

James Dickey
1923–

2 A shudder of joy runs up
The trunk: the needles tingle;
One bird uncontrollably cries.
The wind changes round, and I stir
Within another's life. Whose life?
In the Tree House at Night [1962]

3 And I to my motorcycle
Parked like the soul of the junkyard
Restored, a bicycle fleshed
With power, and tore off
Up Highway 106, continually
Drunk on the wind in my mouth,
Wringing the handlebar for speed,
Wild to be wreckage forever.
Cherrylog Road [1963]

4 All families lie together, though some are burned
alive.
The others try to feel
For them. Some can, it is often said.
The Firebombing [1965]

5   All day I climb myself
Bowlegged up those damned poles   rooster-heeled
in all
Kinds of weather.
Power and Light [1967]

6 And this is the house I pass through on my way
To power and light.
Ibid.

7 We have all been in rooms
We cannot die in.
Adultery [1967]

Robert B. Elliott
1923–
and
Raymond H. Goulding
1922–1990

8   Hang by your thumbs, everybody! Write if you get work!
Bob and Ray radio show [1946], signature closing line

Nadine Gordimer
1923–

9   That was one of the things she held against missionaries: how they stressed Christ's submission to humiliation, and so had conditioned the people of Africa to humiliation by the white man.
Not for Publication [1965], title story

10   She filled her house with blacks, and white parsons who went around preaching Jesus was a revolutionary, and then when the police walked in she was surprised.   *The Conservationist [1974]*

Joseph Heller
1923–

11   He had decided to live forever or die in the attempt, and his only mission each time he went up was to come down alive.   *Catch-22 [1961], ch. 3*

12   There was only one catch and that was Catch-22, which specified that a concern for one's own safety in the face of dangers that were real and immediate was the process of a rational mind. Orr was crazy and could be grounded. All he had to do was ask; and as soon as he did, he would no longer be crazy and would have to fly more missions. . . . If he flew them he was crazy and didn't have to; but if he didn't want to he was sane and had to. . . . "That's some catch, that Catch-22," he [Yossarian] observed. "It's the best there is," Doc Daneeka agreed.   *Ibid. 5*

Henry Alfred Kissinger
1923–

13   Power is the great aphrodisiac.[1]
In the New York Times [January 19, 1971]

14   History knows no resting places and no plateaus.
White House Years [1979], ch. 3

15   The management of a balance of power is a permanent undertaking, not an exertion that has a foreseeable end.   *Ibid. 5*

Denise Levertov
1923–

16 I like to find
what's not found
at once, but lies
within something of another nature
in repose, distinct.
Pleasures [1959]

17 Marvelous Truth, confront us
at every turn,
in every guise.
Matins [1962], VII

18 Two by two in the ark of
the ache of it.
The Ache of Marriage [1964]

[1]Also quoted as: Power is the ultimate aphrodisiac.

Norman Mailer
1923–

1   In the air the Pentagon would then, went the presumption, turn orange and vibrate until all evil emissions had fled this levitation. At that point the war in Vietnam would end.
The Armies of the Night [1968], pt. III, ch. 5

2   A night journey on a bus was one of the few times when everything ambitious, wild, overconceived, hopeless, garish, and suffocatingly technical in American life nonetheless came together long enough to give the citizens a little peace, for it was only when they were on the move that Americans could feel anchored in their memories.
Ibid. IV, 5

3   So we think of Marilyn who was every man's love affair with America, Marilyn Monroe who was blonde and beautiful and had a sweet little rinky-dink of a voice and all the cleanliness of all the clean American backyards. She was our angel, the sweet angel of sex, and the sugar of sex came up from her like a resonance of sound in the clearest grain of a violin.   *Marilyn [1973], ch. 1*

4   Then the Warden said, "Do you have anything you'd like to say?" and Gary looked up at the ceiling and hesitated, then said, "Let's do it." That was it.
The Executioner's Song [1979], ch. 38

Hank Williams
1923–1953

5 Hear that lonesome whippoorwill?
He sounds too blue to fly.
The midnight train is whining low,
I'm so lonesome I could cry.
I'm So Lonesome I Could Cry [1942]

James Baldwin
1924–1987

6   My life, my *real* life, was in danger, and not from anything other people might do but from the hatred I carried in my own heart.
Notes of a Native Son [1955], title essay

7   Harlem had needed something to smash. To smash something is the ghetto's chronic need.
Ibid.

8   If we do not now dare everything, the fulfillment of that prophecy, re-created from the Bible in song by a slave, is upon us: *God gave Noah the rainbow sign, No more water, the fire next time!*
The Fire Next Time [1963], end

Robert Bolt
1924–

9   The law is not a "light" for you or any man to see by; the law is not an instrument of any kind. The law

is a causeway upon which, so long as he keeps to it, a citizen may walk safely.
A Man for All Seasons [1960], act II

George Herbert Walker Bush
1924–

10   Voodoo economics.
Remark, presidential primary campaign [1980]

11   We are a nation of communities, of tens and tens of thousands of ethnic, religious, social, business, labor union, neighborhood, regional and other organizations, all of them varied, voluntary, and unique . . . a brilliant diversity spread like stars, like a thousand points of light in a broad and peaceful sky.[1]
Acceptance speech, Republican National Convention, New Orleans [August 18, 1988]

12   The Congress will push me to raise taxes, and I'll say no, and they'll push, and I'll say no, and they'll push again. And all I can say to them is read my lips: No New Taxes.   *Ibid.*

13   I want a kinder, gentler nation.   *Ibid.*

Truman Capote
1924–1984

14   It was a terrible, strange-looking hotel. But Little Sunshine stayed on: it was his rightful home, he said, for if he went away, as he had once upon a time, other voices, other rooms, voices lost and clouded, strummed his dreams.
Other Voices, Other Rooms [1948], ch. 5

15   [It] isn't writing at all—it's typing.
Comment [1959] on Beat Generation writers.
From GERALD CLARKE, *Capote [1988]*

16   I didn't want to harm the man. I thought he was a very nice gentleman. Soft-spoken. I thought so right up to the moment I cut his throat.
In Cold Blood [1966]

Jimmy [James Earl, Jr.] Carter
1924–

17   No poor, rural, weak, or black person should ever again have to bear the additional burden of being deprived of the opportunity for an education, a job, or simple justice.
Inaugural address as governor, Atlanta [January 12, 1971]

18   We believe that the first time we're born, as children, it's human life given to us; and when we accept

[1]Instantly he could see the town below now, coiling in a thousand fumes of homely smoke, now winking into a thousand points of friendly light its glorious small design, its aching passionate assurances of walls, warmth, comfort, food, and love.—THOMAS WOLFE, *The Web and the Rock [1939]*

Jesus as our Savior, it's a new life. That's what "born again" means.[1]

In an interview with Robert L. Turner [March 16, 1976]

1   I've looked on a lot of women with lust. I've committed adultery in my heart many times. This is something that God recognizes I will do—and I have done it—and God forgives me for it.

Interview in Playboy magazine [October 1976]

2   The first step in providing economic equality for women is to ensure a stable economy in which every person who wants to work can work.

Speech at Women's Agenda Conference, Washington, D.C. [October 2, 1976]

3   We are of course a nation of differences. Those differences don't make us weak. They're the source of our strength. . . . The question is not when we came here . . . but why our families came here. And what we did after we arrived.

Speech at Al Smith Dinner, New York City [October 21, 1976]

4   Two problems of our country—energy and malaise.

Remark at town meeting, Bardstown, Kentucky [July 31, 1979]

Arthur Charles Erickson
1924–

5   North American civilization is one of the ugliest to have emerged in human history, and it has engulfed the world. Asphalt and exhaust fumes clog the villages. . . . This great, though disastrous, culture can only change as we begin to stand off and see . . . the inveterate materialism which has become the model for cultures around the globe.

Speech at Simon Fraser University [1973]

6   What the West has thrown on the waters of the world drifts back to us on a tide of cultural pollution appalling to behold.

Speech at International Congress of Architecture in Iran [1974]

Russell Baker
1925–

7   The only thing I was fit for was to be a writer, and this notion rested solely on my suspicion that I would never be fit for real work, and that writing didn't require any.   *Growing Up [1982], ch. 9*

Yogi [Lawrence Peter] Berra
1925–

8   It ain't over till it's over.

Comment on National League pennant race [1973]

[1]See *John 3:3, 39:43.*

9   How can you think and hit at the same time?
    Remark

10   In baseball, you don't know nothing.   *Remark*

11   Slump? I ain't in no slump. I just ain't hitting.
    Remark

12   You can observe a lot by watching.   *Remark*

13   If people don't want to come out to the ball park, nobody's going to stop them.   *Attributed*

14   It was déjà vu all over again.   *Attributed*

15   When you come to a fork in the road, take it.
    Attributed

Lenny Bruce
1925–1966

16   People should be taught what is, not what should be. All my humor is based on destruction and despair. If the whole world were tranquil, without disease and violence, I'd be standing in the breadline.
    The Essential Lenny Bruce [1967]. Epigraph

17   I'll die young, but it's like kissing God.
    On his drug addiction

Barbara Pierce Bush
1925–

18   Somewhere out in this audience may even be someone who will one day follow in my footsteps, and preside over the White House as the President's spouse. I wish him well!
    Remarks at Wellesley College Commencement [June 1, 1990]

John Daniel Ehrlichman
1925–

19   It'll play in Peoria.[2]   *Phrase [1970]*

20   I think we ought to let him [Patrick Gray] hang there. Let him twist slowly, slowly in the wind.
    Telephone conversation with John Dean [March 7/8, 1973]

Frantz Fanon
1925–1961

21   When I search for man in the technique and the style of Europe, I see only a succession of negations of man, and an avalanche of murders.
    The Wretched of the Earth[3] [1961]. Conclusion

Maxine Kumin
1925–

22 I took the lake between my legs.
    Morning Swim [1965]

[2]Meaning politically acceptable to "middle America."
[3]Translated by CONSTANCE FARRINGTON.
See Pottier, 476:18.

1 Something went crabwise
across the snow this morning.
The Presence [1970]

2 Love, we are a small pond.
We Are [1970]

3 Meanwhile
let us cast one shadow
in air or water.
Turning To [1972]

4 Our daughters and sons have burst
from the marionette show
leaving a tangle of strings
and gone into the unlit audience.
The Absent Ones [1972]

5 Can it be
I am the only Jew residing in Danville, Kentucky,
looking for matzoh in the Safeway and the
A & P?
Living Alone with Jesus [1972]

6 When Sleeping Beauty wakes up
she is almost fifty years old.
Time to start planning her retirement cottage.
The Archaeology of a Marriage [1978]

Malcolm X [El-Hajj Malik El-Shabazz]
1925–1965

7 If you're born in America with a black skin,
you're born in prison.   *Interview [June 1963]*

8 We are not fighting for integration, nor are we
fighting for separation. We are fighting for recognition as human beings. We are fighting for . . .
human rights.
Speech, Black Revolution, New York [1964]

9 The day that the black man takes an uncompromising step and realizes that he's within his rights,
when his own freedom is being jeopardized, to use
any means necessary to bring about his freedom or
put a halt to that injustice, I don't think he'll be by
himself.
*Oxford Union Society debate [December 3,
1964]*

10 [On the assassination of President John F. Kennedy:] It was, as I saw it, a case of "the chickens
coming home to roost." I said that the hate in white
men had not stopped with the killing of defenseless
black people, but that hate, allowed to spread unchecked, had finally struck down this country's
Chief Magistrate.
*Autobiography (as told to ALEX HALEY) [1964],
ch. 16*

Zhores Aleksandrovich Medvedev
1925–

11 Science and technology, and the various forms of
art, all unite humanity in a single and interconnected
system. As science progresses, the worldwide cooperation of scientists and technologists becomes more
and more of a special and distinct intellectual community of friendship, in which, in place of antagonism, there is growing up a mutually advantageous
sharing of work, a coordination of efforts, a common language for the exchange of information, and
a solidarity, which are in many cases independent of
the social and political differences of individual
states.   *The Medvedev Papers [1970], preface*

Mishima Yukio [Kimitake Hiraoka]
1925–1970

12 My solitude grew more and more obese, like a
pig.   *Temple of the Golden Pavilion[1] [1959]*

Flannery O'Connor
1925–1964

13 Does one's integrity ever lie in what he is not able
to do? I think that usually it does, for free will does
not mean one will, but many wills conflicting in one
man. Freedom cannot be conceived simply.
Wise Blood [1952], foreword

14 "She would of been a good woman," The Misfit
said, "if it had been somebody there to shoot her
every minute of her life."
A Good Man Is Hard to Find [1955]

15 The novel is an art form and when you use it
for anything other than art, you pervert it. . . .
If you manage to use it successfully for social, religious, or other purposes, it is because you make it
art first.
*Letter to Father John McCown [May 9,
1956]*

16 I doubt if the texture of Southern life is any more
grotesque than that of the rest of the nation, but it
does seem evident that the Southern writer is particularly adept at recognizing the grotesque; and to
recognize the grotesque, you have to have some notion of what is not grotesque and why.
Talk at Notre Dame University [spring 1957]

17 Knowing who you are is good for one generation
only.
*Everything That Rises Must Converge [1965],
title story*

Frank R. Pierson
1925–

18 What we've got here is failure to communicate.
Cool Hand Luke (screenplay) [1967]

[1]Translated by IVAN MORRIS.

Margaret Hilda Roberts Thatcher
1925–

1   I like Mr. Gorbachev. We can do business together.   *On their meeting [December 17, 1984]*

2   If you lead a country like Britain . . . you have
to have a touch of iron about you.
*On her reputation as The Iron Lady [March 21,
1986]*

3   In politics, if you want anything said, ask a man.
If you want anything done, ask a woman.
Saying

Gore Vidal
1925–

4   The theater needs continual reminders that there
is nothing more debasing than the work of those
who do well what is not worth doing at all.
Quoted in Newsweek [March 25, 1968]

5   Some writers take to drink, others take to audiences.   *Interview in Paris Review [1981]*

6   He turned being a Big Loser into a perfect triumph by managing to lose the presidency in a way
bigger and more original than anyone else had ever
lost it before.
Richard Nixon in Esquire [December 1983]

A. R. Ammons
1926–

7   Though I have looked everywhere
I can find nothing lowly
in the universe.
Still [1972]

8   In nature there are few sharp lines.
Corson's Inlet [1972], l. 31

9   No humbling of reality to precept.
Ibid. l. 116

10   Counting my numberless fingers.
Mountain Talk [1972]

11   Not so much looking for the shape
as being available
to any shape that may be
summoning itself
through me
from the self not mine but ours.
Poetics [1972]

12   I attended the burial of all my rosy feelings:
I performed the rites, simple and decisive.
Transaction [1972]

13   The stones are
prepared: they are round and ready.
Upland [1972]

14   I don't know about you,
but I'm sick of good poems, all those little
rondures
splendidly brought off, painted gourds on a shelf.
Sphere [1974]

Chuck Berry
[Charles Edward Anderson]
1926–

15   Roll over Beethoven
And tell Tchaikovsky the news.
Roll over Beethoven [1956]

16   He never learned to read or write so well
But he could play a guitar just like ringing a bell.
Johnny B. Goode [1958]

Robert Bly
1926–

17   I have wandered in a face, for hours,
Passing through dark fires.
I have risen to a body
Not yet born,
Existing like a light around the body,
Through which the body moves like a sliding
moon.
*The Light Around the Body [1967]. Looking
into a Face*

18   The sound of the rampaging Missouri,
Bending the reeds again and again—something
inside us
Like a ghost train in the Rockies
About to be buried in snow!
Its long hoot
Making the owl in the Douglas fir turn his head.
*Ibid. Asian Peace Offers Rejected Without
Publication*

Mel Brooks
1926–

19   That's it, baby, if you've got it, flaunt it.
The Producers (screenplay) [1968]

20   Springtime for Hitler and Germany,
Deutschland is happy and gay.
We're moving to a faster pace,
Look out, here comes the Master Race!
Ibid. Springtime for Hitler

Fidel Castro
1926–

21   History will absolve me.[1]
*At his trial for raid on Moncada barracks
[October 16, 1953]*

[1]La Historia me absolvera.

1   We are not only a Latin-American nation; we are an Afro-American nation also.
Speech in Havana [1977]

Allen Ginsberg
1926–

2   I saw you, Walt Whitman, childless, lonely old grubber, poking among the meats in the refrigerator and eyeing the grocery boys.
   I heard you asking questions of each: Who killed the pork chops? What price bananas? Are you my Angel?   *A Supermarket in California [1955]*

3 America I'm putting my queer shoulder to the wheel.
America [1956]

4 I saw the best minds of my generation destroyed
       by madness, starving hysterical naked,
   dragging themselves through the negro streets at
       dawn looking for an angry fix
   angelheaded hipsters burning for the ancient
       heavenly connection to the starry dynamo in
       the machinery of night.
Howl [1956]

5   This is the end, the redemption from Wilderness, way for the Wonderer, House sought for All, black handkerchief washed clean by weeping.
Kaddish [1959], I

6 O mother
   what have I left out
   O mother
   what have I forgotten
Ibid. IV

James Ingram Merrill
1926–

7 Again last night I dreamed the dream called
       Laundry.
The Mad Scene [1966]

8 I yearned for the kind of unseasoned telling
       found
   In legends, fairy tales, a tone licked clean
   Over the centuries by mild old tongues,
   Grandam to cub, serene, anonymous.
The Book of Ephraim [1976], sec. A

9 What we dream up must be lived down, I think.
Ibid. I

10   HE PREFERS
   LIVE MUSIC TO A PATRON'S HUMDRUM SPHERES
   Is this permitted? WHEN U ARE MOZART YES
   He's living *now*? As what? A BLACK ROCK STAR
   WHATEVER THAT IS.
Ibid. P

Newton Norman Minow
1926–

11   When television is bad, nothing is worse. I invite you to sit down in front of your television set when your station goes on the air . . . and keep your eyes glued to that set until the station signs off. I can assure you that you will observe a vast wasteland.
Speech as chairman of the Federal Communications Commission to National Association of Broadcasters, Washington, D.C. [May 9, 1961]

Peter Shaffer
1926–

12   We keep saying old people are square. Then when they suddenly aren't—we don't like it!
Equus [1973], act II, sc. 31

William DeWitt Snodgrass
1926–

13 It was the nature of the thing:
   No moon outlives its leaving night,
   No sun its day. And I went on
   Rich in the loss of all I sing
   To the threshold of waking light,
   To larksong and the live, gray dawn.
   So night by night, my life has gone.
Orpheus [1959]

14 The sleek, expensive girls I teach,
   Younger and pinker every year,
   Bloom gradually out of reach.
April Inventory [1959]

15 Though trees turn bare and girls turn wives,
   We shall afford our costly seasons;
   There is a gentleness survives
   That will outspeak and has its reasons.
   There is a loveliness exists,
   Preserves us, not for specialists.
Ibid.

John Ashbery
1927–

16 As I sit looking out of a window of the building
   I wish I did not have to write the instruction
       manual on the uses of a new metal.
The Instruction Manual [1956]

17   You and I
   Are suddenly what the trees try
   To tell us we are:
   That their merely being there
   Means something; that soon
   We may touch, love, explain.
Some Trees [1956]

1 As Parmigianino did it, the right hand
Bigger than the head, thrust at the viewer
And swerving easily away, as though to protect
What it advertises.
Self-Portrait in a Convex Mirror [1975]

2 Something like living occurs, a movement
Out of the dream into its codification.
Ibid.

Cesar Estrada Chavez
1927–

3   Viva la huelga [Long live the strike]!
Slogan of the United Farm Workers [the 1960s]

Günter Grass
1927–

4   You can declare at the very start that it's impossible to write a novel nowadays, but then, behind your
back, so to speak, give birth to a whopper, a novel
to end all novels.
The Tin Drum [1959],[1] *bk. I, The Wide Skirt*

5   Even bad books are books and therefore sacred.
Ibid. Rasputin and the Alphabet

Ronald David Laing
1927–

6   We are born into a world where alienation awaits
us.
The Politics of Experience [1967], introduction

7   Madness need not be all breakdown. It may also
be breakthrough. It is potentially liberation and
renewal as well as enslavement and existential
death.   *Ibid. ch. 6*

William Stanley Merwin
1927–

8 You came back to us in a dream and we were not
here.
Come Back [1967]

9 The dead will think the living are worth it we will
know
Who we are
And we will all enlist again.
When the War Is Over [1967]

10 Every year without knowing it I have passed the
day.
For the Anniversary of My Death [1967]

11 Of course there is nothing the matter with the
stars
It is my emptiness among them

[1]Translated by RALPH MANHEIM.

While they drift farther away in the invisible
morning.
In the Winter of My Thirty-eighth Year [1967]

12 I think I was cold in the womb.
The Forebears [1971]

13 I am the son of the first fish who climbed ashore
but the news has not yet reached my bowels.
Psalm: Our Fathers [1971]

14   Like shadows
of the plumbing
that is all that is left
of the great city.
The Plumbing [1971]

15 Some alien blessing
is on its way to us.
Midnight in Early Spring [1971]

16 Oh pile of white shirts who is coming
to breathe in your shapes.
The Night of the Shirts [1971]

Andy Warhol
1927–1987

17   In the future everyone will be world-famous for
fifteen minutes.
*Catalogue of his photo exhibition in Stockholm
[1968]*

Edward Franklin Albee
1928–

18   *George:* Who's afraid of Virginia Woolf . . .
Martha: I . . . am . . . George . . . I am.
Who's Afraid of Virginia Woolf? [2] *[1962]. The
Exorcism*

19   You gotta have a swine to show you where the
truffles are.   *Ibid. act II, Walpurgisnacht*

[Avram] Noam Chomsky
1928–

20   Colorless green ideas sleep furiously.[3]
Syntactic Structures [1957], ch. 2

Mary Daly
1928–

21   If God is male, then the male is God. The divine
patriarch castrates women as long as he is allowed to
live on in the human imagination.
Beyond God the Father [1973], ch. 1

[2]Who's Afraid of the Big Bad Wolf?—*Title of song,* WALT
DISNEY *film cartoon Three Little Pigs [1933]*
Ellipses are in the original text.
[3]Illustrating how meaning and syntax are independent of
each other.

Gabriel García Márquez
1928–

1   It was foreseen that the city of mirrors (or mirages) would be wiped out by the wind and exiled from the memory of men at the precise moment when Aureliano Babilonia would finish deciphering the parchments, and that everything written on them was unrepeatable since time immemorial and forevermore, because races condemned to one hundred years of solitude did not have a second opportunity on earth.

One Hundred Years of Solitude (Cien Años de Soledad) [1967][1]

Larry Gelbart
1928–
and
Burt Shevelove
1915–

2   A Funny Thing Happened on the Way to the Forum.   *Title of musical comedy [1962]*

Michael Harrington
1928–1989

3   The other America, the America of poverty, is hidden today in a way that it never was before. Its millions are socially invisible to the rest of us. . . . The very development of American society is creating a new kind of blindness about poverty. The poor are increasingly slipping out of the very experience and consciousness of the nation.

The Other America: Poverty in the United States [1962], ch. 1

4   For the urban poor the police are those who arrest you. In almost any slum there is a vast conspiracy against the forces of law and order.   *Ibid.*

Tom [Thomas Andrew] Lehrer
1928–

5   Remember the war against Franco?
That's the kind where each of us belongs.
Though he may have won all the battles,
We had all the good songs.
   The Folk Song Army [1965]

6   "Once the rockets are up, who cares where they
   come down?
That's not my department," says Wernher von
   Braun.
   Wernher von Braun [1965]

7   It is a sobering thought that when Mozart was my age, he had been dead for two years.
   That Was the Year That Was [1965]

Desmond Morris
1928–

8   There are one hundred and ninety-three living species of monkeys and apes. One hundred and ninety-two of them are covered with hair. The exception is a naked ape self-named *Homo sapiens*.
   The Naked Ape [1967], Introduction

Cynthia Ozick
1928–

9   The whole peninsula of Florida was weighted down with regret. Everyone had left behind a real life.   *Rosa [1984]*

10   I wanted to use what I was, to be what I was born to be—not to have a "career," but to be that straightforward obvious unmistakable animal, a writer.   *Metaphor and Memory [1989]*

Robert Maynard Pirsig
1928–

11   Other people can talk about how to expand the destiny of mankind. I just want to talk about how to fix a motorcycle. I think that what I have to say has more lasting value.
   Zen and the Art of Motorcycle Maintenance [1974], pt. III, ch. 25

Anne Sexton
1928–1974

12   You, Doctor Martin, walk
from breakfast to madness. Late August,
I speed through the antiseptic tunnel where the
      moving dead still talk
of pushing their bones against the thrust
of cure. And I am queen of this summer hotel
      or the laughing bee on a stalk
      of death.
   You, Doctor Martin [1960], st. 1

13   I have gone out, a possessed witch,
haunting the black air, braver at night.
   Her Kind [1960]

14   A woman like that is not a woman, quite.
I have been her kind.
   Ibid.

15   Leaving the page of the book carelessly open,
something unsaid, the phone off the hook
and the love, whatever it was, an infection.
   Wanting to Die [1966], last stanza

16   Little Girl, My Stringbean, My Lovely Woman.
   Title of poem [1966]

[1]Translated by GREGORY RABASSA.

1 Beauty is a simple passion,
but, oh my friends, in the end
you will dance the fire dance in iron shoes.
Snow White and the Seven Dwarfs [1971]

2 Though they washed her with wine
and rubbed her with butter
it was to no avail.
She lay as still as a gold piece.
Ibid.

3 I would like a simple life
yet all night I am laying
poems away in a long box.
The Ambition Bird [1973], st. 4

Alvin Toffler
1928–

4 Future shock . . . the shattering stress and disorientation that we induce in individuals by subject-
ing them to too much change in too short a time.
Future Shock [1970], Introduction

James Dewey Watson
1928–
and
Francis Henry Crompton Crick
1916–

5 This [double helix] structure has novel features
which are of considerable biological interest. . . .
It has not escaped our notice that the specific pairing
we have postulated immediately suggests a possible
copying mechanism for the genetic material.
*Molecular Structure of Nucleic Acids, in Nature
[April 25, 1963]*[1]

Elie Wiesel
1928–

6 I was the accuser, God the accused. My eyes were
open and I was alone—terribly alone in a world
without God and without man.   *Night [1958]*[2]

7 You'll try to reveal what should remain hidden,
you'll try to incite people to learn from the past and
rebel, but they will refuse to believe you. They will
not listen to you. . . . You'll possess the truth, you
already do; but it's the truth of a madman.
A Beggar in Jerusalem [1970], ch. 5[3]

8 Rejected by mankind, the condemned do not go
so far as to reject it in turn. Their faith in history
remains unshaken, and one may well wonder why.

[1] We told her [the typist of their article] that she was partici-
pating in perhaps the most famous event in biology since Darwin's book.—WATSON, *The Double Helix* [1968].

[2] Translated by STELLA RODWAY.

[3] Translated by LILY EDELMAN and ELIE WIESEL.

They do not despair. The proof: they persist in sur-
viving not only to survive, but to testify.
The victims elect to become witnesses.
One Generation After [1970]. Readings[3]

Harvey Gallagher Cox
1929–

9 The Secular City.   *Title of book [1965]*

Anne Frank
1929–1945

10 Whoever is happy will make others happy too.
He who has courage and faith will never perish in
misery!
*Anne Frank: The Diary of a Young Girl
[1952].*[4] *March 7, 1944*

11 What *one* Christian does is his own responsibility,
what *one* Jew does is thrown back at all Jews.
Ibid. May 22, 1944

12 [Daddy] said: "All children must look after their
own upbringing." Parents can only give good advice
or put them on the right paths, but the final forming
of a person's character lies in their own hands.
Ibid. July 15, 1944

13 In spite of everything I still believe that people are
really good at heart.   *Ibid.*

X. J. Kennedy
1929–

14 One-woman waterfall, she wears
Her slow descent like a long cape
And pausing, on the final stair
Collects her motions into shape.
Nude Descending a Staircase, last stanza

15 I rang them up while touring Timbucktoo,
Those bosom chums to whom you're known as
"Who?"
To Someone Who Insisted I Look Up Someone

Martin Luther King, Jr.
1929–1968

16 The Negro's great stumblingblock is not the
White Citizen's Counciler or the Ku Klux Klanner,
but the white moderate who is more devoted to
"order" than to justice, . . . who paternalistically
believes he can set the timetable for another man's
freedom.
Letter from Birmingham jail [April 16, 1963]

17 If a man hasn't discovered something that he will
die for, he isn't fit to live.
Speech in Detroit [June 23, 1963]

[4] Translated by B. M. MOOYART.

1   I have a dream that one day on the red hills of Georgia the sons of former slaves and the sons of former slaveowners will be able to sit down together at the table of brotherhood.

Speech at Civil Rights March on Washington [August 28, 1963]

2   I have a dream that my four little children will one day live in a nation where they will not be judged by the color of their skin, but by the content of their character.   *Ibid.*

3   When we let freedom ring, when we let it ring from every village and every hamlet, from every state and every city, we will be able to speed up that day when all of God's children, black men and white men, Jews and Gentiles, Protestants and Catholics, will be able to join hands and sing in the words of the old Negro spiritual, "Free at last! Free at last! Thank God Almighty, we are free at last!"[1]

Ibid.

4   Nonviolence is the answer to the crucial political and moral questions of our time; the need for man to overcome oppression and violence without resorting to oppression and violence.

Man must evolve for all human conflict a method which rejects revenge, aggression and retaliation. The foundation of such a method is love.[2]

Speech accepting the Nobel Peace Prize [December 11, 1964]

5   The tortuous road which has led from Montgomery to Oslo is a road over which millions of Negroes are traveling to find a new sense of dignity. It will, I am convinced, be widened into a superhighway of justice.   *Ibid.*

6   I refuse to accept the idea that the "isness" of man's present nature makes him morally incapable of reaching up for the "oughtness" that forever confronts him.   *Ibid.*

7   I refuse to accept the cynical notion that nation after nation must spiral down a militaristic stairway into the hell of nuclear destruction. I believe that unarmed truth and unconditional love will have the final word in reality.   *Ibid.*

8   The Negro was willing to risk martyrdom in order to move and stir the social conscience of his community and the nation . . . he would force his oppressor to commit his brutality openly, with the rest of the world looking on. . . . Nonviolent resistance paralyzed and confused the power structures against which it was directed.

Why We Can't Wait [1964]

9   Like anybody, I would like to live a long life. Longevity has its place. But I'm not concerned about that now. I just want to do God's will. And He's

allowed me to go up to the mountain. And I've looked over, and I've seen the promised land. I may not get there with you, but I want you to know tonight that we as a people will get to the promised land. . . .

So I'm happy tonight. I'm not worried about anything. I'm not fearing any man.

Address to sanitation workers, Memphis, Tennessee [April 3, 1968], the night before his assassination

Milan Kundera
1929–

10   The struggle against power is the struggle of memory against forgetting.

The Book of Laughter and Forgetting [1980],[3] pt. I, sec. ii

11   The only reason people want to be masters of the future is to change the past.   *Ibid. xvii*

12   Her drama was a drama not of heaviness but of lightness. What fell to her lot was not the burden but the unbearable lightness of being.

The Unbearable Lightness of Being [1984],[3] pt. III

13   Kitsch excludes everything from its purview which is essentially unacceptable in human existence.   *Ibid. VI*

14   The wisdom of the novel comes from having a question for everything. When Don Quixote went out into the world, that world turned into a mystery before his eyes. That is the legacy of the first European novel.

A Talk with the Author by PHILIP ROTH *[1980][4]*

Ursula Kroeber Le Guin
1929–

15   The king was pregnant.

The Left Hand of Darkness [1969], ch. 8

16   He had grown up in a country run by politicians who sent the pilots to man the bombers to kill the babies to make the world safer for children to grow up in.   *The Lathe of Heaven [1971], ch. 6*

Claes Oldenburg
1929–

17   I am for an art that tells you the time of day, or where such and such a street is. I am for an art that helps old ladies across the street.

Statement for exhibition catalogue [1961]

---

[1]King's epitaph, South View Cemetery, Atlanta, Georgia. See Anonymous: Spirituals, 794:12.
[2]See Gandhi, 606:13.

[3]Translated by MICHAEL HENRY HEIM.
[4]Translated by VERA KUNDERA and PETER KUSSI.

John James Osborne
1929–

1   Look Back in Anger.   *Title of play [1956]*

Adrienne Rich
1929–

2 Your mind now, moldering like wedding-cake,
heavy with useless experience, rich
with suspicion, rumor, fantasy,
crumbling to pieces under the knife-edge
of mere fact.
            Snapshots of a Daughter-in-Law [1963], st. 1

3 A thinking woman sleeps with monsters.
The beak that grips her, she becomes.
                                Ibid. 3

4 Piece by piece I seem
to re-enter the world.
                    Necessities of Life [1966]

5 My visionary anger cleansing my sight.
                        The Stranger [1973]

6 I am the androgyne.
                            Ibid.

7 There is a ladder.
The ladder is always there
hanging innocently
close to the side of the schooner.
                    Diving into the Wreck [1973]

8 I came to explore the wreck.
                            Ibid.

9 I came to see the damage that was done
and the treasures that prevail.
I stroke the beam of my lamp
slowly along the flank
of something more permanent
than fish or weed.
                            Ibid.

10   Re-vision—the act of looking back, of seeing
with fresh eyes, of entering an old text from a new
critical direction—is for women more than a chapter in cultural history: it is an act of survival.
    *On Lies, Secrets, and Silence [1979]. When We
    Dead Awaken*

Chinua Achebe
1930–

11   In such a regime, I say, you died a good death if
your life had inspired someone to come forward and
shoot your murderer in the chest—without asking
to be paid.
    A Man of the People [1966], closing sentence

Neil Alden Armstrong
1930–

12   Houston, Tranquility Base here. The Eagle has
landed.   *On reaching the moon [July 20, 1969]*

13   That's one small step for [a] man, one giant leap
for mankind.
        On first stepping on the moon [July 20, 1969]

Buck Henry
1930–
and
Calder Willingham
1922–

14   Ben—I want to say one word to you—just one
word—plastics.
                The Graduate (screenplay) [1967][1]

Ted [Edward J.] Hughes
1930–

15 Stare at the monster: remark
How difficult it is to define just what
Amounts to monstrosity in that
Very ordinary appearance.
                        Famous Poet [1957]

16 My feet are locked upon the rough bark.
It took the whole of Creation
To produce my foot, my each feather:
Now I hold Creation in my foot
Or fly up, and revolve it all slowly—
I kill where I please because it is all mine.
                        Hawk Roosting [1960]

17 Daylong this tomcat lies stretched flat
As an old rough mat, no mouth and no eyes,
Continual wars and wives are what
Have tattered his ears and battered his head.
                        Esther's Tomcat [1960]

18 The rat is in the trap, it is in the trap,
And attacking heaven and earth with a mouthful
        of screeches like torn tin.
                        The Rat's Dance [1967]

Harold Pinter
1930–

19   I said to this monk . . . I heard you got a stock
of shoes here. Piss off, he said to me.
                    The Caretaker [1960], act I

20   If only I could get down to Sidcup! I've been
waiting for the weather to break. He's got my papers, this man I left them with, it's got it all down
there, I could prove everything.   *Ibid.*

[1]From the novel [1962] by CHARLES WEBB [1939–].

1 The earth's about five million years old, at least.
Who can afford to live in the past?
The Homecoming [1965], act III

2 I don't think we don't love each other.
Betrayal [1978], sc. 3

Wilfrid Sheed
1930–

3 If God had died in the blare of the twentieth
century and in houses too new and cheap to be
haunted, one must seek him in the old quiet places,
where he might still live on in retirement.
The Good Word [1978], pt. I, ch. 12

4 Suicide . . . is about life, being in fact the sincerest form of criticism life gets. *Ibid. 15*

Stephen Sondheim
1930–

5 Tonight, tonight, won't be just any night.
Tonight there will be no morning star.
West Side Story [1957].[1] Tonight

6 I like to be in America!
O.K. by me in America!
Ev'rything free in America
For a small fee in America!
Ibid. America

7 Everything's Coming Up Roses.
Gypsy [1959].[2] Title of song

Derek Walcott
1930–

8 I who am poisoned with the blood of both,
Where shall I turn, divided to the vein?
I who have cursed
The drunken officer of British rule, how choose
Between this Africa and the English tongue I love?
A Far Cry from Africa [1962]

9 These palms are greater than Versailles,
for no man made them.
Names [1976], II

10 The tourist archipelagoes of my South
are prisons too, corruptible, and though
there is no harder prison than writing verse,
what's poetry, if it is worth its salt,
but a phrase men can pass from hand to mouth?
Forest of Europe [1979]

11 The Caribbean was borne like an elliptical basin
in the hands of acolytes, and a people were
absolved
of a history which they did not commit.
The Star-Apple Kingdom [1979]

[1]Music by LEONARD BERNSTEIN.
[2]Music by JULE STYNE.

12 I am tired of words,
and literature is an old couch stuffed with fleas.
North and South [1981]

Mikhail Sergeyevich Gorbachev
1931–

13 The guilt of Stalin and his immediate entourage
before the Party and the people for the mass repressions and lawlessness they committed is enormous
and unforgivable.
*Speech on the seventieth anniversary of the
Russian Revolution [November 2, 1987]*

14 The idea of restructuring [perestroika] . . .
combines continuity and innovation, the historical
experience of Bolshevism and the contemporaneity
of socialism. *Ibid.*

John Le Carré
[David John Moore Cornwell]
1931–

15 The Spy Who Came In from the Cold.
Title of novel [1963]

Toni Morrison
[Chloe Anthony Wofford]
1931–

16 I know what every colored woman in this country is doing. . . . Dying. Just like me. But the difference is they dying like a stump. Me, I'm going
down like one of those redwoods. I sure did live in
this world. *Sula [1973], 1940*

17 At no point in my life have I ever felt as though
I were an American.
In the New York Times [January 5, 1986]

Anthony Newley
1931–
and
Leslie Bricusse
1931–

18 Stop the World—I Want to Get Off.
Title of musical [1961]

Mordecai Richler
1931–

19 "I'm world-famous," Dr. Parks said, "all over
Canada." *The Incomparable Atuk [1963], ch. 4*

Tom [Thomas Kennerly, Jr.] Wolfe
1931–

1   The Life—that *feeling*—The Life—the late 1940s early 1950s American Teenage Drive-In Life.
The Electric Kool-Aid Acid Test[1] *[1968], ch. 4*

2   A glorious place, a glorious age, I tell you! A very Neon Renaissance—And the myths that actually touched you at that time—not Hercules, Orpheus, Ulysses and Aeneas—but Superman, Captain Marvel, Batman.   *Ibid.*

3   Radical Chic, after all, is only radical in style; in its heart it is part of Society and its traditions.
Radical Chic & Mau-Mauing the Flak Catchers [1970]

4   The Me Decade and the Third Great Awakening.
Title of essay [1976]

5   The idea was to prove at every foot of the way up that you were one of the elected and anointed ones who had *the right stuff* and could move higher and higher and even—ultimately, God willing, one day—that you might be able to join that special few at the very top, that elite who had the capacity to bring tears to men's eyes, the very Brotherhood of the Right Stuff itself.   *The Right Stuff [1979], ch. 2*

6   On Wall Street he and a few others—how many?—three hundred, four hundred, five hundred?—had become precisely that . . . Masters of the Universe.
The Bonfire of the Vanities [1987], ch. 1, The Master of the Universe

Aharon Appelfeld
1932–

7   The Holocaust is a central event in many people's lives, but it has also become a metaphor for our century. There cannot be an end to speaking and writing about it.
In the New York Times [November 15, 1986]

Carl Perkins
1932–

8 You can do anything,
But don't step on my blue suede shoes.
Blue Suede Shoes [1956]

Sylvia Plath
1932–1963

9   The silence drew off, baring the pebbles and shells and all the tatty wreckage of my life. Then, at the rim of vision, it gathered itself, and in one sweeping tide, rushed me to sleep.
The Bell Jar [1963]

[1]See Kesey, 768:1.

10 A living doll, everywhere you look.
It can sew, it can cook,
It can talk, talk, talk. . . .
My boy, it's your last resort.
Will you marry it, marry it, marry it.
The Applicant [1963]

11 I have done it again.
Lady Lazarus [1963], st. 1

12 Dying
Is an art, like everything else.
I do it exceptionally well.

I do it so it feels like hell.
I do it so it feels real.
I guess you could say I've a call.
Ibid. st. 15, 16

13 Out of the ash
I rise with my red hair
And I eat men like air.
Ibid. last stanza

14 The woman is perfected.
Her dead

Body wears the smile of accomplishment,
The illusion of a Greek necessity

Flows in the scrolls of her toga,
Her bare

Feet seem to be saying:
We have come so far, it is over.
Edge [1963]

15 What a thrill—
My thumb instead of an onion.
Cut [1963]

16 You do not do, you do not do
Any more, black shoe
In which I have lived like a foot
For thirty years, poor and white,
Barely daring to breathe or Achoo.
Daddy [1963], st. 1

17 I have always been scared of *you*,
With your Luftwaffe, your gobbledygoo.
And your neat mustache
And your Aryan eye, bright blue.
Panzer-man, panzer-man, O You—
Ibid. st. 9

18 Every woman adores a Fascist,
The boot in the face, the brute
Brute heart of a brute like you.
Ibid. st. 10

19 White
Godiva, I unpeel—
Dead hands dead stringencies.
Ariel [1965]

20 And now I
Foam to wheat, a glitter of seas.
Ibid.

François Truffaut
1932–1984

1 Airing one's dirty linen never makes for a master-piece.[1]
Bed and Board [1972]

John Updike
1932–

2 Our noise for some seconds passed beyond excitement into a kind of immense open anguish, a cry to be saved. But immortality is nontransferable. The papers said that the other players, and even the umpires on the field, begged him to come out and acknowledge us in some way, but he never had and did not now. Gods do not answer letters.
Hub Fans Bid Kid[2] Adieu, in The New Yorker [October 22, 1960]

3 That's one of my Goddam precious American rights, not to think about politics.
Rabbit Redux [1971]

4 We are cruel enough without meaning to be.
Rabbit Is Rich [1981]

Vine Victor Deloria, Jr.[3]
1933–

5 Tribalism is the strongest force at work in the world today.
Custer Died for Your Sins [1969], ch. 11

6 This country was a lot better off when the Indians were running it.
In the New York Times Magazine, March 3, 1970

Jerry Leiber
1933–
and
Mike Stoller
1933–

7 You ain't nothin' but a hound dog cryin' all the time.
Well, you ain't never caught a rabbit and you ain't no friend of mine.
Hound Dog [1956]

Yoko Ono
1933–

8 Woman Is the Nigger of the World.
Title of song [1972]

[1] Les rendements de contes ne font jamais un chef d'oeuvre.
[2] Ted Williams of the Boston Red Sox, who played his last Fenway Park game on September 28, 1960.
[3] A Standing Rock Sioux.

Joe Orton [John Kingsley]
1933–1967

9 I'd the upbringing a nun would envy and that's the truth. Until I was fifteen I was more familiar with Africa than my own body.
Entertaining Mr. Sloane [1964], act I

10 You were born with your legs apart. They'll send you to the grave in a Y-shaped coffin.
What the Butler Saw [1969], act I

Theodore Roszak
1933–

11 The Making of a Counter Culture.
Title of book [1969]

Philip Roth
1933–

12 Doctor Spielvogel, this is my life, my only life, and I'm living it in the middle of a Jewish joke! I am the son in the Jewish joke—*only it ain't no joke!*
Portnoy's Complaint [1969]. Whacking Off

13 A Jewish man with parents alive is a fifteen-year-old boy, and will remain a fifteen-year-old boy *till they die!*
Ibid. Cunt Crazy

14 So [*said the doctor*]. Now vee may perhaps to begin Yes?
Ibid. Punch Line

Susan Sontag
1933–

15 Camp is a vision of the world in terms of style —but a particular kind of style. It is the love of the exaggerated, the "off," of things-being-what-they-are-not. . . . The ultimate Camp statement: "it's good because it's awful."
Against Interpretation [1966]. Notes on Camp

16 Illness is the night-side of life, a more onerous citizenship. Everyone who is born holds dual citizenship, in the kingdom of the well and in the kingdom of the sick.
Illness as Metaphor [1978]

Andrei Andreevich Voznesenski
1933–

17 I am Goya
of the bare field, by the enemy's beak gouged
till the craters of my eyes gape
I am grief

I am the tongue
of war, the embers of cities
on the snows of the year 1941
I am hunger
I Am Goya [1960],[4] st. 1, 2

[4] Translated by STANLEY KUNITZ.

1 They carried him[1] not to bury him:
They carried him down to crown him. . . .
The poet flourished here, disheveled,
Who would not bow before votive lamps
But to the common spade.
Leaves and Roots [1960][2]

2 The urge to kill, like the urge to beget,
Is blind and sinister. Its craving is set
Today on the flesh of a hare: tomorrow it can
Howl the same way for the flesh of a man.
Hunting a Hare [1964],[3] *st. 5*

3 Along a parabola life like a rocket flies,
Mainly in darkness, now and then on a rainbow.
Parabolic Ballad [1960][3]

Steven Weinberg
1933–

4   It is very hard to realize that this present universe
has evolved from an unspeakably unfamiliar early
condition, and faces a future extinction of endless
cold or intolerable heat. The more the universe
seems comprehensible, the more it also seems pointless.   *The First Three Minutes [1977]. Epilogue*

Yevgeny Alexandrovich Yevtushenko
1933–

5 There is no Jewish blood in my veins,
But I am hated with a scabby hatred
By all the anti-Semites,
      like a Jew.
And therefore
      I am a true Russian.
Babi Yar [1961]

Amiri Baraka [LeRoi Jones]
1934–

6 Lately, I've become accustomed to the way
The ground opens up and envelops me
Each time I go out to walk the dog.
Preface to a Twenty Volume Suicide Note
[1961]

7 Saturday mornings we listened to *Red Lantern* &
his undersea folk.
At 11, *Let's Pretend* / & we did / & I, the poet, still
do, Thank God!
In Memory of Radio [1961]

8 Walk it slow
where you go

walk it slow . . .
We in the world
Poor as dirt
   Don't get some rhythm
Somebody'll get hurt
the world is black
the world is green
the world is red, yellow, brown
the world is mean
3rd World Blues [1979]

James Brown
1934–

9   Say It Loud: "I'm Black and I'm Proud."
Title of song [1968]

Joan Didion
1934–

10   Writers are always selling somebody out.
Slouching Towards Bethlehem [1968], preface

11   San Francisco was where the social hemorrhaging
was showing up. San Francisco was where the missing children were gathering and calling themselves
"hippies."   *Ibid.*

Janet Malcolm
1934–

12   Every journalist who is not too stupid or too full
of himself to notice what is going on knows that
what he does is morally indefensible. He is a kind of
confidence man, preying on people's vanity, ignorance, or loneliness, gaining their trust and betraying
them without remorse.
The Journalist and the Murderer [1990], pt. I

Jonathan Wolfe Miller
1934–

13   I'm not a Jew. I'm Jew-*ish*. I don't go the whole
hog.   *Beyond the Fringe [1960]*

Navarre Scott Momaday
1934–

14   Words were medicine; they were magic and invisible. They came from nothing into sound and meaning. They were beyond price; they could neither be
bought nor sold.
House Made of Dawn[4] *[1968], January 26*

---

[1]Boris Pasternak.
[2]Translated by STANLEY KUNITZ.
[3]Translated by W. H. AUDEN.

[4]See Anonymous: North American Indian, 787:9.

Carl Sagan
1934–

1 We are an intelligent species and the use of our intelligence quite properly gives us pleasure. In this respect the brain is like a muscle. When it is in use we feel very good. Understanding is joyous.

Broca's Brain [1979], ch. 2

Gloria Steinem
1934–

2 Any woman who chooses to behave like a full human being should be warned that the armies of the status quo will treat her as something of a dirty joke; that's their natural and first weapon.

Sisterhood, in Ms. [Spring 1972]

3 I can sometimes deal with men as equals and therefore can afford to like them.   *Ibid.*

4 Some of us are becoming the men we wanted to marry.

Speech at Yale University [September 1981]

Mark Strand
1934–

5 Ink runs from the corners of my mouth.
There is no happiness like mine.
I have been eating poetry.

Eating Poetry [1968]

6 Wherever I am
I am what is missing.

Keeping Things Whole [1969]

7 Nothing could stop you.
Not the best day. Not the quiet. Not the ocean
    rocking.
You went on with your dying.

Elegy for My Father [1970]. 3. Your Dying

8 Nobody knows you. You are the neighbor of
    nothing.

Ibid. 6. The New Year

9 Now you invent the boat of your flesh and set it
    upon the waters
and drift in the gradual swell, in the laboring salt.
Now you look down. The waters of childhood are
    there.

Where Are the Waters of Childhood? [1978]

Woody Allen
1935–

10 Play It Again, Sam.[1]   *Title of film [1969]*

11 Not only is there no God, but try getting a plumber on weekends.

Getting Even [1972]. My Philosophy

[1]See Epstein et al., 726:10.

12 How wrong Emily Dickinson was! Hope is not "the thing with feathers."[2] The thing with feathers has turned out to be my nephew. I must take him to a specialist in Zurich.

Without Feathers [1975]. From the Allen Notebooks

13 It's not that I'm afraid to die. I just don't want to be there when it happens.   *Ibid. Death (A Play)*

14 On the plus side, death is one of the few things that can be done as easily lying down.

Ibid. The Early Essays

15 [Sex:] The most fun I've ever had without laughing.[3]   *Annie Hall (screenplay) [1977][4]*

16 More than any other time in history, mankind faces a crossroads. One path leads to despair and utter hopelessness. The other, to total extinction. Let us pray we have the wisdom to choose correctly.

Side Effects [1980]. My Speech to the Graduates

17 Eighty percent of success is showing up.

Interview

Susan Brownmiller
1935–

18 Man's discovery that his genitalia could serve as a weapon to generate fear must rank as one of the most important discoveries of prehistoric times, along with the use of fire and the first crude stone axe.

Against Our Will: Men, Women, and Rape [1975], ch. 1

[Leroy] Eldridge Cleaver
1935–

19 Rape was an insurrectionary act. . . . I wanted to send waves of consternation throughout the white race.   *Soul on Ice [1968]. On Becoming*

20 You're either part of the solution or part of the problem.   *Speech, San Francisco [1968]*

Ken Kesey
1935–

21 A sound of cornered-animal fear and hate and surrender and defiance . . . like the last sound the treed and shot and falling animal makes as the dogs get him, when he finally doesn't care any more about anything but himself and his dying.

One Flew over the Cuckoo's Nest [1962], pt. IV

[2]See Dickinson, 511:20.
[3]Giving canonical form to a quip already familiar on American college campuses for several decades.
[4]Written with MARSHALL BRICKMAN [1941–].

1 There are going to be times when we can't wait for somebody. Now, you're either on the bus or off the bus. If you're on the bus, and you get left behind, then you'll find it again. If you're off the bus in the first place — then it won't make a damn.

> *Quoted by* Tom Wolfe *in* The Electric
> Kool-Aid Acid Test [1968],[1] *ch. 6*

William P. Kinsella
1935–

2 If you build it, he will come.

> *Shoeless Joe [1982]*[2]

Elvis Presley
1935–1977

3 Well since my baby left me
Well I found a new place to dwell
Well it's down at the end of lonely street
At Heartbreak Hotel.

> *Heartbreak Hotel [1956]*[3]

4 Love me tender, love me sweet,
Never let me go.

> *Love Me Tender [1956]*[4]

Simon Gray
1936–

5 *Stephen: . . .* What have you got against having children?
Simon: Well Steve, in the first place there isn't enough room. In the second place they seem to start by mucking up their parents' lives, and then go on in the third place to muck up their own. In the fourth place it doesn't seem right to bring them into a world like this in the fifth place and in the sixth place I don't like them very much in the first place. OK.

> *Otherwise Engaged [1975], act II*

6 In my experience, the worst thing you can do to an important problem is discuss it. You know, I really do think this whole business of non-communication is one of the more poignant fallacies of our zestfully overexplanatory age. *Ibid.*

Václav Havel
1936–

7 A specter is haunting eastern Europe:[5] the specter of what in the West is called "dissent."

> *The Power of the Powerless [1978]*[6]

8 God—I don't know why—wanted me to be a Czech. It was not my choice. But I accept it, and I try to do something for my country because I live here.

> *Interview [1988]*

Abbie [Abbott] Hoffman
1936–1989

9 Sacred cows make the tastiest hamburger.

> *Remark. Recalled at his death*

Barbara C. Jordan
1936–

10 "We, the people." It is a very eloquent beginning. But when that document[7] was completed on the seventeenth of September in 1787 I was not included in that "We, the people." I felt somehow for many years that George Washington and Alexander Hamilton, just left me out by mistake. But through the process of amendment, interpretation and court decision I have finally been included in "We, the people."

> *Statement at Debate on Articles of
> Impeachment, Committee on the Judiciary,
> House of Representatives, Ninety-third
> Congress [July 25, 1974]*

Kris Kristofferson
1936–
and
Fred Foster

11 Freedom's just another word for nothin' left to lose,
And nothin' ain't worth nothin' but it's free.

> *Me and Bobby McGee [1969]*

Claude Brown
1937–

12 The children of these disillusioned colored pioneers inherited the total lot of their parents—the disappointments, the anger. To add to their misery, they had little hope of deliverance. For where does one run to when he's already in the promised land?

> *Manchild in the Promised Land [1965]*

Thomas Pynchon
1937–

13 Yet who can presume to say *what* the war wants, so vast and aloof it is . . . so *absentee.*

> *Gravity's Rainbow [1973]*

---

[1]See Wolfe, 764:1 and 764:2.
[2]Basis for the movie *Field of Dreams* [1989].
[3]Written with Mae Boren Axton [1907–] and Tommy Durden [1920–].
[4]Written with Vera Matson.
[5]See Marx and Engels, 481:14.
[6]Translated by P. Wilson.

[7]Preamble to the Constitution of the United States. See Bethune, 627:21.

Erich Segal
1937–

1   Love means not ever having to say you're sorry.[1]
Love Story [1970]

Tom Stoppard
1937–

2   You're familiar with the tragedies of antiquity, are you? The great homicidal classics?
Rosencrantz and Guildenstern Are Dead [1967], act I

3   Though an arrow is always approaching its target, it never quite gets there, and Saint Sebastian died of fright.   *Jumpers [1972], act I*

4   If rationality were the criterion for things being allowed to exist, the world would be one gigantic field of soya beans!   *Ibid.*

5   An essentially private man [James Joyce] who wished his total indifference to public notice to be universally recognized.   *Travesties [1975], act I*

6   I learned three things in Zurich during the war. I wrote them down. Firstly, you're either a revolutionary or you're not, and if you're not you might as well be an artist as anything else. Secondly, if you can't be an artist, you might as well be a revolutionary . . . I forget the third thing.   *Ibid. last lines*

John Dean
1938–

7   We have a cancer within, close to the Presidency, that is growing.
From The [Nixon] Presidential Transcripts [March 21, 1973]

A. Bartlett Giamatti
1938–1989

8   [Baseball] breaks your heart. It is designed to break your heart. The game begins in the spring, when everything else begins again, and it blossoms in the summer, filling the afternoons and evenings, and then as soon as the chill rains come, it stops, and leaves you to face the fall alone.
The Green Fields of the Mind [1977]

Joyce Carol Oates
1938–

9   This is a work of history in fictional form—that is, in personal perspective, which is the only kind of history that exists.   *Them [1969]. Author's Note*

[1]Love means never having to say you're sorry.—*Love Story (screenplay) [1970]*, spoken by Ali MacGraw.

Raymond Carver
1939–1988

10   Maybe I just don't understand poetry. I admit it's not the first thing I reach for when I pick up something to read.   *Cathedral [1983]*

Francis Ford Coppola
1939–

11   I love the smell of napalm in the morning. It smells like victory.
Apocalypse Now (screenplay) [1979], spoken by Robert Duvall

Germaine Greer
1939–

12   Is it too much to ask that women be spared the daily struggle for superhuman beauty in order to offer it to the caresses of a subhumanly ugly mate?
The Female Eunuch [1970]. Loathing and Disgust

Seamus Justin Heaney
1939–

13 Between my finger and my thumb
The squat pen rests.
I'll dig with it.
Death of a Naturalist [1966]. Digging

14 I shouldered a kind of manhood
stepping in to lift the coffins
of dead relations.
North [1975]. Funeral Rites, I

15 It all came back to me last night, stirred
By the sootfall of your things at bedtime,
Your head-down, tail-up hunt in a bottom
    drawer
For the black plunge-line nightdress.
Field Work [1979]. The Skunk

16 You lose more of yourself than you redeem
Doing the decent thing.
Station Island [1984], XII

William Least Heat-Moon
[William Lewis Trogdon]
1939–

17   On the old highway maps of America, the main routes were red and the back roads blue. Now even the colors are changing. But in those brevities just before dawn and a little after dark—times neither day nor night—the old roads return to the sky some of its color. Then, in truth, they cast a mysterious shadow of blue, and it's that time when the pull of the blue highway is strongest, when the open

road is a beckoning, a strangeness, a place where a man can lose himself.
Blue Highways [1982]. Preface

James Rado
1939–
and
Gerome Ragni
1942–1991

1 When the moon is in the seventh house
And Jupiter aligns with Mars,
Then peace will guide the planets,
And love will steer the stars;
This is the dawning of the age of Aquarius,
The age of Aquarius.
Hair [1966].[1] *Aquarius*

Grace Slick
1939–

2 One pill makes you taller
And one pill makes you small
And the ones that mother gives you
Don't do anything at all.
Go ask Alice
When she's ten feet tall.
White Rabbit [1967]

Michael Herr
1940–

3   There was a famous story, some reporters asked a door gunner, "How can you shoot women and children?" and he'd answered, "It's easy, you just don't lead 'em so much."
Dispatches [1977]. Breathing In

4   I think Vietnam was what we had instead of happy childhoods.   *Ibid. Colleagues*

5   Out on the street I couldn't tell the Vietnam veterans from the rock and roll veterans. The sixties had made so many casualties, its war and its music had run power off the same circuit for so long they didn't even have to fuse.
Ibid. Breathing Out

John Lennon
1940–1980

6   We're more popular than Jesus now.[2] I don't know which will go first—rock 'n' roll or Christianity.
Interview in London Evening Standard [March 4, 1966]

[1]Music by GALT MacDERMOT.
[2]See Chaplin, 675:18.

John Lennon
1940–1980
and
Paul McCartney
1942–

7   I'll tell you something
I think you'll understand,
Then I'll say that something,
I want to hold your hand.
I Want to Hold Your Hand [1963]

8 There's a shadow hanging over me,
Oh yesterday came suddenly.
Yesterday [1965]

9 All the lonely people, where do they all belong?
Eleanor Rigby [1966]

10 Oh I get by with a little help from my friends
Mmm get high with a little help from my friends.
With a Little Help from My Friends [1967]

11   Lucy in the Sky with Diamonds.
Title of song [1967]

12 How does it feel to be one of the beautiful people?
Baby You're a Rich Man [1967]

13 You say you want a revolution
Well you know
we all want to change the world . . .
But when you talk about destruction
Don't you know that you can count me out
Don't you know it's gonna be alright.
Revolution [1968]

14   Let It Be.   *Title of song [1970]*

Phil Ochs
1940–1976

15 I'm sure it wouldn't interest anybody
Outside of a small circle of friends.
A Small Circle of Friends [1967]

Jack Weinberg
1940–

16   We have a saying in the movement that we don't trust anybody over thirty.
Interview on Free Speech movement at University of California, Berkeley [1964]

Paul Anka
1941–

17 I've lived a life that's full, I traveled each and ev'ry highway,

And more, much more than this, I did it my
way.
My Way [1969][1]

Philip Joseph Caputo
1941–

1   You're going to learn that one of the most brutal
things in the world is your average nineteen-year-old
American boy.   *A Rumor of War [1977]*

Stokely Carmichael [Kwame Toure]
1941–
and
Charles Vernon Hamilton
1929–

2   Black power[2] . . . is a call for black people in
this country to unite, to recognize their heritage, to
build a sense of community. It is a call for black
people to begin to define their own goals, to lead their
own organizations and to support those organizations. It is a call to reject the racist institutions and
values of this society.   *Black Power! [1967], ch. 2*

3   Before a group can enter the open society, it must
first close ranks.   *Ibid.*

Bob Dylan [Robert Zimmerman]
1941–

4 How many roads must a man walk down
Before you call him a man?
Blowin' in the Wind [1962]

5 The answer, my friend, is blowin' in the wind,
The answer is blowin' in the wind.
Ibid.

6   A Hard Rain's A-Gonna Fall.
Title of song [1963]

7 The order is
Rapidly fadin'.
And the first one now

[1]Music by CLAUDE FRANÇOIS, JACQUES REVAUX, and GILES
THIBAUT.
Signature song of FRANK SINATRA [1915–]. In November
1989 Soviet leader Mikhail Gorbachev announced (through a
Foreign Ministry spokesman) that "the Sinatra Doctrine" had
replaced the "Brezhnev Doctrine" for the east bloc nations:
"Hungary and Poland are doing it their way."
[2]Carmichael had used the phrase "Black power" in a speech
in Greenwood, Mississippi [June 17, 1966].
To demand these God-given rights is to seek black power
—what I call audacious power—the power to build black
institutions of splendid achievement.—ADAM CLAYTON PO-
WELL, JR. [1908–1972], *Baccalaureate address at Howard University* [May 29, 1966]
See Langston Hughes, 709:2.

Will later be last[3]
For the times they are a-changin'.
The Times They Are A-Changin' [1963]

8 Hey! Mister Tambourine Man play a song for me,
I'm not sleepy and there is no place I'm goin' to.
Mister Tambourine Man [1964]

9 How does it feel
To be on your own
With no direction home
Like a complete unknown
Like a rolling stone?
Like a Rolling Stone [1965]

10 You don't need a weatherman to know which
way the wind blows.
Subterranean Homesick Blues [1965]

Jesse Jackson
1941–

11   My right and my privilege to stand here before
you has been won—won in my lifetime—by the
blood and the sweat of the innocent.
*Speech at Democratic National Convention,
Atlanta [July 19, 1988]*

12   When I look out at this convention, I see the face
of America, red, yellow, brown, black and white.
We are all precious in God's sight—the real rainbow coalition.   *Ibid.*

Robin Morgan
1941–

13   Sisterhood Is Powerful.   *Title of book [1970]*

Helen Reddy
1941–

14 If I have to, I can do anything.
I am strong, I am invincible, I am woman.
I Am Woman [1972]

Muhammad Ali[4]
1942–

15   I am the greatest.
Slogan, inspired by wrestler Gorgeous George

16   Float like a butterfly, sting like a bee.
*Boxing credo, devised by aide Drew "Bundini"
Brown*

17   Not only do I knock 'em out, I pick the round.
Statement [December 1962]

[3]See *Matthew* 19:30, 35:38.
[4]Formerly Cassius Clay.

1 Keep asking me no matter how long—
On the war in Vietnam I sing this song—
I ain't got no quarrel with the Viet Cong.

On the draft [February 1966]

Stephen William Hawking
1942–

2   If we do discover a complete [unified] theory [of
the universe], it should in time be understandable in
broad principle by everyone, not just a few scientists. Then we shall all, philosophers, scientists, and
just ordinary people, be able to take part in the
discussion of the question of why it is that we and
the universe exist. If we find the answer to that, it
would be the ultimate triumph of human reason
—for then we should know the mind of God.

A Brief History of Time [1988]. Conclusion

Jimi Hendrix [James Marshall]
1942–1970

3 Purple haze was in my brain,
Lately things don't seem the same,
Actin' funny, but I don't know why,
'Scuse me while I kiss the sky.

Purple Haze [1967]

Erica Jong
1942–

4   The zipless fuck is absolutely pure. It is free of
ulterior motives. There is no power game. The man
is not "taking" and the woman is not "giving." No
one is attempting to cuckold a husband or humiliate
a wife. No one is trying to prove anything or get
anything out of anyone. The zipless fuck is the purest thing there is. And it is rarer than the unicorn.

Fear of Flying [1973], ch. 1

Garrison Keillor
1942–

5   That's the news from Lake Wobegon, where all
the women are strong, the men are good-looking,
and all the children are above average.

*A Prairie Home Companion [1974–1987],
signature line*

6   The little town that time forgot, that the decades
cannot improve.   *Ibid.*

Paul Simon
1942–

7 Hello darkness my old friend
I've come to talk with you again.

The Sound of Silence [1964]

8 The words of the prophets
Are written on the subway walls
And tenement halls
And whispered in the sounds of silence.

Ibid.

9 Where have you gone, Joe DiMaggio?
A nation turns its lonely eyes to you.

Mrs. Robinson [1966]

10 I'm empty and aching and I don't know why.
Counting the cars on the New Jersey Turnpike.
They've all come to look for America.

America [1967]

11 Like a bridge over troubled water
I will lay me down.

Bridge over Troubled Water [1969]

Rap [Hubert Gerold] Brown
1943–

12   Violence is as American as cherry pie.

Press conference [July 27, 1967]

Robert Crumb
1943–

13   Keep on truckin'.

Slogan of cartoon character

Nikki Giovanni
1943–

14 show me someone not full of herself and i'll show
   you a hungry person

*Poem for a Lady Whose Voice I Like [1970],
last line*

15   I really hope no white person ever has cause
to write about me
because they never understand
Black love is Black wealth and they'll
probably talk about my hard childhood
and never understand that
all the while I was quite happy.

Nikki-Rosa [1970]

Mick [Michael Philip] Jagger
1943–
and
Keith Richards
1943–

16 I can't get no satisfaction . . .
I can't get no girl with action.

Satisfaction [1965]

17   Two Thousand Light Years from Home.

Title of song [1967]

1 Please allow me to introduce myself,
I'm a man of wealth and taste.
I've been around for long, long years,
Stolen many a man's soul and faith.
Sympathy for the Devil [1968]

2 Well, we all need someone we can lean on,
And if you want it, well, you can lean on me.
Let It Bleed [1969]

3 War, children, is just a shot away, it's just a shot
away.
Gimme Shelter [1969]

4 You can't always get what you want
But if you try sometimes
You just might find
You get what you need.
You Can't Always Get What You Want [1969]

Janis Joplin
1943–1970

5 Down on me, down on me,
Looks like everybody in this whole round world
Is down on me.
Down on Me [1967]

6 Lord, won't you buy me a Mercedes-Benz,
My friends all drive Porsches,
I must make amends.
Mercedes-Benz [1970]

Joni Mitchell
1943–

7 They paved paradise
And put up a parking lot.
Big Yellow Taxi [1969]

8 We are stardust,
We are golden,
And we've got to get ourselves
Back to the garden.
Woodstock [1969]

Bill Griffith
1944–

9 Are we having fun yet?
Zippy the Pinhead (comic strip) [1979]

George W. Lucas, Jr.
1944–

10 Evil Empire.   *Star Wars (screenplay) [1977]*[1]

11 May the Force be with you!
Ibid. spoken by Alec Guinness

[1]March 1983. [President] Reagan tells an evangelical group that the Soviet Union is "the focus of evil in the modern world" and "an evil empire." Two weeks later, he proposes a space-based missile defense system and "Star Wars" is born.—*New York Times*, "The Decade in Review" [December 24, 1989].

Alice Walker
1944–

12 Guided by my heritage of a love of beauty and a respect for strength—in search of my mother's garden, I found my own.
In Search of Our Mothers' Gardens [1974]

13 I think it pisses God off if you walk by the color purple in a field somewhere and don't notice it.
The Color Purple [1982]

14 I'm pore, I'm black, I may be ugly and can't cook, a voice say to everything listening. But I'm here.
Ibid.

Annie Dillard
1945–

15 I had been my whole life a bell, and never knew it until at that moment I was lifted and struck.
Pilgrim at Tinker Creek [1974], ch. 2

16 The second before the sun went out we saw a wall of dark shadow come speeding at us. We no sooner saw it than it was upon us, like thunder. . . . It was as if an enormous, loping god in the sky had reached down and slapped the earth's face.
Teaching a Stone to Talk [1982]. Total Eclipse

Bob Marley
1945–1981

17 We're leaving Babylon
We're going to our Father's land.
Movement of Jah People [1977]

Peter Townshend
1945–

18 Hope I die before I get old.
This is my generation.
My Generation [1965]

August Wilson, Jr.
1945–

19 As long as the colored man look to white folks to put the crown on what he say . . . as long as he looks to white folks for approval . . . then he ain't never gonna find out who he is and what he's about.[2]
Ma Rainey's Black Bottom [1984], act 1

Julian Barnes
1946–

20 Why does the writing make us chase the writer? Why can't we leave well enough alone? Why aren't the books enough?
Flaubert's Parrot [1984], ch. 1

[2]Ellipses are in the original text.

Steve [Stephen Bantu] Biko
1946–1977

1   The most potent weapon in the hands of the oppressor is the mind of the oppressed.
Statement as witness [May 3, 1976][1]

2   The basic tenet of black consciousness is that the black man must reject all value systems that seek to make him a foreigner in the country of his birth and reduce his basic human dignity.   *Ibid.*

David Allen Stockman
1946–

3   None of us really understands what's going on with all these numbers.
On the U.S. budget [1981]

Oliver Stone
1946–

4   Greed is good! Greed is right! Greed works! Greed will save the U.S.A.![2]
Wall Street (screenplay) [1987], spoken by Michael Douglas

Arlo Guthrie
1947–

5 You can get anything you want at Alice's Restaurant.
Alice's Restaurant [1966]

Elton John
1947–
and
Bernie Taupin
1950–

6 They crawled out of the woodwork
And they whispered into your brain.
They set you on a treadmill
And they made you change your name.
And it seems to me you lived your life
Like a candle in the wind.
Candle in the Wind (Goodbye Norma Jean) [1973]

[Ahmed] Salman Rushdie[3]
1947–

7   Literature is the one place in any society where, within the secrecy of our own heads, we can hear

[1]From *Black Consciousness in South Africa* [1979], edited by MILLARD ARNOLD.
[2]"Greed is all right. . . . Greed is healthy. You can be greedy and still feel good about yourself.—IVAN FREDERICK BOESKY [1937–], *commencement address, Berkeley, California [May 18, 1986]*
[3]See Khomeini, 704:13.

voices talking about everything in every possible way.   *Is Nothing Sacred? [1990]*

Joseph C. Stinson
1947–

8   Go ahead, make my day.[4]
Sudden Impact (screenplay) [1983], spoken by Clint Eastwood

Charles Philip Arthur George, Prince of Wales
1948–

9   Give this much to the Luftwaffe. When it knocked down our buildings, it didn't replace them with anything more offensive than rubble. We did that.   *Speech in London [December 1987]*

Jimmy Cliff
1948–

10 As sure as the sun will shine
I'm going to get it, what's mine
And then the harder they come
The harder they fall,
One and all.
The Harder They Come [1972]

Leslie Marmon Silko
1948–

11 It's only a matter of time, Indian
you can't sleep with the river forever.
Storyteller [1981]. Indian Song: Survival

Bruce Springsteen
1949–

12 We gotta get out while we're young
'Cause tramps like us, baby, we were born to run.
Born to Run [1975]

13 Down in the shadow of the penitentiary,
Out by the gas fires of the refinery;
I'm ten years burning down the road,
Nowhere to run, ain't nowhere to go.
Born in the U.S.A. [1984]

Melinda Mathison
1950–

14   E.T., phone home.
E.T.: The Extra Terrestrial (screenplay) [1982]

[4]"I have only one thing to say to the tax increasers: "Go ahead and make my day."—RONALD REAGAN [March 13, 1985]

[Karen] Louise Erdrich
1954–

1   I was in love with the whole world and all that lived in its rainy arms.
> *Love Medicine [1984]. The Good Tears*

James Gleick
1954–

2   Tiny differences in input could quickly become overwhelming differences in output. . . . In weather, for example, this translates into what is only half-jokingly known as the Butterfly Effect —the notion that a butterfly stirring the air today in Peking can transform storm systems next month in New York.
> *Chaos [1987], Prologue*

Michael Jackson
1958–
and
Lionel Richie
1950–

3   We are the world,
We are the children,
We are the ones
To make a better day.
> *We Are the World [1985]*

The Doors
1967

4   Come on, baby, light my fire
Try to set the night on fire.
> *Light My Fire [1967]*

Monty Python's Flying Circus
1969–1974[1]

5   This parrot is no more. It has ceased to be. It's expired and gone to meet its maker. This is a late parrot. It's a stiff. Bereft of life, it rests in peace. If you hadn't nailed it to the perch, it would be pushing up the daisies. It's rung down the curtain and joined the choir invisible. This is an ex-parrot.
> *Episode 8 [1969]*

6   I cut down trees, I skip and jump,
I like to press wild flowers.
I put on women's clothing
And hang around in bars.
> *Episode 9 [1969]*

[1] Series first shown on BBC television between 1969 and 1974. Written and conceived by GRAHAM CHAPMAN, JOHN CLEESE, TERRY GILLIAM, ERIC IDLE, TERRY JONES, and MICHAEL PALIN.

7   I'd like to welcome the pommy bastard to God's own earth and I'd like to remind him that we don't like stuck-up sticky-beaks here.
> *Episode 22 [1970]*

Sesame Street
1969–

8   Me want cookie!
> *Spoken by Cookie Monster[2]*

9   It's not that easy bein' green.
> *Green.[3] Sung by Kermit the Frog*

Anonymous

10 Sumer is icumen in,
Lhude sing cuccu!
Groweth sed, and bloweth med,
And springth the wude nu—
Sing cuccu![4]
> *Cuckoo Song [c. 1250]*

11 A new broom sweeps clean.
> *Saying [13th century]*

12 Ich am of Irlonde
Ant of the holy lande
    Of Irlonde.
Gode sire, pray ich the,
For of saynte charite,
Come ant dance wyth me
    In Irlonde.
> *Ich Am of Irlonde [14th century][5]*

13 When Adam delved and Eve span
Who was then a gentleman?
> *Text used by JOHN BALL for his speech at Blackheath to the men in Wat Tyler's Rebellion [1381]*

14 Hew not too high lest the chips fall in thine eye.
> *Proverb [14th century]*

15 I sing of a maiden
That is makeless;
King of all kings
To her son she ches.
> *Carol. I Sing of a Maiden [15th century]*

16 For in my mind, of all mankind
I love but you alone.
> *The Nut-Brown Maid [15th century], refrain*

[2] Character created by JIM [James Maury] HENSON [1936–1990], FRANK OZ [1944–], and others.
[3] Words and music by JOE RAPOSO [1937–1989].
[4] See Pound, 659:2.
[5] "I am of Ireland, / And the Holy Land of Ireland, / And time runs on," cried she. / "Come out of charity, / Come dance with me in Ireland." — YEATS, *The Winding Stair and Other Poems* [1933], *Words for Music Perhaps, no. 20, "I Am of Ireland," refrain*

1 For I must to the greenwood go,
Alone, a banished man.
The Nut-Brown Maid, refrain

2 No burial this pretty pair
Of any man receives,
Till Robin Redbreast piously
Did cover them with leaves.
The Children in the Wood, st. 16

3   Before you trust a man, eat a peck of salt with
him.   *Proverb*[1]

4   A fool's paradise.
Paston Letters [1462], no. 457

5 Everyman, I will go with thee, and be thy guide,
In thy most need to go by thy side.
Everyman [before 1500], act I, l. 522

6 O Western wind, when wilt thou blow,
That the small rain down can rain?
Christ, that my love were in my arms
And I in my bed again!
O Western Wind [c. 1530]

7 Crabbed age and youth cannot live together.
Youth is full of pleasance, age is full of care.
The Passionate Pilgrim [1599]

8 Love me little, love me long,
Is the burden of my song.
Love Me Little [1569–1570], refrain

9 Multiplication is vexation,
Division is as bad;
The rule of three doth puzzle me,
And practice drives me mad.
Elizabethan MS [1570]

10 Alas, my Love! ye do me wrong
To cast me off discourteously:
And I have loved you so long,
Delighting in your company.
*From A Handful of Pleasant Delights [1584],
st. 1*

11 Greensleeves was all my joy,
Greensleeves was my delight;
Greensleeves was my heart of gold,
And who but Lady Greensleeves.
Ibid. refrain

12 Where griping griefs the heart would wound
And doleful dumps the mind oppress,
There music with her silver sound
With speed is wont to send redress.[2]
A Song to the Lute in Musicke, st. 1

13 The blinded boy that shoots so trim,
From heaven down did hie.
King Cophetua and the Beggar Maid,[3] st. 2

14 It was a friar of orders gray
Walked forth to tell his beads.
The Friar of Orders Gray,[4] st. 1

15 Our joys as winged dreams do fly;
Why then should sorrow last?
Since grief but aggravates thy loss,
Grieve not for what is past.
Ibid. st. 13

16 King Stephen was a worthy peer,
His breeches cost him but a crown.
Take Thy Old Cloak About Thee,[5] st. 7

17 It's pride that puts this country down;
Man, take thine old cloak about thee.
Ibid.

18   A fool and his money are soon parted.
English proverb

19 April is in my mistress' face,
And July in her eyes hath place,
Within her bosom is September,
But in her heart a cold December.
*From THOMAS MORLEY, Madrigals to Four
Voices [1594]*

20   Hobson's choice.[6]   *Phrase for no choice*

21 Lo here a new Aurora!
*From THOMAS MORLEY, The First Book of
Canzonets to Two Voices [1595]*

22 Kill then, and bliss me,
But first come kiss me.
*From THOMAS MORLEY, The First Book of
Ballets to Five Voices [1595]*

23 Shoot, false Love, I care not.
Spend thy shafts and spare not.
Ibid.

24 I was more true to Love than Love to me.
*From JOHN DOWLAND, The First Book of Songs
or Airs [1597]*

25 Jerusalem, my happy home,
When shall I come to thee?
When shall my sorrows have an end?
Thy joys when shall I see?
The Song of Mary [1601]

26 What poor astronomers are they
Take women's eyes for stars!
*From JOHN DOWLAND, The Third Book of
Songs or Airs [1603]*

27 And let all women strive to be
As constant as Penelope.
Constant Penelope, st. 18

[1]An adage originating before Cicero, who quotes a version
of it in *De Amicitia* 19, 67.
[2]Another version is used by Shakespeare in *Romeo and
Juliet, act IV, sc. v.*
[3]See Shakespeare, 174:25, and Tennyson, 456:5.

[4]Composed by THOMAS PERCY [1728–1811] from fragments
of ancient ballads in Shakespeare; published in his *Reliques of
Ancient English Poetry* [1765].
[5]Quoted in Shakespeare, *Othello, act II, sc. iii, l. 93.*
[6]Liveryman Thomas Hobson [1544–1631] obliged customers "to take the horse which stood near the stable door," according to RICHARD STEELE, *The Spectator, no. 509* [October
14, 1712].

1 Turn again, Whittington,
  Lord Mayor of London.[1]
        Refrain of Bow Bells heard by Dick Whittington
        [c. 1605]

2 From the hag and hungry goblin
  That into rags would rend ye,
  And the spirit that stands by the naked man
  In the book of Moons defend ye!
              Tom o' Bedlam [17th century], st. 1

3 The law locks up both man and woman
  Who steals the goose from off the common,
  But lets the greater felon loose
  Who steals the common from the goose.
        From EDWARD POTTS CHEYNEY, Social and
        Industrial History of England [1901],
        introduction

4 There is a lady sweet and kind,
  Was never face so pleased my mind;
  I did but see her passing by,
  And yet I love her till I die.
        From THOMAS FORD, Music of Sundry Kinds
        [1607], st. 1

5 Love not me for comely grace,
  For my pleasing eye or face,
  Nor for any outward part,
  No, nor for a constant heart.
        From JOHN WILBYE, Second Set of Madrigals
        [1609]

6 The silver swan, who living had no note,
  When death approached unlocked her silent
          throat;
  Leaning her breast against the reedy shore,
  Thus sung her first and last, and sung no more:[2]
  Farewell, all joys; O death, come close mine eyes;
  More geese than swans now live, more fools than
          wise.
        From ORLANDO GIBBONS, The First Set of
        Madrigals and Motets of Five Parts [1612], I

7 Stay, O sweet, and do not rise!
  The light that shines comes from thine eyes;
  The day breaks not: it is my heart,
  Because that you and I must part.
  Stay, or else my joys will die,
  And perish in their infancy.[3]
        From JOHN DOWLAND, A Pilgrim's Solace [1612]

8 We gather together to ask the Lord's blessing;
  He chastens and hastens his will to make known;
  The wicked oppressing now cease from
          distressing:[4]
  Sing praises to his Name; he forgets not his own.
              Hymn [1625][5]

   [1]Richard Whittington, son of a London mercer, rose to be
mayor of London three times before his death [1423].
   [2]See Plato, 74:21, and Shakespeare, 170:20 and 181:2.
   [3]Attributed also to JOHN DONNE, and included in a variant
form in the seventh edition of his poems [1669].
   [4]See Job 3:17, 13:36.
   [5]Translated by THEODORE BAKER.
Written by an unknown author in celebration of Dutch free-

9 If there is a paradise on the face of the earth,
  It is this, oh! it is this, oh! it is this.
        Mogul Inscription in the Red Fort at Delhi
        [1640]

10   Hear no evil, see no evil, speak no evil.
        Legend related to the "Three Wise Monkeys"
        carved over door of Sacred Stable, Nikko,
        Japan [17th century]

11 Over the mountains and over the waves,
   Under the fountains and under the graves;
   Under floods that are deepest, which Neptune
           obey,
   Over rocks that are steepest, Love will find out
           the way.
              Love Will Find Out the Way, st. 1

12 Begone, dull Care! I prithee begone from me!
   Begone, dull Care! Thou and I shall never agree.
        From JOHN PLAYFORD, Musical Companion
        [1687]

13 Though little, I'll work as hard as a Turk,
   If you'll give me employ,
   To plow and sow, and reap and mow,
   And be a farmer's boy.
              The Farmer's Boy [before 1689], st. 2

14 Carriages without horses shall go,
   And accidents fill the world with woe.
              Attributed to Mother Shipton[6]

15 Around the world thoughts shall fly
   In the twinkling of an eye.
                                          Ibid.

16 Under water men shall walk,
   Shall ride, shall sleep, and talk;
   In the air men shall be seen
   In white, in black, and in green.
                                          Ibid.

17 Iron in the water shall float
   As easy as a wooden boat.
                                          Ibid.

18 A swarm of bees in May
   Is worth a load of hay;
   A swarm of bees in June
   Is worth a silver spoon;
   A swarm of bees in July
   Is not worth a fly.
                            Old English proverb

19   When poverty comes in at the door, love flies out
   the window.   *Saying [17th century]*

20 Please to remember the fifth of November,
   Gunpowder treason and plot.
              Guy Fawkes rhyme [17th century]

dom from Spanish sovereignty at the end of the sixteenth century.—*The Hymnal 1940 Companion*
   [6]Prophecies ascribed to the fictitious Mother Shipton first
appeared in 1641.

1 A zealous locksmith died of late,
And did arrive at heaven gate,
He stood without and would not knock,
Because he meant to pick the lock.
> *Epitaph upon a Puritanical Locksmith; from*
> WILLIAM CAMDEN, *Remains Concerning Britain*
> [1637]

2   All the brothers were valiant, and all the sisters virtuous.
> *From the inscription on the tomb of the*
> *Duchess of Newcastle in Westminster Abbey*
> [1673]

3 It is so soon that I am done for,
I wonder what I was begun for.
> *For a child aged three weeks, Cheltenham*
> *Churchyard*

4   Live and let live.   *Scottish proverb*

5   When I rest I rust [Rast ich, so rost ich].
> *German proverb*

6   Coming through the rye.[1]
> *The Bob-tailed Lass, refrain*

7 Sabina has a thousand charms
To captivate my heart;
Her lovely eyes are Cupid's arms,
And every look a dart:
But when the beauteous idiot speaks,
She cures me of my pain;
Her tongue the servile fetters breaks
And frees her slave again.
> *From Amphion Anglicus [1700]*

8 God rest you merry, gentlemen,
Let nothing you dismay;
Remember Christ our Savior,
Was born on Christmas Day.
> *Carol*

9 The holly and the ivy,
When they are both full grown,
Of all the trees that are in the wood,
The holly bears the crown:
The rising of the sun
And the running of the deer,
The playing of the merry organ,
Sweet singing in the choir.
> *Carol*

10   Rain cats and dogs.   *Saying*

11   Sister Anne, do you see anyone coming?
> *Bluebeard; the cry of Fatima*

12   Who will change old lamps for new?
> *The Arabian Nights (A Thousand and One*
> *Nights).*[2] *The History of Aladdin*

13   Open sesame!   *Ibid. The History of Ali Baba*

14   Drive a coach and six through an Act of Parliament.
> *Credited to Sir Stephen Rice [1637–1715], Chief*
> *Baron of the Exchequer, by* MACAULAY *in*
> *History of England [1849–1861], ch. 12*

15 The Campbells are comin', oho, oho.
> *Song [c. 1715]*

16 Fools' names, like fools' faces,
Are often seen in public places.[3]
> *Saying*

17 And this is law, I will maintain,
Unto my dying day, sir,
That whatsoever king shall reign,
I'll still be the Vicar of Bray, sir!
> *The Vicar of Bray [1734], chorus*

18 Some talk of Alexander, and some of Hercules;
Of Hector, and Lysander, and such great names
    as these;
But of all the world's brave heroes, there's none
    that can compare
With a tow, row, row, row, row, row for the
    British Grenadier.
> *The British Grenadiers [c. 1750]*

19   The Girl I Left Behind Me.
> *Title of song [1759]*

20   The united voice of all His Majesty's free and loyal subjects in America—liberty and property, and no stamps.
> *Motto of various American colonial newspapers*
> *[1765–1766]*

21 Yankee Doodle came to town
Riding on a pony,
He stuck a feather in his hat
And called it macaroni.

Yankee Doodle, keep it up,
Yankee Doodle dandy,
Mind the music and the step,
And with the girls be handy.
> *Yankee Doodle,*[4] *st. 1 and chorus*

22   It's all in the day's work.
> *Current since the 18th century*

23 Man may work from sun to sun,
But woman's work is never done.
> *Saying*

---

[1]Gin a body meet a body / Coming through the rye; / Gin a body kiss a body, / Need a body cry?—BURNS, *Coming Through the Rye, st. 1*
See Salinger, 747:8.

[2]First European translation (ANTOINE GALLAND), 1704–1717.

[3]Collected by THOMAS FULLER [1654–1734], in *Gnomologia* [1732].

[4]This version was sufficiently popular in America in 1767 to be used in the ballad opera *The Disappointment; or, The Force of Credulity* by ANDREW BARTON.
Father and I went up to camp, / Along with Captain Goodwin; / And there we saw the men and boys, / As thick as hasty pudding. / Yankee doodle do.—*Version used by* ROYALL TYLER [1757–1826], *in The Contrast* [1790]

1 Count that day lost whose low descending sun
Views from thy hand no worthy action done.[1]

Saying

2 Don't tread on me.
*Motto of the first official American flag; first
raised by Lieutenant John Paul Jones in
Commodore Esek Hopkins's flagship Alfred
[December 3, 1775]*

3 Rebellion to tyrants is obedience to God.[2]
Motto on Thomas Jefferson's seal [c. 1776]

4 Lost is our old simplicity of times,
The world abounds with laws, and teems with
crimes.
On the Proceedings Against America,[3] *st. 1*

5 Our cargoes of meat, drink, and clothes beat the
Dutch.
Siege of Boston [1775]

6 There were three gypsies a-come to my door,
And downstairs ran this lady, O!
One sang high and another sang low,
And the other sang bonny, bonny Biscay, O!
The Wraggle-Taggle Gypsies, O!, st. 1

7 She's gone with the wraggle-taggle gypsies, O!
Ibid. st. 2

8 Down in the valley, the valley so low,
Hang your head over, hear the wind blow.
Down in the Valley

9 The goose hangs high.[4]   *Saying*

10 O Paddy dear, an' did ye hear the news that's
goin' round?
The shamrock is by law forbid to grow on Irish
ground!
No more St. Patrick's Day we'll keep, his color
can't be seen,
For there's a cruel law agin the wearin' o' the
Green!
The Wearing o' the Green [c. 1795]

11 For they're hangin' men an' women there for
wearin' o' the Green.
Ibid.

12 With drums and guns, and guns and drums
The enemy nearly slew ye.
My darling dear, you look so queer,
Oh, Johnny, I hardly knew ye.
Irish folk song, st. 1

13 Here we are on Tom Tiddler's ground
Picking up gold and silver.
Children's game

14 Christmas is coming, the geese are getting fat,
Please to put a penny in the old man's hat;
If you haven't got a penny, a ha'penny will do,
If you haven't got a ha'penny, God bless you!
Beggar's rhyme

15 From ghoulies and ghosties and long-leggety
beasties
And things that go bump in the night, Good Lord,
deliver us!
Cornish prayer

16 O God, thy sea is so great, and my boat is so
small.   *Breton fishermen's prayer*

17 Rest and be thankful.
*Inscription on stone seat in the Scottish
Highlands, and title of one of Wordsworth's
poems*

18 The wisdom of many and the wit of one.
Definition of a proverb[5]

19 Don't cross the bridge until you come to it.
Proverb

20 It's gude to be merry and wise,
It's gude to be honest and true;
It's gude to be off with the old love,
Before you are on with the new.[6]
Rhyme

21 Oh, ye'll tak' the high road an' I'll tak' the low
road,
An' I'll be in Scotland before ye;
But me and my true love will never meet again,
On the bonnie, bonnie banks o' Loch Lomond.
Loch Lomond, refrain

22 The woods are full of them.
Quoted by ALEXANDER WILSON, *American
Ornithology [1808], preface*

23 I wooed her in the wintertime
And in the summer too;
And the only, only thing I did that was wrong
Was to keep her from the foggy, foggy dew.
The Foggy, Foggy Dew, st. 1

24 Turkey in the straw, turkey in the hay,
Roll 'em up and twist 'em up a high tuckahaw,
And hit 'em up a tune called Turkey in the Straw.
Turkey in the Straw,[7] *st. 1 and refrain*

---

[1]An earlier version, signed by JAMES BOBART [December 8,
1697], begins "Think" rather than "Count."

[2]The motto of one, I believe, of the regicides of Charles I.
—*Letter from Jefferson to Edward Everett* [February 24, 1823]
   Jefferson's reference probably is to John Bradshaw [1602–
1659].

[3]In the *Pennsylvania Gazette* [February 8, 1775], "from a late
London Magazine."

[4][Meaning:] All is wonderful, 1866. Sometimes said to be
from "The goose honks high," referring to the fact that geese
fly higher in good weather, but there is no evidence this is the
origin of the term.—STUART BERG FLEXNER, *Listening to
America* [1982]

[5]Probably based on the definition of a proverb which LORD
JOHN RUSSELL gave one morning at breakfast at Mardock's:
"One man's wit, and all men's wisdom."—*Memoirs of Sir
James Mackintosh, vol. 1, p. 473*

[6]Quoted as an old song by ANTHONY TROLLOPE in *Barches-
ter Towers* [1857], *ch. 46.*
   See Shaw, 570:9.

[7]The classical American rural tune . . . steps around like
an apple-faced farmhand . . . as American as Andrew Jackson, Johnny Appleseed, and Corn on the Cob.—SANDBURG,
The American Songbag [1927]

1 Sugar in the gourd and honey in the horn,
I never was so happy since the hour I was born.
Turkey in the Straw, st. 6

2 Jimmie crack corn and I don't care,
Old Massa's gone away.
The Blue-tail Fly, chorus

3 Give me that old-time religion,
It's good enough for me.
Hymn

4 It was good for Paul and Silas
And it's good enough for me.
Ibid.

5   I expect to pass through this world but once; any
good thing therefore that I can do, or any kindness
that I can show to any fellow creature, let me do it
now; let me not defer or neglect it, for I shall not
pass this way again.[1]   *Proverbial saying*

6 I've been working on the railroad
All the livelong day,
I've been working on the railroad
To pass the time away.
Don't you hear the whistle blowing?
Rise up so early in the morn.
Don't you hear the captain shouting,
"Dinah blow your horn."
I've Been Working on the Railroad

7   When [or Since] Hector was a pup.
American saying

8   OK.
*Abbreviation for humorous misspelling, "oll
korrect" [1838][2]*

9 'Tis the gift to be simple,
'Tis the gift to be free,
'Tis the gift to come down
Where we ought to be.
Simple Gifts. Shaker song [c. 1848], st. 1

10 Buffalo gals, won't you come out tonight,
And dance by the light of the moon?
Buffalo Gals

11   Women and children first.
The Birkenhead Drill[3] [February 26, 1852]

12   You can't use tact with a Congressman! A Congressman is a hog! You must take a stick and hit him
on the snout!   *Remark[4]*

13 Up and down the City Road,
In and out the Eagle,
That's the way the money goes—
Pop goes the weasel!
Pop Goes the Weasel[5] [c. 1853]

14   Free soil, free men, free speech, Frémont.[6]
Republican party rallying cry [1856]

15   Muscular Christianity.[7]
*Popular term for Christian social reform in
England*

16   It is a newspaper's duty to print the news and
raise hell.   *The Chicago Times [1861]*

17   Dirty work at the crossroads.
*Attributed to WALTER MELVILLE's melodrama
The Girl Who Took the Wrong Turning; or, No
Wedding Bells for Him*

18 The man on horseback.
*Popular term for General Georges Ernest
Boulanger [1837–1891]*

19   All I want of you is a little seevility, and that of
the commonest goddamnedest kind.[8]
*The New Bedford Classic, as reported in
ZEPHANIAH W. PEASE, The History of New
Bedford [1918]. Supposed to be said by the mate
of a whaler to his ill-humored captain*

20 John Henry told his captain,
Says, "A man ain't nothin' but a man,
And before I'd let your steam drill beat me down,
Lord,
I'd die with this hammer in my hand.
John Henry [1873]

21 You-all means a race or section,
Family, party, tribe, or clan;
You-all means the whole connection
Of the individual man.
You-All; from the Richmond Times-Dispatch

22 From the halls of Montezuma,
To the shores of Tripoli,
We fight our country's battles
On the land as on the sea.
The Marines' Hymn [1847],[9] st. 1

23 There is a tavern in the town,
And there my true love sits him down,

---

[1]This saying has been attributed to many authors, most especially to STEPHEN GRELLET [Étienne de Grellet du Mabillier,
1773–1855], although it has not been found in any of Grellet's
writings.
See Addison, 292:19.

[2]For the history of this "most popular typical American
expression," see STUART BERG FLEXNER, *I Hear America Talking* [1976], pp. 261–262.

[3]The women and children were the first to be removed from
the sinking ship *Birkenhead*.

[4]Made by an unidentified cabinet member (possibly Secretary of the Interior JACOB DOLSON COX [1828–1900]), quoted
by HENRY ADAMS, *The Education of Henry Adams, ch. 17.*

[5]The weasel was a hatter's tool, and "pop" was a term
meaning to pawn or "hock." The Eagle was a music hall in the
City Road. The song is attributed to W. R. MANDALE.

[6]John Charles Frémont [1813–1890] was the party's candidate for President.

[7]A term applied (from about 1857) to the ideal of religious
character exhibited in the writings of Charles Kingsley.—
Oxford English Dictionary
His Christianity was muscular.—DISRAELI, *Endymion*
[1880], *ch. 14*

[8]Another traditional version, repudiated by a New Bedford
authority, is that the skipper said: "All I want out of you is
silence, and damn little of that."

[9]See Anonymous, 783:13.

And drinks his wine with laughter and with glee,
And never, never thinks of me.
                    There Is a Tavern in the Town, st. 1

1 Adieu, adieu, kind friends, adieu, adieu, adieu,
I can no longer stay with you.
I'll hang my harp on a weeping willow-tree,
And may the world go well with thee.
                                    Ibid. refrain

2 I belong to that highly respectable tribe
Which is known as the Shabby Genteel . . .
Too proud to beg, too honest to steal.
    *The Shabby Genteel; sung by Sol Smith Russell
    [1848–1901] in A Poor Relation*

3 The sons of the prophet are brave men and bold,
And quite unaccustomed to fear,
But the bravest by far in the ranks of the Shah
Was Abdullah Bulbul Amir.
                Abdullah Bulbul Amir [1877], st. 1

4 Now the heroes were plenty and well known to
    fame
In the troops that were led by the Czar,
And the bravest of these was a man by the name
Of Ivan Petrofski Skevar.
                                        Ibid. st. 3

5 Is that Mr. Reilly, can anyone tell?
Is that Mr. Reilly that owns the hotel?
Well, if that's Mr. Reilly, they speak of so highly,
Upon me soul, Reilly, you're doin' quite well.
                Is That Mr. Reilly?[1] [1882], chorus

6 Sow a thought, and you reap an act;
Sow an act, and you reap a habit;
Sow a habit, and you reap a character;
Sow a character, and you reap a destiny.
    *Quoted by SAMUEL SMILES [1812–1904], in Life
    and Labor [1887]*

7 Now is the time for all good men to come to the
aid of the party.
            Practice sentence used in typewriting[2]

8 The quick brown fox jumps over the lazy dog.
                    Ibid. (using whole alphabet)

9 As Maine goes, so goes the nation.[3]
                    American political maxim [c. 1888]

10 Slide, Kelly, Slide.
                Title of song by J. W. KELLY [1889]

11 Lizzie Borden took an ax
And gave her mother forty whacks;

When she saw what she had done
She gave her father forty-one!
    *Rhyme popular after the murder trial of Lizzie
    Borden, Fall River, Massachusetts [June 1893]*

12 Out in the fields with God!
                                Out in the Fields

13   Remember the Maine![4]
            Slogan in the Spanish-American War [1898]

14 Frankie and Johnny were lovers, my gawd, how
        they could love,
Swore to be true to each other, true as the stars
    above;
He was her man, but he done her wrong.
                        Frankie and Johnny,[5] st. 1

15 The halls of fame are open wide
And they are always full;
Some go in by the door called "push,"
And some by the door called "pull."
    *Quoted by STANLEY BALDWIN [1867–1947] in a
    speech in the House of Commons*

16 The codfish lays ten thousand eggs,
The homely hen lays one.
The codfish never cackles
To tell you what she's done.
And so we scorn the codfish,
While the humble hen we prize,
Which only goes to show you
That it pays to advertise.
                            It Pays to Advertise

17 One white foot—try him,
Two white feet—buy him,
Three white feet—look well about him;
Four white feet—go without him.[6]
                        Rhyme for a horse-buyer

18   An apple a day keeps the doctor away.
                        Current since the 19th century

19   Time is of the essence.   *Saying*

20   All the world is queer save me and thee; and
sometimes I think thee is a little queer.
    Attributed to a Quaker, speaking to his wife

21   Everyone has at least one sermon in him.
                                            Saying

22   You can always tell a Harvard man, but you can't
tell him much.
            Attributed to JAMES BARNES [1866–1936]

23   I seen my duty and I done it.
                        Current since the 19th century

---

[1]Assumed origin of "the life of Riley" (an easy life).

[2]Charles Weller, a court reporter, originated this expression
in . . . 1867 to test the efficiency of the first practical typewriter which his friend Christopher Sholes had constructed.
—*Life* [April 11, 1955]

[3]As Maine goes, so goes Vermont.—JAMES A. FARLEY
[1888–1976], *statement to press* [November 4, 1936], *after pre-
dicting correctly that Roosevelt would carry all but two states
in the presidential election*

[4]Derived from cartoon caption by CLIFFORD K. BERRYMAN
[1869–1949] in *The Washington Post* [April 3, 1898]: If the row
comes, REMEMBER THE MAINE, and show the world how American sailors can fight.

[5]Traditional ballad; there are innumerable versions and
verses.

[6]Three white feet and a white nose, / Rip off his skin and
throw him to the crows.—*New Hampshire version of last two
lines*

1   Keeping up with the Joneses.   *Popular saying*

2   Paying through the nose.
Popular phrase for excessive payment

3   Doesn't amount to Hannah Cook.[1]
Saying common in Maine and on Cape Cod

4   Hit's a lot worse to be soul-hungry than to be body-hungry.
A Kentucky mountain woman asking for her granddaughter to be admitted to Berea College high school [c. 1900]. Quoted by CARL R. WOODWARD *in The Wonderful World of Books, edited by Alfred Stefferud [1953]*

5   There ain't no such animal.
Caption for cartoon of a farmer at the circus looking at a dromedary. From Life [November 7, 1907], credited to Everybody's Magazine

6   How old is Ann?
Popular phrase for "who knows?" [early 20th century][2]

7   The Pyramids first, which in Egypt were laid;
Next Babylon's Gardens, for Amytis made;
Then Mausolos' Tomb of affection and guilt;
Fourth, the Temple of Dian in Ephesus built;
The Colossus of Rhodes, cast in brass, to the Sun;
Sixth, Jupiter's Statue, by Phidias done;
The Pharos of Egypt comes last, we are told,
Or the Palace of Cyrus, cemented with gold.
Seven Wonders of the Ancient World

8   Use it up, wear it out;
Make it do, or do without.
New England maxim

9   Earned a precarious living by taking in one another's washing.   *Saying*

10   Something old, something new,
Something borrowed, something blue,
And a lucky sixpence in her shoe.[3]
Wedding rhyme

11   God looks after fools, drunkards, and the United States.
Epigram

12   Church ain't out till the fat lady sings.[4]
From FABIA RUE SMITH *and* CHARLES RAYFORD SMITH, *Southern Words and Sayings [1976]*

13   Oh, why don't you work
Like other men do?

How the hell can I work
When there's no work to do?
Hallelujah, I'm a Bum [c. 1907]

14   We want bread and roses too.
Slogan of women strikers, Lawrence, Massachusetts [1912]

15   Old soldiers never die;
They only fade away![5]
British Army song [c. 1915]

16   I didn't raise my boy to be a soldier.
A Mother's Plea for Peace [1915]

17   She was poor but she was honest,[6]
And her parents was the same,
Till she met a city feller,
And she lost her honest name.
Song [c. 1915]

18   It's the same the whole world over,
It's the poor wot gets the blame,
It's the rich wot gets the pleasure,
Ain't it all a bloomin' shame?
Ibid. chorus

19   Fifty million Frenchmen can't be wrong.[7]
Saying popular with American soldiers during World War I [1917–1918]

20   Say it ain't so, Joe.
Small boy to "Shoeless Joe" Jackson of the Chicago White Sox, as he emerged from a grand jury session [1920] on corruption in the 1919 World Series

21   One picture is worth a thousand words.
Misattributed "Chinese proverb"[8]

22   Don't sell America short.   *Saying [c. 1925]*

23   Don't lose
Your head
To gain a minute
You need your head
Your brains are in it.
Burma-Shave, roadside advertisement [1925–1963]

24   No woman can be too rich or too thin.
Saying[9]

[5]See MacArthur, 642:5.
[6]See Shakespeare, 203:11.
[7]Sometimes "forty" or "thirty" is heard instead of "fifty." When Texas Guinan and her troupe were refused entry into France [1931], she was quoted as saying: "It goes to show that fifty million Frenchmen *can* be wrong." She promptly renamed her show *Too Hot for Paris,* and toured the United States with it.
[8]"One look is worth a thousand words." Fred R. Barnard, in *Printers' Ink,* 8 Dec., 1921, p. 96. He changed it to "One picture is worth a thousand words" in *Printers' Ink,* 10 March, 1927, p. 114, and called it "a Chinese proverb, so that people would take it seriously."—BURTON STEVENSON, ed., *The Home Book of Proverbs, Maxims, and Familiar Phrases* [1948]
[9]Frequently attributed to the DUCHESS OF WINDSOR and others.
Tell a female she's thin and she's yours for life.—ANNE BERNAYS [1930–], *Professor Romeo* [1989]

[1]Variously explained as a character who once lived on Campobello Island; a corruption of a phrase in Indian dialect; and a comparison with the worthlessness (for navigation) of a cook on board ship.
[2]"Mary is 24 years old. She is twice as old as Ann was when Mary was as old as Ann is now. How old is Ann?"—*Brain-twister in the New York Press* [October 16, 1903]
    Answer: Ann is 18.
[3]There are variants for the less familiar last line, such as: And a silver sixpence in each shoe.
[4]Proverbial lore current in several variant forms, the most familiar and recent of which is: The opera ain't over till the fat lady sings.—DANIEL JOHN COOK [1926–], *television newscast, San Antonio, Texas* [April 1978]

1 No good deed goes unpunished.   *Saying*

2 God is in the details.   *Saying*[1]

3 Tennis, anyone?   *Saying*[2]

4 Lord, through this hour
Be Thou our Guide,
So by Thy power
No foot shall slide.

          Westminster Chimes

5 Climb high
Climb far
Your goal the sky
Your aim the star.

    Inscription on Hopkins Memorial Steps,
    Williams College, Williamstown, Massachusetts

6 Mother, may I go out to swim?
Yes, my darling daughter:
Hang your clothes on a hickory limb
And don't go near the water.

          Rhyme

7 See the happy moron,
He doesn't give a damn.
I wish I were a moron—
My God, perhaps I am!

          Rhyme

8 The difficult we do immediately. The impossible takes a little longer.

    Slogan of United States Army Service Forces

9 Loose lips sink ships.

    Government slogan, World War II

10 Kilroy was here.[3]

    Army saying, World War II

11 SNAFU (Situation Normal All Fouled Up).

          Ibid.

12 G.I. Joe.

    World War II term for infantryman[4]

13 And when he goes to heaven
To Saint Peter he will tell:
Another Marine reporting, sir;
I've served my time in hell![5]

    Epitaph on grave of Pfc. Cameron of the
    Marine Corps, Guadalcanal [1942]

14 Stay with me, God. The night is dark,
The night is cold: my little spark

Of courage dies. The night is long;
Be with me, God, and make me strong.

    A Soldier—His Prayer,[6] *st. 1*

15 We sure liberated the hell out of this place.

    American soldier in the ruins of a French village
    [1944]; quoted by MAX MILLER, *The Far Shore*
    [1945]

16 Spartan simplicity must be observed. Nothing will be done merely because it contributes to beauty, convenience, comfort, or prestige.

    From the Office of the Chief Signal Officer, U.S.
    Army [May 29, 1945]

17 Education is what you have left over after you have forgotten everything you have learned.

          Saying

18 Time is a river without banks.[7]   *Saying*

19 Till Hell freezes over.   *Saying*

20 One man, one vote.   *Civil rights slogan*

21 We shall overcome, we shall overcome,
We shall overcome some day
Oh, deep in my heart I do believe
We shall overcome some day.

    Adapted [1960s] for the civil rights movement
    from an old religious song[8]

22 This is the grave of Mike O'Day
Who died maintaining his right of way.
His right was clear, his will was strong,[9]
But he's just as dead as if he'd been wrong.

    Rhyme [20th century]

23 Do not fold, spindle, or mutilate.

    Instructions on punch cards and computer cards
    [c. 1950s]

24 That's the way the cookie crumbles.

          Saying [1950s]

25 "Murphy's Law": If anything can go wrong, it will.   *Ibid.*

26 Winning isn't everything, it's the only thing.

    Saying [1953], often attributed to Vanderbilt
    University coach Red Sanders[10]

27 What, Me Worry?

    Mad magazine ("Alfred E. Newman") motto
    [1955], adapted from a turn-of-the-century
    advertising slogan

---

[1] A popular aphorism with the architect Ludwig Mies van der Rohe and the art historian Aby Warburg; attributed [*Le bon Dieu est dans le détail*] to GUSTAVE FLAUBERT but without verification.

[2] Frequently attributed to actor HUMPHREY BOGART, who resolutely denied saying it in any play or movie.

[3] See Faulkner, 697:3.

[4] This name, chosen for the soldier in Lieutenant DAVE BREGER's comic strip for *Yank*, the Army weekly, first appeared in the issue of June 17, 1942. Writing in *Time* [February 26, 1945], Lieutenant Breger said: "I decided on 'G.I. Joe,' the 'G.I.' [Government Issue] because of its prevalence in Army talk, and the 'Joe' for the alliterative effect."

[5] From *The Marines' Hymn;* see Anonymous, 780:22.

[6] This poem, found on a scrap of paper in a slit trench in Tunisia during the battle of El Agheila, was printed in *Poems from the Desert,* by members of the British Eighth Army [1944].

[7] Title of a painting by Marc Chagall.
See Marcus Aurelius, 111:10, and Watts, 294:16.

[8] Originating in pre–Civil War days, this song was adapted [c. 1900] by C. ALBERT TINDLEY as a Baptist hymn called "I'll Overcome Some Day." It became famous as a protest theme when sung by black workers on picket lines in Charleston, S.C. [1946].

[9] In some versions: He was right, dead right, as he sped along.

[10] Compare: Winning isn't everything, but wanting to win is.
—VINCE [VINCENT THOMAS] LOMBARDI [1913–1970], *interview* [1962]

1   Black is beautiful.[1]   *Slogan [1960s]*

2   We are the people of this generation, bred in at least modest comfort, housed now in universities, looking uncomfortably to the world we inherit.
> *Students for a Democratic Society, Port Huron Statement [1962], Preamble*

3   Eyeball to eyeball.[2]   *Common expression*

4   Carnation Milk is the best in the land;
Here I sit with a can in my hand—
No tits to pull, no hay to pitch,
You just punch a hole in the son of a bitch.
> *The Virtues of Carnation Milk. From David Ogilvy, Confessions of an Advertising Man [1963]*

5   America, love it or leave it.   *Slogan [1960s]*

6   It became necessary to destroy the town in order to save it.
> *Attributed to an American officer firing on Ben Tre, Vietnam [February 8, 1968]*

7   Here men from the planet Earth first set foot on the moon, July 1969 A.D. We came in peace for all mankind.
> *Plaque on moon marking the U.S. landing there [July 1969]*

8   Today is the first day of the rest of your life.
> *Wall slogan [1970s]*

9   Garbage in, garbage out (GIGO).
> *Computer-users' aphorism [1970s]*

10   Beam me up, Scotty. There's no intelligent life down here.
> *Invented [early 1970s] by fans of Star Trek television series[3]*

11   A mind is a terrible thing to waste.
> *United Negro College Fund advertising slogan [1972][4]*

12   Expletive deleted.
> *White House transcripts [published 1974]*

13   The most fundamental lesson of Three Mile Island, one that must be continually emphasized, is that accidents can happen.
> *Report of Congressional Subcommittee on Energy Research and Production [1980]*

14   A woman without a man is like a fish without a bicycle.   *Feminist slogan [1980s]*

15   What you see is what you get (WYSIWYG).
> *Computer-users' aphorism [1980s]*

---

[1]See Langston Hughes, 708:13.
[2]We're eyeball to eyeball, and I think the other fellow just blinked.—DEAN RUSK [1909–], *Conversation [October 24, 1962] during the Cuban missile crisis*
[3]Catchphrase based on a line from *Star Trek* scripts: Beam us up, Mr. Scott.
For *Star Trek,* see Roddenberry, 749:7.
[4]What a waste it is to lose one's mind or not to have a mind is very wasteful.—DAN [J. DANFORTH] QUAYLE [1947–], *address to United Negro College Fund [May 1989]*

Anonymous: African

16   In the time when Dendid created all things,
He created the sun,
And the sun is born, and dies, and comes again.
> *Old Song (Dinka)*

17   He created man,
And man is born, and dies, and does not come again.
> *Ibid.*

18   Somewhere the Sky touches the Earth, and the name of that place is the End.
> *Saying (Wakamba)*

19   All animals of the forest are alike, though we eat some and not others, because we the Dorobo and the animals all live side by side in the forest.
> *From a Dorobo*

20   Everything has an end.   *Saying (Masai)*

21   When elephants fight it is the grass that suffers.
> *Proverb (Kikuyu)*

22   Haste, haste, has no blessing.
> *Proverb (Swahili)*

23   To the person who seizes two things, one always slips from his grasp!   *Proverb (Swahili)*

24   The lie has seven endings.   *Proverb (Swahili)*

25   Goodness sold itself, badness flaunted itself about.   *Proverb (Swahili)*

26   Speak silver, reply gold.   *Proverb (Swahili)*

27   The prayer of the chicken hawk does not get him the chicken.   *Proverb (Swahili)*

28   Wisdom is not bought.   *Proverb (Akan)*

29   Not even God is wise enough.
> *Proverb (Yoruba)*

30   Leave a log in the water as long as you like: it will never be a crocodile.   *Proverb (Guinea-Bissau)*

Anonymous: Ballads

31   The king sits in Dunfermline town
Drinking the blude-red wine.
> *Sir Patrick Spens, st. 1*

32   To Noroway, to Noroway,
To Noroway o'er the faem;
The king's daughter o' Noroway,
'Tis thou must bring her hame.
> *Ibid. st. 4*

33   I saw the new moon late yestreen
Wi' the auld moon in her arm;
And if we gang to sea, master,
I fear we'll come to harm.
> *Ibid. st. 10*

34   O laith, laith were our gude Scots lords
To wet their cork-heel'd shoon;

But lang or a' the play was play'd
They wat their hats aboon.

Ibid. st. 15

1 Half owre, half owre to Aberdour,
'Tis fifty fathoms deep;
And there lies gude Sir Patrick Spens,
Wi' the Scots lords at his feet!

Ibid. st. 19

2 "And what will ye leave to your ain mither dear,
Edward, Edward?"

Edward, Edward, st. 7

3 "The curse of hell frae me sall ye bear,
Sic counsels ye give to me, O!"

Ibid.

4 Fight on, my merry men all;
For why, my life is at an end.[1]

Chevy Chase

5 A fairer lady there never was seen
Than the blind beggar's daughter of Bethnal
Green.

The Beggar's Daughter of Bethnal Green,[2] st. 33

6 When captains courageous, whom death could not
daunt,
Did march to the siege of the city of Gaunt,
They mustered their soldiers by two and by three,
And the foremost in battle was Mary Ambree.

Mary Ambree,[3] st. 1

7 "I'll rest," said he, "but thou shalt walk";
So doth this wandering Jew
From place to place, but cannot rest
For seeing countries new.

The Wandering Jew, st. 9

8 Glasgerion swore a full great oath,
By oak, and ash and thorn.

Glasgerion, st. 19

9 In Scarlet town, where I was born,
There was a fair maid dwellin',
Made every youth cry Well-a-day!
Her name was Barbara Allen.

All in the merry month of May,
When green buds they were swellin',
Young Jemmy Grove on his deathbed lay,
For love of Barbara Allen.

Barbara Allen's Cruelty, st. 1, 2

10 So slowly, slowly rase she up,
And slowly she came nigh him,

And when she drew the curtain by—
"Young man, I think you're dyin'."

Ibid. st. 4

11 True Thomas lay on Huntlie Bank;
A ferlie he spied wi' his e'e;
And there he saw a lady bright
Come riding down by the Eildon Tree.

Thomas the Rhymer, st. 1

12 "A bed, a bed," Clerk Saunders said,
"A bed for you and me!"
"Fye na, fye na," said may Margaret,
"Till anes we married be!"

Clerk Saunders, st. 2

13 There were twa sisters sat in a bour;
Binnorie, O Binnorie!
There came a knight to be their wooer,
By the bonnie milldams o' Binnorie.

Binnorie, st. 1

14 There were three ravens sat on a tree,
They were as black as they might be.

The one of them said to his mate,
"Where shall we our breakfast take?"

The Three Ravens, st. 1, 2

15 Down there came a fallow doe
As great with young as she might go.

Ibid. st. 6

16 She buried him before the prime,
She was dead herself ere evensong time.

God send every gentleman
Such hounds, such hawks, and such leman.

Ibid. st. 9, 10

17 Mony a one for him maks mane,
But nane sall ken where he is gane:
O'er his white banes, when they are bare,
The wind sall blaw for evermair.

The Twa Corbies, st. 5

18 Ye Highlands and ye Lawlands,
O where hae ye been?
They hae slain the Earl of Murray,
And laid him on the green.

The Bonny Earl of Murray, st. 1

19 O waly, waly, up the bank,
And waly, waly, doun the brae,
And waly, waly, yon burnside,
Where I and my Love wont to gae!

Waly, Waly, st. 1

20 "What gat ye to your dinner, Lord Randal, my
son?
What gat ye to your dinner, my handsome young
man?"
"I gat eels boil'd in broo'; mother, make my bed
soon,
For I'm weary wi' hunting, and fain wald lie
down."

Lord Randal

[1]Says Johnnie, "Fight on, my merry men all, / I'm a little
wounded, but I am not slain; / I will lay me down for to bleed
a while, / Then I'll rise and fight with you again."—*Johnnie
Armstrong's Last Goodnight, st. 18; from* DRYDEN'S *Miscellanies* [1702]

[2]This very house was built by the blind beggar of Bednall
Green, so much talked of and sung in ballads.—SAMUEL
PEPYS, *Diary* [June 26, 1663]

[3]BEN JONSON calls any virago Mary Ambree, and JOHN
FLETCHER alludes to Mary Ambree in *The Scornful Lady*
[1616].

Anonymous: Cowboy Songs

1 As I was a-walking one morning for pleasure,
I spied a cowpuncher a-riding along.
Whoopee Ti Yi Yo, Git Along, Little Dogies

2 Whoopee ti yi yo, git along, little dogies,
It's your misfortune and none of my own,
Whoopee ti yi yo, git along, little dogies,
For you know Wyoming will be your new home.
Ibid.

3 My foot in the stirrup, my pony won't stand,
Good-bye, Old Paint, I'm a-leavin' Cheyenne.
Good-bye Old Paint

4 Foot in the stirrup and hand on the horn,
Best damned cowboy ever was born.
Come-a ti yi youpy, youpy yea, youpy yea,
Come-a ti yi youpy, youpy yea.
The Old Chisholm Trail

5 Last night as I lay on the prairie,
And looked at the stars in the sky,
I wondered if ever a cowboy
Would drift to that sweet bye-and-bye.
The Cowboy's Dream

6 As I walked out in the streets of Laredo,
As I walked out in Laredo one day,
I spied a poor cowboy wrapped up in white
linen,
Wrapped up in white linen as cold as the clay.
The Cowboy's Lament, st. 1

7 Oh, beat the drum slowly[1] and play the fife
lowly,
Play the Dead March as you carry me along;
Take me to the green valley, there lay the sod o'er
me,
For I'm a young cowboy and I know I've done
wrong.
Ibid. refrain

8 Oh bury me not on the lone prairie
Where the wild coyotes will howl o'er me.
The Dying Cowboy

9 Oh, bury me out on the prairie,
Where the coyotes may howl o'er my grave.
Bury Me Out on the Prairie

10   Remember the Red River Valley
And the cowboy that loves you so true.
Red River Valley

11 Oh, give me a home where the buffalo roam,
Where the deer and the antelope play,
Where seldom is heard a discouraging word
And the skies are not cloudy all day.
Home on the Range [1873][2]

[1] Also familiar as: Oh, bang the drum slowly.
[2] Possibly written by BREWSTER HIGLEY.

Anonymous: French

12   Revenons à nos moutons [Let us return to our
sheep—i.e., subject].
Maître Pathelin (15th-century farce)

13   Il ne faut pas être plus royaliste que le roi [One
must not be more royalist than the king].
Saying from the time of Louis XVI

14   Ça ira, ça tiendra [That will be, that will last].
*Revolutionary song, based on a phrase of
Benjamin Franklin's*

15   Liberté! Égalité! Fraternité! [Liberty! Equality!
Fraternity!]
*Phrase from before the French Revolution,
officially adopted in 1793*

16   Tout passe, tout casse, tout lasse [Everything
passes, everything perishes, everything palls].[3]
Proverb

17   Ah, les bons vieux temps où nous étions si malheureux! [Oh, the good old times when we were so
unhappy!]
Saying

18   L'amour, l'amour fait tourner le monde [It's love,
it's love that makes the world go round].[4]
Song

19   On ne saurait faire une omelette sans casser des
oeufs [You can't make an omelet without breaking
eggs].
Proverb

20 Ami, entends-tu
Le vol noir—des corbeaux—sur nos plaines . . .

Ami, entends-tu
Les cris sourds—du pays—qu'on enchaîne.[5]
Song of the Partisans [1940s]

21 Au clair de la lune,
Mon ami Pierrot,
Prête-moi ta plume
Pour écrire un mot.

Au Clair de la Lune[6]

Anonymous: North American Indian

22 Screaming the night away
With his great wing feathers
Swooping the darkness up;
I hear the Eagle bird
Pulling the blanket back
Off from the eastern sky.

Invitation Song (Iroquois)

[3] See Apollinaire, 641:10.
[4] See W. S. Gilbert, 530:16.
[5] Friend, do you hear / The black flight—of our crows—
on our plains . . . / Friend, do you hear / The faint cries—
of the country—in chains.
[6] By the light of the moon, / My friend Pierrot, / Lend me your
pen / To write a word.
This song, with music by JEAN BAPTISTE LULLY [1632–
1687], has been popular since the time of Louis XVI [1638–
1715].

1   Holy Mother Earth, the trees and all nature are witnesses of your thoughts and deeds.
Saying (Winnebago)

2   A people without history is like the wind on the buffalo grass.   *Saying (Sioux)*

3 Out of the earth
I sing for them
a Horse nation . . .
I sing for them
the animals.
I Sing for the Animals (Teton Sioux)

4 O our Mother the Earth, O our Father the Sky,
Your children are we, and with tired backs
We bring you gifts.   *Song of the Sky Loom (Tewa)*

5 May the warp be the white light of morning,
May the weft be the red light of evening,
May the fringes be the falling rain,
May the border be the standing rainbow.
Thus weave for us a garment of brightness.
Ibid.

6 Lovely! See the cloud, the cloud appear!
Lovely! See the rain, the rain draw near!
Who spoke?
It was the little corn ear
High on the tip of the stalk.
Corn-grinding Song (Zuñi)

7 Big Blue Mountain Spirit,
The home made of blue clouds . . .
I am grateful for that mode of goodness there.
Chant (Apache)[1]

8 The black turkey gobbler, the tips of his beautiful
tail; above us the dawn becomes yellow.
The sunbeams stream forward.
Black Turkey Gobbler Chant (Apache)[2]

9 House made of dawn,[3]
House made of evening light,
House made of the dark cloud. . . .
Dark cloud is at the house's door,
The trail out of it is dark cloud,
The zigzag lightning stands high upon it.
Night Chant (Navaho)[4]

10 Happily may I walk.
May it be beautiful before me.
May it be beautiful behind me.
May it be beautiful below me.
May it be beautiful above me.
May it be beautiful all around me.
In beauty it is finished.
Ibid.

11 Lo, the Turquoise Horse of Johano-ai . . .
There he spurneth dust of glittering grains—
How joyous his neigh.
Song of the Horse (Navaho)

12 Hi! ni! ya! Behold the man of flint, that's me!
Four lightnings zigzag from me, strike and return.
War Chant (Navaho)

13 The ancient folk with evil spells, dashed to earth,
plowed under!
Ibid.

14 Quarry mine, blessed am I
In the luck of the chase.
Comes the deer to my singing.
Hunting Song (Navaho)

15 Idlers and cowards are here at home now,
But the youth I love is gone to war, far hence.
Weary, lonely, for me he longs.
Wind Song (Kiowa)

16   In the beginning God gave to every people a cup
of clay, and from this cup they drank their life.
Proverb (Northern Paiute)

17 As long as the moon shall rise,
As long as the rivers shall flow,
As long as the sun shall shine,
As long as the grass shall grow.
Expression for term of a treaty

18 It ended . . .
With his body changed to light,
A star that burns forever in that sky.
The Flight of Quetzalcoatl (Aztec)[5]

19 I was out in my kayak . . .
and the seal came gently toward me.
Why didn't I harpoon him?
Was I sorry for him?
Was it the day, the spring day, the seal
playing in the sun
like me?
Spring Fjord (Eskimo)[6]

Anonymous: Nursery Rhymes

20 A man of words and not of deeds
Is like a garden full of weeds.
A Man of Words and Not of Deeds

21 It's like a lion at the door;
And when the door begins to crack,
It's like a stick across your back;
And when your back begins to smart,
It's like a penknife in your heart;
And when your heart begins to bleed,
You're dead, and dead, and dead, indeed.
Ibid.

[1]Translated by HARRY HOIJER.
[2]Translated by PLINY E. GODDARD.
[3]See Momaday, 766:14.
[4]Translated by WASHINGTON MATTHEWS.

[5]Translated by JEROME ROTHENBERG.
[6]Translated by ARMAND SCHWERNER.

1 Cock a doodle doo!
My dame has lost her shoe;
My master's lost his fiddle stick,
And knows not what to do.

Cock a Doodle Doo

2 Three blind mice, see how they run!
They all ran after the farmer's wife,
She cut off their tails with a carving knife,
Did you ever see such a sight in your life,
As three blind mice?

Three Blind Mice

3 A frog he would a-wooing go.
Sing heigh-ho says Rowley.

A Frog He Would A-Wooing Go

4 With a rowley powley gammon and spinach,
Heigh-ho says Anthony Rowley.

Ibid. chorus

5 Old King Cole
Was a merry old soul,
And a merry old soul was he,
He called for his pipe,
And he called for his bowl,
And he called for his fiddlers three.

Old King Cole

6 The King of France went up the hill
With forty thousand men;
The King of France came down the hill
And ne'er went up again.

The King of France

7 Jack Sprat could eat no fat,
His wife could eat no lean;
And so betwixt them both,
They licked the platter clean.

Jack Sprat

8 Rain, rain, go away,
Come again another day.

Rain, Rain

9 Pat-a-cake, pat-a-cake, baker's man,
Bake me a cake as fast as you can;
Pat it and prick it, and mark it with B,
Put it in the oven for baby and me.

Pat-a-Cake

10 The lion and the unicorn
Were fighting for the crown;
The lion beat the unicorn
All round about the town.
Some gave them white bread,
And some gave them brown;
Some gave them plum cake,
And sent them out of town.

The Lion and the Unicorn

11 Little Jack Horner sat in the corner,
Eating a Christmas pie.
He put in his thumb, and pulled out a plum,
And said, "What a good boy am I!"

Little Jack Horner

12 London Bridge is falling down,
My fair lady.

London Bridge

13 Tell tale tit,
Your tongue shall be slit,
And all the dogs in our town
Shall have a bit.

Tell Tale Tit

14 As I was going to St. Ives,
I met a man with seven wives,
Each wife had seven sacks,
Each sack had seven cats,
Each cat had seven kits:
Kits, cats, sacks, and wives,
How many were there going to St. Ives?

As I Was Going to St. Ives

15 The man in the wilderness asked of me
How many strawberries grew in the sea.
I answered him as I thought good,
"As many as red herrings grow in the wood."

The Man in the Wilderness

16 Ladybug, ladybug, fly away home,
Your house is on fire, and your children will burn.

Ladybug, Ladybug

17 Hickory dickory dock,
The mouse ran up the clock,
The clock struck one,
The mouse ran down;
Hickory dickory dock.

Hickory Dickory Dock

18 Baa, baa, black sheep,
Have you any wool?
Yes, sir, yes, sir,
Three bags full:
One for my master,
And one for my dame,
And one for the little boy
Who lives down the lane.

Baa, Baa, Black Sheep

19 Mary, Mary, quite contrary,
How does your garden grow?
With silver bells, and cockleshells,
And pretty maids all in a row.

Mary, Mary, Quite Contrary

20 Oranges and lemons,
Say the bells of St. Clement's.
You owe me five farthings,
Say the bells of St. Martin's.
When will you pay me?
Say the bells of Old Bailey.
When I grow rich,
Say the bells of Shoreditch.

Oranges and Lemons

21 Here comes a candle to light you to bed,
Here comes a chopper to chop off your head.

Ibid.

1 "Who killed Cock Robin?"
  "I," said the sparrow,
  "With my bow and arrow,
  I killed Cock Robin."[1]

Who Killed Cock Robin?

2 "Who saw him die?"
  "I," said the fly,
  "With my little eye,
  I saw him die."

Ibid.

3 This little pig went to market;
  This little pig stayed home;
  This little pig had roast beef;
  This little pig had none;
  And this little pig cried, Wee, wee, wee!
  All the way home.

This Little Pig

4 Little boy blue, come blow your horn,
  The sheep's in the meadow, the cow's in the corn;
  But where is the boy who looks after the sheep?
  He's under the haystack fast asleep.
  Will you wake him? No, not I,
  For if I do, he'll be sure to cry.

Little Boy Blue

5 Simple Simon met a pieman
  Going to the fair:
  Says Simple Simon to the pieman,
  "Let me taste your ware."

Simple Simon

6 Ding dong bell,
  Pussy's in the well.
  Who put her in?
  Little Johnny Green.

Ding Dong Bell

7 Little Tom Tucker
  Sings for his supper;
  What shall he eat?
  White bread and butter.
  How will he cut it
  Without e'er a knife?
  How will he be married
  Without e'er a wife?

Little Tom Tucker

8 Crosspatch, draw the latch,
  Set by the fire and spin:
  Take a cup and drink it up,
  Then call your neighbors in.

Crosspatch

9 High diddle diddle
  The cat and the fiddle,
  The cow jumped over the moon;
  The little dog laughed
  To see such craft
  And the dish ran away with the spoon.

High Diddle Diddle

[1]See Byron, 403:28.

10 Three wise men of Gotham
   Went to sea in a bowl:
   And if the bowl had been stronger,
   My song had been longer.

Three Wise Men of Gotham

11 Jack and Jill went up the hill
   To fetch a pail of water;
   Jack fell down and broke his crown,
   And Jill came tumbling after.

Jack and Jill

12 Seesaw, Margery Daw,
   Jacky shall have a new master;
   Jacky must have but a penny a day,
   Because he can work no faster.

Seesaw, Margery Daw

13 Taffy was a Welshman, Taffy was a thief;
   Taffy came to my house and stole a piece of beef.
   I went to Taffy's house, Taffy wasn't in;
   Taffy came to my house and stole a silver pin.
   I went to Taffy's house; Taffy wasn't home.
   Taffy came to my house and stole a marrow bone.
   I went to Taffy's house and Taffy was in bed;
   So I picked up the poker and hit him in the head.

Taffy Was a Welshman

14 The Queen of Hearts
   She made some tarts,
   All on a summer's day;
   The Knave of Hearts
   He stole the tarts,
   And took them clean away.

The Queen of Hearts

15 Bye baby bunting,
   Daddy's gone a-hunting.
   Gone to get a rabbit skin
   To wrap the baby bunting in.

Bye Baby Bunting

16 Come, let's to bed,
   Says Sleepyhead;
   Tarry awhile, says Slow;
   Put on the pot,
   Says Greedy-gut,
   We'll sup before we go.

Let's to Bed

17 Four and twenty tailors went to kill a snail,
   The best man among them durst not touch her
     tail.
   She put out her horns like a little Kyloe cow,
   Run, tailors, run, or she'll kill you all e'en now.

Four and Twenty Tailors

18 Goosey goosey gander,
   Whither shall I wander?
   Upstairs and downstairs,
   And in my lady's chamber;
   There I met an old man who wouldn't say his
     prayers;

I took him by the left leg
And threw him down the stairs.

Goosey Goosey Gander

1 Sing a song of sixpence,
  A pocket full of rye,
  Four and twenty blackbirds,
  Baked in a pie;
  When the pie was opened,
  The birds began to sing;
  Wasn't that a dainty dish
  To set before a king?

  The king was in his countinghouse
  Counting out his money;
  The queen was in the parlor
  Eating bread and honey;
  The maid was in the garden
  Hanging out the clothes,
  Along came a blackbird,
  And snipped off her nose.

Sing a Song of Sixpence

2 There was an old woman who lived in a shoe,
  She had so many children she didn't know what
    to do;
  She gave them some broth without any bread,
  She whipped them all soundly and put them to
    bed.

There Was an Old Woman

3 Ride a cockhorse to Banbury Cross,
  To see a fine lady upon a white horse;
  Rings on her fingers and bells on her toes,
  She shall have music wherever she goes.

Ride a Cockhorse

4 Tom, Tom, the piper's son,
  He learned to play when he was young.
  But all the tune that he could play
  Was "Over the hills and far away."[1]

Tom, Tom, the Piper's Son

5 Tom, Tom, the piper's son,
  Stole a pig, and away he run;
  The pig was eat, and Tom was beat,
  And Tom went howling down the street.

Ibid.

6 "Where are you going to, my pretty maid?"
  "I'm going a-milking, sir," she said.

Where Are You Going To, My Pretty Maid?

7 "My face is my fortune, sir," she said.

Ibid.

8 "Nobody asked you, sir," she said.

Ibid.

9 One a penny, two a penny, hot cross buns;
  If you have no daughters, give them to your sons.

Hot Cross Buns

10 Pease-porridge hot, pease-porridge cold,
   Pease-porridge in the pot, nine days old.

Pease-Porridge Hot

[1]See Gay, 297:15, and Tennyson, 456:2.

11 Curlylocks, Curlylocks,
   Wilt thou be mine?
   Thou shalt not wash dishes
   Nor yet feed the swine,
   But sit on a cushion
   And sew a fine seam,
   And feed upon strawberries,
   Sugar and cream.

Curlylocks

12 I had a little nut tree, nothing would it bear
   But a silver nutmeg and a golden pear;
   The king of Spain's daughter came to visit me,
   And all for the sake of my little nut tree.

I Had a Little Nut Tree

13 Humpty Dumpty sat on a wall,
   Humpty Dumpty had a great fall;
   All the king's horses
   And all the king's men
   Couldn't put Humpty Dumpty together again.

Humpty Dumpty

14 Little Bo-peep has lost her sheep,
   And cannot tell where to find them;
   Leave them alone, and they'll come home,
   And bring their tails behind them.

Little Bo-peep

15 Little Polly Flinders
   Sat among the cinders,
   Warming her pretty little toes.
   Her mother came and caught her,
   And whipped her little daughter
   For spoiling her nice new clothes.

Little Polly Flinders

16 There was an old woman tossed in a blanket,
   Seventeen times as high as the moon;
   But where she was going no mortal could tell,
   For under her arm she carried a broom.
   Old woman, old woman, old woman, said I,
   Whither, ah whither, ah whither so high?
   To sweep the cobwebs from the sky,
   And I'll be with you by and by.

There Was an Old Woman

17 The north wind doth blow,
   And we shall have snow,
   And what will poor robin do then,
   Poor thing?
   He'll sit in a barn,
   To keep himself warm,
   And hide his head under his wing,
   Poor thing!

The North Wind Doth Blow

18 Old mother Hubbard
   Went to the cupboard,
   To fetch her poor dog a bone;
   But when she came there
   The cupboard was bare,
   And so the poor dog had none.

Old Mother Hubbard

1 Pussy cat, pussy cat, where have you been?
I've been to London to look at the queen.
Pussy cat, pussy cat, what did you there?
I frightened a little mouse under the chair.

Pussy Cat

2 Peter Piper picked a peck of pickled peppers;
A peck of pickled peppers Peter Piper picked.
If Peter Piper picked a peck of pickled peppers,
Where's the peck of pickled peppers Peter Piper
picked?

Peter Piper

3 Monday's child is fair of face,
Tuesday's child is full of grace,
Wednesday's child is full of woe,
Thursday's child has far to go,
Friday's child is loving and giving,
Saturday's child has to work for its living,
But a child that's born on the Sabbath day
Is fair and wise and good and gay.

Monday's Child Is Fair of Face

4 Solomon Grundy,
Born on a Monday,
Christened on Tuesday,
Married on Wednesday,
Took ill on Thursday,
Worse on Friday,
Died on Saturday,
Buried on Sunday:
This is the end
Of Solomon Grundy.

Solomon Grundy

5 What are little boys made of?
Snips and snails, and puppy dogs' tails;
That's what little boys are made of.

What Are Little Boys Made Of?

6 What are little girls made of?
Sugar and spice, and everything nice;
That's what little girls are made of.

Ibid.

7 Hickety pickety, my black hen,
She lays eggs for gentlemen.
Gentlemen come every day
To see what my black hen doth lay.

Hickety Pickety[1]

8 Little Miss Muffet
Sat on a tuffet,
Eating some curds and whey.
Along came a spider,
And sat down beside her,
And frightened Miss Muffet away.

Little Miss Muffet

9 Peter, Peter Pumpkin-Eater,
Had a wife and couldn't keep her.

He put her in a pumpkin shell,
And there he kept her very well.

Peter, Peter Pumpkin-Eater

10 Jack, be nimble,
Jack, be quick,
Jack, jump over the candlestick.

Jack Be Nimble

11 There was a crooked man, and he went a crooked
mile,
He found a crooked sixpence against a crooked
stile;
He bought a crooked cat, which caught a crooked
mouse,
And they all lived together in a little crooked
house.

There Was a Crooked Man

12 Diddle diddle dumpling, my son John,
He went to bed with his stockings on;
One shoe off, one shoe on;
Diddle diddle dumpling, my son John.

Diddle Diddle Dumpling

13 Rub-a-dub-dub,
Three men in a tub,
And who do you think they be?
The butcher, the baker,
The candlestick-maker;
And all of them went to sea![2]

Rub-a-Dub-Dub

14 I saw three ships come sailing by,
Come sailing by, come sailing by,
I saw three ships come sailing by,
On New Year's Day in the morning.

I Saw Three Ships

15 In fir tar is,
In oak none is.
In mud eel is,
In clay none is.
Goats eat ivy.
Mares eat oats.

In Fir Tar Is

16 Lucy Locket lost her pocket,
Kitty Fisher found it;
There was not a penny in it,
But a ribbon round it.

Lucy Locket

17 There were three jolly huntsmen,
As I have heard them say,
And they would go a-hunting
Upon St. David's Day.

There Were Three Jolly Huntsmen

18 All day they hunted,
And nothing did they find,
But a ship a-sailing,
A-sailing with the wind.

Ibid.

---

[1]Higgledy-piggledy my white hen, / She lays eggs for gentlemen; / She cannot be persuaded by gun or lariat / To come
across for the proletariat.—DOROTHY PARKER

[2]In some editions: Turn 'em out, knaves all three!

1 O do you know the muffin man,
The muffin man, the muffin man,
O do you know the muffin man,
That lives in Drury Lane?

The Muffin Man

2 To market, to market, to buy a fat pig,
Home again, home again, jiggety-jig.

To Market, To Market

3 Doctor Foster went to Gloucester
In a shower of rain;
He stepped in a puddle, up to his middle,
And never went there again.

Doctor Foster

4 There was an old woman
Lived under a hill;
And if she's not gone,
She lives there still.

There Was an Old Woman

5 There was a little man, and he had a little gun,
And his bullets were made of lead, lead, lead;
He went to the brook, and saw a little duck,
And shot it through the head, head, head.

There Was a Little Man

6 Lavender's blue, dilly dilly, lavender's green;
When I am king, dilly dilly, you shall be queen.

Lavender's Blue

7 A dillar, a dollar,
A ten o'clock scholar,
What makes you come so soon?
You used to come at ten o'clock,
And now you come at noon.

A Dillar, a Dollar

8 One flew east, one flew west,
One flew over the cuckoo's nest.

One Flew East

9 I had a little pony,
His name was Dapple Gray;
I lent him to a lady
To ride a mile away.
She whipped him, she slashed him,
She rode him through the mire;
I would not lend my pony now
For all the lady's hire.

I Had a Little Pony

10 Polly, put the kettle on,
We'll all have tea.

Polly, Put the Kettle On, st. 1

11 Sukey, take it off again,
They've all gone away.

Ibid.

12 Little Tommy Tittlemouse
Lived in a little house;
He caught fishes
In other men's ditches.

Little Tommy Tittlemouse

13 The farmer in the dell, the farmer in the dell,
Heigho! the derry oh, the farmer in the dell.

The Farmer in the Dell

14 Hark! Hark! The dogs do bark,
The beggars are coming to town;
Some in rags, some in tags,
And some in velvet gowns.

Hark! Hark!

15 Ten little Indians standing in a line—
One went home, and then there were nine.

Ten Little Indians

16 When good King Arthur ruled this land,
He was a goodly king,
He bought three pecks of barley meal,
To make a bag pudding.

Good King Arthur

17 One misty, moisty morning,
When cloudy was the weather,
I chanced to meet an old man
Clothed all in leather;
He began to compliment,
And I began to grin—
"How do you do?" and "How do you do?"
And "How do you do?" again!

One Misty, Moisty Morning

18 Bobby Shaftoe's gone to sea,
Silver buckles on his knee;
He'll come back and marry me,
Pretty Bobby Shaftoe.

Bobby Shaftoe

19 Fe fi fo fum!
I smell the blood of an Englishman;
Be he alive or be he dead,
I'll grind his bones to make my bread.

Fe Fi Fo Fum

20 Sing, sing! What shall I sing?
The cat's run away with the pudding-bag string.

Sing, Sing! What Shall I Sing?

21 Shoe the horse, shoe the mare,
But let the little colt go bare.

Shoe the Horse

22 There was a man in our town,
And he was wondrous wise;
He jumped into a bramble bush
And scratched out both his eyes.

There Was a Man in Our Town

23 There were two blackbirds,
Sitting on a hill,
The one named Jack,
The other named Jill;
Fly away, Jack! Fly away, Jill!
Come again, Jack! Come again, Jill!

Two Blackbirds

24 This is the farmer sowing the corn,
That kept the cock that crowed in the morn,
That waked the priest all shaven and shorn,

That married the man all tattered and torn,
That kissed the maiden all forlorn,
That milked the cow with the crumpled horn,
That tossed the dog
That worried the cat
That killed the rat
That ate the malt
That lay in the house that Jack built.

The House That Jack Built

Anonymous: Russian

1 Let the woman into Paradise, she'll bring her cow along.   *Proverb*

2 An egg is dear on Easter Day.   *Proverb*

3 To live a life through is not like crossing a field.[1]
                                                        Proverb

4 The eggs do not teach the hen.   *Proverb*

5 Without a shepherd sheep are not a flock.
                                                        Proverb

6 Live with wolves, howl like a wolf.   *Proverb*

7 Don't hang noodles on my ears.   *Saying*

Anonymous: Shanties

8 Whiskey is the life of man,
Whiskey, Johnny!
Oh, I'll drink whiskey while I can,
Whiskey for my Johnny!

Whiskey Johnny

9 Oh, blow the man down, bullies, blow the man down!
To me way-aye, blow the man down.
Oh, blow the man down, bullies, blow him right down!
Give me some time to blow the man down!

Blow the Man Down

10 What shall we do with the drunken sailor,
Early in the morning?

The Drunken Sailor

11 Hooray and up she rises
Early in the morning.

Ibid. chorus

12 Oh, Shenandoah, I long to hear you,
Way-hay, you rolling river!
Oh, Shenandoah, I long to hear you,
Ha-ha, we're bound away,
'Cross the wide Missouri!

Shenandoah

13 A-roving, a-roving,
Since roving's been my ru-i-in,

[1]See Pasternak, 679:17.

I'll go no more a-roving
With you, fair maid!

A-Roving

14 Glos'ter girls they have no combs,
Heave away, heave away!
They comb their hair with codfish bones.

The Codfish Shanty

15 Oh, you New York girls, can't you dance the polka?

Can't You Dance the Polka?

16   Good-bye, fare you well!
We're homeward bound for New York town,
Hurrah, my boys, we're homeward bound!

Good-bye, Fare You Well

17 Oh, the times are hard and the wages low;
Leave her, Johnny, leave her!
I'll pack my bag and go below.
It's time for us to leave her!

Leave Her, Johnny

18 There were two lofty ships, from old England
they set sail,
Blow high, blow low, and so sailed we! . . .
Cruising down along the shores of High Barbaree!

High Barbaree

19 There was a ship came from the north country,
And the name of the ship was the *Golden Vanity*.
And they feared she might be taken by the Turkish
enemy,
That sails upon the Lowland, Lowland, Lowland,
That sails upon the Lowland sea.

The Golden Vanity

20 Then blow ye winds, heigh-ho!
A-roving I will go,
I'll stay no more on England's shore,
To hear the music play.
I'm off on the morning train
To cross the raging main,
I'm taking a trip on a Government ship,
Ten thousand miles away!

Ten Thousand Miles Away

21 There is a flash packet, flash packet of fame,
She hails from New York and the *Dreadnought*'s
her name.

The Dreadnought

22 She's the Liverpool packet—O Lord, let her go!

Ibid.

Anonymous: Spanish

23   A enemigo que huye puente de plata [If your
enemy turns to flee, give him a silver bridge].

Proverb

24   Al que madruga Dios le ayuda [God helps those
who get up early].   *Proverb*

25   Con pan y vino se anda el camino [With bread
and wine you can walk your road].   *Proverb*

1 El pez muere por la boca [The fish dies because he opens his mouth].   *Proverb*

2 El que se sienta en la puerta de su casa verá pasar el cadáver de su enemigo [He who sits at the door of his house will watch his enemy's corpse go by].   *Proverb*

3 En boca cerrada no entran moscas [The closed mouth swallows no flies].   *Proverb*

4 En casa del leñero cuchillo de palo [In the woodsman's house the knives are of wood].   *Proverb*

5 No por mucho madrugar amanece más temprano [Dawn comes no sooner for the early riser].   *Proverb*

6 Quien bien te quiere te hará llorar [Whoever really loves you will make you cry].   *Proverb*

7 El oro y amores eran malos de encubrir [Gold and love affairs are difficult to hide].[1]   *Proverb*

8 Dios te tenga en su santa mano [God keep you in his holy hand].   *A farewell*

Anonymous: Spirituals

9 Nobody knows the trouble I've seen,
Nobody knows but Jesus.
                           Nobody Knows the Trouble I've Seen

10 Joshua fit the battle of Jericho,
And the walls come tumbling down.[2]
                           Joshua Fit the Battle of Jericho

11 Go down, Moses,
Way down in Egypt land,
Tell old Pharaoh,
Let my people go.[3]
                           Go Down, Moses

12 Free at last, free at last,
Thank God Almighty, we're free at last.[4]
                           Free at Last

13 I looked over Jordan, and what did I see? . . .
A band of angels coming after me,
Coming for to carry me home.
                           Swing Low, Sweet Chariot, st. 1

14 Swing low, sweet chariot,
Coming for to carry me home.
                           Ibid. refrain

15 Michael row the boat ashore,
Hallelujah!
                           Michael Row the Boat Ashore

16 Rise and shine[5] and give God the glory
For the year of Jubilee.[6]
                           Rise and Shine

17 My Lord, what a morning,[7]
When the stars begin to fall.
                           My Lord, What a Morning

18 You'll hear the trumpet sound,
To wake the nations underground,
Look in my God's right hand,
When the stars begin to fall.
                           Ibid.

19 One more river,
And that's the river of Jordan,
One more river,
There's one more river to cross.
                           One More River

20 Oh, freedom! Oh, freedom!
Oh, freedom over me!
And before I'd be a slave, I'll be buried in my grave,
And go home to my Lord and be free.
                           Oh, Freedom!

21 Get on board, little children,
There's room for many a more.
                           Get on Board, Little Children

22 The Gospel train's a-coming.
                           Ibid.

23 Just like a tree that's standing by the water,[8]
We shall not be moved.[9]
                           We Shall Not Be Moved[10]

24 O Lord, I want to be in that number
When the saints go marching in.
                           When the Saints Go Marching In

---

[1]See George Herbert, 244:4.
[2]See *Joshua 6:20, 10:34.*
[3]See *Exodus 5:1, 8:29.*
[4]See Martin Luther King, Jr., 761:3.

[5]See *Isaiah 60:1, 28:4.*
[6]See *Leviticus 25:10, 9:27.*
[7]Also written as: mourning.
[8]See *Psalm 1:3, 15:29.*
[9]See *Psalm 46:5, 17:17.*
[10]Later adapted as a labor and civil rights song.

Index

Index

*Please see the Index section of the Guide to
the Use of* Familiar Quotations,
page xiii.

A

A, black A white E, 565:17
  emotions from A to B, 687:13
  first write a crowned A, 129:14
  injures B to improve X, 643:3
  on gown letter A, 435:25
A', for a. that and a. that, 363:23
A-angling, be quiet and go a., 245:31
Aaron's rod, 8:32
Ab Iove principium, 92:*n*4
  ovo, 98:*n*6
  urbe condita, 118:11
Abandon, all hope a. who enter here, 125:6
  do not fear to a. faults, 60:20
  government which kept us free, 344:6
  learning and no sorrow, 57:7
  to cries and lamentations, 104:3
Abandoned, down the a. heaven, 657:17
  God a. these defended, 580:2
  man a. on earth, 717:15
  poem never finished only a., 614:3
Abandonment of force, 650:9
Abased, whoso exalt himself be a., 36:2
Abashed the Devil stood, 259:1
Abatement and low price, 201:17
Abbot of Aberbrothok, 386:10
Abbots purple as their wines, 304:1
A.B.C.'s, droop in a hundred A., 668:10
Abdullah Bulbul Amir, 781:3
Abednego, Shadrach Meshach and A., 29:13
A-begging, truth goes a., 138:9
Abel was keeper of sheep, 7:2
Aberbrothok, Abbot of A., 386:10
Aberdour, half owre to A., 785:1
Abhor detest Sabbath-Day, 527:1
  makers and laws approve, 275:22
Abhorred in my imagination, 199:8
  shears, 253:20
  that senseless tribe, 289:18
Abhors, God a. you, 308:20
  nature a. a vacuum, 277:16
Abide, fates impose that men a., 164:26

Abide (*continued*)
  nowhere did a., 381:20
  others a. our question, 497:4
  tyme nyl no man a., 131:13
  under the shadow of the Almighty, 18:15
  who shall a. in thy tabernacle, 16:4
  with me, 410:17
Abides, in mystery soul a., 497:13
  there a. peace of thine, 497:14
Abideth, earth a. forever, 23:22
  faith hope charity, 43:16
Abiding Leaf, 725:21
  shepherds a. in field, 38:3
Abiezer, vintage of A., 11:9
Abiit ad plures, 105:*n*2
  excessit evasit erupit, 87:*n*4
Abilities below mediocrity rewarded, 385:15
  common opinions uncommon a., 506:10
  from each according to a., 481:11
  possible for others to use a., 734:1
  splendid a. but utterly corrupt, 386:1
Ability, answer question to best of a., 614:10
  charge not soul save to its a., 117:3
  distressed by want of a., 61:28
  laughter a. and Sighing, 513:6
  lean and low a., 203:2
  retain a. to function, 694:17
  they never perform, 200:20
  to get to verge, 667:8
  to register multiple perception, 660:7
Abject are usually ambitious, 278:8
  submission, 336:14
Abjure my so much loved variety, 230:8
  this rough magic I here a., 224:23
Able and willing to pull weight, 576:1
  at least as far as a., 561:8
  be a. for thine enemy, 203:8
  rather a. than learned, 145:16
Ablest navigators, 340:6
Ablution round earth's shores, 417:12
Abner a prince and a great man, 12:4
  smote him under the fifth rib, 12:3
Abode destined Hour, 445:11
  dread a., 322:24

Abode (*continued*)
  Last A. is Life, 117:8
  Olympus a. of the gods, 53:9
  untented Kosmos my a., 561:22
Abodes, peaceful a. of the gods, 53:*n*1
Abolish, English never a. anything, 585:4
  right to alter or a. it, 343:2
  serfdom from above, 479:16
  slavery of half of humanity, 722:10
  tyranny and vice, 337:10
Abolition of private property, 482:4
Abominable, newspapers the most a., 352:33
Abominably, imitated humanity so a., 197:1
Abomination, Mass an a., 138:11
  of desolation, 36:8
Abora, singing of Mount A., 382:24
Aborigines, fell on knees then on a., 481:4
Abortion, men pregnant a. a sacrament, 739:17
  will not give pessary to cause a., 71:1
Abortions will not let you forget, 740:4
Abou Ben Adhem, 397:1
Abound, grace a., 41:42
  joys a. as seasons fleet, 163:23
Abounded, where sin a., 41:42
About about in reel and rout, 381:10
  it and about but evermore, 445:17
Above, at once a. beneath around, 325:10
  economic tyranny a., 661:2
  every good gift is from a., 46:6
  insolence and triviality, 664:7
  may it be beautiful a. me, 787:10
  world stretched the sky, 683:16
Abraham, God of A. not of philosophers, 271:11
  of scientific men, 493:19
  that which has been sent down on A., 116:3
  thy name shall be A., 7:31
  we are coming Father A., 461:11
Abraham's, beggar in A. bosom, 39:2
  liest in A. bosom, 374:16
  sleep in A. bosom, 166:5

Abram dwelled in Canaan, 7:28
  O father A., 180:11
Abreast, one but goes a., 201:1
Abreuve nos sillons, 366:9
Abridging freedom of speech, 346:11
Abridgment of freedom, 352:2
Abroad for good of my country,
    295:14
  know own country before goes a.,
    320:30
  lie a. for commonwealth, 227:12
  obsequious a., 396:3
  purchase great alliance, 164:23
  schoolmaster is a., 390:1
  what should not be published a.,
    71:1
  when he next doth ride a., 334:24
Absalom my son my son, 12:14
Absence, conspicuous by a., 406:7
  cry of A. A. in heart, 674:10
  cure of love, 149:38
  darkness death, 229:9
  diminishes mediocre passions,
    265:28
  dote on his very a., 179:33
  doth breed continual remembrance,
    132:n8
  like a winter my a., 221:18
  love cannot admit a., 229:11
  love rekindled by a., 314:7
  makes heart fonder, 101:2
  of mind we have borne, 388:10
  of occupation not rest, 334:15
  of romance in my history, 71:19
  peace not a. of war, 277:15
  seemed my flame to qualify, 221:24
  Ulysses' a., 218:25
Absent, friends a. speak, 230:14
  from Him I roam, 377:17
  if to be a. were to be away, 267:19
  in body present in spirit, 42:36
  in the spring, 221:19
  let no one speak ill of a., 100:31
  one from another, 7:44
  room of a. child, 170:4
  thee from felicity, 199:27
Absentee, war vast aloof a., 768:13
Absentes, in a. felicior aestus amantes,
    101:n1
Absenti nemo non nocuisse velit,
    100:n15
Absentminded, most a. of men
    plunged in reveries, 486:17
Absents, les a. ont toujours tort,
    295:n5
  presents endear a., 387:32
Absit omen, 118:12
Absolute and in herself complete,
    259:29
  atoms preserved by a. solidity,
    89:10
  be a. for death, 204:8
  built a. trust, 212:27
  dictatorship a. as any other, 649:13
  foreknowledge a., 257:12
  freedom of navigation, 572:13
  how a. the knave is, 199:6
  idea of knowledge, 76:5
  Johannes fac totum, 157:20
  mark you his a. shall, 219:7

Absolute (*continued*)
  natures or kinds, 76:5
  notion of a. beauty, 74:12
  power corrupts absolutely, 521:5
  power in majority, 338:16
  power over wives, 347:2
  security, 713:19
  truth forever a., 462:20
Absolutely, corrupts a., 521:5
Absolutes in Bill of Rights, 661:7
  in world affairs, 713:19
  meant prohibitions to be a., 661:7
  the a. the eternities, 736:19
Absolutism tempered by assassination,
    368:3
Absolve, compensate bad in man a.
    him so, 468:4
  foulness of their fate, 662:7
  history will a. me, 756:21
  pray God a. us all, 134:4
Absolved from allegiance, 336:11
  judge condemned when criminal a.,
    99:22
  people a. of history, 763:11
Absorb as Parallax a Flame, 514:3
Absorbing, reflects images without a.,
    535:23
Absorbs, country a. him affectionately,
    488:12
  tinged by what a. it, 546:20
Abstain from fleshly lusts, 46:22
  from intentional wrongdoing, 71:1
Abstains from words, 484:3
Abstention, faith in a. from faith,
    589:15
Abstinence easy to me, 315:11
  lean and sallow a., 253:8
  lend easiness to next a., 198:6
  sows sand all over, 357:20
Abstinete, a fabis a., 234:15
Abstract concepts, 345:9
  ideas conditioned by time, 585:1
  liberty not found, 331:13
  love of beauty in a., 418:6
  man in the a., 510:13
  words obscene, 701:14
Abstracts and brief chronicles, 196:2
Absurd, death a. also, 728:3
  is essential concept, 732:14
  lick a. pomp, 197:2
  poets creatures most a., 303:11
  question is a., 721:5
  the a. not the improbable, 473:13
  to be believed because a., 112:10
Absurdity, dull without a single a.,
    328:17
  man only subject to a., 239:18
  privilege of a., 239:18
  what to do with this a., 597:11
Abundance, add more to a., 649:8
  full sharers in a., 560:2
  if thou hast a., 30:17
  out of a. mouth speaketh, 35:3
  possesses virtue in a., 57:16
  pray in days of a., 651:14
  will not suffer him to sleep, 24:4
Abundant, more a. life, 648:20
  shower of curates, 476:14
  wretched and a. Russia, 496:20
Abundantly, have life more a., 40:16

Abuse, cry out loudest its a., 278:17
  how long Catiline a. our patience,
    87:6
  land as commodity, 662:2
  of greatness, 187:31
  wicked dreams a., 213:21
  you cause what you a., 284:7
Abused, by himself a. or disabused,
    301:13
Abuses, evils exist only in a., 369:12
  excites hatred to conceal a., 389:14
Abusing, abstain from a. bodies, 71:1
  of God's patience, 182:23
  stop a. my verses or publish, 106:11
Abydos, Sestos and A. of her breasts,
    230:10
Abysm of time, 223:21
Abysmal dark of center, 419:2
Abyss, cradle rocks above a., 702:17
  discovery metamorphosis, 616:19
  look long into a., 552:16
  looks into you, 552:16
  man is rope over a., 552:6
Abysses, dread a. unknown tides,
    547:1
Abyssinia, Rasselas Prince of A., 314:9
Abyssinian maid, 382:24
Academe, groves of A., 97:22
  olive grove of A., 261:1
Academes, they are the books the a.,
    169:4
Academi, inter silvas A., 97:n11
Academic life, 233:15
Academy, Frenchman in A., 315:n7
Accelerated grimace, 659:6
Acceleration proportional to applied
    force, 282:n1
Accents, aged a. untimely words,
    161:1
  caught his clear a., 464:23
  yet unknown, 188:18
Accept, bow and a. end, 622:18
  decline to a. end of man, 696:21
  fall in with what asked to a.,
    625:16
  God a. him, 458:8
  I will not a. if nominated, 492:13
  learn to a. in silence, 558:5
  never a. thing as true, 246:16
  not God I don't a., 495:8
  our thanksgiving a., 532:14
  tamely a., 589:1
  things that cannot be changed,
    684:7
  universe, 461:7
  will for deed a., 140:n3
Acceptability, hallmark of conven-
    tional wisdom a., 723:6
Acceptable, be a. in thy sight, 16:13
  more a. the straightforward man,
    3:15
  offices a. here, 344:3
  safeguards a. to all nations, 655:9
Acceptation, news worthy of a.,
    286:22
Accepted, fellow mortals a. as they
    are, 483:8
  now is a. time, 44:4
  that which a. false, 614:1
  you are a., 662:10

Accepting, charms by a., 300:18
  not by a. favors, 72:5
Access and passage to remorse, 212:29
Accessible, English not a. to Englishmen, 571:18
Accident, by a. got its liberty, 137:3
  counts for much, 535:10
  found out by a., 388:14
  happy a., 237:5
  of sentiment, 523:21
  progress not a. but necessity, 492:14
  shot of a., 207:23
  what seems a. springs from destiny, 365:5
Accidentally, America discovered a., 665:12
  only a. am I French, 304:12
Accidents can happen, 784:13
  chapter of a. very long, 305:15
  confront ridicule a. rebuffs, 488:14
  controlled by a. or by ourselves, 715:11
  fill world, 777:14
  in best-regulated families, 470:33
  miracles propitious a., 588:10
  moving a. by flood, 205:25
  omissions are not a., 664:n2
  shackles a., 218:10
  universe capable of such a., 622:14
Accommodating vice, 269:19
Accommodations, equal but separate a., 682:n3
Accompany old age, 216:9
Accomplice, art a. of love, 575:2
  evening comes like a., 494:8
Accomplish little, 365:21
Accomplished anything except get along, 658:6
  desire a. is sweet, 21:16
  her warfare is a., 27:15
  nothing a. alone, 684:18
  nothing great a. without passion, 372:10
  plan of Zeus was being a., 50:24
Accomplisher, Zeus a., 64:2
Accomplishes without any action, 57:15
Accomplishing, armorers a. the knights, 185:14
  their appointed courses, 70:11
Accomplishment, smile of a., 764:14
Accomplishments, emerges ahead of a., 710:9
  give luster, 305:12
Accord, someone whom we a. with, 349:11
Accordance, activity in a. with excellence, 78:9
According, to every man a. to his work, 17:34
Account, closing your a. and mine, 445:22
  give accurate exhaustive a., 614:6
  of her life to clod, 186:18
  sent to my a., 194:24
  whatever you lose no a., 99:6
Accountability to no one, 656:5
Accounting, death the final a., 119:13
  no a. for tastes, 118:25
Accounts, cross out overpaid a., 490:6

Accumulate, horrors a., 207:11
  sage does not a., 58:7
Accumulated experience, 628:8
  wrong, 589:1
Accumulates, where wealth a., 329:8
Accuracy tried by severe tests, 71:19
Accurate, give a. exhaustive account, 614:6
  in his judgment, 337:n1
Accursed craving for gold, 93:37
  fear most a. of base passions, 163:15
  he that first invented war, 161:19
  night she bore me, 68:5
  opinions are a., 597:5
Accuse, j'a., 541:14
  not a. me before the God, 4:5
  not Nature, 259:30
  not servant to his master, 23:13
Accused, I accuser God a., 760:6
Accuser, I a. God accused, 760:6
  no a. so terrible, 85:11
Accuses, excuses himself a. himself, 144:10
Accusing Spirit, 320:29
Accustomed to deliberate when drunk, 69:23
  to her face, 745:12
  to way ground opens up, 766:6
Aces, confidence in four a., 525:18
  triumphing over kings and a., 680:17
Acetylene, rip-tooth of sky's a., 701:3
Achaeans, brought upon the A. myriad woes, 50:23
  well-greaved A., 51:14
A-changin', times they are a., 771:7
Achates, faithful A., 94:7
  fidus A., 94:n4
Ache, age a. penury, 204:15
  ark of the a. of it, 752:18
  charm a. with air, 187:8
Acheron, fear of A. be sent packing, 89:21
Aches, my heart a., 415:9
  sense a. at thee, 208:1
  when the head a., 150:17
Achieve and cherish peace, 450:11
  some a. greatness, 202:18
  the a. of the thing, 550:21
Achieved by others' death, 170:12
  matchless deed's a., 325:13
  nothing a. without enthusiasm, 432:10
  the a. West, 696:7
Achievement, bring it to a., 68:14
  death of endeavor, 544:12
  of continuous human effort, 704:9
  quality form Man of A., 417:18
  sum of human a., 558:6
  talent in every branch of a., 72:2
  wealth opportunity for a., 72:3
Achievements of intellect everlasting, 91:29
Achieveth, naught n' assaieth naught n' a., 128:24
Achieving, still a. still pursuing, 440:18
Achilles exists only through Homer, 369:16

  not even A. will bring all to fulfillment, 52:18
  O fortunate youth A., 80:23
  see the great A., 455:6
  what name A. assumed, 248:30
  wrath of A., 50:23
Achilles', matter of Troy and A. wrath, 490:6
  stood upon A. tomb, 403:4
  wrath, 299:n9
Aching, bring my a. heart to rest, 86:18
  ease one Life the A., 513:10
  empty and a. and I don't know why, 772:10
  one tooth and it a., 613:9
  spare my a. sight, 323:9
  they have left a. void, 333:21
Achitophel, false A. was first, 274:3
Achoo, barely daring to A., 764:16
Acknowledge and bewail our sins, 49:15
  and confess our sins, 48:15
  I a. the Furies, 611:13
  restraint of reverence, 72:2
  thing of darkness I a. mine, 224:28
  us in some way, 765:2
Acknowledged, governments whose independence a., 360:12
Acknowledgment, transcribed without a., 103:19
A-clickin' like tickin' of a clock, 559:1
A-cold, owl a., 414:21
  poor Tom's a., 210:11
Acolytes, basin in hands of a., 763:11
A-coming, Gospel train's a., 794:22
Acorns, hogs eat a., 262:n4
  oaks from little a., 119:18
Acquaintance, creditable a., 288:23
  in which no new a., 318:1
  should auld a., 362:19
  sneered and slanged, 609:5
  visiting a., 352:12
Acquaintances, make new a., 315:21
Acquainted with grief, 27:35
  with the night, 624:3
Acquaints, misery a. with strange bedfellows, 224:8
Acquent, when we were first a., 362:15
Acquiesce, if we a. in discrimination, 628:2
Acquire and beget a temperance, 196:21
Acquired, fortune has a. him, 82:9
  knowledge a. under compulsion, 75:21
Acquiring and possessing property, 327:1
  ways of a. books, 682:12
Acquisition, desire increases with a., 320:16
Acquisitions or losses by nature, 347:13
Acre in Middlesex, 425:5
  of barren ground, 223:19
Acres, a few paternal a. bound, 298:5
  happy man works ancestral a., 95:13

Acres (*continued*)
    has a. of flutes, 689:9
    over whose a. blessed feet, 176:23
Acrobat, Governor of New York not
    an a., 618:7
Act against Constitution, 327:6
    against natural equity, 327:6
    an a. of survival, 762:10
    and do things accordingly, 707:6
    as if God did exist, 589:12
    as if there were God, 546:15
    beauty and valor and a., 550:22
    between motion and a., 669:10
    both a. and know, 268:12
    bring to light goodly a., 634:17
    but not rely on own ability, 57:2
    has no ethical quality unless chosen,
      545:19
    heaven helps not men who will not
      a., 59:*n*5
    in doubt to a. or rest, 301:13
    in the noon, 357:8
    initial a. of culture, 653:8
    last a. crowns play, 242:13
    lover's or Roman's part, 300:8
    no a. of kindness ever wasted, 58:18
    not afraid of destructive a., 587:8
    not criminal unless intent criminal,
      118:14
    of fear, 193:20
    of God defined, 678:23
    of life, 549:13
    old age play's last a., 88:12
    only on that maxim, 326:12
    our Antipodes, 249:7
    perform every a. as though your
      last, 110:15
    poem of a. of mind, 384:*n*3
    power to live and a., 377:6
    prologues to swelling a., 212:22
    promptly, 570:5
    reap an a., 781:6
    sins they love to a., 219:19
    sleep an a. or two, 226:10
    think himself a. of God, 476:8
    two witnesses to overt a., 346:9
    virtue and prudent a., 331:20
    vote and a. to bring good, 546:11
    Way of sage is to a., 58:7
    what it is to a. or suffer, 670:8
Acta est fabula, 118:13
Actaeon ego sum dominum cognoscite,
    101:*n*15
    I am A., 101:22
Acted, lofty scene be a. o'er, 188:18
Acting is suffering, 670:8
    of dreadful thing, 188:2
    only when off stage he was a.,
      330:12
    people inside your head a., 751:1
    surrender explaining not a., 618:1
Action, accomplishes without any a.,
    57:15
    advantage of taking no a., 57:13
    brave in a. patient under labors,
      522:13
    faithful honor clear, 300:24
    feeling for single good a., 350:1
    fruit of a. not be motive, 84:7
    give a. its character, 74:4

Action (*continued*)
    great end of life a., 505:16
    horse symbol of a., 657:20
    I can't get no girl with a., 772:16
    imitate a. of the tiger, 185:3
    imitation of a. that is serious, 78:31
    impartial in thought and a., 572:2
    in a. how like an angel, 195:28
    in bondage to history, 510:5
    in thought as in a., 723:11
    knowledge must come through a.,
      67:2
    life a. and passion, 542:6
    lose the name of a., 196:10
    lust in a., 222:7
    made to follow path of a., 61:14
    makes the a. fine, 243:26
    man is origin of his a., 78:5
    man of a. forced into thought,
      603:22
    mindless a., 716:1
    moment not of a. or inaction,
      84:*n*7
    no worthy a. done, 779:1
    nor utterance nor speech, 189:10
    nothing more terrible than igno-
      rance in a., 351:10
    of masses of men, 477:10
    on a. alone be thy interest, 84:7
    pious a. sugar o'er, 196:9
    pious fraud as with bad a., 341:10
    predestined from eternity, 510:5
    proud men of a., 420:7
    science guide of a., 554:10
    sense of honor in a., 72:7
    sentiments weigh less than a.,
      486:10
    spectator of a. he describes, 503:5
    suit a. to the word, 196:22
    Tao takes no a., 57:11
    test lies in a., 63:31
    thought too much for a., 537:20
    to every a. equal reaction, 282:3
    vice by a. dignified, 175:16
Actions, decisive a. unconsidered,
    607:4
    exceeds in his a., 61:24
    extreme a. ascribed to vanity, 552:3
    morality of his a., 319:20
    must be his spirit, 79:4
    mutual a. of two bodies, 282:3
    my a. are my ministers', 273:4
    not always a. show man, 300:11
    not always true sons, 263:12
    of the just, 246:21
    society exists for noble a., 78:20
    speaks according to his a., 60:22
    speech is image of a., 55:18
    think beforehand that a. be resolute,
      79:22
    thousand a. once afoot, 184:25
    what a. most excellent, 498:8
    when our a. do not, 215:24
    work good of agent, 278:5
Active, deeply and intensely a., 545:5
    experimentation a. science, 473:3
    free a. individuals, 499:2
    through form and figure, 384:20
    to the vigilant a. brave, 339:9
Activest, his a. part, 264:15

Activities, knowledge of unconscious
    a. of mind, 569:3
Activity in accordance with excellence,
    78:9
    property product of a., 631:14
Actor, better be a. than critic, 619:11
    condemn fault and not a., 203:34
    dreamer is a., 629:2
    pregnant with part, 588:23
    well-graced a. leaves, 172:13
Actors, like a. in ancient plays, 565:14
    these our a. were spirits, 224:21
Acts before he speaks, 60:22
    four a. already past, 296:27
    his a. being seven ages, 191:3
    let a play have five a., 98:14
    nameless unremembered a., 373:1
    no second a. in American lives,
      694:22
    our lives in a. exemplary, 157:10
    psychical a. develop by reflex, 511:1
    to keep good a. refresh with new,
      158:25
    with such a. fill a pen, 161:10
Actual, solid earth a. world, 477:7
    true account of a. is poetry, 477:21
Actuality of thought is life, 77:23
Actus non facit reum, 118:14
Acute inquisitive dexterous, 331:15
Acutely, companion so feel solitude a.,
    614:2
Ad astra per aspera, 118:15
    maiorem Dei gloriam, 143:*n*2
    unguem factus homo, 95:*n*5
Ad infinitum, so proceed a., 289:20
Adage, poor cat i' the a., 213:9
Adam, all that A. had, 431:4
    and his wife, 454:2
    as A. early in morning, 490:2
    called his wife's name Eve, 6:26
    deep sleep upon A., 6:16
    had 'em, 607:7
    in A. all die, 43:20
    offending A., 184:20
    old A., 50:11
    son of A. and Eve, 288:5
    take care A., 652:5
    the goodliest man, 258:14
    was a gardener, 164:10, 593:23
    was but human, 527:7
    when A. delved, 775:13
    wonder what A. and Eve think,
      664:3
    young A. Cupid, 174:25
Adamant for drift, 619:20
    frame of a., 313:18
Adamantine chains, 255:22
Adam's dream, 417:15
    from Pyrrha's pebbles or A. seed,
      414:16
    hold up A. profession, 198:27
    in A. ear left voice, 259:23
    in A. fall sinned, 287:6
    riverrun past Eve and A., 647:18
    since A. fall, 595:15
    sons conceived in sin, 235:4
Adamses vote for Douglas, 582:*n*1
Adaptation, struggle for a., 628:8
Adapted, means plainly a. to end,
    355:12

Adapted (*continued*)
  to my kind of fooling, 625:4
Adazzle dim, 551:1
Add hue to rainbow, 170:9
  more to abundance, 649:8
  one cubit to stature, 33:19
  power to a. or detract, 450:2
  some extra just for you, 750:15
  to these retired Leisure, 252:1
  to those with too much, 649:8
Added, all these things a. unto you,
    33:22
Adder, like the deaf a., 17:29
  stingeth like an a., 22:22
  tread upon the lion and a., 18:16
Adding insult to injury, 318:23
Addison, volumes of A., 314:17
Addled mosses dank, 660:4
Address, prefer to a. myself to one
    man, 122:10
Addressed her winged words, 50:28
  is must a word to be a. to princes,
    145:7
Addressing popular audiences, 78:30
Adds precious seeing to the eye, 169:2
Adelante adelante, 543:*n*4
Adequate, no a. military defense,
    655:8
  strength not a. to resist, 79:8
Adeste fideles, 118:16
Adhere, time nor place did then a.,
    213:11
Adieu, bid you welcome a., 521:13
  chers tableaux, 247:*n*5
  fair day a., 169:29
  forevermore my dear, 362:14
  hand at lips bidding a., 416:18
  kind friends, 781:1
  she cries and waved, 297:4
  tristesse, 691:*n*3
Adjacent, doors of heaven a. identical,
    652:5
Adjective when in doubt strike out,
    527:13
Adjectives, American without qualify-
    ing a., 560:4
  no straddled a., 660:4
Adjoining, lain in a Room, 512:13
Adjunct, learning an a. to ourself,
    168:35
Adjusted in the Tomb, 512:13
Adjustment of colonial claims, 572:13
Adler, Irene A. always the woman,
    577:15
Administer wealth for good, 525:13
Administration, conduct affairs of a.,
    450:8
  during my a. no blood shed, 344:20
  life of this A., 741:6
  said of first A., 649:6
  said of second A., 649:6
Admirable, express and a., 195:28
  something howsoever strange and
    a., 174:2
Admirably, those which most a. flour-
    ish, 221:*n*2
Admiral cheered them holding out
    hope, 134:7
  Dewey was the A., 544:6
  from time to time kill one a., 306:9

Admiration, as great in a. as herself,
    226:8
  from critics, 424:22
  greatness worthy to excite a.,
    500:12
  jumps from a. to love, 386:25
  of the poet, 384:14
  only of weak minds, 260:27
  season your a., 193:17
Admire, many a. few know, 71:15
  most men a. virtue, 260:25
  that riches grow in hell, 256:21
  the world, 731:3
  to a. we should not understand,
    291:6
  too simple to a. it, 424:22
  we like those who a. us, 265:29
  where none a., 318:7
Admired, celerity never more a.,
    217:23
  few a. by own households, 146:17
  that she might a. be, 168:7
  through being misunderstood,
    675:20
Admires, coral lip a., 246:9
  meanly a. mean things, 463:12
Admiring Bog, 511:22
  in gloomy shade, 249:28
  Senate a. its members, 535:14
Admit I'm licked, 678:4
  impediments, 222:2
  never a. them in sight, 387:3
  no kind of traffic would I a., 224:4
Admitted, good pun may be a., 342:1
  no one else a. here, 651:18
  views advanced in volume generally
    a., 444:11
Adonais, soul of A. like star, 409:9
  weep for A., 408:14
Adonis, my A. hath a sweet tooth,
    155:17
  this A. in loveliness, 396:23
Adoo, welcome a., 521:13
Adopt character of octopus, 59:23
Adoption, their a. tried, 193:29
Adopts, finds man misusing money a.
    it, 539:*n*1
Adoration, breathless with a., 374:15
  down in a. falling, 124:6
  for a. all the ranks, 325:11
Adore beauty because disdains to de-
    stroy, 630:6
  command where I a., 202:17
  hand that gives blow, 274:*n*8
  I a. thee implore thee, 147:14
  Jews kiss and infidels a., 299:10
  my gifts instead of me, 243:19
  now I a. my life, 725:21
  seek and a. them, 550:1
Adored, in every clime a., 303:14
  still be a., 391:13
Adoring, I die a. God, 307:5
Adorn, Greece Italy and England did
    a., 275:25
  manners must a. knowledge, 305:5
  modest looks cottage a., 329:22
  nothing he did not a., 316:32
  old England to a., 593:17
  point moral or a. tale, 313:19

Adorned, holy city a. for husband,
    47:37
  I am she who a. herself, 491:7
  in naked beauty more a., 258:24
  when unadorned a. most, 308:7
Adornin', bride in rich a., 555:16
Adornment, some women handsome
    without a., 87:18
Adorns and cheers our way, 328:5
  only itself, 729:1
Adult, world of a. life, 629:1
Adulterers, drunkards liars and a.,
    209:3
Adulteries of art, 232:6
Adultery, committed a. in his heart,
    33:5
  committed a. in my heart, 754:1
  gods call a., 402:8
  psychology of a., 615:13
  Sara could commit a. at one end,
    667:4
  thou shalt not commit a., 9:12
Adulthood, remnants of childhood
    hopes of a., 708:6
Advance in science from audacity of
    imagination, 577:10
  mark out your doings in a., 420:7
  not to go back to a., 303:2
  retrograde if not a., 340:8
  twice set to partners, 518:4
Advanced, death's pale flag not a.,
    176:17
  outdistance a. countries, 610:3
  true friends, 498:1
  work they who fought a., 450:2
Advancement of pure science, 685:19
Advances, Chief who in triumph a.,
    378:21
  in direction of dreams, 478:36
Advantage in the past judged, 79:2
  mixed up for mutual a., 620:11
  nailed for our a., 176:23
  nature to a. dressed, 298:14
  no way of taking a., 550:9
  ocean gain a. on shore, 221:3
  of taking no action, 57:13
  over cleverer boys, 619:17
  them that take a. get a., 483:13
  to whose a., 87:11
Advantages, in hope of fair a., 180:22
  little a. every day, 311:4
  tries to keep a. of life, 614:14
  various qualities and a., 612:19
  wealth not without a., 723:4
Adventure art peace, 584:15
  fair a. of tomorrow, 170:19
  most unto itself, 513:7
  politics greatest a., 628:3
  some for a., 659:8
  this grotesque a. ours, 728:3
  vitality of thought in a., 584:18
Adventurer, no lover and no a.,
    572:24
  Ulysses interminable a., 640:11
  well-wishing a., 220:19
Adventures, embellish a., 341:14
  of Tom Sawyer, 526:19
  way full of a. and experiences,
    587:11
Adventuring, by a. both, 179:24

Age (*continued*)

not by a. is wisdom acquired, 83:8
not numbered by years, 148:8
not of an a. but for all time, 232:22
not one continued faithful until old
  a., 76:17
not only a night an a., 623:22
not profited so much as lost, 478:3
not so well qualified as youth, 478:3
not to be tuneless in old a., 95:*n*24
not weary them, 606:9
of antiquity youth of world, 158:*n*2
of Aquarius, 770:1
of chivalry gone, 332:12
of chivalry past, 484:18
of discord and strife, 163:17
of ease, 329:10
of fear, 703:15
of freedom ended discipline began,
  656:12
of gold, 96:28
of Gold, 250:22
of iron, 305:23
of Miracles, 412:34
of revolution and reformation,
  344:9
of unreason, 724:7
Old A. and Experience, 283:27
Old A. coming bolt door, 118:10
old a. crown of life, 88:12
old a. in universal man, 158:*n*3
old a. is woman's hell, 267:20
old a. lacking neither honor nor
  lyre, 95:30
old a. level light, 683:14
old a. only disease, 432:9
old a. play's last act, 88:12
old a. should burn, 737:20
old a. time of spending, 262:11
old Mr. Senex showing a., 733:6
olives of endless a., 221:23
or grief or sickness, 242:2
outworn buried a., 221:2
pays us with a. and dust, 153:2
peaceful as old a., 466:6
perform promises of youth, 314:9
physician of Iron A., 497:16
prayers which are a. his alms,
  156:15
preferable to youth, 293:21
regret in chilled a., 549:12
restored of the Antonines, 340:*n*1
returns the Golden A., 92:10
shakes rooted folly of a., 280:15
shall be clearer than noonday, 14:13
Shelley of my a., 742:17
sign of old a., 380:22
smack of a. in you, 183:15
soon comes a., 153:11
soul of the a., 232:18
spirit of a., 306:30
tested to extreme old a., 497:3
the a. is dull and mean, 443:7
the harbor of all ills, 82:6
therefore summon a., 467:10
think at your a. it is right, 517:9
thinks better of gilded fool, 227:17
thirty-five attractive a., 567:11
this slaughtered a., 730:7
thou hast nor youth nor a., 204:10

Age (*continued*)

'tis well an old a. is out, 276:22
to age succeeds, 453:20
too late or cold climate, 260:1
toys of a., 301:15
tragedy of the a., 605:1
veracity with old a., 265:41
very staff of my a., 180:16
view a. of poverty, 181:25
war dearth a. agues, 230:20
weak evils a. and hunger, 191:2
what was done in remote a., 431:16
when a. in wit out, 186:40
when Mozart was my a., 759:7
when old a. crept over, 583:11
when old a. shall generation waste,
  416:7
when Thule no more ultimate,
  103:13
will fade beauty's flower, 144:5
with stealing steps, 143:12
without a name, 333:8
wives companions for middle a.,
  159:12
world's great a. begins, 408:10
worst of woes wait on a., 399:17
youth and a. equally a burden, 75:4
youth passed old a. not arrived,
  482:15
Aged, beauty of a. face, 644:12
certain age means a., 403:8
later times more a. than earlier,
  158:*n*3
man paltry thing, 597:8
matched with a. wife, 454:24
thrush frail gaunt, 540:10
youth becomes as a., 204:10
Agenbite of inwit, 647:13
Agent, actions work good of a., 278:5
free a. you were before, 111:22
imagination a. of perception, 384:6
Nature a. and patient at once, 77:17
thus the poor a. despised, 201:15
trust no a., 186:21
Agents of men of thought, 420:7
Age's, poison for a. tooth, 169:17
Ages, all a. believed in gods, 628:12
and ages hence, 623:7
before history, 335:24
cycle of the a. renewed, 92:10
emptiness of a. in face, 563:6
famous to all a., 254:20
God our help in a. past, 294:14
gone a. long ago, 415:8
heir of all a., 455:24
how many a. hence, 188:18
now he belongs to the a., 474:10
Rock of A., 342:3
seven a., 191:3
thousand a. in Thy sight, 294:15
three poets in three a., 275:25
through a. one purpose, 455:20
trace events of a., 420:17
value from esteem of a., 273:1
what thing not thought of a. long
  ago, 350:23
ye unborn a., 323:9
Agglomeration called Holy Roman
  Empire, 306:4

Agglutinative, tonsorial or a. type,
  609:11
Aggrandizement, no a. territorial or
  other, 650:7
Aggravate, I will a. my voice, 172:28
Aggravation of self, 535:17
Aggravations, accept minor a., 558:5
Aggregate efforts of busy multitude,
  503:3
interests of community, 351:21
Aggression of Germany, 676:*n*1
stop their a., 719:8
threaten a., 650:9
Aggressions, when a. require war,
  344:10
Aggressors, quarantine the a., 649:*n*1
Agin, off a. on a., 607:6
Agincourt, affright air at A., 184:19
Aging people in contraction of life,
  628:11
person give attention to self, 628:11
Agir, j'ai trop pensé pour a., 537:*n*3
Agitation, peace at heart of endless a.,
  376:21
those who deprecate a., 480:16
Agitators, rights protected not by
  labor a., 544:8
A-gley, gang aft a., 361:6
Aglow, all a. is the work, 93:6
Agnes, world dear A. is strange,
  268:29
Agnes', St. A. Eve, 414:21
Agnosco veteris vestigia flammae,
  93:*n*20
Agnostic, compliment to be called a.,
  573:19
judges neither Catholic nor a.,
  646:11
Agnosticism, that's all a. means,
  573:19
Agnus Dei, 48:9
A-going out with tide, 470:36
Agonies, exultations a., 374:18
find a. strife of human hearts, 414:4
one of my changes of garments,
  489:19
small talk dies in a., 407:23
voices a. creations and destroyings,
  417:1
Agonizing reappraisal, 743:1
Agony, charm a. with words, 187:8
leave off a., 555:18
of flame that cannot singe, 598:13
strong swimmer in a., 402:17
that a. our triumph, 674:20
Agree, all things differ all a., 299:21
birds in little nests a., 294:8
how a. kettle and pot, 31:31
let mankind a., 276:21
music and poetry a., 233:13
not free thought for those who a.,
  543:10
people have good sense a. with us,
  265:36
two of a trade never a., 297:9
whether they a. or not, 685:10
with her would not a., 594:17
Agreeable, do not want people a.,
  387:12

Agreeable (*continued*)
  impressions of American manners, 393:9
  in conversation, 293:2
  person agrees with me, 435:10
  what is more a. than home, 87:24
Agreed, except they be a., 29:35
  to differ, 386:17
Agreement, living in a. with nature, 82:1
  love is a., 161:7
  on nuclear control, 742:5
  verbal a. isn't worth paper written on, 647:3
  who does not forget old a., 61:22
  with hell, 437:16
  with hell are we at a., 26:33
Agrees, agreeable person a. with me, 435:10
  what a. disagrees, 62:16
Agriculture, navigation commerce a., 338:10
Ague of skeleton, 668:13
Agues, praise doth nourish a., 178:23
  war dearth age a., 230:20
Ahab, all evil to crazy A., 486:25
  he ran before A., 12:38
Ahead, go a. make my day, 774:8
  of the world, 57:22
  sure you're right go a., 398:4
Ahkoond of Swat, 472:*n*1
A-hunting, daddy's gone a., 789:15
  daren't go a., 504:2
  upon St. David's Day, 791:17
  we will go, 311:15
Aid, alliteration's artful a., 333:15
  come to a. of party, 781:7
  expletives feeble a. join, 298:18
  foreign a. of ornament, 308:7
  giving enemies a. and comfort, 346:9
  lend us thine a., 395:16
  mutual a. law of animal life, 547:5
  saints a. if men call, 382:14
  small a. is wealth, 68:23
  super-legal-a. bureau, 646:12
  thine a. supply strength bestow, 124:8
  to interpretation of future, 71:19
  to worker God lends a., 59:*n*5
  vanity give no hollow a., 400:13
  Wisdom's a., 324:18
  wit hope flock to a., 431:15
AIDS disease of defect in immunity, 745:*n*1
Ail, what can a. thee, 417:4
Ailed, what a. us O gods, 533:16
Ailes de géant l'empêchent, 494:*n*2
Ailest here and here, 497:16
Ailments, our a. are the same, 288:22
  selfish clod of a., 570:22
Aim, being's end and a., 301:16
  fixed as an a. or butt, 184:23
  forgotten a., 588:5
  hit only what a. at, 478:7
  malice never was his a., 289:18
  man sets himself, 717:15
  prince have no a. but war, 136:12
  rivalry of a., 535:27
  thought to a. at some good, 77:25

Aim (*continued*)
  two things a. at in life, 594:2
  who a. at great deeds must suffer, 87:4
  your a. the star, 783:5
Aime, je ne vous a. pas Hylas, 286:*n*11
  qui m'a. me suive, 127:*n*4
Aimest, all the ends thou a. at, 225:21
Aiming, slight not what's near by a. far, 68:9
Aimless rhetoric, 505:20
Ain't heard nothing yet, 661:14
  necessarily so, 695:11
  no such animal, 782:5
  nothin' but hound dog, 765:7
  she a. no lady, 604:8
  we got fun, 661:15
Air, affright a. at Agincourt, 184:19
  all a. and nerve, 743:3
  allaying both with its sweet a., 223:31
  always in earth and a., 725:12
  an a. and peculiar grace, 294:21
  awash with angels, 749:15
  babbling gossip of the a., 201:28
  Baldwin simply hole in a., 711:11
  bites shrewdly, 194:7
  blackest a., 749:17
  breathe his native a., 298:5
  breathe the a. again, 492:6
  brightness falls from the a., 227:2
  cast shadow in a. or water, 755:3
  Cervantes' serious a., 303:24
  change of a., 629:9
  charm ache with a., 187:8
  chartered libertine, 184:22
  common a. bathes globe, 489:3
  common sun a. skies, 322:25
  crows that wing midway a., 210:27
  crystallized a. of centuries, 662:8
  dance upon the a., 567:18
  death of a., 671:21
  diviner a., 377:5
  drinks water her keel plows a., 157:13
  earth fire sea a., 541:7
  earth or a., 192:28
  eat men like a., 764:13
  eating a. on promise of supply, 183:25
  emptier ever dancing in a., 172:9
  fairer than evening a., 162:20
  false as a. as water, 200:22
  fields of a., 335:23
  fight with strength in a., 620:7
  flies through a. with ease, 536:20
  fog and filthy a., 212:10
  fowls of the a. shall tell, 14:16
  fowls of the a. sow not, 33:18
  fresh a. sunshine good water, 563:5
  happy good-night a., 540:11
  haunting the black a., 759:13
  he says with solemn a., 361:9
  honor is a., 178:33
  hurtles in darkened a., 323:12
  I drew in the common a., 30:28
  I eat the a., 197:6
  I lived on a., 623:19
  if lungs receive our a., 334:27

Air (*continued*)
  in a. men seen, 777:16
  in a. Pentagon turn orange, 753:1
  inebriate of A., 511:17
  inner a. inner light, 706:11
  is delicate, 213:4
  let out to warm a., 289:12
  melted into thin a., 224:21
  meteor of ocean a., 447:3
  might wash leaves cover me, 533:18
  mock a. with idle state, 323:6
  most excellent canopy a., 195:28
  nimbly and sweetly recommends itself, 213:4
  now a. is hushed, 324:14
  now thoroughly small, 669:14
  of delightful studies, 254:14
  of Seven Dials, 530:9
  on A. Bird stamped, 512:7
  other passions fleet to a., 181:7
  over the plain quiver, 656:9
  prison a., 567:22
  retrace steps to upper a., 94:6
  round ocean and living a., 373:5
  saw the a. with hand, 196:21
  sightless couriers of a., 213:7
  signed with their honor, 727:10
  soft summer a., 507:3
  solemn stillness holds, 322:2
  speche in substaunce ys but a., 128:2
  speed through a. thirty-one, 604:10
  spiders marching through a., 742:12
  stood naked in open a., 562:18
  sweet a. coming into house, 664:4
  sweeter a. where it was made, 665:1
  take into a. my breath, 415:16
  that kills, 579:9
  thin a., 224:21
  trifles light as a., 207:5
  troubled a., 256:*n*1
  underneath him steady a., 550:20
  vans to beat a., 669:14
  walking in a. of glory, 270:10
  wanton in the a., 267:16
  waste sweetness on desert a., 322:13
  water rush to rest in a., 696:3
  way of eagle in a., 23:15
  web of sunny a., 476:10
  whether in earth or a., 192:28
  which way hot a. blows, 586:5
  wild, 551:10
  wild with leaves, 660:12
  word honor is a., 178:33
  world sick for a., 666:20
  world-mothering a., 551:10
  wound with mercy as if a., 551:9
Air-drawn dagger, 215:5
Airly, git up a. to take in God, 485:11
Airmen, soldiers sailors a., 621:18
Airplane, strange high singing of a., 650:16
Airs, all a. make one country, 248:17
  don't give yourself a., 517:11
  melting a., 335:11
  Naiad a., 451:12
  soft Lydian a., 251:19
  sounds and sweet a., 224:18
Airy distance with majestic motion, 400:11

Airy (*continued*)
    ever so a. tread, 458:24
    gold to a. thinness beat, 229:12
    navies, 455:17
    nothing, 174:1
    objects in an a. height, 287:16
    reveries so a., 335:1
    servitors, 254:16
    subtleties in religion, 248:3
    tongues that syllable, 252:24
    unseen within thy a. shell, 252:26
Aisle, long-drawn a., 322:9
Aisles, monastic a., 429:9
    of Christian Rome, 429:10
Ajalon, valley of A., 10:37
Akond of Swat, 472:7
Alabama, all over A. lamps are out,
    726:4
    come from A., 506:17
    moon of A., 698:16
Alabaster box of ointment, 36:20
    grandsire cut in a., 179:18
    smooth as monumental a., 208:9
Alacrity, kind of a. in sinking, 183:2
Aladdin's lamp, 403:14, 485:25
Alamo, remember the A., 437:20
Alarm, give moderate a., 437:14
    ride and spread a., 442:13
Alarming, serious and a. consequences,
    336:18
Alarms, confused a. of struggle,
    499:22
    look of love a., 357:23
    sighs his a., 157:2
    world's a. to Paris, 598:22
Alarums, wars and a. unto nations,
    154:2
Alas, cried in goose A., 674:11
    how love can trifle, 168:8
    I loved you best, 284:4
    my Love, 776:10
    our young affections, 400:23
    poor Yorick, 199:8
    Postumus fleeting years slip by,
    96:10
    say A. but cannot help, 720:6
Albatross, shot the A., 381:5
    thought he saw A., 520:3
Albert, ask me to take message to A.,
    435:20
Albion, perfidious A., 371:5
Alcestis, like A. from the grave,
    255:16
Alchemists, sociologists a., 590:1
Alchemized, shine full a., 414:11
Alchemy, courtesy true a., 508:24
    happy a. of mind, 307:8
    love wrought new a., 229:9
    of the word, 565:24
    richest a., 187:30
Alcides, none equal A. except himself,
    103:11
Alcohol, narcotics a. and Christianity,
    552:28
Alcoran, rather believe fables in A.,
    159:18
Alcuin my name learning I loved,
    120:10
Alderman, agate on forefinger of a.,
    174:20

Ale, belly God send thee good a.,
    144:12
    cakes and a., 202:5
    fame for pot of a., 185:6
    fed purely upon a., 295:11
    ginger a. on the side, 673:13
    man ale's the stuff, 579:15
    nut-brown a., 251:16
    of myghty a. a large quart, 130:25
    pint of English a., 619:6
    shoulder sky and drink a., 579:18
    sleep upon a., 295:11
    take size of pots of a., 263:2
Alea, iacta a. est, 88:n15
Alehouse, an honest a., 245:21
Aleppo, in A. once, 208:17
Alexander, Diogenes asked by A.,
    77:2
    if I were not A., 80:24
    in his tent, 712:18
    of course A. the Great was hero,
    446:20
    some talk of A., 778:18
    trace noble dust of A., 199:9
Alexandria, strange power of A.,
    731:8
Alexandrian, present our A. revels,
    218:13
Alexandrine, needless A. ends song,
    298:19
Algae, delicate a. and sea anemone,
    671:13
Algebra, clock doth strike by a., 263:3
Algiers, dying in A., 444:1
Ali cibus aliis venenum, 90:n6
Alibi, stick to the a., 468:33
Alice, can't explain myself said A.,
    517:8
    go ask A., 770:2
    grave A., 442:10
    replied offended, 517:21
    what use of book thought A., 517:2
Alice's, at A. Restaurant, 774:5
Alien blessing on its way, 758:15
    corn, 415:17
    ism, 649:5
    nothing human is a., 85:16
    something bright and a., 709:n3
    there is none, 584:4
Alienation, world where a. awaits,
    758:6
Alieni appetens sui profusus, 91:n9
Alienum, humani nil a me a. puto,
    85:n13
Alike, all animals of forest a., 784:19
    all places distant from heaven a.,
    235:7
    by nature all a., 235:4
    by nature men nearly a., 62:1
    darkness and light a. to thee, 20:9
    destiny waits a., 63:21
    equals and unequals a., 75:24
    glory and danger a., 72:4
    looks on a., 223:12
    to suffer all a., 217:26
Alimentary canal with big appetite,
    730:14
Alive and so bold O earth, 408:12
    and wagging tail in mud, 80:17
    astonishing thing earth is a., 734:10

Alive (*continued*)
    attitude in which most a., 545:5
    be a. at great time, 700:9
    deeply and intensely a., 545:5
    fight to keep something a., 672:19
    hardly a man now a., 442:12
    how possible that dead be brought
    a., 116:22
    I am a. forevermore, 47:6
    in Christ all made a., 43:20
    in that dawn to be a., 373:12
    is that thing a., 734:14
    looking as if a., 464:11
    mission to come down a., 752:11
    more come through a., 52:8
    not a. enough to know how to kill
    self, 747:2
    remain a. past usual date, 587:3
    since none returned a. I answer,
    125:31
    some burned a., 752:4
    still while thy book live, 232:18
    supreme triumph to be most a.,
    657:21
    the most a. is wildest, 479:8
    was dead and is a., 38:37
All a green willow, 140:12
    aglow is the work, 93:6
    all alone, 381:19
    all are gone, 387:14
    all of a piece throughout, 276:22
    all sleeping on hill, 607:10
    and a. that tribe, 95:4
    are but ministers of Love, 383:3
    be as before Love, 465:8
    bed-time Hal and a. well, 178:32
    best of dark and bright, 401:14
    blind and ignorant in a., 227:14
    changed changed utterly, 596:17
    charity for a., 450:11
    Christ is a. and in a., 44:40
    come out of Gogol's Overcoat,
    495:18
    comes from the mind, 64:18
    cry and no wool, 133:n1
    death closes a., 455:5
    deliberate speed, 682:n4
    did you say a., 215:29
    died to save us a., 479:18
    down come baby and a., 555:4
    driven into same fold, 96:6
    eggs in one basket, 149:34
    else confusion, 456:17
    end crowns a., 201:12
    enough for a., 633:8
    except sun is set, 402:25
    fish that cometh to net, 141:35
    flesh is grass, 27:17
    for a. that and a. that, 363:23
    for best in best of all possible
    worlds, 306:n3
    for love, 153:10
    for one, 427:12
    for our rightfu' King, 362:12
    from a. things one and from one a.
    things, 62:16
    gas and gaiters, 469:23
    Gaul divided into three parts, 88:16
    give a. to love, 429:19
    God for us a., 142:30

Almighty (*continued*)
　shadow of the A., 18:15
　thank God A. free at last, 761:3
　that the A. would answer me, 14:46
Almighty's, arrow from A. bow, 359:4
　form glasses itself, 401:2
　God A. gentlemen, 274:13
　orders to perform, 291:30
Almond, peach once bitter a., 527:8
　tree shall flourish, 24:28
Almoner, best a. keeps nothing,
　　113:21
Almost right word and right word,
　　527:2
　thou persuadest me, 41:36
Alms, beg a. of palsied eld, 204:10
　for oblivion, 200:23
　give a. accordingly, 30:17
　give a. to every one that asks,
　　488:11
　of those who work with joy, 651:13
　when thou doest a., 33:11
Alms-basket of words, 169:6
Almsman's gown, 172:4
Aloft, Death a., 701:7
　invisible in night, 572:21
Aloha oe, 537:1
Alone a banished man, 776:1
　alone all all alone, 381:19
　and palely loitering, 417:4
　art should stand a., 524:1
　as sparrow a. upon house top,
　　18:24
　be a. on earth, 399:17
　being human born a., 660:18
　better to live a., 64:21
　beweep my outcast state, 220:15
　born unto himself a., 242:5
　Britain fight on a., 621:10
　cannot live a. at peace, 650:5
　clouded you will be a., 102:3
　don't live in world a., 630:19
　dwell kings of sea, 497:9
　go it sole a., 624:21
　grief mine a., 404:7
　heaven a. given away, 485:4
　here at gate a., 458:20
　how said I am a., 173:8
　I a. sit lingering here, 270:9
　I am a., 679:17
　I did it, 219:15
　I lie down a., 580:5
　I sleep a., 56:8
　I want to be a., 716:2
　in bee-loud glade, 594:21
　in the midst of the earth, 25:38
　in world without God, 760:6
　Jacob was left a., 7:45
　learn to stand a., 508:1
　leaving me never a., 540:17
　let her a. she will court you, 232:13
　let me a., 14:9
　let us a., 454:9
　long way I tread a., 411:5
　love but you a., 775:16
　love lives not a. in brain, 169:1
　loved him for himself a., 352:22
　man a. at moment of birth, 104:3
　man is a., 717:15
　man not sufficiently a., 614:2

Alone (*continued*)
　man only feels a., 736:13
　man thinking or working is a.,
　　478:26
　man with God strive, 400:13
　never a. accompanied with noble
　　thoughts, 155:24
　never a. with poet in pocket, 338:11
　never less a. than wholly a., 88:3
　never less a. than when a., 367:3
　nor for you for one a., 490:16
　not a. God is within, 108:1
　not good that man be a., 6:15
　not live by bread a., 10:*n*5
　nothing accomplished a., 684:18
　on wide wide sea, 381:19, 382:6
　one minute a. with him, 654:12
　paces about room a., 669:2
　right to be let a., 568:16
　sometimes be a., 242:20
　soon find himself a., 315:21
　strange city lying a., 451:14
　stranger and a., 706:17
　strongest stands a., 508:11
　though in wilderness never a.,
　　108:*n*2
　through seas of thought a., 373:10
　travels fastest a., 591:7
　trodden the winepress a., 28:7
　virtue not left to stand a., 61:7
　we exist a., 613:1
　we live as we dream a., 573:4
　we millions live a., 498:3
　we shall die a., 270:24
　weep and you weep a., 562:15
　white man will never be a., 398:11
　withouten compaignye, 130:22
　you a. are you, 221:10
Along came a spider, 791:8
　to get a. go a., 648:12
Aloof in order to gain reputation,
　　76:10
Aloud, all a. wind doth blow, 169:14
　not winced nor cried a., 557:9
　secrets cry a., 724:10
　think a., 431:37
　to fight a. very brave, 511:13
Alpes, au-delà des A. l'Italie, 98:*n*17
　in conspectu A. alterum latus Ita-
　　liae, 98:*n*17
Alph the sacred river, 382:19
Alpha, I am A. and Omega, 48:4
Alphabet of flowers, 230:5
Alpine mountains cold, 255:14
Alps, beyond A. lies Italy, 98:28
Already with thee, 415:13
Alright, it's gonna be a., 770:13
　listen Christ you did a., 708:16
Altar, even at Thy glowing a., 711:3
　every light focused on high a.,
　　601:12
　family a., 501:15
　great world's a. stairs, 457:20
　of freedom, 450:9
　what green a., 416:5
　with this inscription, 41:15
Altars, their a. their hearths, 91:27
　to unknown gods, 545:9
Alter, circumstances a. cases, 419:10
　ego, 81:*n*13

Alter (*continued*)
　human nature, 583:5
　life garment we a., 697:9
　make and a. constitutions, 337:4
　right to a. or abolish it, 343:2
　when Hills do, 513:4
Alteration, alters when it a. finds,
　　222:2
　world capable of a., 698:19
Altereth, law of the Medes and Per-
　　sians which a. not, 29:17
Alteri seculo, 85:*n*6
Altering, Eye a. all, 725:21
Alters, affliction a., 223:14
　love a. not, 222:2
　when it alteration finds, 222:2
Altitude, what leopard seeking at a.,
　　702:4
Altitudo in bloodstream, 675:4
　O a., 248:4
Alway, I would not live a., 14:9
　Lo I am with you a., 37:16
Always, believed a. everywhere by all,
　　115:4
　fair weather, 589:3
　I am with you a., 37:16
　in earth and air, 725:12
　poor a. with you, 36:22
　suspect everybody, 469:31
　three o'clock, 694:18
Alyosha, not God I don't accept A.,
　　495:8
Am, I a. not what I was, 288:4
　I a. that I a., 8:27
　I a. what I a., 43:19
　I a. what I yam that's all I yam,
　　690:2
　my God perhaps I a., 783:7
　not I a fly, 358:5
　sames of a., 689:1
　tell them I A., 325:10
　what I a. so shall thou be, 120:9
Amanece no más temprano, 794:5
Amantium irae amoris integratio est,
　　85:*n*11
Amaryllis, anger of A. a sad thing,
　　92:7
　sport with A., 253:20
Amassing harmony, 640:1
Amateur, whine of a. for three, 523:18
Amateurs, hell full of musical a.,
　　571:4
　ruined by a., 666:1
Amaze the unlearned, 298:16
Amazed and curious, 363:8
　gazing rustics, 329:18
　I am a. methinks, 170:17
　wise a. temperate furious, 214:16
Amazing grace how sweet the sound,
　　327:4
Amazon, she was an A., 721:12
Ambassador from Britain's crown,
　　461:1
　is an honest man, 227:12
Ambassadors in every quarter, 463:16
Amber, bee preserved in a., 106:14
　flies preserved in a., 106:*n*6
　scent of odorous perfume, 261:16
　waves of grain, 576:19
Amber-dropping hair, 253:11

Ambiguities, smile vehicle for a.,
   487:4
Ambiguous undulations, 638:26
Ambition a species of madness, 278:12
   all the pride cruelty and a., 153:1
   bookish a., 234:2
   choked with a. of meaner sort,
     163:13
   Distraction Uglification, 518:3
   drove men to become false, 91:23
   fling away a., 225:20
   forgo even a., 463:26
   heart's supreme a., 318:5
   let not a. mock, 322:7
   low a. and pride of kings, 301:1
   low a. and thirst of praise, 334:5
   made of sterner stuff, 189:1
   of living like Thoreau, 594:*n*2
   pen instrument to inflame a., 337:11
   public life worthiest a., 628:3
   soldier's virtue, 217:22
   thicksighted, 414:8
   to grasp continent, 503:3
   to reign is worth a., 256:6
   vain the a. of kings, 237:20
   vaulting a., 213:7
   wars that make a. virtue, 207:8
   who doth a. shun, 190:20
   whole possible scope of human a.,
     585:14
Ambition's, young a. ladder, 187:32
Ambitions, let go hold of a., 697:14
   weakens their a., 56:14
   which climb on miseries, 573:15
   whispering a., 668:7
Ambitious, abject usually a., 278:8
   as a. I slew him, 188:26
   become a. for her own sake, 722:12
   finger, 225:1
   man have no satisfaction, 231:14
   materially a., 665:9
   not a. to appear man of letters,
     272:2
   we live in a. poverty, 108:24
Ambitiously, leaders a. contending,
   351:22
Ambles, who Time a. withal, 191:18
Ambree, foremost in battle Mary A.,
   785:6
Ambrosia, streams flow with a., 68:20
Âme, l'â. d'un emploi, 560:*n*1
   quelle â. est sans défauts, 565:*n*14
Amelette Ronsardelette, 110:*n*7
Amelioration, novelty connected to a.,
   438:6
Amemus, vivamus atque a., 90:*n*14
Amen, sound of great A., 506:1
   stuck in my throat, 214:5
   will no man say a., 172:8
Amend your ways, 28:19
Amended, little said soon a., 149:40
Amending, constitutional right of a.,
   449:4
Amendment, Fifth A. old friend,
   698:20
   First A. has erected wall, 661:6
   Fourteenth A. not enact Spencer,
     542:16
   guarantee of First A., 661:8
Amends, I must make a., 773:6

Amends (*continued*)
   no making a. in world, 483:9
America, all lost wild A., 698:13
   America, 576:19
   bad Americans die go to A., 566:26
   beaten by strangers, 694:6
   born in A. black, 755:7
   breach with A. calamity, 564:21
   cannot be ostrich, 572:7
   come to look for A., 772:10
   destiny of A., 480:17
   destiny of republics of A., 486:9
   discovered accidentally, 665:12
   don't sell A. short, 782:22
   everybody in A. soft, 585:13
   friendly dog in small room, 677:9
   furnished Washington, 395:4
   getting on in A., 615:17
   gigantic but giant mistake, 570:1
   glorious morning for A., 325:5
   God bless A., 666:11, 666:12
   God's crucible, 590:6
   gone to degeneration, 542:2
   good evening Mr. Mrs. A., 698:2
   greatest question debated in A.,
     338:4
   half-brother of world, 476:9
   heart and mind of A., 721:11
   huntsmen are up in A., 249:7
   I hear A. singing, 488:15
   I like to be in A., 763:6
   i love you, 688:15
   I see the face of A., 771:12
   I'm putting queer shoulder to wheel,
     757:3
   in A. two classes of travel, 675:13
   in which people still get rich,
     730:15
   is just ourselves, 500:9
   know all people worth knowing in
     A., 461:4
   land of unlimited possibilities, 556:4
   land of wonders, 438:6
   lost in A. shall be found, 706:20
   love it or leave it, 784:5
   Marilyn man's love affair with A.,
     753:3
   melting pot, 590:6
   middle class in A. the nation, 501:2
   my country hardly a nation, 660:8
   my country Paris home town,
     627:11
   my new-found land, 230:12
   named after man, 665:12
   new regions A. we call New World,
     135:15
   nothing less than whole A., 331:12
   of poverty, 759:3
   proclaimed rights of human nature,
     368:15
   put all A. behind him, 479:10
   rejoice that A. resisted, 312:20
   remote from wrangling world,
     340:24
   save soul rather than face, 655:3
   settlement of A. a grand scene,
     337:12
   so happy as A., 340:24
   spend blood and might, 572:12
   such is state of A., 331:3

America (*continued*)
   the other A., 759:3
   true original native of A., 310:24
   ugly A., 748:13
   war in which A. engaged, 341:4
   was primitivism, 653:12
   was promises, 683:12
   what is left of A., 427:*n*1
   would be no longer ruler of own
     spirit, 368:16
   you cannot conquer A., 313:6
   you have it better, 351:13
   young man there is A., 331:7
   youth of A. tradition, 567:1
American bathrooms, 693:12
   born live and die an A., 395:9
   chief business of A. people, 614:17
   children's books, 587:4
   complex fate being A., 548:6
   continents not for colonization,
     360:10
   cradle of A. liberty, 395:10
   credit card good in Europe, 559:7
   crisis in A. leadership, 738:3
   destiny of colored A., 480:17
   experiment of A. people, 337:1
   flag floats from hill, 330:19
   from blues A. music, 612:10
   Goddam precious A. rights, 765:3
   has no sense of privacy, 571:29
   high school closer to core of A. ex-
     perience, 751:14
   how behave toward A. government,
     477:9
   if I were A., 313:6
   imitate Europe not A. literature,
     461:3
   impressions of A. manners, 393:9
   impressive fact about A. women,
     751:7
   jumps into train, 588:13
   life powerful solvent, 588:12
   literature from one book, 702:2
   love mankind except A., 317:7
   most pecksniffian of A. cities,
     642:14
   Muse, 698:8
   names, 698:6
   Negro problem in heart of Ameri-
     can, 700:5
   never felt I were an A., 763:17
   new deal for A. people, 648:16
   nineteen-year-old A. boy, 771:1
   no A. criminal class except Con-
     gress, 527:25
   no second acts in A. lives, 694:22
   North A. civilization engulfed
     world, 754:5
   not about to send A. boys, 723:19
   not Virginian but A., 339:6
   pass to A. strand, 244:3
   Philistine livelier, 501:3
   professors like literature dead, 658:9
   Revolution produced Declaration of
     Independence, 665:13
   right to be treated as wish, 742:2
   says he loves country, 706:11
   sense to A. people, 706:10
   show world how A. sailors fight,
     781:*n*4

American (*continued*)
  smiling aspects of life more A., 532:17
  system rugged individualism, 625:20
  Teenage Drive-In Life, 764:1
  tragedy, 611:14
  underestimating intelligence of A. people, 643:*n*1
  violence is as A. as cherry pie, 772:12
  what dissatisfies in A. civilization, 501:4
  what then is the A., 339:1
  who reads A. book goes to A. play, 379:28
  without qualifying adjectives, 560:4
  women kept from growing, 748:18
  write well of A. things, 548:5
Americanism, hyphenated A., 576:12
Americanization, line of rapid effective A., 584:6
American's guarantee of freedom, 655:17
Americans, brave A. all, 336:10
  disdain to be instruments, 355:3
  do not always explain, 536:6
  first self-constituted People, 683:13
  freemen or slaves, 336:14
  good A. die go to Paris, 566:26
  good at long shot, 398:9
  hope of world, 327:12
  I love the A., 313:4
  in A. spark of idealism, 569:1
  let us all be A., 560:4
  love of wealth in all A. do, 438:11
  must look outward, 541:4
  my people are A., 699:13
  new generation of A., 741:3
  North A. use reality, 736:12
  of African descent, 522:13
  prefer Continent, 605:22
  races didn't bother A., 683:13
  refuse to learn languages, 605:22
  Russians and A., 438:7
  strength of A., 438:10
  this generation of A., 649:3
America's my nation, 697:12
  participate in A. growth, 726:2
  read in A. signs, 340:*n*1
  treatment of Negro A. greatest scandal, 700:6
Amerika du hast es besser, 351:*n*4
Âmes, par de pareils objects les â. blessées, 269:*n*2
Ami entends-tu, 786:20
Amiability, brimstone behind beautiful a., 426:9
Amiable, good a. or sweet, 260:10
  good nature more a. than beauty, 293:2
  how a. are thy tabernacles, 18:5
  lovely death, 170:3
  virtue not always a., 338:8
  weakness, 311:27
  words, 459:20
Amicable, candor and a. relations, 360:12
Amicably if they can, 385:7
Amice gray, 261:5
Amici diem perdidi, 106:*n*12

Amicus Plato sed magis amica veritas, 77:*n*13
A-milking sir she said, 790:6
Amis, le choix fait les a., 341:*n*5
Amiss, better to love a., 457:*n*4
  nothing comes a. so money comes, 167:19
  thou shalt never do a., 31:18
Amittuntur, non a. sed praemittuntur, 102:*n*13
Amity, absolute a., 713:19
'Ammer along 'ard 'igh road, 554:17
Ammiral, mast of some great a., 256:7
Ammunition, praise Lord pass a., 679:7
Amo amas, 348:12
  odi et a., 91:*n*5
Amoebas at start not complex, 611:16
Among them but not of them, 400:8
Amor, and after A. vincit omnia, 129:14
  batallas de a. campo de pluma, 101:*n*6
  l'a. che muove il sole e l'altre stelle, 127:*n*1
  omnia vincit a., 92:*n*10
  vincit insomnia, 722:3
Amores, el oro y a. malos de encubrir, 794:7
Amorous descant sung, 258:19
  excite my a. propensities, 315:14
  from a. causes springs, 299:9
  nightingale a., 533:8
  of their strokes, 217:14
  sweet reluctant a. delay, 258:13
  tangled in a. nets, 260:26
Amorphous, all was vague and a., 86:15
Amortization of heart and soul, 686:21
Amount to Hannah Cook, 782:3
Amounts, spent tremendous a. on army, 643:8
Amour, beginning of an A., 281:21
  doux comme l'a., 354:*n*2
  fait tourner le monde, 786:18
  l'a. l'histoire de la vie des femmes, 368:*n*2
  on ne badine pas avec l'a., 461:*n*4
  un peu d'a., 522:*n*2
Amphibious ill-born mob, 285:15
Amphibium, man that great and true A., 248:10
Amphitryon, I am the true A., 275:29
  true A. gives dinners, 269:21
Ample, cabined a. spirit, 498:15
  knowledge her a. page, 322:12
  room and verge enough, 323:7
Ampler ether, 377:5
Amplified, hand prosperity down a., 576:7
Amplitude, know a. of time, 489:6
Amuck, too discreet to run a., 302:20
Amun give me what I found, 4:8
  obelisks for my father A., 4:10
Amurath, not A. an A. succeeds, 184:5
Amuse his riper stage, 301:15
  television used to delude a. insulate, 724:8

Amuse (*continued*)
  you with stories, 331:7
Amused according to taste, 642:21
  by its presumption, 690:8
  delicately and unceasingly a., 642:21
  we are not a., 488:6
Amusement, let early education be a., 75:22
Amusements, great friend to public a., 316:12
Amusing with numerous errors, 328:17
Amyntas, what if A. is dark, 92:19
Amytis, for A. made, 782:7
Anachronism, periodization of history a., 704:2
Analogy least misleading thing, 525:3
Analysis, last point reached by a., 345:10
  literature a. of character, 715:5
  must lay down its arms, 569:11
  subject men to external a., 558:10
  submit data to a., 351:16
  third of impossible professions, 569:17
Analyze, culture a. itself, 584:19
Ananda, since A. women received permission, 65:4
  the Tathagata, 64:22
Anarch, thy hand great A., 304:2
Anarchic, weeping a. Aphrodite, 720:13
Anarchy, digest of a., 332:9
  freedom cure of a., 331:19
  mere a. loosed on world, 596:19
  of poverty, 654:3
  show me greater evil, 66:15
  threaten free nations, 733:16
  wild a. of drink, 233:2
Anathema Maranatha, 43:30
Anatomizing of motives, 433:4
Anatomy, learn a. from dissections, 236:1
  Pinch a mere a., 166:34
Ancestor, I am my own a., 76:*n*1
  I feel shame in recalling, 505:20
Ancestors, democracy makes man forget a., 438:9
  glory belongs to our a., 107:7
  Great Spirit gave a. lands we possess, 370:5
  hunting wild boar, 434:*n*1
  insult to spirits of a., 502:5
  look backward to a., 332:10
  no need of a., 306:1
  not degenerate from virtues of a., 69:*n*5
  of honorable gentleman, 434:21
  owe it to a., 345:15
  part of Self, 545:20
  regardless of race of a., 634:18
  true picture of a., 425:18
  turned savage wilderness, 331:25
  very good kind of folks, 352:12
  wisdom of our a., 330:22
Ancestral, amidst tall a. trees, 410:10
  happy man works a. acres, 95:13
  in a. Jove Troy's sons rejoice, 94:19
  voices prophesying war, 382:22

Angels (*continued*)
pass in a. say, 429:23
progeny of light, 259:13
sad as a., 320:*n*5
send his a. with trumpet, 36:10
sing thee to thy rest, 199:29
sons of men and a. say, 312:13
sorrow for a., 464:25
swearing I was right, 451:4
tears such as a. weep, 256:18
they have the faces of a., 115:15
tongues of a., 43:13
trumpet-tongued, 213:7
walking in peace, 116:19
we shall hear a., 582:13
where a. fear to tread, 299:6
where a. tremble, 323:4
with a. and archangels, 49:16
with cash-boxes for hearts, 422:14
women are a. wooing, 200:4
wrote of A. and God, 357:2
yield eternal thanks, 325:11
Angels' Bread made Bread of man,
    124:7
man did eat a. food, 18:3
Anger, a God slow to a., 13:23
at clog of his body, 250:9
contempt and a. of lip, 202:25
furious a., 31:24
give vent to millennial a., 747:1
he that is slow to a., 21:27
is a short madness, 97:10
is a weed, 114:31
look back in a., 762:1
monstrous a. of guns, 687:2
more in sorrow than a., 193:21
of Amaryllis, 92:7
of Lord kindled, 12:6
of lovers renews love, 85:*n*11
one of sinews of soul, 250:17
provoke not children to a., 44:41
slow to a., 21:32
take care you strike in a., 571:10
tread them in mine a., 28:7
visionary a. cleansing sight, 762:5
words of pain tones of a., 125:8
Angkor, Machu Picchu Cambridge A.,
    735:8
Anglais s'amusent tristement, 157:*n*9
Angle, brother of the A., 245:16
in every a. greet, 268:22
Angler, honest a., 245:15
no man born an a., 245:14
now with God, 245:23
Anglers, too good for any but a.,
    245:29
Angles, that they were called A.,
    115:15
Angleterre, l'A. la perfide A., 371:*n*4
Angli, non A. sed Angeli, 115:*n*10
Angling, be quiet and go a-a., 245:31
frequent practicer of a., 245:17
like mathematics, 245:13
like virtue of humility, 245:18
never fully learnt, 245:13
of a. as of strawberries, 245:27
produce gentleness, 245:*n*3
reward to itself, 245:17
Anglo-Catholic in religion, 672:18
Angry, be ye a., 44:25

Angry (*continued*)
bellows full of a. wind, 597:5
feel a. because we strike, 546:4
feigned an a. look, 284:4
I was a. with my foe, 358:12
I was a. with my friend, 358:12
like an a. ape, 204:4
looking for a. fix, 757:4
opposition to idea, 629:7
passions rise, 294:7
prayers, 611:18
proud and a. dust, 579:18
tears gone, 596:13
up the blood, 719:12
when a. count four very a. swear,
    527:12
when a. count ten, 345:6
wrenlike vigilance, 743:10
Anguis, latet a. in herba, 92:*n*5
Anguish comes to end, 734:14
divinest a., 480:2
edges of laughter and a., 651:2
immense open a., 765:2
in a. uplift new song, 573:22
lessened by another's a., 174:16
must an a. pay, 511:12
of bereavement, 450:9
of the marrow, 668:13
pain and a. wring brow, 378:14
pale A. keeps gate, 567:22
whatever a. of spirit, 339:7
Anima, dum a. est spes est, 87:*n*12
Animae dimidium meae, 95:*n*13
Animal, aid law of a. life, 547:5
ancient a. symbols of St. John,
    420:9
another armored a., 664:16
bang now the a., 617:6
cow a good a. in field, 316:15
dead and dumb and done, 617:6
external reaction of a. to world,
    558:9
fastened to dying a., 597:9
inescapable a. walks with me, 734:6
information vegetable a. mineral,
    529:12
man a noble a., 249:4
man a political a., 78:12
man a poor bare forked a., 210:6
man a reasoning a., 102:24
man a social a., 278:10
man a successful a., 575:3
man a tool-using a., 411:23
man is raised above a., 722:8
man only a. devours own kind,
    343:13
man the ubiquitous a., 722:14
no a. more invincible than woman,
    73:16
no such a., 782:5
poor bare forked a., 210:6
post coitum omne a. triste, 119:21
press a wild a., 656:5
Public a mean a., 390:10
red a. war, 611:1
rope between a. and Superman,
    552:6
sta'tin' wid new kind of a., 678:4
unmistakable a. a writer, 759:10
we are worrying a., 734:12

Animality, endued with a., 335:24
Animals, all a. equal, 711:12
all a. of forest alike, 784:19
among a., 664:18
beyond a. is man, 690:21
boy most unmanageable of a., 76:14
could turn and live with a., 489:16
feed themselves men eat, 354:13
first a. then intelligences, 508:27
heart of a., 235:25
I sing for them the a., 787:3
infuse themselves, 181:17
interest in a. and athletes, 665:8
love earth sua, 488:11
medicine distinguishes man from a.,
    558:4
merely passage for food, 134:15
placid and self-contained, 489:16
production of higher a., 444:10
tomb for other a., 134:15
warm-blooded a., 335:24
will not look, 720:6
Animate and encourage each other,
    336:13
onion atoms a. whole, 380:17
Animated bust, 322:10
forces by which nature a., 351:16
nature, 380:25
only by faith and hope, 314:18
Animosity, inflamed with mutual a.,
    351:22
slave to a. or affection, 337:6
Animula vagula blandula, 110:*n*7
Animus, dux atque imperator a. est,
    91:*n*15
Anise, tithe of mint and a., 36:3
Ankle, down-gyved to his a., 195:8
Ann, how old is A., 782:6
marry A., 571:3
Anna whom three realms obey, 299:13
Anna Livia, O tell me all about A.,
    647:19
Annabel, I and my A. Lee, 453:8
the beautiful A. Lee, 453:9
Annals of the poor, 322:7
war's a. cloud into night, 540:22
writ your a. true, 219:15
Anne Donne Un-done, 228:*n*1
mother of Mary, 538:6
Sister A. do you see, 778:11
yes by Saint A., 202:5
Anne's, tell 'em Queen A. dead,
    366:13
Annie, witch-tales A. tells, 558:15
Annihilate, army corps a. in one sec-
    ond, 521:2
but space and time, 300:27
Annihilating all that's made, 268:18
means for a. itself, 645:19
Anniversaries, secret a. of heart,
    442:24
Anno aetatis suae, 118:17
domini fatal complaint, 704:12
Announced by trumpets of sky, 429:12
Announcer, victor or a. of victor,
    62:31
Annoy, goyim a. 'im, 656:*n*3
only does it to a., 517:15
Annoyance of good example, 527:17
to his extreme a., 609:7

Annoyed, people a. with Moses, 748:9

Annoying to be honest to no purpose, 102:5

Annoys, buzz witty and fair a., 302:15

Annual upkeep of yacht, 533:3

Annuit coeptis, 92:*n*12

Annuities, enrage those paying your a., 307:1

Annuity, buy a. cheap, 469:40

Anointed, elected and a. ones, 764:5

  I am your a. Queen, 144:16

  Lord's a. temple, 214:13

  sovereign of sighs, 168:28

  wash balm from an a. king, 171:21

Anointest my head with oil, 16:17

Anonymity, passion for a., 635:6

Anonymous, like writin' a. letters, 603:14

Another, absent one from a., 7:44

  and better world, 366:11

  I, 81:22

  love one a., 40:25, 42:21

  one good turn deserves a., 105:3

  such victory and we are undone, 82:11

  thought as well him as a., 647:17

  tomorrow is a. day, 705:3

Another's, burns out a. burning, 174:16

  can I see a. woe, 356:18

  semblance in a. case, 335:22

Answer a fool according to his folly, 22:29

  but is that an a., 420:12

  came there none, 519:7

  Daisy give me a., 600:18

  dat's on'y a. yuh know, 673:16

  dusty a., 508:30

  echoes, 456:11

  Gods do not a. letters, 765:2

  gratified to a. promptly, 526:10

  how could I a. the child, 488:19

  I will give Roosevelt, 620:15

  if find a. know mind of God, 772:2

  is blowin' in the wind, 771:5

  me in one word, 191:14

  not every question deserves a., 100:2

  Pilate would not stay for a., 159:2

  silver a. rang, 438:21

  since none returned alive I a., 125:31

  soft a. turneth away wrath, 21:24

  that the Almighty would a. me, 14:46

  the words of truth, 22:12

  think of Oedipus' a., 706:7

  to Hi or loud cry, 519:19

  to punish they a. prayers, 59:*n*6

  trickled through head, 519:16

  what is the a. what is the question, 627:14

  what shall I a. thee, 15:19

  why did you a. phone, 690:5

  without knowing what question, 617:17

  woods a. and Echo ring, 154:12

Answered as I thought good, 788:15

  calumnies a. best with silence, 232:3

  I came no one a., 616:23

Answered (*continued*)

  jealous souls not a., 207:17

  Lord a. Job out of the whirlwind, 15:6

  slowly a. Arthur, 459:26

  three questions, 517:11

  who rises a better man prayer a., 508:20

Answers, better to know questions than a., 690:17

  she who ne'er a., 300:18

Ant and the grasshopper, 59:6

  go to the a., 20:27

  not so much as weight of a., 116:10

  to ant is dear, 82:15

Antaeus-like grew strong, 599:15

Antagonism between classes, 482:5, 661:2

Antagonist is our helper, 332:20

Antediluvian tone, 519:22

Antelope, deer and a. play, 786:11

Anthem, pealing a. swells, 322:9

Anthems, hollaing and singing of a., 183:21

  service high and a. clear, 252:10

Anthologist, who as an a., 689:4

Anthology dispensary of medicine, 692:3

Anthropology, familiar facts of a., 565:2

Anthropophagi, 205:27

Antibombs, what use bombs and a., 690:22

Antic, dance the a. hay, 162:10

  disposition, 195:4

  old father a. the law, 176:29

Antichrist that denieth the Father, 46:34

Anticipate, what we a. seldom occurs, 434:22

Antidote, she is a. to desire, 291:15

  sweet oblivious a., 216:10

Antipodes, act our A., 249:7

  conquests even to A., 160:*n*5

Antiquas, stare super vias a., 28:*n*2

Antiquated, idea a. once modern, 617:13

Antiquates, time which a. antiquities, 248:29

Antique joy, 594:16

  learning, 503:4

  mask and a. pageantry, 251:19

  more a. Roman than Dane, 199:26

  pen would have expressed, 221:22

  Persians taught, 403:22

  traveler from a. land, 406:13

  ye a. towers, 321:13

Antiquitas saeculi juventus mundi, 158:5

Antiquities, even living men were a., 248:25

  time which antiquates a., 248:29

Antiquity, a little skill in a., 159:*n*8

  age of a. youth of world, 158:*n*2

  beautiful women of a., 538:5

  blasted with a., 183:20

  country with no a., 436:12

  farther from beginning, 158:*n*3

  history brings tidings of a., 87:14

  night shrouds remote a., 290:31

Antiquity (*continued*)

  one who is fond of a., 61:11

  tragedies of a., 769:2

Anti-Semites, hated by a., 766:5

Anti-Semitism, would be no a., 637:3

Antiseptic tunnel, 759:12

Antithesis, himself one vile a., 302:16

Antlers, bringing to his a., 684:11

Antonines, Age restored of the A., 340:*n*1

  united reigns of A., 340:2

Antonio, Stradivari's violins without A., 483:6

Antony brought drunken forth, 218:13

  catch another A., 218:22

  happy horse to bear A., 217:5

  much A. of Hamlet most, 557:7

  my A. is away, 217:4

  my oblivion is a very A., 217:3

  that revels long o' nights, 188:12

  who lost A. the world, 284:15

Ant's centaur in dragon world, 660:1

Ants, belligerent a. claimed boundaries, 370:*n*1

  nothing but a. find living, 633:11

  preserved in amber, 106:*n*6

Anulus in digito tenuatur, 89:*n*6

Anvil laughs at hammers, 634:15

  lay me on a., 634:9

  sword out of stone and a., 133:4

  what the a., 358:7

  when an a. hold still, 244:22

  when you are a. bear, 244:*n*6

Anxiety about livelihood, 626:14

  banquet partaken in a., 59:1

  basic a. cannot be eliminated, 662:11

  born with a. about weather, 532:7

  state of man a., 270:20

  tabooed by a., 530:14

  unrest unhappiness mood of a., 569:12

Anxious, freedom made man a., 704:8

  pleasing a. being, 322:19

Anybody anywhere any time, 614:16

  can be pope, 645:2

  can make history, 567:14

  don't trust a. over thirty, 770:16

  else I knew as well, 477:28

  more space where nobody than a., 627:12

  no one's a., 531:22

  there said Traveler, 616:22

  who goes to psychiatrist, 646:20

Anyone allowed to write like that, 651:*n*1

  lived in pretty how town, 688:22

  tennis a., 783:3

  who hates children, 641:14

Anythin' for quiet life, 469:3

Anything, courage not to believe in a., 482:17

  Everything and A., 650:12

  for a quiet life, 237:6, 469:3

  for good of country, 295:14

  he hasn't got a. on, 437:9

  if a. can go wrong it will, 783:25

  is there a. beyond, 663:1

  man says take with dose of salts, 647:2

Apples *(continued)*
 sure as Lord made little green a.,
  710:12
 sweeter than a., 565:12
Applesauce, politics is a., 637:18
Appleseed, Johnny A., 637:13
Apple-tree, bare branch of mossy a.,
  382:17
Apple-woman, Mr. Whitman's Eve
  drunken a., 535:9
Appliance, by desperate a. relieved,
  198:9
Appliances, with all a. to boot, 183:37
Application, lays in a. on it, 470:18
Applied, acceleration proportional to
  a. force, 282:*n*1
 science not exist, 502:3
Applies west of Rockies, 748:10
Apply our hearts unto wisdom, 18:13
 thine heart unto my knowledge,
  22:11
Applying thought one finds, 433:*n*1
Appointed for my second race, 270:4
 house a. for all living, 14:44
 limits keep, 506:4
 their a. courses, 70:11
Appointeth the moon for seasons,
  19:6
Appointment at end of world, 656:8
 in Samarra, 626:19
 never yields by a., 396:13
Appreciate things left behind, 644:16
 to criticize is to a., 549:6
Appreciates what others comprehend,
  136:17
Apprehend some joy, 174:1
 we a. good clearly, 68:14
Apprehended, next world as closely a.,
  248:27
Apprehension, death most in a.,
  204:11
 in a. how like a god, 195:28
 of the good, 171:3
Apprenticehood, serve long a., 170:32
Appris, rien a. ni rien oublié, 354:*n*3
Approach, drum beats my a. tells thee
  I come, 242:3
 like rugged bear, 215:7
 see a. proud Edward's, 363:19
 snuff a. of tyranny, 331:15
 sweet a. of even or morn, 257:24
 touch me, 490:2
Approaching, arrow always a. target,
  769:3
Approbation, cold a., 313:11
 from Sir Hubert Stanley, 367:10
Appropriate, all means which are a.,
  355:12
 to criticize is to a., 549:6
Approval, colored man looks to white
  folks for a., 773:19
Approve, abhor makers and laws a.,
  275:22
 by his loved mansionry, 213:4
 gods a. the depth, 377:4
 not a. slightest breach, 661:6
Approximate, hated the a., 630:3
Après nous le déluge, 324:19
April, bright cold day in A., 711:15
 eighteenth of A., 442:12

April *(continued)*
 he smells A. and May, 182:31
 hoarfrost spread, 381:21
 how it is with A. day, 624:6
 in mistress' face, 776:19
 is the cruellest month, 668:17
 laugh thy girlish laughter, 576:18
 love resembleth A. day, 168:1
 lovely A. of her prime, 220:9
 men A. when they woo, 192:4
 of A. May of June, 240:16
 proud-pied A., 221:19
 shakes out her hair, 655:2
 showers May flowers, 144:8
 thirty days hath A., 143:13
 those that A. wears, 204:*n*5
 uncertain glory of A. day, 168:1
 with his shoures soote, 129:6
April's breeze unfurled, 429:22
 if you were A. lady, 534:8
 now that A. there, 465:3
Aprons, sewed fig leaves and made a.,
  6:21
Apt alliteration's aid, 333:15
 words have power, 261:11
Aptitude, genius a. for patience, 311:8
Aptitudes, produce according to a.,
  481:*n*4
Aquarium is gone, 743:13
Aquarius, age of A., 770:1
A-quarreling, set them a., 318:15
Aquitaine, Prince of A., 443:23
Arab in desert, 315:*n*7
Arabesque, Lateral A. a pseudo-
  promotion, 747:7
Arabia, all the perfumes of A., 216:5
Arabian, as fast as A. trees, 208:16
Arabs, fold tents like A., 441:12
 no more war between A. Israelis,
  745:22
 of the desert, 117:16
Arahat Buddhas who appear in world,
  64:24
Ararat, always been an A., 625:3
Arbeiten, lieben und a., 570:*n*1
Arbiter is taste, 453:14
 of everyone's fortune, 92:*n*2
 of taste, 109:15
Arbitrary, deliberative forces over a.,
  568:14
Arbitrator, old common a. Time,
  201:12
Arboreal, hairy quadruped probably
  a., 444:13
Arbores, serit a. quae alteri seculo,
  85:*n*6
Arcadia, et in A. ego, 118:31
 I too am in A., 118:31
Arcady, woods of A. dead, 594:16
Arch, broken a. of London Bridge,
  425:7
 experience a. to build upon, 535:12
 experience is an a., 455:1
 of ranged empire fall, 216:25
 sunlit a., 624:6
Archangel a little damaged, 387:22
 angel and a. join, 303:6
 ruined, 256:15
Archangels, with angels and a., 49:16
Arched flood, 429:22

Arched *(continued)*
 heaven-gates not so a., 237:18
Archer, feat of Tell the a., 365:23
 laughs at a., 494:2
 mark a. little meant, 379:5
Arches, fled Him down a. of years,
  581:4
Archetypes of unconscious, 628:12
Archipelago, Gulag a., 746:6
Archipelagoes, starry a. and islands,
  565:16
 tourist a. of South, 763:10
Archipels sidéraux et des îles, 565:*n*11
Architect advise to plant vines, 608:13
 every man a. of his fortune, 92:1
 fate of a., 349:27
 man his own a., 468:9
 of Universe a mathematician, 632:3
 venture to call himself a., 379:7
Architecture adaptation of form,
  487:29
 fashion is a., 651:10
 frozen music, 350:7
 give children right to study a.,
  338:10
 love's a. is his own, 264:19
 man that has taste of a., 292:23
 music in space, 350:*n*1
 new styles of a., 720:4
 wondrous A. of world, 161:21
Archives, language the a. of history,
  432:16
 of memory, 609:11
Archy a cockroach, 633:*n*1
Arcs, on earth broken a., 467:2
Arctic, to wear a. fox, 665:6
Arcturus, guide A. with his sons,
  15:13
Arden, now am I in A., 190:14
Ardent, love of glory most a., 293:20
Ardeur dans mes veines cachée,
  281:*n*5
Ardor gives the charge, 197:32
 learning must be sought with a.,
  347:10
Are and are not, 76:8
 compared with might be, 511:6
 I shall tell you what you a., 354:14
 right you a., 604:3
 we a. the world, 775:3
 we know what we a., 198:18
Area, he who controls a. controls religion, 118:24
Arena, only beast in a. the crowd,
  602:5
Aren't I a woman, 420:22
Arethusa grant me this labor, 92:18
Argent, les affaires l'a. des autres,
  504:*n*1
Argos do without sons of Atreus,
  587:6
 dulces moriens reminiscitur A.,
  94:*n*12
 dying dreams of his A., 94:26
Argosies of magic sails, 455:17
Argue, good man does not a., 58:7
 hard to a. with belly, 85:3
 liberty to a. freely, 255:3
 not against Heaven's hand, 255:15
 not concerning God, 488:11

Argue *(continued)*
   though vanquished a. still, 329:18
Argued each case with wife, 517:10
Argues, not to know me a. yourselves
   unknown, 258:28
   who a. is not a good man, 58:7
Arguing, in a. parson owned skill,
   329:18
   much a. much writing, 254:26
   no a. with Johnson, 330:16
   not a. I am telling, 524:3
   with inevitable, 486:2
Arguit, stilus virum a., 234:8
Argument and intellects too, 328:21
   conduct right a. wrong, 330:11
   exact and priggish a., 436:26
   finer than staple of his a., 169:5
   for a week, 177:14
   heard great a., 445:17
   height of this great a., 255:20
   I have found a., 317:32
   in a. with men, 261:17
   knockdown a., 275:27, 519:14
   knowest thou what a., 429:7
   maintain his a., 185:8
   makes thee beat wings, 89:n10
   metermaking a., 432:15
   necessity a. of tyrants, 364:9
   needs no reason, 58:13
   not stir without great a., 198:14
   of earth, 488:18
   overrefines a. brings self to grief,
     127:9
   sheathed swords for lack of a.,
     185:4
   with east wind, 486:2
Arguments, no time for catch a.,
   449:15
   sure experiments and demonstrated
     a., 148:13
Argus, dark death seized A., 54:5
A-riding, cowpuncher a. along, 786:1
Ariel, deal of A., 557:7
   I A. will be correspondent, 223:28
Ariosto of North, 400:14
A-ripening, greatness is a., 225:16
Aris, pro a. atque focis, 91:n14
Arise, ah for man to a., 458:18
   arise from death, 230:19
   avenger of wrongs, 94:2
   awake a., 256:9
   Barak and lead captivity captive,
     11:2
   from dreams of thee, 407:21
   how shall the dead a., 248:14
   I will a. and go, 594:21
   my lady sweet a., 219:24
   Phoebus 'gins a., 219:24
   prisoners of starvation, 476:18
   shine for thy light is come, 28:4
   soldiers of Christ a., 312:16
   take up thy bed, 37:18
   thoughts that a. in me, 456:7
   wretched of earth, 476:18
Arises, democracy a. out of notion,
   78:23
Ariseth a little cloud like a man's
   hand, 12:37
   sun also a., 23:22
   sun a. they gather themselves, 19:6

Aristocracy, Clover any time A., 514:9
   natural a. among men, 344:15
   not society without a., 653:6
   of Moneybag, 412:21
   untitled a., 447:18
Aristocratic, beast of prey in a. races,
   552:24
Aristotle and all you philosophers,
   404:n4
   assures us man possesses immortal-
     ity, 718:8
   bookes of A. and his philosophie,
     129:21
   is it A. Pliny Buffon, 319:16
Aristotle's, live and die in A. works,
   162:13
Arithmetic, branches of A., 518:3
   wealth a. cannot number, 238:8
Arithmetical, subsistence increases in
   a. ratio, 368:2
Arizona is my land, 510:17
Ark, into Noah's a., 334:17
   make thee an a., 7:16
   of bulrushes, 8:21
   of God is taken, 11:30
   of the ache of it, 752:18
   straight out of a., 380:5
   Uzzah put hand to a., 12:6
Arkansaw, rest anywhere it would be
   in A., 398:6
Arks, these are the a., 161:2
Arm and burgonet of men, 217:6
   brutal a. appear, 599:17
   can honor set to a., 178:33
   clothed in white samite, 133:6
   doth bind restless wave, 506:4
   faithless a., 720:16
   give me your a. old toad, 750:12
   I bit my a., 381:11
   is very long, 70:12
   it in rags, 211:4
   long a. of coincidence, 582:5
   maketh flesh his a., 28:29
   mortal a. and nerve feel, 379:10
   my bended a. for pillow, 61:10
   on bended a. doglike, 63:9
   reared a. crested world, 218:11
   seal upon thine a., 25:22
   short a. to reach to Heaven, 581:14
   slumbering on own right a., 414:5
   some quick to a., 659:8
   soon shall thy a., 335:23
   the obdured breast, 257:14
   under a. carried broom, 790:16
   wreath of hair which crowns my a.,
     229:19
Arma, cedant a. togae, 88:n2
   virumque cano, 93:n7
Armageddon, place called A., 47:33
   we stand at A., 576:10
Armchair, old a., 480:9
Armed at points exactly, 193:19
   Forces in control, 682:11
   goeth on to meet the a. men, 15:16
   goodness a. with power, 684:15
   neutrality, 572:10
   peace, 247:14
   rhinoceros, 215:7
   so strong in honesty, 189:16

Armed *(continued)*
   thrice a. that hath quarrel just,
     164:1
   thy want as an a. man, 20:28
   without innocent within, 303:3
Armenians, who remembers A., 676:9
Armentières, mademoiselle from A.,
   680:8
Armes, aux a. citoyens, 366:9
Armies, anarchy scatters a., 66:15
   disbanding hired a., 411:22
   embattled a. clad in iron, 261:10
   ignorant a. clash by night, 499:22
   mechanized a., 621:1
   of ransomed saints, 460:17
   resisted but not an idea, 427:18
   swore in Flanders, 320:22
   when a. are mobilized, 58:1
Arming me from fear, 480:4
Armistice signed with fate, 696:6
Armor is his honest thought, 227:6
   man in a. slave, 468:7
   no a. against fate, 246:23
   not boast who puts a. on, 442:18
   of light, 42:23
   of righteous cause, 582:2
   person with no social a., 648:4
   put your a. on, 312:16
   whole a. of God, 44:27
Armored, another a. animal, 664:16
Armorers accomplishing knights,
   185:14
Armpits, scent of a. finer than prayer,
   489:10
Arms, a people takes up a., 438:13
   against a sea of troubles, 196:10
   analysis must lay down its a.,
     569:11
   and the man I sing, 93:10, 276:5
   blow trumpet to a., 340:17
   bring to our ears clash of a., 339:10
   by little a. plied, 517:1
   children receive a. race from us,
     748:4
   come to my a., 518:16
   Cupid's a., 778:7
   defy Omnipotent to a., 255:22
   everlasting a., 10:29
   excites us to a., 275:9
   fall into a. not hands, 544:23
   field his a., 157:2
   foes will provide with a., 93:34
   fury provides a., 93:15
   haughty nation proud in a., 252:14
   Helen's a., 598:22
   hold hidden charms, 693:6
   hug it in my a., 204:12
   I never would lay down a., 313:6
   imparadised in one another's a.,
     258:16
   industry, 678:17
   Infinite Goodness has wide a., 126:6
   law stands mute in midst of a.,
     87:10
   laws and a. foundations of states,
     136:11
   let a. yield to toga, 88:2
   lord of folded a., 168:28
   love world and all in its rainy a.,
     775:1

Art (*continued*)

moral sense of work of a., 549:2
more matter with less a., 195:11
my a. negation of society, 541:12
my trade and a. is living, 146:1
mysterious is source of a. and science, 635:12
nature is but a. unknown, 301:12
nature is the a. of God, 248:7
Nature not dull A., 426:21
nature's above a., 210:28
Nature's handmaid A., 273:10
neurotics created great works of a., 612:18
next to Nature A., 388:21
not learned much by a., 237:21
not thou man, 358:5
nothing without form, 496:1
novel is an a. form, 755:15
o' letter-writing, 468:32
of angling, 245:17
of being wise, 546:3
of Biography different from Geography, 627:17
of getting on together, 646:4
of knowing what to overlook, 546:3
of losing not hard, 729:15
of necessities strange, 209:30
of Racine's verse, 613:15
of seeing things invisible, 289:4
of teaching is awakening, 550:10
of telling you nothing, 269:11
of winning games, 705:5
only clean thing, 556:19
only through a. get outside selves, 613:5
personality of a. impersonality of science, 473:6
posterity of work of a., 612:15
practice and thought forge a., 92:24
practiced black a. in Cefalu, 712:6
pretty but is it A., 592:1
production of a. in soul, 584:14
professor of a. of puffing, 352:35
purpose inherent in a. so in nature, 77:17
refuge of a., 703:3
register multiple perception in a., 660:7
removed from contact with life, 705:7
respect for a., 543:7
revolt against fate, 707:11
romantic character in a., 538:12
schoolman's subtle a., 302:18
science and a. unite humanity, 755:11
selfish and perverse, 371:19
should stand alone, 524:1
smaller with their a., 698:8
subjects for a. and exemplars, 665:8
subordinates a. to nature, 384:14
substitute for experience, 746:3
take away a. of writing, 369:16
take love away n ., 575:2
tell thee what thou a., 151:1
tender strokes of a., 299:19
thanks to a. see world multiply, 613:5
that speaks, 707:10

Art (*continued*)

that tells time of day, 761:17
theme of A. and Song, 598:23
then must a. retire, 365:13
'tis all thou a., 300:9
to blot, 303:9
to find mind's construction, 212:27
to make dust of all things, 248:29
too precise in every part, 241:5
transmission of highest feelings, 510:16
unpremeditated a., 408:4
unthinkable without risk, 679:16
upsets, 646:1
war only a. necessary, 136:12
war's glorious a., 296:3
what a. wash guilt away, 328:29
where love of man love of a., 71:5
who comprehends a., 371:18
wise men know a. of eating, 354:13
work of a. corner of creation, 541:11
work of body and soul, 487:16
work that aspires to a., 572:18
works of a. products of danger, 630:13
works of a. turned to wall, 505:2
writer's responsibility to a., 697:2
Arteries, man as old as his a., 271:18
Artery, makes each petty a., 194:14
Artful, alliteration's a. aid, 333:15
careless with a. care, 291:16
Dodger, 469:6
Arthur, good King A., 792:16
King A. not dead, 133:18
knightly endured pain, 133:7
most renowned Christian king, 133:3
slowly answered A., 459:26
Arthur's bosom, 184:30
Article, fundamental a. of political creed, 338:16
snuffed out by a., 403:13
Articles, Christians agree in a., 315:24
Articulate, bleats a. monotony, 376:*n*2
sweet sounds together, 595:14
Artifice of eternity, 597:9
Artificer, great a. made my mate, 561:25
in brass and iron, 7:11
lean unwashed a., 170:14
old father old a., 647:11
Artificers, errors not in art but in a., 281:27
Artificial, all things are a., 248:7
kill in a. manner, 412:17
natural and a., 384:14
objects especially tools, 577:4
refined or a. type, 609:11
speech lacking in a. graces, 87:18
wilderness, 721:2
Artillery, hi-hi-yee for field a., 636:16
to thine A. left a Friend, 513:8
Artilleryman, red-haired a. killed or not, 510:3
Artist, allow a. freedom of choice, 548:14
be free a. and nothing else, 582:7
be more of an a., 418:19
cheat for sake of beauty, 631:4

Artist (*continued*)

create a. do not talk, 351:1
critic helper of a., 548:17
critic when cannot be a., 496:3
curiosity about a. important, 715:4
God only another a., 645:3
grant a. his subject, 548:14
greatest a. greatest ideas, 487:11
if not a. be revolutionary, 769:6
imitate that within, 384:20
is his own fault, 717:6
keep work to himself, 350:8
key to mystery of great a., 744:14
master a. who bids come to heel, 667:1
masterpiece joy to a., 523:21
must paint, 724:2
no home save Paris, 553:10
no man born an a., 245:14
perceives more than fellows, 614:22
progress of a. self-sacrifice, 672:9
range limited as specialist, 582:9
records more than has seen, 614:22
remains within behind handiwork, 647:10
search for subject, 421:11
selects guesses synthesizes, 582:9
speaks to our capacity, 572:19
that queer monster the a., 549:13
what an a. dies with me, 105:18
writes own autobiography, 578:7
Artiste triche pour le beau, 631:*n*1
Artistic, not separate a. from social, 629:23
nothing a. from mere art, 618:16
verisimilitude, 531:7
Artistries in circumstance, 540:13
Artistry, scaled invention or true a., 660:1
Artists, as many worlds as a., 613:5
great a. never Puritans, 642:13
scientists a. and artisans, 738:14
what a. call posterity, 612:15
Artless, full of a. jealousy, 198:15
Art's, art for a. sake, 405:18, 437:2
Arts, Athens mother of a. eloquence, 260:33
babblative and scribblative, 386:19
degrade first the a., 358:14
fashion's brightest a., 329:21
flourishing of the a., 686:16
Imagination with Reason mother of a., 348:*n*1
in the a. style, 600:7
in which wise excel, 284:2
inglorious a. of peace, 268:9
liberal a. study humanizes, 102:6
medicine most distinguished of a., 71:8
no a. no letters no society, 239:22
no relish of those a., 292:23
nurse of a. plenties, 186:1
of war and peace, 525:17
state of our a., 726:2
stomach teacher of a., 104:15
that caused to rise, 302:11
they are the books the a., 169:4
three a. with all things, 76:1
Aryan, neat mustache and A. eye, 764:17

As if, 546:15
  you desire me, 604:6
A-sailing with the wind, 791:18
Ascend, base degrees by which a.,
    187:32
  if I a. up into heaven, 20:8
  into the hill of the Lord, 16:18
  Muse of fire a., 184:18
Ascendancy, capital in a. system of
    plunder, 481:10
Ascended, bright pomp a. jubilant,
    259:22
  into heaven, 48:25
  morning hymns a., 506:16
Ascending, angels a. and descending,
    7:40, 39:37
Ascendit, quanto plus a., 123:n8
Ascends to mountaintops, 399:25
Ascent, no a. too steep for mortals,
    95:17
  of Man, 722:15
Ascetic in unnecessary points, 545:12
  systematically a., 545:12
Asclepius cured the body, 74:n3
  I swear by A., 71:1
  owe a cock to A., 70:25
Ash, oak a. and thorn, 593:17, 785:8
  on old man's sleeve, 671:21
  one adjusting a. heaps, 664:5
  out of a. I rise, 764:13
Ashamed, epitaph of which not a.,
    562:7
  more a. more respectable, 571:2
  naked and were not a., 6:18
  never a. to own wrong, 303:21
  no reason to be a. of ape, 505:20
  not a. to defend a friend, 31:41
  not a. to fail, 313:15
  of death, 248:13
  of having been in love, 265:8
  shame is a. to sit, 176:2
  to be seen with him, 279:22
  to die, 419:5
  to look upon one another, 245:25
  white men ought to be a., 369:7
  workman that needeth not to be a.,
    45:27
Ashen, skies a. and sober, 453:1
Ashes, all a. to taste, 399:23
  am I and dust, 120:9
  beauty for a., 28:6
  cinders a. dust, 414:17
  e'en in our a. live, 322:20
  fell in fire and burnt to a., 625:19
  from his a. made, 457:8
  handful of gray a. at rest, 502:9
  heaven and earth in a., 123:14
  in a. olde is fyr yreke, 130:27
  in a. rather than enslaved, 620:9
  into a. all my lust, 268:16
  new-create another heir, 226:8
  of his fathers, 425:14
  of Napoleon Bonaparte, 371:14
  out of a. life again, 554:13
  past a bucket of a., 634:7
  put on sackcloth with a., 13:24
  speak to your silent a., 91:17
  splendid in a., 249:4
  to ashes, 50:8
  turn to a. on lips, 392:14

Ashes (continued)
  well-wrought urn becomes greatest
    a., 228:16
  yesterday embryo tomorrow a.,
    111:12
Ashore, till last galoot's a., 536:11
Asia and Africa expelled freedom,
    340:21
  peace and stability in A., 733:15
  settlement in A., 677:4
  seven churches in A., 47:2
  vast multitudes of A., 621:1
Asian, do what A. boys ought to be
    doing, 723:19
Aside, not idly stand a., 72:7
  to step a. is human, 362:5
Asinorum, pons a., 82:n3
Ask, all I a. is merry yarn, 633:16
  all I a. is tall ship, 633:14
  and it shall be given, 34:6
  and ye shall receive, 40:34
  cease to a. what morrow will bring,
    95:24
  don't a. me to take none, 469:41
  drink divine, 232:15
  for anything except time, 370:7
  for me tomorrow, 175:27
  for the old paths, 28:18
  how he is he tells you, 601:5
  I do not a. you much, 170:22
  if you got to a. you ain't got it,
    703:n1
  me blessing, 211:13
  me no more, 456:19
  me no more where Jove bestows,
    246:4
  me no questions, 330:8
  never a. refuse resign office, 311:3
  not a dinner to a. a man to, 316:4
  not a. for what you wish you had
    not, 103:1
  not offer people but a. of, 740:20
  not what country can do for you,
    741:7
  not whom sleep beside, 578:21
  nothing want nothing, 123:1
  of him will they a. more, 38:31
  of thee forgiveness, 211:13
  only what they can give, 600:14
  the beasts, 14:16
  the Lord's blessing, 777:8
  us prophet, 750:2
  we a. and a., 497:4
  wealth I a. not, 561:21
  what you can do for country, 741:7
  where a. is have, 325:12
  who could a. for more, 695:4
  why I have no statue, 85:5
  wilt thou go a. the Mole, 357:1
Asked a lithe lady, 357:18
  are you lost I a., 657:5
  for it Georges Dandin, 269:23
  how pearls did grow, 241:3
  no other thing, 512:19
  not come even if a., 624:14
  Oliver a. for more, 469:5
  one another the reason, 192:10
  thief to steal me peach, 357:18
  to be where no storms, 550:15

Askelon, publish it not in the streets
    of A., 11:46
Asking, keep a. over and over, 420:12
  only God had for a., 485:4
  shoot murderer without a. to be
    paid, 762:11
  too much, 372:2
Asks a little of us here, 625:1
  if this be joy, 329:21
  of us certain height, 625:1
Asleep, athwart noses as they lie a.,
    174:20
  awake and a. the same, 62:19
  birds are a. in trees, 351:2
  devil is a., 570:6
  drunk and a. in boots, 638:23
  half a. as they stalk, 540:22
  in lap of legends, 415:2
  is in world of his own, 107:11
  keep it quiet till it falls a., 273:2
  lips of those that are a. to speak,
    25:20
  my Mary's a., 362:21
  on furrow sound a., 416:14
  sucks the nurse a., 218:19
  tide moving seems a., 460:11
  under haystack a., 789:4
  very houses seem a., 374:13
  when men were all a., 549:20
  where winds all a., 497:7
Asparagus stumbling block in girl's
    education, 616:18
Aspect, lend the eye terrible a., 185:3
  meet in her a. and eyes, 401:14
  sweet a. of princes, 225:16
Aspects, relations between a. of expe-
    rience, 656:3
  smiling a. of life, 532:17
Aspen, as a. leef gan to quake, 128:18
  light quivering a., 378:14
Asphalt and exhaust fumes, 754:5
Aspics' tongues, 207:1
Aspiration, social order and thirsty a.,
    726:1
Aspirations, right a., 65:1
Aspire, by due steps a., 252:13
  light and will a., 165:9
  mind a. to higher things, 155:28
  on what wings dare he a., 358:6
  smile we would a. to, 225:16
  there bade me a., 498:19
  to what greater character can mor-
    tal a., 337:10
Aspired to be and was not, 467:9
Aspires, art a. towards condition of
    music, 538:7
Aspiring, all to have a. minds, 161:21
Ass, affectioned a., 202:6
  egregiously an a., 206:13
  enamored of an a., 173:24
  idle to play lyre for a., 113:15
  in three letters, 269:2
  jawbone of an a., 11:15
  knoweth his master's crib, 25:25
  law is a., 469:12
  not covet neighbor's a., 9:12
  opened the mouth of the a., 10:4
  recover and prove an a., 174:10
  riding upon an a., 30:3

Ass (continued)
    sinned against my brother the a.,
        123:11
    Wild A. Stamps o'er Head, 445:12
    will carry load, 151:16
    write me down an a., 187:6
Assail, ills scholar's life a., 313:17
Assailed, everything hard to attain eas-
        ily a., 110:10
    seasons, 608:3
Assassin, forgot copperheads and a.,
        634:8
    kind a. Sleep, 750:6
Assassination, absolutism tempered by
        a., 368:3
    extreme censorship, 571:27
    trammel up consequence, 213:5
Assault, against a. of laughter nothing
        stand, 528:7
    and battery of wind, 597:4
    of thoughts on unthinking, 652:13
Assaulting, early bees a. fumbling
        flowers, 737:4
Assaults, defend in a. of our enemies,
        49:2
    mercy itself, 224:29
Assay so hard, 128:7
Assayed, thrice he a., 256:18
Assayeth, naught n' a. naught n'
        acheveth, 128:24
Assays of bias, 195:7
Assemblage of sloth sleep and little-
        ness, 338:9
Assemble, peaceably to a., 346:11
Assemblies, nails fastened by masters
        of a., 24:29
Assembling, slow in a., 72:1
Assembly, club a. of good fellows,
        314:1
    power in majority of popular a.,
        338:16
    proper office of representative a.,
        439:25
    suppression of free a., 568:15
Assent and you are sane, 512:11
    with civil leer, 302:11
Assert eternal Providence, 255:20
Assertions, convince hearers of own
        a., 75:1
Asses made to bear and you, 167:22
    mankind a. that pull, 403:26
Asses' bridge, 82:n3
Assist him to save face, 692:21
Assistance, gives persecution no a.,
        337:2
    of Thee do we beg a., 116:1
Assisting advancement of science,
        685:19
Associate, the good must a., 330:23
Associated, cannot be a. with govern-
        ment, 477:9
Association, quotations touch chord of
        a., 574:17
Ass's, white curd of a. milk, 302:14
Assuage anguish of bereavement,
        450:9
    words have power to a., 261:11
Assuaged, half a. for Itylus, 533:8
Assume a virtue, 198:5
    honorable style of Christian, 247:16

Assume (continued)
    spirits either sex a., 256:10
    what I a. you a., 488:16
Assumes, no vice but a. some virtue,
        181:5
    the god affects to nod, 276:7
Assuming, start a. that men are bad,
        137:2
Assumptions, most necessary of a.,
        588:4
    not admit a. of superiority, 79:24
Assurance given by looks, 163:3
    make a. double sure, 215:20
    of a man, 197:30
    of recorded history, 671:15
    sufficient for life, 439:13
Assurances of walls warmth comfort
        love, 753:n1
Assure survival of liberty, 741:3
Assured, crown themselves a., 221:23
    ignorant of what he's most a.,
        204:4
Assyria, Sennacherib king of A., 13:12
Assyrian came down like wolf, 401:15
Astern, look a. row ahead, 107:15
Asteroid, hen cackles as if laid a.,
        527:23
Astolat, lily maid of A., 459:12
Astonish, gratify some a. rest, 528:3
Astonished at my own moderation,
        326:13
Astonishing thing about earth, 734:10
Astonishment, curse a. hissing and re-
        proach, 28:34
    thou shalt become an a., 10:22
    wine of a., 17:30
Astonishment's, your a. odd, 673:n1
Astound me wait for you to astound
        me, 614:23
Astra, ad a. per aspera, 118:15
    sic itur ad a., 94:n10
Astray, all likely to go a., 66:17
    black sheep gone a., 592:3
    if world go a., 126:15
    light that led a., 361:15
    light which cannot lead a., 290:31
    one that had been led a., 252:3
    we like sheep have gone a., 27:37
Astrologers, sociologists a., 590:1
Astrology disease not science, 122:9
Astronomer, undevout a. is mad,
        296:21
    when I heard learned a., 490:9
Astronomers, say a. universe must fall,
        748:8
    what poor a., 776:26
Astronomy compels soul to look up-
        wards, 75:18
    geology by day a. night, 690:1
Astrophil, who knew not A., 163:2
Astute and dangerous man, 578:2
Asunder, afar and a., 528:20
    half a life a., 518:13
    let no man put a., 50:6
    let not man put a., 35:35
    put this rogue and whore a., 289:22
    We clave them a., 117:1
    whirl a. and dismember me, 169:29
Asylum, Jesus Christ shut up in a.,
        578:15

Asylum (continued)
    lunatics taken charge of a., 643:16
    optimism in lunatic a., 578:11
    prepare a. for mankind, 340:21
    their last a., 325:6
Asylums, comfortably padded a.,
        650:17
Atahualpa, who strangled A., 425:6
Ate cheeses out of vats, 464:18
    held heart in hands a. of it, 611:7
    the malt, 792:24
    when we were not hungry, 289:14
    with runcible spoon, 472:3
Aten, O living A., 5:2
    shine as A. of daytime, 5:4
Athanasian Creed splendid lyric,
        435:18
Atheism like that of Spinoza, 588:16
    little philosophy inclineth to a.,
        159:19
    owlet A., 382:18
    religion and not a., 331:19
Atheist half believes God, 296:16
    not satisfied with appearances,
        707:12
    superstitious a., 466:10
    town a., 704:1
Atheist-laugh's a poor exchange,
        361:23
Atheists, no a. in foxholes, 711:5
Athena, gray-eyed A., 53:1
Athenian, Thucydides an A., 71:18
Athenians commanded by myself,
        62:26
    crushed gold-bearing Medes, 60:10
    quality of A. lucidity, 500:25
    war between Peloponnesians and A.,
        71:18
Athens, bringing owls to A., 73:9
    divine city, 64:12
    Euripides' land, 67:n9
    fix eyes on greatness of A., 72:7
    maid of A., 399:7
    nigh to Euboea, 74:9
    nurse of men, 67:8
    the eye of Greece, 260:33
    to A. sent ships, 402:n5
    weeds of A. he doth wear, 173:13
    ye men of A., 41:15
Athirst, man a. supposes mirage to be
        water, 117:5
Athis, loved you once long ago A.,
        56:7
Athlete crowned in sweat of brow,
        113:12
Athletes, interest in animals and a.,
        665:8
Athwart men's noses as asleep, 174:20
A-tiptoe, stand a. when day named,
        185:22
Atlanta to the sea, 520:6
Atlantic, dawn on other side of A.,
        323:23
    drag A. for whales, 526:7
    frontier from A. to Pacific, 620:2
    Ocean on my head, 743:4
    steep A. stream, 252:19
    Thulè and A. surge, 308:8
Atlas, Teneriff or A. unremoved,
        259:3

Atmosphere, clear brown twilight a., 436:4
  of Gallup Poll, 621:4
Atom belonging to me belongs to you, 488:16
  changed everything save thinking, 636:8
  intense a. glows, 408:19
  knowledge of stars through a., 646:8
  movements of lightest a., 351:16
  secret powers of a., 601:15
Atomic age, 608:14
  bomb turn of screw, 714:10
  bombs burst in hands, 601:9
  cannot control a. energy, 613:6
  careless handling of a. technology, 645:19
  energy a menace, 636:4
  energy lead to bombs, 636:1
  first moment of a. age, 735:20
  habits of age of a. energy, 686:7
  not take a. weapons to want peace, 714:10
  reduced to a. mechanics, 522:16
  release of a. energy, 655:7
  war fought with a. bomb, 636:3
Atomies, crumbled out again to his a., 230:15
  team of little a., 174:20
Atom's weight of good, 117:25
Atoms and compounds of atoms, 89:10
  cannot be swamped by force, 89:10
  in reality a. and space, 70:28
  onion a. lurk in bowl, 380:17
  or systems, 301:5
  reduction to motions of a., 537:3
  true structure of a., 725:24
  we have seen our a., 680:18
Atoned, microcosm and macrocosm a., 504:17
Atones for later disregard, 624:8
Atreus, Argos do without sons of A., 587:6
  son of A., 51:17
Atrocious crime of being young man, 312:18
Atrocity, doctrines surpass in a., 536:18
Attach golden chain from heaven, 51:28
Attachée, à sa proie a., 281:*n*5
Attachment fabricator of illusions, 727:12
  to government, 331:23
Attack all the more boldly, 94:5
  first to a. neighbors, 269:1
  is the reaction, 316:22
  lawless a. upon liberty, 325:4
  prompt in a., 331:15
  repeat attack, 647:4
  strength in a., 676:5
Attacked, rather a. than unnoticed, 317:11
  United States a., 649:19
Attacking, situation excellent I am a., 562:19
Attacks, sharp a. on government, 719:4

Attacks (*continued*)
  try to answer a., 451:4
Attain, everything hard to a. easily assailed, 110:10
Attainable, is uniformity of opinion a., 343:8
Attainment, Zeus grant a. of sweet delight, 64:2
Attains upmost round, 187:32
Attempt and not the deed, 214:3
  fearing to a., 203:27
  literary a. unfortunate, 318:16
  make voyages a. them, 730:22
  the end, 241:16
  wind rising a. to live, 613:17
Attempted, something a. done, 441:5
Attend men and not women, 76:9
  shooting stars a. thee, 241:12
  to history of Rasselas, 314:9
Attendance, dance a., 226:7
Attendant, am an a. lord, 667:17
  bark a. sail, 302:3
Attended, is on his way a., 375:8
Attending, captive good a. captain ill, 221:6
  softest music to a. ears, 175:13
Attendre, j'ai failli a., 281:*n*3
Attention, dance a. on old age, 599:14
  like deep harmony, 171:5
  must be paid, 738:15
  pen instrument to fix a., 337:11
Attentions, trivial a. men think manly, 365:30
Attentive eyes, 315:2
  sit a. to own applause, 302:11
Attic, beauty crieth in a., 524:13
  bird, 261:1
  not an A. grace, 659:6
  seasoned with A. salt, 269:30
  shape, 416:6
Atticus, if A. were he, 302:12
Attire comely not costly, 155:5
  in halls in gay a., 377:25
  man's a., 31:39
  rich a. creeps rustling, 415:5
Attitude, Fair a., 416:6
  in which most alive, 545:5
Attitudenize, don't a., 317:34
Attorney, Hocus an old cunning a., 307:*n*4
  right to a., 682:10
Attorney's, go to a. office pay for it, 475:16
  office boy to A. firm, 529:6
Attract silver churn, 529:20
Attracted, those far off are a., 61:19
Attraction and affection, 615:13
Attractive, sweet a. grace, 163:3, 258:12
  thirty-five a. age, 567:11
Attracts envy of world, 331:7
Attribute, no a. of superior man greater, 79:9
  to awe and majesty, 181:19
Attributes characters of living creature, 487:13
  God and a. of God eternal, 277:17
Attunement, from things that differ comes a., 62:15
Auber, dank tarn of A., 453:2

Auburn, sweet A., 329:7
Audace, de l'a. encore de l'a., 364:*n*1
Audacia certe laus erit, 100:*n*14
Audacibus annue coeptis, 92:*n*12
Audacious power, 771:*n*2
Audacity more audacity always audacity, 364:6
  of imagination, 577:10
Audentes fortuna iuvat, 94:*n*11
Audi partem alteram, 114:*n*13
Audible, ill-bred as a. laughter, 329:*n*4
Audience, dreamer a. of dream, 629:2
  for sake of crowded a., 71:6
  gone into unlit a., 755:4
  good play a. pleased, 618:12
  how long a. sits, 388:19
  never fail to laugh, 73:20
  participation by a., 730:4
  somewhere out in this a., 754:18
  takes him serious, 638:3
Audiences, addressing popular a., 78:30
  great poets great a., 491:16
  some writers take to a., 756:5
  vaudeville a. give loudest sighs, 733:3
Auf Flügeln des Gesanges, 419:*n*5
Aught that I could ever read, 172:19
Augur misgovernment, 331:15
Augurs mock their own presage, 221:23
Augury, defy a., 199:22
  his powers of a., 51:10
  single best a. is to fight, 51:36
August, day in latter A., 742:12
  winter recommence in A., 403:16
  yellow with A., 659:9
Augustan, next A. age will dawn, 323:23
Augustine, why St. A. thanked God, 628:14
Augustinian doctrine of damnation, 536:18
Auld lang syne, 362:19, 362:20
  moon in her arm, 784:33
  should a. acquaintance, 362:19
Aunt, I am Charley's a. from Brazil, 571:31
  kept regard for truth, 609:3
Aunts, delight of husband a. infant, 674:12
  sisters cousins and a., 529:5
Auream quisquis mediocritatem diliget, 96:*n*7
Aureliano Babilonia finish deciphering, 759:1
Aurochs and angels, 703:3
Aurora, new A., 776:21
Aurora Borealis, bounded on north by A., 460:*n*1
Aurora Leighs, no more A. thank God, 446:11
Aurore, Belle A., 468:6
Auschwitz existed not speak of Providence, 747:3
Auspicious, one a. eye, 192:32
Austere beauty of mathematics, 615:10
  look a. of landscapes, 660:17
Austerlitz, pile bodies at A., 634:6

Australia, unscrupulous rascals A. has evolved, 578:2

Austria, Don John of A., 619:2
  Tom Jones will outlive eagle of A., 340:9

Author and finisher of our faith, 45:39
  choose a. as choose friend, 278:22
  dreamer a. of dream, 629:2
  he was the a., 102:12
  Holy A. of that religion, 287:3
  leaves of any a., 248:11
  neither man nor woman but a., 476:16
  no a. genius to publisher, 420:14
  not bein' a. gr-reat critic, 603:13
  of peace, 49:2
  of Satanic Verses book, 704:13
  ourselves a. and finisher, 448:1
  out from bushes, 651:5
  read by five hundred, 535:24
  relationship of a. to works, 572:22
  revised and corrected by A., 309:5
  same steps as A., 418:4
  select five hundred readers, 535:24
  sent by a. with autograph, 388:12
  shrimp of an a., 323:14
  six characters in search of a., 604:4
  steal from one a. plagiarism, 631:10
  thou Virgil art my master and a., 125:5
  time the a. of authors, 158:3
  what good a. whispers, 594:7
  what I like in good a., 594:7
  when man of rank an a., 317:24
  where any a. teaches such beauty, 168:35
  worst thing do to a., 317:11

Authorities, destruction shows activity of a., 446:21
  nihilist not bow to a., 482:14

Authority, adduces a. uses not intellect, 135:5
  age in virtuous carries a., 293:21
  and show of truth, 187:1
  base a. from others' books, 168:15
  by proving strength in life, 590:4
  by whose a. do you act, 341:15
  children opportunity for display of a., 662:13
  compass of national a., 355:7
  declining a. of establishment, 738:3
  every shadow of a., 331:26
  expected unquestioningly to obey, 693:16
  fit for public a., 66:14
  forgets a dying king, 459:25
  highest spiritual a., 645:1
  little brief a., 204:4
  miracle mystery a., 495:11
  no potential enemy to establish a., 682:11
  obedient to whomsoever in a., 72:2
  of Church moved me, 114:28
  saying No to a., 706:8
  sovereign a. of our partners, 347:11
  throw your a. at our feet, 347:2
  tongue-tied by a., 221:5
  what's that a., 209:5
  without wisdom, 262:12

Author's, sincerely from a. soul, 689:17
  without a. knowing it, 587:4

Authors, among good a. accounted Plagiarè, 255:7
  books like men their a., 288:13
  damn a. they never read, 333:18
  established it as rule, 292:26
  old a. to read, 158:23
  originality exaggerated by a., 723:5
  praise of ancient a., 239:24
  Shakespeare debts to a., 433:20
  steal from many a. research, 631:10
  time the author of a., 158:3
  when a. talk of sublime, 341:11

Authors', judge of a. names, 299:1

Autobiographies begin Chapter Two, 615:16
  nations write a., 488:1

Autobiography, artist writes own a., 578:7

Autocracy, communism a. upside down, 471:25

Autograph, foolish a. at beginning, 388:12

Automatic hand, 669:2

Automaton, mechanized a., 406:8

Automne, violons de l'a., 554:n1

Autonomy, lose individual a., 727:9

Autres, l'enfer c'est les A., 717:n1
  pour encourager les a., 306:n5

Autumn, dull dark day in a., 452:4
  fell like a. fruit, 273:21
  happy a. fields, 456:13
  I saw old A., 422:24
  in everything, 466:2
  in misty morn, 422:24
  leaves fall early this a., 659:3
  no season such delight as a., 240:15
  nodding o'er yellow plain, 308:6
  that grew by reaping, 218:11
  violins of a., 553:24

Autumnal, deep a. tone, 407:17
  face, 230:7
  thick as a. leaves, 256:8

Autumn's, breath of A. being, 407:13

Auxiliary, suffering an a. of creation, 555:5

Available, starving because food isn't a., 730:16
  to any shape, 756:11

Availeth, say not struggle nought a., 483:3

Avalanche of murders, 754:21
  snowflake in a., 726:16

Avarice a species of madness, 278:12
  an incurable disease, 3:7
  and happiness, 309:12
  disease of old men a., 236:20
  good old-gentlemanly vice, 236:n12
  Pride Envy A. three sparks, 125:21
  prudery a kind of a., 396:14
  rich beyond dreams of a., 317:22, 319:1
  seems not so much a vice, 278:n2
  spur of industry, 318:11
  take up with a., 236:n12

Avatar, in Vishnu-land what A., 465:18

Ave atque vale, 91:n6

Ave (*continued*)
  Caesar morituri te salutamus, 110:n6

Avenge O Lord thy slaughtered saints, 255:14
  patriotic gore, 538:20
  wish of some is to a., 72:1

Avenged of Philistines, 11:18
  South is a., 536:5
  1440 times a day, 544:24

Avenger, mightiest still the enemy and a., 15:34
  of these wrongs, 94:2
  time the a., 400:25

Avenues of ill, 430:5

Average man, 649:1
  type hear Tao, 57:12
  where the children are above a., 772:5

Averages, fugitive from law of a., 749:3

Averni, facilis descensus A., 94:n3

Averse, what cat's a. to fish, 321:20

Aversion, in matrimony begin with a., 352:4
  world outlasts a., 497:11

Aversions, man of my a., 642:21

Aviary, mind is an a., 76:12

Avocation, my a. and my vocation, 624:7

Avoid citations from poets, 71:6
  evil do good, 64:20
  fall into Scylla to a. Charybdis, 181:n2
  perils by united forces, 278:11
  ready for war to a. it, 284:12
  reeking herd, 660:15
  self-righteousness, 692:21
  what is to come, 198:3

Avon, swan of A., 233:1

Avowed erect the manly foe, 371:25

Await, wanderer a. it too, 498:10

Awaits alike inevitable hour, 322:8

Awake, all shall a. again, 249:7
  and asleep the same, 62:19
  and sing, 26:29
  arise, 256:9
  Deborah and utter a song, 11:2
  England a., 359:24
  for Morning, 445:4
  for night is flying, 156:11
  keep drowsy Emperor a., 597:10
  lying a. with headache, 530:14
  my lute a., 143:6
  my soul, 308:16
  my soul and with the sun, 280:20
  my St. John, 301:1
  O north wind, 25:13
  only day dawns to which we are a., 478:40
  thy Nightingales a., 502:9
  wide a. the moon and I, 531:1

Awaken, friends for when we a., 247:8

Awakened, living word a. my soul, 641:18
  the A. One (Buddha), 64:20

Awakening, near a. when dream that we dream, 385:6
  third great a., 764:4

A-walking, as I was a., 786:1
    Devil is gone, 386:21
A-waltzing Matilda, 589:5
Aware, mind a. of own rectitude,
    93:23
    myths operate without being a. of
        fact, 724:1
    of damp souls, 667:22
    of slightest bondage mad a., 624:12
    valet not a. of this, 79:7
Awareness, give each moment a.,
    630:1
    women contribute a., 707:20
A-watering last year's crops, 483:10
Away and mock the time, 213:15
    bound a., 793:12
    can't take that a. from me, 695:13
    from men and towns, 409:21
    look a., 475:1
    o'er hills and far a., 456:2
    over hills and far a., 297:15, 790:4
    pass not a., 7:32
    you scullion, 183:29
Awe, attribute to a. and majesty,
    181:19
    devised to keep strong in a., 166:16
    ever-increasing wonder and a.,
        326:10
    imaginative a., 721:10
    lifted hand in a., 296:3
    man from career of humor, 186:31
    of such thing as myself, 187:20
    romantic a. of rich, 702:3
    Sacred A., 652:4
    strike a. into beholders, 289:8
    tradition inspires a., 552:4
    without common power to keep
        them in a., 239:21
Aweary of the sun, 216:15
    she said I am a., 453:17
A-wearyin', jest a. fer you, 574:2
Awed by firmness, 72:9
Awful, anything a. makes me laugh,
    387:21
    beneath a. Hand we hold, 592:25
    felt how a. goodness is, 259:1
    good because it's a., 765:15
    nobody goes it's a., 718:14
    pause prophetic of end, 296:8
    shadow of unseen Power, 406:9
    still and a. red, 381:21
A-whining, born naked and falls a.,
    104:*n*3
A-winding into land of dreams,
    676:17
Awkward, always made a. bow,
    418:20
    historical fact, 637:3
    in their soil, 725:3
Awoke and behold it was dream,
    272:26
    and found it truth, 417:15
    and found myself famous, 401:6
    one night from dream, 397:1
A-wooing, frog a. go, 788:3
Awry, currents turn a., 196:10
    leaning all a., 446:4
Awww, everybody goes A., 750:9
Ax, Lizzie Borden took a., 781:11
    to grind, 393:8

Axe, book a. for frozen sea inside us,
    651:23
    fitter to bruise, 262:12
    laid unto the root, 32:32
    neither hammer nor a., 12:23
Axe's edge did try, 268:10
Axes, talking of a., 517:14
Axiom hatred of bourgeois, 496:12
    old as hills, 610:12
Axioms, derives a. from particulars,
    158:12
    flies from particulars to a., 158:12
    of mathematics, 542:5
    proved upon our pulses, 418:4
Axis of earth sticks out, 447:14
    soft underbelly of A., 621:14
    sword a. of world, 678:8
Axle, glowing a. doth allay, 252:19
Axletree, clot bedded a., 670:14
Ayenbite of inwyt, 647:*n*1
Aylmer, Rose A. whom these eyes,
    388:16
Ayuda, al que madruga Dios a.,
    793:24
Azcan, Chieftain Iffucan of A., 638:27
Azores, behind lay gray A., 543:17
    Flores in the A., 460:6
Aztecs by no means would give up,
    138:17
Azure, arose from out a. main, 308:12
    far in a. deeps, 441:9
    riding o'er a. realm, 323:8
    ringed with a. world, 458:4
    robe of night, 413:19
Azure-lidded, slept an a. sleep, 415:6
Azures, devouring green a., 565:13
Azurs, dévorant les a. verts, 565:*n*8

B

B, emotions from A to B, 687:13
    mark it with B, 788:9
Blame, no use to b. looking-glass,
    446:19
Baa baa baa, 592:3
    baa black sheep, 788:18
Baalim, Peor and B., 251:1
Babbitt, his name was B., 658:4
Babblative, arts b. and scribblative,
    386:19
Babbled of green fields, 184:30
Babbling drunkenness, 203:3
    gossip of the air, 201:28
Babblings, profane and vain b., 45:25
Babe, birth-strangled b., 215:15
    let mighty b. alone, 264:19
    love b. that milks me, 213:12
    pity like new-born b., 213:7
    pretty B. all burning bright, 160:19
    whose birth embraves morn, 264:19
Babel, name of it called B., 7:26
    stir of the great B., 335:4
    voices once Tower of B. knew,
        528:17
Babes, out of the mouth of b., 15:34
Babies, anyone who hates b., 641:*n*8
    bit b. in cradles, 464:18
    feel like doing for b., 711:22
    haven't hair, 679:1
    kill b. make world safer, 761:16

Babies (*continued*)
    wars fought by b., 751:13
Baboon who saved comrade, 444:14
Babs knows what and babs knows
    why, 633:2
Baby and me, 788:9
    bunting, 789:15
    down come b. and all, 555:4
    figure of giant mass, 200:10
    government like big b., 730:14
    looked like mouse, 703:12
    mother laid her b., 479:19
    my b. at my breast, 218:19
    of thee I sing b., 695:7
    rock-a-bye-b., 555:4
    since my b. left me, 768:3
    Tar-b. ain't sayin' nuthin', 556:6
Babylon, ere B. was dust, 406:16
    I was King in B., 557:12
    is fallen, 26:19, 47:31
    king of B. stood at the parting, 29:7
    we're leaving B., 773:17
Babylonish dialect, 263:1
Babylon's Gardens, 782:7
Baby's, know what going on in b.
    mind, 695:18
Bacchus ever fair and ever young,
    276:9
    that first, 252:16
    with pink eyne, 217:21
Bachelor, die a b., 186:31
    got acquainted with a b., 387:19
    one day b. next grampa, 709:17
    see b. of threescore, 186:13
Bachelors, reformers are b., 563:11
Bachelors' prayer, 656:7
Back, African moon lying on b., 656:9
    and side go bare, 144:12
    at b. from time to time hear, 668:23
    at my b. I always hear, 268:15
    begins to smart, 787:21
    borne me on his b., 199:8
    care not who sees your b., 177:23
    carries sky on b., 476:27
    cast-iron b. with hinge, 511:4
    dagger into b. of neighbor, 649:14
    die with harness on our b., 216:16
    eyes and b. turn upward, 669:1
    far b. in soul horse prances, 657:20
    follow and not see its b., 57:5
    got over Devil's b., 236:16
    mermaid on dolphin's b., 173:5
    never came b. to me, 472:5
    nowhere to come but b., 573:24
    on b. burden of world, 563:6
    on bat's b. I do fly, 224:25
    see what boys in b. room will have,
        728:11
    shop entirely free, 145:20
    showed his b. above element,
        218:11
    so much upon his b., 233:14
    speed today put b. tomorrow, 154:5
    think of some way to get him b.,
        705:3
    to Army again, 592:12
    to loneliness of yesterday, 695:22
    to the old drawing board, 712:14
    to you cold father, 647:22
    unto ladder turns his b., 187:32

Barère's, not read B. Memoirs, 425:16

Bares, foeman b. steel tarantara, 529:13

Bargain catch cold and starve, 219:22
in the way of b., 178:6
necessity never good b., 309:14
never better b. driven, 155:26

Bargaining, collective b. bilateral monopoly, 657:4
for wages, 635:5

Barge, Arthur from the b., 459:26
drag the slow b., 335:23
like burnished throne, 217:14

Bark, all dogs of Europe b., 720:10
and bite, 294:6
attendant sail, 302:3
band of exiles moored b., 410:12
bitter b. burning clove, 623:20
fatal and perfidious b., 253:22
feet locked upon rough b., 762:16
hark dogs do b., 792:14
is on the sea, 401:27
let no dog b., 179:20
moor b. with two anchors, 99:3
off shot the specter b., 381:14
seal on cold ice with piteous b., 414:20
see they b. at me, 210:14
star to every wandering b., 222:2
watchdog's honest b., 402:11
worse than bite, 245:8
yond tall anchoring b., 210:27

Barked, dogs b. far from river, 699:6

Barking, crowing of cocks and b. of dogs, 58:6

Barkis is willin', 470:21

Barks, Hylax b. in doorway, 92:14
Nicean b. of yore, 451:12
old dog b. backward, 624:9

Barley, land of wheat and b., 10:16

Barleycorn, inspiring bold John B., 363:7
John B. got up again, 362:3

Barn, hay creaking to b., 742:12
jackass can kick b. down, 648:11
sit in a b., 790:17
stack or the b. door, 251:12

Barnaby, like B. Rudge, 485:8

Barns, neither reap nor gather into b., 33:18

Barometer, poet b. but also weather, 718:6

Barrage, chemical b. against life, 721:14

Barred on account of race, 742:3
recognize good but be b., 64:4

Barrel, beat an empty b., 637:8
inspiration not stored up in b., 732:7
of meal wasted not, 12:34
organs, 650:16

Barrel-house kings, 637:8

Barren, acre of b. ground, 223:19
after summer b. winter, 163:23
among b. crags, 454:24
bosom starves birth, 321:22
bride, 300:14
buds of b. flowers, 534:13
earth b. as moon, 633:13
imagination cold and b., 331:8

Barren (*continued*)
leave this b. spot, 389:8
live a b. sister all your life, 172:18
small model of b. earth, 171:25
superfluity of words, 286:6
'tis all b., 320:34
weep b. tears, 406:17

Barrenness, nature in its b., 654:4

Barricade, disputed b., 674:17

Barrier, escaped b. of your teeth, 51:17

Barriers against tyranny of political, 438:2

Barroom floor, 548:4
Gideon Bibles not in b., 679:15

Bars, contentions are like b. of a castle, 21:40
I hang around in b., 775:6
implacable iron b., 675:10
nor iron b. a cage, 267:18

Barter, government founded on b., 331:20
that horn, 597:5

Bartlett's Familiar Quotations, 619:18

Base, army would be b. rabble, 331:23
authority from others' books, 168:15
battle removes all b., 658:16
beetles o'er his b., 194:13
contagious clouds, 176:37
fall to the b. earth, 171:19
first time caught off b., 701:16
fly from firm b., 378:24
keep down b. in man, 459:20
laws of servitude began, 273:14
like the b. Indian, 208:16
limps after in b. imitation, 171:7
men being in love, 206:12
of b. passions fear most accursed, 163:15
sale of chapmen's tongues, 168:22
scorning the b. degrees, 187:32
small things make b. men proud, 164:5
to what b. uses return, 199:9

Baseball breaks your heart, 769:8
chalk mark b. score, 548:4
eternal importance like b., 658:5
in b. don't know nothing, 754:10
pelicans old men in b. caps, 739:10
to know America learn b., 721:11

Baseless fabric of this vision, 224:21

Basely, spend that shortness b., 179:3

Baseness to write fair, 199:20
we will smite, 607:18

Baser, fellows of b. sort, 41:14

Basest, our b. beggars, 209:21

Bashful, maiden of b. fifteen, 352:29
stream hath seen God, 264:*n*3

Basic element in Constitution, 655:18
hero of books labor, 605:15

Basilisk is sure to kill, 297:19

Basin, elliptical b. in hands of acolytes, 763:11
stare in b., 720:8

Basis of democratic state, 78:27

Basket, eggs in one b., 149:34, 527:15
terrorist and policeman from same b., 573:11
watch that b., 527:15

Bassarid, blatant B. of Boston, 535:2

Bassoon, flute violin b., 458:22
heard the loud b., 381:1

Bastard, soft b. Latin, 402:4
substitute Anesthesia, 584:16
truth comes like b., 254:17
welcome pommy b. to God's earth, 775:7

Bastards, now gods stand up for b., 209:1

Bastille, prisoners in B. couldn't have touched them, 733:3

Bat beats about in caverns, 749:17
black b. night, 458:20
Casey at the b., 588:24
ere b. hath flown, 214:27
mind is like b., 749:17
twinkle little b., 517:20
weak-eyed b., 324:14
wool of b. tongue of dog, 215:14

Bataillons, formez vos b., 366:9

Bate, nor b. one jot of heart, 255:15

Bated breath and whispering humbleness, 180:9

Bath, blood b., 652:19
sore labor's b., 214:6

Bathe in fiery floods, 204:14

Bathed in Poem of Sea, 565:13
like eagles lately b., 178:20

Bathes, common air b. globe, 489:3

Bathing, caught Whigs b., 434:29
large b. machine, 530:15

Bathroom, wicked man in b. cupboard, 739:12

Bathrooms, well-equipped American b., 693:12

Baths, army no private b., 666:14
grand flights Sunday b., 639:12
of all western stars, 455:6
uplifting thoughts in b., 693:12

Batman, not Hercules but B., 764:2

Baton, French soldier carries marshal's b., 371:4

Bat's, on b. back I do fly, 224:25
thin b. squeak of sexuality, 712:7

Bats, bawk of b., 647:20
cast idols to moles and b., 25:31
do b. eat cats, 517:3

Battalions, God for big b., 266:*n*7
God with strongest b., 318:20
sorrows come in b., 198:20

Battening our flocks, 253:17

Batter my heart, 230:26
on your banjos, 634:10

Battered Caravanserai, 445:11
cottage b. and decayed, 250:6
few thousand b. books, 659:10
tattered ears and b. head, 762:17
wrecked old man, 491:5

Battering sandal, 551:4

Battery, assault b. of wind, 597:4

Battiades, tomb of B., 82:19

Battle and the breeze, 388:26
be the b. queen of yore, 538:20
borne the b., 450:11
Britain wins last b., 621:11
common perils of b., 522:13
cry of Freedom, 492:7
day is past, 506:14
drunk delight of b., 455:1

Bear (*continued*)
cow and b. shall feed, 26:11
decision to b. or beget child, 719:5
exit pursued by a b., 222:26
false witness, 9:12
finds he can b. anything, 696:16
flying-chariot, 335:23
for which we b. to live, 301:16
his friend's infirmities, 189:17
his mild yoke, 255:13
his own burden, 44:20
ills we ought to b., 497:23
infirmities of weak, 42:28
it that the opposed beware thee,
193:30
like the Turk, 302:11
melancholy as lugged b., 176:30
more than he can b., 696:16
my tavern the Big B., 565:9
never be on b. side, 533:4
not b. much reality, 670:11
not every soil can b. all, 92:27
nothing he not fitted to b., 111:15
nothing would it b., 790:12
of Very Little Brain, 648:7
pain to the b., 425:19
pleasing punishment women b.,
166:19
punishment greater than I can b.,
7:6
right to keep and b. arms, 346:12
rugged Russian b., 215:7
shade him till he can b., 356:10
sing savageness out of b., 207:21
sweet as I could b., 623:19
sword of heaven will b., 204:20
them we can, 579:18
they shall b. thee up, 18:16, 38:10
those ills we have, 196:10
too tender heart, 300:8
up and steer right onward, 255:15
vapor like b. or lion, 218:3
virgin shall b. a son, 26:5
whatever you stuff men with they
b., 479:15
when you are anvil b., 244:n6
whips and scorns of time, 196:10
who would fardels b., 196:10
with all the faults of man, 226:17
wounded spirit who can b., 21:39
yoke in his youth, 29:4
Bear-baiting, Puritan hated b., 425:19
Beard, built nests in b., 471:27
hath not offended king, 137:19
his b. was grizzled, 193:22
husband with b., 186:16
icicle on Dutchman's b., 202:27
lion in his den, 378:12
long gray b., 380:26
of formal cut, 191:3
Old Man with b., 471:27
plucks dead lions by b., 169:20
plucks off my b., 196:6
white b. decreasing leg, 183:19
wrapped in b. and silence, 698:9
Bearded like the pard, 191:3
soldier's kiss on b. lips, 490:12
Beards, tarry until b. be grown, 12:8
where b. wag all, 144:9
Bearing birthrights proudly, 169:18

Bearing (*continued*)
on excellence of character, 78:8
precious seed, 19:28
Bearings lays in application, 470:18
Bears all its sons away, 294:16
dancing dogs and b., 611:18
each b. his own Hell, 94:14
first born are shapeless, 104:11
greatest names, 261:18
his blushing honors, 225:16
in itself causes of destruction, 319:9
it out to edge of doom, 222:2
rhythms for b. to dance to, 496:6
sorrows with steadfast spirit, 54:7
stamp of human condition, 146:18
strongly it b. us, 383:1
time b. away all things, 92:16
Beast, a very gentle b., 174:6
blond b., 552:24
call this b. to mind, 608:17
caught like b. at bay, 680:7
civilization scarcely b., 611:11
cursed above every b., 6:23
deem himself god or b., 301:13
either a b. or god, 78:14
endeavoring to turn man into b.,
707:14
every b. of the forest is mine, 17:19
first b. like a lion, 47:15
fourth b. like a flying eagle, 47:15
great strong b., 97:n4
in view, 276:22
like wild b. guards way, 358:16
little better than b., 179:32
making b. with two backs, 205:17
man and bird and b., 382:7
man neither angel nor b., 271:4
mark or name of the b., 47:29
maw-crammed b., 467:7
more subtile than any b., 6:19
multitude b. of many heads, 97:n4
no b. so fierce but knows pity,
165:22
no more, 198:12
of prey in aristocratic races, 552:24
only b. in arena the crowd, 602:5
only connect b. and monk, 636:10
owest b. no hide, 210:6
Pellinore followed questing b.,
133:5
people a many-headed b., 97:7
people resemble wild b., 137:3
righteous man regardeth the life of
his b., 21:12
second b. like a calf, 47:15
serpent subtlest b., 260:2
strangest b. ever he saw, 133:5
that wants discourse of reason,
193:11
third b. had a face as a man, 47:15
what rough b., 596:20
with many heads butts me, 219:10
would act angel acts b., 271:4
Beastie, tim'rous b., 361:4
Beasties, long-leggety b., 779:15
Beastly, how b. bourgeois is, 657:16
to the Germans, 700:18
Beast's, man's life cheap as b., 209:21
Beasts, ape vilest of b., 84:18
ask the b., 14:16

Beasts (*continued*)
browse on their herbs, 5:5
coupling of b., 670:21
fly to wilderness, 79:16
four b. had six wings, 47:15
giant of b., 230:17
invent new b. so terrible, 420:9
judgment fled to b., 189:2
man lived with birds and b., 80:13
nature teaches b. to know friends,
218:26
of all wild b. preserve me from tyrant, 232:2
of the forest creep forth, 19:6
pair of very strange b., 192:13
shall be at peace with thee, 14:4
small and great b., 19:6
transform ourselves into b., 206:23
upon earth draw us to kingdom,
112:17
Beasts', not God's not b., 467:14
Beat an empty barrel, 637:8
Blake b. upon wall, 599:11
down baffling foes, 498:1
downward b. thy wings, 89:n10
earth with unfettered foot, 96:2
generation, 750:8
gold to airy thinness b., 229:12
heart hear her and b., 458:24
him when he sneezes, 517:15
his breast, 381:1
man is b. when goes for broke,
750:n2
me and hammer me, 634:9
my people to pieces, 25:34
so we b. on, 694:13
sound trumpet b. drums, 308:23
sound trumpets b. drums, 276:8
swords into plowshares, 25:30
the bush, 140:22, 240:2
the drum slowly, 786:7
the Dutch, 779:5
the ground, 252:23
they b. and Voice b., 581:5
Turk b. a Venetian, 208:17
upon whorled ear, 550:16
water they b., 217:14
waves of science b. in vain, 493:21
with fist instead of stick, 262:17
you b. your pate, 300:26
Beaten at all points, 72:12
poop was b. gold, 217:14
till they know, 263:18
Beatific, enjoyed in vision b., 256:20
vision, 124:n7
Beating, disastrous b. of wings, 611:13
got a hell of a b., 653:27
in void luminous wings, 501:7
way for rising sun, 708:3
Beatitude, ninth b., 300:25
Beatles', between Chatterley ban and
B. first LP, 750:13
Beatrice a light between truth and intellect, 126:10
Beats about in caverns, 749:17
all lies you can invent, 359:9
back envious siege, 171:10
drum b. my approach tells thee I
come, 242:3
light b. on throne, 459:3

Beats (continued)
upon high shore of world, 185:19
Beaumont, not bid B. lie, 232:18
rare B., 240:13
Beaut, when I make mistake it's a b., 648:2
Beauteous, commands the b. files, 270:8
dear b. death, 270:11
evening calm and free, 374:15
eye of heaven to garnish, 170:9
idiot speaks, 778:7
kindness not b. looks, 167:30
love all b. things, 550:1
pearls in b. ladies' eyes, 168:9
prove a b. flower, 175:10
Beauties, glory of honors b. wits, 229:5
in small proportions b. see, 233:3
meaner b. of the night, 227:9
unripened b. of north, 292:7
Beautifier, rank great b., 428:20
Beautiful a faery's child, 417:5
all b. drifts away, 595:16
all b. sentiments in world, 486:10
all once so b. is dead, 675:1
all things bright and b., 479:17
and ineffectual angel, 501:7
and therefore to be wooed, 163:16
art for sake of b., 437:2
as the sky, 490:14
be b. and be sad, 494:11
beauty comes from b. blood b. brain, 488:10
beauty making b. old rime, 221:22
black is b., 784:1
changes as forest, 749:13
childish but divinely b., 364:18
dancing most b. art, 578:10
dreamer, 507:5
face candid brow, 573:2
find each other it's b., 687:16
for spacious skies, 576:19
from perceived harmony, 383:22
how b. they are, 383:6
how b. they stand, 410:10
how b. they stood, 410:n1
I am Negro and b., 708:11
identification with b., 409:24
in faces dress thoughts, 582:12
may it be b. before me, 787:10
mind more b. than earth, 373:14
most b. among gods, 54:17
most b. lady, 616:21
most b. most useless, 487:15
most b. mouth in world, 305:16
most b. thing is mysterious, 635:12
nothing b. makes complete sense, 684:18
nothing in houses not b., 523:9
oh what a b. mornin', 692:8
overmuch, 596:22
palace B., 272:16
pea-green boat, 471:31
people, 770:12
poetry most b. mode, 499:11
Pussy you are, 471:31
quarto page, 352:27
sacrifices of friendship b., 610:20
scorn looks b., 202:25

Beautiful (continued)
small is b., 730:17
so awful ugly becomes b., 491:11
so various so b. so new, 499:22
sorrow more b., 416:20
soup, 518:9
Sredni Vashtar the B., 610:19
swindles b. and simple, 585:17
thing raises man, 137:9
things adorn world, 588:15
this is b. country, 424:6
time of young love, 365:12
too b. to live, 469:16
true words are not b., 58:7
uncut hair of graves, 488:20
upon the mountains, 27:33
what is b. is moral, 496:14
when I was b., 144:2
wise and b., 497:5
women indisputably b. or ugly, 305:7
wonderful world, 503:12
words are not true, 58:7
Beauty, addition of strangeness to b., 538:12
adventure art, 584:15
all b. comes from blood and brain, 488:10
all that b. all that wealth, 322:8
and high degree, 674:12
and majesty of ships, 442:6
and virtue rarely together, 127:12
and wisdom rarely conjoined, 105:7
as b. not great star, 631:18
as feel it indescribable, 588:1
as much b. as could die, 232:12
barbarous in b. stooks, 551:2
beholding b. with eye of mind, 74:13
bereft of b., 167:34
body's b. lives, 639:4
born of own despair, 598:2
bought by judgment of eye, 168:22
brute b. and valor, 550:22
by b. and by fear, 373:7
calls, 285:3
cheat for sake of b., 631:4
clad in b. of thousand stars, 162:20
come near your b. with nails, 163:19
concept of mathematical b., 583:13
convenience comfort, 783:16
creation of B., 453:14
crieth in attic, 524:13
daily b. in his life, 208:7
dead black chaos, 165:16
Death mother of b., 638:25
definition of b., 383:21
doth of itself persuade, 166:35
draws with single hair, 299:12
dreamed life b., 476:17
ease and speed not give work b., 131:n7
elevation and b., 501:4
ever ancient and ever new, 114:25
exists in mind, 318:12
extent of b. and power, 424:18
facts in naked simple b., 161:17
fatal gift of b., 400:15
flattered upon b., 305:7

Beauty (continued)
for ashes, 28:6
fruits of life and b., 357:20
gift of God, 77:11
give b. in the inward soul, 74:10
good nature more amiable than b., 293:2
grows familiar to lover, 292:8
half mad with b., 523:3
half the b. you possess, 368:13
has not been fathomed, 495:4
Helen's b. in brow of Egypt, 174:1
her b. and her chivalry, 399:21
I died for B., 512:13
ill layer-up of b., 186:4
images of b., 74:13
in all things, 418:18
in art economy is b., 549:9
in b. it is finished, 787:10
in eye of beholder, 568:4
in naked b. more adorned, 258:24
is a mystery, 657:18
is a simple passion, 760:1
is there b. in Sodom, 495:5
is there in truth no b., 243:9
is truth, 416:7
is vain, 23:21
keep back b., 551:8
know b. as b., 56:13
left b. on shore, 429:8
light from her own b., 408:3
like hers is genius, 509:24
little concerned with b., 541:10
looked on B. bare, 684:9
love b. truth we seek, 407:9
love built on b., 230:3
loved your b., 595:2
lust not after her b., 20:29
makes b. because outlet, 632:16
making beautiful old rime, 221:22
mathematics supreme b., 615:10
momentary in mind, 639:4
must be truth, 417:14
mystery of b., 594:13
Nature's brag, 253:10
Nature's coin, 253:9
ne'er enjoys, 302:15
neither heat limb nor b., 204:10
no excellent b., 160:5
no spring nor summer b., 230:7
notion of absolute b., 74:12
of aged face, 644:12
of good old cause, 374:14
of great machine, 663:2
of holiness, 16:24
of inflections, 639:6
of innuendoes, 639:6
of minstrel's lyre, 612:6
of own b. mind diseased, 400:24
of the lilies, 484:7
of world has edges, 651:2
one's b. another's ugliness, 432:8
orators dumb when b. pleadeth, 167:1
own excuse for being, 429:15
perception of b. moral test, 476:28
pierce like pain, 629:8
power of b. I remember, 276:26
power of Greek in b., 500:7
principal b. in a building, 250:12

Belly (*continued*)
 noise in the beast's b., 133:5
 secret life of b., 734:6
 shoulder bum, 599:17
 spent under b., 236:16
 upon thy b. shalt thou go, 6:23
 wears his wit in his b., 200:13
 whose God is their b., 44:33
Bellyful, man with b. of classics is
  enemy, 681:10
 of fighting, 219:23
Bellying, broad b. sails, 654:2
Belong, don't care to b., 693:2
 idea does not b. to soul, 538:14
 land to which we b., 662:2
 secret things b. unto the Lord,
  10:24
 to Company G, 524:8
 to oneself, 145:21
 to vanishing race, 695:19
 where do they all b., 770:9
Belonging, atom b. to me belongs to
  you, 488:16
Belongs, death b. to no one else,
  705:20
 kind where each of us b., 759:5
 now he b. to ages, 474:10
Beloved, ah my B. fill Cup, 445:14
 creature that is b., 202:9
 escape me never b., 465:14
 from pole to pole, 381:23
 he giveth his b. sleep, 19:30
 let my b. come into his garden,
  25:13
 never be b. by men, 359:8
 of Abraham Lincoln, 607:14
 our dearly b. brothers, 748:5
 our own b. home, 492:6
 Pan, 74:10
 perfection in b., 396:12
 physician, 45:2
 so is my b. among the sons, 25:4
 Son, 32:34
 this is my b., 25:15
 thought himself b., 597:3
Beloved's, heaped for b. bed, 409:10
 I am my b., 25:21
Below, down and away b., 497:6
 insure position by giving to those
  b., 5:7
 joy to pass to world b., 94:3
 may it be beautiful b. me, 787:10
 my thoughts remain b., 197:26
 no safety here b., 138:*n*2
 serfdom abolish itself from b.,
  479:16
 slave spirit b., 661:2
 thy element's b., 209:17
Belshazzar made a great feast, 29:15
Belt, undo b. look for trouble, 652:3
Belted, prince can mak b. knight,
  363:22
 you an' flayed you, 591:20
Belua multorum es capitum, 97:*n*4
Bemocked, beams b. sultry main,
  381:21
Ben Adhem's name led rest, 397:4
 Bolt, 484:5
 Bulben's head, 600:2
 Jonson his best poetry, 232:11

Ben (*continued*)
 O rare B. Jonson, 231:*n*6
Bench, log hut with simple b., 516:3
Bend, grass must b. when wind blows,
  61:18
 I b. but do not break, 267:26
 if I cannot b. Heaven, 94:20
 shall I b. low, 180:9
 soften rocks or b. oak, 291:7
 woman not breaks will b., 734:14
Bended, on b. arm doglike, 63:9
Bendemeer's stream, 392:11
Bending sickle's compass, 222:2
 to your wool, 144:2
Bends, blue sky b. over all, 382:14
 gallant mast, 396:22
 though she b. him, 441:26
 with remover to remove, 222:2
Beneath, at once above b. around,
  325:10
 married b. me all women do, 635:3
 rung battle shout, 447:3
Benedick the married man, 186:15
Benediction, face like a b., 149:9
Benefaction, calling to mind previous
  b., 71:5
Benefactor, less to blame than b.,
  265:15
Beneficence, private b. inadequate,
  581:16
Beneficent, belief in b. power, 540:2
 mother of gods and men, 5:1
Beneficial, the opposite is b., 62:15
Benefit, find man to b. kingdom, 79:11
 from illnesses, 71:12
 from literary accomplishments in
  women, 347:4
 God made for b. of men, 273:7
 government for common b., 327:2
 human b. and enjoyment, 331:20
 if men stop work at sixty, 558:7
 means of acquiring knowledge
  greatest b., 369:4
 no b. in gifts of bad man, 68:10
 of clergy, 613:*n*2
 of ill, 222:4
 poor b. of bewildering minute,
  234:1
 practical b. in failures, 505:11
 trees to b. another generation, 85:9
 Way of Heaven to b. others, 58:7
Benefits, caution in refusing b., 278:14
 disable b. of your country, 191:28
 doubly b. who gives quickly, 98:30
 gratitude a desire for b., 265:30
 many b. from good read, 732:6
 memory of b. fades, 65:11
 water b. all things, 57:1
Benevolence, beans and b., 434:7
 calls his trusting b., 329:2
 decrees of farseeing b., 492:16
 is man's mind, 79:28
 not from b. of butcher brewer
  baker, 326:1
 not infused from without, 79:27
 peace a disposition for b., 277:15
 tranquil habitation of man, 79:17
 whether b. does good, 506:9
Benevolent, heart b. and kind, 362:4
 people turn to b. rule, 79:16

Benevolent (*continued*)
 stormy patient, 717:3
Benighted, pore b. 'eathen, 591:19
Benign indifference of universe, 732:13
Benison of hot water, 663:2
 to fall, 241:21
Benjamin, little model was B., 657:10
Benjamin's, fell upon B. neck and
  wept, 8:13
 mess five times theirs, 8:9
Bennet called us Quakers, 271:14
 Mrs. B. stirring fire, 386:26
Bent, affection cannot hold b., 202:11
 as twig b. tree's inclined, 300:12
 bow cannot stand b., 150:15
 find out natural b., 75:22
 fool me to top of my b., 197:19
 goldenrod, 669:20
 idly b. on him that enters next,
  172:13
 man who has b. himself, 79:12
 natural b. in accordance with nature's, 538:19
 thoughts downward b., 256:20
 to be b. is to become straight, 57:8
Benumbs, care's a canker that b.,
  531:19
Bequeath my soul to God, 160:12
 myself to dirt, 489:23
Bereaved, black as if b. of light, 356:8
Bereavement, anguish of b., 450:9
Bereft, muddy ill-seeming b. of beauty,
  167:34
Bergère ô tour Eiffel, 641:*n*1
Berkeley, Bishop B. said no matter,
  403:11
Berlin, citizens of B., 742:4
Berliner, ich bin ein B., 742:4
Bermoothes, still-vexed B., 223:27
Bermudas, remote B. ride, 268:23
Bernard had prayers in hall whiskey
  afterwards, 644:9
Berries, pluck your b. harsh and
  crude, 253:14
 sweet b. ripen in wilderness, 638:26
 two b. on one stem, 173:19
Berry, could have made better b.,
  245:27
Berserk, New York has symptoms of
  mind gone b., 715:8
Beseech, lighten our darkness we b.,
  49:7
 thee for all sorts of men, 49:3
 Walrus did b., 519:1
 ye in bowels of Christ, 615:4
 you brethren, 42:12
 you in bowels of Christ, 247:1
 you of your pardon, 207:1
Beset, being woman hard b., 660:18
Beside, leadeth me b. still waters,
  16:17
 thou art b. thyself, 41:33
Besiege, forty winters b. thy brow,
  220:8
Besieged, by flatterers b., 302:11
Bespangling, dew b. herb and tree,
  241:17
Best, a little wise b. fools be, 228:18
 afflict the b., 321:18
 all b. though we doubt, 261:26

Bind (*continued*)

shall my joyful temples b., 249:29
the sweet influences of Pleiades, 15:12
up my wounds, 166:13
up nation's wounds, 450:11
Binding Nature fast in fate, 303:15
Binds brave of all earth, 586:12
he who b. to himself a joy, 357:22
so dear a head, 408:14
vow b. too strictly, 459:18
Binnorie, milldams o' B., 785:13
Biographers, reviewers would have been b., 383:19
Biographies clothes and buttons of man, 528:10
disease of English literature, 484:4
geniuses shortest b., 432:25
history innumerable b., 412:n4
Biography accounts for six or seven selves, 651:1
Art of B. different from Geography, 627:17
art of b. fallen on evil times, 643:17
heroic poem a b., 412:27
history b. and relations between, 740:1
history of world b., 412:32
is about Chaps, 627:17
is ultimately fiction, 736:8
no history only b., 431:17
of man cannot be written, 528:10
Biological, features of b. interest, 760:5
not b. but cultural evolution, 722:15
Biologically, idle b. speaking, 684:5
Biology, most famous event in b., 760:n1
Biped, divide b. class, 77:n2
Birches, swinger of b., 623:9
Bird, a very few a B. or two, 511:14
as b. endearment tries, 329:14
Attic b., 261:1
beat bush another take b., 140:n18
cat versus b. old as time, 706:9
change me to winged b., 68:19
clumsy dirty gray b., 437:11
crop-full b., 467:7
divine b. of Zeus, 63:30
flee as a b., 16:1
forgets dying b., 341:6
gold-feathered b. sings in palm, 640:13
half angel half b., 467:24
heart like singing b., 515:5
here and there b. or butterfly, 623:13
I sing as b. sings, 349:6
if men like wise b., 554:18
immortal B., 415:17
in gilded cage, 609:15
in hand worth two in bush, 107:n5
is on the Wing, 445:6
it was carol of b., 401:23
it's a b. plane Superman, 737:7
Jubjub b., 518:15
know why caged b. sings, 614:24
like b. on wing, 577:6
live like stoic b., 660:15
Loaf to every B., 513:5

Bird (*continued*)

man and b. and beast, 382:7
night's sweet b., 409:6
no b. soars too high, 357:5
no further than wanton's b., 175:14
of bad moral character, 310:24
of dawning, 192:29
of night did sit, 187:28
of Time, 445:6
of wonder dies, 226:8
or devil, 452:19
perhaps singing b. come, 118:5
pinnace like fluttered b., 460:6
rare b. on earth, 108:25
rise up at the voice of the b., 24:27
said b. in musical voice, 703:13
shall carry the voice, 24:22
silence with waking b., 458:22
small hot b., 559:19
soft-sigh me home, 724:17
soul of grandam inhabit b., 181:n3
stamped foot, 512:7
swift as b. or thought, 53:12
that filleth own nest, 135:20
that shunnest noise of folly, 252:2
this her solemn b., 258:22
thou never wert, 408:4
thou warbling b., 362:8
to nest from wandering, 579:22
to others flew, 240:2
turkey a more respectable b., 310:24
uncontrollably cries, 752:2
with B. the abiding Leaf, 725:21
wonderful b. is pelican, 637:14
Birdcage, like summer b. in garden, 146:n10
Bird's, consciousness like b. life, 545:16
night-b. wail, 531:12
sweet b. throat, 190:18
Birds, all could see was sky water b., 727:19
all the tribes of b. sang, 123:4
are asleep in trees, 351:2
as b. caught in snare, 24:20
bees stirring b. on wing, 383:14
began to sing, 790:1
blossoms b. and bowers, 240:16
chant ye little b., 362:8
charm of earliest b., 258:21
days when B. come back, 511:14
do sing, 226:20
eagle suffers little b. to sing, 167:11
fear b. of prey, 203:28
fly from their nests, 5:5
fly over the rainbow, 699:16
fly to calico tree, 472:5
if b. confabulate or no, 335:20
in little nests agree, 294:8
in the trees, 597:7
kinds of knowledge, 76:12
little b. that fly, 295:17
man lived with b. and beasts, 80:13
melodious b. sing madrigals, 162:3
million golden b., 565:16
mind an aviary of b., 76:12
no B. happy as we, 472:16
no b. in last year's nest, 151:19
no b. sing, 417:4

Birds (*continued*)

not only fine feathers make fine b., 59:3
not throw stones at b., 314:28
of a feather, 235:12
of air have nests, 34:17
other men catch b., 140:22
sing like b. i' the cage, 211:13
sit brooding in snow, 169:14
time of the singing of b., 25:6
unperplexed like migratory b., 630:7
warble sweet in springtime, 564:19
we are nest of singing b., 315:13
when b. do sing, 192:12
when small b. sighed, 725:7
where late sweet b. sang, 221:8
without despair to get in, 146:19
Birds', wind full of b. cries, 633:17
Birdsong at morning, 561:23
Birnam wood to Dunsinane, 215:21, 637:13
Birth and copulation and death, 670:2
Angel that presided o'er b., 359:20
as if b. sundered, 477:23
bed for this huge b., 264:18
befits proud b., 65:9
begins to die from b., 319:9
better world's in b., 476:18
between b. and dying, 669:19
boasts his b., 404:4
border nor breed nor b., 591:9
certain is b. for the dead, 84:5
creativeness is conception and b., 588:22
day of one's b., 24:6
death borders upon our b., 233:16
dew of thy b., 153:n6
distinction of b. or fortune, 370:19
embraces this morn, 264:19
false idol or noble true b., 76:9
famous by their b., 171:9
fashion b. intellect, 503:8
foreigner in country of b., 774:2
from b. to age eighteen, 656:1
frowned not on humble b., 322:22
give b. to whopper, 758:4
grievous burden was thy b., 166:6
high b. vigor of bone, 201:3
inquiries about events following b., 110:11
is sorrow, 64:26
land that gave you b., 586:12
life and death, 283:16
mourned at b. not death, 304:8
my love of b. as rare, 268:21
new b. of freedom, 450:2
no cure for b., 588:14
of ancient race by b., 274:15
of morning dew, 153:12
rejoice at b. grieve at funeral, 527:11
repeats story of her b., 292:1
Savior's b. celebrated, 192:29
sleep and a forgetting, 375:7
starves her generous b., 321:22
sunshine a glorious b., 375:5
Birthday of my life, 515:6
Birthplace of valor, 362:16
Birthright, Esau sold his b., 7:37

Blessed *(continued)*

green groves of the b., 94:12
half part of b. man, 169:23
hope whereof he knew, 540:11
horny hands of toil, 484:19
I had lived a b. time, 214:15
is man who expects nothing, 300:25
is the fruit of thy womb, 37:39
is the man that trusteth, 28:29
is the man that walketh not in
    counsel of ungodly, 15:29
judge none b., 31:28
kings may be b., 363:5
little b. with soft phrase, 205:21
Lord b. the latter end of Job, 15:28
love of God had b., 397:4
man who possesses keen mind,
    73:25
memory of the just is b., 21:5
mood, 373:2
more b. to give, 41:23
mother of us all, 345:7
mutter of Mass, 465:7
over whose acres b. feet, 176:23
part to heaven, 226:2
plot this earth, 171:9
quarry mine b. am I, 787:14
seeming b. they grow, 328:11
soul or body more b., 599:9
them unaware, 381:22
they that have not seen, 40:43
thou fallest a b. martyr, 225:21
thrice and four times b., 93:14
to put cares away, 90:24
twice b., 181:19
were but as b. as I, 295:17
who have no talent, 430:20
who having nothing to say, 484:3
whom thou blessest is b., 10:3
with milk and honey b., 482:10
youth becomes as aged, 204:10

Blessedness, perfect b. vision of God,
    124:12
Blesses stars and thinks it luxury,
    292:5
Blessest, whom thou b. is blessed,
    10:3
Blesseth him that gives and him that
    takes, 181:19
Blessing, alien b. on its way, 758:15
and cursing, 10:25
ask me b., 211:13
brother hath taken away thy b.,
    7:39
creations of mind b. not curse,
    635:13
good neighbor is great b., 54:25
haste haste has no b., 784:22
I had most need of b., 214:5
makes a b. dear, 262:10
money cannot buy, 245:30
national debt b., 354:17, 394:12
no harm in b., 304:14
of Saint Peter's Master, 245:31
out of God's b. into sun, 142:16
paid thy utmost b., 617:1
public debt a public b., 354:n10
society is a b., 340:18
unqualified b., 369:12

Blessing *(continued)*

war b. compared with reign of lie,
    680:5
Blessings, free trade one of b., 424:10
God from whom all b. flow, 280:21
health and intellect the two b.,
    81:15
health greatest of b., 71:12
on him who invented sleep, 151:15
on thee little man, 443:5
on this house, 338:13
on your frosty pow, 362:15
one of evils and another of b.,
    52:26
reap b. of freedom, 341:1
secure b. of liberty, 346:7
two supreme b., 68:26
unequal sharing of b., 622:10
upon head of the just, 21:5
use b. of gods with wisdom, 97:2
without number, 294:12
Blest, sanctified by reason b. by faith,
    373:14
Blew, fair breeze b., 381:6
great guns, 470:44
slug-horn to lips set and b., 210:n3
Blight man was born for, 551:6
Blighted, seared and b. heart, 451:8
Blights with plagues, 358:9
Blind and ignorant in all, 227:14
and naked Ignorance, 459:11
as nails upon Cross, 665:19
beggar's daughter, 785:5
Booth died b., 637:5
eyes of the b. shall be opened, 27:9
eyes to the b., 14:43
for being b. God prepare me,
    279:27
Fortune painted b. with muffler,
    160:n2
Fortune though b. not invisible,
    160:3
Fury with abhorred shears, 253:20
guides, 36:4
halt and b., 38:32
he was as often seene, 130:17
hearts, 89:14
Homer sing to me, 162:18
I was b., 40:14
in country of b. one-eyed man king,
    136:6
justice b. deef an' dumb, 602:18
Justice is b., 726:17
leaders of the blind, 35:23
leading blind to pit, 113:11
love is b., 131:20, 180:20
love needs be b., 172:n2
love to faults always b., 357:19
man's ditch, 598:5
mouths, 254:2
none so b., 286:18
oblivion swallowed cities, 200:22
old mad b. despised king, 407:24
right to be b. sometimes, 360:14
three b. mice, 788:2
till some b. hand, 358:5
Tiresias though b., 669:1
to faults a little b., 287:19
urge to kill b., 766:2
was b. but now I see, 327:4

Blind *(continued)*

winged Cupid painted b., 172:21
wretched b. pit ponies, 611:18
Blinded boy, 776:13
Blindly, had we never loved sae b.,
    362:11
Blindness about poverty, 759:3
heathen in his b., 395:20
left to native b., 319:30
we may forgive, 607:18
Blinds, drawing-down of b., 687:3
Blindworms, newts and b. do no
    wrong, 173:12
Blinked, other fellow b., 784:n2
Bliss, beyond happiness is b., 681:11
bought by years, 479:29
contrary bringeth b., 163:17
cuckold lives in b., 206:31
deprived of everlasting b., 162:15
follow your b., 712:16
happy be and have immortal b.,
    153:14
he lives in b., 364:2
heart intoxicated with b., 365:12
in our brows bent, 217:1
in proof, 222:7
kill and b. me, 776:22
mutual and partaken b., 253:9
need of imperishable b., 638:25
never parted b. or woe, 260:11
no right to b., 497:20
not beds of down, 242:6
of dying, 299:8
of solitude, 376:1
perfect b. and sole felicity, 161:21
pneumatic b., 668:14
shadow's b., 180:28
soul in b., 211:9
source of all my b., 329:23
sum of earthly b., 259:28
waking b., 252:28
was it in that dawn, 373:12
where ignorance is b., 321:17
work of fiction affords aesthetic b.,
    703:5
Blisses about my pilgrimage, 539:7
Blissful dreams of long ago, 536:10
Blister, never had b. in hand, 73:5
thirst b. easier, 512:1
Blithe, buxom b. and debonair, 251:7
Irish lad, 388:25
no lark more b. than he, 338:18
spirit, 408:4
Block, chip of old b., 332:1
do not b. way of inquiry, 538:13
each b. cut smooth, 659:14
mind a b. of wax, 76:11
Blockhead, no man but a b., 316:29
Blockheads, Blame-all Praise-all b.,
    309:10
read what blockheads wrote, 305:13
Blocks, stumbling b. in girl's educa-
    tion, 616:18
towns you built of b., 698:4
Blond beast, 552:24
more b. than you, 688:19
Blonde to make bishop kick hole in
    window, 667:6
Blondes, gentlemen prefer b., 686:8

Blood, after book of circulation of b., 271:19
all nations one b., 41:16
bath, 652:19
be on your own heads, 41:18
beauty comes from beautiful b., 488:10
bit arm sucked b., 381:11
blow in cold b., 571:10
by man shall his b. be shed, 7:23
Christ's b. streams, 162:23
courage tastes of b., 731:3
created Man of b. clot, 117:24
created you of b. clot, 117:2
crusted with b., 663:19
cry aloud for b., 492:12
delivered from shipwreck of b., 699:11
devise laws for b., 179:28
drenched in fraternal b., 394:15
drops of b. form on forehead, 678:19
ears gushed b., 414:20
earth one mighty b. spot, 435:22
effusion of b., 586:22
every drop of b. drawn, 450:11
fizz like wine, 633:7
flesh and b. so cheap, 423:8
for this all that b. shed, 596:1
freeze thy young b., 194:17
fried meats angry up b., 719:12
future smells of b., 420:10
glories of our b. and state, 246:23
good enough to shed b., 576:2
guiltless of country's b., 322:14
hand raised to shed b., 301:4
heart dry of b., 417:3
her young suck up b., 15:18
heyday in the b. is tame, 197:31
his b. be on us, 37:8
I that am of your b. taken from you, 236:21
impure b. drench field, 366:n1
in b. stepped in so far, 215:12
in torrents pour, 573:23
inhabits our frail b., 203:3
iron and b., 474:11
is nipped and ways be foul, 169:13
is their thinking, 67:20
it will have b. they say, 215:10
liquors in my b., 190:11
lust for b. and plunder, 621:1
magic to stir men's b., 555:7
make thick my b., 212:29
man whose b. is snow-broth, 203:26
man whose b. is warm, 179:18
meditate on b., 186:2
mingle b. with b. of children, 424:5
more stirs to rouse lion, 177:8
more things move than b. in heart, 696:4
Negro b. sure powerful, 709:2
new testament in my b., 43:12
no Jewish b. in my veins, 766:5
no sure foundation on b., 170:12
nor can b. be in sticks, 90:2
Norman b., 454:1
not a drop of b. shed, 344:20
not against flesh and b., 44:28
not see b. of Ignacio, 699:9

Blood (*continued*)
odor of b. when Christ slain, 597:18
of a poet, 675:21
of an Englishman, 792:19
of Christians is seed, 112:5
of martyrs seed of Church, 112:n2
of our heroes, 344:9
of patriots and tyrants, 343:15
of the lamb, 47:23
of the new testament, 36:28
of the slaughtered, 612:3
of this just person, 37:7
oh b. that freezes b. that burns, 465:10
old man had so much b., 216:3
on hands rather than water, 713:12
one b. ye and I, 592:13
own b. rise against you, 613:n2
pint of sweat save gallon of b., 658:17
poet's feverish b., 498:7
poisoned with b. of both, 763:8
present joys more to flesh and b., 275:21
pure and eloquent b., 230:16
rivers older than flow of b., 708:12
sets gypsy b. astir, 583:17
shed by immortal King, 124:5
shed for you and for many, 48:11
sheds his b. with me, 185:23
sign to know gentle b., 154:15
smell b. of British man, 210:12
souls of b., 658:19
spend her b. and might, 572:12
spill no drop of b., 541:7
sprinkled upon garments, 28:7
still b. is strong, 421:17
stir men's b., 189:10
strong as flesh and b., 376:14
strong wyn reed as b., 130:7
summon up the b., 185:3
sun's o'ercast with b., 169:29
sweat and tear-wrung millions, 620:n1
sweat on drill ground save b. on battlefield, 658:n4
tears sweat or b., 620:n1
that strange mixture of b., 339:1
thick water's thin, 530:16
thicker than water, 272:6
thicks man's b. with cold, 381:12
this is my b., 36:28
till he spouts black b., 486:23
to drink, 436:6
toil tears sweat, 620:5
tree of liberty refreshed with b., 343:15
trilling wire in b., 670:14
up to eyes in b., 331:3
vigor flows into my b., 679:9
voice of thy brother's b., 7:4
wash this b. from hand, 214:9
watered by b. of tyrants, 354:11
weltering in his b., 276:12
what little b. is left, 633:7
when the b. burns, 194:5
whoso sheddeth man's b., 7:23
will have blood, 215:10
without shedding of b., 45:37

Blood (*continued*)
won by b. and sweat of innocent, 771:11
young b. have its course, 484:15
Blood-dimmed tide loosed, 596:19
Blood-hot eyes, 690:20
Bloodless substitute for life, 560:19
week of repose, 73:n7
Blood-red banner, 395:17
sunset glorious b., 465:5
wine, 784:31
Blood's a rover, 578:20
Bloodshed, fear and b., 376:9
no more wars no more b., 732:10
Bloodstream, O Altitudo in b. swims, 675:4
Blood-swollen, war b. god, 611:1
Bloodthirsty guttersnipe, 621:1
Bloody and invisible hand, 214:28
be b. bold and resolute, 215:19
book of law, 205:20
but unbowed, 557:9
dark and b. ground, 492:5
even so my b. thoughts, 207:15
full of blame, 222:7
iron curtain, 622:n1
mothers a b. brood, 693:6
often wipe b. nose, 297:10
sang within the b. wood, 668:16
sweats, 567:20
treason flourished, 189:7
where's the b. horse, 707:1
Bloom along the bough, 578:18
barred clouds b. soft-dying day, 416:15
flowers that b. in spring, 531:8
full on thy b., 361:20
gradually out of reach, 757:14
how can ye b., 362:8
is gone, 499:17
its b. is shed, 363:6
lemon trees b., 349:8
look at things in b., 578:19
now withering in my b., 300:3
of young Desire, 323:1
perfect in bud as in b., 523:21
sight of vernal b., 257:24
sort of b. on woman, 581:23
water lily b., 454:16
well in prison air, 567:22
with the b. go I, 499:17
Bloomed, when lilacs in dooryard b., 490:15
Bloomin' cosmopolouse, 592:22
lyre, 592:11
shame, 782:18
Blooming, left b. alone, 391:16
Blooms each thing, 226:20
o'er folded b., 558:11
Bloomy, nightingale on b. spray, 254:9
Blossom, blossomed Sarah and I b., 734:14
by blossom spring begins, 533:9
desert b. as the rose, 27:8
in purple and red, 458:24
in their dust, 246:21
leaf b. or bole, 598:2
let black flower b., 435:28
letting hundred flowers b., 686:16
May when lusty heart b., 133:11

Blushes into wine, 264:*n*3
  man only animal that b., 527:31
Blushful Hippocrene, 415:11
Blushing, bears his b. honors, 225:16
  flowers shall rise, 298:7
  Religion b. veils fires, 304:2
Blustering, pity from b. wind, 267:19
Blut, Eisen und B., 474:*n*3
  O Haupt vol B. und Wunden,
    250:*n*1
Blynken, Wynken B. and Nod, 559:20
Boanerges, neigh like B., 512:18
Board, back to the old drawing b.,
    712:14
  dim on Bristol b., 729:16
  get on b. little children, 794:21
  heart for bed and b., 742:17
  money in ginger jar, 523:13
  struck the b., 243:16
  well-benched ships, 55:21
Boards, ships are but b., 180:1
Boast, frantic b., 593:4
  having my freedom b. of nothing,
    170:32
  let not him that girdeth on his har-
    ness b., 12:40
  not b. who puts armor on, 442:18
  not of what thou wouldst have
    done, 261:21
  not thyself of tomorrow, 22:32
  now b. thee death, 218:20
  of heraldry, 322:8
  of this I can, 171:4
  such is the patriot's b., 328:8
Boasters, great nations not b., 432:30
Boasteth, when he is gone his way
    then he b., 22:4
Boastful, high and b. neighs, 185:14
  in war daring b., 404:21
Boasting, strength without b., 344:1
Boasts, that which b. his birth, 404:4
Boat, carry Caesar in your b., 88:22
  forefathers met the b., 638:6
  give man b. he can sail, 523:15
  is on the shore, 401:27
  Michael row b. ashore, 794:15
  news of the b., 431:12
  of life be light, 580:11
  of your flesh, 767:9
  pea-green b., 471:31
  sea so great b. so small, 779:16
  sings in b. on bay, 456:7
  slow b. to China, 728:12
  speed bonnie b., 577:6
  they sank my b., 740:18
Boats against the current, 694:13
  messing about in b., 578:16
  oh the little cargo b., 592:19
  shallow bauble b., 200:6
  that are not steered, 220:5
Boatswain, memory of B. a dog,
    398:16
  tight and midshipmite, 528:22
Bobolink for Chorister, 512:4
Bobtail nag, 506:18
Boca, el pez muere por la b., 794:1
  en b. cerrada no entran moscas,
    794:3
Bodes some strange eruption, 192:22
Bodice, loosens fragrant b., 415:5

Bodies a living sacrifice, 42:12
  abstain from abusing b., 71:1
  are buried in peace, 32:15
  as clothes to b., 585:2
  as imagination b. forth, 174:1
  clothes without b., 585:2
  died before b. died, 721:3
  elements or principles of b., 345:10
  freedom of living b., 473:7
  gave b. to commonwealth, 72:7
  ghosts of defunct b. fly, 263:4
  hollow sound same as our b.,
    705:16
  molecules that compose b., 345:10
  movements of largest b., 351:16
  mutual actions of two b., 282:3
  nature works by b. unseen, 89:9
  of unburied men, 237:13
  our b. are our gardens, 205:32
  our selves our souls and b., 49:17
  persons with torn b. happy, 611:2
  pile b. at Austerlitz, 634:6
  princes like to heavenly b., 159:21
  remove weight from heavenly b.,
    751:15
  rough notes and dead b., 606:2
  single soul in two b., 77:13
  soldiers bore dead b. by, 177:3
  these black b., 356:9
  thrown into sea, 706:3
  unclothed, 230:13
  we have seen dead b., 424:2
Bodiless and simple, 749:15
Bodily decrepitude wisdom, 598:23
  exercise when compulsory, 75:21
  form from natural thing, 597:10
  form of them b., 534:19
  states following perception, 546:4
Boding tremblers, 329:17
Bodkin, bare b., 196:10
Body, absent in b. present in spirit,
    42:36
  age and b. of the time, 196:23
  and spirit twins, 535:7
  art work of b. and soul, 487:16
  Asclepius cured the b., 74:*n*3
  be not afraid of my b., 490:2
  book makes b. cold, 514:19
  carry b. for sentimental value, 722:1
  changed to light, 787:18
  clog of his b., 250:9
  continues in state of rest, 282:1
  damned of b. and soul, 591:11
  demd damp b., 469:21
  dies body's beauty lives, 639:4
  distressed in mind b. or estate, 49:4
  each petty artery in b., 194:14
  employ b. to serve, 91:20
  fear made manifest on b., 495:22
  filled and vacant mind, 185:19
  find thy b. by wall, 500:3
  gave b. to country's earth, 172:6
  gin a b. meet a b., 778:*n*1
  give b. to be burned, 43:14
  happiness beneficial for b., 613:4
  having seen his b. borne before her,
    463:21
  health intelligence talent, 582:8
  her b. thought, 230:16
  her dead b. wears smile, 764:14

Body (*continued*)
  here in the b. pent, 377:17
  human b. sacred, 489:24
  I have risen to a b., 756:17
  ideals in one dark b., 605:2
  infirm and exhausted, 134:14
  instrument for art, 584:14
  is his book, 229:16
  is Nature God is soul, 301:11
  is not b. more than raiment, 33:18
  its b. brevity, 383:5
  John Brown's b., 524:7
  joint and motive of b., 201:10
  lean b. and visage, 250:9
  light around the b., 756:17
  light of the b., 33:15
  like b. wholly b., 639:7
  little b. mighty heart, 184:28
  loves world as his b., 57:3
  man member of b., 440:1
  marry my b. to that dust, 242:2
  material fortune associated with b.,
    110:12
  mind or b. to prefer, 301:13
  more familiar with Africa than own
    b., 765:9
  my b. my dungeon is, 561:17
  my good bright dog, 747:13
  my house, 747:12
  no riches above sound b., 32:2
  not b. enough to cover mind, 380:6
  not bruised to pleasure soul, 598:2
  not more than soul, 489:20
  of Benjamin Franklin Printer, 309:5
  of each creature different, 71:16
  of little recruit, 700:8
  of this death, 42:1
  old in b. but never mind, 88:10
  one motion, 725:16
  oppressions of b. and mind, 344:19
  part of man's Self, 545:20
  pass from colder to hotter b., 501:8
  perfectly spherical, 471:30
  piece of b. torn out by root, 726:3
  Poet filling other B., 418:10
  poet of B. poet of Soul, 489:7
  politic like human body, 319:9
  power lies in mind and b., 91:20
  presence of b. in question, 388:10
  pygmy-b., 274:3
  reading to mind as exercise to b.,
    291:31
  remember, 587:12
  Resurrection of the b., 48:25
  ruler having human b. as subject,
    75:5
  sex woven into whole b., 578:6
  sickness-broken b., 250:8
  so young b. with so old head,
    181:18
  soul gentle companion of b., 110:7
  soul is form and doth b. make,
    154:14
  soul its b. off, 599:2
  soul look b. touch, 599:9
  sound mind in sound b., 109:9
  sound of b. and mind, 95:30
  subject to forces of gravity, 738:9
  swayed to music, 598:2
  swung gently, 544:10

Bonhomie, overcame natural b., 627:19

Bonjour, et puis b., 522:*n*2
tristesse, 691:*n*3

Bonnet, war b. of Medicine Hat, 698:6

Bonnets of Bonny Dundee, 379:27

Bonny, am I no a b. fighter, 561:14
banks and braes o' b. Doon, 362:8
banks o' Loch Lomond, 779:21
bonnets of B. Dundee, 379:27
bonny Biscay O, 779:6
brow was brent, 362:15
milldams o' Binnorie, 785:13
speed b. boat, 577:6
thou b. gem, 361:19

Bono, cui b. fuerit, 87:*n*7
pro b. publico, 119:24

Bononcini, some say Signor B., 304:15

Bons mots, laboring to produce b., 269:13

Bonsoir, et puis b., 522:*n*2

Bonum, summum b., 88:*n*1, 90:*n*8

Boo, under the b., 670:3

Boobies, don't count your b., 690:14

Booboisie, 643:7

Booby, give her b. for another, 297:7

Boogie-woogie rumble of dream deferred, 708:18

Boojum, Snark was a B., 519:25

Book, alive while thy b. live, 232:18
all American literature from one b., 702:2
although nothing in 't, 399:2
and heart never part, 287:7
and volume of my brain, 194:28
angel writing in b., 397:2
another damned thick b., 342:22
axe for frozen sea inside us, 651:23
bad b. as much labor, 689:17
bell b. and candle, 170:1
beware man of one b., 118:19
big b. big bore, 82:18
bloody b. of law, 205:20
blot out of b. of life, 47:12
body is his b., 229:16
camerado this is no b., 491:9
chief need is be readable, 476:7
classic b. people praise don't read, 527:30
covers of b. too far apart, 545:2
curse with b. bell and candle, 133:14
dainties bred of a b., 168:29
destroys b. kills reason, 254:23
do not throw b. about, 608:16
doings of mankind subject of my b., 108:18
English dictionary best b., 610:10
face is as a b., 213:2
farewel my b. and my devocioun, 129:4
furnishes no quotations, 397:23
genius when I wrote that b., 290:22
go b. and wish to all, 129:*n*1
go forth my b., 129:*n*1
go litel b. litel myn tragedye, 129:1
go little b., 644:8
go now b. to every place, 129:*n*1
good b. best of friends, 462:5

Book (*continued*)
good reader makes good b., 433:13
I am myself matter of my b., 145:8
I'll drown my b., 224:24
in b. of my memory a rubric, 124:17
in his hand, 272:11
kill man as kill b., 254:23
leaves of Judgment B. unfold, 506:3
lifeblood of spirit, 254:24
like cover of old b., 309:5
liked the b. the better, 330:7
little b. go without me, 129:*n*1
little b. I cast thee on waters, 129:*n*1
Macaulay a b. in breeches, 380:16
makes my body cold, 514:19
may be very amusing, 328:17
mine adversary had written a b., 14:46
nature's infinite b. of secrecy, 216:26
never read b. not year old, 433:2
new era in life from b., 478:23
no b. so bad but some good, 110:2
no Frigate like B., 514:2
no moral or immoral b., 566:10
not at his picture but his b., 232:17
not concerned with Poetry, 687:1
not more in b. than before, 713:1
note it in a b., 27:2
note you in b. of memory, 163:11
of a certain Cicero, 114:22
of deeds words and art, 488:1
of Egoism, 509:4
of female logic, 463:23
of knowledge fair, 257:24
of Life begins, 567:2
of life was opened, 47:36
of moonlight not written, 638:15
of Moons defend ye, 777:2
of Nature, 148:*n*7
of nature, 272:2
of Songs and Sonnets, 182:19
of Verses underneath Bough, 445:9
oh for b. and shady nook, 541:8
one b. furnishes treatise, 319:16
only one b. in them, 380:14
page of b. carelessly open, 759:15
present new b. to Cornelius, 90:14
putting mind's eye in b., 748:10
read b. of fate, 184:1
reads but one b., 245:10
recognizes me in my b., 146:20
same today and forever, 462:5
say in sentences what others in b., 552:32
sealed with seven seals, 47:17
sour misfortune's b., 176:15
take down this b., 595:1
that they were printed in a b., 14:29
that wonderful b., 424:22
the world the b. of God, 227:4
this grand b. the universe, 161:15
thou art the b., 241:22
throw whole b. in fire, 436:19
Time criticized for us, 486:6
to be read in twilight, 436:4
turn over library make b., 316:24
well-chosen b. or friend, 227:7

Book (*continued*)
what is this marvelous b., 319:16
what is use of b., 517:2
what thou seest write in a b., 47:2
what you don't know make b., 380:19
when nobleman writes b., 317:*n*4
which does not sell, 388:12
who reads American b., 379:28
without pictures or conversations, 517:2
works at body of b., 328:1
written in God's b., 116:10

Bookish ambition, 234:2
theoric, 205:10

Bookmen, you two are b., 168:31

Book's a book although nothing in 't, 399:2

Books about books, 147:5
all b. else so poor, 284:3
all good b. alike, 702:1
ambition to be stored with b., 234:2
are weapons, 649:21
as schoolboys from b., 175:11
authority from others' b., 168:15
bear him up, 283:26
belong to eyes, 432:17
best b. universal appeal, 617:10
bloodless substitute, 560:19
borrowers of b., 387:25
burn b. burn human beings, 420:3
by persons in America, 461:3
by which printers have lost, 250:13
children of brain, 288:14
clad in blak or reed, 129:21
consumed midnight oil, 297:6
cover country in b., 551:19
crushed by b., 735:20
deep versed in b., 261:4
do serve some purpose, 717:18
do with friends as b., 432:4
do you read b. through, 316:18
dreams b. each a world, 376:14
drunk on b., 643:6
even bad b. are b., 758:5
feelings beings b. events battles, 714:8
few friends and many b., 266:17
few thousand battered b., 659:10
from b. of honor razed, 220:14
gentleman not in your b., 186:11
God written all the b., 525:6
good b. truer than real, 702:1
Homer all b. you need, 284:3
I cannot live without b., 344:17
I have read all the b., 547:10
I'll burn my b., 162:25
in lighted windows b. kept watch, 612:20
in running brooks, 190:7
knowing I loved my b., 223:26
lard their lean b., 234:5
learn anatomy not from b., 236:1
Learning wiser without b., 335:12
legacies genius leaves, 293:1
like men their authors, 288:13
lineaments of Gospel b., 163:3
live without b., 516:4
magic preservation in b., 412:35
many b. and never use them, 234:2

Born (*continued*)
  not b. under riming planet, 187:12
  not b. woman becomes one, 722:9
  not conscious of being b., 283:16
  not to be b., 160:*n*8
  not to be b. best, 720:5
  not to be b. surpasses thought, 67:9
  of a little sin, 684:4
  of blackest Midnight b., 251:6
  of the Spirit, 39:44
  of the sun, 727:10
  of Virgin Mary, 48:25
  of virgin mother b., 250:19
  old and ugly, 469:34
  on a Monday, 791:4
  on Christmas Day, 778:8
  on Fourth of July, 632:11
  One b. in a manger, 270:8
  out of my due time, 523:7
  poet's made as well as b., 232:24
  posthumously, 553:12
  powerless to be b., 498:20
  risen to body not yet b., 756:17
  soil good to be b. on, 486:1
  some are b. great, 202:18
  strength though of Muses b., 414:6
  sucker b. every minute, 460:18
  sun b. and dies, 784:16
  sun b. over and over, 737:18
  terrible beauty b., 596:17
  they had never been b., 32:14
  thing I was b. to do, 161:4
  things that are b. and die, 718:8
  time to be b., 23:32
  to be king, 577:6
  to be nobly b. now crime, 238:7
  to blush unseen, 322:13
  to set it right, 195:6
  to the manner b., 194:8
  to write, 302:11
  towards Bethlehem to be b., 596:20
  tramps like us were b. to run,
    774:12
  under one law to another bound,
    155:1
  under that was I b., 186:25
  unto us a child is b., 26:8
  unto you is b., 38:3
  we were not b. to sue, 170:27
  went to trouble to be b., 336:8
  wept that he was b., 608:3
  when we are b. we cry, 211:6
  where I was b. unimportant, 665:14
  with anxiety about weather, 532:7
  with gift of laughter, 630:15
  with legs apart, 765:10
  with silver spoon, 151:18
  would thou hadst ne'er been b.,
    208:1
Borne and yet must bear, 406:15
  angel b. on my bosom, 466:28
  back into past, 694:13
  his faculties so meek, 213:7
  like thy bubbles, 401:4
  me on his back, 199:8
  not b. this in my hot youth, 96:22
  oldest hath b. most, 211:21
  the burden, 35:39
  through hatred b. apart, 67:19
  well b. without defeat, 184:25

Borogoves, mimsy were b., 518:15
Borrow army for a while, 449:10
  every changing shape, 667:21
  men who b. men who lend, 387:24
  to live within means, 522:6
Borrowed plumes, 59:2
  something b., 782:10
  wit, 240:3
Borrower is servant to the lender,
  22:10
  neither b. nor lender be, 194:1
  of the night, 214:19
Borrowers always ill-spenders, 487:24
  of books, 387:25
Borrowing accounted Plagiarè, 255:7
  banqueting upon b., 31:36
  dulls edge of husbandry, 194:1
  everything of neighbors, 279:21
  life that depends on b., 507:18
  only lingers it out, 183:24
Boshaft ist er nicht, 636:*n*1
Bosom, Abraham's b., 39:2, 166:5,
  374:16
  angel borne on my b., 466:28
  Arthur's b., 184:30
  barren b. starves birth, 321:22
  beggar in Abraham's b., 39:2
  can a man take fire in his b., 20:30
  carry them in his b., 27:20
  chums, 760:15
  crept into b. of the sea, 164:4
  friend of sun, 416:13
  glory in His b., 484:7
  heart out of b., 578:23
  her hand on her b., 208:4
  I must not see, 269:5
  in ocean's b. unespied, 268:23
  in your fragrant b. dies, 246:6
  let me to Thy b. fly, 312:14
  liest in Abraham's b., 374:16
  loosened from her b. the girdle,
    52:3
  of his Father and his God, 322:24
  of urgent West, 549:19
  sleep in Abraham's b., 166:5
  stuffed b. of perilous stuff, 216:10
  swell b. with thy fraught, 207:14
  third in your b., 175:19
  thorns that in b. lodge, 194:25
  warm cheek and rising b., 323:1
  which thy frozen b. bears, 204:*n*5
  wife of thy b., 10:18
  within b. is September, 776:19
  wring his b., 328:30
  write sorrow on b. of earth, 171:24
Bosomed deep in vines, 304:1
  high in tufted trees, 251:14
Bosoms, hair hang and brush b.,
  466:15
  men's business and b., 159:1
  waters lift their b., 200:9
  white b. of actresses, 315:14
Bossuet, celebrities such as B., 521:4
Boston, a Thucydides at B., 323:23
  blatant Bassarid of B., 535:2
  Cluett Shirt B. Garter, 688:12
  Concord Lexington, 394:13
  Evening Transcript, 667:23, 702:16
  good old B., 582:1

Boston (*continued*)
  in B. ask how much does he know,
    527:19
  just returned from B., 687:21
  marching through B., 743:10
  marriage serious around B., 686:18
  not blue on B., 742:14
  runs to brains, 567:27
  solid man of B., 442:11
  State-House hub, 447:13
  though I am not genuine B., 528:17
Boston-plated, I am B., 528:17
Boston's Marlborough Street, 742:21
Bo'sun tight and midshipmite, 528:22
Botanist, puzzle to b., 523:21
Botanize, peep and b., 374:2
Botany, all their b. Latin, 429:21
Botch of it trying to swap, 450:5
Botched civilization, 659:10
Boteler, Dr. B. said of strawberries,
  245:27
Both, by adventuring b., 179:24
  I am with b., 169:29
  plague o' b. houses, 175:28
  wear b. for b. are thine, 165:23
Bother, long words B. me, 648:7
Bothered, bewitched b. bewildered,
  692:18
  hot and b., 593:26
Bottle, a little for the b., 348:2
  fragrance in whiskey b., 739:4
  friend in need nor b., 470:16
  large cold b., 559:19
  leave b. on chimleypiece, 469:41
  my b. of salvation, 152:16
  of hay, 173:22
  shake and shake catsup b., 718:12
  take b. down from shelf, 732:6
Bottled lightning, 469:22
Bottleneck, president is b., 729:21
Bottles, narrow-necked b., 303:22
  new wine in old b., 34:24
  stay the b. of heaven, 15:14
Bottom, bless thee B., 173:17
  build from b. up, 648:14
  dive into b. of deep, 177:9
  every vat stand upon b., 272:14
  from shore sees sea b., 126:27
  I see not the b. of it, 201:5
  line is in heaven, 726:13
  not in one b. trusted, 179:14
  of the monstrous world, 254:4
  of the worst, 200:14
  sees into b. of my grief, 176:8
  sit on our own b., 147:7
  strike rock and go to b., 360:7
  unknown b. like bay of Portugal,
    192:5
Bottomless, consciousness as b. lake,
  538:18
  in b. nights you sleep, 565:16
  perdition, 255:22
  some ponds thought b., 478:32
Bouchon, plus léger qu'un b., 565:*n*6
Bough, apple reddens on high b.,
  56:10
  bloom along b., 578:18
  blossom that hangs on b., 224:25
  Book of Verses underneath B.,
    445:9

Brave *(continued)*
 none but b. deserves fair, 276:6
 o'erhanging firmament, 195:28
 on ye b., 389:4
 outrage b. man dead, 65:15
 passing b. to be a king, 161:20
 resistance or submission, 336:14
 secret of freedom a b. heart, 72:7
 that are no more, 335:17
 then I was clean and b., 579:2
 they shall be gentle b. strong, 541:7
 to fight aloud b., 511:13
 to the vigilant active b., 339:9
 toll for the b., 335:17
 translunary things, 161:13
 war favored by fortune which loves
   b., 536:15
 war spares not the b., 60:3
 when were b. in majority, 479:1
 world kills the b., 701:15
 world sir, 281:15
 world's b. heroes, 778:18
Bravely fleshed maiden sword, 179:10
 greatly think or b. die, 300:8
Braver at night, 759:13
 I have done one b. thing, 228:8
 to be rebel, 589:1
Bravery never out of fashion, 464:1
 on and tackle trim, 261:16
Bravest, always to be b., 51:24
 by far, 781:3
 who have clearest vision, 72:4
Braw brass collar, 361:16
 brecht moonlecht necht, 609:17
Brawling courts, 457:25
 judgments unashamed, 459:11
 of sparrow in eaves, 594:23
 stormy husky b., 634:4
 woman in a wide house, 22:7
Brawn, abundance result of b., 560:2
Brawny, lean rats b. rats, 464:19
 muscles of b. arms, 441:3
 old sinners have b. consciences,
   262:14
Bray of bragging tongues, 66:3
 Vicar of B., 778:17
Brazen foreheads of defamers, 520:11
 Stentor with b. voice, 51:21
 throat of war, 260:21
Brazil, aunt from B. where nuts come
   from, 571:31
 he twirled a Button, 512:19
Breach, could not approve slightest b.,
   661:6
 imminent deadly b., 205:25
 more honored in b., 194:8
 not a b. but an expansion, 229:12
 once more unto the b., 185:3
 with America calamity, 564:21
Bread and circuses, 109:7
 Angels' B. made B. of man, 124:7
 beans and brown b., 567:27
 better b. with happy heart, 5:15
 bitter b. of banishment, 171:20
 broken life up for b., 533:21
 broth without b., 790:2
 brown b. and the Gospel, 286:17
 cast thy b. upon the waters, 24:23
 country people had no b., 319:25
 crust of b. and liberty, 302:24

Bread *(continued)*
 cursed the b., 608:8
 daily b., 33:12
 dear flesh cheap, 423:8
 distressful b., 185:19
 dry as paper, 659:15
 eat b. in sweat of thy face, 6:26
 eat b. without scarceness, 10:16
 eat dusty b., 696:2
 eaten in secret, 21:3
 eaten your b. and salt, 590:17
 ever more stale rags, 659:15
 feeds me b. of bitterness, 679:9
 from mouth of labor, 344:8
 gave Esau b. and pottage, 7:37
 give thine enemy b., 22:26
 give us our daily b., 33:12
 giver of breath and b., 550:17
 God cannot appear except in form
   of b., 745:3
 grind bones to make b., 792:19
 half-penny-worth of b., 177:34
 how salt is another's b., 126:25
 I am the b. of life, 40:4
 I broke with you, 675:1
 I do like butter to my b., 648:6
 if son ask b., 34:7
 Living B. from heaven, 124:7
 living Homer begged b., 233:*n*4
 Loaf of B. and Thou, 445:9
 looked to Government for b.,
   332:29
 neither yet b. to wise, 24:20
 nor his seed begging b., 17:1
 not live by b. only, 10:14
 of adversity, 27:3
 of affliction, 13:3
 of deceit is sweet, 22:5
 of heaven, 19:7
 of idleness, 23:20
 of life, 40:4
 of life dropped in mouth, 283:8
 on which side b. buttered, 142:25
 peace into poet as flour into b.,
   714:7
 quarrel with b. and butter, 290:5
 ravens brought him b., 12:32
 sauce of happy ending, 548:19
 sell b. buy hyacinth, 118:9
 seven days shall ye eat unleavened
   b., 8:40
 shows b. in other hand, 83:10
 sky daily b. of eyes, 430:17
 some gave white b., 788:10
 staff of life, 286:15
 strengthens man's heart, 286:15
 took b. and blessed it, 36:28
 took b. and brake it, 145:6
 unleavened b. and bitter herbs, 8:37
 we want b. and roses too, 782:14
 went on cutting b. and butter,
   463:21
 white b. and butter, 789:7
 who ne'er his b. in sorrow ate,
   349:7
 whole stay of b., 25:33
 with bitter herbs, 483:20
 with b. and wine walk road, 793:25
 with one fish ball, 503:2
 with you more than bread, 675:1

Bread *(continued)*
 wringing b. from sweat, 450:10
Breadline, if world tranquil I'd be in
   b., 754:16
Breadth, taller by b. of nail, 289:8
Break, bend but do not b., 267:26
 best you get is even b., 644:6
 better to bow than b., 141:13
 bids it b., 215:28
 bloody glass, 722:4
 break break, 456:7
 bruised reed shall he not b., 27:25
 civilizations b. fail to meet challenge, 677:8
 embraces, 720:5
 eternal Sabbath, 274:24
 frame of Nature b., 292:3
 given thee till b. of day, 358:1
 hugest hearts that b., 514:7
 I'll b. my staff, 224:24
 into hundred thousand flaws,
   209:23
 it to our hope, 216:20
 mounting at b. of day, 376:13
 never doubted clouds b., 468:17
 never give sucker even b., 572:17
 never knew land to run away or b.,
   338:14
 O to b. loose like chinook, 743:15
 oath he never made, 263:24
 off last lamenting kiss, 230:1
 onetwothreefourfive pigeons, 688:10
 out rather than surrender, 621:*n*5
 shins against wit, 190:17
 that sole bond, 331:22
 those eyes the b. of day, 204:22
 thou'll b. my heart, 362:8
 time to b. down, 23:32
 true believers b. eggs at convenient
   end, 289:9
 until the day b., 25:8
 up by b. of day, 243:8
 you may b. you may shatter, 392:2
Breakbone, induces condition like b.
   fever, 714:16
Breakdown, madness need not be all
   b., 758:7
Breaker recede but tide coming in,
   424:21
Breakers, more dangerous b., 403:5
 wandering by lone sea b., 553:21
 wantoned with b., 401:4
Breakfalls, holds rolls throws b., 737:5
Breakfast, for her own b. a scheme,
   296:2
 from b. to madness, 759:12
 hope is good b. bad supper, 158:20
 kills seven dozen Scots at b., 177:20
 six impossible things before b.,
   519:12
 where our b. take, 785:14
 with appetite, 225:13
Breakfasts at five-o'clock tea, 519:21
Breakfast-time critical period, 678:22
Breaking, cheerfulness always b. in,
   318:9
 gray dawn b., 424:7, 633:14
 sleep that knows not b., 378:20
 stop Heart from b., 513:10
 through foul and ugly mists, 176:37

Breaking (*continued*)
   tired waves vainly b., 483:3
   waves dashed high, 410:11
   wrestled until b. of day, 7:45
Breaks, bough b. cradle fall, 555:4
   butterfly upon wheel, 302:14
   chains from every mind, 357:19
   jest b. no bones, 317:25
   lance of justice b., 211:4
   law of gravity, 670:19
   light through yonder window b., 174:26
   like Atlantic Ocean, 743:4
   my pate across, 196:6
   rider that b. youth, 244:33
   sorrow b. seasons, 165:32
   sun b. through darkest clouds, 167:31
   world b. everyone, 701:15
Breakthrough, madness may be b., 758:7
Breakup, in b. of marriage take side, 717:8
Breast, arm the obdured b., 257:14
   burn from brain and b., 619:5
   deep in her b. lives silent wound, 93:40
   Hampden with dauntless b., 322:14
   heart at rest within b., 356:17
   hope springs in human b., 301:6
   in thy b. stars of fate, 365:9
   lacerate his b., 598:9
   love lodged in woman's b., 227:5
   Madeline's fair b., 415:4
   marched b. forward, 468:17
   my baby at my b., 218:19
   Nature's learned b., 148:10
   nunnery of thy chaste b., 267:14
   of huge Mississippi, 499:13
   one thought in b. another on tongue, 91:23
   pressed with excitement to b., 719:2
   sail upon her patient b., 200:6
   soft as b. of doves, 661:12
   soothe a savage b., 291:7
   soul wears out b., 402:1
   sweetness flows into b., 598:6
   tamer of human b., 321:18
   that gives rose, 509:1
   thy b. encloseth my heart, 165:23
   trembles in the b., 377:18
   truth hath a quiet b., 170:29
   turtle's b., 670:5
   two souls dwell in my b., 350:13
   wail or knock the b., 261:25
   weariness toss him to my b., 243:20
   Wedding Guest beat b., 381:1
   what his b. forges, 219:9
Breastie, panic's in thy b., 361:4
Breastplate of faith, 45:7
   what stronger b. than heart, 164:1
Breasts, brown b., 683:11
   come to my woman's b., 212:29
   every salesman can fondle her b., 626:5
   feel my b. all perfume, 647:17
   from rocky b. forever flowing, 729:5
   her b. are dun, 222:8
   like two young roes, 25:10

Breasts (*continued*)
   Miss Twye soaping b. in bath, 739:12
   Sestos and Abydos of her b., 230:10
   that feed France, 157:16
   touched her sleeping b., 699:5
Breath, a b. thou art, 204:9
   a little flesh a little b., 110:14
   bated b. and whispering humbleness, 180:9
   boldest held his b., 389:5
   breathes with human b., 453:22
   by the gate of b., 533:22
   call the fleeting b., 322:10
   Chaucer whose sweet b., 454:12
   dirt breathing a small b., 724:13
   draw thy b. in pain, 199:27
   dulcet and harmonious b., 173:5
   ecstasy come to b., 696:1
   every thing that hath b., 20:16
   flattered its rank b., 400:7
   fluttered failed for b., 498:15
   fly away b., 202:13
   from one mother both draw b., 64:9
   give hautboys b. he comes, 276:8
   giver of b. and bread, 550:17
   he giveth b., 41:16
   healthy b. of morn, 416:19
   hearest hardly a b., 351:2
   heaven's b. smells wooingly, 213:4
   hot and cold with same b., 59:12
   if b. terrible as terminations, 186:22
   is in his nostrils, 25:32
   kept b. to cool his pottage, 55:8
   lightly draws its b., 372:17
   love endures for b., 533:10
   make them as breath made, 329:8
   mouth-honor b., 216:9
   my quiet b., 415:16
   never drawn b. of life, 598:3
   no b. at all, 211:19
   of Autumn's being, 407:13
   of life, 6:11, 598:3
   of new-mown hay, 611:15
   of self-respect, 706:11
   of the night-wind, 499:22
   of vernal shower, 323:15
   poetry b. of knowledge, 373:15
   possession outvalues others last b., 527:32
   princes but b. of kings, 361:10
   rides on posting winds, 219:29
   smiles tears of life, 439:1
   some of us out of b., 519:4
   stealing my b. of life, 679:9
   summer's ripening b., 175:10
   sweet is the b.of morn, 258:21
   thought takes b. away, 502:10
   thy b. was shed, 602:7
   to last moment of b., 328:4
   toil of b., 385:5
   took one long slow b., 582:16
   utter sweet b., 173:28
   want of words lack of b., 261:17
   weary of b., 423:9
   whiskey on your b., 724:15
   world gray from thy b., 534:4
   writing holding b. swimming, 695:1
Breathe air again, 492:6

Breathe (*continued*)
   and blow, 456:10
   as though to b. life, 455:2
   daring to b. or Achoo, 764:16
   hate were why men b., 689:2
   hear bronze Negroes b., 743:10
   heart pause to b., 402:1
   his native air, 298:5
   if such there b., 378:1
   not his name, 391:10
   slaves cannot b. in England, 334:27
   thou thereon didst only b., 232:16
   thoughts that b., 323:5
   yearning to b. free, 558:1
   you but knock b. shine, 230:26
Breathed, first true gentleman that b., 227:19
   still b. in sighs, 300:2
Breathes, hell itself b. out, 197:21
   of nations saved, 403:9
   there the man, 378:1
   upon bank of violets, 201:16
   with human breath, 453:22
Breathing, almost hear them b. as they march, 743:*n*2
   closer He than b., 460:4
   health and quiet b., 414:9
   household laws, 374:14
   music b. from her face, 267:*n*5
   revenge, 479:12
   talking coeval with b., 290:28
   whether b. is eating, 73:24
   without a tighter b., 513:12
Breathless, hanging b. on fate, 441:18
   we flung us on hill, 662:17
   with adoration, 374:15
Breath's a ware that will not keep, 578:20
Bred, dainties b. of a book, 168:29
   en bawn in brier-patch, 556:8
   me long ago, 579:11
   where is fancy b., 181:3
Bredon, bells sound on B., 579:4
Breeches, coat red b. blue, 386:22
   cost a crown, 776:16
   hand in b. pocket, 417:19
   Macaulay a book in b., 380:16
   women wear the b., 234:11
Breed and haunt, 213:4
   border nor b. nor birth, 591:9
   feared by their b., 171:9
   happy b. of men, 171:9
   if sun b. maggots, 195:17
   more careful of b. of horses, 282:22
   or England b. again, 161:10
   use doth b. habit, 168:10
Breeding, bad b. and vulgar manner, 73:1
   Burgundy without b., 690:8
   eating drinking and b., 489:9
   lilacs out of dead land, 668:17
   test of man or woman's b., 570:11
   write with ease to show b., 353:2
Breeds, familiarity b. contempt, 58:20
   lesser b. without Law, 593:3
Breeze, Athena sent favorable b., 53:1
   battle and the b., 388:26
   fair b. blew, 381:6
   flag to April's b., 429:22
   folds rippling in b., 463:5

Bronze (*continued*)
up from b. I saw, 696:3
work with breathing b., 94:15
Bronzed lank man, 637:11
Brooch, bow or b. or braid, 551:8
of gold ful sheene, 129:14
Brooches, make you b. and toys,
561:23
Brood, mothers a bloody b., 693:6
of Folly, 251:21
Brooding, birds sit b. in snow, 169:14
on God, 725:19
over bein' dog, 555:9
sad b. on country's fate, 482:20
toads b. in wells, 724:17
Brook, dwelt by the b. Cherith, 12:31
many can b. the weather, 168:30
noise like hidden b., 381:24
smooth water where b. deep,
152:*n*7
went to the b., 792:5
where b. and river meet, 441:7
Brookland, far in western b., 579:11
Brooklyn, from B. over B. Bridge,
729:6
tree grows in B., 715:13
Brooks, as b. make rivers, 276:23
as hart panteth after water b., 17:11
books in running b., 190:7
for fishers of song, 574:13
golden sands crystal b., 229:10
I sing of b., 240:16
shallow b. and rivers wide, 251:14
strow b. in Vallombrosa, 256:8
too broad for leaping, 579:13
Brooks Brothers, man in B. shirt,
732:1
Broom, beat barrel with b., 637:8
new b. sweeps clean, 775:11
under arm carried b., 790:16
Broomstick, write finely upon b.,
289:*n*2
Broomsticks, all their b. and tears,
596:13
Broth without any bread, 790:2
Brothel, world not metaphysical b.,
716:12
Brother, am I not man and b., 333:11
and companion in tribulation, 47:1
be my b. or I kill you, 342:6
Big B. watching, 711:16
came with subtilty, 7:39
can you spare dime, 699:15
critic b. of artist, 548:17
dead divine b. of all, 490:11
Death's b. Sleep, 94:8
every one said to his b., 27:24
every sword against his b., 29:11
far off, 23:3
fight against his b., 26:17
gently scan b. man, 362:5
half-b. of world, 476:9
hypocrite reader my b., 494:1
I am that insect b., 495:4
lawless linsey-woolsey b., 263:17
life sweet b., 428:15
lo'ed him like a b., 363:4
man and b., 333:11
my double my b., 494:1
no b. near the throne, 302:11

Brother (*continued*)
now must I depart from b., 4:8
of the Angle, 245:16
offended is harder to be won, 21:40
Remus and his b. knew this life,
93:2
shall be my b., 185:23
sinned against my b. the ass, 123:11
sleep Death's twin b., 52:*n*1
sleep the b. of death, 52:4
Sleep the B. to Death, 160:21
sticketh closer than a b., 21:42
still to my b. turns, 328:7
Sun who brings us day, 123:7
thy tail hangs down, 592:14
to all creatures, 748:12
to dragons, 14:45
which of us known b., 706:17
would brother cheat, 123:5
Brotherhood, crown good with b.,
576:19
love the b., 46:23
men and women affirm b., 722:11
of the Right Stuff, 764:5
sit down at table of b., 761:1
that binds brave, 586:12
Brotherly, feel it so b., 732:13
love, 42:14, 45:42
Brother's, called b. father dad, 169:24
keeper, 7:3
mote in b. eye, 34:3
murder, 197:23
sad mad b. name, 535:4
voice of thy b. blood, 7:4
what I sowed b. sons gathering,
708:2
Brothers, all men born are my b.,
488:18
all the b. too, 202:15
and Sisters beware, 593:18
are evil, 4:1
as b. live together, 441:23
band of b., 185:23
call from bay, 497:6
forty thousand b., 199:16
goodbye b., 572:21
linsey-woolsey b., 303:28
men become b., 364:13
our dearly beloved b., 748:5
shall b. be for a' that, 363:23
sons kindred slain, 302:*n*6
valiant sisters virtuous, 778:2
ye are b. ye are men, 389:6
Brought, Antony b. drunken forth,
218:13
before the mountains were b. forth,
18:10
daughters of music b. low, 24:27
death into the world, 255:18
forth on this continent, 450:2
me home to glory, 451:12
mouse will be b. forth, 98:10
never b. to min', 362:19
nothing into this world, 45:21
over vast and furious ocean, 240:8
palsy to bed, 659:16
up in this city, 41:25
which b. us hither, 375:13
Brow, athlete crowned in sweat of b.,
113:12

Brow (*continued*)
bonie b. was brent, 362:15
candid b., 573:2
dangerous b. by night, 188:3
flushing his b., 415:3
forty winters besiege thy b., 220:8
grace seated on this b., 197:30
Helen's beauty in b. of Egypt, 174:1
no wrinkle on azure b., 401:1
now your b. is beld John, 362:15
of labor, 582:4
of lip of eye of b., 221:22
pain and anguish wring b., 378:14
parallels in beauty's b., 221:1
pure unclouded b., 518:13
shine upon b. today, 557:1
so grim mouth so prim, 670:6
sweat of b., 478:9
upon his b. shame ashamed, 176:2
view with wrinkled b., 181:25
wet with honest sweat, 441:4
where he got that high b., 108:13
wrinkle deeper on b., 399:17
Brown, baked me too b., 518:8
bread and the Gospel, 286:17
breasts, 683:11
bright nightingale, 533:8
changing from b. suit to gray, 658:5
good man Charlie B., 751:9
hair and speaks small, 182:17
hair over mouth, 669:16
heath and shaggy wood, 378:2
hills melted into spring, 480:1
in b. study, 155:8
Jeanie with light b. hair, 507:3
long and lank and b., 381:18
man's burden, 593:*n*1
meadows b. and sere, 411:8
myrtles b., 253:14
not Old B. any longer, 479:4
prefer philanthropy of Captain B.,
479:2
quick b. fox, 781:8
some gave them b., 788:10
strong b. god, 671:12
world black red yellow b., 766:8
Browne, sedulous ape to Sir Thomas
B., 561:19
Browning, find B. plain, 465:*n*2
hang it all Robert B., 659:12
Meredith prose B., 566:8
Mrs. B. guard silence, 626:10
Browning, entsichere meinen B.,
679:*n*1
Browning's, Mrs. B. death relief,
446:11
Brown's, John B. body, 524:7
Brows, bliss in our b. bent, 217:1
dark rebellious b., 491:5
earned with sweat of b., 149:1
like gathering storm, 363:2
nodded with his darkish b., 51:2
not seen in either of our b., 161:11
of dauntless courage, 256:17
Bruce has aften led, 363:19
Brüder, alle Menschen werden B.,
364:*n*3
Bruise, axe fitter to b., 262:12
better for b. than arnica, 467:23
it shall b. thy head, 6:24

Bruise *(continued)*
  thou shalt b. his heel, 6:24
Bruised, body not b. to pleasure soul,
    598:2
  reed shall he not break, 27:25
  together crushed and b., 299:21
Brunswick, Hamelin town's in B.,
    464:17
Brunt, bear b. pay arrears, 467:19
  stands b. of life, 68:15
Brush, blind hand b. my wing, 358:5
  essential in painting, 120:13
  George B. is my name, 697:12
  painter's b. consumes dreams,
    597:19
  sea's big b. recolors, 731:7
  whether chisel pen b., 596:16
  whitewash and long-handled b.,
    526:2
  work with so fine a b., 387:13
Brushed past palms on staircase,
    718:22
Brushwood sheaf, 465:3
Brutal arm appear, 599:17
  most b. thing nineteen-year-old boy,
    771:1
Brutality, industry without art b.,
    487:27
  oppressor commit b. openly, 761:8
  that special b., 496:4
Brutalizing lower class, 500:23
Brute beauty and valor, 550:22
  chuck 'im out the b., 591:18
  heart of brute like you, 764:18
  love of a b., 452:9
  use wit drive b. off, 750:10
Brute, et tu B., 88:*n* 18, 188:16
Brutes, as we to b. poets to us, 509:15
  exterminate b., 573:7
  nation of b., 573:*n* 2
  not born to live like b., 125:30
  without you, 284:17
Brutish, nasty b. and short, 239:22
Brutus and Cassius not displayed,
    109:12
  Caesar had his B., 339:5
  dear B., 187:22
  is an honorable man, 188:29
  makes mine greater, 189:17
  no orator as B. is, 189:9
  not kill B. not kill sons of B., 137:4
  you also B., 88:26
Bubble, fire burn cauldron b., 215:13
  gonfalon b., 644:5
  life a b., 160:*n*7
  like b. on fountain, 378:22
  now a b. burst, 301:5
  reputation, 191:3
  world's a b., 160:13
Bubbles, borne like thy b. onward,
    401:4
  earth hath b., 212:19
  man and his dwellings as b., 122:16
  millions of B. like us, 445:22
  we buy, 485:4
  winking at brim, 415:11
Bubbling and loud-hissing urn, 335:3
  cry of swimmer, 402:17
  sinks with b. groan, 400:31
Buccaneers of Buzz, 514:8

Buchenwald, believe what I said about
    B., 724:5
Buck in the snow, 684:11
  stops here, 655:20
Bucket down and full of tears am I,
    172:9
  drop of a b., 27:21
  old oaken b., 398:3
  past a b. of ashes, 634:7
  up doun as b. in a welle, 130:15
Buckets into empty wells, 335:1, 380:7
  two b. filling one another, 172:9
Buckhurst, I would B. choose, 283:22
Buckingham, so much for B., 291:21
Buckle, pride plume here b., 550:22
Buckler, his truth thy shield and b.,
    18:15
Buckles, silver b. on knee, 792:18
Bucks, fat black b., 637:8
Bud, canker lives in sweetest b.,
    220:21
  in age I b. again, 243:23
  not as in b. of spring, 231:10
  rose is sweeter in b., 155:18
  this b. of love, 175:10
  worm i' the b., 202:14
Buddha, go for refuge to B., 65:5
  the Awakened One, 64:20
Buddhas, Arahat B. who appear in
    world, 64:24
Budding historians, 665:11
Buddy, Christ Himself b., 747:9
Budge, I'll not b. an inch, 167:13
Buds, cankers in musk-rose b., 173:10
  darling b. of May, 220:12
  green b. they were swellin', 785:9
  of barren flowers, 534:13
Buff and the blue, 364:4
Buffalo Bill's defunct, 688:10
  gals come out tonight, 780:10
  home where b. roam, 786:11
  life breath of b. in wintertime,
    494:21
  my b. have found me, 698:4
  thought he saw B., 520:2
  wind on b. grass, 787:2
Buffaloes, water b. neurasthenic, 665:7
Buffet, not wise who b. against love,
    67:1
Buffets, blows and b. of world, 214:22
  fortune's b. and rewards, 197:3
Buffon, is it Aristotle Pliny B., 319:16
Buffoon and poet, 557:7
  chemist fiddler and b., 274:11
Buffoonery, life piece of b., 604:5
Buffoons, great men not b., 432:30
Buffs, private of B., 461:1
  steady the B., 591:6
Bug, flap b. with gilded wings, 302:15
  snug as a b. in rug, 310:16
Bugle, blow b. blow, 456:11
  one blast upon b. horn, 379:1
  sound upon b. horn, 455:8
Bugles, blow out you b., 663:5
  cry of b. going by, 583:16
  what are b. blowin' for, 591:15
Build beneath stars, 296:19
  except the Lord b. the house, 19:29
  experience arch to b. upon, 535:12
  from bottom up, 648:14

Build *(continued)*
  Great Society, 723:18
  houses and inhabit them, 28:12
  if you b. it he will come, 768:2
  intending to b. tower, 38:33
  lofty rhyme, 253:15
  me nest on greatness of God, 547:7
  me straight, 441:16
  middle-aged b. woodshed, 477:1
  on Fortune build on sand, 240:5
  pair nor b. nor sing, 383:14
  schoolrooms for boy, 480:10
  ship of death, 658:2
  small cabin b. there, 594:21
  takes carpenter to b. barn, 648:11
  that dome in air, 382:25
  thee more stately mansions, 447:11
  therefore your own world, 431:4
  they labor in vain that b. it, 19:29
  throne of bayonets, 583:10
  time to b. up, 23:32
  upon this rock b. my church, 35:28
  youth b. bridge to moon, 477:1
Builded better than knew, 429:10
  was Jerusalem b. here, 359:17
  wisdom hath b. her house, 21:1
Builders, stone which the b. refused,
    19:20
Buildeth on vulgar heart, 183:26
Building castles in Spain, 132:23
  principal beauty in a b., 250:12
  roofs of gold, 184:24
  stole life o' the b., 214:13
  three things in b., 349:23
  we are nation b., 663:7
Buildings he may never enter, 349:27
  leap tall b. at single bound, 737:7
  riding in taxi between tall b.,
    694:15
  when Luftwaffe knocked down b.,
    774:9
  will collapse, 715:8
  you may have all the b., 516:3
Builds, Devil b. chapel there, 285:14
  Heaven in Hell's despair, 358:2
  Hell in Heaven's despite, 358:3
  marsh hen secretly b., 547:7
  phoenix b. phoenix' nest, 264:19
  phoenix b. spicy nest, 246:6
  what man b. has but a day, 631:15
Built absolute trust, 212:27
  against will of gods, 51:35
  before I b. wall, 623:1
  bicycle b. for two, 600:18
  fortress b. by Nature for herself,
    171:9
  God a church, 334:16
  house that Jack b., 792:24
  in such logical way, 447:16
  in the eclipse, 253:22
  love b. on beauty, 230:3
  nests in beard, 471:27
  of just a syllable, 514:7
  Rome must be b. in day, 743:17
  Rome not b. in one day, 141:29
  ruined love when b. anew, 222:5
  science b. with facts, 565:6
  till we have b. Jerusalem, 359:17
  which b. desolate places, 13:35
Bulben's, bare Ben B. head, 600:2

Bull, a Cock and a B., 320:32
be on b. side, 533:4
cloud that looked like b., 73:3
greatest of all is John B., 403:26
handsome as b. that kidnapped
    Europa, 87:25
John B. or Englishman's fireside,
    366:16
moose, 575:13
savage b. bear yoke, 186:14
taking b. by both horns kissed her,
    644:11
Bullen's, dawned from B. eyes, 321:24
Bullet, ballot stronger than b., 448:6
bite b., 591:10
faster than speeding b., 737:7
has its billet, 284:6
that will kill me not cast, 370:13
through his head, 608:8
Bullets made of lead, 792:5
paper b. of the brain, 186:31
seek out where heart lies, 714:5
word as b. flying, 572:23
Bullied into following master artist,
    667:1
out of vice, 434:9
Bullocks, whose talk is of b., 32:12
Bullpen, waiting sentence in b., 742:22
Bulls, plowman's story of b., 100:28
Bulrush, seeking knot in a b., 83:9
Bulrushes, ark of b., 8:21
Bulwark, floating b. of our island,
    325:20
never failing, 138:5
of continuing liberty, 649:11
of Greece famous Athens, 64:12
Bulwarks, Britannia needs no b., 389:1
greatest b. of liberty, 327:3
Bum, belly shoulder b., 599:17
I'll moider de b., 728:6
let's face it I am, 737:6
Bumbast out blank verse, 157:20
Bumble, the law is a ass said Mr. B.,
    469:12
Bumblebee, Moses on b., 698:10
Bump, don't b. into furniture, 700:19
go b. in the night, 779:15
Bumper of good liquor, 352:24
Bumping, love b. against obstacles of
    civilization, 436:16
Bumps along the dusk, 558:11
Bumpy, fasten seatbelts b. night, 727:5
Bunbury, invaluable invalid B., 567:6
Bunch-backed, curse this pois'nous b.
    toad, 165:26
Buncombe and millions mostly fools,
    413:13
Bunghole, stopping a b., 199:9
Bunk, been in his b. below, 545:3
history more or less b., 499:n2
Bunker Hill, there is Boston and B.,
    394:13
Buns, hot cross b., 790:9
Bunting, baby b., 789:15
Buoy too small for sight, 210:27
Burbled as it came, 518:16
Burden, bear any b., 741:3
bear his own b., 44:20
borne the b., 35:39
brown man's b., 593:n1

Burden (*continued*)
changes labor from b. to honor,
    638:9
grasshopper shall be a b., 24:28
great b. upon his back, 272:11
grievous b. was thy birth, 166:6
her lot not b., 761:12
my b. is light, 34:38
not b. our remembrances, 224:27
of his song, 338:19
of incommunicable, 397:13
of my song, 776:8
of nothing to do, 280:19
of the desert of the sea, 26:18
of the mystery, 373:2
of them is intolerable, 49:15
on back b. of world, 563:6
they're a b. for us, 705:18
vapors weep their b., 459:1
weight of another's b., 245:1
White Man's b., 593:5
years are still a b., 67:26
youth and age equally a b., 75:4
Burdens, had such b. on mind, 597:16
they that bare b., 13:21
Burdensome, school in which nothing
    b., 115:9
when life is b., 70:8
Bureau, super-legal-aid b., 646:12
Burgeoning wood brings forth, 51:23
Burglaree, with a little b., 529:15
Burglary, flat b. as ever committed,
    187:4
vary piracee with b., 529:15
Burgonet, arm and b. of men, 217:6
Burgundy, naive domestic B., 690:8
treat wretch with B., 287:1
Burial, no b. this pretty pair, 776:2
of my rosy feelings, 756:12
Buried, bodies are b. in peace, 32:15
body to be b. obscurely, 160:12
Caesar bled, 445:13
dies and is b. with them, 69:12
hatchet, 605:18
here children born one b., 448:16
him before prime, 785:16
lie deep b., 59:24
life, 498:4
not b. in consecrated ground,
    539:18
old Adam b., 50:11
on Sunday, 791:4
outworn b. age, 221:2
putrid corpse of liberty, 652:21
soil good to be b. in, 486:1
they b. him, 612:20
want to be b. among mountains,
    510:17
was crucified dead and b., 48:25
where Michael Furey b., 647:8
Buries empires in common grave,
    340:7
universal darkness b. all, 304:2
Burke great because brings thought,
    499:7
said Reporters' Gallery Fourth Es-
    tate, 411:n1
Burma girl a-settin', 591:22
got run out of B., 653:27
Burn and rave, 737:20

Burn (*continued*)
another Troy to b., 595:18
better to marry than b., 43:2
books burn human beings, 420:3
children will b., 788:16
everything or throw into water,
    138:17
fire b. cauldron bubble, 215:13
flag yet terrific b., 389:2
from brain and breast, 619:5
frost itself doth b., 197:32
great sphere thou movest in, 218:6
heart b. within us, 39:27
I'll b. my books, 162:25
like fabulous roman candles, 750:9
no blazing hearth b., 322:6
old wood b. brightest, 237:11
old wood to b., 158:23
out false shames, 657:14
some b. damp faggots, 596:7
stars that round her b., 292:1
time the fire in which we b., 734:5
to the socket, 376:20
violent fires soon b. out, 171:8
we b. daylight, 174:19
what thou hast worshipped, 115:6
with hard gemlike flame, 538:9
words that b., 323:5
you bid me b. letters, 338:3
Burned, and his feet not be b., 20:30
black with sun, 683:11
bush b. with fire, 8:23
candle b. on the table, 680:2
feared witches and b. women,
    568:15
feet as if b. in a furnace, 47:4
give my body to be b., 43:14
half his Troy was b., 183:10
heart ne'er within b., 378:1
is Apollo's laurel bough, 163:1
Matilda and house b., 609:4
money b. out his purse, 137:15
my life, 696:1
on the water, 217:14
some b. alive, 752:4
take fire and his clothes not be b.,
    20:30
topless towers of Ilium, 162:19
while I was musing the fire b., 17:6
word b. like a lamp, 32:16
worship what thou hast b., 115:6
Burning and shining light, 39:49
bow of b. gold, 359:17
boy stood on b. deck, 410:13
burns out another's b., 174:16
candle b. while sleeping, 234:2
clove, 623:20
fire in mind ever b., 152:10
for ancient connection, 757:4
heaven and earth in ashes b., 123:14
I'm ten years b. down the road,
    774:13
is Paris b., 676:12
keep home fires b., 617:12
lifetime b. in moment, 671:10
marle, 256:7
pretty Babe all b. bright, 160:19
roof and tower, 598:1
Sappho, 402:24
seraphim in b. row, 254:11

Burning *(continued)*
    smell of b. fills air, 608:19
    success worse than house b., 727:4
    three words as with b. pen, 364:14
    Tyger Tyger b. bright, 358:6
    your lights b., 38:30
Burnished, barge like b. throne,
        217:14
    livery of b. sun, 180:13
Burns, blood that freezes blood that
        b., 465:10
    candle b. at both ends, 684:2
    it b. your clothes, 354:10
    not she which b. in 't, 222:23
    one fire b. out another's, 174:16
    Shelley with us, 464:24
    smell fire whose gown b., 244:10
    wasted oil unprofitably b., 334:13
    what b. me now, 725:19
    when the blood b., 194:5
Burnside, waly yon b., 785:19
Burnt, charmed water b. alway,
        381:21
    child fire dreadeth, 142:6
    Christians b. each other, 402:9
    fire of thine eyes, 358:6
    millions of innocent b., 343:8
    night's candles are b. out, 176:6
    offering, 7:34
    offerings, 29:26
Burr, I am a kind of b., 204:26
Burro, no laurel crown for outrunning
        b., 106:23
Burrow, go b. underground, 660:16
Burrs and thorns of life, 414:6
Burst cannon's roar, 447:3
    first that ever b., 381:6
    hot heart's shell, 486:25
    nigh to b. my boilers, 398:5
    now a bubble b., 301:5
Bursts, melodious b., 454:12
Burthen of the mystery, 373:2
    vapors weep their b., 459:1
    weight of another's b., 245:1
Burton, great direction B. left, 317:*n*2
Bury for nothing, 469:43
    Great Duke, 458:5
    I come to b. Caesar, 188:28
    it fathoms in earth, 224:24
    let dead b. their dead, 34:18
    living scarce able to b. dead, 240:10
    marry ancient people to b. them,
        250:15
    me in their buryingplace, 8:16
    me not on lone prairie, 786:8
    me out on prairie, 786:9
    my heart at Wounded Knee, 698:7
    no one to b., 671:5
    physician can b. mistakes, 608:13
    we will b. you, 689:20
Buryingplace, bury me in their b.,
        8:16
Bus, either on b. or off b., 768:1
    Hitler missed b., 606:11
    night journey on b., 753:2
Bush afire with God, 439:7
    beat the b., 140:22, 240:2
    bird in hand worth two in b.,
        107:*n*5
    burned with fire, 8:23

Bush *(continued)*
    fear each b. an officer, 165:6
    good wine needs no b., 100:*n*10
    jumped into bramble b., 792:22
    supposed a bear, 174:1
    thorough b. thorough brier, 172:30
    was not consumed, 8:23
Bushel, put candle under a b., 33:3
    words won't fill b., 310:7
Bushels, wheat in two b. of chaff,
        179:23
Bushes, author out from b., 651:5
Busier, yet semed b. than he was,
        129:23
Business as usual, 619:15
    avoid clergyman who is man of b.,
        113:18
    best b. father's farm, 462:12
    could not make dull, 497:3
    crises at intervals, 559:9
    derned sight better b., 536:13
    diligent in his b., 22:15
    dinner lubricates b., 348:6
    dirty b., 543:9
    dispatch b. quickly, 134:6
    dispatch the soul of b., 305:11
    do b. in great waters, 19:9
    do b. of day in day, 371:11
    economic slavery nobody's b., 649:2
    end of this day's b., 189:24
    everybody's b. nobody's b., 245:19
    fiendishness of b. competition,
        661:2
    great b. of life, 537:8
    he had talents equal to b., 109:13
    Hell where mind own b., 522:*n*1
    I like Mr. Gorbachev we can do b.,
        756:1
    if everybody minded b., 517:13
    in hands of a few, 525:11
    is Business, 644:3
    laid aside b., 245:12
    life's b. choice, 468:4
    love only b. in life, 396:21
    love yields to b., 102:1
    marriage damnably serious b.,
        686:18
    may bring money, 387:9
    men some to b. take, 300:17
    men's b. and bosoms, 159:1
    mind b. and spend less, 279:8
    mind his own b., 149:31
    Monopoly is B. at end of journey,
        555:14
    my Father's b., 38:7
    no better ballast than b., 486:7
    no b. carried on at all, 305:8
    no b. like show b., 666:15
    no feeling of his b., 199:1
    no foreigner do b. here, 134:10
    of American people is business,
        614:17
    of comic poet, 290:35
    one hundred and fifty lawyers do b.,
        345:2
    other people's money, 504:8
    overwise in doing thy b., 31:25
    perpetual devotion to b., 560:20
    study to do your own b., 45:4
    talk of nothing but b., 134:6

Business *(continued)*
    that we love, 217:30
    that's his b., 420:13
    that's true b. precept, 469:39
    to be drunk the b. of day, 276:29
    to know what other people don't,
        577:17
    what b. is it of yours, 349:9
    with income at heels, 334:14
    without some dissimulation no b.,
        305:8
    woman enter active b. of life,
        410:18
Businesslike, more b. than business-
        men, 623:11
Businessmen, all b. sons of bitches,
        741:15
    more businesslike than b., 623:11
Bust, animated b., 322:10
    friendly b., 668:14
    outlasts citadel, 462:11
    pallid b. of Pallas, 452:21
Busting, June b. out all over, 692:11
Bustle in House Morning after Death,
        513:17
Busts, picture placed the b. between,
        296:28
Busy as a bee, 155:14
    as one-armed man, 585:18
    bee improve each hour, 294:9
    curious thirsty fly, 307:9
    hammers closing rivets, 185:14
    haunts of men, 410:15
    housewife ply evening care, 322:6
    how doth the b. bee, 294:9
    hum of men, 251:17
    monster manunkind, 689:5
    old fool unruly Sun, 228:11
    the stop to b. fools, 270:2
    whisper circling round, 329:17
Busybodies, tattlers and b., 45:19
Butcher baker candlestick-maker,
        791:13
    his father was a b., 271:22
    hog b. for world, 634:4
    not from benevolence of b., 326:1
Butchered to make Roman holiday,
        400:26
Butchers, gentle with these b., 188:22
Butchery, work of b. and desolation,
        621:1
Butt and very sea-mark, 208:14
    fixed as an aim or b., 184:23
    knocks you with b. end, 330:16
Butter, guns or b., 697:*n*2
    I do like bit of b. to bread, 648:6
    in a lordly dish, 11:4
    it was the best b., 517:19
    not melt in her mouth, 141:23
    quarrel with bread and b., 290:5
    rubbed her with b., 760:2
    went on cutting bread and b.,
        463:21
    white bread and b., 789:7
    words b. no parsnips, 379:16
    words smoother than b., 17:28
Buttercup, called Little B., 529:2
Buttered, on which side bread b.,
        142:25
    scones and crumpets, 668:10

Butterflies are already yellow, 659:3
  frogs eat b., 639:2
  laugh at gilded b., 211:13
  no b. no bees, 423:1
Butterfly, blue in b., 623:13
  breaks b. upon wheel, 302:14
  dreaming I was a b., 80:9
  Effect, 775:2
  float like a b., 771:16
  in eternity as b. in air, 556:21
  upon road, 590:19
Butterfly's flicker swan's down, 706:3
Butter's spread too thick, 519:5
Butting through the Channel, 634:1
Button, Brazil he twirled B., 512:19
  little b. at top, 324:7
  pray you undo this b., 211:19
Button-cute rapier-keen, 715:1
Buttoned-up and white-chokered,
  547:1
Buttonhole, take you a b. lower, 169:9
Buttons be disclosed, 193:26
  biographies but clothes and b.,
  528:10
  bronze b. stamped with eagle, 694:5
  taken of b. off, 591:16
Buttress nor coign of vantage, 213:4
Butts, beast with many heads b. me,
  219:10
Buxom blithe and debonair, 251:7
Buy a fat pig, 792:2
  a world of happy days, 165:29
  annuity cheap, 469:40
  bubbles we b., 485:4
  cherries which none may b., 226:18
  costly as purse can b., 193:30
  decline to b. repentance, 79:5
  dispraise thing you desire to b.,
  201:6
  full and fair ones come and b.,
  241:1
  hyacinths to feed soul, 118:n2
  I will b. with you, 180:2
  lose it that b. it with care, 179:16
  never b. what you do not want,
  345:5
  no man might b. or sell, 47:29
  nor can b. tomorrow, 228:1
  two white feet b. him, 781:17
  what would you b., 428:14
Buyer, city to perish if it finds b.,
  91:30
  it is naught saith the b., 22:4
  let b. beware, 118:21
  needs a hundred eyes, 244:25
Buying and selling, 478:29
  it's no fish ye're b., 379:8
Buys, who b. a minute's mirth, 166:38
Buzz, buccaneers of B., 514:8
  crowd b. and murmurings, 266:16
  the witty and fair annoys, 302:15
Buzzing world lisping firmament,
  639:18
B.V.D., from every B., 688:12
By and by easily said, 197:20
  and by God caught eye, 697:6
  I get b. with a little help, 770:10
Bye baby bunting, 789:15
Bye-and-bye, sweet b., 786:5
Byron, close thy B., 412:8

Byron (*continued*)
  cuts a figure, 418:11
  from poetry of B. ethics, 424:24
  mad bad dangerous to know,
  397:19
  times B. goes into Texas, 748:10
Byron's struggle cease, 497:15
Byway to heaven, 285:17
Byword, proverb and a b., 12:24
  story and b. through world, 239:27
  thou shalt become a b., 10:22
Byzantium, lords and ladies of B.,
  597:10

C

C Major of this life, 467:5
Caballero, el C. de la Triste Figura,
  149:n9
Cabbage, cauliflower c. with college
  education, 527:8
  cut a c. leaf, 324:7
Cabbages and kings, 519:3
  death find me planting c., 145:11
  happy those who plant c., 140:1
  no c. sprouting out, 448:8
Cabin, enter Logan's c. hungry,
  326:14
  mounted to the c., 610:22
  small c. build there, 594:21
  willow c. at gate, 201:27
Cabined ample spirit, 498:15
  cribbed confined, 215:2
  from her c. loophole peep, 252:22
Cabinet, post offices and c. appointments, 448:n2
Cabinets, make parties as ministers c.,
  483:30
Cable broke anchor lost, 165:2
  no c. draw forcibly as love, 235:13
  on seventh day scrape c., 474:19
  taught me to abhor detest Sabbath,
  527:1
Cabots talk only to God, 582:1
Cackle, don't c. w'en fine wum,
  556:14
Cackles, codfish never c., 781:16
  groans and dies, 410:8
Cadence from man named Yeats,
  725:5
  harsh c. of rugged line, 274:28
  to his verse a smooth c., 280:5
  tremulous c. slow, 499:20
Cadiz, reeking into C. Bay, 465:5
Cadmean victory, 69:24
Caecorum, in regione c. rex est luscus,
  136:n4
Caelia has undone me, 321:11
Caelum, quid si nunc c. ruat, 85:n17
Caesar, all that C. could, 431:4
  appeal unto C., 41:32
  buried C. bled, 445:13
  carry C. in your boat, 88:22
  every wound of C., 189:11
  great C. fell, 189:7
  had his Brutus, 339:5
  I come to bury C., 188:28
  imperious C. dead, 199:10
  not that I loved C. less, 188:25
  O mighty C., 188:19

Caesar (*continued*)
  poor cried C. wept, 189:1
  render unto C., 35:45
  sawdust C., 680:10
  thou art mighty yet, 189:25
  upon what meat C. feed, 187:23
  word of C. stood, 189:3
Caesar's, all is C., 264:13
  dead C. trencher, 217:27
  hand Plato's brain, 430:12
  I am, 143:8
  poison from C. crown, 359:13
  self is God's, 264:13
  wife must be above suspicion,
  88:n14
Café, every street c., 692:7
Caftan of tan with henna, 638:27
Cage, gilded c., 609:15
  nor iron bars a c., 267:18
  put me in a c., 673:16
  robin redbreast in c., 359:6
  sing like birds i' the c., 211:13
  women put not on pedestal but in
  c., 719:6
Caged, know why c. bird sings,
  614:24
Cages, marriage as with c., 146:19
Cain, eye stared at C., 427:20
  land God gave to C., 139:2
  set a mark upon C., 7:7
  terre Dieu donna à C., 139:n2
  was tiller of the ground, 7:2
  went out from presence of the Lord,
  7:8
Caissons go rolling along, 636:15
Caius is a man, 510:13
Cake, bake c. fast as can, 788:9
  eat c. and have it, 142:29
  Heaven's sugar c., 283:7
  let them eat c., 319:25
  see to substance of c., 574:16
  some gave plum c., 788:10
Cakes and ale, 202:5
  bridegrooms brides and bridal c.,
  240:16
Calabash, goodnight Mrs. C., 686:1
Calais, find C. lying in my heart,
  143:16
Calamities of life, 286:3
Calamitous in drawn-out witticism,
  388:17
  necessity of going on, 341:10
  to the conquered, 72:12
Calamity, Child of C., 526:8
  fortune not satisfied with one c.,
  99:11
  in English history, 564:21
  in power of no c., 552:n5
  makes c. of so long life, 196:10
  man's true touchstone, 238:19
  no c. greater than lavish desires,
  57:14
Calamus, hinc quam sic c. saevior ense
  patet, 234:29
Calaveras, celebrated jumping frog of
  C. county, 525:n5
  outjump any frog in C. county,
  525:21
Calcaria, de c. in carbonarium,
  112:n7

Calculate, no wisdom can c. end, 341:5

Calculated, nicely c. less or more, 377:10

    so c. so malignant, 683:3

Calculation shining out of other, 469:36

    sum defies c., 349:24

Calculations, most dangerous c. we call illusions, 666:19

Calculators, age of c., 332:12

Calculus, common sense reduced to c., 351:17

Caldron of dissolute loves, 114:20

Caledonia stern and wild, 378:2

Caledonia's, support C. cause, 364:4

Calendar, a c. look in almanack, 173:16

    striking from C., 445:24

    year of Julian C. 710, 237:23

Calf and young lion together, 26:11

    bring fatted c., 38:36

    false as wolf to c., 200:22

    killed c. in high style, 271:22

    second beast like a c., 47:15

Calf's-skin on recreant limbs, 169:28

Caliban, 'Ban 'Ban Ca-C., 224:11

Calico cat replied Mee-ow, 559:22

    Jam, 472:6

    Pie, 472:5

    tree, 472:5

California, cured of drug taking in C., 712:6

    from C. to New York island, 731:13

    if C. becomes prosperous country, 474:20

    wonderful place to live if orange, 687:22

Californians race of people, 586:3

Caligula's horse made Consul, 385:15

Call, almost like c. to come, 624:14

    back yesterday, 171:22, 233:19

    bawd a bawd, 81:n7

    brothers c. from bay, 497:6

    cattle home, 484:9

    delicate creatures ours, 207:4

    don't c. out National Guard, 655:5

    dunno what to c. 'im, 574:3

    fig a fig, 81:11

    for robin redbreast, 237:13

    forth thundering Aeschylus, 232:21

    gods to witness, 211:23

    grief at not wanting to c. dead back, 629:19

    had c. to literature, 525:19

    heaven and earth to witness, 10:10

    her blessed, 23:20

    how you c. to me c. to me, 540:19

    in and invite God, 231:11

    in thy death's head, 243:17

    let us c. thee devil, 206:22

    let's c. whole thing off, 695:12

    me early mother dear, 454:4

    me horse, 177:24

    me Ishmael, 486:16

    neighbors in, 789:8

    nigh unto them that c., 20:13

    no man foe, 682:13

    none dare c. it treason, 160:16

Call (*continued*)

    nothing c. our own but death, 171:25

    obey the important c., 335:9

    of running tide, 633:15

    one clear c. for me, 460:11

    philosophy down from heavens, 87:30

    please to c. it rush-candle, 167:32

    saints aid if men c., 382:14

    spade a spade, 81:11

    spirits from vasty deep, 178:3

    that backing your friends, 177:23

    that which we c. a rose, 175:2

    the fleeting breath, 322:10

    things by right names, 367:7

    through curtains c. on us, 228:11

    today his own, 274:29

    Truth obeyed c., 599:11

    try first thyself and after c. God, 59:n5

    up your men, 379:27

    upon all who love freedom, 678:16

    upon my soul, 201:27

    when you c. me that smile, 583:14

    wild c. and clear c., 633:15

    will they come when you c., 178:3

    you back dear love, 67:24

    you c. for faith, 466:11

    you c. me misbeliever, 180:8

    you could say I've a c., 764:12

    you Shepherd from hill, 498:9

Calla lilies in bloom again mother, 693:11

Called brother's father dad, 169:24

    fool c. her lady fair, 592:23

    for his pipe, 788:5

    him soft names, 415:16

    it macaroni, 778:21

    Little Cousins C. back, 515:1

    many are c., 35:44

    neither two nor one c., 199:31

    never knew me never c. me mother, 548:1

    New World into existence, 372:3

    out of Egypt c. my son, 32:25

    them untaught knaves, 177:3

    till we are c. to rise, 513:18

    whom he did predestinate he c., 42:5

Calleth, deep c. unto deep, 17:13

    them all by their names, 20:15

Callimachus, tomb of C., 82:19

Calling, dignity of high c., 331:25

    followed mercenary c., 580:1

Callooh callay, 518:16

Calls back lovely April, 220:9

    beauty c., 285:8

    death c. ye to the crowd, 246:22

    fool c. you foolish, 69:1

    if anybody c., 627:18

    Jerusalem thy sister c., 359:24

    me Tom, 233:21

    stated c. to worship, 314:18

    who c. me villain, 196:6

Calm, after storm c., 690:4

    after storm comes c., 286:20

    all c. all bright, 406:5

    all c. as it was bright, 270:7

    cankers of c. world, 178:25

Calm (*continued*)

    contending kings, 167:2

    day so cool so c., 243:10

    drifted in sheepish c., 743:1

    envisage circumstance c., 416:21

    escape into c. regions, 318:15

    evening c. and free, 374:15

    for a c. unfit, 274:3

    great events make me c., 488:4

    he of c. and happy nature, 75:4

    in c. sea every man pilot, 272:3

    my soul's c. retreat, 270:2

    no joy but c., 454:7

    quiet innocent recreation, 245:27

    region where no night, 242:1

    sea is c. tonight, 499:19

    so deep, 374:13

    Soul of all things, 497:14

    stars in their c., 498:2

Calme, luxe c. et volupté, 494:n5

Calmer of thoughts, 245:17

Calumniating, envious and c. time, 201:3

Calumnies answered best with silence, 232:3

Calumnious strokes, 193:26

Calumny, envy c. hate pain, 409:4

    thou shalt not escape c., 196:15

Calvary, place called C., 39:18

Calvin oatcakes and sulphur, 380:1

Calvinistic doctrine of reprobation, 536:18

Cambridge ladies, 688:11

    Machu Picchu C. Angkor, 735:8

    ye fields of C., 267:6

Cambuscan, story of C. bold, 252:8

Cambyses', King C. vein, 177:29

Came back in dream, 758:8

    cut and c. again, 353:18

    fear c. upon me, 13:38

    forth to see again stars, 126:1

    gave a war no one c., 634:n2

    I c. I saw I conquered, 88:25

    I c. like Water, 445:18

    I c. saw and overcame, 184:8

    it all c. back to me, 769:15

    naked c. I out, 13:31

    once a World, 512:1

    out from Egypt, 8:42

    Satan c. also, 13:28

    tell them I c., 616:23

    three thousand miles and died, 485:2

    to dark tower c., 210:12

    to making of man, 533:10

    to scoff, 329:15

    upon midnight clear, 462:2

Camel, cloud in shape of a c., 197:18

    easier for c. to go, 35:37

    nine she-c. hairs aid memory, 665:4

    swallow a c., 36:4

Camelot, brief shining moment C., 745:13

    looked down to C., 454:16

    many-towered C., 454:14

    said he, 527:3

Camels are snobbish, 665:7

    rich folk on c., 469:42

Camera, I am a c., 713:17

Camerado this is no book, 491:9

Camino, con pan y vino se anda c., 793:25

Camlet, my fine c. cloak, 278:27

Camp, concentration c. universe, 732:3
  court the c. the grove, 377:25
  every c. has firmament for roof, 537:18
  father and I to c., 778:n4
  vision of style, 765:15

Campaigning weather, 700:3

Campaigns are emotional orgies, 587:15

Campaspe, Cupid and my C., 155:19

Campbells are comin', 778:15

Camped by billabong, 589:5

Campground, tenting on old c., 523:1

Camping, Fame's eternal c. ground, 492:4

Camps, terrible from c., 717:1

Campus, ceased to notice students on c., 703:6

Campus habet lumen auris acumen, 130:n3

Cam'st, how c. to be siege of this moon-calf, 224:9

Can, come fill up my c., 379:27
  cry I c. no more, 551:11
  guess if you c., 249:20
  he who c. does, 571:8
  here I sit with c. in hand, 784:4
  if poor whenever you c., 77:4
  if we c. we must, 579:18
  live as we c., 81:3
  live we how we c., 164:31
  make us do what we c., 432:40
  pass me the c. lad, 579:17
  something hope wish, 551:11
  youth replies I c., 430:4

Cana, miracles in C., 39:40

Canaan, Abram dwelled in C., 7:28

Canada, imagine C. as vast hunting preserve, 693:15
  war over few acres of snow near C., 306:8
  world-famous all over C., 763:19

Canadian frontier pattern for world, 620:2

Canal, alimentary c. with big appetite, 730:14
  took the Isthmus started the C., 576:9

Canary wine, 416:12

Cancel all our vows, 161:11
  and tear to pieces, 214:28
  half a Line, 445:25
  power to c. captivity, 187:29

Canceled, across c. skies, 683:7

Cancels, end of life c. bands, 178:14
  time c. young pain, 68:8

Cancer, we have a c. within, 769:7

Candid, be c. where we can, 301:2
  brow, 573:2
  save me from C. Friend, 371:25
  ye marshes how c., 547:6

Candidate, not Catholic c. for President, 741:1

Candied, let c. tongue lick pomp, 197:2

Candle, bell book and c., 170:1

Candle (*continued*)
  better to light one c., 654:n2
  book bell and c., 133:14
  burned c. at both ends, 684:n1
  burned on table, 680:2
  burning while sleeping, 234:2
  burns at both ends, 684:2
  feel steady c. flame, 465:7
  highest c. lights dark, 640:9
  hold c. to my shames, 180:21
  hold farthing c. to sun, 235:n4
  how far c. throws beams, 182:11
  light c. to the sun, 270:1
  lights gleaming, 611:15
  lived like c. in wind, 774:6
  not care a farthing c., 388:3
  of understanding, 30:16
  one small c. light a thousand, 240:12
  out out brief c., 216:14
  put c. under a bushel, 33:3
  scarcely fit to hold c., 304:15
  set a c. in the sun, 235:14
  this day light such a c., 138:18
  to be c. or mirror, 586:18
  to light you to bed, 788:21
  two chairs half c., 472:9
  white c. in holy place, 644:12

Candlelight, colors by c., 438:19
  dress by yellow c., 561:7
  sit in early c. of old age, 491:17

Candlelit, old at evening c., 144:2

Candles are all out, 213:17
  blessed c. of night, 182:15
  burn like fabulous roman c., 750:9
  night's c. burnt out, 176:6
  rather light c., 654:n2
  when c. out all women fair, 107:14

Candlestick, jump over c., 791:10
  put candle on a c., 33:3

Candlestick-maker, butcher baker c., 791:13

Candlesticks, seven golden c., 47:3

Candor and amicable relations, 360:12

Candy deal of courtesy, 177:10
  is dandy, 709:6
  not made of sugar c., 621:9

Cane, carrying a small c., 703:12
  wind is in the c., 690:19

Canem, cave c., 118:20

Canker, as killing as c. to rose, 253:19
  galls infants of spring, 193:26
  loathesome c., 220:21
  that benumbs, 531:19
  this c. Bolingbroke, 177:6
  worm c. and grief, 404:7

Cankers in musk-rose buds, 173:10
  of calm world, 178:25

Cannes, Hotel Magnifique at C., 645:16

Cannibal, better sleep with sober c., 486:19

Cannibals that each other eat, 205:27

Cannikin, why clink c., 464:20

Cannon come again, 599:13
  then c. and he comes, 619:2
  to right of them, 458:13

Cannon's, burst c. roar, 447:3
  mouth, 191:3

Cannons taken or saved, 510:3

Cannons (*continued*)
  thundering c. roar, 330:6

Cannon-shot, revolution more c., 599:13

Cannot, he who c. teaches, 571:8

Canoe, paddle own c., 406:4

Canon 'gainst self-slaughter, 193:5

Canopy, most excellent c. the air, 195:28
  my c. the skies, 301:9
  who spread its c., 283:4

Canst, give all thou c., 377:10

Cant, clear your mind of c., 317:30
  nothing but c., 397:22
  of criticism, 320:23
  of hypocrites the worst, 320:23
  of Not men but measures, 330:24

Cantankerous, small speech c., 80:7

Canted in this canting world, 320:23

Canter, little finishing c., 543:11

Canters, as they c. awaäy, 460:2

Cantharides, Hottentot wench under influence of c., 535:9

Cantie wi' mair, 362:7

Canting, canted in this c. world, 320:23

Cants, clear myself of c., 412:11
  which are canted, 320:23

Canvas of heavy foresail, 572:21
  sail even with c. rent, 102:23
  set your full c. flying, 83:2

Canyons, neighing c., 701:6

Cap, feather in his c., 320:26
  for c. and bells lives pay, 485:4
  riband in c. of youth, 198:25

Capability and godlike reason, 198:12
  Negative C., 417:18

Capable, all I am c. of becoming, 673:11
  and wide revenge, 207:15
  become all c. of, 412:24
  created in his mind, 639:13
  hand now warm and c., 417:3
  mathematician c. of reasoning, 75:19
  not all c. of everything, 92:12
  of being in uncertainties, 417:18
  of every wickedness, 573:14
  of greatest vices, 246:15
  of nothing but dumbshows, 196:21

Capacious salad bowl, 561:15

Capacities, growing to full human c., 748:8

Capacity, by c. is wisdom acquired, 83:8
  contribution according to c., 481:n4
  for delight and wonder, 572:19
  for taking pains, 532:2
  for taking trouble, 311:n3, 525:5
  freed c. of thought, 577:9
  functional c., 347:13
  genius is c. to see, 660:7
  of taking trouble, 413:15
  receiveth as the sea, 201:17
  to despise himself, 588:9

Cap-a-pe, 193:19

Caparisons, no c. if you please, 352:13

Cape, nobly C. Saint Vincent, 465:5
  round c. of a sudden, 465:2
  wears descent like long c., 760:14

Cape Cod, man may stand there [C.], 479:10

Caper and shake a leg, 633:7

Capers, he c. he dances, 182:31
  nimbly in lady's chamber, 165:20
  strange c., 190:16

Capes, on dark c. glisten ink wax, 699:7

Capital an' labor git t'gether, 605:19
  Belgium's c. gathered, 399:21
  bring c. into competition, 326:9
  fruit of labor, 449:9
  has its rights, 449:9
  in ascendancy system of plunder, 481:10
  labor not ask patronage of c., 394:7
  labor prior to c., 449:9
  not by savings and c., 723:12
  reasons for scarcity of c., 652:16
  sensitive ear detecting c. letters, 645:15
  ship for ocean trip, 545:3
  where kingly Death, 408:16

Capitalism, contest between c. and socialism over, 746:16
  creates social unrest, 653:25
  inherent vice of c., 622:10
  system where man exploits man, 746:14

Capitalist, more sham than c. democracy, 653:26
  way to destroy c. system, 652:11

Capitalists owners of means of production, 482:n1

Capitol, musing amidst ruins of C., 340:16
  woman betrayed the C., 284:15

Capon, belly with good c. lined, 191:3

Capons, unless minutes c., 176:24
  you cannot feed c. so, 197:6

Capri, three irreconcilable feuds in C., 712:6

Caprice and lifelong passion, 566:16
  lasts a little longer, 566:16
  of minutest event, 487:2

Capricious, gods' c. hand, 716:16

Capriciousness of summer air, 624:12

Caps, threw their c., 218:24

Capsule, finger on c. of truth, 703:10

Captain, captive good attending c. ill, 221:6
  Carpenter rose up, 674:14
  chief c. answered, 41:26
  cook and c. bold, 528:22
  Death old c., 494:10
  don't you hear c. shouting, 780:6
  his c. Christ, 172:6
  no c. do very wrong, 360:16
  O C. my C., 490:19
  of all these men of death, 272:32
  of Hampshire grenadiers, 340:15
  of his soul, 677:7
  of my soul, 557:10
  of second rank, 427:25
  of the Pinafore, 529:3
  of thine own fate, 91:n15
  right good c. too, 529:3
  should be judged as a c., 134:13
  soul the c. of life, 91:28
  walk deck my C. lies, 491:1

Captain's choleric word, 204:5
  crew of c. gig, 528:22
  troubled c. mind, 545:3

Captains and kings depart, 593:1
  courageous, 785:6
  of industry, 413:9
  thunder of the c., 15:17

Captive, carried us away c., 20:6
  good attending captain ill, 221:6
  Israel, 482:11
  jailer another kind of c., 443:22
  lead captivity c., 11:2
  of time, 679:18
  today unbind c., 430:2
  weak minds led c., 260:27

Captivity, home after years in c., 4:4
  is Consciousness, 512:9
  lead c. captive, 11:2
  power to cancel his c., 187:29
  spent many years in c., 4:4

Capture of men by women, 463:n1

Captured, faced enslavement if c., 522:13

Capulet, I'll no longer be a C., 175:1

Car, drive the rapid c., 335:23
  gilded c. of day, 252:19
  radio bleats, 743:6
  rattling o'er stony street, 399:22

Caravan, innumerable c. which moves, 411:4
  put up your c., 611:19

Caravanserai, battered C., 445:11

Carcass fit for hounds, 188:4
  honey in the c. of the lion, 11:11
  of leopard, 702:4
  where c. is eagles gather, 36:9

Carcasses bleed at sight of murderer, 132:n1

Card, clear conscience is sure c., 155:12
  he's a sure c., 274:21
  insipid as queen on c., 459:30
  master to those below, 680:17
  speak by the c., 199:6

Cardozos, can't all have Brandeises C., 713:16

Cards, cheat at c. genteelly, 316:23
  dreaded c. foretell, 720:17
  luck not holding best c., 536:14
  never play c. with man named Doc, 726:6
  nothing but pack of c., 518:12
  patience and shuffle c., 150:43
  played c. for kisses, 155:19
  thrust ivrybody but cut c., 603:6
  world of c., 680:17

Care a farthing candle, 388:3
  age full of c., 776:7
  and not to care, 669:14
  begone dull C., 777:12
  careless with artful c., 291:16
  cast away c., 149:29, 228:1
  dark C. sits enthroned, 96:13
  deliberation and public c., 257:7
  driveth away sleep, 32:5
  feeling c. of law, 155:3
  fig for c. fig for woe, 140:14
  for who shall have borne battle, 450:11
  full of c. no time, 611:10

Care (*continued*)
  golden c., 184:9
  happy whose wish and c., 298:5
  housewife ply evening c., 322:6
  I c. for nobody, 338:19
  I don't c. one straw, 86:7
  I don't c. what they do, 590:7
  I prayed and did God C., 512:7
  I sae weary fu' o' c., 362:8
  I shall not c., 655:2
  insensate c. of mortals, 89:n10
  irks c. the crop-full bird, 467:7
  Jimmie crack corn I don't c., 780:2
  keeps his watch, 175:17
  killed a cat, 187:11
  lose it that buy it with much c., 179:16
  nor c. beyond today, 321:15
  nor for itself hath c., 358:2
  not who sees your back, 177:23
  nought but c. on ev'ry han', 361:24
  of discipline is love, 30:27
  of life and happiness, 344:11
  of the poor, 278:15
  of this world, 35:8
  punch with c., 520:8
  raveled sleave of c., 214:6
  Reason is past c., 222:13
  rest that knows no c., 90:5
  sat on his faded cheek, 256:17
  so wan with c., 176:22
  sought it with c., 519:24
  sounds take c. of themselves, 518:1
  taken better c. of myself, 651:6
  things past redress past c., 171:18
  tiresome verse-reciter C., 409:22
  weep away life of c., 406:15
  what boots it with incessant c., 253:20
  what c. I how fair she be, 240:1
  what is life if full of c., 611:10
  where c. lodges sleep never lie, 175:17
  windy side of c., 186:24
  woman who did not c., 592:23
  wrinkled C. derides, 251:9
  your sex's earliest latest c., 318:5

Care-charmer Sleep, 160:21

Cared as much as Bird, 512:7
  not to be at all, 256:25

Career, awe man from c. of his humor, 186:31
  close military c. fade away, 642:5
  my c. my brilliant c., 636:14
  poetry not c., 673:1
  public life crown of c., 628:3
  this is our c., 674:19
  what they call fine c., 728:4

Careful, be c. what you do, 637:10
  ivry man equal if isn't c., 603:15
  not c. what they mean, 167:11
  o' widders, 468:25
  so c. of type, 457:19
  surgeons must be c., 511:11

Carefulness bringeth age, 32:4

Careless, be not c. in deeds, 111:24
  desolation, 191:20
  ease from tree to tree, 295:17
  first fine c. rapture, 465:4
  I tasted c. then, 512:1

Cast (*continued*)
longing eye on offices, 344:3
lots upon my vesture, 16:16
me not off in the time of old age, 17:40
me off discourteously, 776:10
mine eyes and see, 241:20
off his friends, 330:13
off works of darkness, 42:23
one longing look, 322:19
one's eyes so low, 210:27
over Edom will I c. out my shoe, 17:31
pale c. of thought, 196:10
pearls before swine, 34:5
set exact wealth at one c., 178:19
set my life upon c., 166:18
thy bread upon the waters, 24:23
time to c. away stones, 23:32
tree is c. into the fire, 32:32
unprofitable servant into darkness, 36:16
why art thou c. down, 17:12
wilt c. forth no more, 580:7
Caste, Brahmin c. of New England, 447:1
regard for thine own c. duty, 84:6
Castest, why c. thou off my soul, 18:9
Casteth, perfect love c. out fear, 46:37
Castilian, choose what becomes C., 419:8
Casting body's vest aside, 268:19
dim religious light, 252:10
Cast-iron back with hinge, 511:4
Castle, bores through his c. wall, 172:1
contentions like bars of c., 21:40
Doubting C., 272:23
hath pleasant seat, 213:4
Howth C. and Environs, 647:18
man's house his c., 152:3
splendor falls on c. walls, 456:11
stand in window of c., 89:n9
village belongs to C., 651:20
Castled crag of Drachenfels, 400:1
Castlereagh, mask like C., 407:25
Castle's strength will laugh, 216:12
Castles, building c. in Spain, 132:23
Castrates, divine patriarch c. women, 758:21
Casts, shadow that it c., 377:14
to write a living line, 232:23
Casual creeds, 498:10
flocks of pigeons, 638:26
Casualties, sixties made so many c., 770:5
Cat and fiddle, 789:9
bell the c., 59:11, 127:19
bought crooked c., 791:11
calico c. replied Mee-ow, 559:22
care killed a c., 187:11
Cat's a c. Rolet a knave, 280:9
Cheshire C. vanished slowly, 517:17
consider my C. Jeoffrey, 325:17
differences between c. and lie, 527:9
dog pipe or two, 580:11
endow college or c., 300:22
fog comes on c. feet, 634:5
God invented giraffe elephant c., 645:3

Cat (*continued*)
had seven kits, 788:14
had Tiberius been c., 500:4
harmless necessary c., 181:13
has only nine lives, 527:9
in gloves catches no mice, 310:5
in the hat, 715:3
kitten eventually becomes a C., 709:13
mad if they behold a c., 181:12
made a c. laugh, 419:6
may look on king, 142:18
melancholy as gib c., 176:30
mew and dog have day, 199:18
nine lives like a c., 142:8
not room enough to swing c., 325:3
on hot bakestone, 272:8
on hot tin roof, 272:n4
on tin roof, 731:1
owest c. no perfume, 210:6
pastime to c. more than she to me, 146:3
poor c. i' the adage, 213:9
that sits on hot stove-lid, 527:27
versus bird old as time, 706:9
walked by himself, 593:11
watch mouse, 290:17
who shall bell the c., 59:11
worried the c., 792:24
yellow c. black c. catches mice good c., 712:17
Catalogue, in c. ye go for men, 214:21
no reading more fascinating than c., 550:4
of things necessary, 279:28
read c. than nothing, 626:21
Cataract, faint idea of c., 425:16
leaps in glory, 456:11
sounding c. haunted me, 373:4
Cataracts and hurricanoes, 209:24
Catastrophe, education and c., 601:14
of old comedy, 209:4
tickle your c., 183:29
Catastrophes, unparalleled c., 636:8
Catbird, sitting in c. seat, 690:16
Catch a falling star, 228:5
another Antony, 218:22
as catch can, 324:7
bargain c. cold and starve, 219:22
Christ with worm, 742:11
claws that c., 518:15
conscience of the king, 196:8
earth's heedless sons, 694:1
hard to c. and conquer, 509:10
him once upon hip, 180:4
I have to c. them, 747:8
nets to c. the wind, 237:20
only one c. Catch-22, 752:12
perdition c. my soul, 206:27
springes to c. woodcocks, 194:4
the manners living, 301:2
the nearest way, 212:28
up with advanced countries, 610:3
when pleasure can be had c. it, 316:33
with his surcease success, 213:5
you will never c. up, 600:10
Catch-22, some catch that C., 752:12
Catched, swallow gudgeons ere they're c., 58:n8

Catcher in the rye, 747:8
Catches, slow man c. up with swift, 53:15
Catching, poverty's c., 281:17
Catchwords, man lives by c., 560:15
Catechism, so ends my c., 178:33
Catechist, something of Shorter-C., 557:7
Categorical imperative, 326:12
order c., 529:12
Categories, gripes fall into two c., 745:4
Caterpillar, I don't see said C., 517:8
Caterpillars of the commonwealth, 171:17
Caters for the sparrow, 190:10
Catharsis, tragedy a c., 78:31
Cathay, cycle of C., 456:1
Cathedral, after great c. gong, 598:11
in vast c. leave him, 458:8
mankind inspired made c., 560:11
needs more than opinion to erect c., 420:8
Tunes, 511:21
uplifting thoughts in bathrooms than c., 693:12
Cathedrals, cars equivalent of Gothic c., 738:4
Cather, Willas c., 697:7
Catholic, candidate who happens also to be C., 741:1
C.O., 742:22
Church understands enthusiasts, 425:8
holy C. Church, 48:25
judges neither C. nor agnostic, 646:11
not C. candidate for President, 741:1
Catholicism minus Christianity, 505:8
Catholics and Communists, 713:12
they came for C., 684:19
Catiline, how long C., 87:6
prodigal of own possessions, 91:22
Cato, like C. give Senate laws, 302:11
vanquished had C., 105:19
Cat's a cat and Rolet a knave, 280:9
pull chestnuts with c. paw, 268:26
run away with string, 792:20
what c. averse to fish, 321:20
Cats, all c. gray when candles out, 107:n8
and monkeys monkeys and cats, 548:9
count c. in Zanzibar, 478:34
do c. eat bats, 517:3
each sack had seven c., 788:14
fought dogs killed c., 464:18
have two holes in coat, 342:20
nation of c. wild and tame, 135:22
rain c. and dogs, 778:10
those who'll play with c., 149:32
Catsup, shake and shake c. bottle, 718:12
Cattle beneath shadow of oak, 332:18
call c. home, 484:9
cursed above all c., 6:23
die as c., 687:2
if c. and horses had hands, 60:5
lowly c. shed, 479:19

Cattle *(continued)*
  men the c. of God, 3:15
  upon a thousand hills, 17:19
  would draw gods like cattle, 60:5
Catullus be resolved and firm, 90:21
  worst of all poets, 91:3
  you should cease folly, 90:20
Caucasus, thinking on frosty C., 171:3
Caught, ain't never c. a rabbit, 765:7
  at God's skirts, 464:16
  God c. his eye, 697:6
  hanging around till you've c. on,
    625:18
  him yes I held him, 548:21
  his clear accents, 464:23
  in that sensual music, 597:7
  like beast at bay, 680:7
  man of honor regrets even if not c.,
    642:22
  morning's minion, 550:20
  mother came and c. her, 790:15
  my heavenly jewel, 156:6
  our youth, 663:4
  she c. him by his garment, 8:6
  trout c. with tickling, 202:16
  with his sweet perfections c., 163:4
Cauldron, fire burn c. bubble, 215:13
Cauliflower cabbage with college edu-
    cation, 527:8
Causa latet vis notissima, 101:*n*16
Causation, law of c., 522:16
Cause, armor of righteous c., 582:2
  bad c. bad means, 340:25
  be c. strong or weak, 485:7
  beauty of good old c., 374:14
  calledst me dog before c., 181:10
  common c. decays, 72:1
  common c. to save Union, 449:1
  died in virtue's c., 167:9
  effect defective comes by c., 195:13
  effect whose c. is God, 335:14
  evolution not c. but law, 537:5
  final c. produces motion, 77:22
  full c. of weeping, 209:23
  Germany the c. of Hitler, 666:3
  good old c. is gone, 374:14
  Great First C., 335:24
  griefs we c. ourselves, 65:19
  hear me for my c., 188:24
  hidden but result well known,
    101:23
  idea of oneself as c., 278:3
  if any man show just c., 50:2
  if world astray c. is in you, 126:15
  is there any c. in nature, 210:15
  it is just, 391:3
  Jesus found spiritual c., 495:20
  laws or kings c. or cure, 314:15
  little grace my c., 205:22
  no warrants but upon probable c.,
    346:13
  not a field but a c., 341:2
  not be judge in own c., 99:*n*14
  not jealous for the c., 207:17
  nothing comes without c., 308:21
  obstinacy in bad c., 248:8, 320:12
  of Freedom cause of God, 366:12
  of this effect, 195:13
  or men of Emerald Isle, 354:1
  perseverance in good c., 320:12

Cause *(continued)*
  produces more than one effect,
    493:3
  rebel without a c., 736:3
  report me and my c., 199:25
  sea of C. and Theory, 619:10
  set c. above renown, 586:12
  support Caledonia's c., 364:4
  tenacious of purpose in rightful c.,
    96:15
  try c. condemn to death, 517:6
  turn to c. of policy, 184:22
  water-colors to impaint c., 178:31
  what in effect already in c., 577:3
  when just c. reaches flood tide,
    577:8
  wherein tongue confuted, 250:11
  wit in other men, 183:12
  you c. what you abuse, 284:7
  Zeus first c., 63:17
Caused the widow's heart to sing,
    14:42
Causes célèbres, 294:1
  defend c. which were unpopular,
    724:7
  fight for lost c., 672:19
  flowers as in c. sleep, 246:4
  from amorous c. springs, 299:9
  great c. on move, 620:19
  happy man who could search out c.,
    92:30
  hidden c. of things, 227:16
  home of lost c., 499:10
  investigation of hidden c., 148:13
  of destruction, 319:9
  which impel separation, 343:2
  why and wherefore, 185:25
Causeway, law is a c., 753:9
Caution in refusing benefits, 278:14
  scars of others teach c., 114:3
  upward look of c., 624:19
Cautious people never bring reform,
    491:20
  politic c. and meticulous, 667:17
  seldom err, 61:6
  statistical Christ, 553:2
Cavalry of Woe, 511:13
Cave, courts thee in some pleasant c.,
    95:20
  error correct c., 749:17
  Idols of the C., 158:13
  shadows on opposite wall of c.,
    75:17
  sky will c. in on him, 683:16
  Stygian c. forlorn, 251:6
  vacant interlunar c., 261:8
Cave ab homine unius libri, 118:19
  canem, 118:20
Caveat emptor, 118:21
Cavern, mossy c., 416:12
  Pan's c., 599:17
Caverns, in c. all alone, 749:17
  measureless to man, 382:19
  sand-strewn c. cool and deep, 497:7
  twice ten thousand c., 417:8
Caves, beetles in c., 724:16
  dark unfathomed c., 322:13
  of ice, 382:23, 382:25
Caviar to the general, 196:1
Cavil on ninth part of hair, 178:6

Cawdor, Glamis thou art and C.,
    212:28
  I am Thane of C., 212:23
  shall sleep no more, 214:7
Cease and then again begin, 499:20
  ask whether happy c. to be, 440:6
  Byron's struggle c., 497:15
  Catullus you should c. folly, 90:20
  day and night shall not c., 7:22
  efforts to find where last rose lin-
    gers, 96:4
  fears that I may c., 417:9
  from mental fight, 359:17
  from thine own wisdom, 22:17
  long contention c., 500:2
  man I am c. to be, 458:18
  not c. from exploration, 672:6
  poor shall never c., 10:19
  sing or c. to sing, 303:11
  the wicked c. from troubling, 13:36
  time c. and midnight never come,
    162:22
  to ask what morrow will bring,
    95:24
  to be free for religion, 683:5
  upon the midnight, 415:16
  weeping without c., 554:3
  ye from man, 25:32
Ceased, God created woman boredom
    c., 553:2
  Pnin c. to notice students, 703:6
  this parrot has c. to be, 775:5
  when Lucy c. to be, 373:19
Ceaseless devouring of weak by
    strong, 493:8
  thoughts of roaming, 282:11
  turns with c. pain, 328:7
Ceases, forbearance c. to be virtue,
    330:21
  happiness c. like dream, 247:10
  to be free for irreligion, 683:5
Ceasing, O swiftness never c., 156:14
  pray without c., 45:8
Cedant arma togae, 88:*n*2
Cedar, as c. tall and slender, 348:12
  grow like a c. in Lebanon, 18:17
  lordly c. green with boughs, 563:10
Cedars of Lebanon, 19:5
  roots of c. of Lebanon, 632:16
Cedarwood, sandalwood c., 633:18
Cefalu, practiced black art in C.,
    712:6
Ceiling, Gary looked at c. hesitated,
    753:4
Célébrait, Ronsard me c., 144:*n*2
Celebrate, I c. myself, 488:16
  not c. funeral with weeping, 84:17
Celebrated cultivated Duke of Plaza
    Toro, 531:16
  Savior's birth c., 192:29
Celebrates pale Hecate's offerings,
    213:21
Célèbres, causes c., 294:1
Celebrities, congress of c., 521:4
Celebrity person known for well-
    knowness, 735:16
Celeriter, sat c. fieri satis bene, 98:*n*14
Celerity never more admired, 217:23
Celestial, apparelled in c. light, 375:3
  ennui of apartments, 639:22

Changed (*continued*)
we have c. all that, 269:9
we shall be c., 43:27
whole world have been c., 270:22
ye too c. ye hills, 499:15
Changeful mind of mortals, 64:16
presuming on c. potency, 201:8
Changes, agonies one of my c. of garments, 489:19
cause great c. in the world, 339:1
control our being, 454:22
follow c. of the moon, 206:33
God c. and man and form, 534:19
God c. not people until they change,
116:11
monthly c. in circled orb, 175:7
sky c. when wives, 192:4
woman often c., 94:n1
world's a scene of c., 266:19
Changeth, old order c., 459:26
sweareth to his own hurt and c.
not, 16:5
Changin', times they are a-c., 771:7
Changing, borrow every c. shape,
667:21
scenes of life, 285:3
shallow c. woman, 166:9
stress on not c. mind, 626:12
Chankly Bore, 472:13
Channel, brush c. with sleeve, 521:3
butting through the C., 634:1
crossing C. and tossing, 530:15
man merely c. for food, 134:15
Chant, do use to c. it, 202:12
how can ye c., 362:8
none chanted c. of welcome, 490:18
Chanted, none c. chant of welcome,
490:18
Chanticleer, lungs crow like c., 190:24
Chanting, exaltation in c. of Muses,
68:7
faint hymns to moon, 172:18
Chants doleful hymn, 170:20
Chaos and old Night, 256:13
beauty dead black c., 165:16
bounded by primeval c., 460:n1
breeds life, 535:21
freedom of action without freed
thought c., 577:9
is come again, 206:27
of the sun, 638:26
of thought and passion, 301:13
our policy against c., 642:7
rough unordered mass, 101:19
this is why there is c., 80:15
thy dread empire C., 304:2
what a c. is man, 271:7
Chaos-like together crushed, 299:21
Chapel, afternoon in secluded c.,
672:5
Devil builds c. there, 285:14
Devil would build c., 138:10
God's greenwood c., 637:n3
Chapels had been churches, 179:27
legend of green c., 737:13
Chapfallen, quite c., 199:8
Chaplain, Blue Beard's c., 468:27
Chapman, heard C. speak out loud
and bold, 413:24
Chapmen, you do as c. do, 201:6

Chapmen's, not uttered by c. tongues,
168:22
Chaps, Biography is about C., 627:17
with couple o' guns, 654:13
Chapter, autobiographies begin C.
Two, 615:16
of accidents very long, 305:15
of knowledge very short, 305:15
said he could repeat c., 317:4
say in first c. rifle hanging on wall,
582:n4
write the next c., 723:16
Chapters in art of living, 493:22
of lives to natural end, 557:19
these thirty c., 6:2
Character, accommodatin c., 521:14
adopt c. of octopus, 59:23
analysis of c. highest entertainment,
715:5
bearing on excellence of c., 78:8
best way to define c., 545:5
bird of bad moral c., 310:24
December 1910 human c. changed,
650:15
education for c., 492:15
energy of c., 366:4
family stamped c. on child, 629:1
find well-drawn c., 526:14
formed in world's torrent, 349:20
give action its c., 74:4
good c. remembered, 3:16
habits and manners, 503:5
higher than intellect, 431:8
his c. arbiter of everyone's fortune,
92:n2
liberal arts humanizes c., 102:6
lies in own hands, 760:12
limitations of own c., 537:10
man that makes c., 296:4
man's c. is his fate, 62:22
men of contrary c., 61:5
never mind the c., 468:33
of mistress from dress of maids,
114:1
of perfection, 500:13
poetical c., 418:9
power of Latin in c., 500:7
reap a c., 781:6
simplicity of c., 537:9
Characteristics, have certain mental c.,
574:12
of popular politician, 73:1
of vigorous mind, 313:25
Characterless, mighty states c., 200:22
Characters, attributes c. of living creature, 487:13
fashioning our c. wrong, 545:13
high c. cries one, 262:4
knowledge of c. of rulers, 337:13
most women have no c., 300:13
not in calm that great c. are formed,
347:8
of hell to trace, 323:7
six c. in search of author, 604:4
Charge Chester charge, 378:15
compulsive ardor gives c., 197:32
Cromwell I c. thee, 225:20
give his angels c. over thee, 18:16
give lie to slander c., 398:9
lunatics taken c. of asylum, 643:16

Charge (*continued*)
not soul save to its ability, 117:3
once more be dumb, 500:3
prepared lawyers met, 297:21
such is the c., 74:14
with all thy chivalry, 389:4
within the bosom, 511:13
Charged, language c. with meaning,
660:5
troops of error, 248:1
Charger, John Baptist's head in c.,
35:15
Charges, die to save c., 234:23
Chariest maid prodigal enough,
193:26
Charing Cross, Heaven and C., 581:12
went out to C. to see Harrison
hanged, 279:3
Chariot, appeared a c. of fire, 13:4
flying-c. through air, 335:23
maketh clouds his c., 19:3
of fire, 359:17
of Israel, 13:5
swing low sweet c., 794:14
that bears Human Soul, 514:2
Time's winged c., 268:15
why is his c. so long in coming,
11:6
Chariots, why tarry the wheels of his
c., 11:6
Charisma inner determination inner
restraint, 590:4
Charismatic leader gains authority,
590:4
Charitable, intents wicked or c.,
194:10
men's c. speeches, 160:12
Charite, of saynte c., 775:12
Charities of kiss or smile, 385:4
Charity, affecting c. and devotion,
80:12
and have not c., 43:13
anticipate c. by preventing poverty,
122:8
beareth all things, 43:15
begins at home, 85:15, 248:18
believeth all things, 43:15
come out of c., 775:n5
crawling for c., 80:13
creates multitude of sins, 567:13
degrades, 436:20
edifieth, 43:4
endureth all things, 43:15
envieth not, 43:14
for all, 450:11
greatest is c., 43:16
hopeth all things, 43:15
I am in c. with world, 290:3
in all things c., 266:10
in c. no excess, 159:14
in c. to all mankind, 369:2
in love and c. with neighbors, 49:14
indiscriminate c., 525:14
is kind, 43:14
justice not c. wanting in world,
365:32
little earth for c., 226:1
love friendship c., 201:3
never faileth, 43:15
not puffed up, 43:14

Charity (*continued*)
 now abideth c., 43:16
 of saynte c., 775:12
 pity gave ere c. began, 329:13
 rarity of Christian c., 423:10
 scrimped and iced, 553:20
 shall cover multitude of sins, 46:26
 suffereth long, 43:14
 towards each other, 339:11
 towards others, 248:18
 vaunteth not, 43:14
 where c. neither fear nor ignorance,
  123:9
Charity's golden ladder, 122:8
Charlemagne, world-transforming C.,
 599:5
Charles, gentlehearted C., 387:*n*1
 immense empire of C. the Fifth,
  364:*n*5
 navy of C. the Second, 425:20
 successors of C. the Fifth, 340:9
 the First his Cromwell, 339:5
Charles's, King C. head, 470:29
Charley's, I am C. aunt from Brazil,
 571:31
Charlie is my darling, 368:5
 live and die wi' C., 372:14
 o'er the water to C., 372:14
Charlie Brown, good man C., 751:9
Charlotte true friend good writer,
 703:17
 went on cutting bread and butter,
  463:21
Charm ache with air, 187:8
 by thought supplied, 373:4
 in melancholy, 367:5
 music oft hath such a c., 204:23
 northern c., 742:8
 object in possession seldom retains
  c., 110:1
 of all the Muses, 460:7
 of earliest birds, 258:21
 one native c., 329:20
 quality in others, 493:24
 simplicity and c., 95:9
 smiling at good mouth, 659:10
 some have c. for none, 581:23
 some women c. all, 581:23
 strengthen and teach, 441:22
 touching all the muses' c., 89:11
 wasted on sky, 429:15
 what c. soothe melancholy, 328:29
 witch hath power to c., 192:29
 without c. no literature, 594:14
Charmed alike tilt-yard and bower,
 396:26
 bear a c. life, 216:18
 it with smiles and soap, 519:24
 magic casements, 415:17
 water burnt alway, 381:21
 with foolish whistlings, 267:9
Charmer, were t'other dear c. away,
 297:20
Charmers, will not hearken to voice of
 c., 17:29
Charmian is this well done, 218:21
Charming, be c. with nothing, 560:7
 evening criminal's friend, 494:8
 form of government, 75:24
 friendly and c. relationship, 138:12

Charming (*continued*)
 how c. divine philosophy, 253:3
 left his voice, 259:23
 never so wisely, 17:29
 to totter into vogue, 323:22
Charm's, peace the c. wound up,
 212:15
Charms, Aphrodite with intricate c.,
 56:*n*5
 by accepting, 300:18
 do not all c. fly, 414:18
 endearing young c., 391:13
 freedom has thousand c., 334:3
 icy arms hold c., 693:6
 music has c. to soothe, 291:7
 O Solitude where are c., 334:20
 or ear or sight, 383:10
 other maids' surpass, 353:11
 power obtained by c., 365:31
 Sabina has thousand c., 778:7
Charon could not prevent me, 67:24
Charter, large a c. as wind, 190:27
 this was c. of land, 308:12
Chartered libertine, 184:22
Charybdis, I fall into C., 181:11
 implacable C. guards left, 181:*n*2
 on starboard beam C., 181:*n*2
Chase, blessed in luck of c., 787:14
 glowing hours, 399:22
 had a beast in view, 276:22
 lead a wild-goose c., 149:26
 my gloom away, 367:5
 panting syllable, 334:17
 piteous c., 190:8
 the sport of kings, 295:1
 to c. white whale, 486:23
 unhurrying c., 581:5
 when heated in the c., 285:4
 writing make us c. the writer,
  773:20
Chased shouting wind along, 751:3
Chassis, state o' c., 654:11
Chaste and fair, 231:21
 as ice, 196:15
 as the icicle, 219:12
 as unsunned snow, 219:25
 early bright transient c., 277:*n*1
 fair c. unexpressive she, 191:6
 modest and commonly c., 404:21
 nunnery of thy c. breast, 267:14
 to her husband, 300:14
 was she not c., 107:2
Chasten, power to c. and subdue,
 373:5
Chasteneth, he that loveth c. him,
 21:17
 whom the Lord loveth he c., 45:40
Chastening in hour of pride, 448:14
Chastise, I will c. with scorpions,
 12:29
Chastised, father hath c. you, 12:29
 having been a little c., 30:23
Chastity, give me c. but not now,
 114:23
 my brother Chastity, 253:2
 of honor, 332:14
 scepticism c. of intellect, 588:17
Chat, before we have our c., 519:4
Chat, la patte du c., 268:*n*7
Châteaux, O seasons O c., 565:19

Chatter against bird of Zeus, 63:30
 harebrained c., 435:17
 insignificant c. of world, 475:14
 of transcendental kind, 529:17
 those who have learned art c., 63:30
Chattering voltage, 679:14
Chatterley, between C. ban and Beatles' LP, 750:13
Chatterton marvelous boy, 374:9
Chaucer, Dan C. first warbler, 454:12
 nigh to learned C., 240:13
 not lodge thee by C., 232:18
 well of English, 153:19
 whose sweet breath, 454:12
Chaucer's, corruption since C. days,
 237:4
Chaud comme l'enfer, 354:*n*2
Chaudron, parole humaine comme un
 c. fêlé, 496:*n*3
Chavender or Chub, 245:22
Cheap defense of nations, 332:13
 electrical energy too c. to meter,
  695:21
 flesh and blood so c., 423:8
 good counsel c., 235:5
 greet c. holde at litel prys, 131:6
 hold c. the strain, 467:8
 how potent c. music is, 700:17
 ill ware is never c., 244:5
 life not c. but sacred, 432:39
 man's life c. as beast's, 209:21
 never buy because c., 345:5
 sitting as standing, 290:2
 sleep a c. pleasure, 151:15
 sold c. what is most dear, 221:26
 tin trays, 634:1
 what we obtain too c., 340:22
Cheaper than keep cow, 525:9
Cheapest, man richest whose pleasures
 c., 477:5
Cheat at cards genteelly, 316:23
 came to c. them, 369:7
 for sake of beauty, 631:4
 life 'tis all a c., 273:16
 out of love c. others, 613:1
 pleasure as great as to c., 263:26
 sweet c. gone, 617:2
 undertaken to c. me, 411:11
Cheated, illusion by which c., 613:1
 pleasure of being c., 263:26
Cheater, old bald c. Time, 232:1
Cheating, winning games without c.,
 705:5
Check, care's c. and curb, 270:2
 judicial power a c., 338:7
 rod to c. the erring, 376:3
Checked, be c. for silence, 203:8
Checkerboard of Nights and Days,
 445:23
Checkered shade, 251:15
Checkers, kids loved the dog C.,
 733:11
Checks, as if C. given, 513:15
 handed in his c., 531:25
Cheek, care sat on his faded c., 256:17
 dancing c. to c., 666:10
 feed on her damask c., 202:14
 he that loves a rosy c., 246:9
 I the blow and c., 494:7
 iron tears down Pluto's c., 252:7

Cheek (*continued*)
Jesus of twice-turned c., 711:3
language in her eye her c., 201:10
leans her c. upon her hand, 174:28
of tan, 443:5
she hangs on c. of night, 174:23
that I might touch that c., 174:28
tongue not far from Kilmer c.,
  666:23
turn the other c., 33:7
warm c. and rising bosom, 323:1
withered c. tresses gray, 377:19
yellow c. white beard, 183:19
Cheekbone, short a c. and ear, 492:*n*5
Cheeks, blood spoke in her c., 230:16
blow winds and crack c., 209:24
crimson in lips and c., 176:17
make pale my c. with care, 240:1
of sorry grain, 253:10
rosy lips and c., 222:2
stain my man's c., 209:22
tears on her c., 29:1
wind on our c., 477:7
Cheer, al his c. as in his herte, 130:21
at Christmas make good c., 144:6
be of good c., 35:19, 40:35
but not inebriate, 296:24, 335:3
is best physician, 64:6
our weary hearts, 523:1
piped with merry c., 356:4
sing song of c. again, 685:12
small c. and great welcome, 166:25
three cheers one c. more, 529:4
unite with a c., 340:17
up comrades they come, 492:6
Cheered, Admiral c. them holding out
  hope, 134:7
ship was c., 380:29
up with ends of verse, 263:16
Cheerer of spirits, 245:17
Cheerful, be c. while you are alive,
  3:10
giver, 44:7
godliness, 374:20
looking as c. as any man could do,
  279:3
man of c. yesterdays, 377:2
merry heart maketh a c. countenance, 21:25
warm precincts of c. day, 322:19
ways of men cut off, 257:24
Cheerfully, do evil so c., 271:10
he seems to grin, 517:5
part with life c., 111:12
Cheerfulness always breaking in,
  318:9
keeps daylight in mind, 293:6
Cheering, public men nor c. crowds,
  596:11
Cheerless over hills of gray, 443:13
Cheerly rouse the slumbering morn,
  251:12
Cheers, adorns and c. our way, 328:5
responding to the c., 588:24
silence no worse than c., 579:3
tar's labor, 404:5
three c. one cheer more, 529:4
two c. for Democracy, 636:13
Cheese, apple pie and c., 559:17

Cheese (*continued*)
country with 265 different kinds of
  c., 678:15
dreamed of toasted c., 561:5
moon made of green c., 142:24
Cheeses, ate c. out of vats, 464:18
Cheevy, Miniver C., 608:3
Chef d'oeuvre, les rendements de
  contes ne font jamais c., 765:*n*1
Chemical barrage against life, 721:14
personalities like c. contact, 628:9
Chemist fiddler and buffoon, 274:11
Chemistry, microscopy c. mathematics, 681:13
Cherchez la femme, 427:*n*3
Cherish, achieve and c. peace, 450:11
those hearts that hate thee, 225:21
to love and to c., 50:4
to love c. and obey, 50:12
Cherished, Country c. in hearts,
  460:14
memory of loved and lost, 450:9
Cherishes love of comfort, 61:21
Cherith, dwelt by the brook C., 12:31
Cherries fairly do enclose, 226:19
grow which none may buy, 226:18
Cherry, grew like a double c., 173:19
hung with snow, 578:19
I did cut c., 336:*n*7
now hung with bloom, 578:18
ripe I cry, 241:1
sap make c. red, 664:20
violence is as American as c. pie,
  772:12
Cherry-isle, there's land or c., 241:1
Cherry-ripe themselves do cry, 226:18
Cherub, he rode upon a c., 16:8
Cherubims east of the garden, 7:1
Cherubin, heaven's c. horsed, 213:7
young and rose-lipped c., 207:27
Cherubin's, fyr-reed c. face, 130:6
Cherubins, young-eyed c., 182:8
Ches, to her son she c., 775:15
Cheshire Cat vanished slowly, 517:17
Chess board is the world, 505:6
pieces phenomena of universe,
  505:6
Chest, as if c. a mortar, 486:25
Dead Man's C., 561:1
if it is well with your c., 97:14
of drawers by day, 329:19
voice of iron c. of brass, 94:11
Chester, charge C. charge, 378:15
Chestnut, O c. tree, 598:2
roast c. happiness, 652:2
spreading c. tree, 441:3
Chestnuts, pull c. out of fire, 268:26
sailor's wife had c., 212:12
Chevalier, the young C., 368:5
Chew cud and are silent, 332:18
Chewed, few books to be c., 160:8
Cheweth, whatsoever c. the cud, 9:21
Chewing food of fancy, 192:7
little bits of string, 609:2
Cheyenne, I'm a-leavin' C., 786:3
Chic, radical C. only radical in style,
  764:3
Chicago at northwest gates, 607:17
responsible for Tribune, 666:3

Chicken, champagne and c. at last,
  304:3
in pot every Sunday, 154:20
prayer of hawk not get c., 784:27
she's no c., 290:6
some c. some neck, 621:10
Chickens, all my pretty c., 215:29
as hen gathereth c., 36:6
beside white c., 654:1
coming home to roost, 755:10
count c. before hatched, 58:16
literature or c., 703:11
quit quarrelling over food, 633:8
Chide, fall out and c. and fight, 294:8
God for countenance, 191:28
me for loving armchair, 480:9
trumpets 'gan to c., 414:22
Chides, at fifty c. delay, 296:12
Chiding, better a little c., 183:8
Chief, a c. a rod, 301:18
defect of Henry King, 609:2
good and market, 198:12
hail to the C., 378:21
his c. beside, 464:10
Justice was rich quiet, 425:9
Magistrate hate struck down C.,
  755:10
nourisher in life's feast, 214:6
of the Army, 371:6
sinners of whom I am c., 45:11
Chiefest treasure, 608:16
Chief's, vain the c. pride, 303:13
Chiefs, our c. are killed, 541:2
Chieftain Iffucan of Azcan, 638:27
I'm a tribal c., 745:18
Child's amang you takin' notes,
  363:15
Child, a simple c., 372:17
again just for tonight, 516:13
always say what's true, 561:8
any c. at any stage, 738:11
anything we change in c., 628:13
as yet a c., 302:8
beautiful a faery's c., 417:5
became part of c. who went forth,
  491:3
behold the c., 301:15
better is a poor and wise c., 24:1
burnt c. fire dreadeth, 142:6
christom c., 184:30
cry of c. by roadway, 595:5
decision to bear or beget c., 719:5
do not throw book, 608:16
draws inscrutable house, 729:8
Duty's faithful c., 422:6
Eros Zeus's c., 68:17
every c. may joy to hear, 356:5
family stamped character on c.,
  629:1
fast fold thy c., 551:10
foster-c. of silence, 415:20
get with c. mandrake root, 228:5
give a little love to c., 487:25
great with c. longing for prunes,
  203:31
hasn't got anything on c. said,
  437:9
he became a little c., 356:7
heard one calling C., 243:18
Heaven-born c., 250:20

Child (*continued*)

her innocence a c., 275:6
here a little c. I stand, 241:21
I spake as a c., 43:16
I was a c., 453:8
idiotic c., 583:5
if you strike a c., 571:10
in simplicity a c., 300:28
in the name of this C., 49:21
is father of the man, 374:7
is known by his doings, 22:3
Jesus Christ her little c., 479:19
keeps secret well, 428:2
lie down like tired c., 406:15
life like froward c., 273:2
like three years' c., 380:28
little c. shall lead them, 26:11
look upon a little c., 312:15
lost in unreality, 744:1
Magus Zoroaster my dead c.,
    406:16
make c. able man, 145:16
meet nurse for poetic c., 378:2
Monday's c. fair of face, 791:3
more hideous in a c., 209:10
my c.-wife, 470:40
ne'er spend fury on c., 165:4
of Calamity, 526:8
of my right hand, 232:10
of our grandmother Eve, 168:19
of pure unclouded brow, 518:13
of scorn, 608:3
old man twice a c., 195:32
on a cloud I saw a c., 356:4
painted c. of dirt, 302:15
role to be born, 588:23
room of absent c., 170:4
Rowland to dark tower, 210:12
said What is the grass, 488:19
saving little c., 536:13
seemed a small ungainly c., 56:7
seen a curious c., 376:21
Shakespeare Fancy's c., 251:19
shall play on hole of the asp, 26:11
slayeth c. in womb, 659:16
spare rod and spoil c., 81:*n*6,
    263:21
take me into bright c. of mind,
    689:10
teach c. to doubt, 359:11
thankless c., 209:11
there is a man c. conceived, 13:34
there was a c. went forth, 491:2
thought as a c., 43:16
to mother sheep to fold, 579:22
train up a c. in the way, 22:9
tyrant is c. of Pride, 65:18
understood as a c., 43:16
unto us a c. is born, 26:8
virgin shall be with c., 32:22
warble c., 168:25
when I was a c., 43:16
white as angel English c., 356:8
wise father knows own c., 180:17
would have made ugly c., 517:16
you are like a flower, 420:1
young c. with Mary, 32:24
Childbirth, death taxes c., 705:1
Childhood, barb in arrow of c., 568:6
eye of c. fears painted devil, 214:8

Childhood (*continued*)

in my days of c., 387:14
little world of c., 629:1
make glad heart of c., 538:2
manhood and decrepit age, 242:14
model of greater world, 629:1
one moment in c., 713:5
remnants of c. hopes of adulthood,
    708:6
scenes of my c., 398:2
shows the man, 260:32
talk about my hard c., 772:15
waters of c. are there, 767:9
womanhood and c. fleet, 441:7
wove web in c., 476:10
Childhood's hour, 392:13, 451:9
Childhoods, had Vietnam instead of
    happy c., 770:4
Childish but divinely beautiful, 364:18
practice c. ways, 52:31
put away c. things, 713:19
religion but a c. toy, 162:5
sweet c. days, 374:8
things, 43:16
treble, 191:3
Childishly, sucked on pleasures c.,
    228:2
Childishness, second c., 191:3
Childless and crownless, 400:21
saw Whitman c. lonely, 757:2
Children, age finds us true c. still,
    350:9
all God's c. join hands, 761:3
an' all us other c., 558:15
and fools cannot lie, 141:34
and fools want everything, 279:28
as c. fear in darkness, 90:1
as one would wish c. treated, 742:2
become as little c., 35:31
begin by loving parents, 566:17
believe in good family angels, 715:7
blood on us and on our c., 37:8
bones on which c. sharpen teeth,
    749:11
books c. of brain, 288:14
breed of horses dogs c., 282:22
bring forth c. in sorrow, 6:25
bring up c. in behavioristic freedom,
    635:1
bringing up c., 711:22
bringing-up of c., 569:17
can c. of bridechamber mourn,
    34:23
can't form c. on own concepts,
    349:21
come dear c. let us away, 497:6
don't read to find identity, 715:7
dream that my four c., 761:2
drinkest tears of c., 397:14
even c. followed, 329:16
extensions of our egos, 662:13
familiarity breeds contempt and c.,
    58:*n*10
fear death as c. fear dark, 159:4
forever explaining to grown-ups,
    705:12
freezing to death, 541:2
get on board little c., 794:21
give c. right to study painting,
    338:10

Children (*continued*)

Great Spirit make them all for his
    c., 370:4
had so many c., 790:2
hates c. and dogs can't be all bad,
    641:14
her c. arise up, 23:20
herd c. home to mothers, 56:11
here my c. born, 448:16
how can you shoot women c., 770:3
husband c. friends nothing to that,
    556:20
in days of our c., 576:7
in peace c. inter parents, 69:22
in the foliage, 670:18
in the wood, 776:2
indifferent c. of earth, 195:23
iniquity of the fathers upon the c.,
    9:10
invent a game, 656:9
king over c. of pride, 15:26
laboring c. look out, 631:1
listen my c., 442:12
little c. cried in streets, 474:8
look after own upbringing, 760:12
missing c. were gathering, 766:11
most men are like c., 651:9
my c. glean, 708:2
nature fits c., 485:9
Nature's c. given into slavery,
    135:13
Negro school-c., 743:12
no longer any c., 269:32
nor do c. prattle about his knees,
    51:19
not leave unless I do, 704:5
of an idle brain, 174:21
of disillusioned colored pioneers,
    768:12
of kingdom cast out, 34:16
of larger growth, 305:6
of light, 38:40, 499:12
of light and day, 45:6
of Men full of wiles, 73:11
of the day, 45:6
of this world wiser, 38:40
old men are c., 73:4
parents bore their c., 571:17
peace to our c. when they fall,
    743:16
playthings in playhouse of c.,
    624:17
provoke not c. to anger, 44:41
Rachel weeping for her c., 32:26
receive arms race from us, 748:4
red c. acknowledge no boundaries,
    369:17
remember c. you did not get, 740:4
return ye c. of men, 18:10
Revolution eats own c., 473:10
second wife hateful to c., 67:22
shall wander in the wilderness, 10:1
sins of fathers upon c., 69:17
so act toward c. so toward wife,
    108:12
so are c. of the youth, 20:1
suffer little c., 37:31
swarmed like settlers, 720:19
sweeter than apples to c., 565:12

Children (*continued*)

tale which holdeth c. from play, 156:2

teach them diligently unto thy c., 10:11

terrible c., 435:21

their country their c., 91:27

they shall be called c. of God, 33:1

travel first-class and with c., 675:13

walk on frozen toes, 608:6

war c. is just a shot away, 773:3

we are c. of our landscape, 731:9

we are the c., 775:3

wealth and c. adornment of life, 116:21

weeping O brothers, 438:16

were all thy c. kind, 184:28

what give my c., 740:5

what have you got against c., 768:5

when voices of c., 356:17

where c. above average, 772:5

where did c. vanish, 717:2

wife and c. impediments, 159:11

wife and c. stand afraid, 248:13

will burn, 788:16

will enjoy electrical energy, 695:21

wisdom exalteth her c., 31:7

wisdom justified of c., 34:37

women and c. first, 780:11

words c. of many men, 706:5

world safer for c. grow up in, 761:16

your c. are we, 787:4

Children's, all our c. fate, 593:24

books of my day, 587:4

children think they are alone, 398:11

gratitude woman's love, 598:15

Hour, 442:8

house of make believe, 624:17

lips shall echo, 399:24

my God the C. Crusade, 751:13

teeth set on edge, 28:35

Child's amang you takin' notes, 363:15

credulity c. strength, 387:29

no c. pley to take wyf, 131:19

Child's-heart, not lose his c., 79 23

Chill and drear, 378:3

bitter c. it was, 414:21

in wintry age feel no c., 335:18

mantle of wind and c. and rain, 132:22

penury, 322:12

sun was warm wind c., 624:6

thy dreaming nights, 417:3

wind is c., 378:11

Chilling, on love request for money c., 496:10

Chills, of c. and fever died, 674:12

Chilly, I feel c. and old, 466:15

room grows c., 625:19

Chime, faintly as tolls evening c., 391:8

higher than the sphery c., 253:13

hours to which Heaven c., 270:2

to guide their c., 268:25

Chimera, what a c. is man, 271:7

Chimeras, how many vain c. have you created, 135:12

Chimeras (*continued*)

nothing achieved without c., 503:17

Chimerical, reduction to atoms c. ideal, 537:3

Chimes at midnight, 184:4

little jingle little c., 298:1

Chimleypiece, bottle on c., 469:41

Chimney, as c.-sweepers come to dust, 220:3

hung by c. with care, 391:6

little c. hot in moment, 167:*n*4

makes c. of your nose, 354:10

old men from c. corner, 156:2

Chimneypiece, Buffalo upon c., 520:2

Chimneys, your c. I sweep, 356:11

Chin, close-buttoned to the c., 335:15

dogs shame the gray c., 52:20

new-reaped, 177:2

China, break c. plates of others, 581:18

'crost the bay, 591:23

leave C. convert Christians, 528:8

mankind from C. to Peru, 313:16

not seeking to dominate world, 685:15

slow boat to C., 728:12

though c. fall, 300:19

thought of C. and Greece, 712:18

Chinee, heathen C. is peculiar, 532:1

Chinese, bombing of C. cities, 655:19

great and vital people, 733:15

love jade, 662:8

nightingale, 637:12

people have solidarity, 601:4

sediment of long C. past, 662:8

Chink, importunate c., 332:18

in floor of Wicklow house, 613:8

Chinks of her sickness-broken body, 250:8

that Time has made, 250:6

Chinook, break loose like c. salmon, 743:15

Chip of old block, 332:1

Chips down nation acts helpless, 733:16

lest c. fall in eye, 775:14

Chirurgery, what c. relieve conscience, 235:23

Chisel, whether c. pen or brush, 596:16

Chiseled, down their c. names, 540:23

Chivalrous, proud and c. spirit, 79:4

Chivalry, age of c. gone, 332:12

age of c. past, 484:18

charge with all thy c., 389:4

her beauty and her c., 399:21

smiled c. away, 403:15

Chocolate, no c. to eat, 750:3

Choice and master spirits, 188:20

brave man's c. is danger, 68:24

can I have no other c., 743:19

careful in c. of enemies, 566:13

courage of making c., 614:14

grain into this wilderness, 277:3

Hobson's c., 776:20

in the worth and c., 231:20

it was not my c., 768:8

life's business c., 468:4

of horse and wife, 497:2

of point of view, 653:8

Choice (*continued*)

pays money takes c., 554:15

reckless c., 623:10

small c. in rotten apples, 167:16

with freedom of c. and honor, 136:1

word measured phrase, 374:10

Choir, chorister whose 5c4 preceded c., 640:12

full-voiced c. below, 252:10

invisible, 483:7

of saints, 231:2

sanctuary and c., 672:1

singing in the c., 778:9

St. Stephen's c., 742:10

wailful c., 416:15

Choirs, bare ruined c., 221:8

Choix, le c. fait les amis, 341:*n*5

Choke them amid flowers, 90:8

Choked with ambition of meaner sort, 163:13

Choleric, captain's c. word, 204:5

Chondria, Russia's c. for short, 423:17

Choose, any language you c., 530:14

author as you c. friend, 278:22

between Africa and English tongue, 763:8

between betraying country and friend, 636:12

do not c. to run, 614:18

don't c. to run, 638:4

equality, 500:21

fool multitude c. by show, 180:25

ground and take thy rest, 404:8

if thou must c. c. the odd, 720:21

if you dare, 249:20

intellect forced to c., 598:10

it is time to c., 639:14

let's c. executors, 171:24

likely man in preference to rich, 62:27

not alone proper mate, 335:21

not c. not to be, 551:11

odd of God to c. Jews, 656:14

path leading wherever I c., 490:3

slavery or death, 292:9

the irregular, 554:4

therefore c. life, 10:25

to live without friends, 78:6

Venus here c. dwelling, 275:30

we c. our friends, 341:16

what becomes Castilian, 419:8

Choosers, beggars should be no c., 141:25

Chooses, consciousness c. object, 545:18

intimacy that c. right, 596:22

no man c. evil, 365:25

Choosest not better part, 587:17

Choosing presidential nominee, 655:16

Chop off her head, 517:14

off your head, 788:21

Chopper to chop off your head, 788:21

Chord in melancholy, 422:22

in unison is touched, 335:11

struck c. of music, 506:1

Chords that vibrate pleasure, 362:9

Chorister, bobolink for C., 512:4

whose *c* preceded choir, 640:12

Chortled in his joy, 518:16
Chorus ending from Euripides, 466:9
   from Atlanta to sea, 520:6
   what a c., 388:19
Choruses above guinea's squawk,
   690:19
Chose, David c. him five smooth
   stones, 11:40
Chosen, few are c., 35:44
   I have c. you, 40:32
   Lord hath c. thee, 10:13
   people children of light, 499:12
   people of God, 343:10
   vessel, 41:7
Choses que je conte, 675:*n*5
Choughs that wing air, 210:27
Choux, que la mort me trouve plantant mes c., 145:*n*8
Christ ain't a-going to be too hard,
   536:12
   all at once what C. is, 551:17
   blood when C. slain, 597:18
   born across the sea, 484:7
   born in Bethlehem, 312:17
   bowels of C., 247:1, 615:4
   came from God and a woman,
      421:1
   came to save sinners, 45:11
   catch C. with worm, 742:11
   cautious statistical C., 553:20
   deep did rot O C., 381:9
   Don Quixote and I, 395:15
   everyone in world is C., 630:21
   face is face of C. himself, 490:11
   half a drop ah my C., 162:23
   Himself buddy, 747:9
   his captain C., 172:6
   I believe in Jesus C., 48:25
   in C. all made alive, 43:20
   is all and in all, 44:40
   is C. thy advocate, 283:9
   it is the Inchcape Rock, 386:11
   Jesus C. her little child, 479:19
   Jesus C. the righteous, 46:33
   Jesus C. the same yesterday, 46:1
   joint heirs with C., 42:2
   Judas or Peter who loved C., 713:9
   keep your hearts through C. Jesus,
      44:34
   kingdom and patience of Jesus C.,
      47:1
   kingdoms of his C., 47:26
   listen C. you did alright, 708:16
   Lord C. enter in, 567:23
   our Lord, 49:18
   our Passover sacrificed, 43:1
   our Savior, 778:8
   people who never heard of Jesus C.,
      675:18
   receive him, 458:8
   redemption by Jesus C., 49:5
   risen from dead, 43:20
   rule given by C., 510:8
   save us all, 441:2
   Savior which is C., 38:3
   see the C. stand, 466:22
   show me dear C. Thy spouse, 231:1
   shut up in asylum, 578:15
   so Judas did to C., 172:8
   soldiers of C. arise, 312:16

Christ (*continued*)
   stopped at Eboli, 709:3
   testimony of Jesus C., 47:1
   that it were possible, 458:25
   that my love in my arms, 776:6
   the Lord risen today, 312:13
   the Son took Father's place, 569:18
   thief said last word to C., 467:26
   thou art the C., 35:27
   to live is C., 44:29
   took the kindness, 467:26
   vision of C. thou see, 360:1
   walking on the water, 581:13
   walks on black water, 742:10
   what are patterns for, 626:9
Christendom, christianize C., 486:14
   in C. where Christian, 431:28
   live in any place in C., 144:16
   wisest fool in C., 154:23
Christened on Tuesday, 791:4
Christian, any husband rather than C.,
   182:1
   bear other's misfortunes like C.,
      303:20
   charity, 423:10
   confidence C. feels in four aces,
      525:18
   darkness fell upon C., 272:25
   enterprise for glory of C. religion,
      134:10
   feels repentance on Sunday, 644:2
   fled with a C., 180:24
   forgive them as C., 387:3
   hate him for a C., 180:3
   honorable style of C., 247:16
   I am a C. faithful man, 165:29
   ideal found difficult, 618:15
   if victory I shall become C., 115:7
   in what peace a C. can die, 293:12
   inconsistent with C. religion, 324:9
   meaning of C. life, 678:1
   men control property interests,
      544:8
   not so good a C. as thinks, 562:2
   O my C. ducats, 180:24
   only C. come to these parts, 134:10
   pagan spoiled, 590:5
   persuadest me to be C., 41:36
   practice C. forbearance, 339:11
   principle of suffering, 436:18
   richest monarch in C. world, 364:20
   Scientists some science, 602:13
   scratch C. find pagan, 590:5
   sleep with drunken C., 486:19
   soldiers, 521:10
   what one C. does, 760:11
   where C. in Christendom, 431:28
   witness of soul naturally C., 112:3
   wonders of C. religion, 287:3
   word of gentleman and C., 150:5
   you are Ciceronian not C., 113:14
   you were a C. Slave, 557:12
Christianity blemish of mankind,
   553:4
   Catholicism minus C., 505:8
   cult called C., 540:14
   doctors more C., 602:13
   enormous perversion, 553:4
   genius of C., 707:13
   is an idea, 420:6

Christianity (*continued*)
   muscular C., 780:15
   narcotics alcohol and C., 552:28
   one great curse, 553:4
   religion of the son, 569:18
   since introduction of C., 343:8
   takes great deal of C., 591:1
   which go first rock and roll or C.,
      770:6
Christianize Christendom, 486:14
   Filipinos, 549:18
Christians, all C. agree, 315:24
   blood of C. is seed, 112:5
   good C. good citizens, 394:6
   have burnt each other, 402:9
   have little difference, 316:10
   missionary leave China convert C.,
      528:8
   not born but made, 114:9
   predicted conversion lead to peace,
      536:19
   see how C. love one another, 112:4
   what these C. are, 180:11
Christmas, at C. no more desire rose,
   168:16
   at C. play, 144:6
   born on C. Day, 778:8
   comes but once a year, 144:6
   Day in workhouse, 556:1
   dreaming of white C., 666:13
   Ghost of C. Past, 470:6
   Ghost of C. Present, 470:8
   Ghost of C. Yet to Come, 470:11
   happy C. to all, 391:7
   home C., 604:10
   is coming, 779:14
   it was C. Day, 160:20
   jest 'fore C., 559:23
   keep C. all the year, 470:12
   keep our C. merry still, 378:11
   night before C., 391:6
   one C. much like another, 738:1
   over and Business is Business, 644:3
   pie, 788:11
   won't be Christmas, 516:10
Christom child, 184:30
Christ's blood streams, 162:23
   in C. coach, 283:5
   lady of C. College, 271:21
   loore and his apostles twelve, 130:4
   Lord C. heart, 430:12
   progress and His prayer-time, 270:2
   stamp, 243:4
   submission to humiliation, 752:9
Chromis did not save himself, 51:10
Chronic anxiety about weather, 532:7
   do not weep it's c., 469:37
   hotel guests, 605:23
   melancholy of civilized, 540:2
Chronicle of wasted time, 221:22
   pride his own c., 200:16
   small beer, 206:9
   wars of kites, 261:28
Chronicles, brief c. of the time, 196:2
   transcribe my c., 423:20
Chronology, according to our c.,
   237:23
Chrysanthemum, white c. immaculate,
   282:13
Chuang-tzu, Begone cried C., 80:17

Chub, Chavender or C., 245:22
Chuck 'im out the brute, 591:18
Chuckle, he with c. replied, 644:15
  little kind of low c., 526:20
Chuds, the C. Slavs and Krivchians, 121:1
Chums, bosom c., 760:15
Church ain't out till fat lady sings, 782:12
  and State demand for country, 648:20
  and State separate, 501:15
  authority of C. moved me, 114:28
  bells knolled to c., 190:29
  blood of martyrs seed of C., 112:n2
  built God a c., 334:16
  come to c. good people, 579:4
  get me to c. on time, 745:10
  holy Catholic C., 48:25
  I like a c., 429:9
  I like silent c., 431:26
  keep Sabbath going to C., 512:4
  Mother C., 112:7
  nearer to c. further from God, 141:11
  new and great period in His C., 255:1
  no other C. understood, 425:8
  not forgotten inside of c., 178:15
  not God for father if not C. for mother, 112:18
  novel by Henry James like c., 601:12
  persecuted c. of God, 43:19
  plain as way to parish c., 190:28
  prayers of c. to preserve travel, 290:15
  saw a wedding in the c., 279:13
  see a c. by daylight, 186:19
  sleep and feed at once, 668:11
  some to c. repair, 298:18
  stands c. clock at ten to three, 662:19
  take care of the c., 45:12
  to be of no c. dangerous, 314:18
  to c. and with my mourning very handsome, 279:20
  two lanterns in North C., 339:4
  upon this rock build my c., 35:28
  wall between c. and state, 661:6
  where God built c., 138:10
  wide as a c. door, 175:27
Churches, chapels had been c., 179:27
  head more than c. bibles creeds, 489:10
  in flat countries, 377:n1
  scab of c., 227:13
  seven c. in Asia, 47:2
Churchill, Randolph C. went into hospital, 712:9
Churchman, I that cowled c. be, 429:9
Churchyard abounds with images, 314:14
  Drumcliff c., 600:2
  where Michael Furey buried, 647:8
Churchyards yawn, 197:21
Churlish, reply c., 192:16
Churn, silver c., 529:20
Cibus, ali c. aliis venenum, 90:n6
Cicada, wild c. cried, 679:14

Cicadas, cries of c., 282:12
  like c. so leaders of Trojans, 51:13
  pour out their piping voices, 51:13
Cicala to cicala is dear, 82:15
Cicero, accept views C. Locke Bacon have given, 431:6
  book of a certain C., 114:22
Ciceronian, you are C. not Christian, 113:14
Ciel, j'allais sous le c. Muse, 565:n3
Cigar, good c. is a smoke, 590:20
  good five-cent c., 565:4
  sometimes c. just a c., 570:3
Cilicia, Tarsus in C., 41:24
Cinara, reign of the good C., 96:27
Cincinnatus of the West, 401:12
Cinderella fulfilling herself, 640:2
Cinders ashes dust, 414:17
  sat among the c., 790:15
  somebody's always heaving c., 637:7
Cinnamon, color of c., 731:2
  nutmegs ginger c. cloves, 242:16
  tinct with c., 415:6
  tree, 711:2
Cinzano, another dry C. in sun, 739:8
Cipher, write and c. too, 329:17
Circle, all within this c. move, 249:30
  close the c. of felicities, 344:8
  ever-nearing c. weaves shade, 499:18
  everything Indian does is in a c., 587:5
  glory like a c. in water, 163:8
  if you have formed a c., 359:19
  live in small c. as we will, 349:28
  of potential being, 545:6
  of the golden year, 454:23
  of wedding ring, 291:25
  outside a small c. of friends, 770:15
  perfect c. and vicious c., 731:14
  restricted c. of potential, 545:6
  shock of recognition whole c. round, 486:13
  vicious c., 522:8
  weave c. round him, 382:25
  wheel is come full c., 211:16
Circled, monthly changes in c. orb, 175:7
Circles, power of world works in c., 587:5
  produce perfect c., 79:14
  share decisions of consequences, 739:18
  triangles c. and other geometrical figures, 161:15
Circling, busy whisper c. round, 329:17
  morn waked by c. hours, 259:16
Circuit, his c. unto the ends of it, 16:10
Circulation, after book of c. of blood, 271:19
Circumcised, took by throat the c. dog, 208:17
Circumcision, neither c. nor uncircumcision, 44:40
Circumference, in universe neither center nor c., 151:27

Circumscribed, not c. in one self place, 162:16
Circumspection deliberation fortitude, 325:4
Circumspections, truth has c. and limits, 147:6
Circumstance and proper timing, 74:4
  artistries in c., 540:13
  envisage c. calm, 416:21
  fell clutch of c., 557:9
  of glorious war, 207:8
  some c. to please us, 266:n2
  unsifted in perilous c., 194:3
Circumstances, all classes times c., 474:21
  alter cases, 419:10
  classic survives c., 738:12
  creatures of men, 434:19
  fortuitous c., 379:17
  harmony of temperament and c., 496:7
  man is own c., 700:11
  man not creature of c., 434:19
  people always blaming c., 570:12
  rule men, 70:9
  same c. same phenomena, 290:30
  war train of c., 341:5
Circumstantial, lie c., 192:16
  some c. evidence strong, 476:25
  things essential or things c., 272:19
Circumvent God, 199:3
Circuses, bread and c., 109:7
Cistern contains, 357:7
  wheel broken at the c., 24:28
Cisterns, we have c. and worship them, 705:16
Citadel, did not go to c. of Troy, 55:21
  sacked the holy c. of Troy, 52:27
  towered c. pendant rock, 218:3
Citadels, vain c. not walled, 687:5
Citations, avoid c. from poets, 71:6
Cite, devil can c. Scripture, 180:6
Cité, le buste survit à la c., 462:n1
Cities, anarchy why c. tumble, 66:15
  buries c. in common grave, 340:7
  embers of c., 765:17
  Eros builder of c., 720:13
  government of c. failure of United States, 536:7
  grass in a hundred c., 625:21
  great lost c., 735:8
  hum of c. torture, 400:4
  London flower of C. all, 136:2
  man's skill built c., 87:3
  marble well-governed c., 721:2
  most pecksniffian of c., 642:14
  never have rest from evils, 75:15
  oblivion swallowed c. up, 200:22
  of men and manners, 455:1
  of the plain, 7:28
  our c. badly built, 677:4
  place philosophy in c., 87:30
  remove weight from c., 751:15
  say unto the c. of Judah, 27:19
  shame of the c., 601:2
  towered c. please us then, 251:17
  turned pleasant c. into slums, 694:6
  two c. formed by two loves, 115:3
  warred for Homer dead, 233:22

Citizen consider traveling expenses, 686:20

first requisite of good c., 576:1

free nation great, 428:3

good c. not silent, 507:10

humblest c. of land, 582:2

I am a Roman c., 87:9

in wild weed she is c., 740:12

may walk safely on law, 753:9

nation guarantees maintenance of c., 559:4

obliged to be c., 496:19

of no mean city, 41:24

of the world, 70:24, 159:15

takes stand upon economic theories, 645:12

Citizen's, White C. Counciler, 760:16

Citizens clamoring for what is wrong, 96:15

demean themselves as good c., 337:2

equal before law, 520:10

faction a number of c., 351:21

fat and greasy c., 190:9

force c. to confess, 683:2

frenzy of his fellow c., 96:15

good Christians good c., 394:6

not women or Negroes but c., 475:9

of Berlin, 742:9

of death's land, 662:4

of middle class, 78:22

of the world, 650:5

people born in U.S. are c., 346:18

rights of other c., 351:21

second class c., 685:11

to arms c., 366:*n*1

want to go to Hell I will help them, 543:2

Citizenship anxious about what do for nation, 741:*n*1

illness onerous c., 765:16

Citoyens, aux armes c., 366:9

City, all that is left of c., 758:14

and proud seat of Lucifer, 260:14

Athens divine c., 64:12

Babylon that great c., 47:31

bust survives c., 462:11

defend village town c., 620:9

education to Greece, 72:6

entire c. has suffered, 54:22

except the Lord keep the c., 19:29

failing that the rest of the c., 75:11

famous Hanover c., 464:17

flakes falling on c. brown, 549:20

for sale, 91:30

God made first c., 267:7

grass will grow in streets of every c., 582:3

great c. greatest men, 490:5

happy c. which in peace thinks of war, 235:8

harder to be won than a strong c., 21:40

he that taketh a c., 21:32

hell c. like London, 407:22

honor once at home in c., 239:12

how doth the c. sit solitary, 28:38

in country you praise c., 95:12

in the c. of David, 38:3

is teacher of the man, 60:9

City (*continued*)

like rain falling on c., 554:1

long in populous c. pent, 260:5

looking over harbor and c., 634:5

make glad the c. of God, 17:17

men make the c., 72:10

most glorious c. of God, 115:2

no continuing c., 46:2

no mean c., 41:24

obedient to his will, 75:16

of big shoulders, 634:4

of mirrors, 759:1

of Night perchance Death, 523:16

of the soul, 400:20

one long in c. pent, 413:22

raised on c. land taxes, 511:7

road to the C. of Emeralds, 568:10

Rome a c. of bricks, 98:23

rose-red c., 473:11

royal David's c., 479:19

secular c., 760:9

seen one c. slum seen all, 744:13

set on an hill, 33:3

since the founding of the c., 118:11

speck of light below, 562:12

sweet c. dreaming spires, 499:16

taking in hand a c., 62:23

this c. going to follow you, 587:10

this great hive the c., 266:16

throne in a strange c., 451:14

to the c. and the world, 120:1

up and down C. Road, 780:13

upon a hill, 239:27

what is the c. but people, 219:8

without a c. wall, 479:18

Zion c. of our God, 327:5

City's disinherited, 581:16

feel amid c. jar, 497:14

Civet, give me an ounce of c., 211:2

in the room, 334:11

Civic, some c. manhood, 457:1

Civil, assent with c. leer, 302:11

discord, 292:16

engaged in great c. war, 450:2

founder of c. society, 319:2

fury first grew high, 262:16

in respect of c. rights, 520:10

over violent or over c., 274:12

rights of Englishman, 345:13

sea grew c. at her song, 173:5

text of c. instruction, 344:9

too c. by half, 352:11

Civil War rebirth of Union, 572:5

Civilian control of military, 655:18

Civility, a little c., 780:19

wild c., 241:5

Civilization advances by operations we perform without thinking, 584:8

advances poetry declines, 424:13

botched c., 659:10

bourgeoisie draws nations into c., 482:2

cannot tolerate wrongs, 683:3

civilize c., 486:14

could be restored, 636:3

created under pressure of exigencies, 569:8

curiosity lifeblood of c., 631:16

definition of c., 584:15

elements of modern c., 412:25

Civilization (*continued*)

English c. humanizing, 501:1

farmers founders of c., 395:3

France conquered for c., 503:4

homicidal c., 648:4

ignorant free in state of c., 344:18

in middle stage, 611:11

meeting-point between savagery and c., 584:6

nature and c. literary field, 548:5

New York the collapse of c., 738:8

not conquered from without, 656:13

not wiped out by atomic war, 636:3

obstacles of c., 436:16

poets in our c. difficult, 672:15

progress toward privacy, 717:9

provision for poor is test of c., 316:9

requires slaves, 567:12

resources of c. not exhausted, 446:15

results in deserts, 633:12

speech is c., 629:17

test of c. way cares for helpless, 682:14

theory of true c., 494:16

thin crust over revolution, 578:8

true test of c. is man, 433:6

usual interval of c., 542:2

western c. be feminized, 737:1

what dissatisfies in American c., 501:4

workers mainstay of c., 560:2

Civilizations break down fail to meet challenge, 677:8

grow by responding to challenges, 677:8

Civilize civilization, 486:14

educate Filipinos uplift c. them, 549:18

Civilized, in Japan c. nation, 525:17

man cannot live without cooks, 516:4

man has habits of house, 476:21

no c. life without clothes, 585:2

society five qualities, 584:15

they and I are c., 711:4

valued by c. men, 568:16

Woman last thing c., 508:19

Civilizer, comedy the ultimate c., 509:2

Civilizers, two c. of man, 435:11

Civis Romanus sum, 87:*n*5

Clad in beauty of thousand stars, 162:20

in complete steel, 253:2

in sober livery c., 258:18

morn in russet mantle c., 192:30

naked every day he c., 328:25

with native honor c., 258:11

Claim that our city is education, 72:6

woman takes off c. to respect, 69:21

Claims, adjustment of colonial c., 572:13

of long descent, 454:2

snakeskin titles of mining c., 698:6

Clamor, not in c. of crowded street, 442:21

Clamoring, citizens c. for what is wrong, 96:15

Clamorous owl that nightly hoots, 173:11

Clamors, immortal Jove's dread c., 207:8

venom c. of jealous woman, 166:32

Clan, family party tribe c., 780:21

leaf last of its c., 382:11

Clanging rookery home, 455:11

Clangor, trumpet's loud c., 275:9

Clap, if you believe c. hands, 581:22

padlock on her mind, 287:19

soul c. hands and sing, 597:8

Clapper, his tongue the c., 186:33

Claps, at heaven's gates c. wings, 155:20

Claptrap, art independent of c., 524:1

Claret liquor for boys, 317:13

Clarification, adventure in c. of thought, 584:12

poem ends in c. of life, 625:8

Clarifies, time cools time c., 629:20

Clarinets, has meadows of c., 689:9

Clarion laid away, 695:22

Clarity, culture moment of c., 653:4

give each moment c., 630:1

Clarum et venerabile nomen, 106:*n*1

Clash, bring to our ears c. of arms, 339:10

ignorant armies c., 499:22

Clasp, dare deadly terrors c., 358:7

thrice tried to c. her image, 53:18

Clasps crag with crooked hands, 458:4

Class, brutalizing lower c., 500:23

could've had c. been somebody, 737:6

equal wealth made us one c., 559:8

ideas of ruling c., 482:6

leisure c. replaced by New C., 723:9

materializing upper c., 500:23

middle c. best political community, 78:22

middle c. in America the nation, 501:2

middle c. safety of England, 464:2

no criminal c. except Congress, 527:25

office of leisure c., 574:7

one c. overthrows another, 686:11

ones of middle c. who left home, 744:12

proletariat revolutionary c., 482:3

Rome's decline lay in c. struggle, 656:13

second c. citizens, 685:11

she was in c. by herself, 703:17

struggle, 481:7

struggles, 481:15

taking from one c., 306:17

vulgarizing middle c., 500:23

while lower c. I am in it, 568:2

White-Anglo Saxon-Protestant upper c., 738:3

Classes, all c. times circumstances, 474:21

antagonism between c., 482:5, 661:2

back masses against c., 446:16

bow lower middle c., 530:5

dissolution of all c., 481:7

draw powers into higher c., 345:4

Classes (*continued*)

four c. of Idols, 158:13

let ruling c. tremble, 482:7

no c. among citizens, 520:10

noblest work she c. O, 361:25

of travel first-class and with children, 675:7

other c. decay disappear, 482:3

ruin of contending c., 481:15

tempt upper c., 574:1

tied to historical phases, 481:7

Classic book people praise don't read, 527:30

face, 451:21

Paris our black c., 742:15

reread c., 713:1

survives circumstances, 738:12

tread on c. ground, 291:29

Classical quotation, 317:23

Classicist in literature, 672:18

royalist Anglo-Catholic, 672:18

Classics, great homicidal c., 769:2

in paraphrase, 659:7

man with bellyful of c. enemy, 681:10

Classified, objects c., 350:1

Classless, formation of c. society, 481:7

Clatter of presses, 659:13

they make with his coach, 279:21

Clause, servant with this c., 243:26

two kinds of relative c., 575:1

Clavichord, stately at the c., 466:13

Claw, from c. can tell a lion, 119:1

red in tooth and c., 457:21

Clawed, age c. me in his clutch, 143:12

Claws, neatly spreads c., 517:5

pair of ragged c., 667:14

that catch, 518:15

Clay, beings of mind are not of c., 400:12

bless turf that wraps c., 324:11

dead and turned to c., 199:10

feet of c., 29:12

in c. none is, 791:15

kingdoms are c., 216:25

lies still, 578:20

of c. and wattles made, 594:21

porcelain c. of humankind, 275:26

Potter thumping his wet C., 445:21

power over the c., 42:10

say to him that fashioneth it, 27:26

tenement of c., 274:3

to every people cup of c., 787:16

weak creatures of c., 73:12

white linen cold as c., 786:6

Clean, art only c. thing, 556:19

bid them keep teeth c., 219:4

create in me a c. heart, 17:22

cry that it isn't c., 284:8

he that hath c. hands, 16:18

hearth, 387:26

horse of courage, 750:2

let other people c. up mess, 694:11

passed c. over Jordan, 10:32

pasture spring, 622:19

purge me and I shall be c., 17:21

starved for a look, 221:9

then c. and brave, 579:2

Clean (*continued*)

things holy profane c. obscene, 239:20

think of c. beds, 662:5

tumbler and corkscrew, 469:22

wash blood c. from hand, 214:9

Cleaned windows swept floor, 529:6

Cleaning, yesterday had daily c., 737:3

Cleanliness next to godliness, 309:1

of all clean American backyards, 753:3

who of late for c., 238:2

Cleanly, leave sack and live c., 179:12

not too c. manger, 264:18

room lavender in windows, 245:21

thus so c. I myself can free, 161:11

Cleanse stuffed bosom of perilous stuff, 216:10

thou me from secret faults, 16:12

thoughts of our hearts, 49:13

Cleansed, what God hath c., 41:9

Cleanses, poetry c., 742:6

Clean-shaven, buttoned-up and c., 547:1

Clean-winged hearth, 443:14

Clear, action faithful honor c., 300:24

and cool clear and cool, 484:14

and present danger, 542:24

as a whistle, 304:16

as crystal, 471:24

as nose in face, 140:*n*5

as the sun, 25:16

as you go, 528:19

brown twilight atmosphere, 436:4

but one rule to be c., 396:18

coast was c., 161:12

conscience is sure card, 155:12

deep and absolutely c., 729:4

doctrines plain and c., 263:29

enemy of c. language is insincerity, 711:13

fire clean hearth, 387:26

honor purchased by merit, 180:27

in cool September morn, 443:9

in his great office, 213:7

literature c. and cold, 658:9

my sad thoughts doth c., 270:9

one c. call for me, 460:11

read my title c., 294:18

religion of heaven, 414:11

spouse so bright and c., 231:1

summers wet and winters c., 92:23

they could get it c., 518:24

though deep yet c., 266:11

viol of her memory, 639:5

what is not c. is not French, 353:14

wild call and c. call, 633:15

your mind of cant, 317:30

Cleared, if this were only c., 518:24

ship cheered harbor c., 380:29

Clearer, age c. than noonday, 14:13

view ourselves with c. eyes, 242:1

Clearest of God's creatures, 743:3

way into Universe through forest, 537:15

who have c. vision, 72:4

Clearly, I see so c., 350:12

well conceived c. said, 280:6

Clearness, chief merit of language c., 111:29

Closet, back in C. lays, 445:23
do very well in a c., 305:5
knowledge not in c., 304:19
Closing, busy hammers c. rivets,
185:14
diapason c. full in Man, 275:7
Clot bedded axle-tree, 670:14
created Man of blood c., 117:24
created you of blood c., 117:2
Cloth, cut my coat after my c., 141:10
from moon cloth from another
planet, 735:22
meat drink and c. to us, 140:10
untrue with twisted cue, 531:5
Clothe my naked villainy, 165:27
summer c. general earth, 382:17
with rags, 22:20
Clothed all in leather, 792:17
and in right mind, 37:26
his neck with thunder, 15:15
in white samite held sword, 133:6
in white samite mystic, 459:6
man c. with rags, 272:11
naked and he c. him, 326:14
naked and ye c. me, 36:18
with heavens, 280:22
with integrity, 269:17
Clothes, as c. to bodies, 585:2
biographies but c. and buttons,
528:10
emperor's new c., 437:8
enterprises that require new c.,
478:6
food fuel and c., 487:30
give woman comfortable c., 651:11
good smell of old c., 663:2
hanging out c., 790:1
his old c. a few books, 653:28
it burns your c., 354:10
kindles in c. a wantonness, 241:4
liquefaction of her c., 241:20
loves but their oldest c., 228:9
make the man, 528:14
Mordecai rent his c., 13:24
nothing wears c. but Man, 243:14
on hickory limb, 783:6
part of man's Self, 545:20
slip out of wet c., 675:11
spoiling nice new c., 790:15
stepped out of c., 599:2
swaddling c., 38:2
take fire and his c. not be burned,
20:30
through tattered c., 211:4
thrown on with pitchfork, 290:7
upon c. behind tenement, 679:8
walked away with c., 434:29
wear our c. and what difference,
235:4
when he put on his c., 328:25
Clothing, come in sheep's c., 34:10
I put on women's c., 775:6
of delight, 356:6
softest c. woolly bright, 356:6
strength and honor are her c., 23:19
things in books' c., 388:8
wolf in sheep's c., 58:14
Cloths, heavens' embroidered c., 595:8
Clotilda, God of C. grant victory,
115:7

Cloud, are as a floating c., 61:10
brightest day hath c., 163:23
but c. and like shady grove, 356:9
comes over sunlit arch, 624:6
every c. engenders not storm, 165:1
fair luminous c., 383:9
geese like snow c., 674:11
house made of dark c., 787:9
in c. and clod to Sing, 650:12
in shape of a camel, 197:18
in trousers, 686:19
joy the luminous c., 383:10
lift me as wave leaf c., 407:16
lightning out of dark c., 552:7
like a fiend in a c., 356:2, 358:11
like a man's hand, 12:37
lovely see c. appear, 787:6
of barbarism and despotism, 345:3
of witnesses, 45:39
on a c. I saw a child, 356:4
pillar of c., 8:43
sable c., 252:25
seemed to be local dust c., 735:19
set my bow in the c., 7:24
Son of man coming in c., 39:14
stirred by solitary c., 282:11
stooping through a fleecy c., 252:3
that looked like centaur, 73:3
that's dragonish, 218:3
through dark c. shining, 617:12
wandered lonely as c., 375:19
when c. is scattered, 409:19
Cloud-capped towers, 224:21
Cloud-Cuckoo-Land, 73:13
Clouded, moon rising in c. majesty,
258:19
Cloud-kissing Ilion, 167:5
Cloudless climes starry skies, 401:14
fill sky with c. sunshine, 96:24
scintillant in c. days, 654:2
Clouds and eclipses stain, 220:21
are pedagogues, 639:24
ascribing to c. the flame, 103:15
barred c. bloom soft-dying day,
416:15
base contagious c., 176:37
blue-massing c., 663:2
cannot be in deep sea, 90:2
color that paints morning evening
c., 127:3
creeping quietly over it, 510:3
fill sky with black c., 96:24
he that regardeth the c., 24:24
her life filled with c. of goodness,
347:*n* 1
home made of blue c., 787:7
hung oppressively, 452:4
looks in the c., 187:32
maketh the c. his chariot, 19:3
mountains fleeting as c., 117:6
never doubted c. break, 468:17
new-made c., 737:18
no pity sitting in c., 176:8
nor c. soak with showers, 53:*n* 1
now here now there, 410:7
number the c. in wisdom, 15:14
O c. unfold, 359:17
of June, 515:2
out of c. silence, 554:13
pack c. away, 233:20

Clouds (*continued*)
prince of c., 494:2
return after the rain, 24:27
round setting sun, 375:15
scare white c. on, 623:10
sees God in c., 301:7
ships dim-discovered from c., 308:1
silk-sack c., 551:2
somewhere among c. above, 596:10
spirits of wise sit in c., 183:32
storm-c. brood on heights, 472:13
sun breaks through darkest c.,
167:31
sweep c. no more, 447:3
trailing c. of glory, 375:7
tumult in the c., 596:11
what with all these c., 73:13
white c. on wing, 504:3
wrapt in c. and snow, 399:25
Cloud-topped hill, 301:7
Cloudy, among c. trophies hung,
416:18
flaming opal ring, 594:12
huge c. symbols, 417:10
skies not c. all day, 786:11
tabernacle parted, 419:7
was the weather, 792:17
Clove, burning c., 623:20
Cloven tongues as of fire, 40:45
Clovenfooted, whatsoever is c., 9:21
Clover and one bee, 514:16
any time Aristocracy, 514:9
wind with fragrance of sweet c.,
616:11
Clove's sweet smell, 731:2
Cloves, nutmegs ginger cinnamon c.,
242:16
Clown, emperor and c., 415:17
of spirit's motive, 734:6
Cloy appetites they feed, 217:15
hungry edge of appetite, 171:3
of all meats soonest c., 266:16
Cloyless sauce, 217:12
Club, any c. that will accept me,
693:2
assembly of good fellows, 314:1
not with C. Heart broken, 514:5
spear to thrust c. to strike, 139:5
swamp elm c., 567:27
Clubs typical of strife, 335:6
Clue, singularity almost invariably a
c., 577:16
Cluett, land of the C. Shirt, 688:12
Clusium, Lars Porsena of C., 425:13
Cluster, woes c., 198:*n* 5
Clustered spires of Frederick, 443:10
Clutch, age clawed me in his c.,
143:12
come let me c. thee, 213:20
fell c. of circumstance, 557:9
Clutching inviolable shade, 498:13
C.O., Catholic C.O., 742:22
Coach, Christ's c., 283:5
clatter they make with c., 279:21
come my c., 198:19
rattling of a c., 231:11
through Act of Parliament, 778:14
throw yourself into c., 664:*n* 3
Coal, cargo of Tyne c., 634:1
portable climate, 432:32

Cold (*continued*)

my lodging on c. ground, 297:5

neither c. nor hot, 47:13

neutrality, 332:24

never caught a c., 600:23

night blasts c., 619:2

night is c., 783:14

no such c. thing, 243:21

not more c. to you than I, 454:1

out o' c. an' rain, 592:12

out of dead c. ashes life, 554:13

owl a-c., 414:21

pain darkness and c., 467:19

pease-porridge c., 790:10

poor Tom's a-c., 210:11

principle, 245:*n*2

put it in c. storage, 585:4

side outside, 612:*n*1

sleep in dull c. marble, 225:19

sleep is heat for c., 151:15

snow said c. said sleep, 675:3

so c. no fire warm, 514:19

spy who came in from c., 763:15

sweat bathes me, 56:5

temper leaps over c. decree, 179:28

thicks man's blood with c., 381:12

through dark c. and desolation, 671:11

till sun grows c., 506:3

'tis bitter c., 192:19

to distant misery, 340:5

trembling c. in ghastly fears, 357:17

upon dead Caesar's trencher, 217:27

war getting warmer, 608:15

waters to a thirsty soul, 22:27

way long wind c., 377:19

we are dying of c., 589:16

winter with wrathful nipping c., 163:23

words of tongue or pen, 611:17

years grow c. to love, 93:4

Colder, heat cannot pass from c., 501:8

Coldly furnish forth marriage tables, 193:14

Coldness of my dear, 297:5

Cole, old King C., 788:5

Coleridge poet and philosopher, 501:6

Coliseum, while stands C. Rome stand, 400:27

Collaboration, peculiar illusion of c., 739:13

Collapse, New York the c. of civilization, 738:8

Collapsed, all c. and sea rolled on, 487:1

Collar, braw brass c., 361:16

Collars, Earl & Wilson C., 688:12

Collateral, with intellect only c. relations, 453:14

Collection of facts not science, 565:6

Collections, mutilators of c., 387:25

not c. of pictures but of fruit, 87:1

Collective bargaining is bilateral monopoly, 657:4

unconscious, 628:8

Collective-unit only form, 546:22

Collectors, scientists c. classifiers, 738:14

Collects motions into shape, 760:14

College, aging c. people, 703:6

cauliflower cabbage with c. education, 527:8

endow c. or cat, 300:22

farewell to c. joys, 652:18

intent on getting results, 610:11

it is a small c., 394:5

lady of Christ's C., 271:21

Maud went to c., 740:3

not much between unless c., 624:5

Colleges to do with progress, 603:1

Collied night, 172:20

Collins, Mr. C. had only to change, 386:26

Collision, avoid foreign c., 389:12

Colonel lean as compass-needle, 743:10

Colonel's Lady an' Judy O'Grady, 592:21

Colonels full of corn, 580:15

Colonial, adjustment of c. claims, 572:13

Colonies are and ought to be free, 338:4

commerce with our c., 331:8

religion prevalent in c., 331:14

these united c., 336:11

Colonist, wilderness masters the c., 584:6

Colonization, American continents not for c., 360:10

Colony, dissenting c., 338:4

Coloquintida, bitter as c., 206:1

Color, air quiver with c., 656:9

blue c. delight, 487:17

by convention there is c., 70:28

her c. comes and goes, 539:6

his c. can't be seen, 779:10

horse of different c., 202:*n*2

horse of that c., 202:7

in the cup, 22:22

loves and skin, 228:9

met by c. line, 480:20

no matter c. of skin, 685:10

none knew c. of the sky, 611:6

not judged by c. of skin, 761:2

not superior by c., 520:12

of ground in him, 563:9

prejudice against c., 475:7

prison for c. of hair, 580:9

problem of c. line, 604:19

right to vote not denied on account of c., 346:19

Sergeant said, 591:15

shade without c., 669:9

that paints morning and evening clouds, 127:3

till heart tinged with c., 384:21

walk by c. purple in a field, 773:13

white is their c., 243:24

Colorado, Kansas and C. have quarrel, 655:5

Color-blind, Constitution is c., 520:10

Colored, as long as c. man look to white folks, 773:19

destiny of c. American, 480:17

disillusioned c. pioneers, 768:12

every c. woman is dying, 763:16

ground c. man occupies, 480:15

I am not tragically c., 707:5

Colored (*continued*)

no white or c. signs, 742:3

people understand white people, 612:4

relation between white and c. people, 480:18

skins not c. like your own, 480:14

twopence c., 561:20

Coloring, sober c. from eye, 375:15

Colorless green ideas sleep, 758:20

Colors, all c. suffusion from light, 383:10

changing c. shooting upward, 673:6

coat of many c., 8:4

embroidered girdle of many c., 52:3

hoist c. to peak, 642:3

nailed c. to the mast, 378:4

no c. or crest, 592:7

of imagination, 384:9

oldest c. have faded, 591:13

perfumes c. sounds echo, 494:3

seen by candlelight, 438:19

so like your own, 144:4

that are but skin-deep, 226:*n*1

that never fade, 585:9

their c. and their forms, 373:4

under whose c. he fought so long, 172:6

Colossus, bestride world like C., 187:22

of Rhodes, 782:7

Colt, let little c. go bare, 792:21

Columbia, hail C., 372:15

Columbus enjoyed pure delight, 665:10

Column, fifth c., 664:1

fountain's silvery c., 383:2

rising toward heaven, 394:8

throws up a steamy c., 335:3

took shape of mushroom, 673:7

Columns, proofs figures in c. before me, 490:9

Comb gray hair, 596:8

hair with codfish bones, 793:14

me all to thunder, 526:4

scraped life with fine-tooth c., 740:3

Combat ceased for want of combatants, 249:11

deepens, 389:4

obstacles to get repose, 536:2

reason left free to c. it, 344:5, 345:1

Combatants, dust involves the c., 334:31

want of c., 249:11

Combination and a form indeed, 197:30

no powers of c., 332:28

of fortuitous circumstances, 379:17

Combine, when bad men c., 330:23

Combined, knotted and c. locks part, 194:17

Combs, Glos'ter girls they have no c., 793:14

Combustible, entire c. world, 596:7

Combustion, hideous ruin and c., 255:22

Come again another day, 788:8

again Jack, 792:23

again to Carthage, 182:7

again with rejoicing, 19:28

Come (*continued*)

all things c. of thee, 13:18
all to church good people, 579:4
all you rounders, 610:*n*2
and trip it as you go, 251:9
as chimney-sweepers c. to dust,
    220:3
as the winds come, 379:9
at last the Distinguished Thing,
    549:15
avoid what is to c., 198:3
a-waltzing Matilda, 589:5
away death, 202:13
back to earth begin over, 623:8
beats my approach tells thee I c.,
    242:3
before his presence with singing,
    18:22
before the swallow dares, 223:7
believe in life to c., 718:18
between bid us part, 308:11
blow wind c. wrack, 216:16
blow your horn, 789:4
cannot c. again, 579:9
cannot c. to good, 193:12
cheer up they c., 492:6
children shut up box, 463:11
consider where you c. out, 100:12
cry is still They c., 216:12
dance wyth me, 775:12
days to c. are wisest witnesses,
    63:27
dear children let us away, 497:6
death c. when it will c., 188:11
down redeem us, 533:16
dreaming on things to c., 221:23
ethereal mildness c., 308:3
fill the Cup, 445:6
fill up my cup, 379:27
first c. first served, 123:*n*5
first c. kiss me, 776:22
flee from wrath to c., 32:31
for the life to c., 223:3
forth into light of things, 372:20
friends who plow sea, 529:15
from dying moon, 456:10
from ends of earth, 591:9
from haunts, 458:15
gentle Spring, 308:3
ghost c. back again, 706:18
Ghost of Christmas Yet to C.,
    470:11
give a war and nobody c., 634:12
give us taste of quality, 195:34
harder they c. harder they fall,
    774:10
he slow, 378:6
hither, 190:18
home to roost, 386:12
home with me now, 520:5
hour is not yet c., 39:38
Husband I c., 218:17
I c. quickly, 48:3
I c. to bury Caesar, 188:28
I hear you I will c., 579:4
I will c. again, 40:27
I would not c. in, 624:14
idea whose time c., 427:18
if c. to my house I will c. to yours,
    102:8

Come (*continued*)

if not to c. will be now, 199:22
if now 'tis not to c., 199:22
if you build it he will c., 768:2
in the evening, 474:1
in the rearward of woe, 221:13
in under shadow, 668:18
in we'll keep ye broke, 602:17
into the garden Maud, 458:20
it shall not c. nigh thee, 18:15
I've c. to talk with you again, 772:7
jump the life to c., 213:5
King of glory shall c. in, 16:19
kiss me sweet and twenty, 202:2
knit hands, 252:23
know end ere it c., 189:24
knowledge must c. through action,
    67:2
let me clutch thee, 213:20
let us kiss and part, 161:11
let us mock at great, 597:16
let us sing unto Lord, 18:19
let's away to prison, 211:13
like shadows so depart, 215:22
live with me and be my love, 162:2,
    229:10
Lord is c., 294:17
lovely soothing death, 490:17
men may c. and go, 458:16
Messiah will c. day after arrival,
    651:19
Mr. Watson c. here, 555:11
Muse migrate from Greece, 490:6
my Celia let us prove, 232:4
my coach, 198:19
my lad and drink beer, 315:3
my own c. to me, 532:6
near me while I sing, 594:20
never c. back to me, 456:8
never c. back to us, 464:26
night strike hour, 641:7
not between dragon and wrath,
    208:23
not near our fairy queen, 173:12
not to steal away hearts, 189:9
nothing will c. of nothing, 208:20
now and let us reason, 25:29
nowhere to c. but back, 573:24
O come Emmanuel, 482:11
one come all, 378:24
over into Macedonia, 41:13
over way with tears watered, 612:3
past and to c. seem best, 183:27
past passing or to c., 597:10
perhaps singing bird c., 118:5
season to c. and go, 303:11
seeling night, 214:28
shan't be gone long you c. too,
    622:19
shape of things to c., 601:16
so far it is over, 764:14
soon soon, 409:14
that it should c. to this, 193:6
that it will never c. again, 514:14
that they might have life, 40:16
things past or things to c., 272:19
things to c., 200:12
thou monarch of the vine, 217:21
thou'lt c. no more, 211:19
three corners of world, 170:24

Come (*continued*)

thy kingdom c., 33:12
till boys c. home, 617:12
'tis the gift to c. down, 780:9
to aid of party, 781:7
to lay weary bones among ye, 226:1
to look for America, 772:10
to me my dear Bozzy, 317:20
to my arms, 518:16
to my woman's breasts, 212:29
to pluck your berries, 253:14
to see and be seen, 101:13
to take their ease, 226:10
to thee by moonlight, 643:12
to this favor she must c., 199:8
to this stage of fools, 211:6
treading path through blood, 612:3
unbutton here, 210:6
until I c. in peace, 13:3
unto me ye that labor, 34:38
unto my love, 154:13
unto these yellow sands, 223:30
up and see me sometime, 685:*n*2
up sometime and see me, 685:6
weal come woe, 372:14
what come may, 212:25
what dreams may c., 196:10
what is to c. I know not, 30:14
what may I have been blessed,
    401:8
what may Sinon said, 102:14
wheel is c. full circle, 211:16
when shall I c. to thee, 776:25
when will indifference c., 735:14
whence had they c., 599:5
whistle and I'll c. to you, 362:18
whistle and she'll c. to you, 238:18
will they c. when you call, 178:3
will ye no c. back again, 368:4
with singing unto Zion, 27:30
within a pint of wine, 293:15
within bending sickle's compass c.,
    222:2
without warning, 474:1
women c. and go, 667:10
won't c. back till it's over, 632:13
worst is yet to c., 459:31
ye thankful people, 460:16
ye to the waters, 27:39
you back to Mandalay, 591:22
you spirits that tend, 212:29
Come del morire, 231:*n*7
Come-a ti yi youpy youpy yea, 786:4
Comedian can last till he takes himself
    serious, 638:3
no matter if country need c., 638:4
Comedians extemporally will stage us,
    218:13
Comedy, all I need to make c., 675:17
catastrophe of the old c., 209:4
killing time essence of c., 589:18
most lamentable c., 172:22
said except in second act of musical
    c., 645:18
the c. is finished, 575:4
the ultimate civilizer, 509:2
world is a c., 324:1
Comely, attire c. not costly, 155:5
black but c., 25:1
bowed his c. head down, 268:11

Comely (*continued*)
  grace, 777:5
Comer, grasps in the c., 201:2
Comers, entertain all c., 51:22
Comes apparelled like spring, 219:18
  at one stride c. the dark, 381:14
  at the last, 172:1
  Autumn c. jovial on, 308:6
  conquering hero c., 308:23
  Death who c. at last, 378:6
  effect defective c. by cause, 195:13
  ever 'gainst that season c., 192:29
  fog c. on cat feet, 634:5
  God behind them, 467:22
  God c. as sun at noon, 231:10
  he c. he c., 276:8
  hope never c., 255:24
  in the sweet o' the year, 223:1
  knowledge c. wisdom lingers,
    455:21
  look who c. here, 170:2
  love that c. too late, 203:21
  moment to decide, 485:1
  nearer c. the sun, 657:17
  pat he c., 209:4
  Rainbow c. and goes, 375:4
  something wicked this way c.,
    215:16
  take it as it c., 531:19
  then cannon and he c., 619:2
  thrill that c. once in lifetime, 660:10
  to me o'er and o'er, 504:6
  unlooked for if c. at all, 298:8
  want for one who c. not, 694:20
  wear day out before it c., 557:18
  wine c. in at mouth, 595:20
Comest in such questionable shape,
  194:10
  whence c. thou, 13:29
Cometh, another generation c., 23:22
  behold the day c. that shall burn,
    30:9
  forth like a flower, 14:20
  from afar, 375:7
  from whence c. my help, 19:25
  hour c. and now is, 39:48
  in the name of the Lord, 19:22
  joy c. in the morning, 16:25
  my help c. from the Lord, 19:25
  the night c., 40:13
  this dreamer c., 8:3
  whence it c., 39:44
Comets, discoverers as c., 312:10
  when beggars die no c., 188:10
Comfort and despair, 222:10
  bred in modest c., 784:2
  carrion c., 551:11
  conceited carry c., 483:21
  continual c. in a face, 163:3
  gives c. in despair, 163:21
  giving enemies aid and c., 346:9
  hobbit-hole and that means c.,
    685:3
  I beg cold c., 170:22
  is any c. to be found, 597:14
  like cold porridge, 224:3
  me with apples, 25:5
  nightingale sing of c., 437:10
  of c. no man speak, 171:24

Comfort (*continued*)
  scholar who cherishes love of c.,
    61:21
  she hath none to c. her, 29:1
  so will I c. you, 28:13
  society no c. to one not sociable,
    220:1
  thy rod and thy staff c. me, 16:17
  to my age, 190:10
  values c. or money more, 626:22
  warn to c. and command, 375:18
  what gnashing is not a c., 231:9
  ye my people, 27:14
Comfortable advice, 418:7
  feel free easy c. on a raft, 526:22
  feeling of superiority, 642:21
  give woman c. clothes, 651:11
  minds, 688:11
  newspaper afflicts c., 603:12
  no c. feel, 423:1
  progress a c. disease, 689:5
  words, 459:5
Comfortably in debt, 463:8
  padded lunatic asylums, 650:17
  speak c. to Jerusalem, 27:15
Comforted, be c. for him, 32:11
  folly of being c., 595:11
  they shall be c., 33:1
  would not be c., 32:26
Comforters, miserable c. are ye all,
  14:24
Comforteth, love c. like sunshine,
  165:14
  one whom his mother c., 28:13
Comforting thought when not our
  trouble, 633:10
Comfortless, grim-visaged c. Despair,
  321:16
  not leave you c., 40:29
  through c. despairs, 154:6
Comforts, adversity not without c.,
  159:8
  creature c., 286:12
  flee, 410:17
  of life not indispensable, 478:4
  of weary pilgrimage, 317:27
  what I aspired c. me, 467:9
Comic demands anesthesia of heart,
  577:1
  perception of c. tie, 433:23
  poet paint follies, 290:35
Comical how nature contrive, 530:11
Comin', Campbells are c., 778:15
  in on a wing, 718:7
Coming back and coming back, 640:6
  Campbells are c., 778:15
  cold c. we had of it, 669:12
  events cast shadows, 389:3
  everything's c. up roses, 763:7
  far off his c. shone, 259:18
  for to carry me home, 794:14
  good time c., 474:7
  Gospel train's a-c., 794:22
  gude time c., 379:12
  hither, 211:12
  hold fort I am c., 492:10
  I am c. says Death, 94:30
  I'm c., 507:4
  it's c. yet for a' that, 363:23
  my own my sweet, 458:24

Coming (*continued*)
  night of dark intent c., 623:22
  of the Lord, 46:16, 484:6
  patient unto c. of Lord, 46:16
  preserve thy going out and c. in,
    19:25
  see anyone c., 778:11
  sometimes c. sometimes coy, 281:14
  through the rye, 778:6
  to the sacrifice, 416:5
  together foretaste of resurrection,
    404:14
  way of c. into world, 288:13
  we are c. Father Abraham, 461:11
  Yanks are c., 632:12
Comings-in, what are thy c., 185:18
Command, barking of Germans in c.,
  747:1
  by his c. words cut, 600:3
  correspondent to c., 223:28
  eagle mount at thy c., 15:18
  fit for c., 336:15
  give what you c., 114:26
  Heaven's c., 308:12
  iron fist to c. them, 371:12
  man to c., 456:17
  more invitation than c., 293:18
  move only in c., 216:6
  my heart and me, 264:8
  not born to sue but to c., 170:27
  not full c. of myself, 139:11
  obedient to c. of God, 493:19
  prize of general is c., 542:19
  she might c. him tasks, 207:20
  sneer of cold c., 406:13
  success, 292:4
  take c. of troops, 370:12
  threaten and c., 197:30
  warn to comfort and c., 375:18
  where I adore, 202:17
  who commands sea has c., 62:30
Commanded, do without being c.,
  77:14
  God so c., 260:6
  Hellenes c. by Athenians, 62:26
  nature to be c. must be obeyed,
    158:15
  rain shower of c. tears, 167:14
Commander, Congress is his c., 410:4
  to the people, 27:40
Commander-in-Chief, President is C.,
  410:4
Commandment, a new c., 40:25
  first and great c., 36:1, 678:6
  one unconditional, 546:11
Commandments, aren't no Ten C.,
  591:24
  fear God and keep his c., 24:30
  hearkened to my c., 27:28
  love me and keep my c., 9:10
  on these two c. hang law and
    prophets, 36:1
  set my ten c. in your face, 163:19
  ten c., 9:20
Commands, he that c. sea is at liberty,
  160:7
  I gave c., 464:13
  the beauteous files, 270:8
  those he c. move in command,
    216:6

Commands (*continued*)
  war necessary to one who c., 136:12
  who c. the sea has command, 62:30
Commedia è finita, 575:*n*3
Commemorated as day of deliverance, 338:5
Commencement of history, 335:24
Commend, all our swains c. her, 168:7
  all summer long, 597:7
  blame or to c., 302:11
  my spirit, 39:22
  those who are afflicted, 49:4
  to cold oblivion, 408:13
  to write to to c., 229:18
Commendable, humility a thing c., 141:*n*6
Commendations, paltry c. of mankind, 452:12
Commended yellow stockings, 202:19
Comment, no c. splendid expression, 622:1
Commentary, that is whole Torah rest is c., 102:7
Commerce and honest friendship, 344:9
  between equals, 329:4
  equal to whole of that c., 331:7
  heavens fill with c., 455:17
  in matters of c., 372:2
  navigation c. agriculture, 338:10
  promote c. not betray it, 280:*n*1
  where c. long prevails, 328:9
  with our colonies, 331:8
Commercing, looks c. with the skies, 251:24
Commissar, yogi and the c., 716:14
Commission, sins of c. mortal, 318:8
Commit, follies that themselves c., 180:20
  history they did not c., 763:11
  oldest sins newest ways, 184:13
  shalt not c. a social science, 720:20
  thou shalt not c. adultery, 9:12
Committed, crimes c. in thy name, 354:2
  flat burglary as ever c., 187:4
  sins most grievously c., 49:15
  themselves to God, 240:7
  to whom men have c. much, 38:31
  vices c. genteelly, 316:23
Committee for affairs of bourgeoisie, 482:1
  inquisition, 636:7
Committees, intellectual before c., 636:7
Committing suicide by working, 589:20
Commodities, hateful tax on c., 314:3
Commodity bias of the world, 169:26
  of good names, 176:31
  regard land as c., 662:2
  smooth-faced gentleman C., 169:26
  tickling C., 169:26
Commodius vicus of recirculation, 647:18
Common affairs of life, 390:9
  air bathes globe, 489:3
  as light is love, 407:1
  buries empires in c. grave, 340:7

Common (*continued*)
  bush afire with God, 439:7
  call not thou c., 41:9
  cause decays, 72:1
  cause to save Union, 449:1
  century of c. man, 674:22
  crossing bare c., 430:26
  crowd of c. men, 246:22
  dictate of c. sense, 308:22
  earth and every c. sight, 375:3
  education forms c. mind, 300:12
  faction united by c. impulse, 351:21
  fade into light of c. day, 375:8
  friends have all in c., 74:11
  government for c. benefit, 327:2
  grayness silvers everything, 466:1
  hate the c. herd, 96:12
  I drew in the c. air, 30:28
  I embrace the c., 431:12
  law not omnipresence, 542:22
  law nothing but reason, 152:1
  Law of England, 678:21
  life in c. ideal, 436:22
  life's c. way, 374:20
  make good thing too c., 183:22
  man, 552:23, 674:22
  no c. men, 432:22
  not jump with c. spirits, 180:26
  nothing c. did or mean, 268:10
  old c. arbitrator Time, 201:12
  opinions uncommon abilities, 506:10
  people of the skies, 227:9
  provide for c. defense, 346:7
  right of humanity, 448:11
  roll of c. men, 178:2
  sense and plain dealing, 432:11
  sense appall, 583:9
  sense hasty superficial, 477:21
  sense not so common, 306:16
  sense of next age, 500:20
  sense on ground floor, 447:19
  sense reduced to calculus, 351:17
  sense without genius, 677:3
  steals c. from goose, 777:3
  sun air skies, 322:25
  sweets grown c., 221:20
  talk of the town, 279:6
  the actual world the c. sense, 477:7
  thou knowest 'tis c., 193:1
  touch, 593:20
  uncommon valor c. virtue, 658:14
  universal and c. bond, 146:23
  weal and woe is c., 247:13
  where climate's sultry, 402:8
  witness to c. lot, 675:7
Commonest Man shows grace in quarrel, 418:13
  seevility of c. goddamnedest kind, 780:19
Common-looking people best, 450:3
Commonplace, more featureless c. a crime, 577:16
  never yawn or say c., 750:9
Commons faithful to system, 367:15
Commonwealth, caterpillars of the c., 171:17
  debate of c. affairs, 184:21
  gave bodies to c., 72:7
  in c. by contraries execute, 224:4

Commonwealth (*continued*)
  last thousand years, 620:8
  lie abroad for the c., 227:12
  or human combination, 247:13
  realization of c., 523:10
  wise men refrain to meddle in c., 137:14
Communicate, failure to c., 755:18
  poetry c. before understood, 672:20
  speech given to c., 280:2
  to do good and to c., 46:3
Communicatest with dreams, 222:19
Communication, facilitated means of c., 482:2
  monk's state transcends c., 65:3
  of the dead, 671:20
  poetry c. of pleasure, 383:18
  science c. of truth, 383:18
  theory, 691:3
Communications, evil c., 43:22
Communion, further union deeper c., 671:11
  good marriage a c., 138:12
  of Holy Ghost, 44:13
  of Saints, 48:25
  with her visible forms, 411:1
Communism autocracy upside down, 471:25
  government plus electrification, 610:6
  intellectuals describe journey into C., 721:15
  is vice versa, 746:14
  repudiate support of C., 649:5
  specter of C., 481:14
Communist, because I wasn't C., 684:19
  dictatorship of C. Party, 641:3
  every C. grasp truth, 686:12
  members of C. Party, 724:3
  spent life under C. regime, 746:8
  what is a c., 393:12
Communists, Catholics and C., 713:12
  disdain to conceal views, 482:7
  theory of C., 482:4
Communities divide into few and the many, 355:1
  industrialized c., 644:1
  nation of c., 753:11
  overlook one another, 58:6
Community, aim at c. of goods, 366:8
  best political c., 78:22
  build sense of c., 771:2
  human c., 650:5
  in dissolution, 615:6
  investment for c. as whole, 652:15
  like a ship, 508:8
  permanent interests of c., 351:21
  power of c. mass of powers, 368:17
  property subject to c., 576:8
  quarantine to protect c., 649:9
  rules c. evolved, 626:16
  see land as c., 662:2
  standing in the c., 564:1
  what c. produces, 723:8
Commuter one who spends life, 703:9
Compact between North and South, 437:16
  of imagination all c., 174:1
  spirit all c. of fire, 165:9

Comprehends, intellect which c. by itself, 136:17
some bringer of joy, 174:1
who c. art, 371:18
Comprehensible, universe more c. more pointless, 766:4
Comprehensive, most c. soul, 273:11
most c. of rights, 568:16
poet become more c., 672:15
Comprendre, tout c. tout pardonner, 368:n3
Compromise, government founded on c., 331:20
Compulsion, fools by heavenly c., 209:3
give reason on c., 177:25
knowledge acquired under c., 75:21
put upon writers, 658:7
sweet c. in music lie, 251:5
two gods Persuasion and C., 62:28
Compulsive ardor gives charge, 197:32
icy current and c. course, 207:15
Compulsory, bodily exercise when c., 75:21
education c. on all, 486:9
Compunctious visitings of nature, 212:29
Computation backward from ourselves, 158:5
material c., 620:19
Computer no better than its program, 727:6
Comrades chase e'en now the fliers, 483:3
cheer up c. they come, 492:6
leave me here a little, 455:8
that fight and fall, 682:8
Comte's philosophy, 505:8
Concave, hell's c., 256:13
shores, 187:17
Conceal, always stupid losing ability to c., 733:6
dreary morals like vice, 562:6
half c. Soul within, 457:6
its sex, 709:7
knowing how to c. skill, 265:26
no disguise can c. love, 265:7
speech given to c. mind, 280:2
speech to c. thoughts, 306:21
speech to c. wants, 280:n1
taught to c., 402:20
what c. from reader, 721:9
Concealed beauties of writer, 293:4
in yon smoke c., 483:3
lay c. throughout war, 531:17
Concealing, hazard of c., 361:22
Concealment like worm i' bud, 202:14
Conceit lies in his hamstring, 200:11
man wise in his own c., 22:30
pride and c. original sin, 290:26
Conceited carry their comfort, 483:21
man satisfied with effect on himself, 614:12
throw away love on c., 483:n2
Conceits, wise in your c., 42:16
Conceive, heart to c., 346:3
in sin did my mother c. me, 17:20
many without the one, 76:7
so hopeless to c., 514:13
tongue not able to c., 173:27

Conceive (continued)
virgin shall c., 26:5
wise or stupid thing can man c., 350:23
Conceived by the Holy Ghost, 48:25
greater than God cannot be c., 121:4
in Liberty, 450:2
nation so c., 450:2
there is a man child c., 13:34
well c. is clearly said, 280:6
when Charlemagne was c., 599:5
Concentered, wretch c. all in self, 378:1
Concentrate their energies, 570:5
Concentrates his mind wonderfully, 317:1
Concentration camp universe, 732:3
good writing takes enormous c., 751:10
of business, 525:11
on electric chair, 743:1
Concept, essential c. and first truth, 732:14
of length, 646:3
of time makes possible Day of Judgment, 652:1
portray phenomenon c. needed, 345:9
to call forth c., 345:9
Conception, creativeness is c. and birth, 588:22
makes originally false c. come true, 728:13
Concepts, abstract c., 345:9
can't form children on own c., 349:21
physical c. free creations, 635:15
stairs of c., 710:9
Concern, conduct largest c. of life, 500:19
for man and his fate, 635:13
for unfortunate not socialism, 729:20
our c. be peace of mind, 82:14
your c. Roman to rule under law, 94:15
your c. when neighbor's wall on fire, 97:19
Concerns, entrusted with great c., 61:32
Concessions born of earnest struggle, 480:16
of the weak, 331:6
Conciliate with dignity, 318:22
Conciliation, religion c. of powers, 564:22
Concise, vigorous writing c., 608:9
Conclave of the night's stars, 63:9
Conclude against wall of stone, 749:17
only on edge of grave, 535:13
Concludes with Cupid's curse, 156:13
Conclusion, foregone c., 207:13
lame and impotent c., 206:9
leap to c., 738:10
of the whole matter, 24:30
Conclusions from insufficient premises, 525:1
most impossible of c., 588:4

Conclusions (continued)
necessary c., 451:5
Concord and Lexington, 394:13
give to all nations c., 49:11
give you home and gracious c., 53:10
love-quarrels in c. end, 261:20
lover of c., 49:2
of sweet sounds, 182:10
sweet milk of c., 215:27
traveled a good deal in C., 477:29
wolves and lambs have no c., 52:22
Concordant is discordant, 62:16
Concordia discors, 97:n8
Concrete cases, 542:17
general with c., 384:14
man has one interest, 545:8
Condemn, conscience makes us c. ourselves, 235:22
fault and not actor, 203:34
innocent person, 306:2
neither do I c., 40:9
nor years c., 606:9
these men because few, 479:1
try cause c. to death, 517:6
wrongs we seek to c., 683:3
Condemnation, justice thunders c., 476:18
Condemned alike to groan, 321:17
cells of Newgate, 524:17
into everlasting redemption, 187:5
judge c. when criminal absolved, 99:22
Soul c. to be, 513:7
survive to testify, 760:8
to kill time, 736:15
to repeat past, 588:6
Condemnest, thou c. thyself, 41:37
Condemns, every tale c. me, 166:15
Condensation of sensations, 607:15
Condescend to drop gin scuttle to cellar, 732:8
to take a bit, 289:5
Condescending, not c. to anything within reach, 76:10
Condition, abnormal exhausting c., 571:15
as cheerful as any in that c., 279:3
bears stamp of human c., 146:18
death inviolable c. of life, 629:11
decoyed into our c., 279:13
ideal c. to be right by instinct, 66:17
indispensable c. of freedom, 609:13
living in equality of c., 523:10
of complete simplicity, 672:7
universe evolved from unfamiliar c., 766:4
upon which God given liberty, 351:20
which is called war, 239:21
world in good c., 279:17
Conditioned people of Africa to humiliation, 752:9
Conditions, all sorts and c. of men, 49:3
dat prevail, 686:2
little adjustment in face of new c., 683:6
stars govern our c., 210:25

Conquered (*continued*)
you have c. Galilean, 113:5
Conquering army on border, 474:15
he went forth c., 47:18
hero comes, 308:23
Conqueror creates a muse, 249:26
lie at proud foot of c., 170:23
Worm, 452:8
Conquers, if nature c., 365:13
love c. all things, 92:20
ruling passion c. reason, 300:23
wherever Roman c. he dwells, 103:9
Conquest, horse noblest c. of man,
311:6
of joy of freedom, 682:8
of world by creed, 741:13
right of c., 319:7
shameful c. of itself, 171:11
Conquest's crimson wing, 323:6
Conquests, carnage and c. cease, 401:9
even to Antipodes, 160:n5
honorable c., 331:25
shrunk to this, 188:19
tramplings of three c., 248:28
Conquistadors, language inherited
from C., 714:6
Con's, from pro's and c. they fell,
149:39
Conscience ae thing I cannae bear,
561:18
agenbite of inwit c., 647:13
argue according to c., 255:3
aroused popular c., 646:13
brilliance without c., 685:13
but word cowards use, 166:16
catch c. of the king, 196:8
clear c. is sure card, 155:12
convenient end left to every man's
c., 289:9
courage of c., 422:16
coward c. dost afflict, 166:14
dictates of c., 339:11
does make cowards, 196:10
excused from it as against c., 324:9
freedom of speech freedom of c.,
527:29
gentle beast of good c., 174:6
god to all mortals, 81:17
good c. continual feast, 235:21
guardian of community rules,
626:16
hath thousand tongues, 166:15
Hebraism strictness of c., 500:17
in everything, 320:20
is great ledger book, 235:22
justice temporary but c. eternal,
138:8
liberty of c., 247:13
little grain of c., 456:6
live without c., 516:4
love gets better of c., 540:6
matters of c., 325:6
money in jar c. clear, 523:13
no more to do with gallantry,
352:25
no witness so dreadful as c., 85:11
not cut c. to fit fashions, 716:9
of her worth, 259:27
of people's representatives, 646:13
or vanity appalled, 598:16

Conscience (*continued*)
perfect interpreter of life, 661:1
quiet c. stands brunt of life, 68:15
salve c. by our concurrence, 628:1
science without c. ruin of soul,
139:13
seared with hot iron, 45:14
social c. of nation, 761:8
still and quiet c., 225:17
strict regard to c., 339:3
tongue confuted by c., 250:11
uncreated c. of race, 647:11
upright and stainless, 126:4
use money according to c., 539:2
value it next to good c., 245:30
void of offense, 41:30
warns somebody looking, 643:4
what can assuage c., 235:23
with injustice corrupted, 164:1
with intellect or with c., 453:14
with whole c. listen, 641:12
Conscience-calmed, thou be c., 417:3
Consciences, historian of fine c.,
573:17
old sinners have brawny c., 262:14
Conscientious, sensible and c. men,
315:n7
Conscious, beyond what c. ego can
reach, 629:3
elevate life by c. endeavor, 478:16
in c. virtue bold, 299:19
mind c. of rectitude, 93:n13
mind trained like parrot, 628:14
movements reflex, 511:1
of our own existence, 78:7
that we are perceiving, 78:7
water saw its God, 264:6
Consciously, not try to think c.,
593:27
Consciousness, black c., 774:2
Captivity is C., 512:9
first c. sense of wind, 616:11
freedom stretches to limits of c.,
629:5
Hellenism spontaneity of c., 500:17
inseparable like life and c., 657:19
is disease, 589:10
life c. of what we can do, 653:14
like bird's life, 545:16
national c., 572:5
of freedom, 372:9
one unbroken stream, 545:17
poor slipping out of c., 759:3
religious feeling in c., 493:21
stream of c., 545:16
use small portion of c., 545:6
welcomes or rejects, 545:18
whole past experience in c., 538:18
Consciousnesses melt into each other,
545:17
Conscripted unvictorious ones, 662:7
Consecrate to thee, 388:16
we cannot c., 450:2
with thine own hues, 406:10
Consecrated it above our power,
450:2
not buried in c. ground, 539:18
Consecration and poet's dream, 376:6
from within himself, 691:4
what we did had c., 436:1

Consecutive, two c. moments, 493:17
Consensus, president is c. seeker,
729:21
Consent, deriving powers from c.,
343:2
if sinners entice thee c. not, 20:18
not govern without c., 448:4
not inferior without your c., 654:14
of governed, 343:2
of governors and governed, 338:1
of the governed, 491:25
reference to one c., 184:25
silence gives c., 329:5
taxed without c., 327:n6
whispering I will ne'er c. consented,
402:10
Consented, whispering ne'er consent
c., 402:10
Consents, no injustice to person who
c., 120:4
poverty but not my will c., 176:11
Consequence, applause of great c.,
317:19
deepest c., 212:21
repentance is fear of c., 265:21
servitude c. of crime, 351:20
trammel up the c., 213:5
Consequences I note and enjoy noting,
549:13
logical c. are beacons, 505:14
looking toward c., 546:18
pernicious c., 474:21
power elite share decisions of c.,
739:18
serious and alarming c., 336:18
will be the same, 341:2
Conservation harmony between men
and land, 662:3
Principle of C. of Force, 496:17
Conservatism, meanness in argument
of c., 432:14
Conservative, habit c. agent of society,
545:10
little Liberal or C., 530:11
Conserve what is obsolescent, 574:7
Consider anything don't cry, 519:11
beauty sufficient end, 596:22
her ways and be wise, 20:27
him well, 210:6
how my light is spent, 255:11
in day of adversity c., 24:10
let every man c. last day, 66:2
lilies of field, 33:20
my Cat Jeoffry, 325:17
my traveling expenses, 686:20
one must c. the end, 268:2
question can machines think, 732:5
where you come out, 100:12
wise what they cleave to, 111:9
Consideration like an angel came,
184:20
made arrogant by c., 72:9
of public object, 72:1
wives to be paid in c., 739:14
Considers, no physician c. own good,
75:5
Consimility, wonderful c. of fancy,
238:n3
Consist, by him all things c., 44:37
Consistency, foolish c., 431:23

Contemplation (*continued*)
  he for c. formed, 258:12
  her best nurse C., 252:29
  mind serene for c., 292:n4
  more than reading, 271:20
  right c., 65:1
  sundry c. of my travels, 191:26
Contemplative or saintly life, 719:10
Contemporaries, man lives life of c.,
    629:10
Contempt against majesty of Heaven,
    308:19
  and anger of lip, 202:25
  comes from head, 404:12
  familiarity breeds c., 58:20
  for c. too high, 266:15
  for governor who is afraid, 66:5
  for wildest blow, 545:3
  no weakness no c., 261:25
  of God contempt of self, 115:3
  reading it with perfect c., 664:6
  silence is c., 436:15
  speak of moderns without c., 305:3
  treating with c. all from God,
    138:14
Contemptible, bored more c. than
    bore, 524:11
  rendered United States c., 572:9
  ridiculous c. animal, 312:6
  struggle, 330:23
Contemptuous, discerning reader c.,
    574:17
Contend, gods c. in vain, 365:17
  no more Love, 465:8
  seven towns c. for Homer, 233:n4
  ye powers of heaven, 264:18
Contender, could've been a c., 737:6
Contending, calm c. kings, 167:2
  fierce c. nations, 292:16
  for liberty, 336:13
  leaders ambitiously c., 351:22
  with adversity, 235:2
Content at the last, 671:19
  be c. with your lot, 59:7
  farewell c., 207:8
  good pleasure ease c., 301:16
  humble livers in c., 225:8
  I am c., 369:5
  if reversion nourish, 671:19
  in health and mind's c., 279:18
  in tight hot cell, 696:2
  in whatsoever state to be c., 44:36
  land of lost c., 579:9
  majority of men c., 136:16
  make c. with fortunes fit, 210:1
  mind c. both crown and kingdom,
    157:19
  money means and c., 191:8
  my crown is called c., 164:19
  natural c., 595:19
  nothing less will c. me, 331:12
  poor and c. is rich, 206:32
  shut up in measureless c., 213:19
  that we might procreate like trees,
    248:19
  thoughts that savor of c., 157:18
  to breathe his native air, 298:5
  to entertain lag-end of my life,
    178:29
  to live it all again, 598:5

Content (*continued*)
  travelers must be c., 190:14
  with life retire from world, 95:3
  with my harm, 191:9
  with vegetable love, 529:18
  with your lot, 59:7
Contented, always c. with his life,
    423:15
  live on little with c. mind, 90:9
  men employed best c., 311:5
  most enjoy c. least, 220:16
  slaves howe'er c., 334:3
  white people never c., 370:3
  wi' little, 362:7
Contentedness, procurer of c., 245:17
Contention, let long c. cease, 500:2
  man of strife and c., 28:27
Contentions are like bars of a castle,
    21:40
  fat c., 254:19
  of a wife, 21:44
Contentious, petty wisdom c., 80:7
Contentment fails, 328:9
  in c. still feel need, 638:25
  nor poorest receive c., 231:14
  preaches c. to toad, 590:19
  recover through c. with physician,
    71:5
Contents, inability of mind to corre-
    late all c., 679:6
  torn out and stripped, 309:5
Contest between capitalism and social-
    ism over, 746:16
  end a c. quicker, 352:24
  great c. follows, 334:31
  this is a people's c., 449:8
Contests, what mighty c. rise, 299:9
Context, immediate c. of history,
    684:18
Contiguity, boundless c. of shade,
    334:26
Continence, give me c. but not now,
    114:23
Continent allotted by Providence,
    473:15
  almost a c. hardly a nation, 660:8
  Americans prefer C., 605:22
  brought forth on c., 450:2
  disappoint a C., 524:2
  heart no island but c., 159:15
  iron curtain across C., 622:2
  man home in every c., 722:14
  man is a piece of the c., 231:8
  most momentous question on c.,
    503:2
  our c. the old one, 351:13
  striving to grasp c., 503:3
  untamed c., 503:4
Continental, Jehovah and C. Congress,
    341:15
  never tolerate two c. powers, 676:8
Continents, African giant among c.,
    719:15
  American c. not subjects for coloni-
    zation, 360:10
  dissolve into sea, 721:13
Contingencies, O to be self-balanced
    for c., 488:14
Continual comfort in a face, 163:3

Continual (*continued*)
  contentions of wife are c. dropping,
    21:44
  endeavor in c. motion, 184:23
  feast, 21:26
  live in c. mortification, 308:18
  small have c. plodders won, 168:15
Continually, think c. of truly great,
    727:10
  times change and move c., 154:3
Continuation, thermonuclear war not
    c. of politics, 749:8
Continued, not one c. faithful until
    old age, 76:17
Continues, tree c. to be, 673:5
Continueth, he fleeth and c. not, 14:20
Continuing, faculty of c. to improve,
    335:24
  no c. city, 46:2
Continuity, restructuring combines c.
    innovation, 763:14
  self has c. and sameness, 708:5
Continuous and seems always existing,
    56:16
  as stars that shine, 375:20
  brain changes c., 545:17
  nature one and c., 477:23
  use of any organ, 347:13
Contra naturam, 659:16
Contraceptive, like having totally ef-
    ficient c., 740:16
Contract, passions we inspire c. time,
    612:17
  permanent c. on temporary feeling,
    540:5
  Social C. vast conspiracy, 601:7
  succession bourn none, 224:4
  'twixt Hannah God and me, 521:1
  unspoken c. of wife and her works,
    739:14
Contraction of life, 628:11
Contracts, prisoners cannot enter into
    c., 745:16
  with the people, 655:14
Contradict, do I c. myself, 489:21
  proverbs c. each other, 726:15
Contradiction, phrase long poem c.,
    453:12
  what a c. is man, 271:7
  when we risk no c., 297:8
  woman's a c. still, 300:20
Contradictions exist side by side,
    495:4
Contraption, verbal c., 721:9
Contraries, by c. execute all things,
    224:4
Contrariously, work c., 184:25
Contrariwise, 518:22
Contrary blast proclaims, 261:18
  bringeth bliss, 163:17
  everythink c. with me, 470:20
  Mary quite c., 788:19
  men of c. character, 61:5
  runneth not to the c., 325:21
  Spirit and flesh c., 44:18
  to the c. notwithstanding, 346:10
Contribute to diversion or improve-
    ment of country, 292:19
Contribution according to capacity,
    481:n4

Contribution (*continued*)
to current literature, 525:4
Contributions to peace of world,
655:13
Contrite, broken and c. heart, 17:25
Contrivance of human wisdom,
332:11
to raise prices, 326:3
Contrivances, wisdom of human c.,
331:10
Contrive, head to c., 262:1
our fees to pilfer, 73:5
Contrived corridors, 668:7
double debt to pay, 329:19
Control and communication theory,
691:3
cannot c. atomic energy, 613:6
Chance shall not c., 497:10
civilian c. of military, 655:18
forces of nature, 677:12
grammar c. even kings, 269:29
lease of my true love c., 221:23
man c. the wind, 497:22
men gained c. over nature, 569:12
nuclear c., 742:5
over human behavior, 558:10
stops at the shore, 400:30
straitjacket or club c., 567:27
without c. over ourselves, 351:12
Controlled by world constructed by
men, 715:11
events c. me, 450:4
Controlling intelligence understands,
111:17
Controls, love of other sights c., 228:3
Controversy, hearts of c., 187:21
Contumely, proud man's c., 196:10
Conturbat, Timor Mortis c. me, 136:4
Convenience comfort prestige, 783:16
he that for c. takes oath, 263:24
Convenient, a c. season, 41:31
break eggs at c. end, 289:9
never c. time for any, 705:1
that there be gods, 101:14
Convent of the Sacred Heart, 668:16
Convention, by c. there is color, 70:28
is ruler of all, 64:15
system has faults, 655:16
when I look out at c., 771:12
Conventional, hallmark of c. wisdom
acceptability, 723:6
merely c. signs, 519:20
picture of femininity, 748:17
Conventionality not morality, 476:12
Convent's narrow room, 376:10
solitary gloom, 300:3
Convents, happy c., 304:1
Conversation art of never appearing a
bore, 560:7
for c. well endued, 289:16
good nature agreeable in c., 293:2
hinges in French c., 320:35
is but carving, 289:21
Johnson's c. was mustard, 342:10
of most searching sort, 432:2
of select companions, 292:21
one of greatest pleasures, 626:17
preaching word for dull c., 380:2
smaller excellencies of c., 342:1
socializing instrument, 653:7

Conversation (*continued*)
three cannot take part in c., 432:2
unforced as c. passed, 423:14
wants leisure, 626:17
when you fall into a man's c.,
293:19
where there's half a c., 681:7
writing name for c., 320:17
Conversational or homely type, 609:11
Conversations, without pictures or c.,
517:2
Converse and live with ease, 302:11
formed by thy c., 302:2
high c. with mighty dead, 307:18
Conversing I forget all time, 258:21
Conversion of world lead to perpetual
peace, 536:19
refuse till c. of Jews, 268:14
Convert Bill of Rights, 683:4
you into stew, 670:1
Converted and become as children,
35:31
love c. from thing it was, 220:24
silenced man not c., 537:7
Converting human beings to machines,
481:9
Convey the wise it call, 182:20
Convicted, Daniel had c. them, 32:18
Conviction, do evil from religious c.,
271:10
editor's c., 677:6
faithful to c. to old age, 76:17
impeachment for and c. of high
crimes, 346:8
sadness of c., 542:8
the best lack all c., 596:19
we are loved, 427:22
Convictions, enter c. in open lists,
615:6
people in old times had c., 420:8
Convince hearers of own assertions,
75:1
logic and sermons never c., 489:14
to c. is to weaken, 616:15
Convinced, frightening when c. they
are right, 719:16
of too little, 672:17
Convinces, credit to man who c.
world, 556:3
Convincing while they thought of dining, 330:10
Conviviality, taper of c., 469:26
Convolutions of smooth-lipped shell,
376:21
Convulsions, system liable to c., 559:9
Conwiviality, taper of c., 469:26
Cook, amount to Hannah C., 782:3
and captain bold, 528:22
every c. learn to govern, 610:2
good c. as cooks go, 610:14
ill c. that cannot lick fingers, 176:10
makes his c. his merit, 269:12
Cookery is an art a noble science,
234:16
kissing don't last c. do, 508:22
Cookie, me want c., 775:8
the way c. crumbles, 783:24
Cooks are gentlemen, 234:16
as c. go she went, 610:14
cannot live without c., 516:4

Cooks (*continued*)
Epicurean c., 217:12
God sends meat Devil sends c.,
141:*n*3
guests praise it not c., 160:17
Cooks' own ladles, 464:18
Cool, caverns c. and deep, 497:7
clear and c. clear and c., 484:14
day so c. so calm, 243:10
glassy c. translucent wave, 253:11
in any case keep c., 692:21
in dust in c. tombs, 634:8
in Gardens when eve c., 511:9
keep c. it will be all one, 432:27
kept breath to c. pottage, 55:8
kindliness of sheets, 663:2
Negro c. strong imperturbable,
480:19
of the day, 6:21
one Pain, 513:10
place was c. and pleasant, 735:19
sequestered vale of life, 322:17
we real c., 740:8
winding saxophones, 634:10
Cooled a long age, 415:11
Coolibah tree, 589:5
Coolidge look as if weaned on pickle,
654:9
Cooling streams, 285:4
Coolness, wind to bring c. to men,
53:8
Cools, till husband c., 300:18
time c. time clarifies, 629:20
Coon, gone c., 398:7
Cooped we live and die, 446:1
Cooperate, stay and c., 681:5
Cooperation with Government, 661:10
Coort, supreme c. follows iliction,
602:14
Coot, haunts of c., 458:15
Cope, starry c. of heaven, 259:4
Cophetua loved the beggarmaid,
174:25
sware oath, 456:5
Copious Dryden, 303:9
Copper, beneath her c. a worm,
477:15
Irishman lined with c., 526:16
kettledrums, 619:2
Copperheads, forgot c. and assassin,
634:8
Coppice, leant upon c. gate, 540:9
Copulate in the foam, 599:17
Copulation, action limited to c. of
clichés, 703:4
birth c. and death, 670:2
let c. thrive, 211:1
Copy, create equivalent not c., 665:16
leave the world no c., 201:26
your forefathers, 3:12
Copycat, life is a c., 667:1
Copying, by c. ancient models per-
petuated, 115:8
mechanism for genetic material,
760:5
Copyists, shortened labor of c., 411:22
Coquette, death and i c., 633:3
Cor, j'aime le son du c., 421:*n*1
Cor lacerare nequit, 290:23
Coral is far more red, 222:8

Coral (*continued*)
lip admires, 246:9
of his bones c. made, 223:32
Corbeaux, le vol noir des c., 786:20
Cord, as unto bow c. is, 441:26
no c. draw forcibly as love, 235:13
silver c. be loosed, 24:28
stretch c. however fine, 411:12
threefold c. not quickly broken,
23:35
time consume strongest c., 379:10
Cordelia, such sacrifices my C., 211:14
Cordial, gold in phisik is a c., 129:28
restore with c. fruit, 243:16
Cords, draw iniquity with c. of vanity,
25:40
scourge of small c., 39:41
Core, apple's cleft through c., 365:23
boredom at c. of life, 272:1
hypocrite rotten to the c., 718:11
red heart's c., 414:15
wear him in heart's c., 197:4
Corinth, not everyone can get to C.,
97:17
Corinthian a lad of mettle, 177:19
Coriolanus, have talk with C., 668:9
Corioli, Volscians in C., 219:15
Cork, Drunkard cannot meet C.,
514:10
lighter than c. danced, 565:11
Cork-heeled shoon, 784:34
Corkscrew, clean tumbler and c.,
469:22
Cormorant devouring Time, 168:11
sat like a c., 258:7
Corn, alien c., 415:17
before my tears did drown it,
243:16
colonels full of c., 580:15
cotton c. and taters, 564:19
cow's in the c., 789:4
crop of c. a field of tares, 156:22
ear on tip of stalk, 787:6
farmer sowing the c., 792:24
field of ripe c., 667:23
fields of c. where Troy was, 101:18
full c. in the ear, 37:21
full of kernels, 580:15
high as elephant's eye, 692:9
hope c. in chaff, 399:5
Jimmie crack c., 780:2
licker stop victim's watch, 631:2
like smut in c., 716:18
meadows rich with c., 443:9
never thrust sickle in another's c.,
100:4
night in which c. grows, 479:7
no use of metal c. or wine, 224:4
not move sickle unto neighbor's c.,
10:20
not muzzle ox when treadeth c.,
10:21
out of olde feldes newe c., 128:8
rain on c. a sad thing, 92:7
raise less c. more hell, 560:3
sent not c. for rich men only,
218:23
shock of c. cometh in season, 14:5
staff of life, 286:*n*7
state that raises c., 566:4

Corn (*continued*)
two ears of c. grow, 289:11
was orient, 280:23
whar man gits c. pone, 528:9
Cornelia said these are my jewels,
235:15
Cornelius, my new book to you C.,
90:14
Corner, better to dwell in a c., 22:7
draft fluttered flame, 680:3
driven from every other c., 325:6
head stone of the c., 19:20
in deepest heart, 546:6
in the thing I love, 207:4
never c. opponent, 692:21
of foreign field, 663:3
of nonsense, 385:3
old men from chimney c., 156:2
sits wind in that c., 186:29
thing not done in c., 41:35
work of art c. of creation, 541:11
years around seatown c., 738:1
Cornered-animal fear, 767:21
Corners, belie all c. of world, 219:29
come three c. of world, 170:24
four angels on c. of earth, 47:20
four c. to my bed, 266:*n*3
in his hand are'c. of earth, 48:21
not wholly reap the c., 9:24
old fantastical duke of dark c.,
204:25
round earth's imagined c., 230:19
Cornets, played before Lord on c.,
12:5
Cornfield, o'er green c. did pass,
192:12
Cornish, twenty thousand C. men,
433:31
Corn-rows, between c. held old puissance, 642:23
Corollaries, axioms and c., 542:5
Coromandel, black men fought on C.,
425:11
coast of C., 472:9
Coronation, kind as kings upon c.
day, 275:16
Coronets, kind hearts more than c.,
454:3
Corporal, in c. sufferance, 204:11
Corporation of the Goosequill, 463:16
Corporations cannot commit treason,
152:5
have no souls, 152:5, 555:15
Corps, army c. annihilate each other,
521:2
Corpse, frozen c. was he, 441:1
make a lovely c., 469:44
of Public Credit, 394:18
Politician's c. laid away, 609:5
putrid c. of liberty, 652:21
slovenly unhandsome c., 177:3
watch enemy's c. go by, 794:2
Corpses, behold they were dead c.,
13:12
Corpulent man of fifty, 396:23
Corpus, habeas c., 119:7, 344:9
hoc est c., 307:*n*4
hoc est enim C. meum, 48:10
Corpus Christi, on C. heart, 742:10

Correct, easier to be critical than c.,
435:3
ideas also dubious ideas, 749:10
what all mortals may c., 289:18
Corrected, revised and c. by Author,
309:5
Corrections, error bursting with c.,
556:22
Correctness, passion with c., 547:2
Correggios and stuff, 330:14
Correlate, inability of mind to c. all
contents, 679:6
Correlative, objective c., 672:11
Correspondent to command, 223:28
Corridor, lit c. races through dark
one, 747:17
Corridors, contrived c., 668:7
of power, 718:1
of Time, 441:11
Corroborative, merely c. detail, 531:7
Corrupt a saint, 176:32
abilities utterly c., 386:1
enemies intelligent and c., 713:13
evil communications c., 43:22
influence, 331:26
judge no king can c., 225:11
moth and rust doth c., 33:13
one good custom c. world, 459:26
peace c., 260:22
plea tainted and c., 181:4
power tends to c., 521:5
progeny yet more c., 96:17
unlimited power apt to c., 313:2
word like corrupt tree, 116:13
Corrupted, conscience with injustice
c., 164:1
goodness with power c., 684:15
sun not c., 77:*n*5
traitorously c. youth, 164:11
Corruptible put on incorruption,
43:27
Corruption, guilty of c. and renounce
defense, 158:16
honest words suffered c., 237:4
I have said to c., 14:26
man coffer full of c., 134:15
sown in c., 43:25
strong c. inhabits blood, 203:3
symptom of liberty, 340:4
wins not more than honesty, 225:21
Corruptly, offices not derived c.,
180:27
Corrupts, absolute power c. absolutely, 521:5
power c. poetry cleanses, 742:6
Socrates c. the youth, 74:14
Corse, dead c. in complete steel,
194:11
to rampart we hurried, 405:15
Corsets, Heine loosened c. of German
language, 626:5
Cortesía, la mesma, 150:*n*7
Cortez, stout C., 413:24
Cory, Richard C. one summer night,
608:8
Corydon what madness has caught
you, 92:5
Così è se vi pare, 604:3
Cosmic night, 629:3

Cosmographers, physicians by their love grown c., 231:3
Cosmopolite, best C. loves country, 460:9
Cosmopolouse, bloomin' c., 592:22
Cosmos, energies of c. into cultural manifestation, 712:15
push and pressure of c., 546:17
Cost, every farthing of c., 720:17
give and not count c., 139:3
good words c. little, 244:14
is labor to produce anything, 487:20
little less than new, 291:24
loved and c. me so much, 247:12
of outworn buried age, 221:2
sitteth and counteth c., 38:33
utility or c. of production, 547:15
Costing not less than everything, 672:7
Costly, attire comely not c., 155:5
morality private c. luxury, 535:30
seasons, 757:15
so c. a sacrifice, 450:9
thy habit, 193:30
Costs, good counsel c. nothing, 235:5
nothing to be polite, 622:6
Cottage, hides not visage from our c., 223:12
modest looks c. adorn, 329:22
planning retirement c., 755:6
poor man in mean c., 32:1
poorest man in his c., 312:19
soul's dark c., 250:6
Cottages, poor men's c. palaces, 179:27
Cotton, corn and c. and cockleburs, 566:4
is king, 427:11
land of c., 475:1
spinning noble, 413:6
where c. and taters grow, 564:19
Cottons mather, 697:7
Cottontail and Peter, 600:20
Couch, frowsy c. in sorrow steep, 364:3
literature old c. stuffed with fleas, 763:12
when owls do cry, 224:25
wraps drapery of c., 411:4
Couché, longtemps je me suis c. de bonne heure, 612:n3
Cough, love and a c., 244:4
Coughed and called it fate, 608:4
Coughing drowns parson's saw, 169:14
Could, if youth but knew if old age but c., 144:13
nor even thing I c. be, 364:1
Couleurs, les parfums les c., 494:n3
Council, before ashes of c. fire cold, 502:5
in c. rooms apart, 643:14
outcome of words is in the c., 52:9
power in aristocratical c., 338:16
unapproachable in C. of Ten, 652:7
Zeus god of c., 51:6
Counciler, White Citizen's C., 760:16
Councilor ought not to sleep, 51:5
Councils, takes wisdom from c., 331:26

Counsel, good c. cheap, 235:5
how hard for women to keep c., 188:13
if this c. be of men, 41:1
love overwhelms wise c., 54:17
man who c. can bestow, 299:7
of thine own heart, 32:9
princely c. in his face, 257:7
sometimes c. take, 299:13
spirit of c. and might, 26:10
three keep c. if two away, 142:13
took sweet c. together, 17:27
two may keep c., 142:n7
walketh not in c. of ungodly, 15:29
who darkeneth c. by words, 15:6
Counseled ignoble ease, 257:6
Counselor, name shall be called C., 26:8
Counselors, good c. lack no clients, 203:23
kings and c. of the earth, 13:35
multitude of c., 21:7
wisest of c. Time, 65:6
Counsels, close designs crooked c., 274:3
excellent things in c., 22:12
hate c. not in such quality, 181:1
how monie c. sweet, 363:3
sic c. ye give, 785:3
Count, as long as I c. votes, 504:1
cats in Zanzibar, 478:34
chickens before hatched, 58:16
don't c. your boobies, 690:14
let me c. the ways, 438:23
let us c. our spoons, 315:27
milestones till haze dances, 446:27
myself in nothing else so happy, 171:14
myself king of space, 195:26
only sunny hours, 390:n3
that day lost, 779:1
them over every one apart, 586:17
until nothing else to c., 433:14
when angry c. ten, 345:6
you can c. me out, 770:13
Counted as the small dust, 27:21
them and cursed luck, 579:21
two and seventy stenches, 383:16
Countenance, bright c. of truth, 254:14
cannot lie, 163:3
chide God for c., 191:28
damned disinheriting c., 352:30
did the C. Divine, 359:17
heart changeth his c., 31:34
his c. like richest alchemy, 187:30
human c. composed of ten parts, 104:8
Knight of the Sorrowful C., 149:18
lift up his c. upon thee, 9:28
lift up the light of thy c., 15:32
like lightning, 37:14
merry heart maketh a cheerful c., 21:25
more in sorrow than anger, 193:21
of all Science, 373:15
soon brightened, 376:21
that in your c. would call master, 209:5
tyrant's threatening c., 96:15

Counter, making of c. culture, 765:11
original spare strange, 551:1
stake c. boldly, 466:16
Counteracts Devil who is Death, 325:18
Counterargument, possibility of c., 749:10
Countercheck quarrelsome, 192:16
Counterfeit a gloom, 252:5
Jove's dread clamors c., 207:8
sleep death's c., 214:14
Counterfeited, laughed with c. glee, 329:17
Countermoves, revolution legality c. in same game, 573:11
Counterparts in world of fact, 493:18
Counters, wise men's c., 239:17
Countesses had no outlines, 469:20
Counteth, sitteth and c. cost, 38:33
Counting cars on New Jersey Turnpike, 772:10
my numberless fingers, 756:10
Countinghouse, king in c., 790:1
Countless infinitesimals of feeling, 385:4
thousands mourn, 361:8
Countree, is this mine own c., 382:1
North C. hard, 693:6
Countries, churches in flat c., 377:n1
give themselves to you, 656:10
material out of which c. made, 616:8
outdistance advanced c., 610:3
peace of all c. connected, 644:17
preferreth all c. before his own, 237:22
seek no aggrandizement, 650:7
wandering through many c., 91:17
Country, abroad for good of c., 295:14
absorbs poet, 488:12
all places all airs one c., 248:17
America my c., 627:11, 660:8
American says he loves c., 706:11
anything for good of c., 295:14
as soldier for c., 586:n3
ask not what c. do for you, 741:7
behind people your c., 501:17
belongs to people, 449:4
best c. is at home, 328:8
betraying c. betraying friend, 636:12
better off when Indians running it, 765:6
cannot ask success even for c., 368:14
ceases to be free for irreligion, 683:5
cherished in hearts, 460:14
cover c. in books, 551:19
cries of c. in chains, 786:n5
defamers of his c., 520:11
defended by our hands, 460:14
departed into their own c., 32:24
die but once to serve c., 292:12
die in defense of his c., 52:7
disable benefits of your c., 191:28
diversion, 291:11
divine nature gave us c., 87:3
dreary tract of c., 452:4
epitaph for their c., 588:7

Country (*continued*)
essential service to c., 289:11
every c. but his own, 530:21
every C. hath its Machiavel, 136:*n*5
fame noised throughout c., 10:35
fate of c. not in ballot, 477:27
father of your c., 336:*n*7
fight for one's c., 51:36
fight to set c. free, 341:3
find my c. in the right, 390:*n*4
Flora and c. green, 415:11
foreign troop in my c., 313:6
fornication but in another c., 162:9
fortunes of my c., 370:2
found that famous c., 683:10
friend of every c. but own, 371:23
from yon far c. blows, 579:9
genius is of no c., 333:12
give c. back to Indians, 698:11
God made the c., 334:25
good for c. good for General Motors, 680:15
good news from a far c., 22:27
good to be shifty in new c., 475:3
governed by despot, 317:6
grow up with c., 475:*n*2
half savage c., 659:4
has 265 different kinds of cheese, 678:15
history of c. begins in heart, 616:5
honorable to die for one's c., 96:14
I loathe the c., 291:11
I tremble for my c., 343:9
in c. of blind one-eyed man king, 136:6
in c. you praise city, 95:12
in town, 106:25
is this mine own c., 382:1
King will not leave c., 704:5
know something of own c., 320:30
lead c. like Britain, 756:2
leaving c. for country's sake, 295:*n*2
let who loves c. follow, 440:11
love c. and be poor, 303:18
love of home love of c., 469:28
love sweeping c., 695:6
loved c. as no other man, 501:18
loves native c. best, 460:9
man to all c. dear, 329:12
master of sea Master of every c., 160:*n*5
merchants have no c., 344:16
most beautiful in West C., 616:21
mouth of no other c., 683:11
my c. is Kiltartan Cross, 596:10
my c. is the world, 341:7
my c. 'tis of thee, 444:3
my c. 'tis of you, 688:12
my soul there is a c., 270:8
needs good five-cent cigar, 565:4
new purchaser of c. place, 714:15
no c. for old men, 597:7
no matter if c. need comedian, 638:4
no place in c. where man can be alone, 398:11
North C. hard c., 693:6
not a c. at all, 616:8
of dinginess bleakness, 446:26

Country (*continued*)
of the Gadarenes, 37:23
of worth, 362:16
one c. one constitution, 395:2
one life to lose for my c., 354:16
our C. however bounded, 460:14
our c. right or wrong, 390:22, 510:18
our c. the world, 437:12
peace of each c., 644:17
physical mental health of c., 748:18
pride of c., 463:5
pride puts c. down, 776:17
prophet in his own c., 35:13
punished as enemy of c., 369:8
relinquish life for good of c., 370:14
right or wrong, 390:22
run by politicians, 761:16
Savior of 'is c., 591:18
sell a c., 370:4
serve c. and thy kind, 522:12
she is my c. still, 333:19
shed blood for his c., 576:2
shrink from service of c., 340:22
slow sort of c., 518:19
small c. with few people, 58:6
spirit of government that of c., 564:15
spirit of resistance in c., 345:14
spread over globe, 446:27
stand by c. as mother, 501:17
stranger in a strange c., 67:5
stroll a gallery, 505:2
sucked on c. pleasures, 228:2
take pleasures sadly after fashion of c., 157:17
the past a foreign c., 692:19
their c. their children, 91:27
they've undone his c., 292:11
this c. to preserve liberty, 345:3
this c. with its institutions, 449:4
this happy c., 325:6
this is a beautiful c., 424:6
this slave c., 424:5
touch our c. shackles fall, 334:27
try do something for my c., 768:8
two problems of our c., 754:4
Union is my c., 389:15
vegetate like the c., 390:13
what c. has done for us, 741:*n*1
where liberty is there is my c., 327:8
who serves c. well, 306:1
winters of that c. sharp and violent, 240:9
with no antiquity, 436:12
Countrymen are mankind, 437:12
first in hearts of c., 355:16
friends Romans c., 188:28
Kiltartan's poor, 596:10
rebels our c. again, 501:12
Romans c. and lovers, 188:24
warring on that day, 399:24
what a fall was there my c., 189:7
Country's, all the ends be thy c., 225:21
bold peasantry c. pride, 329:8
brooding on c. fate, 482:20
by all c. wishes blessed, 324:10
fight our c. battles, 780:22

Country's (*continued*)
for c. glory fast, 378:4
guiltless of c. blood, 322:14
leaving country for c. sake, 295:*n*2
never to see my c. ruin, 284:5
pleasant c. earth, 172:6
spare c. flag, 443:11
Countryside, may c. content me, 92:29
smiling and beautiful c., 577:19
Count's, nobody without C. permission, 651:20
Couple, human c. find true form, 722:10
Couples are wholes and not wholes, 62:16
Coupling of man and woman, 670:21
Courage and conduct of this army, 336:14
and devotion of patriot, 522:13
be of good c., 27:24
bear his share with c., 505:1
bear with a good c., 30:15
brows of dauntless c., 256:17
by experience with fear, 654:15
fear nor c. saves us, 668:8
fires us with c. love joy, 297:16
freedom based on c., 618:3
gaiety and quiet mind, 562:9
his c. foes proclaim, 274:7
horse of our c., 750:2
if one only had c., 508:15
mastiffs of unmatchable c., 185:12
May giveth unto lovers c., 133:11
mounteth with occasion, 169:19
my spark of c., 783:14
never to submit or yield, 256:1
not to believe in anything, 482:17
of conscience, 422:16
of heart or holiness, 608:21
of making choice, 614:14
of my companions, 606:2
of New England, 422:16
one man with c. a majority, 369:13
pathos piety c., 636:11
placed decency above c., 586:22
price life exacts, 700:7
red badge of c., 611:2
screw your c., 213:13
secret of liberty, 568:14
spark of c., 783:14
species of c., 278:5
strong and of good c., 10:31
tastes of blood, 731:3
to change what should be, 684:14
to endure, 480:3
to him that can get it, 272:30
to live, 411:20
to live by grace, 588:19
two o'clock in morning c., 370:21
unprepared c., 370:21
was mine, 687:5
were we men of c., 741:2
Western world lost civil c., 746:7
who has c. never perish in misery, 760:10
without ferocity, 398:16
without justice c. weak, 309:9
won by men with c., 72:7
words such as c. obscene, 701:14

Courageous because of deep love,
57:22
captains c., 785:6
intellectual virile c., 605:24
Couriers, sightless c. of the air, 213:7
stays these c., 70:*n*4
upon every road, 463:16
Course, bow to that whose c. run,
323:17
chances change by c., 160:18
earth's diurnal c., 374:1
finished my c., 45:29
great nature's second c., 214:6
I must stand the c., 210:16
icy current compulsive c., 207:15
impediments in fancy's c., 203:22
insisture c. proportion, 200:7
many bees on single c., 653:11
my whole c. of love, 205:22
of empire, 296:27
of impious stubbornness, 193:4
of true love, 172:19
straight c. to highest good, 90:12
turned from one's c. by opinions,
83:5
westward the c. of empire, 296:27
what c. others may take, 339:10
whate'er the c., 203:17
when in c. of human events, 343:2
world's c. will not fail, 503:10
young blood have c., 484:15
Coursers, nor C. like a Page, 514:2
Courses, accomplishing their appointed c., 70:11
Russian and American c. not same,
438:7
stars in their c. fought, 11:3
Court a mistress she denies you,
232:13
attacks upon the C., 542:20
bows to experience, 568:18
bring suit in Supreme C., 655:5
confession in open c., 346:9
English not Turkish c., 184:15
envious c., 190:6
for owls, 27:7
hear rogues talk of c. news, 211:13
in beauty and decay, 408:16
in perpetual session, 652:1
keeps Death his c., 171:25
let her alone she will c. you, 232:13
moderation gone no c. can save,
615:3
no justice in or out of c., 573:21
starry threshold of Jove's C., 252:11
sun that shines upon his c., 223:12
supreme c. follows iliction, 602:14
temper doctrinaire logic, 683:4
the camp the grove, 377:25
though lewdness c. it, 194:22
used against him in c., 682:10
what's the new news at new c.,
189:29
world history is world's c., 364:15
Courte, n'ai pas loisir de la faire plus
c., 270:*n*2
Courted by all the winds, 261:16
Courteous, gracious and c. to strangers, 159:15
intellectual virile, 605:24

Courteous (*continued*)
lowely and servysable, 129:11
retort c., 192:16
Courtesan, word love in mouth of c.,
430:21
Courtesies, sweet c. of life, 321:1
Courtesy, always time for c., 433:16
and self-possession, 600:7
candy deal of c., 177:10
Grace of God in c., 608:21
greater man greater c., 459:17
high-erected thoughts in heart of c.,
155:23
in c. have her learned, 597:2
mirour of alle c., 130:31
mirror of all c., 225:5
pink of c., 150:33, 175:21
true alchemy, 508:24
Courthouse, portals of every c., 615:4
Courtier, heel of c., 199:7
Courtier's soldier's scholar's, 196:17
Courting, stayeth young man's c.,
659:16
Courtliness and desire of fame, 459:20
Courtly nurture, 503:4
Courts, brawling c., 457:25
case still before c., 98:6
day in thy c., 18:7
forsaken c. pale pavilions, 704:11
hollow murmurs through c., 367:12
into his c. with praise, 18:22
laws conflict c. decide, 355:9
shown in c. at feasts, 253:10
thee on roses, 95:20
thrusting on c. nurture of spirit,
615:3
where Jamshyd gloried, 445:12
Cousins, Little C. Called back, 515:1
sisters c. and aunts, 529:5
Coûte, il n'y a que le premier pas qui
c., 307:*n*3
Couvrez ce sein que je ne saurais voir,
269:*n*2
Covenant, token of a c., 7:24
with death, 26:33, 437:16
words of the c., 9:20
Covenanted with him for silver, 36:23
Covenants, open c. of peace, 572:13
Cover country in books, 551:19
cunning sin c. itself, 187:1
her face, 237:19
I c. all, 634:6
like c. of old book, 309:5
only art guilt to c., 328:30
paste and c. to our bones, 171:25
that bosom I must not see, 269:5
thee with his feathers, 18:15
them with leaves, 776:2
Covered up our names, 512:14
Covers of book too far apart, 545:2
out of night that c., 557:9
who c. faults, 208:27
Covert from the tempest, 27:6
Covet, sin to c. honor, 185:21
thou shalt not c., 9:12, 483:5
Coveted her and me, 453:8
Covetous desires of the world, 49:21
man ever in want, 97:9
of others' possessions, 91:22
sordid fellow, 305:1

Covetousness, wealth cause of c.,
162:7
when old guard against c., 62:3
Cow and bear shall feed, 26:11
cheaper than keep c., 525:9
good animal in field, 316:15
jumped over moon, 789:9
little Kyloe c., 789:17
purple c., 600:16
red and white, 561:11
she'll bring her c. along, 793:1
sizzle sells steak not c., 719:17
till the c. comes home, 238:14
with crumpled horn, 792:24
work way c. grazes, 604:1
you do de pullin' Sis C., 556:9
Coward and brave held in same
honor, 51:31
conscience dost afflict, 166:14
does it with kiss, 567:17
had not resolution to fire it, 315:19
never forgave, 320:4
no c. soul mine, 480:4
not so great a c. as thinks, 562:2
sea hates c., 674:5
turns away, 68:24
worth little more than c., 369:9
Cowardice distinguished from panic,
702:7
here all c. be ended, 125:7
that clings, 619:5
Cowardly, war spares the c., 60:3
Cowards, conscience but word c. use,
166:16
conscience does make c., 196:10
die many times, 188:11
hundred c., 676:4
idlers and c. at home, 787:15
in reasoning, 291:27
mannish c., 190:5
plague of all c., 177:21
Public greatest of c., 390:10
Cowboy, best damned c., 786:4
damned c. President of United
States, 575:*n*5
I wondered if ever a c., 786:5
I'm a young c., 786:7
that loves you so true, 786:10
wrapped in white linen, 786:6
Cowl does not make monk, 118:23
I like a c., 429:9
take wife or c., 149:*n*6
Cowled, I that c. churchman be, 429:9
Cowpuncher a-riding along, 786:1
Cow'rin', wee sleekit c., 361:4
Cow's in the corn, 789:4
Cows are my passion, 470:17
sacred c. make tastiest hamburger,
768:9
till the c. come home, 238:*n*5
Cowslip's, hang pearl in c. ear, 173:1
in c. bell I lie, 224:25
sweet c. grace, 348:12
Coxcomb ask two hundred guineas,
524:*n*2
Coxcombs, some made c. nature
meant fools, 298:15
Coy and hard to please, 378:14
denial vain and c. excuse, 253:16

Crooked (*continued*)
Lane, 422:25
Leviathan that c. serpent, 26:31
man went crooked mile, 791:11
roads are roads of genius, 357:11
set c. straight, 523:7
shall be made straight, 27:16
slim and c. genius, 548:8
tell the c. rose, 737:8
Croolty, previntion of c. to money, 539:*n*1
Crop, familiar as c. in summer, 111:11
fungus c. of sentiment, 532:16
of corn a field of tares, 156:22
Crop-full bird, 467:7
Crops are ripe, 617:3
flowery food, 301:4
men want c. without plowing, 480:16
watering last year's c., 483:10
Cross, a sparkling c. she wore, 299:10
blind as nails upon C., 665:19
don't c. bridge until come to it, 779:19
e'en though it be a c., 437:4
he that taketh not his c., 34:35
hot c. buns, 790:9
nailed on bitter c., 176:23
no c. no crown, 242:6, 282:17
of gold, 582:4
of Jesus, 521:10
old rugged c., 616:2
one more river to c., 794:19
out immensely overpaid accounts, 490:6
over river and rest, 504:10
shall come again win Holy C., 133:18
transit where dreams c., 669:19
Crossbow, with my c., 381:5
Crossed, arms about neck c. and rested, 490:12
oyster may be c. in love, 353:3
right hand over left, 582:16
the sierras, 683:10
when I have c. bar, 460:13
with direct eyes, 669:9
Crosses, crooked c. and headstones, 647:8
row on row, 615:7
to fret thy soul with c., 154:6
Cross-gartered, see thee c., 202:19
Crossing Channel and tossing, 530:15
death is but c. world, 282:21
Crosspatch draw latch, 789:8
Crossroads, dirty work at c., 780:17
mankind faces c., 767:16
Crossway, eternity waits at c. of stars, 700:10
Crotchets in thy head, 182:25
Crouch, to fawn to c. to wait, 154:6
to television set, 743:12
Crow beautified with our feathers, 157:20
before the cock c., 37:3
louder in own farmyard, 475:15
lungs c. like chanticleer, 190:24
makes wing to rooky wood, 214:28
many-wintered c., 455:11
safer 'n to c., 485:17

Crow (*continued*)
shook down on me, 623:15
sun risen to hear him c., 483:14
think thy swan a c., 174:17
we'll pluck c. together, 166:27
Crowbar, creation for c., 447:13
hammer me into c., 634:9
Crow-blue mussel shells, 664:5
Crowd, after night I do c., 356:2
all at once I saw a c., 375:19
and buzz and murmurings, 266:16
beauty not comprehended by c., 594:13
faces in the c., 659:1
firm against c., 457:1
for c. they need interpreters, 63:30
great man in c., 431:22
I am the c., 634:3
into a shade, 298:7
not feel the c., 335:4
not on my soul, 323:9
of common men, 246:22
only beast in arena the c., 602:5
out of the c. a mistress or friend, 408:13
will support itself, 510:*n*4
you were a good c., 572:21
Crowded, for sake of c. audience, 71:6
hour of glorious life, 333:8
it's too c., 693:3
not in clamor of c. street, 442:21
world's most c. streets, 498:4
Crowd's, madding c. ignoble strife, 322:17
Crowds, public men nor cheering c., 596:11
talk with c. keep virtue, 593:20
without company, 340:14
Crowed, cock that c. in morn, 792:24
Crowing, faded on c. of the cock, 192:29
of cocks and barking of dogs, 58:6
Crowley, Stuhldreher Miller C. Layden, 643:15
Crown, allegiance to c., 336:11
ambassador from Britain's c., 461:1
becomes monarch better than c., 181:19
breeches cost a c., 776:16
Caesar's laurel c., 359:13
carried him c. him, 766:1
chance may c. me, 212:24
contrary to c. built paper-mill, 164:11
cross for c., 616:2
defiance to forces of the C., 312:19
fell down broke c., 789:11
fighting for c., 788:10
fill me from c. to toe, 212:29
from c. of head to sole, 186:32
golden c. like a deep well, 172:9
good with brotherhood, 576:19
Greece with freedom, 60:12
hairy gold c. on 'ead, 591:21
hath worn the c., 31:26
have I no bays to c. it, 243:16
head that wears a c., 183:38
hoary head a c. of glory, 21:32
hollow c., 171:25

Crown (*continued*)
holly bears the c., 778:9
immortal c., 308:16
is called content, 164:19
is in my heart, 164:19
is love and friendship, 414:12
is of night, 534:20
kingly c. to gain, 395:17
laurel c. yield to praise, 88:2
many a c. spotless now, 365:4
mind content both c. and kingdom, 157:19
no cross no c., 242:6, 282:17
not the king's c. nor sword, 204:1
of glory, 46:27
of life, 46:5, 47:9
of life as it closes, 533:15
of thorns, 413:7
of thorns on brow of labor, 582:4
old age c. of life, 88:12
old Winter's head, 264:11
ourselves with rosebuds, 30:21
quiet mind richer than c., 157:18
small but costly c., 644:10
sorrow's c. of sorrow, 455:13
still the fine's the c., 203:17
sweet fruition of earthly c., 161:21
sword mace c. imperial, 185:19
that seldom kings enjoy, 164:19
the watery glade, 321:13
themselves assured, 221:23
thorns thy only c., 250:7
though they possess c., 285:19
virtuous woman is a c., 21:11
Crowned, due to be c. again, 657:13
Ghost sitting c. upon grave, 239:23
knot of fire, 672:7
Peace c. with smiles, 270:8
with lilies, 684:12
with stars, 280:22
with the sickle, 308:6
Crownest year with thy goodness, 17:36
Crownets, walked crowns and c., 218:11
Crowning, reason God's c. gift, 66:16
Crownless in voiceless woe, 400:21
Crowns and pounds and guineas, 578:22
are empty things, 285:19
end c. all, 201:12
end c. the work, 119:3
end c. us not fight, 241:2
if store of c. be scant, 233:12
in shades like these, 329:10
last act c. play, 242:13
not c. but men, 393:10
walked c. and crownets, 218:11
Crows and choughs that wing air, 210:27
black flight of c., 786:*n*5
throw him to c., 781:*n*6
wars of kites or c., 261:28
Crow's-feet, til c. be growen, 128:15
Cru, j'ai pleuré et j'ai c., 369:*n*7
Crucible, God's c., 590:6
not test faith in c., 558:8
Crucified dead and buried, 48:25
everyone Christ and all c., 630:21
if this woman must be c., 475:10

Crucified *(continued)*
   let him be c., 37:6
   where dear Lord c., 479:18
Crucifixion, living through another c., 700:9
Cruciform shadow, 680:3
Crucify mankind on cross of gold, 582:4
   Son of God afresh, 45:36
Crude, berries harsh and c., 253:14
   no c. surfeit reigns, 253:3
Cruel and unrelenting enemy, 336:14
   and unusual punishment, 346:17
   as death, 307:17
   but composed and bland, 500:4
   crawling foam, 484:10
   death of Pyramus, 172:22
   doubts more c. than truths, 269:15
   enough without meaning to, 765:4
   foam is not c., 487:13
   I must be c. to be kind, 198:7
   jealousy is c. as the grave, 25:22
   mother of sweet loves, 96:27
   never be c., 470:27
   savage extreme rude c., 222:7
   say we are c. to each other, 475:10
   slain by fair c. maid, 202:13
   tender mercies of the wicked are c., 21:12
Cruelest lies told in silence, 560:16
   she alive, 201:26
Cruellest, April c. month, 668:17
   thing happened to Lincoln, 693:13
Cruelly, Fortune c. scratched, 203:18
Cruelty, all the pride c. and ambition, 153:1
   farewell fair c., 201:29
   fear source of c., 615:14
   full of direst c., 212:29
   has human heart, 358:13
   Mr. C., 272:21
   never gauged your c., 680:14
   of pirates, 485:23
   to load falling man, 225:*n*2
   war is c., 492:9
Cruise, all on our last c., 560:17
Cruising down shores of High Bar-baree, 793:18
Crumb, craved no c., 531:14
   just a C. to Me, 513:5
   of madeleine, 612:13
Crumbled out again to his atomies, 230:15
Crumbles, the way cookie c., 783:24
   Time c. things, 77:18
Crumbling, mind c. to pieces, 762:2
Crumbs, dogs eat of c., 35:24
Crumpets, buttered scones and c., 668:10
Crumpetty Tree, 472:8
Crumpled, cow with c. horn, 792:24
Crusade, my God the Children's C., 751:13
Crusader, Franklin Roosevelt no c., 677:1
Cruse, little oil in a c., 12:33
Crush amang the stoure, 361:19
   man shall man no longer c., 353:8
   the infamous thing, 306:15

Crushed, human being c. by books, 735:20
   most fragrant when c., 159:10
   odors c. sweeter still, 159:*n*4
   the sweet poison, 252:16
   to ground diffuse sweets, 159:*n*4
   together c. and bruised, 299:21
   truth c. to earth, 411:10
Crushes, friend supports whom For-tune c., 105:24
Crusoe, Robinson C., 286:3, 319:16
Crust and sugar over, 708:19
   dinosaur death-steps on c., 743:7
   eaten in peace, 59:1
   of bread and liberty, 302:24
   over volcano of revolution, 578:8
   upper c., 405:2, 419:9
   water and c., 414:17
Crusted with blood, 663:19
Cry, all should c. Beware, 382:25
   at a play to laugh or c., 289:15
   battle c. of Freedom, 492:7
   Bellman c. crew reply, 519:20
   bubbling c. of swimmer, 402:17
   but behold a c., 25:38
   caused constantly a c., 639:7
   cherry-ripe themselves do c., 226:18
   consider anything don't c., 519:11
   couch when owls do c., 224:25
   damned don't c., 674:6
   don't you c. for me, 506:17
   every infant's c. of fear, 358:8
   feel sorry because c., 546:4
   for being born, 160:15
   for restful death I c., 221:4
   forgot c. of gulls, 669:3
   God for Harry, 185:5
   great c. in Egypt, 8:41
   harlot's c. from street, 359:15
   Havoc, 188:23
   hear us when we c., 506:4
   heard the dead c., 724:17
   he'll be sure to c., 789:4
   Hi or any loud c., 519:19
   Hold hold, 213:1
   hounds join in glorious c., 311:15
   I can no more, 551:11
   inhuman as hawk's c., 663:19
   is still They come, 216:12
   kitten and c. mew, 178:4
   laugh for fear of having to c., 336:5
   man's image and his c., 594:23
   much c. no wool, 133:1
   mum, 151:*n*4
   my eyes out, 150:2
   need a body c., 778:*n*1
   nor swooned nor uttered c., 456:18
   not when father dies, 315:4
   of Absence Absence in heart, 674:10
   of bugles going by, 583:16
   of child by roadway, 595:5
   of pulleys, 749:15
   onward sailors c., 577:6
   out liberty freedom, 188:17
   out loudest its abuse, 278:17
   out Olivia, 201:28
   raise a hue and c., 149:33
   scarcely c. 'weep, 356:11
   scrawny c. was a chorister, 640:12
   secrets c. aloud, 724:10

Cry *(continued)*
   shake me like a c., 583:16
   so lonesome I could c., 753:5
   stone shall c. out of wall, 29:41
   stones c. out, 39:11
   sudden c. of pain, 650:10
   that was not ours, 639:7
   the more it made them c., 330:7
   there little girl don't c., 558:13
   too big to c., 449:14
   truth c. of all, 296:25
   voice c. Sleep no more, 214:6
   voiced c. of his people, 628:4
   war war still the c., 399:12
   wave c. wind c., 671:11
   we c. that we are come, 211:6
   we still should c., 160:15
   what shall I c., 27:17
   whoever loves you make you c., 794:6
Cryin' all the time, 765:7
   at the lock, 461:12
Crying, first voice was c., 30:28
   in the wilderness, 32:29
   infant c. in night, 457:18
   no more c., 48:1
   spiders c. together, 743:8
   watchmen on the heights are c., 156:11
   with sighing and c., 147:14
Crystal, golden sands c. brooks, 229:10
   river of c. light, 559:20
   soul pure as c., 471:24
Crystallization action of mind, 396:12
Crystallized air of centuries, 662:8
Cub, grandam to c., 757:8
Cubic inch of space a miracle, 491:4
Cubit, add one c. to stature, 33:19
Cuccu, lhude sing c., 775:10
Cuckold lives in bliss, 206:31
   not be c., 656:7
Cuckoo, as c. is in June, 178:12
   Cloud-C.-Land, 73:13
   jug-jug pu-we, 226:20
   lhude sing c., 775:10
   thus sings he C., 169:12
Cuckoo-buds of yellow hue, 169:12
Cuckoo-clock, Switzerland produced c., 739:5
Cuckoo's, one flew over c. nest, 792:8
Cucullus non facit monachum, 118:23
Cucumbers, cold as c., 238:13
   lodge in garden of c., 25:27
   sunbeams out of c., 289:12
Cud, chew c. and are silent, 332:18
   whatsoever cheweth the c., 9:21
Cudgel thy brains no more, 198:28
Cudgel's, know what wood a c. of, 263:18
Cue is villainous melancholy, 209:4
   twisted c., 531:5
Cueillez les roses de la vie, 144:*n*3
   votre jeunesse, 144:*n*5
Cuff, the roses get it says Sergeant C., 504:7
Cui bono fuerit, 87:*n*7
Culled, nosegay of c. flowers, 147:4
Culpa, mea c., 48:6
   O felix c., 48:12

Culprit, stirs C. Life, 511:11
Cult called Christianity, 540:14
  of personality, 689:19
Cultivate peace and harmony, 337:6
  sedulously c. free speech, 621:17
  we must c. our garden, 306:12
Cultivated, celebrated c. Duke, 531:16
Cultivates the golden mean, 96:7
Cultivation, equal in rights and in c.,
    440:5
Cultiver, il faut c. notre jardin,
    306:n7
Cults, clarification c. founded on,
    625:8
Cultural, character of c. environment,
    574:11
  effective c. design, 715:11
  evolution, 722:15
  freedom, 631:14
  ivory tower of c., 629:23
  man's nature c. product, 704:9
  tide of c. pollution, 754:6
Culture, above all believer in c.,
    500:10
  believe only in French c., 553:8
  doesn't save anyone, 717:18
  equal opportunities of c., 559:8
  European c. a misunderstanding,
    553:8
  Germany ruins c., 553:9
  great law of c., 412:24
  great though disastrous c., 754:5
  Greek essential to c., 507:9
  hear word c. reach for pistol, 679:4
  in finest flower, 584:19
  individual creature of his c., 662:12
  initial act of c., 653:8
  knowledge of other c., 707:16
  leaves unsatisfied drives to rebel-
    liousness, 569:10
  making of counter c., 765:11
  mechanics of c., 605:14
  men of c. true apostles, 500:15
  moment of clarity, 653:4
  no better than its woods, 721:6
  no prospect of continued existence,
    569:10
  not function of race, 662:14
  pick out what c. has defined, 676:20
  politics economic development c.,
    749:9
  pursue C. in bands, 586:19
  pursuit of perfection, 500:8
  socialist c. thrive, 686:16
  soul takes nothing but education
    and c., 75:3
  study of perfection, 500:11
  to achieve richer c., 707:17
Cultures, materialism model for c.,
    754:5
Cum grano salis, 104:n11
Cumbered with much serving, 38:25
Cumin, tithe of anise and c., 36:3
Cunard's liners and telegraph, 484:8
Cunning, Esau was a c. hunter, 7:36
  history has c. passages, 668:7
  Hocus old c. attorney, 307:n4
  in war boastful c., 404:21
  livery of hell, 204:13
  men pass for wise, 159:23

Cunning (*continued*)
  more c. to be strange, 175:6
  nature's sweet c. hand, 201:26
  old Fury, 517:6
  punishment sharpens c., 552:25
  right hand forget her c., 20:6
  sin cover itself, 187:1
  truth which c. times put on, 181:6
  what plighted c. hides, 208:27
Cunningest pattern, 208:10
Cunningly, little world made c.,
    230:18
Cup, between c. and lip, 235:6
  come fill the C., 445:6
  come fill up my c., 379:27
  drained c. of Lethe, 95:14
  drowned Glory in C., 446:6
  Etruscan c., 742:15
  fear at heart as at c., 381:15
  giveth his color in the c., 22:22
  he took the c., 36:28
  is new testament in my blood,
    43:12
  leave a kiss but in the c., 232:15
  let this c. pass, 36:30
  life's enchanted c., 399:19
  man in whose hand the c. is found,
    8:12
  my c. runneth over, 16:17
  o' kindness yet, 362:20
  of hot wine, 219:1
  of trembling, 27:31
  sun in golden c., 599:1
  take c. drink it up, 789:8
  that clears today, 445:14
  to every people c. of clay, 787:16
  valley his golden c., 509:5
  woodspurge has c. of three, 509:21
Cupboard, glacier knocks in c., 720:8
  was bare, 790:18
  wicked man in bathroom c., 739:12
Cupboards, keys took and c. opened,
    539:16
Cupid and my Campaspe, 155:19
  bolt of C. fell, 173:6
  has his camps, 101:9
  it has long stood void, 242:9
  paid, 155:19
  senior-junior Dan C., 168:28
  silent note C. strikes, 248:20
  winged C. painted blind, 172:21
  young Adam C., 174:25
Cupiditas, radix malorum est c.,
    45:n3
Cupido upon his shuldres wynges,
    130:17
Cupid's arms, 778:7
  concludes with C. curse, 156:13
Cups, flowing c. run swiftly, 267:17
  that cheer, 335:3
  when they are in their c., 30:12
Cur, ears of the old c., 263:13
Cur ergo haec ipse non facis, 113:n12
Curates, shower of c., 476:14
Curb, care's check and c., 270:2
  use snaffle c. all right, 707:1
  your magnanimity, 418:19
Curd, white c. of ass's milk, 302:14
Curdied by frost from snow, 219:12
Curds and whey, 791:8

Cure, absence c. of love, 149:38
  disease kill patient, 159:28
  freedom c. of anarchy, 331:19
  laws or kings cause or c., 314:15
  no c. for birth and death, 588:14
  not worth the pain, 99:n5
  on exercise depend, 276:19
  past c. I am, 222:13
  past hope past c. past help, 176:9
  tale would c. deafness, 223:23
  the c. is freedom, 424:15
  thrust of c., 759:12
Cured, Asclepius c. the body, 74:n3
  I am frizzled stale, 742:20
  I treated him God c. him, 143:10
  more than Galen c., 244:18
  of every folly but vanity, 319:18
Cures, endure neither evils nor c.,
    98:26
  me of my pain, 778:7
  opposites c. for opposites, 71:7
  to fear worst c. worse, 200:19
Cureth, quiet mind c. all, 235:23
Curfew, far-off c. sound, 252:4
  must not ring tonight, 562:11
  tolls knell, 322:1
Curiosity, culture origin not in c.,
    500:11
  do well in closet by way of c.,
    305:5
  insatiable intellectual c., 587:3
  intellectual c., 631:16
  love c. freckles doubt, 687:7
  natural c. of young, 550:10
  offers to our c., 671:13
  order awakened c., 430:25
  permanent and certain, 313:25
  pleasure to rouse c., 733:5
Curious, amazed and c., 363:8
  busy c. thirsty fly, 307:9
  crime, 468:1
  in unnecessary matters, 31:4
  incident of dog, 577:20
  quaint and c. war is, 540:12
  seen a c. child, 376:21
  volume of forgotten lore, 452:13
Curiouser and curiouser, 517:4
Curl, had a little c., 442:25
  make your hair c., 531:11
Curled, wealthy c. darlings, 205:19
  wonderful water c., 503:12
Curlicues of marijuana, 742:22
Curls done up with bank notes,
    475:12
  Frocks and C., 513:6
  Hyperion's c., 197:30
  natural c., 105:9
Curlylocks wilt be mine, 790:11
Currency, debauch c., 652:11
  no graven images except c., 483:4
Current, azure c. floweth, 474:6
  boats against the c., 694:13
  genial c. of soul, 322:12
  icy c. compulsive course, 207:15
  misleading guide to c. affairs, 652:8
  noiseless c. strong, 500:18
  swollen c. masses of ice, 463:1
  take c. when it serves, 189:20
  time a river of strong c., 111:10
Currents, fresh c. of life, 461:3

D

Dab at an index, 328:1
Dad, called brother's father d., 169:24
 they fuck you up your mum and d.,
  750:15
Daddy, are you lost d., 657:5
 my heart belongs to d., 682:6
Daddy's gone a-hunting, 789:15
Daemon, when your D. in charge,
  593:27
Daffodil sky, 458:21
 surfeit when D. doth, 513:4
Daffodils, fair d. we weep to see,
  241:10
 host of golden d., 375:19
 that come before swallow, 223:7
 what d. were for Wordsworth,
  751:2
Dafter, maybe I couldn't be d., 710:2
Dagger, air-drawn d., 215:5
 into back of neighbor, 649:14
 is this a d. which I see, 213:20
 of the mind, 213:20
 wear not my d. in my mouth, 220:2
Daggers, give me the d., 214:8
 speak d. to her, 197:22
Daily beauty in his life, 208:7
 before us lies in d. life, 259:24
 duly and d. serving him, 325:17
 give us our d. bread, 33:12
 wealth small aid for d. gladness,
  68:23
 with souls that cringe, 485:3
Dainties bred of a book, 168:29
 spiced d., 415:6
 such d. to them, 330:15
Daintiest last to make end sweet,
  170:28
Dainty dish, 790:1
Daiquiris, two d. withdrew, 734:18
Daisies, lie upon the d., 529:17
 meadows trim with d. pied, 251:14
 pied and violets blue, 169:12
 she can hear d. grow, 566:5
 swich as men callen d., 129:5
Daisy by shadow it casts, 377:14
 give me answer do, 600:18
 there's a d., 198:24
Dakotas I am for war, 502:5
Dale, hawthorn in the d., 251:13
 over hill over d., 172:30
Dales, hills and valleys d. and fields,
  162:n1
Dalliance, not give d. rein, 224:20
 primrose path of d., 193:27
 silken d., 184:27
Dallies with innocence of love, 202:12
Dam, all my chickens and their d.,
  215:29
Damage, came to see d. done, 762:9
Damaged, archangel a little d., 387:22
Damaging, nothing more d. than old
  error, 351:4
Damask, feed on her d. cheek, 202:14
Dame, dance in old d. yet, 633:3
 has lost shoe, 788:1
 La Belle D. sans Merci, 417:7
 nothing like a d., 692:15
 one for my d., 788:18
 our sulky sullen d., 363:2
 smiled at the d., 357:18

Dames, ah gentle d., 363:3
 struts his d. before, 251:12
 that Squire of D., 153:15
Damfool, biggest d. mistake, 678:18
Damn authors they never read, 333:18
 devil d. thee black, 216:7
 doesn't give a d., 783:7
 don't care twopenny d., 371:14
 don't give a d., 533:7
 God d. you, 590:n4
 my dear I don't give a d., 705:2
 no general proposition worth d.,
  543:1
 the torpedoes, 426:16
 with faint praise, 302:11
Damnable deceitful woman, 284:15
 iteration, 176:32
Damnably, marriage d. serious business, 686:18
Damnation, deep d. of his taking-off,
  213:7
 distilled d., 367:7
 marriage bed to this d., 231:9
 of unbaptized infants, 536:18
 two fingers' breadth of d., 56:n1
Damned, another d. thick book,
  342:22
 at certain revolutions all the d.,
  257:16
 be him that first cries Hold, 216:22
 better d. than mentioned not,
  341:17
 born by dying and being d., 138:13
 cohort of the d., 592:2
 could have had d. good time,
  701:13
 dear d. distracting town, 299:27
 devilish and d. tobacco, 235:10
 disinheriting countenance, 352:30
 dissolute d. despairful, 627:1
 don't cry, 674:6
 drama whether d. or not, 352:18
 elusive Pimpernel, 594:1
 Faustus must be d., 162:23
 forever d. with Lucifer, 162:14
 from here to Eternity, 592:3
 I will see thee d. first, 371:21
 if goats cannot be d., 230:21
 if I see how helican, 637:14
 if you do or don't, 389:18
 in fair wife, 205:9
 many an old host d., 177:31
 may salute eloquence, 698:12
 music brandy of the d., 571:4
 of body and soul, 591:11
 out d. spot, 216:1
 perpetually, 162:22
 public be d., 496:21
 publish and be d., 371:16
 smiling d. villain, 195:1
 spirits of the d., 448:10
 universal cock, 638:28
 what d. minutes tells he, 206:31
Damning those they have no mind to,
  263:8
Damozel, blessed d., 509:19
Damp, demd d. moist unpleasant
  body, 469:21
 lived in cellar d., 485:25
 nights are very d., 520:3

Damp (*continued*)
 of night drives deeper into soul,
  489:14
 souls of housemaids, 667:22
 tonnage, 701:5
 years d. my intended wing, 260:1
Damsel lay deploring, 297:1
 to every man a d. or two, 11:7
 with dulcimer, 382:24
Damyata (control), 50:n8
 datta dayadhvamiti, 50:n8
Dan, Dangerous D. McGrew, 627:2
 from D. to Beersheba, 11:20
 senior-junior D. Cupid, 168:28
Danaë to the stars, 456:21
Danaos, timeo D. et dona ferentis,
  93:n14
Dance, a god has given the d., 52:1
 and drink and sing, 358:5
 and Provençal song, 415:11
 as often as d. it can, 382:11
 attendance, 226:7
 attention on old age, 599:14
 barefoot on wedding day, 167:21
 by light of moon, 780:10
 can't you d. polka, 793:15
 fire dance in iron shoes, 760:1
 I made them d., 689:9
 in old dame yet, 633:3
 join the d., 518:6, 518:7
 know dancer from d., 598:2
 like wave of sea, 595:10
 maids d. in a ring, 226:20
 mehitabel dance, 633:7
 move easiest who learned to d.,
  298:20
 on with the d., 399:22
 praise him with d., 20:16
 round in ring and suppose, 624:16
 rouses him up to d., 53:28
 sweet d. to violins, 567:18
 the antic hay, 162:10
 there is only the d., 670:16
 time to d., 23:32
 tipsy d. and jollity, 252:20
 to flutes dance to lutes, 567:18
 tossing heads in sprightly d., 375:21
 upon the air, 567:18
 walk before they d., 303:2
 when you do d., 223:9
 while you can, 720:5
 with me in Ireland, 775:n5
 with William Blake, 725:21
 wyth me in Irlonde, 775:12
Danced by light of moon, 472:3
 daughter of Herodias Salome d.,
  35:14
 David d. before the Lord, 12:7
 death fires d., 381:10
 his did, 688:22
 I could have d. all night, 745:9
 like dingledodies, 750:9
 moon on Monan's rill, 378:17
 on waves, 565:11
 Salome d., 35:14
 star d., 186:25
 till doomsday, 291:4
 to see that banner, 447:3
Dancer from dance, 598:2
Dancers all gone under hill, 671:3

Dark (*continued*)
   fate sits on d. battlements, 367:12
   fear death as children fear d., 159:4
   fell of d. not day, 551:15
   go home in d., 586:7
   great leap in the d., 239:26
   hawks hear us, 647:20
   highest candle lights d., 640:9
   horse, 434:20
   hour or twain, 214:19
   hunt it in the d., 334:17
   in d. time eye begins to see, 725:15
   in nightmare of the d., 720:10
   in the d. and silent grave, 153:2
   inscrutable workmanship, 373:8
   iron New England d., 696:18
   irrecoverably d., 261:7
   let d. come upon you, 671:5
   lie in d. weep for sins, 489:16
   life one long struggle in d., 89:15
   Maid and her Lord, 67:24
   mother always gliding near, 490:18
   mutinous Shannon waves, 647:8
   narrowing d. hours, 696:4
   night is d., 426:18, 783:14
   night of d. intent, 623:22
   night of the soul, 147:12, 694:18
   not d. days great days, 621:6
   not put me in d. to die, 564:13
   o'er d. silver mantle threw, 258:19
   old fantastical duke of d. corners,
     204:25
   on d. theme trace verses of light,
     89:11
   pillared d., 624:14
   raging in the d., 598:10
   rebellious brows, 491:5
   road whence no one returns, 90:17
   Satanic mills, 359:17
   sea iridescent and d., 731:4
   some days d. and dreary, 441:6
   soul's d. cottage, 250:6
   sun to me is d., 261:8
   then it is d., 731:5
   they all go into d., 671:4
   things in d. besides Santa Claus,
     625:22
   to d. tower came, 210:12
   unconscious not only d. but light,
     628:15
   unfathomed caves, 322:13
   violets are d. too, 92:19
   wall between us and d., 691:2
   wandering in d. labyrinth, 161:15
   ways that are d., 532:1
   we are for the d., 218:12
   we work in d., 548:18
   what if Amyntas is d., 92:19
   what in me is d. illumine, 255:20
   who art d. as night, 222:14
   with excessive bright, 257:26
   with torment and tears, 479:29
   wood where straight way lost,
     125:3
   woods lovely d. deep, 623:18
   world and wide, 255:11
   world present treatment, 605:5
Darken, never d. threshold of doors,
   492:2
Darkened, blue d. on blueness, 658:1

Darkened (*continued*)
   hurtles in d. air, 323:12
   sun or light be not d., 24:27
   windows be d., 24:27
Darkeneth, who d. counsel by words,
   15:6
Darker and darker stairs, 658:1
   as d. grows the night, 328:5
   the tinge that saddens, 435:27
Darkest before day dawneth, 250:18
   day will have passed, 335:19
   sun breaks through d. clouds,
     167:31
Dark-heaving boundless, 401:3
Darkies how heart grows weary,
   507:1
Darkling I listen, 415:16
   plain, 499:22
   roll d. down torrent, 313:22
   stand varying shore, 218:6
Darkly it knows obstacles, 749:17
   saw through glass eye d., 527:20
   see through glass d., 43:16
   wise and rudely great, 301:13
Darkness, absence d. death, 229:9
   affronts with his own d., 734:6
   again and silence, 442:16
   and light alike to thee, 20:9
   and shadow of death, 14:11, 19:8,
     38:1
   as children fear in d., 90:1
   awake upon dark, 658:1
   awful d. silence reign, 472:12
   blackness of d., 46:38
   cast into outer d., 34:16
   comprehended it not, 39:30
   crown of our life is d., 533:15
   curse the d., 654:*n*2
   dawn on our d., 395:16
   deep but dazzling d., 270:3
   deep things out of d., 14:18
   deepens, 410:17
   distant voice in d., 442:16
   downward to d. on wings, 638:26
   dying of cold not d., 589:16
   embalmed d., 415:14
   encounter d. as a bride, 204:12
   falls at thy behest, 506:16
   falls from wings, 441:10
   fell upon Christian, 272:25
   gives light in d., 163:21
   hello d. my old friend, 772:7
   horror of outer d., 520:9
   hovers earth is silent, 5:4
   how great that d., 33:16
   how in your d. know, 612:6
   if light in thee be d., 33:16
   in d. and with dangers, 259:19
   in d. bind them, 685:4
   in him is no d., 46:31
   in what d. of life spend little span,
     89:14
   instruments of d., 212:21
   into d. peering, 452:17
   into d. they go, 684:12
   into eternal d. fire and ice, 125:12
   jaws of d. do devour it, 172:20
   land of d. and shadow, 14:11
   lead me from d. to light, 50:15
   leaves world to d. to me, 322:1

Darkness (*continued*)
   lest d. come, 40:23
   light excelleth d., 23:29
   light shineth in d., 39:30
   lighten our d., 49:7
   love in spite of d., 229:4
   mainly in d., 766:3
   man ever in d., 117:11
   man in unsearchable d., 550:2
   no d. but ignorance, 203:5
   no d. into light without emotion,
     629:4
   no light but d. visible, 255:23
   not walk in d., 40:10
   of God, 671:5
   of man's heart, 729:18
   outer d., 34:16, 36:16, 520:9
   over spirits of damned, 448:10
   pain d. and cold, 467:19
   peace and d., 580:7
   people that walked in d., 26:7
   people which sat in d., 32:36
   pestilence that walketh in d., 18:15
   prince of d. a gentleman, 210:10
   raven down of d., 252:27
   rulers of the d., 44:28
   scatters rear of d. thin, 251:12
   shaft of light in d., 742:5
   shares the d., 684:6
   sit in d. here, 257:8
   such as sit in d., 19:8
   swooping d. up, 786:22
   them that sit in d., 38:1
   this thing of d., 224:28
   thou makest d., 19:6
   through d. up to God, 457:20
   two eternities of d., 702:17
   universal d. buries all, 304:2
   upon face of the deep, 6:4
   wave of light breaks into d., 662:10
   we are not of d., 45:6
   where d. let me sow light, 123:10
   which may be felt, 8:34
   wind torrent of d., 643:11
   works of d., 42:23
   worms and shrouds, 414:6
   year of now done d., 551:12
Dark-shining Pacific, 663:11
Darky's heart longed to go, 564:19
Darling buds of May, 220:12
   Charlie is my d., 368:5
   daughter, 783:6
   I am growing old, 557:1
   man been mother's undisputed d.,
     569:9
   my d. dear, 779:12
   my d. from the lions, 16:32
   Nature's D., 323:2
   of men and gods, 89:2
   of my heart, 298:2
   of our crew, 348:3
Darlings, we must march my d., 490:7
   wealthy curled d., 205:19
Dart, every look a d., 778:7
   time throw a d. at thee, 240:14
Darts, lay full of d., 414:20
Darwin Abraham of scientific men,
   493:19
   Evolution from Washington to
     Grant upset D., 535:25

Darwin's, most famous event since D.
  book, 760:*n*1
  theory conjectural, 440:10
Dash thy foot against a stone, 18:16,
  38:10
Dashed, breaking waves d. high,
  410:11
  in pieces the enemy, 9:4
  the brains out, 213:12
  through thick and thin, 274:17
Dastard in war, 378:9
Dastardly pitiful Public, 390:10
Dat veniam corvis vexat censura
  columbas, 108:*n*7
Data, submit d. to analysis, 351:16
Date, out of d., 659:4
  will live in infamy, 649:19
Dates, manna and d., 415:6
Datta (give), 50:*n*8
Daubed with slime and pitch, 8:21
Daughter all her life, 506:13
  am I in mother's house, 592:24
  as mother so her d., 29:6
  at point of death, 37:27
  beggar's d. of Bethnal Green, 785:5
  fairer d. of fair mother, 95:27
  harping on my d., 195:18
  have you a d., 195:17
  I have a d., 182:1
  images return O my d., 669:22
  king of Spain's d., 790:12
  light God's eldest d., 250:12
  marry d. when you can, 244:12
  Mrs. Porter and d., 668:23
  my d. O my ducats, 180:24
  of a hundred Earls, 453:25
  of debate, 145:2
  of Elysium, 364:13
  of Herodias Salome danced, 35:14
  of Jove, 321:18
  of Moon Nokomis, 441:24
  of the gods, 454:13
  one fair d., 195:33
  sole d. of his voice, 260:6
  stern d. of voice of God, 376:2
  taken his little d., 440:20
  undaunted d. of desires, 264:16
  whipped her little d., 790:15
  yes my darling d., 783:6
  your d. and the Moor, 205:17
Daughter's daughter all her life,
  506:13
  preaching down d. heart, 455:15
Daughters and sons gone, 755:4
  curses all Eve's d., 183:5
  degenerate sons and d., 607:12
  earth's heedless sons and d., 694:1
  fairest of her d. Eve, 258:14
  have done virtuously, 23:21
  horseleach hath two d., 23:14
  if you have no d., 790:9
  my d. I suppose, 717:2
  none of Beauty's d., 401:24
  O d. of Jerusalem, 25:1, 25:15
  of music brought low, 24:27
  of my father's house, 202:15
  of Time, 430:6
  prayers are d. of Zeus, 51:33
  sage d. of Muses, 64:6
  tigers not d., 210:24

Daughters (*continued*)
  who Shem and Shaun d. of, 647:20
  words are d. of earth, 313:27
Daughtersons, all Livia's d., 647:20
Daunt, death could not d., 785:6
Dauntless, brows of d. courage,
  256:17
  Hampden with d. breast, 322:14
  in war, 378:8
  slug-horn to my lips, 210:*n*3
Dauphin, daylight's d., 550:20
David, and D. his ten thousands,
  11:42
  danced before the Lord, 12:7
  died full of days, 13:20
  in the city of D., 38:3
  in the midst, 325:11
  Josias, 287:8
  King D. and King Solomon, 583:11
  my sling the sling of D., 564:16
  no more behind your scenes D.,
  315:14
  played before the Lord, 12:5
  prevailed over the Philistine, 11:41
  the son of Jesse, 12:16
David's, once in royal D. city, 479:19
  upon St. D. Day, 791:17
Davil, ole D. sea, 673:12
Daw, Margery D., 789:12
  no wiser than a d., 163:10
Dawn becomes yellow, 787:8
  before d. of day, 327:11
  bodiless as false d., 749:15
  comes no sooner for early riser,
  794:5
  comes up like thunder, 591:23
  creation's d. beheld, 401:1
  embraced summer d., 566:1
  gray d. breaking, 424:7, 633:14
  house made of d., 787:9
  in Helen's arms, 598:22
  in that d. to be alive, 373:12
  into silver d., 688:6
  live gray d., 757:13
  Morning Star herald of d., 87:5
  of knowledge false dawn, 696:9
  of morning after, 600:13
  on other side of Atlantic, 323:23
  on our darkness, 395:16
  past is twilight of d., 601:8
  rosy-fingered d., 51:1
  said to d. Be sudden, 581:7
  speeds a man, 54:29
  will dispel night, 405:8
  with silver-sandaled feet, 566:6
Dawned from Bullen's eyes, 321:24
Dawneth, darkest before day d.,
  250:18
Dawning, bird of d., 192:29
  here hath been d., 413:17
  not as d. of day, 231:10
Dawn's early light, 391:2
  light dispersed, 56:11
Dawns, day d. to which we are
  awake, 478:40
Daws, for d. to peck at, 205:14
Day, a little work and good d., 522:10
  a summer's d. and with setting sun,
  256:22
  after wedding night, 616:19

Day (*continued*)
  all days as marriage d., 242:15
  all on summer's d., 789:14
  all the livelong d., 780:6
  all things all d. long, 459:11
  alternation of night and d., 116:8
  and night shall not cease, 7:22
  and way we met, 534:17
  another blue d., 413:17
  apple a d., 781:18
  as it fell upon a d., 233:10
  as morning shows the d., 260:32
  battle d. past, 506:14
  be d. never so long, 142:23
  be she fairer than the d., 240:1
  beneath blue d., 579:1
  best d. first to flee, 93:3
  better d. better deed, 236:14
  beyond night across d., 456:2
  bounded by D. of Judgment,
  460:*n*1
  breaks not it is heart, 777:7
  brief December d., 443:13
  bright cold d. in April, 711:15
  bright d. is done, 218:12
  bright d. not for aye, 479:29
  brought back my night, 255:17
  burden and heat of d., 35:39
  by d. in a pillar of cloud, 8:43
  called feast of Crispian, 185:22
  cares that infest d., 441:12
  chest of drawers by d., 329:19
  children of the d., 45:6
  Christmas D. in workhouse, 556:1
  clear d. see forever, 745:14
  close eye of d., 254:10
  come another d., 788:8
  come not on last d. but very last,
  651:17
  cometh that shall burn as oven,
  30:9
  compare thee to summer's d.,
  220:12
  cool of the d., 6:21
  count that d. lost, 779:1
  creatures of a d., 64:5
  dance barefoot on wedding d.,
  167:21
  darkest before d. dawneth, 250:18
  darkest d., 335:19
  dawns to which we are awake,
  478:40
  death will have his d., 171:23
  dependency of d. and night, 638:26
  dies at the opening d., 294:16
  dim light of immortal d., 407:5
  dines on following d., 519:21
  do business of d. in d., 371:11
  do each d. two things disliked,
  626:15
  dog hath a d., 142:3
  dog will have his d., 199:18
  drink oblivion of d., 508:26
  dying d. sir, 778:17
  each d. like a year, 567:21
  end of perfect d., 585:8
  endures moment or d., 597:19
  entertains the harmless d., 227:7
  ere I had seen that d., 193:14

Day (*continued*)

evening and morning were first d., 6:5
every d. got up and gone to bed, 626:15
every d. hidden growths, 483:24
every d. in every way, 573:18
every d. passed as if our last, 100:6
every dog has his d., 428:17
every dog his d., 484:15
every year passed d., 758:10
everyone has his d., 622:7
exact d.-labor light denied, 255:12
faint in the d. of adversity, 22:24
fair d. adieu, 169:29
famous d. and year, 442:12
fate put heads together, 624:2
fell of dark not d., 551:15
first last everlasting d., 229:5
first spring d., 563:16
fogs prevail upon the d., 274:26
follow as night the d., 194:1
forever and a d., 192:3
frabjous d., 518:16
friends I have lost a d., 106:27
from our immortal d., 356:16
from this d. forward, 50:4
gaudy blabbing remorseful d., 164:4
geology by d., 690:1
gilded car of d., 252:19
given thee till break of d., 358:1
go ahead make my d., 774:8
go to bed by d., 561:7
God is d. night winter summer, 62:13
good to gain d., 489:4
got tired of Me, 512:10
great and dreadful d. of the Lord, 30:11
guest that tarrieth but a d., 30:26
gwine to run all d., 506:18
happiest d. happiest hour, 451:8
hath brightest d. a cloud, 163:23
he that outlives this d., 185:22
health and a d., 431:1
hippopotamus's d., 668:11
home being washing-d., 279:15
how it is with April d., 624:6
I had rued, 623:15
I hate the d., 154:8
I have lived my d., 96:*n*20
idle singer of empty d., 523:6
if she be a d., 290:6
in d. of adversity consider, 24:10
in d. of prosperity be joyful, 24:10
in its hotness, 498:2
in the d. of vengeance, 20:31
in the posteriors of this d., 169:7
in thy courts, 18:7
in which ye came out, 8:42
infinite d. excludes the night, 294:19
is a poem, 663:19
is at hand, 42:23
is done and darkness falls, 441:10
is for honest men, 68:25
is short labor long, 115:16
it is his d., 133:10
it was Christmas D., 160:20
jocund d. stands tiptoe, 176:6
joint-laborer with d., 192:24

Day (*continued*)

July's d. short as December, 222:20
just for one d., 611:19
kings upon coronation d., 275:16
knell of parting d., 322:1
known a better d., 377:19
left alone with our d., 720:6
lengthens not a d., 228:1
let every man consider last d., 66:2
let the d. perish, 13:34
let them have their d., 596:14
light of common d., 375:8
little systems have d., 457:3
long weary d. have end, 154:13
looked into eye of d., 598:3
love resembleth April d., 168:1
maddest merriest d., 454:4
makes d. seep into night, 117:12
meditate d. and night, 15:29
merry as d. is long, 186:17
merry heart goes all d., 223:4
mildewed d. in August, 742:12
most wasted d. of all, 342:4
mounting at break of d., 376:13
night and d. you are the one, 682:1
Night mother of D., 443:2
night of time surpasseth d., 249:3
night thousand eyes d. one, 563:2
not a d. without a line, 81:1
not as dawning of d., 231:10
not look same by d., 438:19
not the best d., 767:7
not to me returns d., 257:24
not up soon as I, 170:19
now d. over, 521:11
now's the d., 363:19
of adversity, 24:10
of affliction, 31:27
of death better than birth, 24:6
of deliverance, 338:5
of Empires come, 528:21
of glory has come, 366:*n*1
of my destiny's over, 401:26
of one's birth, 24:6
of prosperity, 31:27
of small things, 30:2
of spirits, 270:2
of the great reckoning, 4:5
of the locust, 712:12
of the Lord, 45:5
of vengeance, 20:31
of wrath, 123:14
on seventh d. God ended his work, 6:10
on that d. no soul wronged, 117:13
pack clouds away and welcome d., 233:20
past and yet I saw no sun, 156:22
perfect d., 585:8
petty pace from d. to d., 216:14
precincts of cheerful d., 322:19
proper man as see in summer's d., 172:29
rain it raineth every d., 203:7, 210:1
rape of every blessed d., 749:16
rare as d. in June, 485:5
remember the sabbath d., 9:11
returns too soon, 402:1
Rome must be built in d., 743:17
Rome not built in one d., 141:29

Day (*continued*)

rose with delight to us, 242:4
runs through roughest d., 212:25
saw my evil d., 369:6
seize the d., 95:25
set down as gain each d., 95:24
seventh d. thou shalt not work, 9:11
shall declare it, 42:33
shall stand at the latter d., 14:30
she set out one d., 618:14
shineth unto perfect d., 20:24
sleep neither night nor d., 212:13
so cool so calm, 243:10
so foul and fair a d., 212:16
soundless d. in autumn, 452:4
specter night and d., 358:16
spent but one d. thoroughly well, 132:18
St. Patrick's D., 779:10
sufficient unto d. is evil, 34:1
sun anew each d., 664:19
sun gone down while it was d., 28:26
sun shall not smite thee by d., 19:25
sunbeam in winter's d., 307:14
superfluous to demand time of d., 176:24
support us all d. long, 426:22
tender eye of pitiful d., 214:28
thanks to heroes reached this d., 732:9
that is dead, 456:8
that shall burn as oven, 30:9
think every d. your last, 97:11
third d. comes a frost, 225:16
third d. he rose again, 48:25
third d. he will raise us up, 29:24
this d. for a memorial, 8:39
this d. we must part, 424:8
this January D., 514:10
those eyes the break of d., 204:22
those who dream by d., 452:6
thou d. I hour, 530:4
thou gavest Lord is ended, 506:16
thought it Judgment D., 540:21
time makes possible D. of Judgment, 652:1
tire the d. in toil, 242:7
'tis true 'tis d., 229:4
today first d. of rest of life, 784:8
today isn't any other d., 519:9
tomorrow a new d., 151:2
tomorrow as today, 222:16
tomorrow is another d., 705:3
trysting d., 425:13
turn by night or d., 375:3
two nights to every d., 243:13
unpurged images of d., 598:11
until the d. break, 25:8
unto day uttereth speech, 16:9
up by break of d., 243:8
vulgarize d. of judgment, 434:3
was it the spring d., 787:19
we the ones to make better d., 775:3
weakening eye of d., 540:9
wear d. out before comes, 557:18
wedding d. fixed, 312:5
well-spent d. happy sleep, 135:2

Dead (*continued*)

beauty d. chaos comes, 165:16
become lumber of world, 284:1
being d. with him beauty slain,
   165:16
besides the wench is d., 162:9
better to be fool than d., 560:18
bivouac of the d., 492:4
blow bugles over rich d., 663:5
Body my good dog d., 747:13
body without spirit is d., 46:10
brave men living and d., 450:2
breed maggots in d. dog, 195:17
broke spell of d. letter, 680:5
by ships lies a d. man, 52:23
Caesar's trencher, 217:27
called it Bible d. now, 708:16
certain is birth for the d., 84:5
Christ risen from d., 43:20
close wall with English d., 185:3
communication of d., 671:20
corpse of Public Credit, 394:18
corse in complete steel, 194:11
crucified d. buried, 48:25
day that is d., 456:8
days among d. past, 386:15
dead and dead indeed, 787:21
dead dead and never knew me,
   548:1
dear d. women, 466:15
Death once d., 222:12
deathless hour, 509:23
descent of last end on d., 647:8
desire d. be near us, 457:15
dishonor not trouble once I am d.,
   68:2
divine brother of all, 490:11
dooms imagined for d., 414:10
doubled globe of d., 737:10
earth that bears thee d., 179:6
earth to living not d., 344:14
either d. or watch stopped, 728:15
England finished and d., 626:24
envy for the d., 527:28
envy of the d., 68:5
faith d. which does not doubt,
   590:2
faith without works is d., 46:10
fallen cold and d., 491:1
fame sun of d., 422:9
fell at his feet as d., 47:5
for a ducat dead, 197:27
for Love is d., 155:27
for Lycidas sorrow not d., 254:6
forgotten as a d. man out of mind,
   16:26
full of d. men's bones, 36:5
gear of foreign d. men, 671:13
God is d., 552:5
govern living, 421:10
great god Pan is d., 107:16
greatest service or injury to d. man,
   75:3
half d. a living death, 261:9
half regiment d., 743:10
hands dead stringencies, 764:19
harrow house of d., 720:4
heads of d. up line, 700:8
healthy wealthy and d., 690:12
heard the d. cry, 724:17

Dead (*continued*)

heart fell d., 688:7
Hector is d., 201:14
help for living hope for d., 520:14
her d. body wears smile, 764:14
her warrior d., 456:18
herself ere evensong, 785:16
high converse with mighty d.,
   307:18
honor dies man d., 443:4
how fares it with happy d., 457:12
how possible that d. be brought
   alive, 116:22
how shall the d. arise, 248:14
I am every d. thing, 229:9
ideas and dead beliefs, 508:5
if Lucy should be d., 373:18
immortal d. who live again, 483:7
in long run all d., 652:8
in praise of ladies d., 221:22
is at rest, 32:11
is God d., 420:21
is the king d., 166:10
just as d. as if wrong, 783:22
King Pandion he is d., 233:11
kissed by English d., 687:4
knocking when I'm d., 634:17
know not any thing, 24:18
lain for century d., 458:24
land of d., 697:11, 720:8
laughter out of d. bellies, 659:9
law hath not been d., 204:2
left it d. and with head, 518:16
let d. bury their d., 34:18
life is shrunk d. and interred, 229:8
lift coffins of d. relations, 769:14
light in dust lies d., 409:19
like vampire d. many times, 538:6
lilacs out of d. land, 668:17
living and d. are same, 62:19
living dog better than d. lion, 24:18
living scarce able to bury d., 240:10
look at my d. house, 714:3
Lord of living and d., 550:17
loses past and d. for future, 69:16
love never sick old d., 152:10
Magus Zoroaster my d. child,
   406:16
maid not d. but sleepeth, 34:25
man cannot bite, 88:15
Man's Chest, 561:1
men rise up never, 534:15
men tell no tales, 274:23
mie love ys d., 353:6
mighty d., 307:18
mindful of unhonored d., 322:21
Mistah Kurtz he d., 573:9
more d. people than living, 731:15
more to say when d., 608:5
mourn the d., 749:14
mouth of one just d., 632:15
moving d. still talk of pushing
   bones, 759:12
Mozart had been d. two years,
   759:7
my enemy is d. man divine d.,
   490:14
my lady's sparrow is d., 90:16

Dead (*continued*)

nature seems d., 213:21
ne'er said till friend d., 554:11
newspaper buries d., 603:12
no longer mourn when I am d.,
   221:7
noble Living and noble D., 373:13
not a house where not one d., 8:41
not d. but gone before, 102:*n*13
not God of d., 39:12
not interested in living, 697:14
not make war on d., 143:2
not reverence of d. but envy of living, 239:24
now he is d. should I fast, 12:12
O he is d. then, 551:3
objects essentially d., 384:7
of d. nothing but good, 55:*n*5
old bawd is d., 599:19
old men are all d., 541:2
once d. never return, 445:20
one d. other powerless, 498:20
only d. who do not return, 354:12
only good Indians d., 516:8
out of d. cold ashes life, 554:13
outrage brave man d., 65:15
pattern of d. and living, 671:10
people so d. to liberty, 312:20
perfection, 458:17
Phlebas a fortnight d., 669:3
plucks d. lions by beard, 169:20
poetry of earth never d., 414:2
Poets d. and gone, 416:12
poets in misery d., 374:11
praised the d. already d., 23:33
pray for d. fight like hell for living,
   515:3
professors like literature d., 658:9
quick and the d., 48:25
renown and grace is d., 214:15
Respite to be d., 513:13
rest for the d., 521:9
rest her soul she's d., 199:5
resurrection of the d., 43:20
revisit in dreams the dear d., 67:23
right d. right as sped along, 783:*n*9
romantic Ireland's d., 596:1
rough notes and d. bodies, 606:2
rule over the departed d., 53:25
say I'm sick I'm d., 302:6
Sea and Sea of Galilee, 632:16
Sea fruits, 392:14
Sea's shore, 399:23
seek living among d., 39:25
shall be raised, 43:27
shall live living die, 275:11
sheeted d., 192:25
shores will swarm with invisible d.,
   398:11
smiling the boy fell d., 464:10
so dull so d. in look, 183:10
soldiers bore d. bodies by, 177:3
somebody threw d. dog down ravine, 727:3
something d. in each of us, 567:19
soul so d., 378:1
Spartan d., 402:27
speak ill of the d., 55:11
stars are d., 720:6

Dead (*continued*)
stepping-stones of d. selves, 457:5
tell 'em Queen Anne's d., 366:13
there are no d., 586:11
there he fell down d., 11:5
these d. not died in vain, 450:2
these honored d., 450:2
think living worth it, 758:9
thirty is as good as d., 350:22
though d. shall he live, 40:19
three keep secret if two d., 309:15
thy greatest enemy d., 31:19
time is d., 696:11
time you have to spend d., 145:13
told me Heraclitus d., 502:9
took wages and are d., 580:1
topics of sex and the d., 600:4
travel to home among d., 408:13
tree gives no shelter, 668:18
trophies and d. things, 237:20
truth never fell d., 461:17
unhonored d., 322:21
until he is d. do not call man
    happy, 55:20
vast and middle of night, 193:18
voices of d. like torrent's fall, 403:1
warred for Homer being d., 233:22
was d. and is alive, 38:37
what d. had no speech for living,
    671:20
what was d. was Hope, 567:19
when d. put money in coffin, 390:11
when I am d., 655:2
when I am d. my dearest, 515:4
when living might exceed d., 248:25
when only d. could smile, 675:9
where d. men lost bones, 668:20
which die in the Lord, 47:32
which he slew at his death, 11:19
who fed the guns, 662:7
why can't d. die, 674:7
winds' riot, 534:12
word d. when said, 514:1
would that I were d., 453:17
youth stone d., 662:6
Dead March, play D. as you carry me,
    786:7
Dead-born, fell d. from the press,
    318:16
Dead-letter days, 387:23
Deadlock, holy d., 678:20
Deadly, dare d. terrors clasp, 358:7
forfeit should release, 250:19
imminent d. breach, 205:25
more d. than mad dog's tooth,
    166:32
more d. than male, 593:22
pay with a d. blow, 63:22
wither and come to d. use, 210:22
Deadwood and Lost Mule Flat, 698:6
Deaf, ears of the d. shall be un-
    stopped, 27:9
justice blind d. an' dumb, 602:18
like the d. adder, 17:29
live d. to land beneath us, 681:7
music good nor bad to d., 278:9
trouble d. heaven, 220:15
Deafness, tale would cure d., 223:23
Deal, candy d. of courtesy, 177:10
falsely with God, 239:27

Deal (*continued*)
in remnants of remnants, 291:14
infinite d. of nothing, 179:23
intolerable d. of sack, 177:34
new d., 648:16
of scorn looks beautiful, 202:25
square d., 576:2
to d. plainly, 211:10
with men as equals, 767:3
Dealing, common sense plain d.,
    432:11
hard d. teaches them suspect,
    180:11
Dean could write finely upon broom-
    stick, 289:*n*2
Dear as light and life, 363:13
as remembered kisses, 456:14
beauty for earth too d., 174:23
Brutus, 187:22
coldness of my d., 297:5
damned distracting town, 299:27
dead women, 466:15
experience keeps d. school, 309:28
Fatherland, 488:2
friends we love so d., 523:1
God bless you my d., 318:2
how d. to this heart, 398:2
I die, 229:1
is life so d., 339:10
jesses my d. heart-strings, 207:2
land that gave you birth, 586:12
Lord and Father, 443:17
lose their d. delight, 221:20
makes a blessing d., 262:10
makes remembrance d., 203:19
man to all country d., 329:12
my d. times' waste, 220:18
name forever sad forever d., 300:2
nurse of arts, 186:1
pay too d. for what's given freely,
    222:15
Plato and truth are d., 77:26
Sir your astonishment's odd, 673:*n*1
so d. I love him, 260:8
sold cheap what is most d., 221:26
son of memory, 251:2
think on thee d. friend, 220:19
thoughts to memory d., 379:2
to God famous to all ages, 254:20
to me as ruddy drops, 188:8
to me more d., 329:20
too d. for my possessing, 221:11
what restraint to grief for one so d.,
    95:29
Wotton a most d. lover, 245:17
Dearer, honor d. than life, 150:4
yet the brotherhood, 586:12
Dearest, met my d. foe in heaven,
    193:14
nearest and d. enemy, 178:13
throw away d. thing owed, 212:26
when I am dead my d., 515:7
Dearly let or let alone, 242:9
Dearness only gives value, 340:22
Dears, Nature swears the lovely d.,
    361:25
Dearth, war d. age agues, 230:20
Deary, flew o'er me and my d., 363:13
in short my d. kiss me, 304:4
Death a necessary end, 188:11

Death (*continued*)
absence darkness d., 229:9
absurd also, 728:3
after d. better bad epitaph, 196:2
after first d. no other, 737:12
after life does please, 153:9
after life is d., 534:11
aloft gigantically down, 701:7
amiable lovely d., 170:3
and i coquette, 633:3
and Night wash world, 490:14
and sorrow our companions, 620:12
and taxes, 310:27
any man's d. diminishes me, 231:8
anyone's d. releases stupefaction,
    496:11
arise arise from d., 230:19
ashamed of d., 248:13
be absolute for d., 204:8
be not proud, 230:22
because chose to turn, 675:6
become sought-after refuge, 70:8
beggars mounted run horse to d.,
    164:12
better than day of birth, 24:6
birth copulation and d., 670:2
birth life and d., 283:16
Black Widow d., 742:13
blackness of d., 89:21
blaze forth d. of princes, 188:10
body of this d., 42:1
borders upon our birth, 233:16
bridegroom in my d., 218:5
bring d. to a friend, 66:10
bringeth to light the shadow of d.,
    14:18
brought d. into world, 255:18
Bustle in House Morning after D.,
    513:17
by inches, 219:14
by man came d., 43:20
calls ye to the crowd, 246:22
came d. into the world, 30:22
captain of men of d., 272:32
certain is d. for the born, 84:5
certain to all, 184:3
chance d. and mutability, 407:3
chants doleful hymn to d., 170:20
Chromis did not save himself from
    dark d., 51:10
City of Night perchance D., 523:16
closed in d. attentive eyes, 315:2
closes all, 455:5
cold hand of d., 179:5
come away d., 202:13
come close eyes, 777:6
come lovely soothing d., 490:17
cometh soon or late, 425:14
could not daunt, 785:6
counteracts Devil who is D., 325:18
covenant with d., 26:33, 437:16
crossing the world, 282:21
cruel as d., 307:17
cruel d. always near, 287:13
cruel d. of Pyramus, 172:22
darkness and shadow of d., 14:11,
    19:8, 38:1
daughter at point of d., 37:27
dear beauteous d., 270:11

Death (*continued*)

defend to d. your right to say it, 307:4

departure beyond borders d., 680:6

desire father's d., 495:14

desireth not d. of sinner, 48:19

destroyer of worlds, 714:12

devours lovely things, 684:6

die a dry d., 223:20

die not poor d., 230:22

die the d. of the righteous, 10:5

died good d. if life inspired, 762:11

direst shapes of d., 503:4

does not end all, 101:3

done to d. by slanderous tongues, 187:14

draw trigger after his d., 315:19

dread d., 52:21

dread of something after d., 196:10

dull cold ear of d., 322:10

dung and d., 670:21

dusty d., 216:14

each earns his d., 705:20

easeful D., 415:16

eaten to d. with rust, 183:23

Elizabeth-Jane not told of my d., 539:18

eloquent just and mighty D., 153:1

embrace is d., 692:4

ende of worldly soore, 130:23

enviable d. was his, 621:18

equal in presence of d., 98:29

equal piece of justice D., 248:12

ere thou hast slain another, 240:14

escapades of d., 640:2

eternal sleep, 364:8

even D. listened, 437:10

even in Arcadia there am I D., 118:*n*10

everybody's looks of d., 279:11

Exodus of d., 442:4

faithful unto d., 47:9

Falstaff sweats to d., 177:15

Famine Pestilence Destruction D., 643:15

fear and danger of violent d., 239:22

fear d. as children fear dark, 159:4

fear d. feel fog, 467:18

fear of d. more dreaded than d., 99:28

fear of D. troubles me, 136:*n*2

fear of ignominious d., 366:3

fed on fullness of d., 534:4

feed on D., 222:12

fell sergeant d., 199:24

final accounting, 119:13

find me planting cabbages, 145:11

fly down D., 734:3

for restful d. I cry, 221:4

for thirty pence my d., 243:6

foretaste of d., 404:14

fortune favored him in moment of d., 109:23

found d. in life, 385:5

fraternity or d., 342:*n*3

friends enough now for d., 710:8

from d. to immortality, 50:15

from sudden d., 49:10

fruit threw d., 230:21

Death (*continued*)

gallop Pegasus to d., 303:1

gates of dark D. stand wide, 94:6

give me liberty or d., 339:10

giving life by d. of others, 134:15

go down D. bring her, 612:9

go hand in hand to d., 509:27

go with anyone to d., 623:4

gods have neither age nor d., 67:7

gone to her d., 423:9

good d. does honor to whole life, 127:10

good thing to escape d., 66:10

great d., 611:5

grim d., 238:9

grim D. my son and foe, 257:18

had appointment in Samarra, 626:19

had undone so many, 668:19

half dead a living d., 261:9

halls of d., 411:4

has broached him to, 348:3

hath no more dominion, 41:43

hath ten thousand doors, 237:17

he brought them d., 610:19

he taketh all away, 502:9

heaven gives favorites early d., 81:*n*4

here find life in d., 385:5

how can you know about d., 61:15

how little room we take in d., 246:19

how strange a thing is d., 684:11

how they pray for d., 67:26

hungry for life and d., 736:19

I am near to d., 56:5

I here importune d., 218:7

I hung on like d., 724:15

idle and who has done much meet d. alike, 51:31

if D. knew how to forgive, 93:7

immortal D. has taken mortal life, 90:4

in d. daylight finish, 468:12

in d. they were not divided, 11:47

in his d. all things appear fair, 52:20

in itself is nothing, 273:15

in our own power, 552:*n*5

in ranks of d. find him, 391:17

in sterres writen d. of every man, 130:32

in the midst of life d., 50:7

in the pot, 13:7

in the shadow of d., 19:8, 38:1

in vain to wish for d., 66:21

in Venice, 629:21

interest in d. interest in life, 629:15

intricate as d., 231:12

is a sleep, 534:6

is afraid of him, 118:7

is as lover's pinch, 218:18

is dead not he, 409:5

is in my sight today, 4:4

is knowledge, 365:14

is most efficient, 643:2

is not D. at watch, 694:1

is nothing to us, 90:3

is slumber, 406:11

is sorrow, 64:26

Death (*continued*)

is swallowed up, 43:28

is the enemy, 651:4

jaws of d., 148:6, 458:14

judge none blessed before his d., 31:28

just d. kind umpire, 163:12

just that distance from d., 56:1

keeps D. his court, 171:25

keys of hell and d., 47:6

kingly D. keeps court, 408:16

kings did king to d., 737:10

kiss of d., 618:5

land of darkness and shadow of d., 14:11

land of the shadow of d., 26:7

last enemy is d., 43:21

last guerdon of d., 91:17

laugh myself to d., 224:10

lays icy hand on kings, 246:23

leaves body at d., 84:11

Life D. and that For Ever, 484:13

life or d. crave reality, 478:20

life perfected by d., 438:15

life shadow of d., 249:6, 533:10

life that which men call d., 69:15

life well used brings happy d., 135:2

like sleep steal on me, 406:15

like this, 441:2

limbs cold in d., 94:28

lively form of d., 156:17

looks gigantically, 451:16

love better after d., 439:1

love is strong as d., 25:22

Love posterior to D., 513:9

loves shining mark, 296:18

made d. his ladder, 154:9

makes equal high and low, 140:14

makes life live, 468:5

men at point of d., 176:16

men of d., 272:32

milder fate than tyranny, 63:16

Mister D., 688:10

more bitter than d., 24:13

mother of beauty, 638:25

mourned at birth not d., 304:8

naked in d. on unknown shore, 94:4

nativity chance or d., 183:7

neither fear nor long for d., 106:22

never taste of d. but once, 188:11

newspaper d., 535:29

no cure for d., 588:14

no God stronger than d., 534:6

no life by others' d., 170:12

no more d., 48:1

no trouble, 652:3

no work pause for d., 467:28

nor life nor angels, 42:9

not born for d., 415:17

not d. but dying is terrible, 312:3

not D. but Love, 438:21

not D. for I stood up, 512:15

not room for D., 480:5

not stop for D., 513:3

not the worst, 66:21

nothing call our own but d., 171:25

nothing to us, 81:18

now boast thee, 218:20

now to D. devote, 260:10

Death (*continued*)

O d. I will be thy plagues, 29:31
O D. in Life, 456:14
O sane and sacred d., 490:16
of a dear friend, 174:9
of air, 671:21
of democracy, 702:14
of each day's life, 214:6
of endeavor birth of disgust, 544:12
of friends inspire us, 477:18
of hope and despair, 671:21
of one god death of all, 639:21
of the most noblest knights, 133:15
of water and fire, 672:1
old captain, 494:10
on else immortal us, 230:21
on his pale horse, 260:16
on life on d., 600:3
once dead, 222:12
one in life and d. are we, 530:4
one of few things done easily,
    767:14
one of things Nature wills, 111:25
one studied in his d., 212:26
one talent d. to hide, 255:11
or dreamful ease, 454:10
our souls survive d., 101:*n*2
out of jaws of d., 148:*n*5
owe God a d., 184:5
pale horse and on him was D.,
    47:19
pang preceding d., 328:4
part and parcel of life, 629:11
parting foretaste of d., 404:14
past so he waited, 466:18
people given over to d., 90:13
perfected being survives after d.,
    65:3
play to you d. to us, 266:12
posterior to D., 513:9
precious is the d. of his saints,
    19:19
preferred d. before slavery, 105:17
protracting life not deduct from d.,
    90:6
proud d., 199:30
proud to take us, 218:9
quick even in d., 151:25
quiet us in d. so noble, 261:25
read d. of Little Nell, 567:25
reared himself throne, 451:14
reasonable moderator D., 248:12
redeem them from d., 29:31
remain until d. do part, 571:15
remembered kisses after d., 456:14
rendezvous with D., 674:17
report of my d. an exaggeration,
    528:2
ribs of D., 253:5
ride not free horse to d., 151:16
right to d. or liberty, 493:14
sad stories of d. of kings, 171:25
seized Argus, 54:5
sense of d. in apprehension, 204:11
sentence of Versailles, 676:10
set before you life and d., 10:25
set d. i' the other, 187:19
setter up and plucker down of
    kings, 164:17
shall be no more, 230:24

Death (*continued*)

shall be surely put to d., 9:14
shall have no dominion, 737:11
ship of d., 658:2
sickened and nigh to d., 491:5
side of life away from us, 630:9
silent halls of d., 411:4
single d. tragedy, 638:13
sit in shadow of d., 19:8, 38:1
slavery or d., 292:9
sleep brother of d., 52:4
Sleep Brother to D., 160:21
sleep of d., 196:10
sleep the sleep of d., 359:24
slew at d. more than in life, 11:19
slew not him, 154:9
someone's d., 466:9
soul sorrowful unto d., 36:29
stalk of d., 759:12
state of nothingness, 74:16
storm desertion d., 419:8
strange that d. should sing, 170:20
strict in his arrest, 199:24
stroke of d. eclipsed gaiety, 314:22
strong lean upon d., 663:15
struck sharp on d., 439:2
sudden d. best, 88:24
Sudden D. General Desolation,
    526:7
suffuses all with blackness of d.,
    89:21
sure as d., 231:15
swallow up d. in victory, 26:27
swallowed up in d., 74:20
taxes childbirth, 705:1
think not disdainfully of d., 111:25
those who died so cruel a d., 139:4
thou shalt die, 230:24
thou wilt bring me to d., 14:44
thought of that late d., 596:9
till d. us do part, 50:4
time of d. every moment, 84:*n*7
to accept d. is to die, 371:*n*7
touch the great d., 611:5
tramples it to fragments, 409:8
true to thee till d., 474:2
truly longed for d., 453:22
try cause condemn d., 517:6
twitches my ear, 94:30
two fates of dread d., 52:21
ugly fact Nature hides, 515:16
unknown song sounded by d.,
    405:10
useless life is early d., 349:14
valley of d., 458:9
valley of shadow of d., 16:17
vasty hall of d., 498:15
veil called life, 407:2
visit us with d., 240:10
wages of sin is d., 41:45
way to dusty d., 216:14
Webster possessed by d., 668:12
what should it know of d., 372:17
what sights of ugly d., 165:30
what we fear of d., 204:15
when is d. not within ourselves,
    62:19
where is thy sting, 43:28
who comes at last, 378:6
will have his day, 171:23

Death (*continued*)

windpipe throttled in fakes of d.,
    489:12
with impartial tread, 95:18
world easily reconciles to d., 436:9
worse things than d., 533:22
worst is d., 171:23
your d. Heraclitus, 82:20
your Loveliness and my d., 418:17
Deathbed, Jemmy Grove on d. lay,
    785:9
Death-bedde, gon to hys d., 353:6
Death-fires danced at night, 381:10
Deathless Aphrodite on your throne,
    56:4
    dead d. hour, 509:23
    his mansions are d., 53:6
    music, 607:13
Deathly slumber, 617:1
Death's a debt, 352:20
    beg d. pardon now, 749:14
    brother Sleep, 94:8
    call in thy d. head, 243:17
    fell d. untimely frost, 363:14
    gray land, 662:4
    ironic scraping, 639:5
    other Kingdom, 669:9
    pale flag not advanced, 176:17
    sleep d. counterfeit, 214:14
    sleep D. twin brother, 52:*n*1
Deaths, after so many d., 243:23
    all d. could endure, 260:8
    brutal lives ugly d., 690:22
    by feigned d. to die, 228:19
    die many times before d., 188:11
    glorious in thy Defense, 292:*n*2
    happen at ebb tide, 564:20
    million d. statistic, 638:13
    more d. than one, 567:20
    ye died watched beside, 590:17
Death-steps, dinosaur d., 743:7
Death-world claws at everything,
    82:20
Debases, virtue d. in justifying, 305:22
Debasing work to do well what not
    worth doing, 756:4
Debate, Congress not to d. Canal d.
    me, 576:9
    daughter of, 145:2
    of commonwealth affairs, 184:21
    on public issues uninhibited, 719:4
    profound thoughts arise in d.,
    749:10
    Roman senate long d., 292:9
Debated, greatest question ever d.,
    338:4
Debauch currency, 652:11
    friend's wife genteelly, 316:23
Debauchee of Dew, 511:17
Debonair, buxom blithe and d., 251:7
Deborah arose, 11:1
    awake D. and utter a song, 11:2
Deboshed, thou d. fish thou, 224:14
Debt, by no means run in d., 243:1
    comfortably in d., 463:8
    death's a d., 352:20
    discharged through eternity, 349:24
    double d. to pay, 329:19
    how well live in d., 463:8
    life that depends on d., 507:18

Debt *(continued)*
   millions of d., 331:26
   national d. blessing, 354:17, 394:12
   pay every d., 430:5
   public d. public blessing, 354:*n*10
   put future in d. to ourselves, 628:2
   remember to pay the d., 70:25
   run in d. by disputation, 262:20
   to die a d. we must discharge, 242:*n*3
   to imagination, 628:7
   to Nature's quickly paid, 242:10
   which cancels all others, 393:6
Debtors, as we forgive our d., 33:12
   we are d. or creditors, 349:28
Debts, forgive us our d., 33:12
   he that dies pays all d., 224:17
   new way to pay old d., 238:10
   words pay no d., 200:18
Decade, before d. out landing man on moon, 741:9
   me d., 764:4
Decades, town that d. cannot improve, 772:6
Decay, court in beauty and d., 408:16
   degeneracy and d., 425:17
   feeling's dull d., 401:17
   fondest hope d., 392:13
   fretted the pygmy-body to d., 274:3
   human things subject to d., 274:25
   in House on Hill, 608:2
   inherent in all component things, 64:25
   love sicken and d., 189:12
   man dupe deceiver d., 407:5
   muddy vesture of d., 182:8
   no flood, 595:4
   of that colossal wreck, 406:13
   on D. greenest mosses cling, 443:2
   our love hath no d., 229:5
   riches hasten to d., 133:19
   state falls into d., 395:13
   thoughts of men d., 154:4
   Time makes these d., 246:9
   wealth accumulates and men d., 329:3
   woods d. and fall, 459:1
Decayed, cottage battered and d., 250:6
   think sufficiently d., 531:10
Decays, common cause d., 72:1
   mere glimmering and d., 270:10
   unconscious of d., 273:*n*5
Deceased, Ghost of d. Roman Empire, 239:23
   he first d., 227:10
   name of late d., 591:12
Deceit, bread of d. is sweet, 22:5
   hug the dear d., 309:3
   look of soft d., 357:23
   men favor d., 273:16
   noble and incapable of d., 379:24
   picture requires knavery trickery d., 522:7
   rumor of oppression and d., 334:26
   smile of d., 359:3
   threshold high to turn d., 563:14
Deceitful, damnable d. woman, 284:15
   favor is d., 23:21
   heart is d., 28:30

Deceitful *(continued)*
   kisses of enemy d., 23:1
Deceitfully, who hath not sworn d., 16:18
Deceitfulness of riches, 35:8
Deceits, from all d. of the world, 49:9
Deceive, dreams at length d. 'em, 288:2
   falsehood no longer d., 346:1
   not thy physician, 244:7
   pleasure to d. deceiver, 267:27
   practice to d., 378:13
   we d. ourselves, 46:32, 319:15
Deceived, be not d., 44:21
   good sense in country not d., 345:14
   more ignominious to mistrust than be d., 265:12
   the mother of mankind, 255:21
   true way to be d., 265:18
   world wants to be d., 135:16
Deceiver, gay d., 366:19
   man dupe d. decay, 407:5
   man's d. never mine, 580:4
   pleasure to deceive d., 267:27
Deceivers, men were d. ever, 186:28
Deceives, everything that d. enchants, 75:10
   nature never d. us, 319:15
   with whispering ambitions, 668:7
Deceiveth, serpent d. whole world, 47:28
Deceiving, appearances often are d., 58:15
December, brief D. day, 443:13
   from May to D., 666:4
   in heart cold D., 776:19
   in the bleak D., 452:14
   July's day short as D., 222:20
   love you in D., 547:4
   1910 human character changed, 650:15
   seek roses in D., 399:5
   wallow naked in D. snow, 171:3
   when they wed, 192:4
   yesterday D. 7, 1941, 649:19
Decembers, fifteen wild D., 480:1
Decency, no sense of d. sir, 680:14
   placed d. above courage, 586:22
   want of d. want of sense, 278:23
Decent and manly examination, 385:13
   docent doesn't doze, 697:8
   doing the d. thing, 769:16
   easy men, 340:10
   fall cloths over high income, 735:7
   provision for poor, 316:9
   respect to opinions, 343:2
Decently and in order, 43:18
Deception, lying is d. not words, 487:14
   military operation involves d., 80:18
Deceptive, masterpieces less d. than life, 612:16
Decide, comes moment to d., 485:1
   laws conflict courts d., 355:9
   wise men speak fools d., 56:3
Decided, matter d. considered true, 119:27
   on what they will not do, 79:21

Decided *(continued)*
   only to be undecided, 619:20
   to live forever, 752:11
Decides, doctors differ who d., 300:*n*1
Deciding not to be bitch, 701:12
Deciphered, stones that cannot be d., 671:10
Decision by majorities expedient, 446:12
   heroic d. not from cowards, 676:4
   once a d. made, 655:11
   valley of d., 29:33
   woman's d. to terminate pregnancy, 722:13
Decisions, careful resolutions unerring d., 108:8
   great d. of life, 628:10
   more of instincts than will, 628:10
   political d. under pressure, 590:9
Decisive, performed rites simple and d., 756:12
   struggle goes on, 700:5
   the d. moment, 722:17
Deck, boy stood on burning d., 410:13
   of cards hierarchies, 680:17
   walk d. my Captain lies, 491:1
Decked, bride-bed to have d., 199:14
   crown not d. with diamonds, 164:19
Decks, holystone d., 474:19
   turtle 'twixt plated d., 709:7
Declamation, New World favorable to d., 573:10
   roared Passion slept, 313:12
Declaration, for support of this d., 343:4
   make real D. of Independence, 627:21
   Revolution produced D. of Independence, 665:13
Declare, day shall d. it, 42:33
   fishes shall d. unto thee, 14:16
   heavens d. glory of God, 16:9
   if thou hast understanding, 15:7
   older men d. war, 626:1
Decline and fall of Rome, 340:16
   of belief, 540:2
   to accept end of man, 696:21
   to buy repentance, 79:5
Declined election some years ago, 658:7
   into vale of years, 207:3
   star of fate d., 401:26
Declines, glow of early thought d., 401:17
Declineth, shadow when it d., 19:12
Declining, without d. West, 228:4
Déclose, la rose qui avoit d., 144:*n*4
Decompose, not yet been able to d., 345:10
Decomposing in eternity of print, 650:18
Decorum, dulce et d. est, 96:*n*12
Découvrir saint Pierre pour couvrir saint Paul, 141:*n*12
Decoy, fashion's brightest arts d., 329:21
Decoyed into our condition, 279:13
Decreasing leg increasing belly, 183:19
Decree, God and man d., 579:19

Defeated, destroyed but not d., 702:10
  History to the d., 720:6
  warriors go to war first, 80:19
Defeats, terrible incantations of d.,
  639:19
Defect, cause of this d., 195:13
  chief d. of Henry King, 609:2
  of modern literature, 498:18
  pay in affliction or d., 614:11
  satire points at no d., 289:18
Defective, effect d. comes by cause,
  195:13
Defects as nation tendency to use weasel words, 576:13
  faith for all d. supplying, 124:6
Defend, book of Moons d. ye, 777:2
  dog foremost to d., 398:17
  every village town city, 620:9
  from all perils, 49:7
  God d. the right, 163:22
  me from my friends, 372:n1
  ministers of grace d. us, 194:9
  neighbor he promised to d., 425:11
  newspapers not d. if can help it,
    642:12
  not ashamed to d. a friend, 31:41
  our island whatever cost, 620:7
  ourselves and henroosts, 479:3
  ready to d. liberty, 395:1
  refuses to d. rights, 369:8
  to death your right to say it, 307:4
  us thy humble servants, 49:2
  will d. what's mine, 152:n2
  you from seasons, 210:3
  your departed friend, 276:3
Defended, Country d. by hands,
  460:14
  God abandoned these d., 580:2
Defender, Faith's D., 304:14
Defenders, no error fails to find d.,
  521:4
  truth suffers by heat of d., 282:19
Defending not field but cause, 341:2
Defense, as well for d. as repose,
  152:4
  at one gate to make d., 261:14
  cheap d. of nations, 332:13
  Deaths glorious in thy D., 292:n2
  die in d. of his country, 52:7
  friend is strong d., 31:15
  guilty of corruption and renounce
    d., 158:16
  he is my d., 17:33
  immodest words admit no d.,
    278:23
  millions for d., 367:13
  navy its greatest d., 325:20
  no adequate military d., 655:8
  no d. against reproach, 292:24
  of our Liberty Tree, 340:17
  provide for common d., 346:7
  ready in d., 331:15
  strength not in d. but attack, 676:5
  think about d. of England, 601:18
  vain to look for d. against lightning,
    100:15
Defensive, moat d. to a house, 171:9
Defer, not d. kindness, 780:5
  not to be wise, 291:17
  'tis madness to d., 296:10

Deference, out of d. cheat others,
  613:1
Deferential glad to be of use, 667:17
Deferred, dream d., 708:18
  hope d. maketh the heart sick,
    21:14
Defiance, fear hate surrender d.,
  767:21
  in defeat d., 622:4
  in their eye, 328:13
  to all forces of the Crown, 312:19
Deficiency, easier discover d. than see
  value, 372:11
Defile, vengeance presume to d., 354:1
Defiled, he that toucheth pitch d.,
  31:30
  his father's grave, 98:19
  they that touch pitch d., 186:38
Defilement, purity ability to contemplate d., 727:13
Defileth, not that which goeth into
  mouth d., 35:22
  that which cometh out of mouth d.,
    35:22
Define, hold good d. it well, 457:16
  how difficult to d., 762:15
  to d. is to exclude, 653:9
Defined, pick out what culture has d.,
  676:20
Definite, change not sudden d., 650:15
  evolution from vague to d., 538:17
Definition of criticism, 499:9
  of gentleman, 427:1
  of individual, 716:13
  of oats meant to vex, 314:n1
  of style, 289:6
  self-fulfilling prophecy false d.,
    728:13
Definitions, I hate d., 434:15
Deflower, age that will pride d.,
  153:11
Deflowered and now to Death devote,
  260:10
Defoe, sedulous ape to D., 561:19
Defraud not the poor, 31:6
Defunct, Buffalo Bill's d., 688:10
  ghosts of d. bodies fly, 263:4
Defy augury, 199:22
  man know how to d. opinion,
    368:11
  Power which seems omnipotent,
    407:6
  the Omnipotent to arms, 255:22
  tooth of time, 296:5
Degeneracy and decay, 425:17
Degenerate, poor d. from ape, 689:18
  power to d. into lower forms, 136:1
  sons and daughters, 607:12
Degenerates, extensive state d., 395:13
  in hands of man, 319:11
Degeneration, from barbarism to d.,
  542:2
Degradation not to overcome poverty,
  72:3
  of idea of liberty, 733:1
Degrade first the arts, 358:14
Degraded, women d. by trivial attentions, 365:30
Degrades, charity d., 436:20

Degrading anxiety about livelihood,
  626:14
Degree, beauty and high d., 674:12
  curs of low d., 328:26
  exalted them of low d., 37:42
  no best in kind but d., 441:22
  only difference lies in d., 280:11
  priority and place, 200:7
  take but d. away, 200:9
  unless d. preserved place not safe,
    100:22
  when d. is shaked, 200:8
Degrees, boil at different d., 433:9
  by d. dwindle into a wife, 291:13
  crime like virtue has d., 281:12
  estates d. and offices, 180:27
  grows up by d., 238:15
  ill habits gather by unseen d.,
    276:23
  one battle or by d., 341:2
  scorning the base d., 187:32
  what wound heal but by d., 206:26
Dehumanizing the Negro, 448:10
Dei, Agnus D., 48:9
Deified, by our own spirits d., 374:9
Deify me as if blithe wine I had
  drunk, 417:1
Deign on passing world, 313:17
Deity, design of D. preservation of
  species, 366:6
  everlastingly appointed by D.,
    487:17
  offended, 361:23
Déjà vu, it was d. all over again,
  754:14
Dejected Mariana, 204:18
  most d. thing of fortune, 210:18
Dejectedly, takes d. his seat, 498:11
Delacroix, recipe for making D., 544:1
Delay, in d. no plenty, 202:2
  infamous d., 296:12
  law's d., 196:10
  preferable to error, 343:19
  reproved each dull d., 329:14
  sweet reluctant amorous d., 258:13
Delayed, justice d. justice denied,
  446:18
  till I am indifferent, 315:17
Delaying, by d. preserved state, 84:16
  make gift rich by d., 476:2
Delays breed dangers, 155:7
  dangerous in war, 155:n1
  disease gained strength by d.,
    101:29
  have dangerous ends, 163:14
  life admits not of d., 316:33
Delectable Mountains, 272:24
  not because troubles are d. joy,
    89:13
Delegated, scholar is d. intellect, 431:5
Delenda est Carthago, 85:n4
Deleted, expletive d., 784:12
Deliberate, accustomed to d. when
  drunk, 69:23
  derangement of senses, 566:3
  shaping of things, 600:7
  speed, 581:5, 682:n4
Deliberately, live d., 478:17
  read as d. as written, 478:22
  shield d. planned, 661:5

Deliberates, woman that d. is lost, 292:10

Deliberation fortitude perseverance, 325:4

sat and public care, 257:7

Deliberations, chose after endless d., 612:19

Deliberative forces over arbitrary, 568:14

Delicate, air is d., 213:4

algae and sea anemone, 671:13

and rare, 567:18

creatures ours, 207:4

fare in another's house, 32:1

relationship of author to works, 572:22

sooner or later d. death, 490:17

Delicately gelded, 688:13

Delicious moan, 416:8

torment, 431:34

Delight, aim of oratory to d., 87:21

all love all liking all d., 241:19

and wonder of our stage, 232:18

appetite makes eating d., 262:8

bind another to its d., 358:3

blue color d., 487:17

brief dreamy d., 595:12

capacity for d. and wonder, 572:19

clothing of d., 356:6

commonest d. of race, 511:2

desire that outruns d., 533:14

dogs d. to bark and bite, 294:6

enjoy d. with liberty, 154:7

followed d. with heart unsatisfied, 120:9

from the whole, 384:11

give d. and hurt not, 224:18

go to it with d., 217:30

Greensleeves my d., 776:11

hear thy shrill d., 408:6

impulse of d., 596:11

in conceiving Iago, 418:9

in singing, 388:20

is in law of the Lord, 15:29

labor we d. in physics pain, 214:12

lady of my d., 555:17

land of pure d., 294:19

lo she that was world's d., 533:17

love with d. discourses, 125:2

lulled with dances and d., 173:9

Moon of my D., 446:2

my ever new d., 259:6

never d. in another's misfortune, 99:25

no season such d. can bring, 240:15

of battle, 455:1

of husband aunts infant, 674:12

paint the meadows with d., 169:12

phantom of d., 375:16

playing Idiot's D., 695:20

plaything gives youth d., 301:15

poem begins in d., 625:8

rebirth brings d., 64:26

spirit of D., 409:15

stars gave the first d., 249:28

stretches of pure d., 665:10

strongest tower of d., 487:2

studies a d. to the old, 87:12

such deep d. 'twould win me, 382:25

Delight *(continued)*

sweets grown common lose d., 221:20

temple of D., 416:18

that consumes desire, 533:14

these virtues of d., 356:12

to d. paid blessing, 617:1

to do things I ought, 394:4

toys for your d., 561:23

unrest men miscall d., 409:4

weighing d. and dole, 192:32

what d. without Aphrodite, 55:6

with silent d., 356:15

Zeus grant sweet d., 64:2

Delighted spirit, 204:14

us long enough, 387:1

Delighteth, speech finely framed d., 32:21

whom the king d. to honor, 13:25

Delightful, both wise both d., 266:17

delicious de-lovely, 682:5

in this d. garden grows, 153:14

still air of d. studies, 254:14

task rear tender thought, 308:4

Delighting and instructing at the same time, 98:16

best poetry d. us, 501:5

in your company, 776:10

Delights, all d. are vain, 168:13

all thoughts passions d., 383:3

anarchy of poverty d. me, 654:3

fleeting d. of days, 405:7

from heart of fountain of d., 90:8

hence all you vain d., 236:13

joy d. in joy, 220:10

man d. not me, 195:29

misery still d. to trace, 335:22

reader and instructs too, 280:15

scorn d., 253:20

speak of banqueting d., 226:14

supremest of d. sexual intercourse, 528:11

these d. if thou canst give, 251:20

violent d. have violent ends, 175:23

were dolphin-like, 218:11

winter his d., 226:16

Delineation, happiest d., 387:10

Delinquency, trying to control feline d., 706:9

Delinquents, beg d. for life, 743:14

Delirium, all that d. of brave, 596:1

Deliver, from winter plague Lord d. us, 227:1

good Lord d. us, 49:8, 779:15

I will d. him to you, 36:23

me from body of death, 42:1

me from phlegmatic preachers, 347:3

no human efforts d. them, 336:14

round unvarnished tale d., 205:22

thee from the snare, 18:15

us from evil, 33:12

Deliverance, day of d., 338:5

little hope of d., 768:12

Delivered from perils and miseries, 240:8

upon mellowing of occasion, 168:32

Deliverer, Lord is my d., 12:15

Delivering improvements by generation, 335:24

Dell, farmer in the d., 792:13

De-lovely, delightful delicious d., 682:5

Delude, television used to distract d., 724:8

Deluding, vain d. Joys, 251:21

Deluge, after us the d., 324:19

pedigree far back as D., 463:22

Déluge, après nous le d., 324:19

Delusion, give up liberties under d., 332:3

Solon was under a d., 75:20

to the philanthropist, 523:21

trial by jury a d., 391:1

Delusive, most d. of passions, 571:15

Delved, Adam d., 775:13

Delves parallels in beauty's brow, 221:1

Delving in patient industry, 541:5

Demand, heroes created by popular d., 679:2

superflous to d. time of day, 176:24

supply of truth in excess of d., 479:24

Demanded an image, 659:6

Demands, heavenly race d. zeal, 308:16

rebellion makes upon us, 732:16

Demd damp moist unpleasant body, 469:21

dowager's a d. outline, 469:20

horrid grind, 469:24

Demean themselves as good citizens, 337:2

Demented, not one is d., 489:16

Demesne, deep-browed Homer ruled as d., 413:24

Demeter, goddess D. or Earth, 68:26

Demi-Atlas of this earth, 217:6

Demi-paradise, this other Eden d., 171:9

Demirep that loves, 466:10

Demitasses, villainous d., 574:1

Demmed elusive Pimpernel, 594:1

Demnition bowwows, 469:25

Democracies cannot dispense with hypocrisy, 666:18

security to d. against despots, 351:n7

Democracy, American d. discover middle ground, 744:10

appropriate for economic surplus, 728:16

arises out of notion, 78:23

arsenal of d., 649:16

associate d. with freedom of action, 577:9

charming form of government, 75:24

constitution named a d., 72:2

cycle d. built on, 730:18

death of d., 702:14

direct self-government, 461:n5

egg of d., 486:8

government of people, 461:18

if liberty and equality found in d., 78:21

is a great word, 491:13

ism change American d., 649:5

Democracy (*continued*)
more unsafe than ever, 587:16
my idea of d., 448:9
neither despotism nor d., 355:2
passes into despotism, 75:25
recurrent suspicion, 703:14
self-canceling business, 412:22
shuts past opens future, 438:8
socialist d. may be sham, 653:26
Switzerland years of d. and peace,
739:5
true d. never existed, 319:8
two cheers for D., 636:13
United States not proclaimed d.,
618:13
whatever differs from this no d.,
448:9
world safe for d., 572:11, 587:16
Democrat, no person called self d.,
618:13
Democratic, basis of d. state, 78:27
cherished ideal of d. society, 745:15
created new d. world, 411:22
establishes d. regime kill sons of
Brutus, 137:4
nations not care for past, 438:8
party ain't on speakin' terms,
602:16
Party like mule, 516:1
Party's candidate for President,
741:1
public men, 571:25
secrecy and d. government, 655:22
society like ours, 646:13
thou great d. God, 486:22
utter word D., 488:13
Democrats, afford a few D., 704:1
all saloon keepers D., 462:14
raises corn and D., 566:4
Demon, when your D. in charge,
593:27
you have roused, 448:10
Demoniac frenzy, 260:17
Demonic, semihuman and d., 628:15
Demonisms, subtle d. of life, 486:25
Demon-lover, wailing for her d.,
382:20
Demons down under sea, 453:9
Demonstrandum, quod erat d., 82:4
Demonstrating careless desolation,
191:20
Demonstration, full monstrous d.,
549:16
Demonstrative or persuasive type,
609:11
Demoralizing, human slavery d.,
567:12
nothing so d. as money, 66:7
Demur you're dangerous, 512:11
Demure, sober steadfast and d.,
251:23
Demurrer, no bail no d., 352:20
Den, beard lion in his d., 378:12
cast Daniel into the d. of lions,
29:18
cockatrice' d., 26:11
living in underground d., 75:17
made it a d. of thieves, 35:42
seven sleepers' d., 228:2

Dendid, when D. created all things,
784:16
Denial vain and coy excuse, 253:16
Denied, call may not be d., 633:15
exact day-labor light d., 255:12
justice delayed justice d., 446:18
no other was d., 512:19
Peter d. Lord, 287:9
the faith, 45:18
this only d. to God, 74:2
Denies, court a mistress she d. you,
232:13
heaven to gaudy day d., 401:14
Spirit that always d., 350:14
voyager further sailing, 68:20
Denieth, antichrist d. the Father,
46:34
Denmark, ne'er villain in D., 195:2
something rotten in D., 194:16
sure it may be so in D., 195:1
Denoted foregone conclusion, 207:13
Denouncing someone or something
else, 642:12
Dens and fastnesses of barbarism,
503:4
lay them down in their d., 19:6
Denunciation in place of evidence,
615:6
Deny, easier to believe than d., 532:9
me thrice, 37:3
oh was no d., 357:17
participation of freedom, 331:22
poor heart would fain d., 216:9
themselves nothing, 463:8
thy father, 175:1
us for our good, 217:11
Denying, to allure by d., 476:2
Deo erexit Voltaire, 334:*n*2
gloria in excelsis D., 48:8
Deos fortoribus adesse, 109:*n*12
Depart, ah she doth d., 357:17
be off, 87:*n*4
captains and kings d., 593:1
come like shadows so d., 215:22
from evil, 16:31
I d. from materials, 491:10
I say let us have done, 247:2
loth to d., 287:23
ready to d., 388:21
servant d. in peace, 38:5
this vale, 642:15
to be to do to d., 537:8
to d. from evil is understanding,
14:41
to serve better, 522:12
when old he will not d. from it,
22:9
when ye d. shake off dust, 34:29
Departed, all but he d., 392:8
defend your d. friend, 276:3
ghosts of d. quantities, 296:23
glory is d. from Israel, 11:30
he has d. withdrawn gone away,
87:8
his spirit is d., 32:11
into their own country, 32:24
minds me o' d. joys, 362:8
never to return, 362:8
rule over the d. dead, 53:25
sacred to d. spirit, 118:28

Departed (*continued*)
souls d. shadows of living, 249:6
Departeth, heart d. from the Lord,
28:29
Departing, knolling d. friend, 183:11
leave behind us, 440:17
Department, duty of judicial d., 355:9
fair sex your d., 578:1
that's not my d., 759:6
Departure beyond borders death,
680:6
hour of d. has arrived, 74:18
is taken for misery, 30:23
Depend, all rest on us d., 490:7
Depended, always d. on kindness of
strangers, 730:19
Dependence, in marriage d. mutual,
410:18
of art on felt life, 549:2
upon militia, 336:16
women educated for d., 365:28
Dependency, old d. of day and night,
638:26
Dependent, mortals live d. upon another, 89:16
Depends, happiness d. as Nature
shows, 334:2
so much d. upon, 654:1
Deplore, though still I do d., 231:4
Deploring, damsel lay d., 297:1
Deportment, model of D., 471:4
Depose my state but not my griefs,
172:10
Deposed, ghosts they have d., 171:25
some have been d., 171:25
Deposit for substantial virtue, 343:10
little cell by cell, 538:5
Deposited, near this spot d., 398:16
Depository of public interests, 345:4
of truth, 271:7
safe d. of ultimate powers, 344:22
Deposits of accumulated experience,
628:8
Depot eleven miles away, 606:3
Depravations of Europe, 287:3
Depraved, no one becomes d. in mo-
ment, 108:20
Depraves all good dispositions, 343:11
Depravity, perverse d. of nature,
284:14
within classes, 661:2
Depressed, fine weather heavier on d.,
746:13
heart d. with cares, 297:17
Deprivation for me what daffodils for
Wordsworth, 751:2
Deprive or divest posterity, 327:1
Deprived, female d. of voice in legislation, 347:11
of everlasting bliss, 162:15
poor man d. of power, 75:23
without due process of law, 346:14
Depth, far beyond my d., 225:16
gods approve d. not tumult, 377:4
height nor d., 42:9
in philosophy bringeth to religion,
159:19
of all being God, 662:9
of divine despair, 456:13

Depth (*continued*)
  to weep make less d. of grief, 164:14
  truth lies in the d., 70:27
  walked in the search of the d., 15:10
Depths congealed in heart of sea, 9:5
  Germans like women haven't d., 553:14
  go down again to the d., 19:10
  of height, 689:1
  out of the d. have I cried, 20:2
Deputed sword, 204:1
Derangement, nice d. of epitaphs, 352:9
  of all senses, 566:3
Derby, Justice Bennet of D., 271:14
Dérèglement de tous les sens, 566:n2
Derides, shame them d., 208:27
  wrinkled Care d., 251:9
Derision, Uglification and D., 518:3
Derive from women's eyes this doctrine, 169:4
Derives axioms from particulars, 158:12
Deriving just powers from consent, 343:2
Derned sight better business, 536:13
Dervishes, barefoot d., 430:6
Descant, amorous d. sung, 258:19
Descartes, seen further than D., 281:25
Descend, ready to d. throne, 370:14
  terrible simplifiers going to d., 480:8
  to meet, 431:35
  we d. from Jove, 94:19
  we too into Dust d., 445:16
Descendants, democracy hides d., 438:9
  shall gather your fruits, 92:15
Descended, Curtius Rufus d. from himself, 76:n1
  desirable to be well d., 107:7
  from a god, 395:22
  from heroic monkey, 444:14
  into hell, 48:25
  of so many kings, 218:21
Descending, angels ascending and d., 7:40, 39:37
  black and white, 742:14
  like a dove, 32:33
  low d. sun, 779:1
Descends, new generation d. from on high, 92:10
Descent, Americans of African d., 522:13
  claims of long d., 454:2
  from certain group of people, 574:12
  if d. from heroic sires, 280:13
  of last end on living, 647:8
  to Hades is same, 64:17
  trace d. through ape, 505:n1
  wears d. like long cape, 760:14
Describe undescribable, 400:16
  world of today, 698:19
Description, beggared all d., 217:14
  of nature, 656:3
  short d. of happy state, 277:10

Description (*continued*)
  theory of d. matters most, 639:18
Descriptions of the fairest wights, 221:22
Dese are conditions dat prevail, 686:2
Desegregation with all deliberate speed, 682:n4
Desert, Arab in d., 315:n7
  from d. I come to thee, 506:2
  heath in the d., 28:29
  in d. saw creature naked bestial, 611:7
  in service, 201:3
  inaccessible, 190:29
  legs of stone in d., 406:13
  make a d. call it peace, 109:21
  make straight in the d. a highway, 27:15
  mice d. building about to fall, 104:10
  my dwelling place, 400:28
  never d. Mr. Micawber, 470:24
  of a thousand lines, 303:8
  of the sea, 26:18
  rats d. sinking ship, 104:n9
  shall rejoice, 27:8
  sighs in bed, 720:8
  these gardens of d., 411:9
  until D. knows Water grows, 514:4
  use every man after d., 196:3
  waste sweetness on d. air, 322:13
  water but the d., 400:23
  wildernesses, 252:24
  you for creeds that refuse, 533:16
Deserted at his utmost need, 276:12
  banquet hall d., 392:8
  old people not to be d., 682:14
Desertion, storm d. death, 419:8
Deserts, beyond this nothing but sandy d., 107:1
  civilization results in d., 633:12
  man making d., 633:11
  of vast eternity, 268:15
  or his d. are small, 264:4
  when she d. the night, 261:8
Deserve all these kittens, 633:6
  better of mankind, 289:11
  neither liberty nor safety, 310:13
  Sempronius we'll d. it, 292:4
  success in war, 622:5
Deserved, least d. such a fate, 72:11
  less at country's hands, 501:18
  so mighty a Redeemer, 48:12
Deserves, government it d., 353:12
  love and thanks, 340:22
  none but brave d. fair, 276:6
  one good turn d. another, 105:3
  to be a slave, 369:8
Deserving, lost without d., 206:21
  of freedom he only is d., 350:26
Design, grand d. in providence, 337:12
  of all his words, 640:7
  of all parts helpful to motive, 502:1
  to make haste to be gone, 247:6
Designed, great masterpiece d., 363:1
  to make people stumble, 651:21
Designing St. Paul's, 627:18
Designs, close d. crooked counsels, 274:3
  ladder to all high d., 200:8

Designs (*continued*)
  Nature full of d., 546:15
  were strictly honorable, 311:28
Desirable, more d. than fortunate hour, 91:8
Desire, a' the learning I d., 361:11
  accomplished is sweet, 21:16
  antidote to d., 291:15
  arrows of d., 359:17
  as you d. me, 604:6
  beholding face of d., 572:24
  bloom of young D., 323:1
  dead be near us, 457:15
  death end of man's d., 534:11
  delight that consumes d., 533:14
  difficult to tell from despair, 639:17
  dispraise thing you d., 201:6
  drink provokes d., 214:11
  father's death, 495:14
  follow your d., 3:6
  from fairest creatures d. increase, 220:7
  gratified plants fruits, 357:20
  hast given him his heart's d., 16:14
  Heart's D., 446:8, 595:4
  his d. is toward me, 25:21
  in it was love and d., 52:3
  kindle soft d., 276:15
  know what he ought to d., 124:10
  lineaments of Gratified D., 357:24
  lose your heart's d., 571:6
  love and d. and hate, 602:10
  love distills d., 68:17
  men by nature d. knowledge, 77:21
  men d. the good, 78:18
  mixing memory and d., 668:17
  more love and knowledge, 190:1
  my d. is that the Almighty answer me, 14:46
  nature of d. not to be satisfied, 78:16
  no more d. rose, 168:16
  not mortal what you d., 101:20
  of discipline, 30:27
  of fame, 459:20
  of knowledge increases, 320:16
  of moth for star, 409:12
  of power in excess, 159:16
  one shore beyond d., 701:4
  outlive performance, 183:35
  perpetual rack, 234:21
  prayer soul's sincere d., 377:18
  pure and just d. of man, 137:9
  remold it nearer to D., 446:8
  satisfiest the d. of every living thing, 20:12
  second silence of d., 442:22
  shall fail, 24:28
  sick with d., 597:9
  speed of my d., 506:2
  that outruns delight, 533:14
  those who d. slavery, 451:1
  to a bottle of hay, 173:22
  to appear natural, 265:43
  to get on in world, 665:9
  to live again, 553:5
  to live beyond income, 525:2
  train noble natures not to d. more, 78:16
  under the elms, 674:1

Desire *(continued)*
    unspeakable d., 498:4
    vain d. vain regret, 509:27
    vanquished by d., 56:9
    we may be better strangers, 191:16
    what I've tasted of d., 623:14
    what we ought not to have, 99:34
    which of us has his d., 463:11
    without hope we live in d., 125:13
    without knowledge or d., 56:14
    wonder and wild d., 467:24
    yearning in d., 455:3
Desired and timely things, 579:22
    more to be d. than gold, 16:11
    not one to be d., 453:25
    pinch which hurts and is d., 218:18
    that which most d., 284:14
    who hath d. sea, 593:13
Desires and dreams and powers,
        534:13
    and petitions of thy servants, 49:6
    be for what is good, 61:18
    covetous d. of the world, 49:21
    from Death fulfillment to d., 638:25
    grant all things your heart d., 53:10
    have few d., 57:6
    heart's d. be with you, 189:34
    liberty doing what one d., 439:23
    limited nature infinite d., 405:9
    mastery of d., 552:25
    no calamity greater than lavish d.,
        57:14
    nurse unacted d., 357:12
    painting gives form to d., 645:4
    reviving old D., 445:5
    sinful d. of the flesh, 49:21
    submitting things to d. of mind,
        158:7
    those d. glowing openly, 587:12
    two d. toss about, 498:7
    undaunted daughter of d., 264:16
    unto whom all d. known, 49:13
    weaned heart from low d., 137:10
    weight of chance d., 376:4
Desireth not death of sinner, 48:19
Desiring this man's art, 220:16
Desirous, aught else on earth d.,
        297:16
Desist, I shall ask leave to d., 249:24
Desk, but a d. to write upon, 263:20
    turn upward from d., 669:1
Desolate and sick of old passion,
        602:7
    dark weeks, 654:4
    home of mirth made d., 435:23
    shores, 417:8
    which built d. places, 13:35
    Winter's dregs made d., 540:9
    without you all is d., 675:1
Desolation, abomination of d., 36:8
    blood vengeance d., 492:12
    butchery and d., 621:1
    careless d., 191:20
    dark cold and empty d., 671:11
    intellectual d., 481:9
    seat of d. void of light, 256:4
    Sudden Death General D., 526:7
Despair at not having found joy,
        631:3
    beauty born of own d., 598:2

Despair *(continued)*
    begotten by d., 268:21
    beyond hope and d., 669:16
    carrion comfort D., 551:11
    comfort and d., 222:10
    comfortless D., 321:16
    death of hope and d., 671:21
    desire difficult to tell from d.,
        639:17
    divine d., 456:13
    dying and in d., 510:13
    ending is d., 224:29
    endure my own d., 287:5
    fiercer by d., 256:24
    from d. high uplifted, 256:23
    Giant D., 272:23
    gives comfort in d., 163:21
    Hell's d., 358:7
    humor based on destruction d.,
        754:16
    imagined d. fallen upon me, 419:14
    in d. comes wisdom, 63:11
    infinite wrath and d., 258:5
    law chance hath slain, 230:20
    melancholy and d., 235:20
    my only hope lies in d., 281:8
    never d., 95:21
    no more d. or loss of faith, 745:22
    path leads to d. utter hopelessness,
        767:16
    procures extremity of bitterness,
        235:20
    rash-embraced d., 181:7
    result of fatal situations, 443:21
    reveals own folly and d., 696:13
    seraphs might d., 399:10
    shall I wasting in d., 240:1
    Shame D. her teachers, 436:2
    toils d. to reach, 288:1
    Warder is D., 567:22
    where d. let me sow hope, 123:10
    White Sustenance d., 513:1
    ye Mighty and d., 406:13
    you with unpaid bill D., 409:22
Despairful, dissolute damned d., 627:1
Despairing songs loveliest, 461:15
Despairs, leaden-eyed d., 415:12
    through comfortless d., 154:6
Desperandum, nil d., 95:*n*17
Desperate, beware of d. steps, 335:19
    by d. appliance relieved, 198:9
    diseases d. grown, 198:9
    marriage a d. thing, 239:4
    seas long wont to roam, 451:12
    slave to d. men, 230:23
    tempt not d. man, 176:14
    wisdom not to do d. things, 478:1
Desperately, deceitful and d. wicked,
        28:30
Desperation, our policy against d.,
        642:7
    quiet d. confirmed d., 477:32
Despicable, wretched d. creature,
        308:19
Despise, a contrite heart thou wilt not
        d., 17:25
    capacity to d. himself, 588:9
    force human beings to d. them-
        selves, 707:15
    hold to one d. other, 33:17

Despise *(continued)*
    ignorant d. education, 99:35
    not thy mother, 22:21
    pity ignorance d. him, 469:17
    riches, 488:11
    Shakespeare when I measure my
        mind, 571:14
    what female heart gold d., 321:20
    with work you d., 605:6
Despised and dying king, 407:24
    and rejected of men, 27:35
    being unarmed be d., 136:13
    day of small things, 30:2
    poor infirm d. old man, 209:26
    race, 522:13
    straight, 222:7
    thus the poor agent d., 201:15
Despises, husband frae wife d., 363:3
Despising, myself almost d., 220:16
Despite, Heaven's d., 358:3
Despitefully, them which d. use you,
        33:8
Despond, slough was D., 272:13
Despondency and madness, 374:9,
        742:16
Despondently, sprouting d. at gates,
        667:22
Desponding view of present, 425:17
Despot, country governed by d., 317:6
    custom d. of mankind, 423:16
    man once d. and slave, 407:5
Despotism, cloud of barbarism and d.,
        345:3
    degenerates into d., 395:13
    democracy passes into d., 75:25
    feeble engines of d., 345:3
    France d. tempered by epigrams,
        412:12
    in majority of popular assembly,
        338:16
    neither d. nor democracy, 355:2
    Rome's decline lay in d., 656:13
    to liberty in featherbed, 343:17
    whatever crushes individuality is d.,
        439:19
    will destroy all good, 471:26
Despots, security against d., 351:*n*7
Destination, Heaven's my d., 697:12
Destined, his d. Hour, 445:11
Destinies, sway d. of half the globe,
        438:7
Destiny, chosen his d., 716:4
    exercises influence, 552:1
    expand the d. of mankind, 759:11
    hanging and wiving go by d.,
        141:*n*1
    man forges for himself, 717:15
    manifest d., 473:15
    not by material computation,
        620:19
    obscure, 322:7
    of colored American, 480:17
    one country one d., 395:2
    reap a d., 781:6
    rendezvous with d., 649:3
    repose not d. of man, 542:9
    shady leaves of d., 264:9
    waits alike, 63:21
    wedding is d., 141:1

Destiny (*continued*)
what seems accident springs from
d., 365:5
with Men for Pieces plays, 445:23
Destiny's, day of d. over, 401:26
Destitute of emotional warmth, 546:4
Destroy, beauty disdains to d. us,
630:6
does thy life d., 358:4
evil they set out to d., 676:1
farms grass will grow in streets,
582:3
for one grape vine d., 166:38
many monsters to d., 706:7
natural resources, 576:7
nor sword nor age d., 101:28
not come to d. law, 33:3
not to d. but fulfill, 33:3
one to d. is murder, 296:3
power of reasoning, 76:6
power to tax involves power to d.,
355:13
power to tax not power to d., 543:8
surely not in Wrath d., 446:3
they shall not hurt nor d., 26:11
those who hate and d., 564:11
thought would d. paradise, 321:17
town to save it, 784:6
whom God wishes to d., 69:18,
119:25
winged life d., 357:22
worms d. this body, 14:30
Destroyed but not defeated, 702:10
by each other, 284:11
by madness, 757:4
Carthage must be d., 85:6
flower of kings and knights d.,
133:16
great civilization d. within, 656:13
if men are d., 65:7
last enemy d. is death, 43:21
love without power d., 684:15
Medici created and d. me, 135:14
nations are d. or flourish, 359:22
poetry painting music d., 359:22
the very ruins d., 106:3
things violently d., 373:16
when once d., 329:8
Destroyer and preserver hear, 407:14
become Death d. of worlds, 714:12
force that blasts trees is my d.,
737:8
time d. time preserver, 671:16
Destroying, not by d. but promoting,
331:25
prison soul d., 712:2
Destroyings, creations and d., 417:1
Destroys good book kills reason,
254:23
habit d. first nature, 347:*n*5
nothing d. us but time, 117:14
outrage when man d. nature, 631:15
use d. beauty, 589:21
whoever d. single life is guilty,
115:17
Destruction, all other to d. draw,
229:5
brought her dowry d., 63:12
causes of d., 319:9
creation same as d., 80:8

Destruction (*continued*)
Famine Pestilence D. Death, 643:15
fool's mouth is his d., 21:38
for d. ice suffice, 623:14
forces of nuclear d., 742:5
genocide d. of nation ethnic group,
704:14
give enemies means of our d., 59:19
hell of nuclear d., 761:7
humor based on d. despair, 754:16
I will be thy d., 29:31
if d. be our lot, 448:1
means of d. hitherto unknown,
655:8
of life and happiness, 344:11
of Nazi tyranny, 650:8
of Tao and virtue, 80:13
of tea so bold, 337:17
pride goeth before d., 21:31
set him apart for d., 277:*n*8
shows activity of authorities, 446:21
that wasteth at noonday, 18:15
their going seemed utter d., 30:23
thou turnest man to d., 18:10
way that leadeth to d., 34:9
when you talk about d., 770:13
whose end is d., 44:33
word deals d., 572:23
world peace or world d., 608:14
Destructions, rescue my soul from
their d., 16:32
Destructive damnable woman, 284:15
not afraid of d. act, 587:8
smiling d. man, 285:9
Detached, reality attained only by d.,
727:12
Detail, frittered away by d., 478:18
merely corroborative d., 531:7
Details, God is in the d., 783:2
so many incidents so many d.,
587:13
Detection, traitors escape d., 615:5
Detective novel art-for-art's sake of
Philistinism, 705:7
Detectives, scientists d. and explorers,
738:14
Detector, built-in shock-proof shit d.,
702:11
Deteriorating, shabby equipment d.,
671:9
Determinate, every thing has d. idea,
76:6
Determination, charisma inner d.,
590:4
enough in mighty enterprises,
100:30
Determine, education will d. future
life, 75:13
men d. gods dispose, 235:*n*1
people seldom d. right, 355:1
Determined by what lies outside it,
483:29
dared and done, 325:13
so long d. not to do it, 278:7
to know beans, 478:28
Determines, way world imagined d.
what men do, 676:19
Detest, abhor d. Sabbath-Day, 527:1
begin to d. him, 346:4
I d. what you write, 307:*n*2

Detest (*continued*)
love offender d. offense, 276:*n*4
pageantry of king, 346:2
phrases I d., 580:18
Detesting, die d. superstition, 307:5
Detract, power to add or d., 450:2
Detraction will not suffer it, 178:33
Deus, Domine D. Agnus Dei, 48:9
ex machina, 81:10
homo proponet D. disponit, 132:*n*7
vult, 118:27
Deutschland is happy and gay, 756:20
über Alles, 421:14
Devastation, slaughter pillage d.,
621:1
Develop, men free to d. faculties,
568:14
Development, great unital continuous
d., 522:16
in language development of feeling,
672:13
psychic d. of individual, 569:6
Develops and enlarges organ, 347:13
Deviates, Shadwell never d. into sense,
274:26
Deviation from truth is multiplied,
77:19
Device, banner with strange d., 441:8
brain d. to keep ears from grating,
728:5
miracle of rare d., 382:23
no work nor d. nor knowledge,
24:19
Devil, abashed the D. stood, 259:1
an angel too, 589:17
apology for D., 525:6
a-walking the D. is gone, 386:21
became woman, 427:16
beggar will outride the D., 164:*n*4
bird or d., 452:19
black as the d., 354:3
builds a chapel there, 285:14
can cite Scripture, 180:6
cannot make Hawthorne say yes,
486:15
come and Faustus damned, 162:23
counteracts D. who is Death,
325:18
created in man's image, 495:7
damn thee black, 216:7
drink and d. had done, 561:1
eat with d. have long spoon, 131:*n*8
envy of the d., 30:22
every man God or D., 274:12
fears a painted d., 214:8
from deceits of the d., 49:9
from d. does proceed, 354:10
give d. his due, 149:15
go poor d., 320:18
God and d. fighting, 495:5
God sends meat D. sends cooks,
141:*n*3
hath not arrow, 403:21
having nothing else to do, 609:7
having trouble with wife, 570:6
heart place d. dwells in, 248:15
he's a very d., 203:1
if d. doesn't exist, 495:7
if the d. dress her not, 218:14
is a gentleman, 210:*n*2

Devil (*continued*)
  is asleep, 570:6
  is ever God's ape, 138:10
  knows how to row, 382:4
  let the d. wear black, 197:7
  let us call thee d., 206:22
  Love a mischievous d., 525:7
  man for himself D. for all, 142:*n*17
  match for d., 698:11
  Nazarite conjured the d., 180:2
  needs go whom d. drive, 142:20
  not serve God if d. bid, 205:16
  old serpent called the D., 47:28
  ole d. sea, 673:12
  puritan that he is, 202:6
  renounce the d., 49:21
  resist the d., 46:14
  sarcasm language of D., 412:2
  seem saint when most play d.,
    165:27
  showed him kingdoms, 38:9
  speak truth and shame D., 140:5
  sugar o'er d. himself, 196:9
  take her, 262:3
  take the hindmost, 238:17
  thou wast made d., 236:6
  to pay, 150:10
  walketh about as roaring lion,
    46:28
  what the d. was he doing in that
    galley, 269:28
  whispered behind leaves, 592:1
  why d. have all good tunes, 347:12
  wi' usquebae face the d., 363:7
  would build chapel, 138:10
  your father the d., 40:12
Devil-and-all to pay, 150:10
Devilish and damned tobacco, 235:10
  excused his d. deeds, 258:15
  sly, 470:15
  this wisdom is d., 46:13
Devil's, got over D. back, 236:16
  had final say, 734:7
  pundit d. advocate enthusiast,
    703:19
  true poet and of D. party, 357:2
  who cleft the D. foot, 228:5
Devils, as many d. in Worms as tiles,
    138:15
  being offended, 206:5
  fight like d., 185:13
  in twists of road, 613:9
  more d. than hell hold, 174:1
  not so black as painted, 156:21
  seven and seventy d., 613:9
  to ourselves, 201:8
  wrote at liberty when of D., 357:2
Devils', one more d.-triumph, 464:25
Devise, for thirty pence my death d.,
    243:6
  laws for blood, 179:28
  wit write pen, 168:21
Devised to keep strong in awe, 166:16
  who d. torment, 672:4
Deviseth, man's heart d. his way,
    21:30
Devoid of sense and motion, 257:2
Devote himself to life, 630:17
  now to Death d., 260:10

Devotion, affecting charity and d.,
    80:12
  farewel my bok and my d., 129:4
  ignorance mother of d., 235:17
  increased d. to cause, 450:2
  last full measure of d., 450:2
  no concern with art, 524:1
  of patriot soldier, 522:13
  to something afar, 409:12
Devotion's visage, 196:9
Devotions, I beheld your d., 41:15
Devour, crocodiles shed tears when
    would d., 159:26
  entire hostile army, 620:9
  jaws of darkness do d. it, 172:20
  seeking whom he may d., 46:28
  which d. widows' houses, 37:32
Devoured, great ones d. the small,
    219:*n*6
  when I was a worm I d., 725:9
Devourer, time d. of all things, 101:27
Devouring, cormorant d. Time, 168:11
  green azures, 565:13
  of weak by strong, 493:8
Devours, animal which d. own kind,
    343:13
  death d. lovely things, 684:6
Devoutly to be wished, 196:10
Dew, as sun the morning d., 277:1
  begotten drops of d., 15:11
  bespangling herb and tree, 241:17
  breeze dried the d., 624:11
  Daffodil doth of D., 513:4
  Debauchee of D., 511:17
  fearfully o'ertrip the d., 182:7
  foggy foggy d., 779:23
  ghastly d., 455:17
  gold and bramble d., 561:25
  honey-heavy d. of slumber, 188:6
  I D. not think we D., 544:6
  into a sea of d., 559:20
  like d. on mountain, 378:22
  liquid d. of youth, 193:26
  of thy birth, 153:*n*6
  of yon high eastern hill, 192:30
  of youth, 19:13, 193:26
  pour sweet d. on his tongue, 54:16
  smell d. and rain, 243:23
  thaw and resolve into a d., 193:5
  timely d. of sleep, 258:20
  which in sleep fallen on you, 408:2
  will rust them, 205:18
  womb of morning d., 153:12
Dewdrop, lingering d., 377:14
  starlight and d., 507:5
Dewdrops, seek some d. here, 173:1
  with showers and d. wet, 515:7
Dewey feel discouraged, 544:6
  was the morning, 544:6
Dew-pearled, hillside's d., 464:4
Dews, fresh d. of night, 253:17
  of evening shun, 305:18
  silence fall like d., 660:14
Dewy, from noon to d. eve, 256:22
  morn to dewy night, 523:5
  shakes his d. wings, 249:23
Dexterous, acute inquisitive d., 331:15
Dhamma, hold fast to d. as a lamp,
    64:23
Dhrink is nicissry evil, 603:16

Dhry, wet eye d. heart, 603:3
Diable, noir comme le d., 354:*n*2
  que d. allait-il faire dans cette
    galère, 269:*n*8
  s'est fait femme, 427:*n*4
Diadems and fagots, 430:6
Diagrams, charts d. to add divide
    measure, 490:9
  in midst of d. and equations, 635:13
Dial, drew d. from his poke, 190:22
  laugh an hour by his d., 190:24
  true as d. to sun, 263:31
Dialect, Babylonish d., 263:1
  purify d. of tribe, 672:3
Dialogue, wooden d. and sound,
    200:11
Dial's, many lines in d. center, 184:25
Dials signs of leaping houses, 176:24
Diamond cut diamond, 239:13
  done on a d., 747:16
  goodness what lovely d., 685:*n*1
  immortal d. is immortal d., 551:17
  in the sky, 394:2
  lacks glitter of d., 662:8
  lasts forever, 686:10
  O D. thou little knowest the mis-
    chief done, 282:6
  point of a d., 28:28
  rough d., 305:5
  sixty d. minutes, 419:4
  spots of d. form, 335:6
Diamonds, crown not decked with d.,
    164:19
  girl's best friend, 705:10
  graven with d. in letters plain,
    143:8
  Lucy in the sky with d., 770:11
  sky sparkling with d., 582:13
Dian, Temple of D., 782:7
Diana of the Ephesians, 41:22
Diana's foresters, 176:25
Dian's, hangs on D. temple, 219:12
Diapason closing full in Man, 275:7
Diary, never travel without d., 567:10
Diastole, great systole and d. of his-
    tory, 656:12
Dice, God plays d. with world, 636:5
  human bones, 404:3
  never abolish chance, 547:12
Dicers', false as d. oaths, 197:28
Dick, evil assailable in Moby D.,
    486:25
  the shepherd blows his nail, 169:13
Dickens, not have any D. today, 712:4
  what the d. his name is, 182:30
Dickinson, how wrong Emily D. was,
    767:12
Dickon thy master bought and sold,
    153:*n*7
Dick's, Dirty D., 720:18
Dickybird why do you sit, 531:9
Dictate direction work must take,
    687:19
  of common sense, 308:22
  terms between old and new world,
    355:3
Dictates of conscience, 339:11
Dictator, German d., 620:1
Dictators ride on tigers, 619:21

Die (*continued*)

sail until I d., 455:6
seem though I d. old, 599:4
seems rich to d., 415:16
shall never d., 40:19
shall Trelawny d., 433:31
sink or swim live or d., 394:9
soil good to d. for, 486:1
something he will d. for, 760:17
spirit d. of inanition, 499:8
Tamburlaine must d., 162:1
teach men to d., 145:12
teach us how to d., 400:13
tells me I must d., 417:2
the death of the righteous, 10:5
theirs but to do and d., 458:12
there smothered, 657:7
they seemed to d., 30:23
things that are born and d., 718:8
thou shalt surely d., 6:14
time to d., 23:32
to d. a debt we must discharge, 242:*n*3
to d. honorably greatest virtue, 60:12
to d. is gain, 44:29, 74:16
to d. to sleep, 196:10
to itself it live and d., 221:15
to leave to d. a little, 570:4
to make men free, 484:7
to save charges, 234:23
toddle home d. in bed, 662:6
trust that when we d., 522:10
unlamented let me d., 298:6
unsung noblest deed will d., 64:13
unto the Lord, 42:26
we about to d. salute you, 110:6
we d. and we live, 117:14
we d. only once, 268:27
we d. soon, 740:8
we must, 164:31
we must be free or d., 375:1
we must needs d., 12:13
we shall d. alone, 270:24
we will d. free men, 348:1
weep or she will d., 456:18
went abroad to d., 648:3
when beggars d., 188:10
when good men d., 69:12
when he shall d. cut him in stars, 176:1
when I came to d., 478:17
who saw him d., 789:2
who would wish to d., 428:15
why can't dead d., 674:7
wisdom shall d. with you, 14:14
with face to sun, 564:13
with hammer in hand, 780:20
with harness on our back, 216:16
with honor, 584:1
with you ready to d., 96:19
without benefit of clergy, 613:*n*2
without visiting one another, 58:6
Wolf that break it d., 592:15
world a place to d. in, 248:21
Xerxes did d., 287:11
ye shall d. like men, 18:4
youth fight and d., 626:1
Died as one studied in death, 212:26
as soldier for his country, 586:*n*3

Died (*continued*)

before bodies died, 721:3
before god of love born, 229:17
Booth d. blind, 637:5
came three thousand miles d., 485:22
David d. full of days, 13:20
deaths ye d., 590:17
die as my fathers d., 534:5
dog it was that d., 328:28
far away before his time, 586:*n*3
for Beauty, 512:13
for God and to procure wealth, 139:4
for this Fitzgerald d., 596:1
gloriously on field, 450:9
good death if life inspired, 762:11
had I d. hour before, 214:15
had no poet and d., 303:13
he that d. o' Wednesday, 178:33
in boots like pioneer, 698:3
in harness, 621:18
in hollow murmurs d., 324:17
in virtue's cause, 167:9
land where fathers d., 444:3
last night of my physician, 287:22
learn from having d., 625:5
like wise one d., 151:21
liked it not and d., 227:10
maintaining right of way, 783:22
man that d. for men, 536:12
men d. but not for love, 192:2
Mithridates he d. old, 579:16
Mother to day, 732:12
never knew worth till he d., 607:19
no one d. of laughter, 614:13
of chills and fever d., 674:12
of no blast he d., 273:21
on Saturday, 791:4
One who d. for Truth, 512:13
playing ukelele, 727:1
queens have d. young and fair, 227:2
she d. young, 237:19
she should have d. hereafter, 216:14
some pro patria, 659:8
that ever d. so young, 452:1
there d. a myriad, 659:10
these dead not d. in vain, 450:2
those who d. with thee for right, 615:1
to have d. once enough, 94:22
to make men holy, 484:7
to northwest d. away, 465:5
to save us all, 479:18
unmarked unknown, 674:19
when I d. last, 229:1
when my mother d., 356:11
withered when my father d., 198:24
would God I had d. for thee, 12:14
would we had d. in the land of Egypt, 9:6
youngest critic d., 591:13
zealous locksmith d., 778:1
Die'll, them that d. be lucky ones, 561:6
Diem adimere aegritudinem homini-bus, 85:*n*15
carpe d., 95:*n*21

Dies, after many a summer d. swan, 459:1
all that was theirs d., 69:12
an honest fellow, 236:*n*3
as when a giant d., 204:11
at the opening day, 294:16
begotten born and d., 597:7
bird of wonder d., 226:8
body d. body's beauty lives, 639:4
cackles groans and d., 410:8
cry not when father d., 315:4
ere he knows it, 465:24
fish d. because he opens mouth, 794:1
fling stone giant d., 307:7
he d. and makes no sign, 164:2
he that d. pays all debts, 224:17
if tree d. plant another, 312:12
in your fragrant bosom d., 246:6
irae dies illa, 123:*n*7
kicks the dust, 478:10
language d., 588:2
light d. before thy word, 304:2
light d. with dying sun, 563:2
like a dog, 443:12
love built on beauty d., 230:3
man d. in pain, 283:16
ne'er like angels till passion d., 227:20
no gossip ever d. away, 55:2
noblest lives and d., 494:20
not how man d. but lives, 316:6
nulla d. sine linea, 81:*n*1
on wind like memories, 641:10
optima d. prima fugit, 93:*n*2
reputation d., 299:14
reputation d. quickly, 278:13
re-resolves then d., 296:12
rich dies disgraced, 525:15
Sahara d., 514:4
something in us never d., 362:23
swan, 459:1
tumult and shouting d., 593:1
what an artist d. with me, 105:18
when lovely flame d., 617:16
who d. if England live, 593:25
whom gods love d. young, 81:5
youth grows pale and d., 415:12
Diet, Doctor D., 290:13
scrip of joy immortal d., 152:16
sober in d., 304:4
Dieth, how d. the wise man, 23:31
man d. and wasteth away, 14:21
no man d. to himself, 42:26
Dieu a donc oublié, 281:*n*2
est dans le détail, 783:*n*1
mesure le froid à la brebis tondue, 144:*n*8
s'est fait homme, 427:*n*4
Dieux, l'homme forge D. à douzaines, 146:*n*4
Differ, agreed to d., 386:17
all things d. all agree, 299:21
from things that d. comes attune-ment, 62:15
when doctors d., 300:*n*1
Difference between lightning bug and lightning, 527:2
distinction without d., 311:25
extent of d. no democracy, 448:9

Difference (*continued*)
   is important, 546:12
   makes d. whose ox gored, 138:16
   night makes no d., 241:7
   no other d. than age and sex, 366:7
   of opinion divide, 247:17
   of opinion makes horse-races,
     527:18
   of taste in jokes, 484:1
   oh the d. to me, 373:19
   only d. lies in degree, 280:11
   principal d. between dog and man,
     527:16
   sameness with d., 384:14
   that made all the d., 623:7
   the d. to him, 373:n2
   they wear our clothes and what d.,
     235:4
   wear rue with a d., 198:24
Differences among experts, 586:9
   between cat and lie, 527:9
   settle d. before war, 710:2
   source of strength, 754:3
   tiny d. in input overwhelming,
     775:2
   trivial and political, 315:24
   world made safe for d., 662:16
Different drummer, 478:37
   hatched o'er an' hatched d., 483:11
   men are created d., 727:9
   mob not ask better only d., 138:4
   names after they are produced,
     56:12
   prayin' it tuh be d. wid you, 707:7
   something d. from either, 668:18
   Sunday d. from another day, 314:28
   to d. minds, 430:13
   zeal for d. opinions, 351:22
Differentiation, through natural d. affirm brotherhood, 722:11
Differently, freedom for one who
   thinks d., 610:9
   they do things d. there, 692:19
Differeth, one star d., 43:24
Differs, true love d. from gold and
   clay, 408:13
   whatever d. from this is no democracy, 448:9
Difficile est saturam non scribere,
   108:n4
   Latin was no more d., 262:18
Difficilis facilis fucundus acerbus,
   106:n9
Difficult, as easy as temperance d.,
   315:11
   criticism easy art d., 295:22
   do immediately, 783:8
   dreams surely are d., 54:9
   even those d. to please, 246:13
   excellent things d. as rare, 278:19
   fascination of what's d., 595:19
   found d. left untried, 618:15
   in d. are friendly forces, 630:12
   judgment d., 71:13, 349:12
   living up to it d., 463:17
   nothing so d. but may be found,
     85:19
   of things known most d., 596:2
   Olympian is a d. foe, 51:3
   people d. to govern, 57:21

Difficult (*continued*)
   poetry d. to read, 467:27
   poets must be d., 672:15
   remark how d. to define, 762:15
   to believe people starving, 730:16
   to flee from reality, 653:19
   to lay aside long-cherished love,
     91:14
   to speak, 332:6
   to write good life as to live one,
     643:17
   too d. to think nobly, 319:23
   when you do it reluctantly, 86:2
Difficulties of any individual, 387:8
Difficulty and danger, 346:1
   daunted by no d., 463:26
   govern tongues with d., 277:22
   makes d. his first business, 61:9
Diffused knowledge immortalizes,
   367:14
Diffuses, dissolves d. dissipates, 384:7
   numbness d. my senses, 95:14
Diffusion, increase and d. of knowledge, 367:18
Dig deep trenches in beauty's field,
   220:8
   forbear to d. dust enclosed here,
     226:11
   grave and let me lie, 561:16
   I cannot d., 38:39
   I'll d. with it, 769:13
   them up again, 237:14
Digest, edible wholesome to d., 544:16
   inwardly d. the Scriptures, 49:20
   more beliefs than can d., 578:12
   no more than able to d., 289:21
   of anarchy, 332:9
   some writers cannot them d.,
     160:17
   something to d., 633:n3
Digested, few books to be d., 160:8
Digestion, give me good d. Lord,
   633:n3
   god on side of best d., 633:9
   good d. wait on appetite, 215:3
   prove in d. sour, 170:31
   sleep from pure d. bred, 259:5
   with sound d. man may front much,
     412:4
Digestions, unquiet meals make ill d.,
   166:33
Digests experiences as digests meats,
   552:27
Diggeth a pit, 22:31
Dight, storied windows richly d.,
   252:10
Dignified, anything but d. English,
   622:15
   better go down d., 624:8
   vice by action d., 175:16
Dignitate, otium cum d., 87:n8
Dignities, earthly d., 225:17
Dignity and worth of person, 655:23
   conciliate with d., 318:22
   contrary to d. built paper-mill,
     164:11
   human d., 774:2
   in effort of patriots, 337:17
   in tilling field, 571:33
   last vestige of human d., 702:15

Dignity (*continued*)
   leisure with d., 87:13
   Negroes find new sense of d., 761:5
   of high calling, 331:25
   of history, 295:8, 425:18
   of truth lost with protesting, 232:7
   reach the d. of crimes, 348:5
   restores man to d., 588:19
   true d. of man, 588:9
   wear undeserved d., 180:27
Digression, began a lang d., 361:17
Digressions, eloquent d., 505:20
   sunshine of reading, 320:14
Dike, last d. of prevarication, 332:7
Dilemma, here lay the d., 663:9
   horns of my d., 320:25
Diligence, best of me is d., 209:6
   keep thy heart with all d., 20:25
   learning must be attended to with
     d., 347:10
   mother of good fortune, 151:10
   observe physician with same d.,
     231:5
   work out salvation with d., 64:25
Diligent dispensation of pleasure,
   396:7
   in his business, 22:15
Diligently, teach them d. unto thy children, 10:11
   they d. practice it, 57:12
Dillar, a d. a dollar, 792:7
Dim and joyless if not shared, 392:15
   behind d. unknown, 485:2
   forsake their temples d., 251:1
   in intense inane, 407:3
   on Bristol board, 729:16
   religious light, 252:10
   spot which men call earth, 252:12
   sun in d. eclipse, 256:16
   windows of the soul, 360:3
DiMaggio, where have you gone Joe
   D., 772:9
   worthy of great D., 702:9
Dim-discovered, ships d., 308:1
Dime, brother can you spare d.,
   699:15
Dimension, sickness enlarges d. of self,
   388:9
Dimensions, hath not a Jew d., 180:30
Dim-glimmering, moon d. through
   window-pane, 383:17
Diminish, joys with age d., 468:12
   some nations increase others d.,
     89:16
Diminished, force in Nature not d.,
   496:17
   hide your d. rays, 258:n1
   stars hide their d. heads, 258:3
   to her cock, 210:27
Diminishes, any man's death d. me,
   231:8
   functional capacity, 347:13
Diminution of original sin, 494:16
   without increase or d., 385:9
Diminutives, lovely d., 725:3
Dimitri, Long live D. Ivanovich, 424:2
Dimmycratic party ain't on speakin'
   terms, 602:16
Dimness, most experience sunk to d.,
   538:18

Din, cock with lively d., 251:12
 hear the merry d., 380:27
 of strife, 498:4
Dinah blow your horn, 780:6
Dine at journey's end, 596:12
 at ten sup at six, 428:6
 going to d. with men, 627:18
 hang that jurymen d., 299:15
 when Noah sat down to d., 619:8
 with some men, 627:18
Dined, I have d. today, 380:18
 on mince, 472:3
 upon cold meat, 279:15
 when Jefferson d. alone, 741:14
Diners-out from whom we guard
 spoons, 425:2
Dines on following day, 519:21
Ding dong bell, 789:6
 hey d. a d. d., 192:12
Dinge, make sure not a d. boys, 694:5
Dinginess, country of d., 446:26
Dingledodies, danced like d., 750:9
Dining and dancing begin, 709:11
 while they thought of d., 330:10
Dinner, after d. is after d., 288:24
 among old soakers, 279:10
 better is a d. of herbs, 21:26
 good d. and feasting, 279:12
 his life d. wife, 423:15
 lubricates business, 348:6
 man always willing to come to d.,
 655:1
 man who came to d., 676:15
 much depends on d., 403:18
 nap after d. silver before d. golden,
 510:2
 not a d. to ask a man to, 316:4
 revolution not same as inviting to
 d., 686:11
 that we expect our d., 326:1
 three hours' march to d., 390:15
 what gat ye to d., 785:20
 write with no d., 674:13
Dinner's, glasses' edge when d. done,
 466:7
Dinners, true Amphitryon gives d.,
 269:21
 visits his d. not him, 269:12
Dinosaur death-steps, 743:7
Diogenes, if not Alexander would be
 D., 80:24
 plucked a cock, 77:3
 struck father when son swore,
 235:16
Diomede, this sodeyn D., 128:27
Dios te tenga en su mano, 794:8
Diplomacy is to do and say, 663:8
Diplomats, pens of d. not ruin, 342:12
Dipped into the future, 455:17
 Jonathan d. rod in honeycomb,
 11:35
Dirck galloped, 465:1
Dire, beckoning shadows d., 252:24
 effects from civil discord, 292:16
 gorge of salt sea tide, 181:n2
 offense from amorous causes, 299:9
Direct and honest not safe, 207:12
 eminently plain and d., 498:22
 him where to look for it, 230:15
 leaving to d. themselves, 685:19

Direct (continued)
 lie d., 192:16
 relations with good joke, 619:1
 understanding to d., 346:3
Direction, advances in d. of dreams,
 478:36
 chief source of d., 727:8
 dictate d. work must take, 687:19
 great thing is what d., 447:10
 in which education starts, 75:13
 new critical d., 762:10
 new d. of Time, 657:8
 of right line, 282:2
 which thou canst not see, 301:12
Directions, by indirections find d.,
 195:7
 rode off in all d., 607:8
Director, can be d. of opponent's fate,
 80:21
Directs the storm, 291:30, 303:29
Direful spring of Grecian woes,
 299:23
Direst, full of d. cruelty, 212:29
 shapes of death, 503:4
Dirge, by forms unseen d. sung,
 324:11
 for most lovely dead, 452:1
 in marriage, 192:32
 of dying year, 407:15
Dirt, bequeath myself to d., 489:23
 breathing a small breath, 724:13
 eyes of you and me full of d.,
 689:10
 instead of d. and poison, 288:17
 loss of wealth loss of d., 140:13
 painted child of d., 302:15
Dirty, airing d. linen never masterpiece, 765:1
 all d. and wet, 290:20
 British coaster, 634:1
 business wiretapping, 543:9
 Dick's and Sloppy Joe's, 720:18
 treat woman as d. joke, 767:2
 wash d. linen at home, 370:11
 work at crossroads, 780:17
Dis, by gloomy D. was gathered,
 258:10
Dis aliter visum, 93:n17
 manibus sacrum, 118:28
Disable benefits of your country,
 191:28
Disabused, by himself abused or d.,
 301:13
Disaffection, nonconformity mark of
 d., 615:6
Disagree, doctors d., 300:21
Disagreeable, such a d. man, 530:17
Disagreements, scholarship record of
 d., 586:9
Disagrees, what agrees d., 62:16
Disappearance, law master after my
 d., 64:27
Disappeared, sun would have d.,
 578:14
Disappoint a Continent, 524:2
Disappointed in monkey, 528:4
 unhoused d. unaneled, 194:24
 who expects nothing never d.,
 300:25

Disappointment, boredom and d.,
 710:16
 mathematics commence in d., 584:7
Disappointments, too familiar with d.,
 447:21
Disappoints, man appoints God d.,
 132:n7
Disapprove of what you say, 307:4
Disarmament is essential, 650:9
Disaster clouded Union cause, 522:13
 evil gains equivalent of d., 54:26
 exaltation from d. and ruin, 619:13
 'gainst all d., 272:n9
 loss is no d., 729:15
 no greater d. than greed, 57:14
 success like d., 727:4
 Triumph and D., 593:19
Disasters, day's d. in morning face,
 329:17
 make guilty of our d., 209:3
 middle station fewest d., 286:3
 weary with d., 214:23
Disastrous beating of wings, 611:13
 born to d. end, 154:6
 spake of d. chances, 205:25
 twilight sheds, 256:16
Disbanded, funeral done and d., 734:7
Disbelief in great men, 412:31
 suspension of d., 384:10
Disbranch, sliver and d., 210:22
Discard knowledge, 80:14
Discarded, welcome home d. faith,
 170:18
Discern infinite passion, 465:13
 innocence of neighbors, 478:33
Discerner of the thoughts, 45:34
Discerning, gives genius better d.,
 330:1
 to a d. Eye, 512:11
Discharge, no d. in war, 24:16, 593:15
 to die a debt we must d., 242:n3
Discharged, at once indebted and d.,
 258:4
 debt d. through eternity, 349:24
 with greater ease, 242:10
Discharging less than tenth, 200:20
Disciple not above master, 34:32
 true teacher has no d., 422:2
Disciples, gave bread to d., 36:28
 masters ashamed to become d.,
 227:3
 threatening against d., 41:4
Discipline, age of d. began, 656:12
 care of d. is love, 30:27
 desire of d., 30:27
 Doric d. vain, 597:18
 organization and d. of war, 136:12
 soul of army, 336:12
 that I have established, 64:27
Disciplined by peace, 741:3
 inaction, 367:17
Disciplines, I know d. of wars, 185:9
Disclose, merits to d., 322:24
 not d. essence of phenomena, 656:3
Disclosed, before buttons be d.,
 193:26
Discobolus standeth face to wall,
 524:13
Discomforts accompany my being
 blind, 279:27

Discontent, but only want and d., 264:3
    want of self-reliance, 431:27
    waste nights in d., 154:5
    wealth and poverty parents of d., 75:12
    winter of our d., 165:18
    yields nothing but d., 331:3
Discontented, stirs of d. strife, 233:15
Discontentment, no greater guilt than d., 57:14
Discord, age of d. and strife, 163:17
    civil d., 292:16
    danger in d., 441:23
    eke d. doth sow, 145:2
    harmony in d., 97:15
    harmony not understood, 301:12
    in my Kosmis no feeva of d., 641:17
    music must investigate d., 107:5
    so musical a d., 173:25
    what d. follows, 200:9
Discordant, concordant is d., 62:16
    reconciles d. elements, 373:8
    reconciliation of d. qualities, 384:14
    wavering multitude, 183:9
Discourage and abolish tyranny and vice, 337:10
Discouraged, Dewey feel d., 544:6
    lest they be d., 44:41
    never get d., 733:19
Discouragement, there's no d., 272:29
Discouraging, which more d. literature or chickens, 703:11
Discourse according to learning, 184:*n*2
    bid me d., 165:8
    everybody's d. of death, 279:11
    excellent dumb d., 224:19
    good company good d., 245:20
    in novel phrases, 529:17
    made us with large d., 198:12
    of fools is irksome, 31:43
    of reason, 193:11
    of the elders, 31:20
    rather thy d. than play, 235:11
    showers of sweet d., 264:11
Discourteously, cast me off d., 776:10
Discover everybody's face but own, 288:16
    I had no talent, 675:15
    I had not lived, 478:17
    never d. land of nowadays, 608:11
    who could d. God, 103:16
    you are human as I, 744:2
Discovered, America d. accidentally, 665:12
    I was not God, 543:12
    plant whose virtues not d., 433:24
    poets philosophers d. unconscious, 569:20
    when d. not wanted, 665:12
    wicked man in bathroom cupboard, 739:12
Discoverer, exultation only d. can experience, 665:10
Discoverers among them as comets, 312:10
    ill d. think there is no land, 158:8
    sea-d. to new worlds, 228:3
Discovereth, he d. deep things, 14:18

Discovering, only two ways of d. truth, 158:12
Discovers, flute in dying notes d., 275:10
    fresh perfection, 396:12
Discovery, abyss d. metamorphosis, 616:19
    errors portals of d., 647:16
    man's d. genitalia a weapon, 767:18
    mistaking paradox for d., 613:14
    new dish does more than d. of star, 354:15
    seeing what everybody seen nobody thought, 687:20
    terra firma of accomplished d., 635:2
Discredit what they do not excel in, 80:15
Discreditable, regrets d. act, 642:22
Discreet, too d. to run amuck, 302:20
Discreetest, virtuousest d. best, 259:29
Discreetly blot, 250:5
    entered into reverently d. advisedly, 50:1
Discretion, better part of valor d., 179:9
    dronkenesse sepulture of his d., 131:30
    fair woman without d., 21:8
    inform their d., 344:22
    should be thrown aside, 81:6
    to the young man knowledge and d., 20:17
Discriminate between important and negligible, 635:2
Discriminating, keen d. sight, 371:24
Discrimination, art d. and selection, 549:3
    nation has history of sex d., 719:6
    protest d. and slander, 628:1
    sophisticated modes of d., 646:9
Discuss freely settle question, 424:20
    worst for problem is d. it, 768:6
Discussing duty to God, 489:16
Disdain, for thee to d. it, 409:11
    give me more love or more d., 246:7
    Lady D., 186:12
    to be instruments, 355:3
Disdained, one feeling d., 409:11
Disdainful smile, 322:7
Disdainfully, think not d. of death, 111:25
Disdaining littlenesses, 76:10
Disdains all things above his reach, 237:22
    beauty d. to destroy us, 630:6
Disease, AIDS d. of defect in immunity, 745:*n*1
    as physician observes d., 231:5
    astrology d. not science, 122:9
    bad rhyming a d., 303:12
    biographies d. of English literature, 484:4
    brought on by boredom, 710:16
    called lack of money, 139:14
    consciousness d., 589:10
    cure d. kill patient, 159:28
    cured yesterday of my d., 287:22

Disease (*continued*)
    dreaded scandal more than d., 586:22
    experience of mortal mind, 495:22
    fee bestow upon foul d., 208:24
    gained strength by delays, 101:29
    greater toll on health than any d., 748:18
    I have Bright's D. and he mine, 714:13
    interest in d. interest in life, 629:15
    is sorrow, 64:26
    life is an incurable d., 267:5
    long d. my life, 302:9
    medicine has to examine d., 107:5
    meet d. at first stage, 104:18
    of modern life, 498:12
    of not listening, 183:16
    of old men avarice, 236:20
    old age only d., 432:9
    or sorrows strike him, 483:2
    part in developing man, 532:11
    people given over to d., 90:13
    physician hath favorite d., 311:22
    remedies worse than d., 99:16
    remedy too strong for d., 67:12
    shapes of foul d., 457:30
    specialists in mental d., 652:12
    success our national d., 545:7
    the d. is incurable, 183:24
    to pretend to know is a d., 58:2
    tyranny's d., 63:4
    wine cause of d., 284:13
    writing a contagious d., 121:7
Diseased, mind d. always illusion., 473:9
    minister to mind d., 216:10
    nature breaks forth, 178:1
    of own beauty mind d., 400:24
Dis-eased, thou shalt not be d., 128:1
Diseased, words are physicians of mind d., 63:5
Diseases, as to d. make habit of two things, 71:2
    desperate grown, 198:9
    for extreme d. extreme strictness, 71:14
Disembodied, as one d. triumphant dead, 491:10
    bones, 660:16
    emotion a nonentity, 546:5
Disfigure, in a moment so d. us, 248:13
Disgrace and ignominy of natures, 248:13
    impatient of d., 274:3
    in d. with fortune and men's eyes, 220:15
    intellectual d., 720:11
    lived without d. without praise, 125:9
    no d. to be poor, 605:16
    not without d. associated, 477:9
    vice-prisidincy a d., 603:14
Disgraced, dies rich dies d., 525:15
Disgraces, labor d. no man, 501:16
Disgruntled, if not actually d., 645:17
Disguise, again in this identical d., 740:6
    fair nature with rage, 185:3

Disguise (*continued*)
no d. can conceal love, 265:7
profession is to d., 137:13
to go naked best d., 291:2
Disguises, gods go in various d., 54:6
troublesome d. we wear, 258:25
Disgust, achievement birth of d.,
544:12
not exist where hunger is, 573:6
Dish, as a man wipeth a d., 13:14
butter in a lordly d., 11:4
chameleon's d., 197:6
dainty d., 790:1
discovery of new d., 354:15
feast of joy a d. of pain, 156:22
fit for gods, 188:4
he will to his Egyptian d. again,
217:20
of meat too good, 245:29
other men serving d., 601:4
ran away with spoon, 789:9
thirty-two religions one d., 354:6
woman a d. for the gods, 218:14
Dishes, shalt not wash d., 790:11
shattered d. underneath pine,
624:17
Disheveled, poet flourished here d.,
766:1
Dishonor, by honor and d., 44:5
fears d. worse than death, 97:2
honor rooted in d., 459:15
no d. to halt at second place, 87:17
vessel unto d., 42:10
will not trouble me, 68:2
Dishonorable graves, 187:22
Dishonorably, to speak d. is pardonable, 67:13
Dishonored fragments of Union,
394:15
shroud, 668:16
Disiecti membra poetae, 95:n4
Disillusion, one d. mankind, 652:6
Disillusionment that woman has brain,
704:15
Disinherited, city's d., 581:16
Disinheriting, damned d. countenance,
352:30
Disinterested as being who made him,
337:n1
commerce between equals, 329:4
endeavor to learn, 499:9
intellectual curiosity, 631:16
patriotism in female most d. of virtues, 347:11
Disinterestedness, self-interest plays d.,
265:4
Disjoins remorse from power, 187:31
Dislike, hesitate d., 302:11
I too d. it, 664:6
same things is friendship, 91:25
Disliked, each day do two things d.,
626:15
person who d. gravy, 269:n7
Dislocate language into meaning,
672:15
Disloyal or subversive, 716:8
Disloyalty, not confuse dissent with d.,
724:6
Dismal, at d. treatise rouse, 216:13
headache, 530:14

Dismal (*continued*)
Science, 413:12
tidings when he frowned, 329:17
universal hiss, 260:15
Waterloo d. plain, 427:19
Dismantle, man d. structures, 723:21
Dismay, let nothing you d., 778:8
Dismayed her crew, 545:3
neither be d., 10:31
ran d. away, 182:7
was there man d., 458:10
Dismember or overthrow it, 449:4
whirl asunder and d. me, 169:29
Dismembered poet, 95:5
Dismissed, at length d. from thee,
397:14
Dismount, rides tiger afraid to d.,
619:n3
Disobedience, discontent disorder d.,
331:3
of Man's first d., 255:18
Disobedient, even if d. I shall follow,
82:3
Disorder, all prodigality and d.,
331:26
and early sorrow, 629:22
democracy full of d., 75:24
discontent d. disobedience, 331:3
domestic d., 284:13
great d. is order, 639:11
sweet d. in the dress, 241:4
violent order d., 331:26
Disordered, men d. like you, 317:n2
Disorders, all ruinous d., 209:2
medicine for mental d., 692:3
wisdom to recognize d., 122:13
Disorientation, shattering stress and
d., 760:4
Disparagement, words in Yiddish gradations of d., 714:17
Dispatch in putting end to it, 79:13
the soul of business, 305:11
Dispatchful looks, 259:10
Dispelled, live tongue all d., 750:2
mist d. when woman appears,
297:17
Dispelling, gleams through fog with-
out d., 321:5
Dispensary, anthology a d., 692:3
Dispensation of pleasure, 396:7
Dispense with life's necessaries, 474:9
with trifles, 182:24
Dispensing equality, 75:24
Disperse, by spreading d. to naught,
163:8
Display, electrical d. of God, 674:3
extended to d. its patterns, 62:29
Human Form D., 359:16
ridiculous d., 609:5
Displayed, flower d. doth fall, 202:11
Displeasing, misfortune of our friends
not d., 266:3
ten thousand fools, 122:10
Dispoged, lips to it when d., 469:41
Dispose, men determine gods d.,
235:n1
unsearchable d., 261:26
Disposed, tyrant has d. of foreign ene-
mies, 75:28
Disposer of other men's stuff, 147:n4

Disposes, man proposes God d.,
132:14
Disposition, antic d., 195:4
flag of my d., 488:19
horridly to shake our d., 194:11
I know d. of women, 86:10
patronizing d., 483:12
to be pleased, 316:33
truant d., 193:13
unfriendly d. toward U.S., 360:12
Dispossessed, his little heart d., 548:21
Dispraise, no d. or blame, 261:25
thing you desire to buy, 201:6
Dispraised no small praise, 260:29
Dispraises, praising most d., 302:n7
Disprized, pangs of d. love, 196:10
Disputable, dispute upon everything
d., 282:23
Disputandi pruritus ecclesiarum scabies, 227:n5
Disputants put me in mind of skuttle
fish, 293:8
Disputation, feeling d., 178:8
run in debt by d., 262:20
Disputations, doubtful d., 42:24
Dispute confute change hands, 262:19
it like a man, 215:30
my right none to d., 334:19
scholars d. and case still before
courts, 98:6
'twixt Tweedledum and Tweedledee, 304:15
upon everything disputable, 282:23
will you d. with Muhammad,
117:18
Disputed barricade, 674:17
ground colored man occupies d.,
480:15
Disputes, equal justice in private d.,
72:2
Disputing, itch of d., 227:13
warmer way of d., 149:39
Disquieted, never to be d., 242:2
they are d. in vain, 17:9
why art thou d. in me, 17:12
Disquietly, follow d. to our graves,
209:2
Disquiets, almighty time d., 67:7
Disregard, atones for later d., 624:8
Dissatisfied, I am troubled I'm d.,
664:15
not one is d., 489:16
Socrates d., 439:27
with what I learn, 625:5
writers d. with books they could
buy, 682:12
Dissatisfies, what d. in American civilization, 501:4
Dissections, learn anatomy from d.,
236:1
Dissemble, right to d. your love, 360:6
Dissembling, play one scene of excellent d., 217:2
Dissension, in d. never judge, 68:21
Dissent, dissidence of d., 331:14
in few days I should d., 247:17
not confuse d. with disloyalty,
724:6
orthodoxy chokes d., 615:6
specter in West called d., 768:7

Divided (*continued*)
   Gaul d. into three parts, 88:16
   have they not d. the prey, 11:7
   house d. against itself, 37:20, 448:7
   in death they were not d., 11:47
   mankind into parties, 351:22
   thy kingdom is d., 29:16
   we fall, 336:*n*5
Dividends, comfortable man with d.,
   442:11
Dividing asunder of soul and spirit,
   45:34
   by d. we fall, 336:10
   lover and lover, 533:9
   your sweet d. throat, 246:5
Divine, against thy D. Majesty, 49:15
   all things by law d., 407:20
   and terrible radiance, 427:23
   ask a drink d., 232:15
   Athens d. city, 64:12
   bird of Zeus, 63:30
   comfortable words, 459:5
   Countenance D. shine forth, 359:17
   dead d. brother of all, 490:11
   despair, 456:13
   discovery of d. truths, 295:9
   drink d., 232:15
   event, 458:3
   fear of some d. powers, 235:18
   fellowship d., 414:11
   God the Father a school-d., 303:6
   good amiable or sweet, 260:10
   Hand that made us is d., 292:2
   human face d., 257:24
   I myself more d., 461:2
   illusion, 500:24
   Love the human form d., 356:13
   love which greybeards call d., 165:7
   Majority, 512:2
   makes drudgery d., 243:26
   man d. as myself is dead, 490:14
   nature gave us country, 87:3
   no government by d. right, 385:12
   nor glimpse d., 304:2
   one who shares in the d., 103:16
   philosophy, 253:3
   Philosophy, 457:16
   reborn into highest forms which are
     d., 136:1
   relations with good joke, 619:1
   reliance on d. providence, 343:4
   Right D. of Kings, 303:31
   right of kings, 448:11
   sign indicates future, 70:21
   superhuman spiritual and d., 628:15
   tale of Troy d., 252:6
   Terror the human form d., 358:13
   thought thinks of itself, 77:24
   to forgive d., 299:4
   tobacco d. rare, 235:10
   truth is precious and d., 263:23
   utterance, 509:15
   what the form d., 388:15
   whatever poet writes with d. inspi-
     ration, 70:26
Divinely, childish but d. beautiful,
   364:18
   in the wrong, 296:1
   tall, 454:13

Divineness, Poesy participation of d.,
   158:7
Diviner air, 377:5
Divinest anguish, 480:2
   Madness d. Sense, 512:11
   Melancholy, 251:22
Divining, takes d. rod to find, 569:1
Divinities, new d. of his own, 74:14
Divinity, all the d. I understand,
   150:38
   doth hedge a king, 198:22
   dry volumes of d., 342:23
   gives wealth even to wicked man,
     59:21
   gossip a kind of d., 55:2
   in odd numbers, 183:7
   man own doctor of d., 560:12
   nature full of d., 477:3
   piece of d. in us, 248:22
   stirs within us, 292:14
   that shapes our ends, 199:19
   wingy mysteries in d., 248:3
Divisa, Gallia est omnis d. in partes
   tres, 88:*n*11
Division, equal d. of unequal earnings,
   393:12
   is as bad, 776:9
   salvation not in d., 609:12
   same as creation, 80:8
   saw d. grow together, 200:1
Divisions, how many d. has Pope got,
   638:11
Divorce, long d. of steel, 225:6
Divorced from eye and bone, 696:1
Divulge, I will never d. such things,
   71:1
Dix, French word d. on reverse,
   475:*n*1
Dixie comes from ten-dollar notes,
   475:*n*1
   Land, 475:1
   lib and die in D., 475:2
Dixit, ipse d., 119:10
Dizziness, two people shaken by d.,
   736:17
Dizzy, how fearful and d., 210:27
   make a small boy d., 724:15
Do, a' is done that men can d., 362:13
   all the good you can, 309:2
   anything you can d. I can d., 666:16
   as chapmen do, 201:6
   as I say not as I do, 239:10
   as you would be done by, 304:21
   boys do, 556:17
   damned if you d., 389:18
   decided on what they will not d.,
     79:21
   don't d. it in street, 590:7
   each day two things disliked, 626:15
   go and d. likewise, 38:24
   great right do little wrong, 181:20
   his arms might d. what this has
     done, 249:29
   how not to d. it, 471:8
   I dare d. all, 213:10
   I d. it more natural, 202:3
   if to d. as easy as to know, 179:27
   it after high Roman fashion, 218:9
   it as for thee, 243:25
   it with thy might, 24:19

Do (*continued*)
   just as one pleases, 390:14
   justice, 3:14
   justly and love mercy, 29:38
   know not what they d., 39:19
   know what he ought to d., 124:10
   let's d. it, 753:4
   make it d. or d. without, 782:8
   nastiest thing in nicest way, 663:8
   never d. today what can put off,
     503:11
   no one knows what he can d.,
     100:14
   noble things not dream, 484:13
   not as some pastors, 193:27
   not choose to run, 614:18
   not do thing they most do show,
     221:14
   not do to others, 61:30
   not do what we want, 717:14
   not go gentle, 737:20
   not kill, 3:14
   not we wanderer await, 498:10
   not what we ought, 497:21
   nothing we d. wiped out, 545:14
   now I'll d. 't, 197:24
   O what men dare d., 186:41
   one must be to d., 350:5
   or die, 236:12, 363:20, 689:16
   other men for they do you, 469:39
   reckless what I d., 214:22
   seeks little thing to d., 465:24
   so much to d., 457:23, 564:18
   that thou doest d. quickly, 40:24
   the evil I d., 41:46
   the very best I can, 451:4
   theirs but to d. and die, 458:12
   they d. things we can't, 725:25
   they know not what they d., 39:19
   thing I was born to d., 161:4
   thing that ends other deeds, 218:10
   thing think you cannot, 654:15
   things I did not d., 598:16
   things worth the writing, 309:23
   this in remembrance, 39:15
   this one thing I d., 44:32
   this will never d., 376:*n*3
   thou but thine, 259:30
   to be to d. to d. without, 537:8
   to will and to d. his pleasure, 44:31
   two things is to do neither, 98:31
   unto others as would have others
     do, 34:*n*1
   we d. what we can, 548:18
   well what not worth doing, 756:4
   what country d. for you, 741:7
   what d. about it, 504:1
   what have you or I to d. with it,
     320:8
   what he may, 199:18
   what I will with mine, 35:40
   what man would d. exalts, 466:21
   what manhood bids, 494:20
   what then thou would'st, 261:21
   what thou wilt, 139:12
   what will I d. when you fallen,
     747:12
   what you can d. for country, 741:7
   what you d. still betters what is
     done, 223:8

Do (*continued*)

 what you have to do, 108:11

 whatsoever thy hand findeth to d., 24:19

 will to d., 378:19

 without being commanded, 77:14

 write what men d., 158:10

 ye even so unto them, 34:8

 you d. not d., 764:16

Doc, never play cards with man named D., 726:6

Docent, decent d., 697:8

Doch-an'-dorris, wee d., 609:17

Docile and omnipotent, 512:18

Doctor and Saint, 445:17

 apple keeps d. away, 781:18

 Diet Quiet Merryman, 290:13

 every man own d. of divinity, 560:12

 fee d. for nauseous draught, 276:19

 Foster went to Gloucester, 792:3

 kills more than general, 283:19

 Livingstone I presume, 544:5

 while runnin' for d., 654:12

Doctor's, outlived the d. pill, 297:19

Doctors, believe d. nothing wholesome, 515:14

 best d. in the world, 290:13

 if d. had more Christianity, 602:13

 is all swabs, 561:2

 we d. know hopeless case, 689:7

 when d. disagree, 300:21

Doctrinaire logic, 683:4

Doctrine, all the winds of d., 255:4

 Augustinian d. Calvinistic d., 536:18

 every wind of d., 44:24

 from women's eyes this d., 169:4

 go for refuge to D., 65:5

 hidden under strange verses, 125:23

 involving pernicious consequences, 474:21

 little difference in d., 316:10

 not for d. but music, 298:18

 of pathological generation, 497:1

 of separate but equal, 682:9

 of strenuous life, 575:11

 or practice or interpretation, 111:23

 prove their d. orthodox, 263:7

 so illogical and dull, 652:9

 that each one select, 408:13

 yesterday fact today d., 345:12

Doctrines, makes d. plain and clear, 263:29

Documents, historian wants d., 549:7

Dodger, artful D., 469:6

Dodo never had a chance, 654:5

Doe, came a fallow d., 785:15

 life looking out from eyes of d., 684:11

Doer, speaker of words and d. of deeds, 51:32

Doers of the word, 46:8

 talkers no good d., 165:28

Does, dogged as d. it, 476:1

 he who can d., 571:8

 sees it and d. it, 465:24

 two reasons for what man d., 533:2

 what man d. based not on knowledge, 676:19

Doeth, what thy right hand d., 33:11

Doeth (*continued*)

 whatsoever he d. shall prosper, 15:29

 with youre owene thyng, 131:14

Doff it for shame, 169:28

Doffed, lightly d. hat, 588:24

Dog, absolutely unselfish friend is d., 515:17

 Almighty gave d., 379:24

 America friendly d. in small room, 677:9

 and your little d. too, 730:2

 better than his d., 455:10

 beware of d., 118:20

 bites man not news, 554:7

 Boatswain a d., 398:16

 Body my good bright d., 747:13

 breed maggots in dead d., 195:17

 broodin' over bein' d., 555:9

 cat d. pipe or two, 580:11

 circumcised d., 208:17

 commends himself to our favor, 574:6

 cut-throat d., 180:8

 did nothing in nighttime, 577:20

 dies like a d., 443:12

 door what d. on wrong side of, 709:16

 drunken d. ragged head, 387:15

 each time I walk the d., 766:6

 every d. his day, 484:15

 faithful d. bear him company, 301:8

 fall in grave like old d., 738:15

 fetch poor d. a bone, 790:18

 gingham d. went Bow-wow, 559:22

 grim king's d., 67:24

 hair of d. that bit us, 142:4

 has his day, 428:17

 hath a day, 142:3

 heart to d. to tear, 593:18

 hold-fast the only d., 185:2

 hound d. cryin' all the time, 765:7

 I am his Highness' d., 303:16

 I'm a lean d. keen d., 681:9

 in life firmest friend, 398:17

 in the manger, 59:5

 is thy servant a d., 13:8

 it was that died, 328:28

 jumps over lazy d., 781:8

 kids loved the d., 733:11

 let no d. bark, 179:20

 libelous statements about d., 650:2

 like d. hunts in dreams, 455:14

 little d. laughed, 789:9

 living d. better than dead lion, 24:18

 man bites d., 554:7

 mine enemy's d., 211:8

 offers drowning d. drink, 244:6

 old d. barks backward, 624:9

 old d. Tray, 388:n3

 old wife old d. ready money, 309:22

 pick up starving d., 527:16

 poor d. Tray, 388:25

 rather be d. and bay the moon, 189:14

 returneth to his vomit, 22:30

 since I am a d. beware, 181:10

 so poor he could not keep a d., 113:2

Dog (*continued*)

 somebody threw dead d. down ravine, 727:3

 starved at master's gate, 359:7

 suspicious of buried bone, 549:3

 this d. my d., 174:7

 thou calledst me d., 181:10

 to gain private ends, 328:27

 to this d. praise, 438:18

 tossed d. that worried cat, 792:24

 toy d. covered with dust, 559:21

 truth's a d. must to kennel, 209:7

 turned to his own vomit, 46:30

 whose d. are you, 303:16

 why should a d. have life, 211:19

 will have his day, 199:18

 wool of bat tongue of d., 215:14

Dogged as does it, 476:1

 strength, 605:2

 strong d. unenlightened, 499:12

Doggedly, set himself d. to it, 315:15

Doggerel, rym d., 132:2

Dogies, git along little d., 786:2

Doglike, on bended arm d., 63:9

Dogma, Bible literature not d., 588:11

Dogmatism, greater ignorance greater d., 558:2

 puppyism its full growth, 434:2

Dog's, more deadly than mad d. tooth, 166:32

 walking on hinder legs, 316:3

Dogs, all d. of Europe bark, 720:10

 all the d. in town, 788:13

 as many d. there be, 328:26

 black d. bay at moon, 531:12

 crowing of cocks and barking of d., 58:6

 dancing d. and bears, 611:18

 delight to bark and bite, 294:6

 drink running at the Nile, 102:13

 eat of crumbs, 35:24

 fought d. killed cats, 464:18

 hark d. do bark, 792:14

 hates babies and d., 641:n8

 hates children and d., 641:14

 horizon of d., 699:6

 leave Now for d. and apes, 465:22

 let slip d. of war, 188:23

 lies with d. riseth with fleas, 244:23

 little d. and all, 210:14

 loathe people who keep d., 559:2

 mad d. and Englishmen, 700:15

 more careful of breed of d., 282:22

 more I admire my d., 405:11

 not live as d. in manger, 650:5

 rain cats and d., 778:10

 shall eat Jezebel, 12:42

 shame the gray head, 52:20

 sleeping d. lie, 470:38

 strained anxious lives d. lead, 693:16

 straw d., 56:15

 terrible for old woman to outlive her d., 730:21

 throw physic to the d., 216:10

 which hath deeper mouth, 163:10

Dogs', puppy d. tails, 791:5

Dog-star rages, 302:6

Doing, cease to think about d., 390:19

 do well what not worth d., 756:4

Doing (*continued*)
  good one of professions which are
    full, 478:11
  is another thing, 146:13
  it all takes d. and I do, 549:13
  joy's soul lies in d., 200:4
  learn by d., 78:2
  manners happy ways of d., 432:36
  miserable d. or suffering, 256:2
  secure friends by d. favors, 72:5
  the decent thing, 769:16
  up and d., 440:18
Doings, amend your ways and your
    d., 28:19
  child known by his d., 22:3
  mark out your d. in advance, 420:7
  of mankind subject of my book,
    108:18
Dolabella's Cleopatra, 273:18
Dolce far niente, 110:n 4
  vita, 126:n 11
Dole, happy man be his d., 141:n 2
  happy man happy d., 141:2
  unequal laws, 454:24
  weighing delight and d., 192:32
Doleful, chants d. hymn, 170:20
  dumps, 167:n 2, 776:12
  shades, 255:24
Doll in the doll's house, 471:20
  living d. can sew cook, 764:10
  put youth away like d., 747:15
  your d. wife, 507:19
Dollar, a dillar a d., 792:7
  almighty d., 396:10
  broken never dollar agin, 479:20
Dollars, bought St. Louis for six mil-
    lion d., 526:15
  hours and minutes d. and cents,
    310:n 3
Dolls cloths tobacco crumbs, 740:7
  the children my d., 507:19
Dolore, nessun maggior d., 125:n 8
Dolores, splendid and sterile D.,
    533:13
Dolphin-like, his delights were d.,
    218:11
Dolphin's, mermaid on d. back, 173:5
Dolphin-torn gong-tormented sea,
    598:14
Dolts, three greatest d., 395:15
Domain France conquered, 503:4
  has d. of violins, 689:9
Dome, build that d. in air, 382:25
  of many-colored glass, 409:8
  of vast sepulcher, 407:15
  Orchard for a D., 512:4
  rounded Peter's d., 429:10
  stately pleasure d., 382:19
  sunny d., 382:25
  sunny pleasure d., 382:23
Domestic disorder, 284:13
  insure d. tranquillity, 346:7
  internal d. empire, 696:7
  malice d. foreign levy, 214:26
  naive d. Burgundy, 690:8
Domestica, quae est d. sede iucundior,
    87:n 13
Domina mater ecclesia, 112:n 3
Dominate, China not seeking to d.
    world, 685:15

Dominated, horse d. mind of early
    races, 657:20
Domination, fought against white d.
    black d., 745:15
  no Soviet d. of Eastern Europe,
    733:9
Dominations, Thrones D. Princedoms,
    259:13
Domine Deus Agnus Dei, 48:9
  Deus speravi in te, 147:n 11
Dominion, between Grand Army and
    d. of world, 541:3
  death hath no more d., 41:43
  death shall have no d., 737:11
  good old D., 345:7
  no such strange d., 410:7
  over every living thing, 6:9
  over palm and pine, 592:25
  tired of dark d., 509:7
  truly sorry man's d., 361:5
Dominions, sun in d. never sets,
    364:20
Dominus illuminatio mea, 16:n 5
  vobiscum, 48:5
Domus tutissimum refugium, 152:3
Don John of Austria, 619:2
  Quixote and I, 395:15
  when D. Quixote went out into
    world, 761:14
Done, a' is d. that men can do, 362:13
  because we are too menny, 540:7
  bright day is d., 218:12
  by the rule, 217:16
  Charmian is this well d., 218:21
  dared and d., 325:13
  dead and dumb and d., 617:6
  do as you would be d. by, 304:21
  foolish thing well d., 316:17
  game is d. I've won, 381:13
  God's will be d., 341:18
  her wrong, 781:14
  him who has d. deed to suffer,
    63:22
  I have d. it again, 764:11
  I have d. the state service, 208:16
  if d. when 'tis d., 213:5
  it couldn't be d., 644:15
  it unto the least, 36:19
  I've d. it from my youth, 353:16
  knowing when to have d., 413:10
  let what will be d., 343:18
  long day's task is d., 218:4
  much to be d., 314:27
  my dancing days are d., 174:n 4
  my story being d., 205:28
  my task is smoothly d., 253:12
  nay I have d., 161:11
  no sooner said than d., 84:14
  no worthy action d., 779:1
  not my will be d., 39:16
  one braver thing, 228:8
  reward of thing well d., 432:21
  servant of God well d., 259:17
  sight of means makes ill deeds d.,
    170:15
  so little d., 457:23, 564:18
  some villain hath d. me wrong,
    167:n 1
  still betters what is d., 223:8

Done (*continued*)
  surprised to find it d. at all, 316:3
  take honor and my life is d., 170:26
  that which is d. is that which shall
    be d., 23:25
  there shall be d. a deed, 214:27
  things that are d., 61:1
  things we ought not to, 48:17
  things won are d., 200:4
  thou hast d. thou hast not d., 231:4
  to deserve kittens, 633:6
  to have loved thought d., 498:1
  treason has d. his worst, 214:26
  'twere well d. quickly, 213:5
  want anything d. ask woman, 756:3
  we have d. this before, 739:9
  well begun is half d., 78:26
  well d. is quickly d., 98:22
  what another would have d. as well,
    607:3
  what have I d. unto thee, 10:4
  what have you d. to me, 510:4
  what have you d. with your youth,
    554:3
  what without Zeus is d., 63:17
  what you do not want d. to your-
    self, 61:30
  what's d. is d., 214:24
  when the hurlyburly's d., 212:9
  who has begun has half d., 97:8
  work may yet be d., 455:5
  worldly task hast d., 220:3
Donkey like horse translated into
    Dutch, 342:15
Donna è mobile, 94:n 1
Donne, John D. Anne D. Un-done,
    228:n 1
  whose muse on dromedary trots,
    383:12
  with Landor and with D., 596:12
Donnée, subject idea d., 548:14
Donner un sens plus pur, 672:n 1
Don't, Advice to Persons About to
    Write History D., 521:6
  advice to persons about to marry
    D., 554:14
  be gentle to your wife, 53:23
  damned if you d., 389:18
  fire until you see whites of eyes,
    327:10
  give up the ship, 393:n 3
  go near water, 783:6
  I d. think we d. love each other,
    763:2
  look back, 719:12
  sell America short, 782:22
  sell steak sell sizzle, 719:17
  tell her everything, 53:23
  tread on me, 779:2
Doodle handlebar moustaches, 742:18
Dooley, I think said Mr. D., 602:13
Doom, edge of d., 222:2
  feeling has force of d., 435:27
  Felicity or D., 514:17
  forfeit to a confined d., 221:23
  involve others in our d., 325:4
  regardless of their d., 321:15
  stretch out to crack of d., 215:23
Doomed conscripted ones, 662:7
  story ephemeral and d., 696:20

Doomed (*continued*)
  to company with pain, 376:9
Dooms imagined for mighty dead,
    414:10
  of love, 689:1
Doomsday, danced till d., 291:4
  is near, 178:24
Doomsters, purblind D., 539:7
Doon, banks and braes o' bonny D.,
    362:8
Dooney, play on fiddle in D., 595:10
Door, at its own stable, 512:18
  at the d. of life, 533:22
  at this d. England stands sentry,
    539:3
  before his cottage d., 386:3
  begins to crack, 787:21
  called push, 781:15
  came out by same, 445:17
  clicked behind d., 329:19
  dark cloud at house's d., 787:9
  dream hidden d. of soul, 629:3
  ever-open d., 51:n6
  foot wear steps of his d., 31:17
  form from off d., 452:20
  golden d., 558:1
  handle of big front d., 529:6
  he who sits at d. of house, 794:2
  hell of good universe next d., 689:7
  I am the d., 40:15
  know grass beyond d., 509:29
  leave world by natural d., 564:13
  lion at the d., 787:21
  moonlit d., 616:22
  no d. is shut, 584:4
  no right to open d., 74:19
  nor so wide as church d., 175:27
  of all subtleties, 56:12
  Old Age coming bolt d., 118:10
  open d., 536:16
  open to remedy, 149:12
  opening of a D., 514:17
  opens and lets future in, 713:5
  over that same d. was writ, 153:17
  put in his hand by the hole of the
    d., 25:14
  rapping at chamber d., 452:13
  shut shut the d., 302:6
  sits on horse at hostess' d., 169:22
  stack or the barn d., 251:12
  stand at the d. and knock, 47:14
  steed stolen shut stable d., 141:22
  stone leaf unfound d., 706:16
  then shuts the D., 512:2
  three gypsies a-come to d., 779:6
  to which no Key, 445:19
  turn in d. once only, 669:6
  up to old inn-d., 643:11
  we never opened, 670:13
  what dog on wrong side of, 709:16
  what is wind in that d., 133:8
  whining of a d., 231:11
  wide as a church d., 175:27
  wolf from d., 135:19
  wolf is at the d., 583:8
  world make path to d., 430:n2
  younger generation knocking at d.,
    508:18
Doorkeeper in the house of my God,
    18:7

Doors are widely flung, 724:10
  as yet shut upon me, 418:5
  be ye lift up ye everlasting d., 16:19
  for men to take their exits, 237:17
  if no d. or windows, 736:7
  in to the upper d., 429:23
  never darken threshold of d., 492:2
  of heaven adjacent identical, 652:5
  open d. of his face, 15:22
  open your living d., 259:22
  pictures out of d., 206:5
  shut d. against setting sun, 212:1
  shut in the streets, 24:27
  shut-in homes closed d., 607:2
  ten thousand several d., 237:17
  to let out life, 237:n4
  unscrew d. themselves from jambs,
    489:9
  unscrew locks from d., 489:9
Doorway, Hylax barks in d., 92:14
Doorways, unjoined person who hung
    in d., 744:6
Dooryard, lilacs last in d. bloomed,
    490:15
Dorian mood of flutes, 256:14
Doric discipline, 597:18
  lay, 254:7
Dorking, Hens of D., 472:10
Dormons, veillons dormants et veil-
    lants d., 146:n6
Dorobo and animals live side by side,
    784:19
Dorure en reste aux mains, 496:n4
Dose, anything man says take with d.
    of salts, 647:2
Dostoevski's realism, 653:17
Dotages, plagues and d. of human
    kind, 234:25
Dote, I d. on myself, 489:11
  on his very absence, 179:33
  on scraps of learning d., 295:24
Dotes yet doubts, 206:31
Double debt to pay, 329:19
  double toil and trouble, 215:13
  ducats stolen by daughter, 180:24
  eyes upon d. string, 229:14
  for all her sins, 27:15
  Giant hit into d., 644:5
  grew like a d. cherry, 173:19
  halve rights d. duties, 404:11
  health to thee, 401:27
  helix structure, 760:5
  hypocrite reader my d., 494:1
  life's fading space, 106:n8
  make assurance d. sure, 215:20
  of orient pearl a d. row, 226:19
  palter with us in d. sense, 216:20
  pleasure to deceive deceiver, 267:27
  single nature's d. name, 199:31
  snakes with d. tongue, 173:12
Double-consciousness peculiar sensa-
    tion, 605:2
Doubled globe of dead, 737:10
Double-faced, fame if not d., 261:18
Double-lived in regions new, 416:11
Double-mouthed, fame is d., 261:18
Doubly benefits who gives quickly,
    98:30
  dying, 378:1

Doubly (*continued*)
  seconded with will and power,
    200:10
Doubt, all best though oft d., 261:26
  doubter and d., 430:11
  explain till all men d., 303:32
  faith dead which does not d., 590:2
  faith in honest d., 457:26
  frets d. maw-crammed beast, 467:7
  grows with knowledge, 351:5
  hesitation and pain, 464:26
  I d. it said Carpenter, 518:24
  I d. some foul play, 193:24
  I show you d., 466:11
  ignorant taught to d., 542:20
  in d. to act or rest, 301:13
  iron time of d., 497:17
  let us not pretend to d., 538:16
  loop to hang d. on, 207:10
  love curiosity freckles d., 687:7
  modest d. called beacon, 200:14
  more d. stronger faith, 466:11
  my days of endless d., 152:8
  never d. I love, 195:14
  never stand to d., 241:16
  new philosophy calls all in d.,
    230:15
  night of d. and sorrow, 521:12
  no freedom of thought without d.,
    712:20
  no manner of d., 531:18
  one may prove a fool, 436:10
  our d. is our passion, 548:18
  read to d., 379:19
  road to resolution lies by d., 242:11
  sun and moon should d., 359:14
  sunnier side of d., 460:8
  teach child to d., 359:11
  that sun doth move, 195:14
  thou stars are fire, 195:14
  time d. of Rome, 403:4
  to be once in d., 206:33
  to d. everything or believe, 565:5
  true science teaches d., 589:11
  truth to be liar, 195:14
  when in d. tell truth, 527:22
  when in d. win trick, 293:13
  where d. let me sow faith, 123:10
  wherefore didst thou d., 35:20
Doubted, never d. clouds break,
    468:17
Doubter and the doubt, 430:11
Doubtful disputations, 42:24
  dreams of dreams, 534:12
  in d. things liberty, 266:10
  nice hazard of d. hour, 178:19
  thinking about thing no longer d.,
    439:15
  thoughts, 181:7
Doubting Castle, 272:23
  dreaming dreams, 452:17
  liberty is possibility of d., 706:8
Doubtless come again with rejoicing,
    19:28
  God never did, 245:27
Doubts are traitors, 203:27
  begin with certainties end in d.,
    158:4
  begin with d. end in certainties,
    158:4

Draweth out thread of his verbosity, 169:5

Drawing, back to the old d. board, 712:14
from no less kindled earth, 404:4
no unnecessary lines, 608:9
nothing up, 335:1

Drawing-down of blinds, 687:3

Drawn in pearly monotones, 660:17
linked sweetness long d. out, 251:19
never curtain d., 624:1
never d. breath of life, 598:3
see Harrison hanged d. quartered, 279:3
wine of life is d., 214:15
with team of atomies, 174:20
yet were they d. swords, 17:28

Draws, beauty d. with single hair, 299:12
lightly d. its breath, 372:17

Drayhorse, great gray d., 551:4

Dread abode, 322:24
and fear of kings, 181:19
back from the d. fray, 51:19
close eyes with holy d., 382:25
empire Chaos, 304:2
fifty above, 623:21
Inferno, 466:28
innocence has nothing to d., 281:11
Jove's d. clamors, 207:8
nothing more d. and shameless, 53:21
of mother-in-law, 565:2
of something after death, 196:10
two fates of d. death, 52:21
walk in fear and d., 381:26
what d. grasp, 358:7
whence this secret d., 292:14

Dreadeth, burnt child fire d., 142:6

Dreadful, acting of d. thing, 188:2
called thee mighty and d., 230:22
deed of d. note, 214:27
done a thousand d. things, 167:12
endured something more d., 54:10
gathers samphire d. trade, 210:27
knowledge of truth, 65:17
lion among ladies d., 173:15
no witness so d., 85:11
noise of water, 165:30
note of preparation, 185:14
Past, 454:9
pleasing d. thought, 292:14
silence that d. bell, 206:17
summit of the cliff, 194:13

Dreading e'en fools, 302:11

Dreadnought's her name, 793:21

Dream, Adam's d., 417:15
all dreams of other dreamers, 491:6
awakened from d. of life, 409:3
behind a d., 222:7
behold it was a d., 272:26
beholding shape of d., 572:24
beneath tamarind tree, 451:10
boldness to d., 713:15
came back in d. and we not here, 758:8
closes within d., 602:10
compared life to a d., 146:9
deep d. of peace, 397:1
deferred, 708:18

Dream (*continued*)
deferred dry up like raisin, 708:19
disturb not her d., 362:21
dreamed d. called Laundry, 757:7
eye hath not heard what my d. was, 173:27
fly forgotten as a d., 294:16
ghost fled like d., 93:36
glory and freshness of a d., 375:3
glory and the d., 375:6
Greeks have dreamt d. of life best, 351:11
happiness ceases like d., 247:10
happiness you may never feel, 611:12
hidden door of soul, 629:3
hope a waking d., 77:9
hope beyond shadow of d., 414:13
horrid dreams, 487:3
how I'll d. fast asleep, 487:10
I d. and say Why not, 571:24
I have a d., 761:1, 761:2
impossible dream, 740:17
in my d. saw lost cities, 735:8
into her d. he melted, 415:7
is a theater, 629:2
is the truth, 707:6
life as lake dreams sky, 589:20
life but empty d., 440:15
life is a d., 247:7
like a shadow like a d., 53:18
loosed from d. of life, 735:21
love's young d., 391:14
mankind is d. of a shadow, 64:5
might be all we d. of, 407:9
movement out of d. into codification, 758:2
near awakening when d. that we d., 385:6
no mortal dared d. before, 452:17
nor Homer nods but we d., 298:12
not all a dream, 401:25
not d. all day long, 484:13
not so wild a d., 435:26
nothing happens unless first d., 634:11
of battled fields, 378:20
of home, 617:12
of Jeanie, 507:3
of joye all but in vayne, 132:*n*12
of Spring, 383:14
of things that were, 399:13
old men shall d. dreams, 29:32
out of misty d., 602:10
past the wit of man, 173:26
phantasma or hideous d., 188:2
poet's d., 376:6
President had d., 450:3
republic is a d., 634:11
short as any d., 172:20
sight to d. of not tell, 382:13
sits as new-risen from d., 167:28
sleep not d. not, 479:29
somnambulist of vanished d., 427:24
strange things, 435:24
sweet d. when trick's over, 633:16
taught me this wisdom, 247:10
that I forget, 534:10

Dream (*continued*)
that it fades from kiss to kiss, 595:12
that we dream, 385:6
the d. is one, 8:7
those who d. by day, 452:6
to sleep perchance to d., 196:10
too is from Zeus, 50:25
translators between d. and reality, 665:20
vision in higher d., 669:17
vision or waking d., 415:19
warned in a d., 32:24
we live as we d. alone, 573:4
what we d. up, 757:9
within dream, 451:7
writing nothing more than guided d., 700:14
you are crossing Channel, 530:15
youthful poets d., 251:19

Dreamcrossed twilight, 669:19

Dreamed, crack-pated when we d., 597:15
dream called Laundry, 757:7
Greece might be free, 402:26
he d. and behold a ladder, 7:40
I dwelt in marble halls, 419:1
life was beauty, 476:17
never d. wrong triumph, 468:17
of in any philosophy, 683:1
of in your philosophy, 195:3
of toasted cheese, 561:5

Dreamer, beautiful d., 507:5
behold this d. cometh, 8:3
of dreams, 10:17, 523:7
scene actor prompter, 629:2

Dreamers of dreams, 553:21
other d., 491:6
soldiers are d., 662:5

Dreamful ease, 454:10

Dreaming dreams no mortal dared, 452:17
eyes of wonder, 518:13
false or honest d., 749:14
I was a butterfly, 80:9
my excuse for d., 683:1
of white Christmas, 666:13
on both, 204:10
on things to come, 221:23
pool, 484:14
spires, 499:16
with strange whale eyes, 657:22
world on d. fed, 594:16

Dreamless, deep and d. sleep, 524:9

Dreams abuse curtained sleep, 213:21
advances in direction of d., 478:36
all my nightly d., 452:3
arise from d. of thee, 407:21
at length deceive 'em, 288:2
before us like land of d., 499:22
being poor have only d., 595:9
blissful d. of long ago, 536:10
books each a world, 376:14
communicatest with d., 222:19
desires d. and powers, 534:13
doubtful d. of d., 534:12
dream d. of other dreamers, 491:6
dream horrid d., 487:3
dreamer of d., 10:17, 523:7
dying d. of his Argos, 94:26

Dreams (*continued*)
    forgotten d., 453:21
    from Death fulfillment to d., 638:25
    gate of ivory for false d., 94:17
    have two gates, 54:9
    hunters of d., 574:13
    hunts in d., 455:14
    I have bad d., 195:26
    in d. begins responsibility, 595:22
    in d. behold Hebrides, 421:17
    interpretation of d. road to knowl-
        edge, 569:3
    jailer envious of prisoner's d.,
        443:22
    joys as d. do fly, 776:15
    land of my d., 676:17
    lies down to pleasant d., 411:4
    man's best d. to shame, 438:22
    men in exile feed on d., 63:19
    necessary to life, 711:8
    night full of ghastly d., 165:29
    no mortal dared before, 452:17
    not responsible for d., 628:14
    old men shall dream d., 29:32
    painter's brush consumes d., 597:19
    pleasing d. slumbers light, 378:16
    revisit in d. the dear dead, 67:23
    rich beyond d. of avarice, 317:22,
        319:1
    sleep full of sweet d., 414:9
    spread d. under your feet, 595:9
    stuff as d. are made on, 224:21
    surely are difficult, 54:9
    than this world d. of, 459:27
    that blister sleep, 712:15
    themselves are only dreams, 247:7
    thought of old best d., 709:n3
    to sell, 428:14
    torn by d., 639:19
    transit where d. cross, 669:19
    tread softly on d., 595:9
    true I talk of d., 174:21
    vain hopes like d. of those who
        wake, 105:12
    voices strummed his d., 753:14
    we are dreamers of d., 553:21
    what d. may come, 196:10
Dreamt I went to Manderley again,
        721:16
    past never past redeeming, 749:14
Dreamy, brief d. delight, 595:12
    lullaby, 530:18
Drear, chill and d., 378:3
    epitaph d., 591:12
    vast edges d., 499:22
Dreariest and longest journey, 408:13
Dreary, all world sad d., 507:1
    if your morals make you d., 562:6
    midnight d., 452:13
    some days dark and d., 441:6
    these d. dumps, 167:10
    to be Somebody, 511:22
    tract of country, 452:4
Dregs, drunken the d., 27:31
    of Romulus, 87:22
Drenched in fraternal blood, 394:15
    our steeples, 209:24
Dress, all this fleshly d., 270:5
    as nation don't d. well, 570:17
    by yellow candlelight, 561:7

Dress (*continued*)
    if the devil d. her not, 218:14
    Peace the human d., 356:13
    plain in d. sober in diet, 304:4
    Secrecy the human d., 358:13
    she is more than d. on ironing
        board, 733:22
    style the d. of thoughts, 305:10
    sweet disorder in the d., 241:4
    tatter in mortal d., 597:8
Dressed, all d. up nowhere to go,
        606:7
    April d. in all his trim, 221:19
    closest to naked when well d.,
        651:11
    fine as I will, 294:11
    good spirits when well d., 469:35
    in brief authority, 204:4
    lord neat trimly d., 177:2
    nature to advantage d., 298:14
    out in all her finery, 330:3
    still to be d., 232:5
    walks to funeral d. in shroud,
        489:20
    world beautifully d., 503:12
Dressing nursing praying and all's
        over, 402:20
Drew, Creator d. his spirit, 277:1
    everything that begins with M,
        517:22
    from out boundless deep, 460:11
    Jew that Shakespeare d., 303:19
    many-colored life he d., 313:10
    men as they ought to be, 65:n7
    one angel, 466:28
    she d. an angel down, 276:16
    them with bands of love, 29:29
Dried frozen carcass of leopard, 702:4
    sap out of veins, 595:19
    tubes twisted and d., 591:13
Drift, adamant for d., 619:20
    everything begins to d., 717:12
    go with d. of things, 622:18
    in gradual swell, 767:9
    not d. or lie at anchor, 447:10
    outside tent whirling d., 606:3
    tell you my d., 186:26
    toward unparalleled catastrophes,
        636:8
    wait and obey, 593:27
    we know your d., 186:n2
Drifted in sheepish calm, 743:1
    on crooked crosses, 647:8
Drifts, all beautiful d. away, 595:16
    life at ease d., 509:18
Drill, before steam d. beat me down,
        780:20
    drop of sweat on d. ground, 658:n4
Drink, a little in d., 293:16
    ale's stuff to d., 579:15
    and be whole again, 624:18
    and devil done for rest, 561:1
    and forget poverty, 23:16
    as he brews so shall he d., 231:16
    as oft as ye d. it, 43:12
    ask a d. divine, 232:15
    blood to d., 436:6
    cannot make horse d., 141:28
    come my lad and d. beer, 315:3
    dance and d. and sing, 358:5

Drink (*continued*)
    deep or taste not, 298:13
    divine, 232:15
    eat d. be merry, 24:17, 38:28
    every creature d. but I, 267:1
    felony to d. small beer, 164:7
    five reasons we should d., 283:20
    follow strong d., 25:39
    for tomorrow we die, 26:21
    for your lips to d., 533:21
    give me to d. mandragora, 217:4
    goes in wit goes out, 244:16
    good men eat and d. to live, 70:23
    herbs to d. smoke thereof, 134:9
    is nicissry evil, 603:16
    it up, 789:8
    it with pleasure, 31:21
    Jesus saith give me to d., 39:47
    let him d. merrily, 228:1
    life to the lees, 454:25
    light is lion comes to d., 639:10
    man takes d. d. takes man, 544:3
    many companions for food and d.,
        59:20
    meat d. and cloth to us, 140:10
    more than enough to d., 580:11
    never taste who always d., 233:n1
    nevermore to d. again, 617:6
    no longer water, 45:20
    nor any drop to d., 381:8
    not d. fruit of the vine, 36:28
    not meat nor d., 684:13
    not my design to d., 247:6
    not the third glass, 242:18
    not to elevation, 311:2
    oblivion of a day, 508:26
    offers drowning dog d., 244:6
    old wine to d., 158:23
    one can d. too much, 333:4
    one more d. be under host, 687:14
    provokes desire, 214:11
    Russians' joy to d., 121:3
    shoulder sky d. ale, 579:18
    sleep is d. for the thirsty, 151:15
    snake came to d. there, 657:12
    snewed of mete and d., 129:25
    some writers take to d., 756:5
    stagger but not with strong d., 27:1
    strive mightily d. as friends, 167:20
    strong d. is raging, 22:1
    sweetest d. be sorrow, 613:n2
    taken to d., 608:10
    think that I can d., 144:11
    thirsty and ye gave d., 36:18
    tippled d. more fine, 416:12
    to general joy of table, 215:6
    to me only with thine eyes, 232:15
    to the lass, 352:29
    today and drown sorrow, 236:3
    unto him that is ready to perish,
        23:16
    water of gall, 29:n1
    when men d. they are rich, 72:14
    while you live d., 445:20
    wild anarchy of d., 233:2
    will not d. with you, 180:2
    willing to taste any d. once, 635:7
    wine of astonishment, 17:30
    with me and drink as I, 307:9

Dumb (*continued*)
    shallow murmur but deep are d.,
        152:13
    to d. forgetfulness a prey, 322:19
    to tell crooked rose, 737:8
    tongue of the d. shall sing, 27:9
Dumbs, now is one of the d., 471:29
Dumbshows, inexplicable d., 196:21
Dump, what a d., 704:3
Dumpling, diddle diddle d., 791:12
Dumps, doleful d. mind oppress,
        167:*n*2, 776:12
    these dreary d., 167:10
Dumpy, hate a d. woman, 402:7
Dun, her breasts are d., 222:8
Duncan, fatal entrance of D., 212:29
    hath borne his faculties, 213:7
    hear it not D., 214:1
    is in his grave, 214:26
Dunce kept at home, 334:8
    sent to roam, 334:8
    with wits, 303:30
Dunces, wit with d., 303:30
Dundee, bonnets of Bonny D., 379:27
Dunfermline town, 784:31
Dung and death, 670:21
Dungeon, live upon vapor of d., 207:4
    my body my d. is, 561:17
    scourged to his d., 411:4
    so dark as own heart, 436:8
Dungeons, brightest in d. Liberty,
        401:22
Dunghill, cock has great influence on
        own d., 99:17
    sun shineth upon d., 77:*n*5
Dunsinane, Birnam wood to D.,
        215:21
    Birnam Wood to D., 637:13
Dunstable, Miss D. curls pass muster,
        475:12
Dupe, man d. deceiver decay, 407:5
    mind is d. of heart, 265:16
Dupes, what d. needed was a new
        deal, 648:*n*4
Dupree, Weatherby George D., 648:5
Durable, make recollection d., 311:1
    odors of ointments more d., 159:13
    true love a d. fire, 152:10
Durance vile, 364:3
Duration, not deduct from d. of death,
        90:6
Dürer in a town like this, 664:3
Durst defy the Omnipotent, 255:22
Dusk, bumps along the d., 558:11
    each slow d., 687:3
    faces with silken turbans, 260:31
    out of d. shadow, 554:13
    owl of Minerva spreads wings with
        d., 372:5
    skin like d. on horizon, 690:18
    thwarted by d., 664:19
Dusky night rides down sky, 311:15
    rear my d. race, 455:23
    trusty d. vivid true, 561:25
Dust and silence of shelf, 424:12
    and soot of complaints, 558:5
    as chimney-sweepers come to d.,
        220:3
    as d. that drives, 557:8
    as we are, 373:8

Dust (*continued*)
    ashes am I and d., 120:9
    awake and sing ye that dwell in d.,
        26:29
    blossom in their d., 246:21
    blowing of dry d., 659:13
    cinders ashes d., 414:17
    created you of d., 117:2
    darkness fruit there of d., 533:15
    earth and grave and d., 153:2
    equal but in d., 231:14
    even while d. moves, 670:18
    excuse my d., 687:15
    forbear to dig d. enclosed here,
        226:11
    formed man of d. of the ground,
        6:11
    guilty of d. and sin, 244:1
    handful of d., 668:18
    hath closed Helen's eye, 227:2
    heap called history, 559:13
    heap of d. alone remains, 300:9
    hear her and beat, 458:24
    hearts dry as summer d., 376:20
    I shall lie in the d., 52:15
    if as they say some d., 624:4
    in air suspended, 671:21
    in the d. the cool tombs, 634:8
    into D. and under D., 445:16
    kicks d., 478:10
    lay mightily in whirl of d., 52:10
    lick the d., 17:42
    light in d. lies, 409:19
    limns on water writes in d., 160:14
    love reachest but to d., 155:28
    make d. of all things, 248:29
    make d. our paper, 171:24
    maniac scattering d., 457:14
    marry my body to that d., 242:2
    mouth filled with d., 231:14
    much learned d., 334:31
    mysteries beyond thy d., 270:11
    name not perish in d., 386:16
    noble d. of Alexander, 199:9
    not without d. and heat, 254:25
    of creeds outworn, 406:19
    of glittering grains, 787:11
    of snow, 623:15
    of systems and creeds, 453:20
    on marble pavement d. grows,
        86:18
    pays us with age and d., 153:2
    plummets to d. of hope, 65:18
    pride that licks the d., 302:17
    proud and angry d., 579:18
    quaint honor turn to d., 268:16
    quintessence of d., 195:29
    rain in d. on her shoulders, 683:11
    return to the earth, 24:28
    returneth to d. again, 520:9
    seemed to be local d. cloud, 735:19
    shake off d. of your feet, 34:29
    shalt thou eat, 6:23
    silent d., 322:10
    small d. of the balance, 27:21
    so nigh grandeur to d., 430:4
    that is a little gilt, 201:4
    that is blown away, 30:26
    this quiet D., 513:6
    thou art to dust returneth, 440:15

Dust (*continued*)
    thou art unto dust return, 6:26
    thrown in my eyes, 624:4
    to dust, 50:8
    toy dog covered with d., 559:21
    unto d. return, 6:26
    valiant d., 186:18
    vile d. whence he sprung, 378:1
    was Gentlemen and Ladies, 513:6
    we are but d. and shadow, 96:29
    we too into D. descend, 445:16
    weighed me D. by D., 514:12
    what a d. I raise, 411:16
    what is pomp but earth and d.,
        164:31
    with d. is dark and dim, 373:*n*2
    write good in d., 137:17
    you are not worth the d., 210:21
    you've long been d., 82:20
Duster, tomorrow feather d., 617:7
Dustman, Golden D., 471:19
Dusty answer, 508:30
    cobweb-covered maimed, 524:13
    eat d. bread, 696:2
    grated to d. nothing, 200:22
    hit the d. trail, 636:15
    purlieus of law, 457:25
    way to d. death, 216:14
Dutch, beat the D., 779:5
    donkey like horse translated into D.,
        342:16
    fault of the D., 372:2
Dutchman, see Flying D., 553:18
Dutchman's, icicle on D. beard,
        202:27
Duties, brace ourselves to d., 620:8
    halve rights double d., 404:11
    live without d. obscene, 433:25
    property has d., 434:27
Duty, astray from d. and interest,
        337:6
    better one's own d., 84:8
    brave man inattentive to d., 369:9
    cannot exist without faith, 434:30
    daily stage of d. run, 280:20
    dare do d. as we understand it,
        448:15
    dead then my d. ended, 551:3
    discussing d. to God, 489:16
    divided d., 205:29
    do your d., 249:12
    doing d. unfitted one for anything
        else, 587:1
    done my d. and no more, 311:11
    essence of judicial d., 355:9
    expects every man will do d.,
        360:17
    fight required of d., 84:6
    gratifying d. done, 531:20
    knowledge of their d., 72:7
    laid on me a sinner, 423:20
    lies in what is near, 79:18
    limping with d., 80:13
    lively sense of filial d., 342:23
    love is then our d., 297:18
    my d. to obey orders, 504:9
    neatness a d., 309:1
    no concern with d. or truth, 453:14
    nor law nor d. bade fight, 596:11
    not to be silent, 507:10

Duty (*continued*)
of being happy, 560:21
of judicial department, 355:9
of younger Negro artist, 708:11
out of d. cheat others, 613:1
performing public d., 501:14
rule of joy and d. one, 542:11
sacred d. to myself, 508:2
seen d. and done it, 781:23
some sense of d., 457:1
stern daughter of voice of God,
  376:2
subject's d. is king's, 185:17
such d. as subject owes, 167:35
thank God I have done d., 361:1
to love those who wrong him,
  111:20
to worship sun, 537:4
transforms obedience into d., 319:6
trespasses against d., 331:2
we owe Creator, 339:11
whispers low, 430:4
whole d. of man, 24:30
woke found life d., 476:17
Duty's, constabulary d. to be done,
  529:14
faithful child, 422:6
Dux femina facti, 93:*n*11
O vitae philosophia d., 87:*n*15
vitae animus est, 91:*n*15
Dwarf on shoulders of giant, 234:7
Dwarfed and abased below, 563:*n*4
Dwarfish thief, 216:6
whole, 383:5
Dwell a weeping hermit, 324:11
awake and sing ye that d. in dust,
  26:29
better to d. in a corner, 22:7
critic d. on excellencies, 293:4
House we d. in every day, 514:11
I but in suburbs of your pleasure,
  188:7
I found a new place to d., 768:3
in house of the Lord, 16:17
in midst of people of unclean lips,
  26:2
in the tents of wickedness, 18:7
in the uttermost parts of the sea,
  20:8
not d. in temples, 271:12
nothing ill d. in such a temple,
  224:2
on heights of mankind, 365:16
peace and rest never d., 255:24
shall I like a hermit d., 152:18
such as d. in tents, 7:9
to perdition there to d., 255:22
together in unity, 20:5
two souls d. in my breast, 350:13
where Israfel, 451:13
who shall d. in thy holy hill, 16:4
with vilest worms to d., 221:7
world and they that d. therein,
  16:18
Dwelled, Abram d. in Canaan, 7:28
Lot d. in the cities, 7:28
Dwellers by the sea, 564:20
sur la branche, 605:23
Dwelleth in the secret place, 18:15
not in temples, 41:16

Dwellin', fair maid d., 785:9
Dwelling, desert my d. place, 400:28
much on right, 280:17
of the blest, 94:12
single soul d. in two bodies, 77:13
there God is d. too, 356:14
thou hast been our d. place, 18:10
Venus here choose d., 275:30
whose d. is light of suns, 373:5
Dwells, heart place devil d. in, 248:15
in me d. no greatness, 459:14
water d. in lowly places, 57:1
wherever Roman conquers he d.,
  103:9
with gods above, 200:21
Dwelt among untrodden ways, 373:19
by the brook Cherith, 12:31
child who d. upon tract, 376:21
in marble halls, 419:1
Judah and Israel d. safely, 12:20
like star and d. apart, 374:20
too long have d. on thee, 229:6
unerring wisdom never d., 280:11
where Israfel d., 451:13
Word d. among us, 39:33
Dwindle, days d. down, 666:5
into a wife, 291:13
peak and pine, 212:14
Dwindles, man only growth that d.,
  328:10
Dyer's hand, 222:1
Dyin', young man you're d., 785:10
Dying and in despair, 510:13
at my d. hour, 584:5
behold you again in d., 562:1
between birth and d., 669:19
bless hand that gave blow, 274:20
bliss of d., 299:8
born by d. and being damned,
  138:13
come from d. moon, 456:10
day sir, 778:17
despised and d. king, 407:24
dirge of d. year, 407:15
doubly d., 378:1
dreams of his Argos, 94:26
echoes d. d., 456:11
every colored woman d., 763:16
fall, 201:16
fastened to d. animal, 597:9
flute in d. notes, 275:10
forgets d. bird, 341:6
generations, 597:7
green and d., 737:19
groans of love like those of d.,
  727:2
has made us rarer gifts, 663:5
himself and his d., 767:21
I am d. Egypt d., 218:7
if d. don't think much of it, 643:18
in Algiers, 444:1
in d. we are born, 123:10
in hotel room, 674:9
is a trifle, 513:13
is an art, 764:12
light dies with d. sun, 563:2
lives and unborn smiles, 731:7
living indisposeth for d., 248:31
man to dying men, 266:9
men enforce attention, 171:5

Dying (*continued*)
more survivors' affair, 629:18
multifold, 513:13
no more d. then, 222:12
not death but d. is terrible, 312:3
not d. for faith hard, 463:17
not grasp thought of d., 510:13
of cold, 589:16
of thirst by the fountain, 132:21
rage against d. of light, 737:20
separate d. ember, 452:14
so great an experiment as d., 249:24
stay d. here all night, 353:1
strike so he may feel is d., 103:17
tomorrow will be d., 241:9
truth on lips of d., 498:17
unconscionable time d., 273:6
whether living is d., 73:24
yet fancy ourselves eternal, 114:7
you went on with d., 767:7
young man you're d., 785:10
Dynamo, starry d., 757:4
Dynasties, carved new d., 649:2
go onward though d. pass, 540:22
Dyspepsy ruin of most things, 397:17

E

E equals mc², 635:11
pur si muove, 161:*n*4
white E red I, 565:17
Each bears his own Hell, 94:14
from e. according to abilities,
  481:11
hath one and is one, 228:3
man for hymself, 130:11
one's himself yet everyone, 725:8
singing e. to e., 667:19
slow dusk, 687:3
to e. according to needs, 481:11
Each-form, pluralism lets exist in e.,
  546:22
Eager, don't be e., 354:8
keep guest back who is e., 53:29
mount e. and quick, 747:13
soul biting for anger, 250:9
Eagle and me, 699:17
bald e. not chosen, 310:24
buttons stamped with screaming e.,
  694:5
by all the e. in thee, 264:17
does the E. know, 357:1
fly as e. toward heaven, 22:18
forgotten, 637:6
fourth beast like flying e., 47:15
from e. in his flight, 441:10
has landed, 762:12
I hear E. bird, 786:22
in a dovecote, 219:15
in and out the E., 780:13
like sick E. looking at sky, 417:2
mewing her mighty youth, 255:2
mount up at thy command, 15:18
never lark nor e. flew, 751:3
of house of Austria, 340:9
of the rock, 660:15
old man's e. mind, 599:12
or the snake, 592:9
suffers little birds to sing, 167:11

Eagle (*continued*)
Tom Jones outlive imperial e., 340:9
way of an e. in the air, 23:15
with e. eyes, 413:24
Eagle's fate and mine are one, 59:*n*8
feathered with e. plumes, 59:19
Eagles, baited like e., 178:20
mount up with wings as e., 27:23
of Ngong look out, 656:9
prey where e. dare not perch, 165:25
swifter than e., 11:47
where carcass is e. gather, 36:9
Ear, as mind pitched e. pleased, 335:11
bow down thine e., 22:11
came o'er my e. like sweet sound, 201:16
deaf adder that stoppeth her e., 17:29
Death twitches my e., 94:30
drowsy e. of night, 399:8
dull cold e. of death, 322:10
dull e. of drowsy man, 170:5
first blade then e., 37:21
flattery lost on poet's e., 377:26
flea in mine e., 139:17
give every man thy e., 193:30
hang pearl in cowslip's e., 173:1
heard of thee by hearing of the e., 15:27
hearing e. seeing eye, 22:3
I have no e., 387:27
I was all e., 253:5
I will enchant thine e., 165:8
in Adam's e. left voice, 259:23
in one e. out other, 128:*n*6
incline thine e., 27:12
jest's prosperity lies in e., 169:11
keep word of promise to our e., 216:20
more meant than meets e., 252:9
never e. did hear that tongue, 163:4
nor e. heard, 42:30
nor the e. filled with hearing, 23:24
of Faith, 376:21
of jealousy heareth all, 30:19
of man hath not seen, 173:27
oon e. herde at tothir out, 128:20
open vowels tire, 298:18
piercing night's dull e., 185:14
reasonable good e. in music, 173:21
rich jewel in Ethiop's e., 174:23
short a cheekbone and e., 492:*n*5
soothe thine e., 324:13
sweetness through mine e., 252:10
to my e. morning brings, 430:1
toad at e. of Eve, 258:27
unpleasing to a married e., 169:12
whorled e., 550:16
won the e. of Pluto, 251:20
wood has a sharp e., 130:*n*3
wrong sow by e., 142:26
'Ear my 'erse's legs, 460:2
Earl, slain E. of Murray, 785:18
Earlier and other creation, 671:13
later times more aged than e., 158:*n*3
Earliest, charm of e. birds, 258:21

Earliest (*continued*)
drops e. to ground, 181:16
Earls, daughter of hundred E., 453:25
Early and latter rain, 46:16
bright transient chaste, 277:*n*1
call me e. mother, 454:4
git up e. to take in God, 485:11
God helps those who get up e., 793:24
good die e. bad late, 286:2
had it been e. had been kind, 315:17
happy those e. days, 270:4
in the morning, 793:10
late and e. pray, 227:7
leaves fall e., 659:3
let e. education be amusement, 75:22
nipt my flower sae e., 363:14
not rise e. never do good, 314:29
those that seek me e., 20:33
to bed early to rise, 309:17
to rise early to bed, 690:12
too e. seen unknown, 174:24
used to go to bed e., 612:12
vote e. and often, 501:21
Early-born, dawn the e., 51:1
Earn, I e. that I eat, 191:9
little to e., 484:11
living by sweat of brow, 478:9
Earned, hearts are e., 597:2
night's repose, 441:5
with sweat of brows, 149:1
Earnest about these objects, 658:5
between jest and e., 149:42
frogs die in e., 82:10
I am in e., 437:15
in seeking knowledge, 61:11
intermingle jest with e., 160:1
life is art gay, 365:1
life real life e., 440:15
those who are really in e., 491:20
Earnestness, sincerity e. and kindness, 62:2
Earnings, division of unequal e., 393:12
Earns, each e. his death, 705:20
whate'er he can, 441:4
Ear-piercing fife, 207:8
Ears, belly has no e., 85:3
blast of war in e., 185:3
brain device to keep e. from grating, 728:5
bring to our e. clash of arms, 339:10
compliments reaching proper e., 591:2
don't hang noodles on my e., 793:7
earth has stopped e., 579:3
give your e., 5:11
gushed blood, 414:20
have e. and hear not, 28:15
have e. but hear not, 19:17
have heard Holy Word, 357:25
having e. hear not, 339:7
he has e. and two eyes, 471:29
he that hath e., 34:36
hearing with sharper e., 750:1
hum about mine e., 224:18
I have e. in vain, 415:16

Ears (*continued*)
lend me your e., 188:28
let music creep in our e., 182:8
look with thine e., 211:3
my e. hum, 56:5
noise of water in my e., 165:30
of people attentive unto law, 13:22
of the deaf shall be unstopped, 27:9
of the old cur, 263:13
only for what experience gives access, 553:13
porches of mine e., 194:23
seven empty e., 8:7
seven good e., 8:7
shout about my e., 619:9
small pitchers have wide e., 142:14
softest music to attending e., 175:13
sound lifts me by e., 476:23
speech delighteth the e., 32:21
split e. of groundlings, 196:21
tail and pointed e., 444:13
to hear, 34:36
trust e. less than eyes, 69:20
walls have e., 130:*n*3
with ravished e., 276:7
wode hath e., 130:14
woods have e., 130:*n*3
word of earth in e. of world, 534:21
Earth, a little e. whereon to grow, 361:3
abideth forever, 23:22
after e. stopped ears, 579:3
all Danaë to stars, 456:21
all e. forgot, 392:3
all e. o'erwhelm them, 193:25
all the corners of e., 48:21
all things in e., 44:37
all ye know on e., 416:7
alone on e. as I am now, 399:17
always in e. and air, 725:12
and every common sight, 375:3
and grave and dust, 153:2
and high heaven, 579:10
and water strive again, 299:21
Angels bending near e., 462:2
argument of e., 488:18
as showers that water the e., 17:41
astonishing thing about e., 734:10
attacking heaven and e., 762:18
axis of e. sticks out, 447:14
barren as moon, 633:13
beat e. with unfettered foot, 96:2
beauty for e. too dear, 174:23
belongs to living, 344:9
best of men that e'er wore e., 227:19
bleeding piece of e., 188:22
blessed are peacemakers on e., 163:20
bodies thrown into e., 706:3
brave of all the e., 586:12
bridal of e. and sky, 243:10
brightens when you dawn, 5:4
bringeth forth fruit, 37:21
call heaven and e. to witness, 10:10
call to e. and sea, 489:8
center of my sinful e., 222:11
cloud enveloping the e., 383:9
cold in the e., 480:1

Earth (*continued*)
too wonderful to realize you, 697:15
touch of e., 459:13
truth crushed to e., 411:10
two kinds of people on e., 562:14
unfolds both heaven and e., 172:20
upon e. there is not his like, 15:25
walk not on e. exultantly, 116:17
walk the e. unseen, 258:23
was bountiful, 606:4
weaned away from e., 697:14
welcome pommy bastard to God's e., 775:7
what e. and its interests, 477:24
what is pomp but e. and dust, 164:31
when I am laid in e., 284:18
when I laid the foundations of the e., 15:7
whether in e. or air, 192:28
which made heaven and e., 19:25
while the e. remaineth, 7:22
whole e. and all time, 373:16
whole e. our hospital, 671:7
why on e. except to grow, 466:23
winds lashing e., 634:14
with her thousand voices, 383:4
without form and void, 6:4
word of e. in ears of world, 534:21
words are daughters of e., 313:27
would know no adventurer, 572:24
wretched of e., 476:18
write sorrow on bosom of e., 171:24
you made e. as you wished, 5:6
yours is the E., 593:21
Earthen, kettle and e. pot, 31:31
Earthly ball a peopled garden, 349:11
city formed by love of self, 115:3
dignities, 225:17
fancies, 458:8
godfathers of heaven's lights, 168:15
paragon, 219:32
power then likest God's, 181:19
sum of e. bliss, 259:28
sweet fruition of e. crown, 161:21
things heavenly or things e., 272:19
this wisdom is e., 46:13
thoughts of e. men, 54:7
touch of e. years, 374:1
very honey of all e. joy, 266:16
who mind e. things, 44:33
Earthquake, dam'd by e., 526:7
gloom of e. and eclipse, 406:14
Lord was not in the e., 12:39
Earth's, ablution round e. shores, 417:12
crammed with heaven, 439:7
diurnal course, 374:1
five million years old, 763:1
foundations fled, 580:1
foundations stand, 580:8
god reached down slapped e. face, 773:16
heedless sons, 694:1
human shores, 417:12
last picture painted, 591:13
lid, 659:10
returns, 465:10

Earth's (*continued*)
right place for love, 623:8
round e. imagined corners, 230:19
round e. shore, 499:22
shadows fly, 409:8
smoothness rough, 467:8
Earth-star and snow-star, 477:4
Earthworm, feeble e., 271:7
Earthworms, land plowed by e., 444:16
Earthy and cold hand of death, 179:5
earth in e. bed, 458:24
of the earth e., 43:26
Ease after war, 153:9
an age of e., 329:10
and speed not give work beauty, 131:*n*7
at e. in my generation, 541:10
at e. in Zion, 29:36
but for another gives e., 358:2
careless e., 295:17
darbies at wrist, 487:10
death or dreamful e., 454:10
done with so much e., 274:2
equal e. unto my pain, 246:7
flies through air with e., 536:20
for e. from Heaven, 359:21
full-throated e., 415:10
gently sways at e., 624:11
gives happiness or leaves e., 303:12
good pleasure e. content, 301:16
greater e. than hogs eat, 262:*n*4
ignoble e., 93:8, 575:11
ignoble e. and peaceful sloth, 257:6
joys in another's loss of e., 358:3
lest we rest in e., 454:22
life at e. drifts, 509:18
life of e. not for man, 413:6
live at home at e., 247:11
live with e., 302:11
Nature bent to e. us, 266:*n*2
never desire worldly e., 308:18
no healthful e., 423:1
one Life the Aching, 513:10
prodigal of e., 274:4
rots in e. on Lethe wharf, 194:19
some come to take their e., 226:10
take mine e. in mine inn, 141:8
take thine e., 38:28
true e. in writing, 298:20
with e. and You beside, 512:20
Woman in hours of e., 378:14
words flow with e., 280:6
write with e. to show breeding, 353:2
Easeful Death, 415:16
Eases, time e. all things, 65:20
Easier go through eye of needle, 35:37
grass-blade's no e. than oak, 485:6
nothing e. than rest, 535:29
nothing e. than self-deceit, 79:3
played on than pipe, 197:17
swallowed than flap-dragon, 169:6
sweats e. than I, 478:9
Thirst blister e., 512:1
to be critical than correct, 435:3
to believe than deny, 532:9
to get favor from Fortune, 99:15
to get into enemy's toils, 59:18
to make war than peace, 542:3

Easier (*continued*)
to resist at beginning, 135:8
Easiest, move e. who learned to dance, 298:20
Easily, by and by e. said, 197:20
never have come back so e., 570:6
Easiness, lend a kind of e., 198:6
property of e., 199:2
Easing, they call it e. Spring, 737:4
East and West will pinch heart, 683:16
argument with e. wind, 486:2
blasted with the e. wind, 8:7
cherubims e. of the garden, 7:1
fill his belly with e. wind, 14:23
from e. to western Ind, 191:10
gorgeous e. in fee, 374:17
gorgeous E. with richest hand, 256:23
i' the E. my pleasure lies, 217:17
is East and West is San Francisco, 586:3
is East and West is West, 591:9
it is the e. Juliet the sun, 174:26
of Suez, 591:24
one flew e., 792:8
one ship e. another west, 562:13
or west Phoenix builds, 246:6
Side West Side, 585:7
somewheres e. of Suez, 591:24
star in the e., 32:23
tried to hustle the E., 591:12
west south north, 425:13
wicked Witch of the E., 568:9
wind never blow, 245:15
youth who from e. travel, 375:8
Easter, egg dear on E. Day, 793:2
Easter-day, no sun upon an E., 262:5
Eastern, blabbing e. scout, 252:22
dew of yon high e. hill, 192:30
dusk on e. horizon, 690:18
foul guilt of E. kings, 302:*n*6
no Soviet domination of E. Europe, 733:9
not by e. windows only, 483:3
pulling blanket off e. sky, 786:22
specter haunting e. Europe, 768:7
wipe out E. instincts, 591:1
Eastward, a garden e. in Eden, 6:12
I go only by force, 479:5
to the sea, 591:22
Easy, abstinence e. to me, 315:11
all zeal Mr. E., 406:1
as e. to marry rich woman, 463:15
as grass grows on weirs, 594:18
bid me take love e., 594:17
criticism e. art difficult, 295:22
decent e. men, 340:10
evil is e., 271:5
false man does e., 214:17
give throne would be e., 79:11
how e. bush supposed a bear, 174:1
if to do as e. as to know, 179:27
it's not e. bein' green, 775:9
jolly and e. in minds, 463:8
leap to pluck bright honor, 177:9
live quiet die, 379:15
my yoke is e., 34:38
nothing so e. but becomes difficult, 86:2

Easy (*continued*)

poetry e. to write, 523:2
Rabelais' e. chair, 303:24
road to Hades e. to travel, 82:8
smooth e. inoffensive down to Hell, 82:n6
so e. and so plain a stop, 183:9
summertime and livin' e., 695:8
there life is supremely e., 53:8
to blow and swallow not e., 84:2
to go down into Hell, 94:6
words are e. like the wind, 233:12
writing's curst hard reading, 353:2
young and e., 737:14

Eat bread in sweat of thy face, 6:26

bread without scarceness, 10:16
cake and have it, 142:29
Cannibals that each other e., 205:27
cannot e. but little meat, 144:11
cones under his pines, 622:21
dare to e. a peach, 667:19
did e. and were filled, 35:17
dogs shall e. Jezebel, 12:42
don't e. your heart, 58:10
drink be merry, 24:17, 38:28
drink for tomorrow we die, 26:21
dust shalt thou e., 6:23
dusty bread, 696:2
eat me soul, 283:8
enough to e. and wear, 580:11
fine women e. crazy salad, 597:1
frogs e. butterflies, 639:2
great ones e. up little ones, 219:21
he hath not e. paper, 168:29
his pleasant fruits, 25:13
I earn that I e., 191:9
I e. and e. I swear, 185:26
I e. the air, 197:6
I e. what I see, 517:18
I'll e. my head, 469:9
in orchard enough to e., 297:24
in the evening, 357:8
it in haste, 8:38
let them e. cake, 319:25
like wolves fight like devils, 185:13
men like air, 764:13
Nebuchadnezzar did e. grass, 29:14
neither e. it nor make flannel, 657:18
never e. at place called Mom's, 726:6
nevermore to e. again, 617:6
no beans, 234:15
no fat, 788:7
no onions nor garlic, 173:28
not to dullness, 311:2
not to e. not for love, 430:14
of fish that fed of worm, 198:10
of the habitation, 180:2
of the tree I did e., 6:22
peck of salt with him, 776:3
people who e. the earth, 716:5
plant vineyards and e. the fruit, 28:12
poor when anything to e., 77:n3
so I did sit and e., 244:2
some hae meat canna e., 363:16
some s. I will not e., 688:18
strive mightily e. as friends, 167:20

Eat (*continued*)

take e. this is my body, 36:28, 43:11
tell me what you e., 354:14
that shall ye e., 9:21
that they may live, 70:23
the fat of the land, 8:14
their flesh shall ye not e., 9:22
they shall e. the flesh, 8:37
thou shalt not e. of it, 6:14
to e. thy heart, 154:6
to e. with apple tart, 561:11
to live and live to eat, 70:n8
to live not live to eat, 269:20, 309:6
up himself, 200:10
wad e. that want it, 363:16
we hae meat we can e., 363:16
will not e. with you, 180:2
worm that e. of a king, 198:10

Eaten a sour grape, 28:35

crust e. in peace, 59:1
God made and e., 465:7
have we e. on insane root, 212:20
me out of house and home, 183:30
thee for a word, 169:6
they'd e. every one, 519:7
to death with rust, 183:23
worms have e. them, 192:2
your bread and salt, 590:17

Eater, great e. of beef, 201:21

out of the e. came meat, 11:12

Eateth grass as an ox, 15:20

'Eathen, pore benighted 'e., 591:19

Eating air on promise of supply, 183:25

appetite comes with e., 139:9
appetite makes e. delight, 262:8
bitter bread of banishment, 171:20
bread and honey, 790:1
cares, 251:19
Christmas pie, 788:11
curds and whey, 791:8
drinking and breeding, 489:9
drinking dung death, 670:21
poetry, 767:5
produce of the land, 52:19
proof of pudding in e., 150:12
Son of man came e., 34:37
whether breathing is e., 73:24
wise men know art of e., 354:13
worn out with e. time, 273:21

Eats, believes he e. God, 321:7

proud e. up himself, 200:16
Revolution e. own children, 473:10
seeking the food he e., 190:20
she-wolf's young, 382:3
soles offen shoes, 698:5
thing that e. heart, 716:17
whatever Miss T. e., 617:5

Eau verte pénétra ma coque de sapin, 565:n7

Eave-drops, whether e. fall heard in trances, 382:17

Eaves, brawling of sparrow in e., 594:23

gilded e., 456:15

Ebb and flow by the moon, 211:13

ceaseless e. and flow, 564:20
deaths at e. tide, 564:20
ne'er e. to humble love, 207:15

Ebb (*continued*)

ne'er feels retiring e., 207:15
where beauty has no e., 595:4

Eboli, Christ stopped at E., 709:3

Ebon throne in rayless majesty, 296:7

Ecbatana, here in mid-plain of E., 74:9

Ecce homo, 40:n5

Eccentric propositions of its fate, 639:19

Eccentricities of genius, 468:29

Ecclesiarum, disputandi pruritus e. scabies, 227:n5

Ecclesiastic, pulpit drum e., 262:17

tyranny's worst, 285:18

Ecclesiastical influence increased number of wars, 536:19

Échasses, sur des é. marcher de nos jambes, 147:n5

Echo and light unto eternity, 408:15

applaud thee to the very e., 216:11
began to undermine, 636:11
catch e. of infinite, 542:10
children's lips e., 399:24
distant footsteps e., 441:11
footfalls e. in memory, 670:13
my speech to a T, 140:n2
ne'er sink while e. left, 404:4
of your mournful song, 446:26
perfumes colors sounds e., 494:3
sound an e. to sense, 298:20
sounds that e. still, 454:12
sublimity the e. of noble mind, 106:5
sweet E. sweetest nymph, 252:26
where is E., 509:22
woods answer and E. ring, 154:12

Echoes, answer e., 456:11

of that voice, 383:10
wild e. flying, 456:11

Eclipse, built in the e., 253:22

earthquake and e., 406:14
first the rest nowhere, 324:8
irrecoverably dark total e., 261:7
moon hath her e. endured, 221:23
sun in dim e., 256:16

Eclipsed gaiety of nations, 314:22

Eclipses, clouds and e. stain, 220:21

of moon and other experiments, 134:12

Ecology, sensitive science of e., 748:13

Economic, democracy appropriate for e. surplus, 728:16

distress teach men, 615:18
equality for women, 754:2
figures referring to e. events, 645:13
freedom, 631:14
freedom means to political freedom, 731:11
politics e. development culture, 749:9
position, 581:17
principle of e. production, 635:9
pulse of modern life e., 635:9
pyramid, 648:14
royalists, 649:2
slavery nobody's business, 649:2
strongest of e. motives, 574:5
tyranny above, 661:2
vital e. interests, 727:15

Elephants endorsed with towers, 260:30
  kings ride e. over mountains, 731:5
  place e. for want of towns, 107:*n*1
  when e. fight grass suffers, 784:21
  women and e., 610:15
Elephone tried to use telephone, 560:10
Elevate condition of men, 449:8
  life by conscious endeavor, 478:16
Elevated, joy of e. thoughts, 373:5
Elevation and beauty, 501:4
  drink not to e., 311:2
  removal of hindrances to her e., 410:18
Eleven, possession e. points, 291:19
Elfin from green grass, 451:10
Elfland, horns of E., 456:12
Elginbrodde, here lie I Martin E., 504:14
Elgin's, stands in E. place, 461:1
Eli Eli lama sabachthani, 37:12
Elijah, mantle of E., 13:6
  the prophet, 30:11
  went up by a whirlwind, 13:4
Eliminated impossible, 577:13
Eliot, meet Mr. E., 670:6
Elisha took up mantle of Elijah, 13:6
Elite had capacity to bring tears, 764:5
  minority, 653:6
  power e. decide national events, 739:18
Elixir, bright e. peerless I had drunk, 417:1
Eliza made desperate retreat, 463:1
Elizabeth, from Jane to E., 386:26
  great E., 454:12
  Servant to Queen E., 155:2
Elizabeth-Jane Farfrae not told of my death, 539:18
Ell, give an inch take an e., 142:28
Ellen, wed fair E., 378:9
Elliptical billiard balls, 531:5
  Caribbean borne like e. basin, 763:11
Elm, expect pears from an e., 100:*n*5
  old as yonder e., 647:20
  round e. tree bole, 465:3
  tell me tell me e., 647:20
Elms, desire under the e., 674:1
  immemorial e., 456:22
Elocution, wherefore waste e., 531:19
Elongated-yellow-fruit school of writing, 702:16
Eloquence, army not halted by e., 474:15
  fill winepress of e., 114:11
  frothy e., 566:4
  gods do not give all men e., 53:14
  mother of arts and e., 260:33
  of Mr. Webster, 698:12
  silence more e., 462:4
  take e. wring neck, 554:5
  talking and e. not same, 233:8
  thou has inspired with, 121:5
  true e. takes no heed of e., 270:15
Éloquence, prends l'é. tords-lui son cou, 554:*n*6
Eloquent but 'tis not true, 498:5

Eloquent (*continued*)
  digressions, 505:20
  epitaph for country, 588:7
  feeling and imagination make us e., 105:13
  just and mighty Death, 153:1
  pure and e. blood, 230:16
  what an e. manikin, 91:5
Else, leave all e. to the gods, 95:23
Elusive, The Vague and E., 57:5
Elves, make my small e. coats, 173:10
  whose little eyes glow, 241:12
Elysian, send you to E. plain, 53:8
Elysium as far as nearest Room, 514:17
  daughter of E., 364:13
  palpable E., 659:17
  what E. known, 416:12
Emanation, my e. far within, 358:16
Emancipates, everything that e. spirit, 351:12
Emancipating all nations, 347:2
Emancipation, African fight for e., 681:4
  of individual, 471:26
  of slavish part of mankind, 337:12
  of woman, 699:*n*8
Embalmed and treasured up to life, 254:24
  darkness, 415:14
Embalms, precedent e. principle, 435:2
Embark, firs cloaked as if to e., 557:15
Embarras des richesses, 306:*n*13
Embarrassment of riches, 306:28
  to my e. born in bed with lady, 631:13
Embassies, saris go by me from e., 735:22
Embattled armies clad in iron, 261:10
  farmers stood, 429:22
Embellish adventures, 341:14
Embellished, no part Nature has not e., 111:31
Ember, each separate dying e., 452:14
Embers, glowing e. through the room, 252:5
  O joy that in our e., 375:10
  of cities, 765:17
Emblem, shears and pastepot e., 609:11
Emblems of untimely graves, 335:6
  those things they were e. of, 599:21
Embodiment of everything excellent, 530:6
Embody the Law, 530:6
Emboldens, nothing e. sin as mercy, 212:3
Embosomed in the deep, 328:12
Embrace, arms take your last e., 176:18
  as to e. me she inclined, 255:17
  endure then pity then e., 301:14
  is death, 692:4
  my dead mother's ghost, 53:18
  none do there e., 268:16
  Pole as Frenchman, 146:23
  possibilities I didn't e., 549:12
  principles or mistresses, 327:13
  rest that knows no care, 90:5

Embrace (*continued*)
  simplicity, 57:6
  time to e., 23:32
Embraced, ghost e. fled, 93:36
  summer dawn, 566:1
Embraces, break e., 720:5
  sorcery of hot e., 679:19
  your e. give life, 4:8
Embraves this morn, 264:19
Embroidered, heavens' e. cloths, 595:8
  loosened the e. girdle, 52:3
  speech like e. tapestries, 62:29
Embroideries, coat covered with e., 596:4
Embroil earth about fancied line, 280:17
Embryo, yesterday e. tomorrow ashes, 111:12
Emerald, cause or men of E. Isle, 354:1
  green as e., 381:3
Emeralds, road to the City of E., 568:10
Emergencies, government in e., 450:7
  great e. show resources, 545:6
  presence of mind in e., 485:24
Emerges ahead of accomplishments, 710:9
  path e. then closes, 602:10
  with verb in mouth, 527:4
Emetic, Ulysses somewhat e., 632:6
Emily set doors ajar and slam them, 626:10
Eminence, raised to that bad e., 256:23
Eminent, censure is tax for being e., 289:1
Eminently noble, 498:22
  plain and direct, 498:22
Emissions, until all evil e. had fled, 753:1
Emits a brighter ray, 328:5
Emmanuel, call his name E., 32:22
  O come O come E., 482:11
Emmet, Robert E. and Wolfe Tone, 596:1
Emotion, disembodied e. a nonentity, 546:5
  expressing e. in art, 672:11
  formula of that particular e., 672:11
  intellect is to e. as clothes, 585:2
  laughter has no greater foe than e., 577:1
  more than usual e., 384:14
  motion fact made e., 701:20
  no transforming without e., 629:4
  poetry escape from e., 672:10
  poetry express every e., 721:10
  recollected in tranquillity, 373:17
  source of becoming-conscious, 629:4
  undisciplined squads of e., 671:9
  weave e. thought sound, 423:19
Emotional, destitute of e. warmth, 546:4
  orgies, 587:15
  subtlety and toughness, 722:15
Emotions, expression of e., 123:2
  foreign to art, 524:1
  from A to B, 687:13

Emotions (*continued*)
   metaphysical brothel for e., 716:12
   no longer diverted by e., 604:1
   of the Spaniards, 419:7
   those who have e., 672:10
Empêchent, ailes de géant l'e., 494:*n*2
Emperor and clown, 415:17
   big stealin' makes you e., 673:15
   hasn't anything on, 437:9
   in mine own house, 152:*n*2
   keep drowsy E. awake, 597:10
   of ice-cream, 638:22
   pope and e., 427:15
   power in single e., 338:16
   subject to no one but God, 122:5
   you are E. yet you weep, 281:7
Emperor's, at midnight on E. pave-
      ment, 598:12
   drunken soldiery abed, 598:11
   new clothes, 437:8
   she might lie by e. side, 207:20
Emperors, pomp of e. ridiculous,
      431:1
   purple of e., 592:10
   souls of e. and cobblers, 146:4
Emphatic facts of history, 431:17
Empire, British E. and United States,
      620:11
   course of e., 296:27
   England an e., 421:15
   entrusted with e., 57:3
   Evil E., 773:10
   for raising customers, 326:7
   great e. and little minds, 331:24
   Holy Roman E., 306:4
   how is the E., 590:13
   internal domestic e., 696:7
   is a prison, 405:4
   is e. unpossessed, 166:10
   last thousand years, 620:8
   liquidation of British E., 621:13
   loungers of E. drained, 577:12
   neither holy nor e., 306:4
   power in trust, 274:8
   preserve unity of e., 331:22
   rod of e., 322:11
   sun never sets on e., 364:*n*5
   this is alone Life Joy E. Victory,
      407:6
   thy dread e. Chaos, 304:2
   vast e. of human society, 373:16
   westward the course of e., 296:27
   wide arch of ranged e. fall, 216:25
   wilderness into e., 331:25
Empire's lamentation, 458:5
Empires, buries e. in common grave,
      340:7
   day of E. come, 528:21
   dyspepsy ruin of e., 397:17
   game was e., 404:3
   hatching vain e., 257:8
   vaster than e. and more slow,
      268:14
Emploi, le physique d'un e., 560:*n*1
Employ, how fit to e., 466:17
   means requisite to ends, 355:6
Employed, age e. in edging steel,
      353:9
   men e. best contented, 311:5

Employee rise to level of incompe-
      tence, 747:5
Employees required to state beliefs,
      703:15
Employment, rising prices full e.,
      635:5
Emptied some dull opiate, 415:9
Emptier ever dancing in air, 172:9
Emptiness, dull privations and lean e.,
      229:9
   my e. among stars, 758:11
   of ages in face, 563:6
   produced the universe, 86:15
Emptor, caveat e., 118:21
Empty, a little louder but as e., 301:15
   and aching and I don't know why,
      772:10
   bag cannot stand, 309:26
   beat an e. barrel, 637:8
   buckets into e. wells, 335:1
   buckets into wells, 380:7
   crowns are e. things, 285:19
   fame nothing but e. name, 333:16
   go not e. unto thy mother-in-law,
      11:25
   her e. room is cold, 86:18
   idle singer of e. day, 523:6
   is the chair e., 166:10
   life an e. dream, 440:15
   no life moves in e. passageways,
      65:16
   no patriot on e. stomach, 371:*n*2
   rich sent e. away, 37:43
   room my heart keeps e., 242:2
   seek e. world again, 480:2
   seven e. ears, 8:7
   solid pudding e. praise, 303:25
   tigers or roaring sea, 176:13
   to be e. is to be full, 57:8
   turn down e. Glass, 446:9
   vessel greatest sound, 185:24
   words are e. thanks, 291:20
Empty-vaulted night, 252:27
Emulation, propensity for e., 574:5
   shouting their e., 218:24
Enable socialist culture to thrive,
      686:16
Enacted, history unwritten yet to be
      e., 491:13
Enacting laws like drinking songs,
      72:13
Enactments, wicked cruel e., 424:5
Enameled, makes music with e. stones,
      168:3
   snake throws e. skin, 173:9
Enameling, hammered gold and gold
      e., 597:10
Enamored of an ass, 173:24
Encamp, though an host should e.,
      16:22
Enchafed flood, 206:3
Enchains us to permitted ill, 407:9
Enchant, I will e. thine ear, 165:8
   Unity doth e. me, 151:25
   what deceives may be said to e.,
      75:10
Enchanted, enter e. woods, 509:9
   holy and e., 382:20
   life's e. cup, 399:19
   Medea gathered e. herbs, 182:7

Enchanted (*continued*)
   mind is e. thing, 665:2
   some e. evening, 692:12
Enchanter, ghosts from e. fleeing,
      407:13
Enchanting, mind is e. thing, 665:2
Enchantment, distance lends e., 388:22
Enchantments, last e. of Middle Age,
      499:10
Enchants my sense, 200:17
Enclose, cherries fairly do e., 226:19
Enclosed, forbear to dig dust e. here,
      226:11
Encloseth, thy breast e. my heart,
      165:23
Enclosing, mistake of e. envelope,
      657:6
Encompass, poetic fields e. me, 291:29
   unencompassable, 479:13
Encompassed by horrors, 486:27
Encompasseth, my ring e. thy finger,
      165:23
Encounter darkness as a bride, 204:12
   Truth in free and open e., 255:4
Encountering Fly this January Day,
      514:10
Encourage, animate and e., 336:13
   to e. the others, 306:9
Encouraged, examination of govern-
      ment e., 385:13
   he ought to be e., 317:*n*4
Encouragement for cultivation of her
      powers, 410:18
Encourager, pour e. les autres, 306:*n*5
Encouraging clever pupil, 312:10
Encroach, habit will e., 380:13
Encroaching, white people always e.,
      370:3
Encroachments, gradual and silent e.,
      352:2
Encumbers him with help, 315:17
Encumbrance, periodization of history
      e., 704:2
Encyclopedia of Error, 521:4
End a contest quicker, 352:24
   accept e. of love or season, 622:18
   apathetic e., 454:21
   appointment at e. of world, 656:8
   at his e. shall be a fool, 28:31
   at the e. take your fill, 54:28
   at their wit's e., 19:11
   attempt the e., 241:16
   beauty sufficient e., 596:22
   began to draw to our e., 30:25
   begin with certainties e. in doubts,
      158:4
   beginning and the e., 48:4
   beginning of the e., 354:5
   being's e. and aim, 301:16
   better is the e. of a thing, 24:9
   blessed the latter e. of Job, 15:28
   born to disastrous e., 154:6
   break eggs at convenient e., 289:9
   by opposing e. them, 196:10
   by sleep we e. heartache, 196:10
   chapters of lives come to natural e.,
      557:19
   commit adultery at one e., 667:4
   crowns all, 201:12
   crowns the work, 119:3

End (continued)

crowns us not the fight, 241:2
death a necessary e., 188:11
decline to accept e. of man, 696:21
despondency and madness, 374:9
dine at journey's e., 596:12
dispatch in putting e. to it, 79:13
easier to resist at beginning than e.,
    135:8
even unto e. of world, 37:16
everything has e., 784:20
experience itself the e., 538:8
fairest things fleetest e., 581:1
go till the e., 518:10
go with me to my e., 225:6
God will put an e. to these, 93:16
going forth is from the e. of the
    heaven, 16:10
good beginning good e., 141:21
good of subjects e. of kings, 285:19
great e. of learning, 79:29
guide original and e., 115:13
hair to stand an e., 194:17
heartache, 196:10
here at life's e., 599:10
hope to the e., 46:19
if e. brings me out, 451:4
in e. despondency and madness,
    742:16
in my beginning is my e., 670:20
in my e. my beginning, 147:13,
    671:11
in one purpose, 184:25
in the e. truth will conquer, 127:20
is bitter as wormwood, 20:26
is not yet, 36:7
is the renown, 203:17
journey's e., 208:14
journeys e. in lovers meeting, 202:1
justifying means by the e., 113:16
keep e. in view, 105:21
keeps e. from being hard, 624:8
knocks you with butt e., 330:16
last e. be like his, 10:5
latter e. of a fray, 178:27
laws e. tyranny begins, 313:2
let e. try the man, 183:31
let the e. be legitimate, 355:12
liberty as e. and means, 568:14
long weary day have e., 154:13
losses restored and sorrows e.,
    220:19
love hath an e., 534:3
made finer e. and went away,
    184:30
make me to know mine e., 17:7
makes a swanlike e., 181:2
mankind must put e. to war, 741:10
minutes hasten to their e., 220:26
must justify the means, 287:17
my wrath did e., 358:12
New York the e. of the world,
    738:8
no e. in wandering mazes, 257:12
no e. of it the voiceless wailing,
    671:14
no e. to withering, 671:14
no prospect of an e., 327:9
not e. to writing about Holocaust,
    764:7

End (continued)

not forsake me in my e., 278:25
of every man's desire, 534:11
of exploring to arrive, 672:6
of fight tombstone white, 591:12
of journey too, 585:8
of life cancels bands, 178:14
of life is action, 505:16
of making many books there is no
    e., 24:30, 644:7
of perfect day, 585:8
of that man is peace, 17:3
of the beginning, 621:12
of the tunnel, 741:16
of the unending, 672:2
of the world, 37:16
of this day's business, 189:24
one must consider the e., 268:2
only when life comes to e., 63:14
pleasure the beginning and e., 81:19
pursue the unknown e., 543:3
quiet-colored e. of evening, 465:9
remember the e., 31:18
right true e. of love, 230:9
sans E., 445:16
served no private e., 300:24
sleep itself must e., 249:7
snow swept world e. to e., 680:2
some say world e. in fire, 623:14
something ere the e., 455:5
stay a while e. the sooner, 158:22
stick it out to e., 606:3
their words to the e. of the world,
    16:10
there's an e. of May, 579:17
there's an e. on 't, 316:21
this is not the e., 621:12
Time will one day e. it, 201:12
to all an e., 594:11
to beginnings of wars, 650:6
to make the e. most sweet, 170:28
to pause to make e., 455:2
to war, 650:6
true beginning of our e., 174:4
true lover therefore had good e.,
    133:12
truth to the e. of reckoning, 205:3
up somewhere else, 747:6
war put e. to mankind, 741:10
war that will e. war, 601:11
we shall go on to e., 620:7
when e. of world comes, 626:4
where e. knows God, 708:10
where Sky touches Earth is E.,
    784:18
where you begun, 331:3
whole has beginning middle and e.,
    78:32
whose e. is destruction, 44:33
world without e., 48:22, 335:24
End-all, be-all and e., 213:5
Endanger, power to e. public liberty,
    337:16
Endearing elegance of female friend-
    ship, 314:14
    with e. wile, 329:16
    young charms, 391:13
Endearment, each fond e. tries, 329:14

Endeavor, achievement death of e.,
    544:12
    by no e. can magnet, 529:20
    disinterested e. to learn, 499:9
    elevate life by conscious e., 478:16
    in continual motion, 184:23
    it were a vain e., 383:7
Endeavors to live life imagined,
    478:36
Ended, God be praised Georges e.,
    627:n5
    his cares now all e., 184:14
    our revels now are e., 224:21
    so e. Sicilian expedition, 72:12
    with his body changed to light,
    787:18
Endin, now sees de e., 696:12
Ending, all lovely things have e., 675:2
    bad beginning makes bad e., 69:7
    bread sauce of happy e., 548:19
    hard beginning good e., 141:4
    is despair, 224:29
    O bitter e., 647:22
    of interminable night, 672:2
Endings, beginnings and e. untidy,
    603:23
    lie has seven e., 784:24
Endless, humility is e., 671:1
    in e. error hurled, 301:13
    my days of e. doubt, 152:8
    night, 241:19, 323:4
    olives of e. age, 221:23
    perpetual posterity, 389:16
    pure and e. light, 270:7
    regret or happiness, 557:17
    road you tread, 579:14
    summer days, 511:17
    time an e. song, 595:4
    whole vocation e. imitation, 375:9
Endlessly, cradle e. rocking, 490:8
Endorsed, elephants e. with towers,
    260:30
Endow college or cat, 300:22
    with all my goods I thee e., 50:13
Endowed by ruined millionaire, 671:7
    by their creator, 343:2
Ends, all well that e. well, 141:20
    all's well that e. well, 203:17
    candle burns at both e., 684:2
    come from e. of earth, 591:9
    consult our private e., 266:n2
    delays have dangerous e., 163:14
    dog to gain private e., 328:27
    filled with e. of worms, 685:3
    formula for making e. meet, 646:4
    game that never e., 695:20
    his circuit unto the e. of it, 16:10
    Law e. Tyranny begins, 277:9
    man's glory most begins and e.,
    599:16
    means requisite to e., 355:6
    needless Alexandrine e. song,
    298:19
    of Being and ideal Grace, 438:23
    of world come, 538:5
    one e. other begins, 452:10
    smile upon fingers' e., 184:30
    strange eventful history, 191:3
    thing that e. other deeds, 218:10
    thou aimest at, 225:21

Enfranchisement, liberty freedom e., 188:17

Engaged in great civil war, 450:2

Engagement, get loose from honorable e., 330:24
  positive e. to marry, 426:7

Engenders, every cloud e. not storm, 165:1
  not white hair that e. wisdom, 81:14
  shudder in loins e., 598:1
  so much more, 696:16

Engine, clock not steam-e., 693:4
  great e. never sleeps, 463:16
  human e. waits, 669:1
  power alone, 604:10
  steam e. in trousers, 380:11
  two-handed e. at door, 254:3
  which drives Enterprise, 652:10
  wit's an unruly e., 243:2

Engineer, give me the e., 484:8
  hoist with own petar, 198:8
  sometimes striking the e., 243:2
  story of brave e., 610:n2

Engineers of soul, 605:14

Enginer hoist with own petar, 198:8

Engines, feeble e. of despotism, 345:3
  O you mortal e., 207:8

England, always be an E., 736:11
  an empire, 421:15
  and Saint George, 185:5
  at this door E. stands sentry, 539:3
  awake, 359:24
  be E. what she will, 333:19
  bound with triumphant sea, 171:10
  breeds valiant creatures, 185:12
  cliffs of E. stand, 499:19
  Common Law of E., 678:21
  corner of field forever E., 663:3
  dress in E., 570:17
  expects, 360:17
  from old E. they set sail, 793:18
  further off from E., 518:7
  gentlemen of E., 247:11
  Greece Italy and E. did adorn, 275:25
  has no name for prairies, 411:9
  hath given warning, 340:21
  hath need of thee, 374:19
  high road to E., 315:25
  history is now and E., 672:5
  I am in E. everywhere, 248:17
  if E. to itself true, 170:24
  in E. I've mate, 472:11
  in E. now, 465:3
  Ireland gives E. generals, 509:14
  keep my bones, 170:16
  know Kings of E., 529:12
  knuckle-end of E., 380:1
  let not E. forget precedence, 254:18
  light candle in E., 138:18
  many a peer of E. brews, 579:15
  mariners of E., 388:26
  martial airs of E., 394:19
  men of E. wherefore plow, 407:19
  meteor flag of E., 389:2
  middle class in E., 501:2
  middle class safety of E., 464:2
  model to inward greatness, 184:28
  navy of E., 325:20

England (*continued*)
  neck wrung like chicken, 621:10
  never at foot of conqueror, 170:23
  nor E. did I know, 374:6
  of a king of E. too, 144:15
  oh to be in E., 465:3
  old E. to adorn, 593:17
  or E. breed again, 161:10
  paradise of women, 154:18
  poorest he in E., 239:16
  rightwise king of E., 133:4
  roast beef of E., 311:12
  roast beef of old E., 311:n4
  sea once made E. secure, 626:23
  shower of curates on E., 476:14
  slaves cannot breathe in E., 334:27
  St. George for E., 619:6
  stately homes of E., 410:10, 650:17
  such night in E., 425:4
  there I find flag of E., 370:16
  think about defense of E., 601:18
  this realm this E., 171:9
  what is left of E., 427:n1
  who dies if E. live, 593:25
  who only E. know, 592:5
  whoever wakes in E., 465:3
  wins last battle, 621:11
  with all thy faults, 333:n6
  wont to conquer others, 171:11
  world where E. dead, 626:24
  youth of E. are on fire, 184:27

England's green and pleasant land, 359:17
  mountains green, 359:17
  old E. winding sheet, 359:15
  pleasant pastures, 359:17
  song forever, 586:14
  stay no more on E. shore, 793:20

English, among E. Poets after death, 418:8
  anyone been to E. public school, 712:2
  attain E. style, 314:17
  biographies disease of E. literature, 484:4
  can't think of E., 518:20
  Chaucer well of E., 153:19
  children spoke bad E., 587:4
  civilization humanizing, 501:1
  close wall with E. dead, 185:3
  dictionary best reading, 610:10
  father of E. criticism, 314:19
  for suppressing other, 499:6
  God had never spoken anything but E., 622:15
  Good Soldier finest French novel in E., 617:8
  his E. sweete upon his tonge, 129:18
  in an E. lane, 465:11
  in favor of boys learning E., 619:17
  king's E., 182:23
  kissed by E. dead, 687:4
  language of E. poet, 672:21
  most beautiful words in E. language, 549:17
  mother made moan, 485:22
  never abolish anything, 585:4
  not accessible even to Englishmen, 571:18
  not Turkish court, 184:15

English (*continued*)
  one pair of E. legs, 185:10
  pint of E. ale, 619:6
  principle of E. constitution, 325:22
  strung on E. thread, 486:3
  take their pleasures sadly, 157:17
  tongue I love, 763:8
  trick of our E. nation, 183:22
  up with which not put, 622:13
  we E. nation of brutes, 573:n2
  white as angel E. child, 356:8
  winter ending in July, 403:16

Englishman beat three Frenchmen, 293:7
  blood of an E., 792:19
  content to say nothing, 317:16
  either for E. or Jew, 360:4
  every E. paid his way, 326:n1
  hangdog look of E. about to talk French, 645:16
  he is an E., 529:9
  if I were American as I am E., 313:6
  impossible for E. to open mouth, 571:18
  last great E., 458:6
  prejudices of true E., 293:7
  rights of E., 345:13
  stirred heart of E., 606:2
  thinks moral when uncomfortable, 571:5
  true-born E., 171:4
  vain ill-natured E., 285:15

Englishman's, part of every E. education, 501:19
  thoughts, 499:8

Englishmen, mad dogs and E., 700:15
  O when shall E., 161:10
  reveal first to His E., 255:1

English-speaking, clearer understanding of E. audiences, 586:20
  union of E. peoples, 564:17

Engraven, deep on his front e., 257:7

Enhance, rubs e. value of favors, 328:19

Enigma, riddle in mystery inside e., 620:3

Enisled, in sea of life e., 498:3

Enjoy both operations at once, 667:4
  crown that seldom kings e., 164:19
  delight with liberty, 154:7
  don't have to go e. it, 594:10
  get what want and e. it, 594:2
  grudge what they cannot e., 59:5
  her while she's kind, 275:2
  honey-heavy dew of slumber, 188:6
  ice cream while it's on plate, 697:16
  indifferent and cannot e. it, 315:17
  interval, 588:14
  most e. contented least, 220:16
  neither e. nor suffer, 575:12
  other people's sufferin', 603:11
  private men e., 185:18
  prize not whiles we e. it, 187:2
  resources within thy reach, 64:3
  things we ought, 78:8

Enjoyed, hours I once e., 333:21
  in vision beatific, 256:20
  much endured little e., 314:11
  no sooner but despised, 222:7

Enjoyed *(continued)*
supinely e. gifts of founder, 340:10
the lady, 357:18
to have e. sun, 498:1
Enjoyment, communal e. of fruits of
earth, 366:8
human benefit and e., 331:20
intellectual e., 581:17
life not from e. to e., 316:30
of life and liberty, 327:1
of riches parade of riches, 326:4
variety mother of E., 434:16
Enjoyments, occasional e. lighting
pain, 584:11
seasoning of all e., 269:18
Enjoys, beauty ne'er e., 302:15
Enlaced are fallen among grass,
736:17
Enlarge, circle never ceaseth to e.,
163:8
my life, 313:20
Enlarges, develops and e. organ,
347:13
Enlighten people generally, 344:19
Enlightened enough to exercise control, 344:22
his eyes were e., 11:35
who knows himself is e., 57:9
Enlist, we will all e. again, 758:9
Enlisted, is there view for e. men,
749:5
En-Masse, utter word E., 488:13
Enmity between thee and the woman,
6:24
three classes of friendship and e.,
110:13
Enna, not that fair field of E., 258:10
Ennoble, we must e. our works,
124:16
Ennobled by own exertions, 365:29
Ennui, celestial e. of apartments,
639:22
Enoch walked with God, 7:12
Enormous, guilt is e., 763:13
knowledge e., 417:1
writing takes e. concentration,
751:10
Enough as good as feast, 142:33
damned that cries Hold e., 216:22
for all, 633:8
for my life, 31:10
if something, 377:6
know what is more than e., 357:10
love is e., 523:8
never know what is e., 357:10
not e. to fight, 642:8
not e. to help feeble up, 211:22
of children's gratitude, 598:15
or too much, 357:14
the living are not e., 706:1
time e. for that, 223:17
'tis e. 'twill serve, 175:27
to have died once e., 94:22
why aren't the books e., 773:20
word to wise e., 151:9
Enrage those paying your annuities,
307:1
Enrich yourselves, 398:12
Enriched, pension never e. young man,
244:29

Enriches, that which not e. him,
206:30
Enrichissez-vous, 398:*n*5
Ensanguined hearts, 335:6
Ensign, beauty's e. yet is crimson,
176:17
full high advanced, 256:12
tear tattered e., 447:3
Enskyed, thing e. and sainted, 203:25
Enslave, man alone e. man, 727:14
people impossible to e., 390:4
we fight not to e., 341:3
Enslaved, baptism e. me, 565:22
destiny alike for free and e., 63:21
London in ruins rather than e.,
620:9
tamely and abjectly e., 620:9
Enslavement and existential death,
758:7
certainty of worse, 733:2
faced e. if captured, 522:13
Ensnare, man's imperial race e.,
299:12
Ensured release, 580:8
Entails, when truth e. ruin, 67:13
Entangling alliances, 344:9
what so e. as death, 231:12
Enter, all hope abandon who e. here,
125:6
enchanted woods, 509:9
into his gates with thanksgiving,
18:22
into joy, 36:14
into kingdom of heaven, 34:13
Lord Christ e. in, 567:23
nation which keepeth truth may e.,
26:28
not into temptation, 36:31
storm rain may e., 312:19
they that e. must go on knees,
237:18
to grow in wisdom, 522:12
ye shall not e. into heaven, 35:31
Entered, I have e. on enterprise,
319:21
into springs of sea, 15:10
into unadvisedly, 50:1
Entergraft our hands, 229:14
Enterprise for glory of Christian,
134:10
heroic e. gone, 332:13
is sick, 200:8
life-blood of our e., 178:18
more e. in walking naked, 596:4
private e. not yet tried, 649:12
Profit engine of E., 652:10
set habits of age, 686:7
voyages of starship E., 749:7
want of e. and faith, 478:29
without precedent, 319:21
Enterprises, in mighty e. determination
enough, 100:30
of great pith, 196:10
that require new clothes, 478:6
Enters, idly bent on him that e. next,
172:13
nought e. there, 201:17
war seldom e. but where wealth allures, 275:18
Entertain all comers, 51:22

Entertain *(continued)*
lag-end of my life, 178:29
strangers, 45:42
this starry stranger, 264:18
Entertained angels unawares, 45:42
spirit once e. you, 725:2
Entertainer who understood his time,
645:5
Entertaining, more e. than half the
novels, 626:21
Entertainment, analysis of character
highest e., 715:5
Entertains harmless day, 227:7
Enthroned, dark Care sits e., 96:13
mercy e. in hearts of kings, 181:19
Enthusiasm, faith an excitement and
e., 436:26
nothing great without e., 432:10
whatever poet writes with e., 70:26
Enthusiasts, how to deal with e.,
425:8
Entice, if sinners e. thee, 20:18
Entière, Vénus toute e., 281:*n*5
Entire, that ye may be perfect and e.,
46:4
Entities not multiplied unnecessarily,
127:7
Entitled, more no man e. to, 576:2
Entity and quiddity, 263:4
Entrails, in our own proper e., 189:25
webs from e. spin, 148:*n*4
Entrance, all men have one e. into life,
30:29
beware e. to quarrel, 193:30
fatal e. of Duncan, 212:29
give God e. ticket, 495:8
Entrances, exits and their e., 191:3
Entrap, seeming truth to e. wisest,
181:6
Entrapped, love of you e. me, 4:7
Entreats, Hesperus e. thy light, 231:21
Entrepreneur, what e. contributes,
653:23
Entrepreneurial profit, 653:23
Entreprise, c'est une épineuse e.,
145:*n*16
Entrusted, man to whom populace is
e., 51:5
with great concerns, 61:32
Entrusts life to one hole only, 83:13
Entwine itself verdantly, 391:13
Envelope, mistake of enclosing e.,
657:6
Enveloping earth, 383:9
Envelops, ground opens and e. me,
766:6
Enviable death was his, 621:18
Envied, better e. than pitied, 70:2
Envieth, charity e. not, 43:14
love e. not, 43:14
Envious and calumniating time, 201:3
beggar is e. of beggar, 54:20
Casca, 189:5
humble are usually e., 278:8
more free than e. court, 190:6
regarded wounded soldiers in e.
way, 611:2
serpents e., 230:21
siege of watery Neptune, 171:10
silence e. tongues, 225:21

Envious *(continued)*
   ungrateful Public, 390:10
Environ, what perils do e., 153:*n*3
Environment, ancestry and cultural e.,
   574:11
   change e. not man, 691:16
   freedom in relation to e., 473:7
   inequality of e., 525:11
   internal e., 473:8
   is all excepting me, 691:22
   man not locked into e., 722:15
Environs, Howth Castle and E.,
   647:18
Envisage circumstance all calm, 416:21
Envoys, her e. ubiquitous, 463:16
   two punctilious e. Thine and Mine,
   280:17
Envy and wrath shorten life, 32:4
   attracts e. of world, 331:7
   born from the start, 70:3
   calumny hate pain, 409:4
   dared not hate, 401:12
   for the dead, 527:28
   from e. hatred and malice, 49:8
   golden mean avoids e. of palace,
   96:7
   honor without e. friend who prospered, 63:13
   no man's happiness, 191:9
   not reverence of dead but e. of living, 239:24
   of less happier lands, 171:9
   of the dead, 68:5
   of the devil, 30:22
   Pride E. Avarice three sparks,
   125:21
   slayeth the silly, 14:1
   slays itself by own arrows, 118:2
   stirred up with e., 255:21
   strongly rooted as e., 352:32
   toil e. want, 313:17
   too low for e., 266:15
   void of e. guile lust, 308:14
   whim e. or resentment, 333:18
Envying, strife and e., 42:23
Enwrought with gold and silver, 595:8
Eon, lie down for e. or two, 591:13
Épater le bourgeois, 494:*n*12
Epecho [Επεχω], 146:5
Ephemeral, fame is e., 111:8
   story e. and doomed, 696:20
Ephesus, Temple of Dian in E., 782:7
Ephraim, gleaning of grapes of E.,
   11:9
Epicure, serenely full e. say, 380:18
Epicurean cooks sharpen his appetite,
   217:12
Epicurus, he was E. owene sone,
   129:24
   set forth highest good, 90:12
Epicurus', hog of E. herd, 97:11
Epidemic of world lawlessness, 649:9
Epidemical love of flattery, 293:22
Epigram, what is an e., 383:5
Epigrams, France despotism tempered
   by e., 412:12
   your e. are shorter, 106:12
Epigram-surprise, or with e., 423:14
Epilogue, no e. I pray you, 174:11

Episode, love an e. in man's life,
   368:10
Episodes, Renaissance and Reformation e., 704:2
Epitaph, believe woman or e., 399:5
   better bad e., 196:2
   drear, 591:12
   for their country, 588:7
   me who am their e., 229:8
   not remembered in thy e., 179:7
   of those who fell, 621:16
   of which not ashamed, 562:7
   to be my story, 624:15
Epitaphs, let's talk of e., 171:24
   nice derangement of e., 352:9
Epithet belongs to gentleman, 387:15
   his surname e. for knave, 136:*n*5
Epithets, stuffed with e. of war, 205:8
Epitome, all mankind's e., 274:11
Epoch, coincide with e. or differ,
   564:7
   man lives life of e., 629:10
   no one immune to spirit of e., 629:5
   spirit of e., 629:5
Epocha in history, 337:17
Equal, admitted to that e. sky, 301:8
   all animals e., 711:12
   all evils e. when extreme, 249:13
   all men and women created e.,
   475:5
   all men created e., 343:2, 450:2
   and exact justice, 344:9
   before the law, 520:10
   born free and e., 343:*n*2
   but in dust, 231:14
   chance to obtain rights, 627:21
   division of unequal earnings, 393:12
   I am e. and whole, 534:19
   in e. scale weighing, 192:32
   in marriage independence e., 410:18
   in presence of death, 98:29
   in rights and in cultivation, 440:5
   inferiors revolt to be e., 78:24
   ivry man e. if isn't careful, 603:15
   justice for all, 72:2
   male cannot tolerate living with e.,
   440:3
   mutual actions e., 282:3
   nature with e. mind, 497:22
   none e. Alcides except himself,
   103:11
   Pay for Equal Work, 491:22
   piece of justice Death, 248:12
   protection of laws, 346:18
   rate with unequal weights, 89:18
   sees with e. eye as God, 301:5
   separate and e. station, 343:2
   separate but e., 682:9
   sharing of miseries, 622:10
   some more e. than others, 711:12
   syllables require, 298:18
   taken with e. thanks, 197:3
   talked long enough about e. rights,
   723:16
   those e. in any respect, 78:23
   to a god sitting opposite you, 91:4
   to all things, 330:10
   to Him is not anyone, 117:26
   to whole of that commerce, 331:7
   upstairs, 581:21

Equal *(continued)*
   want to be e. in man's world,
   722:12
   wealth and opportunities, 559:8
   when favor of gods was e., 69:19
Equaling, think of e. men of worth,
   61:5
Equality, apostles of e., 500:15
   believe in e. of man, 341:9
   choose e., 500:21
   dispensing e., 75:24
   economic e. for women, 754:2
   if e. found in democracy, 78:21
   intimate e. of the Four, 652:7
   law in majestic e., 550:13
   liberty e. fraternity, 786:15
   living in e., 523:10
   never e. in servants' hall, 581:21
   of property, 438:1
Equally, because e. free absolutely
   equal, 78:23
   entitled to protection, 369:11
   youth and age e. a burden, 75:4
Equals and unequals alike, 75:24
   commerce between e., 329:4
   deal with men as e., 767:3
   energy e. mass times speed of light
   squared, 635:*n*3
   first among e., 119:23
   peace between e., 572:8
   revolt to be superior, 78:24
   virtue only flourish amongst e.,
   365:26
Equations, in midst of diagrams and
   e., 635:13
Equators, North Poles and E., 519:20
Equi et poetae alendi, 151:*n*11
   lente currite noctis e., 101:*n*7,
   162:23
   noli e. dentes inspicere donati,
   114:*n*7
Equilibrium from within, 653:10
Equinox, who knows when was the e.,
   249:3
Equinoxes, precession of e., 460:*n*1
Equipment, shabby e. deteriorating,
   671:9
Equitable, aim at something more e.,
   366:8
Equity, act against natural e., 327:6
   law of humanity justice e., 332:8
Equivalent, create e. for what I felt,
   665:16
   evil gains e. of disaster, 54:26
   no moral e. of war, 546:23
Equivocate, I will not e., 437:15
Equivocation, poetry purged of e.,
   613:18
   will undo us, 199:6
Era, new e. in life from reading,
   478:23
Eradicated, savage in man never e.,
   477:6
Erased, guilt of Germany not e., 704:7
Ercles' vein, 172:24
Erebus, dark as E., 182:10
Erect, avowed e. manly foe, 371:25
   godlike e., 258:11
   sprang to feet stood e., 464:16
Erected, fleshed fair e., 729:2

Europe *(continued)*
  fifty years of E., 456:1
  glory of E. extinguished, 332:12
  governments of E., 343:13
  if clod washed away E. less, 231:8
  lamps going out over E., 585:15
  liberation of E., 678:16
  liberties of E., 345:3
  longest kingly line in E., 306:*n*1
  new order in E., 638:10
  no Soviet domination of Eastern E.,
    733:9
  noblest river in E., 293:7
  of ancient parapets, 565:15
  old tyrannical governments of E.,
    379:28
  pass over to E. between sun and
    sun, 393:7
  people of Western E., 678:16
  powers of old E., 481:14
  prison of nations, 638:10
  races of E. melting, 590:6
  really a swarm, 653:11
  regards her like stranger, 340:21
  Russia's future a danger for E.,
    471:26
  settlement in E., 677:4
  simplifiers going to descend upon
    E., 480:8
  specter haunting eastern E., 768:7
  specter haunting E., 481:14
  superstitious valuation of E., 548:6
  technique and style of E., 754:21
  thrilled with joy, 373:11
  two continental powers in E., 676:8
  under his heel, 621:1
  United States of E., 428:7
  window on E., 424:3
European, colonization by E. powers,
    360:10
  descendant of E., 339:1
  instruments of E. greatness, 355:3
  legacy of first E. novel, 761:14
  Mozart last of great E. taste, 552:21
  narcotics, 552:28
  nose, 750:3
  periodization of E. history, 704:2
  philosophical tradition footnotes to
    Plato, 584:13
  United States and E. power, 360:12
  wars of E. powers, 360:11
Europeans often ask, 536:6
Eurydice, half-regained E., 251:20
Eutrapelia happy flexibility, 500:25
Euxine, more dangerous breakers than
    E., 403:5
Evade erump, 87:*n*4
Evanescent, velocities of e. increments,
    296:23
Evangelical, things moral or things e.,
    272:19
Evasion of what white men set them,
    696:14
Evasit, abiit excessit e. erupit, 87:*n*4
Eve, called his wife's name E., 6:26
  child of our grandmother E., 168:19
  fairest of daughters E., 258:14
  from noon to dewy e., 256:22
  like toad at ear of E., 258:27
  motherless E., 612:1

Eve *(continued)*
  Mr. Whitman's E. drunken apple-
    woman, 535:9
  obey voice at e., 430:9
  oh had simple E., 611:20
  pensive E., 324:13
  riverrun past E. and Adam's, 647:18
  said to e. Be soon, 581:7
  since E. ate apples, 403:18
  son of Adam and E., 288:5
  span, 775:13
  St. Agnes' E., 414:21
  stag at e., 378:17
  warblest at e., 254:9
  wonder what Adam and E. think,
    664:8
Even, approach of e. or morn, 257:24
  as you and I, 592:23
  break, 572:17, 644:6
  deep and crisp and e., 482:8
  don't get mad get e., 673:4
  such is time, 153:2
  waters stilled at e., 509:19
  would God it were e., 10:23
Even-balanced soul, 497:3
Even-handed justice, 213:6
Evening and morning were first day,
    6:5
  beauteous e. calm free, 374:15
  Boston E. Transcript, 667:23,
    702:16
  bright exhalation in the e., 225:14
  charming e. criminal's friend, 494:8
  come in the e., 474:1
  dews of e. carefully shun, 305:18
  die in e. without regret, 61:3
  eat in the e., 357:8
  expects his e. prey, 323:8
  fairer than e. air, 162:20
  gracious e. star, 473:16
  grateful e. mild, 258:22
  hate to see e. sun go down, 617:15
  house made of e. light, 787:9
  housewife ply e. care, 322:6
  in afternoon, 683:14
  in the e. it is cut down, 18:10
  is come rise up, 91:7
  isolation of sky at e., 638:26
  it was a summer e., 386:3
  light first light of e., 640:8
  like an e. gone, 294:15
  love morning and e. star, 658:8
  man that was in e. made, 249:28
  morning incense e. meal, 353:15
  must usher night, 408:21
  now came still e. on, 258:18
  of their lives, 503:4
  open house in e., 619:4
  quickly come as the E. Star, 87:5
  quiet-colored end of e., 465:9
  rainy e. to read this discourse,
    245:15
  red light of e., 787:5
  rest at pale e., 708:14
  shades of e. drew on, 452:4
  shades prevail, 292:1
  shadow at e. rising, 668:18
  shadows of the e., 521:11
  shut of e. flowers, 260:4
  slight sound at e., 476:23

Evening *(continued)*
  some enchanted e., 692:12
  soup of the e., 518:9
  spread out against sky, 667:9
  star love's harbinger, 260:20
  star you shine on dead, 408:*n*3
  sunset and e. star, 460:11
  to his labor until e., 19:6
  twilight and e. bell, 460:12
  until e. comes, 426:22
  walks at e. on three feet, 66:*n*1
  welcome peaceful e. in, 335:3
  when it is e. fair weather, 35:25
  withhold not thine hand in the e.,
    24:25
Evenings, we have had summer e.,
    660:12
Evensong, at last ring to e., 142:23
  at length ringeth to e., 142:*n*12
  dead ere e., 785:16
Event, caprice of minutest e., 487:2
  divine e., 458:3
  greatest e. in war, 72:12
  haunt spot of great e., 435:27
  Holocaust central e., 764:7
  how much the greatest e., 348:16
  men labels that name e., 510:5
  one e. happeneth to all, 23:30
  prophets make sure of e., 324:2
  thinking too precisely on e., 198:13
  unveil third e. to me, 514:13
  verity is an e., 546:21
Eventful, strange e. history, 191:3
Eventide, fast falls e., 410:17
Events cast shadows before, 389:3
  controlled me, 450:4
  course of human e., 343:2
  great e. make me calm, 488:4
  names deeds legends e., 417:1
  national e. decided by power elite,
    739:18
  signs should prefigure e., 87:26
  some great e. some mean hypocri-
    sies, 338:9
  spirits of great e., 389:*n*1
  study e. in bearings, 503:5
  three e. in life, 283:16
Ever-during dark surrounds me,
    257:24
  power, 376:21
  sleep one e. night, 226:13
Everest, square root of E., 748:10
Ever-fixed mark, 222:2
Ever-increasing wonder and awe,
    326:10
Everlasting, achievements of intellect
    e., 91:29
  bonfire, 214:10
  composed to be e. possession, 71:19
  condemned into e. redemption,
    187:5
  deprived of e. bliss, 162:15
  doors, 16:19
  eyes of Pierrot, 701:2
  farewells, 397:16
  Father, 26:8
  first last e. day, 229:5
  from e. to e. thou art God, 18:10
  funeral marches round your heart,
    738:17

Everlasting (*continued*)
God the E. Refuge, 117:26
had not fixed canon, 193:5
here set up my e. rest, 176:18
hills, 8:19
his mercy is e., 18:22
life, 39:46
no, 412:3
open ye e. gates, 259:22
stood from e. to e., 280:23
the e. arms, 10:29
yea, 412:6
Everlastingness, bright shoots of e.,
270:5
Ever-living, our e. poet, 220:*n*1
Evermore, probing through you O e.,
701:7
Ever-nearing circle weaves shade,
499:18
Ever-returning spring, 490:15
Ever-rolling, time like e. stream,
294:16
Evers, Tinker to E. to Chance, 644:5
Ever-whirling wheel, 154:1
Every day in every way, 573:18
day's news, 204:19
inch a king, 210:29
man architect of his fortune, 92:1
man for himself, 142:30
war of e. man against e. man,
239:21
Everybody, everything happens to e.,
571:26
goes Awww, 750:9
hard to please e., 100:9
he who praises e., 341:20
if e. minded business, 517:13
looks like e. is down on me, 773:5
most e. climbs into graves married,
697:13
partner has had it with, 745:1
suspect e., 469:31
wants to be Cary Grant, 713:2
Everybody's business nobody's business, 245:19
Everyday, refinement of e. thinking,
635:14
Everyman I will go with thee, 776:5
Everyone, each one's himself yet e.,
725:8
Future something e. reaches, 700:2
has one sermon, 781:21
in world is Christ, 630:21
is a moon has dark side, 528:1
love come to e., 685:16
not e. can get to Corinth, 97:17
satisfying life for e., 715:9
understandable by e. not just scientists, 772:2
upon which e. has sat, 689:3
went over e. nobody's missing,
735:1
when e. is somebodee, 531:22
will say, 529:18
world breaks e., 701:15
Everyone's tired of turmoil, 743:9
true worship, 74:5
Everything, a bore to tell e., 305:26
and Anything, 650:12
autumn in e., 466:2

Everything (*continued*)
belongs to fatherland, 364:5
conscience in e., 320:20
costing not less than e., 672:7
custom reconciles to e., 330:20
deed e. glory nothing, 350:25
don't tell her e., 53:23
else is still, 356:17
esteem e. esteem nothing, 269:10
exists nothing has value, 636:11
fearlessness of those who lost e.,
746:2
feeling not always e., 496:1
for e. missed gained something,
431:31
for poetry idea e., 500:24
glory of e., 703:16
God not willing to do e., 137:1
good for something, 274:22
good in e., 190:7
grayness silvers e., 466:1
grows old under power of Time,
77:18
had e. I wanted, 694:15
happens to everybody, 571:26
hard to attain easily assailed, 110:10
has an end, 784:20
has two handles, 108:14
he is superior to e. he possesses,
306:10
he wants nothing you want, 501:20
hear voices talking about e., 774:7
I could prove e., 762:20
I have e. yet nothing, 86:5
I touch mean and farcical, 508:17
in its place, 528:18
in relation to nothing, 270:18
includes itself in power, 200:10
is A-OK, 751:5
is for the best, 306:5
is gratuitous, 717:12
is up to date in Kansas City, 692:10
know e. forgive e., 368:*n*3
lived in me, 504:17
man esteems, 597:19
man grows used to e., 495:2
mean between nothing and e.,
270:18
men ask for e., 746:19
moments when e. goes well, 589:7
not all capable of e., 92:12
now dare e., 753:8
of one hidden stuff, 431:32
passes, 786:16
passes art alone eternal, 462:11
practice is e., 99:*n*11
public opinion e., 448:13
sans e., 191:3
smattering of e., 468:19
spirit of youth in e., 221:19
that emancipates spirit, 351:12
that pretty is, 219:24
that's lovely is, 595:12
tries e. before arms, 86:9
understand e. makes tolerant,
368:12
was rainbow, 729:3
we look upon blest, 598:6
what else to say but e., 740:9
what is God e., 64:14

Everything (*continued*)
winning isn't e. it's only thing,
783:26
worth what purchaser will pay,
100:16
Everything's coming up roses, 763:7
got a moral, 517:24
Everywhere he is in chains, 319:5
his place, 267:3
I roam, 507:1
one little room an e., 228:3
that Mary went, 404:10
the same as e., 349:3
water water e., 381:8
we have need of Zeus, 82:12
who lives e. lives nowhere, 106:19
Eve's, curses all E. daughters, 183:5
one star, 416:19
Eves, flies on summer e., 415:15
now for October e., 660:12
summer e. by haunted stream,
251:19
Evidence, denunciation in place of e.,
615:6
for God, 546:19
growth only e. of life, 426:19
of immortality, 430:23
of servile status, 574:8
of things not seen, 45:38
passions cannot alter e., 337:15
some circumstantial e. strong,
476:25
take everything on e., 471:17
Evil, all e. to crazy Ahab, 486:25
all means permitted to fight e.,
676:1
ancient folk with e. spells, 787:13
art of biography fallen on e. times,
643:17
atom's weight of e., 117:25
avoid e. do good, 64:20
banality of e., 718:9
be not overcome of e., 42:19
be thou my good, 258:6
believe no e. till done, 267:21
bent on e. never want occasion,
99:24
brothers are e., 4:1
by e. and good report, 44:5
communications, 43:22
days come not, 24:27
deeds do no prosper, 53:15
deeds religion prompt, 89:5
deliver us from e., 33:12
depart from e., 16:31
do e. so completely, 271:10
do not seek e. gains, 54:26
Empire, 773:10
entire city suffered because of e.
man, 54:22
every e. hath good, 431:30
extravagance of her e., 53:22
eye that looks to mood apart,
624:20
fallen on e. days, 259:19
find means of e., 256:3
generation, 38:27
good comes out of e., 532:11
good e. reward punishment, 277:11

Evil *(continued)*

good indistinguishable from e., 676:1

good or e. side, 485:1

goodness in things e., 185:16

Government necessary e., 340:18

hacking at branches of e., 478:13

hear no e. see no e., 777:10

hope in the day of e., 28:32

I will fear no e., 16:17

idleness dragged toward e., 71:11

if dhrink e. not nicissry, 603:16

ill deeds doubled with e. word, 166:30

imagination of man's heart is e., 7:21

in life of worms, 505:1

inadvertently said some e. thing, 76:19

infect the soul with e., 75:2

is easy, 271:5

judge should have learned to know e., 75:9

keep thy tongue from e., 16:31

knowing good and e., 6:20

Lord shall preserve thee from all e., 19:25

maketh sun rise on e. and good, 33:9

manners live in brass, 226:5

many e. men are rich, 55:15

marriage a necessary e., 81:13

marriage an e. most men welcome, 81:n9

met me in e. hour, 361:19

necessary for triumph of e., 332:30

never suffer e. in future, 54:7

news rides post, 261:23

no e. can happen to good man, 74:17

no e. deed live on, 544:7

no man chooses e., 365:25

not into e. wrought, 532:14

notion of E. One, 721:9

obscures the show of e., 181:4

of moral e. and of good, 372:21

on ground of expediency, 575:14

one e. ignorance, 70:20

one that eschewed e., 13:27

overcome e. with good, 42:19

partial e. universal good, 301:12

perceive e. where exists, 719:13

perplexity of radical e., 718:11

plan is most harmful to planner, 54:23

political good carried to extreme productive of e., 366:2

punish world for their e., 26:13

rash hand in e. hour, 260:7

recognition of e., 56:13

recompense no e. for e., 42:16

resist not e., 33:7

return good for e., 288:8

rewarded e. for good, 8:10

rewardeth e. for good, 21:35

root of all e., 45:22

saw my e. day, 369:6

say e. against you, 33:1

show me a greater e., 66:15

Evil *(continued)*

snake stood for e. in Garden, 623:12

Socrates a doer of e., 74:14

spinning fates good or e., 545:14

stifling opinion is e., 439:16

stubborn heart shall fare e., 31:5

submit to present e., 102:11

sufficient unto day is e., 34:1

supernatural source of e., 573:14

that men do lives after them, 188:28

the e. I do, 41:46

them that call e. good, 25:41

thing of e., 452:19

to depart from e. is understanding, 14:41

to him who evil thinks, 127:13

tongue an unruly e., 46:12

tree of knowledge of good and e., 6:14

unconscious not only e. but good, 628:15

until all e. emissions had fled, 753:1

vanish like e. spirits, 344:19

vice lost half its e., 332:15

what e. I intend to do, 68:13

whether it be good or e., 24:30

wi' tippenny fear nae e., 363:7

will bless, 429:11

with indifference notes e., 424:1

with lent money e. done, 487:24

withstand in the e. day, 44:28

write e. in marble, 137:17

wrought by want of thought, 422:23

Evildoers, seeing e. taken to execution, 143:9

Evildoing, greatest penalty of e., 76:13

Evil's, believe no evil till e. done, 267:21

Evils, all e. equal when extreme, 249:13

avoided powers exercised, 108:8

between two e. pick one never tried, 685:9

cities no rest from e., 75:15

compel philosophy to inquire about e., 87:30

Congress has right to prevent, 542:24

draw men together, 78:29

endure neither e. nor cures, 98:26

greatest of our e. is poverty, 571:12

he must expect new e., 159:27

knowledgeable of e., 63:1

least of the e., 78:4

least of two e., 52:n3

most preferable of e., 52:12

newly acquired freedom produces, 424:15

no necessary e. in government, 369:12

one of e. and another of blessings, 52:26

philosophy triumphs over past e., 264:24

present e. triumph over philosophy, 264:24

suffering e. of long peace, 109:2

they say e. come from us, 52:29

Evils *(continued)*

three great e., 306:11

two e. monstrous either one, 674:10

weak e. age and hunger, 191:2

when e. most free, 188:3

yield not to e., 94:5

Evolution, cultural e., 722:15

from vague to definite, 538:17

general theory of e., 522:16

leisure class in social e., 574:7

not a force but a process, 537:5

of thought, 498:22

progress of E. from Washington to Grant, 535:25

Evolutionary, from e. point of view man stopped moving, 645:8

Evolved, endless beautiful forms e., 444:10

universe e. from unfamiliar, 766:4

Ev'rythin's up to date in Kansas City, 692:10

Ewe, lilting at e. milking, 327:11

tupping your white e., 205:15

Ewes, milk my e. and weep, 223:13

Ewig-Weibliche, das E. zieht uns hinan, 350:n11

Ex pede Herculem, 70:n2

ungue leonem, 119:1

Exact, aim of e. science, 516:6

equal and e. justice, 344:9

knowledge of the past, 71:19

set e. wealth of states, 178:19

writing maketh an e. man, 160:9

Exactitude, judgment and e. enter him, 3:3

l'e. la politesse des rois, 355:n2

Exactness, facts detailed with e., 503:5

Exaggerated, love of the e., 765:15

originality easily e., 723:5

stress on not changing mind, 626:12

Exaggeration, chargeable with no e., 390:2

report of my death an e., 528:2

Exalt him above all, 32:17

himself shall be abased, 36:2

will to live, 630:17

Exaltation from proximity of disaster, 619:13

in chanting of Muses, 68:7

Exalted, both will be e., 636:10

every valley shall be e., 27:16

God an e. father, 569:7

no very e. opinion, 331:5

Satan e. sat, 256:23

them of low degree, 37:42

whoso humble himself be e., 36:2

Exalteth, righteousness e. a nation, 21:23

wisdom e. her children, 31:7

Exalts, not what man does e., 466:21

Examination, decent and manly e., 385:13

of acts of government, 385:13

Examine, crime to e. laws of heat, 537:4

turn inwards and e., 61:5

Examined, ought to have head e., 646:20

Example, annoyance of good e., 527:17

Example (*continued*)
from others take e., 86:14
from the monkey, 123:15
Homer is my e., 598:17
if lower orders don't set good e.,
567:4
is school of mankind, 332:26
more efficacious than precept,
314:13
profit by their e., 339:5
salutary influence of e., 314:18
Examples, no longer able to provide
bad e., 265:14
Excalibur, so fell the brand E., 454:18
Exceed, flies worms e. me still, 294:11
never e. your rights, 319:3
reach e. grasp, 466:5
Exceedeth, thy wisdom and prosperity
e. the fame, 12:26
Exceeding, grind e. small, 247:15
honest e. poor man, 180:15
wise fair-spoken, 226:6
Exceeds, far e. all earthly bliss,
148:n2
man's might, 200:21
Excel, arts in which wise e., 284:2
bees for government, 148:3
discredit what they do not e. in,
80:15
not e. because they labor, 390:20
teach who themselves e., 298:10
thou shalt not e., 8:17
useless to e., 318:7
Excellence, activity in accordance with
e., 78:9
bearing on e. of character, 78:8
fair divided e., 169:23
fame of her e., 54:12
in front of e. gods put sweat, 54:24
long time to bring e. to maturity,
100:13
mental e. a splendid possession,
91:21
not exchange e. for riches, 55:15
not only know e. but use it, 78:11
stewards of their e., 221:15
to few men comes e., 59:21
Excellencies, smaller e. of conversation, 342:1
true critic dwell on e., 293:4
Excellent angler now with God,
245:23
dumb discourse, 224:19
everything that's e., 530:6
fancy, 199:8
first e. second good, 136:17
foppery of the world, 209:3
hard to be truly e., 60:8
how e. is thy name, 15:35
how e. is thy lovingkindness, 16:33
I cried, 577:23
if you were a village, 627:10
man of understanding is of e. spirit,
21:37
most e. canopy the air, 195:28
parts of it are e., 555:3
situation e. I am attacking, 562:19
so e. a king, 193:7
so so is e. good, 192:8
the e. lies before us, 368:1

Excellent (*continued*)
thing in woman, 211:18
things difficult as rare, 278:19
things in counsels, 22:12
things that are more e., 41:39
to have giant's strength, 204:3
to make a poet e., 264:3
well a fishmonger, 195:15
what actions most e., 498:8
wretch, 206:27
Excellently, goddess e. bright, 231:21
Excellest, thou e. them all, 23:21
Excelleth, light e. darkness, 23:29
wisdom e. folly, 23:29
Excelling, cunningest pattern of e. nature, 208:10
Isle all isles e., 275:30
Excels dunce kept at home, 334:8
quirks of blazoning pens, 206:4
Excelsior, 441:8
Excelsis, gloria in e. Deo, 48:8
Except a man be born again, 39:43
it die, 43:23
the Lord build the house, 19:29
the Lord keep the city, 19:29
the present company, 348:13
thou bless me, 8:1
Exception, in your case make e., 693:1
no rule admits not some e., 234:17
proves rule, 234:n8
Exceptional, glorious to be e., 461:16
Excess, blasted with e. of light, 323:4
desire of power in e., 159:16
don't regret a single e., 549:12
give me e. of it, 201:16
in charity no e., 159:14
moderation even in e., 434:17
not drinking but e., 238:24
nothing in e., 119:15
of glory obscured, 256:15
of wealth cause of covetousness,
162:7
reform carried to e. needs reforming, 384:3
reproach to religion, 282:20
road of e. leads to palace of wisdom, 357:3
such e. of stupidity, 316:2
surprise by fine e., 418:1
wasteful and ridiculous e., 170:9
when love is in e., 68:11
Excessit, abiit e. evasit erupit, 87:n4
Excessive, bail nor e. fines, 346:17
dark with e. bright, 257:26
good fortune, 507:11
if national debt not e., 354:17
laughter, 31:39
Exchange, atheist-laugh's a poor e.,
361:23
by just e. one for other, 155:26
cross for crown, 616:2
excellence for riches, 55:15
Exchequer of the poor, 171:15
Excise hateful tax, 314:3
those to whom e. paid, 314:3
Excitabat enim fluctus in simpulo,
88:n5
Excite my amorous propensities,
315:14
Excited abnormal condition, 571:15

Excited (*continued*)
passions not at will e., 452:12
reverie, 596:21
Excitement, beyond e. into anguish,
765:2
faith an e. and enthusiasm, 436:26
spiritual e., 500:5
Excites us to arms, 275:9
Exciting, found it less e., 531:15
politics almost e. as war, 619:16
Exclamation, by way of e., 135:22
Exclude, to define is to e., 653:9
Excluded, law of e. middle, 748:10
Excludes, kitsch e. everything, 761:13
Excommunicate, corporations cannot
be e., 152:5
Excrement, place of e., 598:21
Excursion same for sorrow as joy,
727:18
Excuse, any e. will serve tyrant, 59:9
came prologue, 260:9
denial vain and coy e., 253:16
fault worse by e., 170:10
for the glass, 352:29
I will not e., 437:15
my dust, 687:15
never e., 174:11
play needs no e., 174:11
Excused from it as against my conscience, 324:9
his devilish deeds, 258:15
Excuses himself accuses himself,
144:10
ignorance e. no man, 238:25
Excusing, love shows by e. nothing,
269:14
make fault worse, 170:10
Execrable shape, 257:17
sum of all villainies, 308:25
Execute, by contraries e., 224:4
hand to e., 262:1, 346:3
orders, 332:21
to e. laws royal office, 332:21
villainy you teach me, 180:32
Executed, successfully e., 349:23
Execution of final solution of Jewish
question, 686:5
seeing evildoers taken to e., 143:9
Executioner, hire e. to throw switch,
694:6
I victim and e., 494:7
man his own e., 248:18
mine own e., 231:6
the master e., 58:4
Executioners would be most learned,
138:2
Executions far from useful examples,
366:3
for the master executioner, 58:4
Executive, judicial distinct from e.,
338:7
legislative nominated by e., 340:1
of modern state, 482:1
political e. magistracy, 332:21
Executors, let's choose e., 171:24
Exegi monumentum aere perennius,
96:n21
Exemplary, our lives in acts e., 157:10
Exemplum de simia, 123:n8
Exempt from public haunt, 190:7

Experience (*continued*)
  substitute for e. is art and literature, 746:3
  tells in every soil, 328:15
  travel part of e., 159:20
  triumph of hope over e., 316:8
  what e. and history teach, 372:6
  whole past e. in consciousness, 538:18
  wisdom acting upon e., 315:6
  write from e. only, 548:13
Experienced, nothing real till e., 418:14
Experiences, evidence for God in inner e., 546:19
  in solitude, 546:13
  shared e., 370:8
  strong man digests e., 552:27
  way full of adventures and e., 587:11
Experiencing suffering to full, 613:3
Experientia docet, 470:*n*1
  does it, 470:22
Experiment, all life is e., 542:25
  convinced of imbecility by e., 314:26
  entrusted to American people, 337:1
  every e. like weapon, 139:5
  mad and lamentable e., 588:3
  reason and e. indulged, 343:6
  so great an e. as dying, 249:24
  to me every one I meet, 513:16
  treacherous, 71:13
  we are not the only e., 691:21
Experimental, all poetry e. poetry, 640:26
  philosophy, 281:26
  youth is wholly e., 562:10
Experimentation active science, 473:3
  bold persistent e., 648:15
Experiments, eclipses of moon and other e., 134:12
  I love fools' e., 445:2
  sure e. and demonstrated arguments, 148:13
Expert, believe an e., 94:27
  knows more about less, 585:10
Experto credite, 94:*n*13
Experts, differences among e., 586:9
Expire, lamps e., 602:9
Expires, unawares Morality e., 304:2
Explain, can't e. myself said Alice, 517:8
  his explanation, 402:5
  law is but let me e. once more, 720:14
  never apologize and never e., 724:9
  spoil it by trying to e., 352:15
  till all men doubt, 303:32
  time will e. all, 69:8
  we may touch love e., 757:17
  you e. nothing O poet, 604:14
Explained, not die before we have e. ourselves, 338:15
  shut up he e., 657:5
  simplicity itself once e., 577:21
Explainer, Ezra Pound was village e., 627:10
Explaining, surrender e. not acting, 618:1

Explanation, explain his e., 402:5
  inaccuracy saves e., 610:21
  unintelligible, 632:4
Expletive deleted, 784:12
Expletives their feeble aid do join, 298:15
Explicable, thanks to poet things e., 604:14
Explicitness not necessary virtue, 594:13
Explode, or does it e., 708:19
Exploitation, ultimate sanction of e., 686:6
Exploited, many e. by few, 686:6
Exploits, capable of noble e., 496:9
  capitalism system where man e. man, 746:14
  fond of relating own e., 278:4
Exploration, not cease from e., 672:6
Explore all options, 716:1
  came to e. wreck, 762:8
  falter or e., 749:17
  unconscious, 577:2
Explorer, man e. of nature, 722:14
Explorers, old men ought to be e., 671:11
  old men should be e., 725:11
  scientists detectives and e., 738:14
Exploring, end of e. to arrive, 672:6
Exponent of Earth, 513:9
Exposed, intellect improperly e., 380:6
  left e. a Friend, 513:8
  on bare earth e. he lies, 276:12
Exposition of sleep upon me, 173:23
Expounding, it is a constitution we are e., 355:10
Express flowery tale, 415:20
  it in numbers, 504:11
  speech not to e. but conceal, 280:*n*1
Expressed even such a beauty, 221:22
  monitor e., 376:21
  ne'er so well e., 298:14
  not e. in fancy, 193:30
  whatever is felicitously e., 368:1
Expresses, this young man e. himself, 529:17
Expressing emotion in art, 672:11
  itself beyond expression, 232:9
Expression, borrow shape to find e., 667:21
  expressing itself beyond e., 232:9
  freedom of e. matrix, 609:13
  freedom of speech and e., 649:17
  impassioned e., 373:15
  individuality of e. end of art, 351:3
  monk's state transcends e., 65:3
  natural e. of villainy, 526:1
  of mediocrity of apparatus, 641:4
  of working of mind, 505:4
  scream e. of vestige of human dignity, 702:15
Expressive silence, 308:9
Expunge, fool enough to e., 317:12
Expunged, Nature's works to me e., 257:24
Exquisite passions, 538:5
  pleasure so e. almost pain, 397:8
Extend freedom to everyone, 685:10
  system to this hemisphere, 360:12
Extended to display its patterns, 62:29

Extensive and honorable conquests, 331:25
Extenuate, it is vain sir to e., 339:10
  nothing e., 208:16
Exterior, fair e. silent recommendation, 99:10
  less on e. things, 334:2
Exterminate all the brutes, 573:7
Exterminating one another to last man, 569:12
Extermination camps intimated, 707:14
  threat of common e., 748:4
External artistries in circumstance, 540:13
  differ in e. forms, 316:10
  falseness in impressions of e., 487:13
  reaction to external world, 558:9
  reimpressed by e. ordinances, 314:18
  these e. regions, 640:2
  world super-ego and id, 569:14
Extinct, Dodo invented for becoming e., 654:5
  our name not become e., 510:17
Extinction, continual e. of personality, 672:9
  from apathy, 702:14
  path leads to total e., 767:16
  universe faces future e., 766:4
Extinguish hope from soul, 565:21
Extinguished, fire which seems e., 249:19
  his soul, 448:10
  nature seldom e., 160:2
  prey of fear he e., 664:19
  theologians, 505:3
Extol, how shall we e. thee, 585:5
Extolling past, 380:22
Extra, add some e. just for you, 750:15
Extract laws from nature, 646:6
Extracted from many objects, 191:26
Extracting sunbeams of cucumbers, 289:12
Extraordinary, results of idealism e., 569:1
  youth the time for e. toil, 75:20
Extravagance, beauty without e., 72:3
  calls his e. generosity, 329:2
  if e. but little is left, 85:1
  of her evil, 53:22
Extravagant and erring spirit, 192:28
  flaunting e. quean, 352:29
Extreme actions ascribed to vanity, 552:3
  all evils equal when e., 249:13
  fear neither fight nor fly, 166:39
  for e. diseases e. strictness, 71:14
  in quest to have e., 222:7
  justice extreme injustice, 119:32
  justice often injustice, 86:*n*1
  law often extreme injustice, 86:1
  of wickedness or folly, 449:6
  perplexed in the e., 208:16
  political good carried to e., 366:2
  reformers have been bachelors, 563:11
  savage e. rude cruel, 222:7

Face *(continued)*

baseball leaves you f. fall alone, 769:8
beautiful f. candid brow, 573:2
beauty of aged f., 644:12
beheld God nature f. to f., 430:24
blows it in my f., 196:6
boot stamping on human f. forever, 711:19
but then f. to f., 43:16
change in my f., 558:17
climber-upward turns f., 187:32
continual comfort in a f., 163:3
cover her f., 237:19
darkness upon f. of the deep, 6:4
downward in sun, 683:9
dust blows in your f., 210:21
emptiness of ages in f., 563:6
everybody's f. but own, 288:16
fall flat on your f., 690:13
false f. must hide, 213:15
fierce fur soft to f., 750:1
final f. of love, 750:4
find f. you loved when young, 484:16
garden in her f., 226:18
gazed on f. of Agamemnon, 502:6
give me a f., 232:6
God f. to f., 8:2
God has given you one f., 196:16
God moved upon f. of the waters, 6:4
god reached down slapped earth's f., 773:16
grace and music of her f., 267:13
hides smiling f., 334:1
honest labor bears a lovely f., 227:18
how am I to f. the odds, 579:20
how silently with how wan f., 156:5
human f. divine, 257:24
husband with beard on f., 186:16
I have wandered in a f., 756:17
I never forget a f., 693:1
if I lie spit in my f., 177:24
if your f. is awry, 446:19
in sweat of thy f., 6:26
in thy f. see map of honor, 163:25
is as a book, 213:2
is face of Christ himself, 490:11
is my fortune, 790:7
Jealousy a human f., 358:13
Jezebel painted her f., 13:11
kind and northern f., 701:2
kissed her on dainty f., 644:11
knew thy f. or name, 229:3
lifts f. all unashamed, 740:11
like a benediction, 149:9
like hoosier Michael Angelo, 491:11
look fear in the f., 654:15
look on her f., 299:11
magic of a f., 246:12
make f. of heaven so fine, 176:1
mind's construction in f., 212:27
mirror of mind, 114:2
mist in my f., 467:18
moment that his f. I see, 382:5
morning f., 329:17
Moses hid his f., 8:25
music breathing from her f., 267:n5

Face *(continued)*

my f. I don't mind it, 631:18
my f. in thine eye, 228:4
negative in slate window, 747:17
never eye did see that f., 163:4
night's starred f., 417:10
no more spoil upon my f., 186:4
no stranger's wing shielded my f., 675:7
nose on man's f., 168:2
of God shine through, 683:16
on barroom floor, 548:n2
open doors of his f., 15:22
open f. of heaven, 413:22
pardoned all except f., 403:7
Pity has a human f., 356:13
plain as nose in f., 140:6
poor lean lank f., 448:8
prism and silent f., 373:10
round jolly fruitful f., 448:n2
sages have seen in thy f., 334:20
saw manners in f., 315:2
sea's f. and gray dawn, 633:14
sees other's umbered f., 185:14
set my ten commandments in your f., 163:19
she has a lovely f., 454:17
shining morning f., 191:3
smiling f. dream of Spring, 383:14
smiling in my f., 213:12
so pleased my mind, 777:4
socialism with human f., 748:16
soft f. of a girl, 66:18
something in a f., 294:21
sorrows of changing f., 595:2
strong men f. to f., 591:9
surrenders his f. to God, 117:9
that drove me mad, 548:4
that launched a thousand ships, 162:19
this fair f. the cause, 162:n7
this sunburnt f., 356:9
thou canst not see my f., 9:19
thy classic f., 451:12
touched f. of God, 751:3
truth has such f. and mien, 275:13
truth showing its f. undisguised, 64:8
turned f. with ghastly pang, 381:17
visit her f. too roughly, 193:7
whole f. of world changed, 270:22
why hidest thou thy f. from me, 18:9
wish I loved silly f., 584:3
with twain he covered his f., 25:42
worst thing about him, 203:33
you could not see, 472:8

Face's, viewed in her fair f. field, 166:36

Faces all gather blackness, 29:39
bid them wash their f., 219:4
draw living f. from marble, 94:15
dusk f. with silken turbans, 260:31
estranged f., 581:11
fools' names like fools' f., 778:16
grind the f. of the poor, 25:34
hearts do in the f. rest, 228:4
in the crowd, 659:1
lords and owners of their f., 221:15
millions of f. none alike, 104:n7

Faces *(continued)*

of coffee-pickers, 656:9
of Negro school-children, 743:12
old familiar f., 387:14
put on two several f., 279:5
sea of upturned f., 379:11
sweat of other men's f., 450:10
Thracian ships foreign f., 533:8

Facets, iceberg cuts f. from within, 729:1

Facias ipse quod faciamus suades, 84:n2

Facile, plus f. de faire la guerre, 542:n1

Facilis descensus Averni, 94:n3

Facility of octosyllabic verse, 401:10

Facing fearful odds, 425:14
man who sits f. you, 56:5

Façon, je veux qu'on m'y voit en ma f., 145:n4

Fact, awkward historical f., 637:3
belief help create f., 546:9
Caspian F., 514:4
death ugly f. Nature hides, 515:16
falsehood more miraculous than f., 318:14
fatal futility of F., 549:4
firm ground of F., 619:10
frontiers wherever man fronts f., 477:20
idea is the f., 500:24
impressive f. about American women, 751:7
irritable reaching after f., 417:18
knife-edge of mere f., 762:2
natural f. spiritual f., 431:2
slaying of hypothesis by ugly f., 505:9
state one f. belie another, 431:18
superiority in f. of conservatism, 432:14
thought counterparts in f., 493:18
yesterday f. today doctrine, 345:12

Fact-finding more effective than fault-finding, 615:18

Faction a number of citizens, 351:21
danger of f., 352:1

Factions, old religious f., 332:23

Factor, timing is most important f., 55:1

Factories may make end of war, 521:2

Factors, gods as psychic f., 628:12
women economic f. in society, 583:3

Factory windows always broken, 637:7

Facts alarm more than principles, 346:5
all f. when come to brass tacks, 670:2
alone wanted in life, 471:5
are sacred, 555:8
are stubborn things, 290:29, 337:15
at first seem improbable, 161:17
collection of f. not science, 565:6
detailed with exactness, 503:5
drop cloak stand forth naked, 161:17
emphatic f. of history, 431:17
front essential f. of life, 478:17

Facts (*continued*)
  if Lord knew f. iv case, 603:4
  ignorance inert f., 535:32
  imagination baffled by f., 620:16
  imagination for f., 353:4
  inert f., 535:32
  judges of f. not laws, 296:22
  looking toward f., 546:18
  passions cannot alter f., 337:15
  personages appear twice, 481:6
  politics ignoring f., 535:31
  power most serious of f., 535:33
  science built with f., 565:6
  we poor passing f., 744:4
  what I want is F., 471:5
Faculties, borne his f. so meek, 213:7
  men free to develop f., 568:14
  t' affections and to f., 229:15
  whose f. can comprehend, 161:21
Faculty, Eleazer was f., 589:4
  infinite in f., 195:28
  of continuing to improve, 335:24
  unshackled exercise of every f., 427:10
Fade as a leaf, 28:8
  colors that never f., 585:9
  far away, 415:12
  first to f. away, 392:13
  into light of common day, 375:8
  loveliness f., 391:13
  lovely things f. and die, 675:2
  may flourish or may f., 329:8
  nothing of him that doth f., 223:32
  old soldiers f. away, 642:5, 782:15
  thy eternal summer not f., 220:13
Faded and gone, 391:16
  but still lovely woman, 694:19
  care sat on his f. cheek, 256:17
  flowers of friendship f., 627:7
  friendship f., 627:7
  insubstantial pageant f., 224:21
  oldest colors f., 591:13
  on crowing of the cock, 192:29
Fades glimmering landscape, 322:2
  out from kiss to kiss, 595:12
Fadeth, crown of glory that f. not, 46:27
  flower f., 27:18
Fadin', order is rapidly f., 771:7
Fading, bestows the f. rose, 246:4
  down the river, 586:14
  fading, 669:16
  in music, 181:2
  life f. fast away, 557:1
Faery, Land of F., 595:3
  lands forlorn, 415:17
Faery's child, 417:5
Faggot, flames no f. feeds, 598:12
Faggots, some burn damp f., 596:7
Fagots, diadems and f., 430:6
Fail, audience never f. to laugh, 73:20
  desire shall f., 24:28
  from eternity shall not f., 579:18
  if we should f., 213:13
  let no man's heart f., 11:38
  no such word as f., 429:1
  not ashamed to f., 313:15
  not f. that rendezvous, 674:18
  not flag or f., 620:7
  possible to f. in many ways, 78:3

Fail (*continued*)
  sooner f. than not among greatest, 418:7
  this could not f., 449:16
  we'll not f., 213:13
Failed, fluttered f. for breath, 498:15
  if cannot use talent, 706:19
  most editors f. writers, 673:2
  therefore turn critics, 383:19
  tried a little f. much, 562:7
Faileth, enemy faints not nor f., 483:3
  forsake me not when strength f., 17:40
Failing, bulwark never f., 138:5
  from f. hands throw, 615:8
  tell aloud greatest f., 289:16
  that the rest of the city, 75:11
Failings leaned to Virtue's side, 329:13
Fails, contentment f., 328:9
  if heart f. climb not, 152:*n*6
  my voice f. me, 331:3
  oft expectation f., 203:12
  persuades when speaking f., 222:22
Failure, government of cities conspicuous f., 536:7
  heaven's success or earth's f., 465:23
  hell f. in great object, 414:7
  I'll show you f., 674:15
  might have died a f., 674:19
  minute's success pays f., 468:16
  never afraid of f., 418:7
  to communicate, 755:18
Failures, benefit in f. early, 505:11
  haste brings f., 70:7
  history of masterwork not f., 660:2
  of all f. witticism worst, 388:17
Fain climb yet fear to fall, 152:12
  wald lie down, 785:20
Faint, chanting f. hymns to moon, 172:18
  cygnet to pale f. swan, 170:20
  damn with f. praise, 302:11
  heart ne'er won fair lady, 150:29
  heart never won fair lady, 530:16
  in light she loves, 458:21
  in the day of adversity, 22:24
  man so f. so spiritless, 183:10
  to some f. meaning make pretense, 274:26
  walk and not f., 27:23
  whole heart is f., 25:26
  with envy of the dead, 68:5
Faintest, water hears thy f. word, 264:*n*3
Fainting Robin, 513:10
Faintly then he praises, 302:*n*7
Fair adventure of tomorrow, 170:19
  all f. is good, 154:15
  all's f. in love and war, 482:13
  always f. weather, 589:3
  ambition to be f., 318:5
  and f. and twice so f., 156:12
  and flagrant things, 264:14
  and foul near kin, 598:20
  and learned and good as she, 240:14
  and softly goes far, 128:*n*8
  and stately palace, 452:5
  and unpolluted flesh, 199:11

Fair (*continued*)
  and wise good and gay, 791:3
  angels are painted f., 284:17
  anything possible except f. play, 539:15
  anything to show more f., 374:12
  as a star, 373:19
  as f. as any may be, 156:12
  as the moon, 25:6
  at first when our day f., 540:19
  attitude, 416:6
  Bacchus ever f. and young, 276:9
  baseness to write f., 199:20
  bevy of f. women, 260:19
  book of knowledge f., 257:24
  breeze blew, 381:6
  buzz witty and f. annoys, 302:15
  chaste and f., 231:21
  chaste unexpressive she, 191:6
  daffodils we weep to see, 241:10
  damned in a f. wife, 205:9
  day adieu, 169:29
  day's wages for work, 413:4
  die because a woman's f., 240:1
  disguise f. nature, 185:3
  divided excellence, 169:23
  Elaine the f., 459:12
  Ellen of brave Lochinvar, 378:9
  exterior a silent recommendation, 99:10
  fairer daughter of f. mother, 95:27
  fallen unto me in a f. ground, 16:*n*1
  farewell f. cruelty, 201:29
  fat f. and forty, 348:14
  field full of folk, 127:18
  find how to make it f., 466:8
  fleshed f. erected, 729:2
  fool called her lady f., 592:23
  forever love and she f., 416:3
  forfeit f. renown, 378:1
  from foul to f., 160:18
  going to f., 789:5
  guerdon we hope to find, 253:20
  hand that made you f., 204:16
  Harvard, 405:12
  holy f. and wise is she, 168:7
  hot wench in taffeta, 176:24
  house upon another man's ground, 182:28
  how sweet and f. she seems, 250:1
  I have sworn thee f., 222:14
  I was also, 350:20
  if it prove f. weather, 262:9
  if ladies but young and f., 190:26
  in hope of f. advantages, 180:22
  is foul and foul is fair, 212:10
  it isn't f. isn't right, 739:15
  it will be f. weather, 35:25
  justice in f. round belly, 191:3
  laughs the morn, 323:8
  luminous cloud, 383:9
  Madeline's f. breast, 415:4
  maid dwellin', 785:9
  maidens commonly fortunate, 155:15
  means or foul, 649:5
  mistress moderately f., 266:18
  Montague I am too fond, 175:5
  most divinely f., 454:13

Fair (*continued*)
my f. lady, 788:12
my own f. hands, 288:21
never fight f. with stranger, 738:16
none but brave deserves f., 276:6
not to fancy what f. in life, 466:8
nothing f. alone, 429:7
one f. daughter, 195:33
open face of heaven, 413:22
play f. just and patient, 505:6
power of one f. face, 137:10
practices to fair notions, 74:12
queens have died young and f.,
227:2
rise up my f. one, 25:6
Sabrina f., 253:11
sae fresh and f., 362:8
Science frowned not, 322:22
seedtime had my soul, 373:7
sex, 150:27
sex your department, 578:1
she a f. divided excellence, 169:23
she that was ever f., 206:8
slain by f. cruel maid, 202:13
so f. a house, 224:2
so foul and f. a day, 212:16
so lovely f., 208:1
so sweet and pure and f., 420:1
stood wind for France, 161:9
tale of a tub, 137:16
terms and villain's mind, 180:12
their very memory is f., 270:9
thou art all f., 25:11
though f. and wise, 408:13
tide full moon lies f., 499:19
to me f. friend never old, 221:21
trees that grow so f., 593:17
tresses race ensnare, 299:12
view f. Melrose, 377:23
viewed in her f. face's field, 166:36
wants us to fight f., 654:13
was she not f., 107:2
weather cometh out of the north,
15:5
what care I how f. she be, 240:1
what's right and f., 501:20
when Love and Life f., 567:18
wild and f., 379:4
wisly f. and softe, 128:23
woman true and f., 228:6
women and brave men, 399:21
words shall prevail, 592:16
young and so f., 423:9
Faire, laissez f. laissez passer, 305:21
Fairer, be she f. than the day, 240:1
daughter of fair mother, 95:27
grows f. than at first, 222:5
herself a f. flower, 258:10
lady never seen, 785:5
than evening air, 162:20
when we look back, 486:4
Fairest, descriptions of f. wights,
221:22
from f. creatures desire increase,
220:7
Isle all isles excelling, 275:30
joys give most unrest, 414:14
mock time with f. show, 213:15
of creation, 260:10
of her daughters Eve, 258:14

Fairest (*continued*)
things fleetest end, 581:1
thou f. among women, 25:2
Fair-haired Rhadamanthys, 53:8
Fairies at bottom of garden, 632:1
do you believe in f., 581:22
rewards and f., 238:1
sweets of F. Peris Goddesses, 414:16
Fairies' midwife, 174:20
Fairing, ah Tam thou'll get thy f.,
363:11
Fair-spoken and persuading, 226:6
Fairy, by f. fiction dressed, 323:10
by f. hands knell rung, 324:11
come not near our f. queen, 173:12
fruits and flowers, 452:2
gifts fading away, 391:13
gold, 222:27
love-gift of f. tale, 518:13
no f. takes, 192:29
queen, 173:12
story of simians, 622:14
'tis almost f. time, 174:12
wide enough to wrap a f., 173:9
Fais ce que voudras, 139:*n*12
Faith, alternative to f. we lose, 713:12
an excitement and enthusiasm,
436:26
and fire within us, 540:20
and justice toward nations, 337:6
and morals hold, 375:1
animated by f. and hope, 314:18
be alone and f. renew, 544:2
become intuition, 376:22
begets heretics, 606:5
blind f. unpardonable sin, 505:5
breastplate of f., 45:7
confess f. therein, 683:2
creed of our political f., 344:9
dead which does not doubt, 590:2
denied the f., 45:18
duty cannot exist without f., 434:30
dying for f. not hard, 463:17
for all defects supplying, 124:6
for the sake of f. in f., 589:15
fresh and full of f., 435:1
fruit of Spirit is f., 44:19
good fight of f., 45:23
guardians of the f., 668:1
have f. and pursue end, 543:3
he mauna fa' that, 363:22
he who has courage and f., 760:10
holy f., 474:2
humor prelude to f., 684:17
if f. o'ercomes doubt, 466:11
if it want for f., 479:28
if scholar have not f., 80:2
if strong f. indulge in skepticism,
552:30
illogical belief in improbable,
642:20
in result makes result, 546:7
in some nice tenets, 267:12
in this f. I will live and die, 134:2
is her own scourge, 105:*n*16
is sight and knowledge, 476:20
is the substance of things hoped for,
45:38
kept the f., 45:29
many a man's soul and f., 773:1

Faith (*continued*)
martyrs create f., 589:13
more f. in honest doubt, 457:26
mountain whom only f. can move,
732:8
no f. in immortality, 443:21
no more despair or loss of f.,
745:22
nonviolence article of f., 606:12
nor love nor law, 406:21
not create martyrs, 589:13
not f. but philosophy, 248:14
not for all his f. see, 429:9
not yet entered your hearts, 117:16
nothing more wonderful than f.,
558:8
now abideth f., 43:16
O thou of little f., 35:20
O ye of little f., 34:19
of our fathers, 474:2
passive or hereditary f., 393:2
pin f. in things not seen, 111:30
pity their want of f., 341:13
plain and simple f., 189:12
Punic f., 91:31
quality cannot dispense with, 575:9
reaffirm f. in human rights, 655:23
reason greatest enemy f. has, 138:14
room from which f. gone, 713:10
sanctified by reason blest by f.,
373:14
save myself by work and f., 717:19
saved by f., 684:18
sea of f., 499:22
shatter f. of men, 589:15
shell universe is to ear of F., 376:21
shines equal arming me, 480:4
show doubt prove f., 466:11
simple f. than Norman blood, 454:3
something of a f., 457:1
staff of f. to walk upon, 152:16
stand fast in f., 43:29
still by f. he trod, 637:5
that could remove mountains, 43:14
that yields to none, 101:7
thy f. hath saved thee, 38:14
triumphant o'er fears, 441:19
under another mask, 713:12
unfaithful, 459:15
walk by f. not sight, 44:3
want of enterprise and f., 478:29
wears f. as fashion of hat, 186:10
welcome home discarded f., 170:18
when f. lost honor dies, 443:4
where f. in reason timid, 615:6
without works, 46:10
ye must have f., 575:9
you call for f., 466:11
Faithful Achates, 94:7
action f. honor clear, 300:24
among the faithless f., 259:15
are the wounds of a friend, 23:1
at all times f. husband, 293:16
Christian f. man, 165:29
dog bear him company, 301:8
Duty's f. child, 422:6
elephant's f. one hundred per cent,
715:2
ever f., 119:29
falling out of f. friends, 85:*n*11

Faithful (*continued*)
  fierce wars and f. loves, 153:4
  friend is medicine, 31:16
  friend is strong defense, 31:15
  friends hard to find, 233:12
  good and f. servant, 36:14
  in least faithful in much, 39:1
  in love, 378:8
  love is f., 132:20
  O come all ye f., 118:16
  Penelope, 54:12
  three f. friends, 309:22
  to conviction to old age, 76:17
  to thee Cynara, 602:7
  to what exists in yourself, 607:3
  unto death, 47:9
  women all alike, 646:16
Faithfully to serve State, 246:25
Faithfulness, His infinite f., 287:3
  hold f. and sincerity, 60:18
  to truth of history, 503:5
Faithless, among the f. faithful, 259:15
  arm, 720:16
  as a smile, 668:4
  as winds or seas, 281:14
  be not f., 40:42
  but f. was she, 497:9
  in friendship but f. haven, 65:13
Faith's Defender, 304:14
Faiths, fighting f., 542:25
  men's f. wafer-cakes, 185:2
  old f. loosen and fall, 534:4
Fakes, windpipe throttled in f. of
    death, 489:12
Fakir, powers of levitation make f.
    stare, 670:19
Falcon, dapple-dawn-drawn F., 550:20
  gentle as f., 135:23
  like a f. swooping, 4:6
  not hear falconer, 596:19
  red rose a f., 553:19
  towering in her pride, 214:18
Falconer, falcon not hear f., 596:19
Falconer's, O for a f. voice, 175:12
Falcons, hopes like towering f., 287:16
Fall, a thousand shall f. at thy side,
    18:15
  Anarch lets curtain f., 304:2
  as wrong as to f. short, 61:16
  baseball leaves you face f. alone,
    769:8
  benison to f., 241:21
  bigger they come harder f., 70:n3
  both f. into ditch, 35:23
  by dividing we f., 336:10
  cradle will f., 555:4
  decline and f. of Rome, 340:16
  desire of power caused angels to f.,
    159:16
  divided we f., 336:n5
  down can f. no lower, 263:15
  dying f., 201:16
  fain climb yet fear to f., 152:12
  fear no f., 272:28
  flat on your face, 690:13
  flower displayed doth f., 202:11
  forts of folly f., 500:3
  fruit that can f. without shaking,
    304:6
  glass f. forever, 722:4

Fall (*continued*)
  good to gain day good to f., 489:4
  half to rise half to f., 301:13
  hard rain's a-gonna f., 771:6
  harder they come harder they f.,
    774:10
  haughty spirit before a f., 21:31
  he that trusteth in riches shall f.,
    21:9
  hero perish or sparrow f., 301:5
  Humpty Dumpty had f., 790:13
  I f. into Charybdis, 181:11
  I with shuddering f., 509:1
  if Freedom f., 593:25
  if you stay price will f., 159:22
  in love with Athens, 72:7
  in with what asked to accept,
    625:16
  into a habit, 589:14
  into arms not hands, 544:23
  into hands of Carl Sandburg,
    693:13
  into Scylla to avoid Charybdis,
    181:n2
  leaves f. early, 659:3
  let f. the curtains, 335:3
  let sword of France f., 678:10
  let them f. in over pigs, 650:14
  lie talking of f. of man, 479:9
  like a bright exhalation, 225:14
  like one of the princes, 18:4
  liquid siftings f., 668:16
  not a sparrow f., 34:33
  O what a f. was there, 189:7
  of a sparrow, 199:22
  one by one, 330:23
  out and chide and fight, 294:8
  pride will have a f., 65:n11
  Satan as lightning f., 38:20
  silence f. like dews, 660:14
  since Adam's f., 595:15
  soar not too high to f., 238:5
  some by virtue f., 203:30
  some rain must f., 441:6
  stars begin to f., 794:17
  sweet music's melting f., 323:15
  take heed lest he f., 43:7
  things f. apart, 596:19
  though china f., 300:19
  though heaven f. thy will be done,
    119:28
  through air of true wise friend,
    729:18
  to reprobation, 208:13
  to the base earth, 171:19
  tyrants f. in every foe, 363:20
  universe must one day f., 748:8
  unless billboards f., 709:10
  upon gilded eaves, 456:15
  upon thorns of life, 407:16
  water reach rest and f., 696:3
  we f. to rise, 468:17
  what if sky were to f., 85:20
  wide arch of ranged empire f.,
    216:25
  wit on other souls may f., 274:26
  woods decay and f., 459:1
Fall, die Welt ist alles was der F. ist,
    677:n2
Fallacies, poignant f. of our age, 768:6

Fallacy, Pathetic F., 487:13
Fallen at length that tower, 458:7
  Babylon is f., 26:19, 47:31
  be forever f., 256:9
  by the edge of the sword, 31:44
  by the tongue, 31:44
  cold and dead, 491:1
  fallen fallen fallen, 276:12
  from grace, 44:17
  from his high estate, 276:12
  god who remembers heavens, 405:9
  how are mighty f., 12:1
  how art thou f., 26:14
  imagined despair f. upon me,
    419:14
  into the sere, 216:9
  lines are f. unto me, 16:6
  lot is f. unto me, 16:n1
  moon stars f. on me, 655:4
  on evil days, 259:19
  prince and great man f., 12:4
  so f. so lost, 443:3
  soldier's pole is f., 218:8
  speak for f. and weak, 484:20
  splendid tear, 458:23
  strength like f. angel, 414:6
  what will I do when you f., 747:12
Fallest a blessed martyr, 225:21
  if thou f. O Cromwell, 225:21
Fallible men governed by bad pas-
    sions, 343:7
  will of another f. being, 365:28
Falling, adjusted to beams f., 689:12
  catch a f. star, 228:5
  cruelty to load f. man, 225:n2
  dropped like f. star, 256:22
  gently f. on thy head, 294:12
  horror of f. into naught, 292:14
  in love at first sight, 591:1
  in melody back, 383:2
  of a leaf, 487:2
  on dark central plain, 647:8
  out of faithful friends, 85:n11
  press not f. man, 225:15
  salmon jumping f. back, 743:15
  secure amidst f. world, 292:3
  softly on Bog of Allen, 647:8
  what's this am I f., 510:3
  when heaven f., 580:1
  with f. oars kept time, 268:25
Falling-off, what a f. was there,
    194:21
Fallow, came a f. doe, 785:15
Falls, as long divorce of steel f., 225:6
  brightness f. from the air, 227:2
  Coliseum Rome fall, 400:27
  force without wisdom f. of own
    weight, 96:16
  howls hoo and f., 639:23
  into abatement, 201:17
  like Lucifer, 225:16
  monotonously f. rain, 700:8
  nature f. into revolt, 184:10
  nips his root then he f., 225:16
  ripest fruit first f., 171:12
  splendor f. on castle, 456:11
  the Shadow, 669:10
  thy shadow Cynara, 602:9
  with leaf in October, 236:4
False Achitophel was first, 274:3

False *(continued)*

ambition drove men to become f., 91:23

and hollow, 257:1

as air as water, 200:22

as common fame, 283:24

as Cressid, 200:22

as dicers' oaths, 197:28

as tears of crocodiles, 157:*n*3

as water, 208:12

betrayed by f. within, 508:28

burn out f. shames, 657:14

by philosopher equally f., 339:12

creation from brain, 213:20

distinguish true from f., 277:19

face must hide, 213:15

fictions only and f. hair, 243:9

framed to make women f., 206:2

from f. to f., 200:22

gallop of verses, 191:11

history must be f., 295:5

how f. the argument, 89:*n*10

idea of what true and f., 277:19

idle and f. imposition, 206:21

idol or noble true birth, 76:9

if I be f. or swerve, 200:22

in friendship f., 274:6

little better than f. knaves, 187:3

maids in love, 200:22

man does easy, 214:17

man f. man, 285:9

never be f., 470:27

never say I was f. of heart, 221:24

not f. to others, 159:24

or honest dreaming, 749:14

philosophy, 257:13

prophet, 684:16

prophets, 34:10

proved true before prove f., 263:29

punishment if one swears f. oath, 52:17

ring out the f., 457:29

sea shows f. alluring smile, 89:19

shoot f. Love, 776:23

that which accepted f., 614:1

to any man, 194:1

to object, 720:5

to two or three, 228:7

understanding is f. mirror, 158:14

what f. heart doth know, 213:15

witness against thy neighbor, 9:12

witness by their own mouth, 32:18

words infect the soul, 75:2

Falsehood, flattery and f., 346:1

God's mouth knows not f., 63:7

goodly outside f. hath, 180:7

has to be invented, 646:2

history belief in f., 499:*n*2

let her and F. grapple, 255:4

Mississippi of f., 499:13

more miraculous than fact, 318:14

no f. lingers to old age, 67:16

no word to express lying and f., 289:13

not veil truth with f., 116:2

of the tongue, 343:11

stick the heart of f., 200:22

strife of Truth with F., 485:1

time's glory to unmask f., 167:2

truth f. to world beyond, 146:8

Falsehood *(continued)*

upbraid my f., 200:22

your bait of f., 195:7

Falsehoods, we know how to speak f., 54:15

Falsely, deal f. with God, 239:27

paint f. and add accent of nature, 522:7

science f. so called, 45:25

true, 459:15

Falseness in impressions of external, 487:13

Falser than vows made in wine, 191:25

tomorrow's f. than former day, 273:16

Falstaff in Arthur's bosom, 184:30

sweats to death, 177:15

Falter life away, 498:10

my heart grow sick f., 711:3

neither to change nor f. nor repent, 407:6

or explore, 749:17

when the Sun, 513:4

Fama volat, 93:*n*19

Fame created something of nothing, 250:16

desire of f., 459:20

enjoying timeless f., 60:12

estate good f., 429:19

fair F. inspires, 302:11

flash packet of f., 793:21

fool to f., 302:8

foolish and false as f., 283:24

for his f. the ocean sea, 233:9

for pot of ale, 185:6

from zone to zone, 544:9

great heir of f., 251:2

Hall o' F. when you croaks, 673:15

halls of f., 781:15

heard of the f. of Solomon, 12:25

if not double-faced, 261:18

is ephemeral, 111:8

is no plant, 253:21

is the spur, 253:20

lives in f. died in virtue's cause, 167:9

lost to f., 92:29

love and f. to nothingness, 417:11

nor F. I slight, 298:8

nor yet fool to f., 302:8

nothing but empty name, 333:16

of her excellence, 54:12

only to myself, 249:22

over living head bent, 408:22

poets' food love and f., 407:12

pursues f. at risk of losing self, 80:11

rage for f., 341:17

rather than love money f., 478:39

Riches F. and Pleasure, 278:20

ruins of another's f., 297:11

sun of dead, 422:9

thirst of youth, 400:6

to fortune and f. unknown, 322:22

trust to common f., 430:22

was noised throughout the country, 10:35

well known to f., 781:4

what is end of f., 402:15

Fame *(continued)*

while f. elates thee, 391:9

wisdom and prosperity exceedeth the f., 12:26

Famed in song famous Athens, 64:12

Troy walls f. in battle, 93:30

Fame's eternal beadroll, 153:19

eternal camping ground, 492:4

Familiar acts beautiful, 407:4

as his garter, 184:22

as rose in spring, 111:11

be thou f., 193:29

beauty grows f. to lover, 292:8

more f. with Africa, 765:9

new things are made f., 314:23

old and f. objects, 384:14

old f. faces, 387:14

sit at feet of the f., 431:12

style f. but not coarse, 314:17

things are made new, 314:23

wine a good f. creature, 206:24

with tragedies of antiquity, 769:2

Familiarity breeds contempt, 58:20

breeds contempt and children, 58:*n*10

Families, best-regulated f., 470:33

God setteth the solitary in f., 17:39

great f. of yesterday, 285:16

happy f. alike, 510:11

I hate you, 607:2

lie together, 752:4

rooks in f. go, 540:25

Familles je vous hais, 607:*n*3

Family, about man that left f., 526:21

children of one f., 294:8

church and private school, 501:15

father of a f., 110:3

greatest thing in f. life, 625:15

history begins with me, 76:18

join the f., 624:5

nobody not in f., 387:8

of Man, 634:14

party tribe or clan, 780:21

refuse to help f., 602:12

root of the state, 79:15

stamped character on child, 629:1

supporting f. paying taxes, 541:5

unhappy f. unhappy in own way, 510:11

Famine, die by f. die by inches, 286:13

Pestilence Destruction Death, 643:15

seven years of f., 8:7

Famished, I hear a f. howl, 734:14

Fam'ly, refuse to help f., 602:12

Famous Athens divine city, 64:12

awoke and found myself f., 401:6

by my sword, 264:5

by their birth, 171:9

couldn't give up writing too f., 675:15

day and year, 442:12

earth sepulcher of f. men, 72:7

forgotten for want of writers, 97:*n*1

found that f. country, 683:10

Hanover city, 464:17

harmony of leaves, 594:23

high top-hat, 637:11

island descending, 619:22

let us praise f. men, 32:13

Famous (*continued*)
maiden f. to all time, 96:20
make thee f. by my pen, 264:*n*2
most f. event in biology, 760:*n*1
remarks seldom quoted correctly, 641:1
to all ages, 254:20
victory, 386:7
Washington full of f. men, 541:1
world-f. for fifteen minutes, 758:17
Famoused, painful warrior f. for fight, 220:14
Fan, brain him with lady's f., 177:17
cool gales f. the glade, 298:7
like an injured f., 664:5
with her f. spread, 291:10
Fanatic can't change mind, 622:9
does what Lord wud do, 603:4
Fanatical, my f. will power, 676:10
Fanaticism redoubling efforts, 588:5
to barbarism one step, 320:3
Fancier, Moses should have f. stick, 748:9
Fancies, high region of f., 254:12
lay earthly f. down, 458:8
our f. are more giddy, 202:10
realities less dangerous than f., 615:18
Fanciful, no test which is not f., 67:2
Fancy, ever let f. roam, 416:10
excellent f., 199:8
from flower bell, 466:9
full of shapes is f., 201:17
hopeless f. feigned, 456:14
is mode of memory, 384:8
motives of more f., 203:22
my f. flies, 328:12
not expressed in f., 193:30
not to f. what fair in life, 466:8
now f. passes by, 579:2
sweet and bitter f., 192:7
when I go to rest, 634:17
where is f. bred, 181:3
whispers of f., 314:9
work of the brain and f., 280:3
young man's f., 455:9
Fancy-free, maiden meditation f., 173:6
Fancy's, impediments in f. course, 203:22
misled by f. meteor ray, 361:15
more witnesseth than f. images, 174:2
Shakespeare F. child, 251:19
Faneuil Hall cradle of liberty, 395:10
Fanged, fields f. with flints, 708:7
Fangs, beware my f., 181:10
Fanny's, pretty F. way, 295:19
Fans, pelicans collapsed like f., 739:10
Fantasies, thousand f. begin to throng, 252:24
Fantastic century move, 353:9
light f. round, 252:23
light f. toe, 251:9
plays such f. tricks, 204:4
reveries, 538:5
summer's heat, 171:3
tripped light f., 585:7
Fantastical, high f., 201:17
old f. duke of dark corners, 204:25

Fantasy, begot of vain f., 174:21
goes for walk returns with bride, 736:9
master of f., 565:23
neurotic possessed by f., 718:2
poet in command of f., 718:2
suspicion rumor f., 762:2
Far and few, 472:4
and near unite, 340:17
as coin would stretch, 176:28
be it from God, 15:3
brother f. off, 23:3
do not peer too f., 63:29
do not set eyes on things f. off, 63:*n*11
down within dim West, 451:14
fair and softly goes f., 128:*n*8
fierce hour and sweet, 619:9
forward since we have come so f., 167:32
from fiery noon, 416:19
from madding crowd's, 322:17
from old folks at home, 507:1
from the sun, 323:2
green hill f. away, 479:18
how f. candle throws beams, 182:11
I can be pushed so f., 604:9
in the pillared dark, 624:14
in western brookland, 579:11
much too f. out all my life, 710:6
not too f. from yew, 671:19
o'er hills and f. away, 456:2
on ringing plains of Troy, 455:1
over hills and f. away, 297:15, 790:4
peace to him that is f. off, 28:3
side of baldness, 594:9
slight not what's near by aiming f., 68:9
so f. only should we hate, 65:13
so f. trust thee Kate, 177:18
so near yet so f., 457:27
those f. off are attracted, 61:19
whistles f. and wee, 688:8
why art thou so f. from helping me, 16:15
Far East, those who brought war to F., 655:6
Far West, seek gold in F., 502:5
Farce, facts personages appear second as f., 481:6
is played, 140:11
Farced title 'fore king, 185:19
Farcical, everything I touch f., 508:17
Fardels, who would f. bear, 196:10
Fare, bread and Gospel good f., 286:17
delicate f. in another's house, 32:1
forward, 84:*n*7
forward voyagers, 671:17
good-bye f. you well, 793:16
hard very hard is my f., 297:5
last of Romans f. thee well, 189:26
like my peers, 467:19
thee well if forever, 401:20
when you receive f., 520:8
Fares, how f. it with happy dead, 457:12
ill f. the land, 329:8
Farewell all joys, 777:6

Farewell (*continued*)
also called F., 509:26
and then forever, 362:10
bid f. to every fear, 294:18
bid joys f., 414:4
content, 207:8
dear paintings, 247:12
distracting town f., 299:27
fair cruelty, 201:29
fear farewell remorse, 258:6
forever f. Cassius, 189:23
goes out sighing, 201:2
hail and f. my brother, 91:18
hope, 258:6
Horace whom I hated, 400:19
king, 172:1
Leicester Square, 627:15
lobster-nights f., 300:1
Monsieur Traveler, 191:28
Morning Star, 87:5
my bok and my devocioun, 129:4
neighing steed, 207:8
only feel f., 398:15
Othello's occupation's gone, 207:8
plumed troop, 207:8
renowned Eretria, 74:9
rewards and fairies, 238:1
sadness, 691:10
sweets to the sweet f., 199:13
the tranquil mind, 207:8
thou art too dear, 221:11
thou child of my right hand, 232:10
to all my greatness, 225:16
to college joys, 652:18
to Lochaber, 297:25
to the Highlands, 362:16
to thee farewell, 537:1
Farewells, as many f. as stars, 201:7
everlasting f., 397:16
should be sudden, 403:24
Far-flung battle line, 592:25
Farfrae, Elizabeth-Jane F. not told of my death, 539:18
Farm, best business father's f., 462:12
crouched on hillside, 708:7
is like a man, 85:1
keep 'em down on f., 658:3
Middlesex village and f., 442:13
snug little f. the world, 386:21
Farmer in the dell, 792:13
sowing the corn, 792:24
Farmer's boy, 777:13
on f. land may fall, 554:8
wife, 788:2
Farmers, ah too fortunate f., 92:28
embattled f. stood, 429:22
founders of civilization, 395:3
gentlemen f., 403:10
mechanics and laborers, 369:11
pray that summers be wet, 92:23
Farmhand, apple-faced f., 779:*n*7
Farmhouse, stop without f. near, 623:17
Farms, destroy f. grass will grow in streets, 582:3
houses and f. pillaged, 336:14
what spires what f., 579:9
Farmsteads, when people inspect f., 87:1

Farmyard, cock louder in own f.,
    475:15
Far-off curfew sound, 252:4
    divine event, 458:3
    spies a f. shore, 164:21
    touch of greatness, 459:14
Farquhar, Peyton F. was dead, 544:10
Far-reaching ancestry, 503:4
Farrier, Felix Randal the f., 551:3
Farrow, Ireland old sow that eats f.,
    647:9
Far-stretched, all the f. greatness,
    153:1
Farther away on either hand, 683:16
    off from heaven, 422:20
Farthest Thule, 92:21
    Thulè, 308:8
    way home's the f. way, 242:11
Farthing, do not care a f. candle,
    388:3
    every f. of cost, 720:17
    hold f. candle to sun, 235:n 4
    two sparrows sold for f., 34:33
Farthings, Latin word for three f.,
    168:26
    owe me five f., 788:20
Fas est et ab hoste doceri, 101:n 17
Fascinate, blandishments not f. us,
    348:1
Fascinates, work f. me, 580:12
Fascination frantic, 531:10
    of what's difficult, 595:19
    war regarded wicked will have f.,
    566:9
Fascist, woman adores F., 764:18
Fashion birth intellect, 503:8
    bravery never out of f., 464:1
    faithful in my f., 602:7
    glass of f. mould of form, 196:18
    high Roman f., 218:9
    is architecture, 651:10
    like rusty mail, 200:24
    mayest f. thyself in whatever shape,
    136:1
    of these times, 190:13
    of this world passeth, 43:3
    out of world out of f., 291:18
    seen in my natural f., 145:8
    take pleasures sadly after f. of coun-
    try, 157:17
    true to you in my f., 682:7
    wears faith as f. of hat, 186:10
    wears out more apparel, 186:39
    worn-out poetical f., 670:23
Fashionable, other f. topics, 328:24
    supersede f. novel, 425:10
    time like f. host, 201:2
Fashioned, gods f. by men, 588:16
    Providunce f. us holler, 485:12
    so slenderly, 423:9
Fashion's brightest arts, 329:21
    word is out, 599:4
Fashions in proud Italy, 171:7
    not cut conscience to fit f., 716:9
    old f. please best, 167:24
Fast and furious, 363:8
    driveth onward to f., 454:9
    hit f. hit often, 647:5
    how f. shadows fall, 608:20
    ill weed groweth f., 141:24

Fast (*continued*)
    men die f. enough, 284:11
    now he is dead should I f., 12:12
    or come he f., 378:6
    ship that does not sail f., 348:9
    stumble that run f., 175:18
    they follow, 198:n 5
    thick and f. came at last, 519:2
    thine arrows stick f. in me, 17:4
    wit speeds too f., 168:24
Fasted forty days and nights, 32:35
Fasten him as a nail, 26:22
    your seatbelts bumpy night, 727:5
Fastened me flesh, 550:17
    to dying animal, 597:9
    Venus f. to prey, 281:10
Faster, beat to follow f., 217:14
    faster, 518:18
    speed far f. than light, 618:14
    than speeding bullet, 737:7
    travel f. than stagecoach, 329:24
    walk a little f., 518:5
    world would go round f., 517:13
Fastest, travels f. alone, 591:7
Fastidious, most f. critics, 424:22
Fastidiousness, unconscious f., 664:12
Fasting, lives on hope die f., 310:8
    thank heaven f., 191:23
    when full talk of f. easy, 114:5
Fat, all of us are f., 519:4
    and bean-fed horse, 173:2
    and greasy citizens, 190:9
    and sleek a true hog, 97:11
    black bucks, 637:8
    church ain't out till f. lady sings,
    782:12
    contentions, 254:19
    duller than f. weed, 194:19
    eat the f. of the land, 8:14
    fair and forty, 348:14
    feast of f. things, 26:26
    feed f. the ancient grudge, 180:4
    geese are getting f., 779:14
    if to be f. be hated, 177:31
    in every f. man a thin one, 711:1
    is in the fire, 140:19
    Jack Sprat eat no f., 788:7
    Jeshurun waxed f., 10:27
    laugh and grow f., 187:n 1
    men about me that are f., 187:24
    more f. than bard beseems, 308:14
    no sweeter f. than sticks to bones,
    489:5
    of others' works, 234:5
    oily man of God, 308:15
    one is f. and grows old, 177:22
    outside every f. man an even fatter
    man, 711:n 1
    resolved to grow f., 348:n 2
    Seymour's F. Lady, 747:9
    sharp names never f., 698:6
    should himself be f., 317:31
    take f. with lean, 470:42
    Venus grown f., 397:6
    white woman, 661:12
    who drives f. oxen, 317:31
Fatal and perfidious bark, 253:22
    bellman, 214:2
    bowels of deep, 166:3
    complaint, 704:12

Fatal (*continued*)
    entrance of Duncan, 212:29
    facility of octosyllabic, 401:10
    futility of Fact, 549:4
    gift of beauty, 400:15
    vision, 213:20
    Waterloo, 399:24
    yes I am f. man, 463:14
Fatality of seeing things too well,
    640:5
Fate, all our children's f., 593:24
    can be director of opponent's f.,
    80:21
    cannot harm me, 380:18
    certain of his f., 206:31
    chooses our relatives, 341:16
    complex f. being American, 548:6
    coughed and called it f., 608:4
    death milder f. than tyranny, 63:16
    determines or indicates f., 477:30
    eagle's f. and mine are one, 59:n 8
    eccentric propositions of its f.,
    639:19
    fears his f. too much, 264:4
    fixed f. free will, 257:12
    forced by f., 276:5
    foulness of their f., 662:7
    gave his sad lucidity, 497:10
    gave whate'er denied, 485:27
    had imagination about, 624:2
    hanging breathless on f., 441:18
    has cursed you, 68:6
    have conquered F., 497:12
    heart for any f., 440:18
    heart for every f., 401:27
    hung on razor's edge, 60:13
    I feel my f., 725:6
    I thy f. shall overtake, 242:2
    is handspike, 486:28
    lead me Zeus and F., 82:3
    man identifies with his f., 700:11
    man's character is his f., 62:22
    man's f., 707:11
    master of f., 459:9, 677:7
    master of my f., 557:10
    masters of our own f., 700:4
    meet f. among clouds, 596:10
    men cannot suspend f., 286:2
    my f. cries out, 194:14
    no armor against f., 246:23
    no f. misunderstand me, 623:8
    nobly born must nobly meet f.,
    69:10
    not decide single human f., 717:22
    of all extremes, 300:10
    of architect, 349:27
    of nation in own power, 426:4
    of nation riding, 442:14
    of new truths, 505:19
    of unborn millions, 336:14
    proud captain of thine own f.,
    91:n 15
    Providence will and f., 257:12
    rave no more 'gainst f., 532:6
    read book of f., 184:1
    seemed to wind him up, 273:21
    seize f. by the throat, 371:17
    sits on dark battlements, 367:12
    slave to f., 230:23
    stars of thy f., 365:9

Fate (*continued*)
    stronger than anything, 68:7
    summons monarchs obey, 274:25
    take a bond of f., 215:20
    take F. by throat., 516:12
    thy f. and mine sealed, 456:19
    torrent of his f., 313:22
    what f. predestined, 370:20
    why know their f., 321:17
Fateful lightning, 484:6
Fates have given a patient soul, 52:25
    impose that men abide, 164:26
    masters of their f., 187:22
    of dread death, 52:21
    spinning our own f., 545:14
Father Abraham, 461:11
    alone is God, 392:17
    and I went to camp, 778:*n*4
    and mither gae mad, 362:18
    answered never word, 441:1
    antichrist denieth the F., 46:34
    author of play, 588:23
    baptizing in the name of F., 37:15
    bosom of his F., 322:24
    called brother's f. dad, 169:24
    child f. of man, 374:7
    cold mad f., 647:22
    dear f. come home, 520:5
    deny thy f., 175:1
    disappointed in monkey, 528:4
    eternal F. strong to save, 506:4
    far greater than his f., 51:26
    fear was my f., 725:1
    fell back behind Christ, 569:18
    foolish son calamity of f., 21:44
    forgive my injuries, 743:7
    full fathom five thy f. lies, 223:32
    gave f. forty-one, 781:11
    ghost of Hamlet's f., 584:7
    glorify your F. in heaven, 33:3
    glory be to the F., 48:22
    God an exalted f., 569:7
    God F. even more Mother, 731:17
    Great F. building forts among us,
        502:5
    Great Spirit is my f., 370:1
    greatness in f. overwhelms son,
        233:6
    happy to be f. unto many sons,
        164:20
    hath chastised you, 12:29
    have we not all one f., 30:7
    heard my f. say, 338:14
    held out golden scales, 52:21
    honor thy f. and thy mother, 9:12
    in my youth said f., 517:10
    in thy gracious keeping, 506:15
    into thy hands, 39:22
    liar and f. of it, 40:12
    lived his soul, 689:2
    mad feary f., 647:22
    man shall leave f. and mother, 6:18
    many talks from great f., 333:7
    more than hundred schoolmasters,
        244:35
    moved through dooms, 689:1
    my f. feeds flocks, 325:8
    my f. paints summer, 749:12
    my f. sold me, 356:11
    my f. wept, 358:11

Father (*continued*)
    my God my F. and Friend, 278:25
    name called everlasting F., 26:8
    no one like one's f. ever lived,
        743:18
    not God for f. if not Church for
        mother, 112:18
    of a family, 110:3
    of all in every age, 303:14
    of English criticism, 314:19
    of lights, 46:6
    of mankind, 443:17
    of many nations, 7:31
    of such as dwell in tents, 7:9
    of such as handle harp, 7:10
    of Waters unvexed to sea, 449:18
    of your country, 336:*n*7
    old f. antick the law, 176:29
    old f. old artificer, 647:11
    old F. William, 386:8, 517:9
    omnipotent F. with his thunder,
        53:*n*4
    our F. the Sky, 787:4
    please world and f., 268:1
    prince subject F. Son, 230:15
    rather have turnip than f., 315:4
    resembled my f. as he slept, 214:4
    ruffian, 177:30
    Scylla your f., 181:11
    seek f. who need son, 739:6
    smile at his f., 91:6
    Son and Holy Ghost, 37:15, 280:21
    struck f. when son swore, 235:16
    to corruption thou art my f., 14:26
    told me businessmen sons of
        bitches, 741:15
    true-begotten f., 180:14
    used to say, 664:10
    was a butcher, 271:22
    which art in heaven, 33:12
    will of my F., 34:13
    wise son maketh a glad f., 21:4
    wish f. to thought, 184:11
    withered when my f. died, 198:24
    without f. bred, 251:21
    would strangle f., 319:30
    you think your f. does not, 68:1
    your f. the devil, 40:12
Fathered, so f. and so husbanded,
    188:9
Fatherland, die for friends or f., 97:2
    everything belongs to f., 364:5
    no danger thine, 488:2
    O f. O Ilium, 93:30
Fatherless, judge the f., 25:29
Father-Mother God, 495:19
Father's, about my F. business, 38:7
    daughters of my f. house, 202:15
    desire f. death, 495:14
    drink in my F. kingdom, 36:28
    grave, 98:19
    house not house of merchandise,
        39:42
    in my f. house, 40:26
    joy mother's pride, 379:3
    lean in joy upon F. knee, 356:10
    looked into f. heart, 706:17
    must be about His F. business,
        694:9
    my f. theory, 557:5

Father's (*continued*)
    my land my f. land, 510:17
    sword girded on, 391:17
    we're going to our F. land, 773:17
    without f. word, 410:14
Fathers, ashes of his f., 425:14
    brought forth nation, 450:2
    desire not merely what f. had, 78:18
    faith of our f., 474:2
    God of f. known of old, 592:25
    good mothers and f., 711:22
    have eaten a sour grape, 28:35
    iniquity of the f., 9:10
    land where f. died, 444:3
    lie with my f., 8:16
    pardon old f., 595:23
    provoke not your children, 44:41
    scenes f. loved, 711:2
    sins of f. upon children, 69:17
    sojourner as all my f. were, 17:10
    sons similar to their f., 52:32
    that begat us, 32:13
    victory hundred f., 710:15
    worshipped stocks and stones,
        255:14
    your f. where are they, 29:43
Fathers-forth whose beauty past
    change, 551:1
Fathom, full f. five, 223:32
    line could never touch, 177:9
    scarcely f. their depths, 553:14
Fathomed, beauty not been f., 495:4
    the fathomable, 351:6
Fathoms, down f. down, 487:10
    fifty f. deep, 785:1
Fatigue of judging for themselves,
    352:36
    of supporting freedom, 341:1
    without f. of traveling, 150:25
Fatling, lion and f. together, 26:11
Fatness of these pursy times, 198:4
Fatted calf, 38:36
Fattenin' hogs ain't in luck, 556:16
Fattening, immoral illegal or f., 666:2
Fatter, outside fat man f. man trying
        to close in, 711:*n*1
    valley sheep f., 397:21
Fatti maschii parole femine, 244:*n*9
Fatuus, ignis f. of mind, 283:25
Faucet, writing f. upstairs, 625:14
Faulkner sole owner, 696:19
Fault, all f. who hath no f., 459:13
    artist is his own f., 717:6
    by her f. dropped like flower, 90:22
    condemn f. and not actor, 203:34
    every man has his f., 212:2
    faultless to f., 467:31
    feed on for f. not mine, 403:27
    fellow f. came to match, 191:19
    grows two thereby, 242:19
    if f. only on one side, 266:2
    if sack and sugar be f., 177:31
    just hint a f., 302:11
    knows how to confess f., 309:25
    no f. or flaw, 530:6
    not in our stars, 187:22
    O happy f., 48:12
    of penetrating wit, 265:39
    of the Dutch, 372:2
    one f. at first, 242:*n*8

Fault *(continued)*

only f. that he has no f., 110:5
seeming monstrous, 191:19
talk and find f., 149:10
through my f., 48:6
weariness and f., 623:20
worse by excuse, 170:10

Fault-finding, fact-finding more effective than f., 615:18

Faultily faultless, 458:17

Faultless monster world ne'er saw, 262:*n*1
to a fault, 467:31

Faults, all his f. observed, 189:18
all men make f., 220:21
bear with all the f. of man, 226:17
best men molded of f., 205:6
cleanse me from secret f., 16:12
do not fear to abandon f., 60:20
frees all f., 224:29
greatest of f. to be conscious of none, 110:*n*5
if no f. of our own, 265:2
lie gently on him, 226:3
love to f. always blind, 357:19
loves him better for f., 329:3
man must have f., 105:4
mum dad fill you with f. they had, 750:15
not for thy f. but mine, 400:19
persuade ourselves we have no great f., 265:34
pleasure in f. of others, 265:2
to f. a little blind, 287:19
to scan, 329:13
vile ill-favored f., 182:32
who covers f., 208:27
with all her f., 333:19
with all thy f. I love thee, 333:*n*6

Fauna, flora f. geography, 729:13

Faustus must be damned, 162:23

Faut, il f. cultiver notre jardin, 306:*n*7

Faute, pire qu'un crime c'est une f., 366:17

Favor, flattery in return for f., 371:19
found f. in thy sight, 7:32
from Fortune easier to get, 99:15
in that same way grant f., 84:9
increased in f., 38:8
is deceitful, 23:21
look with f. on bold beginning, 92:22
men f. deceit, 273:16
nor f. to men of skill, 24:20
obedience to law right not f., 576:3
render praise and f., 438:18
those who f. fire, 623:14
to this f. she must come, 199:8
truths in and out of f., 623:5
well bestowed, 293:24
when f. of gods was equal, 69:19
with God and man, 38:8

Favorite has no friend, 321:21
physician hath f. disease, 311:22
that f. subject Myself, 341:19

Favorites, all Kings and their f., 229:5
heaven gives its f., 81:*n*4
Way has no f., 58:5

Favoritism in public life, 572:22

Favors, conferring rather than accepting f., 72:*n*4
error to expect f., 337:8
fortune f. the brave, 86:*n*8, 94:25
hangs on princes' f., 225:16
lively sense of future f., 265:*n*2
nor for her f. call, 298:8
not by accepting f., 72:5
not won by trifling f., 392:16
rime into ladies' f., 186:3
rubs enhance value of f., 328:19
shower f. alike, 369:12

Fawn, to f. to crouch to wait, 154:6

Fawning greyhound did proffer, 177:10
publican, 180:3
thrift may follow f., 197:2

Fawns, when lion f. upon lamb, 164:30

Fe fi fo fum, 792:19

Fear, act of f., 193:20
afraid of f., 371:9
age of f., 703:15
all-powerful should f. everything, 249:15
and bloodshed, 376:9
and danger of violent death, 239:22
and distrust the people, 345:4
angels f. to tread, 299:6
arming me from f., 480:4
as children f. in darkness, 90:1
at my heart as at cup, 381:15
be just and f. not, 225:21
be not afraid of sudden f., 20:22
better is little with the f. of the Lord, 21:26
bid farewell to every f., 294:18
birds of prey, 203:28
boys that f. no noise, 330:6
by beauty and by f., 373:7
came upon me, 13:38
cannot be without hope, 278:6
concessions of f., 331:6
conquer f. beginning of wisdom, 615:14
cornered-animal f., 767:21
death as children fear dark, 159:4
death feel fog, 467:18
do not f. to abandon faults, 60:20
doth Job f. God for nought, 13:30
every infant's cry of f., 358:8
extreme f. neither fight nor fly, 166:39
fain climb yet f. to fall, 152:12
farewell f., 258:6
Father F., 725:1
feel fate in what I cannot f., 725:6
for f. very stones prate, 213:22
freedom from f., 649:17, 650:8
frighted out of f., 217:29
from hope and f. set free, 534:15
glad to brink of f., 430:26
God and keep his commandments, 24:30
God and take own part, 428:16
God honor the king, 46:23
Greeks even when they bring gifts, 93:27
hair stand up in panic f., 67:11
I am not in perfect mind, 211:10

Fear *(continued)*

I cannot taint with f., 215:*n*1
I will f. no evil, 16:17
imagining some f., 174:1
in handful of dust, 668:18
is sharp-sighted, 149:20
keeps men in obedience, 235:18
let them hate so long they f., 86:17
littlest doubts are f., 197:11
livid loneliness of f., 700:7
look f. in the face, 654:15
love and f. hardly together, 136:10
made manifest on body, 495:22
made without f., 15:25
mean actions ascribed to f., 552:3
mercy toward them that f. him, 19:1
my heart shall not f., 16:22
natural f. increased with tales, 159:4
never f. to negotiate, 741:5
never negotiate out of f., 741:5
no fall, 272:28
no f. stand up to hunger, 573:6
no more heat o' the sun, 220:3
nor courage saves us, 668:8
not I bring good tidings, 38:3
not lest Existence, 445:22
not to touch the best, 152:15
not well-fed long-haired men I f., 89:1
nothing terrible except f. itself, 158:18
nothing to be feared as f., 476:26
nothing you carry Caesar, 88:22
o' hell's a hangman's whip, 235:*n*5
O word of f., 169:12
of Acheron be sent packing, 89:21
of censure, 659:8
of change, 256:16
of death more dreaded than death, 99:28
of having to cry, 336:5
of ignominious death, 366:3
of kings, 181:19
of little men, 504:2
of some divine powers, 235:18
of suffering injustice, 265:10
of the Lord, 26:10
of the Lord is beginning of wisdom, 19:14
of the Lord is wisdom, 14:41
of weakness, 659:8
only thing to f. is f., 648:18
pale hungry-looking men, 89:1
perfect love casteth out f., 46:37
pine with f. and sorrow, 154:5
possess them not with f., 185:20
prey of f., 664:19
punishment increases f., 552:25
Puritanism haunting f. someone happy, 643:5
quite unaccustomed to f., 781:3
repentance is f. of consequence, 265:21
shuddering f. green-eyed jealousy, 181:7
source of superstition cruelty, 615:14
spirit of f., 45:26

Fervor, stranger moral f., 284:8
  with measure, 547:2
Fester like a sore, 708:19
  lilies that f., 221:16
Festina lente, 98:*n*13
Festively she puts forth, 376:13
Festivity, Two Lands are in f., 5:4
Fetch pail of water, 789:11
  poor dog a bone, 790:18
  the Age of Gold, 250:22
Fetter in shackles of historian, 249:25
Fettered, poetry f. fetters race, 359:22
  so free we seem so f. are, 466:3
  to her eye, 267:16
Fetters, no f. in Bay State, 443:1
  poetry fettered f. race, 359:22
  reason Milton wrote in f., 357:2
  servile f. breaks, 778:7
Fettle for great gray drayhorse, 551:4
Feuds, rent with civil f., 394:15
  three irreconcilable f. in Capri,
  712:6
Fever called Living, 453:6
  induces condition like breakbone f.,
  714:16
  is Nature's instrument, 271:16
  life's fitful f., 214:26
  of chills and f. died, 674:12
  of life over, 426:22
  of temptation, 680:3
  of the bone, 668:13
  passion a f. in mind, 283:2
  weariness f. fret, 415:12
  youth bent by wintry f., 737:8
Feverish preoccupation with riches,
  644:1
  selfish little clod, 570:22
Fever-trees, set about with f., 593:9
Few admired by own households,
  146:17
  and far between are the Tathagatas,
  64:24
  are chosen, 35:44
  business in hands of a f., 525:11
  companions f. in serious business,
  59:20
  condemn men because f., 479:1
  could know when Lucy ceased,
  373:19
  days precious f., 666:5
  err grossly as the f., 274:14
  far and f., 472:4
  give but f. thy voice, 193:30
  happy f., 185:23
  how f. know own good, 276:4
  if bees are f., 514:16
  immortal names, 405:6
  in hands not of f. but many, 72:2
  in science the f. dictate, 429:4
  join f. if any, 624:5
  join special f. at top, 764:5
  know how to be old, 265:42
  laborers are f., 34:26
  let thy words be f., 24:2
  many admire f. know, 71:15
  many exploited by f., 686:6
  men of f. words best, 185:7
  much in f. words, 32:6
  philosophy is for the f., 148:12
  small country with f. people, 58:6

Few (*continued*)
  so much owed to so f., 620:10
  sold the many on the f., 689:4
  some f. books to be chewed, 160:8
  that f. is all the world, 161:3
  the f. and the many, 355:1
  the notes are f., 356:3
  there be that find, 34:9
  to f. men comes excellence, 59:21
  very f. to love, 373:19
  ye are many they are f., 408:2
  yellow leaves or none or f., 221:8
Fewest, having f. wants, 70:19
Fezziwig, Mrs. F. one vast smile,
  470:7
ffinch-ffarrowmere corrected the visitor, 645:15
Fiamma, conosco i segni dell' antica f.,
  126:*n*6
Fiat justitia pereat coelum, 368:14
  justitia ruat coelum, 119:2
  lux, 6:*n*7
  ruat coelum f. voluntas tua, 119:28
Fiber, show food in minutest f.,
  384:21
Fibers, made of multitude of f., 427:27
Fibs, I'll tell you no f., 330:8
Fickle, whatever is f. freckled, 551:1
  woman always a f. thing, 94:1
Fickleness of women I love, 570:10
Fico, a f. for the phrase, 182:20
Fiction, biography is ultimately f.,
  736:8
  by fairy f. dressed, 323:10
  final belief in f., 639:14
  lags after truth, 331:8
  poetry supreme f., 638:21
  tongue to deal in f., 297:8
  truth stranger than f., 403:20
  work of f. affords aesthetic bliss,
  703:5
  writing f. developed respect for unknown, 727:20
Fictional, work of history in f. form,
  769:9
Fictions only and false hair, 243:9
  supreme f. of life, 640:16
Fiddle, cat and f., 789:9
  de-dee, 472:14
  master's lost f. stick, 788:1
  play on f. in Dooney, 595:10
  robes riche or f., 129:21
  we know is diddle, 535:8
Fiddle-de-dee, French for f., 519:17
Fiddler, in came a f., 470:7
  statesman and buffoon, 274:11
Fiddlers three, 788:5
Fide, Punica f., 91:*n*17
Fidelity, gossamer f. of Man, 452:9
  think of f. not husbands, 646:16
Fidget, no f. and no reformer, 583:15
Fidus Achates, 94:*n*4
Fie fie upon her, 201:10
  foh and fum, 210:12
  my lord fie, 216:2
  upon this quiet life, 177:20
Field, accidents by flood and f.,
  205:25
  as a flower of the f., 19:2
  betokened tempest to f., 165:12

Field (*continued*)
  consider lilies of f., 33:20
  cow a good animal in f., 316:15
  crop of corn a f. of tares, 156:22
  dedicate portion of f., 450:2
  dignity in tilling f., 571:33
  Esau was a man of the f., 7:36
  fair f. full of folk, 127:18
  gigantic f. of soya beans, 769:4
  goodliness as the flower of the f.,
  27:17
  Goya of the bare f., 765:17
  happy f. mossy cavern, 416:12
  has sight, 130:*n*3
  hath eyen wode eres, 130:14
  hi-hi-yee for f. artilleree, 636:16
  his arms, 157:2
  in league with stones of f., 14:4
  lay f. to f., 25:38
  life is not like crossing f., 793:3
  little f. well tilled, 309:13
  man for the f., 456:17
  man tills f. lies beneath, 459:1
  market economy's f. is world,
  645:11
  not a f. but a cause, 341:2
  not that fair f. of Enna, 258:10
  not wholly reap corners of f., 9:24
  of human conflict, 620:10
  of ripe corn, 667:23
  potter's f., 37:4
  Prussia hurried to the f., 353:*n*5
  ring with importunate chink, 332:18
  roamed from f. to f., 355:17
  she is as in a f., 624:11
  shepherds abiding in f., 38:3
  six Richmonds in the f., 166:18
  so Truth be in the f., 255:4
  thy beauty's f., 220:8
  to live not as simple as cross f.,
  679:17
  viewed in her fair face's f., 166:36
  what though f. be lost, 256:1
Fields, as long as f. green, 408:21
  babbled of green f., 184:30
  battle won on playing f., 371:15
  carrying you into f. of light, 67:24
  dream of battled f., 378:20
  earth's green f., 474:3
  fanged with flints, 708:7
  fight in f. and streets, 620:7
  flowering of His f., 459:22
  gone into the f., 409:22
  happy autumn f., 456:13
  have eyes woods have ears, 130:*n*3
  hills and valleys dales and f.,
  162:*n*1
  hunt in f. for health, 276:19
  in Flanders f., 615:7
  in those holy f., 176:23
  lie with nothing at work in them,
  726:4
  little tyrant of his f., 322:14
  of air, 335:23
  of corn where Troy was, 101:18
  once tall with wheat, 703:13
  out in f. with God, 781:12
  out of olde f. newe corn, 128:8
  plows in the f., 656:9
  poetic f. encompass me, 291:29

Fields (continued)
  they have not sown, 708:2
  unshorn f. boundless, 411:9
  valleys groves hills f., 162:2
  walk through f. in gloves, 661:12
Fiend, foul F. Apollyon, 272:18
  frightful f., 381:26
  like a f. in a cloud, 356:2, 358:11
  long spoon eat with f., 131:23
  marble-hearted f., 209:10
  so spake the F., 258:15
  swung the f., 509:7
Fiendishness of business competition,
    661:2
Fiends, juggling f., 216:20
  that plague thee thus, 381:5
Fierce and accustomed to woods,
    137:3
  change of f. extremes, 257:16
  composition and f. quality, 208:29
  contending nations know, 292:16
  extremes by change more f., 257:16
  far f. hour, 619:9
  four champions f. strive, 257:19
  fur soft to face, 750:1
  generous true and f., 619:19
  grew more f. and wild, 243:18
  light beats on throne, 459:3
  lion not so f. as they paint him,
    244:19
  look not so f. on me, 162:24
  more f. and inexorable far, 176:13
  no beast so f. but knows pity,
    165:22
  Spirit f., 407:17
  though little she is f., 173:20
  wars and faithful loves, 153:4
  wretchedness that glory brings,
    212:6
Fierceness, swalloweth the ground
    with f., 15:17
Fiercer, now f. by despair, 256:24
Fiercest, strongest and f. spirit, 256:24
Fiery, bathe in f. floods, 204:14
  far from f. noon, 416:19
  furnace, 29:13
  mind very f. particle, 403:13
  Pegasus, 178:22
  soul, 274:3
Fiery-footed steeds, 175:30
Fife, clamor of f. and drum, 507:10
  ear-piercing f., 207:8
  Elephant practiced on f., 520:1
  play f. lowly, 786:7
  Thane of F. had a wife, 216:4
  wry-necked f., 180:18
Fifteen apparitions seen, 599:20
  I was f. f., 636:14
  Jewish man remain f.-year-old boy,
    765:13
  maiden of bashful f., 352:29
  men on Dead Man's Chest, 561:1
  speak for f. minutes need three
    days, 572:15
  until I was, 765:9
  wild Decembers, 480:1
Fifth Amendment old friend, 698:20
  column, 664:1
  of November, 777:20
  shall close drama, 296:27

Fifth (continued)
  smote him under the f. rib, 12:3
Fifths, three f. genius, 485:8
Fifties, tranquilized F., 742:22
Fiftieth, hallow f. year, 9:27
Fifty, at f. chides delay, 296:12
  corpulent man of f., 396:23
  dread f. above more than f. below,
    623:21
  forty till f. man stoic or satyr, 568:5
  here's to the widow of f., 352:29
  million Frenchmen, 782:19
  not care to live after f., 603:2
  only leaves me f. more, 578:19
  Sleeping Beauty f. years old, 755:6
  springs little room, 578:19
  wise at f., 244:24
  years of Europe, 456:1
Fifty-four forty or fight, 428:12
Fifty-fourth Regiment, 522:13
Fifty-minute, the f. hour, 736:4
Fifty-score strong, 464:14
Fifty-three, we have sighted f., 460:6
Fig bear fruit then ripen, 108:2
  call f. a f., 81:11
  every man under his f. tree, 12:20
  for care fig for woe, 140:14
  land of vines and f. trees, 10:16
  sewed f. leaves together, 6:21
Figements, de longs f. violets, 565:n9
Fight, African f. for emancipation,
    681:4
  against his brother, 26:17
  all means permitted to f. evil, 676:1
  aloud very brave, 511:13
  and conquer again, 323:18
  and not heed wounds, 139:3
  back from eyes tears, 674:21
  baffled to f. better, 468:17
  beyond your strength, 52:2
  cannot f. future, 446:13
  don't f. forces use them, 691:11
  don't want to f., 507:6
  Duke great f. did win, 386:7
  end crowns us not f., 241:2
  end of f. tombstone white, 591:12
  extreme fear neither f. nor fly,
    166:39
  fall out and chide and f., 294:8
  fifty-four forty or f., 428:12
  fire and ice within me f., 579:6
  for lost causes, 672:19
  for love and glory, 689:16
  for one's country, 51:36
  fought a good f., 45:29
  fought the better f., 259:17
  gods f. against necessity, 55:12
  gone to f. French, 366:20
  good fight of faith, 45:23
  harder matter to f., 460:1
  her till she sinks, 393:13
  I will f. no more forever, 541:2
  in fields and streets, 620:7
  in France and on seas, 620:7
  it out on this line, 501:10
  like devils, 185:13
  like hell for living, 515:3
  love as much as good f., 648:13
  man who runs may f. again, 81:16
  mental f., 359:17

Fight (continued)
  never f. fair with stranger, 738:16
  never wear best trousers to f.,
    508:10
  nor law nor duty bade f., 596:11
  not yet begun to f., 348:10
  nothing sure in sea f., 360:15
  on beaches fields streets, 620:7
  on merry men all, 785:4
  opinions not survive without f.,
    629:14
  our country's battles, 780:22
  painful warrior famoused for f.,
    220:14
  people f. for their law, 62:20
  perish in the f., 444:2
  required of duty, 84:6
  rise and f. again, 785:n1
  those I f. I do not hate, 596:10
  through perilous f., 391:2
  till last gasp, 163:6
  to keep something alive, 672:19
  to maintain freedom, 649:18
  too proud to f., 572:4
  wants us to f. fair, 654:13
  we f. not to enslave, 341:3
  when f. begins within, 466:12
  whenever I must, 678:11
  why f. what's decisive, 423:16
  youth f. and die, 626:1
Fighter, am I no a bonny f., 561:14
  dull f. and keen guest, 178:27
  that means to have been a f., 350:4
Fighters, woke to black flak nightmare
    f., 735:21
Fightin', first-class f. man, 591:19
  runnin' away and f., 603:10
  show you're up to f., 485:19
Fighting, Aztecs would die f., 138:17
  bellyful of f., 219:23
  best to win without f., 80:20
  faiths, 542:25
  first-class f. man, 591:19
  for human rights, 755:8
  for the crown, 788:10
  God and devil f., 495:5
  in forefront of the Greeks, 60:10
  runnin' away and f., 603:10
  show you're up to f., 485:19
  Téméraire, 586:14
  words braver than f., 3:11
  world worth f. for, 702:6
Fights, best part of married life f.,
    698:1
  historical, 529:12
Figs, love long life better than f.,
    216:27
  of thistles, 34:11
Figurative, figure not f., 418:11
Figure a poem makes, 625:8
  baby f. of giant mass, 200:12
  but not figurative, 418:11
  human f. interests me most, 607:16
  in the carpet, 548:20
  in the landscape, 722:14
  is handsome, 536:20
  make me a fixed f., 207:26
  of a Nut, 513:16
  quaint great f., 637:11

Flat (*continued*)
he whose soul is f., 683:16
hev it plain an' f., 485:10
how weary stale f., 193:5
I their map lie f., 231:3
in f. sea sunk, 252:29
on your face, 690:13
strike f. thick rotundity, 209:24
the wall fell down f., 10:34
with broad f. nails, 77:3
Flatter, more we love less we f.,
269:14
Neptune for his trident, 219:9
not f. me at all, 247:5
Flattered, being then most f., 188:5
himself on being without prejudices,
550:6
into virtue, 434:9
not f. its rank breath, 400:7
upon understandings, 305:7
Flatterer can risk everything, 290:25
of all tame a f., 232:2
scoundrel hypocrite f., 359:23
Flatterers, by f. besieged, 302:11
self-love greatest of f., 264:22
solitude hath no f., 400:13
tell him he hates f., 188:5
Flattereth, meddle not with him that
f., 22:6
Flattering, now with f. tongue, 597:17
some with f. word, 567:17
unction, 198:2
Flatters, everyone that f., 233:12
Fortune f. to betray, 99:13
wolf hates when it f., 114:32
Flattery and falsehood, 346:1
art not submit to f., 371:19
guarding oneself against f., 136:18
imitation sincerest f., 393:5
in return for favor, 371:19
lost on poet's ear, 377:26
love of f., 293:22
proud taken in by f., 278:16
sincere f., 336:9
soothe ear of death, 322:10
woman gained by f., 305:14
Flattery's the food of fools, 289:5
Flaubert, true Penelope was F., 659:5
write novel about nothing, 748:7
Flaunt, if you've got it f. it, 756:19
Flaunted, badness f. itself, 784:25
Flaunting extravagant quean, 352:29
Flavor absorbed remains, 392:*n*1
you f. everything, 380:8
Flaw, conceal f. world will imagine
worst, 106:13
man without a f., 95:6
no kind of fault or f., 530:6
Flaws, heart break into f., 209:23
what soul without f., 565:19
Flax, smoking f. shall he not quench,
27:25
Flayed, belted you an' f. you, 591:20
Flea in mine ear, 139:17
naturalists observe f., 289:20
though he kill none, 231:7
Fleas, literature old couch stuffed with
f., 763:12
reasonable amount o' f. good, 555:9
riseth with f., 244:23

Fleas (*continued*)
smaller f. on him prey, 289:20
Fled, a life which has f., 58:12
across margent of world f., 581:6
as if that soul were f., 391:12
earth's foundations f., 580:1
from this vile world, 221:7
ghost f. from grasp, 93:36
Him down the nights, 581:4
I waked she f., 255:17
is that music, 415:19
judgment f. to beasts, 189:2
soul has f., 443:4
visionary gleam, 375:6
whence all but he f., 410:13
with a Christian, 180:24
Flee as a bird, 16:1
best day first to f., 93:3
from me that did me seek, 143:7
from reality, 653:19
from those who f. no glory, 52:8
from wrath to come, 32:31
if your enemy f., 793:23
let sound of it f., 340:17
resist devil and he will f., 46:14
shadows f. away, 25:8
sorrow and sighing shall f. away,
27:10
to f. vice is beginning of virtue,
97:5
whither shall I f. from thy presence,
20:8
wicked f. when no man pursueth,
23:5
Fleece white as snow, 404:10
white but 'tis too cold, 153:*n*7
Fleecy, stooping through a f. cloud,
252:3
Flees, who f. will fight again, 81:*n*10
Fleet, all in Downs f. moored, 297:3
away with wings, 401:19
dull in F. Street, 387:17
in my arms, 391:13
joys abound as seasons f., 163:23
of life like tree leaves, 73:12
other passions f. to air, 181:7
retiring toward Japanese f., 647:6
say to the f., 360:*n*4
such sweet things f., 534:16
the time carelessly, 189:30
though time be f., 518:13
Fleetest, fairest things f. end, 581:1
Fleeth as a shadow, 14:20
Fleeting, a few f. hours I would be as
old, 636:14
Art long Time f., 440:16
call the f. breath, 322:10
fable song or f. shade, 241:19
ghost fled like f. dream, 93:36
how f. the estate of man, 111:12
mountains f. as clouds, 117:6
opportunity f., 71:13
renown is f. and frail, 91:21
years slip by, 96:10
Fleets, ten thousand f. sweep, 400:30
Flere, si vis me f., 98:*n*4
Flesh, all f. is as grass, 46:21
all f. is grass, 27:17
and blood so cheap, 423:8
boat of your f., 767:9

Flesh (*continued*)
brought him bread and f., 12:32
consorteth according to kind, 31:32
contact possible to f., 668:13
every living thing of all f., 7:17
every part of f. Nature makes f.,
111:31
fair and unpolluted f., 199:11
fastened me f., 550:17
fish f. or fowl, 597:7
fish nor f. nor good red herring,
141:19
from deceits of the f., 49:9
gross f. sinks downward, 172:17
hair of my f. stood up, 13:39
how art thou fishified, 175:20
howl for f. of man, 766:2
in f. beauty immortal, 639:4
in my f. shall I see God, 14:30
is sad alas, 547:10
is weak, 36:31
little f. little breath, 110:14
lusteth against Spirit, 44:18
make not provision for f., 42:23
maketh f. his arm, 28:29
marriage makes one f., 291:1
more f. more worms, 102:10
more f. than another man, 178:17
much study is weariness of the f.,
24:30
my f. longeth for thee, 17:35
neither f. nor fleshless, 670:15
of flesh bone of bone, 260:11
of my flesh, 6:17
of thy flesh, 148:11
present joys more to f. and blood,
275:21
profiteth nothing, 40:5
set today on f. of hare, 766:2
sinful desires of the f., 49:21
star stone f. soul, 466:19
strong as f. and blood, 376:14
swift red f., 701:6
that f. is heir to, 196:10
their f. shall ye not eat, 9:22
these set our f. upright, 230:11
they shall be one f., 6:18
they shall eat the f., 8:37
this f. of mine might be, 533:18
this too too solid f., 193:5
thorn in f., 44:11
wants to make f. creep, 468:23
watching for riches consumeth f.,
32:5
way of all f., 237:12
we are one f., 260:12
we wrestle not against f., 44:28
Word was made f., 39:33
world-wearied f., 176:18
Fleshed fair erected, 729:2
maiden sword, 179:10
Fleshless, neither flesh nor f., 670:15
Fleshly, all this f. dress, 270:5
lusts, 46:22
school of poetry, 541:15
Fleshpots, sat by the f., 9:6
Fleshy, turbulent f. sensual eating
drinking, 489:9
Flew, bird to others f., 240:2
down almost touching craft, 709:5

Flew (*continued*)
  o'er me and my dearie, 363:13
  one f. over cuckoo's nest, 792:8
  white foam f., 381:6
Flexibility, happy gracious f., 500:25
Flicker, moment of greatness f.,
    667:16
Flickered, in past our light f., 621:7
Flickering, dove with f. tongue, 672:2
Fliers, comrades chase e'en now the f.,
    483:3
Flies, ain't no f. on me, 559:23
  as f. to wanton boys, 210:20
  bees for f. hornets for bees, 138:4
  closed mouth swallows no f., 794:3
  follow shadow it f. you, 232:13
  from particulars to axioms, 158:12
  happiness too swiftly f., 321:17
  hope f. with swallow's wings,
    166:11
  in night in howling storm, 358:4
  kisses joy as it f., 357:22
  laws catch small f., 288:18
  my fancy f., 328:12
  on summer eves, 415:15
  preserved in amber, 106:*n*6
  rumor f., 93:38
  see where it f., 162:19
  shoot folly as it f., 301:2
  through air with ease, 536:20
  time's f., 212:4
  unto you at last she f., 246:6
  verse find who sermon f., 242:17
  who f. can fight anew, 81:*n*10
  wings of Time grief f., 268:4
  worms and flowers, 294:11
Flieth, arrow that f. by day, 18:15
Flight, beetle wheels droning f., 322:2
  black f. of crows, 786:*n*5
  fellow of selfsame f., 179:24
  flown his cloistered f., 214:27
  from afar to view f., 287:16
  his wild airy f., 261:18
  life like f. of sparrow, 120:6
  never-ending f. of days, 257:5
  puts Stars to f., 445:4
  soul of youth taken f., 657:2
  struggle and f., 499:22
  Sun scattered into f., 445:3
  swift be thy f., 409:14
  through sky thy certain f., 411:5
  time and world in f., 595:6
  time arrest f., 405:7
  Time in your f., 516:13
Flights and perchings, 545:16
  four f. Thursday, 604:10
  grand f. Sunday baths, 639:12
  of angels sing thee, 199:29
Flinch, we did not f., 60:13
Flinders, little Polly F., 790:15
Fling away ambition, 225:20
  garment of Repentance f., 445:6
  stone giant dies, 307:7
Flint, behold man of f., 787:12
  firmest f. doth in continuance wear,
    89:*n*6
  weariness snore upon f., 219:31
Flints, fields fanged with f., 708:7
Flirt, money won't surrender to f.,
    603:17

Flirtation, significant word f., 305:16
Flit on wings of borrowed wit, 240:3
Flits by on leathern wing, 324:14
Flitter dip and soar, 749:17
Flitting, Raven never f., 452:21
Float, how sweetly did they f., 252:27
  iron in water f., 777:17
  like a butterfly, 771:16
Floated into inmost soul, 486:18
  web f. wide, 454:16
Floating bulwark of our island, 325:20
  hair, 382:25
  ice mast-high came f. by, 381:3
  like vapor on air, 507:3
  many bells down, 688:22
  on the floor, 452:22
  over Harvard Square, 699:14
  spar to men that sink, 684:13
Floats on high o'er vales, 375:19
  though unseen among us, 406:9
Flock, birds of a feather f. together,
    235:*n*2
  feed his f. like a shepherd, 27:20
  keeping watch over their f., 38:3
  of bridges bleating, 641:6
  shun the polluted f., 660:15
  silent f. in fold, 414:21
  without shepherd sheep not f.,
    793:5
Flocks, bad herdsmen ruin their f.,
    54:3
  battening our f., 253:17
  casual f. of pigeons, 638:26
  my father feeds f., 325:8
  or herds or human face, 257:24
  while shepherds watched f., 285:1
Flogged, man never f. never taught,
    81:7
  she f. herself, 446:23
Flogging, habit of f. me constantly,
    476:4
Flood, accidents by f. and field,
    205:25
  arched the f., 429:22
  carriest them away as with a f.,
    18:10
  decay no f., 595:4
  enchafed f., 206:3
  giant race before the f., 276:1
  half our sailors swallowed in f.,
    165:2
  land of mountain and f., 378:2
  Milton Proteus of f., 384:16
  of mortal ills, 138:5
  of words drop of reason, 309:18
  taken at the f., 189:19
  ten years before the F., 268:14
  thorough f. thorough fire, 172:30
  torn Naiad from f., 451:10
  when just cause reaches f. tide,
    577:8
Floods, bathe in fiery f., 204:14
  haystack in f., 523:4
  he hath established it upon the f.,
    16:18
  neither can f. drown it, 25:23
  passions like f. and streams, 152:13
  rimless f., 701:1
  stood upright as an heap, 9:5
  that are deepest, 777:11

Floor, bar-room f., 548:4
  careless on granary f., 416:14
  cleaned windows swept f., 529:6
  common sense on ground f., 447:19
  forest's ferny f., 616:22
  front of this small f., 264:21
  mystery on bestial f., 596:3
  nicely sanded f., 329:19
  of heaven is inlaid, 182:8
  reorganized upon f., 668:15
  scratching at the f., 583:8
  starry f., 358:1
  sunk beneath watery f., 254:6
  two jars on f. of Zeus, 52:26
  wrought ghost upon f., 452:14
Floors of silent seas, 667:14
Flopsy Mopsy Cottontail Peter, 600:20
Flora and country green, 415:11
  fauna geography, 729:13
  Lady F. lovely Roman, 509:22
Flores in the Azores, 460:6
Florida weighted with regret, 759:9
Flots, léger j'ai dansé sur les f.,
    565:*n*6
Floundered enjoyed suffered, 549:12
Flour, peace into poet as f. into bread,
    714:7
Flourish, almond tree shall f., 24:28
  first onion f. there, 561:15
  may f. or may fade, 329:8
  men f. only for a moment, 54:8
  nations are destroyed or f., 359:22
  poetry painting music f., 359:22
  righteous shall f., 18:17
  set on youth, 221:1
  those which most admirably f.,
    221:*n*2
  where you turn eyes, 298:7
Flourished, bloody treason f., 189:7
  hoop unbroken people f., 587:5
Flourishes, society where moderation
    f., 615:3
Flourisheth as flower of the field, 19:2
  in the morning it f., 18:10
Flourishing like a green bay tree,
    17:*n*1
  of the arts, 686:16
Flours, no f. on grave, 539:18
Flout, banners f. the sky, 212:11
  'em and scout 'em, 224:16
Flow, all pleasant fruits do f., 226:18
  ceaseless ebb and f., 564:20
  ebb and f. by the moon, 211:13
  from discord f., 292:16
  from my lips would f., 408:8
  from whom all blessings f., 280:21
  gently sweet Afton, 362:21
  how well soe'er it f., 302:13
  I within did f., 281:2
  its one will f., 701:5
  of soul, 302:21
  oh could I f. like thee, 266:11
  salt tides seaward f., 497:6
  streams f. with ambrosia, 68:20
  with tears of gold, 356:16
  words to say it f., 280:6
Flower, age will fade beauty's f.,
    144:5
  as a f. of the field, 19:2
  bee does not hurt f., 65:2

Fly (*continued*)

little birds that f., 295:17
little F., 358:5
long-legged f. upon stream, 599:18
make fur f., 263:13
my words f. up, 197:26
neglect God for noise of a f., 231:11
no longer wings to f., 669:14
on bat's back I do f., 224:25
riches f. away as an eagle, 22:18
rode upon a cherub and did f., 16:8
seem to f. it, 232:13
shoo f., 524:8
soon cut off and we f. away, 18:12
sounds too blue to f., 753:5
Spider to F., 423:11
stir her lawn canapie, 148:4
that sips treacle, 297:19
then f. betimes, 246:11
this rock shall f., 378:24
thrain lobsters to f., 603:7
Timothy learnt sin to f., 287:10
to her, 456:15
to others we know not of, 196:10
to war and arms I f., 267:14
up above world you f., 517:20
upon the wings of the wind, 16:8
way I f. is hell, 258:5
when me they f., 430:11
which way shall I f., 258:5
white sails f. seaward, 669:20
willingly as kill a f., 167:12
with arms outstretched would f., 201:2
with twain he did f., 25:42
Flyin' fishes play, 591:23
Flying, banner torn but f., 400:22
chariot through air, 335:23
Dutchman, 553:18
fishes play, 591:23
from Brooklyn please come f., 729:6
hoping lingering f., 299:8
mind f. abroad, 76:10
old Time still a-f., 241:9
pluck out f. feather, 534:9
sea-crow, 491:3
seaward f., 669:20
snow came f., 549:20
time f. never to return, 93:5
trapeze, 536:20
wild echoes f., 456:11
Foal, likeness of filly f., 173:2
Foam, born and die like f., 122:16
copulate in f., 599:17
cruel crawling f., 484:10
is not cruel, 487:13
like f. on river, 378:22
now f. to wheat, 764:20
oceans white with f., 666:12
of flowers, 533:18
opening on the f., 415:17
poetry new as f., 430:18
sea folk turn into f., 437:7
too full for sound and f., 460:11
weeds and f., 429:8
white f. flew, 381:6
Foam-bell no consequence, 499:13
Foaming out their own shame, 46:38
Foams, my sad heart f. at stern, 565:10

Focis, pro aris atque f., 91:*n*14
Fodder's in the shock, 559:1
Foe, angry with my f., 358:12
at another gate let in the f., 261:14
avowed erect manly f., 371:25
call no man f., 682:13
comes with fearless eyes, 586:12
foils f. by effusion of ink, 325:15
friend to her f., 369:8
grim Death my son and f., 257:18
heat not furnace for f., 225:3
idleness sorrow friend f., 687:6
laughter has no greater f. than emotion, 577:1
make one worthy man f., 302:13
meet insulting f., 353:7
met dearest f. in heaven, 193:14
never made a f., 459:16
Olympian a difficult f., 51:3
overcome but half his f., 256:19
perhaps a jealous f., 408:13
scratch lover find f., 687:8
someday to prove our f., 65:13
sternest knight to f., 133:17
support friend oppose f., 741:3
thou that seemest f., 138:*n*2
timorous f., 302:11
to favoritism, 572:22
tyrants fall in every f., 363:20
unrelenting f. to love, 308:11
wolf that's f. to men, 237:14
Foeman bares steel tarantara, 529:13
Foeman's, beneath f. frown, 461:1
Foemen worthy of steel, 378:25
Foes, ah my f., 684:2
beat down baffling f., 498:1
his courage f. proclaim, 274:7
learning's barbarous f., 313:10
man that makes character makes f., 296:4
not know friends from f., 477:14
now have neither f. nor friends, 684:*n*1
our f. press on, 124:8
so far only hate our f., 65:13
thrice he routed f., 276:11
what their f. liked was done, 721:3
will provide with arms, 93:34
Fog and filthy air, 212:10
comes on cat feet, 634:5
feel f. in throat, 467:18
gleams through f., 321:5
London particular a f., 471:2
patience everywhere like f., 713:10
woodthrush singing through f., 669:22
Foggy foggy dew, 779:23
Fogs, his rising f. prevail, 274:26
Foh a fico for the phrase, 182:20
Fie f. and fum, 210:12
Foibles, half our misery from f., 348:4
Foiled, after thousand victories f., 220:14
Foils foe by effusion of ink, 325:15
Fold, all driven into same f., 96:6
do not f. spindle or mutilate, 783:23
flock in woolly f., 414:21
hands and wait, 532:6
home fast f. thy child, 551:10
sheep not of this f., 40:18

Fold (*continued*)

sheep to f., 579:22
star that bids shepherd f., 252:18
tents like Arabs, 441:12
walking round the f., 356:16
wolf in f. sad thing, 92:7
Folded her hair expectantly, 491:7
lord of f. arms, 168:28
Folding of the hands to sleep, 20:28
Folds, lost f. of damasked gown, 144:4
lull distant f., 322:2
of bright girdle furled, 499:22
rippling in breeze, 463:5
Foliage, children in f., 670:18
silver light on f., 699:6
Folio, whole volumes in f., 168:21
Folk, ancient f. with evil spells, 787:13
best literature becomes f. literature, 718:4
black f. say America been stronger, 726:2
dance like wave of sea, 595:10
down there sea f. live, 437:6
fair field full of f., 127:18
messenger with language of his f., 116:12
queerest f. of all, 583:9
songs from soul sounds, 690:20
Folks, as long as colored man look to white f., 773:19
O yonge fresshe f., 129:2
rail against other folks, 311:20
there's where old f. stay, 506:19
think you lack, 693:9
Folks', lazy f. stummucks, 556:11
Follies and misfortunes of mankind, 340:3
and wickedness, 717:22
cease with youth, 312:18
of town crept slowly, 329:24
perished by their own f., 52:28
that themselves commit, 180:20
vices and f. of human kind, 290:35
woes because of their own f., 52:29
Follow a shadow, 232:13
admire virtue f. not her lore, 260:25
after peace, 42:27
and will not see its back, 57:5
as night the day, 194:1
beat to f. faster, 217:14
even if disobedient I shall f., 82:3
good to fire but not into it, 146:15
goodness and mercy shall f. me, 16:17
grasp subject words will f., 85:7
him who sets you right, 111:22
I f. but myself, 205:13
if thou f. thy star, 125:26
knowledge like star, 455:3
lamb will never cease to f., 164:30
let who loves country f., 440:11
loves me let him f. me, 127:8
me fishers of men, 32:37
me let dead bury dead, 34:18
nature, 105:21
so fast they f., 198:*n*5
spirit of men who f., 658:15
still changes of the moon, 206:33
the Gleam, 460:10

Fool (*continued*)

when he holdeth his peace, 21:37
when we play the f., 388:19
wise enough to play f., 202:21
wise man dieth as the f., 23:31
wise man knows himself f., 192:9
wisest f. in Christendom, 154:23
with f. no companionship, 64:21
with foolish play the f., 81:6
with judges, 105:*n*8

Fooled with hope, 273:16

Foolery governs whole world, 239:6
that wise men have, 189:32
walk about like sun, 202:20

Fool-gudgeon opinion, 179:22

Fooling, adapted to my f., 625:4

Foolish, an' f. notion, 361:18
and false as fame, 283:24
consistency, 431:23
fond old man, 211:10
fool calls you f., 69:1
forgive f. ways, 443:17
frantic boast f. word, 593:4
gets f. or wife does, 603:9
God hath chosen f. things, 42:29
hold that mortal f., 69:5
I being young and f., 594:17
lean and f. knight, 619:3
learned fool more f., 269:31
man built house on sand, 34:15
man who trusts woman, 94:*n*1
men who accuse a woman, 284:7
never said a f. thing, 283:21
newspaper marries f., 603:12
old and f. king, 24:1
passionate man, 599:4
penny wise pound f., 234:10
people without understanding,
28:15
seem f. among wise, 105:14
son heaviness of his mother, 21:4
son is calamity of his father, 21:44
studied in my f. youth, 133:20
thing but a toy, 203:7
thing well done, 316:17
things to confound wise, 42:29
to make long prologue, 32:19
virgins, 36:13
when he had not pen, 317:18
whistlings of a name, 267:9
with f. play the fool, 81:6
women f. to match men, 483:17
wrath killeth the f., 14:1
young and f., 594:17

Foolishness, not fools but f., 238:4

Fool's errand, 320:11
mouth is his destruction, 21:38
paradise, 776:4

Fools, a little wise best f. be, 228:18
all f. on our side, 526:25
amongst f. a judge, 105:*n*8
are my theme, 399:1
but f. caught it, 596:4
by follies they perished the f., 52:28
by heavenly compulsion, 209:3
children and f. cannot lie, 141:34
children and f. want everything,
279:28
crabbed as dull f. suppose, 253:3
discourse of f. is irksome, 31:43

Fools (*continued*)

displeasing ten thousand f., 122:10
do not imitate successes, 85:4
do not know how much more is
half than whole, 54:21
dreading e'en f., 302:11
effect of coercion to make f., 343:8
fill world with f., 493:11
flanneled f. at wicket, 593:7
food of f., 289:5
for I also had my hour, 619:9
God looks after f. and United
States, 782:11
great stage of f., 211:6
greatest f. most satisfied, 280:12
hundred f. not make wise man,
676:4
I am two f. I know, 228:17
illusion of f., 696:13
in all tongues called f., 192:13
in idle wishes f. stay, 353:17
laugh at men of sense, 283:15
learn in no other, 309:28
leaves 'em still two f., 291:1
let f. use talents, 201:24
lighted f. way to dusty death,
216:14
make a mock at sin, 21:18
millions mostly f., 413:13
more f. than wise, 777:6
ninety-nine percent of people f.,
697:17
no more I'll tease, 299:27
not f. but foolishness, 238:4
of fortune, 212:4
of nature, 194:11
old men know young men f., 157:3
Paradise of F., 258:1
play the f. with time, 183:32
poems made by f. like me, 662:1
poor f. decoyed, 279:13
rush in, 299:6
say man has or has not principles,
422:11
scarecrows of f., 505:14
shoal of f. for tenders, 291:10
so deep-contemplative, 190:24
some made coxcombs nature meant
f., 298:11
suckle f., 206:9
suffer f. gladly, 44:9
tedious old f., 195:22
the stop to busy f., 270:2
too green and only good for f.,
58:*n*9
we f. of nature, 194:11
what f. call Nature, 468:2
what f. these mortals be, 102:18,
173:18
who came to scoff, 329:15
wise men profit more from f., 85:4
wise men speak f. decide, 56:3
wish to appear wise among f.,
105:14
words are money of f., 239:17
young men think old men f., 157:3

Fools' experiments, 445:2
names like f. faces, 778:16

Foos, my f. won't moos, 647:20

Foot, accent of coming F., 514:17

Foot (*continued*)

and hand go cold, 144:12
beat earth with unfettered f., 96:2
beggar on f., 599:13
better f. before, 170:13
cannot put shoe on every f., 100:5
crown to sole of f., 186:32
dash f. against stone, 38:10
dash thy f. against a stone, 18:16
for foot, 9:15
from f. to Hercules, 70:5
her f. speaks, 201:10
her f. was light, 417:5
here men first set f. on moon, 784:7
I hold Creation in my f., 762:16
in the stirrup, 786:3, 786:4
it featly, 223:30
lived like f. for thirty years, 764:16
my f. on my native heath, 379:13
no f. of unfamiliar men, 499:15
no f. slide, 783:4
noiseless f. of time, 203:20
of hand of f. of lip, 221:22
one f. already in grave, 107:9
one f. in sea one on shore, 186:28
one white f. try him, 781:17
print of naked f., 286:4
proud f. of conqueror, 170:23
put forward best f., 170:*n*4
rest for the sole of her f., 7:19
stamped f. and cried, 512:7
suffer thy f. to be moved, 19:25
thy soul the fixt f., 229:13
wear steps of his door, 31:17
who cleft Devil's f., 228:5
wishing his f. equal with eye,
164:21
with naked f. stalking my chamber,
143:7

Foot-and-a-half-long words, 98:7

Football, in life as in f., 575:15

Footfalls echo in memory, 670:13

Foothold tenoned and mortised in
granite, 489:6

Footing, 'twixt his stretched f., 200:11

Foot-in-the-grave young man, 530:2

Footless halls of air, 751:3

Footman, eternal F. snicker, 667:16

Footnotes to Plato, 584:13

Footpads, when f. quail, 531:12

Footpath, jog on the f. way, 223:4

Footprint, Zuleika looking for man's
f., 614:7

Footprints of gigantic hound, 577:25
on the sands of time, 440:17

Footstep, where thy f. gleams, 452:3

Footsteps, distant f. echo, 441:11
home his f. turned, 378:1
plants his f. in the sea, 333:22
someone follow in my f., 754:18

Footstool, earth as f., 601:15
earth is his f., 33:6
God's f. may be throne, 622:14
my f. earth, 301:9

Foppery, excellent f. of the world,
209:3

Fops, whole tribe of f., 208:29

Forbade me to put off my hat, 271:13
to wade through slaughter, 322:16

Forbear and persevere, 562:9

Forbear (*continued*)
  be not too bold, 153:*n*7
  cruel mother, 96:27
  to dig dust enclosed here, 226:11
  to judge, 164:3
Forbearance ceases to be virtue,
  330:21
  practice Christian f., 339:11
Forbid, God f., 8:11
  it Almighty God, 339:10
  them not, 37:31
Forbidden by Constitution, 355:7
  tree whose mortal taste, 255:18
  wanted apple because was f., 527:7
  whatever not f. is permitted, 365:2
Forbids, my mind f. to crave, 148:2
  rich as well as poor, 550:13
Force, abandonment of f., 650:9
  acceleration proportional to applied
    f., 282:*n*1
  adaptation of form to resist f.,
    487:29
  Allied Expeditionary F., 678:16
  and beauty of process, 549:14
  change from liberty to f., 368:16
  citizens to confess faith, 683:2
  Conservation of F., 496:17
  constant f. for muddlement, 549:5
  eastward I go only by f., 479:5
  elemental f. freed, 673:6
  evolution not a f., 537:5
  from which sun draws power, 655:6
  had not f. to shape, 459:23
  in Nature not increased, 496:17
  knowing f. of words, 62:6
  knowledge more than f., 158:*n*1
  language into meaning, 672:15
  love f., 606:13
  may the F. be with you, 773:11
  moment to its crisis, 667:15
  no f. however great, 411:12
  no motion has she no f., 374:1
  no place where need of skill, 70:4
  not by f. or violence, 339:11
  not remedy, 462:7
  of heaven-bred poesy, 168:6
  of his own merit, 225:2
  of righteousness, 606:13
  of temporal power, 181:19
  oppressor to commit brutality
    openly, 761:8
  paralyzed f., 669:9
  passion spent novel f., 455:10
  produce according to f., 481:*n*4
  proportional to motive f., 282:2
  secret f. driving me, 446:26
  some patient f., 457:1
  soul f., 606:13
  spiritual f. stronger, 433:18
  terror and f., 676:3
  that through green fuse, 737:8
  them in spite of Nature, 263:11
  them to write, 263:11
  too revolutionary for old ideas,
    655:7
  tribalism strongest f., 765:5
  uncomprehended which was his life,
    510:7
  use of f. but temporary, 331:11
  when one by f. subdues, 79:8

Force (*continued*)
  who overcomes by f., 256:19
  without wisdom falls of own
    weight, 96:16
  world f. not presence, 640:30
  worship God not constrained by f.,
    105:15
Forced by fate, 276:5
  gait of shuffling nag, 178:5
  praise on our part, 464:26
  the sound is f., 356:3
  to surrender truth, 248:2
  wedlock f. a hell, 163:17
Forces, Armed F. in control, 682:11
  avoid perils by united f., 278:11
  by which nature animated, 351:16
  deliberative f., 568:14
  determination of f., 504:12
  don't fight f. use them, 691:11
  imagination one of f. of nature,
    640:28
  impressed upon it, 282:1
  in the difficult are friendly f., 630:12
  irresistible f. for uniformity, 661:10
  man who f. opportunity, 354:7
  natural and moral f., 496:18
  one to repeat No, 553:16
  our f. stand on Philippine soil,
    642:2
  politics struggle of f., 536:1
  these f. met master, 649:6
  which threaten soul, 648:4
Forcible, how f. are right words, 14:6
Forcibly if we must, 385:*n*1
Ford, I'm a F. not a Lincoln, 733:7
Fordoes, makes me or f. me quite,
  208:8
Forearmed, forewarned f., 150:30
Forecast, others f. the rising stars,
  94:15
Foredoomed, innocent and f., 714:15
Forefathers, contemplate our f., 325:4
  copy your f., 3:12
  had no books but score, 164:11
  met the boat, 638:6
  never forget laws of f., 105:16
  rude f. of hamlet, 322:4
  were warriors, 370:2
Forefinger, agate on f. of alderman,
  174:20
  of all Time, 456:9
Forefront, fighting in f. of the Greeks,
  60:10
  set Uriah in f. of battle, 12:9
Forego, propensity to f., 545:1
Foregoing generations beheld God nature, 430:24
Foregone conclusion, 207:13
Forehead, drops of blood form on f.,
  678:4
  of humanity, 414:12
  of the age to come, 414:1
  of the morning sky, 254:6
  right in middle of her f., 442:25
Foreheads of defamers, 520:11
  villainous low, 224:22
Foreign aid of ornament, 308:7
  apprenticehood to f. passages,
    170:32
  avoid f. collision, 389:12

Foreign (*continued*)
  banners of f. independence, 368:16
  boys not sent into f. wars, 649:15
  corner of f. field, 663:3
  disposed of f. enemies, 75:28
  gear of f. dead men, 671:13
  intercourse with f. nations, 390:22
  levy, 214:26
  life is a f. language, 679:12
  nations and the next age, 160:12
  no f. sky protected me, 675:7
  the past a f. country, 692:19
  things f. or things at home, 272:19
  troop in my country, 313:6
  wandering on f. strand, 378:1
Foreigner in country of birth, 774:2
  no f. do business here, 134:10
Foreigners spell better than pronounce,
  525:22
Foreknow, for whom he did f., 42:5
Foreknowledge absolute, 257:12
Forelock, by f. take time, 154:11
Foremost files of time, 455:24
Forensic, aim of f. oratory, 87:21
Forepangs, pangs schooled at f.,
  551:13
Forest, beasts of the f. creep forth,
  19:6
  beautiful changes as f., 749:13
  cutting through the f., 637:9
  every beast of the f. is mine, 17:19
  flowers of the f., 327:11
  I believe in the f., 479:7
  lyre even as f. is, 407:17
  met a fool i' the f., 190:21
  primeval, 441:15
  vast wastes of f. verdure, 503:4
  way into Universe through f.,
    537:15
  wild f. green mansions, 543:15
Foresters, Diana's f., 176:25
Forest's ferny floor, 616:22
Forests are rended, 379:9
  helmets gleamed in f., 503:4
  in the f. of the night, 358:6
  Pelion with its leafy f., 53:19
Foretold that danger lurks within,
  164:28
Forever, ae farewell and then f.,
  362:10
  and a day, 192:3
  boot stamping on human face f.,
    711:19
  can't sleep with the river f., 774:11
  clear day see f., 745:14
  corner of field f. England, 663:3
  diamond lasts f., 686:10
  do you want to live f., 318:*n*4
  fare thee well, 401:20
  farewell Cassius, 189:23
  Fortune wilt thou prove, 308:11
  good jest f., 177:14
  he is mine f., 493:25
  his time is f., 267:3
  I go on f., 458:16
  Life Death and that F., 484:13
  live f. or die in attempt, 752:11
  man has F., 465:22
  may be f., 424:8
  piping songs, 416:4

Form (*continued*)

each of like f. from everlasting, 110:17

earth was without f., 6:4

essential thing in f., 640:15

ever follows function, 571:30

expediency determines f., 664:9

follows but for f., 209:18

follows function, 571:30

free f. not assure freedom, 640:15

free in whatever f. used, 640:15

freedom regardless of f., 640:15

from off my door, 452:20

harmony manifest in F., 583:13

human couple find true f., 722:10

human thought or f., 406:10

in f. in moving, 195:28

Love the human f. divine, 356:13

mould of f., 196:18

new government that suits better, 448:3

of popular government, 352:1

proportion season f., 200:7

quiet at heart of f., 725:10

shape without f., 669:9

soul is f. and doth body make, 154:14

Terror the human f. divine, 358:13

work of history in fictional f., 769:9

Formal, beard of f. cut, 191:3

feeling comes, 512:6

Formalities, in statesmanship get f. right, 527:34

Formed but one such man, 401:21

by thy converse, 302:2

for ruin of our sex, 325:1

his hands f. the dry land, 18:19

if you have f. a circle, 359:19

man was f. for society, 325:19

moment when friendship f., 341:21

of joy and mirth, 359:20

of various stuff, 363:1

or ever thou hadst f. the earth, 18:10

visible f. in love invisible f. in fright, 486:26

Former, get rid of f. bear latter, 310:14

latter and f. rain, 29:25

no remembrance of f. things, 23:26

one jot of f. love retain, 161:11

people, 605:9

things grow old, 241:13

thy f. light restore, 208:10

Formez vos bataillons, 366:9

Formidable, makes small numbers f., 336:12

Formless ruin of oblivion, 201:11

Formlessness, be subtle to point of f., 80:21

Forms all produced by laws, 444:8

by f. unseen dirge sung, 324:11

degenerate into lower f. of life, 136:1

differ in external f., 316:10

endless f. most beautiful, 444:10

evil has infinite f., 271:5

from outward f. to win passion life, 383:7

more real than living, 406:20

Forms (*continued*)

of things unknown, 174:1

reborn into highest f., 136:1

their colors and their f., 373:4

waves with purple f., 565:14

Formula for making ends meet, 646:4

in same f. largest and lightest, 351:16

of that particular emotion, 672:11

Formulas, clear myself of f., 412:11

Fornicated, he f. and read papers, 732:20

Fornication but in another country, 162:9

Forsake, do not f. me in my end, 278:25

her Cyprian groves, 275:30

let the wicked f. his way, 28:1

me like memory lost, 410:5

me not when my strength faileth, 17:40

not an old friend, 31:21

their temples dim, 251:1

Forsaken beliefs, 499:10

courts pale pavilions, 704:11

have not seen the righteous f., 17:1

my God why hast thou f. me, 16:15, 37:12

old f. bough, 447:20

town like place f., 279:11

Forsaking all others, 50:3

Forsan et haec olim meminisse iuvabit, 93:*n*10

Forsitan et nomen miscebitur istis, 101:*n*12

Forspent, clean f., 547:9

Forsworn, that so sweetly were f., 204:22

Fort, hold f. I am coming, 492:10

Forted residence, 205:2

Forth, child went f., 491:2

went f. will always go f., 491:3

Forties, in f. know they won't save us, 694:24

Fortieth, laugh never granted before f. day, 104:4

Fortify thy name against old age, 161:2

Fortitude and perseverance, 325:4

great f. of mind, 315:12

what F. Soul contains, 514:17

Fortnight, to be hanged in a f., 317:1

Fortress built by Nature for herself, 171:9

he is my refuge and my f., 18:15

house is as f., 152:4

Lord is my f., 12:15

mighty f. is our God, 138:5

thou art my f., 138:*n*2

vast gray f., 527:3

Forts, Great Father building f. among us, 502:5

of folly, 500:3

Fortuitous circumstances, 379:17

Fortunatam natam me consule Romam, 88:*n*3

Fortunate, fair maidens commonly f., 155:15

farmers, 92:28

first king f. soldier, 306:1

Fortunate (*continued*)

more desirable than f. hour, 91:8

senex, 92:*n*3

youth to have found Homer, 80:23

Fortunatus et ille deos, 93:*n*1

Fortune and men's eyes, 220:15

any occurrence of special good f., 430:26

arbiter of everyone's f., 92:*n*2

ask not good f., 490:3

brings in some boats, 220:5

carry Caesar and his f., 88:22

charge f. with partiality, 389:11

come up I'll tell your f., 685:6

diligence mother of good f., 151:10

distinction of birth or f., 370:19

each day that F. grants, 95:24

every man architect of his f., 92:1

excessive good f., 507:11

face is my f., 790:7

favor from F. easier to get, 99:15

favored him in moment of death, 109:23

favors the brave, 86:*n*8, 94:25

flatters to betray, 99:13

fools of f., 212:4

friend supports whom F. crushes, 105:24

good f. is god among men, 63:20

good F. may be short-lived, 240:5

good night, 209:16

great f. great slavery, 103:8

grow out at heels, 209:15

has acquired him, 82:9

he has not acquired a f., 82:9

helps the brave, 86:12

hostages to f., 159:11

I am maker of my own f., 370:2

if farmers knew own f., 92:28

if thou f. bereft, 118:*n*2

in disgrace with f., 220:15

in home of man without f., 53:25

in West build f., 462:12

insults of F., 312:1

judge men by good f., 265:23

leads on to f., 189:19

leaves door to remedy, 149:12

like glass easily broken, 99:14

like the market, 159:22

made f. send for friends, 73:26

man in possession of f., 386:23

man whom F. scratched, 203:18

man's f. in own hands, 160:4

method of making f., 323:13

most dejected thing of f., 210:18

not satisfied with one calamity, 99:11

out of suits with f., 189:35

outrageous f., 196:14

painted blind with muffler, 160:*n*2

popular when F. on our side, 99:12

prey at f., 207:2

ready for F. as she wills, 125:27

rob lady of f. by marriage, 311:28

seize good f., 350:29

shifts of F. test friends, 88:8

shows herself more kind, 181:25

sick in f., 209:3

sustain good f., 265:1

though blind not invisible, 160:3

Founding, since the f. of the city, 118:11

Fount Bandusian more sparkling than glass, 96:21

Fountain and a shrine, 452:2
dying of thirst by the f., 132:21
even f. have rest, 479:14
from f. wells up bitter taste, 90:8
like bubble on f., 378:22
pitcher broken at the f., 24:28
rise like f. for me, 459:27
the f. overflows, 357:7
troubled like f. stirred, 201:5
woman moved like f. troubled, 167:34

Fountain's silvery column, 383:2

Fountains, Afric's sunny f., 395:18
are within, 383:7
fraught with tears, 156:17
mountains are f. of men, 537:16
silver f. have mud, 220:21
under f. and graves, 777:11
where the pleasant f. lie, 165:10

Four, age best in f. things, 158:23
and twenty tailors, 789:17
angels to my bed, 266:8
ducks on a pond, 504:3
freedoms, 649:17
grant that twice two not f., 482:19
hands are f., 689:18
horsemen of Apocalypse, 602:6
Horsemen rode again, 643:15
intimate equality of the F., 652:7
lean hounds, 688:7
not f. friends in world, 270:19
snakes gliding, 430:14
spend in prayer, 152:7
things better without, 687:7
things wiser to know, 687:6
two and two mathematician makes f., 523:18
undergraduates right number, 610:11
what F. Freedoms establish, 627:21
winds of the heaven, 29:44

Fourfold, threefold f. tomb, 240:13

Four-in-hand, fiery f., 385:3

Fours, crawling on all f., 306:14

Fourscore and seven years ago, 450:2
and upward, 211:10
if by reason of strength they be f., 18:12
wind him up for f. years, 273:21

Foursquare in hand and foot, 60:8
to winds that blew, 458:7

Fourteen hundred years ago nailed, 176:23

Fourteenth Amendment not enact Spencer, 542:16

Fourth, born on F. of July, 632:11
Estate, 411:18
estate, 424:17, 463:16
estate in politics, 390:6
Estate more important than all, 411:n1
generation of them that hate me, 9:10
safe and sane F., 600:19
this is the F., 345:8

Fourth (*continued*)
what to slave your F. of July, 480:13

Fowl, dominion over f. of the air, 6:9
elegant f., 472:1
fish flesh or f., 597:7

Fowler, snare of the f., 18:15

Fowls, May comen I here f. synge, 129:4
of air draw us to kingdom, 112:17
of the air shall tell, 14:16
of the air sow not, 33:18

Fox, Aesop's f., 234:12
be f. to recognize traps, 136:15
Brer F. he lay low, 556:6
build nest on hearthstone, 613:n2
false as f. to lamb, 200:22
from lair in morning, 413:20
has many tricks, 55:n1
knows many things, 55:5
prince imitate f. and lion, 136:15
prince must know how to play f., 107:n3
quick brown f., 781:8
says they are not ripe, 58:n9
sleep in earth like tired f., 698:4
to wear arctic f., 665:6
treason trusted like f., 179:1

Foxes, fellow f. cut off theirs, 234:12
have holes, 34:17
honored among f., 737:18
little f. that spoil vines, 25:7

Foxey, maxim with F., 469:31

Foxholes, no atheists in f., 711:5
no white or colored signs on f., 742:3

Fox's, patch lion's skin with f., 107:3

Frabjous day, 518:16

Fractions, happiness made of f., 385:4

Fragment, ship f. detached, 572:20
truth f. by f., 711:10

Fragmentary blue, 623:13

Fragments, broken dishonored f., 394:15
Death tramples it to f., 409:8
gather up f., 40:3
live in f. no longer, 636:10
of the f. twelve baskets, 35:17
shored against ruins, 669:7

Fragrance, as metal keeps f., 625:10
jar will keep f., 392:n1
no spicy f. while they grow, 159:n4
of salt marsh shore mud, 491:3
perfect flower without f., 594:14
tobacco's f. greet, 750:3
wind with f. of hot sun, 616:11

Fragrant bodice, 415:5
centuries loaded f., 432:39
in your f. bosom dies, 246:6
most f. when crushed, 159:10
thousand f. posies, 162:4

Frail gaunt and small, 540:10
inhabits our f. blood, 203:3
may be f. its roof may shake, 312:19
renown is fleeting and f., 91:21
so f. a thing man, 287:13
that I may know how f. I am, 17:7
to f. mortality trust, 160:14

Frailties from dread abode, 322:24

Frailty, in f. consider last day, 66:2
more flesh therefore more f., 178:17
noblest f. of mind, 282:7
tempt f. of our powers, 201:8
thy name is woman, 193:9

Frame, heavens a shining f., 291:32
I f. no hypotheses, 281:26
mind mingles with whole f., 94:13
of adamant, 313:18
of Nature break, 292:3
out of three sounds f. star, 467:1
quit this mortal f., 299:8
stirs this mortal f., 383:3
this goodly f. earth, 195:28
this universal f. began, 275:7
thy fearful symmetry, 358:6
universal f. without mind, 159:18

Framed her last best work, 363:1
Nature hath f. strange fellows, 179:3
nature that f. us, 161:21
speech finely f., 32:21
to make women false, 206:2

Framers, wisdom of f. of treaty, 590:9

Français, je parle f. aux hommes, 143:n1

France a person, 421:15
breasts that feed F., 157:16
conquered for civilization, 503:4
despotism tempered by epigrams, 412:12
fair stood wind for F., 161:9
fight in F. and on seas, 620:7
forward sons of F., 366:n1
get out of F. quickly, 321:n2
glories of F., 543:7
half of F. in mourning for other, 436:24
has more need of me, 370:11
has not lost the war, 678:9
is invaded, 370:12
King of F. went up hill, 788:6
landing on coast of F., 678:16
let sword of F. fall, 678:10
nearer is to F., 518:7
never go to F., 422:26
not France without greatness, 678:12
one illusion F., 652:6
order matter better in F., 320:33
save squadron honor F., 468:6
shall F. remain here, 503:7
son of F. never lack statue, 605:21
standing on top of golden hours, 373:11
want to know what F. thinks, 678:14
when you march into F., 521:3

Francesca da Rimini miminy piminy, 530:1

Franchise, women to secure elective f., 475:6

Franco, remember war against F., 759:5

Frank, friendly and f., 462:6
if heart just f. kindly, 269:17
to all beside, 300:14

Frankfurters, can't all have Cardozos F., 713:16

Frankie and Johnny, 781:14

Freedom (*continued*)

black f. jeopardized, 755:9
born to f., 649:18
born to give you your name F., 691:9
brought independence and rationality, 704:8
cause of F. cause of God, 366:12
chance to be better, 733:2
competition afford f. to individual, 657:3
crown Greece with f., 60:12
cultural f., 631:14
cure is f., 424:15
deny f. to others, 448:12
deny participation of f., 331:22
deprived of f. by authorities, 682:10
deserving of f. and life, 350:26
drawing f. and peace, 404:4
economic f., 631:14
every man who lives without f., 716:6
fight for f. and truth, 508:10
fight to maintain f., 649:18
fills space 'twixt marsh, 547:7
flame of f. in souls, 541:6
for all poor workers, 682:8
for one who thinks differently, 610:9
for thought we hate, 543:10
free form not assure f., 640:15
free press without f. bad, 733:2
friends of f. doubt our sincerity, 448:5
from every B.V.D. f. ring, 688:12
from fear, 649:17, 650:8
from mountain height, 413:19
from prejudice, 500:25
from violence and lies, 582:8
from want, 649:17, 650:8
greater f. for average man, 649:1
greatest gift f. of will, 126:24
gret Press's f., 485:13
has a thousand charms, 334:3
having my f. boast of nothing, 170:32
history progress of f., 372:9
hunted round the globe, 340:21
idea of F., 461:18
if F. fall, 593:25
if I have f. in my love, 267:18
in economic arrangements, 731:11
in highest position least f., 91:26
indispensable condition of f., 609:13
indivisible word, 685:10
infringement of human f., 364:9
intellectual f. only guarantee, 749:9
is slavery, 711:17
is the prize, 368:18
law can only bring f., 350:30
let f. ring, 444:3, 761:3
liberal institutions enemies of f., 552:31
liberty f. enfranchisement, 188:17
life pure transparent f., 722:6
light in which f. lives, 706:11
lose f. if value anything more, 626:22
lose social f. individual autonomy, 727:9

Freedom (*continued*)

love not f. but license, 255:8
made man isolated anxious powerless, 704:8
nation which enjoys most f., 368:17
new birth of f., 450:2
no f. in borrowing, 507:18
no f. of thought without doubt, 712:20
none love f. but good men, 255:8
not conceived simply, 755:13
obedience bane of f., 406:8
of choice and with honor, 136:1
of expression matrix, 609:13
of f. he only is deserving, 350:26
of knyghthod and of f. flour, 132:4
of my mind, 253:7
of navigation, 572:13
of person, 344:9
of press, 344:9
of press bulwarks of liberty, 327:3
of press guaranteed those who own one, 714:2
of press has suffered most, 733:1
of religion, 344:9
of speech and expression, 649:17
of speech freedom of conscience, 527:29
of speech may be taken, 336:18
of thought, 325:6
of worship, 649:17
oh f. over me, 794:20
on mountains is f., 365:19
only to limits of consciousness, 629:5
people f. light, 680:7
political f., 631:14
political f. business of Government, 649:2
private property guaranty of f., 701:9
reap blessings of f., 341:1
reason salvation of f., 706:15
regardless of form, 640:15
religious f., 631:14
rhymes suggest wildest f., 430:15
safeguards of individual f., 701:10
secret of f. a brave heart, 72:7
secret of happiness, 72:7
seven-pillared house, 673:8
shall awhile repair, 324:11
shrieked as Kosciusko fell, 388:23
slaves fought for f., 427:6
so celestial article as F., 340:22
spirit of truth and f., 507:17
state exists is no f., 610:5
striking blow for f., 664:2
system based on courage, 618:3
those who profess to favor f., 480:16
to speak, 485:7
to think, 485:7
unchartered f. tires, 376:4
values anything more than f., 626:22
wars which usurp standard of f., 368:16
wealth and f. reign, 328:9
what is F., 419:3
whose service is perfect f., 49:2

Freedom (*continued*)

with great sum obtained f., 41:26
yet F. yet thy banner, 400:22
Freedom's, bled in F. cause, 372:15
holy light, 444:4
just another word, 768:11
Freedoms, four f., 649:17
insensible to f. of Constitution, 646:11
what Four F. establish, 627:21
Freeloader confirmed guest, 655:1
Freely give, 34:28
lives at ease that f. lives, 127:15
offer itself to you, 651:22
serve because we freely love, 259:11
too dear for what's given f., 222:15
ye have received, 34:28
Freeman contending for liberty, 336:13
no f. taken except by legal judgment, 123:12
slave patrician plebeian, 481:15
Freemen, Americans f. or slaves, 336:14
nation of f., 448:1
who rules o'er f., 317:*n*5
Freer, nowhere is speech f., 621:17
Frees all faults, 224:29
her slave again, 778:7
one word f. us, 67:10
Freethinking of one age, 500:20
Freeze, mountain-tops that f., 225:10
thy young blood, 194:17
Freezes, till Hell f. over, 783:19
Freight, nation's f. handler, 634:4
proportioned to groove, 514:18
Freiheit, nur der verdient sich F., 350:*n*9
Frémont, free speech F., 780:14
French, believe only in F. culture, 553:8
Englishman about to talk F., 645:16
for fiddle-de-dee, 519:17
for suppressing one, 499:6
German text of F. operas, 586:20
gone to fight the F., 366:20
Good Soldier finest F. novel, 617:8
hinges in F. conversation, 320:35
I speak F. to men, 143:3
new F. books, 466:10
of Parys to hir unknowe, 129:12
on F. coast light gleams, 499:19
only accidentally F., 304:12
only peril can bring F. together, 678:15
or Turk or Proosian, 529:10
phrase for hotel guests, 605:23
Radicals and German police spies, 481:14
Revolution began at top, 503:8
soldier carries marshal's baton, 371:4
spak ful faire and fetisly, 129:12
speak F. when can't think of English, 518:20
stormed Ratisbon, 464:9
struggle of F. soldiers, 510:3
true German can't stand F., 350:17
what is not clear is not F., 353:14
word impossible not F., 370:10

Friendly (*continued*)

hath friends must show himself f., 21:42

in difficult are f. forces, 630:12

mingles with f. bowl, 302:21

open and f. in private, 72:2

social f. honest man, 361:12

universe not hostile nor f., 637:4

Friend's, bear his f. infirmities, 189:17

debauch f. wife genteelly, 316:23

Friends, a little help from my f., 770:10

absent speak, 230:14

adieu kind f., 781:1

adversity tries f., 100:18

age leaves f. and wine, 392:9

all thy f. lapped in lead, 233:11

are exultations, 374:18

become bitter enemies, 234:9

behave as we wish f. to behave, 77:15

born not made, 535:15

call that backing your f., 177:23

choose men f., 600:6

death of f. inspire us, 477:18

defend me from my f., 372:n1

die adoring God loving f., 307:5

distresses of our f., 266:n2

do with f. as books, 432:4

enemies in war in peace f., 343:3

enough now for death, 710:8

ever been best of f., 471:15

faithful f. hard to find, 233:12

falling out of faithful f., 85:n11

few f. and many books, 266:17

forget love to f. and brethren, 30:12

forsake me like memory, 410:5

gain f. for when we awaken, 247:8

golden f. I had, 579:12

good book best of f., 462:5

had been f. in youth, 382:15

has thousand f. not friend to spare, 115:18

have all in common, 74:11

have no place in graveyard, 477:18

he cast off his f., 330:13

he that repeateth a matter separateth f., 21:34

held up of his f., 31:33

his truth proclaim, 274:7

honor truth above f., 77:26

humblest f., 377:14

husband children f. nothing to that, 556:20

in thirties want f., 694:24

joy to their f., 53:10

just f. and brave enemies, 344:10

kindred days, 429:19

lay down life for f., 40:31

live without f., 516:4

look with love as f., 279:5

made fortune send for f., 73:26

man that hath f., 21:42

misfortune of our f., 266:3

misfortune shows who not really f., 79:1

multitude of f., 231:20

my glory was I had such f., 599:16

Friends (*continued*)

nature teaches beasts to know f., 218:26

nearest f. can go, 623:4

never f. with roses, 534:2

no one would choose to live without f., 78:6

not be four f. in world, 270:19

not equal to yourself, 60:19

of freedom doubt our sincerity, 448:5

of my youth where are they, 118:8

of today unlovable, 4:1

oh my f., 684:2

old f. are best, 238:22

old f. times manners, 329:25

old f. to trust, 158:23

ornament of house f., 433:11

ought to forgive our f., 158:24

outside a small circle of f., 770:15

part of man's Self, 545:20

people people have for f., 583:9

preachers politicians f., 347:3

precious all things from f., 82:17

prosperity makes f., 100:18

Romans countrymen, 188:28

second glass for my f., 293:3

secure f. by doing favors, 72:5

secure you count many f., 102:3

share all things, 58:9

shifts of fortune test f., 88:8

soul remembering my good f., 171:14

spare to us our f., 562:9

State not know f. from foes, 477:14

strive mightily eat as f., 167:20

those f. thou hast, 193:29

three faithful f., 309:22

three f. hardly possible, 535:27

thrust away by his f., 31:33

to have advanced f., 498:1

trencher-f., 212:4

troops of f., 216:9

two f. in lifetime many, 535:27

tyranny's disease to trust no f., 63:4

we choose our f., 341:16

we love so dear, 523:1

wealth maketh many f., 21:43

were poor but honest, 203:11

what became of f. I loved so, 124:3

who go with the wind, 124:4

who no longer know how to die, 705:18

who plow sea, 529:15

wife and children afraid, 248:13

win f. and influence people, 667:2

without three good f., 191:8

women find few f., 318:4

wounded in house of my f., 30:6

wretched have no f., 273:17

you and I long f., 310:17

Friendship, author demands your f., 388:12

boughten f., 624:8

commerce between equals, 329:4

constant save in love, 186:21

crown is love and f., 414:12

elegance of female f., 314:14

faded, 627:7

Friendship (*continued*)

from wine sudden f., 297:13

hardly ever brings money, 387:9

highest kind of f., 739:13

holy passion of F., 527:10

in appearance at f. with me, 279:25

in f. but faithless haven, 65:13

in f. false, 274:6

is the strongest, 551:21

keep f. in repair, 315:21

let f. die, 317:27

Levin wanted f. got friendliness, 736:6

like and dislike same things is f., 91:25

love f. charity, 201:3

Love without wings, 398:14

moment when f. formed, 341:21

needs no reason, 58:13

needs parallelism of life, 535:27

of the many, 523:19

only solitary know joys of f., 616:12

out of f. cheat others, 613:1

paltry f. of Man, 452:9

peace and honest f., 344:9

pious frauds of f., 312:4

rural quiet f. books, 308:5

sacrifices of f., 610:20

sets f. above public welfare, 66:5

sheltering tree, 383:3

sounds too cold, 392:10

swear an eternal f., 269:26

that can cease never real, 113:7

three classes of f. and enmity, 110:13

time strengthens f., 283:13

true f. never serene, 271:23

two chairs for f., 478:27

wing of f. never moults, 469:26

with a man, 79:24

Friendship's, true f. laws, 299:26

Friendships invalidated by marriage, 524:22

keep f. in repair, 315:n6

Frieze, no jutty f. buttress, 213:4

Frigate, no F. like Book, 514:2

Fright, invisible spheres formed in f., 486:26

power of f. and lust, 692:4

Saint Sebastian died of f., 769:3

Frighted out of fear, 217:29

sleep I have f. thee, 183:36

the reign of Chaos, 256:13

Frighten, don't do it and f. horses, 590:7

mountain cannot f. one born on it, 365:20

Frightened, crept like f. girl, 566:6

don't be f. it won't last, 589:7

little mouse under chair, 791:1

Miss Muffet away, 791:8

to death, 434:10

Frightening when convinced they are right, 719:16

Frightful fiend, 381:26

vice a monster of f. mien, 301:14

Frights, it f. the isle, 206:17

Frigid, beat down f. Rome, 599:5

Fringe, lunatic f., 576:11

Fringed curtains of thine eye, 223:33
Fringes be falling rain, 787:5
Frippery, a little f. necessary, 347:9
Frisk i' the sun, 222:17
Frisson nouveau, 427:n7
Fritter my wig, 519:19
Frittered away by detail, 478:18
Frittering away his age, 380:7
Frivolity, irresponsible f., 435:17
Frivolous, one who is f. all day, 3:9
 work of polished idleness, 367:16
Frizzled stale and small, 742:20
Fro, going to and f. in the earth, 13:29
 many shall run to and f., 29:21
 reel to and f., 19:11
Frocks and Curls, 513:6
Frog better'n any other frog, 525:20
 eye of newt toe of f., 215:14
 has drink enough to spare, 82:16
 how public like a F., 511:22
 leaping in, 282:15
 outjump any f., 525:21
 thus use your f., 245:28
 would a-wooing go, 788:3
Frog's life is most jolly, 82:16
Frogs die in earnest, 82:10
 drone their lament, 92:26
 eat butterflies, 639:2
 in the marsh mud, 92:26
Frogs', spawning islands like f. eggs, 729:13
Frog-spawn of ditch, 598:5
Frolic wine, 241:15
Front, all quiet on western f., 700:8
 cannon in f., 458:13
 of Jove himself, 197:30
 of this small floor, 264:21
 only essential facts, 478:17
 see f. o' battle lour, 363:19
 smoothed his wrinkled f., 165:19
Frontier from Atlantic to Pacific, 620:2
 grave far away, 586:13
 New F., 740:20
 outer edge of wave, 584:6
 Rhine where f. lies, 601:18
 space the final f., 749:7
Frontiers, aggression outside f., 650:9
 economy not respect political f., 645:11
 wherever man fronts fact, 477:20
Frost, curdied by f. from snow, 219:12
 fell death's untimely f., 363:14
 is on the punkin, 559:1
 itself doth burn, 197:32
 not night kills but f., 589:16
 performs secret ministry, 382:16
 prime of youth a f. of cares, 156:22
 secret ministry of f., 382:17
 Six weeks to f., 679:14
 snow congealed with biting f., 53:n1
 third day comes a f., 225:16
 was specter-gray, 540:9
 which binds so dear head, 408:14
Frosted September, 658:1
Frosts are slain, 533:9
Frost-wind, meantime the f. blows, 415:7

Frosty, blessings on your f. pow, 362:15
 but kindly, 190:12
 Caucasus, 171:3
 wind made moan, 515:10
Frothy, hopping through f. waves, 519:2
Froward, life like a f. child, 273:2
Frowned, Critic you have f., 377:13
 dismal tidings when he f., 329:17
 fair Science f. not, 322:22
Frowning, behind f. providence, 334:1
Frowns o'er wide Rhine, 400:1
 sits on battlements and f., 367:12
Frowsy couch in sorrow steep, 364:3
Froze genial current, 322:12
 hunched in belly till wet fur f., 735:21
Frozen, children walk on f. toes, 608:6
 corpse was he, 441:1
 grass, 414:21
 milk comes f. home in pail, 169:13
 music, 350:7
 Naked Lunch a f. moment, 735:17
 sea inside us, 651:23
 toes, 608:6
 torrid or f. zone, 246:7
 tunes f. up in horn, 341:12
 which thy f. bosom bears, 204:n5
 wind off f. peak, 624:6
Fructify in lives of others, 84:n7
Frugal, how f. the Chariot, 514:2
 mind, 334:22
 swain, 325:8
 wise and f. government, 344:8
Frugality, second is f., 57:22
Fruit, bound as f. to tree, 502:3
 bringeth forth his f. in season, 15:29
 brought forth f., 35:7
 cease from yielding f., 28:29
 collections of f., 87:1
 earth bringeth forth f., 37:21
 feed on bitter f., 708:2
 fell like autumn f., 273:21
 forth reaching to the f. she plucked, 260:7
 hang like f. my soul, 220:6
 husbandman waiteth for precious f., 46:16
 I bore was sun, 107:n11
 its f. sweet its shade delightful, 5:13
 life f. ripe on plate, 717:4
 man stole the f., 243:7
 no f. but untimely grave, 246:8
 of action not be motive, 84:7
 of experience, 538:8
 of her hands, 23:21
 of loyal nature, 459:19
 of sense beneath, 298:15
 of Spirit, 44:19
 of that forbidden tree, 255:18
 of the vine, 36:28
 of thy womb, 37:39
 plant vineyards and eat the f., 28:12
 reach ripest f. of all, 161:21
 restore with cordial f., 243:16
 ripest f. first falls, 171:12
 that can fall without shaking, 304:6
 that your seasons bring, 111:5

Fruit (*continued*)
 tree bringeth not forth f., 32:32
 tree known by f., 35:2
 tree whose f. threw death, 230:21
 weakest f. drops earliest, 181:16
Fruited, above f. plain, 576:19
Fruitful, be f. and multiply, 6:9
 error full of seeds, 556:22
 of golden deeds, 257:25
 vineyard in a very f. hill, 25:37
 was she not f., 107:2
Fruition, prospects more pleasing than f., 110:n1
 sweet f. of earthly crown, 161:21
Fruitless, cold f. moon, 172:18
 weak and f. words, 450:9
 wishes, 284:14
Fruits, all pleasant f. do flow, 226:18
 by their f. know them, 34:12
 Dead Sea f., 392:14
 descendants shall gather your f., 92:15
 eat his pleasant f., 25:13
 fairy f. and flowers, 452:2
 green f. of world, 638:20
 here are f. flowers leaves, 554:2
 judge but by f., 403:27
 kindly f. of the earth, 49:12
 know them by f., 34:11
 let not f. of action be motive, 84:7
 no f. no flowers, 423:1
 of earth are for everyone, 366:8
 of life and beauty, 357:20
 of love gone, 404:7
 outdo what flowers promised, 156:9
Fruit-stall, rotten refuse of overturned f., 535:9
Fruit-tree, tips with silver f. tops, 175:7
Frumious Bandersnatch, 518:15
Frustrate, not f. of his hope, 254:15
Fry in owene grece, 131:3
 me or Fritter my wig, 519:19
Frying, out of f. pan into fire, 112:12
Fuck you up your mum and dad, 750:15
 zipless f. is absolutely pure, 772:4
Fudge, two fifths sheer f., 485:8
Fuehrer, Constitution will of F., 704:6
Fuel, adding f. to the flame, 261:22
 to maintain his fires, 246:9
Fugit inreparabile tempus, 93:n3
Fugitive and cloistered virtue, 254:25
 from law of averages, 749:3
 receive the f., 340:21
 shalt thou be, 7:5
 what was so f., 375:10
Fugue, folly alone stays f. of Youth, 136:7
Fulfill desires of thy servants, 49:6
 not to destroy but f., 33:3
 to f. lusts, 42:23
Fulfilled, see f. prophets' warning, 123:14
 till all be f., 33:4
Fulfilling, love is f. of law, 42:22
Fulfillment, all men's plans to f., 52:16
 bring all his words to f., 52:18
 give each moment f., 630:1
Fulfills, God f. in many ways, 459:26

Fulfills (*continued*)
 great Nature's plan, 361:12
Full, age f. of care, 776:7
 bloody f. of blame, 222:7
 cause of weeping, 209:23
 earth is f. of his glory, 26:1
 earth is f. of thy riches, 19:6
 fathom five, 223:32
 hell f. of good intentions, 121:10
 I am f. of matter, 15:1
 isle is f. of noises, 224:18
 little knowest that hast not tried,
  154:5
 man that hath quiver f., 20:1
 meridian of my glory, 225:14
 moon throw shadow, 656:9
 night f. of ugly sights, 165:29
 not the f. four seasons, 684:7
 o' beans and benevolence, 434:7
 o' milk of human kindness, 212:28
 of artless jealousy, 198:15
 of direst cruelty, 212:29
 of few days and f. of trouble, 14:20
 of grace and truth, 39:33
 of high sentence, 667:17
 of number of things, 561:12
 of quarrels as egg of meat, 175:25
 of shapes is fancy, 201:17
 of smiles in early days, 75:27
 of sound and fury, 216:14
 of spirit as month of May, 178:20
 of strange oaths, 191:3
 of wiles full of guile, 73:11
 of wise saws, 191:3
 reading maketh a f. man, 160:9
 sea is not f., 23:23
 sea of faith at f., 499:22
 someone not f. of herself, 772:14
 speed ahead, 426:16
 supped f. with horrors, 216:13
 that your joy may be f., 40:34
 to be empty is to be f., 57:8
 too f. for sound and foam, 460:11
 wasna f. but had plenty, 362:2
 wheel is come f. circle, 211:16
 woods are f. of them, 779:22
 youth f. of pleasance, 776:7
Full-blown rose, 415:3
Full-dazzling, all his beams f., 490:13
Fullness, earth and f. thereof, 16:18,
  43:9
 of all things, 51:38
 of perfection in him, 169:23
Full-throated ease, 415:10
Full-voiced choir below, 252:10
Fulmen, eripuit coelo f., 309:*n*1
 eripuitque Jovi f., 103:*n*11
Fum, Fie foh and f., 210:12
Fumble with the sheets, 184:30
Fumbling, early bees assaulting f.
  flowers, 737:4
Fume of poppies, 416:14
Fumes, coiling in thousand f. of
  smoke, 753:*n*1
Fun, ain't we got f., 661:15
 allowed himself f. and relaxation,
  70:1
 animal dead what f., 617:6
 are we having f. yet, 773:9
 has the mostest f., 558:15

Fun (*continued*)
 mirth and f. fast furious, 363:8
 sex most f. without laughing,
  767:15
 taken f. where found it, 592:20
 to match sorrow, 522:10
 What jolly f., 584:3
Function, form follows f., 571:30
 immotions f. in hominy kind feelings, 641:17
 judicial f., 568:18
 retain ability to f., 694:17
 to live is to f., 543:11
Functional capacity, 347:13
Functions, man in divers f., 184:23
Fund of good sense, 345:14
Fundamental article of political creed,
  338:16
 human rights, 655:23
 principle of constitution, 325:22
 things apply, 689:15
Funeral, aftermath of relative's f.,
  744:8
 baked meats, 193:14
 done and disbanded, 734:7
 everlasting f. marches round your
  heart, 738:17
 into silent f., 671:5
 marches to grave, 440:16
 mirth in f., 192:32
 misbehaved once at f., 387:21
 nobody's f., 671:5
 not a f. note, 405:15
 not celebrate f. with weeping, 84:17
 present at your f., 690:*n*1
 rejoice at birth grieve at f., 527:11
 victory won by f. establishment,
  744:8
 walks to own f. drest in shroud,
  489:20
Funerals, go to other men's f., 622:16
Fungus crop of sentiment, 532:16
Funnier, nothing f. than unhappiness,
  718:19
Funny, actin' f. but I don't know why,
  772:3
 if happening to somebody else,
  638:1
 thing happened on way to forum,
  759:2
Fur, fierce f. soft to face, 750:1
 hunched in belly till wet f. froze,
  735:21
 make f. fly, 263:13
 oh my f. and whiskers, 517:7
Furey, churchyard where Michael F.
  buried, 647:8
Furies, I acknowledge the F., 611:13
Furious anger, 31:24
 fast and f., 363:8
 to be frighted out of fear, 217:29
 vast and f. ocean, 240:8
 winter blowing, 674:10
 winter's rages, 220:3
 wise amazed temperate f., 214:16
Furiously, green ideas sleep f., 758:20
 Jehu driveth f., 13:10
Furled, battle flags were f., 455:18
 bright girdle f., 499:22
Furlongs, thousand f. of sea, 223:19

Furnace, burning fiery f., 29:13
 feet as if burned in a f., 47:4
 heat not f. for foe, 225:3
 in what f. thy brain, 358:7
 lover sighing like f., 191:3
 of affliction, 27:27
Furnish forth marriage tables, 193:14
 means of acquiring knowledge,
  369:4
 you f. pictures I f. war, 587:14
 you with argument and intellects,
  328:21
Furnished, live in f. souls, 688:11
 me from mine own library, 223:26
Furnishes oil for own wheels, 334:14
Furniture, don't bump into f., 700:19
 for man's upper chamber, 447:19
 science first-rate f., 447:19
Furrow followed free, 381:6
 half-reaped f., 416:14
Furrows, smite sounding f., 455:6
Furs to touch, 663:2
Furside is outside, 612:11
Further, get a little f. you are too
  near, 333:7
 hitherto shalt thou come but no f.,
  15:9
 nearer to church f. from God,
  141:11
Furtive, crept look of f. shame, 645:16
Fury, allaying their f., 223:31
 blind F. with abhorred shears,
  253:20
 civil f. first grew high, 262:16
 cunning old F., 517:6
 full of sound and f., 216:14
 in your words, 207:24
 like woman scorned, 291:9
 ne'er spend f. on child, 165:4
 of patient man, 274:16
 provides arms, 93:15
 Queen crimson with f., 517:23
 slinging flame, 457:14
 stronger than afterthoughts, 68:13
 trample them in my f., 28:7
Fuse, through green f. drives flower,
  737:8
 war and music not have to f., 770:5
Fust in us unused, 198:12
Fustest, git thar f. with mostest,
  496:*n*6
Fustian's so sublimely bad, 302:10
Fustilarian, you rampallian you f.,
  183:29
Futility, fatal f. of Fact, 549:4
 utility of f., 80:10
Future, aid to interpretation of f.,
  71:19
 all concerned about f., 631:6
 always says Not yet, 736:16
 America was past not f., 653:12
 Arthur the once and f. king, 133:*n*6
 as past would be present, 351:16
 been into f. and it works, 601:3
 cannot fight f., 446:13
 democracy shuts past opens f.,
  438:8
 dipped into the f., 455:17
 divine sign indicates f., 70:21
 door opens and lets f. in, 713:5

Girl (*continued*)
I can't get no g. with action, 772:16
I left behind me, 778:19
I like to see, 719:1
little g. had making of poet, 576:17
little g. my stringbean, 759:16
need park policeman pretty g., 675:17
needs good parents, 656:1
nice g. won't give an inch, 106:16
soft face of a g., 66:18
Spearmint G., 688:12
sweetest g. I know, 627:15
then spoke I to my g., 241:3
there little g. don't cry, 558:13
there was a little g., 442:25
unlessoned g. unschooled, 181:8
wild solitary g. Rima, 543:16
wink at homely g., 642:15
Girlish glee, 530:22
laughter, 576:18
Girl's, diamonds g. best friend, 705:10
stumbling blocks in g. education, 616:18
Girls, all g. he can please, 536:20
boys and g. level with men, 218:8
boys and g. together, 585:7
Dust was Lads and G., 513:6
Glos'ter g. they have no combs, 793:14
golden lads and g., 220:3
hear what servant g. said, 613:8
little g. made of, 791:6
little g. recognize your prime, 746:12
of all g. so smart, 298:2
oh you New York g., 793:15
sleek g. I teach, 757:14
turn wives, 757:15
what shall I do for pretty g., 599:19
which g. hath merriest eye, 163:10
who wear glasses, 687:9
with g. be handy, 778:21
wretched un-ideaed g., 315:16
Git thar fustest with mostest, 496:n6
Gitche Gumee, shores of G., 441:24
Gits, them that has g., 555:10
Give a little love to child, 487:25
a man enough rope, 140:n7
a new commandment, 40:25
all that a man hath will he g., 13:32
all thou canst, 377:10
all to love, 429:19
an inch take an ell, 142:n15
and not count cost, 139:3
ask only what they can g., 600:14
Aztecs by no means would g. up, 138:17
bouquets while I'm living, 634:17
countries g. themselves to you, 656:10
country back to Indians, 698:11
cried G. Me, 512:7
crowns pounds guineas, 578:22
Dayrolles a chair, 305:19
delight and hurt not, 224:18
enemies means of our destruction, 59:19
every man thy ear, 193:30
fame for pot of ale, 185:6

Give (*continued*)
freely received freely g., 34:28
Galilee gets to g., 632:16
great meals of beef, 185:13
hand and heart, 394:9
hautboys breath he comes, 276:8
haves of g., 689:1
him a little earth, 226:1
him death by inches, 219:14
his angels charge, 18:16
I generally had to g. in, 370:18
I will g. you rest, 34:38
I will not g. sleep to mine eyes, 20:4
if can g. that you are a writer, 702:1
in life did harbor g., 232:12
it an understanding, 193:23
kiss better than you g., 201:9
lady what she wants, 522:14
man horse can ride boat can sail, 523:15
me a kiss, 241:8
me a look, 232:6
me a thousand kisses, 90:19
me a torch, 658:1
me ae spark, 361:11
me again my hollow tree, 302:24
me an ounce of civet, 211:2
me another horse, 166:13
me back my heart, 399:7
me back my legions, 98:20
me but that, 149:28
me excess of it, 201:16
me good digestion Lord, 633:n3
me hand that is honest, 377:16
me handfuls of lilies, 94:16
me health and a day, 431:1
me John Baptist's head, 35:15
me liberty or give me death, 339:10
me liberty to know, 255:3
me more love or more disdain, 246:7
me my scallop shell, 152:16
me ocular proof, 207:9
me quoth I, 212:12
me that man, 197:4
me that old-time religion, 780:3
me the daggers, 214:8
me to drink mandragora, 217:4
me today take tomorrow, 118:4
me truth, 478:39
me where to stand, 83:4
me your answer do, 600:18
me your arm old toad, 750:12
me your tired your poor, 558:1
meanest flower can g., 375:15
more blessed to g., 41:23
mother g. me sun, 508:6
my regards to Broadway, 632:10
name to every fixed star, 168:15
Nature a chance, 147:8
never g. all heart, 595:12
never g. in never, 621:5
no more g. the people straw, 8:30
no more to every guest, 289:21
not a windy night rainy morrow, 221:13
oh g. me a home, 786:11
peace I g. unto you, 40:30
peace in our time, 50:10

Give (*continued*)
reason on compulsion, 177:25
sop to Cerberus, 118:3
sorrow words, 215:28
thee peace, 9:28
them meat in due season, 19:6
these delights if thou canst g., 251:20
throne would be easy, 79:11
thy thoughts no tongue, 193:28
thy worst of thoughts, 206:29
to a thief, 725:23
to get esteem, 328:11
to spend to g. to want, 154:6
to the poor, 35:36
two daughters crying g. g., 23:14
up verse my boy, 659:11
us a song to cheer, 523:1
us grace and strength, 562:9
us grace to accept, 684:14
us our daily bread, 33:12
us rest or death, 454:10
us taste of your quality, 195:34
us the tools, 620:15
warning to world, 221:7
we g. what we have, 548:18
we receive but what we g., 383:8
what shall I g. my children, 740:5
what we g. and preserve, 449:16
what you command, 114:26
while we have praise to g., 232:18
world assurance of a man, 197:30
world the lie, 152:5
you some violets, 198:24
your heart to hawks, 663:16
Given, as if Checks g., 513:15
ask and it shall be g., 34:6
gladly not to be standing here, 723:15
God has g. you one face, 196:16
hast thou g. the horse strength, 15:15
heart change of mood, 623:15
heaven alone g. away, 485:4
I have g. suck and know, 213:12
more g. less work, 510:15
much g. much required, 38:31
not have g. it for monkeys, 180:33
nothing g. nothing required, 311:16
of thine own have we g. thee, 13:18
our hearts away, 376:11
pay for what gods g., 614:11
take what is g., 625:16
thee till break of day, 358:1
them the slip, 286:9
thou hast g. him his heart's desire, 16:14
too dear for what's g. freely, 222:15
unto everyone that hath be g., 36:15
what scanted in hair g. in wit, 166:24
Giver, cheerful g., 44:7
keep modest as g., 552:8
Givers, when g. prove unkind, 196:12
Gives, blesseth him that g., 181:19
but for another g. ease, 358:2
but greater feeling to worse, 171:3
doubly benefits who g. quickly, 98:30
'er all she needs, 592:19

Gives (*continued*)
   he that lends g., 244:39
   heart and soul away, 579:1
   lovely light, 684:2
   new meaning, 665:20
   no man a sinecure, 659:11
   secure whate'er he g., 313:23
   sternest good-night, 214:2
   the more he g. to others, 58:7
   thoughts nature g. way to, 213:18
   time takes all g. all, 151:24
   to airy nothing, 174:1
   twice who gives promptly, 118:18
Giveth his beloved sleep, 19:30
   land the Lord g. thee, 9:12
   life and breath, 41:16
   man g. up the ghost, 14:21
   not as world g., 40:30
   unto the poor, 23:8
Giving enemies the slip, 320:10
   heart to dog to tear, 593:18
   in g. we receive, 123:10
   insure position by g. generously, 5:7
   manner of g. worth more, 249:17
   not g. life but risking life, 722:8
   not in g. vein today, 166:4
   stealing and g. odor, 201:16
Gizzard, something in her g., 279:24
Glacier knocks in cupboard, 720:8
   woman, 701:6
Glad did I live gladly die, 561:16
   heart too soon g., 464:12
   kindness, 597:3
   let us live and be g., 119:6
   make g. the city of God, 17:17
   me with soft black eye, 392:13
   moments of g. grace, 595:2
   never g. confident morning, 464:26
   New Year, 454:4
   not born before tea, 380:21
   of other men's good, 191:9
   Olaf g. and big, 688:16
   sad g. brother's name, 535:4
   show ourselves g., 48:20
   some have what others would be g. of, 311:20
   tidings of great joy, 285:2
   to be of use, 667:17
   to brink of fear, 430:26
   to sleep with Aphrodite, 53:16
   weep for what could make them g., 624:17
   when they said unto me, 19:26
   wine that maketh g. the heart, 19:4
   wise son maketh a g. father, 21:4
   with all my heart, 161:11
   you like adverbs, 549:11
Glade, bee-loud g., 594:21
   cool gales fan the g., 298:7
   crown the watery g., 321:13
   points to yonder g., 300:7
Gladly, be your wife g., 472:11
   beyond any experience, 688:20
   die, 561:16
   lerne and gladly teche, 129:22
   suffer fools g., 44:9
Gladness, begin in g., 374:9
   garments of g., 30:18
   I that in heill wes and g., 136:4
   notes of g., 389:10

Gladness (*continued*)
   of the heart, 32:3
   serve the Lord with g., 18:22
   teach me half g., 408:8
   wealth small aid for daily g., 68:23
Gladsome light of jurisprudence, 152:2
Glamis hath murdered sleep, 214:7
   thou art and Cawdor, 212:28
Glamour, moment of romance of g., 573:1
Glance from heaven to earth, 174:1
   glum, 531:14
   O brightening g., 598:2
   of the Lord, 401:16
   she will not g. up at bomber, 732:8
   ten thousand saw I at a g., 375:21
   without a g. my way, 512:19
Glances, casting backward g., 491:17
   gray eye g., 452:3
Glare, moths caught by g., 399:10
   rockets' red g., 391:2
   sunburnt by g. of life, 439:5
   surrounds king hides him, 146:21
Glareth, not all gold that g., 122:n6
Glasgerion swore great oath, 785:8
Glass, bishop kick hole in stained g. window, 667:6
   break bloody g., 722:4
   dome of many-colored g., 409:8
   drink not the third g., 242:18
   excuse for the g., 352:29
   falling hour by hour, 722:4
   fill every g., 297:16
   first g. for myself, 293:3
   Fortune like g. easily broken, 99:14
   fount more sparkling than g., 96:21
   get thee g. eyes, 211:5
   grief with g. that ran, 533:10
   if your windows g., 309:21
   made mouths in a g., 209:27
   obscured or broken, 750:2
   of brandy and water, 367:7
   of fashion mould of form, 196:18
   of years is brittle, 534:5
   people in g. houses, 244:n4
   pride is his own g., 200:16
   satire a sort of g., 288:16
   saw through g. eye darkly, 527:20
   see through g. darkly, 43:16
   shown g. flowers, 664:10
   swift sandy g., 233:19
   third g. thou canst not tame, 242:18
   thou art thy mother's g., 220:9
   Time turn up his g., 233:19
   turn down empty G., 446:9
   Venus take my votive g., 288:4
   wherein noble youth dress, 183:33
   whose house is g., 244:17
Glasses, fill all the g. there, 267:1
   girls who wear g., 687:9
   itself in tempests, 401:2
   Shakespeare and the musical g., 328:24
Glasses', peeps over g. edge, 466:7
Glassy cool translucent wave, 253:11
   his g. essence, 204:4
Glaze on katydid-wing, 665:2
Glazed with rain water, 654:1
Glazen, upon the g. shelves, 668:1
Gleam, bright g. of noble deeds, 64:10

Gleam (*continued*)
   fled visionary g., 375:6
   follow the G., 460:10
Gleamed upon my sight, 375:16
Gleaming, like g. taper's light, 328:5
   twilight's last g., 391:2
Gleams, light g. and is gone, 499:19
   of remoter world, 406:11
   on whom pale moon g., 553:21
   through fog, 321:5
   thy footstep g., 452:3
   untraveled world, 455:1
Glean, let me g. after the reapers, 11:24
   shalt not g. thy vineyard, 9:24
Gleaned my teeming brain, 417:9
Gleaning of grapes of Ephraim, 11:9
Gleanings, shalt not gather the g., 9:24
Glee, counterfeited g., 329:17
   girlish g., 530:22
   piping songs of pleasant g., 356:4
Glen, down the rushy g., 504:2
Glenartney's, lone G. hazel shade, 378:17
Glib and oily art, 208:25
Glide, in sunny beams did g., 355:17
   leisurely we g., 517:1
   safe into haven g., 312:14
   soul into boughs does g., 268:19
   to wind tossing water, 654:2
Glided, mourns that day has g. by, 413:23
Glideth at own sweet will, 374:13
Gliding, dark mother always g. near, 490:18
   snakes g. up hollow, 430:14
Glimmer of twilight, 464:26
   women have g. of loyalty to Truth, 556:20
Glimmering, gone g., 399:13
   hold g. tapers to sun, 235:n4
   mere g. and decays, 270:10
   now fades g. landscape, 322:2
   river lake g. pool, 503:4
Glimpse, nor g. divine, 304:2
   same old g. of Paradise, 580:14
Glimpses make me less forlorn, 376:12
   of forgotten dreams, 453:21
   revisitest g. of the moon, 194:11
   thousand g. wins, 497:18
Glint, in g. old gold, 619:2
Glisten, all silence an' g., 485:15
Glister me forward, 724:17
Glistering grief, 225:8
Glisters, all that g. not gold, 122:n6
Glitter of seas, 764:20
Glittered when he walked, 608:7
Glittering, ancient g. eyes, 599:8
   eye, 380:26
   how that g. taketh me, 241:20
Glitters, all that g. is not gold, 122:n6
Gloamin', roamin' in the g., 609:18
Global, my wars g. from the start, 737:5
   village, 730:5
Globe, common air bathes g., 489:3
   country spread over half g., 446:27
   distracted g., 194:27
   doubled g. of dead, 737:10

Globe (*continued*)
flames have spread over g., 345:3
freedom hunted round the g., 340:21
great g. itself, 224:21
interior of solid g., 420:17
power dotted over g., 394:19
sop of all this solid g., 200:9
sway destinies of half the g., 438:7
Glocca Morra, how are things in G., 699:18
Gloire, le jour de g. est arrivé, 366:9
Gloom, chase my g. away, 367:5
convent's solitary g., 300:3
counterfeit a g., 252:5
deep thicket's g., 349:8
encircling g., 426:18
in g. black-purple, 619:2
moral g. of world, 435:23
nor g. of night, 70:n4
of earthquake and eclipse, 406:14
tempted her out of g., 453:4
Glooms, beetle booms adown g., 558:11
welcome kindred g., 307:16
Gloomy, deep and g. wood, 373:4
view of future, 632:2
Gloria in excelsis Deo, 48:8
mundi, 132:12
Gloriam, ad maiorem Dei g., 143:n2
Gloried and drank deep, 445:12
Glories, conquests g. triumphs spoils, 188:19
Heaven's g. shine, 480:4
my g. and state depose, 172:10
of our blood and state, 246:23
of the winter moon, 454:19
strung like beads, 490:4
with their triumphs and their g., 465:10
Glorieth, let him that g. glory in me, 28:23
Glorified, whom he justified he g., 42:5
Glorify Father in heaven, 33:3
Glorious blood-red, 465:5
by my sword, 264:n2
circumstance of g. war, 207:8
crowded hour of g. life, 333:8
Deaths g. in thy Defense, 292:n2
full many a g. morning, 220:20
gifts of the gods, 51:11
heaven's g. sun, 168:15
honorable and g., 336:17
how g. and painful, 461:16
institution, 331:23
king's daughter all g. within, 17:15
made g. summer by sun of York, 165:18
make thee g. by my pen, 264:5
making city g. and great, 62:23
mirror, 401:2
mission of trade unions, 560:2
morning for America, 325:5
most g. city of God, 115:2
most g. to victors, 72:12
necessity to g. gain, 376:9
place glorious age, 764:2
right hand is become g., 9:4
shadow of g. name, 105:20

Glorious (*continued*)
song of old, 462:2
sun in Heaven, 382:18
sunshine a g. birth, 375:5
Tam was g., 363:5
the g. Ninety-two, 339:3
the more g. the triumph, 340:22
thing to be Pirate King, 529:11
things g. had no glory, 701:14
things of thee are spoken, 327:5
war's g. art, 296:3
Gloriously drunk, 335:9
he hath triumphed g., 9:2
perjured, 96:20
succeeded, 706:19
Glory, a light a g., 383:9
and danger alike, 72:4
and freshness of a dream, 375:3
and nothing of a name, 401:18
and shame of universe, 271:7
and the dream, 375:6
be the Perfect One, 513:4
be to the Father, 48:22
belongs to our ancestors, 107:7
cataract leaps in g., 456:11
crown of g., 46:27
day of g. has come, 366:n1
days of youth days of g., 403:23
deed everything g. nothing, 350:25
desire for g. clings, 109:18
desirous of honor and g., 278:17
die in g. never old, 579:5
doesn't mean argument, 519:14
drowned G. in Cup, 446:6
excess of g. obscured, 256:15
fight for love and g., 689:16
for country's g. fast, 378:4
from gray hairs gone, 443:3
from the earth, 375:5
full meridian of my g., 225:14
go where g. waits thee, 391:9
guards bivouac of dead, 492:4
heavens declare the g. of God, 16:9
hoary head a crown of g., 21:32
Homer herald of your g., 80:23
hope of g., 49:5
in His bosom, 484:7
in one day fill stage, 242:14
in the flower, 375:14
is departed from Israel, 11:30
is in their shame, 44:33
jest and riddle of world, 301:13
King of g. shall come in, 16:19
land of hope and g., 585:5
left him alone with g., 405:17
let him that glorieth g. in me, 28:23
like a circle in water, 163:8
like a shooting star, 171:19
long hair g. to woman, 43:10
love of g. most ardent, 293:20
my gown of g., 152:16
myn the travaille thyn the g., 130:20
no more Hope no more G., 617:11
nothing so expensive as g., 380:3
O what joy and g. must be, 121:6
of Christian religion, 134:10
of coming of Lord, 484:6
of Europe extinguished, 332:12
of everything, 703:16

Glory (*continued*)
of Him who moves everything, 126:21
of his country, 394:8
of honors beauties wits, 229:5
of Lord shone, 38:3
of old story is forever, 94:21
of the Lord is risen, 28:4
of their times, 32:14
of thy people Israel, 38:6
of war moonshine, 492:12
of winning were she won, 509:10
of woman who occasions least talk, 72:8
Old G., 429:5
one star differeth in g., 43:24
or grave, 389:4
pacing alone, 421:19
paths of g., 322:8
pomp and g. of this world, 225:16
power and g., 39:14
power and the g., 13:17
precious forever, 69:3
pride of peacock g. of God, 357:6
pursuit of human g., 246:8
race of g. run, 261:15
rainbow's g. is shed, 409:19
search their own g., 22:28
set stars of g. there, 413:19
shone around, 285:1
shows the way, 285:8
sing tongue the Savior's g., 124:5
sittest throned in g., 520:4
so passes g. of world, 132:12
Solomon in all his g., 33:21
such g. over everything, 493:13
sudden g. maketh laughter, 239:19
summers in a sea of g., 225:16
take away our free will and g., 137:1
that was Greece, 451:12
they to g. ride therein, 283:5
thine is the g., 33:12
things glorious had no g., 701:14
time's g. calm contending kings, 167:2
to God for dappled things, 550:23
to God in highest, 38:4, 48:8
to Man in highest, 535:1
to newborn King, 312:17
to the greater g. of God, 143:4
trailing clouds of g., 375:7
trembles before your g., 66:18
triumph without g., 249:9
'twas my one G., 513:14
uncertain g. of April day, 168:1
vain pomp and g., 49:21
visions of g., 323:9
walked in g. and joy, 374:9
walking in an air of g., 270:10
was I had such friends, 599:16
what price g., 666:6
who is this King of g., 16:20
wonder and g. of universe, 444:12
words such as g. obscene, 701:14
wretchedness that g. brings, 212:6
you probably take away g., 369:16
Glory's small change, 427:17
Gloss, all the g. of art, 329:20

Goal (*continued*)

grave not life's g., 440:15

is living in agreement with nature, 82:1

pint people to the g., 485:13

progress our g., 421:8

rider deciding on g., 569:13

riders not stop at g., 543:11

the sky, 783:5

Goals, black people define g., 771:2

muddied oafs at g., 593:7

Goat, lust of g. bounty of God, 357:6

splashing with hoofs of g., 439:8

with g. feet dance antic hay, 162:10

Goat-head, foul g., 599:17

Goats, divideth sheep from g., 36:17

eat ivy, 791:15

lecherous g., 230:21

you herd g., 56:11

Gobbledygoo, your Luftwaffe your g., 764:17

Gobbler, black turkey g., 787:8

Gobble-uns 'at gits you, 558:15

Goblet, upon first g., 427:28

Goblin, hag and hungry g., 777:2

Goblins 'at gits you, 558:15

sprites and g., 222:21

God, a G. ready to pardon, 13:23

a sea of infinite substance, 120:7

abandoned these defended, 580:2

abhors you, 308:20

accept him, 458:8

act as if G. exist, 589:12

act as if there were G., 546:15

act of G., 476:8

Act of G. defined, 678:23

afraid to look upon G., 8:25

all mercy is God unjust, 296:15

all service same with G., 464:8

Almighty has hung sign, 395:11

Almighty's gentlemen, 274:13

alone knows, 532:3

am I a g. I see so clearly, 350:12

and angels as surety, 116:19

and attributes eternal, 277:17

and devil fighting, 495:5

and history remember, 681:2

and I knew once, 532:3

and imagination one, 640:9

and man decree, 579:19

and nature do nothing uselessly, 78:n5

and sinners reconciled, 312:17

angler now with G., 245:23

announced selves descended from a g., 395:22

answers sharp, 439:4

Appears and God is Light, 359:16

argue not concerning G., 488:11

as G. alone Jesus not saved us, 711:6

as G. gives us to see right, 450:11

as I would do were I Lord G., 504:14

as if G. wrote bill, 430:5

as revealed to vicars, 717:3

assumes the g., 276:7

atheist half believes G., 296:16

attribute to G. himself, 181:19

be good to the man, 745:17

God (*continued*)

be merciful, 39:9

be praised Georges ended, 627:n5

be still and know that I am G., 17:18

be thanked, 663:4

beauty the gift of G., 77:11

became man devil woman, 427:16

behold your G., 27:19

bein' G. ain't bed of roses, 678:5

being with thee, 374:16

believe in one G. and no more, 341:9

believes he eats G., 321:7

bequeath my soul to G., 160:12

bless America, 666:11, 666:12

bless Captain Vere, 487:9

bless the Pretender, 304:14

bless us every one, 470:10

bless you, 779:14

bless you my dear, 318:2

body Nature G. soul, 301:11

brewed waters into gale, 486:20

brooding on G., 725:19

built G. a church, 334:16

bush afire with G., 439:7

but for grace of G., 143:9

by G. Mr. Chairman, 326:13

by G. she'd better, 461:n1

by grace of G. forces on Philippine soil, 642:2

Cabots talk only to G., 582:1

Cabots walk with G., 582:n1

cannot appear except in form of bread, 745:3

cast all cares on G., 459:29

caught his eye, 697:6

cause of Freedom cause of G., 366:12

caused a deep sleep, 6:16

changes and man and form, 534:19

changes not people until they change, 116:11

charged with grandeur of G., 550:18

chide G. for countenance, 191:28

chosen people of G., 343:10

Christ came from G. and a woman, 421:1

circumvent G., 199:3

city of G., 115:2

closer walk with G., 333:20

comes as sun at noon, 231:10

comes G. behind them, 467:22

committed themselves to G., 240:7

Communism vision of Kingdom of G. on earth, 721:15

conscience a g. to all mortals, 81:17

contempt of G. love of G., 115:3

could have made a better berry, 245:27

course of Nature art of G., 248:n2

created heaven and earth, 6:4

created woman and boredom ceased, 553:2

curse G. and die, 13:33

damn you, 590:n4

darkness of G., 671:5

dazzled by ways of G., 637:5

dear G. the very houses, 374:13

God (*continued*)

dear G. who loveth us, 382:8

dear to G. famous to all ages, 254:20

death of one g. death of all, 639:21

deem himself g. or beast, 301:13

defend the right, 163:22

depth of all being is G., 662:9

did G. Care, 512:7

die adoring G. loving friends, 307:5

die young like kissing G., 754:17

died before g. of love was born, 229:17

discovered I was not G., 543:12

discussing duty to G., 489:16

don't believe in G. or Mother Goose, 573:20

doth G. exact day-labor, 255:12

dwells there among men, 121:2

ef you want to take in G., 485:11

effect whose cause is G., 335:14

either a beast or a g., 78:14

electrical display of G., 674:3

Enoch walked with G., 7:12

enormous loping g. in sky, 773:16

enter into kingdom of G., 35:37

equal to a g. sitting opposite you, 91:4

erects house of prayer, 285:14

eternal G. is thy refuge, 10:29

every g. set his seal, 197:30

every man G. or Devil, 274:12

evidence for G. in inner experiences, 546:19

except for G. our only lord, 161:8

face of G. shine through, 683:16

far be it from G., 15:3

Father-Mother G., 495:19

favor with G. and man, 38:8

fear G. and keep commandments, 24:30

fear G. and take own part, 428:16

fear G. honor the king, 46:23

fear G. nothing else, 474:18

fell upon knees and blessed G., 240:8

finding man not sufficiently alone, 614:2

finger of G., 8:33

first planted garden, 160:6

for G. sake hold your tongue, 228:14

for Harry, 185:5

for us all, 142:30

forbid it Almighty G., 339:10

foregoing generations beheld G., 430:24

forgive you but I never, 145:3

forgives me for it, 754:1

forgotten all I have done, 281:4

formed matter, 282:4

from the machine, 81:10

from whom blessings flow, 280:21

fulfills in many ways, 459:26

gave every people cup of clay, 787:16

gave Loaf to Bird, 513:5

gave me my money, 539:2

gave Noah rainbow sign, 753:8

gave the increase, 42:31

God (*continued*)

give him blood to drink, 436:6
give them wisdom, 201:24
give us grace to accept, 684:14
giver of breath and bread, 550:17
giveth both mouth and meat,
141:*n*3
glory to G., 38:4, 48:8
good fortune is g. among men,
63:20
good G. prepare me, 279:27
grace is given of G., 482:21
Grace of G. in courtesy, 608:21
grant you find one face, 484:16
granted it, 306:22
grants liberty, 395:1
great G. I'd rather be, 376:12
great G. our King, 444:4
great g. Pan, 107:16, 439:8
great G. to thee we tend, 115:13
greater than G. cannot be conceived, 121:4
greatness of G., 547:7
guideth whom He will, 117:7
ha' mercy on such as we, 592:3
had I but studied, 133:20
had never spoken anything but English, 622:15
hand of G. spirit of G., 488:18
handiwork you give G., 563:7
Hannah G. and me, 521:1
happiness not gift of G., 635:10
has brought us this peace, 92:2
has given you one face, 196:16
has G. sent a mortal as messenger,
116:19
has no real style, 645:3
has written all the books, 525:6
hates bray of bragging, 66:3
hath chosen foolish things, 42:29
hath given liberty, 351:20
hath made man upright, 24:15
hath made them so, 294:6
hath no better praise, 550:1
hath not given spirit of fear, 45:26
hath not one G. created us, 30:7
hath numbered thy kingdom, 29:16
hath said there is no G., 16:3
hath sifted a nation, 277:3
have mercy on sinner, 674:13
have mercy on such as we, 592:3
he for G. only, 258:12
he was a son of G., 694:9
heirs of, 42:2
help us we knew worst too young,
592:4
helps them that help selves, 309:20
helps those who get up early,
793:24
herdsman goads, 594:19
here I stand G. help me, 138:3
hid fossils in rocks, 557:5
Himself can't kill words, 97:*n*10
himself from G. not free, 429:10
himself scarce seemed to be, 382:6
his Father and his G., 322:24
honest G. noblest work, 520:15
honest man noblest work of G.,
301:18, 361:10
how odd of God, 656:14

God (*continued*)

how would man exist if G. did not
need him, 632:8
I accuser G. accused, 760:6
I am a G., 406:18
I am a jealous G., 9:10
I am part or particle of G., 430:27
I am the Lord thy G., 9:8
I bless G. in libraries, 325:14
I think it pisses G. off, 773:13
I treated him G. cured him, 143:10
I who saw face of G., 162:15
I wretch wrestling with G., 551:12
if find answer know mind of G.,
772:2
if G. be for us, 42:6
if G. did not exist, 306:25
if G. died, 763:3
if G. is male, 758:21
if G. were not necessary, 273:7
if G. will, 116:20
if it be of G., 41:1
if triangles had g., 304:9
I'll leap up to my G., 162:23
in apprehension like a g., 195:28
in G. dazzling darkness, 270:3
in G. is our trust, 391:3
in mercy lend grace, 454:17
in name of most merciful G., 116:1
in the image of G., 7:23
in Three Persons, 395:21
in works and in word, 295:9
in youth remembered my G., 386:9
inclines to think there is G., 483:2
incomprehensibility of G., 422:13
insult to G., 464:25
invite G. and his angels, 231:11
is a Mother, 674:2
is a verb, 691:12
is an exalted father, 569:7
is an in order to, 589:19
is and all well, 443:16
is and is not voice of G., 303:5
is day night winter summer, 62:13
is dead, 552:5
is G. blunder of man, 552:29
is G. dead, 420:21
is in heaven, 24:2
is in me or does not exist, 640:29
is in the details, 783:2
is in the midst of her, 17:17
is light, 46:31
is love, 46:36
is Love I dare say, 525:7
is man blunder of G., 552:29
is no respecter of persons, 41:10
is not a because, 589:19
is not a man, 10:6
is not mocked, 44:21
is our refuge and strength, 17:16
is seen God, 466:19
is swift at the reckoning, 117:5
is their belly, 44:33
is they are, 467:14
it is a g. who gave you this gift,
50:27
it's not G. I don't accept, 495:8
jealous G., 9:10
just are the ways of G., 261:12
justify ways of G. to men, 255:20

God (*continued*)

keep you in his holy hand, 794:8
keeps thee from G., 426:20
Kingdom of G. within you, 39:5
kissing carrion, 195:17
know what G. and man is, 460:5
know ye that the Lord he is G.,
18:22
knowledge and love of G., 49:18
knowledge makes G. of me, 417:1
knows which God God recognizes,
717:3
land G. gave to Cain, 139:2
laws of G. are forever, 66:11
laws of G. laws of man, 579:19
laws of nature and nature's G.,
343:2
lay me on anvil O G., 634:9
let not G. speak with us, 9:13
let us worship G., 361:9
life of ease not for a g., 413:6
light is shadow of G., 249:6
light of heavens and earth, 117:4
light prime work of G., 257:*n*6
live innocently G. is here, 312:11
livin' G. that made you, 591:20
living G., 17:11
looks after fools, 782:11
looks up to Nature's G., 302:1
Lord G. Almighty, 395:21
Lord G. formed man, 6:11
Lord G. is subtle, 636:6
Lord G. made them all, 479:17
Lord G. of Hosts, 592:25
Lord G. planted a garden, 6:12
Lord G. send high wave, 613:9
Lord G. walking in garden, 6:21
love not Pleasure love G., 412:9
love of G. had blessed, 397:4
loveth cheerful giver, 44:7
lust of goat bounty of G., 357:6
made him let him pass for man,
179:31
made integers, 503:1
made the country, 334:25
made the world, 41:16
make me strong, 783:14
make straight a highway for our G.,
27:15
makes sech nights, 485:15
makes those who believe stand firm,
116:13
man fallen g., 405:9
man g. in ruins, 431:3
man proposes G. disposes, 132:14
man sent from G., 39:31
man with G. always in majority,
143:15
man with G. strive, 400:13
man's word G. in man, 459:4
Masai House of G., 702:4
men G. made mad, 618:17
men the cattle of G., 3:15
mighty fortress is our G., 138:5
mills of G. grind slowly, 247:15
most glorious city of G., 115:2
moved upon face of the waters, 6:4
moves in mysterious way, 333:22
music sent up to G., 467:3

God (*continued*)

must think it exceedingly odd, 673:5
my G. and King, 243:25
my G. Father and Friend, 278:25
my G. have mercy, 147:9
my G. look not so fierce, 162:24
my G. why hast thou forsaken me, 16:15, 37:12
my soul thirsteth for G., 17:11
nakedness of woman work of G., 357:6
name called the mighty G., 26:8
name of G. upon lips, 319:12
Nature and Nature's G., 295:9
nature is the art of G., 248:7
Nature's G., 302:1
nature's G. commands slave to rise, 368:18
nearer my G. to thee, 437:4
nearer to church further from G., 141:11
nest on greatness of G., 547:7
never made work for man to mend, 276:19
never spoke with G., 513:15
next to of course g., 688:15
no G. and Mary His Mother, 588:21
no g. higher than truth, 607:1
no G. stronger than death, 534:6
no man hath seen G., 39:34
no more Aurora Leighs thank G., 446:11
no society bring Kingdom of G., 645:9
noblest work of G., 301:18
none other but the house of G., 7:42
not alone G. is within, 108:1
not even G. is wise enough, 784:29
not G. for father if not Church for mother, 112:18
not G. in Gardens, 511:9
not G. of dead, 39:12
not only no G., 767:11
not serve G. if devil bid, 205:16
not willing to do everything, 137:1
O G. O Montreal, 524:13
O G. that bread so dear, 423:8
O G. that it were possible, 233:19
O Lamb of G., 48:9
of battles, 185:20
of Clotilda grant victory, 115:7
of fathers known of old, 592:25
of God, 49:1
of my idolatry, 175:8
of Nature, 243:19
of Nature placed in power, 339:9
of such is kingdom of G., 37:31
of the Congo, 637:10
of truth, 10:26
of universal laws, 546:16
Oh G. put back universe, 562:20
on right hand of G., 48:25
on seventh day G. ended his work, 6:10
on side of best digestion, 633:9
on side of big squadrons, 266:13
one G. even the Father, 392:17

God (*continued*)

one g. greatest among gods, 60:6
one G. law element, 458:3
one G. one principle of being, 111:19
One God the Everlasting Refuge, 117:26
one nation under G., 568:12
one that feared G., 13:27
only another artist, 645:3
only G. and angels lookers on, 158:9
only G. can make tree, 662:1
only G. had for asking, 485:4
only G. my dear, 598:8
only knows which is which, 535:7
our help in ages past, 294:14
out in fields with G., 781:12
out of me G. and man, 534:19
owe G. a death, 184:5
pairs off like with like, 54:2
patriarch obedient to G., 493:19
peace of G. passeth understanding, 44:34
Peace of G. which passeth all understanding, 49:18
perfect blessedness vision of G., 124:12
perhaps G. resembles etchings of Goya, 735:10
plays dice with world, 636:5
pleased G. to visit us with death, 240:10
poor dear G., 695:20
poor Mexico so far from G., 511:10
praise be to G., 116:1
presume not G. to scan, 301:13
pride of peacock glory of G., 357:6
purlieu of g. of love, 229:18
put hand to ark of G., 12:6
rather believe G. not exist, 437:3
read New Yorker trust in G., 720:21
reason in man like G. in world, 124:13
rebellion obedience to G., 779:3
reflect that G. is just, 343:9
register of G., 249:2
reigns Government lives, 516:2
remains dead, 552:*n*2
render unto G., 35:45
rest you merry, 778:8
rib which Lord G. had taken, 6:16
rise and shine give G. glory, 794:16
round fat oily man of G., 308:15
said I am tired, 430:1
said Let Newton be, 303:17
said Let there be light, 6:4
said Let us make man, 6:7
saint if G. does not exist, 732:17
save the king, 11:32, 298:3
save the king say amen, 172:8
save the mark, 177:5
save the people, 393:11
save thee ancient Mariner, 381:5
saw that it was good, 6:6
say first of G. above, 301:3
says there is no G., 319:12
says why did they put you in prison, 689:9

God (*continued*)

Scourge of G., 162:1
secluded from sight of G., 231:9
see G. made and eaten, 465:7
seek G. in old quiet places, 763:3
seen G. face to face, 8:2
sees G. in clouds, 301:7
self-reliance is reliance on G., 432:29
send every gentleman, 785:16
send them sorrow and shame, 135:22
sends meat Devil sends cooks, 141:*n*3
servant of G. well done, 259:17
servant of Living G., 325:17
served my G. with half the zeal, 225:22
service greater than the g., 200:15
sets nothing but riddles, 495:4
setteth the solitary in families, 17:39
shall any teach G., 14:34
shall smite thee, 41:27
shall wipe away tears, 48:1
she for G. in him, 258:12
shed grace on thee, 576:19
shield us, 173:15
shows sufficient light, 467:30
so commanded, 260:6
so loved the world, 39:46
so near is G. to man, 430:4
sole G. beside whom is none, 5:6
some lesser g. made world, 459:23
Son of G. goes forth, 395:17
Son of the living G., 35:27
sons of G. shouted for joy, 15:8
sons of the living G., 29:22
Soul of each G. of all, 380:25
souls are in the hand of G., 30:23
souls mounting up to G., 509:20
Spirit of G. descending, 32:33
spirit shall return unto G., 24:28
standeth G. within shadow, 485:2
stands winding horn, 595:6
stay with me G., 783:14
stepped out on space, 612:7
stern daughter of voice of G., 376:2
strong brown g., 671:12
subject to G. and Justice, 122:5
sufficeth me, 116:7
surrenders his face to G., 117:9
sways G. nearby, 734:14
take in G., 485:11
tempers wind, 144:14, 321:2
temple of G. is holy, 42:34
thank G. Almighty, 794:12
thank G. Almighty free at last, 761:3
thank G. for tea, 380:21
thank G. I have done duty, 361:1
the Father a school-divine, 303:6
the Father fell back behind Christ, 569:18
the first garden made, 267:7
the herdsman goads, 594:19
the most resembles G., 362:4
the unknown g., 41:15
the word spake it, 145:6
the world the book of G., 227:4
there G. is dwelling too, 356:14

God *(continued)*

there is no G. but He, 116:7
these old men, 67:26
they shall be called children of G.,
33:1
they shall see G., 33:1
think himself act of G., 476:8
think not G. at all, 261:12
this nation under G., 450:2
this only is denied to G., 74:2
this thing is G., 534:20
those G. loves do not live long,
81:*n* 4
those G. wishes to destroy, 69:18
those whom G. hath joined together, 50:6
thou art the Son of G., 35:21
thou great democratic G., 486:22
thought and thought, 612:8
three-personed G., 230:26
through darkness up to G., 457:20
throws himself on G., 465:24
thy G. shall be my G., 11:23
'tis G. gives skill, 483:6
to begin new and great period,
255:1
to kirk nearer from G. more far,
153:3
to the greater glory of G., 143:4
to whom G. assigns no light, 117:5
too full of G. to speak, 594:15
took spinning-jenny, 597:21
touched face of G., 751:3
towards G. the other towards Satan,
494:13
trust in G. hope for best, 380:4
trust in G. keep powder dry, 389:20
two halves of G., 427:15
two not without G., 112:16
unchanging law of G., 461:18
unto G. is the sequel, 117:9
very G. of very G., 49:1
vindicate ways of G. to man, 301:2
voice of people is voice of G., 120:8
walk humbly with thy G., 29:38
wanted me to be Czech, 768:8
wants nothing of a g. but eternity,
219:13
war blood-swollen g., 611:1
was it G. was it man, 534:21
was the holy Lamb of G., 359:17
ways of G. justifiable, 261:12
we believe in G., 116:3
we praise thee O G., 48:23
what G. hath joined, 35:35
what hath G. wrought, 10:7
what I call G., 468:2
what is G. everything, 64:14
what kind of g. art thou, 185:18
what man not know of G., 712:19
what we have instead of G., 701:12
when you ask G. to send trials,
555:6
where end knows G., 708:10
where G. built church, 138:10
who brought over ocean, 240:8
who could discover G., 103:16
who gave life gave liberty, 343:1
who G. doth late and early pray,
227:7

God *(continued)*

who is able to prevail, 245:11
who is not we see, 535:8
who is our home, 375:7
who made him sees, 593:23
who made thee mighty, 585:5
whole armor of G., 44:27
whom G. wishes to destroy, 119:25
whom science recognizes, 546:16
whom we see not is, 535:8
whose puppets are we, 464:8
why St. Augustine thanked G.,
628:14
will not let us fall, 237:10
will of G. prevail, 500:14
will provide himself a lamb, 7:34
will put an end to these, 93:16
will take you to task for your
hearts, 116:5
wills it, 118:27
wills us free, 341:18
wisdom by awful grace of G., 63:11
with G. nothing impossible, 37:38
with strongest battalions, 318:20
with thousand voices praises G.,
383:4
with us, 32:22
word of G. is quick, 45:34
word of our G. shall stand, 27:18
Word was with G., 39:29
Words of G. not exhausted, 117:10
worketh in you, 44:31
works in mysterious way, 668:11
world's G. is treacherous, 663:12
worship G. according to own inclinations, 105:15
worship G. in own way, 649:17
would G. this flesh might be,
533:18
would have three sides, 304:9
wrath of G., 47:35
wrath of lion wisdom of G., 357:6
wrongs not men, 116:9
wrote of Angels and G., 357:2
yearning like G., 415:1
you need G. G. needs you, 632:8
your false g. dim rememoring,
674:21
Yours Faithfully G., 673:*n* 1
Zion city of our G., 327:5
Goddam precious American rights,
765:3
Goddamm, Lhude sing G., 659:2
Goddamnedest, seevility of commonest
g. kind, 780:19
Goddess, bitch-g. Success, 545:7
consult concerning great g., 371:18
Demeter or Earth, 68:26
excellently bright, 231:21
Liberty white G., 528:16
moves a g., 299:24
night sable g., 296:7
of Grecian woes O g. sing, 299:23
of the silver lake, 253:11
to thy shrine we come, 364:13
walk revealed her as true g., 93:19
White G., 692:4
write about it G., 303:32
Goddesses, even if g. too should be
looking, 53:16

Goddesses *(continued)*

sweets of Fairies Peris G., 414:16
take hold ye gods and g., 51:28
Godfathers of heaven's lights, 168:15
God-fearing, signs for a g. people,
116:8
God-given rights, 437:18
God-intoxicated man, 277:*n* 8
Godiva, white G. I unpeel, 764:19
Godlessness, future smells of g.,
420:10
Godlike, capability and g. reason,
198:12
erect, 258:11
man with g. intellect, 444:15
Godliness, cheerful g., 374:20
cleanliness next to g., 309:1
Godly, old and g. and grave, 595:3
God's above all, 206:16
abusing of G. patience, 182:23
arrest, 283:10
blessing said Sancho Panza, 151:*n* 5
Caesar's self is G., 264:13
capricious hand, 716:16
crucible, 590:6
dare ask just G. assistance, 450:10
Devil is ever G. ape, 138:10
do deed without G. knowledge,
63:28
earthly power then likest G., 181:19
elect, 42:7
finger touched him, 457:24
first creature light, 257:*n* 6
first temples, 411:6
fool, 526:6
footstool may be throne, 622:14
for G. sake sit upon ground, 171:25
gifts put dreams to shame, 438:22
great Judgment Seat, 591:9
greenwood chapel, 637:*n* 3
hand folks over to G. mercy, 483:16
heaven is G. throne, 33:6
help and their valor, 370:12
here is G. plenty, 276:24
I'm under G. arrest, 283:10
in G. wildness hope of world,
537:14
in his heaven, 464:4
instant men call years, 467:29
issue is in G. hands, 64:1
justify G. ways to man, 579:15
last Put out the Light, 623:22
light G. eldest daughter, 250:12
look in my G. right hand, 794:18
love G. ultimate gift, 466:20
man's bedevilment and G., 579:20
mill grinds slow, 244:38
mouth knows not falsehood, 63:7
not G. not beasts', 467:14
one on G. side majority, 462:17
Park specimen of G. handiwork,
502:2
reason G. crowning gift, 66:16
skirts, 464:16
spies, 211:13
things which are G., 35:45
thy country's thy G. and truth's,
225:21
to Indian all days are G., 575:7
voice of G. creatures, 451:*n* 2

God's (*continued*)
  want to do G. will, 761:9
  ways to man, 579:15
  we are in G. hand, 185:11
  will be done, 341:18
  woman G. second mistake, 553:2
  word Be, 116:14
  written in G. book, 116:10
  ye are G. husbandry, 42:32
Gods, all ages believed in g., 628:12
  all men have need of g., 53:3
  altars to unknown g., 545:9
  angels would be g., 159:*n*7
  approve the depth, 377:4
  are just, 211:15
  are on side of stronger, 109:19
  arrive, 429:20
  as flies to boys we to g., 210:20
  as psychic factors, 628:12
  believe in g. of state, 74:14
  built against will of g., 51:35
  by Nine G. he swore, 425:13
  call the g. to witness, 211:23
  calling on the g., 71:17
  contend in vain, 365:17
  convenient that there be g., 101:14
  darling of men and g., 89:2
  daughter of g., 454:13
  dish fit for g., 188:4
  do not answer letters, 765:2
  do not give all men gifts, 53:14
  dwells with g. above, 200:21
  even if g. should be looking, 53:16
  execute judgment against g. of
    Egypt, 8:38
  fashioned by men, 588:16
  fight against necessity, 55:12
  glorious gifts of the g., 51:11
  go in various disguises, 54:6
  good g. how he will talk, 285:6
  grant me this, 91:15
  graven images of her g., 26:19
  hail to you g., 4:5
  happy who knows rural g., 93:1
  have neither age nor death, 67:7
  have their own rules, 101:26
  help them that help themselves,
    59:15
  immortal g. I crave no pelf, 211:26
  in lap of the g., 52:*n*5
  in likeness of men, 41:11
  kings it makes g., 166:11
  knees of the g., 52:30
  laughter among the g., 51:4
  leave all else to the g., 95:23
  Little Tin G. on Wheels, 590:18
  live with the g., 111:16
  love rules the g., 67:1
  make G. to whom to impute ills,
    497:23
  makes g. by the dozen, 146:7
  may g. grant you all things, 53:10
  men determine g. dispose, 235:*n*1
  men that strove with g., 455:5
  might of g. slow but sure, 69:2
  minds of g. not changed, 53:4
  mortals are blaming the g., 52:29
  most beautiful among the immortal
    g., 54:17
  mother of g. and men, 5:1

Gods (*continued*)
  nearest to g., 70:19
  no other g. before me, 9:9
  not fit that men be compared with
    g., 91:10
  not know much about g., 671:12
  not similar are immortal g. and
    men, 51:20
  now g. stand up for bastards, 209:1
  O nights and feasts of g., 95:11
  of the Congo, 637:10
  Olympus abode of the g., 53:9
  opinion that there are no g., 76:17
  pay for what g. given, 614:11
  right idea of the g., 76:16
  search out purposes of g., 64:11
  sent not corn for rich men only,
    218:23
  so many g. so many creeds, 562:16
  spun the thread for mortals, 52:26
  take hold ye g. and goddesses,
    51:28
  temples of his g., 425:14
  that wanton in the air, 267:16
  themselves throw incense, 211:14
  thought otherwise, 93:35
  two g. Persuasion and Compulsion,
    62:28
  victor had g. the vanquished had
    Cato, 105:19
  visit sins of fathers upon children,
    69:17
  voice of g. makes heaven drowsy,
    169:3
  what ailed us O g., 533:16
  what men or g. are these, 416:1
  whatever g. may be, 534:15, 557:9
  when favor of g. was equal, 69:19
  whoever obeys the g., 50:29
  whom the g. love, 81:5
  whom the G. would destroy,
    69:*n*11
  woman a dish for g., 218:14
  would draw g. like horses, 60:5
  would g. made thee poetical, 191:21
  ye shall be as g., 6:20
Gods' custom to bring low greatness,
    70:6
Godunov, Maria G. and son poisoned,
    424:2
Goes down with great shout, 563:10
  from great deep he g., 459:28
  in and out with me, 561:10
  much against my stomach, 191:7
  naked to naked g., 599:2
  no one g. and comes back, 3:2
  nobody g. there anymore, 693:3
  one but g. abreast, 201:1
  one never g. so far, 350:2
  Rainbow comes and g., 375:4
  see how world g., 211:3
  so it g., 751:12
  the further one g. the less one
    knows, 57:15
  where tooth point g., 590:19
Goest, whither g. thou, 40:33
  whither thou g. I will go, 11:23
  with thee whithersoever thou g.,
    10:31
Goeth forth and weepeth, 19:28

Goeth (*continued*)
  he g. after her straightway, 20:32
  light from wisdom never g. out,
    30:30
  man g. forth unto his work, 19:6
  on to meet the armed men, 15:16
  pride g. before a fall, 65:*n*11
  whither it g., 39:44
Goethe has done pilgrimage, 497:16
  in Weimar sleeps, 497:15
  open thy G., 412:8
Gogol's Overcoat, 495:18
Going a journey, 390:12
  a-milking sir, 790:6
  down the wind, 279:2
  endure their g. hence, 211:12
  from g. to and fro, 13:29
  from rising of the sun unto g.
    down, 19:15
  his g. forth is from end of the
    heaven, 16:10
  if don't know where g., 747:6
  I'm g. all along, 512:5
  I'm g. to get what's mine, 774:10
  know world without g. outdoors,
    57:15
  learn by g., 725:6
  long and loath at g., 674:10
  none understands what's g. on,
    774:3
  order of your g., 215:9
  out to clean spring, 622:19
  out with tide, 470:36
  preserve thy g. out and coming in,
    19:25
  sage knows without g. about, 57:15
  speed the g. guest, 302:22
  sun knoweth his g. down, 19:6
  the way of all the earth, 10:39
  to St. Ives, 788:14
  to the fair, 789:5
  true order of g., 74:12
  way of all flesh, 237:12
  we're g. to our Father's land,
    773:17
  what's it g. to be then eh, 740:14
  year is g. let him go, 457:29
Gold, accurst craving for g., 93:37
  age of g., 96:28
  Age of G., 250:22
  all g. goose could give, 59:13
  all that glisters not g., 122:*n*6
  all that glitters not g., 122:*n*6
  almighty g., 232:14
  and frankincense, 32:24
  and love affairs difficult to hide,
    794:7
  and silver ivory and apes, 12:27
  and silver light, 595:8
  and the lust, 693:6
  apples of g. in pictures of silver,
    22:25
  as good as American g., 559:7
  bar of Heaven, 509:19
  barbaric pearl and g., 256:23
  be it gash or g., 740:6
  beauty provoketh sooner than g.,
    190:4
  becomes her object, 184:10
  blazing in G., 511:19

Gone (*continued*)

they've g. about as fur as c'n go, 692:10
thou art g. and forever, 378:22
Thursday come and week g., 244:32
to her death, 423:9
under earth's lid, 659:10
where have you g. Joe DiMaggio, 772:9
wind passeth over it and it is g., 19:2
with the wind, 602:8
yes thou art g., 499:18
Gonfalon bubble, 644:5
Gong, after great cathedral g., 598:11
Gongs, strong g. groaning, 619:2
Gong-tormented sea, 598:14
Good, a little fun and g. morrow, 522:10
a little work and g. day, 522:10
a thing moderately g., 341:8
abroad for g. of country, 295:14
all g. men, 781:7
all g. to me is lost, 258:6
Americans die go to Paris, 566:26
amiable or sweet, 260:10
and bad angel, 234:14
and bad of every land, 476:9
and faithful servant, 36:14
any g. thing I can do, 780:5
any g. thing out of Nazareth, 39:36
apothecary, 211:2
apprehension of the g., 171:3
arrived in a g. harbor, 240:8
art for sake of g., 437:2
as all no better than any, 717:20
as gold, 470:9
as g. almost kill man as g. book, 254:23
as g. be out of world, 291:18
as g. in the dark, 241:7
as g. luck would have it, 183:3
as I can be, 559:23
as seems beforehand, 483:23
ask not g. fortune, 490:3
atom's weight of g., 117:25
bad book as much labor as g., 689:17
bad indifferent, 278:9, 320:21
bad worst best, 451:14
be g. and be lonesome, 527:21
be g. and happy today, 380:23
be g. sweet maid, 484:13
be of g. cheer, 35:19, 40:35
because it's awful, 765:15
becomes indistinguishable from evil, 676:1
befriend themselves, 67:6
best is enemy of g., 306:19
best is g. enough, 349:18
better made by ill, 159:*n*4
bid me G. morning, 342:21
book best of friends, 462:5
book lifeblood of spirit, 254:24
bringer of g. tidings, 116:6
bringeth thee into a g. land, 10:15
but not religious-good, 539:9
by evil and g. report, 44:5
by quiet natures understood, 597:5
call this Friday g., 671:8

Good (*continued*)

cannot come to g., 193:12
can't say anything g., 654:10
captive g. attending captain ill, 221:6
catches mice g. cat, 712:17
character remembered, 3:16
charm to make bad g., 204:23
cheer is best physician, 64:6
chief g. and market, 198:12
cigar is a smoke, 590:20
circumstance makes action g. or bad, 74:4
club assembly of g. fellows, 314:1
comes out of evil, 532:11
commodity of g. names, 176:31
company good discourse, 245:20
constituted for practice of g., 79:26
corn wood boards to sell, 430:22
counselors lack no clients, 203:23
crown g. with brotherhood, 576:19
day's work, 311:5
deed in naughty world, 182:11
deed to say well, 225:12
demean themselves as g. citizens, 337:2
deny us for our g., 217:11
depart from evil and do g., 16:31
desires be for what is g., 61:18
devil have all g. tunes, 347:12
die early bad late, 286:2
die first, 376:20
digestion wait on appetite, 215:3
dinner and feasting, 279:12
do all the g. I can, 530:17
do all the g. you can, 309:2
do g. purify mind, 64:20
do g. the right way, 537:6
do g. to them that hate you, 33:8
doing g. one of professions full, 478:11
enough for me, 780:3
enough to shed blood, 576:2
Epicurus set forth highest g., 90:12
evening Mr. Mrs. America, 698:2
every creature of God is g., 45:15
every evil hath g., 431:30
every g. gift, 46:6
everything in world g. for something, 274:22
evil be thou my g., 258:6
evil reward punishment, 277:11
fair and learned and g. as she, 240:14
fair is by nature g., 154:15
faith toward nations, 337:6
familiar creature, 206:24
fell into g. ground, 35:7
fellows get together, 589:3
fences make good neighbors, 622:21
fight of faith, 45:23
five-cent cigar, 565:4
follow g. side to fire, 146:15
for a man that he bear the yoke, 29:4
for country good for General Motors, 680:15
for sore eyes, 290:1
fortune is god among men, 63:20
Fortune may be short-lived, 240:5

Good (*continued*)

fought a g. fight, 45:29
free press g. or bad, 733:2
friend for Jesus' sake, 226:11
general g. is plea of scoundrel, 359:23
gentle beast of a g. conscience, 174:6
glad of other men's g., 191:9
go gentle into that g. night, 737:20
go with me like g. angels, 225:6
God saw that it was g., 6:6
gods do not give all men g. looks, 53:14
gods how he will talk, 285:6
great poet so g. friend, 276:17
greed is g. greed is right, 774:4
half so g. a grace, 204:1
hand that made you g., 204:16
hanging too g. for him, 272:21
happiness the only g., 520:16
hard beginning g. ending, 141:4
have no need of advocate, 77:1
hay sweet hay, 173:22
he our g. will sever, 232:4
he who would do g., 359:23
hearkeners seldom hear g., 286:16
hell full of g. intentions, 121:10
hell full of g. meanings, 244:15
hell paved with g. intentions, 121:*n*7, 244:*n*3
highest g., 88:1, 90:*n*8
him that bringeth g. tidings, 27:33
hold fast that which is g., 45:9
hold thou the g., 457:16
honest painful sermon, 279:4
how few know own g., 276:4
how g. and how pleasant, 20:5
how g. man's life, 466:17
I am the g. shepherd, 40:17
I have g. eye uncle, 186:19
I will be g., 488:3
if all g. people clever, 541:9
if g. why do I yield, 212:23
if he had not been born, 36:27
ill wind bloweth no man g., 142:27
in congruity of thing, 383:22
in everything, 190:7
in which mind at rest, 126:16
is it g. friend, 611:7
jest forever, 177:14
joke cannot be criticized, 619:1
judge men by g. fortune, 265:23
keep g. tongue in head, 224:15
King Arthur, 792:16
King Wenceslas, 482:8
kissing carrion, 195:*n*1
know g. as g., 56:13
know what were g. to do, 179:27
knowing g. and evil, 6:20
lad of mettle a g. boy, 177:19
lady be g. to me, 695:2
largest universe of g., 546:11
law is g., 45:10
law is good order, 78:28
laws lead to better, 319:10
laws where state armed, 136:11
leave while looking, 686:9
leaves aside g. and bad, 333:10
left country for country's g., 295:*n*2

Good (*continued*)

lie and humbug for general G., 601:7
life of battle g., 586:12
life or good place, 721:9
Life waiting for us, 715:9
like a g. thing die, 564:13
live in world g. or bad, 477:11
Lord deliver us, 49:8, 779:15
Lord is g., 18:22
lose g. we oft might win, 203:27
loser, 674:15
love as much as g. fight, 648:13
love g. pursue the worst, 101:*n*18
love sought is g., 202:26
loves what he is g. at, 282:10
luck in odd numbers, 183:7
luxury was doing g., 286:7
maintain g. government, 355:1
make g. thing too common, 183:22
maketh sun rise on evil and g., 33:9
man and a just, 39:24
man does not argue, 58:7
man's fortune, 209:15
man's g. knowing he is bad, 467:25
man's love, 191:23
man's sin, 320:*n*5
man's treasure, 57:19
many g. men are poor, 55:15
marriage, 630:10
Master of All G. Workmen, 591:13
meaning g. or bad, 274:17
men and true, 186:35
men desire the g., 78:18
men eat that they may live, 70:23
men of g. will, 38:*n*2, 48:8
men of ill judgment ignore g., 65:14
men to do nothing, 332:30
mingled yarn g. and ill, 203:15
moral what you feel g. after, 701:19
Morning Midnight coming Home, 512:10
morning sadness, 691:10
morrow to our waking souls, 228:3
mothers and fathers, 711:22
mouth-filling oath, 178:10
music g. to melancholy, 278:9
must associate, 330:23
my g. vain hope of gain, 156:22
my religion is to do g., 341:7
name better than precious ointment, 24:6
name in man and woman, 206:30
name is rather to be chosen, 22:8
name like precious ointment, 159:13
nature in conversation, 293:2
neighbor is great blessing, 54:25
neighbor policy, 648:19
neighbors, 655:23
neither honesty nor g. fellowship, 176:35
never bad man g. service, 332:4
never g. to bring bad news, 217:19
never g. war or bad peace, 310:23
news baits, 261:23
news worthy of acceptation, 286:22
no evil can happen to g. man, 74:17
no physician considers own g., 75:5
noble be man helpful and g., 349:5
noble to be g., 454:3

Good (*continued*)

noble type of g., 442:7
not enough to do g., 537:6
not enough to have g. mind, 246:14
not g. for swarm not g. for bee, 111:18
not g. that man should be alone, 6:15
not three g. men unhanged, 177:22
not to make g. place to live, 477:11
not too g. to be true, 286:22
nothing either g. or bad, 195:25
nothing g. alone, 429:7
nothing g. makes complete sense, 684:18
obstinacy in bad cause constancy in g., 248:8
of moral evil and of g., 372:21
of subjects end of kings, 285:19
oft interred with bones, 188:28
old age, 7:29
old Boston, 582:1
old paths where is the g. way, 28:18
old times are gone, 404:2
old times when unhappy, 786:17
one g. custom corrupt, 459:26
one g. knowledge, 70:20
one g. turn deserves another, 105:3
only what is g. in man, 567:22
or evil side, 485:1
orator a g. man skilled in speaking, 85:8
out of g. find evil, 256:3
overcome evil with g., 42:19
panics produce as much g., 340:23
Parent of g., 259:7
partial evil universal g., 301:12
people all with one accord, 328:2
people really g. at heart, 760:13
people's g. the highest law, 88:5
perseverance in g. cause, 320:12
philosophy a g. horse, 329:1
phrase g. and bad at same time, 688:1
play audience pleased, 618:12
pleasure ease content, 301:16
poet's made as well as born, 232:24
political g. carried to extreme, 366:2
portion of g. man's life, 373:1
poverty parts g. company, 379:21
prospect of distant g., 275:21
provoke to harm, 204:23
public g., 119:24
public g. and private rights, 352:1
pun may be admitted, 342:1
put on g. behavior, 403:6
quiet wise and g., 409:17
really a very g. man, 568:11
recognize g. but be barred, 64:4
relinquish life for g. of country, 370:14
reputation valuable, 99:2
return g. for evil, 288:8
rewarded evil for g., 8:10
rewardeth evil for g., 21:35
rich in g. works, 45:24
right reader of g. poem, 625:7
ripe and g. scholar, 226:6
sat at g. man's feast, 190:29

Good (*continued*)

sat too long for any g., 247:2
Scots lords, 784:34
second class of intellect g., 136:17
see your g. works, 33:3
seize g. fortune, 350:29
sense equally distributed, 246:13
sense in country, 345:14
seven g. kine, 8:7
seven hundred pounds g. gifts, 182:18
shall not see when g. cometh, 28:29
share the g. man's smile, 329:16
shepherd, 40:17
smell of old clothes, 663:2
smiled and said G. Night, 609:8
so absolutely g. is truth, 468:8
Soldier finest French novel, 617:8
some g. some so-so, 106:9
some said It might do g., 272:9
so so is g., 192:8
soul remembering my g. friends, 171:14
speech more hidden than malachite, 3:4
speed to your youthful valor, 94:24
spinning fates g. or evil, 545:14
strong and of g. courage, 10:31
strong thick stupefying, 465:7
substantial world pure and g., 376:14
sum of g. government, 344:8
sustain g. fortune, 265:1
taste and see that the Lord is g., 16:30
tendency to g. like water, 79:25
the g. I do not, 41:46
the G. lies so near, 350:29
them that call evil g., 25:41
thing when an't woman's, 468:24
things fruits of originality, 439:18
things not had singly, 388:13
things strive to dwell, 224:2
things which belong to prosperity, 159:6
third glass for g. humor, 293:3
this time like all times g., 431:11
this world's g., 46:35
thought to aim at some g., 77:25
time coming, 379:12, 474:7
to be born on, 486:1
to be merry and wise, 140:16, 364:4, 779:20
to do g. and to communicate, 46:3
to gain day good to fall, 489:4
to love the unknown, 387:31
today better tomorrow, 438:5
too g. for any but anglers, 245:29
too much of g. thing, 149:4
traced lives of g. men, 377:8
tree of knowledge of g. and evil, 6:14
trust that somehow g., 457:17
two nations g. bad, 268:20
unconscious source of highest g., 628:15
undefined g. thirsted for, 393:1
universal license to be g., 419:3
value it next to g. conscience, 245:30

Gothic (*continued*)
　more than G. ignorance, 311:26
Gottbetrunkener, ein G. Mensch,
　277:*n*8
Göttingen, University of G., 371:22
Gouged, by enemy's beak g., 765:17
Gourd, sugar in the g., 780:1
Gourds, painted g. on a shelf, 756:14
Gout kills more rich than poor,
　271:17
Govern, angels to g., 344:7
　another without consent, 448:4
　dead g. living, 421:10
　easy to g. not to enslave, 390:4
　every cook learn to g., 610:2
　how can tyrants safely g., 164:23
　legitimate right to g., 385:12
　most make least noise, 239:7
　no man g. another, 448:4
　others first master himself, 238:6
　people difficult to g., 57:21
　reflect how you are to g., 331:3
　reigns but does not g., 148:1
　Right of Kings to g. wrong, 303:31
　stars g. our conditions, 210:25
　syllables g. the world, 239:8
　those that think must g., 328:15
　tongues with difficulty, 277:22
Governed, consent of g., 338:1
　consent of the g., 343:2, 491:25
　governments result of nature of g.,
　　290:32
　grant of power from g., 385:12
　with how little wisdom world g.,
　　239:*n*1
Governing governor, 395:23
Government, all persons share in g.,
　78:21
　at Washington lives, 516:2
　attachment to g., 331:23
　balance of natural elements, 564:15
　basis of g. opinion, 343:12
　behave toward g. today, 477:9
　behind g. and people, 501:17
　best g. make people happy, 424:9
　British g. best model, 354:18
　by crony, 626:2
　by means of his virtue, 60:21
　charming form of g., 75:24
　complain of injustice of g., 369:11
　consists in taking money, 306:17
　contrivance of wisdom, 332:11
　cooperation with G., 661:10
　excel the bees for g., 148:3
　excess a reproach to g., 282:20
　exigencies of g., 474:21
　first duty of g., 487:30
　first office of g. splendid misery,
　　344:2
　for common benefit, 327:2
　form of g. never take root, 370:8
　forming a republican g., 355:2
　founded on compromise, 331:20
　free to people, 282:18
　gives bigotry no sanction, 337:2
　good g. obtains, 61:19
　great writer second g., 746:1
　happiness end of g., 338:6
　happiness sole object of g., 340:2
　in carrying on your g., 61:18

Government (*continued*)
　in flag g. and truths, 473:1
　in g. deliberative forces prevail,
　　568:14
　includes all the people, 437:19
　increase of his g., 26:8
　influenced by shopkeepers, 326:7
　institute new g., 343:2
　is a trust, 389:13
　it deserves, 353:12
　kept sheep rather than undertaken
　　g., 247:4
　lawful foundations of g., 368:15
　legitimate object of g., 344:11
　like big baby, 730:14
　looked to G. for bread, 332:29
　luxury of liberal g., 474:12
　made for people, 394:14
　maintain good g., 355:1
　maintain in emergencies, 450:7
　make alter constitutions of g., 337:4
　make it an article of faith, 343:6
　make life livable, 543:7
　monarchy an intelligible g., 506:6
　necessary evil, 340:18
　newspapers without g., 343:12
　no administration injure g., 449:6
　no g. by divine right, 385:12
　no g. provides for termination,
　　449:2
　no necessary evils in g., 369:12
　not at war with rights, 343:16
　not endure half slave, 448:7
　not too strong for liberties, 450:7
　object of British g., 354:18
　of by and for people, 450:2, 461:18
　of cities failure of United States,
　　536:7
　of eternal justice, 461:18
　of laws not men, 337:18
　of nations, 569:17
　of others, 344:7
　of people, 410:4
　of statesmen or clerks, 434:24
　of the sage, 56:14
　old forms of g. oppressive, 493:5
　only maxim of free g., 337:16
　organize civil g. of community,
　　369:3
　petition g. for redress, 346:11
　petticoat g., 395:23
　play ignoble part, 543:9
　political freedom business of G.,
　　649:2
　political understanding to run g.,
　　655:15
　poverty a reproach to g., 282:20
　power in g. sovereign, 355:6
　power of making laws, 355:4
　relaxing pressure, 438:13
　Republican highest g., 493:10
　republican model of g., 337:1
　resting on property, 75:23
　result of shared experiences, 370:8
　secrecy and free g., 655:22
　shake off existing g., 448:3
　shall be upon his shoulder, 26:8
　sharp attacks on g., 719:4
　sovereign control over g., 649:11
　Soviet g. plus electrification, 610:6

Government (*continued*)
　spirit and form of popular g., 352:1
　strong enough to protect, 649:11
　sum of good g., 344:8
　the less g. the better, 432:18
　this g. best hope, 344:6
　to first class share in g., 355:1
　trip on G. ship, 793:20
　virtue of paper g., 331:5
　watch and control g., 439:25
　weary of existing g., 449:4
　which imprisons unjustly, 477:13
　which kept us free, 344:6
　whose object is to elevate, 449:8
　why g. at all, 355:5
　will ever maintain good g., 355:1
　wise and frugal g., 344:8
　wise g. enforce conciliate, 318:22
　without newspapers, 343:12
　women without share in g., 365:33
　workings of g. that led to Vietnam
　　War, 661:9
Governmental, right to be free from g.
　intrusion, 719:5
Governments, climates councils g.,
　455:1
　confiscate wealth, 652:11
　instituted among men, 343:2
　liberty is in moderate g., 355:2
　never learned from history, 372:6
　old tyrannical g. of Europe, 379:28
　pro-labor policies of g., 645:10
　result of nature of governed, 290:32
　whose independence acknowledged,
　　360:12
Governor, contempt for g. who is
　afraid, 66:5
　governing g., 395:23
　of New York not an acrobat, 618:7
　of South Carolina said, 562:4
Governors, consent of g. and gov-
　erned, 338:1
　supreme g. the mob, 323:20
Governs, foolery g. whole world,
　239:6
　law which g. all law, 332:8
　like a king, 319:27
　opinion g. world, 572:3
Gowd, man's g. for a' that, 363:21
Gower, O moral G., 129:3
Gown, chose wife as she wedding g.,
　328:18
　my g. of glory, 152:16
　on g. appeared letter A, 435:25
　plucked his g., 329:16
　smell fire whose g. burns, 244:10
　unclose damask g. to sun, 144:4
Gowns, furred g. hide all, 211:4
　some in velvet g., 792:14
Goya of the bare field, 765:17
　perhaps God resembles etchings of
　　G., 735:10
Goyim annoy 'im, 656:*n*3
Grace a summer queen, 379:4
　abound, 41:42
　amazing g. how sweet the sound,
　　327:4
　an air and peculiar g., 294:21
　and music of her face, 267:13
　and strength to forbear, 562:9

Grace *(continued)*
   as smart ship grew in stature g., 540:18
   awful g. of God, 63:11
   beauty without g., 433:1
   but for g. of God, 143:9
   comely g., 777:5
   courage to live by g., 588:19
   does it with better g., 202:3
   fallen from g., 44:17
   full of g. and truth, 39:33
   get wealth with g., 303:4
   given of God, 482:21
   God in mercy lend g., 454:17
   God shed g. on thee, 576:19
   gods do not give all men gifts of g., 53:14
   great g. with little gift, 82:17
   half so good a g., 204:1
   heart that lives in g., 126:7
   heaven such g. did lend her, 168:7
   her strong toil of g., 218:22
   ideal G., 438:23
   inward and spiritual g., 49:22
   little g. my cause, 205:22
   love brings bewitching g., 68:17
   makes simplicity a g., 232:6
   me no grace, 171:16
   ministers of g. defend us, 194:9
   moments of glad g., 595:2
   more of his g. than gifts, 227:7
   never mind did mind his g., 163:4
   no spring beauty hath such g., 230:7
   not an Attic g., 659:6
   of day that is dead, 456:8
   of God in courtesy, 608:21
   of Lord Jesus Christ, 44:13
   renown and g. is dead, 214:15
   seated on this brow, 197:30
   silence gives proper g. to women, 65:8
   speech be alway with g., 45:1
   strikes when in pain, 662:10
   sways in wicked g., 740:11
   sweet attractive g., 163:3, 258:12
   sweet cowslip's g., 348:12
   tender g. of day dead, 456:8
   thanks for means of g., 49:5
   unbought g. of life, 332:13
   under pressure, 701:18
   unshy beautiful full of g., 731:4
   will to g. as horse to rider, 114:18
   yield with g. to reason, 622:18
Graced, proud to have memory g., 675:10
Graces, beauty or g., 305:7
   lead these g. to grave, 201:26
   mourn ye G. and Loves, 90:16
   speech lacking in artificial g., 87:18
Gracing, either other sweetly g., 226:15
Gracious, a God g. and merciful, 13:23
   and be g. unto thee, 9:28
   and courteous to strangers, 159:15
   evening star, 473:5
   God save our g. king, 298:3
   good g. loser, 674:15
   happy g. flexibility, 500:25

Gracious *(continued)*
   heaven's all-g. King, 462:2
   keeping, 506:15
   Lord bomb Germans, 718:23
   my g. silence hail, 219:2
   remembers me his g. parts, 170:4
   seasoned with g. voice, 181:4
   so hallowed and so g., 192:29
   swear by thy g. self, 175:8
   this is our g. will, 137:5
Gradual and silent encroachments, 352:2
   degradation of idea of liberty, 733:1
   road to Hell g., 700:1
Gradually extricate babe from fire, 437:14
   let go earth, 697:14
Gradualness, inevitability of g., 581:15
Grain, amber waves of g., 576:19
   cheeks of sorry g., 253:10
   clearest g. of violin, 753:3
   Demeter gave nourishment of g., 68:26
   of manhood, 261:13
   of mustard seed, 35:9
   of poetry season a century, 564:8
   say which g. will grow, 212:17
   see world in g. of sand, 359:5
   send g. into wilderness, 277:3
   spirits of land and g., 80:6
   with a g. of salt, 104:13
Grains, little g. of sand, 502:8
   two g. of wheat in chaff, 179:23
Grainy wood, 663:2
Grammar control even kings, 269:29
   corrupted youth in erecting g.-school, 164:11
   I am above g., 269:*n*9
   lesson on g. impertinence, 502:10
   nonsense and learning, 330:1
   prefer geniality to g., 574:15
Grammarian rhetorician geometrician, 108:21
Grammaticam, rex et supra g., 269:*n*9
Grammatici certant sub iudice lis est, 98:*n*2
Gramophone, puts record on g., 669:2
Grampa, one day bachelor next g., 709:17
Grampian, on the G. hills, 325:8
Granary, sitting on g. floor, 416:14
Grand, dumb inscrutable g., 500:4
   hooded phantom, 486:18
   Meaulnes the wanderer, 661:13
   O Ireland g. you look, 555:16
   Panjandrum, 324:7
   seek a g. perhaps, 140:11
   statues and pictures g., 523:14
   style, 499:1
   sweet song, 484:13
   they said it would be g., 518:24
   this g. book the universe, 161:15
   'tis g. 'tis solemn, 405:1
Grand Army, between G. and dominion, 541:3
Grandam, soul of g. inhabit a bird, 181:*n*3
   to cub, 757:8
Grandchild heir of the first, 233:6

Grandchildren come into world with thick skin, 420:10
Grande Ourse, mon auberge à la G., 565:*n*4
Grandest lesson On sail on, 543:18
   of all sepulchers, 72:7
Grandeur, feel every kind of g., 422:1
   hear with disdainful smile, 322:7
   in this view of life, 444:10
   indivisible, 678:8
   of God, 550:18
   of the dooms, 414:10
   remains without intensity, 106:6
   Scotia's g. springs, 361:10
   size is not g., 505:15
   so nigh g. to dust, 430:4
   that was Rome, 451:12
Grandfather, ape for his g., 505:20
Grandfather's house, 427:7
   rule was safer, 485:17
Grandmother, ape as his g., 505:*n*1
   child of our g. Eve, 168:19
   sings to stove, 729:8
Grandsire cut in alabaster, 179:18
   proverbed with g. phrase, 174:18
Grandsires', sires' age worse than g., 96:17
Grange, moated g., 204:18, 453:16
Granite into which it reaches, 671:13
   one block of hard g., 4:10
   tenoned and mortised in g., 489:6
Grant, everybody wants to be Cary G., 713:2
   Evolution from Washington to G., 535:25
   half g. what I wish, 623:8
   I may never prove so fond, 211:26
   may gods g. you all things, 53:10
   me old man's frenzy, 599:11
   me this last labor, 92:18
   O gods g. me this, 91:15
   of power from governed, 385:12
   old Cary G. fine, 713:3
   that twice two not four, 482:19
   us safe lodging, 426:22
   youth's heritage, 467:10
Granted, and God g. it, 306:22
   to behold you again, 562:1
Gran'ther's rule safer, 485:17
Granting our wish one of Fate's jokes, 59:*n*6
Grants, each day that Fortune g., 95:24
Grape, a little more g., 397:11
   burst Joy's g., 416:18
   eaten a sour g., 28:35
   first from out the purple g., 252:16
   for one g. the vine destroy, 166:38
   peel me a g., 685:7
   rich g. juice of good sense, 114:11
   shalt not gather every g., 9:24
Grapes are sour, 58:17
   gleaning of the g. of Ephraim, 11:9
   of thorns, 34:11
   our vines have tender g., 25:7
   where g. of wrath stored, 484:6
Grapeshot, whiff of g., 412:15
Grapple, let her and Falsehood g., 255:4
   them to thy soul, 193:29

Graven image, 9:9
  images of her gods, 26:19
Grave's a fine and private place,
  268:16
Graves, beautiful uncut hair of g.,
  488:20
  climbs into g. married, 697:13
  dishonorable g., 187:22
  follow disquietly to g., 209:2
  from g. of our slain, 421:18
  let's talk of g., 171:24
  sacred g. plowed for corn, 502:5
  stood tenantless, 192:25
  under fountains and g., 777:11
  untimely g., 335:6
  watch from their g., 464:24
Graveyard, Europe a precious g.,
  495:6
  friends have no place in g., 477:18
Graveyards, no white or colored signs
  on g., 742:3
Gravitation, Newtonian principle of
  g., 343:6
Gravity, body subject to forces of g.,
  738:9
  breaks law of g., 670:19
  out of his bed, 177:27
  settled g., 220:24
  sometimes man of g., 138:1
  to practice g., 62:2
Gravy, no g. no grub, 674:13
  person who disliked g., 269:*n*7
Gray, all cats g. when candles out,
  107:*n*8
  all theory is g., 350:15
  amice g., 261:5
  beginning of years, 534:21
  behind lay g. Azores, 543:17
  bring down my g. hairs, 8:8
  changing from brown suit to g.,
  658:5
  cheerless over hills of g., 443:13
  cold g. stones O Sea, 456:7
  comb g. hair, 596:8
  dawn breaking, 424:7, 633:14
  dawn of morning after, 600:13
  death's g. land, 662:4
  dogs shame the g. head, 52:20
  flannel suit, 748:14
  friar of orders g., 776:14
  glory from g. hairs gone, 443:3
  great g. drayhorse, 551:4
  handful of g. ashes at rest, 502:9
  head grown g. in vain, 409:4
  iniquity, 177:30
  little g. cells, 677:14
  locks left are g., 386:8
  long g. beard, 380:26
  mist on sea's face, 633:14
  name was Dapple G., 792:9
  night is growing g., 540:20
  old and g. full of sleep, 595:1
  pilgrim g., 324:11
  red spirits and g., 237:9
  sad last g. hairs, 415:12
  set g. life, 454:21
  spires of Oxford, 648:3
  spirit yearning, 455:3
  still evening and twilight g., 258:18
  Truth her painted toy, 594:16

Gray (*continued*)
  where thy g. eye glances, 452:3
  wing upon every tide, 596:1
  withered cheek tresses g., 377:19
  world g. from thy breath, 534:4
Gray-eyed Athena, 53:1
Gray-fly winds her sultry horn, 253:17
Gray-green greasy Limpopo, 593:9
Gray-haired Saturn, 416:19
Gray-headed, old and g. error, 248:24
Grayness silvers everything, 466:1
Graze, as long as stars g., 93:24
  neither g. nor pierce, 207:23
  on my lips, 165:10
Grazes, work way cow g., 604:1
Grazing, men like satyrs g., 162:10
  tilling and g. feed France, 157:16
Grease, frye in owene g., 131:3
  lust melted him in own g., 131:*n*1
  servility slides by on g., 743:13
  wheel that squeaks gets g., 479:26
Greased worm, 742:11
Greasy, fat and g. citizens, 190:9
  gray-green g. Limpopo, 593:9
  Joan doth keel pot, 169:13
  top of g. pole, 435:6
Great age begins anew, 408:10
  Amen, 506:1
  and mighty resolutions, 263:12
  and original writer, 376:18
  and wide sea, 19:6
  apostle of Philistines, 499:14
  Architect of Universe mathematician, 632:3
  army of pointed firs, 557:15
  artificer made my mate, 561:25
  Babel, 335:4
  ball of fire, 673:6
  be g. be misunderstood, 431:24
  Beginning produced emptiness,
  86:15
  Birnam wood, 215:21
  blew g. guns, 470:44
  Britain going to war, 568:13
  build a G. Society, 723:18
  burden upon his back, 272:11
  Caesar fell, 189:7
  ceremony that to g. ones 'longs,
  204:1
  compare g. things with small, 92:3,
  257:20
  creatures g. and small, 479:17
  death, 611:5
  deeds wrought at great risks, 70:10
  deep to great deep, 459:28
  desire to bottle of hay, 173:22
  dissolved into something g., 616:9
  do business in g. waters, 19:9
  do g. right do little wrong, 181:20
  duration of g. sentiments makes g.
  men, 552:14
  Elizabeth, 454:12
  empire and little minds, 331:24
  Father building forts among us,
  502:5
  feast of languages, 169:6
  fell g. oaks, 310:4
  finds pang as g., 204:11
  First Cause, 335:24
  fortune great slavery, 103:8

Great (*continued*)
  Gaels of Ireland, 618:17
  globe itself, 224:21
  God our King, 444:4
  god Pan, 107:16, 439:8
  gray-green greasy Limpopo, 593:9
  Gromboolian plain, 472:12
  gulf fixed, 39:3
  have seen the wicked in g. power,
  17:2
  he is a g. observer, 187:25
  hedgehog knows one g. thing, 55:5
  heir of fame, 251:2
  here thou g. Anna, 299:13
  horse of gold, 688:6
  how g. that darkness, 33:16
  ice also g. would suffice, 623:14
  ill can he rule the g., 153:21
  illusion, 614:4
  impotently g., 299:20
  in admiration as herself, 226:8
  indispensable unique g., 587:7
  interests at stake, 78:25
  is Diana, 41:22
  is glory of the woman, 72:8
  is truth, 30:13
  is truth and shall prevail, 30:*n*3
  know well I am not g., 459:14
  leap in the dark, 239:26
  let us mock at g., 597:16
  live at level of g. men, 565:3
  lives of g. men remind us, 440:17
  making city glorious and g., 62:23
  malefactors of g. wealth, 576:5
  man does not lose child's-heart,
  79:23
  man does not think beforehand,
  79:22
  man's memory, 197:8
  many talks from g. father, 333:7
  manye smale maken a g., 132:8
  mast of some g. ammiral, 256:7
  matter or small, 31:13
  meals of beef iron steel, 185:13
  men are not always wise, 14:47
  men can't be ruled, 717:10
  men contending with adversity,
  235:2
  men great nations not boasters,
  432:30
  men not scholars, 447:15
  men texts of Revelation, 412:5
  mother of big apples, 730:10
  names as these, 778:18
  nature's second course, 214:6
  Neptune's ocean wash, 214:9
  nice customs curtsy to g. kings,
  186:5
  none unhappy but g., 294:2
  nose great man, 605:24
  not g. pleasure to bring death,
  66:10
  nothing g. accomplished without
  passion, 372:10
  nothing g. created suddenly, 108:2
  O God thy sea is so g., 779:16
  O that I were as g., 172:3
  office not filled by great men, 536:6
  ones eat up little ones, 219:21
  only g. man write history, 567:14

Greeks, fear G. even when they bring gifts, 93:27
first westerners, 603:25
had modesty we have cant, 397:22
had word for it, 660:22
have dreamt dream of life best, 351:11
known what G. did not uncertainty, 700:13
led us to where they worship, 121:2
seeking land of G., 349:13
were right, 567:12
when G. joined G., 285:7
Green, all a g. willow, 140:12, 208:4
all in g. went my love, 688:6
among thy g. braes, 362:21
and dying, 737:19
and pleasant land, 359:17
and yellow melancholy, 202:14
as emerald, 381:3
babbled of g. fields, 184:30
banks of Shannon, 388:25
bay tree, 17:2
be the g. grass above me, 515:7
be turf above thee, 405:5
beechen g., 415:10
casque has outdone elegance, 660:1
colorless g. ideas sleep, 758:20
crammers of green fruits, 638:20
devouring g. azures, 565:13
do these things in g. tree, 39:17
doors of heaven both g., 652:5
drives my g. age, 737:8
dry smooth-shaven g., 252:3
Elfin from g. grass, 451:10
Flora and country g., 415:11
Gatsby believed in the g. light, 694:12
girl, 194:3
golden lamps in g. night, 268:24
good crier of g. sauce, 139:16
Greta woods are g., 379:4
groves of the blest, 94:12
grow the rashes O, 362:1
happy as grass was g., 737:14
heads g. hands blue, 472:4
heard on the g., 356:17
hill far away, 479:18
how much I want you green, 699:3
in hamlets dances on g., 377:25
in judgment, 217:10
in thy g. lap, 323:2
isle in sea, 452:2
it's not easy bein' g., 775:9
keep g. tree in heart, 118:5
keep memory g., 391:11
laid him on the g., 785:18
laurel g. for season, 534:4
lavender's g., 792:6
leaf shall be g., 28:29
learn of g. world, 660:1
legend of g. chapels, 737:13
lie down in g. pastures, 16:17
life once lived there, 728:14
little Johnny G., 789:6
little vaulter, 396:25
making the g. one red, 214:9
mansions, 543:15
mantle of standing pool, 210:8
Meander's margent g., 252:26

Green (*continued*)
memory be g., 192:31
moon made of g. cheese, 142:24
o'er g. corn-field did pass, 192:12
old age, 273:20
on ilka g. loaning, 327:11
out of hopeful g. stuff woven, 488:19
pastures, 16:17
remain g. forever, 365:12
sea's g. crying towers, 701:4
sing all a g. willow, 208:4
snow on g. grass, 674:11
soul bright invisible g., 477:16
swell in havens dumb, 550:15
text old orator too g., 165:15
the golden tree of life, 350:15
thought in a green shade, 268:18
through g. fuse drives flower, 737:8
to what g. altar, 416:5
too g. and only good for fools, 58:*n*9
tossing g. water, 654:2
U blue O, 565:17
underwood and cover, 533:9
water spurted through hull, 565:12
wearin' o' the G., 779:10, 779:11
when all trees g., 484:15
with boughs, 563:10
Greenery-yallery, 530:2
Greenest of our valleys, 452:5
Green-eyed jealousy, 181:7
monster, 206:31
Greenhouse, loves a g. too, 335:2
Greenish, eyes g. and remote, 712:8
Greenland's icy mountains, 395:18
Greenly, we have done but g., 198:21
Greenness, clothe general earth with g., 382:17
heart recovered g., 243:22
Greensleeves all my joy, 776:11
Green-walled by hills of Maryland, 443:10
Greenwood chapel, 637:*n*3
must to g. go, 776:1
under the g. tree, 190:18
Greet, in every angle g., 268:22
it gars me g., 363:3
me with that sun thine eye, 220:24
offspring from camps, 717:1
two solitudes g., 630:4
Greeting, 'change one g. and part, 494:18
Gregor Samsa awoke from uneasy dreams, 651:17
Gregory, John Synge and Augusta G., 599:15
Grenadier, British G., 778:18
she strode like g., 573:2
Grenadiers, captain of Hampshire g., 340:15
Grenville, Sir Richard G. lay, 460:6
Greta woods are green, 379:4
Greville Servant to Queen Elizabeth, 155:2
Grew, as ship g. in stature grace and hue, 540:18
autumn that g. by reaping, 218:11
lean assailed seasons, 608:3
miles around wonder g., 579:2

Grew (*continued*)
still the wonder g., 329:18
together like double cherry, 173:19
up fostered by beauty, 373:7
where one g. before, 289:11
within this learned man, 163:1
Greybeards, love which g. call divine, 165:7
Greyhound, fawning g. did proffer, 177:10
puppies, 446:22
Greyhound's gentle tautness, 743:10
Greyhounds, stand like g. in slips, 185:5
Gridley, fire when ready G., 532:13
Grief, acquainted with g., 27:35
age or g. or sickness, 242:2
aggravates loss, 776:15
at not wanting to call dead back, 629:19
beguile you from g., 450:9
but for g. as if not been, 408:20
can honor take away g., 178:33
can I see another's g., 356:18
develops mind, 613:4
divine radiance, 427:23
drug which takes away g., 53:7
each substance of a g., 171:13
everyone can master g., 186:34
fills room of absent child, 170:4
for every g. to physician, 244:20
forgotten, 533:9
glistering g., 225:8
great as my g., 172:3
hair turned quite gold from g., 567:5
hopeless g. passionless, 438:17
I am g., 765:17
in much wisdom is much g., 23:28
is proud, 169:27
itself be mortal, 408:20
journeyman to g., 170:32
make carnival of g., 605:13
makes owner stoop, 169:27
melts away, 243:21
mortals live in, 52:26
my joy my g., 249:30
past help should be past g., 222:25
pitched past pitch of g., 551:13
plague of sighing and g., 177:28
put in words g., 457:6
reason unhinged by g., 487:13
returns with revolving year, 408:18
sees into bottom of my g., 176:8
smiling at g., 202:14
sure to come to g., 624:21
teaches to waver, 66:12
that does not speak, 215:28
think you can shut g. in, 653:29
to weather as to g., 653:29
to weep make less depth of g., 164:14
unmanly g., 193:4
was ever g. like mine, 243:5
what greater g., 68:12
what restraint to g. for one so dear, 95:29
wings of Time g. flies, 268:4
with glass that ran, 533:10

Grief (*continued*)

with g. and shame bowed down,
250:7

worm canker and g., 404:7

you must first feel g., 98:8

Griefs, all my g. are gone, 160:22

beware the easy g., 740:13

drinking my g., 172:9

even his g. are a joy, 54:1

fresh tears over old g., 69:9

griping g., 776:12

he hath borne our g., 27:36

my state depose but not my g.,
172:10

patch g. with proverbs, 187:7

private g., 189:8

purify and prepare man, 564:5

some g. are med'cinable, 219:26

sufferest mortal g., 185:18

that harass distressed, 313:8

we cause ourselves, 65:19

Grievance, no g. redress by mob law,
448:2

way of establishing g. for the day,
673:10

Grievances, clod of ailments and g.,
570:22

inferior g. lose force, 345:16

redress of g., 346:11

Grieve at funeral, 527:11

his heart, 215:22

not for what past, 776:15

not g. over inevitable, 84:5

one suffer than nation g., 274:9

who g. for this woman, 675:6

woman to be over-mastered, 186:18

Grieved, by wind g. ghost, 706:18

Grieves, that which g. me more, 297:5`

Grieving, Margaret are you g., 551:5

Grievous burden was thy birth, 166:6

gossip is g. to bear, 55:2

my most g. fault, 48:6

remembrance of them is g., 49:15

roar, 385:8

Grievously, sins most g. committed,
49:15

Griffith, met by Mr. G., 293:15

Grim and ancient Raven, 452:18

brow g. mouth prim, 670:6

death, 238:9

Death my son and foe, 257:18

hushed in g. repose, 323:8

king's dog, 67:24

shape towered up, 373:9

wolf with privy paw, 254:3

Grimace, accelerated g., 659:6

Grimaces called laughter, 239:19

Grim-visaged comfortless Despair,
321:16

war smoothed his front, 165:19

Grin, all Nature wears one g., 311:9

ending with the g., 517:17

how cheerfully seems to g., 517:5

remained after rest gone, 517:17

universal g., 311:9

Grind, ax to g., 393:8

bones to make bread, 792:19

demd horrid g., 469:24

exceeding small, 247:15

faces of the poor, 25:34

Grind (*continued*)

in mill of truism, 431:15

in the prison house, 11:17

laws g. the poor, 328:16

mills of God g. slowly, 247:15

with water that's past, 244:13

Grinders cease, 24:27

Grinding, sound of the g. is low,
24:27

Grinds, God's mill g. slow, 244:38

Grindstone, hold noses to g., 141:9

tightfisted hand at g., 470:3

Grinning, mock your own g., 199:8

Griping griefs heart wound, 776:12

Grisilda, in trust to fynde G., 131:18

Grisly gang, 621:2

Gristle, a people still in the g., 331:9

Grizzled, his beard was g., 193:22

his hair just g., 273:20

Groan, condemned alike to g., 321:17

hear each other g., 415:12

of martyr's woe, 359:4

scarcely howl or g., 519:22

sinks with bubbling g., 400:31

spirit fled with g., 94:28

weep no more nor g., 236:8

Groaned, my mother g., 358:11

Groaneth, whole creation g., 42:3

Groaning, strong gongs g., 619:2

Groans, cackles g. and dies, 410:8

of love like those of dying, 727:2

shrieks and g. of wounded, 492:12

sovereign of sighs and g., 168:28

Grocery, eyeing the g. boys, 757:2

Groined aisles of Rome, 429:10

Grolle, ich g. nicht, 419:*n*6

Gromboolian, great G. plain, 472:12

Groove, freight proportioned to g.,
514:18

Grooves, ringing g. of change, 455:25

Gross and scope of my opinion,
192:22

flesh sinks downward, 172:17

gratitude not among g. people,
315:1

not g. to sink but light, 165:9

scarce so g. as beetles, 210:27

things rank and g., 193:6

two g. broken statues, 659:10

Grossest iridescence of ocean, 639:23

superstitions, 444:14

Grossly, decay doth g. close it in,
182:8

err as g. as the few, 274:14

Grossness, lost evil by losing g.,
332:15

Grosvenor Gallery young man, 530:2

Grotesque, so striking and g., 425:12

what is not g. and why, 755:16

Grotesques, all had become g., 630:20

Grotius, celebrities such as G., 521:4

Ground, accustomed to way g. opens
up, 766:6

acre of barren g., 223:19

all seated on the g., 285:1

another man's g., 182:28

as water spilt on the g., 12:13

beat the g., 252:23

between two stools sits on g.,
140:*n*16

Ground (*continued*)

betwixt stirrup and g., 151:29

bit of g. to call own, 511:3

Cain was tiller of g., 7:2

cannot dedicate this g., 450:2

cast it to g. regardlessly, 236:21

choose g. take thy rest, 404:8

colored man occupies, 480:15

crushed to g. diffuse sweets, 159:*n*4

dark and bloody g., 492:5

drops earliest to g., 181:16

exiled on g. in jeers, 494:2

fallen unto me in a fair g., 16:*n*1

Fame's camping g., 492:4

fell into good g., 35:7

four thousand miles deep, 511:3

gain little patch of g., 198:11

gazes on the g., 563:6

grow on Irish g., 779:10

hallowed g., 685:18

haunted holy g., 399:16

into the sea upon dry g., 9:1

kings sat down upon the g., 31:26

lose g. won today, 498:10

miles of fertile g., 382:19

more malign with bad seed, 126:19

my lodging is on cold g., 297:5

my tail go to the g., 140:18

not buried in consecrated g., 539:18

of all being God, 662:9

passion that left g., 467:3

place whereon thou standest is holy
g., 8:24

plat of rising g., 252:4

rope just above g., 651:21

stand your g., 333:5

stood firm on dry g., 10:32

swalloweth g. with fierceness, 15:17

till thou return unto the g., 6:26

to own a bit of g., 511:2

Tom Tiddler's g., 779:13

tract of inland g., 376:21

tread on classic g., 291:29

vantage g. of truth, 89:*n*9

vapors weep burthen to g., 459:1

where sorrow holy g., 567:24

Groundlings, split ears of g., 196:21

Grounds, fight on landing g., 620:7

Group, before g. enter open society,
771:3

genocide destruction of nation ethnic g., 704:14

of willful men, 572:9

Grove, but cloud and like shady g.,
356:9

court the camp the g., 377:25

Jemmy G. on deathbed lay, 785:9

meadow g. and stream, 375:3

no quiet g., 353:9

olive g. of Academe, 261:1

shade which g. of myrtles made,
233:10

spicy g. cinnamon tree, 711:2

Grovel, mediocre and you g., 336:7

Groveling, he who goeth g., 117:22

Groves are of laurel, 349:8

forsake her Cyprian g., 275:30

God's first temples, 411:6

green g. of the blest, 94:12

o'er shady g. they hover, 237:13

Groves (*continued*)
  of Academe, 97:22
  valleys g. hills fields, 162:2
Grow, asked how pearls did g., 241:3
  cannot g. by inch, 599:7
  consider lilies how they g., 33:20
  corn and taters g., 564:19
  enter to g. in wisdom, 522:12
  from grass I love, 489:23
  grass will g. in streets, 625:21
  green g. the rashes O, 362:1
  hatched would g. mischievous,
    188:1
  heads g. beneath shoulders, 205:27
  in place of one, 289:n3
  into likeness of bad men, 76:13
  learn but not wiser g., 288:12
  libraries not made they g., 559:12
  like a cedar in Lebanon, 18:17
  like savages, 186:2
  lopped tree may g. again, 65:n6
  love's mysteries in souls g., 229:16
  makes not fresh nor g. again, 236:8
  my wrath did g., 358:12
  oaks from acorns g., 119:18
  old along with me, 467:6
  on Irish ground, 779:10
  out at heels, 209:15
  pastime and happiness g., 376:14
  pinks that g., 204:n5
  poets by sufferings g., 264:3
  riches g. in hell, 256:21
  roses and white lilies g., 226:18
  say which grain will g., 212:17
  she can hear daisies g., 566:5
  so be it when I g. old, 374:7
  straight in strength of spirit, 534:20
  to what they seem, 328:11
  trees g. up again quickly, 65:7
  trees that g. fair, 593:17
  two blades of grass g., 289:11
  up with the country, 475:n2
  vegetable love g. vaster, 268:14
  virtuously into knowledge, 587:8
  why on earth except to g., 466:23
Growed, I 'spect I g., 463:2
Groweth, like grass which g. up,
    18:10
  sed, 775:10
Growing and a becoming, 500:13
  close upon the g. boy, 375:7
  darling I am g. old, 557:1
  iron rungs of g. up, 744:1
  loves life like him g. old, 67:17
  old in drawing nothing, 335:1
  sorrow of day's g., 522:10
  tender and g. night, 489:8
  toil of g. up, 598:4
  tree g. when ye're sleeping, 379:14
  we have a cancer that is g., 769:7
  women kept from g. to capacities,
    748:18
Growled, cracked g. roared howled,
    381:4
Grown, age g. so picked, 199:7
  both full g., 778:9
  by what it fed on, 193:8
  diseases desperate g., 198:9
  if it had g. up, 517:16
  old before my time, 515:11

Grown (*continued*)
  old in love, 359:21
  sweets g. common, 221:20
  that he is g. so great, 187:23
Grown-up nation, 713:19
Grown-ups never understand anything,
    705:12
Grows, each thing that in season g.,
    168:16
  everything that g., 220:11
  fairer than at first, 222:5
  great love g. there, 197:11
  home where small experience g.,
    167:17
  immortal spirit g., 373:8
  in this delightful garden g., 153:14
  marble wastes statue g., 137:8
  no profit g. where no pleasure,
    167:15
  nodding violet g., 173:9
  one is fat and g. old, 177:22
  since when it g. and smells, 232:16
  that which is g., 111:32
  up by degrees, 238:15
  weed that g. in every soil, 331:21
  what soon g. old, 77:10
  when watered by blood, 354:11
Growth, children of larger g., 305:6
  confidence plant of slow g., 313:1
  moral soil for aesthetic g., 618:16
  only evidence of life, 426:19
  participate in America's g., 726:2
  self-help root of g., 472:17
  shadow kills the g., 233:6
Growths, every day hidden g., 483:24
Grub first then ethics, 698:15
  no gravy no g., 674:13
Grubber, Whitman lonely old g.,
    757:2
Grubstreet inhabited by writers, 314:4
Grudge, dare never g. throe, 467:8
  feed fat the ancient g., 180:4
  potter bears g. against potter, 54:20
  what they cannot enjoy, 59:5
Grudging worshipper of the gods,
    96:1
Grumble, we g. about weather,
    528:n1
Grundy, Solomon G., 791:4
  tyranny of Mrs. G., 493:4
  what will Mrs. G. say, 367:11
Grunt and sweat under weary life,
    196:10
Gruntin', I'll do de g., 556:9
Gruntled, far from being g., 645:17
Guanahani, called G. in Indians'
    tongue, 134:8
Guarantee, Bill of Rights g. of free-
    dom, 655:17
  no one g. success in war, 622:5
  of First Amendment, 661:8
  of freedom, 655:17
  of scientific-democratic approach,
    749:9
Guaranteed, freedom of press g. those
    who own one, 714:2
Guarantees, mutual g. of independ-
    ence, 572:14
  not worth paper, 440:7
Guard and keep them, 57:22

Guard (*continued*)
  Browning g. silence, 626:10
  don't call out National G., 655:5
  grow weak keeping on g., 553:11
  holy angels g. thy bed, 294:12
  our native seas, 388:26
  ready to g. liberty, 395:1
  those I g. I do not love, 596:10
  time every minute, 630:1
  who is to g. the guards, 109:3
Guarded by neighborly respect, 620:2
  with ships, 249:27
Guardian angels sung this strain,
    308:12
  conscience g. of community rules,
    626:16
  Naiad of strand, 378:18
  necessity g. of nature, 135:9
  need a guardian, 109:n3
  of other's solitude, 630:10
Guardians of the faith, 668:1
Guards bivouac of dead, 492:4
  die but never surrender, 371:20
  like wild beast g. way, 358:16
  Scylla g. right side, 181:n2
  who is to guard the g., 109:3
Gude nicht and joy, 368:7
  Scots lords, 784:34
  to be merry and wise, 779:20
Gudgeons, swallow g. ere they're
    catch'd, 58:n8
Guenever for whom I make mention,
    133:12
Guerdon, fair g. we hope to find,
    253:20
  last g. of death, 91:17
Guérit, je le soignay Dieu le g.,
    143:n4
Guerre, magnifique mais pas la g.,
    460:n2
  plus facile de faire la g., 542:n1
  trop grave pour la confier à des
    militaires, 354:n6
Guess each sweet, 415:14
  if you can, 249:20
  now who holds thee, 438:21
  shrewd g. valuable, 738:10
Guessed, ghost g., 551:6
Guesses, secrets everybody g., 570:13
Guessing, pleasure of poem g., 547:13
Guest, after three days weary of g.,
    309:7
  dear old Carian g., 502:9
  dull fighter and keen g., 178:27
  earth receive honored g., 720:9
  freeloader confirmed g., 655:1
  give no more to every g., 289:21
  love is but a g., 227:5
  make welcome the present g., 53:29
  no g. welcome after three days,
    83:14
  remembrance of a g., 30:26
  retire like g. sated, 90:5
  retire like satisfied g., 95:3
  shakes parting g. by hand, 201:2
  soul g. of body, 110:7
  speed the going g., 302:22
  speed the parting g., 299:26
  speeds parting g., 597:17
  this g. of summer, 213:4

Habitation, benevolence the tranquil
h., 79:17
  eat of the h., 180:2
  giddy and unsure, 183:26
  heart h. large enough, 435:26
  local h. and name, 174:1
  of dragons, 27:7
Habits, character h. and manners,
503:5
  civilized man has h. of house,
476:21
  follow other men's h., 506:11
  form second nature, 347:14
  ill h. gather by degrees, 276:23
  my other h. air good, 521:18
  of age of atomic energy, 686:7
  of peace and patience, 245:17
  reforming other people's h., 527:14
  well pursued betimes, 348:5
Habitual hatred or fondness, 337:6
  lie becomes h., 343:11
  nothing h. but indecision, 545:11
Hack, somebody to hew and h., 263:9
Hacking at branches of evil, 478:13
Hackles, henna h. halt, 638:27
Hackney, starved h. sonneteer, 299:2
Hackneyed phrases, 574:16
Had having and in quest to have,
222:7
Hades, descent to H. is same, 64:17
  hateful as gates of H., 51:30
  is relentless, 51:29
  no man takes wealth to H., 59:25
  pass gates of H., 59:24
  road to H. easy to travel, 82:8
  sent to H. many valiant souls, 50:23
Hag and hungry goblin, 777:2
Haggard, if I do prove her h., 207:2
Haggards ride no more, 580:17
Hags, secret black midnight h., 215:17
Ha-ha we're bound away, 793:12
Hail and farewell my brother, 91:18
  Columbia, 372:15
  congenial horrors h., 307:16
  divinest Melancholy, 251:22
  Emperor we who are about to die,
110:6
  fellow well met, 290:20
  hail gang's all here, 529:n1
  holy light, 257:23
  let others h. rising sun, 323:17
  Liberty hail, 421:18
  love-gift of fairy tale, 518:13
  Master, 36:33
  thou highly favored, 37:37
  to the Chief, 378:21
  to thee blithe spirit, 408:4
  to you gods, 4:5
  wedded love, 258:26
  ye small sweet courtesies, 321:1
Hailed, so proudly we h., 391:2
Haine, un peu de h., 522:n2
Hair, amber-dropping h., 253:11
  as free, 232:6
  babies haven't h., 679:1
  beautiful uncut h. of graves, 488:20
  beauty draws with single h., 299:12
  bindest in wreaths thy golden h.,
95:20
  blown h. is sweet, 669:16

Hair (*continued*)
  bracelet of bright h., 229:20
  brown h. and speaks small, 182:17
  burned black with sun, 683:11
  comb gray h., 596:8
  divide a h., 262:19
  draw you with single h., 235:n3
  Edith with golden h., 442:10
  fictions only and false h., 243:9
  folded her h. expectantly, 491:7
  hank of h., 592:23
  has become very white, 517:9
  his floating h., 382:25
  horrid image unfix h., 212:23
  hyacinth h., 451:12
  Jeanie with light brown h., 507:3
  lie tangled in her h., 267:16
  lilac and brown h., 669:16
  live h. shining and free, 663:2
  long h. glory, 43:10
  Love with streaming h., 695:22
  lute strung with his h., 169:3
  make your h. curl, 531:11
  my fell of h., 216:13
  ninth part of a h., 178:6
  not white h. that engenders wisdom,
81:14
  not your yellow h., 598:8
  of dog that bit us, 142:4
  of my flesh stood up, 13:39
  of yon gray head, 443:12
  part my h. behind, 667:19
  prison for color of h., 580:9
  rain-drenched h., 655:2
  recover h. that grows bald, 166:23
  rise with my red h., 764:13
  ruddy limbs flaming h., 357:20
  sacred h. dissever, 299:18
  scent of her h., 683:11
  smooths h. with automatic hand,
669:2
  soft-lifted, 416:14
  species covered with h., 759:8
  stand up, 67:11
  stars in h. seven, 509:19
  stroke his silver h., 356:10
  subtle wreath of h., 229:19
  sugar my h., 518:8
  swerve a h. from truth, 200:22
  tangles of Neaera's h., 253:20
  to stand an end, 194:17
  turned quite gold from grief, 567:5
  vine leaves in h., 508:16
  was long, 417:5
  wash that man outa my h., 692:14
  weave sunlight in h., 668:3
  what scanted in h. given in wit,
166:24
  with such h. too, 466:15
Hairbreadth missings of happiness,
312:1
  'scapes, 205:25
Haircut and a shave, 679:1
Hairs, bring down my gray h., 8:8
  glory from gray h. gone, 443:3
  how ill white h. become fool,
184:16
  if h. be wires, 222:8
  nine she-camel h. aid memory,
665:4

Hairs (*continued*)
  of your head numbered, 34:33
  sad last gray h., 415:12
  stand on end, 692:4
  superfluity sooner by white h.,
179:26
  those set our h. upright, 230:11
Hairy gold crown on 'ead, 591:21
  man from east, 606:4
Hal, 'tis my vocation H., 176:34
  would it were bed-time H., 178:32
Halcyon days, 73:14
  expect h. days, 163:7
Hale Father William, 386:8
Half a drop ah my Christ, 162:23
  a league, 458:9
  a life asunder, 518:13
  a loaf, 141:32
  angel half bird, 467:24
  as old as Time, 367:4
  as old as time, 473:11
  better be ignorant than h. know,
100:17
  better h., 155:25
  dead a living death, 261:9
  grant what I wish, 623:8
  he's still h. with us, 727:11
  his Troy was burned, 183:10
  how much more is h. than whole,
54:21
  how the other h. lives, 245:4
  in love with Death, 415:16
  light half shade, 454:20
  more than h. people right, 703:14
  of my own soul, 95:16
  of one order half another, 263:17
  one h. of the world, 387:6
  overcome but h. his foe, 256:19
  owre to Aberdour, 785:1
  part of blessed man, 169:23
  proper gardener's work, 593:23
  reveal half conceal, 457:6
  revolutions put h. of France in
mourning, 436:24
  savage country, 659:4
  seas over, 290:4
  see with h. an eye, 151:3
  served God with h. the zeal, 225:22
  speak h. an hour need two days,
572:15
  the wit for half the beauty, 368:13
  they h. believe in it, 57:12
  to rise and half to fall, 301:13
  use h. talent, 706:19
  was not told me, 12:26
  well begun is h. done, 78:26
  who has begun has h. done, 97:8
Half-acre tombs, 228:16
Half-a-crown, help to h., 540:12
Half-alligator, half-horse h. breed,
398:6
Half-believers of casual creeds, 498:10
Half-brother of world, 476:9
Half-dozen, six of one h. of other,
406:3
Half-gods, when h. go, 429:20
Half-horse half-alligator breed, 398:6
Half-ignorant they turned an easy
wheel, 414:20

Half-know, better know nothing than
  h., 479:*n*4
Half-look, backward h. over shoulder,
  671:15
Half-reaped furrow, 416:14
Half-regained Eurydice, 251:20
Half-truth, aphorism a h., 626:6
Half-truths, all truths are h., 584:17
  Nature hints and h., 532:8
Half-witted, old h. sheep, 376:*n*2
  saw State was h., 477:14
Half-world, o'er one h. nature dead,
  213:21
Halicarnassian, my H. friend, 82:20
Hall, bride paced into the h., 381:2
  dazzlingly lighted h., 473:4
  Douglas in his h., 378:12
  equality in servants' h., 581:21
  flowers in garden meat in h.,
    129:*n*1
  in h. or bower, 252:15
  Liberty H., 330:4
  o' Fame when you croaks, 673:15
  'tis merry in h., 144:9
  Tom bears logs into the h., 169:13
  vasty h. of death, 498:15
  waiter roars through h., 503:2
Hallelujah, Michael row boat ashore
  H., 794:15
Halloo halloo loo loo, 210:4
Hallow the fiftieth year, 9:27
  we cannot h., 450:2
  words such as h. obscene, 701:14
Hallowed be thy name, 33:12
  ground, 685:18
  relics should be hid, 251:2
  so h. and so gracious, 192:29
Halls, footless h. of air, 751:3
  in h. in gay attire, 377:25
  marble h., 419:1
  my ho head h., 647:20
  of fame, 781:15
  of hell, 659:17
  of Montezuma, 780:22
Hallucinations of poets, 642:16
Halt and blind, 38:32
  henna hackles h., 638:27
  how long h. ye between opinions,
    12:35
  I pray you make a little stay, 120:9
  no dishonor to h. at second place,
    87:17
  put a h. to injustice, 755:9
Halted, army not h. by eloquence,
  474:14
Halter, hope one will cut h., 250:15
  threats of h., 348:1
Halters, ill talking of h., 149:44
Halve rights double duties, 404:11
Halves, two h. of God, 427:15
Ham, Noah begat H., 7:14
Haman, they hanged H., 13:26
Hamburger, gladly pay you Tuesday
  for h. today, 690:3
  sacred cows make tastiest h., 768:9
Hamelin town's in Brunswick, 464:17
Hamlet, Bacon not written H., 413:18
  I am not Prince H., 667:17
  much Antony of H. most, 557:7
  O H. what a falling-off, 194:21

Hamlet (*continued*)
  rambles Lear rages, 599:7
  rude forefathers of h., 322:4
  there struts H., 599:6
Hamlet's, ghost of H. father, 584:7
Hamlets, in h. dances on green,
  377:25
  they have H. we Karamazovs,
    495:15
Hammer along 'ard 'igh road, 554:17
  die with h. in hand, 780:20
  iron when hot, 99:8
  me into crowbar, 634:9
  neither h. nor axe, 12:23
  what the h., 358:7
  when you are a h. strike, 244:22
Hammered gold and gold enameling,
  597:10
Hammers, busy h. closing rivets,
  185:14
  laughs at broken h., 634:15
Hammock, future not a comfortable
  h., 691:5
  me they'll lash in h., 487:10
Hampden, some village H., 322:14
Hampering with ceremonies and
  music, 80:12
Hampshire, captain of H. grenadiers,
  340:15
Hamstring, conceit lies in his h.,
  200:11
Han', prentice h. tried on man, 361:25
Hand against every man, 7:30
  against Heaven's h., 255:15
  and heart to this vote, 394:9
  and lash that beat Rome, 599:5
  as arrows in the h., 20:1
  automatic h., 669:2
  beneath awful H. we hold, 592:25
  bird in h. worth two in bush,
    107:*n*5
  bite h. that fed, 332:29
  bless h. that gave blow, 274:20
  bloody and invisible h., 214:28
  bondman in h. bears power, 187:29
  book in his h., 272:11
  books you hold in h., 315:9
  Caesar's h., 430:12
  capped withered heart, 712:18
  child of my right h., 232:10
  close h. out of love, 552:8
  cloud like a man's h., 12:37
  cold h. of death, 179:5
  death lays icy h. on kings, 246:23
  died by the h. of the Lord, 9:6
  do not saw air with h., 196:21
  dry h. yellow cheek, 183:19
  dyer's h., 222:1
  each army hath a h., 169:29
  East with richest h., 256:23
  even I be in Somebody's h., 539:17
  every man's h. against him, 7:30
  eye see for h. not mind, 477:26
  farther away on either h., 683:16
  fear thy skinny h., 381:18
  findeth to do, 24:19
  foot and h. go cold, 144:12
  for hand, 9:15
  from h. no worthy action, 779:1
  God keep you in his h., 794:8

Hand (*continued*)
  gods' capricious h., 716:16
  handle toward my h., 213:20
  having put h. to plow, 38:16
  heart in h., 462:6
  heaving up my either h., 241:21
  her h. on her bosom, 208:4
  here's my h., 224:13
  his hat in his h., 315:10
  hold fire in his h., 171:3
  hold infinity in palm of h., 359:5
  hold your h. victorious, 69:3
  hop a little from her h., 175:14
  hour is at h., 36:32
  hurts my h., 207:20
  I want to hold your h., 770:7
  if thy right h. offend thee, 33:5
  in every honest h. a whip, 208:2
  in hand Americans all, 336:10
  in hand on edge of sand, 472:3
  in hand with wandering, 260:24
  in her left h. riches and honor,
    20:20
  in his h. are the deep places, 18:19
  in one h. a stone, 83:10
  individual led by invisible h., 326:6
  infection and h. of war, 171:9
  iron h. in velvet glove, 143:1
  kingdom of heaven is at h., 32:28
  kissing h. may feel good, 686:10
  leans her cheek upon her h., 174:28
  left h. know what right h. doeth,
    33:11
  left his garment in her h., 8:6
  lends h. to honest boldness, 81:12
  length of days in her right h., 20:20
  lifted h. in awe, 296:3
  like base Indian, 208:16
  like this hand, 466:22
  living from h. to mouth, 148:5
  made all to prosper in his h., 8:5
  man himself lend a h., 71:17
  man's h. not able to taste, 173:27
  medieval h., 529:18
  mortality's strong h., 170:11
  my thoughtless h., 358:5
  my times are in thy h., 16:27
  nature's sweet cunning h., 201:26
  never had blister in h., 73:5
  nonchalance of h., 596:16
  not h. but understanding, 150:16
  not leave my h. without light, 663:6
  of all that hate us, 37:45
  of God promise of my own, 488:18
  of h. of foot of lip, 221:22
  of Potter shake, 446:4
  Old Age and Experience h. in h.,
    283:27
  on the horn, 786:4
  orders in his h., 610:22
  our h. finished it, 102:12
  our times in his h., 467:6
  phrase men pass h. to mouth,
    763:10
  prentice h. tried on man, 361:25
  put in his h. by the hole of the
    door, 25:14
  raised to shed blood, 301:4
  rash h. in evil hour, 260:7
  red right h., 257:3

Handsome (*continued*)
wee thing, 363:12
with my mourning very h., 279:20
Handsomely, have merit h. allowed,
317:24
Handspike, Fate is h., 486:28
Handwriting on the wall, 679:13
Handy, with girls be h., 778:21
Handy-dandy which is the justice,
211:3
Hang by your thumbs, 752:8
calf's-skin on limbs, 169:28
caps on horns o' the moon, 218:24
clothes on hickory limb, 783:6
enough rope h. himself, 140:*n*7
feel his title h. loose, 216:6
go h. yourselves critics, 140:8
I h. around in bars, 775:6
in their own straps, 201:20
it all Robert Browning, 659:12
let him h. there, 754:20
like icicle on beard, 202:27
loop to h. doubt on, 207:10
my harp on willow-tree, 781:1
out our banners, 216:12
pearl in cowslip's ear, 173:1
she would h. on him, 193:8
so fretted you would h. yourself,
316:14
sorrow, 187:*n*1
that jurymen may dine, 299:15
them up in silent icicles, 382:17
themselves in hope one will cut halter, 250:15
there like fruit my soul, 220:6
together or hang separately, 310:18
up philosophy, 176:4
upon his pent-house lid, 212:13
us every mother's son, 172:27
when icicles h. by the wall, 169:13
yellow leaves do h., 221:8
your head over, 779:8
yourself brave Crillon, 154:22
Hangdog, shifty h. look, 645:16
Hanged, house of a man h., 149:44
I'll be h., 177:12
knows he is to be h., 317:1
longed to see him h., 609:5
men h. that horses not be stolen,
280:1
millstone h. about neck, 39:4
my poor fool is h., 211:19
our harps upon willows, 20:6
they h. Haman, 13:26
went out to see Harrison h., 279:3
when skies are h., 689:8
Hangin' Danny Deever, 591:16
men and women there, 779:11
Hanging and wiving by destiny,
141:*n*1
around till you've caught on, 625:18
breathless on thy fate, 441:18
Danny Deever, 591:16
in a golden chain, 257:22
likewise destiny, 141:1
men and women there, 779:11
no man not deserve h., 147:1
shadow h. over me, 770:8
too good for him, 272:21
worst use for man, 227:11

Hangman's, fear o' hell's a h. whip,
235:*n*5
Hangout, talking about certain h.,
693:3
Hangover became part of day, 694:16
Hangs as mute on Tara's walls,
391:12
blossom that h. on bough, 224:25
bodiless as false dawn, 749:15
goose h. high, 779:9
he h. between in doubt, 301:13
in shades the orange bright, 268:24
in uncertain balance, 157:21
on Dian's temple, 219:12
on princes' favors, 225:16
tail h. down behind, 592:14
thereby h. a tale, 190:23
upon cheek of night, 174:23
Hank of hair, 592:23
Hannah, amount to H. Cook, 782:3
God and me, 521:1
Hannibal is at the gates, 119:8
know how to win victory H., 84:4
put H. in the scales, 109:8
Hanover, famous H. city, 464:17
Saint George's H. Square, 524:17
Hansom, helped to h. outside, 718:22
Hap, from better h. to worse, 160:18
my hope my h. my love, 148:9
Ha'penny will do, 779:14
Haphazardly, ideas blow h., 601:17
Haply I think on thee, 220:16
Happen, accidents can h., 784:13
it can't h. here, 658:10
know what will h. next, 702:12
lies at last letting it h., 750:1
melting pot did not h., 590:*n*2
things you do not hope h., 84:1
we's nuts and things h., 673:14
what would h. if one woman told
truth, 734:4
Happened, good books feel all h. to
you, 702:1
nothing ever h. at all, 526:20
put down what really h., 701:20
remember anything whether h. or
not, 528:13
this could have h. once, 467:21
Happening, being and h., 721:10
funny if h. to somebody else, 638:1
Happens, don't want be there when
h., 767:13
future in us before it h., 630:5
nothing h. unless first a dream,
634:11
too much h., 696:16
truth h. to idea, 546:21
unexpected always h., 84:*n*1
whatever h. we have Maxim Gun,
608:18
Happier, envy of less h. lands, 171:9
I am h. than I know, 259:26
in passion we feel, 265:27
people capable of becoming h.,
677:7
Pobbles h. without toes, 472:15
remembering h. things, 455:13
those who feel love most are h.,
407:1
Happiest day happiest hour, 451:8

Happiest (*continued*)
intellection, 749:17
martini one of h. marriages, 696:8
of all men, 306:10
time of New Year, 454:4
treatise of natural education, 319:16
women nations have no history,
483:22
Happily may I walk, 787:10
Happiness activity in accordance with
excellence, 78:9
avarice and h., 309:12
beauty that comes from h., 496:7
being's end and aim, 301:16
beneficial for body, 613:4
beyond h. is bliss, 681:11
care of life and h., 344:11
ceases like dream, 247:10
consume h. without producing it,
570:15
counting upon H., 417:17
depends less on exterior things,
334:2
dream h. you may never feel,
611:12
enjoy h., 100:*n*2
envy no man's h., 191:9
freedom secret of h., 72:7
great step towards h., 396:11
greatest degree of h., 327:2
greatest h. for greatest numbers,
305:20
greatest h. for thinking man, 351:6
Greatest H. Principle, 439:26
habit takes place of h., 423:18
hairbreadth missings of h., 312:1
health foundation of h., 435:13
hope for h. beyond life, 341:9
how simple and frugal is h., 652:2
ideal of h., 436:22
in hands of others, 390:9
in married estate, 250:14
is of retired nature, 292:21
is warm puppy, 751:8
jealous possessions of h., 607:2
liberty secret of h., 568:14
lifetime of h. hell, 571:1
look into h. through another's eyes,
192:11
made of minute fractions, 385:4
make ourselves worthy of h., 326:11
makes up in height, 624:13
man mistakes evil for h., 365:25
mistaken path to h., 404:19
new dish does more for human h.,
354:15
no h. like mine, 767:5
no h. perfect as martyr's, 585:16
no h. where no wisdom, 66:20
no one can arrange another's h.,
713:7
not in multitude of friends, 231:20
of human race, 331:25
of peoples, 550:7
of society end of government, 338:6
on earth no sure h., 153:24
on surer ground of mutual h., 436:3
only one h. in life, 436:25
pastime and our h., 376:14
politics art of human h., 590:12

Happiness (*continued*)
    principles to effect h., 343:2
    produced by good tavern, 316:28
    pursuing and obtaining h., 327:1
    pursuit of h., 343:2
    regret or secret h., 557:17
    result h., 470:25
    result of man's effort, 635:10
    rhyming gives men h., 303:12
    secret of h. freedom, 72:7
    she does not find, 313:24
    sole object of government, 340:2
    sum of human h., 646:4
    supreme h. of life, 427:22
    take life-lie away take h., 508:13
    that makes heart afraid, 422:21
    the only good, 520:16
    the only sanction of life, 588:3
    thirst after h., 319:26
    to be dissolved into something
        great, 616:9
    to crave h. is revolt, 508:4
    too swiftly flies, 321:17
    two foes of human h., 404:16
    what right have we to h., 508:4
    wherein lies h., 414:11
Happy a man as any in world, 279:9
    accident, 237:5
    age when idle with impunity, 396:5
    alchemy of mind, 307:8
    all the while I was h., 772:15
    and I wrote my h. songs, 356:5
    as grass was green, 737:14
    as heart was long, 737:18
    as kings, 561:12
    as we imagine, 265:5
    ask yourself whether h., 440:6
    autumn fields, 456:13
    be and have immortal bliss, 153:14
    be good and h. today, 380:23
    best government make people h.,
        424:9
    bread sauce of h. ending, 548:19
    breed of men, 171:9
    bridegroom Hesper brings, 579:22
    call that man h., 63:14
    Christmas to all, 391:7
    combination of circumstances,
        379:17
    convents, 304:1
    created you while h., 587:13
    days here again, 685:12
    deep down, 673:11
    description of h. state, 277:10
    duty of being h., 560:21
    families alike, 510:11
    fault, 48:12
    few, 185:23
    field mossy cavern, 416:12
    genius of my household, 653:30
    good government when those near
        made h., 61:19
    good to be just plain h., 681:11
    good-night air, 540:11
    had Vietnam instead of h. child-
        hoods, 770:4
    hail Columbia h. land, 372:15
    he of calm and h. nature, 75:4
    heart that sighed, 160:22
    high majestical, 407:9

Happy (*continued*)
    highways where I went, 579:9
    horse to bear Antony, 217:5
    hour wherein man might be h.,
        245:9
    house shelters friend, 431:36
    how h. he who crowns, 329:10
    how h. vestal's lot, 300:5
    how h. with either, 297:20
    how we make ourselves h., 326:11
    if all h. as we, 358:10
    if ever wife h. in man, 262:15
    I'm h. again, 689:11
    I'm h. tonight, 761:9
    in arms of chambermaid, 317:10
    in being and knowing, 681:11
    in even bad movie, 740:2
    in nothing else so h., 171:14
    in small ways, 587:3
    in sorrow, 151:25
    is he born and taught, 227:6
    Isles, 455:6
    Jerusalem h. home, 776:25
    laugh before we are h., 283:14
    let a lord once own the h. lines,
        299:2
    let us be h. as we can, 317:20
    liking what they do, 321:6
    little h. if say how much, 186:23
    little needed to make h. life, 111:21
    living things, 381:22
    lucid intervals and h. pauses, 158:17
    make fellow creatures h., 341:9
    make two lovers h., 300:27
    man be his dole, 141:*n*2
    man happy dole, 141:2
    man that hath his quiver full, 20:1
    man who could search out causes,
        92:30
    man who works ancestral acres,
        95:13
    man's without a shirt, 140:13
    master of himself a h. man, 96:24
    mindful of h. time in misery, 125:18
    moron, 783:7
    never was so h., 780:1
    no lad so h. as I, 388:25
    no lot is altogether h., 96:11
    no man h. who does not think so,
        100:3
    no one h. till all h., 493:2
    not h. unless free, 405:4
    not to seem too h., 467:16
    object of making men h., 495:9
    old man, 92:4
    pair, 258:17
    people whose annals blank, 413:16
    persons with torn bodies h., 611:2
    place green groves of blest, 94:12
    place to be h. here, 520:16
    policeman's lot not h., 529:14
    ports and h. havens, 171:1
    possessor of talent, 717:19
    prologues to swelling act, 212:22
    prospects more pleasing than frui-
        tion, 110:*n*1
    Puritanism haunting fear someone
        h., 643:5
    rarely find a h. life, 95:3
    realize been h. was h. still, 732:13

Happy (*continued*)
    remote from the h., 721:1
    ring h. bells, 457:29
    so h. as America, 340:24
    that we are not over happy, 195:24
    the h. that have called thee so,
        386:14
    the man and happy he alone,
        274:29
    the man who void of cares, 295:2
    the man whose wish, 298:5
    they h. are and love, 250:2
    thing to be father unto many sons,
        164:20
    this h. country, 325:6
    this the h. morn, 250:19
    those early days when I, 270:4
    those who plant cabbages, 140:1
    those whose walls already rise,
        93:20
    time to be h. is now, 520:16
    to be alone last work done, 727:11
    to be h. be well fed, 642:21
    to be h. make others so, 520:16
    to have been h. most unhappy,
        115:10
    'twere now to be most h., 206:11
    until dead not call man h., 55:20
    Warrior, 376:8, 618:*n*2
    was he free was he h., 721:5
    where h. wing-beats are, 364:13
    where one is h. there's homeland,
        119:35
    which of us h. in world, 463:11
    who hath this only, 55:9
    who in verse steer, 280:4
    who knows rural gods, 93:1
    who uses blessings with wisdom,
        97:2
    whoever h. make others h., 760:10
    whom unbroken bond unites, 95:26
    world not making you h., 570:22
    world of h. days, 165:29
    would never be so h. again, 694:15
Harangue, telling nothing in great h.,
    269:11
Harbinger, evening star love's h.,
    260:20
Harbingers are come, 243:24
    to heaven, 250:8
Harbor, age the h. of all ills, 82:6
    arrived in a good h., 240:8
    bar be moaning, 484:11
    cleared, 380:29
    in life did h. give, 232:12
    looking over h. and city, 634:5
    run into a safe h., 55:24
    ship comes into the h., 240:11
    ship of state safely to h., 66:4
Hard as a piece of nether millstone,
    15:23
    as nails, 469:7
    beginning good ending, 141:4
    cause that makes these h. hearts,
        210:15
    Christ ain't a-going to be too h.,
        536:12
    curst h. reading, 353:2
    dealing teaches them suspect,
        180:11

Hard (*continued*)
  for women to keep counsel, 188:13
  gemlike flame, 538:9
  heroic for earth too h., 467:3
  hit h. fast often, 647:5
  hit the line h., 575:15
  it is well I die h., 337:9
  it shall go h., 180:32
  keeps end from being h., 624:8
  latent value, 549:3
  like tip of wedge, 657:9
  makes them soft where we are h.,
    694:14
  not to write satire, 108:15
  nothing's so h. but search will find,
    241:16
  prove him with h. questions, 12:25
  rain's a-gonna fall, 771:6
  sloth finds down pillow h., 219:31
  solid massy h. particles, 282:4
  stairs, 126:25
  things that are too h. for thee, 31:3
  this is my h. time, 724:17
  times h. and wages low, 793:17
  to argue with belly, 85:3
  to catch and conquer, 509:10
  to kick against pricks, 41:6
  to please everybody, 100:9
  very hard is my fare, 297:5
  was their lodging, 286:7
  way of transgressors is h., 21:15
Hard-boiled as picnic egg, 693:7
Hardened, he h. Pharaoh's heart, 8:32
Hardens, charity hardens, 436:20
  it h. a' within, 361:22
Harder, heart h. than stone, 54:11
  they come harder they fall, 774:10
Hardest, first hundred years h., 631:8
  first step is h., 307:11
  knife ill-used, 221:17
  of all to close hand, 552:8
  softest things overcome h., 57:13
Hard-favored rage, 185:3
Hardihood, cure for soft is h., 585:13
  dauntless h., 503:4
  endurance courage, 606:2
Harding not bad man just a slob,
    654:8
Hardship, godlike h., 417:2
  meet any h., 741:3
  our garment, 620:12
Hardships, to stars through h., 118:15
  unknown h. we suffered, 683:10
Hard-working ancestry, 686:17
Hardy as Nemean lion's nerve, 194:14
  kiss me H., 361:2
Hardy-handsome, big-boned and h.,
    551:3
Hare and tortoise, 58:19
  hold with h. run with hound,
    141:18
  limped trembling, 414:21
  mad March h., 135:17
  March H. went on, 517:18
  of whom proverb goes, 169:20
  rouse lion than start h., 177:8
  today on the flesh of a h., 766:2
Harebells, heath and h., 480:7
Harebrained chatter, 435:17
Hares, little hunted h., 611:18

Hares (*continued*)
  pull dead lions by beard, 169:*n*2
Hark deep sound strikes, 399:21
  do you hear sea, 417:*n*3
  hark dogs do bark, 792:14
  hark my soul, 474:3
  hark the lark, 219:24
  the herald angels sing, 312:17
Harlem needed something to smash,
    753:7
Harlot's cry, 359:15
  youthful h. curse, 358:9
Harlots, ye h. sleep at ease, 299:27
Harm, content with my h., 191:9
  didn't want to h. the man, 753:16
  do h. to other nations, 708:1
  do me no h., 394:3
  do no h., 71:2
  do not h. subtle wreath of hair,
    229:19
  do sick no h., 492:3
  does h. to another, 54:23
  does h. to my wit, 201:21
  fate cannot h. me, 380:18
  flea does all h. he can, 231:7
  good provoke to h., 204:23
  I abstain from intentional h., 71:1
  no one h. man who does self no
    wrong, 114:16
  none shall h. Macbeth, 215:19
  nothing do much h., 690:4
  once h. has been done, 52:11
  to one harm to all, 523:10
  whether benevolence good or h.,
    506:9
  win us to our h., 212:21
Harmful, everything without control
    over selves h., 351:12
  more h. than reasoned errors,
    505:18
Harmless as doves, 34:30
  drudge, 314:5
  entertains the h. day, 227:7
  inoffensive aristocracy, 447:18
  necessary cat, 181:13
  only h. great thing, 230:17
  pleasure, 314:22
Harmonicas, has territory of h., 689:9
Harmonies, tumult of mighty h.,
    407:17
Harmonious and humane life, 501:1
  dulcet and h. breath, 173:5
  Father-Mother God all-h., 495:19
  madness from my lips, 408:8
Harmoniously confused, 299:21
Harmonizes natural and artificial,
    384:14
Harmony, absolute h., 713:19
  attention like deep h., 171:5
  between men and land, 662:3
  between tides and life, 564:20
  cultivate peace and h., 337:6
  disposed to h., 387:28
  for you my Universe, 111:5
  from h. from heavenly h., 275:7
  I don't want h., 495:8
  in bad taste elegance, 728:7
  in discord, 97:15
  in h. with universe, 484:8
  is pure love, 161:7

Harmony (*continued*)
  like h. in music, 373:8
  makes heaven drowsy with h.,
    169:3
  manifest in Form and Number,
    583:13
  more h. in her bright eye, 267:13
  music wherever there is h., 248:20
  not live in h., 716:11
  not understood, 301:12
  of leaves, 594:23
  of temperament and circumstances,
    496:7
  of the whole universe, 137:6
  perceived h. of object, 383:22
  power of h., 373:3
  such h. in immortal souls, 182:8
  too high price for h., 495:8
  touches of sweet h., 182:8
  whole complicate amassing h.,
    640:1
Harm's, in h. way, 348:9
Harms, beg often our own h., 217:11
  himself who does harm, 54:23
  lesse of two h., 52:*n*3
  took not for thy h., 581:9
Harness, die with h. on our back,
    216:16
  died in h., 621:18
  him that girdeth on his h., 12:40
Harold stands on place of skulls,
    399:20
Harp, as harper lays palm on h.,
    442:17
  hang h. on willow-tree, 781:1
  no h. like my own, 388:25
  not all who own h. are harpers,
    87:2
  not on that string, 166:8
  once the h. of Innisfail, 389:10
  praise him with h., 20:16
  such as handle h., 7:10
  that once through Tara's halls,
    391:12
  tuning lyre and handling h., 62:23
  wild h. slung behind him, 391:17
Harper, as h. lays palm on harp,
    442:17
Harpers, not all who own harp are h.,
    87:2
Harping, still h. on my daughter,
    195:18
Harpoon, why didn't I h. him, 787:19
Harps, hanged h. upon willows, 20:6
  of gold, 462:2
  organic h. diversely framed, 380:25
  played before the Lord on h., 12:5
Harris, words she spoke of Mrs. H.,
    470:2
Harrison, went out to see H. hanged,
    279:3
Harrow house of dead, 720:4
  rust to the h., 617:3
  toad beneath h., 590:19
  up thy soul, 194:17
Harrowing clods, 540:22
Harry, cry God for H., 185:5
  Harry succeeds, 184:15
  little touch of H., 185:15
  such a King H., 161:10

Harry (*continued*)
these were swift to h., 658:19
young H. with beaver on, 178:21
Harsh as truth, 437:14
berries h. and crude, 253:14
cadence of a rugged line, 274:28
in this h. world, 199:27
life teaches us to be less h., 349:17
nor h. nor grating, 373:5
out of tune and h., 196:19
philosophy not h., 253:3
school in which nothing h., 115:9
words of Mercury are h., 169:15
Harsher, qualify war in h. terms, 492:9
Harshly, do not judge us too h., 698:17
strings untouched will h. jar, 162:12
Harshness, no h. gives offense, 298:20
Hart, as h. panteth after water brooks, 17:11
as pants the h., 285:4
be thou like to a young h., 25:24
lame man leap as an h., 27:9
ungalled play, 197:15
Harvard, always tell H. man, 781:22
fair H., 405:12
glass flowers at H., 664:10
Law School, 646:14
whale-ship was my Yale College and H., 486:21
Harvard Square, Greek islands over H., 699:14
Harvest, all the H. I reaped, 445:18
gathereth her food in the h., 20:27
God comes as sheaves in h., 231:10
home, 177:2, 460:16
is past, 28:20
moon, 286:8
no h. but a thorn, 243:16
of a quiet eye, 374:4
reap the h. of your land, 9:24
seedtime and h., 7:22
shalt not gather the gleanings of h., 9:24
time of h., 670:21
truly is plenteous, 34:26
your hour, 144:5
Harvests, wholesome h. reaps, 422:3
Harwich, steamer from H., 530:15
Has, what man h. he's sure of, 151:11
Hasard, coup de dés n'abolira le h., 547:*n*4
l' h. ne favorise que les esprits pré-parés, 502:*n*3
Hash, couldn't eat h. with enny safety, 479:28
Haste, always in h., 308:26
away so soon, 241:10
brings failures, 70:7
come time and h. day, 353:8
eat it in h., 8:38
haste has no blessing, 784:22
I said in my h., 19:18
in paying obligation, 265:25
in wikked h. no profit, 140:*n*14
make h. better foot before, 170:13
make h. my beloved, 25:24
maketh waste, 140:15

Haste (*continued*)
married in h. repent at leisure, 290:34
more h. less speed, 98:21
now to my setting, 225:14
of fool slowest thing, 282:8
still pays haste, 205:5
thee Nymph, 251:8
this sweaty h., 192:24
without h. but without rest, 351:14
wooed in h. wed at leisure, 167:25
Hasten, minutes h. to their end, 220:26
to be drunk, 276:29
Hastening, to h. ills a prey, 329:8
Hastens, midnight strikes and h., 580:5
Hastily, no werkman may werke wel and h., 131:22
nothing can be done h. and pru-dently, 99:33
Hasty, common sense takes h. view, 477:21
man in his h. days, 550:1
marriage seldom proveth well, 164:25
orisons, 687:2
Pudding, 353:15
pudding, 778:*n*4
start awa sae h., 361:4
Hat, cat in the h., 715:3
cockle h. and staff, 198:16
he can't think without h., 718:15
his h. in his hand, 315:10
lightly doffed h., 588:24
Lord forbade me to put off my h., 271:13
my h. upon my head, 315:10
not worse for wear, 334:23
off with your h., 568:1
on account of Beaver H., 472:8
penny in old man's h., 779:14
runcible h., 471:30
stuck feather in h., 778:21
wears faith as fashion of h., 186:10
Hatched, count chickens before h., 58:16
don't count boobies until h., 690:14
o'er an' hatched different, 483:11
silent when eggs h., 250:14
would grow mischievous, 188:1
Hatchet, buried h., 605:18
I did cut it with my h., 336:*n*7
Hatching vain empires, 257:8
Hate, cherish hearts that h. thee, 225:21
common herd, 96:12
counsels not in such quality, 181:1
creative h., 616:7
do good to them that h. you, 33:8
dumpy woman, 402:7
envy calumny h. pain, 409:4
envy dared not h., 401:12
families I h. you, 607:2
fear h. surrender defiance, 767:21
fly from not h. mankind, 400:2
for arts, 302:11
found only on stage, 403:3
freedom for thought we h., 543:10
gods h. the obvious, 50:18

Hate (*continued*)
hand of all that h. us, 37:45
him for a Christian, 180:3
I dont h. it, 696:18
I h. and I love, 91:16
I h. definitions, 434:15
I h. nobody, 290:3
I h. quotation, 430:19
I h. slavery, 448:5
I h. the day, 154:8
I h. war, 649:4
I h. ye all, 267:8
I h. you I h. you cried Madeline, 645:18
I know enough of h., 623:14
I shall h. all women, 229:2
immortal h., 256:1
implacable in h., 274:6
in white men, 755:10
inaccuracy, 525:10
ingratitude, 203:3
Juno's unrelenting h., 276:5
let them h. so long they fear, 86:17
love and desire and h., 602:10
love as though someday h., 65:*n*9
love treason but h. traitor, 88:18
loved him too much not to h., 281:6
making other Englishman h. him, 571:18
mankind, 212:7
matter whether you h. self, 663:18
my verses, 663:17
no h. lost between us, 237:8
no sport in h., 409:18
nor love thy life nor h., 260:18
nought I did in h., 208:15
of those below, 399:25
one and love other, 33:17
one another and know it, 279:25
only love sprung from only h., 174:24
only those who h. Negro, 564:14
owe no man h., 191:9
Persian luxury I h., 96:3
rage and h. from Adam down, 486:25
religion enough to make us h., 288:25
scourge laid upon your h., 176:20
skins not like your own, 480:14
smile to those who h., 401:27
so far only should we h., 65:13
strength erect against her h., 679:9
the tree, 114:31
things we ought, 78:8
those I fight I do not h., 596:10
those who h. and destroy, 564:11
those who h. you don't win, 733:19
time to h., 23:32
to be unquiet at home, 279:26
to leave world, 702:6
to see evenin' sun go down, 617:15
traitors and treason love, 275:22
tyrants, 488:11
war, 649:4
were why men breathe, 689:2
whom they fear they h., 84:21
whom they have injured they h., 103:6

Hate (*continued*)

   why do you h. the South, 696:18

Hated for my name's sake, 34:31

   if to be fat be h., 177:31

   past reason h., 222:7

   quarrel in streets to be h., 418:13

   the approximate, 630:3

   to be h. needs but be seen, 301:14

   way she had of waking him, 673:10

   with hate found on stage, 403:3

   with scabby hatred, 766:5

Hateful art how to forget, 242:4

   as the gates of Hades, 51:30

   pride is h. before God, 31:22

   second wife h. to children, 67:22

   self is h., 271:8

   what h. to you do not to neighbor, 102:7

   woman once loved h., 614:9

Hater, very good h., 315:5

Hates, anyone who h. babies, 641:*n*8

   children can't be all bad, 641:14

   God h. bray of bragging, 66:3

   him that would stretch him, 211:20

   tell him he h. flatterers, 188:5

   thing he would not kill, 181:14

Hath, unto everyone that h., 36:15

Hating, die not h. enemies, 307:5

Hatred, all h. driven hence, 597:6

   carried in my heart, 753:6

   ceases by love, 64:19

   comes from heart, 404:12

   envy h. and malice, 49:8

   excites h. to conceal abuses, 389:14

   habitual h. or fondness, 337:6

   hate Negro see h. in him, 564:14

   hated with scabby h., 766:5

   healthy h. of scoundrels, 413:14

   I must have no h., 590:8

   if no h. in mind, 597:4

   intellectual h. worst, 597:5

   love to h. turned, 291:9

   made law, 716:18

   not cease by hatred, 64:19

   of bourgeois beginning of wisdom, 496:12

   renders votaries credulous, 319:24

   stalled ox and h. therewith, 21:26

   stirreth up strifes, 21:6

   through h. borne apart, 67:19

   where h. let me sow love, 123:10

Hats off gentlemen a genius, 462:1

   Seraphs swing snowy H., 511:18

   wat their h. aboon, 784:34

Hatter, can't take less said H., 517:21

Haughtiness of soul, 292:6

   of the terrible, 26:13

Haughty, discountenance h. and law-less, 337:10

   Juno's unrelenting hate, 276:5

   nation proud in arms, 252:14

   spirit before a fall, 21:31

   vigilant resolute, 425:12

Haul up the flag, 734:7

Hauling, crazy as h. timber into woods, 95:8

Haunch and hump is Obey, 592:17

Haunches, sits on silent h., 634:5

Haunt, breed and h., 213:4

   exempt from public h., 190:7

Haunt (*continued*)

   ghostlike the spot, 435:27

   murmurous h. of flies, 415:15

   so h. thy days, 417:3

Haunted, beneath waning moon h., 382:20

   by ghosts, 171:25

   holy ground, 399:16

   me like a passion, 373:4

   passage in Lear h. me, 417:*n*3

   summer eves by h. stream, 251:19

Haunters of cavern lake waterfall, 414:16

Haunting black air, 759:13

   Puritanism h. fear someone may be happy, 643:5

Haunts about thy shape, 415:20

   busy h. of men, 410:15

   of coot and hern, 458:5

   suspicion h. guilty mind, 165:6

   tempest laughs at archer, 494:2

Haupt, O H. vol Blut und Wunden, 250:*n*1

Hautboys, give h. breath he comes, 276:8

Havana, our man in H., 713:11

Have, all I h. would h. given gladly, 723:15

   all we h. and are, 593:24

   curtsied when you h., 223:30

   desire what we ought not to h., 99:34

   everything yet nothing, 86:5

   House of H., 538:3

   in quest to h. extreme, 222:7

   more than thou showest, 209:8

   thee not yet see thee still, 213:20

   these for yours, 580:8

   to h. and to hold, 50:4

   to h. to hold and let go, 590:15

   to h. what we would h., 204:6

   try to h. and use excellence, 78:11

   we h. Maxim Gun they h. not, 608:18

   what others would be glad of, 311:20

   what we h. we prize not, 187:2

   where ask is h., 325:12

Haven, in friendship but faithless h., 65:13

   in sunny Palestine, 633:18

   safe into h. glide, 312:14

   under the hill, 456:7

Have-nots, Haves and H., 150:37

Havens, in h. dumb, 550:15

   ports and happy h., 171:1

Haves and Have-Nots, 150:37

   of give, 689:1

Having, are we h. fun yet, 773:9

   fewest wants, 70:19

   had h. and in quest to have, 222:7

   love not h. to say sorry, 769:1

   not a h. and resting, 500:13

   nothing possessing all, 44:6

Havoc, cry H., 188:23

Hawk, gentle as falcon or h. of tower, 135:23

   know h. from handsaw, 195:31

   prayer of h. does not get chicken, 784:27

Hawk (*continued*)

   sooner kill man than h., 663:13

Hawked, by mousing owl h. at, 214:18

Hawk's, inhuman as h. cry, 663:19

Hawks, dark h. hear us, 647:20

   give your heart to h., 663:16

   such hounds such h., 785:16

   which h. flies higher pitch, 163:10

Hawthorn in the dale, 251:13

Hawthorne says NO in thunder, 486:15

   sedulous ape to H., 561:19

Hay, antic h., 162:10

   bottle of h., 173:22

   came creaking to barn, 742:12

   good h. sweet h., 173:22

   make h. when sun shineth, 140:20

   needle in bottle of h., 150:31

   new-mown h., 611:15

   no tits to pull no h. to pitch, 784:4

   work and pray live on h., 637:1

   world bundle of h., 403:26

Haydn, some cry up H., 388:3

Haystack in the floods, 523:4

   needle in h., 150:*n*6

   under h. asleep, 789:4

Hazard, men that h. all, 180:22

   nice h. of doubtful hour, 178:19

   of concealing, 361:22

   of new fortunes, 169:18

   of the die, 166:18

Haze, purple h. was in my brain, 772:3

Hazel, lone Glenartney's h. shade, 378:17

Hazlitt, sedulous ape to H., 561:19

Hé Dieu si j'eusse étudié, 133:*n*7

He for God only, 258:12

   forget the H. and She, 228:10

   if you build it h. will come, 768:2

   is risen, 37:35, 48:14

   is the Rock, 10:26

   poorest h. in England, 239:16

   was he and I was I, 145:17

Head and hoof of Law, 592:17

   anointest my h. with oil, 16:17

   apples on Newton's h., 625:11

   at his h. a grass-green turf, 198:17

   bare Ben Bulben's h., 600:2

   behold my h., 243:24

   bending low, 507:4

   binds so dear a h., 408:14

   black wires grow on her h., 222:8

   blessings upon the h. of the just, 21:5

   bloody but unbowed, 557:9

   bowed comely h. down, 268:11

   bullet through his h., 608:8

   call in thy death's h., 243:17

   chop off her h., 517:14

   chop off your h., 788:21

   crotchets in thy h., 182:25

   crown in my heart not on h., 164:19

   crown of h. to sole, 186:32

   desolate and bowed h., 602:7

   dogs shame the gray h., 52:20

   don't lose your h., 782:23

   drunken dog ragged h., 387:15

Head (*continued*)
eat my h., 469:9
feel as if top of h. off, 514:19
four angels round my h., 266:8
from heels up to h., 561:10
from the fair h. forever, 299:18
full of quarrels, 175:25
gently falling on thy h., 294:12
grown gray in vain, 409:4
guts in his h., 200:13
hairs of h. numbered, 34:33
hang your h. over, 779:8
heap coals of fire upon his h., 22:26
heart runs away with h., 366:17
heaven to weary h., 423:3
her h. on her knee, 208:4
here rests his h., 322:22
hers is the h., 538:5
hide h. under his wing, 790:17
hitteth nail on h., 142:32
hoary h. a crown of glory, 21:32
if she'd but turn her h., 595:11
imperfections on my h., 194:24
in heart or in h., 181:3
incessantly stand on h., 517:9
it shall bruise thy h., 6:24
Jezebel tired her h., 13:11
John Baptist's h., 35:15
keep good tongue in h., 224:15
King Charles's h., 470:29
lay sleeping h. my love, 720:16
make you shorter by the h., 145:1
man with the h., 456:17
meet and not see its h., 57:5
more than churches bibles creeds,
489:10
my hat upon my h., 315:10
my ho h. halls, 647:20
no bigger than his h., 210:27
no roof to shroud his h., 233:22
not sound the rest not well, 150:n2
not yet has heart or h., 711:4
not yet silvered, 334:29
O sacred h. now wounded, 250:7
off with her h., 517:23
off with his h., 166:2, 291:21
on horror's h. horrors, 207:11
one small h. could carry, 329:18
ought to have h. examined, 646:20
over h. and heels, 90:23
picked up poker hit him in h.,
789:13
precious jewel in his h., 190:7
right hand bigger than h., 758:1
root of family is person of its h.,
79:15
sacred h. of thine, 253:22
shake of his poor little h., 531:9
shot it through the h., 792:5
show my h. to the people, 364:7
singe my white h., 209:24
slide into lover's h., 373:18
so young body with so old h.,
181:18
some once lovely H., 445:13
Son of man nowhere to lay h.,
34:17
stone of the corner, 19:20
strike stars with my exalted h.,
95:15

Head (*continued*)
stuff the h. with reading, 303:32
sudden if thing comes in his h.,
165:5
that wears crown, 183:38
this old gray h., 443:11
threw back fierce young h., 628:4
to contrive, 262:1
trickled through h., 519:16
turns no more his h., 381:26
useful lesson to h., 335:12
very staid h., 181:n4
well-made rather than well-filled h.,
145:16
when the h. aches, 150:17
whole h. is sick, 25:26
wisdom of h. and heart, 471:6
with its h. went galumphing, 518:16
your h. concerned with outer
weather, 624:2
Headache, dismal h., 530:14
Head-down tail-up hunt, 769:15
Headings, good reduced to three h.,
278:20
Headline, best h. ever wrote, 730:6
Headlong, hurled h. flaming, 255:22
Headpiece filled with straw, 669:8
Heads, beast of many h., 97:n4
beast with many h., 219:10
blood be on your h., 41:18
brains of better h., 248:3
day fate put h. together, 624:2
diminished h., 258:3
erect instead of bowing necks, 114:6
green hands blue, 472:4
grow beneath shoulders, 205:27
heaven over our h., 478:31
hills whose h. touch heaven, 205:26
houseless h., 210:3
lift up your h. O ye gates, 16:19
monster with uncounted h., 183:9
not seat on others' h., 552:11
o'ertaxed, 498:12
old h. on young shoulders, 746:10
old men's h. bare, 679:1
saw h. black and gold in water,
731:4
so many h. so many wits, 86:n9
tossing h. in sprightly dance, 375:21
two h. better than one, 141:15
when trees bow h., 515:12
within secrecy of our own h., 774:7
Headstones, crooked crosses and h.,
647:8
Headstrong as an allegory, 352:10
liberty lashed with woe, 166:21
Heal blows of sound, 447:4
physician h. thyself, 38:11
time to h., 23:32
wound h. by degrees, 206:26
Healed of suffering by experiencing it,
613:3
Healer, Plato h. of soul, 74:n3
Healing in his wings, 30:10
matter of time, 71:3
Heals, time h. all wounds, 85:n15
Health and a day, 431:1
and intellect the two blessings,
81:15
and quiet breathing, 414:9

Health (*continued*)
and wealth missed me, 397:5
best physic to preserve h., 159:30
blessing money cannot buy, 245:30
by his h. sickness, 356:16
double h. to thee, 401:27
foundation of happiness, 435:13
greatest of blessings, 71:12
I swear by H., 71:1
I that in h. was and gladness, 136:4
in h. and mind's content, 279:18
in perfect state of h., 109:n17
in sickness and in h., 50:4
innocence and h., 329:9
intelligence talent, 582:8
nobody in good h. if not fresh air,
563:5
physical mental h. of country,
748:18
protect h. homes firesides, 560:2
recover h. through contentment,
71:5
taken from you for your better h.,
236:21
that mocks doctor's rules, 443:6
their h. it might hurt, 330:15
trusts in horse's h., 210:13
unbought, 276:19
universal sickness implies idea of h.,
718:5
unto all nations, 49:3
wait on both, 215:3
war is h. of state, 661:10
Healthful, sober h. with his wits,
266:7
Healthy and wealthy and dead, 690:12
breath of morn, 416:19
free the world before me, 490:3
sick danger for h., 552:26
wealthy wise, 309:17
Heap coals of fire, 22:26
dust h. called history, 559:13
o' livin', 644:16
of broken images, 668:18
of dust alone remains, 300:9
of loose sand, 601:4
of stones not a house, 565:6
on more wood, 378:11
struck all on a h., 352:23
worn out before thrown on scrap
h., 570:22
Heapeth, he h. up riches, 17:9
Heaps of miser's treasure, 253:1
Hear a little song, 349:10
all ye Angels, 259:13
angels sing, 462:2
at back from time to time h.,
668:23
at my back I always h., 268:15
be silent that you may h., 188:24
bronze Negroes breathe, 743:10
by tale or history, 172:19
can't h. with bawk of bats, 647:20
conclusion of the whole matter,
24:30
destroyer and preserver h., 407:14
did ye not h. it, 399:22
dust h. her and beat, 458:24
each other groan, 415:12
'erse's legs, 460:2

Hear (*continued*)

every child may joy to h., 356:5
falcon cannot h. falconer, 596:19
far-off curfew sound, 252:4
few love to h. sins they act, 219:19
friend do you h., 786:*n*5
hate enough to h. your prayers,
59:*n*6
have ears and h. not, 28:15
have ears but h. not, 19:17
having ears h. not, 339:7
he wept to h., 356:4
heart h. her and beat, 458:24
him prate, 509:16
hungry stomach cannot h., 268:8
I h. America singing, 488:15
I h. you I will come, 579:4
in chamber above me, 442:9
incline thine ear and h., 27:12
it not Duncan, 214:1
know the man that must h. me,
382:5
lady sing in Welsh, 178:9
let him h., 34:36
listen and do not h. it, 57:4
listen and you shall h., 442:12
Lord h. me out, 725:20
me for my cause, 188:24
mermaids singing, 228:5
mind-forged manacles I h., 358:8
music everyone should h., 641:12
my voice approach, 490:2
never merry when h. sweet music,
182:9
no evil, 777:10
none h. beside the singer, 388:20
not my steps, 213:22
now this, 27:32
now this foolish people, 28:15
old Triton, 376:12
one to speak another h., 477:17
other side, 114:27
public does not h. what I say, 626:3
replication of your sounds, 187:17
right way in the morning, 61:3
rogues talk of court news, 211:13
Shenandoah I long to h. you,
793:12
still stood fixed to h., 259:23
strike but h. me, 62:25
sudden cry of pain, 650:10
surly sullen bell, 221:7
swift to h., 46:7
that lonesome whippoorwill, 753:5
the word of the Lord, 28:33
the words of the wise, 22:11
therefore h. now this, 27:32
those things ye h., 38:21
through midnight steets I h., 358:9
thy shrill delight, 408:6
Time's winged chariot, 268:15
to see moves more than to h., 167:4
us when we cry to Thee, 506:4
voice in every wind, 321:14
voice of the Bard, 357:25
whatsoever I shall see or h., 71:1
why snorer can't h. himself snore,
527:5
wind blow, 779:8
wooden dialogue and sound, 200:11

Hear (*continued*)

word culture reach for pistol, 679:4
you or you hear him, 293:19
you this Triton, 219:7
Heard, ain't h. nothing yet, 661:14
by each let this be h., 567:17
cannot be h. so high, 210:27
chimes at midnight, 184:4
eye of man hath not h., 173:27
have ye not h., 27:22
heavens fill with shouting, 455:17
her massive sandal, 684:9
I have h. key turn, 669:6
I will be h., 437:15
in ancient days, 415:17
it on the Aegean, 499:21
laugh h. when nobody else laughing,
733:4
laughing h. on hill, 356:17
long after h. no more, 375:2
loud bassoon, 381:1
melodies are sweet, 416:2
more he h. less he spoke, 554:18
music h. so deeply, 671:18
music I h. with you, 675:1
never h. so musical discord, 173:25
nor ear h., 42:30
not regarded, 178:12
of thee by hearing of the ear, 15:27
of wonderful one-hoss shay, 447:16
of your paintings, 196:16
old old men say, 595:16
other side, 68:21
people who never h. of Jesus Christ,
675:18
satisfaction of being h., 585:14
shot h. round the world, 429:22
sing songs not h. before, 96:12
sweetest song ever h., 401:23
the dead cry, 724:17
the mermaids singing, 667:19
then is h. no more, 216:14
trumpet be h. on high, 275:11
voice cry Sleep no more, 214:6
voices of children h. on the green,
356:17
we should certainly have h., 721:5
whether there be Holy Ghost, 41:21
wise man say, 578:22
wished she had not h. it, 205:28
Hearers, convince h. of own assertions, 75:1
not h. only, 46:8
readers and h. like my books,
160:17
too deep for his h., 330:10
Hearest thou hardly a breadth, 351:2
why h. thou music sadly, 220:10
Heareth, thy servant h., 11:28
Hearing ear and the seeing eye, 22:3
grass grow, 483:27
heard of thee by h. of the ear, 15:27
make passionate my h., 168:25
mentioned in your h., 387:3
nor ear filled with h., 23:24
of a voice, 487:2
Hearings, smallest sights and h., 490:4
Hearken, will not h. to voice of
charmers, 17:29

Hearkened, old men h. when he was
young, 98:25
to my commandments, 27:28
Hearkeners seldom hear good, 286:16
Hears different drummer, 478:37
ear of him that h., 169:11
him in the wind, 301:7
monarch h., 276:7
neither h. nor sees, 374:1
other mainly h. the No, 349:15
step to music he h., 478:37
sun which h. all things, 51:16
you nearby sweetly speaking, 56:5
Hearse, gilded h., 669:17
marriage h., 358:9
underneath this sable h., 240:14
Heart, a man's h. deviseth his way,
21:30
absence makes h. grow fonder,
101:2
abundance of the h., 35:3
aimed at public's h. hit it in stomach, 634:16
all that mighty h., 374:13
all the h. soul senses, 466:17
all thy h. open, 456:21
although my h. is torn, 419:13
amortization of h. and soul, 686:21
and mind of America, 721:11
and voice oppressed, 482:10
apple rotten at the h., 180:7
apply h. unto my knowledge, 22:11
as he thinketh in his h., 22:19
baseball breaks your h., 769:8
batter my h., 230:26
battlefield h. of man, 495:5
because it is my h., 611:7
because my h. is pure, 456:3
begins to bleed, 787:21
benevolent and kind, 362:4
betray h. that loved her, 373:6
black spot in any h., 507:16
blessed are the pure in h., 33:1
blood around men's h., 67:20
book and h. never part, 287:7
bread strengthens man's h., 286:15
break into flaws, 209:23
bring my aching h. to rest, 86:18
broken and contrite h., 17:25
brute h. of brute like you, 764:18
buildeth on vulgar h., 183:26
bullets seek out where h. lies, 714:5
burn within us, 39:27
bury my h. at Wounded Knee,
698:7
by sorrow of the h. the spirit is broken, 21:25
can push sea and land, 683:16
candle of understanding in thine h.,
30:16
captivate my h., 778:7
caused the widow's h. to sing,
14:42
change of h., 720:4
clean hands and a pure h., 16:18
command my h. and me, 264:8
committed adultery in his h., 33:5
committed adultery in my h., 754:1
congenial to my h., 329:20
consume my h. away, 597:9

Heaven (*continued*)

if earth be shadow of h., 259:12
if H. looked on riches, 289:7
if I ascend up into h., 20:8
if I cannot bend H., 94:20
in heart a little h., 287:18
in h. perfect round, 467:2
in Hell's despair, 358:2
in which no horses, 563:4
is above all yet, 225:11
is he in h., 594:1
is love, 377:25
it smells to h., 197:23
itself points out hereafter, 292:14
itself we seek in our folly, 95:17
itself would stoop to her, 253:13
keys of kingdom of h., 35:28
kingdom of h. is at hand, 32:28
kingdom of h. like mustard seed,
   35:9
kingdom of h. like a net, 35:11
kingdom of H. within you, 112:17
knows how to put price, 340:22
lay up treasures in h., 33:13
leave her to h., 194:25
leave the rest to h., 249:12
leaving mercy to h., 311:23
let justice be done though h. fall,
   119:2
lies about us in infancy, 375:7
lift my soul to h., 225:6
light from h., 361:15
like egg earth like yolk, 110:8
Lord of h. and earth, 41:16
love is h., 377:25
made h. and earth, 3:15, 19:25
made thee neither of h. nor of
   earth, 136:1
majesty of H., 308:19
make a h. of hell, 256:5
make face of h. so fine, 176:1
Maker of h. and earth, 48:25
makes h. drowsy with harmony,
   169:3
man is as H. made him, 150:20
marriages made in h., 155:22
matches made in h., 141:n1
measuring earth and h., 76:10
met my dearest foe in h., 193:14
more things in h. and earth, 195:3,
   683:1
mount up to h., 19:10
near h. by sea as by land, 147:11
needs such men more than H. does,
   342:17
new h. and new earth, 47:37
no humor in h., 527:26
not enter into kingdom of h., 35:31
not h. if we knew what it were,
   262:10
not h. itself upon past has power,
   275:1
not want Honor in H., 668:9
nurseries of H., 581:3
of whales in waters, 657:22
offspring of h. firstborn, 257:23
on earth, 258:8
open face of h., 413:22
or near it, 408:4
ordinances of h., 62:4

Heaven (*continued*)

our Father which art in h., 33:12
parting all we know of h., 514:13
peep through blanket, 213:1
Persian's h. easily made, 392:6
places eye of h. visits, 171:1
plays such tricks before h., 204:4
presents the solid hue, 623:13
prove that I and she ride together,
   465:21
puts all H. in rage, 359:6
rains pennies from H., 722:16
reach port of h., 447:10
rejects the lore, 377:10
remembrance fallen from h., 533:10
rich man enther H., 603:5
ring bells of H., 611:18
same world hell h., 430:13
see h. in wildflower, 359:5
see h. open, 39:37
sends love of her, 4:6
serve in h., 256:6
short arm to reach to H., 581:14
silent finger points to h., 377:1
sincerity the way of h., 79:19
single Dram of H., 514:12
smells to h., 197:23
so he goes to h., 197:24
some call it Tree of H., 715:13
spark from h., 498:10
spark from H. immortal, 364:13
spirit that fought in h., 256:24
star of unascended h., 407:3
starry cope of h., 259:4
stay the bottles of h., 15:14
steep and thorny way to h., 193:27
strange interesting astonishing grotesque, 528:11
such grace did lend her, 168:7
summons thee to h. or hell, 214:1
Sun drives Night from H., 445:3
swear neither by h. nor earth, 33:6
symbol of power of H., 665:5
take my soul, 170:16
tasted eternal joys of H., 162:15
tell little Greek to go to h., 108:21
thank h. fasting, 191:23
that leads men to hell, 222:7
theirs is the kingdom of h., 33:1
then Summer Then H. of God,
   512:16
therefore doth h. divide, 184:23
things are sons of h., 313:27
though h. fall thy will be done,
   119:28
till h. and earth pass, 33:4
to be young was very h., 373:12
to gaudy day denies, 401:14
to h. being gone, 229:19
to throne in, 219:13
toward H. advancing, 364:13
treasure in h., 35:36
treasures in h., 33:13
trouble deaf h., 220:15
under feet as well as over heads,
   478:31
unextinguishable laugh in h., 249:5
unfolds both h. and earth, 172:20
vain war with h., 256:23
visited in H., 513:15

Heaven (*continued*)

war in h., 47:27
watered h. with tears, 358:7
way to h. of like length, 147:n8
what's a h. for, 466:5
when h. was falling, 580:1
wherever bright sun of h., 226:9
which giant Atlas upholds, 68:20
who know h. save by heaven's gift,
   103:16
who sword of h. will bear, 204:20
will most incorrect to h., 193:4
will protect working girl, 574:1
wind from blue h. blows, 349:8
winds of h. through our land,
   676:18
winds of h. visit face roughly, 193:7
winged seraphs of H., 453:8
wished Hell for ease from H.,
   359:21
with all splendors lie, 485:3
with the company of h., 49:16
words never to h. go, 197:26
Heaven-born band, 372:15
   child, 250:20
Heaven-bred poesy, 168:6
Heaven-gates not so arched, 237:18
Heaven-kissing hill, 197:30
Heavenly blessings without number,
   294:12
can h. minds yield, 93:11
caught my h. jewel, 156:6
city formed by love of God, 115:3
connection, 757:4
Father disappointed in monkey,
   528:4
fools by h. compulsion, 209:3
gift of poesy, 275:5
harmony, 275:7
paradise is that place, 226:18
pen wherewith thou h. sing, 377:n2
Powers, 349:7
princes like to h. bodies, 159:21
race demands zeal, 308:16
refuse h. mansion, 598:10
remove weight from h. bodies,
   751:15
rhetoric of thine eye, 168:34
Rosalind, 190:2
things h. or things earthly, 272:19
Heaven-rescued land, 391:3
Heaven's, against h. hand, 255:15
all-gracious King, 462:2
at h. gates claps wings, 155:20
breath smells wooingly, 213:4
cherubin horsed, 213:7
command, 308:12
despite, 358:3
eternal King, 250:19
eternal year is thine, 275:4
glories shine, 480:4
godfathers of h. lights, 168:15
great lamps do dive, 226:13
in h. high bower, 356:15
lark at h. gate sings, 219:24
last best gift, 259:6
light forever shines, 409:8
my destination, 697:12
net is indeed vast, 58:3
nothing situate under h. eye, 166:21

Hell (*continued*)
  is to love no longer, 666:17
  itself breathes out, 197:21
  keys of h. and death, 47:6
  lead apes in h., 167:21
  liberated the h. out of place, 783:15
  limbecks foul as h., 222:3
  madness risen from h., 533:10
  make a heaven of h., 256:5
  make my bed in h., 20:8
  more devils than h. hold, 174:1
  myself am h., 258:5
  never married that's his h., 234:31
  no fury like woman scorned, 291:9
  of a good universe, 689:7
  of nuclear destruction, 761:7
  old age is woman's h., 267:20
  on earth, 571:1
  out of h. leads to light, 257:10
  passage broad to h., 82:*n*6
  paved with good intentions, 121:*n*7, 244:*n*3
  paved with priests' skulls, 114:15
  pour milk of concord into h., 215:27
  print news and raise h., 780:16
  procurress to Lords of H., 457:16
  Puritan's idea of H., 522:*n*1
  raise less corn more h., 560:3
  rebellious h., 197:32
  reign in h., 256:6
  riches grow in h., 256:21
  rising from thousand thrones, 451:17
  road to H. gradual, 700:1
  same world h. heaven, 430:13
  served my time in h., 783:13
  spinach and the h. with it, 703:8
  summons thee to heaven or h., 214:1
  take curtains, 653:29
  tell him to go to h., 397:12
  this is h. nor am I out, 162:15
  though h. bar way, 643:12
  till H. freezes, 783:19
  tyranny like h., 340:22
  very respectable H., 604:16
  walked eye-deep in h., 659:8
  war is h., 492:12
  way I fly is h., 258:5
  we make ourselves, 545:13
  wedlock forced a h., 163:17
  what h. in suing long, 154:5
  what I call h., 707:15
  what in h. have i done, 633:6
  when one is in h., 306:7
  where h. is there must we be, 162:16
  where we are is h., 162:16
  whip all h. yet, 492:*n*5
  whole body not be cast into h., 33:5
  with h. are we at agreement, 26:33
  with work which bores you life h., 605:6
  within him, 258:2
  within myself, 248:15
  wrote of Devils and H., 357:2
Hellas, confounded H., 72:13
  of Hellas, 67:*n*9

Hellenes, boy is most powerful of H., 62:26
Hellenism spontaneity of consciousness, 500:17
Hellespont, Propontic and H., 207:15
Hell-kite, O h., 215:29
Hello darkness my old friend, 772:7
  sucker, 654:6
Hell's broke loose in Georgia, 698:5
  broken loose, 157:22
  concave, 256:13
  despair, 358:2
  fear o' h. a hangman's whip, 235:*n*5
Hells, tormented with ten thousand h., 162:15
Helm, everyone prepared to take h., 508:8
  hold h. when sea calm, 99:18
  Pleasure at the h., 323:8
Helmet and the plume, 454:16
  for h. the hope of salvation, 45:7
  now hive for bees, 156:15
Helmets gleamed in forests, 503:4
Help, a little h. from my friends, 770:10
  a very present h. in trouble, 17:16
  between hindrance and h., 374:5
  cannot h. or pardon, 720:6
  could not hope for h., 721:3
  encumbers him with h., 315:17
  feeble up, 211:22
  for living hope for dead, 520:14
  from whence cometh my h., 19:25
  go love without the h., 359:20
  God our h. in ages past, 294:14
  God's h. and their valor, 370:12
  her and that right early, 17:17
  here I stand God h. me, 138:3
  into Macedonia and h. us, 41:13
  man endure, 697:1
  man is without h., 717:15
  me down Cemetery Road, 750:12
  mutual h. as often as warfare, 704:4
  my h. cometh from the Lord, 19:25
  no h. came, 721:3
  nothing will h., 690:4
  of the helpless, 410:17
  one fainting Robin, 513:10
  only h. her to know, 733:22
  others out of fellow-feeling, 234:4
  past hope past cure past h., 176:9
  since there's no h., 161:11
  them that help themselves, 59:15
  thou mine unbelief, 37:30
  thyself, 59:*n*5
  to half-a-crown, 540:12
  to h. or do no harm, 71:2
  use treatment to h. sick, 71:1
  what's gone past h., 222:25
  when no h. in truth, 65:17
  with h. of surgeon recover, 174:10
Helped every one his neighbor, 27:24
  to hansom outside, 718:22
Helper, antagonist our h., 332:20
  Lord is my h., 45:43
Helpers fail and comforts flee, 410:17
Helpful, noble be man h. and good, 349:5

Helping, God h. me I can do no other, 138:*n*1
  men to practice virtue, 79:9
  so far from h. me, 16:15
Helpless before the iron, 733:22
  justice without strength is h., 271:2
  man in ignorance sedate, 313:22
  naked piping loud, 358:11
  rendered United States h., 572:9
  test of civilization way cares for h., 682:14
Helpmeet, make him an h., 6:15
Helps, art h. old ladies across street, 761:17
  fortune h. the brave, 86:12
  God h. them that help selves, 309:20
  God h. those who get up early, 793:24
Hemisphere, extend system to this h., 360:12
Hemispheres, where find two better h., 228:4
Hemlock I had drunk, 415:9
  snow from h. tree, 623:15
Hemlocks, murmuring pines and h., 441:15
Hemmed, since I have h. thee here, 165:10
Hemorrhaging, San Francisco where social h., 766:11
Hemp, molders h. and steel, 379:10
Hempen, sing in a h. string, 236:5
Hen, as h. gathereth chickens, 36:6
  cackles as if laid asteroid, 527:23
  egg's way of making egg, 524:12
  eggs do not teach h., 793:4
  has right to set, 522:1
  homely h. lays one, 781:16
  laid an egg, 650:15
  marsh h. secretly builds, 547:7
  my black h., 791:7
  my white h., 791:*n*1
  two owls and h., 471:27
  yard in printing house, 659:13
Hence all you vain delights, 236:13
  endure their going h., 211:12
  horrible shadow, 215:8
  loathed Melancholy, 251:6
  stay far h. you prudes, 101:11
  these tears, 85:13
  vain deluding Joys, 251:21
  with denial vain, 253:16
  ye profane, 267:8
Henna hackles halt, 638:27
Henpecked, fraternity of h., 293:9
  you all, 402:6
Henroosts, defend ourselves and h., 479:3
Henry, never did H. end anyone, 735:1
  pried open for all to see, 734:16
  unappeasable H. sulked, 734:15
Hens, milk-white H. of Dorking, 472:10
Hent, merrily h. the stile-a, 223:4
Heraclitus, told me H. dead, 502:9
  your death H., 82:20
Herald, hark the h. angels sing, 312:17

Herald (*continued*)
  Homer h. of your glory, 80:23
  lark h. of the morn, 176:5
  Morning Star h. of dawn, 87:5
  of tomorrow, 590:14
  owl night's h., 165:13
  silence perfectest h. of joy, 186:23
  station like h. Mercury, 197:30
  three years we waited for h., 705:14
Herald Square, remember me to H.,
  632:10
Heraldry, boast of h., 322:8
  new h. hands not hearts, 207:16
Herb, dew bespangling h. and tree,
  241:17
Herba, latet anguis in h., 92:*n*5
Herbs and trees flourish in May,
  133:11
  better is a dinner of h., 21:26
  bitter h., 8:37
  bread with bitter h., 483:20
  Medea gathered enchanted h., 182:7
  men with h. to smoke, 134:9
  of every joyous kind, 117:2
Hercules and Goth bequeathed us,
  539:3
  behind Gates of H., 543:17
  from the foot H., 70:5
  let H. do what he may, 199:18
  not H. but Superman, 764:2
  snakes beside cradle of H., 505:3
Herd, avoid reeking h., 660:15
  groups individuals lack h. sense,
  661:10
  hate the common h., 96:12
  Hesperus you h. homeward, 56:11
  imitators you slavish h., 97:21
  lowing h. wind slowly, 322:1
  of elephant traveling, 656:8
  ran into sea, 37:25
  that only sleep and feed, 198:*n*3
Herds, flocks or h. or human face,
  257:24
Herdsman, God the h. goads, 594:19
Herdsmen, bad h. ruin flocks, 54:3
Here a little child I stand, 241:21
  a little there a little, 26:32
  a sheer hulk, 348:3
  am I, 11:27
  am I send me, 26:3
  and now cease to matter, 671:11
  and now is happiness, 652:2
  but I'm h., 773:14
  comes the trout, 202:16
  from h. to Eternity, 592:3
  gone h. and there, 221:26
  he lies where he longed, 561:16
  I am and here I stay, 443:20
  I have been h. before, 509:29
  I stand, 138:3
  in the body pent, 377:17
  is God's plenty, 276:24
  is my space, 216:25
  is no water, 669:4
  it can't happen h., 658:10
  Kilroy was h., 697:3, 783:10
  Lafayette we are h., 580:16
  lies a King that ruled, 246:3
  lies a truly honest man, 264:21
  lies lady of beauty, 674:12

Here (*continued*)
  lies Matthew Prior, 288:5
  lies my wife let her lie, 277:2
  no intelligent life down h., 784:10
  rests his head, 322:22
  thou ailest h. and h., 497:16
  today gone tomorrow, 281:20
  where wind north-northeast, 608:6
  where world is quiet, 534:12
Hereafter, heaven points out h.,
  292:14
  she should have died h., 216:14
  what is love 'tis not h., 202:2
  what may come h., 534:13
Hereditary, virtue is not h., 340:20
Here's looking at you kid, 726:11
Heresies, no h. in dead religion, 606:5
  truths begin as h., 505:19
Heresy lifeblood of religions, 606:5
  overcome h. with fire, 138:2
Heretic that makes the fire, 222:23
  they will proclaim me h., 136:8
Heretics, faith begets h., 606:5
Heritage, guided by my h., 773:12
  I have a goodly h., 16:6
  of woe, 401:13
  proud of ancient h., 741:3
  what thou lovest thy true h., 659:17
  youth's h., 467:10
Hermit crab whale's backbone, 671:13
  dwell a weeping h., 324:11
  old h. of Prague, 203:4
  poor in place obscure, 152:8
  shall I like a h. dwell, 152:18
Hermitage, give palace for h., 172:4
  take that for h., 267:18
Hermon, heights of H., 632:16
Hern, coot and h., 458:15
Hero, A H. of Our Time, 474:4
  basic h. of books labor, 605:15
  conquering h. comes, 308:23
  Conqueror Worm, 452:8
  every h. becomes bore, 432:24
  keeps getting in bed with women,
  685:2
  killed h. in man, 717:11
  millions a h., 336:2
  must drink brandy, 317:13
  of course Alexander h., 446:20
  perish or sparrow fall, 301:5
  show me a h., 694:21
  to his valet, 249:8
  Truth h. of my tale, 510:1
Herod, born in the days of H., 32:23
  out-herods H., 196:21
  Salome pleased H., 35:14
  should not return to H., 32:24
Herodias, daughter of H. danced,
  35:14
Heroes as well as idealists, 542:8
  blood of our h., 344:9
  broods on her shining h., 421:19
  created by popular demand, 679:2
  hail ye h., 372:15
  hand in hand with my h., 446:25
  if we will, 497:5
  many valiant souls of h., 50:23
  of that kidney, 668:9
  peers h. of old, 467:19
  seeds of patriots and h., 327:*n*5

Heroes (*continued*)
  statesmen philosophers, 347:4
  thanks to our fallen h., 732:9
  thin red h., 591:17
  thin red line of h., 492:*n*4
  were plenty, 781:4
  world's brave h., 778:18
Heroic decision not from cowards,
  676:4
  enterprise is gone, 332:13
  for earth too hard, 467:3
  giving man h. fiber, 532:11
  little monkey, 444:14
  obstacle to being h., 436:10
  pleasures of h. poesy, 249:25
  poem a biography, 412:27
  sires, 280:13
  systematically h., 545:12
  womanhood, 442:7
Heroically mad, 274:17
Heroism endurance for moment more,
  554:12
  feels never reasons, 432:6
  labor matter of h., 638:9
  truest h. to resist doubt, 436:10
  vices fathered by h., 668:8
Héros pour les valets de chambre,
  249:*n*1
Herring, fish nor flesh nor good red
  h., 141:19
  in hell roast like h., 363:11
Herrings, not stored in barrel like salt
  h., 732:7
  red h., 788:15
Herself, show me someone not full of
  h., 772:14
Hertford Hereford Hampshire, 745:8
Herz, mein H. ist schwer, 350:*n*6
  und wenn das H. auch bricht,
  419:*n*6
Hesiod, Homer and H. attributed to
  gods, 60:4
  might have kept his breath, 55:8
  taught H. beauteous song, 54:14
Hesitate and falter life away, 498:10
  dislike, 302:11
Hesitation, doubt h. pain, 464:26
Hesper loves to lead home, 579:22
Hesperian, apple-bearing H. coast,
  68:20
Hesperides, we shall find H., 657:9
Hesperus entreats thy light, 231:21
  it was schooner H., 440:20
  that led the starry host, 258:19
  you herd homeward, 56:11
Hessians, yonder are the H., 330:19
Heterodoxy another man's doxy,
  307:13
  Thy-doxy, 412:19
Hew, not h. as carcass, 188:4
  somebody to h. and hack, 263:9
Hewers of wood, 10:36
Hewing wood for master carpenter,
  58:4
Hewn on Norwegian hills, 256:7
  tree is h. down, 32:32
  wisdom hath h. out her seven pil-
  lars, 21:1
Hexameter, in the h. rises, 383:2
Hey for boot and horse, 484:15

Hi-hi-yee, 636:16

Hill, all all sleeping on h., 607:10
and house live together, 608:12
ascend into the h. of the Lord, 16:18
below the kirk below the h., 380:29
city set on an h., 33:3
city upon a h., 239:27
cloud-topped h., 301:7
dancers all gone under h., 671:3
flung us on windy h., 662:17
green h. far away, 479:18
haven under h., 456:7
heaven-kissing h., 197:30
high Dunsinane h., 215:21
house should be of h., 608:12
hunter home from h., 561:16
hunts on lonely h., 568:8
is this the h., 382:1
Jack and Jill went up h., 789:11
King of France up h., 788:6
laughing heard on h., 356:17
lived under a h., 792:4
on Richmond H. a lass, 353:11
over h. over dale, 172:30
over h. to poorhouse, 554:9
Pillicock h., 210:4
round it was upon a h., 639:1
ruin decay in House on H., 608:2
shall be made low, 27:16
some liken fame to climbing up h., 402:15
they call you Shepherd from the h., 498:9
vineyard in a very fruitful h., 25:37
who shall dwell in thy holy h., 16:4
yon high eastern h., 192:30

Hills, alter when H. do, 513:4
and valleys dales and fields, 162:n1
as old as h., 379:18
blue remembered h., 579:9
brown h. melted into spring, 480:1
cattle upon thousand h., 17:19
everlasting h., 8:19
fight in the h., 620:7
Grampian h., 325:8
great shout upon h., 563:10
hewn on Norwegian h., 256:7
hide h. of snow, 204:n5
if those h. be dry, 165:10
Israel scattered upon the h., 13:2
lift up mine eyes unto the h., 19:25
little h. like lambs, 19:16
ocean of h. and hollows, 83:2
o'er h. and far away, 456:2
o'er vales and h., 375:19
of Chankly Bore, 472:13
of Habersham, 547:8
of Highlands, 362:16
of home, 562:1
of Maryland, 443:10
old as h., 610:12
out of h. thou mayest dig brass, 10:16
over h. and far away, 297:15, 790:4
reverberate h., 201:28
rock-ribbed and ancient, 411:3
shine forth upon clouded h., 359:17
sleep among lonely h., 376:17
snow on treeless h., 647:8

Hills (continued)
strength of h. is his, 18:19, 48:21
vales woodland plain, 299:21
valleys groves h. fields, 162:2
whose heads touch heaven, 205:26
ye too changed ye h., 499:15

Hillside, crouched on bleak h., 708:7

Hillside's dew-pearled, 464:4

Hilltops, o'er all the h. is quiet, 351:2

Him first him last, 259:8
President's spouse I wish h. well, 754:18

Himself, above h. erect h., 161:5
black man not by h., 755:9
ech man for h., 130:11
every man for h., 142:30
go outside h. to reveal h., 564:10
got the better of h., 151:17
he h. said it, 119:10, 529:9
into h. Eternity changed him, 547:11
knows universe not h., 268:7
lives unto h., 242:5
lord of h., 227:8, 401:13
loved him for h. alone, 352:22
man count on no one but h., 717:15
man lost nothing if he has h., 145:19
master of h., 238:6
no man born unto h., 242:5
no man dieth to h., 42:26
no man wise by h., 83:15
none liveth to h., 42:26
out of reputation by h., 286:9
savage he who saves h., 135:7
special people unto h., 10:13
witness against h., 346:14
yet everyone, 725:8

Hinc illae lacrimae, 85:n10
quam sic calamus saevior ense patet, 234:29

Hind, false as pard to h., 200:22
that would be mated, 203:10

Hindmost, devil take the h., 238:17

Hindrance, between h. and help, 374:5

Hindrances, luxuries h., 478:4

Hindside-before-ness, 660:4

Hinge, cast-iron back with h., 511:4
no h. nor loop, 207:10

Hinges in French conversation, 320:35
liberty of conscience upon two h., 247:13
pregnant h. of the knee, 197:2

Hinky dinky parley-voo, 680:8

Hint, before Franklin took h., 625:11
beholding at a h., 572:24
just h. a fault, 302:11
take h. when h. intended, 625:15
upon this h. I spake, 205:28
we take the h., 625:11

Hinter, she was a h., 733:5

Hinting, nature always h., 625:11

Hints for better ordering of universe, 124:2
Nature h. and half-truths, 532:8
nature h. over and over, 625:11
of earlier creation, 671:13
to literary craftsmanship, 665:11

Hip, catch him once upon h., 180:4
I have thee on the h., 182:3

Hip (continued)
smote them h. and thigh, 11:14

Hipparchia, where is H., 509:22

Hippies, children calling themselves h., 766:11

Hippocrene, blushful H., 415:11

Hippopotamus's day, 668:11

Hips, when your h. stick, 709:15

Hipsters, angelheaded h., 757:4

Hire, for all lady's h., 792:9
idiots to paint, 358:14
laborer worthy of h., 38:19
shall win lover's h., 357:23
this gun for h., 713:4
those who lied for h., 659:13

Hired, oblivion not to be h., 249:2
tears, 248:26
the money didn't they, 614:20
wretches h., 314:3

Hiroshima boiling, 743:11
bomb on H., 655:6

Hiss, dismal universal h., 260:15
now becoming a roar, 675:3
of love, 716:21
roasted crabs h. in bowl, 169:14

Hissing, curse astonishment h. and reproach, 28:34

Histoire vieille dame exaltée, 560:n2

Historia me absolvera, 756:n1

Historian, first law for h., 87:15
Goldsmith Poet H., 316:32
of fine consciences, 573:17
of the Roman Empire, 340:15
prophet in reverse, 385:11
shackles of a h., 249:25
sylvan h., 415:20
wants more documents, 549:7

Historians, hints to budding h., 665:11
of opinion, 652:9
reviewers would have been h., 383:19
their tyrants their h., 427:6

Historical, fights h., 529:12
statistical figures are h. data, 645:13

Histories make men wise, 160:10
writers of small h., 314:4

History a nightmare, 647:14
absence of romance in my h., 71:19
absolved of h. they did not commit, 763:11
action in bondage to h., 510:5
ages before commencement of h., 335:24
all h. modern h., 640:25
anybody can make h., 567:14
assurance of recorded h., 671:15
attests happiness depends on dinner, 403:18
bear witness to his patriotism, 369:1
becomes a race, 601:14
Bible has blood-drenched h., 528:12
biography and relations between, 740:1
biography of great men, 412:32
cannot escape h., 449:16
completed chapter of Revelation named H., 412:5
consider an epocha in h., 337:17

Hold (*continued*)
makes nice of no vile h., 170:7
me but safe again, 467:20
me in thy heart, 199:27
mirror up to nature, 196:23
more devils than hell can h., 174:1
net to h. the wind, 237:*n*5
nozzle agin the bank, 536:11
opinion with Pythagoras, 181:17
out relief is coming, 492:*n*5
own with whatever's going, 625:16
speak or forever h. his peace, 50:2
that you know it, 60:24
thou the good, 457:16
thy right hand shall h. me, 20:8
to have and to h., 50:4
to have to h. and let go, 590:15
to one despise other, 33:17
up Adam's profession, 198:27
water, 291:23
with hare run with hound, 141:18
world but as world, 179:17
world wide enough to h. both, 320:18
you as thing enskyed, 203:25
you here root and all, 460:5
your hand victorious, 69:3
your tongue and let me love, 228:14
yours to h. it high, 615:8
Hold, so h. und schön und rein, 420:*n*1
Hold-fast the only dog, 185:2
Holding mental problem in mind, 652:14
pocket-handkerchief, 519:6
writing is h. your breath, 695:1
Holds, guess now who h. thee, 438:21
him with glittering eye, 380:28
in perfection but moment, 220:11
nature her custom h., 198:26
rolls throws breakfalls, 737:5
that anchor h., 459:29
Hole, Baldwin simply h. in air, 711:11
child shall play on h. of the asp, 26:11
entrusts life to one h., 83:13
hobbit-h., 685:3
if you knows of a better h., 666:7
in a' your coats, 363:15
in space small black h., 748:8
mouse that hath one h., 83:*n*10
not a nasty dirty wet h., 685:3
old swimmin' h., 558:17
pessimist sees h., 632:5
poisoned rat in h., 289:17
punch h. in son of a bitch, 784:4
put in his hand by the h. of the door, 25:14
stop h. to keep wind away, 199:10
weasels fighting in h., 597:13
where tail came through, 386:22
Holes, cats have two h. in coat, 342:20
foxes have h., 34:17
of different shapes, 379:29
Holiday, he speaks h., 182:31
regular h. to them, 469:2
Roman h., 400:26
specters' h., 531:12
sunshine h., 251:15

Holiday-rejoicing spirit, 388:2
Holidays, holiest of all h., 442:24
if year playing h., 176:37
put away youth take out on h., 747:15
vague penitence h. awaken, 469:29
Holier, richer man held to be h., 113:10
than thou, 28:10
Holies, my holy of h., 582:8
Holiest of all holidays, 442:24
Holiness, art only clean thing except h., 556:19
courage or h., 608:21
in the beauty of h., 16:24
of Heart's affections, 417:14
Holla your name to hills, 201:28
Hollaing and singing of anthems, 183:21
Holland, where H. lies, 328:12
Holler, Providence fashioned us h., 485:12
Hollow, all was false and h., 257:1
blasts of wind, 297:1
crown, 171:25
from each h. of Spain, 714:4
give me again my h. tree, 302:24
in h. murmurs died, 324:17
life h. existence burden, 526:2
meet thee in h. vale, 242:2
men, 669:8, 669:9
Providence fashioned us h., 485:12
snakes up and down h., 430:14
view with h. eye, 181:25
voice in h. murmurs, 367:12
Hollow-eyed sharp-looking wretch, 166:34
Hollowness, machinations h. treachery, 209:2
never more h. of heart, 491:12
Hollows, dripping water h. stone, 89:8
ocean of hills and h., 83:2
pour into wide h. of brain, 417:1
where flowers grew, 544:2
Holly and the ivy, 778:9
Hollywood induces condition like breakbone fever, 714:16
Holmes, my name is Sherlock H., 577:17
Sherlock H., 577:20
to Sherlock H. always the woman, 577:15
Holocaust central event, 764:7
metaphor for century, 764:7
Holy alliance to exorcise specter, 481:14
and enchanted, 382:20
and meek she cries, 357:18
angels guard thy bed, 294:12
as h. as severe, 204:20
Author of that religion, 287:3
Catholic Church, 48:25
citadel of Troy, 52:27
city new Jerusalem, 47:37
close eyes with h. dread, 382:25
coming to that h. room, 231:2
deadlock, 678:20
died to make men h., 484:7
divine good or sweet, 260:10

Holy (*continued*)
ears have heard H. Word, 357:25
every thing that lives is H., 357:16
fair and wise is she, 168:7
ground, 8:24, 399:16
hail h. light, 257:23
holding such things to be h. secrets, 71:1
holy holy, 26:1, 47:15
Holy Holy, 395:21
I will keep pure and h., 71:1
in those h. fields, 176:23
knight of h. spirit, 420:2
Lamb of God, 359:17
Land of Ireland, 775:*n*5
land of Irlonde, 775:12
land of Walsinghame, 152:9
let him be h. still, 48:3
Mother Earth, 63:8, 787:1
mouth of h. prophets, 37:45
my h. mountain, 26:11
my h. of holies, 582:8
neither h. nor Roman, 306:4
odd old ends stolen of h. writ, 165:27
pebbles of h. streams, 737:17
place whereon thou standest is h. ground, 8:24
proofs of h. writ, 207:5
remember sabbath to keep it h., 9:11
revered h. simplicity, 114:4
Roman Empire, 306:4
sages once did sing, 250:19
shall come again win H. Cross, 133:18
silent night h. night, 406:5
simplicity, 132:11
stand in his h. place, 16:18
take not thy h. spirit from me, 17:23
temple of God is h., 42:34
text of pike and gun, 263:6
things h. profane clean obscene, 239:20
things h. revealed only to men h., 71:10
time quiet as nun, 374:15
tradition becomes h., 552:4
what is gold doing in h. place, 104:16
where sorrow h. ground, 567:24
who shall dwell in thy h. hill, 16:4
Holy Ghost, communion of H., 44:13
conceived by the H., 48:25
Father Son and H., 37:15, 280:21
filled with H., 40:45
glory be to the H., 48:22
I believe in the H., 48:25
incarnate by the H., 49:1
sedentary life sin against H., 553:15
sin against H., 537:12
whether there be any H., 41:21
Holystone decks scrape cable, 474:19
Homage, owes no h. unto sun, 248:22
vice pays to virtue, 265:24
won by lavish h., 392:16
Homard a l'Américaine, 616:18
Home, about h. and run, 747:16
afraid to go h. in dark, 586:*n*2

Home (*continued*)

after years in captivity, 4:4
again jiggety-jig, 792:2
all the way h., 789:3
and being washing-day, 279:15
any more at h. like you, 563:17
art gone and ta'en wages, 220:3
artist no h. save Paris, 553:10
best be getting h. he said, 520:3
best country is at h., 328:8
call cattle h., 484:9
charity begins at h., 85:15, 248:18
Christmas, 604:10
come h. to roost, 386:12
coming for to carry me h., 794:14
day's march nearer h., 377:17
dunce kept at h., 334:8
eaten out of house and h., 183:30
father come h. with me, 520:5
fly away h., 788:16
give you husband and h., 53:10
go h. in dark, 586:7
God who is our h., 375:7
Good Morning Midnight coming
    H., 512:10
harvest-h., 177:2, 460:16
hate to be unquiet at h., 279:26
heaven and h., 377:12
Hesper loves to lead h., 579:22
hills of h., 562:1
his footsteps turned, 378:1
homely features to keep h., 253:10
homely h. simple pleasures, 580:11
hotel refuge from h. life, 570:18
how can tyrants govern h., 164:23
hunter h. from hill, 561:16
I am far from h., 426:18
I came h. forever, 388:1
I keep Sabbath staying at H., 512:4
I'm going h., 429:6
in minds of men, 72:7
in our own beloved h., 492:6
is home, 405:n7
is on the deep, 389:1
is safest refuge, 152:n2
is the sailor, 561:16
is where one starts from, 671:10
it was his rightful h., 753:14
Jerusalem happy h., 776:25
keep h. fires burning, 617:12
keep only son at h., 325:8
knock as you please nobody h.,
    300:26
knows when to go h., 536:14
life that depends on borrowing,
    507:18
longest way round shortest h.,
    242:n4
love of h. love of country, 469:28
made of blue clouds, 787:7
make house h., 644:16
man desires to see h., 4:4
man goeth to his long h., 24:28
merriest when from h., 184:26
my h. sweet h., 666:12
my songs draw Daphnis h., 92:13
Naiad airs brought h., 451:12
nearer h. today, 504:6
never change when love has found
    h., 100:27

Home (*continued*)

no h. like raft, 526:22
no place like h., 405:14
of bean and cod, 582:1
of lost causes, 499:10
of love, 221:25
of the brave, 391:2, 678:7
of wild mirth, 435:23
old Kentucky h., 507:2
our eternal h., 294:14
outlives day and comes safe h.,
    185:22
Paris my h. town, 627:11
place they have to take you in,
    623:3
pleasure never at h., 416:10
returned h. previous night, 618:14
returns h. to find needs, 563:13
seek fortunes further than h.,
    167:17
send h. my long strayed eyes, 229:6
shall men come, 619:4
show piety at h., 45:18
sick for h., 415:17
song of h. and friends, 523:1
tavern for friends, 604:18
they brought warrior, 456:18
they'll come h., 790:14
things foreign or things at h.,
    272:19
this pig stayed h., 789:3
till boys come h., 617:12
till the cow comes h., 238:14
to a lie, 659:8
to my Lord and be free, 794:20
toddle safely h., 662:6
turns again h., 460:11
two thousand light years from h.,
    772:17
welcome h. discarded faith, 170:18
what does it leave at h., 474:5
what is more agreeable than h.,
    87:24
when you knock it never is h.,
    334:12
where buffalo roam, 786:11
wherever that may be, 729:7
wish him safe at h., 366:20
with no direction h., 771:9
Wyoming will be your new h.,
    786:2
Home-keeping youth homely wits,
    167:36
Homeland of patience, 434:13
    where happy there's h., 119:35
    wherever he prospers, 74:1
Homeless near thousand homes,
    372:16
    permission to enter h. state, 65:4
    tempest-tost, 558:1
Homely beauty of good old cause,
    374:14
    conversational or h. type, 609:11
    definitions, 385:1
    features to keep home, 253:10
    hen lays one, 781:16
    home be it never so h., 405:n7
    home simple pleasures, 580:11
    home-keeping youth h. wits, 167:36
    joys, 322:7

Homely (*continued*)

men who charmed women, 586:1
slighted shepherd's trade, 253:20
was their food, 286:7
wink at h. girl, 642:15
Homemade but aren't we all, 729:12
Homer, Achilles exists only through
    H., 369:16
all the books you need, 284:3
and Hesiod attributed to the gods,
    60:4
and Whitman roared in pines,
    607:11
deep-browed H. ruled as demesne,
    413:24
even good old H. nods, 98:17
found H. herald of your glory,
    80:23
is my example, 598:17
learned root of H., 233:n4
liken H. to setting sun, 106:6
living H. begged bread, 233:n4
made blind H. sing to me, 162:18
new and fresh, 618:2
nods, 98:17, 298:12
our poets steal from H., 234:6
read H. once, 284:3
smote bloomin' lyre, 592:11
there were poets before H., 87:20
translator of H., 498:22
warred for H. being dead, 233:22
with single exception of H., 571:14
you must not call it H., 286:10
Homère noveau ce matin, 618:n1
Homer's rule best, 302:22
Homerus, quandoque dormitat H.,
    98:n10
Home's, way h. the farthest way,
    242:11
Homes, homeless near thousand h.,
    372:16
introduce philosophy into h., 87:30
poverty keeps h. together, 610:18
protect health h. firesides, 560:2
shut-in h. closed doors, 607:2
stately h. of England, 410:10,
    650:17
think of firelit h., 662:5
Homesickness, poem begins as h.,
    625:6
Homeward bound for New York
    town, 793:16
Hesperus you herd h., 56:11
look h. Angel, 254:5
plowman h. plods, 322:1
rooks in families h. go, 540:25
Homicidal civilization, 648:4
great h. classics, 769:2
Homines, quot h. tot sententiae,
    86:n9
Homing, horizon of his h., 672:2
Hominy, immotions function in h.
    kind feelings, 641:17
white man filled with Indians' h.,
    333:n5
Homme avec Dieu dans la majorité,
    143:n7
    chaque h. porte la forme de l'hu-
    maine condition, 146:n9
    condition de l'h., 270:n4

Homme (*continued*)
  d'entendement n'a rien perdu,
    145:*n*13
  la vraie étude de l'h., 301:*n*5
  le style c'est l'h. même, 311:*n*2
  l'h. c'est un roseau pensant, 271:*n*1
  l'h. est né libre, 319:*n*3
  l'h. ni ange ni bête, 271:*n*2
  ne saurait forger un ciron, 146:*n*4
  n'y a point h. nécessaire, 648:*n*5
  qu'est-ce que l'h. dans la nature,
    270:*n*3
  vain divers et ondoyant, 145:*n*6
Hommes sont toujours sincères,
    600:*n*2
Homo, ad unguem factus h., 95:*n*5
  ecce h., 40:*n*5
  naked ape H. sapiens, 759:8
  proponet Deus disponit, 132:*n*7
  sum humani nil a me alienum puto,
    85:*n*13
Homos, became one of stately h. of
    England, 410:*n*1
Honest, a few h. men, 246:24
  ale-house, 245:21
  and wise men rule, 338:13
  angler, 245:15
  anglers or very h. men, 245:29
  armor is his h. thought, 227:6
  as world goes, 195:16
  day is for h. men, 68:25
  depository of public interests, 345:4
  dies an h. fellow, 236:*n*3
  direct and h. not safe, 207:12
  doubt, 457:26
  exceeding poor man, 180:15
  George Third h. dullard, 564:21
  God noblest work of man, 520:15
  good h. painful sermon, 279:4
  good to be h. and true, 364:4
  gude to be h. and true, 779:20
  hand that is h. and hearty, 377:16
  hard-working ancestry, 686:17
  here lies a truly h. man, 264:21
  I one of few h. people, 694:8
  in every h. hand a whip, 208:2
  labor bears lovely face, 227:18
  looking for h. man, 77:5
  man close-buttoned, 335:15
  man looked h. enough, 526:1
  man sent to lie abroad, 227:12
  man's aboon his might, 363:22
  man's the noblest work of God,
    301:18, 361:10
  merry and yet h. too, 183:6
  nation secure only while h., 481:1
  no such thing as h. man, 296:26
  not h. that filleth own nest, 135:20
  not so h. more h., 466:*n*1
  peace and h. friendship, 344:9
  politician stays bought, 422:15
  politicians long step from h. men,
    447:22
  poor but h., 203:11, 782:17
  prejudices of Englishman, 293:7
  religion made h. woman of super-
    natural, 722:2
  room for h. men, 341:3
  six h. servingmen, 593:8
  social friendly h. man, 361:12

Honest (*continued*)
  soul that can be h., 236:7
  tale speeds plainly told, 166:7
  taught in intellectually h. form,
    738:11
  thief tender murderer, 466:10
  tired of h. things, 684:10
  to no purpose, 102:5
  too h. to steal, 781:2
  twelve h. men, 296:22
  water, 211:25
  whatsoever things are h., 44:35
  win us with h. trifles, 212:21
  words suffered corruption, 237:4
Honesta turpitudo est pro causa bona,
    99:*n*2
Honestly, let us walk h., 42:23
Honesty, armed so strong in h.,
    189:16
  corruption wins not more than h.,
    225:21
  is his fault, 212:2
  is praised and starves, 108:16
  love paradox without losing h.,
    432:12
  manhood nor fellowship, 176:35
  rich h. dwells like miser, 192:15
  root of h. in good education, 107:6
  thy h. and love, 206:19
Honesty's best policy, 151:5
Honey and plenty of money, 471:31
  eating bread and h., 790:1
  fill hives with h. and wax, 288:17
  gather h. all the day, 294:9
  I just forgot to duck, 691:8
  in the carcass of the lion, 11:11
  in the horn, 780:1
  land flowing with milk and h., 8:26
  land of h., 10:16
  locusts and wild h., 32:30
  milk and h., 8:26, 482:10
  no go my h. love, 722:4
  nor h. make nor pair, 383:14
  Pedigree of H., 514:9
  speech sweeter than h., 50:30
  still for tea, 662:19
  surfeited with h., 178:11
  sweeter than h. and honeycomb,
    16:11
  this Self is h. of all beings, 50:17
  very h. of earthly joy, 266:16
  with milk and h. blessed, 482:10
Honeybee, hive for the h., 594:21
Honeybees, so work the h., 184:23
Honeycomb, dipped rod in h., 11:35
  lips of a strange woman drop as h.,
    20:26
  sweeter than honey and the h.,
    16:11
  Will H. calls ladies, 293:23
  wrath sweeter than h., 52:14
Honeydew, on h. hath fed, 382:25
Honeyed, filled thicket with h. song,
    73:8
  Muses gave me h. gift, 83:1
  steeped amid h. morphine, 489:12
  words like bees, 660:21
Honey-heavy dew of slumber, 188:6
Honeyless, leave them h., 189:22
Honi soit qui mal y pense, 127:13

Honks, goose h. high, 779:*n*4
Honor, accompany old age as h.,
    216:9
  action faithful h. clear, 300:24
  all lost save h., 139:6
  all men, 46:23
  and greatness of his name, 226:9
  as valiant I h. him, 188:26
  bards have a share of h., 53:17
  before h. is humility, 21:29
  belongs to soul, 110:12
  bright, 200:24
  by h. and dishonor, 44:5
  can h. set a leg, 178:33
  changes labor from burden to h.,
    638:9
  chastity of h., 332:14
  Christmas in heart, 470:12
  comes a pilgrim gray, 324:11
  comes from Zeus, 51:6
  dearer than life, 150:4
  depends on opinion of mob, 278:13
  desirous of h. and glory, 278:17
  die with h., 584:1
  done with Hope and H., 592:4
  favor well bestowed an h., 293:24
  foe while you strike, 586:12
  free man abide with h., 477:13
  friend who prospered, 63:13
  from books of h. razed, 220:14
  full of days riches and h., 13:20
  giving h. unto the wife, 46:25
  good death does h. to whole life,
    127:10
  his memory, 233:5
  hurt that H. feels, 455:16
  if we can vertical man, 720:2
  in her left hand riches and h., 20:20
  is a mere scutcheon, 178:33
  jealous in h., 191:3
  lacking neither h. nor lyre, 95:30
  let it look like perfect h., 217:2
  life and h. in hands, 522:13
  like an island, 280:16
  louder talked of h., 425:*n*1
  love in excess brings nor h., 68:11
  loved I not h. more, 267:15
  make one vessel unto h., 42:10
  maligners of his h., 520:11
  man of h. regrets discreditable act,
    642:22
  man willing to sink, 485:7
  map of h. in thy face, 163:25
  may we h. law, 395:8
  men who have a sense of h., 52:8
  mine h. is my life, 170:26
  national h. national property, 360:9
  neither property nor h. touched,
    136:16
  new-made h. doth forget, 169:16
  no h. in sure success, 673:9
  no longer live with h., 584:1
  not least in h. or applause, 154:*n*2
  not pay h. with tears, 84:17
  nought in hate all in h., 208:15
  of striking blow for freedom, 664:2
  or dishonor to last generation,
    449:16
  our sacred h., 343:4
  peace with h., 435:14, 606:10

Honor (*continued*)

peace without h. not peace, 406:6
peasants carry h. in their hands, 239:12
peereth in meanest habit, 167:31
perseverance keeps h. bright, 200:24
physician, 32:10
pluck bright h. from moon, 177:9
pluck up drowned h., 177:9
post of h. is private station, 292:13
pricks me on, 178:33
prophet not without h., 35:13
purchased by merit, 180:27
quaint h. turn to dust, 268:16
rooted in dishonor, 459:15
sense of h. in action, 72:7
set h. in one eye, 187:19
shall uphold the humble, 23:11
signed with their h., 727:10
sin to covet h., 185:21
sin to prefer life to h., 109:6
sinks, 328:9
so long shall your h. endure, 93:24
stain in thine h., 32:8
strength and h. are her clothing, 23:19
subject of my story, 187:20
take h. from me and life done, 170:26
that h. would thee do, 184:28
the king, 46:23
those they have slain, 495:12
through his h. I conquered him, 239:12
thy father and mother, 9:12
to whom honor due, 42:21
travels in strait so narrow, 201:1
truth above friends, 77:26
what is h. a word, 178:33
what is left when h. lost, 99:9
when faith lost h. dies, 443:4
whom king delighteth to h., 13:25
with native h. clad, 258:11
words such as h. obscene, 701:14
Honorable, all h. men, 188:29
ancient and h., 26:9
and glorious, 336:17
Brutus is an h. man, 188:29
conquests, 331:25
designs were strictly h., 311:28
get loose from h. engagement, 330:24
have that which is truly h., 80:1
intentions h., 336:6
murderer, 208:15
no title more h., 646:14
not h. to tell lies, 67:13
object only of war h., 341:4
obstinate truthful man, 471:1
politics most h. adventure, 628:3
retreat, 191:12
style of Christian, 247:16
to die for one's country, 96:14
true and h. wife, 188:8
yet write verse badly, 269:16
Honorably, to die h. greatest virtue, 60:12
Honored among foxes, 737:18
among wagons, 737:15
bones, 251:2

Honored (*continued*)

custom more h. in breach, 194:8
followed him h. him, 464:23
how loved how h. once, 300:9
in their generations, 32:14
man in hasty days h. for them, 550:1
of them all, 455:1
these h. dead, 450:2
Honorificabilitudinitatibus, 169:6
Honoring, not so much h. thee, 232:16
Honor's, can h. voice provoke, 322:10
listen for dear h. sake, 253:11
when h. at the stake, 198:14
Honors acquired by unrighteousness, 61:10
bears his blushing h., 225:16
beauties wits, 229:5
female sex excluded from h. and offices, 347:11
gave his h. to the world, 226:2
mindless of its just h., 377:13
people I cannot win with h., 271:15
Hood, him that wears a h., 144:11
more than a h. to make monk, 118:*n*7
Hooded, one grand h. phantom, 486:18
Hoodoo, Mumbo-Jumbo will h. you, 637:10
Hoof, head and h. of Law, 592:17
whatsoever parteth the h., 9:21
Hoofs of swinish multitude, 332:17
Hook, bait the h. well, 186:30
draw out leviathan with a h., 15:21
spares next swath, 416:14
without bait, 433:1
Hook-nosed fellow of Rome, 184:8
Hooks, silver h., 229:10
Hoop of the nation, 587:5
Hoops, grapple with h. of steel, 193:29
Hooray and up she rises, 793:11
Hoosier, face like h. Michael Angelo, 491:11
Hooting and shrieking, 187:28
at glorious sun, 382:18
Hoots, owl that nightly h., 173:11
Hop, lets it h. a little, 175:14
light ladies, 556:17
Hope, Admiral cheered them holding out h., 134:7
against h. believed in h., 41:41
all h. abandon who enter here, 125:6
all we h. in Heaven, 451:6
all will yet be well, 448:16
Americans h. of world, 327:12
animated by faith and h., 314:18
because I do not h., 669:13
beyond h. and despair, 669:16
beyond shadow of dream, 414:13
blessed h. whereof he knew, 540:11
break it to our h., 216:20
certain h. of Resurrection, 50:8
cradle of h., 634:14
days are spent without h., 14:7
death of h. and despair, 671:21

Hope (*continued*)

deferred maketh the heart sick, 21:14
Democratic Party without h. of posterity, 516:1
done with H. and Honor, 592:4
extinguish h. from soul, 565:21
farewell h., 258:6
fear cannot be without h., 278:6
feed on h., 154:5
fondest h. decay, 392:13
fooled with h., 273:16
for a season, 388:23
for helmet the h. of salvation, 45:7
for the best, 380:4
for years to come, 294:14
forks and h., 519:24
from h. and fear set free, 534:15
frustrate of his h., 254:15
full of immortality, 30:23
good breakfast bad supper, 158:20
help for living h. for dead, 520:14
I die before I get old, 773:18
if youth season of h., 483:28
illusions of h., 339:7
in the day of evil, 28:32
in trembling h. repose, 322:24
is there any better h., 449:5
is to expect something for nothing, 564:2
is waking dream, 77:9
land of h. and glory, 585:5
last best h. of earth, 449:16
lies to mortals, 580:4
like taper's light, 328:5
lined himself with h., 183:25
little h. of deliverance, 768:12
lives on h. die fasting, 310:8
look forward with h., 623:2
memory outlive his life, 197:8
men in exile feed on h., 63:19
my good vain h. of gain, 156:22
my h. my hap my love, 148:9
my h. my love, 249:30
never comes, 255:24
never to h. again, 225:16
no more H. no more Glory, 617:11
no other medicine but h., 204:7
nor love nor friend, 561:21
not endure another's h., 287:5
not h. and no help came, 721:3
not thing with feathers, 767:12
now abideth h., 43:16
nursing unconquerable h., 498:13
of fair advantages, 180:22
of glory, 49:5
of pride and power, 451:8
of the ungodly, 30:26
on h. wretch relies, 328:4
one jot of heart or h., 255:15
one will cut halter, 250:15
only h. lies in despair, 281:8
past h. past cure past help, 176:9
phantoms of h., 314:9
plummets to dust of h., 65:18
prisoners of h., 30:4
ray of h. blown out, 448:10
safety to h. not safety, 93:33
saved by h., 684:18
sin was too much h., 232:10

Hope (*continued*)
springs eternal, 301:6
that there it not withered be, 232:16
the thing with feathers, 511:20
things you do not h. happen, 84:1
this government best h., 344:6
to h. till H. creates, 407:6
to see Pilot, 460:13
to the end, 46:19
to turn again, 669:13
triumph of h. over experience, 316:8
true h. is swift, 166:11
understood terror and h., 744:9
virtue flock to their aid, 431:15
what was dead was H., 567:19
whence this pleasing h., 292:14
which guides changeful mind, 64:16
while life there's h., 86:3, 87:23
whose h. the Lord is, 28:29
without all h. of day, 261:7
without h. we live in desire, 125:13
without object cannot live, 383:15
work without H., 383:15
Hoped, substance of things h. for, 45:38
we were broken-hearted, 534:17
Hopeful, elders h. about us, 483:28
green stuff woven, 488:19
hey but I'm h., 529:19
Hopeless fancy feigned, 456:14
grief passionless, 438:17
passion, 463:14
so huge so h., 514:13
we doctors know h. case, 689:7
woes of h. lovers, 275:10
Hopelessness of early youth, 483:19
path leads to despair utter h., 767:16
Hope's true gage, 152:16
Hopes, adversity not without h., 159:8
and fears of all years, 524:9
hearts h. prayers tears, 441:19
if h. were dupes fears may be liars, 483:3
life's span forbids us enter on h., 95:19
like towering falcons, 287:16
no more change name, 376:4
of future years, 441:18
remnants of childhood h. of adult-hood, 708:6
stirred up with high h., 254:20
tender leaves of h., 225:16
that resemble regrets, 482:15
that St. Nicholas, 391:6
vain h. like dreams of those who wake, 105:12
vanity of human h., 313:26
wholly h. to be, 467:14
Hoping, tender yearning sweet h., 365:12
trembling h. lingering, 299:8
Hopkins, Mark H. on one end, 516:3
Hopping, meager shriveled h., 332:18
through frothy waves, 519:2
Horace, studied spontaneity of H., 105:8
whom I hated so, 400:19
Horatii curiosa felicitas, 105:*n*3

Horatio, I knew him H., 199:8
in my mind's eye H., 193:15
more things in heaven H., 195:3
speak to it H., 192:21
thrift thrift H., 193:14
to what base uses we may return H., 199:9
Horde, society one polished h., 403:17
Horeb, Moses in H. struck rock, 748:9
Horizon, dusk on eastern h., 690:18
of dogs, 699:6
of his homing, 672:2
our h. never at our elbows, 478:25
Horizon's edge, 491:3
Horizontal, cord into h. line, 411:12
one, 720:2
Horn, barter that h., 597:5
beetle winds sullen h., 324:14
blow wreathed h., 376:12
come blow h., 789:4
cow with crumpled h., 792:24
Dinah blow your h., 780:6
gate of h., 54:9, 94:17
God winding lonely h., 595:6
gray-fly winds sultry h., 253:17
hand on h., 786:4
honey in the h., 780:1
hounds and h., 251:12
huntsman winds his h., 311:15
lusty h., 192:6
mouth of Plenty's h., 597:5
of hunter on hill, 424:7
one blast upon bugle h., 379:1
poured through mellow h., 324:16
Roland sound your h., 121:12
sound of h. at night, 421:3
sound upon bugle h., 455:8
tunes frozen up in h., 341:12
with his hounds and h., 413:20
Horned Moon with one bright star, 381:16
Horner, little Jack H., 788:11
Hornets, bees for flies and h. for bees, 138:4
cobwebs let h. through, 288:18
Horns, hang caps on h. o' the moon, 218:24
like Kyloe cow, 789:17
of Elfland, 456:12
of my dilemma, 320:25
sound of h. and motors, 668:23
sound of hunting h., 641:10
taking bull by both h. kissed her, 644:11
Horny hands of toil, 484:19
Horresco referens, 93:*n*15
Horrible, hence h. shadow, 215:8
imaginings, 212:23
invention the bourgeois, 496:2
that lust and rage, 599:14
voice, 73:1
Horribly, I will h. revenge, 185:26
live by medicine live h., 312:8
stuffed with epithets, 205:8
Horrid, blow h. deed in every eye, 213:7
dream h. dreams, 487:3
hideous notes of woe, 403:19
image doth unfix hair, 212:23

Horrid (*continued*)
life demd h. grind, 469:24
shapes and shrieks, 251:6
when bad she was h., 442:25
Horridly to shake our disposition, 194:11
Horror, Dead Sea makes h., 632:16
fell upon Christian, 272:25
lived through this h., 654:15
of falling into naught, 292:14
of outer darkness, 520:9
of that moment, 518:14
screams of h. rend, 299:18
soul of plot, 452:7
the h. the h., 573:8
this h. is ours, 728:3
universal h. unbend, 645:6
Horror's, on h. head horrors, 207:11
Horrors accumulate, 207:11
congenial h. hail, 307:16
of half known life, 486:27
sunset stained with mystic h., 565:14
supped full with h., 216:13
Horrorshow, shut her up h. and lovely, 740:15
Horse stood near stable door, 776:*n*6
a dog a h. a rat, 211:19
and his rider hath he thrown, 9:2
bean-fed h. beguile, 173:2
beggars mounted run h. to death, 164:12
body my h. my hound, 747:12
boot saddle to h. and away, 464:15
brewer's h., 178:15
bring h. to water, 141:28
Caligula's h. made Consul, 385:15
call me h., 177:24
cart before h., 142:21
choice of h. and wife, 497:2
dark h., 434:20
dearer than his h., 455:10
death on his pale h., 260:16
difference of opinion makes h.-races, 527:18
dominated mind of early races, 657:20
donkey like h. translated into Dutch, 342:16
ego's relation to id as rider to h., 569:13
far back in soul h. prances, 657:20
fine lady upon white h., 790:3
flung himself on h., 607:8
foot an' artillery, 654:13
for want of h. rider lost, 244:28, 310:10
for want of shoe h. lost, 244:28, 310:10
give man h. he can ride, 523:15
give me another h., 166:13
great h. of gold, 688:6
guide h. along path it wants to go, 569:13
happy h. to bear Antony, 217:5
hast thou given the h. strength, 15:15
hey for boot and h., 484:15
horsewhip you if had a h., 654:7
I am not so poor a h., 450:5

Horse (*continued*)

in silence champed, 616:22
in the mountain, 699:3
know two things about the h.,
 630:14
knows the way, 427:7
leene as is a rake, 129:20
lord if you had h., 657:20
love and marriage like h. and carriage, 732:11
must think it queer, 623:17
my h. my wife my name, 434:8
my kingdom for a h., 166:17
nation, 787:3
never look gift h. in mouth, 114:14
noblest conquest of man, 311:6
nothing but talk of his h., 179:29
O for a h. with wings, 219:27
of different color, 202:n2
of our courage, 750:2
of that color, 202:7
old h. stumbles and nods, 540:22
pale h., 47:19, 260:16
philosophy a good h., 329:1
shoe the h., 792:21
short h. soon curried, 141:16
sits on h. at hostess' door, 169:22
spur not unbroken h., 379:20
Turquoise H. of Johano-ai, 787:11
uses folly like stalking h., 192:18
when h. stolen fool shuts stable,
 141:n10
where's the bloody h., 707:1
Horseback, beggar on h., 164:n4
beggar upon h., 599:13
man on h., 780:18
on h. through dreary tract, 452:4
Horsed upon sightless couriers, 213:7
Horseleach hath two daughters, 23:14
Horseman pass by, 600:3
Horsemanship, forgetful of his h.,
 52:10
witch world with noble h., 178:22
Horsemen, chariot and h. of Israel,
 13:5
four h. of Apocalypse, 602:6
Four H. of Notre Dame, 643:n5
Horsemill, desire a h., 234:21
Horse's, 'ear h. legs, 460:2
trusts in h. health, 210:13
Horses, all the king's h., 790:13
and poets not overfed, 151:28
as fed h. in the morning, 28:14
black are the h., 699:7
carriages without h. go, 777:14
chariot and h. of fire, 13:4
come saddle your h., 379:27
don't do it and frighten h., 590:7
England hell of h., 154:18
handling of blooded h., 496:4
heaven in which no h., 563:4
if cattle and h. had hands, 60:5
if wishes were h., 272:4
men hanged that h. not be stolen,
 280:1
more careful of breed of h. than
 children, 282:22
not swap h., 450:5
oats in England given to h., 314:6
of instruction, 357:9

Horses (*continued*)

price of thousand h., 613:7
run slowly h. of night, 101:10
slowly run O h. of night, 162:n9
they shoot h. don't they, 697:10
watered our h. in Helicon, 157:15
which h. bear him best, 163:10
wild white h. play, 497:6
women h. economic factors in society, 583:3
would draw gods like horses, 60:5
Horses' heels over paving, 670:4
Horseshoes, laws flung like h., 681:8
Horsewhip, I'd h. you if had a horse,
 654:7
Horus non numero nisi serenas,
 390:17
Hose, washed me out of turret with
 h., 735:21
youthful h. well saved, 191:3
Hospitable, in peace generous h.,
 404:21
on h. thoughts intent, 259:10
Hospital, first requirement in H.,
 492:3
tray of narcotics, 730:20
whole earth our h., 671:7
world not inn but h., 248:21
Hospitality, given to h., 42:15
Host, Hesperus led starry h., 258:19
many an old h. damned, 177:31
of golden daffodils, 375:19
one more drink be under h., 687:14
praise Him heavenly h., 280:21
though an h. should encamp, 16:22
tie of h. and guest, 63:23
time like fashionable h., 201:2
with angelic h. proclaim, 312:17
Hostage, you are eternity's h., 679:18
Hostages to fortune, 159:11
Hostess', sits on horse at h. door,
 169:22
Hostesses make parties as ministers
 cabinets, 483:30
Hostile, universe not h. nor friendly,
 637:4
Hostilities, victory when opponent
 surrenders before h., 80:20
Hostility, eternal h. against tyranny,
 344:4
sorrow to disarm h., 442:1
Host's Canary wine, 416:12
Hosts, holy is the Lord of h., 26:1
Lord God of H., 592:25
Lord of h. King of glory, 16:20
of Error, 582:2
Hot and bothered, 593:26
and cold and moist and dry, 257:n5
and rebellious liquors, 190:11
as hell, 354:3
blow h. and cold, 59:12
can one go upon h. coals, 20:30
cat on h. tin roof, 272:n4
cold and h. moist and dry, 275:7
cold light and h. shade, 358:14
cold moist and dry, 257:19
conscience seared with h. iron,
 45:14
cross buns, 790:9
fair h. wench in taffeta, 176:24

Hot (*continued*)

feel h. and think cold, 667:3
for certainties, 508:30
ginger h. i' the mouth, 202:5
hammer iron when h., 99:8
heat flow from h. to cold object,
 501:n1
I would thou wert cold or h., 47:13
in my h. youth, 96:22
Just Add H. Water, 688:12
lead effective from linotype, 717:5
little pot and soon h., 167:27
long h. summer, 696:10
my heart was h. within me, 17:6
my love was so h., 398:5
neither cold nor h., 47:13
pease-porridge h., 790:10
sleep is cold for the h., 151:15
small h. bird, 559:19
snake came on h. h. day, 657:12
so h. that it singe yourself, 225:3
temper leaps over, 179:28
time in old town tonight, 589:2
w'en stew smokin' h., 615:2
when iron is h. strike, 99:n3
which way h. air blows, 586:5
why sea boiling h., 519:3
your wit's too h., 168:24
Hotel, back to h. in rain, 701:17
born in goddam h. room dying in h.
 room, 674:9
Heartbreak H., 768:3
instead of hymns, 640:6
queen of this summer h., 759:12
refuge from home life, 570:18
smoke-filled room in h., 582:18
terrible strange-looking h., 753:14
Hotels, big peppermint h., 739:7
people in h., 605:23
Hothouse, no h. flowers, 653:28
Hotness, day in its h., 498:2
Hotspur of the North, 177:20
Hottentot, Mr. Whitman's Venus H.
 wench, 535:9
Hotter, pass from colder to h., 501:8
Hound dog cryin' all the time, 765:7
footprints of gigantic h., 577:25
hold with hare run with h., 141:18
mongrel puppy whelp h., 328:26
my horse my h., 747:12
single H., 513:7
Hounds and horn, 251:12
carcass fit for h., 188:4
four lean h., 688:7
join in glorious cry, 311:15
moon men and barking h., 690:20
noise like questing of thirty h.,
 133:5
of spring, 533:8
such h. such hawks, 785:16
with his h. and horn, 413:20
Hour before dawn silent, 632:15
books of the h., 487:23
childhood's h., 392:13, 451:9
Children's H., 442:8
cometh and now is, 39:48
crowded h. of glorious life, 333:8
dark h. or twain, 214:19
destined H., 445:11
eternity in an h., 359:5

Hour (*continued*)
    every h. a miracle, 491:4
    every h. that passes O, 361:24
    fall that very h., 202:11
    far fierce h. and sweet, 619:9
    fluster of h. badly spent, 729:15
    fools for I also had my h., 619:9
    for one short h. see, 458:25
    from h. to h. we ripe, 190:23
    had I died h. before, 214:15
    happiest day happiest h., 451:8
    hazard of doubtful h., 178:19
    I have had my h., 275:1
    I was born, 780:1
    improve each shining h., 294:9
    inevitable h., 322:8
    is at hand, 36:32
    is not yet come, 39:38
    its h. come round at last, 596:20
    last h. of my life, 308:17
    laugh an h. by his dial, 190:24
    lives its little h., 411:7, 644:8
    living at this h., 374:19
    look on you when last h. comes,
        101:4
    look thy last every h., 617:1
    Lord through this h., 783:4
    matched us with His h., 663:4
    met me in evil h., 361:19
    more desirable than fortunate h.,
        91:8
    nighing his h., 579:21
    not an h. more or less, 211:10
    not showpiece of an h., 71:19
    nothing can bring back h., 375:14
    now's the h., 363:19
    of adversity, 396:2
    of departure has arrived, 74:18
    of thoughtless youth, 373:5
    of truth now always, 630:18
    one bare h. to live, 162:22
    one dead deathless h., 509:23
    our h. is marked, 370:20
    rash hand in evil h., 260:7
    ripe, 184:12
    serve the future h., 377:6
    speak an h. ready now, 572:15
    stay longer in h., 533:1
    struts and frets his h., 216:14
    takes away things, 316:33
    that turns back longing of seafarers,
        126:11
    the fifty-minute h., 736:4
    the wished the trysted h., 363:17
    this was their finest h., 620:8
    thou the day I the h., 530:4
    time and the h., 212:25
    torturing h., 321:18
    two hundred fifty words every quar-
        ter h., 476:6
    uncertain h. before morning, 672:2
    violet h., 669:1
    watch with me one h., 36:31
    what sweet h. yields, 409:22
    wherein man might be happy, 245:9
    who drowsy at that h., 249:7
    wonder of an h., 399:14
Hour's, never spent h. talk withal,
    168:23
    sleep before midnight, 245:2

Hours, age not numbered by h., 148:8
    and minutes dollars and cents,
        310:*n*3
    arrest your course, 405:7
    better three h. too soon, 182:29
    count only sunny h., 390:*n*3
    creeping h. of time, 190:29
    entertain lag-end with quiet h.,
        178:29
    golden h. on angel wings, 363:13
    his brief h. and weeks, 222:2
    I once enjoyed, 333:21
    I spent with thee, 586:17
    life short quiet h. few, 487:22
    mournful midnight h., 349:7
    narrowing dark h., 696:4
    nor h. days months, 228:12
    redeem these h., 233:19
    seven h. to law, 152:*n*3
    six h. in sleep, 152:7
    sixteen h. ago Hiroshima, 655:6
    sorrow breaks reposing h., 165:32
    steal h. from night, 392:1
    success unexpected in common h.,
        478:36
    sweetest h. e'er I spend, 362:1
    three h. a day what man ought to
        write, 476:5
    Time in h. days years, 270:7
    to which Heaven doth chime, 270:2
    two golden h., 419:4
    unless h. cups of sack, 176:24
    waked by circling h., 259:16
    weary of days and h., 534:13
    what h. O what black h., 551:15
    Woman in our h. of ease, 378:14
House, all the h. of Israel played, 12:5
    all through the h., 391:6
    appointed for all living, 14:44
    bear witness to his piety, 369:1
    blessings on this h., 338:13
    body my h. my horse my hound,
        747:12
    built on sand, 34:15
    Bustle in a H. Morning after Death,
        513:17
    by the side of the road, 51:22,
        574:14
    call upon my soul within the h.,
        201:27
    child draws inscrutable h., 729:8
    children's h. of make believe,
        624:17
    civilized man's h. prison, 476:21
    clergyman so much about h., 524:19
    covet thy neighbor's h., 9:12
    crooked h., 791:11
    daughter in mother's h., 592:24
    daughters of my father's h., 202:15
    divided against itself, 37:20, 448:7
    doll in the doll's h., 471:20
    doorkeeper in h. of my God, 18:7
    dust inbreathed was h., 671:21
    dwell in h. of the Lord, 16:17
    eaten out of h. and home, 183:30
    Eden old-fashioned H., 514:11
    emperor in mine own h., 152:*n*2
    evil shall not depart from his h.,
        21:35
    except the Lord build the h., 19:29

House (*continued*)
    fell not, 34:14
    filled her h. with blacks, 752:10
    for future prison for present, 736:16
    God erects h. of prayer, 285:14
    great h. of Tarquin, 425:13
    half of h. be pulled down, 587:8
    harrow h. of dead, 720:4
    he that troubleth own h., 21:10
    he who sits at door of h., 794:2
    heap of stones not h., 565:6
    heart keeps open h., 724:10
    hill and h. live together, 608:12
    hog whole h., 742:21
    I pass through on way, 752:6
    if come to my h. I will come to
        yours, 102:8
    in my Father's h., 40:26
    in woodsman's h. knives wood,
        794:4
    is as fortress, 152:4
    is in village though, 623:16
    keepers of the h. shall tremble,
        24:27
    keeps his h. in hand, 66:14
    kept h. the Past and I, 540:17
    labor of women in h., 583:3
    let us go into the h. of the Lord,
        19:26
    lilting h., 737:14
    lion in thy h., 31:9
    little h. of my own, 644:13
    little h. well filled, 309:13
    lived in little h., 792:12
    look at my dead h., 714:3
    machine for living in, 663:21
    made of dawn, 787:9
    make h. home, 644:16
    make my h. your inn, 664:11
    man so in way in h., 461:8
    man's h. his castle, 152:3
    master of the h. cometh, 37:34
    Matilda and h. burned, 609:4
    moat defensive to a h., 171:9
    moon in seventh h., 770:1
    my Father's h. not h. of merchan-
        dise, 39:42
    my h. called h. of prayer, 35:42
    my h. though small, 244:26
    no legal slaves except mistress of h.,
        440:4
    no tool heard in h., 12:23
    nor my h. now my h., 699:4
    not a h. where there was not one
        dead, 8:41
    of bondage, 8:42
    of feasting, 24:7
    of God, 7:42
    of good stone, 659:14
    of Have, 538:3
    of marriage, 716:22
    of mourning, 24:7
    of Peers throughout war, 530:13
    of prayer, 35:42, 285:14
    of Representatives, 339:3
    of the Lord, 19:26
    of Usher, 452:4
    of Want, 538:3
    on fire children burn, 788:16
    open h. in evening, 619:4

House *(continued)*
   ornament of h. friends, 433:11
   our h. a playroom, 507:19
   out of the h. of bondage, 8:42
   part of man's Self, 545:20
   peace to this h., 38:18
   quit h. never darken threshold,
     492:2
   return no more to his h., 14:8
   rich honesty in poor h., 192:15
   rose up like scenery, 612:13
   ruin decay in H. on Hill, 608:2
   rule his own h., 45:12
   set h. on fire to roast eggs, 159:25
   set thine h. in order, 13:13
   seven-pillared worthy h., 673:8
   shelters friend, 431:36
   should be of hill, 608:12
   sky flows into h., 700:10
   small h. and large garden, 266:17
   so fair a h., 224:2
   sought for All, 757:5
   sweet air coming into h., 664:4
   that Jack built, 792:24
   them that join h. to h., 25:38
   to be let for life, 242:9
   to lodge friend, 302:23
   upon another man's ground, 182:28
   wandering about from h. to h.,
     45:19
   we all dwell in h. of world, 537:18
   where I was born, 422:19
   whose h. is glass, 244:17
   wisdom hath builded her h., 21:1
   wounded in h. of my friends, 30:6
   you take my h., 182:5
Housed where it gets possession,
   166:28
Household, breathing h. laws, 374:14
   happy genius of my h., 653:30
   keep h. in oneness, 53:10
   of Impulse mourns, 720:13
   permission to go out from h., 65:4
   she looketh well to ways of her h.,
     23:20
Households, clergymen's h. unhappy,
   524:19
   few admired by own h., 146:17
Houseless heads and unfed sides,
   210:3
Housemaids, damp souls of h., 667:22
Houses all gone under sea, 671:2
   and farms pillaged, 336:14
   build h. and inhabit them, 28:12
   destroyed by rats, 281:22
   devour widows' h., 37:32
   great h. rain down, 66:15
   nimble in selling h., 658:4
   old h. mended, 291:24
   people in glass h., 244:*n*4
   plague o' both h., 175:28
   signs of leaping h., 176:24
   too new to be haunted, 763:3
   useful or beautiful in h., 523:9
   very h. seem asleep, 374:13
Housetop, as a sparrow alone upon
   the h., 18:24
Housewife, here's to the h. that's
   thrifty, 352:29
   ply evening care, 322:6

Housewifery, players in your h., 206:5
Housewife's, tease the h. wool, 253:10
Housewives, good h. now may say,
   238:1
   in your beds, 206:5
   mothers and h. vacationless, 719:11
Houston Tranquility Base here, 762:12
Hovel, golden mean avoids poverty of
   h., 96:7
Hover, o'er shady groves they h.,
   237:13
   through fog and filthy air, 212:10
Hovered, through all tasks it h. nigh,
   540:17
How and Where and Who, 593:8
   can these things be, 39:45
   do you do again, 792:17
   feel to be on your own, 771:9
   had I come to be here, 729:11
   long Catiline, 87:6
   many ages hence, 188:18
   much more is half than whole,
     54:21
   not to do it, 471:8
   odd of God, 656:14
   should man be just, 14:10
How-de-do, pretty h., 531:2
Howl howl howl howl, 211:17
   I hear a famisht h., 734:14
   Lady h. in Irish, 178:9
   live with wolves h. like wolf, 793:6
   same way for flesh of man, 766:2
   scarcely a h. or groan, 519:22
Howled, cracked growled roared h.,
   381:4
Howling as of a hen-yard, 659:13
   down the street, 790:5
   flies in night in h. storm, 358:4
   neither yield to h. of wolf, 157:6
   no more hear tempest h., 348:3
   village of H., 708:7
   woe, 356:2
Howls hoo and rises, 639:23
Howth Castle and Environs, 647:18
Hub, Boston State-House h., 447:13
Hubbard, old mother H., 790:18
Huckleberry Finn, 702:2
Huddled masses, 558:1
Hue, add another h. to rainbow,
   170:9
   as smart ship grew in stature grace
     h., 540:17
   country represented wild and savage
     h., 240:9
   cuckoo-buds of yellow h., 169:12
   flowers of all h., 258:9
   heaven presents solid h., 623:13
   like when great painter dips, 406:14
   native h. of resolution, 196:10
   now turn different h., 59:23
   raise a h. and cry, 149:33
Huelga, viva la h., 758:3
Huffy Henry hid, 734:15
Hug dear deceit, 309:3
   it in my arms, 204:12
Huge, bed for this h. birth, 264:18
   cloudy symbols, 417:10
   so h. so hopeless, 514:13
   walk under his h. legs, 187:22
Hugest hearts that break, 514:7

Hugest *(continued)*
   Leviathan h. of living, 259:21
Hugged offender forgave offense,
   276:28
Hugger-mugger to inter him, 198:21
Hulk, here a sheer h., 348:3
Hull, water spurted through h.,
   565:12
Hulls, ships are only h., 65:16
Hum, busy h. of men, 251:17
   my ears h., 56:5
   of either army, 185:14
   of human cities torture, 400:4
   of mighty workings, 414:1
   still steeples h., 579:4
   thousand instruments h., 224:18
Human, Adam was but h., 527:7
   all h. life in monkeys and cats,
     548:9
   all h. must retrograde, 340:8
   all must love h. form, 356:14
   all right for woman to be h., 711:7
   all that h. hearts endure, 314:15
   alter h. nature, 583:5
   applause of single h. being, 317:19
   as I am if I am, 744:2
   bears stamp of h. condition, 146:18
   being crushed by books, 735:20
   being dissatisfied, 439:27
   being h. born alone, 660:18
   being h. though boys, 608:11
   being more or less, 738:6
   being through descent from group,
     574:12
   beings ever realize life, 697:15
   beings in underground den, 75:17
   beings into machines, 481:9
   beings live and progress, 605:7
   beings never more frightening,
     719:16
   bellyful of classics enemy to h. race,
     681:10
   benefit and enjoyment, 331:20
   best work the h. mind, 363:1
   body politic like h. body, 319:9
   body sacred, 489:24
   brain device to keep ears from grat-
     ing, 728:5
   burn books burn h. beings, 420:3
   Chariot that bears H. Soul, 514:2
   civilization scarcely h., 611:11
   combination or society, 247:13
   community, 650:5
   condition, 146:18
   conspiracy of h. beings, 601:7
   contrivance of h. wisdom, 332:11
   couple find true form, 722:10
   course of h. events, 343:2
   creatures' lives, 423:3
   crises of h. affairs, 355:11
   Cruelty has h. heart, 358:13
   custom guide of h. life, 318:13
   December 1910 h. character
     changed, 650:15
   dignity, 774:2
   distances between h. beings, 630:11
   each h. gift find place, 707:17
   earth's h. shores, 417:12
   engine waits, 669:1
   everything h. pathetic, 527:26

Human (*continued*)
  face divine, 257:24
  features composed of ten parts, 104:8
  felicity produced by little advantages, 311:4
  field of h. conflict, 620:10
  fighting for h. rights, 755:8
  figure interests me most, 607:16
  force h. beings to despise themselves, 707:15
  Form Display, 359:16
  four essential h. freedoms, 649:17
  free the h. will, 303:15
  fundamental h. rights, 655:23
  future of h. race, 632:2
  happiness of h. race, 331:25
  he served h. liberty, 598:9
  heart by which we live, 375:15
  heart has treasures, 476:11
  hearts to chew, 408:1
  highest type of h. nature, 493:10
  hope springs in h. breast, 301:6
  hum of h. cities, 400:4
  I had no h. fears, 374:1
  identify myself with something h., 736:2
  in h. life much endured, 314:11
  inextinguishable rights of h. nature, 368:15
  informer poor weak h. being, 695:17
  infringement of h. freedom, 364:9
  Jealousy has a h. face, 358:13
  kind not bear much reality, 670:11
  king's might greater than h., 70:12
  knowledge of h. nature, 387:10, 535:19
  life a Mansion, 418:5
  life might be pure freedom, 722:6
  life transient, 584:11
  live in h. imagination, 758:21
  Love the h. form divine, 356:13
  march of h. mind slow, 331:18
  Mercy has a h. heart, 356:13
  milk of h. kindness, 212:28
  more than h. arms, 645:6
  my Treatise of H. Nature, 318:16
  nature finer, 418:3
  nature made arrogant by consideration, 72:9
  nature seeming born again, 373:11
  nature weak in bookstore, 472:20
  no h. being understand another, 713:7
  no h. creature give orders to love, 436:17
  no h. thing of importance, 76:2
  no other difference between h. beings, 366:7
  nor h. spark is left, 304:2
  nothing h. is alien, 85:16
  O h. love, 451:6
  observer of h. nature, 468:21
  on my faithless arm, 720:16
  Peace the h. dress, 356:13
  Pity has a h. face, 356:13
  politics art of h. happiness, 590:12
  position in universe as h. being, 562:17

Human (*continued*)
  power cannot remove, 672:4
  predatory h. hands, 578:14
  primary h. affections, 498:8
  provide for h. wants, 332:11
  pursuit of h. glory, 246:8
  race born to fly upward, 126:14
  race has means for annihilating itself, 645:19
  race never have rest from evils, 75:15
  recognition as h. beings, 755:8
  relations perfectly exhibited, 79:14
  reverence h. nature, 392:18
  rights, 655:23
  rights over h. beings or monuments, 349:26
  rights to which committed, 741:3
  ruler having h. body as subject, 75:5
  same way with h. race, 633:8
  scientific thought h. progress, 554:10
  Secrecy the h. dress, 358:13
  socialism with h. face, 748:16
  solitude at depth of h. condition, 736:13
  sorrow of h. existence, 333:10
  species of two races, 387:24
  speech like cracked kettle, 496:6
  stares from every h. face, 720:11
  stars of h. race, 334:7
  stories repeating selves, 616:4
  subtlety never devise more than nature, 135:10
  subtracting from h. knowledge, 539:1
  suffering h. race, 497:16
  sum of h. things, 348:4
  tale of h. life, 333:10
  tamer of h. breast, 321:18
  Terror the h. form divine, 358:13
  things subject to decay, 274:25
  thought or form, 406:10
  three words for h. race, 568:7
  till H. nature came, 514:3
  to err is h., 107:18, 118:30, 299:4
  to step aside is h., 362:5
  understanding is false mirror, 158:14
  vanity of h. hopes, 313:26
  vast empire of h. society, 373:16
  voices wake us, 667:20
  weakness of h. mind, 277:21
  whole possible scope of h. ambition, 585:14
  wholeness of h. problem, 629:23
  wisdom of h. contrivances, 331:10
  wish I loved h. race, 584:3
  woman behave like full h. being, 767:2
  women's training in h. relations, 707:20
  world began without h. race, 723:21
Humane, harmonious and h. life, 501:1
  heaven and earth are not h., 56:15
Humani nil a me alienum puto, 85:n13

Humanité, il n'y a de réel que l'h., 421:n3
Humanity, address ourselves not to their h., 326:1
  common right of h., 448:11
  exalts delights adorns h., 397:22
  forehead of h., 414:12
  history life of h., 510:10
  idiom of frightened hopeful h., 715:6
  imitated h. so abominably, 197:1
  justice equity, 332:8
  law of h., 332:8
  nothing real except h., 421:9
  only three days old, 632:2
  reason and justice, 331:17
  science and art unite h., 755:11
  services of Europe to h., 629:16
  silence real crime against h., 702:15
  slavery of half of h., 722:10
  still sad music of h., 373:5
  there is one race h., 563:12
  victory for h., 419:5
  wearisome condition of h., 155:1
  with all its fears, 441:18
Humanized, deep distress hath h. my Soul, 376:7
Humanizes, liberal arts study h., 102:6
Humanizing, power of h. nature, 384:19
  whole body of society, 501:1
Humankind, lords of h. pass by, 328:13
  not bear much reality, 670:11
  of all tyrannies on h., 275:14
  porcelain clay of h., 275:26
  vices and follies of h., 290:35
Humble and hearty thanks, 49:5
  appearance of telephone, 516:7
  are usually envious, 278:8
  be it ever so h., 405:14
  frowned not on h. birth, 322:22
  heyday in blood is h., 197:31
  himself shall be exalted, 36:2
  honor shall uphold the h., 23:11
  livers in content, 225:8
  members of society, 369:11
  ne'er ebb to h. love, 207:15
  not only h. but umble, 470:n2
  pie, 470:37
  soft meek patient h., 227:19
  son of h. laborer, 645:1
  the greater the more h., 31:1
  through vainglory, 146:11
  very h. person, 470:28
  wisdom is h., 335:13
  with lure of the real, 640:19
Humbleness, whispering h., 180:9
Humbler heaven, 301:7
Humblest citizen of land, 582:2
  friends, 377:14
  peer of powerful, 520:10
Humbling, no h. of reality to precept, 756:9
Humbly beseech you of pardon, 207:1
  walk h. with thy God, 29:38
Humbug, bah h., 470:4
  conspiracy to lie and h., 601:7
  government of H. or Humdrum, 434:24

Hurt (*continued*)
  enemy and friend h. you to heart,
    527:33
  give delight and h. not, 224:18
  he who shall h. wren, 359:8
  if I don't h. her, 394:3
  man keenest in self-love, 507:12
  more afraid than h., 141:6
  no h. found upon Daniel, 29:19
  not the earth, 47:21
  panics produce as much good as h.,
    340:23
  power to h., 221:14
  somebody'll get h., 766:8
  sweareth to his own h., 16:5
  that Honor feels, 455:16
  their health it might h., 330:15
  they h. me I grow older, 659:3
  they shall not h. nor destroy, 26:11
  too badly h. to laugh, 449:14
  why should I h. thee, 320:18
Hurtles in darkened air, 323:12
Hurtless breaks, 211:4
Hurts, fellows it h. to think, 579:15
  it h. my hand, 207:20
  pinch which h. and is desired,
    218:18
  truth never h. teller, 468:8
Husband and wife keep a household,
  53:10
  any her h. rather than Christian,
    182:1
  at all times faithful h., 293:16
  being h. whole-time job, 602:2
  chaste to her h., 300:14
  children friends nothing to that,
    556:20
  delight of h. aunts infant, 674:12
  doth safely trust in her, 23:17
  easier to be lover than h., 422:7
  frae wife despises, 363:3
  give you h. and home, 53:10
  holy city adorned for h., 47:37
  I come, 218:17
  is known in the gates, 23:18
  light wife heavy h., 182:14
  lover in h. lost, 318:6
  Man-o'-War's 'er h., 592:19
  no worse a h. than best of men,
    217:13
  shape a h. out of, 463:n1
  sovereynetee over h., 131:10
  thankless h., 402:20
  till h. cools, 300:18
  virtuous woman a crown to her h.,
    21:11
  with beard, 186:16
  woman oweth duty to h., 167:35
  women stimulated by news wife left
    h., 717:7
Husbanded, so fathered and so h.,
  188:9
Husbandman waiteth for precious
  fruit, 46:16
Husbandry, edge of h., 194:1
  in heaven, 213:17
  ye are God's h., 42:32
Husband's, level in her h. heart,
  202:10

Husbands at chirche dore hadde fyve,
  130:1
  friends lovers h., 347:3
  think of fidelity not h., 646:16
  unlimited power into hands of h.,
    347:1
Hush hark deep sound strikes, 399:21
  my dear, 294:12
  with setting moon, 458:22
Hushed be every thought, 377:11
  in grim repose, 323:8
  in silence h. his soul, 376:21
  now air is h., 324:14
Hushing traffic of drowsy town,
  549:20
Husks, dead h. of life, 721:13
  strewed with h., 201:11
Husky, stormy h. brawling, 634:4
Hustle, tried to h. the East, 591:12
Hustled, Indian summer never h.,
  536:4
Huswife's, tease the h. wool, 253:10
Hut, love in h., 414:17
Hutchinson, isn't fair Mrs. H.
  screamed, 739:15
Huts, ragged h. greatest city, 490:5
Hyacinth, breasts like spikes of h.,
  699:5
  hair, 451:12
  sell bread and buy h., 118:9
  the Garden wears, 445:13
Hyacinths are dark too, 92:19
  to feed thy soul, 118:n2
Hybla, words rob H. bees, 189:22
Hybrid, Alexandria a h., 731:8
Hyde, Dr. Jekyll and Mr. H., 561:13
Hydra, monstrosity more prodigious
  than H., 97:n4
Hydrant, talking is a h. in the yard,
  625:13
Hydroptic earth hath drunk, 229:8
Hyena, man who sold h. skin, 621:15
  song of siren nor voice of h., 157:6
Hylas, je ne vous aime pas H.,
  286:n11
Hylax barks in doorway, 92:14
Hymn Brahmin sings, 430:11
  chants doleful h., 170:20
  sober as a h., 557:6
Hymns, chanting faint h. to moon,
  172:18
  hotel instead of h., 640:6
  psalms h. and spiritual songs, 44:26
  that fall out of wind, 640:6
  to thee morning h. ascended, 506:16
Hyperboles, three-piled h., 169:8
Hyperion to a satyr, 193:7
Hyperion's curls, 197:30
Hyphenated Americanism, 576:12
Hypocisies, some great events some
  mean h., 338:7
Hypocrisy, democracies cannot dispense with h., 666:18
  drowns in Pharisees' h., 679:17
  from pride vainglory and h., 49:8
  has ample wages, 138:9
  homage vice pays to virtue, 265:24
  of bishop, 346:2
  panics touchstones of h., 340:23
  speaking lies in h., 45:14

Hypocrisy (*continued*)
  vice of vices, 718:11
Hypocrite lecteur, 494:1
  reader, 494:1
  rotten to the core, 718:11
  scoundrel h. flatterer, 359:23
  sometimes more sometimes less,
    422:11
  thou h., 34:4
Hypocrites, cant of h. the worst,
  320:23
  effect of coercion to make h., 343:8
  enemies taunt us as h., 448:5
  not h. in sleep, 390:21
  scribes and Pharisees h., 36:3
Hypocritic Days, 430:6
Hypotheses, I frame no h., 281:26
Hypothesis, fertile h., 738:10
  no need of that h., 351:18
  slaying of h. by ugly f., 505:9
  whatever not deduced is h., 281:26
Hyrcan tiger, 215:7
Hyssop, purge me with h., 17:21
Hysterias trench confessions, 659:9
Hysterica passio, 209:17
Hysterical patients suffer from reminiscences, 569:5
  starving h. naked, 757:4

I

I accept the universe, 461:7
  am, 8:27
  am a Jew, 180:30
  am a Liberal, 500:10
  am a Roman citizen, 87:9
  am Actaeon, 101:22
  am Alpha and Omega, 48:4
  am always about in the Quad,
    673:n1
  am Duchess of Malfi still, 237:16
  am dying Egypt dying, 218:7
  am Fortune's fool, 175:29
  am from Missouri, 566:4
  am guilty of corruption, 158:16
  am he that liveth, 47:6
  am Heathcliff, 480:6
  am I you are you, 465:14
  am innocent of the blood, 37:7
  Am Jehovah said, 325:10
  am Madame Bovary, 496:15
  am master of my fate, 557:10
  am no more I, 699:4
  am not as other men, 39:8
  am not what I was, 96:27
  am only guinea pig I have, 691:18
  am quite myself again, 579:2
  am rising to a man's work, 111:13
  am Sir Oracle, 179:20
  am that I am, 8:27
  am that which began, 534:19
  am the androgyne, 762:6
  am the bread of life, 40:4
  am the door, 40:15
  am the good shepherd, 40:17
  am the grass, 634:6
  am the greatest, 771:15
  am the light of the world, 40:10
  am the Lord thy God, 9:8
  am the people, 634:3

Ignorant *(continued)*
far rather be i., 63:1
illumination of i., 337:12
in spite of experience, 312:18
learned fool more foolish than i.
one, 269:31
loved and were i., 598:23
malady of i., 422:5
many i. men are sure, 573:19
nation i. and free, 344:18
not that men are i., 605:1
of his understanding, 384:4
of ignorance, 113:22, 422:5
of ourselves, 217:11
of what before what to follow i.,
120:6
of what he's most assured, 204:4
only i. despise education, 99:35
science teaches to be i., 589:11
taught to doubt, 542:20
worst enemies not i., 713:13
Ignore, men of ill judgment i. good,
65:14
Ignoring all you reject, 433:26
I-ity, annihilate my I., 426:8
Île triste et noire, 494:*n*9
Iliction, supreme coort follows i.,
602:14
tu-rrned into angels be i., 603:7
Ilion, cloud-kissing I., 167:5
Ilium, O fatherland O I., 93:30
topless towers of I., 162:19
I'll not budge an inch, 167:13
Ill, as i. luck would have it, 183:*n*1
avenues of i., 430:5
benefit of i., 222:4
best things confused with i., 406:17
can he rule the great, 153:21
captive good attending captain i.,
221:6
cook that cannot lick fingers,
176:10
deeds doubled with evil word,
166:30
fares the land, 329:8
fit instruments of i., 299:17
good better made by i., 159:*n*4
good final goal of i., 457:17
habits gather by degrees, 276:23
how i. white hairs become fool,
184:16
layer-up of beauty, 186:4
love presst with i., 335:18
luck seldom alone, 149:25
means to do i. deeds, 170:15
men of i. judgment ignore good,
65:14
met by moonlight, 173:3
mingled yarn good and i., 203:15
ne'er wants occasion, 244:8
no malice or i. will, 369:2
not lived i. who passed unknown,
97:16
not speak i. of another, 117:15
nothing i. can dwell in such temple,
224:2
power to do me i., 225:*n*5
rather speak i. of ourselves than not
talk, 265:19
report while you live, 196:2

Ill *(continued)*
run to meet i. luck, 434:4
speak i. of the dead, 55:11
spirit have so fair a house, 224:2
things i. got had bad success,
164:16
took i. on Thursday, 791:4
unquiet meals make i. digestions,
166:33
ware is never cheap, 244:5
weary and i. at ease, 505:22
weed groweth fast, 141:24
wind bloweth no man good, 142:27
Ill-advised, quotations i., 574:17
Ill-born, amphibious i. mob, 285:15
Ill-bred as audible laughter, 329:*n*4
scenes, 586:22
this age how i., 91:1
Ill-clad, ill-housed i., 649:7
Illegal, immoral i. or fattening, 666:2
when President does it not i.,
733:20
Ill-favored thing but mine own,
192:14
vile i. faults, 182:32
Ill-housed ill-clad ill-nourished, 649:7
Illiberal as audible laughter, 329:*n*4
Illinois not control feline delinquency,
706:9
Illiterate him from your memory,
352:3
Ill-natured, vain i. Englishman, 285:15
Illness is night-side of life, 765:16
psychoanalysis is mental i., 626:7
with which smitten, 423:17
Illnesses, benefit from i., 71:12
Ill-nourished, ill-housed ill-clad i.,
649:7
Illogical belief in improbable, 642:20
doctrine so i. and dull, 652:9
Ills, age the harbor of all i., 82:6
bear those i. we have, 196:10
flood of mortal i. prevailing, 138:5
forgetfulness of all i., 53:7
medicos marveling on i., 674:12
mighty i. done by woman, 284:15
no sense of i. to come, 321:15
o'er i. o' life victorious, 363:5
scholar's life assail, 313:17
to hastening i. a prey, 329:8
we ought to bear, 497:23
what i. you are free from, 89:13
Ill-seeming, muddy i. thick, 167:34
Ill-spenders, borrowers i., 487:24
Ill-spirit sob in blood cell, 743:6
Ill-tempered and queer, 471:28
Illuminatio, dominus i. mea, 16:*n*5
Illumination of ignorant, 337:12
truth by instant i., 711:10
Illuminations, bonfires and i., 338:5
Illumine, sunset i. rolling waves,
565:14
what in me is dark i., 255:20
Illumines, history i. reality, 87:14
Ill-used, hardest knife i., 221:17
Illusion by which cheated, 613:1
certainty generally i., 542:9
Clemenceau had one i., 652:6
give reality to i., 631:5
great i., 614:4

Illusion *(continued)*
in love i. reaches zenith, 553:1
life is an i., 247:7
mind diseased always i., 473:9
of philosophers, 696:13
religion an i., 569:16
that times were better, 462:13
world of divine i., 500:24
Illusions, attachment fabricator of i.,
727:12
most dangerous calculations we call
i., 666:19
natural to indulge in i., 339:7
poetry purged of i., 613:18
Illusory, reality reveals itself to be i.,
604:5
Illustrate all shadows, 231:10
Illustrious acts high raptures infuse,
249:26
name i. and revered, 106:1
predecessors, 312:7
Ilych, Ivan I. dying, 510:13
Ilych's, Ivan I. life most simple, 510:12
I'm mad as hell, 752:1
not a Jew I'm Jew-ish, 766:13
OK you're OK, 728:10
Image, age demanded an i., 659:6
constant i. of the creature, 202:9
consumed in i. if not in usage,
738:4
culture offers man i., 717:18
graven i., 9:9
his own i. walking in garden,
406:16
horrid i. doth unfix hair, 212:23
idea with i., 384:14
in the i. of God, 7:23
make man in our i., 6:7
man is God's i., 243:4
man's i. and his cry, 594:23
of Eternity, 401:3
of his own eternity, 30:22
of revolution, 5:5
of splitting apart, 5:7
of war without guilt, 295:1
of what we actually see, 537:22
scorn her own i., 196:23
speech is i. of actions, 55:18
that blossoms a rose, 595:5
thrice tried to clasp her i., 53:18
time the i. of eternity, 112:1
Images, both i. regard, 243:4
deposits of accumulated experience,
628:8
draw from ourselves i., 707:9
find mirror in every mind, 314:21
graven i. of her gods, 26:19
heap of broken i., 668:18
more witnesseth than fancy's i.,
174:2
no graven i. worshipped, 483:4
of beauty, 74:13
of collective unconscious, 628:8
prisoners tattoo, 706:2
receives i. without absorbing,
535:23
reflect before throwing i., 675:19
what i. return O my daughter,
669:22

Imaginary gardens with real toads, 664:7
necessities, 247:3
relish is so sweet, 200:17
Imagination, a really grasping i., 548:5
abandoned by Reason, 348:*n*1
abhorred in my i., 199:8
Adam's dream, 417:15
as i. bodies forth, 174:1
audacity of i., 577:10
baffled by facts, 620:16
bare i. of feast, 171:3
cold and barren, 331:8
colors of i., 384:9
dwell most on woman won or lost, 597:12
fate had i. about her, 624:2
gifted with egotistical i., 435:16
God and i. one, 640:9
in balance or reconciliation, 384:14
in i. of their hearts, 37:42
incalculable debt to i., 628:7
indebted to i. for facts, 353:4
instrument of moral good is i., 409:24
judgment and i., 383:22
lady's i. rapid, 386:25
literalists of the i., 664:7
live in human i., 758:21
living power prime agent, 384:6
loose i., 599:10
makes us eloquent, 105:13
man without i., 653:21
master of art, 573:16
of boy healthy, 414:8
of i. all compact, 174:1
of man's heart, 7:21
one of forces of nature, 640:28
poet make his i. the people's, 640:18
political ideas and i., 718:3
primary i. living power, 384:6
reconciling mediatory power, 384:1
regulate i. by reality, 315:7
resemblance striking i., 341:6
secondary i. dissolves, 384:7
sociological i., 740:1
such tricks hath strong i., 174:1
suspend i., 702:7
sweeten my i., 211:2
synthetical and magical i., 384:13
takes abundance of i., 626:8
trace dust of Alexander, 199:9
truth of I., 417:14
truth only in i., 573:16
were it not for i., 317:10
wings of ostrich, 424:19
Imaginations, Lord understandeth all the i., 13:16
my i. are as foul, 197:5
Imaginative awe, 721:10
Imagine himself pleasing to all, 278:2
more felicity than can i., 594:9
people i. a vain thing, 15:30
to i. is everything, 550:5
too bold to i., 335:24
you are creating human destiny, 495:9
Imagined, each i. pinnacle, 417:2
exhausted worlds i. new, 313:10

Imagined (*continued*)
land, 639:13
live life he has i., 478:36
one chose person one loved, 612:19
republics and principalities, 136:14
round earth's i. corners, 230:19
way world i. determines what men do, 676:19
world i. ultimate good, 640:8
Imagines he cannot do this or that, 278:7
Imagining in excited reverie, 596:21
some fear, 174:1
Imaginings, horrible i., 212:23
Imbeciles, three generations of i., 543:6
Imbecility, convinced of i., 314:26
Imbres, cur i. ruerent, 103:*n*11
Imitate action of the tiger, 185:3
fools do not i. successes, 85:4
him if you dare, 598:9
immature poets i., 672:12
original writer one nobody can i., 369:15
the sun, 176:37
Imitated humanity so abominably, 197:1
Imitates, art i. Nature, 104:*n*13
third art i. them, 76:1
Imitation, art i. of nature, 102:28
limps after in base i., 171:7
of action that is serious, 78:31
sincerest flattery, 393:5
to do opposite is form of i., 342:15
whole vocation endless i., 375:9
Imitator, without precedent and i., 319:21
Imitators, no garlands for i., 364:22
you slavish herd, 97:21
Imiter, celui que personne ne peut i., 369:*n*8
Immaculate, look i. of landscapes, 660:17
white chrysanthemum i., 282:13
Immanent Will and its designs, 540:13
Immanuel, call his name I., 26:5
Immature poets imitate, 672:12
Immediate context of history, 684:18
jewel of souls, 206:30
Immediately, difficult do i., 783:8
they'd i. go out, 359:14
Immemorial elms, 456:22
most i. year, 453:1
Immense, at twelve I felt i., 600:12
error is i., 295:6
long derangement, 566:3
silkworm size or i., 665:5
Immensity of first power, 368:2
of life, 446:25
Immigrants, all i. except Indians, 650:3
Imminent, contagious blastments i., 193:26
deadly breach, 205:25
Immoderate, unseasonable and i. sleep, 314:25
Immodest, no more modest than i., 489:9
words admit no defense, 278:23
Immoral illegal or fattening, 666:2

Immoral (*continued*)
no moral or i. book, 566:10
thing for moral reasons, 540:8
what you feel bad after, 701:19
Immorality, schools nurseries of i., 311:19
what majority dislike, 584:20
Immortal, and so become i., 417:1
bee to be i., 639:25
beings of mind essentially i., 400:12
Bird, 415:17
Christianity indestructible and i., 420:6
crown, 308:16
dead who live again, 483:7
Death has taken mortal life, 90:4
diamond is immortal diamond, 551:17
dim light of this i. day, 407:5
driven away from i. day, 356:16
else i. us, 230:21
God created man to be i., 30:22
gods I crave no pelf, 211:26
grow i. as they quote, 295:24
happy be and have i. bliss, 153:14
hate, 256:1
he is i., 696:23
in flesh beauty i., 639:4
Jove's dread clamors, 207:8
land is i., 745:19
lay plans as if i., 546:15
locks fell forward, 51:2
longings in me, 218:16
look, 467:20
made thee neither mortal nor i., 136:1
make me i. with a kiss, 162:19
married to i. verse, 251:19
names not born to die, 405:6
no i. work behind, 418:18
not similar are i. gods and men, 51:20
now is i. life, 556:21
part of myself, 206:20
reason i. all else mortal, 58:11
scrip of joy i. diet, 152:16
Shakespeare rose, 313:10
sight of i. sea, 375:9
songs composed of tears, 461:15
soul and all, 657:10
soul of man i., 76:3
spark from Heaven i., 364:13
spirit grows, 373:8
such harmony in i. souls, 182:8
unrecorded laws of God, 66:11
verse boasts to be i., 588:2
what i. hand or eye, 358:6
wheat, 280:23
where saints i. reign, 294:19
wound, 625:7
youth to mortal maids, 388:18
Immortality, evidence of i., 430:23
from death to i., 50:15
hope full of i., 30:23
if you destroy belief in i., 495:3
is nontransferable, 765:2
labor at eternal task, 503:16
longing after i., 292:14
man possesses i., 718:8
mortal put on i., 43:27

Impulse (*continued*)
  household of I. mourns, 720:13
  lonely i. of delight, 596:11
  natural i. God gave me, 284:10
  one i. from vernal wood, 372:21
  to see it tried, 451:1
Impulses, instinctual wishful i., 569:16
  primitive i. of heart, 452:*n*1
Impunity, no one provokes me with i., 119:14
Impure, although it passes among i., 77:*n*5
Impurities, no room for i. in essay, 650:19
Impute, make Gods to whom i., 497:23
In and out the Eagle, 780:13
  birds without despair to get i., 146:19
  harm's way, 348:9
  hoc signo vinces, 113:*n*2
  marriage wish to get out, 432:28
  when age i. wit out, 186:40
  who's i. who's out, 211:13
Inability of mind to correlate all contents, 679:6
Inaccessible, desert i., 190:29
  tower of past, 486:4
  valley of reveries, 617:14
Inaccuracy, not mind lying hate i., 525:10
  saves explanation, 610:21
Inaction, disciplined i., 367:17
  moment not of action or i., 84:*n*7
  nor be thy attachment to i., 84:7
  saps vigor of mind, 135:6
Inactivity, wise and masterly i., 367:15
Inadvertently said some evil thing, 76:19
Inalienable rights, 343:*n*2
Inane, intense i., 407:3
Inanimate, mortality of i. things, 532:18
Inanition, spirit die of i., 499:8
Inarticulate, raid on i., 671:9
Inartistic, Thoreau i., 548:8
Inattention, patient i., 509:16
Inattentive, brave man i. to duty, 369:9
Inaudible and noiseless foot, 203:20
  its name is The I., 57:4
  sexuality i. to any but me, 712:7
Inauspicious stars, 176:18
Incantations of defeats, 639:19
Incapable, noble and i. of deceit, 379:24
Incarnadine, seas i., 214:9
Incarnate by the Holy Ghost, 49:1
  Well I told you so, 442:15
Incense, gods themselves throw i., 211:14
  my morning i., 353:15
  soft i. hangs, 415:14
  stupefying i. smoke, 465:7
Incense-breathing Morn, 322:5
Incensed, blows and buffets have i., 214:22
  most fragrant when i., 159:10
Incertainties now crown themselves, 221:23

Incessant, what boots it with i. care, 253:20
Incessantly stand on head, 517:9
  weeps i. for my sin, 358:16
  work i. to the last, 350:6
  world joked i., 531:23
Inch, cannot grow by i., 599:7
  cubic i. of space a miracle, 491:4
  every i. a king, 210:29
  every i. not fool is rogue, 274:18
  give an i. take an ell, 142:28
  I'll not budge an i., 167:13
  no painful i. to gain, 483:3
  paint an i. thick, 199:8
  queen it no i. further, 223:13
Inchcape Rock, 386:11
Inches, death by i., 219:14
  die by famine die by i., 286:13
Incident, curious i. of dog in night-time, 577:20
Incidents, so many i. so many details, 587:13
Incidis in Scyllam cupiens, 181:*n*2
Incipit Vita Nova, 124:17
Incisions, underneath fine i., 511:11
Incisors, writers divided into i. and molars, 506:5
Incite people to learn from past, 760:7
Incited, pseudo-event someone i., 735:15
Incitement, every idea an i., 543:5
Inciters of servile insurrection, 522:13
Incivility and procrastination, 397:18
Inclement, raw i. summers, 289:12
Inclination, read as i. leads, 315:26
  thoughts according to i., 184:*n*2
  to hear you, 293:19
Inclinations cannot alter evidence, 337:15
  worship God according to own i., 105:15
Incline thine ear O Lord, 27:12
Inclined, as to embrace me she i., 255:17
  as twig bent tree's i., 300:12
  sins they are i. to, 263:8
  to notice ruin in things, 739:1
  to snap like vixens, 660:20
Inclines to think there is God, 483:2
Include me out, 646:17
  things that included whole, 640:1
Included in We the people, 768:10
Includes itself in power, 200:10
Inclusion, life i. and confusion, 549:3
Income, annual i. twenty pounds, 470:25
  business with i. at heels, 334:14
  decent fall cloths over high i., 735:7
  devote i. labor to others, 488:11
  good i. of no avail, 594:5
  he has i. she pattable, 709:14
  however great i., 85:1
  just man will pay more i. tax, 75:6
  live beyond i., 525:2
  rent is sorrow i. tears, 242:9
  solvency not matter of i., 594:4
  twenty expenditure nineteen, 470:25
Incommunicable, burden of i., 397:13
Incomparable, Clemens sole i., 532:19

Incompatibility established between them, 616:16
  spice of life, 709:14
Incompetence, rise to level of i., 747:5
Incompetent, though competent appear i., 80:18
Incomplete and unfit for view, 523:20
Incomprehensibility of God, 422:13
Incomprehensible, history i. without Jesus, 503:13
Incomprehension, mutual i., 717:21
Inconceivable idea of sun, 639:20
Incongruous moonlight shines, 679:8
  with intelligence, 493:20
Inconsistencies in principle, 539:10
  of opinion justifiable, 395:6
Inconsolé, je suis le veuf l'i., 443:*n*5
Inconstancy, constant in Nature i., 266:19
  nothing constant but i., 288:19
  state of man i., 270:20
Inconstant, mob is varied and i., 278:13
  moon, 175:7
Inconvenience, go with show of i., 653:29
Inconveniences, modern i., 526:17
Incorrect, will most i. to heaven, 193:4
Incorruptible, dead raised i., 43:27
  sea-green I., 412:20
Incorruption, corruptible put on i., 43:27
  raised in i., 43:25
Increase and diffusion of knowledge, 367:18
  as if i. of appetite, 193:8
  from fairest creatures desire i., 220:7
  God gave i., 42:31
  his tribe i., 397:1
  of his government, 26:8
  some nations i. other diminish, 89:16
  without i. or diminution, 385:9
Increased devotion to cause, 450:2
  force in Nature not i., 496:17
  Jesus i. in wisdom, 38:8
  knowledge shall be i., 29:21
  means and leisure, 435:11
Increasers, one thing to say to tax i., 774:*n*4
Increases, absence i. great passions, 265:28
  in geometrical ratio, 368:2
  necessity of being ready i., 449:7
Increaseth, he that i. knowledge i. sorrow, 23:28
Increasing belly, 183:19
  purpose runs, 455:20
  store with loss, 221:3
  youth waneth by i., 156:14
Increment, unearned i., 439:24
Increments, velocities of evanescent i., 296:23
Incumbent, care of poor i. on society, 278:15
Incurable, disease is i., 183:24
  life is an i. disease, 267:5
  old age is an i. disease, 432:*n*1

Ind, from east to western I., 191:10
    wealth of Ormus and I., 256:23
Indebted, at once i. and discharged,
    258:4
    to memory for his jests, 353:4
Indecency, prejudicial as public i.,
    150:40
Indecent, sent down for i. behavior,
    712:1
Indecision, nothing habitual but i.,
    545:11
Indeed, friend in need friend i.,
    83:*n*12
Indefatigable pursuit of unattainable,
    594:6
Indefensible, journalist morally i.,
    766:12
Indemnify, literature effort to i.,
    432:13
Indemnity for the past, 313:*n*3
Indenture, this oath and this i., 71:1
Independence, banners of foreign i.,
    368:16
    forever, 394:*n*5
    freedom brought i. rationality,
        704:8
    governments whose i. acknowl-
        edged, 360:12
    in marriage i. will be equal, 410:18
    individual i. economic principle,
        635:9
    magnanimity trust, 478:5
    make real Declaration of I., 627:21
    mutual guarantees of, 572:14
    now Independence forever, 394:10
    of solitude, 431:22
    Revolution produced Declaration of
        I., 665:13
Independent and have inherent rights,
    327:1
    free and i. states, 336:11
    free and i. States, 338:4
    scientist, 691:4
    support renders i., 336:15
Indescribable, beauty i., 588:1
Indestructible, Christianity i. and im-
    mortal, 420:6
    Union indestructible States, 443:18
Indeterminable, life-form i., 628:10
Index, a dab at an i., 328:1
    marble i. of a mind, 373:10
Indexes baby figure of giant mass,
    200:12
Indian, I'll be an I., 725:11
    knows his village, 707:2
    like the base I., 208:16
    lo the poor I., 301:7
    morn on the I. steep, 252:22
    not decked with I. stones, 164:19
    only a matter of time I., 774:11
    stands free in Nature, 476:21
    summer of life, 536:4
    to I. all days are God's, 575:7
    to wilderness to teach I., 589:4
    wilderness, 287:3
Indians, all immigrants except I.,
    650:3
    country better when I. running it,
        765:6
    give country back to I., 698:11

Indians (*continued*)
    know better how to live, 563:5
    only good I. dead, 516:8
    ten little I., 792:15
    thanks f'r bein' presarved fr'm I.,
        602:20
Indians', called Guanahaní in I.
        tongue, 134:8
    white man warmed before I. fire,
        333:6
India's coral strand, 395:18
Indicates, determines or i. man's fate,
    477:30
Indictment against whole people,
    331:16
Indies, had come to the I., 134:7
    wealth of I., 317:8
    went to I. to conquer a people,
        134:13
Indifference, benign i. of universe,
    732:13
    extinction from i., 702:14
    morn and cold i., 294:3
    total i. to public notice, 769:5
    tragedy of love i., 626:18
    when will i. come, 735:14
Indifferent, artist i. paring fingernails,
    647:10
    children of earth, 195:23
    delayed till I am i., 315:17
    good bad i., 278:9, 320:21
    rather than believe God i., 437:3
    stood aside been i., 713:12
    to be i. essence of inhumanity,
        570:21
    to each i., 679:8
    universe is i., 637:4
Indifferently, look on both i., 187:19
Indigested, irregular i. piece, 314:2
Indignant, no one such liar as i. man,
    552:13
    spirit fled i. to shades, 94:28
Indignatio, ubi saeva i., 290:23
Indignation, provoking thy wrath and
    i., 49:15
    savage i., 290:23, 598:9
    unsatisfied i., 495:8
    until the i. be overpast, 26:30
    will produce verses, 108:17
Indignity, the i. of it, 724:14
Indirect, persecution i. way to plant
    religion, 248:9
    poet become more i., 672:15
Indirections, by i. find directions,
    195:7
Indiscretion, lover without i., 539:11
Indiscriminate charity, 525:14
Indispensable, as loved we are i.,
    562:5
    comforts not i., 478:4
    condition of freedom, 609:13
    make yourself i., 607:3
    no i. man, 648:17
    titles such as I., 587:7
Indisposeth, living i. for dying, 248:31
Indisputable, nothing more i. than
    senses, 323:16
Individual, affirmation of i., 541:12
    balance of i. with representative,
        384:14

Individual (*continued*)
    competition afford freedom to i.,
        657:3
    competition hard for i., 525:11
    connection of i. man, 780:21
    definition of i., 716:13
    development of i. repetition of race,
        569:6
    difficulties of i. of family, 387:8
    emancipation of i., 471:26
    first and foremost I am i., 508:3
    free from governmental intrusion,
        719:5
    idea due to i., 644:14
    independence economic principle,
        635:9
    labors to render annual revenue,
        326:6
    liberty individual power, 368:17
    liberty of i., 439:17
    lose i. autonomy, 727:9
    monopoly granted to i., 326:2
    must remain supreme, 705:4
    no i. could resent, 289:18
    no progress except in i., 494:12
    no such creature as i., 734:9
    not accountable to society, 439:21
    not i. but species, 311:17
    ontogenesis development of i.,
        522:15
    person sacrificed to i., 648:4
    public strength i. security, 354:18
    relations as i. to world, 562:17
    savage i. man, 601:7
    serves industrial system, 723:12
    taken into custody, 682:10
    way of seeing, 546:17
    who refuses to defend, 369:8
Individualism, rugged i., 625:20
Individuality, components of i. are
    sorrow, 64:26
    draw chalk circle round i., 426:10
    of expression beginning of art,
        351:3
    whatever crushes i. is despotism,
        439:19
Individuals, coercing into obedience i.,
    661:10
    if i. have no virtues, 346:6
    not accommodate to conveniences
        of i., 546:16
    numerous free active, 499:2
    of all nations melted into new race,
        339:1
    preservation of species not i., 366:6
    reproduction to new i., 347:13
    worth of state worth of i., 439:22
    Yiddish words pinpoint i., 714:17
Indivisibility of peace, 631:*n*2
Indivisible, fleshed fair erected i.,
    729:2
    freedom i. word, 685:10
    grandeur i., 678:8
    one nation i., 568:12
    peace i., 631:7
Indolence, wealth the parent of i.,
    75:12
Indolent but agreeable doing nothing,
    110:4
    readers become more i., 328:3

Inform (*continued*)
  their discretion, 344:22
Information, can find i., 316:26
  vegetable animal mineral, 529:12
  woman of little i., 386:24
Informed, correctly i. as to past,
    425:17
  people well enough i., 649:11
Informer poor weak human being,
    695:17
Infrequent, sighs short and i., 668:19
  worshipper of gods, 96:1
Infringement of human freedom, 364:9
Infuse, illustrious acts high raptures i.,
    249:26
  souls of animals i. into men, 181:17
Infuses that liberal obedience, 331:23
Infusing thoughts and passions, 384:19
Ingiuria, chi fa i. non perdona, 103:*n*3
Inglorious arts of peace, 268:9
  mute i. Milton, 322:14
Ingrateful man, 209:24
Ingratitude, haste in paying is i.,
    265:25
  hate i. more than lying, 203:3
  man's i., 191:4
  thou marble-hearted fiend, 209:10
Inhabit, build houses and i. them,
    28:12
  country belongs to people who i. it,
    449:4
  house and all that i. it, 338:13
  parched places, 28:29
  soul of grandam i. bird, 181:*n*3
Inhabitant, Indian is Nature's i.,
    476:21
Inhabitants, Californians a race not i.,
    586:3
  not only i. of field, 332:18
  number of portraits as great as i.,
    643:9
  proclaim liberty to all i., 9:27
Inhabits our frail blood, 203:3
  poem, 721:9
Inherent, decay i. in all component
    things, 64:25
  purpose i. in art so in nature, 77:17
  rights, 327:1
Inherit, all which it i. dissolve, 224:21
  flow'rets of Eden i., 392:12
  looking uncomfortably to world we
    i., 784:2
  meek shall i. the earth, 16:34, 33:1
  the wind, 21:10
  tonight doth i., 498:15
  with pain purchased i. pain, 168:13
Inheritance, divided an i. with him,
    342:7
  not be destroyed, 345:15
Inherited total lot of parents, 768:12
  tradition cannot be i., 672:8
Inheritor, president is i., 729:21
Inhuman as hawk's cry, 663:19
  of the veritable ocean, 639:7
  reign of lie, 680:5
Inhumanity, indifferent is essence of i.,
    570:21
  man's i. to man, 361:8
Inimies, keep our i., 602:11
Iniquities, judge allow i., 543:9

Iniquity, bond of i., 41:3
  draw i. with cords of vanity, 25:40
  gray i., 177:30
  I was shapen in i., 17:20
  is pardoned, 27:15
  of oblivion, 249:1
  of the fathers, 9:10
  punish wicked for their i., 26:13
  reaped i., 29:28
  religious know more about i., 591:3
Initial of Creation, 513:9
Iniuria, volenti non fit i., 120:4
Injure, to benefit and not i., 58:7
Injured, forgiveness to i. does belong,
    103:*n*3
  like i. fan, 664:5
  minds i. by hunger and thirst, 80:5
  no one i. save by himself, 114:*n*8
  party, 532:5
  those I have i., 743:7
  whom they have i. they hate, 103:6
Injures, never pardons those he i.,
    103:*n*3
Injuries, forgive me my i., 743:7
  saints in your i., 206:5
Injuring, at expense of i. their virtue,
    61:26
  kill time without i. eternity, 477:31
  rarely escapes i. own hands, 58:4
  restrain men from i., 344:8
Injurious, beauty though i., 261:19
Injury, add insult to i., 102:16
  adding insult to i., 318:23
  fear of serious i., 568:15
  greatest service or greatest i., 75:3
  never forget i., 610:15
  never use treatment with view to i.,
    71:1
  recompense i. with justice, 61:25
  returns on him who began, 90:11
  sooner forgotten than insult, 304:20
  such i. vex a saint, 167:26
  where i. let me sow pardon, 123:10
Injustice, bear with patience i., 269:17
  complain of i. of government,
    369:11
  conscience with i. corrupted, 164:1
  easy to bear, 642:18
  extreme justice extreme i., 119:32
  extreme justice often i., 86:*n*1
  extreme law often extreme i., 86:1
  fear of suffering i., 265:10
  man ever in darkness of i., 117:11
  mankind censure i., 75:7
  no i. to person who consents, 120:4
  nothing so felt as i., 471:14
  one man's justice another's i., 432:8
  put a halt to i., 755:9
  sometimes service to public, 346:5
Injustices, heaped i. upon us, 606:4
Injye other people's sufferin', 603:11
Ink, effusion of i., 325:15
  essential in painting, 120:13
  every drop of i. ran cold, 323:21
  gall enough in thy i., 202:28
  galley slave to i., 422:8
  hath not drunk i., 168:29
  never saw pen and i., 203:4
  runs from mouth, 767:5
  seven seas of i., 117:10

Inky, not alone my i. cloak, 193:2
Inlaid with patines of bright gold,
    182:8
Inland island, 535:5
  though i. far we be, 375:13
Inn, gain timely i., 215:1
  happiness produced by i., 316:28
  make my house your i., 664:11
  no room in the i., 38:2
  remember i. Miranda, 609:1
  take mine ease in mine i., 141:8
  up to old i.-door, 643:11
  warmest welcome at an i., 316:*n*8
  world not i. but hospital, 248:21
Inner air inner light, 706:11
  light will shine forth, 351:*n*5
  man, 44:23
  mine with i. weather, 624:2
  Temple's i. shrine, 374:16
  weather, 624:2
Innisfail, harp of I., 389:10
Innisfree, go to I., 594:21
Innocence and health, 329:9
  ceremony of i., 596:19
  changed i. for i., 222:17
  confession next thing to i., 100:23
  fearful i., 374:14
  has nothing to dread, 281:11
  her i. a child, 275:6
  ignorance not i., 468:11
  murderous i. of sea, 596:21
  never blossom into license, 281:12
  of love, 202:12
  of our neighbors, 478:33
  our peace our i., 374:14
  Ralph wept for end of i., 729:18
  recovered i., 478:33
  silence often of pure i., 222:22
  soul recovers i., 597:6
  what is our i., 664:13
Innocent and foredoomed, 714:15
  armed without i. within, 303:3
  as new-laid egg, 529:1
  believe theologians nothing i.,
    515:14
  calm quiet i. recreation, 245:27
  children's souls not i., 114:19
  condemn an i. person, 306:2
  coursed down his i. nose, 190:8
  he that maketh haste to be rich not
    i., 23:6
  look like i. flower, 213:3
  man sent to legislature, 605:20
  merriment, 531:4
  millions of i. burnt tortured, 343:8
  minds i. and quiet, 267:18
  no i. wit be suppressed, 342:1
  of the blood, 37:7
  officious i. sincere, 317:26
  skin of i. lamb parchment, 164:9
  sleep, 214:6
  than one i. suffer, 325:23
  who perished being i., 13:37
  women i. and pure, 224:4
  won by blood and sweat of i.,
    771:11
Innocently, live i. God here, 312:11
Innovation, restructuring combines
    continuity i., 763:14

Interminable night, 672:2
  Ulysses i. adventurer, 640:11
Intermingle jest with earnest, 160:1
Intermission, laugh sans i., 190:24
  pleasure is i. of pain, 239:5
Internal domestic empire, 696:7
  environment, 473:8
  medium, 473:7
International, bring order to i. affairs,
  636:4
  nuclear control, 742:5
  spirit of science in i. affairs, 708:1
Internationally, bring suit in court i.,
  655:5
Interpose, who in quarrels i., 297:10
Interpret interpretatons, 147:5
Interpretation, aid to i. of future,
  71:19
  doctrine or practice or i., 111:23
  of dreams road to knowledge, 569:3
  science right i. of nature, 411:13
  this is the i. of the thing, 29:16
Interpreter, critic i. of artist, 548:17
  hardest understood of the two,
  352:34
  in marriage room for i., 716:22
  man i. of nature, 411:13
  perfect i. of life, 661:1
Interpreters, for crowd they need i.,
  63:30
Interprets, poet i. poem, 600:5
Interracial tension has focus, 700:5
Interred, good oft i. with bones,
  188:28
  life is shrunk dead and i., 229:8
Interrupt with such silly question,
  320:7
Interrupted by dying, 249:24
Interstellar, vacant i. spaces, 671:4
Interstitially, judges legislate i., 542:21
Intertissued robe of gold, 185:19
Interval, enjoy i., 588:14
  lucid i., 274:26
Intervals, full of lucid i., 150:35
  lucid i. and happy pauses, 158:17
Interview, not train wreck earthquake
  but i., 735:15
  with Satan, 578:15
Intestines, prejudices traced to i.,
  553:15
Intimacy, gay i. of slums, 712:2
  heart-revealing i., 596:22
Intimate equality of the Four, 652:7
Intimates are predestined, 535:20
  eternity to man, 292:14
Intimations, reason's icy i., 423:13
Intimidate human race into order,
  636:4
  threats of halter i., 348:1
Intolerable, burden of them is i., 49:15
  deal of sack, 177:34
  in worst state i., 340:18
  music falls, 599:17
  shirt of flame, 672:4
  wrestle with words and meanings,
  670:23
Intolerant, learned toleration from i.,
  651:15
Intoxicate the brain, 298:13
Intoxicated, heart i. with bliss, 365:12

Intoxication, best of life i., 402:19
Intractable, sullen untamed i., 671:12
Intricate as death, 231:12
Intricated, poor i. soul, 231:13
Intrigue, spotless through i., 463:26
Intrinsic value of knowledge, 305:5
Introduce philosophy into homes,
  87:30
  please allow me to i. myself, 773:1
Introduced, cut anyone i. to, 519:18
  when I'm i. to one, 584:3
Introspection, prone to i., 665:9
Introversion, tendency to i., 433:4
Intrudes, society where none i., 400:29
Intrusion, right to be free from gov-
  ernmental i., 719:5
Intuition, feminine i., 707:20
  intelligence which goes with sex is
  i., 657:19
  more subtle than premise, 542:17
  passionate i., 376:22
  reliance on i., 628:6
Intuitive, beautiful always i., 383:22
  calculation transcended mathematics, 628:6
Inurned, weep a people i., 425:n2
Invade, religion allowed to i. private
  life, 391:5
Invaded, France is i., 370:12
Invalid, invaluable permanent i. Bunbury, 567:6
Invalidated, friendships i. by marriage,
  524:22
Invasion can be resisted, 427:18
  l'i. des idées, 427:n5
  waiting for i. so are fishes, 620:13
Invent boat of your flesh, 767:9
  lies you can i., 359:9
  necessary to i. him, 306:25
  would children i. game, 656:9
Invented an invaluable invalid, 567:6
  Dodo i. for becoming extinct, 654:5
  falsehood i., 646:2
  first i. sleep, 151:15
  first i. war, 161:19
  first i. work, 388:2
  fool i. kissing, 290:12
  history, 307:10
  time someone i. plot, 651:5
Invention arises from idleness, 677:17
  brightest heaven of i., 184:18
  equal license in bold i., 98:3
  greatest i. of century, 584:10
  horrible i. the bourgeois, 496:2
  is unfruitful, 331:8
  necessity mother of i., 104:n13,
  119:12
  necessity not mother of i., 677:17
  noble i., 342:19
  of method of invention, 584:10
  scaled i., 660:1
  stomach dispenser of i., 104:15
  war is an i., 653:16
Inventions by which man remade environment, 722:15
  in nature's i. nothing lacking,
  135:10
  sought out many i., 24:15
Inventories, statistics and history i.,
  432:26

Inventors, seldom or never i., 306:20
Invents, modern man i. museum,
  693:5
Inversion, negative i., 720:3
Inverted, country an i. cone, 317:6
  Winter ruler of i. year, 335:5
Investigation of hidden causes, 148:13
  scientific i., 505:4
Investment, liquidity of i., 652:15
Inveterate scars, 670:14
Invigorated and reimpressed, 314:18
Invincible, I am i. I am woman,
  771:14
  no animal more i. than woman,
  73:16
  shaking her i. locks, 255:2
  within me i. summer, 732:18
Inviolable shade, 498:13
Invisible, all things visible and i.,
  44:37
  aloft i. in night, 572:21
  artist i. refined out of existence,
  647:10
  at times i., 665:5
  authentic tidings of i. things, 376:21
  bloody i. hand, 214:28
  choir i., 483:7
  essential is i. to eye, 705:13
  Fortune though blind not i., 160:3
  individual led by i. hand, 326:6
  its name is The I., 57:4
  jest unseen inscrutable i., 168:2
  labor, 428:1
  man, 735:18
  other world i., 248:10
  power of visible is i., 664:14
  shores will swarm with i. dead,
  398:11
  skuttle fish becomes i., 293:8
  soap, 423:2
  soul bright i. green, 477:16
  spheres formed in fright, 486:26
  spirit of wine, 206:22
  vision art of seeing i., 289:4
  world full of i. things, 748:10
  world i. we view, 581:10
  worm, 358:4
  wounds i., 191:22
Invisibly, silently i., 357:17
Invitation, more i. than command,
  293:18
Invite, all occasions i. his mercies,
  231:1
  God and his angels, 231:11
Invites, bell i. me, 214:1
  his wit i. you, 334:12
  my steps and points, 300:7
Invocation, true poem an i., 692:4
Invoke genius of Constitution, 313:7
Involuntary, it was i., 740:18
Involve us in wrong war, 685:15
Involved, dogs emotionally i. in world
  of men, 693:16
  in mankind, 231:8
  not person i., 527:11
Inward and spiritual grace, 49:22
  as men of i. light are wont, 263:28
  beauty in i. soul, 74:10
  draw i. quality after, 217:26
  eye, 376:1

Israel (*continued*)
glory departed from I., 11:30
glory of thy people I., 38:6
he that keepeth I., 19:25
in I. believe in miracles, 661:4
Judah and I. dwelt safely, 12:20
lost sheep of house of I., 34:27
no king in I., 11:22
scattered upon the hills, 13:2
sweet psalmist of I., 12:16
thy tabernacles O I., 10:8
to your tents O I., 12:30
Israelis, no more war between Arabs
I., 745:22
Israfel, dwell where I. dwelt, 451:13
whose heartstrings a lute, 451:*n*2
Issue is in God's hands, 64:1
judged in light of final i., 79:2
Issues, contrived corridors and i.,
668:7
debate on public i. uninhibited,
719:4
distract attention from i., 587:15
out of it are the i. of life, 20:25
when i. are joined, 58:1
Isthmus of a middle state, 301:13
took the I. started the Canal, 576:9
It, believe i. or not, 687:17
can't happen here, 658:10
is finished, 40:40
it's just I., 593:16
let's do i., 753:4
Ita in maxima fortuna minima licentia,
91:*n*13
Italia who hast fatal gift, 400:15
Italian, I speak I. to women, 143:3
operas translated into I., 586:20
perhaps I., 529:10
proletariat, 652:19
Italien, je parle i. aux femmes, 143:*n*1
Italy, beyond Alps lies I., 98:28
far from I. I lie, 83:1
fashions in proud I., 171:7
graved inside of it I., 465:12
Greece I. and England did adorn,
275:25
had warfare terror murder, 739:5
notice ruin because born in I., 739:1
Paradise of exiles, 407:8
Itch, incurable i. for writing, 109:4
of disputing, 227:13
Itchez, Ah i. Ah scratchez, 709:12
Itching palm, 189:13
Iteration, damnable i., 176:32
Ithaca, fill I. full of moths, 218:25
setting out on voyage to I., 587:11
Ithers, see ourselves as i. see us,
361:18
Itself, illness which regards i. as therapy, 626:7
is it true in and for i., 372:13
love is most nearly i., 671:11
no relevance to anything but i.,
748:2
thou art the thing i., 210:6
Itylus, half assuaged for I., 533:8
Iucundior, quae est domestica sede i.,
87:*n*13
Iudex damnatur ubi nocens absolvitur,
99:*n*10

Iudicaret, ne supra crepidam sutor i.,
81:*n*2
Iura, sunt superis sua i., 101:*n*19
Ius est ars boni et aequi, 119:11
summum saepe summa est malitia,
86:*n*1
Ivan Ilych dying, 510:13
Ilych's life most simple, 510:12
Petrofski Skevar, 781:4
Ives, going to St. I., 788:14
Ivory apes and peacocks, 12:27,
633:18
bit of i. on which I work, 387:13
gate of i., 54:9, 94:17
neck is as a tower of i., 25:19
tower, 629:23
tower of i., 436:14
Ivy, goats eat i., 791:15
holly and the i., 778:9
myrtle and i., 403:23
not hang i. over wine, 100:20
pluck i. branch for me, 515:11
with i. never sere, 253:14
Ivy-mantled tower, 322:3, 644:8

J

Jabal father of such as dwell in tents,
7:9
Jabberwock, beware J., 518:15
J'accuse, 541:14
Jack and Jill, 789:11
banish plump J., 177:32
be nimble, 791:10
house that J. built, 792:24
joke poor potsherd, 551:17
little J. Horner, 788:11
makes J. a dull boy, 246:2
one named J. fly away J., 792:23
Sprat eat no fat, 788:7
Jackass can kick barn down, 648:11
Jackknife, just a j. has Macheath,
698:14
Jackknives, pelicans flew like j.,
739:10
Jackson standing like stone wall,
504:4
Stonewall J. wrapped in beard,
698:9
who didst pick up Andrew J. from
pebbles, 486:22
Jacky have new master, 789:12
Jacob gave the place Peniel, 8:2
gave Esau bread and pottage, 7:37
God of J. not philosophers, 271:11
served seven years, 7:43
sold his birthright unto J., 7:37
that which has been sent down on
J., 116:3
thy tents O J., 10:8
was a plain man, 7:36
was left alone, 7:45
wrestled as Angel with J., 245:11
Jacob's ladder, 581:12
talk of J. ladder, 434:5
voice is J. voice, 7:38
Jade, arrant j. on a journey, 329:1
Chinese love j., 662:8
let galled j. wince, 197:14
Jael brought forth butter, 11:4

Jael (*continued*)
took a nail, 10:41
J'ai vécu, 348:15
Jail, all we know who lie in j., 567:21
can't be sint to j. for it, 603:14
like living in j., 725:25
little stealin' gits you in j., 673:15
patron and the j., 313:17
with chance of being drowned,
315:23
Jailed for telling lies to young, 716:10
Jailer another kind of captive, 443:22
inexorable as self, 436:8
Jake, Yukon J., 693:7
Jam, Calico J., 472:6
every other day, 519:8
tomorrow jam yesterday, 519:9
Jamaicas of Remembrance, 514:10
Jambs, unscrew doors from j., 489:9
James could almost hear the bronze
Negroes, 743:1
Councillor to King J., 155:2
I James II Old Pretender, 676:2
James Morrison Morrison, 648:5
King J. used to call for old shoes,
238:22
let J. rejoice, 325:15
novel by Henry J. like church,
601:12
work of Henry J., 676:2
James's, ladies of St. J., 539:6
Jamshyd gloried drank deep, 445:12
Jane, from J. to Elizabeth, 386:26
John Thomas marryin' Lady J.,
657:15
me Tarzan you J., 628:*n*2
Jangled, sweet bells j., 196:19
Jangling, keep juices flowing by j.
around, 719:12
January, a Fly this J. Day, 514:10
Japan, create in J. civilized nation,
525:17
forces of Empire of J., 649:19
from Paris to J., 280:14
what they say in J., 544:3
Japanese reliance on intuition, 628:6
Japheth, Noah begat J., 7:14
Jar, feel amid city's j., 497:14
in Tennessee, 639:1
people in front get j., 631:18
retains odor, 392:*n*1
strings untouched will harshly j.,
162:12
wine j. when molding began, 98:4
Jardin, il faut cultiver notre j., 306:*n*7
Jargon of the schools, 287:15
Jars, two j. on floor of Zeus, 52:26
Jasper of jocundity, 136:3
Jaundice, jealousy j. of the soul,
275:20
Jaundiced eye, 299:5
Jaunts, Jorrocks' j. and jollities, 434:6
Javan, bound for J. or Gadire, 261:16
Jaw, muscular strength to j., 517:10
Jawbone of an ass, 11:15
Jaw-jaw better than to war-war, 622:8
Jaws, gently smiling j., 517:5
of darkness do devour it, 172:20
of death, 148:6, 458:14
of sea and earth, 706:3

Jewels (*continued*)
  unclasps warmed j., 415:5
Jewish, being J. trouble enough, 738:7
  choose a J. God, 656:*n*3
  establishment of home for J. people,
    556:2
  final solution of J. question, 686:5
  gaberdine, 180:8
  living in middle of J. joke, 765:12
  man with parents alive, 765:13
  no J. blood in my veins, 766:5
Jew-ish, I'm not a Jew I'm J., 766:13
Jews, Jesus king of J., 37:10
  King of the J., 32:23
  kiss and infidels adore, 299:10
  odd of God to choose the J., 656:14
  Papists Protestants J. Turks in one
    ship, 247:13
  refuse till conversion of J., 268:14
  right and status of J. in any coun-
    try, 556:2
  spurn the J., 656:*n*3
  thrown back at all J., 760:11
Jezebel, dogs shall eat J., 12:42
  painted her face, 13:11
Jiggety-jig, home again j., 792:2
Jigsaw, Rosebud missing piece in j.
    puzzle, 697:5
Jill, Jack and J., 789:11
  other named J. fly away J., 792:23
Jim, poor J. Jay, 617:4
  simple child dear brother J., 372:*n*6
Jimmie crack corn, 780:2
Jinetes, los cuatro j. del Apocalipsis,
    602:6
Jingle, little j. little chimes, 298:1
  triumph and the j., 650:16
Jingling of guinea, 455:16
Jingly, Lady J. Jones, 472:10
Jingo, by j. if we do, 507:6
  repent by j., 422:26
Joan as my Lady, 241:7
  Darby same to old wife J., 557:2
  greasy J. keel pot, 169:13
Job, blessed the latter end of J., 15:28
  doth J. fear God for nought, 13:30
  give tools finish j., 620:15
  go to Hell will help them is my j.,
    543:2
  no person deprived of j., 753:17
  patience of J., 46:17
  poor as J., 183:17
Joblillies, Picninnies and the J., 324:7
Jobs, right people in right j., 474:17
Jockey of Norfolk not too bold,
    153:*n*7
Jocund, cocks and lions j. be, 230:2
  day stands tiptoe, 176:6
  rebecks sound, 251:15
  such a j. company, 375:22
  then be thou j., 214:27
Jocundity, jasper of j., 136:3
Joe, G.I. J., 783:12
  Old Black J., 507:4
  say it ain't so J., 782:20
  where have you gone J. DiMaggio,
    772:9
Joe's, Sloppy J., 720:18
Jog on the footpath way, 223:4

Johannes, absolute J. fac totum,
    157:20
Johano-ai, Turquoise Horse of J.,
    787:11
John and I are quit, 288:3
  Anderson my jo, 362:15
  awake my St. J., 301:1
  Baptist's head, 35:15
  Barleycorn got up again, 362:3
  Brown's body, 524:7
  Bull or Englishman's fireside, 366:16
  Don J. of Austria, 619:2
  Donne Anne Donne Un-done,
    228:*n*1
  greatest of all is J. Bull, 403:26
  I J., 47:1
  I J. saw the holy city, 47:37
  inspiring bold J. Barleycorn, 363:7
  Matthew Mark Luke and J., 266:8
  my son J., 791:12
  or Shaun, 647:20
  Peel with coat so gay, 413:20
  shut the door good J., 302:6
  some said J. print it, 272:9
  speak for yourself J., 442:3
  Stuart Mill, 627:19
  there St. J. mingles, 302:21
  Thomas marryin' Lady Jane, 657:15
  who killed J. Keats, 403:28
  whose name was J., 39:31
John Henry told his captain, 780:20
Johnny, Frankie and J., 781:14
  I hardly knew ye, 779:12
  leave her J. leave her, 793:17
  little J. Green, 789:6
  whiskey J., 793:8
John's, bounded by St. J., 460:14
Johnson, great Cham of literature
    Samuel J., 325:2
  no arguing with J., 330:16
Join, children j. hands and sing, 761:3
  choir invisible, 483:7
  don't j. too many gangs, 624:5
  few gangs if any, 624:5
  hand in hand Americans, 336:10
  now j. your hands and hearts,
    164:27
  the family, 624:5
  them that j. house to house, 25:38
  triumph of skies, 312:17
  union and say Equal Pay, 491:22
  United States, 624:5
  will you j. dance, 518:6
Joined, he has j. great majority, 105:1
  lawfully j. together, 50:2
  make third j. former two, 275:25
  my name j. to theirs, 101:17
  rogue and whore together, 289:22
  what God hath j., 35:35
  when issues are j., 58:1
  whom God hath j., 50:6
Joint, every j. and motive, 201:10
  heirs with Christ, 42:2
  remove the j., 519:18
  time is out of j., 195:6
Joint-laborer, night j. with day,
    192:24
Joints, dividing j. and marrow, 45:34
  of all gin j. in all towns in world,
    726:9

Joke, ain't no j., 765:12
  every j. long ago made, 531:23
  forgive Thy j. on me, 625:2
  good j. not criticized, 619:1
  Jack j. poor potsherd, 551:17
  living in middle of Jewish j., 765:12
  loses everything when joker laughs,
    364:11
  many a j. had he, 329:17
  treat woman as dirty j., 767:2
Joked about every prominent man,
    638:7
  world j. incessantly, 531:23
Joker, joke loses everything when j.
    laughs, 364:11
Jokes, crack any of these old j., 73:20
  difference of taste in j., 484:1
  Fate's saddest j., 59:*n*6
  little j. on Thee, 625:2
  standing j., 292:17
  ten j. an hundred enemies, 320:9
Jollities, Jorrocks' jaunts and j., 434:6
Jollity, jest and youthful j., 251:8
  tipsy dance and j., 252:20
  upon my yowthe and my j., 131:2
Jolly and easy in minds, 463:8
  miller, 338:18
  red nose, 242:16
  swagman, 589:5
  three j. huntsmen, 791:17
  What j. fun, 584:3
Jonah was in the belly of the fish,
    29:37
Jonathan heard not his father's oath,
    11:35
  loved him as his own soul, 11:43
Jones, Casey J., 610:22
  Lady Jingly J., 472:10
  this is the army Mr. J., 666:14
Joneses, keeping up with J., 782:1
Jonson, Ben J. his best poetry, 232:11
  O rare Ben J., 231:*n*6
Jonson's learned sock, 251:19
Jordan, fertilize J. plain, 632:16
  I looked over J., 794:13
  stood in midst of J., 10:32
  that's the river of J., 794:19
Joris and he, 465:3
Jorrocks' jaunts and jollities, 434:6
Joseph, king which knew not J., 8:20
  stript J. of his coat, 8:4
Joshua fit battle of Jericho, 794:10
  like J. commanded sun, 310:21
Jostle, though Philistines may j.,
    529:18
Jostling, no man lives without j.,
    412:28
  not done by j. in street, 359:18
Jot, one j. of former love retain,
    161:11
  one j. of heart or hope, 255:15
  or tittle, 33:4
Jour, le j. de gloire est arrivé, 366:9
Journal, aussi vieux que le j. d'au-
    jourd-hui, 618:*n*1
Journalism, responsible j., 677:6
Journalist, bribe or twist British j.,
    660:13
  knows is morally indefensible,
    766:12

Journey, arrant jade on a j., 329:1
  begin j. on Sundays, 290:15
  dawn speeds a man on j., 54:29
  death and sorrow on our j., 620:12
  end of j. too, 585:8
  going a j., 390:12
  he is in a j. or sleepeth, 12:36
  in middle of j. of life, 125:3
  intellectuals describe j. into Communism, 721:15
  life is its own j., 719:14
  long day's j. into night, 674:8
  longest j. go, 408:13
  longest j. inwards, 716:4
  longest part of j., 86:19
  Monopoly Business at end of j., 555:14
  night j. on a bus, 753:2
  of a thousand miles, 57:20
  some point of pointless j., 750:6
  soul of j. liberty, 390:14
  to oblivion, 658:2
  to promised land, 610:22
  to unknown, 686:20
  universe in map, 150:25
  with my strange heroes, 446:25
Journeyed across centuries, 621:9
Journeyman to grief, 170:32
Journeymen, delicate art relegated to j., 643:17
  nature's j., 197:1
Journey's, dine at j. end, 596:12
  here is my j. end, 208:14
  when j. over, 578:20
Journeys end in lovers meeting, 202:1
Journeywork of stars, 489:15
Jours s'en vont je demeure, 641:*n*3
Jove, daughter of J., 321:18
  for his power to thunder, 219:9
  front of J. himself, 197:30
  in ancestral J. Troy's sons rejoice, 94:19
  Jehovah J. or Lord, 303:14
  laughs at lovers' perjuries, 175:4
  Rain-giver, 101:6
  we descend from J., 94:19
  where J. bestows, 246:4
  with J. I begin, 92:6
Jove's, immortal J. dread clamors, 207:8
  of J. nectar sup, 232:15
  starry threshold of J. Court, 252:11
Jovi, eripuitque J. fulmen, 103:*n*11
Jovial, Autumn comes j. on, 308:6
  three j. huntsmen, 311:*n*5
Joy, all that j. can give, 300:15
  although our last, 208:19
  always to j. inclined, 357:19
  and Love triumphing, 257:25
  antique j., 594:16
  apprehend some j., 174:1
  asks if this be j., 329:21
  at weeping, 186:7
  be unconfined, 399:22
  be wi' you a', 368:7
  bed of crimson j., 358:4
  before a j. proposed, 222:7
  bitter j., 700:7
  brightened with j., 376:21
  bringer of that j., 174:1

Joy (*continued*)
  chortled in his j., 518:16
  cometh in the morning, 16:25
  courage love j., 297:16
  deep power of j., 373:3
  delights in joy, 220:10
  dreme of j. all but in vayne, 132:*n*12
  enter into j., 36:14
  Europe thrilled with j., 373:11
  even his griefs are a j., 54:1
  every child may j. to hear, 356:5
  excursion same for sorrow as j., 727:18
  father's j. mother's pride, 379:3
  feast of j. a dish of pain, 156:22
  formed of j. and mirth, 359:20
  fruit of Spirit is j., 44:19
  gem of all j., 136:3
  general j. of whole table, 215:6
  glad tidings of great j., 285:2
  good tidings of great j., 38:3
  Greensleeves all my j., 776:11
  have j. or power, 430:16
  he who binds to himself a j., 357:22
  honey of all earthly j., 266:16
  I wish you j. of the worm, 218:15
  in trouble and in j., 285:3
  is the sweet voice, 383:10
  is wisdom, 595:4
  kisses j. as it flies, 357:22
  lean in j. upon Father's knee, 356:10
  man made for j. and woe, 359:10
  marriage has more j. than pain, 67:21
  masterpiece j. to artist, 523:21
  meet with j. in sweet Jerusalem, 165:3
  my j. my grief, 249:30
  my life my j., 148:9
  no j. but calm, 454:7
  no j. but lacks salt, 623:20
  no j. in Mudville, 588:25
  nor love nor light, 499:22
  not because troubles are delectable j., 89:13
  not carol of j. or glee, 614:24
  not intermeddle with his j., 21:19
  now 'tis little j., 422:20
  O j. that in our embers, 375:10
  O what j. and glory must be, 121:6
  Ocean and my j., 401:4
  of elevated thoughts, 373:5
  of life is variety, 314:7
  of love too short, 133:9
  of sex, 748:1
  oil of j. for mourning, 28:6
  pain short j. eternal, 365:18
  perfect j. therein I find, 148:*n*2
  Phyllis is my only j., 281:14
  pity planet all j. gone, 743:16
  pleasance revel, 206:23
  poet's j. conceals despair, 631:3
  politics of j., 729:19
  pray in j. and abundance, 651:14
  pure and complete j. impossible, 510:9
  reveal itself when transformed in us, 630:8

Joy (*continued*)
  riding's a j., 465:20
  rule of j. and duty one, 542:11
  scrip of j. immortal diet, 152:16
  senses forever in j., 466:17
  shall reap in j., 19:28
  shudder of j. runs up, 752:2
  silence perfectest herald of j., 186:23
  silly j. at silly things, 329:*n*4
  snatch a fearful j., 321:14
  sons of God shouted for j., 15:8
  source of Humor not j. but sorrow, 527:26
  spontaneous j., 595:19
  stern j. warriors feel, 378:25
  strength through j., 679:5
  surprised by j., 377:3
  Tahiti full of peace and j., 486:27
  that your j. be full, 40:34
  the luminous cloud, 383:10
  thing of beauty j. forever, 414:9
  this is alone Life J. Empire Victory, 407:6
  this torment my j., 725:17
  thou spark from Heaven, 364:13
  to pass to world below, 94:3
  to the world, 294:17
  to their friends, 53:10
  true j. in life, 570:22
  walked in glory and j., 374:9
  was never sure, 534:14
  weep at j., 186:7
  where poverty and j., 123:9
  whose hand is ever at lips, 416:18
  work with j., 651:13
  world can give, 401:17
Joyance everywhere, 380:24
Joyce, private man James J., 769:5
Joyful all ye nations rise, 312:17
  births, 186:1
  in day of prosperity be j., 24:10
  make a j. noise, 17:37, 18:19, 18:22
  shall my j. temples bind, 249:29
Joyfulness prolongeth his days, 32:3
Joyless, sin to be j., 687:18
Joyous, how j. his neigh, 787:11
  understanding is j., 767:1
Joyously, flowers through grass j. sprang, 123:4
Joyousness, lends j. to a wall, 543:19
Joy's, burst J. grape, 416:18
  soul lies in doing, 200:4
Joys abound as seasons fleet, 163:23
  as winged dreams, 776:15
  be j. three parts pain, 467:8
  bid j. farewell, 414:4
  fairest j. give unrest, 414:14
  fall not to rich alone, 97:16
  homely j., 322:7
  in another's loss of ease, 358:3
  kill your j. with love, 176:20
  let j. be as May, 242:15
  minds me o' departed j., 362:8
  nakedness all j. are due to thee, 230:13
  only solitary know j. of friendship, 616:12
  our youth our j. our all, 153:2
  perish in infancy, 777:7

Joys (*continued*)

present j. more to flesh and blood, 275:21
raise j. and triumphs high, 312:13
summer hath his j., 226:16
taste whole j., 230:13
tasted eternal j. of Heaven, 162:15
tenderness its j. and fears, 375:15
thy j. when shall I see, 776:25
to this are folly, 234:3
vain deluding J., 251:21
with age diminish, 468:12
youth's season for j., 297:18
Jubal father of such as handle harp, 7:10
Jubilant, bright pomp ascended j., 259:22
Jubilee, bring the J., 520:6
fiftieth year j., 9:27
sons to thy J. throng, 405:12
year of J., 794:16
Jubjub bird, 518:15
Judah and Israel dwelt safely, 12:20
say unto the cities of J., 27:19
sin of J., 28:28
Judaism religion of the father, 569:18
Judas had given them the slip, 286:19
if J. had not been born, 36:27
jealous J. cowardly Peter, 713:9
saith Why is ointment not sold, 40:22
so J. did to Christ, 172:8
Judea, Bethlehem of J., 32:23
Judge above his last, 81:2
allow iniquities, 543:9
amongst fools a j., 105:*n*8
by sample we j. whole, 149:2
children j. parents, 566:17
condemned when criminal absolved, 99:22
do not j. us too harshly, 698:17
forbear to j., 164:3
I j. not thee, 151:29
I'll be j. I'll be jury, 517:6
impartial j., 332:24
justice j. or vicar, 352:24
law says j. as looks down nose, 720:14
listening like j. supreme, 423:14
cannot j. lot good or evil, 66:*n*2
my friend j. not me, 151:29
my witness and my j., 236:2
never j. until other side heard, 68:21
no king can corrupt, 225:11
no one should j. own case, 99:31
none blessed, 31:28
not according to appearance, 40:6
not play before done, 242:15
not that we be not judged, 450:10
not that ye be not judged, 34:2
of all things, 271:7
of authors' names, 299:1
out of thy mouth will I j., 39:10
people j. men by success, 265:23
people seldom j. right, 355:1
quick and the dead, 48:25
rain influence and j. prize, 251:18
right j. judges wrong, 66:8
setting yourself up as j., 76:15

Judge (*continued*)

should not be young, 75:9
sober as j., 311:13
sole j. of truth, 301:13
the fatherless, 25:29
to j. events sanely, 396:11
upright j. learned j., 182:2
Judged in light of final issue, 79:2
intellectual product j. from age produced, 538:4
judge not that we be not j., 450:10
judge not that ye be not j., 34:2
not to have lived, 542:6
should be j. as a captain, 134:13
Judge's robe, 204:1
Judges, a fool with j., 105:*n*8
all ranged, 297:21
as j. neither Jew nor Gentile, 646:11
common j. of property, 314:3
Constitution what j. say, 586:8
do and must legislate, 542:21
hungry j. sentence sign, 299:15
in every state bound thereby, 346:10
lots of mediocre j., 713:16
of facts not laws, 296:22
right judge j. wrong, 66:8
Judgest, thou j. another, 41:37
Judging for themselves, 352:36
no way of j. future, 339:8
people by appearances, 268:3
Judgment, accurate in his j., 337:*n*1
and exactitude enter him, 3:3
and imagination, 383:22
beauty bought by j. of eye, 168:22
bounded by Day of J., 460:*n*1
bring every work into j., 24:30
complains of his j., 265:13
Daniel come to j., 181:21
defend against your j., 276:3
difficult, 71:13, 349:12
do not wait for last j., 732:19
ever awake, 384:14
execute j. against gods of Egypt, 8:38
fled to brutish beasts, 189:2
God and history remember j., 681:2
God's great J. Seat, 591:9
green in j., 217:10
hard to found j. on man, 145:9
he looked for j., 25:38
his ways are j., 10:26
I suspend my j., 146:5
leaves of J. Book unfold, 506:3
men of ill j. ignore good, 65:14
no comparison no j., 332:28
nor people's j. always true, 274:14
not industry only but j., 331:4
or intuition more subtle, 542:17
power out of thy soul's j., 136:1
practical j. of Americans, 438:3
private j., 325:6
prophet under j. he preaches, 684:16
reserve thy j., 193:30
seek j., 25:29
shallow spirit of j., 163:10
time makes possible Day of J., 652:1
vulgarize day of j., 434:3
we thought it J. Day, 540:21

Judgment (*continued*)

were we men of j., 741:2
young in limbs in j. old, 180:23
Judgments, brawling j., 459:11
men's j. parcel of their fortunes, 217:26
of Lord righteous, 16:11, 450:11
with j. as watches, 298:9
Judicial, duty of j. department, 355:9
function, 568:18
power distinct from legislative, 338:7
types of j. writing, 609:11
Judiciary safeguard of liberty, 586:8
Judicious, a little j. levity, 562:3
swearin' keeps temper, 603:10
wales portion with j. care, 361:9
Jug of Wine Loaf of Bread, 445:9
one old j. without handle, 472:9
w'en it gits loose fum j., 556:13
Jugement, je suspends mon j., 146:*n*2
Juggler of Day is gone, 511:19
threadbare j. fortune-teller, 166:34
Juggling fiends no more believed, 216:20
Jug-jug, cuckoo j. pu-we, 226:20
Jugular, nearer unto him than his j. vein, 117:17
Juice, write until still have j., 702:12
Juices, keep j. flowing by jangling around, 719:12
Julia, in silks my J. goes, 241:20
Julian, remembered poor J., 702:3
year of J. Calendar 710, 237:23
Julia's, where my J. lips smile, 241:1
Juliet and her Romeo, 176:21
is the sun, 174:26
unless philosophy make a J., 176:4
Julius Caesar thou art mighty yet, 189:25
mightiest J. fell, 192:25
July, born on Fourth of J., 632:11
English winter ending in J., 403:16
in her eyes, 776:19
June and J. flowers, 240:16
March J. October May, 143:*n*6
second day of J. 1776, 338:5
swarm of bees in J., 777:18
what to slave your Fourth of J., 480:13
July's day short as December, 222:20
Jumblies, lands where J. live, 472:4
Jump, good wits j., 151:9
I cut down trees skip and j., 775:6
I see him j. before me, 561:10
not j. with common spirits, 180:26
over the candlestick, 791:10
thought j. sea and land, 220:23
we'd j. life to come, 213:5
Jumped into bramble bush, 792:22
Jumping, chinook salmon j. falling back, 743:15
from chair she sat in, 397:5
Jumps in after train started, 588:13
over lazy dog, 781:8
June and July flowers, 240:16
as cuckoo is in J., 178:12
bustin' out all over, 692:11
knee-deep in J., 558:16
leafy month of J., 381:24

Kick (*continued*)
  I get k. out of you, 682:2
  jackass can k. barn down, 648:11
  wheel's k., 633:14
  why k. me down stairs, 360:6
  won't have Nixon to k., 733:12
  you downstairs, 517:11
Kicked and torn and beaten out, 410:8
  until they can feel, 263:18
  waxed fat and k., 10:27
Kicks dust, 478:10
Kid, here's looking at you k., 726:11
  leopard shall lie down with the k.,
    26:11
Kiddo, take it from me k., 688:12
Kidney, heroes of that k., 668:9
  man of my k., 183:4
Kids loved the dog, 733:11
  playing game in rye, 747:8
  thank you k., 710:1
Kike, make sure not a guinea or k.,
    694:5
Kilimanjaro highest mountain, 702:4
Kill, almost k. man as k. book, 254:23
  and bliss me, 776:22
  basilisk is sure to k., 297:19
  be my brother or I k. you, 342:6
  best to k. him right away, 350:22
  bullet that will k. me, 370:13
  cankers in musk-rose buds, 173:10
  care k. a cat, 187:*n*1
  cure disease k. patient, 159:28
  do not k., 3:14
  establishes tyranny k. Brutus, 137:4
  flea though he k. none, 231:7
  hates thing he would not k., 181:14
  him in the shell, 188:1
  in artificial manner, 412:17
  joys with love, 176:20
  kill kill kill kill kill, 211:7
  learn him or k. him, 526:13
  let's k. all the lawyers, 164:8
  nor yet canst thou k. me, 230:22
  not alive enough to know how to k.
    self, 747:2
  one admiral to encourage others,
    306:9
  reverence you've killed hero, 717:11
  sooner k. man than hawk, 663:13
  strike at king must k. him, 433:30
  things they do not love, 181:14
  thou shalt not k., 9:12
  thy physician, 208:24
  time to k., 23:32
  time which man trying to k., 493:12
  time without injuring eternity,
    477:31
  to know to k. to create, 494:14
  to wear fox have to k. it, 665:6
  truths which can k. nation, 646:15
  urge to k., 766:2
  us for their sport, 210:20
  when you have to k., 622:6
  where I please, 762:16
  why k. her policeman asked, 697:10
  wife with kindness, 167:29
  willingly as k. a fly, 167:12
  you if you quote it, 600:17
Killed, before he k. dragon, 619:6
  books not k. by fire, 649:21

Killed (*continued*)
  by overwork, 591:8
  calf in high style, 271:22
  care k. a cat, 187:11
  dragons have to be k., 735:13
  effort nearly k. her, 609:3
  fought dogs k. cats, 464:18
  hawked at and k., 214:18
  hunting hyena, 621:15
  I'm k. sire, 464:10
  many times in politics, 619:16
  more k. by suppers, 244:18
  only once in war, 619:16
  scotched snake not k. it, 214:25
  some sleeping k., 171:25
  than frightened to death, 434:10
  the rat, 792:24
  two thirds of people k., 636:3
  we have k. God, 552:*n*2
  who k. Cock Robin, 789:1
  who k. John Keats, 403:28
  who k. the pork chops, 757:2
  you first time off base, 701:16
Killer kings on Etruscan cup, 742:15
Killeth, letter k., 43:31
  wrath k. the foolish man, 14:1
Killing as canker to rose, 253:19
  by simply exerting will, 495:*n*2
  defenseless black people, 755:10
  eternity essence of tragedy, 589:18
  frost, 225:16
  time ends in k. man, 493:12
  time essence of comedy, 589:18
  treat for Ossete, 681:8
  why use k. at all, 61:18
Kills, air that k., 579:9
  destroys book k. reason, 254:23
  doctor k. more, 283:19
  gout k. more rich than poor, 271:17
  not night that k., 589:16
  shadow k. the growth, 233:6
  six or seven dozen Scots, 177:20
  superiority to sex that k., 722:8
  thing he loves, 567:17
  world k. the good, 701:15
Kilmer tongue not far from cheek,
    666:23
Kilroy was here, 697:3, 783:10
Kiltartan, my country K. Cross,
    596:10
Kiltartan's poor, 596:10
Kimono, woman in k., 713:17
Kin, fair and foul near k., 598:20
  little more than k., 192:34
  makes whole world k., 201:3
Kind, adieu k. friends, 781:1
  and northern face, 701:2
  art of being k., 562:16
  as kings upon coronation, 275:16
  be k. to my remains, 276:3
  be to her virtues k., 287:19
  be too k. to be k. enough, 298:4
  blundering k. of melody, 274:17
  charity is k., 43:14
  consorteth according to k., 31:32
  could not ourselves be k., 698:17
  cruel only to be k., 198:7
  enjoy her while she's k., 275:2
  Fortune more k. than her custom,
    181:25

Kind (*continued*)
  had it been early had been k.,
    315:17
  heart benevolent and k., 362:4
  hearts more than coronets, 454:3
  human k. not bear much reality,
    670:11
  I am a k. of burr, 204:26
  I have been her k., 759:14
  kindness not therefore k., 300:11
  lady sweet and k., 777:4
  less than k., 192:34
  love is k., 43:14
  no best in k. but degree, 441:22
  not seek for k. relief, 356:18
  plenty of the k., 453:19
  serve country and thy k., 522:12
  thief said last k. word, 467:26
  through fire for k. heart, 183:1
  two almost divide the k., 300:16
  war is k., 611:8
  were all thy children k., 184:28
  where each of us belongs, 759:5
  yet he was k., 329:17
Kinder, a little k. than necessary,
    581:20
  gentler nation, 753:13
Kindle, cannot k. when will, 497:13
  soft desire, 276:15
  truths k. light for t., 89:12
Kindled, anger of Lord k., 12:6
  at taper of conwiviality, 469:26
  earth, 404:4
  light here k., 240:12
  man like light k. and put out, 62:18
  world Fire k., 62:12
Kindles, fires true Genius k., 302:11
  in clothes a wantonness, 241:4
  love kindled by virtue k. another,
    126:17
Kindleth, how great a little fire k.,
    46:11
Kindliness of sheets, 663:2
Kindling her undazzled eyes, 255:2
Kindly, be k. affectioned, 42:14
  earth slumber, 455:19
  frosty but k., 190:12
  fruits of the earth, 49:12
  had we never loved sae k., 362:11
  if heart just frank k., 269:17
  Light, 426:18
  Nature's k. law, 301:15
  stopped for me, 513:3
  to his fellow men, 51:22
  word goodly act, 634:17
  words do not enter so deeply, 80:4
Kindness, a God of great k., 13:23
  acts of k. and of love, 373:1
  always depended on k. of strangers,
    730:19
  and lies, 713:6
  begets kindness, 65:11
  Christ took k., 467:26
  cup o' k. yet, 362:20
  glad k., 597:3
  in women not looks, 167:30
  kill wife with k., 167:29
  learned k. from unkind, 651:15
  lose natural k., 596:22
  milk of human k., 212:28

Kingdom (*continued*)
of the shore, 221:3
of well kingdom of sick, 765:16
other k., 732:*n*1
remember me when in thy k., 39:20
rich man enter into k., 35:37
root of the k., 79:15
teach order to peopled k., 184:23
theirs is the k. of heaven, 33:1
thine is the k., 13:17, 33:12
thy k. come, 33:12
to find man to benefit k., 79:11
who draw us to k., 112:17
Kingdoms, all the k. of world, 38:9
are but cares, 133:19
are clay, 216:25
destroyed by bandits, 281:22
did shake k., 26:15
goodly states and k., 413:24
kissed away k., 217:24
of this world, 47:26
sifted three k., 277:*n*2
Kingfisher, blue k. dives, 742:10
Kingfishers, as k. catch fire, 551:7
Kingly crown to gain, 395:17
his state is k., 255:13
King's, all the k. horses, 790:13
daughter is all glorious within,
17:15
daughter o' Noroway, 784:32
English, 182:23
First Minister, 621:13
grim k. dog, 67:24
marched by k. name, 683:10
might greater than human, 70:12
name a tower of strength, 166:12
not the k. crown nor sword, 204:1
our only lord, 161:8
rides hobbyhorse along k. highway,
320:8
subject's duty is k., 185:17
Kings, all be happy as k., 561:12
all K. and their favorites, 229:5
all k. mostly rapscallions, 526:24
alone dwell k. of sea, 497:9
and counselors of the earth, 13:35
and princes have philosophy, 75:15
angels in forms of k., 344:7
barrel-house k., 637:8
cabbages and k., 519:3
calm contending k., 167:2
captains and k. depart, 593:1
change state with k., 220:17
crown that seldom k. enjoy, 164:19
death beats at palaces of k., 95:18
death lays icy hand on k., 246:23
descended of so many k., 218:21
did king to death, 737:10
divine right of k., 448:11
dread and fear of k., 181:19
flower of k. and knights, 133:16
glory to King of k., 312:*n*3
good of subjects end of k., 285:19
grammar control k., 269:29
have sat down, 31:26
he shall stand before k., 22:15
heart's ease must k. neglect, 185:18
in golden suits ride elephants, 731:5
it makes gods, 166:11

Kings (*continued*)
kind as k. upon coronation day,
275:16
king of all k., 775:15
King of k., 47:34, 312:*n*3
know K. of England, 529:12
laws or k. cause or cure, 314:15
like stars, 408:9
mad world mad k., 169:25
may be blest, 363:5
may love treason but traitor hate,
88:*n*13
meaner creatures k., 166:11
mercy enthroned in hearts of k.,
181:19
Nature's little k., 227:14
nice customs curtsy to great k.,
186:5
not k. and lords but nations, 393:10
on Etruscan cup, 742:15
Ozymandias king of k., 406:13
pale k. and princes, 417:7
peasants born k. of earth, 436:21
plucker down of k., 164:17
politeness of k., 355:8
pretend to watch over economy,
326:5
pride of k., 301:1
princes but breath of k., 361:10
prophets and k., 38:21
Right Divine of K., 303:31
royal throne of k., 171:9
sad stories of death of k., 171:25
setter up of k., 164:17
showers on her k. barbaric pearl,
256:23
slave to fate chance k., 230:23
spirit of Zeus-fostered k., 51:6
sport of k., 295:1
tax heavier than k., 310:14
teeming womb of royal k., 171:9
they are no k., 285:19
tired of k., 430:1
triumphing over k. and aces, 680:17
tyrants from policy, 332:16
until philosophers are k., 75:15
vain the ambition of k., 237:20
walk with K., 593:20
what have k. that privates have not,
185:18
would not play at, 335:10
Kinquering Congs their titles take,
553:22
Kinship with the stars, 508:25
Kinsmen, as K. met a Night, 512:14
Kipling, Rudyards cease from K.,
580:17
Kirk, below the k., 380:29
is this the k., 382:1
nearer God more far, 153:3
Kiss, ae fond k., 362:10
afresh, 241:8
after k. comes throttle, 720:5
and cling, 520:*n*3
and tell, 291:5
come k. me, 776:22
come let us k. and part, 161:11
coward does it with k., 567:17
fades out from k. to k., 595:12
gin a body k. a body, 778:*n*1

Kiss (*continued*)
give me a k., 241:8
is still a kiss, 689:15
Jews k. infidels adore, 299:10
keep k. in refrigerator, 696:8
Kiss Bang Bang, 746:17
last lamenting k., 230:1
leave a k. but in the cup, 232:15
long as my exile, 219:11
make me immortal with a k.,
162:19
me and be quiet, 304:4
me Hardy, 361:2
me Kate, 167:23
me sweet and twenty, 202:2
not a k. nor look be lost, 720:17
not k. your f.ing flag, 688:17
of death, 618:5
part without k., 523:4
place to make well, 394:1
rough male k. of blankets, 663:2
'scuse me while I k. the sky, 772:3
so k. on, 241:8
soldier's k. dwells on lips, 490:12
some that shadows k., 180:28
till the cow comes home, 238:14
what is a k., 240:17
with one long k. my soul, 162:*n*8
you take is better, 201:9
Kissed, came to Jesus and k. him,
36:33
curtsied when you have and k.,
223:30
good-bye I have k. it, 710:1
here hung lips I have k., 199:8
Jenny k. me, 397:5
lovely grass, 662:17
maiden all forlorn, 792:24
not k. in forty years, 680:8
O sad k. mouth, 533:19
pacified Psyche k. her, 453:4
righteousness and peace have k.
each other, 18:8
stones k. by English dead, 687:4
taking bull by horns k. her violently, 644:11
them and put them there, 559:21
toyed and k., 297:14
we have k. away kingdoms, 217:24
Kisses, between k. and wine, 602:7
bring again bring again, 204:22
from female mouth, 402:4
give me a thousand k., 90:19
I understand thy k., 178:8
joy as it flies, 357:22
many thousand k., 218:7
more than k. letters mingle souls,
230:14
of enemy deceitful, 23:1
played cards for k., 155:19
remembered k. after death, 456:14
you have forgotten my k., 534:18
Kissing, die young like k. God, 754:17
don't last cookery do, 508:22
fool invented k., 290:12
god k. carrion, 195:17
had to stop, 466:14
hand may feel good, 686:10
no more k. after, 520:*n*3
Kit, your old k.-bag, 641:11

Know (*continued*)

dancer from dance, 598:2
determined to k. beans, 478:28
disciplines of wars, 185:9
disposition of women, 86:10
do not k. much about gods, 671:12
do you k. me my lord, 195:15
does one really want to k., 736:8
doesn't k. what he likes, 690:7
don't k. where go better, 623:8
dost k. who made thee, 356:6
dost thou k. me fellow, 209:5
enough who k. how to learn,
    535:28
every wise man's son k., 202:1
everything forgive everything,
    368:n3
for whom bell tolls, 231:8
four things wiser to k., 687:6
gallanter I k., 511:13
go we k. not where, 204:14
God with thee k. it not, 374:16
greater than we k., 377:7
have the gift to k. it, 190:26
hawk from handsaw, 195:31
heartily k., 429:20
how in your darkness k., 612:6
how should I true love k., 198:16
how tender 'tis to love babe, 213:12
how to grow old, 493:22
how to speak falsehoods, 54:15
I am but summer, 684:7
I am happier than I k., 259:26
I k. a bank, 173:9
I k. all worth knowing in America,
    461:4
I k. myself a man, 227:15
I k. not seems, 193:2
I k. not the man, 37:3
I k. that is poetry, 514:19
I k. thy pride, 11:37
I k. what I like, 614:8
I k. you all, 176:37
I said I didn't k., 526:10
I shall meet fate, 596:10
if cuckold may not k., 656:7
if don't k. where going, 747:6
if find answer k. mind of God,
    772:2
if to do as easy as to k., 179:27
if you gotta ask you'll never k.,
    703:20
if you want to k. yourself, 364:21
I'm farther from heaven, 422:20
in baseball don't k. nothing, 754:10
in Boston ask how much does he k.,
    527:19
in mathematics never k. what about,
    615:9
in part prophesy in part, 43:16
in truth we k. nothing, 70:27
it no more, 19:2
Jesus loves me this I k., 507:13
knows not how to k., 494:19
less than all unknown, 235:26
less understand more, 650:13
let him not k. 't, 207:7
let not left hand k., 33:11
liberty to k., 255:3

Know (*continued*)

like love don't k. where or why,
    720:15
living k. no bounds, 246:19
lucky to die and I k. it, 489:1
make me to k. mine end, 17:7
man not k. of God, 712:19
many admire few k., 71:15
men k. so little of men, 605:1
much say little, 319:13
my methods Watson, 577:22
my soul hath power to k., 227:14
neither shall his place k. him, 14:8
never k. how high we are, 513:18
never k. what is enough, 357:10
never k. when succeeded best, 590:3
never prophesy onless k., 485:17
never see nor k. nor miss me,
    647:22
no such liberty, 267:16
none of them k. one half as much,
    578:17
not enough to k., 78:11
not k. I am a woman, 191:15
not subtle ways, 430:10
not utter what dost not k., 177:18
not what they do, 39:19
not what they mean, 456:13
not what we may be, 198:18
not whether laws be right, 567:21
nothing except my ignorance, 70:22
one thing I k. is land, 648:10
only broken images, 668:18
only k. we loved in vain, 398:15
only that he nothing knew, 261:3
others that we k. not of, 196:10
parting all we k. of heaven, 514:13
people you k. yet can't name, 751:1
place for first time, 672:6
pleasure none but madmen k.,
    274:19
pools I used to k., 579:11
power to k. all things, 227:14
reason from what we k., 301:3
rest who does not k., 101:8
safer to k. too little, 524:16
say not you k. another, 342:7
saying all we did not k., 661:3
shall never k. how to Reply, 359:12
she thinks o' me, 591:22
shore of what we k., 750:5
something of own country, 320:30
strive to grasp what they do not k.,
    80:15
study great deal to k. little, 304:13
subject of knowledge is to k., 76:12
tell me what you k., 430:19
that age to age succeeds, 453:20
that I may k. how frail I am, 17:7
that man might k. end, 189:24
that men are like children, 651:9
that my redeemer liveth, 14:30
that the Lord is God, 18:22
that you do not know, 58:2
the best thought and said, 500:8
the like no more, 445:22
the right moment, 55:13
them by their fruits, 34:11
there is cause for her to k., 733:22
they k. and do not k., 670:8

Know (*continued*)

this I k. full well, 286:25
thought so now I k. it, 297:22
thyself, 55:7, 301:13
till then what love I bore thee,
    374:6
to k. is nothing, 550:5
to k. men thoroughly, 396:11
to k. to kill to create, 494:14
to k. well involves ignorance,
    487:12
too much convinced of too little,
    672:17
trick worth two of that, 177:11
we all k. Anna Livia, 647:19
we are eternal, 278:18
we k. the good, 68:14
we k. what we are, 198:18
well I am not great, 459:14
what do I k., 146:6
what false heart doth k., 213:15
what God and man is, 460:5
what I know and write it, 736:19
what I like, 614:8
what I read in papers, 637:17
what is past I k., 30:14
what is to come I k. not, 30:14
what no other man can k., 573:5
what other people don't know,
    577:17
what should it k. of death, 372:17
what should they k. of England,
    592:5
what 'tis to pity, 190:29
what to do with this time, 431:11
what want to prove, 604:12
what wood a cudgel's of, 263:18
what you don't k. make book,
    380:19
when one doesn't k. where going,
    350:2
where'er I go, 375:5
who only England k., 592:5
who speaks does not k., 57:17
who we are enlist again, 758:9
whose prayers make whole, 591:11
whose woods I think I k., 623:16
world unknowable we k., 581:10
world without going outdoors,
    57:15
worst and provide for it, 339:7
wot lays afore us, 469:47
ye not there is a prince fallen, 12:4
you k. we French, 464:5
you k. what I was, 736:1
Knowed, know all there is to be k.,
    578:17
Knowest, speak less than thou k.,
    209:8
thou k. my downsitting, 20:7
thou k. thy estimate, 221:11
thou k. 'tis common, 193:1
thou the land, 349:8
Knoweth, He k. all things, 117:20
he k. not who shall gather them,
    17:9
no man k. of his sepulcher, 10:30
sun k. his going down, 19:6
Knowing I loved my books, 223:26
not k. what they do, 186:41

Knowing (*continued*)
　of Devil's party without k. it, 357:2
　secret of happiness freedom, 72:7
　when to have done, 413:10
　who you are, 755:17
　without author's k. it, 587:4
Knowledge, absolute idea of k., 76:5
　acquired under compulsion, 75:21
　after such k., 668:7
　all k. and wonder is pleasure, 158:2
　all k. my province, 157:23
　and love of God, 49:18
　apply thine heart unto my k., 22:11
　ask it for k. of lifetime, 524:4
　birds are kinds of k., 76:12
　book of k. fair, 257:24
　born in possession of k., 61:11
　born to follow k., 125:30
　but no power, 70:13
　by suffering, 438:15
　causes to be without k., 56:14
　chapter of k. very short, 305:15
　climbing after k. infinite, 161:21
　comes wisdom lingers, 455:21
　conformity of object and intellect, 122:6
　dawn of k. false dawn, 696:9
　death is k., 365:14
　desirable of itself, 426:23
　desire more love and k., 190:1
　desire of k. caused man to fall, 159:16
　desire of k. increases, 320:16
　diffused k. immortalizes, 367:14
　diffusion of k. advantageous, 438:5
　discard k., 80:14
　do deed without God's k., 63:28
　doubt grows with k., 351:5
　dreadful of truth, 65:17
　earth full of k. of Lord, 26:11
　end of life not k. but action, 505:16
　enormous makes God of me, 417:1
　essential k., 473:14
　every sluice of k. opened, 337:14
　exact k. of the past, 71:19
　excellent things in counsels and k., 22:12
　extraordinary collection of k., 741:14
　faith sight and k., 476:20
　fence against world is k., 277:14
　follow k. like star, 455:3
　foundations of k. in mathematics, 124:1
　furnish means of acquiring k., 369:4
　grow from more to more, 457:4
　grow virtuously into k., 587:8
　he that hath k. spareth his words, 21:37
　he that increaseth k., 23:28
　her ample page, 322:12
　highest point not K., 652:4
　if a little k. dangerous, 505:17
　improver of natural k., 505:5
　in traveling carry k., 317:8
　increase and diffusion of k., 367:18
　increaseth strength, 22:23
　is bought in market, 482:21
　is of two kinds, 316:26
　is power, 158:1

Knowledge (*continued*)
　is proud, 335:13
　is sufficient to attain, 61:31
　is the one only good, 70:20
　liberty not preserved without k., 337:13
　light of k. in eyes, 541:6
　like what we imagine k. to be, 729:5
　manners must adorn k., 305:5
　may give weight, 305:12
　meager and unsatisfactory, 504:11
　men by nature desire k., 77:21
　money power, 730:18
　monk's state transcends k., 65:3
　more than force, 158:n 1
　much k. a curse, 80:16
　multiplieth words without k., 15:4
　must come through action, 67:2
　never learned of schools, 443:6
　night unto night showeth k., 16:9
　no k. beyond experience, 277:6
　no work nor device nor k., 24:19
　not arrogant because of k., 3:4
　not infused from without, 79:27
　not true k. but only belief, 117:14
　of atom through stars, 646:8
　of God more than burnt offerings, 29:26
　of Greek thought, 507:9
　of human nature, 387:10, 535:19
　of itself a treasure, 426:23
　of nothing, 468:19
　of other culture appreciate our own, 707:16
　of our buried life, 498:4
　of their duty, 72:7
　of unconscious activities of mind, 569:3
　of women of his own family, 440:2
　of world not in closet, 304:19
　opinion is k. in making, 254:26
　out-topping k., 497:4
　peace and k. pass argument, 488:18
　poetry finer spirit of k., 373:15
　profess not the k., 31:5
　puffeth up, 43:4
　rich storehouse, 158:6
　science achieve perfect k., 496:18
　science begets k., 71:9
　search for k. a passion, 615:15
　shall any teach God k., 14:34
　shall be increased, 29:21
　should be his guide, 75:9
　show tracks of k., 89:17
　sorrow is k., 402:2
　spirit of k. and fear of the Lord, 26:10
　subject of k. is to know, 76:12
　subjective and objective in k., 384:5
　subtracting from human k., 539:1
　sweetly uttered k., 156:1
　they have too much k., 57:21
　this is k., 60:24
　to be possessed of all this k., 337:10
　to the young man k. and discretion, 20:17
　too much k. for skeptic, 301:13
　tree of k. of good and evil, 6:14
　under difficulties, 390:3

Knowledge (*continued*)
　virtue harder than k., 277:13
　what man does not based on k., 676:19
　wise man has no extensive k., 58:7
　wise man utter vain k., 14:23
　you have been given little k., 116:18
Knowledgeable of evils, 63:1
Knowledges, general k. idiots possess, 358:15
Known a better day, 377:19
　all writer had k. become grotesques, 630:20
　among leaves never k., 415:12
　and do not want it, 315:17
　because of all things k., 596:2
　believed what is least k., 145:18
　best k. and thought, 499:9
　by company he keeps, 69:n 7
　by people never heard of Jesus Christ, 675:18
　cause hidden result well k., 101:23
　God of fathers k. of old, 592:25
　have ye not k., 27:22
　if k. going to live this long, 651:6
　know as I am k., 43:16
　lady k. as Lou, 627:2
　letters should not be k., 224:4
　much to be done little k., 314:27
　must have k. me had he seen me, 476:4
　no more than other men, 271:20
　searched me and k. me, 20:7
　too late, 174:24
　unto whom all desires k., 49:13
　what do to be forever k., 266:14
　what Greeks did not uncertainty, 700:13
　you're k. as who, 760:15
Knows, all this the world well k., 222:7
　babs k. what and babs k. why, 633:2
　but world end tonight, 465:19
　each exercise art he k., 73:6
　expert k. more about less, 585:10
　God's mouth k. not falsehood, 63:7
　greatness k. itself, 178:28
　happy who k. rural gods, 93:1
　how to confess, 309:25
　if you k. of a better 'ole, 666:7
　it k. not what it is, 597:9
　man says what he k., 319:19
　no beast but k. some pity, 165:22
　no one k. masterpiece, 659:11
　no one k. till he tries, 100:14
　not also to un-know, 494:19
　not draw out more than already k., 553:13
　not how other half lives, 245:4
　not what to do, 788:1
　now God alone k., 532:3
　reason k. nothing of, 270:25
　sage k. without going about, 57:15
　Secret sits in middle and k., 624:16
　sleep that k. not breaking, 378:20
　tale every schoolboy k., 321:12
　tell wife all he k., 250:10
　the less one k., 57:15
　the universe not himself, 268:7

Laconic or sententious type, 609:11
Lacrimae, hinc illae l., 85:*n*10
  rerum, 93:*n*12
Lad, blithe Irish l., 388:25
  born to be king, 577:6
  come to you my l., 362:18
  lightfoot l., 579:12
  of mettle a good boy, 177:19
  pass me the can l., 579:17
  up l. when journey's over, 578:20
  well for sailor l., 456:7
  when all world young l., 484:15
  when I was a l., 529:6
Ladder always close to schooner,
    762:7
  behold a l., 7:40
  charity's golden l., 122:8
  down l. rung by rung, 592:4
  Jacob's l., 434:5, 581:12
  made death his l., 154:9
  make a l. of our vices, 114:30
  talk of Jacob's l., 434:5
  to all high designs, 200:8
  unto l. turns his back, 187:32
  young ambition's l., 187:32
Ladders, lie down where l. start,
    599:22
Laddie, your Highland l. gone, 366:20
Laden, with rue heart l., 579:12
Ladies, art helps old l. across street,
    761:17
  Cambridge l., 688:11
  Dust was Gentlemen and L., 513:6
  good night sweet l., 198:19
  Grecian Urn worth old l., 697:2
  if l. be but young and fair, 190:26
  in praise of l. dead, 221:22
  intellectual, 402:6
  lion among l., 173:15
  lords and l. of Byzantium, 597:10
  novel on tables of l., 425:10
  of St. James's, 539:6
  over-offended l., 293:23
  remember the l., 347:1
  whose bright eyes, 251:18
  wild witches noble l., 596:13
Ladies', for l. love unfit, 276:26
  kindling smiles in l. eyes, 423:14
  pearls in beauteous l. eyes, 168:9
  rime into l. favors, 186:3
Ladles, cooks' own l., 464:18
Lads, Dust was L. and Girls, 513:6
  golden l. and girls, 220:3
  pure-minded l. and lasses, 516:11
  that die in glory, 579:5
  though l. far away, 617:12
  thought no more behind, 222:16
Lady be good to me, 695:2
  born in bed with a l., 631:13
  Bountiful, 295:12
  by yonder blessed moon I swear,
    175:7
  church ain't out till fat l. sings,
    782:12
  Colonel's L. an' Judy O'Grady,
    592:21
  Disdain, 186:12
  doth protest too much, 197:13
  downstairs ran l. O, 779:6
  enjoyed the l., 357:18

Lady (*continued*)
  faint heart ne'er won fair l., 150:29
  faint heart never won fair l., 530:16
  fairer l. never seen, 785:5
  fine l. upon white horse, 790:3
  fool called her l. fair, 592:23
  for secrecy no l. closer, 177:18
  garmented in light, 408:3
  give l. what she wants, 522:14
  he saw a l. bright, 785:11
  hear l. sing in Welsh, 178:9
  here lies l. of beauty, 674:12
  here lies most beautiful l., 616:21
  history excitable old l., 560:8
  I asked a lithe l., 357:18
  if you got to ask, 703:*n*1
  if you were April's l., 534:8
  in the case, 297:12
  Jingly Jones, 472:10
  Joan as my L., 241:7
  John Thomas marryin' L. Jane,
    657:15
  lent him to a l., 792:9
  Liner she's a l., 592:19
  longing for that lovely l., 86:18
  longing to be a lazy l., 665:18
  many many l. friends, 583:11
  met l. in meads, 417:5
  my fair l., 788:12
  my l. sweet arise, 219:24
  O l. we receive what we give, 383:8
  of certain age, 403:8
  of Christ's College, 271:21
  of my delight, 555:17
  of Shalott, 454:16, 454:17
  old l. from Dubuque, 684:20
  Old L. of Threadneedle Street,
    360:5
  or the tiger, 523:12
  Our L. of Pain, 533:13
  rather hear L. howl in Irish, 178:9
  rob l. by marriage, 311:28
  Seymour's Fat L., 747:9
  sighed for love of l., 531:14
  sweet and kind, 777:4
  talking to Hens of Dorking, 472:10
  that's known as Lou, 627:2
  that's why l. is tramp, 692:17
  the brach may stand, 209:7
  weep no more my l., 507:2
  who was that l., 604:8
  with Lamp, 442:7
  you are the cruelest she, 201:26
  young l. named Bright, 618:14
Ladybug fly away home, 788:16
Lady's, brain him with l. fan, 177:17
  for all l. hire, 792:9
  get you to l. chamber, 199:8
  he capers nimbly in l. chamber,
    165:20
  imagination rapid, 386:25
  in my l. chamber, 789:18
  in the case, 297:12
  love learned in l. eyes, 169:1
Ladyships, lordships sold to maintain
    l., 234:1
Lady-smocks all silver-white, 169:12
Lafayette we are here, 580:16
Lag-end of my life, 178:29

Lager, give Irishman l. for month,
    526:16
Laggard in love, 378:9
Lags, fiction l. after truth, 331:8
  superfluous l. veteran, 313:21
Laid aside business, 245:12
  bait l. to make taker mad, 222:7
  him on the green, 785:18
  in a manger, 38:2
  in sad cypress l., 202:13
  me down with a will, 561:16
  my heart open to indifference,
    732:13
  on with a trowel, 189:33
  sun is l. to sleep, 231:21
  when I am l. in earth, 284:18
  where wast thou when I l. founda-
    tions, 15:7
Lain for a century dead, 458:24
  should I have l. still, 13:35
Lair, deep his midnight l. made,
    378:17
  rouse lion from his l., 379:23
  slugs leave their l., 383:14
Laisse un peu de soi-même, 570:*n*2
Laissez faire laissez passer, 305:21
Laith were gude Scots lords, 784:34
Laity, paintings the Bible of l., 121:14
Lake, consciousness as bottomless l.,
    538:18
  dream life as l. dreams sky, 589:20
  fire in the l., 5:8
  goddess of the silver l., 253:11
  in l. an arm, 133:6
  Lebarge, 627:3
  lo the level l., 454:19
  Pilot of Galilean l., 254:1
  river l. glimmering pool, 503:4
  sedge withered from l., 417:4
  to Rydal L. that lead, 373:*n*2
  took l. between my legs, 754:22
  wind over l. image, 5:9
Lake Wobegon, that's the news from
    L., 772:5
Lakes, great l. of North America,
    425:11
  light shakes across l., 456:11
Lalun member of ancient profession,
    591:5
Lama, Eli Eli l. sabachthani, 37:12
Lamb, blood of the l., 47:23
  false as fox to l., 200:22
  go to bed with l., 155:13
  God will provide himself a l., 7:34
  he who made thee, 358:7
  little L. I'll tell thee, 356:7
  little L. who made thee, 356:6
  Mary had a little l., 404:10
  of God, 39:35, 48:9
  of God although I speak, 711:3
  pipe song about a L., 356:4
  quiet as a l., 170:8
  save one little ewe l., 12:10
  sedulous ape to L., 561:19
  shall be without blemish, 8:36
  skin of innocent l. parchment, 164:9
  tempers wind to shorn l., 144:14,
    321:2
  to the slaughter, 27:38
  was the holy L. of God, 359:17

Lamb (*continued*)

when lion fawns upon l., 164:30
will never cease to follow, 164:30
wolf shall dwell with the l., 26:11
Lambs could not forgive, 470:2
gather the l. with his arm, 27:20
little hills like l., 19:16
loud bleat from hilly bourn, 416:15
poor little l. lost way, 592:3
we were as twinned l., 222:17
wolves and l. have no concord,
52:22
Lame and impotent conclusion, 206:9
feet to the l., 14:43
little l. balloonman, 688:8
man leap as an hart, 27:9
wrinkled and slanting-eyed, 51:33
Lament, come to dark and l., 624:14
for Madame Blaize, 328:2
frogs drone their l., 92:26
have I not reason to l., 372:18
mistakes of good man, 346:4
wild l., 712:18
Lamentable, most l. comedy, 172:22
that skin of lamb parchment, 164:9
Lamentation, empire's l., 458:5
Lamentations, sighs l. and wailings,
125:8
Lamenting, last l. kiss, 230:1
Lamp, Aladdin's l., 403:14, 485:25
beside the golden door, 558:1
confusing beams from memory's l.,
709:17
fluttered round l., 520:3
God's light like a l., 117:4
I have but one l., 339:8
Lady with L., 442:7
of experience, 339:8
smell of the l., 80:22
stroke beam of my l., 762:9
swallowed lighted l., 631:2
unto my feet, 19:23
when l. is shattered, 409:19
word burned like a l., 32:16
writing smelling of l., 609:11
Lamps, all over Alabama l. are out,
726:4
be l. unto yourselves, 64:23
bright l. shone o'er, 399:21
expire, 602:9
going out over Europe, 585:15
golden l. in green night, 268:24
heaven's great l. dive, 226:13
like hidden l., 334:13
not bow before votive l., 766:1
old l. for new, 778:12
virgins took l., 36:13
Lance, never had oar or l., 73:5
strong l. of justice, 211:4
threw his shining l., 520:11
Lancelot mused a space, 454:17
sang Sir L., 454:15
through L. war wrought, 133:15
Land, after all a poor l., 494:9
already in promised l., 768:12
America my new-found l., 230:12
and the pleasant l., 502:8
appeared at two leagues, 134:8
as near by sea as by l., 147:11
bourn bound of l., 224:1

Land (*continued*)

bringeth thee into a good l., 10:15
death's gray l., 662:4
Dixie L., 475:1
dry and thirsty l., 17:35
ethic for tomorrow, 748:13
fat of the l., 8:14
fenced in piece of l., 319:2
flowing with milk and honey, 8:26
free l. in beloved home, 492:6
go to l. of poetry, 350:3
God gave to Cain, 139:2
gone into silent l., 515:8
good and bad of every l., 476:9
grass grows wherever l. water is,
489:3
grasses in ruined l., 421:19
great rock in a weary l., 27:6
green and pleasant l., 359:17
hail Columbia happy l., 372:15
harmony between men and l., 662:3
he became a l., 720:19
Heaven-rescued l., 391:3
his hands formed the dry l., 18:19
holy l. of Irlonde, 775:12
holy l. of Walsinghame, 152:9
hour later I saw l., 709:5
huge l. will lie revealed, 103:13
I will pass through the l., 8:38
if by l. one lantern, 339:4
ill discoverers think there is no l.,
158:8
ill fares the l., 329:8
imagined l., 639:13
in which always afternoon, 454:5
is immortal, 745:19
it cometh from a terrible l., 26:18
it is promised l., 419:7
law of the l., 123:12
leans against the l., 328:12
light shines over l. and sea, 621:7
lilacs out of dead l., 668:17
live deaf to l. beneath us, 681:7
long l. be bright, 444:4
Lord's song in strange l., 20:6
loss of native l., 68:12
marching to promised l., 521:12
murder l. for private profit, 726:7
my children leastwise of l., 740:5
my l. my father's l., 510:17
my new-found l., 230:12
my own my native l., 378:1
never knew l. to run away, 338:14
never was on sea or l., 376:6
no slave upon our l., 443:1
nothing but l., 616:8
o' the leal, 368:9
ocean surrounds verdant l., 486:27
o'er all the pleasant l., 410:10
of brown heath, 378:2
of Calvin and oatcakes, 380:1
of cotton, 475:1
of darkness and shadow, 14:11
of dead, 697:11, 720:8
of dreams, 499:22
of drowsyhead, 308:13
of Faery, 595:3
of Goshen, 8:15
of Heart's Desire, 595:4
of hope and glory, 585:5

Land (*continued*)

of Just Add Water, 688:12
of Lincoln and Pinkham, 688:12
of living, 697:11
of lost content, 579:9
of mountain and flood, 378:2
of my dreams, 676:17
of nowadays, 608:11
of pilgrims' and so forth, 688:15
of pilgrims' pride, 444:3
of pure delight, 294:19
of scholars, 328:14
of the Arrow Ide, 688:12
of the Cluett Shirt, 688:12
of the free, 391:2, 678:7
of the living, 14:39
of unlimited possibilities, 556:4
of wheat and barley, 10:16
on l. as on the sea, 780:22
one if by l., 442:13
one thing I know is l., 648:10
or cherry-isle, 241:1
our l. before we her people, 624:10
our l. great but no order in it, 121:1
ours before we the land's, 624:10
owes nothing to l., 319:20
Pacific leans on the l., 663:11
pass like night from l. to l., 382:5
peace more precious than piece of
l., 745:21
piece of l. with a garden, 95:10
plowed before man, 444:16
poet's l., 350:3
post o'er l. and ocean, 255:13
prepared the dry l., 48:21
proclaim liberty throughout l., 9:27
Promised L. beyond wilderness,
578:13
raised on city l. taxes, 511:7
rats and water-rats, 180:1
reap the harvest of your l., 9:24
rent with civil feuds, 394:15
rock in weary l., 27:6
salt l. and not inhabited, 28:29
scatter plenty o'er smiling l., 322:15
search l. of living men, 378:5
see l. as community, 662:2
seeking l. of Greeks, 349:13
seems a moving l., 259:21
seen promised l., 761:9
sees across weary l., 619:3
sent to spy out the l., 9:29
sing by l. and sea, 592:11
six feet of l., 510:14
sky and sea and l., 580:8
somewhere in favored l., 588:25
spirits of l. and grain, 80:6
stranger in a strange l., 8:22
stubble l. at harvest-home, 177:2
Supreme Law of the l., 346:10
sweet l. of liberty, 444:3
that gave you birth, 586:12
that I love, 666:11
thieves and water-thieves, 180:1
this l. is your l., 731:13
this was charter of l., 308:12
thought jump sea and l., 220:23
too deep into new l., 379:20
turning back without sighting l.,
543:n4

Land (*continued*)
  unwillingly I left your l., 94:10
  various as your l., 698:8
  violet of native l., 457:8
  voice of the turtle is heard in our l., 25:6
  we're going to our Father's l., 773:17
  westward look the l. is bright, 483:3
  where Bong-tree grows, 472:1
  where lemon trees bloom, 349:8
  where lies the l., 376:13
  where my fathers died, 444:3
  wherein thou shalt eat bread, 10:16
  which the Lord giveth thee, 9:12
  Woman a foreign l., 503:9
  wretched he who bound l. to himself, 3:13
Landed, Eagle has l., 762:12
Landing, fight on l. grounds, 620:7
  on coast of France, 678:16
Landmark, remove not the ancient l., 22:14
Landmarks in man's struggle, 698:20
Landor, with L. and with Donne, 596:12
Land's, land ours before we the l., 624:10
  sea l. edge also, 671:13
Lands and horses part of Self, 545:20
  beyond the sea, 374:6
  envy of less happier l., 171:9
  faery l. forlorn, 415:17
  Great Spirit gave ancestors l., 370:5
  lord of himself not l., 227:8
  men in all l., 650:8
  rulers in all l., 563:7
  sun in lonely l., 458:4
  take us L. away, 514:2
  these l. are ours, 369:17
  voyager at last, 506:14
  where are Sioux l., 516:9
  where Jumblies live, 472:4
  white men take away l., 369:7
Landscape, man shaper of l., 722:14
  now fades glimmering l., 322:2
  we are children of our l., 731:9
Landscapes drawn in monotones, 660:17
  of the moon, 613:5
Lane, boy who lives down l., 788:18
  in an English l., 465:11
  lives in Drury L., 792:1
  long l. knows no turnings, 464:21
  straight down Crooked L., 422:25
  to land of dead, 720:8
Lang, auld l. syne, 362:19
Language, best part of human l., 384:18
  betrayers of l., 659:13
  charged with meaning, 660:5
  chief merit of l. clearness, 111:29
  clearness propriety of l., 500:25
  confound the l. of all earth, 7:26
  conveyed in best chosen l., 387:10
  dictionary best book in l., 610:10
  dies, 588:2
  dissociate l. from science, 345:9

Language (*continued*)
  enemy of clear l. is insincerity, 711:13
  everything in l. perish, 424:18
  for exchange of information, 755:11
  force l. into meaning, 672:15
  high thoughts must have high l., 73:23
  I love the l., 402:4
  in her eye, 201:10
  inherited from Conquistadors, 714:6
  is archives of history, 432:16
  learned his great l., 464:23
  learning me your l., 223:29
  life is a foreign l., 679:12
  loosened corsets of German l., 626:5
  manners laws customs, 373:16
  messenger with l. of his folk, 116:12
  money l. nations understand, 281:18
  my l. is plain, 532:1
  mystery of l. revealed to me, 641:18
  no l. but a cry, 457:18
  no l. like Irish, 613:12
  of Dante common language, 672:21
  of English poet, 672:21
  of the heart, 302:18
  of the living, 671:20
  of truth language of creation, 613:18
  perverters of l., 659:13
  political l. make lies sound truthful, 711:14
  remove weight from l., 751:15
  sarcasm l. of Devil, 412:2
  seeking symbolical l., 383:17
  silent l. of peak, 675:5
  soothing l., 343:18
  speaks a various l., 411:1
  that would make hair curl, 531:11
  things used as l. are attractive, 432:26
  touched by poetry, 736:14
  traveleth before he hath l., 159:20
  universe in l. of mathematics, 161:15
  use any l. you choose, 530:14
  use in measured l., 457:7
  vital development in l., 672:13
  we have l., 734:11
  we praise thee for perspicuity of l., 121:5
  Yiddish wise humble l. of all, 715:6
Languages, Americans not learn l., 605:22
  great feast of l., 169:6
  skilled in works of both l., 96:18
Langueur monotone, 554:n1
Languid strings scarcely move, 356:3
Languor, pierce heart with l., 553:24
Languors, lilies and l. of virtue, 533:12
Lank, bronzed l. man, 637:11
  long and l. and brown, 381:18
  poor lean l. face, 448:8
Lantern, if by land one l., 339:4
  Red L. and his undersea folk, 766:7
Lanterns, eyes like agate l., 701:7
  in North Church, 339:4
Lanthorn is the moon, 174:7

Lap, chestnuts in her l., 212:12
  dropt in her L., 445:13
  in l. of the gods, 52:n5
  in thy green l., 323:2
  me in soft Lydian airs, 251:19
  of Earth, 322:22
  of legends, 415:2
  sat Beauty in my l., 565:20
  see it l. the Miles, 512:17
Lapel, plucked lint from l., 586:2
Lapidary inscriptions, 316:27
Lapidem, stilicidi casus l. cavat, 89:n6
Lapped in lead, 233:11
Lapping, water l. the bow, 669:22
Lapse, forgotten through l. of Time, 77:18
  of murmuring streams, 259:25
Lapses, bards gild l. of time, 413:21
Larceny, sparkle with l., 631:11
Lard their lean books, 234:5
Lards lean earth, 177:15
Laredo, streets of L., 786:6
Large a charter as wind, 190:27
  and smooth and round, 386:4
  as life twice as natural, 519:15
  as store, 243:16
  cold bottle, 559:19
  discourse, 198:12
  divine comfortable words, 459:5
  I am l. contain multitudes, 489:21
  kingdom for little grave, 172:5
  limbo l. and broad, 258:1
  small house and l. garden, 266:17
  was his bounty, 322:23
Large-brained woman large-hearted man, 438:14
Larger, children of l. growth, 305:6
Largest and most comprehensive soul, 273:11
  movements of l. bodies, 351:16
  those of l. size, 519:6
Lark at heaven's gate sings, 219:24
  bisy l. messenger of day, 130:12
  clouds silence then l., 554:13
  fresh as a l., 376:13
  hark hark the l., 219:24
  herald of the morn, 176:5
  never l. nor eagle flew, 751:3
  no l. more blithe than he, 338:18
  now leaves his wat'ry nest, 249:23
  rise with l., 155:13
  that soars singing, 127:1
  when a l. I sang, 725:9
Lark's on the wing, 464:4
Larks, four l. and wren, 471:27
Lars Porsena of Clusium, 425:13
Lasciate ogni speranza voi ch'entrate, 125:n4
Lasciva est nobis pagina vita proba, 106:n4
Lascivious pleasing of a lute, 165:20
  would make anchorite l., 399:n1
Lash, blood drawn with l., 450:11
  I could bear the l., 420:22
  Magic Creature, 514:5
  that beat down Rome, 599:5
  the l. goes on, 599:13
  the rascals naked, 208:2
Lashed, headstrong liberty l. with woe, 166:21

Laugh (*continued*)
  who but must l., 302:12
  yet all these seem to l., 229:8
  yourselves into stitches, 202:29
Laughed consumedly, 295:13
  day on which not l., 342:4
  he l. because knew what next, 733:4
  His word to scorn, 334:16
  in the sun, 662:17
  little dog l., 789:9
  no man who l. bad, 411:21
  upright man l. to scorn, 14:15
  with counterfeited glee, 329:17
Laughing Allegra, 442:10
  at yourselves, 446:24
  bee on stalk, 759:12
  fellow rover, 633:16
  he l. said to me, 356:4
  heard on the hill, 356:17
  in your sleeve, 352:7
  leave them l., 632:9
  quaffing unthinking time, 276:20
  read death of Little Nell without l., 567:25
  sets a wise man to l., 53:28
  sex most fun without l., 767:15
  shallow dreaming pool, 484:14
  somewhere men are l., 588:25
  split sides with l., 150:3
  sports and plays, 356:1
  sweetly speaking and softly l., 56:5
  up her sleeve, 269:3
  Water, 441:25
Laughingstock, make myself l., 150:24
Laughs at archer, 494:2
  at broken hammers, 634:15
  best who laughs last, 288:9
  fair l. the morn, 323:8
  joke loses everything when joker l., 364:11
  Jove l. at lovers' perjuries, 175:4
  Jupiter l. at perjuries of lovers, 101:5
  laugh and world l., 562:15
Laughter, a little time for l., 520:*n*3
  against assault of l. nothing stand, 528:7
  and ability and Sighing, 513:6
  arose among gods, 51:4
  beginning of prayer, 684:17
  better last smile than first l., 288:*n*2
  born with gift of l., 630:15
  can blow it to rags atoms, 528:7
  edges of l. and anguish, 651:2
  enjoy l. at right moment, 82:19
  excessive l., 31:39
  feast is made for l., 24:21
  for a month, 177:14
  has no greater foe than emotion, 577:1
  heart is sorrowful even in l., 21:20
  hidden l. of children, 670:18
  holding both his sides, 251:9
  I'll use you for my l., 189:15
  ill-bred as audible l., 329:*n*4
  laugh thy girlish l., 576:18
  love and l., 520:9
  myriad l. of ocean waves, 63:3
  no one died of l., 614:13
  no time for mirth and l., 600:13

Laughter (*continued*)
  of Gargantua the l., 701:2
  of her heart, 692:7
  of the fool, 24:8
  out of dead bellies, 659:9
  present l., 202:2
  seriously scribbling to excite l., 525:19
  sudden glory maketh l., 239:19
  that all can see, 446:25
  tinkled among teacups, 668:2
  tired of tears and l., 534:13
  under running l., 581:4
  weeping and the l., 602:10
  when her lovely l. shows, 226:19
  wine women mirth l., 402:18
  with pain fraught, 408:7
Laughter-silvered wings, 751:3
Launched, face that l. a thousand ships, 162:19
  forth filament, 491:8
Laundry, dreamed dream called L., 757:7
  nothing but l., 749:16
Laura, grave where L. lay, 152:17
  if L. Petrarch's wife, 402:22
  rose-cheeked L. come, 226:15
Laurea, concedat l. laudi, 88:*n*2
Laurel and myrtle and rose, 349:8
  burned is Apollo's l. bough, 163:1
  crown yield to praise, 88:2
  crowned with l., 684:12
  for perfect prime, 515:11
  green for a season, 534:4
  no l. crown for outrunning burro, 106:23
  outlives not May, 534:4
  poison from Caesar's l. crown, 359:13
Laurels all are cut, 502:7
  in chains or in l., 462:19
  Northern l. not change, 336:1
  worth all your l., 403:23
  yet once more O ye l., 253:14
Lavender in the windows, 245:21
  mints savory marjoram, 223:6
Lavender's blue dilly dilly lavender's green, 792:6
Laver son linge sale, 370:*n*5
Lavish, liar always l. of oaths, 249:18
  no calamity greater than l. desires, 57:14
Lavvy Minx or Sphinx, 471:21
Law agin wearin' o' Green, 779:10
  all things by l. divine, 407:20
  and order pay, 542:20
  and the prophets, 34:8, 36:1
  army of unalterable l., 509:8, 668:1
  bloody book of l., 205:20
  book of the l., 13:22
  born under one l. to another bound, 155:1
  broken every human l., 670:19
  by transgressing kept l., 255:5
  can only bring freedom, 350:30
  common l. not omnipresence, 542:22
  common l. nothing but reason, 152:1
  Common L. of England, 678:21

Law (*continued*)
  Congress shall make no l., 346:11
  conspiracy against l. and order, 759:4
  craving to go to l., 532:5
  curses in Book of L., 277:*n*8
  delight is in l. of the Lord, 15:29
  despair l. chance hath slain, 230:20
  do as adversaries in l., 167:20
  due process of l., 346:14, 346:18
  dusty purlieus of l., 457:25
  embodies nation's development, 542:5
  embody the L., 530:6
  ends Tyranny begins, 277:9
  equal before l., 520:10
  eternal l., 64:19
  evolution not cause but l., 537:5
  extreme l. often extreme injustice, 86:1
  faith nor love nor l., 406:21
  first is l. the last prerogative, 275:15
  first l. for historian, 87:15
  for man law for thing, 429:18
  for rulers and people, 474:21
  fugitive from l. of averages, 749:3
  future lays l. of today, 552:1
  gave l. air of science, 325:*n*4
  good l. is good order, 78:28
  good l. would have stood fast, 65:4
  great cases make bad l., 542:15
  great l. of culture, 412:24
  has honored us, 395:8
  hath not been dead, 204:2
  hatred made l., 716:18
  having not the l., 41:38
  head and hoof of L., 592:17
  hint of universal l., 542:10
  hocus-pocus science, 307:12
  I my Lords embody L., 530:6
  ignorance of the l., 238:25
  in his l. doth he meditate, 15:29
  in l. what plea so tainted, 181:4
  in majestic equality, 550:13
  is a ass a idiot, 469:12
  is a jealous mistress, 392:16
  is good, 45:10
  is order, 78:28
  is The Law, 720:14
  justice the l. my ducats, 180:24
  lapped in universal l., 455:19
  last result of wisdom, 315:6
  lesser breeds without L., 593:3
  life of l. is experience, 542:4
  locks up man and woman, 777:3
  love is fulfilling of l., 42:22
  love l. to itself, 115:14
  master after my disappearance, 64:27
  mighty mightier necessity, 350:21
  mob l., 448:2
  moral l. within me, 326:10
  murder by the l., 296:3
  mysterious l. true source, 258:26
  natural l. old nonsense, 396:17
  Nature's kindly l., 301:15
  nature's l. man made to mourn, 361:7
  necessity has no l., 114:29
  necessity hath no l., 247:3

Law (*continued*)

necessity knows no l. except prevail, 99:32

nice sharp quillets of l., 163:10

no l. more binding than custom, 577:7

no l. of history, 487:21

no man above or below l., 576:3

no such thing as natural l., 396:17

nor l. bade me fight, 596:11

not a light to see by, 753:9

not come to destroy l., 33:3

not concerned with trifles, 118:26

not exempted from power of l., 155:3

not l. so much as right, 477:8

not make scarecrow of l., 203:28

not one jot pass from l., 33:4

nothing l. that is not reason, 152:*n*1

obedience to l. demanded, 576:3

of competition, 525:11

of excluded middle, 748:10

of humanity, 332:8

of musical world, 586:20

of nature and nations, 332:8

of our Creator, 332:8

of the Jungle, 592:15

of the land, 123:12

of the Medes and Persians, 29:17

of the Yukon, 627:1

old father antick the l., 176:29

old l. sad but not bitter, 631:15

one God l. element, 458:3

one l. and one truth, 111:19

one l. for all, 332:8

one L. for Lion and Ox, 357:15

ordinance of reason for common good, 124:11

others will plead at l., 94:15

ought to weed it out, 159:5

our reason is our l., 260:6

people fight for their l., 62:20

people's good the highest l., 88:5

perfection of reason, 152:1

Poetry not matured by l., 418:7

possession eleven points in l., 291:19

precedents constitute l., 345:12

primary l. of every work of art, 502:1

principles of l. and applications, 586:9

Professor of Harvard L. School, 646:14

protection by l., 369:11

public opinion in advance of l., 603:20

reason the life of the l., 152:1

remoter aspects of l., 542:10

rich men rule the l., 328:16

rule nations under l., 94:15

same l. shapes earth-star and snow-star, 477:4

say what l. is, 355:9

says judge as looks down nose, 720:14

school no more than school of fencing, 574:10

seat of l. bosom of God, 155:3

seven hours to l., 152:*n*3

Law (*continued*)

so general a study, 331:15

sociability l. of nature, 547:5

stable but not stand still, 610:13

stands mute in midst of arms, 87:10

Supreme L. of the land, 346:10

sword of war or of l., 344:20

this is l. I maintain, 778:17

to windward of l., 333:17

tongue is the l. of kindness, 23:20

took to the l., 517:10

translating into living l., 661:5

true embodiment, 530:6

universal l., 326:12

unto themselves, 41:38

voice of l. harmony of world, 155:3

what others do from fear of l., 77:14

where no l. no transgression, 41:40

which governs all law, 332:8

who to himself is l., 157:11

windy side of the l., 186:*n*1

write in books of l., 723:16

Lawd, gangway for de L., 678:2

Lawful, all ambitions l., 573:15

all things l. for me, 43:8

guns aren't l., 687:10

is it not l., 35:40

without some l. recreation, 150:15

Lawfully, if a man use it l., 45:10

Lawlands, ye Highlands and L., 785:18

Lawless attack upon liberty, 325:4

discountenance haughty and l., 337:10

linsey-woolsey brother, 263:17

winged unconfined, 357:19

Lawlessness, world l., 649:9

Lawn, rivulets through l., 456:22

white as driven snow, 223:10

Lawns, like satyrs grazing on the l., 162:10

Law's delay, 196:10

in l. grave study six, 152:7

to take care o' raskills, 483:18

Laws, abhor makers and their l. approve, 275:22

abounds with l. teems with crimes, 779:4

acting around us, 444:8

and arms foundations of states, 136:11

and constitution of country, 346:3

are like cobwebs, 288:18

are sand customs rock, 528:5

bad l. bring about worse, 319:10

base l. of servitude, 273:14

best l. teach to trample bad l., 462:16

breathing household l., 374:14

conflict courts decide, 355:9

Constitution and l. of U.S., 346:10

crime to examine l. of heat, 537:4

devise l. for blood, 179:28

doing what l. permit, 304:10

end tyranny begins, 313:2

equal protection of the l., 346:18

fewer l. less power, 432:18

flung at head, 681:8

for themselves not me, 579:19

Laws (*continued*)

forms all produced by l., 444:8

found state and give it l., 137:2

give little Senate l., 302:11

God of universal l., 546:16

good l. lead to better, 319:10

government free where l. rule, 282:18

government of l. not men, 337:18

grind the poor, 328:16

human mind put in nature, 646:6

in which we have no voice, 347:1

judges of facts not l., 296:22

know not whether l. right, 567:21

language manners l. customs, 373:16

like spiders' webs, 56:2

Nature and Nature's l. hid, 303:17

never forget l. of forefathers, 105:16

not assume physical l. exist, 575:8

not care who make l., 285:11

not good l. where not armed, 136:11

not violate l. of justice, 326:9

obedient to their l. we lie, 60:11

of God are forever, 66:11

of God laws of man, 579:19

of nature and nature's God, 343:2

of the Jungle, 592:17

one by one forging l., 681:8

or kings cause or cure, 314:15

ought not to remain unaltered, 78:17

physical l. and l. of numbers, 516:6

power of making l., 355:4

right from which l. derive authority, 345:16

rules of game l. of Nature, 505:6

secure equal justice, 72:2

self-made l., 494:20

sweeps a room as for thy l., 243:26

the more l. are made prominent, 57:18

three l. of righteousness, 63:2

to execute l. royal office, 332:21

true friendship's l., 299:26

two l. discrete, 429:18

unequal l. to savage race, 454:24

useless l. weaken necessary l., 304:11

which ran like drinking songs, 72:13

Lawsuit machine you go into, 544:19

mania, 532:5

Lawsuits, win l. and are happy, 72:14

Lawyer, deceive not thy l., 244:7

has peasant inside, 589:22

nor for every quarrel to l., 244:20

not what l. tells me, 331:17

peasant has l. inside, 589:22

prairie-l. master of all, 637:11

skull of a l., 199:4

without history a mechanic, 379:7

Lawyers, charge prepared l. met, 297:21

let's kill all the l., 164:8

no l. among them, 137:13

one hundred and fifty l. do business, 345:2

Lay aside long-cherished love, 91:14

Leaping, brooks too broad for l., 579:13
  frog l. in, 282:15
  signs of l. houses, 176:24
Leaps, cataract l. in glory, 456:11
  my heart l. up, 374:7
  nature not proceed by l., 312:9
Lear, Hamlet rambles L. rages, 599:7
  passage in L. haunted me, 417:*n*3
  pleasant to know Mr. L., 471:28
  reading King L., 342:23
  there Hamlet there L., 599:6
  till I am Timon and L., 599:11
Learn about one thing from another, 112:20
  and propagate best, 499:9
  at no other, 332:26
  by doing, 78:2
  by going, 725:6
  craft so long to l., 128:7
  fools l. in no other, 309:28
  from having died, 625:5
  from our enemies, 101:24
  from those who teach, 66:17
  gladly he l. and gladly teche, 129:22
  him or kill him, 526:13
  how to forget, 242:4
  I l. from you guess you l. from me, 709:1
  in suffering teach in song, 407:11
  Irish poets l. trade, 600:1
  know how to l., 535:28
  lines don't bump into furniture, 700:19
  live and l., 288:12
  man l. nothing without being taught, 104:5
  neither shall they l. war, 25:30
  never had time to l., 701:16
  nor account pang, 467:8
  not yet so old but she may l., 181:8
  of the green world, 660:1
  read mark l., 49:20
  they l. to be idle, 45:19
  to be policeman, 645:2
  to bear beams of love, 356:9
  to do well, 25:29
  to labor and wait, 440:18
  we were crack-pated, 597:15
  what life had to teach, 478:17
  when will they ever l., 747:10
  wise l. from enemies, 73:10
Learned, all l. all drunk, 335:8
  although men say he has not l., 60:17
  and conned by rote, 189:18
  angling never fully l., 245:13
  fair and l. and good as she, 240:14
  fool more foolish, 269:31
  forgotten everything l., 783:17
  grew within this l. man, 163:1
  his great language, 464:23
  in courtesy have her l., 597:2
  Jonson's l. sock, 251:19
  judge should have l. to know evil, 75:9
  know best things not l., 321:10
  libraries of the l., 325:14
  love first l. in lady's eyes, 169:1
  love trade you have l., 111:7

Learned (*continued*)
  make the l. smile, 298:16
  more l. from Dante, 672:21
  much l. dust, 334:31
  never l. to read, 756:16
  nothing forgotten nothing, 354:4
  rather able than l., 145:16
  root of Homer, 233:*n*4
  thoughts of many men, 52:27
  to look on nature, 373:5
  to melt at others' woe, 321:19
  upright judge l. judge, 182:2
  we should have l. women, 347:4
  when I heard l. astronomer, 490:9
  without sense, 333:13
  writer wishes to show he is l., 574:17
Learning, a' the l. I desire, 361:11
  abandon l. and no sorrow, 57:7
  Alcuin my name l. I loved, 120:10
  angel's wit and singular l., 138:1
  blundering people live on, 634:13
  but an adjunct to ourself, 168:35
  cast into mire, 332:17
  discourse according to l., 184:*n*2
  enough l. to misquote, 399:4
  grammar nonsense and l., 330:1
  great end of l., 79:29
  grow old l. many things, 55:17
  hath gained most, 250:13
  how to use eyes, 437:1
  if I should not be l. now, 83:6
  inclination towards l. strong, 284:10
  inflamed with study of l., 254:20
  knows all he is capable of l., 122:11
  labored for them that seek l., 32:7
  leadership and l., 742:7
  little l. dangerous, 298:13
  love he bore to l., 329:17
  love of l., 442:19
  love of slaughter, 659:8
  much l. make mad, 41:33
  much l. not teach understanding, 62:11
  not attained by chance, 347:10
  on scraps of l. dote, 295:24
  pause from l. to be wise, 313:17
  polite l., 286:21
  red plague rid you for l. me your language, 223:29
  royal road to l., 82:*n*4
  secretary of Nature and all l., 246:1
  steeped in antique l., 503:4
  thought without l., 60:23
  wear l. like watch, 305:4
  weight of l., 458:2
  whence is thy l., 297:6
  who so neglects l. in youth, 69:16
  wiser without books, 335:12
  without liberty in vain, 741:17
  without thought, 60:23
Learning's triumph o'er her foes, 313:10
Learns, who l. must suffer, 63:11
Lease of my true love, 221:23
  summer's l. too short, 220:12
Leash, slow on the l., 658:19
Leash-men, pallid the l., 658:19
Least deserved such a fate, 72:11
  faithful in l., 39:1

Least (*continued*)
  I am l. of apostles, 43:19
  joy last not l., 208:19
  last not l. in love, 188:21
  love l. that let men know, 167:38
  most enjoy contented l., 220:16
  myself not l. but honored, 455:1
  not l. in honor or applause, 154:*n*2
  nothing so l. as truth, 689:2
  of the evils, 78:4
  of these my brethren, 36:19
  of two evils, 52:*n*3
  promise most given when l. said, 157:1
  said soonest mended, 149:*n*13
  though last not l., 154:10
  unjust in l., 39:1
  woman who occasions l. talk, 72:8
Leather, clothed all in l., 792:17
  future smells of Russian l., 420:10
  rest all l. or prunella, 301:17
  Spanish or neat's l., 263:18
  trod upon neat's l., 187:16
Leathern, flits by on l. wing, 324:14
  silken or l. purse, 295:2
  war with rere-mice for l. wings, 173:10
Leave all else to the gods, 95:23
  all meaner things, 301:1
  America love or l. it, 784:5
  at point of bayonets, 351:19
  behind bit of ourselves, 570:4
  bottle on chimleypiece, 469:41
  by next town drain, 553:23
  do not need l. your room, 651:22
  give themselves when you l., 656:10
  her Johnny leave her, 793:17
  her to heaven, 194:25
  him for religion, 746:9
  I must l. all that, 247:12
  King not l. country, 704:5
  kiss but in the cup, 232:15
  living name behind, 237:20
  man shall l. father and mother, 6:18
  me a little, 455:8
  me O Love, 155:28
  me to repose, 323:11
  monument behind, 597:16
  no stone unturned, 68:22
  not a rack behind, 224:21
  not a stain, 32:8
  not l. unless father does, 704:5
  not l. you comfortless, 40:29
  off agony leave off style, 555:18
  off wishing to deserve thanks, 91:12
  peace I l. with you, 40:30
  religion to family, 501:15
  sack and live cleanly, 179:12
  something to after-times, 254:13
  the rest to heaven, 249:12
  thee in the storm, 209:18
  them alone they'll come home, 790:14
  them for the poor and stranger, 9:24
  them honeyless, 189:22
  them in midst of his days, 28:31
  them laughing, 632:9
  them while looking good, 686:9
  to l. to die a little, 570:4

Leave (*continued*)

took l. but was loth to depart, 287:23
we thy servant sleeping, 506:15
world no copy, 201:26
Leaven, a little l., 42:37
pain for l., 533:10
Leaveneth the whole lump, 42:37
Leaves, air wash l. cover me, 533:18
air wild with l., 660:12
among l. never known, 415:12
cane l. swaying, 690:19
cover them with l., 776:2
cover with l. and flowers, 237:13
crisped and sere, 453:1
dead driven like ghosts, 407:13
easy as l. grow on tree, 594:17
fall early, 659:3
generation of men like l., 51:23
harmony of l., 594:23
lisp of l., 533:8
mankind fleet of life like l., 73:12
me fifty more, 578:19
must walk over the l., 148:*n*7
naturally as L. to tree, 418:2
no l. no birds, 423:1
oak l. horses' heels, 670:4
of any author, 248:11
of Judgment Book unfold, 506:3
of Life keep falling, 445:7
piled against doors, 86:18
sewed fig l. together, 6:21
shady l. of destiny, 264:9
shatter your l., 253:14
stop to rake l. away, 622:19
stuck out tongues, 724:17
swayed my l. and flowers, 595:21
tender l. of hopes, 225:16
thick as autumnal l., 256:8
though l. many the root is one, 595:21
tomb of green l., 564:13
vine l. in hair, 508:16
what if my l. falling, 407:17
where l. the rose, 445:8
words are like l., 298:15
world to darkness, 322:1
yellow l. or none or few, 221:8
Leaving all that here win us, 540:20
country for country's sake, 295:*n*2
Love behind, 513:8
me never alone, 540:17
nothing became him like l., 212:26
to direct themselves, 685:19
to take command of troops, 370:12
we're l. Babylon, 773:17
Lebanon, cedars of L., 19:5, 632:16
grow like a cedar in L., 18:17
silken Samarcand to cedared L., 415:6
Lebarge, Lake L., 627:3
Lecher, gilded fly does l., 211:1
Lecherous goats, 230:21
Lecteur, hypocrite l., 494:1
Lecture, if you wish to hold a l., 71:6
Lectured, astronomer l. with applause, 490:9
Led, Bruce has aften l., 363:19
dumb and silent be l., 336:18
neither saint- nor sophist-l., 497:19

Led (*continued*)

regiment from behind, 531:15
to believe a lie, 360:*n*1
Leda mother of Helen, 538:6
Lee, between windward and l., 535:5
I and my Annabel L., 453:8
shore of age, 557:17
the beautiful Annabel L., 453:9
Leek, by this l., 185:26
Leeks, wel loved he garleek oynons l., 130:7
Leer, assent with civil l., 302:11
Lees, drink life to l., 454:25
mere l. is left, 214:15
stirs up l. of things, 486:25
wines on the l., 26:26
Leewardings, unfettered l., 701:1
Left behind a real life, 759:9
better to be l., 457:*n*4
booming surge of Aegean, 74:9
cannon to l. of them, 458:13
country for country's good, 295:*n*2
fair Scotland's strand, 362:12
for handful of silver l. us, 464:22
his garment in her hand, 8:6
implacable Charybdis guards l., 181:*n*2
in her l. hand riches and honor, 20:20
let not l. hand know, 33:11
lies on her l. side, 683:11
ne'er l. man i' mire, 211:25
O mother what have I l. out, 757:6
one taken the other l., 36:12
the warm precincts, 322:19
the web left the loom, 454:16
thou hast l. thy first love, 47:7
vivid air signed with honor, 727:10
Leg, can honor set to l., 178:33
caper and shake l., 633:7
decreasing l. increasing belly, 183:19
justice has wooden l., 602:18
never breaks l., 588:13
one old timber l., 613:9
took him by left l., 789:18
Legacies, books l. genius leaves, 293:1
Legacy alleviates sorrow, 151:20
charm in a good l., 151:20
of first European novel, 761:14
Legal justice art of good and fair, 119:11
no l. slaves except mistress of house, 440:4
society without objective l. scale, 746:8
super-l.-aid bureau, 646:12
unanimity on l. questions, 586:9
Legality, revolution l. counter-moves in same game, 573:11
Legalizer, time great l., 642:10
Legend, ghost of ancient l., 419:14
leaf-fringed l., 415:20
of green chapels, 737:13
Legend's, qui procul hinc l. writ, 586:13
Legends, asleep in lap of l., 415:2
fairy tales tone licked clean, 757:8
names deeds gray l. events, 417:1
rather believe fables in l., 159:18
Leges, silent enim l. inter arma, 87:*n*6

Leggemmo, quel giorno più non vi l. avante, 125:*n*9
Legible, thoughts l. in eye, 163:3
Legion, my name is L., 37:24
of lost ones, 592:2
soldier of the L., 444:1
that never was 'listed, 592:7
Legiones redde, 98:*n*12
Legions, give me back my l., 98:20
Legislate, judges do and must l., 542:21
Legislation, female deprived of voice in l., 347:11
great problem of l., 369:3
solve problem of cat versus bird by l., 706:9
Legislative, every l. body in U.S., 615:4
judicial distinct from l., 338:7
nominated by executive, 340:1
Legislators, poets l. of world, 410:3
Legislature, innocent man sent to l., 605:20
newspaper conthrols l., 603:12
Legitimate, let the end be l., 355:12
object of government, 344:11
Legs, born with l. apart, 765:10
'ear 'erse's l., 460:2
giving way under me, 510:3
his l. bestrid the ocean, 218:11
if go high use own l., 552:11
not natural to walk on two l., 342:19
of iron, 29:12
on his last l., 237:2
on stilts we walk on our own l., 147:7
one pair of English l., 185:10
slimy things crawl with l., 381:9
that bird never on l., 470:13
took lake between my l., 754:22
vast trunkless l., 406:13
walk under his huge l., 187:22
Leibniz, monads of L., 658:12
Leicester, farewell L. Square, 627:15
Leisure answers leisure, 205:5
be doon at l. parfitly, 131:22
class replaced by New Class, 723:9
conversation wants l., 626:17
gentleman of l., 574:4
has utility as evidence of l., 574:9
means and l. civilizers, 435:11
no l. who useth it not, 245:3
office of l. class, 574:7
repent at l., 290:34
retired L., 252:1
to grow wise, 498:6
with dignity, 87:13
wooed in haste wed at l., 167:25
Leisurely, full l. we glide, 517:1
Leman, such l., 785:16
Lemon, be with you in squeezing of l., 330:2
Martini with slice of l. peel, 723:2
trees bloom, 349:8
twelve miles from a l., 380:10
Lemonade, black eyes and l., 392:6
Lemons, oranges and l., 788:20
Lend a kind of easiness, 198:6
eye a terrible aspect, 185:3

Letters, ass in three l., 269:2
  Gods do not answer l., 765:2
  graven with diamonds in l. plain,
    143:8
  in your l. speak of me, 208:16
  like writin' anonymous l., 603:14
  man of l., 272:2
  mingle souls, 230:14
  no arts no l. no society, 239:22
  republic of l., 312:2
  sensitive ear detecting capital l.,
    645:15
  should not be known, 224:4
  you bid me burn l., 338:3
Letter-writing, the great art o' l.,
    468:32
Letting hundred flowers blossom,
    686:16
  I dare not, 213:9
Lettres, un sot en trois l., 269:*n*1
Level, boys and girls l. with men,
    218:8
  in her husband's heart, 202:10
  levelers wish to l. down, 316:1
Leveled together by Tao, 80:8
Levelers wish to level down, 316:1
Leveling, cannot bear l. up, 316:1
  rancorous mind, 598:7
  wind, 597:16
Levels all ranks, 428:21
Lever you can only turn once, 688:1
Leviathan, draw out l. with a hook,
    15:21
  hugest of creatures, 259:21
  that crooked serpent, 26:31
  whom thou hast made to play, 19:6
Levin wanted friendship got friendli-
    ness, 736:6
Levitation, evil emissions fled l., 753:1
  powers of l. would make fakir stare,
    670:19
Levity, a little judicious l., 562:3
  say it with utmost l., 570:8
  soul ruled by l. pure, 738:9
  there should be no l., 314:28
Levy, foreign l., 214:26
Levying war, 346:9
Lewd fellows, 41:14
  the sinful and l., 693:6
Lewdness, though l. court it, 194:22
Lex, de minimis non curat l., 118:26
  salus populi suprema l., 88:*n*4
Lexicographer writer of dictionaries,
    314:5
Lexicography, not yet so lost in l.,
    313:27
Lexicon of youth, 429:1
Lexington and Bunker Hill, 394:13
Lhude sing cuccu, 775:10
  sing Goddamm, 659:2
Liable, all men are l. to error, 277:8
Liar always lavish of oaths, 249:18
  and the father of it, 40:12
  best l., 524:21
  doubt truth to be l., 195:14
  either l. or madman, 319:12
  no one such l. as indignant man,
    552:13
  of first magnitude, 291:3
  should have good memory, 105:11

Liar (*continued*)
  show me a l., 244:34
  they answered Little l., 609:4
Liars, all Cretans are l., 58:8
  all men are l., 19:18
  drunkards l. adulterers, 209:3
  fears may be l., 483:5
  when they speak truth, 77:8
Libelous statements about dog, 650:2
Liber, vade salutatem pro me l.,
    129:*n*1
Liberal arts study humanizes, 102:6
  education, 286:21
  emphasizing rights ∪ɪ individual,
    705:4
  I am a L., 500:10
  infuses that l. obedience, 331:23
  institutions cease being liberal,
    552:31
  little L., 530:11
  luxury of l. government, 474:12
  tempered by experience, 500:10
  to love her is l. education, 293:18
Liberality in gifts well timed, 283:12
Liberate, men and women l., 691:1
Liberated, I have l. my soul, 121:9
  the hell out of place, 783:15
Liberates, neither shoots nor l. me,
    479:2
Liberation, madness potentially l.,
    758:7
  of energies of men, 741:13
  of Europe, 678:16
Liberavi animam meam, 121:*n*6
Liberis, pro patria pro l., 91:*n*14
Libertas, in dubiis l., 266:*n*4
  ubi l. ibi patria, 327:8
Libertate, sub l. quietem, 269:*n*10
Liberté, je suis né pour te nommer L.,
    691:*n*2
Liberties, dramatist wants l., 549:7
  liberty above all l., 255:3
  not too strong for l., 450:7
  people never give up l., 332:3
  science and l. of Europe, 345:3
Libertine, chartered l., 184:22
  freedom of the l., 635:1
  puffed and reckless l., 193:27
Libertines, self-love makes more l.,
    319:17
Liberty, abstract l. not found, 331:13
  Americans love l., 313:4
  and glory of his country, 394:8
  and Union, 394:16
  arduous struggle for l., 339:7
  as end and means, 568:14
  assert and maintain l. and virtue,
    337:10
  basis of democratic state is l., 78:27
  brightest in dungeons L., 401:22
  bulwark of continuing l., 649:11
  bulwarks of l., 327:3
  by accident got its l., 137:3
  cannot be preserved without knowl-
    edge, 337:13
  Captivity is Consciousness so's L.,
    512:9
  change from l. to force, 368:16
  condition upon which given l.,
    351:20

Liberty (*continued*)
  contending for l., 336:13
  corruption symptom of l., 340:4
  cost of l., 605:3
  courage secret of l., 568:14
  cradle of l., 395:10
  crust of bread and l., 302:24
  degradation of idea of l., 733:1
  deprive of life l. or property, 346:18
  deprived of life l. or property,
    346:14
  doing what laws permit, 304:10
  doing what one desires, 439:23
  enjoy delight with l., 154:7
  enjoy such l., 267:18
  enjoyment of life and l., 327:1
  equality fraternity, 786:15
  establish our real l., 145:20
  extremism in defense of l., 341:*n*1
  freedom enfranchisement, 188:17
  from despotism to l. in featherbed,
    343:17
  give me l. or death, 339:10
  God who gave life gave l., 343:1
  hail L. hail, 421:18
  he served human l., 598:9
  he that commands sea is at l., 160:7
  headstrong l., 166:21
  highest political end, 521:7
  history of l. history of safeguards,
    646:10
  history of progress of human l.,
    480:16
  I must have l. withal, 190:27
  if l. found in democracy, 78:21
  in doubtful things l., 266:10
  in moderate governments, 355:2
  in mouth of Webster, 430:21
  in proportion to restraint, 395:7
  individual l. individual power,
    368:17
  inspire our Souls, 292:*n*2
  interfering with l., 439:11
  is possibility of doubting, 706:8
  judiciary safeguard of l., 586:8
  know no such l., 267:16
  knows nothing but victories, 462:19
  lawless attack upon l., 325:4
  life l. pursuit of happiness, 343:2
  little is achieved through L., 468:15
  love of l. love of others, 390:18
  man establish reign of l., 722:11
  mocks my loss of l., 356:1
  most power least l., 273:8
  mountain nymph sweet l., 251:10
  my Soul at L., 512:8
  nation conceived in L., 450:2
  natural l. establishes itself, 326:9
  neither in despotism or democracy,
    355:2
  neither l. nor safety, 310:13
  of a poet, 249:25
  of conscience, 247:13
  of individual, 439:17
  of press, 345:13, 438:4
  of thought life of soul, 307:2
  only to those who love it, 395:1
  peace l. and safety, 344:9
  people so dead to l., 312:20
  placid repose under l., 269:34

Liberty (*continued*)

plucks justice by nose, 203:24
possessions take away l., 588:15
power to endanger public l., 337:16
precious must be rationed, 610:7
price of l., 351:*n*7
proclaim l. throughout land, 9:27
property no stamps, 778:20
putrid corpse of l., 652:21
quick with seed of l., 486:8
right to death or l., 493:14
sacred fire of l., 337:1
secret of happiness, 568:14
secure blessings of l., 346:7
seeking l. which is so dear, 126:3
so loving-jealous of his l., 175:14
soul of journey is l., 390:14
spirit of l., 331:10
survival of l., 741:3
sweet land of l., 444:3
taken with Nature, 536:9
this country to preserve l., 345:3
this is L. Hall, 330:4
to know, 255:3
to think feel do, 390:14
trains for liberty, 605:4
Tree, 340:17
tree of l. refreshed, 343:15
tree of l. watered by blood, 354:11
what crimes in thy name, 354:2
where l. there is my country, 327:8
where Slavery is L. cannot be, 463:4
white Goddess, 528:16
with l. and justice for all, 568:12
without learning is peril, 741:17
wrote at l. when of Devils, 357:2
Liberty's in every blow, 363:20
Libraries, have well-furnished l., 234:2
I bless God in l., 325:14
meek young men grow up in l., 431:6
not made they grow, 559:12
Library, furnished me from mine own l., 223:26
public l. affords conviction, 313:26
turn over half a l., 316:24
was dukedom large enough, 223:24
whereon I look, 241:22
Libre, l'homme est né l., 319:*n*3
Libri, cave ab homine unius l., 118:19
Lice tethered, 724:16
License, equal l. in bold invention, 98:3
innocence never blossom into l., 281:12
love not freedom but l., 255:8
poetic l., 87:16
universal l. to be good, 419:3
Licensing and prohibiting, 255:4
Licentiae, poetarum l. liberiora, 87:*n*9
Licentious, newspapers the most l., 352:33
soldiery, 332:2
Lick absurd pomp, 197:2
ill cook that cannot l. fingers, 176:10
it into form, 104:*n*10
the dust, 17:42
Valleys up, 512:17
Licked, admit I'm l., 678:4

Licked (*continued*)

platter clean, 788:7
soup from ladles, 464:18
Licker, corn l. stop victim's watch, 631:2
talks mighty loud, 556:13
Licks, bear l. them into proper shape, 104:11
hand raised to shed blood, 301:4
pride that l. the dust, 302:17
Lid, earth's l., 659:10
pent-house l., 212:13
Lids, drops blue-fringed l., 382:18
eternal l. apart, 417:12
Lie a thought more nigh, 240:13
abroad for commonwealth, 227:12
all the Dead l. down, 512:15
asked lady to l. her down, 357:18
asks no questions isn't told l., 330:*n*1
at proud foot of conqueror, 170:23
athwart noses as they l. asleep, 174:20
becomes habitual, 343:11
before us like land of dreams, 499:22
big l., 676:7
by emperor's side, 207:20
can't pray a l., 526:26
children and fools cannot l., 141:34
circumstantial, 192:16
contrive one noble l., 75:11
countenance cannot l., 163:3
credit his own l., 223:22
deep buried, 59:24
differences between cat and l., 527:9
dig grave let me l., 561:16
direct, 192:16
dost thou l. so low, 188:19
down because 'twas night, 229:4
down for eon or two, 591:13
down in green pastures, 16:17
down like tired child, 406:15
down till leaders spoken, 592:16
down where ladders start, 599:22
every word she writes is l., 732:2
fain wald l. down, 785:20
families l. together, 752:4
faults l. gently on him, 226:3
for a moment l. becomes truth, 495:17
give the world the l., 152:15
half a truth blackest, 460:1
handle which fits all, 447:12
has seven endings, 784:24
heaven with splendors l., 485:3
here let her l., 277:2
here obedient to their laws we l., 60:11
home to a l., 659:8
how l. through centuries, 465:7
how still we see thee l., 524:9
I can't tell a l., 336:*n*7
I l. down alone, 580:5
I shall l. in the dust, 52:15
I their map l. flat, 231:3
if I l. spit in my face, 177:24
in cold obstruction, 204:14
in cowslip's bell I l., 224:25
in dark weep for sins, 489:16

Lie (*continued*)

in your throat, 183:14
inhuman reign of l., 680:5
leads you to believe a l., 360:3
lightly gentle earth, 238:16
like bill on Nature's Reality, 412:13
nicer to l. in bed, 609:16
not a man that he should l., 10:6
not know what it is to l., 425:16
nothing can need a l., 242:19
on knees of the gods, 52:30
on Mother's bed, 743:2
one daiquiri told the other a l., 734:18
permits himself to tell l., 343:11
rather l. in woollen, 186:16
sergeant's widow told l., 446:23
shall rot, 503:10
sleep will never l., 175:17
sleeping dogs l., 470:38
still and slumber, 294:12
still ye thief, 178:9
stone tell where I l., 298:6
sweet compulsion in music l., 251:5
sweets compacted l., 243:11
talking of fall of man, 479:9
tangled in her hair, 267:16
thought uttered is l., 434:11
to me tell me you've waited, 734:13
truth in masquerade, 403:12
underneath this stone doth l., 232:12
unless statistics l., 688:19
upon the daisies, 529:17
violence intertwined with l., 746:5
what is a l., 403:12
where'er she l., 264:9
which is all a lie, 460:1
who loves to l. with me, 190:18
with a purpose worst, 602:15
with my fathers, 8:16
worse things than l., 476:3
yonder all before us l., 268:15
young shall l. down together, 26:11
Liebchen with whom should I quarrel, 716:21
Lieben und arbeiten, 570:*n*1
Lied, never seen anybody but l., 526:19
those who l. for hire, 659:13
Lief not be as be in awe, 187:20
Liege of loiterers, 168:28
we are men my l., 214:21
Lies are mortar, 601:7
at last as always, 750:1
believe her though she l., 222:9
Bible has thousand l., 528:12
cruelest l. told in silence, 560:16
dalliance in wardrobe l., 184:27
death l. on my tongue, 179:5
exposed he l., 276:2
Fool l. here, 591:12
freedom from l., 582:8
full fathom five thy father l., 223:32
great Prince in prison l., 229:15
half truth blackest of l., 460:1
heaven l. about us, 375:7
here again he l., 490:11
here food for worms, 309:5
here l. a King that ruled, 246:3

Lies *(continued)*

here l. beautiful lady, 616:21
here l. Matthew Prior, 288:5
here l. my wife, 277:2
here l. one who meant well, 562:7
here l. one whose name, 418:21
here l. our good Edmund, 330:10
here l. truly honest man, 264:21
Hope l. to mortals, 580:4
in his bed walks with me, 170:4
in the rude manger l., 250:20
jailed for telling l. to young, 716:10
kindness and l., 713:6
long time l. in one word, 170:30
make l. sound truthful, 711:14
Matilda told dreadful l., 609:3
matters I relate are true l., 675:22
music on spirit l., 454:6
now l. he there, 189:3
old men's l., 659:8
on chaliced flowers that l., 219:24
on her left side, 683:11
poets tell many l., 55:16
religion of slaves, 605:11
speaking l. in hypocrisy, 45:14
steep my speech in l., 63:31
tells l. without attending, 343:11
that way madness l., 210:2
to hide it, 242:*n*8
to tell l. not honorable, 67:13
truth to cover l., 291:2
uneasy l. head that wears crown, 183:38
where he longed to be, 561:16
with dogs riseth with fleas, 244:23
you can invent, 359:9

Life a battle and sojourning, 110:19
a bubble, 160:*n*7
a Fury slinging flame, 457:14
a man's real l., 573:12
academic l., 233:15
accept Jesus new l., 753:18
account of her l. to clod, 186:18
actuality of thought is l., 77:23
admits not of delays, 316:33
adore my l. with Bird, 725:21
affirmation of l., 630:17
after l. is death, 534:11
ain't all beer and skittles, 469:*n*1
all a man hath will he give for l., 13:32
all his l. in the wrong, 283:27
all human l. in monkeys and cats, 548:9
all I care about is l., 541:10
all inclusion and confusion, 549:3
all l. an experiment, 542:25
all l. is a dream, 247:7
all l. 6 to 5 against, 654:17
along parabola l. flies, 766:3
American l. solvent, 588:12
among people who love each other, 436:22
and Death and For Ever, 484:13
and memory of it, 729:16
and power of increase, 277:4
and what's a l., 242:14
anyone whose l. married to sea, 618:11
anything for a quiet l., 237:6

Life *(continued)*

anythin' for a quiet l., 469:3
art long l. short, 349:12
art makes l., 549:14
art of drawing conclusions, 525:1
as for future l. man judge, 445:1
as much as my l. was worth, 320:24
as to bed's-feet l. shrunk, 229:8
as to breathe were l., 455:2
at ease drifts, 509:18
at no point in l. felt American, 763:17
at the door of l., 533:22
awful wretched mess of l., 718:21
bagatelle of transient experience, 584:11
bankrupt of l., 274:4
be it l. or death crave reality, 478:20
be not afraid of l., 546:9
bear a charmed l., 216:18
before us lies in daily l., 259:24
beg delinquents for l., 743:14
begins perpetually, 601:15
believe in l., 605:7
believe in l. to come, 718:18
best of l. intoxication, 402:19
best part of married l. fights, 698:1
best portion of man's l., 373:1
best things in l. free, 685:16
birth l. and death, 283:16
birthday of my l., 515:6
bitterness of feelings about modern l., 731:6
bitterness of L., 520:1
blameless l., 459:3
blot out of book of l., 47:12
boat of l. be light, 580:11
Book of L. begins, 567:2
book of l. opened, 47:36
books substitute for l., 560:19
boredom at core of l., 272:1
bread called staff of l., 286:15
bread of l., 40:4
bread of l. in mouth, 283:8
breath of l., 6:11
breathed by Creator, 444:10
breathtakingly serious, 680:4
brief l. our portion, 482:9
brisking about the l., 325:18
broad margin to my l., 478:24
broken l. up for bread, 533:21
buried l., 498:4
burrs and thorns of l., 414:6
but a span, 287:13
C Major of this l., 467:5
calamity of so long l., 196:10
cannot tear out page of l., 436:19
care of l. and happiness, 344:11
careless of single l., 457:19
care's an enemy to l., 201:19
cast cold eye on l. on death, 600:3
chain of l., 748:13
change we think we see in l., 623:5
changing scenes of l., 285:3
chaos breeds l., 535:21
charmed l., 216:18
clock stops time come to l., 696:11
closed twice before close, 514:13

Life *(continued)*

comes a time in every man's l., 680:12
comes before literature, 524:10
comes to end in prosperity, 63:14
comes to him with love, 710:8
compared l. to a dream, 146:9
compel philosophy to inquire about l., 87:30
conduct three-fourths of l., 500:19
consciousness of what we can do, 653:14
consists with wildness, 479:8
contraction of l., 628:11
control nature and human l., 564:22
controlling circumstances of l., 492:1
cool sequestered vale of l., 322:17
count l. of battle good, 586:12
crowded hour of l., 333:8
crown of l., 46:5, 47:9
crown of l. as it closes, 533:15
Culprit L., 511:11
custom guide of human l., 318:13
daily beauty in his l., 208:7
dancing is l. itself, 578:10
dead husks of l., 721:13
dear as light and l., 363:13
death after l. does please, 153:9
death makes l. live, 468:5
death nor l. nor angels, 42:9
death of each day's l., 214:6
death part of l., 629:11
death side of l. away from us, 630:9
defeat my l., 208:3
demd horrid grind, 469:24
deprive of l. liberty or property, 346:18
deprived of l. liberty or property, 346:14
destroys single l. rescues single l., 115:17
devote his l. in serving his prince, 60:17
difficult to write good l. as live one, 643:17
digressions l. of reading, 320:14
dim origins of l., 721:13
disease of modern l., 498:12
does thy l. destroy, 358:4
done their song and dance in your l., 728:2
dost thou love l., 310:1
doth l. in tendance spend, 154:6
dream l. as lake dreams sky, 589:20
dream of l., 409:3
dreamed l. was beauty, 476:17
dreams necessary to l., 711:8
drink l. to lees, 454:25
earnest art gay, 365:1
ease one L. the Aching, 513:10
echo undermine hold on l., 636:11
education not preparation for l. is l., 577:11
education will determine future l., 75:13
effective therapist, 657:1
elevate l. by conscious endeavor, 478:16
empty dream, 440:15

Life (*continued*)

end in itself, 542:12
end of l. cancels bands, 178:14
enjoyment of l. and liberty, 327:1
enlarge my l., 313:20
enough for my l., 31:10
entrusts l. to one hole, 83:13
envy and wrath shorten l., 32:4
eternal l. gift of God, 41:45
eternal l. in knowledge of God, 49:2
everlasting l., 39:46
everything in political l., 500:16
evidence of vicarious l., 574:8
exempt from public haunt, 190:7
exile's l. no l., 83:1
experience of this sweet l., 126:28
fabric of l., 721:14
fall upon thorns of l., 407:16
falter l. away, 498:10
fear of Acheron which troubles l., 89:21
feels l. in every limb, 372:17
felt l. in producing art, 549:2
fever of l. over, 426:22
fie upon this quiet l., 177:20
for l. six hundred pounds, 302:23
for l. to come, 223:3
for the living, 521:9
for why my l. at end, 785:4
force uncomprehended was his l., 510:7
fought for l., 727:10
free to develop hostile forms as friendly, 532:11
friend is medicine of l., 31:16
frittered away by detail, 478:18
from this cup they drank their l., 787:16
front essential facts of l., 478:17
fruit she longs to hand you, 717:4
fruits of l. and beauty, 357:20
gale of l. high, 579:7
game is l., 705:20
game that must be played, 608:1
garment we alter, 697:9
gates of new l. to thee, 466:22
gave thee l. bid thee feed, 356:6
give to eat of the tree of l., 47:8
give us luxuries of l., 474:9
giveth his l. for sheep, 40:17
giving l. by death of others, 134:15
God gave l. gave liberty, 343:1
golden tree of l., 350:15
good death does honor to whole l., 127:10
Good L. waiting for us, 715:9
grants nothing without work, 95:7
great business of l., 537:8
great end of l. is action, 505:16
greater price than l., 705:11
greatest thing in family l., 625:15
Greek thought and l., 507:9
Greeks have dreamt dream of l. best, 351:11
green l. once lived there, 728:14
growth only evidence of l., 426:19
grunt and sweat under weary l., 196:10
half a l. asunder, 518:13

Life (*continued*)

half spent before we know, 245:5
happy all his l., 245:9
harder toward summit, 553:3
harmonious and humane l., 501:1
have the light of l., 40:10
have you found l. distasteful, 468:12
he giveth l., 41:16
he that findeth l., 34:35
he that loveth her loveth l., 31:7
he who knows l., 284:11
here find l. in death, 385:5
high l., 328:24
high l. mistaken path, 404:19
his l. a breath of God, 476:8
his l. dinner wife, 423:15
his l. was gentle, 189:28
his l. was in the right, 267:12
honor dearer than l., 150:4
hope for happiness beyond l., 341:9
horrors of half known l., 486:27
hot for certainties in l., 508:30
house to be let for l., 242:9
how good man's l., 466:17
human l. a large Mansion, 418:5
human l. a state in which much endured, 314:11
human l. priceless, 705:11
hungry for l. and death, 736:19
I am the bread of l., 40:4
I believe in l. everlasting, 48:25
I burned my l., 696:1
I have painted my l., 665:15
I haven't a literary l., 727:16
I would like simple l., 760:3
if it be l. to pitch, 598:5
if l. bitter pardon, 535:6
if one had courage l. livable, 508:15
if woman told truth about her l., 734:4
if you haven't had l., 549:1
ills scholar's l. assail, 313:17
imagination master of l., 573:16
immortal Death has taken mortal l., 90:4
in internal environment, 473:8
in l. as in football, 575:15
in l. courtesy, 600:7
in l. did harbor give, 232:12
in London all l. can afford, 317:2
in middle of journey of l., 125:3
in our l. Nature live, 383:8
in sea of l. enisled, 498:3
in struggle for l. find love, 682:8
in the midst of l. death, 50:7
in whom standeth eternal l., 49:2
Indian summer of l., 536:4
inseparable like l. and consciousness, 657:19
intend to lead new l., 49:14
interest in death interest in l., 629:15
into each l. rain fall, 441:6
irremediable poverty of l., 640:27
is a copycat, 667:1
is a foreign language, 679:12
is a jest, 297:22
is a wave, 493:17
is action and passion, 542:6
is all beer and skittles, 469:*n*1

Life (*continued*)

is an incurable disease, 267:5
is boring, 734:17
is but a span, 287:13
is fading fast away, 557:1
is its own journey, 719:14
is l. so dear, 339:10
is not l. more than meat, 33:18
is only error, 365:14
is painting picture, 542:18
is real life is earnest, 440:15
is short art long, 71:13
is supremely easy for men, 53:8
is the thing, 594:8
is thorny, 382:15
is trouble Zorba continued, 652:3
is unfair, 741:12
is what we make it, 546:8
isn't all beer and skittles, 501:19
it pretends to build on, 705:7
it takes l. to love l., 607:12
it would be L., 512:21
joy of l. is variety, 314:7
jump the l. to come, 213:5
jury passing on l., 203:29
keep pure both l. and art, 71:1
keep way of the tree of l., 7:1
lag-end of my l., 178:29
large as l. twice as natural, 519:15
Last Abode is L., 117:8
last hour of my l., 308:17
last of l. best, 467:6
lasted the rest of my l., 517:10
lay down l. for friends, 40:31
lay hold on eternal l., 45:23
Leaves of L. falling, 445:7
left behind a real l., 759:9
length of l. leading among inquiries, 110:11
let thy l. be sincere, 31:12
liberty pursuit of happiness, 343:2
light l. pleasure pain, 520:9
light of l., 40:10
light of whole l. dies, 563:2
like a dome of many-colored glass, 409:14
like a froward child, 273:2
like living l. over, 311:1
like runners pass on torch of l., 89:16
little l. rounded with sleep, 224:21
little needed to make happy l., 111:21
live all days of your l., 290:14
live l. he has imagined, 478:36
live l. not simple, 679:17
live l. through not like crossing field, 793:3
live out thy l. as light, 534:20
lived in scene it composes, 640:17
lived l. talking at street corners, 674:19
lively form of death, 156:17
Lolita light of my l., 703:1
London this moment, 650:16
long disease my l., 302:9
long littleness of l., 661:11
looking out from eyes of doe, 684:11
lose l. shall find it, 35:30

Life (*continued*)

love an episode in man's l., 368:10
love anterior to L., 513:9
love long l. better than figs, 216:27
love of wisdom guide of l., 360:8
love only business in l., 396:21
love the history of woman's l.,
　　368:10
loveth her loveth l., 31:7
lust for l., 508:14
made of marble and mud, 436:7
making ends meet in l., 646:4
man lives l. of epoch, 629:10
mankind fleet of l. like leaves, 73:12
man's l. cheap as beast's, 209:21
many-colored l. he drew, 313:10
married to sea, 618:11
married to single l., 264:12
material of l., 653:17
may perfect be, 233:3
measured l. with coffee spoons,
　　667:13
medicine for l. which has fled,
　　58:12
memory without pain, 66:2
messed up l. for nothing, 673:1
mine honor is my l., 170:26
miserable mortals flame with l.,
　　52:19
money as means to l., 652:12
more abundant l., 648:20
more lost than l., 105:23
more sweet than painted pomp,
　　190:6
more than he slew in his l., 11:19
most loathed worldly l., 204:15
much too far out all my l., 710:6
my l. has gone, 757:13
my l. is preserved, 8:2
my l. my joy, 148:9
my l. my real l. in danger, 753:6
my l. poem I would have writ,
　　477:22
my lines and l. are free, 243:16
my poems naughty my l. pure,
　　106:7
my way of l. is fallen, 216:9
near bone sweetest, 478:38
never know what l. means till you
　　die, 468:5
never to have drawn breath of l.,
　　598:3
new era in l. from book, 478:23
new l. begins, 124:17
new l. when sin no more, 474:3
nightmare L.-in-Death was she,
　　381:12
no bonds attached him to l., 127:6
no life but death, 156:17
no l. by others' death, 170:12
no l. can be recaptured wholly,
　　736:8
no l. lives forever, 534:15
no l. moves in empty passageways,
　　65:16
no man loses other l. than that he
　　lives, 110:16
no man loves l. like old, 67:17
no no no l., 211:19
no wealth but l., 487:18

nobody write l. of man, 316:11
nor love thy l. nor hate, 260:18
not cheap but sacred, 432:39
not doing a sum, 542:18
not giving l. but risking l., 722:8
not keep advantages of l., 614:14
not l. alone makes man, 707:14
not L. for which they stand, 523:14
not long l. by fire, 583:19
not take his own l., 74:19
not to fancy what fair in l., 466:8
nothing give up l., 724:13
nothing in his l., 212:26
nothing much to lose, 580:6
novel attempt to represent l., 548:11
now I live now l. is done, 156:22
now is immortal l., 556:21
O Death in L., 456:14
O for L. of Sensations, 417:16
o' the building, 214:13
occupations few tranquil l., 111:6
ocean of l., 442:16
o'er ills o' l. victorious, 363:5
of jealousy, 206:33
of law not logic, 542:4
of l. he only is deserving, 350:26
of man heroic poem, 412:27
of man solitary, 239:22
of peoples and humanity, 510:10
of poor man in mean cottage, 32:1
of Riley, 781:*n*1
of significant soil, 671:19
of simplicity independence magna-
　　nimity, 478:5
of soul, 307:2
of this world, 117:14
old age crown of l., 88:12
on earth passes away, 3:13
on this unavailing star, 594:6
one Draught of L., 514:12
one entrance into l., 30:29
one in l. and death are we, 530:4
one l. to lose for country, 354:16
one long struggle in dark, 89:15
only one happiness in l., 436:25
out of ashes l. again, 554:13
out of it are the issues of l., 20:25
outlive his l. half a year, 197:8
over my long l., 584:5
over there behind Shelf, 512:21
part with l. cheerfully, 111:12
pass them for nobler l., 414:4
perceivers of terror of l., 432:30
perfect interpreter of l., 661:1
perfected by death, 438:15
perfection of l. or work, 598:10
period in l. when work comes first,
　　604:1
philosophy you leader of l., 87:29
piece of buffoonery, 604:5
poem ends in clarification of l.,
　　625:8
poem part of sense of l., 640:23
poet gives l. to fictions, 640:16
present l. a diversion and sport,
　　117:2
present l. like flight of sparrow,
　　120:6
pressure of exigencies of l., 569:8

price l. exacts for peace, 700:7
progress from want to want, 316:30
progress to fuller l., 605:7
prolong l. only when shorten miser-
　　ies, 726:18
protracted is protracted woe, 313:20
protracting l. not deduct from
　　death, 90:6
public l. crown of career, 628:3
public l. situation of power, 331:2
pulse of l. stood still, 296:8
pulse of modern l. economic, 635:9
pure in l. free from sin, 95:28
ran gaily as Thames, 498:12
rarely find a happy l., 95:3
realize l. while live it, 697:15
reason the l. of the law, 152:1
rejoice in l. mark of Greek spirit,
　　603:26
religion reaction upon l., 546:14
religious feeling toward l., 607:16
relinquish l. for good of country,
　　370:14
rest of his dull l., 238:11
resurrection and the l., 40:19
resurrection unto eternal l., 50:8
Reverence for L., 630:16
reward of labor is l., 523:11
rights to a better l., 560:2
rounded with a sleep, 224:21
rule of l. from tonight, 581:20
sated with banquet of l., 90:5
save l. shall lose it, 35:30
saw l. steadily saw it whole, 497:3
science of l. superb hall, 473:4
scraped l. with fine-tooth comb,
　　740:3
seas of l. like wine, 281:2
secret l. of belly and bone, 734:6
sedentary l. sin, 553:15
see into l. of things, 373:3
seek not l. of immortals, 64:3
sense of what l. means, 546:17
set before you l. and death, 10:25
set gray l., 454:21
set l. at pin's fee, 194:12
set my l. on any chance, 214:23
set my l. upon cast, 166:18
sex pattern of process of l., 578:6
shadow of death, 249:6, 533:10
shape of l., 653:17
sharpened l. commands course,
　　509:18
she is mine for l., 746:11
sheltered l. can be daring l., 728:1
short l. in saddle, 583:19
short quiet hours few, 487:22
sin to prefer l. to honor, 109:6
slits the thin-spun l., 253:20
smooth road of l., 321:1
so short craft so long, 128:7
so was it when l. began, 374:7
soul the captain of l., 91:28
sound which tells of l., 387:*n*1
space of l. between, 414:8
spare all I have take l., 295:16
spend l. your own way, 679:11
spirit giveth l., 43:31
staff of l. bread, 286:*n*7

Lifted, hath not l. his soul unto vanity,
  16:18
    moment I was l. and struck, 773:15
    nevermore, 452:22
Lifting, help by l. his heart, 697:1
Light a glory a fair cloud, 383:9
    a little warmth a little l., 522:10
    a little while is l., 40:23
    afraid of l. all of us, 508:5
    all was l., 303:17
    and life pleasure pain, 520:9
    and will aspire, 165:9
    Angels progeny of l., 259:13
    appareled in celestial l., 375:3
    armor of l., 42:23
    around the body, 756:17
    a-roving by l. of moon, 402:1
    at end of tunnel, 741:n2
    be not darkened, 24:27
    be the earth, 67:25
    because it lendeth l., 154:8
    better to l. one candle, 654:n2
    black as if bereaved of l., 356:8
    body changed to l., 787:18
    breaks where no sun shines, 737:9
    bringeth to l. the shadow of death,
      14:18
    broke upon brain, 401:23
    buried under chains, 699:11
    burning and shining l., 39:49
    by her own radiant l., 252:29
    by l. of moon, 786:n6
    candle and put it under bushel, 33:3
    candle of understanding, 30:16
    candle to the sun, 270:1
    carrying you into fields of l., 67:24
    certain Slant of l., 511:21
    children of l., 38:40, 499:12
    children of l. and day, 45:6
    cold l. and hot shade, 358:14
    come on baby l. my fire, 775:4
    comes from thine eyes, 777:7
    common as l. is love, 407:1
    consider how l. is spent, 255:11
    danced by l. of moon, 472:3
    darkness and l. alike to thee, 20:9
    dawn's early l., 391:2
    dear as l. and life, 363:13
    dies before thy word, 304:2
    dim religious l., 252:10
    doth trample on my days, 270:10
    echo and l. unto eternity, 408:15
    enough for wot I've to do, 469:11
    everlasting L., 524:9
    exact day-labor l. denied, 255:12
    excelleth darkness, 23:29
    excess of l., 323:4
    existence brief crack of l., 702:17
    fade from eyes, 613:n2
    fade into l. of common day, 375:8
    fails on winter's afternoon, 672:5
    faintly muddy l., 662:8
    fantastic round, 252:23
    fantastic toe, 251:9
    fierce l. beats on throne, 459:3
    flash of l. cut across sky, 735:19
    former l. restore, 208:10
    forward the L. Brigade, 458:10
    freedom's holy l., 444:4
    from grave to l., 280:4

Light (*continued*)
    gains make heavy purses, 157:4
    garmented in l., 408:3
    gates of l., 259:16
    Gatsby believed in the green l.,
      694:12
    gives a lovely l., 684:2
    gives l. in darkness, 163:21
    gladsome l. of jurisprudence, 152:2
    gleams and is gone, 499:19
    God Appears and God is L., 359:16
    God guideth to His l., 117:4
    God is l., 46:31
    God l. of heavens and earth, 117:4
    God shows sufficient l., 467:30
    God's eldest daughter, 250:12
    God's first creature l., 257:n6
    gold and silver l., 595:8
    gone into world of l., 270:9
    gospel l. first dawned, 321:24
    guide by l. of reason, 568:17
    hail holy l., 257:23
    half l. half shade, 454:20
    half-believers, 498:10
    have l. of life, 40:10
    he is angel of l., 479:4
    heaven to day denies, 401:14
    heaven's l. forever shines, 409:8
    here kindled, 240:12
    Hesperus entreats thy l., 231:21
    hop l. ladies, 556:17
    I am l. of the world, 40:10
    if l. in thee be darkness, 33:16
    if once we lose this l., 232:4
    in despite of l. keep us together,
      229:4
    in minds of others, 640:18
    in present l. flames, 621:7
    in ragged luck, 557:7
    in room by artificial l., 749:12
    in sound sound-like power in light,
      380:24
    in the dust lies dead, 409:19
    in which freedom lives, 706:11
    infant crying for l., 457:18
    inner l. will shine forth, 351:n5
    is lion comes to drink, 639:10
    is shadow of God, 249:6
    it giveth l. unto all, 33:3
    judged in l. of final issue, 79:2
    law not a l. to see by, 753:9
    lead kindly L., 426:18
    lead me from darkness to l., 50:15
    let the Big L. in, 690:21
    let there be l., 6:4
    let your l. shine, 33:3
    lift up the l. of thy countenance,
      15:32
    like gleaming taper's l., 328:5
    listened, 725:14
    little drops of l., 249:28
    live and love in God's l., 137:11
    live out thy life as l., 534:20
    lived l. in spring, 498:1
    Lolita l. of my life, 703:1
    long l. shakes, 456:11
    made l. of it, 35:43
    man like l. kindled and put out,
      62:18
    many hands make l. work, 142:15

Light (*continued*)
    mass times speed of l. squared,
      635:n3
    men of inward l., 263:28
    mocks at it and sets it l., 171:2
    moralists put tale in edifying l.,
      705:8
    more by number than your l., 227:9
    more l., 351:15
    my burden is l., 34:38
    neither joy nor love nor l., 499:22
    night shadow of l., 533:10
    no darkness into l. without emotion,
      629:4
    no l. but darkness visible, 255:23
    Noose of L., 445:4
    not leave my hand without l., 663:6
    of bright world dies, 563:2
    of Light, 49:1
    of light beguile, 168:14
    of my understanding, 284:10
    of oncoming train, 741:n2
    of setting suns, 373:5
    of step and heart, 616:21
    of the body, 33:15
    of the world, 33:3, 40:10
    of things, 372:20
    of thy sword, 421:18
    of whole life dies, 563:2
    old age level l., 683:14
    on dark theme trace verses of l.,
      89:11
    once set is our little l., 226:13
    one small candle l. a thousand,
      240:12
    out of hell leads to l., 257:10
    people have seen a great l., 26:7
    people in darkness saw great l.,
      32:36
    place void of all l., 125:14
    pleasing dreams slumbers l., 378:16
    power and l., 752:6
    prime work of God, 257:n6
    progeny of l., 259:13
    pure and endless l., 270:7
    purple l. of Love, 323:1
    put out the l., 208:10, 576:14
    Put out the L., 623:22
    radiant l. rests on men, 64:5
    rage against dying of l., 737:20
    rather l. candles than curse dark-
      ness, 654:n2
    river of crystal l., 559:20
    roving by l. of moon, 402:1
    sadder l. than moon, 443:13
    seeking light, 168:14
    shaft of l. in darkness, 742:5
    she loves, 458:21
    she treads on it so l., 165:17
    shines over land and sea, 621:7
    shineth in darkness, 39:30
    shower of l. is poesy, 414:5
    something of angelic l., 375:18
    speed far faster than l., 618:14
    stand in your own l., 142:11
    steeps of l., 460:17
    strikes Sultan's Turret with L.,
      445:3
    strong shadow where much l., 349:1
    suffusion from that l., 383:10

Light (*continued*)

sun gives l. soon as he rises, 310:25
suns to l. me rise, 301:9
sweetness and l., 288:17, 500:14
teach l. to counterfeit a gloom, 252:5
that cometh from her wisdom, 30:30
that green l. that lingers, 383:7
that led astray, 361:15
that lies in woman's eyes, 392:4
that loses night that wins, 533:9
that never was, 376:6
that shineth more and more, 20:24
the first light of evening, 640:8
the Lord is my l., 16:21
the true L., 39:32
thickens and crow makes wing, 214:28
things holy profane grave and l., 239:20
those that rebel against the l., 14:35
thousand points of l., 753:11
threshold of waking l., 757:13
thy l. is come, 28:4
thy l. relume, 208:10
time's glory bring truth to l., 167:2
to guide, 376:3
to lighten Gentiles, 38:6
to them in darkness, 38:1
to those in darkness, 139:4
to whom God assigns no l., 117:5
tracings of eternal l., 364:14
travel l., 722:1
trifles l. as air, 207:5
tripped l. fantastic, 585:7
truth not sought for comes to l., 81:8
truth will come to l., 132:n1
truths kindle l. for truths, 89:12
two thousand l. years from home, 772:17
two ways of spreading l., 586:18
unconscious not only dark but l., 628:15
unto my path, 19:23
unveiled her peerless l., 258:19
upon them hath the l. shined, 26:7
us down in honor or dishonor, 449:16
Vesper now raising his l., 91:7
void of l., 256:4
waited for the l., 608:8
walk while ye have l., 40:23
wave of l. breaks into darkness, 662:10
we fear in the l., 90:1
we shall need no other l., 351:n5
what l. is to painting, 563:3
what l. through yonder window, 174:26
when daylight comes comes in l., 483:3
when my l. low, 457:13
when our brief l. has set, 90:19
which lighteth every man, 39:32
white l. of morning, 787:5
why rise because 'tis l., 229:4
wife make heavy husband, 182:14
winning make prize light, 224:1

Light (*continued*)

withdrawn which once he wore, 443:3
world but thickened l., 433:28
Lighted fools way to dusty death, 216:14
old is having l. rooms in head, 751:1
Lighten our darkness, 49:7
Lightened, thundered and l., 72:13
weight of world l., 373:2
Lightens, cease to be ere it l., 175:9
Lighter than cork danced on waves, 565:11
town is l. than vanity, 272:20
Lightest, movements of l. atom, 351:16
sovereign is the l., 80:6
word harrow soul, 194:17
Lightfoot, many a l. lad, 579:12
Light-hearted, afoot and l., 490:3
Lighthouse, below the l. top, 380:29
took sitivation at l., 469:3
Lightland, rise in heaven's l., 5:2
set in western l., 5:3
Lightly draws its breath, 372:17
earth rest l. on you, 119:31
entered into unadvisedly or l., 50:1
lie l. gentle earth, 238:16
rest, 67:25
soul of my youth taken flight, 657:2
tread l. she is near, 566:5
we esteem too l., 340:22
Lightness, drama not of heaviness but of l., 761:12
Lightning, bottled l., 469:22
countenance like l., 37:14
does the work, 528:6
done like l., 231:17
fateful l., 484:6
flashed the living l., 299:18
he thence had riven, 404:4
he's a l. pilot, 526:12
in collied night, 172:20
in thunder l. or in rain, 212:9
like writing history with l., 572:16
makes awful l., 439:2
mirth like flash of l., 293:6
outstare the l., 217:29
Satan as l. fall, 38:20
scratch head with l., 526:7
strikes mountaintop, 96:8
Superman the l., 552:7
too like the l., 175:9
vain to look for defense against l., 100:15
zigzag l. stands high, 787:9
Lightnings, four l. zigzag from me, 787:12
in the splendor of the moon, 454:18
veiling l. of song, 408:22
Light-o'-love lady known as Lou, 627:2
Lights around the shore, 509:29
Father of l., 46:6
fled garlands dead, 392:8
godfathers of heaven's l., 168:15
highest candle l. dark, 640:9
love is keeper of warm l., 66:18
moon l. up the earth, 56:6

Lights (*continued*)

Northern L. seen sights, 627:3
of the world, 334:7
ridicule one of principal l., 291:28
that do mislead the morn, 204:22
turn up l., 586:7
water closing over sleepy l., 730:8
your l. burning, 38:30
Light-winged Dryad, 415:10
Ligislachure, newspaper conthrols l., 603:12
Like a winter my absence, 221:18
ape how l. to us, 84:18
can afford to l. them, 767:3
doth quit like, 205:5
find their l. again, 378:5
God pairs l. with l., 54:2
how do you l. your blueeyed boy, 688:10
I don't l. them much, 768:5
I don't l. you Sabidius, 106:10
I know what I l., 614:8
I l. to be in America, 763:6
look upon his l. again, 193:16
lose freedom autonomy seeking to become l., 727:9
me from heels to head, 561:10
more ye see better l. it, 602:21
never met one I didn't l., 638:7
not fair terms, 180:12
of each thing, 168:16
one that stands on promontory, 164:21
people like priest, 29:23
poor cat i' the adage, 213:9
same things is friendship, 91:25
tell me what you l., 487:26
those who admire us, 265:29
to an hermit poor, 152:8
to like, 54:n3
to see it lap Miles, 512:17
upon earth there is not his l., 15:25
very l. a whale, 197:18
very very l. me, 561:10
want it most l. it least, 305:2
we don't l. it, 757:12
what he loves never l. too much, 232:11
will to like, 141:5
Liked, all people need be l. by some people, 727:8
book the better, 330:7
it not and died, 227:10
several women, 224:12
way it walks, 584:3
Likely impossibility preferable, 78:34
man in preference to rich, 62:27
we are all l. to go astray, 66:17
Likeness, devil erected in man's l., 495:7
gods in l. of men, 41:11
grow into l. of bad men, 76:13
let us make man after our l., 6:7
of filly foal, 173:2
very l. of roasted crab, 173:2
Likenesses, they are l. of Him, 3:15
Likes, doesn't know what he l., 690:7
nobody l. man who brings bad news, 66:6
Likewise, go and do l., 38:24

Liking, all love all l. all delight,
241:19
  grounds other than l., 483:30
  happy l. what they do, 321:6
  saves me trouble of l., 387:12
Lilac all over New England, 626:11
  and brown hair, 669:16
  lost l., 669:20
  time, 643:10
Lilacs last in dooryard bloomed,
490:15
  out of dead land, 668:17
Lilies and languors of virtue, 533:12
  beauty of the l., 484:7
  breaking golden l., 439:8
  calla l. in bloom again mother,
693:11
  crowned with l., 684:12
  feed among the l., 25:10
  handfuls of l. to scatter, 94:16
  of the field, 33:20
  peacocks and l., 487:15
  roses and white l. grow, 226:18
  silent war of l., 166:36
  that fester, 221:16
  three l. in her hand, 509:19
  twisted braids of l., 253:11
  wheat set about with l., 25:18
Lilting house, 737:14
  I've heard them l., 327:11
Lily maid of Astolat, 459:12
  of the valleys, 25:3
  paint the l., 170:9
  poppy or a l., 529:18
  take silver and buy l., 118:*n*2
  thick with l. and rose, 523:5
  trembles to a l., 539:6
  water l. bloom, 454:16
Lily-livered boy, 216:8
Lima, curious traveler from L., 323:23
Limb, feels life in every l., 372:17
  neither heat affection l., 204:10
  sound wind and l., 150:42
  tail's a l., 689:18
Limbecks foul as hell, 222:3
Limbo large and broad, 258:1
Limbs, gentle l. undress, 382:12
  his l. cold in death, 94:28
  I the l. and wheel, 494:7
  lopped l., 724:11
  melter of l., 54:17
  of a dismembered poet, 95:5
  recreant l., 169:28
  ruddy l. flaming hair, 357:20
  these l. her provinces, 229:19
  young in l. judgment old, 180:23
Lime, madeleine soaked in l. flowers,
612:13
  of love, 240:17
Limestone quarried near spot, 600:3
Limit, fixes solemn l. of Heaven,
68:20
  of becoming mirth, 168:23
  quiet l. of world, 459:2
  use me to the l., 575:13
  what l. to grief for one so dear,
95:29
Limitations, in l. the master, 350:30
  no man climb beyond l., 537:10

Limitless, swelling and l. billows,
383:1
Limits, hell hath no l., 162:16
  no l. but sky, 149:14
  of own field limits of world, 404:13
  own appointed l. keep, 506:4
  stony l. cannot hold love, 175:3
  truth has its l., 147:6
Limns on water writes in dust, 160:14
Limousine, one perfect l., 687:11
Limp and damp as tendrils, 725:4
  into scalding grave, 613:9
Limped, hare l. trembling, 414:21
Limping with duty, 80:13
Limpopo, greasy L. River, 593:9
Limps after in base imitation, 171:7
Lincoln belongs to ages, 474:10
  beloved of Abraham L., 607:14
  Clemens the L. of our literature,
532:19
  cruellest thing that happened to L.,
693:13
  I'm a Ford not a L., 733:7
  land of L. and Pinkham, 688:12
  shoveled into tombs, 634:8
Line, bottom l. is in heaven, 726:13
  cadence of a rugged l., 274:28
  cancel half a L., 445:25
  creep in one dull l., 298:18
  custom in all l. of order, 200:7
  embroil about fancied l., 280:17
  far-flung battle l., 592:25
  fathom l. could never touch, 177:9
  fight it out on this l., 501:10
  hit l. hard, 575:15
  horizontal l. straight, 411:12
  I had crossed that l., 493:13
  in nature is not found, 429:11
  in which force impressed, 282:2
  is gone out through all the earth,
16:10
  Marlowe's mighty l., 232:19
  met by color l., 480:20
  most insincere l. written, 666:23
  not a day without a l., 81:1
  second l. sublime third bombast,
106:4
  Shakespeare never blotted l., 233:4
  stepped across l., 419:8
  take us hours maybe, 595:13
  the l. must terminate, 743:20
  thin red l. of 'eroes, 492:*n*4
  thin red-l. streak, 492:8
  three hundred hours in l., 675:10
  uniform motion in right l., 282:1
  upon line, 26:32
  waiting in l. outside prison, 675:8
  will stretch out, 215:23
  write a living l., 232:23
Linea, nulla dies sine l., 81:*n*1
Lineaments, molded changing l., 538:6
  of Gospel books, 163:3
  of Gratified Desire, 357:24
Lined himself with hope, 183:25
Linen, airing dirty l. never masterpiece, 765:1
  all for l. undulation, 706:3
  not l. wearing out, 423:7
  old l. wash whitest, 237:11
  smooth and lavendered, 415:6

Linen (*continued*)
  wash dirty l. at home, 370:11
Liner she's a lady, 592:19
Lines are fallen unto me, 16:6
  as l. so loves oblique, 268:22
  deep-cut criss-cross l., 491:11
  desert of a thousand l., 303:8
  in nature few sharp l., 756:8
  learn l. don't bump into furniture,
700:19
  let lord once own happy l., 299:2
  many l. in dial's center, 184:25
  my l. and life are free, 243:16
  silken l. silver hooks, 229:10
  town-crier spoke my l., 196:21
  Zones and Meridian L., 519:20
Linge, laver son l. sale, 370:*n*5
Linger, do not live but l., 234:20
  out a purposed overthrow, 221:13
Lingered under benign sky, 480:7
Lingering bays, 313:11
  dewdrop, 377:14
  hoping l. flying, 299:8
  I alone sit l. here, 270:9
  longing l. look behind, 322:19
Lingers, borrowing only l. it out,
183:24
  find where last rose l., 96:4
  green light that l., 383:7
  no falsehood l. to old age, 67:16
  one who l. behind, 51:31
  wisdom l., 455:21
Lingo, unless you know l., 422:26
Linguistics an ever eerier area, 710:4
Lining, look for silver l., 645:14
  silver l. on the night, 252:25
  there's a silver l., 617:12
Link, I feel the l. of nature, 260:11
Linked sweetness long drawn out,
251:19
  to radiant angel l., 194:22
Links, golf l. lie so near mill, 631:1
Linnet, never tear l. from leaf, 597:4
Linnets, pipe but as l., 457:9
Linotype, lead effective from l., 717:5
Linsey-woolsey brother, 263:17
  brothers, 303:22
Lint, invisible strand of l., 586:2
Lintel low to keep out pride, 563:14
Lion among ladies, 173:15
  and fatling together, 26:11
  and Lizard keep, 445:12
  and unicorn, 788:10
  as l. woos his brides, 325:7
  at the door, 787:21
  be l. to frighten wolves, 136:15
  beard l. in his den, 378:12
  devil as roaring l., 46:28
  every l. comes from den, 5:4
  first beast like a l., 47:15
  first l. thought last a bore, 385:8
  from his claw can tell a l., 119:1
  he has heart of a l., 118:7
  honey in the carcass of the l., 11:11
  hungry l. grievous roar, 385:8
  in the way, 22:30
  in thy house, 31:9
  is in the streets, 22:30
  light is the l. that comes to drink,
639:10

Live (*continued*)

alone in bee-loud glade, 594:21
and die in Aristotle's works, 162:13
and die in Dixie, 475:2
and die r-r-rich, 471:22
and die wi' Charlie, 372:14
and learn, 288:12
and let live, 778:4
and love in God's light, 137:11
as if God beheld you, 102:20
as long as you please, 145:13
as men not ostriches, 650:5
as we can, 81:3
at home at ease, 247:11
at level of great men, 565:3
because I l. here, 768:8
begins to l. that day, 514:1
better l. rich, 317:9
better to l. alone, 64:21
bid me to l., 240:18
by medicine live horribly, 312:8
by squeezing from stone, 660:18
can these bones l., 29:9
cannot l. without cooks, 516:4
can't l. with them or without, 73:17
can't l. without or with you, 101:12
ceases to l. unreflectively, 630:17
converse and l. with ease, 302:11
courage to l., 411:20
date l. in infamy, 649:19
dead l. the living die, 275:11
decided to l. forever, 752:11
deeds by which we l., 157:10
deliberately, 478:17
desire to l. again, 553:5
desire to l. beyond income, 525:2
difficult to write good life as l. one,
    643:17
do not l. but linger, 234:20
do you want to l. forever, 318:*n*4
easy l. quiet die, 379:15
eat to l. not l. to eat, 269:20, 309:6
evil manners l. in brass, 226:5
exalt will to l., 630:17
for more than one century, 90:15
for what l. but make sport, 387:4
for which we bear to l., 301:16
Gilpin long l. he, 334:24
glad l. and gladly die, 561:16
gray dawn, 757:13
hair shining and free, 663:2
haven't knowledge how to l., 567:9
Hope without object not l., 383:15
how to l. well on nothing, 463:9
how we l. far from how we ought,
    136:14
human heart by which we l., 375:15
I cannot l. with You, 512:21
I cannot l. without books, 344:17
I still l., 395:12
I sure did l. in this world, 763:16
I to die and you to l., 74:18
I would not l. alway, 14:9
if I l. I will fight, 678:11
if I should l. to be, 447:20
if man die shall he l. again, 14:22
ill report while you l., 196:2
in divided and distinguished worlds,
    248:10
in fragments no longer, 636:10

Live (*continued*)

in furnished souls, 688:11
in him we l., 41:17
in house by side of road, 574:14
in human imagination, 758:21
in old chaos of sun, 638:26
in our life Nature l., 383:8
in restricted circle, 545:6
in small circle as we will, 349:28
in this faith I will l. and die, 134:2
in world as spectator, 292:18
in world good or bad, 477:11
Indians know better how to l.,
    563:5
innocently God is here, 312:11
isn't fit to l., 760:17
it all again, 598:5
known going to l. this long, 651:6
leave sack l. cleanly, 179:12
let me l. unseen unknown, 298:6
let us l. and love, 90:19, 226:13
life he has imagined, 478:36
life through not like crossing field,
    793:3
like stoic bird, 660:15
like to l. a long life, 761:9
like velvet mole, 660:16
like wretch and die rich, 234:24
long l. our noble king, 298:3
long l. the strike, 758:3
love wisdom l. accordingly, 478:5
loves to l. i' the sun, 190:20
mad to l. mad to be saved, 750:9
make war to l. in peace, 78:10
man born to l., 680:4
man desires to l. long, 289:2
man does not l. by GNP alone,
    739:3
man forgets to l., 283:16
martyrdom to l., 248:27
marvel how fishes l. in sea, 219:21
merrily shall I l. now, 224:25
mirth with thee I mean to l., 251:20
more virtue than doth l., 232:12
name shall l. behind me, 199:27
no evil deed l. on, 544:7
no longer l. here, 584:1
no man shall see me and l., 9:19
no picture made to l. with, 659:15
nobly to l., 65:9
not both l. and utter it, 477:22
not in myself, 400:4
not l. by bread only, 10:14
not l. if England finished, 626:24
not l. unto oneself, 81:9
not l. with living, 178:33
not three good men unhanged,
    177:22
not to l. but to make war, 727:15
now I l. now life is done, 156:22
on knees, 632:7, 649:18
one bare hour to l., 162:22
only by risking we l., 546:7
or die, 394:9
out thy life as light, 534:20
peaceably, 42:17
pleasurably without living wisely,
    81:20
power to l. and act, 377:6
prophets do they l. forever, 29:43

Live (*continued*)

proudly, 584:*n*1
pure speak true, 459:7
rage to l., 300:15
rationally for time assigned, 111:12
realize life while l. it, 697:15
says Death, 94:30
sea folk l. three hundred years,
    437:7
see so much nor l. so long, 211:21
shall not l. in Vain, 513:10
she tried to l. without him, 227:10
so l. that when summons comes,
    411:4
so long as ye both shall l., 50:3
so we'll l. pray sing, 211:13
so wise young never l. long, 166:1
soil good to l. on, 486:1
something that doth l., 375:10
take means whereby I l., 182:5
teach men to l., 145:12
teaching nations how to l., 254:18
ten times ten, 428:6
that nation might l., 450:2
that they may eat, 70:23
that thou desire to live again, 553:5
their wonted fires, 322:20
thou hast no more to l., 535:6
though dead shall he l., 40:19
through time or die by suicide,
    448:1
till tomorrow, 335:19
to be in awe, 187:20
to be show and gaze, 216:21
to extent they coincide with epoch,
    564:7
to fight another day, 81:*n*10
to itself it l. and die, 221:15
to l. is Christ, 44:29
to l. is to function, 543:11
to l. not as simple as cross field,
    679:17
to please must please to live, 313:14
today, 106:8
together in peace, 655:23
too beautiful to l., 469:16
true as I l., 236:17
unable to l. in society, 78:14
undo belt look for trouble, 652:3
until next day when hit it again,
    702:12
unto the Lord, 42:26
upon daily rations, 470:14
upon vapor of dungeon, 207:4
we die and we l., 117:14
we how we can, 164:31
we l. as we dream alone, 573:4
we l. here they l. there, 725:25
we must attempt to l., 613:17
we only l. only suspire, 672:4
we shall l. in his sight, 29:24
what thou livest l. well, 260:18
while ye may, 258:17
who dies if England l., 593:25
with ease, 302:11
with her and live with thee, 251:11
with me and be my love, 162:2,
    229:10
with the gods, 111:16
with thee and be thy love, 152:11

Live (*continued*)
with wolves howl like wolf, 793:6
with you love to l., 96:19
within no power to l. long, 102:22
within reach to l. nobly, 102:22
within sense they quicken, 409:10
without conscience, 516:4
without duties obscene, 433:25
without playing knave, 279:5
without poetry music art, 516:4
world not to l. but to die in, 248:21
would you l. forever, 318:18
you might as well l., 687:10
you will know how to l., 350:16
Live-and-help-live logic, 748:13
Lived, back above element they l. in, 218:11
discover I had not l., 478:17
everything l. in me, 504:17
for all times, 364:23
had we l. tale to tell, 606:2
how I have l. unimportant, 665:14
I had l. a blessed time, 214:15
I have l. long enough, 216:9, 534:3
I have l. my day, 96:*n*20
I have l. today, 274:29
I have not l. in vain, 292:19
I l. on air, 623:19
in cellar damp, 485:25
in his mild magnificent eye, 464:23
in little house, 792:12
in Paris as young man, 702:13
in practice of every virtue, 72:11
in pretty how town, 688:22
in tide of times, 188:22
I've l. a life that's full, 770:17
judged not to have l., 542:6
life l. in scene it composes, 640:17
light in spring, 498:1
like foot for thirty years, 764:16
long on alms-basket of words, 169:6
loved cursed floundered, 549:12
men l. like fishes, 219:*n*6
must be l. down, 757:9
my father l. his soul, 689:2
never to have l. is best, 598:3
nightly drank daily, 727:1
on River Dee, 338:18
she l. unknown, 373:19
some l. long and l. little, 145:14
through this horror, 654:15
together in crooked house, 791:11
under a hill, 792:12
under my woodside, 247:4
without disgrace without praise, 125:9
Livelier liquor than Muse, 579:15
plaything gives youth delight, 301:15
Livelihood, anxiety about l., 626:14
right l., 65:1
Lively, cock with l. din, 251:12
from l. to severe, 302:2
life l. form of death, 156:17
sense of filial duty, 342:23
understandable spirit, 725:2
Liver, as well speak of female l., 583:4
Liverpool, she's the L. packet, 793:22
Livers, humble l. in content, 225:8

Livery, cunning l. of hell, 204:13
in his l. walked crowns, 218:11
in sober l. clad, 258:18
of burnished sun, 180:13
Lives at ease that freely lives, 127:15
body's beauty l., 639:4
brutal l. ugly deaths, 690:22
cat has only nine l., 527:9
competency l. longer, 179:26
cuckold l. in bliss, 206:31
do our best and live our l., 716:11
every thing that l. is Holy, 357:16
evil men do l. after them, 188:28
for cap and bells l. pay, 485:4
fructify in l. of others, 84:*n*7
gave l. that nation live, 450:2
gave our l. to save Greece, 60:13
goodness l. though they are gone, 69:12
he l. he wakes, 409:5
he l. in bliss, 364:2
here or passes night, 651:20
history in all men's l., 184:2
Holocaust central event in l., 764:7
how the other half l., 245:4
human creatures' l., 423:7
in eternity's sunrise, 357:22
in fame died in virtue's cause, 167:9
in our alley, 298:2
in purer l. service find, 443:17
it's men's l. ye're buying, 379:8
like drunken sailor, 166:3
look into l. as into mirror, 86:14
lovely and pleasant in their l., 11:47
make our l. sublime, 440:17
merry merry l., 583:11
more lives than one, 567:20
music of men's l., 172:14
nine l. like a cat, 142:8
no second acts in American l., 694:22
noblest l. and dies, 494:20
noon and evening of l., 503:4
not alone in brain, 169:1
not how man dies but l., 316:6
not long who battles immortals, 51:19
not mounting and unfolding, 628:11
of great men, 440:17
of quiet desperation, 477:32
of shoemaker and peddler, 674:20
on a leaf, 724:16
on hope die fasting, 310:8
one l. but once, 349:2
our l. grow together, 534:7
our l. in acts exemplary, 157:10
our pilot still, 165:2
part as ships, 442:*n*3
pledge our l. our fortunes, 343:4
poet help people live their l., 640:18
preaches well that l. well, 150:38
public supreme judge of l., 396:15
sacrifice l. to preserve virtue, 61:26
Santa Claus l. forever, 538:2
slander l. upon succession, 166:28
spend rest of l. in future, 631:6
spending l. like serfs, 478:29
spoil l. of better people, 562:6
strained anxious l. dogs lead, 693:16

Lives (*continued*)
talk not of other men's l., 31:38
there still, 792:4
throbbing between two l., 669:1
traced l. of good men, 377:8
two lives who relives past, 106:21
went in jeopardy of their l., 12:17
what textures of our l., 726:2
who l. everywhere l. nowhere, 106:19
who l. unto himself, 242:5
who well l. long l., 148:8
woman true and fair, 228:6
worry away our l., 734:12
ye led were mine, 590:17
Livest, be useful where thou l., 243:3
Liveth and believeth in me, 40:19
I am he that l., 47:6
know that my redeemer l., 14:30
name l. forevermore, 32:15
none l. to himself, 42:26
Livia's daughtersons, 647:20
Livid loneliness of fear, 700:7
Livin', heap o' l., 644:16
life not worth l., 602:11
Living, all the l. and the dead, 647:8
and dead are same, 62:19
and partly living, 670:7
as black rock star, 757:10
at this hour, 374:19
bouquets while I'm l., 634:17
brave men l. and dead, 450:2
catch the manners l., 301:2
dead govern l., 421:10
dead live the l. die, 275:11
dead not interested in l., 697:14
dead think l. worth it, 758:9
desire of every l. thing, 20:12
difficult chapters in art of l., 493:22
dog better than dead lion, 24:18
doll can sew cook, 764:10
earn l. by sweat of brow, 478:9
earned precarious l., 782:9
earth belongs to l., 344:14
end of world want to be l. in retirement, 626:4
every l. thing of all flesh, 7:17
fever called L., 453:6
from hand to mouth, 148:5
glowed with l. sapphires, 258:19
God, 35:27, 325:17
God of l., 39:12
habit of l., 248:31
half dead a l. death, 261:9
heap o' l., 644:16
help for l. hope for dead, 520:14
Homer begged his bread, 233:*n*4
house a machine for l. in, 663:21
house appointed for all l., 14:44
how good mere l., 466:17
I advise you to go on l., 307:1
I make war on the l., 143:2
in a garret, 324:4
in agreement with nature, 82:1
in living seasons, 670:21
in underground den, 75:17
in Yorkshire, 380:10
include dying multifold, 513:13
it is for us the l., 450:2
know no bounds, 246:19

Living (*continued*)
know they shall die, 24:18
Lady Disdain are you yet l., 186:12
land of the l., 14:39, 697:11
language of the l., 671:20
law, 661:5
leave a l. name behind, 237:20
leave l. to servants, 537:19
life for the l., 521:9
life not worth l., 602:11
life worth l., 546:8, 588:4
lightning from her eyes, 299:18
like l. in jail, 725:25
Lord of l. and dead, 550:17
lyre, 322:11
more dead than l. l. getting rarer,
   731:15
mother of all l., 6:26
Mother of All L., 692:4
motion like l. thing, 373:9
my trade and art l., 146:1
no l. near her, 186:22
no l. with you or without, 106:24
no speech for when l., 671:20
noble L. and noble Dead, 373:13
not live with l., 178:33
not measured by length but use,
   145:14
not reverence of dead but envy of l.,
   239:24
object in l. to unite, 624:7
one thinks to get a l., 319:23
pattern of dead and l., 671:10
pity for the l., 527:28
plain l. high thinking, 374:14
pleasure the beginning and end of l.,
   81:19
pray for dead fight like hell for l.,
   515:3
precarious l., 782:9
question whether worth l., 542:12
recollection like l. over, 311:1
riotous l., 38:35
round ocean and l. air, 373:5
sacrifice, 42:12, 49:17
scarce able to bury dead, 240:10
search land of l. men, 378:5
seek l. among dead, 39:25
servant of L. God, 325:17
shake l. out of Fate, 516:12
shall forfeit renown, 378:1
something like l. occurs, 758:2
Son of the l. God, 35:27
sons of the l. God, 29:22
sorcery of embraces, 679:19
souls departed shadows of l., 249:6
summertime and l. easy, 695:8
take no notice if he were l., 390:11
the l. are not enough, 706:1
theologian born by l., 138:13
this life worth l., 546:8
this l. hand, 417:3
throne, 323:4
to one's self, 390:8
too much love of l., 534:15
translating into l. law, 661:5
up to it difficult, 463:17
well best revenge, 244:31
when l. might exceed dead, 248:25
whether l. is dying, 73:24

Living (*continued*)
which are yet alive, 23:33
who l. had no note, 777:6
who l. had no roof, 233:22
with us even in silence, 349:11
would be no l. in world, 479:28
write a l. line, 232:23
yet we have gone on l., 670:7
Living-dead man, 166:34
Livingstone, Dr. L. I presume, 544:5
Livre, je suis moi-même la matière de
   mon l., 145:*n*4
Lizard, Lion and L. keep, 445:12
seen the good l., 699:2
time slips away like l., 630:1
Lizzie Borden took ax, 781:11
Llorar, quien te quiere te hará l.,
   794:6
Lo Christ walking on the water,
   581:13
I am with you always, 37:16
the poor Indian, 301:7
virtue is at hand, 61:12
Load, ass will carry l., 151:16
cruelty to l. falling man, 225:*n*2
every rift of subject, 418:19
would sink a navy, 225:18
Loaded, centuries l. fragrant, 432:39
not put l. rifle on stage, 582:10
Loads, laid many heavy l. on thee,
   288:*n*1
Loaf, better half a l., 141:32
of Bread and Thou, 445:9
to every Bird, 513:5
Loafe, I l. and invite my soul, 488:16
Loafing around The Throne, 536:13
Loan oft loses friend, 194:1
Loaning, on ilka green l., 327:11
Loath, long and l. at going, 674:10
to lay out money on rope, 234:23
what maidens l., 416:1
Loathe, I l. the country, 291:11
people who keep dogs, 559:2
sweet tunes, 534:2
taste of sweetness, 178:11
Loathed Melancholy, 251:6
most l. worldly life, 204:15
Loathes, all outward l., 228:9
Loathing, deepest l. brings, 173:14
Loathsome canker in sweetest bud,
   220:21
Loaves, five l. and two fishes, 35:16
Lobotomized, flabby bald l., 743:1
Lobster, voice of the L., 518:8
Lobster-nights, luxurious l., 300:1
Lobsterpot, shattered l., 671:13
Lobsters, change l. and retire, 518:4
thrain l. to fly, 603:7
Local cult Christianity, 540:14
habitation and name, 174:1
seemed to be l. dust cloud, 735:19
Loch, banks o' L. Lomond, 779:21
Lochaber, farewell to L., 297:25
Lochinvar, young L., 378:7
Lock, cryin' at l., 461:12
meant to pick l., 778:1
sure l. me up, 673:16
Locke, accept views Cicero L. Bacon
   have given, 431:6
sank into swoon, 597:21

Locked and frozen in eye, 720:11
feet l. upon rough bark, 762:16
lettered collar, 361:16
man and woman two l. caskets,
   656:11
naked though l. up in steel, 164:1
razor, 742:19
'tis in my memory l., 194:2
up from mortal eye, 264:9
Locket, Lucy L. lost pocket, 791:16
Locks are like the snaw, 362:15
immortal l. fell forward, 51:2
knotted and combined l., 194:17
open l. whoever knocks, 215:16
pluck drowned honor by l., 177:9
shake thy gory l. at me, 215:4
shaking her invincible l., 255:2
time to silver turned, 156:14
unscrew l. from doors, 489:9
were like the raven, 362:15
which are left are gray, 386:8
yellow as gold, 381:12
Locksmith, zealous l. died, 778:1
Locomotive, more powerful than l.,
   737:7
Locust, day of the l., 712:12
of soul unshelled, 750:2
tossed up and down as the l., 19:12
Locusts and wild honey, 32:30
food as luscious as l., 206:1
like in Bible with l., 716:5
Lodge, house to l. friend, 302:23
in garden of cucumbers, 25:27
in some vast wilderness, 334:26
not l. thee by Chaucer, 232:18
thorns that in bosom l., 194:25
where thou lodgest I will l., 11:23
Lodged, love l. in woman's breast,
   227:5
with me useless, 255:11
Lodges, where care l. sleep never lie,
   175:17
Lodgest, where thou l. I will lodge,
   11:23
Lodging, grant us safe l., 426:22
hard was their l., 286:7
my l. is on cold ground, 297:5
Phoebus' l., 175:30
place of wayfaring men, 28:22
Lo'ed, better l. ye canna be, 368:4
Loftier race than known, 541:6
raise somewhat l. strain, 92:9
Loftiest peaks most wrapt, 399:25
Loftiness of thought surpassed, 275:25
Lofty and sour, 226:6
build the l. rhyme, 253:15
scene be acted o'er, 188:18
sky immeasurably l., 510:3
Log hut with simple bench, 516:3
Mark Hopkins at end of l., 516:*n*1
roll my l. I roll yours, 103:10
tough wedge for tough l., 100:10
will never be crocodile, 784:30
Logan's, enter L. cabin hungry, 326:14
Logic and rhetoric able to contend,
   160:10
and sermons never convince, 489:14
book of female l., 463:23
doctrinaire l., 683:4
is logic, 447:17

Logic (*continued*)
of mind overtasked, 447:7
page of history worth volume of l.,
543:4
that's l., 518:22
Logical, built in such l. way, 447:16
consequences scarecrows of fools,
505:14
Logs, Tom bears l. into the hall,
169:13
Loins, fire of my l., 703:1
gird up thy l. like a man, 15:6
he girded up his l., 12:38
let your l. be girded, 38:30
shudder in l., 598:1
with your l. girded, 8:38
Lois, built on order of L. De Fee,
714:14
Loiterers, liege of all l., 168:28
Loitering, alone and palely l., 417:4
Lolita, immortality you and I share L.,
703:3
light of my life, 703:1
Loman never made money, 738:15
Lomond, bonnie banks of Loch L.,
779:21
London Bridge falling down, 585:7,
788:12
broken arch of L. Bridge, 425:7
don't send poet to L., 420:5
flower of Cities all, 136:2
great cesspool, 577:12
hell city much like L., 407:22
in ruins rather than enslaved, 620:9
isn't far from L., 643:10
Lord Mayor of L., 777:1
loved life L., 650:16
particular a fog, 471:2
sea at best at L., 618:10
this is L., 724:4
tired of L. tired of life, 317:2
to L. to look at queen, 791:1
vilest alleys of L., 577:19
Lone Glenartney's hazel shade, 378:17
lorn creetur, 470:20
not in l. splendor, 417:12
poor l. woman, 183:28
sheiling, 421:17
walking by wild l., 593:12
worker makes first advance, 644:14
Lonelier, make each other l., 716:7
Loneliness, die of l., 600:6
intense l. ignorance, 568:6
of yesterday, 695:22
our l. our love our bodies, 705:16
people's ignorance or l., 766:12
Lonely, all the l. people, 770:9
and poor of old, 663:5
and swift like planet, 572:20
dark and l. hiding place, 382:18
down at end of l. street, 768:3
flowering in l. word, 460:7
God winding l. horn, 595:6
heart l. hunter, 568:8, 744:5
hunts on l. hill, 568:8
I'm l. I'll make world, 612:7
impulse of delight, 596:11
more l. among men, 478:26
nation turns its l. eyes to you, 772:9
people talking to each other, 716:7

Lonely (*continued*)
rapture on l. shore, 400:29
sea and sky, 633:14
sleep among l. hills, 376:17
so l. 'twas that God, 382:6
sun in l. lands, 458:4
thing that shone, 598:18
tramp l. fellow, 675:16
wandered l. as a cloud, 375:19
Lonelyhearts, Miss L., 712:10
Lonesome, be good and be l., 527:21
like one that on l. road, 381:26
October, 453:1
place against sky, 563:10
road, 381:26
whippoorwill, 753:5
Lonesomeness, starlight lit l., 539:8
Lonesome's a bad place, 730:13
Long and ghastly kitchen, 473:4
and lank and brown, 381:18
and loath at going, 674:10
and steep is the way, 54:24
and terrible way, 725:20
apprenticehood, 170:32
arm of coincidence, 582:5
art l. life short, 349:12
as l. as ever you can, 309:2
as l. as moon rise, 787:17
be day never so l., 142:23
calamity of so l. life, 196:10
cool winding saxophones, 634:10
day's journey into night, 674:8
day's task is done, 218:4
deliberate derangement, 566:3
divorce of steel, 225:6
for imperishable quiet, 725:10
for l. time used to go to bed early,
612:12
from l. to l. in solemn sort, 383:11
Gilpin l. live he, 334:24
gray beard glittering eye, 380:26
hair glory to woman, 43:10
happy as heart was l., 737:18
his arm is very l., 70:12
hot summer, 696:10
how l. a time in one word, 170:30
how l. to obtain vote, 751:7
how l. wilt thou forget me, 16:2
I have lived l. enough, 216:9
I loved you once l. ago, 56:7
I speak not loud or l., 154:*n*5
in l. run all dead, 652:8
it shan't be l., 305:17
it wont be l. now, 633:11, 633:13
kiss l. as my exile, 219:11
labor l. workers idle, 115:16
lane knows no turnings, 464:21
life how l. or short, 260:18
life is short art l., 71:13
life well spent is l., 135:3
light shakes, 456:11
littleness of life, 661:11
live our noble king, 298:3
live the strike, 758:3
long ago, 419:11
long thoughts, 442:5
long trail a-winding, 676:17
long wintry nights, 472:12
Lord how l., 26:4

Long (*continued*)
love me little love me l., 241:6,
776:8
may land be bright, 444:4
mechanic pacings, 454:21
melancholy l. withdrawing roar,
499:22
merry as day is l., 186:17
never make l. visits, 664:10
nor that little l., 296:14
nor wants that little l., 328:22
not l. life by fire, 583:19
not l. the weeping and the laughter,
602:10
poem does not exist, 453:12
pray that way be l., 587:11
pull strong pull, 470:35
run misleading guide to affairs,
652:8
see so much nor live so l., 211:21
seven l. year, 210:9
short and l. of it, 182:27
short meaning of l. speech, 365:7
small showers last l., 171:8
suits, 680:17
that thy days may be l., 9:12
think life too l., 284:11
thought the travel l., 163:4
three l. mountains, 683:15
time between drinks, 562:4
to talk with lover's ghost, 229:17
trick's over, 633:16
Trochee trips from l. to short,
383:11
way l. wind cold, 377:19
way to Tipperary, 627:15
within no power to live l., 102:22
words Bother me, 648:7
Long Island, Jay Gatsby of West Egg
L., 694:9
Long-drawn aisle, 322:9
Longed, lies where l. to be, 561:16
to embrace mother's ghost, 53:18
truly l. for death, 453:22
Longer, impossible takes l., 783:8
letter l. than usual, 270:14
no l. stay with you, 781:1
smile dwells l., 616:13
some days l., 622:7
song had been l., 789:10
stretch him out l., 211:20
words have l. life than deeds, 64:7
Longest fifty-nine minutes, 604:10
journey go, 408:13
journey inwards, 716:4
journey to oblivion, 658:2
nights are l. there, 203:32
part of the journey, 86:19
way round shortest home, 242:*n*4
Longest-lived and shortest-lived die
same, 110:18
Longeth, my flesh l. for thee, 17:35
Longevity has its place, 761:9
Longfellow's, shown L. grave, 664:10
Long-haired, not these l. men I fear,
89:1
Longing after immortality, 292:14
cast l. eye on offices, 344:3
for stewed prunes, 203:31
for that lovely lady, 86:18

Looks (*continued*)
    more elder than thy l., 181:22
    never l. nor 'eeds, 592:19
    not deep-searched with saucy l., 168:15
    old man l. before and after, 51:12
    on alike, 223:12
    on tempests, 222:2
    patron l. with unconcern, 315:17
    poet l. at world as man at woman, 640:24
    puts on his pretty l., 170:4
    quite through deeds of men, 187:25
    she l. with threatening eye, 170:6
    she needs good l., 656:1
    through Nature up, 302:1
    toward school with heavy l., 175:11
    war of l. between them, 165:11
    were free, 381:12
    whole world in face, 441:4
Loom, I cannot ply the l., 56:9
    left the web left the l., 454:16
Loon, thou cream-faced l., 216:7
Loop to hang doubt on, 207:10
Looped and windowed raggedness, 210:3
Loophole, from her cabined l. peep, 252:22
    no l. in case drafted, 638:4
Loopholes of retreat, 335:4
Loose, all hell broke l., 259:2
    as the wind, 243:16
    feel his title hang l., 216:6
    hell's broken l., 157:22
    imagination, 599:10
    lips sink ships, 783:9
    the bands of Orion, 15:12
    w'en it gits l. fum jug, 556:13
Loosed, arrows l. several ways, 184:25
    blood-dimmed tide l., 596:19
    fateful lightning, 484:6
    silver cord be l., 24:28
Loosen, old faiths l. and fall, 534:4
    old foundations, 634:9
Loosened, Heine l. corsets of German language, 626:5
Loosens fragrant bodice, 415:5
Lopped limbs, 724:11
    tree may grow again, 65:*n*6
Lord, all ye works of the L., 32:17
    am an attendant l., 667:17
    among wits, 315:18
    and Father of mankind, 443:17
    angel of L. came down, 285:1
    angel of L. came upon them, 38:3
    anger of L. kindled, 12:6
    answered Job out of the whirlwind, 15:6
    be thankit, 363:16
    be with you, 48:5
    better is little with the fear of the L., 21:26
    bless thee and keep thee, 9:28
    bless ye the L., 32:17
    blessed be L. God, 37:44
    blessed the latter end of Job, 15:28
    blot out his name, 277:*n*8
    bringeth thee into good land, 10:15
    Cain went out from presence of the L., 7:8

Lord (*continued*)
    Christ the L. risen today, 312:13
    Christ's heart, 430:12
    climb tree L. to see, 287:12
    coming of the L., 484:6
    Dark Maid and her L., 67:24
    day of the L., 45:5
    day thou gavest L. is ended, 506:16
    day which the L. hath made, 19:21
    dead which die in the L., 47:32
    died by the hand of the L., 9:6
    directeth his steps, 21:30
    disciples of the L., 41:4
    do if He knew facts, 603:4
    fear of the L. is beginning of wisdom, 19:14
    fear of the L. is wisdom, 14:41
    feast to the L., 8:39
    for the erring thought, 532:14
    forbade me to put off my hat, 271:13
    forgive O L. my jokes, 625:2
    from winter plague L. deliver us, 227:1
    gangway for L., 678:2
    gave and hath taken away, 13:31
    glory of the L. is risen, 28:4
    go and the L. be with thee, 11:39
    go home to my L. and be free, 794:20
    God Almighty, 47:15
    God caused a deep sleep, 6:16
    God formed man, 6:11
    God is subtle, 636:6
    God made them all, 479:17
    God of Hosts, 592:25
    God planted a garden, 6:12
    God send high wave, 613:9
    God walking in garden, 6:21
    good L. deliver us, 49:8, 779:15
    good L. had only ten, 542:1
    good works better in sight of L., 116:21
    Gracious L. bomb Germans, 718:23
    great and dreadful day of the L., 30:11
    hath chosen thee, 10:13
    have mercy on us, 48:7, 227:2
    hear me out, 725:20
    hear word of the L., 28:33
    holy is the L. of hosts, 26:1
    how discourse is of death, 279:11
    how long, 26:4
    how world given to lying, 179:11
    I am the L. thy God, 9:8
    I believe, 37:30
    I heard the voice of the L., 26:3
    I replied My L., 243:18
    I want to be in that number, 794:24
    I were l. in May, 534:8
    I will sing unto the L., 9:2
    if you had horse, 657:20
    in glance of the L., 401:16
    is a man of war, 9:3
    is come, 294:17
    is good, 18:22
    is in his holy temple, 29:42
    is in this place, 7:41
    is it I, 36:26
    is my helper, 45:43

Lord (*continued*)
    is my light, 16:21
    is my rock, 12:15
    is my shepherd, 16:17
    is my strength and shield, 16:23
    is my strength and song, 9:2
    is nigh unto them that call, 20:13
    is risen, 48:14
    is risen indeed, 39:28
    is the strength of my life, 16:21
    is thy keeper, 19:25
    is thy shade, 19:25
    is with thee, 37:37
    Jehovah Jove or L., 303:14
    kingdoms of our L., 47:26
    King's our only l., 161:8
    know ye that the L. he is God, 18:22
    land which the L. giveth thee, 9:12
    lendeth unto the L., 21:45
    lift up his countenance, 9:28
    looketh on the heart, 11:36
    love is my l. and king, 458:1
    love the L. with all thine heart, 10:11
    made all to prosper, 8:5
    make a joyful noise unto the L., 18:22
    make his face shine upon thee, 9:28
    make me an instrument, 123:10
    make my enemies ridiculous, 306:22
    Mayor of London, 777:1
    mercy on Thy People L., 593:4
    methought what pain to drown, 165:30
    more brain O L., 508:29
    my help cometh from the L., 19:25
    my L. what a morning, 794:17
    my soul doth magnify L., 37:40
    name of the L. in vain, 9:10
    neat and trimly dressed, 177:2
    not everyone that saith L., 34:13
    not in wind earthquake fire, 12:39
    not tempt the L. your God, 10:12
    not the weight of an ant escapes the L., 116:10
    O L. if there is a L., 503:14
    O L. let her go, 793:22
    O L. my God I have trusted, 147:14
    of all Being, 116:1
    of all yet prey to all, 301:13
    of far-flung battle line, 592:25
    of folded arms, 168:28
    of heaven and earth, 41:16
    of himself, 227:8, 401:13
    of hosts he is the King of glory, 16:20
    of living and dead, 550:17
    of lords, 47:34
    of the Ocean, 68:72
    of yourself, 276:18
    once own happy lines, 299:2
    our maker, 18:19
    oure l. dooth with youre owene thing, 131:14
    patient unto coming of L., 46:16
    peace in our time O L., 50:10
    praise L. pass ammunition, 679:7
    pray L. soul to keep, 287:14

Lost (*continued*)

Bo-peep has l. sheep, 790:14
but ane twa behin', 363:24
causes, 499:10, 672:19
defaced deflowered, 260:10
every other friend, 450:8
for him I am not l., 84:10
for want of nail shoe l., 244:28, 310:10
found my wits you l. yours, 239:14
found sheep which was l., 38:34
France not l. war, 678:9
friends I have l. a day, 106:27
generation, 627:5
haven't l. battle yet, 735:12
he is not l. for Me., 84:10
heart stiffens, 669:20
her honest name, 782:17
holding anchor l., 165:2
I have l. my reputation, 206:20
I once was l. now am found, 327:4
in America shall be found, 706:20
in convent's gloom, 300:3
in the sweets, 297:19
in wandering mazes l., 257:12
it with hollaing and singing, 183:21
lacked and l., 187:2
lambs who l. way, 592:3
land of l. content, 579:9
legion of l. ones, 592:2
Lenore, 452:15
loved and l., 457:11
memory of loved and l., 450:9
men have l. their reason, 189:2
missed it l. it forever, 467:21
more l. than life, 105:23
Mule Flat, 698:6
no friend, 300:24
no hate l. between us, 237:8
no love l., 150:41, 231:19
no one ever l. money, 643:1
not a kiss nor look be l., 720:17
not l. but gone before, 102:27
not profited so much as l., 478:3
not that you won or l., 643:13
nothing except battle l., 371:7
nothing l. but money, 723:3
old nonchalance of hand, 596:16
old simplicity of times, 779:4
on roundabouts, 614:15
only Playboy of Western World, 613:10
or won game, 426:2
pain wanders like l. fire, 725:19
people on whom nothing l., 548:13
praising what is l., 203:19
principles of free constitution l., 340:1
reputation, 206:20
sea smell, 669:20
seek for the l. mind, 79:29
sheep of house of Israel, 34:27
so fallen so l., 443:3
sooner l. and worn, 202:10
sun is l. and the earth, 230:15
swallowed up and l., 257:2
things filled with intent to be l., 729:15
time never found, 310:2
to fame, 92:29

Lost (*continued*)

to Love and Truth, 592:4
to memory nothing really l., 727:20
violent souls, 669:9
virtue l. seldom recovered, 277:13
war and carnage be utterly l., 490:14
was l. and is found, 38:37
what is left when honor l., 99:9
what though field be l., 256:1
when battle's l. and won, 212:9
when faith is l., 443:4
when I had l. one shaft, 179:24
without deserving, 206:21
woman that deliberates l., 292:10
woman won or woman l., 597:12
wreath has l. rose, 379:6
year only l. to me, 243:16
yesterday, 419:4

Lot, blameless vestal's l., 300:5
dwelled in the cities, 7:28
inherited total l. of parents, 768:12
is fallen unto me, 16:*n*1
no l. is altogether happy, 96:11
no man content with l., 94:31
policeman's l., 529:14
this l. is bitterest, 64:4

Lothario, gay L., 294:4

Lot'll, none will come then a l., 718:12

Lot's, remember L. wife, 39:6

Lots, cast l. upon my vesture, 16:16

Lou, lady known as L., 627:2

Loud, could have got l. but hadn't, 729:11
had tongue yet never l., 206:8
heard the l. bassoon, 381:1
helpless naked piping l., 358:11
I speak not l. or long, 154:*n*5
laugh spoke vacant mind, 329:11
licker talks mighty l., 556:13
play skillfully with a l. noise, 16:29
say l. I'm black I'm proud, 766:9
shout out l. and strong, 636:16
sing cuckoo, 775:10
sing Goddamm, 659:2
troublesome insects, 332:18
trumpet's l. clangor, 275:9
uplifted angel trumpets, 254:11

Louder, a little l. but as empty, 301:15
cock l. in own farmyard, 475:15
he talked of honor, 425:*n*1

Loud-hissing, bubbling and l. urn, 335:3

Loungers of Empire drained, 577:12

Loup, comme un complice à pas de l., 494:*n*8

Lousy, poor and very l., 310:24
unethical and l., 712:13

Lovable, Elaine the l., 459:12
to be loved be l., 101:15

Love a ballad in print, 223:11
a feeling and a l., 373:4
a kind of warfare, 101:*n*6
a lover, 431:33
absence cure of l., 149:38
acts of kindness and of l., 373:1
alas how l. can trifle, 168:8
all beauteous things, 550:1
all for l. a little for bottle, 348:2

Love (*continued*)

all for l. nothing for reward, 153:10
all in green went my l. riding, 688:6
all l. all liking all delight, 241:19
all love of other sights controls, 228:3
all l. sweet, 407:1
all must l. human form, 356:14
all policy's allowed in l., 482:*n*4
all she loves is l., 402:21
all trust a few, 203:8
all we know of L., 514:18
all's fair in l. and war, 482:13
almost too much l., 623:20
alters not, 222:2
am like to l. three more, 262:9
America l. or leave it, 784:5
Americans because they love liberty, 313:4
and a cough, 244:4
and all his pleasures toys, 226:16
and be loved by forever, 466:22
and be loved by me, 453:7
and be wise, 98:32
and desire and hate, 602:10
and fame to nothingness, 417:11
and fear hardly together, 136:10
and glory, 689:16
and good company, 295:15
and have not l., 43:*n*4
and laughter, 520:9
and man's unconquerable mind, 374:18
and marriage go together, 732:11
and scandal, 311:21
and still to l., 335:18
and thanks, 340:22
and War same thing, 150:39
and we will teach them how, 373:14
anger of lovers renews l., 85:*n*11
anterior to Life, 513:9
art accomplice of l., 575:2
ashamed of having been in l., 265:8
at first sight, 591:1
at the lips, 623:19
babe that milks me, 213:12
bade me welcome, 244:1
base men being in l., 206:12
beareth all things, 43:15
beautiful time of young l., 365:12
begets love, 725:17
believeth all things, 43:15
better is thy l. than wine, 25:12
beyond the world, 282:21
bid me take l. easy, 594:17
Black l. is Black wealth, 772:15
born with pleasure of looking, 564:3
bout with l., 60:1
boy's l., 210:13
breastplate of faith and l., 45:7
bridge is l., 697:11
brief as woman's l., 197:10
bright particular star, 203:9
brings bewitching grace, 68:17
brook weather that l. not wind, 168:30
brotherly l., 42:14, 45:42

Love (*continued*)

built on beauty, 230:3
bumping against obstacles of civilization, 436:16
business that we l., 217:30
but her love forever, 362:11
but I do l. thee, 206:27
but you alone, 775:16
by heaven I do l., 168:33
calls to war, 157:2
can come to everyone, 685:16
care of discipline is l., 30:27
careless l., 743:6
cement glue and lime of l., 240:17
change old l. for new, 156:13
cherish and obey, 50:12
children's gratitude woman's l., 598:15
close hand out of l., 552:8
clouds of goodness and l., 347:*n* 1
collaborating in private way of l., 739:13
come unto my l., 154:13
comes in at eye, 595:20
comforteth like sunshine, 165:14
common as light is l., 407:1
concluded with impossibility of separation, 564:3
conquer L. that run away, 246:11
conquers all things, 92:20
contend no more L., 465:8
converted from thing it was, 220:24
corporations can l. each other, 555:15
could you and I conspire, 446:8
countless ties of l., 624:12
courage l. joy, 297:16
course of true l., 172:19
covereth all sins, 21:6
crime to l. too well, 300:8
crown is l. and friendship, 414:12
curiosity freckles doubt, 687:7
dare l. that and say so too, 228:10
dark secret l., 358:4
deep as first l., 456:14
demanded of genius l. of truth, 351:7
desire more l. and knowledge, 190:1
die for l., 203:10
die to what we l., 570:4
died before god of l. was born, 229:17
dinner of herbs where l. is, 21:26
distills desire, 68:17
do justly and l. mercy, 29:38
do not trifle with l., 461:14
doesn't l. a wall, 622:20
dooms of l., 689:1
draw as l. with thread, 235:13
drew them with bands of l., 29:29
dropped like a flower, 90:22
dull sublunary lovers' l., 229:11
earth sun animals, 488:11
earth's place for l., 623:8
end of l. or season, 622:18
endureth all things, 43:15
envieth not, 43:14
episode in man's life, 368:10
eternity in l. with production of time, 357:4

Love (*continued*)

eyes silent tongues of L., 149:8
faith nor l. nor law, 406:21
faithful in l., 378:8
fall in l. with Athens, 72:7
falling out renewing is of l., 85:*n* 11
false maids in l., 200:22
false or true, 595:2
fed with necessity of seeing, 564:3
few l. to hear sins they act, 219:19
fickleness of women I l., 570:10
final face of l., 750:4
first is deep l., 57:22
first learned in lady's eyes, 169:1
fitter l. for me, 228:19
flies out window, 777:19
food of l., 201:16
for ladies' l. unfit, 276:26
for l. lead apes in hell, 167:21
for l. of Barbara Allen, 785:9
for Love's sake, 725:21
forbearance l. charity, 339:11
force, 606:13
forever lost, 419:13
forever wilt thou l., 416:3
forget l. to friends and brethren, 30:12
forgive us, 414:17
forspent with l. and shame, 547:9
foundation is l., 761:4
freedom in my l., 267:18
freely serve because we freely l., 259:11
friendship charity, 201:3
from eyelids dripped l., 54:18
fruit of Spirit is l., 44:19
fruits of l. gone, 404:7
fullness even of l., 51:38
game beyond prize, 586:12
gather Rose of l., 153:11
gilds the scene, 352:18
give a little l. to child, 487:25
give all to l., 429:19
give me more l. or more disdain, 246:7
go l. without the help, 359:20
God is l., 46:36
God is L. I dare say, 525:7
gods l. the obscure, 50:18
goes toward love, 175:11
gold and l. affairs difficult to hide, 794:7
golden time of first l., 365:12
good man's l., 191:23
good to l. the unknown, 387:31
great l. grows there, 197:11
great secret of morals is l., 409:24
greater l. hath no man, 40:31
greater l. the more false, 720:5
greatest is l., 43:16
greatness worthy to excite l., 500:12
groans of l. like those of dying, 727:2
grown old in l., 359:21
grows bitter with treason, 534:4
gude to be off with old l., 779:20
hail wedded l., 258:26
half in l. with Death, 415:16
happiness to l. and be loved, 436:25
hardly worth thinking of, 595:12

Love (*continued*)

harmony is pure l., 161:7
hate as though someday l., 65:*n* 9
hate foes as far as we soon might l. them, 65:13
hate one and l. other, 33:17
hate traitors treason l., 275:22
hath an end, 534:3
hath so long possessed me, 125:1
hatred as well as l., 319:24
hatred ceases by l., 64:19
he bore to learning, 329:17
he will then l. me, 356:10
hearts in l. use own tongues, 186:21
heaven is l., 377:25
heaven sends l. of her, 4:6
hell is to l. no longer, 666:17
her till I die, 777:4
hid in heart of l., 594:22
Highlands for ever I l., 362:16
him most for enemies, 507:8
him who in l. of Nature, 411:1
his banner over me was l., 25:5
hiss of l., 716:21
history of woman's life, 368:10
hold your tongue and let me l., 228:14
hollow sound same as our l., 705:16
hope nor l. nor friend, 561:21
hopeth all things, 43:15
how do I l. thee, 438:23
how should I true l. know, 198:16
how they could l., 781:14
human l. seen at its height, 636:10
hunt down l. together, 534:9
I am sick of l., 25:5
I both l. and do not l., 60:2
I do not l. thee Doctor Fell, 286:25
I don't think we don't l. each other, 763:2
I hate and I l., 91:16
I l. a lass, 348:12
I l. a lassie, 609:19
I l. broad margin to life, 478:24
I l. everything old, 329:25
I taught thee to l., 230:4
I told my l., 357:17
I was in l. with the whole world, 775:1
I'd l. to get you on slow boat, 728:12
idea of two sexes, 690:6
if ever thou shalt l., 202:9
if I l. you what business of yours, 349:9
if l. were what rose is, 534:7
if music food of l., 201:16
if no l. is what feel I so, 128:12
if she will not l., 262:3
if world and l. were young, 152:11
if you l. you suffer, 678:1
I'm savin' my l. for you, 693:8
impossible not to l. all things, 380:24
in a golden bowl, 357:1
in a hut, 414:17
in it was l. and desire, 52:3
in l. and charity with neighbors, 49:14
in l. illusion reaches zenith, 553:1

Love (*continued*)

in l. two solitudes touch, 630:4
in l. with American names, 698:6
in l. with loving, 114:21
in l. woman more barbarous, 552:15
in my bosom like a bee, 156:20
in others they l. l., 266:1
in our will to l. or not, 259:11
in spite of darkness, 229:4
in struggle for life find l., 682:8
in summer's wonderland, 643:10
inestimable l., 49:5
innocence of l., 202:12
inspiration l. and freedom, 582:8
instill l. of you into world, 3:16
is a boy, 263:21
is a sickness full of woes, 161:6
is agreement, 161:7
is all there is, 514:18
is best, 465:10
is blind, 180:20
is blynd, 131:20
is dead, 155:27
is enough, 523:8
is flower-like, 383:13
is fulfilling of law, 42:22
is heaven, 377:25
is intercourse between tyrants and slaves, 329:4
is kind, 43:14
is most beautiful among gods, 54:17
is most nearly itself, 671:11
is not all, 684:13
is not love which alters, 222:2
is strong as death, 25:22
is sweeping the country, 695:6
is the whole, 689:2
is then our duty, 297:18
it and who shall dare, 480:9
itself have rest, 402:1
itself slumber on, 409:10
iz like meazles, 479:21
jealousy born with l., 265:37
Joy and L. triumphing, 257:25
joy nor l. nor light, 499:22
joy of l. too short, 133:9
jumps from admiration to l., 386:25
keep corner in thing I l., 207:4
kelson of creation is l., 488:18
kill things they do not l., 181:14
kill your joys with l., 176:20
kindled by virtue, 126:17
kindness shall win my l., 167:30
King of l. my shepherd is, 493:25
King without the woman I l., 691:6
know the l. betwixt us, 267:6
knowledge and l. of God, 49:18
known l. how bitter, 533:20
knows nothing of order, 113:9
labor of l., 45:3
laggard in l., 378:9
land that I l., 666:11
last not least in l., 188:21
law to itself, 115:14
lay aside long-cherished l., 91:14
learn to bear beams of l., 356:9
lease of my true l., 221:23
least that let men know, 167:38
leave me O L., 155:28

Love (*continued*)

leaving L. behind, 513:8
lest thy l. prove variable, 175:7
let l. who never loved, 118:22
let me l. river and woodland, 92:29
let thy l. be younger, 202:11
let us be true, 499:22
let us live and l., 90:19, 226:13
let us surrender to l., 92:20
let warm L. in, 416:9
life among people who l. each other, 436:22
light dies when l. done, 563:2
like Death levels, 428:21
like everybody not in l., 612:19
like l. don't know where or why, 720:15
live and l. in God's light, 137:11
live with me and be my l., 162:2, 229:10
live with thee and be thy l., 152:11
lodged in woman's breast, 227:5
long life better than figs, 216:27
long l. doth so, 175:24
longing for l. a passion, 615:15
look at enemies with l., 279:5
look at was to l., 455:12
look of l. alarms, 357:23
looked as she did l., 417:6
looks not with eyes, 172:21
Lord with all thy heart, 36:1
lore of l. deep learned, 414:15
lost to L. and Truth, 592:4
lovers' quarrels renewal of l., 85:14
Lyric L. half angel, 467:24
makes world go round, 530:16, 786:18
man in l. endures more, 553:1
man in l. with suffering, 495:1
man is in l., 597:14
mankind except American, 317:7
man's l. apart from life, 402:14
many waters cannot quench l., 25:23
Marilyn man's l. affair with America, 753:3
marriage from which l. gone, 713:10
marriage without l., 309:11
martyrs honor slain, 495:12
may perfectly l. thee, 49:13
me and keep my commandments, 9:10
me and my true l., 779:21
me in December, 547:n1
me little love me long, 241:6, 776:8
me not for grace, 777:5
me sure to die, 392:13
me tender, 768:4
means not having to say sorry, 769:1
medicines to make me l. him, 177:12
men died but not for l., 192:2
Mercy Pity Peace and L., 356:12
mercy unto them that l. me, 9:10
met you not with my true L., 152:9
mie l. ys dedde, 353:6
mighty pain to l., 267:2
ministers of L., 383:3

Love (*continued*)

mischievous devil, 525:7
moderately, 175:24
money rage and l., 716:16
money the sinew of l., 88:n9
moody food of l., 217:18
more libertines than l., 319:17
more l. less we flatter, 269:14
more than love, 453:8
more true than L. to me, 776:24
morning and evening star, 658:8
most important business, 396:21
music food of l., 217:18
musick thing I l. most, 279:16
my home of l., 221:25
my hope my hap my l., 148:9
my hope my l., 249:30
my lord and king, 458:1
my l. and I did meet, 594:17
my l. he purloined away, 536:20
my l. is come to me, 515:6
my L. like red red rose, 362:6
my L. like the melodie, 362:6
my l. of birth as rare, 268:21
my whole course of l., 205:22
mysterious by this l., 228:15
ne'er ebb to humble l., 207:15
neighbor as thyself, 9:26
neighbor yet pull not down hedge, 244:11
never any that could escape l., 113:1
never change when l. has found home, 100:27
never doubt I l., 195:14
never faileth, 43:15
never l. stranger, 682:13
never l. unless you can, 226:17
never see what you l., 613:n2
never seek to tell thy l., 357:17
never seeketh own, 132:20
never sick old dead, 152:10
never taint my l., 208:3
never told her l., 202:14
no concern with art, 524:1
no creature give orders to l., 436:17
no disguise conceal l., 265:7
no go my honey l., 722:4
no l. but vanity, 397:7
no l. lost, 150:41, 231:19
no more dear l., 456:19
no season knows, 228:12
noght oold as whan newe, 131:15
none but L. find me out, 152:8
none knew thee but to l., 405:5
nor l. thy life nor hate, 260:18
not a gaping pig, 181:12
not Death but L., 438:21
not enough religion to make us l., 288:25
not found thing to l., 630:22
not freedom but license, 255:8
not l. thee dear so much, 267:15
not man the less, 400:29
not my l. to see, 154:8
not Pleasure love God, 412:9
not puffed up, 43:14
not to be loved but to l., 123:10
not to eat not for l., 430:14
not to l. when we l., 149:23

Love (*continued*)

not wise who buffet against l., 67:1
nothing I l. as much as fight, 648:13
nothing in l., 216:6
nourished without denying l., 749:1
now abideth l., 43:16
now l. is over, 594:11
now warm in l., 300:3
now who never loved before, 295:20
now with l. now in colde grave, 130:22
O human l., 451:6
O ye that l. mankind, 340:21
obedience troops of friends, 216:9
of a brute, 452:9
of beauty, 60:17
of British people, 331:23
of flattery, 293:22
of gentle woman, 731:3
of glory the most ardent, 293:20
of God, 44:13
of God in Christ, 42:9
of home love of country, 469:28
of justice simply fear, 265:10
of learning, 442:19
of money as possession, 652:12
of money impulse to effort, 559:5
of money the root of evil, 45:22
of old for old, 580:13
of pleasure, 300:16
of praise, 295:23
of self love of God, 115:3
of slaughter, 659:8
of spiders, 703:16
of sway, 300:16
of the exaggerated, 765:15
of the virtuous, 60:17
of virtue, 319:20
of wisdom guide of life, 360:8
of you has entrapped me, 4:7
of young for young, 580:13
offender detest offense, 276:n4
on l. request for money chilling, 496:10
one another, 40:25, 42:21
one jot of former l. retain, 161:11
one of best things about l., 616:17
only l. sprung from only hate, 174:24
open rebuke better than secret l., 23:1
our l. hath no decay, 229:5
our occupations, 470:14
our principle, 421:8
out of l. cheat others, 613:1
out of l. with your nativity, 191:28
oyster may be crossed in l., 353:3
pain to l. in vain, 267:2
pains of l. sweeter far, 273:13
pangs of disprized l., 196:10
pardon to extent we l., 265:35
passed muse appeared, 423:19
passing the l. of women, 12:2
path to deepest mystery path of l., 707:13
paths to woman's l., 236:9
people and things I l., 727:16
perfect l. casteth out fear, 46:37
perhaps right to dissemble l., 360:6

Love (*continued*)

pest of l., 414:14
physicians by their l. grown cosmographers, 231:3
pitched his mansion, 598:21
planet of L. on high, 458:21
Platonic l., 149:43
pleasure and l. are pinions, 349:16
pleasure drives l. away, 597:19
pleasure of l. in loving, 265:27
poets' food l. and fame, 407:12
possesses heart fall in l., 612:14
pray that l. may never come, 68:17
prophet of soul, 429:9
prosperity's very bond of l., 223:14
purlieu of god of l., 229:18
purple light of L., 323:1
Pussy my l., 471:31
putting L. away, 513:17
quaint figure men l., 637:11
quantity of l., 199:16
quarrels in concord end, 261:20
quick-eyed L., 244:1
radiant with splendor, 123:8
rather than l. than money than fame, 478:39
regain l. once possessed, 261:19
regent of l.-rimes, 168:28
rekindled by absence, 314:7
resembleth April day, 168:1
respect or natural l., 573:12
right true end of l., 230:9
rose of our l., 750:2
ruined l. when built anew, 222:5
rules the court, 377:25
rules the gods, 67:1
satisfied, 669:15
saved by l., 684:18
seals of l., 204:22
see how Christians l. one another, 112:4
seeketh not itself to please, 358:2
seeketh self to please, 358:3
seized this man for fair form, 125:16
separate us from l. of Christ, 42:8
servant in l. lord in marriage, 131:27
sets l. task like that, 397:7
shackles of old l., 459:15
shadow of power, 629:6
shall know no quarrels, 95:26
she whom I l. hard to catch, 509:10
shoot false L., 776:23
sigh to those who l. me, 401:27
sighed for l. of lady, 531:14
silence in l. bewrays woe, 152:14
sin who tell us l. die, 386:13
sit down says L., 244:2
sleep on my L., 242:2
smile of l., 359:3
so dear I l. him, 260:8
so full in my nature, 466:20
so hot as nigh to burst my boilers, 398:5
so long as we l. we serve, 562:5
someone to l. and l. you, 580:11
something tells me but not l., 181:1
sorrow of l. dureth overlong, 133:9
sought is good, 202:26

Love (*continued*)

speak low if you speak l., 186:20
spirit all compact of fire, 165:9
spirit of l., 45:26
spirit of l. how quick and fresh, 201:17
sports of l., 232:4
spring of l. gushed from heart, 381:22
steer stars, 770:1
stony limits cannot hold l., 175:3
study way to l. each other, 242:4
such I believe my l., 137:9
suffereth long, 43:14
swears she is made of truth, 222:9
sweet as l., 354:3
sweet for a day, 534:4
sweet lovers l. spring, 192:12
sweetest l. I do not go, 228:19
take l. away no art, 575:2
take l. together to sky, 544:2
takes life to l. life, 607:12
tale without l., 550:14
teach monarch to be wise, 321:24
that can be reckoned, 216:24
that comes too late, 203:21
that dare not speak its name, 609:14
that endures for breath, 533:10
that L. is all is all we know of L., 514:18
that moves sun and other stars, 127:4
that my l. were in my arms, 776:6
that never seen twice, 421:6
that never told can be, 357:17
that winged seraphs coveted, 453:8
that word is l., 67:10
the brotherhood, 46:23
the good pursue the worst, 101:n18
the human form divine, 356:13
the look of landscapes, 660:17
the Lord with all thine heart, 10:11
the only meaning, 697:11
the only priest, 520:16
the wild swan, 663:16
thee better after death, 439:1
thee to the depth, 438:23
them as God gives them, 349:21
them that love me, 20:33
there are those who l. it, 394:5
they do not l. that do not show, 167:38
they happy are and l., 250:2
they l. a train, 198:n5
this bud of l., 175:10
this cultured hell, 679:9
those I guard I do not l., 596:10
those who always loved l. more, 295:20
those who l. and create, 564:11
those who l. want wisdom, 406:17
those who love you, 306:15
those who wrong him, 111:20
those who yearn for impossible, 350:24
thou wast all to me l., 452:2
though presst with ill, 335:18
through l. come together into one, 67:19

Love (*continued*)

through our l. is my lord slain, 133:15
throw away l. on conceited, 483:*n*2
thy first l., 47:7
thy honesty and l., 206:19
thy l. to me was wonderful, 12:2
thy neighbor, 9:26
thy neighbor as thyself, 36:1
thy sweet l. remembered, 220:17
thyself last, 225:21
till I prince of l. beheld, 355:17
time to l., 23:32
time weakens l., 283:13
tired of L., 609:6
to be wise and l., 200:21
to be worst of company, 288:23
to begin journey on Sundays, 290:15
to faults always blind, 357:19
to hatred turned, 291:9
to lose myself, 388:6
to lose myself in a mystery, 248:4
to l. and to cherish, 50:4
to l. and to work, 570:2
to l. her a liberal education, 293:18
to matrimony in a moment, 386:25
to say how much l. is little l., 127:11
to see her was to l. her, 362:11
too much l. of living, 534:15
took all my l., 599:21
trade you have learned, 111:7
tragedy of l. indifference, 626:18
treason but hate traitor, 88:18
true l. a durable fire, 152:10
true l. differs from gold and clay, 408:13
true l. is like ghosts, 265:9
true l. sits him down, 780:23
truth pardon error, 305:27
try thinking of l., 722:3
tunes shepherd's reed, 377:25
turns to thoughts of l., 455:9
unconditional l., 761:7
unconquerable waster, 66:18
unfamiliar Name, 672:4
unrelenting foe to l., 308:11
unsatisfied, 669:15
unsought is better, 202:26
up groweth with youre age, 129:2
vaunteth not, 43:14
vegetable l. grow, 268:14
vegetable l. not suit me, 529:18
very ecstasy of l., 195:9
very few to l., 373:19
Virtue she alone is free, 253:13
visible world formed in l., 486:26
waft her l. to Carthage, 182:7
we are a small pond, 755:2
we may touch l. explain, 757:17
weathered storms of life, 580:13
what I l. near at hand, 725:12
what is l., 658:8
what is l. 'tis not hereafter, 202:2
what l. I bore to thee, 374:6
whatever is l. was an infection, 759:15
when I l. thee not, 206:27
when I was in l. with you, 579:2
when L. and Life fair, 567:18

Love (*continued*)

when l. begins to sicken, 189:12
when l. is in excess, 68:11
when L. speaks, 169:3
when my l. swears, 222:9
when we love not, 149:23
where I and my L. wont to gae, 785:19
where is l. beauty truth, 407:9
where l. and need one, 624:7
where l. is great, 197:11
where l. of man l. of art, 71:5
where l. rules no will to power, 629:6
where Mercy L. and Pity dwell, 356:14
where power predominates l. lacking, 629:6
which greybeards call divine, 165:7
white rose breathes of l., 553:19
whom the gods l., 81:5
why is all l. speak, 514:7
why L. needs be blind, 172:*n*2
wife Belle Aurore, 468:6
wilder shores of l., 721:12
will find out way, 777:11
wisdom live accordingly, 478:5
with all thy faults I l. thee, 333:*n*6
with delight discourses, 125:2
with streaming hair, 695:22
with you l. to live, 96:19
without bitterness, 683:14
without dissimulation, 42:13
without his wings, 398:14
without marriage, 309:11
without power destroyed, 684:15
women l. lovers, 266:1
word l. in mouth of courtesan, 430:21
words of l. then spoken, 392:7
work is l. made visible, 651:13
world in l. with night, 176:1
world outlasts l., 497:11
worms eaten but not for l., 192:2
would be dried up, 495:3
write of hunger writing about l., 723:1
wroth with one we l., 382:15
wrought new alchemy, 229:9
ye do me wrong, 776:10
years grow cold to l., 93:4
yes I'm in l., 321:11
yields to business, 102:1
you as New Englanders love pie, 633:1
you for yourself alone, 598:8
you in December, 547:4
you l. me so much, 657:7
you l. the daylight, 68:1
you ten years before the Flood, 268:14
your enemies, 33:8
your eyes that can see, 663:18
youth gave l. and roses, 392:9
Zeus's bed of l., 68:20

Loved, alas I l. you best, 284:4
alas that all we l. of him, 408:20
Alcuin my name learning I l., 120:10
and lost, 450:9, 457:11

Loved (*continued*)

and thought himself beloved, 597:3
as l. we are indispensable, 562:5
at first sight, 162:11
at home revered abroad, 361:10
betray heart that l. her, 373:6
better l. ye canna be, 368:4
better to be l. than feared, 136:10
better to have l. and lost, 457:11
burning Sappho l., 402:24
conviction we are l., 427:22
country as no other man, 501:18
cursed floundered, 549:12
did till we l., 228:2
each other and were ignorant, 598:23
God so l. world, 39:46
happiness to love and be l., 436:25
him because he was he, 145:17
him for himself alone, 352:22
him like a brother, 363:4
him so followed him, 464:23
him that l. rose, 581:1
him too much not to hate him, 281:6
how l. how honored once, 300:9
I have l. beauty, 418:15
I have l. thee Ocean, 401:4
I l. her that she did pity, 205:28
I l. Ophelia, 199:16
I not honor more, 267:15
I saw and l., 340:12
if ever man l. by wife, 262:15
if I had a friend that l. her, 205:28
Jonathan l. him as his own soul, 11:43
King Cophetua l. beggarmaid, 174:25
know we l. in vain, 398:15
knowing I l. my books, 223:26
life London this moment, 650:16
love and be l. by me, 453:7
love now who never l., 295:20
love of being l., 540:6
mansionry, 213:4
memory of l. and lost, 450:9
moments of glad grace, 595:2
money with affliction, 603:17
Muses l. me, 83:1
needs only to be seen, 275:13
never l. tree or flower, 392:13
never time place l. one, 468:14
never to have l., 457:11
no man ever l., 222:2
no sooner looked but l., 192:10
not l. world nor world me, 400:7
not that I l. Caesar less, 188:25
not wisely but too well, 208:16
one blotted from page, 399:17
out upon it I have l., 262:9
pale hands I l., 590:16
passing well, 195:33
Pharaoh's lean kine l., 177:31
pilgrim soul in you, 595:2
produces motion through being l., 77:22
remember not only how l., 587:12
Rome more, 188:25
safer to be feared than l., 136:10
scenes his fathers l., 711:2

Loved (*continued*)

see souls we l., 458:25
she l. me for dangers, 205:28
she l. much, 38:13
sighed to many l. one, 399:9
so much cost me so much, 247:12
Solomon l. many strange women, 12:28
some we l. loveliest, 445:15
the man and honor memory, 233:5
those who always l. love more, 295:20
thou hast not l., 190:15
to be l. be lovable, 101:15
to have l. to have thought, 498:1
too late I l. you, 114:25
too much hope of thee l. boy, 232:10
twice or thrice had I l. thee, 229:3
use him as though you l. him, 245:28
we never l. sae kindly, 362:11
what did L. One pass on from, 712:8
when all was young, 484:16
wish I l. human race, 584:3
with more than love, 453:8
woman once l. hateful, 614:9
you once long ago, 56:7
you so I drew tides of men, 673:8
Love-darting eyes, 253:10
Love-gift of fairy tale, 518:13
Love-in-idleness, 173:6
Loveliest and best, 445:15
and best said Good Night, 609:8
despairing songs l., 461:15
of lovely things, 411:7
of trees, 578:18
village of the plain, 329:7
woman born, 597:5
Loveliness exists, 757:15
its l. increases, 414:9
lay down in her l., 382:12
let thy l. fade, 391:13
needs not ornament, 308:7
portion of the l., 409:7
this Adonis in l., 396:23
within, 228:9
your L. and my death, 418:17
Lovely, a single l. action, 486:10
all l. things have ending, 675:2
amiable l. death, 170:3
and pleasant in their lives, 11:47
apparition sent, 375:16
April of her prime, 220:9
as l. so be various, 692:1
as woman so be l., 692:1
billboard l. as a tree, 709:10
come l. soothing death, 490:17
corpse, 469:44
devours all l. things, 684:6
diminutives, 725:3
everything that's l. is, 595:12
faded but still l. woman, 694:19
flowers are l., 383:13
gentleman-like man, 172:29
gives a l. light, 684:2
go l. rose, 250:1
go l. Rose, 644:8
he is altogether l., 25:15

Lovely (*continued*)

honest labor bears a l. face, 227:18
in her bones, 725:7
is the Rose, 375:4
ladies dead and l. knights, 221:22
look last on things l., 617:1
loveliness he made more l., 409:7
Mary Morison, 363:18
monster, 716:15
more l. and more temperate, 220:12
more l. than Pandora, 258:24
most l. dead, 452:1
Nature swears l. dears, 361:25
nothing but truth is l., 280:18
poem l. as a tree, 661:16
Richard sweet l. rose, 177:6
see cloud appear, 787:6
shut her up horrorshow and l., 740:15
so l. fair, 208:1
some once l. Head, 445:13
two l. berries on one stem, 173:19
virtue how l., 259:1
whatsoever things are l., 44:35
when her l. laughter shows, 226:19
wise and the l., 684:12
with me is to be l. still, 335:18
woman stoops to folly, 328:29, 669:2
woods l. dark and deep, 623:18
your eyes, 705:17
Lover all as frantic, 174:1
and sensualist, 557:7
angel appear to l., 295:18
beauty familiar to l., 292:8
cannot having been l., 594:11
dividing l. and l., 533:9
easier to be l. than husband, 422:7
every l. a warrior, 101:9
faithless l., 402:20
fond l., 262:2
found my l. on his bed, 4:9
give repentance to her l., 328:30
I am l., 630:22
in husband lost, 318:6
it was a l. and his lass, 192:12
Jesus l. of my soul, 312:14
love a l., 431:33
lunatic the l. the poet, 174:1
magnetic peripatetic l., 529:20
music sent up by l. and bard, 467:3
my truant l. has come, 491:7
no l. and no adventurer, 572:24
of all plagues l. bears, 287:4
of concord, 49:2
of men the sea, 534:1
scratch l. find foe, 687:8
sighed as l. obeyed as son, 340:13
sighing like furnace, 191:3
threw wild hands toward sky, 611:8
true l. therefore had good end, 133:12
wild Jack for a l., 598:19
without indiscretion no lover, 539:11
woman loves her l., 402:21
woman wailing for demon-l., 382:20
Wotton a most dear l., 245:17
you l. of trees, 465:11

Loverly, wouldn't it be l., 745:5
Lover's, act l. or Roman's part, 300:8
death as l. pinch, 218:18
quarrel with world, 624:15
run into it as to l. bed, 218:5
shall win l. hire, 357:23
slide into l. head, 373:18
some old l. ghost, 229:17
Lovers always talking about themselves, 265:32
among all her l. none to comfort, 29:1
bodies of l. drowned, 641:9
cannot see follies, 180:20
falling out of l. renewing of love, 85:*n*11
fled away into storm, 415:8
Frankie and Johnny l., 781:14
friends l. husbands, 347:3
journeys end in l. meeting, 202:1
lying two and two, 578:21
make two l. happy, 300:27
never tired of each other, 265:32
not of two l. but two loves, 230:10
of beauty without extravagance, 72:3
of virtue, 245:31
of wisdom without unmanliness, 72:3
old l. soundest, 237:11
other l. estranged or dead, 598:23
perjuries of l., 101:5
Romans countrymen and l., 188:24
star-crossed l., 174:14
such as I all true l., 202:9
swear more performance, 200:20
sweet l. love the spring, 192:12
thy l. were all untrue, 276:22
to bed, 174:12
true l. run into strange capers, 190:16
woes of hopeless l., 275:10
women born my sisters and l., 488:18
women love l., 266:1
world will welcome l., 689:16
Lovers', at l. perjuries Jove laughs, 175:4
dull sublunary l. love, 229:11
pure l. souls descend, 229:15
quarrels renewal of love, 85:14
seasons run, 228:11
silver-sweet sound l. tongues, 175:13
sonnets turned psalms, 156:15
Love's architecture is his own, 264:19
evening star l. harbinger, 260:20
fires glow longest, 551:21
keen arrows, 191:22
my l. richer than tongue, 208:18
mysteries in souls grow, 229:16
not Time's fool, 222:2
passives, 264:15
pleasure drives love, 597:19
purple with l. wound, 173:6
stricken why, 514:7
such ever l. way, 467:12
young dream, 391:14
Loves, all she l. is love, 402:21
an inner air, 706:11

Loves (*continued*)

as lines so l. oblique, 268:22
but their oldest clothes, 228:9
caldron of dissolute l., 114:20
change everything except l., 306:26
color l. and skin, 228:9
cowboy that l. you so true, 786:10
cruel mother of sweet l., 96:27
demirep that l., 466:10
faint in light she l., 458:21
fat woman nobody l., 661:12
fierce wars and faithful l., 153:4
he that l. a rosy cheek, 246:9
he that l. sorrow, 228:1
heart of woman he l., 612:14
him better for faults, 329:3
his fellow men, 397:3
I have reigned with your l., 145:4
if our l. remain, 465:11
kills thing he l., 567:17
man l. what he is good at, 282:10
me best that calls me Tom, 233:21
me let him follow me, 127:8
mourn ye Graces and L., 90:16
muse l. the race of bards, 53:17
no man l. life like old, 67:17
not his wronger, 206:31
of two l. the nests, 230:10
seat of pleasures and l., 275:30
silence somewhat platonically,
    412:*n*1
suspects yet soundly l., 206:31
to hear himself talk, 175:22
to live i' the sun, 190:20
to sit and hear me sing, 356:1
two cities formed by two l., 115:3
two l. I have, 222:10
what he l. never like too much,
    232:11
who l. a garden, 335:2, 422:3
who l. to lie with me, 190:18
whoever really l. you, 794:6
world as his body, 57:3
Lovesick, twenty l. maidens, 529:16
winds were l., 217:14
Lovesickness, poem begins as l., 625:6
Lovesome, Garden l. thing, 511:8
wee thing, 363:12
Lovest, canst not guide whom thou l.,
    117:7
what thou l. well, 659:17
Loveth cheerful giver, 44:7
dear God who l. us, 382:8
he that l. her l. life, 31:7
he that l. not knoweth not God,
    46:36
him whom my soul l., 25:9
prayeth best who l. best, 382:8
well both man bird beast, 382:7
whom the Lord l. he chasteneth,
    45:40
Loving, after l. you so much, 743:19
can't help l. that man of mine,
    692:6
children begin l. parents, 566:17
die adoring God l. friends, 307:5
distance between human beings,
    630:11
for l. and for saying so, 228:17
give a l. heart to thee, 240:18

Loving (*continued*)

in love with l., 114:21
mercy, 341:9
night made for l., 402:1
pardon for too much l. you, 207:1
pleasure of love is in l., 265:27
rapid merciless, 743:4
shutting away of l. hearts, 684:12
so l. to my mother, 193:7
take heed of l. me, 229:21
that old armchair, 480:9
Loving-jealous of his liberty, 175:14
Loving-kindness, goodness and l., 49:5
Lovingkindness, how excellent is thy
    l., 16:33
Low, abatement and l. price, 201:17
ambition and pride of kings, 301:1
ambition and thirst of praise, 334:5
Brer Fox he lay l., 556:6
cast one's eyes so l., 210:27
death makes equal high and l.,
    140:14
descending sun, 779:1
dost thou lie so l., 188:19
exalted them of l. degree, 37:42
foreheads villainous l., 224:22
gods' custom to bring l. greatness,
    70:6
high and l. rich and poor, 369:12
I'll tak' the l. road, 779:21
last great Englishman l., 458:6
lean and l. ability, 203:2
low breathe and blow, 456:10
man adding one to one, 465:24
one sang high another l., 779:6
speak l., 186:20
sweet and l., 456:10
swing l. sweet chariot, 794:14
swinging l. with sullen roar, 252:4
talk l. talk slow, 722:5
ten l. words, 298:18
too l. for envy, 266:15
too l. they build, 296:19
valley so l., 779:8
voice was gentle and l., 211:18
what is l. raise and support, 255:20
when my light l., 457:13
Lowells talk to Cabots, 582:1
Lower, a little l. than angels, 15:34
brutalizing l. class, 500:23
down can fall no l., 263:15
middle classes, 530:5
night beginning to l., 442:8
orders don't set good example,
    567:4
part of mankind, 286:3
prevent l. from getting more, 78:16
see front o' battle l., 363:19
take you a button-hole l., 169:9
while there is a l. class, 568:2
Lowered, sash l. when night, 624:1
Lowest and most dejected thing,
    210:18
type hear Tao, 57:12
Lowing herd wind slowly, 322:1
Lowland, between l. and highland,
    535:5
sails upon L. sea, 793:19
Lowlands, ye Highlands and L.,
    785:18

Lowliness, man of l. and affability,
    138:1
young ambition's ladder, 187:32
Lowly air of Seven Dials, 530:9
and riding upon an ass, 30:3
better to be l. born, 225:8
man bears stamp of l. origin,
    444:15
meek and l. in heart, 34:38
nothing l. in universe, 756:7
organized creatures, 444:16
Lowry, Malcolm L. of Bowery, 727:1
Low-vaulted past, 447:11
Loyal and neutral in a moment,
    214:16
nature noble mind, 459:19
to a trust, 570:5
Loyalties, impossible l., 499:10
Loyalty, map of l. in thy face, 163:25
women have l. to Truth to yourself,
    556:20
Lubricates, dinner l. business, 348:6
Lucan, line in which L. meant to rise,
    106:4
Lucasta, then my L. might I crave,
    267:19
Lucent, softly l. as moon, 486:3
Lucid, full of l. intervals, 150:35
interval, 274:26
intervals and happy pauses, 158:17
moments, 420:11
Lucidity of thought, 500:25
sad l. of soul, 497:10
Lucifer, he falls like L., 225:16
Prince L. uprose, 509:7
proud seat of L., 260:14
son of the morning, 26:14
spirits that fell with L., 162:14
Luck, as good l. would have it, 183:3
blessed l. of chase, 787:14
counted and cursed his l., 579:21
fattenin' hogs ain't in l., 556:16
for good l. cast old shoe, 141:12
good l. in odd numbers, 183:7
had l. met monster, 716:15
ill l. seldom alone, 149:25
in odd numbers, 183:7, 420:16
I've got the L. with me, 531:24
light in ragged l., 557:7
little bit of l., 745:6
not holding best cards, 536:14
run to meet ill l., 434:4
shallow men believe in l., 432:38
spit on us for l., 82:14
struck streak of bad l., 531:25
watching l. his light-o'-love, 627:2
Luckiest knows when to go home,
    536:14
people in the world, 751:4
Lucky, not call man happy but l.,
    55:20
sixpence in shoe, 782:10
them that die'll be l. ones, 561:6
to be alive at great time, 700:9
to be born, 489:1
to die and I know it, 489:1
to have lived in Paris, 702:13
Lucre, filthy l., 45:13
Lucrece swears he did her wrong,
    167:6

Machiavel, every Country hath its M., 136:*n*5
  much beholden to M., 158:10
  Nick M. had ne'er trick, 263:30
Machina, deus ex m., 81:10
Machinations hollowness treachery, 209:2
Machine, bathing m., 530:15
  beauty of great m., 663:2
  created to serve us, 723:11
  for living in, 663:21
  for turning wine into urine, 656:6
  god from the m., 81:10
  justice is a m., 603:19
  man is a m., 318:3
  no unnecessary parts, 608:9
  pulse of the m., 375:17
  slavery of the m., 567:12
  time m., 601:6
  you're not man you're m., 570:20
Machine-à-habiter, 663:*n*3
Machinery of night, 757:4
Machines, can m. think, 732:5
  human beings into m., 481:9
  not whether m. think but men, 715:10
  slaves not masters, 578:9
Macht, der Wille zur M., 553:*n*4
Mächte, ihr himmlischen M., 349:*n*3
Machu Picchu Cambridge Mass. Angkor, 735:8
Mackerel, stinks like rotten m., 386:1
Mackerel-crowded seas, 597:7
Macrocosm, microcosm and m. atoned, 504:17
Macte nova virtute puer, 94:*n*10
Mad, all poets are m., 234:13
  am m. and am not m., 60:2
  and lamentable experiment, 588:3
  as Bedlam, 470:26
  as March hare, 135:*n*3
  bad and dangerous, 397:19
  cold m. father, 647:22
  dogs and Englishmen, 700:15
  don't call a man m., 321:7
  don't get m. get even, 673:4
  face that drove me m., 548:4
  father and mither gae m., 362:18
  go m. or unstable, 70:1
  half m. with beauty, 523:3
  he first makes m., 69:18
  heroically m., 274:17
  I am not m., 41:34
  idolatry, 200:15
  if they behold a cat, 181:12
  I'm m. as hell, 752:1
  in pursuit, 222:7
  laid to make taker m., 222:7
  makes men m., 208:11
  man must be a little m., 147:2
  March days, 634:1
  March hare, 135:17
  men God made m., 618:17
  more deadly than m. dog's tooth, 166:32
  much learning make m., 41:33
  naked summer night, 489:8
  nobly wild not m., 241:14
  north-northwest, 195:31
  O fool I shall go m., 209:23

Mad (*continued*)
  old m. blind despised king, 407:24
  pleasure in being m., 274:19
  practice drives m., 776:9
  prose run m., 302:10
  provided man not m., 319:18
  pursuit, 416:1
  sad and bad and m., 467:17
  sad m. brother's name, 535:4
  sense that world was m., 630:15
  some born m. some remain so, 718:16
  that he is m. 'tis true, 195:12
  that trusts in wolf, 210:13
  to live mad to be saved, 750:9
  undevout astronomer is m., 296:21
  we are m. nationally, 103:2
  went m. and bit the man, 328:27
  whom God wishes to destroy he makes m., 119:25
  world, 470:26
  world mad kings, 169:25
Madam is there nothing else, 512:19
Madame Bovary had beauty, 496:7
  hell M. is to love no longer, 666:17
  I am M. Bovary, 496:15
  poetry the supreme fiction m., 638:21
Madcap, once in my days be a m., 176:36
Maddens, all that m. torments, 486:25
  Trees m. me, 666:23
Madder music stronger wine, 602:9
Maddest merriest day, 454:4
Madding, far from m. crowd's strife, 322:17
Made a rural pen, 356:5
  and loveth all, 382:8
  annihilating all that's m., 268:18
  as he is so was he m., 550:2
  begotten not m., 49:1
  by whom all things m., 49:1
  Christians not born but m., 114:9
  confusion m. masterpiece, 214:13
  day which the Lord hath m., 19:21
  did he who m. Lamb, 358:7
  fearfully and wonderfully m., 20:10
  friends born not m., 535:15
  God m. and eaten, 465:7
  God m. him let him pass for man, 179:31
  him a little lower than angels, 15:34
  his pendent bed, 213:4
  in wisdom hast thou m. all, 19:6
  incarnate and was m. man, 49:1
  it is he that hath m. us, 18:22
  little Lamb who m. thee, 356:6
  Lord God m. them all, 479:17
  marriages m. in heaven, 155:22
  men and not made them well, 197:1
  mouths in a glass, 209:27
  my song a coat, 596:4
  myself a motley, 221:26
  of sterner stuff, 189:1
  poet's m. as well as born, 232:24
  sea is his and he m. it, 18:19
  stuff as dreams are m. on, 224:21
  swears she is m. of truth, 222:9
  the best of this, 364:2
  this parting well m., 189:23

Made (*continued*)
  us with large discourse, 198:12
  what man has m. of man, 372:18
  when or you or I are m., 241:19
  without fear, 15:25
  world I never m., 579:20
  world m. safe for democracy, 572:11
  world of m. not world of born, 689:6
Madeleine soaked in lime flowers, 612:13
  upon bar-room floor, 548:4
Madeline, I hate you I hate you cried M., 645:18
Madeline's fair breast, 415:4
Mademoiselle from Armenteers, 680:8
  from St. Nazaire, 680:9
Madest, creature that thou m., 580:7
Madly, stars shot m. from spheres, 173:5
  twirled fingers m., 472:11
Madman, either liar or m., 319:12
  if he like m. lived, 151:21
  that is the m., 174:1
  truth of a m., 760:7
Madmen in authority distilling frenzy, 652:17
  which none but m. know, 274:19
Madness, a little M. in Spring, 514:6
  anger a short m., 97:10
  avarice a piece of m., 278:*n*2
  despondency and m., 374:9, 742:16
  destroyed by m., 757:4
  from breakfast to m., 759:12
  go you may call it m., 367:5
  great wits to m. allied, 274:3
  harmonious m. flow, 408:8
  in brain, 382:15
  let us have m. openly, 730:7
  life is a m., 247:7
  midsummer m., 202:31
  moon-struck m., 260:17
  much M. divinest Sense, 512:11
  much of M., 452:7
  need not be all breakdown, 758:7
  no genius without touch of m., 103:7
  of many for gain of few, 303:23
  risen from hell, 533:10
  Sense starkest M., 512:11
  species of m., 278:12
  sudden m. came upon Orpheus, 93:7
  that fine m., 161:14
  that way m. lies, 210:2
  the rest is m. of art, 548:18
  though this be m., 195:21
  'tis m. to defer, 296:10
  to let private enterprise set habits, 686:7
  to live like wretch, 234:24
  what m. has caught you, 92:5
Madonnas, Rafael of dear M., 466:28
Madrigal, woeful stuff this m., 299:2
Madrigals, melodious birds sing m., 162:3
Madruga, al que m. Dios ayuda, 793:24
Madrugar, no por mucho m., 794:5

Major (*continued*)
   silicon been gas I a m. general,
      524:6
Majorities, decision by m. expedient,
   446:12
   not entirely wrong, 493:6
Majority deprive minority of right,
   449:3
   divine M., 512:2
   fools big enough m., 526:25
   he has joined great m., 105:1
   man with God always in m., 143:15
   morality what m. like, 584:20
   never replace man, 676:4
   not leave right to m., 477:10
   of one, 477:12
   one man with courage a m., 369:13
   one on God's side m., 462:17
   power in m. of popular assembly,
      338:16
   questions not decided by m., 474:11
   silent m., 733:14
   'tis M. prevail, 512:11
   when were good and brave in m.,
      479:1
Make a joyful noise, 17:37, 18:22
   angels weep, 204:4
   be and m. new nations, 226:9
   can't find circumstances m. them,
      570:12
   conscience m. cowards, 196:10
   content with his fortunes, 210:1
   fault worse by excuse, 170:10
   fears m. us traitors, 215:24
   felicity we m. or find, 314:15
   ghost of him that lets me, 194:15
   go ahead m. my day, 774:8
   haste better foot before, 170:13
   he himself his quietus m., 196:10
   her laugh at that, 199:8
   I could not well m. out, 386:6
   I shall m. reckless choice, 623:10
   it do or do without, 782:8
   it over your way, 625:16
   life what we m. it, 546:8
   me a child again, 516:13
   me a fixed figure, 207:26
   me a willow cabin, 201:27
   me immortal with a kiss, 162:19
   me to know mine end, 17:7
   men m. the city, 72:10
   mighty ocean, 502:8
   money by any means, 97:6
   most of what may spend, 445:16
   my bed in hell, 20:8
   my bed soon, 785:20
   my house your inn, 664:11
   my seated heart knock, 212:23
   my small elves coats, 173:10
   not m. can not mar, 497:14
   not m. graven image, 9:9
   not m. scarecrow of law, 203:28
   of your prayers one sacrifice, 225:6
   only God can m. tree, 662:1
   right to m. alter constitutions, 337:4
   so much of fragmentary blue,
      623:13
   soul is form and doth body m.,
      154:14

Make (*continued*)
   straight a highway for our God,
      27:15
   sudden sally, 458:15
   the Lord m. his face shine upon
      thee, 9:28
   the most of it, 339:5
   thee an ark, 7:16
   thee mightier yet, 585:5
   thick my blood, 212:29
   unless philosophy m. a Juliet, 176:4
   up my sum, 199:16
   us do what we can, 432:40
   us heirs of all eternity, 168:12
   war to live in peace, 78:10
   waves m. towards pebbled shore,
      220:26
   world safe for diversity, 742:1
   worse appear the better, 73:2
   yourselves another face, 196:16
Make-believe, children's house of m.,
   624:17
   Eve seen through m., 611:20
Makeless, maiden that is m., 775:15
Maker, as though m. and molder of
      thyself, 136:1
   Lord our m., 18:19
   more pure than his m., 13:40
   of Heaven and earth, 48:25
   reproacheth his M., 21:33
   rests in lightland, 5:4
   tool m., 634:4
Makers, abhor m. and their laws ap-
      prove, 275:22
Makes, another which m., 76:1
   heaven drowsy with harmony,
      169:3
   heretic that m. the fire, 222:23
   me or fordoes me quite, 208:8
   me poor indeed, 206:30
   men mad, 208:11
   night hideous, 194:*n*3
   one little room an everywhere,
      228:3
   or mars us, 208:5
   swanlike end, 181:2
   sweet music with stones, 168:3
   thinking m. it so, 195:25
   tongue of him that m. it, 169:11
   whole world kin, 201:3
Makest, thou m. darkness, 19:6
   what m. thou, 27:26
Maketh clouds his chariot, 19:3
   he m. me to lie down, 16:17
   the deep to boil, 15:24
Making green one red, 214:9
   many books, 24:30, 644:7
   news better than taking it, 619:11
   night hideous, 194:11
   shaping and controlling life, 492:1
Mal, honi soit qui m. y pense, 127:13
Malachite, good speech more hidden
      than m., 3:4
Maladies, soul with all its m., 538:5
Maladministration, secured against m.,
   327:2
Malady, greatest m. is poverty, 281:24
   he smiles it is a m., 90:25
   medicine worse than m., 99:*n*5
   of not marking, 183:16

Malaise, two problems energy and m.,
   754:4
Malapropism, concocting m. passing it
      off, 646:*n*1
Malcontents, liege of m., 168:28
   Mars of m., 182:22
Male and female created he, 6:8
   and female fuse into one solid,
      71:16
   cannot tolerate living with equal,
      440:3
   difference of education between m.
      and female, 347:5
   especially m. of species, 657:16
   healthy wealthy and dead, 690:12
   if God is m., 758:21
   kiss of blankets, 663:2
   more deadly than m., 593:22
Malefactors of great wealth, 576:5
Malfi, I am Duchess of M. still,
   237:16
Malherbe, at last comes M., 280:5
   what M. writes will endure, 156:10
Malheur, de son âge tout le m.,
   306:*n*14
Malheureux, où nous étions si m.,
   786:17
Malice domestic, 214:26
   from envy hatred and m., 49:8
   much m. little wit, 275:19
   never was his aim, 289:18
   no m. or ill will, 369:2
   no rampart against m., 268:30
   no suspicion of m. in his writing,
      87:15
   nor set down aught in m., 208:16
   ridicule without m., 450:1
   toward none, 450:11
   truth with m. in it, 486:25
Malicious ferocity, 637:*n*1
   he is not, 636:6
   wisdom entereth not in m. mind,
      139:13
Malignant and turbaned Turk, 208:17
   so m. so devastating, 683:3
   trouble was not m., 712:9
Maligners of his honor, 520:11
Malignity, motiveless m., 383:20
Malitia, ius summum saepe summa est
      m., 86:*n*1
Mallecho, miching m., 197:9
Malorum, radix m. est cupiditas,
   45:*n*3
Malt, ate the m., 792:24
   does more than Milton can, 579:15
Maltreat, shouldn't m. our idols,
   496:8
Mama, we've lost good old m., 698:16
Mamas, last of red-hot m., 656:*n*2
Mammon, cannot serve God and m.,
   33:17
   is like fire, 413:*n*2
   the least erected spirit, 256:20
   wins his way, 399:10
Man, a certain m. went down, 38:22
   a little mad if not stupid, 147:2
   a little worse than a m., 179:32
   a m. like me, 358:4
   a m. zealous for nothing, 317:12
   a social animal, 278:10

Man (*continued*)

actions show m. we find, 300:11
Adam the goodliest m., 258:14
after his own heart, 11:33
aged m. paltry thing, 597:8
ah for m. to arise, 458:18
ah when to heart of m., 622:18
ain't nothin' but a man, 780:20
all that a m. hath will he give, 13:32
all that makes m., 459:20
all that may become a m., 213:10
alone abandoned on earth, 717:15
alone can enslave man, 727:14
always tell Harvard m., 781:22
am I not a m. and brother, 333:11
ambitious m. have no satisfaction, 231:14
an ape or angel, 435:4
and bird and beast, 382:7
and brother, 333:11
and his fate, 635:13
and what he loves have but day, 631:15
and woman in garden, 567:2
and woman two locked caskets, 656:11
animal which devours own, 343:13
apparel oft proclaims m., 193:30
arms and the m. I sing, 93:10, 276:5
Art mediatress between nature and m., 384:19
as a m. wipeth a dish, 13:14
as happy a m. as any, 279:9
as M. alone Jesus not saved us, 711:6
as m. looks at woman, 640:24
as nature made him, 319:21
as old as his arteries, 271:18
Ascent of M., 722:15
assurance of a m., 197:30
at thirty m. suspects himself fool, 296:12
at wheel taught to feel, 545:3
average m., 649:1
baker's m., 788:9
battered wrecked old m., 491:5
battlefield heart of m., 495:5
be a friend to m., 574:14
be m. be nonconformist, 431:21
bear with all the faults of m., 226:17
bears stamp of lowly origin, 444:15
beautiful thing raises m., 137:9
became a living soul, 6:11
become ignorant m. again, 639:20
been mother's undisputed darling, 569:9
before you call him a m., 771:4
before you trust a m., 776:3
behold m. of flint, 787:12
behold the m., 40:38
being his own physician, 77:17
being reasonable must get drunk, 402:19
belief woman made for m., 475:8
believe in equality of m., 341:9
Benedick the married m., 186:15
best m. like water, 57:1

Man (*continued*)

best m. worst-natured muse, 283:22
better m. than I Gunga Din, 591:20
better spared better m., 179:8
beware m. of one book, 118:19
beyond m. is universe, 690:21
bites dog, 554:7
blessings on thee little m., 443:5
blest m. that spares these stones, 226:11
blood of a British m., 210:12
blow the m. down, 793:9
bold bad m., 153:6, 225:7
bold m. first eat oyster, 290:8
born dies and does not come again, 784:17
born to live not prepare for life, 680:4
boyhood changing into m., 598:4
brave m. inattentive to duty, 369:9
brave m. with a sword, 567:17
breathes there the m., 378:1
bronzed lank m., 637:11
Brutus is an honorable m., 188:29
but be a m., 497:19
butterfly dreaming I am a m., 80:9
by m. came death, 43:20
by m. came resurrection, 43:20
by m. shall his blood be shed, 7:23
by nature political animal, 78:12
Caius is a m., 510:13
call no m. foe, 682:13
came to making of m., 533:10
can a m. take fire in his bosom, 20:30
can die but once, 184:5
can raise thirst, 591:24
cannot emerge from himself, 613:1
can't hold m. down without staying, 572:1
capable of becoming true m., 677:7
cause of work, 613:15
caverns measureless to m., 382:19
cease ye from m., 25:32
cells and gibbets for m., 480:10
century of common m., 674:22
certain way to hold a m., 746:9
certainly crazy, 146:7
change environment not m., 691:16
child conceived, 13:34
child father of m., 374:7
childhood shows the m., 260:32
Christian faithful m., 165:29
city is teacher of the m., 60:9
civilized m. cannot live without cooks, 516:4
civilized m. has habits of house, 476:21
clothed with rags, 272:11
comes with his torment, 365:19
common m. has triumphed, 552:23
commonest M. shows grace in quarrel, 418:13
composed of all men, 717:20
concern for m. himself, 635:13
concrete m. has one interest, 545:8
conference maketh a ready m., 160:9
confidence in tall m. merited, 723:10

Man (*continued*)

connection of individual m., 780:21
control the wind, 497:22
count on no one but himself, 717:15
country turns out, 433:6
coupling of m. and woman, 670:21
created M. of blood clot, 117:24
crime of being young m., 312:18
crooked m., 791:11
cruelty to load falling m., 225:*n*2
daring young m. on trapeze, 536:20
dark as world of m., 665:19
dark cloud m., 552:7
delights not me, 195:29
desire for desire of m., 385:2
desire of knowledge caused m. to fall, 159:16
diapason closing in M., 275:7
did not make can not mar, 497:14
dieth and wasteth away, 14:21
dignity of m. capacity to despise self, 588:9
dispute it like a m., 215:30
does not live by GNP alone, 739:3
does what he must, 740:19
doth not live by bread only, 10:14
dream past wit of m., 173:26
drest in brief authority, 204:4
drink takes m., 544:3
drove out the m., 7:1
dull ear of drowsy m., 170:5
each m. act of God, 476:8
ear of m. hath not seen, 173:27
either m. obsolete or war is, 691:17
end of that m. is peace, 17:3
endeavoring to turn m. into beast, 707:14
errs as long as he strives, 350:10
Esau was a m. of the field, 7:36
escape from rope and gun, 297:19
establish reign of liberty, 722:11
even such a m. so faint, 183:10
every cry of every m., 358:8
every m. a piece of the continent, 231:8
every m. architect of his fortune, 92:1
every m. at his best state, 17:8
every m. for himself, 142:30
every m. has his fault, 212:2
every m. hath a good and bad angel, 234:14
every m. his greatest enemy, 248:18
every m. is wanted, 432:20
every m. own architect, 468:9
every m. satisfied there is truth, 538:15
every m. under his vine, 12:20
every m. was God or Devil, 274:12
every m. will do duty, 360:17
expatiate o'er scene of m., 301:1
eye of m. hath not heard, 173:27
fallen god, 405:9
false m., 285:9
false m. does easy, 214:17
false to any m., 194:1
Family of M., 634:14
fashion wears out more than m., 186:39
favor with God and m., 38:8

Man (*continued*)

first m. among these than second in Rome, 88:20
first-class fightin' m., 591:19
fit night for m. or beast, 641:13
foolish fond old m., 211:10
foolish passionate m., 599:4
foot-in-the-grave young m., 530:2
for all seasons, 138:1
for m. as for flower beast bird, 657:21
for the field, 456:17
for the sword, 456:17
forgotten as a dead m. out of mind, 16:26
Forgotten M., 541:5
forgotten m., 648:14
formed for society, 325:19
formed m. of dust, 6:11
free as Nature made m., 273:14
free to do evil as good, 532:11
frees himself from bonds, 436:18
fresh from Natur's mold, 469:46
Friday, 286:5
frontiers wherever m. fronts fact, 477:20
fury of patient m., 274:16
gently scan brother m., 362:5
get a new m., 224:11
girl up thy loins like a m., 15:6
give every m. thy ear, 193:30
giveth up the ghost, 14:21
glory to M. in highest, 535:1
go west young m., 475:4
goal of landing m. on moon, 741:9
God above or m. below, 301:3
God and m. decree, 579:19
God became m. devil woman, 427:16
god in ruins, 431:3
God is not a m., 10:6
God's ways to m., 579:15
goes riding by, 561:9
goeth forth unto his work, 19:6
goeth to his long home, 24:28
good for a m. that he bear the yoke, 29:4
good m. and just, 39:24
good m. does not argue, 58:7
good name in m. and woman, 206:30
great m. great ganglion, 542:13
great nose great m., 605:24
greater m. greater courtesy, 459:17
greatest fool is m., 280:14
greatest m. ever seen, 330:*n*5
greatness of work inside m., 748:3
grew within this learned m., 163:1
ground colored m. occupies, 480:15
grows beyond his work, 710:9
grows used to everything, 495:2
half part of blessed m., 169:23
hand of a mighty m., 20:1
hand will be against every m., 7:30
happy citizen free, 428:3
happy m. be his dole, 141:*n*2
happy m. happy dole, 141:2
happy m. works ancestral acres, 95:13
happy old m., 92:4

Man (*continued*)

happy the m. and he alone, 274:29
hardly a m. now alive, 442:12
harrowing clods, 540:22
has Forever, 465:22
has two primal passions, 558:3
has will woman way, 447:8
hath penance done, 381:25
having put hand to plow, 38:16
he created m., 784:17
he was a m., 611:5
he was a m. take him for all in all, 193:16
he was her m., 781:14
heard wise m. say, 578:22
heart of m. place devil dwells in, 248:15
hearty old m., 386:8
her wit was more than m., 275:6
himself important creation, 704:9
himself lend a hand, 71:17
his answer was M., 706:7
his own executioner, 248:18
honest exceeding poor m., 180:15
honest m. close-buttoned, 335:15
honest m. noblest work of God, 301:18, 361:10
honest m. sent to lie abroad, 227:12
horse noblest conquest of m., 311:6
how dieth the wise m., 23:31
how many roads m. walk down, 771:4
how marvelous is M., 605:12
how poor a thing is m., 161:5
how proud word M. rings, 605:12
how would m. exist if God did not need him, 632:8
howl for flesh of m., 766:2
humiliation by white m., 752:9
hungry m. not free, 706:12
hungry sinner, 403:18
I am cease to be, 458:18
I am first a m., 304:12
I am the m., 489:18
I appeal to any white m., 326:14
I got my m., 695:4
I have been a m., 350:4
I know thee not old m., 184:16
I loved the m. and honor memory, 233:5
I must feel it as a m., 215:30
I never writ nor no m. loved, 222:2
I the m. in the moon, 174:7
identifies with his fate, 700:11
if a m. die shall he live, 14:22
if a m. has talent, 706:19
if not wedding day absolutely fixed on, 312:5
if such a m. there be, 302:12
I'll make me a m., 612:8
I'm m. of wealth and taste, 773:1
improvable reason of M., 420:18
in armor slave, 468:7
in arms wish to be, 376:8
in Brooks Brothers shirt, 732:1
in every fat m. a thin one, 711:1
in every m. two postulations, 494:13
in gray flannel suit, 748:14
in his hasty days, 550:1

Man (*continued*)

in love endures more, 553:1
in love with suffering, 495:1
in mind of m. a motion, 373:5
in our town, 792:2
in subjection to white Saxon m., 475:7
in unsearchable darkness, 550:2
in whose hand cup is found, 8:12
in wilderness, 788:15
in wit a m., 300:28
incarnate and was made m., 49:1
ingrateful m., 209:24
inner m., 44:23
insignificant and aware of it, 616:1
intellect of m. choose, 598:10
interpreter of nature, 411:13
intimates eternity to m., 292:14
invented m. because disappointed in monkey, 528:4
invisible m., 735:18
is a machine, 318:3
is a prisoner, 74:19
is a reasoning animal, 102:24
is a thinking reed, 271:3
is as Heaven made him, 150:20
is born for uprightness, 61:8
is born free, 319:5
is born unto trouble, 14:2
is God blunder of m., 552:29
is man and master, 459:9
is m. blunder of God, 552:29
is m. no more than this, 210:6
is not so good a Christian, 562:2
is not so great a coward, 562:2
is one soul many tongues, 112:6
is origin of his action, 78:5
is raised above animal, 722:8
is singular creature, 722:14
is the hunter, 456:16
je-ne-sais-quoi young m., 530:1
Jewish m. with parents alive, 765:13
joked about every prominent m., 638:7
killed hero in m., 717:11
kills thing he loves, 567:17
know how to defy opinion, 368:11
know myself a m., 227:15
know the m. that must hear me, 382:5
know what God and m. is, 460:5
knoweth not his time, 24:20
known by company he keeps, 69:*n*7
lame m. leap as an hart, 27:9
large-hearted m., 438:14
last m. on right brush channel, 521:3
last strands of m., 551:11
laugh to scorn power of m., 215:19
law for m., 429:18
laws of God beyond m., 66:11
laws of God laws of m., 579:19
least considerable m., 346:3
leave his father and mother, 6:18
lengthened shadow of one m., 431:25
less no m. have, 576:2
let end try the m., 183:31
let him pass for a m., 179:31

Man (*continued*)

let m. outlive his wealth, 181:25
let no such m. be trusted, 182:10
let us make m. in our image, 6:7
life of m. solitary, 239:22
lightning out of cloud m., 552:7
like light kindled and put out, 62:18
little difference between m. and m.,
  546:12
little m. had little gun, 792:5
lived with birds and beasts, 80:13
lives by catchwords, 560:15
lives life of epoch, 629:10
living-dead m., 166:34
long as colored m. look to white
  folks, 773:19
look no way but downwards,
  272:27
looketh on the outward appearance,
  11:36
looking for honest m., 77:5
Lord is a m. of war, 9:3
Lord seeth not as m. seeth, 11:36
lose what he never had, 245:26
lot of m. but once to die, 242:12
love not m. the less, 400:29
lovely gentleman-like m., 172:29
loves what vanishes, 597:14
lovin' that m. of mine, 692:6
low m. seeks little thing, 465:24
made for joy and woe, 359:10
made her such a m., 205:28
made of ordinary things, 365:3
made the town, 334:25
made to mourn, 361:7
majority never replace m., 676:4
makes gods by the dozen, 146:7
making deserts of earth, 633:11
manners maketh m., 127:16
man's inhumanity to m., 361:8
man's word God in m., 459:4
marks earth with ruin, 400:30
master of fate, 459:9, 677:7
master of himself a happy m., 96:24
may fish with worm, 198:10
measure of all things, 70:15
mere M., 452:9
merely a passage for food, 134:15
middle-aged m. build woodshed,
  477:1
military m., 185:8
mind's the standard of m., 294:5
misfortunes of m. occasioned by m.,
  104:6
mistakes evil for happiness, 365:25
Mister Tambourine M. play a song,
  771:8
Moby Dick whale or m., 685:1
mollusk cheap edition of m., 433:15
more no m. entitled to, 576:2
more right than neighbors, 477:12
more sinned against, 209:29
muffin m., 792:1
must have faults, 105:4
my m. of men, 217:9
native metal of m., 485:24
Nature formed one such m., 401:21
nature in form of m., 725:24
necessarily a m., 304:12
needs go outside himself, 564:10

Man (*continued*)

needs to suffer, 564:5
ne'er left m. i' mire, 211:25
negations of m., 754:21
neither angel nor beast, 271:4
neither m. nor woman but author,
  476:16
never bad m. good service, 332:4
never is blest, 301:6
never met m. I didn't like, 638:7
never saw m. who looked, 567:15
new m. raised up in him, 50:11
nice m., 289:3
no angel, 422:11
no benefit in gifts of bad m., 68:10
no indispensable m., 648:17
no m. above or below law, 576:3
no m. born an angler, 245:14
no m. born unto himself, 242:5
no m. content with lot, 94:31
no m. deserved less at country's
  hands, 501:18
no m. do for your sake, 533:21
no m. hero to his valet, 249:8
no m. is an island, 231:8
no m. not deserve hanging, 147:1
no m. remember me, 539:18
no m. see me more, 225:14
no m. should marry, 435:8
no m. takes wealth with him, 59:25
no m. useless who has friend, 562:5
no m. worth having true, 288:7
no reasonable m. expected, 678:23
no sin for m. to labor in vocation,
  176:34
no such thing as honest m., 296:26
noble animal, 249:4
noble be m. helpful and good, 349:5
noblest work of m., 520:15
none more wonderful than m., 66:9
not a just m. upon earth, 24:12
not a m. but cloud, 686:19
not creature of circumstances,
  434:19
not good that m. be alone, 6:15
not happy unless free, 405:4
not lifetime of one m. only, 671:10
not locked into environment, 722:15
not materials that counts, 686:13
not passion's slave, 197:4
not sum of what he has, 717:13
not take goods with him, 3:2
not what kind of paper but m.,
  477:27
nothing feebler than a m., 54:7
nothing more wretched than a m.,
  52:13
nothing to do with just m., 37:5
nothing wears clothes but M.,
  243:14
O that m. might know end, 189:24
of action forced into thought,
  603:22
of an unbounded stomach, 226:4
of cheerful yesterdays, 377:2
of comfort no m. speak, 171:24
of dust, 6:11
of genius had to pay, 614:11
of honor regrets discreditable act,
  642:22

Man (*continued*)

of letters, 272:2
of many resources, 52:27
of many wiles, 299:25
of morals tell me why, 267:1
of my kidney, 183:4
of my peculiar weakness, 642:21
of nasty ideas, 289:3
of sorrows, 27:35
of strife and contention, 28:27
of talent sees two or three, 660:7
of unclean lips, 26:2
of understanding, 31:17
of understanding is of excellent
  spirit, 21:37
of understanding lost nothing,
  145:19
of virtue, 61:9
of words not deeds, 787:20
Ol' M. River, 692:5
old age in universal m., 158:*n*3
old m. broken, 226:1
old m. had so much blood, 216:3
old m. in dry month, 668:6
old m. to whom old men hearkened,
  98:25
old m. twice a child, 195:32
old m. who will not laugh, 588:18
Old M. with beard, 471:27
old m. with something of young,
  88:10
old m. wouldn't say prayers, 789:18
on horseback, 780:18
once a man who said God, 673:5
once to every m. and nation, 485:1
one m. among a thousand, 24:14
one m. crossing bridge, 638:14
one m. one vote, 783:20
one m. plays many parts, 191:3
one m. with courage a majority,
  369:13
one more wrong to m., 464:25
one small step for m., 762:13
one-book m., 380:14
only animal that blushes, 527:31
only feels alone, 736:13
only great m. write history, 567:14
only m. harrowing clods, 540:22
only m. is vile, 395:19
only one that knows nothing, 104:5
organization m., 744:12
organized by labor, 605:15
our m. in Havana, 713:11
out of me God and m., 534:19
out of one m. a race, 259:20
outrage a brave m. dead, 65:15
outrage when m. destroys nature,
  631:15
outside every fat m., 711:*n*1
owes not any m., 441:4
palms greater no m. made them,
  763:9
Parliament of m., 455:18
particularly pure young m., 529:18
partly is, 467:14
people arose as one m., 11:21
perceives it die away, 375:8
perhaps this is the m., 746:18
picked out of ten thousand, 195:16
pig edible to m., 544:16

Man (*continued*)

pious m. not less a m., 269:6
place and means for every m., 203:16
plain blunt m., 189:9
Plato's m., 77:3
play is tragedy M., 452:8
play the m. Master Ridley, 138:18
poetry inner calling in m., 714:9
poor despised old m., 209:26
poor m. accustomed to small things, 731:18
poor m. being down, 31:33
poor m. get out iv Purgatory, 603:5
poor m. had nothing, 12:10
poor m. is Christ's stamp, 243:4
poor m. poor mankind, 696:15
poor m. that has loved, 597:3
poorest m. in his cottage, 312:19
possesses immortality, 718:8
power of m. and moment, 499:4
powers superior to m., 564:22
prayer of righteous m., 46:18
preached as dying m., 266:9
prejudiced reasonable m., 471:1
prentice han' tried on m., 361:25
press not falling m., 225:15
primitive m. tactile m., 653:22
private m. James Joyce, 769:5
privilege to help m. endure, 697:1
projects himself into culture, 717:18
proper m. as see in summer's day, 172:29
proper study of mankind is m., 301:13
proposes God disposes, 132:14
prosperity comes to bad m., 59:22
proud yet wretched thing, 227:15
prudent m. looketh well to his going, 21:21
rather be worm than son of m., 663:20
reading maketh a full m., 160:9
ready money makes the m., 294:20
ready to believe what is told, 105:2
really a very good m., 568:11
Reasonable M. mythical figure, 678:21
rebuke a wise m., 21:2
recovered of the bite, 328:28
register of God not record of m., 249:2
rejoice O young m. in youth, 24:26
rejoiceth as a strong m., 16:10
rich in things he can let alone, 478:15
rich m. beginning to fall, 31:33
rich m. enter into kingdom, 35:37
rich m. enther Hiven, 603:5
richest pleasures cheapest, 477:5
righteous m. regardeth the life of his beast, 21:12
righteous m. to make fall, 153:8
rights of m., 332:9
rope between animal and Superman, 552:6
round fat oily m. of God, 308:15
rousing like strong m., 255:2
ruined m., 672:22
ruins of the noblest m., 188:22

Man (*continued*)

rule will show the m., 55:14
sabbath made for m., 37:19
said to universe, 611:9
savage in m. never eradicated, 477:6
savage individual m., 601:7
says what he knows, 319:19
scholar is M. Thinking, 431:5
seeks for what is remote, 79:18
seems the only growth, 328:10
seen how m. made slave slave made m., 480:12
self-made m. and worships creator, 462:9
sent from God, 39:31
serve time to every trade, 399:3
setting m. free from men, 717:9
seven women shall take hold of one m., 25:36
severe he was, 329:17
shall m. be more pure than maker, 13:40
shall man no longer crush, 353:8
shall mortal m. be more just, 13:40
she knows her m., 235:*n*3
sight make old m. young, 454:20
significance of m., 616:1
silliest woman manage m., 591:4
single sentence for modern m., 732:20
singularly deep young m., 529:17
slothful m. saith, 22:30
small m. may not be entrusted, 61:32
smiling destructive m., 285:9
smiteth a m. so that he die, 9:14
so can any m., 178:3
so frail a thing m., 287:13
so in way in house, 461:8
so is it now I am a m., 374:7
so much one m. can do, 268:12
so near is God to m., 430:4
so unto m. woman, 441:26
so various, 274:11
social friendly honest m., 361:12
social world work of m., 290:31
solid m. of Boston, 442:11
something m. will die for, 760:17
son of m. that thou visitest him, 15:34
sooner kill m. than hawk, 663:13
soul of m. imperishable, 76:3
soul of m. larger, 419:2
spares neither m. nor his works, 340:7
speech open m. to m., 280:*n*1
spirit stands by naked m., 777:2
sprang to his feet, 464:16
stage where every m. play part, 179:17
stagger like a drunken m., 19:11
state of m. like kingdom, 188:2
stole the fruit, 243:7
stopped moving if ever did move, 645:8
strives for someone to worship, 495:10
strong m. digests experiences, 552:27
strongest m. stands alone, 508:11

Man (*continued*)

style is the m., 311:7
subtle knot which makes us m., 229:15
successful animal, 575:3
such a disagreeable m., 530:17
such master such m., 144:7
sum of all he has acquired, 321:4
superior m. acts before he speaks, 60:22
superior m. is modest, 61:24
sweet slumbers of virtuous m., 292:15
system where m. exploits m., 746:14
takes drink drink takes man, 544:3
teach you more of m., 372:21
tempt not desperate m., 176:14
temptation but for m. to master, 468:3
that died for men, 536:12
that great and true Amphibium, 248:10
that hangs on favors, 225:16
that has mind and knows it, 571:28
that hath his quiver full, 20:1
that hath no music, 182:10
that hath tongue no man, 168:4
that is a worm, 14:37
that is born of a woman, 14:20
that makes character, 296:4
that m. to man the world o'er, 363:23
that mocks and sets it light, 171:2
that trusteth in man, 28:29
that trusteth in the Lord, 28:29
that was in evening made, 249:28
that's marred, 203:14
the third m., 713:8
there did meet another m., 315:10
there is a m. child conceived, 13:34
thin m., 689:13
think mortal thoughts, 68:4
thinking or working is alone, 478:26
third beast had a face as a m., 47:15
this is Plato's m., 77:3
this is the state of m., 225:16
this m. shall be myself, 319:21
this was a m., 189:28
thou art the m., 12:11
though old m. young gardener, 344:13
thought young m. brings forth, 76:9
tills field lies beneath, 459:1
time ends in killing m., 493:12
time whereof memory of m., 325:21
Time you old gypsy m., 611:19
to a wise m. ports, 171:1
to all country dear, 329:12
to be a great m., 494:15
to be m. with thy might, 534:20
to command, 456:17
to every m. a damsel or two, 11:7
to every m. according to his work, 17:34
to every m. upon earth, 425:14
to laugh proper to m., 139:8

Man (*continued*)

to man so oft unjust always to women, 402:20
to match mountains, 563:8
to men m. is mind, 544:11
to the young m. knowledge and discretion, 20:17
tool-using animal, 411:23
totality of what he might have, 717:13
tree of m. never quiet, 579:7
truly honest m., 264:21
trust m. on his oath or bond, 211:26
try fortunes to last m., 184:7
two words for m., 568:7
tyranny over mind of m., 344:4
unaccommodated m., 210:6
unfinished m. and his pain, 598:4
use every m. after desert, 196:3
use money for good of fellow m., 539:2
vain diverse undulating, 145:9
various M., 363:1
vertical m., 720:2
very unclubable m., 316:5
victory shifts from m. to m., 51:25
vindicate ways of God to m., 301:2
violent m. come down on everyone, 4:2
want anything said ask m., 756:3
wants but little, 296:14, 328:22
war as is of every m. against every m., 239:21
was it God was it m., 534:21
was there m. dismayed, 458:10
wash that m. outa my hair, 692:14
way of m. with maid, 23:15, 592:9
We created M., 117:17
wealth even to a wicked m., 59:21
well-bred m. knows how to confess, 309:25
well-favored m., 186:36
went mad and bit the m., 328:27
went to Bar as very young m., 530:10
what a chimera is m., 271:7
what a piece of work is m., 195:28
what is American this new m., 339:1
what is m. in nature, 270:18
what is m. that thou art mindful, 15:34
what is m. what is he not, 64:5
what is significance of M., 616:1
what m. can be he must be, 724:2
what m. dare I dare, 215:7
what m. has made of m., 372:18
what m. not know of God, 712:19
what manner of m., 37:22
what may m. within hide, 204:21
what mean m. seeks, 61:29
what signifies life o' m., 361:24
what treaty white m. kept, 516:9
when honor dies m. dead, 443:4
when I get to be m., 608:11
when I search for m., 754:21
when m. can help fellow m., 698:17
when m. of rank an author, 317:24
when m. of real talent dies, 342:17

Man (*continued*)

when right m. rings them, 561:24
where love of m. love of art, 71:5
whiskey life of m., 793:8
white m. warmed before Indians' fire, 333:6
who brings bad news, 66:6
who broke bank, 560:1
who came to dinner, 676:15
who craves more is poor, 102:19
who expects nothing, 300:25
who had been promised, 683:12
who has city obedient, 75:16
who has found himself out, 581:24
who is not himself mean, 667:7
who looks part has soul of part, 560:6
who never fought pilfers, 73:5
who owes nothing to land, 319:20
who runs may fight again, 81:16
who said This is mine, 319:2
who sits facing you, 56:5
who sold hyena skin, 621:15
who touches this touches a m., 491:9
who turnips cries, 315:4
who was a key a m., 740:10
who wasn't there, 630:2
who wert once despot, 407:5
whole duty of m., 24:30
whole relation between m. and woman, 436:3
whom Fortune scratched, 203:18
whom king delighteth to honor, 13:25
who's master who's m., 290:20
whose blood is snow-broth, 203:26
whose blood warm within, 179:18
why can't woman be more like m., 745:11
wicked m. in bathroom cupboard, 739:12
will cleave to like, 31:32
will no m. say amen, 172:8
will not merely endure, 696:22
wills us slaves, 341:18
wind sweep m. away, 497:22
wine a peep-hole on a m., 55:23
wise and moral m., 65:2
wise in his own conceit, 22:30
wise m. has no extensive knowledge, 58:7
wise m. is strong, 22:23
wise m. knows himself fool, 192:9
wise m. not leave right to chance, 477:10
wise m. speaks, 233:8
wisest m. does not fancy he is, 280:8
with God always in majority, 143:15
with God strive, 400:13
with great thing to pursue, 465:24
with seven wives, 788:14
with the head, 456:17
without a flaw, 95:6
without a tear, 389:9
without imagination, 653:21
without money rather than money without man, 62:27

Man (*continued*)

witness unto his deeds, 117:23
wolf to man, 674:21
woman lesser m., 455:22
woman more barbarous than m., 552:15
woman not depend on protection of m., 491:23
woman without m. cannot meet m., 746:18
woman without m. like fish without bicycle, 784:14
women looking-glasses reflecting m., 651:3
wonder and glory of universe, 444:12
word m. defines all rights, 564:12
words guard shape of m., 706:6
work for m. to mend, 276:19
work from sun to sun, 778:23
world without God and m., 760:6
worst use a m. could be put to, 227:11
worth makes the m., 301:17
wrathful m. stirreth up strife, 21:27
writing maketh exact m., 160:9
writing master to world, 664:17
yes I am fatal m., 463:14
you drop from chamber, 477:27
you shall find me grave m., 175:27
you'll be a M. my son, 593:21
young m. I think I know you, 490:11
young m. in whom something of old, 88:10
young m. married is marred, 203:14
young m. there is America, 331:7
young m. who has not wept, 588:18
you're a good m. Charlie Brown, 751:9
you're not m. you're machine, 570:20
Manacles, mind-forged m., 358:8
Manage this matter to a T, 140:*n*2
Management of balance of power, 752:15
Man-at-arms now serve on knees, 156:15
Mandalay, back to M., 591:22
road to M., 591:23
Mandamus binds all alike, 352:20
Mandarin, my thirty-third m., 495:*n*2
Manderley, dreamt I went to M. again, 721:16
Mandragora, give me to drink m., 217:4
not poppy nor m., 207:6
Mandrake, get with child a m. root, 228:5
Mane, laid hand upon thy m., 401:5
Manes, whirlwind home in m., 446:27
Mangent, qu'ils m. de la brioche, 319:*n*4
Manger, cold and not cleanly m., 264:18
dog in the m., 59:5
for his bed, 479:19
in the rude m. lies, 250:20
laid in a m., 38:2
not live as dogs in m., 650:5

Man's (*continued*)
  image and his cry, 594:23
  imagination of m. heart, 7:21
  imperial race ensnare, 299:12
  in theater of m. life, 158:9
  ingratitude, 191:4
  inhumanity to man, 361:8
  life allegory, 418:11
  life cheap as beast's, 209:21
  looking for m. footprint, 614:7
  love an episode in m. life, 368:10
  love of man's life apart, 402:14
  nature cultural product, 704:9
  no m. enemy, 720:3
  no m. pie is freed, 225:1
  old m. eagle mind, 599:12
  old m. frenzy, 599:11
  old m. gold, 609:15
  one m. will all men's misery, 155:4
  own resinous heart, 597:20
  plant m. lordship, 541:7
  practically inexterminate, 625:3
  print of m. foot, 286:4
  proud m. contumely, 196:10
  reach exceed grasp, 466:5
  rising to a m. work, 111:13
  share the good m. smile, 329:16
  skill built cities, 87:3
  sorrow not mine but m., 580:3
  stain my m. cheeks, 209:22
  take each m. censure, 193:30
  thirty years in m. life, 75:14
  truly sorry m. dominion, 361:5
  unconquerable mind, 374:18
  village is his peace of mind, 745:20
  want to be equal in m. world,
    722:12
  watch o'er m. mortality, 375:15
  way to m. heart, 462:10
  White M. burden, 593:5
  word God in man, 459:4
  work portrait of himself, 524:18
  young m. fancy, 455:9
Manservant, not covet neighbor's m.,
  9:12
Mansion, back to its m. call, 322:10
  human life a M., 418:5
  Jove's Court my m., 252:11
  Love has pitched his m., 598:21
  refuse heavenly m., 598:10
Mansionry, approve by his loved m.,
  213:4
Mansions, build more stately m.,
  447:11
  green m., 543:15
  his m. deathless, 53:6
  in Father's house many m., 40:26
  in the skies, 294:18
Manslaughter, check m. but what of
  war, 103:2
Mantle, green m. of standing pool,
  210:8
  like a standing pond, 179:19
  morn in russet m. clad, 192:30
  of Elijah, 13:6
  of wind and chill and rain, 132:22
  silver m. threw, 258:19
  twitched his m. blue, 254:8
Mantled in mist, 721:1
Manual on uses of new metal, 757:16

Manufactures, monopoly same as secret in m., 326:2
Manunkind, busy monster m., 689:5
Manure, natural m., 343:15
Manus haec inimica tyrannis, 269:n10
Many a one for him maks mane,
    785:17
  admire few know, 71:15
  and mighty are they, 592:17
  are called, 35:44
  as the sand by the sea, 12:19
  beast with m. heads, 219:10
  beguile m. beguiled by one, 207:18
  can brook the weather, 168:30
  conceive the m. without one, 76:7
  daughters have done virtuously,
    23:21
  done because we are too m., 540:7
  exploited by few, 686:6
  hands make light work, 142:15
  in hands not of few but m., 72:2
  in literature the m. force judgment,
    429:4
  inventions, 24:15
  I've had m. of them, 680:12
  must labor for one, 401:11
  mutable rank-scented m., 219:6
  not how m. enemy are but where,
    70:17
  not m. but much, 119:16
  one composed of m., 94:29
  play of the m., 584:4
  reason Lord makes so m., 450:3
  receive advice few profit, 99:4
  savings of m., 568:3
  shall run to and fro, 29:21
  so much owed by so m., 620:10
  sold the m. on the few, 689:4
  strokes overthrow the oaks, 155:9
  that are first, 35:38
  the few and the m., 355:1
  there be which go in thereat, 34:9
  to keep, 484:11
  we are m., 37:24
  what are they among m., 40:2
  wisdom of m., 779:18
  ye are m. they are few, 408:2
Many-colored glass, 409:8
  life he drew, 313:10
Many-headed monster of pit, 303:10
  multitude, 97:n4, 219:3
  people a m. beast, 97:7
Many-splendored thing, 581:11
Many-wintered crow, 455:11
Map, I their m., 231:3
  journey universe in m., 150:25
  of honor in thy face, 163:25
Maple Leaf forever, 515:4
Maples, scarlet of m. shake me,
  583:16
Maps, geographers crowd edges of m.,
  107:1
  Geography is about M., 627:17
  on old highway m. of America,
    769:17
  to other world, 228:3
Mar, not make can not m., 497:14
  striving to better we m., 209:12
  this fair garden, 508:29
  your fortunes, 208:21

Marathon, Athenians crushed at M.
  the Medes, 60:10
  looks on the sea, 402:26
  patriotism gain force upon M.,
    314:16
  to Waterloo, 529:12
Marble, draw living faces from m.,
  94:15
  dwelt in m. halls, 419:1
  enduring as m. to retain, 151:23
  hills full of m., 524:10
  index of a mind, 373:10
  left Rome a city of m., 98:23
  life made of m. and mud, 436:7
  nor gilded monuments, 220:25
  on m. pavement dust grows, 86:18
  poets that lasting m. seek, 250:3
  Priapus made of m., 92:11
  say more than many a braver m.,
    264:21
  sleep in dull cold m., 225:19
  sweep through m. halls, 440:14
  to retain, 402:3
  wastes statue grows, 137:8
  well-governed cities, 721:2
  write evil in m., 137:17
Marble-hearted fiend, 209:10
Marbles, like m. touching but separate, 537:17
March, alluvial m. of days, 701:5
  almost hear breathing as they m.,
    743:n2
  beware ides of M., 187:18
  day's m. nearer home, 377:17
  droghte of M. perced to roote,
    129:6
  Hare went on, 517:18
  her m. o'er mountain waves, 389:1
  Ides of M., 88:23, 187:18
  July October May, 143:n6
  mad M. days, 634:1
  mad M. hare, 135:17
  men who m. away, 540:20
  of human mind slow, 331:18
  of intellect, 386:20
  of this retreating world, 687:5
  on he said, 443:12
  take winds of M. with beauty,
    223:7
  three Frenchmen, 185:10
  three hours' m. to dinner, 390:15
  trees that would m., 637:13
  truth is on m., 541:13
  two months back in M., 624:6
  we must m. my darlings, 490:7
  worse than sun in M., 178:23
Marche, le Congrès ne m. pas, 339:n2
Marched breast forward, 468:17
  by a king's name, 683:10
  forth he m. far beyond heavens,
    89:4
  rank on rank, 509:8
Märchen aus alten Zeiten, 419:n7
Marches, Africa m. patiently through
  time, 719:15
  army m. on stomach, 371:3
  funeral m. to grave, 440:16
Marching along, 464:14
  as to war, 521:10
  boys are m., 492:6

Marching *(continued)*
His truth is m. on, 484:6
single in file, 430:6
soul m. on, 524:7
through Boston, 743:10
through Georgia, 520:6
to promised land, 521:12
when saints go m. in, 794:24
Marchons Marchons, 366:9
Mare, look of bay m. shames silliness, 489:2
shoe the m., 792:21
Mares eat oats, 791:15
Margalo, my name is M., 703:13
Margaret are you grieving, 551:5
fye na said may M., 785:12
merry M., 135:23
you mourn for, 551:6
Marge of Lake Lebarge, 627:3
Margent, Meander's m. green, 252:26
of the world, 581:6
Margery Daw, 789:12
some went upstairs with M., 720:18
Margin, broad m. to my life, 478:24
meadow of m., 352:27
Margins, outmost m., 663:11
Mariana, dejected M., 204:18
Marian's nose looks red, 169:14
Marigold goes to bed wi' the sun, 223:6
Marijuana, curlicues of m., 742:22
Marilyn every man's love affair with America, 753:3
Marine, another m. reporting sir, 783:13
Mariner, ancient M., 380:26
fear thee ancient M., 381:18
hath his will, 380:28
if Ancient M. called Old Sailor, 525:8
Mariners of England, 388:26
rest ye brother m., 454:11
Marines, tell that to the m., 379:22
that will do for the m., 379:*n*2
Marionette, burst from m. show, 755:4
Marjoram, lavender mints savory m., 223:6
Mark archer little meant, 379:5
as arrows fly to one m., 184:25
coming and look brighter, 402:11
could man outlook that m., 270:11
death loves shining m., 296:18
ever-fixed m., 222:2
fault of wit to go beyond m., 265:39
go m. him well, 378:1
God save the m., 177:5
how my fame rings, 544:9
how plain tale put you down, 177:26
I press toward the m., 44:32
man's distinctive m., 467:14
Matthew M. Luke and John, 266:8
no drowning m. upon him, 223:18
of the beast, 47:29
Philosophy push beyond m., 457:16
read m. learn, 49:20
see see their m., 243:24
set a m. upon Cain, 7:7

Mark *(continued)*
some m. of virtue, 181:5
the perfect man, 17:3
three quarks for Muster M., 647:21
where his carnage, 401:9
you his absolute shall, 219:7
Mark Antony, woman lost M. the world, 284:15
Mark Twain, book by M., 702:2
book by Mr. M., 526:19
Marked him for her own, 322:22
him for his own, 245:17
Him in flowering, 459:22
I where bolt of Cupid fell, 173:6
our hour is m., 370:20
Markers, do not move m. on border, 5:14
Market competition afford freedom, 657:3
do you know considering m., 623:11
economy not respect political frontiers, 645:11
existence m. price, 514:12
fortune like the m., 159:22
knowledge bought in m., 482:21
little pig to m., 789:3
of his time, 198:12
prees at m. maketh deere ware, 131:6
to m. to buy fat pig, 792:2
truth accepted in m., 542:25
Marketplace, bird of night upon m., 187:28
Idols of the M., 158:13
Markets, you are not for all m., 191:24
Marking, malady of not m., 183:16
Marks I carry with me, 272:30
not won or lost, 643:13
Marl, clod of wayward m., 186:18
over the burning m., 256:7
Marlborough Street, hardly passionate M., 742:21
Marlowe's mighty line, 232:19
Marmion, last words of M., 378:15
Marquis duke and a' that, 363:22
Marred, young man m., 203:14
Marreth what he makes, 302:*n*7
Marriage a necessary evil, 81:13
a noose, 150:36
accident counts in m., 535:10
all thy days as m. day, 242:15
an evil most men welcome, 81:*n*9
and hanging go by destiny, 141:*n*1
as with cages, 146:19
buys them in m., 402:20
community of two slaves, 544:20
damnably serious business, 686:18
desperate thing, 239:4
dirge in m., 192:32
disparity in m., 470:41
field of battle, 560:14
friendships invalidated by m., 524:22
from which love gone, 713:10
good m. a communion, 138:12
good m. each guardian, 630:10
has many pains, 314:12
has more joy than pain, 67:21

Marriage *(continued)*
hasty m. seldom proveth well, 164:25
hearse, 358:9
in break-up of m. take side, 717:8
in Cana of Galilee, 39:*n*5
in m. husband and wife equal, 410:18
in m. room for interpreter, 716:22
in m. wish to get out, 432:28
is popular, 571:9
keep eyes open before m., 309:24
love and m. go together, 732:11
love without m., 309:11
luxury not necessity, 492:1
makes one flesh, 291:1
merry as m. bell, 399:21
negative feelings about m., 284:9
not bed of roses, 560:14
O curse of m., 207:4
of true minds, 222:2
only actual bondage, 440:4
resembles shears, 380:15
rob lady of fortune by m., 311:28
servant in love lord in m., 131:27
stylish m., 600:18
tables, 193:14
that's been our m., 507:19
though I make this m. for my peace, 217:17
triumphal procession air to m., 426:14
what Adam and Eve think of m., 664:8
what torment not a m. bed, 231:9
without love, 309:11
Marriages made in heaven, 155:22
martini one of happiest m., 696:8
Married and that's his plague, 234:31
Benedick the m. man, 186:15
best part of m. life fights, 698:1
everybody climbs into graves m., 697:13
happiness in m. estate, 250:14
how m. without wife, 789:7
I m. beneath me, 635:3
I would be me, 264:12
if be m. not be cuckold, 656:7
imprudently m. barber, 324:7
in haste, 290:34
life m. to sea, 618:11
man tattered and torn, 792:24
mocks m. men, 169:12
most m. man I ever saw, 522:3
never m. that's his hell, 234:31
no taste when you m. me, 352:28
not live till I were m., 186:31
O let us be m., 472:1
on Wednesday, 791:4
reader I m. him, 476:13
saints rarely m. women, 719:10
strange as if m. a great while, 291:12
sum m. people owe, 349:24
till anes we m. be, 785:12
to immortal verse, 251:19
to single life, 264:12
unpleasing to a m. ear, 169:12
we will be m. o' Sunday, 167:23
well-bred as if not m., 291:12

Married (*continued*)

women they m. when young, 541:1
young man m. is marred, 203:14
Marries, doesn't signify whom one m.,
    367:6
Marrons, tirer les m. du feu, 268:n7
Marrow, anguish of m., 668:13
    dividing joints and m., 45:34
    suck substantific m., 139:7
Marrowbone, thinks in a m., 599:3
Marrowbones, better down on m.,
    595:13
Marry, advice to persons about to m.,
    554:14
    ancient people, 250:15
    Ann, 571:3
    as easy to m. rich woman, 463:15
    becoming men we wanted to m.,
        767:4
    better to m. than burn, 43:2
    boy will you m. it, 764:10
    certain person at certain time, 426:7
    error to m. with poets, 735:6
    every woman should m., 435:8
    God let Carlyle and Mrs. Carlyle
        m., 524:15
    he'll come back and m. me, 792:18
    is to halve rights double duties,
        404:11
    maiden will you m. me, 529:19
    may m. whom she likes, 463:6
    my body to that dust, 242:2
    people people m., 583:9
    prepared to m. again, 530:8
    proper time to m., 335:21
    this is miching mallecho, 197:9
    your son when you will, 244:12
Marryin', John Thomas m. Lady Jane,
    657:15
Marrying left maiden name disused,
    750:11
Mars, an eye like M., 197:30
    Jupiter aligns with M., 770:1
    makes us or m. us, 208:5
    of malcontents, 182:22
    this seat of M., 171:9
Marsh, fragrance of salt m., 491:3
    frogs in the m. mud, 92:26
    hen secretly builds, 547:7
    space 'twixt m. and skies, 547:7
Marshall Plan one of greatest contri-
    butions, 655:13
Marshal's, French soldier carries m.
    baton, 371:4
    truncheon, 204:1
Marshes how candid and simple,
    547:6
    of Glynn, 547:7
Martha was cumbered with serving,
    38:25
Martial, airs m. brisk or grave, 335:11
    airs of England, 394:19
    cloak around him, 405:16
    sounds, 256:13
    swashing and m. outside, 190:5
Martin Elginbrodde, 504:14
    you Doctor M., 759:12
Martini, into dry M., 675:11
    medium Vodka dry M., 723:2

Martini (*continued*)

one of happiest marriages on earth,
    696:8
something about m., 709:11
Martin's, bells of St. M., 788:20
    expect Saint M. summer, 163:7
Martlet, temple-haunting m., 213:4
Martyr, deye a m. go to heaven,
    128:21
    saint and M. rule from tomb, 670:9
    thou fallest a blessed m., 225:21
Martyrdom, all have not gift of m.,
    275:17
    Negro willing to risk m., 761:8
    not at all fond of m., 306:27
    to live, 248:27
    torches of m., 344:12
Martyrdoms have crowned church,
    112:n2
Martyr's, groan of m. woe, 359:4
    no happiness perfect as m., 585:16
Martyrs, blood of m. seed of Church,
    112:n2
    create faith, 589:13
    faith not create m., 589:13
    love m. honor slain, 495:12
    noble army of m., 48:24
    noisy set m. call world, 595:14
Martyrs', out of m. bones elegance,
    639:13
Marvel how fishes live in sea, 219:21
    more and more, 608:17
    not Ulysses but Captain M., 764:2
Marveling sweetly on her ills, 674:12
Marvelous, Chatterton m. boy, 374:9
    how m. is Man, 605:12
    in all nature something m., 77:20
    's wonderful 's m., 695:3
    Truth confront us, 752:17
    unknown taken for m., 109:20
    what does not first appear m., 104:7
    what is this m. book, 319:16
Marvels of man's labor, 723:18
Marx case in point, 723:13
Marxian Socialism portent to histori-
    ans, 652:9
Marxism product of bourgeois mind,
    653:24
Marxist, all I know is I am not M.,
    481:13
Mary at thy window be, 363:17
    born of the Virgin M., 48:25
    call cattle home, 404:9
    had a little lamb, 404:10
    hath chosen good part, 38:26
    incarnate of the Virgin M., 49:1
    my M., 335:18
    my sweet Highland M., 363:13
    no God and M. His Mother, 588:21
    quite contrary, 788:19
    Saint Anne mother of M., 538:6
    was that mother mild, 479:19
    young child with M., 32:24
Mary-buds, winking M. begin, 219:24
Maryland, hills of M., 443:10
    my Maryland, 538:20
Mary's, my M. asleep, 362:21
Masai House of God, 702:4
Masculine, the usual m. disillusion-
    ment, 704:15

Mask and antique pageantry, 251:19
faith under another m., 713:12
how recognized under m., 728:4
like Castlereagh, 407:25
no m. like truth, 291:2
off reality remains, 89:22
strike strike through m., 486:24
Masks and revels sweet youth make,
    226:14
Mason, mere working m., 379:7
Masonry, lies mortar that bind man
    into social m., 601:7
Masons building roofs of gold, 184:24
Masquerade, truth in m., 403:12
Masquerades as cream, 529:8
Mass and majesty of world, 721:3
    baby figure of giant m., 200:12
    blessed mutter of M., 465:7
    chaos a rough unordered m., 101:19
    I am the m., 634:3
    lead lives of quiet desperation,
        477:32
    novelty stains ancient m., 546:20
    of London itself, 620:9
    of the people, 355:1
    Paris well worth a M., 154:21
    particle of general m., 629:5
    rough unordered m., 101:19
    skies and earth a solid m., 117:1
    spirit which goes through m., 629:5
    the greatest blasphemy, 138:11
    times speed of light squared, 635:n3
    world terrible in m., 540:1
Massachusetts, here's to M., 582:n1
    House of Representatives of M.
        Bay, 339:3
    rampant Maenad of M., 535:2
    there she is, 394:13
Massage, medium is m., 730:5
Massa's, old M. gone away, 780:2
Masses, as to what are called the m.,
    432:22
    back m. against classes, 446:16
    bow ye m., 530:5
    easily fall victims to lie, 676:7
    huddled m., 558:1
    little virtue in action of m., 477:10
    long suits, 680:17
Massive, heard her m. sandal, 684:9
Massy, solid m. hard particles, 282:4
    two m. keys he bore, 254:1
Mast, bends gallant m., 396:22
    like drunken sailor on m., 166:3
    nailed colors to the m., 378:4
    of some great ammiral, 256:7
    what though m. blown overboard,
        165:2
Master, accuse not a servant unto his
    m., 23:13
    artist who bids come to heel, 667:1
    behold m., 307:3
    blessing of Saint Peter's M., 245:31
    calls no man m., 393:2
    card m. to those below, 680:17
    disciple not above m., 34:32
    everyone can m. grief, 186:34
    executioner, 58:4
    fire what a m., 413:5
    follow the M., 272:n9
    great M. said I see, 441:22

Master (*continued*)
  has a new m., 224:11
  hewing wood for m. carpenter, 58:4
  I am m. of fantasy, 565:23
  in limitations the m., 350:30
  into the woods my M. went, 547:9
  Jacky have new m., 789:12
  law m. after my disappearance,
    64:27
  lifeblood of m. spirit, 254:24
  look out here comes M. Race,
    756:20
  Man is m. of things, 535:1
  man writing m. to world, 664:17
  mistress two slaves, 544:20
  need more to be m., 548:5
  no more subtle m., 459:20
  nor master's man, 523:10
  not be slave not be m., 448:9
  O worthy M., 441:16
  of All Good Workmen, 591:13
  of himself, 238:6
  of himself a happy man, 96:24
  of his fate, 459:9, 677:7
  of my fate, 557:10
  of sea Master of every country,
    160:n5
  of the day of judgment, 116:1
  of us all, 637:11
  one for my m., 788:18
  past m. of genre of silence, 688:3
  recognize Actaeon your m., 101:22
  Shallow I owe thousand pound,
    184:17
  spirits of this age, 188:20
  strong enough to be m., 319:6
  such beauty as you m., 221:22
  such m. such man, 144:7
  that which I would fain call m.,
    209:5
  these forces met m., 649:6
  thou Virgil art my m. and author,
    125:5
  to lead but not m. them, 57:2
  urgent, 115:16
  which is to be m., 519:14
  who's m. who's man, 290:20
  ye know not when m. cometh,
    37:34
Mastering, thou m. me God, 550:17
Masterly, wise and m. inactivity,
    367:15
Masterpiece, airing dirty linen never
    m., 765:1
  appear as flower, 523:21
  confusion made m., 214:13
  great m. designed, 363:1
  joy to artist, 523:21
  Nature's great m., 230:17
  nature's m. writing well, 284:2
  no one knows m., 659:11
  of Nature, 432:1
  place in chain of being, 433:8
Masterpieces, adventures among m.,
    550:11
  not give best at beginning, 612:16
Master's, dog starved at m. gate,
    359:7
  lost fiddle stick, 788:1
  neither master nor m. man, 523:10

Masters ashamed to become disciples,
    227:3
  done away with, 552:23
  ego serves three severe m., 569:14
  free ourselves subdue our m., 347:2
  lords and rulers, 563:7
  machines slaves not m., 578:9
  nails fastened by m., 24:29
  no man can serve two m., 33:17
  of future, 761:11
  of our own fate, 700:4
  of the Universe, 764:6
  of their fates, 187:22
  of things they write, 239:2
  Old M. never wrong, 720:7
  sleep that m. all, 65:12
  spread yourselves, 172:23
  we cannot all be m., 205:11
  worthy valets, 336:4
Masters', crumbs from m. table, 35:24
Masterwork, creation of m., 499:4
  history of m. not failures, 660:2
  of wisdom, 493:22
Mastery, achieve of m. of, 550:21
  I had m., 687:5
  of desires, 552:25
  of subject, 629:13
  propensity for m., 574:6
  strive here for m., 257:19
Mast-high, ice m., 381:3
Mastiffs of unmatchable courage,
    185:12
Masts, sail-yards tremble m. crack,
    157:13
  though her m. firm, 477:15
Masturbation, woman substitute for
    m., 626:8
Mat, tomcat flat as old rough m.,
    762:17
Match for the devil, 698:11
  forces of selfishness met m., 649:6
  I cannot blow out m., 744:3
Matched, passions m. with mine,
    455:22
  us with His hour, 663:4
  with aged wife, 454:24
Matches made in heaven, 141:n1
Matchless deed's achieved, 325:13
Matchwood immortal diamond,
    551:17
Mate, caresses of subhumanly ugly m.,
    769:12
  choose not alone proper m., 335:21
  great artificer made m., 561:25
  in England I've m., 472:11
  of Nancy brig, 528:22
Mated by the lion, 203:10
Mater artium necessitas, 119:12
  saeva Cupidinum, 96:n23
Material and obvious things, 280:3
  computation, 620:19
  copying mechanism for genetic m.,
    760:5
  disbranch from her m. sap, 210:22
  fortune associated with body,
    110:12
  objects of two kinds, 89:10
  of life, 653:17
  out of which countries made, 616:8
  raw m. of opinion, 572:3

Material (*continued*)
  spiritual stronger than m., 433:18
  sublime, 384:22
  surface of things, 495:20
Materialism model for cultures, 754:5
Materialistic, far from having m. tend-
    ency, 420:18
Materializing upper class, 500:23
Materially ambitious, 665:9
Materials, I depart from m., 491:10
  man not m. that counts, 686:13
  work with m. I am made of, 714:8
  youth gets together m., 477:1
Mates, moves and m. and slays,
    445:23
Mathematical, concept of m. beauty,
    583:13
  sciences founded, 516:6
Mathematician, Architect of Universe
    m., 632:3
  capable of reasoning, 75:19
  two and two m. makes four, 523:18
  union of m. with poet, 547:2
Mathematics, angling like m., 245:13
  axioms of book of m., 542:5
  chemistry m. electronics, 681:13
  commence in disappointment, 584:7
  draws necessary conclusions, 451:5
  foundations of knowledge in m.,
    124:1
  fruits of m., 135:11
  in m. never know what talking
    about, 615:9
  in region of necessity, 615:11
  intuitive calculation transcended m.,
    628:6
  my sons ought to study m., 338:10
  poets witty m. subtile, 160:10
  possesses beauty, 615:10
  pure m. original creation, 584:9
  queen of sciences, 389:19
  universe in language of m., 161:15
Mather, Cottons m., 697:7
Matilda and house burned, 609:4
  a-waltzing M., 589:5
  told dreadful lies, 609:3
Matin, glowworm shows m. near,
    194:26
Matre pulchra filia pulchrior, 95:n22
Matrimonial, error of m. union, 540:5
Matrimony, critical period in m.,
    678:22
  in m. begin with aversion, 352:4
  jumps from love to m., 386:25
  road to wealth, 475:13
Matrix, freedom of expression m.,
    609:13
Matron's, mutine in m. bones, 197:32
Matter, Berkeley said no m., 403:11
  carry on m. for own sake, 473:17
  daily to be shown m., 477:7
  for a May morning, 202:32
  for virtuous deeds, 157:10
  goes to root of m., 546:12
  great m. or small, 31:13
  hear the conclusion of the whole
    m., 24:30
  here and now cease to m., 671:11
  his m. and ideas, 498:22
  I am full of m., 15:1

Matter (*continued*)

make a Star Chamber m., 182:16
meaning doesn't m., 529:17
mince the m., 148:15, 206:19
mind over m., 420:18
more m. with less art, 195:11
nervous m., 535:22
no m. from the heart, 201:13
no m. what he said, 403:11
order m. better in France, 320:33
poetry does not m., 670:23
root of the m. found in me, 14:31
solid hard particles, 282:4
state of m. at given moment, 504:12
subordinates manner to m., 384:14
totally different m., 446:22
unalterable as quantity of m., 496:17
unreal and temporal, 495:21
waking no such m., 221:12
what does it m. to me, 741:*n*1
what is M. Never mind, 554:16
whether you hate self, 663:18
wings shall tell the m., 24:22
Matters I relate are true lies, 675:22
read strange m., 213:2
to do well is what m., 247:8
what m. what anybody thinks, 432:*n*2
Matthew and Waldo guardians, 668:1
man named M., 34:20
Mark Luke and John, 266:8
Mattresses, princess felt pea through m., 437:5
Mature poets steal, 672:12
Maturing sun, 416:13
Maturity sacred to ease and relaxation, 559:3
Matzoh, only Jew in Danville looking for m., 755:5
Maud, come into garden M., 458:20
went to college, 740:3
Mausolos' Tomb, 782:7
Mauve and rosy sky, 694:15
Maw-crammed beast, 467:7
Mawkishness and thousand bitters, 414:8
Maxim, act only on that m., 326:12
general m. useless, 424:16
Gun, 608:18
of British people, 619:15
old m. in the schools, 289:5
only m. of free government, 337:16
with Foxey, 469:31
Maxima debetur puero reverentia, 109:*n*9
Maxims, little hoard of m., 455:15
Maximum temptation maximum opportunity, 571:9
May, April showers M. flowers, 144:8
as you do in M., 547:*n*1
come what come m., 212:25
come what m., 102:14, 401:8
darling buds of M., 220:12
flowery meads in M., 240:1
flush as M., 197:25
fressh as month of M., 129:9
from M. to December, 666:4
full of spirit as month of M., 178:20

May (*continued*)

gather ye rosebuds while ye m., 241:9
he smells April and M., 182:31
I were lord in M., 534:8
in M. when sea winds, 429:14
joys as month of M., 242:15
laurel outlives not M., 534:4
like snow in M., 243:21
love I gave in M., 547:4
lusty month of M., 133:11
maids M. when maids, 192:4
March July October M., 143:*n*6
matter for M. morning, 202:32
merry month of M., 233:10, 785:9
month before month of M., 382:10
nightingale when M. is past, 246:5
of April M. of June, 240:16
one month on in M., 624:6
Queen o' the M., 454:4
swarm of bees in M., 777:18
the Force be with you, 773:11
there's an end of M., 579:17
welcome faire fresshe M., 130:13
when month of M. is comen, 129:4
with thy floures and grene, 130:13
wol have no slogardie anyght, 130:10
Mayakovski's, last years of M. life, 680:1
Mayday, more bright than M. morn, 353:11
Mayflower, forefathers not on M., 638:6
including those on M., 650:3
Mayor, Lord M. of London, 777:1
Mayors, make m. but not scholars, 234:28
Maypoles Hock-carts wassails, 240:16
May's newfangled mirth, 168:16
Maze, mighty m., 301:1
of schools, 298:11
Mazes, in wandering m. lost, 257:12
Mazy, eye intent on mazy plan, 363:1
five miles with m. motion, 382:21
mc², E equals m., 635:11
McClellan's, army is M. bodyguard, 449:10
McGee, cremated Sam M., 627:3
McGregor's, Mr. M. garden, 600:21
McGrew, Dangerous Dan M., 627:2
Me, Day got tired of M., 512:10
decade, 764:4
deprivation is for m., 751:2
does Africa know song of m., 656:9
if you don't go down with m., 648:5
lilac in m. I am New England, 626:11
raise stone and find M., 112:16
self-subsisting self-seeking m., 426:8
some little talk of M., 445:19
Tarzan you Jane, 628:*n*2
this is the real m., 545:5
universe is all including m., 691:22
want cookie, 775:8
what m. worry, 783:27
who am as a nerve, 407:10
who sees M. in all, 84:10
woe is m., 26:2

Me (*continued*)

ye have not always, 36:22
you get no more of m., 161:11
Mea culpa, 48:6
Mead, by stream and o'er m., 356:6
groweth seed bloweth m., 775:10
of al floures in the m., 129:5
Meadow grove and stream, 375:3
I believe in the m., 479:7
mother of months in m., 533:8
of margin, 352:27
rivulets overflow, 540:25
sheep's in m., 789:4
Meadow's, dropped like flower on m. edge, 90:22
Meadows brown and sere, 411:8
has m. of clarinets, 689:9
paint the m. with delight, 169:12
strangers who fenced off m., 694:6
trim with daisies pied, 251:14
up from the m., 443:9
Meadowsweet, vales of m., 703:13
Meads, flowery m. in May, 240:1
met lady in m., 417:5
Meager knowledge, 504:11
shriveled m. hopping, 332:18
Meal, barrel of m. wasted not, 12:34
handful of m. in a barrel, 12:33
in the firkin, 431:12
morning incense evening m., 353:15
Meal-drift molded ever, 551:2
Meals of beef iron steel, 185:13
unquiet m. make ill digestions, 166:33
Mealy boys, 469:10
Mean actions ascribed to fear, 552:3
as a panther, 745:17
between nothing and everything, 270:18
don't m. a thing if ain't got swing, 701:8
down m. streets man must go, 667:7
everything I touch m. and farcical, 508:17
few say all they m., 536:3
golden m., 96:7
I m. what I say, 517:18
if conduct m. and paltry, 79:4
if they m. to have war, 333:5
keep golden m., 96:*n*7
know not what they m., 456:13
man full of distress, 61:13
man who is not himself m., 667:7
means what I choose it to m., 519:14
never be m., 470:27
not careful what they m., 167:11
nothing common did or m., 268:10
or wish to mean, 750:2
poem should not m. but be, 683:8
stupid Public, 390:10
suspicion companion of m. souls, 340:19
they may not m. to but do, 750:15
we speak not what we m., 204:6
what may this m., 194:11
what m. man seeks, 61:29
woman of m. understanding, 386:24
world is m., 766:8

Meddling, every fool will be m., 22:2
Medea gathered enchanted herbs,
 182:7
Medes, crushed the gold-bearing M.,
 60:10
 law of the M. and Persians, 29:17
Media, hot m. low in participation,
 730:4
Medias, in m. res, 98:*n*7
Mediator, painting m. between world
 and us, 645:4
 president mostly a m., 729:21
Mediatory, reconciling m. power,
 384:1
Mediatress, Art m. between nature
 and man, 384:19
Medici created and destroyed me,
 135:14
Medicinable gum, 208:16
 some griefs are m., 219:26
Medicine distinguishes man from animals, 558:4
 doeth good like m., 21:36
 for life which has fled, 58:12
 for mental disorders, 692:3
 for misery, 68:26
 has to examine disease, 107:5
 in m. sins of commission mortal,
 318:8
 live by m. live horribly, 312:8
 most distinguished of arts, 71:8
 my lawful wife, 582:6
 no m. but hope, 204:7
 of life, 31:16
 thee to sweet sleep, 207:6
 words were m., 766:14
 worse than malady, 99:*n*5
Medicine Hat, war bonnet of M.,
 698:6
Medicines to make me love him,
 177:12
Medicos marveling sweetly, 674:12
Medieval hand, 529:18
Medio tutissimus ibis, 101:*n*14
Mediocre, if you are m. and grovel,
 336:7
 lots of m. judges people lawyers,
 713:16
 minds, 265:38
 passions, 265:28
Mediocrities, single genius hundred
 m., 532:4
Mediocrity, abilities below m. rewarded, 385:15
 gratified with m., 368:1
 history of masterwork not m., 660:2
 of apparatus, 641:4
 solitude safeguard of m., 432:35
Meditate, in his law doth he m., 15:2⁹
 on blood, 186:2
 thankless Muse, 253:20
Meditating, in path good lizard m.,
 699:2
 upon whatsoever state, 84:11
Meditation and water wedded forever,
 486:17
 let us all to m., 164:3
 maiden m. fancy-free, 173:6
 of my heart, 16:13

Meditation (*continued*)
 where m. neither anxiety nor doubt,
 123:9
Mediterranean, bagful of blue M.,
 719:15
Mediterraneans see clearly, 653:3
Medium, hot m. like radio cool like
 telephone, 730:4
 internal m., 473:7
 is massage, 730:5
 is message, 730:3
Meek and gentle with these butchers,
 188:22
 blessed are the m., 33:1
 borne his faculties so m., 213:7
 gentle Jesus m. and mild, 312:15
 he is m. he is mild, 356:7
 holy and m. she cries, 357:18
 I am m. and lowly, 34:38
 mysteries revealed unto m., 31:2
 ornament of m. spirit, 46:24
 shall inherit the earth, 16:34
 soft m. patient humble, 227:19
 young men grow up in libraries,
 431:6
Meekest man and gentlest, 133:17
Meek-eyed parents, 717:1
Meekness, fruit of Spirit is m., 44:19
 Wrath by his m., 356:16
Meet, beauteous flower when next we
 m., 175:10
 bold I can m., 371:25
 descend to m., 431:35
 experiment to me is everyone I m.,
 513:16
 extremes m., 342:2
 him with one tooth, 613:9
 if we do m. again, 189:23
 in her aspect and eyes, 401:14
 in one spirit m. mingle, 407:20
 it and not see its head, 57:5
 many ways m. in one town, 184:25
 Mr. Eliot, 670:6
 never twain m., 591:9
 on bridge of Time, 494:18
 political greatness and wisdom m.,
 75:15
 shadow rising to m. you, 668:18
 Spirit with Spirit m., 460:4
 thee in that hollow vale, 242:2
 though infinite never m., 268:22
 two smiles m., 359:3
 until we m. again, 537:1
 we shall m. but miss him, 473:19
 we three m. again, 212:9
 when men and mountains m.,
 359:18
 where brook and river m., 441:7
 with champagne and chicken, 304:3
 with joy in sweet Jerusalem, 165:3
 your visage here, 701:7
Meeter to carry off latter, 397:21
Meeting, journeys end in lovers m.,
 202:1
 soul may pierce, 251:19
 speaks to me as if I were public m.,
 488:7
Meeting-point between savagery and
 civilization, 584:6
Meets in oppugnancy, 200:9

Meets (*continued*)
 less than m. eye, 710:13
 life m. all motion becomes its soul,
 380:24
 more meant than m. ear, 252:9
Mehitabel, dance m. dance, 633:7
Meilleur, ce m. des mondes possibles,
 306:*n*3
Melancholia of everything completed,
 552:22
Melancholy and despair, 235:20
 as battle won, 371:7
 as gib cat, 176:30
 bait, 179:22
 black sun of M., 443:23
 charm in m., 367:5
 chord in m., 422:22
 chronic m. of civilized, 540:2
 days are come, 411:8
 divinest M., 251:22
 dull-eyed m., 219:20
 fears without cause, 235:20
 green and yellow m., 202:14
 House of Usher, 452:4
 loathed M., 251:6
 long withdrawing roar, 499:22
 marked him for her own, 322:22
 men eat no beans, 234:15
 men most witty, 235:1
 moping m., 260:17
 most m. of reflections, 506:9
 most musical most m., 252:2
 music is good to the m., 278:9
 naked m. isles, 308:8
 naught so sweet as m., 234:3
 never give way to m., 380:13
 O sweetest m., 236:13
 of mine own, 191:26
 pale M. sate retired, 324:16
 purge m., 223:16
 rare recipe for m., 387:17
 rime and be m., 168:33
 shade of m. boughs, 190:29
 slow, 328:6
 suck m. out of song, 190:19
 villainous m., 209:4
 what charm soothe m., 328:29
Meliorist, not optimist but m., 578:*n*1
Mellow, fruit too m. for me, 304:6
 he who goes to bed m., 236:*n*3
Mellowed, fruit that m. long, 273:21
 to tender light, 401:14
Mellowing, delivered upon m. of occasion, 168:32
 year, 253:14
Melodies echoes of that voice, 383:10
 heard m. sweet, 416:2
Melodious birds sing madrigals, 162:3
 bursts that fill, 454:12
 plot, 415:10
Melody, blundering kind of m.,
 274:17
 could you view the m., 267:13
 falling in m. back, 383:2
 mortal m., 451:13
 my Luve is like the m., 362:6
 pretty girl love, 666:9
 singing and making m., 44:26
 smale foweles maken m., 129:7
Melrose, view fair M., 377:23

Melt at others' woe, 321:19
    butter not m. in mouth, 141:23
    in her own fire, 197:32
    let Rome in Tiber m., 216:25
    too solid flesh would m., 193:5
    with ruth, 254:5
Melted, brown hills m. into spring,
    480:1
    into air, 224:21
    into new race of men, 339:1
    like snow, 401:16
Melter of limbs, 54:17
Melting airs, 335:11
    mood, 208:16
    poem ride on own m., 625:10
    point about m. pot, 590:*n*2
    pot, 590:6
    sweet music's m. fall, 323:15
Melts, grief m. away, 243:21
    like kisses, 402:4
    then m. forever, 363:6
Member, club that will accept me as
    m., 693:2
    not a m. was m. of nothing, 744:6
Members, list of m. of Communist
    Party, 724:3
    of human community, 650:5
    one of another, 44:25
    that one of thy m. should perish,
    33:5
Membrane of bright blue sky, 734:10
Même, plus ça change plus la m.,
    443:*n*3
Memento, some common m. better,
    653:28
Mémoire, il faut bonne m. après qu'on
    a menti, 105:*n*6
Memoirs, not read Barère's M.,
    425:16
    we will write our m., 370:17
Memorable, days m. in history, 621:6
    moments in their lives, 740:2
    sentences, 515:15
Memorandum, make a m. of it,
    518:14
Memorial from soul's eternity, 509:23
    Passover shall be for a m., 8:39
    some have no m., 32:14
Memories, anchored in m., 753:2
    dies on wind like m., 641:10
    encrusted with sublime thoughts,
    477:18
    more m. than if thousand years old,
    494:6
    mother of m., 494:4
    night of m. and sighs, 388:16
    youth has no long m., 483:19
Memory, adduces authority uses m.,
    135:5
    archives of m., 609:11
    be green, 192:31
    complains of his m., 265:13
    dear son of m., 251:2
    emancipated from time, 384:8
    exiled from m. of man, 759:1
    fills m. with natural objects, 350:1
    fond M. brings light, 392:7
    footfalls echo in m., 670:13
    Franklin's quiet m., 404:4
    from false to false, 200:22

Memory (*continued*)
    good m. to keep promises, 552:2
    green, 391:11
    grows fainter relaxes bonds, 613:1
    hands of m. weave, 536:10
    he shall have a noble m., 219:17
    history vitalizes m., 87:14
    honor his m., 233:5
    how sweet their m. still, 333:21
    illiterate him from your m., 352:3
    in book of my m. a rubric, 124:17
    indebted to m. for jests, 353:4
    keep m. green, 391:11
    liar should have good m., 105:11
    life a m. without pain, 66:2
    life and m. of it, 729:16
    literature m. of nation, 746:4
    mixing m. and desire, 668:17
    mousetraps moon m. muchness,
    517:22
    my name and m. I leave, 160:12
    nine she-camel hairs aid m., 665:4
    no force abolish m., 649:21
    no m. of having starred, 624:8
    not necessary for love, 697:11
    note you in book of m., 163:11
    of all he stole, 303:26
    of all that, 695:13
    of benefits fades, 65:11
    of Boatswain a dog, 398:16
    of loved and lost, 450:9
    of Paris inexhaustible, 681:12
    of the just is blessed, 21:5
    of them is forgotten, 24:18
    outlive his life, 197:8
    painted perfect day, 585:9
    pluck from m. rooted sorrow,
    216:10
    poor m. that only works backwards,
    519:10
    pray bring me to men's m., 125:22
    proud to have m. graced, 675:10
    sinner of his m., 223:22
    some women stay in m., 593:16
    struggle of m. against forgetting,
    761:10
    table of my m., 194:27
    tablet a gift of M., 76:11
    their very m. is fair, 270:9
    thoughts to m. dear, 379:2
    throng into my m., 252:24
    'tis in my m. locked, 194:2
    to m. nothing really lost, 727:20
    ventricle of m., 168:32
    vibrates in m., 409:10
    viol of her m., 639:5
    warder of the brain, 213:14
    while m. holds a seat, 194:27
    wit at expense of m., 290:24
Memory's, confusing beams from m.
    lamp, 709:17
Men, a few honest m., 246:24
    about me that are fat, 187:24
    above reach of ordinary m., 374:10
    adversity test of strong m., 103:4
    all are m. condemned, 321:17
    all honorable m., 188:29
    all m. and women had become gro-
    tesques, 630:20
    all m. are liars, 19:18

Men (*continued*)
    all m. be free, 451:1
    all m. born are my brothers, 488:18
    all m. born free, 255:9
    all m. created equal, 343:2, 450:2
    all m. liable to error, 277:8
    all m. make faults, 220:21
    all m. of a size, 432:22
    all m. would be tyrants, 286:1,
    347:1
    all sorts and conditions of m., 49:3
    all the king's m., 790:13
    all the same, 626:20
    and boys thick as hasty pudding,
    778:*n*4
    and women affirm brotherhood,
    722:11
    and women created equal, 475:5
    and women liberate, 691:1
    and women merely players, 191:3
    animals infuse into trunks of m.,
    181:17
    April when they woo, 192:4
    are men, 206:18
    are m. born to go down like this,
    690:22
    are my teachers, 301:*n*5
    are products reflections, 564:7
    are quick to flare up, 53:13
    are where they are, 478:29
    arm and burgonet of m., 217:6
    as in a theater eyes of m., 172:13
    ask for everything, 746:19
    at point of death, 176:16
    attend m. and not women, 76:9
    bad cause bad means bad m.,
    340:25
    be read as books too much, 300:10
    beacons of wise m., 505:14
    become brothers, 364:13
    becoming m. we wanted to marry,
    767:4
    below and saints above, 377:25
    best m. molded of faults, 205:6
    best of m., 217:13
    best of m. that e'er wore earth,
    227:19
    black m. are pearls, 168:9
    blaspheme what they do not know,
    271:9
    bodies of unburied m., 237:13
    books like m., 288:13
    boys and girls level with m., 218:8
    brave m. and worthy patriots,
    254:20
    brave m. brave from the first,
    249:10
    brave m. lived before Agamemnon,
    97:1
    brave m. living and dead, 450:2
    busy haunts of m., 410:15
    busy hum of m., 251:17
    by nature desire knowledge, 77:21
    by nature equally free, 327:1
    call up your m., 379:27
    capable of wickedness, 573:14
    captain of m. of death, 272:32
    capture of m. by women, 463:*n*1
    cause or m. of Emerald Isle, 354:1
    cheerful ways of m., 257:24

Men (*continued*)

children of M. full of wiles, 73:11
Christian m. control property interests, 544:8
circumstances rule m., 70:9
cities of m. and manners, 455:1
condemn m. because few, 479:1
Constitution for all m., 474:21
created different, 727:9
created free equal true and misleading, 727:9
creatures that once were m., 605:9
creep not walk, 443:7
crowd of common m., 246:22
cunning m. pass for wise, 159:23
darling of m. and gods, 89:2
day is for honest m., 68:25
dead m. rise up never, 534:15
dead m. tell no tales, 274:23
deal with m. as equals, 767:3
Death that feeds on m., 222:12
decay, 329:8
deceivers ever, 186:28
decent easy m., 340:10
desire the good, 78:18
Destiny with M. for Pieces plays, 445:23
determine gods dispose, 235:*n*1
die like m., 18:4
die to make m. free, 484:7
died as m. before their bodies died, 721:3
died to make m. holy, 484:7
difference between m. and women, 707:18
difference of forty thousand m., 371:8
dine with some m., 627:18
disbelief in great m., 412:31
disease of old m. avarice, 236:20
disgrace labor, 501:16
done with roofs and m., 583:18
doors for m. to take their exits, 237:17
duration of great sentiments makes great m., 552:14
dying m. enforce attention, 171:5
eat hogs, 639:2
eat m. like air, 764:13
Education is Making M., 516:*n*1
eight or nine elderly m., 590:10
elevate condition of m., 449:8
England is purgatory of m., 154:18
equal right of m. and women, 655:23
evil m. do lives after them, 188:28
evils draw m. together, 78:29
fair women and brave m., 399:21
fallible m. governed by bad passions, 343:7
fear of little m., 504:2
feared witches, 568:15
fell out knew not why, 262:16
fifteen m. on Dead Man's Chest, 561:1
Filipinos our fellow-m., 549:18
filthy dirty pigs, 626:20
finds too late m. betray, 328:29
first subjects afterward, 477:8
fishers of m., 32:37

Men (*continued*)

flourish only for a moment, 54:8
foolery wise m. have, 189:32
foolish m. who accuse a woman, 284:7
fools laugh at m. of sense, 283:15
foot of unfamiliar m., 499:15
forty thousand m., 788:6
free m. free speech, 780:14
gear of foreign dead m., 671:13
get there first with most m., 496:16
given to m. of middle age, 223:6
God justifiable to m., 261:12
God made mad, 618:17
God these old m., 67:26
God wrongs not m., 116:9
gods fashioned by m., 588:16
gods in likeness of m., 41:11
goeth on to meet the armed m., 15:16
good m. and true, 186:35
good m. eat that they may live, 70:23
good m. to do nothing, 332:30
good will to m., 462:2
good will toward m., 38:4
government of laws not m., 337:18
great city greatest m. women, 490:5
great m. are not always wise, 14:47
great m. can't be ruled, 717:10
great m. contending with adversity, 235:2
great m. not boasters, 432:30
great m. not scholars, 447:15
great m. texts of Revelation, 412:5
grow into likeness of bad m., 76:13
hanged that horses may not be stolen, 280:1
hangin' m. and women, 779:11
happiest of all m., 306:10
happy breed of m., 171:9
harmony between m. and land, 662:3
hate in white m., 755:10
have died from time to time, 192:2
have lost their reason, 189:2
have their price, 295:4
heard old old m. say, 595:16
heart of oak our m., 323:18
heaven that leads m. to hell, 222:7
His ways with m., 459:22
history biography of great m., 412:32
hit only what they aim at, 478:7
hollow m., 669:8, 669:9
homely m. charmed women, 586:1
honor all m., 46:23
if all m. were just, 74:3
if m. are destroyed, 65:7
if m. could get pregnant, 739:17
if m. like that wise bird, 554:18
in catalogue ye go for m., 214:21
in m. we various passions find, 300:16
inflation few m. remit, 739:14
is there view for enlisted m., 749:5
keeping m. off keep them on, 297:14
knocking around with m., 349:4
know so little of men, 605:1

Men (*continued*)

labels that give name to event, 510:5
Lake Wobegon where m. are good-looking, 772:5
lead lives of quiet desperation, 477:32
let us die like m., 444:2
let us praise famous m., 32:13
let your light shine before m., 33:3
like m. undergo fatigue, 341:1
like satyrs grazing, 162:10
little group of willful m., 572:9
live as m. not ostriches, 650:5
live at level of great m., 565:3
lived like fishes, 219:*n*6
lives of great m. remind us, 440:17
lodging place of wayfaring m., 28:22
looks quite through deeds of m., 187:25
love is waster of rich m., 66:18
made m. and not made them well, 197:1
made spectacle to m., 42:35
make the city, 72:10
man that died for m., 536:12
masters of their fates, 187:22
may come men may go, 458:16
may read strange matters, 213:2
measures not m., 304:17, 329:6
melancholy m. eat no beans, 234:15
melancholy m. most witty, 235:1
men's m., 484:2
merriest when from home, 184:26
merry m. all, 785:4
mice and m., 361:6
mighty m. of valor, 10:33
mighty m. which were of old, 7:15
mocks married m., 169:12
moon m. and barking hounds, 690:20
more fortunate than mothers, 559:6
more lonely among m., 478:26
more m. killed by overwork, 591:8
most m. are like children, 651:9
mountains are fountains of m., 537:16
must be decided, 79:21
must endure their going, 211:12
must work women weep, 484:11
my man of m., 217:9
natives of rain rainy m., 638:17
naturally in two parties, 345:4
need of world of m., 465:2
never be beloved by m., 359:8
no common m., 432:22
no compacts between lions and m., 52:22
no country for old m., 597:7
no two m. cannot be distinguished, 104:8
no worse husband than best of m., 217:13
nor blame the writings but the m., 299:1
not ashamed of age, 749:11
not descended from fearful m., 724:7

Men (*continued*)
  wise m. cast down rods, 8:32
  wise m. from the east, 32:23
  wise m. in great struggle, 339:7
  wise m. know art of eating, 354:13
  wise m. of Gotham, 789:10
  wise m. profit more from fools, 85:4
  wise m. refrain to meddle, 137:14
  wise m. shun mistakes of fools, 85:4
  wise m. speak fools decide, 56:3
  wish m. everywhere free, 449:12
  with firebrand in hand, 134:9
  with knives in brains, 433:4
  with mothers and wives, 423:7
  with muckrakes indispensable, 576:4
  with sisters dear, 423:7
  women and clergymen, 380:9
  women better or worse than m., 283:18
  women foolish to match m., 483:17
  women wiser than m., 650:13
  won by m. with courage, 72:7
  wonder m. trust themselves with m., 211:24
  words are women deeds m., 244:40
  words children of many m., 706:5
  working m. of all countries unite, 482:7
  worth a thousand m., 379:1
  would be angels, 159:n7
  write what m. do not what they ought, 158:10
  ye are brothers ye are m., 389:6
  ye m. of Athens, 41:15
  ye shall die like m., 18:4
  you are m. of stones, 211:17
  young m. need stiffening, 570:5
  young m. regarding elders senile, 535:18
  young m. shall see visions, 29:32
  young m. think it is, 580:6
  young m. think old m. fools, 157:3
  youngsters read m. understand, 150:18
Mena, di qua di là di giù di su li m., 125:n6
Menace, accents of m. alien to air, 528:16
  atomic energy a m., 636:4
Menaces, insolent m. of villains, 339:3
Mend it or be rid on 't, 214:23
  knock breathe seek to m., 230:26
  never made for man to m., 276:19
  the heart, 299:19
  we dreamed to m., 597:15
  your speech a little, 208:21
Mendacities, better m., 659:7
Mendax, splendide m., 96:n15
Mended, all is m., 174:13
  least said soonest m., 149:n13
  old houses m., 291:24
Mene Mene Tekel Upharsin, 29:16
Menny, done because we are too m., 540:7
Men's, all m. good, 454:23
  athwart m. noses as asleep, 174:20
  business and bosoms, 159:1

Men's (*continued*)
  evil manners live in brass, 226:5
  faiths wafer-cakes, 185:2
  fortune and m. eyes, 220:15
  history in all m. lives, 184:2
  it's m. lives, 379:8
  judgments parcel of their fortunes, 217:26
  men, 484:2
  music of m. lives, 172:14
  old m. heads are bare, 679:1
  old m. lies, 659:8
  one man's will all m. misery, 155:4
  poor m. cottages palaces, 179:27
  sweat of other m. faces, 450:10
  talk not of other m. lives, 31:38
  times that try m. souls, 340:22
  wives young m. mistresses, 159:12
Mens sana in corpore sano, 109:n8
Mensch, es irrt der M., 350:n2
  Studium der Menschheit ist der M., 301:n5
Menschen, alle M. werden Bruder, 364:n3
Menschheit, Studium der M. ist der Mensch, 301:n5
Mensonges, choses que je conte sont m., 675:n5
Mental excellence a splendid possession, 91:21
  fight, 359:17
  have certain m. characteristics, 574:12
  medicine for m. disorders, 692:3
  never influences physical, 473:9
  obesity m. state, 710:16
  obscure unconscious m. processes, 569:2
  psychoanalysis is m. illness, 626:7
  specialists in m. disease, 652:12
  suffering in Hanover Square, 524:17
Mentality, origin of modern m., 704:2
Mention, Kremlin's mountaineer get m., 681:7
  making m. of thee always, 45:32
Mentioned, better damned than m. not, 341:17
Mépris, silence seul est le souverain m., 436:n2
Mer allée avec le soleil, 565:n13
  la m. toujours recommencée, 613:n4
Mercator's North Poles and Equators, 519:20
Mercedes-Benz, Lord buy me M., 773:6
Mercenary, followed m. calling, 580:1
  slavish m., 336:13
Merces, ipsa quidem virtus sibimet pulcherrima m., 245:n2
Merchandise, not an house of m., 39:42
Merchant, Mighty M. sneered, 512:19
  overpolite to customers, 393:8
Merchantman, monarchy is a m., 360:7
Merchants are princes, 26:23
  have no country, 344:16
Merci, La Belle Dame sans M., 417:7

Mercies, all occasions invite his m., 231:10
  tender m. of the wicked are cruel, 21:12
Merciful, a God gracious and m., 13:23
  and Mighty, 395:21
  as constant, 692:1
  be m. to broken reed, 158:16
  blessed are the m., 33:1
  give be m., 50:19
  God be m. to this drinker, 122:14
  most m. God, 116:1
  most m. thing in world, 679:6
  powers, 213:18
  to me a fool, 544:4
  to me a sinner, 39:9
Merciless, loving rapid m., 743:4
  Nature a m. stepmother, 104:2
Mercury, station like herald M., 197:30
  words of M. are harsh, 169:15
Mercy and truth are met together, 18:8
  assaults m. itself, 224:29
  betwixt stirrup and ground, 151:29
  do justly and love m., 29:38
  doing justice loving m., 341:9
  full of compassion and m., 30:33
  God all m. is God unjust, 296:15
  goodness and m. shall follow me, 16:17
  ha no I cry her m., 291:10
  hae m. o' my soul Lord God, 504:14
  half so good a grace as m., 204:1
  hand folks to God's m., 483:16
  has a human heart, 356:13
  have m. on us, 48:9
  his m. endureth for ever, 13:15
  his m. is everlasting, 18:22
  how can he m. have, 153:22
  I asked and found, 151:29
  I desired m., 29:26
  is above sceptered sway, 181:19
  leaving m. to heaven, 311:23
  Lord have m. on parents, 116:16
  Lord have m. on us, 48:7, 227:2
  no more could be, 358:10
  nobility's true badge, 167:7
  not m. unto others show, 153:22
  nothing emboldens sin as m., 212:3
  of a rude stream, 225:16
  of his means, 737:16
  on my poor people, 147:9
  on such as we, 592:3
  on Thy People Lord, 593:4
  peace on earth m. mild, 312:17
  Pity Peace and Love, 356:12
  quality of m. not strained, 181:19
  render the deeds of m., 181:19
  seasons justice, 181:19
  show no m. ourselves, 483:16
  shut gates of m., 322:16
  so great is his m., 19:1
  stood at m. of the sun, 562:18
  temper justice with m., 260:13
  tender m. of God, 38:1
  they shall obtain m., 33:1
  to forgive, 275:15

Mercy *(continued)*
to myself I cried, 373:18
unto them that love me, 9:10
we do pray for m., 181:19
where M. Love and Pity dwell,
  356:14
wound with m. round, 551:9
Merde le mot de Cambronne, 371:n7
Mere, honor a m. scutcheon, 178:33
Mère des souvenirs, 494:n4
Meredith prose Browning, 566:8
Meretricious, vast vulgar m. beauty,
  694:9
Meridian, in England under any m.,
  248:17
  of my glory, 225:14
  Zones and M. Lines, 519:20
Meridians reel thy purpose, 701:4
Merit, by m. raised to that bad emi-
    nence, 256:23
  handsomely allowed, 317:24
  makes his cook his m., 269:12
  makes his way, 225:2
  of perpetuity, 249:1
  oft got without m., 206:21
  patient m. takes, 196:10
  purchased by m. of wearer, 180:27
  to particularize is m., 358:15
  unassisted m., 313:n5
  whoever rescues single life earns m.,
    115:17
Merits, goodness result of one's own
    m., 121:11
  or faults to scan, 329:13
  seek his m. to disclose, 322:24
Merlin had strange laugh, 733:4
  I am M., 460:10
Mermaid on dolphin's back, 173:5
  Tavern, 416:12
  what things done at the M., 238:11
Mermaids, heard the m. singing,
    667:19
  singing, 228:5
Merrier man never spent talk withal,
    168:23
  the more the m., 142:22
Merriest, maddest m. day, 454:4
  when they are from home, 184:26
Merrily did we drop, 380:29
  die all die m., 178:24
  fly after summer m., 224:25
  hent the stile-a, 223:4
  let him drink m., 228:1
  shall I live now, 224:25
Merriment, flashes of m., 199:8
  innocent m., 531:4
Merry, all their wars m., 618:17
  as cricket, 141:26
  as day is long, 186:17
  as marriage bell, 399:21
  eat drink be m., 24:17, 38:28
  God rest you m. gentlemen, 778:8
  good to be m. and wise, 140:16
  gude to be m. and wise, 779:20
  guid to be m. and wise, 364:4
  he that is of a m. heart, 21:26
  heart doeth good, 21:36
  heart goes all the day, 223:4
  heart maketh cheerful countenance,
    21:25

Merry *(continued)*
I am not m., 206:7
if to be old and m. be sin, 177:31
keep our Christmas m. still, 378:11
led m. m. lives, 583:11
Margaret, 135:23
may'st hear the m. din, 380:27
measure, 409:16
men all, 785:4
men at point of death m., 176:16
merry lives, 583:11
merry merry roundelay, 156:13
monarch scandalous and poor,
  283:23
month of May, 233:10
never m. when hear sweet music,
  182:9
obstinate pliant m. morose, 106:24
old soul, 788:5
playing of m. organ, 778:9
rather have fool make me m.,
  191:27
small cheer makes m. feast, 166:25
three m. boys are we, 236:5
'tis m. in hall, 144:9
turn his m. note, 190:18
tu-who a m. note, 169:13
very m. dancing drinking, 276:20
wanderer of the night, 173:2
we were very m., 684:3
wine maketh m., 24:21
wives may be m., 183:6
yarn from fellow rover, 633:16
Merryman, Doctor M., 290:13
  moping mum, 531:14
Meshach, Shadrach M. and Abednego,
    29:13
Meshes, though its m. are wide, 58:3
Mess, awful wretched m. of life,
    718:21
  Benjamin's m., 8:9
  cleanin' up whole m. of 'em, 678:4
  let other people clean up m., 694:11
  of imprecision of feeling, 671:9
Message, ask me to take m. to Albert,
    435:20
  knowing how to reply to m., 5:10
  many a m. from skies, 362:23
  medium is m., 730:3
  messenger makes m. clear, 116:12
  to Garcia, 570:5
Messed up life for nothing, 673:1
Messenger, bisy lark m. of day,
    130:12
  don't shoot the m., 66:n5
  has God sent a mortal as m.,
    116:19
  I will send my m., 30:8
  with language of his folk, 116:12
Messenger-boy Presidency, 744:10
Messengers, bade m. ride forth,
    425:13
Messiah come only when no longer
    necessary, 651:19
Messing about in boats, 578:16
Met, day and way we m., 534:17
  dearest foe in heaven, 193:14
  guests are m., 380:27
  hail fellow well m., 290:20
  lovely monster, 716:15

Met *(continued)*
man who wasn't there, 630:2
me in evil hour, 361:19
mercy and truth are m. together,
  18:8
never m. one I didn't like, 638:7
never m. or never parted, 362:11
no sooner m. but looked, 192:10
part of all I have m., 455:1
true when you m. her, 228:7
we have m. enemy, 398:1
you not with my true Love, 152:9
Metal, as m. keeps fragrance, 625:10
  manual on uses of new m., 757:16
  no use of m., 224:4
  of man tested, 485:24
  sonorous m. blowing, 256:13
  there on shining m., 721:2
Metals, keys of m. twain, 254:1
Metamorphosis separated me from
    day before, 616:19
Metaphor fertile power, 653:20
  Holocaust m. for century, 764:7
  mistaking m. for proof, 613:14
Metaphysical, world not m. brothel
    for emotions, 716:12
Mete and dole laws, 454:24
  with what measure ye m., 34:3
Meteor flag of England, 389:2
  misled by fancy's m. ray, 361:15
  of ocean air, 447:3
  poem is m., 640:21
  streamed like a m., 256:n1
  streaming to the wind, 256:12
Meter ballad-mongers, 178:4
  electrical energy too cheap to m.,
    695:21
  prose opposed to m., 383:18
Meter-making, not meters but m.,
    432:15
Method by which unconscious studied,
    569:20
  for choosing presidential nominee,
    655:16
  in man's wickedness, 238:15
  invention of m. of invention, 584:10
  madness yet m. in't, 195:21
  new psychoanalytic m. irreplaceable,
    569:2
  of drawing up indictment, 331:16
  of making a fortune, 323:13
  of scientific investigation, 505:4
  take m. and try it, 648:15
  what pragmatic m. means, 546:18
  which rejects revenge, 761:4
Methods, know my m. Watson,
    577:22
  sociology with greatest number of
    m., 565:7
Methought I heard one calling Child,
    243:18
  I saw late espoused saint, 255:16
  I saw the grave, 152:17
Methuselah, days of M., 7:13
Meticulous, politic cautious and m.,
    667:17
Métier, c'est son m., 420:13
  mon m. et mon art c'est vivre,
    146:n1

Metternich, Pope Czar M. Guizot,
481:14

Mettle enough to kill care, 187:11
grasp it like a man of m., 297:23
lad of m. a good boy, 177:19

Metuant, oderint dum m., 86:*n*12

Meum est propositum in taberna
mori, 122:*n*5

Meurs, je m. de soif auprès de la fontaine, 132:*n*10

Meurt, la Garde m. mais ne se rend
pas, 371:*n*7

Mew, cat m. and dog have day,
199:18
kitten and cry m., 178:4

Me-wards, to m. your affection's
strong, 241:6

Mewing her mighty youth, 255:2

Mewling and puking, 191:3

Mexico, a Virgil at M., 323:23
poor M. so far from God so close
to U.S., 511:10

Micawber's favorite expression,
470:23

Mice and men, 361:6
and rats and such small deer, 210:9
cat catches m. good cat, 712:17
cat in gloves catches no m., 310:5
desert building about to fall, 104:10
fishermen appear like m., 210:27
like little m. stole in and out, 262:5
three blind m., 788:2

Michael and his angels fought, 47:27
face like hoosier M. Angelo, 491:11
row the boat ashore, 794:15

Michelangelo, Italy produced M. Leonardo, 739:5
talking of M., 667:10

Miching mallecho, 197:9

Mickle, every little makes a m.,
150:28

Microcosm and macrocosm atoned,
504:17
heart sun of their m., 235:25
of public school, 434:14

Microscope begins where telescope
ends, 428:5

Microscopes of the press, 590:10

Microscopy chemistry mathematics,
681:13

Midday, kindling eyes at m. beam,
255:2
sweat, 242:7

Middle age time of improving, 262:11
beware the m. mind, 660:20
class best political community,
78:22
class in America the nation, 501:2
class the safety of England, 464:2
dead vast and m. of night, 193:18
enchantments of M. Age, 499:10
flowers of m. summer men of m.
age, 223:6
in politics m. way none at all, 338:2
in the m. be sparing, 54:28
isthmus of a m. state, 301:13
law of excluded m., 748:10
of the night, 518:23
ones of m. class who left home,
744:12

Middle (*continued*)
safest in the m., 101:21
son of m. border, 583:1
station fewest disasters, 286:3
vulgarizing m. class, 500:23
wheel in the m. of a wheel, 29:5
whole has beginning m. and end,
78:32
wives companions for m. age,
159:2

Middle-aged build woodshed, 477:1
prosperity adversity, 700:3

Middlesex, acre in M., 425:5
village and farm, 442:13

Midnight, cease upon the m., 415:16
Cerberus and blackest M., 251:6
clear, 462:2
deep m. lair made, 378:17
dreary, 452:13
Good Morning M. coming Home,
512:10
gravity out of bed at m., 177:27
hags, 215:17
heard chimes at m., 184:4
hour's sleep before m., 245:2
iron tongue of m., 174:12
it is m. and time passes, 56:8
moan upon m. hours, 416:8
mournful m. hours, 349:7
Ninth-month m., 490:8
oil, 242:7, 297:6
on Emperor's pavement, 598:12
once upon m. dreary, 452:13
owl songs or m. blast, 403:19
ride of Paul Revere, 442:12
shout and revelry, 252:20
strikes and hastens, 580:5
through m. streets, 358:9
time cease and m. never come,
162:22
train whining low, 753:5
troubled m. and noon's repose,
668:5
year's m., 229:7

Midshipmite, bo'sun tight and m.,
528:22

Midst, him first last m., 259:8
I am in m. of eternity, 556:21
I am in the m. of them, 35:33
in m. of life we are in death, 50:7
in the m. of things, 98:12
into the m. of the sea upon dry
ground, 9:1
stood in m. of Jordan, 10:32

Midsummer, gorgeous as sun at m.,
178:20
madness, 202:31
merry Margaret as m. flower,
135:23

Midwife, she is the fairies' m., 174:20

Midwifery, my m. like theirs, 76:9

Midwinter, bleak m., 515:10

Mien, monster of frightful m., 301:14
truth has such face and m., 275:13

Mieux, je vais de m. en m., 573:*n*4
le m. est l'ennemi du bien, 306:*n*9
tant pis et tant m., 320:35
tout est au m., 306:*n*3

Might, dear m. of him that walked,
254:6

Might (*continued*)
do it with thy m., 24:19
exceeds man's m., 200:21
half slumbering, 414:5
honest man's aboon his m., 363:22
is right, 123:5
It m. have been, 443:8
king's m. greater than human, 70:12
love the Lord with all thy m., 10:11
mighty man not glory in m., 28:23
not by m. nor by power, 30:1
of gods slow but sure, 69:2
of the Gentile, 401:16
protect us by thy m., 444:4
right makes m., 448:15
sadness of her m., 416:18
shining with all m., 518:23
spend her blood and m., 572:12
spirit of counsel and m., 26:10
to be man with thy m., 534:20

Might-have-been, name is M., 509:26

Mightier, cometh one m. than I, 37:17
make thee m. yet, 585:5
pen m. than sword, 428:22
than the noise of many waters,
18:18
than they in arms, 259:17

Mightiest in the mightiest, 181:19
Julius fell, 192:25

Mightily, lay m. in whirl of dust,
52:10
strive m. eat as friends, 167:20

Mighty above all things, 30:13
all proud and m. have, 307:14
all that m. heart lying still, 374:13
Caesar thou art m. yet, 189:25
dead, 307:18
each a m. voice, 376:16
eagle mewing her m. youth, 255:2
fortress is our God, 138:5
God who made thee m., 585:5
great and m. resolutions, 263:12
hand of m. man, 20:1
he that is slow to anger is better
than the m., 21:32
hear the m. crack, 292:3
how are the m. fallen, 12:1
I am m. world-destroying Time,
84:13
in the Scriptures, 41:20
lak' a rose, 574:3
law m. mightier necessity, 350:21
let m. babe alone, 264:19
little body m. heart, 184:28
look on my works ye M., 406:13
make m. ocean, 502:8
man not glory in might, 28:23
many and m. are they, 592:17
Marlowe's m. line, 322:19
maze not without plan, 301:1
men of valor, 10:33
men which were of old, 7:15
Merchant sneered, 512:19
Merciful and M., 395:21
minds of old, 386:15
name shall be called the m. God,
26:8
O m. Caesar, 188:19
pain to love, 267:2
poets in misery dead, 374:11

Mighty (*continued*)
put down the m., 37:42
scourge of war, 450:11
so m. a Redeemer, 48:12
some have called thee m., 230:22
sound of m. wind, 40:44
states characterless, 200:22
things from small beginnings grow, 273:10
true free Russian speech, 482:20
weak and m. Russia, 496:20
weak things to confound m., 42:29
Mighty One, splendor of M. Krishna, 84:12
Mignonne allons voir si la rose, 144:*n*4
Migrate, come Muse m. from Greece, 490:6
Migration of the soul, 74:16
Migratory, unperplexed like m. birds, 630:7
Mild and magnificent eye, 464:23
gentle Jesus meek and m., 312:15
grateful evening m., 258:22
he is meek he is m., 356:7
Mary was mother m., 479:19
peace on earth mercy m., 312:17
Milder fate than tyranny is death, 63:16
term to governments, 343:13
Mildewed day in August, 742:12
silo, 631:2
Mildness, ethereal m. come, 308:3
Mile, crooked m., 791:11
every m. two in winter, 245:6
lesson of Three M. Island, 784:13
miss as good as m., 379:25
Mile-a, your sad tires in a m., 223:4
Miles around wonder grew, 579:2
of fertile ground, 382:19
sed m. sed pro patria, 586:13
see it lap the M., 512:17
six m. from earth, 735:21
three thousand m. and died, 485:22
to go before I sleep, 623:18
twelve m. from a lemon, 380:10
Milestones, counting m. count on, 446:27
road to Hell without m., 700:1
Milieu, un m. entre rien et tout, 270:*n*3
Milishy, newspaper commmands m., 603:12
Militaristic stairway, 761:7
Military, civilian control of m., 655:18
establishment, 678:17
man, 185:8
mind, 601:13
no adequate m. defense, 655:8
now close m. career fade away, 642:5
operation involves deception, 80:18
risks sacrifices of m. encounter, 713:20
war too serious for m., 354:9
Military-industrial complex, 678:17
Militia, newspaper commmands m., 603:12
place dependence upon m., 336:16
well-regulated m. necessary, 346:12

Milk, adversity's sweet m. philosophy, 176:3
and honey blessed, 482:10
Carnation M. best in land, 784:4
comes frozen home in pail, 169:13
find trout in m., 476:25
gin was mother's m. to her, 571:22
in the pan, 431:12
land flowing with m. and honey, 8:26
likely to be watered, 525:9
my ewes and weep, 223:13
of human kindness, 212:28
of Paradise, 382:25
skim m. masquerades as cream, 529:8
sweet m. of concord, 215:27
take my m. for gall, 212:29
takes m. cheaper than keep cow, 525:9
white curd of ass's m., 302:14
Milked cow with crumpled horn, 792:24
Milking, going a-m. sir she said, 790:6
lilting as she went, 327:11
time of m., 670:21
Milks, love babe that m. me, 213:12
Milk-white, before m. now purple, 173:6
Hens of Dorking, 472:10
Milky, all the m. sky, 594:23
over Sado the M. Way, 282:16
solar walk or m. way, 301:7
twinkle on m. way, 375:20
Way sister in whiteness, 641:9
Mill, at the m. with slaves, 261:6
cannot grind with water that's past, 244:13
does m. make water run, 603:1
God's m. grinds slow, 244:38
golf links so near m., 631:1
John Stuart M., 627:19
much water goeth by m., 142:19
of the mind, 599:10
of truism, 431:15
Milldams o' Binnorie, 785:13
Mille, plus de souvenirs que si m. ans, 494:*n*6
Millennial, give vent to m. anger, 747:1
Millennium, war usher in new m., 676:11
Miller, honest m. hath golden thumb, 130:*n*1
knoweth not of water, 142:19
sees not all the water, 142:*n*11
Stuhldreher M. Crowley Layden, 643:15
there was a jolly m., 338:18
Milliard-headed throng, 300:*n*1
Milliner, perfumed like a m., 177:2
Million, bought St. Louis for six m. dollars, 526:15
earth's five m. years old, 763:1
golden birds, 565:16
high man aiming at m., 465:24
make that thousand up a m., 241:8
multitude of m. divided by m., 716:13
play pleased not the m., 196:1

Million (*continued*)
second m., 319:4
Millionaire, I am a M. that is my religion, 571:13
right of m. to millions, 525:12
ruined m., 671:7
Millions, fate of unborn m., 336:14
for defense, 367:13
of Bubbles like us, 445:22
of debt, 331:26
of spiritual creatures, 258:23
of tongues record, 399:24
one murder made villain m. a hero, 336:2
ready saddled and bridled, 425:21
right of millionaire to m., 525:12
tear-wrung m., 620:*n*1
there's m. in it, 525:23
we mortal m. live alone, 498:3
with m. under his care, 4:11
yearly multiplying m., 473:15
yet unborn, 325:4
Millionth, encounter for m. time, 647:11
Mills, dark Satanic m., 359:17
of God grind slowly, 247:15
Millstone hanged about neck, 39:4
hard as a piece of nether m., 15:23
look through a m., 155:16
Milquetoast, Caspar M., 660:9
Milton aggravated dissociation, 672:14
attracts into unity of ideal, 384:16
faith hold which M. held, 375:1
function as M., 642:16
malt does more than M., 579:15
mute inglorious M., 322:14
reason M. wrote in fetters, 357:2
test of M. to function as M., 642:16
thou shouldst be living, 374:19
was for us, 464:24
Miltonic, balanced and M. style, 551:18
Milton's wormwood words, 254:*n*3
Miltons, no mute inglorious M., 642:16
Miltown, tamed by M., 743:2
Mimic motion made cry, 639:7
Mimics, we are the m., 639:24
Mimsy were borogoves, 518:15
Mince, not to m. the matter, 148:15
this matter, 206:19
Mincing poetry, 178:5
walking and m. as they go, 25:35
Mind, a certain unsoundness of m., 424:14
absence of m. we have borne, 388:10
accurate m. overtasked, 447:7
acts of m. itself, 384:18
all comes from the m., 64:18
allus on yer m., 644:16
and soul according, 457:4
as a dead man out of m., 16:26
as m. pitched ear pleased, 335:11
aspire to higher things, 155:28
aware of own rectitude, 93:23
balloon of the m., 596:15
beauty exists in m., 318:12
beauty momentary in m., 639:4
become aware of itself, 433:4

Mind (*continued*)

beholding beauty with eye of m., 74:13

beings of m. are not of clay, 400:12

benevolence is man's m., 79:28

best work the human m., 363:1

beware the middle m., 660:20

blessed man who possesses keen m., 73:25

block of wax, 76:11

body filled and vacant m., 185:19

bonds only in m., 613:1

breaks chains from every m., 357:19

bright child of m., 689:10

celestial Wisdom calms m., 313:24

chance favors prepared m., 502:4

changeful m. of mortals, 64:16

characteristics of vigorous m., 313:25

chaste breast quiet m., 267:14

clap padlock on her m., 287:19

clear your m. of cant, 317:30

clothed and in right m., 37:26

companion none like unto m., 143:11

complicated state of m., 529:17

concentrates his m. wonderfully, 317:1

conscious m. trained like parrot, 628:14

contemplate itself from without, 558:10

content, 157:19

courage gaiety quiet m., 562:9

creations of m. be blessing, 635:13

dagger of the m., 213:20

daylight in the m., 293:6

disdaining littlenesses, 76:10

disease experience of mortal m., 495:22

diseased always illusion, 473:9

distressed in m. body or estate, 49:4

dupe of the heart, 265:16

education forms common m., 300:12

employ m. to rule, 91:20

enabled to number worlds, 420:17

essay a loose sally of m., 314:2

exercises his m. with suffering, 80:3

extract laws from nature, 646:6

eye see for hand not m., 477:26

face so pleased my m., 777:4

face the mirror of the m., 114:2

fanatic can't change m., 622:9

farewell the tranquil m., 207:8

feed this m. of ours, 372:19

fiery particle, 403:13

first destroys their m., 69:*n*11

first from m. banish understanding, 69:*n*11

fool uttereth all his m., 23:9

free m. guards rights, 393:2

free play of m., 499:8

freedom of m., 253:7

frugal m., 334:22

gentle m. by gentle deeds, 153:23

gentle sensitive m., 596:16

gentleness of spirit serenity of m., 245:*n*3

golden m. stoops not, 180:22

Mind (*continued*)

good in which m. at rest, 126:16

good m. possesses kingdom, 103:14

grateful m. by owing owes not, 258:4

great fortitude of m., 315:12

greatest powers of m., 387:10

grief develops m., 613:4

had such burdens on m., 597:16

happy alchemy of m., 307:8

has mountains cliffs, 551:14

has thousand eyes, 563:2

he that wants anger hath maimed m., 250:17

heart and m. of America, 721:11

heavy with useless experience, 762:2

her m. to be attached like garden, 548:10

his eyes are in his m., 172:*n*2

his own business, 149:31

household in oneness of m., 53:10

human m. invents Puss-in-Boots, 707:12

I am not in perfect m., 211:10

idle m. knows not what it wants, 84:20

if find answer know m. of God, 772:2

if I am to know may not m., 656:7

if no hatred in m., 597:4

impatient, 193:4

impressions of free m., 600:7

in adversity keep an even m., 96:5

in another Zeus puts a good m., 52:1

in m. of man a motion, 373:5

in my m. of mankind, 775:16

in purest play like bat, 749:17

in the m. ever burning, 152:10

inability of m. to correlate, 679:6

inaction saps vigor of m., 135:6

Indian whose untutored m., 301:7

is an aviary, 76:12

is an enchanting thing, 665:2

is its own place, 256:5

is stayed on thee, 26:28

keep m. steady on keel, 486:7

know what going on in baby's m., 695:18

knowledge of unconscious activities of m., 569:3

known m. of the Lord, 42:11

labyrinthine ways of m., 581:4

last infirmity of noble m., 253:20

laugh that spoke vacant m., 329:11

let dauntless m. still ride, 164:22

let your m. alone, 690:11

leveling rancorous m., 598:7

live on little with contented m., 90:9

lives on the Heart, 265:*n*1

look clean through the m., 155:16

love looks with the m., 172:21

love Lord with all thy m., 36:1

loyal nature noble m., 459:19

makes body rich, 167:31

man that has m. and knows it, 571:28

man's unconquerable m., 374:18

Mind (*continued*)

man's village is his peace of m., 745:20

marble index of a m., 373:10

march of human m. slow, 331:18

Marxism product of bourgeois m., 653:24

measure my mind against Shakespeare's, 571:14

military m., 601:13

mill of the m., 599:10

mingles with whole frame, 94:13

minister to m. diseased, 216:10

mirror in every m., 314:21

mode of working of human m., 505:4

moldering like wedding-cake, 762:2

movement so wandering as that of m., 145:22

moves upon silence, 599:18

my m. forbids to crave, 148:2

my m. is troubled, 201:5

narrowed his m., 330:10

nature of m. mortal, 90:3

nature with equal m., 497:22

never brought to m., 362:19

never m. did m. his grace, 163:4

noble m. here o'erthrown, 196:17

nobler in m. to suffer, 196:10

noblest frailty of m., 282:7

nor mouth had no nor m. expressed, 551:6

not body enough to cover m., 380:6

not enough to have good m., 246:14

not rival save with m., 689:18

not set m. for or against, 61:4

not sex-typed, 707:19

not to be changed, 256:5

not yet of Percy's m., 177:20

nothing so irrevocable as m., 588:2

of man becomes more beautiful, 373:14

of own beauty m. diseased, 400:24

old in body but never m., 88:10

old man's eagle m., 599:12

one just suited to our m., 389:7

openness of m., 500:25

opinionated m., 597:5

oppressions of body and m., 344:19

or body to prefer, 301:13

our concern be peace of m., 82:14

out of sight out of m., 132:17

over matter, 420:18

overset m. with reading, 557:13

painter's m. with viewer, 421:13

palm at end of m., 640:13

passion a fever in m., 283:2

passion wholly of m., 696:1

peace is a state of m., 277:15

persecutes the m., 275:14

persuaded in his m., 42:25

poem of act of m., 384:*n*3

poetry fine-spun from m. at peace, 102:2

power lies in m. and body, 91:20

presence of m., 86:8, 485:24

presence of m. in danger, 278:5

prudent m. can see room, 66:22

purify the m., 64:20

quiet m. cureth all, 235:23

Mind (*continued*)
quiet m. richer than crown, 157:18
raise and erect the m., 158:7
reading to m. as exercise to body, 291:31
reason ignis fatuus of m., 283:25
reclothe us in our rightful m., 443:17
reeled the m., 708:9
rest to m. cheerer of spirits, 245:17
seek for the lost m., 79:29
serene for contemplation, 292:*n*4
sound m. in sound body, 109:9, 277:10
sound of body and m., 95:30
spirit of a sound m., 45:26
Spirit of chainless M., 401:22
steal fire from m., 399:19
stops and steps of m., 669:16
stress on not changing m., 626:12
sublimity the echo of a noble m., 106:5
submitting things to desires of m., 158:7
subsoil of the m., 577:2
Sumner's m. contained itself, 535:23
suspicion haunts guilty m., 165:6
sweet to let m. unbend, 97:3
tact a kind of m.-reading, 557:16
terrible thing to waste, 784:11
that can hear music, 663:18
the music and the step, 778:21
the music breathing, 267:*n*5
time out of m., 148:17
to me a kingdom is, 148:2
to men man is m., 544:11
to m. shameful to heart beauty, 495:5
torpid in old age, 317:3
tranquil m. a m. well ordered, 111:1
troubled captain's m., 545:3
troubled m. be stranger, 242:15
tumors of a troubled m., 261:11
tyranny over m. of man, 344:4
universal frame without m., 159:18
unsuitability of m. and purpose, 470:41
untutored m., 301:7
vacant is mind distressed, 334:15
villain's m., 180:12
was still unpledged, 68:18
water never formed to m., 639:7
weakness of human m., 277:21
weapon of oppressor m. of oppressed, 774:1
wet m. and say something clever, 72:14
what I am taught, 394:4
what is M. No matter, 554:16
what pleased to call m., 426:6
where is love but in m., 407:9
wisdom entereth not in malicious m., 139:13
words are physicians of m. diseased, 63:5
your m. and you, 658:18
your m. tossing on ocean, 179:13
Minded what they were about, 320:6
Mind-forged manacles I hear, 358:8

Mindful of unhonored dead, 322:21
what is man that thou art m., 15:34
Mindfulness, right m., 65:1
Mindless action, 716:1
of its just honors, 377:13
Mind-reading, tact a kind of m., 557:16
Mind's adventures among masterpieces, 550:11
find the m. construction, 212:27
in my m. eye Horatio, 193:15
my m. not right, 743:6
opaque depths of m. folds, 145:22
putting m. eye in book, 748:10
the standard of man, 294:5
Minds, admiration only of weak m., 260:27
affect hearts and m., 682:9
all their m. transfigured, 174:2
all to have aspiring m., 161:21
balm of hurt m., 214:6
becks m. to fellowship, 414:11
best m. of my generation, 757:4
can heavenly m. yield, 93:11
comfortable m., 688:11
danger spur of great m., 157:14
great empire and little m., 331:24
greatest m. capable of greatest vices, 246:15
grow in spots, 546:20
hearts and m., 49:18
hobgoblin of little m., 431:23
home in m. of men, 72:7
injured by hunger and thirst, 80:5
innocent and quiet, 267:18
keep your hearts and m., 44:34
let our m. be bold, 568:17
little things affect little m., 434:28
lose self in other m., 388:6
made better by presence, 483:7
marriage of true m., 222:2
me o' departed joys, 362:8
mediocre m., 265:38
men of other m., 328:12
mighty m. of old, 386:15
naturally affirmative, 532:9
never do more than imperfectly reach, 693:16
O miserable m. of men, 89:14
of different generations, 658:12
of gods not changed, 53:4
only function when open, 545:4
paper-weight sat upon men's m., 601:17
reason freed men's m., 103:15
record of best m., 410:1
refuge of weak m., 305:9
religion of feeble m., 332:19
show how myths operate in m., 724:1
so many men so many m., 86:*n*9
speak m. of others to speak my own better, 145:15
stay our m. be staid, 625:1
steadiest m. to waver, 66:12
strongest m. world hears least, 376:19
themselves our m. impress, 372:19
to different m., 430:13

Minds (*continued*)
young men's m. are changeable, 51:12
Mine, because it is all mine, 762:16
every beast of the forest is m., 17:19
eyes have seen glory, 484:6
fatal words M. and Thine, 149:7
I am Tarzan I am yours you are m., 628:5
I'm going to get what's m., 774:10
lives ye led were m., 590:17
lovin' that man of m., 692:6
mother o' m., 591:11
she is m. for life, 746:11
was always that, 718:18
was ever grief like m., 243:5
what is yours is m., 83:7
what's m. is yours, 205:7
why shouldst thou have m., 262:7
will defend what's m., 152:*n*2
with my heart in it, 224:13
Mineral, information vegetable animal m., 529:12
Minerals, poisonous m. and that tree, 230:21
Minerva, owl of M. spreads wings, 372:5
Mingle blood with blood of children, 424:5
in one spirit meet m., 407:20
letters m. souls, 230:14
you that m. may, 237:9
Mingled, respect m. with surprise, 378:25
yarn good and ill, 203:15
Mingles, mind m. with whole frame, 94:13
with friendly bowl, 302:21
with her cares sweet bitterness, 91:9
Mingling, understanding distorts by m., 158:14
Minikin won't set fire to Thames, 324:5
Minimum guarantee of First Amendment, 661:8
searcher for fecund m., 638:16
Mining, titles of m. claims, 698:6
Minion, morning's m., 550:20
Minions of the moon, 176:25
Minister, King's First M., 621:13
patient must m. to himself, 216:10
thou flaming m., 208:10
to mind diseased, 216:10
Ministering angel shall my sister be, 199:12
angel thou, 378:14
Ministers, maketh m. flame of fire, 45:33
of grace defend us, 194:9
of Love, 383:3
you murdering m., 212:29
Ministers', my actions are my m., 273:4
Ministry, by the m. of the prophets, 29:30
frost performs secret m., 382:16
secret m. of frost, 382:17
Miniver Cheevy, 608:3
Minnehaha Laughing Water, 441:25

Minnesotan, young M. did heroic
   thing, 709:n3
Minnows, Triton of the m., 219:7
Minorities are qualified individuals,
   653:13
Minority always right, 508:9
   coercing into obedience m. groups,
      661:10
   elite m., 653:6
   majority deprive m., 449:3
   most vilified m. in history, 646:11
Minstrel Boy to war has gone, 391:17
   infirm and old, 377:19
   no M. raptures swell, 378:1
   wandering m. I, 530:18
Minstrel's, power of m. lyre, 612:6
Mint, tithe of m., 36:3
Mints, lavender m. savory marjoram,
   223:6
Minute, do good in m. particulars,
   359:23
   don't lose head to gain m., 782:23
   one m. with him, 654:12
   poor benefit of bewildering m.,
      234:1
   speak more in m., 175:22
   sucker born every m., 460:18
   too late, 182:29
Minutely organized particulars, 359:23
Minute's success pays failure, 468:16
   who buys a m. mirth, 166:38
Minutes, five m. with that man,
   330:n5
   hasten to their end, 220:26
   hours and m. dollars and cents,
      310:n3
   my thoughts are m., 172:15
   round earth in forty m., 173:7
   sixty diamond m., 419:4
   speak for ten m. need week, 572:15
   unless m. capons, 176:24
   what damned m. tells he, 206:31
   world-famous for fifteen m., 758:17
Minutiae of deeds never suggested,
   491:15
Minx, don't care whether a M. or
   Sphinx, 471:21
Miracle, cubic inch of space a m.,
   491:4
   every hour a m., 491:4
   man always prays for m., 482:19
   monstrosity and m. myself, 147:3
   mystery and authority, 495:11
   no testimony establish m., 318:14
   of rare device, 382:23
   r'ar back pass m., 678:3
Miracles, Age of M., 412:34
   are past, 203:13
   did Jesus in Cana, 39:40
   in Israel you must believe in m.,
      661:4
   laughed at, 603:8
   propitious accidents, 588:10
Miraculous, falsehood more m. than
   fact, 318:14
Mirage of social justice, 701:10
   works of unbelievers a m., 117:5
Mirages, city of m., 759:1
Miranda, remember inn M., 609:1
Mire, learning cast into m., 332:17

Mire (continued)
   ne'er left man i' m., 211:25
   rode him through m., 792:9
Mirror, best m. an old friend, 244:21
   cracked from side to side, 454:16
   critical m. of culture, 717:18
   face the m. of the mind, 114:2
   hold m. up to nature, 196:23
   in every mind, 314:21
   look into lives as into m., 86:14
   man's manners a m., 351:8
   novel a m. that strolls along high-
      way, 396:16
   of all courtesy, 225:5
   of alle curteisye, 130:31
   speech a m. of soul, 100:25
   that reflects candle, 586:18
   thou glorious m., 401:2
   understanding is false m., 158:14
   you who dirty the m., 284:8
Mirroring, windborne m. soul, 497:18
Mirrors, city of m., 759:1
   of shadows futurity casts, 410:2
   should reflect, 675:19
Mirth admit of thy crew, 251:11
   and fun fast furious, 363:8
   as does not make ashamed, 245:25
   bards of Passion and M., 416:11
   formed of joy and m., 359:20
   he is all m., 186:32
   home of m. made desolate, 435:23
   I'll use you for my m., 189:15
   in funeral, 192:32
   like flash of lightning, 293:6
   limit of becoming m., 168:23
   man of marvelous m. and pastimes,
      138:1
   May's newfangled m., 168:16
   no time for m. and laughter, 600:13
   present m., 202:2
   required of us m., 20:6
   resort of m., 252:5
   songs of sadness and m., 441:21
   string attuned to m., 422:22
   sunburnt m., 415:11
   tragical m., 174:3
   tumbling m. of sun-split clouds,
      751:3
   vexed with m. ear of night, 399:8
   who buys a minute's m., 166:38
   wine women m. laughter, 402:18
   with thee I mean to live, 251:20
Misanthropos, I am M., 212:7
Misanthropy and voluptuousness,
   424:24
Misapplied, virtue turns vice being m.,
   175:16
Misbehaved once at funeral, 387:21
Misbehavin', ain't m. savin' love,
   693:8
Misbeliever, you call me m., 180:8
Miscalled, simple truth m. simplicity,
   221:6
Mischance, ride in triumph over m.,
   164:22
Mischief, it means m., 197:9
   little neglect great m., 310:10
   mend whatever m., 597:15
   O Diamond thou little knowest m.,
      282:6

Mischief (continued)
   Satan finds m., 294:10
   that is past and gone, 205:30
   virtuous do, 463:19
   when to m. mortals bend, 299:17
Mischiefs, dreadful m. from wine,
   284:13
Mischievous, gossip is m., 55:2
   hatched would grow m., 188:1
   Love a m. devil, 525:7
Misdeeds, murder and m., 156:17
Misdemeanors, high crimes and m.,
   346:8
Misdoings, heartily sorry for m.,
   49:15
Miser, rich honesty like m., 192:15
Miserable comforters are ye all, 14:24
   have no other medicine, 204:7
   I have passed m. night, 165:29
   made neighbors m., 550:7
   me m., 258:5
   mercy on us m. offenders, 48:18
   minds of men, 89:14
   mortals like leaves, 52:19
   nothing m. but what is thought so,
      115:12
   now made m. by white people,
      370:3
   render last part m., 283:17
   sharers of the event, 325:4
   sinners, 49:19
   to be weak is m., 256:2
   train, 376:9
Miserere, 17:n4
   nobis, 48:9
Miseries, ambitions which climb on
   m., 573:15
   bound in shallows and m., 189:19
   death umpire of men's m., 163:12
   delivered from perils and m., 240:8
   equal sharing of m., 622:10
   getting idea of m., 483:25
   of world are misery, 417:13
   prolong life only when shorten m.,
      726:18
Miser's, heaps of m. treasure, 253:1
Misery acquaints with strange bedfellows, 224:8
   companions in m., 100:21
   departure is taken for m., 30:23
   distant m., 340:5
   drink and remember m. no more,
      23:16
   gave to m. all he had, 322:23
   half our m. from foibles, 348:4
   in m. mindful of happy time,
      125:18
   loves company, 272:7
   medicine for m., 68:26
   mighty poets in m. dead, 374:11
   miseries of world are m., 417:13
   no friend in m., 233:12
   one man's will all men's m., 155:4
   result m., 470:25
   so full of m., 453:18
   splendid m., 344:2
   still delights to trace, 335:22
   vow eternal m. together, 284:16
Misfit, good woman The M. said,
   755:14

Misfortune, bad neighbor is m., 54:25
  in other countries poverty m., 428:19
  it's your m. none of my own, 786:2
  lose one parent m., 567:8
  made throne her seat, 294:2
  never delight in another's m., 99:25
  of our best friends, 266:3
  remembrance of former m., 149:37
  shows who not really friends, 79:1
  to have been happy is most unhappy m., 115:10
  war national m., 426:5
Misfortune's, sour m. book, 176:15
Misfortunes, bear another's m. perfectly, 303:20
  by speaking relieve m., 249:16
  come from wrong notions, 396:11
  crimes and m., 306:23
  endure m. of others, 264:23
  follies and m. of mankind, 340:3
  not unacquainted with m., 53:26
  of man occasioned by man, 104:6
Misgiving, room for m., 66:22
Misgivings, not view process with m., 620:11
Misgovernment, augur m., 331:15
Mishaps like knives, 486:5
Mislead, lights that m. morn, 204:22
Misleading, analogy least m. thing, 525:3
  long run m. guide, 652:8
Misled by fancy's meteor ray, 361:15
  simplicity no longer m., 346:1
Mislike me not for complexion, 180:13
  not my speeches you m., 163:18
Misprint, poet not survive m., 566:7
Mispronounce, all men m. it, 679:12
Misquote, enough learning to m., 399:4
Miss as good as mile, 379:25
  many-splendored thing, 581:11
  march of retreating world, 687:5
  mine he cannot m., 155:26
  Nature cannot m., 276:25
  pain that pain to m., 267:2
  see nor know nor m. me, 647:22
Miss Lonelyhearts priests of twentieth-century, 712:11
Miss T., whatever M. eats, 617:5
Missed, for everything m. gained something, 431:31
  I wouldn't have m. it, 710:1
  it lost it forever, 467:21
  mr u will not be m., 689:4
  never would be m., 530:20
  stars might not have m., 624:19
  woman much m., 540:19
  wonder what you've m., 720:8
Misses an unit, 465:24
  Heaven's net m. nothing, 58:3
  man who m. opportunity, 354:7
Missing, I am what is m., 767:6
  nobody is ever m., 735:1
  Rosebud m. piece in jigsaw puzzle, 697:5
  so much and so much, 661:12
  what m. at the man's heart, 735:9
Mission, glorious m. of unions, 560:2

Mission (*continued*)
  to come down alive, 752:11
Missionaries, things she held against m., 752:9
Missionary leave China convert Christians, 528:8
  not visited our planet, 486:14
  stew, 670:1
Mississippi, commence travels in M. steamboat, 393:9
  of falsehood called History, 499:13
  rolling mile-wide tide along, 526:9
Missouri, 'cross the wide M., 793:12
  I am from M., 566:4
  sound of rampaging M., 756:18
Misspending time a self-homicide, 279:30
Mist, came both m. and snow, 381:3
  dispelled when woman appears, 297:17
  gray m. on sea's face, 633:14
  in my face, 467:18
  mantled in m., 721:1
  of tears, 581:4
  only m. is real, 736:18
  Scotch m., 486:11
  swoln with rank m., 254:3
  white in blue m. on foam, 474:5
  wrecked in m. of opium, 501:6
Mistake, America giant m., 570:1
  biggest damfool m., 678:18
  blue and gold m., 511:14
  in translation, 288:8
  is has been shall be no m., 371:13
  never overlooks m., 505:6
  not to close eyes, 586:10
  of enclosing envelope, 657:6
  of my life, 526:15
  pardon Thy M., 718:23
  pray make no m., 531:1
  when I make m. it's a beaut, 648:2
  woman God's second m., 553:2
Mistaken, I pronounce m., 265:n3
  intuitive calculation, 628:6
  over-zealous piety, 332:5
  think that we may be m., 615:4
  think that ye may be m., 247:1, 615:4
Mistakes, experience name for m., 566:24
  if you make m. I will protect, 686:4
  man of genius no m., 647:16
  of good man, 346:4
  physician can bury m., 608:13
Mistaking paradox for discovery, 613:14
Mister Death, 688:10
  Tambourine Man play a song, 771:8
Mistress, art a jealous m., 432:34
  as with maid so with her m., 26:24
  character of m. from dress of maids, 114:1
  court a m. she denies you, 232:13
  in my own, 592:24
  law a jealous m., 392:16
  literature my m., 582:6
  moderately fair, 266:18
  my m. the open road, 561:22
  necessity m. of nature, 135:9

Mistress (*continued*)
  no casual m. but wife, 457:22
  no legal slaves except m. of house, 440:4
  O m. mine, 201:30
  of herself, 300:19
  of mistresses, 494:4
  or a friend, 408:13
  pensive m., 725:18
  riches good handmaid worst m., 158:19
  such m. such Nan, 144:7
  teeming m. barren bride, 300:14
Mistress' eyebrow, 191:3
  my m. eyes nothing like the sun, 222:8
  orders to perform, 303:29
Mistresses, embrace principles or m., 327:13
  hardly any m., 610:17
  mistress of m., 494:4
  others go to bed with m., 564:9
  wives young men's m., 159:12
Mistrust, more ignominious to m., 265:12
Mists, errors wanderings m. and tempests, 89:n9
  foul and ugly m., 176:37
  mothlike in m., 654:2
  season of m., 416:13
  the Apennine, 511:15
Misty moisty morning, 792:17
  mountaintops, 176:6
  out of m. dream, 602:10
  sheiling of m. island, 421:17
Misunderstand, no fate willfully m., 623:8
Misunderstanding, culture a m. if not French, 553:8
Misunderstands, how often he m. others, 349:29
Misunderstood, admired through being m., 675:20
  to be great to be m., 431:24
Misuse, oft happeth to m. wit, 132:5
Misused, sweet poison of m. wine, 252:16
Mite, can't make m. makes gods, 146:7
Mites, widow threw in two m., 37:33
Mither, father and m. gae mad, 362:18
  leave to m. dear, 785:2
Mithridates, half M., 425:12
  he died old, 579:16
Mitte sectari rosa, 96:n4
Mixed, elements so m. in him, 189:28
  in wrong that's all, 673:14
Mixing memory and desire, 668:17
Mixture, good things come in m., 388:2
  that strange m. of blood, 339:1
Mizpah, name of it called M., 7:44
Moab is my washpot, 17:31
Moan, delicious m., 416:8
  English mother made m., 485:22
  frosty wind made m., 515:10
  made sweet, 417:6
  of doves in elms, 456:22
  paid with m., 581:2

Moananoaning, moyles of it m., 647:22

Moaning, harbor bar m., 484:11
no m. of the bar, 460:11
now they are m., 327:11

Moans, amid no earthly m., 451:17
round with many voices, 455:6

Moat defensive to a house, 171:9

Moated grange, 204:18, 453:16

Mob, amphibious ill-born m., 285:15
at times m. swayed, 625:1
honor depends on opinion of m., 278:13
I am the m., 634:3
is varied and inconstant, 278:13
not ask better only different, 138:4
of gentlemen, 303:7
redress of m. law, 448:2
supreme governors the m., 323:20

Mobile, donna è m., 94:n1

Mobilized, when armies are m., 58:1

Mobs, best university gauntlet of m., 433:10

Moby Dick whale or man, 685:1
evil assailable in M. Dick, 486:25

Mock, after I have spoken m. on, 14:33
air with idle state, 323:6
at the great, 597:16
fools make a m. at sin, 21:18
meat it feeds on, 206:31
on Voltaire Rousseau, 359:2
spirits of wise m. us, 183:32
their own presage, 221:23
their useful toil, 322:7
time with fairest show, 213:15
Turtle, 518:2, 518:3
your own grinning, 199:8

Mocked, God is not m., 44:21
my sense is m., 227:15
smiles as if he m. himself, 187:26

Mocker, wine is a m., 22:1

Mockery king of snow, 172:12
monumental m., 200:24
of monumental stone, 409:2
unreal m. hence, 215:8

Mocketh, whoso m. the poor, 21:33

Mockingbird, listen to the m., 507:14

Mockingbird's, out of m. throat, 490:8

Mocks, man that m. and sets it light, 171:2
married men, 169:12
my loss of liberty, 356:1

Model, Americans may become m., 327:12
British government best m., 354:18
little m. was Benjamin, 657:10
of Deportment, 471:4
of man from Natur's mold, 469:46
of modern Major-General, 529:12
republican m. of government, 337:1
small m. of barren earth, 171:25
to thy inward greatness, 184:28

Models, ancient m. perpetuated, 115:8
turn pages of Greek m., 98:15

Moderate, give m. alarm, 437:14
liberty is in m. governments, 355:2
white m. devoted to order, 760:16

Moderately, a thing m. good, 341:8

Moderately (*continued*)
love m., 175:24
mistress m. fair, 266:18
rescue wife, 437:14

Moderation, astonished at my own m., 326:13
even in excess, 434:17
gone no court can save, 615:3
in all things, 85:12
in justice no virtue, 341:n1
in principle a vice, 341:8
in temper a virtue, 341:8
keep to m., 105:21
spirit of m. flourishes, 615:3
stoutness in m., 530:3
urge me not to m., 437:14

Moderator of passions, 245:17
reasonable m. Death, 248:12

Modern, all history m., 640:25
American literature from one book, 702:2
disease of m. life, 498:12
feelings about m. life, 731:6
idea antiquated once m., 617:13
inconveniences, 526:17
key-machine of m. industrial age, 693:4
life economic, 635:9
man invents museum, 693:5
old or m. bard, 252:15
one must be absolutely m., 565:26
origin of m. world, 704:2
single sentence for m. man, 732:20
something for m. stage, 659:6
spirit Greek discovery, 603:25
wise saws and m. instances, 191:3

Moderns only have opinions, 420:8
speak of m. without contempt, 305:3

Modest and commonly chaste, 404:21
coy submission m. pride, 258:13
doubt, 200:14
front of this small floor, 264:21
in speech, 61:24
keep m. as giver, 552:8
looks cottage adorn, 329:22
no more m. than immodest, 489:9
quip m., 192:16
stillness and humility, 185:3
the m. near to virtue, 61:20
wee m. crimson-tipped, 361:19
woman dressed in finery, 330:3

Modesty a species of nobility, 278:5
ancient sculpture true m., 397:22
and unselfishness, 658:13
mine is blushing m., 101:7
o'erstep not m. of nature, 196:22
speaks without m., 61:23

Modification, bad plan admits no m., 99:26

Modified, single substance variously m., 318:3

Modifying colors of imagination, 384:9

Modo liceat vivere est spes, 86:n2

Modum, servare m., 105:n13

Modus, est m. in rebus, 95:n2

Möglichen, Politik ist die Lehre von M., 474:n4

Moi, le m. est haïssable, 271:n5

Moi (*continued*)
l'état c'est m., 281:n1

Moider, I'll m. de bum, 728:6

Moi-même, je suis m. la matière de mon livre, 145:n4

Moist, cold and hot m. and dry, 275:7
eye dry hand, 183:19
hot cold m. and dry, 257:19
in mystical m. night-air, 490:9
unpleasant body, 469:21

Moisty morning, 792:17

Molar to molecular motions, 542:21

Molars, writers divided into incisors and m., 506:5

Mold, fresh from Natur's m., 469:46
made him and then broke m., 137:7
of form, 196:18
splashing wintry m., 595:5

Molded, best men m. of faults, 205:6
changing lineaments, 538:6
heart m. as she pleases, 151:23
two berries m. on one stem, 173:19

Moldering, a-m. in grave, 524:7
mind m. like wedding-cake, 762:2

Molders hemp and steel, 379:10

Molding, wine jar when m. began, 98:4

Molds, crack nature's m., 209:24
musket m. in his hands, 559:21

Mole, live like velvet m., 660:16
wilt thou go ask the M., 357:1

Molecular motions, 542:21

Molecule, propensity to unite even in m., 645:7

Molecules, by mathematics m. counted, 584:7
simple and indivisible m., 345:10

Moles, cast his idols to m., 25:31

Molle atque facetum, 95:n7

Mollify it with tears, 620:n1

Mollusk cheap edition of man, 433:15

Molly Stark a widow, 330:19

Moloch sceptered king, 256:24

Molten, inns of M. Blue, 511:17
tears scald like m. lead, 211:9

Mome raths outgrabe, 518:15

Moment, brief shining m. Camelot, 745:13
culture m. of clarity, 653:4
endurance for m. more, 554:12
endures m. or day, 597:19
eternity was in that m., 290:33
exhaust the little m., 740:6
first m. of atomic age, 735:20
force m. to its crisis, 667:15
great pith and m., 196:10
hide thyself for a little m., 26:30
hold every m. sacred, 630:1
I cut his throat, 753:20
in a m. of time, 38:9
intense m. isolated, 671:10
knew precise m. to say nothing, 566:15
know the right m., 55:13
last m. belongs to us, 674:20
lifetime burning in m., 671:10
loyal and neutral in m., 214:16
men flourish only for a m., 54:8
not of action or inaction, 84:n7
nothing startles beyond M., 417:17

Moment (*continued*)
  of difficulty and danger, 346:1
  of greatness flicker, 667:16
  of strength of romance, 573:1
  of time fleeting by, 537:22
  only a m., 573:1
  only m. here and m. there, 625:12
  perfection but m., 220:11
  power of man and m., 499:4
  present m. of time, 546:1
  psychological m., 566:15
  that his face I see, 382:5
  the decisive m., 722:17
  this m. in June, 650:16
  this which you deem of no m.,
    76:16
  time of death every m., 84:*n*7
  to decide, 485:1
  trap m. before ripe, 357:21
  work of a m., 149:5
Momentary, beauty m. in mind, 639:4
Moment's monument, 509:23
  seem a m. thought, 595:13
  sent to be m. ornament, 375:16
Moments, art gives quality to m.,
    538:10
  best and happiest m., 410:1
  hardly dared pass, 704:11
  history pattern of timeless m., 672:5
  lucid m., 420:11
  no two m. the same, 493:17
  of high exultation, 665:10
  when everything goes well, 589:7
Momentum, psychological m., 566:*n*3
Mom's, never eat at place called M.,
    726:6
Mona Lisa, you're the smile on M.,
    682:3
Monads of Leibniz, 658:12
Monan's, moon on M. rill, 378:17
Monarch, becomes throned m. better
    than crown, 181:19
  but would give his crown, 249:29
  hears, 276:7
  love teach m. to be wise, 321:24
  merry m. scandalous and poor,
    283:23
  morsel for a m., 217:8
  of all I survey, 334:19
  of the vine, 217:21
  richest m. in world, 364:20
Monarchs, fate summons m. obey,
    274:25
  perplexes m., 256:16
Monarchy, British m. mystery is life,
    506:7
  intelligible government, 506:6
  is a merchantman, 360:7
  universal m. of wit, 246:3
Monastic aisles, 429:9
Monday, born on a M., 791:4
  going to do on M., 644:2
  morning press reports, 717:3
  snatched on M. night, 176:26
  unromantic as M. morning, 476:15
Monday's child fair of face, 791:3
Monde, l'amour fait tourner le m.,
    786:18
  tard dans m. trop vieux, 461:*n*3

Mondes, ce meilleur des m. possibles,
    306:*n*3
Money, a little wanton m., 137:15
  and goods best references, 471:18
  answereth all things, 24:21
  beautiful as roses, 432:19
  begets money, 272:5
  bet my m. on bobtail nag, 506:18
  billion here there talking real m.,
    694:4
  blessing m. cannot buy, 245:30
  board m. in ginger jar, 523:13
  business may bring m., 387:9
  business other people's, 504:8
  by you all the while, 555:18
  counting out m., 790:1
  disease called lack of m., 139:14
  doänt marry for m., 460:3
  fool and his m., 776:18
  Friendship last if not asked to lend
    m., 527:10
  gives me pleasure, 609:6
  goä wheer m. is, 460:3
  government consists in taking m.,
    306:17
  hain't the m. but the principle,
    605:17
  having more credit than m., 349:4
  hired the m. didn't they, 614:20
  honey and plenty of m., 471:31
  how painful to keep m., 279:23
  is like muck, 159:17
  is trash, 228:1
  keeps m. movin' around, 603:9
  knowlege m. power, 730:18
  lay out m. on a rope, 234:23
  like sixth sense, 626:14
  love of m. as possession, 652:12
  love of m. impulse to effort, 559:5
  love of m. root of evil, 45:22
  love of m. taken hold, 438:1
  made m. because loved it, 603:17
  make m. by any means, 97:6
  making m. like bee, 65:2
  man without m. rather than m.
    without man, 62:27
  may rub off on you, 654:16
  means and content, 191:8
  much m. as 'twill bring, 263:19
  no m. no change of routine, 713:14
  no one ever lost m., 643:1
  not good unless spread, 159:17
  not pay for anything, 610:12
  nothing lost but m., 723:3
  nothing so demoralizing as m., 66:7
  old wife old dog ready m., 309:22
  on love request for m. chilling,
    496:10
  pays m. takes choice, 554:15
  people who have m., 651:8
  power to make m. is gift from God,
    539:2
  pretty to see what m. will do,
    279:19
  prose of life, 432:19
  put m. in thy purse, 205:33
  put m. in trust, 447:9
  rage and love, 716:16
  ready m. Aladdin's lamp, 403:14
  ready m. makes the man, 294:20

Money (*continued*)
  reputation more valuable than m.,
    99:2
  retreated back into m., 694:11
  rich have more m., 702:*n*2
  rich possessed by m., 234:22
  rub up against m., 654:16
  seed of money, 319:4
  sets world in motion, 100:7
  silk suit cost much m., 278:27
  sinew of love, 88:*n*9
  sinews of affairs, 88:*n*9
  sinews of war, 88:13
  society for previntion of crooIty to
    m., 539:*n*1
  speaks sense, 281:18
  store m. in stomachs of needy,
    114:12
  they have more m., 702:3
  thy m. perish with thee, 41:2
  time is m., 310:12, 427:*n*1
  times hard m. scarce, 433:12
  to even get beat with, 638:5
  use m. for good of fellow man,
    539:2
  values comfort or m. more, 626:22
  voice is full of m., 694:10
  war begun without m., 139:10
  waste of public m., 537:12
  way the m. goes, 780:13
  we've got the m. too, 507:6
  Willy Loman never made m.,
    738:15
  with lent m. evil done, 487:24
  won't surrinder to flirt, 603:17
  words are m. of fools, 239:17
  world his who has m., 432:33
  wrote except for m., 316:29
Moneybag, Aristocracy of M., 412:21
Moneychanger, morals of m., 606:8
Moneychangers, tables of the m.,
    35:41
Money-lust before senses, 659:13
Moneymaker, not a mere m., 75:5
Mongrel, I like a bit of a m., 571:16
  puppy whelp hound, 328:26
  son and heir of m. bitch, 209:13
Mongrels, Europe continent of m.,
    590:11
Monism thinks all-form only form,
    546:22
Monitor expressed, 376:21
Monk bring to light my toil, 423:20
  cowl does not make m., 118:23
  enlightened m. is free, 65:3
  I said to this m., 762:19
  only connect beast and m., 636:10
Monkey, as soon be descended from
    m., 444:14
  disappointed in m., 528:4
  heroic little m., 444:14
  higher m. climbs more see of be-
    hind, 123:15
  never look long on m., 444:*n*3
  wine, 427:28
Monkeys, army of m. strumming on
    typewriters, 646:7
  cats and m. m. and cats, 548:9
  New and Old World m., 444:12
  species of m. and apes, 759:8

Monkeys (*continued*)
  wilderness of m., 180:33
Monopoly Business at end of journey,
    555:14
  collective bargaining bilateral m.,
    657:4
  has same effect as trade secret,
    326:2
  no single nation have m., 655:8
Monotones, drawn in pearly m.,
    660:17
Monotonous languor, 553:24
  nothing so m. as sea, 485:23
Monotonously falls the rain, 700:8
Monotony, bleats articulate m.,
    376:n2
Monroe, Marilyn M. blonde beautiful,
    753:3
Monroe Doctrine, 360:10
  will go far, 575:16
Monsieur, farewell M. Traveler,
    191:28
Monster begot upon itself, 207:17
  faultless m., 262:n1
  green-eyed m., 206:31
  I had created, 420:20
  I have lived in the m., 564:16
  lovely m., 716:15
  made m. me, 716:15
  man-hero not exceptional m., 640:3
  manunkind, 689:5
  many-headed m. of pit, 303:10
  more hideous than sea m., 209:10
  of wickedness, 621:1
  queer m. the artist, 549:13
  see to it not become m., 552:16
  simple word destroyed m., 706:7
  stare at m., 762:15
  vice m. of frightful mien, 301:14
  what a m. is man, 271:7
  with uncounted heads, 183:9
Monsters, Imagination abandoned by
    Reason produces m., 348:n1
  many m. to destroy, 706:7
  sleep of reason produces m., 348:8
  thinking woman sleeps with m.,
    762:3
  whoever fights m., 552:16
Monstrosity and miracle myself, 147:3
  in ordinary appearance, 762:15
  more prodigious than Hydra, 97:n4
Monstrous anger of guns, 687:2
  big river down there, 526:23
  bottom of m. world, 254:4
  demonstration, 549:16
  every fault seeming m., 191:19
  little voice, 172:25
  O m., 177:34
  regiment of women, 143:14
  two evils m. either, 674:10
Monstruos, sueño de la razón m.,
    348:8
Montague, fair M. I am too fond,
    175:5
Montaigne, book of M. world en-
    dorsed, 145:n5
  in his tower, 712:18
  sedulous ape to M., 561:19
Monte Carlo, broke bank at M.,
    560:1

Montes, parturient m. nascetur mus,
    98:n5
Montesquieu, celebrities such as M.,
    521:4
Montezuma, halls of M., 780:22
  who imprisoned M., 425:6
Montgomery to Oslo, 761:5
Month, April cruellest m., 668:17
  difference sometimes a m., 563:16
  follow month with woe, 408:21
  full of spirit as m. of May, 178:20
  laughter for a m., 177:14
  leafy m. of June, 381:24
  merry m. of May, 233:10
  no trumpets for new m., 629:12
  old man in dry m., 668:6
  one m. on in May, 624:6
  stand to in a m., 175:22
  this is the m., 250:19
  'tis m. before m. of May, 382:10
Monthly changes in circled orb, 175:7
Months add themselves make years,
    459:21
  mother of m., 533:8
  nor hours days m., 228:12
  not to eat an oyster, 147:10
  travelers of eternity, 282:11
  twelve dreary m., 491:5
  two m. back in March, 624:6
Montreal, O God O M., 524:13
Monument, all Greece Euripides' m.,
    67:n9
  early but enduring m., 408:22
  leave some m. behind, 597:16
  like fishbone, 743:10
  make your m. in love, 3:12
  moment's m., 509:23
  more lasting than bronze, 96:25
  Patience on m., 202:14
  placed where I endured, 675:10
  to see m. look around, 278:21
  vote m. an' refuse help, 602:12
  without a tomb, 232:18
Monumental mockery, 200:24
  smooth as m. alabaster, 208:9
Monuments, mountains earth's m.,
    436:13
  not marble nor gilded m., 220:25
  of men overgrown with moss,
    477:18
  of safety, 344:5
  of unaging intellect, 597:7
  of wit survive monuments of power,
    157:24
  rights over human beings or m.,
    349:26
Monumentum, exegi m. aere peren-
    nius, 96:n21
  si m. requiris circumspice, 278:21
Mony a one for him, 785:17
Monyment, vote m. an' refuse help,
    602:12
Mood apart, 624:20
  blessed m., 373:2
  given heart change of m., 623:15
  listening m. seemed to stand, 378:18
  melting m., 208:16
  no m. maintained through hours,
    629:20
Moody food of love, 217:18

Moon, African m. lying on back,
    656:9
  and I keep this up forever, 644:8
  and stars thou hast ordained, 15:34
  appointeth the m. for seasons, 19:6
  a-roving by light of m., 402:1
  as long as m. rise, 787:17
  be not darkened, 24:27
  be still as bright, 402:1
  behold the wandering m., 252:3
  beneath waning m. was haunted,
    382:20
  black dogs bay m., 531:12
  body moves like a sliding m.,
    756:17
  brilliant m. milky sky, 594:23
  by light of m., 786:n6
  by yonder blessed m. I swear, 175:7
  close by the m., 257:22
  cloth from m. from another planet,
    735:22
  cold fruitless m., 172:18
  come from the dying m., 456:10
  cow jumped over m., 789:9
  dance by light of m., 780:10
  danced by light of m., 472:3
  daughter of M. Nokomis, 441:24
  dwelleth in cold of m., 467:15
  earth barren as m., 633:13
  earth viewed from m., 734:10
  ebb and flow by the m., 211:13
  eclipses of m. and other experi-
    ments, 134:12
  error of the m., 208:11
  everyone is a m. has a dark side,
    528:1
  fair as the m., 25:16
  follow changes of the m., 206:33
  full m. throw shadow, 656:9
  ghostly galleon, 643:11
  goal of landing man on m., 741:9
  hang caps on horns o' the m.,
    218:24
  harvest m., 286:8
  has set, 56:8
  hath her eclipse endured, 221:23
  here men first set foot on m., 784:7
  his head rested on m., 333:6
  horned M. with one star, 381:16
  hush with setting m., 458:22
  I the man in the m., 174:7
  if m. shine full or no, 263:27
  in seventh house, 770:1
  in silver bag, 599:1
  inconstant m., 175:7
  is down, 213:16
  Jerry don't ask for m., 711:21
  kneaded by the m., 539:14
  landscapes of m., 613:5
  lanthorn is the m., 174:7
  lies fair upon the straits, 499:19
  like a flower, 356:15
  long glories of winter m., 454:19
  lucent as rounded m., 486:3
  made of green cheese, 142:24
  make guilty the m., 209:3
  minions of the m., 176:25
  moping owl to m. complain, 322:3
  Mountains of M., 453:5

Moon (*continued*)

mousetraps m. memory muchness, 517:22

moving m. went up sky, 381:20

new m. wi' auld in arm, 784:33

no m. outlives night, 757:13

no Moravians in M., 486:14

nor the m. by night, 19:25

nothing remarkable beneath visiting m., 218:8

of Alabama, 698:16

of my Delight, 446:2

on casement wintry m., 415:4

on Monan's rill, 378:17

on whom pale m. gleams, 553:21

one revolving m., 274:11

only you beneath m., 682:1

or sun or what you please, 167:32

pluck honor from pale-faced m., 177:9

rather be dog and bay m., 189:14

revisitest glimpses of m., 194:11

rising in clouded majesty, 258:19

sadder light than m., 443:13

said Wind to M., 504:13

seventeen times high as m., 790:16

shines bright, 182:7

shining to quiet m., 382:17

shone on Mrs. Porter, 668:23

silent as the m., 261:8

silver apples of m., 595:7

slowly silently now the m., 616:20

splendor of the m., 454:18

stain both m. and sun, 220:21

stand still in the valley, 10:37

stars about the lovely m., 56:6

stars planets fallen on me, 655:4

subordinated sun and m., 117:12

sun and m. in flat sea sunk, 252:29

sun and m. should doubt, 359:14

swear not by the m., 175:7

takes up wondrous tale, 292:1

tell m. to come, 699:9

the m. and I, 531:1

this night of no m., 120:12

tree etched by m., 285:10

unmask her beauty to m., 193:26

whenever m. and stars set, 561:9

white m. beams, 676:17

with how sad steps O M., 156:5

would have disappeared, 578:14

youth build bridge to m., 477:1

Moon-calf, how cam'st to be siege of this m., 224:9

Moonlecht, braw brecht m. necht, 609:17

Moonless night in small town, 738:2

Moonlight, book of m. not written, 638:15

come to thee by m., 643:12

ghost along m. shade, 300:7

how sweet the m. sleeps, 182:8

ill met by m., 173:3

incongruous strange m., 679:8

music m. feeling are one, 409:23

ribbon of m., 643:11

softest in Kentucky, 551:21

unto sunlight, 455:22

visit it by pale m., 377:23

Moonlight's fair along Wabash, 611:15

Moonlit door, 616:22

Moons, book of M. defend ye, 777:2

Moonshine an' snow, 485:15

find out m., 173:16

glory of war m., 492:12

Moon-struck madness, 260:17

Moor bark with two anchors, 99:3

Goth and M. bequeathed us, 539:3

never saw a M., 513:15

over the purple m., 643:11

your daughter and the M., 205:17

Moore, before I go Tom M., 401:27

Moored, in Downs fleet m., 297:3

Moos, my foos won't m., 647:20

Moose, bull m., 575:13

Moping melancholy, 260:17

merryman m. mum, 531:14

owl to moon complain, 322:3

Mops, seven m., 518:24

Mopsy Cottontail Peter, 600:20

Moquer, se m. de la philosophie, 271:*n*3

Moral attitude in which most alive, 545:5

author provided with m., 436:5

bird of bad m. character, 310:24

depravity within classes, 661:2

difference in m. life, 546:15

equivalent of war, 546:23

everything's got a m., 517:24

find m. in narrative be banished, 526:18

flabbiness, 545:7

gloom of world, 435:23

immoral thing for m. reasons, 540:8

law within me, 326:10

man and man of honor, 642:22

natural and m. forces, 496:18

natural philosophy deep m. grave, 160:10

no m. or immoral book, 566:10

no one m. till all m., 493:2

of m. evil and of good, 372:21

perception of beauty m. test, 476:28

point a m. or adorn tale, 313:19

positive m. sense, 535:11

real progress is m. progress, 494:12

regeneration of mankind, 440:5

saintliness a m. procedure, 728:9

satire ever m. ever new, 280:15

sense of work of art, 549:2

soil for aesthetic growth, 618:16

spark out of stone easier than m., 532:10

stranger m. fervor, 284:8

terror overwhelming, 484:17

things m. or things evangelical, 272:19

thinks is m. when uncomfortable, 571:5

what is beautiful is m., 496:14

what you feel good after, 701:19

will ends by settling m., 535:11

wise and m. man, 65:3

Moralists, come from set of m., 705:8

tampering to put in edifying light, 705:8

Moralities, never mind about m., 527:34

Morality, conventionality not m., 476:12

courage of making choice, 614:14

enliven m. with wit, 292:20

for morality's sake, 405:18

I who dispensed with m., 565:25

ignorance of m., 270:17

not doctrine of how we make ourselves happy, 326:11

of common man, 552:23

of his actions, 319:20

periodical fits of m., 424:23

private costly luxury, 535:30

taste is the only m., 487:26

temper wit with m., 292:20

true m. takes no heed of m., 270:15

unawares M. expires, 304:2

veracity heart of m., 505:13

what majority like, 584:20

Moralize my song, 153:4

Moralized his song, 153:*n*2

Morally, journalist m. indefensible, 766:12

Morals, code of modern m., 408:13

conventional m., 615:13

faith and m. hold, 375:1

great secret of m. is love, 409:24

have you no m. man, 571:20

if your m. make you dreary, 562:6

man of m. tell me why, 267:1

man of rigid m., 281:23

of moneychanger, 606:8

Rome's decline lay in m., 656:13

time legalizer of m., 642:10

Moravians, no M. in Moon, 486:14

Morbidity, somewhat disgusting m., 652:12

Mordecai rent his clothes, 13:24

More and more about less and less, 585:10

and more and more, 519:2

cantie wi' m., 362:7

Cawdor shall sleep no m., 214:7

celebrities such as M., 521:4

come through alive, 52:8

easy to take m. than nothing, 517:21

for I have m., 231:4

grow from m. to m., 457:4

how much m. is half than whole, 54:21

is man of angel's wit, 138:1

know what is m. than enough, 357:10

less he spoke m. he heard, 554:18

little m. than kin, 192:34

loved Rome m., 188:25

Macbeth shall sleep no m., 214:7

matter with less art, 195:11

meant than meets ear, 252:9

nicely calculated less or m., 377:10

no man entitled to, 576:2

no m. dear love, 456:19

no m. of that, 208:16

Oliver asked for m., 469:5

say m. than this rich praise, 221:10

sleep no m., 214:6

the m. he uses for others, 58:7

Mortal (*continued*)

raised a m. to the skies, 276:16
reason immortal all else m., 58:11
shall m. man be more just, 13:40
shuffled off this m. coil, 196:10
sins of commission m., 318:8
stakes, 624:7
struck a deep m. blow, 63:15
sufferest m. griefs, 185:18
temples of king, 171:25
tend on m. thoughts, 212:29
therefore Caius is m., 510:13
things doth sway, 154:1
think all men m. but themselves, 296:13
think m. thoughts, 68:4
tree whose m. taste, 255:18
what m. heard good of George the Third, 627:*n*5
Mortalem vitam mors cum immortalis, 90:*n*3
Mortality, faint squeak of m., 703:10
nothing serious in m., 214:15
of inanimate things, 532:18
pilgrims of m., 666:22
to frail m. trust, 160:14
touches the heart, 93:21
watch o'er man's m., 375:15
weighs on me like sleep, 417:2
Mortality's strong hand, 170:11
Mortal's lot good or evil, 66:*n*2
Mortals are blaming the gods, 52:29
changeful mind of m., 64:16
fellow m. accepted as they are, 483:8
Hope lies to m., 580:4
make earth bitter, 412:16
miserable m. like leaves, 52:19
no ascent too steep for m., 95:17
not in m. to command success, 292:4
what all m. may correct, 289:18
what fools these m. be, 102:18, 173:18
when to mischief m. bend, 299:17
Mortar, as if chest a m., 486:25
lies m. that bind, 601:7
Mortgage beats 'em all, 554:8
Mortification, live in continual m., 308:18
Mortify a wit, 303:10
Mortifying reflections, 444:*n*3
when woman considers difference of education, 347:5
Mortis, Timor M. conturbat me, 136:4
Mortised, tenoned and m. in granite, 489:6
Mortuis, de m. nil nisi bonum, 55:*n*5
Mosaic, truth like a laborious m., 711:10
Moscas, en boca cerrada no entran m., 794:3
Moscow, to M. to M., 582:14
Moses, go down M., 794:11
greeted M. from Pisgah, 419:7
hid his face, 8:25
in Horeb struck rock, 748:9
ridin' on bumblebee, 698:10
smote the rock twice, 10:2

Moses (*continued*)

that which was given to M., 116:3
was there forty days, 9:20
Moses' sepulcher, 10:30
Moslems, ask M. to execute them, 704:13
Moss, rolling stone gathers no m., 99:29
until M. reached lips, 512:14
Moss-covered bucket, 398:3
Mosses, addled m. dank, 660:4
greenest m. cling, 443:2
Mossy cavern, 416:12
violet by m. stone, 373:19
Most enjoy contented least, 220:16
fails where m. it promises, 203:12
make the m. of it, 339:5
may err grossly as few, 274:14
thing they m. do show, 221:14
who is it that says m., 221:10
Mostest, git thar fustest with m., 496:*n*6
Mot, fait des vers avec des m., 547:*n*6
pour écrire m., 786:21
Mote in thy brother's eye, 34:3
Motes, thikke as m. in sonne-beem, 131:9
Moth and rust doth corrupt, 33:13
desire of m. for star, 409:12
Mother accursed the night she bore me, 68:5
actor pregnant with part, 588:23
and lover the sea, 534:1
arose a m. in Israel, 11:1
as m. so her daughter, 29:6
blessed m. of us all, 345:7
boy's best friend is m., 751:11
call me early m., 454:4
came and caught her, 790:15
Charybdis your m., 181:11
child to m. sheep to fold, 579:22
Church, 112:7
cruel m. of sweet loves, 96:27
dark m. always gliding near, 490:18
Death m. of beauty, 638:25
despise not thy m., 22:21
died today, 732:12
diligence m. of good fortune, 151:10
earth is my m., 370:1
earth no more a m., 104:*n*2
English m. made moan, 485:22
experience M. of Sciences, 149:27
fairer daughter of fair m., 95:27
father and m. gae mad, 362:18
Father-M. God, 495:19
first you are wife and m., 508:3
foolish son the heaviness of his m., 21:4
from one m. both draw breath, 64:9
gave m. forty whacks, 781:11
give me the sun, 508:6
God Father even more M., 731:17
God is a M., 674:2
great m. of big apples, 730:10
holy M. Earth, 63:8
Holy M. Earth, 787:1
honor thy father and thy m., 9:12
if writer rob m., 697:2
ignorance m. of devotion, 235:17
in sin did my m. conceive me, 17:20

Mother (*continued*)

laid her baby, 479:19
leave to m. dear, 785:2
make my bed soon, 785:20
man shall leave father and m., 6:18
Mary was that m. mild, 479:19
may I go out to swim, 783:6
Memory m. of Muses, 76:11
my m., 394:1
my m. bore me, 356:8
my m. groaned, 358:11
myself commanded by boy's m., 62:26
Named is m. of all things, 56:12
nature by her m. wit, 153:20
Nature called m., 421:5
Nature tender and benignant m., 135:13
necessity m. of invention, 104:*n*13, 119:12
never knew me never called me m., 548:1
no God and Mary His M., 588:21
no one like one's m. ever lived, 743:18
not God for father if not Church for m., 112:18
o' mine, 591:11
O m. what have I left out, 757:6
of Aeneas and his race, 89:2
of all living, 6:26
of All Living, 692:4
of arts and eloquence, 260:33
of five sons who died, 450:9
of gods and men, 5:1
of mankind, 255:21
of memories, 494:4
of months, 533:8
of the free, 585:5
old m. Hubbard, 790:18
one whom his m. comforteth, 28:13
ones m. gives don't do anything, 770:2
our M. the Earth, 787:4
Pembroke's m., 240:14
Russia, 496:20
so loving to my m., 193:7
stand by country as m., 501:17
sweet m. I cannot ply, 56:9
took great care of his M., 648:5
walked with his m., 737:13
wedded maid virgin m., 250:19
whales lie dreaming, 657:22
when my m. died, 356:11
who'd give her booby for another, 297:7
wit, 153:20
worm thou art my m., 14:26
would sleep with m., 319:30
Mother Goose, don't believe in God or M., 573:20
Mother-in-law, go not empty unto thy m., 11:25
savage contemplates m., 565:2
Motherless, poor m. Eve, 612:1
Mother's, botanize upon m. grave, 374:2
cannot bear a m. tears, 94:23
daughter in m. house, 592:24
embrace my dead m. ghost, 53:18

Mounted (*continued*)
Troilus m. Troyan walls, 182:7
Mounteth, courage m. with occasion, 169:19
Mounting at break of day, 376:13
lives not m. and unfolding, 628:11
souls m. to God, 509:20
Mounts, in war m. warrior's steed, 377:25
Mourir, partir c'est m. un peu, 570:n2
Mourn, all beings thou shouldst not m., 84:6
blessed are they that m., 33:1
can children of bridechamber m., 34:23
countless thousands m., 361:8
I will not m., 419:13
man was made to m., 361:7
Margaret you m. for, 551:6
mischief past and gone, 205:30
music bad to those who m., 278:9
must m. the deepest o'er fatal truth, 402:2
no longer m. for me, 221:7
small gnats m., 416:15
the dead, 749:14
time to m., 23:32
ye Graces and Loves, 90:16
Mourned at birth not death, 304:8
I m. and shall mourn, 490:15
Mourners go about the streets, 24:28
haul up flag you m., 734:7
no m. walk behind me, 539:18
Mournful ditty to merry measure, 409:16
I with m. tread, 491:1
midnight hours, 349:7
numbers, 440:15
Mourning becomes Electra, 674:4
don't waste time m., 637:2
grief at not wanting to call back, 629:19
house of m., 24:7
let m. shows be spread, 155:27
music in m., 31:40
my Lord what a m., 794:n7
O day of m., 123:14
oil of joy for m., 28:6
she will move from m. into morning, 732:8
through night of m., 612:20
with my m. very handsome, 279:20
Mourns his yet unbroken chains, 353:8
household of Impulse m., 720:13
that day has glided by, 413:23
Mourra, on m. seul, 270:n6
Mouse, baby looked like m., 703:12
cat watch m., 290:17
caught crooked m., 791:11
consider the little m., 83:13
frightened m. under chair, 791:1
I am magical m., 730:12
in a trappe if deed or bledde, 129:13
mountains brought forth m., 98:10
not a m. stirring, 192:20
not even a m., 391:6
pleasant shy manner of m., 703:12
prevails in the Latin, 325:16

Mouse (*continued*)
ran up clock, 788:17
studying to be rat, 631:12
that hath one hole, 83:n10
tiny m. came forth, 59:8
town m. country m., 59:1
Mouse's, holde a m. herte nat worth leek, 83:n10
Mousetrap, make better m., 430:n2
Mousetraps moon memory muchness, 517:22
Mousing, by m. owl hawked at, 214:18
Mouth, bread from m. of labor, 344:8
bread of life in m., 283:8
brown hair over m. blown, 669:16
butter not melt in m., 141:23
cane-lipped scented m., 690:20
closed m. swallows no flies, 794:3
cold hard m. of world, 729:5
false witness by their own m., 32:18
filled with dust, 231:14
filled with gravel, 22:5
find m. a rein, 534:9
fish dies because he opens m., 794:1
fool's m. is his destruction, 21:38
from m. flow gentle words, 54:16
ginger hot i' the m., 202:5
God's m. knows not falsehood, 63:7
heart in my m., 105:6
her m. is smoother than oil, 20:26
his heart's his m., 219:9
his m. is most sweet, 25:15
impossible for Englishman to open m., 571:12
in cannon's m., 191:3
in her m. was an olive leaf, 7:20
ink runs from m., 767:5
it as many players do, 196:21
kisses from female m., 402:4
living from hand to m., 148:5
most beautiful m. in world, 305:16
my m. shall show forth thy praise, 17:24
nay an thou'lt m., 199:17
never look gift horse in m., 114:14
nor m. had no nor mind expressed, 551:6
not that which goeth into m., 35:22
not thine own m., 22:33
O sad kissed m., 533:19
of hell, 458:14
of his holy prophets, 37:45
of no other country, 683:11
of one just dead, 632:15
of Plenty's horn, 597:5
ope his m. out flew trope, 262:21
opened the m. of the ass, 10:4
out of the m. of babes, 15:34
out of thine own m., 39:10
phrase men pass hand to m., 763:10
proceedeth out of the m. of the Lord, 10:14
pure of m., 4:5
purple-stained m., 415:11
reasons made m. water, 263:14
sendeth m. sendeth meat, 141:3
silver spoon in m., 151:18
smiling at the good m., 659:10
so prim, 670:6

Mouth (*continued*)
speaketh out of abundance, 35:3
spew thee out of my m., 47:13
strange m., 491:11
that which cometh out of m., 35:22
tongue cleave to the roof of my m., 20:6
violence covereth the m. of the wicked, 21:5
wear not my dagger in my m., 220:2
which dogs hath deeper m., 163:10
wickedness sweet in his m., 14:32
wine comes in at m., 595:20
words of his m. were smoother than butter, 17:28
words of my m. be acceptable, 16:13
Mouth-honor breath, 216:9
Mouths, blind m., 254:2
enemy in their m., 206:23
had I a hundred m., 94:11
handful of earth stops m., 420:12
have m. but speak not, 19:17
made m. in a glass, 209:27
never open m., 539:1
not if I had ten m., 51:9
Moutons, revenons à nos m., 786:12
Movable feasts, 48:13
impenetrable m. particles, 282:4
Move, aim of oratory to m., 87:21
but if the other do, 229:13
but it does m., 161:16
did thee feel earth m., 702:5
doubt that sun doth m., 195:14
fantastic century m., 353:9
gentle wind does m., 357:17
great affair is to m., 560:13
I by backward steps m., 270:6
I shall m. Hell, 94:20
I will m. the earth, 83:4
languid strings scarcely m., 356:3
man stopped moving if ever did m., 645:8
on m. Americans feel anchored, 753:2
only in command, 216:6
pretty pleasures might me m., 152:11
social conscience of nation, 761:8
stars m. still time runs, 162:23
stones known to m., 215:10
stones of Rome to mutiny, 189:11
times change and m. continually, 154:3
we live and m., 41:17
what can I do but m., 750:4
when looking well can't m. her, 262:2
Moveable feast, 702:13
Moved, have not m. from there to here, 738:17
I shall not be m., 17:33
like a vast shadow m., 270:7
more ways than one, 725:7
not m. with concord, 182:10
not suffer thy foot to be m., 19:25
she shall not be m., 17:17
through dooms of love, 689:1
to smile at anything, 187:26

Moved (*continued*)
virtue never will be m., 194:22
we shall not be m., 794:23
woman m. like fountain troubled, 167:34
Movement, Establishment and the M., 433:3
most magnificent m., 337:17
no apathy into m. without emotion, 629:4
out of dream into codification, 758:2
retard the m., 574:7
so wandering as that of mind, 145:22
symbol of power of m., 657:20
Movements, conscious m. reflex, 511:1
of the largest bodies, 351:16
Mover, Zeus prime m., 63:17
Movers and shakers, 553:21
Moves a goddess, 299:24
and mates and slays, 445:23
curst be he that m. my bones, 226:11
glory of Him who m. everything, 126:21
God m. in mysterious way, 333:22
Love that m. sun and other stars, 127:4
no life m. in empty passageways, 65:16
she stirs she starts she m., 441:17
sits looking then m. on, 634:5
to see sad sights m. more, 167:4
where I move, 734:6
whole creation m., 458:3
Movest, great sphere thou m. in, 218:6
Movie, happy in even bad m., 740:2
hot medium like m., 730:4
Movies, at m. the only modern mystery, 694:3
basic appeal of m., 746:17
Movin' up and down again, 593:15
Moving accidents by flood and field, 205:25
always m. as restless Spheres, 161:21
finger writes, 445:25
forward to greater freedom, 649:1
his slow and m. finger, 207:26
in m. how express, 195:28
into another intensity, 671:11
man has stopped m. if ever did move, 645:8
nightly pitch m. tent, 377:17
others themselves as stone, 221:14
push on keep m., 367:9
tide as m. seems asleep, 460:11
up and down again, 593:15
waters at priestlike task, 417:12
Mown, like rain upon m. grass, 17:41
we multiply whenever m. down, 112:5
Moyles and moyles of it, 647:22
Mozart last chord of European taste, 552:21
some cry up M., 388:3
when M. was my age, 759:7
when u are M., 757:10

Much, and this is m., 399:24
by m. too m., 178:11
don't say too m., 722:5
drinking little thinking, 288:24
enough or too m., 357:14
faithful in m., 39:1
given much required, 38:31, 741:2
have I seen and known, 455:1
have I traveled, 413:24
I do not ask you m., 170:22
in few words, 32:6
is force of heaven-bred poesy, 168:6
know too m. convinced of too little, 672:17
lady doth protest too m., 197:13
learning doth make thee mad, 41:33
learning not teach understanding, 62:11
little happy if I could say how m., 186:23
missing so m. and so m., 661:12
no man wanted m., 432:20
not many but m., 119:16
nothing too m., 55:10
of a muchness, 288:10, 484:2, 517:22
of Madness, 452:7
once that seemed too m., 623:19
safer too little than too m., 524:16
see so m. nor live so long, 211:21
so little time to do so m., 649:20
so m. depends upon, 654:1
so m. for him, 192:33
so m. owed by so many, 620:10
so m. to do, 457:23, 564:18
talk too m., 274:10
those who have too m., 649:8
too m. of good thing, 149:4
unjust in m., 39:1
what he loves never like too m., 232:11
wrested from sure defeat, 673:9
Muchness, much of a m., 288:10, 484:2, 517:22
Muck, all of a m. of sweat, 328:23
know when to stop raking m., 576:4
money is like m., 159:17
whole world is m., 576:4
Mucking up parents' lives, 768:5
Muckle, twice as m. 's a' that, 363:24
Muckrake in his hand, 272:27
Muckrakes, men with m. indispensable, 576:4
Mud, alive and wagging tail in m., 80:17
flies from wings, 742:10
fragrance of salt marsh shore m., 491:3
frogs in the marsh m., 92:26
garlic and sapphires in m., 670:14
in Black M. kingfisher, 742:10
in m. eel is, 791:15
life made of marble and m., 436:7
silk stocking filled with m., 371:2
silver fountains have m., 220:21
Muddied oafs at goals, 593:7
Muddle through, 462:8
Muddled, Don Quixote's a m. fool, 150:35

Muddled (*continued*)
state sharpest of realities, 549:5
Muddlement, constant force for m., 549:5
Muddy ill-seeming thick, 167:34
vesture of decay, 182:8
waist deep in Big M., 747:11
Mud-luscious, world is m., 688:8
Mudville, no joy in M., 588:25
Muffet, little Miss M., 791:8
Muffin man, 792:1
Muffins, no more inspiration than plate of m., 571:3
Muffled and dumb, 430:6
oars, 386:2
Muffler, Fortune painted blind with m., 160:*n*2
Mug's, poetry m. game, 673:1
Mugwump educated beyond intellect, 533:5
Muhammad, heart of M., 117:18
I M. am only a warner, 116:6
Mule, Democratic Party like m., 516:1
nigger woman m. uh de world, 707:7
Multa, non m. sed multum, 119:16
Multeity in Unity, 383:21
Multifold, dying m., 513:13
Multiple, register m. perception in art, 660:7
Multiplication is vexation, 776:9
Multiplied, deviation from truth is m., 77:19
entities not m. unnecessarily, 127:7
visions, 29:30
Multiplieth words without knowledge, 15:4
Multiply, be fruitful and m., 6:9
in us a brighter ray, 400:12
survive and m., 444:9
thanks to art see world m., 613:5
thoughts, 726:14
we m. whenever mown down, 112:5
Multitude a Hydra, 97:*n*4
always in the wrong, 278:24
as the sand by the sea in m., 12:19
barbarous m., 180:26
beast of many heads, 97:*n*4
charity creates m. of sins, 567:13
charity shall cover m. of sins, 46:26
could not name the m., 51:9
discordant wavering m., 183:9
efforts of busy m., 503:3
many-headed m., 97:*n*4, 219:3
of counsellors, 21:7
of days, 313:20
of friends, 231:20
of million divided by million, 716:13
of rulers, 51:7
of sins, 46:26
rude m. call afternoon, 169:7
swinish m., 332:17
that choose by show, 180:25
Multitudes, against revolted m., 259:17
I am large contain m., 489:21
in the valley of decision, 29:33
pestilence-stricken m., 407:13
vast m. of Russia, 621:1

Multitudinous seas incarnadine, 214:9

Multiversity, university become m., 729:21

Mum, cry m., 151:*n*4
  merryman moping m., 531:14
  they fuck you up your m. and dad, 750:15

Mumbo-Jumbo God of the Congo, 637:10

Mumbo jumbos, soot-smeared M., 411:17

Mummers, grave m., 303:28

Mummy, yesterday embryo tomorrow a m., 111:12

Mum's the word, 151:13

Munch your good dry oats, 173:22

Munched and munched and munched, 212:12

Mundi, flammantia moenia m., 89:*n*3
  Stupor M., 742:10

Mundus, fiat justitia et pereat m., 119:*n*2
  quantilla prudentia m. regatur, 139:*n*1

Munich, wave M. all thy banners, 389:4

Munny, doänt marry for m., 460:3
  goä wheer m. is, 460:3

Muove, e pur si m., 161:*n*4

Murder and misdeeds, 156:17
  brother's m., 197:23
  cannot be hid, 132:*n*1
  contrived husband's m., 53:21
  from battle and m., 49:10
  how easily m. discovered, 132:*n*1
  I'll m. de bum, 728:6
  indulges himself in m., 397:18
  infant in cradle, 357:12
  land for private profit, 726:7
  Macbeth does m. sleep, 214:6
  make m. respectable, 711:14
  met M. on the way, 407:25
  most foul, 194:18
  one m. made a villain, 336:2
  one to destroy is m., 296:3
  sacrilegious m., 214:13
  shrieks out, 132:*n*1
  speak with miraculous organ, 132:*n*1
  thousands, 296:3
  time to m. and create, 667:11
  war I call it m., 485:10
  wol out, 132:1

Murdered, all m., 171:25
  Glamis hath m. sleep, 214:7

Murderer, an honorable m., 208:15
  carcasses bleed at sight of m., 132:*n*1
  inspired someone to shoot your m., 762:11
  is somebody's old friend, 677:15
  tender m., 466:10

Murdering, you m. ministers, 212:29

Murderous innocence of sea, 596:21
  love come with m. intent, 68:17
  perjured m. bloody, 222:7
  water buffaloes even m., 665:7

Murders, avalanche of m., 754:21
  check m. but what of war, 103:2

Murmur, ever importunate m., 549:8

Murmur (*continued*)
  shallow m. but deep are dumb, 152:13

Murmured to Picasso, 627:8

Murmuring, asleep by thy m. stream, 362:21
  lapse of m. streams, 259:25
  of innumerable bees, 456:22
  pines and hemlocks, 441:15
  surge cannot be heard, 210:27

Murmurings, crowd and buzz and m., 266:16
  from within heard m., 376:21

Murmurous haunt of flies, 415:15

Murmurs, in hollow m. died, 324:17
  voice in hollow m., 367:12

Murners, no m. walk behind me, 539:18

Murphy's Law, 783:25

Murray, slain Earl of M., 785:18

Mus prevails in the Latin, 325:16

Muscle, brain is like a m., 767:1

Muscles of brawny arms, 441:3
  she had m. of panther, 714:14

Muscular Christianity, 780:15
  strength it gave to jaw, 517:10

Muse, American M., 698:8
  be thou the tenth M., 220:22
  come M. migrate from Greece, 490:6
  conqueror creates a m., 249:26
  dear to me the M. and song, 82:15
  Fool said my m. to me, 156:4
  has taught them songs, 53:17
  I was your vassal, 565:8
  livelier liquor than M., 579:15
  love passed m. appeared, 423:19
  meditate the thankless M., 253:20
  O for a M. of fire, 184:18
  on dromedary trots, 383:12
  on Nature with poet's eye, 388:24
  plans credit and the M., 429:19
  silence m. His praise, 308:9
  tell me m., 52:17
  tell me M., 299:25
  tenth M. governs press, 475:11
  Tragic M. trod stage, 299:19
  why M. speak when unhappy, 710:7
  worst-natured m., 283:22

Mused, many a m. rhyme, 415:16

Muses, all charm of all M., 460:7
  exaltation in chanting of M., 68:7
  loved me, 83:1
  Memory mother of M., 76:11
  of Helicon, 54:13
  recorded by M. live for ay, 154:4
  sacrifice to the M., 55:19
  sage daughters of M., 64:6
  some say there are nine m., 56:*n*4
  strength though of M. born, 414:6

Muses', I the M. priest sing, 96:12
  touching all the m. charm, 89:11

Museum, modern man invents m., 693:5
  monkeys write books in British M., 646:7

Mushroom, supramundane m., 673:7

Music above all, 554:4
  and sweet poetry agree, 233:13

Music (*continued*)
  and the step, 778:21
  and women I give way to, 279:14
  arose with voluptuous swell, 399:21
  art aspires towards condition of m., 538:7
  bad m. people don't talk, 567:7
  body swayed to m., 598:2
  brandy of damned, 571:4
  breathing from her face, 267:*n*5
  caught in that sensual m., 597:7
  crept by me upon waters, 223:31
  daughters of m. brought low, 24:27
  deathless m., 607:13
  die in m., 74:*n*8
  don't know anything about m., 614:8
  everyone should hear, 641:12
  fading in m., 181:2
  fingers on keys make m., 639:3
  fled is that m., 415:19
  food of love, 201:*n*2, 217:18
  from blues American m., 612:10
  from the spheres, 202:22
  frozen m., 350:7
  give children right to study m., 338:10
  good m. people don't listen, 567:7
  good to the melancholy, 278:9
  grace and m. of her face, 267:13
  hampering with ceremonies and m., 80:12
  has charms to soothe, 291:7
  heard so deeply, 671:18
  heard with you more than m., 675:1
  his voice in all her m., 409:6
  how potent cheap m. is, 700:17
  how sour sweet m. is, 172:14
  I care to hear, 550:16
  I got m., 695:4
  I heard with you, 675:1
  I shall be made thy m., 231:2
  if m. be the food of love, 201:16
  in heart I bore, 375:2
  in its roar, 400:29
  in mourning, 31:40
  in space, 350:*n*1
  intolerable m. falls, 599:17
  let m. creep in our ears, 182:8
  like harmony in m., 373:8
  like m. on the waters, 401:24
  live without m., 516:4
  loud and long, 382:25
  madder m., 602:9
  mads me, 172:16
  make m. mute, 459:10
  make one m. as before, 457:4
  makes sweet m. with stones, 168:3
  man that has taste of m., 292:23
  man that hath no m., 182:10
  mind that can hear m., 663:18
  moody food, 217:18
  moonlight feeling are one, 409:23
  must investigate discord, 107:5
  never merry when hear sweet m., 182:9
  night filled with m., 441:12
  no m. in nightingale, 168:5
  not for doctrine but m., 298:18
  of flute, 669:16

Music *(continued)*
of men's lives, 172:14
of poem as well as words, 613:13
of the spheres, 202:*n*3, 248:20
of the Union, 422:17
of yonder pine, 82:13
oft hath such a charm, 204:23
on spirit make m. too, 639:3
one chord of m., 506:1
poetry painting and m., 359:22
prefers live m. to humdrum spheres, 757:10
raise and quell, 275:8
reasonable good ear in m., 173:21
sent up to God, 467:3
setting sun and m. at close, 171:6
silence sank like m., 382:2
softest m. to attending ears, 175:13
soul of m. shed, 391:12
sphere-descended maid, 324:18
step to the m. he hears, 478:37
still sad m. of humanity, 373:5
stop da m., 686:3
Susanna's m., 639:5
sweet compulsion in m. lie, 251:5
that gentlier lies, 454:6
that will melt stars, 496:6
thing I love most, 279:16
thou hast thy m. too, 416:15
thrush m. went, 624:14
to hear m. play, 793:20
to hear sea-maid's m., 173:5
true m. repeat thought of time, 699:13
unreality and loud m., 744:1
untune the sky, 275:11
vibrations of deathless m., 607:13
Wagner's m. better than it sounds, 560:9
war and m. run off same circuit, 770:5
we have m., 734:11
when soft voices die, 409:10
wherever she goes, 790:3
wherever there is harmony, 248:20
why hearest thou m. sadly, 220:10
with silver sound, 776:12
with thy beauty's silent m., 226:15
yearning like a God, 415:1
you are m. while m. lasts, 671:18
Musical as bright Apollo's lute, 169:3
as is Apollo's lute, 253:3
law of m. world, 586:20
most m. most melancholy, 252:2
said except in second act of m. comedy, 645:18
Shakespeare and the m. glasses, 328:24
shuttle, 490:8
so m. a discord, 173:25
Musically, so m. wells, 453:11
Musician must make music, 724:2
Music-makers, we are the m., 553:21
Music's melting fall, 323:15
power obey, 275:7
Musing there an hour alone, 402:26
while I was m. the fire burned, 17:6
Musique, de la m. avant toute chose, 554:*n*5
Musk, cankers in m.-rose buds, 173:10

Musk *(continued)*
sweet m.-roses and eglantine, 173:9
swirls of m., 558:11
Musket molds in his hands, 559:21
Mussel, crow-blue m. shells, 664:5
Mussolini, even M. against war, 681:6
Must a word to be addressed to princes, 145:7
calm observer of m., 583:15
die we m., 164:31
forget because we m., 498:21
if we can we m., 579:18
shoot if you m., 443:11
Thou m., 430:4
to greenwood go, 776:1
Mustache, neat m. and Aryan eye, 764:17
Mustaches, doodle m. on last Czar, 742:18
Mustard, beef without m., 550:14
heaven like to m. seed, 35:9
Johnson's conversation was m., 342:10
Muster, three quarks for M. Mark, 647:21
Mutabile, varium et m. femina, 94:*n*1
Mutability, chance death and m., 407:3
in large republics, 395:13
nought endure but M., 406:12
Mutable rank-scented many, 219:6
Mute, by and by music m., 459:10
hangs as m., 391:12
inglorious Milton, 322:14
law stands m. in midst of arms, 87:10
unchanged to hoarse or m., 259:19
Mutilate, do not fold spindle or m., 783:23
Mutilators of collections, 387:25
Mutine in matron's bones, 197:32
Mutinous and quarrelsome, 311:5
Shannon waves, 647:8
Mutiny, move stones of Rome to m., 189:11
Mutter, blessed m. of Mass, 465:7
unmentionable thoughts, 487:3
Mutual aid law of animal life, 547:5
and partaken bliss, 253:9
envy of the living, 239:24
guarantees of independence, 572:14
in marriage dependence m., 410:18
incomprehension, 717:21
inflamed with m. animosity, 351:22
meet m. heart, 308:7
prevention of m. crime, 78:20
Muzzle, not m. ox when treadeth corn, 10:21
My, I did it m. way, 770:17
Lord what a morning, 794:17
My-doxy, Orthodoxy M., 412:19
Myriad laughter of ocean waves, 63:3
there died a m., 659:10
Myriad-minded Shakespeare, 384:17
Myriads of rivulets hurrying, 456:22
Myrrh, gold and frankincense and m., 32:24
Myrtle and ivy of two-and-twenty, 403:23
laurel and m. and rose, 349:8

Myrtles, once more ye m. brown, 253:14
which a grove of m. made, 233:10
Myself, all by m., 132:23
am hell, 258:5
answer questions about m., 716:8
awe of such thing as m., 187:20
coming down shift for m., 137:18
commanded by boy's mother, 62:26
feel it so like m., 732:13
first glass for m., 293:3
garden city and m., 717:12
hell within m., 248:15
his only son m., 325:8
I am m. and what is around me, 653:2
I celebrate m. sing m., 488:16′
I contradict m., 489:21
I live not in m., 400:4
I m. am hell, 743:6
I owe my fame to m., 249:22
I pray for no man but m., 211:26
I was at last becoming m., 717:17
if not for m. who is, 102:9
it is m. I portray, 145:8
it is m. I remake, 595:17
know all except m., 134:5
know how to kill m., 747:2
monstrosity and miracle m., 147:3
must I remake, 599:11
not least honored of all, 455:1
not talk so much about m., 477:28
quite m. again, 579:2
sacred duty to m., 508:2
taken better care of m., 651:6
that favorite subject M., 341:19
this man shall be m., 319:21
understanding of m., 508:1
when young, 445:17
with Yesterday's Years, 445:14
Mysteries are revealed unto the meek, 31:2
land harbors m. of creation, 745:19
lie beyond thy dust, 270:11
love's m. in souls grow, 229:16
power in m. of thought, 68:7
talk of m., 477:7
wingy m. in divinity, 248:3
Mysterious, be m. to point of sound-lessness, 80:21
beauty m. as well as terrible, 495:5
by this love, 228:15
God moves in m. way, 333:22
God works in m. way, 668:11
independent variable, 505:12
law true source, 258:26
O m. priest, 416:5
past of sea, 721:13
source of art and science, 635:12
thing in soul, 487:3
union with native sea, 376:21
Mystery, at movies the only modern m., 694:3
beauty is a m., 657:18
blessings of Great M., 606:4
British monarchy m. is life, 506:7
burthen of the m., 373:2
I had m., 687:5
I show you a m., 43:27
in m. soul abides, 497:13

Name (*continued*)
  my n. and memory I leave, 160:12
  my n. endure for eternity, 4:10
  my n. is Legion, 37:24
  my n. is MacGregor, 379:13
  my n. joined to theirs, 101:17
  my n. survives me, 83:1
  my 'oss my wife my n., 434:8
  nature but n. for effect, 335:14
  no n. of magistrate, 224:4
  no profit but the n., 198:11
  not the eternal n., 56:12
  object take away pleasure of poem,
    547:13
  of friendless n. the friend, 317:26
  of God upon lips, 319:12
  of late deceased, 591:12
  of one was Obstinate, 272:12
  of scorn, 459:21
  of the beast, 47:29
  of the Lord thy God in vain, 9:10
  of the star is Wormwood, 47:25
  of the wicked shall rot, 21:5
  our n. not become extinct, 510:17
  owl calls n. of man who is to die,
    707:2
  people you know yet can't quite n.,
    751:1
  problem that has no n., 748:18
  proud his n., 378:1
  refuse thy n., 175:1
  rose by any n. as sweet, 175:2
  rouse at n. of Crispian, 185:22
  Sacco's n. live, 674:21
  sad bad brother's n., 535:4
  see n. in print, 399:2
  shadow of glorious n., 105:20
  shall be called Wonderful, 26:8
  shall live behind me, 199:27
  sing praises to his N., 777:8
  single nature's double n., 199:31
  so long shall your n. endure, 93:24
  somewhere a rare n., 73:13
  synonym for devil, 136:n5
  teach but to n. tools, 262:22
  tell one's n. livelong June, 511:22
  that can be named, 56:12
  that will not perish, 386:16
  thy n. shall be Abraham, 7:31
  to all ages cursed, 274:3
  weak witness of thy n., 251:2
  what a wounded n., 199:27
  what n. Achilles assumed, 248:30
  what the dickens his n. is, 182:30
  what thy lordly n. is, 452:18
  what's in a n., 175:2
  whispering still her n., 611:20
  woman's n. in print twice, 656:4
  writ in water, 418:21
  writing is a n. for conversation,
    320:17
Named, a tip-toe when day n., 185:22
  constitution n. a democracy, 72:2
  is mother of all things, 56:12
  thee but to praise, 405:5
  you n. him not I, 281:9
Nameless deed, 367:12
  the N. is the origin, 56:12
  unremembered acts, 373:1
Name's, for his n. sake, 16:17

Name's (*continued*)
  hated for my n. sake, 34:31
Names, American n., 698:6
  bears greatest n., 261:18
  call things by right n., 367:7
  called him soft n., 415:16
  calleth them all by their n., 20:15
  commodity of good n., 176:31
  deeds legends events, 417:1
  different n. after they are produced,
    56:12
  down their chiseled n., 540:23
  fools' n. like fools' faces, 778:16
  great n. as these, 778:18
  judge of authors' n., 299:1
  Moss covered up our n., 512:14
  never allow n. mentioned, 387:3
  new-made honor forget men's n.,
    169:16
  not born to die, 405:6
  of those who fought for life, 727:10
  sharp n. never get fat, 698:6
  their botany Latin n., 429:21
  tongues that syllable men's n.,
    252:24
  two most sacred n., 267:11
  unpopular n. impossible loyalties,
    499:10
  What and Why and When, 593:8
  whom love of God blessed, 397:4
  written in letters of gold, 139:4
Naming, to-day we have n. of parts,
    737:3
Nan, such mistress such N., 144:7
Nancy, mate of N. brig, 528:22
Nane sall ken where he is gane,
    785:17
Nap after dinner silver before dinner
    golden, 510:2
Napalm, smell of n. in morning,
    769:11
Napoleon, ashes of N. Bonaparte,
    371:14
  celebrities such as N., 521:4
  mighty somnambulist, 427:24
  Moriarty the N. of crime, 577:24
  sole obstacle to peace, 370:14
Napping, nodded nearly n., 452:13
Narcotics alcohol and Christianity,
    552:28
  hospital tray of n., 730:20
  numbing pain, 457:7
  two great European n., 552:28
Narrative as whole untrue, 503:5
  bald and unconvincing n., 531:7
  motive in this n., 526:18
Narrator imbue self with the time,
    503:5
Narrow, bestride the n. world, 187:22
  convent's n. room, 376:10
  creep into n. bed, 500:1
  every bed is n., 684:6
  Fellow in the Grass, 513:11
  honor in strait so n., 201:1
  in n. cell forever laid, 322:4
  into its n. shed, 596:15
  is the way, 34:9
  measure spans, 580:3
  track to highest good, 90:12
  two n. words Hic jacet, 153:1

Narrow (*continued*)
  when find road n., 122:10
Narrowed his mind, 330:10
Narrowing lust of gold, 457:30
Narrow-mindedness, superior man will
    not manifest n., 79:10
Narrow-necked bottles, 303:22
Narrow-souled people, 303:22
Narvus, I have been rather n., 417:n3
Nascitur, poeta n. non fit, 110:n9
Nassau, can Bourbon or N. go higher,
    288:5
Nastiest thing in nicest way, 663:8
Nastily, live meanly and n., 279:21
Nasty brutish and short, 239:22
  man of n. ideas, 289:3
  not n. dirty hole, 685:3
  something n. in woodshed, 708:8
Natal, Rome n. neath my consulship,
    88:4
Natchez, belle of old N., 709:12
Nation, America's my n., 697:12
  as Maine so goes n., 781:9
  better one suffer than n. grieve,
    274:9
  commit to landing man on moon,
    741:9
  conceived in Liberty, 450:2
  darlings of our n., 205:19
  defects as n. to use weasel words,
    576:13
  fate of n. in own power, 426:4
  fate of n. riding, 442:14
  favors from n. to n., 337:8
  from single crime know n., 93:28
  genocide destruction of n. ethnic
    group, 704:14
  Germany a n. a race, 421:15
  God hath sifted a n., 277:3
  greatness of British N., 293:7
  grown-up n., 713:19
  guarantees maintenance of citizen,
    559:4
  guiding-star of whole brave n.,
    474:8
  hardly yet a n., 660:8
  has government it deserves, 353:12
  has history of sex discrimination,
    719:6
  haughty n. proud in arms, 252:14
  hoop of n., 587:5
  Horse n., 787:3
  ignorant and free, 344:18
  in Japan civilized n., 525:17
  institutions create n., 435:5
  judged by best not worst, 612:5
  kinder gentler n., 753:13
  light shone to whole n., 240:12
  like pitiful helpless giant, 733:16
  literature memory of n., 746:4
  look beyond n. and race, 744:9
  make all ballads of n., 285:11
  middle class in America the n.,
    501:2
  most important element in n., 80:6
  moving toward two societies,
    723:20
  ne'er would thrive, 287:20
  no n. greater than any other, 681:2
  no n. ruined by trade, 310:22

Nation (*continued*)
  no single n. have monopoly, 655:8
  not flag only but n., 473:1
  not only Latin-American n., 757:1
  of brutes, 573:*n*2
  of communities, 753:11
  of freemen, 448:1
  of shopkeepers, 326:7
  once to every man and n., 485:1
  one n. under God, 568:12
  one-third of a n., 649:7
  paramount question for n., 480:18
  perpetually to be conquered, 331:11
  plant a n., 237:10
  preserved us a n., 391:3
  publish it to all the n., 288:3
  puissant n., 255:2
  righteousness exalteth a n., 21:23
  rise against nation, 36:7
  secure only while honest, 481:1
  serve my n. ruin another, 304:12
  shall not lift up sword, 25:30
  shopkeeping n., 319:28
  small one become a strong n., 28:5
  so conceived so dedicated, 450:2
  social prosperity means n. great,
    428:3
  supports Wall Street, 603:8
  tardy apish n., 171:7
  territory not make n., 505:15
  that that n. might live, 450:2
  this n. under God, 450:2
  trick of our English n., 183:22
  truths which can kill n., 646:15
  turns its lonely eyes to you, 772:9
  values anything more than freedom,
    626:22
  vengeance ask and cry on whole n.,
    135:22
  we are here by will of n., 351:19
  we are n. building, 663:7
  we are n. of differences, 754:3
  what it can do for n., 741:*n*1
  which enjoys most freedom most
    powerful, 368:17
  which keepeth the truth, 26:28
  worthy of mighty n., 695:7
National, Chinese not have n. spirit,
    601:4
  compass of n. authority, 355:7
  consciousness, 572:5
  debt national blessing, 354:17,
    394:12
  don't call out N. Guard, 655:5
  events decided by power elite,
    739:18
  honor is national property, 360:9
  motto root hog, 703:21
  nightmare over, 733:8
  rock of n. resources, 394:18
  stain washed clean, 678:11
  there is N. flag, 463:5
Nationalism, orthodox in n., 683:2
Nationalities, squabbling n., 576:12
Nation's, bind up n. wounds, 450:11
  freight handler, 634:4
  law embodies n. development, 542:5
  read history in n. eyes, 322:15
  spirit die of inanition, 499:8
  ultimate judicial tribunal, 646:12

Nations abandon use of force, 650:9
  all n. and kindreds, 47:22
  all n. gathered, 36:17
  all n. one blood, 41:16
  are as a drop of a bucket, 27:21
  are destroyed or flourish, 359:22
  astonishment among all n., 10:22
  be and make new n., 226:9
  belong to other n., 529:10
  breathes of n. saved, 403:9
  cheap defense of n., 332:13
  civilized n. will recoil from war,
    521:2
  day of small n. past, 528:21
  dwelling in safety, 650:8
  eclipsed gaiety of n., 314:22
  equal right of n., 655:23
  Europe prison of n., 638:10
  father of many n., 7:31
  fierce contending n., 292:16
  foreign n. and the next age, 160:12
  free n. and free men, 741:13
  general association of n., 572:14
  get better of other n., 708:1
  go and teach all n., 37:15
  government of n., 569:17
  great n. not boasters, 432:30
  great when ideal higher, 499:2
  happiest n. have no history, 483:22
  individuals of all n., 339:1
  intercourse with foreign n., 390:22
  joyful all ye n. rise, 312:17
  justice toward all n., 337:6
  kept alive by program, 653:5
  know these two n. war over acres
    of snow, 306:8
  large and small, 655:23
  law of nature and n., 332:8
  like men have infancy, 295:7
  listen ye n. and be dumb, 414:1
  money language n. understand,
    281:18
  Niobe of n., 400:21
  not kings but n., 393:10
  other n. step aside, 446:27
  ourselves and all n., 450:11
  prison of n., 638:*n*3
  rule n. under law, 94:15
  safeguards acceptable to all n.,
    655:9
  service fairer than other n., 121:2
  shall rush like many waters, 26:16
  some n. increase others diminish,
    89:16
  sovereign n. possessing power,
    636:2
  sword united n. drew, 399:24
  teaching n. how to live, 254:18
  twilight sheds on half the n., 256:16
  two great n. in world, 438:7
  two n. the rich and poor, 434:26
  united n., 399:24
  wake n. underground, 794:18
  wars and alarums unto n., 154:2
  which threaten aggression, 650:9
  world doth two n. bear, 268:20
  write autobiographies, 488:1
Nations' airy navies, 455:17
Native, breathe his n. air, 298:5
  fast by their n. shore, 335:17

Native (*continued*)
  foot on my n. heath, 379:13
  good will complacency, 588:12
  his own n. shore, 451:12
  hue of resolution, 196:10
  I am a n. in this world, 639:9
  loss of n. land, 68:12
  my own my n. land, 378:1
  nobility more than is n., 206:12
  one n. charm, 329:20
  think as n. thinks, 639:9
  though I am n. here, 194:8
  true n. of America, 310:24
  union with n. sea, 376:21
  violet of n. land, 457:8
  with n. honor clad, 258:11
  wood-notes wild, 251:19
Native American shared elemental
    ethic, 748:12
Natives of rain rainy men, 638:17
Nativity, in n. chance or death, 183:7
  out of love with your n., 191:28
Natura, divina n. dedit agros, 87:*n*1
  il fece e poi ruppe la stampa,
    137:*n*5
  non facit saltus, 312:*n*2
  si n. negat facit indignatio versum,
    108:*n*6
Natural, act against n. equity, 327:6
  ancient and n. strength, 325:20
  and moral forces, 496:18
  aristocracy among men, 344:15
  balance of n. elements, 564:15
  belief in particular n. law, 710:5
  bodily form from n. thing, 597:10
  chapters come to n. end, 557:19
  children kind and n., 184:28
  considerable revolution in n. his-
    tory, 444:11
  desire to appear n., 265:43
  destroy n. resources, 576:7
  essential rights, 343:*n*2
  fact symbol of spiritual, 431:2
  fear increased with tales, 159:4
  find out n. bent, 75:22
  I do it more n., 202:3
  improver of n. knowledge, 505:5
  large as life twice as n., 519:15
  liberty establishes itself, 326:9
  lose n. kindness, 596:22
  man has two passions, 558:3
  manure, 343:15
  my n. ordinary fashion, 145:8
  no such thing as n. law, 396:17
  old-type n. fouled-up guys, 750:14
  phenomena subject to causation,
    522:16
  philosophy deep moral grave,
    160:10
  Philosophy embodied in mathemati-
    cal beauty, 583:13
  piety, 374:7
  price of labor, 385:9
  propensities, 332:25
  revolution n., 462:15
  right to use pens, 306:18
  science involves three things, 345:9
  sciences aim never reach, 504:12
  Selection, 444:5
  selection, 493:9

Natural (*continued*)

simple affecting, 330:12
skilled poet through n. gift, 63:30
something more than n., 195:30
study n. history, 338:10
thousand n. shocks, 196:10
to indulge in illusions, 339:7
to please, 274:2
treating Psychology like n. science, 547:3
treatise of n. education, 319:16
uninstructed in n. history, 505:2
wants the n. touch, 215:25
wealth and beauty, 741:8
what is n. is need, 396:17
Naturalist, Goldsmith Poet N., 316:32
Naturalists, so n. observe a flea, 289:20
Naturalized, flag of man n. yesterday, 560:5
people n. in U.S., 346:18
Naturam, contra n., 659:16
Naturamque sequi, 105:*n*13
Nature a grave, 421:5
a kind parent, 104:2
a merciless stepmother, 104:2
abhors a vacuum, 277:16
abhors the old, 432:9
accuse not N., 259:30
acquisitions by n., 347:13
adherence to truth of n., 384:9
against the use of n., 212:23
agayns proces of n., 131:28
agent and patient at once, 77:17
all N. seems at work, 383:14
all N. wears one grin, 311:9
all the powers of N., 431:32
allow not n. more, 209:21
alter human n., 583:5
always does contrive, 530:11
always hinting at us, 625:11
and books belong to eyes, 432:17
and civilization literary field, 548:5
and Nature's God, 295:9
and Nature's laws hid, 303:17
animated n., 380:25
art imitates N., 104:*n*13
art imitation of n., 102:28
Art mediatress between n. and man, 384:19
assures being-forever, 718:8
be your teacher, 372:20
begins to recognize itself, 725:24
beings which compose n., 351:16
binding N. fast in fate, 303:15
body N. God soul, 301:11
book of N., 148:*n*7
book of n., 272:2
but name for effect, 335:14
by a rule in n. teach, 184:23
by her mother wit, 153:20
by n. all alike, 235:4
by n. men nearly alike, 62:1
by n. wise, 237:21
by viewing N., 273:10
called mother, 421:5
cannot miss, 276:25
change stamp of n., 198:6
common goal of n., 734:11
compunctious visitings of n., 212:29

Nature (*continued*)

constant in N. inconstancy, 266:19
could no further go, 275:25
course of N. art of God, 248:*n*2
custom almost second n., 168:*n*2
death one of things N. wills, 111:25
death ugly fact N. hides, 515:16
description of n., 656:3
direct and control course of n., 564:22
diseased n. breaks forth, 178:1
disguise fair n., 185:3
divine n. gave us country, 87:3
does not depend on us, 691:21
does nothing uselessly, 78:13
drive out N. with a pitchfork, 97:12
enough till Human nature came, 514:3
equals stupidity of man, 654:4
excelling n., 208:10
exposed to method of questioning, 707:4
falls into revolt, 184:10
finest spectacles in n., 310:15
finest woman in n., 293:17
fits all her children, 485:9
follow n., 105:21
fools of n., 194:11
force in N. not increased, 496:17
forces by which n. animated, 351:16
forces in n., 504:12
foregoing generations beheld n., 430:24
fortress built by N. for herself, 171:9
foster-nurse of n., 210:26
frame of N. break, 292:3
free as N. first made man, 273:14
friend masterpiece of N., 432:1
Friendship sweet steady n., 527:10
fruit your seasons bring N., 111:5
full of designs, 546:15
full of genius full of divinity, 477:3
generous n. take own way, 331:10
good n. agreeable in conversation, 293:2
habits form second n., 347:14
happiness depends as N. shows, 334:2
happiness of retired n., 292:21
hath framed strange fellows, 179:15
he is great who is from N., 432:23
he of calm and happy n., 75:4
heaven and n. sing, 294:17
her custom holds, 198:26
her masterpiece designed, 363:1
highest type of human n., 493:10
hints and half-truths, 532:8
hold mirror up to n., 196:23
human n. finer, 418:3
human n. made arrogant by consideration, 72:9
human n. seeming born again, 373:11
I fear thy n., 212:28
I feel the link of n., 260:11
I loved, 388:21
I was escaping from N., 717:17
if n. conquers, 365:13

Nature (*continued*)

imagination one of forces of n., 640:28
impartiality of N. best, 532:11
in her inventions, 135:10
in love of N. holds, 411:1
in n. few sharp lines, 756:8
in our life N. live, 383:8
in perfect n. no distinction of kind, 80:13
in state of war by n., 289:19
in terms of cylinder sphere cone, 537:21
in you stands on verge, 209:19
Indian unconstrained in N., 476:21
is but art unknown, 301:12
is the art of God, 248:7
is there any cause in n., 210:15
is wont to hide herself, 62:10
kindly bent to ease us, 266:*n*2
knowledge of human n., 387:10, 535:19
knows her business better than we do, 147:8
law of n. and nations, 332:8
laws of n. and nature's God, 343:2
laws which mind put into n., 646:6
learned to look on n., 373:5
liberty taken with N., 536:9
lies within something of another n., 752:16
limited n. infinite desires, 405:9
line in n. is not found, 429:11
link of n., 260:11
little we see in N., 376:11
living in agreement with n., 82:1
living N. not Art, 426:21
looking at objects of N., 383:17
looks through N. up, 302:1
losses wrought by n., 347:13
lost their original n., 80:12
loyal n. noble mind, 459:19
lusty stealth of n., 208:29
made a pause, 296:8
made him then broke mold, 137:7
made one with N., 409:6
made thee to temper man, 284:17
man as n. made him, 319:21
man by n. political animal, 78:12
man explorer of n., 722:14
man's efforts to control n., 677:12
man's n. cultural product, 704:9
means God of N. placed in our power, 339:9
men by n. desire knowledge, 77:21
men by n. equally free, 327:1
men gained control over n., 569:12
might stand up and say, 189:28
mingling its n. with n. of things, 158:14
mistress and guardian of n., 135:9
modesty of n., 196:22
more than n. needs, 209:21
mortal n. did tremble, 375:11
muse on N. with poet's eye, 388:24
must obey necessity, 189:21
my n. is subdued, 222:1
my Treatise of Human N., 318:16
needed not books to read N., 273:12

Nature (*continued*)
never deceives us, 319:15
never did betray, 373:6
never makes blunders, 479:22
no arrogant wonders of n., 446:26
no chance of understanding n.,
 538:19
no part N. has not touched, 111:31
no such thing in N., 262:*n*1
noble and incapable of deceit,
 379:24
noble n. poetically gifted, 499:1
not from philosophers but n., 236:1
not man less but N. more, 400:29
not proceed by leaps, 312:9
nothing at prompting of n. but
 weep, 104:5
nothing in n. without purpose,
 440:9
nothing purposeless trivial unnecessary, 122:12
observer of human n., 468:21
of desire not to be satisfied, 78:16
of mind mortal, 90:3
of the thing, 757:13
often hidden, 160:2
once out of n., 597:10
one and continuous, 477:23
one touch of n., 201:3
outrage when man destroys n.,
 631:15
owes me another existence, 350:6
paint falsely add accent of n., 522:7
passing through n. to eternity, 193:1
passion could not shake, 207:23
pattern of excelling n., 208:10
peevish N., 287:18
progress part of n., 492:14
prophets of N., 373:14
qu'est-ce que l'homme dans la n.,
 270:*n*3
recover hair bald by n., 166:23
red in tooth and claw, 457:21
reduce problems of n. to numbers,
 516:6
reduction of n. to mechanics,
 504:12
renews annual round untired,
 631:15
rest in N. not God, 243:19
reverence human n., 392:18
rich with spoils of N., 248:5
rules of game laws of N., 505:6
science of N., 280:3
science right interpretation of n.,
 411:13
secret of study of n., 437:1
secretary of N., 246:1
seems dead, 213:21
sighing through her works, 260:7
silent energy of n., 426:15
simple n. to his hope given, 301:7
simple News N. told, 512:12
sloping to southern side, 485:27
so priketh n. in hir corages, 129:7
sociability law of n., 547:5
some made coxcombs n. meant
 fools, 298:11
something marvelous in all n., 77:20
such stupidity not in N., 316:2

Nature (*continued*)
suffers n. of insurrection, 188:2
sullenness against N., 254:22
swears lovely dears, 361:25
teaches beasts to know friends,
 218:26
teaches more than preaches, 532:10
tendency of man's n. to good, 79:25
that framed us, 161:21
things rank and gross in n., 193:6
think of our life in n., 477:7
thou and n. so gently part, 218:18
thoughts n. gives way to, 213:18
thrust into n. like wedge, 477:23
to advantage dressed, 298:14
to be commanded must be obeyed,
 158:15
to him who in love of N., 411:1
to read N. he looked inwards,
 273:12
to white man n. wilderness, 606:4
to write and read comes by n.,
 186:36
too noble for world, 219:9
trees and all n., 787:1
trying to make us succeed, 691:21
understanding distorts n. of things,
 158:14
universal n. say, 312:*n*3
usura sin against n., 659:15
vicaire of almyghty lorde, 128:9
voice of n. cries, 322:20
voice of N. cries, 362:23
war of n., 444:10
we fools of n., 194:11
what fools call N., 468:2
what is man in n., 270:18
what put into world to rise above,
 726:5
what tell you about n. of life, 736:8
when n. makes fool she means it,
 479:22
wherefore thus partial, 135:13
with equal mind, 497:22
without voice or sound, 325:10
words like N. half reveal, 457:6
works by means of bodies unseen,
 89:9
write in spite of N., 263:11
yet do I fear thy n., 212:28
yet remembers, 375:10
you've conquered human n., 469:14
Nature-faker, 576:6
Nature's above art, 210:28
beauty is N. brag, 253:10
beauty is N. coin, 253:9
chief masterpiece, 284:2
crack n. molds, 209:24
Darling, 323:2
debt to N. quickly paid, 242:10
discipline enjoins mutual help,
 704:4
eye N. walks, 301:2
fever is N. instrument, 271:16
fresh from N. mold, 469:46
fulfills great N. plan, 361:12
God, 302:1
great masterpiece, 230:17
great n. second course, 214:6
handmaid Art, 273:10

Nature's (*continued*)
infinite book of secrecy, 216:26
journeymen, 197:1
kindly law, 301:15
law man made to mourn, 361:7
laws of nature and n. God, 343:2
lay idiot, 230:4
learned breast, 148:10
like bill on N. Reality, 412:13
list to N. teachings, 411:2
little kings, 227:14
looks up to N. God, 302:1
masterpiece writing well, 284:2
natural bent in accordance with n.,
 538:19
Nature and N. God, 295:9
Nature and N. laws hid, 303:17
own Nobleman, 462:6
own sweet cunning hand, 201:26
patient sleepless Eremite, 417:12
pleasing themes, 308:14
single n. double name, 199:31
social union, 361:5
soft nurse, 183:36
spark o' N. fire, 361:11
still is N. priest, 375:8
tired n. sweet restorer, 296:6
trees in N. workshops, 537:16
works to me expunged, 257:24
Natures, absolute n. or kinds, 76:5
by quiet n. understood, 597:5
how call n. forth, 750:2
ignominy of our n., 248:13
nobility in their n., 206:12
train noble n. not to desire more,
 78:16
Naught but care on ev'ry han', 361:24
but vast sorrow there, 617:2
by spreading disperse to n., 163:8
carry on dread n., 620:4
doth Job fear God for n., 13:30
enters there, 201:17
it is n. saith the buyer, 22:4
it will come to n., 41:1
shall make us rue, 170:24
so sweet as melancholy, 234:3
stitching and unstitching n., 595:13
venture nought have, 141:33
Naughtiness of thine heart, 11:37
Naughty, good deed in n. world,
 182:11
my poems n. but life pure, 106:7
night to swim in, 210:7
Nausea, that's n., 717:12
Nauseate, I n. walking, 291:11
Nauseous, fee doctor for n. draught,
 276:19
sham goodfellowship, 571:25
Naval, study n. architecture, 338:10
without n. force nothing, 336:17
Navee, Ruler of Queen's N., 529:6
Navies, airy n., 455:17
are stranded, 379:9
Navigation commerce agriculture,
 338:10
freedom of n., 572:13
truce to n., 529:15
Navigators, winds on side of ablest n.,
 340:6
Navy but rotten timber, 331:23

Needless Alexandrine ends song, 298:19
  omit n. words, 608:9
  Show, 512:16
  to blame things past, 61:1
  to speak about things done, 61:1
Needs, country n. and demands, 648:15
  fair n. foul I cried, 598:20
  gives 'er all she n., 592:19
  go whom devil drive, 142:20
  man in search of what n., 563:13
  more than nature n., 209:21
  to each according to n., 481:11
  we must n. die, 12:13
Needy hollow-eyed sharp-looking wretch, 166:34
  I am poor and n., 19:12
  make not n. eyes to wait, 31:6
  not for n. but for greedy, 650:1
  store money in stomachs of n., 114:12
  strength to the n., 26:25
Negate, to define is to n., 653:9
Negation, faith in n., 589:15
  my art n. of society, 541:12
Negations of man, 754:21
Negative Capability, 417:18
  feelings about marriage, 284:9
  inversion, 720:3
Neglect creeping hours, 190:29
  easier to mend n. than quicken love, 113:8
  God and his angels, 231:11
  heart's ease must kings n., 185:18
  little n. great mischief, 310:10
  monuments of unaging intellect, 597:7
  perpetual n. of things, 560:20
  sweet n. more taketh me, 232:6
  wise and salutary n., 331:10
Neglectful Nature wherefore thus partial, 135:13
Neglects, whoso n. learning in youth, 69:16
Negligence, let friendship die by n., 317:27
Negligences, noble n., 288:1
Negligent, celerity admired by n., 217:23
Negligible, discriminate between important and n., 635:2
Negotiate, every eye n. for itself, 186:21
  never fear to n., 741:5
  never n. out of fear, 741:5
  only free men can n., 745:16
Negro, American N. problem in heart of American, 700:5
  blood sure powerful, 709:2
  boy with curlicues, 742:22
  cool strong imperturbable, 480:19
  dehumanizing the N., 448:10
  duty of younger N. artist, 708:11
  I am a N., 708:13
  I am N. and beautiful, 708:11
  school-children, 743:12
  those who hate N. see hatred in N., 564:14
  through n. streets, 757:4

Negro (*continued*)
  treatment of N. greatest scandal, 700:6
  two-ness an American a N., 605:2
  what does N. want, 627:21
  willing to risk martyrdom, 761:8
Negroes, hear bronze N. breathe, 743:10
  not women or N. but citizens, 475:9
Negro's great stumblingblock, 760:16
  skin prima facie evidence, 475:7
Neiges, où sont les n. d'antan, 134:*n*1
Neigh, how joyous his n., 787:11
  like Boanerges, 512:18
Neighbor, bad n. is misfortune, 54:25
  better a n. that is near, 23:3
  dagger into back of n., 649:14
  eye n. as enemy, 615:6
  false witness against thy n., 9:12
  good n. policy, 648:19
  hate your n., 424:24
  he promised to defend, 425:11
  helped every one his n., 27:24
  let n. carve for you, 289:21
  love n. yet pull not down hedge, 244:11
  love thy n., 36:1
  love thy n. as thyself, 9:26
  not look to see what n. does, 111:3
  of nothing, 767:8
  tyranny of next-door n., 506:11
  what hateful to you do not to n., 102:7
Neighboring communities overlook one another, 58:6
  cynosure of n. eyes, 251:14
Neighbor's, life to n. creed lent, 429:7
  neighed after his n. wife, 28:14
  not covet thy n. wife, 9:12
  not covet thy n. house, 9:12
  not move sickle unto n. corn, 10:20
  your concern when n. wall on fire, 97:19
Neighbors, borrowing everything of n., 279:21
  call n. in, 789:8
  first to attack their n., 269:1
  good fences good n., 622:21
  innocence of our n., 478:33
  live as good n., 655:23
  made n. miserable, 550:7
  make sport for n., 387:4
  more right than n., 477:12
  who practices virtue will have n., 61:7
Neighed after his neighbor's wife, 28:14
Neighing canyons, 701:6
  farewell the n. steed, 207:8
  in likeness of filly foal, 173:2
Neighs, high and boastful n., 185:14
Neither, do two things at once do n., 98:31
Nell, death of Little N. without laughing, 567:25
Nelly, let not poor N. starve, 273:5
Nelson touch, 586:16
Nemean, hardy as N. lion's nerve, 194:14

Nemo me impune lacessit, 119:14
  repente fuit turpissimus, 108:*n*8
Neon Renaissance, 764:2
Nephew of my Uncle Sam's, 632:11
  turned out to be my n., 767:12
Neptune, envious siege of watery N., 171:10
  flatter N. for trident, 219:9
  floods which N. obey, 777:11
  sink ship on even keel, 102:30
Neptune's ocean wash this blood, 214:9
Neque semper arcum, 96:*n*8
Nero, tyranny of N., 506:11
Nerve, all air and n., 743:3
  hardy as Nemean lion's n., 194:14
  iron n., 458:7
  mortal arm and n. feel, 379:10
  o'er which do creep, 407:10
  stretch every n., 308:16
Nerves, ganglion in n. of society, 542:13
  my firm n. never tremble, 215:7
  strengthens n., 332:20
  trifles irritate my n., 488:4
Nervous, I have been rather n., 417:*n*3
  renewal of relations n. matter, 535:22
  tough but n., 665:9
Nessus, shirt of N. upon me, 218:2
  shirts, 412:11
Nest, bird that filleth own n., 135:20
  builds phoenix' n., 264:19
  eagle make n. on high, 15:18
  feathered his n. well, 236:19
  good to keep n. egg, 150:28
  help Robin unto N. again, 513:10
  jaybird don't rob own n., 556:12
  no birds in last year's n., 151:*n*6
  of singing birds, 315:13
  on greatness of God, 547:7
  phoenix builds spicy n., 246:6
  wat'ry n., 249:23
Nests, birds in little n. agree, 294:8
  birds of air have n., 34:17
  built n. in beard, 471:27
  of two loves the n., 230:10
  whatever special n. we make, 537:18
Net, all fish that cometh to n., 141:35
  as fishes taken in evil n., 24:20
  heaven's n. is vast, 583:3
  kingdom of heaven like a n., 35:11
  on wall when fish eaten, 743:20
  play tennis with the n. down, 625:17
  to hold the wind, 237:*n*5
Nether, hard as n. millstone, 15:23
Nets, heart is snares and n., 24:13
  not fall into same n. twice, 113:23
  tangled in amorous n., 260:26
  to catch the wind, 237:20
Nettings, till n. are legion, 665:2
Nettle, out of this n. danger, 177:16
  tender-handed stroke n., 297:23
  the world's a n., 297:*n*4
Nettle-rash, one-armed man with n., 585:2
Neues, im westen nichts n., 700:8

Neurasthenic, water buffaloes n., 665:7

Neurotic possessed by fantasy, 718:2

Neurotics, great things from n., 612:18

Neutral in fact as well as name, 572:2
  loyal and n. in a moment, 214:16
  studiously n., 572:6
  to one n. thing both sexes fit, 228:15

Neutrality, armed n., 572:10
  cold n., 332:24
  just for a word n., 568:13

Neutralize intellectual element, 588:12
  white not n. black, 468:4

Never be mean false cruel, 470:27
  better late than n., 98:27
  blows so red, 445:13
  came back to me, 472:5
  come back to me, 456:8
  despair, 95:21
  do what can put off, 503:11
  excuse, 174:11
  give all the heart, 595:12
  give in never never, 621:5
  go to sea, 529:7
  in field of human conflict, 620:10
  less idle than wholly idle, 88:3
  love a stranger, 682:13
  love means n. having to say sorry, 769:n1
  love unless you can, 226:17
  man spake like this, 40:7
  never never never, 211:19
  no n. what n., 529:4
  now or n., 320:27
  saw wild thing sorry, 657:11
  seek to tell thy love, 357:17
  shake thy gory locks, 215:4
  so little time to do so much, 649:20
  story of more woe, 176:21
  thinks of me, 780:23
  this will n. do, 376:n3
  to be disquieted, 242:2
  to have lived is best, 598:3
  to hope again, 225:16
  too late to give up prejudices, 478:2
  twain meet, 591:9
  whispered she, 436:1

Never-ending flight of future days, 257:5

Nevermore, quoth Raven N., 452:18, 452:20
  shall be lifted n., 452:22

New, adversity blessing of N. Testament, 159:7
  all the glad N. Year, 454:4
  always something n. out of Africa, 104:9
  Aurora, 776:21
  be and make n. nations, 226:9
  birth of freedom, 450:2
  blood of the n. testament, 36:28
  brave n. world, 224:26
  called N. World into existence, 372:3
  change old love for n., 156:13
  commandment I give, 40:25
  cost little less than n., 291:24
  deal for American people, 648:16

New (*continued*)
  direction of Time, 657:8
  draw n. mischief on, 205:30
  emperor's n. clothes, 437:8
  era in life from reading, 478:23
  exhausted worlds imagined n., 313:10
  familiar things made n., 314:23
  first by whom n. is tried, 298:17
  force too revolutionary, 655:7
  fresh woods and pastures n., 254:8
  friend is as new wine, 31:21
  Frontier, 740:20
  generation descends from on high, 92:10
  generation of Americans, 741:3
  has a n. master get a n. man, 224:11
  hazard of n. fortunes, 169:18
  heaven and new earth, 47:37
  heavens and a new earth, 28:11
  heraldry hands not hearts, 207:16
  Homer n. and fresh, 618:2
  how strange it seems and n., 465:16
  Jerusalem, 47:37
  leisure class replaced by N. Class, 723:9
  life begins, 124:17
  love noght oold as whan n., 131:15
  man raised up in him, 50:11
  nation conceived in Liberty, 450:2
  no n. acquaintance, 318:1
  No N. Taxes, 753:12
  no n. thing under the sun, 23:25
  not criticize N. Testament, 585:11
  nothing more perilous than n. order, 136:9
  nothing quite n. is perfect, 87:19
  off with old love before on with n., 779:20
  off with Old Woman before N., 570:9
  old lamps for n., 778:12
  old offenses of affections n., 221:26
  old woes n. wail, 220:18
  only thing n. in world, 655:21
  opinions always suspected, 277:5
  order in Europe, 638:10
  pain of n. idea, 506:8
  philosophy calls all in doubt, 230:15
  piping songs forever n., 416:4
  plants still awkward, 725:3
  regions we call New World, 135:15
  reproduction to n. individuals, 347:13
  ring in the n., 457:29
  satire ever moral ever n., 280:15
  sea-discoverers to n. worlds, 228:3
  so various so beautiful so n., 499:22
  something n., 782:10
  stand upon threshold of the n., 250:6
  terms between old and n. world, 355:3
  things are made familiar, 314:23
  things succeed, 241:13
  time to begin a n., 276:22
  time was when toy dog n., 559:21
  to keep good acts refresh with n., 158:25

New (*continued*)
  tomorrow a n. day, 151:2
  too deep into n. land, 379:20
  turn over a n. leaf, 150:34
  wail my dear times' waste, 220:18
  way to pay old debts, 238:10
  what is n. not valuable what valuable not n., 389:21
  what's the n. news at n. court, 189:29
  wine in old bottles, 34:24
  World favorable to declamation, 573:10
  Year's Day in morning, 791:14
  years ruin and rend, 534:4
  yielding place to n., 459:26
  you will see something n., 715:3

New England, Brahmin caste of N., 447:18
  courage of N., 422:16
  growth of N., 503:3
  heart-leaves of lilac all over N., 626:11
  iron N. dark, 696:18
  weather, 526:5
  rum, 589:4
  wild N. shore, 410:12

New Englanders, as N. love pie, 633:1

New France, expansion of N., 503:3

New Hampshire, up in mountains of N., 395:11

New Hampshiremen, two N., 698:11

New Jersey, counting cars on N. Turnpike, 772:10

New Mexico, in N. he awoke young, 616:11

New York, a Xenophon at N., 323:23
  butterfly in Peking storm systems in N., 775:2
  dawn has mud, 699:10
  from California to N. island, 731:13
  Governor of N. not an acrobat, 618:7
  has symptoms of mind gone berserk, 715:8
  homeward bound for N. town, 793:16
  in N. ask how much worth, 527:19
  little old N., 586:4
  makes one think of collapse, 738:8
  oh you N. girls, 793:15
  only credential N. asked, 713:15
  present in N. powerful, 585:12
  she hails from N., 793:21
  sidewalks of N., 585:7
  way of taking life, 586:22

New Yorker not edited for old lady, 684:20
  read the N. trust in God, 720:21

New Zealand, traveler from N., 425:7

Newborn, glory to n. King, 312:17
  infant's tear, 358:9
  pity like naked n. babe, 213:7

Newcastle, carrying coals to N., 95:n6

New-create another heir, 226:8

Newest, oldest sins n. ways, 184:13

Newfangled, May's n. mirth, 168:16
  theories, 435:4

Newfangledness, men loven n., 131:24

New-fledged, tempt its n. offspring, 329:14

New-found, America my n. land, 230:12

Newgate, condemned cells of N., 524:17

New-laid, innocent as n. egg, 529:1

New-lighted on heaven-kissing hill, 197:30

Newly, bee had stung it n., 262:6

New-made clouds, 737:18
    honor doth forget, 169:16

New-mown hay, 611:15

New-reaped, chin n., 177:2

New-risen, sits as n. from dream, 167:28

News, all n. fit to print, 575:6
    better making n. than taking it, 619:11
    bitter n. to hear, 502:9
    bringer of unwelcome n., 183:11
    evil n. rides post, 261:23
    good n. baits, 261:23
    good n. from a far country, 22:27
    hear talk of court n., 211:13
    literature n. that stays n., 660:6
    man bites dog that's n., 554:7
    man who brings bad n., 66:6
    never good to bring bad n., 217:19
    not yet reached my bowels, 758:13
    of the boat, 431:12
    office of newspaper gathering n., 555:8
    one to slander other to get n. to you, 527:33
    print n. and raise hell, 780:16
    simple N. Nature told, 512:12
    suspense in n. is torture, 261:24
    tell Tchaikovsky the n., 756:15
    that's goin' round, 779:10
    this n. is old enough, 204:19
    what n. on Rialto, 180:2
    what's the new n. at new court, 189:29
    worthy of acceptation, 286:22

New-spangled ore, 254:6

Newspaper death, 535:29
    does ivrything for us, 603:12
    ghosts between lines of n., 508:5
    never look into n., 352:33
    office of n. gathering news, 555:8
    today's n. old and tired, 618:2

Newspaper's duty to print news, 780:16

Newspapers ceaselessly querulous, 642:12
    did that which Founders hoped, 661:9
    government without n., 343:12
    r-reads thirty millyon n., 603:8
    the most villainous, 352:33
    without government, 343:12

Newt, eye of n. toe of frog, 215:14

Newton, a N. at Peru, 323:23
    God said Let N. be, 303:17
    with his prism, 373:10

Newtonian principle of gravitation, 343:6

Newton's, apples on N. head, 625:11
    peculiar gift, 652:14

Newts and blind-worms do no wrong, 173:12
    beetles n. stone-deaf fishes, 724:16

Next, laughed because knew what n., 733:4

Ngàje Ngài, 702:4

Ngong, eagles of N. look out, 656:9

Niagara, leap of whale up N., 310:15
    never looked on N., 425:16

Nice, be n. to people on way up, 631:9
    customs curtsy to great kings, 186:5
    girl won't give an inch, 106:16
    guys finish last, 715:15
    hazard of doubtful hour, 178:19
    little missionary stew, 670:1
    makes n. of no vile hold, 170:7
    man a man of nasty ideas, 289:3
    new clothes, 790:15
    sugar spice everything n., 791:6
    to get up in mornin', 609:16
    too n. for a statesman, 330:10
    work if you can get it, 695:14

Nicean barks of yore, 451:12

Nicely calculated less or more, 377:10

Nicer to lie in bed, 609:16

Nicest, nastiest thing in n. way, 663:8

Nicholas, St. N. soon be there, 391:6

Nicht, gude n. and joy, 368:7

Nichts, im westen n. neues, 700:8

Nicias least deserved such fate, 72:11

Nicissry, if dhrink evil not n., 603:16

Nick, gave name to our Old N., 263:30

Nickel, good five-cent n., 565:*n*1

Nickname for Providence, 342:5

Niece of King Gorboduc, 203:4
    sister's husband's n., 520:2

Niggard earth, 321:22

Nigger, woman is n. of the world, 765:8
    woman mule uh de world, 707:7

Niggerization result of oppression, 739:16

Niggerized, old people poor people students get n., 739:16

Nigh, Athens n. to Euboea, 74:9
    Lord is n. unto them that call, 20:13
    so n. is grandeur, 430:4

Nighing his hour, 579:21

Night, a little warmth and good n., 522:10
    accursed the n. she bore me, 68:5
    acquainted with the n., 624:3
    admits no ray, 274:26
    afraid for the terror by n., 18:15
    after n. I do crowd, 356:2
    all n. jessamine stirred, 458:22
    all n. long in dark and wet, 561:9
    all n. roses heard, 458:22
    all the story of the n. told over, 174:2
    alternation of n. and day, 116:8
    and day sweet things, 428:15
    and day you are the one, 682:1
    and silence who is here, 173:13
    as darker grows the n., 328:5
    as I in hoary winter n., 160:19
    ask of thee beloved N., 409:14

Night (*continued*)
    at n. hippopotamus hunts, 668:11
    awake for n. is flying, 156:11
    azure robe of n., 413:19
    bare-bosomed n., 489:8
    be by Silvia in the n., 168:5
    bed by n. chest of drawers by day, 329:19
    before Christmas, 391:6
    beginning to lower, 442:8
    beneath suffocating n., 579:6
    beyond n. across day, 456:2
    bird of dawning singeth all n., 192:29
    bird of n. did sit, 187:28
    black as n. is black, 708:13
    black bat n., 458:20
    black hours spent this n., 551:15
    blasts cold, 619:2
    blessed candles of n., 182:15
    borrower of the n., 214:19
    Bowl of N., 445:4
    braver at n., 759:13
    braw brecht moonlecht n., 609:17
    breath of n.-wind, 499:22
    bridegroom all n. through, 578:21
    but daylight sick, 182:13
    by n. atheist half believes a God, 296:16
    by n. in a pillar of fire, 8:43
    by night my life gone, 757:13
    by n. on my bed I sought him, 25:9
    calm region where no n., 242:1
    carried His servant by n., 116:15
    Chaos and old N., 256:13
    cheek of n., 174:23
    City of N. perchance Death, 523:16
    closed eyes in endless n., 323:4
    collied n., 172:20
    come n. strike hour, 641:7
    come seeling n., 214:28
    cometh, 40:13
    coming tenderly, 708:14
    confront n. storms hunger, 488:14
    councilor ought not sleep whole n., 51:5
    country astronomy by n., 690:1
    crown is of n., 534:20
    Cynthia regent of n., 297:2
    damp of n. drives deeper into soul, 489:14
    dark and stormy n., 429:2, 751:10
    dark n. of the soul, 147:12
    day after wedding n., 616:19
    day and n. shall not cease, 7:22
    day brought back my n., 255:17
    dead vast and middle of n., 193:18
    dear N. world's defeat, 270:2
    Death and N. wash world, 490:14
    deep of n. crept, 189:21
    defend us from dangers of n., 49:7
    dependency of day and n., 638:26
    desire of n. for the morrow, 409:12
    dewy morn to dewy n., 523:5
    did we lie down because 'twas n., 229:4
    drowsy ear of n., 399:8
    dusky n. rides down sky, 311:15
    empty-vaulted n., 252:27
    endless n., 241:19, 323:4

Night (*continued*)

eternity only a single n., 74:16
evening mild silent n., 258:22
fasten seatbelts bumpy n., 727:5
filled with music, 441:12
firebell in the n., 344:21
fit n. for man or beast, 641:13
flies in n. in howling storm, 358:4
follow as n. the day, 194:1
for thieves, 68:25
forests of the n., 358:6
fresh dews of n., 253:17
gaudy n., 217:28
gentle into that good n., 737:20
gets through bad n., 552:17
go bump in the n., 779:15
God is day n. winter summer, 62:13
golden lamps in green n., 268:24
goodbye N. Goodbye, 573:1
hangs on cheek of n., 174:23
Harry in the n., 185:15
has a thousand eyes, 563:2
hath a thousand eyes, 155:21
hear this passing n., 415:17
heart plunges lower than n., 654:4
hoary winter n., 160:19
horses of the n., 101:10, 162:n9
hung aloft the n., 417:12
I could have danced all n., 745:9
I have passed miserable n., 165:29
I saw Eternity the other n., 270:7
ignorant armies clash by n., 499:22
in her silence, 498:2
in lonesome October, 453:1
in n. imagining some fear, 174:1
in which corn grows, 479:7
in winter get up at n., 561:7
infant crying in n., 457:18
infinite day excludes n., 294:19
interminable n., 672:2
into the n. go one and all, 557:8
is dark, 426:18, 783:14
is drawing nigh, 521:11
is far spent, 42:23
is growing gray, 540:20
is thine, 602:9
it will not last the n., 684:2
joint-laborer with day, 192:24
journey on bus, 753:2
kingdom of perpetual n., 165:31
last n. ah yesternight, 602:7
last n. among fellow roughs, 461:1
last out n. in Russia, 203:32
late in n. fires are out, 561:9
lies upon the deep, 93:13
like fountain n. and day, 459:27
lives here or passes n., 651:20
long day's journey into n., 674:8
lovers' tongues by n., 175:13
machinery of n., 757:4
made for loving, 402:1
makes n. seep into day, 117:12
makes no difference, 241:7
making n. hideous, 194:11
many a watchful n., 184:9
meaner beauties of the n., 227:9
meditate day and n., 15:29
merry wanderer of the n., 173:6
middle of the n., 518:23
moonless n. in small town, 738:2

Night (*continued*)

morning and noontide night, 165:32
mother of Day, 443:2
motions of spirit dull as n., 182:10
mystical moist n.-air, 490:9
Nature's laws hid in n., 303:17
naughty n. to swim in, 210:7
night my ho head halls, 647:20
no moon outlives n., 757:13
not n. that kills, 589:16
not only a n. an age, 623:22
not snow nor rain nor heat nor n.,
    70:11
not spend another such n., 165:29
nothing but the n., 579:14
now tell me elm, 647:20
of cloudless climes, 401:14
of dark intent, 623:22
of doubt and sorrow, 521:12
of memories and sighs, 388:16
of the soul, 694:18
of time surpasseth day, 249:3
oft in the stilly n., 392:7
on a starred n., 509:7
on marge of Lake Lebarge, 627:3
one calm summer n., 608:8
out of n. that covers me, 557:9
perpetual n., 90:19, 232:4
Portals alternate N. and Day,
    445:11
praise at morning blame at n.,
    299:3
preceding twenty third day of Octo-
    ber, 237:23
primeval cosmic n., 629:3
proof through the n., 391:2
resonance recedes, 598:11
returned home previous n., 618:14
revelry by n., 399:21
round me too the n., 499:18
run slowly horses of n., 101:10
sable goddess, 296:7
sash lowered when n., 624:1
say to n. Pass slowly, 405:8
screaming n. away, 786:22
set the n. on fire, 775:4
shadow of light, 533:10
shadow of n. comes on, 683:9
ships that pass in n., 442:16
show dangerous brow by n., 188:3
shrouds remote antiquity, 290:31
silent n. holy n., 406:5
silver lining on the n., 252:25
singeth all n. long, 192:29
sits and smiles on the n., 356:15
sleep in the n., 357:8
sleep neither n. nor day, 212:13
sleep of perpetual n., 90:19
sleep one ever-during, 226:13
slowly run O horses of n., 162:n9
smiled and said Good N., 609:8
snatched on Monday n., 176:26
soft stillness and the n., 182:8
soon comes the n., 426:2
sorrow makes n. morning, 165:32
specter and day, 358:16
Spirit of N., 409:13
Stars from Field of n., 445:3
stars of summer n., 441:9
starshine at n., 561:23

Night (*continued*)

steal hours from n., 392:1
stilly n., 392:7
such a n. as this, 182:7
such n. in England, 425:4
suffocating n., 579:6
sweat with terror, 597:13
tell me elm n. n., 647:20
tender and growing n., 489:8
tender is the n., 415:13
that hides things from us, 127:2
that makes or fordoes me, 208:8
that n. that year, 551:12
that wins, 533:9
there shall be no n., 48:2
thief in the n., 45:5
this n. of no moon, 120:12
those poor Souls who dwell in N.,
    359:16
those who dream at n., 452:6
thou makest darkness and it is n.,
    19:6
thy tempests fell all n., 243:23
tire the n. in thought, 242:7
tired with one spend n. with other,
    582:6
to remember, 742:9
trailing garments of N., 440:14
troubled n. depart, 389:2
turn by n. or day, 375:3
unto n. showeth knowledge, 16:9
unwept in eternal n., 97:1
urge the morrow, 408:21
walks n. in silver shoon, 616:20
war's annals cloud into n., 540:22
watch in the n., 18:10
watch that ends n., 294:15
watches of n., 442:23
we are not of the n., 45:6
weepeth sore in the n., 29:1
weeping may endure for a n., 16:25
what hath n. to do with sleep,
    252:21
what is the n., 215:11
what of the n., 26:20
whatever flames upon n., 597:20
when no man can work, 40:13
when she deserts the n., 261:8
where kings in golden suits ride,
    731:5
who art dark as n., 222:14
windy n. rainy morrow, 221:13
wings of N., 441:10
witching time of n., 197:21
with great gift of sleep, 557:11
with n. we banish sorrow, 233:20
with n. will go, 356:2
with train of stars, 557:11
womb of uncreated n., 257:2
world in love with n., 176:1
world's last n., 230:25
year plunges into n., 654:4
yield day to n., 163:5
Night-bird's wail, 531:12
Nightdress, black plunge-line n.,
    769:15
Nightingale, brown bright n. amorous,
    533:8
    Chinese n., 637:12
    no music in n., 168:5

Noble *(continued)*
    efforts in last war, 313:4
    eightfold path, 65:1
    eminently n., 498:22
    false idol or n. true birth, 76:9
    he shall have a n. memory, 219:17
    hearts of the n. may be turned, 52:6
    horsemanship, 178:22
    in reason, 195:28
    invention, 342:19
    is he no more, 65:11
    last infirmity of n. mind, 253:20
    Living and noble Dead, 373:13
    long live our n. king, 298:3
    man a n. animal, 249:4
    mind here o'ethrown, 196:17
    nature passion not shake, 207:23
    nature poetically gifted, 499:1
    nature too n. for world, 219:9
    negligences teach, 288:1
    never alone accompanied with n.
      thoughts, 155:24
    not rebellion which is n., 732:16
    not think n., 716:11
    now cracks a n. heart, 199:29
    person attracts noble people, 349:19
    quiet us in death so n., 261:25
    repressed their n. rage, 322:12
    savage, 273:14
    sentiments, 607:5
    silence n. till end, 533:11
    society exists for n. actions, 78:20
    to be good, 454:3
    train n. natures, 78:16
    truth of sorrow, 64:26
    type of good, 442:7
    work is alone n., 413:6
    work of n. note, 455:5
Nobleman, interest equal to n., 346:3
    nature's own N., 462:6
    underrated n., 531:16
    when n. writes book, 317:*n*4
Nobleness, no security in n. of an-
    other, 616:3
Nobler in mind to suffer, 196:10
    pass them for n. life, 414:4
    two of far n. shape, 258:11
    yet in his own worth, 274:15
Nobles and heralds by your leave,
    288:5
    by earlier creation, 424:11
Noblesse oblige, 367:8
Noblest deed will die if unsung, 64:13
    frailty of mind, 282:7
    function of object, 589:21
    horse n. conquest of man, 311:6
    lives and noblest dies, 494:20
    prospect a Scotchman sees, 315:25
    Roman of them all, 189:27
    ruins of the n. man, 188:22
    Thames n. river, 293:7
    time's n. offspring, 296:27
    two n. of things, 288:17
    work of God, 301:18, 361:10
    work of man, 520:15
    work she classes O, 361:25
Nobly born must nobly meet fate,
    69:10
    Cape Saint Vincent, 465:5
    deeds die however n. done, 154:4

Nobly *(continued)*
    perfect woman n. planned, 375:18
    save or meanly lose, 449:16
    to be n. born now crime, 238:7
    to die, 65:9
    to live, 65:9
    too difficult to think n., 319:23
    wild not mad, 241:14
    within reach to live n., 102:22
    work they so n. advanced, 450:2
Nobody, are you N. too, 511:22
    asked you, 790:8
    cares for me, 338:*n*9
    come because nobody does, 540:4
    comes nobody goes, 718:14
    does anything about weather,
      528:15
    expected me to be President, 448:8
    fat white woman n. loves, 661:12
    gets old and crafty, 595:3
    give a war and n. come, 634:12
    goes there anymore, 693:3
    helps me over puddles, 420:22
    I care for n., 338:19
    I hate n., 290:3
    I'm N. who are you, 511:22
    is ever missing, 735:1
    knock as you please n. home,
      300:26
    knows trouble I've seen, 794:9
    knows you, 767:8
    likes man who brings bad news,
      66:6
    more space where n. than anybody,
      627:12
    never made me, 463:2
    not even the rain, 688:21
    praises everybody praises n., 341:20
    shoots at Santa Claus, 618:8
    tells me anything, 603:18
    who does not rise early, 314:29
Nobody's enemy but own, 470:32
    everybody's business n. business,
      245:19
    funeral, 671:5
    going to stop them, 754:13
    here, 743:6
Nocere, primum non n., 71:*n*2
Noche oscura del alma, 147:*n*9
Noctes, O n. cenaeque deum, 95:*n*10
Noctis, lente currite n. equi, 101:*n*7,
    162:23
Nod, affects to n., 276:7
    Cain dwelt in land of N., 7:8
    ready with every n. to tumble,
      166:3
    Wynken Blynken and N., 559:20
Nodded nearly napping, 452:13
Nodding o'er yellow plain, 308:6
    rests and n. places in writer, 292:26
    violet grows, 173:9
Nods a little that's all, 295:10
    and becks, 251:8
    even good old Homer n., 98:17
    nor is it Homer n., 298:12
    old horse stumbles and n., 540:22
Nohow, 518:21
Noir, A n. E blanc, 565:*n*12
    comme le diable, 354:*n*2
Noise, above n. and danger, 270:8

Noise *(continued)*
    boys that fear no n., 330:6
    dangerous who make no n., 268:6
    dreadful n. of water, 165:30
    folly n. and sin, 465:10
    govern most make least n., 239:7
    he who sleeps in n., 532:15
    in the beast's belly, 133:5
    inexplicable dumbshows and n.,
      196:21
    like of hidden brook, 381:24
    loudest n. in New Rolls-Royce,
      730:6
    make a joyful n., 17:37, 18:19,
      18:22
    makes no n. over good deed, 111:14
    narrow-souled people make n.,
      303:22
    neglect God for n. of a fly, 231:11
    of battle rolled, 459:24
    of folly, 252:2
    of many waters, 18:18
    of tongues and deeds, 453:20
    passed beyond excitement, 765:2
    play skillfully with a loud n., 16:29
    proves nothing, 527:23
    those who make the n., 332:18
    what n. soever ye hear, 162:21
Noised, fame n. throughout country,
    10:35
Noiseless current strong obscure,
    500:18
    foot of time, 203:20
    patient spider, 491:8
    tenor of their way, 322:17
Noises in a swound, 381:4
    isle is full of n., 224:18
    of the northern sea, 454:18
Noisome pestilence, 18:15
    unsightly n. things, 429:8
Noisy bells be dumb, 579:4
    keys, 505:22
    thought idler by n. set, 595:14
    world hears least, 376:19
Nokomis, wigwam of N., 441:24
Noli me tangere, 40:*n*6
    me tangere for Caesar's I am, 143:8
Noll, for shortness called N., 323:19
No-man-fathomed, cliffs frightful n.,
    551:14
Nominated, if n. will not run, 492:*n*6
    so n. in the bond, 181:23
Nominative, her n. case, 348:12
Nominee, choosing presidential n.,
    655:16
Nommé, c'est toi qui l'a n., 281:*n*4
No-more, also called N., 509:26
Non dulce non et decor, 659:8
    effugies meos iambos, 91:*n*7
    omnia possumus omnes, 92:*n*8
    omnis moriar, 96:*n*22
    semper ea sunt quae videntur,
      102:*n*8
    sum qualis eram, 96:*n*23
Non-action, ruler takes n. as his way,
    86:16
Non-being, anxiety about threat of n.,
    662:11
    being comes from n., 57:11
    let there always be n., 56:12

Notes *(continued)*

as warbled to the string, 252:7
by distance made sweet, 324:16
chield's amang you takin' n., 363:15
curls done up with bank n., 475:12
flute in dying n., 275:10
he listens well who takes n., 125:28
liquid n. close day, 254:10
of gladness, 389:10
rough n. and dead bodies, 606:2
thrill deepest n. of woe, 362:9
through all compass of n., 275:7
trills thick-warbled n., 261:1
with many a winding bout, 251:19
write N. from Olympus, 652:7
Nothing, a man zealous for n., 317:12
a worm a mere n., 308:19
a year, 463:9
achieved without chimeras, 503:17
ain't heard n. yet, 661:14
ain't worth nothin' but it's free,
    768:11
airy n., 174:1
all for love n. for reward, 153:10
all or n., 507:15
before and nothing behind, 383:1
begins and nothing ends, 581:2
begot of n. but vain fantasy, 174:21
beside remains, 406:13
better know useless things than n.,
    102:32
blessed man who expects n., 300:25
book's a book though n. in 't, 399:2
bring peace but yourself, 431:29
brought n. into world, 45:21
burden of n. to do, 280:19
but hath been said, 234:6
but pack of cards, 518:12
but talk of his horse, 179:29
but the night, 579:14
but the truth, 150:8
call our own but death, 171:25
can be accomplished alone, 684:18
can be created from nothing, 89:6
can be done hastily and prudently,
    99:33
can bring back hour, 375:14
can need a lie, 242:19
can rescue me, 162:21
can touch him further, 214:26
cannot create when n. to say,
    707:10
certain except death and taxes,
    310:27
comes amiss so money comes,
    167:19
comes out, 431:15
comes without cause, 308:21
common law n. but reason, 152:1
constant but inconstancy, 288:19
could stop you, 767:7
death in itself is n., 273:15
death is n. to us, 81:18, 90:3
deed everything glory n., 350:25
did n. in particular, 530:13
do much harm, 690:4
do n. be a gentleman, 157:5
done merely for beauty, 783:16
done while anything remained,
    105:22

Nothing *(continued)*

dusty n., 200:22
easier than self-deceit, 79:3
easy to take more than n., 517:21
either good or bad, 195:25
else is, 228:13
emboldens sin as mercy, 212:3
endures but change, 62:8
esteem everything esteem n., 269:10
everything in relation to n., 270:18
except battle lost, 371:7
exists without some effect, 277:18
expect something for n., 564:2
extenuate, 208:16
eyes n. like the sun, 222:8
fair alone, 429:7
fame created something of n.,
    250:16
fear God n. else, 474:18
fear n. you carry Caesar, 88:22
Flaubert write novel about n., 748:7
for which no standard, 510:8
funnier than unhappiness, 718:19
give your services for n., 71:5
given nothing required, 311:16
glory and n. of a name, 401:18
good men to do n., 332:30
goodness had n. to do with it,
    685:5
grated to dusty n., 200:22
great without enthusiasm, 432:10
greater than one's self, 489:20
griefs that fuel n., 740:13
had n. can't take more, 517:21
half so sweet in life, 391:14
happens nobody comes, 718:14
happens unless first dream, 634:11
happens which he is not fitted to
    bear, 111:15
has value, 636:11
have value but object of utility,
    481:8
having n. n. can he lose, 164:24
having n. possessing all, 44:6
having n. to say, 484:3
he wants n. you want, 501:20
he who believes n., 343:5
heaven's net misses n., 58:3
her wishes and ways be as n.,
    539:16
human is alien, 85:16
I am n., 43:14
I am n. I see all, 430:27
I ask n. want n., 123:1
I do n. upon myself, 231:6
I had seen n. sacred, 701:14
I have everything yet n., 86:5
I know these are n., 106:26
I love as good fight, 648:13
I n. lack if I am his, 493:25
I regret n., 718:*n*2
if not critical, 206:6
in baseball don't know n., 754:10
in excess, 119:15
in his life, 212:26
in nature's inventions n. lacking,
    135:10
in n. else so happy, 171:14
in relation to infinite, 270:18
in Stupidity Street, 612:2

Nothing *(continued)*

in the pot, 615:2
in truth we know n., 70:27
in world single, 407:20
indolent but agreeable doing n.,
    110:4
infinite deal of n., 179:23
is had for nothing, 483:1
is here for tears, 261:25
is it n. to you, 29:2
is secret, 38:15
it profiteth me n., 43:14
knew moment to say n., 566:15
know n., 479:27
know n. except my ignorance, 70:22
know only that he n. knew, 261:3
lasts save eternal change, 240:4
law that is not reason, 152:*n*1
learned n. forgotten n., 354:4
left remarkable, 218:8
left to lose, 768:11
less will content me, 331:12
life grants n. without work, 95:7
like a dame, 692:15
like the sun, 222:8
lost but money, 723:3
love shows by excusing n., 269:14
lowly in universe, 756:7
make no use of n. nuncle, 209:9
man n. before We created him,
    116:22
mean between n. and everything,
    270:18
miserable but what is thought so,
    115:12
more indisputable than our senses,
    323:16
more perilous than new order,
    136:9
more silly than silly laugh, 90:26
more terrible than ignorance,
    351:10
more wretched than a man, 52:13
move in command n. in love, 216:6
neck or n., 465:23
neighbor of n., 767:8
nothing at all, 683:7
of him that doth fade, 223:32
of n. am I in want, 86:5
off time you spend dead, 145:13
people on whom n. lost, 548:13
perfect and entire wanting n., 46:4
plenty of n., 695:10
poor man had n., 12:10
quite new is perfect, 87:19
quite so least as truth, 689:2
real except humanity, 421:9
real till experienced, 418:14
refuse, 429:19
reputed wise for saying n., 179:21
said that has not been said, 86:4
say n. in dangerous times, 239:9
scoured to n., 183:23
seen n. yet, 149:41
serious in mortality, 214:15
shall be impossible, 37:38
she speaks yet says n., 174:27
signifying n., 216:12
situate under heaven's eye, 166:21
sleep in that cellar, 724:12

Nothing (*continued*)
　so demoralizing as money, 66:7
　so good as beforehand, 483:23
　so irrevocable as mind, 588:2
　so ridiculous but philosopher said it, 87:27
　sole or whole, 598:21
　soul takes n. with her, 75:3
　stranger ever happened, 729:10
　stronger than habit, 101:16
　succeeds like success, 427:13
　sure in sea fight, 360:15
　take n. of his labor, 24:5
　take n. on looks, 471:17
　telling n. in great harangue, 269:11
　terrible except fear itself, 158:18
　thank you for n., 149:13
　there is n. hid from the heat, 16:10
　there is n. more to say, 608:2
　they that starve with n., 179:25
　think n. done, 367:2
　'tis something n., 206:30
　to be feared as fear, 476:26
　to be thus is n., 214:20
　to do with case, 531:8
　to do with just man, 37:5
　to have yet think enow, 233:15
　to it n. uncertain, 351:16
　to look backward to, 623:2
　to lose but chains, 482:7
　to offer but blood, 620:5
　to say say nothing, 393:4
　to write about, 109:25
　too much, 55:10
　true writer has n. to say, 751:6
　trust that man in n., 320:20
　useless is or low, 441:20
　venture nothing win, 530:16
　we can carry n. out, 45:21
　we do is wiped out, 545:14
　wears clothes but Man, 243:14
　whatsoever to do, 744:7
　will come of nothing, 208:20
　will help, 690:4
　will remain, 579:2
　worth doing completed, 684:18
　would give up life, 724:13
　yields n. but discontent, 331:3
　you couldn't actually say, 660:4
Nothingness, death a state of n., 74:16
　death irruption of n., 496:11
　pass into n., 414:9
　quintessence even from n., 229:9
　to n. do sink, 417:11
　we deny our n., 707:9
Nothingnesses of human beings, 76:10
Nothing's so hard but search will find it out, 241:16
Nothings, labored n., 298:16
Nothing-withholding and free, 547:6
Nothin's plenty for me, 695:10
Notice ruin in things, 739:1
　total indifference to public n., 769:5
　walk by color purple don't n. it, 773:13
　would they take n., 390:11
　you take of my labors, 315:17
Notion, an' foolish n., 361:18
　of absolute beauty, 74:12
　of good life, 721:9

Notions about things that happen to us, 396:11
　fair practices to fair n., 74:12
Notre Dame, Four Horsemen of N., 643:*n*5
Nourish, praise doth n. agues, 178:23
　show contain and n. all world, 169:4
Nourished, both male and female n. in both, 71:16
　how begot how n., 181:3
　in womb of pia mater, 168:32
　without denying love, 749:1
Nourisher, chief n. in life's feast, 214:6
Nourishes, spirit within n., 94:13
　war n. war, 365:8
Nourishing, magnetic n. night, 489:8
Nourishment, Demeter gave n. of grain, 68:26
　little n. I get, 660:18
　which is called supper, 168:17
Nous avons changé tout cela, 269:*n*3
Novel a mirror that strolls along highway, 396:16
　about nothing, 748:7
　anything that happens subject of n., 120:16
　attempt to represent life, 548:11
　boom in petroleum but not in n., 737:2
　by Henry James like church, 601:12
　detective n. Philistinism, 705:7
　Good Soldier finest French n., 617:8
　happens because storyteller moved to passion, 120:15
　is an art form, 755:15
　obligation of n. be interesting, 548:12
　only a n., 387:10
　passion spent its n. force, 455:10
　supersede fashionable n., 425:10
　to end all novels, 758:4
　wisdom of n., 761:14
Novelists concern themselves with smiling aspects, 532:17
Novels, in pornographic n. action limited, 703:4
　more entertaining than half the n., 626:21
Novelties, world full of untold n., 505:7
Novelty and freshness with familiar, 384:14
　connected with amelioration, 438:6
　interest of n., 384:9
　stains ancient mass, 546:20
　what a n. is man, 271:7
November, 423:1
　fifth of N., 777:20
　now in N. nearer comes, 657:17
　thirty days hath N., 143:13
　what is late N. doing, 670:22
November's sky leaf, 378:3
Novus ordo seclorum, 92:*n*7
Now, eternal n., 267:4
　gods stand up for bastards, 209:1
　he is dead should I fast, 12:12
　here and n. cease to matter, 671:11
　history is n. and England, 672:5

Now (*continued*)
　if n. 'tis not to come, 199:22
　is eternity immortal life, 556:21
　is the accepted time, 44:4
　is the time, 44:4
　is the winter of our discontent, 165:18
　is time for drinking, 96:2
　laborer's task o'er, 506:14
　leave N. for dogs, 465:22
　now cried the Queen, 518:18
　or never, 320:27
　the day is over, 521:11
　there is merely silence, 661:3
　vee may perhaps to begin, 765:14
　what man wants he wants n., 736:16
Nowadays, land of n., 608:11
Nowhere did abide, 381:20
　dressed up n. to go, 606:7
　Eclipse first the rest n., 324:8
　to go but out, 573:24
　who lives everywhere lives n., 106:19
Now's the day, 363:19
Nox est perpetua una dormienda, 90:*n*14
Noxiae poena, 88:*n*6
Nozzle, hold n. agin bank, 536:11
Nuclear control, 742:5
　giants ethical infants, 685:13
　hell of n. destruction, 761:7
Nudgers, numb n., 724:16
Nuisance, guest a n. after three days, 83:14
　not a n. to others, 439:17
　relating exploits a n., 278:4
　universal n., 278:2
　violetflavored, 688:14
Nuit, je dis à cette n., 405:*n*5
　vienne n. sonne l'heure, 641:*n*3
Null, splendidly n., 458:17
Nullifies, amendment n. discrimination, 646:9
Numb nudgers, 724:16
Number, god delights in odd n., 104:*n*12
　greatest happiness of greatest n., 305:*n*4
　harmony manifest in N., 583:13
　he telleth the n. of the stars, 20:15
　if I called wrong n., 690:5
　Lord I want to be in that n., 794:24
　more by your n. than light, 227:9
　teach us to n. our days, 18:13
　the clouds in wisdom, 15:14
　wagers sum on single n., 750:*n*2
　wealth arithmetic cannot n., 238:8
　wealth n. and happiness, 331:25
Numbered, God hath n. thy kingdom, 29:16
　hairs of head n., 34:33
　that which is wanting cannot be n., 23:27
Numbering, time made me n. clock, 172:15
Numberless are world's wonders, 66:9
　infinities of souls, 230:19
　shadows n., 415:10

Numbers, a few honest men better than n., 246:24

came, 302:8

determination of quantities by n., 516:6

divinity in odd n., 183:7

express it in n., 504:11

good luck in odd n., 183:7

greatest happiness for greatest n., 305:20

I lisped in n., 302:8

if opposed n. pluck hearts, 185:20

in n. warmly pure, 324:12

luck in odd n., 420:16

magic n., 291:8

makes small n. formidable, 336:12

mournful n., 440:15

odd n. most effectual, 104:14

physical laws and laws of n., 516:6

slight acquaintance with n., 368:2

vast n. of disinherited, 581:16

what's going on with all these n., 774:3

wise words taught in n., 154:4

Numbing, narcotics n. pain, 457:7

Numbness diffuses my senses, 95:14

drowsy n. pains, 415:9

Numerical precision soul of science, 583:12

Numerous free active individuals, 499:2

same shape very n., 583:2

writers become more n., 328:3

Nun, holy time quiet as n., 374:15

I became a n., 284:9

upbringing n. would envy, 765:9

Nuncle, make no use of nothing n., 209:9

Nunnery, get thee to a n., 196:13

of thy chaste breast, 267:14

Nuns fret not, 376:10

Nurse, Athens n. of men, 67:8

best n. Contemplation, 252:29

habit is his n., 365:3

if ye had a good n., 602:13

into greatness, 75:26

meet n. for poetic child, 378:2

nature's soft n., 183:36

of arms, 328:14

of full-grown souls, 484:22

of manly sentiment, 332:13

Peace dear n. of arts, 186:1

sucks the n. asleep, 218:19

this n. this teeming womb, 171:9

unacted desires, 357:12

Nursed dear gazelle, 392:13

Nurseries of Heaven, 581:3

schools n. of vice, 311:19

Nurse's, mewling in n. arms, 191:3

Nurses, wives old men's n., 159:12

Nursing, dressing n. praying and all's over, 402:20

unconquerable hope, 498:13

wrath to keep it warm, 363:2

Nurslings of immortality, 406:20

Nurture, courtly n., 503:4

Nurturing Venus, 89:2

Nut, Figure of a N., 513:16

little n. tree, 790:12

Nut-brown maid, 775:16

Nut-brown (*continued*)

spicy n. ale, 251:16

Nutmeg, silver n., 790:12

Nutmegs ginger cinnamon cloves, 242:16

Nutritive truth, 549:2

Nuts, Brazil where n. come from, 571:31

we's all poor n., 673:14

Nutshell, bounded in a n., 195:26

Nymph, haste thee N., 251:8

in thy orisons, 196:11

mountain n. sweet liberty, 251:10

sweet Echo sweetest n., 252:26

Nympha pudica Deum vidit, 264:*n*3

Nymphets, creatures I designate n., 703:2

Nymphic, maidens not human but n., 703:2

Nymph's, twitch N. garment off, 465:6

Nymphs and satyrs, 599:17

O

O altitudo, 248:4

Altitudo in bloodstream, 675:4

blue O, 565:17

Captain my Captain, 490:19

fortunatam natam me consule Romam, 88:*n*3

my prophetic soul, 194:20

O O O Shakespeherian Rag, 668:21

quanta qualia sunt illa sabbata, 121:*n*3

tell me all about Anna Livia, 647:19

tempora O mores, 87:7

terque quaterque beati, 93:*n*9

wooden O, 184:19

Oafs, muddied o. at goals, 593:7

Oak and ash and thorn, 593:17, 785:8

bend knotted o., 291:7

grass-blade's no easier than o., 485:6

heart of o. our ships, 323:18

hearts of o., 140:7

in o. none is, 791:15

many strokes fell the o., 155:*n*2

owl lived in o., 554:18

revolution growth natural as o., 462:15

shadow of British o., 332:18

under o. in stormy weather, 289:22

Oak-cleaving thunderbolts, 209:24

Oaken, old o. bucket, 398:3

Oakhurst, body of John O., 531:25

Oakland California no there there, 627:13

Oakleaves, stone steel stone o., 670:4

Oaks, fell great o., 310:4

from little acorns, 119:18

many strokes overthrow o., 155:9

Oar, broken o. and gear of dead, 671:13

never had o. or lance, 73:5

no better companion than o., 503:6

put in her o., 150:26

wind and wave and o., 454:11

Oars, both o. with little skill, 517:1

falling o. kept time, 268:25

Oars (*continued*)

keep time, 391:8

muffled o., 386:2

were silver, 217:14

Oasis in air of lost connections, 743:1

Oatcakes, Calvin o. and sulphur, 380:1

Oaten, if aught of o. stop, 324:13

Oath, blushed as he gave o., 320:29

break o. he never made, 263:24

Cophetua sware o., 456:5

good mouth-filling o., 178:10

he that imposes o., 263:24

in lapidary inscriptions not upon o., 316:27

punishment if one swears false o., 52:17

swore full great o., 785:8

this o. and this indenture, 71:1

trust man on o. or bond, 211:26

whore's o., 210:13

Oaths are but words, 263:22

are straws, 185:2

false as dicers' o., 197:28

God not take you to task for o., 116:5

liar always lavish of o., 249:18

strange o., 191:3

Oats, definition of o. meant to vex, 314:*n*1

grain given to horses, 314:6

mares eat o., 791:15

munch your good dry o., 173:22

Obadias, young O., 287:8

Obdured, arm the o. breast, 257:14

Obedience bane of genius, 406:8

coercing into o., 661:10

enforced o., 209:3

fear keeps men in o., 235:18

infuses that liberal o., 331:23

love o. troops of friends, 216:9

makes slaves of men, 406:8

principle of rule or o., 338:1

rebellion o. to God, 779:3

to law demanded, 576:3

to which is fixed o., 184:23

transforms o. into duty, 319:6

Obedient, city o. to his will, 75:16

compulsion to become o., 658:7

to their laws we lie, 60:11

to truth, 493:19

to whomsoever in authority, 72:2

Obelisk, strong upright like o., 573:2

Obelisks, these two great o., 4:10

Obermann, sedulous ape to O., 561:19

Oberon, I jest to O., 173:2

my O. what visions, 173:24

Obese, solitude grew o., 755:12

Obesity mental state, 710:16

Obey, Anna whom three realms o., 299:13

drift wait and o., 593:27

fate summons monarchs o., 274:25

haunch and hump is O., 592:17

I but o. urge of song, 625:5

in silence tyrannous word, 507:10

Music's power o., 275:7

my duty to o. orders, 504:9

nature must o. necessity, 189:21

thy heart, 429:19

Offer (*continued*)
 itself to be unmasked, 651:22
 not o. to people but ask, 740:20
 nothing to o. but blood, 620:5
 yourselves to sea, 547:6
Offered, I o. Being for it, 512:19
Offering, a lamb for a burnt o., 7:34
 too little asking too much, 372:2
Offerings, knowledge of God more
  than burnt o., 29:26
 pale Hecate's o., 213:21
Office and affairs of love, 186:21
 and custom, 200:7
 boy to Attorney's firm, 529:6
 Circumlocution O., 471:8
 great o. not filled by great men,
  536:6
 Heaven about to confer great o.,
  80:3
 I shall return to the o., 293:14
 insolence of o., 196:10
 never ask refuse resign o., 311:3
 perpetual o. seekers, 677:2
 prisidincy highest o., 603:14
 public o. public trust, 532:n3
 serves it in o. of a wall, 171:9
 so act toward o. so toward wealth,
  108:12
 so clear in his great o., 213:7
 to execute laws royal o., 332:21
 to o. and so to bed, 644:4
 unfit to hold an o., 83:5
 vice-presidency most insignificant o.,
  338:12
 vice-prisidincy next highest an' lowest o., 603:14
 which false man does easy, 214:17
Officeholder, president is o., 729:21
Officer, drunken o. of British rule,
  763:8
 fear each bush an o., 165:6
Officers, behind o. government people,
  501:17
 civil o. removed on impeachment,
  346:8
 her o. march with armies, 463:16
 make o. but not scholars, 234:28
 white o. cast lot, 522:13
Offices acceptable as elsewhere, 344:3
 cast longing eye on o., 344:3
 estates degrees and o., 180:27
 female sex excluded from honors
  and o., 347:11
 people I cannot win with o., 271:15
 post o. and cabinet appointments,
  448:n2
 sensitive to mass sentiment, 677:2
Official, no o. high or petty, 683:2
 not just an elected o., 745:18
Officials, sharp attacks on public o.,
  719:4
Officious innocent sincere, 317:26
Offspring of heaven firstborn, 257:23
 tempt its new-fledged o., 329:14
 terrible from camps, 717:1
 time's noblest o., 296:27
 true source of human o., 258:26
 we are also his o., 41:17, 82:12
 we are your o., 82:2
Oft in the stilly night, 392:7

Often, hit o., 647:5
Ogalala Iroquois, 725:11
O'Grady, Colonel's Lady an' Judy O.,
  592:21
 Lily O. silly and shady, 665:18
Oh say can you see, 391:2
 what a beautiful mornin', 692:8
Oil, everything soothed by o., 104:1
 for its own wheels, 334:14
 her mouth is smoother than o.,
  20:26
 land of o. olive, 10:16
 little o. in a cruse, 12:33
 midnight o., 242:7, 297:6
 no use of o., 224:4
 of joy for mourning, 28:6
 pouring o. on the sea, 104:n1
 thou anointest my head with o.,
  16:17
 vinegar sugar, 330:9
 wasted o. unprofitably burns,
  334:13
 wisdom out of midnight o., 598:2
 woe to him who seeks to pour o.
  upon waters, 486:20
 words were softer than o., 17:28
Oily, glib and o. art, 208:25
 round fat o. man of God, 308:15
Ointment, at three hundred pence o.
  prize, 243:6
 better than precious o., 24:6
 box of precious o., 36:20
 good name like precious o., 159:13
 not sold for three hundred pence,
  40:22
Ointments, odors of o. more durable,
  159:13
OK, 780:8
 I'm O. you're O., 728:10
O.K. by me in America, 763:6
Okie means scum, 710:10
Oklahoma, Okie mean from O.,
  710:10
Olaf glad and big, 688:16
Old abusing of God's patience, 182:23
 accompany o. age, 216:9
 acquaintance be forgot, 362:19
 Adam, 50:11
 Age and Experience, 283:27
 Age coming bolt door, 118:10
 age crown of life, 88:12
 age ill layer-up of beauty, 186:4
 age, in a good o., 7:29
 age in universal man, 158:n3
 age is woman's hell, 267:20
 age lacking neither honor nor lyre,
  95:30
 age level light, 683:14
 age play's last act, 88:12
 age should burn, 737:20
 age the harbor of all ills, 82:6
 age the only disease, 432:9
 age time of spending, 262:11
 all times o. are good, 404:2
 always wanted to be o., 735:11
 and bitter of tongue, 595:3
 and crafty and wise, 595:3
 and foolish king, 24:1
 and godly and grave, 595:3
 and gray full of sleep, 595:1

Old (*continued*)
 and gray-headed error, 248:24
 and haughty nation, 252:14
 and old sad and old, 647:22
 and remember only what not happened, 528:13
 and stricken in years, 10:38
 and young on last cruise, 560:17
 apple tree, 627:16
 armchair, 480:9
 as I am for love unfit, 276:26
 as the hills, 379:18, 610:12
 as we left grow o., 606:9
 as yonder elm, 647:20
 ash on o. man's sleeve, 671:21
 ask for the o. paths, 28:18
 at evening candlelit, 144:2
 authors to read, 158:23
 bald cheater Time, 232:1
 ball game, 827:16
 battered wrecked o. man, 491:5
 bawd is dead, 599:19
 beats off louring O. Age, 136:7
 beauty making beautiful o. rime,
  221:22
 before we grow o. and die, 595:20
 being o. having lighted rooms,
  751:1
 bellows full of angry wind, 597:5
 bells of O. Bailey, 788:20
 bitch gone in teeth, 659:10
 Black Joe, 507:4
 black ram tupping ewe, 205:15
 books wines, 329:25
 born o. and ugly, 469:34
 busy o. fool unruly Sun, 228:11
 Cary Grant fine, 713:3
 cast me not off in the time of o.
  age, 17:40
 change o. love for new, 156:13
 chaos of sun, 638:26
 chilly and grown o., 466:15
 chip of o. block, 332:1
 custom made life sweet, 190:6
 dance attention on o. age, 599:14
 dance in o. dame yet, 633:3
 darling I am growing o., 557:1
 despise not thy mother when she is
  o., 22:21
 disease of o. men avarice, 236:20
 dog barks backward, 624:9
 dog Tray, 388:n3
 dogs shame nakedness of o. man,
  52:20
 early candle-light of o. age, 491:17
 education best provision for o. age,
  77:16
 ends stolen of holy writ, 165:27
 England to adorn, 593:17
 England's winding sheet, 359:15
 every o. man's eye, 175:17
 faiths loosen and fall, 534:4
 familiar faces, 387:14
 fashions please best, 167:24
 father antick the law, 176:29
 father old artificer, 647:11
 Father William, 386:8, 517:9
 few know how to be o., 265:42
 foolish fond o. man, 211:10
 former things grow o., 241:13

Old (*continued*)

weary and o. with service, 225:16
weeping philosopher when o., 179:30
when he is o. he will not depart, 22:9
when he's o. cashiered, 205:12
when o. age crept over, 583:11
when o. men gather, 608:11
when thou art o. and rich, 204:10
when time is o., 200:22
wine to drink, 158:23
wine wholesomest, 237:11
wines, 329:25
winter hangs on till o., 616:10
with o. woes new wail, 220:18
wives' fables, 45:16
wives' tale, 602:1
woman lived in shoe, 790:2
woman lived under hill, 792:4
woman tossed in blanket, 790:16
women should not be perfumed, 55:4
wood burn brightest, 237:11
wood to burn, 158:23
words when short best, 622:11
world not grow o. at all, 279:17
World overrun with oppression, 340:21
world too o., 461:13
you never can be o., 221:21
young and o. come forth to play, 251:15
young and o. the same, 62:19
young in limbs judgment o., 180:23
young men think o. men fools, 157:3

Older men declare war, 626:1
place than Eden, 619:4
realize he was growing o., 616:11
she is o. every minute, 544:24
than the rocks, 538:6
they hurt me I grow o., 659:3
we grow o. world stranger, 671:10
you're o. and white and free, 709:1
Oldest hath borne most, 211:21
loves but their o. clothes, 228:9
sins newest ways, 184:13
two o. professions, 666:1
Old-fashioned House we dwell in, 514:11
poetry choicely good, 245:24
Old-time, that o. religion, 780:3
Old-timers, we are o., 742:19
Old-type natural fouled-up guys, 750:14
'Ole, if you knows of a better o., 666:7
O'Leary, with O. in grave, 596:1
Oligarchical, power in o. junto, 338:16
Oligarchy government resting on property, 75:23
Oliphant, Roland sonnez de votre o., 121:n9
Olive grove of Academe, 261:1
in her mouth was an o. leaf, 7:20
land of oil o., 10:16
leaf pacific sign, 260:23
vines and o. trees, 721:2

Oliver, a Roland for an O., 121:n10
Roland valorous O. wise, 121:13
Twist asked for more, 469:5
Olives of endless age, 221:23
Olivia, cry out, 201:28
Olympian, in wrath the O. Pericles, 72:13
is a difficult foe, 51:3
Olympic, victor in O. games or announcer, 62:31
Olympus ever unchanging, 53:9
made O. tremble, 51:2, 53:n4
Notes from O., 652:7
pile Ossa on O., 53:19
roll up leafy O., 92:25
shady O., 53:n4
Om, 50:21
Omar, diver O. plucked from bed, 486:3
inclined to agree with O., 710:3
Omega, I am Alpha and O., 48:4
Omelet, can't make o. without breaking eggs, 786:19
Omelette, ne saurait faire o. sans casser des oeufs, 786:19
Omen, may it not be an o., 118:12
Omens, barbaric o., 663:19
sits watching for o., 73:15
'Omer smote bloomin' lyre, 592:11
Omission, sins of o. venial, 318:8
Omissions are not accidents, 664:n2
Omit needless words, 608:9
Omitted all voyage of their life, 189:19
Omne ignotum pro magnifico est, 109:n13
post coitum o. animal triste, 119:21
Omnes eodem cogimur, 96:n6
eodem patre nati, 235:4
Omnia vincit amor, 92:n10
Omnibuses, carriages and o., 650:16
Omnipotence, sea creation of O., 618:11
Omnipotent but friendless to reign, 406:21
defy the O. to arms, 255:22
docile and o., 512:18
Father with his thunder, 53:n4
Omnipresence, brooding o. in sky, 542:22
Omnipresent process of sex, 578:6
Omnis cellula a cellula, 497:1
Omnivorous, I am o., 714:8
On bus or off bus, 768:1
off agin o. agin, 607:6
Stanley on, 378:15
with New Woman, 570:9
with the dance, 399:22
ye brave, 389:4
Once and future king, 133:n6
in a lifetime, 660:10
man can die but o., 184:5
more unto the breach, 185:3
more upon waters, 399:18
one lives but o., 349:2
to every man and nation, 485:1
to have died o. enough, 94:22
Ondoyant, l'homme vain divers et o., 145:n6
One a penny, 790:9

One (*continued*)

acquainted with night, 624:3
all for o., 166:37, 427:12
all o. a hundred years hence, 432:27
all things are o., 62:9
alone I am with him, 112:16
among a thousand, 15:2
and inseparable, 394:16
and the same thing, 278:9
bell strikes o., 296:9
born in a manger, 270:8
by one two by two, 408:1
clear call for me, 460:11
composed of many, 94:29
conceive many without the o., 76:7
country one constitution, 395:2
crowded hour, 333:8
dead deathless hour, 509:23
each hath o. and is o., 228:3
enemy is too much, 244:30
ere herde at tothir out, 128:20
fair daughter and no more, 195:33
fall o. by o., 330:23
far-off divine event, 458:3
fire burns out another's, 174:16
fish ball, 503:2
flew over cuckoo's nest, 792:8
food to o. poison to others, 90:7
foot in sea one on shore, 186:28
for all, 166:37, 427:12
for my master, 788:18
for o. sweet grape vine destroy, 166:38
found truth in all but o., 172:8
from all, 112:21
from all things o. and from o. all things, 62:16
god greatest among gods, 60:6
God law element, 458:3
good knowledge, 70:20
good turn deserves another, 105:3
hearts that beat as o., 439:9
hundred years of solitude, 759:1
I am party of o., 703:15
if by land, 442:13
if ever two were o., 262:15
in life and death, 530:4
is fat and grows old, 177:22
is or is not, 76:8
just o. of those things, 682:4
less than tenth part of o., 200:20
little o. shall become a thousand, 28:5
live as two, 670:3
lost but o. twa behin', 363:24
low man adding o. to o., 465:24
majority of o., 477:12
man among a thousand, 24:14
man of o. book, 118:19
man one vote, 783:20
man's meat another's poison, 90:n6
man's will all men's misery, 155:4
minute with him, 654:12
more river, 794:19
more unfortunate, 423:9
my little o. pretty o., 456:10
nature o. and continuous, 477:23
never lose touch of the o., 584:4
not o. for putting off proof, 624:4
on God's side majority, 462:17

One (*continued*)
   our two souls which are o., 229:12
   pain lessened by another's, 174:16
   parted between twelve and o.,
      184:30
   pay for o. by o., 592:6
   people arose as o. man, 11:21
   perfect limousine, 687:11
   perfect rose, 687:11
   road up and road down o. and
      same, 62:17
   shock of recognition, 486:13
   small o. a strong nation, 28:5
   small step for man, 762:13
   spot where I made O., 446:9
   striking at root of evil, 478:13
   swallow not a summer, 78:1
   sweet sacrifice, 225:6
   sweetly solemn thought, 504:6
   that loved not wisely, 208:16
   the o. and the many, 76:4
   the other will contain, 512:20
   Thing O. and Thing Two, 715:3
   third of a nation, 649:7
   this o. thing I do, 44:32
   three centuries removed, 711:2
   to succeed possible only o. way,
      78:3
   touch of nature, 201:3
   two and third in your bosom,
      175:19
   two one two, 518:16
   two three strikes you're out, 637:16
   twothreefourfive pigeons, 688:10
   we are o. flesh, 260:12
   what did Loved O. pass on from,
      712:8
   who died for Truth, 512:13
   word frees us, 67:10
   word plastics, 762:14
   world's life and mine o., 504:17
One-and-a-half, aphorism o. truths,
   626:6
One-and-twenty, when I was o.,
   578:22
One-armed man pasting wallpaper,
   585:18
One-book man, 380:14
One-eyed, in country of blind o. man
   is king, 136:6
One-hoss shay, 447:16, 447:17
Oneness, household in o. of mind,
   53:10
Ones, great o. eat up little o., 219:21
Oneself, belong to o., 145:21
   idea of o. as cause, 278:3
   little one knows o., 678:13
   look better into o., 586:10
   mistaking o. for oracle, 613:14
   not live unto o., 81:9
   to be saint for o., 494:15
One's-Self I sing, 488:13
One-third of a nation, 649:7
One-upmanship, 705:6
One-woman waterfall, 760:14
Onion atoms lurk in bowl, 380:17
   let first o. flourish, 561:15
   thumb instead of o., 764:15
   will do well for such shift, 167:14
Onions, eat no o. nor garlic, 173:28

Onions (*continued*)
   wel loved he garleek o. lekes, 130:7
Onlie begetter of insuing sonnets,
   220:*n*1
Only love sprung from only hate,
   174:24
   that it is your o. one, 78:15
   winning isn't everything o. thing,
      783:26
Onset, stand aside from enemy's o.,
   72:7
Ontogenesis recapitulation of phylogenesis, 522:15
Ontogeny recapitulates phylogeny,
   522:*n*4
Onward Christian soldiers, 521:10
   goes pilgrim band, 521:12
   half a league o., 458:9
   sailors cry, 577:6
   steer right o., 255:15
Ootah, Eskimo O. had explanation,
   570:6
Oozing out at palm of my hands,
   352:16
Oozy weeds about me twist, 487:10
Opal, cloudy flaming o. ring, 594:12
Ope his mouth out flew trope, 262:21
   their golden eyes, 219:24
   when I o. my lips, 179:20
Open and friendly in private, 72:2
   covenants of peace, 572:13
   door, 536:16
   doors of his face, 15:22
   ear the o. vowels tire, 298:18
   ever-o. door, 51:*n*6
   eyes o. before marriage, 309:24
   face facts with both eyes o., 137:6
   free and o. encounter, 255:4
   locks whoever knocks, 215:16
   my heart, 465:12
   my mistress the o. road, 561:22
   no right to o. door, 74:19
   page of book carelessly o., 759:15
   ports of slumber o., 184:9
   rebuke better than secret love, 23:1
   road, 561:22
   sentence is for o. war, 256:26
   sesame, 778:13
   speech o. man to man, 280:*n*1
   thou my lips, 17:24
   Time and let him pass, 583:18
   unto whom all hearts are o., 49:13
   war, 256:26
   where knock is o. wide, 325:12
   ye everlasting gates, 259:22
   ye the gates, 26:28
Opened, door we never o., 670:13
   he o. us, 740:10
   knock and it shall be o., 34:6
   Lord o. mouth of the ass, 10:4
   my heart new o., 225:16
   your eyes shall be o., 6:20
Openest, thou o. thine hand, 20:12
Open-eyed Conspiracy, 224:6
Opening eyelids of the morn, 253:17
   myth is secret o., 712:15
   of a Door, 514:17
Open-minded impartial adjustment,
   572:13

Opera ain't over till fat lady sings,
   782:*n*4
Operas, German text of French o.,
   586:20
Operate, show how myths o. in
   minds, 724:1
Operation, military o. involves deception, 80:18
   preparing us for fatal o., 730:20
Operations by which length determined, 646:3
   enjoy both o. at once, 667:4
   we perform without thinking, 584:8
Ophelia, I loved O., 199:16
Ophir, distant O., 633:18
Opiate, emptied dull o., 415:9
Opinion, backed o. with quotations,
   287:21
   basis of government o., 343:12
   custom supported by popular o.,
      577:7
   determined by feelings, 493:1
   difference of o., 247:17
   difference of o. makes horse-races,
      527:18
   endeavoring to stifle, 439:16
   error of o. tolerated, 344:5
   governs world, 572:3
   gross and scope of my o., 192:22
   having no o. at all, 342:14
   historians of o., 652:9
   hold o. with Pythagoras, 181:17
   honor depends on o. of mob,
      278:13
   inconsistencies of o., 395:6
   individual given freedom of o.,
      648:4
   intelligence of public o., 522:11
   is knowledge in making, 254:26
   is of his own o. still, 264:1
   is truth filtered, 462:20
   is uniformity of o. attainable, 343:8
   live after world's o., 431:22
   luxury of own o., 474:16
   man know how to defy o., 368:11
   no o. but their own, 572:9
   no very exalted o., 331:5
   of Pythagoras concerning wildfowl,
      181:*n*3
   of strongest always best, 267:23
   only one of contrary o., 439:12
   orthodox in o., 683:2
   public o. everything, 448:13
   public o. exacts obedience, 506:11
   public o. in advance of law, 603:20
   Public O. variable, 505:12
   public o. weak tyrant, 477:30
   public o. welcomes talent, 72:2
   raw material of o., 572:3
   researchers into Public O., 721:4
   sacrifices it to your o., 331:4
   science and o., 71:9
   stifling o. is evil, 439:16
   subject o. to coercion, 343:7
   that there are no gods, 76:17
   think last o. right, 299:3
   this fool-gudgeon this o., 179:22
   unanimity of o., 586:9
   vagrant o. without support, 544:21
   whole climate of o., 720:12

Over (*continued*)
 hill over dale, 636:15
 June bustin' out all o., 692:11
 me bright April, 655:2
 opera ain't o. till fat lady sings,
  782:*n*4
 over there, 632:13
 prologues are o., 639:14
 the river, 427:7
Overboard, what though mast blown
  o., 165:2
Overcame, I came saw and o., 184:8
Over-canopied with luscious woodbine, 173:9
Overcoat, Gogol's O., 495:18
 put on your o., 486:2
Overcome, be not o. of evil, 42:19
 but half his foe, 256:19
 difficulty to be o., 61:9
 evil with good, 42:19
 finitude is o., 588:8
 I have o. the world, 40:35
 nature sometimes o., 160:2
 oppression without oppression,
  761:4
 softest things o. hardest, 57:13
 strong by what we o., 532:11
 terror at own finitude, 588:8
 thou shalt not be o., 128:1
 we shall o., 783:21
Overcomes, who o. by force, 256:19
Overcometh, to him that o., 47:8
Overexpecting happiness in married
  estate, 250:14
Overexplanatory, our zestfully o. age,
  768:6
Overfed, horses and poets not o.,
  151:28
Overflow, meadow rivulets o., 540:25
 of powerful feelings, 373:17
Overflows, the fountain o., 357:7
Overgrow, suffer them and they'll o.
  garden, 163:24
Overhanging, brave o. firmament,
  195:28
Overhear cry of pain, 729:11
Overlook, communities o. one an-
  other, 58:6
 knowing what to o., 546:3
Overmastered with piece of dust,
  186:18
Over-offended ladies, 293:23
Overpast, until the indignation be o.,
  26:30
Overrefines argument brings self to
  grief, 127:9
Overseer, no guide o. or ruler, 20:27
Overserious, reindeer seem o., 665:7
Overset mind with reading, 557:13
Overstep not modesty of nature,
  196:22
Overt, two witnesses to o. act, 346:9
Overtake, I thy fate shall o., 242:2
Overthrew the tables of moneychang-
  ers, 35:41
Overthrow, forcible o. of social condi-
  tions, 482:7
 linger out a purposed o., 221:13
 revolutionary right to o., 449:4
 whom thou thinkest thou o., 230:22

Overthrow (*continued*)
 ye cannot o. it, 41:1
Overwhelm myself in poesy, 414:3
Overwhelming, let it be o., 624:4
 loss so o., 450:9
 tiny differences in input o., 775:2
Overwhelms, greatness of name o.
  son, 233:6
Overwise in doing thy business, 31:25
 keep talk from getting o., 624:4
Overwork, killed by o., 591:8
Overworked, neither idle nor o.,
  523:10
Overzealous, mistaken o. piety, 332:5
Ovid, Venus clerk O., 128:3
Ovo, ab o., 98:*n*6
Owe, duty we o. Creator, 339:11
 fame only to myself, 249:22
 God a death, 184:5
 I o. a cock, 70:25
 if I can't pay I can o., 140:14
 it to posterity, 345:15
 me five farthings, 788:20
 no man anything, 42:21
 no man hate, 191:9
 Shallow I o. thousand pound,
  184:17
 sum married people o., 349:24
 to this place I o. everything, 448:16
Owed, so much o. by so many, 620:10
 throw away dearest thing he o.,
  212:26
Owedst, sleep which thou o., 207:6
Owes, by owing o. not, 258:4
 duty subject o. prince, 167:35
 me another existence, 350:6
 no homage unto sun, 248:22
 not any man, 441:4
 nothing to land, 319:20
 your representative o. you, 331:4
Owest, lend less than thou o., 209:8
 worm no silk, 210:6
Owing, by o. owes not, 258:4
Owl and Pussycat, 471:31
 by mousing o. hawked at, 214:18
 calls name of man who is to die,
  707:2
 clamorous o., 173:11
 Creek bridge, 544:10
 for all his feathers, 414:21
 in Douglas fir turn head, 756:18
 lived in an oak, 554:18
 nightly sings the staring o., 169:13
 night's herald, 165:13
 of Minerva spreads wings, 372:5
 Pussy said to O., 472:1
 sadder than o. songs, 403:19
 that shrieked, 214:2
 to moon complain, 322:3
Owlet Atheism, 382:18
 whoops to wolf below, 382:3
Owls, bringing o. to Athens, 73:9
 companion to o., 14:45
 couch when o. do cry, 224:25
 court for o., 27:7
 no o. in whole island, 317:*n*1
 two o. and hen, 471:27
Own a bit of ground, 511:2
 he forgets not his o., 777:8
 how feel to be on your o., 771:9

Own (*continued*)
 if any provide not for his o., 45:18
 ill-favored thing but mine o., 192:14
 my o. my native land, 378:1
 my o. shall come to me, 532:6
 of thine o. have we given, 13:18
 poor thing but mine o., 192:*n*1
 the soft impeachment, 352:17
 thing that is your o., 78:15
Owned, dearest thing he o., 212:26
 I was o. of Thee, 513:14
Owner of the sphere, 430:12
 ox knoweth his o., 25:25
Owners, lords and o. of their faces,
  221:15
Ownership, woman proclaim o., 586:2
Owning, mania of o. things, 489:16
Ox, as an o. goeth to the slaughter,
  20:32
 eateth grass as an o., 15:20
 knoweth his owner, 25:25
 lion eat straw like the o., 26:11
 makes difference whose o. gored,
  138:16
 not covet neighbor's o., 9:12
 not muzzle o. when treadeth corn,
  10:21
 of the wrongdoer, 3:15
 one Law for Lion and O., 357:15
 stalled o. and hatred therewith,
  21:26
 stands on my tongue, 63:10
 tired o. treads with firmer step,
  114:10
Oxen, draw more than hundred pair
  of o., 235:*n*3
 of his own breeding, 95:13
 who drives fat o., 317:31
 years like great black o., 594:19
Oxford, clever men at O., 578:17
 from O. up pathway strays, 499:15
 leave O. by town drain, 553:23
 spires of O., 648:3
 Street stony-hearted, 397:14
Oxlips and nodding violet grows,
  173:9
Oyster, bold man first eat o., 290:8
 may be crossed in love, 353:3
 pearl in your foul o., 192:15
 sharpening my o. knife, 707:5
 solitary as o., 470:3
 unseasonable to eat an o., 147:10
 world's mine o., 182:26
Oyster-bank, shelving in o., 433:15
Oysters come walk with us, 519:1
 wait a bit the O. cried, 519:4
Oz, feel like I'm in O., 710:4
Ozymandias king of kings, 406:13

P

Pace, creeps in this petty p., 216:14
 moving to faster p., 756:20
 not keep p. with companions,
  478:37
 requiescat in p., 119:26
 thoughts with violent p., 207:15
 traveling all same p., 446:10
 unperturbed p., 581:5
Paced into the hall, 381:2

Pacem, desiderat p. praeparet bellum, 114:*n*9
in terris, 644:17
Paces about room again alone, 669:2
three p. through room, 454:16
time travels in divers p., 191:18
Pacific, frontier from Atlantic to P., 620:2
in his name to great P., 637:13
leans on the land, 663:11
olive leaf p. sign, 260:23
stared at the P., 413:24
Pacified Psyche and kissed her, 453:4
Pacify stomach with cool thoughts, 719:12
touchy tribe of poets, 98:2
Pacis, nunc patimur longae p. mala, 109:*n*2
Pack, as huntsman his p., 330:13
clouds away, 233:20
hear baying of p., 680:7
meets with Pack in Jungle, 592:16
nothing but p. of cards, 518:12
relations a tedious p., 567:9
up your troubles, 641:11
when it begins to rain, 209:18
Packard, first P. had whipstock, 683:6
Packet, flash p. of fame, 793:21
Liverpool p., 793:22
Packs and sets of great ones, 211:13
Padded lunatic asylums, 650:17
Paddle, doves p. in putrescent waters, 699:10
in cold streams, 596:6
own canoe, 406:4
Paddling palms and pinching fingers, 222:18
Paddocks, cold as p., 241:21
Paddy dear did ye hear, 779:10
Padlock, clap p. on her mind, 287:19
Padua, come to wive it wealthily in P., 167:18
Pagan, Christian p. spoiled, 590:5
poor p. planet of ours, 486:14
suckled in creed outworn, 376:12
tenets admitted into p. creed, 536:18
who defends religion, 611:4
Page, beautiful quarto p., 352:27
cannot tear out p. of life, 436:19
don't know which writing this p., 700:12
excels at title p., 328:1
history's purchased p., 399:27
knowledge her ample p., 322:12
life's p., 399:17
of book carelessly open, 759:15
of prancing Poetry, 514:2
refine her sterling p., 280:15
shone not on poet's p., 97:*n*1
Pageant, became like piece of p., 582:16
insubstantial p. faded, 224:21
Pageantry, mask and antique p., 251:19
of a king, 346:2
Pages, like volume of blank p., 436:4
picture shows what p. expound, 482:18
turn p. of Greek models, 98:15

Pagoda, old Moulmein P., 591:22
Paid, attention must be p., 738:15
debt to Nature's quickly p., 242:10
in his own coin, 149:17
shoot murderer without asking to be p., 762:11
soul bought and p. for, 463:3
tell you what I p., 514:12
well p. that is satisfied, 182:6
with moan, 581:2
with sighs aplenty, 578:23
Paige, inclined to agree with Satchel P., 710:3
Pail, milk comes frozen home in p., 169:13
Pain, after great p. formal feeling, 512:6
and anguish wring brow, 378:14
and boredom foes of happiness, 404:16
and evil in life of worms, 505:1
and pleasure rudders, 277:*n*6
aromatic p., 301:10
as readily blisses as p., 539:7
assuage unforgotten p., 509:27
beauty pierce like p., 629:8
bitterest p. among men, 70:13
born in other's p., 581:2
cease upon midnight with no p., 415:16
cool one P., 513:10
cry of p. that could have got worse, 729:11
cure not worth the p., 99:*n*5
cures me of my p., 778:7
darkness and cold, 467:19
dashed with p., 623:20
die of rose in aromatic p., 301:10
disposed to one another by p., 110:13
doomed to company with p., 376:9
doubt hesitation and p., 464:26
draw thy breath in p., 199:27
envy calumny hate p., 409:4
equal ease unto my p., 246:7
eternal p., 498:16
feast of joy a dish of p., 156:22
for leaven, 533:10
full of p. this intellectual being, 257:2
gentleman never inflicts p., 427:1
great p. and restlessness, 662:10
has Element of Blank, 513:2
heart rapture then p., 554:13
history of wound beguiles p., 320:15
I know my life's a p., 227:15
joys three parts p., 467:8
king of p., 534:9
labor we delight in physics p., 214:12
laughter with p. fraught, 408:7
life a memory without p., 66:2
light life pleasure p., 520:9
man dies in p., 283:16
marriage has more joy than p., 67:21
mighty p. to love, 267:2
narcotics numbing p., 457:7
neither any more p., 48:1

Pain (*continued*)
occasional enjoyments lighting p., 584:11
of a new idea, 506:8
of bone spur in heel, 702:9
of finite hearts, 465:13
oh the p. the bliss, 299:8
older connotation of p., 723:9
one p. lessened by another's, 174:16
Our Lady of P., 533:13
painful pleasure to pleasing p., 153:16
peace nor help for p., 499:22
pleasure is intermission of p., 239:5
pleasure so exquisite almost p., 397:8
pleasures banish p., 294:19
records of heart in p., 423:13
sense of pity beauty p., 572:19
short joy eternal, 365:18
sudden cry of p., 650:10
sweet pleasure after p., 276:10
tender for another's p., 321:17
that cannot forget, 63:11
time cancels young p., 68:8
'tis p. that p. to miss, 267:2
to the bear, 425:19
tongueless vigil and all the p., 533:8
travaileth in p., 42:3
turns with ceaseless p., 328:7
unfinished man and his p., 598:4
wanders through bones, 725:19
weight and p. of life, 67:10
what p. it was to drown, 165:30
which cost Ceres all that p., 258:10
with p. purchased inherit p., 168:13
words of p. tones of anger, 125:8
world p., 367:*n*1
yearning like God in p., 415:1
you purchase p., 300:15
Painful, good honest p. sermon, 279:4
how glorious and p., 461:16
how p. to keep money, 279:23
it's p. and difficult, 706:1
pleasure to pleasing pain, 153:16
seem no p. inch to gain, 483:3
to excess, 663:19
truth, 339:7
warrior famoused for fight, 220:14
Pains, capacity for taking p., 532:2
disciplined state of pleasures and p., 277:*n*6
genius capacity for getting into p., 525:5
marriage has many p., 314:12
members partake of p., 150:17
nothing but labor for p., 148:16
nothing without p., 148:*n*11
numbness p. sense, 415:9
of all p. the greatest, 267:2
of love be sweeter far, 273:13
she gave me for my p., 205:28
stings you for your p., 297:23
Paint an inch thick, 199:8
capture its reality in p., 537:22
does he p., 466:26
flinging pot of p. in public's face, 524:*n*2
fresh as p., 482:12
good-bye Old P., 786:3

Paint (*continued*)

he best can p. them, 300:6

here was something to p., 700:9

hire idiots to p., 358:14

lily, 170:9

lion not so fierce as they p. him, 244:19

meadows with delight, 169:12

my picture truly like me, 247:5

vices and follies, 290:35

Painted, angels are p. fair, 284:17

child of dirt, 302:15

Duchess p. on wall, 464:11

Earth's last picture p., 591:13

fears a p. devil, 214:8

gourds on a shelf, 756:14

I have p. my life, 665:15

love things we see p., 466:24

memory p. perfect day, 585:9

not so black as p., 156:21

not so young as p., 614:5

players and p. stage, 599:21

pomp, 190:6

ship upon painted ocean, 381:7

to the eyes, 539:6

veil call Life, 407:*n*1

winged Cupid p. blind, 172:21

Painter, great p. dips pencil, 406:14

trainer soothsayer, 108:21

Painter's brush consumes dreams, 597:19

mind with that of viewer, 421:13

Painters and poets have equal license, 98:3

boldest p. cannot trace, 294:21

Painting, as in p. so in poetry, 98:18

bridge linking painter's mind, 421:13

feast for eyes, 421:12

give children right to study p., 338:10

gives form to terrors, 645:4

is silent poetry, 60:14

man that has taste of p., 292:23

mediator between world and us, 645:4

poetry is p. that speaks, 60:14

poetry p. and music, 359:22

six essentials in p., 120:13

that lends joyousness, 543:19

what light is to p., 563:3

Paintings Bible of the laity, 121:14

farewell dear p., 247:12

heard of your p., 196:16

Pair, no burial this pretty p., 776:2

nor build nor sing, 383:14

of ragged claws, 667:14

of sparkling eyes, 531:21

of star-crossed lovers, 174:14

of very strange beasts, 192:13

one p. of English legs, 185:10

then there's a p. of us, 511:22

yet happy p., 258:17

Paired butterflies yellow, 659:3

Pairing suggests copying mechanism, 760:5

Paisley, cutty sark o' P. harn, 363:9

Paix, plus facile de faire la guerre que la p., 542:*n*1

Pajamas fresh from washer, 742:21

Pajamas (*continued*)

how got into p. never know, 693:10

I in p. for heat, 657:12

shot elephant in my p., 693:10

Palace and prison on each hand, 400:9

Beautiful, 272:16

cypress in p. walk, 456:20

fair and stately p., 452:5

give p. for hermitage, 172:4

golden mean avoids envy of p., 96:7

of Cyrus, 782:7

of Eternity, 252:13

of the soul, 250:4

road of excess leads to p. of wisdom, 357:3

Palaces, cottages princes' p., 179:27

Death beats at p. of kings, 95:18

gorgeous p., 224:21

'mid pleasures and p., 405:14

my body parks and p., 561:17

not so arched as princes' p., 237:18

prosperity within thy p., 19:27

Paladins, knights and p. aged accents, 161:1

Palate, burst Joy's grape against p. fine, 416:18

Pale and specter-thin, 415:12

Anguish keeps gate, 567:22

bond which keeps me p., 214:28

cast of thought, 196:10

cygnet to this p. swan, 170:20

death on his p. horse, 260:16

Death with impartial tread, 95:18

death's p. flag, 176:17

fear p. and hungry-looking men, 89:1

Galilean, 534:4

hands I loved, 590:16

Hecate's offerings, 213:21

his uneffectual fire, 194:26

horse, 47:19, 260:16

kings and princes, 417:7

leaves yellow black p., 407:13

lies shadow of tomb, 508:27

make p. my cheeks with care, 240:1

Melancholy sate retired, 324:16

name at which world grew p., 313:19

over park over p., 172:30

rest at p. evening, 708:14

so thin so p. yet gold, 353:19

turn not p. beloved snail, 518:7

unripened beauties, 292:7

visit it by p. moonlight, 377:23

why so p. and wan, 262:2

with breath of cloister, 503:4

within circuit of ivory p., 165:10

Pale-faced, pluck honor from p. moon, 177:9

Palely loitering, 417:4

Paleozoic time, 576:15

Paler than grass, 56:5

Palestine national home for Jewish people, 556:2

sunny P., 633:18

Palfrey, his p. broun as is a berye, 129:15

Pall, black p. of nothing, 683:7

in sceptered p. sweeping by, 252:6

Palladium of rights, 345:13

Pallas, pallid bust of P., 452:21

Pallid, angels all p. and wan, 452:8

bust of Pallas, 452:21

the leash-men, 658:19

Palls, everything p., 786:16

upon the sense, 292:8

Palm at end of mind, 640:13

dominion over p. and pine, 592:25

hold infinity in p. of hand, 359:5

itching p., 189:13

oozing out at p. of hands, 352:16

righteous flourish like the p. tree, 18:17

strife with the p., 498:2

touch p. of hand to my body, 490:2

under p. tree at noon, 670:5

wind is in p. trees, 591:22

Palms before my feet, 619:9

on the staircase, 718:22

other p. are won, 375:15

paddling p. and pinching fingers, 222:18

these p. greater than Versailles, 763:9

Palmy, high and p. state of Rome, 192:25

Palmyra, editions of Balbec and P., 323:23

Palo, cuchillo de p., 794:4

Palpable obscure, 257:9

thus p. Elysium, 659:17

Palpitation, came winglike p., 739:4

Palsied, beg alms of p. eld, 204:10

crippled p. slain, 627:1

Palsy, brought p. to bed, 659:16

shakes gray hairs, 415:12

Palter with us in double sense, 216:20

Paltry, aged man p. thing, 597:8

compensations of mankind, 452:12

friendship of Man, 452:9

if conduct mean and p., 79:4

Paly flames, 185:14

Pan, beloved P., 74:10

great god P., 439:8

great god P. is dead, 107:16

milk in the p., 431:12

out of frying p. into fire, 112:12

twitch Nymph's garment off, 465:6

Panacea, I swear by P., 71:1

Panaceas, tobacco goes beyond all p., 235:10

Panama and its poverty, 419:8

Pandemonium city and proud seat, 260:14

Panders, reason p. will, 197:32

Pandion, King P. he is dead, 233:11

Pandora, more lovely than P., 258:24

Panegyric, practitioner in p., 352:35

Panem et circenses, 109:*n*6

Pang, finds p. as great, 204:11

ghastly p., 381:17

learn nor account p., 467:8

preceding death, 328:4

Pange lingua gloriosi, 124:*n*4

Pangolins hornbills pitchers catchers, 665:1

Pangs, in sweet p. remember me, 202:9

more p. and fears, 225:16

more p. wilder wring, 551:13

Pangs (*continued*)
  of disprized love, 196:10
Panic, cowardice distinguished from
    p., 702:7
  hair stand up in p. fear, 67:11
  idiocy during p., 723:3
  shouting fire causing p., 542:24
Panic's in thy breastie, 361:4
Panics have their uses, 340:23
Panjandrum, grand P., 324:7
Pan's cavern, 599:17
Pansies for thoughts, 198:23
Pantaloon, lean and slippered p.,
    191:3
Panteth, as hart p. after water brooks,
    17:11
Panther, mean as a p., 745:17
Panting, chase p. syllable, 334:17
  Time toiled after him, 313:10
Pants, as p. the hart, 285:4
  neither vest nor p., 524:14
Panza, God's blessing said Sancho P.,
    151:n5
  so Sancho P. said, 644:7
Panzer-man panzer-man you, 764:17
Papa, as P. used to say, 470:22
  potatoes poultry, 471:9
Papacy Ghost of Roman Empire,
    239:23
Paper, bread dry as p., 659:15
  bullets of the brain, 186:31
  dry dust and stray p., 659:13
  fill certain portion of uncertain p.,
    402:15
  hand that signed the p., 737:10
  he hath not eat p., 168:29
  make dust our p., 171:24
  name never in p., 738:15
  not what kind of p. but man,
    477:27
  not worth p. written on, 440:7
  receipt of little bit of p., 487:2
  scrap of p., 568:13
  stare at p. until blood on forehead,
    678:19
  unpleasantest words that blotted p.,
    181:9
  verbal agreement isn't worth p.
    written on, 647:3
  virtue of p. government, 331:5
  you drop in ballot box, 477:27
Paper-mill, contrary to king built p.,
    164:11
Papers, fornicated and read p., 732:20
  he's got my p., 762:20
  know what I read in p., 637:17
  turns over your p., 342:8
Paperweight, Queen Victoria like great
    p., 601:17
Papists Jews Turks in one ship,
    247:13
  or Protestants, 315:24
Paquin pull down, 660:1
Par, below p. to extent of two whisk-
    ies, 604:2
Parable, God coined a p., 116:13
Parables, God setteth forth p., 117:4
  of sunlight, 737:13
Parabola, along p. life flies, 766:3
Parachutes, minds like p., 545:4

Parade, Files-on-P., 591:15
  of riches, 326:4
  solemnized with pomp and p.,
    338:5
Parades, no more p. for you and me,
    617:11
Paradise, drunk milk of P., 382:25
  England is p. of women, 154:18
  fool's p., 776:4
  heavenly p. is that place, 226:18
  if p. on face of earth, 777:9
  is where I am, 305:24
  itself were dim, 392:15
  keys of P. O opium, 397:15
  let woman into P., 793:1
  lost Angel of ruined P., 408:17
  mechanics p. of mathematical
    sciences, 135:11
  mount to p., 429:23
  not only in my eyes is P., 126:26
  of exiles Italy, 407:8
  of Fools to few unknown, 258:1
  on earth, 604:16
  same old glimpse of P., 580:14
  stood formed in her yën, 128:25
  they paved, 773:7
  thought would destroy p., 321:17
  to him are opening p., 322:25
  to what we fear of death, 204:15
  Wilderness were P., 445:9
  with me in p., 39:21
Paradox, love p. without losing wit,
    432:12
  mistaking p. for discovery, 613:14
  not p. but truism, 76:4
Paragon, earthly p., 219:32
Paragraph no unnecessary sentences,
    608:9
Parallax, as P. a Flame, 514:3
Parallel, none but himself his p.,
    103:n5
  ours so truly p., 268:22
Parallelism, friendship needs p.,
    535:27
Parallels in beauty's brow, 221:1
Paralyze, campaigns p. cerebration,
    587:15
Paralyzed force, 669:9
  power structures, 761:8
Parameters, slip through p. of skies,
    117:19
Paramount object to save Union,
    449:11
  question for nation, 480:18
Parapets, Europe of ancient p., 565:15
Paraphrase, classics in p., 659:7
Parasite, like any P., 265:n1
Parcel of boilers and vats, 317:22
  of their fortunes, 217:26
  of vain strivings, 476:19
Parcels of dreadful Past, 454:9
Parched, inhabit the p. places, 28:29
Parchment, from p. shaking dust,
    423:20
  should undo a man, 164:9
  skin of innocent lamb p., 164:9
Parchments, everything written on p.
    unrepeatable, 759:1
Parcus deorum cultor et infrequens,
    96:n1

Pard, bearded like the p., 191:3
  false as p. to hind, 200:22
Pardlike spirit, 409:1
Pardon, a God ready to p., 13:23
  beg death's p. now, 749:14
  cannot help or p., 720:6
  for too much loving you, 207:1
  if life bitter to thee p., 535:6
  love truth p. error, 305:27
  me thou bleeding piece of earth,
    188:22
  old fathers, 595:23
  one offense encourage many, 100:11
  pity though not p., 166:20
  remorseful p., 203:21
  to spirit of liberty, 331:10
  virtue of vice p. beg, 198:4
  we p. to extent we love, 265:35
Pardonable, to speak dishonorably is
    p., 67:13
Pardoned all except her face, 403:7
  her iniquity is p., 27:15
Pardoning, in p. we are pardoned,
    123:10
Pardonner, tout comprendre tout p.,
    368:n3
Pardonnera, bien sûr, il me p., 420:13
Pardons, never p. those he injures,
    103:n3
Paree, after they've seen P., 658:3
Parent, lose one p. misfortune, 567:8
  Nature a kind p., 104:2
  of good, 259:7
  poverty is p. of meanness, 75:12
  see his boy as he really is, 607:9
  wealth is p. of luxury, 75:12
Parental, mild p. sway, 503:4
Parents bones on which children
    sharpen teeth, 749:11
  bore their children, 571:17
  children begin loving p., 566:17
  girl needs good p., 656:1
  if in serving his p., 60:17
  in peace children inter p., 69:22
  in Philadelphia ask who were p.,
    527:19
  insist on being obeyed, 366:1
  Jewish man with p. alive, 765:13
  meek-eyed p., 717:1
  reverence for p., 63:2
  show kindness to p., 116:16
  was the same, 782:17
  were Lord knows who, 285:16
  who weighed measured priced,
    471:7
Parents, le sort fait les p., 341:n5
Parents', children mucking up p. lives,
    768:5
Pares, primus inter p., 119:23
Parfums, les p. les couleurs, 494:n3
Paring, artist indifferent p. fingernails,
    647:10
Paris, after they've seen P., 658:3
  Americans die go to P., 566:26
  artist no home save P., 553:10
  from P. to Japan, 280:14
  il n'est bon bec que de P., 134:n2
  is a moveable feast, 702:13
  is P. burning, 676:12
  is well worth a Mass, 154:21

Paris (*continued*)

last time I saw P., 692:7

last time I see P., 681:12

mighty P. when he found, 598:22

my home town, 627:11

no good speech save in P., 134:3

our black classic, 742:15

vaut bien une messe, 154:*n*6

Parish, look upon world as p., 308:24

plain as way to p. church, 190:28

Park, come out to ball p., 754:13

I'll be a p. thou shalt be my deer, 165:10

need p. policeman pretty girl, 675:17

over p. over pale, 172:30

Parked, motorcycle p. like soul of junkyard, 752:3

Parking, paved paradise put up p. lot, 773:7

Parks, I'm world-famous Dr. P. said, 763:19

my body p. and palaces, 561:17

Parley, no truce or p., 621:2

Parley-voo, hinky dinky p., 680:8

Parliament, coach through Act of P., 778:14

of man, 455:18

speaking to Buncombe, 413:13

Three Estates in P., 411:*n*1

Parliaments, kings and p., 310:14

Parlor, queen in p., 790:1

walk into p., 423:11

Parlors, bells in your p., 206:5

Parlous boy, 165:33

Parmigianino did it, 758:1

Parnassus, rocks of your snowy P., 490:6

Parochial, worse than provincial p., 548:8

Parole, classical quotation p. of literary men, 317:23

Parole humaine comme chaudron fêlé, 496:*n*3

Parrot, conscious mind trained like p., 628:14

this p. is no more, 775:5

Parsimony not economy, 332:27

requires no providence, 332:28

Parsnips, words butter no p., 379:16

Parson, if P. lost senses, 611:18

in arguing p. owned skill, 329:18

Parson's, coughing drowns p. saw, 169:14

Parsons, white p. preaching Jesus, 752:10

Part, act lover's or Roman's p., 300:8

art too precise in every p., 241:5

beginning most important p., 75:8

better p. of valor, 179:9

book and heart never p., 287:7

choosest not better p., 587:17

come between bid us p., 308:11

come let us kiss and p., 161:11

death p. of life, 629:11

each play p. in memorable days, 621:6

every man must play a p., 179:17

from yours will not p., 262:7

half p. of blessed man, 169:23

Part (*continued*)

his blessed p. to heaven, 226:2

I am p. of all met, 455:1

I play double p., 711:3

immortal p. of myself, 206:20

know in p., 43:16

looks p. has soul of p., 560:6

love's passives his activest p., 264:15

maid of Athens ere we p., 399:7

Mary hath chosen good p., 38:26

my garments among them, 16:16

my hair behind, 667:19

Nature hath done her p., 259:30

ninth p. of a hair, 178:6

none shall p. us, 530:4

of solution or part of problem, 767:20

of wisdom, 335:7

prophesy in p., 43:16

read p. all through, 646:19

some p. of day I had rued, 623:15

take my own p., 428:16

that which is in p., 43:16

thou and nature so gently p., 218:18

till death us do p., 50:4

we sadly in troublous world, 165:3

which laws or kings cause, 314:15

without kiss, 523:4

you and I must p., 777:7

Partake gale, 302:3

Partaken, banquet p. in anxiety, 59:1

mutual and p. bliss, 253:9

Parted are those singing today, 528:20

between twelve and one, 184:30

fool and money p., 776:18

from others as nail from flesh, 122:2

never be p. bliss or woe, 260:11

never met or never p., 362:11

remember way we p., 534:17

Partes, Gallia est omnis divisa in p. tres, 88:*n*11

Parteth the hoof, 9:21

Parthenope nourished me, 93:8

Partial evil universal good, 301:12

for observer's sake, 300:10

Nature wherefore thus p., 135:13

Partiality, charge fortune with p., 389:11

no p. in his writing, 87:15

Participate in America's growth, 726:2

Participation, deny them p. of freedom, 331:22

hot media low in p. cool media high, 730:4

Particle, each of us p. of mass, 629:5

mind very fiery p., 403:13

part of God, 430:27

Particles, impenetrable movable p., 282:4

not composed of same p., 493:17

straining at p. of light, 418:12

Particular, each p. hair to stand, 194:17

London p. a fog, 471:2

love a bright p. star, 203:9

Particularize, to p. is merit, 358:15

Particulars, do good in minute p., 359:23

Particulars (*continued*)

flies from p. to axioms, 158:12

minutely organized p., 359:23

Parties, always two p., 433:3

divided mankind into p., 351:22

men naturally in two p., 345:4

Parting all we know of heaven, 514:13

foretaste of death, 404:14

if not this p. well made, 189:23

is such sweet sorrow, 175:15

king stood at p. of way, 29:7

shakes p. guest by hand, 201:2

speed the p. guest, 299:26

speeds the p. guest, 597:17

Partir c'est mourir un peu, 570:*n*2

Partisan cares nothing about rights, 75:1

Partition, union in p., 173:19

Partitions, thin p., 274:3

Partner, everybody p. has had it with, 745:1

take side of p. with most vitality, 717:8

Partners, our property subject to control of p., 347:11

set to p. change lobsters, 518:4

Partridge sitteth on eggs, 28:31

Parts, Gaul divided into three p., 88:16

here the p. shift, 466:20

of good natural p., 149:30

of it are excellent, 555:3

one man plays many p., 191:3

only Christian come to these p., 134:10

remembers me his gracious p., 170:4

to-day we have naming of p., 737:3

uttermost p. of the sea, 20:8

virtue on outward p., 181:5

Parturient montes nascetur mus, 98:*n*5

Party, come to aid of p., 781:7

comes from grass roots, 585:6

fire tolerable third p., 477:2

guilt of Stalin before P., 763:13

I am p. of one, 703:15

injured p., 532:5

is madness of many, 303:23

joining political p. casting ballot, 645:12

of Past party of Future, 433:3

of revolution civilization, 428:7

offices not for p., 393:14

platforms are contracts, 655:14

print strongest weapon of p., 638:8

spirit of p., 337:5

that does not carry flag, 422:17

that works both sides of street, 650:4

to p. gave up, 330:10

tribe or clan, 780:21

true poet and of Devil's p., 357:2

unshackled by p., 377:16

p. wants to see people still get rich, 730:15

what that p. has done for women, 491:24

Party-spirit at best madness, 299:22

Parvis e glandibus quercus, 119:18

Pas, du sublime au ridicule il n'y a
    qu'un p., 370:*n*3
  premier p. qui coûte, 307:*n*3
Pasarán, no p., 692:20
Pascal, celebrities such as P., 521:4
Pass, all which will not p. away,
    399:24
  all ye that p. by, 29:2
  and turn again, 430:10
  by me as idle wind, 189:16
  by sight so touching, 374:12
  gates of Hades, 59:24
  he brings to p. every word, 63:7
  heaven and earth p., 33:4
  horseman p. by, 600:3
  I p. a willful stranger, 561:22
  in angels say, 429:23
  in naked breadths of ocean, 442:*n*3
  into nothingness, 414:9
  joy to p. to world below, 94:3
  let him p. for a man, 179:31
  let it be let it p., 305:*n*5
  let the toast p., 352:29
  like night from land to land, 382:5
  loveliest soonest p. away, 411:7
  me the can lad, 579:17
  my words not p. away, 36:11
  not away, 7:32
  not p. save with My authority,
    117:19
  not p. this way again, 780:5
  O let him p., 211:20
  o'er green corn-field did p., 192:12
  on let us pass, 641:10
  onward though dynasties p., 540:22
  open Time let him p., 583:18
  praise Lord p. ammunition, 679:7
  ships that p. in night, 442:16
  strangely p., 220:24
  these things come to p., 36:7
  they shall not p., 570:7, 692:20
  this too shall p. away, 448:14
  through land of Egypt, 8:38
  virtues men praise and p. by, 658:13
  we p. the gate, 602:10
  what cannot speak about p. over,
    677:11
Passage broad to Hell, 82:*n*6
  fret p. through it, 250:9
  man merely p. for food, 134:15
  Northwest P. to intellectual world,
    320:28
  of angel's tear, 413:23
  over the river, 490:4
  to remorse, 212:29
  we did not take, 670:13
  you think particularly fine, 316:19
Passages, apprenticehood to foreign p.,
    170:32
  history has cunning p., 668:7
  which seem confidences, 433:13
Passageways, no life moves in empty
    p., 65:16
Passe, on ne p. pas, 570:*n*4
  tout p., 786:16
Passé, hiverné dans mon p., 641:*n*4
Passed away glory from earth, 375:5
  below horizon of homing, 672:2
  clean over Jordan, 10:32
  for dangers I had p., 205:28

Passed (*continued*)
  fortunes that I have p., 205:24
  over on dry ground, 10:32
  so he p. over, 272:31
  we've p. a lot of water since then,
    647:1
Passenger e'er pukes in, 403:5
Passengers are just that distance from
    death, 56:1
Passenjare, punch in presence of p.,
    520:8
Passer deliciae meae puellae, 90:*n*11
Passer, laissez faire laissez p., 305:21
  ne les laisserez pas p., 570:*n*4
Passeront, ils ne p. pas, 570:*n*4
Passes among the impure, 77:*n*5
  bright youth p. swiftly, 59:26
  every hour that p. O, 361:24
  everything p. art eternal, 462:11
  everything p. perishes palls, 786:16
  men seldom make p., 687:9
  now fancy p. by, 579:2
  rise to feet as He p. by, 591:14
Passest, tell Spartans thou who p. by,
    60:11
Passeth, fashion of world p., 43:3
  one generation p. away, 23:22
  peace which p. understanding,
    44:34
  that within which p. show, 193:3
  wind p. over it, 19:2
Passing, all is p., 641:10
  bells for these who die, 687:2
  longest part of journey p. of gate,
    86:19
  out O bitter ending, 647:22
  past or p. or to come, 597:10
  power p. from the earth, 376:15
  see her p. by, 777:4
  speak each other in p., 442:16
  the love of women, 12:2
  through nature to eternity, 193:1
  tribute of a sigh, 322:18
  wind is p. by, 515:12
Passio, hysterica p., 209:17
Passion, all p. spent, 261:27
  and death of a friend, 174:9
  bards of P., 416:11
  beauty is a simple p., 760:1
  by p. driven, 361:15
  caprice and lifelong p., 566:16
  chaos of thought and p., 301:13
  connect prose and p., 636:10
  cows my p., 470:17
  drug which takes away p., 53:7
  eternal p. eternal pain, 498:16
  fever in mind, 283:2
  for a scarlet coat, 289:15
  for anonymity, 635:6
  for hunting something, 469:8
  for righteousness, 665:9
  gratification of every p., 496:4
  grown man's p., 319:30
  happier in p. we feel, 265:27
  haunted me like a p., 373:4
  holy p. of Friendship, 527:10
  hopeless p., 463:14
  I must speak in p., 177:29
  impulse of p. or interest, 351:21

Passion (*continued*)
  in first p. woman loves lover,
    402:21
  in first p. women love lovers, 266:1
  infinite p. and pain, 465:13
  intellectual p. drives out sensuality,
    135:1
  interpret story of P., 713:9
  Justice forever in p., 463:23
  life action and p., 542:6
  maiden p. for maid, 459:20
  ne'er like angels till p. dies, 227:20
  no longer a p. hidden, 281:10
  nor p. wild, 497:3
  nothing great without p., 372:10
  novel happens because storyteller
    moved to p., 120:15
  of resentment, 553:7
  one p. expel another, 157:7
  our p. is our task, 548:18
  Poet binds together by p., 373:16
  poetry not purpose but p., 452:12
  rebirth brings delight and p., 64:26
  red rose whispers of p., 553:19
  ruling p., 300:23
  sick of an old p., 602:7
  slept, 313:12
  spent its novel force, 455:10
  strongly rooted as envy, 352:32
  talking is p. of woman, 290:28
  tear a p. to tatters, 196:21
  that left ground, 467:3
  their fury and my p., 223:31
  utmost p. of her heart, 435:29
  what p. cannot music raise, 275:8
  which maketh laughter, 239:19
  whirlwind of p., 196:21
  wholly of mind, 696:1
  whom p. could not shake, 207:23
  win p. and life, 383:7
  with correctness, 547:2
  worst sin p. commit, 687:18
Passionate, foolish p. man, 599:4
  full of p. intensity, 596:19
  hardly p. Marlborough Street,
    742:21
  intuition, 376:22
  make p. my hearing, 168:25
  simple sensuous and p., 254:21
  women, 595:12
Passion-flower at gate, 458:23
Passionless, hopeless grief p., 438:17
Passion's slave, 197:4
Passions, all other p. fly, 386:13
  all p. all delights, 383:3
  cannot alter facts, 337:15
  capable of boundless p., 496:9
  exquisite p., 538:5
  hath not a Jew p., 180:30
  held in reverence, 452:12
  infusing p., 384:19
  like floods and streams, 152:13
  matched with mine, 455:22
  mediocre p., 265:28
  men governed by bad p., 343:7
  men of like p., 41:12
  minutiae of deeds and p., 491:15
  moderator of p., 245:17
  most transient of p., 571:15
  natural man has two p., 558:3

Patience (*continued*)
    may compass anything, 140:3
    means self-suffering, 606:13
    my p. are exhausted, 647:15
    no p. wear hunger out, 573:6
    no wedded man assaille wyves p.,
        131:18
    of Job, 46:17
    on a monument, 202:14
    pattern of all p., 209:28
    perseverance and soothing, 343:18
    possess soul in p., 39:13
    possess soul with p., 275:24
    preached up p., 287:21
    run with p., 45:39
    Russia homeland of p., 434:13
    stubborn p. as with triple steel,
        257:14
    thou cherubin, 207:27
    Time and P. strongest of warriors,
        510:6
    where p. neither anger nor vexation,
        123:9
    you tread upon my p., 177:1
Patient, be p. therefore, 46:16
    cure disease kill p., 159:28
    etherized upon table, 667:9
    fates have given a p. soul, 52:25
    fury of p. man, 274:16
    inattention, 509:16
    looker-on, 242:13
    love is p., 132:20
    merit takes, 196:10
    must minister to himself, 216:10
    Nature agent and p. at once, 77:17
    noiseless p. spider, 491:8
    or out of sorts, 717:3
    play fair just and p., 505:6
    poor as Job but not p., 183:17
    sail upon her p. breast, 200:6
    sleepless Eremite, 417:12
    soft meek p. humble, 227:19
    some p. force, 457:1
    sons before me stand, 328:12
Patientia, quo usque Catilina abutere
    p., 87:n3
Patients, hysterical p. suffer from remi-
    niscences, 569:5
Patines of bright gold, 182:8
Patio heaven's watercourse, 700:10
Patmos, isle that is called P., 47:1
Patre, omnes eodem p. nati, 235:4
Patrem, non deum p. ecclesiam non
    matrem, 112:n11
Patria, died some pro p., 659:8
    pro p. mori, 96:n12
    pro p. pro liberis, 91:n14
    sed miles sed pro p., 586:13
    ubi bene ibi p., 119:35
    ubi libertas ibi p., 327:8
Patriarch, divine p. castrates, 758:21
    obedient to God, 493:19
Patriarchs, had she lived to age of P.,
    347:n1
Patrician plebeian lord and serf,
    481:15
Patrick, gude Sir P. Spens, 785:1
Patrick's, St. P. Day, 779:10
Patrie, enfants de la p., 366:9
Patrimony, that was all his p., 630:15

Patriot a fool in every age, 302:25
    devotion of p. soldier, 522:13
    no p. on empty stomach, 371:n2
    steady p. of world alone, 371:23
    sunshine p., 340:22
Patriotic, avenge p. gore, 538:20
Patriotism gain force upon Marathon,
    314:16
    in female most disinterested of vir-
        tues, 347:11
    is not enough, 590:8
    last refuge of scoundrel, 316:25
    no concern with art, 524:1
Patriot's, such is the p. boast, 328:8
Patriots, blood of p. and tyrants,
    343:15
    brave men and worthy p., 254:20
    last effort of p., 337:17
    seeds of p. and heroes, 327:n5
    so to be p., 331:1
Patris, Filius P., 48:9
Patroclus, unwept unburied P., 52:23
Patron and the jail, 313:17
    is not a p. my lord, 315:17
Patronizing has meaner side, 483:12
Patrons, best of all p., 91:3
Pattable, if she p., 709:14
Patte, la p. du chat, 268:n7
Patter of little feet, 442:9
    out hasty orisons, 687:2
Pattern, behind outside p. dim shapes,
    583:2
    called war, 626:9
    cunningest p. of nature, 208:10
    made him our p., 464:23
    more complicated of dead and liv-
        ing, 671:10
    of all patience, 209:28
    of celestial peace, 163:17
    to live and to die, 464:23
    which controls phenomena, 632:4
Patterns, Christ what are p. for, 626:9
    extended to display its p., 62:29
Paul, good for P. and Silas, 780:4
    I P. a Jew of Tarsus, 41:24
    I P. a Pharisee, 41:29
    leave Saint P. nothing, 141:n12
    rarely Saul becomes P., 575:10
    rob Peter pay P., 141:27
    said But I was free born, 41:26
    thou art beside thyself, 41:33
Paulo maiora canamus, 92:n6
Paul's, designing St. P., 627:18
    ruins of St. P., 323:23, 425:7
Paunch, fat p. never breeds fine
    thoughts, 113:19
Paunches, fat p. have lean pates,
    113:n14
Pauper in midst of wealth, 96:23
    whom nobody owns, 423:12
Pauper-poor, wafer-thin p., 715:1
Pause for a reply, 188:27
    from learning to be wise, 313:17
    in day's occupation, 442:8
    must give us p., 196:10
    Nature made a p., 296:8
    no work p. for death, 467:28
    to p. to make end, 455:2
Pauses, lucid intervals and happy p.,
    158:17

Paved, hell p. with good intentions,
    121:n7, 244:n3
    they p. paradise, 773:7
Pavement, Emperor's p., 598:12
    on marble p. dust grows, 86:18
    riches of heaven's p., 256:20
    scrub kitchen p., 595:13
    stand on highest p., 668:3
Pavilions, pale p., 704:11
Paving, horses' heels over p., 670:4
Paw, cat's p., 268:26
    grim wolf with privy p., 254:3
Paweth, he p. in the valley, 15:16
Pax, in terra p., 48:8
Pay, business in life is p., 541:5
    devil to p., 150:10
    double debt to p., 329:19
    Equal P. for Equal Work, 491:22
    every debt, 430:5
    for it first or last, 475:16
    for one by one, 592:6
    for what gods given him, 614:11
    Forgotten Man p. for all, 541:5
    glad life's arrears, 467:19
    gladly p. you Tuesday for ham-
        burger, 690:3
    great deal too dear, 222:15
    I p. thy poverty not thy will, 176:11
    I will p. you in grave, 409:22
    if I can't p. I can owe, 140:14
    just man will p. more tax, 75:6
    law and order p., 542:20
    make me able to p. for it, 278:27
    man of genius had to p., 614:11
    money not p. for anything, 610:12
    new way to p. old debts, 238:10
    no worship to garish sun, 176:1
    not p. honor with tears, 84:17
    only things we can p., 566:19
    our lives we p., 485:4
    piper, 291:4
    remember to p. the debt, 70:25
    rob Peter p. Paul, 141:27
    served without p., 522:13
    taxes p. for civilized society, 542:14
    vow and not p., 24:3
    we must anguish p., 511:12
    we shall p. any price, 741:3
    when will you p. me, 788:20
    with a deadly blow, 63:22
    with ratiocination, 262:20
    words p. no debts, 200:18
    you ought to p. you know, 518:21
Paying, enrage those p. your annuities,
    307:1
    through nose, 782:2
Pays, he that dies p. all debts, 224:17
    he who p. piper, 291:n1
    him in own coin, 290:18
    money takes choice, 554:15
    to advertise, 781:16
    us with age and dust, 153:2
Pays, du p. qu'on enchaine, 786:20
    fameux dans les chansons, 494:n9
Pea, looking as one p. does another,
    140:9
    princess felt p. through mattresses,
        437:5
    tearing up p. patch, 690:16
Peace, abides a p. of thine, 497:14

Peace (*continued*)

above all earthly dignities, 225:17
adventure art p., 584:15
all her paths are p., 20:21
and knowledge pass argument, 488:18
and rest can never dwell, 255:24
armed p., 247:14
as a river, 27:28
at p. with himself, 724:2
at the last, 426:22
author of p., 49:2
be American without threatening p., 662:16
be at p. henceforward, 441:23
be within thy walls, 19:27
beasts shall be at p. with thee, 14:4
between effect and it, 212:29
between equals, 572:8
bodies are buried in p., 32:15
bring p. to others, 132:19
calm world and long p., 178:25
cannot live alone at p., 650:5
carry gentle p., 225:21
cease not to advocate p., 310:n5
central p. at heart, 376:21
commerce honest friendship, 344:9
Constitution law in war and p., 474:21
contributions to p. of world, 655:13
conversion of world perpetual p., 536:19
corrupt, 260:22
crimes against p., 683:3
crowned with smiles, 270:8
crust eaten in p., 59:1
cultivate p. and harmony, 337:6
dangerous to p. and safety, 360:12
deep dream of p., 397:1
depart in p., 398:10
easier to make war than p., 542:3
end of that man is p., 17:3
enemies called for p., 610:19
enemies in war in p. friends, 343:3
first in war first in p., 355:16
follow after p., 42:27
fool when he holdeth p., 21:37
for our time, 606:10
fruit of Spirit is p., 44:19
gentlemen may cry P., 339:10
give citizens little p., 753:2
give to all nations p., 49:11
go in p., 38:14, 120:2
go sleep with Turks, 172:7
god has brought this p., 92:2
God is war p. surfeit hunger, 62:13
guide planets, 770:1
habits of p. and patience, 245:17
hard and bitter p., 741:3
hath her victories, 255:10
hope to see p. established, 650:8
I am for p., 19:24
I give unto you, 40:30
I leave with you, 40:30
if you want p., 485:19
imperishable p., 580:8
in His will is our p., 126:23
in our time, 50:10
in p. children inter parents, 69:22
in p. goodwill, 622:4

Peace (*continued*)

in p. just generous, 404:21
in p. Love tunes, 377:25
in p. nothing so becomes man, 185:3
in p. thinks of war, 235:8
in p. ye critics dwell, 299:27
in their hearts, 746:2
in what p. a Christian can die, 293:12
indivisibility of p., 631:n2
indivisible, 631:7
inglorious arts of p., 268:9
into poet as flour into bread, 714:7
is in grave, 406:18
is not absence of war, 277:15
is p. so sweet, 339:10
is poor reading, 540:16
its ten thousands, 336:3
it's wonderful, 646:5
just and lasting p., 450:11
justice made for sake of p., 138:7
keep him in perfect p., 26:28
keep p. within yourself, 132:19
lay me down in p., 15:33
let us have p., 501:13
liberty and safety, 344:9
live together in p., 655:23
make a desert call it p., 109:21
make war to live in p., 78:10
makes solitude calls it p., 401:9
man's village is his p. of mind, 745:20
may he rest in p., 119:26
means of preserving p., 337:3
Mercy Pity P. and Love, 356:12
more important than justice, 138:7
more precious than piece of land, 745:21
my p. is gone, 350:19
naked poor mangled P., 186:1
Napoleon sole obstacle to p., 370:14
never good war or bad p., 310:23
no p. unto the wicked, 27:29
nor help for pain, 499:22
nor shall this p. sleep with her, 226:8
not made for justice, 138:7
not p. but a sword, 34:34
not take atomic weapons to want p., 714:10
nothing bring p. but self, 431:29
nothing contributes more to p. of soul, 342:14
object of war p., 492:11
of all countries connected, 644:17
of God which passeth all understanding, 49:18
of p. there shall be no end, 26:8
on earth mercy mild, 312:17
on earth p. and good will, 38:4
on the earth, 462:2
order security and p., 644:17
our concern be p. of mind, 82:14
our p. in His will, 669:21
our p. our innocence, 374:14
passes into Anesthesia, 584:16
pattern of celestial p., 163:17
perpetual p., 250:19

Peace (*continued*)

poetry act of p., 714:7
poetry fine-spun from mind at p., 102:2
price life exacts for p., 700:7
Prince of P., 26:8
proclaims olives of age, 221:23
publisheth p., 27:33
rest in soft p., 232:11
righteousness and p. have kissed each other, 18:8
running wild all over, 698:18
seek p. and pursue it, 16:31
separate p., 701:11
servant depart in p., 38:5
sinews of p., 622:3
slept in p., 226:2
snow said p., 675:3
soft phrase of p., 205:21
speak or forever hold his p., 50:2
star of p. return, 389:2
suffering evils of long p., 109:2
Tahiti full of p. and joy, 486:27
take chances for p., 667:8
the charm's wound up, 212:15
the human dress, 356:13
there is no p., 339:10
they are in p., 30:23
though make this marriage for my p., 217:17
thousand years of p., 457:30
time of p., 23:32
to him that is far off, 28:3
to men of good will, 38:n2, 48:8
to our children when they fall, 743:16
to this house, 38:18
universal p., 454:23
unjust p. before just war, 310:n5
until I come in p., 13:3
unto you shalom salaam forever, 732:10
uproar the universal p., 215:27
war is p., 711:17
we came in p. for all mankind, 784:7
we now to p. and darkness, 580:7
we shall find p., 582:13
weak piping time of p., 165:21
what hast thou to do with p., 13:9
when there is no peace, 28:17
when there was p. he was for p., 721:4
where p. neither anxiety nor doubt, 123:9
which America treasured, 572:12
which passeth understanding, 44:34
who desires p. prepare for war, 114:17
with honor, 435:14, 606:10
without honor not peace, 406:6
without victory, 572:8
work us a perpetual p., 250:19
world p. or destruction, 608:14
Peaceably along highway, 320:8
if we can, 385:n1
live p., 42:17
to assemble, 346:11
Peaceful abodes of the gods, 53:n1
as old age tonight, 466:6

Peaceful (*continued*)
coexistence, 715:16
generous just, 449:16
revolution impossible, 741:11
sloth, 257:6
welcome p. evening in, 335:3
what p. hours enjoyed, 333:21
Peacemaker, if is the only p., 192:17
Peacemakers, blessed are the p., 33:1,
163:20
Peach, asked thief to steal me p.,
357:18
dare to eat a p., 667:19
once bitter almond, 527:8
ripest p. highest, 558:12
Peacock Pie, 617:3
pride of p. glory of God, 357:6
Peacocks and lilies, 487:15
ivory apes and p., 12:27, 633:18
Pea-green boat, 471:31
Peak, dwindle p. and pine, 212:14
frozen p., 624:6
ice silent language of p., 675:5
in Darien, 413:24
Peaks most wrapt in clouds, 399:25
Peal, rung night's yawning p., 214:27
wildest p. for years, 611:18
Pealing anthem swells, 322:9
let the p. organ blow, 252:10
Peanuts, buy p. and cracker-jack,
637:15
Pear, go to p. tree for pears, 100:8
golden p., 790:12
Pearl, barbaric p. and gold, 256:23
for carnal swine, 263:23
hang p. in cowslip's ear, 173:1
in your foul oyster, 192:15
of great price, 35:10
of orient p. a double row, 226:19
quarelets of p., 241:3
robe of gold and p., 185:19
Tankards scooped in P., 511:16
threw a p. away, 208:16
Pearls and vermin, 425:22
asked how p. did grow, 241:3
black men are p., 168:9
cast p. before swine, 34:5
of thought, 486:3
string of p. to me, 586:17
string p. strung on, 548:20
that were his eyes, 223:32
Pearly monotones, 660:17
shows teeth p. white, 698:14
Pears, go to pear tree for p., 100:8
Peas, tame pigeons p., 262:n4
with first salmon and first green p.,
442:11
Peasant has lawyer inside, 589:22
have chicken in pot, 154:20
lawyer has p. inside, 589:22
rogue and p. slave, 196:4
toe of p., 199:7
Peasantry, bold p., 329:8
dictatorship of proletariat and p.,
609:20
Peasants born kings of earth, 436:21
call bachelors' prayer, 656:7
carry honor in their hands, 239:12
Pease-porridge hot, 790:10
Pebble, finding smoother p., 282:5

Pebbled, waves make towards p.
shore, 220:26
Pebbles, didst pick up Andrew Jackson
from p., 486:22
grating roar of p., 499:20
of holy streams, 737:17
unnumbered idle p., 210:27
Peccata, qui tollis p. mundi, 48:9
Peck, for daws to p. at, 205:14
of pickled peppers, 791:2
truly a p. of provender, 173:22
Pecks, three p. of barley meal, 792:16
Pecksniff, said Mr. P. tenderly, 469:37
Pecksniffian, Philadelphia p., 642:14
Pectus est enim quod disertos facit,
105:n7
Peculiar, an air and p. grace, 294:21
deposit for virtue, 343:10
God's p. light, 137:11
heathen Chinee is p., 532:1
Pedagogues, clouds are p., 639:24
Pedantical, figures p., 169:8
Pedants, learned p. much affect, 263:1
Peddler, lives of shoemaker and fish
p., 674:20
Pede, ex p. Herculem, 70:n2
Pedestal, on p. these words appear,
406:13
women put not on p. but in cage,
719:6
Pedestaled in triumph, 468:3
Pedigree as far back as Deluge, 463:22
lass wi' lang p., 368:8
of Honey, 514:9
Peel, d'ye ken John P., 413:20
me a grape, 685:7
set sharp racks to pinch and p.,
414:20
Peeled patched and piebald, 303:28
Peep about to find graves, 187:22
and botanize, 374:2
at such a world, 335:4
from her cabined loophole p.,
252:22
heaven p. through blanket, 213:1
nevermore to p. again, 617:6
treason can but p., 198:22
Peephole, wine is a p., 55:23
Peeping in at morn, 422:19
Peeps over glasses' edge, 466:7
primrose p. beneath thorn, 329:22
Peer, do not p. too far, 63:29
King Stephen worthy p., 776:16
many a p. of England brews, 579:15
Peereth, honor p. in meanest habit,
167:31
Peering, into darkness p., 452:17
littlenesses, 459:3
Peerless, unveiled her p. light, 258:19
Peers, drunk delight of battle with p.,
455:1
heroes of old, 467:19
House of P. throughout war, 530:13
judgment of his p., 123:12
powerful amidst p., 551:4
Peevish Nature, 287:18
Peg, square p. in round hole, 379:n3
Pegasus, gallop P. to death, 303:1
turn and wind a fiery P., 178:22
Peignoir, complacencies of p., 638:24

Peine, la p. de naître, 336:n4
Peinture, la lumière à p., 563:n1
Pejorist, not pessimist but p., 578:n1
Peking, butterfly stirring air in P.,
775:2
improved relations with P., 733:15
Peleus', wrath of P. son, 50:23, 299:23
Pelf, I crave no p., 211:26
titles power and p., 378:1
Pelican jee, 472:16
Lord Jesu blessed P., 124:9
wonderful bird is p., 637:14
Pelicans, all of sudden came p., 739:10
Pelion, from Ossa hurled P., 53:n4
pile Ossa on P., 92:25
with its leafy forests, 53:19
Pellet with poison's in flagon, 736:10
Pellinore followed questing beast,
133:5
Peloponnesians, war between P. and
Athenians, 71:18
Pelops', Thebes or P. line, 252:6
Pelting of pitiless storm, 210:3
Pembroke's mother, 240:14
Pen, and I made a rural p., 356:5
antique p. would have expressed,
221:22
breathing revenge, 479:12
cold words of tongue or p., 611:17
excellent instrument, 337:11
feather whence p. shaped, 377:8
galley slave to p., 422:8
gleaned teeming brain, 417:9
in hand, 317:18
lend me your p., 786:n6
Lord taught by the P., 117:24
make famous by my p., 264:n2
make glorious by my p., 264:5
mightier than sword, 428:22
my tongue is the p. of a ready
writer, 17:14
need far less brilliant p. than mine,
614:6
never saw p. and ink, 203:4
nose as sharp as p., 184:30
poet's p. turns to shapes, 174:1
preferable to sword, 150:13
sad words of tongue or p., 443:8
squat p. rests, 769:13
through every other word, 380:20
wherewith thou heavenly sing,
377:n2
whether chisel p. brush, 596:16
with such acts fill a p., 161:10
words as with burning p., 364:14
worse than the sword, 234:29
write p. for I am volumes, 168:21
written with a p. of iron, 28:28
Penal, chains and p. fire, 255:22
Penalty, greatest p. of evildoing, 76:13
paying p. for no idealism, 585:3
Penance, hath p. done, 381:25
more will do, 381:25
Pence, eternal lack of p., 456:4
eternal want of p., 139:n13
for thirty p. my death, 243:6
take care of p., 305:1
three hundred p., 40:22
Pendent, blown about p. world,
204:14

People (*continued*)

naked p. have little influence, 528:14
narrow-souled p., 303:22
never give up liberties, 332:3
never learned from history, 372:6
new deal for American p., 648:16
ninety-nine percent of p. fools, 697:17
no doubt but ye are the p., 14:14
no more give the p. straw, 8:30
not always what seem, 333:1
numerous and warlike, 134:13
O stormy p., 131:17
oats supports p., 314:6
of his pasture, 18:19
of p. by p. for p., 450:2, 461:18
of unclean lips, 26:2
of Western Europe, 678:16
old p. are square, 757:12
old p. not to fear young or be deserted, 682:14
old p. poor p. also get niggerized, 739:16
on whom nothing lost, 548:13
on world not in it, 537:17
one man die for p., 40:21
one of beautiful p., 770:12
one should like to drop, 317:21
one thing besides p. I know, 648:10
only p. for me mad, 750:9
our land before we her p., 624:10
our sovereign the p., 394:*n*8
people have for friends, 583:9
people marry, 583:9
planned obsolescence of p., 732:4
poet help p. live their lives, 640:18
power from the p., 434:18
protection of p., 327:2
put up with oppressive rule, 438:13
really good at heart, 760:13
relation between white and colored p., 480:18
religion opium of p., 481:5
remove weight from p., 751:15
representatives of p., 405:11
resemble wild beast, 137:3
retain virtue and vigilance, 449:6
right of p. to make alter constitutions, 337:4
right of trampling on p., 427:5
right p. in right jobs, 474:17
Rome's decline lay in p., 656:13
Sacco's name in hearts of p., 674:21
safe depository of powers, 344:22
say life is the thing, 594:8
seldom judge right, 355:1
sensed by p. expressed by p., 503:15
should be beautiful, 582:12
should be taught what is, 754:16
should fight for their law, 62:20
shouted with a great shout, 10:34
show my head to the p., 364:7
showed thy p. hard things, 17:30
signs for a god-fearing p., 116:8
small country with few p., 58:6
so dead to liberty, 312:20
so many hungry, 745:3
special p. unto himself, 10:13
spoil lives of better p., 562:6

People (*continued*)

still in the gristle, 331:9
such tongue to great p., 482:20
sum married p. owe, 349:24
talebearer among thy p., 9:25
talk sense to American p., 706:10
that once bestowed commands, 109:7
that p. may require leader, 75:28
the p. will live on, 634:13
there is a p. risen, 271:15
thy p. shall be my p., 11:23
to all the p. you can, 309:2
to these p. I owe everything, 448:16
tricked and sold, 634:13
turn to benevolent rule, 79:16
two kinds of p., 562:14
two p. miserable instead of four, 524:15
two p. shaken by dizziness, 736:17
two thirds of p. killed, 636:3
under violent passions, 571:15
underestimating intelligence of p., 643:1
visited and redeemed his p., 37:44
voice of p. is voice of God, 120:8
want to be masters of future, 761:11
watch over economy of private p., 326:5
we are his p., 18:22
we p. will get to promised land, 761:9
we the p., 346:7
were passed clean over Jordan, 10:32
what did you do to the p., 689:9
what is the city but p., 219:8
what kind of p. do they think we are, 621:8
what p. are like here, 349:3
what p. say behind back, 564:1
what p. say of us true, 594:3
where no vision the p. perish, 23:10
which sat in darkness, 32:36
who eat the earth, 716:5
who have money, 651:8
who know little, 319:13
who lift people who lean, 562:14
who love each other, 436:22
who need people, 751:4
win friends influence p., 667:2
wish p. to think well of you, 270:16
wishes of p. concerned, 650:7
with no weaknesses, 550:9
with rights in hands, 437:19
without history, 672:5, 787:2
witness to the p., 27:40
would die for my p., 516:9
would that Roman p. had single neck, 103:18
you know yet can't name, 751:1
Peopled, earthly ball a p. garden, 349:11
teach order to p. kingdom, 184:23
world must be p., 186:31
People's good is highest law, 88:5
in p. eyes life, 650:16
nor p. judgment always true, 274:14
not seat self on other p. backs, 552:11

People's (*continued*)

other p. money, 504:8
reforming other p. habits, 527:14
sits high in p. hearts, 187:30
soil of p. necessities, 585:6
state worst of all states, 249:14
this is a p. contest, 449:8
voice odd, 303:5
Peoples, English-speaking p., 564:17
happiness of p., 550:7
history life of p., 510:10
mos p. gonna lose, 735:4
of United Nations, 655:23
sink or swim together, 609:12
who have courage to face war, 652:20
Peopling the void air, 497:23
Peor and Baalim, 251:1
Peoria, it'll play in P., 754:19
Peppercorn, I am a p., 178:15
Peppered two of them, 177:24
Peppermint, big p. hotels, 739:7
Peppers, peck of pickled p., 791:2
Per caputque pedesque, 90:*n*15
Perceive here a divided duty, 205:29
in form stereotyped by culture, 676:20
ye are too superstitious, 41:15
yourself sole heir of world, 280:22
Perceived harmony of object, 383:22
Perceivers of terror of life, 432:30
Perceives, artist p. more than fellows, 614:22
it die away, 375:8
Perceiving, conscious that we are p., 78:7
genius p. in unhabitual way, 546:2
Percent, eighty p. of success, 767:17
Percents, elegant simplicity of three p., 348:7
Perception, imagination agent of p., 384:6
of beauty moral test, 476:28
pale colorless, 546:4
register multiple p. in art, 660:7
Perch, custom make it their p., 203:28
if you hadn't nailed parrot to p., 775:5
where eagles dare not p., 165:25
Perches in the soul, 511:20
Perchings, flights and p., 545:16
Percy, old song of P. and Douglas, 156:3
Percy's, not yet of P. mind, 177:20
Perdition, bottomless p., 255:22
catch my soul, 206:27
Perdu, tout p. fors l'honneur, 139:*n*6
Perdue, une génération p., 627:*n*1
Pereant qui nostra ante nos dixerunt, 119:19
Pereat, fiat justitia et p. mundus, 119:*n*2
Peremptory, would not with p. tone, 334:10
Perennial pleasures plants, 422:3
spring of prodigality, 331:26
Perestroika combines continuity innovation, 763:14
Perfect and entire, 46:4
be ye therefore p., 33:10

Perfect *(continued)*
circle and vicious circle, 731:14
end of p. day, 585:8
every p. gift, 46:6
form a more p. Union, 346:7
Glory be the P. One, 513:4
happiness p. as martyr's, 585:16
his work is p., 10:26
I am not in p. mind, 211:10
in bud as in bloom, 523:21
in heaven p. round, 467:2
in p. nature no distinction of kind,
    80:13
interpreter of life, 661:1
keep him in p. peace, 26:28
let patience have her p. work, 46:4
life may p. be, 233:3
love casteth out fear, 46:37
made p. in weakness, 44:12
mark the p. man, 17:3
move in p. phalanx, 256:14
nothing quite new is p., 87:19
one p. limousine, 687:11
only p. man, 236:7
practice makes p., 99:*n*11
produce p. circles, 79:14
shineth unto the p. day, 20:24
spirits of just men made p., 45:41
then if ever p. days, 485:5
visit p. in being too short, 387:7
when that which is p., 43:16
woman nobly planned, 375:18
world p. everywhere, 365:19
Perfected, woman is p., 764:14
Perfectest, silence p. herald of joy,
    186:23
Perfectibility of man, 438:5
Perfection as culture conceives it,
    500:13
culture study of p., 500:11
dead p., 458:17
discovers p. in beloved, 396:12
fullness of p. in him, 169:23
holds in p. but moment, 220:11
law is p. of reason, 152:1
little concerned with p., 541:10
of life or of work, 598:10
of mathematics, 615:10
pink of p., 329:26
rides upon p. of his officials, 86:16
right praise true p., 182:12
spiritual p. of man, 122:11
stern p. as greatest art, 615:10
unattainable p., 594:6
vowing p. of ten, 200:20
Perfections, sweet p. caught, 163:4
Perfidious Albion, 371:5
fatal and p. bark, 253:22
Perform, ability they never p., 200:20
Almighty's orders to p., 291:30
every act as though it were your
    last, 110:15
his wonders to p., 333:22
never promise more than p., 99:30
Performance, desire outlive p., 183:35
lovers swear more p., 200:20
takes away the p., 214:11
Performed, look for deed soul p.,
    117:21
rites simple decisive, 756:12

Performed *(continued)*
to a T, 140:2
Performs, man p. engenders, 696:16
Perfume, amber scent of odorous p.,
    261:16
feel my breasts all p., 647:17
owest cat no p., 210:6
puss-gentleman all p., 334:11
throw p. on violet, 170:9
Perfumed like milliner, 177:2
old women should not be p., 55:4
sea, 451:12
so p. that winds love-sick, 217:14
Perfumes, all the p. of Arabia, 216:5
colors sounds echo, 494:3
Perhaps, seek a grand p., 140:11
Pericles calls quality lucidity, 500:25
in wrath the Olympian P., 72:13
Periculum ex aliis facito, 85:*n*14
Periculum in mora, 155:*n*1
Periit, qui ante diem p., 586:13
Peril, in p. mask is off, 89:22
those in p. on sea, 506:4
use our pens at our p., 306:18
woods more free from p., 190:6
Perilous, cleanse bosom of p. stuff,
    216:10
fight, 391:2
nothing more p. than new order,
    136:9
seas in faery lands forlorn, 415:17
thought without learning is p.,
    60:23
turns to p. waters, 125:4
unsifted in p. circumstance, 194:3
Perils, avoid p. by united forces,
    278:11
defend us from all p., 49:7
how many p. do enfold, 153:8
of camp march and battle, 522:13
when our p. are past, 372:1
Period at the right moment, 688:2
new and great p. in His Church,
    255:1
of effectiveness of generation,
    653:15
Periodic, success to p. sentence,
    693:14
Periodization of European history,
    704:2
Peripatetic lover, 529:20
Periphrastic study, 670:23
Peris, sweets of Fairies P. Goddesses,
    414:16
Perish, city to p. if it finds buyer,
    91:30
drink unto him that is ready to p.,
    23:16
fame of her excellence will never p.,
    54:12
hero p. or sparrow fall, 301:5
if it had to p. twice, 623:14
if we must p. in fight, 444:2
in our own, 581:2
in their infancy, 777:7
let justice be done though world p.,
    119:*n*2
let the day p., 13:34
may they p. who used our words,
    119:19

Perish *(continued)*
name not p. in dust, 386:16
or catch up, 610:3
shall not p. from earth, 450:2
should not p., 39:46
spirit of moderation will p., 615:3
surely weak p., 627:1
survive or p., 394:9
that one of thy members should p.,
    33:5
the thought, 291:22
their goodness does not p., 69:12
thy money p., 41:2
truths wake to p. never, 375:12
twice, 623:14
weakly p. at another moment, 52:19
where no vision the people p., 23:10
with the sword, 37:1
Perished as they had never been, 32:14
by own follies they p., 52:28
in his pride, 374:9
the weapons of war p., 12:2
who p. being innocent, 13:37
Perishes, everything p., 786:16
Periuria ridet amantum Iupiter,
    101:*n*4
Periwig, new p. make a great show,
    279:20
Periwig-pated, robustious p. fellow,
    196:21
Perjured, gloriously p., 96:20
murderous bloody, 222:7
Perjuries, at lovers' p. Jove laughs,
    175:4
of lovers, 101:5
Perjury, Jove laughs at lovers' p.,
    175:*n*2
Perked up in glistering grief, 225:8
Permanence sea cannot claim, 539:14
Permanent alliances, 337:7
and certain characteristics, 313:25
and the same, 498:8
contract on temporary feeling,
    540:5
disuse of any organ, 347:13
feelings p. and the same, 498:8
interests of community, 351:21
more p. than fish or weed, 762:9
nothing ought to be p., 438:5
share in government, 355:1
system of security, 650:9
Permission, nobody without Count's
    p., 651:20
to go out from household, 65:4
Permit base contagious clouds, 176:37
doing what laws p., 304:10
how long p. to Heaven, 260:18
Permitte divis cetera, 95:*n*19
Permitted to shuffle in slippers, 590:10
whatever not forbidden is p., 365:2
Pernicious consequences, 474:21
love of flattery, 293:22
race of odious vermin, 289:10
Perpetual, court in p. session, 652:1
desire a p. rack, 234:21
devotion to business, 560:20
feast of nectared sweets, 253:3
kingdom of p. night, 165:31
neglect of other things, 560:20
night, 90:19, 232:4

Perpetual (*continued*)
  office seekers, 677:2
  our interests eternal and p., 397:9
  scoured with p. motion, 183:23
  sleep of p. night, 90:19
  speculators about p. motion, 135:12
  work us a p. peace, 250:19
Perpetually, life begins p., 601:15
  nation p. to be conquered, 331:11
  one hour then damned p., 162:22
  saves itself p., 729:1
Perpetuate, any way to p. the World,
    248:19
Perpetuated, ancient models p., 115:8
Perpetuity, merit of p., 249:1
Perplexed in the extreme, 208:16
  labyrinthical soul, 231:13
  to have plenty is to be p., 57:8
Perplexes and affronts, 734:6
  monarchs, 256:16
Perplexity of radical evil, 718:11
Persecute, despitefully use and p. you,
    33:8
  you for my sake, 33:1
Persecuted church of God, 43:19
  for righteousness' sake, 33:1
  most p. minority, 646:11
Persecutes the mind, 275:14
Persecutest, why p. thou me, 41:5
Persecution bad way to plant religion,
    248:9
  gives p. no assistance, 337:2
  object of p. is p., 711:18
  religious p. shield itself, 332:5
Persecutions have made Church grow,
    112:*n*2
Persephone, even where P. goes, 658:1
Persepolis, ride in triumph through P.,
    161:20
Persever in obstinate condolement,
    193:4
Perseverance and soothing language,
    343:18
  fortitude and p., 325:4
  in good cause, 320:12
  keeps honor bright, 200:24
  more prevailing than violence, 107:4
Persevere, forbear and p., 562:9
Persia, past first sleep in P., 249:7
Persian, how can anyone be P., 304:7
  luxury I hate, 96:3
  pearls of thought in P. gulfs bred,
    486:3
Persian's heaven easily made, 392:6
Persians accustomed to deliberate
    when drunk, 69:23
  law of the Medes and P., 29:17
  taught three things, 403:22
Persicos odi puer apparatus, 96:*n*3
Person, aging p. give attention to self,
    628:11
  agreeable p. agrees with me, 435:10
  attention must be paid to p., 738:15
  beggared all description, 217:14
  blood of this just p., 37:7
  dignity and worth of p., 655:23
  don't believe no sich p., 470:1
  France a p., 421:15
  freedom of p., 344:9
  get up so white p. could sit, 734:2

Person (*continued*)
  may have many thousand selves,
    651:1
  no more a p. now, 720:12
  no p. must have to, 332:32
  no sich p., 470:1
  noble p. attracts noble people,
    349:19
  not p. involved, 527:11
  of contrary opinion, 439:12
  of its head root of family, 79:15
  portrayed and portrait, 653:18
  produce the p., 119:7
  really hope no white p., 772:15
  sacrificed to individual, 648:4
  show you hungry p., 772:14
  simple separate p., 488:13
  touch my p. to someone else's,
    489:13
  very umble p., 470:28
  who seizes two things, 784:23
  with no social armor, 648:4
  young p. occupied with self, 628:11
Personages, facts p. appear twice,
    481:6
Personal considerations in public duty,
    501:14
  inner p. experiences, 546:19
  knowledge not p. experience, 75:9
  none can regard it as p., 447:22
  perspective only kind of history,
    769:9
Personalities, meeting of p. chemical
    contact, 628:9
  trivial p. decomposing, 650:18
Personality, continual extinction of p.,
    672:9
  cult of p., 689:19
  needs a good p., 656:1
  of art impersonality of science,
    473:6
  poetry escape from p., 672:10
  taint of p., 509:6
Personified, evil to Ahab p., 486:25
Personne, celui que p. ne peut imiter,
    369:*n*8
Persons About to Write History, 521:6
  advice to p. about to marry, 554:14
  all p. born in U.S. citizens, 346:18
  all p. share in government, 78:21
  divers paces with divers p., 191:18
  God in Three P., 395:21
  God no respecter of p., 41:10
  great p. great kindnesses, 151:4
  neither p. nor property safe, 481:2
  respect of place p. time, 202:4
  without respect of p., 46:20
Perspective, cylinder sphere cone in p.,
    537:21
  personal p. only kind of history,
    769:9
  youth forge central p., 708:6
Perspicuity, we praise thee for p. of
    language, 121:5
Perspiration, ninety-nine percent p.,
    555:13
Persuade, beauty doth of itself p.,
    166:35
  even if you p. me, 73:28
  if possible the rulers, 75:11

Persuade (*continued*)
  tongue to p., 262:1
Persuaded, burnt each other quite p.,
    402:9
  cannot be p. by gun or lariat,
    791:*n*1
  in his own mind, 42:25
  none could advise thou p., 153:1
Persuader, president is p., 729:21
Persuades, truth p. by teaching, 112:8
  when speaking fails, 222:22
Persuadest, almost p. me to be a
    Christian, 41:36
Persuading, fair-spoken and p., 226:6
Persuasion and belief, 376:22
  companion's words of p., 51:34
  hung upon his lips, 320:13
  in it was blandishing p., 52:3
  two gods P. and Compulsion, 62:28
  whatever race creed or p., 661:5
Persuasive, demonstrative or p. type,
    609:11
  sound, 291:8
Pert as schoolgirl can be, 530:22
Perturbation, polished p., 184:9
Perturbed, rest p. spirit, 195:5
Peru, a Newton at P., 323:23
  mankind from China to P., 313:16
  there lies P., 419:8
Perverse, art selfish and p., 371:19
  imp of the p., 452:23
  mankind by p. depravity, 284:14
  tugging at p. life, 724:14
  widows most p. creatures, 293:5
Perverseness primitive impulse, 452:*n*1
Perversion, Christianity enormous p.,
    553:4
Pervert, use novel not for art you p. it,
    755:15
Perverted, woman's cold p. will, 410:7
Perverters of language, 659:13
Perverts who set money-lust before
    pleasures, 659:13
Pessary, will not give wman p., 71:1
Pessimism agreeable as optimism,
    602:3
Pessimist, difference between optimist
    and p., 632:5
  fears this is true, 635:8
  I am not p., 719:13
  not p. but pejorist, 578:*n*1
  sees hole, 632:5
Pest that fairest joys give unrest,
    414:14
Pestered with a popinjay, 177:4
Pestilence, Famine P. Destruction
    Death, 643:15
  noisome p., 18:15
  power like desolating p., 406:8
  that walketh in darkness, 18:15
  winter plague and p., 227:1
Pestilence-stricken multitudes, 407:13
Pestilent, foul and p., 195:28
Pestle, vessel with p. has brew, 736:10
Petal, now sleeps crimson p., 456:20
Petals on wet black bough, 659:1
Petar, hoist with his own p., 198:8
Peter and Wendy, 581:26
  denied Lord and cried, 287:9
  Flopsy Mopsy Cottontail P., 600:20

Peter (*continued*)

give not Saint P. so much, 141:*n*12

jealous Judas cowardly P., 713:9

Piper picked peck, 791:2

Pumpkin-Eater, 791:9

remembered word of Jesus, 37:3

rob P. pay Paul, 141:27

thou art P., 35:28

wept bitterly, 37:3

Peterkin, quoth little P., 386:7

Peter's, blessing of Saint P. Master, 245:31

dome, 429:10

Petersburg most theoretical town, 494:22

Petite, oh my P., 743:3

Petition government for redress, 346:11

Petitions, desires and p. of thy servants, 49:6

Petrarch's, if Laura P. wife, 402:22

Petrel, waters of p. and porpoise, 671:11

Petrifies the feeling, 361:22

Petticoat, feet beneath her p., 262:5

government, 395:23

tempestuous p., 241:5

turned out of Realm in my p., 144:16

Petty, creeps in this p. pace, 216:14

makes each p. artery, 194:14

never be p., 733:19

official high or p., 683:2

we p. men, 187:22

Peuple, pitié de mon pauvre p., 147:*n*6

Peur, de p. d'en pleurer, 336:*n*3

le plus de p. que la p., 145:*n*7

Peut-être, chercher un grand p., 140:*n*9

Pewter, no p. no pub, 674:13

Pez muere por la boca, 794:1

Phalanx, move in perfect p., 256:14

Phantasma, like p. or hideous dream, 188:2

Phantom deer arise, 698:13

of delight, 375:16

one grand hooded p., 486:18

Pharaoh, one more plague upon P., 8:35

tell old P., 794:11

Pharaoh's, he hardened P. heart, 8:32

lean kine loved, 177:31

wise men cast down rods, 8:32

Pharisee, one a P. the other a publican, 39:7

the son of a P., 41:29

Pharisees, scribes and P., 36:3

Pharisees', drowns in P. hypocrisy, 679:17

Pharos of Egypt, 782:7

Phases, definite historical p. of production, 481:7

Phenomena, concepts call p. to mind, 345:9

natural p. subject to causation, 522:16

new p. lead to bombs, 636:1

not deduced from p. is hypothesis, 281:26

Phenomena (*continued*)

not disclose essence of p., 656:3

pattern which controls p., 632:4

predict p., 411:14

same circumstances same p., 290:30

sequence of p., 345:9

Phenomenon, felicitous p., 665:5

infant p., 469:18

portray p. concept needed, 345:9

Phidias, by P. done, 782:7

unable to reach all the material, 111:31

Philadelphia, I'd rather be in P., 641:15

in P. ask who were parents, 527:19

pecksniffian, 642:14

Philanthropist, masterpiece delusion to p., 523:21

Philanthropy of Captain Brown, 479:2

only virtue appreciated, 478:14

which forgives, 392:18

which neither shoots nor liberates, 479:2

Philippine, our forces stand on P. soil, 642:2

Philistia triumph thou because of me, 17:31

Philistine, American P. livelier, 501:3

David prevailed over the P., 11:41

strong dogged unenlightened, 499:12

what is called a p., 404:17

Philistines, apostle of P. Macaulay, 499:14

avenged of P., 11:18

Barbarians P. Populace, 500:9

be upon thee, 11:16

put out Samson's eyes, 11:17

though P. may jostle, 529:18

Philistinism, detective novel P., 705:7

Philologists who chase syllable, 334:17

Philomène a dainty thing, 714:14

Philosopher, anything implausible already said by p., 246:17

doesn't think in vacuum, 585:1

endure toothache, 187:9

great poet profound p., 384:15

guide p. and friend, 302:4, 644:7

I have tried too to be p., 318:9

not aloof to gain reputation, 76:10

nothing so ridiculous but p. said it, 87:27

scold jester raconteur, 703:19

thinks like a p., 319:27

to be p. to love wisdom, 478:5

was a p. yet hadde but litel gold, 129:21

weeping p. when old, 179:30

what are sinews of p., 108:8

worship considered by p., 339:12

Philosopher's stones, 235:10

Philosophers come down from mountains, 537:16

discovered unconscious, 569:20

God of Abraham not p., 271:11

great economists called worldly p., 746:15

heroes statesmen p., 347:4

illusion of p., 696:13

Philosophers (*continued*)

interpreted world in various ways, 481:12

not from p. but nature, 236:1

quotidian saps p., 638:19

until p. are kings, 75:15

verse and sayings of p., 263:16

Philosopher-scientists, there are p., 738:14

Philosophia biou kybernetes, 360:*n*3

O vitae p. dux, 87:*n*15

Philosophic ideals altars to unknown gods, 545:9

poetry more p., 78:33

Philosophical, European p. tradition footnotes to Plato, 584:13

speculators of common sort, 148:13

Philosophize, to ridicule philosophy is to p., 271:6

Philosophy, adversity's sweet milk p., 176:3

bladders of p., 283:26

call p. down from heavens, 87:30

clip angel's wings, 414:19

Comte's p., 505:8

depth in p. bringeth to religion, 159:19

divine p., 253:3

divine P., 457:16

dreamed of in any p., 683:1

dreamt of in your p., 195:3

errors in p. ridiculous, 318:10

experimental p., 281:26

false p., 257:13

gained this by p., 77:14

good horse in stable, 329:1

guide of life, 360:8

handmaid to religion, 158:11

hang up p., 176:4

hast any p. in thee, 191:7

history is p. learned from examples, 100:26

I have no p. myself, 683:1

if p. could find it out, 195:30

in p. experts differ, 586:9

in p. most worldly of activities, 746:15

is for the few, 148:12

little p. inclineth to atheism, 159:19

make a Juliet, 176:4

my sons ought to study p., 338:10

natural p. deep moral grave, 160:10

Natural P. embodied in mathematical beauty, 583:13

new p. calls all in doubt, 230:15

new p. proceeds from world, 227:4

not faith but mere p., 248:14

not pretend to doubt in p., 538:16

not technical matter, 546:17

obscure regions of p., 318:15

pieced thoughts into p., 597:13

right in saying life understood backward, 473:12

sense of what life means, 546:17

spirit and power of p., 75:15

to get rid of self-conceit, 108:9

to ridicule p., 271:6

touch of cold p., 414:18

triumphs over past evils, 264:24

written in universe, 161:15

Piper (continued)
  Peter P. picked peck, 791:2
  pipe song again, 356:4
Piper's son, 790:4
Pipers, wi' a hundred p. an' a', 368:6
Pipes and timbrels, 416:1
  and whistles in his sound, 191:3
Piping, cicadas pour out their p. voices, 51:13
  down valleys wild, 356:4
  helpless naked p. loud, 358:11
  songs forever new, 416:4
  songs of pleasant glee, 356:4
  weak p. time of peace, 165:21
Pippins, old p. toothsomest, 237:11
Piracee, vary p., 529:15
Piracy, let's vary p., 529:15
Pirate King, 529:11
Pirates, wonder at cruelty of p., 485:23
Pis, tant p. and tant mieux, 320:35
Pisa, you're the Tower of P., 682:3
Piscem natare doces, 119:20
Pisgah, greeted Moses from P., 419:7
Piss off he said to me, 762:19
  vice-presidency not worth pitcher of warm p., 605:8
Pisses, I think it p. God off, 773:13
Pistol, hear word culture reach for my p., 679:4
  if his p. misses fire, 330:16
  pun a p. not feather, 388:11
Pistols, fire p. for new century, 629:12
  put on p. went riding, 674:14
Pit, black as the P., 557:9
  Eagle know what is in p., 357:1
  many-headed monster of p., 303:10
  ponies, 611:18
  they'll fill a p., 178:26
  whoso diggeth a p., 22:31
Pitch, daubed with slime and p., 8:21
  he that toucheth p., 31:30
  into frog-spawn, 598:5
  nightly p. moving tent, 377:17
  pitched past p. of grief, 551:13
  they that touch p. defiled, 186:38
  what validity and p., 201:17
  which hawks flies higher p., 163:10
Pitch-black, night p. upon the deep, 93:13
Pitched, as mind p. ear pleased, 335:11
  betwixt Heaven and Charing Cross, 581:12
  his tent toward Sodom, 7:28
  Love p. mansion, 598:21
  past pitch of grief, 551:13
Pitcher, as wheel runs why water p., 98:4
  broken at the fountain, 24:28
  vice-presidency not worth p. of warm piss, 605:8
Pitchers, small p. have wide ears, 142:14
Pitchfork, clothes thrown on with p., 290:7
  drive out Nature with p., 97:12
  use wit as p., 750:10
Piteous, coursed down in p. chase, 190:8

Piteous (continued)
  thing among wretched mortals, 52:20
Pitfalls, snares traps gins p., 463:*n*1
Pith, enterprises of great p., 196:10
Pitiable, world p. in units, 540:1
Pitied, better envied than p., 70:2
  how they p. Eve, 612:1
  lost respect and p. it, 477:14
  pity and be p., 190:29
Pities plumage, 341:6
Pitiful helpless giant, 733:16
  long-suffering and very p., 30:33
  selfish Public, 390:10
  tender eye of p. day, 214:28
  'twas wondrous p., 205:28
Pitiless, pelting of p. storm, 210:3
Pitt, celebrities such as P., 521:4
Pity a human face, 356:13
  beyond all telling, 594:22
  deserveth double p., 152:14
  for suffering mankind, 615:15
  for the living, 527:28
  from blustering wind, 267:19
  gave ere charity began, 329:13
  hid in heart of love, 594:22
  his ignorance, 469:17
  know what 'tis to p., 190:29
  knows not wrath nor p., 424:1
  like naked new-born babe, 213:7
  loved her that she did p., 205:28
  Mercy P. Peace and Love, 356:12
  my simplicity, 312:15
  no beast but knows touch of p., 165:22
  no concern with art, 524:1
  no p. sitting in clouds, 176:8
  of it Iago, 207:22
  of War, 687:1
  Poetry is in the p., 687:1
  renneth soone in gentil herte, 130:1
  seas of p. lie, 720:11
  sense of p. beauty pain, 572:19
  she's a whore, 239:15
  showing an outward p., 172:11
  straightest path to love, 236:9
  the planet all joy gone, 743:16
  their want of faith, 341:13
  then embrace, 301:14
  this busy monster, 689:5
  thou never come for p., 409:16
  'tis 'tis true, 195:12
  upon the poor, 21:45
  we may p. though not pardon, 166:20
  what are p. conscience fear, 679:19
  where Mercy Love and P. dwell, 356:14
  would be no more, 358:10
Pitying the tender cries, 356:16
Pity-pat, heart goin' p., 485:16
Pity's straightest of paths, 236:9
Pity-Zekle, hern went p., 485:16
Pix, sticks nix hick p., 704:10
Pixy, time slips away like p. wife, 630:1
Pizarro traced line with sword, 419:8
Placard removed and to let, 490:6
Place, all other things give p., 297:12

Place (continued)
  always seemed to put in wrong p., 737:5
  and means for every man, 203:16
  bounds of p. and time, 323:4
  California wonderful p. to live if orange, 687:22
  called Armageddon, 47:33
  called Calvary, 39:18
  called Golgotha, 37:9
  candle in holy p., 644:12
  degree priority and p., 200:7
  dwelleth in the secret p., 18:15
  for everything, 528:18
  get wealth and p., 303:4
  grave's fine private p., 268:16
  he that stands on slippery p., 170:7
  heavenly paradise is that p., 226:18
  hideous and untenable p., 714:16
  hiding p. from the wind, 27:6
  his p. is everywhere, 267:3
  home p. they have to take you, 623:3
  I found a new p. to dwell, 768:3
  I go to prepare a p., 40:26
  if man aspires to highest p., 87:17
  in the first p., 768:5
  in the sun, 557:3
  know p. for first time, 672:6
  lodging p. of wayfaring men, 28:22
  lonesome p. against sky, 563:10
  lonesome's a bad p., 730:13
  many are in high p., 31:2
  mind is its own p., 256:5
  neither shall his p. know him, 14:8
  new purchaser of country p., 714:15
  none of new spiders took her p., 703:17
  nor time nor p., 213:11
  nor to one p. trusted, 179:14
  not circumscribed in one self p., 162:16
  not safe unless degree preserved, 100:22
  of a skull, 37:9
  of excrement, 598:21
  of skulls, 399:20
  older p. than Eden, 619:4
  philosophy in cities, 87:30
  prayed to genius of the p., 94:18
  pseudo-promotion a new work p., 747:7
  rain upon p. beneath, 181:19
  remote and islanded, 557:17
  respect of p. persons time, 202:4
  resting p. for those who gave lives, 450:2
  rivers of water in a dry p., 27:6
  running to keep in p., 518:19
  savage p. holy enchanted, 382:20
  shall know it no more, 14:*n*1
  stand in his holy p., 16:18
  sunshine in the shady p., 153:7
  the Lord is in this p., 7:41
  thereof shall know it no more, 19:2
  this is the p., 427:4
  thou hast been our dwelling p., 18:10
  till there be no p., 25:38
  time p. loved one, 468:14

Pleure dans mon coeur, 554:*n*2
Pleuré, j'ai p. et j'ai cru, 369:*n*7
Pleurer, de peur d'en p., 336:*n*3
Pleut, comme il p. sur la ville, 554:*n*2
   doucement sur la ville, 566:*n*1
Pliable, name of other P., 272:12
Pliant, obstinate p. merry morose,
   106:24
Plied, by little arms p., 517:1
   myself to fruitless poetry, 156:19
Plighted, what p. cunning hides,
   208:27
Pliny, is it Aristotle P. Buffon, 319:16
Plis, les p. de sa robe pourprée,
   144:*n*4
Plodders, small have p. won, 168:15
Plods, plowman homeward p., 322:1
Ploffskin Pluffskin Pelican jee, 472:16
Plot, blessed p. this earth, 171:9
   find p. in narrative be shot, 526:18
   gunpowder treason and p., 777:20
   Horror soul of p., 452:7
   melodious p., 415:10
   passions spin p., 508:28
   souls that cringe and p., 485:3
   thickens, 273:3
   time someone invented p., 651:5
   women guide the p., 352:18
Plotted, foul deed which she p., 53:21
Plow ancient and valuable, 444:16
   following p. along mountainside,
   374:9
   for lords who lay ye low, 407:19
   friends who p. sea, 529:15
   having put hand to p., 38:16
   sow reap mow, 777:13
   speed his p., 157:9
Plowed, dashed to earth p. under,
   787:13
   I have p. and planted, 420:22
   if ye had not p. with my heifer,
   11:13
   land p. before man, 444:16
   sea, 395:14
   wickedness, 29:28
Plowing, men want crops without p.,
   480:16
Plowman, heavy steps of p., 595:5
   homeward plods, 322:1
Plowman's story is of bulls, 100:28
Plows, drinks water her keel p. air,
   157:13
   in the fields, 656:9
Plowshare, drives p. o'er creation,
   296:20
   put not p. too deep, 379:20
   stern Ruin's p., 361:20
Plowshares, beat swords into p., 25:30
Pluck a crow together, 166:27
   bright honor from moon, 177:9
   from memory rooted sorrow,
   216:10
   I come to p. your berries, 253:14
   it out and cast it from thee, 33:5
   love not flower they p., 429:21
   out heart of my mystery, 197:16
   out his flying feather, 534:9
   sworn to weed and p. away, 171:17
   their hearts from them, 185:20
   this flower safety, 177:16

Pluck (*continued*)
   till time and times done, 595:7
   time to p. up, 23:32
   up drowned honor, 177:9
   you out of crannies, 460:5
Plucked, an olive leaf p. off, 7:20
   Diogenes p. a cock, 77:3
   fruit she p. she eat, 260:7
   his gown, 329:16
   lint from lapel, 586:2
   my nipple from his gums, 213:12
   violets p., 236:8
Plucker down of kings, 164:17
Plucks dead lions by beard, 169:20
   liberty p. justice, 203:24
   off my beard, 196:6
   with a thread p. it back, 175:14
Plum, pulled out p., 788:11
   some gave p. cake, 788:10
   survives its poems, 638:18
Plumage, pities p., 341:6
Plumber, try getting p. on weekends,
   767:11
Plumbing, shadows of p. left of city,
   758:14
Plume, blast-beruffled p., 540:10
   helmet and the p., 454:16
Plume, prête-moi ta p., 786:21
Plumed, farewell p. troop, 207:8
   helmets gleamed in forests, 503:4
   knight, 520:11
   war bonnet, 698:6
Plumes, borrowed p., 59:2
   feathered with eagle's p., 59:19
   her feathers, 252:29
Plummet, deeper than p. sound,
   224:24
Plummets to dust of hope, 65:18
Plump, banish p. Jack, 177:32
Plumpskin Ploshkin Pelican jill, 472:16
Plumpy Bacchus with pink eyne,
   217:21
Plums, life's a pudding full of p.,
   531:19
Plunder, capital in ascendancy system
   of p., 481:10
   lust for blood and p., 621:1
   public p., 393:*n*4
   years p. one thing after another,
   98:1
Plunge hands in water, 720:8
Plunged, be p. in deepest reveries,
   486:17
Plunge-line, black p. nightdress,
   769:15
Plunges, heart p. lower than night,
   654:4
   into scientific questions, 505:20
   Orion p. prone, 580:5
   year p. into night, 654:4
Plural, unity is p., 691:20
Pluralism lets exist in each-form,
   546:22
Plus ça change plus la même, 443:*n*3
   est quam vita salusque, 105:*n*15
Pluto, won the ear of P., 251:20
Plutonian shore, 452:18
Pluto's, iron tears down P. cheek,
   252:7
Ply, I cannot p. the loom, 56:9

Ply (*continued*)
   the sampler, 253:10
Plyin', boats a-p. up and down,
   592:19
Plying needle and thread, 423:4
Plymouth, pious ones of P., 481:4
Pneumatic bliss, 668:14
Pnin ceased to notice students, 703:6
Po, wandering P., 328:6
Pobble who has no toes, 472:14
Pobbles happier without toes, 472:15
Pocket full of rye, 790:1
   learning in private p., 305:4
   Lucy Locket lost p., 791:16
   never alone with poet in p., 338:11
   not scruple to pick p., 285:12
   plates dropped from his p., 218:11
   put me in your p., 657:7
   save their own p., 72:1
Pocket-handkerchief, holding p., 519:6
Pockets, contents of his p., 658:5
Pod, seeds in dry p. tick, 607:11
Poe with his raven, 485:8
Poem a poem and nothing more,
   453:13
   bathed in P. of Sea, 565:13
   begins as lump in throat, 625:6
   day is a p., 663:19
   dignity in writing p., 571:33
   does P. not merely says P., 413:11
   don't make p. with ideas, 547:14
   fain write p., 466:26
   feeling for single good p., 350:1
   figure a p. makes, 625:8
   finds the thought, 625:6
   for poem's sake, 453:13
   heroic p. a biography, 412:27
   immediate object pleasure not truth,
   384:11
   is a meteor, 640:21
   language touched by poetry is p.,
   736:14
   lovely as a tree, 661:16
   metermaking argument makes p.,
   432:15
   music of p. in translation, 613:13
   my life p. I would have writ, 477:22
   never finished only abandoned,
   614:3
   of any length not all poetry, 384:12
   of the act of the mind, 384:*n*3
   of world, 712:19
   ought himself to be true p., 254:15
   part of sense of life, 640:23
   phrase long p. contradiction, 453:12
   pleasure of p. guessing, 547:13
   poetry subject of p., 639:8
   pretty p. Mr. Pope, 286:10
   questions when reading p., 721:9
   read a good p., 349:10
   ride on own melting, 625:10
   right reader of good p., 625:7
   rooted in awe, 721:10
   should not mean, 683:8
   suggestibility of p., 600:5
   that took place of mountain, 640:10
   to which we return, 384:2
   true p. an invocation, 692:4
   United States greatest p., 488:9
   way to tell if p. lasting, 625:7

Policy's, all p. allowed in war and
    love, 482:*n*4
Polis, newspaper runs p. foorce,
    603:12
Polish, fitter to bruise than p., 262:12
Polished handle of big front door,
    529:6
    idleness, 367:16
    perturbation, 184:9
    satire like p. razor, 304:5
Polisher, comedy the civilizer the p.,
    509:2
Polite, compulsion to become p.,
    658:7
    costs nothing to be p., 622:6
    learning, 286:21
Politeness, out of p. cheat others,
    613:1
    pineapple of p., 352:8
    punctuality p. of kings, 355:8
Politesse, l'exactitude la p. des rois,
    355:*n*2
Politic, body p. like human body,
    319:9
    cautious and meticulous, 667:17
Political affairs, 446:17
    beginning and end of p. education,
    535:19
    best p. community, 78:22
    campaigns emotional orgies, 587:15
    creed of our p. faith, 344:9
    dissolve p. bands, 343:2
    economic freedom means to p. free-
    dom, 731:11
    economy not respect p. frontiers,
    645:11
    everything in p. life, 500:16
    executive magistracy, 332:21
    freedom, 631:14
    freedom business of Government,
    649:2
    fundamental article of p. creed,
    338:16
    give me p. economist, 484:8
    good carried to extreme, 366:2
    greatness and wisdom meet, 75:15
    ideas and imagination, 718:3
    joining p. party casting ballot,
    645:12
    language make lies sound truthful,
    711:14
    liberty highest p. end, 521:7
    man a p. animal, 78:12
    opportunities around for p. pull,
    548:3
    power out of barrel of gun, 686:12
    Principles of P. Economy, 627:19
    rather p. than religious, 315:24
    rebellion in p. world, 343:14
    society exists for noble actions,
    78:20
    tyranny of p. assemblies, 438:2
    understanding to run government,
    655:15
    variable of p. calculation, 505:12
Politician, being p. myself, 447:22
    characteristics of popular p., 73:1
    honest p. stays bought, 422:15
    I'm not a p., 521:18
    is an arse, 689:3

Politician (*continued*)
    scurvy p., 211:5
    under every stone lurks p., 73:18
    who steals is a fool, 548:3
    would circumvent God, 199:3
Politician's corpse laid away, 609:5
Politicians, country run by p., 761:16
    friends lovers husbands, 347:3
    have interests aside from people's,
    447:22
    tinhorn p., 606:6
    whole race of p., 289:11
Politics almost exciting as war, 619:16
    applesauce, 637:18
    art of happiness, 590:12
    Cobbett a fourth estate in p., 390:6
    customs p. and tongue, 503:9
    economic development culture,
    749:9
    education part of p., 421:16
    expensive, 638:5
    greatest adventure, 628:3
    I must study p. and war, 338:10
    in p. if you want anything, 756:3
    in p. middle way none at all, 338:2
    is art of possible, 474:14
    killed many times in p., 619:16
    like ours profess, 307:6
    like religion, 344:12
    magnanimity in p., 331:24
    makes strange bedfellows, 511:5
    must not bring Queen into p., 506:7
    my p. like my religion, 521:14
    no more with gallantry than p.,
    352:25
    not engaged in domestic p., 663:7
    not think about p., 765:3
    of accommodatin character, 521:14
    of joy, 729:19
    orthodox in p., 683:2
    practical p., 446:14, 535:31
    royalist in p., 672:18
    saturates p. with thought, 499:7
    struggle of forces, 536:1
    thermonuclear war not continuation
    of p., 749:8
    war not separated from p., 686:14
    world of pure power p., 680:17
Politik ist die Lehre von Möglichen,
    474:*n*4
Polity, ideal p., 75:16
Polka, can't you dance p., 793:15
Poll, talked like poor P., 323:19
Pollertics of accommodatin character,
    521:14
Polliwogs of islands, 729:13
Polluted, not p. though it passes
    among impure, 77:*n*5
    shun the p. flock, 660:15
    sun not p. by privies, 77:6
Pollutes whate'er it touches, 406:8
Pollution, tide of cultural p., 754:6
Pollutions, sun remains pure through
    p., 77:*n*5
Polly, little P. Flinders, 790:15
    put kettle on, 792:10
    you might have toyed, 297:14
Poltagrue, Devil went off to tempt
    Lady P., 609:7

Polygamy, before p. was made a sin,
    274:1
Pomegranate, sweet p. wine, 4:8
Pomegranates, land of p., 10:16
Pommy, welcome p. bastard to God's
    earth, 775:7
Pomp and circumstance, 207:8
    and feast and revelry, 251:19
    and glory of this world, 225:16
    and pride, 563:14
    blot out p. check impulse, 111:27
    bright p. ascended, 259:22
    happiness enemy to p., 292:21
    lick absurd p., 197:2
    lintel low to keep out p., 563:14
    lo p. of yesterday, 593:2
    of emperors ridiculous, 431:1
    of power, 322:8
    painted p., 190:6
    solemnized with p. and parade,
    338:5
    Sultan after Sultan with P., 445:11
    take physic p., 210:3
    tide of p. that beats, 185:19
    vain p. and glory, 49:21
    what is p. rule reign, 164:31
Pompous in the grave, 249:4
Pond, an old p., 282:15
    fish have their stream and p., 663:1
    four ducks on p., 504:3
    love we are a small p., 755:2
    mantle like a standing p., 179:19
Ponder, first p. then dare, 426:3
Pondered weak and weary, 452:13
Ponds, some p. thought bottomless,
    478:32
Pone, whar man gits corn p., 528:9
Poniards, she speaks p., 186:22
Ponies, wretched blind pit p., 611:18
Pons asinorum, 82:*n*3
Pontellier, Mrs. P. beginning to realize
    position, 562:17
Pontic, like to the P. sea, 207:15
Pontius Pilate, suffered under P., 48:25
Pony, had a little p., 792:9
    won't stand, 786:3
    Yankee Doodle on p., 778:21
Pool, dreaming p., 484:14
    green mantle of standing p., 210:8
    rhymes with P stands for P., 710:11
    river lake glimmering p., 503:4
Pools I used to know, 579:11
    where it offers to curiosity, 671:13
Poop was beaten gold, 217:14
Poor agent despised, 201:15
    alas p. Yorick, 199:8
    and content is rich, 206:32
    and maimed, 38:32
    and often very lousy, 310:24
    annals of the p., 322:7
    apt the p. to be proud, 202:23
    as dirt don't get rhythm, 766:8
    as Job, 183:17
    bare forked animal, 210:6
    beetle we tread upon, 204:11
    being p. have only dreams, 595:9
    benighted 'eathen, 591:19
    better is a p. and wise child, 24:1
    blessed are p. in spirit, 33:1
    but honest, 203:11

Poor (*continued*)

but she was honest, 782:17
cannot help many who are p., 741:4
care of the p., 278:15
cat i' the adage, 213:9
cried Caesar wept, 189:1
dear God, 695:20
Death beats at p. man's door, 95:18
decent provision for p., 316:9
defraud not the p., 31:6
degenerate from ape, 689:18
die not p. death, 230:22
dog Tray, 388:25
exchequer of the p., 171:15
few save p. feel for p., 428:8
fools decoyed, 279:13
for urban p. police arrest, 759:4
foundest p. and keepest so, 329:23
freedom to rich or p., 685:10
get poorer, 661:15
give me your tired your p., 558:1
give to the p., 35:36
giveth unto the p., 23:8
gout kills more rich than p., 271:17
grind the faces of the p., 25:34
grow p. staying in one place, 122:4
hear p. rogues talk of news, 211:13
heart would fain deny, 216:9
high and low rich and p., 369:12
honest exceeding p. man, 180:15
how p. a thing is man, 161:5
I am even p. in thanks, 195:27
I am p. and needy, 19:12
if p. whenever you can, 77:4
if we not make somebody p.,
    358:10
I'm p. I'm black, 773:14
in behalf of despised p., 424:5
infirm weak old man, 209:26
intricated soul, 231:13
Jim Jay, 617:4
Kiltartan's p., 596:10
last I lay upon thy lips, 218:7
law forbids rich as well as p.,
    550:13
laws catch the weak and p., 56:2
laws grind the p., 328:16
lean lank face, 448:8
leave them for the p. and stranger,
    9:24
little lambs lost way, 592:3
lo the p. Indian, 301:7
lone woman, 183:28
lonely and p. of old, 663:5
love country and be p., 303:18
makes me p. indeed, 206:30
man accustomed to small things,
    731:18
man being down, 31:33
man deprived of power, 75:23
man get out iv Purgatory, 603:5
man had nothing, 12:10
man is Christ's stamp, 243:4
man poor mankind, 696:15
man that hangs on favors, 225:16
man who craves more is p., 102:19
many a p. man that loved, 597:3
many good men are p., 55:15
men's cottages palaces, 179:27
my children who are p., 740:5

Poor (*continued*)

my p. fool is hanged, 211:19
my wife p. wretch, 279:7
naked p. mangled Peace, 186:1
naked wretches, 210:3
neither rich nor p., 523:10
no disgrace to be p., 605:16
no p. person be deprived, 753:17
none so p. to do him reverence,
    189:3
not p. who has enough to use,
    97:14
obliged wealthy and relieved p.,
    51:n6
one of the undeserving p., 571:21
outrage of p., 430:1
pity upon the p., 21:45
player that struts, 216:14
prey of rich on p., 343:13
purses proud garments p., 167:31
relation irrelevant, 388:5
rich gifts wax p., 196:12
rich honesty in p. house, 192:15
rich rob p., 421:2
rob not the p., 22:13
rob one another, 421:2
scandalous and p., 283:23
scandals of th' p., 602:19
shall never cease, 10:19
slipping out of consciousness, 759:3
so p. he could not keep a dog,
    113:2
sold the p. for a pair of shoes,
    29:34
solitary p. nasty, 239:22
sort of memory, 519:10
soul sat sighing, 208:4
soul the center, 222:11
splendid wings, 535:3
strength to the p., 26:25
that have not patience, 206:26
thing but mine own, 192:n1
Tom's a-cold, 210:11
too p. for bribe, 323:13
two nations the rich and p., 434:26
unhappy brains for drinking, 206:14
what will p. robin do, 790:17
when anything to eat, 77:n3
whoso mocketh the p., 21:33
why not given to p., 40:22
with hunger rich and p. as one,
    68:23
world said I, 264:18
wot gets blame, 782:18
ye have p. always, 36:22
Poorer, for richer for p., 50:4
Poorest he that is in England, 239:16
in p. thing superfluous, 209:21
man in his cottage, 312:19
nor p. receive contentment, 231:14
this Traverse p. take, 514:2
Poorhouse, over hill to p., 554:9
Poorly satisfy our eyes, 227:9
Pop goes the weasel, 780:13
Pope and emperor, 427:15
anybody can be p., 645:2
better err with P., 399:6
Czar Metternich Guizot, 481:14
how many divisions has P. got,
    638:11

Pope (*continued*)

pretty poem Mr. P., 286:10
Popery, inclines a man to P., 159:n8
Popinjay, pestered with a p., 177:4
Popinjays, reverences gilt P., 411:17
Pop'lar, dead always p., 602:12
Poplars stand and tremble, 579:11
Poppet, no go my p., 722:4
Poppies, fume of p., 416:14
in Flanders p. blow, 615:7
pleasures like p. spread, 363:6
Poppy, not p. nor mandragora, 207:6
oblivion blindly scattereth p., 249:1
or a lily, 529:18
Populace, Barbarians Philistines P.,
    500:9
man to whom p. is entrusted, 51:5
Popular, addressing p. audiences,
    78:30
characteristics of p. politician, 73:1
conscience, 646:13
custom supported by p. opinion,
    577:7
dead always p., 602:12
heroes created by p. demand, 679:2
power in majority of p. assembly,
    338:16
propaganda has to be p., 676:6
spirit and form of p. government,
    352:1
truth not so p. as fiction, 403:n3
war will cease to be p., 566:9
we're more p. than Jesus now,
    770:6
when Fortune on our side, 99:12
Popularity glory's small change,
    427:17
is a crime, 279:29
Population unchecked increases, 368:2
Populi, salus p. suprema lex, 88:n4
vox p. vox Dei, 120:8
Populous and smoky city, 407:22
long in p. city pent, 260:5
Porcelain clay of humankind, 275:26
give children right to study p.,
    338:10
precious p. of human clay, 275:n7
Porches of mine ears, 194:23
Porcupine, quills upon fretful p.,
    194:17
Pore benighted 'eathen, 591:19
I'm p. I'm black, 773:14
Porgy and Bess, 695:n3
Pork, yes to smell p., 180:2
Pork chops, who killed the p., 757:2
Pornographic, in p. novels action lim-
    ited, 703:4
Porpentine, quills upon fretful p.,
    194:17
Porphyry font, 456:20
Porpoise close behind us, 518:5
waters of petrel and p., 671:11
Porridge, comfort like cold p., 224:3
pease p. hot, 790:10
spare breath to cool p., 55:n3
Porsches, my friends all drive P.,
    773:6
Porsena, Lars P. of Clusium, 425:13
Port after stormy seas, 153:9
bomb might destroy whole p., 636:1

Port (*continued*)
   is near bells I hear, 490:19
   liquor for men, 317:13
   pride in their p., 328:13
   Scylla to p., 181:*n*2
Portable, get hold of p. property,
   471:16
Portal, fitful tracing of p., 639:4
   opens to receive me, 367:12
Portals alternate Night Day, 445:11
   errors p. of discovery, 647:16
   of church and school, 615:4
Portas, Hannibal ad p., 119:8
Portent of fate awaiting Nazi tyranny,
   621:3
   of new atomic age, 608:14
Portentous phrase I told you so,
   403:19
   sight, 382:18
Porter, all p. and skittles, 469:2
   Mrs. P. in the spring, 668:23
Portion, best p. of man's life, 373:1
   brief life our p., 482:9
   dedicate p. of field, 450:2
   equal p. for who lingers, 51:31
   fill certain p. of uncertain paper,
   402:15
   he wales a p., 361:9
   no p. in us after, 602:10
   of that around me, 400:4
   worst p. in this life, 725:18
Portions and parcels of Past, 454:9
Portrait, Hero of Our Time a p.,
   474:4
   manners mirror which shows p.,
   351:8
   man's work p. of himself, 524:18
   of Gertrude Stein, 627:8
   of person one knows, 349:25
   of vices of generation, 474:4
   person portrayed and p., 653:18
   two styles of p. painting, 469:15
Portraits of Franz Joseph, 643:9
Portray, it is myself I p., 145:8
Portrayed, person p. and portrait,
   653:18
Ports and happy havens, 171:1
   of slumber open, 184:9
Portugal, like bay of P., 192:5
Posies, thousand fragrant p., 162:4
Position, in highest p. least freedom,
   91:26
   not certain of own p., 629:7
   Stalin rose to his p., 641:4
   those above insure p., 5:7
Positive economics can be objective,
   731:10
Possess, but for you p. the field, 483:3
   decisive marks of opulence, 326:4
   find lose but never p., 716:3
   general knowledges idiots p., 358:15
   let us p. one world, 228:3
   origin of poems, 488:17
   rich p. and enjoy early, 694:14
   soul with patience, 275:24
   souls in patience, 39:13
   them not with fear, 185:20
   things rank and gross p. it, 193:6
   to have little is to p., 57:8
Possessed, I die but have p., 401:8

Possessed (*continued*)
   object p., 509:4
   of no value p., 284:14
   regain love once p., 261:19
   rich p. by money, 234:22
   two evils p. me, 674:10
   Webster p. by death, 668:12
Possesses, he is superior everything he
   p., 306:10
   heart fall in love, 612:14
   more he gives more he p., 58:7
   virtue in abundance, 57:16
Possessing, acquiring and p. property,
   327:1
   having nothing p. all, 44:6
   heart of woman, 612:14
   too dear for my p., 221:11
Possession, best p. is sympathetic wife,
   69:11
   composed to be everlasting p.,
   71:19
   each person born to one p., 527:32
   eleven points in law, 291:19
   fy on p., 131:25
   housed where it gets p., 166:28
   loads us with weariness, 487:28
   love of money as p., 652:12
   mad in pursuit and in p., 222:7
   object in p. seldom retains charm,
   110:1
   of truth as of a city, 248:2
   of woman not as precious as truths,
   613:2
   put him in p. of truth, 277:7
   take intellectual p., 549:6
   virtue that p. would not show,
   187:2
   without obligation, 509:4
Possessions, covetous of others' p.,
   91:22
   his p. are deathless, 53:6
   jealous p. of happiness, 607:2
   more p. more worry, 102:10
   take away liberty, 588:15
Possibilities, believe only p., 248:14
   land of unlimited p., 556:4
   seven hundred pounds and p.,
   182:18
Possibility, even p. can transform us,
   553:6
   preferable to unconvincing p., 78:34
   State have p. of life, 75:15
Possible, anything p. except fair play,
   539:15
   best of all p. worlds, 306:5, 635:8
   Christ that it were p., 458:25
   Father if it be p., 36:30
   make p. things not so held, 222:19
   no p. doubt whatever, 531:18
   O God that it were p., 233:19
   politics is art of p., 474:14
   shadow of doubt, 531:18
   to fail in many ways, 78:3
   you may be mistaken, 247:1
Post, hope to die at my p., 610:8
   o'er land and ocean, 255:13
   offices and cabinet appointments,
   448:*n*2
Post coitum omne animal triste,
   119:21

Post (*continued*)
   equitem sedet atra cura, 96:*n*11
   hoc ergo propter hoc, 119:22
Post-coaches, good old days of p.,
   393:7
Posteras, et maiores vestros et p. cogitate, 109:*n*15
Posteriora, tanto plus apparent p.,
   123:*n*8
Posteriors of this day, 169:7
Posterity bear witness to his mind,
   369:1
   Constitution for p., 389:16
   contemplate forefathers and p.,
   325:4
   Democratic Party without hope of
   p., 516:1
   deprive or divest p., 327:1
   do something for us, 293:11
   evoke one's p., 688:5
   look forward to p., 332:10
   of work of art, 612:15
   of yet unborn, 293:1
   ourselves and our p., 346:7
   owe it to p., 345:15
   plant tree for p., 85:*n*6
   say of Washington, 310:20
   think of p., 109:22
   to have no p., 79:20
   to p. world without end, 335:24
   unlimited undefined, 389:16
   weaves no garlands, 364:22
   when we are planning for p., 340:20
Posters of the sea and land, 212:15
Posthumously, some born p., 553:12
Posting, breath rides on p. winds,
   219:29
Posts, up men to your p., 505:21
Postulations, two simultaneous p.,
   494:13
Postumus, alas P. fleeting years slip
   by, 96:10
Posture of a whore, 218:13
Pot calls kettle black, 151:12
   chicken in p. every Sunday, 154:20
   crackling of thorns under a p., 24:8
   death in the p., 13:7
   fame for p. of ale, 185:6
   go to p., 330:18
   greasy Joan doth keel p., 169:13
   kettle and earthen p., 31:31
   little p. and soon hot, 167:27
   maketh the deep boil like a p.,
   15:24
   melting p., 590:6
   melting p. did not happen, 590:*n*2
   nor for every thirst to p., 244:20
   nuffin' in de p., 615:2
   pease-porridge in p., 790:10
   put on p. says Greedy-gut, 789:16
   who is Potter who P., 446:5
Potable gold, 235:10
Potations pottle deep, 206:15
Potatoes, small p., 511:6
Potency, presuming on changeful p.,
   201:8
   symbol of surging p., 657:20
Potent, how p. cheap music is, 700:17
   make p. more powerful, 369:11
   poet p. figure, 640:16

Power (*continued*)

nations possessing great p., 636:2

no one fit to be trusted with p., 717:22

nonviolence paralyzed p. structures, 761:8

not by might nor by p., 30:1

not means is end, 711:18

not now in fortune's p., 263:15

object of p. is p., 711:18

obtained by weakness, 365:31

of beauty I remember yet, 276:26

of fright and lust, 692:4

of making laws, 355:4

of man and moment, 499:4

of one fair face, 137:10

of public plunder, 393:*n*4

of surplus in banks, 393:15

of sustaining and delighting, 501:5

of the atom, 636:8

of visible is invisible, 664:14

of world works in circles, 587:5

only prize for powerful is p., 542:19

over the clay, 42:10

passing from the earth, 376:15

plants will stop generating, 715:8

poesy supreme of p., 414:5

political p. out of barrel of gun, 686:12

pomp of p., 322:8

possesses the genuine p., 384:2

pre-eminence and p., 351:22

pride of p. sink, 331:10

proud Edward's p., 363:19

public life situation of p., 331:2

ransom them from the p. of the grave, 29:31

rather in p. than use, 203:8

relentless p., 321:18

rich have p. and poor deprived, 75:23

riches and p. gifts of fate, 121:11

right hand is glorious in p., 9:4

rise of misplaced p., 678:17

same in all countries, 389:14

shadow of love, 629:6

shadow of unseen P., 406:9

some p. giftie gie us, 361:18

sorrow hath less p. to bite, 171:2

spare thee past my p., 361:19

spirit of p., 45:26

strange p. of speech, 382:5

struggle against p., 761:10

surpassed others but had no more p., 98:24

symbol of p. of Heaven, 665:5

symbol of p. of movement, 657:20

tends to corrupt, 521:5

the great aphrodisiac, 752:13

thine is the p., 33:12

thou shalt have p. to degenerate, 136:1

titles p. and pelf, 378:1

to add or detract, 450:2

to be silent, 277:22

to build black institutions, 771:*n*2

to cancel his captivity, 187:29

to chasten and subdue, 373:5

to do me ill, 225:*n*5

to drink or rise, 397:20

Power (*continued*)

to hurt and will do none, 221:14

to know all things, 227:14

to live and act, 377:6

to say Behold, 172:20

to tax not power to destroy, 543:8

to tax power to destroy, 355:13

to undo the past, 74:2

to which Rome not compared, 394:19

transfiguring p., 553:1

trust no man with p. to endanger liberty, 337:16

unlimited p. corrupt, 313:2

unlimited p. into hands of husbands, 347:1

upon the past has p., 275:1

villains in p., 339:3

waits upon him who earns it, 532:11

we here hold the p., 449:16

weird p. in spoken word, 572:23

where love rules no will to p., 629:6

where p. predominates love lacking, 629:6

which men call Chance, 253:6

wielded by abnormal energy, 535:33

will and p., 200:10

will to p., 553:17

wisdom goodness, 287:3

witch hath p. to charm, 192:29

with p. and glory, 39:14

witty beauty a p., 509:11

Powerful amidst peers, 551:4

black is p., 709:2

boy is most p. of Hellenes, 62:26

goodness want, 406:17

has power over self, 139:*n*11

humblest peer of most p., 520:10

impulse to punish, 552:9

make potent more p., 369:11

more p. than locomotive, 737:7

nation which enjoys most freedom most p., 368:17

only prize for p. is power, 542:19

oppressed and p. Russia, 496:20

outlive this p. rime, 220:25

overflow of p. feelings, 373:17

sisterhood is p., 771:13

word of God is p., 45:34

Powerless, freedom made man anxious p., 704:8

to be born, 498:20

Powerlessness, to have no cash means p., 436:23

Powers, against principalities and p., 44:28

colonizations by European p., 360:10

cultivation of her p., 410:18

deem that there are P., 372:19

deny us for our good, 217:11

depository of ultimate p., 344:22

desires dreams and p., 534:13

draw p. into higher classes, 345:4

evils avoided p. exercised, 108:8

fear of divine and supreme p., 235:18

just p. from consent, 343:2

knows you not Heavenly P., 349:7

Powers (*continued*)

lay waste our p., 376:11

men fear p. principalities of air, 642:23

merciful p., 213:18

never two continental p., 676:8

of augury, 51:10

of combination, 332:28

Princedoms Virtues P., 259:13

principalities nor p., 42:9

remaining second weakest among great p., 643:8

specified p., 355:7

superior to man, 564:22

tempt frailty of our p., 201:8

that be, 42:20

wars of European p., 360:11

Pox, die on gallows or of p., 327:13

Practical politics, 446:14

politics ignoring facts, 535:31

Practicality never even suggested, 491:15

Practice and thought forge art, 92:24

best of instructors, 99:23

by p. get to be wide apart, 62:1

childish ways, 52:31

Christian forbearance, 339:11

constituted for p. of good, 79:26

doctrine or p. or interpretation, 111:23

drives me mad, 776:9

five things, 62:2

good p. to verify references, 355:15

he fell mightily in his p., 271:19

helping men p. virtue, 79:9

humility all preach none p., 238:23

is everything, 99:*n*11

little proceed to greater, 108:5

lived in p. of every virtue, 72:11

makes perfect, 99:*n*11

selfish in p. not principle, 387:5

success in p., 539:10

they diligently p. Tao, 57:12

this without me, 353:1

to deceive, 378:13

what you preach, 84:3, 113:17

world of p., 499:6

Practicer, frequent p. of angling, 245:17

Practices, fair p. to fair notions, 74:12

who p. virtue will have neighbors, 61:7

Practitioner in panegyric, 352:35

Praevalet, magna est veritas et p., 30:*n*3

Pragmatic method attitude of orientation, 546:18

Pragmatism first introduced, 546:*n*2

Prague, as old hermit of P. said, 203:4

Prairie, bury me not on lone p., 786:8

bury me out on p., 786:9

last night as I lay on p., 786:5

to make a p., 514:16

Prairie-lawyer master of all, 637:11

Prairies for which speech no name, 411:9

from mountains to p., 666:12

Praise, ask criticism want p., 626:13

at morning blame at night, 299:3

be to God, 116:1

Praise *(continued)*

boldness certain to win p., 100:30
book people p. don't read, 527:30
bury Caesar not p. him, 188:28
damn with faint p., 302:11
dispraised no small p., 260:29
famous men, 32:13
firm restraint with which write, 707:1
for being and happening, 721:10
forced p. on our part, 464:26
forms no part of beauty, 111:4
from Sir Hubert Stanley, 367:10
garment of p., 28:6
God from whom all blessings flow, 280:21
God hath no better p., 550:1
guests p. it not cooks, 160:17
he fathers-forth p. him, 551:1
her own works p. her, 23:21
him and exalt him, 32:17
I p. the Frenchman, 334:18
if there be any p., 44:35
in country you p. city, 95:12
in deeper reverence p., 443:17
in p. of ladies dead, 221:22
into his courts with p., 18:22
kind of strife man might p., 54:19
laurel crown yield to p., 88:2
let another man p. thee, 22:33
let every thing p. the Lord, 20:16
lived without disgrace without p., 125:9
Lord pass ammunition, 679:7
love of p., 295:23
low ambition and thirst of p., 334:5
maid whom none to p., 373:19
my mouth shall show forth thy p., 17:24
named thee but to p., 405:5
never p. sister to sister, 591:2
nor blame the writings, 299:1
nourish agues, 178:23
of ancient authors, 239:24
only to be praised, 265:20
or blame momentary, 418:6
or blame too far, 625:1
poets lose half the p., 250:5
Power that hath made, 391:3
right p. and true perfection, 182:12
sacrament of p., 639:5
say more than this rich p., 221:10
scarce could p., 313:11
scarcely can p. it, 330:10
sea on shore remain, 154:19
see how man receives p., 102:26
shall sanctify our rest, 506:16
silence muse His p., 308:9
sing thee a song in thy p., 362:21
solid pudding empty p., 303:25
swells note of p., 322:9
that will never die, 72:7
thirst of p., 334:5
those who follow other paths, 94:31
those who spoke her p., 328:2
to give, 232:18
verses but read something else, 106:15
virtues men p. and pass by, 658:13

Praise *(continued)*

we p. thee for perspicuity of language, 121:5
we p. thee O God, 48:23
your p. not worth dying for, 106:20
Praise-all, Blame-all and P. block-heads, 309:10
Praised, honesty is p. and starves, 108:16
Lord's name is to be p., 19:15
praise only to be p., 265:20
the dead already dead, 23:33
woman that feareth the Lord shall be p., 23:21
Praiser of past time, 98:13
Praises, earth with voices p. God, 383:4
everybody praises nobody, 341:20
faintly then he p., 302:*n*7
might be reported, 32:14
sing p. to his Name, 777:8
so long shall your p. endure, 93:24
with enthusiastic tone, 530:21
Praising, advantage of p. oneself, 524:20
lean and sallow abstinence, 253:8
most dispraises, 302:*n*7
what is lost, 203:19
Prances, far back in soul horse p., 657:20
Prancing Poetry, 514:2
Prate, hear him p., 509:16
stones p. of whereabout, 213:22
Prates, all she p. has nothing in it, 289:15
Prattle, nor do children p. about his knees, 51:19
thinking his p. tedious, 172:13
Praxed, Saint P. in a glory, 465:6
Praxiteles unable to reach all the material, 111:31
Pray, after this manner p. ye, 33:12
all p. in their distress, 356:12
as if to die tomorrow, 310:6
can't p. a lie, 526:26
farmers p. that summers be wet, 92:23
for dead fight like hell for living, 515:3
for me and come not, 162:21
for no man but myself, 211:26
for repose of his soul, 582:17
for them which despitefully use you, 33:8
God absolve us all, 134:4
God to keep me from being proud, 278:26
goes to bed and does not p., 243:13
how they p. for death, 67:26
I p. you in your letters, 208:16
in distress and need, 651:14
in fullness of joy, 651:14
late and early p., 227:7
Lord soul to keep, 287:14
make me able to pay for it, 278:27
make no mistake, 531:1
never learned to p., 716:20
one to watch one to p., 266:8
place men can p., 619:7
remained to p., 329:15

Pray *(continued)*

so we'll live p. sing, 211:13
that love may never come, 68:17
that the way be long, 587:11
to p. is to work, 119:17
two went to p., 264:7
watch and p., 36:31
we do p. for mercy, 181:19
will not p. with you, 180:2
without ceasing, 45:8
work and p. live on hay, 637:1
you now forget, 211:11
you undo this button, 211:19
Prayed, caught God's skirts p., 464:16
of Course I p., 512:7
to genius of the place, 94:18
Prayer, be relieved by p., 224:29
be sure p. will be granted, 555:6
Christ's progress and His p.-time, 270:2
comes round again, 599:4
effectual fervent p., 46:18
every p. reduces to this, 482:19
fool there was made p., 592:23
for S.T.C., 385:5
four spend in p., 152:7
from heart's deep core, 614:24
God erects house of p., 285:14
indeed good, 71:17
laughter beginning of p., 684:17
more wrought by p., 459:27
my house a house of p., 35:42
never made but one p., 306:22
of hawk not get chicken, 784:27
rises better man p. answered, 508:20
sadness touches me with a p., 420:1
same p. doth teach us all, 181:19
scent of arm-pits finer than p., 489:10
soul's sincere desire, 377:18
which rises from heart in grace, 126:7
wing and p., 718:7
Prayerbooks, beads and p., 301:15
Prayers, among p. a piece of land, 95:10
angry p., 611:18
are daughters of Zeus, 51:33
Bernard had p. in hall whiskey afterwards, 644:9
fall to thy p., 184:16
for a pretense make p., 37:32
God answers sharp some p., 439:4
hate enough to hear your p., 59:*n*6
make of your p. one sacrifice, 225:6
mention of thee in my p., 45:32
profit by losing our p., 217:11
to preserve travel, 290:15
to punish they answer p., 59:*n*6
which are age his alms, 156:15
whose p. make me whole, 591:11
wouldn't say p., 789:18
Prayeth best who loveth best, 382:8
well who loveth well, 382:7
Prayin' it tuh be different wid you, 707:7
Praying, dressing nursing p. and all's over, 402:20
now he is p., 197:24

Present (*continued*)
  evils triumph, 264:24
  except the p. company, 348:13
  extolling past at expense of p.,
    380:22
  fears less than imaginings, 212:23
  Ghost of Christmas P., 470:8
  gone in instant of becoming, 546:1
  had I been p. at the creation, 124:2
  Happiness in p. hour, 417:17
  house for future prison for p.,
    736:16
  in New York powerful, 585:12
  in p. light flames, 621:7
  in time future, 670:12
  it is p. that matters, 688:5
  joys more to flesh and blood,
    275:21
  mirth hath present laughter, 202:2
  morose view of p., 425:17
  no time like the p., 287:2
  our Alexandrian revels, 218:13
  Past Future sees, 357:25
  previous benefaction or p. satisfac-
    tion, 71:5
  submit to the p. evil, 102:11
  the P. teaches in vain, 615:1
  things p. nor things to come, 42:9
  things p. worst, 183:27
  those not p. always wrong, 295:21
  time p. and time past, 670:12
  to divine Majority p. no more,
    512:2
  to whom p. my new book, 90:14
  unbirthday p., 519:13
  unto thee O Lord our selves, 49:17
  what if p. were world's last night,
    230:25
Presentation copy does not sell, 388:12
Presented with a universal blank,
    257:24
Presents endear absents, 387:32
  not Christmas without p., 516:10
Preservation, in wildness p. of world,
    479:6
  magic p. in books, 412:35
  of species, 366:6
  ruin rather than p., 136:14
  we bless thee for our p., 49:5
Preserve as chiefest treasure, 608:16
  Canada a vast hunting p., 693:15
  entire those rights, 345:15
  he shall p. thy soul, 19:25
  me from a tyrant, 232:2
  me from unseasonable sleep, 314:25
  prayers to p. travel, 290:15
  reform that you may p., 425:1
  sacrifice lives to p. virtue, 61:26
  stars from wrong, 376:5
  the Lord shall p. thee, 19:25
  this country to p. liberty, 345:3
  thy going out and coming in, 19:25
  unity of empire, 331:22
  wants energy to p. itself, 344:6
  what we give and p., 449:16
  within wild sanctuary, 617:14
  your sangfroid, 343:18
Preserved, atoms p. by solidity, 89:10
  bee p. in amber, 106:14
  by delaying he p. state, 84:16

Preserved (*continued*)
  by reproduction, 347:13
  his gore O, 531:17
  liberty not p. without knowledge,
    337:13
  my life is p., 8:2
  reputation not p. dies, 278:13
  that long p. virginity, 268:16
  to yield is to be p., 57:8
  Union must be p., 369:10
  unless degree p. place not safe,
    100:22
  us a nation, 391:3
Preserver, Creator and P., 49:3
  destroyer and p. hear, 407:14
  time destroyer time p., 671:16
Preserves us not for specialists, 757:15
Preserving conditions of life, 473:8
  peace, 337:3
  sweetness of proportion, 232:9
Preside over liquidation of Empire,
    621:13
Presided, Angel that p. o'er birth,
    359:20
Presidency has followed change,
    729:21
  highest office, 603:14
  lose p. in a way bigger, 756:6
  runaway P. not messenger-boy P.,
    744:10
  we have a cancer close to P., 769:7
President be removed on impeach-
    ment, 346:8
  damned cowboy P. of United States,
    575:*n*5
  had a dream, 450:3
  is Commander-in-Chief, 410:4
  man who would like to be P., 677:1
  needs political understanding,
    655:15
  nobody expected me to be P., 448:8
  not Catholic candidate for P., 741:1
  of multiversity, 729:21
  of the Immortals, 540:3
  ordains bee to be, 639:25
  rather be right than P., 389:17
  telling off p., 742:22
  when P. does it not illegal, 733:20
  whether P. is a crook, 733:18
  Wintergreen for P., 695:5
Presidential, choosing p. nominee,
    655:16
President's spouse I wish him well,
    754:18
Press acknowledges accountability to
    no one, 656:5
  close bare-bosomed night, 489:8
  corporation of p., 463:16
  fell dead-born from p., 318:16
  free p. good or bad, 733:2
  free p. necessity, 677:5
  freedom of p., 344:9
  freedom of p. bulwarks of liberty,
    327:3
  freedom of p. guaranteed those who
    own one, 714:2
  freedom of p. has suffered most,
    733:1
  freedom of speech or of p., 346:11
  I like to p. wild flowers, 775:6

Press (*continued*)
  inform p. home Christmas, 604:10
  let's go to p., 698:2
  liberty of p., 345:13, 438:4
  microscopes and telescopes of p.,
    590:10
  Monday p. reports, 717:3
  my last p. conference, 733:12
  not falling man, 225:15
  not p. upon brow of labor, 582:4
  sort of wild animal, 656:5
  stir p. feel with fingers, 489:13
  tenth Muse governs p., 475:11
  toward the mark, 44:32
  with vigor on, 308:16
Pressed into service out of shape,
    623:6
  love though p. with ill, 335:18
Presses, clatter of p., 659:13
Presseth, thy hand p. me sore, 17:4
Press's, gret P. freedom, 485:13
Pressure, form and p., 196:23
  government relaxing p., 438:13
  grace under p., 701:18
  hardly feel p. of age, 75:4
  of cosmos, 546:17
  of exigencies of life, 569:8
  opening first p. off second, 625:14
Pressures, in spite of dangers p.,
    740:19
Prestige, convenience comfort p.,
    783:16
Presume, Dr. Livingstone I p., 544:5
  not God to scan, 301:13
  yourself ignorant, 384:4
Presuming on changeful potency,
    201:8
Presumption, amused by its p., 690:8
  in kings and ministers, 326:5
  in wisdom, 331:10
Presumptions, art flying in face of p.,
    548:14
Pretend, let us not p. to doubt, 538:16
  Let's P. and we did, 766:7
  to know when you do not, 58:2
Pretender, God bless the P., 304:14
  had she known p. he was, 611:20
  James I James II and Old P., 676:2
  who P. or who King, 304:14
Pretends, life it p. to build on, 705:7
Pretense, for a p. make prayers, 37:32
  to faint meaning make p., 274:26
Pretenses to break known rules by,
    247:3
Pretension, this p. a prejudice, 550:6
Pretentiousness, correcting of p., 509:2
Prêtre guerrier poète, 494:*n*11
Prettier, pebble or p. shell, 282:5
Prettiest little parlor, 423:11
Pretty, all my p. ones, 215:29
  Babe all burning bright, 160:19
  birds do sing, 226:20
  Bobby Shaftoe, 792:18
  but is it Art, 592:1
  everything that p. is, 219:24
  Fanny's way, 295:19
  feet like snails, 241:11
  follies themselves commit, 180:20
  how town, 688:22
  how-de-do, 531:2

Pretty (*continued*)
    I'll get you my p., 730:2
    it is a p. world, 730:10
    kettle of fish, 530:12
    little toes, 790:15
    maids all in row, 788:19
    my p. maid, 790:6
    need park policeman p. girl, 675:17
    no burial this p. pair, 776:2
    only p. ring time, 192:12
    pleasures might me move, 152:11
    poem Mr. Pope, 286:10
    puts on his p. looks, 170:4
    state of things, 531:2
    tell me p. maiden, 563:17
    to see what money will do, 279:19
    to think so, 701:13
    what do for p. girls, 599:19
    young wards, 530:7
Prevail, conditions dat p., 686:2
    evening shades p., 292:1
    fair words p., 592:16
    gates of hell not p., 35:28
    God who is able to p., 245:11
    his rising fogs p., 274:26
    make best ideas p., 499:5
    man will p., 696:22
    necessity knows no law except p., 99:32
    'tis the Majority p., 512:11
    truth shall p., 30:*n*3
    truth shall p. when none cares, 503:10
    will looking ill p., 262:2
Prevailed, David p. over the Philistine, 11:41
    the dragon p. not, 47:27
    with double sway, 329:15
Prevails, when vice p., 292:13
    where commerce long p., 328:9
Prevalent, religion most p., 331:14
Prevarication, last dike of p., 332:7
Prevent, enjoy religion p. others, 522:5
    lower from getting more, 78:16
    me from carrying you up, 67:24
    surest way to p. war, 385:14
Prevention, anthology used for p., 692:3
    of mutual crime, 78:20
    society for p. of croolty to money, 539:*n*1
Prevents our being natural, 265:43
Previous, calling to mind p. benefaction, 71:5
    returned home p. night, 618:14
Prey, animals and athletes not p., 665:8
    at fortune, 207:2
    beast of p. in aristocratic races, 552:24
    eagle seeketh p., 15:18
    expects his evening p., 323:8
    fear birds of p., 203:28
    great lord yet p. to all, 301:13
    greater p. upon less, 307:6
    have they not divided the p., 11:7
    of fear, 664:19
    of rich on poor, 343:13
    of rival imperialisms, 681:4
    on garbage, 194:22

Prey (*continued*)
    people easily becomes p., 137:3
    smaller fleas on him p., 289:20
    to dumb forgetfulness a p., 322:19
    to hastening ills a p., 329:8
    universal p., 200:10
    Venus fastened to p., 281:10
    where eagles dare not perch, 165:25
    young lions roar after p., 19:6
Preying on people's vanity ignorance, 766:12
Priam's curtain, 183:10
Priapus, it is I P. crying, 83:2
    made of marble, 92:11
Price, abatement and low p., 201:17
    for precocity p. demanded, 461:5
    great p. for wisdom, 508:25
    greater p. than life, 705:11
    greet cheep holde at litel p., 131:6
    heaven put p. upon goods, 340:22
    is far above rubies, 23:17
    is labor in exchange for anything, 487:20
    life exacts for peace, 700:7
    market p. they said, 514:12
    men have their p., 295:4
    natural and market p., 385:9
    of everything, 566:23
    of justice eternal publicity, 602:4
    of liberty, 351:*n*7
    of thousand horses, 613:7
    of wisdom is above rubies, 14:40
    pay any p., 741:3
    pearl of great p., 35:10
    too high p. for harmony, 495:8
    weighed for my p., 30:5
    what p. bananas, 757:2
    what p. glory, 666:6
    will fall, 159:22
    words beyond p., 766:14
Priced, weighed measured p. everything, 471:7
Priceless, human life p., 705:11
Prices, contrivance to raise p., 326:3
    spiral of rising p., 635:5
Prick and sting her, 194:25
    if you p. us do we not bleed, 180:31
    it mark it with B., 788:9
    sides of my intent, 213:7
Pricking, gentle knight p. on plain, 153:5
    gonfalon bubble, 644:5
    of my thumbs, 215:16
Pricks, honor p. me on, 178:33
    kick against the p., 41:6, 63:18
    to subsequent volumes, 200:12
Pride, age that will p. deflower, 153:11
    aiming at blest abodes, 159:*n*7
    all the p. cruelty and ambition, 153:1
    and conceit original sin, 290:26
    and courage of patriot, 522:13
    bold peasantry country's p., 329:8
    chastening in hour of p., 448:14
    coy submission modest p., 258:13
    Democratic Party without p. of ancestry, 516:1
    Envy Avarice three sparks, 125:21
    fell with my fortunes, 189:36

Pride (*continued*)
    from p. vainglory and hypocrisy, 49:8
    goeth before destruction, 21:31
    he that is low no p., 272:28
    I know thy p., 11:37
    idleness and p., 310:14
    in Casey's bearing, 588:24
    in occupation, 526:11
    in their port, 328:13
    is hateful before God, 31:22
    is his own glass, 200:16
    is therefore pleasure, 278:1
    king over children of p., 15:26
    land of pilgrims' p., 444:3
    lintel low to keep out p., 563:14
    look backward with p., 623:2
    mother's p. father's joy, 379:3
    my high-blown p. broke under me, 225:16
    of country, 463:5
    of kings, 301:1
    of peacock glory of God, 357:6
    of power sink, 331:10
    of those who have survived, 621:16
    perished in his p., 374:9
    plume here buckle, 550:22
    pomp and circumstance, 207:8
    pomp and p., 563:14
    rank p., 292:6
    rid earth of him in my p., 607:19
    shall bring him low, 23:11
    soldier's p., 464:10
    solemn p. yours, 450:9
    speak with p. of our doings, 664:2
    stoic's p., 301:13
    tasted all the summer's p., 355:17
    that licks the dust, 302:17
    that puts country down, 776:17
    they lost their p., 721:3
    to relieve wretched his p., 329:13
    touched to quick, 464:10
    towering in p. of place, 214:18
    tyrant is child of P., 65:18
    vain the sage's p., 303:13
    was not made for men, 31:24
    will have a fall, 65:*n*11
Priest all shaven and shorn, 792:24
    free me from turbulent p., 122:7
    God's high p., 41:28
    I the Muses' p. sing, 96:12
    like people like p., 29:23
    love the only p., 520:16
    no difference 'twixt P. and Clerk, 241:7
    O mysterious p., 416:5
    of most authentic creed, 520:13
    soldier poet, 494:14
    still is Nature's p., 375:8
    the true God's p., 246:3
    well ought p. example give, 193:*n*4
    while runnin' for p., 654:12
Priestcraft, pious times ere p., 274:1
Priestlike, waters at p. task, 417:12
Priestly vestments evidence of servile status, 574:8
    vestments in dens, 503:4
Priests, ancestors p. in temple, 434:21
    bless her when she is riggish, 217:15
    by mightier hand, 424:11

Priests (*continued*)
Miss Lonelyhearts p., 712:11
not merit praise of poets, 564:6
poets not yet p., 564:6
stood firm on dry ground, 10:32
Priests', hell paved with p. skulls,
114:15
Priez Dieu que tous nous veuille absoudre, 134:*n*3
Prim, mouth so p., 670:6
Primal eldest curse, 197:23
Primary, great p. human affections,
498:8
imagination, 384:6
Prime, buried him before p., 785:16
gather Rose whilst p., 153:11
give him always of p., 289:21
laurel for perfect p., 515:11
light the p. work of God, 257:*n*6
lovely April of her p., 220:9
obeyed at p., 430:9
of youth a frost of cares, 156:22
one's p. elusive, 746:12
rose up in his p., 674:14
what is the p. of life, 75:14
wisdom, 259:24
Zeus p. mover, 63:17
Prime Minister returned, 606:10
what war said P., 712:3
Primer, armed with his p., 390:1
Primeval cosmic night, 629:3
forest p., 441:15
mountains in p. sleep, 503:4
Primitive impulses of heart, 452:*n*1
man tactile man, 653:22
North America, 703:21
people not waken sleeper, 565:1
terror, 671:15
unattached state, 629:9
Primitivism, America was p., 653:12
Primordial images of collective unconscious, 628:8
Primrose path of dalliance treads,
193:27
sweet as the p., 329:22
way, 214:10
Primum non nocere, 71:*n*2
Primus inter pares, 119:23
Prince, advise the p., 667:17
can mak belted knight, 363:22
duty subject owes p., 167:35
first servant of state, 318:19
good night sweet p., 199:29
great P. in prison lies, 229:15
have no study but war, 136:12
I am not P. Hamlet, 667:17
I warn you, 717:2
imitate fox and lion, 136:15
in serving his p., 60:17
keeps tortoise enclosed, 80:17
Lucifer uprose, 509:7
must be lion, 107:*n*3
my p. you'd soon forget, 292:7
not propose it to my p., 304:12
of apple towns, 737:15
of Aquitaine, 443:23
of clouds haunts tempest, 494:2
of darkness a gentleman, 210:10
of Peace, 26:8

Prince (*continued*)
of Wales in small but costly crown,
644:10
Rasselas P. of Abyssinia, 314:9
semblable au p. des nuées, 494:*n*2
subject Father Son, 230:15
there is a p. fallen, 12:4
till I p. of love beheld, 355:17
Princedoms Virtues Powers, 259:13
Princely counsel in his face, 257:7
Princerple, don't believe in p., 485:14
Princes, all p. I, 228:13
ancestors p. of earth, 434:*n*1
and lords may flourish, 329:8
blaze forth death of p., 188:10
but breath of kings, 361:10
contentment in being equal to p.,
231:14
fall like one of the p., 18:4
find few real friends, 318:4
gilded monuments of p., 220:25
hate traitor but love treason,
88:*n*13
kings and p. have philosophy, 75:15
like to heavenly bodies, 159:21
must a word to be addressed to p.,
145:7
orgulous, 402:*n*5
pale kings and p., 417:7
put not your trust in p., 20:14
sweet aspect of p., 225:16
whose merchants are p., 26:23
Princes', cottages p. palaces, 179:27
hangs on p. favors, 225:16
not so arched as p. palaces, 237:18
Princess descended of kings, 218:21
felt pea through mattresses, 437:5
thoughtless saying of p., 319:25
three days afterwards p. buried,
510:4
Principal translators between dream
and reality, 665:20
wisdom is the p. thing, 20:23
Principalities, against p. and powers,
44:28
men fear power p. of air, 642:23
never known to exist, 136:14
nor powers, 42:9
Principality in Utopia, 425:5
Principle, active p. of literature,
613:18
but a cold p., 245:*n*2
don't believe in p., 485:14
general p. gives no help, 372:7
Greatest Happiness P., 439:26
hain't money but p., 605:17
inconsistencies in p., 539:10
love our p., 421:8
moderation in p. a vice, 341:8
necessary and fundamental p.,
325:22
nihilist takes no p. on trust, 482:14
o' the thing, 605:17
of Conservation of Force, 496:17
of resistance, 331:14
old but true as fate, 88:*n*13
on which society not founded,
321:6
one God one p. of being, 111:19

Principle (*continued*)
one p. make universe single creature, 112:21
precedent embalms p., 435:2
rebels from p., 332:16
same p. in whatever shape, 448:11
strange p. as first requirement,
492:3
Principles, elements or p. of bodies,
345:10
embrace p. or mistresses, 327:13
facts alarm more than p., 346:5
faithfulness and sincerity as first p.,
60:18
first p. take deepest root, 347:4
fools say man has or has not p.,
422:11
guide his life by true p., 90:9
important p. inflexible, 451:2
less than chaff, 573:6
looking away from p., 546:18
might p. swaller, 485:12
of Political Economy, 627:19
renounce his p., 346:4
restless unfixed in p., 274:3
that gave America birth, 572:12
to effect safety, 343:2
Print, all news fit to p., 575:6
eternity of p., 650:18
faith he'll p. it, 363:15
gentlehearted in p., 387:15
I love a ballad in p., 223:11
news and raise hell, 780:16
of a man's naked foot, 286:4
see name in p., 399:2
sharpest weapon, 638:8
some said John p. it, 272:9
woman's name in p. twice, 656:4
Printed, that they were p. in a book,
14:29
Printer, Benjamin Franklin P., 309:5
Printers, books by which p. have lost,
250:13
Printing and Protestant religion,
412:25
and the Reformation, 629:16
caused p. to be used, 164:11
invented art of p., 411:22
Printing-house, hen-yard in p., 659:13
Prior, what was Matthew P., 288:5
Priority, degree p. and place, 200:7
Prisidincy highest office, 603:14
Prism and silent face, 373:10
prunes and p., 471:9
Prison, beast brought up in p., 137:3
bloom in p. air, 567:22
born black born in p., 755:7
civilized man's house p., 476:21
come let's away to p., 211:13
die in the streets or in p., 610:8
each confirms a p., 669:6
each in his p., 669:6
Europe p. of nations, 638:10
feel at home in p., 712:2
for color of his hair, 580:9
great Prince in p. lies, 229:15
grind in the p. house, 11:17
house for future p. for present,
736:16
in p. and ye came unto me, 36:18

Prodigal (*continued*)
enemy be p., 720:3
how p. the soul, 194:5
of ease, 274:4
son, 38:35
Prodigality, spring of p., 331:26
Prodigies, all Africa and her p., 248:6
Prodigy, what a p. is man, 271:7
Produce according to aptitudes, 481:*n*4
but not take possession, 57:2
eating p. of the land, 52:19
laboring to p. bons mots, 269:13
my foot my feather, 762:16
perfect circles and squares, 79:14
the person, 119:7
things and to rear them, 57:2
Produced, after they are p., 56:12
intellectual product judged from age p., 538:4
Producer, promoting interest of p., 326:8
Produces, final cause p. motion, 77:22
what community p., 723:8
Producing, consume without p., 570:15
Product, happiness not spontaneous p., 635:10
man's nature cultural p., 704:9
Production, consumption sole end of all p., 326:8
entrepreneur contributes to p., 653:23
eternity in love with p. of time, 357:4
improvement of instruments of p., 482:2
means of social p., 482:*n*1
principle of economic p., 635:9
utility or cost of p., 547:15
Profanation to keep in, 241:18
Profane and old wives' fables, 45:16
and vain babblings, 45:25
for me to p. it, 409:11
hence ye p., 267:8
things holy p. clean obscene, 239:20
things sacred or things p., 272:19
Profaned heavenly gift of poesy, 275:5
one word too often p., 409:11
Profess not the knowledge, 31:5
politics like ours p., 307:6
Profession, hold up Adam's p., 198:27
is to disguise, 137:13
most ancient p., 591:5
Professions, analysis third of impossible p., 569:17
one of p. which are full, 478:11
satisfied to have two p., 582:6
Professor encouraging clever pupil, 312:10
of art of puffing, 352:35
of Harvard Law School, 646:14
profit p. naught, 156:19
Professors like literature dead, 658:9
of Dismal Science, 413:12
Proffer, fawning greyhound did p., 177:10
Profit, and the p. and loss, 669:3
between p. and the loss, 669:19
by folly of others, 104:12

Profit (*continued*)
by losing our prayers, 217:11
by their example, 339:5
engine of Enterprise, 652:10
entrepreneurial p., 653:23
few p. by advice, 99:4
in all labor there is p., 21:22
murder land for private p., 726:7
no more p. of shining nights, 168:15
no p. but the name, 198:11
no p. where no pleasure, 167:15
private enterprise for p., 649:12
professor naught, 156:19
title and p. I resign, 292:*n*4
truth as opposeth no p., 239:25
what p. of all his labor, 23:22
winds blow p., 722:4
wise men p. more from fools, 85:4
Profitable, lie with purpose most p., 602:15
Profited, age not p. so much as lost, 478:3
what is a man p., 35:30
Profits, keeping p. up by keeping wages down, 385:10
little p. that idle king, 454:24
Profound, both may be called p., 56:12
in his view, 337:*n*1
man thinks woman p., 553:*n*2
subtle and p. female, 56:16
thoughts arise in debate, 749:10
Profoundness of yearning for more vivid world, 731:6
Profuse strains of unpremeditated art, 408:4
Progeny, Angels p. of light, 259:13
give world corrupt p., 96:17
of learning, 352:5
Prognostics not always prophecies, 324:2
Program, computer no better than its p., 727:6
for tomorrow, 653:5
Progress based on universal desire, 525:2
call P. Tomorrow, 427:26
Christ's p. and His prayer-time, 270:2
comfortable disease, 689:5
competition essential for p., 525:11
condition of social p., 522:11
from want to want, 316:30
history p. of freedom, 372:9
in human virtue, 365:27
man's mark, 467:14
no p. except individual, 494:12
no struggle no p., 480:16
not accident but necessity, 492:14
not real cannot be permanent, 538:3
of all countries connected, 644:17
of artist self-sacrifice, 672:9
our goal, 421:8
part of nature, 492:14
Pilgrim's P. about man left family, 526:21
promote p. of science, 686:16
rake's p., 463:13
scientific thought human p., 554:10

Progress (*continued*)
separate yet one in mutual p., 571:32
social p. of each country, 644:17
swell a p., 667:17
test of our p., 649:8
to fuller life, 605:7
Prohibited, means which are not p., 355:12
Prohibiting free exercise thereof, 346:11
licensing and p., 255:4
Prohibitions, meant p. to be absolutes, 661:7
Proie, à sa p. attachée, 281:*n*5
Project for extracting sunbeams, 289:12
Pro-labor policies of governments, 645:10
Proletarian state, 605:14
suppression of bourgeois state by p., 610:4
Proletarians have nothing to lose, 482:7
Proletariat class of wage laborers, 482:*n*2
come across for p., 791:*n*1
dictatorship of the p., 481:7, 609:20
Italian p., 652:19
product of industry, 482:3
revolutionary class, 482:3
Prologue, excuse came p., 260:9
make a long p., 32:19
what's past is p., 224:5
Prologues, happy p. to swelling act, 212:22
over, 639:14
Prolongeth, joyfulness p. his days, 32:3
Promethean heat, 208:10
sparkle right P. fire, 169:4
Prominent, the more laws are made p., 57:18
Promise, broke no p., 300:24
eating air on p. of supply, 183:25
keep word of p. to our ear, 216:20
most given when least said, 157:1
never p. more than perform, 99:30
none relies on, 283:21
of pneumatic bliss, 668:14
oh p. me, 544:2
only to do our best, 716:11
years of p. rapidly roll round, 368:18
Promise-crammed, I eat the air p., 197:6
Promised, already in p. land, 768:12
fruits outdo what flowers p., 156:9
land, 419:7, 521:12
Land beyond wilderness, 578:13
Man who had been p., 683:12
seen p. land, 761:9
shalt be what thou art p., 212:28
Promises, age perform p. of youth, 314:9
America was p., 683:12
fails where most it p., 203:12
good memory to keep p., 552:2
to keep, 623:18

Putrid corpse of liberty, 652:21
Puts all Heaven in a rage, 359:6
    forth tender leaves of hopes, 225:16
    he who p. armor off, 442:18
    record on gramophone, 669:2
Puttees, pair of roll p., 694:5
Putting, dispatch in p. end to it, 79:13
    Love away, 513:17
    mind's eye in book, 748:10
    off the proof, 624:4
    on breastplate of faith, 45:7
    queer shoulder to wheel, 757:3
Puzzle, Rosebud missing piece in jig-
    saw p., 697:5
    rule of three p., 776:9
    schoolmasters p. brain, 330:1
    to botanist, 523:21
Puzzled, thou art more p. than Egyp-
    tians, 203:5
Puzzles the will, 196:10
Puzzling, though p. not beyond conjec-
    ture, 248:30
Pye, shine with P., 399:6
Pygmy body, 274:3
Pyramid, bottom of economic p.,
    648:14
    star-y-pointing p., 251:2
Pyramids first, 782:7
    from summit of p., 370:6
Pyramus and Thisby, 172:22
    cruel death of P., 172:22
Pyre, ghost escapes from vanquished
    p., 101:3
Pyrrha for whom bindest thou thy
    hair, 95:20
Pyrrha's, from P. pebbles, 414:16
Pyrrhic victory, 82:*n*8
Pythagoras, hold opinion with P.,
    181:17
    opinion of P. concerning wildfowl,
    181:*n*3
    said to his scholars, 234:15
Pythagoreans, rather wrong with Plato
    than right with P., 87:28

Q

Q.E.D., 82:4
Quad, I am always about in Q.,
    673:*n*1
    when no one about in the Q., 673:5
Quadrangular, spots q. of diamond,
    335:6
Quadrille, war not q. in ball-room,
    491:15
Quadruped, hairy q. with tail, 444:13
Quae est domestica sede iucundior,
    87:*n*13
Quaffed, jested q. and swore, 461:1
Quaffing, laughing q. unthinking time,
    276:20
Quail and shake the orb, 218:11
    when footpads q., 531:12
    whistle about us, 638:26
Quails, he brought q., 19:7
Quaint and curious volume, 452:13
    and curious war is, 540:12
    great figure, 637:11
    honor turn to dust, 268:16
    wonders at q. spirits, 173:11

Quake, earth did q., 37:13
Quakers, first called us Q., 271:14
Qualifications, adverbs only q. I re-
    spect, 549:11
    without any important q. for office,
    677:1
Qualified, I am q., 209:6
    masses are not q., 653:13
Qualify, my flame to q., 221:24
Qualis artifex pereo, 105:*n*10
Qualities, chose on various q., 612:19
    such q. as would wear, 328:18
Quality, composition and fierce q.,
    208:29
    draw inward q. after, 217:26
    hate counsels not in such a q.,
    181:1
    not quantity but q., 119:*n*8
    of mercy not strained, 181:19
    rather than quantity, 102:25
    royal banner and all q., 207:8
    taste of your q., 195:34
    true-fixed and resting q., 188:14
Qualms, many many q., 583:11
Quanch my heart trobling, 674:21
Quangle Wangle, 472:8
Quantities, determination of q. by
    numbers, 516:6
    ghosts of departed q., 296:23
    such q. of sand, 518:24
Quantity, not q. but quality, 119:*n*8
    of force in Nature eternal, 496:17
    of love, 199:16
    of matter unalterable, 496:17
    quality rather than q., 102:25
Quantum, waive q. o' the sin, 361:22
Quarantine aggressors, 649:*n*1
    to protect community, 649:9
Quarelets of pearl, 241:3
Quarks, three q. for Muster Mark,
    647:21
Quarrel, beware entrance to q.,
    193:30
    find q. in a straw, 198:14
    how they behave in q., 570:11
    in streets to be hated, 418:13
    lover's q. with world, 624:15
    no q. with Viet Cong, 772:1
    nor for every q. to lawyer, 244:20
    over water, 655:5
    pretty q. as it stands, 352:15
    sudden and quick in q., 191:3
    thrice armed that hath q. just, 164:1
    with bread and butter, 290:5
    with whom should I q., 716:21
Quarreling, chickens quit q. over food,
    633:8
    set them a-q., 318:15
Quarrels, dove loves when it q.,
    114:32
    full of q. as egg of meat, 175:25
    love know no sundering q., 95:26
    love-q. in concord end, 261:20
    lovers' q. renewal of love, 85:14
    who in q. interpose, 297:10
    wine cause of q., 284:13
    would not last long, 266:2
Quarrelsome, countercheck q., 192:16
    mutinous and, 311:5

Quarrelsomeness, when strong guard
    against q., 62:3
Quarried, limestone q. near spot,
    600:3
Quarries of Sicily, 706:4
Quarry, go not like q.-slave, 411:4
    mine blessed am I, 787:14
Quartered, see Harrison hanged drawn
    q., 279:3
Quarterly, I says the Q., 403:28
Quarto, beautiful q. page, 352:27
Que sais-je, 146:*n*3
Quean, flaunting extravagant q.,
    352:29
Queen and huntress, 231:21
    be drunk as we, 311:10
    be the battle q. of yore, 538:20
    beggar maid my q., 456:5
    British warrior q., 334:21
    come not near our fairy q., 173:12
    every lass a q., 484:15
    grace a summer q., 379:4
    I am your anointed Q., 144:16
    I would not be a q., 225:9
    it no inch further, 223:13
    Mab hath been with you, 174:20
    mathematics q. of sciences, 389:19
    moves a goddess looks a q., 299:24
    must not bring Q. into politics,
    506:7
    now·now cried the Q., 518:18
    o' the May, 454:4
    of Hearts, 789:14
    of pleasure, 534:9
    of Sheba heard of Solomon, 12:25
    of this summer hotel, 759:12
    poor memory the Q. remarked,
    519:10
    tell 'em Q. Anne's dead, 366:13
    to London to look at q., 791:1
    turned crimson with fury, 517:23
    unveiled peerless light, 258:19
    upon a card, 459:30
    Victoria like great paper-weight,
    601:17
    was in parlor, 790:1
    you shall be q., 792:6
    you will though Q. said, 518:14
Queen's, Ruler of Q. Navee, 529:6
Queens, dreamed of Oriental q., 496:9
    have died young and fair, 227:2
Queer, all q. save me and thee, 781:20
    horse must think it q., 623:17
    how strange and q., 465:*n*2
    ill-tempered and q., 471:28
    monster the artist, 549:13
    Northern Lights seen q. sights,
    627:3
    putting q. shoulder to wheel, 757:3
    thee a little q., 781:20
    you look so q., 779:12
Queerer, universe q. than we suppose,
    683:1
Queerest folk of all, 583:9
    they ever did see, 627:3
Quell, music raise and q., 275:8
Quelle est cette île triste et noire,
    494:*n*9
Quem deus vult perdere, 119:25
Quench, fire rivers cannot q., 164:29

Quench (*continued*)
  if I q. thee, 208:10
  many waters cannot q. love, 25:23
  smoking flax shall he not q., 27:25
Quenched in most cold repose, 408:19
Quenching in Purple, 511:19
Querulous, newspapers q. and bellicose, 642:12
  usual q. serenity, 387:2
Quest, go Soul the body's q., 152:15
  in q. to have extreme, 222:7
  whither and what thy q., 549:19
Questing, passes the q. vole, 712:5
  Pellinore followed q. beast, 133:5
  Snail, 725:21
Question, answer q. to best of ability,
  614:10
  broach q. begin to quote, 430:19
  consider q. can machines think,
  732:5
  final solution of Jewish q., 686:5
  greatest q. ever debated, 338:4
  he would not ask any q., 538:15
  if His Glory, 513:4
  important q. what you think, 499:3
  in that case what is the q., 627:14
  interrupt with silly q., 320:7
  is absurd, 721:5
  is which is to be master, 519:14
  know what France thinks q. myself,
  678:14
  let history answer q., 344:7
  momentous q. like firebell, 344:21
  most momentous q. on continent,
  503:7
  not been able to answer, 569:19
  not every q. deserves answer, 100:2
  not harm nor q. much, 229:19
  now of final belief, 639:14
  others abide our q., 497:4
  settle q. discuss it, 424:20
  that is the q., 196:10
  two sides to every q., 70:16
  what q. you desire to answer,
  617:17
  why did you do that, 569:4
  why we and universe exist, 772:2
  wisdom of novel q. for everything,
  761:14
  young embarrassed to q. older, 53:2
Questionable, comest in such q. shape,
  194:10
  superfluity small beer, 164:*n3*
Questioned me story of my life,
  205:24
Questioner who sits so sly, 359:12
Questioning, drew nearer sweetly q.,
  244:1
  nature exposed to method of q.,
  707:4
  needs no q. before he speaks, 69:8
  warned prior to q., 682:10
Questions, answer q. about myself,
  716:8
  answer q. intelligently, 520:13
  answered three q., 517:11
  ask me no q., 330:8
  attempt to answer q., 617:17
  better to know some q., 690:17

Questions (*continued*)
  came to prove him with hard q.,
  12:25
  heard you asking q., 757:2
  no q. unanswerable, 430:25
  them that asks no q., 330:*n1*
  though puzzling q. not beyond conjecture, 248:30
  unanimity on legal q., 586:9
Quhat say thai, 154:24
Qui ante diem periit, 586:13
  procul hinc legend's writ, 586:13
  s'excuse s'accuse, 144:*n7*
Quibbles, in q. angel and archangel,
  303:6
Quick and dead, 48:25
  brown fox, 781:8
  even in death, 151:25
  eyes gone, 659:10
  her q. look, 725:4
  how did I get old so q., 709:17
  how q. and fresh art thou, 201:17
  Jack be q., 791:10
  now here now always, 670:18
  so q. bright things come to confusion, 172:20
  sudden and q. in quarrel, 191:3
  to arm, 659:8
  to flare up, 53:13
  true apothecary thy drugs q., 176:19
  word of God is q., 45:34
Quicken, live within sense they q.,
  409:10
Quickened, not q. except it die, 43:23
Quickeneth, spirit that q., 40:5
Quickens to rebel, 669:20
Quicker, end a contest q., 352:24
  liquor is q., 709:6
Quick-eyed Love observing me, 244:1
Quickly, behold I come q., 48:3
  bring me beaker of wine, 72:14
  do q. that thou doest, 40:24
  doubly benefits who gives q., 98:30
  little fire q. trodden, 164:29
  nature falls into revolt, 184:10
  to pass gates of Hades, 59:24
  turn away, 598:3
  'twere well it were done q., 213:5
  well done is q. done, 98:22
Quickness, too much q. to be taught,
  300:15
Quicksands, Soundings q. rocks, 418:7
Quid datur a divis felici optatius hora,
  91:*n4*
  si nunc caelum ruat, 85:*n17*
Quiddities, quips and q., 176:27
  where be his q. now, 199:4
Quiddity, entity and q., 263:4
Quien bien te quiere, 794:6
Quiet, all q. along Potomac, 507:7
  all q. on western front, 700:8
  anything for a q. life, 237:6
  as a lamb, 170:8
  as a stone, 416:19
  be q. and go a-angling, 245:31
  bower q. for us, 414:9
  breath, 415:16
  by q. natures understood, 597:5
  calm q. innocent recreation, 245:27
  chaste breast and q. mind, 267:14

Quiet (*continued*)
  conscience stands brunt of life,
  68:15
  consummation have, 220:4
  courage gaiety q. mind, 562:9
  desperation, 477:32
  Doctor Q., 290:13
  easy live q. die, 379:15
  enforced from q. sphere, 184:6
  entertain lag-end with q. hours,
  178:29
  eye made q. by power, 373:3
  fie upon this q. life, 177:20
  harvest of a q. eye, 374:4
  here where world q., 534:12
  holy time q. as nun, 374:15
  hours few, 487:22
  imperishable q., 725:10
  in q. she reposes, 498:14
  kiss me and be q., 304:4
  lain still and been q., 13:35
  limit of world, 459:2
  mind cureth all, 235:23
  mind richer than crown, 157:18
  minds innocent and q., 267:18
  my temptation q., 599:10
  not the q., 767:7
  o'er hilltops is q. now, 351:2
  ornament of q. spirit, 46:24
  retirement rural q. friendship, 308:5
  rich q. and infamous, 425:9
  richness q. and pleasure, 494:5
  scallop shell of q., 152:16
  shining to the q. moon, 382:17
  singeth a q. tune, 381:24
  sleep when the long trick's over,
  633:16
  sleepers in q. earth, 480:7
  spirit so still and q., 205:23
  still and q. conscience, 225:17
  study to be q., 45:4
  tree of man never q., 579:7
  truth hath a q. breast, 170:29
  wise and good, 409:17
Quiet-colored end of evening, 465:9
Quieting, soothing and q., 613:12
Quietly shining to quiet moon, 382:17
Quietness, bride of q., 415:20
  handful with q., 23:34
  richness q. and pleasure, 494:5
Quietness', king made for q. sake,
  239:11
Quietus, he himself his q. make,
  196:10
Quill from angel's wing, 377:*n2*
Quillets, his q. his cases, 199:4
  nice sharp q. of law, 163:10
Quills, stops of various q., 254:7
  upon fretful porpentine, 194:17
Quince, slices of q., 472:3
Quinquireme of Nineveh, 633:18
Quintessence even from nothingness,
  229:9
  morning q. of life, 404:20
  of dust, 195:29
Quintilian, made Q. stare and gasp,
  255:6
Quintilius give me back my legions,
  98:20
Quip modest, 192:16

Quippe secundae res sapientium
  animos fatigant, 91:*n*11
Quips and cranks, 251:8
  and quiddities, 176:27
  shall q. and sentences awe, 186:31
Quire of bad verses, 425:12
Quiring to young-eyed cherubins,
  182:8
Quirks of blazoning pens, 206:4
Quis custodiet ipsos custodes, 109:*n*3
Quislings, vile race of q., 620:18
Quit certainty for uncertainty, 314:8
  house never darken threshold, 492:2
  John and I are q., 288:3
  oh quit this mortal frame, 299:8
  quit for shame, 262:3
  rats have q. it, 223:25
  you like men, 43:29
  yourselves like men, 11:29
Quitter, il faut q. tout cela, 247:*n*5
Quiver, air q. with a color, 656:9
  happy is the man that hath his q.
  full, 20:1
Quivering, light q. aspen, 378:14
  ratio, 511:12
Quiver's choice, 403:21
Quixote, Don Q. a muddled fool,
  150:35
  when Don Q. went out into world,
  761:14
Quixote's, youngsters read Don Q.
  story, 150:18
Quo usque Catilina abutere patientia,
  87:*n*3
  vadis, 40:*n*4
Quod erat demonstrandum, 82:4
  semper quod ubique quod ab omnibus, 115:*n*1
Quos deus vult perdere, 119:25
Quot homines tot sententiae, 86:*n*9
Quotation, classical q., 317:23
  I hate q., 430:19
Quotations, backed opinion with q.,
  287:21
  Bartlett's Familiar Q., 619:18
  book furnishes no q., 397:23
  good to read books of q., 619:18
  ill-advised, 574:17
  pretentious q. tedium, 574:17
  wrapped himself in q., 592:10
Quote fights historical, 529:12
  grow immortal as they q., 295:24
  kill you if you q. it, 600:17
  we all q., 433:21
  wise reader q. wisely, 422:4
Quoted, famous remarks seldom q.
  correctly, 641:1
  odes and jewels, 456:9
Quoter, next to originator first q.,
  433:19
Quoth, give me q. I, 212:12
  Raven Nevermore, 452:18, 452:20
Quotidian saps philosophers, 638:19

R

R, months that have no r, 147:10
Rabbit, ain't never caught a r., 765:7
  in a snare, 650:10
  ole man R. say scoot, 556:10

Rabbit (*continued*)
  skin to wrap baby, 789:15
  thoughts of r. are rabbits, 433:29
Rabbits, four little r., 600:20
  thoughts of rabbit are r., 433:29
Rabble, army would be base r.,
  331:23
Rabelais' easy chair, 303:24
Race, a simple r., 377:26
  all run in r., 43:6
  another r. hath been, 375:15
  appointed for my second r., 270:4
  arms r., 748:4
  barred on account of r., 742:3
  bellyful of classics enemy to human
  r., 681:10
  between education and catastrophe,
  601:14
  Californians a r., 586:3
  competition essential for r., 525:11
  conscience of my r., 647:11
  consternation throughout white r.,
  767:19
  culture not function of r., 662:14
  despised r., 522:13
  development of individual repetition
  of r., 569:6
  dusky r., 455:23
  fair chance in r. of life, 449:8
  feelings permanently in r., 498:8
  friend to human r., 51:*n*6
  future of human r., 632:2
  Germany a r., 421:15
  giant r. before the flood, 276:1
  happiness of human r., 331:25
  heavenly r. demands zeal, 308:16
  history of our r., 621:6
  human r. born to fly upward,
  126:14
  human r. has means for annihilating
  itself, 645:19
  human r. never have rest from evils,
  75:15
  in conversation see capacities of r.,
  653:7
  is to the swift, 573:22
  judged by best not worst, 612:5
  laborers perpetuate r., 385:9
  laws unto savage r., 454:24
  loftier r. than known, 541:6
  look out here comes Master R.,
  756:20
  man's imperial r. ensnare, 299:12
  melted into new r. of men, 339:1
  mother of Aeneas and his r., 89:2
  my lot bound up with human r.,
  392:18
  no matter what r., 685:10
  no r. monopoly on virtue, 750:7
  no special right to one r., 564:12
  not similar are r. of gods and men,
  51:20
  not superior by r., 520:12
  not to the swift, 24:20
  of ancient r. by birth, 274:15
  of glory run, 261:15
  of shame, 261:15
  once they were happy r., 370:3
  out of one man a r., 259:20
  over work never done, 543:11

Race (*continued*)
  pernicious r. of vermin, 289:10
  poetry fettered fetters r., 359:22
  purity of r. does not exist, 590:11
  rejoiceth as a strong man to run a
  r., 16:10
  ride over obstacles win r., 470:34
  right to vote not denied on account
  of r., 346:19
  run r. set before us, 45:39
  same way with human r., 633:8
  sceptered r., 388:15
  slaughters of r. writ, 540:15
  slow and steady wins the r., 58:19
  stars of human r., 334:7
  suffering human r., 497:16
  there is one r. humanity, 563:12
  to separate because of r., 682:9
  type of all her r., 461:1
  vanishing r., 695:19
  vile r. of quislings, 620:18
  whatever r. creed or persuasion,
  661:5
  where immortal garland, 254:25
  whole r. is a poet, 639:19
  whole r. of politicians, 289:11
  win r. runs by himself, 591:*n*1
  winding-sheet of Edward's r., 323:7
  wish I loved human r., 584:3
  world began without human r.,
  723:21
  worn out quite, 403:10
  you-all means r., 780:21
Racehorse, breed r. in few generations,
  544:1
Races, beast of prey in aristocratic r.,
  552:24
  condemned to one hundred years of
  solitude, 759:1
  didn't bother Americans, 683:13
  difference of opinion makes horse-r.,
  527:18
  horse dominated mind of early r.,
  657:20
  preservation of favored r., 493:9
  quick to flare up we r. of men,
  53:13
  youthful sinewy r., 490:7
Rachel, Jacob served seven years for
  R., 7:43
  weeping for her children, 32:26
Racial, not r. affiliation but ancestry,
  574:11
Racine, facts about life of R., 613:15
  will go out of style, 271:24
Racine's, art of R. verse, 613:15
Racism is dogma, 662:15
Racist, reject r. institutions and values,
  771:2
Rack, desire a perpetual r., 234:21
  leave not a r. behind, 224:21
  no R. torture me, 512:8
  of this tough world, 211:20
  ship weathered every r., 490:19
  then we r. the value, 187:2
Racker, ihr R. wollt ihr ewig leben,
  318:*n*4
Racket, would I were r. pressed, 719:2
Racks, set sharp r. at work, 414:20
Radar, this is writer's r., 702:11

Raise (*continued*)
  the genius, 299:19
  what is low r. and support, 255:20
Raised a mortal to the skies, 276:16
  dead shall be r., 43:27
  in incorruption, 43:25
  new man r. up in him, 50:11
  not a stone, 405:17
Raiseth, cross that r. me, 437:4
Raisin in the sun, 708:19
Raising, empire for r. customers,
    326:7
Raisons, le coeur a ses r., 270:*n*7
Rake among scholars, 425:15
  every woman at heart r., 300:17
  hors leene as is a r., 129:20
  stop to r. leaves away, 622:19
Rake's progress, 463:13
Rakes, scholar among r., 425:15
Raking, know when to stop r. muck,
    576:4
Rally round the flag boys, 492:7
Ralph wept for end of innocence,
    729:18
Ram, black r. tupping your ewe,
    205:15
  caught in a thicket, 7:35
  how wind doth r., 659:2
Rambles, Hamlet r., 599:7
Rambling, be not r. in thought,
    111:24
Ramm, how wind doth r., 659:2
Rampallian, away you r., 183:29
Rampant for spoil and victory, 552:24
  Maenad of Massachusetts, 535:2
Rampart, corse to r. we hurried,
    405:15
  no r. against malice, 268:30
Ramparts we watched, 391:2
Ramps, hasten down r., 717:1
Rams, mountains skipped like r.,
    19:16
Ran a hundred years to a day, 447:16
  before Ahab, 12:38
  dismayed away, 182:7
  grief with glass that r., 533:10
  my heedless ways, 737:18
  neighing canyons, 701:6
  on ten winters more, 273:21
  sunset r. one glorious blood-red,
    465:5
Rancor outpouring of inferiority,
    653:1
  will out, 163:18
Rancorous rational mind, 598:7
Randal, Felix R. the farrier, 551:3
  Lord R. my son, 785:20
Randolph Churchill went into hospi-
    tal, 712:9
  thy wreath has lost rose, 379:6
Random grim forge, 551:4
  I am writing at r., 418:12
  shaft at r. sent, 379:5
  we thrown down here at r., 707:9
Rang, sabbath r. slowly, 737:17
  them while touring Timbucktoo,
    760:15
Range with humble livers, 225:8
Ranged his tropes, 287:21
  if I have r., 221:25

Ranged (*continued*)
  wide arch of r. empire fall, 216:25
Ranges, something lost behind the r.,
    593:14
Rank, battle of the first r., 427:25
  black r. and file, 522:13
  but guinea's stamp, 363:21
  great beautifier, 428:20
  has its obligations, 367:8
  keep no r. nor station, 742:20
  marched r. on r., 509:8
  me with barbarous multitude,
    180:26
  my offense is r., 197:23
  swoln with r. mist, 254:3
  things r. and gross, 193:6
  when man of r. an author, 317:24
Rankers, gentlemen r., 592:3
Ranks, close r., 771:3
  for adoration all the r., 325:11
  of death, 391:17
  the same with God, 464:8
Rank-scented many, 219:6
Ransom captive Israel, 482:11
  them from the power of the grave,
    29:31
Rant, I'll r. as well as thou, 199:17
  when you r. and swear, 235:*n*3
Rapacious and licentious soldiery,
    332:2
Rape an insurrectionary act, 767:19
  of every day, 749:16
Raphael made a century of sonnets,
    466:25
Raphaels, talked of their R., 330:14
Rapid, drive the r. car, 335:23
  Homer eminently r., 498:22
  lady's imagination r., 386:25
Rapier-keen, button-cute r., 715:1
Rapping at chamber door, 452:13
Rapscallions, all kings mostly r.,
    526:24
Rapt ship run on side so low, 157:13
  soul sitting in thine eyes, 251:24
Rapture, first fine careless r., 465:4
  on lonely shore, 400:29
  then a pain, 554:13
Raptures and roses of vice, 533:12
  illustrious acts high r. infuse, 249:26
  no Minstrel r. swell, 378:1
  no poetic r. feel, 353:9
R'ar back an' pass a miracle, 678:3
Rara avis in terris, 108:*n*11
Rare and bloodless week of repose,
    73:*n*7
  and radiant maiden, 452:15
  are solitary woes, 198:*n*5
  as day in June, 485:5
  Beaumont, 240:13
  Ben Jonson, 231:*n*6
  bird on earth, 108:25
  delicate and r., 567:18
  excellent things r., 278:19
  few rid selves of friendship, 523:19
  my love of birth as r., 268:21
  somewhere a r. name, 73:13
  to meet man outdoors, 477:25
  tobacco divine, 235:10
Rarely rarely comest thou, 409:15
Rarer gifts than gold, 663:5

Rarer (*continued*)
  the living are getting r., 731:15
Rarity of Christian charity, 423:10
Rascal, biggest r. that walks, 109:24
  if r. have not given medicines,
    177:12
Rascally yea-forsooth knave, 183:13
Rascals, lash the r. naked, 208:2
  law's to take care o' r., 483:18
  one of most unscrupulous r., 578:2
  would you live forever, 318:18
Rase, slowly r. she up, 785:10
Rash hand in evil hour, 260:7
  not splenetive and r., 199:15
  too r. too unadvised, 175:9
  who reckons on morrow, 67:3
Rash-embraced despair, 181:7
Rashes, green grow the r. O, 362:1
Rashly charged troops of error, 248:1
  importunate, 423:9
Rashness, beware of r., 449:17
Raskills, law's to take care o' r.,
    483:18
Rasselas Prince of Abyssinia, 314:9
Rast ich so rost ich, 778:5
Rat, a dog a horse a r., 211:19
  begin to smell a r., 150:11
  giant r. of Sumatra, 578:3
  how now a r., 197:27
  is in the trap, 762:18
  killed the r., 792:24
  mouse studying to be r., 631:12
  poisoned r. in hole, 289:17
Raths, mome r. outgrabe, 518:15
Ratio, keen and quivering r., 511:12
  population increases in geometrical
    r., 368:2
  subsistence in arithmetical r., 368:2
Ratiocination, pay with r., 262:20
Rational ethics, 588:7
  I am r. therefore sing hymns, 108:4
  one r. voice dumb, 720:13
  rancorous r. mind, 598:7
  world presents r. aspect, 372:8
Rationalism adventure in clarification
    of thought, 584:12
Rationality, freedom brought indepen-
    dence r., 704:8
  if r. were criterion, 769:4
Rationally, him who looks on world
    r., 372:8
  live r. for time assigned, 111:12
  till women more r. educated, 365:27
Rationed, so precious must be r.,
    610:7
Rations, live upon daily r., 470:14
Ratisbon, stormed R., 464:9
Rats came tumbling, 464:19
  desert sinking ship, 104:*n*9
  have quit it, 223:25
  houses destroyed by r., 281:22
  land-r. and water-r., 180:1
  mice r. and such small deer, 210:9
  nearness of r., 703:16
  they fought dogs, 464:18
Rats' alley, 668:20
Rattle his bones over stones, 423:12
  pleased with a r., 301:15
  rifles' rapid r., 687:2
Rattling good history, 540:16

Ready (*continued*)

my tongue is the pen of a r. writer, 17:14

necessity of being r., 449:7

no r. way to virtue, 248:16

old wife old dog r. money, 309:22

rough sir but r., 470:19

to ride spread alarm, 442:13

to try our fortunes, 184:7

we always are r., 323:18

with every nod to tumble, 166:3

with you be r. to die, 96:19

Ready-made, critics all r., 399:3

Real, a man's r. life, 573:12

coming back to r., 640:6

dark night of soul, 694:18

do it so feels r., 764:12

lead me from unreal to r., 50:15

life r. life earnest, 440:15

lure of the r., 640:19

never fit for r. work, 754:7

nothing r. except humanity, 421:9

nothing r. till experienced, 418:14

only mist is r., 736:18

Simon Pure, 288:11

spirit r. and eternal, 495:21

that is moral, 494:12

thing which made the emotion, 701:20

this is the r. me, 545:5

War Will Never Get in Books, 491:14

what is r. is reasonable, 372:4

Realism, Dostoevski's r., 653:17

Realist, in Israel to be r., 661:4

Realities and creators, 431:9

less dangerous than fancies, 615:18

muddled state sharpest of r., 549:5

not images of beauty but r., 74:13

Reality, appearance never attain r., 365:13

attained only by detached, 727:12

between idea and r., 669:10

capture its r. in paint, 537:22

criticism parts company with r., 620:14

final word in r., 761:7

fine r. of hunger satisfied, 723:1

flee from r., 653:19

give r. to illusion, 631:5

history illumines r., 87:14

human kind not bear much r., 670:11

in r. atoms and space, 70:28

is things as they are, 640:17

mask off r. remains, 89:22

no humbling of r. to precept, 756:9

of distress, 341:6

of experience, 647:11

regulate imagination by r., 315:7

the more threatening r. appears, 645:6

three mirror same r., 345:9

translators between dream and r., 665:20

use r. rather than know it, 736:12

we crave only r., 478:20

your own r. for yourself, 573:5

Realize bitterness of Life, 520:1

Realize (*continued*)

earth too wonderful to r. you, 697:15

I'd been happy, 732:13

Mrs. Pontellier to r. position, 562:1

Realized, design of all his words r., 640:7

they and I civilized, 711:4

Realm, invade borders of my r., 144:15

mysterious r., 411:4

riding o'er azure r., 323:8

this r. this England, 171:9

turned out of R. in my petticoat, 144:16

Realms above, 382:15

and islands as plates, 218:11

Anna whom three r. obey, 299:13

of gold, 413:24

those who Dwell in R. of day, 359:16

whatever r. to see, 328:7

Reap an act, 781:6

as you sow ye r., 263:25

blessings of freedom, 341:1

harvest of your land, 9:24

he that regardeth the clouds not r., 24:24

in joy, 19:28

men that sow and r., 534:13

not wholly r. the corners, 9:24

sow not neither r., 33:18

that shall he also r., 44:21

the whirlwind, 29:27

we r. our sowing, 522:10

Reaped, all the harvest I r., 445:18

iniquity, 29:28

wheat never r. nor sown, 280:23

Reaping, autumn that grew by r., 218:11

Reappraisal, agonizing r., 743:1

Reaps, wholesome harvests r., 422:3

Rear my dusky race, 455:23

tender thought, 308:4

to produce and to r. them, 57:2

Reared arm crested the world, 218:11

himself a throne, 451:14

Rearward of a conquered woe, 221:13

Reason and experiment have been indulged, 343:6

and will of God prevail, 500:14

argument needs no r., 58:13

art has r. for being, 433:7

asked one another the r., 192:10

beast that wants discourse of r., 193:11

but from what we know, 301:3

by r. of strength, 18:12

capability and godlike r., 198:12

common law nothing but r., 152:1

deeply when forcibly feel, 366:5

destroys book kills r., 254:23

discourse of r., 193:11

feast of r. flow of soul, 302:21

flood of words drop of r., 309:18

freed men's minds, 103:15

give r. on compulsion, 177:25

God's crowning gift, 66:16

greatest enemy faith has, 138:14

Reason (*continued*)

guide by light of r., 568:17

have I not r. to lament, 372:18

humanity r. and justice, 331:17

ignis fatuus of mind, 283:25

Imagination abandoned by R., 348:n1

immortal all else mortal, 58:11

improvable r. of Man, 420:18

in images of sense, 384:1

in itself confounded, 200:1

in man like God in world, 124:13

is of no use to us, 336:18

is past care, 222:13

keep r. under control, 111:27

know truth not only by r., 271:1

knows nothing of, 270:25

law is perfection of r., 152:1

law ordinance of r. for common good, 124:11

left free to combat error, 344:5

left free to combat it, 345:1

let my will take place of r., 109:1

let us r. together, 25:29, 723:14

lies between spur and bridle, 244:36

life of the law, 152:1

make worse appear better r., 73:2

men have lost their r., 189:2

Milton wrote in fetters, 357:2

most sovereign r., 196:19

no other but woman's r., 167:37

noble in r., 195:28

not listen to r., 461:10

not yet guided by r., 611:11

nothing law that is not r., 152:n1

of this thusness, 522:4

or any other r. why, 283:20

our r. is our law, 260:6

panders will, 197:32

passions not conform to r., 355:5

past r. hunted, 222:7

psychological r., 548:15

pursue my R. to O altitudo, 248:4

rather to feel than r., 365:31

reaching after fact and r., 417:18

rhyme nor r., 154:17

right deed for wrong r., 670:10

ruling passion conquers r., 300:23

salvation of freedom, 706:15

sanctified by r. blest by faith, 373:14

shall enforce her sway, 353:8

sleep of r. produces monsters, 348:8

still keeps its throne, 295:10

takes the r. prisoner, 212:20

teach thy necessity to r., 171:1

tell me the r. I pray, 386:8

theirs not to r. why, 458:12

themselves out again, 186:3

to rule mercy to forgive, 275:15

two worlds to r., 248:10

victory over r., 676:3

we bicker creates war, 146:4

what someone else has to say, 461:10

where faith in r. timid, 615:6

why I cannot tell, 286:25

with reasonable r., 437:17

worse appear better r., 257:1

yield with grace to r., 622:18

Reasonable amount o' fleas good for
dog, 555:9
good ear in music, 173:21
holy and living sacrifice, 49:17
man being r. must get drunk,
402:19
Man mythical, 678:21
moderator Death, 248:12
no r. man expected, 678:23
nothing r. from pure reason, 618:16
speak a few r. words, 349:10
what is real is r., 372:4
Reasonableness, will and well-meaning
r., 628:10
Reasoned errors, 505:18
Reasonest, Plato thou r. well, 292:14
Reasoning but to err, 301:13
cowards in r., 291:27
destroy power of r., 76:6
infant's r., 319:30
like all Holmes's r., 577:21
man is a r. animal, 102:24
mathematician capable of r., 75:19
self-sufficing thing, 374:3
Reasonings, versed in r. of men, 68:7
Reason's icy intimations, 423:13
in erring r. spite, 301:12
words clothed in r. garb, 257:6
Reasons, and he had r., 608:3
as two grains of wheat, 179:23
find of settled gravity, 220:24
for scarcity of capital, 652:16
heart has its r., 270:25
heroism never r., 432:6
immoral thing for moral r., 540:8
made his mouth water, 263:14
man always has two r., 533:2
plenty as blackberries, 177:25
private as well as public r., 343:7
Reassures, science r., 646:1
Rebecks, jocund r. sound, 251:15
Re-begot, ruined me and I am r.,
229:9
Rebel, aspiring to angels men r.,
159:n7
I'm a good old r., 533:6
in act and deed, 589:1
learn from past and r., 760:7
quickens to r., 669:20
those that r. against the light, 14:35
without a cause, 736:3
Rebellion, a little r. a good thing,
343:1
against United States, 449:13
century and half without r., 343:15
determined to foment r., 347:1
lay in his way, 178:30
not r. which is noble, 732:16
now and then good, 343:14
rude eye of r., 170:18
Rum Romanism R., 468:18
to tyrants, 779:3
Rebellions, legends events r. majesties,
417:1
Rebellious, dark r. brows, 491:5
hell, 197:32
hot and r. liquors, 190:11
revolting and r. heart, 28:16
storms it wooeth, 474:6
stubborn and r. generation, 18:2

Rebelliousness, culture drives to r.,
569:10
Rebels from principle, 332:16
our countrymen again, 501:12
Rebirth, craving leads to r., 64:26
of Union, 572:5
Reborn, power to be r. into highest
forms, 136:1
Rebounds, hit hard it r., 316:22
Rebuff, welcome each r., 467:8
Rebuffs, confront accidents r., 488:14
Rebuilding of backward countries,
677:4
Rebuke a wise man, 21:2
is better than secret love, 23:1
recoils, 622:12
Rebus, cedit amor r., 102:n1
est modus in r., 95:n2
Recall a stone thrown, 97:n10
Recalled, word cannot be r., 97:18
Recant, if I do not r., 136:8
Recapitulation, ontogenesis r. of phy-
logenesis, 522:15
Recapture, never could r., 465:4
Recede, unpurged images r., 598:11
Recedes, orgiastic future that r. before
us, 694:12
Receipt of little bit of paper, 487:2
sitting at r. of custom, 34:20
Receive, ask and ye shall r., 40:34
Christ r. him, 458:8
hand stretched out to r., 31:9
if lungs r. our air, 334:27
more blessed to give than r., 41:23
my soul at last, 312:14
the fugitive, 340:21
wax to r., 402:3
we r. but what we give, 383:8
Received, freely ye have r., 34:28
Receives comfort like cold porridge,
224:3
reproach of being, 222:6
Receiveth, one r. prize, 43:6
Recessions, predicted nine of last five
r., 739:2
Recht, yer a' r. that's a', 609:17
Recipe for making Delacroix, 544:1
rare r. for melancholy, 387:17
Reciprocal enforceable safeguards,
655:9
in marriage obligations r., 410:18
Recirculation, commodius vicus of r.,
647:18
Recite In the name of thy Lord,
117:24
Reck the rede, 193:n4
Reckless, make r. choice, 623:10
puffed and r. libertine, 193:27
what I do to spite world, 214:22
Recklessness, never gauged your cruelty r., 680:14
Reckon ill who leave me out, 430:11
when I count at all, 512:16
Reckoned, love that can be r., 216:24
Reckoning, day of great r., 4:5
God swift at the r., 117:5
honor a trim r., 178:33
no r. made, 194:24
sense of r., 185:20
truth to the end of r., 205:3

Reckons, rash who r. on morrow,
67:3
up by dozens, 529:5
Recks not his own rede, 193:27
Reclined, all on a rock r., 297:1
Reclothe us in rightful mind, 443:17
Recognition of evil, 56:13
of ugliness, 56:13
shock of r., 486:13
Recognize a wise man, 60:7
did not r. me by my face, 476:4
gods' hand, 716:16
good but be barred, 64:4
relations to world, 562:17
Recognized, wished indifference universally r., 769:5
Recognizes, man r. himself in culture,
717:18
my book in me, 146:20
which God God r., 717:3
Recognizing man's step, 616:17
Recoiled, warmest heart r. at war,
688:16
Recoils, rebuke r., 622:12
Recollect, cannot r. ignorance in
which born, 321:3
cannot r. when it begun, 513:2
that Almighty gave dog, 379:24
Recollected, emotion r. in tranquillity,
373:17
Recollection, fond r. presents them,
398:2
like living life over, 311:1
Recommencée, la mer toujours r.,
613:n4
Recommendation, fair exterior a silent
r., 99:10
Recommends, nimbly and sweetly r.
itself, 213:4
Recompense as largely send, 322:23
injury with justice, 61:25
no evil for evil, 42:16
service beyond all r., 249:21
Reconciled, God and sinners r.,
312:17
Reconciles, custom r. to everything,
330:20
discordant elements, 373:8
forgotten wars, 670:14
good dinner r., 279:12
world easily r. to death, 436:9
Reconciliation of opposite qualities,
384:14
Reconciling mediatory power, 384:1
Reconstructed, won't be r., 533:7
Reconstruction, demand in R. suffrage,
475:9
Record, dreadful r. of sin, 577:19
let's look at the r., 618:6
one more the final r., 423:20
poetry r. of best happiest moments,
410:1
puts r. on gramophone, 669:2
register of God not r. of man, 249:2
weep to r., 320:n5
Recorded, assurance of r. history,
671:15
by Muses live for ay, 154:4
last syllable of r. time, 216:14
Recorders, flutes and soft r., 256:14

Recording Angel dropped a tear, 320:29
  make ourselves r. plate, 537:22
  man shaving, 713:17
Records that defy tooth of time, 296:5
  trivial fond r., 194:27
Recount, such bickerings to r., 261:28
Recover and prove an ass, 174:10
  hair that grows bald, 166:23
  health through contentment, 71:5
  that I may r. strength, 17:10
Recovered innocence, 478:33
  man r. of the bite, 328:28
  virtue if lost seldom r., 277:13
Recreant limbs, 169:28
Recreation, calm quiet innocent r., 245:27
  without some lawful r., 150:15
Recruit, body of little r., 700:8
Recruits in worldly warfare, 262:n3
Rectitude, marks of God in r., 392:18
  mind aware of own r., 93:23
Recure, woes time cannot r., 152:8
Recurrent end of unending, 672:2
Red animal war, 611:1
  as a rose is she, 381:2
  as stones kissed by dead, 687:4
  badge of courage, 611:2
  beauty whose r. and white, 201:26
  beholding myself rosy r., 606:1
  blossom in purple and r., 458:24
  China not seeking to dominate world, 685:15
  coat r. breeches blue, 386:22
  coral is far more r., 222:8
  cow all r. and white, 561:11
  fair weather for sky is r., 35:25
  fortunes of my r. people, 370:2
  heart's core, 414:15
  her lips were r., 381:12
  herrings, 788:15
  I green U blue O, 565:17
  in him the r. earth, 563:9
  in r. cloth appeared letter A, 435:25
  in tooth and claw, 457:21
  jolly r. nose, 242:16
  Lantern and his undersea folk, 766:7
  leaf r. and sear, 378:3
  life stream again, 417:3
  lips not so red, 687:4
  lips r. and one was thin, 262:6
  making the green one r., 214:9
  Marian's nose looks r., 169:14
  men scalped each other, 425:11
  morn that betokened, 165:12
  my Luve like a r. r. rose, 362:6
  my sin is r., 283:10
  my skin is r., 516:9
  nose makes me ashamed, 279:22
  pale and hectic r., 407:13
  plague rid you, 223:29
  remember R. River Valley, 786:10
  right hand, 257:3
  rise with my r. hair, 764:13
  rose is a falcon, 553:19
  Rose proud Rose, 594:20
  rose whispers of passion, 553:19
  roses r. and violets blue, 153:13
  sap make cherry r., 664:20

Red (*continued*)
  shadow under r. rock, 668:18
  slayer, 430:10
  so r. the Rose, 445:13
  soldier r. with rust, 559:21
  spirits and gray, 237:9
  still and awful r., 381:21
  sun pasted in sky, 611:3
  swift r. flesh, 701:6
  tape, 470:39
  thin r. 'eroes, 591:17
  thin r.-line streak, 492:8
  thoughts were r. thoughts, 610:19
  tigers in r. weather, 638:23
  wheel barrow, 654:1
  when last r. man has vanished, 398:11
  wine when it is r., 22:22
Redbreast, call for robin r., 237:13
  robin r. in cage, 359:6
  Robin R. piously, 776:2
  sit and sing, 382:17
  whistles from garden-croft, 416:15
Reddens, as an apple r., 56:10
Rede, reck the r., 193:n4
  recks not his own r., 193:27
Redeem, lose more of yourself than r., 769:16
  the time, 669:17
  them from death, 29:31
  these hours, 233:19
  unread vision, 669:17
  us from virtue, 533:16
Redeemed of the Lord shall return, 27:30
  visited and r., 37:44
Redeemer, know that my r. liveth, 14:30
  my strength and my r., 16:13
  so mighty a R., 48:12
Redeeming, past never past r., 749:14
Redemption, condemned into everlasting r., 187:5
  from above did bring, 250:19
  from Wilderness, 757:5
  inestimable love in r., 49:5
Redemptorem, tantum meruit habere R., 48:12
Red-handed, 119:4
Red-hot, last of r. mamas, 656:n2
Rediscover gods as psychic factors, 628:12
Red-leaved table of my heart, 233:17
Red-letter days, 387:23
Red-line streak, 492:8
Redoubling efforts, 588:5
Redress balance of the Old, 372:3
  I will r. that wrong, 484:18
  music send r., 776:12
  no r. by mob law, 448:2
  of grievances, 346:11
  procure r. of wrongs, 337:10
  things past r. now past care, 171:18
Reduce selfishness, 57:6
Reduction of physical processes, 537:3
Redwood, from r. forest to Gulf Stream waters, 731:13
Redwoods, I'm going down like r., 763:16

Reed, be merciful to broken r., 158:16
  bruised r. shall he not break, 27:25
  Love tunes shepherd's r., 377:25
  man is a thinking r., 271:3
  staff of this broken r., 27:11
Reeds, bending r. again and again, 756:18
  down in r. by river, 439:8
Reedy shore, 777:6
Reef of Norman's Woe, 441:2
Reeking herd, 660:15
  into Cadiz Bay, 465:5
Reel, about in r. and rout, 381:10
  to and fro, 19:11
Réel, il n'y a de r. que l'humanité, 421:n3
Reeled mind, 708:9
  sagged and r., 637:8
Reeling, send me r. in, 514:10
  through summer days, 511:17
Re-enter, I r. world, 762:4
Reference to one consent, 184:25
References, money and goods best r., 471:18
  verify your r., 355:15
Refine, cannot r. war, 492:9
  if good sense r. her page, 280:15
  it ne'er so much, 232:8
Refined, artist r. out of existence, 647:10
  gild r. gold, 170:9
  or artificial type, 609:11
  pleasures too r., 300:15
  thee but not with silver, 27:27
Refinement of everyday thinking, 635:14
  on resistance, 331:14
Refinery, out by gas fires of the r., 774:13
Refines, how the style r., 299:2
Refining, still went on r., 330:10
Reflect before throwing images, 675:19
  how awful to r., 594:3
  how you are to govern, 331:3
Reflecting man twice natural size, 651:3
Reflection, dispense with necessity of r., 565:5
  Liberal tempered by r., 500:10
  on acts of mind, 384:18
  remembrance and r. allied, 274:n2
  you may come tomorrow, 409:22
Reflections, except r. escapades of death, 640:2
  mortifying r., 444:n3
Reflects, novel r. blue of skies, 396:16
  who r. too much, 365:21
Reflex, conscious movements r., 511:1
Reform carried to excess needs reforming, 384:3
  cautious people never bring r., 491:20
  is not to equalize property, 78:16
  let us r. schools, 487:19
  that you may preserve, 425:1
Reformation mere episode, 704:2
  printing and the R., 629:16
  reforming of R. itself, 255:1
  revolution and r., 344:9

Relations (*continued*)
fundamental of social r., 440:5
human r. perfectly exhibited, 79:14
lift coffins of dead r., 769:14
renewal of r. nervous, 535:22
squire and his r., 470:14
tedious pack of people, 567:9
with intellect only collateral r.,
    453:14
women's training in human r.,
    707:20
Relationship, essential r. to existence,
    473:14
friendly and charming r., 138:12
of author to works, 572:22
Relative, set out in r. way, 618:14
that r. pronoun, 575:1
Relatives, fate chooses our r., 341:16
Relaxation, allowed himself fun and
    r., 70:1
maturity sacred to r., 559:3
only r. from labor, 550:8
there may be r., 314:28
Release, deadly forfeit should r.,
    250:19
ensured r., 580:8
from little things, 700:7
of atomic energy, 655:7
Relent, shall make him once r., 272:29
Relenting fool, 166:9
Relentless, Hades is r., 51:29
power, 321:18
war r., 610:3
Relents, my rigor r., 331:10
Relevance, sermon no r. to anything,
    748:2
Reliability, shifts of Fortune test r. of
    friends, 88:8
Reliance on divine providence, 343:4
self-reliance r. on God, 432:29
Relics, hallowed r. should be hid,
    251:2
unhonored his r. laid, 391:10
Relief, cricket no r., 668:18
for greedy, 650:1
for this r. much thanks, 192:19
hold out r. coming, 492:n5
not seek for kind r., 356:18
to dig him up throw stones at him,
    571:14
too proud for r., 624:21
Relies, on hope wretch r., 328:4
Relieve misfortunes by speaking,
    249:16
the oppressed, 25:29
to r. wretched his pride, 329:13
what wealth r. conscience, 235:23
Relieved, by desperate appliance r.,
    198:9
obliged wealthy and r. poor, 51:n6
unless I be r. by prayer, 224:29
Religio, tantum r. potuit suadere
    malorum, 89:n4
Religion, airy subtleties in r., 248:3
allowed to invade private life, 391:5
and not atheism, 331:19
Anglo-Catholic in r., 672:18
any r. keeping masses satisfied,
    677:7
behold clear r., 414:11

Religion (*continued*)
blunderbuss against r., 315:19
blushing veils fires, 304:2
breathing household laws, 374:14
but a childish toy, 162:5
Christianity r. of the son, 569:18
depth in philosophy bringeth to r.,
    159:19
different opinions concerning r.,
    351:22
duty we owe Creator, 339:11
enjoy r. prevent others, 522:5
enough to make us hate, 288:25
enterprise for glory of Christian r.,
    134:10
errors in r. dangerous, 318:10
establishment of r., 346:11
evil deeds r. prompt, 89:5
excess a reproach to r., 282:20
feelings in solitude, 546:13
for religion's sake, 405:18
free exercise of r., 339:11
free for r., 683:5
freedom of r., 344:9
he who controls area controls r.,
    118:24
I am a Millionaire that is my r.,
    571:13
in r. so uneven, 285:17
inconsistent with Christian r., 324:9
is an illusion, 569:16
Judaism r. of the father, 569:18
knavery and change, 281:15
leave him for r., 746:9
leave r. to family, 501:15
lies r. of slaves, 605:11
literature substitute for r., 672:17
made honest woman, 722:2
most prevalent in colonies, 331:14
my r. is to do good, 341:7
no heresies in dead r., 606:5
no part of r. to compel r., 112:14
not popular error, 503:15
of feeble minds, 332:19
of inequality, 500:22
of well-doing and daring, 315:n7
of which rewards distant, 314:18
one r. hundred versions, 570:19
one r. true as another, 235:19
one's r. neither harms nor helps an-
    other, 112:13
opium of people, 481:5
orthodox in r., 683:2
pagan who defends r., 611:4
persecution bad way to plant r.,
    248:9
philosophy handmaid to r., 158:11
politics like r., 344:12
poverty a reproach to r., 282:20
powerless to bestow, 433:17
printing and Protestant r., 412:25
propitiation of powers, 564:22
protestantism of Protestant r.,
    331:14
restores man to dignity, 588:19
rum and true r., 402:16
self-righteousness not r., 476:12
sensible men of same r., 435:19
slovenliness no part of r., 309:1
stands on tiptoe, 244:3

Religion (*continued*)
superstition incongruous r., 493:20
that old-time r., 780:3
total reaction upon life, 546:14
we too have our r., 520:14
will not last so long, 65:4
wonders of Christian r., 287:3
your r. is Success, 581:25
Religions, from poetry r., 714:9
heresy lifeblood of r., 606:5
neurotics founded r., 612:18
thirty-two r. one dish, 354:6
vicissitude of sects and r., 160:11
Religious, appeals to r. prejudice,
    505:20
dim r. light, 252:10
do evil from r. conviction, 271:10
duties consist in justice, 341:9
feeling a verity, 493:21
feeling toward life, 607:16
freedom, 631:14
old r. factions, 332:23
people suspicious, 591:3
persecution, 332:5
rather political than r., 315:24
seed of r. liberty, 486:8
suspended r. inquiries, 340:11
vision our ground for optimism,
    584:11
waves of r. emotion, 665:9
way to think of death, 629:11
Religious-good, good but not r., 539:9
Relinquish, time does not r. rights,
    349:26
Relish him more in soldier, 206:10
imaginary r. is so sweet, 200:17
love of gentle woman, 731:3
no r. of those arts, 292:23
of saltness of time, 183:15
versing, 243:23
Relished, taste by which r., 376:18
Reluctant feet, 441:7
sweet r. amorous delay, 258:13
Reluctantly, difficult when you do it
    r., 86:2
Relume, Promethean heat thy light r.,
    208:10
Rem tene verba sequentur, 85:n5
Remain, if our loves r., 465:11
laws ought not to r. unaltered,
    78:17
my thoughts r. below, 197:26
nothing will r., 579:2
shall France r. here, 503:7
sitting at your table, 651:22
some born mad some r. so, 718:16
thou shalt r., 416:7
until death do part, 571:15
with unavenged suffering, 495:8
Remained to pray, 329:15
Remaineth, while the earth r., 7:22
Remaining second weakest among
    great powers, 643:8
Remains, be kind to my r., 276:3
heap of dust alone r., 300:9
nothing done while aught r., 367:2
the One r., 409:8
what r. is bestial, 206:20
what thou lovest well r., 659:17
Remake, it is myself I r., 595:17

Render (*continued*)
  praise and favor, 438:18
  to all their dues, 42:21
  unto Caesar, 35:45
Renderest, thou r. to every man according to his work, 17:34
Rendezvous, shall not fail r., 674:18
  with Death, 674:17
  with destiny, 649:3
Renew a right spirit within me, 17:22
  herbs that did r. Aeson, 182:7
  their strength, 27:23
  tinker more than r., 546:20
  unspeakable sorrow you bid me r., 93:26
Renewal, lovers' quarrels r. of love, 85:14
  of relations nervous, 535:22
  plant seeds watch r., 511:2
Renewed, cycle of the ages r., 92:10
  sum of things ever being r., 89:16
  to be worn out is to be r., 57:8
Renewing, falling out of friends r. is, 85:*n*11
  the ever r. sea, 613:16
Renounce, guilty of corruption and r. defense, 158:16
  the devil, 49:21
Renouncement, Liberal tempered by r., 500:10
Renown and grace is dead, 214:15
  end is the r., 203:17
  forfeit fair r., 378:1
  in high place and of r., 31:2
  let me win noble r., 52:15
  men of r., 7:15
  naught but breath of wind, 126:13
  purchased not by violence, 396:7
  set cause above r., 586:12
  some for r., 295:24
  speak no more of his r., 458:8
  win high r., 53:10
Renowned be thy grave, 220:4
  farewell r. Eretria, 74:9
  Spenser, 240:13
Rent, blood and sweat for r., 620:*n*1
  envious Casca made, 189:5
  is sorrow income tears, 242:9
  Mordecai r. his clothes, 13:24
  nothing whole that has not been r., 598:21
  spontaneous joy, 595:19
  the rocks r., 37:13
  veil of temple r., 37:13
Rents, what are thy r., 185:18
Reorganized upon the floor, 668:15
Repair, Freedom shall awhile r., 324:11
  keep friendship in r., 315:21
  some to church r., 298:18
Reparation for rights at home, 313:5
Repay, I will r., 42:18
  shut when thou shouldest r., 31:9
  tomorrow will r., 273:16
Repeat, condemned to r. past, 588:6
  No again and again, 553:16
Repeateth, he that r. a matter, 21:34
Repeating, human stories r., 616:4
  oft r. they believe 'em, 288:2
Repeats his words, 170:4

Repent at leisure, 290:34
  neither to change nor falter nor r., 407:6
  restore should I r. me, 208:10
  we do earnestly r., 49:15
  what's past, 198:3
  ye kingdom is at hand, 32:28
  ye who do truly and earnestly r., 49:14
  you will r. by jingo, 422:26
Repentance, call sinners to r., 34:22
  decline to buy r., 79:5
  fear of consequence, 265:21
  garment of R., 445:6
  give r. to her lover, 328:30
  on a Sunday, 644:2
  tears of r. you'll wipe, 357:21
Repented, strove and much r., 402:10
Repetition, of r. most master, 640:3
Repine, do not r. my friends, 469:37
Replace, no one could r. Franklin, 309:*n*1
Replenish the earth, 6:9
Replication of your sounds, 187:17
Replied Fish fiddle de-dee, 472:14
  O Lord Thou art, 325:10
  shade r., 453:5
  with chuckle r., 644:15
Replies, heart r., 335:11
Reply churlish, 192:16
  pause for a r., 188:27
  reply, 181:3
  shall never know how to R., 359:12
  sing ye heavens earth r., 312:13
  theirs nor to r., 458:12
Report, by evil r. and good r., 44:5
  ill r. while you live, 196:2
  me and cause aright, 199:25
  nor heart to r., 173:27
  of fashions in proud Italy, 171:7
  of my death an exaggeration, 528:2
  true r. to him who sent you, 22:*n*2
  vexation only to understand the r., 26:34
  whatsoever things are of good r., 44:35
  who knows how he may r., 261:22
Reported, their praises might be r., 32:14
Reporters sit in fourth estate, 424:17
Reporters' Gallery Fourth Estate, 411:*n*1
Repose, as well for defense as r., 152:4
  earned night's r., 441:5
  find r. reveal self, 564:10
  foster-nurse of nature is r., 210:26
  hushed in grim r., 323:8
  in r. distinct, 752:16
  in trembling hope r., 322:24
  leave me to r., 323:11
  long for a r., 376:4
  not destiny of man, 542:9
  placid r. under liberty, 269:34
  pray for r. of his soul, 582:17
  quenched in cold r., 408:19
  rare and bloodless week of r., 73:*n*7
  spirit of r., 426:15
  tabooed by anxiety, 530:14

Repose (*continued*)
  that ever is the same, 376:4
  thoughts nature gives way to in r., 213:18
  when got r. insupportable, 536:2
  worship but no r., 408:9
Reposes, in quiet she r., 498:14
Reposing, sorrow breaks r. hours, 165:32
Reprehend, if I r. anything in world, 352:9
Represent, effort to see and r., 549:5
  Muhammad did not falsely r., 117:18
Representation, laws in which we have no r., 347:1
  mediocre people entitled to r., 713:16
  taxation without r., 327:7
Representative, individual with r., 384:14
  of highest spiritual authority, 645:1
  owes you, 331:4
  proper office of r. assembly, 439:25
Representatives, conscience of r., 646:13
  House of R., 339:3
  more I see r. of people, 405:11
  women ought to have r., 365:33
Repressed their noble rage, 322:12
Repression, price of r., 605:3
Repressions, mass r. and lawlessness, 763:13
Reproach, cheerfully bear r., 425:18
  curse astonishment hissing and r., 28:34
  everything that is a r. among men, 60:4
  mine ways without r., 101:7
  no defense against r., 292:24
  people talking about themselves, 550:12
  receives r. of being, 222:6
Reproached me in public, 370:11
Reproacheth his Maker, 21:33
Reproaching, without r. brethren, 392:17
Reprobate, who such r. as I, 539:17
Reprobation, doctrine of r., 536:18
  fall to r., 208:13
Reproduction, preserved by r., 347:13
Reproof on her lip, 420:15
  valiant, 192:16
Reprove, check erring and r., 376:3
  not a scorner, 21:2
  sager sort our deeds r., 226:13
Reproved each dull delay, 329:14
Reptiles, no r. found there, 120:5
Republic a raft, 360:7
  for which it stands, 568:12
  if you can keep it, 310:26
  is a dream, 634:11
  of letters, 312:2
  they died to save, 450:9
Republican, deprives r. example of just influence, 448:5
  eternal importance like R. Party, 658:5
  forming a r. government, 355:2
  highest government, 493:10

Republican (*continued*)
model of government, 337:1
only form of government, 343:16
party broke ye, 602:17
work for R. party, 491:24
Republicans, we are all R., 344:5
we are R., 468:18
Republics, destiny of r. settled, 486:9
in small r. is stability, 395:13
never known to exist, 136:14
Repudiate support of Communism,
649:5
Repulsive, free speech in r. form,
621:17
Reputation an idle imposition, 206:21
at every word r. dies, 299:14
better than my r., 365:15
bubble r., 191:3
kindness enters deeply, 80
gain forever r. among men
I have lost my r., 206:20
men who survive their r., 10
more valuable than money, 99:2
not aloof in order to gain r., 76:10
not carefully preserved, 278:13
part of man's Self, 545:20
reputation reputation, 206:20
sold R. for Song, 446:6
spotless r., 170:25
written out of r., 286:9
Repute, sink present r. for freedom,
485:7
thing of good r., 574:6
Reputed wise for saying nothing,
179:21
Request deed in silence, 125:29
Requiem, to thy high r., 415:16
Requiescat in pace, 119:26
Require, that people may r. leader,
75:28
thought 'e might r., 592:11
what is it men in women r., 357:24
Required, much given much r., 38:31,
741:2
nothing given nothing r., 311:16
of us a song, 20:6
of us mirth, 20:6
this night soul shall be r., 38:29
Requirement, first r. in Hospital,
492:3
Requisite, first r. of good citizen,
576:1
Meat r. to Squirrels, 513:16
right to means r., 355:6
Reread classic, 713:1
Rere-mice, some war with r., 173:10
Re-resolves then dies, 296:12
Rerum, sunt lacrimae r., 93:n12
Res iudicata pro veritate habetur,
119:27
Rescind, voted not to r., 339:3
Rescue me protect me, 4:5
my soul from their destructions,
16:32
nothing can r. me, 162:21
trump of r. sound, 430:2
Rescues, whoever r. single life earns
merit, 115:17
Research contribution to ideas, 738:13

Research (*continued*)
steal from many authors is r.,
631:10
Researchers into Public Opinion,
721:4
Resemblance neglects spirit of objects,
120:14
showy r. of distress, 341:6
Resembled my father as he slept,
214:4
Resembles, the most r. God, 362:4
Resembleth, love r. April day, 168:1
Resent, do not r. criticism, 620:14
Resentment consumes a man, 553:7
whim envy or r., 333:18
Reserve back shop all our own,
145:20
side of last r., 266:n7
thy judgment, 193:30
Reservedly, read books as r. as written, 478:22
Réserver une arrière boutique toute
notre, 145:n14
Reside in thrilling region, 204:14
Residence, forted r., 205:2
Residences, inns not r., 664:11
Resides, fire that in heart r., 497:13
Resign, never ask refuse r. office,
311:3
title and profit I r., 292:n4
Resignation is confirmed desperation,
477:32
please accept r., 693:2
Resigned, I am not r., 684:12
pleasing being e'er r., 322:19
to shutting away, 684:12
trees more r. than other things,
616:6
Resinous heart has fed, 597:20
Resist beginnings, 101:29
boots not to r. wind and tide,
164:26
easier to r. at beginning, 135:8
everything except temptation,
566:20
not evil, 33:7
strength not adequate to r., 79:8
the devil, 46:14
Resistance, diminished r. to that disease, 745:n1
nonviolent r. paralyzed, 761:8
or abject submission, 336:14
Passive R., 606:13
principle of r., 331:14
spirit of r., 345:14
Resistances, breaking down half-
hearted r., 496:4
Resisted, rejoice that America r.,
312:20
Resolute, be bloody bold and r.,
215:19
haughty vigilant r., 425:12
think beforehand that actions be r.,
79:22
Resolutely, purse most r. snatched,
176:26
Resolution, in war r., 622:4
native hue of r., 196:10
passed without dissenting, 338:4
road to r., 242:11

Resolutions, careful r. unerring decisions, 108:8
great and mighty r., 263:12
keep r., 314:26
Resolve is not to seem but be, 63:24
itself into a dew, 193:5
not only way to r. conflicts, 657:1
not shaken from his firm r., 96:15
pushes his purpose to r., 296:12
to conquer or die, 336:14
we here highly r., 450:2
Resolved, Catullus be r. and firm,
90:21
is once to be r., 206:33
so they r. to proceed, 240:7
to be irresolute, 619:20
to die in last dike, 332:7
to live a fool, 238:11
to ruin or rule state, 274:6
to take Fate by throat, 516:12
Resolves and re-resolves, 296:12
Resonance of sound in violin, 753:3
sinister r., 573:n1
Resort of mirth, 252:5
Resound in another street, 736:18
Resources, enjoy r. within thy reach,
64:3
full of r., 331:15
greater vital r. than supposed, 545:6
man of many r., 52:27
of civilization not exhausted, 446:15
oneness of r., 748:13
rock of national r., 394:18
small portion of soul's r., 545:6
wagers sum of r., 750:n2
waste natural r., 576:7
Respect, but you lose their r., 136:18
decent r. to opinions, 343:2
developed r. for unknown in lifetime, 727:20
have his son r. him, 277:12
I can't get no r., 748:15
idle wind which I r. not, 189:16
mingled with surprise, 378:25
neighborly r., 620:2
no r. of persons with God, 41:n2
not law so much as right, 477:8
of place persons time, 202:4
or natural love, 573:12
strength without fearing, 344:1
that makes calamity of life, 196:10
those equal in any r., 78:23
three worthy of r., 494:14
too much r. upon world, 179:16
woman takes off claim to r., 69:21
you in my r. are world, 173:8
Respectable, great artists seldom r.,
642:13
Hell, 604:16
highly r. tribe, 781:2
make murder r., 711:14
more ashamed more r., 571:2
not one r. or unhappy, 489:16
Professors of Dismal Science, 413:12
since when genius r., 439:6
turkey a more r. bird, 310:24
Respectables, n'existe que trois êtres
r., 494:n11
Respecter, God no r. of persons,
41:10, 424:5

Respectful to his elders, 60:16
Respectfully return Him ticket, 495:8
Respite from long year's watch, 63:9
　to be dead, 513:13
Responding, successfully r. to chal-
　lenges, 677:8
Responsibilities, fulfilled r. to state,
　741:2
　infinite r. of man, 717:15
　who has many r., 51:5
Responsibility, at summit r. increases,
　553:3
　first step in responsibility, 605:4
　in dreams begins r., 595:22
　intellectual r., 681:3
　no r. at other end, 730:14
　without woman I love, 691:6
　writer's only r., 697:2
Responsible, Chicago r. for Tribune,
　666:3
　for what we are, 717:14
　journalism, 677:6
　no snowflake in avalanche feels r.,
　726:16
　not r. for dreams, 628:14
　through time and eternity, 449:15
Rest, absence of occupation not r.,
　334:15
　and be thankful, 779:17
　and faith we need it, 591:13
　body continues in state of r., 282:1
　cannot r. for seeing countries, 785:7
　choose ground and take r., 404:8
　choose their place of r., 260:24
　cities never have r. from evils, 75:15
　could r. anywhere would be in Ar-
　kansaw, 398:6
　die or r. at last, 408:11
　dove found no r., 7:19
　embrace r. that knows no care, 90:5
　even fountain have r., 479:14
　failing that the r. of the city, 75:11
　far far better r., 471:13
　for the dead, 521:9
　from their labors, 47:32
　gets him to r., 185:19
　God r. you merry, 778:8
　gone to eternal r., 451:14
　good in which mind at r., 126:16
　grant us holy r., 426:22
　hearts do in the faces r., 228:4
　her soul she's dead, 199:5
　here set up my everlasting r., 176:18
　I will give you r., 34:38
　if England r. but true, 170:24
　I'll r. but thou walk, 785:7
　in doubt to act or r., 301:13
　in Nature not God, 243:19
　in soft peace, 232:11
　is dross, 659:17
　is silence, 199:28
　lay me down and take my r., 15:n2
　let his remembrance r., 32:11
　lightly r., 67:25
　long long ago at r., 502:9
　long r. or death, 454:10
　may he r. in peace, 119:26
　miseries not let them r., 417:13
　much veneration but no r., 159:21
　my heart is at r., 356:17

Rest *(continued)*
　peace and r. never dwell, 255:24
　perturbed spirit, 195:5
　profound as grave, 535:29
　said Good Night gone to r., 609:8
　shall shortly be at r., 261:15
　she's at r. and so am I, 277:2
　sing thee to thy r., 199:29
　so may he r., 226:3
　soldier r., 378:20
　Swift sailed into his r., 598:9
　then had I been at r., 13:35
　then would I fly away and be at r.,
　17:26
　there the weary be at r., 13:36
　thou too shalt r., 351:2
　thy praise sanctify our r., 506:16
　to mind cheerer of spirits, 245:17
　toil and not seek r., 139:3
　under the trees, 504:10
　unto your souls, 34:38
　water rush to r. in air, 696:3
　wear ourselves and never r., 161:21
　when I r. I rust, 778:5
　where peace and r. can never dwell,
　255:24
　where's r. of me, 711:20
　who does not know, 101:8
　who sink to r., 324:10
　William Yeats laid to r., 720:9
　without haste but without r., 351:14
　ye brother mariners, 454:11
Restaurant, at Alice's R., 774:5
Reste, j'y suis j'y r., 443:n4
Rested, arms about neck crossed and
　r., 490:12
Restful, for r. death I cry, 221:4
Resting, history knows no r. places,
　752:14
　not a having and r., 500:13
　place for those who gave lives,
　450:2
　true-fixed and r. quality, 188:14
Restless, blown with r. violence,
　204:14
　press r. gigantic, 656:5
　tenacious but r., 665:9
　unfixed in principles, 274:3
Restlessness, great pain and r., 662:10
Restore, thy former light r., 208:10
　to earth and thee r., 580:7
Restored, all losses are r., 220:19
　Chaos is r., 304:2
　civilization could be r., 636:3
　O divinely r., 421:18
Restorer, tired nature's sweet r., 296:6
Restoreth, he r. my soul, 16:17
Restrain, creeds that r., 533:16
　in me cursed thoughts, 213:18
　men from injuring, 344:8
Restraint, acknowledge r. of reverence,
　72:2
　charisma inner determination inner
　r., 590:4
　not silence but r., 664:11
　praise firm r. with which write,
　707:1
　systems of preference or r., 326:9
　what r. to grief for one so dear,
　95:29

Restraint *(continued)*
　wholesome r., 395:7
　Zeus grant grave r., 64:2
Restricted circle of potential, 545:6
Restructuring combines continuity in-
　novation, 763:14
Rests and nodding places, 292:26
　here r. his head, 322:22
　mountain r. on earth, 5:7
Resty sloth finds down pillow hard,
　219:31
Result, cause hidden r. well known,
　101:23
　faith in r. makes r., 546:7
　firm ground of R., 619:10
　happiness, 470:25
　misery, 470:25
　shot at without r., 619:12
Results, sociology science with least r.,
　565:7
　sure of unsatisfying r., 569:17
Resurrection and the life, 40:19
　books symbol of his r., 612:20
　by man came r., 43:20
　foretaste of r., 404:14
　in doubt as to the R., 117:2
　newspaper r. rare, 535:29
　of dry sticks, 724:11
　of the body, 48:25
　of the dead, 43:20
　unto eternal life, 50:8
Resuscitate dead art, 659:4
Retail, God who does wholesale not
　r., 546:16
Retailer of phrases, 291:14
Retain ability to function, 694:17
　enduring as marble to r., 151:23
　marble to r., 402:3
　not r. all rare works, 612:16
Retake, go back and r. Burma, 653:27
Retire, anecdotage sign to r., 435:7
　like guest sated, 90:5
　like satisfied guest, 95:3
　then must art r., 365:13
Retired, happiness of r. nature, 292:21
　Leisure, 252:1
　pale Melancholy sate r., 324:16
　sweet r. solitude, 252:29
Retirement, end of world want to be
　living in r., 626:4
　Plato's r., 261:1
　rural quiet friendship, 308:5
　Sleeping Beauty planning r., 755:6
　urges sweet return, 260:3
Retiring at high speed toward Japa-
　nese, 647:6
　in r. draw hearts after, 260:26
　ne'er feels r. ebb, 207:15
Retort courteous, 192:16
Retreat, friend in my r., 334:18
　honorable r., 191:12
　loopholes of r., 335:4
　my soul's calm r., 270:2
　not r. a single inch, 437:15
Retreated back into money, 694:11
Retreating to the breath, 499:22
　world, 687:5
Retrograde if not advance, 340:8
Retrouvée, l'Éternité r., 565:n13

Revolution (*continued*)
  party of r. civilization, 428:7
  peaceful r., 741:11
  produced Declaration of Independence, 665:13
  scientific r., 704:2
  served r. plowed sea, 395:14
  Sire it is a r., 348:11
  stop r. at beginning, 706:13
  suppression impossible without r., 610:4
  to establish dictatorship, 711:18
  tremble at communist r., 482:7
  true r. would succeed, 663:9
  you say you want a r., 770:13
Revolutionaries, mad r. will run in streets, 715:8
Revolutionary, atomic energy r. force, 655:7
  bourgeoisie historically r., 482:1
  either r. or not, 769:6
  higher ideals r., 546:10
  if not r. be artist, 769:6
  in r. times, 679:3
  parsons preaching Jesus a r., 752:10
  proletariat alone r., 482:3
  reconstitution of society, 481:15
  right to overthrow, 449:4
Revolutionary-democratic, establishment of r. dictatorship, 609:20
Revolution's victory over tsarism, 609:20
Revolutions, collapse of r. of 1848, 587:16
  in r. great interests at stake, 78:25
  never go backward, 462:21
  not made they come, 462:15
  put half of France in mourning, 436:24
  state which creates r., 78:24
Revolve it all slowly, 762:16
Revolving, grief with r. year, 408:18
  in course of one r. moon, 274:11
Reward according to his works, 45:30
  all for love nothing for r., 153:10
  angling r. to itself, 245:17
  good evil r. punishment, 277:11
  great Master urgent, 115:16
  if thou not thine own r., 245:n2
  labor not ask for r., 139:3
  neither have they any more a r., 24:18
  no r. offered, 419:4
  of knowing we do Thy will, 139:3
  of labor is life, 523:11
  of thing to have done it, 432:21
  of virtue is virtue, 432:3
  rather than punishment, 424:4
  virtue is her own r., 245:n2
Rewarded, abilities below mediocrity r., 385:15
  evil for good, 8:10
  for that which ye have done, 117:13
  they shall be greatly r., 30:23
Rewarder, who now will be my r., 272:30
Rewardeth evil for good, 21:35
Rewards and fairies, 238:1
  and punishments in cards, 680:17
  fortune's buffets and r., 197:3

Rewards (*continued*)
  religion of which r. distant, 314:18
Rewrite, don't r. what moving finger writ, 710:3
Rex, ego sum r., 269:n9
  quondam rexque futurus, 133:18
Rhadamanthys, fair-haired R., 53:8
Rhapsody in blue, 699:12
  of words, 197:29
Rhein, die Wacht am R., 488:n1
Rhetoric able to contend, 160:10
  for r. he could not ope, 262:21
  heavenly r. of thine eye, 168:34
  obscure by aimless r., 505:20
  of rule of Plato, 254:21
Rhetorician, grammarian r. geometrician, 108:21
  sophisticated r., 435:16
Rhetorician's rules, 262:22
Rheumatics, unless down with r., 84:15
Rhine frontier of England, 601:18
  watch along the R., 488:2
  wide and winding R., 400:1
Rhinoceros, armed r., 215:7
Rhodes, Colossus of R., 782:7
Rhodora, fresh R. in woods, 429:14
Rhone, arrowy R., 400:3
Rhyme, beauty making beautiful old r., 221:22
  into ladies' favors, 186:3
  it hath taught me to r., 168:33
  lofty r., 253:15
  many a mused r., 415:16
  more sweetly than r., 415:20
  nor reason, 154:17
  outlive this powerful r., 220:25
  rudder of verses, 263:10
  Runic r., 453:11
  tired of Love more tired of R., 609:6
  unattempted yet in prose or r., 255:19
Rhymed dogerel, 132:2
Rhymes, Namby Pamby's little r., 298:1
  no r. in my verse, 604:15
  regent of love-r., 168:28
  suggest freedom, 430:15
  that r. with P, 710:11
Rhyming, bad r. a disease, 303:12
  planet, 187:12
Rhythm essential in painting, 120:13
  I got r., 695:4
  in all thought, 380:24
  keeping r. in dancing, 670:21
  one of principal translators, 665:20
  poor as dirt don't get r., 766:8
  to world of sound what light is, 665:20
Rhythmical creation of Beauty, 453:14
Rhythms measureless and wild, 68:17
  we tap crude r. for bears, 496:6
Rialto, what news on R., 180:2
Rib, smote him under the fifth r., 12:3
  which Lord God had taken, 6:16
Riband in cap of youth, 198:25
  to stick in coat, 464:22
Ribbed sea sand, 381:18
Ribbon, a R. at a time, 512:3

Ribbon (*continued*)
  in cap of youth, 198:25
  road r. of moonlight, 643:11
  round it, 791:16
Ribs, he took one of his r., 6:16
  heart knock at my r., 212:23
  of Death, 253:5
Rice, not stir r. though it sticks, 151:8
  same old r., 580:14
  with coarse r. to eat, 61:10
Rich, abundance of the r., 24:4
  America in which people still get r., 730:15
  and poor all as one, 68:23
  are different from you and me, 694:14
  as easy to marry r. woman, 463:15
  attire creeps rustling, 415:5
  beauty too r. for use, 174:23
  better live r. than die r., 317:9
  beyond dreams of avarice, 317:22, 319:1
  blow bugles over r. dead, 663:5
  cannot save few who are r., 741:4
  choose likely man in preference to r., 62:27
  company of just men better than r. estate, 69:6
  dies r. dies disgraced, 525:15
  difference between r. and other people, 702:n2
  different from you and me, 702:3
  dull and drank, 702:3
  few are r. and wellborn, 355:1
  flames and hired tears, 248:26
  folk ride on camels, 469:42
  freedom to r. or poor, 685:10
  get rich, 661:15
  gifts wax poor, 196:12
  gout kills more r. than poor, 271:17
  greater part of r. people, 326:4
  had I interfered for r., 424:4
  have more money, 702:n2
  have power and poor deprived, 75:23
  high and low r. and poor, 369:12
  honesty dwells like miser, 192:15
  if r. gets foolish, 603:9
  if r. whenever you please, 77:4
  in good works, 45:24
  in loss of all I sing, 757:13
  in poverty, 151:25
  in things he can let alone, 478:15
  is better, 656:2
  jewel in Ethiop's ear, 174:23
  joys fall not to r. alone, 97:16
  knowledge a r. storehouse, 158:6
  labor not to be r., 22:17
  law forbids r. as well as poor, 550:13
  laws broken by mighty and r., 56:2
  let him be r. and weary, 243:20
  live and die r-r-r., 471:22
  live like a wretch and die r., 234:24
  make r. richer, 369:11
  maketh haste to be r., 23:6
  man beginning to fall, 31:33
  man enther Hiven, 603:5
  man not glory in riches, 28:23
  man to enter into kingdom, 35:37

Ridiculous (*continued*)

bitter poverty makes men r., 108:22
contemptible animal, 312:6
display, 609:5
don't make me r., 387:15
engagement to marry r., 426:7
errors in philosophy r., 318:10
excess, 170:9
from sublime to r., 370:9
made arms r., 261:10
make my enemies r., 306:22
mouse will be brought forth, 98:10
no spectacle so r., 424:23
nothing so r. but philosopher said
  it, 87:27
pomp of emperors r., 431:1
sublime borders on r., 341:11
waste sad time, 670:18

Riding, cowpuncher a-r. along, 786:1
down by Eildon Tree, 785:11
eyes through your side, 701:7
fate of nation r., 442:14
highwayman came r., 643:11
in his r. of rolling level, 550:20
in taxi between tall buildings,
  694:15
man goes r. by, 561:9
near her highest noon, 252:3
o'er azure realm, 323:8
put on pistols went r., 674:14
to and from wife, 703:9
upon an ass, 30:3
went my love r., 688:6

Riding's a joy, 465:20

Ridley, play the man Master R.,
  138:18

Rien appris ni rien oublié, 354:n3
au monde ne dure, 240:n1
de plus, 336:n4
milieu entre r. et tout, 270:n3
ne réussit comme le succès, 427:n2

Rifle, no better companion than r.,
  503:6
not put loaded r. on stage, 582:10

Rifles' rapid rattle, 687:2

Rift, every r. of subject, 418:19
within lute, 459:10

Rigged with curses dark, 253:22

Riggish, bless her when she is r.,
  217:15

Right against unreasonable searches
  and seizures, 346:13
all's r. with the world, 464:4
almost-r. word and r. word, 527:2
always do r., 528:3
are and of r. ought to be, 336:11
as a trivet, 469:4
aspirations, 65:1
be sure r. go ahead, 398:4
born to set it r., 195:6
cannon to r., 458:13
chiefly with the strong, 280:17
child of my r. hand, 232:10
common r. of humanity, 448:11
conduct, 65:1
conduct r. argument wrong, 330:11
constitutional r. of amending, 449:4
contemplation, 65:1
dead right as sped along, 783:n9
deed for wrong reason, 670:10

Right (*continued*)

defend r. to say it, 307:4
did that which was r. in his own
  eyes, 11:22
Divine of Kings, 303:31
divine r. of kings, 448:11
do great r. do little wrong, 181:20
dwelling much on r., 280:17
effort, 65:1
every single one is r., 592:8
firmness in the r., 450:11
fool now and then r., 334:9
frightening when convinced they are
  r., 719:16
give Rus r. of way, 446:27
God defend the r., 163:22
great Power make me do r., 505:10
hand forget her cunning, 20:6
hand is become glorious, 9:4
hand offend thee, 33:5
hands of fellowship, 44:14
he who maintains he's r., 350:18
his life was in the r., 267:12
how forcible are r. words, 14:6
idea of the gods, 76:16
if thy r. eye offend, 33:5
in r. with two or three, 484:21
it must be r., 353:16
judge judges wrong, 66:8
kind of victory, 655:19
know not whether laws r., 567:21
length of days in her r. hand, 20:20
little island, 377:15
livelihood, 65:1
makes might, 448:15
man more r. than neighbors, 477:12
may country be always r., 368:14
may she always be r., 390:22
men should be r. by instinct, 66:17
might is r., 123:5
mindfulness, 65:1
minority always r., 508:9
more than half people r., 703:14
most valued by civilized, 568:16
my mind's not r., 743:6
my r. and my privilege, 771:11
my r. none to dispute, 334:19
natural r. to use pens, 306:18
no r. consume happiness, 570:15
no r. to bliss, 497:20
no r. to open door, 74:19
not law so much as r., 477:8
not leave r. to chance, 477:10
not leave r. to majority, 477:10
obedience to law r. not favor, 576:3
obtain r. to vote, 751:7
of conquest, 319:7
of laborer to savings, 525:12
of millionaire to millions, 525:12
of people to assemble, 346:11
of trial by jury, 346:16
of way, 783:22
on r. hand of God, 48:25
original r. of the people, 345:16
our country r. or wrong, 390:22,
  510:18
people have r. to knowledge, 337:13
people have r. to rise up, 448:3
people in right jobs, 474:17
perhaps r. to dissemble love, 360:6

Right (*continued*)

praise and true perfection, 182:12
procure advancement of r., 337:10
rather be r. than President, 389:17
rather wrong with Plato than r.
  with these, 87:28
reader of good poem, 625:7
red r. hand, 257:3
revolutionary r. to overthrow, 449:4
rule of r. and wrong, 510:8
rule of r. fitness of things, 311:24
sacred r. of elective franchise, 475:6
Scylla guards r. side, 181:n2
simply does what is r., 79:22
sparkle r. Promethean fire, 169:4
speech, 65:1
speech after silence r., 598:23
struggle between r. and wrong,
  448:11
Stuff, 764:5
that which they will is r., 535:11
think at your age r., 517:9
those who died with thee for r.,
  615:1
though r. worsted, 468:17
thy r. hand shall hold me, 20:8
to be free from governmental intrusion, 719:5
to be let alone, 568:16
to be r. is art of arts, 545:8
to keep and bear arms, 346:12
to make alter constitutions, 337:4
to means requisite, 355:6
to remain silent, 682:10
to say what one pleases, 661:8
to speedy and public trial, 346:15
to strike, 614:16
to vote denied, 491:25
to vote not denied on account of
  sex, 346:20
to vote not denied or abridged,
  346:19, 346:20
transforms strength into r., 319:6
true end of love, 230:9
views, 65:1
wars for r. thing, 655:19
what is r. he will follow, 61:4
what thy r. hand doeth, 33:11
whatever is is r., 301:12
what's r. and fair, 501:20
when r. man rings them, 561:24
when r. to be kept r., 510:18
wrong follow King, 459:7
yer a' r. that's a', 609:17
you are, 604:3

Righteous are bold as a lion, 23:5
armor of r. cause, 582:2
be not r. over much, 24:11
company of just and r., 69:6
die the death of the r., 10:5
flourish like palm, 18:17
have not seen the r. forsaken, 17:1
I am not come to call r., 34:22
judgments of Lord r., 16:11, 450:11
let him be r. still, 48:3
man regardeth the life of his beast,
  21:12
man to make fall, 153:8
nation which keepeth the truth,
  26:28

Righteous (*continued*)
    prayer of r. man, 46:18
    sold the r. for silver, 29:34
    souls of the r. are in hand of God,
       30:23
    where were the r. cut off, 13:37
Righteousness and peace have kissed,
    18:8
    as waves of sea, 27:28
    exalteth a nation, 21:23
    force of r., 606:13
    found in the way of r., 21:32
    he looked for r., 25:38
    his straight path, 79:17
    hunger and thirst after r., 33:1
    in view of gain thinks of r., 61:22
    is man's path, 79:28
    king shall reign in r., 27:5
    leadeth me in paths of r., 16:17
    not infused from without, 79:27
    not r. to outrage man dead, 65:15
    three laws of r., 63:2
    wrath worketh not r., 46:7
    wrongdoing and r. of men, 54:6
Righteousness', persecuted for r. sake,
    33:1
Righteousnesses are as filthy rags,
    28:8
Rightful, tenacious of purpose in r.
    cause, 96:15
Rightly to be great, 198:14
Rights, at war with r. of mankind,
    343:16
    become accumulated wrong, 589:1
    Bill of R. into suicide pact, 683:4
    black man within his r., 755:9
    certain unalienable r., 343:2
    civil r. citizens equal, 520:10
    equal in r. and in cultivation, 440:5
    essential unalienable r., 343:*n*2
    fighting for human r., 755:8
    fundamental human r., 655:23
    God-given r., 437:18
    halve r. double duties, 404:11
    individual given equality of r., 648:4
    inextinguishable r. of human nature,
       368:15
    inherent in human being, 437:18
    inherent r., 327:1
    make real the Bill of R., 627:21
    man's idea of sexual r., 475:8
    never exceed your r., 319:3
    no more suffering or denial of r.,
       745:22
    of children not respected, 662:13
    of Englishman, 345:13
    of existing non-Jewish communities,
       556:2
    of laboring man, 544:8
    of man, 332:9
    partisan cares nothing about r.,
       75:1
    people with r. in hands, 437:19
    preserve entire r., 345:15
    public good and private r., 352:1
    refuses to defend r., 369:8
    reparation for r. at home, 313:5
    slow undoing of human r., 741:3
    talked long enough about equal r.,
       723:16

Rights (*continued*)
    time does not relinquish its r.,
       349:26
    wilderness bill of r., 699:1
    women have as much r. as man,
       421:1
    word man defines all r., 564:12
Rightwise king of England, 133:4
Rigid, man of r. morals, 281:23
Rigor, my r. relents, 331:10
    of the game, 387:26
Rigorous teachers seized my youth,
    498:19
Riley, life of R., 781:*n*1
Rill, moon on Monan's r., 378:17
Rim, beyond utmost purple r., 456:2
    sun over mountain's r., 465:2
    sun's r. dips, 381:14
Rima wild solitary girl, 543:16
Rime, beauty making beautiful old r.,
    221:22
    into ladies' favors, 186:3
    it hath taught me to r., 168:33
    outlive this powerful r., 220:25
    was on the spray, 539:8
Rimes, regent of love-r., 168:28
Riming planet, 187:12
Rimini miminy piminy, 530:1
Rimless floods, 701:1
Ring at end of nose, 472:1
    at last r. to even-song, 142:23
    becomes thin by wearing, 89:8
    bells of Heaven, 611:18
    bright the r. of words, 561:24
    circle of wedding r., 291:25
    cloudy flaming opal r., 594:12
    curfew not r. tonight, 562:11
    dance in r. and suppose, 624:16
    impression as from seal of r., 76:11
    let freedom r., 444:3
    maids dance in a r., 226:20
    my r. encompasseth thy finger,
       165:23
    O bells, 491:1
    of pure and endless light, 270:7
    one R. to rule, one R. to find them,
       685:4
    only pretty r. time, 192:12
    out the old, 457:29
    out wild bells, 457:28
    out your bells, 155:27
    the r. so worn, 353:19
    what shall we do for r., 472:1
    when we let freedom r., 761:3
    with importunate chink, 332:18
    with this r. I thee wed, 50:5
    woods answer and Echo r., 154:12
Ring-a-rosie, tots sang R., 585:7
Ringed with azure world, 458:4
Ringing grooves of change, 455:25
    just like r. a bell, 756:16
    plains of Troy, 455:1
Rings, tumbling in twenty r., 611:20
    when right man r. them, 561:24
Rinky-dink, sweet r. voice, 753:3
Rio, rolling down to R., 593:10
Riot, purple r., 415:3
    spent waves' r., 534:12
    woods in r., 579:7

Rioting, not in r. and drunkenness,
    42:23
Riotous living, 38:35
Riotously, flung roses r., 602:8
Ripe and good scholar, 226:6
    cherry r. I cry, 241:1
    Crops are r., 617:3
    field of r. corn, 667:23
    from hour to hour we r., 190:23
    hour r., 184:12
    once let r. moment go, 357:21
    trap moment before it's r., 357:21
    what shelter to grow r., 498:6
Ripeness is all, 211:12
Ripening, his greatness is a-r., 225:16
    summer's r. breath, 175:10
Riper, amuse his r. stage, 301:15
Ripest fruit first falls, 171:12
    fruit of all, 161:21
    peach highest, 558:12
Ripped, from mother's womb un-
    timely r., 216:19
Ripple of rain, 533:8
Rippling, folds r. in breeze, 463:5
Rip-tooth of sky's acetylene, 701:3
Rire de tout, 336:*n*3
    est le propre de l'homme, 139:*n*8
Rise alone and drink more, 397:20
    and fight again, 785:*n*1
    and shine give God glory, 794:16
    and walk with him, 67:26
    at six dine at ten, 428:6
    by sin, 203:30
    caused himself to r., 302:11
    constellations when they r., 63:9
    created half to r., 301:13
    early to r., 309:17, 690:12
    evening is come r. up, 91:7
    expectation r., 328:4
    foul deeds will r., 193:25
    happy those whose walls already r.,
       93:20
    I caused sun to r., 606:1
    in heaven's lightland, 5:2
    in the heart, 456:13
    joyful all ye nations r., 312:17
    kings r. and set, 408:9
    light to r. by and I r., 467:30
    like fountain for me, 459:27
    like Lions after slumber, 408:2
    maketh sun r. on evil and good,
       33:9
    move stones of Rome to r., 189:11
    my Shakespeare r., 232:18
    not r. early never do good, 314:29
    out of ash I r., 764:13
    out of wreck r., 468:13
    people have right to r. up, 448:3
    stoop to, 238:5
    sun sets to r. again, 468:12
    suns that set may r. again, 232:4
    then we shall r., 242:1
    though war should r. against me,
       16:22
    till we are called to r., 513:18
    to feet as He passes by, 591:14
    to r. love stoops, 467:12
    tomorrow's sun may never r.,
       291:17
    truth crushed will r. again, 411:10

Rise (*continued*)
  up at the voice of the bird, 24:27
  up my love, 25:6
  up so early in morn, 780:6
  we die and r. the same, 228:15
  we fall to r., 468:17
  what are you when sun shall r., 227:9
  why r. because 'tis light, 229:4
  wilt thou therefore r. from me, 229:4
  with lark, 155:13
  woe unto them that r. up early, 25:39
Risen, Christ r. from dead, 43:20
  Christ the Lord r. today, 312:13
  He is r., 37:35
  he is r., 48:14
  Jesus Christ r. today, 285:5
  Lord is r. indeed, 39:28
  the Lord is r., 48:14
  there is a people r., 271:15
Riser, dawn comes no sooner for early r., 794:5
Rises from prayer better man, 508:20
  hidden laughter, 670:18
  hooray up she r., 793:11
  howls hoo and r., 639:23
  my gorge r. at it, 199:8
  soul that r. with us, 375:7
  sun gives light soon as he r., 310:25
  unspeakable desire, 498:4
Riseth from feast with keen appetite, 180:19
  late trot all day, 309:27
  with fleas, 244:23
Rising, beating way for r. sun, 708:3
  before the r. sun, 294:15
  every land rejoices at his r., 5:1
  fogs prevail upon day, 274:26
  from r. of the sun unto going down, 19:15
  I see them r., 647:22
  let others hail r. sun, 323:17
  listen the wind is r., 660:12
  more worship r. than setting sun, 88:14
  of the sun, 778:9
  plat of r. ground, 252:4
  Proteus r. from sea, 376:12
  revolution of r. expectations, 745:2
  shadow r. to meet you, 668:18
  through change and storm, 405:13
  warm cheek and r. bosom, 323:1
  wind is r., 613:17
Risk, art unthinkable without r., 679:16
  conquer without r., 249:9
  flatterer r. everything, 290:25
  I had to take and took, 624:19
  of reigns of terror, 493:5
  t'other half for freedom, 485:7
Risking, not giving life but r. life, 722:8
  only by r. we live, 546:7
Risks, great deeds wrought at great r., 70:10
Rites, performed r. simple decisive, 756:12
Rival, cannot r. for one hour, 515:2

Rival (*continued*)
  know I may not r. him, 689:18
  remains to r. what they have done, 72:7
Rivalry of aim, 535:27
Rivals are the worst, 287:4
  jealousy of r. near throne, 347:5
Rivalship of wisest men, 293:17
River, Alph the sacred r., 382:19
  among r. sallows, 416:15
  at my garden's end, 302:23
  can't sleep with the r. forever, 774:11
  cross r. rest under trees, 504:10
  down in reeds by r., 439:8
  drifting down r., 526:20
  Eliza across r., 463:1
  glideth at own sweet will, 374:13
  great r. take me to main, 456:19
  in the ocean, 439:10
  lake glimmering pool, 503:4
  let me love r. and woodland, 92:29
  Lethe the r. of oblivion, 257:15
  like foam on r., 378:22
  like snow falls in r., 363:6
  lived on R. Dee, 338:18
  met character on r., 526:14
  monstrous big r. down there, 526:23
  not step twice into same r., 62:n2
  Oceanus the ocean r., 721:13
  of crystal light, 559:20
  of oblivion, 257:15
  Ol' Man R., 692:5
  on a tree by a r., 531:9
  one more r. to cross, 794:19
  over r. through wood, 427:7
  passage over the r., 490:4
  peace as a r., 27:28
  pilot cares about nothing but r., 526:11
  see one r. and see all, 234:30
  she's fading down r., 586:14
  spreadeth out her roots by the r., 28:29
  strong brown god, 671:12
  swap horses crossing r., 450:5
  Thames noblest r., 293:7
  there is a r., 17:17
  time a r. of strong current, 111:10
  time r. without banks, 783:18
  tirra lirra by r., 454:15
  water of r. never the same, 122:16
  way-hay you rolling r., 793:12
  weariest r., 534:15
  where brook and r. meet, 441:7
River City gonna have Boys Band, 710:12
  trouble here in R., 710:11
Rivering, beside r. waters of, 647:20
Riverrun past Eve and Adam's, 647:18
Rivers, as brooks make r., 276:23
  as long as r. flow, 787:17
  as long as r. shall run, 93:24
  at their source, 660:16
  by shallow r. birds sing, 162:3
  by the r. of Babylon, 20:6
  deepest r. least sound, 152:n7
  drain pent-up r. of myself, 490:1
  fire r. cannot quench, 164:29

Rivers (*continued*)
  I've known r., 708:12
  my soul deep like r., 708:12
  no r. no wells no springs, 705:16
  not step twice into same r., 62:14
  of water in a dry place, 27:6
  rains return in r., 721:13
  run into the sea, 23:23
  run to seas, 276:23
  shallow brooks and r. wide, 251:14
  tree planted by r., 15:29
Rivets, busy hammers closing r., 185:14
Rivulet, neat r. of text, 352:27
Rivulets hurrying through lawn, 456:22
  meadow r. overflow, 540:25
Road, 'ammer along 'ard 'igh r., 554:17
  backward glances over traveled r., 491:17
  broad hard-beaten r., 430:22
  but one r. leads to Corinth, 97:n9
  butterfly upon r., 590:19
  by r. his ever-open door, 51:n6
  come to fork in r. take it, 754:15
  dark r. whence no one returns, 90:17
  divils in twists of r., 613:9
  free as the r., 243:16
  from Montgomery, 761:5
  heaven above r. below, 561:21
  help me down Cemetery R., 750:12
  high r. to England, 315:25
  house by side of r., 51:22, 574:14
  if r. could not make it out, 616:8
  I'm ten years burning down the r., 774:13
  is smooth, 54:24
  lonesome r., 381:26
  matrimony r. to wealth, 475:13
  no r. or ready way to virtue, 248:16
  no royal r. to geometry, 82:5
  of excess leads to palace of wisdom, 357:3
  open r., 561:22
  poor slaves tread, 408:13
  rail pig lead, 634:1
  ribbon of moonlight, 643:11
  right r. to Ireland, 709:5
  rough r. leads to greatness, 102:29
  royal r. to Thebes, 716:15
  smooth r. of life, 321:1
  straggling r. in Spain, 619:3
  take to open r., 490:3
  takes no private r., 302:1
  to City of Emeralds, 568:10
  to Hades easy to travel, 82:8
  to Hell gradual, 700:1
  to resolution, 242:11
  to stars through atom, 646:8
  Tobacco R., 710:14
  up and down City R., 780:13
  up and road down one and same, 62:17
  virtue demands thorny r., 146:2
  when find r. narrow, 122:10
  which leads to peace, 344:9
  will be less tedious, 92:17
  winding r. before me, 390:15

Road (*continued*)
  with bread and wine walk r., 793:25
  ye'll take the high r., 779:21
Roads, crooked r. are r. of genius, 357:11
  how many r. man walk down, 771:4
  improvement makes straight r., 357:11
  lie with nothing to use them, 726:4
  old r. return to sky some color, 769:17
  open when you rise, 5:5
  two r. diverged, 623:7
Roadway, cry of child by r., 595:5
Roam, absent from Him I r., 377:17
  all morning sends to r., 579:22
  dunce sent to r., 334:8
  ever let fancy r., 416:10
  ev'rywhere I r., 507:1
  home where buffalo r., 786:11
  long wont to r., 451:12
  not their hearts that r., 592:18
  soar but never r., 377:12
  though we may r., 405:14
  where'er I r., 328:7
  wish to r. farther, 350:29
Roamed, how sweet I r., 355:17
  with my Soul, 453:3
Roamin' in the gloamin', 609:18
Roaming, ceaseless thoughts of r., 282:11
  mistress mine where r., 201:30
Roar, grating r. of pebbles, 499:20
  grievous r., 385:8
  hiss now becoming r., 675:3
  melancholy long withdrawing r., 499:22
  men want ocean without r., 480:16
  music in its r., 400:29
  of only beast in arena, 602:5
  other side of silence, 483:27
  set table on a r., 199:8
  swinging low with sullen r., 252:4
  think lion sleeping because he didn't r., 364:12
  thundering cannons r., 330:6
  welkin r., 183:34
  you as any nightingale, 172:28
  you gently as sucking dove, 172:28
  young lions r. after prey, 19:6
Roared, cracked growled r. howled, 381:4
  Declamation r., 313:12
  Homer and Whitman r., 607:11
  well r. Lion, 174:8
Roaring, devil as r. lion, 46:28
  empty tigers or r. sea, 176:13
  with hollow blasts, 297:1
  words of my r., 16:15
Roars it through the hall, 503:2
Roast beef of England, 311:12
  in hell r. you like herrin, 363:11
  rules the r., 135:*n*4
  set house on fire to r. eggs, 159:25
  with fire, 8:37
Roasted crabs hiss in bowl, 169:14
  very likeness of r. crab, 173:2

Roasts, newspaper buries dead r. thim aftherward, 603:12
Rob, if writer r. mother, 697:2
  jaybird don't r. own nes', 556:12
  lady by marriage, 311:28
  neighbor he promised to defend, 425:11
  not the poor, 22:13
  Peter pay Paul, 141:27
  rich r. poor, 421:2
  starve ere I'll r. further, 177:13
  words r. Hybla bees, 189:22
Robbed, he's not r. at all, 207:7
  not wanting what stolen, 207:7
  that smiles, 205:31
  we wuz r., 695:15
Robber, Barabbas a r., 40:37
Robbers, the more r. there will be, 57:18
  what makes r. bold but lenity, 164:18
Robbing, live by sharping and r., 310:24
  think little of r., 397:18
Robe, giant's r., 216:6
  intertissued r. of gold, 185:19
  judge's r., 204:1
  sa r. de poupre au soleil, 144:*n*4
Robert, believe R. who has tried it, 94:*n*13
Robes and furred gowns, 211:4
  garland and singing r., 254:12
  loosely flowing, 232:6
  mountain in azure hue, 388:22
  riche or fithele, 129:21
  sky-r. spun of Iris' woof, 252:17
  washed r. in blood, 47:23
Robespierre sea-green Incorruptible, 412:20
Robin, call for r. redbreast, 237:13
  fainting R., 513:10
  redbreast in a cage, 359:6
  redbreast piously, 776:2
  what will poor r. do., 790:17
  who killed Cock R., 789:1
Robin Hood, old wives' tales of R., 602:*n*1
Robinson Crusoe, 286:3, 319:16
Robot, waited upon by r. slaves, 691:5
Robots, Rossum's Universal R., 677:13
Robs me of that which not enriches him, 206:30
Robust, debate on public issues r., 719:4
Robustious periwig-pated fellow, 196:21
Rock, all on a r. reclined, 297:1
  cradle will r., 555:4
  crag of the r., 15:18
  dwell on r. or in cell, 152:18
  eagle dwelleth on r., 15:18
  eagle of the r., 660:15
  founded upon r., 34:14
  he is the R., 10:26
  he only is my r., 17:33
  it is the Inchcape R., 386:11
  knew the perilous r., 386:10
  laws are sand customs r., 528:5

Rock (*continued*)
  lean upon death as on r., 663:15
  living as black r. star, 757:10
  Lord is my r., 12:15
  Moses in Horeb struck r., 748:9
  Moses smote r. twice, 10:2
  no water only r., 669:4
  of Ages, 342:3
  of offense, 26:6
  of our salvation, 18:19
  poetry old as r., 430:18
  sails well but strike r., 360:7
  shadow under red r., 668:18
  shadows of a great r. in a weary land, 27:6
  small r. holds back great wave, 53:5
  takes on appearance of nearby r., 59:23
  that is higher than I, 17:32
  the tall r. the mountain, 373:4
  this r. shall fly, 378:24
  towered citadel pendant r., 218:3
  upon this r. I will build, 35:28
  way of a serpent upon a r., 23:15
  which Hercules bequeathed, 539:3
  will split, 657:9
Rock-a-bye-baby, 555:4
Rock and roll, not tell Vietnam from r. veterans, 770:5
  which go first r. or Christianity, 770:6
Rockbound, stern and r. coast, 410:11
Rocked in cradle of deep, 398:13
Rocket, life like r. flies, 766:3
Rockets, once r. are up, 759:6
Rockets' red glare, 391:2
Rockies, applies west of R., 748:10
  ghost train in R. buried in snow, 756:18
Rocking, cradle endlessly r., 490:8
  in your r. chair by window, 611:12
Rock-ribbed, hills r., 411:3
Rocks and stones and trees, 374:1
  cries of cicadas sink into r., 282:12
  even among these r., 669:21
  hand that r. cradle, 488:8
  nor can sap be in r., 90:2
  older than r., 538:6
  over r. wood and water, 426:15
  seas laugh when r. near, 237:15
  soften r. or bend oak, 291:7
  Soundings quicksands r., 418:7
  that are steepest, 777:11
  the r. rent, 37:13
  trees wind, 477:7
  walled round with r., 535:5
  what gray r., 669:22
  whereon greatest men wrecked, 260:28
Rocky shore beats back siege, 171:10
Rod, a chief a r., 301:18
  Aaron's r., 8:32
  and blows not much good, 138:6
  cast thy r. before Pharaoh, 8:31
  creed is a r., 534:20
  he that spareth his r., 21:17
  Jonathan put forth the r., 11:35
  not pious longer than r., 138:6
  of empire, 322:11
  of iron, 47:10

Rudge, like Barnaby R., 485:8
Rudis indigestaque moles, 101:*n*13
Rudyards cease from Kipling, 580:17
Rue, nought shall make us r., 170:24
  rosemary and r., 223:5
  sold for endless r., 578:23
  wear r. with a difference, 198:24
  with r. heart laden, 579:12
Rued, day I had r., 623:15
Ruerent, cur imbres r., 103:*n*11
Ruffian, father r., 177:30
Ruffles, giving pair of laced r., 287:1
  like sending them r., 330:15
Rufus, Curtius R. descended from
    himself, 76:*n*1
Rug, snug as bug in r., 310:16
Rugged and without a beach, 280:16
  cadence of a r. line, 274:28
  individualism, 625:20
  old r. cross, 616:2
  Russian bear, 215:7
Ruh', meine R. ist hin, 350:*n*6
Ruin and combustion, 255:22
  around the dear r., 391:13
  bad herdsmen r. flocks, 54:3
  decay in House on Hill, 608:2
  dyspepsy r. of most things, 397:17
  exaltation from disaster and r.,
    619:13
  final R. fiercely drives, 296:20
  formless r. of oblivion, 201:11
  he stared at r. r. stared back, 735:2
  he that tastes woman r. meets,
    297:19
  here meets rain wind r., 705:21
  I'll r. you, 411:11
  in r. and confusion hurled, 292:3
  into r. hurled, 301:5
  majestic though in r., 257:7
  man marks earth with r., 400:30
  my country's r., 284:5
  new years r. and rend, 534:4
  notice r. in things, 739:1
  of our sex, 325:1
  pens of diplomats not r., 342:12
  predicts r. of the state, 359:7
  princes and their r., 225:16
  rather than preservation, 136:14
  science without conscience r. of
    soul, 139:13
  seize thee ruthless King, 323:6
  serve my nation r. another, 304:12
  since roving's been my r., 793:13
  spreading r. scattering ban, 439:8
  that was my r., 350:20
  that's romantic, 531:10
  upon ruin rout on rout, 257:21
  when truth entails r., 67:13
  whom God to r. has designed,
    69:*n*11
Ruined, archangel r., 256:15
  bare r. choirs, 221:8
  by amateurs, 666:1
  love when built anew, 222:5
  me and I am re-begot, 229:9
  men that are r., 332:25
  millionaire, 671:7
  no nation r. by trade, 310:22
  spend wealth at once you are r.,
    422:10

Ruined (*continued*)
  threshold of r. tenement, 312:19
  to be r. man a vocation, 672:22
Ruinous, all r. disorders, 209:2
Ruin's, stern R. plowshare, 361:20
Ruins, fragments shored against r.,
    669:7
  Germany r. culture, 553:9
  in r. rather than enslaved, 620:9
  man is a god in r., 431:3
  musing amidst r. of Capitol, 340:16
  of another's fame, 297:11
  of St. Paul's, 323:23, 425:7
  of the noblest man, 188:22
  the very r. destroyed, 106:3
  winter's rains and r., 533:9
Rule, a little r. a little sway, 307:14
  authors established it as r., 292:26
  bring world under r., 597:13
  Britannia, 308:12
  but one r. to be clear, 396:18
  by r. in nature teach, 184:23
  capable of r. if he had not ruled,
    109:17
  circumstances r. men, 70:9
  divide and r., 118:29
  done by the r., 217:16
  employ mind to r., 91:20
  exception proves r., 234:*n*8
  from tomb, 670:9
  given by Christ, 510:8
  Golden R., 34:*n*1
  golden r. is no golden rules, 571:7
  golden r. will fit everybody, 523:9
  government free where laws r.,
    282:18
  gran'ther's r. safer, 485:17
  his own house, 45:12
  Homer's r. best, 302:22
  ill can he r. the great, 153:21
  my heart, 426:21
  never look into newspaper, 352:33
  new r. from tonight, 581:20
  no r. admits not exception, 234:17
  of joy and duty one, 542:11
  of right, 311:24
  of right and wrong, 510:8
  of three puzzle me, 776:9
  one Ring to r. them all, 685:4
  over all the departed dead, 53:25
  people put up with oppressive r.,
    438:13
  people turn to benevolent r., 79:16
  reason to r., 275:15
  rich men r. the law, 328:16
  ruin or r. state, 274:6
  sage Homer's r. best, 302:22
  should r. who r. best, 78:19
  the rost, 135:*n*4
  them with rod of iron, 47:10
  thoughts r. world, 433:18
  too fond to r. alone, 302:11
  under law your proper skill, 94:15
  under this roof, 338:13
  wel thyself, 132:9
  what is pomp r. reign, 164:31
  will show the man, 55:14
Ruled as he thought fit, 246:3
  genius for not being r., 426:11
  great men can't be r., 717:10

Ruled (*continued*)
  man willingly r. ruleth safely,
    132:16
  roast, 395:23
  with little understanding world r.,
    139:1
Ruler, convention is r. of all, 64:15
  having human body as subject, 75:5
  let there be one r., 51:7
  no guide overseer or r., 20:27
  no longer r. of own spirit, 368:16
  of Queen's Navee, 529:6
  of the waters, 400:11
  soul the r. of life, 91:28
  takes non-action as his way, 86:16
  Winter r. of inverted year, 335:5
Rulers in all lands, 563:7
  knowledge of characters and con-
    duct of r., 337:13
  law for r. and people, 474:21
  multitude of r., 51:7
  of the darkness, 44:28
  persuade if possible the r., 75:11
Rules community evolved, 626:16
  gods have their own r., 101:26
  love r. the gods, 67:1
  never shows she r., 300:18
  of game laws of Nature, 505:6
  of propriety, 62:5
  pretenses to break r. by, 247:3
  rhetorician's r., 262:22
  rocks cradle r. world, 488:8
  threw you in told you r., 701:16
  where love r. no will to power,
    629:6
Ruleth all the roost, 135:18
  he that r. his spirit, 21:32
Ruling ideas of age, 482:6
  ideas of r. class, 482:6
  passion, 300:23
  various r. passions find, 300:16
Rum and true religion, 402:16
  curriculum was r., 589:4
  influence of adulterated r., 535:9
  Romanism Rebellion, 468:18
  yo-ho-ho and bottle of r., 561:1
Rumble of distant Drum, 445:10
Rumbling, wild dark times r. toward
    us, 420:9
Ruminate, as thou dost r., 206:29
Ruminating, learn from kine r.,
    552:10
Rumination, by often r., 191:26
Rumor flies, 93:38
  history distillation of r., 412:18
  in place of inquiry, 615:5
  is a pipe, 183:9
  of oppression and deceit, 334:26
  suspicion r. fantasy, 762:2
Rumors, wars and r. of wars, 36:7
Rump-fed ronyon cries, 212:12
Rum-tumming, drums r. everywhere,
    632:12
Run, about home and r., 747:16
  and not be weary, 27:23
  beggars mounted r. horse to death,
    164:12
  bow to that whose course r., 323:17
  Congress doesn't r. it waltzes, 339:2
  do not choose to r., 614:18

Sacrament, men pregnant abortion a
  s., 739:17
  of praise, 639:5
  virtue of s. like light, 77:*n*5
Sacred, Alph the s. river, 382:19
  Awe, 652:4
  cod, 582:*n*1
  cows make tastiest hamburger,
  768:9
  drama heaved, 599:5
  duty to myself, 508:2
  even bad books are s., 758:5
  facts are s., 555:8
  feed his s. flame, 383:3
  fire of liberty, 337:1
  hair dissever, 299:18
  head now wounded, 250:7
  head of thine, 253:22
  history a s. thing, 150:19
  hold every moment s., 630:1
  hoop of the nation, 587:5
  human body s., 489:24
  let there be s. silence, 96:12
  life not cheap but s., 432:39
  lips touch s. fire, 612:6
  nothing s., 701:14
  our s. honor, 343:4
  sane and s. death, 490:16
  source of sympathetic tears, 323:3
  they lack a s. poet, 97:1
  things s. or things profane, 272:19
  to departed spirit, 118:28
  to oblivion, 233:23
  two most s. names, 267:11
  veils her s. fires, 304:2
Sacredness of property, 525:12
Sacrifice acceptable to God, 42:12
  coming to s., 416:5
  living s., 42:12, 49:17
  make one sweet s., 225:6
  mercy and not s., 29:26
  too long a s., 596:18
  you make for sentiment, 603:21
Sacrificed, certainty precedent not
  lightly s., 609:10
  Christ our Passover s., 43:1
  person s. to individual, 648:4
Sacrifices it to your opinion, 331:4
  like stockyards, 701:14
  of friendship, 610:20
  such s. my Cordelia, 211:14
  with such s. God is pleased, 46:3
Sacrilegious murder hath broke ope,
  214:13
Sacrum, oblivioni s., 233:23
Sad, a little sunny a little s., 536:4
  all their songs s., 618:17
  all world s. dreary, 507:1
  and bad and mad, 467:17
  and weary I go back, 647:22
  as angels, 320:*n*5
  augurs mock own presage, 221:23
  bad brother's name, 535:4
  be beautiful and be s., 494:11
  companion dull-eyed melancholy,
  219:20
  created you while s., 587:13
  cypress, 202:13
  experience make me s., 191:27
  flesh is s. alas, 547:10

Sad (*continued*)
  heart foams at stern, 565:10
  heart of Ruth, 415:17
  how s. our Russia, 447:1
  is Eros builder of cities, 720:13
  kissed mouth, 533:19
  last gray hairs, 415:12
  lucidity of soul, 497:10
  make man look s., 174:9
  mechanic exercise, 457:7
  mine a s. one, 179:17
  my verse s. no wonder, 580:3
  name forever s., 300:2
  no s. songs for me, 515:7
  old law s. not bitter, 631:15
  or singing weather, 534:7
  remember and be s., 515:9
  Rose of all my days, 594:20
  say I'm s., 397:5
  soul s. glance glum, 531:14
  sound of horn, 421:4
  still s. music of humanity, 373:5
  stories of death of kings, 171:25
  sullen and s., 307:15
  tale's best for winter, 222:21
  tires in a mile-a, 223:4
  to see s. sights moves, 167:4
  'twas s. by fits, 324:15
  uncertain rustling, 452:16
  vicissitude of things, 320:5
  visit my s. heart, 188:3
  weight of this s. time, 211:21
  words of tongue or pen, 443:8
Sadder and wiser man, 382:9
  light than waning moon, 443:13
  than owl songs, 403:19
  those who hear s. than I, 522:2
Saddest are these, 443:8
  of the year, 411:8
  story ever heard, 617:9
  sweetest songs s. thought, 408:7
  when I sing, 522:2
Saddle, boot s. to horse, 464:15
  come s. your horses, 379:27
  no better place than s., 503:6
  put Germany in s., 474:13
  short life in s., 583:19
  things are in s., 429:17
Saddled, millions s. and bridled,
  425:21
Sadie stayed home, 740:3
  Thompson answer, 626:20
Sadly, part we s. in troublous world,
  165:3
  why hearest thou music s., 220:10
Sadness, begin in s., 742:16
  diverter of s., 245:17
  eternal note of s., 499:20
  farewell s., 691:10
  humorous s., 191:26
  more prevailing s., 389:10
  of a vale, 416:19
  of conviction, 542:8
  songs of s. and mirth, 441:21
  soul taste s. of might, 416:18
  sweet though in s., 407:17
  touches me with a prayer, 420:1
  unmannerly s. in youth, 179:30
  where s. let me sow joy, 123:10
  wraps me in humorous s., 191:26

Sado, over S. the Milky Way, 282:16
Safe and sane Fourth, 600:19
  believe soldiers nothing s., 515:14
  compulsion to become s., 658:7
  depository of public interests, 345:4
  direct and honest not s., 207:12
  for democracy, 587:16
  he that's secure is not s., 310:3
  hold me but s., 467:20
  none is s., 664:13
  run into a s. harbor, 55:24
  see me s. up, 137:18
  shall wooden wall continue, 62:*n*4
  weariest river s. to sea, 534:15
  wish him s. at home, 366:20
  world s. for democracy, 572:11
  world s. for diversity, 742:1
Safeguard, judiciary s. of liberty,
  586:8
  of the west, 374:17
Safeguards acceptable to all nations,
  655:9
  history of procedural s., 646:10
Safely, but to be s. thus, 214:20
  citizen may walk s. on law, 753:9
  Judah and Israel dwelt s., 12:20
  ship of state s. to harbor, 66:4
  toddle s. home, 662:6
Safer to be feared than loved, 136:10
  world s. for children, 761:16
Safest, home is s. refuge, 152:*n*2
  in the middle, 101:21
  just when s. sunset touch, 466:9
  road to Hell, 700:1
Safety, as if s. in stupidity, 478:35
  concern for s. in face of dangers,
  752:12
  dangerous to peace and s., 360:12
  fame for ale and s., 185:6
  greatest degree of s., 327:2
  in multitude of counsellors, 21:7
  in s. within boundaries, 650:8
  in skating s. is speed, 432:5
  neither liberty nor s., 310:13
  no s. here below, 138:*n*2
  no strike against public s., 614:16
  obtaining happiness and s., 327:1
  peace liberty and s., 344:9
  pluck this flower s., 177:16
  principles to effect s., 343:2
  to hope not safety, 93:33
  unite for public s., 370:15
  with which error tolerated, 344:5
Sagacious blue-stocking, 425:12
  bold and turbulent of wit, 274:3
  how s. the mouse, 83:13
Sagacity, no s. no powers, 332:28
Sage, by saint by savage by s., 303:14
  daughters of Muses, 64:6
  does not accumulate, 58:7
  government of the s., 56:14
  hoary S. replied, 315:3
  hold tongue pass for s., 100:19
  Homer's rule best, 302:22
  knows without going about, 57:15
  lengthened s. advices, 363:3
  Milton's wormwood words, 254:*n*3
  never strives for the great, 57:10
  Way of s. is to act, 58:7

Sage, que m'importe que tu sois s., 494:*n*10
Sagebrush, wind with fragrance of s., 616:11
Sager sort our deeds reprove, 226:13
Sage's, vain the s. pride, 303:13
Sages appeared crawling for charity, 80:13
  by s. perfectly exhibited, 79:14
  error of the S., 80:13
  have seen in thy face, 334:20
  holy s. once did sing, 250:19
  superior only in cleverness, 333:9
  than all the s. can, 372:21
  wisdom of our s., 344:9
Sagged and reeled, 637:8
Sags like heavy load, 708:19
Sahara dies, 514:4
Said, by and by easily s., 197:20
  fool hath s. in his heart, 16:3
  he himself has s. it, 529:9
  he was against sin, 614:19
  I kept my word he s., 616:23
  I meant what I s. s. what I meant, 715:2
  I s. in my haste, 19:18
  I to myself said I, 530:10
  in grief or pride, 684:10
  inadvertently s. some evil thing, 76:19
  least s. soonest mended, 149:*n*13
  let no more be s., 500:1
  let what will be s., 343:18
  little s. soon amended, 149:40
  much s. on both sides, 292:25
  never to himself hath s., 378:1
  no sooner s. than done, 84:14
  nothing s. that has not been s., 86:4
  so Sancho Panza s., 644:7
  the best thought and s., 500:8
  thing that is s. is s., 132:7
  thing which was not, 289:13
  'tis well s. again, 225:12
  to my soul be still, 671:5
  too late to say anything not s., 283:11
  want anything s. ask man, 756:3
  well as if I had s. it, 290:9
  who s. Peacock Pie, 617:3
  word dead when s., 514:1
Sail, all s. no anchor, 426:1
  at break of day, 652:18
  bark attendant s., 302:3
  beyond sunset and stars, 455:6
  cried A s. a s., 381:11
  even with canvas rent, 102:23
  give man boat he can s., 523:15
  here she comes full s., 291:10
  hoist s. while gale, 140:*n*17
  more s. than ballast, 283:1
  on, 543:18
  on O Ship of State, 441:18
  out on your trades again, 83:2
  sea-mark of my utmost s., 208:14
  shallow bauble boats dare s., 200:6
  solitary s. that rises, 474:5
  soul s. leagues beyond, 509:25
  time to take in s., 430:8
  tomorrow s. the Ocean Sea, 95:22
  two lofty ships set s., 793:18

Sail (continued)
  we must s. not drift, 447:10
  wet seas roun', 592:19
  white and rustling s., 396:22
  with unshut eye, 497:8
Sailed away year and day, 472:1
  off in wooden shoe, 559:20
  Swift s. into rest, 598:9
Sailing celestial spaces, 537:18
  denies voyager further s., 68:20
  great whales s. by, 497:8
  like a stately ship, 261:16
  on obscene wings, 382:18
  ship a-s. with the wind, 791:18
Sailor, drunken s. on mast, 166:3
  here and there old s., 638:23
  home is the s., 561:16
  if Ancient Mariner called Old S., 525:8
  soldier an' s. too, 592:22
  staring s. that shakes watch, 729:9
  well for s. lad, 456:7
  what shall we do with drunken s., 793:10
Sailor's wife had chestnuts, 212:12
Sailors but men, 180:1
  half our s. swallowed, 165:2
  images s. tattoo, 706:2
  onward s. cry, 577:6
  show world how American s. fight, 781:*n*4
  soldiers an airmen, 621:18
  Spanish s. with bearded lips, 442:6
  won't believe it, 379:22
Sail's shaking, 633:14
Sails, argosies of magic s., 455:17
  biased by full s., 701:4
  broad bellying s., 654:2
  filled streamers waving, 261:16
  filled with lusty wind, 157:13
  handed all s. and set treo, 134:8
  purple the s., 217:14
  set of s. not gales, 562:13
  swell full, 428:13
  thy white s. crowding, 549:19
  vessel of my genius now hoists s., 126:2
  well but strike rock, 360:7
  white s. fly seaward, 669:20
Sail-yards tremble masts crack, 157:13
Saint and Martyr rule from tomb, 670:9
  by s. by savage by sage, 303:14
  corrupt a s., 176:32
  dead sinner revised, 544:22
  Doctor and S., 445:17
  if God does not exist, 732:17
  lips would temp a s., 399:*n*1
  looked out of eye of s., 598:7
  neither s.- nor sophist-led, 497:19
  old s. in forest, 552:5
  poet and s. to thee alone, 267:11
  saw my late espoused s., 255:16
  Sebastian died of fright, 769:3
  seem s. when most play devil, 165:27
  strained so much, 724:11
  such injury vex a s., 167:26
  threadbare s., 227:17
  to be a s. for oneself, 494:15

Saint Agnes' Eve, 414:21
  moon hath set, 415:7
Saint Anne mother of Mary, 538:6
  yes by S., 202:5
Saint Augustine thanked God, 628:14
Saint Clement's, bells of S., 788:20
Saint George, England and S., 185:5
  for England, 619:6
  that swinged dragon, 169:22
Saint George's Hanover Square, 524:17
Saint Ives, going to S., 788:14
Saint James's, ladies of S., 539:6
Saint John, awake my S., 301:1
  ancient animal symbols of S., 420:9
  there S. mingles, 302:21
Saint John's, whether bounded by the S., 460:14
Saint Louis bought it for six million dollars, 526:15
Saint Martin's, expect S. summer, 163:7
Saint Nazaire, mademoiselle from S., 680:9
Saint Nicholas soon would be there, 391:6
Saint Paul's, designing S., 627:18
  ruins of S., 323:23, 425:7
Saint Peter's, blessing of S. Master, 245:31
Saint Stephen's choir, 742:10
Saint Theresa in wild lament, 712:18
Saint Vincent, nobly Cape S., 465:5
Sainted, thing enskyed and s., 203:25
Sainte-Terrer, there goes a S., 476:*n*4
Saintliness not a state, 728:9
Saintly, woman's normal occupations counter s. life, 719:10
Saints aid if men call, 382:14
  choir of s., 231:2
  Communion of S., 48:25
  for all the s., 502:11
  heroes if we will, 497:5
  in your injuries, 206:5
  men below and s. above, 377:25
  precious is the death of his s., 19:19
  rarely married women, 719:10
  slaughtered s., 255:14
  sweetly sing, 283:5
  take your s. and virgins, 484:8
  to windows run, 511:18
  when s. go marching in, 794:24
  where s. immortal reign, 294:19
Saint-seducing gold, 174:15
Saintship of an anchorite, 399:11
Sairey, oh S. S. little do we know, 469:47
Sais, que s.-je, 146:*n*3
Saisons, O s. O châteaux, 565:*n*14
Saith, he s. among the trumpets, 15:17
Sake, for God's s. sit upon ground, 171:25
  for his name's s., 16:17
  good friend for Jesus' s., 226:11
  hated for my name's s., 34:31
  love for Love's s., 725:21
  persecute you for my s., 33:1
  poem for poem's s., 453:13
  wine for thy stomach's s., 45:20
Sakes, Heaven and future's s., 624:7

Saki, eternal S. from Bowl poured, 445:22
 O S. you pass, 446:9
Salaam, peace unto you shalom s. forever, 732:10
Salad, capacious s. bowl, 561:15
 crazy s. with meat, 597:1
 days, 217:10
 Garrick's a s., 330:9
Salads, ho 'tis time of s., 320:31
Salaputtium disertum, 91:*n*3
Salary, draw s. before spending, 600:11
Sale, base s. of chapmen's tongues, 168:22
 city for s., 91:30
Salesman, every s. can fondle her breasts, 626:5
 lazy insolence of shoe s., 714:14
Salley, down by s. gardens, 594:17
Sallied flesh, 193:*n*1
Sallow, lean and s. abstinence, 253:8
Sallows, among river s., 416:15
Sally in our alley, 298:2
 loose s. of mind, 314:2
 make a sudden s., 458:15
 none like pretty S., 298:2
Salmon, like chinook s. jumping, 743:15
 wasn't wine was s., 468:22
 with first s. and first green peas, 442:11
Salmon-falls, 597:7
Salome danced, 35:14
Saloon, all s. keepers Democrats, 462:14
Salt, became a pillar of s., 7:33
 drift in laboring s., 767:9
 eat peck of s. with him, 776:3
 eaten your bread and s., 590:17
 fragrance of s. marsh, 491:3
 how s. is another's bread, 126:25
 if s. have lost savor, 33:2
 land and not inhabited, 28:29
 no joy but lacks s., 623:20
 not worth his s., 105:5
 of the earth, 33:2
 one s. sea, 184:25
 seasoned with Attic s., 269:30
 speech seasoned with s., 45:1
 tides seaward flow, 497:6
 upon their tails, 288:15
 water unbounded, 593:13
 with a grain of s., 104:13
Salt-caked smokestack, 634:1
Salted, wherewith shall it be s., 33:2
Saltness of time, 183:15
 sugar and s. agree, 330:9
Salts, anything man says take with dose of s., 647:2
Saltsick, seasilt s., 647:22
Saltus, natura non facit s., 312:*n*2
Salus extra ecclesiam non est, 112:*n*12
 populi suprema lex, 88:*n*4
Salutary influence of example, 314:18
 wise and s. neglect, 331:10
Salute, we about to die s. you, 110:6
Salutes everyone in early days, 75:27
Salvaged, ships s. and retiring, 647:6
Salvation, concern temporal s., 339:7

Salvation (*continued*)
 for helmet the hope of s., 45:7
 for him there is s., 350:27
 for our s. came down, 49:1
 Genius work out s., 418:7
 he is become my s., 9:2, 26:12
 he only is my rock and s., 17:33
 in union, 609:12
 my bottle of s., 152:16
 my light and my s., 16:21
 no s. outside Church, 112:19
 none should see s., 181:19
 rock of our s., 18:19
 three things necessary for s., 124:10
 waited for thy s., 8:18
 work out own s., 44:30
 work out s. with diligence, 64:25
Sam, play it again S., 767:10
 play it S., 726:10
Samarcand, silken S. to cedared Lebanon, 415:6
Samaria, woman of S., 39:47
Samaritan had compassion, 38:23
Samarra, appointment in S., 626:19
Same, Darby always s. to Joan, 557:2
 descent to Hades is s., 64:17
 ever the s., 145:5
 men all the s., 626:20
 not be then the s., 426:2
 permanent and the s., 498:8
 repose that ever is the s., 376:4
 self was not the s., 199:31
 the more they remain s., 443:19
 the s. as everywhere, 349:3
 think and hit s. time, 754:9
 whole world over, 782:18
 yesterday today and forever, 46:1
Sameness of sheep, 703:16
 self has continuity and s., 708:5
 with difference, 384:14
Sames of am, 689:1
Samite, arm clothed in white s., 133:6
 clothed in white s. mystic, 459:6
Samphire, one that gathers s., 210:27
Sample, by s. we judge whole, 149:2
Sampler, serve to ply the s., 253:10
Sam's, nephew of my Uncle S., 632:11
Samsa, Gregor S. awoke from uneasy dreams, 651:17
Samson, Philistines be upon thee S., 11:16
 Philistines brought S. to Gaza, 11:17
San Francisco bay center of prosperity, 474:20
 West is S., 586:3
 where social hemorrhaging, 766:11
San Salvador, island called S., 134:8
Sancho Panza, God's blessing said S., 151:*n*5
 so S. said so say I, 644:7
Sanctified by reason blest by faith, 373:14
Sanctify, thy praise s. our rest, 506:16
Sanction, gives bigotry no s., 337:2
 happiness the only s. of life, 588:3
 laws with s., 355:4
 ultimate s. of exploitation, 686:6
Sanctity, untrespassed s. of space, 751:3

Sanctuary, of s. and choir, 672:1
 wild s., 617:14
Sanctum of the soul, 629:3
Sand, abstinence sows s. all over, 357:20
 as the s. by the sea, 12:19
 blood of Ignacio on s., 699:9
 build on Fortune build on s., 240:5
 heap of loose s., 601:4
 house built on s., 34:15
 laws are s. customs rock, 528:5
 little grains of s., 502:8
 number the s. of the sea, 30:31
 on edge of s., 472:3
 ostrich with head in s., 572:7
 ribbed sea s., 381:18
 roll down golden s., 395:18
 see world in grain of s., 359:5
 such quantities of s., 518:24
 sun s. wild uproar, 429:8
 throw s. against the wind, 359:2
 weaving s., 433:27
Sandal, battering s., 551:4
 heard her massive s., 684:9
 shoon, 198:16
Sandalwood cedarwood, 633:18
Sandburg, fall into hands of Carl S., 693:13
Sanded, nicely s. floor, 329:19
Sands and shores, 252:24
 come unto these yellow s., 223:30
 crucified the George S., 475:10
 footprints on s. of time, 440:17
 ghosts countless as s., 508:5
 golden s. crystal brooks, 229:10
 lone level s. stretch, 406:13
 of Dee, 484:9
 of time, 440:17
 steer too nigh s., 274:3
 suffice, 514:4
Sand-strewn caverns, 497:7
Sandwich men shuffling, 650:16
Sandy, false as s. earth, 200:22
 swift s. glass, 233:19
Sane and had to fly, 752:12
 and sacred death, 490:16
 assent you are s., 512:11
 only s. thing to do if up there [Boston], 687:21
 safe and s. Fourth, 600:19
Saner to be rebel, 589:1
Sang, all we said or s., 599:15
 beyond genius of sea, 639:7
 bonny bonny Biscay O, 779:6
 from morn till night, 338:18
 ful weel s. service dyvyne, 129:12
 his didn't, 688:22
 in my chains like sea, 737:19
 light listened when she s., 725:14
 morning stars s. together, 15:8
 perhaps it may turn out s., 361:21
 Sir Lancelot, 454:15
 summer s. in me, 684:8
 Tilly-loo, 472:5
 to small guitar, 471:31
 what song the Sirens s., 248:30
 when a lark I s., 725:9
 where late sweet birds s., 221:8
 Willow titwillow, 531:9
 within bloody wood, 668:16

Sang, qu'un s. impur, 366:9
Sangfroid, preserve your s., 343:18
Sanglots longs des violons, 554:*n*1
Sangreal, noble history of S., 133:3
Sanguinis, hic est enim Calix S. mei,
   48:11
Sanitary, give me s. reformer, 484:8
Sanity virtue of ancient literature,
   498:18
Sank my boat, 740:18
   sighted sub s. same, 733:10
Sans teeth eyes everything, 191:3
   Wine Song Singer, 445:16
Santa Claus, nobody shoots at S.,
   618:8
   things in dark besides S., 625:22
   yes Virginia there is a S., 538:2
Sap, dried s. out of veins, 595:19
   make cherry red, 664:20
   material s., 210:22
   nor can s. be in rocks, 90:2
   world's whole s. is sunk, 229:8
Sapiens, naked ape Homo s., 759:8
Sapless, earth s. as bone, 633:13
Sapphire bracelet lasts forever, 686:10
   heaven's deep repose, 415:7
   the s. blaze, 323:4
Sapphires, garlic and s., 670:14
   glowed with living s., 258:19
Sappho, burning S., 402:24
   of Lesbos tenth muse, 56:*n*4
   would speak openly, 626:10
Sapping solemn creed, 400:5
Sarah, blossomed S. and I blossom,
   734:14
Sarcasm language of Devil, 412:2
Sargasso, your mind and you S. Sea,
   658:18
Saris go by me from embassies, 735:22
Sash lowered night comes, 624:1
Sashes, Billy in one of nice new s.,
   625:19
Sat among the cinders, 790:15
   at good man's feast, 190:29
   by the fleshpots, 9:6
   like a cormorant, 258:7
   like Patience on monument, 202:14
   on a tuffet, 791:8
   on Pillicock-hill, 210:4
   Satan exalted s., 256:23
   so Tiberius might have s., 500:4
   upon which everyone has s., 689:3
   you have s. too long, 247:2
Satan as lightning fall, 38:20
   came also, 13:28
   exalted sat, 256:23
   finds mischief, 294:10
   get thee behind me S., 35:29
   interview with S., 578:15
   old serpent called S., 47:28
   that waiteth to bigile, 131:1
   towards God the other towards S.,
   494:13
Satanic, dark S. mills, 359:17
   school, 386:18
Satanic Verses, author of S., 704:13
Satchel, whining school-boy with s.,
   191:3
Sate itself in celestial bed, 194:22

Sated with banquet of life, 90:5
Satire a sort of glass, 288:16
   be my song, 399:1
   ever moral ever new, 280:15
   hard not to write s., 108:15
   like polished razor, 304:5
   or sense can Sporus feel, 302:14
   points at no defect, 289:18
   what closes Saturday, 676:13
Satire's my weapon, 302:20
Satisfaction, ambitious man have no
   s., 231:14
   cost of s. of instincts, 569:8
   get s. of being heard, 585:14
   I can't get no s., 772:16
   in making it possible for others,
   734:1
   previous benefaction or present s.,
   71:5
   that I have not lived in vain, 292:19
   work brings, 605:6
Satisfactory, plant seeds most s., 511:2
Satisfied, charm makes us more s.,
   493:24
   fine reality of hunger s., 723:1
   greatest fools oft most s., 280:12
   I can't be s., 708:15
   love s. greater torment, 669:15
   nature of desire not to be s., 78:16
   pig s., 439:27
   retire like s. guest, 95:3
   superior man s. and composed,
   61:13
   to live in hunger, 677:7
   well paid that is well s., 182:6
Satisfies, makes hungry where most s.,
   217:15
Satisfiest desire of every living thing,
   20:12
Satisfy, poorly s. our eyes, 227:9
   your greed, 593:*n*1
Satisfying curiosity of young, 550:10
   full and s. life, 715:9
Saturam, difficile est s. non scribere,
   108:*n*4
Saturates politics with thought, 499:7
Saturday, died on S., 791:4
   mornings we listened to Red Lantern, 766:7
   satire closes S., 676:13
   what he did on S., 644:2
Saturday's child, 791:3
Saturn, gray-haired S., 416:19
   Revolution like S., 473:10
Saturnians through life's Tempe led,
   487:8
Satya truth, 607:1
Satyagraha, term S. coined by me,
   606:13
Satyr, forty till fifty man a s., 568:5
   Hyperion to a s., 193:7
Satyrs, men like s. grazing, 162:10
   nymphs and s., 599:17
Sauce, bread s. of happy ending,
   548:14
   cloyless s., 217:12
   good crier of green s., 139:16
   no s. like hunger, 150:21
Saucy doubts and fears, 215:2

Saucy (*continued*)
   not deep-searched with s. looks,
   168:15
Saul and Jonathan were lovely and
   pleasant, 11:47
   becomes Paul, 575:10
   hath slain his thousands, 11:42
   is S. among the prophets, 11:31
   why persecutest thou me, 41:5
   yet breathing slaughter, 41:4
Saunders, a bed Clerk S. said, 785:12
Saunter, great art to s., 476:22
Sauntering from à la Sainte Terre,
   476:*n*4
Sausage, in as pig out as s., 544:19
Sausages, men are like s., 479:15
Savage and Tartarly, 403:28
   breast, 291:7
   bull bear the yoke, 186:14
   by saint by s. by sage, 303:14
   contemplates mother-in-law, 565:2
   delights to torture, 444:14
   dole laws unto s. race, 454:24
   extreme rude cruel, 222:7
   half s. country, 659:4
   if little s. left to himself, 319:30
   in man never eradicated, 477:6
   indignation, 290:23, 598:9
   individual man, 601:7
   is he who saves himself, 135:7
   men and uncouth manners, 331:7
   noble s., 273:14
   place as holy and enchanted, 382:20
   ruled s. hordes, 503:4
   servility slides by, 743:13
   soothe a s. breast, 291:7
   take some s. woman, 455:23
   thrown on s. shore, 491:5
   wilderness into empire, 331:25
   young man who wept s., 588:18
Savage-creating fellow, 73:22
Savageness, sing s. out of a bear,
   207:21
Savagery, meeting-point between s.
   and civilization, 584:6
Savages, grow like s., 186:2
   in unknown island, 434:21
Savage-wild, time and intents are s.,
   176:13
Save, assist him to s. face, 692:21
   came to s. sinners, 45:11
   conquer but to s., 389:6
   destroy town to s. it, 784:6
   died to s. us all, 479:18
   eternal Father strong to s., 506:4
   God s. the king, 11:32, 172:8,
   298:3
   God s. the mark, 177:5
   greed will s. the U.S.A., 774:4
   himself he cannot s., 37:11
   listen and s., 253:11
   me from Candid Friend, 371:25
   me from therrble prongs, 647:22
   my soul if I have soul, 503:14
   myself by work and faith, 717:19
   nobly s. or meanly lose, 449:16
   not s. it it not s. me, 653:2
   old worth saving, 603:24
   one drop would s. my soul, 162:23
   squadron honor France, 468:6

Save (*continued*)

thee ancient Mariner, 381:5
what is around me, 653:2
whosoever s. life shall lose it, 35:30
wish to s. their own pocket, 72:1

Saved by hope faith love, 684:18
harvest is past and we are not s., 28:20
he s. others, 37:11
I have s. myself, 55:3
part of day rued, 623:15
there be souls must be s., 206:16
youthful hose well s., 191:3

Saves, humor s. a few steps, 664:18
itself perpetually, 729:1
savage he who s. himself, 135:7
soul in new French books, 466:10

Savin', I'm s. love for you, 693:8

Saving, not s. but selection, 332:28
save old worth s., 603:24

Savings, not by s. and capital, 723:12
of many in hands of one, 568:3

Savior at his sermon on mount, 465:6
Christ our S., 778:8
of 'is country, 591:18
which is Christ, 38:3

Savior's birth celebrated, 192:29
sing tongue the S. glory, 124:5

Savoir être à soi, 145:*n*15
tuer et créer, 494:*n*11

Savor, filths s. but themselves, 210:23
fleeting delights, 405:7
if salt have lost s., 33:2
seeming and s. all winter, 223:5
thoughts that s. of content, 157:18

Savory, lavender mints s. marjoram, 223:6

Saw, all at once I s. a crowd, 375:19
coughing drowns parson's s., 169:14
do not s. the air, 196:21
first one another s., 229:5
heavens fill, 455:17
him with my own eyes, 269:8
I at a glance, 375:21
I came I s. I conquered, 88:25
I came s. and overcame, 184:8
I s. and loved, 340:12
last time I s. Paris, 692:7
life steadily saw it whole, 497:3
man clothed with rags, 272:11
manners in face, 315:2
ne'er s. I never felt, 374:13
never s. a man who looked, 567:15
never s. a Moor, 513:15
never s. purple cow, 600:16
not seen as others s., 451:9
on a cloud I s. a child, 356:4
skull beneath skin, 668:12
spiders marching, 742:12
spires of Oxford, 648:3
then I s. the Congo, 637:9
three ships, 791:14
through glass eye darkly, 527:20
water lily bloom, 454:16
who was that lady I s., 604:8
young Harry with beaver on, 178:21

Sawdust Caesar, 680:10

Saws, full of wise s., 191:3

Sawyer, Adventures of Tom S., 526:19

Saxa, in spatio pertundere s., 89:*n*6

Saxon I am Roderick Dhu, 378:23
in subjection to white S. man, 475:7

Saxophones, long cool winding s., 634:10

Say, cannot create when nothing to s., 707:10
canst not s. I did it, 215:4
can't s. anything good, 654:10
defend right to s. it, 307:4
disapprove of what you s., 307:4
Do as I s. not as I do, 239:10
don't s. too much, 722:5
everything interestingly, 560:7
find right thing to s., 570:8
first of God above, 301:3
good deed to s. well, 225:12
good night till it be morrow, 175:15
I don't s. what public wants, 626:3
I shall have less to s., 623:10
it ain't so Joe, 782:20
it as you understand it, 365:10
it loud I'm black and proud, 766:9
it with utmost levity, 570:8
know much s. little, 319:13
light stream of what we s., 500:18
love not having to s. sorry, 769:1
more to s. when dead, 608:5
nastiest thing in nicest way, 663:8
never s. I was false of heart, 221:24
never s. more than necessary, 352:6
not struggle nought availeth, 483:3
not what we ought to s., 211:21
not what you s. but how, 515:15
nothin' without compelled, 485:21
nothin' you can be held to, 485:21
nothing but what said, 234:6
nothing to s., 484:3
nothing to s. nothing, 393:4
nothing you couldn't actually s., 660:4
one may s. what one thinks, 109:16
person who could not s. no, 726:8
remember what we s. here, 450:2
right to s. what one pleases, 661:8
secure within can s., 274:29
see what I s., 576:17
shall my little bark, 302:3
shame s. what it will, 198:26
shudder to s. it, 93:29
so long as we can s., 210:19
some s. world end in fire, 623:14
style of what man has to s., 500:5
tale as said to me, 377:24
temple bells they s., 591:22
that's all I s., 447:17
there is no more to s., 201:14
there is nothing more to s., 608:2
they s. my verse sad, 580:3
things I did not do or s., 598:16
this with presence of mind, 86:8
though I s. it that should not, 238:20
to all the world, 189:28
to the fleet, 360:*n*4
too late to s. anything not said, 283:11
way they s. it, 710:10
wet mind and s. something clever, 72:14

Say (*continued*)

what else to s. but everything, 740:9
what everyone else does not s., 552:32
what law is, 355:9
what more is there to s., 597:14
what others s. of them, 270:19
what people s. behind back, 564:1
what s. they let them s., 154:*n*10
what will Mrs. Grundy s., 367:11
what you mean, 517:18
what you would be, 108:11
which can s. more, 221:10
which grain will grow, 212:17
will it not be the same, 426:2
wouldn't s. so till tried, 644:15

Sayer, always seer is a s., 431:14

Saying all we did not know, 661:3
for loving and for s. so, 228:17
goodbye to statue, 701:17
is one thing, 146:13
mode of s. things, 499:11
reputed wise for s. nothing, 179:21
thoughtless s. of princess, 319:25
wise and old, 153:*n*7
Wrath by his meekness, 356:16

Sayings full of knowledge and advice, 22:*n*2

Says a lot in vain refusing, 349:15
no one means all he s., 536:3
she speaks yet s. nothing, 174:27
what he s. least important, 537:13
who is it that s. most, 221:10
who s. it what he s., 537:13

Scab of churches, 227:13

Scabbard, sword of justice has no s., 353:13
sword within the s. keep, 276:21

Scabby, hated with s. hatred, 766:5

Scabies, disputandi pruritus ecclesiarum s., 227:*n*5

Scaffold sways the future, 485:2
Truth forever on s., 485:2

Scaffoldage, 'twixt footing and s., 200:11

Scald, tears s. like molten lead, 211:9

Scalding grave, 613:9

Scale, every golden s., 517:5
he by geometric s., 263:2
in equal s. weighing, 192:32
lapping scale with regularity, 664:16
Poetic Justice with lifted s., 303:25
so shall you s. the stars, 94:24
society without objective legal s., 746:8

Scaled invention or artistry, 660:1

Scales are his pride, 15:22
father held out golden s., 52:21
fell from his eyes, 41:8
put Hannibal in the s., 109:8
waves as formal as s. on fish, 664:4

Scallop shell of quiet, 152:16

Scalped each other, 425:11

Scan, gently s. brother man, 362:5
merits or faults to s., 329:13
presume not God to s., 301:13

Scandal, dreaded s. more than disease, 586:22
greatest s. waits on greatest state, 167:3

Scandal (*continued*)
love and s., 311:21
public s. is wicked, 269:7
tea and s., 290:36
treatment of Negro greatest s.,
700:6
Scandalous and poor, 283:23
Scandals of th' poor, 602:19
short an' simple s., 602:19
Scant, if store of crowns be s., 233:12
Scanted, what s. in hair given in wit,
166:24
Scanter of your maiden presence,
194:6
Scanty, in longitude tho' s., 363:9
'Scape, who should 's. whipping,
196:3
'Scaped, heart 's. this sorrow, 221:13
Scapegoat, let him go for a s., 9:23
'Scapes, hair-breadth 's., 205:25
Scar, virtue or vice leaves s., 545:14
wound heals s. disappears, 477:23
Scarcely greet me with that sun,
220:24
Scarceness, eat bread without s., 10:16
Scarcity, on first s. will turn, 332:29
reasons for s. of capital, 652:16
Scare, Don't let them s. you, 678:6
white clouds on, 623:10
Scarecrow, not make s. of law, 203:28
Scarecrows of fools, 505:14
Scared, always been s. of you, 764:17
to go to brink, 667:8
Scarf up tender eye of day, 214:28
Scarfs garters gold, 301:15
Scarlet, in S. town, 785:9
letter her passport, 436:2
line slender rigid exact, 492:*n*4
of maples shake me, 583:16
passion for a s. coat, 289:15
sins s. books read, 609:9
though your sins be as s., 25:29
Scars, he jests at s., 174:26
I carry with me, 272:30
inveterate s., 670:14
of others teach caution, 114:3
Scat, w'en Miss Rabbit say s., 556:10
Scatted, Miss Rabbit say scat they s.,
556:10
Scatter plenty o'er smiling land,
322:15
Scattered, he hath s. the proud, 37:42
Israel s. upon the hills, 13:2
to the wind, 453:19
when cloud s., 409:19
Scattering, maniac s. dust, 457:14
Scatters, anarchy s. armies, 66:15
deep surmise s., 477:24
rear of darkness thin, 251:12
Scene, dreamer is dream s., 629:2
last s. of all, 191:3
live o'er each s., 299:19
lofty s. be acted o'er, 188:18
love gilds the s., 352:18
not ask to see distant s., 426:18
play one s. of excellent dissembling,
217:2
speaks a new s., 242:13
start a s. or two, 667:17
Scenery essential in painting, 120:13

Scenery (*continued*)
fine human nature finer, 418:3
Scenes, changing s. of life, 285:3
from s. like these, 361:10
gay gilded s., 291:29
his fathers loved, 711:2
ill-bred s., 586:22
no more behind your s. David,
315:14
of my childhood, 398:2
shifted on stage of history, 559:10
Scent, amber s. of perfume, 261:16
of arm-pits aroma finer than prayer,
489:10
of her hair, 683:11
of pine, 669:22
of roses hang round it, 392:2
rose's s. bitterness, 581:1
survives their close, 581:1
Scepter, balm s. and ball, 185:19
leaden s., 296:7
shepherd's crook beside s., 428:21
shows force of power, 181:19
snatched with unruly hand, 170:7
Sceptered, in s. pall sweeping by,
252:6
isle, 171:9
mercy above s. sway, 181:19
Moloch s. king, 256:24
what avails the s. race, 388:15
Scheldt, lazy S. or wandering Po,
328:6
Scheme, for breakfast a s., 296:2
of weal and woe, 467:4
Sorry S. of Things, 446:8
yields no revenue, 331:3
Schemes, best laid s., 361:6
Schiller has material sublime, 384:22
Scholar among rakes, 425:15
determined s. and man of virtue,
61:26
he was a s., 226:6
if s. have not faith, 80:2
is delegated intellect Man Thinking,
431:5
more in soldier than s., 206:10
showed him gentleman an' s.,
361:16
ten o'clock s., 792:7
thou art a s., 192:21
who cherishes love of comfort,
61:21
who pursues fame not s., 80:11
Scholar's, courtier's soldier's s., 196:17
ills s. life assail, 313:17
Scholars dispute and case still before
courts, 98:6
God of Abraham not s., 271:11
land of s., 328:14
make mayors but not s., 234:28
not great men, 447:15
Pythagoras said to his s., 234:15
Scholarship record of disagreements,
586:9
Schön, so hold und s. und rein,
420:*n*1
war ich auch, 350:*n*7
School, anyone been to English public
s., 712:2

School (*continued*)
corrupted youth in erecting s.,
164:11
creeping like snail to s., 191:3
elongated-yellow-fruit s. of writing,
702:16
experience keeps dear s., 309:28
fleshly s. of poetry, 541:15
high s. closer to core of experience,
751:14
in joyful s. days, 387:14
in my s.-days, 179:24
in which nothing harsh, 115:9
Intelligence make it a soul, 418:16
law s. no more than s. of fencing,
574:10
leave religion to private s., 501:15
microcosm of public s., 434:14
of mankind, 332:26
of Stratford atte Bowe, 129:12
Satanic s., 386:18
stealthy s. of criticism, 509:28
tales out of s., 141:17
threadbare saint in wisdom's s.,
227:17
three little maids from s., 530:22
time the s. in which we learn, 734:5
to s. not to travel, 159:20
toward s. with heavy looks, 175:11
we left s., 740:8
Schoolboy, every s. knows it, 266:5
every s. knows, 425:6
tale every s. knows, 321:12
whining s. with satchel, 191:3
Schoolboy's tale, 399:14
Schoolboys, as s. from books, 175:11
Schoolchildren, Negro s., 743:12
School-divine, God the Father a s.,
303:6
Schoolgirl, pert as s. can be, 530:22
Schooling, in and outdoor s., 625:4
Schoolman's subtle art, 302:18
Schoolmaster, becoming a s. sir, 712:1
is abroad, 390:1
Schoolmasters, bankers s. clergymen,
595:14
father more than hundred s., 244:35
let s. puzzle brain, 330:1
Schoolrooms, better s. than cells,
480:10
Schools, hundred s. of thought contend, 686:16
jargon of the s., 287:15
knowledge never learned of s.,
443:6
let us reform s., 487:19
maze of s., 298:11
nurseries of vice, 311:19
old maxim in the s., 289:5
Schooner Hesperus, 440:20
ladder close to s., 762:7
Schweigen ist golden, 412:10
Science achieve perfect knowledge,
496:18
advance in s. audacity of imagination, 577:10
advancement of pure s., 685:19
aim of exact s., 516:6
and applications together, 502:3
and opinion, 71:9

Scourge (*continued*)
  laid upon your hate, 176:20
  mighty s. of war, 450:11
  of God, 162:1
  of small cords, 39:41
  of war, 655:23
Scourged to his dungeon, 411:4
Scout, blabbing eastern s., 252:22
  flout 'em and s. 'em, 224:16
Scramble, great s. and big divide,
    541:5
Scrambling to the shore, 519:2
Scrap of paper, 568:13
  worn out before on s. heap, 570:22
Scrape cable, 474:19
Scraping, Death's ironic s., 639:5
Scraps, on s. of learning dote, 295:24
  stolen the s., 169:6
Scratch Christian find pagan, 590:5
  it with a hoe, 511:2
  lover find foe, 687:8
  on wall of oblivion, 697:3
Scratched, expect to be s., 149:32
  head kept thinking, 608:4
  man whom Fortune s., 203:18
  out both eyes, 792:22
Scratchez, Ah itchez Ah s., 709:12
Scratching at the floor, 583:8
Scrawls, few hundred s., 654:13
Scrawny cry was a chorister, 640:12
Scream, better to s., 702:15
  not a shriek not a s., 519:22
  suddenly s. pierced the air, 751:10
Screamed, Mrs. Hutchinson s., 739:15
Screaming, buttons stamped with s.
    eagle, 694:5
  night away, 786:22
Screams message to outside world,
    702:15
  of horror rend, 299:18
Screeches, mouthful of s. like torn tin,
    762:18
Screen, world vast s. of snow, 675:3
Screw, atomic bomb turn of s., 714:10
  your courage, 213:13
Scribblative, babblative and s., 386:19
Scribble scribble scribble, 342:22
  we all s. poetry, 98:9
Scribbled, parchment s. o'er undo a
    man, 164:9
Scribbler, distilling frenzy from aca-
    demic s., 652:17
Scribbling, seriously s. to excite laugh-
    ter, 525:19
Scribe worthy to be courtier, 6:3
Scribes and Pharisees, 36:3
Scrimped, charity s. and iced, 553:20
Scrip and scrippage, 191:12
  nor s. nor shoes, 38:17
  of joy immortal diet, 152:16
Scrippage, scrip and s., 191:12
Scripture, devil can cite S., 180:6
  moveth us, 48:15
Scriptures, let us look at the s., 238:21
  mighty in S., 41:20
  search S., 40:1
Scrolls, flows in s. of toga, 764:14
Scrooge, bah said S. humbug, 470:4
  covetous old sinner, 470:3

Scrooge (*continued*)
  Ghost of Christmas Yet to Come
    said S., 470:11
Scrotumtightening sea, 647:12
Scrub kitchen pavement, 595:13
Scrunch or be scrunched, 471:23
Scrunched, scrunch or be s., 471:23
Scruple, not s. to pick pocket, 285:12
  some craven s., 198:13
Scrutamini scripturas, 238:21
Scullion, away you s., 183:29
Sculptor well those passions read,
    406:13
Scum of the earth, 371:10
  Okie means s., 710:10
Scurvy politician, 211:5
Scutcheon, blot in thy s., 151:7
  honor a mere s., 178:33
Scuttlefish, disputants like s., 293:8
  rejoice with s., 325:15
Scuttling across floors of seas, 667:14
Scylla guards right side, 181:*n*2
  to port, 181:*n*2
  when I shun S., 181:11
Scythe, work the s. of time, 370:17
Scythian, Barbarian S. bond nor free,
    44:40
Sea, all our s. our own, 249:27
  all returns to s., 721:13
  all the rivers run into the s., 23:23
  all went to s., 791:13
  alone dwell kings of s., 497:9
  alone on wide wide s., 381:19
  as long as rivers run to s., 93:24
  as near by s. as by land, 147:11
  as the sand by the s., 12:19
  Atlanta to the s., 520:6
  bark is on s., 401:27
  bathed in Poem of S., 565:13
  beetles o'er base into s., 194:13
  being smooth, 200:6
  best in chair before fire, 618:10
  better cast into s., 39:4
  beyond genius of s., 639:7
  beyond leagues more s., 509:25
  bodies thrown into s., 706:3
  born across the s., 484:7
  bound with triumphant s., 171:10
  bred to the s., 406:2
  by the deep s., 400:29
  changed Egdon remained, 539:14
  cold gray stones O S., 456:7
  creation of Omnipotence, 618:11
  crept into bosom of the s., 164:4
  dance like wave of s., 595:10
  deep s. swell, 669:3
  delicate algae and s. anemone,
    671:13
  demons down under s., 453:9
  depths congealed in heart of s., 9:5
  desert of the s., 26:18
  do you not hear s., 417:*n*3
  dolphin-torn s., 598:14
  down there s. folk live, 437:6
  dragon that is in the s., 26:31
  dwellers by the s., 564:20
  earth fire s. air, 541:7
  eastward to the s., 591:22
  empty tigers or roaring s., 176:13
  ever renewing s., 613:16

Sea (*continued*)
  far-heard whisper o'er the s., 381:14
  Father of Waters unvexed to s.,
    449:18
  firm-footed by s., 424:3
  fishes of the s. shall declare, 14:16
  from s. to shining s., 576:19
  frozen s. inside us, 651:23
  ghost of garden fronts s., 535:5
  glitter of s., 764:20
  go down to the s. in ships, 19:9
  God a s. of infinite substance, 120:7
  goes to s. for nothing, 230:9
  gone with the sun, 565:18
  grasped eastern and western s.,
    333:6
  great and wide s., 19:6
  great shroud of s. rolled on, 487:1
  green isle in s., 452:2
  grew civil at her song, 173:5
  half-held by night, 489:8
  has many voices, 671:13
  hast thou entered into the springs of
    the s., 15:10
  hates a coward, 674:5
  he that commands s. is at liberty,
    160:7
  herd ran into s., 37:25
  hold helm when s. calm, 99:18
  houses all gone under s., 671:2
  how many strawberries in s., 788:15
  hurt not the s., 47:21
  if we gang to s. master, 784:33
  in calm s. every man pilot, 272:3
  in flat s. sunk, 252:29
  in peril on the s., 506:4
  influence of s. power, 541:3
  into the s. upon dry ground, 9:1
  iridescent and dark, 731:4
  is calm tonight, 499:19
  is his and he made it, 18:19
  is land's edge also, 671:13
  is not full, 23:23
  itself floweth in veins, 280:22
  kingdom by s., 453:8
  lands beyond the s., 374:6
  lies all about us, 721:13
  light over land and s., 621:7
  like stars on the s., 401:15
  like to drink whole s., 714:8
  lonely s. and sky, 633:14
  lost s. voices, 669:20
  love it you cannot, 618:11
  lover of men the s., 534:1
  made for his tomb, 233:9
  magic of the s., 442:6
  man not afraid of s., 613:11
  man to match the s., 563:8
  Marathon looks on s., 402:26
  marvel how fishes live in s., 219:21
  master of s. Master of every coun-
    try, 160:*n*5
  monotonous as s., 485:23
  more hideous than s. monster,
    209:10
  mountains by the winter s., 459:24
  murderous innocence of s., 596:21
  never loved by anyone married to it,
    618:11
  never never sick at s., 529:4

Seas (continued)
　roaring with blasts, 297:1
　roll to waft me, 301:9
　sail wet s. roun', 592:19
　seven s. of ink, 117:10
　shoreless s., 543:17
　strange s. of thought, 373:10
　tossed upon cloudy s., 643:11
　unsuspected isle in s., 464:6
　untamed s., 721:2
　wandering over many s. to these
　　obsequies, 91:17
　waste of s., 421:17
　what s. what shores, 669:22
Seashore, like boy playing on s., 282:5
Seaside stroll a gallery, 505:2
Seasilt saltsick, 647:22
Season, a convenient s., 41:31
　be instant in s., 45:28
　bringeth forth his fruit in s., 15:29
　each thing that in s. grows, 168:16
　end of love or s., 622:18
　ever 'gainst that s., 192:29
　for wild oats, 586:21
　grain of poetry s. century, 564:8
　incompatibility like new s., 616:16
　little s. of love laughter, 520:9
　love no s. knows, 228:12
　meat in due s., 19:6
　my scope had not this s., 225:n5
　no s. such delight can bring, 240:15
　of love and laughter, 520:9
　of mists, 416:13
　of ships is here, 83:2
　of snows and sins, 533:9
　open s. and no limit to bag, 714:15
　proportion s. form, 200:7
　shock of corn cometh in s., 14:5
　tale out of s., 31:40
　things by s. seasoned, 182:12
　to come and go, 303:11
　to every thing there is a s., 23:32
　word spoken in due s., 21:28
　your admiration, 193:17
　youth's s. for joys, 297:18
Seasoned, speech s. with salt, 45:1
　things by season s., 182:12
　timber never gives, 243:12
　with a gracious voice, 181:4
　with Attic salt, 269:30
Seasoning of all enjoyments, 269:18
Seasons, afford costly s., 757:15
　all s. shall be sweet, 382:17
　all times are his s., 231:10
　appointeth moon for s., 19:6
　as swift s. roll, 447:11
　assailed the s., 608:3
　defend you from s., 210:3
　he makes the s., 5:1
　joys abound as s. fleet, 163:23
　lovers' s. run, 228:11
　man for all s., 138:1
　mercy s. justice, 181:19
　not the full four s., 684:7
　O s. O châteaux, 565:19
　sorrow breaks s., 165:32
　time of s. and constellations, 670:21
　vernal s. of year, 254:22
　with the year s. return, 257:24
　yin and yang became four s., 86:15

Seat, castle hath pleasant s., 213:4
　God's great Judgment S., 591:9
　of desolation, 256:4
　of Mars, 171:9
　of pleasures and loves, 275:30
　of sensation stomach, 580:10
　proud s. of Lucifer, 260:14
　sitteth in the s. of the scornful,
　　15:29
　sitting in catbird s., 690:16
　thy s. is up on high, 172:17
　upon intellectual throne, 498:11
　while memory holds a s., 194:27
　wild sequestered s., 324:16
Seatbelts, fasten s. bumpy night, 727:5
Seated, all s. on the ground, 285:1
　grace s. on this brow, 197:30
　heart knock at my ribs, 212:23
　in thy silver chair, 231:21
　one day at organ, 505:22
Sea-tides tossing free, 442:6
Seatown, years around s. corner,
　738:1
Seats, put down mighty from s., 37:42
Seaward flying unbroken wings,
　669:20
　from the town, 396:24
　salt tides s. flow, 497:6
　trees seemed to march s., 557:15
Sebastian, Saint S. died of fright,
　769:3
Secluded chapel, 672:5
　eternally from God, 231:9
Second, appointed for my s. race,
　270:4
　best to go back quickly, 67:9
　best's gay goodnight, 598:3
　childishness, 191:3
　children for s. time, 73:4
　class citizens, 685:11
　custom almost s. nature, 168:n2
　Daniel, 182:4
　first among these than s. in Rome,
　　88:20
　friend is a s. self, 88:9
　great nature's s. course, 214:6
　in war no s. prize, 685:14
　is frugality, 57:22
　mads him, 201:25
　nature, 347:14
　no dishonor to halt at s. place,
　　87:17
　no s. acts in American lives, 694:22
　office of government easy, 344:2
　thoughts are best, 68:16
　What's on s., 691:7
　wife hateful to children, 67:22
Secondary imagination, 384:7
Second-class intellect first-class tem-
　perament, 543:14
Seconded with will and power, 200:10
Secrecy and free government, 655:22
　for s. no lady closer, 177:18
　nature's infinite book of s., 216:26
　the human dress, 358:13
　within s. of our own heads, 774:7
Secret, and his dark s. love, 358:4
　anniversaries of heart, 442:24
　as grave, 151:14
　be s. and exult, 596:2

Secret (continued)
　black midnight hags, 215:17
　bread eaten in s., 21:3
　cleanse me from s. faults, 16:12
　courage s. of liberty, 568:14
　dwelleth in s. place, 18:15
　every creature s. to other, 471:12
　guilt by silence betrayed, 275:23
　keeps s. well as child, 428:2
　liberty s. of happiness, 568:14
　life of belly and bone, 734:6
　ministry, 382:16, 382:17
　not secret if confided, 479:20
　nothing is s., 38:15
　of being a bore, 305:26
　of freedom a brave heart, 72:7
　of happiness freedom, 72:7
　of my success, 543:12
　of study of nature, 437:1
　of success constancy, 435:12
　only s. is Immortality, 514:15
　open rebuke better than s. love,
　　23:1
　powers of atom, 601:15
　self-contained solitary, 470:3
　single s. will still be man, 689:8
　sits in middle and knows, 624:16
　tell you a great s., 732:19
　things belong unto the Lord, 10:24
　though s. it rolls, 391:11
　thoughts run over all things, 239:20
　three keep s. if two dead, 309:15
　trade s., 326:2
　treasures in s. kept, 476:11
　Vereker's s., 548:20
　waters, 694:1
　whence this s. dread, 292:14
　whispers of other's watch, 185:14
　with every s. thing, 24:30
Secretary of Nature, 246:1
Secretly, how swift how s., 683:9
Secret's safe 'twixt you and me,
　468:10
Secrets cry aloud, 724:10
　dark s. of ocean, 420:17
　everybody guesses, 570:13
　from whom no s. are hid, 49:13
　holding such things to be holy s.,
　　71:1
　learned s. of grave, 538:6
　trust not him with s., 342:8
Sect, know neither s. nor idolatry,
　134:11
　never attached to that s., 408:13
　slave to no s., 302:1
Section, you-all means s., 780:21
Sects, clarification s. founded on,
　625:8
　vicissitude of s. and religions,
　160:11
Secular city, 760:9
Seculo, alteri s., 85:n6
Secure amidst falling world, 292:3
　and now never mourn, 409:4
　blessings of liberty, 346:7
　friends by doing favors, 72:5
　he that's s. is not safe, 310:3
　he who s. within can say, 274:29
　you count many friends, 102:3

Secured against maladministration, 327:2
Securely founded, 349:23
Security, absolute s., 713:19
  against future violations, 313:5
  culture moment of s., 653:4
  for average man, 649:1
  for the future, 313:n3
  how little s. we have, 390:9
  in old book, 486:6
  maintain peace and s., 655:23
  militia necessary to s. of free State, 346:12
  no s. in nobleness of another, 616:3
  of all countries connected, 644:17
  of people, 327:2
  order s. and peace, 644:17
  public strength individual s., 354:18
  system of general s., 650:9
  to democracies against despots, 351:n7
Sed haec prius fuere, 90:n12
Sedate, ignorance s., 313:22
Sedentary life sin, 553:15
Sedge withered from lake, 417:4
Sediment of long Chinese past, 662:8
Sedition, wine cause of s., 284:13
Sedulous ape, 561:19
Sedulously cultivate free speech, 621:17
See a fine picture, 349:10
  all could s. was sky water birds, 727:19
  all we s. or seem, 451:7
  and be seen, 101:13
  bachelor of threescore again, 186:13
  best not to s. beams of sun, 59:24
  blind now I s., 40:14
  bosom I must not s., 269:5
  can I s. another's woe, 356:18
  change we think we s., 623:5
  cherry hung with snow, 578:19
  Christ stand, 466:22
  church by daylight, 186:19
  clear day s. forever, 745:14
  dagger I s. before me, 213:20
  direction which thou canst not s., 301:12
  dwarf on giant s. farther, 234:7
  eye begins to s., 725:15
  eye to eye, 27:34
  eyes and s. not, 28:15
  eyes have they but s. not, 19:17
  eyes that can s., 663:18
  eyes weep but never s., 388:16
  from where I stood, 683:15
  full plain I s., 382:4
  girl I like to s., 719:1
  God made and eaten, 465:7
  God whom we s. not is, 535:8
  gold that I never s., 579:8
  happy moron, 783:7
  have thee not yet s. thee still, 213:20
  Heaven's glories shine, 480:4
  here it is, 417:3
  here shall he s. no enemy, 190:18
  how she leans her cheek, 174:28
  how they run, 788:2
  how world goes, 211:3

See (*continued*)
  how world wags, 190:22
  how yond justice rails, 211:3
  how you would do, 359:19
  I don't s. said Caterpillar, 517:8
  I s. not feel how beautiful, 383:6
  I s. what I eat, 517:18
  I'll s. you again, 700:16
  image of what we actually s., 537:22
  in all things thee to s., 243:25
  in my flesh shall I s. God, 14:30
  in small proportions beauties s., 233:3
  into life of things, 373:3
  it clearly in the idea, 639:20
  it lap the Miles, 512:17
  it shining plain, 579:9
  it yet remains to s., 514:13
  kings have desired to s., 38:21
  let mine eyes not s., 201:18
  little Tippler, 511:18
  lovers cannot s. follies, 180:20
  may I be there to s., 334:24
  me safe up, 137:18
  Mediterraneans s. clearly, 653:3
  meet and not s. its head, 57:5
  more people s. than weigh, 305:12
  more ye s. better like it, 602:21
  never s. nor know nor miss me, 647:22
  never s. tree at all, 709:10
  no evil, 777:10
  no man s. me more, 225:14
  none should s. salvation, 181:19
  none so blind as not s., 286:18
  not my love to s., 154:8
  not s. me stopping here, 623:16
  not the bottom of it, 201:5
  not worth going to s., 317:14
  O can't you s. it, 690:18
  object as it really is, 498:23
  oh say can you s., 391:2
  one mountain and see all, 234:30
  one-third of nation ill-housed, 649:7
  only their own shadows, 75:17
  only with heart one can s., 705:13
  other whole against sky, 630:11
  oursels as ithers see us, 361:18
  people refuse to s. me, 735:18
  really do not s. signal, 360:14
  sad sights moves, 167:4
  see their mark, 243:24
  seem s. things thou dost not, 211:5
  she stirs, 441:17
  Shelley plain, 465:16
  smile his work to s., 358:7
  so much nor live so long, 211:21
  sons what things you are, 184:10
  sun with ignorant eye, 639:20
  taste and s. that the Lord is good, 16:30
  ten things where ordinary man sees one, 660:7
  the conquering hero, 308:23
  the Way of Heaven, 57:15
  there shall no man s. me, 9:19
  they bark at me, 210:14
  they shall s. God, 33:1

See (*continued*)
  things as they are, 315:7
  things seen I s. no more, 375:3
  things through his eyes, 692:21
  think I shall never s., 661:16, 709:10
  those things ye see, 38:21
  thou canst not s. my face, 9:19
  through glass darkly, 43:16
  to s. her was to love her, 362:11
  Veil through which not s., 445:19
  Venus let me never s., 288:4
  was blind but now I s., 327:4
  we are as much as we s., 476:20
  what a rent, 189:5
  what can not s. over is infinite, 412:1
  what I say, 576:17
  what I see, 196:20
  what s. elsewhere not here, 132:15
  what you s. is what you get, 784:15
  whatever you s. is Jupiter, 106:2
  whatsoever I shall s. or hear, 71:1
  where Christ's blood streams, 162:23
  where it flies, 162:19
  where she comes apparelled like spring, 219:18
  Winter comes, 307:15
  with half an eye, 151:3
  with not through the eye, 360:3
  world in grain of sand, 359:5
  you s. more in you, 713:1
  you s. things, and say Why, 571:24
  you s. what I am, 736:1
  young men shall s. visions, 29:32
  your good works, 33:3
Seed, bearing precious s., 19:28
  blood of Christians is s., 112:5
  blood of martyrs s. of Church, 112:n2
  broadcast catch somewhere, 461:17
  de first en last de beginnin, 696:12
  enmity between thy s. and her s., 6:24
  ground more malign with bad s., 126:19
  groweth s., 775:10
  heaven like to mustard s., 35:9
  money the s. of money, 319:4
  nor his s. begging bread, 17:1
  of religious liberty, 486:8
  searching to rediscover first s., 705:15
  sow thy s. in the morning, 24:25
  wonder the s. of knowledge, 158:2
  work is s. sown, 411:19
Seeds, fruitful error full of s., 556:22
  in dry pod tick, 607:11
  of godlike power, 497:5
  of patriots and heroes, 327:n5
  of time, 212:17
  plant s. watch renewal, 511:2
  some s. fell by way side, 35:5
  treason sows secret s., 123:5
Seedtime and harvest, 7:22
  fair s. had my soul, 373:7
  regret my s., 742:22
Seeing, adds precious s. to the eye, 169:2

Selection (*continued*)
Natural S., 444:5
natural s., 493:9
not saving but s., 332:28
Selects, artist observes s. guesses, 582:9
Soul s. her own Society, 512:2
Self, applause from none but s., 494:20
concentered all in s., 378:1
earthly city formed by love of s., 115:3
experience one's s., 708:5
for my single s., 187:20
friend is a second s., 88:9
is hateful, 271:8
is honey of all beings, 50:17
love seeketh s. to please, 358:3
luminous island of s., 731:7
not mine but ours, 756:11
nothing greater than one's s., 489:20
One's-S. I sing, 488:13
only prison, 563:15
swear by thy gracious s., 175:8
through eyes of others, 605:2
to thine own s. be true, 194:1
toll me back from thee to my sole s., 415:18
total of all he can call his, 545:20
try to speak hidden s., 498:5
was not the same, 199:31
what jailer inexorable as s., 436:8
Self-affrighting, learns it is s., 597:6
Self-appeasing, learns it is s., 597:6
Self-appointed inspector of snow-storms, 476:24
Self-balanced, O to be s. for contingencies, 488:14
Self-blinding, nothing so s., 692:21
Self-canceling, democracy a, 412:22
Self-circling energies, 384:1
Self-complacency is pleasure, 278:3
Self-conceit may lead to self-destruction, 59:4
philosophy to get rid of s., 108:9
Self-conscious, not make us s., 665:8
Self-constituted, Americans first s. People, 683:13
Self-contained, placid and s., 489:16
Self-control, self-knowledge s., 453:24
Self-deceit, nothing easier than s., 79:3
Self-delighting, learns it is s., 597:6
Self-denial indulgence, 545:1
Self-denying, in war ruthless s., 404:21
Self-destruction, self-conceit may lead to s., 59:4
Self-devoted, in war s., 404:21
Self-dissection introversion, 433:4
Self-evident, hold these truths s., 475:5
hold truths to be s., 343:2
Self-fulfilling prophecy false definition, 728:13
Self-government, democracy direct s., 461:n5
Self-help root of growth, 472:17
Self-homicide, misspending time a s., 279:30
Self-idealization childish, 713:19
Self-interest speaks all tongues, 265:4

Selfish, art s. and perverse, 371:19
being all my life, 387:5
feverish s. little clod, 570:22
spiteful Public, 390:10
very old most s., 463:25
Selfishness, forces of s. met match, 649:6
reduce s., 57:6
systems perverted by s., 645:9
Self-knowledge self-control, 453:24
Self-love, address ourselves to their s., 326:1
and social be made the same, 369:3
and social the same, 302:5
greatest of flatterers, 264:22
in jealousy more s., 265:33
makes more libertines, 319:17
strike at s., 507:12
Self-made from elements, 729:2
laws, 494:20
man and worships creator, 462:9
Self-observation, psychology based on s., 520:7
Self-perpetuating, mind soul of s. institutions, 744:12
Self-possession, courtesy and s., 600:7
Self-preservation, instinct of s., 574:5
Self-protection sole end for interfering, 439:11
Self-reliance aversion to society, 431:20
discontent want of s., 431:27
reliance on God, 432:29
Self-respect, draw breath of s., 706:11
never break word or lose s., 110:20
not manifest want of s., 79:10
Self-revelation, terrible fluidity of s., 549:10
Self-reverence self-knowledge, 453:24
Self-righteousness, avoid s., 692:21
not religion, 476:12
Self-sacrifice, progress of artist s., 672:9
risk and spiritual s., 679:16
vocation demands s., 691:4
Self-sacrificing love of brute, 452:9
Selfsame, shot fellow's way, 179:24
song that found path, 415:17
sun that shines upon court, 223:12
winds that blow, 562:13
Self-slaughter, his canon 'gainst s., 193:5
Self-subsisting self-seeking me, 426:8
Self-suffering, patience means s., 606:13
Self-sufficing, reasoning s. thing, 374:3
Self-trust, in s. all virtues comprehended, 431:9
teacher inspires s., 422:2
Sell a country, 370:4
buy with you s. with you, 180:2
did s. himself to work wickedness, 13:1
don't s. America short, 782:22
don't s. steak s. sizzle, 719:17
for a shilling, 472:2
go and s. that thou hast, 35:36
made to s. and s. quickly, 659:15
no branch over wine that will s., 100:20

Sell (*continued*)
no man might buy or s., 47:29
not here to s. boilers, 317:22
precious as stuff they s., 446:7
to none s. right or justice, 123:13
when you can, 191:24
Willie is no good I'll s. him, 607:9
Seller needs not one eye, 244:25
Selling, buying and s. spending lives, 478:29
nimble in s. houses, 658:4
writers are always s. somebody out, 766:10
Sells eternity to get toy, 166:38
Selva, mi ritrovai per una s. oscura, 125:n2
Selves, beautiful in thoughts in s., 582:12
biography accounts for six or seven s., 651:1
our s. our souls and bodies, 49:17
Semblable au prince des nuées, 494:n2
hypocrite lecteur mon s. mon frère, 494:1
Semblance in another's case, 335:22
Semel emissum volat irrevocabile verbum, 97:n10
Semen est sanguis christianorum, 112:n2
Semi-criminal semi-pathological, 652:12
Semihuman and demonic, 628:15
Semi-pathological propensities, 652:12
Semper eadem, 145:5
fidelis, 119:29
Sempronius, we'll do more S., 292:4
Senate admiring its members, 535:14
like Cato give S. laws, 302:11
Roman s. long debate, 292:9
Senator seldom proclaims inferiority, 535:14
Send an Angel before thee, 9:16
choice grain into this wilderness, 277:3
fortune will s. it, 228:1
here am I s. me, 26:3
home my long strayed eyes, 229:6
homeless tempest-tost, 558:1
me reeling in, 514:10
more grace than gifts to s., 227:7
never s. to know for whom bell tolls, 231:8
recompense as largely s., 322:23
them that s. unto thee, 22:12
whom shall I s., 26:3
Senex, old Mr. S. showing age, 733:6
Senex, fortunate s., 92:n3
Senile, regarding elders as s., 535:18
Senior-junior giant-dwarf, 168:28
Sennacherib king of Assyria departed, 13:12
Sens, donner un s. plus pur, 672:n1
Sensation instinct intelligence, 420:18
Sensational event changing from brown suit, 658:5
something s. to read, 567:10
Sensations, condensation of s., 607:15
rather than Thoughts, 417:16
Sense aches at thee, 208:1
common s. appall, 583:9

Sense *(continued)*
  common s. hasty superficial, 477:21
  common s. not so common, 306:16
  common s. on ground floor, 447:19
  common s. plain dealing, 432:11
  common s. reduced to calculus,
    351:17
  common s. without genius, 677:3
  devoid of s. and motion, 257:2
  dictate of common s., 308:22
  divinest S., 512:11
  enchants my s., 200:17
  find people have good s., 265:36
  fools laugh at men of s., 283:15
  from thought divide, 274:n2
  fruit of s. beneath, 298:15
  genius s. and wit, 334:4
  good s. equally distributed, 246:13
  good s. in country, 345:14
  good s. of Americans, 438:3
  good s. refine her page, 280:15
  humility s. of reverence, 69:4
  in larger s. cannot dedicate, 450:2
  learned without s., 333:13
  lively s. of filial duty, 342:23
  money like sixth s., 626:14
  money speaks s., 281:18
  moral s. of work of art, 549:2
  much S. starkest Madness, 512:11
  my s. is mocked, 227:15
  no s. of decency sir, 680:14
  no s. of ills to come, 321:15
  not s. enough to come in, 137:n7
  nothing good makes complete s.,
    684:18
  of death in apprehension, 204:11
  of future favors, 265:n2
  of honor in action, 72:7
  of it is anyhow, 467:27
  of life, 640:23
  of obligation, 611:9
  of reckoning, 185:20
  of what life means, 546:17
  one has s. of humor, 664:18
  one that has another s., 292:23
  one world to s., 248:10
  palls upon the s., 292:8
  palter with us in double s., 216:20
  Pickwickian s., 468:20
  poem part of s. of life, 640:23
  rich grape juice of good s., 114:11
  satire or s., 302:14
  seal s. in slumber, 617:1
  Shadwell never deviates into s.,
    274:26
  sound an echo to s., 298:20
  stings and motions of s., 203:26
  sublime, 373:5
  sublime in old s., 659:4
  take care of s., 518:1
  talk s. to a fool, 69:1
  talk s. to American people, 706:10
  through s. and nonsense, 274:17
  want of decency want of s., 278:23
  whose soul is s., 229:11
Senseless, abhorred that s. tribe,
    289:18
  kind of s. wit, 749:17
Senses, derangement of all s., 566:3
  diffuses s. with oblivion, 95:14

Senses *(continued)*
  flies from s. and particulars to axi-
    oms, 158:12
  forever in joy, 466:17
  hath not a Jew s., 180:30
  if Parson lost s., 611:18
  indisputable existence of s., 323:16
  money-lust before s., 659:13
  our gentle s., 213:4
  so long as I keep my s., 426:13
  steep s. in forgetfulness, 183:36
Sensibility, dissociation of s., 672:14
  inexhaustible s., 549:13
  soil of subject, 549:2
Sensible and conscientious men,
    315:n7
  impressions of free mind, 600:7
  men never tell, 435:19
  this s. warm motion, 204:14
  to feeling as to sight, 213:20
Sensitive, gentle s. mind, 596:16
Sensitivity, chief area of s., 727:8
Sensual, caught in s. music, 597:7
  lust a tempest, 495:4
  this wisdom is s., 46:13
  turbulent fleshy s. eating drinking,
    489:9
Sensualist, lover and s., 557:7
Sensuality, intellectual passion drives
    out s., 135:1
Sensuous, simple s. and passionate,
    254:21
Sent, him that s. me, 40:13
  thee late a rosy wreath, 232:16
  to my account, 194:24
  to spy out the land, 9:29
Sentence, death s. of Versailles, 676:10
  every s. victory, 115:5
  first verdict afterwards, 518:11
  full of high s., 667:17
  German dives into s., 527:4
  hungry judges s. sign, 299:15
  I catch every s., 582:11
  my s. is for open war, 256:26
  no unnecessary words, 608:9
  not understand words apart from s.,
    510:7
  originator of good s., 433:19
  single s. for modern man, 732:20
  structure of British s., 619:17
  success to periodic s., 693:14
  true in all times, 448:14
  waiting s. in bull pen, 742:22
Sentenced, author sentenced to death,
    704:13
Sentences, backward ran s., 708:9
  memorable s., 515:15
  paragraph no unnecessary s., 608:9
  say in ten s. what others in book,
    552:32
  shall quips and s. awe, 186:31
  that stir bile, 580:18
Sententiae, quot homines tot s., 86:n9
Sententious, laconic or s. type, 609:11
Sentest, thou s. forth thy wrath, 9:5
Sentient, critic s. and restless, 548:17
Sentiment and alliteration, 523:21
  fungus crop of s., 532:16
  in s. public crude, 396:15
  living s. and dying s., 394:10

Sentiment *(continued)*
  nurse of manly s., 332:13
  offices sensitive to mass s., 677:2
  read Richardson for s., 316:14
  sacrifice you make for s., 603:21
Sentimental, carry body for s. value,
    722:1
Sentimentalist, no s. no stander above,
    489:9
Sentimentality failure of feeling,
    640:22
Sentimentally disposed to harmony,
    387:28
Sentiments, duration of great s.,
    552:14
  precluded from offering s., 336:18
  them's my s., 463:7
  to which bosom echo, 314:21
  weigh less than action, 486:10
  with noble s. bad literature, 607:5
Sentinels almost receive, 185:14
Sentry are you there, 487:10
  at this door England stands s.,
    539:3
  stands a winged s., 270:8
Separate and equal station, 343:2
  and unequal, 723:20
  but equal, 682:9
  church and State s., 501:15
  dying ember, 452:14
  educational facilities unequal, 682:9
  from forces to repeat No, 553:16
  he shall s. them, 36:17
  like marbles touching but s., 537:17
  peace, 701:11
  people s. rigidly alone, 537:17
  quite quite s., 510:13
  simple s. person, 488:13
  to s. because of race, 682:9
  us from love of Christ, 42:8
Separated, war not s. from politics,
    686:14
Separately, hang together or hang s.,
    310:18
Separateness of all things, 725:3
Separateth, he that repeateth a matter
    s. friends, 21:34
Separation, causes which impel s.,
    343:2
  not fighting for s., 755:8
  prepare definitely for s., 385:7
  yield who will to s., 624:7
September, from frosted S. to sightless
    realm, 658:1
  morn, 443:9
  thirty days hath S., 143:13
  when you reach S., 666:4
  within bosom S., 776:19
Sepulcher, night dome of vast s.,
    407:15
  no man knoweth of his s., 10:30
  there by the sea, 453:10
  whole earth s. of famous men, 72:7
Sepulchers, grandest of all s., 72:7
  shrouds and s. delight, 414:6
  whited s., 36:5
Sepulchral, old s. urns, 334:13
Sequel, unto God is the s., 117:9
Sequence, natural s. of unnatural be-
    ginning, 387:11

Sequence (*continued*)
  of phenomena, 345:9
Sequestered, her wild s. seat, 324:16
  nooks, 442:19
  vale of life, 322:17
Seraphically, song s. free, 509:6
Seraphim, bright s. in burning row,
    254:11
Seraphims, above it stood the s., 25:42
Seraphs swing snowy Hats, 511:18
  where s. might despair, 399:10
  winged s. of Heaven, 453:8
Sere, fallen into the s., 216:9
  leaf red and s., 378:3
  leaves crisped and s., 453:1
  meadows brown and s., 411:8
  with ivy never s., 253:14
Serene before direst death, 503:4
  count only hours s., 390:*n*3
  I fold my hands, 532:6
  mind s. for contemplation, 292:*n*4
  pure s., 413:24
  purest ray s., 322:13
  see with eye s., 375:17
  true friendship never s., 271:23
Serenely eternity waits at crossway of
    stars, 700:10
  full epicure would say, 380:18
Serenity, gentleness of spirit s. of
    mind, 245:*n*3
  grace to accept with s., 684:14
  steady and perpetual s., 293:6
  sweet s. of books, 442:19
  usual querulous s., 387:2
Serf, labor as another's s., 53:25
  patrician plebeian lord and s.,
    481:15
Serfdom, abolish s. from above,
    479:16
  African not accept s. forever, 681:4
Serfs, spending lives like s., 478:29
  vassals and s., 419:1
Sergeant, back to Army again s.,
    592:12
  Color-S. said, 591:15
  this fell s. death, 199:24
Sergeant Cuff, the roses get it says S.,
    504:7
Sergeant's widow told lie, 446:23
Serious and alarming consequences,
    336:18
  and the smirk, 469:15
  audience takes him s., 638:3
  Cervantes' s. air, 303:24
  comedian takes himself s., 638:3
  companions few in s. business,
    59:20
  I never was more s., 387:15
  imitation of action that is s., 78:31
  insisted always on being s., 70:1
  life breathtakingly s., 680:4
  marriage damnably s. business,
    686:18
  no human thing of s. importance,
    76:2
  nothing s. in mortality, 214:15
  one who is s. all day, 3:9
  strenuous and s., 673:11
  war too s. for military, 354:9
Sermon, all one asks of s., 748:2

Sermon (*continued*)
  calls it a s., 380:2
  everyone has one s., 781:21
  good honest painful s., 279:4
  perhaps turn out a s., 361:21
  verse find who s. flies, 242:17
  whole of her s., 636:10
Sermons and soda water, 402:18
  in stones, 190:7
  logic and s. never convince, 489:14
  no s. in stones, 532:10
Serpent, be the s. under 't, 213:3
  beguiled me, 6:23
  biteth like a s., 22:22
  infernal s. whose guile, 255:21
  Leviathan that crooked s., 26:31
  more s. than dove, 162:8
  of old Nile, 217:7
  old s. called Devil, 47:28
  rod shall become a s., 8:31
  sharpened their tongues like a s.,
    20:11
  sting thee twice, 181:15
  subtlest beast, 260:2
  trail of s. over all, 392:12
  was more subtile, 6:19
  way of a s. upon a rock, 23:15
  wise as s., 34:*n*2
Serpent's egg, 188:1
  sharper than s. tooth, 209:11
Serpents, all the s. bite, 5:4
  be wise as s., 34:30
  envious, 230:21
  rods became s., 8:32
  there's no pleasing them, 517:12
Servant, accuse not a s. unto his mas-
    ter, 23:13
  borrower is s. to the lender, 22:10
  carried His s. by night, 116:15
  good and faithful s., 36:14
  he shall be my s., 8:12
  hear what s. girls said, 613:8
  in love lord in marriage, 131:27
  individual make state his s., 705:4
  is thy s. a dog, 13:8
  lettest thy s. depart, 38:5
  not above lord, 34:32
  of God well done, 259:17
  of Living God, 325:17
  prince first s. of state, 318:19
  thy s. heareth, 11:28
  thy s. sleeping, 506:15
  unprofitable, 36:16
  virtues expected of s., 336:4
  with this clause, 243:26
Servants, desires and petitions of thy
    s., 49:6
  fire best of s., 413:5
  frantic among thy s., 31:9
  gods s. of human interest, 588:16
  leave living to s., 537:19
  of the machine, 723:11
  public s. serve you right, 706:14
  reveal Himself to His s., 255:1
Servants', never equality in s. hall,
    581:21
Servare modum, 105:*n*13
Serve, also s. who only stand, 255:13
  as Thou deservest, 139:3
  as we love we s., 562:5

Serve (*continued*)
  because we freely love, 259:11
  cannot s. God and mammon, 33:17
  country and thy kind, 522:12
  employ body to s., 91:20
  faithfully to s. State, 246:25
  future hour, 377:6
  if elected I will not s., 492:*n*6
  in heaven, 256:6
  knives that s. or cut, 486:5
  long apprenticehood, 170:32
  my nation ruin another, 304:12
  no man can s. two masters, 33:17
  not s. God if devil bid, 205:16
  the Lord with gladness, 18:22
  they also s., 255:13
  'tis enough 'twill s., 175:27
  while not able to s. men, 61:15
  whom should we s., 347:7
  you right, 706:14
Served, first come first s., 123:*n*5
  God with half zeal, 225:22
  human liberty, 598:9
  my time in hell, 783:13
  no private end, 300:24
  public will be s., 283:3
  youth will be s., 428:17
Serves it in office of a wall, 171:9
  sir which s. and seeks for gain,
    209:18
  take current when it s., 189:20
Serveth not another's will, 227:6
Service, all s. same with God, 464:8
  beyond all recompense, 249:21
  desert in s., 201:3
  do a friend s., 65:13
  done the state some s., 208:16
  essential s. to country, 289:11
  fairer than other nations, 121:2
  ful weel soong s. dyvyne, 129:12
  greater than the god, 200:15
  greatest s. or greatest injury, 75:3
  high and anthems clear, 252:10
  in purer lives s., 443:17
  injustice sometimes s. to public,
    346:5
  is perfect freedom, 49:2
  lay out ourselves in s. of mankind,
    347:7
  never bad man good s., 332:4
  of vast meretricious beauty, 694:9
  pressed into s., 623:6
  riches poverty and use of s., 224:4
  shrink from s. of country, 340:22
  small s. is true s., 377:14
  strong for s. still, 334:29
  weary and old with s., 225:16
  yeoman's s., 199:21
Serviceable, fool be made s., 573:13
  substitute for masturbation, 626:8
Services, give your s. for nothing, 71:5
  goods and s. paid with goods and
    s., 610:12
  of Europe to humanity, 629:16
Servile, evidence of s. status, 574:8
  fetters breaks, 778:7
  inciters of s. insurrection, 522:13
  to all skyey influences, 204:9
Servility, savage s. slides by, 743:13
Serving, betrays instead of s., 331:4

Shakespeare (*continued*)
  darts himself forth, 384:16
  debts to authors, 433:20
  despise S. when I measure my mind, 571:14
  Fancy's child, 251:19
  had largest soul, 273:11
  immortal S. rose, 313:10
  Jew that S. drew, 303:19
  life of Allegory, 418:11
  my S. rise, 232:18
  myriad-minded S., 384:17
  never blotted line, 233:4
  room for S. in your tomb, 240:13
  tongue S. spake, 375:1
  unlocked heart, 377:13
  was naturally learned, 273:12
  was of us, 464:24
  what needs my S., 251:2
Shakespeare's strain, 430:12
Shakespeherian Rag, 668:21
Shaking, fall without s., 304:6
  her invincible locks, 255:2
  sail's s., 633:14
Shalimar, pale hands beside S., 590:16
Shall, all that is and s. be, 66:13
  mark you his absolute s., 219:7
Shallow bauble boats, 200:6
  brooks and rivers wide, 251:14
  by s. rivers birds sing, 162:3
  changing woman, 166:9
  draughts intoxicate, 298:13
  I owe thousand pound, 184:17
  in himself, 261:4
  laughing s. dreaming pool, 484:14
  men believe in luck, 432:38
  murmur but deep are dumb, 152:13
  spirit of judgment, 163:10
  surface stream s. light, 500:18
  weeds are s.-rooted, 163:24
  woman not even s., 553:*n*2
Shallows, bound in s. and miseries, 189:19
Shalom, peace unto you s. salaam forever, 712:10
Shalott, Lady of S., 454:16, 454:17
Sham, Fourth of July celebration a s., 480:13
  nauseous s. goodfellowship, 571:25
Shame all worst could wish, 721:3
  avoid s. but not seek glory, 380:3
  bloomin', 782:18
  cast s. when cast off smok, 131:8
  cometh behind, 65:*n*11
  crept look of furtive s., 645:16
  Despair her teachers, 436:2
  doff it for s., 169:28
  everything that is a s. among men, 60:4
  forspent with love and s., 547:9
  glory and s. of universe, 271:7
  God send them sorrow and s., 135:22
  he was not born to s., 176:2
  hide s. from every eye, 328:30
  is ashamed to sit, 176:2
  of the cities, 601:2
  on herself and all women, 53:22
  proclaim no s., 197:32
  put him to open s., 45:36

Shame (*continued*)
  quit quit for s., 262:3
  race of s., 261:15
  say what it will, 198:26
  secret thoughts without s., 239:20
  speak truth and s. Devil, 140:5
  them derides, 208:27
  transgression brings admitted s., 72:2
  waste of s., 222:7
  waves foaming out their s., 46:38
  where is thy blush, 197:32
  whose glory is in their s., 44:33
  with grief and s. bowed down, 250:7
Shameful conquest of itself, 171:11
  to mind s. to heart beauty, 495:5
Shameless, nothing more s., 53:21
  nothing worse than s. woman, 73:19
Shame's, thy tongue thy s. orator, 166:29
Shames, burn out false s., 657:14
  hold candle to my s., 180:21
  look of bay mare s. silliness, 489:2
Shamest to show dangerous brow, 188:3
Shamrock by law forbid, 779:10
  Thistle S. Rose entwine, 515:4
Shangri-La, serenity of S., 704:11
Shank, shrunk s., 191:3
Shannon, green banks of S., 388:25
  mutinous S. waves, 647:8
Shanti, 50:22
Shape, always same s. very numerous, 583:2
  Attic s., 416:6
  bear licks them into proper s., 104:11
  borrow every changing s., 667:21
  cloud in s. of a camel, 197:18
  collects motions into s., 760:14
  contemplate my flaccid s., 689:18
  court it in s. of heaven, 194:22
  execrable s., 257:17
  grim s. towered up, 373:9
  haunts about thy s., 415:20
  it as he would, 459:23
  let it keep one s., 203:28
  may be summoning itself, 756:11
  no bigger than agate-stone, 174:20
  of life, 653:17
  of things to come, 601:16
  pressed out of s., 623:6
  questionable s., 194:10
  take any s. but that, 215:7
  two of far nobler s., 258:11
  without form, 669:9
  words guard s. of man, 706:6
Shaped, feather whence pen was s., 377:8
Shapen, I was s. in iniquity, 17:20
Shapes and gives new meaning, 665:20
  behind outside pattern dim s., 583:2
  bright container can contain, 725:7
  calling s. and beckoning shadows, 252:24
  divinity that s. our ends, 199:19
  full of s. is fancy, 201:17
  horrid s. and shrieks, 251:6

Shapes (*continued*)
  of foul disease, 457:30
  poet's pen turns to s., 174:1
  ring out old s., 457:30
  shirts who coming to breathe s., 758:16
Shaping, deliberate s. of things, 600:7
Shard-borne beetle, 214:27
Share, all persons s. in government, 78:21
  bear own s. with courage, 505:1
  friends s. all things, 58:9
  good man's smile, 329:16
  no man's opinions, 482:16
  passion and action of time, 542:6
  threatened with railway s., 519:24
Shared experiences, 370:8
  joyless if not s. with him, 392:15
Sharer of action he describes, 503:5
Sharers, full s. in abundance, 560:2
  miserable s. of the event, 325:4
Shares the darkness, 684:6
Sharing, equal s. of miseries, 622:10
  unequal s. of blessings, 622:10
Shark has pretty teeth, 698:14
  went all naked to hungry s., 414:20
Sharon, rose of S., 25:3
Sharp as a two-edged sword, 20:26
  in nature few s. lines, 756:8
  names never get fat, 698:6
  necessity's s. pinch, 209:20
  nice s. quillets of law, 163:10
  nose as s. as pen, 184:30
  without s. North, 228:4
  wood has s. ear, 130:*n*3
Sharpen with cloyless sauce his appetite, 217:12
Sharpened life commands course, 509:18
  their tongues like a serpent, 20:11
Sharpeneth, iron s. iron, 23:4
Sharpening, busy s. my oyster knife, 707:5
Sharpens skill, 332:20
Sharper, slander whose edge s. than sword, 219:29
  than a serpent's tooth, 209:11
  than two-edged sword, 45:34
Sharpest, time rush s. sword, 379:10
Sharping, live by s. and robbing, 310:24
Sharp-looking, hollow-eyed s. wretch, 166:34
Sharp-sighted, fear is s., 149:20
Shatter faith of men, 589:15
  it to bits and then, 446:8
  possibility can s. us, 553:6
  vase if you will, 392:2
  your leaves, 253:14
Shattered lobsterpot, 671:13
  visage lies, 406:13
  when lamp is s., 409:19
Shaun, tale of S. or Shem, 647:20
Shave, began to s. realize growing older, 616:11
  haircut and a s., 679:1
  rides back to s. again, 703:9
Shaven, all s. and shorn, 792:24
Shavers, two of a thousand s., 104:*n*7
Shaves and takes train, 703:9

Shine (_continued_)

face of God s. through, 683:16
for thy light is come, 28:4
forever singing as they s., 292:2
forth upon clouded hills, 359:17
full alchemized and free, 414:11
Heaven's glories s., 480:4
if moon s. at full or no, 263:27
inner light will s. forth, 351:_n_5
let your light s., 33:3
make his face s. upon thee, 9:28
nor public flame dares s., 304:2
not to s. in use, 455:2
rise and s. give God glory, 794:16
traffic of Jacob's ladder, 581:12
upon my brow today, 557:1
vessels oft handled brightly s.,
162:12
wherever bright sun shall s., 226:9
wind's feet s. along sea, 533:18
wit will s., 274:28
with Pye, 399:6
you but knock breathe s., 230:26

Shined, although not s. upon, 263:31
eye of heaven s. bright, 153:7
in my angel-infancy, 270:4
upon them hath the light s., 26:7

Shines and stinks, 386:1
faith s. equal arming me, 480:4
foolery s. everywhere, 202:20
gold s. like fire, 63:26
good deed, 182:11
incongruous moonlight s., 679:8
light where no sun s., 737:9
moon s. bright, 182:7
simile that solitary s., 303:8
upon court and cottage, 223:12
wise moral man s. like fire, 65:2
wit s. at expense of memory, 290:24

Shineth everlasting Light, 524:9
light s. in darkness, 39:30
light that s. unto perfect day, 20:24
when sun s. make hay, 140:20

Shingles, naked s. of world, 499:22

Shining Big-Sea-Water, 441:24
burning and s. light, 39:49
death loves s. mark, 296:18
eyes s. for me, 673:8
improve each s. hour, 294:9
improve s. tail, 517:5
live hair s. and free, 663:2
look s. at architecture, 720:4
morning face, 191:3
no more profit of s. nights, 168:15
nowhere but in the dark, 270:11
of the stars, 459:22
on broken fragments, 394:15
on the sea, 518:23
only one s. in sky, 373:19, 644:7
path of the just is as s. light, 20:24
prospects rise, 291:29
sea to s. sea, 576:19
see it s. plain, 579:9
spangled heavens s. frame, 291:32
through dark cloud s., 617:12
to the quiet moon, 382:17
with all his might, 518:23

Shins, break s. against wit, 190:17

Ship, anchor heaves s. swings free,
428:13

Ship (_continued_)

and I took off suddenly, 709:4
as the smart s. grew, 540:18
being in s. is being in jail, 315:23
build s. of death, 658:2
came from north country, 793:19
capital s. for ocean trip, 545:3
comes into the harbor, 240:11
community like s., 508:8
don't give up the s., 393:_n_3
fragment from earth, 572:20
idle as painted s., 381:7
land to which s. must go, 376:13
me east of Suez, 591:24
name of s. Golden Vanity, 793:19
never sink except on even keel,
102:30
not to give up s., 393:13
of state, 55:_n_13, 66:4
of State, 441:18
of Union, 449:1
one s. drives east, 562:13
Papists Protestants Jews Turks in
one s., 247:13
places s. alongside enemy, 360:16
rapt s. run on side so low, 157:13
rats desert sinking s., 104:_n_9
sailing like a stately s., 261:16
tall s. and star to steer, 633:14
trip on Government s., 793:20
unstable pilot steers leaking s.,
113:11
upon the sea, 699:3
was cheered, 380:29
way of a s. in the sea, 23:15
weathered every rack, 490:19
whither O splendid s., 549:19
whose weal and woe is common,
247:13
wish to have no connection with
any s., 348:9

Shipped, and this is what ye have s.
for, 486:23

Ship's huge shadow, 381:21
way upon the sea, 592:9

Ships are but boards, 180:1
are only hulls, 65:16
are swift as a bird, 53:12
beauty and majesty of s., 442:6
believe these s. from sky, 134:11
board the well-benched s., 55:21
by s. lies a dead man, 52:23
dim-discovered, 308:1
distant storm-beaten s., 541:3
face that launched a thousand s.,
162:19
fare north, fare south, 5:5
go down to the sea in s., 19:9
guarded with s., 249:27
heart of oak our s., 323:18
how many s. my presence worth,
79:6
like s. steer courses, 263:10
loose lips sink s., 783:9
Mr. Mrs. America all s. at sea,
698:2
of war at sea, 460:6
salvaged and retiring, 647:6
saw three s. come sailing, 791:14
season of s. is here, 83:2

Ships (_continued_)

shoes s. sealing wax, 519:3
stately s. go on, 456:7
that pass in night, 442:16
there go the s., 19:6
there were two lofty s., 793:18
Thracian s. foreign faces, 533:8
upon untamed seas, 721:2
we've got the s., 507:6
wooden wall is your s., 62:24

Shipwreck, delivered from s. of blood,
699:11

Shipwrecked before I got aboard,
102:31

Shiraz, wine of S. into urine, 656:6

Shirt, essayist can pull on any s.,
703:19
happy man's without s., 140:13
land of the Cluett S., 688:12
man in Brooks Brothers s., 732:1
naked truth is I have no s., 169:10
never s. on back, 287:1
not dignify with name of stuffed s.,
711:11
of flame, 672:4
of Nessus upon me, 218:2
Song of the S., 423:5
when wanting a s., 330:15

Shirtless, sleeveless some s. others,
303:28

Shirts, Nessus s., 412:11
who is coming to breathe shapes,
758:16

Shirtsleeves, three generations s. to s.,
525:16

Shit, built-in shock-proof s. detector,
702:11

Shiver runs down spine, 692:4
sunset breezes s., 586:14

Shivering, stood in snow, 160:19

Shivering-sweet to touch, 661:12

Shoal, bank and s. of time, 213:5
of fools for tenders, 291:10

Shock disturbing delicate balance,
726:1
fodder's in the s., 559:1
future s., 760:4
like s. of corn cometh, 14:5
of recognition, 486:13
strikes with shivering s., 386:11
we shall s. them, 170:24
you must s. bourgeois, 494:17

Shocks, thousand natural s., 196:10

Shod, worse s. than shoemaker's wife,
142:1

Shoe, cannot put s. on every foot,
100:5
dame has lost s., 788:1
fits one pinches another, 628:10
for want of nail s. lost, 244:28,
310:10
none tell where s. pinches me, 107:2
not do any more black s., 764:16
old s. for good luck, 141:12
old woman lived in s., 790:2
one s. off one s. on, 791:12
over Edom will I cast out my s.,
17:31
sailed in wooden s., 559:20
sixpence in her s., 238:2, 782:10

Shoe (*continued*)
the horse, 792:21
whether s. be Spanish, 263:18
Shoemaker, lives of s. and fish peddler, 674:20
Shoemaker's, worse shod than s. wife,
142:1
Shoes and ships and sealing wax,
519:3
blue suede s., 764:8
dance fire dance in iron s., 760:1
eats soles offen s., 698:5
heard you got stock of s., 762:19
him that makes s. go barefoot,
142:*n*1
King James used to call for old s.,
238:22
latchet of whose s., 37:17
nor scrip nor s., 38:17
put off thy s., 8:24
put yourself in his s., 692:21
sold the poor for a pair of s., 29:34
surgeon to old s., 187:15
walk in velvet s., 660:14
well then o'er s. o'er boots, 530:*n*4
with your s. on your feet, 8:38
Shoestring, careless s. in whose tie,
241:5
Shone, eyes that s. now dimmed,
392:7
far off his coming s., 259:18
glory s. around, 285:1
glory s. round about them, 38:3
light here kindled s. unto many,
240:12
like meteor streaming, 256:12
moon s. on Mrs. Porter, 668:23
princely counsel s., 257:7
they s. not on poet's page, 97:*n*1
with preeminent luster, 109:12
Shoo fly, 524:8
Shook all our coffins, 540:21
softening chalk of bones, 724:17
ten days that s. world, 665:17
Shoon, cork-heeled s., 784:34
sandal s., 198:16
silver s., 616:20
Shoot, cannot s. with butter, 697:4
do not s. pianist, 566:18
don't s. Colonel, 398:7
don't s. the messenger, 66:*n*5
false Love, 776:23
fellow down, 540:12
first inquire afterwards, 686:4
folly as it flies, 301:2
guns begin to s., 591:18
her every minute, 755:14
how can you s. women children,
770:3
if you must, 443:11
inspired someone to s. your murderer, 762:11
teach young idea to s., 308:4
they s. horses don't they, 697:10
Shootin', what's all s. for, 632:14
Shooting, glory like a s. star, 171:19
stars attend thee, 241:12
Shoots, boy that s. so trim, 776:13
his wit, 192:18
neither s. nor liberates, 479:2

Shoots (*continued*)
nobody s. at Santa Claus, 618:8
of everlastingness, 270:5
Shop, back s. our own free, 145:20
closed for other business, 451:4
keep s. and s. keep thee, 157:4
said you were coming from s.,
520:5
she-bear pops head into s., 324:7
Shopkeeper, what is true of s., 319:28
Shopkeepers, government influenced
by s., 326:7
nation of s., 326:7
Shopkeeping nation, 319:28
Shops, in s. nothing to eat, 612:2
Shore, Afric's burning s., 385:8
beats back envious siege, 171:10
boat is on s., 401:27
breast on reedy s., 777:6
fast by their native s., 335:17
fragrance of salt marsh s. mud,
491:3
from s. sees sea bottom, 126:27
gaze from s. on another's tribulation, 89:13
high s. of world, 185:19
his own native s., 451:12
I on opposite s., 442:13
kingdom of the s., 221:3
lee s. of age, 557:14
left beauty on s., 429:8
lights around s., 509:29
man's control stops at s., 400:30
naked in death on unknown s., 94:4
never reach the s., 553:18
Nightly s., 452:18
ocean's wave-beat s., 474:3
of what we know, 750:5
one foot in sea one on s., 186:28
one s. beyond desire, 701:4
Plutonian s., 452:18
praise sea on s. remain, 154:19
rapture on lonely s., 400:29
refuse of teeming s., 558:1
roar echoed along s., 385:8
round earth's s., 499:22
scrambling to the s., 519:2
spies a far-off s., 164:21
stayed upon green s., 418:7
sunshine on strange s., 573:1
then on s. of world, 417:11
thrown on savage s., 491:5
unknown and silent s., 387:18
upon farther s., 506:14
upon the Irish s., 362:14
varying s. o' the world, 218:6
watery s., 358:1
waves make towards pebbled s.,
220:26
wide-watered s., 252:4
wild New England s., 410:12
Shoreditch, bells of S., 788:20
Shoreless seas, 543:17
watery wild, 498:3
Shores and desert wildernesses, 252:24
concave s., 187:17
exult O s., 491:1
not ghost of s., 543:17
of Gitche Gumee, 441:24
of Tripoli, 780:22

Shores (*continued*)
pure ablution round s., 417:12
what seas what s., 669:22
whisperings around desolate s.,
417:8
wilder s. of love, 721:12
will swarm with invisible dead,
398:11
Shoreward, great winds s. blow, 497:6
Shorn, tempers wind to s. lamb,
144:14
Short an' simple scandals, 602:19
and long of it, 182:27
and simple annals, 322:7
arm to reach to Heaven, 581:14
art long life s., 349:12
as any dream, 172:20
as watch that ends night, 294:15
as wrong as to fall s., 61:16
cut to everything, 314:30
day s. labor long, 115:16
full description of happy state,
277:10
in s. I was afraid, 667:16
in s. measures life perfect be, 233:3
in the story itself, 32:19
joy of love too s., 133:9
July's day s. as December, 222:20
lack time to make it s., 270:14
let thy speech be s., 32:6
life how long or s., 260:18
life in saddle Lord, 583:19
life is s. art long, 71:13
life s. quiet hours few, 487:22
life too s. to bore ourselves, 552:19
meaning of long speech, 365:7
my scope had not been so s.,
225:*n*5
nasty brutish and s., 239:22
nearest comes so far s., 623:4
not make sentences s., 608:9
of seeming arms s. essay, 276:29
one ready for my own, 624:15
one s. sleep past, 230:24
pain s. joy eternal, 365:18
panics duration s., 340:23
perfect in being too s., 387:7
shrill shriek, 324:14
sighs s. and infrequent, 668:19
sudden storms are s., 171:8
summer's lease too s., 220:12
take s. views, 380:4, 720:21
time of life is s., 179:3
trips from long to s., 383:11
woman's time of opportunity s.,
73:15
words are best, 622:11
Shorten, envy and wrath s. life, 32:4
stature of my soul, 508:26
tedious nights, 226:16
Shorter, Cleopatra's nose s., 270:22
make you s. by the head, 145:1
your epigrams are s., 106:12
Shorter-Catechist, something of S.,
557:7
Shortest, longest way round s. home,
242:*n*4
Shortest-lived, longest-lived and s. die
same, 110:18

Simplicity (*continued*)
simple truth miscalled s., 221:6
Spartan s., 783:16
treats with s. or severity, 499:1
Simplificateurs, terribles s., 480:8
Simplification first step to mastery of
subject, 629:13
Simplify simplify, 478:18
Simulacrum, sun the dark s. of God,
249:6
Simulate, no disguise can s. love,
265:7
Sin, Adam's sons conceived in s.,
235:4
against Holy Ghost, 537:12, 553:15
against s., 614:19
be ye angry and s. not, 44:25
before polygamy made a s., 274:1
behoved that there should be s.,
127:21
blossoms of my s., 194:24
born of a little s., 684:4
by that s. fell the angels, 225:20
choose one s., 476:3
cunning s. cover itself, 187:1
draw s. with cart rope, 25:40
dreadful record of s., 577:19
feared no danger knew no s.,
275:12
fight with death and s., 460:17
folly noise and s., 465:10
fools make a mock at s., 21:18
go and s. no more, 40:9
good man's s., 320:n5
guilty of dust and s., 244:1
has many tools, 447:12
he that is without s., 40:8
hold it half a s., 457:6
human sympathy for s., 435:22
if old and merry be s., 177:31
ignorance not innocence but s.,
468:11
in private not sin, 269:7
in s. did my mother conceive me,
17:20
in this be free from s., 418:12
is Behovely, 127:n7
learnt s. to fly, 287:10
much of Madness more of S., 452:7
my s. is red, 283:10
my s. my soul, 703:1
neatness a duty not s., 309:1
no s. but ignorance, 162:5
no s. to labor in vocation, 176:34
nothing emboldens s. as mercy,
212:3
of Judah, 28:28
original s., 494:16
original s. of man, 290:26
physicists have known s., 714:11
plate s. with gold, 211:4
pleasure's a s., 402:13
poverty is no s., 244:41
private s. not so prejudicial, 150:40
pure in life free from s., 95:28
sedentary life s., 553:15
shall be no more, 474:3
some rise by s., 203:30
sure your s. will find you out, 10:9
taketh away s. of world, 39:35

Sin (*continued*)
that I s. not with my tongue, 17:5
'tis s. nay profanation, 241:18
to covet honor, 185:21
to prefer life to honor, 109:6
usura s. against nature, 659:15
wages of s. is death, 41:45
waive quantum o' the s., 361:22
was too much hope, 232:10
we sing s., 740:8
weeps incessantly for my s., 358:16
where s. abounded, 41:42
who tell us love can die, 386:13
wilt thou forgive that s., 231:4
without s., without guilt, 4:5
worst s. passion can commit, 687:18
worst s. towards fellow creatures,
570:21
ye do by two and two, 592:6
Sinai, Wilson write Notes from S.,
652:7
Sinais, we S. climb, 485:3
Sincere flattery, 336:9
friend person with whom s., 431:37
his soul, 322:23
if his words are s., 60:17
let thy life be s., 31:12
love is s., 132:20
men always s., 600:15
not s. even when saying not s.,
589:8
of soul s., 300:24
officious innocent s., 317:26
prayer soul's s. desire, 377:18
think beforehand that words be s.,
79:22
work give reality to illusion, 631:5
Sincerely from author's soul, 689:17
Sincerest, our s. laughter, 408:7
Sincérité, changent de s., 600:n2
Sincerities, men change s., 600:15
Sincerity, friends of freedom doubt
our s., 448:5
hold faithfulness and s., 60:18
panics touchstones of s., 340:23
tell young men with great s., 314:29
to practice s., 62:2
way of heaven, 79:19
wrought in sad s., 429:10
Sinecure, gives no man a s., 659:11
Sinew, money the s. of love, 88:n9
Sinews, coin is s. of war, 139:10
cracks s. cakes brain, 486:25
exercises s. with toil, 80:3
money s. of war, 88:13
of peace, 622:3
of soul, 250:17
of virtue, 245:20
stiffen s. summon blood, 185:3
wealth the s. of affairs, 82:7
what are s. of philosopher, 108:8
Sinewy, youthful s. races, 490:7
Sinful, center of my s. earth, 222:11
desires of the flesh, 49:21
greedy the s. and lewd, 693:6
Sing, a little time to s., 520:n3
all a green willow, 208:4
ancient ways, 594:20
and build the lofty rhyme, 253:15
and louder sing, 597:8

Sing (*continued*)
arms and the man I s., 93:10, 276:5
awake and s., 26:29
because I must, 457:9
bid soul of Orpheus s., 252:7
bow themselves when he did s.,
225:10
by land and sea, 592:11
caused the widow's heart to s.,
14:42
charmingly sweet you s., 472:1
dance and drink and s., 358:5
do not think they s. to me, 667:19
eagle suffers little birds to s., 167:11
elected Silence s. to me, 550:16
for Horse nation, 787:3
Grecian woes goddess s., 299:23
hark the herald angels s., 312:17
hear angels s., 462:2
hear lady s. in Welsh, 178:9
heaven and nature s., 294:17
heavenly s., 377:n2
heigh-ho says Rowley, 788:3
holy sages once did s., 250:19
I can't s., 522:2
I s. as bird sings, 349:6
I s. myself, 488:16
I s. of brooks, 240:16
I s. with mortal voice, 259:19
I will s. unto the Lord, 9:2
in a hempen string, 236:5
in my brain I s. it, 466:28
let others s. of knights, 161:1
lhude s. cuccu, 775:10
Lhude s. Goddamm, 659:2
like birds i' the cage, 211:13
Long live king, 334:24
loss of all I s., 757:13
me your song O, 531:13
nightingale came to s., 437:10
no birds s., 417:4
no sad songs for me, 515:7
nor pair nor build nor s., 383:14
of a maiden, 775:15
of days that are gone, 536:17
of Everything and Anything, 650:12
of Olaf glad and big, 688:16
of thee I s., 444:3
of thee I s. baby, 695:7
of you i s., 688:12
one of the songs of Zion, 20:6
One's-Self I s., 488:13
or cease to sing, 303:11
pipe as linnets s., 457:9
praises to his Name, 777:8
pretty birds do s., 226:20
riding's a joy, 465:20
saddest when I s., 522:2
saints sweetly s., 283:5
savageness out of a bear, 207:21
set upon bough to s., 597:10
sit and hear me s., 356:1
so we'll live pray s., 211:13
so wildly well, 451:13
song of cheer again, 685:12
song of sixpence, 790:1
songs not heard before, 96:12
still wouldst thou s., 415:16
strange that death should s., 170:20
the Lord's song, 20:6

Sing (*continued*)

thee a song in thy praise, 362:21
thee to thy rest, 199:29
thou smoothly, 226:15
tongue the dumb shall s., 27:9
tongue the Savior's glory, 124:5
unto him a new song, 16:29
unto the Lord a new song, 18:20
we must laugh and s., 598:6
we s. sin, 740:8
what shall I s., 792:20
whatever well made, 600:1
when birds do s., 192:12
willow willow willow, 208:4
wrath of Achilles, 50:23
ye heavens earth reply, 312:13

Singe, flame that cannot s. sleeve, 598:13
my white head, 209:24
so hot that it s. yourself, 225:3

Singe, ich s. wie der Vogel singt, 349:*n*2

Singer accompany the king, 365:16
he the s. passes, 509:17
idle s. of empty day, 523:6
none hear beside the s., 388:20
sans Wine Song S., 445:16
thou s. I song, 530:4

Singers, God sent S. on earth, 441:21
long ago was one of the s., 471:29

Singest of summer, 415:10
soaring after, 408:5

Singeth all night long, 192:29
quiet tune, 381:24

Singin' in the rain, 689:11

Singing and making melody, 44:26
as they shine, 292:2
come before his presence with s., 18:22
come with s. unto Zion, 27:30
comes deer to my s., 787:14
delight in s., 388:20
each morning, 689:1
garland and s. robes, 254:12
go s. as far as we go, 92:17
hear mermaids s., 228:5
heard the mermaids s., 667:19
heart like s. bird, 515:5
hollaing and s. of anthems, 183:21
I hear America s., 488:15
in the choir, 778:9
in the Wilderness, 445:9
locust of soul, 750:2
masons building roofs, 184:24
of Mount Abora, 382:24
perhaps s. bird come, 118:5
sad or s. weather, 534:7
sets even a wise man s., 53:28
songs of expectation, 521:12
still dost soar, 408:5
those who are s. today, 528:20
till his heaven fills, 509:5
time of the s. of birds, 25:6
we are nest of s. birds, 315:13
where nightingales s., 676:17
where weeping willows, 507:14
with muses of Helicon begin s., 54:13
woodthrush s. through fog, 669:22

Singist, as s. not success, 522:2

Single, beauty draws with s. hair, 299:12
best augury is to fight, 51:36
Dram of Heaven, 514:12
draw you with s. hair, 235:*n*3
eternity only a s. night, 74:16
every s. one is right, 592:8
for my s. self, 187:20
from s. crime know nation, 93:28
Hound, 513:7
man in possession of fortune, 386:23
married to s. life, 264:12
must begin with a s. step, 57:20
nature's double name, 199:31
no s. nation have monopoly, 655:8
no such creature as s. individual, 734:9
not a s. kind of strife, 54:19
nothing in world s., 407:20
secret will be man, 689:8
soul in two bodies, 77:13
spies, 198:20

Single-minded like migratory birds, 630:7

Sings at grave-making, 199:1
below inveterate scars, 670:14
church ain't out till fat lady s., 782:12
each song twice, 465:4
for his supper, 789:7
he that s. lasting song, 599:3
in boat on bay, 456:7
know why caged bird s., 614:24
lark at heaven's gate s., 219:24
like an angel s., 182:8
morn not waking till she s., 155:20
nightingale s. all day, 392:11
nightly s. the staring owl, 169:13
on orchard bough, 465:3
this truth poet s., 455:13
thus s. he Cuckoo, 169:12
tune without the words, 511:20
yonder pine that s., 82:13

Singularity almost invariably a clue, 577:16
poetry surprise not by S., 418:1

Singulars, statements of history are s., 78:33

Sinister resonance, 573:*n*1
urge to kill s., 766:2

Sink downward to darkness, 638:26
heart and voice oppressed, 482:10
hold you as I s., 101:4
load would s. a navy, 225:18
loose lips s. ships, 783:9
Neptune s. ship on even keel, 102:30
not gross to s. but light, 165:9
of uncertainty and error, 271:7
or swim, 177:7
or swim live or die, 394:9
or swim together, 609:12
present repute for freedom, 485:7
pride of power s., 331:10
raft which will never s., 360:7
to nothingness do s., 417:11
tosses but doesn't s., 119:5
who s. to rest, 324:10

Sinking into inferiority, 393:16

Sinking (*continued*)

kind of alacrity in s., 183:2
knowledge like s. star, 455:3
rats desert s. ship, 104:*n*9
someone s. today, 563:1

Sinks and I am ready to depart, 388:21
day-star in ocean bed, 254:6
gross flesh s. downward, 172:17
honor s., 328:9
with bubbling groan, 400:31

Sinn, das kommt mir nicht aus dem S., 419:*n*7

Sinned against my brother the ass, 123:11
in Adam's fall s., 287:6
more s. against than sinning, 209:29
we have s. against thee, 28:25

Sinner, dead s. revised and edited, 544:22
desireth not death of s., 48:19
forgive some s., 642:15
merciful to me a s., 39:9
of his memory, 223:22
too weak to be a s., 211:25
whether he be s., 40:14
who write with no dinner, 674:13

Sinners, call s. to repentance, 34:22
came to save s., 45:11
God and s. reconciled, 312:17
if s. entice thee, 20:18
miserable s., 49:19
old s. have brawny consciences, 262:14
publicans and s., 34:37
Son of man betrayed to s., 36:32
standeth in the way of s., 15:29
we are s. all, 164:3

Sinning, more sinned against than s., 209:29

Sin's, sometimes s. a pleasure, 402:13

Sins, acknowledge our manifold s., 49:15
be all my s. remembered, 196:11
charity creates multitude of s., 567:13
double for all her s., 27:15
few love to hear s. they act, 219:19
forgiveness of s., 48:11
Forgiveness of s., 48:25
forgiveth s. and saveth, 30:33
her s. which are many, 38:13
lie in dark weep for s., 489:16
love covereth all s., 21:6
manifold s. and wickedness, 48:15
multitude of s., 46:26
of commission mortal, 318:8
of fathers upon children, 69:17
of omission venial, 318:8
of whole world, 46:33
oldest s. newest ways, 184:13
other s. only speak, 132:*n*1
remembrance of precedent s., 235:22
scarlet books read, 609:9
shed for remission of s., 36:28
snows and s., 533:9
takest away s. of the world, 48:9
they are inclined to, 263:8
though your s. be as scarlet, 25:29

Sins (*continued*)
  weep for her s. at other, 667:4
Sion, never climbed Mount S., 743:7
  wept when we remembered S.,
    20:*n*2
Sioux owned the world, 516:9
Sip, can't be tasted in s., 469:30
  lifeblood seemed to s., 381:15
Sipped no sup, 531:14
Sir Oracle, 179:20
Siren, listen to song of s., 339:7
  song of s. nor voice of hyena, 157:6
  tears, 222:3
Sirens, what song the S. sang, 248:30
Sires, heroic s., 280:13
Sires' age worse than grandsires',
    96:17
Sisera, mother of S. looked out win-
    dow, 11:6
  stars fought against S., 11:3
Sister Anne do you see, 778:11
  art my mother and my s., 14:26
  Caroline, 612:9
  Jerusalem thy s. calls, 359:24
  live a barren s. all your life, 172:18
  Milky Way s. in whiteness, 641:9
  ministering angel my s., 199:12
  never praise s. to s., 591:2
  poverty is s. of beggary, 73:27
  shouts with s., 456:7
  Sidney's s. Pembroke's mother,
    240:14
  still gentler s. woman, 362:5
Sisterhood is powerful, 771:13
Sister's husband's niece, 520:2
Sisters, all s. virtuous, 778:2
  Brothers and S. beware, 593:18
  cousins and aunts, 529:5
  Death and Night, 490:14
  twa s. sat in bour, 785:13
  under skins, 592:21
  wayward s. depart, 398:10
  weird s. hand in hand, 212:15
  women born my s. and lovers,
    488:18
Sisyphus, believe S. happy, 732:15
Sit and hear me sing, 356:1
  bird of night did s., 187:28
  dicky-bird why do you s., 531:9
  down says Love, 244:2
  get up so white person could s.,
    734:2
  here will we s., 182:8
  in a barn, 790:17
  in darkness, 38:1, 257:8
  Jessica look, 182:8
  let us s. upon the ground, 171:25
  like grandsire in alabaster, 179:18
  nor s. nor stand but go, 467:8
  not s. on throne of bayonets, 583:10
  on a cushion, 790:11
  on our own bottom, 147:7
  openly to weather, 653:29
  right here by me, 654:10
  shalt not s. with statisticians,
    720:20
  shame is ashamed to s., 176:2
  so I did s. and eat, 244:2
  such as s. in darkness, 19:8
  teach us to s. still, 669:14

Sit (*continued*)
  thee down sorrow, 168:20
  their strength is to s. still, 27:2
  them that s. in darkness, 38:1
  thou a patient looker-on, 242:13
  though I s. down now, 434:23
  trees where you s., 298:7
  unable to s. still, 270:21, 734:12
Sit tibi terra levis, 119:31
Sits and smiles on the night, 356:15
  as one new-risen from dream,
    167:28
  high in people's hearts, 187:30
  looking over harbor, 634:5
  on horse at hostess' door, 169:22
  Secret s. in middle, 624:16
  truth s. on lips of dying, 498:17
  watching for omens, 73:15
  wind in that corner, 186:29
  with keen appetite he s. down,
    180:19
Sittest throned in glory, 520:4
Sitteth in the seat of the scornful,
    15:29
Sitting, as cheap s. as standing, 290:2
  by desolate streams, 553:21
  careless on floor, 416:14
  equal to a god s. opposite you, 91:4
  in a pleasant shade, 233:10
  in catbird seat, 690:16
  in the sun, 386:3
  listen where thou art s., 253:11
  no pity s. in clouds, 176:8
  remain s. at your table, 651:22
  still is s., 452:21
  well in order smite, 455:6
Situation excellent I am attacking,
    562:2
  inwardness of s., 546:23
  normal all fouled up, 783:11
Six characters in search of author,
    604:4
  days shalt thou labor, 9:11, 474:19
  essentials in painting, 120:13
  everything left at s. and seven,
    128:*n*7
  feet of land, 510:14
  honest servingmen, 593:8
  hours in sleep, 152:7
  hundred pounds a year, 302:23
  impossible things before breakfast,
    519:12
  of one half-dozen other, 406:3
  or seven dozen Scots, 177:20
  Richmonds in the field, 166:18
  rode the s. hundred, 458:9
  sette world on s. and sevene, 128:21
  snowed s. days and s. nights, 738:1
  weeks to frost, 679:14
Sixes, things go at s. and sevens,
    128:*n*7
Sixpence, found crooked s., 791:11
  I give thee s., 371:21
  in her shoe, 238:2, 782:10
  not a s. sir, 367:*n*4
  song of s., 790:1
Sixteen hours ago Hiroshima, 655:6
Sixth, every s. man a slave, 379:28
Sixties made so many casualties, 770:5

Sixty, at s. miles an hour loudest
    noise, 730:6
  minutes an hour, 700:2
Sixtyfold, brought forth fruit s., 35:7
Sixty-three, intercourse began in nine-
    teen s., 750:13
Size, all men are of a s., 432:22
  near sight of mere s. of him, 647:22
  no virtue with s., 430:3
  not grandeur, 505:15
  silkworm s. or immense, 665:5
  take s. of pots of ale, 263:2
  those of largest s., 519:6
Sizzle, sell s. s. sells steak, 719:17
Skating, in s. safety is speed, 432:5
Skeleton, ague of s., 668:13
  found s. and clothed it, 325:*n*4
Skeptic, too much knowledge for s.,
    301:13
Skepticism chastity of intellect, 588:17
  highest of duties, 505:5
  luxury of s., 552:30
  more clearly understood, 146:6
  wise s. is good critic, 486:12
Skeptics' way of speaking, 146:5
Sketch ruins of St. Paul's, 425:7
Skevar, Ivan Petrofski S., 781:4
Skewered with office pens, 470:39
Skies above clear again, 685:12
  and earth a solid mass, 117:1
  are hanged, 689:8
  as long as s. are blue, 408:21
  ashen and sober, 453:1
  change s. above them, 592:18
  cloudless climes starry s., 401:14
  common people of the s., 227:9
  common sun air s., 322:25
  danced the s., 751:3
  distant deeps or s., 358:6
  fear can see more in s., 149:20
  heifer lowing at s., 416:5
  islands whose raving s. opened,
    565:16
  join triumph of the s., 312:17
  ladder to s., 154:9
  look up at s., 550:19
  looks commercing with the s.,
    251:24
  mansions in the s., 294:18
  many a message from s., 362:23
  molded and melted across s., 551:2
  moon climbest s., 156:5
  my canopy the s., 301:9
  not cloudy all day, 786:11
  parameters of s. and earth, 117:19
  raised mortal to the s., 276:16
  rend the affrighted s., 299:18
  resume sophistries of June, 511:14
  spacious s., 576:19
  statures touch s., 513:18
  suns s. clouds of June, 515:2
  tempt offspring to s., 329:14
  watcher of the s., 413:24
  wings across canceled s., 683:7
Skill, a little s. in antiquity, 159:*n*8
  baseball is game of s., 680:11
  force no place where need of s.,
    70:4
  honor hath no s. in surgery, 178:33
  man's s. built cities, 87:3

Skill (*continued*)

nor favor to men of s., 24:20

oars plied with little s., 517:1

pass days in that where s. greatest, 100:29

sharpens s., 332:20

simple truth his utmost s., 227:6

'tis God gives s., 483:6

to conceal skill, 265:26

to him that can get it, 272:30

Skilled in works of both languages, 96:18

orator a good man s. in speaking, 85:8

poet through natural gift, 63:30

Skillful, all s. in the wars, 270:8

be s. in speech, 3:11

Skillfully, play s. with a loud noise, 16:29

Skim milk masquerades, 529:8

Skimble-skamble stuff, 178:7

Skin, after my s. worms destroy, 14:30

beauty's but s. deep, 226:12

because my s. is red, 516:9

born with black s., 755:7

calf's-s. on recreant limbs, 169:28

can the Ethiopian change his s., 28:24

chameleon's tuning s., 749:13

color loves and s., 228:9

come into world with thick s., 420:10

come off with whole s., 149:19

deep, 226:*n*1

for skin, 13:32

like dusk on horizon, 690:18

man who sold hyena s., 621:15

Negro's s. prima facie evidence, 475:7

no matter color of s., 685:10

not judged by color of s., 761:2

of innocent lamb parchment, 164:9

patch lion's s. with fox's, 107:3

rip off s., 781:*n*6

skull beneath the s., 668:12

snake throws enamelled s., 173:9

squeeze orange throw away s., 306:3

white as leprosy, 381:12

with the s. of my teeth, 14:28

worth not related to color of s., 750:7

Skinny, fear thy s. hand, 381:18

Skins not colored like your own, 480:14

sisters under s., 592:21

Skinside is inside, 612:11

Skip, I cut down trees s. and jump, 775:6

Skipped, mountains s. like rams, 19:16

Skipper had taken daughter, 440:20

Skirmish of wit, 186:9

Skirt, sound of her silk s., 86:18

Skirts, God's s., 464:16

Skittish, unstaid and s. in motions, 202:9

Skittles, beer and s., 469:*n*1, 501:19

porter and s., 469:2

Skoal to the Northland, 440:19

Skugg, here S. lies, 310:16

Skull beneath the skin, 668:12

of a lawyer, 199:4

place of s., 37:9

some poor fellow's s., 386:5

Skulls, hell paved with priests' s., 114:15

leaden they don't weep, 699:7

place of s., 399:20

Skuttle-Fish, rejoice with S., 325:15

Sky, above the vaulted s., 410:6

above world stretched the s., 683:16

admitted to that equal s., 301:8

against pearl-gray s., 648:3

all could see was s. water birds, 727:19

all the milky s., 594:23

and sea and land, 580:8

banners flout the s., 212:11

beautiful as the s., 490:14

believe power and goodness in s., 134:11

believe these ships from s., 134:11

blue ethereal s., 291:32

blue s. bends over all, 382:14

blue s. of spring, 504:3

blue s. over my head, 390:15

bluebird carries s., 476:27

Brain wider than S., 512:20

bridal of earth and s., 243:10

broad and peaceful s., 753:11

changes when wives, 192:4

daffodil s., 458:21

daily bread of eyes, 430:17

descending black and white, 742:14

diamond in the s., 394:2

dusky night rides down s., 311:15

Eagle looking at s., 417:2

equal s., 301:8

ethereal s., 255:22

fair weather for s. is red, 35:25

forehead of morning s., 254:6

go forth under open s., 411:2

goal the s., 783:5

guides through s. thy flight, 411:5

immeasurably lofty, 510:3

inverted Bowl we call S., 446:1

isolation of s., 638:26

like lead, 721:2

lingered under benign s., 480:7

living air and blue s., 373:5

lonely sea and s., 633:14

lonesome place against s., 563:10

lose itself in s., 467:3

Lucy in the s. with diamonds, 770:11

lyre within s., 451:13

mauve and rosy s., 694:15

measure pathways of s., 94:15

membrane of bright blue s., 734:10

moving moon went up s., 381:20

Music shall untune s., 275:11

no bright reversion in s., 300:8

no foreign s. protected me, 675:7

no limits but s., 149:14

none knew color of the s., 611:6

nothing but hath bound in s., 166:21

nothing but s. and the ocean, 383:1

November's s., 378:3

old and true as s., 592:15

Sky (*continued*)

only one shining in s., 373:19, 644:7

only regret leaving the s., 127:6

our Father the S., 787:4

peopling earth waters s., 280:14

pie in s., 637:1

prisoners call the s., 567:15

publish yourselves to s., 547:6

pulling blanket off eastern s., 786:22

rain from dirty s., 746:13

rainbow in the s., 374:7

ring out to wild s., 457:28

robes spun of Iris' woof, 252:17

'scuse me while I kiss the s., 772:3

sea rising nor s. clouding, 549:19

sent him down the s., 502:9

shoulder s. drink ale, 579:18

silence in starry s., 376:17

slope down which s. flows, 700:10

somewhere S. touches Earth, 784:18

soul larger than s., 419:2

sparkling with diamonds, 582:13

split the s. in two, 683:16

spread out against s., 667:9

squired glacier woman down s., 701:6

stand at Judgment Seat, 591:9

star drooped in western s., 490:15

star that burns forever in s., 787:18

steal across the s., 521:11

sweep cobwebs from s., 790:16

take love together to s., 544:2

tears of s., 305:18

teatray in the s., 517:20

threw wild hands toward s., 611:8

tree cannot grow in s., 90:2

tree struggles to reach s., 715:13

under wide and starry s., 561:16

went out under s. Muse, 565:8

what if s. were to fall, 85:20

wide s. above me, 698:3

will cave in on him, 683:16

wrote across s. in stars, 673:8

Skye, over sea to S., 577:5

Skyey, servile to s. influences, 204:9

Sky's, rip-tooth of s. acetylene, 701:3

the limit, 149:*n*8

whatever s. above me, 401:27

Skyscrapers, send s. toppling, 726:1

Slack, observing me grow s., 244:1

Slain a thousand men with jawbone, 11:15

all whom war hath s., 230:20

brothers sons kindred s., 302:*n*6

by fair cruel maid, 202:13

crippled palsied s., 627:1

death ere thou s. another, 240:14

Earl of Murray, 785:18

from graves of our s., 421:18

frosts are s., 533:9

her own eyes see him s., 523:4

honor those they have s., 495:12

if s. thinks he is s., 50:20

Jabberwock, 518:16

more come through alive than are s., 52:8

Saul hath s. his thousands, 11:42

some s. in war, 171:25

think he is slain, 430:10

Sleep *(continued)*

covers man like cloak, 151:15
curtained s., 213:21
death an eternal s., 364:8
death is a s., 534:6
death like s. steal, 406:15
Death's brother S., 94:8
death's counterfeit, 214:14
Death's twin brother, 52:*n*1
deep and dreamless s., 524:9
Do I wake or s., 415:19
even in our s. pain, 63:11
exposition of s. upon me, 173:23
first sweet s. of night, 407:21
flowers as in causes s., 246:4
folding of the hands to s., 20:28
freed from everlasting s., 249:7
friend of woe, 386:14
from mother's s. fell into State, 735:21
full of sweet dreams, 414:9
fullness even of s., 51:38
gates of S., 94:17
gentle s., 183:36
Glamis hath murdered s., 214:7
go home and get s., 606:10
God bless man who invented s., 151:*n*5
great gift of s., 557:11
green ideas s. furiously, 758:20
he giveth his beloved s., 19:30
Homer may s., 98:*n*10
hour's s. before midnight, 245:2
how s. the brave, 324:10
I always s. upon ale, 295:11
I s. alone, 56:8
I will not give s. to mine eyes, 20:4
ignominy s. with thee, 179:7
in Abraham's bosom, 166:5
in dull cold marble, 225:19
in exile, 565:16
in s. a king, 221:12
in soot I s., 356:11
in the night, 357:8
in the shade, 391:10
innocent s., 214:6
is drink for the thirsty, 151:15
is meat for the hungry, 151:15
it is a gentle thing, 381:23
itself must end, 249:7
kind assassin S., 750:6
lay me down in peace and s., 15:33
lay me down to s., 287:14
Lord God caused a deep s., 6:16
Macbeth does murder s., 214:6
Macbeth shall s. no more, 214:7
medicine thee to sweet s., 207:6
men such as s. o' nights, 187:24
miles to go before s., 623:18
most gentle s., 183:*n*6
most things s. lying, 243:15
mountains in primeval s., 503:4
nature's soft nurse, 183:36
neither night nor day, 212:13
neither slumber nor s., 19:25
never s. with anyone with worse troubles, 726:6
nevermore to s. again, 617:6
nice quiet s., 606:10
no more, 214:6

Sleep *(continued)*

no s. till morn, 399:22
nor shall this peace s. with her, 226:8
not dream not, 479:29
not hypocrites in s., 390:21
not my design to s., 247:6
nothing s. in that cellar, 724:12
of a laboring man, 24:4
of death, 196:10
of Lethe, 95:14
of perpetual night, 90:19
of reason produces monsters, 348:8
old and gray full of s., 595:1
on my Love in thy cold bed, 242:2
one ever-during night, 226:13
one short s. past, 230:24
only s., 465:8
out the thought of it, 223:3
out this great gap, 217:4
past first s. in Persia, 249:7
perchance to dream, 196:10
quiet s. when trick's over, 633:16
rounded with a s., 224:21
rude forefathers s., 322:4
sets fool and wise even, 151:15
shake off this downy s., 214:14
shall our gratitude s., 372:1
shall we s. after all, 534:4
silence rushed me to s., 764:9
six hours in s., 152:7
sleeping wake and waking s., 146:9
snow said s., 675:3
softly eagle forgotten, 637:6
some must watch some s., 197:15
son of sable Night, 160:21
sooner over sooner to s., 484:12
soundly as wretched slave, 185:19
spirited from s., 749:15
strong man after s., 255:2
sun is laid to s., 231:21
sword s. in my hand, 359:17
task done we must s., 218:4
that knits up ravelled sleave, 214:6
that knows not breaking, 378:20
that masters all, 65:12
the sleep of death, 359:24
they are as a s., 18:10
they s. and it is lifted, 407:2
time enough to s., 578:20
time for s., 53:20
timely dew of s., 258:20
to die to s., 196:10
to wake, 468:17
turned aside to s., 228:21
two gates of S., 94:17
under bridges beg and steal, 550:13
unseasonable immoderate s., 314:25
upon golden bed, 598:22
visit soul in s., 406:11
voices that make me s. again, 224:18
wake to s., 725:6
waked after long s., 224:18
was airy light, 259:5
we shall not all s., 43:27
weary of everything but s., 534:13
weighs like unwilling s., 417:2
well-spent day happy s., 135:2

Sleep *(continued)*

what hath night to do with s., 252:21
why wilt thou s., 359:24
will never lie, 175:17
with golden Aphrodite, 53:16
with Turks and infidels, 172:7
without wink of s., 149:11
would s. with his mother, 319:30
ye harlots s. at ease, 299:27
yet a little s., 20:28
Sleeper, primitive people not waken s., 565:1
Sleepers in that quiet earth, 480:7
numb nudgers, 724:16
Sleepers', seven s. den, 228:2
Sleepeth, not dead but s., 34:25
peradventure he s., 12:36
Sleeping, all all s. on hill, 607:10
and the dead as pictures, 214:8
at last, 515:13
Beauty wakes up, 755:6
candle burning while s., 234:2
dogs lie, 470:38
he find you s., 37:34
is a wool blanket, 73:24
some s. killed, 171:25
think lion s. because he didn't roar, 364:12
thy servant s., 506:15
tree growing when ye're s., 379:14
wake and waking sleep, 146:9
wakened us from s., 663:4
woods all night, 381:24
Sleepless Eremite, 417:12
soul that perished, 374:9
through suburbs s. people, 699:11
vigilance, 449:17
watches of night, 442:23
Sleeps, after life's fever s., 214:26
creation s., 296:8
Goethe in Weimar s., 497:15
great engine never s., 463:16
in continual noise, 532:15
moonlight s. upon this bank, 182:8
now s. crimson petal, 456:20
on watch, 331:2
remorse s., 319:22
there s. Titania, 173:9
till tired he s., 301:15
while my little one s., 456:10
Sleepy and proud, 674:11
I am s. and weeds twist, 487:10
I'm not s. and no place I'm goin', 771:8
Sleepyhead, let's to bed says S., 789:16
Sleet, iron s., 323:12
pattering sharp s., 415:7
Sleeve, ash on old man's s., 671:21
brush channel with s., 521:3
flame that cannot singe s., 598:13
laughing in your s., 352:7
laughing up her s., 269:3
ravelled s. of care, 214:6
wear heart upon my s., 205:14
Sleeveless some shirtless others, 303:28
Sleeves, fluttering empty s., 639:7
Sleigh, carry the s., 427:7
Sleight, tricks by s. of hand, 291:6
Slender, as cedar tall and s., 348:12

Slender (*continued*)
  debt to Nature's, 242:10
  thy s. stem, 361:19
  waist confined, 249:29
Slenderly, fashioned so s., 423:9
Slept azure-lidded sleep, 415:6
  dreamed life beauty, 476:17
  George Washington s. here, 676:16
  I should have s., 13:35
  in peace, 226:2
  law not dead though it s., 204:2
  one wink, 219:30
  Passion s., 313:12
  resembled my father as he s., 214:4
  touched him and he s., 457:24
Slew, as ambitious I s. him, 188:26
  dead which he s. at his death, 11:19
  death s. not him, 154:9
  enemy nearly s. ye, 779:12
  thrice he s. the slain, 276:11
  who s. warriors, 516:9
Slice, no matter how thin s. it, 618:9
Slices of quince, 472:3
Slide into lover's head, 373:18
  Kelly slide, 781:10
  let world s., 140:14
  no foot shall s., 783:4
Slight, nor Fame I s., 298:8
  not what's near, 68:9
Slightest, rememberest not s. folly,
    190:15
Slightly shakes parting guest, 201:2
Slime, daubed with s. and pitch, 8:21
  in grains of State, 716:18
Slimy things did crawl with legs,
    381:9
Sling, my s. the s. of David, 564:16
  prevailed with a s. and with a stone,
    11:41
Slinging, fury s. flame, 457:14
Slings and arrows of fortune, 196:10
Slinks out of race, 254:25
Slip away before they're up, 647:22
  given them the s., 286:19
  giving enemies s., 320:10
  let it s. useless away, 413:17
  let s. dogs of war, 188:23
  'twixt cup and lip, 235:*n*1
  Waring gave us all the s., 465:17
Slipped surly bonds of Earth, 751:3
  thrice it s. through my hands, 53:18
Slippered, lean and s. pantaloon,
    191:3
Slippers, same old s., 580:14
  shuffle about in s., 590:10
Slippery, he that stands on s. place,
    170:7
  words s. thought viscous, 536:3
Slippy-sloppy, water s. in larder,
    600:23
Slips, greyhounds in s., 185:5
  remember black wharves and s.,
    442:6
  seizes two things one s., 784:23
Slit, tongue be s., 788:13
Slithy toves, 518:15
Slits the thin-spun life, 253:20
Sliver and disbranch, 210:22
Slob, Harding not bad man just a s.,
    654:8

Slop Over, 521:19
  staineth s., 659:2
Slope, patio s. down which sky flows,
    700:10
  through darkness to God, 457:20
Sloping to southern side, 485:27
Sloppy Joe's, 720:18
Sloth and cowardice that clings, 619:5
  assemblage of s. sleep and littleness,
    338:9
  finds down pillow hard, 219:31
  peaceful s., 257:6
Slothful man saith, 22:30
Slouches towards Bethlehem, 596:20
Slough was Despond, 272:13
Slovenliness is no part of religion,
    309:1
Slovenly unhandsome corpse, 177:3
  wilderness, 639:1
Slow, a God s. to anger, 13:23
  and moving finger, 207:26
  and silent stream Lethe, 257:15
  and steady wins, 58:19
  as tardy as too s., 175:24
  be s. to speak s. to wrath, 46:7
  boat to China, 728:12
  but sure, 244:38
  but sure moves might, 69:2
  cold and to temptation s., 221:14
  come he s., 378:6
  confidence plant of s. growth, 313:1
  drag of days, 67:26
  drag the s. barge, 335:23
  drags its s. length along, 298:19
  drip over stones, 724:17
  he that is s. to anger, 21:27
  how s. shadow creeps, 608:20
  I am s. of speech, 8:28
  I am s. of study, 172:26
  in assembling, 72:1
  man catches up with swift, 53:15
  march of human mind s., 331:18
  Meander's margent green, 252:26
  melancholy s., 328:6
  of a s. tongue, 8:28
  on the leash, 658:19
  rises worth, 313:9
  silent walk, 540:22
  sort of country, 518:19
  Spondee stalks, 383:11
  swift s. sweet sour, 551:1
  talk low talk s., 722:5
  tarry awhile says S., 789:16
  tremulous cadence s., 499:20
  vaster than empires and more s.,
    268:4
  walk it s. where you go, 766:8
  wisely and s., 175:18
Slow-breathing unconscious Kosmos,
    547:1
Slowest, haste of fool s. thing, 282:8
Slowly, ever forward but s., 342:11
  follies of town crept s., 329:24
  let him twist s. in wind, 754:20
  lowing herd wind s., 322:1
  mills of God grind s., 247:15
  night Pass more s., 405:8
  rase she up, 785:10
  run O horses of night, 162:*n*9
  run s. horses of night, 101:10

Slowly (*continued*)
  silently now moon, 616:20
Slug-a-bed, sweet S., 241:17
Sluggard, go to the ant thou s., 20:27
  voice of the s., 294:13
Sluggardy, May wol have no s. an-
    yght, 130:10
Slughorn to my lips I set, 210:*n*3
Slugs leave their lair, 383:14
Sluice, every s. of knowledge opened,
    337:14
Slum, see one city s. seen all, 744:13
Slumber, death is s., 406:11
  did my spirit seal, 374:1
  he that keepeth thee will not s.,
    19:25
  honey-heavy dew of s., 188:6
  I must s. again, 294:13
  kindly earth s., 455:19
  lie still and s., 294:12
  love itself s. on, 409:10
  more sweet than toil, 454:11
  neither s. nor sleep, 19:25
  nor s. nor a roof, 684:13
  ports of s. open, 184:9
  seal sense in s., 617:1
  to mine eyelids, 20:4
  to soothing s. seven, 152:*n*3
  where s. abbots, 304:1
  yet a little s., 20:28
Slumbered, you have but s. here,
    174:13
Slumbering in open air, 383:14
  might half s., 414:5
  rouse the s. morn, 251:12
  scepter o'er s. world, 296:7
  thoughts, 249:7
Slumber's chain bound me, 392:7
Slumbers, fire extinguished often s.,
    249:19
  how imagine unquiet s., 480:7
  pleasing dreams s. light, 378:16
  soul dead that s., 440:15
  sweet s. of virtuous, 292:15
  what s. in background, 364:17
Slump, ain't in no s., 754:11
Slums, gay intimacy of s., 712:2
  turned cities into s., 694:6
Sly, Questioner who sits so s., 359:12
  tough and devilish s., 470:15
Smack and tang of elemental things,
    563:9
  my life s. sweet, 468:12
  of age in you, 183:15
Small, air thoroughly s. and dry,
    669:14
  all things how s. soever, 277:4
  and could not hope, 721:3
  and great beasts, 19:6
  buoy too s. for sight, 210:27
  but sullen horn, 324:14
  cabin build there, 594:21
  candle light a thousand, 240:12
  cannot reach the s., 153:21
  choice in rotten apples, 167:16
  chronicle s. beer, 206:9
  compare great things with s., 92:3,
    257:20
  country with few people, 58:6
  creatures great and s., 479:17

Small (*continued*)
day of s. nations past, 528:21
day of s. things, 30:2
felony to drink s. beer, 164:7
frizzled stale and s., 742:20
gray coffee pot, 660:11
great matter or s., 31:13
grind exceeding s., 247:15
have plodders won, 168:15
home where s. experience grows, 167:17
hot bird, 559:19
house and large garden, 266:17
how s. of all hearts endure, 314:15
in s. proportions beauties see, 233:3
is beautiful, 730:17
is it so s. a thing, 498:1
Latin and less Greek, 232:20
make my s. elves coats, 173:10
man may not be entrusted, 61:32
manye s. maken a greet, 132:8
men afraid of writings, 336:9
mice and such s. deer, 210:9
mighty things from s. beginnings grow, 273:10
model of barren earth, 171:25
my house though s., 244:26
nobody has such s. hands, 688:21
one a strong nation, 28:5
one pill makes you s., 770:2
out of s. beginnings, 240:12
potatoes, 511:6
questionable superfluity s. beer, 164:*n*3
rain down can rain, 776:6
rock holds back great wave, 53:5
sea so great boat so s., 779:16
service is true service, 377:14
showers last long, 171:8
speaks s. like a woman, 182:17
still s. voice, 12:39
still s. voice of gratitude, 323:15
sweet courtesies of life, 321:1
thing analogy of great things, 89:17
things and silence, 731:18
things both great and s., 382:8
things make base men proud, 164:5
vices do appear, 211:4
Smaller and dryer than will, 669:14
behavior better than that of s. man, 723:10
fleas that on him prey, 289:20
made s. with art, 698:8
Smallest orb like angel sings, 182:8
star of s. magnitude, 257:22
Small-knowing, unlettered s. soul, 168:18
Smart, as the s. ship grew, 540:18
girls that are so s., 298:2
shall s. for it, 21:7
some will s. for it, 187:10
Smarts so little as fool, 302:7
Smash, Harlem needed something to s., 753:7
why s. the chairs, 446:20
Smashed up things, 694:11
Smattering of everything, 468:19
Smell, ancient and fish-like s., 224:7
begin to s. a rat, 150:11
blood of British man, 210:12

Smell (*continued*)
blood of Englishman, 792:19
dew and rain, 243:23
far worse than weeds, 221:16
fire whose gown burns, 244:10
flowers along the way, 682:15
good s. of old clothes, 663:2
I love the s. of napalm, 769:11
lilies that fester s. worse, 221:16
lost sea s., 669:20
of burning fills air, 608:19
of the lamp, 80:22
rose by any name s. as sweet, 175:2
sweet and blossom in dust, 246:21
sweet keen s., 509:29
yes to s. pork, 180:2
Smellest so sweet, 208:1
Smelleth the battle afar off, 15:17
Smelling of the lamp, 609:11
Smells, gas s. awful, 687:10
he s. April and May, 182:31
heaven's breath s. wooingly, 213:4
like gangrene, 631:2
not of itself but thee, 232:16
to heaven, 197:23
Smelt heaviest ore of body, 657:14
Smile, affliction s. again, 168:20
and be a villain, 195:1
as I do now, 447:20
at claims of descent, 454:2
better last s., 288:*n*2
did he s. work to see, 358:7
disdainful s., 322:7
dwells longer, 616:13
faithless as a s., 668:4
forget and s., 515:9
horror unbend and s. at us, 645:6
if we meet we shall s., 189:23
in her eye, 420:15
jest to Oberon make him s., 173:2
loving s. surely hail, 518:13
make the learned s., 298:16
of accomplishment, 764:14
of deceit, 359:3
of love, 359:3
of smiles, 359:3
on Casey's face, 588:24
on lips tear in eye, 378:10
on the Mona Lisa, 682:3
once more turn thy wheel, 209:16
one vast substantial s., 470:7
sea shows false alluring s., 89:19
share the good man's s., 329:16
sidelong pickerel s., 725:4
smile smile, 641:11
social s., 321:23
sweet s. at his father, 91:6
to those who hate, 401:27
upon fingers' ends, 184:30
vain tribute of a s., 377:26
vehicle for ambiguities, 487:4
we would aspire to, 225:16
when only dead could s., 675:9
when you call me that s., 583:14
where my Julia's lips s., 241:1
world seems to s. upon me, 279:9
Smiled, all sat back and s., 583:5
and said Good Night, 609:8
at the dame, 357:18
he never s. again, 410:16

Smiled (*continued*)
of darkness till it s., 252:27
Spain's chivalry away, 403:15
Smiler with knyf, 130:18
Smiles, all s. stopped together, 464:13
and soap, 519:24
as if he mocked himself, 187:26
down from height at me, 719:1
dying lives and unborn s., 731:7
full of s. in early days, 75:27
he s. it is a malady, 90:25
in which two s. meet, 359:3
kindling s. in ladies' eyes, 423:14
Peace crowned with s., 270:8
quiet-colored evening s., 465:9
same flower that s. today, 241:9
seldom he s., 187:26
sits and s. on the night, 356:15
smile of s., 359:3
sweet strains pensive s., 429:9
tears of boyhood's years, 392:7
the robbed that s., 205:31
welcome ever s., 201:2
wreathed s., 251:8
Smilest and art still, 497:4
Smiling aspects of life more American, 532:17
at grief, 202:14
at the good mouth, 659:10
damned villain, 195:1
destructive man, 285:9
from world's snare, 218:1
gently s. jaws, 517:5
hides s. face, 334:1
in my face, 213:12
scatter plenty o'er s. land, 322:15
the boy fell dead, 464:10
through tears, 51:27
Smirk, serious and the s., 469:15
Smite all the firstborn, 8:38
baseness we will s., 607:18
God shall s. thee, 41:27
once and smite no more, 254:3
sounding furrows, 455:6
the sun shall not s. thee, 19:25
thee on thy right cheek, 33:7
without hands to s., 533:10
Smiteth so that he die, 9:14
Smith mighty man, 441:3
Sydney S. a molar, 506:5
Smithsonian, to found S. Institution, 367:18
Smithy of soul, 647:11
village s. stands, 441:3
Smitten, illness with which s., 423:17
with our own feathers, 59:*n*8
Smock, cast shame when cast off s., 131:8
Smoke and stir of this dim spot, 252:12
consume own s., 413:2, 558:5
days are consumed like s., 18:23
days gone up in s., 581:8
gets in your eyes, 617:16
good cigar is a s., 590:20
good strong incense s., 465:7
herbs to drink s. thereof, 134:9
in yon s. concealed, 483:3
no fire without s., 142:17
thin s. without flame, 540:22

Smoke (*continued*)
w'at do wid de s., 556:15
Smoke-filled room, 582:18
Smokes, wretcheder one s. more,
522:8
Smokestack, salt-caked s., 634:1
Smoking flax shall he not quench,
27:25
Smoky, populous and s. city, 407:22
Smooth as monumental alabaster,
208:9
away trouble, 663:2
billows s. and bright, 518:23
block s. and well fitting, 659:14
chose him five s. stones, 11:40
easy inoffensive down to Hell,
82:*n*6
large and s. and round, 386:4
road is s., 54:24
road of life, 321:1
runs water where brook deep,
152:*n*7
sea being s., 200:6
the ice, 170:9
true love never did run s., 172:19
Smoothed his wrinkled front, 165:19
Smoother, finding s. pebble, 282:5
her mouth is s. than oil, 20:26
words were s. than butter, 17:28
Smoothest, stream s. water deepest,
152:*n*7
Smooth-faced gentleman Commodity,
169:26
Smoothing the raven down, 252:27
Smooth-lipped, convolutions of s.
shell, 376:21
Smoothly, my task is s. done, 253:12
Smoothness, temperance may give it
s., 196:21
turns s. rough, 467:8
Smooths hair with automatic hand,
669:2
oil s. what is rough, 104:1
Smooth-shaven, dry s. green, 252:3
Smote him thus, 208:17
him under the fifth rib, 12:3
Jael s. the nail into his temples,
10:41
'Omer s. bloomin' lyre, 592:11
them hip and thigh, 11:14
Smother up his beauty, 176:37
Smothered, I should die there s., 657:7
Smothery, cramped up and s., 526:22
Snaffle, they use s. curb all right,
707:1
SNAFU, 783:11
Snail, creeping like s. to school, 191:3
glister me forward, 724:17
questing S., 725:21
turn not pale beloved s., 518:7
went to kill s., 789:17
whiting to a s., 518:5
Snail's on the thorn, 464:4
Snails, pretty feet like s., 241:11
snips and s., 791:5
Snake came to water trough, 657:12
eagle or s., 592:9
earth like s. renew, 408:10
in the grass, 92:8
like a wounded s., 298:19

Snake (*continued*)
no s. can live there, 120:5
stood up for evil, 623:12
things are of the s., 429:16
throws enamelled skin, 173:9
toad edible to s., 544:16
we have scotched the s., 214:25
Snakes eat frogs, 639:2
gliding up hollow, 430:14
hogs eat s., 639:2
no s. to be met with, 317:4
spotted s. with double tongue,
173:12
strangled s. beside Hercules, 505:3
Snakeskin titles of claims, 698:6
Snap like vixens at truth, 660:20
Snapper-up of unconsidered trifles,
223:2
Snaps, vow s. itself, 459:18
Snare of the fowler, 18:15
rabbit in a s., 650:10
trial by jury a s., 391:1
world's great s., 218:1
Snares, heart is s. and nets, 24:13
riches are ready s., 133:19
traps gins pitfalls, 463:*n*1
Snark was a Boojum, 519:25
Snarling, silver s. trumpets, 414:22
Snatch a fearful joy, 321:14
me away not to return, 623:8
Snatched, purse most resolutely s.,
176:26
scepter s. with unruly hand, 170:7
spear but left shield, 353:*n*5
Snatches, ballads songs s., 530:18
Snatching victuals from table, 620:1
Snaw, locks are like the s., 362:15
Sneaking, valor is s. off, 352:16
Sneer at me for leaning, 446:4
of cold command, 406:13
sapping creed with s., 400:5
who can refute a s., 345:11
without sneering teach to s., 302:11
Sneered, acquaintance s., 609:5
Mighty Merchant s., 512:19
Sneering, born s., 530:19
without s. teach to sneer, 302:11
Sneezed, not to be s. at, 366:14
Sneezes, beat him when he s., 517:15
Snicker, eternal Footman s., 667:16
Snicker-snack, blade went s., 518:16
Snickersnee, I drew my s., 531:6
Sniffs round the mass as dog, 549:3
Snips and snails, 791:5
Snob, admires mean things is S.,
463:22
Snobbish, camels are s., 665:7
Snodgrass, murmured Mr. S., 468:22
Snore, weariness s. upon flint, 219:31
why snorer can't hear himself s.,
527:5
Snorted we in seven sleepers' den,
228:2
Snotgreen sea, 647:12
Snout, jewel of gold in a swine's s.,
21:8
take stick hit him on s., 780:12
Snow, arrives the s., 429:12
bells across the s., 457:29
birds sit brooding in s., 169:14

Snow (*continued*)
buck in the s., 684:11
came both mist and s., 381:3
came flying, 549:20
chaste as unsunned s., 219:25
cherry hung with s., 578:19
dripping s. on grass, 674:11
dust of s., 623:15
fallen s. on s., 515:10
falling faintly through universe,
647:8
falling s. silent, 632:15
fare wel s. of ferne yere, 128:28
fleece white as s., 404:10
frost from purest s., 219:12
geese like s. cloud, 674:11
general over Ireland, 647:8
hide hills of s., 204:*n*5
I shall be whiter than s., 17:21
if s. be white, 222:8
lay round about, 482:8
like s. falls in river, 363:6
like s. hill in the air, 486:18
like s. in May, 243:21
locks are like s., 362:15
melted like s., 401:16
mockery king of s., 172:12
moonshine an' s., 485:15
no s. is there, 53:8
nor does s. come near it, 53:9
not s. nor rain nor heat, 70:11
pure as s., 196:15
raiment white as s., 37:14
rosebuds filled with s., 226:19
said peace cold sleep, 675:3
she is near under s., 566:5
sins shall be white as s., 25:29
something crabwise across s., 755:1
step softly under s., 619:7
stood shivering in s., 160:19
swept world end to end, 680:2
swooned as he heard s., 647:8
try s. of heaven, 690:4
tufts of s. on bare branch, 382:17
wallow naked in December s., 171:3
war over a few acres of s., 306:8
we shall have s., 790:17
white and drifted s., 427:7
white as driven s., 223:10
wish s. in May's mirth, 168:16
woods fill with s., 623:16
world vast screen of s., 675:3
wrapt in clouds and s., 399:25
year rich year, 244:9
Snow-broth, man whose blood is s.,
203:26
Snowed, it s. of mete amd drynke,
129:25
six days and six nights, 738:1
whole world over, 680:2
Snowflake in avalanche, 726:16
not a s. escapes fashioning hand,
477:3
Snowflakes, words like winter s.,
51:15
Snows and sins, 533:9
of the year 1941, 765:17
where are s. of yesteryear, 134:1
where s. of yesteryear, 509:22
Snow-star, earth-star and s., 477:4

Snowstorms, inspector of s., 476:24
Snow-white, little s. feet, 594:17
Snowy, Seraphs swing s. Hats, 511:18
   summits old in story, 456:11
Snub, hard to s. beautiful woman,
   622:12
Snuff approach of tyranny, 331:15
   shifted his trumpet took s., 330:14
Snuffbox, fill his s., 287:1
Snuff-colored, Doctor Franklin s. little
   man, 657:10
Snuffed out by article, 403:13
Snug as bug in rug, 310:16
   little farm the world, 386:21
   little island, 377:15
So can any man, 178:3
   if it was s. it might be, 518:22
   if she be not s. to me, 240:1
   it goes, 751:12
   it has been, 684:12
   life boring must not say s., 734:17
   much for him, 192:33
   runs world away, 197:15
Soakers, old s., 279:10
Soaking in comfortable baths, 693:12
Soap, invisible s., 423:2
   smiles and s., 519:24
   what no s., 324:7
Soaping, Miss Twye s. breasts in bath,
   739:12
Soar, angels alone that s. above,
   267:18
   but never roam, 377:12
   flitter dip and s., 749:17
   not too high to fall, 238:5
   run though not s., 424:19
   singing still dost s., 408:5
Soaring ever singest, 408:5
   in high region of fancies, 254:12
Soars, if he s. with own wings, 357:5
   no bird s. too high, 357:5
Sob as you spin, 721:1
   heavy world, 721:1
   on the saxophones, 634:10
Sober as a hymn, 557:6
   as a judge, 311:13
   be s. be vigilant, 46:28
   certainty of waking bliss, 252:28
   healthful and with his wits, 266:7
   in s. livery clad, 258:18
   plain in dress s. in diet, 304:4
   skies ashen and s., 453:1
   sleep with s. cannibal, 486:19
   steadfast and demure, 251:23
   studious days, 300:1
   take s. coloring from eye, 375:15
   to bed go s., 236:4
Sobering thought when Mozart my
   age, 759:7
Soberly, entered into s., 50:1
Soberness, speak truth and s., 41:34
Sobers, drinking s. again, 298:13
Sobriety a species of courage, 278:5
   something said for s., 735:3
Sobs of violins of autumn, 553:24
   with s. and tears sorted out, 519:6
Sociability law of nature, 547:5
Sociable ez baskit er kittens, 556:7
   society no comfort to one not s.,
   220:1

Social armor, 648:4
   capitalism creates s. unrest, 653:25
   conscience of nation, 761:8
   Contract vast conspiracy, 601:7
   friendly honest man, 361:12
   fundamental of s. relations, 440:5
   in things purely s. separate, 571:32
   leisure class in s. evolution, 574:7
   less arbitrary s. fabric, 707:17
   lies mortar that bind man into s.
     masonry, 601:7
   lived in s. intercourse, 316:11
   lose s. freedom individual auton-
     omy, 727:9
   man is a s. animal, 278:10
   mirage of s. justice, 701:10
   Nature's s. union, 361:5
   order and thirsty aspiration, 726:1
   our s. arrangements unsatisfactory,
     677:4
   overthrow of s. conditions, 482:7
   process of s. change, 683:6
   progress of each country, 644:17
   prosperity, 428:3
   ramble ain't restful, 719:12
   self-love and s. be made the same,
     369:3
   self-love and s. the same, 302:5
   shalt not commit a s. science,
     720:20
   smile, 321:23
   state natural to man, 440:1
   Statics, 542:16
   world work of man, 290:31
Socialism, combines Bolshevism s.,
   763:14
   concern for unfortunate not s.,
     729:20
   contest between capitalism and s.
     over, 746:16
   inherent virtue of s., 622:10
   Marxian S. portent to historians,
     652:9
   what I mean by S., 523:10
   with human face, 748:16
Socialist competition, 638:9
   culture to thrive, 686:16
   democracy may be sham, 653:26
   proceed to construct s. order, 610:1
Socializing, conversation s. instrument,
   653:7
Socially invisible, 759:3
Societies, two s. one black one white,
   723:20
Society, before group enter open s.,
   771:3
   build a Great S., 723:18
   care of poor incumbent on s.,
     278:15
   cling together in one s., 373:8
   complicated urban s., 677:5
   conspiracy against manhood, 431:20
   democratic s. like ours, 646:13
   distributes itself, 500:9
   established s., 713:12
   exists for noble actions, 78:20
   for previntion of croolty to money,
     539:*n*1
   formation of classless s., 481:7

Society (*continued*)
   full of women who remained thirty-
     five, 567:11
   great s., 576:16
   Great S. here at home, 677:4
   great s. on earth, 373:13
   had s. been well organized, 366:4
   happiness of s. end of government,
     338:6
   human combination or s., 247:13
   humanizing body of s., 501:1
   humble members of s., 369:11
   ideal of democratic free s., 745:15
   if free s. cannot help poor, 741:4
   in our factitious s., 436:23
   individual not accountable to s.,
     439:21
   individual promotes interest of s.,
     326:6
   is a blessing, 340:18
   is no comfort, 220:1
   man was formed for s., 325:19
   my art negation of s., 541:12
   naked people little influence in s.,
     528:14
   nerves of s., 542:13
   no arts no letters no s., 239:22
   no one would talk much in s.,
     349:29
   no s. bring Kingdom of God, 645:9
   of neither rich nor poor, 523:10
   offenders, 530:20
   one polished horde, 403:17
   part of S. and traditions, 764:3
   pillars of s., 507:17
   principle on which s. not founded,
     321:6
   protection of s., 439:20
   revolutionary reconstitution of s.,
     481:15
   so riven that moderation gone,
     615:3
   solitude best s., 260:3
   Soul selects her S., 512:2
   state not a mere s., 78:20
   such s. as is quiet, 409:17
   suspicion bane of good s., 340:19
   taxes pay for civilized s., 542:14
   three chairs for s., 478:27
   till s. differently constituted, 366:1
   true founder of civil s., 319:2
   unable to live in s., 78:14
   vanilla of s., 380:8
   vast empire of human s., 373:16
   where none intrudes, 400:29
   without aristocracy not society,
     653:6
   without objective legal scale, 746:8
   women horses economic factors in
     s., 583:3
   wonderfully delightful, 567:3
Sociological imagination, 740:1
Sociologists astrologers, 590:1
Sociology, children detest s., 715:7
   science with greatest number of
     methods, 565:7
Sock, Jonson's learned s., 251:19
Socket, burn to the s., 376:20
Socrates and two great disciples, 588:7
   corrupts the youth, 74:14

Socrates (*continued*)
  dissatisfied, 439:27
  first to call philosophy down, 87:30
  is a doer of evil, 74:14
  not because S. said so, 146:23
  wisest of men, 261:2
Socratic manner not a game, 614:10
Sod, beneath s. poet lies, 385:5
  builds on watery s., 547:7
  lay s. o'er me, 786:7
  roots grass sends in s., 547:7
  to thy requiem a s., 415:16
Soda, sermons and s. water, 402:18
  wash feet in s. water, 668:23
  water the day after, 402:18
Sodom, is there beauty in S., 495:5
  pitched his tent toward S., 7:28
Soeur, voie lactée ô s. lumineuse,
    641:n5
Sofa, wheel s. round, 335:3
Soft answer turneth away wrath,
    21:24
  as breast of doves, 661:12
  bastard Latin, 402:4
  complaining flute, 275:10
  everyone in America s., 585:13
  eyes looked love, 399:21
  face of a girl, 66:18
  flutes and s. recorders, 256:14
  her voice was ever s., 211:18
  in s. regions born s. men, 70:14
  look of s. deceit, 357:23
  Lydian airs, 251:19
  makes them s. where we are hard,
    694:14
  meek patient humble, 227:19
  nature's s. nurse, 183:36
  own the s. impeachment, 352:17
  phrase of peace, 205:21
  rest in s. peace, 232:11
  stillness and the night, 182:8
  summer air, 507:3
  summer season when s. was sun,
    127:17
  underbelly of Axis, 621:14
  what s. incense, 415:14
  zephyr blows, 323:8
Soften rocks or bend oak, 291:7
  to us our enemies, 562:9
Softened, cultivation of taste s. me,
    728:8
Softening chalk of my bones, 724:17
Softer, words were s. than oil, 17:28
Softest clothing woolly bright, 356:6
  music to attending ears, 175:13
  overcome the hardest, 57:13
Soft-lifted by winnowing wind, 416:14
Softly, fair and s. goes far, 128:n8
  go s. all my years, 27:13
  she was going up, 381:20
  sleep s. eagle forgotten, 637:6
  speak s. carry big stick, 575:16
  step s. under snow, 619:7
  sweet Thames run s., 154:16
  sweetly speaking and s. laughing,
    56:5
  tread s. on dreams, 595:9
Softness, she for s. formed, 258:12
Soft-sigh me home, 724:17
Soil, awkward in their s., 725:3

Soil (*continued*)
  contact with s., 599:15
  deserve precious bane, 256:21
  difference of s. and climate, 373:16
  for aesthetic growth, 618:16
  free s. free men, 780:14
  good to be born on, 486:1
  grows on mortal s., 253:21
  life of significant s., 671:19
  not every s. can bear all, 92:27
  of people's necessities, 585:6
  of which such men made, 486:1
  our forces stand on Philippine s.,
    642:2
  roots of lilac under s., 626:11
  weed that grows in every s., 331:21
  win of watery main, 221:3
Soiled, poor wings so s., 535:3
  truth impossible to be s., 77:n5
  wash s. world, 490:14
Soi-même, on laisse un peu de s.,
    570:n2
  si l'homme a s., 145:n13
Soir, voici le s. charmant, 494:n8
Sojourner as all my fathers were,
    17:10
Sojourners, we are s. on planet,
    420:17
Sojourning, life a battle and s., 110:19
Solace, freedom all s. to man gives,
    127:15
Solar, hub of s. system, 447:13
  walk or milky way, 301:7
Sold cheap what is most dear, 221:26
  Dickon thy master s., 153:n7
  Esau s. his birthright, 7:37
  even to cloak I wore, 134:14
  for endless rue, 578:23
  for old man's gold, 609:15
  goodness s. itself, 784:25
  my father s. me, 356:11
  neither bought nor s., 766:14
  pleasing ware is half s., 244:5
  Reputation for Song, 446:6
  righteous for silver, 29:34
  the many on the few, 689:4
  virtue now is s., 232:14
Soldat, tout s. français porte le bâton,
    371:n3
Soldier, a s. and afeard, 216:2
  an' sailor too, 592:22
  as s. for his country, 586:n3
  come back British s., 591:22
  devotion of patriot s., 522:13
  didn't raise boy to be a s., 782:16
  first king fortunate s., 306:1
  French s. carries marshal's baton,
    371:4
  full of strange oaths, 191:3
  gallant old s., 385:n2
  Good S. finest French novel, 617:8
  in full military array, 390:1
  in s. is flat blasphemy, 204:5
  no s. in gallant band, 531:17
  priest s. poet, 494:14
  relish him more in s., 206:10
  rest, 378:20
  stool pigeon when cannot be s.,
    496:3
  summer s. sunshine patriot, 340:22

Soldier (*continued*)
  tells his wounds, 100:28
  toy s. red with rust, 559:21
Soldier's, ambition s. virtue, 217:22
  courtier's s. scholar's, 196:17
  grave best, 404:8
  history of s. wound, 320:15
  kiss dwells on bearded lips, 490:12
  many a s. loving arms, 490:12
  pole is fallen, 218:8
  pride touched to quick, 464:10
  sound of white s. axe, 502:5
Soldiers are dreamers, 662:5
  believe s. nothing safe, 515:14
  bore dead bodies by, 177:3
  by two and by three, 785:6
  Christian s., 521:10
  citizens of death's land, 662:4
  French s. with artilleryman, 510:3
  grow like savages as s. will, 186:2
  Ireland gives England s., 509:14
  of Christ arise, 312:16
  old s. never die, 642:5, 782:15
  old s. surest, 237:11
  regarded wounded s. in envious
    way, 611:2
  sailors and airmen, 621:18
Soldiers', steel my s. hearts, 185:20
Soldiery, Emperor's drunken s., 598:11
  licentious s., 332:2
Sole arbiter is taste, 453:14
  crown of head to s., 186:32
  go it s. alone, 624:21
  God beside whom is none, 5:6
  rest for the s. of her foot, 7:19
  unbusy thing, 383:14
Soleil bas taché d'horreurs mystiques,
    565:n9
Solemn drifting down river, 526:20
  fillet, 430:7
  gorgeous palaces s. temples, 224:21
  he says with s. air, 361:9
  one sweetly s. thought, 504:6
  pride yours, 450:9
  sapping s. creed, 400:5
  stillness lay, 462:2
  suits of s. black, 193:2
  this her s. bird, 258:22
Solemnest of industries, 513:17
Solemnities, feasts and high s., 253:10
Solemnized their obsequies, 248:26
  with pomp and parade, 338:5
Soles, eats s. offen shoes, 698:5
Soliciting, still s. eye, 208:26
Solid earth actual world, 477:7
  for fluidity, 619:20
  heaven presents s. hue, 623:13
  man of Boston, 442:11
  massy hard particles, 282:4
  nothing s. is its s. self, 639:18
  pudding empty praise, 303:25
  sop of all this s. globe, 200:9
  this too too s. flesh, 193:5
  virtue, 207:23
Solidarity, family and clan s., 601:4
  independent of differences, 755:11
  loses s. with other women, 722:12
Solidity, atoms preserved by absolute
    s., 89:10

Solidity (*continued*)
  give appearance of s. to pure wind,
    711:14
Solitary and cannot impart it, 315:17
  as oyster, 470:3
  be not s. be not idle, 235:24
  convent's s. gloom, 300:3
  God setteth the s. in families, 17:39
  how doth the city sit s., 28:38
  if idle be not s. if s. be not idle,
    317:15
  love all s. places, 407:7
  men know friendship, 616:12
  poor nasty brutish, 239:22
  quite still and s., 651:22
  rare are s. woes, 198:*n*5
  sail that rises, 474:5
  shriek, 402:17
  simile that s. shines, 303:8
  stirred by s. cloud, 282:11
  took their s. way, 260:24
Solitude at depth of human condition,
    736:13
  bliss of s., 376:1
  companion so feel s. more, 614:2
  companionable as s., 478:26
  drives poet to s., 498:7
  each guardian of other's s., 630:10
  friend to genius, 432:35
  grew more obese, 755:12
  how sweet is s., 334:18
  I love tranquil s., 409:17
  independence of s., 431:22
  is sweet, 334:18
  island s. unsponsored free, 638:26
  makes s. calls it peace, 401:9
  not exchange s. for anything,
    733:21
  nurse of souls s., 484:22
  O S. where are charms, 334:20
  of his own heart, 438:9
  one chair for s., 478:27
  one hundred years of s., 759:1
  religion experiences in s., 546:13
  safeguard to mediocrity, 432:35
  sometimes best society, 260:3
  Soul to S. retires, 445:5
  sweet retired s., 252:29
  teach us to die, 400:13
Solitudes, in love two s. touch, 630:4
  pierced our s., 429:14
Solo game, 627:2
Solomon, behold a greater than S.,
    35:4
  curtains of S., 25:1
  Grundy, 791:4
  in all his glory, 33:21
  King David and King S., 583:11
  loved many strange women, 12:28
  priests in temple of S., 434:21
  Proverbs of S., 470:16
  wisdom of S., 12:22
Solomon's, song of songs which is S.,
    24:31
Solon was under a delusion, 75:20
Solution, dissatisfaction with other s.,
    430:23
  final s. of Jewish question, 686:5
  for world peace, 642:6
  of international problems, 708:1

Solution (*continued*)
  part of s. or of problem, 767:20
  waste elocution on s., 531:19
Solutions, two equally convenient s.,
    565:5
Solvency a matter of temperament,
    594:4
Solvent, American life powerful s.,
    588:12
Somber, I am the s. one, 443:23
Some are born great, 202:18
  born mad some remain so, 718:16
  born posthumously, 553:12
  come to take their ease, 226:10
  for adventure, 659:8
  gave white bread, 788:10
  must watch some sleep, 197:15
  of you with Pilate, 172:11
  quick to arm, 659:8
  said John print it, 272:9
  say world will end in fire, 623:14
  talk of Alexander, 778:18
  that shadows kiss, 180:28
  to kill cankers, 173:10
  war with rere-mice, 173:10
  will smart for it, 187:10
Somebody, could've had class been s.,
    737:6
  how dreary to be S., 511:22
  may be looking, 643:4
  necessary to s., 432:41
  said it couldn't be done, 644:15
  to hew and hack, 263:9
  when everyone is s., 531:22
Somebody's always throwing bricks,
    637:7
  even I be in S. hand, 539:17
Someday I must go into that, 625:3
  inner light shine forth, 351:*n*5
  love as though s. hate hate as
    though s. love, 65:*n*9
  to prove our foe, 65:13
Someone better be prepared, 623:22
  find next morning it was s. else,
    367:6
  gently rapping, 452:13
  had blundered, 458:11
  is sinking today, 563:1
  not be something but s., 651:7
  someone else begat, 625:3
  to love and someone to love you,
    580:11
  touch my person to s. else's, 489:13
  we can lean on, 773:2
Something about a martini, 709:11
  attempted something done, 441:5
  bright and alien, 709:*n*3
  cool s. flowing over hand, 641:18
  crabwise across snow, 755:1
  dead in each of us, 567:19
  ere the end, 455:5
  everything good for s., 274:22
  expect s. for nothing, 564:2
  fame created s. of nothing, 250:16
  far more interfused, 373:5
  for modern stage, 659:6
  good and bad of every land, 476:9
  had greater price than life, 705:11
  have in me s. dangerous, 199:15
  he prized and is known by, 653:28

Something (*continued*)
  hidden behind things, 636:9
  hidden go and find it, 593:14
  in her gizzard, 279:24
  in the wind, 166:26
  in this more than natural, 195:30
  in us never dies, 362:23
  like a star, 625:1
  lost behind Ranges, 593:14
  might be gaining on you, 719:12
  must be left to chance, 360:15
  nasty in woodshed, 708:8
  no reasonable man expected, 678:23
  not be s. but someone, 651:7
  of Shorter-Catechist, 557:7
  old something new, 782:10
  one must be s. to do s., 350:5
  rich and strange, 223:32
  right in world something we trust,
    744:14
  rotten in state of Denmark, 194:16
  tells me but not love, 181:1
  that doesn't love a wall, 622:20
  that doth live, 375:10
  there is s. in a face, 294:21
  time for a little s., 648:8
  'tis s. nothing, 206:30
  to do, 485:9
  too much of this, 197:4
  try do s. for my country, 768:8
  very like Him, 483:2
  what is that s., 705:11
  would turn up, 435:1
  wrong with something human,
    736:2
  you do s. to me, 681:14
  you will see s. new, 715:3
Sometime, come up and see me s.,
    685:*n*2
  come up s. and see me, 685:6
  did me seek, 143:7
  woman a s. thing, 695:9
Somewhat, I have s. against thee, 47:7
Somewhere ages hence, 623:7
  beyond the curtain, 598:18
  end up s. else, 747:6
  in favored land, 588:25
  over the rainbow, 699:16
  people freedom light, 680:7
  set forth for s., 623:10
  what with all these clouds, 73:13
Somewheres east of Suez, 591:24
Somnambulist of vanished dream,
    427:24
Son, Absalom my s. my s., 12:14
  and heir of mongrel bitch, 209:13
  antichrist denieth Father and S.,
    46:34
  be a Man my s., 593:21
  bring forth a s., 32:22
  brought forth firstborn s., 38:2
  Christ the S. took Father's place,
    569:18
  crucify S. of God afresh, 45:36
  David the s. of Jesse, 12:16
  dear s. of memory, 251:2
  every s. hoped to do, 569:18
  every wise man's s. doth know,
    202:1
  false as stepdame to s., 200:22

Son (*continued*)

Father S. and Holy Ghost, 37:15, 280:21
foolish s. calamity of father, 21:44
foolish s. the heaviness of his mother, 21:4
glory be to the S., 48:22
greatness in father overwhelms s., 233:6
grim Death my s. and foe, 257:18
hang us every mother's s., 172:27
have his s. respect him, 277:12
he was a s. of God, 694:9
his only s. myself, 325:8
if s. ask bread, 34:7
in the Jewish joke, 765:12
knew my s. was mortal, 74:7
Lord Randal my s., 785:20
man is s. of own works, 92:*n*2
marry s. when you will, 244:12
my beloved S., 32:34
of a Pharisee, 41:29
of Atreus, 51:17
of Bharata, 84:6
of first fish ashore, 758:13
of God goes forth to war, 395:17
of Heaven's eternal king, 250:19
of humble laborer, 645:1
of Kronos, 51:2
of man came eating and drinking, 34:37
of man coming in cloud, 39:14
of man is betrayed, 36:32
of man nowhere to lay head, 34:17
of man that thou visitest him, 15:34
of man which is a worm, 14:37
of the living God, 35:27
of the middle border, 583:1
of the morning, 26:14
of the Sun, 79:7
only begotten S., 39:46
out of Egypt called my s., 32:25
prince subject Father S., 230:15
prodigal s., 38:35
punch hole in s. of a bitch, 784:4
rather be worm than s. of man, 663:20
reverence for his s., 277:12
seek father who need s., 739:6
sighed as lover obeyed as s., 340:13
struck father when s. swore, 235:16
the carpenter's s., 35:12
this is my s. Telemachus, 455:4
this my s. was dead, 38:37
thou art ever with me, 38:38
thou art the S. of God, 35:21
till he gets wife, 506:13
to her s. she ches, 775:15
Tom the piper's s., 790:5
unfeathered thing a s., 274:5
unto us a s. is given, 26:8
virgin shall bear a s., 26:5
where one s. only, 613:7
wise s. maketh a glad father, 21:4
woman behold thy s., 40:39
wrath of Peleus' S., 299:23
you are young my s., 76:15
Son, j'aime le s. du cor, 421:*n*1
Song, a god has given the lyre and s., 52:1

Song (*continued*)

all my s. would be, 437:4
burden of my s., 776:8
burthen of his s., 338:19
dance and Provençal s., 415:11
does Africa know s. of me, 656:9
echo of mournful s., 446:26
fable s. or fleeting shade, 241:19
famed in s. famous Athens, 64:12
filled thicket with honeyed s., 73:8
fishers of s., 574:13
from beginning to end, 441:14
full lasting is s., 509:17
gentlemen singing this s., 464:14
give us s. to cheer, 523:1
glorious s. of old, 462:2
good s. ringing clear, 589:3
had been longer, 789:10
hear a little s., 349:10
heel on throat of my s., 686:22
in England's s. forever, 586:14
in thy praise, 362:21
Jehovah is my s., 26:12
learn suffering teach in s., 407:11
let satire be my s., 399:1
let them take it, 596:4
listen to s. of siren, 339:7
Lord is my strength and s., 9:2
made s. a coat, 596:4
moralize my s., 153:4
needless Alexandrine ends s., 298:19
never heard in tale or s., 252:15
new unhallowed s., 573:22
night-walkers' s., 598:11
oaten stop or pastoral s., 324:13
of a merryman, 531:14
of Africa, 656:9
of faithful Penelope, 54:12
of Harvest-home, 460:16
of night's sweet bird, 409:6
of siren nor voice of hyena, 157:6
of sixpence, 790:1
of songs, 24:31
of the Shirt, 423:5
on wings of s., 419:12
one grand sweet s., 484:13
perhaps it may turn out s., 361:21
perhaps self-same s., 415:17
pipe s. about a Lamb, 356:4
play a s. for me, 771:8
read s. not sermon, 242:*n*7
remake a s., 595:17
required of us a s., 20:6
revive her symphony and s., 382:25
sans Wine S., 445:16
sea grew civil at her s., 173:5
seraphically free, 509:6
shall rise to Thee, 395:21
sing one s. for old Kentucky home, 507:2
sing the Lord's s., 20:6
sing unto him a new s., 16:29
sing unto the Lord a new s., 18:20
sings lasting s., 599:3
sings s. twice over, 465:4
sold Reputation for a S., 446:6
sounded by death, 405:10
spur me into s., 599:14
suck melancholy out of s., 190:19
sweetest s. ever heard, 401:23

Song (*continued*)

taught Hesiod beauteous s., 54:14
theme of Art and S., 598:23
thou singer I s., 530:4
till I end my S., 154:16
time an endless s., 595:4
to sing O, 531:13
unlike subject frame s., 305:17
urge of a s., 625:5
what s. the Sirens sang, 248:30
when this s. sung and past, 143:6
whose note sounded by death, 405:10
wind's s. sail's shaking, 633:14
wine women and s., 353:5
wrote one s., 466:28
Songe, la vie apparié a un s., 146:*n*6
Songs, all their s. sad, 618:17
and I wrote my happy s., 356:5
angelic s. swelling, 474:3
ballads s. snatches, 530:18
Book of S. and Sonnets, 182:19
composed of tears, 461:15
despairing s. loveliest, 461:15
folk s. from soul sounds, 690:20
forever new, 416:4
harsh after s. of Apollo, 169:15
his s. were a thousand and five, 12:21
I who once played shepherds' s., 93:9
laws which ran like drinking s., 72:13
leave to sing own s., 589:1
make and well endyte, 129:10
muse has taught them s., 53:17
my s. draw Daphnis home, 92:13
no sad s. for me, 515:7
of expectation, 521:12
of pleasant glee, 356:4
of sadness and mirth, 441:21
of slaves testimony, 480:11
of Zion, 20:6
psalms hymns and spiritual s., 44:26
sage daughters of Muses, 64:6
sing s. not heard before, 96:12
song of s., 24:31
strongest and sweetest s. remain, 491:18
sweetest s. saddest thought, 408:7
we had all good s., 759:5
where are s. of Spring, 416:15
without words best, 522:9
your gambols s., 199:8
Sonitum ventis concessit, 103:*n*11
Sonnet a moment's monument, 509:23
scorn not the s., 377:13
Sonneteer, starved hackney s., 299:2
Sonnets, Book of Songs and S., 182:19
century of s., 466:25
lovers' s. turned psalms, 156:15
onlie begetter of insuing s., 220:*n*1
prophetic s., 703:3
written s. all his life, 402:22
Sonorous metal blowing, 256:13
Son's son till he gets wife, 506:13
Sons, Adam's s. conceived in sin, 235:4
all her s. at play, 497:22
anchors of mother's life, 67:14

Sons (*continued*)
bears all its s. away, 294:16
brother's s. gathering stalk and root, 708:2
brothers s. kindred slain, 302:*n*6
businessmen s. of bitches, 741:15
degenerate s. and daughters, 607:12
earth's heedless s., 694:1
five s. died gloriously, 450:9
forward s. of France, 366:*n*1
give them to your s., 790:9
guide Arcturus with his s., 15:13
happy to be father unto many s., 164:20
her patient s., 328:12
kill s. of Brutus, 137:4
more worthless than sires, 96:17
now we are all s. of bitches, 714:*n*3
of Atreus, 587:6
of Belial, 256:11
of bitches do you want to live forever, 318:*n*4
of dark and bloody ground, 492:5
of Edward sleep, 166:5
of former slaves, 761:1
of God shouted for joy, 15:8
of men and angels say, 312:13
of the living God, 29:22
of the morning, 395:16
of the prophet, 781:3
of toil, 503:4
see s. what things you are, 184:10
similar to their fathers, 52:32
that my s. may have liberty to study, 338:10
things are s. of heaven, 313:27
to thy Jubilee throng, 405:12
who Shem and Shaun s. of, 647:20
Soon as once set is our little light, 226:13
better three hours too s., 182:29
late and s., 376:11
little pot and s. hot, 167:27
said to eve Be s., 581:7
shall thy arm, 335:23
Sooner it's over sooner to sleep, 484:12
kill man than hawk, 663:13
stay a while end the s., 158:22
Soonest, least said s. mended, 149:*n*13
Soot, dust and s. of complaints, 558:5
in s. I sleep, 356:11
Sootfall, stirred by s. of your things, 769:15
Sooth, silly s., 202:12
Soothe a savage breast, 291:7
cares lift thoughts, 414:6
flattery s. ear of death, 322:10
or wound heart, 379:5
songs s. with their touch, 64:6
thine ear, 324:13
what charm s. melancholy, 328:29
Soothed by unfaltering trust, 411:4
Soothing, come lovely s. death, 490:17
Irish language for s., 613:12
language, 343:18
Soothsayer, painter trainer s., 108:21
Soothsayers make better living than truthsayers, 342:18
Sop, give s. to Cerberus, 118:3

Sop (*continued*)
of all this solid globe, 200:9
Sophist, saint- nor s.-led, 497:19
Sophisters, age of s., 332:12
Sophisticated modes of discrimination, 646:9
three on 's are s., 210:6
Sophistries, old old s. of June, 511:14
Sophocles drew men as they ought to be, 65:*n*7, 67:*n*9
long ago, 499:21
Sophonisba, O S. S. O, 308:10
Sorbonne, straight one day at S., 640:4
Sorcerer, I who fashioned myself s., 565:25
Sorcery of hot embraces, 679:19
Sordello, can but be one S., 659:12
Sordid boon, 376:11
covetous s. fellow, 305:1
Sore, good for s. eyes, 290:1
laborers have hard hands, 262:14
labor's bath, 214:6
stiff with toils, 491:5
task, 192:23
thy hand presseth me s., 17:4
thy so s. loss, 581:12
Sore-eyed, he's dropsical she s., 557:*n*2
Sorrow, a little fun to match s., 522:10
abandon learning and no s., 57:7
and sighing shall flee away, 27:10
bitterest cup of s., 613:*n*2
bread in s. ate, 349:7
breaks seasons, 165:32
bring forth children in s., 6:25
by s. of the heart the spirit is broken, 21:25
calls no time that's gone, 236:8
death and s. our companions, 620:12
disorder and early s., 629:22
down thou climbing s., 209:17
drink today and drown s., 236:3
enough to disarm, 442:1
ere s. comes with years, 438:16
excursion same for s. as joy, 727:18
find s. near at hand, 61:27
for angels, 464:25
for lost Lenore, 452:15
for Lycidas s. not dead, 254:6
frowsy couch in s. steep, 364:3
give s. words, 215:28
glut s. on rose, 416:17
God send them s. and shame, 135:22
hang s. care'll kill cat, 187:*n*1
happy in s., 151:25
hath less power to bite, 171:2
he that increaseth knowledge increaseth s., 23:28
he that loves s., 228:1
I had a little s., 684:4
I have known s., 93:25
idleness s. friend foe, 687:6
is knowledge, 402:2
keep thy s. to thyself, 30:15
legacy alleviates s., 151:20
more beautiful, 416:20

Sorrow (*continued*)
more in s. than anger, 193:21
naught but vast s. there, 617:2
never comes too late, 321:17
night of doubt and s., 521:12
no great s. dammed up in soul, 707:5
no more s., 48:1
no old age only s., 587:2
noble truth of s., 64:26
not be in s. too, 356:18
not mine but man's, 580:3
of human existence, 333:10
of love dureth overlong, 133:9
parting is such sweet s., 175:15
pine with fear and s., 154:5
pure and complete s. impossible, 510:9
regions of s., 255:24
rent is s. income tears, 242:9
rooted s., 216:10
Russian people make s. a diversion, 605:13
see if there be s. like unto my s., 29:2
sickness and troubled mind, 242:15
sing away s., 149:29
sit by fireside with S., 409:22
sit thee down s., 168:20
sorrow's crown of s., 455:13
source of Humor not joy but s., 527:26
sphere of our s., 409:12
stranger to s., 68:6
sweet that teaches, 750:4
to think full of s., 415:12
unfelt s., 214:17
unspeakable s. you bid me renew, 93:26
veiling song in s., 408:22
we are not sure of s., 534:14
wear a golden s., 225:8
what s. was bad'st her know, 321:19
when my heart 'scaped this s., 221:31
where s. is holy ground, 567:24
why should s. last, 776:15
wilt Thou live with me, 457:22
with night we banish s., 233:20
with s. to the grave, 8:8
write s. on bosom of earth, 171:24
year wake year to s., 408:21
yet is their strength labor and s., 18:12
Sorrowful, even in laughter the heart is s., 21:20
O sad kissed mouth how s., 533:19
soul s. unto death, 36:29
they were exceeding s., 36:26
Sorrow's crown of sorrow, 455:13
Sorrows, carried our s., 27:36
come not single spies, 198:20
disease or s. strike him, 483:2
few s. in which income no avail, 594:5
instruct s. to be proud, 169:27
losses restored and s. end, 220:19
man of s., 27:35
of your changing face, 595:2

Sorrows (*continued*)
    when gods bring s., 54:7
    when s. have end, 776:25
    women plunged into s., 365:31
Sorry, cheeks of s. grain 253:10
    feel s. because we cry, 546:4
    heartily s. for misdoings, 49:15
    if our wishes were gratified, 59:16
    love not having to say s., 769:1
    man who is s. will win, 58:1
    now I wrote it, 600:17
    Scheme of Things, 446:8
    truly s. man's dominion, 361:5
    union of very s. men, 51:37
    wild thing s. for itself, 657:11
Sort, ambition of meaner s., 163:13
    sager s. our deeds reprove, 226:13
    two of every s., 7:17
Sort, le s. fait les parents, 341:n5
Sorted out largest size, 519:6
Sorts, all s. and conditions of men,
        49:3
    all s. of people, 213:8
Soshubble ez baskit er kittens, 556:7
So-so is good, 192:8
    rest of married life s., 698:1
    some good some s., 106:9
Sot, vous êtes un s., 269:n1
Soudan, home in the S., 591:19
Sought, by night on my bed I s. him,
        25:9
    he s. the storms, 274:3
    I never s. world, 317:29
    it with thimbles, 519:24
    less often s. than found, 404:8
    love s. is good, 202:26
    many a thing I s., 220:18
    not s. support of Communism,
        649:5
    out many inventions, 24:15
    popularity crime when s., 279:29
    the remedy, 192:10
    to men that s. him sweet, 226:6
    truth not s. for, 81:8
    unknowing what he s., 276:27
Soul, adventure most unto itself S.,
        513:7
    America save s. rather than face,
        655:3
    amortization of heart and s., 686:21
    and in my s. am free, 267:18
    architect expends s., 349:27
    art in life of s., 584:14
    art work of body and s., 487:16
    astounded s., 749:15
    astronomy compels s. to look up-
        wards, 75:18
    awake my s., 280:20, 308:16
    beauty in inward s., 74:10
    belongs to the idea, 538:14
    bequeath my s. to God, 160:12
    beyond ego reach, 629:3
    bitterness of my s., 27:13
    body brevity wit s., 383:5
    body Nature is and God the s.,
        301:11
    brevity the s. of wit, 195:10
    call upon my s., 201:27
    calm S. of all things, 497:14
    can split sky in two, 683:16

Soul (*continued*)
    captain of his s., 677:7
    captain of life, 91:28
    captain of my s., 557:10
    chainless s., 480:3
    charge not s. save to its ability,
        117:3
    Chariot that bears Human S., 514:2
    clap hands and sing, 597:8
    cold waters to a thirsty s., 22:27
    condemned to be, 513:7
    crowd not on my s., 323:9
    damned of body and s., 591:11
    damp of night drives deeper into s.,
        489:14
    dare call s. my own, 439:3
    dark night of the s., 147:12
    dead that slumbers, 440:15
    deep distress humanized my S.,
        376:7
    digressions s. of reading, 320:14
    discipline s. of army, 336:12
    dissever my s. from s. of Annabel
        Lee, 453:9
    dividing s. and spirit, 45:34
    dream is hidden door of s., 629:3
    dull would he be of s., 374:12
    dusty answer gets s., 508:30
    eager s. biting for anger, 250:9
    eat eat me s., 283:8
    engineers of s., 605:14
    eternally unslayable, 84:6
    even-balanced, 497:3
    extinguish hope from s., 565:21
    extinguished his s., 448:10
    fair seedtime had my s., 373:7
    false words infect the s., 75:2
    far back in s. horse prances, 657:20
    fates have given a patient s., 52:25
    fiery s., 274:3
    find prison s. destroying, 712:2
    floated into my inmost s., 486:18
    flow of s., 302:21
    folk songs from s. sounds, 690:20
    for which s. did pine, 452:2
    force, 606:13
    forces which threaten s., 648:4
    from out that shadow, 452:22
    gain world lose s., 35:30
    genial current of s., 322:12
    gives heart and s. away, 579:1
    go S. the body's quest, 152:15
    God changes I am the s., 534:19
    grapple them to thy s., 193:29
    grave unto a s., 170:2
    half conceal S. within, 457:6
    half of my own s., 95:16
    hang like fruit my s., 220:6
    hark hark my s., 474:3
    harrow up thy s., 194:17
    has fled, 443:4
    has many motions, 725:16
    has to itself decreed, 414:3
    hath been alone, 382:6
    hath elbow-room, 170:21
    hath not lifted his s. unto vanity,
        16:18
    hath power to know all things,
        227:14
    haughtiness of s., 292:6

Soul (*continued*)
    he restoreth my s., 16:17
    he shall preserve thy s., 19:25
    he whose s. is flat, 683:16
    heart and s. and senses forever,
        466:17
    heaven take my s., 170:16
    height my s. can reach, 438:23
    her lips suck forth my s., 162:19
    him whom my s. loveth, 25:9
    his s. sincere, 322:23
    honor belongs to s., 110:12
    Horror s. of plot, 452:7
    hyacinths to feed s., 118:n2
    I have liberated my s., 121:9
    I hope his s. be in glorie, 131:4
    icebergs behoove the s., 729:2
    idea does not belong to s., 538:14
    if you would keep s., 660:16
    immortal because has s., 696:23
    immortal s. and all, 657:10
    in bliss, 211:9
    in mystery s. abides, 497:13
    in prison I am not free, 568:2
    in s. of man one insular Tahiti,
        486:27
    in the s. and the clod, 466:19
    intercourse from s. to s., 300:4
    into boughs does glide, 268:19
    iron entered into his s., 50:9
    is form and doth body make,
        154:14
    is his own, 185:17
    is in a ferment, 414:8
    is marching on, 524:7
    is the concern of my Lord, 116:18
    its body off, 599:2
    jaundice of the s., 275:20
    Jesus lover of my s., 312:14
    Jonathan loved him as his own s.,
        11:43
    joy's s. lies in doing, 200:4
    kindled at conwiviality, 469:26
    kiss my whole s., 162:n8
    knows no release, 700:7
    larger than sky, 419:2
    largest and most comprehensive s.,
        273:11
    lay not unction to s., 198:2
    lends tongue vows, 194:5
    life meets all motion becomes its s.,
        380:24
    life of s., 307:2
    lift my s. to heaven, 225:6
    like cloudy opal ring, 594:12
    listened intensely, 376:21
    little s. wandering guest, 110:7
    loafe and invite my s., 488:16
    locust of s. unshelled, 750:2
    look and body touch, 599:9
    look for deed s. performed, 117:21
    looks part has s. of part, 560:6
    love the Lord with all thy s., 10:11
    made up of wants, 483:19
    man became a living s., 6:11
    many a man's s. and faith, 773:1
    measured by my s., 294:5
    meeting s. may pierce, 251:19
    merry old s., 788:5
    migration of the s., 74:16

Soul (*continued*)

mind and s. according, 457:4
mirroring s., 497:18
more stately mansions O s., 447:11
most offending s. alive, 185:21
motorcycle parked like s. of junkyard, 752:3
mount mount my s., 172:17
my father lived his s., 689:2
my sin my s., 703:1
my s. an't yours Mas'r, 463:3
my S. at Liberty, 512:8
my s. bright invisible green, 477:16
my s. deep like rivers, 708:12
my s. doth magnify the Lord, 37:40
my s. there is a country, 270:8
my s. thirsteth for thee, 17:35
my s. waiteth for the Lord, 20:3
my unconquerable s., 557:9
mysterious thing in s., 487:3
never taught to stray, 301:7
new depths broken in s., 393:1
no coward s. mine, 480:4
no higher than s. high, 683:16
Northland s., 693:6
not bruised to pleasure s., 598:2
not more than body, 489:20
not spoken of the s., 440:15
nothing contributes more to peace
of s., 342:14
numerical precision s. of science,
583:12
O my prophetic s., 194:20
O my s. is white, 356:8
O s. be changed to waterdrops,
162:24
of Adonais like star, 409:9
of business, 305:11
of each God of all, 380:25
of fire, 313:18
of friend we've made, 585:9
of goodness in things evil, 185:16
of grandam inhabit a bird, 181:*n*3
of man immortal, 76:3
of music shed, 391:12
of my youth, 657:2
of sleeper away, 565:1
of s. sincere, 300:24
of the age, 232:18
of the plot, 452:7
of wit, 195:10
offends me to the s., 196:21
on that day no s. wronged, 117:13
one s. though many tongues, 112:6
palace of the s., 250:4
pensive s., 324:16
perches in the s., 511:20
perdition catch my s., 206:27
pilgrim s. in you, 595:2
Plato healer of s., 74:*n*3
poet brings s. into activity, 384:13
poet of Body poet of S., 489:7
poetry should enter one's s., 417:19
poor intricated s., 231:13
poor s. sat sighing, 208:4
poor s. the center, 222:11
possess s. with patience, 275:24
pouring forth s., 415:16
pray for repose of his s., 582:17
pray Lord my s. keep, 287:14

Soul (*continued*)

prison that can bind s., 563:15
prophet of the s., 429:9
prophetic s. of world, 221:23
Psyche my S., 453:3
pure and clear as crystal, 471:24
rapt s. in thine eyes, 251:24
receive my s. at last, 312:14
recovers radical innocence, 597:6
rejoices in truth uttered, 475:8
remembering my good friends,
171:14
rescue my s. from their destructions,
16:32
research into feminine s., 569:19
rest her s. she's dead, 199:5
richness of s., 77:7
riddling perplexed s., 231:13
roamed with my S., 453:3
ruled by levity pure, 738:9
sad glance glum, 531:14
sad lucidity of s., 497:10
said to s. be still, 671:5
sail leagues and leagues, 509:25
same in all creatures, 71:16
sanctum of the s., 629:3
save my s. if I have s., 503:14
saves s. in new French books,
466:10
School Intelligence make it a s.,
418:16
science without conscience ruin of
s., 139:13
seeking with s. land of Greeks,
349:13
selects her Society, 512:2
shall be required of thee, 38:29
shorten stature of s., 508:26
shrinks from all to remember,
749:16
sighed s. toward Grecian tents,
182:7
sincerely from author's s., 689:17
sinews of s., 250:17
single s. in two bodies, 77:13
sleepless s. that perished, 374:9
smithy of s., 647:11
so dead, 378:1
so panteth my s. after thee, 17:11
sorrowful unto death, 36:29
speech a mirror of s., 100:25
stirred s. to inmost depths, 426:15
strains that might create a s., 253:5
strong is the s., 497:5
sun steadies my s., 664:19
sweet and virtuous s., 243:12
swell the s. to rage, 276:15
swooned slowly, 647:8
takes nothing with her, 75:3
taste sadness of might, 416:18
that can be honest, 236:7
that rises with us, 375:7
the hungry s., 23:2
the Timid S., 660:9
thirst that from s. doth rise, 232:15
thirsteth for God, 17:11
this that oppresses s., 519:23
thou hast much goods, 38:28
thoughtful S. to Solitude, 445:5
thy s. the fixt foot, 229:13

Soul (*continued*)

time the s. of this world, 107:19
'tis my outward s., 229:19
to dare, 378:19
tumult of the s., 377:4
two to bear my s. away, 266:8
unlettered small-knowing s., 168:18
unto captain Christ, 172:6
upon my s. between kisses, 602:7
variety s. of pleasure, 281:16
wake s. by tender strokes, 299:19
was like a star, 374:20
wears out breast, 402:1
weddings of the s., 639:12
what Fortitude S. contains, 514:17
what of s. left I wonder, 466:14
what s. without flaws, 565:19
whispereth within him, 117:17
whose s. is sense, 229:11
why art thou cast down O my s.,
17:12
why castest thou off my s., 18:9
why shrinks the s., 292:14
windows of the s., 360:3
wine-scented poetic s., 561:15
with all its maladies, 538:5
with all thy heart and s., 36:1
with my whole s., 28:36
witness of s. naturally Christian,
112:3
yet my s. drew back, 244:1
Soul-hungry, worse to be s., 782:4
Soul-making, vale of S., 418:15
Soul's arrest, 619:5
dark cottage, 250:6
for s. good do things disliked,
626:15
my s. calm retreat, 270:2
prayer s. sincere desire, 377:18
whole s. tasking, 485:4
Souls are in the hand of God, 30:23
beams of wit on other s., 274:26
beyond reaches of our s., 194:11
boundless as we wish our s., 407:7
conscience grinds our s., 235:22
corporations have no s., 152:5,
555:15
damp s. of housemaids, 667:22
departed shadows of living, 249:6
flame of freedom in s., 541:6
great s. suffer in silence, 364:19
have sight of sea, 375:13
immediate jewel of their s., 206:30
in s. sympathy with sounds, 335:11
jealous s. not answered, 207:17
left your s. on earth, 416:11
letters mingle s., 230:14
Liberty inspire our S., 292:*n*2
live in furnished s., 688:11
look after s. in labor, 76:9
love's mysteries in s. grow, 229:16
many valiant s. of heroes, 50:23
memory green in our s., 391:11
miserable state wretched s., 125:9
mounting up to God, 509:20
must not be saved, 206:16
numberless infinities of s., 230:19
nurse of full-grown s., 484:22
of animals infuse themselves, 181:17
of blood, 658:19

Sow a thought, 781:6
  as you s. ye reap, 263:25
  he that observeth wind not s., 24:24
  Ireland old s. that eats farrow, 647:9
  men that s. and reap, 534:13
  they s. not, 33:18
  they that s. in tears, 19:28
  thy seed in the morning, 24:25
  wrong s. by ear, 142:26
Sowed, what I s. what orchard yields, 708:2
Sowest, that which thou s., 43:23
Soweth, whatsoever a man s., 44:21
Sowing, farmer s. the corn, 792:24
Sown in corruption, 43:25
  never reaped nor was s., 280:23
  the wind, 29:27
  wild oats not s. more than once, 586:21
Soya, gigantic field of s. beans, 769:4
Space, alchemized and free of s., 414:11
  annihilate s. and time, 300:27
  chained to point in s., 420:17
  cubic inch of s. a miracle, 491:4
  duty beyond s. and time, 620:19
  engenders forgetfulness, 629:9
  eye vanquished by s., 151:26
  God stepped on s., 612:7
  here is my s., 216:25
  in reality atoms and s., 70:28
  king of infinite s., 195:26
  memory emancipated from s., 384:8
  much rychnesse in lytell s., 162:n4
  music in s., 350:n1
  non-being penetrates no s., 57:13
  objects extended in s., 640:17
  out of S. out of Time, 452:11
  put on earth a little s., 356:9
  seas of s. and time, 666:22
  the final frontier, 749:7
  untrespassed sanctity of s., 751:3
Spaces in togetherness, 651:12
  sailing celestial s., 537:18
  silence of infinite s., 270:23
  vacant interstellar s., 671:4
Spaceship, automated S. Earth, 691:13
Spacious firmament on high, 291:32
  skies, 576:19
  times of Elizabeth, 454:12
Spade, call s. a s., 81:11
  part Sam S. liked, 689:12
  poet bow to common s., 766:1
Spaded, delicately gelded or s., 688:13
Spades emblems of graves, 335:6
  let s. be trumps, 299:16
Spaghetti, ticker tape ain't s., 648:1
Spain, building castles in S., 132:23
  comes forth, 714:4
  from each hollow of S., 714:4
  is become richest of countries, 134:13
  look at broken S., 714:3
  rain in S., 745:7
Spain's, king of S. daughter, 790:12
Spake as a child, 43:16
  never man s. like this, 40:7
  of disastrous chances, 205:25
  so s. the Fiend, 258:15

Spake (*continued*)
  Solomon s. three thousand proverbs, 12:21
  upon this hint I s., 205:28
Spam, he wanted steak they offered s., 736:6
Span, eternity shut in a s., 264:20
  Eve s., 775:13
  life is but s., 287:13
  life less than s., 160:13
  life's brief s. forbids us, 95:19
  life's but a s., 227:15
Spangled heavens a shining frame, 291:32
Spaniard, I am a S., 653:21
  man without imagination, 653:21
Spaniards, emotions of S., 419:7
Spanish, I speak S. to God, 143:3
  or neat's leather, 263:18
  sailors with bearded lips, 442:6
  ships of war at sea, 460:6
  sun never sets in S. dominions, 364:n5
Spanish-American War splendid little war, 536:15
Spans, narrow measure s., 580:3
Spar to men that sink, 684:13
Spare all I have take my life, 295:16
  brother can you s. dime, 699:15
  establish peace s. conquered, 94:15
  he will not s. in day of vengeance, 20:31
  me that I may recover strength, 17:10
  my aching sight, 323:9
  rod and spoil child, 81:n6, 263:21
  spend shafts s. not, 776:23
  thee past my power, 361:19
  to us our friends, 562:9
  women for Thy Sake, 718:23
  woodman s. beechen tree, 389:8
  woodman s. that tree, 428:10
  your country's flag, 443:11
Spared, better s. better man, 179:8
  lashed vice s. name, 289:18
Spares, blest man that s. these stones, 226:11
  neither man nor his works, 340:7
  war s. not the brave, 60:3
Spareth, he that s. his rod, 21:17
Sparing, in the middle be s., 54:28
Spark, dusk shadow then s., 554:13
  from heaven, 498:10
  from Heaven immortal, 364:13
  gie me ae s., 361:11
  great flame follows little s., 126:22
  my little s. of courage, 783:14
  nor human s. is left, 304:2
  of heavenly fire, 396:2
  of that ancient flame, 93:39
  out of stone easier than moral, 532:10
  vital s. of heavenly flame, 299:8
Sparkle, on forefinger of Time s., 456:9
  out among fern, 458:15
  still right Promethean fire, 169:4
  with larceny, 631:11
Sparkles near the brim, 399:19
Sparkling cross she wore, 299:10

Sparkling (*continued*)
  fount more s. than glass, 96:21
  pair of s. eyes, 531:21
Sparks, as the s. fly upward, 14:2
  like s. of fire befriend thee, 241:12
  that set these hearts on fire, 125:21
Sparrer-grass, hit look lak s., 556:5
Sparrow, brawling of s., 594:23
  caters for s., 190:10
  come before Window, 417:17
  hero perish or s. fall, 301:5
  I said the s., 789:1
  I watch and am as a s., 18:24
  Lesbia with her s., 684:6
  life like flight of s., 120:6
  my lady's s. is dead, 90:16
  old king to s., 617:3
  providence in fall of s., 199:22
Sparrows, as boys do s., 288:15
  two s. sold for farthing, 34:33
Spartan, remnant of S. dead, 402:27
  simplicity, 783:16
Spartans, go tell the S., 60:11
Speak a few reasonable words, 349:10
  after manner of men, 41:44
  all that love can s., 514:7
  although s. with mouth thus, 711:3
  arrows which s. to the wise, 63:30
  by the card, 199:6
  causing lips of those asleep to s., 25:20
  comfortably to Jerusalem, 27:15
  daggers to her, 197:22
  did he stop s. to you, 465:16
  difficult to s., 332:6
  don't s. well of self, 270:16
  each other in passing, 442:16
  for ten minutes need week, 572:15
  for yourself John, 442:3
  free to think s. write, 345:4
  freedom to s., 485:7
  friends absent s., 230:14
  gently she can hear, 566:5
  grief that does not s., 215:28
  hands for me, 188:15
  have mouths but s. not, 19:17
  how to s. true things, 54:15
  I must s. in passion, 177:29
  I only s. right on, 189:10
  I s. Spanish to God, 143:3
  I will s. to thee, 194:10
  if any s., 188:27
  ill of the dead, 55:11
  in monstrous little voice, 172:25
  less than thou knowest, 209:8
  let no one s. ill of absent, 100:31
  let not God s. with us, 9:13
  let us not s. of them, 125:10
  liars when they s. truth, 77:8
  live pure s. true, 459:7
  Lord for thy servant heareth, 11:28
  Love that dare not s. its name, 609:14
  low if you speak love, 186:20
  masters of things they s., 239:2
  minds of others to speak my own better, 145:15
  more in minute, 175:22
  needless to s. about things done, 61:1

Speak (continued)
   no evil, 777:10
   no man s. to him, 277:n 8
   no more of his renown, 458:8
   no one left to s. up, 684:19
   no one should s. of Providence,
      747:3
   not loud or long, 154:n 5
   of comfort no man s., 171:24
   of me as I am, 208:16
   of moderns without contempt,
      305:3
   of one that loved, 208:16
   one to s. another hear, 477:17
   or forever hold his peace, 50:2
   power to s., 277:22
   rather of sterner days, 621:6
   rather s. ill of ourselves, 265:19
   Reilly they s. of so highly, 781:5
   roughly to little boy, 517:15
   Sappho would s. openly, 626:10
   silver reply gold, 784:26
   slaves who fear to s., 484:20
   slow to s., 46:7
   softly carry big stick, 575:16
   suffer me that I may s., 14:33
   tears that s., 267:10
   the affirmative, 433:26
   the speech I pray you, 196:21
   time to s., 23:32
   to be silent better than to s., 107:8
   to God as if men listening, 102:20
   to him again, 465:16
   to Him for He hears, 460:4
   to it Horatio, 192:21
   to me as to thy thinkings, 206:29
   to me not of me, 464:5
   to s. and purpose not, 208:25
   to s. and s. well are two things,
      233:8
   to s. dishonorably is pardonable,
      67:13
   to the earth, 14:16
   to whom can I s. today, 4:1, 4:2,
      4:3
   to your silent ashes, 91:17
   too full of God to s., 594:15
   trees known to s., 215:10
   truth and shame Devil, 140:5
   truth more as I grow old, 146:16
   we s. not what we mean, 204:6
   we to them will s., 373:14
   what cannot s. about must pass
      over, 677:11
   what we feel, 211:21
   when I s. they are for war, 19:24
   when I think I s., 191:15
   when spoken to, 561:8
   who knows does not s., 57:17
   with pride of our doings, 664:2
   with tongues of men, 43:13
   woe when men s. well, 38:12
   write s. associate, 724:7
   you s. like a green girl, 194:3
Speakest, think before thou s., 150:6
Speaketh, out of abundance of the
   heart mouth s., 35:3
Speaking, distant s. of voices, 738:1
   hears you nearby sweetly s., 56:5
   idle biologically s., 684:5

Speaking (continued)
   in s. for myself, 205:22
   judge s. clearly most severly, 720:14
   keep thy lips from s. guile, 16:31
   lies in hypocrisy, 45:14
   measure what s. about, 504:11
   orator a good man skilled in s.,
      85:8
   persuades when s. fails, 222:22
   prose without knowing it, 269:24
   terms with itsilf, 602:16
   things which they ought not, 45:19
Speaks a new scene, 242:13
   according to his actions, 60:22
   acts before he s., 60:22
   as man s. so is he, 100:25
   for Family of Man, 634:14
   heart thinks tongue s., 186:33
   her foot s., 201:10
   hides one thing and s. another,
      51:30
   holiday, 182:31
   infinite deal of nothing, 179:23
   money s. sense, 281:18
   needs no questioning before he s.,
      69:8
   poetry is painting that s., 60:14
   she s. poniards, 186:22
   she s. yet says nothing, 174:27
   small like a woman, 182:17
   to me as if I were public meeting,
      488:7
   when he s. air is still, 184:22
   when Love s., 169:3
   who s. does not know, 57:17
   wise man s., 233:8
   without modesty, 61:23
Spear, bring me my s., 359:17
   idle s. and shield, 250:21
   mangled by the bronze s., 52:20
   observing s. of summer grass,
      488:16
   to equal tallest pine, 256:7
   to thrust club to strike, 139:5
   took s. but left shield, 353:7
Spearmint Girl, 688:12
Spears into pruninghooks, 25:30
   sheen of their s., 401:15
   stars threw down s., 358:7
Special people unto himself, 10:13
   providence, 199:22
Specialist, take him to s. in Zurich,
   767:12
   train him to become any type of s.,
      634:18
Specialists in mental disease, 652:12
   preserves us not for s., 757:15
Species, especially male of s., 657:16
   female of s., 593:22
   not individual but s., 311:17
   of monkeys and apes, 759:8
   one s. of superstition, 318:15
   preservation of s., 366:6
Specious, murder takes s. name, 296:3
Speckled band, 577:18
Spectacle unto the world, 42:35
Spectacles, finest s. in nature, 310:15
   of books, 273:12
   on nose pouch on side, 191:3

Spectator, blood and disposition of s.,
   462:20
   live as s. of mankind, 292:18
   of action he describes, 503:5
   of mighty scene, 390:8
Spectators, pleasure to s., 425:19
   some must be s., 233:7
Spectatum veniunt veniunt spectentur,
   101:n 10
Specter bark, 381:14
   haunting eastern Europe, 768:7
   haunting Europe, 481:14
   my s. around me, 358:16
Specter-gray, when Frost was s., 540:9
Specters' holiday, 531:12
Specter-thin, pale and s., 415:12
Speculating, theologian not born by s.,
   138:13
Speculation, everybody watches s.,
   469:40
   rouse s. about dangerous things,
      733:5
Speculators about perpetual motion,
   135:12
   philosophical s., 148:13
Sped, right dead right as s. along,
   783:n 9
Speech, abridging freedom of s.,
   346:11
   after long silence, 598:23
   be alway with grace, 45:1
   be skillful in s., 3:11
   day unto day uttereth s., 16:9
   dead had no s. for, 671:20
   ere Thought wed with S., 457:10
   finely framed, 32:21
   first silence of s., 442:22
   free men from bondage, 568:15
   free s. Frémont, 780:14
   free s. in repulsive form, 621:17
   freedom of s. and expression,
      649:17
   freedom of s. freedom of conscience,
      527:29
   freedom of s. taken, 336:18
   from him never real s., 413:8
   given to communicate, 280:2
   good s. more hidden than malachite,
      3:4
   great s. impassioned, 80:7
   I am slow of s., 8:28
   I wrote in a garret, 312:n 4
   impelled us, 672:3
   in substaunce ys but air, 128:2
   is civilization, 629:17
   is image of actions, 55:18
   is like tapestries, 62:29
   is small change of Silence, 508:23
   let thy s. be short, 32:6
   like cracked kettle, 496:6
   make s. to maggots, 688:5
   many harmed by s., 143:11
   mend your s. a little, 208:21
   mighty true free Russian s., 482:20
   mirror of soul, 100:25
   modest in s., 61:24
   never taxed for s., 203:8
   no good s. save in Paris, 134:3
   not to express but conceal, 280:n 1
   nowhere is s. freer, 621:17

Speech (*continued*)

our concern was s., 672:3

plainness of s., 44:1

poetry of s., 400:18

protection of free s., 542:24

regretted s. never silence, 100:24

right s., 65:1

rude am I in my s., 205:21

rude in s., 44:8

short meaning of long s., 365:7

Silence golden S. silvern, 412:10

silence more eloquence than s., 462:4

small s. cantankerous, 80:7

speak the s. I pray you, 196:21

steep my s. in lies, 63:31

strange power of s., 382:5

subtle s. delights us, 87:18

suppression of free s., 568:15

sweeter than honey, 50:30

Tennysonianness of s., 660:4

thy s. bewrayeth thee, 37:2

to conceal thoughts, 306:21

to stir men's blood, 189:10

took all heart for s., 596:9

what s. escaped your teeth, 51:17

Speeches, men's charitable s., 160:12

no one hears our s., 681:7

not my s. you mislike, 163:18

questions not decided by s., 474:11

Speed, all deliberate s., 682:*n*4

at rate of six miles an hour, 393:7

be wise with s., 295:25

bonnie boat, 577:6

deliberate s., 581:5

ease and s. not give work beauty, 131:*n*7

far faster than light, 618:14

full s. ahead, 426:16

good s. to your youthful valor, 94:24

his plow, 157:9

in skating safety is s., 432:5

mass times s. of light squared, 635:*n*3

more haste less s., 98:21

of my desire, 506:2

retiring at high s. toward Japanese, 647:6

the going guest, 302:22

the parting guest, 299:26

the plow, 157:*n*6

the soft intercourse, 300:4

thousands at his bidding s., 255:13

through the antiseptic tunnel, 759:12

today put back tomorrow, 154:5

wrong to s. a guest, 53:29

Speeding, Rus whither are you s., 446:27

unreeling tirelessly s. them, 491:8

wall of dark shadow came s. at us, 773:16

Speeds, dawn s. a man, 54:29

parting guest, 597:17

tale is best plainly told, 166:7

wit s. too fast, 168:24

Speedy and public trial, 346:15

Spell, foreigners s. better than pronounce, 525:22

Spell (*continued*)

soon fades the s., 426:2

Spencer, expression used by S., 444:6

Spencer's, Mr. S. Social Statics, 542:16

Spend, doth life in tendance s., 154:6

he that will s. it, 228:1

life your own way, 679:11

mind business s. less, 279:8

ne'er s. fury on child, 165:4

not s. another such night, 165:29

not then his gifts in vain, 232:4

shafts and spare not, 776:23

sweetest hours e'er I s., 362:1

that shortness basely, 179:3

time most valuable thing man can s., 81:21

to s. to give to want, 154:6

we s. our years as a tale that is told, 18:11

wealth at once you are ruined, 422:10

what we yet may s., 445:16

whatever you have s. less, 317:28

wherewith to s., 233:12

Spending, draw salary before s., 600:11

getting and s., 376:11

lives like serfs, 478:29

old age time of s., 262:11

riches are for s., 159:29

youth now bravely s., 675:2

Spendthrifts, kings and ministers greatest s., 326:5

Spens, gude Sir Patrick S., 785:1

Spenser, not lodge thee by S., 232:18

renowned S., 240:13

Spent, all passion s., 261:27

but one day thoroughly well, 132:18

confess this world's s., 230:15

consider how light is s., 255:11

days are s. without hope, 14:7

dissolutely s. Tuesday morning, 176:26

enough to assure remaining second weakest, 643:8

hours s. with thee, 586:17

life half s. before we know, 245:5

life well s. is long, 135:3

never s. hour's talk withal, 168:23

under belly, 236:16

waves' riot, 534:12

Sperm, created you of s. drop, 117:2

Spes, dum anima est s. est, 87:*n*12

modo liceat vivere est s., 86:*n*2

Spew thee out of my mouth, 47:13

Sphere, enforced from quiet s., 184:6

great s. thou movest in, 218:6

motion in one s., 179:4

nature in terms of s., 537:21

owner of s., 430:12

storm-troubled s., 480:4

Sphere-descended, Music s. maid, 324:18

Spheres, driven by the s., 270:7

ever-moving s. of Heaven, 162:22

invisible s. formed in fright, 486:26

moving as the restless S., 161:21

music from the s., 202:22

music of the s., 248:20

Spheres (*continued*)

prefers live music to humdrum s., 757:10

seems to shake the s., 276:7

stars shot madly from their s., 173:5

start from their s., 194:17

tuned s., 218:11

Spherical, body perfectly s., 471:30

predominance, 209:3

read that world was s., 134:12

Sphery chime, 253:13

Sphinx, don't care whether a Minx or S., 471:21

Oedipus met S., 706:7

riddle of the S., 66:1

Spice, sugar and s., 791:6

variety's s. of life, 334:28

Spices thereof may flow out, 25:13

young hart upon mountains of s., 25:24

Spicy grove cinnamon tree, 711:2

no s. fragrance while they grow, 159:*n*4

nut-brown ale, 251:16

Phoenix builds s. nest, 246:6

Spider, almost like a s., 148:4

along came a s., 791:6

confined in web's center, 148:4

much as one holds s., 308:20

noiseless patient s., 491:8

subtle s., 148:*n*4

to Fly, 423:11

Spider-like we feel the touch, 148:*n*4

Spider's net is heavy, 726:4

touch how fine, 148:*n*4

Spiders crying together, 743:8

like s. across stars, 750:9

love of s., 703:16

marching through air, 742:12

none of new s. took her place, 703:17

preserved in amber, 106:*n*6

Spiders', laws like s. webs, 56:2

Spielvogel, Doctor S. this is my life, 765:12

Spies a far-off shore, 164:21

God's s., 211:13

single s., 198:20

Spill, all germens s. at once, 209:24

Spilled, as water s. on the ground, 12:13

fearing to be s., 198:15

Spills in fearing to be spilt, 198:15

Spin, great world s. forever, 455:25

set by fire and s., 789:8

sob as you s., 721:1

toil not neither s., 33:20

webs from entrails s., 148:*n*4

Spinach and the hell with it, 703:8

gammon and s., 470:31, 788:4

Spindle, do not fold s. or mutilate, 783:23

Spinnage, gammon and s., 470:31

Spinning our own fates, 545:14

Spinning-jenny and railroad, 484:8

out of side, 597:21

Spinning-wheel, make me O Lord thy s., 283:6

Spinoza, atheism like that of S., 588:16

Spins, hither and thither s., 497:18

Spinsters and knitters in the sun, 202:12

Spiral down militaristic stairway, 761:7

Spires, dreaming s., 499:16
   of Oxford, 648:3
   what s. what farms, 579:9
   whose silent finger, 377:1
   ye distant s., 321:13

Spirit, absent in body present in s., 42:36
   Accusing S., 320:29
   actions must be his s., 79:4
   against flesh, 44:18
   all compact of fire, 165:9
   and with your s., 48:5
   animating universe, 420:17
   be thou S. fierce, 407:17
   Big Blue Mountain S., 787:7
   blessed are poor in s., 33:1
   blithe s., 408:4
   bloweth and is still, 497:13
   body and s. twins, 535:7
   body without s. is dead, 46:10
   born of the S., 39:44
   by my s. saith the Lord, 30:1
   by sorrow s. broken, 21:25
   cabined ample s., 498:15
   capable of compassion, 696:23
   Chinese not have national s., 601:4
   Creator drew his s., 277:1
   decides issue, 642:8
   delighted s., 204:14
   descending like dove, 32:33
   dividing soul and s., 45:34
   erring s., 192:28
   essential in painting, 120:13
   eternal S. of chainless Mind, 401:22
   everything that emancipates s., 351:12
   expense of s. in waste of shame, 222:7
   fled indignant to the shades, 94:28
   follow your s., 185:5
   fruit of the S., 44:19
   full of s. as month of May, 178:20
   gentleness of s. serenity of mind, 245:n3
   gentlier on s. lies, 454:6
   given on Earth, 451:6
   giveth life, 43:31
   haughty s. before a fall, 21:31
   he that ruleth his s., 21:32
   holiday-rejoicing s., 388:2
   humble in s., 23:11
   humble tranquil s., 227:19
   I commend my s., 39:22
   ill s. have so fair a house, 224:2
   immortal s. grows, 373:8
   in one s. meet mingle, 407:20
   in s. and truth, 39:48
   invisible s. of wine, 206:22
   is departed, 32:11
   is willing, 36:31
   knight of holy s., 420:2
   letter and s. of constitution, 355:12
   lifeblood of master s., 254:24

Spirit (*continued*)
   lively understandable s., 725:2
   Mammon least erected s., 256:20
   man of understanding is of excellent s., 21:37
   mark of Greek s., 603:26
   meek and quiet s., 46:24
   modern s. Greek discovery, 603:25
   motion and a s., 373:5
   motions of his s. dull, 182:10
   my s. too weak, 417:2
   nation's s. die of inanition, 499:8
   naught so much s. calms, 402:16
   no longer ruler of own s., 368:16
   no s. can walk abroad, 192:29
   not letter but s., 43:31
   of age, 306:30
   of Beauty that dost consecrate, 406:10
   of counsel and might, 26:10
   of Delight, 409:15
   of fear, 45:26
   of God brother of my own, 488:18
   of God moved upon face of the waters, 6:4
   of government must be of country, 564:15
   of his own epoch, 629:5
   of knowledge and fear of the Lord, 26:10
   of liberty, 331:10
   of love how quick and fresh, 201:17
   of men who follow, 658:15
   of moderation, 615:3
   of Night, 409:13
   of party, 337:5
   of popular government, 352:1
   of prophecy in me, 74:21
   of repose, 426:15
   of science, 708:1
   of suspicion and distrust, 615:5
   of the time, 503:5
   of the valley never dies, 56:16
   of wisdom and understanding, 26:10
   of youth in everything, 221:19
   of Zeus-fostered kings, 51:6
   original creation of s., 584:9
   pardlike s. beautiful swift, 409:1
   passed before my face, 13:39
   perturbed s., 195:5
   poetry finer s. of knowlege, 373:15
   proud and chivalrous s., 79:4
   real and eternal, 495:21
   renew a right s. within me, 17:22
   resemblance neglects s. of objects, 120:14
   revenge delight of mean s., 109:10
   sacred to departed s., 118:28
   scorned his s., 187:26
   self-same sounds on s., 639:3
   shall rest upon him, 26:10
   shall return unto God, 24:28
   shallow s. of judgment, 163:10
   slave s. below, 661:2
   slumber did my s. seal, 374:1
   so still and quiet, 205:23
   spur the clear s. doth raise, 253:20
   straight in strength of s., 534:20
   strongest and fiercest s., 256:24

Spirit (*continued*)
   that always denies, 350:14
   that on life's rough sea, 157:13
   that quickeneth, 40:5
   that stands by naked man, 777:2
   thy s. walks abroad, 189:25
   too much s. to be at ease, 300:15
   tool carries s. by which created, 707:3
   travail and vexation of s., 23:34
   truth shows s. and substance, 120:14
   vanity and vexation of s., 23:27
   vital s., 577:5
   weak s. quickens, 669:20
   whatever anguish of s., 339:7
   which goes through mass, 629:5
   whither shall I go from thy s., 20:8
   wild S. moving everywhere, 407:14
   with Spirit can meet, 460:4
   within me constraineth me, 15:1
   within nourishes, 94:13
   wounded s. who can bear, 21:39
   yearning in desire, 455:3
   yet a S. still and bright, 375:18

Spiriting, do my s. gently, 223:28

Spiritless, man so faint so s., 183:10

Spirit's, clown of s. motive, 734:6

Spirits, all s. and melted into air, 224:21
   apothecary never out of s., 352:19
   be free all worthy s., 157:12
   black s. and white, 237:9
   blast drives wicked s., 125:15
   by our own s. defied, 374:9
   call s. from vasty deep, 178:3
   can either sex assume, 256:10
   cheerer of s., 245:17
   day of s., 270:2
   good s. when well dressed, 469:35
   her wanton s. look out, 201:10
   how can you serve s., 61:15
   I summoned up, 349:22
   insult to s. of ancestors, 502:5
   like two s. suggest me, 222:10
   maketh his angels s., 45:33
   master s. of this age, 188:20
   not jump with common s., 180:26
   of great events, 389:n1
   of just men, 45:41
   of land and grain, 80:6
   of the damned, 448:10
   of wise mock us, 183:32
   other s. standing apart, 414:1
   red s. and gray, 237:9
   that fell with Lucifer, 162:14
   that tend thoughts, 212:29
   throng with returning s., 398:11
   tribe of s. and of men, 117:19
   unclean s. entered swine, 37:25
   unhappy s. fell with Lucifer, 162:14
   vanish like evil s., 344:19
   we are s. not animals, 620:19
   who live in twilight, 575:12
   wonders at quaint s., 173:11

Spirit-stirring drum, 207:8

Spiritu, et cum s. tuo, 48:5

Spiritual excitement, 500:5
   found s. cause, 495:20
   highest s. authority, 645:1

Spiritual (*continued*)
inward and s. grace, 49:22
millions of s. creatures, 258:23
natural fact symbol of s., 431:2
Negro s. free at last, 761:3
perfection of man, 122:11
psalms hymns and s. songs, 44:26
risk and s. self-sacrifice, 679:16
stronger than material, 433:18
superhuman s. and divine, 628:15
wickedness in high places, 44:28
Spirochete, without little s., 750:3
Spit, if I lie s. in my face, 177:24
on us for luck, 82:14
upon my Jewish gaberdine, 180:8
Spite, force in s. of Nature, 263:11
in erring reason's s., 301:12
O cursed s., 195:6
of cormorant devouring Time, 168:11
the world, 214:22
Spiteful envious animal the Public, 390:10
Splashing wintry mold, 595:5
Spleen, in a s. unfolds heaven and earth, 172:20
that scourge of Britain, 423:17
Splendid abilities utterly corrupt, 386:1
and sterile Dolores, 533:13
by the vision s., 375:8
give me s. silent sun, 490:13
in ashes, 249:4
little war, 536:15
misery, 344:2
poor s. wings, 535:3
Shilling, 295:2
tear, 458:23
you rise, 5:2
Splendide mendax, 96:n15
Splendidly null, 458:17
Splendor falls on castle walls, 456:11
guilty s., 334:30
in the grass, 375:14
not in lone s., 417:12
of the Mighty One Krishna, 84:12
on earth no such s., 121:2
your s. like heaven's s., 4:11
Splendors, heaven with s. lie, 485:3
Splenetive and rash, 199:15
Split ears of groundlings, 196:21
mountains with thunderbolt, 92:25
sides with laughing, 150:3
the sky in two, 683:16
world would s. open, 734:4
Splits, who s. wood warms twice, 478:n1
Splitting, image of s. apart, 5:7
warmed while s. stumps, 478:30
Spoil it by trying to explain, 352:15
little foxes that s. the vines, 25:7
lives of better people, 562:6
no more s. upon my face, 186:4
rampant for s. and victory, 552:24
spare rod and s. child, 81:n6, 263:21
villainous company s. of me, 178:16
Spoiled, Christian a pagan s., 590:5
Spoiling nice new clothes, 790:15

Spoils, conquests glories triumphs s., 188:19
of time, 322:12
rich with s. of Nature, 248:5
to victor belong s., 398:8
treasons stratagems and s., 182:10
victor belongs to s., 694:7
Spoke, man who knew more s. less, 107:12
more he heard less he s., 554:18
never s. with God, 513:15
of disastrous chances, 205:25
town-crier s. my lines, 196:21
Spoken, glorious things of thee s., 327:5
God had never s. anything but English, 622:15
God's last Put out Light s., 623:22
lie down till leaders s., 592:16
not s. of soul, 440:15
Rome has s. case closed, 114:33
speak when s. to, 561:8
weird power in s. word, 572:23
word at random s., 379:5
word comes not back, 97:n10
Spondee, slow S. stalks, 383:11
Spontaneity, Hellenism s. of consciousness, 500:17
studied s. of Horace, 105:8
Spontaneous, happiness not s. product, 635:10
joy and natural content, 595:19
overflow of feelings, 373:17
Spoon, dish ran away with s., 789:9
hire long s. eat with feend, 131:23
runcible s., 472:3
silver s. in mouth, 151:18
Spoons, faster counted s., 425:n1
guard our s., 425:2
let us count our s., 315:27
measured life with coffee s., 667:13
woman with silver s., 477:14
Sport, boys throw stones in s., 82:10
ended his s. with Tess, 540:3
make s. for neighbors, 387:4
no s. in hate, 409:18
of kings, 295:1
present life a diversion and s., 117:8
that wrinkled Care derides, 251:9
they kill us for their s., 210:20
to have enginer hoist, 198:8
with Amaryllis, 253:20
would be tedious, 176:37
Sported on the green, 386:3
Sports and plays with me, 356:1
joy of youthful s., 401:4
of love, 232:4
shows games s. guns, 338:5
Sporus, let S. tremble, 302:14
Spot, black s. to keep concealed, 507:16
certain am I of s., 513:15
dim s. men call earth, 252:12
do in that remote s., 370:17
earth one mighty blood s., 435:22
out damned s., 216:1
stand on right s., 349:23
there is no s. in thee, 25:11
what is Black S., 561:3
Spotless reputation, 170:25

Spots, leopard change his s., 28:24
minds grow in s., 546:20
quadrangular of diamond, 335:6
Spotted sight or sound, 660:16
snakes with double tongue, 173:12
Spouse, President's s. I wish him well, 754:18
so bright and clear, 231:1
Spout till you have drenched, 209:24
Spouted arms, 701:6
Spouts black blood and rolls fin out, 486:23
trunk s. out a sea, 259:21
Sprang to the stirrup, 465:1
Sprat, Jack S. eat no fat, 788:7
Sprawling in slush and gutter, 535:9
Spray, never a s. of yew, 498:14
nightingale on bloomy s., 254:9
rime was on the s., 539:8
toss in the s., 497:6
Spread alarm, 442:13
dreams under your feet, 595:9
masters s. yourselves, 172:23
money not good unless s., 159:17
out against sky, 667:9
silent tents s., 492:4
truth from pole to pole, 292:1
with her fan s., 291:10
Spreading, by broad s. disperse, 163:8
chestnut tree, 441:3
himself like a green bay tree, 17:2
Spreads, wrath s. through hearts of men, 52:14
Sprechen ist silbern, 412:10
wovon man nicht s. kann, 677:n3
Spree, gentlemen rankers on s., 592:3
Sprightly, tossing heads in s. dance, 375:21
Spring, a little Madness in S., 514:6
absent in the s., 221:19
apparelled like the s., 219:18
blossom by blossom s. begins, 533:9
blue sky of s., 504:3
breaks through again, 700:16
brings back balmy warmth, 91:2
brown hills melted into s., 480:1
call it easing the S., 737:4
came on forever, 637:12
can s. be far behind, 407:18
clean pasture s., 622:19
come gentle S., 308:3
comes slowly up this way, 382:10
comes with rustling shade, 674:17
direful s., 299:23
disturbance of the s., 670:22
ever-returning s., 490:15
first day of s. one thing first s. day another, 563:16
flowers that bloom in s., 531:8
from her may violets s., 199:11
full of sweet days, 243:11
game begins in the s., 769:8
hounds of s., 533:8
in Just-s., 688:8
in s. young man's fancy, 455:9
in the fire of S., 445:6
infants of s., 193:26
last leaf in s., 447:20
lived light in s., 498:1
makest a s. to gush forth, 116:19

Spring (*continued*)

Mrs. Porter in s., 668:23
no season such delight as s., 240:15
no s. nor summer beauty, 230:7
not as in bud of s., 231:10
of ever-flowing water, 95:10
of love gushed from heart, 381:22
of love resembleth April day, 168:1
of prodigality, 331:26
Pierian s., 298:13
ran canyons all s., 701:6
season of s. comes on, 51:23
silent s., 721:14
starless and bible-black, 738:2
stirring roots with s. rain, 668:17
summer autumn winter, 688:22
sweet lovers love the s., 192:12
targeted trod like S., 598:18
time abhorrent to nihilist, 638:16
'tis s. and weeds shallow-rooted,
    163:24
where are songs of S., 416:15
Winter mother of S., 443:2
would not be so pleasant, 262:13
year's at s., 464:4
year's pleasant king, 226:20
Springes to catch woodcocks, 194:4
Springs, beside the s. of Dove, 373:19
entered into s. of sea, 15:10
every thought that s., 377:11
fifty s. little room, 578:19
from seventy s. a score, 578:19
hope s. eternal, 301:6
of behavior hidden, 618:11
root from which tyrant s., 75:26
Scotia's grandeur s., 361:10
steeds to water at those s., 219:24
we have no s., 705:16
Springth the wude nu, 775:10
Springtime, birds warble sweet in s.,
    564:19
for Hitler and Germany, 756:20
fragrance of all s., 739:4
in s. every day growths, 483:24
only pretty ring time, 192:12
younger than s., 692:13
Sprinkled, blood s. upon my garments,
    28:7
Sprite, angelic s., 230:18
Sprites and goblins, 222:21
Sprouting despondently at gates,
    667:22
no cabbages s. out, 448:8
Spruce affectation, 169:8
cone regularity, 664:16
Sprung, vile dust whence he s., 378:1
Spun, gods have s. the thread, 52:26
of Iris' woof, 252:17
yarn s. in Ulysses' absence, 218:25
Spur, avarice s. of industry, 318:11
between s. and bridle, 244:36
fame is the s., 253:20
me into song, 599:14
my dull revenge, 198:12
no s. to my intent, 213:7
not unbroken horse, 379:20
pain of bone s. in heel, 702:9
reward and punishment s., 277:11
studies a s. to young, 87:12

Spurn, choose Jewish God s. Jews,
    656:n3
existence saw him s. reign, 313:10
Spurned, youth s. in vain, 156:14
Spurns that patient merit takes,
    196:10
Spurred boldly on and dashed, 274:17
ready booted and s., 425:21
Spurs, let boy win his s., 127:14
now s. lated traveler, 215:1
Spy, prettiest little parlor you did s.,
    423:11
sent to s. out the land, 9:29
who came in from cold, 763:15
Squabbling nationalities, 576:12
Squadron, save s. honor France, 468:6
Squadrons, God on side of big s.,
    266:13
Squads, undisciplined s. of emotion,
    671:9
Squalid cash interpretation, 545:7
Squander, do not s. time, 310:1
faith treasure we must not s.,
    436:26
Square, all around the S., 422:25
damned thick s. book, 342:22
deal, 576:2
everything upon the s., 150:23
gathered on public s., 587:9
I have not kept my s., 217:16
old people are s., 757:12
person in round hole, 379:29
produces perfect squares, 79:14
root of Everest, 748:10
triangular person in s. hole, 379:29
Squared, mass times speed of light s.,
    635:n3
Squares, produce perfect s., 79:14
Squat like toad at ear of Eve, 258:27
pen rests, 769:13
toad work s. on my life, 750:10
Squatting upon ground held heart in
    hands, 611:7
Squeak and gibber, 192:25
faint s. of mortality, 703:10
speak Greek naturally as pigs s.,
    262:18
thin bat's s. of sexuality, 712:7
Squeaking Cleopatra, 218:13
Squeaks, wheel that s. gets grease,
    479:26
Squealing of wry-necked fife, 180:18
Squeeze orange throw away skin,
    306:3
Squeezing, be with you in s. of lemon,
    330:2
from a stone, 660:18
Squire, that S. of Dames, 153:15
Squired glacier woman, 701:6
Squirmed and struggled, 531:6
Squirmers in bogs, 724:16
Squirrel, like coffee pot sits s., 660:11
Squirrel's heart beat, 483:27
Squirrels, requisite to S. and to Me,
    513:16
Sredni Vashtar went forth, 610:19
Stability in small republics, 395:13
of internal medium, 473:7
Stable earth proper element, 240:8
ensure s. economy, 754:2

Stable (*continued*)

good horse in s., 329:1
its own s. door, 512:18
law s. but not stand still, 610:13
steed stolen shut s. door, 141:22
Stabs, every word s., 186:22
intention s. the center, 222:19
Stack or the barn door, 251:12
Stacker of wheat, 634:4
Staff, bread called s. of life, 286:15
cockle hat and s., 198:16
I'll break my s., 224:24
of faith to walk upon, 152:16
of life bread, 286:n7
of life ease of burdens, 149:35
of this broken reed, 27:11
resting upon broken s., 336:16
stay and the s., 25:33
thy rod and thy s., 16:17
very s. of my age, 180:16
with your s. in your hand, 8:38
Stag at eve, 378:17
Stage, all the world's a s., 191:3
daily s. of duty run, 280:20
dreamer is s. manager, 629:2
earth a s., 191:n1
frets his hour upon s., 216:14
glory in one day doth fill s., 242:14
great s. of fools, 211:6
hate found only on s., 403:3
lags the veteran on s., 313:21
meet disease at first s., 104:18
not put loaded rifle on s., 582:10
of history, 559:10
on the s. he was natural, 330:12
players and painted s., 599:21
something for modern s., 659:6
Tragic Muse trod s., 299:19
well-graced actor leaves s., 172:13
well-trod s., 251:18
where every man play part, 179:17
wonder of our s., 232:18
world's a s., 191:n1
Stagecoach, travel faster than s.,
    329:24
Stages, hundred thousand s., 599:7
Stagger but not with strong drink,
    27:1
like a drunken man, 19:11
Staggered and terrible-eyed, 718:22
Stagnant, fen of s. waters, 374:19
water loses purity, 135:6
Staid, stay our minds be s., 625:1
very s. head, 181:n4
Stain all my raiment, 28:7
both moon and sun, 220:21
crave s. of tears, 623:20
felt s. like wound, 332:14
in thine honor, 32:8
left s. upon the silence, 718:21
my man's cheeks, 209:22
national s. washed clean, 678:11
stiff dishonored shroud, 668:16
world's slow s., 409:4
Stained, and I s. the water clear, 356:5
bishop kick hole in s. glass window,
    667:6
with mystic horrors, 565:14
Staineth slop, 659:2

Stainless, conscience upright and s., 126:4

Stains white radiance of eternity, 409:8

Stair, as I was going up s., 630:2
  climbing the third s., 669:16
  pausing on final s., 760:14

Staircase, palms on s., 718:22
  wit, 320:2

Stairs, down darker and darker s., 658:1
  great world's altar s., 457:20
  how hard the way up another's s., 126:25
  of concepts, 710:9
  recognizing man's step when climbs s., 616:17
  threw him down the s., 789:18

Stairway leads to dark gulf, 619:22
  militaristic s., 761:7
  of surprise, 429:23

Stake counter boldly, 466:16
  great interests at s., 78:25
  I am tied to the s., 210:16
  in glorious institution, 331:23
  when honor's at the s., 198:14

Stakes, mortal s., 624:7
  were thrones, 404:3

Stale, bread ever more s. rags, 659:15
  dull s. tired bed, 208:29
  frizzled s. and small, 742:20
  how weary s. flat, 193:5
  nor custom s., 217:15
  stench of s. oranges, 659:13
  winter hangs on till s., 616:10

Stalin, guilt of S. and entourage, 763:13
  rose to his position, 641:4

Stalk, corn ear on tip of s., 787:6
  gathering s. and root, 708:2
  half asleep as they s., 540:22
  of death, 759:12

Stalking, uses folly like s. horse, 192:18
  with naked foot s. my chamber, 143:7

Stalks, slow Spondee s., 383:11

Stalled ox and hatred therewith, 21:26

Stallion, like a s. on the track, 4:6
  shod with fire, 506:2
  watersmooth-silver s., 688:10

Stalls above like elephant, 743:5

Stamp and esteem of ages, 273:1
  change s. of nature, 198:6
  man bears s. of lowly origin, 444:15
  of human condition, 146:18
  penny postage s., 520:3
  poor man is Christ's s., 243:4
  rank but guinea's s., 363:21

Stamped foot cried Give Me, 512:7
  on these lifeless things, 406:13

Stamping, boot s. on human face forever, 711:19

Stamps, liberty property no s., 778:20
  wrinkle deeper, 399:17

Stand a little out of my sun, 77:2
  a tip-toe when day named, 185:22
  alone and think, 417:11
  and look at them long, 489:16
  and wait, 255:13

Stand (*continued*)
  at the door and knock, 47:14
  by the fire and stink, 209:7
  by uniting we s., 336:10
  darkling s. varying shore, 218:6
  earth's foundations s., 580:8
  fast in faith, 43:29
  give me where to s., 83:4
  hair s. up, 67:11
  hair to s. an end, 194:17
  having done all to s., 44:28
  hazard of the die, 166:18
  he shall s. at the latter day, 14:30
  here a little child I s., 241:21
  here I s., 138:3
  house divided cannot s., 37:20
  how beautiful they s., 410:10
  I must s. the course, 210:16
  if you can't s. heat, 655:10
  in his holy place, 16:18
  in your own light, 142:11
  incessantly s. on head, 517:9
  law not s. still, 610:13
  learn to s. alone, 508:1
  like an anvil, 244:*n*6
  like Druids of old, 441:15
  like greyhounds in slips, 185:5
  man may s. there, 479:10
  me now in good stead, 647:11
  my right to s. here has been won, 771:11
  Nature s. up and say, 189:28
  never s. to doubt, 241:16
  no time to s. and stare, 611:10
  nor sit nor s. but go, 467:8
  not idly s. aside, 72:7
  not upon order of going, 215:9
  now gods s. up for bastards, 209:1
  on highest pavement, 668:3
  on right spot, 349:23
  poplars s. and tremble, 579:11
  still ever-moving spheres, 162:22
  sun s. still upon Gibeon, 10:37
  then I'll s. and stroke, 356:10
  to in a month, 175:22
  to the main chance, 155:10
  too near one another, 233:3
  undisturbed as monuments, 344:5
  united we s. divided we fall, 336:*n*5
  up and take war, 593:24
  up for stupid and crazy, 488:11
  up stand up for Jesus, 481:3
  up straight, 731:3
  upon threshold of the new, 250:6
  virtue not left to s. alone, 61:7
  who only s. and wait, 255:13
  with us now, 678:16
  word of our God shall s., 27:18
  ye in the ways, 28:18
  your ground, 333:5

Standard, mind's the s. of man, 294:5
  nothing for which no s., 510:8
  unfurled s. to air, 413:19

Standards, compel philosophy to inquire about s., 87:30

Stander, no sentimentalist no s. above, 489:9

Standest, place whereon thou s. is holy, 8:24

Standeth God within shadow, 485:2

Standeth (*continued*)
  in the way of sinners, 15:29

Standing, as cheap sitting as s., 290:2
  given gladly not to be s. here, 723:15
  green mantle of s. pool, 210:8
  in the community, 564:1
  jokes, 292:17
  mantle like a s. pond, 179:19
  on pleasant lea, 376:12
  things s. thus unknown, 199:27
  upon shoulders of Giants, 281:25
  with reluctant feet, 441:7

Stands, as the case s., 237:1
  bigly under unruly scrutiny, 740:12
  brunt of life, 68:15
  church clock at ten to three, 662:19
  elephant leans or s., 243:15
  great ox s. on my tongue, 63:10
  he that s. it now, 340:22
  in Elgin's place, 461:1
  like one that s. on promontory, 164:21
  Massachusetts there she s., 394:*n*7
  nature s. on very verge, 209:19
  on slippery place, 170:7
  ringed with world he s., 458:4
  there she s. childless, 400:21
  tiptoe on misty mountaintops, 176:6
  what s. if Freedom fall, 593:25
  while s. the Coliseum, 400:27
  who Time s. still withal, 191:18
  world s. out on either side, 683:16

Stanley, approbation from Sir Hubert S., 367:10
  on S. on, 378:15

Staple, finer than s. of his argument, 169:5

Star, Adonais like a s., 409:9
  as a beauty I'm not a s., 631:18
  bright particular s., 203:9
  bright s. would I were steadfast, 417:12
  catch a falling s., 228:5
  Chamber matter, 182:16
  compared to north polar s., 60:21
  constant as northern s., 188:14
  danced, 186:25
  desire of moth for s., 409:12
  dropped like falling s., 256:22
  elevation of North S. north to south, 134:12
  evening s. love's harbinger, 260:20
  evening s. you shine on dead, 408:*n*3
  eve's one s., 416:19
  fair as a s., 373:19
  farewell Morning S., 87:5
  feel like morning s., 524:8
  fixed s. in constitutional constellation, 683:2
  for every State, 460:15
  give him the morning s., 47:11
  give name to every fixed s., 168:15
  glory like a shooting s., 171:19
  gracious evening s., 473:16
  great s. early drooped, 490:15
  high s. of Truth, 498:19
  hitch your wagon to a s., 433:5
  if thou follow thy s., 125:26

Star-spangled banner, 391:2
Start from their spheres, 194:17
  rouse lion than s. hare, 177:8
  straining upon the s., 185:5
  world all over at, 625:3
  wrong from the s., 659:4
Started, arrive where we s., 672:6
  jumps in after train s., 588:13
  like a guilty thing, 192:26
Starting-point, Russian and American
  s. different, 438:7
Startle it or amaze it with subject,
  417:19
  statements that s. like a wound,
    61:17
Startled air, 608:19
Starts, by s. 'twas wild, 324:15
  direction in which education s.,
    75:13
  everything by s., 274:11
  home is where one s., 671:10
  she s. she moves, 441:17
Starvation of the idle, 492:16
  prisoners of s., 476:18
  scientist ready to bear s., 687:19
Starve, bargain catch cold and s.,
  219:22
  ere I'll rob further, 177:13
  let not poor Nelly s., 273:5
  neither s. nor stuff, 289:21
  they that s. with nothing, 179:25
Starved at master's gate, 359:7
  clean s. for a look, 221:9
  hackney sonneteer, 299:2
Starves her generous birth, 321:22
  honesty is praised and s., 108:16
Starving, difficult to believe people s.,
  730:16
  hysterical naked, 757:4
  pick up s. dog, 527:16
Star-y-pointing pyramid, 251:2
Stat magni nominis umbra, 105:*n*12
State, basis of democratic s., 78:27
  beweep my outcast s., 220:15
  body continues in s. of rest, 282:1
  by delaying preserved s., 84:16
  change my s. with kings, 220:17
  Church and S. demand for country,
    648:20
  church and S. separate, 501:15
  compelled to change s., 282:1
  completely ready s., 474:12
  death a s. of nothingness, 74:16
  done the s. some service, 208:16
  every man at his best s. is vanity,
    17:8
  exists is no freedom, 610:5
  faithfully to serve S., 246:25
  for every star, 460:15
  found s. and give it laws, 137:2
  from mother's sleep fell into S.,
    735:21
  glories of our blood and s., 246:23
  gods of the s., 74:14
  have possibility of life, 75:15
  high and palmy s. of Rome, 192:25
  his s. is kingly, 255:13
  I am the s., 281:3, 370:11
  in whatsoever s. to be content,
    44:36

State (*continued*)
  in wonted manner keep, 231:21
  independent of everybody but S.,
    336:15
  individual make s. his servant,
    705:4
  initiation into new s., 483:15
  isthmus of a middle s., 301:13
  make men free to develop faculties,
    568:14
  managing affairs of bourgeoisie,
    482:1
  may be given up as lost, 741:*n*1
  mock air with idle s., 323:6
  my glories and s. depose, 172:10
  no fetters in Bay S., 443:1
  no S. abridge privileges or immuni-
    ties, 346:18
  not a mere society, 78:20
  o' chassis, 654:11
  of Denmark, 194:16
  of man inconstancy, 270:20
  of man like kingdom, 188:2
  pack of scoundrels Order of S.,
    716:19
  peace is a s. of mind, 277:15
  people's s., 249:14
  pillar of s., 257:7
  predicts ruin of the s., 359:7
  primitive unattached s., 629:9
  prince first servant of s., 318:19
  proletarian s., 605:14
  renders service to s., 289:*n*3
  root of kingdom the s., 79:15
  ruin or rule s., 274:6
  saintliness not a s., 728:9
  saw that S. was half-witted, 477:14
  scandal waits on greatest s., 167:3
  ship of s., 55:*n*13, 66:4
  Ship of S., 441:18
  slime in grains of S., 716:18
  social s. natural to man, 440:1
  something rotten in s., 194:16
  storms of s., 226:1
  strange eruption to our s., 192:22
  struggle to found Roman s., 93:12
  such is s. of America, 331:3
  suppression by proletarian s., 610:4
  takes no notice of opinions, 246:25
  this is the s. of man, 225:16
  traduced the s., 208:17
  wall between church and s., 661:6
  war is health of state, 661:10
  when freedom no s., 610:5
  worth of s. worth of individuals,
    439:22
State Department, working shaping
  policy of S., 724:3
Stated calls to worship, 314:18
State-House, Boston S. the hub,
  447:13
Stately homes of England, 410:10,
  650:17
  pleasure dome decree, 382:19
  sailing like a s. ship, 261:16
  ships go on, 456:7
Statement, complete s. which is literature, 650:20
  manic s., 742:22

Statements of poetry are universals,
  78:33
Staten Island, the Bronx and S. too,
  692:16
States dissevered discordant, 394:15
  foundations of s. laws and arms,
    136:11
  free and independent s., 336:11
  free and independent S., 338:4
  goodly s. and kingdoms, 413:24
  indestructible S., 443:18
  mighty s. characterless, 200:22
  set exact wealth of s., 178:19
  she is all s., 228:13
  sink or swim together, 609:12
  thirteen S. bound together, 355:3
  unborn and accents yet unknown,
    188:18
  worst of all s. is people's state,
    249:14
Statesman, chemist s. and buffoon,
  274:11
  constitutional s., 506:10
  too nice for a s., 330:10
  yet friend to truth, 300:24
Statesmanship, in s. get formalities
  right, 527:34
Statesmen, adored by little s., 431:23
  heroes s. philosophers, 347:4
Station like herald Mercury, 197:30
  middle s. fewest disasters, 286:3
  no rank nor s., 742:20
  post of honor is private s., 292:13
  separate and equal s., 343:2
  take another s., 529:15
  when s. goes on keep eyes glued,
    757:11
Stations, in order to s. leap, 275:7
  know our proper s., 470:14
  planets in s. listening, 259:22
Statistic, million deaths s., 638:13
Statistical, cautious s. Christ, 553:20
  figures historical data, 645:13
Statisticians, shalt not sit with s.,
  720:20
Statistics, unless s. lie, 688:19
Statists, hold it as our s. do, 199:20
Statuary, give children right to study
  s., 338:10
Statue, ask why I have no s., 85:5
  embraced the cold s., 325:*n*4
  Jupiter's S., 782:7
  like saying goodbye to s., 701:17
  marble wastes s. grows, 137:8
  son of France never lack s., 605:21
  stood of Newton, 373:10
  sum of all it has acquired, 321:4
Statues pictures verse grand, 523:14
  two gross broken s., 659:10
  world blooms with s., 524:10
Stature, add one cubit to s., 33:19
  as smart ship grew in s., 540:18
  increased in wisdom and s., 38:8
  shorten of soul, 508:26
  what s. is she of, 191:17
Statures touch the skies, 513:18
Status, evidence of servile s., 574:8
  inferiority as to s., 682:9
Status quo, woman be warned of s.,
  767:2

Statute, power to pronounce s. uncon-
    stitutional, 438:2
Staunch strong goodly vessel, 441:16
    sturdy and s. he stands, 559:21
Stay a little the price will fall, 159:22
    a while end the sooner, 158:22
    and cooperate, 681:5
    and the staff, 25:33
    far hence you prudes, 101:11
    here I am here s., 443:20
    I wish he'd s. away, 630:2
    longer in hour than week, 533:1
    me with flagons, 25:5
    momentary s. against confusion,
        625:8
    neither have hearts to s., 264:2
    no longer s. with you, 781:1
    O sweet, 777:7
    of water, 25:33
    shakes wings and not s., 275:2
    star to s. our minds on, 625:1
    the bottles of heaven, 15:14
    whole s. of bread, 25:33
    will you not s., 611:19
    with me God, 783:14
Stayed, here shall thy proud waves be
    s., 15:9
    joyous time not be s., 154:11
    should we have s. at home, 729:7
Stayeth young man's courting, 659:16
S.T.C., prayer for S., 385:5
Stead, stand me ever in good s.,
    647:11
Steadfast as thou art, 417:12
    bears sorrows with s. spirit, 54:7
    sober s. and demure, 251:23
Steadiest minds to waver, 66:12
Steadily, saw life s., 497:3
Steady boys steady, 323:18
    candle flame, 465:7
    of heart, 377:22
    patriot of world alone, 371:23
    slow and s. wins, 58:19
    the Buffs, 591:6
Steak, don't sell s. sell sizzle, 719:17
    he wanted s. they offered spam,
        736:6
    to tavern to eat s., 293:14
    tough as a s., 693:7
Steal a few hours from night, 392:1
    across the sky, 521:11
    asked thief to s. me peach, 357:18
    away their brains, 206:23
    cannot s. from you, 725:23
    come not to s. away hearts, 189:9
    fire from mind, 399:19
    foh a fico for phrase, 182:20
    from many authors research, 631:10
    from one author plagiarism, 631:10
    mature poets s., 672:12
    my thunder, 285:13
    our poets s. from Homer, 234:6
    silently s. away, 441:12
    sleep under bridges beg and s.,
        550:13
    thou shalt not s., 9:12
    too honest to s., 781:2
    where thieves break through and s.,
        33:13

Stealin', big s. makes you emperor,
    673:15
    little s. gits you in jail, 673:15
Stealing and giving odor, 201:16
    I feel it s. now, 487:10
    little s. big s., 673:15
    no excuse for s. a cent, 548:3
Steals goose from common, 777:3
    mind even of the wise, 52:3
    politician who s. is a fool, 548:3
    something from the thief, 205:31
    who s. my purse s. trash, 206:30
Stealth, good action by s., 388:14
    lusty s. of nature, 208:29
Stealthy school of criticism, 509:28
Steam, clock not s.-engine, 693:4
    drill beat me down Lord, 780:20
    engine in trousers, 380:11
    gas s. or table turning, 494:16
    rosy hands in s., 749:16
    thy arm unconquered s., 335:23
Steamboat, commence travels in Mis-
    sissippi s., 393:9
Steamer from Harwich, 530:15
Steamy, throws up a s. column, 335:3
Steed, affrighted s. ran on alone, 611:8
    farewell the neighing s., 207:8
    in war mounts warrior's s., 377:25
    that knows his rider, 399:18
    threatens steed, 185:14
    was the best, 378:7
Steeds, fiery-footed s., 175:30
    strange s., 446:27
    to water at those springs, 219:24
Steel, again in complete s., 194:11
    age employed in edging s., 353:9
    clad in complete s., 253:2
    foeman bares s. tarantara, 529:13
    foemen worthy of s., 378:25
    grapple with hoops of s., 193:29
    long divorce of s., 225:6
    meals of beef iron s., 185:13
    molders hemp and s., 379:10
    my soldiers' hearts, 185:20
    naked though locked up in s., 164:1
    no s. pierce heart so chillingly,
        688:2
    nor poison, 214:26
    nor s. has lit, 598:12
    stone bronze stone s., 670:4
    tipped with line of s., 492:8
    trewe as s., 128:26
    triple s., 257:14
Steele, Richard S. rake among schol-
    ars, 425:15
Steel-true and blade-straight, 561:25
Steep and thorny way to heaven,
    193:27
    Atlantic stream, 252:19
    frowsy couch in sorrow s., 364:3
    long and s. is the way, 54:24
    morn on the Indian s., 252:22
    my speech in lies, 63:31
    no ascent too s. for mortals, 95:17
    of godlike hardship, 417:2
    senses in forgetfulness, 183:36
Steeped amid honeyed morphine,
    489:12
    me in poverty to lips, 207:25

Steeple, unseen as weathercock on s.,
    168:2
Steeples, drenched our s., 209:24
    stacked to reach surface of sea,
        437:6
    still s. hum, 579:4
Steepy, woods or s. mountain yields,
    162:2
Steer clear of permanent alliances,
    337:7
    from grave to gay, 302:2
    in verse s. from grave to light,
        280:4
    right onward, 255:15
    star to s. her by, 633:14
    too nigh sands, 274:3
Steered, boats that are not s., 220:5
Steersman, Cybernetics from Greek s.,
    691:3
Stein on table, 589:3
    portrait of Gertrude S., 627:8
Stelle, a riveder le s., 126:n1
    l'amor che muove il sole e l'altre s.,
        127:n1
    puro e disposto a salire alle s.,
        126:n7
Stem or stone, 647:20
    rod out of the s. of Jesse, 26:10
    thy slender s., 361:19
    two berries on one s., 173:19
Stemming with hearts of controversy,
    187:21
Stems, cut s. struggling, 724:11
Stench of stale oranges, 659:13
Stenches, two and seventy s., 383:16
Stentor, great-hearted S., 51:21
Step, don't s. on my blue suede shoes,
    764:8
    fanaticism to barbarism one s.,
        320:3
    first s. is hardest, 307:11
    from sublime to ridiculous, 370:9
    highest s. of charity's golden ladder,
        122:8
    keep s. obey in silence, 507:10
    light of s. and heart, 616:21
    mind music and s., 778:21
    must begin with single s., 57:20
    not s. twice into same rivers, 62:14
    one small s. for man, 762:13
    one s. enough for me, 426:18
    recognizing man's s., 616:17
    softly under snow, 619:7
    to music he hears, 478:37
    to s. aside is human, 362:5
Stepdame, false as s. to son, 200:22
Stephen, feast of S., 482:8
    King S. worthy peer, 776:16
Stephen's, St. S. choir, 742:10
Stepmother, Nature a merciless s.,
    104:2
    Nature cruel and ruthless s., 135:13
    poverty s. ov genius, 479:25
    stony-hearted s., 397:14
Stepped down to the Four, 652:7
    in a puddle, 792:3
    in blood s. in so far, 215:12
    out of their clothes, 599:2
Stepping-stones of dead selves, 457:5

Steppingstones to understanding, 635:2

Steps, age with stealing s., 143:12
beware of desperate s., 335:19
by due s. aspire, 252:13
came forth with pilgrim s., 261:5
foot wear s. of his door, 31:17
hear not my s., 213:22
heavy s. of plowman, 595:5
humor saves a few s., 664:18
I by backward s. move, 270:6
invites my s. and points, 300:7
lead my s. aright, 411:5
Lord directeth his s., 21:30
my s. along this street, 736:18
same s. as Author, 418:4
stops and s. of mind, 669:16
wandering s. and slow, 260:24
with how sad s. O Moon, 156:5

Stereotyped, perceive in form s. by culture, 676:20

Sterile, compulsion to become s., 658:7
earth seems a s. promontory, 195:28
splendid and s. Dolores, 533:13
truth for yourself, 556:22

Sterling, refine her s. page, 280:15

Stern, a s. a true-born Englishman, 171:n2
and rock-bound coast, 410:11
Caledonia s. and wild, 378:2
custom spreads afar, 364:13
daughter of voice of God, 376:2
joy warriors feel, 378:25
man s. to view, 329:17
my sad heart foams at s., 565:10
Ruin's plowshare, 361:20

Sterner, ambition of s. stuff, 189:1
days not darker days, 621:6

Sternest, gives s. good-night, 214:2
knight to foe, 133:17

Stew, convert you into missionary s., 670:1
w'en s. smokin' hot, 615:2

Stewards of their excellence, 221:15

Stewed, longing for s. prunes, 203:31

Stick across your back, 787:21
carry a big s., 575:16
coat upon a s., 597:8
hips s., 709:15
I am a burr I shall s., 204:26
Moses should have fancier s., 748:9
take s. hit him on snout, 780:12
there I'll s., 149:28
thine arrows s. fast in me, 17:4
to s. the heart of falsehood, 200:22
to your last, 81:n2
with fist instead of s., 262:17

Sticketh closer than a brother, 21:42

Sticking, ay s. in a tree, 379:14

Sticking-place, screw your courage to s., 213:13

Sticks nix hick pix, 704:10
no sweeter fat than s. to bones, 489:5
resurrection of dry s., 724:11

Sticky, gilded and s., 660:21

Sticky-beaks, we don't like stuck-up s., 775:7

Stiff dishonored shroud, 668:16

Stiff (*continued*)
flags straining, 619:2
in opinions, 274:11
sore s. with toils, 491:5
twin compasses, 229:13
upper lip, 504:5

Stiffen sinews summon blood, 185:3

Stiffening of vertebrae, 570:5

Stiffens, heart s. and rejoices, 669:20

Stiffish cock-tail, 467:23

Stiffnecked, a s. people, 9:17

Stiffness and soul's arrest, 619:5
freedom from s., 500:25

Stifle, opinion endeavoring to s., 439:16

Stile, over hedge before s., 149:16

Stile-a, merrily hent the s., 223:4

Still and awful red, 381:21
and quiet conscience, 225:17
as a gold piece, 760:2
as a maid, 357:18
be s. and know that I am God, 17:18
be s. wait, 725:2
beside the s. waters, 16:17
everything else is s., 356:17
falls the Rain, 665:19
how s. we see thee lie, 524:9
lute be s. I have done, 143:6
mightest s. the enemy, 15:34
mighty heart lying s., 374:13
point of turning world, 670:5, 670:15
quite s. and solitary, 651:22
sad music of humanity, 373:5
should I have lain s., 13:35
small voice, 12:39
small voice of gratitude, 323:15
sound of voice that is s., 456:7
spirit bloweth and is s., 497:13
spirit so s. and quiet, 205:23
take heed of s. waters, 152:n7
to be neat, 232:5
we must be s. and s. moving, 671:11
when all woods are s., 254:9
when sun out wind s., 624:6

Stille Nacht Heilige Nacht, 406:n1

Stillness, air solemn s. holds, 322:2
modest s. and humility, 185:3
soft s. and the night, 182:8
solemn s. lay, 462:2
such s., 282:12
talent formed in s., 349:20

Still-vexed Bermoothes, 223:27

Stilly, army s. sounds, 185:14

Stilts, no matter walk on s., 147:7

Stilus virum arguit, 234:8

Stimulated by news wife left husband, 717:7

Sting, cold doth not s., 226:20
death where is thy s., 43:28
each s. that bids, 467:8
how bitter a s. a little fault, 126:4
like a bee, 771:16
prick at her, 194:25
serpent s. thee twice, 181:15
with a little s., 660:21

Stinger, 'tis a s., 237:3

Stingeth like an adder, 22:22

Stings, stinks and s., 302:15
wanton s. of sense, 203:26
what s. is justice, 642:18
you for your pains, 297:23

Stingy, don't be s. baby, 673:13

Stink, fish and visitors s., 83:n11
like rotten meat, 708:19
stand by the fire and s., 209:7

Stinks and stings, 302:15
like rotten mackerel, 386:1
several s., 383:16

Stir, all hell s. for this, 185:27
at dismal treatise rouse and s., 216:13
crown me without my s., 212:24
Jamaicas of Remembrance s., 514:10
men's blood, 189:10
not s. rice though it sticks, 151:8
now s. the fire, 335:3
of the great Babel, 335:4
press feel with fingers, 489:13
smoke and s. of this dim spot, 252:12
without great argument, 198:14

Stirred by solitary cloud, 282:11
by the sootfall of your things, 769:15
casement jessamine s., 458:22
heart of Englishman, 606:2
Martini shaken and not s., 723:2
troubled like fountain s., 201:5
up with envy and revenge, 255:21
up with high hopes, 254:20

Stirring, always s. up some war, 75:28
butterfly s. air in Peking, 775:2
dull roots, 668:17
not a creature s., 391:6
not a mouse s., 192:20

Stirrup, betwixt s. and ground, 151:29
foot in s., 786:3, 786:4
sprang to s., 465:1

Stirs, blood more s. to rouse lion, 177:8
Culprit Life, 511:11
divinity that s. within, 292:14
of discontented strife, 233:15
see she s., 441:17
this mortal frame, 383:3

Stitch in time saves nine, 104:n14
stitch stitch, 423:4

Stitches, laugh yourselves into s., 202:29

Stitching and unstitching naught, 595:13

Stithy, foul as Vulcan's s., 197:5

Stock of Barabbas, 182:1
see how his s. went on, 386:21
words once my s. wanting, 276:17

Stocking, silk s. filled with mud, 371:2
yawns and draws s. up, 668:15

Stockings, commended yellow s., 202:19
hung by chimney, 391:6
silk s. and white bosoms, 315:14
to bed with s. on, 791:12

Stocks, worshipped s. and stones, 255:14

Stockyards, sacrifices like s., 701:14

Stoic, every S. was a S., 431:28

Stoic (*continued*)
  forty till fifty man a s., 568:5
  live like s. bird, 660:15
  of the woods, 389:9
Stoicism, Romans call it s., 292:6
Stoic's pride, 301:13
Stole, like little mice s. in and out,
    262:5
  man s. the fruit, 243:7
  memory of all he s., 303:26
  pig and away run, 790:5
  tarts and took them away, 789:14
  thence life i' o' building, 214:13
Stolen, ducats s. by my daughter,
    180:24
  enough to be s., 297:24
  many a man's soul and faith, 773:1
  men hanged that horses not be s.,
    280:1
  my three-and-twentieth year, 251:3
  not wanting what is s., 207:7
  odd old ends s. of holy writ, 165:27
  steed s. shut stable door, 141:22
  sweets are best, 291:26
  the scraps, 169:6
  waters are sweet, 21:3
Stolidity, she had s. of water buffalo,
    714:14
Stomach, aimed at public's heart hit it
    in s., 634:16
  army marches on s., 371:3
  dispenser of invention, 104:15
  disputes you, 719:12
  full talk of fasting easy, 114:5
  goes much against my s., 191:7
  good-humored s., 103:3
  hungry s. cannot hear, 268:8
  is not good, 144:11
  loathing to s. brings, 173:14
  man of an unbounded s., 226:4
  no patriot on empty s., 371:*n*2
  seat of sensation s., 580:10
  teacher of arts, 104:15
  thought depends on s., 306:24
  way to heart through s., 462:10
Stomachaches, tuned like fifty s.,
    470:7
Stomach's, wine for thy s. sake, 45:20
Stomachs, lazy fokes' s., 556:11
  store money in s. of needy, 114:12
  who have best s. not best thinkers,
    306:24
Stone, ask bread and give s., 34:7
  at his heels a s., 198:17
  better pillow than visions, 663:14
  bows to wood and s., 395:20
  bronze stone steel, 670:4
  cold as any s., 185:1
  conscious s. to beauty grew, 429:10
  dash foot against s., 38:10
  dash thy foot against a s., 18:16
  dripping water hollows s., 89:8
  dry s. no water, 668:18
  fling s. giant dies, 307:7
  flung S. puts Stars to flight, 445:4
  he that rolleth a s., 22:31
  head s. of the corner, 19:20
  heart firm as s., 15:23
  heart harder than s., 54:11

Stone (*continued*)
  heart of s. to read death of Little
    Nell, 567:25
  heart turned to s., 207:20
  heavy as yonder s., 647:20
  house of good s., 659:14
  if any have s. to throw, 660:19
  in one hand a s., 83:10
  Jackson like s. wall, 504:4
  leaf unfound door, 706:16
  leave no s. unturned, 68:22
  legs of s., 406:13
  let him first cast s., 40:8
  like a rolling s., 771:9
  live by squeezing from s., 660:18
  make s. of heart, 596:18
  mark with white or black s., 150:32
  mockery of monumental s., 409:2
  moving others themselves as s.,
    221:14
  no bigger than agate-s., 174:20
  nosing up to impossible s., 743:15
  not to conclude against s., 749:17
  not with Club nor S., 514:5
  of stumbling, 26:6
  precious s. set in silver sea, 171:9
  pulleth sword out of s., 133:4
  quiet as s., 416:19
  raise s. cleave wood, 112:16
  rolling s. gathers no moss, 99:29
  shall cry out of wall, 29:41
  sleep softly eagle under s., 637:6
  spark out of s. easier than moral,
    532:10
  star s. flesh soul, 466:19
  stem or s., 647:20
  strange lump of s., 662:8
  strength of past, 663:10
  tell where I lie, 298:6
  that puts Stars to flight, 445:4
  turn s. start wing, 581:11
  under every s. a politician, 73:18
  underneath this s. lie, 232:12
  violet by mossy s., 373:19
  walls do not prison make, 267:18
  water like a s., 515:10
  we raised not a s., 405:17
  which the builders refused, 19:20
  written of me on my s., 624:15
  youth s. dead, 662:6
Stone Age, bomb them into S., 719:8
Stone-deaf fishes, 724:16
Stonefence sherry cobbler, 396:1
Stone's, within a s. throw, 149:36
Stones are iron, 10:16
  blest man that spares these s.,
    226:11
  boys throw s. at frogs, 82:10
  chose him five smooth s., 11:40
  cold gray s. O Sea, 456:7
  cry out, 39:11
  dig him up throw s. at him, 571:14
  don't throw s. if your windows
    glass, 309:21
  have been known to move, 215:10
  heap of s. a witness, 7:44
  heap of s. not house, 565:6
  his look drained s., 725:1
  house glass not throw s., 244:17
  in league with s. of field, 14:4

Stones (*continued*)
  kissed by English dead, 687:4
  labor of an age in piled s., 251:2
  makes music with enamelled s.,
    168:3
  move s. of Rome, 189:11
  no sermons in s., 532:10
  not decked with Indian s., 164:19
  not throw s. at birds, 314:28
  of Troy, 200:22
  philosopher's s., 235:10
  prate of my whereabout, 213:22
  prepared round ready, 756:13
  rocks and s. and trees, 374:1
  roots of trees and s., 660:16
  scrub pavement or break s., 595:13
  sermons in s., 190:7
  shows that wood s. are one, 76:4
  slow drip over s., 724:17
  that cannot be deciphered, 671:10
  time to cast away s., 23:32
  trees and s. will teach you, 121:8
  worshipped stocks and s., 255:14
  you are men of s., 211:17
Stonest them sent unto thee, 36:6
Stonewall, want you to s. it, 733:17
Stony British stare, 458:19
  limits cannot hold love out, 175:3
Stony-hearted stepmother, 397:14
Stood against world, 189:3
  among them not of them, 400:8
  apart studiously neutral, 572:6
  aside been indifferent, 713:12
  for country's glory, 378:4
  from everlasting to everlasting,
    280:23
  graves s. tenantless, 192:25
  hair of my flesh s. up, 13:39
  in tears amid alien corn, 415:17
  in whirling summer, 712:18
  long I s. there, 452:17
  naked in open air, 562:18
  not Death for I s. up, 512:15
  see from where I s., 683:15
  should of s. in bed, 695:16
  snake s. up for evil, 623:12
  that night against fire, 211:8
  where none before him s., 237:10
Stool pigeon when cannot be soldier,
    496:3
Stools, between two s., 140:18
Stoop, grief makes owner s., 169:27
  heaven itself s. to her, 253:13
  to action, 537:20
  to become friend, 594:11
  to rise, 238:5
Stooping, like woman s. down creep-
    ing about, 583:2
  shows sufficient of His light, 467:30
  through a fleecy cloud, 252:3
Stoops, golden mind s. not, 180:22
  grass s. not, 165:17
  to folly, 328:29, 669:2
  to rise love s., 467:12
Stop da music, 686:3
  day and night with me, 488:17
  did he s. speak to you, 465:16
  docile and omnipotent, 512:18
  gangsters will s., 80:14
  go to end then s., 518:10

Stop (*continued*)
got to s. their aggression, 719:8
hole to keep wind away, 199:10
if aught of oaten s., 324:13
kissing had to s., 466:14
nobody's going to s. them, 754:13
not s. for Death, 513:3
one Heart from breaking, 513:10
revolution at beginning, 706:13
so easy and so plain a s., 183:9
sound what s. she please, 197:4
the s. to busy fools, 270:2
up access and passage, 212:29
where are we to s., 365:28
without farmhouse near, 623:17
world I want to get off, 763:18
Stopped, either he's dead or watch s.,
728:15
he kindly s. for me, 513:3
Stoppest, wherefore s. thou me,
380:26
Stoppeth, deaf adder that s. her ear,
17:29
one of three, 380:26
Stopping a bung-hole, 199:9
noble truth of s. of sorrow, 64:26
not see me s. here, 623:16
tricking and s., 674:11
Stops and steps of mind, 669:16
as chill rains come it s., 769:8
buck s. here, 655:20
never s. at all, 511:20
of various quills, 254:7
Storage, put it in cold s., 585:4
Store, increasing s. with loss, 221:3
large as s., 243:16
oft amid thy s., 416:14
Stored, grapes of wrath s., 484:6
with books, 234:2
Storehouse, knowledge a rich s., 158:6
lock words in literary s., 582:11
Tao is s. of all things, 57:19
Storied urn or animated bust, 322:10
windows richly dight, 252:10
Stories, amuse you with s., 331:7
how much believe my s., 396:9
only two or three human s., 616:4
remove weight from structure of s.,
751:15
sad s. of death of kings, 171:25
Storm, after s. calm, 286:20, 690:4
and stress, 353:10
brows like gathering s., 363:2
butterfly can transform s. systems,
775:2
calm rising through s., 405:13
clouds brood on heights, 472:13
directs the s., 291:30, 303:29
every cloud engenders not s., 165:1
flies in night in howling s., 358:4
in a teapot, 88:6
leave thee in the s., 209:18
let s. rage stronger, 605:10
like wagon crossing bridge, 727:17
lovers fled into s., 415:8
nor ever heavy winter s., 53:8
on that side s. desertion death,
419:8
pelting of pitiless s., 210:3
pilot that weathered s., 372:1

Storm (*continued*)
rides upon the s., 333:22
till s. of life past, 312:14
try s., 690:4
tumultuous privacy of s., 429:13
where s. drives I shelter, 97:4
Stormed Ratisbon, 464:9
Storms, as if s. give repose, 474:6
confront night s. hunger, 488:14
country subject to cruel fierce s.,
240:9
ere winter s. begin, 460:16
he sought the s., 274:3
of state, 226:1
rebellion necessary as s., 343:14
sudden s. are short, 171:8
where no s. come, 550:15
Storm-troubled sphere, 480:4
Stormy blast, 294:14
dark and s. night, 429:2, 751:10
Hebrides, 254:4, 308:8
husky brawling, 634:4
O s. peple, 131:17
patient out of sorts, 717:3
weather, 289:22
Story and byword through world,
239:27
ephemeral and doomed, 696:20
epitaph to be my s., 624:15
ere their s. die, 540:22
fairy s. of simians, 622:14
for which world not prepared,
578:3
ghosted you up a swell s., 708:16
honor the subject of my s., 187:20
if you read Richardson for s.,
316:14
illusion shadow s., 247:7
my s. being done, 205:28
never was a s. of more woe, 176:21
not that s. need be long, 270:*n*2
of Cambuscan bold, 252:8
of my life, 205:24
place where s. ended, 671:21
repeats s. of her birth, 292:1
saddest s. ever heard, 617:9
seaman's s. is of tempest, 100:28
short in the s. itself, 32:19
shuts up s. of our days, 153:2
some pretty s. tell, 394:1ˈ
still same old s., 689:16
summits old in s., 456:11
teach him to tell my s., 205:28
tell my s., 199:27
that's another s., 320:19
will never go down, 311:14
Story-dressers do as much, 234:6
Story's about you, 95:1
Storyteller, novel happens because s.
moved to passion, 120:15
Storytellers changing the tale, 705:8
come from set of s., 705:8
Stoure, crush amang the s., 361:19
Stout of hand, 377:22
so s. a gentleman, 179:6
Stoutly struts his dames before, 251:12
Stoutness in moderation, 530:3
Stove, grandmother sings to s., 729:8
ice on hot s., 625:10

Stove-lid, cat that sits on hot s.,
527:27
Stowed away in Montreal, 524:13
Straddled, no s. adjectives, 660:4
Stradivari's violins, 483:6
Stradivarius, efforts to reproduce S.,
681:13
Straggling road in Spain, 619:3
Straight, branch that might have
grown, 163:1
build me s., 441:16
course to highest good, 90:12
crooked cannot be made s., 23:27
crooked shall be made s., 27:16
despised s., 222:7
down Crooked Lane, 422:25
I called unto mind, 160:20
improvement makes s. roads,
357:11
in strength of spirit, 534:20
line accurately s., 411:12
make his paths s., 32:29
make s. a highway for our God,
27:15
never able to make others s., 79:12
one day at Sorbonne, 640:4
righteousness his s. path, 79:17
set crooked s., 523:7
teach crab to walk s., 73:7
to be bent is to become s., 57:8
walketh upright in a s. way, 117:22
was path of gold, 465:2
Straightest, pity's the s., 236:9
Straightforward man more acceptable,
3:15
Straightway, he goeth after her s.,
20:32
Strain at a gnat, 36:4
continuous unbroken s., 394:19
great s. on affections, 484:1
guardian angels sung this s., 308:12
hold cheap the s., 467:8
raise somewhat loftier s., 92:9
Shakespeare's s., 430:12
that s. again, 201:16
unpremeditated s., 308:14
Strained anxious lives dogs lead,
693:16
quality of mercy not s., 181:19
Straining at particles of light, 418:12
in night blasts cold, 619:2
upon the start, 185:5
Strains as would have won the ear,
251:20
blessed s. telling, 474:3
of unpremeditated art, 408:4
sweet s. pensive smiles, 429:9
that might create a soul, 253:5
Strait, honor in s. so narrow, 201:1
is the gate, 34:9
Straitjacket or club, 567:27
Straits, moon fair upon s., 499:19
stranger in financial s., 71:5
Strand, guardian Naiad of s., 378:18
India's coral s., 395:18
left fair Scotland's s., 362:12
pass to American s., 244:3
walked along the S., 315:10
wandering on foreign s., 378:1

Streets (*continued*)
    of Laredo, 786:6
    publish it not in the s. of Askelon,
        11:46
    through midnight s., 358:9
    through negro s., 757:4
    truth never fell dead in s., 461:17
    world's most crowded s., 498:4
Strength, all your s. in union, 441:23
    all your s. is weakness, 66:11
    alone of Muses born, 414:6
    ancient and natural s., 325:20
    and honor are her clothing, 23:19
    as thy days so thy s., 10:28
    beyond hope and despair, 669:16
    by experience with fear, 654:15
    castle's s. will laugh, 216:12
    collected s. and struck, 579:21
    credulity child's s., 387:29
    culture moment of s., 653:4
    differences source of s., 754:3
    disease gained s. by delays, 101:29
    dogged s., 605:2
    erect against her hate, 679:9
    exert his utmost s., 60:17
    feeling his cold s., 663:11
    fight beyond your s., 52:2
    forsake me not when my s. faileth,
        17:40
    giant's s., 204:3
    God is our refuge and s., 17:16
    growing s. in air, 620:7
    hast thou given the horse s., 15:15
    hast thou ordained s., 15:34
    he flourishes in his s., 54:7
    he rejoiceth in his s., 15:16
    if by reason of s. they be fourscore,
        18:12
    ignorance is s., 711:17
    in life, 590:4
    in union even of sorry men, 51:37
    is as strength of ten, 456:3
    is to sit still, 27:2
    Jehovah is my s., 26:12
    justice without s., 271:2
    king's name a tower of s., 166:12
    knowledge increaseth s., 22:23
    lies in attack, 676:5
    Lord is my s. and song, 9:2
    Lord is my s. and my shield, 16:23
    Lord is the s. of my life, 16:21
    moment of s. of romance, 573:1
    muscular s. to jaw, 517:10
    my s. and my redeemer, 16:13
    new ways to use s., 656:5
    not given s. to be artist, 582:7
    not s. of sentiment but duration,
        552:14
    of the ancient giants, 53:*n*4
    of the hills is his, 18:19, 48:21
    of twenty men, 176:12
    perfect in weakness, 44:12
    public s. individual security, 354:18
    renew their s., 27:23
    respect s. without fearing, 344:1
    search things above thy s., 31:3
    stone s. of past, 663:10
    submit because s. not adequate,
        79:8
    that I may recover s., 17:10

Strength (*continued*)
    they go from s. to s., 18:6
    through joy, 679:5
    to forbear and persevere, 562:9
    to force the moment, 667:15
    to the needy, 26:25
    to the poor, 26:25
    tower of s., 458:7
    transforms s. into right, 319:6
    union gives s., 59:17
    unite s. to maintain peace, 655:23
    what though s. fails, 100:30
    without boasting, 344:1
    without hands to smite, 533:10
    without insolence, 398:16
    without justice, 271:2
Strengthen, charm s. and teach, 441:22
    me only this once, 11:18
Strengthens, bread s. man's heart,
        286:15
    nerves, 332:20
    time s. friendship, 283:13
Strenuous life, 575:11
    sounds s. and serious, 673:11
    tongue, 416:18
Stress and disorientation, 760:4
    on not changing mind, 626:12
    storm and s., 353:10
    strives against s. of necessity, 69:5
Stretch every nerve, 308:16
    far as coin would s., 176:28
    him out longer, 211:20
    nor does Apollo always s. bow,
        96:9
    will line s. out, 215:23
    yourselves for greatness, 157:12
Stretched, above world s. the sky,
        683:16
    forefinger of Time, 456:9
    pia mater of mine, 248:3
    tomcat lies s. flat, 762:17
    'twixt his s. footing, 200:11
    walk with s. forth necks, 25:35
Stretches of pure delight, 665:10
    out my golden wing, 356:1
Stretching before and after, 670:18
Strew, flowers to s. Thy way, 243:8
    on her roses, 498:14
Strewed thy grave, 199:14
    with husks, 201:11
Stricken deer go weep, 197:15
    love's s. why, 514:7
    old and s. in years, 10:38
Strict, death s. in his arrest, 199:24
    regard to conscience, 339:3
Strictly held by none, 624:12
    meditate thankless Muse, 253:20
    vow binds too s., 459:18
Strictness, for extreme diseases ex-
        treme s., 71:14
    Hebraism s. of conscience, 500:17
Stride, at one s. comes dark, 381:14
    right in middle of s., 750:6
Striding high there how he rung,
        550:20
    shadow s. behind you, 668:18
    the blast, 213:7
Strife, age of discord and continual s.,
        163:17
    all things born through s., 62:15

Strife (*continued*)
    and envying, 42:23
    appeaseth s., 21:27
    clubs typical of s., 335:6
    din of s., 498:4
    find agonies s. of human hearts,
        414:4
    from the s. of tongues, 16:28
    honor for a man to cease from s.,
        22:2
    ignoble s., 322:17
    man of s. and contention, 28:27
    no s. between me and thee, 7:27
    none worth my s., 388:21
    not a single kind of s., 54:19
    of love, 101:*n*6
    of Truth with Falsehood, 485:1
    stirs of discontented s., 233:15
    with the palm, 498:2
    wrathful man stirreth up s., 21:27
Strifes, hatred stirreth up s., 21:6
Strike, adjective when in doubt s. out,
        527:13
    afraid to s., 302:11
    at self-love, 507:12
    awe into beholders, 289:8
    but hear me, 62:25
    clock doth s. by algebra, 263:3
    clock will s. Devil will come, 162:23
    disease or sorrows s. him, 483:2
    feel angry because we s., 546:4
    flat thick rotundity, 209:24
    honor foe while you s., 586:12
    it and it hurts my hand, 207:20
    long live the s., 758:3
    mine eyes but not my heart, 232:6
    out fine passage, 316:19
    right to s. against public safety,
        614:16
    sails well but s. rock, 360:7
    so he may feel he is dying, 103:17
    spear to thrust club to s., 139:5
    stars with my exalted head, 95:15
    take care you s. in anger, 571:10
    the tent, 440:13
    then no planets s., 192:29
    through the mask, 486:24
    truth may s. out his teeth, 152:20
    we s. straight, 740:8
    when a hammer s., 244:22
    when iron is hot, 99:*n*3
    when s. at king must kill him,
        433:30
Strikes, lightning s. mountaintop, 96:8
    like rising knell, 399:21
    midnight s. and hastens, 580:5
    one two three s. you're out, 637:16
    silent note Cupid s., 248:20
Striking blow for freedom, 664:2
    great office not filled by great s.
        men, 536:6
    so s. and grotesque, 425:12
    sometimes a friend, 243:2
String attuned to mirth, 422:22
    chewing bits of s., 609:2
    dead kitten egg-shell bit of s.,
        601:12
    eyes upon double s., 229:14
    harp not on that s., 166:8
    kite cut from s., 657:2

String (*continued*)
   notes as warbled to the s., 252:7
   of pearls to me, 586:17
   pearls strung on, 548:20
   pudding-bag s., 792:20
   sing in a hempen s., 236:5
   untune that s., 200:9
Stringbean, little girl my s., 759:16
Stringencies, dead hands dead s.,
   764:19
Stringent protection of free speech,
   542:24
Strings, bawdy s. of elders, 639:5
   better not wibrated, 469:33
   languid s. scarcely move, 356:3
   leaving tangle of s., 755:4
   like untuned s. women are, 162:12
   many s. to bow, 141:30
Stripes, broad s. and bright stars,
   391:2
   cut his s. away, 591:16
   forty s. save one, 44:10
Strive, alone man with God s., 400:13
   and hold cheap the strain, 467:8
   earth and water s. again, 299:21
   here for mastery, 257:19
   mightily eat as friends, 167:20
   nor weep, 465:8
   not possible to fight even if you s.,
    52:2
   on to finish work, 450:11
   seven cities s. for Homer, 233:*n*4
   to grasp what they do not know,
    80:15
   to set crooked straight, 523:7
   to s. to seek to find, 455:7
Strives against stress of necessity, 69:5
   man errs as long as he s., 350:10
   sage never s. for the great, 57:10
   to touch the stars, 153:3
   who s. always to utmost, 350:27
Striving, my s. eye dazzles, 270:12
   no s. against stream, 150:14
   to better oft we mar, 209:12
   to grasp continent, 503:3
Strivings, parcel of vain s., 476:19
   two unreconciled s., 605:2
Strode after me, 373:9
Stroke, Constitution produced at single s., 446:17
   his silver hair, 356:10
   of death as lover's pinch, 218:18
   tender-handed s. nettle, 297:23
   tune of flutes kept s., 217:14
Strokes, amorous of their s., 217:14
   calumnious s., 193:26
   little s. fell great oaks, 310:4
   many s. overthrow the oaks, 155:9
   tender s. of art, 299:19
Stroll, country s. is a gallery, 505:2
Strong and diverse heart, 698:8
   Antaeus-like grew s., 599:15
   armed so s. in honesty, 189:16
   as a bull moose, 575:13
   as flesh and blood, 376:14
   as iron bands, 441:3
   as proofs of holy writ, 207:5
   battle not to the s., 24:20, 339:9
   battle to the s., 573:22
   be s. and of good courage, 10:31

Strong (*continued*)
   be s. and quit yourselves, 11:29
   be s. stand fast on faith, 43:29
   brown god, 671:12
   cause s. or weak, 485:7
   corruption inhabits blood, 203:3
   devised to keep s. in awe, 166:16
   devouring of weak by s., 493:8
   dogged opponent of light, 499:12
   drink is raging, 22:1
   enough to be master, 319:6
   fifty-score s., 464:14
   follow s. drink, 25:39
   for service still, 334:29
   founded s., 579:10
   friend is a s. defense, 31:15
   gentleness my s. enforcement,
    190:29
   give s. drink unto him that is ready
    to perish, 23:16
   God make me s., 783:14
   gongs groaning, 619:2
   harder to be won than a s. city,
    21:40
   harm to s. from weakest, 552:26
   heavens fresh and s., 376:5
   I am s. I am woman, 771:14
   is the soul, 497:5
   keep s. if possible, 692:21
   know the wall is s., 567:21
   Lake Wobegon where women are s.,
    772:5
   lance of justice, 211:4
   lean upon death, 663:15
   life too s. for you, 607:12
   long pull and s. pull, 470:35
   love built anew more s., 222:5
   love is s., 132:20
   made what is s. just, 271:2
   man digests experiences, 552:27
   meat to them of full age, 45:35
   men rust, 693:6
   men shall bow themselves, 24:27
   mortality's s. hand, 170:11
   Negro cool s. imperturbable, 480:19
   nor s. at thirty, 244:24
   obscure and deep, 500:18
   only s. thrive, 627:1
   out of the s. came sweetness, 11:12
   pull, 470:35
   pure and sweetly s., 324:12
   rejoiceth as a s. man, 16:10
   remedy too s. for disease, 67:12
   right chiefly with the s., 280:17
   rousing like s. man, 255:2
   shadow where much light, 349:1
   shoulderings aside of weak by s.,
    492:16
   small one become a s. nation, 28:5
   some circumstantial evidence s.,
    476:25
   stagger but not with s. drink, 27:1
   they shall be gentle brave s., 541:7
   thick stupefying incense, 465:7
   to me-wards your affection's s.,
    241:6
   to save, 506:4
   toil of grace, 218:22
   tricks hath s. imagination, 174:1
   two s. men face to face, 591:9

Strong (*continued*)
   we that are s., 42:28
   wise man is s., 22:23
   without rage, 266:11
   yet I am s. and lusty, 190:11
Stronger, America would have been s.,
   726:2
   by weakness, 250:6
   Fate s. than anything, 68:7
   gods are on side of s., 109:19
   handclasp's s., 616:13
   if bowl had been s., 789:10
   let storm rage s., 605:10
   madder music s. wine, 602:9
   more doubt s. faith, 466:11
   Negroes s. than we are, 696:14
   no s. than my sex, 188:9
   nothing s. than habit, 101:16
   than all afterthoughts, 68:13
   than hosts of Error, 582:2
   than lions, 11:47
   what s. breastplate, 164:1
   win because we are s., 634:2
Strongest and sweetest songs remain,
   491:18
   and the fiercest spirit, 256:24
   God with s. battalions, 318:20
   man stands alone, 508:11
   never strong enough, 319:6
   not from s. harm comes, 552:26
   opinion of s. always best, 267:23
   poison ever known, 359:13
   right of s., 319:7
   time consume s. cord, 379:10
   tower of delight, 487:2
Strongly it bears us along, 383:1
Strove, a little still she s., 402:10
   against stream, 456:19
   to resuscitate dead art, 659:4
   with none, 388:21
Strow brooks in Vallombrosa, 256:8
Struck all on a heap, 352:23
   collected strength and s., 579:21
   father when son swore, 235:16
   finger on the place, 497:16
   hate s. down Chief Magistrate,
    755:10
   I am s. a deep mortal blow, 63:15
   I was lifted and s., 773:15
   mighty Casey s. out, 588:25
   Moses in Horeb s. rock, 748:9
   one chord of music, 506:1
   streak of bad luck, 531:25
   the board, 243:16
Structure, double helix s., 760:5
   of British sentence, 619:17
   remove weight from s. of stories,
    751:15
Structures, inquisitor of s., 640:7
   man dismantle s., 723:21
Struggle against limitations of our intelligence, 691:5
   against power, 761:10
   all I care about is s., 541:10
   and flight, 499:22
   and horror past, 515:13
   arduous s. for liberty, 339:7
   Byron's s. cease, 497:15
   class s., 481:7
   contemptible s., 330:23

Suage, words have power to s., 261:11
Sub, sighted s. sank same, 733:10
Sub rosa, 248:*n*7
Subdue appetites my dears, 469:14
  force may s. for moment, 331:11
  free ourselves s. our masters, 347:2
  power to chasten and s., 373:5
  replenish the earth and s. it, 6:9
Subdued, be s., 50:19
  eyes, 208:16
  my nature is s., 222:1
  not s. for want of necessaries,
    105:17
Subdues, surpasses or s. mankind,
    399:25
  when one by force s., 79:8
Subduing, necessity of s. again, 331:11
Subject, any s. taught to any child,
    738:11
  being good neighbor bad s., 648:*n*7
  duty s. owes prince, 167:35
  everything is a s., 421:11
  fanatic won't change s., 622:9
  from ancient s. newest science,
    559:14
  grant artist his s., 548:14
  grasp s. words will follow, 85:7
  honor the s. of my story, 187:20
  idea donnée, 548:14
  know a s. ourselves, 316:26
  matter of poetry life, 640:17
  of all verse, 240:14
  of it is War, 687:1
  of knowledge is to know, 76:12
  poetry s. of poem, 639:8
  prince s. Father Son, 230:15
  ruler having human body as s., 75:5
  sensibility soil of s., 549:2
  that favorite s. Myself, 341:19
  treats serious s. with simplicity,
    499:1
  unlike s. I frame song, 305:17
Subjection to white Saxon man, 475:7
Subjective, all history s., 431:17
  creation s., 629:2
  objective and s. united, 384:5
  stream of s. life, 545:15
Subjectivity and objectivity, 694:2
Subject's duty is king's, 185:17
Subjects, free and loyal s., 778:20
  good of s. end of kings, 285:19
  men first s. afterward, 477:8
  of which soul speaks same every-
    where, 112:6
  rebels from principle, 332:16
  were their s. wise, 335:10
Subjugation, foreign conquest and s.,
    394:19
Sublime, aim at something more s.,
    366:8
  bards s., 441:11
  boundless endless and s., 401:3
  dashed to pieces, 385:3
  from s. to ridiculous, 370:9
  great and s. fool, 526:6
  lieth s., 452:11
  maintain the s., 659:4
  make our lives s., 440:17
  material s., 384:22
  object all s., 531:3

Sublime (*continued*)
  second line s. third bombast, 106:4
  sense s., 373:5
  tobacco, 404:5
  when authors talk of s., 341:11
Sublimely, fustian's so s. bad, 302:10
Sublimity echo of a noble mind, 106:5
  in effort of patriots, 337:17
Sublunary lovers' love, 229:11
Submission, bear his share with s.,
    505:1
  Christ's s. to humiliation, 752:9
  lower the wing of s., 116:16
  no wisdom but in s., 66:20
  resistance or abject s., 336:14
  yielded with coy s., 258:13
Submit because strength not adequate,
    79:8
  courage never to s., 256:1
  I s. let it be done, 424:5
  to be oppressed, 345:14
  woman know how to s., 368:11
Submits, man in love s. to everything,
    553:1
Submitting, by s. sways, 300:18
Subordinates art to nature, 384:14
Subsequent, pricks to s. volumes,
    200:12
Subsist, beg leave to s., 589:1
Subsistence in arithmetical ratio, 368:2
Subsoil of the mind, 577:2
Substance, direct in s. of thought,
    498:22
  each s. of a grief, 171:13
  God a sea of infinite s., 120:7
  lose s. by grasping at shadow, 59:10
  of things hoped for, 45:38
  one s. with the Father, 49:1
  single s. variously modified, 318:3
  truth shows spirit and s., 120:14
  wasted his s., 38:35
Substances, extract healing s., 122:13
  not able to decompose, 345:10
Substantial and genuine virtue, 343:10
  shadows not s. things, 246:23
  world pure and good, 376:14
Substitute, bloodless s. for life, 560:19
  drunken dog, 387:15
  for experience is art, 746:3
  in war no s. for victory, 642:4
  manner is s. for genius, 334:4
  no s. for hard work, 555:12
  woman s. for masturbation, 626:8
Subterranean weeds, 724:16
Subtle and profound female, 56:16
  be s. to point of formlessness, 80:21
  but malicious he is not, 636:6
  its name is The S., 57:4
  knot which makes us man, 229:15
  know not s. ways, 430:10
  Lord God is s., 636:6
  manner of speech delights us, 87:18
  no more s. master, 459:20
  poetry less s. and fine, 254:21
  poets witty mathematics s., 160:10
  schoolman's s. art, 302:18
  serpent was more s., 6:19
  thief of youth, 251:3
  words full of s. flame, 238:11
  wreath of hair, 229:19

Subtlest, serpent s. beast, 260:2
Subtleties, airy s. in religion, 248:3
  door of all s., 56:12
Subtlety, brother came with s., 7:39
  simplicity no hindrance to s., 537:9
  to give s. to the simple, 20:17
Subtract work of men above forty,
    558:6
Subtracting, without s. from human
    knowledge, 539:1
Subtraction, mend a wrong s., 483:9
Suburbs, asylum in s. of Jerusalem,
    578:15
  dwell I but in s. of your pleasure,
    188:7
  through s. sleepless people, 699:11
Subversion, reason is not s., 706:15
Subversive, disloyal or s., 716:8
Subway, Bagdad-on-the-S., 585:19
  words written on s. walls, 772:8
Succeed, I s. him not replace, 309:*n*1
  if at first you don't s., 393:17
  if mediocre you s., 336:7
  nature trying to make us s., 691:21
  new things s., 241:13
  other means may s., 449:16
  to s. add water to wine, 589:6
  to s. in the world appear successful,
    265:6
  to s. possible only one way, 78:3
Succeeded, never know when s. best,
    590:3
  use whole talent gloriously s.,
    706:19
Succeeds, age to age s., 453:20
  nothing s. like success, 427:13
Success, as long as gods give s., 54:7
  as singist not a s., 522:2
  beauty that comes from s., 496:7
  bitch-goddess S., 545:7
  cannot ask of heaven s., 368:14
  cash interpretation of s., 545:7
  catch with surcease s., 213:5
  command s., 292:4
  confidence in s., 569:9
  depends on three things, 537:13
  four flights, 604:10
  heaven's s. or earth's failure, 465:23
  is showing up, 767:17
  like horrible disaster, 727:4
  makes s. only subsequent, 61:9
  no honor in sure s., 673:9
  no one guarantee s. in war, 622:5
  nothing succeeds like s., 427:13
  only one s., 679:11
  owes s. to inconsistencies, 539:10
  people judge men by s., 265:23
  secret of my s., 543:12
  secret of s. constancy, 435:12
  things ill got had bad s., 164:16
  to periodic sentence, 693:14
  to the weak, 336:12
  unexpected in common hours,
    478:36
  writer not want s., 697:3
  your religion is S., 581:25
Successful, everything to appear s.,
    265:6
  man s. animal, 575:3

Sun (*continued*)

force from which s. draws power, 655:6

frisk i' the s., 222:17

from rising of the s. unto going down, 19:15

fruit I bore was the s., 107:*n*11

gather round setting s., 375:15

give me splendid silent s., 490:13

gives light soon as he rises, 310:25

glorious s. in Heaven, 382:18

go out in midday s., 700:15

golden apples of s., 595:7

gorgeous as s. at midsummer, 178:20

greater none beneath S., 593:17

he set a tabernacle for the s., 16:10

heap o' s. and shadder, 644:16

heart s. of their microcosm, 235:25

himself at center of universe, 137:6

himself fair hot wench, 176:24

hold farthing candle to s., 235:*n*4

hold glimmering tapers to s., 235:*n*4

I myself caused s. to rise, 606:1

I saw under the s., 24:20

if s. breed maggots, 195:17

images where s. beats, 668:18

imitate the s., 176:37

in bowling alley bowled s., 283:4

in dim eclipse, 256:16

in dominions never sets, 364:20

in front s. climbs slow, 483:3

in golden cup, 599:1

in lonely lands, 458:4

inconceivable idea of s., 639:20

is but a morning star, 478:40

is gone down while it was day, 28:26

is laid to sleep, 231:21

is lost and the earth, 230:15

itself which makes times, 229:5

Juliet is the s., 174:26

knitters in s., 202:12

knoweth his going down, 19:6

laughed in the s., 662:17

leaning against S., 511:18

leaves and flowers in s., 595:21

let not the s. go down, 44:25

let others hail rising s., 323:17

light candle to the s., 270:1

light dies with dying, 563:2

light where no s. shines, 737:9

like ball of fire, 369:6

like Joshua commanded s., 310:21

liken Homer to setting s., 106:6

little window where s., 422:19

livery of burnished s., 180:13

looked over mountain's rim, 465:2

loss of s., 305:18

love earth s. animals, 488:11

Love that moves s. and other stars, 127:4

loves to live i' the s., 190:20

low descending s., 779:1

made summer by s. of York, 165:18

make guilty the s., 209:3

make our s. stand still, 268:17

maketh s. rise on evil and good, 33:9

Sun (*continued*)

man work s. to s., 778:23

marigold goes to bed wi' the sun, 223:6

maturing s., 416:13

moon or s. or what you please, 167:32

moon stars sweet, 428:15

more worship rising than setting s., 88:14

mother give me s., 508:6

my mistress' eyes nothing like the s., 222:8

nearer comes the s., 657:17

neither shall s. light on them, 47:24

never sets on empire, 364:*n*5

no better thing under the s., 24:17

no new thing under the s., 23:25

no s. its day, 757:13

no s. upon an Easter-day, 262:5

of righteousness arise, 30:10

only you under s., 682:1

out of God's blessing into s., 142:16

owes no homage unto s., 248:22

part of the colossal s., 640:12

pasted in sky, 611:3

pay no worship to garish s., 176:1

penetrates privies, 77:6

place in the s., 557:3

protects dewdrop from s., 377:14

question if His Glory, 513:4

raisin in the s., 708:19

ran s. down with talk, 82:20

remains pure through pollutions, 77:*n*5

risen to hear him crow, 483:14

rising of the s., 778:9

rose and set on Sioux land, 516:9

sand and wild uproar, 429:8

sea gone with s., 565:18

second before s. went out, 773:16

see s. with ignorant eye, 639:20

seemed a sheet of s., 735:19

self-same s. on court and cottage, 223:12

set a candle in the s., 235:14

sets to rise again, 468:12

setting s. and music at close, 171:6

setting s. set to rights, 417:17

shall not smite thee, 19:25

shineth upon dunghill, 77:*n*5

shut doors against setting s., 212:1

sitting in the s., 386:3

somewhere s. is shining, 588:25

Son of the S., 79:7

stain both moon and s., 220:21

stand a little out of my s., 77:2

stand still upon Gibeon, 10:37

steadies my soul, 664:19

study like heaven's glorious s., 168:15

subordinated s. and moon, 117:12

summer season when soft was s., 127:17

tell you how S. rose, 512:3

thank heavens s. gone in, 594:10

that brief December day, 443:13

that is young once only, 737:16

that s. thine eye, 220:24

till s. grows cold, 506:3

Sun (*continued*)

tired s. with talking, 502:9

to have enjoyed s., 498:1

to me is dark, 261:8

tomorrow's s. may never rise, 291:17

traveled short while towards s., 727:10

true as dial to s., 263:31

unruly S., 228:11

walk in the s., 195:17

was shining on the sea, 518:23

was warm wind chill, 624:6

what are you when s. shall rise, 227:9

when s. goes down, 690:18

when s. out wind still, 624:6

when s. shineth make hay, 140:20

wherever bright s. of heaven, 226:9

which sees all things, 51:16

who scattered into flight, 445:3

wind with fragrance of hot s., 616:11

wing subdivided by s., 665:2

wishes lengthen as our s. declines, 296:17

works done under the s., 23:27

worse than s. in March, 178:23

would have disappeared, 578:14

yesternight s. went hence, 228:20

Sunbeam impossible to be soiled, 77:*n*5

in winter's day, 307:14

thikke as motes in s., 131:9

Sunbeams, chances like s. pass, 309:*n*6

out of cucumbers, 289:12

stream forward, 787:8

Sunburnt by glare of life, 439:5

mirth, 415:11

this s. face, 356:9

Sunday, buried on S., 791:4

chicken in pot every S., 154:20

different from another day, 314:28

grand flights S. baths, 639:12

not divide S. from week, 192:23

repentance on a S., 644:2

we will be married o' S., 167:23

Sundays, begin journey on S., 290:15

Sundered, as if birth s., 477:23

Sundering, love know no s. quarrels, 95:26

Sundial, motto of s., 390:17

Sundown, elected between s. and sunup, 638:2

Sundry contemplation of my travels, 191:26

moveth us in s. places, 48:15

Sung, by forms unseen dirge s., 324:11

first and last sung no more, 777:6

guardian angels s. this strain, 308:12

her amorous descant s., 258:19

Sappho loved and s., 402:24

strongest sweetest songs to be s., 491:18

Sunk, all s. beneath waves, 335:17

beneath watery floor, 254:6

in flat sea s., 252:29

Lethe-wards had s., 415:9

Sunk (*continued*)
  so low that sacred head, 253:22
  world's whole sap is s., 229:8
Sunless sea, 382:19
Sunlight, golden s. glows, 474:6
  moonlight unto s., 455:22
  parables of s., 737:13
  sudden in shaft of s., 670:18
  weave s. in hair, 668:3
Sunlit arch, 624:6
Sunnier side of doubt, 460:8
Sunny, a little s. a little sad, 536:4
  count only s. hours, 390:*n*3
  dome, 382:25
  in s. beams did glide, 355:17
  Palestine, 633:18
  pleasure dome, 382:23
  side of life, 645:14
  side up, 685:17
  web of s. air, 476:10
Sunrise, lives in eternity's s., 357:22
  lost between s. and sunset, 419:4
Sun's o'ercast with blood, 169:29
  rim dips, 381:14
Suns, light of setting s., 373:5
  process of the s., 455:20
  radiance of a thousand s., 84:12
  skies clouds of June, 515:2
  systemed s. globed and lit, 540:15
  that set may rise again, 232:4
  to light me rise, 301:9
Sunset and evening star, 460:11
  between sunrise and s., 419:4
  breezes shiver, 586:14
  I have seen s., 565:14
  life little shadow in s., 494:21
  of life gives me lore, 389:3
  ran one glorious blood-red, 465:5
  sail beyond the s., 455:6
  stained with horrors, 565:14
  touch, 466:9
Sunsets, I eat s. and trees, 730:12
Sunshine and good water, 563:5
  comforteth like s. after rain, 165:14
  digressions s. of reading, 320:14
  eternity about me in s., 556:21
  fill sky with cloudless s., 96:24
  glorious birth, 375:5
  holiday, 251:15
  if opened in s., 436:4
  in the shady place, 153:7
  Little S. stayed on, 753:14
  on strange shore, 573:1
  patriot, 340:22
  white town drowsing in s., 526:9
Sun-split, tumbling mirth of s. clouds,
    751:3
Sunt lacrimae rerum, 93:*n*12
Sun-thaw, thatch smokes in s., 382:17
Sunup, elected between sundown and
    s., 638:2
Sunward I've climbed, 751:3
Sup at six sleep at ten, 428:6
  before we go, 789:16
  of Jove's nectar s., 232:15
  sipped no s., 531:14
Superannuated idol, 292:22
Supercilious hypocrisy of bishop,
    346:2

Superego, external world s. and id,
    569:14
Superexcellent, tobacco divine rare s.,
    235:10
Superficial, common sense hasty s.,
    477:21
Superfluity, barren s. of words, 286:6
  questionable s. small beer, 164:*n*3
  sooner white hairs, 179:26
Superfluous, in nature's inventions
    nothing s., 135:10
  in poorest thing s., 209:21
  lags the veteran on stage, 313:21
  to demand time of day, 176:24
  to many the s. is necessary, 543:7
  to point out this is war, 440:8
  very necessary thing, 305:25
Superflux, shake s. to them, 210:3
Superhighway of justice, 761:5
Superhuman, daily struggle for s.
    beauty, 769:12
  spiritual and divine, 628:15
Superintend sick, 71:5
Superior, educated men s., 77:12
  equals revolt to be s., 78:24
  intelligence, 632:4
  man, 61:32
  man acts before he speaks, 60:22
  man distressed by want of ability,
    61:28
  man is modest in speech, 61:24
  man satisfied and composed, 61:13
  man will not manifest narrow-
    mindedness, 79:10
  no attribute of s. man greater, 79:9
  not s. by reason of race, 520:12
  people never make long visits,
    664:10
  powers s. to man, 564:22
  sages s. only in cleverness, 333:9
  three things s. man guards against,
    62:3
  to slavish mercenary, 336:13
  what s. man seeks, 61:29
Superiority, dogma of ethnic s.,
    662:15
  feeling of s., 642:21
  not admit assumptions of s., 79:24
  of their women, 438:10
  Senate s. invisible, 535:14
  to sex that kills, 722:8
Superiors, between s. and inferiors,
    61:18
Super-legal-aid bureau, 646:12
Superman, it's a bird plane S., 737:7
  lightning out of dark cloud, 552:7
  not Hercules but S., 764:2
  rope between animal and S., 552:6
Supernatural, existence of s. probable,
    588:20
  honest woman of s., 722:2
  nothing impossible in s., 588:20
Supersede last fashionable novel,
    425:10
Superseded, life-form not s., 628:10
Superstition constructive religion,
    493:20
  die detesting s., 307:5
  fear source of s., 615:14
  has ample wages, 138:9

Superstition (*continued*)
  infamous thing, 306:15
  less than chaff, 573:6
  opposing one s. to another, 318:15
  religion of feeble minds, 332:19
  true remedy for s., 331:19
Superstitions, haunted by grossest s.,
    444:14
  truths end as s., 505:19
Superstitious atheist, 466:10
  in all things too s., 41:15
  modest chaste, 404:21
  valuation of Europe, 548:6
Supinely enjoyed gifts of founder,
    340:10
  fools s. stay, 353:17
Supped full with horrors, 216:13
Supper, hope good breakfast bad s.,
    158:20
  nourishment which is called s.,
    168:17
  sings for his s., 789:7
  when s. things is done, 558:15
Suppers, more killed by s., 244:18
Suppliant, thus the s. prays, 313:20
Supplied, can never be s., 329:8
  charm by thought s., 373:4
Supply, all just s. and all relation,
    230:15
  eating air on promise of s., 183:25
  no man will s. thy want, 233:12
  of truth in excess of demand,
    479:24
Support Caledonia's cause, 364:4
  it will s. itself, 510:*n*4
  that renders independent, 336:15
  to s. him after, 211:22
  visible means of s., 544:21
  what is low raise and s., 255:20
Supporting, fatigue of s. freedom,
    341:1
  stop s. that crowd, 510:*n*4
Suppose, dance in ring and s., 624:16
  do you s. Walrus said, 518:24
  Lenin died of typhus Hitler killed,
    744:11
  less than most s., 334:2
  my daughters I s., 717:2
  they gave a war no one came,
    634:*n*2
  universe queerer than we s., 683:1
Supposed as forfeit to confined doom,
    221:23
Supposing, no ground for s. it true,
    615:12
Suppress nothing that is true, 87:15
Suppressed, neither world to be s.,
    499:6
  no innocent wit s., 342:1
Suppressing, French for s. one, 499:6
Suppression of bourgeois state by
    proletarian, 610:4
  of free speech, 568:15
Supramundane mushroom, 673:7
Suprema, salus populi s. est lex, 88:*n*4
Supreme, bring suit in S. Court, 655:5
  coort follows iliction, 602:14
  find alone Necessity s., 523:17
  governors the mob, 323:20
  heart's s. ambition, 318:5

Supreme (*continued*)
  Law of the land, 346:10
  poetry s. fiction, 638:21
  self-sacrifice, 691:4
  silence s., 519:22
  theme of Art and Song, 598:23
  triumph to be most alive, 657:21
Surcease, catch with his s. success,
    213:5
Surcingles, Gilt S., 514:8
Sure and firm-set earth, 213:22
  as death, 231:15
  as s. as sun will shine, 774:10
  be s. give ocular proof, 207:9
  be s. your sin will find you out,
    10:9
  clear conscience is s. card, 155:12
  he's a s. card, 274:21
  it may be so in Denmark, 195:1
  joy was never s., 534:14
  make assurance double s., 215:20
  more s. of all I thought, 622:17
  no s. foundation on blood, 170:12
  nothing s. in sea fight, 360:15
  slow but s., 244:38
  slow but s. moves might, 69:2
  sweet cement of love, 240:17
  this Jesus will not do, 360:4
  what man has he's s. of, 151:11
Surely every man walketh in a vain
    show, 17:9
  goodness and mercy shall follow
    me, 16:17
Surest, old soldiers s., 237:11
  way to get a thing, 426:12
Surety, he that is s. for a stranger,
    21:7
Surface and shadow, 662:8
  below s. stream, 500:18
  fine glossy s., 328:18
  go where we will on s., 477:19
  material s. of things, 495:20
  setting right s. of things, 427:2
Surfeit begets insolence, 59:22
  God is war peace s. hunger, 62:13
  no crude s. reigns, 253:3
  of our own behavior, 209:3
  sick that s. with too much, 179:25
  when the Daffodil, 513:4
Surfeited with honey, 178:11
Surfeiting appetite may sicken, 201:16
Surge and thunder of Odyssey, 551:20
  booming s. of Aegean, 74:9
  laces just reveal s., 511:15
  murmuring s., 210:27
  Thulè and Atlantic s., 308:8
Surgeon to old shoes, 187:15
  with help of s. recover, 174:10
Surgeons must be careful, 511:11
Surgery, honor hath no skill in s.,
    178:33
Surging immensity of life, 446:25
  symbol of s. potency, 657:20
Surly bonds of Earth, 751:3
  hear the s. sullen bell, 221:7
Surmise, deep s. pierces, 477:24
  wild s., 413:24
Surmises jealousies conjectures, 183:9
Surname, his s. epithet for knave,
    136:n5

Surpass, charms other maids' s.,
    353:11
Surpassed, loftiness of thought s.,
    275:25
  others but had no more power,
    98:24
Surpasses, not to be born s. thought,
    67:9
  or subdues mankind, 399:25
Surpasseth, night of time s. day, 249:3
Surplus, democracy appropriate for ec-
    onomic s., 728:16
  power of s. in banks, 393:15
  wealth sacred trust, 525:13
Surpluses, get off fat s., 724:8
Surprise, come as welcome s., 97:11
  meaning unfolded by s., 625:10
  poetry should s., 418:1
  respect mingled with s., 378:25
  stairway of s., 429:23
  unfolded by s., 625:10
Surprised by joy, 377:3
  guilty thing s., 375:11
  police walked in she s., 752:10
  sore s. them all, 362:3
  to find it done at all, 316:3
  was I with sudden heat, 160:19
Surrender, break out rather than s.,
    621:n5
  explaining instead of acting, 618:1
  fear hate s. defiance, 767:21
  Guards die but never s., 371:20
  let us s. to love, 92:20
  man may be forced to s., 248:2
  of life nothing, 393:16
  shameful to s. to first comer, 588:17
  to Him we s., 116:3
  unconditional s., 501:9
  we shall never s., 620:7
Surrenders, victory when opponent s.
    before hostilities, 80:20
  whosoever s. his face to God, 117:9
Surrounding, how to explore vacant
    vast s., 491:8
Surrounds, ever-during dark s. me,
    257:24
Survey mankind, 313:16
  monarch of all I s., 334:19
  time takes s. of world, 179:5
Survival, assure s. of liberty, 741:3
  love the only s., 697:11
  of Fittest, 444:6
  of fittest, 493:9, 525:11
  of wildlife in Africa, 749:6
  re-vision an act of s., 762:10
  without victory no s., 620:6
Survive and multiply, 444:9
  cannot s. wrongs repeated, 683:3
  monuments of wit s. monuments of
    power, 157:24
  only the fit s., 627:1
  opinions not s. without fight,
    629:14
  or perish, 394:9
  our souls s. death, 101:n2
  passions which yet s., 406:13
Survived, don't see how Henry s.,
    734:16
  I s., 348:15
  pride of those who have s., 621:16

Survives, classic s. circumstances,
    738:12
  plum s. its poems, 638:18
  Thomas Jefferson still s., 338:17
Survivor, many a stung s., 744:8
  of that time that place, 675:7
Survivors', dying more s. affair,
    629:18
Susanna, O S., 506:17
Susanna's music, 639:5
Suspect everybody, 469:31
  once s. Caspian Fact, 514:4
  thoughts of others, 180:11
Suspected, new opinions always s.,
    277:5
  wished wife not so much as s.,
    88:19
Suspecting, without s. our abode,
    514:11
Suspects himself of virtues, 694:8
  round up the usual suspects, 726:12
  yet soundly loves, 206:31
Suspend functioning of imagination,
    702:7
  I s. my judgment, 146:5
  men cannot s. fate, 286:2
Suspended, I s. religious inquiries,
    340:11
  'twixt heaven and earth s., 562:12
Suspense in news is torture, 261:24
Suspension of disbelief, 384:10
Suspicion always haunts guilty mind,
    165:6
  Caesar's wife must be above s.,
    88:n14
  companion of mean souls, 340:19
  general s. and distrust, 615:5
  jealousy feeds upon s., 265:3
  more than half right, 703:14
  no s. of partiality in his writing,
    87:15
  rumor fantasy, 762:2
  stuck full of eyes, 179:1
Suspicions, fresh s., 206:33
Suspicious friend, 302:11
  religious people s., 591:3
Suspire, we only live only s., 672:4
Sustain, prop that doth s. house,
    182:5
Sustenance, White S. despair, 513:1
Swabs, doctors is all s., 561:2
Swagman, jolly s., 589:5
Swain, frugal s., 325:8
Swains, that all our s. commend her,
    168:7
Swaller, principles s., 485:12
Swallow a camel, 36:4
  blow and s. at same moment, 84:2
  come before s. dares, 223:7
  flying South, 456:15
  gudgeons ere they're catch'd, 58:n8
  more beliefs than digest, 578:12
  one s. makes a summer, 78:n1
  one s. not a summer, 78:1
  principles s., 485:12
  revenge s. them up, 207:15
  Swallow flying, 456:15
  up death in victory, 26:27
Swallowed, Aaron's rod s. their rods,
    8:32

Sweet (*continued*)

food of knowledge, 156:1
for s. grape vine destroy, 166:38
for thy more s. understanding,
168:19
Genevieve, 536:10
glideth at own s. will, 374:13
good amiable or s., 260:10
good night s. prince, 199:29
great s. mother, 534:1
guess each s., 415:14
he makes s. music with stones,
168:3
heard melodies s., 416:2
Helen make me immortal, 162:19
his mouth is most s., 25:15
how monie counsels s., 363:3
how sour s. music is, 172:14
how s. and fair she seems, 250:1
how s. I roamed, 355:17
how s. is solitude, 334:18
how s. their memory still, 333:21
if life s. give thanks, 535:6
imaginary relish is so s., 200:17
in s. pangs remember me, 202:9
influences of Pleiades, 15:12
is breath of vernal shower, 323:15
is every sound, 456:22
is peace so s., 339:10
is pleasure after pain, 276:10
is revenge, 402:12
is the breath of morn, 258:21
is the whispering music, 82:13
keen smell, 509:29
lady s. and kind, 777:4
land of liberty, 444:3
life s. brother, 428:15
loathe s. tunes, 534:2
look s. upon seat, 600:18
love me s., 768:4
love s. for a day, 534:4
lovers love the spring, 192:12
made s. moan, 417:6
magic brings together, 364:13
medicine thee to s. sleep, 207:6
meet in s. Jerusalem, 165:3
mercy nobility's badge, 167:7
milk of concord, 215:27
mingles s. bitterness with her cares,
91:9
more s. than painted pomp, 190:6
mountain nymph s. liberty, 251:10
music's melting fall, 323:15
musk-roses and eglantine, 173:9
my Adonis hath a s. tooth, 155:17
my home s. home, 666:12
my lady s. arise, 219:24
my life smack s., 468:12
my s. Highland Mary, 363:13
nature's s. cunning hand, 201:26
naught so s. as melancholy, 234:3
neglect more taketh me, 232:6
never merry when hear s. music,
182:9
not s. to dance on air, 567:18
notes by distance made s., 324:16
o' the year, 223:1
oblivious antidote, 216:10
of bitter bark, 623:20
one s. sacrifice, 225:6

Sweet (*continued*)

Parthenope nourished me, 93:8
parting is such s. sorrow, 175:15
Peace is crowned, 270:8
perfections caught, 163:4
poison for age's tooth, 169:17
poison of misused wine, 252:16
pour s. dew on his tongue, 54:16
psalmist of Israel, 12:16
reluctant amorous delay, 258:13
retired solitude, 252:29
retirement urges s. return, 260:3
Richard s. lovely rose, 177:6
Roman hand, 202:30
rose by any name as s., 175:2
serenity of books, 442:19
showers of s. discourse, 264:11
silent thought, 220:18
singing in the choir, 778:9
sleep of laboring man s., 24:4
Slug-a-bed, 241:17
slumbers of virtuous, 292:15
smell s. and blossom in dust, 246:21
smellest so s., 208:1
solitude is s., 334:18
sounds and s. airs, 224:18
sounds together, 595:14
spring full of s. days, 243:11
spring year's pleasant king, 226:20
stay O s., 777:7
stolen waters are s., 21:3
such fleet things s., 534:16
such s. thunder, 173:25
summer's flower to summer s.,
221:15
swan of Avon, 233:1
sweets to the s., 199:13
sweets with s. war not, 220:10
tell not s. I am unkind, 267:14
Thames run softly, 154:16
the coming on of evening, 258:22
the moonlight sleeps, 182:8
then how it was s., 467:17
thing to revisit in dreams, 67:23
things s. to taste prove sour, 170:31
though in sadness, 407:17
though wickedness be s., 14:32
thoughts that savor of content,
157:18
thy s. love remembered, 220:17
to dance to violins, 567:18
to know eye will mark, 402:11
to let mind unbend, 97:3
to look into fair, 413:22
to make the end most s., 170:28
took s. counsel together, 17:27
touches of s. harmony, 182:8
two-and-twenty, 403:23
utter s. breath, 173:28
wee wife o' mine, 363:12
what makes life so s., 514:14
where late s. birds sang, 221:8
white wine, 633:18
world not s. in end, 534:4
your most s. voices, 219:5
Zeus grant s. delight, 64:2
Sweeten my imagination, 211:2
this little hand, 216:5
Sweeteners of tea, 311:21
Sweeter air where it was made, 665:1

Sweeter (*continued*)

mountain sheep s., 397:21
no s. fat than sticks to bones, 489:5
odors crushed s. still, 159:*n*4
pains of love be s. far, 273:13
rose is s. in bud, 155:18
speech s. than honey, 50:30
than apples to children, 565:12
than honey and the honeycomb,
16:11
than sound of instrument, 248:20
world hath not a s. creature, 207:20
wrath s. than honeycomb, 52:14
yet is gratitude, 323:15
Sweetes' li'l' feller, 574:3
Sweetest, canker lives in s. bud,
220:21
girl I know, 627:15
hours e'er I spend, 362:1
last taste s. last, 171:6
Lesbia, 226:13
life near bone s., 478:38
li'l' feller, 574:3
love I do not go, 228:19
melancholy, 236:13
rain makes not fresh, 236:8
Shakespeare Fancy's child, 251:19
song ear ever heard, 401:23
songs saddest thought, 408:7
strongest and s. songs remain,
491:18
surfeit of the s. things, 173:14
sweet Echo s. nymph, 252:26
vibrate s. pleasure, 362:9
voice of God's creatures, 451:*n*2
way to me, 592:9
Sweetheart come see if the rose, 144:4
stay my s. never go, 544:11
that old s. of mine, 558:14
Tray Blanch and S., 210:14
Sweetly, hears you nearby s. speaking,
56:5
how s. did they float, 252:27
marveling s. on ills, 674:12
methinks how s. flows, 241:20
more s. than rhyme, 415:20
nimbly and s. recommends, 213:4
one s. solemn thought, 504:6
played in tune, 362:6
pure and s. strong, 324:12
so s. were forsworn, 204:22
worm feed s. upon me, 231:14
worm shall feed s. on him, 14:36
Sweetness and light, 288:17, 500:14
by convention s., 70:28
flows into breast, 598:6
keeps with perfect s., 431:22
linked s. long drawn out, 251:19
loathe taste of s., 178:11
of proportion, 232:9
out of the strong came s., 11:12
through mine ear, 252:10
waste s. on desert air, 322:13
Sweets, brought'st Thy s. along, 243:8
compacted lie, 243:11
diffuse balmy s. around, 159:*n*4
feast of nectared s., 253:3
grown common lose delight, 221:20
into your list, 397:5
last taste of s., 171:6

Take *(continued)*
my yoke, 34:38
no thought for morrow, 34:1
not able to t. the lead, 52:1
not t. his own life, 74:19
not t. it any more, 752:1
not thy holy spirit from me, 17:23
note O world, 207:12
nothing of his labor, 24:5
nothing on looks, 471:17
O take those lips away, 204:22
pair of sparkling eyes, 531:21
passage we did not t., 670:13
physic pomp, 210:3
pray Lord soul t., 287:14
risk I had to t. and took, 624:19
some come to t. their ease, 226:10
the wings of the morning, 20:8
thee with her eyelids, 20:29
them he cannot t., 502:9
they have to t. you in, 623:3
thine ease, 38:28
thine old cloak about thee, 776:17
this cadence from Yeats, 725:5
this cannot t. her, 262:3
thy rod, 8:31
to open road, 490:3
triple ways to t., 592:9
up read, 114:24
up thy bed, 37:18
upon's mystery of things, 211:13
we must t. the current, 189:20
what course others may t., 339:10
what is given, 625:16
what sweet hour yields, 409:22
will for the deed, 140:4
winds of March, 223:7
you a button-hole lower, 169:9
you t. my house, 182:5
Taken, ark of God is t., 11:30
at the flood, 189:19
away that which he hath, 36:15
better care of myself, 651:6
from you for your better health, 236:21
fun where found it, 592:20
hath t. away thy blessing, 7:39
home gone and t. thy wages, 220:3
no profit where no pleasure t., 167:15
one t. the other left, 36:12
the Lord hath t. away, 13:31
to drink, 608:10
when t. to be shaken, 366:15
worth's unknown although height t., 222:2
Taker, laid to make t. mad, 222:7
Takes away the performance, 214:11
blesseth him that t., 181:19
no fairy t., 192:29
no man t. wealth with him, 59:25
no private road, 302:1
soul t. nothing with her, 75:3
the reason prisoner, 212:20
time t. all gives all, 151:24
Takest, bringing in secret whom thou t. away, 87:5
whatsoever thou t. in hand, 31:18
Taketh away sin of world, 39:35
he t. wise in craftiness, 14:3

Taketh *(continued)*
sweet neglect more t. me, 232:6
Taking from one class to give to other, 306:17
in hand a city, 62:23
in one another's washing, 782:9
Talcum always walcum, 709:9
Tale, as a t. that is told, 18:11
every schoolboy knows, 321:12
every t. condemns me, 166:15
every tongue brings in t., 166:15
fair t. of a tub, 137:16
flowery t. more sweetly, 415:20
hear by t. or history, 172:19
I could a t. unfold, 194:17
love-gift of fairy t., 518:13
moon takes up wondrous t., 292:1
never heard in t. or song, 252:15
of hardihood endurance, 606:2
of human life, 333:10
of Shaun or Shem, 647:20
of Troy divine, 252:6
old wives' t., 602:1
out of season, 31:40
plain t. put you down, 177:26
point moral or adorn t., 313:19
round unvarnished t., 205:22
say t. as said to me, 377:24
schoolboy's t., 399:14
shepherd tells his t., 251:13
speeds best plainly told, 166:7
tell t. tit, 788:13
telle a t. after a man, 130:9
that I relate, 335:21
thereby hangs a t., 190:23
thus the t. ended, 440:19
to him my t. I teach, 382:5
told by an idiot, 216:14
Truth hero of my t., 510:1
twice-told t., 170:5
which holdeth children from play, 156:2
without love, 550:14
would cure deafness, 223:23
yet often told a t., 389:10
Talebearer, go up and down as a t., 9:25
Talebearers as bad as tale-makers, 352:26
Tale-makers, tale-bearers as bad as t., 352:26
Talent, blessed who have no t., 430:20
blessed with each t., 302:11
contribution according to t., 481:n4
discover I had no t., 675:15
does what it can, 516:5
extraordinary collection of t., 741:14
formed in stillness, 349:20
grieved when man of t. dies, 342:17
happy possessor of t., 717:19
has t. cannot use it, 706:19
honors t. in every branch, 72:2
inspiration love, 582:8
man of t. sees two or three, 660:7
of meat-packer, 606:8
succeeded using whole t., 706:19
to see what under nose, 721:8
which is death to hide, 255:11
Talents equal to business, 109:13

Talents *(continued)*
grounds are virtue and t., 344:15
la carrière ouverte aux t., 370:19
let fools use t., 201:24
reviewers tried t. failed, 383:19
Tale's, sad t. best for winter, 222:21
Tales already plainly told, 53:27
dead men tell no t., 274:23
natural fear increased with t., 159:4
of an old wife, 602:n1
out of school, 141:17
tell old t. and laugh, 211:13
to me so dear, 419:11
witch-t. Annie tells, 558:15
words as idle t., 39:26
Talk a little wild, 225:4
after-dinner t., 453:23
always t. who never think, 233:n1
and never think, 233:2
bad music people don't t., 567:7
Cabots t. only to God, 582:1
cane leaves rusty with t., 690:19
cannot t. with civet in room, 334:11
come after me let people t., 126:8
create do not t., 351:1
fishes t. like whales, 330:17
fool may t. wise man speaks, 233:8
from getting overwise, 624:4
good gods how he will t., 285:6
hear t. of court news, 211:13
innocent of t. or action, 716:8
is of bullocks, 32:12
I've come to t. with you again, 772:7
let's t. of graves, 171:24
let's t. of wills, 171:24
living doll can t. t. t., 764:10
loves to hear himself t., 175:22
low talk slow, 722:5
never spent hour's t. withal, 168:23
night crept upon our t., 189:21
no one would t. much in society, 349:29
not of other men's lives, 31:38
not to me of name, 403:23
nothing but t. of his horse, 179:29
of crabbed old men, 90:19
of degeneracy and decay, 425:17
of many things, 519:3
of mysteries, 477:7
of nothing but business, 134:6
of pushing their bones, 759:12
of things heavenly, 272:19
only to conceal the mind, 280:n1
pleasant walk pleasant t., 519:1
ran sun down with t., 82:20
save us, 647:20
sense to a fool, 69:1
sense to American people, 706:10
small t. dies in agonies, 407:23
so much about myself, 477:28
some little t. awhile, 445:19
some t. of Alexander, 778:18
telephone really able to t., 516:7
tendeth only to penury, 21:22
'tisn't beauty nor good t., 593:16
to him of Jacob's ladder, 434:5
tongues have their t., 149:n6
too much, 274:10
true I t. of dreams, 174:21

Talk (*continued*)

two t. one hear, 432:2
ways of making men t., 680:16
what common t. of town is, 279:6
with crowds keep virtue, 593:20
with lover's ghost, 229:17
with you walk with you, 180:2
woman who occasions least t., 72:8

Talkative, learned silence from t., 651:15

Talked between the Rooms, 512:14
I believe they t. of me, 295:13
like poor Poll, 323:19
long enough about rights, 723:16
of their Raphaels, 330:14
worse than being t. about, 566:12

Talker, time is a t., 69:8

Talkers, know little great t., 319:13
no good doers, 165:28

Talking and eloquence not same, 233:8
Frenchman always t., 317:16
he is t. or is pursuing, 12:36
he will be t., 186:40
hear voices t. about everything, 774:7
hydrant in yard, 625:14
in mathematics never know what t., 615:9
is passion of woman, 290:28
keep people from t., 149:n6
know what we are t. about, 549:12
lived life t. at street corners, 674:19
lonely people t. to each other, 716:7
of axes, 517:14
of fall of man, 479:9
of Michelangelo, 667:10
people t. about themselves, 550:12
tired sun with t., 502:9
to Hens of Dorking, 472:10

Talks, don't care how much man t., 479:23
wish I liked way it t., 584:3

Tall, as cedar t. and slender, 348:12
ask Alice when ten feet t., 770:2
confidence in t. man merited, 723:10
divinely t., 454:13
ship and star to steer, 633:14
to reach the pole, 294:5
yond t. anchoring bark, 210:27

Taller by breadth of nail, 289:8
one pill makes you t., 770:2
town than Rome, 619:4

Tallest pine, 256:7

Tally, no books but score and t., 164:11

Talmud, rather believe fables in T., 159:18

Tam, ah T. thou'll get thy fairin, 363:11
lo'ed him like brither, 363:4
was glorious, 363:5

Tamarind, dream beneath t. tree, 451:10

Tambourine, Mister T. Man play a song, 771:8

Tamburlaine must die, 162:1
the Scourge of God, 162:1

Tame a shrew, 235:9

Tame (*continued*)

glass thou canst not t., 242:18
heyday in the blood is t., 197:31
of all t. a flatterer, 232:2
though I seem t., 143:8
tongue can no man t., 46:12

Tamed and shabby tigers, 611:18
by Miltown, 743:2

Tamely, suffer t. lawless attack, 325:4

Tameness, trusts in t. of a wolf, 210:13

Tamer of human breast, 321:18

Tames, punishment t. man, 552:25

Tammie, as T. glowered, 363:8

Tan, caftan of t., 638:27
cheek of t., 443:5

Tangere, noli me t., 40:n6
noli me t. for Caesar's I am, 143:8

Tangle of squabbling nationalities, 576:12

Tangled in amorous nets, 260:26
lie t. in her hair, 267:16
web we weave, 378:13

Tangles of Neaera's hair, 253:20

Tankards scooped in Pearl, 511:16

Tant pis and tant mieux, 320:35
pour tant, 142:n6

Tantum religio potuit suadere malorum, 89:n4

Tao, action of T., 57:11
destruction of T. and virtue, 80:13
function of T., 57:11
is storehouse of all things, 57:19
leveled together by T., 80:8
look at T. and do not see it, 57:4
takes no action, 57:11
that can be told of, 56:12
when average hear T., 57:12
when highest hear T., 57:12
when lowest hear T., 57:12
why it is so near to T., 57:1

Tape, Krapp's last t., 718:20
red t., 470:39
ticker t. ain't spaghetti, 648:1

Taper of conwiviality, 469:26

Taper-light, with t. garnish heaven, 170:9

Taper's, like gleaming t. light, 328:5

Tapers, hold glimmering t. to sun, 235:n4

Tapestries, speech like embroidered t., 62:29

Tapestry, give children right to study t., 338:10

Tappertit, strings said Mr. T., 469:33

Tapping, suddenly there came t., 452:13

Tar, in fir t. is, 791:15
water proportioned, 296:24

Tarantara tarantara, 529:13

Ta-ra-ra-boom-de-ay, 601:1

Tara's halls, 391:12

Tar-baby ain't sayin' nuthin', 556:6

Tard dans un monde trop vieux, 461:n3

Tardy apish nation, 171:7
as t. as too slow, 175:24

Tarentum, far from my native T., 83:1

Tares, crop of corn a field of t., 156:22
of mine own brain, 248:11

Targeted trod like Spring, 598:18

Tarn, dank t. of Auber, 453:2

Tarnish late on Wenlock Edge, 579:8

Tarquin, great house of T., 425:13
viewed in her face's field, 166:36

Tarried, too long we t., 472:1

Tarrieth, guest that t. but a day, 30:26
tide t. no man, 140:21
time nor tide t., 140:n17

Tarry at Jericho until beards be grown, 12:8
awhile says Slow, 789:16
why t. the wheels of his chariots, 11:6

Tar's labor or Turkman's rest, 404:5

Tarsus, a Jew of T., 41:24
stately ship of T., 261:16

Tart, to eat with apple t., 561:11

Tartan, beneath the t. plaid, 472:18

Tartarly, savage and T., 403:28

Tarts, made some t., 789:14

Tarzan, I am T. of the Apes, 628:5
me T. you Jane, 628:n2
of the Apes, 628:4

Task, delightful t., 308:4
labor at eternal t., 503:16
laborer's t. o'er, 506:14
long day's t. is done, 218:4
my t. is smoothly done, 253:12
of pure ablution, 417:12
of twentieth century to explore unconscious, 577:2
remaining before us, 450:2
sore t., 192:23
there's the rub the t., 94:6
though hard be t., 504:5
what he reads as t., 315:26
worldly t. hast done, 220:3

Tasking, whole soul's t., 485:4

Taskmaster's, my great T. eye, 251:4

Taskmasters, lies religion of t., 605:11

Tassel-gentle, lure this t. back, 175:12

Taste, all ashes to the t., 399:23
and see that the Lord is good, 16:30
arbiter of t., 109:15
by which relished, 376:18
from fountain wells up bitter t., 90:8
good strong thick smoke, 465:7
is the only morality, 487:26
last t. of sweets, 171:6
liquor never brewed, 511:16
loathe t. of sweetness, 178:11
man of wealth and t., 773:1
man's hand not able to t., 173:27
never t. who always drink, 233:n1
no t. when you married me, 352:28
not Pierian spring, 298:13
of death but once, 188:11
of your quality, 195:34
prosperity with more t., 290:27
refusing to have t., 728:2
sans t. sans everything, 191:3
sit down and t. my meat, 244:2
sole arbiter is t., 453:14
things sweet to t. prove sour, 170:31

Taste (*continued*)
  touch not t. not, 44:38
  tree whose mortal t., 255:18
  whole joys, 230:13
  whole of it, 467:19
  wild vicissitudes of t., 313:13
  willing to t. any drink once, 635:7
  wretched t., 368:1
  your ware, 789:5
Tasted all the summer's pride, 355:17
  can't be t. in sip, 469:30
  eternal joys of Heaven, 162:15
  I t. careless then, 512:1
  of desire, 623:14
  some books to be t., 160:8
  two worms, 553:23
Tasteless, this age how t., 91:1
Tastes like wrath to come, 631:2
  no accounting for t., 118:25
  wit ne'er t., 302:15
  woman ruin meets, 297:19
Tastiest, sacred cows make t. hamburger, 768:9
Tasting of Flora and country, 415:11
Tat, tit for t., 142:12
Taters, corn and t. grow, 564:19
Tathagata has no closed fist, 64:22
Tathagatas, few and far between are T., 64:24
Tatter in mortal dress, 597:8
Tattered coat upon stick, 597:8
  ears and battered head, 762:17
  ensign, 447:3
  married man t. and torn, 792:24
  through t. clothes, 211:4
Tatters, tear a passion to t., 196:21
Tattlers and busybodies, 45:19
Tattoo, images prisoners t., 706:2
Tatty wreckage of my life, 764:9
Taught, character t. learnt, 500:7
  dream t. me this wisdom, 247:10
  first he wroghte afterward t., 130:2
  folly's all they t. me, 392:5
  genius never can be t., 276:2
  happy is he born and t., 227:6
  hearts t. to conceal, 402:20
  I t. thee to love, 230:4
  it hath t. me to rime, 168:33
  man never flogged never t., 81:7
  Man that he knew not, 117:24
  me all I knew, 593:8
  mind what I am t., 394:4
  should be t. what is, 754:16
  three useful things, 403:22
  Tortoise because he t. us, 518:2
  wise words t. in numbers, 154:4
  you t. me language, 223:29
Taut, by going slightly t., 624:12
Tautness, greyhound's gentle t., 743:10
Tavern, happiness produced by t., 316:28
  I am come to t. alone, 293:14
  in the town, 780:23
  intend to die in t., 122:14
  Mermaid T., 416:12
  my t. the Big Bear, 565:9
  opened t. for friends, 604:18
Taverns, knew t. wel in every toun, 129:17

Tawny, gray rats t. rats, 464:19
Tax, excise hateful t., 314:3
  for being eminent, 289:1
  heavier than kings, 310:14
  I t. not you you elements, 209:25
  just man will pay more income t., 75:6
  not t. bill but t. relief bill, 650:1
  one thing to say to t. increasers, 774:*n*4
  power to t. not power to destroy, 543:8
  power to t. power to destroy, 355:13
  where no revenue found, 331:3
Taxation without representation, 327:7
Taxed, never t. for speech, 203:8
  without consent, 327:*n*6
Taxes, death and t., 310:27
  death t. childbirth, 705:1
  generally raised on city land, 511:7
  No New T., 753:12
  pay for civilized society, 542:14
  Rome's decline in stifling t., 656:13
  true as t., 470:30
  war certain to increase t., 341:5
Taxi throbbing waiting, 669:1
Tchaikovsky, tell T. the news, 756:15
Te deum laudamus, 48:23
  spectem te teneam, 101:*n*3
Te Deum before battle begun, 426:14
Tea, after t. and cakes and ices, 667:15
  and comfortable advice, 418:7
  and scandal, 290:36
  and sometimes t., 299:13
  breakfasts at five-o'clock t., 519:21
  destruction of t. so bold, 337:17
  glad not born before t., 380:21
  honey still for t., 662:19
  put kettle on all have t., 792:10
  sweeteners of t., 311:21
  take some more t., 517:21
  thank God for t., 380:21
  without stratagem, 296:2
Teach act of order to kingdom, 184:23
  aim of oratory to t., 87:21
  basest thing is to be afraid, 696:20
  beasts shall t. thee, 14:16
  charm strengthen and t., 441:22
  child to doubt, 359:11
  crab to walk straight, 73:7
  eggs do not t. hen, 793:4
  gladly lerne and gladly t., 129:22
  go and t. all nations, 37:15
  he who shall t. child, 359:11
  high thought, 459:20
  him to tell my story, 205:28
  him what said in past, 3:3
  his feet a measure, 534:9
  learn from those who can t., 66:17
  learn suffering t. in song, 407:11
  learn what it had to t., 478:17
  let such t. others, 298:10
  me half the gladness, 408:8
  me my God and King, 243:25
  me to hear mermaids singing, 228:5
  men sense of existence, 552:7

Teach (*continued*)
  noble negligences t., 288:1
  nothing but Facts, 471:5
  nothing but to name tools, 262:22
  order to peopled kingdom, 184:23
  same prayer doth t. us all, 181:19
  shall any t. God, 14:34
  sleek girls I t., 757:14
  still pleased to t., 299:7
  the earth shall t. thee, 14:16
  them diligently unto thy children, 10:11
  thy necessity to reason, 171:1
  to him my tale I t., 382:5
  trees and stones will t. you, 121:8
  unforgetful to forget, 509:27
  us good Lord to serve Thee, 139:3
  us how to die, 400:13
  us to care, 669:14
  us to have aspiring minds, 161:21
  us to number our days, 18:13
  us to sit still, 669:14
  villainy you t. me, 180:32
  without sneering t. to sneer, 302:11
  ye how to climb, 253:13
  you more of man, 372:21
  young idea to shoot, 308:4
Teacher affects eternity, 535:26
  city is t. of the man, 60:9
  closed fist of t., 64:22
  Nature be your t., 372:20
  passed for a good t., 136:*n*4
  true t. has no disciple, 422:2
  value of true t., 516:3
  who can arouse feeling, 350:1
Teachers, men are my t., 301:*n*5
  seized my youth, 498:19
  Shame Despair her t., 436:2
  ungrateful to those t., 651:15
Teaches, experience t., 470:*n*1
  grief t. to waver, 66:12
  hard dealing t. them suspect, 180:11
  he who cannot t., 571:8
  life t. us to be less harsh, 349:17
  nature t. beasts to know friends, 218:26
  nature t. more than preaches, 532:10
  standing on toes, 697:8
  such beauty as woman's eye, 168:35
  time t. all things, 63:6
  us to see, 750:4
Teaching a fish to swim, 119:20
  for life, 5:10
  hold fast to t. as a lamp, 64:23
  is awakening curiosity, 550:10
  nations how to live, 254:18
  only t. on Tuesdays, 742:21
  thank thee Jew for t. word, 182:4
  truth persuades by t., 112:8
  well-established truth, 122:10
  what t. is and was, 697:8
Teachings, Nature's t., 411:2
Teacup, crack in t. opens, 720:8
Teacups, tinkled among t., 668:2
Team of little atomies, 174:20
Teapot, storm in a t., 88:6
Tear a passion to tatters, 196:21
  all he had a t., 322:23
  cannot t. out page of life, 436:19

Tear *(continued)*
each other's eyes, 294:7
from eyelids wiped t., 190:29
heart to dog to t., 593:18
intellectual thing, 359:4
man without a t., 389:9
never t. linnet from leaf, 597:4
newborn infant's t., 358:9
passage of angel's t., 413:23
Recording Angel dropped a t.,
320:29
shed bitter t., 518:24
smile on lips t. in eye, 378:10
splendid t., 458:23
still ushered with t., 300:2
sympathetic t., 321:23
tattered ensign, 447:3
to pieces that great bond, 214:28
we shed though secret, 391:11
Tearing up pea patch, 690:16
Tears, angry t. gone, 596:13
are on her cheeks, 29:1
before my t. did drown it, 243:16
big round t. coursed down, 190:8
bitter t. to shed, 502:9
blood toil t. sweat, 620:5
blotted all over with t., 463:23
broomsticks and t., 596:13
bucket full of t. am I., 172:9
cannot bear a mother's t., 94:23
crave stain of t., 623:20
crocodile t., 157:*n*3
crocodiles shed t. when would devour, 159:26
crying but without t., 743:8
dark with torment and t., 479:29
drop t. as fast, 208:16
fight from eyes t., 674:21
flow with t. of gold, 356:16
fountains fraught with t., 156:17
from wrath-bearing tree, 668:8
girlish t., 576:18
hence these t., 85:13
here are the t. of things, 93:21
hired t., 248:26
idle tears, 456:13
if you have t., 189:4
in t. amid alien corn, 415:17
iron t. down Pluto's cheek, 252:7
like Niobe all t., 193:10
Lord God will wipe away t., 26:27
mine own t. do scald, 211:9
mist of t., 581:4
no t. in writer no t. in reader, 625:9
nor all your T. wash out, 445:25
not pay honor with t., 84:17
nothing is here for t., 261:25
now am full of t., 594:18
of eternity, 580:3
of one tiny creature, 495:9
of repentance you'll wipe, 357:21
of sky for loss of sun, 305:18
of things, 93:21
rain shower of commanded t.,
167:14
remember with t., 504:3
rent is sorrow income t., 242:9
shall drown the wind, 213:7
Siren t., 222:3
smiles t. of boyhood's years, 392:7

Tears *(continued)*
smiling through t., 51:27
songs composed of t., 461:15
such as angels weep, 256:18
sweat or blood, 620:*n*1
sympathetic t., 323:3
that speak, 267:10
thaw not frost, 408:14
they that sow in t., 19:28
thoughts too deep for t., 375:15
time to plant t., 729:8
time with gift of t., 533:10
tired of t. and laughter, 534:13
unseen and unknown, 446:25
waste not fresh t., 69:9
watered heaven with t., 358:7
way with t. watered, 612:3
weep barren t., 406:17
wipe away all t., 48:1
with sobs and t. sorted, 519:6
your death brought me t., 82:20
Tear-wrung millions, 620:*n*1
Teas where small talk dies, 407:23
Tease, fools no more I'll t., 299:27
the huswife's wool, 253:10
Teases, he knows it t., 517:15
mind over for years, 557:20
Teatray, like t. in sky, 517:20
Technique and style of Europe, 754:21
Techniques to create full life, 715:9
Technologies with vast power to manipulate, 715:12
Technology knack of arranging world,
729:17
Tecum vivere amem tecum obeam libens, 96:*n*14
Tedious as twice-told tale, 170:5
old fools, 195:22
relations t. pack, 567:9
returning as t. as go o'er, 215:12
road will be less t., 92:17
shorten t. nights, 226:16
sport would be t., 176:37
thinking his prattle t., 172:13
to tell tales already told, 53:27
Tedium, pretentious quotations t.,
574:1
Teeming brain, 417:9
mistress barren bride, 300:14
refuse of t. shore, 558:1
womb of kings, 171:9
Teenage, American T. Drive-In Life,
764:1
Teeth, bid them keep t. clean, 219:4
bitch gone in the t., 659:10
children's t. set on edge, 28:35
red thoughts t. white, 610:19
sans t. sans eyes, 191:3
shark has pretty t., 698:14
terrible round about, 15:22
truth may strike out his t., 152:20
weeping and gnashing of t., 34:16
what speech escaped your t., 51:17
who made t. shall give bread,
141:*n*3
with the skin of my t., 14:28
writers like t. incisors molars, 506:5
Teetotaler, beer t. not champagne t.,
570:16
Tehee quod she, 130:26

Tekel, Mene Mene T. Upharsin, 29:16
Telegraph, Cunard's liners and t.,
484:8
Telemachus, mine own T., 455:4
Teleology is theology, 589:19
Telephant, elephant tried to use t.,
560:10
Telephone, cool medium like t., 730:4
elephone tried to use t., 560:10
really able to talk, 516:7
Telephones, army no private baths or
t., 666:14
Telescope ends microscope begins,
428:5
Telescopes of the press, 590:10
Television, chief citadel of t., 714:16
crouch to t. set, 743:12
used to distract delude amuse insulate, 724:8
vast wasteland, 757:11
Tell, a bore to t. everything, 305:26
aloud greatest failing, 289:16
can't t. him much, 781:22
dead can t. you being dead, 671:20
dead men t. no tales, 274:23
don't t. they'd advertise, 511:22
dream of not t., 382:13
'em Queen Anne's dead, 366:13
every word t., 608:9
feat of T. the archer, 365:23
fowls shall t. thee, 14:16
her one thing and keep another,
53:23
her that wastes her time, 250:1
her what I tell to thee, 456:15
him he hates flatterers, 188:5
him to go to hell, 397:12
how it really was, 418:22
if one but t. a thing well, 64:10
I'll t. you no fibs, 330:8
it like it is, 710:*n*1
it like it was, 710:4
it not in Gath, 11:46
kiss and t., 291:5
little Lamb I'll t. thee, 356:7
me all these years you've waited,
734:13
me I ought to do, 331:17
me muse, 52:27
me Muse, 299:25
me not in mournful numbers,
440:15
me not sweet I am unkind, 267:14
me of John or Shaun, 647:20
me tales to me dear, 419:11
me tell me elm, 647:20
me thy company, 151:1
me what thy name is, 452:18
me what you eat, 354:14
me what you know, 430:19
me what you like, 487:26
me where all past years are, 228:5
me where fancy bred, 181:3
my story, 199:27
never seek to t. thy love, 357:17
O t. me all about Anna Livia,
647:19
old tales and laugh, 211:13
sad stories of death of kings, 171:25
tale tit, 788:13

Tell (*continued*)
  tales already told, 53:27
  Tchaikovsky the news, 756:15
  teach him to t. my story, 205:28
  that I cannot t. said he, 386:7
  that to the marines, 379:22
  the crooked rose, 737:8
  the world, 179:2
  them I Am, 325:10
  them I came, 616:23
  those who sent you, 351:19
  truth and shame devil, 140:*n*4
  us your phobias, 675:12
  what and where they be, 458:25
  what thou art, 151:1
  wife all he knows, 250:10
  you a great secret, 732:19
  you my drift, 186:26
  you what you are, 354:14, 487:26
  young men, 314:29
Teller, truth never hurts t., 468:8
Telleth number of the stars, 20:15
Telling, blessed strains t., 474:3
  I am not arguing I am t., 524:3
  nothing in great harangue, 269:11
  off state and president, 742:22
  pity beyond all t., 594:22
  this with sigh, 623:7
Tells lies without attending, 343:11
  nobody t. me anything, 603:18
  of a nameless deed, 367:12
  when too much lipstick, 709:15
Telmetale of stem or stone, 647:20
Téméraire, Fighting T., 586:14
Tempe, through life's T. led, 487:8
Temper doctrinaire logic, 683:4
  enforce with t., 318:22
  hot t. leaps over, 179:28
  judicious swearin' keeps t., 603:10
  justice with mercy, 260:13
  made thee to t. man, 284:17
  moderation in t. a virtue, 341:8
  slander result of hot t., 3:8
  unless I mistake its t., 648:15
  which blades bears better t., 163:10
  wit with morality, 292:20
  woman of uncertain t., 386:24
Temperament, creation seen through
    t., 541:11
  harmony of t. and circumstances,
    496:7
  second-class intellect first-class t.,
    543:14
  solvency matter of t., 594:4
Temperamental atmosphere of Gallup
    Poll, 621:4
Temperance a species of courage,
    278:5
  acquire and beget a t., 196:21
  as easy as t. difficult, 315:11
  fruit of Spirit is t., 44:19
Temperate affords me none, 246:7
  more lovely and more t., 220:12
  wise amazed t. furious, 214:16
Temperature, poll taking t., 621:4
Tempered, absolutism t. by assassina-
    tion, 368:3
  by war, 741:3
Tempers wind to shorn lamb, 144:14,
    321:2

Tempest, betokened t. to field, 165:12
  covert from the t., 27:6
  haunts t., 494:2
  in a teapot, 88:*n*5
  in the very torrent t., 196:21
  no more hear t. howling, 348:3
  on me t. falls, 63:8
  seaman's story is of t., 100:28
  sensual lust t., 495:4
  still is high, 312:14
Tempested, thou shalt not be t., 128:1
Tempests, errors wanderings mists and
    t., 89:*n*9
  fell all night, 243:23
  glasses itself in t., 401:2
  looks on t., 222:2
Tempest-tost, send t. to me, 558:1
Tempestuous petticoat, 241:5
Temple bells they say, 591:22
  drove out of t., 39:41
  hangs on Dian's t., 219:12
  his people were his t., 271:12
  his train filled the t., 25:42
  Lord is in his holy t., 29:42
  Lord's anointed t., 214:13
  many a t. half as old, 367:4
  no sooner t. built to God, 138:*n*3
  nothing ill in such t., 224:2
  of Delight, 416:18
  of Dian, 782:7
  of God is holy, 42:34
  of Jerusalem, 116:15
  of science, 575:9
  sacred t. of Mecca, 116:15
  singing vespers in T. of Jupiter,
    340:16
  two went into t. to pray, 39:7
  veil of t. rent, 37:13
Temple-haunting martlet, 213:4
Temple's inner shrine, 374:16
Temples, forsake their t. dim, 251:1
  God's first t., 411:6
  gorgeous palaces solemn t., 224:21
  made with hands, 41:16
  mortal t. of king, 171:25
  of his gods, 425:14
  shall my joyful t. bind, 249:29
  smote the nail into his t., 10:41
  which men had commanded, 271:12
Tempora mutantur nos et mutamur,
    119:33
  O t. O mores, 87:7
Temporal, concern t. salvation, 339:7
  force of t. power, 181:19
  matter unreal and t., 495:21
  reversion, 671:19
  things seen are t., 44:2
Temporary, dictionaries and t. poems,
    314:4
  obtain a little t. safety, 310:13
  permanent contract on t. feeling,
    540:5
  use of force but t., 331:11
Temps, ah les bons vieux t., 786:17
  au t. de ma jeunesse folle, 133:*n*7
  le t. a laissé son manteau, 132:*n*11
  O t. suspends vol, 405:*n*4
Tempt, Devil went off to t. Lady Pol-
    tagrue, 609:7
  frailty of our powers, 201:8

Tempt (*continued*)
  its new-fledged offspring, 329:14
  not desperate man, 176:14
  shall not t. the Lord, 10:12
  upper classes, 574:1
Temptation, blessed the man that en-
    dureth t., 46:5
  cold and to t. slow, 221:14
  comes in fine gay colors, 226:*n*1
  enter not into t., 36:31
  last t. greatest treason, 670:10
  lead us not into t., 33:12
  maximum of t., 571:9
  my t. is quiet, 599:10
  resist everything except t., 566:20
  to get rid of t. yield, 566:14
  to the editor, 657:6
  white fever of t., 680:3
  why t. but for man to meet, 468:3
Temptations, rid of t. by yielding,
    422:1
  to belong to other nations, 529:10
Tempted her out of gloom, 453:4
  My Lady t. by a private whim,
    609:7
Tempus edax rerum, 101:*n*20
  omnia t. revelat, 103:*n*2
Ten, and David his t. thousands,
    11:42
  aren't no T. Commandments,
    591:24
  ask Alice when t. feet tall, 770:2
  better t. guilty escape, 325:23
  Council of T., 652:7
  days that shook world, 665:17
  death hath t. thousand doors,
    237:17
  good Lord had only t., 542:1
  I'm t. years burning down the road,
    774:13
  it's now t. o'clock, 461:12
  jokes an hundred enemies, 320:9
  little Indians, 792:15
  live t. times t., 428:6
  low words, 298:18
  men who haven't and don't, 571:28
  not if I had t. tongues, 51:9
  o'clock scholar, 792:7
  only one summer that I was t.,
    747:14
  set my t. commandments in your
    face, 163:19
  speak for t. minutes need week,
    572:15
  strength as strength of t., 456:3
  thousand miles away, 793:20
  thousand saw I at a glance, 375:21
  thousand times ten thousand,
    460:17
  thousand to go out of it, 288:13
  to the world allot, 152:*n*3
  vowing perfection of t., 200:20
  when angry count t., 345:6
  wrote words of t. commandments,
    9:20
Tenacious but restless, 665:9
  of purpose in rightful cause, 96:15
Tenanted, by good angels t., 452:5
Tenantless, graves stood t., 192:25
  save to wind, 399:26

Tend, great God to thee we t., 115:13
  on mortal thoughts, 212:29
Tendance, doth life in t. spend, 154:6
Tendencies, containment of Russian
  expansive t., 713:18
Tendency to good like water, 79:25
Tender and true, 506:12
  eye of pitiful day, 214:28
  for another's pain, 321:17
  grace of day dead, 456:8
  irreproachably t., 686:19
  is the night, 415:13
  know how t. 'tis, 213:12
  leaves of hopes, 225:16
  love me t., 768:4
  Majesty, 512:12
  mercies of the wicked are cruel,
    21:12
  murderer, 466:10
  our vines have t. grapes, 25:7
  pitying the t. cries, 356:16
  rear t. thought, 308:4
  stops of various quills, 254:7
  strokes of art, 299:19
  the t. mercy of God, 38:1
  too t. or too firm heart, 300:8
  walks with t. growing night, 489:8
  yearning sweet hoping, 365:12
Tender-handed stroke a nettle, 297:23
Tenderly, night coming t., 708:14
Tenderness its joys and fears, 375:15
  shape of t., 705:21
  thanks to its t., 375:15
Tenders, shoal of fools for t., 291:10
Tendrils, limp and damp as t., 725:4
  strong, 376:14
Ténébreux, je suis le t., 443:*n*5
Tenement of clay, 274:3
  threshold of ruined t., 312:19
  upon clothes behind t., 679:8
  words written on tenement halls,
    772:8
Teneriff or Atlas unremoved, 259:3
Tenets admitted into pagan creed,
  536:18
  faith in some nice t., 267:12
  surpass in atrocity any t., 536:18
Tennessee, placed jar in T., 639:1
Tennis anyone, 783:3
  play t. with the net down, 625:17
Tennyson not Tennysonian, 549:16
  out-babying Keats, 429:3
Tennysonianness of speech, 660:4
Tenoned, foothold t. and mortised in
  granite, 489:6
Tenor, noiseless t. of their way,
  322:17
Tenpence, seven pounds t. a man,
  330:19
Tense for first losing, 735:12
Tension, interracial t. has focus, 700:5
Tent, Alexander in his t., 712:18
  I rede you t. it, 363:15
  in field silken t., 624:11
  little t. of blue, 567:15
  nightly pitch moving t., 377:17
  outside t. whirling drift, 606:3
  pitched his t. toward Sodom, 7:28
  prize of general not t., 542:19
  strike the t., 440:13

Tent (*continued*)
  that searches bottom of worst,
    200:14
Tenth, be thou the t. Muse, 220:22
  less than t. part of one, 200:20
  Muse governs press, 475:11
Tenting tonight, 523:1
Tents, dwell in the t. of wickedness,
  18:7
  dwelling in t., 7:36
  fold t. like Arabs, 441:12
  how goodly are thy t., 10:8
  of Kedar, 25:1
  sighed soul toward Grecian t., 182:7
  silent t. spread, 492:4
  such as dwell in t., 7:9
  to your t. O Israel, 12:30
Tenure, public men no sure t., 677:2
Tenures, his t. and his tricks, 199:4
Tepee warm in winter cool in summer, 563:5
Tepid, never distract reader from t.
  lust, 703:4
Term, served a t., 529:6
Termagant, whipped for o'erdoing T.,
  196:21
Terminate torment, 669:15
  woman's decision to t. pregnancy,
    722:13
Termination, no government provides
  for its own t., 449:2
Terminations, terrible as her t., 186:22
Terminological inexactitude, 619:14
Terms between old and new world,
  355:3
  fair t. and villain's mind, 180:12
  litigious t., 254:19
  of armistice with fate, 696:6
  silken t. precise, 169:8
  too deep for me, 529:17
  unconditional surrender, 501:9
  unfamiliar t., 111:29
Terra firma of accomplished discovery,
  635:2
  in t. pax, 48:8
Terrace walk and half rood, 302:23
Terre, c'est une pauvre t., 494:*n*9
  Dieu donna à Caïn, 139:*n*2
Terrestrial, written on t. things,
  540:11
Terrible as an army with banners,
  25:16
  as her terminations, 186:22
  beauty born, 596:17
  beauty mysterious t., 495:5
  beauty t. and awful, 495:4
  burden of nothing to do, 280:19
  children, 435:21
  each angel is t., 630:6
  fluidity of self-revelation, 549:10
  for old woman to outlive her dogs,
    730:21
  from a t. land, 26:18
  from camps, 717:1
  gift lifted from hearts, 495:11
  haughtiness of the t., 26:13
  invent new beasts so t., 420:9
  judges all ranged a t. show, 297:21
  lend the eye t. aspect, 185:3
  life ordinary most t., 510:12

Terrible (*continued*)
  long and t. way, 725:20
  mind t. thing to waste, 784:11
  no accuser so t., 85:11
  not death but dying is t., 312:3
  nothing more t. than ignorance,
    351:10
  nothing t. except fear itself, 158:18
  sociologists, 590:1
  swift sword, 484:6
  thing happening to him, 738:15
  times, 564:6
  years of Yezhov terror, 675:8
Terrible-eyed, staggered and t., 718:22
Terribles, enfants t., 435:21
  simplificateurs, 480:8
Terribly, armies swore t., 320:22
Terrified, bored and t., 739:9
Terrifies, silence of spaces t. me,
  270:23
Terrify, heart they ought to t., 366:3
Territorial aggrandizement, 650:7
  integrity, 572:14
  no t. changes, 650:7
Territories, occupied t., 621:3
Territory, has t. of harmonicas, 689:9
  not make nation, 505:15
Terror, afraid for the t. by night,
  18:15
  and force, 676:3
  at own finitude, 588:8
  Beauty's beginning of T., 630:6
  human form divine, 358:13
  night sweat with t., 597:13
  no t. Cassius, 189:16
  perceivers of t. of life, 432:30
  perch and not t., 203:28
  primitive t., 671:15
  reigns of t., 493:5
  science frees from bodily t., 484:17
  strike t. in Swede, 424:3
  understood t. and hope, 744:9
  victory in spite of t., 620:6
Terrorist and policeman from same
  basket, 573:11
Terrors, dare deadly t. clasp, 358:7
  king of t., 14:27
  painting gives form to t., 645:4
Tertullian, every word of T. a sentence, 115:5
Tess, ended his sport with T., 540:3
Test, habit with him t. of truth,
  353:16
  lies in action, 63:31
  no t. which is not fanciful, 67:2
  not t. faith in crucible, 558:8
  of civilization, 682:14
  of first-rate intelligence, 694:17
  of leader, 677:3
  of man or woman's breeding,
    570:11
  of ridicule, 291:27
  of true theories to predict, 411:14
  perception of beauty moral t.,
    476:28
  to t. man proofs shift, 467:13
  true t. of civilization, 316:9, 433:6
  untrained to stand t., 545:12
Testament, blood of the new t., 36:28
  new t. in my blood, 43:12

This (*continued*)

is my beloved, 25:15
is my beloved Son, 32:34
is my body, 36:28
is my friend, 25:15
is my own my native land, 378:1
is our gracious will, 137:5
is the place, 427:4
is the real me, 545:5
is the way, 27:4
is the worst, 210:19
it is t. oh it is t., 777:9
that it should come to t., 193:6
too shall pass away, 448:14
was a man, 189:28
Thisbe fearfully o'ertrip dew, 182:7
Thisby, Pyramus and T., 172:22
Thistle Shamrock Rose entwine, 515:4
Thistles, figs of t., 34:11
Thither, hither and t. spins, 497:18
Thomas, John T. marryin' Lady Jane, 657:15
saith he to T., 40:42
true T., 785:11
Thompson, Sadie T. answer, 626:20
Thonx, Bronx no t., 709:8
Thor, da stehe ich nun ich armer T., 350:*n*3
Thoreau, living like T., 594:*n*2
unperfect unfinished, 548:8
Thoreau's, no question of T. genius, 548:8
Thorn in the flesh, 44:11
no harvest but a t., 243:16
oak and ash and t., 593:17, 785:8
plant this t. this canker, 177:6
primrose peeps beneath t., 329:22
rose without a t., 353:11
snail's on t., 464:4
wantons thro' flowering t., 362:8
without t. the rose, 258:9
Thornbush, this t. my t., 174:7
Thorns and dangers of this world, 170:17
burrs and t. of life, 414:6
crown of t. on labor, 582:4
fall upon t. of life, 407:16
grapes of t., 34:11
in your sides, 10:40
noble crown is of t., 413:7
rose among t., 113:4
roses have t. fountains mud, 220:21
snow on barren t., 647:8
that in bosom lodge, 194:25
thy only crown, 250:7
under a pot, 24:8
Thorny hedge-hogs, 173:12
life is t., 382:15
undertaking to follow mind, 145:22
virtue demands t. road, 146:2
way to heaven, 193:27
Thou art that, 50:14
art the man, 12:11
beside me singing, 445:9
Duty whispers T. must, 430:4
holier than t., 28:10
shalt not sit with statisticians, 720:20
Though an host should encamp, 16:22
Thought, actuality of t. is life, 77:23

Thought (*continued*)

adorns nature with new thing, 432:15
adventure in clarification of t., 584:12
agents of men of t., 420:7
all I t. was true, 622:17
all objects of all t., 373:5
armor is his honest t., 227:6
as a child, 43:16
believe own t. genius, 431:19
beneath slight film, 511:15
best known and t., 499:9
beyond utmost bound of t., 455:3
brightest t. incomplete, 493:18
by t. word and deed, 49:15
chaos of t. and passion, 301:13
charm by t. supplied, 373:4
community of t., 535:27
depends on stomach, 306:24
divine t. thinks of itself, 77:24
divorced from eye, 696:1
energy of t., 426:20
erring t., 532:14
essential in painting, 120:13
even t. can shatter us, 553:6
every t. that springs, 377:11
evolution of t., 498:22
finds the words, 625:6
flashes in world of t., 493:18
free t., 543:10
freed capacity of t., 577:9
freedom of t., 325:6
glow of early t. declines, 401:17
God t. and t., 612:8
gods t. otherwise, 93:35
Greek t. and life, 507:9
green t. in green shade, 268:18
he t. they were old friends, 735:2
her body t., 230:16
high t. amiable words, 459:20
his mind a t. of God, 476:8
his who says it best, 485:26
human t. or form, 406:10
in you boundless t. born, 446:26
independent of labor, 477:25
is free, 224:16
lean upon the t., 497:21
leaped to wed with Thought, 457:10
learning without t., 60:23
liberty of t. life of soul, 307:2
lies like burden, 431:14
like full-blown rose, 415:3
lived with no other t., 453:7
loftiness of t. surpassed, 275:25
lucidity of t., 500:25
man of action forced into t., 603:22
near to be t. so shortly, 187:3
nimble t. can jump, 220:23
no freedom of t. without doubt, 712:20
nor t. of leveling wind, 597:16
not a t. be lost, 720:17
not t. death undone so many, 668:19
not t. of own in head, 573:2
of China and Greece, 712:18
of kindnesses done, 91:13
often original, 447:6

Thought (*continued*)

old man had so much blood, 216:3
one t. in breast another on tongue, 91:23
pale cast of t., 196:10
passes swiftly as a t., 59:26
pearls of t., 486:3
penny for your t., 142:9
perish the t., 291:22
pleasing dreadful t., 292:14
plunged into sea of words, 650:21
power in mysteries of t., 68:7
practice and t. forge art, 92:24
principle of free t., 543:10
rear tender t., 308:4
rhythm in all thought, 380:24
Roman t. hath struck him, 216:28
saturates politics with t., 499:7
scientific t. human progress, 554:10
seem a moment's t., 595:13
sense from t. divide, 274:*n*2
servants in t. as in action, 723:11
she pined in t., 202:14
sleep out the t. of it, 223:3
sow a t., 781:6
strange seas of t., 373:10
stream of t., 545:15
style dress of t., 286:24
sweet silent t., 220:18
sweetest songs saddest t., 408:7
sweetly solemn t., 504:6
swift as a bird or t., 53:12
take no t. about what is distant, 61:27
take no t. for morrow, 34:1
taking t. add one cubit, 33:19
the best t. and said, 500:8
thee bright, 222:14
think so then t. so still, 472:16
thinking what nobody t., 687:20
third silence of t., 442:22
tire the night in t., 242:7
to have loved t. done, 498:1
to justify wrongdoings, 306:21
too much thinking to have common t., 300:15
too much to stoop to action, 537:20
traversed universe in t., 89:4
tremble into t., 380:25
troubled seas of t., 723:7
two souls with single t., 439:9
uffish t., 518:16
understandest my t. afar off, 20:7
unmeaning thing they call a t., 298:10
uttered a lie, 434:11
vitality of t., 584:18
want of t. and heart, 422:23
weave emotion t. sound, 423:19
wed with Thought, 457:10
What jolly fun, 584:3
what oft was t., 298:14
what thing not t. of ages long ago, 350:23
when t. takes breath away, 502:10
whistled for want of t., 276:27
wish father to t., 184:11
without learning, 60:23
words slippery t. viscous, 536:3
would destroy paradise, 321:17

Thought (*continued*)
　young man brings forth, 76:9
Thought-executing fires, 209:24
Thoughtless, hour of t. youth, 373:5
　my t. hand, 358:5
　saying of great princess, 319:25
Thoughtlessness and optimism, 588:12
Thought's slave of life, 179:5
Thoughts according to inclination,
　184:*n*2
　all intelligent t. already thought,
　　351:9
　all t. all passions, 383:3
　and intents of heart, 45:34
　assault of t. on unthinking, 652:13
　beautiful in t., 582:12
　beyond reaches of souls, 194:11
　calmer of t., 245:17
　ceaseless t. of roaming, 282:11
　discerner of the t., 45:34
　doubtful t., 181:7
　fat paunch never breeds fine t.,
　　113:19
　fly in twinkling of eye, 777:15
　fond and wayward t., 373:18
　fresh t. along shores, 461:3
　give thy t. no tongue, 193:28
　give thy worst of t., 206:29
　gored mine own t., 221:26
　great t. come from heart, 321:8
　high t. must have high language,
　　73:23
　high-erected t. in heart of courtesy,
　　155:23
　holy profane clean obscene, 239:20
　in these t. myself despising, 220:16
　joy of elevated t., 373:5
　leave to think own t., 589:1
　legible in the eye, 163:3
　long long t., 442:5
　multiply t., 726:14
　my bloody t., 207:15
　my sad t. doth clear, 270:9
　my t. are minutes, 172:15
　my t. my trollops, 319:29
　my t. not your t., 28:2
　never alone accompanied with noble
　　t., 155:24
　never spoken or written, 426:13
　of a turtle turtles, 433:29
　of earthly men, 54:7
　of men decay, 154:4
　of men widened, 455:20
　of other men, 573:12
　of youth long, 442:5
　on hospitable t. intent, 259:10
　pansies for t., 198:23
　pieced t. into philosophy, 597:13
　pious t. as harbingers, 250:8
　profound t. arise in debate, 749:10
　quotations give good t., 619:18
　remain below, 197:26
　rule the world, 433:18
　second t. are best, 68:16
　secret t. run over all things, 239:20
　Sensations rather than T., 417:16
　shroud of t., 400:8
　slumbering t., 249:7
　so thy t. when thou gone, 409:10
　soothe cares lift t., 414:6

Thoughts (*continued*)
　speech to conceal t., 306:21
　style the dress of t., 305:10
　suspect the t. of others, 180:11
　tend on mortal t., 212:29
　that arise in me, 456:7
　that breathe, 323:5
　that nature gives way to, 213:18
　that savor of content, 157:18
　think mortal t., 68:4
　think other men's t., 506:11
　to memory dear, 379:2
　to think great t. be heroes, 542:8
　too deep for tears, 375:15
　turns to t. of love, 455:9
　understandeth all imaginations of
　　the t., 13:16
　unexpressed fall dead, 97:*n*10
　unmentionable t., 487:3
　unrighteous man forsake his t., 28:1
　unthinkable t., 716:1
　uplifting t. in baths, 693:12
　wander through eternity, 257:2
　were always downward bent,
　　256:20
　were red thoughts, 610:19
　what sweet t. what longing, 125:17
　which were not their thoughts,
　　400:8
　with sea's boundlessness, 705:21
　words without t., 197:26
　wrapped in my t., 132:23
Thousand, a t. shall fall at thy side,
　18:15
　actions once afoot, 184:25
　after t. victories foiled, 220:14
　ages in Thy sight, 294:15
　cattle upon t. hills, 17:19
　conscience hath t. tongues, 166:15
　day in thy courts better than a t.,
　　18:7
　death hath ten t. doors, 237:17
　difference of forty t. men, 371:8
　done a t. dreadful things, 167:12
　doors that lead to death, 237:*n*4
　earth with t. voices, 383:4
　few t. battered books, 659:10
　first t. days, 741:6
　forty t. brothers, 199:16
　fragrant posies, 162:4
　freedom has a t. charms, 334:3
　furlongs of sea, 223:19
　give me a t. kisses, 90:19
　hacking at branches of evil, 478:13
　hearts beat happily, 399:21
　Hell rising from t. thrones, 451:17
　his songs were a t. and five, 12:21
　homeless near t. homes, 372:16
　hundred t. thrained men, 654:13
　I in twelve t. none, 172:8
　journey of a t. miles, 57:20
　leagues a thousand years, 310:20
　little one shall become a t., 28:5
　man picked out of ten t., 195:16
　men that fishes gnawed, 165:30
　more memories than if t. years old,
　　494:6
　natural shocks, 196:10
　near a t. tables, 372:16
　night has t. eyes, 563:2

Thousand (*continued*)
　night hath a t. eyes, 155:21
　of t. kisses the poor last, 218:7
　one among a t., 15:2
　one man among a t., 24:14
　one picture worth t. words, 782:21
　one small candle light a t., 240:12
　peering littlenesses, 459:3
　person may have many t. selves,
　　651:1
　points of friendly light, 753:*n*1
　points of light, 753:11
　radiance of a t. suns, 84:12
　saw a t. fearful wracks, 165:30
　Shallow I owe t. pound, 184:17
　slain a t. men with jawbone, 11:15
　Solomon spake three t. proverbs,
　　12:21
　ten t. saw I at a glance, 375:21
　ten t. times ten t., 460:17
　ten t. to go out of it, 288:13
　three hundred t. more, 461:11
　to that hundred, 241:8
　torture word ten t. ways, 274:27
　twangling instruments, 224:18
　two t. light years from home,
　　772:17
　wars of old, 457:30
　worth a t. men, 379:1
　would he had blotted a t., 233:4
　years are as yesterday, 18:10
　years of peace, 457:30
　years pass guilt of Germany not
　　erased, 704:7
Thousands, and David his ten t.,
　11:42
　at his bidding speed, 255:13
　countless t. mourn, 361:8
　equally were meant, 289:18
　mercy unto t. that love me, 9:10
　murder t., 296:3
　Peace its ten t., 336:3
　Saul hath slain his t., 11:42
　slave to t., 206:30
　war its t. slays, 336:3
Thracian ships and foreign faces,
　533:8
Thrained, hundhred thousand t. men,
　654:13
Thrall, free though t., 151:25
　hath thee in t., 417:7
　to least and vilest things am t.,
　　227:14
Thread, draw as love with t., 235:13
　feels at each t., 148:*n*4
　nothing my own but the t., 147:4
　of his verbosity, 169:5
　our eyes upon double string, 229:14
　spun the t. for wretched mortals,
　　52:26
　strung on English t., 486:3
　that ties them together, 147:4
　touch the utmost t., 148:*n*4
　weave their t. with bones, 202:12
　with a t. plucks it back, 175:14
Threadbare juggler fortune-teller,
　166:34
　saint, 227:17
Threadneedle, Old Lady of T. Street,
　360:5

Threads, silver t. among gold, 557:1
  where to look for t., 727:20
Threaten aggression, 650:9
  and command, 197:30
  life of soul, 648:4
Threatened life with railway share,
  519:24
Threatening, looks with t. eye, 170:6
  tyrant's t. countenance, 96:15
Threatenings and slaughter, 41:4
Threatens, steed t. steed, 185:14
Threats, no terror in your t., 189:16
  of halter, 348:1
Three, after t. days weary of guest,
  309:7
  always t. o'clock, 694:18
  arts with all things, 76:1
  at t. hundred pence ointment prize,
    243:6
  bags full, 788:18
  beings worthy of respect, 494:14
  better t. hours too soon, 182:29
  blind mice, 788:2
  come t. corners of world, 170:24
  fiddlers t., 788:5
  fifths of him genius, 485:8
  for t. years out of key, 659:4
  galloped all t., 465:1
  Gaul divided into t. parts, 88:16
  generations of imbeciles, 543:6
  generations shirtsleeves, 525:16
  god would have t. sides, 304:9
  great elemental sounds, 666:21
  hours a day what man ought to
    write, 476:5
  hour's sleep before midnight worth
    t. after, 245:2
  hundred hours in line, 675:10
  I have t. treasures, 57:22
  in right with two or t., 484:21
  jolly huntsmen, 791:17
  jovial huntsmen, 311:n5
  keep counsel if two away, 142:13
  keep secret if two dead, 309:15
  Latin word for t. farthings, 168:26
  laws of righteousness, 63:2
  lesson of T. Mile Island, 784:13
  little maids from school, 530:22
  long mountains, 683:15
  men in a tub, 791:13
  merry boys are we, 236:5
  no guest welcome after t. days,
    83:14
  not t. good men unhanged, 177:22
  on 's are sophisticated, 210:6
  pecks of barley meal, 792:16
  poets in three ages born, 275:25
  ravens on a tree, 785:14
  removes as bad as fire, 310:9
  rule of t., 776:9
  ships come sailing, 791:14
  silent things, 632:15
  stink in t. days, 83:n11
  stoppeth one of t., 380:26
  these t. alone lead life, 453:24
  things in building, 349:23
  things unfilial, 79:20
  things which are too wonderful,
    23:15
  though he was only t., 648:5

Three *(continued)*
  two live as t., 670:3
  we t. meet again, 212:9
  whine of amateur for t., 523:18
  whole days together, 262:9
  wise men of Gotham, 789:10
  without t. good friends, 191:8
  woodspurge has cup of t., 509:21
  years we waited for herald, 705:14
Three-and-twentieth year, 251:3
Threefold cord not quickly broken,
  23:35
  fourfold tomb, 240:13
Three-fourths, conduct t. of life,
  500:19
Three-personed God, 230:26
Three-piled hyperboles, 169:8
Threescore, of my t. years and ten,
  578:19
  our years are t. and ten, 18:12
  see bachelor of t., 186:13
Threshold high to turn deceit, 563:14
  men that stumble at t., 164:28
  never darken t. of doors, 492:2
  of Jove's Court, 252:11
  of ruined tenement, 312:19
  of waking light, 757:13
  stand upon t. of the new, 250:6
  whining at t., 583:8
Threw down their spears, 358:7
  him down the stairs, 789:18
  pearl away, 208:16
  somebody t. dead dog down ravine,
    727:3
  their caps, 218:24
  warm gules, 415:4
  you in told you rules, 701:16
Thrice and four times blessed, 93:14
  and four times happy, 140:1
  armed that hath quarrel just, 164:1
  deny me t., 37:3
  gorgeous ceremony, 185:19
  he assayed, 256:18
  he slew the slain, 276:11
  to thine and thrice to mine, 212:15
  tried to clasp her image, 53:18
Thrift may follow fawning, 197:2
  thrift Horatio, 193:14
Thrifty, here's to housewife that's t.,
  352:29
  to prepare today, 59:6
Thrill deepest notes of woe, 362:9
  new t., 427:21
  of life along keel, 441:17
  that comes once in lifetime, 660:10
Thrilled, Europe at that time t. with
  joy, 373:11
Thrilling region of ice, 204:14
Thrive, let copulation t., 211:1
  only strong t., 627:1
Throat, Amen stuck in my t., 214:5
  as if my hand at t., 743:6
  brazen t. of war, 260:21
  coat from heel to t., 596:4
  constricted, 692:4
  fishbone in city's t., 743:10
  fog in t. mist in face, 467:18
  heel on t. of my song, 686:22
  lie in your t., 183:14
  moment I cut his t., 753:16

Throat *(continued)*
  out of mocking-bird's t., 490:8
  poem begins as lump in t., 625:6
  put a knife to thy t., 22:16
  seize fate by the t., 371:17
  sweet bird's t., 190:18
  taking life by t., 625:13
  took by t. circumcised dog, 208:17
  unlocked silent t., 777:6
  your sweet dividing t., 246:5
Throats, engines whose rude t., 207:8
Throbbed, war drum t. no longer,
  455:18
Throbbing between two lives, 669:1
  taxi t. waiting, 669:1
Throe, dare never grudge t., 467:8
Throne, Aphrodite on your rich-
  wrought t., 56:4
  barge like burnished t., 217:14
  Death reared t., 451:14
  didst thunder him higher than t.,
    486:22
  died to keep Past upon t., 485:22
  down to Gehenna up to T., 591:7
  ebon t. in rayless majesty, 296:7
  for King George upon t., 366:20
  give t. would be easy, 79:11
  God's footstool may be t., 622:14
  heaven is God's t., 33:6
  heaven to t. in, 219:13
  intellectual t., 498:11
  jealousy of rivals near t., 347:5
  light beats on t., 459:3
  loafing around The T., 536:13
  Lord sitting upon a t., 25:42
  Misfortune made t. seat, 294:2
  name t. in possession, 451:11
  no brother near t., 302:11
  nor tide of pomp, 185:19
  of bayonets, 583:10
  of royal state, 256:23
  on highest t. we sit on our own bot-
    tom, 147:7
  ready to descend t., 370:14
  reason keeps its t., 295:10
  royal t. of kings, 171:9
  something behind t., 313:3
  the living t., 323:4
  through slaughter to t., 322:16
  what is the t., 370:11
  Wrong forever on t., 485:2
Throned, becomes t. monarch better,
  181:19
  in glory, 520:4
  on hundred isles, 400:10
Thrones Dominations Princedoms,
  259:13
  Hell rising from thousand t., 451:17
  not t. and crowns, 393:10
  stakes were t., 404:3
Throng, flung roses with t., 602:8
  into my memory, 252:24
  plaudits of t., 442:21
  thou idol I t., 530:4
Throttle, after kiss comes t., 720:5
Throttled, windpipe t. in fakes of
  death, 489:12
Through, muddle t., 462:8
Through-and-through universe, 547:1

Tilling and grazing feed France, 157:16

　dignity in t. field, 571:33

Tills, man t. field lies beneath, 459:1

Tilly-loo, sang T., 472:5

Tilt at all I meet, 302:20

Tilth vineyard none, 224:4

Tilting at windmills, 149:*n*3

Tilt-yard, charmed alike t. and bower, 396:26

Tim, Tiny T. last of all, 470:10

Timber, crazy as hauling t. into woods, 95:8

　navy would be rotten t., 331:23

　one old t. leg, 613:9

　seasoned t. never gives, 243:12

Timbrel is stilled, 695:22

　praise him with t., 20:16

Timbrels, pipes and t., 416:1

　played before the Lord on t., 12:5

Timbucktoo, rang them while touring T., 760:15

Time, a little t. for laughter, 520:*n*3

　a t. when it was not, 513:2

　abysm of t., 223:21

　Africa marches patiently through t., 719:15

　age and body of the t., 196:23

　almighty t. disquiets, 67:7

　always t. for courtesy, 433:16

　an endless song, 595:4

　and chance happeneth to all, 24:20

　and intents are savage-wild, 176:13

　and Patience strongest of warriors, 510:6

　and the hour, 212:25

　and world ever in flight, 595:6

　annihilate space and t., 300:27

　arrest your flight, 405:7

　Art long T. fleeting, 440:16

　art that tells t. of day, 761:17

　as one born out of t., 43:19

　as t. goes by, 689:15, 689:16

　ask for anything except t., 370:7

　at hands of T. and Chance, 539:15

　at same t. good bad indifferent, 278:9

　author of authors, 158:3

　ay fleeth t., 131:13

　bank and shoal of t., 213:5

　bears away all things, 92:16

　beautiful t. of young love, 365:12

　bid t. return, 171:22

　Bird of T. has little way, 445:6

　book T. criticized for us, 486:6

　books of all t., 487:23

　born out of my due t., 523:7

　bounds of place and t., 323:4

　bridge of T., 494:18

　brief chronicles of the t., 196:2

　but little at a t., 289:21

　cancels young pain, 68:8

　captive of t., 679:18

　cease and midnight never come, 162:22

　chinks that T. has made, 250:6

　chronicle of wasted t., 221:22

　come t. and haste day, 353:8

　comes a t. in every man's life, 680:12

Time (*continued*)

　condemned to kill t., 736:15

　consume strongest cord, 379:10

　convinced of imbecility by t., 314:26

　cools time clarifies, 629:20

　cormorant devouring T., 168:11

　corridors of T., 441:11

　could have had damned good t., 701:13

　cracks in furious flower, 740:11

　creeping hours of t., 190:29

　crumbles things, 77:18

　daughters of T., 430:6

　Death old captain it is t., 494:10

　defy tooth of t., 296:5

　destroyer time preserver, 671:16

　devourer of all things, 101:27

　die for such a long t., 268:27

　died far away before his t., 586:*n*3

　discovers truth, 103:5

　do not squander t., 310:1

　does not relinquish its rights, 349:26

　done his best for his t., 364:23

　don't waste t. mourning, 637:2

　doth transfix flourish, 221:1

　driveth onward fast, 454:9

　duty beyond space and t., 620:19

　eases all things, 65:20

　engenders forgetfulness, 629:9

　enough for sleep, 578:20

　enough for that, 223:17

　entertainer who understood his t., 645:5

　envious and calumniating t., 201:3

　eternity in love with production of t., 357:4

　ever-flowing stream of t., 721:13

　falling oars kept t., 268:25

　feet in ancient t., 359:17

　fire in which we burn, 734:5

　fleet the t. carelessly, 189:30

　flying never to return, 93:5

　fool some people all the t., 451:3

　footprints on sands of t., 440:17

　for a change, 708:4

　for a little something, 648:8

　for all good men, 781:7

　for long t. used to go to bed early, 612:12

　for many words, 53:20

　for sleep, 53:20

　for such a word, 216:14

　for us to leave her, 793:17

　foremost files of t., 455:24

　future in time past, 670:12

　get me to church on t., 745:10

　goes you say, 539:5

　good t. coming, 474:7

　great legalizer, 642:10

　great poet writes his t., 672:16

　grown old before my t., 515:11

　gude t. coming, 379:12

　half as old as T., 367:4

　half as old as t., 473:11

　happiest t. of New Year, 454:4

　has come Walrus said, 519:3

　has no divisions, 629:12

　hath taming hand, 426:17

　hath to silver turned, 156:14

　hath wallet at his back, 200:23

Time (*continued*)

　haven't t. to take our t., 731:16

　healing a matter of t., 71:3

　heals all wounds, 85:*n*15

　held me green and dying, 737:19

　his t. is forever, 267:3

　history the witness to passing t., 87:14

　history triumphed over t., 152:19

　hold fast the t., 630:1

　holy t. quiet as nun, 374:15

　hot t. in old town, 589:2

　how long a t. in one word, 170:30

　hurry up please its t., 668:22

　I am mighty world-destroying T., 84:13

　I had lived a blessed t., 214:15

　idea whose t. come, 427:18

　image of eternity, 112:1

　in a moment of t., 38:9

　in hours days years, 270:7

　irreparable ravages of t., 281:13

　is a very shadow, 30:20

　is dead, 696:11

　is elastic, 612:17

　is Lethe, 629:9

　is man's angel, 365:6

　is money, 310:12, 427:*n*1

　is of essence, 781:19

　is on our side, 446:13

　is out of joint, 195:6

　is still a-flying, 241:9

　is that wherein is opportunity, 71:4

　it is t. to choose, 639:14

　it's only a matter of t., 774:11

　joyous t. not be stayed, 154:11

　keeping t., 670:21

　kill t. injuring eternity, 477:31

　killing t. essence of comedy, 589:18

　lack t. to make it short, 270:14

　laid hand on my heart, 442:17

　last syllable of recorded t., 216:14

　last t. I see Paris, 681:12

　least thing we have of, 702:8

　let me play, 737:16

　life and spirit of t., 503:5

　like ever-rolling stream, 294:16

　like fashionable host, 201:2

　liked by some people some of t., 727:8

　lilac t., 643:10

　little town that t. forgot, 772:6

　long t. between drinks, 562:4

　lost t. never found, 310:2

　lucky to be alive at great t., 700:9

　machine, 601:6

　made me his numbering clock, 172:15

　makes possible Day of Judgment, 652:1

　makes these decay, 246:9

　man knoweth not his t., 24:20

　maniac scattering dust, 457:14

　market of his t., 198:12

　memory emancipated from t., 384:8

　misspending t. a kind of self-homicide, 279:30

　mock t. with fairest show, 213:15

　moment of t. fleeting by, 537:22

　most valuable thing, 81:21

Time (*continued*)
youth the t. for toil, 75:20
Timed, gifts well t., 283:12
Time-honored bread sauce, 548:19
Timeless, pattern of t. moments, 672:5
Timely, desired and t. things, 579:22
dew of sleep, 258:20
gain t. inn, 215:1
Timeo Danaos et dona ferentis, 93:*n*14
Time-pleaser, anything constantly but a t., 202:6
Time's fell hand, 221:2
flies, 212:4
glory calm contending kings, 167:2
life t. fool, 179:5
love's not T. fool, 222:2
noblest offspring, 296:27
winged chariot, 268:15
Times, all classes t. circumstances, 474:21
all old t. good, 404:2
all t. are his seasons, 231:10
are in his hand, 467:6
at all the t. you can, 309:2
at t. almost ridiculous, 667:17
background of the t., 364:17
before you, 248:25
best of t. worst of t., 471:11
brisk and giddy-paced t., 202:8
change and move continually, 154:3
change and we change with them, 119:33
cowards die many t., 188:11
fashion of these t., 190:13
glory of their t., 32:14
go by turns, 160:18
good old t. when unhappy, 786:17
hard and wages low, 793:17
hard money scarce, 433:12
illusion that t. were better, 462:13
in the morning of the t., 158:*n*3
in which a genius would live, 347:8
later t. more aged than earlier, 158:*n*3
lived for all t., 364:23
my t. are in thy hand, 16:27
necessity of the t., 325:4
O what fine t., 305:23
of great Elizabeth, 454:12
oh the t. the customs, 87:7
old simplicity of t., 779:4
old t. manners books, 329:25
old t. not forgotten, 475:1
past t. preserve themselves, 693:5
people in old t. had convictions, 420:8
purest treasure mortal t. afford, 170:25
pursy t., 198:4
signs of the t., 35:26
sun itself which makes t., 229:5
terrible t., 564:6
that try men's souls, 340:22
these t. are ancient t., 158:5
these unhappy t., 648:14
they are a-changin', 771:7
thus t. do shift, 241:13
tide of t., 188:22
till time and t. done, 595:7

Times (*continued*)
truth which cunning t. put on, 181:6
truths not for all t., 306:13
wild dark t. rumbling toward us, 420:9
Times', my dear t. waste, 220:18
Timetable, read t. than nothing, 626:21
set t. for another's freedom, 760:16
Timid Soul, 660:9
State t. as lone woman, 477:14
Timing, circumstance and proper t., 74:4
is most important factor, 55:1
Timon, till I am T. and Lear, 599:11
Timor Mortis conturbat me, 136:4
nil terribile nisi ipse t., 158:*n*5
Timorous beastie, 361:4
foe, 302:31
Timothy learnt sin to fly, 287:10
O T. keep thy trust, 45:25
Tim'rous beastie, 361:4
Tin, cat on hot t. roof, 272:*n*4
cat on t. roof, 731:1
cheap t. trays, 634:1
in t. factory human being crushed, 735:10
Little T. Gods, 590:18
screeches like torn t., 762:18
Tincture, best virtue has t. of vice, 146:12
Tinged by what absorbs it, 546:20
eyelids and hands, 538:6
Tinhorn politicians, 606:6
Tinker more than renew, 546:20
to Evers to Chance, 644:5
Tinkled among teacups, 668:2
Tinkling with their feet, 25:35
Tinklings, drowsy t. lull, 322:2
Tintinnabulation musically wells, 453:11
Tiny, little t. boy, 203:7
little t. wit, 210:1
round bole in t. leaf, 465:3
Tim last of all, 470:10
violetflavored nuisance, 688:14
Tip, star within nether t., 381:16
Tiphys disclose new worlds, 103:13
Tippecanoe and Tyler too, 385:*n*2
iron-armed soldier of T., 385:*n*2
Tipped with line of steel, 492:8
Tippenny, wi' t. fear nae evil, 363:7
Tipperary, long way to T., 627:15
Tippled drink more fine, 416:12
Tippler, little T. leaning, 511:18
Tips with silver fruit-tree tops, 175:7
Tipsy dance and jollity, 252:20
Tiptoe on misty mountaintops, 176:6
religion stands on t., 244:3
stand a t. when day named, 185:22
thru' the tulips with me, 681:1
Tirade, your old-fashioned t., 743:4
Tire day in toil, 242:7
ear the open vowels t., 298:18
night in thought, 242:7
of all creation, 447:13
speeds too fast 'twill t., 168:24
Tired, became t. and sick, 490:9
dull stale t. bed, 208:29

Tired (*continued*)
eyelids upon tired eyes, 454:6
give me your t. your poor, 558:1
he was so t., 582:17
nature's sweet restorer, 296:6
of his dark dominion, 509:7
of honest things, 684:10
of kings, 430:1
of London tired of life, 317:2
of Love, 609:6
of my turmoil, 743:9
of ruling over slaves, 318:21
of tears and laughter, 534:13
of words, 763:12
on day of victory no one t., 118:6
Sister Caroline t., 612:9
stummucks don't git t., 556:11
sun with talking, 502:9
till t. he sleeps, 301:15
today's newspaper t., 618:2
we were very t., 684:3
with all these, 221:4
Tirelessly, unreeling t. speeding them, 491:8
Tirer les marrons du feu, 268:*n*7
Tires, sad t. in a mile-a, 223:4
unchartered freedom t., 376:4
Tiresias, I T. though blind, 669:1
Tiresome verse-reciter Care, 409:22
Tirlin' at the window, 461:12
Tirra lirra by the river, 454:15
Tit for tat, 142:12
tell tale t., 788:13
Titan, like thy glory T., 407:6
Titania, ill met by moonlight proud T., 173:3
there sleeps T., 173:9
Titanic, alley T., 453:3
Tithe of mint and anise, 36:3
Title and profit I resign, 292:*n*4
excels at t. page, 328:1
farced t. 'fore king, 185:19
feel his t. hang loose, 216:6
gained no t., 300:24
no t. I deem more honorable, 646:14
pseudo-promotion a new t., 747:7
read my t. clear, 294:18
Titles are shadows, 285:19
gratuities privileges, 369:11
high though his t., 378:1
kinquering Congs t. take, 553:22
of mining claims, 698:6
power and pelf, 378:1
such as Indispensable Unique, 587:7
Tits, no t. to pull no hay to pitch, 784:4
Titter w'en stew smokin' hot, 615:2
Tittle, jot or t., 33:4
Tittlemouse, Tommy T., 792:12
Titwillow, willow t., 531:9
Tityrus, once sang of you T., 93:9
To, going t. and fro in earth, 13:29
many shall run t. and fro, 29:21
reel t. and fro, 19:11
the unknown god, 41:15
Toad beneath harrow knows, 590:19
curse this pois'nous bunch-backed t., 165:26
give me your arm old t., 750:12

Toad (*continued*)
I had rather be a t., 207:4
intelligent Mr. T., 578:17
like t. at ear of Eve, 258:27
like t. ugly and venomous, 190:7
preaches contentment to t., 590:19
why should I let t. work, 750:10
worm to a t., 544:16
Toads brooding in wells, 724:17
imaginary gardens with real t., 664:7
Toast attributed to one of naval heroes, 368:14
let the t. pass, 352:29
Toasted, dreamed of t. cheese, 561:5
Toasts of the young men, 348:14
Tobacco crumbs vases fringes, 740:7
devilish and damned t., 235:10
divine rare, 235:10
for thy sake T., 388:4
is a filthy weed, 354:10
nothing compared with t., 404:n4
Road, 710:14
sublime t., 404:5
this night leave off t., 387:20
Tobacco's fragrance greet, 750:3
Toby, my uncle T., 320:22
Toccatas, sat and played t., 466:13
Today a king, 31:23
and yet is here t., 228:20
be good and happy t., 380:23
be wise t., 296:10
beneath foeman's frown, 461:1
call t. his own, 274:29
describe world of t., 698:19
first day of rest of life, 784:8
flower that smiles t., 241:9
future lays law of t., 552:1
give me t. take tomorrow, 118:4
he puts forth tender leaves, 225:16
here t. gone tomorrow, 281:20
I have dined t., 380:18
I have lived t., 274:29
in t. walks tomorrow, 389:n1
isn't any other day, 519:9
live t., 106:8
lose ground won t., 498:10
made heart cry T. t. like child's, 616:11
Mother died t., 732:12
never do t. what you can put off, 503:11
never jam t., 519:9
nor care beyond t., 321:15
not have any Dickens t., 712:4
nothing else show T., 512:19
our pleasure to be drunk, 311:10
pay you Tuesday for hamburger t., 690:3
same yesterday t. and forever, 46:1
shalt thou be with me, 39:21
speed t. put back tomorrow, 154:5
such a day tomorrow as t., 222:16
thrifty to prepare t., 59:6
Today's t., 68:3
tomorrow is not until t. past, 67:3
voice of t., 590:14
wasn't there again t., 630:2
we have naming of parts, 737:3
weep no more t., 507:2

Today (*continued*)
what he is doing t., 431:16
what you can do t., 503:n2
wiser t. than yesterday, 303:21
Today's newspaper old, 618:2
today, 68:3
Toddle safely home, 662:6
Toe, eye of newt t. of frog, 215:14
fill me from crown to t., 212:29
light fantastic t., 251:9
of peasant, 199:7
Toes, bells on her t., 790:3
frozen t., 608:6
Pobble who has no t., 472:14
Pobbles happier without t., 472:15
pretty little t., 790:15
teaches on t., 697:8
turn out your t., 518:20
Toga, let arms yield to t., 88:2
scrolls of her t., 764:14
Together achieve victory, 678:16
articulate sweet sounds t., 595:14
bring us t. again, 733:13
damned good time t., 701:13
evils draw men t., 78:29
for brethren to dwell t., 20:5
gathered t. in my name, 35:33
gathered t. on public square, 587:9
getting on t., 646:4
good fellows get t., 589:3
hang t. or hang separately, 310:18
let us reason t., 25:29, 723:14
pull all t., 470:35
ride t. forever, 465:21
time place loved one t., 468:14
took sweet counsel t., 17:27
vow an eternal misery t., 284:16
we gather t., 777:8
we'll pluck crow t., 166:27
Togetherness, spaces in t., 651:12
Toil and not seek rest, 139:3
and trouble cauldron bubble, 215:13
blood t. tears sweat, 620:5
consumed midnight oil, 297:6
envy want, 313:17
exercises sinews and bones with t., 80:3
govern those that t., 328:15
her strong t. of grace, 218:22
horny hands of t., 484:19
hunger nakedness, 419:8
mock their useful t., 322:7
not neither spin, 33:20
of breath, 385:5
of growing up, 598:4
sleep after t., 153:9
slumber more sweet than t., 454:11
sons of t., 503:4
tire the day in t., 242:7
unrequited t., 450:11
waste their t., 377:26
youth the time for extraordinary t., 75:20
zealous nameless t., 423:20
Toiled, forgot for which he t., 220:14
so hard and late, 597:16
Toils, backward goes who t. most, 126:12
despair to reach, 288:1

Toils (*continued*)
easier to get into enemy's t., 59:18
pleasures and t., 379:24
sore stiff with t., 491:5
Toilsome way into upper air, 419:7
Toilsomely, can we follow t., 641:9
Token of a covenant, 7:24
Tokens, show him of Our t., 116:15
Told, as a tale that is t., 18:11
but he never t. anybody, 593:12
hath it not been t. you, 27:22
I t. her all my heart, 357:17
I t. my love, 357:17
I t. you so, 403:19, 442:15
I would have t. you, 40:26
if t. to get up so white person sit, 734:2
love that never t. can be, 357:17
me Heraclitus, 502:9
my wrath, 358:12
never t. her love, 202:14
tale speeds best plainly t., 166:7
tale t. by an idiot, 216:14
tales already plainly t., 53:27
Toledo trusty, 263:9
Tolerable, fire most t. third party, 477:2
Tolerance, Platonic t. vain, 597:18
practice t., 655:23
work for t. for justice, 674:19
Tolerant, understand everything makes t., 368:12
Tolerate, not afraid to t. error, 345:1
Tolerated, error of opinion t., 344:5
not only t. but encouraged, 385:13
Toleration, learned t. from intolerant, 651:15
Toll for the brave, 335:17
greater t. on health of country, 748:18
me back from thee, 415:18
oppress of T., 514:2
Tolle lege tolle lege, 114:n12
Tolled, sexton t. bell, 422:18
Tolls, curfew t. knell, 322:1
faintly t. evening chime, 391:8
for whom the bell t., 231:8
it t. for thee, 231:8
Tom appeared on sidewalk, 526:2
bears logs into the hall, 169:13
before I go T. Moore, 401:27
Fool's errand, 320:11
little T. Tucker, 789:7
loves me best that calls me T., 233:21
o' Bedlam, 209:4
O T. Thumb, 175:n1
poor T. Bowling, 348:3
Tom piper's son, 790:4
Tom Jones, more knowledge of heart than in all T., 316:13
will outlive Escurial, 340:9
Tomb, Achilles' t., 403:4
adjusted in the T., 512:13
by sounding sea, 453:10
distant shadow of t., 508:27
earth t. of rest, 634:14
e'en from t. nature cries, 322:20
icy silence of t., 417:3
man t. for other animals, 134:15

Tongues (*continued*)
  not uttered by chapmen's t., 168:22
  of Douglas and myself, 448:11
  of dying men, 171:5
  of fire, 40:45
  of flame infolded, 672:7
  of men and angels, 43:13
  one soul though many t., 112:6
  self-interest speaks all t., 265:4
  sharpened their t. like a serpent,
    20:11
  silence envious t., 225:21
  silver-sweet sound lovers' t., 175:13
  slanderous t., 187:14
  speak with other t., 40:45
  strange t. are loud, 528:16
  that syllable men's names, 252:24
  whispering t. can poison truth,
    382:15
  woods have t., 130:*n*3
Tongue-tied by authority, 221:5
Tonight, child again just for t., 516:13
  curfew not ring t., 562:11
  from Oxford strays, 499:15
  hot time in old town t., 589:2
  met in thee t., 524:9
  refrain t., 198:6
  tenting t. on campground, 523:1
  tonight won't be just any night,
    763:5
  world may end t., 465:19
Tonnage, damp t., 701:5
Tonsorial or agglutinative type,
    609:11
Tonstant Weader Fwowed up, 687:12
Took all heart for speech, 596:9
  all which I t. from thee, 581:9
  by throat circumcised dog, 208:17
  great care of his Mother, 648:5
  not men you t. them for, 186:37
  one Draught of Life, 514:12
  one less traveled by, 623:7
  seen my opportunities and t. 'em,
    548:2
  suffering human race, 497:16
  to my heels, 86:11
  to the law, 517:10
  wages and are dead, 580:1
  went and t. same as me, 592:11
Tool carries spirit, 707:3
  grows keener with use, 396:4
  maker, 634:4
  nor any t. of iron, 12:23
Too-late, also called T., 509:26
Tools, give us the t., 620:15
  no jesting with edge t., 236:11
  sin has many t., 447:12
  teach but to name t., 262:22
  to make tools, 577:4
  with t. he is all, 411:23
Tool-using animal, 411:23
Tooth, defy t. of time, 296:5
  for tooth, 9:15
  hadde alwey coltes t., 131:7
  more deadly than mad dog's t.,
    166:32
  my Adonis hath a sweet t., 155:17
  of time, 205:2
  one t. and it aching, 613:9
  poison for age's t., 169:17

Tooth (*continued*)
  purrs and never shows t., 660:20
  red in t. and claw, 457:21
  sharper than serpent's t., 209:11
  sinks into throat tiger's t., 679:9
  where each t. point goes, 590:19
Toothache, philosopher endure t.,
    187:9
Toothpaste and dandruff ads, 701:7
Toothsomest, old pippins t., 237:11
Tootings at weddings of soul, 639:12
Top, die at the t., 290:21
  fool me to t. of my bent, 197:19
  o' the mornin', 555:16
  of head taken off, 514:19
  of sovereignty, 416:21
  Revolution began at t., 503:8
  special few at very t., 764:5
  struggle to reach t., 732:15
  you're the t., 682:3
Top-hat, famous high t., 637:11
Topics, only two serious t., 600:4
  other fashionable t., 328:24
  two t. yourself and me, 316:31
  while serious t. disputing, 423:14
Topless towers of Ilium, 162:19
Toppling, send skyscrapers t., 726:1
Tops, tips with silver fruit-tree t.,
    175:7
[Topsy] 'spect growed, 463:2
Torah, whole T. rest is commentary,
    102:7
Torch, bright t. and casement, 416:9
  give me a t., 658:1
  like runners pass on t. of life, 89:16
  of a flower, 658:1
  passed to new generation, 741:3
  throw t. hold it high, 615:8
  truth is t., 321:5
Torchbearing outrider, 548:17
Torches of martyrdom, 344:12
Torchlight crimson on kettledrums,
    619:2
Tore, shout t. hell's concave, 256:13
Torment, dark with t. and tears,
    479:29
  delicious t., 431:34
  I feel it and am in t., 91:16
  is my joy, 725:17
  man comes with his t., 365:19
  measure of our t., 592:4
  of love unsatisfied, 669:15
  there shall no t. touch them, 30:23
  what t. not a marriage bed, 231:9
  who devised the t., 672:4
Tormented with ten thousand hells,
    162:15
Tormenting, cant of criticism most t.,
    320:23
Torments in wedding ring, 291:25
  most maddens and t., 486:25
Torn and beaten out he lies, 410:8
  between passion for righteousness,
    665:9
  by dreams, 639:19
  Naiad from flood, 451:10
  persons with t. bodies happy, 611:2
  screeches like t. tin, 762:18
  seine shattered lobsterpot, 671:13
  wings frayed soiled and t., 535:3

Torpedoes, damn the t., 426:16
Torpid, mind t. in old age, 317:3
Torquatus stretching his baby hands,
    91:6
Torrent, character formed in world's
    t., 349:20
  in the very t. tempest, 196:21
  of his fate, 313:22
  rough t. of occasion, 184:6
  wind t. of darkness, 643:11
Torrent's, voices of dead like t. fall,
    403:1
Torrents, blood in t. pour, 573:23
Torrid or frozen zone, 246:7
Tortoise because he taught us, 518:2
  hare and t., 58:19
  prince keeps t. enclosed, 80:17
Tortuous road from Montgomery,
    761:5
Torture, hum of cities t., 400:4
  no rack T. me, 512:8
  object of t. is t., 711:18
  one poor word, 274:27
  one tiny creature, 495:9
  suspense in news is t., 261:24
  touch him not t. not again, 409:4
Tortured, millions of innocent t.,
    343:8
  with history, 701:5
Torturing hour, 321:18
Toss in the spray, 497:6
  tut tut good enough to t., 178:26
  weariness t. him to my breast,
    243:20
Tossed, I am t. up and down, 19:12
  old woman t. in blanket, 790:16
  the dog, 792:24
  them human hearts, 408:1
Tosses but doesn't sink, 119:5
  up our losses, 671:13
Tossing aloft invisible, 572:21
  crossing Channel t., 530:15
  green water, 654:2
  heads in sprightly dance, 375:21
  mind is t. on the ocean, 179:13
  sea of Cause and Theory, 619:10
  so as to scare clouds, 623:10
Total grandeur of total edifice, 640:7
  irrecoverably dark t. eclipse, 261:7
Totalitarianism threaten free nations,
    733:16
Totality of what he might have,
    717:13
Toto I've feeling not in Kansas any-
    more, 730:1
Tots sang Ring-a-rosie, 585:7
Totter into vogue, 323:22
Touch, approach t. me t. palm of
    hand, 490:2
  at t. I yield, 456:19
  common t., 593:20
  fear not to t. the best, 152:15
  furs to t., 663:2
  great death, 611:5
  Happy Isles, 455:6
  harps of gold, 462:2
  have to have t. of iron, 756:2
  he wants the natural t., 215:25
  hills whose heads t. heaven, 205:26
  it and do not find, 57:4

Trapeze, daring young man on t., 536:20

Trappings, these but t. of woe, 193:3

Traps, be fox to recognize t., 136:15
  not fall into same t. twice, 113:23
  snares t. gins pitfalls, 463:*n*1

Trash, money is t., 228:1
  steals my purse steals t., 206:30

Traurig, dass ich so t. bin, 419:*n*7

Travail and vexation of spirit, 23:34
  great t. so gladly spent, 143:5
  le t. éloigne de nous trois grands maux, 306:*n*6
  my labor for my t., 200:3
  myn the t. thyn the glorie, 130:20

Travailed, thou shalt not be t., 128:1

Travaileth, groaneth and t., 42:3

Travel, dangerous to t. to known places, 240:9
  faster than stagecoach, 329:24
  first-class and with children, 675:13
  for travel's sake, 560:13
  from Dan to Beersheba, 320:34
  hopefully better than arrive, 560:22
  light, 722:1
  never t. without diary, 567:10
  not to go anywhere, 560:13
  on life's common way, 374:20
  part of education, 159:20
  prayers to preserve t., 290:15
  road to Hades easy to t., 82:8
  thought the t. long, 163:4
  to home among dead, 408:13
  to school not to t., 159:20
  wherever I t. Greece wounds me, 705:19
  youth who from east t., 375:8

Traveled a good deal in Concord, 477:29
  among unknown men, 374:6
  backward glances over t. road, 491:17
  I t. each and ev'ry highway, 770:17
  much have I t., 413:24
  short while towards sun, 727:10
  somewhere i have never t., 688:20
  took one less t. by, 623:7
  whoe'er has t., 316:*n*8

Traveler, a t. came by, 357:17
  anybody there said T., 616:22
  farewell Monsieur T., 191:28
  from antique land, 406:13
  from cradle to grave, 407:5
  from New Zealand, 425:7
  has right to embellish, 341:14
  hour pierces new t. with love, 126:11
  no t. returns, 196:10
  spurs lated t. apace, 215:1
  swiftest t. afoot, 478:8
  world-besotted t., 598:9

Travelers, fellow t. of Revolution, 641:2
  must be content, 190:14
  of eternity, 282:11

Traveleth before he hath language, 159:20
  poverty come as one that t., 20:28

Traveling all same pace, 446:10
  consider my t. expenses, 686:20

Traveling (*continued*)
  in t. carry knowledge, 317:8
  through dense forest, 656:8
  to regulate imagination, 315:7
  without fatigue of t., 150:25

Travels, commence t. in Mississippi steamboat, 393:9
  fastest travels alone, 591:7
  in strait so narrow, 201:1
  like him that t., 221:25
  sundry contemplation of t., 191:26
  time t. in divers paces, 191:18
  world search of needs, 563:13

Traverse, this T. poorest take, 514:2

Tray Blanch and Sweetheart, 210:14
  dog T., 388:25

Trays, cheap tin t., 634:1

Treacherous, dog never t., 515:17
  experiment t., 71:13
  generals, 714:3
  world's God is t., 663:12

Treachers by spherical predominance, 209:3

Treachery is all their trust, 402:20
  machinations hollowness t., 209:2
  wedlock-t., 261:20

Treacle, fly that sips t., 297:19

Tread, close behind him t., 381:26
  Death with impartial t., 95:18
  don't t. on me, 779:2
  each other's heel, 198:*n*5
  endless road you t., 579:14
  ever so airy t., 458:24
  far-off shore where he would t., 164:21
  hungry generations t., 415:17
  I with mournful t., 491:1
  lightly she is near, 566:5
  men t. underfoot what feared, 90:10
  on classic ground, 291:29
  poor beetle we t. upon, 204:11
  shine by side of path we t., 335:16
  softly t. on dreams, 595:9
  them in mine anger, 28:7
  thou shalt t. upon the lion, 18:16
  upon another's heel, 198:*n*5
  upon brink of meaning, 314:20
  upon my patience, 177:1
  where angels fear to t., 299:6
  where'er we t. haunted, 399:16
  where'er you t., 298:7
  years like oxen t. world, 594:19

Treadeth, not muzzle ox when t. corn, 10:21
  winepress of wrath, 47:35

Treading course of virtue, 61:33
  on my tail, 518:5

Treadmill, set you on a t., 774:6

Treads, one who t. alone, 392:8
  primrose path of dalliance t., 193:27
  she t. on it so light, 165:17

Treason against the United States, 346:9
  bloody t. flourished, 189:7
  bribery or other high crimes, 346:8
  but trusted like fox, 179:1
  can but peep, 198:22
  corporations cannot commit t., 152:5
  cried the Speaker, 339:5

Treason (*continued*)
  doth never prosper, 160:16
  ever less than t., 622:18
  gunpowder t. and plot, 777:20
  has done his worst, 214:26
  hate traitors and t. love, 275:22
  if this be t., 339:5
  last temptation greatest t., 670:10
  love bitter with t., 534:4
  love t. but hate traitor, 88:18
  none dare call it t., 160:16
  of the intellectuals, 601:19
  past traitor no longer needed, 247:9
  sows secret seeds, 123:5

Treasons stratagems and spoils, 182:10

Treasure, buried t., 548:20
  chiefest t., 608:16
  considers impartiality as his t., 86:7
  danger or t., 747:13
  good man's t., 57:19
  great t. and trouble, 21:26
  hath found a t., 31:15
  heaps of miser's t., 253:1
  purest t. mortal times afford, 170:25
  rich the t., 276:10
  thou shalt have t., 35:36
  where your t. is, 33:14
  witty woman a t., 509:11

Treasured, embalmed and t. up, 254:24

Treasures, bee's collected t., 323:15
  heart has hidden t., 476:11
  I have three t., 57:22
  lay not up t., 33:13
  lay up t. in heaven, 33:13
  sea-born t., 429:8
  see t. that prevail, 762:9

Treasury, our heart is a t., 422:10

Treat as dogs do the Nile, 102:*n*7
  friend as if he might become enemy, 99:20
  killing t. for Ossete, 681:8
  nature in terms of cylinder, 537:21
  two impostors same, 593:19
  you'd t. if met where bar, 540:12

Treated as wish to be treated, 742:2
  I t. him God cured him, 143:10

Treaties under authority of U.S., 346:10

Treatise, at dismal t. rouse, 216:13
  my T. of Human Nature, 318:16
  of natural education, 319:16

Treatment, dark world present t., 605:5
  extreme diseases extreme strictness of t., 71:14
  of Negro greatest scandal, 700:6
  stomach endure rough t., 103:3
  use t. to help sick, 71:1

Treaty, if t. serves ten years, 590:9
  what t. white man kept, 516:9

Treble, childish t., 191:3

Tree, against blue a pine t., 285:10
  almond t. shall flourish, 24:28
  apple t. among the trees, 25:4
  as twig bent t. inclined, 300:12
  at my window, 624:1
  beneath the tamarind t., 451:10

Tree (*continued*)

billboard lovely as t., 709:10
boughs off many a t., 243:8
but I must climb the t., 243:7
cannot grow in sky, 90:2
cinnamon t., 711:2
coolibah t., 589:5
Crumpetty T., 472:8
cut cherry t., 336:*n*7
dead t. no shelter, 668:18
dew bespangling herb and t., 241:17
do these things in green t., 39:17
down to calico t., 472:5
easy as leaves grow on t., 594:17
elm t. bole, 465:3
fleet of life like t. leaves, 73:12
forbidden t. whose mortal taste,
   255:18
friendship a sheltering t., 383:13
give me my hollow t., 302:24
give to eat of the t. of life, 47:8
go to pear t. for pears, 100:8
golden t. of life, 350:15
good word like good t., 116:13
growing when ye're sleeping, 379:14
grows in Brooklyn, 715:13
had a peach from the t., 357:18
hang harp on willow-t., 781:1
hang there till t. die, 220:6
hate the t., 114:31
I shall be like t., 290:21
if t. dies plant another, 312:12
is hewn down, 32:32
is known by fruit, 35:2
keep green t. in heart., 118:5
keep way of the t. of life, 7:1
last leaf upon t., 447:20
Liberty T., 340:17
lighted from a blessed t., 117:4
like a t. planted by rivers, 15:29
like t. grown in meadow, 5:13
like t. standing by water, 794:23
little nut t., 790:12
lopped t. may grow again, 65:*n*6
loved t. or flower, 392:13
man plants t. for posterity, 85:*n*6
never see t. at all, 709:10
not too far from yew t., 671:19
O chestnut t., 598:2
of Knowledge is not that of life,
   402:2
of knowledge of good and evil, 6:14
of liberty refreshed, 343:15
of liberty watered by blood, 354:11
of life, 6:13
of Life, 258:7
of man never quiet, 579:7
old apple t., 627:16
on a t. by a river, 531:9
only God can make it, 662:1
planted by the waters, 28:29
poem lovely as a t., 661:16
poisonous minerals and that t.,
   230:21
presents upon a T., 513:16
riding by Eildon T., 785:11
righteous like palm t., 18:17
shady cypress t., 515:7
she gave me of the t., 6:22
sighing by a sycamore t., 208:4

Tree (*continued*)

snow from hemlock t., 623:15
some call it T. of Heaven, 715:13
spreading chestnut t., 441:3
spreading himself like a green bay
   t., 17:2
swimming from t. to t., 742:12
tall slim t., 708:14
this t. continues to be, 673:5
thou t. I flower, 530:4
under the bamboo t., 670:3
under the gallows t., 236:5
under the greenwood t., 190:18
which did not know, 267:6
will continue to be, 673:*n*1
window t., 624:1
with ease from t. to t., 295:17
woodman spare beechen t., 389:8
woodman spare that t., 428:10
wrath-bearing t., 668:8
you have grown to be a mighty t.,
   361:3
Zaccheus climb t., 287:12
Tree's, as twig bent t. inclined, 300:12
Trees, all the t. green, 484:15
amidst tall ancestral t., 410:10
among gusty t., 643:11
and all nature, 787:1
and fields tell nothing, 301:*n*5
and stones will teach you, 121:8
Arabian t. their med'cinable gum,
   208:16
axe laid unto root of the t., 32:32
birds are asleep in t., 351:2
birds in the t., 597:7
blasts roots of t., 737:8
blue promontory with t., 218:3
bosomed high in tufted t., 251:14
cannot see wood for t., 142:10
cross river rest under t., 504:10
Dryad of the t., 415:10
grow up again quickly, 65:7
grown strong with forest t., 537:16
he that plants t. loves others, 85:*n*6
herbs and t. flourish in May, 133:11
herbs are sprouting, 5:5
hurt not the t., 47:21
I cut down t. skip and jump, 775:6
if t. in earth were pens, 117:10
known to speak, 215:10
land of vines and fig t., 10:16
lemon t. bloom, 349:8
loveliest of t., 578:18
maddens me, 666:23
men as t. walking, 37:29
more resigned, 616:6
my apple t. never eat cones, 622:21
of all t. that grow so fair, 593:17
Orpheus with lute made t., 225:10
procreate like t., 248:19
rocks and stones and t., 374:1
roots of t. and stones, 660:16
seemed to march seaward, 557:15
set about with fever-t., 593:9
shall be my books, 191:5
sunsets and tops of t., 730:12
that would march, 637:13
to benefit another generation, 85:9
tongues in t., 190:7
turn bare, 757:15

Trees (*continued*)

uptorn, 414:6
vines and olive t., 721:2
walked among ancient t., 357:25
what t. tell us we are, 757:17
when t. bow down heads, 515:12
where you sit, 298:7
wind in t. a sad thing, 92:7
wind is in palm t., 591:22
you lover of t., 465:11
Treetop, baby on t., 555:4
Treetops, in all t. hardly a breath,
   351:2
Trelawny, shall T. die, 433:31
Tremble, afraid because we t., 546:4
at word of Lord, 271:14
enemies of blacks t., 437:13
I t. for my country, 343:9
into thought, 380:25
keepers of the house shall t., 24:27
let men t. to win woman, 435:29
let Sporus t., 302:14
like guilty thing surprised, 375:11
made the earth to t., 26:15
my firm nerves never t., 215:7
poplars stand and t., 579:11
Quakers because we bid them t.,
   271:14
sail-yards t. masts crack, 157:13
under her feet, 458:24
while they gaze, 323:4
Trembled, Tiber t. underneath banks,
   187:17
Trembler, no t. in world's sphere,
   480:4
Tremblers, boding t., 329:17
Trembles before your glory, 66:18
in the breast, 377:18
to be so understood, 640:5
Trembling cold in ghastly fears,
   357:17
cup of t., 27:31
fear came upon me and t., 13:38
for you in voices, 587:12
hare limped t., 414:21
hoping lingering, 299:8
in t. hope repose, 322:24
seizes me all over, 56:5
work out salvation with fear and t.,
   44:30
Tremendous object of creation, 330:3
Tremulous cadence slow, 499:20
Trench confessions, 659:9
Trenchant blade Toledo trusty, 263:9
Trencher, dead Caesar's t., 217:27
Trencher-friends, 212:4
Trencherman, valiant t., 186:8
Trenches in beauty's field, 220:8
Treo, handed all sails and set t., 134:8
Trespass, those who t. against us,
   33:*n*3
Trespasses against duty, 331:2
forgive us all our t., 650:11
forgive us our t., 33:*n*3
Tresses, fair t. race ensnare, 299:12
like the morn, 253:10
withered cheek t. gray, 377:19
Trial, always on t. for political lives,
   677:2
and error, 568:18

Troika, Rus similar to nimble t., 446:27
  winged t. who invented you, 446:27
Troilus mounted Troyan walls, 182:7
Trojan gestes as they felle, 128:11
  no distinction between T. and Tyrian, 93:22
Trojans, no reason to blame T., 51:14
  we have been T., 93:32
  were sitting on the tower, 51:13
Trollops, my thoughts my t., 319:29
Trône, au plus élevé t. assis sur notre cul, 147:*n*5
Troop, farewell plumed t., 207:8
  foreign t. in my country, 313:6
Troops, charged t. of error, 248:1
  hoist colors to peak, 642:3
  led by the Czar, 781:4
  of Allied Expeditionary Force, 678:16
  of friends, 216:9
  pass through seek gold, 502:5
  take command of t., 370:12
  what t. he considered best, 371:1
  wherever enemy goes our t. go, 501:11
Trope, out flew a t., 262:21
Tropes, ranged his t., 287:21
Trophies, among cloudy t. hung, 416:18
  and dead things, 237:20
  these are the arks the t., 161:2
  unto enemies of truth, 248:1
Tropic for your balm, 690:4
Tropics Zones and Meridian Lines, 519:20
Trot, riseth late t. all day, 309:27
Troth, I wonder by my t., 228:2
Trots, who Time t. withal, 191:18
Trouble, a very present help in t., 17:16
  and turmoil over, 515:13
  being Jewish t. enough, 738:7
  comforting thought when not our t., 633:10
  days begin with t., 287:13
  deaf heaven, 220:15
  dishonor will not t. me, 68:2
  genius capacity for taking t., 311:*n*3
  genius capacity of taking t., 413:15
  great treasure and t., 21:26
  here where all t. seems, 534:12
  in t. and in joy, 285:3
  life is t. Zorba continued, 652:3
  man is born unto t., 14:2
  my presence that doth t. ye, 163:18
  nobody knows t. I've seen, 794:9
  not bring t. to people, 716:8
  of few days and full of t., 14:20
  smooth away t., 663:2
  take utmost t., 570:2
  time of is not our t., 633:10
  toil and t. cauldron bubble, 215:13
  undo belt look for t., 652:3
  went to t. to be born, 336:8
  with a capital T, 710:11
  with kitten, 709:13
  with peace is no organization, 698:18
  words weighty with t., 644:5

Trouble (*continued*)
  ya got t. folks, 710:11
Troubled air, 256:*n*1
  be not t., 36:7
  bridge over t. water, 772:11
  by this beauty, 538:5
  captain's mind, 545:3
  fish in t. waters, 286:14
  gold gateways of stars, 581:6
  I am t., 664:15
  let not heart be t., 40:26, 40:30
  mind, 242:15
  my mind is t., 201:5
  see that ye be not t., 36:7
  tumors of a t. mind, 261:11
  woman moved like fountain t., 167:34
Troubles, fear of Acheron which t. life, 89:21
  never sleep with anyone with worse t., 726:6
  of proud and angry dust, 579:18
  pack up your t., 641:11
  sea of t., 196:10
  wide and dark, 414:20
  written t. of the brain, 216:10
Troublesome disguises which we wear, 258:25
  effort of thinking t., 536:8
  loud and t. insects, 332:18
Troubling, the wicked cease from t., 13:36
Troublous, part we sadly in t. world, 165:3
Trough, snake came to water t., 657:12
Trousers, cloud in t., 686:19
  never wear best t. to fight, 508:10
  steam engine in t., 380:11
  wear bottoms of t. rolled, 667:18
  wear white flannel t., 667:19
Trout, find t. in milk, 476:25
  here comes the t., 202:16
Trowel, laid on with a t., 189:33
Troy, did not go to citadel of T., 55:21
  fields of corn where T. was, 101:18
  fired another T., 276:14
  fires of T., 706:4
  half his T. was burned, 183:10
  has been, 93:32
  heard T. doubted, 403:4
  sacked the holy citadel of T., 52:27
  tale of T. divine, 252:6
  that matter of T., 490:6
  walls famed in battle, 93:30
  was there another T., 595:18
  why Grecians sacked T., 162:*n*7
  windy T., 455:1
  woman laid T. in ashes, 284:15
  worn the stones of T., 200:22
Troyan, Troilus mounted T. walls, 182:7
Truant disposition, 193:13
  every t. knew, 329:17
  my t. lover has come, 491:7
Truce, no t. or parley with Hitler, 621:2
  to navigation, 529:15
Truckin', keep on t., 772:13

Trudge, swing tramp and t., 650:16
Trudged unknowing what he sought, 276:27
Trudgin' my weary way, 554:9
True, advanced t. friends, 498:1
  all I thought was t., 622:17
  and honorable wife, 188:8
  and righteous altogether, 450:11
  apothecary thy drugs quick, 176:19
  art for sake of t., 437:2
  as dial to sun, 263:31
  as I live, 236:17
  as needle to pole, 263:*n*7
  as stars above, 781:14
  as stiel, 128:26
  as taxes, 470:30
  as turnips, 470:30
  beautiful words are not t., 58:7
  beggar true king, 333:2
  beginning of our end, 174:4
  best not expected to go t., 315:8
  blue, 263:5
  both t. both wise, 266:17
  brew that is t., 736:10
  child always say what's t., 561:8
  children and fools speak t., 141:*n*16
  considered by people equally t., 339:12
  course of t. love, 172:19
  dare to be t., 242:19
  definition of style, 289:6
  democracy never existed, 319:8
  distinguish t. from false, 277:19
  ease in writing, 298:20
  eloquent but 'tis not t., 498:5
  every t. man's apparel, 204:24
  everyone's t. worship, 74:5
  false idol or noble t. birth, 76:9
  falsely t., 459:15
  first t. gentleman, 227:19
  for you true for all, 431:19
  founder of civil society, 319:2
  free Russian speech, 482:20
  generous t. and fierce, 619:19
  good men and t., 186:35
  great Power make me think t., 505:10
  gude to be honest and t., 779:20
  guid to be honest and t., 364:4
  happiness not in multitude of friends, 231:20
  how should I t. love know, 198:16
  how to speak t. things, 54:15
  I am a t. laborer, 191:9
  I am t. Russian, 766:5
  I have gone here and there, 221:26
  I talk of dreams, 174:21
  I to my pledged word t., 674:18
  idea of what t. and false, 277:19
  if England rest but t., 170:24
  if we are t. to plan, 513:18
  I'll prove more t., 175:6
  in mathematics never know what t., 615:9
  in print sure they are t., 223:11
  is it t. in and for itself, 372:13
  judgments of Lord t., 16:11, 450:11
  lease of my t. love, 221:23
  live pure speak t., 459:7
  love a durable fire, 152:10

True *(continued)*
  love is like ghosts, 265:9
  love sits him down, 780:23
  lovers run into strange capers, 190:16
  makes false conception come t., 728:13
  marriage of t. minds, 222:2
  matter decided considered t., 119:27
  matters I relate are t. lies, 675:22
  me and my t. love, 779:21
  Milton was a t. poet, 357:2
  more t. than Love to me, 776:24
  music repeat thought of people, 699:13
  mysterious law t. source, 258:26
  never accept thing as t., 246:16
  no ground for supposing it t., 615:12
  no man worth having t., 288:7
  nobility exempt from fear, 164:6
  not too good to be t., 286:22
  nothing t. makes complete sense, 684:18
  nothing t. that may not seem false, 146:5
  Oh 'tis t. 'tis t., 578:23
  one religion t. as another, 235:19
  only regret is that all so terribly t., 572:16
  order of going, 74:12
  Penelope was Flaubert, 659:5
  people's judgment t., 274:14
  pessimist fears this is t., 635:8
  pity 'tis 'tis t., 195:12
  plain hearts, 228:4
  poem an invocation, 692:4
  proved t. before prove false, 263:29
  right praise t. perfection, 182:12
  right t. end of love, 230:9
  ring in the t., 457:29
  small service is t. service, 377:14
  so t. to thyself, 159:24
  so young my lord and t., 208:22
  strange but t., 403:20
  such as I all t. lovers, 202:9
  tender and t., 506:12
  that he is mad 'tis t., 195:12
  the blushful Hippocrene, 415:11
  the t. Light, 39:32
  theory of t. civilization, 494:16
  think of companions t., 371:22
  Thomas, 785:11
  'tis t. 'tis day, 229:4
  'tis t. 'tis pity, 195:12
  to kindred points, 377:12
  to thee till death, 474:2
  to thine own self be t., 194:1
  to t. occasion t., 458:7
  to you in my fashion, 682:7
  trusty dusky vivid t., 561:25
  way but yet untried, 158:12
  way goes over rope, 651:21
  what each wishes he believes t., 79:3
  what is t. of shopkeeper, 319:28
  what people say of us t., 594:3
  whatsoever things are t., 44:35
  when you met her, 228:7
  wit nature to advantage, 298:14

True *(continued)*
  woman t. and fair, 228:6
  words are not beautiful, 58:7
  worshippers shall worship, 39:48
  writ your annals t., 219:15
  writer has nothing to say, 751:6
True-begotten father, 180:14
True-born Englishman, 171:4
True-fixed and resting quality, 188:14
True-love, my t. hath my heart, 155:26
  pokers into t. knots, 383:12
Truer to be rebel, 589:1
Truffles, swine show you where t. are, 758:19
Truism, not paradox but t., 76:4
Truly a peck of provender, 173:22
  here lies t. honest man, 264:21
  those who were t. great, 727:10
Trump, farewell the shrill t., 207:8
  last t., 43:27
  of rescue sound, 430:2
  tell truth or t., 527:6
Trumpet, believeth that it is sound of the t., 15:17
  blow t. to arms, 340:17
  cock the t. to the morn, 192:27
  first blast of the t., 143:14
  give uncertain sound, 43:17
  great sound of a t., 36:10
  hear t. sound, 794:18
  heart moved more than with t., 156:3
  of his own virtues, 187:13
  of prophecy O Wind, 407:18
  praise him with t., 20:16
  pride his own t., 200:16
  shall be heard on high, 275:11
  shall sound, 43:27
  shifted his t., 330:14
  sound t. beat drums, 308:23
  when people heard sound of t., 10:34
Trumpet's loud clangor, 275:9
Trumpets, blow your t. angels, 230:19
  he saith among the t., 15:17
  loud uplifted angel t., 254:11
  no t. for new year, 629:12
  of the sky, 429:12
  silver snarling t., 414:22
  sound t. beat drums, 276:8
  sounded for him, 272:31
  tuckets then t., 619:2
Trumpet-tongued, angels t., 213:7
Trumps, let spades be t. and t. they were, 299:16
Truncheon, marshall's t., 204:1
Trunk, joy up t. needles tingle, 752:2
  so large a t. before, 608:17
  spouts out a sea, 259:21
Trunkless legs of stone, 406:13
Trunks, animals infuse into t. of men, 181:17
Trust, a little t., 522:10
  before you t. a man, 776:3
  brains t., 707:8
  built absolute t., 212:27
  did not t. own impressions, 71:19
  don't t. anybody over thirty, 770:16
  ears less than eyes, 69:20

Trust *(continued)*
  empire power in t., 274:8
  everybody but cut ca-ards, 603:6
  government is a t., 389:13
  hope for best t. in God, 380:4
  husband doth safely t. in her, 23:17
  in God is our t., 391:3
  in God keep powder dry, 389:20
  in Him I put my t., 116:7
  in him will I t., 18:15
  in Providence, 245:31
  in the Lord, 731:3
  life of magnanimity and t., 478:5
  Lord shall raise me up I t., 153:2
  love all t. a few, 203:8
  magistracy is great t., 332:21
  man bore this t., 117:11
  man on his oath or bond, 211:26
  no agent, 186:21
  no man with power to endanger liberty, 337:16
  none, 185:2 .
  not him with secrets, 342:8
  not one night's ice, 244:27
  not t. in money, 447:9
  old friends to t., 158:23
  power a t., 434:18
  public office public t., 532:n3
  put no t. in the morrow, 95:25
  put not your t. in princes, 20:14
  put their t. in him, 30:24
  read New Yorker t. in God, 720:21
  rude cruel not to t., 222:7
  something right in world we t., 744:14
  soothed by unfaltering t., 411:4
  surplus wealth sacred t., 525:13
  that man in nothing, 320:20
  that somehow good, 457:17
  thee gentle Kate, 177:18
  they that put their t. in him, 15:31
  though he slay me yet will I t., 14:19
  time that takes in t., 153:2
  to frail mortality t., 160:14
  tomorrow will repay, 273:16
  treachery is all their t., 402:20
  try to t. one another, 681:5
  tyranny's disease to t. no friends, 63:4
  under his wings shalt thou t., 18:15
  wonder men t. themselves with men, 211:24
  yourself, 350:16
Trusted, Founders t. they would do, 661:9
  I have t. in thee, 147:14
  let no such man be t., 182:10
  not in one bottom t., 179:14
  to thy billows, 401:5
  treason but t. like fox, 179:1
  with government of others, 344:7
Trustees, officers of government t., 389:13
Trustest in staff of this broken reed, 27:11
Trusteth, he that t. in his riches, 21:9
  in his own heart, 23:7
  in man, 28:29
  in the Lord, 28:29

Trustful, makes them cynical where
    we are t., 694:14
Trusting, calls his t. benevolence,
    329:2
    no more t. in women, 53:24
Trusts, foolish man who t. woman,
    94:*n*1
    in tameness of wolf, 210:13
    offices public t., 393:14
Trusty, ancient t. drouthy crony,
    363:4
    dusky vivid true, 561:25
    Toledo t., 263:9
Truth about Life, 716:3
    absurd is the first t., 732:14
    adherence to t. of nature, 384:9
    affirm what seems to be t., 76:8
    all we know for t., 595:20
    always strange, 403:20
    and all that makes man, 459:20
    and nonviolence inseparable, 607:1
    aphorism never coincides with t.,
      626:6
    as opposeth no profit, 239:25
    authority and show of t., 187:1
    awoke and found it t., 417:15
    be in the field, 255:4
    beauty, 416:7
    beauty adventure, 584:15
    Beauty must be t., 417:14
    being truth tell it, 140:*n*4
    best test of t., 542:25
    bright countenance of t., 254:14
    bring to light, 167:2
    by instant illumination, 711:10
    call upon him in t., 20:13
    capsule of t., 703:10
    carp of t., 195:7
    certainty of the words of t., 22:12
    comes like bastard, 254:17
    cry of all game of few, 296:25
    crushed to earth, 411:10
    demanded of genius love of t.,
      351:7
    depository of t., 271:7
    deviation from t. is multiplied,
      77:19
    dignity of t. lost with protesting,
      232:7
    does not blush, 112:9
    doubt t. to be liar, 195:14
    draw bow ride and speak t., 403:22
    dreadful knowledge of t., 65:17
    dream is the t., 707:6
    enemies of t., 248:1
    error more dangerous the more t.,
      493:23
    every man satisfied there is t.,
      538:15
    exists falsehood invented, 646:2
    fiction lags after t., 331:8
    follow t. too near heels, 152:20
    follow t. wherever it may lead,
      345:1
    for a moment lie becomes t., 495:17
    forever absolute, 462:20
    forever on scaffold, 485:2
    found t. in all but one, 172:8
    fragment by fragment, 711:10
    friend to t., 300:24

Truth (*continued*)
    friends his t. proclaim, 274:7
    from his lips prevailed, 329:15
    from shadows into t., 427:3
    full of grace and t., 39:33
    gate of horn for t., 94:17
    give them raw t., 585:13
    God of t., 10:26
    goes a-begging, 138:9
    great and shall prevail, 503:10
    great is t., 30:13
    great is t. and shall prevail, 30:*n*3
    habit with him test of t., 353:16
    half t. blackest lie, 460:1
    happens to idea, 546:21
    has limits, 147:6
    has such face and mien, 275:13
    hath a quiet breast, 170:29
    heart fed upon t., 384:21
    hero of my tale, 510:1
    high star of T., 498:19
    Him who is T. itself, 287:3
    his t. endureth, 18:22
    His t. is marching on, 484:6
    his t. shall be thy shield, 18:15
    holding on to t., 606:13
    honor t. above friends, 77:26
    hour of t. now always, 630:18
    hyest thyng men kepe, 131:29
    I am very fond of t., 306:27
    I have preached the t., 64:22
    I will be harsh as t., 437:14
    if life be t., 247:8
    image of inner t., 5:9
    impossible to be soiled, 77:*n*5
    in masquerade, 403:12
    in peril t. drawn from heart, 89:22
    in shepherd's tongue, 152:11
    in spirit and t., 39:48
    in the end t. will conquer, 127:20
    in t. we know nothing, 70:27
    in wine is t., 55:*n*12, 119:9
    is great and endures, 3:5
    is not in us, 46:32
    is precious and divine, 263:23
    is there in t. no beauty, 243:9
    is torch, 321:5
    is truth to the end, 205:3
    kept strict regard for t., 609:3
    language of t., 613:18
    liars when they speak t., 77:8
    lie which is half t., 460:1
    lies in the depth, 70:27
    light between t. and intellect,
      126:10
    like bastard comes into world,
      254:*n*3
    look for t. not find it, 320:1
    lost to Love and T., 592:4
    love t. pardon error, 305:27
    loyalty to T. to yourself, 556:20
    maintained cause of t., 259:17
    make strange things look like t.,
      435:24
    make the t. known, 599:10
    map of t. in thy face, 163:25
    marvelous T. confront us, 752:17
    mathematics possesses t., 615:10
    may bear all lights, 291:28
    may strike out his teeth, 152:20

Truth (*continued*)
    mercy and t. are met together, 18:8
    most valuable thing economize it,
      527:24
    naked t. is I have no shirt, 169:10
    nation which keepeth the t., 26:28
    never fell dead in streets, 461:17
    never hurts teller, 468:8
    never understood and not believed,
      357:13
    new t. would be revealed, 436:3
    no concern with duty or t., 453:14
    no eternal t., 681:3
    no god higher than t., 607:1
    no greatness where no t., 510:8
    no special time of own, 630:18
    no t. dies, 412:30
    no t. in him, 40:12
    no t. to be discovered, 642:17
    noble t. of sorrow, 64:26
    nor grave nor bed denied, 598:20
    not better for showing face, 64:8
    not conceal t. knowingly, 116:2
    not offend you by speaking t.,
      136:18
    not only by reason, 271:1
    not sought for, 81:8
    not veil t. with falsehood, 116:2
    nothing but the t., 150:8
    nothing but t. is lovely, 280:18
    nothing more damaging to new t.,
      351:4
    nothing so least as t., 689:2
    now her painted toy, 594:16
    nutritive or suggestive t., 549:2
    obedience bane of t., 406:8
    obeyed his call, 599:11
    object of science t., 383:18
    ocean of t. undiscovered, 282:5
    of a madman, 760:7
    of history, 503:5
    of Imagination, 417:14
    on march nothing can stop, 541:13
    one law and one t., 111:19
    one t. is clear, 301:12
    One who died for T., 512:13
    only in imagination, 573:16
    only two ways of discovering t.,
      158:12
    opinion is t. filtered, 462:20
    painful t., 339:7
    peeps over glasses' edge, 466:7
    persuades by teaching, 112:8
    Plato and t. are dear, 77:26
    Plato dear t. dearer, 77:*n*13
    poet sings, 455:13
    possession of t. as city, 248:2
    put in possession of t., 277:7
    put to the worse, 255:4
    rather than love give me t., 478:39
    receives t. as angel, 393:2
    religion instinctive t., 503:15
    Satya t., 607:1
    science search for t., 708:1
    searcher obedient to t., 493:19
    seek t. in groves of Academe, 97:22
    severe, 323:10
    shall be thy warrant, 152:15
    shall make you free, 40:11
    shall prevail, 30:*n*3

Turbulent (*continued*)
  sagacious and t. of wit, 274:3
Turc, la galère d'un T., 269:*n*8
Turf, bless t. that wraps clay, 324:11
  grass-green t., 198:17
  green be t. above thee, 405:5
  green t. beneath feet, 390:15
Turk, bear like the T., 302:11
  human form in heathen t. or jew,
    356:14
  malignant and turbaned T., 208:17
  or Proosian, 529:10
  out-paramoured the T., 210:5
  work hard as T., 777:13
Turkey a more respectable bird,
    310:24
  black t. gobbler, 787:8
  in the straw, 779:24
  it was a t., 470:13
Turkish, be taken by T. enemy,
    793:19
  English not T. court, 184:15
Turkman's rest, 404:5
Turk's, on board a T. galley, 269:*n*8
Turks, Papists Protestants Jews T. in
    one ship, 247:13
  sleep with T. and infidels, 172:7
Turmoil, tired of my t., 743:9
Turn again Whittington, 777:1
  away no more, 358:1
  backward O Time, 516:13
  currents t. awry, 196:10
  dark cloud inside out, 617:12
  death because chose to t., 675:6
  do not hope to t. again, 669:13
  do not t. back at goal, 100:1
  down empty Glass, 446:9
  each thing his t. does hold, 241:13
  good t. asketh another, 142:2
  him to cause of policy, 184:22
  his merry note, 190:18
  in door once turn once only, 669:6
  Lordship t. it over, 426:6
  now t. different hue, 59:23
  on tune in drop out, 748:6
  one good t. deserves another, 105:3
  out your toes, 518:20
  over a new leaf, 150:34
  over half a library, 316:24
  pass and t. again, 430:10
  quickly t. away, 598:3
  smile once more t. thy wheel,
    209:16
  something t. up, 435:1
  stone start a wing, 581:11
  the other cheek, 33:7
  thee behind me, 13:9
  to t. you out t. you out, 591:15
  up the lights, 586:7
  where shall I t., 763:8
  wheresoe'er I may, 375:3
  why wilt thou t. away, 358:1
  worm will t., 164:15
Turned aside to sleep, 228:21
  dead and t. to clay, 199:10
  face with ghastly pang, 381:17
  from one's course by opinions, 83:5
  having once it walks on, 381:26
  he t. up his eyes, 357:18
  heart is t. to stone, 207:20

Turned (*continued*)
  him right and round about, 362:14
  home his footsteps t., 378:1
  in case anything t. up, 470:23
  one who never t. back, 468:17
  round and round in world, 486:28
  suddenly cried and t. away, 662:18
  sword which t. every way, 7:1
  them inside outside, 612:*n*1
  world t. upside downward, 234:11
Turnest, thou t. man to destruction,
    18:10
Turning, from itself never t., 152:10
  gas steam or table t., 494:16
  in widening gyre, 596:19
  neither shadow of t., 46:6
  o' the tide, 184:30
  still point of t. world, 670:5
  to gold all it touches, 508:24
  wine into urine, 656:6
Turnings, long lane knows no t.,
    464:21
Turnip, rather have t. than father,
    315:4
Turnips, man who t. cries, 315:4
  true as t., 470:30
Turnpike, counting cars on New Jer-
    sey T., 772:10
Turns again home, 460:11
  climber-upward t. face, 187:32
  earth's smoothness rough, 467:8
  giddy thinks world t. round, 167:33
  his necessity to gain, 376:9
  into Miss T., 617:5
  lightly t. to love, 455:9
  no more his head, 381:26
  over your papers, 342:8
  poet's pen t. to shapes, 174:1
  times go by t., 160:18
  to thoughts of love, 455:9
  unto ladder t. his back, 187:32
  with ceaseless pain, 328:7
Turpissima bestia, 84:*n*12
Turquoise Horse of Johano-ai, 787:11
Turret, Sultan's T. with Light, 445:3
  washed me out of t. with hose,
    735:21
Turtle, clever of t., 709:7
  lives 'twixt decks, 709:7
  Mock T., 518:2, 518:3
  thoughts of t. turtles, 433:29
  voice of the t. is heard, 25:6
Turtledove, voice of the t., 4:9
Turtle's breast, 670:5
Tut done thousand dreadful things,
    167:12
Tut tut child said Duchess, 517:24
Tu-whit tu-who, 169:13
TV, cool medium like T., 730:4
Twa, lost but ane t. behin', 363:24
  sisters sat in bour, 785:13
Twain, book made by Mr. Mark T.,
    526:19
  from one book by Mark T., 702:2
  never t. meet, 591:9
Twangling, thousand t. instruments,
    224:18
Tweedledee, contrariwise continued
    T., 518:22
Tweedledum and Tweedledee, 304:15

Twelve good men, 390:2
  honest men, 296:22
  I in t. thousand none, 172:8
  in sworn t. have thief, 203:29
  in t. found truth in all but one,
    172:8
  iron tongue hath told t., 174:12
  parted between t. and one, 184:30
  snowed t. days and t. nights, 738:1
Twelvemonth's, run t. length again,
    362:22
Twentieth, party make t. century,
    428:7
  what would t. century look like,
    744:11
Twenty ballads stuck about wall,
    245:21
  cannot live on t. pound, 243:1
  love-sick maidens, 529:16
  men crossing bridge, 638:14
  not handsome at t., 244:24
  strength of t. men, 176:12
  substance of grief hath t. shadows,
    171:13
  sweet and t., 202:2
  to that t. add hundred more, 241:8
  understand life at t., 589:9
  will not come again, 578:19
  years in woman's life, 75:14
Twenty-eight, came to serve at t.,
    134:14
Twenty-five, between t. and forty,
    558:6
  first t. years worth all, 428:18
Twenty-nine, she had a long t.,
    566:*n*5
  when there are pink shades, 566:25
Twenty-one, confidence of t., 315:22
Twenty-seven, woman of t., 694:19
Twenty-third day of October in Julian
    Calendar, 237:23
Twice as muckle 's a' that, 363:24
  blessed, 181:19
  life closed t. before close, 514:13
  love that never seen t., 421:6
  not step t. into same rivers, 62:14
  old man t. a child, 195:32
  or thrice had I loved thee, 229:3
  serpent sting thee t., 181:15
  who splits wood warms t., 478:*n*1
  woman's name in print t., 656:4
  wood stumps warmed me t., 478:30
Twice-told tale, 170:5
Twice-turned, Jesus of t. cheek, 711:3
Twig and a pillar, 80:8
  as t. bent tree's inclined, 300:12
Twilight and evening bell, 460:12
  between birth and dying, 669:19
  brown t. atmosphere, 436:4
  disastrous t. sheds, 256:16
  glimmer of t., 464:26
  live in gray t., 575:12
  of things that began, 534:21
  past is t. of dawn, 601:8
  pilots of purple t., 455:17
  still evening and t. gray, 258:18
Twilight's last gleaming, 391:2
Twin, stiff t. compasses, 229:13
Twined flowers, 416:14
Twinkle little bat, 517:20

Twinkle (*continued*)
  little star, 394:2
  on milky way, 375:20
Twinkling of an eye, 43:27
Twinklings, remembering with t. and
    twinges, 740:7
Twinned, we were as t. lambs, 222:17
Twins, body and spirit t., 535:7
  two young roes that are t., 25:10
Twirled, Brazil he t. Button, 512:19
  fingers madly, 472:11
Twist, cannot hope to bribe or t.,
    660:13
  'em up, 779:24
  let him t. slowly in wind, 754:20
  no more t., 600:22
  Oliver T. asked for more, 469:5
  oozy weeds about me t., 487:10
  secret lies in invisible t., 688:1
  wolf's-bane, 416:16
Twisted braids of lilies, 253:11
  cue, 531:5
  our eye-beams t., 229:14
  prisoner in his t. gyves, 175:14
  tubes t. and dried, 591:13
Twisting, character of t. octopus,
    59:23
Twitched his mantle blue, 254:8
Twitches, Death t. my ear, 94:30
Two and one are three, 376:n2
  and two mathematician makes four,
    523:18
  as stiff twin compasses, 229:13
  bicycle built for t., 600:18
  blackbirds, 792:15
  by two in ark of ache, 752:18
  can t. walk together, 29:35
  cheers for Democracy, 636:13
  do t. things do neither, 98:31
  fifths sheer fudge, 485:8
  gods Persuasion and Compulsion,
    62:28
  grains of wheat in chaff, 179:23
  grant that twice t. not four, 482:19
  gross of broken statues, 659:10
  I am t. fools I know, 228:17
  if by sea, 442:13
  if ever t. were one, 262:15
  in right with t. or three, 484:21
  irons in the fire, 238:12
  kinds of people, 562:14
  lads that thought no more behind,
    222:16
  lanterns in North Church, 339:4
  live as one, 670:3
  lost but ane t. behin', 363:24
  love idea of t. sexes, 690:6
  lovely berries on one stem, 173:19
  loves I have, 222:10
  may keep counsel, 142:n7
  may talk one hear, 432:2
  not without God, 112:16
  o'clock in morning courage, 370:21
  of every sort, 7:17
  of far nobler shape, 258:11
  of trade never agree, 297:9
  oldest professions, 666:1
  one t. and third in your bosom,
    175:19
  or three gathered together, 35:33

Two (*continued*)
  our t. souls which are one, 229:12
  reasons good one real one, 533:2
  roads diverged in wood, 623:7
  seizes t. things one slips, 784:23
  sides to every question, 70:16
  sin ye do by t. and t., 592:6
  single soul in t. bodies, 77:13
  sisters sat in a bour, 785:13
  sleep an act or t., 226:10
  souls dwell in my breast, 350:13
  stars keep not motion, 179:4
  strings to bow, 141:n14
  supreme blessings, 68:26
  takes t. to speak truth, 477:17
  Thing One and Thing T., 715:3
  things believed of any man, 608:10
  thousand light years from home,
    772:17
  unity at minimum is t., 691:20
  voices are there, 376:16
  we t. alone will sing, 211:13
  went to pray, 264:7
Two Lands are in festivity, 5:4
Two-and-twenty, I am t., 578:23
  sweet t., 403:23
Two-edged, sharp as a t. sword, 20:26
  sharper than t. sword, 45:34
Two-handed engine, 254:3
Two-legged, unfeathered t. thing,
    274:5
Two-ness an American a Negro, 605:2
Twopence a week and jam, 519:8
  colored, 561:20
Twopenny, don't care t. damn, 371:14
  wi' t. fear nae evil, 363:7
Twye, Miss T. soaping breasts in
    bath, 739:12
Tyger Tyger burning bright, 358:6
Tygers of wrath, 357:9
Tyler, Tippecanoe and T., 385:n2
Tyne, cargo of T. coal, 634:1
Type, highest t. of human nature,
    493:10
  I am T., 590:14
  of all her race, 461:1
  of the wise, 377:12
  so careful of t., 457:19
Types, movable t., 411:22
  of judicial writing, 609:11
Typewriters, monkeys strumming on
    t., 646:7
Typical, clubs t. of strife, 335:6
Typing, it isn't writing it's t., 753:15
Tyrannical, strength without justice is
    t., 271:2
  three t. masters, 569:14
Tyrannies, of all t. on human kind,
    275:14
  war dearth age agues t., 230:20
Tyrannis, sic semper t., 536:5
Tyrannous to use strength like giant,
    204:3
  word of command, 507:10
Tyranny and oppressions vanish,
    344:19
  death a milder fate than t., 63:16
  destruction of Nazi t., 650:8
  discourage and abolish t. and vice,
    337:10

Tyranny (*continued*)
  economic t. above, 661:2
  establishes t. kill Brutus, 137:4
  fate awaiting Nazi t., 621:3
  fortune's wayward t., 65:10
  government transformed to t.,
    395:13
  Law ends T. begins, 277:9
  laws end t. begins, 313:2
  like hell not easily conquered,
    340:22
  not only t. but tyrant, 340:21
  of Mrs. Grundy, 493:4
  of next-door neighbor, 506:11
  of one literature, 564:4
  over mind of man, 344:4
  snuff approach of t., 331:15
  struggle to be free of t., 698:20
  taxation without representation t.,
    327:7
  toss gauntlet before feet of t.,
    747:18
Tyranny's disease, 63:4
  ecclesiastic t. worst, 285:18
Tyrant, any excuse will serve t., 59:9
  conform to t. custom, 148:7
  is child of Pride, 65:18
  little t. of fields, 322:14
  not only tyranny but t., 340:21
  old man weds t., 69:13
  preserve me from a t., 232:2
  public opinion weak t., 477:30
  root from which t. springs, 75:26
  when t. has disposed of enemies,
    75:28
Tyrant's, Ercles' vein a t. vein, 172:24
  necessity the t. plea, 258:15
  threatening countenance, 96:15
Tyrants, all men would be t., 286:1,
    347:1
  and slaves, 329:4
  argument of t., 364:9
  blood of patriots and t., 343:15
  controlled by t. or by ourselves,
    715:11
  fall in every foe, 363:20
  hand unfriendly to t., 269:34
  hate t., 488:11
  how can t. govern home, 164:23
  kings t. from policy, 332:16
  rebellion to t., 779:3
  their t. their historians, 427:6
  thunderbolts and t., 309:n1
  thus always to t., 119:30
  to t. no quarter, 437:17
  watered by blood of t., 354:11
Tyre, one with Nineveh and T., 593:2
Tyrian, no distinction between Trojan
    and T., 93:22

U

U, green U blue O, 565:17
  will not be missed, 689:4
Ubi bene ibi patria, 119:35
  libertas ibi patria, 327:8
  saeva indignatio, 290:23
Ubiquitous, her envoys u., 463:16
  man u. animal, 722:14
Ucalegon's afire next door, 93:31

Uffish thought, 518:16
Ugliest man who came to Ilium, 51:8
  North American civilization one of
    u., 754:5
Uglification and Derision, 518:3
Ugliness, one's beauty another's u.,
  432:8
  recognition of u., 56:13
Ugly America, 748:13
  born old and u., 469:34
  caresses of subhumanly u. mate,
    769:12
  dirty bird u. and offensive, 437:11
  fact Nature hides, 515:16
  foul and u. mists, 176:37
  I may be u. and can't cook, 773:14
  like toad u. and venomous, 190:7
  night full of u. sights, 165:29
  so awful u. becomes beautiful,
    491:11
  what sights of u. death in eyes,
    165:30
  woman not u., 305:7
  women indisputably u., 305:7
  Yahoo tricks, 637:7
Ukelele, died playing u., 727:1
Ultima Thule, 92:*n*11, 103:*n*7
Ultimate, depository of u. powers,
  344:22
  mystery works sadly, 546:6
  power u. aphrodisiac, 752:*n*1
  sanction of exploitation, 686:6
Ulysses admitted into U.S., 632:6
  is it U. that approaches, 640:11
  like U. made glorious voyage, 144:1
Ulysses' absence, 218:25
Umbered, sees other's u. face, 185:14
Umble, very u. person, 470:28
Umbrella against Scotch mist, 486:11
Umbris, ex u. in veritatem, 427:3
Umpire, death u. of men's miseries,
  163:12
Umpires, players and u. begged, 765:2
Unable, people u. to find work,
  614:21
  to live in society, 78:14
  to sit still in a room, 270:21
Unacceptable in human existence,
  761:13
Unaccommodated man, 210:6
Unaccountable, how soon u., 490:9
Unaccustomed to fear, 781:3
Unacquainted, not u. with misfor-
  tunes, 53:26
Unacted, nurse u. desires, 357:12
Unadorned, beauty u., 281:19
  when u. adorned most, 308:7
Unadvised, too rash too u., 175:9
Unadvisedly, entered into u., 50:1
Unaffected, affecting to seem u.,
  291:16
Unafraid, gentlemen u., 591:14
  of change, 587:3
Unaging intellect, 597:7
Unalienable, certain u. rights, 343:2
  essential and u. rights, 343:*n*2
Unalterable, army of u. law, 509:8,
  668:1
  quantity of force u., 496:17

Unaltered, laws ought not to remain
  u., 78:17
Unaneled, unhouseled disappointed u.,
  194:24
Unanimity, feel way toward u., 590:10
  on legal questions, 586:9
Unapproachable in White House,
  652:7
Unarm Eros, 218:4
Unarmed, being u. be despised, 136:13
  truth, 761:7
Unashamed, brawling judgments u.,
  459:11
Unassisted merit advances slowly,
  313:*n*5
Unattainable perfection, 594:6
Unattempted yet in prose or rhyme,
  255:19
Unavailing star, 594:6
Unavenged suffering, 495:8
Unaware, hope he knew and I u.,
  540:11
  some morning u., 465:3
Unawares, entertained angels u., 45:42
Unbarred gates of light, 259:16
Unbearable lightness of being, 761:12
Unbeautiful and have comfortable
  minds, 688:11
Unbecoming, not u. men that strove,
  455:5
Unbelief, help thou mine u., 37:30
Unbelievers, do not the u. see, 117:1
  works of u. a mirage, 117:5
Unbelieving came home, 659:8
Unbend, sweet to let mind u., 97:3
  universal horror u., 645:6
Unbidden guests welcomest when
  gone, 163:9
Unbirthday present, 519:13
Unblighted unredeemed wilderness,
  537:14
Unbodied, souls u., 230:13
Unborn, fate of u. millions, 336:14
  millions yet u., 325:4
  posterity of those u., 293:1
  states u., 188:18
  ye u. ages, 323:9
Unborrowed, interest u. from the eye,
  373:4
Unbought grace of life, 332:13
  health u., 276:19
Unbound, so are ye u., 430:2
Unbounded, man of an u. stomach,
  226:4
  salt water u., 593:13
Unbowed, head bloody but u., 557:9
Unbreathed, virtue unexercised and u.,
  254:25
Unbribed, what man will do u.,
  660:13
Unbroken, seaward flying u. wings,
  669:20
  spur not u. horse, 379:20
Unburied, bodies of u. men, 237:13
  unwept u. Patroclus, 52:23
Unburnished, rust u., 455:2
Unbusy, sole u. thing, 383:14
Unbutton, come u. here, 210:6
Uncaught, from world's snare u.,
  218:1

Uncertain balance of proud time,
  157:21
  coy hard to please, 378:14
  fill certain portion of u. paper,
    402:15
  glory of April day, 168:1
  hour before morning, 672:2
  life's u. voyage, 212:8
  rustling of curtain, 452:16
  to it nothing u., 351:16
  trumpet give u. sound, 43:17
Uncertainties, capable of u., 417:18
Uncertainty, dazzling u. of New England weather, 526:5
  known what Greeks did not u.,
    700:13
  quit certainty for u., 314:8
  sink of u. and error, 271:7
Unchanging, no u. truth, 681:3
  Olympus ever u., 53:9
Uncharitable to ourselves, 248:18
Uncharitableness, from all u. deliver,
  49:8
Unchartered freedom tires, 376:4
Unchecked, population u. increases,
  368:2
Unchristened, Homer and his u. heart,
  598:17
Uncircumcision, neither circumcision
  nor u., 44:40
Uncivilized Eastern instincts, 591:1
Unclasps her warmed jewels, 415:5
Uncle, I have good eye u., 186:19
  me no uncle, 171:16
  my prophetic soul my u., 194:20
  nephew of my U. Sam's, 632:11
Unclean, man of u. lips, 26:2
  people of u. lips, 26:2
  spirits entered swine, 37:25
  swine is u., 9:22
Unclose, began to u. damask gown,
  144:4
Unclothed, bodies u. must be, 230:13
Unclouded, pure u. brow, 518:13
Unclubable, very u. man, 316:5
Uncoffined and unknown, 400:31
Uncomely, things u. and broken,
  595:5
Uncomfortable feel tarantara, 529:13
  moral when only u., 571:5
Uncommon, common opinions u.
  abilities, 506:10
  valor common virtue, 658:14
Uncompromising as justice, 437:14
Unconcern, patron looks with u.,
  315:17
Unconcerned hear mighty crack, 292:3
Unconditional and immediate surrender, 501:9
  love, 761:7
  right to say what one pleases, 661:8
Unconfined, lawless winged u., 357:19
  let all her ways be u., 287:19
  let joy be u., 399:22
Unconquerable, love u. waster, 66:18
  man's u. mind, 374:18
  nursing u. hope, 498:13
  soul, 557:9
  will, 256:1, 621:3

Unconquered, thy arm u. steam, 335:23

Unconscionable time dying, 273:6

Unconscious, archetypes of u., 628:12
  collective u., 628:8
  explore u., 577:2
  fastidiousness, 664:12
  humor, 525:4
  knowledge of u. activities of mind, 569:3
  Kosmos, 547:1
  not only evil by nature, 628:15
  obscure u. mental processes, 569:2
  part of man's life, 412:29
  poetry, 500:24
  poets philosophers discovered u., 569:20
  source of highest good, 628:15
  studied, 569:20

Unconsidered, decisive actions often u., 607:4
  snapper-up of u. trifles, 223:2

Unconsoled widower, 443:23

Unconstitutional, power to pronounce u., 438:2

Uncontrollable laughter, 51:4
  mystery, 596:3

Unconvincing, preferable to u. possibility, 78:34

Uncorseted her friendly bust, 668:14

Uncounted, monster with u. heads, 183:9

Uncouth, savage men u. manners, 331:7

Uncreated conscience of race, 647:11
  wide womb of u. night, 257:2

Uncreating word, 304:2

Uncrowned in the underworld, 657:13

Unction, flattering u., 198:2

Uncumbered with a wife, 276:18

Uncut, beautiful u. hair of graves, 488:20

Undaunted by villains in power, 339:3
  daughter of desires, 264:16
  we must be u., 620:12

Undazzled, kindling her u. eyes, 255:2

Undecided, decided only to be u., 619:20

Undefeated because we have gone on trying, 671:19

Undefiled, well of English u., 153:19

Under blossom that hangs on bough, 224:25
  every stone a politician, 73:18
  one more drink be u. host, 687:14
  the greenwood tree, 190:18

Underbelly, soft u. of Axis, 621:14

Underestimating, lost money by u. intelligence of people, 643:1

Underfoot, men tread u. what feared, 90:10

Undergraduates limited to four, 610:11

Underground, go burrow u., 660:16
  living in u. den, 75:17
  might well be u., 530:20
  wake nations u., 794:18

Underjaw, most things move u., 243:15

Underlings, that we are u., 187:22

Undermine, echo u. her hold on life, 636:11

Undermining prosperity, 576:7

Underneath are the everlasting arms, 10:29
  in uplifting get u., 600:9
  this sable hearse, 240:14
  this stone doth lie, 232:12

Undernourishment, extinction from u., 702:14

Underrated nobleman, 531:16

Understand and control nature, 677:12
  at last to u., 640:5
  Black love is Black wealth, 772:15
  both these do not u., 50:20
  everything makes tolerant, 368:12
  fury in your words, 207:24
  Gettysburg you cant u., 696:17
  grown-ups never u., 705:12
  how little we need, 581:19
  I and public u. each other, 626:3
  I u. thy kisses, 178:8
  if I could u., 460:5
  know less u. more, 650:13
  life at forty, 589:9
  mankind u. Monarchy, 506:6
  may not be made to u. it, 61:14
  maybe I just don't u. poetry, 769:10
  ne'er quite u. customs, 503:9
  no human being u. another, 713:7
  not to be understood but to u., 123:10
  say it as you u. it, 365:10
  so many tried to u., 698:8
  that he should u., 639:16
  they that trust in him shall u., 30:24
  to admire we should not u., 291:6
  vexation only to u. the report, 26:34
  want to u. others, 364:21, 673:11
  writer's ignorance, 384:4
  youngsters read men u., 150:18

Understandable by everyone not just scientists, 772:2
  spirit, 725:2

Understandest my thought afar off, 20:7

Understandeth, Lord u. all the imaginations, 13:16

Understanding action of forces, 496:18
  begged Him to take away my u., 284:10
  candle of u., 30:16
  declare if thou hast u., 15:7
  first from mind banish u., 69:*n*11
  foolish people without u., 28:15
  for thy more sweet u., 168:19
  give it an u., 193:23
  gone a-woolgathering, 236:*n*10
  ignorant of his u., 384:4
  in length of days u., 14:17
  is false mirror, 158:14
  is joyous, 767:1
  man of u., 31:17
  man of u. is of excellent spirit, 21:37
  man of u. lost nothing, 145:19
  men of u., 24:20
  much learning not teach u., 62:11
  myself, 673:11

Understanding (*continued*)
  no full u. of own epoch, 629:5
  not hand but u., 150:16
  not obliged to find u., 317:32
  of myself and things around me, 508:1
  Peace of God passeth all u., 49:18
  peace which passeth u., 44:34
  political u. to run government, 655:15
  spirit of wisdom and u., 26:10
  steppingstones to u., 635:2
  to depart from evil is u., 14:41
  to direct, 346:3
  where is the place of u., 14:38
  wife, 237:21
  wise and u. heart, 12:18
  with all thy getting get u., 20:23
  with little u. world ruled, 139:1
  woman of mean u., 386:24

Understandings, best flattered upon u., 305:7

Understands, none of us really u., 774:3
  relentlessly she u. you, 717:4
  without seeing, 57:15

Understood as a child, 43:16
  by quiet natures u., 597:5
  harmony not u., 301:12
  his time, 645:5
  interpreter hardest to be u., 352:34
  poetry communicate before u., 672:20
  trembles to be so u., 640:5
  truth never u. and not believed, 357:13

Undertake executions for master executioner, 58:4

Undertaken, work we have u., 239:27

Undertaker, manners of u., 606:8

Undertaking, thorny u. to follow movement of mind, 145:22

Underwear, never heard of u., 680:9

Underwood, green u. and cover, 533:9

Underworld, uncrowned in the u., 657:13

Undescribable, describe u., 400:16

Undeserved, wear u. dignity, 180:27

Undeservedly forgotten, 721:7

Undeserving, one of the u. poor, 571:21

Undesirable to believe proposition, 615:12

Undetected, organizer of nearly all u., 577:24

Undevout astronomer is mad, 296:21

Undiminished natural wealth, 741:8

Undisciplined squads of emotion, 671:9

Undiscovered, bring to light otherwise u., 340:23
  country from whose bourn, 196:10
  ocean of truth lay all u., 282:5

Undisguised, truth showing face u., 64:8

Undismayed unintimidated inquiry, 615:5

Undisturbed, stand u. as monuments, 344:5

Undo, equivocation will u. us, 199:6

Undo (*continued*)
  parchment scribbled o'er u. a man, 164:9
  power to u. the past, 74:2
  pray you u. this button, 211:19
  so much of either may u. thee, 238:3
  things done, 233:19
Undone, another such victory and we are u., 82:11
  death u. so many, 668:19
  I am u., 26:2
  John Donne Anne Donne U., 228:*n*1
  left u. those things, 48:17
  wish estate o' world u., 216:15
  wrongdoer often left something u., 111:26
  yet is nothing left u., 57:11
Undress, gentle limbs u., 382:12
Undulate round the world, 490:17
Undulating, man vain diverse u., 145:9
Undulations, ambiguous u., 638:26
Unearned increment, 439:24
Uneasy lies head that wears crown, 183:38
Uneducated, educated superior to u., 77:12
  simplicity makes u. effective, 78:30
Uneffectual, pale his u. fire, 194:26
Unemployment outcome of pro-labor policies, 645:10
  unable to find work u. results, 614:21
Unencompassable, encompass u., 479:13
Unending, end of the u., 672:2
Unendurable, prospect of future war u., 714:10
Unenlightened, strong dogged u., 499:12
Unequal distribution of property, 351:22
  laws unto savage race, 454:24
  separate and u., 723:20
  separate inherently u., 682:9
  sharing of blessings, 622:10
Unequals, equals and u. alike, 75:24
Unerringly, sniffs u. as dog, 549:3
Unespied, in ocean's bosom u., 268:23
Unethical and lousy, 712:13
Unexamined, life which is u., 74:15
Unexercised, virtue u. and unbreathed, 254:25
Unexpected, absurd not the u., 473:13
  always happens, 84:*n*1
Unexpressed, uttered or u., 377:18
Unexpressive, fair chaste u. she, 191:6
Unextinguishable laugh in heaven, 249:5
Unfair, life is u., 741:12
Unfaithful, faith u., 459:15
Unfamiliar, foot of u. men, 499:15
  love u. Name, 672:4
  nothing detracts so much as u. terms, 111:29
  universe evolved from u., 766:4
Unfathomable, revere the u., 351:6
Unfathomed center, 419:2

Unfathomed (*continued*)
  dark u. caves, 322:13
Unfeathered two-legged thing, 274:5
Unfed sides, 210:3
Unfeeling, the u. for his own, 321:17
Unfelt, show an u. sorrow, 214:17
Unfettered, afford all u. start, 449:8
  beat earth with u. foot, 96:2
  leewardings, 701:1
Unfilial, three things u., 79:20
Unfinished man and his pain, 598:4
  work they nobly advanced, 450:2
Unfirm, fancies more giddy and u., 202:10
Unfit, for a calm u., 274:3
  for all things u., 330:10
  for ladies' love u., 276:26
  for nation of shopkeepers, 326:7
  picture u. for view, 523:20
  to hold an office, 83:5
Unfitted, doing duty u. for anything else, 587:1
Unfix, horrid image doth u. hair, 212:23
Unfixed in principles, 274:3
Unfold, I could a tale u., 194:17
  leaves of Judgment Book u., 506:3
  O clouds u., 359:17
  such companions thou'dst u., 208:2
  what cunning hides, 208:27
Unfolded by surprise, 625:10
Unfolds both heaven and earth, 172:20
Unforeseen, absurd not the u., 473:13
  French Revolution completely u., 438:12
  happiness, 396:13
Unforgetful, teach u. to forget, 509:27
Unforgivable, guilt is u., 763:13
Unforgiving, an u. eye, 352:30
Unfortified, heart u., 193:4
Unfortunate, concern for u. not socialism, 729:20
  literary attempt u., 318:16
  Miss Bailey, 366:18
  one more u., 423:9
Unfound door, 706:16
Unfriended, remote u. melancholy, 328:6
Unfriendly disposition toward U.S., 360:12
  this hand u. to tyrants, 269:34
Unfruitful, invention is u., 331:8
Unfurled, to April's breeze u., 429:22
Ungained, men prize the thing u., 200:5
Ungalled, hart u. play, 197:15
Ungartered and down-gyved to ankle, 195:8
Ungodly are like chaff, 15:29
  hope of the u., 30:26
  walketh not in counsel of u., 15:29
Ungracious, as some u. pastors, 193:27
Ungrateful, dog never u., 515:17
  man to blame, 265:15
  Public, 390:10
  to those teachers, 651:15
Unguarded, well to leave gates u., 528:16

Ungue, ex u. leonem, 119:1
Unhabitual, genius perceiving in u. way, 546:2
Unhallowed, uplift a new u. song, 573:22
Unhand me gentlemen, 194:15
Unhandsome, slovenly u. corpse, 177:3
Unhanged, not three good men u., 177:22
Unhappiness comes of greatness, 412:7
  nothing funnier than u., 718:19
  of his age has the u., 306:30
  of person who not say no, 726:8
  unrest u. mood of anxiety, 569:12
Unhappy as we imagine, 265:5
  brains for drinking, 206:14
  clergymen's households generally u., 524:19
  family u. in own way, 510:11
  good old times when u., 786:17
  how much more u. he might be, 293:10
  lot finds no enemies, 99:27
  none u. but great, 294:2
  not one respectable or u., 489:16
  these u. times, 648:14
  to have been happy u. misfortune, 115:10
  why Muse speak when u., 710:7
  wight, 154:6
Unhatched egg greatest challenge, 703:18
Unheard beyond ocean tide, 485:22
  those u. sweeter, 416:2
Unhelped by any wind, 382:16
Unheroic dead who fed guns, 662:7
Unhinged brains of better heads, 248:3
Unholy pleasure, 608:16
  shrieks and sights u., 251:6
Unhonored, mindful of u. dead, 322:21
  unwept u. unsung, 378:1
Unhounded by sordid cares, 642:21
Unhouseled disappointed unaneled, 194:24
Unhurrying chase, 581:5
Unicorn, lion and u., 788:10
  rarer than the u., 772:4
Unicorns, jeweled u., 469:17
Un-ideaed, wretched u. girls, 315:16
Uniform motion in right line, 282:1
  that band's gonna be in u., 710:12
Uniformity, irresistible forces for u., 661:10
  is u. of opinion attainable, 343:8
  not lightly sacrificed, 609:10
Unify, secondary imagination struggles to u., 384:7
Unimaginable touch of Time, 377:9
Unimpaired, strong and u., 334:29
Unimportant, interesting because u., 677:16
  where I was born u., 665:14
Uninhibited, debate on public issues u. robust, 719:4
Unintelligent, sheep u., 665:7
Unintelligible, find explanation u., 632:4
  weight of u. world, 373:2

Universe *(continued)*
  snow falling faintly through u., 647:8
  spirit animating u., 420:17
  Sun himself at center of U., 137:6
  systematic procession of U., 137:6
  this grand book the u., 161:15
  through-and-through u., 547:1
  traversed u. in thought, 89:4
  true piety towards u., 588:16
  unit and u. are round, 429:11
  way into U. through forest, 537:15
Universities, housed now in u., 784:2
University a collection of books, 413:1
  become multiversity, 729:21
  best u. gauntlet of mobs, 433:10
  he who enters u., 685:18
  law school no more belongs in u., 574:10
Unjoined, Frankie had become u. person, 744:6
Unjust, God all mercy is God u., 296:15
  in least unjust in much, 39:1
  let him be u. still, 48:3
  peace before just war, 310:*n*5
  sendeth rain on just and u., 33:9
  war protracted, 487:24
  will pay less tax, 75:6
Unkind, learned kindness from u., 651:15
  tell me not I am u., 267:14
  thou art not so u., 191:4
  when givers prove u., 196:12
Unkindest cut of all, 189:6
Unkindness, I tax not you with u., 209:25
  may defeat my life, 208:3
  may do much, 208:3
Unkissed, unknowe u. and lost, 128:13
Unknelled uncoffined, 400:31
Unknow, knows not also to u., 494:19
Unknowable, world u. we know, 581:10
Unknown, accents yet u., 188:18
  affection hath u. bottom, 192:5
  altars to u. gods, 545:9
  and silent shore, 387:18
  behind dim u., 485:2
  black and u. bards, 612:6
  critics shouting He's u., 544:9
  developed respect for u. in lifetime, 727:20
  enemy is the u., 629:13
  forms of things u., 174:1
  good to love the u., 387:31
  hardships we suffered, 683:10
  know less than all u., 235:26
  let me live unseen, 298:6
  like a complete u., 771:9
  loss no loss, 99:1
  means of destruction hitherto u., 655:8
  naked in death on u. shore, 94:4
  nature is but art u., 301:12
  not lived ill who passed u., 97:16
  not to know me argues yourselves u., 258:28
  out of me unworthy u., 607:13
  poetry journey to u., 686:20

Unknown *(continued)*
  she lived u., 373:19
  taken for marvelous, 109:20
  things standing thus u., 199:27
  to fortune and fame u., 322:22
  to the u. god, 41:15
  too early seen u., 174:24
  traveled among u. men, 374:6
  unkist and lost, 128:13
  unknelled uncoffined u., 400:31
  worth's u. although height taken, 222:2
Unlamented let me die, 298:6
Unlearned, amaze the u., 298:16
Unleashed power of the atom, 636:8
Unleavened bread and bitter herbs, 8:37
  seven days shall ye eat u. bread, 8:40
Unleaving, Goldengrove u., 551:5
Unless statistics lie, 688:19
Unlessoned girl unschooled, 181:8
Unlettered small-knowing soul, 168:18
Unlimited, land of u. possibilities, 556:4
  power apt to corrupt, 313:2
  rights will become u., 319:3
Unlocked, Shakespeare u. heart, 377:13
  silent throat, 777:6
Unloose, Gordian knot u., 184:22
  not worthy to u., 37:17
Unlovely, keep u. things afar, 82:14
Unlucky, these u. deeds relate, 208:16
Unmake, people can u. Constitution, 355:14
Unmanageable, most u. of all animals, 76:14
Unmanliness, wisdom without u., 72:3
Unmanly, 'tis u. grief, 193:4
Unmannerly, called them untaught u., 177:3
  sadness in youth, 179:30
Unmask her beauty to moon, 193:26
  time's glory to u. falsehood, 167:2
Unmasked, offer itself to be u., 651:22
Unmatchable, mastiffs of u. courage, 185:12
Unmeaning thing they call a thought, 298:19
Unmentionable thoughts, 487:3
Unmotived herd, 198:*n*3
Unmoved cold and to temptation slow, 221:14
Unnat'ral, poetry's u., 468:31
Unnatural, nothing u. that is not impossible, 352:37
  vices fathered by heroism, 668:8
Unnecessarily, entities not multiplied u., 127:7
Unnecessary, curious in u. matters, 31:4
  heroic in u. points, 545:12
  in Nature nothing u., 122:12
  sentence no u. words, 608:9
Unnerved and untrained, 545:12
Unnoticed, rather attacked than u., 317:11
Unnumbered idle pebbles, 210:27

Unobtrusive, poetry should be u., 417:19
Unofficial force Baker Street irregulars, 577:14
Unordered, Chaos a rough u. mass, 101:19
Unpaid, you with u. bill, 409:22
Unparalleled catastrophes, 636:8
  in thought u., 390:17
  lass u., 218:20
Unpassioned beauty of great machine, 663:2
Unpeel, white Godiva I u., 764:19
Unperiphrastic, 73:22
Unperplexed like migratory birds, 630:7
  seeking find Him, 465:24
Unperturbed pace, 581:5
Unpitied sacrifice, 330:23
  unrespited u. unreprieved, 257:4
Unpleasant, demd u. body, 469:21
  to meet Mr. Eliot, 670:6
Unpleasantest words that blotted paper, 181:9
Unpleased, in power u., 274:3
Unpleasing to a married ear, 169:12
Unpledged, mind was still u., 68:18
Unpoetical, poet u., 418:10
Unpolluted, fair and u. flesh, 199:11
Unpopular, free trade u., 424:10
  names impossible loyalties, 499:10
Unpossessed, is empire u., 166:10
Unpracticed, unlessoned girl u., 181:8
Unpremeditated art, 408:4
  lay, 377:20
  strain, 308:14
  verse, 259:31
Unprepared courage, 370:21
  magnificently u., 661:11
Unprincipled for good of unprincipled, 61:18
Unprofitable, how weary stale flat u., 193:5
  servant, 36:16
Unprofitably, wasted oil u. burns, 334:13
Unpunished, no good deed goes u., 783:1
Unpurged images of day, 598:11
Unqualified blessing, 369:12
Unquenchable, gleam of noble deeds ever u., 64:10
Unquiet, hate to be u. at home, 279:26
  heart and brain, 457:7
  how imagine u. slumbers, 480:7
  meals make ill digestions, 166:33
Unravished bride of quietness, 415:20
Unread his works, 373:*n*2
  vision, 669:17
Unreadable forty years from now, 396:20
Unreal, lead me from u. to real, 50:15
  matter u. and temporal, 495:21
  mockery hence, 215:8
Unreality and loud music, 744:1
Unreason, age of u., 724:7
  and anti-intellectualism, 706:15
  world's God full of u., 663:12

Unredeemed, unblighted u. wilderness, 537:14

Unredressed, so long as wrong u. on earth, 484:18

Unreeling tirelessly speeding them, 491:8

Unreflectively, ceases to live u., 630:17

Unregarded time slips away, 630:1

Unregenerate, more about iniquity than u., 591:3

Unrelenting foe to love, 308:11
haughty Juno's u. hate, 276:5
our cruel and u. enemy, 336:14

Unremembered, nameless u. acts, 373:1

Unreprieved, unrespited unpitied u., 257:4

Unreproved pleasures free, 251:11

Unrequited toil, 450:11

Unrespited unpitied unreprieved, 257:4

Unrest, attacks on Court expression of u., 542:20
capitalism creates social u., 653:25
fairest joys give u., 414:14
frantic-mad with evermore u., 222:13
large part of current u., 569:12
men miscall delight, 409:4

Unrighteous, if you know a thing is u., 79:13
man forsake his thoughts, 28:1

Unrighteousness, riches and honors by u., 61:10

Unripened beauties of north, 292:7

Unroll, page did ne'er u., 322:12

Unromantic as Monday morning, 476:15

Unruly, scepter snatched with u. hand, 170:7
Sun, 228:11
tongue an u. evil, 46:12
wit's an u. engine, 243:2

Unsafe, democracy u., 587:16

Unsaid, something u., 759:15

Unsatisfied, culture leaves u. drives to rebelliousness, 569:10
indignation, 495:8
love u., 669:15

Unschooled, unlessoned girl u., 181:8

Unscottified, most u. of your countrymen, 316:20

Unscrew locks from doors, 489:9

Unscrupulous, one of most u. rascals, 578:2

Unsearchable dispose, 261:26

Unseasonable and immoderate sleep, 314:25
to eat an oyster, 147:10

Unseasoned telling found in legends, 757:8

Unseemly, not u. to die in defense, 52:7

Unseen, born to blush u., 322:13
by forms u. dirge sung, 324:11
counsel of the U. and Silent, 413:8
down u. full of water, 172:9
I walk u., 252:3
ill habits by u. degrees, 276:23
jest u. inscrutable, 168:2
let me live u. unknown, 298:6

Unseen (continued)
nature works by bodies u., 89:9
thou art u. yet I hear, 408:6
walk the earth u., 258:23
within thy airy shell, 252:26

Unselfish, absolutely u. friend is dog, 515:17
love of brute, 452:9

Unselfishness, modesty and u., 658:13

Unsettled, precedent not u. overnight, 609:10

Unsex me here, 212:29

Unshackled by party, 377:16
exercise of every faculty, 427:10

Unshorn fields boundless beautiful, 411:9

Unshut eye, 497:8

Unsifted in perilous circumstance, 194:3

Unsightly noisome things, 429:8

Unslayable, soul eternally u., 84:6

Unsmote by the sword, 401:16

Unsought, love u. is better, 202:26

Unsoundness of mind, 424:14

Unspeakable, citadel of television u., 714:16
desire, 498:4
is sorrow you bid me renew, 93:26

Unspoken, words which were better u., 53:28

Unsponsored, solitude u. free, 638:26

Unspotted from the world, 46:9

Unstable as water, 8:17
become u. without knowing it, 70:1
feet u., 637:8
woman always fickle u. thing, 94:1

Unstaid and skittish in motions, 202:9

Unsteadiness of second class, 355:1

Unstilled world whirled, 669:18

Unsubstantial as shadows, 73:12

Unsuccessful or successful war, 334:26

Unsung noblest deed will die, 64:13
unwept unhonored u., 378:1

Unsunned, chaste as u. snow, 219:25
heaps of miser's treasure, 253:1

Unsure, habitation giddy and u., 183:26
what's to come still u., 202:2

Unsuspected isle in far-off seas, 464:6

Unswayed, is the sword u., 166:10

Untainted, what stronger breastplate than heart u., 164:1

Untamed continent, 503:4
seas, 721:2
sullen u. intractable, 671:12

Untaught, called them u. knaves, 177:3

Untell the days, 233:19

Untender, so young and so u., 208:22

Untented Kosmos my abode, 561:22

Unthinkable, dare to think u. thoughts, 716:1

Unthinking, assault of thoughts on u., 652:13
time, 276:20

Unthread rude eye of rebellion, 170:18

Untidy, beginnings and endings u., 603:23

Until the day break, 25:8

Untimely, from mother's womb u. ripped, 216:19
grave, 246:8
graves, 335:6

'Unting, ain't 'u. as 'urts 'un, 554:17

Untitled aristocracy, 447:18

Untouched, strings u. will harshly jar, 162:17

Untrained to stand test, 545:12

Untraveled, gleams u. world, 455:1
heart u. turns to thee, 328:7

Untrespassed sanctity of space, 751:3

Untried emergencies, 485:24
found difficult left u., 618:15

Untrodden, dwelt among u. ways, 373:19

Untroubling and untroubled where I lie, 410:6

Untrue, cloth u. twisted cue, 531:5
might telle his tale u., 130:9
narrative as a whole u., 503:5
thy lovers were all u., 276:22
unsad and evere u., 131:17

Untruth, never dare utter u., 87:15

Untune, Music shall u. the sky, 275:11
that string, 200:9

Untuned, like u. strings women are, 162:12

Untutored, Indian whose u. mind, 301:7

Untwist last strands of man, 551:11

Unum, E pluribus u., 94:n14

Unus, E pluribus u., 94:n14

Unused, fust in us u., 198:12
to the melting mood, 208:16

Unusual, cruel and u. punishment, 346:17

Unutterable, looked u. things, 308:2

Unuttered part of man's life, 412:29

Unvanquishable, in u. number, 408:2

Unvanquished, I u. and unyielding, 651:4

Unvarnished, round u. tale deliver, 205:22

Unveil, Immortality u. third event, 514:13

Unveiled her peerless light, 258:19

Unveiling, uprising u. affirm, 452:8

Unvexed to the sea, 449:18

Unvictorious, conscripted u. ones, 662:7

Unwashed, great u., 390:5
lean u. artificer, 170:14
platters ride, 701:7

Unwastefully, manage affairs u., 523:10

Unwearied still lover by lover, 596:6

Unwelcome, bringer of u. news, 183:11

Unwept in eternal night, 97:1
unburied Patroclus, 52:23
unhonored unsung, 378:1

Unwilling I left your land, 94:10
to school, 191:3

Unwomanly rags, 423:4

Unworthy, merit of the u. takes, 196:10
out of me u. unknown, 607:13

Unwritten, history u. because yet to be enacted, 491:13

Unwritten (*continued*)
ordinances, 72:2
written and u. law, 112:2
Unwrung, our withers are u., 197:14
Unyielding, Hades is u., 51:29
I unvanquished and u., 651:4
Unyoked humor of idleness, 176:37
Up and down City Road, 780:13
cannot bear leveling u., 316:1
game is u., 219:28
go u. and down as a talebearer,
9:25
lad when journey's over, 578:20
look not down but u., 467:11
men to your posts, 505:21
nice to people on way u., 631:9
road u. and road down one and
same, 62:17
roos sonne and up roose Emelye,
130:19
Satan walking u. and down, 13:29
so floating many bells, 688:22
success is showing u., 767:17
sunny side u., 685:17
you've got to get u., 666:8
Upbraid my falsehood, 200:22
Upbringing, children look after own
u., 760:12
nun would envy, 765:9
Upharsin, Mene Mene Tekel U., 29:16
Upholds, giant Atlas u., 68:20
Upkeep, annual u. of yacht, 533:3
Uplift, educate Filipinos u. civilize
them, 549:18
Uplifted, from despair thus high u.,
256:23
loud u. angel trumpets, 254:11
Uplifting, in u. get underneath, 600:9
thoughts in baths, 693:12
Upmost, attains u. round, 187:32
Upon, and then they were u. her,
739:15
me soul Reilly, 781:5
Upper crust, 405:2, 419:9
materializing u. class, 500:23
part of mankind, 286:3
stiff u. lip, 504:5
Upraised, eyes u. as inspired, 324:16
Upright, behold the u., 17:3
God hath made man u., 24:15
judge learned judge, 182:2
man is laughed to scorn, 14:15
these set our flesh u., 230:11
walketh u. in a straight way, 117:22
Uprightness, man is born for u., 61:8
Uprising, my downsitting and mine u.,
20:7
unveiling affirm, 452:8
Uproar, in bellow and u., 650:16
sand and wild u., 429:8
universal peace, 215:27
Uprose, Prince Lucifer u., 509:7
Upset, progress of Evolution u. Darwin, 535:25
Upsets, art u., 646:1
Upside, world turned u. downward,
234:11
Upstairs and downstairs, 461:12
downstairs in lady's chamber,
789:18

Upstairs (*continued*)
equal u., 581:21
Upstart crow beautified with our
feathers, 157:20
Upstream, only gamefish swims u.,
575:5
Upswept angel wings, 680:3
Upturned, sea of u. faces, 379:11
Upward, as the sparks fly u., 14:2
human race born to fly u., 126:14
look of caution, 624:19
Upwards, astronomy compels soul to
look u., 75:18
Uranium new source of energy, 635:16
Uranus, it may be in U., 476:23
Urban, complicated u. society, 677:5
for u. poor police arrest, 759:4
Urbi et orbi, 120:1
Urge of a song, 625:5
to kill, 766:2
wrestle resurrection, 724:11
Urgent, Master is u., 115:16
Uriah, set ye U. in forefront of battle,
12:9
Urine, turning wine into u., 656:6
Urn, bubbling loud-hissing u., 335:3
Grecian U. worth old ladies, 697:2
lean on garden u., 668:3
storied u., 322:10
well-wrought u. becomes greatest
ashes, 228:16
Urns, old sepulchral u., 334:13
U.S.A., greed will save the U., 774:4
Usage, consumed in image if not in u.,
738:4
tristement selon l'u. de leur pays,
157:n9
'Usband, Man-o'-War's 'er 'u., 592:19
Use a little wine for stomach's sake,
45:20
again until Eternity, 513:17
against the u. of nature, 212:23
all gently, 196:21
almost change nature, 198:6
any language you choose, 530:14
beauty too rich for u., 174:23
cannot u. talent, 706:19
come to deadly u., 210:22
doth breed habit, 168:10
every man after desert, 196:3
find but seldom u. them, 432:4
frequent u. of any organ, 347:13
glad to be of u., 667:17
God made for u. of men, 273:7
harms beauty, 589:21
him as though loved him, 245:28
I'll u. you for my mirth, 189:15
in measured language, 457:7
it and never wear it out, 56:16
it up wear it out, 782:8
know not how to u. victory, 84:4
living measured by u., 145:14
main thing is u. it well, 246:14
make proper u. of victories, 85:10
many books and never u. them,
234:2
me to the limit, 575:13
no u. of metal, 224:4
not poor who has enough to u.,
97:14

Use (*continued*)
not to shine in u., 455:2
of force but temporary, 331:11
of him more than I see, 561:10
rather in power than u., 203:8
ring worn thin by u., 89:n6
speak daggers but u. none, 197:22
sure to find u. for it, 379:26
treatment to help sick, 71:1
try to have and u. excellence, 78:11
tyrannous to u. strength like giant,
204:3
want of u. mind torpid, 317:3
what's the u., 617:7
worship he found in u., 74:5
worst u. a man could be put to,
227:11
Used, I am u. to it, 450:1
I have u. similitudes, 29:30
key always bright, 309:29
man grows u. to everything, 495:2
my credit, 176:28
only witchcraft I have u., 205:28
wine good if well u., 206:24
Useful, be u. where thou livest, 243:3
books you may carry most u., 315:9
by magistrate equally u., 339:12
lesson to head, 335:12
mock their u. toil, 322:7
nothing in houses not u., 523:9
villain would have been u., 366:4
Usefulness common goal of nature,
734:11
power of u. gone, 576:4
Useless, art quite u., 566:11
better know u. things than nothing,
102:32
each without other, 441:26
general maxim u., 424:16
gold in itself u., 137:12
if object u. labor u., 481:8
laws weaken necessary laws, 304:11
life is early death, 349:14
lodged with me u., 255:11
most beautiful most u., 487:15
no man u. who has friend, 562:5
nothing u. is, 441:20
other virtues would be u., 269:17
second good third u., 136:17
slip u. away, 413:17
to excel, 318:7
to poet nothing u., 314:10
Uselessly, nature does nothing u.,
78:13
Uselessness of men above sixty, 558:7
Uses, corner for others' u., 207:4
one art which u. things, 76:1
panics have u., 340:23
seem all u. of this world, 193:5
sweet are u. of adversity, 190:7
the more he u. for others, 58:7
to what base u. return, 199:9
Usher, House of U., 452:4
Ushered, still u. with tear, 300:2
Ushers in the morn, 311:15
Usquebae, wi' u. face the devil, 363:7
Usura sin against nature, 659:15
slayeth child in womb, 659:16
with U., 659:14

Valor (*continued*)
  good speed to your youthful v., 94:24
  he for v. formed, 258:12
  mighty men of v., 10:33
  my v. is certainly going, 352:16
  no need of v., 74:3
  plucks dead lions, 169:20
  thy v. prevail, 421:18
  uncommon v. common virtue, 658:14
  who would true v. see, 272:29
Valorous, Roland v. Oliver wise, 121:13
Valuable coin of thinker, 738:10
  if riches v. to Heaven, 289:7
  reputation more v. than money, 99:2
  time most v. thing, 81:21
  what v. not new, 389:21
Valuation, government resting on v. of property, 75:23
  superstitious v. of Europe, 548:6
Value at a penny talk of old men, 90:19
  carry body for its sentimental v., 722:1
  cynic knows v. of nothing, 566:23
  dearness only gives v., 340:22
  easier discover deficiency than see v., 372:11
  from stamp of ages, 273:1
  governed by utility or cost, 547:15
  hard latent v., 549:3
  is life-giving power of anything, 487:20
  it next to good conscience, 245:30
  men of less v. than gold, 137:12
  no v. when possessed, 284:14
  none but horizontal, 720:2
  nothing has v., 636:11
  nothing v. but object of utility, 481:8
  of sentiment is sacrifice, 603:21
  of what entrepreneur contributes, 653:23
  of what poet has written, 673:1
  rubs enhance v. of favors, 328:19
  supreme v. not future but present, 736:16
  then we rack the v., 187:2
  what gives life v., 716:3
  what I say more lasting v., 759:11
Valueless, reading v. books, 487:22
Values anything more than freedom, 626:22
  not single feature in heaven he v., 528:11
Vampire, like v. dead many times, 538:6
Vanbrugh's, dead Sir John V. house of clay, 288:*n*1
Vanessa extraordinary woman, 289:*n*2
Vanilla of society, 380:8
Vanish like evil spirits, 344:19
  where did children v., 717:2
Vanished and shrunk away, 160:20
  Cheshire Cat v. slowly, 517:17
  touch of v. hand, 456:7

Vanishes, man loves what v., 597:14
Vanisheth, life a vapor that v., 46:15
Vanishing, keep beauty from v., 551:8
  race, 695:19
Vanitas vanitatum, 463:11
Vanities, guides us by v., 668:7
  man of my v., 642:21
Vanity, all is v., 23:22
  all others but v., 386:13
  and vexation of spirit, 23:27
  beauty without v., 398:16
  conscience or v. appalled, 598:16
  cords of v., 25:40
  cry out v. of world, 278:17
  cured of every folly but v., 319:18
  dispel v. with v., 112:15
  every man at his best state is v., 17:8
  extreme actions ascribed to v., 552:3
  Fair, 272:20, 463:8
  give no hollow aid, 400:13
  Golden V., 793:19
  hath not lifted his soul unto v., 16:18
  in years, 177:30
  my days are v., 14:9
  no love but v., 397:7
  of human hopes, 313:26
  of vanities, 23:22
  preying on people's v. ignorance, 766:12
  pull down thy v., 660:1
  repeyreth hom fro worldly v., 129:2
  tickle one's v., 496:4
  town is lighter than v., 272:20
Vanquished by desire, 56:9
  had Cato, 105:19
  Macbeth never v. be, 215:21
  one safety to v., 93:33
  though v. argue still, 329:18
Vans, omnibuses and v., 650:16
  to beat the air, 669:14
Vantage, coign of v., 213:4
  ground of truth, 89:*n*9
Vapor, floating like v. on air, 507:3
  life a v. that vanisheth, 46:15
  like bear or lion, 218:3
  live upon v. of dungeon, 207:4
  summit lost in v., 402:15
Vapors both away, 230:1
  congregation of v., 195:28
  strangle him, 176:37
  weep their burthen, 459:1
Variable as the shade, 378:14
  lest thy love prove v., 175:7
  mysterious independent v., 505:12
Variableness, with whom is no v., 46:6
Variation if useful preserved, 444:5
Varied, mob is v. and inconstant, 278:13
  rule the v. year, 307:15
Variety, abjure my so much loved v., 230:8
  about New England weather, 526:5
  Democracy admits v., 636:13
  democracy full of v., 75:24
  in spite of v. and power, 498:18
  infinite v., 217:15

Variety (*continued*)
  joy of life is v., 314:7
  mother of Enjoyment, 434:16
  no pleasure unseasoned by v., 99:21
  order in v. we see, 299:21
  soul of pleasure, 281:16
Variety's spice of life, 334:28
Various, a man so v., 274:11
  as lovely so be v., 692:1
  as your land, 698:8
  constant as v., 692:1
  distribution of property, 351:22
  gift to each, 441:22
  of v. stuff the v. Man, 363:1
  so v. so beautiful so new, 499:22
  speaks a v. language, 411:1
  stops of v. quills, 254:7
Varium et mutabile femina, 94:*n*1
Varnished clock, 329:19
Varying shore o' the world, 218:6
Vase, shatter v. if you will, 392:2
Vases, beads dolls cloths v., 740:7
Vassal, God how fine a v., 122:1
  Muse I was your v., 565:8
Vassals and serfs at side, 419:1
Vast and furious ocean, 240:8
  dead v. and middle of night, 193:18
  deserts of v. eternity, 268:15
  edges drear, 499:22
  heaven's net is v., 58:3
  intelligence were v. enough, 351:16
  like a v. shadow moved, 270:7
  lodge in v. wilderness, 334:26
  mass of London itself, 620:9
  more devils than v. hell, 174:1
  plastic and v. one intellectual breeze, 380:25
  slow-breathing unconscious, 547:1
  struggle to found Roman state, 93:12
  wings across skies, 683:7
Vaster, grow v. than empires, 268:14
Vasty, call spirits from v. deep, 178:3
  hall of death, 498:15
Vat, every v. stand upon bottom, 272:14
Vaterland, lieb V. magst ruhig sein, 488:*n*1
Vats, cheeses out of v., 464:18
  parcel of boilers and v., 317:22
Vaudeville audiences give loudest sighs, 733:3
Vault, fretted v., 322:9
  left this v. to brag of, 214:15
Vaulter in sunny grass, 396:25
Vaulting ambition, 213:7
Vaults, heaven's v. should crack, 211:17
Vaunt-couriers to thunderbolts, 209:24
Vaunteth, charity v. not, 43:14
Vauntie, her best and she was v., 363:9
Vaward of our youth, 183:18
Vécu, j'ai v., 348:15
  rose a v. ce que vivent les roses, 156:*n*5
Vegetable, information v. animal mineral, 529:12
  love not suit me, 529:18
  my v. love should grow, 268:14

Vesprée, a point perdu cette v., 144:*n*4

Vessel, a chosen v., 41:7
empty v. greatest sound, 185:24
gilded v. goes, 323:8
goodly v., 441:16
He that V. made, 446:3
I am like a broken v., 16:26
of more ungainly make, 446:4
of my genius now hoists sails, 126:2
one v. unto honor, 42:10
strikes with shivering shock, 386:11
though masts be firm, 477:15
wife the weaker v., 46:25
with pestle has brew, 736:10

Vessels oft handled brightly shine, 162:12
pass close to each other, 442:*n*3

Vest, casting the body's v., 268:19
neither v. nor pants, 524:14

Vestal's, blameless v. lot, 300:5

Vestige, last v. of human dignity, 702:15
no v. of a beginning, 327:9

Vestigia, agnosco veteris v. flammae, 93:*n*20

Vestments, priestly v. evidence of servile status, 574:8
priestly v. in dens, 503:4

Vesture, cast lots upon my v., 16:16
muddy v. of decay, 182:8

Veteran, lags the v. on stage, 313:21

Veterans, not tell Vietnam v. from rock v., 770:5

Veuf, le v. l'inconsolé, 443:*n*5

Vex and oppress each other, 351:22
definition of oats meant to v., 314:*n*1
not his ghost, 211:20
such injury v. a saint, 167:26

Vexation, multiplication is v., 776:9
only to understand the report, 26:34
travail and v. of spirit, 23:34
vanity and v. of spirit, 23:27

Vexed with mirth ear of night, 399:8

Vexes public men, 456:4

Vexing dull ear of drowsy man, 170:5

Viands, what v. he preferred, 559:19

Vias, stare super v. antiquas, 28:*n*2

Vibrate, Pentagon turn orange and v., 753:1
sweetest pleasure, 362:9

Vibrates in memory, 409:10

Vibration, brave v. each way free, 241:20

Vibrations, deaden its v., 442:17
of deathless music, 607:13

Vicar, justice judge or v., 352:24
of Bray, 778:17

Vicarious, evidence of v. life, 574:8

Vicars, God as revealed to v., 717:3

Vice, accommodating v., 269:19
amusements keep people from v., 316:12
any taint of v., 203:3
avarice not so much a v., 278:*n*2
best virtue has tincture of v., 146:12
boredom v. and poverty, 306:11
bullied out of v., 434:9
by action dignified, 175:16

Vice (*continued*)
conceal dreary morals like v., 562:6
creature of heejous mien, 602:21
discourage and abolish tyranny and v., 337:10
distinction between virtue and v., 315:27
extremism in defense of liberty no v., 341:*n*1
good old-gentlemanly v., 236:*n*12
homage v. pays to virtue, 265:24
hypocrisy v. of vices, 718:11
inherent v. of capitalism, 622:10
lashed v. spared name, 289:18
lost half its evil, 332:15
moderation in principle a v., 341:8
monster of frightful mien, 301:14
no v. so simple, 181:5
prosperity best discover v., 159:9
raptures and roses of v., 533:12
reverend v., 177:30
schools nurseries of v., 311:19
to flee v. beginning of virtue, 97:5
virtue is not desiring v., 571:11
virtue itself turns v., 175:16
virtue of v. pardon beg, 198:4
virtue or v. leaves scar, 545:14
virtue sold and almost every v., 232:14
when v. prevails, 292:13

Vice-presidency most insignificant office, 338:12
next highest an' lowest office, 603:14
not worth pitcher of warm piss, 605:8

Vice-President be removed on impeachment, 346:8

Vice-prisidincy next highest an' lowest office, 603:14

Viceroy, outward soul v., 229:19

Vices, all v. of our generation, 474:4
and follies of human kind, 290:35
aped from white men, 696:14
capable of greatest v., 246:15
committed genteelly, 316:23
fathered by heroism, 668:8
go light on the v., 719:12
make a ladder of our v., 114:30
may be of use, 346:6
our pleasant v., 211:15
small v. do appear, 211:4
virtues of Man without v., 398:16

Vici, veni vidi v., 88:*n*17

Vicious circle, 522:8
display their v. nature, 137:2
perfect circle and v. circle, 731:14
spiral of rising prices, 635:5

Viciousness, poverty the parent of v., 75:12

Vicissitude, greatest v. of things, 160:11
of sects and religions, 160:11
sad v. of things, 320:5

Vicissitudes in all things, 86:6
of fortune, 340:7
wild v. of taste, 313:13

Vicisti Galilaee, 113:*n*4

Victim, I v. and executioner, 494:7
must be found, 530:20

Victim (*continued*)
o' connubiality, 468:27
O saving V. opening wide, 124:8
power marks its v., 389:14

Victime et bourreau, 494:*n*7

Victim's, tumor killing v. sympathies, 535:17

Victims become witnesses, 760:8
little v. play, 321:15
masses easily fall v. to lie, 676:7

Victis, vae v., 120:3

Victor belongs to spoils, 694:7
eventual v., 639:13
had gods vanquished had Cato, 105:19
or announcer of the victor, 62:31
to v. belong spoils, 398:8

Victoria, Queen V. like great paperweight, 601:17
uti nescis, 84:*n*3

Victories, after thousand v. foiled, 220:14
eight v. over Syracusans, 69:19
go forward give us v., 449:17
Liberty knows nothing but v., 462:19
make proper use of v., 85:10
peace hath her v., 255:10

Victorious, hold your hand v., 69:3
o'er ills o' life v., 363:5
rejoice we are v., 63:25
those which are v., 371:1
warriors win first then go to war, 80:19

Victors, let v. in, 460:17
let v. when they come, 500:3
most glorious to v., 72:12

Victory, another such v. and we are undone, 82:11
at all costs, 620:6
best kind of v., 151:17
blessed with v. and peace, 391:3
by bombing Chinese cities, 655:19
Cadmean v., 69:24
death swallowed in v., 43:28
defeat preface to v., 672:19
fell in the great v., 386:5
for humanity, 419:5
God of Clotilda grant v., 115:7
gory bed or to v., 363:19
grave where is thy v., 43:28, 744:8
highest point not V., 652:4
hundred fathers, 710:15
if not v. is yet revenge, 256:27
illusion of philosophers, 696:13
in spite of terror, 620:6
in v. magnanimity, 622:4
in war no substitute for v., 642:4
know how to win v. Hannibal, 84:4
MacArthur had in mind, 655:19
morale wins v., 642:8
napalm smells like v., 769:11
not v. nor defeat, 575:12
on day of v. no one tired, 118:6
over reason, 676:3
peace without v., 572:8
Pyrrhic v., 82:*n*8
rampant for spoil and v., 552:24
revolution's v. over tsarism, 609:20
right and wrong kind of v., 655:19

Victory (*continued*)
shifts from man to man, 51:25
spirit that gains v., 658:15
swallow up death in v., 26:27
terror wins easiest v., 676:3
thine O Lord is the v., 13:17
this is alone Life Joy Empire V.,
407:6
together achieve v., 678:16
'twas a famous v., 386:7
Westminster Abbey or v., 360:13
when opponent surrenders before
hostilities, 80:20
without v. no survival, 620:6
won by funeral establishment, 744:8
Victrix deis victa Catoni, 105:*n*11
Victuals, not difficult to please about
v., 469:*n*1
served v. course by course, 620:1
Vicus, commodius v. of recirculation,
647:18
Vida, toda la v. es sueño, 247:*n*4
Video meliora deteriora sequor,
101:*n*18
Vidi, veni v. vici, 88:*n*17
Vie with Zeus, 53:6
Vie apparié à un songe, 146:*n*6
la v. est vaine, 522:*n*2
Vieille, quand vous serez bien v.,
144:*n*2
Vieillesse est l'enfer des femmes,
267:*n*8
si v. pouvait, 144:13
Vienna, cured of Oedipus complex in
V., 712:16
Viet Cong, no quarrel with V., 772:1
Vietnam, couldn't tell V. veterans,
770:5
declare unilaterally V. war over,
682:11
had V. instead of happy childhoods,
770:4
on war in V., 772:1
war in V. would end, 753:1
workings of government that led to
V. War, 661:9
Vieux, aussi v. que le journal d'au-
jourd-hui, 618:*n*1
bons v. temps, 786:17
View, beast in v., 276:22
beautiful v., 749:5
both worlds at once they v., 250:6
choice of point of v., 653:8
fair Melrose, 377:23
gloomy v. of future, 632:2
keep end in v., 105:21
made myself motley to the v.,
221:26
man stern to v., 329:17
observation with extensive v.,
313:16
ourselves with clearer eyes, 242:1
Prejudice cut off v., 583:7
recollection presents to v., 398:2
which has grander v., 428:5
with hollow eye, 181:25
world invisible we v., 581:10
worm's-eye v., 705:9
Viewed in her face's field, 166:36
View-hollo, Peel's v., 413:20

Viewing, by v. Nature, 273:10
Viewless, imprisoned in v. winds,
204:14
Views, accept v. Cicero Locke Bacon
have given, 431:6
adopt new v. if true v., 449:12
right v., 65:1
take short v., 380:4, 720:21
Vigil in soft face of girl, 66:18
tongueless v., 533:8
Vigilance, energy and sleepless v.,
449:17
eternal v., 351:20
while people retain v., 449:6
wrenlike v., 743:10
Vigilant, be sober be v., 46:28
haughty v. resolute, 425:12
to the v. active brave, 339:9
Vigny more secret, 436:14
Vigor, exist in undiminished v., 425:7
flows like tides, 679:9
from the limb, 399:19
in what they ought to do, 79:21
inaction saps v. of mind, 135:6
O future V., 565:16
of bone, 201:3
press with v. on, 308:16
takes v. from arms, 331:26
what v. it will give style, 380:20
Vigorous, characteristics of v. mind,
313:25
survive and multiply, 444:9
writing concise, 608:9
Vigueur, ô future V., 565:*n*11
Vile antithesis, 302:16
behold I am v., 15:19
better v. than v. esteemed, 222:6
blows and buffets, 214:22
durance v., 364:3
dust whence he sprung, 378:1
fled from this v. world, 221:7
George the First v., 627:*n*5
ill-favored faults, 182:32
insect that has risen up, 308:19
make so v. a pun, 285:12
make v. things precious, 209:30
makes nice of no v. hold, 170:7
only man is v., 395:19
out v. jelly, 210:19
phrase beyond others v., 580:18
race of quislings, 620:18
squealing of wry-necked fife, 180:18
wisdom and goodness to v., 210:23
Vilely, show v. to desire small beer,
164:*n*3
Vileness, if one had spoken v., 636:11
Viler George the Second, 627:*n*5
Vilest, ape v. of beasts, 84:18
deeds like poison weeds, 567:22
things become themselves, 217:15
to v. things am thrall, 227:14
with v. worms to dwell, 221:7
Vilified, most v. minority, 646:11
Villa submit to idea of revolution,
663:9
Village all declared how much he
knew, 329:17
any well-established v., 704:1
belongs to Castle, 651:20
crossing bridge into v., 638:14

Village (*continued*)
defend v. town city, 620:9
every Middlesex v., 442:13
Ezra Pound was v. explainer,
627:10
global v., 730:5
his house in v. though, 623:16
Indian knows his v., 707:2
loveliest v. of the plain, 329:7
man's v. is his peace of mind,
745:20
of Howling, 708:7
smithy stands, 441:3
some v. Hampden, 322:14
Villain, every tale condemns me for v.,
166:15
ne'er v. in Denmark, 195:2
no v. need be, 508:28
one murder made a v., 336:2
Pinch a hungry lean-faced v., 166:34
play the v., 206:25
smile and be a v., 195:1
some v. hath done me wrong,
167:*n*1
still pursued her, 555:19
who calls me v., 196:6
would have been useful, 366:4
Villainies, execrable sum of all v.,
308:25
Villainous company spoil of me,
178:16
demitasses, 574:1
foreheads v. low, 224:22
my cue v. melancholy, 209:4
newspapers the most v., 352:33
Villain's mind, 180:12
Villains by necessity, 209:3
in power, 339:3
Villainy, clothe my naked v., 165:27
natural expression of v., 526:1
you teach me, 180:32
Ville, comme il pleut sur la v., 554:*n*2
il pleut doucement sur la v., 566:*n*1
Villon our sad bad brother's name,
535:4
Vincere scis Hannibal, 84:*n*3
Vinces, in hoc signo v., 113:*n*2
Vinchy, spell Vinci pronounce it V.,
525:22
Vinci, spell V. pronounce it Vinchy,
525:22
Vindicate ways of God to man, 301:2
Vindication of truth, 606:13
truth v. against slander, 450:6
Vine, every man under his v., 12:20
for one grape v. destroy, 166:38
fruit of the v., 36:28
leaves in his hair, 508:16
thou monarch of the v., 217:21
viol violet and v., 451:15
Vinegar, oil v. sugar, 330:9
Vines and olive trees, 721:2
architect advise to plant v., 608:13
bosomed deep in v., 304:1
land of v. and fig trees, 10:16
little foxes that spoil the v., 25:7
our v. have tender grapes, 25:7
Vineyard, bound of land tilth v.,
224:4
my well-beloved hath a v., 25:37

Virtue (*continued*)
  substantial and genuine v., 343:10
  sufficient of herself, 245:*n*2
  talk with crowds keep v., 593:20
  that possession would not show,
    187:2
  though in rags, 275:3
  to die honorably greatest v., 60:12
  to flaming youth v. wax, 197:32
  to flee vice beginning of v., 97:5
  treading the course of v., 61:33
  uncommon valor common v.,
    658:14
  unexercised unbreathed, 254:25
  vice assumes some v., 181:5
  while people retain v., 449:6
  wickedness easier than v., 314:30
Virtue's, died in v. cause, 167:9
  failings leaned to V. side, 329:13
Virtues, be to her v. very kind, 287:19
  curse on his v., 292:11
  expected of servant, 336:4
  for several v. several women, 224:12
  forced upon us by crimes, 668:8
  great necessities call out great v.,
    347:8
  greatest vices as well as v., 246:15
  if individuals no v., 346:6
  in self-trust all v. comprehended,
    431:9
  men praise and pass by, 658:13
  of Man without his vices, 398:16
  other v. would be useless, 269:17
  Princedoms V. Powers, 259:13
  suspects himself of v., 694:8
  these v. of delight, 356:12
  to sustain good fortune, 265:1
  trumpet of his own v., 187:13
  we write in water, 226:5
  will plead like angels, 213:7
  world to hide v. in, 201:23
Virtuous, because v. no more cakes
    and ale, 202:5
  hated what was not v., 61:2
  I wish to be v., 61:12
  love of the v., 60:17
  matter for v. deeds, 157:10
  mischief v. do, 463:19
  nation secure only while v., 481:1
  outrageously v., 293:23
  sisters v., 778:2
  sweet and v. soul, 243:12
  sweet slumbers of v., 292:15
  who can find a v. woman, 23:17
  who moost v. alway, 131:11
  woman is a crown, 21:11
  wrongdoing v. for good cause, 99:7
Virtuousest discreetest best, 259:29
Virtuously, many daughters have done
    v., 23:21
Virulence of appetite for revelation,
    642:9
Virum, stilus v. arguit, 234:8
Visage, hides not v. from cottage,
    223:12
  lean body and v., 250:9
  meet your v. here, 701:7
  shattered v. lies, 406:13
  with devotion's v., 196:9
Visages cream and mantle, 179:19

Viscous, words slippery thought v.,
    536:3
Vishnu-land what Avatar, 465:18
Visibility, from him never real v.,
    413:8
Visible, all things v. and invisible,
    44:37
  all v. objects pasteboard masks,
    486:24
  communion with v. forms, 411:1
  elements least v., 729:2
  labor, 428:1
  no light but darkness v., 255:23
  one world v., 248:10
  outward and v. sign, 49:22
  poem of world, 712:19
  power of v. is invisible, 664:14
  tall man more v., 723:10
  work is love made v., 651:13
  world seems formed in love, 486:26
Vision art of seeing invisible, 289:4
  baseless fabric of this v., 224:21
  beatific, 256:20
  boundless v. grows upon us, 503:4
  by the v. splendid, 375:8
  fatal v., 213:20
  I am afoot with my v., 489:17
  I saw in v., 612:2
  in v. once I saw, 382:24
  of all that is ordinary, 483:27
  of Christ thou dost see, 360:1
  of the world, 455:17
  on inward v. close eyes, 587:17
  or waking dream, 415:19
  perfect blessedness v. of God,
    124:12
  religious v. ground for optimism,
    584:11
  unread v. in higher dream, 669:17
  where there is no v., 23:10
  who have clearest v., 72:4
  write the v., 29:40
Visionary anger cleansing sight, 762:5
  gleam, 375:6
  theoretic and v. fear, 344:6
Vision's, my v. greatest enemy, 360:1
Visions, I have multiplied v., 29:30
  of glory, 323:9
  stone better pillow than v., 663:14
  what v. have I seen, 173:24
  while these v. did appear, 174:13
  young men shall see v., 29:32
Visit, delightful v. too short, 387:7
  drops that v. heart, 188:8
  her face too roughly, 193:7
  it by pale moonlight, 377:23
  only here for short v., 682:15
  sins of fathers upon children, 69:17
  us with death, 240:10
Visited, dayspring hath v. us, 38:1
  he hath v. and redeemed, 37:44
  nor v. in Heaven, 513:15
  sick and ye v. me, 36:18
Visitest, son of man that thou v. him,
    15:34
Visiting acquaintance, 352:12
  nothing remarkable beneath v.
    moon, 218:8
  the iniquity of the fathers, 9:10

Visitings, compunctious v. of nature,
    212:29
Visits his dinners not him, 269:12
  never make long v., 664:10
  places eye of heaven v., 171:1
Vita brevis est, 71:*n*6
  Incipit V. Nova, 124:17
  nel mezzo del cammin di nostra v.,
    125:*n*2
Vitae, cursores v. lampada tradunt,
    89:*n*11
  philosophia dux, 87:*n*15
  summa brevis spem vetat, 95:*n*15
Vital, élan v., 577:5
  mechanisms one object, 473:8
  resources, 545:6
  secondary imagination v., 384:7
  spark of heavenly flame, 299:8
  spirit, 577:5
Vitality of thought in adventure,
    584:18
  take side of partner with most v.,
    717:8
Vitalizes, history v. memory, 87:14
Vitalizing work between twenty-five
    and forty, 558:6
Viva la huelga, 758:3
Vivamus atque amemus, 90:*n*14
Vivere, nec sine te nec tecum v. pos-
    sum, 101:*n*9
Vivez n'attendez à demain, 144:*n*3
Vivid air signed with honor, 727:10
  trusty dusky v. true, 561:25
Vivi-mus, bibi-mus v. oremus, 325:16
Vivito, si fueris Romae v. Romano
    more, 113:*n*5
Vivre, il faut tenter de v., 613:*n*5
  serviteurs feront cela, 537:*n*2
Vixens, snap like v. at truth, 660:20
Vixi, ille potens sui dixisse V., 96:*n*20
Vocation, avocation and v., 624:7
  demands self-sacrifice, 691:4
  no sin to labor in v., 176:34
  'tis my v. Hal, 176:34
  to be ruined man is a v., 672:22
  whole v. endless imitation, 375:9
Vodka, medium V. dry Martini, 723:2
Vogel, ich singe wie der V. singt,
    349:*n*2
Vogue, totter into v., 323:22
Voice, all with one v., 41:22
  arrow like sweet v., 403:21
  as sound of many waters, 47:4
  beat and a V. beat, 581:5
  behind me whispered low, 567:16
  bird shall carry the v., 24:22
  can honor's v. provoke, 322:10
  cry Sleep no more, 214:6
  crying in the wilderness, 32:29
  distant v. in darkness, 442:16
  each a mighty v., 376:16
  give but few thy v., 193:30
  hear my v. approach, 490:2
  hear v. in every wind, 321:14
  hear v. of the Bard, 357:25
  heard the v. of the Lord, 26:3
  hearing of a v., 487:2
  heart and v. oppressed, 482:10
  her v. was ever soft, 211:18
  his big manly v., 191:3

Voice (*continued*)
his v. in all her music, 409:6
his v. was propertied, 218:11
horrible v. a politician, 73:1
I hear this night, 415:17
I sing with mortal v., 259:19
I will aggravate my v., 172:28
in every v. every ban, 358:8
in hollow murmurs, 367:12
in v. and tossing, 623:10
is and is not voice of God, 303:5
is full of money, 694:10
is Jacob's voice, 7:38
Israfel has sweetest v., 451:*n*2
joy is the sweet v., 383:10
laws in which we have no v., 347:1
look in that tone of v., 555:2
love's v. wearies not, 407:1
melodies echoes of that v., 383:10
monstrous little v., 172:25
my v. fails me, 331:3
my v. I have lost it, 183:21
my v. is still for war, 292:9
nature without v. or sound, 325:10
no v. but of the silence, 382:2
not because has inexhaustible v.,
    696:23
O for a falconer's v., 175:12
obey v. at eve, 430:9
of charmers charming, 17:29
of gods makes heaven drowsy,
    169:3
of him that crieth in the wilderness,
    27:15
of iron, 94:11
of law harmony of world, 155:3
of many waters, 47:30
of my heart, 424:8
of nature cries, 322:20
of Nature loudly cries, 362:23
of people is voice of God, 120:8
of protest warning appeal, 507:10
of the Lobster, 518:8
of the Lord God walking in garden,
    6:21
of the sluggard, 294:13
of the turtle is heard, 25:6
of the turtledove, 4:9
of the wild goose, 4:7
of thy brother's blood, 7:4
of today herald of tomorrow,
    590:1
one rational v. dumb, 720:13
only a look and a v., 442:16
Orpheus' v. and poetry, 67:24
people's v. odd, 303:5
rise like fountain, 459:27
rise up at the v. of the bird, 24:27
said Cry, 27:17
said I want I want, 738:5
say to everything listening, 773:14
seasoned with gracious v., 181:4
so charming left his v., 259:23
sole daughter of his v., 260:6
song of siren nor v. of hyena, 157:6
Stentor with brazen v., 51:21
stern daughter of v. of God, 376:2
still small v., 12:39, 453:18
still small v. of gratitude, 323:15
sweet rinky-dink v., 753:3

Voice (*continued*)
sweeter thy v., 456:22
that breathed o'er Eden, 405:19
that is still, 456:7
thy sweet v. to me, 401:24
unwearying, 51:9
watchdog's v., 329:11
water never formed to v., 639:7
wherefore let thy v., 459:27
which I uttered was crying, 30:28
whose sound like sea, 374:20
wisdom uttereth her v., 20:19
Voiceless wailing, 671:14
woe, 400:21
Voices, ancestral v. prophesying war,
    382:22
cicadas pour out their piping v.,
    51:13
deep moans with many v., 455:6
distant speaking of v., 738:1
earth with thousand v., 383:4
gentle v. calling, 507:4
hear v. talking about everything,
    774:7
human v. wake us, 667:20
I thank you for your v., 219:5
keep tune oars time, 391:8
lost sea v., 669:20
music when soft v. die, 409:10
of dead sound like torrent's fall,
    403:1
of dissent, 716:1
once Tower of Babel knew, 528:16
other v. other rooms, 753:14
sea has many v., 671:13
sovran v., 417:1
still thy pleasant v., 502:9
that make me sleep again, 224:18
to thee all v. pray, 520:4
trembling for you in v., 587:12
two v. are there, 376:16
when v. of children, 356:17
Voici des fruits des fleurs, 554:*n*3
Void, act against Constitution v.,
    327:6
act against natural equity v., 327:6
conscience v. of offense, 41:30
earth without form and v., 6:4
it has long stood v., 242:9
of envy guile lust, 308:14
of light, 256:4
they have left aching v., 333:21
Voie lactée ô soeur lumineuse, 641:*n*5
Vol, la propriété c'est le v., 453:15
Volcanic, joy gone from sweet v. cone,
    743:16
Volcano, dancing on v., 411:15
of revolution, 578:8
Volcanoes, old factions are v., 332:23
Vole, passes the questing v., 712:5
Volenti non fit iniuria, 120:4
Volitional and portals of discovery,
    647:16
Volleyed and thundered, 458:13
Volontade, e'n la sua v. e nostra pace,
    126:*n*9
Volscians, fluttered your V., 219:15
Voltage, chattering v., 679:14
Voltaire invented history, 307:10
mock on V., 359:2

Volume of forgotten lore, 452:13
views advanced by me in this v.,
    444:11
within v. of my brain, 194:28
Volumes, creators of odd v., 387:25
dry v. of ethics, 342:23
I prize above dukedom, 223:26
might be written, 493:7
of Addison, 314:17
pricks to subsequent v., 200:12
whole v. in folio, 168:21
Voluminous writer, 292:26
Voluntas, ruat coelum fiat v. tua,
    119:28
Voluntatis, hominibus bonae v., 48:8
Volunteered when disaster clouded,
    522:13
Volupté, luxe calme et v., 494:*n*5
Voluptuous, music with v. swell,
    399:21
Voluptuousness, misanthropy and v.,
    424:24
Vomit, dog returneth to his v., 22:30
dog turned to his own v., 46:30
Voodoo economics, 753:10
Vorpal blade, 518:16
Votaress, imperial v. passed on, 173:6
Votaries, hatred renders v. credulous,
    319:24
Vote and act to bring good, 546:11
early vote often, 501:21
give hand and heart to v., 394:9
monyment refuse to help fam'ly,
    602:12
not live to see women v., 427:8
obtain right to v., 751:7
one man one v., 783:20
right to v. denied, 491:25
right to v. not denied on account of
    race, 346:19
right to v. not denied on account of
    sex, 346:20
straw v., 586:5
supporting church and school,
    541:5
Voted not to rescind, 339:3
Voter exercises public trust, 532:12
Votes, as long as I count v., 504:1
Votive, Venus take my v. glass, 288:4
Voulu, vous l'avez v. Georges Dandin,
    269:*n*6
Vow, better that thou not v., 24:3
eternal misery together, 284:16
it shall be so for me, 167:32
that binds too strictly, 459:18
Vowels, ear the open v. tire, 298:18
I recount your births, 565:17
only consonants and v., 674:13
Vowing more than perfection, 200:20
Vows, cancel all our v., 161:11
made in wine, 191:25
soul lends tongue v., 194:5
write woman's v. upon wave, 67:18
Vox populi vox Dei, 120:8
Voyage, all v. of their life, 189:19
finish of a v., 603:23
I am about to take last v., 239:26
like Ulysses made glorious v., 144:1
people complained of long v., 134:7

Voyage (*continued*)
save ship of Union on v., 449:1
to Ithaca, 587:11
Voyager, denies v. further sailing, 68:20
lands v. at last, 506:14
raving skies opened to v., 565:16
Voyagers, fare forward v., 671:17
years are v., 282:11
Voyages, make v. attempt them, 730:22
of the starship Enterprise, 749:7
selecting v. you never make, 618:10
Voyaging through strange seas, 373:10
Voyant, se faire v., 566:*n*2
Voyelles je dirai vos naissances, 565:*n*12
Vrai, le v. n'être pas vraisemblable, 403:*n*3
Vulcan's, foul as V. stithy, 197:5
Vulgar, both great v. and small, 267:8
bourgeois thinking v., 496:13
buildeth on v. heart, 183:26
Discobolus, 524:14
familiar but by no means v., 193:29
manner popular politician, 73:1
tune becomes v. insupportable, 556:18
vast v. meretricious beauty, 694:9
war looked on as v., 566:9
worse than wicked it's v., 555:1
Vulgarize day of judgment, 434:3
Vulgarizing middle class, 500:23
Vuoi, come tu mi v., 604:6

W

Wabash, banks of W., 611:15
Wabe, gimble in the w., 518:15
Wachet auf ruft uns die stimme, 156:*n*7
Wacht am Rhein, 488:*n*1
Wade, should I w. no more, 215:12
through slaughter to throne, 322:16
Wading up to eyes in blood, 331:3
Wafer, sun pasted like w., 611:3
Wafer-cakes, men's faiths w., 185:2
Wafer-thin, rapier-keen w., 715:1
Waft her love to Carthage, 182:7
seas roll to w. me, 301:9
sigh from Indus to Pole, 300:4
Wag, let world w., 141:8
where beards w. all, 144:9
Wage laborers having no means of production, 482:*n*2
Wägen, erst w. dann wagen, 426:*n*1
Wagers sum of resources, 750:*n*2
Wages are value expression, 653:23
bargaining for w., 635:5
home gone and ta'en thy w., 220:3
keeping profits up by keeping w. down, 385:10
of sin is death, 41:45
times hard and w. low, 793:17
took w. and are dead, 580:1
Wagging, alive and w. tail in mud, 80:17
Wagner's music better than it sounds, 560:9
Wagon, hitch your w. to star, 433:5

Wagon (*continued*)
storm like w. crossing bridge, 727:17
water-w. place for me, 600:13
Wagons, honored among w., 737:15
Wags, see how world w., 190:22
so w. the world, 190:*n*2
tail knocks over chair, 677:9
Wail, new w. times' waste, 220:18
night bird's w., 531:12
or knock the breast, 261:25
to w. such woes, 152:8
who buys mirth to w. a week, 166:38
Wailful choir, 416:15
Wailing, voiceless w., 671:14
winds naked woods, 411:8
woman w. for demon-lover, 382:20
Wailings, sighs lamentations and w., 125:8
Waist deep in Big Muddy, 747:11
slender w. confined, 249:29
Wait a bit Oysters cried, 519:4
a man should w., 74:19
all things come to who w., 431:*n*2
be still w., 725:2
digestion w. on appetite, 215:3
do not listen simply w., 651:22
do not w. be still, 651:22
do not w. for last judgment, 732:19
drift w. and obey, 593:27
fold hands and w., 532:6
for wisest of counselors, 65:6
I almost had to w., 281:5
labor and to w., 440:18
stand and w., 255:13
these w. all upon thee, 19:6
times we can't w. for somebody, 768:1
to fawn to crouch to w., 154:6
to watch water clear, 622:19
upon I would, 213:9
upon the Lord, 27:23
who only stand and w., 255:13
why w. until next year, 79:13
Waited, death past so he w., 466:18
for billy-boil, 589:5
for the light, 608:8
for thy salvation, 8:18
three years w. for herald, 705:14
Waiter roars it through hall, 503:2
Waitest for spark from heaven, 498:10
Waiteth, my soul w. for the Lord, 20:3
Waiting for invasion so are fishes, 620:13
for rain, 668:6
taxi throbbing w., 669:1
what are we all w. for, 587:9
worse things w. than death, 533:22
Waits, destiny w. alike, 63:21
human engine w., 669:1
Waive quantum o' the sin, 361:22
Wake and call me early, 454:4
and feel fell of dark, 551:15
awake for night is flying, 156:11
die before I w., 287:14
Do I w. or sleep, 415:19
eternally, 230:24
for the Sun, 445:3

Wake (*continued*)
him no not I, 789:4
human voices w. us, 667:20
in durance vile I w., 364:3
nations underground, 794:18
sleep to w., 468:17
sleeping w. and waking sleep, 146:9
thou wilt not w., 242:2
to sleep, 725:6
truths w. to perish never, 375:12
unto me, 507:5
Waked after long sleep, 224:18
by the circling hours, 259:16
I w. she fled, 255:17
priest all shaven, 792:24
to ecstasy living lyre, 322:11
you have w. me too soon, 294:13
Wakeful nightingale, 258:19
Waken, not w. sleeper soul is away, 565:1
thou with me, 456:20
Wakened by silence, 532:15
us from sleeping, 663:4
Wakens, firefly w., 456:20
Wakes, Maypoles Hock-carts wassails w., 240:16
Sleeping Beauty w. up, 755:6
whoever w. in England, 465:3
Waketh, watchman w. but in vain, 19:29
Waking bliss, 252:28
hope is w. dream, 77:9
morn not w. till she sings, 155:20
nights of w., 378:20
no such matter, 221:12
silence with w. bird, 458:22
sleeping wake and w. sleep, 146:9
souls, 228:3
take my w. slow, 725:6
threshold of w. light, 757:13
vision or w. dream, 415:19
way she had of w. him, 673:10
Walcum, talcum always w., 709:9
Waldo, Matthew and W. guardians, 668:1
Wales, prince of W. in small but costly crown, 644:10
Walk a little faster, 518:5
amidst beautiful things, 588:15
and not faint, 27:23
and wot not what they are, 168:15
ask for old paths and w. therein, 28:18
before they dance, 303:2
by faith, 44:3
can two w. together, 29:35
citizen may w. safely on law, 753:9
closer w. with God, 333:20
crust where I must w., 743:7
cypress in palace w., 456:20
deck my Captain lies, 491:1
down Piccadilly, 529:18
fantasy goes for w. returns with bride, 736:9
fishermen that w. beach, 210:27
foolery does w. about, 202:20
from breakfast to madness, 759:12
happily may I w., 787:10
how many roads man w. down, 771:4

Walk *(continued)*
humbly with thy God, 29:38
I w. unseen, 252:3
I'll rest but thou w., 785:7
in fear and dread, 381:26
in the street, 490:4
in velvet shoes, 660:14
into my parlor, 423:11
it slow where you go, 766:8
let her not w. in the sun, 195:17
let us w. honestly, 42:23
make running water w., 648:9
no spirit can w. abroad, 192:29
not natural to w. on two legs, 342:19
not on earth exultantly, 116:17
on eggs, 233:18
Oysters come w. with us, 519:1
people may w. but not throw stones, 314:28
pleasant w. pleasant talk, 519:1
race of men who w. upon earth, 51:20
revealed her as true goddess, 93:19
rise and w. with him, 67:26
shall not w. in darkness, 40:10
slow silent w., 540:22
solar w. or milky way, 301:7
take up bed and w., 37:18
talk with you w. with you, 180:2
teach crab to w. straight, 73:7
the earth unseen, 258:23
through fields in gloves, 661:12
through valley of shadow, 16:17
under water men w., 777:16
upon England's mountains, 359:17
upon the beach, 667:19
where'er you w., 298:7
which way they w., 213:22
while ye have light, 40:23
with Kings, 593:20
with stretched forth necks, 25:35
ye in it, 27:4
your ghost will w., 465:11
your mystic way, 529:17
Walked along the Strand, 315:10
among ancient trees, 357:25
Cat w. by himself, 593:11
crowns and crownets, 218:11
Enoch w. with God, 7:12
eye-deep in hell, 659:8
glittered when he w., 608:7
him that w. the waves, 254:6
in glory and in joy, 374:9
in the search of the depth, 15:10
people that w. in darkness, 26:7
straight out of ark, 380:5
through wilderness of world, 272:10
to hotel in rain, 701:17
with his mother, 737:13
without upward look, 624:19
Walketh, devil w. about, 46:28
every man w. in a vain show, 17:9
he who w. upright, 117:22
not in counsel of ungodly, 15:29
pestilence that w. in darkness, 18:15
upon the wings of the wind, 19:3
Walking and mincing as they go, 25:35

Walking *(continued)*
as Adam w. forth from bower, 490:2
as I was a-w., 786:1
by wild lone, 593:12
Christ w. on the water, 581:13
close at hand, 518:24
Devil is gone a-w., 386:21
dog's w. on hinder legs, 316:3
enterprise in w. naked, 596:4
giant wings prevent w., 494:2
have ye not seen us w., 267:6
I nauseate w., 291:11
in an air of glory, 270:10
life's but a w. shadow, 216:14
men as trees w., 37:29
on the sea, 35:18
round the fold, 356:16
up and down in it, 13:29
Walking-stick utility as evidence of leisure, 574:9
Walks, all gin joints in world she w. into mine, 726:9
at noon upon two feet, 66:*n*1
biggest rascal that w., 109:24
eye Nature's w., 301:2
God w. in mine, 511:9
having once turned w. on, 381:26
he w. through a wall, 736:7
in beauty, 401:14
in w. it seems to me, 608:21
lards lean earth as he w., 177:15
night in silver shoon, 616:20
o'er dew on eastern hill, 192:30
on hallowed ground, 685:18
she w. lady of delight, 555:17
third who w. beside you, 669:5
thy spirit w. abroad, 189:25
two luxuries in my w., 418:17
up and down with me, 170:4
up stairs of concepts, 710:9
wish I liked way it w., 584:3
Wall, ballads stuck about w., 245:21
before I built a w., 623:1
between church and state, 661:6
Blake beat upon w., 599:11
bores through his castle w., 172:1
broken w. burning tower, 598:1
close w. up with English dead, 185:3
crannied w., 460:5
doesn't love a w., 622:20
down W. from girder into street, 701:3
even w. fell down, 679:13
faces turned to w., 505:2
fell down flat, 10:34
fight for law as for w., 62:20
find the body by w., 500:3
he walks through a w., 736:7
Humpty Dumpty sat on w., 790:13
Jackson like stone w., 504:4
know the w. is strong, 567:21
must be kept high, 661:6
not conclude against w. of stone, 749:17
of oblivion, 697:3
painting lends joyousness to w., 543:19
serves it in office of a w., 171:9

Wall *(continued)*
shadows on opposite w. of cave, 75:17
St. lays egg, 618:4
stone shall cry out of w., 29:41
they which builded on w., 13:21
thou whited w., 41:27
wainscot and mouse, 671:21
waters were a w., 9:1
weakest goes to w., 150:14
when icicles hang by the w., 169:13
whitewashed w., 329:19
wit is the only w., 691:2
without a city w., 479:18
wooden w. is your ships, 62:24
your concern when neighbor's w. on fire, 97:19
Wall Street, nation that supports W., 603:8
on W. had become Masters, 764:6
predicted nine of last five recessions, 739:2
Wallace, wi' W. bled, 363:19
Walled round with rocks, 535:5
vain citadels not w., 687:5
wear out in a w. prison, 211:13
Wallet at his back, 200:23
Walling in or walling out, 623:1
Walloping Window Blind, 545:3
Wallow naked in December snow, 171:3
Wallpaper and I fighting duel, 567:26
one-armed man pasting w., 585:18
things in that w., 583:2
Walls and towers girdled round, 382:19
are nothing, 65:16
close her from ancient w., 359:24
come tumbling down, 794:10
down the mountain w., 599:17
falls on castle w., 456:11
flaming r. of heavens, 89:4
hang banners on outward w., 216:12
happy those whose w. already rise, 93:20
have ears, 130:*n*3
peace be within thy w., 19:27
pry loose old w., 634:9
stone w. not prison make, 267:18
Troilus mounted Troyan w., 182:7
Troy w. famed in battle, 93:30
watches from mountain w., 458:4
Walnuts and wine, 453:23
Walrus and the Carpenter, 518:24
weep for you W. said, 519:6
Walsinghame, holy land of W., 152:9
Walt, I saw you W. Whitman, 757:2
Walter, this is W. Winchell in New York, 698:2
Waltzes, Congress doesn't run it w., 339:2
Waltzing, a-w. Matilda, 589:5
such w. not easy, 724:15
Waly waly up the bank, 785:19
Wan, angels pallid and w., 452:8
how silently with how w. face, 156:5
so w. with care, 176:22
why so pale and w., 262:2

Wander, children shall w. in the wil-
    derness, 10:1
    forth sons of Belial, 256:11
    hand in hand, 643:10
    if I might, 523:5
    thoughts that w. through eternity,
        257:2
    we will not w. more, 454:11
    where'er I w. boast of this, 171:4
    wherever I w. wherever I rove,
        362:16
    whither shall I w., 789:18
Wandered, fingers w. idly, 505:22
    I have w. in a face, 756:17
    lonely as cloud, 375:19
    rising gliding w. off by myself,
        490:9
Wanderer, ah do not we w., 498:10
    Grand Meaulnes the w., 661:13
    merry w. of the night, 173:2
    the w., 661:13
    weary wayworn w., 451:12
Wandering about from house to
    house, 45:19
    between two worlds, 498:20
    by lone sea breakers, 553:21
    from Nightly shore, 452:18
    in w. mazes lost, 257:12
    Jew, 785:7
    lazy Scheldt or w. Po, 328:6
    minstrel I, 530:18
    moon, 252:3
    movement so w. as that of mind,
        145:22
    on foreign strand, 378:1
    planet's course, 161:21
    star to every w. bark, 222:2
    stars, 46:38
    steps and slow, 260:24
    through many countries, 91:17
    to nest from w. wide, 579:22
Wanderings, Aeneas' Odyseus' w.,
    490:6
    errors w. mists and tempests, 89:n9
    to guide, 517:1
Wane, constellations when they w.,
    63:9
    Moon who knowest no w., 446:2
Waneth, youth w. by increasing,
    156:14
Wangle, Quangle W., 472:8
Waning, beneath w. moon haunted,
    382:20
    sadder than w. moon, 443:13
Want, can't always get what you w.,
    773:4
    climacteric of his w., 743:5
    covetous man ever in w., 97:9
    don't w. to be there when happens,
        767:13
    for one who comes not, 694:20
    for w. of nail shoe lost, 244:28,
        310:10
    freedom from w., 649:17, 650:8
    get what you w., 594:2
    House of W., 538:3
    I am Tarzan I w. you, 628:5
    I shall not w., 16:17
    I w. I w. I w., 738:5
    I w. to get off, 763:18

Want (continued)
    in politics if you w. anything, 756:3
    it most like it least, 305:2
    labor with reference to w., 372:12
    me w. cookie, 775:8
    never buy what you do not w.,
        345:5
    no cash means frightful w., 436:23
    no man will supply thy w., 233:12
    nothing you w., 501:20
    of coincidence between accounts,
        71:19
    of decency want of sense, 278:23
    only w. and discontent, 264:3
    progress from w. to w., 316:30
    prove what we w. to prove, 604:12
    thy w. as an armed man, 20:28
    to be alone, 716:2
    to be masters of own fate, 700:4
    to spend to give to w., 154:6
    toil envy w., 313:17
    we do not do what we w., 717:14
Wanted, every man is w., 432:20
    never done single thing I w. to,
        658:6
    never w. a good word, 328:2
    when discovered not w., 665:12
Wanting, not w. what is stolen, 207:7
    perfect and entire w. nothing, 46:4
    that which is w. cannot be num-
        bered, 23:27
    tried and found w., 618:15
    weighed in the balances and found
        w., 29:16
    winning isn't everything but w. to
        is, 783:n10
    words once my stock w., 276:17
Wanton, as flies to w. boys, 210:20
    boys that swim on bladders, 225:16
    Frere ther was w. and merye,
        129:16
    gods that w. in the air, 267:16
    her w. spirits look out, 201:10
    stings of sense, 203:26
    stretched forth necks and w. eyes,
        25:35
    wiles, 251:8
Wantoned with thy breakers, 401:4
Wantonness, chambering and w.,
    42:23
    kindles in clothes a w., 241:4
Wanton's, no further than w. bird,
    175:14
Wantons thro' flowering thorn, 362:8
Wants, everything he w., 501:20
    getting what one w., 566:22
    give lady what she w., 522:14
    has more than he w., 293:10
    having fewest w., 70:19
    man w. but little, 296:14, 328:22
    nor w. that little long, 296:14,
        328:22
    not getting what one w., 566:22
    nothing but eternity, 219:13
    provide for human w., 332:11
    speech not to express w., 280:n1
    the natural touch, 215:25
    to make flesh creep, 468:23
    what man w. he w. now, 736:16
    what other Americans want, 627:21

War, a god has given deeds of w.,
    52:1
    a just w., 310:n5, 341:4
    aftermath of w., 626:1
    all policy's allowed in w., 482:n4
    all's fair in love and w., 482:13
    alone brings nobility, 652:20
    always stirring up some w., 75:28
    an invention, 653:16
    and deeds of carnage be lost, 490:14
    and music run off same circuit,
        770:5
    annihilating itself in big w., 645:19
    as much and as little of w., 160:7
    battlefield of that w., 450:2
    becoming impossible, 601:9
    begun without money, 139:10
    between men and women, 690:9
    blast of w. in ears, 185:3
    blessing compared with reign of lie,
        680:5
    blood-swollen god, 611:1
    brazen throat of w., 260:21
    breeds war again, 573:23
    chance of w., 200:2
    check murders but what of w.,
        103:2
    circumstance of glorious w., 207:8
    coin is sinews of w., 139:10
    cold w. getting warmer, 608:15
    concealed throughout w., 531:17
    condition which is called w., 239:21
    Constitution is law in w. and peace,
        474:21
    contagion, 649:10
    continuation of political relations,
        393:3
    dastard in w., 378:9
    dauntless in w., 378:8
    dearth age agues, 230:20
    defeated warriors go to w. first,
        80:19
    delays dangerous in w., 155:n1
    deserve success in w., 622:5
    dogs of w., 188:23
    Don John going to w., 619:2
    drum throbbed no longer, 455:18
    each w. creation of preceding w.,
        631:n2
    ease after w., 153:9
    easier to make w. than peace, 542:3
    either man obsolete or w., 691:17
    end to w., 650:6
    enemies in w. in peace friends,
        343:3
    engaged in great civil w., 450:2
    epithets of w., 205:8
    even to the knife, 399:12
    everybody against w., 681:6
    factories may make end of w.,
        521:2
    first in w. first in peace, 355:16
    first invented w., 161:19
    for scrap of paper make w., 568:13
    fought with atomic bomb, 636:3
    France has not lost w., 678:9
    garland of the w., 218:8
    generator of wars, 631:n2
    give a w. nobody come, 634:12
    glorious art, 296:3

War (*continued*)

God is w. peace surfeit hunger, 62:13
Great Britain going to w., 568:13
has actually begun, 339:10
hath smoothed his front, 165:19
health of state, 661:10
how much w. seen, 749:4
I am for w., 502:5
I am the tongue of w., 765:17
I call it murder, 485:10
I have seen w. I hate w., 649:4
I make w. on the living, 143:2
if they mean to have w., 333:5
I'll furnish the w., 587:14
image of w. without guilt, 295:1
in heaven, 47:27
in his heart, 17:28
in peace thinks of w., 235:8
in state of w. by nature, 289:19
in this w. books are weapons, 649:21
in Vietnam would end, 753:1
in w. daring boastful, 404:21
in w. mounts warrior's steed, 377:25
in w. no second prize, 685:14
in w. no substitute for victory, 642:4
in w. parents inter children, 69:22
in w. resolution, 622:4
in Zurich during the w., 769:6
infection and hand of w., 171:9
is a contagion, 649:10
is a game, 335:10
is at best barbarism, 492:12
is cruelty, 492:9
is hell, 492:12
is inevitable, 636:2
is just a shot away, 773:3
is kind, 611:8
is peace, 711:17
is still the cry, 399:12
its thousands slays, 336:3
killed only once in w., 619:16
let slip dogs of w., 188:23
levying w., 346:9
liberty to begin and end W., 160:*n*5
lived peacefully without w., 370:*n*1
Lord is a man of w., 9:3
love and W. same thing, 150:39
love calls to w., 157:2
love of w. for itself, 422:16
luxury more deadly than w., 109:2
magnificent but not w., 460:19
make w. to live in peace, 78:10
makes rattling good history, 540:16
mankind must put end to w., 741:10
marching as to w., 521:10
men unproved in w., 522:13
money sinews of w., 88:13
moral equivalent of w., 546:23
my voice is still for w., 292:9
national misfortune, 426:5
neither shall they learn w., 25:30
never good w. or bad peace, 310:23
never slays bad man, 67:4
no discharge in w., 24:16, 593:15

War (*continued*)

no more w. between Arabs Israelis, 745:22
no w. or battle's sound, 250:21
noble efforts in last w., 313:4
not an instinct, 653:16
not quadrille in ball-room, 491:15
not separated from politics, 686:14
not to live but to make w., 727:15
nourishes war, 365:8
object of w. peace, 492:11
object only of w. honorable, 341:4
of looks between them, 165:11
of nature, 444:10
older men declare w., 626:1
on w. in Vietnam, 772:1
only art necessary, 136:12
open or secret w., 343:16
outcome of the w. in our hands, 52:9
pattern called w., 626:9
peace better than most just w., 310:*n*5
peace corrupt w. waste, 260:22
peace not absence of w., 277:15
political relations by other means, 393:3
politics almost exciting as w., 619:16
prepared for w., 337:3
prince have no study but w., 136:12
prophesying w., 382:22
prospect of future w. unendurable, 714:10
purple testament of bleeding w., 172:2
put end to mankind, 741:10
quaint and curious w. is, 540:12
ready for w. to avoid it, 284:12
Real W. Never Get in Books, 491:14
reason we bicker creates w., 146:4
red animal, 611:1
regarded as inevitable probable, 714:1
regarded as wicked, 566:9
relentless, 610:3
remember w. against Franco, 759:5
result of mistaken calculation, 628:6
scourge of w., 450:11, 655:23
seek no wider w., 723:17
seldom enters but where wealth allures, 275:18
sentence is for open w., 256:26
silent w. of lilies, 166:36
sinews of w., 88:13
small w. on heels of small w., 743:16
some slain in w., 171:25
Son of God goes forth to w., 395:17
Spanish ships of w., 460:6
Spanish-American W. splendid little w., 536:15
spares not the brave, 60:3
stand up and take w., 593:24
study politics and w., 338:10
subject of it is W., 687:1
suppose they gave a w., 634:*n*2
sweets with sweet w. not, 220:10
sword of w. or of law, 344:20

War (*continued*)

tempered by w., 741:3
that will end war, 601:11
the w. is over, 501:12
there was w. in heaven, 47:27
thermonuclear w. means to suicide, 749:8
they could do with good w., 698:18
this is w., 440:8
this w. one of elemental conflicts, 676:11
those who brought w. to Far East, 655:6
though w. should rise against me, 16:22
Thucydides wrote history of w., 71:18
time of w. time of peace, 23:32
to make world safe, 587:16
to prevent w. not fear it, 385:14
to w. and arms I fly, 267:14
too serious for military, 354:9
train of circumstances, 341:5
ultimate sanction of exploitation, 686:6
unjust peace before just w., 310:*n*5
unjust w. protracted, 487:24
unsuccessful or successful w., 334:26
vain w. with heaven, 256:23
vast aloof absentee, 768:13
victorious warriors win go to w., 80:19
warmest heart recoiled at w., 688:16
wasn't fought that way, 685:2
weapons important in w., 686:13
weapons of w. perished, 12:2
well that w. so terrible, 440:12
what w. said Prime Minister, 712:3
when aggressions require w., 344:10
when I speak they are for w., 19:24
when w. he went, 721:4
when w. is done, 662:6
who desires peace prepare for w., 114:17
with rere-mice, 173:10
with rights of mankind, 343:16
woman cause of ten years' w., 284:15
wrong w. at wrong time, 685:15
youth I love gone to w., 787:15
War bonnet of Medicine Hat, 698:6
Warble child, 168:25
native wood-notes wild, 251:19
sweet in springtime, 564:19
Warbled to the string, 252:7
Warbler, Dan Chaucer first w., 454:12
mysterious w. followed me, 543:16
Warblest at eve, 254:9
Warbling his Doric lay, 254:7
thou w. bird, 362:8
Warden said do you have anything to say, 753:4
Warder is Despair, 567:22
memory the w. of brain, 213:14
Wardrobe, dalliance in w. lies, 184:27
Wards, pretty young w. in Chancery, 530:7
Ware, ill w. is never cheap, 244:5

Ware (continued)
    pleasing w. is half sold, 244:5
    taste your w., 789:5
    that will not keep, 578:20
Wares harder to get rid of, 623:11
Warfare is accomplished, 27:15
    Italy years of w. terror murder,
        739:5
    love a kind of w., 101:n6
    mutual help as often as w., 704:4
    thy w. o'er, 378:20
War-horse, didst hurl him upon a w.,
    486:22
Waring, what's become of W., 465:17
Warlike, people numerous and w.,
    134:13
Warm and capable of grasping, 417:3
    cheek and rising bosom, 323:1
    heart within, 335:15
    her coat is so w., 394:3
    into the w. sun, 142:16
    keeper of w. lights, 66:18
    keeps w. her note, 246:5
    let out to w. air, 289:12
    man whose blood is w., 179:18
    now w. in love, 300:3
    nursing wrath to keep it w., 363:2
    precincts of cheerful day, 322:19
    ruddy drops that w. heart, 188:n1
    so cold no fire w., 514:19
    sun was w. wind chill, 624:6
    this sensible w. motion, 204:14
    virtue keep me w., 275:3
    weather in bed, 288:20
    wind the west wind, 633:17
    without heating, 296:24
Warm-blooded animals from one
    filament, 335:24
Warmed, glow has w. the world,
    654:n2
    hands before fire of life, 388:21
    unclasps w. jewels, 415:5
    wood stumps w. me twice, 478:30
Warmest heart recoiled at war, 688:16
    welcome at an inn, 316:n8
Warming pretty little toes, 790:15
Warmly, in numbers w. pure, 324:12
Warms, who splits wood w. twice,
    478:n1
Warmth, a little w. a little light,
    522:10
    no w. no cheerfulness, 423:1
    spring brings back balmy w., 91:2
    warmth more warmth, 589:16
    writing about w., 723:1
Warn, all poet can do is w., 687:1
    to comfort and command, 375:18
Warned in a dream, 32:24
    prior to questioning, 682:10
    woman be w., 767:2
Warner, I am only a w., 116:6
Warning, come without w., 474:1
    give w. to world, 221:7
    voice of w. needed, 507:10
Warp, may w. be light of morning,
    787:5
    weave the w., 323:7
Warrant him heart-whole, 192:1
    she'll prove an excuse, 352:29
    truth shall be thy w., 152:15

Warrants, no w. but upon probable
    cause, 346:13
Warred for Homer dead, 233:22
Warring within breasts, 161:21
Warrior, better thing exists not for w.,
    84:6
    British w. queen, 334:21
    every lover a w., 101:9
    Happy W. of political battlefield,
        618:n2
    home brought her w., 456:18
    lay like w. taking rest, 405:16
    like an armed w., 520:11
    of North America, 404:21
    painful w. famoused for fight,
        220:14
    who is the happy W., 376:8
Warrior's, in war mounts w. steed,
    377:25
Warriors, defeated w. go to war first,
    80:19
    female w., 306:20
    my forefathers were w., 370:2
    pale w. death-pale, 417:7
    stern joy w. feel, 378:25
    Time and Patience strongest of w.,
        510:6
    victorious w. win first go to war,
        80:19
    where are Sioux w., 516:9
War's a game, 335:10
    annals cloud into night, 540:22
    disciplinary function, 546:23
    glorious art, 296:3
Wars, all skillful in the w., 270:8
    all their w. merry, 618:17
    all w. boyish fought by boys, 487:7
    and alarums unto nations, 154:2
    and rumors of wars, 36:7
    boys not sent into foreign w.,
        649:15
    brought nothing about, 276:22
    chronicle the w. of kites, 261:28
    continual w. and wives, 762:17
    disciplines of w., 185:9
    ecclesiastic influence increased w.,
        536:19
    fierce w. and faithful loves, 153:4
    for right thing, 655:19
    forgotten w., 670:14
    fought by babies, 751:13
    global from the start, 737:5
    more pangs than w. or women,
        225:4
    no more w. no more bloodshed,
        732:10
    of European powers, 360:11
    of interest and intrigue, 368:16
    part in developing man, 532:11
    planned by old men, 643:14
    Rome's decline in consuming w.,
        656:13
    Star W., 773:n1
    that make ambition virtue, 207:8
    thousand w. of old, 457:30
    want end to beginnings of w., 650:6
    won by men, 658:15
    wrong from every standpoint,
        655:19
Warts and all, 247:n3

Warts (continued)
    pimples w. and everything, 247:5
War-war, jaw-jaw better than to w.,
    622:8
Was, he is or w. or has to be, 307:3
    I am not what I w., 288:4
    tell it like it w., 710:4
    which w. and is and is to come,
        47:15
Wash, air w. leaves cover me, 533:18
    balm from anointed king, 171:21
    bid them w. their faces, 219:4
    Death and Night w. world, 490:14
    dirty linen at home, 370:11
    feet in soda water, 668:23
    gulfs w. us down, 455:6
    makes me w., 526:4
    me and I shall be whiter than snow,
        17:21
    old linen w. whitest, 237:11
    that man outa my hair, 692:14
    this blood from my hand, 214:9
    what art w. guilt away, 328:29
    with Pilate w. your hands, 172:11
Washed her with wine, 760:2
    if clod w. away, 231:8
    Pilate w. hands, 37:7
    robes in blood, 47:23
    when died w. me out of turret,
        735:21
Washing hands with invisible soap,
    423:2
    home and being w.-day, 279:15
    one another's w., 782:9
Washington, America furnished W.,
    395:4
    bequeathed name of W., 401:12
    city of southern efficiency, 742:8
    Evolution from W. to Grant, 535:25
    full of famous men women they
        married, 541:1
    George W. slept here, 676:16
    Government at W. lives, 516:2
    in clear upper sky, 394:11
    Leonidas and W., 403:9
    like Joshua of old, 310:21
    never slopt over, 521:19
    task greater than W., 448:16
    what posterity say of W., 310:20
Washington's a watchword, 404:4
Washpot, Moab is my w., 17:31
WASP upper class, 738:3
Waspish, when you are w., 189:15
Wasps and hornets break through,
    288:18
Wassails, Maypoles Hock-carts w.,
    240:16
Waste and solitary places, 407:7
    don't w. time mourning, 637:2
    haste maketh w., 140:15
    his flames must w. away, 246:9
    lay w. our powers, 376:11
    mind terrible thing to w., 784:11
    my dear times' w., 220:18
    natural resources, 576:7
    nights in discontent, 154:5
    not fresh tears, 69:9
    now doth time w. me, 172:15
    of public money, 537:12
    of seas, 421:17

Wax, fill hives with honey and w., 288:17
  mind a block of w., 76:11
  my heart is w., 151:23
  rich gifts w. poor, 196:12
  shoes ships sealing w., 519:3
  snapped like sealing w., 470:13
  to flaming youth virtue w., 197:32
  to receive, 402:3
Waxed, Jeshurun w. fat, 10:27
Waxworks, if we're w. you pay, 518:21
Way, abode Hour and went his w., 445:11
  all the w. home, 789:3
  broad is the w., 34:9
  catch the nearest w., 212:28
  come all the w. for this, 523:4
  crow shook snow, 623:15
  died maintaining right of w., 783:22
  down upon Swanee River, 506:19
  every day in every w., 573:18
  every one his own w., 86:13
  every w. makes my gain, 208:6
  everything's going my w., 692:8
  for woman to hold a man, 746:9
  go not into every w., 31:11
  God moves in mysterious w., 333:22
  going the w. of all the earth, 10:39
  great white w., 584:2
  he should go, 22:9
  hear right w. in the morning, 61:3
  heaven's wide pathless w., 252:3
  home's the farthest way, 242:11
  Hungary Poland doing it their w., 771:n1
  I did it my w., 770:17
  in dark wood where straight w. lost, 125:3
  in whatsoever w. any come to Me, 84:9
  is plain peaceful just, 449:16
  I've a long w. to go, 716:20
  jog on the footpath w., 223:4
  king stood at parting of w., 29:7
  lambs who lost w., 592:3
  let each go his own w., 101:1
  let the wicked forsake his w., 28:1
  life's common w., 374:20
  like wild beast guards w., 358:16
  long and steep is the w., 54:24
  long is the w. and hard, 257:10
  long w. to Tipperary, 627:15
  long wind cold, 377:19
  longest w. round shortest home, 242:n4
  love find w., 777:11
  make it over your w., 625:16
  merit makes his w., 225:2
  met you not my Love by the w., 152:9
  my w. of life is fallen, 216:9
  narrow is the w., 34:9
  new w. to pay old debts, 238:10
  no ready w. to virtue, 248:16
  no w. out for me, 680:7
  noiseless tenor of their w., 322:17
  not pass this w. again, 780:5
  of a fool, 21:13

Way (*continued*)
  of a man with a maid, 23:15, 592:9
  of a serpent upon a rock, 23:15
  of a ship in the sea, 23:15
  of all flesh, 237:12
  of an eagle in the air, 23:15
  of coming into world, 288:13
  of Heaven has no favorites, 58:5
  of Heaven to benefit others, 58:7
  of ignorance, 671:6
  of sage is to act, 58:7
  of the tree of life, 7:1
  of transgressors is hard, 21:15
  old paths where is the good w., 28:18
  out of hell leads up, 257:10
  out of wind's and rain's w., 644:13
  plods his weary w., 322:1
  prepare the w. before me, 30:8
  prepare the w. of the Lord, 27:15, 32:29
  pretty Fanny's w., 295:19
  primrose w., 214:10
  rebellion lay in his w., 178:30
  roses all the w., 464:27
  see the W. of Heaven, 57:15
  set out in relative w., 618:14
  ship's w. upon sea, 592:9
  so plain we may lose way, 619:7
  solar walk or milky w., 301:7
  Spring comes slowly up this w., 382:10
  such ever love's w., 467:12
  sweetest w. to me, 592:9
  tells us the w. to go, 562:13
  that can be told of, 56:12
  that w. madness lies, 210:2
  that's the w. it is, 739:11
  that's the w. to do it, 397:10
  the money goes, 780:13
  the truth and the life, 40:28
  there is a lion in the w., 22:30
  they say it, 710:10
  this is w. world ends, 669:11
  this the w. walk ye in it, 27:4
  thorny w. to heaven, 193:27
  though hell bar w., 643:12
  thoughts nature gives w. to, 213:18
  to bliss, 242:6
  to draw new mischief, 205:30
  to dusty death, 216:14
  to keep thee in the w., 9:16
  to man's heart, 462:10
  to tell if poem lasting, 625:7
  took their solitary w., 260:24
  trudgin' weary w., 554:9
  true w. but yet untried, 158:12
  true w. goes over rope, 651:21
  twinkle on milky w., 375:20
  unlikely to be undone, 682:9
  what counts is w. writer says it, 751:6
  win my w. to the coast, 68:20
  wisdom finds a w., 353:17
  with tears watered, 612:3
  world ends, 669:11
Wayfarer world renowned, 120:9
Wayfaring, lodging place of w. men, 28:22
Way-hay you rolling river, 793:12

Ways, amend your w., 28:19
  blood nipped and w. be foul, 169:13
  consider her w. and be wise, 20:27
  dazzled by w. of God, 637:5
  dwelt among untrodden w., 373:19
  from cheerful w. of men, 257:24
  God's w. to man, 579:15
  her w. are w. of pleasantness, 20:21
  his w. are judgment, 10:26
  I will take heed to my w., 17:5
  in all the w. you can, 309:2
  in His w. found Him not, 459:22
  just are the w. of God, 261:12
  keep thee in all thy w., 18:16
  labyrinthine w., 581:4
  many w. meet in one town, 184:25
  nine and sixty w., 592:8
  of God justifiable, 261:12
  of God to man, 301:2
  of God to men, 255:20
  of making men talk, 680:16
  oldest sins newest w., 184:13
  possible to fail in many w., 78:3
  practice childish w., 52:31
  sing ancient w., 594:20
  stand ye in the w., 28:18
  that are dark, 532:1
  to lengthen our days, 392:1
  to make thy w. known, 49:3
  triple w. to take, 592:9
  your w. are not my w., 28:2
Wayside, seeds fell by w., 35:5
Wayward, clod of w. marl, 186:18
  fond and w. thoughts, 373:18
  fortune's w. tyranny, 65:10
  purblind w. boy, 168:28
  sisters depart, 398:10
  tetchy and w. thy infancy, 166:6
Wayworn, weary w. wanderer, 451:12
We about to die salute you, 110:6
  are Ancients of the earth, 158:n3
  are as much as we see, 476:20
  are his offspring, 41:17, 82:12
  are his people, 18:22
  are many, 37:24
  are not amused, 488:6
  are the hollow men, 669:8
  are the world, 775:3
  be brethren, 7:27
  content at the last, 671:19
  gather together, 777:8
  happy few, 185:23
  have ways of making men talk, 680:16
  must needs die, 12:13
  my ship and I., 709:4
  real cool, 740:8
  shall not be moved, 794:23
  shall overcome, 783:21
  that had loved him so, 464:23
  the peoples of United Nations, 655:23
  thought we would try, 709:4
  were very tired, 684:3
  would and would not, 205:1
Weader, Tonstant Weader Fwowed up, 687:12
Weak and beggarly elements, 44:15
  and fruitless words, 450:9

Well *(continued)*
learn to do w., 25:29
loved not wisely but too w., 208:16
mania for saying things are w., 306:7
moments when everything goes w., 589:7
not so deep as a w., 175:27
of true wit truth, 509:13
paid that is satisfied, 182:6
poetry must be w. written as prose, 660:3
preaches w. that lives w., 150:38
pussy's in w., 789:6
roared Lion, 174:8
servant of God w. done, 259:17
sing so wildly w., 451:13
spent but one day thoroughly w., 132:18
till the w. runs dry, 309:n6
to do w. is what matters, 247:8
work done by men who not feel w., 723:13
worth doing is worth doing w., 304:18
Well-a-day, youth cry W., 785:9
Well-being dependent on well-being of others, 650:5
instructions for, 5:10
Well-beloved, my w. hath a vineyard, 25:37
Well-benched, board the w. ships, 55:21
Wellborn, few are rich and w., 355:1
Well-bred man knows how to confess, 309:25
very strange and w., 291:12
Well-chosen anthology, 692:3
book or friend, 227:7
Well-conducted, like a w. person, 463:21
Well-doing, be not weary in w., 44:22
religion of w. and daring, 315:n7
Well-drawn, find w. character, 526:14
Well-dressed, sense of being perfectly w., 433:17
Well-favored man, 186:36
Well-fed, not these w. men I fear, 89:1
Well-filled, well-made rather than w. head, 145:16
Well-furnished libraries, 234:2
Well-governed, marble w. cities, 721:2
Well-graced actor leaves, 172:13
Well-greaved Achaeans, 51:14
Wellington's army, 326:n1
Well-knownness, celebrity person known for w., 735:16
Well-made rather than well-filled head, 145:16
Well-read, writer to show he is w., 574:17
Well's, when the w. dry, 309:30
Wells, buckets into empty w., 335:1, 380:7
toads brooding in w., 724:17
we have no w., 705:16
Well-spent, rare as w. Life, 412:23
Well-trod stage, 251:19
Well-wishing adventurer, 220:n1
Well-written Life rare, 412:23

Well-wrought urn becomes greatest ashes, 228:16
Welsh, hear lady sing in W., 178:9
Welshman, Taffy was a W., 789:13
Welt, die W. ist alles was der Fall ist, 677:n2
Weltering in his blood, 276:12
Weltgeschichte ist das Weltgericht, 364:n4
Weltschmerz, 367:1
Wenceslas, good King W., 482:8
Wench, besides the w. is dead, 162:9
fair hot w. in taffeta, 176:24
one w. in the house, 238:n3
weary of w. guest weather, 309:7
Wendy, Peter and W., 581:26
Wenlock, tarnish late on W. Edge, 579:8
Went, as cooks go she w., 610:14
in jeopardy of their lives, 12:17
Lord w. before them, 8:43
ne'er w. up again, 788:6
same door wherein I w., 445:17
to bed with stockings on, 791:12
to woods to live deliberately, 478:17
Wept as I remembered, 502:9
he w. to hear, 356:4
I w. and I believed, 369:14
I w. for I longed to see him hanged, 609:5
Jesus w., 40:20
like anything to see, 518:24
my father w., 358:11
Peter w. bitterly, 37:3
remembering he w. bitterly, 52:24
that he was born, 608:3
when the poor cried Caesar w., 189:1
when we remembered Zion, 20:6
young man who has not w., 588:18
Were, Euripides drew men as they w., 65:n7
now you are not as you w., 540:19
Werewolf's painful change, 750:1
Wernher, not my department says W. von Braun, 759:6
West begins where rainfall drops, 696:5
bosom of urgent W., 549:19
Cincinnatus of W., 401:12
East and W. will pinch heart, 683:16
East is East W. W., 591:9
east or w. Phoenix builds, 246:6
East Side W. Side, 585:7
far down within dim W., 451:14
go w. young man, 475:4
is San Francisco, 586:3
Lochinvar out of the W., 378:7
most beautiful lady in W. Country, 616:21
one flew w., 792:8
one ship east another w., 562:13
open the W. Port, 379:27
safeguard of w., 374:17
specter in W. called dissent, 768:7
spirit of w. Greek discovery, 603:25
that's where W. begins, 616:13
the achieved W., 696:7
turn to great W., 462:12

West *(continued)*
what W. has thrown on waters, 754:6
Wild W. began, 606:4
wild W. Wind, 407:13
wind and the swallows, 83:2
wind full of cries, 633:17
without declining W., 228:4
West Egg, Jay Gatsby of W. Long Island, 694:9
Westen, im w. nichts neues, 700:8
Wester, rainy Pleiads w., 580:5
Western, all quiet on w. front, 700:8
brookland, 579:11
civilization be feminized, 737:1
custom of one wife, 610:17
equipped as W. world, 525:17
from east to w. Ind, 191:10
little w. flower, 173:6
many w. islands, 413:24
Playboy of the W. World, 613:10
walk o'er w. wave, 409:13
wind of w. sea, 456:10
wind when wilt thou blow, 776:6
world lost civil courage, 746:7
Westerners, Greeks first w., 603:25
Westminster Abbey or victory, 360:13
Westward I go free, 479:5
look the land is bright, 483:3
the course of empire, 296:27
Westward-ho, 202:24
Wet, all dirty and w., 290:20
all night in dark and w., 561:9
black bough, 659:1
eye manes dhry heart, 603:3
farmers pray that summers be w., 92:23
liked getting feet w., 600:23
my mind and say something clever, 72:14
nor ever w. with rain, 53:9
not nasty dirty w. hole, 685:3
sail w. seas roun', 592:19
sheet and flowing sea, 396:22
slip out of w. clothes, 675:11
wild woods, 593:12
Whacks, forty w., 781:11
Whale, endless processions of the w., 486:18
eyes wide open in waters, 657:22
leap of w. up Niagara, 310:15
Moby Dick w. or man, 685:1
to chase that white w., 486:23
very like a w., 197:18
Whale's backbone, 671:13
white hump, 486:25
Whales, drag Atlantic Ocean for w., 526:7
great w. sailing by, 497:8
in mid-ocean, 657:22
talk like w., 330:17
Whaleship was my Yale College and Harvard, 486:21
Wharf, rots in ease on Lethe w., 194:19
Wharves, remember black w. and slips, 442:6
What a dump, 704:3
ain't so, 479:27
and Why and When, 593:8

What (*continued*)
　are they among many, 40:2
　are you when sun shall rise, 227:9
　art thou idol ceremony, 185:18
　can I do for her, 741:*n*1
　could she have done, 595:18
　did Hand of Potter shake, 446:4
　do I know, 146:6
　does a woman want, 569:19
　find out who he is w. he's about,
　　773:19
　God hath joined, 35:35
　hath God wrought, 10:7
　have I done unto thee, 10:4
　have I to do with thee, 39:38
　I am so shall thou be, 120:9
　I have done with where I have been,
　　665:14
　is a man profited, 35:30
　is Africa to me, 711:2
　is city but people, 219:8
　is left when honor lost, 99:9
　is love 'tis not hereafter, 202:2
　is man, 656:6
　is so rare as day in June, 485:5
　is that something, 705:11
　is the night, 215:11
　is this quintessence of dust, 195:29
　is truth, 40:36
　is truth said jesting Pilate, 159:2
　is your life, 46:15
　is yours is mine, 83:7
　know wot's w., 469:1
　makest thou, 27:26
　me worry, 783:27
　needs my Shakespeare, 251:2
　news on the Rialto, 180:2
　no soap, 324:7
　of the night, 26:20
　price glory, 666:6
　say they let them say, 154:*n*10
　shall I cry, 27:17
　the anvil, 358:7
　the devil was he doing in that gal-
　　ley, 269:28
　the hammer, 358:7
　thou seest write, 47:2
　we did after we arrived, 754:3
　who why which w., 472:7
　you have let it suffice, 6:1
　you see is what you get, 784:15
Whatever begotten born and dies,
　597:7
　gods may be, 534:15, 557:9
　I tried to write was verse, 102:4
　is fickle freckled, 551:1
　is in its causes just, 273:19
　is is right, 301:12
　Miss T. eats, 617:5
　stirs this mortal frame, 383:3
　you have spend less, 317:28
　you lose reckon no account, 99:6
Whatever's, hold own with w. going,
　625:16
What's done is done, 214:24
　gone and what's past help, 222:25
　Hecuba to him, 196:5
　her history, 202:14
　in a name, 175:2
　it going to be then eh, 740:14

What's (*continued*)
　past and what's to come, 201:11
　past is prologue, 224:5
　the shootin' for, 632:14
　use of worrying, 641:11
Whatsoever, in w. way any come to
　Me, 84:9
　ye would men do, 34:8
What-was-his-name, 519:19
What-you-may-call-um, 519:19
Wheat, belly is like a heap of w.,
　25:18
　fields tall with w., 703:13
　foam to w. glitter of seas, 764:20
　for this planting, 277:*n*2
　gasoline more than w. cause of con-
　　flict, 727:15
　hid in two bushels of chaff, 179:23
　immortal w., 280:23
　land of w. and barley, 10:16
　stacker of w., 634:4
　worm in the w., 612:2
Wheaten, sickle and w. sheaf, 308:6
Wheel, as w. runs why water pitcher,
　98:4
　bound upon w. of fire, 211:9
　breaks butterfly upon w., 302:14
　broken at the cistern, 24:28
　ever-whirling w., 154:1
　I the limbs and w., 494:7
　in the middle of a wheel, 29:5
　is come full circle, 211:16
　man at w. taught to feel, 545:3
　queer shoulder to the w., 757:3
　shoulder to the w., 59:14
　smile once more turn thy w., 209:16
　sofa round, 335:3
　that squeaks gets grease, 479:26
　turned an easy w., 414:20
Wheelbarrow, red w. glazed with rain,
　654:1
Wheelock, Eleazer W. pious man,
　589:4
Wheel's kick and winds' song, 633:14
Wheels, beetle w. droning flight, 322:2
　clicked off by little w., 696:11
　Little Tin Gods on W., 590:18
　of weary life, 273:21
　oil for its own w., 334:14
　why tarry the w. of his chariots,
　11:6
Whelming, under the w. tide, 254:4
Whelp, mongrel puppy w. hound,
　328:26
When I heard learned astronomer,
　490:9
　I knew him w., 611:17
　men drink they are rich, 72:14
　not w. but why families came,
　　754:3
　or how I cannot tell, 509:29
　shall we three meet again, 212:9
　that I was little tiny boy, 203:7
　What and Why and W., 593:8
　will they ever learn, 747:10
Whence and what art thou, 257:17
　comest thou, 13:29
　cradle asks w., 520:13
　had they come, 599:5

Whenever, if poor w. you can if rich
　w. you please, 77:4
Whensoever called to make exit, 348:1
Where and Oh where, 366:20
　are snows of yesteryear, 134:1
　are you going to, 790:6
　cries out W. is it, 382:18
　fear to be we know not w., 273:15
　go without my mount, 747:13
　have all the flowers gone, 747:10
　hell is there must we be, 162:16
　How and W. and Who, 593:8
　I am there ye may be, 40:27
　is fancy bred, 181:3
　is it now the glory, 375:6
　is she now, 216:4
　not how many but w. they are,
　　70:17
　was Roderick then, 379:1
　wast thou when I laid the founda-
　　tions, 15:7
　we are is hell, 162:16
　who are we w. are we, 477:7
　your treasure is, 33:14
Whereabout, stones prate of my w.,
　213:22
Whereas I was blind, 40:14
Where'er she lie, 264:9
　you walk, 298:7
Wherefore are these things hid, 201:22
　art thou Romeo, 175:1
　causes why and w., 185:25
　every why hath a w., 166:22
　stopp'st me, 380:26
Wherein lies happiness, 414:11
Where's my serpent of old Nile, 217:7
　rest of me, 711:20
Wheresoever called to make exit,
　348:1
Wherever, home w. that may be,
　729:7
　I am, 767:6
　they burn books, 420:3
Whetstone, finest edge with blunt w.,
　155:6
　of wits, 189:31
Whetted, wind's like w. knife, 633:16
Whey, curds and w., 791:8
Which, at odds with morning w. is w.,
　215:11
　God only knows w. is w., 535:7
　is the justice, 211:3
　of us has known brother, 706:17
　that and w., 575:1
　who why what, 472:7
Whiff of grapeshot, 412:15
Whiffling through tulgey wood, 518:16
Whiggery, what is W., 598:7
Whigs, caught the W. bathing, 434:29
While there's life there's hope, 86:3,
　87:23
Whim envy or resentment, 333:18
　just as the w. bites, 388:3
　tempted by a private w., 609:7
Whimper, not bang but w., 669:11
Whine, sweat and w. about condition,
　489:16
Whining at threshold, 583:8
　born naked and falls a-w., 104:*n*3
　of a door, 231:11

Whining (*continued*)
poetry, 228:17
school-boy with satchel, 191:3
wimpled w. purblind, 168:28
Whip all hell yet, 492:*n*5
fear o' hell's a hangman's w., 235:*n*5
in every honest hand a w., 208:2
so small you could not see, 514:5
weight in wildcats, 559:16
Whipped for overdoing Termagant, 196:21
he must be w. out, 209:7
her little daughter, 790:15
offending Adam, 184:20
she w. him, 792:9
them all soundly, 790:2
Whipping, future smells of w., 420:10
who should 'scape w., 196:3
Whippoorwill, hear that lonesome w., 753:5
Whips and scorns of time, 196:10
my father chastised you with w., 12:29
Whipstock, first Packard had w. on dashboard, 683:6
Whirl asunder and dismember me, 169:29
lay mightily in w. of dust, 52:10
Whirled in an arch, 454:18
unstilled world w., 669:18
Whirligig of time, 203:6
Whirling summer, 712:18
Whirls, expectation w. me round, 200:17
Northern ocean in vast w., 308:8
Whirlwind, Elijah went up by a w., 13:4
home in your manes, 446:27
Lord answered Job out of the w., 15:6
of passion, 196:21
reap the w., 29:27
rides in the w., 291:30, 303:29
Whirlwind's, sweeping w. sway, 323:8
Whirlwinds in the south, 26:18
Whiskers, oh my fur and w., 517:7
Whiskey for my Johnny, 793:8
gimme a w. ginger ale on side, 673:13
must have w. you know why, 698:16
on your breath, 724:15
polishes copper, 526:16
prayers in hall w. afterwards, 644:9
say boys another w., 548:4
Whiskies, born two w. below par, 604:2
Whisper, breathed the husky w., 562:11
busy w. circling round, 329:17
far-heard w. o'er the sea, 381:14
not a w. be lost, 720:17
Whispered, Devil w. behind leaves, 592:1
in sounds of silence, 772:8
into your brain, 774:6
voice behind me w. low, 567:16
Whispereth, soul w. within him, 117:17

Whispering ambitions, 668:7
bayed the w. wind, 329:11
from Oxford towers, 499:10
humbleness, 180:9
I will ne'er consent, 402:10
maid and wight w. by, 540:22
music of yonder pine, 82:13
still her name, 611:20
tongues can poison truth, 382:15
Whisperings, keeps eternal w., 417:8
Whispers, Duty w. low, 430:4
listen to w. of fancy, 314:9
o'er-fraught heart, 215:28
of each other's watch, 185:14
what good author w., 594:7
Whist, wild waves w., 223:30
Whistle and I'll come to you, 362:18
and she'll come to you, 238:18
blackbird 'tis to w., 262:18
clear as a w., 304:16
don't you hear w. blowing, 780:6
go w. for the rest, 149:24
hir joly w. wel ywet, 130:30
I love to w., 703:13
I'd w. her off, 207:2
let it w. as it will, 378:11
maybe just w., 673:3
pay too much for w., 310:19
quail w. about us, 638:26
them back, 330:13
Whistled for want of thought, 276:27
Whistles far and wee, 688:8
pipes and w. in his sound, 191:3
thrice, 381:13
Whistling, blackbird w. or just after, 639:6
to bear courage up, 275:*n*8
to keep from being afraid, 275:28
Whistlings, foolish w. of a name, 267:9
White, a moment w., 363:6
and drifted snow, 427:7
as angel English child, 356:8
as driven snow, 223:10
as leprosy, 381:12
as long as colored man look to w. folks, 773:19
beard decreasing leg, 183:19
beautiful when it helps, 750:7
beauty whose red and w., 201:26
black and w. separate as fingers, 571:32
Black Hawk fought against w. men, 369:7
black spirits and w., 237:9
black where I read w., 360:2
bosoms of actresses, 315:14
bread and butter, 789:7
candle in holy place, 644:12
chickens, 654:1
chrysanthemum immaculate, 282:13
Citizen's Counciler, 760:16
cliffs of Dover, 626:23
clothed in w. samite, 133:6, 459:6
clouds on wing, 504:3
colored people understand w. people, 612:4
consternation throughout w. race, 767:19
cow all red and w., 561:11

White (*continued*)
crimson petal now w., 456:20
dreaming of w. Christmas, 666:13
end of fight tombstone w., 591:12
fat w. woman, 661:12
fever of temptation, 680:3
fleece w. but 'tis too cold, 153:*n*7
flower of blameless life, 459:3
foam flew, 381:6
fought against w. domination, 745:15
get up so w. person could sit, 734:2
Goddess, 692:4
Godiva I unpeel, 764:19
great w. way, 584:2
hair become very w., 517:9
hate in w. men, 755:10
how ill w. hairs become fool, 184:16
humiliation by w. man, 752:9
I appeal to any w. man, 326:14
if snow be w., 222:8
in subjection to w. Saxon man, 475:7
in w. black and green, 777:16
is their color, 243:24
little missionary stew, 670:1
made w. in blood, 47:23
man warmed before Indians' fire, 333:6
man will never be alone, 398:11
Man's burden, 593:5
moderate devoted to order, 760:16
moon beams, 676:17
nights all w. an' still, 485:15
nor w. so very w., 371:24
not neutralize black, 468:4
O my soul is w., 356:8
o'er his w. banes, 785:17
officers cast lot, 522:13
one w. foot try him, 781:17
or colored signs, 742:3
parsons preaching Jesus, 752:10
played black or w., 426:2
prisoner to w. man, 369:6
radiance of eternity, 409:8
radiance stretches above it, 53:9
raiment w. as snow, 37:14
really hope no w. person, 772:15
red thoughts teeth w., 610:19
relation between w. and colored people, 480:18
rose breathes of love, 553:19
rose is a dove, 553:19
roses and w. lilies grow, 226:18
sails still fly seaward, 669:20
samite, 133:6, 459:6
scare w. clouds on, 623:10
seas show w. when rocks near, 237:15
silence below, 660:14
singe my w. head, 209:24
sins shall be w. as snow, 25:29
sound of w. soldier's axe, 502:5
superfluity comes by w. hairs, 179:26
Sustenance despair, 513:1
sweet w. wine, 633:18
thunders of w. silence, 438:20
to chase that w. whale, 486:23

White (*continued*)
to w. man nature wilderness, 606:4
tupping your w. ewe, 205:15
two societies one black one w.,
    723:20
ugly when oppresses blacks, 750:7
we black and they w., 725:25
wear w. flannel trousers, 667:19
what treaty w. man kept, 516:9
why should I want to be w., 708:11
wild w. horses play, 497:6
wings one black other w., 261:18
you're older and w. and free, 709:1
White House, preside over W., 754:18
unapproachable in W., 652:7
White-Anglo Saxon-Protestant upper
    class, 738:3
White-chokered and clean-shaven,
    547:1
Whited sepulchers, 36:5
thou w. wall, 41:27
Whiteness, Milky Way sister in w.,
    641:9
restore to w. wool dyed purple,
    114:8
Whiter, I shall be w. than snow, 17:21
Whites of their eyes, 318:17, 327:10
Whitest, old linen wash w., 237:11
Whitewash, bucket of w. and long-
    handled brush, 526:2
Whitewashed wall, 329:19
Whither, advice not to inquire why or
    w., 697:16
away fair rover, 549:19
coffin asks w., 520:13
fled visionary gleam, 375:6
goest thou, 40:33
shall I go from thy spirit, 20:8
so high, 790:16
thou goest I will go, 11:23
Whithersoever, with thee w. thou
    goest, 10:31
Whiting, as w. said with tail in
    mouth, 342:n1
to a snail, 518:5
Whitman, Homer and W. roared in
    pines, 607:11
I saw you Walt W., 757:2
Walt W. a kosmos, 489:9
Whitman's, Mr. W. Eve Mr. W.
    Venus, 535:9
Whittington, turn again W., 777:1
Who are these coming, 416:5
are we where are we, 477:7
can hold fire in his hand, 171:3
doesn't desire father's death, 495:14
doth ambition shun, 190:20
ever got out of winding sheet,
    231:12
ever loved not at first sight, 162:11
find out w. he is what he's about,
    773:19
follows in His train, 395:17
has seen the wind, 515:12
hath desired sea, 593:13
hath known mind of Lord, 42:11
How and Where and W., 593:8
I'm Nobody w. are you, 511:22
is in who's out, 211:13
is Silvia what is she, 168:7

Who (*continued*)
is the happy Warrior, 376:8
is the third, 669:5
is this King of glory, 16:20
killed Cock Robin, 789:1
killed John Keats, 403:28
knows but world may end, 465:19
loses and who wins, 211:13
night and silence w. is here, 173:13
ran to help me, 394:1
said Peacock Pie, 617:3
shall ascend into the hill of the
    Lord, 16:18
shall bell cat, 59:11
shall deliver me, 42:1
shall stand in his holy place, 16:18
should 'scape whipping, 196:3
then devised torment, 672:4
to himself law no law doth need,
    157:11
touches a hair, 443:12
why which what, 472:7
will bell cat, 127:19
would have thought so much blood,
    216:3
you're known as w., 760:15
Whoe'er has traveled, 316:n8
she be, 264:8
Whoever really loves you, 794:6
wishes to attain English style,
    314:17
you are behold your master, 307:3
Whole America nothing less, 331:12
armor of God, 44:27
by sample we judge w., 149:2
climate of opinion, 720:12
complicate amassing harmony,
    640:1
drink and be w. again, 624:18
duty of man, 24:30
earth is sepulcher of famous men,
    72:7
earth our hospital, 671:7
First Comprehend W., 512:16
general joy of w. table, 215:6
has beginning middle and end,
    78:32
how much more is half than w.,
    54:21
I am equal and w., 534:19
indictment against w. people,
    331:16
love is the w., 689:2
makes w. world kin, 201:3
man composed of all men, 717:20
my w. course of love, 205:22
need not physician, 34:21
never sees a w., 497:18
nothing sole or w., 598:21
one stupendous w., 301:11
prayers make me w., 591:11
saw life w., 497:3
soul's tasking, 485:4
taste w. of it, 467:19
tribe of fops, 208:29
volumes in folio, 168:21
wide sky above me, 698:3
willing to know w. truth, 339:7
Wholeness of human problem, 629:23

Wholes, couples are w. and not w.,
    62:16
Wholesale, God who does w. business,
    546:16
Wholesome, believe doctors nothing
    w., 515:14
even for King, 514:6
harvests reaps, 422:3
nights are w., 192:29
Wholesomest, old wine w., 237:11
Whole-time, husband a w. job, 602:2
Wholly, I shall not w. die, 96:26
Whom shall I fear, 16:21
they fear they hate, 84:21
Whoopee ti yi yo git along little do-
    gies, 786:2
Whooping, out of all w., 191:13
Whoops, owlet w. to wolf below,
    382:3
Whopper, give birth to w., 758:4
Whore, joined this rogue and w.,
    289:22
pity she's a w., 239:15
posture of a w., 218:13
the woman's a w., 316:21
Whore's oath, 210:13
Whores, till all w. burnt alive, 287:20
Whorled ear, 550:16
Who's afraid of Virginia Woolf,
    758:18
in who's out, 211:13
master who's man, 290:20
on first, 691:7
Whose, to w. advantage, 87:11
world or mine or theirs, 659:17
Why, causes w. and wherefore, 185:25
did you do that, 569:4
don't you speak for yourself, 442:3
every w. hath a wherefore, 166:22
I can't say w. I don't like you,
    106:10
I can't think w., 530:17
I dream and say W. not, 571:24
is plain as way to church, 190:28
is this thus, 522:4
love's stricken w., 514:7
man of morals tell me w., 267:1
men fell out knew not w., 262:16
not inquire w. or whither, 697:16
not when but w. families came,
    754:3
persecutest thou me, 41:5
then oh why can't I, 699:16
though I could never tell w., 529:2
we and universe exist, 772:2
What and W. and When, 593:8
who w. which what, 472:7
you see things and say W., 571:24
Wibrated, strings better not w.,
    469:33
Wicked are wicked no doubt, 463:19
blast drives w. spirits, 125:15
deceitful and desperately w., 28:30
dreams abuse sleep, 213:21
flee when no man pursueth, 23:5
forsake his way, 28:1
God help the w., 177:31
I have seen the w. in great power,
    17:2
intents w. or charitable, 194:10

Wind (*continued*)

    made heart cry To-day to-day, 616:11

    man control w., 497:22

    mantle of w. and chill and rain, 132:22

    meteor streaming to w., 256:12

    net to hold the w., 237:*n*5

    nets to catch the w., 237:20

    no 'twas but the w., 399:22

    nor tide nor sea, 532:6

    north w. doth blow, 790:17

    O w. weder gynneth clere, 128:14

    of criticism, 317:33

    of doctrine, 44:24

    of western sea, 456:10

    on buffalo grass, 787:2

    over lake inner truth, 5:9

    pass by me as idle w., 189:16

    passeth over it, 19:2

    paths that w. and w., 562:16

    pines keep shape of w., 706:6

    renown but breath of w., 126:13

    rising attempt to live, 613:17

    said W. to Moon, 504:13

    sails filled with lusty w., 157:13

    sall blaw for evermair, 785:17

    scattered to w., 453:19

    scatters some leaves, 51:23

    sits w. in that corner, 186:29

    something in the w., 166:26

    sound of rushing w., 40:44

    sound w. and limb, 150:42

    sown the w., 29:27

    stop hole to keep w. away, 199:10

    straw see which way w. is, 239:3

    sun was warm w. chill, 624:6

    sway in w. like corn, 667:23

    sweep man away, 497:22

    swoln with w. and mist, 254:3

    tears shall drown the w., 213:7

    tempers w. to shorn lamb, 144:14, 321:2

    that blows through me, 657:8

    that follows fast, 396:22

    through woods in riot, 579:7

    throw sand against w., 359:2

    thunderstorm against w., 400:22

    to know which way w. blows, 771:10

    torrent of darkness, 643:11

    unhelped by any w., 382:16

    warm w. the west w., 633:17

    wave cry w. cry, 671:11

    way long w. cold, 377:19

    west w. and the swallows, 83:2

    Western w. when wilt thou blow, 776:6

    what is w. in that door, 133:8

    what woman says written in w., 91:11

    when she dances in the w., 275:2

    when sun out w. still, 624:6

    when w. southerly know hawk, 195:31

    whenever w. is high, 561:9

    where a w. ever soft, 349:8

    who has seen w., 515:12

    wild West W., 407:13

    wings of the w., 16:8, 19:3

Wind (*continued*)

    winnow not with every w., 31:11

    winnowing w., 416:14

    wiped out by w., 759:1

    words are but w., 263:22

    words are easy like the w., 233:12

Windborne mirroring soul, 497:18

Winding, God w. lonely horn, 595:6

    long cool w. saxophones, 634:10

    long trail a-w., 676:17

    notes with many a w. bout, 251:19

Winding-sheet of Edward's race, 323:7

    old England's w., 359:15

    waters were his w., 233:9

    who ever got out of w., 231:12

Windlass, turned round like w., 486:28

Windlasses and assays of bias, 195:7

Windmills, tilting at w., 149:*n*3

Window, bishop kick hole in stained glass w., 667:6

    clapte the w. to, 130:26

    face negative in slate w., 747:17

    in your rocking chair by w., 611:12

    Jezebel looked out at a w., 13:11

    light through yonder w., 174:26

    little w. where sun, 422:19

    love flies out w., 777:19

    Mary at thy w. be, 363:17

    on Europe, 424:3

    sit looking out of w., 757:16

    tirlin' at w., 461:12

    tree, 624:1

    Walloping W. Blind, 545:3

Windowed, looped and w. raggedness, 210:3

Windows be darkened, 24:27

    cleaned w. swept floor, 529:6

    dim w. of the soul, 360:3

    factory w. always broken, 637:7

    if no doors or w., 736:7

    if your w. are glass, 309:21

    in lighted w. books kept watch, 612:20

    lavender in the w., 245:21

    not by eastern w. only, 483:3

    Saints to w. run, 511:18

    see without looking through w., 57:15

    storied w. richly dight, 252:10

    through w. call on us, 228:11

Windpipe throttled in fakes of death, 489:12

Wind's feet shine along sea, 533:18

    like whetted knife, 633:16

    out of w. and rain's way, 644:13

    will, 442:5

Winds are left behind, 506:2

    ascribing to w. the noise, 103:15

    beetle w. sullen horn, 324:14

    beteem w. of heaven, 193:7

    blow profit, 722:4

    blow w. crack your cheeks, 209:24

    blow ye w. heigh-ho, 793:20

    breath rides on posting w., 219:29

    come as the w. come, 379:9

    courted by all the w., 261:16

    cradled on sea, 721:13

    faithless as w. or seas, 281:14

    four w. of the heaven, 29:44

Winds (*continued*)

    four-square to w., 458:7

    gray-fly w. sultry horn, 253:17

    great w. shoreward blow, 497:6

    huntsman w. his horn, 311:15

    imprisoned in viewless w., 204:14

    lashing corners of earth, 634:14

    neither shaken by w. nor wet, 53:9

    of doctrine, 255:4

    of heaven through our land, 676:18

    on side of ablest navigators, 340:6

    over great sea w. trouble waters, 89:13

    rough w. do shake, 220:12

    sea w. pierced solitudes, 429:14

    selfsame w. that blow, 562:13

    somewhere safe to sea, 534:15

    take w. of March with beauty, 223:7

    time w. th' exhausted chain, 362:22

    wailing w. naked woods, 411:8

    were love-sick, 217:14

    when w. breathing low, 407:21

    where w. are all asleep, 497:7

Winds' and spent waves' riot, 534:12

Windsor, Widow at W., 591:21

Windswept, topped w. heights with grace, 751:3

Wind-walks, what w., 551:2

Windward, between w. and lee, 535:5

    to w. of law, 333:17

Windy, flung us on w. hill, 662:17

    night rainy morrow, 221:13

    shadows and w. places, 533:8

    side of care, 186:24

    side of law, 186:*n*1

    Troy, 455:1

Wine, age leaves friends and w., 392:9

    and women go together, 234:25

    and women mirth laughter, 402:18

    as water unto w., 455:22

    best w. that goeth down sweetly, 25:20

    better is thy love than w., 25:12

    between kisses and w., 602:7

    blood fizz like w., 633:7

    blushes into w., 264:*n*3

    bored with good w., 434:25

    bring me beaker of w., 72:14

    bring water bring w., 60:1

    Canary w., 416:12

    come within pint of w., 293:15

    comes in at mouth, 595:20

    days of w. and roses, 602:10

    dear boy and truth, 55:22

    did not know the W., 512:1

    drinking blude-red w., 784:31

    drinks w. with laughter, 780:23

    drunk your water and w., 590:17

    drunken but not with w., 27:1

    enjoy laughter over the w., 82:19

    for thy stomach's sake, 45:20

    frolic w., 241:15

    from w. sudden friendship, 297:13

    glass of w. happiness, 652:2

    good w. a friend or being dry, 283:20

    good w. a good creature, 206:24

    good w. needs no bush, 100:*n*10

Wisdom (*continued*)
    without unmanliness, 72:3
    wrath of lion w. of God, 357:6
Wisdom's aid, 324:18
    self oft seeks, 252:29
    threadbare saint in w. school,
        227:17
Wise, a little too w. ne'er live long,
        166:*n*1
    and beautiful, 497:5
    and frugal government, 344:8
    and masterly inactivity, 367:15
    and moral man, 65:2
    and salutary neglect, 331:10
    and the lovely, 684:12
    and understanding heart, 12:18
    and wonderful, 479:17
    arrows which speak to the w.,
        63:30
    art of being w., 546:3
    be w. as serpents, 34:30
    be w. today, 296:10
    be w. with speed, 295:25
    beacon of the w., 200:14
    beacons of w. men, 505:14
    better is a poor and w. child, 24:1
    both true both w., 266:17
    by nature w., 237:21
    consider her ways and be w., 20:27
    consider w. what they cleave to,
        111:9
    cunning men pass for w., 159:23
    dare to be w., 97:8
    darkly w., 301:13
    defer not to be w., 291:17
    enough to play fool, 202:21
    every w. man's son know, 202:1
    exceeding w. fair-spoken, 226:6
    father that knows child, 180:17
    folly to be w., 321:17
    fool counted w., 21:37
    fool doth think he is w., 192:9
    fool talks w. man speaks, 233:8
    foolery w. men have, 189:32
    foolish things to confound w., 42:29
    full of w. saws, 191:3
    good to be merry and w., 140:16
    gout kills more w. than simple,
        271:17
    government knows how to enforce,
        318:22
    great men are not always w., 14:47
    gude to be merry and w., 779:20
    guid to be merry and w., 364:4
    he that kan hymselven knowe,
        132:3
    he was wondrous w., 792:22
    healthy wealthy w., 309:17
    hear the words of the w., 22:11
    heard w. man say, 578:22
    histories make men w., 160:10
    holy fair and w. is she, 168:7
    honest and w. men rule, 338:13
    how dieth the w. man, 23:31
    if w. gets rich, 603:9
    in his own conceit, 22:30
    in old age learn to be w., 66:20
    in your own conceits, 42:16
    learn from enemies, 73:10
    leisure to grow w., 498:6

Wise (*continued*)
    like w. one died, 151:21
    love and be w., 98:32
    love teach monarch to be w.,
        321:24
    man has no extensive knowledge,
        58:7
    man is a school for magnates, 3:11
    man is strong, 22:23
    man knows himself fool, 192:9
    man not glory in wisdom, 28:23
    man not leave right to chance,
        477:10
    man utter vain knowledge, 14:23
    men from the East, 32:23
    men in great struggle, 339:7
    men know art of eating, 354:13
    men of Gotham, 789:10
    men profit more from fools, 85:4
    men refrain to meddle, 137:14
    men shun mistakes of fools, 85:4
    men speak fools decide, 56:3
    more fools than w., 777:6
    more w. master simpler work,
        124:15
    neither yet bread to w., 24:20
    no man w. by himself, 83:15
    none is born w., 3:3
    nor ever did a w. one, 283:21
    nor w. at fifty, 244:24
    not even God is w. enough, 784:29
    not wisdom to be only w., 587:17
    not w. who buffet against love, 67:1
    not worldly w., 242:8
    old and crafty and w., 595:3
    on exercise depend, 276:19
    passiveness, 372:19
    pause from learning to be w.,
        313:17
    penny w. pound foolish, 234:10
    powers deny us for our good,
        217:11
    prosperity tries souls even of w.,
        91:24
    quiet w. and good, 409:17
    rebuke a w. man, 21:2
    reputed w. for saying nothing,
        179:21
    Roland valorous Oliver w., 121:13
    saying w. and old, 153:*n*7
    skepticism of critic, 486:12
    so w. so young, 166:1
    son maketh a glad father, 21:4
    speech given to w. men, 280:2
    spirits of w. mock us, 183:32
    steals mind even of the w., 52:3
    takes w. man to recognize w. man,
        60:7
    taketh the w. in craftiness, 14:3
    thinks himself w. is great fool,
        306:29
    thrush, 465:4
    to be w. and love, 200:21
    to listen to the Word, 62:9
    to w. man are ports and havens,
        171:1
    type of the w., 377:12
    virgins, 36:13
    want love, 406:17
    wealthy, 74:10

Wise (*continued*)
    were their subjects w., 335:10
    what w. or stupid thing, 350:23
    when he had pen in hand, 317:18
    who are a little w., 228:18
    who can be w. amazed, 214:16
    who knows others is w., 57:9
    who tries everything before arms,
        86:9
    wine sets w. man singing, 53:28
    wish to appear w. among fools,
        105:14
    without folly not so w., 265:22
    woman never yields, 396:13
    word to w. enough, 151:9, 310:7
    words are w. men's counters,
        239:17
    words of the w. are as goads, 24:29
    words taught in numbers, 154:4
    wretch, 300:15
Wisely and slow, 175:18
    charming never so w., 17:29
    faire and softe, 128:23
    live pleasurably without living w.,
        81:20
    loved not w. but too well, 208:16
    worldly, 242:8
Wiser, four things w. to know, 687:6
    learn but not w. grow, 288:12
    no w. than a daw, 163:10
    no w. than before, 350:11
    sadder and w. man, 382:9
    scientist w. not to withhold, 350:8
    than children of light, 38:40
    than our ordinary selves, 500:16
    today than yesterday, 303:21
    tygers of wrath w., 357:9
    without books, 335:12
    women w. than men, 650:13
Wisest, days to come are w. witnesses,
        63:27
    fool in Christendom, 154:23
    man does not fancy he is, 280:8
    of counselors Time, 65:6
    of mankind enjoy life, 594:2
    prophets make sure, 324:2
    rivalship of w. men, 293:17
    seeming truth to entrap w., 181:6
    silence w. thing to heed, 64:8
    Socrates w. of men, 261:2
    these are w., 69:4
    virtuousest discreetest, 259:29
Wish all men everywhere free, 449:12
    believe we what we w., 273:19
    each w. of my heart, 391:13
    every man in arms w. to be, 376:8
    father to thought, 184:11
    half grant what I w., 623:8
    happy whose w. and care, 298:5
    heart dry of blood, 417:3
    him safe at home, 366:20
    I liked way it talks, 584:3
    I loved human race, 584:3
    I thought What jolly fun, 584:3
    I was in land of cotton, 475:1
    I were a moron, 783:7
    I w. he'd stay away, 630:2
    I'd said that, 524:5
    in vain to w. for death, 66:21
    men believe what they w., 88:17

Wish (*continued*)
  my days to be, 374:7
  of some is to avenge, 72:1
  snow in May's mirth, 168:16
  to be virtuous, 61:12
  to save their own pocket, 72:1
  what is it gentlemen w., 339:10
  you a wave o' the sea, 223:9
Wished heaven made her such a man,
    205:28
  I oft w. for Hell, 359:21
  she had not heard it, 205:28
  the w. the trysted hour, 363:17
  to see thee cross-gartered, 202:19
Wishes, by country's w. blessed,
    324:10
  cannot alter facts, 337:15
  expressed w. of people, 650:7
  for that beyond reach, 284:14
  her w. and ways be as nothing,
    539:16
  if w. were horses, 272:4
  in idle w. fools stay, 353:17
  lengthen as our sun declines, 296:17
  never learned to stray, 322:17
  sorry if w. were gratified, 59:16
  what each w. he believes, 79:3
  whom God w. to destroy, 69:18
Wishful, instinctual w. impulses,
    569:16
Wishing He I served were black, 711:3
  his foot equal with eye, 164:21
Wishings, hell full of good w., 244:15
Wist ye not, 38:7
Wistful, such a w. eye, 567:15
Wit, a w. is a feather, 301:18
  all your Piety nor W., 445:25
  among Lords, 315:18
  and wisdom born with man, 239:1
  beams of w. on other souls, 274:26
  beauty w. high birth, 201:3
  boast his w., 274:3
  bold and turbulent of w., 274:3
  borrowed w., 240:3
  brevity the soul of w., 195:10
  cause w. in other men, 183:12
  craves a kind of w., 202:21
  devise w. write pen, 168:21
  does harm to my w., 201:21
  dream past the w. of man, 173:26
  drink goes in w. goes out, 244:16
  dronkenesse is sepulture of w.,
    131:30
  enliven morality with w., 292:20
  enough to run away, 264:2
  every age has its w., 280:7
  fancy w. will come, 300:26
  fault of penetrating w., 265:39
  genius sense and w., 334:4
  good nature more agreeable than
    w., 293:2
  half the w. credited, 368:13
  her w. was more than man, 275:6
  hope flock to aid, 431:15
  how the w. brightens, 299:2
  in w. a man, 300:28
  invites you by his looks to come,
    334:12
  is wall between us and dark, 691:2
  kind of senseless w., 749:17

Wit (*continued*)
  lasts two centuries, 396:19
  levels all distinctions, 433:22
  little tiny w., 210:1
  liveliest effusions of w., 387:10
  love paradox without losing w.,
    432:12
  makes its own welcome, 433:22
  men of w., 289:5
  monuments of w. survive monu-
    ments of power, 157:24
  mortify a w., 303:10
  much malice little w., 275:19
  my w. is thynne, 131:21
  nature by her mother w., 153:20
  ne'er tastes, 302:15
  no innocent w. suppressed, 342:1
  no man's w. can well direct him,
    230:15
  nor too much wealth nor w., 238:3
  nor words nor worth, 189:10
  of one wisdom of many, 779:18
  one man's w., 779:n5
  Phoenix riddle hath more w.,
    228:15
  plentiful lack of w., 195:20
  put his whole w. in a jest, 238:11
  shines at expense of memory,
    290:24
  shoots his w., 192:18
  skirmish of w., 186:9
  soul of epigram, 383:5
  soul of w., 195:10
  staircase w., 320:2
  temper w. with morality, 292:20
  that can creep, 302:17
  the noblest frailty, 282:7
  too proud for a w., 330:10
  true w. is nature to advantage
    dressed, 298:14
  universal monarchy of w., 246:3
  use w. as pitchfork, 750:10
  ware of mine own w., 190:17
  wears his w. in his belly, 200:13
  well of true w. truth, 509:13
  whan man hath over-greet a w.,
    132:5
  what scanted in hair given in w.,
    166:24
  when age in w. out, 186:40
  will shine, 274:28
  Wisdom and W., 296:28
  with dunces, 303:30
Witch, aroint thee w., 212:12
  hath power to charm, 192:29
  I have gone out a w., 759:13
  wicked W. of the East, 568:9
  world with noble horsemanship,
    178:22
Witchcraft celebrates, 213:21
  only w. I have used, 205:28
Witches, feared w. burned women,
    568:15
  wild w. noble ladies, 596:13
Witching time of night, 197:21
Witch-tales Annie tells about, 558:15
Withal, money comes w., 167:19
Withdrawing, melancholy long w.
    roar, 499:22

Withdrawn, he has departed w. gone
    away, 87:8
Wither, age cannot w. her, 217:15
  and come to deadly use, 210:22
  his leaf shall not w., 15:29
  into the truth, 595:21
Withered because no root, 35:6
  before they be w., 30:21
  cheek tresses gray, 377:19
  flowers w. while I spent my days,
    120:11
  hand capped w. heart, 712:18
  is garland of the war, 218:8
  sedge w. from lake, 417:4
  there it could not w. be, 232:16
  when my father died, 198:24
  withering of w. flowers, 671:14
Withereth, grass w., 27:18, 46:21
Withering, leaves w. and sere, 453:1
  now w. in my bloom, 300:3
  of withered flowers, 671:14
Withers, our w. are unwrung, 197:14
  wastes and w. there, 567:22
Withhold not thine hand in the eve-
    ning, 24:25
  scientist wiser not to w., 350:8
Within, birds w. despair, 146:19
  consecration from w. himself, 691:4
  foretold that danger lurks w.,
    164:28
  fountains are w., 383:7
  I have that w., 193:3
  serious daring starts from w., 728:1
Without, birds w. despair to get in,
    146:19
  can't live with them or w., 73:17
  can't live w. or with you, 101:12
  four things better w., 687:7
  mind contemplate itself from w.,
    558:10
  prepared for doing w., 426:12
Withstand in the evil day, 44:28
Withstood, little tyrant of fields w.,
    322:14
Witness against himself, 346:14
  call heaven and earth to w., 10:10
  call the gods to w., 211:23
  false w. by their own mouth, 32:18
  for me that I have fought, 272:30
  God appointed me w., 423:20
  heap of stones a w., 7:44
  heaven and earth to w., 10:10
  history the w. to passing time,
    87:14
  I stand w. to common lot, 675:7
  man w. unto his deeds, 117:23
  no w. so dreadful, 85:11
  of soul naturally Christian, 112:3
  shalt not bear false w., 9:12
  single w. is no w., 119:34
  to the people, 27:40
  weak w. of thy name, 251:2
  without w. against me, 4:5
  your eyes my w., 236:2
Witnesses, cloud of w., 45:39
  days to come are wisest w., 63:27
  to same overt act, 346:9
  trees and all nature w., 787:1
  victims become w., 760:8
Wit's, a w. a feather, 301:18

Womanhood and childhood fleet,
441:7
  heroic w., 442:7
Womanly, manly deeds w. words,
244:*n*9
Woman's a contradiction, 300:20
  body is the woman, 544:11
  brief as w. love, 197:10
  children's gratitude w. love, 598:15
  cold perverted will, 410:7
  come to my w. breasts, 212:29
  desire for desire of man, 385:2
  die because a w. fair, 240:1
  gift to rain tears, 167:14
  life history of affections, 396:6
  light lies in w. eyes, 392:4
  love lodged in w. breast, 227:5
  love of being loved, 540:6
  love the history of w. life, 368:10
  love w. whole existence, 402:14
  name in print twice, 656:4
  no other but w. reason, 167:37
  normal occupations, 719:10
  old age is w. hell, 267:20
  only books w. looks, 392:5
  paths to w. love, 236:9
  right of privacy encompass w. deci-
    sion, 722:13
  sex prima facie evidence, 475:7
  spark in w. heart, 396:2
  such beauty as w. eye, 168:35
  the w. a whore, 316:21
  tiger's heart in w. hide, 164:13
  time of opportunity short, 73:15
  tongue good when an't w., 468:24
  twenty years in w. life, 75:14
  vows write upon wave, 67:18
  will, 169:21
  work never done, 778:23
Womb, came forth of mother's w.,
  24:5
  cold in the w., 758:12
  from mother's w. untimely ripped,
    216:19
  fruit of thy w., 37:39
  naked out of my mother's w., 13:31
  of morning dew, 153:12
  of pia mater, 168:32
  of uncreated night, 257:2
  shall forget him, 14:36
  since black w. held, 734:6
  slayeth child in w., 659:16
  teeming w. of royal kings, 171:9
Women, accord w. equal power, 492:1
  all men and w. had become gro-
    tesques, 630:20
  American w. kept from growing,
    748:18
  American w. to obtain right to vote,
    751:7
  and children first, 780:11
  and elephants, 610:15
  and wine, 297:16
  are angels wooing, 200:4
  are as roses, 202:11
  are like tricks, 291:6
  are seldom inventors, 306:20
  as workers not as w., 491:21
  attend men and not w., 76:9

Women (*continued*)
  be spared struggle for beauty,
    769:12
  better or worse than men, 283:18
  bevy of fair w., 260:19
  blessed among w., 37:37
  brought shame on all w., 53:22
  capture of men by w., 463:*n*1
  children of larger growth, 305:6
  come and go, 667:10
  compare with me ye w., 262:15
  complain about sex more than men,
    745:4
  dear dead w., 466:15
  degraded by trivial attentions,
    365:30
  desiren sovereynetee, 131:10
  die of loneliness but for w., 600:6
  difference between men and w.,
    707:18
  divine patriarch castrates w., 758:21
  duty of w. to secure francise, 475:6
  economic equality for w., 754:2
  economic factors in society, 583:3
  educated for dependence, 365:28
  England is paradise of w., 154:18
  equal right of men and w., 655:23
  especially to w., 402:12
  fair w. and brave men, 399:21
  fairest among w., 25:2
  faithful w. alike, 646:16
  feared witches burned w., 568:15
  feel weariness of battle, 749:2
  fickleness of w. I love, 570:10
  find few real friends, 318:4
  fine w. eat crazy salad, 597:1
  foolish to match men, 483:17
  for w. act of survival, 762:10
  forget what don't want to remem-
    ber, 707:6
  framed to make w. false, 206:2
  gave what other w. gave, 599:2
  Germans are like w., 553:14
  getting along with w., 349:4
  given deplorable education, 436:18
  great city greatest men w., 490:5
  guide the plot, 352:18
  hangin' men and w., 779:11
  happiest w. no history, 483:22
  hate all w. when thou art gone,
    229:2
  have as much rights as man, 421:1
  have glimmer of loyalty to Truth,
    556:20
  have no characters, 300:13
  have no wilderness, 696:2
  have positive moral sense, 535:11
  haven't any depths, 553:14
  hero keeps getting in bed with w.,
    685:2
  hid himself among w., 248:30
  homely men charmed w., 586:1
  how can you shoot w. children,
    770:3
  how hard for w. to keep counsel,
    188:13
  I know disposition of w., 86:10
  if w. had not received permission,
    65:4

Women (*continued*)
  impressive fact about American w.,
    751:7
  in w. two divide, 300:16
  indisputably beautiful, 305:7
  innocent and pure, 224:4
  kindness in w. not looks, 167:30
  know jealous readiest to forgive,
    495:13
  know less understand more, 650:13
  knowledge of w. of his own family,
    440:2
  labor of w. in house, 583:3
  Lake Wobegon where w. are strong,
    772:5
  let w. into your life, 571:19
  like to be conquered, 463:24
  like untuned golden strings, 162:12
  liked several w., 224:12
  literary accomplishments in w.,
    347:4
  looking-glasses reflecting man,
    651:3
  loses solidarity with other w.,
    722:12
  love lovers, 266:1
  make public judge, 396:15
  man always unjust to w., 402:20
  married beneath me all w. do,
    635:3
  men and w. affirm brotherhood,
    722:11
  men and w. created equal, 475:5
  men and w. liberate, 691:1
  men and w. merely players, 191:3
  men w. and clergymen, 380:9
  men work w. weep, 484:11
  monstrous regiment of w., 143:14
  more pangs than wars or w., 225:16
  musick and w. give way to, 279:14
  my sisters and lovers, 488:18
  no more trusting in w., 53:24
  not so young as painted, 614:5
  not w. or Negroes but citizens,
    475:9
  old w. should not be perfumed,
    55:4
  other w. cloy appetites, 217:15
  ought to have representatives,
    365:33
  passing the love of w., 12:2
  passionate w., 595:12
  pleasing punishment w. bear,
    166:19
  plunged into cares and sorrows,
    365:31
  pursuit of loose w., 496:4
  put not on pedestal but in cage,
    719:6
  remember what don't want to for-
    get, 707:6
  run to extremes, 283:18
  saints were rarely married w.,
    719:10
  seven w. take hold of one man,
    25:36
  silence gives grace to w., 65:8
  Solomon loved many strange w.,
    12:28
  some w. charm all, 581:23

Women (*continued*)
some w. handsome without adornment, 87:18
some w. stay in memory, 593:16
spare w. for Thy Sake, 718:23
special contribution awareness, 707:20
stimulated by news wife left husband, 717:7
superiority of their w., 438:10
text of Men and W., 578:5
that's the nature of w., 149:23
these impossible w., 73:17
they married when young, 541:1
thou fairest among w., 25:2
till w. more rationally educated, 365:27
trained to place others' needs first, 734:1
upset everything, 571:19
war between men and w., 690:9
watched naked w. walk out of sea, 731:4
we should have learned w., 347:4
wear the breeches, 234:11
what a woman thinks of w., 509:12
what is it men in w. require, 357:24
what that party promises w., 491:24
when candles out all w. fair, 107:14
who knows what w. can be, 749:1
who remained thirty-five, 567:11
wine and w. go together, 234:25
wine w. and song, 353:5
wine w. mirth laughter, 402:18
words are w. deeds men, 244:40
Women's eyes for stars, 776:26
from w. eyes this doctrine, 169:4
I put on w. clothing, 775:6
intelligence nourished, 749:1
sooner lost than w. are, 202:10
weapons waterdrops, 209:22
Won, battles lost in spirit in which w., 489:4
battles that should been w., 749:2
by captain of second rank, 427:25
by men with courage, 72:7
capitalism has w., 746:16
game is done I've w., 381:13
glory of winning were she w., 509:10
lose ground w. today, 498:10
lost or w. game, 426:2
not that you w. or lost, 643:13
on playing fields of Eton, 371:15
other palms are w., 375:15
prize we sought is w., 490:19
she that with poetry w., 263:20
small have plodders w., 168:15
so melancholy as battle w., 371:7
the ear of Pluto, 251:20
things w. are done, 200:4
though he w. all battles, 759:5
wars w. by men, 658:15
was woman in this humor w., 165:24
when battle's lost and w., 212:9
woman therefore to be w., 163:16
woman w. or woman lost, 597:12
wooed and not unsought be w., 259:27

Won (*continued*)
world made to be w. by youth, 619:19
Wonder, all knowledge and w. is pleasure, 158:2
all w. that would be, 455:17
and glory of universe, 444:12
and wild desire, 467:24
at so grotesque a blunder, 627:20
at the workmanship, 253:10
bird w. dies, 226:8
capacity for w., 572:19
Do I dare, 667:12
dreaming eyes of w., 518:13
ever-increasing w. and awe, 326:10
how I w. what you're at, 517:20
I w. by my troth, 228:2
if same way with human race, 633:8
men trust themselves, 211:24
miles around w. grew, 579:2
my verse sad no w., 580:3
of an hour, 399:14
of our stage, 232:18
still the w. grew, 329:18
what I was begun for, 778:3
what you are, 394:2
what you've missed, 720:8
Wonderer, way for the W., 757:5
Wonderful, all things wise and w., 479:17
bird is pelican, 637:14
grass upon breast, 503:12
mystic w., 459:6
name shall be called W., 26:8
none more w. than man, 66:9
one-hoss shay, 447:16
peace it's w., 646:5
's w. 's marvelous, 695:3
seasoning of enjoyments, 269:18
three things which are too w., 23:15
thy love to me was w., 12:2
wide beautiful w. world, 503:12
wonderful most wonderful, 191:13
Wonderfully, fearfully and w. made, 20:10
Wondering fearing doubting dreaming, 452:17
Wonderland, summer's w., 643:10
Wonders, America land of w., 438:6
at our quaint spirits, 173:11
carry with us w. we seek, 248:6
his w. to perform, 333:22
numberless are world's w., 66:9
of all w. I have heard, 188:11
of Christian religion, 287:3
welcome all w., 264:20
Wonder-working earth puts forth sweet flowers, 89:3
Wondrous Architecture of world, 161:21
days have been w. free, 295:17
he was w. wise, 792:22
it grew w. cold, 381:3
moon takes up w. tale, 292:1
'twas w. pitiful, 205:28
Wont, more near earth than w., 208:11
Won't, when you will they w., 86:10
will you w. you, 518:6

Wonted, live their w. fires, 322:20
Woo her as lion, 325:7
men April when they w., 192:4
that would w. her, 205:28
Wood, an ark of gopher w., 7:16
beyond these a bit of w., 95:10
Birnam w. to Dunsinane, 215:21
Birnam W. to Dunsinane, 637:13
bows to w. and stone, 395:20
brown heath and shaggy w., 378:2
burgeoning w. brings forth, 51:23
cannot see w. for trees, 142:10
children in the w., 776:2
cleave w. there am I, 112:16
crow makes wing to rooky w., 214:28
dark w. where straight way lost, 125:3
deep and gloomy w., 373:4
feeld hath eyen w. eres, 130:14
grainy w., 663:2
has a sharp ear, 130:*n*3
heap on more w., 378:11
hewers of w., 10:36
hewing w. for master carpenter, 58:4
in w. a Piggy-wig, 472:1
in w. furious winter blowing, 674:10
in woodsman's house knives w., 794:4
into a different w., 727:11
know what w. cudgel's of, 263:18
land set out to plant w., 302:23
mountains and a w., 683:15
old w. burn brightest, 237:11
old w. to burn, 158:23
one impulse from vernal w., 372:21
over river through w., 427:7
red herrings in w., 788:15
sang within bloody w., 668:16
stumps warmed me twice, 478:30
throne is bit of w. gilded, 370:11
to wild w. and downs, 409:21
tulgey w., 518:16
two roads diverged in w., 623:7
wherever w. can swim, 370:16
who splits w. warms twice, 478:*n*1
Woodbine, luscious w., 173:9
Woodcocks, springes to catch w., 194:4
Wooden dialogue and sound, 200:11
float easy as w. boat, 777:17
justice has w. leg, 602:18
O, 184:19
wall is your ships, 62:24
water through my w. hull, 565:12
Wooden-shoes, Round-heads and W., 292:17
Woodland, hills vales w. plain, 299:21
let me love river and w., 92:29
of Weir, 453:2
Woodlands, about w. I will go, 578:19
Woodlawn, at W. heard dead cry, 724:17
Woodman spare beechen tree, 389:8
spare that tree, 428:10
Wood-notes, native w. wild, 251:19
Woods against stormy sky, 410:11
are full of them, 779:22

Work (*continued*)

be made manifest, 42:33

beginning most important part of w., 75:8

best w. the human mind, 363:1

between twenty-five and forty, 558:6

bring every w. into judgment, 24:30

by w. one knows workman, 267:25

Central Park single w. of art, 502:1

comes first, 604:1

contrariously, 184:25

dawn speeds him in his w., 54:29

day's wages for day's w., 413:4

debasing w. to do what not worth doing, 756:4

dictate direction w. must take, 687:19

did sell himself to w. wickedness, 13:1

dirty w. at crossroads, 780:17

end crowns the w., 119:3

entire land sets to w., 5:5

Equal Pay for Equal W., 491:22

establish the w. of our hands, 18:14

every person who wants to w., 754:2

expands to fill time, 727:7

extra draught of hard w., 558:5

frivolous w., 367:16

from sun to sun, 778:23

get so much w. done looking dissipated, 675:14

good day's w., 311:5

greatness of w. inside man, 748:3

grows beyond his w., 710:9

half proper gardener's w., 593:23

hands from day to day, 722:4

hands that w. on us, 630:12

harder yet thought idler, 595:14

he can w. no faster, 789:12

his six days' w. a world, 259:22

his w. is perfect, 10:26

how the hell can I w., 782:13

I am rising to a man's w., 111:13

I don't like w., 573:5

I like what is in w., 573:5

I like w. it fascinates me, 580:12

I want w., 177:20

if this w. be of men, 41:1

incessantly to the last, 350:6

is seed sown, 411:19

judgeth according to w., 46:20

Kaspar's w. was done, 386:3

keeps us from three evils, 306:11

labor and do all thy w., 9:11

leave w. sit at temple, 651:13

less w. more poverty, 510:15

let patience have her perfect w., 46:4

light prime w. of God, 257:*n*6

like madness in brain, 382:15

love made visible, 651:13

lovely dears her noblest w., 361:25

man goeth forth unto his w., 19:6

many hands make light w., 142:15

men w. women weep, 484:11

more wise master simpler w., 124:15

Work (*continued*)

nakedness of woman w. of God, 357:6

never fit for real w., 754:7

never made w. for man to mend, 276:19

nice w. if you can get it, 695:14

night when no man can w., 40:13

no immortal w. behind me, 418:18

no substitute for hard w., 555:12

no werkman may w. wel and hastily, 131:22

no w. begun shall pause, 467:28

no w. nor device nor knowledge, 24:19

no w. to do, 782:13

noblest w. of God, 301:18, 361:10

noblest w. of man, 520:15

none of older connotation of pain, 723:9

nor fire nor age shall destroy, 101:28

nothing without hard w., 95:7

of a moment, 149:5

of art corner of creation, 541:11

of Henry James, 676:2

of noble note, 455:5

of thy hand, 28:9

on seventh day God ended his w., 6:10

others w. better with bronze, 94:15

out own salvation, 44:30

partly done, 664:31

people unable to find w., 614:21

perfection of life or w., 598:10

play for mortal stakes, 624:7

portrait of self, 524:18

posterity of w. of art, 612:15

pseudo-promotion a new w. place, 747:7

put us to w. anew, 591:13

race over w. never done, 543:11

save myself by w. and faith, 717:19

scythe of time, 370:17

seventh day thou shalt not w., 9:11

shall not be lost, 309:5

shovel under let me w., 634:6

sincere w. give reality to illusion, 631:5

slaves to do ugly w., 567:12

smile his w. to see, 358:7

so w. the honeybees, 184:23

social world w. of man, 290:31

soon as your day's w. done, 520:5

sport tedious as to w., 176:37

spur whereby mankind w., 277:11

stops expenses run on, 85:2

strive on to finish w., 450:11

studies in which w. dies with worker, 135:4

that aspires to art, 572:18

those who w. with joy, 651:13

to every man according to his w., 17:34

to love and to w., 570:2

to pray is to w., 119:17

to w. to w. wolf at door, 583:8

together for good, 42:4

unfinished w. they advanced, 450:2

until our w. done, 426:22

Work (*continued*)

us a perpetual peace, 250:19

we are w. of thy hand, 28:9

we have corrected Thy w., 495:11

we have undertaken, 239:27

we w. in the dark, 548:18

what a piece of w. is man, 195:28

whatever body obliged to do, 526:3

whether his w. be pure, 22:3

which bores you, 605:6

who first invented w., 388:2

why don't you w., 782:13

why should I let toad w., 750:10

with materials I have, 714:8

with one hand wrought in w., 13:21

with so fine a brush, 387:13

without Hope, 383:15

woman's w. never done, 778:23

work work, 423:6

works of him that sent me, 40:13

world's need of w., 605:6

world's w. by men who not feel well, 723:13

write if you get w., 752:8

your wicked will, 621:1

Worked and sang, 338:18

and waited for light, 608:8

Worker, lone w. makes first advance, 644:14

studies in which work dies with w., 135:4

to w. God lends aid, 59:*n*5

value of what w. produces, 653:23

Workers, as w. not as women, 491:21

brain-sick brain w., 523:10

freedom for all poor w., 682:8

heart-sick hand w., 523:10

idle reward great, 115:16

mainstay of civilization, 560:2

of world unite, 482:*n*3

Park to supply w. God's handiwork, 502:2

Worketh, wrath w. not righteousness, 46:7

Workhouse, Christmas Day in w., 556:1

Working, committing suicide by w., 589:20

Heaven protect w. girl, 574:1

man thinking or w. is alone, 478:26

men of all countries unite, 482:7

mere w. mason, 379:7

necessary mode of w. of mind, 505:4

on the railroad, 780:6

Working-day world, 190:3

Workings, hum of mighty w., 414:1

Workman, by work one knows w., 267:25

no w. may werke wel and hastily, 131:22

that needeth not to be ashamed, 45:27

Workmanship, dark inscrutable w., 373:8

most may wonder at w., 253:10

Workmen, Master of All Good W., 591:13

Works, all ye w. of the Lord, 32:17

authors' names not w., 299:1

Works (*continued*)

be silent as to his w., 317:11
been into future it w., 601:3
best of all God's w., 260:10
both sides of street, 650:4
done under the sun, 23:27
faith without w., 46:10
fat of others' w., 234:5
for sweetness and light, 500:14
God in w. and in word, 295:9
good w. better in sight of Lord, 116:21
her own w. praise her, 23:21
how manifold are thy w., 19:6
I know thy w., 47:13
live and die in Aristotle's w., 162:13
look on my w. ye Mighty, 406:13
man is son of own w., 92:*n*2
move immediately upon your w., 501:9
Nature's w. expunged, 257:24
neurotics created great w. of art, 612:18
not retain rare w., 612:16
of art products of danger, 630:13
of darkness, 42:23
of him that sent me, 40:13
of unbelievers a mirage, 117:5
our w. do not ennoble us, 124:16
part of man's Self, 545:20
poets reading from own w., 703:7
relationship of author to w., 572:22
renounce the devil and his w., 49:21
reward according to his w., 45:30
rich in good w., 45:24
see your good w., 33:3
seen future and it w., 601:*n*1
sighing through all her w., 260:7
skilled in w. of both languages, 96:18
spares man nor his w., 340:7
subdued to what it w. in, 222:1
these are thy glorious w., 259:7
unread his w., 373:*n*2
Workshop, best business father's w., 462:12
of serious inquirer, 537:3
Workshops, trees in Nature's w., 537:16
World abounds with laws, 779:4
above w. stretched the sky, 683:16
absolutes in w. affairs, 713:19
age of antiquity youth of w., 158:*n*2
all kingdoms of the w., 38:9
all the w. and his wife, 290:19
all this the w. well knows, 222:7
all w. here to look on me, 173:8
all w. sad and dreary, 507:1
all's right with w., 464:4
always been man's w., 722:7
Americans hope of w., 327:12
and all her train, 270:7
and my being were one, 504:17
and they that dwell therein, 16:18
another and better w., 366:11
any way to perpetuate the W., 248:19
appointment at end of w., 656:8

World (*continued*)

Arahat Buddhas who appear in w., 64:24
as fresh as at first day, 505:7
as good out of w., 291:18
attracts envy of w., 331:7
banish Jack banish all w., 177:32
beautifully dressed, 503:12
began without human race, 723:21
being by w. oppressed, 597:17
being kind all sad w. needs, 562:16
belie all corners of w., 219:29
best known and thought in w., 499:9
bestride the narrow w., 187:22
better w. than this, 190:1
bigger w. of adult life, 629:1
black green red yellow, 766:8
blooms with statues, 524:10
blows and buffets of w., 214:22
book of Montaigne w. endorsed, 145:*n*5
bottom of monstrous w., 254:4
brave new w., 224:26
brave w. sir, 281:15
breaks everyone, 701:15
breathes contagion to this w., 197:21
bring me back the w., 689:14
bring them into w. like this, 768:5
bring w. under rule, 597:13
broad highway of w., 408:13
brothers in w. too, 630:19
brought death into w., 255:18
build therefore your own w., 431:4
bundle of hay, 403:26
busy w. and I ne'er agree, 266:16
but thurghfare of woe, 130:23
by meeting friend new w. born, 711:9
call w. if you Please, 418:15
came death into the w., 30:22
came once a W., 512:1
cankers of calm w., 178:25
cannot hold thee close enough, 684:1
cannot live at level of great, 565:3
canted in this canting w., 320:23
capable of alteration, 698:19
care of this w., 35:8
changed if two people shaken, 736:17
charged with grandeur of God, 550:18
chess board the w., 505:6
children of w. wiser, 38:40
citizen of the w., 70:24, 159:15
citizens of the w., 650:5
cognition of modern w., 628:6
cold accretion called w., 540:1
cold hard mouth of w., 729:5
come three corners of w., 170:24
Commodity bias of the w., 169:26
concepts not uniquely determined by w., 635:15
conquest of w. by creed, 741:13
content with setting right surface, 427:2
contributions to peace of w., 655:13

World (*continued*)

conversion of w. lead to perpetual peace, 536:19
crumbles to nothing, 396:18
cry out vanity of w., 278:17
dark as w. of man, 665:19
dark w. and wide, 255:11
dark w. present treatment, 605:5
dead become lumber of w., 284:1
dear Agnes is strange, 268:29
death is but crossing w., 282:21
destroyed entire w. rescued entire w., 115:17
do not grow old at all, 279:17
don't live in w. alone, 630:19
doth two nations bear, 268:20
dragon w., 660:1
dreaming on things to come, 221:23
dreams books each a w., 376:14
drives poet to w., 498:7
drowsy syrups of w., 207:6
easily reconciles to death, 436:9
end in fire, 623:14
ends of w. are come, 538:5
enough and time, 268:13
even unto end of w., 37:16
every force maintaining w., 495:3
every woman gift of w. to me, 420:4
everybody in w. down on me, 773:5
everyone in w. is Christ, 630:21
external w. super-ego and id, 569:14
false w. but transitory, 136:5
fashion of w. passeth, 43:3
Federation of the w., 455:18
feeling something right in w., 744:14
fill w. with fools, 493:11
find w. beautiful and delightful, 603:26
fine place worth fighting for, 702:6
fled from this vile w., 221:7
foolery governs whole w., 239:6
foppery of the w., 209:3
forgetting by world forgot, 300:5
founded on four freedoms, 649:17
freedom everywhere in w., 649:17
frippery necessary towards looking like rest of w., 347:9
from all deceits of the w., 49:9
full of invisible things, 748:10
full of number of things, 561:12
full of untold novelties, 505:7
gain whole w., 35:30
gained w. gave w. lesson, 543:18
gave his honors to the w., 226:2
getting on in w., 615:17
ghosts all over w., 508:5
giddy thinks w. turns round, 167:33
give the w. the lie, 152:15
give w. another heart, 414:1
give w. assurance of a man, 197:30
given to lying, 179:11
gleams of remoter w., 406:11
gleams untraveled w., 455:1
glow has warmed the w., 654:*n*2
go into the w., 37:36
go well with thee, 781:1
God made w., 41:16

World (*continued*)

God plays dice with w., 636:5
God so loved w., 39:46
golden w., 189:30
good deed in naughty w., 182:11
good w. to live in, 622:14
good-bye proud w., 429:6
great wonderful w., 503:12
great w. spin forever, 455:25
green fruits of w., 638:20
grown gray, 534:4
half w. knows not how other lives,
  245:4
half w. not understand pleasures of
  other, 387:6
half-brother of w., 476:9
harmoniously confused, 299:21
harmony of w. Form and Number,
  583:13
has joked incessantly, 531:23
hath not a sweeter creature, 207:20
healthy free the w. before me, 490:3
here in this w. changed his life,
  133:18
high shore of this w., 185:19
his six days' work a w., 259:22
his who has money to go, 432:33
history is world's court, 364:15
history of w. biography, 412:32
history of w. progress of freedom,
  372:9
hog butcher for w., 634:4
hold w. but as w., 179:17
honest as w. goes, 195:16
house with firmament for roof,
  537:18
how w. originated, 440:10
huge w. come to him, 431:13
I am in charity with w., 290:3
I am light of w., 40:10
I have overcome w., 40:35
I never made, 579:20
I never sought w., 317:29
I re-enter w., 762:4
I sure did live in this w., 763:16
I was in love with the whole w.,
  775:1
if there's another w., 364:2.
if w. and love were young, 152:11
I'll make me a w., 612:7
imagined ultimate good, 640:8
in arms, 425:12
in image of global village, 730:5
in love with night, 176:1
in one small room, 596:7
in part constructed by men, 715:11
in solemn stillness, 462:2
in this harsh w., 199:27
in wildness preservation of w.,
  479:6
in w. not of it, 390:8
intangible we touch, 581:10
into dangerous w. leapt, 358:11
invisible we view, 581:10
is a bubble, 160:13
is a comedy, 324:1
is a force not presence, 640:30
is a king, 371:19
is all that is case, 677:10
is but thickened light, 433:28

World (*continued*)

is ever-living Fire, 62:12
is grown so bad, 165:25
is mean, 766:8
is mine oyster, 182:26
it is a pretty w., 730:10
it is a w. to see, 155:11
it was whole morning w., 727:19
joy to pass to w. below, 94:3
joy to the w., 294:17
justice is wanting in w., 365:32
kill babies make w. safer, 761:16
knew w. would not be same, 714:12
knowledge of w. acquired in w.,
  304:19
lash rascals through w., 208:2
laugh and w. laughs, 562:15
law of musical w., 586:20
lawlessness, 649:9
leaden army that conquers w.,
  590:14
learn of green w., 660:1
leave the w. no copy, 201:26
leave w. by natural door, 564:13
leaves w. to darkness, 322:1
lesser god made w., 459:23
let justice be done though w. perish,
  119:n2
let the w. mind him, 465:24
let us possess one w., 228:3
let w. slide, 140:14
let w. wag., 141:8
letter to W., 512:12
life of this w., 117:14
light of bright w. dies, 563:2
light of the w., 33:3, 40:10
lights of the w., 334:7
limits of vision limits of w., 404:13
listen then as I now, 408:8
little friend of all w., 593:6
little note nor long remember, 450:2
little w. made cunningly, 230:18
little w. of childhood, 629:1
live in w. as spectator, 292:18
look round habitable w., 276:4
look upon w. as parish, 308:24
looking uncomfortably to w. we inherit, 784:2
looks on w. rationally, 372:8
looks whole w. in face, 441:4
love all things in w. so filled, 380:24
love beyond w., 282:21
Love makes w. go round, 530:16
love makes w. go round, 786:18
lover's quarrel with w., 624:15
loves w. as his body, 57:3
luckiest people in the w., 751:4
mad as Bedlam, 470:26
mad w. mad kings, 169:25
made in six days, 370:7
made safe for democracy, 572:11
made safe for differences, 662:16
made to be won by youth, 619:19
maintain before whole w., 269:27
make w. safe for democracy, 587:16
makes whole w. kin, 201:3
margent of w., 581:6
market economy's field is w.,
  645:11
mass and majesty of w., 721:3

World (*continued*)

mass of public wrongs, 156:17
may end tonight, 465:19
mere anarchy loosed on w., 596:19
money sets w. in motion, 100:7
more overwork than w. justifies,
  591:8
morning of the w., 464:7
most people on w. not in it, 537:17
movers and shakers of w., 553:21
mud-luscious, 688:8
must be peopled, 186:31
must conform to necessity, 615:11
my all the w., 148:n6
my country is the w., 341:7
naked shingles of w., 499:22
native in this w., 639:9
nature too noble for w., 219:9
needs men of real talent, 342:17
never enjoy w. aright, 280:22
New W. favorable to declamation,
  573:10
next w. as closely apprehended,
  248:27
no living in this w., 479:28
no world but wrongs, 156:17
noisy set martyrs call w., 595:14
Northwest Passage to intellectual
  w., 320:28
not a joy the w. can give, 401:17
not as w. giveth, 40:30
not be queen for all w., 225:9
not inn but hospital, 248:21
not loved w. nor w. me, 400:7
not metaphysical brothel, 716:12
not sweet in the end, 534:4
not to live but die in, 248:21
not to live in physical w., 639:17
not worth while to go round the w.,
  478:34
now bubble burst now w., 301:5
O w. invisible intangible, 581:10
O W. thou choosest not, 587:17
O w. w. w., 201:15
of cards, 680:17
of compensations, 448:12
of fashion birth intellect, 503:8
of future a struggle, 691:5
of happy days, 165:29
of ideas, 499:6
of light, 270:9
of made, 689:6
of men for me, 465:2
of nuclear giants, 685:13
of Pains and troubles, 418:16
of sighs, 205:28
of this bad w., 609:8
of vile faults, 182:32
of words, 640:28
on back burden of w., 563:6
on dreaming fed, 594:16
on w. to turn thine eyes, 313:17
one custom corrupt w., 459:26
one w. at a time, 479:11
only fence against the w., 277:14
only thing new in w., 655:21
opinion governs w., 572:3
origin of modern w., 704:2
our country the w., 437:12

World (*continued*)

outlasts aversion outlasts love, 497:11
pain, 367:*n*1
part we sadly in troublous w., 165:3
pass through w. once, 780:5
peace or world destruction, 608:14
peace reversal of record, 642:6
peep at such a w., 335:4
pendant w., 204:14, 257:22
perfect everywhere, 365:19
place I do not care to be, 735:5
Playboy of the Western W., 613:10
please w. and father, 268:1
pleases w. cannot please himself, 280:10
poet creates w., 640:16
poet looks at w., 640:24
poets legislators of w., 410:3
point is to change it, 481:12
poor w. said I, 264:18
power of w. works in circles, 587:5
presents rational aspect, 372:8
puddle-wonderful, 688:9
queer save me and thee, 781:20
quiet limit of w., 459:2
rack of this tough w., 211:20
reaction to external w., 558:9
read that w. was spherical, 134:12
reared arm crested the w., 218:11
rebellion in political w., 343:14
recognize relations to w. within, 562:17
regions we call New W., 135:15
remote from wrangling w., 340:24
retire from w. satisfied, 95:3
retreating w., 687:5
rhythm to w. of sound, 665:20
richest monarch in w., 364:20
riddle of the w., 301:13
ringed with azure w., 458:4
rivers ancient as w., 708:12
rocks cradle rules w., 488:8
roofs of w., 489:22
round w. forever and aye, 497:8
sad and dreary, 507:1
safe for democracy, 587:16
safe for diversity, 742:1
same whole w. over, 782:18
same w. a hell a heaven, 430:13
say to all the w., 189:28
secure amidst falling, 292:3
see how w. goes, 211:3
see w. in grain of sand, 359:5
seek a newer w., 455:6
seek empty w. again, 480:2
seem all uses of this w., 193:5
seems to smile upon me, 279:9
sense that w. was mad, 630:15
serpent deceiveth whole w., 47:28
shore of the wide w., 417:11
shot heard round w., 429:22
should he need next w., 465:24
show contain and nourish all w., 169:4
shut in from w. without, 443:14
sins of whole w., 46:33
slumbering w., 296:7
smother up beauty from w., 176:37

World (*continued*)

snow swept w. end to end, 680:2
snug little farm the w., 386:21
so passes glory of w., 132:12
so runs w. away, 197:15
so wags the w., 190:*n*2
sob heavy w., 721:1
social w. work of man, 290:31
solid earth actual w., 477:7
spectacle unto w., 42:35
stands out, 683:16
start w. all over at, 625:3
steady patriot of w. alone, 371:23
still point of turning w., 670:5, 670:15
stood against w., 189:3
stop w. I want to get off, 763:18
story and byword through w., 239:27
strongest force in w. today, 765:5
strongest minds w. hears least, 376:19
struggle with w. calls forth faculties, 365:24
sword axis of w., 678:8
syllables govern the w., 239:8
take note O w., 207:12
taketh away sin of w., 39:35
technology knack of arranging w., 729:17
tell the w., 179:2
ten days that shook w., 665:17
ten hours to w. allot, 152:*n*3
terms between old and new w., 355:3
terrible in mass, 540:1
that few is all the w., 161:3
that I have had my w. as in my tyme, 131:2
the w. the book of God, 227:4
their words to end of w., 16:10
thick rotundity o' the w., 209:24
this little w., 171:9
this war shake w., 676:11
thorns and dangers of w., 170:17
thoughts rule w., 433:18
through all w. she followed him, 456:2
through art w. multiply, 613:5
thus one goes through w., 349:4
time and w. in flight, 595:6
time takes survey of w., 179:5
time the soul of this w., 107:19
to hide virtues in, 201:23
to seek her through the w., 258:10
to succeed in the w., 265:6
to the city and the w., 120:1
to win, 482:7
today sick, 666:20
tone of some w. far from ours, 409:23
too much respect upon w., 179:16
too much with us, 376:11
too old, 461:13
too wide for shrunk shank, 191:3
triple pillar of the w., 216:23
true and human w., 727:16
turned round in w., 486:28
turned upside downward, 234:11
undulate round the w., 490:17

World (*continued*)

United States of W., 428:7
unknowable we know, 581:10
unspotted from the w., 46:9
unstilled w. whirled, 669:18
up above w. fly, 517:20
up above w. so high, 394:2
varying shore o' the w., 218:6
vast screen of snow, 675:3
visible poem of w., 712:19
visible w. formed in love, 486:26
Vision of the w., 455:17
visits his dinners not him, 269:12
void the w. can never fill, 333:21
wags, 190:22
want to be equal in man's w., 722:12
wants to be deceived, 135:16
was all before them, 260:24
was not to seek me, 317:29
wash soiled w., 490:14
wave to wash him from w., 613:9
way of coming into w., 288:13
way w. ends, 669:11
way w. imagined determines what men do, 676:19
we are the w., 775:3
weary of past, 408:11
weight of unintelligible w., 373:2
what an age what a w., 279:5
what I do to spite w., 214:22
what is this w., 130:22
what thrown on waters of w., 754:6
when all the w. dissolves, 162:17
when all w. young lad, 484:15
when Don Quixote when out into w., 761:14
when end of w. comes, 626:4
when Rome falls the w., 400:27
where alienation awaits, 758:6
where England dead, 626:24
where is any author in w., 168:35
where much to be done, 314:27
where nothing for nothing, 483:1
which seems before us, 499:22
whole face of w. changed, 270:22
whom w. flattered thou despised, 153:1
whose w. or mine or theirs, 659:17
wide enough to hold both, 320:18
wilderness of this w., 272:10
will freely offer itself, 651:22
will welcome lovers, 689:16
wish estate o' w. undone, 216:15
with old w. to the grave, 557:12
without end, 48:22, 335:24
without God and man, 760:6
woman is nigger of the w., 765:8
wondrous Architecture of w., 161:21
word freed from w., 727:11
word making of a w., 639:18
word of earth in ears of w., 534:21
work of w. done through me, 634:3
workers of w. unite, 482:*n*3
working-day w., 190:3
would be field of soya beans, 769:4
would be nicer than ever, 541:9
would go round faster, 517:13
would split open, 734:4

Wrack, betokened w. to seaman,
165:12
 blow wind come w., 216:16
Wracks, thousand fearful w., 165:30
Wraggle-taggle gypsies O, 779:7
Wrang, may gang a kennin w., 362:5
Wrangling, remote from w. world,
340:24
Wrap baby bunting in, 789:15
 thousand onward years, 490:1
 wide enough to w. a fairy, 173:9
Wrapped, child all meanly w., 250:20
 himself in quotations, 592:10
 in clouds and snow, 399:25
 in five-pound note, 471:31
 in swaddling clothes, 38:2
 tiger's heart w. in woman's hide,
 164:13
Wraps me in humorous sadness,
191:26
Wrath, Achilles' w., 299:*n*9
 between dragon and w., 208:23
 by his meekness, 356:16
 day of w. O day of mourning,
 123:14
 did grow, 358:12
 envy and w. shorten life, 32:4
 flee from w. to come, 32:31
 grapes of w., 484:6
 in w. the Olympian Pericles, 72:13
 infinite w. and despair, 258:5
 killeth the foolish man, 14:1
 knows not w. nor pity, 424:1
 let not sun go down on w., 44:25
 matter of Troy and Achilles' w.,
 490:6
 my w. did end, 358:12
 neither w. of love nor fire, 101:28
 nursing w., 363:2
 of Almighty God, 47:35
 of lion wisdom of God, 357:6
 of Peleus' son, 50:23, 299:23
 provoking most justly thy w., 49:15
 sentest forth thy w., 9:5
 slow to w., 46:7
 soft answer turneth away w., 21:24
 surely not in W. destroy, 446:3
 sweeter than honeycomb, 52:14
 tastes like w. to come, 631:2
 towards you burns like fire, 308:20
 tygers of w., 357:9
 winepress of w., 47:35
 worketh not righteousness, 46:7
Wrath-bearing, tears from w. tree,
668:8
Wrathful man stirreth up strife, 21:27
 winter with w. nipping cold, 163:23
Wreath, Don John home with w.,
619:3
 has lost rose, 379:6
 rosy w., 232:16
 subtle w. of hair, 229:19
Wreathe iron pokers into knots,
383:12
Wreathed, blow w. horn, 376:12
 smiles, 251:8
 with fairy fruits, 452:2
 with silken turbans w., 260:31
Wreaths, bindest in w. thy golden
 hair, 95:20

Wreaths (*continued*)
 no w. please, 653:28
Wreck, came to explore w., 762:8
 decay of colossal w., 406:13
 Hope creates from its own w.,
 407:6
 out of the w. I rise, 468:13
Wreckage, tatty w. of my life, 764:9
 wild to be w. forever, 752:3
Wrecked, battered w. old man, 491:5
 greatest men oftest w., 260:28
 in mist of opium, 501:6
 on lee shore of age, 557:14
Wrecks of slavery, 532:16
Wren, four larks and w., 471:27
 goes to 't, 211:1
 hurt the little w., 359:8
 robin redbreast and w., 237:13
 Sir Christopher W., 627:18
Wrenlike vigilance, 743:10
Wrens make prey where eagles dare
 not, 165:25
Wrested from sure defeat, 673:9
Wresting from Jupiter his thunder,
103:15
Wrestle, this urge w. resurrection,
724:11
 we w. not against flesh, 44:28
 with words and meanings, 670:23
Wrestled as Angel with Jacob, 245:11
 until breaking of day, 7:45
Wrestles, he that w. with us, 332:20
Wrestling for world axeth a fal,
132:10
 with my God my God, 551:12
Wretch, beware of robbing w., 5:12
 concentered all in self, 378:1
 excellent w., 206:27
 hollow-eyed sharp-looking w.,
 166:34
 I beheld the w., 420:20
 I w. lay wrestling, 551:12
 live like a w., 234:24
 my wife poor w., 279:7
 on hope w. relies, 328:4
 saved a w. like me, 327:4
 treat poor w., 287:1
 whip to haud w. in order, 235:*n*5
 wise w., 300:15
Wretched and abundant Russia,
496:20
 blind pit ponies, 611:18
 companions consolation to w.,
 100:21
 despicable creature, 308:19
 grief transfigures w., 427:23
 have no friends, 273:17
 is he who bound land to himself,
 3:13
 learned to aid w., 93:25
 man outlive wealth, 181:25
 man w. whom no man pleases,
 106:18
 men cradled into poetry, 407:11
 nothing more w. than a man, 52:13
 of the earth, 476:18
 poor man that hangs on princes' favors, 225:16
 proud yet w. thing, 227:15
 refuse of teeming shore, 558:1

Wretched (*continued*)
 sleep soundly as w. slave, 185:19
 taste gratified with mediocrity,
 368:1
 to relieve w. his pride, 329:13
 un-ideaed girls, 315:16
Wretcheder one is the more one
 smokes, 522:8
Wretchedness, consigned to state of
 w., 336:14
 that glory brings, 212:6
Wretches, feel what w. feel, 210:3
 hang that jurymen dine, 299:15
 hired, 314:3
 poor naked w., 210:3
 who never were alive, 125:11
Wrights, crucified the Fanny W.,
475:10
Wrigley, Spearmint Girl With W.
 Eyes, 688:12
Wring his bosom, 328:30
 pain and anguish w. brow, 378:14
 pangs wilder w., 551:13
Wringing bread from sweat, 450:10
 handlebar for speed, 752:3
Wrings, wearer knows where shoe w.,
107:*n*2
Wrinkle, no w. on azure brow, 401:1
 stamps w. deeper, 399:17
Wrinkled Care derides, 251:9
 lame w. and slanting-eyed, 51:33
 sea, 458:4
 smoothed his w. front, 165:19
 view with w. brow, 181:25
Wrinkles, eyes mid many w., 599:8
Wrist, ease darbies at w., 487:10
 hands in up to w., 720:8
Writ, having w. moves on, 445:25
 I never w., 222:2
 in remembrance, 171:6
 name w. in water, 418:21
 odd old ends stolen of holy w.,
 165:27
 proofs of holy w., 207:5
 slaughters of race w., 540:15
 with me in misfortune's book,
 176:15
 your annals true, 219:15
Write about it Goddess, 303:32
 all books in British Museum, 646:7
 anyone allowed to w. like that,
 651:*n*1
 as much as man ought to w., 476:5
 as soon w. free verse, 625:17
 baseness to w. fair, 199:20
 better neither read nor w., 390:7
 born to w., 302:11
 can't w. can review, 485:9
 casts to w. living line, 232:23
 devise wit w. pen, 168:21
 difficult to w. good life as live one,
 643:17
 does he w., 466:26
 evil in marble, 137:17
 finely upon broomstick, 289:*n*2
 firm restraint with which they w.,
 707:7
 free to think speak w., 345:4
 from worm's-eye view, 705:9
 good in dust, 137:17

Write (*continued*)

History Don't, 521:6
I detest what you w., 307:*n*2
I do not think I can w. more, 606:3
I live and w., 243:23
I w. nothing other than images, 706:2
I w. Poets All, 512:16
I w. wonders of religion, 287:3
if you get work, 752:8
impossible to w. a novel, 758:4
in books of law, 723:16
in de blotter I was born, 673:16
in spite of Nature, 263:11
in youth men w. wisely, 436:11
instruction manual, 757:16
know what I know and w. it, 736:19
last till you w. your letter, 228:7
look in thy heart and w., 156:4
man may w. at any time, 315:15
masters of things they w., 239:2
me as one that loves, 397:3
me down an ass, 187:6
never learned to w., 756:16
nothing to w. about, 109:25
of hunger, 723:1
only great man w. history, 567:14
poem for money, 716:16
poetry very easy to w., 523:2
right to w. badly was privilege, 688:4
sorrow on bosom of the earth, 171:24
speak associate, 724:7
the next chapter, 723:16
the vision, 29:40
things worthy reading, 309:23
three lessons I would w., 364:14
to rage to lust to w. to, 229:18
to w. and read comes by nature, 186:36
'twas certain he could w., 329:17
until still have juice, 702:12
virtues we w. in water, 226:5
well in laudable things, 254:15
well of American things, 548:5
whatever I tried to w. was verse, 102:4
with ease to show breeding, 353:2
with no dinner, 674:13
with watch before me, 476:6
woman's vows upon wave, 67:18
yet w. verse badly, 269:16
you a tragedy, 694:21
Writer, all w. had known become grotesques, 630:20
character of w. in writings, 412:26
concealed beauties of w., 293:4
doesn't want success, 697:3
excels at title page, 328:1
fit to be a w., 754:7
give that you are a w., 702:1
great and original w., 376:18
great w. second government, 746:1
moment here and there w. has, 625:12
most essential gift for good w., 702:11

Writer (*continued*)

my tongue is the pen of a ready w., 17:14
no eminent w. whom I can despise, 571:14
no tears in w. no tears in reader, 625:9
nodding places in w., 292:26
of dictionaries, 314:5
original w. one nobody can imitate, 369:15
problem of creative w., 569:11
someone true friend good w., 703:17
Southern w. adept at recognizing grotesque, 755:16
teach basest thing to be afraid, 696:20
true w. has nothing to say, 751:6
unmistakable animal a w., 759:10
who came from sheltered life, 728:1
writing make us chase the w., 773:20
Writer's only responsibility is to art, 697:2
privilege to help man endure, 697:1
understand w. ignorance, 384:4
Writers, ancient w. say, 598:3
are always selling somebody out, 766:10
become more numerous, 328:3
compulsion put upon w., 658:7
dissatisfied with books they could buy, 682:12
divided into incisors and molars, 506:5
editors are failed w. but so are w., 673:2
forgotten for want of w., 97:*n*1
gifted energetic wives of w., 739:13
habit of accurate w., 521:8
make mistake of enclosing envelope, 657:6
of small histories, 314:4
some w. cannot them digest, 160:17
some w. take to drink, 756:5
transcribed from former works, 103:19
Writes, great poet w. his time, 672:16
limns on water w. in dust, 160:14
Moving Finger w., 445:25
verses speaks holiday, 182:31
very well for a gentleman, 294:*n*5
whatever poet w. with enthusiasm, 70:26
Writing a name for conversation, 320:17
books praiseworthy method, 682:12
couldn't give up w. too famous, 675:15
creative reading creative w., 431:7
didn't require real work, 754:7
do things worth the w., 309:23
elongated-yellow-fruit school of w., 702:16
faucet upstairs, 625:14
get w., 665:11
good w. takes concentration, 751:10
I'd do no w. here, 726:3
in book of gold, 397:2

Writing (*continued*)

in w. himself writes his time, 672:16
incurable itch for w., 109:4
is easy, 678:19
it isn't w. it's typing, 753:15
judicial w., 609:11
make us chase the writer, 773:20
maketh an exact man, 160:9
master to this world, 664:17
Mr. Clemens had best stop w., 516:11
much w. many opinions, 254:26
nature's masterpiece w. well, 284:2
no harder prison than w. verse, 763:10
no partiality in his w., 87:15
nothing more than guided dream, 700:14
precautions against disease of w., 121:7
putting it down in w., 311:1
rid of things by w. them, 701:21
swimming under water holding breath, 695:1
take away art of w., 369:16
that was written, 29:16
true ease in w. 298:20
vigorous w. concise, 608:9
would have started w. long ago, 651:*n*1
Writing's, easy w. curst hard reading, 353:2
Writings, character of writer in w., 412:26
praise nor blame w., 299:1
small men afraid of w., 336:9
Written and unwritten law, 112:2
as it is w., 42:30
biography of man himself cannot be w., 528:10
books well w. or badly w., 566:10
censure who have w. well, 298:10
isn't worth paper w. on, 647:3
most insincere line w., 666:23
of me on my stone, 624:15
out of reputation, 286:9
poetry well w. as prose, 660:3
read books as deliberately as w., 478:22
sonnets all his life, 402:22
that mine adversary had w. a book, 14:46
that my words were w., 14:29
troubles of the brain, 216:10
volumes might be w., 493:7
what woman says w. in wind, 91:11
words w. on subway walls, 772:8
Wrong, accumulated w., 589:1
all his life in the w., 283:27
always in the w., 274:11
citizens clamoring for what is w., 96:15
conduct right argument w., 330:11
cradled into poetry by w., 407:11
divinely in the w., 296:1
do great right do little w., 181:20
do w. to none, 203:8
done my credit w., 446:6
dreary morals w., 562:6
dwelling much on w., 280:17

Wrong *(continued)*
even if I were w., 495:8
faith in nice tenets w., 267:12
fashioning characters w. way,
545:13
forever on throne, 485:2
Frenchmen can't be w., 782:19
friends have it I do w., 595:17
from the start, 659:4
gloomy w., 436:12
had anything been w., 721:5
he done her w., 781:14
he who believes what is w., 343:5
I know I've done wrong, 786:7
if anything can go w. it will, 783:25
if end brings me out w., 451:4
if I called w. number, 690:5
if you w. us shall we not revenge,
180:31
just as dead as if w., 783:22
kind of victory, 655:19
king can do no w., 325:22
Lucrece swears he did her w., 167:6
majorities not entirely w., 493:6
may gang a kennin w., 362:5
mixed in w. that's all, 673:14
multitude always in w., 278:24
ne'er pardon who have done w.,
103:*n*3
never ashamed to own w., 303:21
never dreamed w. triumph, 468:17
never w. Old Masters, 720:7
newts and blind-worms do no w.,
173:12
no end to w., 4:3
no one harm man who does self no
w., 114:16
one idea and that w., 316:7
one more w. to man, 464:25
oppressor's w., 196:10
our country right or w., 390:22,
510:18
poem begins as sense of w., 625:6
preserve stars from w., 376:5
rather be w. with Plato, 87:28
right judge judges w., 66:8
Right of Kings to govern w., 303:31
right w. follow King, 459:7
rule of right and w., 510:8
side of thirty, 290:6
so long as w. unredressed on earth,
484:18
some villain hath done me w.,
167:*n*1
something w. something human,
736:2
sow by ear, 142:26
struggle between right and w.,
448:11
suffer w. no more, 425:13
that which they reject is w., 535:11
themselves men w., 116:9
those not present w., 295:21
to speed a guest, 53:29
unless w. I but obey, 625:5
war at wrong time, 685:15
wars w. from every standpoint,
655:19
when w. to be put right, 510:18
whether laws w., 567:21

Wrong *(continued)*
which roams earth, 4:3
wrongest in Kentucky, 551:21
ye do me w., 776:10
Wrongdoer often left something undone, 111:26
ox of w., 3:15
Wrongdoing, abstain from intentional
w., 71:1
and righteousness of men, 54:6
for great w. great punishments,
69:25
never with view to w., 71:1
of one generation, 436:5
virtuous for good cause, 99:7
Wrongdoings, thought to justify w.,
306:21
Wronged, I am w., 63:8
on that day no soul w., 117:13
woman who has w. you, 544:24
Wronger, loves not his w., 206:31
Wronging your image that blossoms,
595:5
Wrongs, arise avenger of w., 94:2
God w. not men, 116:9
mass of public w., 156:17
procure redress of w., 337:10
we seek to condemn, 683:3
Wrote, and I w. my happy songs,
356:5
blockheads read what blockheads
w., 305:13
ever w. except for money, 316:29
gentlemen who w. with ease, 303:7
like an angel, 323:19
one song, 466:28
Purple Cow, 600:17
reason Milton w. in fetters, 357:2
Thucydides w. history of war, 71:18
upon tables words of covenant,
9:20
will across sky, 673:8
World that never w. to Me, 512:12
Wroth with one we love, 382:15
Wrought, being w. perplexed, 208:16
first he w. afterward taughte, 130:2
ghost upon floor, 452:14
in sad sincerity, 429:10
love w. new alchemy, 229:9
more w. by prayer, 459:27
not into evil w., 532:14
remembers all that he w., 54:1
so distinctly w., 230:16
what hath God w., 10:7
wore as though they w. it, 596:4
Wrung life dry for your lips, 533:21
Wry-necked fife, 180:18
Wum, rooster don't cackle w'en fine
w., 556:14
Wyllowe-tree, al under the w., 353:6
Wynken Blynken and Nod, 559:20
Wyoming will be your new home,
786:2
WYSIWYG, 784:15

X

Xanadu, in X. did Kubla Khan,
382:19

Xenophon, a X. at New York, 323:23
Xerxes did die, 287:11

Y

Yacht and bank account man's Self,
545:20
annual upkeep of y., 533:3
Yahoo tricks, 637:7
Yahoos, Hollywood populated by Y.,
714:16
Yale, whale-ship was my Y. College
and Harvard, 486:21
Yam, I y. what I y. that's all I y.,
690:2
Yang, yin and y., 86:15
Yankee Doodle, 778:21
I'm a Y. Doodle dandy, 632:11
Yankees tough but nervous, 665:9
Yanks are coming, 632:12
Yarn, merry y. from rover, 633:16
mingled y. good and ill, 203:15
spun in Ulysses' absence, 218:25
Yawn, churchyards y., 197:21
never y. or say commonplace, 750:9
yawning make another y., 234:19
Yawning make another yawn, 234:19
rung night's y. peal, 214:27
Yawns and draws stocking up, 668:15
Yawp, sound my barbaric y., 489:22
Yea, everlasting y., 412:6
Yea-forsooth, rascally y. knave,
183:13
Year and a day, 472:1
circle of golden y., 454:23
dirge of dying y., 407:15
every y. passed day, 758:10
famous day and y., 442:12
fare wel snow of ferne y., 128:28
fiftieth y. jubilee, 9:27
firstling of the infant y., 246:10
food for seven long y., 210:9
grief with revolving y., 408:18
heaven's eternal y., 275:4
if y. playing holidays, 176:37
in y. of his age, 118:17
is going let him go, 457:29
live well on nothing a y., 463:9
mellowing y., 253:14
most immemorial y., 453:1
New Y. reviving Desires, 445:5
no trumpets for new y., 629:12
not every y. a king or poet born,
110:9
only lost to me, 243:16
outlive his life half a y., 197:8
plunges into night, 654:4
proper opinions for time of y.,
721:4
rich with forty pounds a y., 329:12
ruler of inverted y., 335:5
saddest of the y., 411:8
sailed away y. and a day, 472:1
seven stars solar y., 430:12
six hundred pounds a y., 302:23
snow y. a rich y., 244:9
sun is elder by a y., 229:5
sweet o' the y., 223:1
that night that y. of now, 551:12
that time of y. in me behold, 221:8

Yours (*continued*)
they won't go to y., 622:16
what is y. is mine, 83:7
what's mine is y., 205:7
Yourself, be greedy feel good about y., 774:*n*2
cannot make y. as you wish, 132:13
don't speak well of y., 270:16
first keep peace in y., 132:19
if you want to know y., 364:21
keep y. to y., 468:30
love you for y. alone, 598:8
loyalty to Truth i.e. y., 556:20
so hot that it singe y., 225:3
speak for y. John, 442:3
your subject is y., 421:11
Yourselves, be lamps unto y., 64:23
quit y. like men, 11:29
Youth a stuff will not endure, 202:2
age not so well qualified as y., 478:3
age of antiquity y. of world, 158:*n*2
age perform promises of y., 314:9
age preferable to y., 293:21
and age equally a burden, 75:4
bear the yoke in his y., 29:4
becomes as aged, 204:10
bedewed with liquid odors, 95:20
bent by wintry fever, 737:8
bourgeois in ferment of y., 496:9
bright y. passes swiftly, 59:26
build bridge to moon, 477:1
caught our y., 663:4
crabbed age and y., 776:7
dew of y., 19:13, 193:26
don't regret excess of y., 549:12
eyes of y., 182:31
fame thirst of y., 400:6
fight and die, 626:1
flaming y., 197:32
flourish set on y., 221:1
follies cease with y., 312:18
forge central perspective, 708:6
freakish y., 334:29
friends of my y. where are they, 118:8
from y. to extreme old age, 497:3
full of pleasance, 776:7
'gainst time and age, 156:14
gave love and roses, 392:9
gives y. delight, 301:15
glass wherein y. dress, 183:33
grows pale, 415:12
had been friends in y., 382:15
heart is evil from his y., 7:21
hell that tests my y., 679:9
home-keeping y. homely wits, 167:36
hopelessness of early y., 483:19
hour of thoughtless y., 373:5
I love gone to war, 787:15
if y. but knew if old age but could, 144:13
if y. season of hope, 483:28
immortal y. to mortal maids, 388:18
in my hot y., 96:22
in my y. said his father, 517:10
in the days of my y., 386:9
in y. hearts touched with fire, 542:7

Youth (*continued*)
in y. it sheltered me, 428:10
in y. men write wisely, 436:11
is given, 747:15
is vain, 382:15
I've done it from my y., 353:16
knew phoenix in y., 596:14
lexicon of y., 429:1
liquid dew of y., 193:26
lying days of y., 595:21
many a y. and many a maid, 251:15
masks and revels sweet y. make, 226:14
measure of our y., 592:4
mewing her mighty y., 255:2
moment of glamor of y., 573:1
much depends upon education of y., 347:4
now bravely spending, 675:2
of America tradition, 567:1
of England are on fire, 184:27
of labor, 329:10
of pleasure wasteful, 468:12
on the prow, 323:8
our y. our joys our all, 153:2
passed old age not arrived, 482:15
Poets in y. begin in gladness, 374:9
poets in y. begin in sadness, 742:16
prime of y. a frost of cares, 156:22
rejoice O young man in y., 24:26
remember thy Creator in days of thy y., 24:27
remembreth me upon my y., 131:2
replies I can, 430:4
riband in cap of y., 198:25
rider that breaks y., 244:33
rose of y., 217:25
roses for flush of y., 515:11
sacred to education, 559:3
season for enjoyment, 428:18
season made for joys, 297:18
season of credulity, 313:1
should be filial, 60:16
so are children of the y., 20:1
Socrates corrupts the y., 74:14
soul of my y., 657:2
spirit of y. in everything, 221:19
stone dead, 662:6
studied in my foolish y., 133:20
thou hast nor y. nor age, 204:10
thoughts of y. long, 442:5
time for extraordinary toil, 75:20
time of getting, 262:11
Time subtle thief of y., 251:3
to fortune and fame unknown, 322:22
traitorously corrupted y., 164:11
unmannerly sadness in y., 179:30
vaward of our y., 183:18
waneth by increasing, 156:14
what done with your y., 554:3
when Y. and Pleasure meet, 399:22
while life abloom with y., 144:5
who daily farther travel, 375:8
wholly experimental, 562:10
will be served, 428:17
world made to be won by y., 619:21
Youthful harlot's curse, 358:9
hose well saved, 191:3

Youthful (*continued*)
jest and y. jollity, 251:8
sights as y. poets dream, 251:19
sinewy races, 490:7
Youth's a stuff will not endure, 202:2
heritage, 467:10
the season made for joys, 297:18
You've got to get up, 666:8
Y-shaped, send to grave in Y. coffin, 765:10
Yukon Jake, 693:7
Law of the Y., 627:1
Will of the Y., 627:1

Z

Zaccheus he did climb tree, 287:12
Zanzibar, count cats in Z., 478:34
Zarathustra said to his heart, 552:5
Zeal, all z. Mr. Easy, 406:1
for different opinions, 351:22
half the z. I served my king,, 225:22
heavenly race demands z., 308:16
Zealous, a man z. for nothing,, 317:12
locksmith died, 778:1
Zealously affected in good thing, 44:16
Zeiten, ein Märchen aus alten Z., 419:*n*7
Zek, country inhabited by Z. people, 746:6
Zekle, hern went pity-Z., 485:16
Zèle, pas de z., 354:*n*5
Zenith, dropped from the z.,, 256:22
illusion reaches its z., 553:1
Zephyr, soft z. blows, 323:8
Zero at the Bone, 513:12
Zeus accomplisher, 64:2
all strangers and beggars are from Z., 53:11
divine bird of Z., 63:30
does not bring all plans to fulfillment, 52:16
drag Z. from heaven to earth, 51:28
dream too is from Z., 50:25
first cause, 63:17
from Z. let us begin, 82:12
god of council loves them, 51:6
lead me Z. and Fate, 82:3
might change me to bird, 68:19
no mortal could vie with Z., 53:6
plan of Z., 50:24
prayers are daughters of Z., 51:33
takes half a man's worth, 54:4
two jars on floor of Z., 52:26
wide-sounding Z., 52:1, 54:4
Zeus-fostered, proud is spirit of Z. kings, 51:6
Zeus's bed of love, 68:20
Eros Z. child, 68:17
Zigzag, four lightnings z. from me, 787:12
lightning stands high, 787:9
Zion, at ease in Z., 29:36, 642:21
city of our God, 327:5
come with singing unto Z., 27:30
songs of Z., 20:6

Zion (*continued*)
  wept when we remembered Z., 20:6
Zipless fuck is absolutely pure, 772:4
Zitronen, das Land wo die Z. blihn,
  349:*n*4
Zone, he who from z. to z., 411:5
  torrid or frozen z., 246:7

Zones and Meridian Lines, 519:20
Zorba, life trouble Z. continued,
  652:3
Zoroaster, holy prophet Z. said,
  141:*n*3
  Magus Z. my dead child, 406:16
Zounds never so bethumped, 169:24

Zuleika on desert island, 614:7
Zurich, learned three things in Z.,
  769:6
  take him to specialist in Z., 767:12
Zwei Sellen und en Gedanke, 439:*n*2
Zweigen, der in den Z. wohnet,
  349:*n*2